Psychotherapeutic Drug Identification Guide

This guide contains color reproductions of some commonly prescribed major psychotherapeutic drugs. This guide mainly illustrates tablets and capsules. A † symbol preceding the name of the drug indicates that other doses are available. Check directly with the manufacturer. *(While the photos are intended as accurate reproductions of the drugs, the guide should be used only as a quick identification aid.)*

†ANAFRANIL®

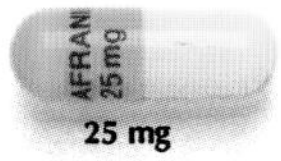

25 mg
clomipramine HCl
CIBA

ANTABUSE®

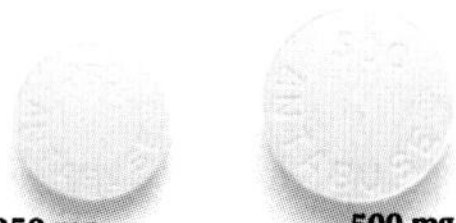

250 mg *disulfiram* 500 mg
Wyeth-Ayerst

ASENDIN®

25 mg 50 mg
100 mg 150 mg 
amoxapine Lederle

†ATARAX®

10 mg 25 mg
50 mg 100 mg 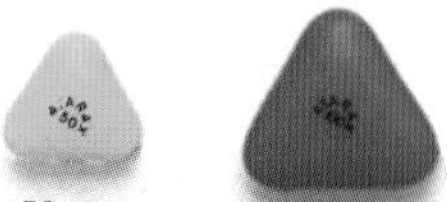
hydroxyzine hydrochloride
Roerig

ATIVAN®

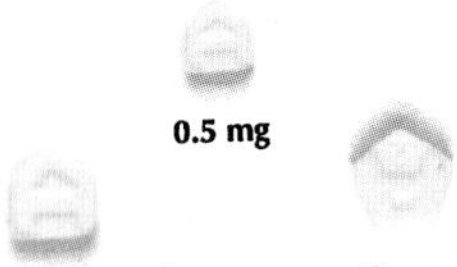

0.5 mg
1 mg *lorazepam* 2 mg
Wyeth-Ayerst

BUSPAR®

5 mg 10 mg
buspirone HCl Mead-Johnson

†CLOZARIL®

100 mg
clozapine
Sandoz

†COGENTIN®

0.5 mg 1 mg 2 mg 
benztropine mesylate
Merck Sharp & Dohme

†COMPAZINE®

5 mg
proclorperazine
Smith Kline & French

†CYLERT®

18.75 mg
pemoline
Abbott

***DALMANE®**

15mg
30mg 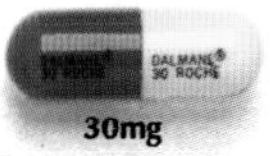
flurazepam HCL
Roche

†DEPAKENE®

250 mg
valproic acid
Abbott

DESYREL®

50 mg 100 mg
trazodone HCl Mead Johnson

†DESYREL® DIVIDOSE®

150 mg
trazodone HCl
Mead Johnson

†DEXEDRINE®

5 mg
dextroamphetamine sulfate
Smith Kline & French

WILLIAMS AND WILKINS ©

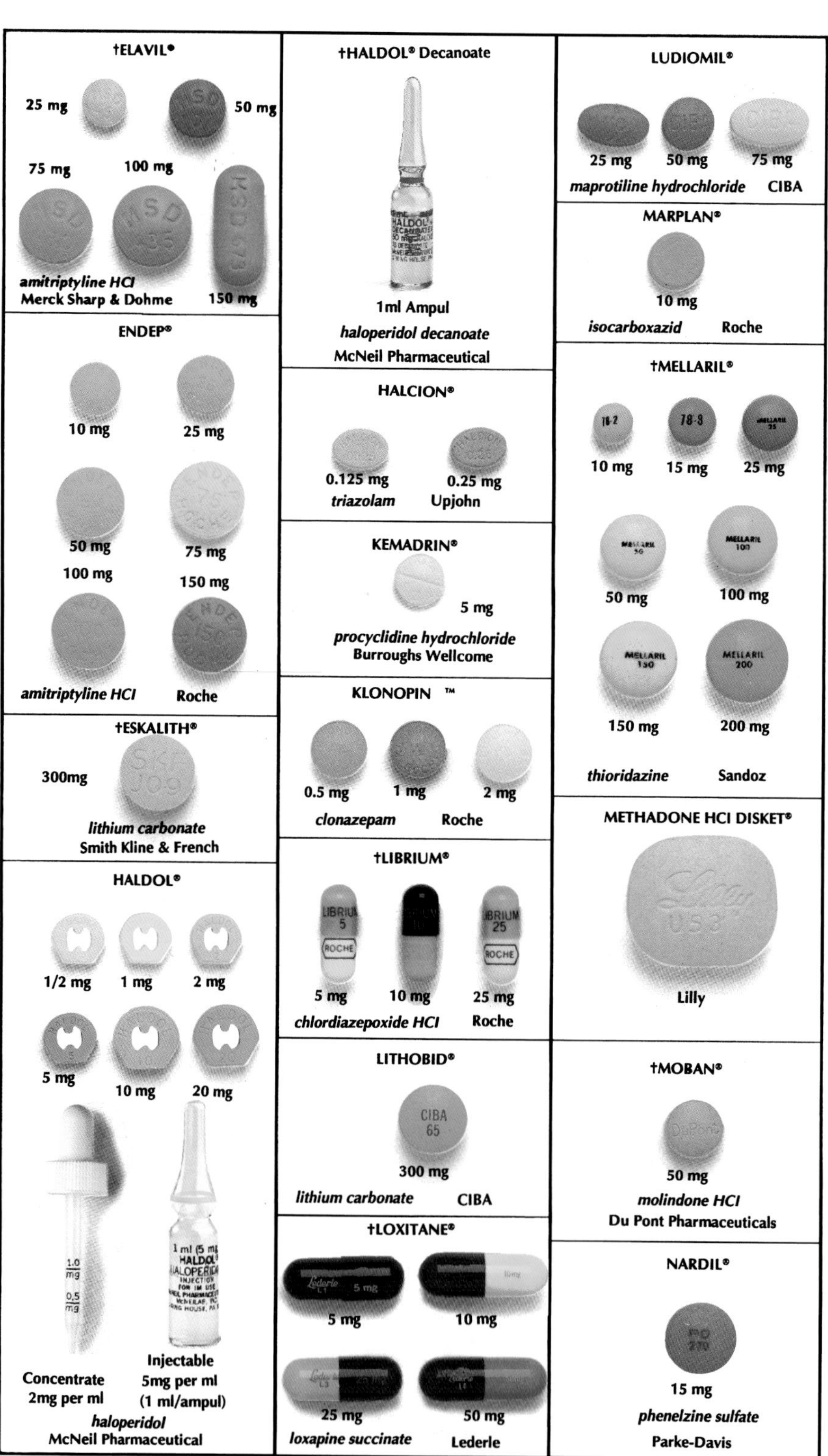

WILLIAMS AND WILKINS ©

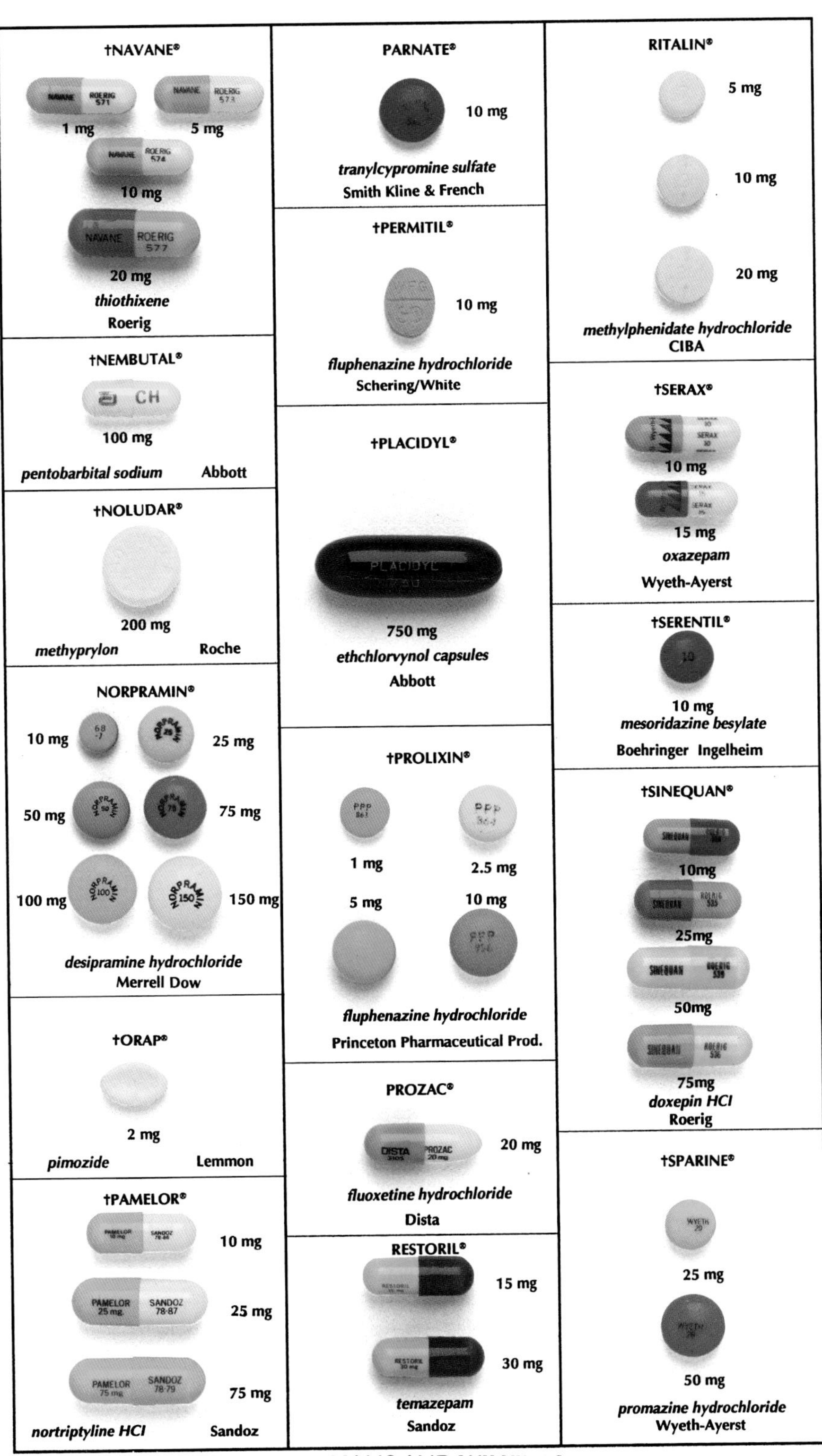

†NAVANE®
1 mg
5 mg
10 mg
20 mg
thiothixene
Roerig
†NEMBUTAL®
100 mg
pentobarbital sodium
Abbott
†NOLUDAR®
200 mg
methyprylon
Roche
NORPRAMIN®
10 mg
25 mg
50 mg
75 mg
100 mg
150 mg
desipramine hydrochloride
Merrell Dow
†ORAP®
2 mg
pimozide
Lemmon
†PAMELOR®
10 mg
25 mg
75 mg
nortriptyline HCl
Sandoz
PARNATE®
10 mg
tranylcypromine sulfate
Smith Kline & French
†PERMITIL®
10 mg
fluphenazine hydrochloride
Schering/White
†PLACIDYL®
750 mg
ethchlorvynol capsules
Abbott
†PROLIXIN®
1 mg
2.5 mg
5 mg
10 mg
fluphenazine hydrochloride
Princeton Pharmaceutical Prod.
PROZAC®
20 mg
fluoxetine hydrochloride
Dista
RESTORIL®
15 mg
30 mg
temazepam
Sandoz
RITALIN®
5 mg
10 mg
20 mg
methylphenidate hydrochloride
CIBA
†SERAX®
10 mg
15 mg
oxazepam
Wyeth-Ayerst
†SERENTIL®
10 mg
mesoridazine besylate
Boehringer Ingelheim
†SINEQUAN®
10mg
25mg
50mg
75mg
doxepin HCl
Roerig
†SPARINE®
25 mg
50 mg
promazine hydrochloride
Wyeth-Ayerst

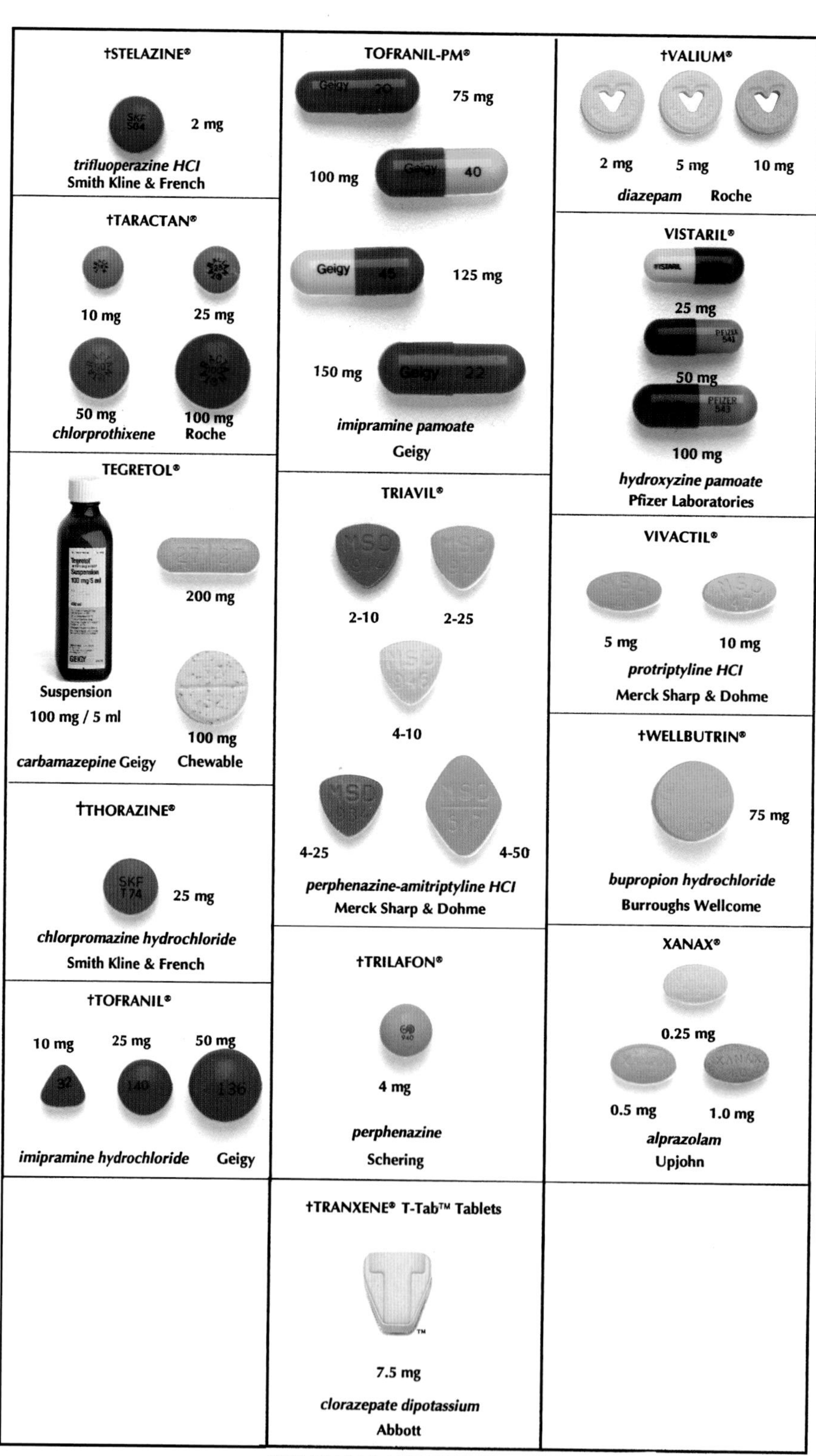

†STELAZINE®
2 mg
trifluoperazine HCl
Smith Kline & French
†TARACTAN®
10 mg
25 mg
50 mg
100 mg
chlorprothixene
Roche
TEGRETOL®
200 mg
Suspension
100 mg / 5 ml
100 mg
Chewable
carbamazepine Geigy
†THORAZINE®
25 mg
chlorpromazine hydrochloride
Smith Kline & French
†TOFRANIL®
10 mg
25 mg
50 mg
imipramine hydrochloride
Geigy
TOFRANIL-PM®
75 mg
100 mg
125 mg
150 mg
imipramine pamoate
Geigy
TRIAVIL®
2-10
2-25
4-10
4-25
4-50
perphenazine-amitriptyline HCl
Merck Sharp & Dohme
†TRILAFON®
4 mg
perphenazine
Schering
†TRANXENE® T-Tab™ Tablets
7.5 mg
clorazepate dipotassium
Abbott
†VALIUM®
2 mg
5 mg
10 mg
diazepam
Roche
VISTARIL®
25 mg
50 mg
100 mg
hydroxyzine pamoate
Pfizer Laboratories
VIVACTIL®
5 mg
10 mg
protriptyline HCl
Merck Sharp & Dohme
†WELLBUTRIN®
75 mg
bupropion hydrochloride
Burroughs Wellcome
XANAX®
0.25 mg
0.5 mg
1.0 mg
alprazolam
Upjohn

J Hirsch

SIXTH EDITION

SYNOPSIS OF PSYCHIATRY

Behavioral Sciences

Clinical Psychiatry

SENIOR CONTRIBUTING EDITOR

ROBERT CANCRO, M.D., MED.D.Sc.

Professor and Chairman, Department of Psychiatry,
New York University School of Medicine;
Director, Department of Psychiatry, Tisch Hospital,
the University Hospital of the New York University Medical Center, New York, New York;
Director, Nathan S. Kline Institute for Psychiatric Research, Orangeburg, New York

CONTRIBUTING EDITORS

REBECCA M. JONES, M.D.

Research Assistant Professor of Psychiatry,
New York University School of Medicine;
Director of Behavioral Sciences and Psychopathology,
Department of Psychiatry, New York University
School of Medicine, New York, New York

PETER M. KAPLAN, M.D.

Clinical Instructor of Psychiatry,
New York University School of Medicine;
Attending Psychiatrist, Manhattan Psychiatric Center,
New York, New York

RICHARD PERRY, M.D.

Clinical Associate Professor of Psychiatry,
New York University School of Medicine;
Assistant Attending Psychiatrist, Tisch Hospital,
the University Hospital of the New York University Medical Center;
Assistant Attending Psychiatrist, Bellevue Hospital,
New York, New York

VIRGINIA A. SADOCK, M.D.

Clinical Professor of Psychiatry and
Director of Graduate Education in Human Sexuality,
Department of Psychiatry, New York University School of Medicine;
Attending Psychiatrist, Tisch Hospital,
the University Hospital of
the New York University Medical Center;
Attending Psychiatrist, Bellevue Hospital,
New York, New York

SIXTH EDITION

SYNOPSIS OF PSYCHIATRY

Behavioral Sciences

Clinical Psychiatry

HAROLD I. KAPLAN, M.D.

Professor of Psychiatry, New York University School of Medicine;
Attending Psychiatrist, Tisch Hospital, the University Hospital of the New York University Medical Center;
Attending Psychiatrist, Bellevue Hospital, New York, New York

BENJAMIN J. SADOCK, M.D.

Professor and Vice Chairman, Department of Psychiatry,
New York University School of Medicine;
Attending Psychiatrist, Tisch Hospital, the University Hospital of the New York University Medical Center;
Attending Psychiatrist, Bellevue Hospital, New York, New York

Assistant to the Authors

JACK A. GREBB, M.D.

Assistant Professor of Psychiatry, New York University School of Medicine;
Associate Attending Psychiatrist, Bellevue Hospital;
Guest Investigator, Laboratory of Cellular and Molecular Neuroscience,
The Rockefeller University, New York, New York;
Research Scientist, Nathan S. Kline
Institute for Psychiatric Research, Orangeburg, New York

Editor: Michael G. Fisher
Associate Editor: Carol Eckhart
Designer: Norman W. Och
Illustration Planner: Lorraine Wrzosek
Production Coordinator: Charles E. Zeller
Project Editor: Lynda Abrams, M.A., NYU School of Medicine

Williams & Wilkins
428 East Preston Street
Baltimore, Maryland 21202, USA

Accurate indications, adverse reactions, and dosage schedules for drugs are provided in this book, but it is possible that they will change. The reader is urged to review the package information data of the manufacturers of the medications mentioned.

Printed in the United States of America

First Edition 1972
Spanish
Second Edition 1976
Italian
Third Edition 1981
Spanish
Portuguese
Fourth Edition 1985
Spanish
Portuguese
Fifth Edition 1988

Library of Congress Cataloging-in-Publication Data

Kaplan, Harold I., 1927–
Synopsis of psychiatry: behavioral sciences, clinical psychiatry
Harold I. Kaplan, Benjamin J. Sadock; assistant to the authors,
Jack A. Grebb.—6th ed.
p. cm.
Includes bibliographical references.
Includes index.
ISBN 0-683-04529-6
1. Mental illness. 2. Psychiatry.
I. Sadock, Benjamin J., 1933–.
II. Grebb, Jack A. III. Title.
[DNLM: 1. Mental Disorders. WM 100 K172s]
RC454.K35 1991
616.89—dc20
DLC
for Library of Congress 90-12955
CIP

92 93 94 95
7 8 9 10

Dedicated to our wives,
Nancy Barrett Kaplan
and
Virginia Alcott Sadock,
without whose help and sacrifice
this textbook would not have been possible

Preface

This is the sixth edition of *Synopsis of Psychiatry* to appear within a span of almost 20 years. The timing of its publication represents a departure from previous editions in that only three years instead of the usual four years have elapsed since the last edition. The reasons for this change are several: New advances in the neural sciences have occurred at an especially rapid pace, particularly in the areas of neurochemistry, neurophysiology, psychoimmunology, and psychoendocrinology; significant data about the nosology, diagnosis, and treatment of mental illness have emerged; and the number of therapeutic methods, particularly in the area of psychopharmacology, have grown rapidly. Because of these changes and advances, a new edition of *Synopsis* was deemed necessary at this time.

An eclectic and multidisciplinary approach is the hallmark of this book and all other books by the authors and shall remain so. Accordingly, biological, psychological, and sociological factors are integrated and presented as they affect the person in health and disease. Modern psychiatry must emphasize the humane and compassionate aspects of medicine; this textbook is dedicated to the humanism that is unfortunately often lost in technically based modern medical education, training, and practice. Of equal importance, the interactions between medical school faculty and students require a high level of mutual empathic concern if America is to avoid producing computerlike robotic physicians.

In the United States psychiatry is one of the few medical school courses consistently included throughout the four years of the curriculum. If taught properly, with quality and sensitivity, psychiatry should be a dramatic and continuing reminder to all in medicine of their mission—the diagnosis, treatment, and elimination of pain, suffering, and disease through the treatment of the whole patient.

The authors believe that textbooks of medicine have an obligation to provide a forum for a discussion of some of the sociopolitical forces that affect medical practice. Some doctors in today's complex society wear many hats—for example, physician and administrator and politician. In those roles controversy may arise regarding decisions in which they participate: managed care; third-party insurance reimbursement for medical and psychiatric care; Medicare and Medicaid; the use and classification of the boundaries and the definition of controlled substances; the use of triplicate prescriptions; poverty, homelessness, and deinstitutionalization; and the working conditions and number of hours on duty of medical house staff are but a few. The authors believe that the time has arrived when medical educators should make observations about these and other controversial areas, and the reader will find such comments in this book. Psychiatrists, who are involved in the humane and psychological aspect of medical care, have a special obligation to discuss all issues that affect the physical and psychological well-being of their patients and their own freedom to exercise their best medical judgment in their work.

CHANGES IN THIS EDITION

New and updated sections. The chapter "The Brain and Behavior" has been updated to provide thorough coverage of the fields of neurochemistry, neurophysiology, and psychoendocrinology, which represent the cutting edge of psychiatry. Other new and extensively changed areas include geriatric psychiatry, the doctor-patient relationship, psychiatric interviewing techniques, history taking and mental status examination, brain-imaging techniques, ethics, neuropsychiatric tests and rating scales, the role of laboratory tests in psychiatry, psychiatry and acquired immune deficiency syndrome (AIDS), neuropsychiatry, behavioral medicine, and the psychiatric aspects of immunology. The chapters on child psychiatry have been heavily rewritten. The chapter on the life cycle has been greatly expanded, with a new discussion of pregnancy and childbirth, among other issues. In addition, the authors have included many clinical case vignettes to illustrate the various psychiatric disorders. These cases have been adapted from the revised third edition of *DSM-III-R Case Book,* published by the American Psychiatric Press, Inc., from which permission was obtained.

Biological therapies. A major change has been introduced in the organization of the chapter on biological therapies. The authors discuss drugs used in the treatment of psychiatric illness in a unique and novel manner through the use of a new pharmacological classification. This represents a departure from the discussion of psychiatric drug therapy under the rubrics of antidepressants, antipsychotics, and the like. This was done to provide the student with a deeper and more comprehensive understanding not only of the general principles of psychopharmacology but also of the use of psychotherapeutic drugs according to their pharmacological activity as discrete drugs, rather than as one of a family of drugs. This edition has expanded information about the uses, caution, interactions, and dosages of drugs, including color illustrations of all the major drugs of use in psychiatry in their various dosage forms. A tinted page contains an index to guide the reader to the section of the book where each of the drugs used in psychiatry are discussed.

Teaching system. *Synopsis* forms one part of a comprehensive system developed by the authors to facilitate the teaching of psychiatry and the behavioral sciences. The keystone of the system is *Comprehensive Textbook of Psychiatry,* now in its fifth (1989) edition, which is global in its depth and scope and encyclopedic in its breadth of information. Another segment is *Study Guide and Self-Examination Review for Synopsis of Psychiatry and Comprehensive Textbook of Psychiatry,* which consists of multiple-choice questions and answers derived from and keyed to this edition of *Synopsis of Psychiatry* and to the fifth edition of *Comprehensive Textbook of Psychiatry*; this application of *Study Guide* to *Comprehensive Textbook* is done for the first time. The authors recognize the importance and contributions of the National Board of Medical Examiners and the American Board of Psychiatry and Neurology, on whose published curricula all our books are based. Their examinations are given in multiple-choice-question format; this is the type of teaching technique used in *Study Guide,* which the authors recommend as a companion volume to be used with the textbooks. The next part of the system is *Pocket Handbook of Clinical Psychiatry,* a new book by the authors with several collaborators from New York University School of Medicine. *Pocket Handbook of Clinical Psychiatry* covers the diagnosis and treatment of psychiatric disorders and is compactly designed and concisely written to be carried in the pocket by the clinical clerk or practicing physician to provide a quick ready reference. Finally, the authors' newly published *Comprehensive Glossary of Psychiatric and Psychological Terms* provides simply written definitions of terms of interest for psychiatrists and other physicians, psychologists, students, other mental health professionals, and the general public.

Two caveats to the reader: First, although the authors recognize the enormous importance and positive contributions of the National Board of Medical Examiners and the American Board of Psychiatry and Neurology to medical education, there is continuing controversy about the growing influence, power, and centralization of these organizations and the effect, albeit mostly constructive, on our psychiatric educational system. Second, the nosology used in this textbook is based totally on DSM-III-R, which is the law of the land in American psychiatry. The student must know DSM-III-R until it is changed when the next version, DSM-IV, is published. The publication of DSM-IV in 1993 is to be coordinated with the publication of the tenth revision of *International Classification of Diseases* (ICD-10). It is expected that ICD-10 and DSM-IV will be published simultaneously. The authors have tried to anticipate as many of these changes as possible.

Synopsis is not a review book, a nosology, or an outline of psychiatry, and it is much more than a diagnostic manual. It is a comprehensive, thoroughly eclectic, timely, and fully integrated medical textbook, which is what the field of psychiatry both deserves and requires.

ACKNOWLEDGMENTS

In the preparation of this edition we have been especially fortunate to enlist the assistance of Jack Grebb, M.D., Assistant Professor of Psychiatry at New York University Medical Center, who served in the newly created role of Assistant to the Authors. Dr. Grebb is an outstanding academic, research, and clinical psychiatrist.

In addition, a major innovation in this edition is the introduction of several outstanding contributing editors—all from the faculty of New York University School of Medicine—who played major roles in the complex revision of this book. These include Rebecca M. Jones, M.D., Peter M. Kaplan, M.D., Richard Perry, M.D., and Virginia A. Sadock, M.D. We thank them for their outstanding help.

The authors also wish to thank the American Psychiatric Press, Inc. for permission to use case histories from the *DSM-III-R Case Book.* Unless otherwise indicated, all cases are from that book.

The production of this book was a major undertaking that involved the efforts of many coworkers. Lynda Abrams, M.A., Education Coordinator of the Department of Psychiatry at New York University School of Medicine, was key to the successful preparation and completion of this book. She deserves our deepest gratitude and appreciation for her skilled editing and for her prodigious work in coordinating many aspects of this textbook. She was the Project Editor and was responsible for continually and intensively assisting the authors in their work. She carried out her many duties with enthusiasm, dedication, and consummate skill.

Robin Segal, M.D., who is Contributing Editor of *Study Guide* and Director of the Clinical Clerkship in Psychiatry at New York University Medical Center, made many helpful suggestions and modifications in the preparation of this revision, for which we thank her.

We also want to thank Bennett Cohen, M.D., Philip Kaplan, M.D., Nancy Barrett Kaplan, James Sadock, and Victoria Sadock for their personal assistance in our efforts.

The authors express their appreciation to Jay E. Kantor, Ph.D., Research Associate Professor of Humanities at New York University School of Medicine, for his help in the ethics section of the book and to Norman Sussman, M.D., Clinical Associate Professor of Psychiatry and Director of Residency Training in Psychiatry at New York University Medical Center, for his assistance in the sleep disorders section. We also especially wish to thank Doris Lowe, Reference Librarian at the Frederick L. Ehrman Medical Library of New York University School of Medicine, for her invaluable assistance in bibliographic research throughout this project.

The authors also want to take this opportunity to acknowledge those who have translated this and other works by the authors into foreign languages. Current translations include Italian, Portuguese, Spanish, and German, in addition to a special Asian and International Student Edition of *Synopsis*.

Robert Cancro, M.D., Professor and Chairman of the Department of Psychiatry at New York University Medical Center, participated as Senior Contributing Editor of this edition. Dr. Cancro's commitment to psychiatric education and psychiatric research is recognized throughout the world. He has been an important source of great inspiration to the authors and has contributed immeasurably to this and previous editions. Dr. Cancro is renowned as a researcher, clinician, and educator. He is a much valued and highly esteemed mentor, collaborator, and dear friend to the authors, and it is a very special privilege to work closely with him. Dr. Cancro has developed a department that represents the very best in American psychiatry. The fruitful and stimulating exchange of ideas among Dr. Cancro and the faculty, residents, medical students, and other professionals at New York University creates a unique blend of academic and clinical psychiatry for which he is responsible and that is continuously growing under his leadership. Our collaboration and association with this outstanding American educator has contributed immeasurably to the new ideas and directions shaping this textbook.

Harold I. Kaplan, M.D.
Benjamin J. Sadock, M.D.

New York University Medical Center
New York, New York
February 1991

Contents

The Doctor-Patient Relationship

The relationship between doctors and patients connotes a variety of conflicting impressions, ranging from romantically idealized to despairingly cynical. Stripped to its basics, the relationship is characterized by the perceptions each participant has of the other's interests, motivations, capacity for understanding, and respect. How each participant plays his or her respective role is based on different expectations, which can form the basis for either a satisfying and productive relationship or one that is infused with suspicion, frustration, and disappointment.

Patients are typically tolerant of the therapeutic limitations of medicine within a context of feeling respected and genuinely heard by the doctor. Physicians work with sick people, not disease syndromes, and sick people bring into the doctor-patient relationship a complex interplay of biological factors, psychological forces, and social conditioning. A doctor who does not understand the inevitability of this interplay may disregard or even completely miss critical information relevant to diagnosis, treatment, compliance, and prognosis.

BIOPSYCHOSOCIAL MODEL

George Engel has been the most prominent proponent of the biopsychosocial model of disease, which stresses an integrated systems approach to human behavior and disease. The biopsychosocial model is derived from general systems theory. The biological system emphasizes the anatomical, structural, and molecular substrate of disease and its impact on the patient's biological functioning; the psychological system emphasizes the impact of psychodynamic factors, motivation, and personality on the experience of and reaction to illness; and the social system emphasizes cultural, environmental, and familial influences on the expression and experience of illness. Engel postulated that each system may affect and be affected by every other system. Engel's model does not assert that medical illness is a direct result of a person's psychological or sociocultural makeup but, rather, encourages a more comprehensive understanding of disease and treatment. A dramatic example of Engel's conception of the biopsychosocial model was a 1971 study of the relationship between sudden death and psychological factors. After investigating 170 sudden deaths over approximately six years, he observed that serious illness or even death may be associated with psychological stress or trauma. Among the potential triggering events Engel listed are the following: the death of a close friend, grief, anniversary reactions, loss of self-esteem, personal danger or threat and the letdown after the threat has passed, and reunions or triumphs.

The doctor-patient relationship is a critical component of the biopsychosocial model. All physicians must not only have a working knowledge of the patient's medical status but also be familiar with how the patient's individual psychology and sociocultural milieu affect the medical condition, the emotional responses to the condition, and involvement with the doctor.

ILLNESS BEHAVIOR

Illness behavior is the term used to describe a patient's reactions to the experience of being sick. Some describe aspects of this illness behavior as the sick role. The *sick role* is, more specifically, the role society ascribes to the sick person because he or she is ill. Characteristics of the sick role include such factors as being excused from certain responsibilities and being expected to want to obtain help to get well. Edward Suchman describes five stages of illness behavior, as follows:

1. *The symptom experience stage,* in which a decision is made that something is wrong
2. *The assumption of the sick role stage,* in which a decision is made that one is sick and needs professional care
3. *The medical care contact stage,* in which a decision is made to seek professional care
4. *The dependent-patient role stage,* in which a decision is made to transfer control to the doctor and to follow prescribed treatment
5. *The recovery or rehabilitation stage,* in which a decision is made to give up the patient role

Illness behavior and the sick role are affected by a person's previous experience with illness and by a person's cultural beliefs about disease. The influence of culture on the reporting and presentations of symptoms must be evaluated. The relationship of illness to family processes, class status, and ethnic identity are all important. The person's and the culture's attitudes about dependency and helplessness greatly influence how and if a person will ask for help, as do such psychological factors as personality type and the personal meaning attributed to the experience of being ill. For instance, different persons react to illness in different ways, depending on their habitual modes of thinking, feeling, and behaving. Some persons may experience illness as an overwhelming loss, whereas others may see in the same illness a challenge to be overcome or a punishment for something they feel guilty about. Table 1-1 lists essential areas to be addressed in the assessment of illness

Table 1-1
Assessment of Individual Illness Behavior in Becoming a Patient and Seeking Care

Prior illness episodes, especially illnesses of standard severity (childbirth, renal stones, or surgery)
Cultural degree of stoicism
Cultural beliefs concerning the specific problem
Personal meaning or beliefs about the particular problem

Specific questions to ask to elicit the patient's explanatory model are:

1. What do you call your problem? What name does it have?
2. What do you think caused your problem?
3. Why do you think it started when it did?
4. What does your sickness do to you? How does it work?
5. How severe is it? Will it have a short or long course?
6. What do you fear most about your sickness?
7. What are the chief problems that your sickness has caused for you?
8. What kind of treatment do you think you should receive? What are the most important results you hope to receive from treatment?
9. What have you done so far to treat your sickness?

Table from M Lipkin Jr: Psychiatry and medicine. In *Comprehensive Textbook of Psychiatry,* ed 5, H I Kaplan and B J Sadock, editors, p 1280. Williams & Wilkins, Baltimore, 1989.

behavior and outlines nine questions that are helpful in making this assessment.

MODELS OF THE DOCTOR-PATIENT RELATIONSHIP

There are a number of potential models of the doctor-patient relationship. Often, neither the doctor nor the patient is fully conscious of actually choosing one or another. The models most often derive from the personalities, expectations, and needs of both doctor and patient. The fact that these personalities, expectations, and needs are largely unspoken and may be quite different for doctor and patient may lead to miscommunication and disappointment for both participants in the relationship. The doctor must be consciously aware of which model is operating with which patient and be able to shift models, depending on the particular needs of specific patients and on the treatment requirements of specific clinical situations.

Specific Models

Models of the doctor-patient relationship include the active-passive model, the teacher-student (or parent-child, guidance-cooperation) model, the mutual participation model, and the friendship (or socially intimate) model.

The *active-passive model* implies the complete passivity of the patient and the taking over by the physician that necessarily results. In this model the patient assumes virtually no responsibility for his or her own care and takes no part in treatment. This model is appropriate when a patient is unconscious, immobilized, or delirious.

In the *teacher-student model,* the dominance of the physician is assumed and emphasized. The role of the physician is paternalistic and controlling; the role of the patient is essentially one of dependence and acceptance. This model is often observed during a patient's recovery from surgery.

The *mutual participation model* implies equality between doctor and patient; both participants require and depend on each other's input. The need for a doctor-patient relationship based on a model of mutual, active participation is most obvious in the treatment of such chronic illnesses as renal failure and diabetes, in which a patient's knowledge and acceptance of treatment ramifications are critical to the success of treatment. It may also be effective in more subtle situations—for example, in pneumonia.

The *friendship model* of the doctor-patient relationship is generally considered dysfunctional if not unethical. It most often represents a primary, underlying psychological problem in the physician, who may have an emotional need to turn the care for the patient into a relationship of mutual sharing of personal information and love. This model often involves indeterminate perpetuation of the relationship, rather than an appropriate ending, and a blurring of boundaries between professionalism and intimacy.

ESTABLISHING RAPPORT

In one survey of 700 patients, there was substantial agreement that physicians do not have the time or inclination to listen to and consider the patient's feelings, that they do not have enough knowledge of the emotional problems and socioeconomic background of the family, and that they increase fear by giving explanations in too technical language. As psychosocial and economic factors exert a profound influence on human relations, the physician should have as much understanding as possible of the patient's subculture.

Failure of the physician to establish good rapport with the patient accounts for much of the ineffectiveness in care. The presence of rapport implies that there is understanding and trust between doctor and patient. Differences in social, intellectual, and educational status interfere seriously with rapport. Understanding—or lack of understanding—of the patient's beliefs, use of language, and attitudes toward illness influences the character of the physician's examination.

Evaluating the social pressures in the patient's earlier life helps the doctor better understand the patient. Emotional reactions, healthy or unhealthy, are the result of a constant interplay of biological, sociological, and psychological forces. Each stress leaves behind some trace of its influence and continues to manifest itself throughout life in proportion to the intensity of its effect and the susceptibility of the particular human being. These stresses and strains should be determined to the extent possible. The significant point may be not the stress itself but the person's reactions to it.

The establishment of genuine rapport also depends on a basic understanding of such complex interpersonal factors as transference and countertransference.

Transference

Transference is generally defined as the set of expectations, beliefs, and emotional responses that a patient brings into the doctor-patient relationship. They are based not necessarily on who the doctor is or how the doctor acts in reality but, rather, on persistent experiences the patient has had with other important authority figures throughout life.

Transferential attitudes. The patient's attitude toward the physician is apt to be a repetition of the attitude he or she has had toward authority figures. This attitude may range from one of a realistic basic trust with an expectation that the doctor has the patient's best interest at heart through one of over-idealization and even eroticized fantasy to one of basic mistrust, with an expectation that the doctor will be contemptuous and potentially abusive. A patient may expect the doctor to do something—for example, prescribe medication or perform surgery—and can only accept a doctor's care as sufficient and competent if these actions occur. Inherent in this attitude is the patient's role as a passive recipient in relation to the doctor's role as an active bestower of help. A patient in whom these expectations are established will feel uncomfortable if the doctor has different expectations. Another patient may be more active and expect to participate more fully in treatment and correspondingly will feel at odds with a doctor who does not want patient participation.

Role of the psychiatric versus nonpsychiatric physician. In many respects the role of the psychiatrist is different from that of a nonpsychiatric physician, and yet many patients expect the same from the psychiatrist as they do from other physicians. If they expect a doctor to take action, give advice, and prescribe medication to cure an illness, they may well expect this same interaction with a psychiatrist and be disappointed or angry if it does not occur. Transference reactions may be strongest with psychiatrists for a number of reasons. For example, as part of intensive, insight-oriented psychotherapy, the encouragement of transference feelings is an integral part of treatment. In some types of therapy, a psychiatrist is more or less neutral. The more neutral or less known the psychiatrist is, the more a patient's transferential fantasies and concerns are mobilized and projected onto the doctor. Once the fantasies are stimulated and projected, the psychiatrist can help patients gain insight into how these fantasies and concerns affect all the important relationships in their lives. Although a nonpsychiatrist does not utilize or even need to understand transference attitudes in this intensive way, a solid understanding of the power and manifestations of transference is necessary for optimal treatment results in any doctor-patient relationship.

The words and deeds of the doctor have a power far beyond the commonplace because of his or her unique authority and the patient's dependence on the doctor. How a particular physician behaves and interacts has a direct bearing on the emotional and even the physical reactions of the patient. One patient repeatedly had high blood pressure when examined by a physician he considered cold, aloof, and stern. He had normal blood pressure, however, when seen by a doctor he regarded as warm, understanding, and sympathetic.

Countertransference

Just as the patient brings transferential attitudes to the doctor-patient relationship, doctors themselves often develop countertransferential reactions to their patients. Countertransference may take the form of negative feelings, disruptive to the doctor-patient relationship, but it may also encompass disproportionately positive, idealizing, or even eroticized reactions. Just as patients have expectations for physicians—for example, competence, lack of exploitation, objectivity, comfort, and relief—physicians often have unconscious or unspoken expectations of patients. Most commonly, patients are thought of as good patients if their expressed severity of symptoms correlates with an overtly diagnosable biological disorder, if they are compliant and generally nonchallenging with treatment, if they are emotionally controlled, and if they are grateful. If these expectations are not met, even if this is a result of unconsciously unrealistic needs on the part of the physician, the patient may be blamed and experienced as unlikable, unworkable, or bad.

Disliking a patient. A physician who actively dislikes a patient is apt to be ineffective in dealing with him or her. Emotion breeds counteremotion. For example, if the physician is hostile, the patient becomes more hostile; the physician then becomes even angrier, and there is rapid deterioration of the relationship. If the physician can rise above such emotions and handle the resentful patient with equanimity, there may be a shift in the interpersonal relationship from one of mutual overt antagonism to one of at least increased acceptance and grudging respect. Rising above such emotions involves being able to step back from the intense, countertransferential reactions and more dispassionately explore why the patient is reacting to the doctor in such an apparently self-defeating way. After all, the patient needs the doctor, and the hostility ensures that the needed help will not occur. If the doctor can understand that the patient's antagonism is in some ways defensive or self-protective and most likely reflects transferential fears of disrespect, abuse, and disappointment, the doctor may be less angry and more empathic.

Doctors who have strong unconscious needs to be all-knowing and all-powerful may have particular problems with certain types of patients. These patients may actually be difficult for most physicians to handle, but, if the physician is as aware as possible of his or her own needs, capabilities, and limitations, these patients will be less threatening. These patients include the following: those who appear to repeatedly defeat attempts to help them (e.g., patients with severe heart disease who continue to smoke or drink); those who are perceived as uncooperative (e.g., patients who question or refuse treatment); those who request a second opinion; those who fail to recover in response to treatment; those who use physical or somatic complaints to mask emotional problems (e.g., patients with somatization disorder, somatoform pain disorder, hypochondriasis, or factitious disorder); those with chronic organic mental syndromes (e.g., patients with senile dementia); and those who are dying or in chronic pain (e.g., patients who represent a professional failure and are, thus, a threat to the physician's identity and self-esteem).

Sexuality and the physician. Physicians are bound to like some patients more than others. However, if the physician feels a strong attraction to a patient and is tempted to act on the attraction, stepping back and dispassionately assessing the situation is essential. In some medical specialties in which the doctor-patient relationship is not particularly intimate or intense, the prohibition against romantic involvement with patients may not be very strong. In certain other specialties, however, especially psychiatry, the ethical and even legal prohibition is very important. The doctor is a powerful figure in this country's culture and may trigger many unconscious fantasies in patients of being rescued, taken care of, and loved. Doctors themselves may have their own unconscious fantasies of being and needing to be all-powerful, rescuing, and lovable. These fantasies are inherently unrealistic and dehumanizing and are bound to be inevitably disappointed. The disappointments, if realized in an actual romantic relationship between doctor and patient, can be destructive, especially for the patient.

Sexual history. Another aspect of sexuality as it pertains to countertransference issues relates to asking patients about sexual issues or obtaining a sexual history. A reluctance may often reflect the physician's own anxiety about sexuality. Moreover, the omission of these types of questions generally tells patients that the doctor is uncomfortable with the subject, thus leading to a general inhibition about discussing any number of other sensitive subjects.

Self-monitoring of countertransference feelings. Countertransference feelings do not always have to be perceived in solely negative terms. They also have the potential, if recognized and analyzed, to help the doctor better understand the patient who has stimulated the feelings. For instance, if a doctor feels bored and restless when with a particular patient and has ascertained that the boredom is not secondary to his or her own preoccupations, the doctor may surmise that the patient is speaking about trivial or insignificant concerns in order to avoid the real, more frightening, and disturbing concerns.

Physicians as patients. A special example of countertransference issues occurs when the patient being treated is a physician. Problems that can arise in this situation include an expectation that the physician-patient will take care of his or her own medications and treatment and the fear on the part of the physician-doctor of criticism of his or her skills or competence. Ill physicians are notoriously poor patients, most likely because physicians are trained to be in control of medical situations and to be the masters in the doctor-patient relationship. For a physician, being a patient may mean giving up control, becoming dependent, and appearing vulnerable and frightened—all of which most physicians are professionally trained to suppress. Physician-patients may be reluctant to become what they perceive as burdens to overworked colleagues, or they may be embarrassed to ask pertinent questions for fear of appearing ignorant or incompetent. Physician-patients may stimulate fear in the treating physicians who see themselves in the patient, an attitude that can lead to denial and avoidance on the part of the treating physicians.

GENERAL CONSIDERATIONS: THE RELATIONSHIP

Gaining conscious insight into the relationship between physicians and patients requires constant evaluation. The better understanding that doctors have of themselves, the more secure they feel, the better able they are to modify destructive attitudes. Doctors need to empathize but not to the point of assuming the burdens of their patients or unrealistically fantasizing that only they can be the patients' saviors. They should be able to leave behind the problems of their patients when away from the office or the hospital and not use their patients as substitutes for an intimacy or relationship that may be missing in their personal lives. Otherwise, they will be handicapped in their efforts to help sick people, who need sympathy and understanding but not sentimentality or overinvolvement.

The physician is prone to some defensiveness, partly with good reason, for many innocent doctors have been sued, attacked, and even killed because they did not give some patients the satisfaction they desired. Consequently, the physician may assume a defensive attitude toward all patients. Although such rigidity may create the image of thoroughness and efficiency, it is frequently inappropriate. Greater flexibility leads to a responsiveness to the subtle interplay between two persons. It also assumes a certain tolerance for the real uncertainty present in any clinical situation with any patient. The doctor must learn to accept the fact that, as much as he or she may wish to control everything in the care of a patient, this wish can never be fully realized. There are situations in which—no matter how conscientious, competent, or caring a physician may be—a disease cannot be controlled, and death cannot be prevented.

Physicians must also avoid sidestepping issues that they find difficult to deal with because of their own sensitivities, prejudices, or peculiarities when these issues are important to the patient.

For example, one medical student insisted on questioning a patient about her relationship with her 23-year-old son. It was evident from the playback of a tape-recorded interview that the patient wished to talk about her problems with her husband. When the patient was later interviewed by the supervising doctor, she said, "The medical student was a nice fellow, but I could see he was having trouble with his mother. It made me understand my own son more."

In such a complex interaction as the doctor-patient relationship, mistakes are usually not disastrous to the relationship if they are relatively infrequent. When the patient senses interest, enthusiasm, and goodwill on the part of the interviewer, the patient is apt to tolerate considerable inexperience.

INTERVIEWING

One of the most critical tools a physician has is the ability to interview effectively. A skillful interviewer is able to gather the data necessary to understand and treat the patient and in the process to increase the patient's understanding of and compliance with the physician's advice. There are three main components of any interview, all of which require special techniques and skills: the beginning of the interview, the interview itself, and the closing of the interview. Interviewers use their own empathic responses to facilitate the development of rapport. In general, an interviewer must convey an attitude that is nonjudgmental, interested, concerned, and kind; otherwise, potentially crucial information may not be obtained.

Many factors influence both the content and the process of the interview: (1) The patient's personality and character style significantly influence transference reactions and the emotional context in which the interview unfolds. (2) Different clinical situations—including whether the patient is seen on a general hospital ward, on a psychiatric ward, in the emergency room, or as an outpatient—shape the types of questions asked and the recommendations offered. (3) Technical factors—such as telephone interruptions, the use of an interpreter, note taking, and the physical space and comfort of the room—affect the interview. (4) The timing of the interview in the patient's illness, be it in the most acute stage or during a remission, influences the content and the process of the interview. (5) The interviewer's style, orientation, and experience have a significant influence on the interview. Even the timing of interjections, such as "uh-huh," can influence what a patient will or will not say and when, as he or she tries unconsciously to follow the subtle leads and cues provided by the doctor.

Format of the Standard Psychiatric-Medical History

One goal of most interviews is to obtain specific and comprehensive information regarding the patient's immediate presenting complaints and the patient's pertinent history. The data involved in the psychiatric-medical history and mental status examination are discussed in Section 7.1.

Psychiatric versus Medical-Surgical Interviews

Similarities

Functions of the interview, coping mechanisms, and psychological versus medical symptoms. Mack Lipkin and associates describe three functions of the medical interview: to assess the nature of the problem, to develop and maintain a therapeutic relationship, and to communicate information and implement a treatment plan (Table 1-2). These functions are exactly the same as those of the psychiatric and surgical interviews. Also universal are the predominant coping mechanisms, both adaptive and maladaptive. These include such reactions as anxiety, depression, regression, denial, anger, and dependency (Table 1-3). These reactions must be anticipated, recognized, and addressed by every physician if any treatment or intervention is to be effective. Many psychiatric problems present as medical illness, and, conversely, many medical or surgical problems present with psychiatric symptoms. For this reason alone, all physicians must recognize the importance of obtaining a comprehensive, biopsychosocial history on each of their patients.

Psychogenic syndromes and medical syndromes with psychiatric presentations. Lipkin defines psychogenic syndromes as "illnesses presenting as medical problems but characterized by strong evidence to suggest that the dominant role in the timing, etiology, and nature of the syndrome is that of psychological or social events, rather than biological ones." Examples include somatization disorder, factitious disorder with physical symptoms, somatoform pain disorder, and hy-

Table 1-2
Three Functions of the Medical Interview

Functions	Objectives	Skills
I. Determining the nature of the problem	1. To enable the clinician to establish a diagnosis or recommend further diagnostic procedures, suggest a course of treatment, and predict the nature of the illness.	1. Knowledge base of diseases, disorders, problems, and clinical hypotheses from multiple conceptual domains: biomedical, sociocultural, psychodynamic, and behavioral. 2. Ability to elicit data for the above conceptual domains (encouraging the patient to tell his or her story; organizing the flow of the interview, the form of questions, the characterization of symptoms, the mental status examination). 3. Ability to perceive data from multiple sources (history, mental status exam, physician's subjective response to patient, nonverbal cues, listening at multiple levels). 4. Hypothesis generation and testing. 5. Developing a therapeutic relationship (function II).
II. Developing and maintaining a therapeutic relationship	1. The patient's willingness to provide diagnostic information. 2. Relief of physical and psychological distress. 3. Willingness to accept treatment plan or a process of negotiation. 4. Patient satisfaction. 5. Physician satisfaction.	1. Defining the nature of the relationship. 2. Allowing the patient to tell his or her story. 3. Hearing, bearing, and tolerating the patient's expression of painful feelings. 4. Appropriate and genuine interest, empathy, support, and cognitive understanding. 5. Attending to common patient concerns over embarrassment, shame, and humiliation. 6. Elicitation of the patient's perspective. 7. Determining the nature of the problem (function I). 8. Communicating information and recommending treatment (function III).
III. Communicating information and implementing a treatment plan	1. The patient's understanding of the nature of the illness. 2. The patient's understanding of suggested diagnostic procedures. 3. The patient's understanding of the treatment possibilities. 4. Achievements of consensus between physician and patient over the above items 1–3. 5. Achievement of informed consent. 6. Improve coping mechanisms. 7. Life-style change.	1. Determining the nature of the problem (function I). 2. Developing a therapeutic relationship (function II). 3. Establishing the differences in perspective between physician and patient. 4. Educational strategies. 5. Clinical negotiations for conflict resolutions.

Table from A Lazare, J Bird, M Lipkin Jr, S Putnam: Three functions of the medical interview: An integrative conceptual framework. In *The Medical Interview,* M Lipkin Jr, S Putnam, and A Lazare, editors. Springer, New York, 1989, with permission.

Table 1-3
Predictable Reactions to Illness

Intrapsychic	Clinical
Lowered self-image → loss → grief	Anxiety
Threat to homeostasis → fear	Denial
Failure of (self) care → helplessness/hopelessness	Depression
Sense of loss of control → shame (guilt)	Bargaining and blaming
	Regression
	Isolation
	Dependency
	Anger
	Acceptance

Table from M Lipkin Jr: Psychiatry and medicine. In *Comprehensive Textbook of Psychiatry,* ed 5, H I Kaplan and B J Sadock, editors, p 1280. Williams & Wilkins, Baltimore, 1989.

pochondriasis. Medical problems that can present with psychiatric symptoms include acquired immune deficiency syndrome (AIDS) (depression, anxiety, cognitive deficits), hypoglycemia (fear and dread, depression, fatigue), intracranial tumors (depression, anxiety, personality changes), multiple sclerosis (personality changes, mood swings, depression), and hypothyroidism (irritability, depression, paranoia, delusions, hallucinations).

Differences

Patients with psychiatric disorders. A psychiatric patient must often contend with stresses and pressures different from those suffered by the patient who does not have a psychiatric disorder. These include the stigma this culture attaches to being a psychiatric patient (it is more acceptable to have a medical or surgical problem than to have a mental one); difficulties communicating because of disorders in thinking, which can include delusions, hallucinations, and disorganized thought processes; oddities of behavior; and impairments of insight and judgment that make compliance with treatment particularly difficult. Because it is often difficult for psychiatric patients to describe fully what is going on, the physician must be prepared to obtain information from other sources. Family members, friends, and the spouse can provide critical pieces of information about the patient—such as past psychiatric history, responses to medication, and precipitating stresses—which the patient may not be able to provide.

Psychiatric patients may not be able to tolerate a traditional interview format, especially in the most acute stages of a disorder. For instance, a psychiatric patient suffering from increased agitation, paranoia, or depression may not be able to sit for 30 to 45 minutes of discussion or questioning. In this case the physician must be prepared to conduct multiple brief interactions over a period of time, sitting or standing with the patient for as long as the patient is able, then stopping and returning when the patient appears able to tolerate more.

Physicians must be particularly prepared to utilize their powers of observation with psychiatric patients who are unable to communicate well verbally. The specific skills of observation, which are fully discussed in Section 7.1, include observations of the patient's general appearance, behavior, and body language and how all these factors provide diagnostic clues.

Many nonpsychiatric physicians see psychiatric patients. Studies show that about 60 percent of patients with mental disorders visit a nonpsychiatric physician during any six-month period, and patients with mental disorders are twice as likely to visit a primary care physician as are other patients. Nonpsychiatric physicians should be knowledgeable about the special problems of and specific techniques utilized with psychiatric patients.

Beginning the Interview

How a physician begins an interview provides a powerful first impression to patients, and the manner in which a doctor opens communication with a patient has potentially powerful effects on how the remainder of the interview will proceed. Patients are often extremely anxious on first encounters with physicians, feeling both vulnerable and intimidated. A physician who can establish rapport quickly, put the patient at ease, and show respect is well on the way to conducting a productive exchange of information. This exchange is critical to formulating a correct diagnosis and to establishing treatment goals.

The physician should initially make sure that he or she knows the patient's name and that the patient knows the physician's name. The physician should introduce him- or herself to any other people who are present with the patient. If relatives or friends accompany the patient, the physician should ascertain whether the patient would like them to be present during the initial interview. If the patient states an emphatic desire for the presence of another person during the interview, this request should be respected, as it may alleviate the patient's anxiety about the interview. It may also be an initial step in the direction of gaining the trust of significant people in the patient's life, people who may be essential to the patient's continued compliance with and acceptance of the doctor. However, the physician should also attempt to speak to the patient individually to make sure that the patient has a chance to say anything he or she may not want to say in front of others. One way to do this is to see the patient along with a family member or friend first, then to say, "I very much appreciate speaking with you both and getting all your thoughts and input about what is going on with Mr. X. At this point, let me give Mr. X a chance to speak with me alone, since he and I are going to work together closely in the coming weeks. If you would like to meet together with me again in the future, I would be happy to arrange such a meeting."

Patients have the right to know the position and the professional status of the persons involved with their care. For example, medical students should introduce themselves as such, not as doctors, and physicians should make it clear whether they are consultants (called in by another physician to see the patient), covering for another physician, or involved in the interview in order to teach students, rather than to treat the patient.

Opening Questions

Once the introductions and other initial assessments have occurred, a useful and appropriate opening remark is, "Can you tell me about the troubles that bring you in today?" or "Tell me about the problems you have been having," Following up this remark with a second one, such as, "What else?" often elicits further information that the patient was reluctant to give initially. It also indicates to the patient that the doctor is interested in hearing as much as the patient wants to say.

A less directive approach is to ask the patient, "Where shall we start?" or "Where would you prefer to begin?" If a patient has been referred by another doctor for consultation, the initial remarks can indicate that the consulting doctor already knows something about the patient. For example, the consulting doctor might say, "Your doctor has told me something about what has been troubling you [e.g., cardiovascular symptoms, depression], but I'd like to hear from you in your own words what is troubling you." Most patients do not speak freely unless they have privacy and are sure that their conversations cannot be overheard. A physician who makes sure at the beginning of an interview that such factors as privacy, quiet, and lack of interruptions are attended to conveys to the patient that what the patient has to say is important and worthy of serious consideration.

A patient may appear frightened or resistant at the beginning of an interview and may not want to answer questions. If this seems to be the case, it can be helpful for the physician to comment on this directly in a gentle and supportive way, encouraging the patient to talk about his or her feelings regarding the interview itself. Acknowledging the patient's anxiety may be the first step in delineating what the anxiety is about, which will enable the physician to offer appropriate reassurance. An example of what could be said is, "I can't help but notice that you seem to be feeling anxious about talking with me, and I wonder if there is anything I can do or any question I can answer that will make it easier for you." Or, "I know that it can be difficult or frightening to talk to a doctor, especially one you have never met before, but I would like to make it as comfortable for you as possible. Is there anything that you can put your finger on that is making it tough for you to talk to me?"

Another important initial question is, "Why now?" The physician should be clear about why the patient has chosen this particular time to ask for help. The reason may be as simple as that this was the first available appointment time. Very often, however, people seek out doctors as the result of particular events in their lives that have led to an increase in stress. These stressful events may be thought of as precipitants and are often significant contributors to the patient's current problems. Examples of stressful precipitants include real or symbolic losses (e.g., death or separations), milestone events (e.g., significant birthdays), and physical changes (e.g., initiation of a new diet, intake of a new drug). Physicians who are unaware of such stresses in a person's life may miss unspoken fears and questions that can compromise the patient's care and well-being.

The Interview Proper

In the interview proper the physician discovers in greater detail what is troubling the patient. The physician must do this in a systematic way that facilitates the identification of relevant problems in the context of an ongoing empathic working alliance with the patient.

Content versus process. The *content* of an interview is literally what is said between the doctor and the patient: the topics discussed, subjects mentioned. The *process* of the interview is what is occurring nonverbally between the doctor and the patient, what is happening in the interview beneath the surface. Process involves feelings and reactions that are unacknowledged or unconscious. For example, a patient may use body language to express feelings he or she cannot express verbally—a clenched fist or nervous tearing at a tissue in the face of an apparently calm outward demeanor. A patient may shift the interview away from an anxiety-provoking subject onto a more neutral topic without realizing that he or she is doing so. A patient may return again and again to a particular topic, regardless of what direction the interview appeared to be taking. Trivial remarks and apparently casual asides may reveal much more serious underlying concerns—for example, "Oh, by the way, a neighbor of mine tells me that he knows someone with the same symptoms as my son, and that person has cancer."

Specific interview techniques

1. Open-ended versus closed-ended questions. The early part of the interview is generally the most open-ended, in that the physician allows the patient to speak as much as possible in his or her own words. A closed-ended question or more directive question is one that asks for specific information and that does not allow the patient many options in answering. Too many closed-ended questions, especially in the early part of an interview, can lead to a restriction of the patient's responses. Sometimes directive questions are necessary to obtain important data, but, if they are used too often, the patient may think that information is to be given only in response to direct questioning by the doctor. An example of an open-ended question is, "Can you tell me more about that?" A closed-ended question, if the patient states that he or she has been feeling depressed, might be, "Your mother died recently, didn't she?" This question can be answered only by a yes or no response, and the mother's death may or may not be the reason the patient is depressed. More information is likely to be obtained if the doctor responds with, "Tell me more about what you're feeling and what you think may be causing it."

2. Reflection. In this technique the doctor repeats to the patient in a supportive manner something that the patient has said. The purpose of reflection is twofold: to assure the doctor that he or she has correctly understood what the patient is trying to say and to let the patient know that the doctor is perceiving what is being said. It is an empathic response meant to allow the patient to know that the doctor is both listening to and understanding the patient's concerns. For example, the patient is speaking about fears of dying and the impact of talking about these fears with his or her family. The doctor may say, "It seems as though you are concerned with becoming a burden to your family." This reflection is not an exact repetition of what the patient has said but, rather, a paraphrase that indicates that the doctor has perceived what the patient is trying to say.

3. Facilitations. The doctor helps the patient continue in the interview by providing both verbal and nonverbal cues that encourage the patient to keep talking. Nodding one's head, leaning forward in one's seat, saying, "Yes, and then. . . ?" or, "Uh-huh, go on" are all examples of facilitations.

4. Silence. Silence can be used in many ways in normal conversations, even to indicate disapproval or disinterest. However, in the doctor-patient relationship, silence may be constructive in certain situations to allow the patient to contemplate, to cry, or just to sit in an accepting, supportive environment where it is made clear that not every moment must be filled with talk.

5. Confrontations. This technique is meant to point out to a patient something that the doctor feels the patient is not paying attention to, is missing, or is in some way denying. Confrontation must be done in a skillful way, so that the patient is not forced to become hostile and defensive. The confrontation is meant to help the patient face whatever needs to be faced in a direct but respectful way. For example, a patient who has just made a suicidal gesture but is telling the doctor that it is not serious may be confronted with the statement, "What you have done may not have killed you, but it's telling me that you are in serious trouble right now and that you need help so that this doesn't happen again."

6. Clarifications. Here the doctor attempts to get more details from the patient about what the patient has already said: "You are feeling depressed. When is it that you feel most depressed?"

7. Interpretations. This technique is most often used when the doctor states something about the patient's behavior or thought that the patient may not be aware of. It follows up on the doctor's careful listening to underlying themes and patterns in the patient's story. Interpretations usually help to clarify interrelationships that the patient may not have been seeing. This technique is a sophisticated one and should generally be utilized only after the doctor has established some rapport with the patient and has a reasonably good idea of what some of the interrelationships are. An example is, "When you talk about how angry you are that your family has not been supportive, I think you're also telling me how worried you are that I won't be there for you either. What do you think?"

8. Summations. Periodically during the interview, the doctor can take a moment and briefly summarize what the patient has said thus far. This assures the patient and the doctor that the information the doctor has heard is the same as what the patient has actually said: "Okay, I just want to make sure that I've gotten everything right up to this point. . . ."

9. Explanations. The doctor explains the treatment plan to the patient in easily understandable language and allows the patient to respond and ask questions: "It is critical that you come into the hospital now because of the seriousness of your condition. You will be admitted tonight through the emergency room, and I will be there to make all the arrangements. You will be given a small dose of medication that will make you sleepy. The medication is called Halcion, and the dose you will be getting is 0.125 mg. I will see you again first thing in the morning, and we'll go over all the procedures that will be required before anything else happens [etc., etc.]. . . Now, what are your questions? I know you must have some."

10. Transitions. This technique allows the doctor to convey the idea that enough information has been obtained on one subject; it encourages the patient to continue on to another subject. For example, "You've given me a very good sense of that particular time in your life. It would be good now if you told me a bit more about an even earlier time in your life."

11. Self-revelations. Limited, discreet self-disclosure by the physician may be useful in certain situations. It is important for the physician to feel natural and to communicate a sense of self-comfort. Conveying this may involve answering questions from the patient about whether he or she is married and where he or she comes from. However, a doctor who practices self-revelation excessively is using the patient to fulfill certain unfilled needs in his or her own life and is abusing the role of physician. If the doctor feels that some piece of information will help the patient be more comfortable, the doctor can decide in each case whether to be self-revealing. It depends on whether the information will further the patient's care or whether it will provide nothing useful. Even if the doctor decides that self-revelation is not warranted, he or she should be careful not to make the patient feel embarrassed for asking: "I'm not sure whether you are really asking if I'm married. Let's talk about it a little more so that I can understand why that information is important to you. Maybe it has more to do with some concerns you have about my commitment to your care." Or, "I am married, but let's talk a little about why it was important for you to know that. If we talk about it, I'll have a bit more information about who you are and what your concerns are regarding me and my involvement in your care." Perhaps the important point here is not to take questions from patients just at face value. Many questions, especially personal ones, besides conveying natural curiosity about the doctor, often contain hidden concerns that should not be ignored.

12. Positive reinforcement. This technique allows the patient to feel comfortable telling the doctor anything, even about such things as noncompliance with treatment. The doctor encourages the patient to feel that the doctor will not be upset by whatever the patient has to say and thereby facilitates an open exchange: "I appreciate your telling me that you have stopped taking your medication. Can you tell me what the problem was with the medication? The more I know what's going on with you, the better I'll be able to treat you in a way that you will feel comfortable with."

13. Reassurance. Truthful reassurance of a patient can lead to increased trust and compliance and can be experienced as an empathic response of a concerned physician. False reassurance, on the other hand, means, essentially, lying to the patient and can badly impair trust and compliance. False reassurance is often given in the desire to make a patient feel better, but, once a patient knows that the doctor has not told the truth, he or she is less likely to accept or believe truthful reassurance. In an example of false reassurance, a patient with a terminal illness asks, "Am I going to be all right, doctor?" and the doctor responds, "Of course, you'll be all right; everything is fine." In an example of truthful reassurance, the doctor responds, "I am going to do everything I can to make you feel as comfortable as possible, and part of being comfortable is for you to know as much as I know about what is going on with you. We both know that what you have is very serious. I'd like to know exactly what you think is happening to you and to clarify any questions or confusion you have."

14. Advice. In many situations it is not only acceptable but desirable for the physician to give advice to a patient. To be effective and to be perceived as empathic, rather than as inappropriate or intrusive, this advice should be given only after the patient is allowed to talk freely about whatever the problem is in order to give the physician an adequate information base from which to make suggestions. At times, after the doctor has listened carefully to a patient, it is clear that the patient does not, in fact, want advice as much as an objective, caring, nonjudgmental ear. Giving advice too quickly can lead the patient to feel that the doctor is not really listening but, rather, is responding either out of anxiety or from the belief that the doctor inherently knows better than the patient what should be done in a particular situation. In an example of advice given too quickly, the patient states, "I cannot take this medication; it's bothering me," and the physician responds, "Fine. I think you should stop taking it, and I'll start you on something new." A more appropriate response would be, "I'm sorry to hear that. Tell me what about the medication is bothering you so that I have a better idea of what we may do to make you feel more comfortable." In another example the patient states, "I've really been feeling down lately," and the doctor responds, "Well, I think in that case it would be a good idea for you to go out and really do some things that are fun, like going to the movies or walking in the park." In this case a more appropriate and helpful response would be, "Tell me what you mean by 'feeling down.' The more I know about what you're feeling, the more likely it will be that I can help."

Interviewing Psychotic Patients

Psychotic patients often have limited insight, are more concrete than abstract in their thinking, and are not always psychologically minded or introspective. In fact, many psychotic patients experience insight and introspection as very frightening and threatening, because their perceptions are distorted and they are unable to integrate certain feelings, fantasies, and ideas about themselves without decompensating (becoming more psychotic). Their internal psychological makeup is fragile or vulnerable, and certain psychological insights can impose too much stress for them. If a psychotic person can tolerate certain degrees of insight and introspection, this should be encouraged, although for the most part the physician's role with a psychotic person is a supportive, rather than an insight-oriented, one. This support, in part, involves increasing the person's ability to reality-test (to differentiate between fantasy and reality). Insight-oriented interventions often trigger disturbing fantasies. Psychotic patients also often experience what has been termed the "need-fear dilemma," in which they experience both an overwhelming loneliness and need for contact with others and a profound fear that contact with others is dangerous, overwhelming, and destructive.

Specific therapy techniques to be used with psychotic patients are discussed at greater length in Chapter 29, "Psychotherapies," and in the chapters on the psychotic disorders. Some of these techniques involve the following: (1) Do not attempt to talk a person out of a delusional belief. (2) Do not laugh at bizarre, psychotic material that may sound funny but is clearly not meant to be funny. (3) Maintain a certain formality with the patient, such that he or she does not feel threatened by what is perceived as frightening closeness. (4) Focus on concrete, day-to-day survival and social skills. (5) Decrease pressure on the patient to achieve more than he or she may feel capable of achieving (including answering interview questions). (6) Structure the interview sessions so that the patient knows what to expect and is not left, for instance, with long periods of silence if these periods seem to increase anxiety. (7) Be extremely sensitive to how easily humiliated or shamed these patients may feel over relatively minor inadequacies (such as the inability to remember a past medication).

Concluding the Interview

The doctor wants the patient to leave the interview feeling understood and respected and feeling that all the pertinent and important information has been conveyed to an informed, empathic listener. To that end, the doctor should give the patient a chance to ask questions and should let the patient know as much as possible about the plans for the future. The doctor should thank the patient for sharing the necessary information and let the patient know that the information conveyed has been helpful in clarifying the next steps. Any prescription of medication should be clearly and simply spelled out, and the doctor should ascertain whether the patient understands the prescription and how to take it. The doctor should make another appointment or give a referral and give some indication as to how the patient can reach help quickly if it is necessary before the next appointment.

COMPLIANCE

Compliance, also known as adherence, is the degree to which a patient carries out the clinical recommendations of the treating physician. Examples include keeping appointments, entering into and completing a treatment program, taking medications correctly, and following recommended changes in behavior or diet. Compliance behavior depends on the specific clinical situation, the nature of the illness, and the treatment program. In general, approximately one-third of patients comply with treatment, one-third sometimes comply with certain aspects of treatment, and one-third never comply with treatment. An overall figure assessed from a number of studies indicates that 54 percent of patients comply with treatment at any given time. One study found that up to 50 percent of hypertensive patients do not follow up at all with treatment and that 50 percent of those who do follow up leave treatment within one year.

In an attempt to understand why such a high percentage of patients fail to comply regularly, a number of variables have been investigated. For example, an increased complexity of regimen, plus an increased number of required behavioral changes, appear to be associated with noncompliance. Psychiatric patients also exhibit a higher degree of noncompliant behavior than do medical patients. However, there is no clear association between compliance and the patient's sex, marital status, race, religion, socioeconomic status, intelligence, or educational level. Compliance is increased by such physician characteristics as enthusiasm, permissiveness, age, experience, time spent talking to the patient, and short waiting room time.

The doctor-patient relationship, or what has been termed the doctor-patient "match," is the most important factor in compliance issues. When the doctor and the patient have different priorities and beliefs, different styles of communication (including a different understanding of medical advice), and different medical expectations, the patient's compliance diminishes. Compliance can be increased if the physician explains the value to the patient of a particular treatment outcome and that following the recommendation will produce that outcome. Compliance can also increase if the patient knows the names and the effects of each drug he or she is taking. A highly significant factor in compliance seems to be the patient's subjective feeling of distress or illness, as opposed to the doctor's often more objective, medical estimate of the disease and required therapy. The patient must believe that he or she is ill. Thus, asymptomatic patients, such as those with hypertension, are at greater risk for noncompliance than are patients with symptoms. Simply stated, when there are problems in communciation, compliance decreases; when there is effective communication, coupled with close patient supervision and the patient's subjective sense of satisfaction that the doctor has met expectations, compliance increases.

Studies have shown that noncompliance is associated with doctors who are perceived as rejecting and unfriendly. Noncompliance is also associated with asking a patient for information without giving feedback and with failing to explain a diagnosis or the cause of the presenting symptoms. A doctor who is aware of the patient's belief system, feelings, and habits and who enlists the patient in establishing a treatment regimen will increase compliant behavior.

Strategies suggested to improve compliance include asking patients directly to describe what they themselves believe is wrong with them, what they believe should be done, what they understand about what the doctor believes should be done, and what they believe to be the risks and benefits of following the prescribed treatment. Common errors are patients' not taking medications as often or as long as they are supposed to and not taking the right number of pills or treatments. Patients are generally noncompliant if they have to take more than three types of medications a day or if their medications must be taken more than four times a day. Purely verbal instructions by the doctor or the presentation of treatment prescriptions to the patient in the few hours immediately before being discharged from the hospital is associated with increased error and noncompliance. Elderly persons who may have trouble hearing or reading small type may become noncompliant if they cannot hear verbal instructions or read prescription labels. In these instances, it has proved helpful to print the instructions on a piece of paper, ask the patient to read them back, ask if there are any questions, and ask the patient to explain when specifically and in what amounts the medication is to be taken. Sometimes instead of making errors, patients deliberately change the treatment regimen—for example, by not showing up for appointments or by taking medications in a manner different from that recommended. In these instances, in which there may be competing pressures from family or work or lack of understanding about the details of the doctor's advice, the doctor needs to negotiate a compromise with the patient, what has been termed a "patient contract." In this case, the doctor and the patient together specify what they can expect from each other. Implicit in this approach is the idea that the contract can be renegotiated, and the patient can be assured that suggestions can be made by either the doctor or the patient to improve compliance.

SPECIFIC ISSUES

Fees

Before an ongoing relationship with a patient can be established, certain issues must be addresed by the physician. For instance, the matter of payment or fees must be openly discussed from the beginning: the doctors' charges; whether the doctor is willing to accept insurance company payments directly (known as assignment); the doctor's policy concerning payment for missed appointments; and whether the doctor utilizes a sliding scale based on ability to pay. Discussing these questions and any others about fees from the very beginning of the relationship between doctor and patient can minimize misunderstandings later.

Confidentiality

The doctor should discuss the extent and the limitations of confidentiality with the patient, so that the patient is clear about what can and cannot remain confidential. As much as one must legally and ethically respect a patient's confidentiality, in some situations confidentiality may be either partially or wholly broken. The doctor must make the patient aware of these situations in order to avoid mistrust. For instance, if a patient makes clear that he or she intends to harm another person violently, the doctor has a legal responsibility to warn the intended victim. (See Chapter 46, "Forensic Psychiatry," for further discussion of the issue of confidentiality.) Other examples of issues related to confidentiality involve the patient's medical record and who has access to it; the extent of the information required by particular insurance companies (which may be highly detailed); and the degree, if any, to which a patient's case will be used in teaching medical students, residents, or others. In all such situations the patient must give prior permission.

Use of Supervisors

It is both commonplace and necessary for doctors in training to receive supervision from more experienced physicians. In large teaching hospitals this is the norm, and most patients are aware of this. If a young doctor is receiving supervision from a senior physician, the patient should know this from the beginning. This is particularly important in psychiatry, in which the supervision of individual psychotherapy cases is a routine and established practice, and the psychiatric resident is required to present verbatim accounts of an entire therapy session (process notes) to a senior supervisor. If a patient is curious about the level of experience of the doctor, the doctor or medical student should respond honestly and not mislead the patient. If the doctor is less than truthful and the patient discovers this later, the relationship between doctor and patient may become untenable.

Session Length and Missed Appointments

Patients need to be informed about the doctor's policies regarding the length of each session and the issue of missed appointments. Psychiatrists, for example, generally see patients in regularly scheduled blocks of 20 to 45 minutes; at the end of that time, it is expected that the patient will accept the fact that the session is over. Nonpsychiatric physicians may schedule somewhat differently, putting aside 30 minutes to an hour for an initial visit, then perhaps scheduling patient visits every 15 to 20 minutes for follow-up appointments. A psychiatrist who is treating a psychotic inpatient may determine that the patient cannot tolerate a lengthy session and decide to see the patient in a series of 10-minute sessions throughout the day. Whatever the doctor's policy is, the patient must be made aware of it, so that misunderstandings do not occur.

The same can be said for the doctor's policy on missed appointments, about which the patient must be informed. Some doctors deal with the issue of missed appointments by asking the patient to give 24 hours' notice to avoid being billed for a missed session. Other doctors bill for missed sessions regardless of notice. Still other doctors decide on a case-by-case basis, perhaps stating a 24-hour rule but making exceptions when warranted. Some doctors state that, if they receive notice and can fill the vacated time with another patient, they will not charge for the missed appointment; some doctors do not charge for missed appointments at all. The decision is up to the individual physician, but the patient must know the doctor's policy in advance so that an informed decision can be made about whether to accept the policy or to choose another doctor.

Doctor-Patient Interaction Between Scheduled Appointments

What is the doctor's obligation to be available to patients in between scheduled appointments? Is it incumbent on the physician to be available 24 hours a day? Once a patient enters into a contract to receive care from a particular physician, it is the physician's responsibility to have a mechanism in place by which the patient can receive help if an emergency occurs outside the time of scheduled appointments. The patient should be explicitly informed what this mechanism is, whether it is an emergency phone number or a covering physician. If a physician is going to be away for any length of time, coverage by another physician must be obtained and the patient informed as to how to reach the covering doctor. It is always well advised to let patients know that the doctor will be available between appointments to answer pressing questions and that, if necessary, extra appointments can be scheduled. Within these general parameters, however, physicians must make their own individual decisions about their availability to specific patients. In some cases it may be necessary for the doctor to place firm limits on availability between sessions. For instance, patients who repeatedly call at all hours with concerns that are best addressed in the context of a regularly scheduled appointment should be gently but definitely encouraged to bring up their concerns during scheduled sessions. The doctor in such a case might reassure the patient that all concerns will be addressed and that, if there is not enough time during the regularly scheduled time, another appointment can be made but that nonemergency concerns will be postponed until the appointment.

Continuing Care

Many events can occur to disrupt the continuity of the doctor-patient relationship; some of these events are quite routine (such as when a resident ends training and moves on to another hospital); others are more out of the ordinary and thus less predictable (such as when the physician becomes ill and can no longer take care of his or her patients). The patient must be able to feel assured that, regardless of what occurs in the course of a particular doctor-patient relationship, the patient's care will be ongoing. If the doctor is a resident and will be serving as the patient's doctor for a finite amount of time, the doctor should be explicit about this at the beginning of treatment. At the same time the resident can make clear to the patient that, when he or she moves on, the patient's care will continue, albeit with a new doctor. It may help in terms of a sense of continuity if the departing resident introduces the incoming resident to the patient.

A more complex situation arises when a physician becomes ill and is unable to continue caring for patients. If the physician knows in advance that he or she is going to have to interrupt therapy, clear arrangements for referral to and coverage by other physicians can be made. Although there are arguments for both revealing and not revealing the physician's illness to patients, it seems best to inform patients truthfully why the doctor is discontinuing therapy. This information can and should be conveyed in as calm and nonthreatening a way as possible. The risk in not telling patients the truth is that many patients may develop fantasies to explain why the doctor has stopped seeing them, including the fear that something about them made the doctor want to leave. Nontruthfulness in this situation also encourages the view that there is something shameful or very frightening about being ill and the feeling that a doctor who cannot discuss or handle his or her own illness should not expect the patient to be able to. However, it is not the role of a patient to take care of his or her doctor; informing patients should not carry with it any sense that the doctor's illness is the patient's burden.

Difficult Patients

In the subsection on countertransference earlier in this chapter, some types of patients who may be particularly problematic for physicians were discussed. In addition to these patients, a number of other types of patients require particular skill on the part of any physician. These patients can create undue stress if they are not managed effectively. Inherent in the management of all these patients is the doctor's understanding of the covert emotions, fears, and conflicts that the patient's overt behavior represents. An appropriate understanding of what is hidden behind a particular patient's difficult behavior will lead the doctor away from responding with anger, contempt, or anxiety and toward responding with helpful interventions. Some examples follow.

1. Histrionic. These patients are often seductive with doctors out of an unconscious need for reassurance that they are still attractive even if ill and out of fear that they will not be taken seriously unless they are found to be sexually desirable. They often appear overly emotional and intimate in their interactions with doctors. The physician needs to be calm, reassuring, firm, and nonflirtatious. These patients do not really want to seduce the physician, but they may not know any other way to get what they feel they need. Further issues related to sexuality and the physician were discussed earlier in the subsection on countertransference.

2. Demanding and dependent. These patients need a tremendous amount of reassurance and yet are often resistant to any and all offers of such. These are the patients who are most likely to make repeated, urgent calls in between scheduled appointments and to demand that the doctor provide special attention. They often become angry or frightened if they perceive that the doctor is not taking their concerns seriously. The doctor must be prepared to set necessary limits but within the context of an expressed willingness to listen to and care for the patient.

3. Demanding and impulsive. These patients have a difficult time delaying gratification and may become extremely demanding about having their discomfort eliminated immediately. They are easily frustrated and may become petulant or even angry and aggressive if they do not get what they want as soon as they want it. These patients may impulsively do something self-destructive if they feel thwarted by the doctor and may appear manipulative and attention-seeking. What they may be feeling underneath these surface manifestations includes the fear that they will never get what they need from others and, thus, must act in this inappropriately aggressive way. These can be particularly difficult patients for any doctor to treat; the doctor must set firm, nonangry limits from the outset, defining clearly acceptable and unacceptable behavior. The patient will be treated with respect and care but will also be held responsible for his or her actions.

4. Narcissistic. These patients act as though they were superior to everyone around them, including the doctor. They have a tremendous need to appear perfect and are contemptuous of others, whom they perceive to be imperfect. They may be rude, abrupt, arrogant, or demeaning. They may initially overidealize the physician in their need to have their doctor be as perfect as they are, but the overidealization may quickly turn to disdain when they discover the doctor to be human. Underneath their surface arrogance, these patients often feel inadequate, helpless, and empty, and they fear that others will see through them.

5. Obsessive and controlling. These patients are very orderly, punctual, and overconcerned with detail. They often appear unemotional, even aloof, especially with regard to anything potentially disturbing or frightening. They may be resistant to any perceived control on the part of the doctor, as they have such a strong need of their own to be in control of everything in their environment. Underneath, these patients are, in reality, often frightened of losing control and of being dependent and helpless. Physicians must be prepared to strengthen these patients' sense of control by including them as much as possible in their own care and treatment. Doctors should explain in detail what is going on and what is being planned.

6. Hypervigilant and paranoid. These patients fear that people want to hurt them and are out to do them harm. They may misperceive cues in their environment to the degree that they see conspiracies in neutral events. They are critical, evasive, and suspicious. They are often called grievance-seekers, because they tend to blame others for everything bad that happens in their lives. They are extremely mistrustful and may question everything the doctor says needs to be done. The doctor must remain somewhat formal, albeit always respectful and courteous, with these patients, as expressions of warmth and empathy are often viewed with suspicion ("what does he want from me?"). As with the obsessive patient, the doctor should be prepared to explain in detail every decision and planned procedure and should react nondefensively to the patient's suspicions.

7. Isolated and solitary. Termed "schizoid personalities," these patients appear detached and reclusive, not appearing to need or want much contact with other human beings. Intimate contact with a doctor is viewed with distaste by these patients, who would prefer to take care of themselves entirely on their own if they could. The doctor should treat these patients with as much respect for privacy as possible and should not expect them to respond to his or her concern in kind.

8. Complaining, martyrlike, and passive-aggressive. These patients appear to communicate solely through a litany of complaints and disappointments. They often covertly blame others for all their problems, and they make others feel guilty about not doing or caring enough. They are often not able to express angry feelings directly and thus express them indirectly or passively by being late for appointments or not making their payments on time. They often perceive themselves as being extremely self-sacrificing and as being taken advantage of by others, who are selfish. These patients may, in fact, unconsciously believe that the only way to be taken seriously or to be cared for or loved is to be sick. The doctor must attempt to be patient and tolerant with these patients, as difficult as it can sometimes be. Doctors should take such patients' concerns seriously but without encouraging the sick role; this most often means that firm limits must be set on the doctor's availability (just as with the overly dependent patient). At the same time, doctors should reassure these patients that they will listen to them during frequent, regularly scheduled appointments. With this type of patient, the doctor must often be involved with the patient's family; family members are dealing with the patient's difficult style every day and are likely to be angry, frustrated, and guilty themselves.

9. Sociopathic and malingering. Sociopathic patients are those described in psychiatric terminology as being antisocial personalities; these people appear not to experience appropriate guilt and, in fact, may not even be consciously aware of what it means to be guilty. On the surface they may appear quite charming, socially adept, and intelligent, but they have over many years perfected the behaviors they know to be appropriate, and they perform them almost as an actor would. They often have histories of criminal acts, and they get by in the world through lying and manipulation. They are often self-destructive, harming not only others but themselves in perhaps an unacknowledged expression of self-punishment. Sociopathic patients often malinger, which is the term for consciously feigning illness for some clear secondary gain (for example, to obtain drugs, to get a bed for the night, or to hide out from people pursuing them). Obviously, these people get sick, just as nonsociopathic people do, and, when they are sick, they need to be cared for in the same ways others do. They must be treated with respect but with a heightened sense of vigilance on the doctor's part. These patients can inspire fear in others, often legitimately so, as many have violent histories. Doctors who feel threatened by patients should unashamedly seek assistance and not feel compelled to see the patients alone. Firm limits must be set as to appropriate behavior (e.g., no drugs in the hospital, no sexual activity with other patients), and the consequences of transgressing must be firmly stated and adhered to (e.g., discharge from the hospital if medically stable, isolation if not). If inappropriate behavior is discovered, these patients must be confronted directly and nonangrily, and they must be held responsible for their actions.

SPECIFIC STRESSES ON PHYSICIANS

A trained physician not only has learned the knowledge base and the techniques of the profession but also must confront, resolve, and incorporate a number of significant attitudinal issues involved in becoming a skilled and effective physician. These issues encompass the ideals of balancing compassionate concern with dispassionate objectivity; the wish to relieve pain and distress with the ability to make difficult, often painful decisions; and the desire to cure or control with the acceptance of the limits on what one can realistically accomplish. Learning to balance these interrelated aspects of the physician's role is essential in allowing the doctor to withstand, in a graceful and life-affirming way, daily work that involves continual confrontation of illness, pain, sadness, fear, suffering, vulnerability, and death. A lack of balance can lead a physician to feel overwhelmed, depressed, and burned-out. A sense of futility and failure can begin to permeate the physician's attitude, setting the stage for anger and frustration about one's profession, patients, and self. Many physicians are at risk for developing this lack of balance because of particular personality and coping styles prevalent among those drawn to the practice of medicine. For instance, many medical students have been observed to be perfectionistic, controlling, and obsessive. These traits can certainly be adaptive for physicians if balanced with healthy doses of self-knowledge, humility, humor, and kindness. If the balance is absent, many physicians travel the path of dispassion at the expense of compassion, willingness to be in charge at the expense of being supportive, and have a diminished capacity to tolerate the limits of what one can realistically and honestly accomplish.

References

Balint M: *The Doctor, the Patient, and the Illness.* International Universities Press, New York, 1964.

Billings J A, Stoeckle J D: *The Clinical Encounter: A Guide to the Medical Interview and Case Presentation.* Year Book Medical Publishers, Chicago, 1989.

Brett A S, et al.: When patients request specific interventions: Defining the limit of the physician's obligation. N Engl J Med *315*: 315, 1986.

Engel G L: The clinical application of the biopsychosocial model. Am J Psychiatry, *137*: 535, 1980.

Freud S: The dynamics of transference. In *The Standard Edition of the Complete Works of Sigmund Freud. 12*: 99, Hogarth Press, London, 1958.

Freud S: Recommendations to physicians practicing psychoanalysis (1912). In *The Standard Edition of the Complete Psychological Works of Sigmund Freud. 12*: 109, Hogarth Press, London, 1974.

Hall, J A, Dornan M C: What patients like about their medical care and how often they are asked: A meta-analysis of the satisfaction literature. Soc Sci Med *27*: 935, 1988.

Korsch B, Negrete V: Doctor-patient communication. Sci Am, *227*: 66, 1972.

Lane F E: Utilizing physician empathy with violent patients. Am J Psychother *40*: 448, 1986.

Leigh H, Reiser M F: *The Patient: Biological, Psychological, and Social Dimensions of Medical Practice.* Plenum, New York, 1980.

Leon R L: *Psychiatric Interviewing: A Primer,* ed 2. Elsevier, New York, 1989.

Lipkin M Jr: Psychiatry and medicine, In *Comprehensive Textbook of Psychiatry,* ed 5, H I Kaplan and B J Sadock, editors, p 1280. Williams & Wilkins, Baltimore, 1989.

Mishler E G, Clark J A, Ingelfinger J, Simon M P: The language of attentive patient care: A comparison of two medical interviews. J Gen Intern Med *4*: 325, 1989.

Omer H: Enhancing the impact of therapeutic interventions. Am J Psychother *44*: 218, 1990.

Quill T: Partnerships in patient care: a contractual approach. Ann Intern Med *98*: 228, 1983.

Reiser D E, Rosen D H: *Medicine as a Human Experience.* University Park Press, Baltimore, 1984.

Reiser D E, Schroder A K: *Patient Interviewing: The Human Dimension.* Williams & Wilkins, Baltimore, 1980.

Roter D L, Hall J A: Studies of doctor-patient interaction. Annu Rev Public Health *10*: 163, 1989.

Shea S C: *Psychiatric Interviewing: The Art of Understanding.* Saunders, Philadelphia, 1988.

Stoffelmayr B, Hoppe R B, Weber N: Facilitating patient participation: The doctor-patient encounter. Prim Care *16*: 265, 1989.

Wilson J: Patients' wants vs. patients' interests. J Med Ethics *12*: 127, 1986.

Human Development Throughout the Life Cycle

2.1 / Overview of the Life Cycle and Normality

The life cycle represents the stages through which all humans pass from birth to death. The fundamental assumption of all life cycle theories is that development occurs in successive, clearly defined stages. This sequence is invariant; that is, it occurs in a particular order in every person's life, whether or not all stages are completed. A second assumption of life cycle theory is the *epigenetic principle*, which maintains that each stage is characterized by events or crises that must be satisfactorily resolved in order for development to proceed smoothly. According to the epigenetic model, if resolution is not achieved within a given life period, all subsequent stages reflect that failure in the form of physical, cognitive, social, or emotional maladjustment. A third assumption is that each phase of the life cycle contains a dominant feature, a complex of features, or a crisis point that distinguishes it from phases that either preceded or will follow it.

The charting of the life cycle lies within the study of developmental psychology and involves such diverse elements as biological maturity, psychological capacity, adaptive techniques, defense mechanisms, symptom complexes, role demands, social behavior, cognition, perception, language development, and interpersonal relationships. The various models of the life cycle describe the major developmental phases but emphasize different elements. Taken together, however, they demonstrate that there is an order in the course of human life, despite the fact that each person's life is unique. As Theodore Lidz, a major exponent of life cycle theory, commented: "The journey from the womb to adulthood and then through maturity into old age is lengthy, circuitous, and beset by countless contingencies."

No common language clearly defines the stages of the life cycle, and no standard vocabulary describes the major developmental phases. A phase of the cycle may be described by various terms, including stage, season, period, era, epoch, and life stage. These terms are conceptually congruent in general and can be used interchangeably.

CONTRIBUTIONS TO LIFE CYCLE THEORY

Current thinking about the human life cycle has been shaped by a handful of highly influential sources. The dominant work on the subject remains the developmental scheme introduced by Sigmund Freud in 1915. Freud's theory, which focused on the childhood period, was organized around his libido theory. According to Freud, childhood phases of development correspond to successive shifts in the investment of sexual energy to areas of the body usually associated with eroticism: the mouth, the anus, and the genitalia. He discerned developmental periods that were accordingly classified as follows: oral phase, birth to 1 year; anal phase, age 1 to 3 years; and phallic phase, age 3 to 5 years.

Freud also described a fourth period, latency, which extends from age 5 to 6 years until puberty. Latency is marked by a diminution of sexual interest, which is reactivated at puberty. The basic outlook expressed by Freud was that the successful resolution of these childhood phases is essential to normal adult functioning. By comparison, what happens in adulthood is of relatively little consequence.

Many followers of Freud modified or built on his conceptualizations while adhering to his focus on sexual energy as the quality that distinguishes the stages of development. Karl Abraham, for example, subdivided the phases of psychosexual development and linked certain adult personality types to difficulties in resolving one of these specific periods.

Although Melanie Klein adhered to Freud's basic formulations, she saw developmental events as occurring more rapidly. The basic premise of Klein's work—like that of Freud's and Abraham's—is that internal processes are the fundamental determinants of personality development and, thus, are the moving forces in the human life cycle.

Alternatively, Carl Jung viewed external factors as playing an important role in personal growth and adaptation. He further held that personality development occurs throughout life and is not firmly determined by early childhood experiences.

Harry Stack Sullivan took that view even further. He approached the issue of the life cycle by stating that human development is largely shaped by external events, specifically by social interaction. His influential model of the life cycle states that each phase of development is marked by a need for interaction with certain other people. The quality of that interaction influences the personality of the individual. Sullivan distinguished the stages or eras of normal development as follows: Infancy, birth to the beginning of language (1½ to 2 years); childhood, language to the need for compeers (2 to 5 years); juvenile era, the need for peers and the beginning of formal education to preadolescence (5 to 9 years); preadolescence, the beginning of the capacity for intimate relationships with peers of the opposite or same sex until genital maturity (9 to 12 years); adolescence, the eruption of true genital interest to the patterning of sexual behavior; and maturity, the establishment of a fully human or mature repertoire of interpersonal relationships, the development of self-respect, and the capacity for intimate and collaborative relationships and loving attitudes.

Erik Erikson (Figure 2.1-1) accepted Freud's theory of infantile sexuality but also saw developmental potentials at all stages of life. Indeed, Erikson constructed a model of the life cycle consisting of eight stages that extend into adulthood and old age (Figure 2.1-2). Erikson's succession of stages is summarized below, along with the dominant issue or maturational crisis that arises during each period.

1. Oral-sensory stage: trust versus mistrust
2. Muscular-anal stage: autonomy versus shame and doubt
3. Locomotor-genital stage: initiative versus guilt
4. Stage of latency: industry versus inferiority
5. Stage of puberty and adolescence: ego identity versus role confusion
6. Stage of young adulthood: intimacy versus isolation
7. Stage of adulthood: generativity versus stagnation
8. Stage of maturity: ego integrity versus despair

Figure 2.1-1. Erik Erikson.

Margaret Mahler, who studied early childhood object relations, made a significant contribution to the understanding of personality development. She described the separation-individuation process, resulting in a person's subjective sense of separateness from the world around him or her. The separation-individuation phase of development begins in the fourth or fifth month of life and is completed by age 3 years. Mahler delineated four subphases of the separation-individuation process:

1. Differentiation. The child is able to distinguish between self and other objects (5 to 10 months).

2. Practicing period. In the early phase, the children discover the ability to physically separate themselves from their mothers by crawling and climbing but still require their mothers' presence for security. The later phase is characterized by free, upright locomotion (10 to 16 months).

3. Rapprochement. Increased need and desire for the mother to share the child's new skills and experiences. Also, a great need for the mother's love (16 to 24 months of age).

4. Consolidation and object constancy. Achievement of a definite individuality and attainment of a certain degree of object-constancy (24 to 36 months).

Jean Piaget's developmental psychology also influenced the study of the life cycle and had interesting similarities to both the psychoanalytic and the academic disciplines. In deriving general principles from the intensive study of a relatively few children, he used an approach resembling that of psychoanalytic inquiry. By concentrating on normal development and using structured tasks (e.g., multiple experiments with each case), he used a scientific method. Jean Piaget's stages of sensorimotor development, preoperational thinking, and concrete and formal operational thought have been a dominant theory of cognition and are discussed in detail in Section 4.1.

Daniel Levinson and his coworkers at Yale University focused on personality development over the life course. In a major study they set out to clarify the issues and the characteristics of male personality development in early and middle adulthood. A total of 40 men were studied; their ages at the start of the investigation ranged from 35 to 45 years. The resulting observations caused Levinson to postulate a new scheme of the adult phases of the life cycle. He suggested that the life cycle is composed of four major eras, each lasting about 25 years, with some overlap, so that a new era is starting as the previous one is ending. Levinson was able to identify a typical age of onset—that is, the age at which an era most frequently begins. The evolving sequence of eras and their age spans as described by Levinson are childhood and adolescence, birth to 22 years; early adulthood, 17 to 45 years; middle adulthood, 40 to 65 years; and late adulthood, 65 years and beyond. Levinson also identified four- to five-year transitional periods between eras that function as boundary zones during which a person terminates the outgoing era and initiates the incoming one.

George Vaillant and his group studied a cohort of men for over 35 years, starting when they were freshmen at Harvard University. A happy childhood was found to correlate significantly with positive traits in middle life. That was mani-

VIII							INTEGRITY vs. DESPAIR
VII						GENERATIV-ITY vs. STAGNATION	
VI					INTIMACY vs. ISOLATION		
V Temporal Perspective vs. Time Confusion	Self-Certainty vs. Self-Consciousness	Role Experi-mentation vs. Role Fixation	Apprenticeship vs. Work Paralysis	IDENTITY vs. IDENTITY CONFUSION	Sexual Polarization vs. Bisexual Confusion	Leader- and Followership vs. Authority Confusion	Ideological Commitment vs. Confusion of Values
IV			INDUSTRY vs. INFER-IORITY	Task Identi-fication vs. Sense of Futility			
III		INITIATIVE vs. GUILT		Anticipation of Roles vs. Role Inhibition			
II	AUTONOMY vs. SHAME, DOUBT			Will to Be Oneself vs. Self-Doubt			
I TRUST vs. MISTRUST				Mutual Recognition vs. Autistic Isolation			
1	2	3	4	5	6	7	8

Figure 2.1-2. A rather complete formulation of Erikson's view of the components and antecedents of identity. Note how identity takes a central place in the diagram. Row V illustrates both what remains of earlier stages in a successful identity formation and the possible disturbances. Column 5 shows both the successful and the negative forerunners of identity in earlier stages. (From E Erikson: *Identity: Youth and Crisis,* p 94, Norton, New York, 1968, with permission.)

fested by few oral-dependent traits, little psychopathology, the capacity to play, and good object relations.

Vaillant noted that a hierarchy of ego mechanisms was constructed as the men advanced in age. Defenses were organized along a continuum that reflected two aspects of the personality: immaturity versus maturity and psychopathology versus mental health. It was found that the maturity of defenses was related to both psychopathology and objective adaptation to the external environment. Moreover, there were shifts in defensive style as a person matured.

Vaillant concluded that adaptive styles mature over the years and that the maturation depends more on development from within than on changes in the interpersonal environment. He also corroborated Erikson's model of the life cycle.

NORMALITY IN PSYCHIATRY

Recently, psychiatrists have made a concerted effort to define mental health and normality. It was understood implicitly that mental health could be defined as the opposite of mental illness. With such an assumption, the absence of gross psychopathology was often equated with normal behavior. A number of recent trends have cast doubt on the usefulness of this assumption and have made it increasingly important for psychiatrists to provide more precise concepts and definitions of mental health and normality.

The many theoretical and clinical concepts of normality seem to fall into four functional perspectives. Although each perspective is unique and has its own definition and description, the perspectives complement each other, and together they represent the totality of the behavioral- and social-science approaches to normality. The four perspectives of normality as formulated by Daniel Offer and Melvin Sabshin are: normality as health, normality as utopia, normality as average, and normality as process.

Normality as Health

The first perspective is basically the traditional medical-psychiatric approach to health and illness. Most physicians equate normality with health and view health as an almost universal phenomenon. Behavior is assumed to be within normal limits when no manifest psychopathology is present. If all behavior were to be put on a scale, normality would encompass the major portion of the continuum, and abnormality would be the small remainder.

This definition of normality correlates with the traditional model of the doctor who attempts to free his patient from grossly observable signs and symptoms. To this physician, the lack of signs or symptoms indicates health. In other words, health in this context refers to a reasonable, rather than an optimal, state of functioning.

Normality as Utopia

The second perspective conceives of normality as that harmonious and optimal blending of the diverse elements of the mental apparatus that culminates in optimal functioning. Such a definition clearly emerges when psychiatrists or psychoanalysts talk about the ideal person or when they discuss their criteria for successful treatment. This approach can be traced directly back to Freud, who, when discussing normality, stated, "A normal ego is like normality in general, an ideal fiction."

Normality as Average

The third perspective is commonly employed in normative studies of behavior and is based on the mathematical principle of the bell-shaped curve. This approach conceives of the middle range as normal and of both extremes as deviant. The normative approach based on this statistical principle describes each person in terms of general assessment and total score. Variability is described only within the context of total groups, not within the context of one person.

Although this approach is more commonly used in psychology and biology than in psychiatry, psychiatrists have recently been using standardized personality pencil-and-paper tests to a much larger extent than in the past. In this model, one assumes that the typologies of character can be statistically measured.

Normality as Process

The fourth perspective stresses that normal behavior is the end result of interacting systems. On the basis of this definition, temporal changes are essential to a complete definition of normality. In other words, the normality-as-process perspective stresses changes or processes, rather than a cross-sectional definition of normality.

Investigators who subscribe to this approach can be found in all the behavioral and social sciences. Most typical of the concepts in this perspective are Erikson's conceptualization of epigenesis of personality development and the eight developmental stages essential in the attainment of mature adult functioning.

Other Parameters of Normality

Efforts are increasing to develop empirical research in the area of normality. Along with their growing involvement in linking normality and social process, psychoanalysts are continuing their long-term interest in elucidating the vicissitudes of the normal psychopathology of everyday life. Psychoanalysts are increasingly demonstrating their interest in normal adaptation to the social environment. For a summary of psychoanalytic concepts of normality, see Table 2.1-1.

Table 2.1-1
Psychoanalytic Concepts of Normality

Theorist	Characteristics
Sigmund Freud	Normality is an ideal fiction.
Kurt Eissler	Absolute normality cannot be obtained because the normal person must be totally aware of his or her thoughts and feelings.
Melanie Klein	Normality is characterized by strength of character, the capacity to deal with conflicting emotions, the ability to experience pleasure without conflict, and the ability to love.
Erik Erikson	Normality is the ability to master the periods of life: trust vs. mistrust; autonomy vs. doubt; initiative vs. guilt; industry vs. inferiority; identity vs. role confusion; intimacy vs. isolation; generativity vs. stagnation; and ego integrity vs. despair.
Laurence Kubie	Normality is the ability to learn by experience, to be flexible, and to adapt to a changing environment.
Heinz Hartmann	Conflict-free ego functions represent the person's potential for normality; the degree the ego can adapt to reality and be autonomous is related to mental health.
Karl Menninger	Normality is the ability to adjust to the external world with contentment and to master the task of acculturation.
Alfred Adler	The person's capacity to develop social feeling and to be productive is related to mental health; the ability to work heightens self-esteem and makes one capable of adaptation.
R. E. Money-Kryle	Normality is the ability to achieve insight into one's self, which is never fully accomplished.
Otto Rank	Normality is the capacity to live without fear, guilt, or anxiety and to take responsibility for one's own actions.

Heinz Hartmann has been a prime mover of this trend by conceptualizing autonomous functions of the ego and the ego's conflict-free sphere. The concept of autonomous and conflict-free functions of the ego has intensified clinical exploration of the mechanisms whereby some persons lead a relatively normal life in the presence of extraordinary external experiential trauma. Discussing the average expectable environment, Hartmann has provided a framework in which the molding of character structure in specific contexts is more easily understood.

Erikson's work also serves as a bridge linking developmental stages and social process. His concept of modal adaptive tasks at phase-specific stages of life provides a process analysis of normal behavior and a cross-sectional analysis of behavior throughout life. Thus, it becomes possible to establish specific modes of adaptation.

Table 2.1-2
A Synthesis of Developmental Theorists

Age (Years)	Margaret Mahler	John Bowlby	Sigmund Freud	Erik Erikson	Jean Piaget
0–1	Normal autistic phase (birth to 4 weeks) • State of half-sleep, half-wake • Major task of phase is to achieve homeostatic equilibrium with the environment Normal symbiotic phase (3–4 weeks to 4–5 months) • Dim awareness of caretaker, but infant still functions as if he or she and caretaker were in state of undifferentiation or fusion • Social smile characteristic (2–4 months) The subphases of separation-individuation proper First subphase: differentiation (5–10 months) • Process of hatching from autistic shell (i.e., developing more alert sensorium that reflects cognitive and neurological maturation) • Beginning of comparative scanning (i.e., comparing what is and what is not mother) • Characteristic anxiety: stranger anxiety, which involves curiosity and fear (most prevalent around 8 months)	Phase I (birth to 8–12 weeks) • Infant's ability to discriminate one person from another is limited to olfactory and auditory stimuli • To any person in infant's vicinity, infant will: –orient to that person –have tracking movements of the eyes –grasp and reach –smile –babble –stop crying on hearing voice or seeing face • These behaviors, by influencing the adult's behavior, are likely to increase time the baby is in proximity to mother (adult) Phase II (8–12 weeks to 6 months or much later, according to circumstances) • Continuation of phase I activities but more marked in relation to mother more specifically Phase III (6–7 months and continues throughout second and into third year) • Attachment to mother figure evident • Following departing mother • Greeting her on her return • Using her as base from which to explore • Waning of friendly, undifferentiated responses	Oral phase (birth to 1 year) • Major site of tension and gratification is the mouth, lips, tongue –includes biting and sucking activities	Basic trust vs. basic mistrust (oral sensory) (birth to 1 year) • Social mistrust demonstrated via ease of feeding, depth of sleep, bowel relaxation • Depends on consistency and sameness of experience provided by caretaker • Second 6-months teething and biting moves infant "from getting to taking" • Weaning leads to "nostalgia for lost paradise" • If basic trust is strong, child maintains hopeful attitude	Sensorimotor phase (birth to 2 years) • Intelligence rests mainly on actions and movements coordinated under "*schemata*," (Schema is a pattern of behavior in response to a particular environmental stimulus.) • Environment is mastered through *assimilation* and *accommodation*. (Assimilation is the incorporation of new environmental stimuli. Accommodation is the modification of behavior to adapt to new stimuli.) • *Object permanence* is achieved by age 2 years. Object still exists in mind if disappears from view: search for hidden object • Reversibility in action begins
1–2	Second subphase: practicing (10–16 months) • Beginning of this phase marked by upright locomotion—child has new perspective and also mood of elation		Anal phase (1-3 years) • Anus and surrounding area are major source of interest • Acquisition of voluntary sphincter control (toilet training)	Autonomy vs. shame and doubt (muscular-anal) (1–3 years) • Biologically includes learning to walk, feed self, talk • Muscular maturation sets	

	• Mother used as home base • Characteristic anxiety: separation anxiety Third subphase: rapprochement (16–24 months) • Infant now a toddler—more aware of physical separateness, which dampens mood of elation • Child tries to bridge gap between self and mother—concretely seen as bringing objects to mother • Mother's efforts to help toddler often not perceived as helpful, temper tantrums typical • Characteristic event: rapprochement crisis: wanting to be soothed by mother and yet not being able to accept her help • Symbol of rapprochement: child standing on threshold of door not knowing which way to turn in helpless frustration • Resolution of crisis occurs as child's skills improve and child is able to get gratification from doing things	to others • Treating strangers with caution, alarm, withdrawal	stage for holding on and letting go • Need for outer control, firmness of caretaker before development of autonomy • *Shame* occurs when child is overtly self-conscious via negative exposure • *Self-doubt* can evolve if parents overly shame child (e.g., about elimination)	
2–3	Fourth subphase: consolidation and object constancy (24–36 months) • Child better able to cope with mother's absence and to engage substitutes • Child can begin to feel comfortable with mother's absences by knowing she will return • Gradual internalization of image of mother as reliable and stable • Through increasing verbal skills and better sense of time, child can tolerate delay and endure separations	Phase IV (from 24 months and beyond) • Mother figure seen as independent • Object seen as persistent in time and space • More complex relationship with mother develops—partnership between mother and child develops, in which child acquires insight into mother's feelings and motives • Child observes mother's behavior and what influences it		Preoperational phase (2–7) years) • Appearance of *symbolic* functions, associated with language acquisition. • *Egocentrism:* child understands everything exclusively from own perspective • Thinking is illogical and magical • Nonreversible thinking with absence of conservation –*Animism:* belief that inanimate objects are alive (i.e., have feelings and intentions –*Immanent justice:* belief that punishment for bad deeds is inevitable

Table 2.1-2
continued

Age (Years)	Margaret Mahler	John Bowlby	Sigmund Freud	Erik Erikson	Jean Piaget
3–4 4–5			Phallic-oedipal phase (3–5 years) • Genital focus of interest, stimulation, and excitement • Penis is organ of interest for both sexes • Genital masturbation common • Intense preoccupation with *castration anxiety* (fear of genital loss or injury) • *Penis envy* (discontent with one's own genitals and wish to possess genitals of male) seen in girls in this phase • *Oedipus complex* universal: child wishes to have sex with and marry parent of opposite sex and simultaneously be rid of parent of same sex	Initiative vs. guilt (locomotor genital) (3–5 years) • *Initiative* arises in relation to tasks for the sake of activity, both motor and intellectual • *Guilt* may arise over goals contemplated (especially aggressive) • Desire to mimic adult world; involvement in oedipal struggle leads to resolution via social role identification • Sibling rivalry frequent	
5–6			Latency phase (from 5–6 years to 11–12 years) • State of relative quiescence of sexual drive with resolution of oedipal complex • Sexual drives channeled into more socially appropriate aims (i.e., schoolwork and sports)		

6–11		• Formation of *superego:* one of three psychic structures in mind that is responsible for moral and ethical development, including conscience • (Other two psychic structures are *ego*, which is a group of functions mediating between the drives and the external environment, and • the *id*, repository of sexual and aggressive drives • The id is there at birth, and the ego develops gradually from rudimentary structure present at birth)	Industry vs. inferiority (latency) (6–11 years) • Child is busy building, creating, accomplishing • Receives systematic instruction and fundamentals of technology • Danger of sense of inadequacy and inferiority if child despairs of his tools, skills, and status among peers • Socially decisive age	Concrete (operational) phase (7–11 years) • Emergence of logical (cause-effect) thinking, including reversibility and ability to sequence and serialize • Understanding of part and whole relationships and classifications • Child able to take other's point of view • Conservation of number, length, weight, and volume
11+		Genital phase (from 11–12 years and beyond) • Final stage of psychosexual development—begins with puberty and the biological capacity for orgasm but involves the capacity for true intimacy	Identity vs. role diffusion (11 years through end of adolescence) • Struggle to develop *ego identity* (sense of inner sameness and continuity) • Preoccupation with appearance, hero worship, ideology • *Group identity* (peers) develops • Danger of *role confusion,* doubts about sexual and vocational identity • *Psychosocial moratorium*, stage between morality learned by the child and the ethics to be developed by the adult	Formal (abstract) phase (11 years through end of adolescence) • Hypothetical-deductive reasoning, not only on basis of objects but also on basis of hypotheses or of propositions • Capable of thinking about one's thoughts • Combinative structures emerge, permitting flexible grouping of elements in a system • Ability to use two systems of reference simultaneously • Ability to grasp concept of probabilities

Table by Sylvia Karasu, M.D., and Richard Oberfield, M.D.

In the area of human development, Anna Freud delineated aspects of normal growth and development in children. Like Erikson, she has been interested in empirical research directed toward helping to clarify how children cope with the variety of adaptive tasks. The understanding of child development has been advanced by a number of longitudinal studies.

The studies by Offer and Sabshin on adolescents are prototypical of this trend. These investigators have studied a group of young adolescents throughout their high school years and have identified three normal types of development: *continuous growth, surgent growth,* and *tumultuous growth.* Although persons typical of these types are different, they are placed along a continuum of normality. Offer and Sabshin have formulated an operational definition of normality that is not absolute but, rather, is descriptive of one type of middle-class adolescent population. The criteria best describing the teenagers are (1) almost complete absence of gross psychopathology, severe physical defects, and severe physical illness; (2) mastery of previous developmental tasks without serious setbacks; (3) ability to experience affects flexibly and to resolve their conflicts actively with reasonable success; (4) relatively good object relationships with parents, siblings, and peers; and (5) feeling a part of a larger cultural environment and being aware of its norms and values.

The developmental approach is also being used by Vaillant and others for adults. Studies of adaptation to marriage, parenthood, work, and leisure activities have become increasingly prominent. Precise empirical studies are being conducted regarding developmental problems in the period of involution and decline.

A controversial view has been taken by Thomas Szasz, who believes that the concept of mental illness should be abandoned entirely. He also states that normality can be measured only in terms of what people do or do not do and that it is actually a problem of ethics.

The development of geriatrics has moved in a more normative direction. The deficit-focused orientation of earlier studies in gerontology has been replaced, to a significant extent, by a normative framework that asks, in effect, "How do older people cope with the adaptational tasks of the 60s, the 70s, and beyond?"

Normal Child Development

Normal child development may be approached from a variety of perspectives. Freud's theories, discussed in detail in Section 6.1, described five psychosexual stages of development—oral, anal, phallic, latency, and genital—derived from the analysis of adults with various types of psychopathology. On the basis of direct observations of children, other psychoanalysts elaborated on many of Freud's theories. For Erik Erikson, one of these theorists, human development can be understood only if one takes into account the social forces that influence and interact with the developing person. Erikson's five childhood psychosocial stages of trust, initiative, autonomy, industry, and identity correlate with Freud's psychosexual stages. In addition, Erikson added three stages—intimacy, generativity, and integrity—that extend beyond young adulthood into old age (Figure 2.1-2). These eight stages have both positive and negative aspects, have specific emotional crises, and are affected by the interaction of the person's biology, culture, and society. Each stage has two possible outcomes, one positive or healthy and the other negative or unhealthy. Under ideal circumstances, the crisis is resolved when the person achieves a new and higher level of functioning at the positive end of the particular stage. According to Erikson, most persons do not achieve perfect positive polarity but fall more toward the positive than toward the negative pole. A third major model is Jean Piaget's theory of cognitive (intellectual) development. By conducting intensive studies of the way children think and behave, Piaget formulated a theory of cognition, which he divided into four stages—sensorimotor, preoperational, concrete, and formal operational.

According to Erikson, Freud, and Piaget, the infant grows by predetermined steps through various stages. In this epigenetic view of development, each stage has its own characteristics and needs, and it must be negotiated successfully before it is possible to go on to the next level. The sequence of stages is not automatic; rather, it depends on both central nervous system growth and life experience. There is ample evidence that an unfavorable environment can delay some of the developmental stages; however, particularly favorable environmental stimulators can accelerate one's progress through the stages.

In view of the several different models for conceptualizing the phases of development (Table 2.1-2), it has become customary to organize the developmental stages in chronological order as follows: infancy; toddler period; preschool period; school period or middle years; early, middle, and late adolescence; and early, middle, and late adulthood (old age). Each developmental stage outlined by these and other workers is discussed in detail in the sections that follow.

References

Adler L L, ed: *Cross-Cultural Research in Human Development.* Praeger, New York, 1989.

Colorusso C A, Nemiroff R A: *Adult Development: A New Dimension in Psychodynamic Theory and Practice.* Plenum, New York, 1981.

Erikson E: *Childhood and Society.* Norton, New York, 1959.

Fagan J R, et al.: Selective screening device for the early detection of normal or delayed cognitive development in infants at risk for later mental retardation. Pediatrics *78*: 1021, 1986.

Freud A: *The Ego and the Mechanisms of Defense.* International Universities Press, New York, 1966.

Freud S: Analysis terminable and interminable (1937). In *Standard Edition of the Complete Psychological Works of Sigmund Freud.* vol 23. Hogarth Press, London, 1974.

Hartmann H: *Ego Psychology and the Problem of Adaptation.* International Universities Press, New York, 1958.

Kellam S E, Branch J D: *Mental Health and Going to School: The Woodlawn Program of Assessment, Early Intervention, and Evaluation.* University of Chicago Press, Chicago, 1975.

Leighton D C, MacMillan A M, Harding J S, et al.: *The Stirling Country Study of Psychiatric Disorders and Socio-Cultural Environment.* vol 3, *The Character of Danger.* Basic Books, New York, 1963.

Lidz T: *The Person: His and Her Development Throughout the Life Cycle.* Basic Books, New York, 1976.

Maccoby E E: The role of gender identity and gender constancy in sex-differentiated development. New Dir Child Dev *47*: 5, 1990.

Maziadi M, Cote R, Boutin P, et al.: *Temperament and Intellectual Development: A Longitudinal Study from Infancy to Four Years.* Am J Psychiatry *144*: 144, 1987.

Notman M T: Menopause and adult development. Ann N Y Acad Sci *592*: 149, 1990.

Offer D, Sabshin M: *Normality and the Life Cycle.* Basic Books, New York, 1984.

Robins L N, Rutter M, eds: *Straight and Devious Pathways from Childhood to Adulthood.* Cambridge University Press, Cambridge, 1989.

Seiden A M: Psychological issues affecting women throughout the life cycle. Psychiatr Clin North Am *12*: 1, 1989.

Vaillant G E, ed: *Empirical Studies of Ego Mechanism and Defense.* American Psychiatric Association Press, Washington, DC, 1986.

Wolff S: Attachment and morality: Developing themes with different values. Br J Psychiatry *156*: 266, 1990.

2.2 / Pregnancy, Childbirth, and the Prenatal Period

PREGNANCY

Pregnancy produces marked biological, physiological, and psychological changes in a woman. Most women have a positive attitude toward pregnancy, especially if it was planned in conjunction with a loving partner. A woman's psychological conflicts concerning pregnancy most often involve her assumption of the mothering role. If her own mother was a poor role model, the woman's sense of maternal competence may be impaired, and a lack of confidence before and after the birth of her baby may result.

Twenty to 40 percent of women report some emotional disturbance or cognitive dysfunction in the postpartum period. Many experience the so-called *postpartum blues,* a normal state of sadness, dysphoria, frequent tearfulness, and clinging dependency. These feelings, which may last several days, have been ascribed to the rapid change in hormonal levels, the stress of childbirth, and the awareness of the increased responsibility motherhood brings. A somewhat similar syndrome has been described in fathers who develop mood changes during their wives' pregnancies or after the baby is born. Such fathers are affected by several factors: added responsibility, diminished sexual outlets, decreased attention from their wives, and the belief that the child represents a binding force in an unsatisfactory marriage. In rare cases (1 to 2 in 1,000 deliveries), a postpartum psychosis may develop in the mother; it is characterized by severe anxiety, hallucinations, or delusions. See Section 15.2, "Other Psychotic Disorders," for further discussion of this disorder.

Biology of Pregnancy

Extensive biological changes occur during pregnancy. Figure 2.2-1 describes the major landmarks of each trimester.

Pregnancy and Sexual Behavior

The effects of pregnancy on sexual behavior vary among women. Some women experience an increased sex drive as pelvic vasocongestion produces a more sexually responsive state. Others are more responsive because they no longer fear becoming pregnant. Some have diminished desire or lose interest in sexual activity altogether either because of physical discomfort or because of a psychological mind set that associates motherhood with asexuality. That association can also occur in men with a Madonna complex, who view pregnant women as sacred and not to be defiled by the sexual act. Some men find the pregnant body ugly. Intercourse may be erroneously regarded by either person as potentially harmful to the developing fetus and may be avoided for that reason as well. Studies have shown that, if a man has an extramarital affair during his wife's pregnancy, it will most likely occur during the last trimester.

Coital prohibitions. Most obstetricians place no prohibitions on coitus until four to five weeks antepartum. If bleeding occurs early in pregnancy, it is usually, though not invariably, followed by spontaneous abortion. In those cases,

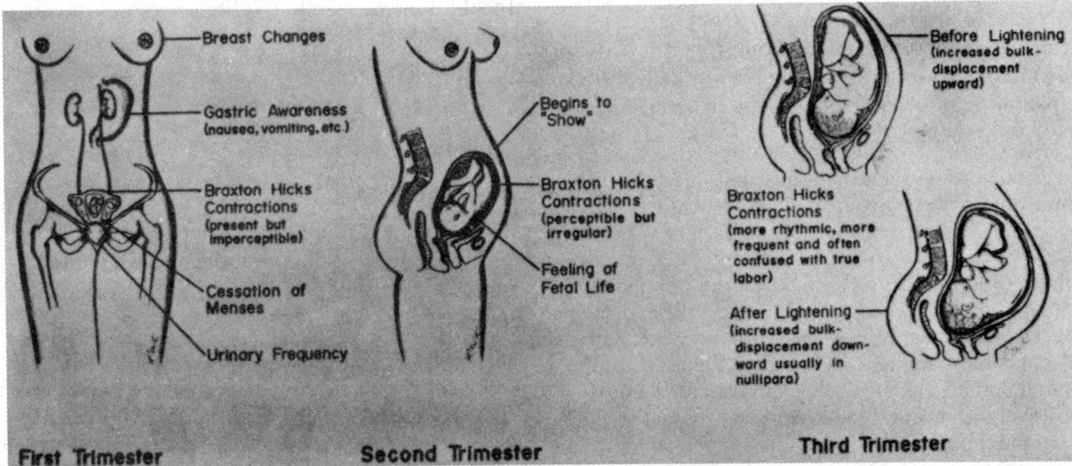

Figure 2.2-1. The symptoms most common to each trimester of pregnancy. The hormonally determined symptoms of pregnancy are often placed in the secondary service of emotional determinants. Thus, the nausea and vomiting of early pregnancy may become overly determined to the extent that hospitalization is required (hyperemesis gravidarum). Braxton Hicks contractions are apparently physiological and occur throughout most of pregnancy. Usually imperceptible in early pregnancy and painless in midpregnancy, these contractions, although expulsively ineffective, are frequently and at times exasperatingly confused with true labor during the last weeks of pregnancy. Lightening occurs during the last weeks of pregnancy and is due to downward descent and accommodation of the fetal head into the pelvic inlet. Upward displacement of the diaphragm by the encroaching uterus is correspondingly reduced, resulting in greater ease of respiration. With this downward displacement of the abdominal bulk, symptoms become targeted to the pelvic girdle, the lumbosacral area, and the lower extremities. Lightening is more obvious in first pregnancies and may not occur in multiparas until the onset of labor. Table from E C Mann, T N Armistead: Pregnancy and sexual behavior. In *The Sexual Experience,* B J Sadock, H I Kaplan, and A M Freedman, editors, p 238. Williams & Wilkins, Baltimore, 1976.

the obstetrician will prohibit coitus on a temporary basis as a therapeutic measure. This abstinence may put a strain on the marriage.

Pregnancy and Medications

Teratogenic syndromes related to medication or drug use do occur in pregnancy. In spite of warnings, pregnant women take an average of 3.8 drugs per pregnancy, mostly prescription drugs. In general, the fetus is most vulnerable during the first trimester of pregnancy. Psychotropic drugs, including sedatives and hypnotics, are used by about one-third of pregnant women. In addition, pregnant women take over-the-counter medications that are self-prescribed and more difficult to monitor.

Medications and lactation. Lactation is influenced by many factors. The wish to nurse may be an ideal that some women feel they should meet, or it may be imposed by others—the husband, friends, relatives, or physicians. In these cases there may be guilt feelings if the woman chooses not to nurse or is unable to do so for physical reasons. There is no evidence of better psychological or physical adjustment in breast-fed infants and children than in bottle-fed infants. Currently, over 50 percent of babies are breast-fed, and of that number about 30 percent are breast-fed for three months or longer.

Many drugs can be transferred to the infant through breast milk. Although most drugs are generally compatible with breast feeding, some can produce signs and symptoms in the newborn infant (e.g., antibiotics can produce rashes; narcotics can produce sedation).

Pregnancy and Marriage

In the psychologically healthy woman, pregnancy is one expression of her sense of self-realization and identity as a woman. Negative attitudes about pregnancy are associated with the fear of childbirth or the mothering role. Some women view pregnancy as a way of diminishing self-doubts about their femininity or as a means of reassuring themselves that they are able to conceive.

The prospective wife-mother and husband-father have to redefine their roles both as a couple and as individuals. They face readjustments in their relationships with friends and relatives, and they must deal with new responsibilities as caregivers to the newborn and to each other. The new parents must reevaluate how they choose to earn and to spend their income. Accustomed to gratifying each other's dependency needs, the couple must attend to the unremitting needs of the newborn infant and developing child. Although most couples respond positively to meeting these demands, some do not. Under ideal conditions, the desire to become pregnant and to have a child should be a decision that is agreed on by both partners to meet a generative need for creative self-realization. Altogether too often, however, it is rationalized as a way to achieve intimacy in a conflicted marriage or to avoid having to deal with other life-circumstance problems.

Attitudes toward the pregnant mother. In general, attitudes toward the pregnant mother reflect a variety of factors: intelligence, temperament, cultural practices, and myths of the society and the subculture into which both parents were born. Married men's responses to pregnancy are generally positive. For some men, however, reactions vary from a misplaced sense of pride that they are able to impregnate the woman to fear of increased responsibility and subsequent termination of the relationship. Small children react to a mother's obvious pregnancy with curiosity about the origin of babies, particularly about where the baby will exit and how it originally got there.

Family Planning and Contraception

Family planning is the term used to describe the process of choosing when and if to bear children. *Contraception* is the prevention of fecundation or fertilization of the ovum—it is just one form of family planning. Current methods of contraception are listed in Table 2.2-1.

The choice of contraception varies with a person's cultural, religious, and political beliefs. The success of contraceptive technology has enabled career-minded couples to delay childbearing into their 30s and 40s. Such a delay, however, may increase infertility problems. Consequently, many women with careers feel this biological clock ticking and plan to have children in their early 30s to avoid the risk of not being able to have them at all.

Midlife Pregnancy

Women who become pregnant after age 35 have higher rates of maternal and infant mortality than women age 20 to 29, who have the lowest rates. (The most complications of all age groups occur in women age 16 or younger.) Women over age 35 are also more prone to obstetric-gynecological disorders, such as eclampsia, hypertension of pregnancy, uterine leiomyomas, and chromosomal abnormalities. The risk of trisomy syndromes (e.g., Down's syndrome) increases about seven times from age 35 to 45. In addition, women in midlife are more often delivered by cesarean section than vaginally in an effort to decrease infant morbidity.

Genetic Counseling

This type of counseling provides patients and their families with direct medical knowledge in the field of genetics. This type of counseling is indicated when there is even the remotest possibility of a genetically based disorder in the family.

For example, a person whose father has Huntington's chorea may be concerned about getting the disease. Huntington's chorea follows Mendelian rules of inheritance; therefore, a person whose parent has the disorder has a 50 percent chance of getting the disease. Because the age of onset varies, the longer one lives without becoming ill, the lower the risk. A chemical test for determining gene carriers for Huntington's chorea was recently developed, so persons can now use this knowledge when deciding whether to have children.

Genetic counseling requires the clinician to be aware of a person's level of maturity, individual conflicts, defense mechanisms, and ego strengths and weaknesses. The counselor has to be ready to deal with depression, anger, anxiety, and other complex emotions related to the issues at hand.

Table 2.2-1
Current Methods of Contraception

Type	Method of Action	Effectiveness	Advantages	Disadvantages	Potential Complications
Rhythm	Time abstinence	Low	No cost Always available No professional help required	Imposed coital timing (lack of spontaneity)	Essentially none
Withdrawal Coitus interruptus	Prevention of insemination	Low (but theoretically high)	No cost Always available No professional help required	Regular coital use required Requires considerable attention and control	Essentially none
Intravaginal foams, creams, jellies, and suppositories	Spermicidal	Low	Inexpensive Generally available No professional help required	Regular coital use required Possible messiness Possible interference with enjoyment	Essentially none; possible allergies
Condom	Sperm barrier	Medium	Inexpensive; latex condom protects against AIDS Generally available No professional help required Decreased acquisition of coitally transmitted diseases	Regular coital use required Possible interference with enjoyment	Essentially none; may tear 3:1,000 defective manufacture rate
Diaphragm, cervical cap, sponge	Sperm barrier (plus spermicidal with jelly)	Medium to high	Inexpensive	Regular coital use required Possible interference with enjoyment	Essentially none
				Requires professional fitting Not anatomically adaptable to everyone	Diaphragm can dislodge during coitus; sponge is for one-time use over 24-hour period
Intrauterine device (IUD)	Unknown (possibly prevents zygote implantation)	Medium	Inexpensive Only single decision required Not coitally connected	Possible increase in bleeding and cramping Requires professional insertion	Uterine perforation, pelvic infection, spontaneous expulsion
Oral (hormonal)	Prevention of ovulation (possible interference with sperm mobility)	High (most commonly used method)	Inexpensive Potential absolute efficiency Not coitally connected	Possible side effects Daily ingestion Requires professional visit (Rx)	Thromboembolism, neuro-ocular disturbances, hypertension, depression
Postcoital hormonal method (RU 486)	Prevention of implantation of fertilized ovum	High	Cited as ideal contraceptive Can be used after coitus without contraception, after rape, incest	Not legal in United States, developed and used in France	Unknown
Male sterilization	Surgical interruption of vas deferens so sperm cannot travel from testes to penis	High	Failure very rare; 20-minute office procedure	Morbidity in 1–2% of patients includes infections, clots	Can be reversed in only 50% of cases; rare neurotic impotence reaction

Table adapted after data by Eugene C. Sandberg, M.D.
Effectiveness is rated roughly as follows: low: more than 20 pregnancies for 100 women-years of use; medium: 1 to 20 for 100 women-years of use; high: less than 1 pregnancy for 100 women-years of use.

Prenatal diagnosis and its implications. In many cases genetic counseling depends on prenatal diagnosis. Techniques used include amniocentesis (transabdominal aspiration of fluid from the amniotic sac), ultrasound examinations, X-rays, fetoscopy (the direct visualization of the fetus), fetal blood and skin sampling, and chorionic villus biopsy. About 2 percent of the total number of cases tested are positive for some abnormality, including X-linked disorders, neural tube defects, chromosomal disorders (trisomy 21), and various inborn errors of metabolism (e.g., Tay-Sachs disease, lipoidoses). In addition to a family history of a disorder with genetic loading, prenatal diagnosis is commonly offered to pregnant women over age 35. A problem in the routine use of diagnostic tests is that some carry a risk; for example, about 5 percent of women who undergo fetoscopy have a miscarriage. Amniocentesis, which is usually performed between the 14th and the 15th week of pregnancy, causes fetal damage or miscarriage in less than 1 percent of cases.

Other Issues in Pregnancy

Abortion. Over 1 million abortions are performed in the United States each year. That figure represents about 350 abortions for every 1,000 live births. Most women who obtain abortions are unmarried, white, and over age 25. However, married women obtain about 20 percent of all abortions, and women 19 and under obtain about 25 percent of all abortions. Fifty percent of abortions are performed under 8 weeks of gestation, 25 percent between 9 and 10 weeks, and 10 percent between 11 and 12 weeks. The remainder occur after 13 weeks, with 1 percent occurring after 21 weeks. Ninety percent of abortions are performed by suction curettage, 5 percent by surgical (sharp) curettage, and the remainder by intraamniotic installation (salting-out) and other procedures.

Attitudes of the patient toward abortion vary. Before the 12th week of gestation, abortion may come as a relief and may produce less emotional reaction than later pregnancy loss or giving up the baby for adoption. Second-trimester abortion is more emotionally traumatic and is usually performed after an abnormal factor in the fetus has been found. Women denied abortions may seek out illegal abortions or abort themselves, which can lead to illness or death. Some women become suicidal if denied an abortion for whatever reason.

Abortion is also a significant experience for men. Those who impregnate women with whom they have had long-term relationships usually want to play an active role; they may accompany their partners to the hospital or abortion center and, in most instances, view the abortion in much the same way as their partners. In general, however, most men are passive in preventing the unwanted pregnancy and in planning for and learning about abortion.

Pregnancy and teenagers. Each year about 1 million teenagers become pregnant. Teenagers obtain 400,000 legal abortions and give birth to about 600,000 babies each year. In certain subcultures, teenagers view pregnancy as a rite of passage into adulthood. The adolescent who is depressed, insecure about her attractiveness, or the product of a conflicted or divorced home is more likely to become pregnant than the adolescent from a more stable background.

Most teenagers elect to have abortions with their parents' consent; however, there are two competing rights regarding mandatory parental consent: the child's claim to privacy and a parent's need to know. Most adults believe teenagers should have parental permission for an abortion. In cases in which parents refuse consent, however, most states prohibit the parents vetoing the teenager's decision. A law called the Maine Compromise requires consent from an adult family member, judge, physician, or counselor.

Pregnancy loss. Intrauterine fetal death can occur at any time during the pregnancy and is most often an emotionally traumatic experience. In the early months of pregnancy, the mother is usually unaware of fetal death and only learns of it from her doctor. Later in pregnancy, after fetal movements and heart tones have been present, the mother may be able to detect fetal demise. When given the diagnosis, most women want the dead fetus removed, and, depending on the trimester, labor may be induced or the patient may have to wait for the spontaneous expulsion of uterine contents. Many couples view sexual relations during this period as not only undesirable but psychologically unacceptable.

Pregnancy loss can also occur in the case of a stillborn child or as a result of an induced abortion when an antenatal diagnosis detects an abnormal fetus. Attachment to the unborn child begins before the actual birth, and grief and mourning can occur at any time. The grief experienced during third-trimester loss, however, is generally greater than during first-trimester loss. Some parents do not wish to view a stillborn child, and their wishes should be respected. Others may wish to hold the stillborn, which can assist the mourning process. A subsequent pregnancy may diminish overt feelings of grief, but does not eliminate the need to mourn. These so-called replacement children are at risk for overprotection and future emotional problems.

Pseudocyesis. First described by Hippocrates in 300 B.C., pseudocyesis refers to false pregnancy accompanied by the classic symptoms of pregnancy—complete cessation of menstruation, nausea, enlargement and pigmentation of the breasts, abdominal distention, and simulated labor pains. The patient suspects or is certain that she is pregnant.

Pseudocyesis occurs at all ages. It has been reported in a girl of 7, and one case has even been reported in a man. In pseudocyesis, the objective signs of pregnancy derive from the pathological wish for and fear of pregnancy. These symptoms may serve as an expression of conflicting attitudes regarding childbearing and related female sexual functions. It may be perceived as a reaffirmation of the woman's youth, potency, and desirability. Pseudocyesis is found in severely disturbed women. Pseudocyesis may also occur as a psychiatric complication of a hysterectomy or sterilization in an effort to deny the loss of the childbearing function. Treatment approaches and results vary. At times, the patient has a true somatic delusion not subject to reality testing. Some patients actually go into "labor." Often, the negative pregnancy test cures the somatic symptoms, and the patient can then undergo psychotherapy.

A syndrome called "couvade" occurs in some primitive cultures and is characterized by the father's taking to his bed during or shortly after the birth of his child, as though he himself had given birth to the child.

CHILDBIRTH

According to the U.S. National Center for Health Statistics, 3,829,000 babies were born in the United States in 1989, with a birth rate of 15.9 per 1,000 population. Advances in prenatal and perinatal care have reduced the infant death rate to 10.4 per 1,000 live births in 1989 (down from 20 infant deaths per 1,000 live births in 1970). The fertility rate was 67.3 live births per 1,000 women age 15 to 44 years, which is an increase over previous years.

The overwhelming majority of babies are born in a hospital with a physician in attendance, but free-standing birthing centers with access to a hospital are an alternative for some couples. There has been a steady increase in the number of babies born by cesarean section—from about 5 percent in the 1960s to about 20 percent in the 1980s. Some of this increase is the result of the doctor's fear of malpractice suits. This fear is understandable, because malpractice suits are emotionally traumatic for both patient and physician. Prolonged labor, which is sometimes hazardous to the fetus, is also avoided with a cesarean section. Analgesic drugs given to the mother during labor enter the fetal bloodstream and sedate the newborn infant. A drug that depresses the mother's nervous system affects the sucking reflex of the infant, sometimes for a few days.

Premature Births

Childbirth is a potentially hazardous time for both mother and child. Although most premature infants develop normally, a premature birth increases the risk of mental retardation, behavior problems, emotional disorders, and sensorimotor problems, such as dyslexia. Also, premature babies are at greater risk for suffering child abuse. Prematurity occurs when the birth weight is under 2,500 g or when the gestation period is less than 34 weeks. Prematurity is correlated with low socioeconomic status, poor maternal nutrition, and teenage pregnancy; it accounts for 7 percent of all births. High socioeconomic status correlates negatively with infant mortality.

PRENATAL PERIOD

Prenatal events have great relevance to psychiatry because the development of the embryo and fetus can go awry from a variety of causes and affect future behavior in a variety of ways. The person's genotype or genes exert their effect throughout life. By birth, there may be a predisposition at the genetic level to the development of an abnormal state, which can appear at any time during the life span. A predisposition to anxiety may occur because of cerebral disorganization, which manifests itself in perceptual motor dysfunctions and impulse control problems. Genetic factors can have delayed effects: Huntington's chorea first becomes manifest in middle adulthood, and life events play no part in the development of the disease.

Any view of emotional disorder must consider the uteroplacental environment of the fetus and its neurobiological substrate. There is an interplay between genetics (nature) and environment (nurture) with variable effects, depending on the extent of each. In general, most disorders are considered to be multifactorial—the result of a combination of effects, some of which may be additive. Damage at the fetal stage is usually more global than damage after birth; rapidly growing organs are most vulnerable. Boys are more vulnerable to developmental damage than girls, and geneticists recognize that, in humans and animals, females show a propensity for greater biological vigor, possibly related to the second X chromosome.

Embryology and Fetology

After implantation, the growth and development of the embryo occurs at a rapid pace. By the end of eight weeks, a recognizable human shape is present, and the embryo is called a *fetus*. Small fetuses, which are defined as those with a birth weight below the 10th percentile for gestational age, occur in about 5 percent of pregnancies. The average newborn weighs about 3,400 g (7½ pounds). By the 26th to 28th week of gestation, the prematurely born fetus has a good chance of survival. With each 100-g increment of weight, beginning at about 1,000 g, there is a progressively better chance for survival; therefore, *premature infants* are usually defined as those infants weighing between 1,000 and 2,500 g. A 36-week-old fetus has less of a chance for survival than does the 3,000-g fetus born close to term.

Postmaturity is generally defined as born two weeks or more beyond the expected date of birth. Since pregnancy at term is calculated as being 40 weeks from the last menstrual period and since the exact time of fertilization varies, the incidence of postmaturity is high when based on menstrual history alone. The postmature baby typically has long nails, scanty lanugo hair, more than the usual scalp hair, and increased alertness. Figure 2.2-2 describes the uterofetal relationships as they develop during pregnancy.

Central Nervous System Development

The nervous system arises from the neural plate, which is a dorsal ectodermal thickening that appears at about the 16th day of gestation. By the 6th week, part of the neural tube becomes the cerebral vesicle, which later becomes the cerebral hemisphere. The cortex begins to develop by the 10th week, but layers do not appear until the 6th month; the sensory cortex and the motor cortex are formed before the association cortex. In utero, some brain function has been detected by the response of the fetal encephalogram to sound. The weight of the human brain is about 350 g in an infant and 1,450 g at full development; this represents a fourfold increase mainly made up by the neocortex. During fetal life and early infancy, there is enormous growth in the number and the branching of dendrites and in the multiplication of synaptic junctions.

Infants are born with a number of reflexes, many of which are present in utero: the grasp reflex appears at 17 weeks, Moro's reflex at 25 weeks, and the sucking reflex at about 28 weeks. Other reflexes present at birth are the rooting reflex (search for the nipple in response to perioral stimulation), grasp reflex, plantar (Babinski's) reflex, knee jerk, abdominal reflex, startle reflex, and tonic neck reflex. In a normal child, the grasp reflex, startle reflex, and tonic neck reflex disappear by the fourth month.

The fetus can be set into total body motion by in utero stimulation of its ventral skin surfaces by the 14th week; at about this time, fetal movements can be felt by the mother (quickening). Survival systems—breathing, sucking, swallowing, and circulatory and temperature homeostasis—are relatively functional at birth. Sensory organs, however, are incompletely developed. Further differentiation of neurophysiological functions depends on an active automatic process of stimulatory reinforcement.

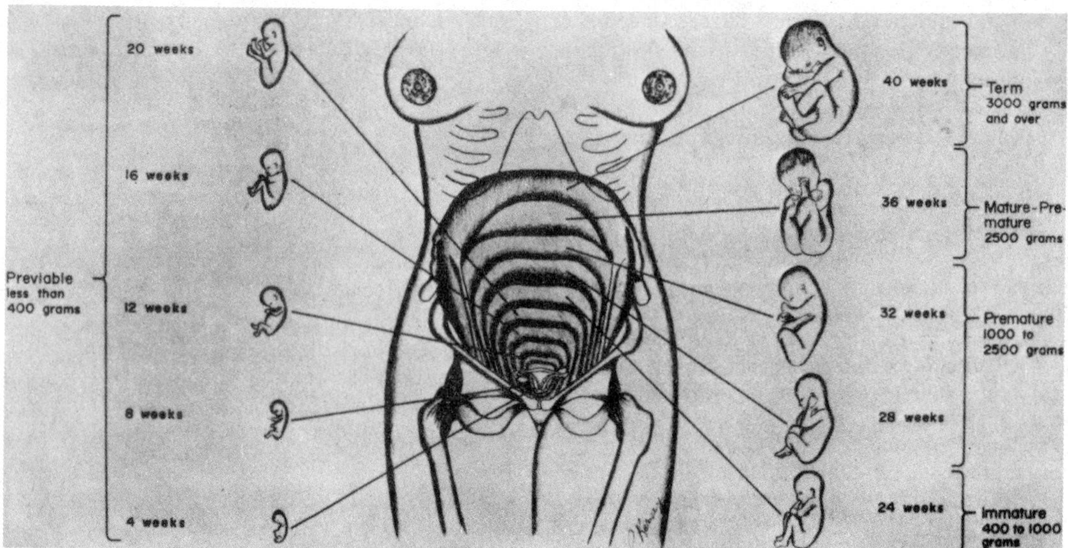

Figure 2.2-2. Uterofetal relationships as they develop during pregnancy. In the world literature there is only one recorded instance of a conceptus weighing less than one pound (397 g) that survived. In most premature and intensive care nurseries, the chance for survival of a fetus weighing even 800 g is minimal. Table from E C Mann, T N Armistead: Pregnancy and sexual behavior. In *The Sexual Experience,* B J Sadock, H I Kaplan, and A M Freedman, editors, p 238. Williams & Wilkins, Baltimore, 1976.

Antepartum Maternal Health and Fetal Development

The fetal nervous system is highly susceptible to damage from a variety of causes. Maternal infectious diseases can cause fetal death, perinatal infection, or congenital defects; maternal toxoplasmosis, the result of a parasite found in the common house cat, can cause anomalies in the newborn. Rubella (German measles) contracted during the first trimester produces severe mental retardation, deafness, and microcephaly in 50 percent of infants. A live virus vaccine against rubella, which has been available for 20 years, is given to young children but not to pregnant women. Cytomegalovirus and herpes simplex virus (HSV) are other causes of intrauterine infection and fetal abnormalities. HSV is acquired during delivery through the infected cervix or vagina and can be prevented by cesarean section. Acquired immune deficiency syndrome (AIDS) is transmitted from the infected mother to the fetus. About 1 percent of all AIDS cases are in children under age 13, most of whom were born to AIDS-infected mothers.

Malnutrition is a major cause of perinatal morbidity. Total caloric intake directly influences fetal weight. Nutritional deficiencies in protein are associated with growth defects, mental retardation, and prematurity; over 150 identified inborn errors of metabolism (e.g., galactosemia and phenylketonuria) have been identified in neonates. Severe maternal malnutrition is the major cause of growth-retarded newborns and stillbirths in third-world countries.

Other factors that influence intrauterine development include an excess or a deficiency of maternal circulating hormones. Chromosomal abnormalities, such as Down's syndrome and Tay-Sachs disease, may occur but are subject to intrauterine diagnosis and therapeutic abortion. Congenital hypothyroidism occurs in infants whose mothers are thryoid deficient; the condition is reversible. The administration of androgens to the mother affects sex differentiation in the fetus, so that female infants may have masculinized organs, such as an enlarged clitoris or a hypoplastic uterus. There is no conclusive evidence that male children are affected. Diethylstilbestrol (DES), once given to pregnant women to prevent miscarriages, has been found to produce cervical dysplasia in female children born to these mothers. Lithium is associated with infant malformation in 10 percent of exposed fetuses.

Fetal alcohol syndrome affects about one-third of all infants born to alcoholic mothers and is characterized by delayed growth and developmental abnormalities. Smok-

Table 2.2-2
Causes of Human Malformations Observed during the First Year of Life

Suspected Cause	Percentage of Total
Genetic	
Autosomal genetic disease	15–20
Cytogenetic (chromosomal abnormalities)	5
Unknown	65
Polygenic	
Multifactorial (genetic-environmental interactions)	
Spontaneous error of development	
Synergistic interactions of teratogens	
Environmental	
Maternal conditions: diabetes; endocrinopathies; nutritional deficiencies, starvation; drug and substance addictions	4
Maternal infections: rubella, toxoplasmosis, syphilis, herpes, cytomegalic inclusion disease, varicella, Venezuelan equine encephalitis, parvovirus B 19	3
Mechanical problems (deformations): abnormal cord constrictions, disparity in uterine size and uterine contents	1–2
Chemicals, drugs, radiation, hyperthermia	<1
Preconception exposures (excluding mutagens and infectious agents)	

Table from R L Brent, D A Beckman: Environmental teratogens. Bull N Y Acad Med *66*: 125, 1990, with permission.

ing during pregnancy is associated with lower-than-average infant birth weight. Infants born to mothers addicted to narcotics go through a true withdrawal syndrome at birth. If the mother is exposed to severe radiation during the first 20 weeks of her pregnancy, the baby will be born with gross deformities. Estimates are that about 3 to 6 percent of all newborns have some sort of birth defect that is fatal at birth or causes permanent disability. Table 2.2-2 lists malformations that occur during the first year of life.

Maternal stress. The fetus may be responsive to emotions in the mother. Mothers with high anxiety levels are likely to produce babies who are hyperactive and irritable, have sleep disorders and low birth weight, and feed poorly. Maternal stress may influence the newborn through the placental transfer of adrenal hormones, such as epinephrine and cortisol.

References

Annas G J: Protecting the liberty of pregnant patients, editorial. N Engl J Med *316*: 1213, 1987.

Apfel R J, Mazor M D: Psychiatry and reproductive medicine. In *Comprehensive Textbook of Psychiatry*, ed 5, H I Kaplan and B J Sadock, editors, p 1331. Williams & Wilkins, Baltimore, 1989.

Briggs G G, Freeman R K, Yaffee S J: *Drugs in Pregnancy and Lactation: A Reference Guide to Fetal and Neonatal Risk.* Williams & Wilkins, Baltimore, 1986.

Cath S H, Gurwitt A R, Ross J M, eds: *Father and Child; Developmental and Clinical Perspectives.* Little, Brown, Boston, 1982.

Colman A, Colman L: *Pregnancy: The Psychological Experience.* Seabury Press, New York, 1973.

Cook R J: Abortion laws and policies: Challenges and opportunities. Int J Gynecol Obstet *3*(Suppl): 61, 1989.

Friedman R, Gradstein B: *Surviving Pregnancy Loss.* Little, Brown, Boston, 1982.

Group for the Advancement of Psychiatry: *The Joys and Sorrows of Parenthood.* Scribner's, New York. 1973.

Hechtman L: Teenage mothers and their children: Risks and problems: A review. Can J Psychiatry *34*: 569, 1989.

Hoffman N S: Stress factors related to antenatal testing during high-risk pregnancy. J Perinatol *10*: 195, 1990.

Mahler M S, Pine F, Bergman A: *The Psychological Birth of the Human Infant.* Basic Books, New York, 1975.

McCormick M C, Brooks-Gunn J, Shorter T, Holmes J H, Wallace C Y, Heagarty M C: Factors associated with smoking in low-income pregnant women: Relationship to birth weight, stressful life events, social support, health behaviors and mental distress. J Clin Epidemiol *43*: 441, 1990.

Molfese V J, Holcomb L C: Predicting learning and other developmental disabilities: Assessment of reproductive and caretaking variables. Birth Defects *25*: 1, 1989.

Rosett H L, Weiner L: *Alcohol and the Fetus: A Clinical Perspective.* Oxford University Press, New York. 1984.

Rothstein, A A: Men's reactions to their partners' elective abortions. Am J Obstet Gynecol April: 832, 1977.

Youngs D D, Ehrhardt A A: *Psychosomatic Obstetrics and Gynecology.* Appleton-Century-Crofts, New York, 1980.

2.3 / Infancy and Childhood

Current views of infant and child development are, for the most part, balanced; they respect the impact of both genetic endowment and environmental experience. They take into account the organism's capacity to structure and restructure experience at each stage of development according to maturational capacities and adaptive goals. However, the controversy regarding nature and nurture continues. This is because certain aspects of development, although influenced by environmental experience, are closely tied to the maturation of the central nervous system (CNS) (i.e., gross motor functioning) and only in extreme situations are seriously undermined by the environment. Other aspects of development are sensitive to day-to-day experiences, such as the ability to experience and show pleasure and to trust human relationships.

INFANCY

Attachment

As sensory development proceeds, there is for all social organisms a parallel task of fashioning a tie between the newborn and its species. It has been shown that infants in the first months after birth have some capacity for self-regulation and become attuned to social and interpersonal interaction. They show a rapidly increasing responsivity to the external environment and an ability to form a special relationship with significant primary caretakers—that is, to form an attachment.

Ethologists have demonstrated, primarily in birds, that there is a critical period shortly after birth during which the newborn becomes imprinted on a moving, sound-producing object. This bond elicits following behavior from the newborn. For all its undoubted importance, imprinting has not been demonstrated conclusively in human beings or in other primates.

Harry Harlow. Harry Harlow studied social learning and the effects of social isolation in monkeys. Harlow placed newborn rhesus monkeys with two different types of surrogate mothers—one wire-mesh and the other wire-mesh covered with terry cloth. The monkeys preferred the terry cloth mothers, which provided contact and comfort. When frightened, cloth-mother-raised monkeys showed intense clinging behavior and appeared to be comforted, whereas wire-mother-raised monkeys gained no comfort and appeared disorganized. Both types of surrogate-reared monkeys were subsequently unable to adjust to life in a monkey colony and had extraordinary difficulty in learning to mate. When impregnated, the females failed to mother their young. These behavioral peculiarities were attributed to the isolates' lack of mothering in infancy. For further discussion, see Section 4.5.

John Bowlby. John Bowlby studied the attachment of infants to mothers and concluded that early separation of infants from their mothers had severe negative effects on the child's emotional and intellectual development. He described attachment behavior, which develops during the first year of life; it is characterized by the maintenance of physical contact between the mother and the child when the child is hungry, frightened, or in distress. Bowlby's theories are further discussed in Section 4.2.

Social deprivation syndromes and maternal neglect. Investigators, especially René Spitz, have long documented the severe developmental retardation that accompanies maternal rejection and neglect. Infants in institutions, characterized by low staff-to-infant ratios and frequent turnover of personnel, tend to display marked developmental retardation, even with adequate physical care and freedom from infection. The same infants, placed in adequate foster or adoptive care, undergo marked acceleration in development.

Fathers and attachment. Babies become attached to fathers, as well as to mothers, but the attachment is different. Generally, mothers hold babies for caregiving, and fathers hold babies for purposes of play. Given a choice of either parent after separation, infants usually go to the mother, but if the mother is unavailable, they turn to the father for comfort.

Stranger anxiety. A fear of strangers is first noted in infants at about 26 weeks of age but does not develop fully until about 32 weeks. At the approach of a stranger, infants cry and cling to the mother. Babies exposed to only one caretaker are more likely to have stranger anxiety than those exposed to a variety of caretakers.

Separation anxiety, which occurs between 10 and 16 months, is related to stranger anxiety but is not identical to it. Separation from the person to whom the infant is attached precipitates separation anxiety. Stranger anxiety, however, occurs even when the infant is in the mother's arms. The infant learns to separate as it starts to crawl and move away from the mother, but the infant constantly looks back and frequently returns to the mother for reassurance.

Margaret Mahler described a developmental phase called symbiosis, during which the infant feels fused with the mother or the mother's breast. It extends from the age of 3 or 4 weeks to 4 or 5 months, at which point the separation-individuation phase begins. Individuation is characterized by the child's perception of himself or herself as a distinct person, separate from the mother.

Temperamental Differences

There are strong suggestions of inborn differences and wide variability among individual infants in autonomic reactivity and temperament. Stella Chess and Alexander Thomas (husband and wife psychiatric collaborators) identified the following nine behavioral dimensions from which reliable differences can be obtained:

1. Activity level—the motor component present in a given child's functioning
2. Rhythmicity—the predictability of such functions as hunger, feeding pattern, elimination, and sleep-wake cycle
3. Approach or withdrawal—the nature of the response to a new stimulus, such as a new food, toy, or person
4. Adaptability—the speed and ease with which a current behavior is able to be modified in response to altered environmental structuring
5. Intensity of reaction—the amount of energy used in mood expression
6. Threshold of responsiveness—the intensity level of stimulation required to evoke a discernible response to sensory stimuli, environmental objects, and social contacts
7. Quality of mood—pleasant, joyful, friendly behavior as contrasted with unpleasant, crying, unfriendly behavior
8. Distractibility—the effectiveness of extraneous environmental stimuli in interfering with or in altering the direction of ongoing behavior
9. Attention span and persistence—the length of time a particular activity is pursued by the child (attention span) and the continuation of an activity in the face of obstacles (persistence)

The ratings on individual children showed considerable stability over a 25-year follow-up period. Researchers were able to discern connections among the initial characteristics of the infant, the mode of parental management, and the subsequent appearance of symptoms.

Effects of Infant Care

Clinicians are starting to view the infant as an important actor in the family drama, one who, in part, determines its course. The behavior of the infant serves to control the behavior of the mother, just as the mother's behavior modulates the infant's. The calm, smiling, predictable, good infant is a powerful reward for tender maternal care. The jittery, irregular, irritable infant tries a mother's patience. If a mother's capacities for giving are marginal, such traits may cause her to turn away from her child and thus complicate the child's already inadequate beginnings.

Parental fit. The concept of parental fit refers to how well the mother or father relates to the newborn or developing infant and takes into account temperamental characteristics of both parent and child. As mentioned, each newborn has innate psychophysiological characteristics, which are known collectively as temperament. Stella Chess and Alexander Thomas also identified a range of normal temperamental patterns from the *difficult child* at one end of the spectrum to the *easy child* at the other end. Difficult children, who make up 10 percent of all children, have a hyperalert physiological makeup. They react intensely to stimuli (cry easily at loud noises), sleep poorly, eat at unpredictable times, and are difficult to comfort. Easy children, who make up 40 percent of all children, are regular in eating, eliminating, and sleeping; are flexible; are able to adapt to change and to new stimuli with a minimum of distress; and are easily comforted when they cry. The other 50 percent of children are mixtures of these two types. The difficult child is harder to raise and places greater demands on the parent. Chess and Thomas used the term *goodness of fit* to characterize the harmonious and consonant interaction between a mother and a child in their motivations, capacities, and styles of behavior. *Poorness of fit* is characterized by dissonance between parent and child, which is likely to lead to distorted development and maladaptive functioning. The difficult child must be recognized because parents of such infants often develop feelings of inadequacy and believe that something they are doing wrong accounts for the difficulty in sleeping and eating and problems in comforting the child. In addition, a majority of such children develop emotional disturbances later in life.

Good-enough mothering. D.W. Winnicott provided a blend of Freudian and Kleinian thought in the form of a radically different developmental theory. Winnicott believed that the infant begins life in a state of unintegration, with unconnected and diffuse experiences, and that the mother provides the relationships that enable the incipient self of the infant to emerge. A holding environment is supplied by the mother, within which the infant is contained and experienced. During the last trimester of pregnancy and for the first few months of the baby's life, the mother is in a state of primary maternal preoccupation, absorbed in fantasies of and experiences with her baby. The mother need not be perfect, but she must provide "good-enough mothering." She plays a vital role in bringing the world to the child and in offering empathic anticipations of the infant's needs. If the mother is able to resonate with the infant's needs, the baby can become attuned to its own bodily functions and drives that afford the basis for the gradually evolving sense of self.

Spacing of Children

For women in the United States, 10 percent of conceptions that lead to live births are considered to be unwanted, and 20 percent are wanted but considered to be ill-timed. The implications of these figures are that some couples may be poorly prepared or may feel guilty about not wanting to be parents at that particular time. It is desirable to plan the pregnancy and to have mutual agreement on the spacing of children. The typical number of children in a present-day family is two, half the typical number at the beginning of the century. Repeated childbearing prevents adequate recuperation from the birth process and places the mother at risk for complications and injury. The new mother requires time to adapt; this period may range from a few weeks to several months. The demands of other children at home can be extremely taxing, and the family may be stressed beyond its capacity if these children are also young.

Studies of children from large families (four or five children) show that they are more likely to develop conduct disorders and have a slightly lower level of verbal intelligence than children from small families. Decreased parental interaction and discipline may account for these findings.

Birth order. The effects of birth order are variable. Firstborn children are more achievement-oriented and perform better academically than second and third children. Parents tend to be more involved, but they are also more anxious about caregiving with firstborn children than with later children. Second and third children have the advantage of their parents' previous experience. If children are spaced too closely together, however, there may not be enough lap time for each. Finally, the arrival of new children in the family affects not only the parents but the siblings as well. Firstborn children may resent the birth of a new sibling, who threatens their sole claim on parental attention. In some cases, such regressive behavior as enuresis or thumb sucking occurs.

In general, the oldest child achieves the most and is the most authoritarian; the middle child usually receives the least attention in the home and may develop strong peer relationships to compensate; and the youngest child may receive too much attention and be spoiled.

Developmental Landmarks

Arnold Gesell described developmental schedules that outline the qualitative sequence of motor, adaptive, and personal-social behavior of the child from birth to 6 years. These milestones of development allow for comparison between the development of a particular child and a normative standard. Gesell's schedules are widely used in both pediatrics and child psychiatry. Table 2.3-1 details the sequence of normal behavioral development from birth through the preschool period.

In the first year, normal milestones include turning toward a stimulus, being able to grab an item in the midline; sitting up; turning over; standing and eventually beginning to walk; vocalizing more clearly, including an occasional word or two (e.g., mama, dada); and simple causal means-ends interactions. By 2 to 4 months, infants start to respond to social cues, rather than internal sensations, with an increasing capacity to focus, concentrate, and interact in a cause-and-effect manner.

Language and cognitive development. At birth, infants are able to make noises such as crying, but they do not vocalize until about 8 weeks. At that time, guttural or babbling sounds occur spontaneously, especially in response to the mother. The persistence and further evolution of the child's vocalizations depend on parental reinforcement. Language development occurs in well-delineated stages, as outlined in Table 2.3-2.

Piaget's view of cognition from birth to 2 years. Jean Piaget formulated a theory of intellectual development that views cognition as a special instance of biological adaptation. In Table 2.3-3, the sensorimotor period is discussed. Piaget divided this period from birth to 2 years into six subgroups or stages.

Personal, emotional, and social development. The stages of emotional development parallel those of cognitive development. Indeed, it is the caretaking person who provides the major stimulus for both aspects of mental growth. The human infant is totally dependent on adult caretakers for sheer survival. Through this regular and predictable interaction, an affectional tie between infant and caretaker develops. The infant's behavioral repertoire expands as a consequence of the caretaker's social responses to its behaviors (Figure 2.3-1).

In the first year, an infant's mood is highly variable and is intimately related to internal states, such as hunger. Toward the second two-thirds of the first year, mood is increasingly related to external social cues (e.g., a parent can get even a

Table 2.3-1
Landmarks of Normal Behavioral Development

Age	Motor and Sensory Behavior	Adaptive Behavior	Personal and Social Behavior
Birth to 4 weeks	Hand to mouth reflex, grasping reflex, Rooting reflex (turning cheek toward touch) Moro's reflex (digital extension when startled), sucking reflex, Babinski's reflex (toes spread when sole of foot is touched) Differentiates sounds (orients to human voice) and sweet and sour tastes Visual tracking Fixed focal distance of 8 inches	Anticipatory feeding approach behavior at 4 days	Responsiveness to mother's face, eyes, and voice within first few hours of life Endogenous smile Independent play (until 2 years)

Table 2.3-1 continued

Age	Motor and Sensory Behavior	Adaptive Behavior	Personal and Social Behavior
Under 4 weeks	Makes alternating crawling movements Moves head laterally when placed in prone position	Responds to sound of rattle and bell Regards moving objects momentarily	Quiets when picked up Impassive face
4 weeks	Tonic neck reflex positions predominate Hands fisted Head sags but can hold head erect for a few seconds Visual fixation stereoscopic vision (12 weeks)	Follows moving objects to the midline Shows no interest and drops objects immediately	Regards face and diminishes activity Responds to speech Smiles preferentially to mother
16 weeks	Symmetrical postures predominate Holds head balanced Head lifted 90 degrees when prone on forearm Visual accommodation	Follows a slowly moving object well Arms activate on sight of dangling object	Spontaneous social smile (exogenous) Aware of strange situations
28 weeks	Sits steadily, leaning forward on hands Bounces actively when placed in standing position	One-hand approach and grasp of toy Bangs and shakes rattle Transfers toys	Takes feet to mouth Pats mirror image Starts to imitate mother's sounds and actions
40 weeks	Sits alone with good coordination Creeps Pulls self to standing position Points with index finger	Matches two objects at midline Attempts to imitate scribble	Separation anxiety manifest when taken away from mother Responds to social play, such as pat-a-cake and peek-a-boo Feeds self cracker and holds own bottle
52 weeks	Walks with one hand held Stands alone briefly	Seeks novelty	Cooperates in dressing
15 months	Toddles Creeps up stairs		Points or vocalizes wants Throws objects in play or refusal
18 months	Coordinated walking, seldom falls Hurls ball Walks up stairs with one hand held	Builds a tower of three or four cubes Scribbles spontaneously and imitates a writing stroke	Feeds self in part, spills Pulls toy on string Carries or hugs a special toy, such as a doll Imitates some behavioral patterns with slight delay
2 years	Runs well, no falling Kicks large ball Goes up and down stairs alone Fine motor skills increase	Builds a tower of six or seven cubes Aligns cubes, imitating train Imitates vertical and circular strokes Develops original behaviors	Pulls on simple garment Domestic mimicry Refers to self by name Says "no" to mother Separation anxiety begins to diminish Organized demonstrations of love and protest Parallel play (plays side by side but does not interact with other children)
3 years	Rides tricycle Jumps from bottom steps Alternates feet going up stairs	Builds tower of 9 or 10 cubes Imitates a three-cube bridge Copies a circle and a cross	Puts on shoes Unbuttons buttons Feeds self well Understands taking turns
4 years	Walks down stairs one step to a tread Stands on one foot for five to eight seconds	Copies a cross Repeats four digits Counts three objects with correct pointing	Washes and dries own face Brushes teeth Associative or joint play (plays cooperatively with other children)
5 years	Skips, using feet alternately Usually has complete sphincter control Fine coordination improves	Copies a square Draws a recognizable man with a head, a body, limbs Counts 10 objects accurately	Dresses and undresses self Prints a few letters Plays competitive exercise games
6 years	Rides two-wheel bicycle	Prints name Copies triangle	Ties shoelaces

Table adapted from Arnold Gesell, M.D., and Stella Chess, M.D.

Table 2.3-2
Language Development

Age and Stage of Development	Mastery of Comprehension	Mastery of Expression
0–6 months	Shows startle response to loud or sudden sounds Attempts to localize sounds, turning eyes or head Appears to listen to speakers, may respond with smile Recognizes warning, angry, and friendly voices Responds to hearing own name	Has vocalizations other than crying Has differential cries for hunger, pain Makes vocalizations to show pleasure Plays at making sounds Babbles (repeats a series of sounds)
7–11 months *Attending to language stage*	Shows listening selectivity (voluntary control over responses to sounds) Listens to music or singing with interest Recognizes "no," "hot," own name Looks at pictures being named for up to one minute Listens to speech without being distracted by other sounds	Responds to own name with vocalizations Imitates the melody of utterances Uses jargon (own language) Has gestures (shakes head for no) Has exclamation ("oh-oh") Plays language games (pat-a-cake, peek-a-boo)
12–18 months *Single word stage*	Shows gross discriminations between dissimilar sounds (bell *vs.* dog *vs.* horn *vs.* mother's or father's voice) Understands basic body parts, names of common objects Acquires understanding of some new words each week Can identify simple objects (baby, ball, etc.) from a group of objects or pictures Understands up to 150 words by age 18 months	Uses single words (mean age of first word is 11 months; by age 18 months, child is using up to 20 words) "Talks" to toys, self, or others, using long patterns of jargon and occasional words Approximately 25% of utterances are intelligible All vowels articulated correctly Initial and final consonants often omitted
12–24 months *Two-word messages stage*	Responds to simple directions ("Give me the ball") Responds to action commands ("Come here," "Sit down") Understands pronouns (me, him, her, you) Begins to understand complex sentences ("When we go to the store, I'll buy you some candy")	Uses two-word utterances ("mommy sock," "all gone," "ball here") Imitates environmental sounds in play ("moo," "rrmm, rrmm," etc.) Refers to self by name, begins to use pronouns Echoes two or more last words of sentences Begins to use three-word telegraphic utterances ("all gone ball," "me go now") Utterances 26% to 50% intelligible Uses language to ask for needs
24–36 months *Grammar formation stage*	Understands small body parts (elbow, chin, eyebrow) Understands family name categories (grandma, baby) Understands size (the little one, big one) Understands most adjectives Understands functions (why do we eat, why do we sleep)	Uses real sentences with grammatical function words (can, will, the, a) Usually announces intentions before acting "Conversations" with other children, usually just monologues Jargon and echolalia gradually drop from speech Increased vocabulary (up to 270 words at 2 years, 895 at 3 years) includes slang Speech 50% to 80% intelligible P, b, m articulated correctly Speech may show rhythmic disturbances
36–54 months *Grammar development stage*	Understands prepositions (under, behind, between) Understands many words (up to 3,500 at 3 years, 5,500 at 4 years) Understands cause and effect (What do you do when you're hungry?, cold?) Understands analogies (Food is to eat, milk is to ______)	Correct articulation of n,w,ng,h,t,d,k,g Uses language to relate incidents from the past Uses wide range of grammatical forms: plurals, past tense, negatives, questions Plays with language: rhymes, exaggerates Speech 90% intelligible, occasional errors in the ordering of sounds within words Able to define words Egocentric use of language rare Can repeat a 12-syllable sentence correctly Some grammatical errors still occur
55 months on *True communication stage*	Understands concepts of number, speed, time, space Understands left and right Understands abstract terms Is able to categorize items into semantic classes	Uses language to tell stories, share ideas, and discuss alternatives Increasing use of varied grammar; spontaneous self-correction of grammatical errors Stabilizing of articulation of f,v,s,z,l,r,th, and consonant clusters Speech 100% intelligible

Reprinted with permission from M Rutter, L Hersov eds, *Child and Adolescent Psychiatry*. Blackwell, London, 1985.

Table 2.3-3
Overview of Piaget's Sensorimotor Period of Cognitive Development

Age	Characteristics
1. Birth–2 months	Uses inborn motor and sensory reflexes (sucking, grasping, looking) to interact and accommodate to the external world
2. 2–5 months	Primary circular reaction—coordinates activities of own body and five senses (e.g., sucking thumb); reality remains subjective—does not seek stimuli outside of its visual field; displays curiosity.
3. 5–9 months	Secondary circular reaction—seeks out new stimuli in the environment; starts both to anticipate consequences of own behavior and to act purposefully to change the environment; beginning of intentional behavior
4. 9 months–1 year	Shows preliminary signs of object permanence; has a vague concept that objects exist apart from itself; plays peek-a-boo; imitates novel behaviors
5. 1 year–18 months	Tertiary circular reaction—seeks out new experiences; produces novel behaviors
6. 18 months–2 years	Symbolic thought—uses symbolic representations of events and objects; shows signs of reasoning (e.g., uses one toy to reach for and get another); attains object permanence

Table adapted from H P Ginsburg: Jean Piaget. In *Comprehensive Textbook of Psychiatry,* ed 4, H I Kaplan and B J Sadock, editors, p 179. Williams & Wilkins, Baltimore, 1985.

hungry infant to smile). When the child is internally comfortable, a sense of interest and pleasure in the world and in primary caretakers should prevail. The development of the infant's personal and social behavior is outlined in Table 2.3-1.

Erikson's stage of basic trust versus basic mistrust (birth to 1 year). Erikson wrote in *Growth and Crisis of the Healthy Personality*: "For the first component of a healthy personality I nominate a sense of basic trust which I think is an attitude toward oneself and the world derived from the experience of the first year of life. Trust is the expectation that one's needs will be taken care of and that the world or outer providers can be relied upon."

This period coincides with Freud's oral stage of development, in which the mouth is the most sensitive zone of the body. Finding the nipple, sucking, and taking in nutrients fill the infant's primary needs. The trust-inducing mother attends to these needs assiduously, thus laying the groundwork for the infant's future positive expectation of the world. The loving parent also attends to the infant's other senses—sight, touch, and hearing. Through this interaction, either infants develop the feeling of trust that their wants will be satisfied, or, if the mother is not attentive, infants develop the mistrustful sense that they are not going to get what they want.

Toward the second half of the first year, the oral crisis occurs. At this point, infants' teeth develop, and a drive to bite occurs. Infants progress from simply being passive to becoming active. If the infants bite too aggressively, however, the nipple is taken away. As a result, infants learn that they can influence the environment and begin to develop a sense of themselves as individuals separate from the environment. In today's culture, weaning from the breast or bottle begins toward the end of this phase. Erikson believed that this separation is the basis of a sense of sorrow or nostalgia. However,

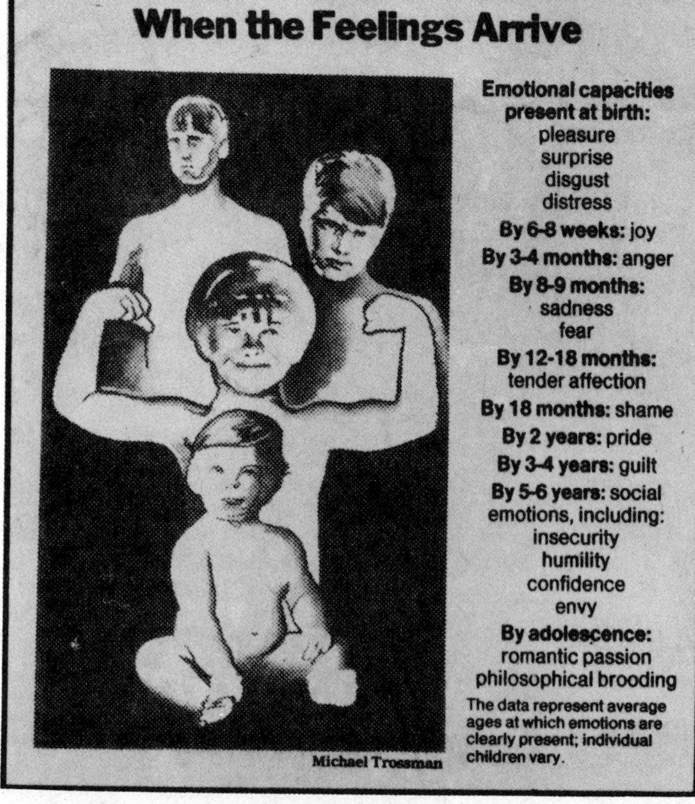

Figure 2.3-1. Emotional development from infancy through adolescence. From Joseph Campas at the University of Denver and other researchers. Used with permission of the New York Times Company, 1984.

if basic trust is strong, the child develops a sense of hope and optimism.

An impairment of basic trust leads to basic mistrust. An affectionate, loving mother or surrogate mother who gives consistent, high-quality care provides the basis for the development of trust. Prolonged separation from the mother at this time can lead to depression, hospitalism, anaclitic depression, or a depressive tone that becomes part of the person's adult character structure.

TODDLER PERIOD (15 MONTHS TO 2½ YEARS)

The second year of life is marked by acceleration of motor and intellectual development. The ability to walk confers on toddlers a degree of control over their own actions; this mobility enables children to determine when to approach and when to withdraw. The acquisition of speech profoundly extends their horizons. Typically, children learn to say "no" before they learn to say "yes." Toddlers' negativism plays a vital part in the development of independence. If persistent, however, this oppositional behavior connotes a problem.

Developmental Landmarks

Normal milestones include progressing from clumsy to coordinated walking and even running and climbing steps. Fine-motor capacities grow (e.g., toddlers can scribble). Learning language is a crucial task of the toddler period. Vocalizations become more distinct, with the ability to name a few objects and to make needs known in one or two words. Near the end of the second year and into the third year, toddlers can sometimes use short sentences. They can begin to reason and to listen to explanations that can help them tolerate delay. Toddlers can create new behaviors from old ones (originality) and engage in symbolic activities (e.g., using words, playing with dolls when the dolls represent something, such as a feeding sequence). They have variable capacities for concentration and self-regulation.

Personal, emotional, and social development. In the second year, affects of pleasure and displeasure become further differentiated. Observed are excited explorations, assertive pleasure, pleasure in discovery and in developing new behavior (e.g., new games), including teasing and surprising or fooling the parent (e.g., hiding). There are capacities for an organized demonstration of love (e.g., running up and hugging, smiling, and kissing the parent at the same time) and protest (e.g., turning away, crying, banging, biting, hitting, yelling, and kicking). Comfort with family and apprehension with strangers may increase. Anxiety appears to be related to disapproval and the loss of a loved caretaker, and it can be disorganizing. For additional information see Table 2.3-1.

Erikson's stage of autonomy versus shame and doubt (1 to 3 years). Children in the second and third years of life learn to walk alone, to feed themselves, to control the anal sphincter, and to talk. It is this muscular maturation that sets the tone for this stage of development. Autonomy refers to children's sense of mastery over themselves and over drives and impulses. Toddlers gain a sense of their separateness from others. "I," "you," "me," and "mine" are common words used by children during this period. Children have a choice of holding on or letting go, of being cooperative or stubborn. The term "terrible twos" refers to the willfulness of children in this stage of development.

This period coincides with Freud's anal stage of development. For Erikson, this is the time for the child either to retain feces—holding in—or to eliminate feces—letting go—both behaviors having an effect on the mother. Too rigorous toilet training—which is commonplace in today's society and requires a clean, punctual, and deodorized body—can produce an overly compulsive personality that is stingy, meticulous, and selfish. Known as anal personalities, such persons are parsimonious, punctual, and perfectionistic.

Parenting. If parents permit the child to function with some autonomy and are supportive without being overprotective, toddlers gain self-confidence and feel they can control themselves and their world. But if toddlers either are punished for being autonomous or are overcontrolled, they feel angry and ashamed. If parents show approval when the child shows self-control, self-esteem is enhanced, and a sense of pride develops. Parental overcontrol or loss of self-control, also called muscular and anal impotence by Erikson, produces a sense of doubt and shame. Shame implies that one is looked down on by the outside world. It exploits the child's sense of being small as one stands upright for the first time. Feeling small, the child is easily shamed by poor parenting experiences. Too much shaming causes the child to feel evil or dirty and may pave the way for delinquent behavior. In effect, the child is saying, "If that's what they think of me, that's the way I'll behave."

Cognitive development. According to Piaget, the toddler period spans the sensorimotor and preoperational stages of development (Table 2.3-3.)

Sexual development. The forerunners of sexual differentiation are evident from birth, when parents start dressing and treating infants differently because of the expectations evoked by sex typing. Through imitation, reward, and coercion, the child assumes the behaviors that the culture defines as appropriate for its sexual role. The child exhibits curiosity about anatomical sex. If this curiosity is recognized as healthy and is met with honest and age-appropriate replies, children acquire a sense of the wonder of life and are comfortable with their own role in it. If the subject of sex is taboo and the child's questions are rebuffed, shame and discomfort result. By the age of 2½ years, children develop a sense of gender identity—that is, whether they are a boy or a girl. In general, play is determined by gender; boys play with guns, and girls play with dolls and doll houses.

Sphincter control and sleep. The second year of life is a period of increasing social demands on the child. Toilet training serves as a paradigm of the family's general training practices; that is, the parent who is overly severe in this area is likely to be punitive and restrictive in other areas as well. Control of daytime urination is usually complete by the age of 2½ years and control of nighttime urination by the age of 4 years. Bowel control is usually accomplished by the age of 4 years.

Toddlers may have sleep difficulties related to fear of the dark, which can often be managed by the use of a nightlight. In general, most toddlers sleep about 12 hours, including a two-hour nap. Parents need to be aware that children at this age may need reassurance prior to going to bed and that it takes the average 2-year-old about 30 minutes to fall asleep.

Parenting during the Toddler Period

Parallel to the changing tasks for the child are changing tasks for the parents. In infancy, the major responsibility for parents is to meet the infant's needs in a sensitive and consistent fashion, without anticipating and fulfilling all the needs so that the child never experiences tension. Some tension is desirable. The parental task at the toddler stage requires firmness about the boundaries of acceptable behavior and encouragement of the progressive emancipation of the child. Parents must be careful not to be too authoritarian at this stage. Children must be allowed to operate for themselves and be able to learn from their mistakes. And they must be protected and assisted when the challenges are beyond their abilities.

At this stage, children are likely to struggle for the exclusive affection and attention of their parents. This struggle includes rivalry both with siblings and with one or another parent for the star role in the family. Although children are beginning to be able to share, they do so with reluctance. If the demands for exclusive possession are not effectively resolved, the result is likely to be jealous competitiveness in relations with peers and lovers. The fantasies aroused by the struggle lead to fear of retaliation and displacement of fear onto external objects. In an equitable, loving family, the child elaborates a moral system of ethical rights. Parents need to set realistic limits on the toddler's behavior, balancing between punishment and permissiveness.

PRESCHOOL PERIOD (2½ TO 6 YEARS)

This period is characterized by marked physical and emotional growth. Somewhere between 2 and 3 years of age, children reach half of their adult height. The 20 baby teeth are in place at the beginning of this stage, and by the end they begin to fall out. Children are ready to enter school by the time the stage ends at age 5 or 6. They have mastered the tasks of primary socialization—to control their bowels and urine, to dress and feed themselves, and to control their tears and temper outbursts, at least most of the time.

The term "preschool" for the age group of 2½ to 6 years may be a misnomer because many of these children are in preschool nurseries. Many working mothers must place their children in such nurseries or in day care centers. Preschool education can be of value; however, too great a stress on academic advancement beyond the capabilities of the child can be counterproductive.

Developmental Landmarks

Cognitive development. For Piaget, this is the preoperational phase (more specifically, 2 to 7 years), during which children begin to think symbolically. In general, however, their thinking is egocentric, as in the sensorimotor period; they cannot place themselves in the position of another child and are incapable of empathy. Preoperational thought is also intuitive and prelogical; children in this stage do not understand cause-effect relationships.

Personal, emotional, and social behavior. At the start of the preschool period, children can express such complex affects as love, unhappiness, jealousy, and envy at both preverbal and verbal levels. The child's emotions are still easily influenced by somatic events, such as tiredness and hunger. Although affects are still mostly at an egocentric level, the child's capacity for cooperation and sharing are emerging. Anxiety is related to the loss of a loved and depended-on person and to the loss of approval and acceptance. Although still potentially disorganizing, anxiety can be better tolerated now than at age 2.

Four-year-olds are learning to share and to have concern for others. Feelings of tenderness are sometimes expressed. Anxiety over bodily injury and the loss of a loved person's approval is sometimes disruptive.

By the end of the preschool period, children have many emotions that are relatively stable. Expansiveness, curiosity, pride, and a gleeful excitement related to the self and the family are balanced with coyness, shyness, fearfulness, jealousy, and envy. Shame and humiliation are evident. Capacities for empathy and love are better developed but fragile and easily lost if competitive or jealous strivings intervene. Anxiety and fears are related to bodily injury and loss of respect, love, and emerging self-esteem. Guilt feelings are possible. For additional information, see Table 2.3-1.

Children between ages 3 and 6 years are very aware of the genitalia and of the differences between the sexes. In their play, doctor-nurse games allow children to act out their sexual fantasies. Their awareness of their bodies extends beyond the genitalia. There is a preoccupation with illness or injury, so much so that this period has been called the Band-Aid phase; every injury needs to be examined and taken care of by a parent.

Freud described this phase as the phallic stage of development; infancy represented the oral phase; toddlerhood, the anal stage. During this phase, pleasure is connected with the genital area. It is the time of the Oedipus complex, when children have sexual impulses toward the opposite-sex parent and want to eliminate the same-sex parent—wishes for which punishment is expected (the talion principle). The punishment feared by boys is castration. Castration anxiety leads the boy to give up his mother as a love object, to repress his impulses toward her, to identify with his father, and in the process to form a superego. The Electra complex holds that the girl wishes to have the exclusive love of her father and to replace her mother; the daughter resolves this conflict by identifying with her mother. Lack of a penis is considered evidence of castration. Freud believed that girls develop penis envy as a result and want to possess their father in order to obtain his penis. The little girl's urge to marry the father and have a baby therefore represents the desire for a penis.

Observational research of children over the past two decades has yielded data that contradict some of Freud's theories of gender identity. Normatively, gender identity is a process that evolves over the first few years of life. It does not occur precipitously in boys with resolution of the Oedipus complex, nor is penis envy a normal or universal determinant of female gender identity.

Erikson's stage of initiative versus guilt (3 to 5 years). As children approach the end of the third year, they are able to initiate both motor and intellectual activity. Whether this initiative is reinforced depends on how much physical freedom children are given and how well their intellectual curiosity is satisfied. If toddlers are made to feel inadequate about their behavior or interests, they may emerge from this period with a sense of guilt about self-initiated activity. Conflicts over initiative can prevent developing children from experiencing their full potential and can interfere with their sense of ambition, which develops during this stage.

During this period, the child's growing sense of sexual curiosity is manifested by engaging in group sex play or touching one's own genitalia or those of a peer. If parents do not make an issue of these childhood impulses (Erikson gives the example, "If you touch it, the doctor will cut it off"), they are eventually repressed and reappear during adolescence as part of puberty. If too much is made of these impulses by the parent, the child may become sexually inhibited.

The child is able to move independently and vigorously by the end of this stage. By playing with peers, the child learns how to interact with others. If aggressive fantasies have been managed properly (neither punished nor encouraged), the child develops a sense of initiative and ambition.

At the end of this stage of initiative versus guilt, the child's conscience (Freud's superego) becomes established. The child learns not only that there are limits to one's behavioral repertoire (for example, that a boy cannot sleep with his mother or murder his father) but that aggressive impulses can be expressed in constructive ways, such as healthy competition, playing games, and using toys. The development of a conscience sets the tone for the moral sense of right and wrong. Excessive punishment, however, can restrict the child's imagination and initiative. The child who develops too strong a superego, with an all-or-nothing quality, may insist as an adult that other persons adhere to his moral code and, therefore, may become a great potential danger to himself and to his fellow men. If the crisis of initiative is successfully resolved, a sense of responsibility, dependability, and self-discipline develops in the personality.

Sibling rivalry. The child relates to others in new ways. The birth of a sibling (a common occurrence during this period) tests the preschool child's capacity for further cooperation and sharing. It may also evoke sibling rivalry, which is most likely to occur at this time. Sibling rivalry is dependent on child-rearing practices. Favoritism, for any reason, is a common outcome of such rivalry. Children who get special treatment because they are gifted, defective in some way, or of a preferred gender are likely to be the recipient of angry feelings from siblings. The experience with siblings may influence the growing child's relationships with peers and authority. If, for example, the needs of the new baby prevent the mother from attending the firstborn child's needs, a problem may result. If not handled properly, the displacement of the firstborn can be a traumatic event.

Play. In the preschool years, the child begins to distinguish reality from fantasy, and play reflects this growing awareness. Games of "let's pretend" are popular and help test real-life situations in a playful manner. Dramatic play in which the child acts out a role, such as that of a housewife or truck driver, is common. One-to-one play relationships advance to more complicated patterns with rivalries, secrets, and two-against-one intrigues. A child's play behavior reflects his or her level of social development.

Between 3 and 6 years of age, growth can be traced through drawings. The first drawing of a person is a circular line with marks for mouth, nose, and eyes; ears and hair are added later; next, arms and sticklike fingers appear; then legs. The last to appear is a torso in proportion to the rest of the body. The intelligent child is able to deal with greater detail. Drawings express creativity throughout the child's development. They are representational and formal in early childhood, make use of perspective in middle childhood, and become abstract and affect-laden in adolescence. Drawings also reflect a person's body image concepts and sexual and aggressive impulses.

Imaginary companions. Imaginary companions most often appear during the preschool years, usually in children with above-average intelligence and usually in the form of persons. Imaginary companions may also be things, such as toys that are anthropomorphized. Some studies indicate that up to 50 percent of children between the ages of 3 and 10 years have imaginary companions at one time or another. Their significance is not clear, but they are usually friendly, relieve loneliness, and reduce anxiety in the child. In most instances, imaginary companions disappear by age 12, but they may occasionally persist into adulthood.

MIDDLE YEARS (6 TO 12 YEARS)

During this period, the child enters kindergarten and elementary school. The formal demands for academic learning and accomplishment become major determinants of further personality development.

Developmental Landmarks

Motor and sensory behavior. Improved gross motor coordination and greater muscle strength enable the child to write with fluency and draw more artistically. The child is also capable of complex motor tasks and activities, such as tennis, gymnastics, golf, baseball, and skateboarding.

Language and cognitive development. Language is used to express complex ideas with relationships among a number of elements. There is a tendency for logical exploration to dominate fantasy, increased interest in rules and orderliness, and an increased capacity for self-regulation. The ability to concentrate is well established by age 9 or 10.

From Piaget's perspective, this phase is the stage of concrete operations, during which a child's conceptual skills develop and thinking becomes more organized and logical. Toward the end of this period, the child begins to think in more abstract terms.

Personal, emotional, and social behavior. This is a stage that Freud called the latency period, resulting from resolution of the Oedipus complex and an assumed quiescence of the sexual drive. Oedipal resolution also accounts for superego development, the formation of which enables the child to make moral judgments. In recent years, evidence has shown that latency results from maturational changes in the brain. The child is now capable of greater independence, learning, and socialization. In contrast to Freud, recent theorists consider moral development a gradual, stepwise process spanning childhood, adolescence, and young adulthood. The child in latency is able to deal with the emotional and intellectual demands that are being placed on him or her by the environment, particularly in the school. See Section 2.4, "Adolescence," for additional information on moral development.

According to Freud, the girl has identified with her mother. Instead of wanting the father as a love object, the daughter now directs her energy toward wanting somebody like him. It is still culturally acceptable, however, for the girl to remain attached to the father during latency, although not with the same degree of emotional intensity.

In latency, both girls and boys make new identifications with other adults, such as teachers and counselors. These identifications may so influence the girl that her goals of wanting to marry and have babies, as her mother did, may be combined with a desire for a career, postponed, or abandoned entirely.

Some girls in latency act as if they were still in the oedipal stage. A girl who is unable to identify with the mother or whose father is overly attached may become fixated at a 6-year-old level and, as a result, may fear men or women or both or become seductively close to them. In either case, she will not be seen as normal during these school-age years. A similar situation may occur in the boy who enters latency without having resolved his Oedipus complex. The child may have been unable to identify successfully with his father because the father was aloof, brutal, or absent. Perhaps the mother prevented the boy from identifying with his father by being overprotective or by binding the son too closely to herself. As a result, the child may enter latency with a variety of problems. The male child may be fearful of men, unsure of his sense of masculinity, or unwilling to leave the mother (which may be manifested by a school phobia), or he may lack initiative and be unable to master school tasks, which then present as academic problems.

The school-age period is a time in which peer interaction assumes major importance. Interest in relationships outside the family take precedence over those within the family. A special relationship exists, however, with the same-sex parent, with whom the child identifies and who is now a role model. At this time, the child idealizes the same-sex parent and wants to be like that parent.

Empathy and a concern for others begin to emerge early in this stage, so by the time children are 9 or 10, they have well-developed capacities for love, compassion, and sharing. There is a capacity for long-term, stable relationships with family, peers, and friends, including best friends. Although sexual feelings are repressed, emotions regarding sexual differences begin to emerge as either excitement or shyness with the opposite sex. The school-age child prefers to interact with children of the same sex. This period has also been referred to as a psychosexual and psychosocial moratorium—a lull between the preschool child's oedipal strivings and the adolescent's pubescent sexual impulses. The moratorium is characterized by an absence of overt sexual behavior, which, according to Freud, is sublimated and expressed in other abilities, such as sports, studies, and nonsexual peer activities.

The chum period. Harry Stack Sullivan postulated that a chum or buddy is an important phenomenon during this period. By about 10 years of age, a close same-sex relationship develops, which Sullivan believed is necessary for further healthy psychological growth. Moreover, Sullivan believed an early harbinger of schizophrenia is the absence of a chum during the middle years of childhood.

School refusal. In some children, the refusal to go to school occurs at this time, generally as a result of separation anxiety. A fearful mother may transmit her own fear of separation to the child, or a child who has not resolved dependency needs panics at the idea of separation. School refusal is usually not an isolated problem; children with the problem typically avoid many other social situations.

Erikson's stage of industry versus inferiority (6 to 11 years). Erikson's fourth stage is the school-age period, during which the child begins to participate in an organized program of learning. In all cultures, children receive formal instruction at about the age of 6; in Western culture, the child learns to be literate and technical. In other societies, learning may involve becoming familiar with tools and weapons.

Industry, the ability to work and to acquire adult skills, is the keynote of the stage. Children learn that they are able to make things and, most important, able to master and complete a task. If too great an emphasis is placed on rules, regulations, shoulds, or oughts, the child will develop a sense of duty at the expense of a natural desire to work. The productive child learns the pleasure of work completion and the pride of doing something well.

A sense of inadequacy and inferiority, the potential negative outcome of this stage, results from several sources: The child may be discriminated against at school; the child may be told he or she is inferior; the child may be overprotected at home or excessively dependent on the emotional support of the family; or the child may compare himself or herself unfavorably with the same-sex parent. Good teachers and good parents who encourage their children to value diligence and productivity and to persevere in a difficult enterprise are bulwarks against a sense of inferiority.

To Erikson, this stage is socially decisive because the child learns how to work with others and develops a sense of division of labor and equality of opportunity. It is equivalent to Freud's latency period because biological drives are dormant and peer interaction prevails.

OTHER ISSUES IN CHILDHOOD

Dreams and Sleep

Dreams in children can have a profound effect on behavior. During the child's first year of life, when the differentiation between reality and fantasy is not yet fully achieved, the dream may be experienced as if it were or could be true. The child has strong reactions to dreams; they are viewed either with pleasure or, as is most often reported, with fear. The dream content is to be seen in connection with the life experience, the developmental stage, the mechanisms used during dreaming, and the sex of the child.

Disturbing dreams peak when the child is 3, 6, and 10 years old. The 2-year-old child may dream about being bitten or chased; at the age of 4, there are many animal dreams, and people are introduced who either protect or destroy. At age 5 or 6, dreams of being killed or injured, of flying and being in cars, and of ghosts become more prominent, exposing the role of conscience, moral values, and increasing conflicts around these themes. In early childhood, aggressive dreams rarely seem to occur; instead, it is the dreamer who is in danger, which may reflect the child's dependent position. By about the age of 5, children realize that their dreams are not real; before that time, they believe dreams are real events. By age 7, children know that dreams are created by themselves.

At certain periods, a child wakes from sleep disturbed by the content of the dream and is extremely frightened; the child is unwilling to return to sleep unless comforted by a parent. *Pavor nocturnus* (night terrors) is a severe form of fright in which the content of the dream overwhelms reality, so that the child remains frightened by the dream for an extended period of time. During night terrors, which occur during nonrapid eye movement (NREM) sleep Stages 3 and 4, children remain in an in-between state from which they cannot be fully aroused. Children do not appear to recognize the people in the room, and, even though their eyes are open, the dream seems to continue.

Between the ages of 3 and 6 years, it is normal for children to want to keep the bedroom door open or a light on, so that they can either maintain contact with their parents or view the room in a more realistic and less fearful way. At times, children resist going to sleep in order to avoid dreaming. Disorders associated with falling asleep, therefore, are often connected with the dream experience. Rituals are set up as protective devices designed to make safer the withdrawal from the world of reality into the world of sleep.

Somnambulism, sleepwalking, may occur. Very often,

the content of the dream seems to release motor discharge, and children go to those persons and places that can offer them protection.

Periods of rapid eye movement (REM) take place about 60 percent of the time during the first few weeks of life, during which the infant sleeps two-thirds of the time. Premature babies spend even more time asleep. The sleep-wake cycle of newborns is about three hours long. The dream-to-sleep ratio is quite stable among adults: 20 percent of sleeping time is spent dreaming. Even in newborns, there is brain activity similar to that of the dreaming state. It is doubtful, however, that dreaming is possible before speech—that is, before the existence of mental representation of the outside world.

Effects of Divorce on Children

Many children live in homes in which divorce has occurred. Over 20 percent of all children in America live in homes in which one parent (usually the mother) is the sole head of household. Forty-five percent of all children born in any given year can expect to live with only one parent before they reach the age of 18 years. The age of the child at the time of divorce affects the reaction to the divorce. Immediately after the divorce, there is an increase in behavioral and emotional disorders in all age groups. Three- to 6-year-old children do not understand what is actually happening, and those who do often assume that they are responsible for the divorce in some way. If divorce occurs when the child is between 7 and 12 years, school performance generally declines. Older children, especially adolescents, comprehend the situation and believe that they could have prevented the divorce had they intervened in some way—in effect, serving as a surrogate marriage therapist—but they are still hurt, angry, and critical of their parents' behavior. Some children harbor the fantasy that their parents will be reunited at some future date. Such children show animosity toward a parent's real or potential new mate because they are forced to recognize that a reconciliation will not take place. Recovery from and adaptation to the effects of divorce usually take three to five years, but about one-third of children from divorced homes have lasting psychological trauma. Among boys, physical aggression is a common sign of distress. Adolescents tend to spend more time away from the parental home after divorce. Suicide attempts may occur as a direct result of the divorce; one of the predictors of suicide in adolescence is the recent divorce or separation of the parents. Children who adapt well to divorce do so if each parent makes an effort to continue to relate to the child in spite of the child's anger. To facilitate this recovery, the divorced couple must avoid arguing with one another and must demonstrate consistent behavior toward the child.

Stepparents. When remarriage occurs, the child must learn to adapt to the stepparent and the so-called reconstituted family. This adaptation is usually difficult, especially if the stepparent is nonsupportive or resentful of the stepchild or favors his or her own natural children. A natural child born to the new mother or father—a stepsibling—sometimes receives more attention than a stepchild and, as a result, is the object of sibling rivalry.

Adoption

Adoption is defined as the process by which a child is taken into a family by one or more adults who are not the biological parents but are recognized by law as the child's parents. In 1981, it was estimated that approximately 2.5 million persons under 18 years of age were adopted. Fifty-two percent of the children were adopted by persons not related to them by birth or marriage, and the remainder were adopted by relatives or stepparents. The majority of adopted children were born out of wedlock, and 40 percent of all such children were born to mothers age 15 to 19 years.

Adoptive parents most often tell their children between the ages of 2 and 4 years of their status, to reduce the possibility that their children will learn of their adoption from extrafamilial sources, which might cause them to feel betrayed by their adoptive parents and abandoned by their biological ones.

Emotional and behavior disorders have been reported to be higher among adopted children than nonadopted children; aggressive behavior, stealing, and learning disturbances are higher among adopted children as well. The later the age of adoption, the higher the incidence and the more severe the degree of behavior problems.

Throughout childhood and adolescence, children may be preoccupied with fantasies of two sets of parents. The adopted child may split the two sets of parents into good parents and bad parents. There is usually a strong desire to know the biological parents, and some children pattern themselves after their fantasies of their absent biological parents, creating a conflict with their adoptive parents. In most cases in which adopted children have sought out and met their biological parents (and vice versa), the experience has been generally positive, especially if the child is in late adolescence or early adulthood.

Other Family Influences

In childhood and adolescence, the death of a parent is associated with adverse effects. There is an increase in later emotional problems, particularly a greater susceptibility to depression and divorce.

This finding is in sharp contrast to separations that result from less traumatic events. There is no evidence, for example, that working mothers raise children who are less healthy than those raised by mothers in the home. Home caretakers can act as surrogate mothers, and in such cases the children do not become more attached to the caretaker than to the parent.

The role of day care centers for children is under continuous investigation. Some studies show that children placed in day care centers before the age of 5 years are less assertive and less effectively toilet trained than a home-reared group. Such studies need to take into account the quality of both the day care center and the home from which the child comes. For example, the child from a disadvantaged home may be better off in a day care center than the child from an advantaged home. Similarly, a woman who wishes to leave the home to work for financial or other reasons and is unable to do so may resent being forced to remain in the home in a child-rearing role and, thus, may adversely affect the child.

Parenting styles. Michael Rutter described four types of parenting styles: (1) authoritarian, characterized by rigidity and strict rules, which can lead to depression in the child; (2) permissive, characterized by indulgence and no limit setting, which can lead to poor impulse control; (3) indifferent, characterized by neglect and lack of involvement, leading to aggressive behavior; and (4) reciprocal, characterized by shared decision making with behavior directed in a rational manner, which results in a sense of self-reliance.

In general, experimental studies indicate that the most effective parenting involves consistency and reward for good behavior and punishment for undesirable behavior, both of which should occur within the context of a warm, loving environment.

References

Ainsworth M, Bell S M, Stayton D: Infant-mother attachment and social development: Socialization as a product of reciprocal responsiveness to signals. In *The Integration of the Child into a Social World,* M Richards, editor. Cambridge University Press, Cambridge, England, 1974.

Bowlby J: *Attachment and Loss,* vol. I: *Attachment.* Basic Books, New York, 1969.

Brodzinksy D M, Schechter D, eds: *The Psychology of Adoption.* Oxford University Press, New York, 1988.

Brodzinsky D M, Schechter D, Brodzinsky A M: Children's knowledge of adoption: Developmental change and implications for adjustment. In *Thinking about the Family: View of Parents and Children.* R Ashmore and D. Brodzinsky, editors. Erlbaum, Hillsdale, NJ, 1986.

Butler J A: Child health and the family. Bull NY Acad Med *65*: 285, 1989.

Call J D, ed: Normal development. In *Basic Handbook of Child Psychiatry,* J D Noshpitz, editor, vol. 1. Basic Books, New York, 1979.

Call J D, Galenson, E. Tyson, R L, eds: *Frontiers of Infant Psychiatry,* vols. 1, 2. Basic Books, New York, 1983, 1984.

Chehrazi S, ed: *Psychosocial Issues in Day Care.* American Psychiatric Press, Washington, DC, 1990.

Dworkin P H: Behavior during middle childhood: Developmental themes and clinical issues. Pediatr Ann *18*: 347, 1989.

Erikson E H: *Childhood and Society,* ed 2, Norton, New York, 1963.

Feldman H: The development of thinking skills in school age children. Pediatr Ann *18*: 356, 1989.

Field T: Individual and maturational differences in infant expressivity. New Dir Child Dev *44*: 9, 1989.

Greenspan S I: Normal child development. In *Comprehensive Textbook of Psychiatry,* ed 5, H I Kaplan and B J Sadock, editors, p 1695.Williams & Wilkins, Baltimore, 1989.

Greenspan S I, Greenspan, N T: *First Feelings: The Emotional Care of Infants and Young Children.* Viking Press, New York, 1985.

Kohnstamm G A, Bates J E, Rothbart M K, eds: *Temperament in Childhood.* Wiley, New York, 1989.

Lewis M: Emotional development in the preschool child. Pediatr Ann *18*: 316, 1989.

Lidz T: *The Person: His and Her Development Throughout the Life Cycle,* Basic Books, New York, 1976.

Parke R D: Social development in infancy: A 25-year perspective. Adv Child Dev Behav *21*: 1, 1989.

Tse W Y, Hindmarsh P C, Brook C G: The infancy-childhood-puberty model of growth: Clinical aspects. Acta Paediatr Scand [Suppl] *356*: 38, 1989.

2.4. / Adolescence

Adolescence is the period between childhood and adulthood that is characterized by biological, psychological, and social developmental changes. The biological onset of adolescence is signaled by the rapid acceleration of skeletal growth and the beginnings of sexual development; the psychological onset is characterized by an acceleration of cognitive development and personality formation; and socially, it is a period of intensified preparation for the forthcoming role of young adulthood. Adolescence is a period of variable onset and duration.

It is useful to distinguish between puberty, which is a physical process of change characterized by the development of secondary sex characteristics, and adolescence, which is more a psychological process of change. Under ideal circumstances, the processes are synchronous; when they do not occur simultaneously, as they often do not, the adolescent has to cope with that as an added stress.

In many cultures the onset of adolescence is clearly signaled by puberty rites, usually involving the adolescent's performance of feats of strength and courage. In technologically advanced societies, however, the end of childhood and the requirements for adulthood are not clearly defined. In these cultures the adolescent undergoes a more prolonged and, in some cases, confused struggle to attain independent adult status.

The end of adolescence occurs when the adolescent is accorded full adult prerogatives, the timing and length of which vary among societies. In the United States the long period of specialized study required for occupational roles delays for many the age of self-support, the opportunity for marriage, and the creative contribution to society—all attributes of the adult role.

Adolescence is commonly divided into three periods: (1) early (ages 11 to 14), (2) middle (ages 14 to 17), and (3) late (ages 17 to 20).

EARLY ADOLESCENCE (11 TO 14 YEARS)

Early adolescence is marked by the onset of puberty. The biological changes of puberty are initiated and controlled by complex interactions between the gonadal and adrenal systems and the hypothalamic-pituitary axis. Hormonal activity produces the manifestations of puberty, which are traditionally categorized as primary and secondary sex characteristics. The primary characteristics are those directly involved in coitus and reproduction: the reproductive organs and the external genitalia. The secondary characteristics include breast development and hip enlargement in girls and facial hair growth and change of voice pitch in boys. The characteristic increase in height and weight occurs earlier in girls than in boys, so that, by age 12, girls are generally both taller and heavier than boys.

Precocious or delayed growth, acne, obesity, and enlarged mammary glands in boys and inadequate or overabundant breast development in girls are some examples of deviations from the expected patterns of maturation. Although these conditions may not be medically significant, they often lead to psychological damage. During this period adolescents are extremely sensitive to the opinions of peers and are constantly comparing themselves with others. Any deviation, real or imagined, can lead to feelings of inferiority, low self-esteem, and loss of confidence.

Hormonal Changes

Most adult levels of hormones are achieved by age 16, but girls begin puberty two years earlier than boys; the average age is 11 for girls and 13 for boys. Sex hormones increase slowly throughout adolescence and correspond to the bodily changes. Follicle-stimulating hormone (FSH) and luteinizing hormone (LH) also increase throughout adolescence, but LH frequently is elevated above adult values between age 17 and 18. LH levels characteristic of adult functioning begin in late adolescence. From age 16 to 17, there seems to be a large increase in average testosterone levels, which then decrease to stabilize at the adult level. See Table 2.4-1 for a summary of pubertal changes.

Psychosexual Development

Freud referred to adolescence as the period of genitality in which the libido or sexual energy, which has remained latent during the preadolescent years, is revived. The sex drive is triggered by certain androgens, such as testosterone, which are at higher levels during adolescence than at any other time of life. According to William Masters and Virginia Johnson, the peak of the male sex drive occurs between 17 and 18 years of age. The early adolescent vents libidinal urges most often through masturbation, a safe way to satisfy sexual impulses.

Because girls enter puberty two years earlier than boys, they may begin dating and having sexual intercourse at an earlier age; however, girls at this age are less sexually active than boys. Boys are easily aroused by stimuli, and erections are frequent. For girls, the sexual impulse is more closely associated with other feelings: Girls tend to view sex and love as related, whereas boys find desire or lust and love to be more separable.

The early adolescent is still attached to the family, and there is sometimes a resurgence of oedipal feelings and even sexual fantasies toward the opposite-sex parent. In general, these thoughts and feelings are repressed, and the adolescent's sexuality is directed outward; crushes, hero-worship, and idealization of movie and music stars are characteristic of this stage.

The school experience also accelerates and intensifies the degree of separation from the family. More and more, the adolescent exists in a world with which the parents are unfamiliar and in which they do not share. Home is only a base. The real world is the school, and the most important relationships are with those persons of similar ages and interests.

Cognitive Development

According to Jean Piaget, the child's thinking at the beginning of adolescence becomes more abstract, conceptual, logical, and future-oriented. The child is entering the stage of formal operations, which comes to fruition during adolescence. With the ability for formal thought and abstract reasoning, the adolescent discovers new facts, experiences, and feelings. Many adolescents are stimulated by this awakening and show remarkable creativity.

Some may write poetry, possibly for the only time in their lives. Others may find expression in writing, music, art, or other forms of creativity. The personal diary is a common creative outlet for adolescents. Often brilliant and talented young people lose this excitement and creativity by adulthood. Creativity may also manifest itself in such areas as gymnastic and athletic ability, abstract mathematics, philosophy, debating, and journalism. As with other expressions, these avenues of creativity may disappear with the end of adolescence. In some instances, the unusual ability may be more precocity than talent; that is, the adolescents perform in an amazingly

Table 2.4-1
Pubertal Stages

	Characteristics		
Stage	**Genital Development***	**Pubic Hair Development*†**	**Breast Development†**
1	Testes, scrotum, and penis are about the same size and shape as in early childhood	The vellus over the pubes is not further developed than over the abdominal wall (i.e., no pubic hair).	There is elevation of the papilla only.
2	Scrotum and testes are slightly enlarged. The skin of the scrotum is reddened and changed in texture. There is little or no enlargement of the penis at this stage.	There is sparse growth of long, slightly pigmented, tawny hair, straight or slightly curled, chiefly at the base of the penis or along the labia.	Breast bud stage. There is elevation of the breast and papilla as a small mound. Areolar diameter is enlarged over that of stage 1.
3	Penis is slightly enlarged, at first mainly in length. Testes and scrotum are further enlarged than in stage 2.	The hair is considerably darker, coarser, and more curled. It spreads sparsely over the function of the pubes.	Breast and areola are both enlarged and elevated more than in stage 2 but with no separation of their contours.
4	Penis is further enlarged, with growth in breadth and development of glans. Testes and scrotum are further enlarged than in stage 3; scrotum skin is darker than in earlier stages.	Hair is now adult in type, but the area covered is still considerably smaller than in the adult. There is no spread to the medial surface of the thighs.	The areola and papilla form a secondary mound projecting above the contour of the breast.
5	Genitalia are adult in size and shape.	The hair is adult in quantity and type, with distribution of the horizontal (or classically feminine) pattern. Spread is to the medial surface of the thighs, but not up the linea alba or elsewhere above the base of the inverse triangle.	Mature stage. The papilla only projects, with the areola recessed to the general contour of the breast.

Table by R W Brunstetter, L B Silver: Normal adolescent development. In *Comprehensive Textbook of Psychiatry,* ed 4, H I Kaplan and B J Sadock, editors, p. 1609. Williams & Wilkins, Baltimore, 1985.
*For boys.
†For girls.

competent fashion at a much earlier age than their peers. This creativity may no longer appear outstanding, however, when their peers finally catch up.

MIDDLE ADOLESCENCE (14 TO 17 YEARS)

Two major biological events occur during this period of transition between early and late adolescence: (1) Boys finally catch up to and surpass girls in height and weight, and (2) menarche (the onset of menstruation) takes place in the majority of girls. Consequently, issues of sexuality, body image, pregnancy, male and female stereotypical roles, popularity, and identity are among the myriad and often overwhelming preoccupations and concerns of the adolescent during this stage.

Psychosexual Development

In middle adolescence sexual behavior and experimentation with a variety of sexual roles are common. Masturbation occurs about equally in both sexes at this time as a normal activity; however, a strict religious upbringing may engender strong feelings of guilt. Heterosexual crushes, often with an unattainable person of the same or older age, are common. Homosexual experiences may also occur at this time but are usually transient. Many adolescents need reassurance about the normality of an isolated homosexual experience and confirmation that it is not an indication of a permanent homosexual orientation.

Although many adolescents experiment with sex at an early age, recent surveys indicate that the average age for first sexual intercourse in both sexes is 16 years. There is a trend in this society toward greater and more frequent sexual activity at earlier ages. A decade ago, for example, the average age for first sexual intercourse was 18, and only 55 percent of women had had sexual intercourse by that time. Currently, 80 percent of men and 70 percent of women have engaged in coitus by age 19.

Peer Group

Middle adolescence is the time when the peer group assumes a major role. The peer group—its membership constantly shifting and its roles never formally defined—is a vital agency for social growth and change. Here, for the first time, the adolescent forms significant relationships that lack the familiarity and security of those with parents and siblings. The peer group represents challenge and opportunity to a powerful degree.

The peer group is an informal institution, different for each adolescent. For most adolescents, there is a core made up of a small number of sustained and emotionally significant friendships; emanating from that core are numbers of less-well-defined contacts with persons who may come and go and who are of some importance in the adolescent's life. Sometimes, the peer group has a defined nature—the gang, the athletic team, the social club—but more often it is only a loose confederation held together by shared interests and the strength of friendship pairings. With distinctive jokes and phrases and unique ways of dressing and thinking, the peer group is an anticipation of the experience of individual identity that lies ahead. For the time being, however, there is the safety in numbers and the protection that the group affords its members.

Inherent in the nature of the peer group is the capacity for great social pressure carried out in a context of basic acceptance and support. This social pressure is a powerful force that does much to shape adolescent character and values. The demand for conformity to the group ideal is extreme.

LATE ADOLESCENCE (17 TO 20 YEARS)

This period lasts for about three to four years and ends when young adult relationships are established. It is a period of strong feelings and emotions with intense opposite-sex relationships. Two major tasks during this period are (1) moving from a dependent to an independent person and (2) establishing an identity. Both tasks are undertaken during adolescence but extend into adulthood and must be reworked throughout the life cycle.

Dependence to Independence

A major task of adolescence is to move from being a dependent to being an independent person. The initial struggles often revolve around the established concepts of sex roles and identification. Old techniques that the child used earlier to master separation may return.

Negativism reappears. "No, I can do it myself. Don't tell me how long my hair can be. Don't tell me how short my skirt can be." This negativism is a renewed attempt to tell, first, parents and then the world that these growing persons have minds of their own. Again, negativism becomes an active verbal way of expressing anger. Adolescents may seize almost any issue to show that they have a mind separate from that of their parents. Parents and adolescents may argue about the choice of friends, peer groups, school plans and courses, or points of philosophy and etiquette. Members of each generation recall how clothes, hairstyles, and other external badges—the more shocking the better—were used to show parents that their children now had minds of their own.

Slowly, adolescents begin to blend many different values from all kinds of sources into their own existing values. By young adulthood, a new conscience or superego is established. The compatibility and the flexibility of this new superego strengthen the ability to handle and express feelings and emotions in relationships. All through life one's superego has to be able to change and grow in order to accommodate new life situations.

As adolescents begin to feel independent of their families and as the families support and encourage this emerging maturity, the question of the 3- to 6-year-old is heard once again: "Who am I?"

Erikson's Stage of Identity versus Role Diffusion (11 to 20 Years)

Developing a sense of identity is the main task of this period, which coincides with puberty and adolescence. Identity is defined as the characteristics that establish who a person is and where he or she is going. Healthy identity is built on the person's success in passing through the first three psychosocial stages and identifying with either healthy parents or parent surrogates.

Identity implies a sense of inner solidarity with the ideas and values of a social group. The adolescent is in a psychosocial moratorium between childhood and adulthood during which various roles are tested. The adolescent may make several false starts before deciding on an occupation or may drop out of school to return at a later date to complete a course of study. Moral values may change, but eventually an ethical system is consolidated into a coherent organizational framework.

An *identity crisis* occurs at the end of adolescence. Erik Erikson calls this a normative crisis because it is a normal event. But failure to negotiate this stage is abnormal and leaves the adolescent without a solid identity. The person suffers from identity diffusion or role confusion, characterized by not having a sense of self and by confusion about one's place in the world. Role confusion may manifest itself in behavioral abnormalities, such as running away, criminality, and overt psychosis. The adolescent may defend against role diffusion by joining cliques or cults or by identifying with folk heroes.

Adolescent turmoil. The normative identity crisis of adolescence described by Erikson is called adolescent turmoil by some investigators. This manifestation of the adolescent's struggle with developmental tasks is characterized by mild anxiety and depression and by minor disagreements with authority figures. Symptoms such as delinquent or acting-out behavior, rebelliousness, and academic failure are often indicative of psychiatric illness that may warrant professional attention. Adolescent turmoil, therefore, should be distinguished from a diagnosable psychiatric illness. Although it may intensify coexisting psychiatric diagnoses, adolescent turmoil is not, by itself, an abnormal state. About 20 percent of adolescents have a diagnosable psychiatric illness. The most common diagnosis is personality disorder, and the second most common is adjustment disorder.

Cognitive Development

The major cognitive event of adolescence is the development of the capacity for abstract logical thought, which Piaget called formal operations. It begins in early adolescence at age 11 or 12 and reaches its peak by late adolescence, when a person is able to make deductions—to take separate facts and bits of data and derive general concepts from them. Thinking is no longer limited to the immediate, concrete environment but is concerned with the larger world.

Piaget understood intelligence to result from the interaction between the growing organism and the changing environment. By late adolescence, the neural structure of the adolescent is complete, and a person constantly accommodates to the changing environment, not only of things but also of ideas. Consequently, the adolescent is concerned with humanitarian issues, morals, ethics, religion, judgment, and world issues. The potential for formal operational thought is limitless in terms of a person's ability to understand the world and one's place in it, but only a few reach their full potential. Most adolescents and adults function somewhere between the concrete and the formal operational stage. In general, those adolescents who go on to college are stimulated to function on a formal operational level, whereas those who enter the work force after high school are less likely to have a need for the abstract conceptualization of that type of thinking.

Moral Development

For most people, developing a well-defined sense of morality is a major accomplishment of late adolescence and adulthood. *Morality* is defined as conformity to shared standards, rights, and duties. There is, however, the possibility of conflict between two socially accepted standards, and the person learns to make judgments based on an individualized sense of conscience. There is a moral obligation to abide by established norms but only to the degree that they serve human ends. This stage of development internalizes ethical principles and the control of conduct.

Piaget described morality as developing gradually, in conjunction with the stages of cognitive development. In the preoperational stage, the child simply follows rules set forth by the parents; in the stage of concrete operations, rules are accepted by the child, but there is an inability to allow for exceptions; and in the stage of formal operations, rules are recognized in terms of what is good for the society at large.

Lawrence Kohlberg integrated Piaget's concepts and described three major levels of morality. The first level is *premorality,* in which punishment and obedience to the parent are the determining factors; the second level is *morality of conventional role-conformity,* in which the child tries to conform to gain approval and to maintain good relations with others; and the third and highest level is *morality of self-accepted moral principles,* in which there is a voluntary compliance to rules based on a concept of ethical principles and in which exceptions can be made to rules in certain circumstances.

Occupational Choice

Occupational choice stems from the question, "Where am I going?" Both men and women need to feel independent, autonomous, and content with their vocational choices. The adolescent is beleaguered by peers, parents, teachers, and counselors, as well as subconscious forces, in attempting to decide on a vocation. Whether opportunities exist for further schooling certainly plays a role in the decision. Among college graduates, 30 percent go on to some type of postcollege graduate education. Those adolescents who are unable to continue schooling are severely hampered in establishing a satisfactory vocational identity. Many are fated for lives of economic and emotional depression.

The psychological basis for a sense of individual worth as an adult rests on the acquisition of competence during adolescence. A sense of competence is acquired by experiencing success in a task that today's society views as important. The sustained motivation necessary for mastering a difficult work role is possible only when there is a real likelihood of fulfilling that role in adult life and of having it respected by others.

END OF ADOLESCENCE

The end of adolescence occurs when the person begins to assume the tasks of young adulthood, which involve choosing an occupation and developing a sense of intimacy that leads, in most cases, to marriage and parenthood. Daniel Levinson described an early-adult transition between adolescence and adulthood in which the young person begins to leave home and live more independently. During this period there is a peaking of biological development, the assumption of new social roles, the socialization into those roles that involves learning skills and attitudes required to perform the roles well, and the eventual assumption of an adult self and life structure.

OTHER ISSUES IN ADOLESCENCE

Risk-Taking Behavior

Risk-taking behavior in adolescence involves drug, alcohol, and tobacco use; promiscuous sexual activity—especially dangerous in view of acquired immune deficiency syndrome (AIDS)—and accident-prone behavior, such as fast driving, skydiving, and hang gliding. Most mortality statistics for teenagers cite accidents as the leading cause of death, with vehicular accidents accounting for about 40 percent of all deaths. The reasons for risk-taking behavior are varied and relate to counterphobic dynamics, fears of inadequacy, the need to affirm a masculine identity, and group dynamics, such as peer pressure. It may also be a reflection of the omnipotent fantasies held by some adolescents, in which they view themselves as invulnerable to harm or injury.

Parenting

The concept of the generation gap between parents and children developed from the experience of being parents of adolescents. The gap represents the difference in life experience and perceptions of life events. In addition to having to deal with the turmoil that accompanies adolescent development, parents of adolescents are usually middle-aged and have to make adjustments at that time to work, to marriage, and to their own parents. Many difficulties surround the adolescent's need to assume greater independence from the home, which can be threatening to parents who cannot let go and who need to maintain control of their children. Some parents may be unable to set limits on behavior; others act out their hidden or unconscious fantasies through the lives of their children. Superego lacunae (gaps or holes in the conscience) in the parent may engender similar lacunae in the child, which are then acted out. Moreover, the strong emerging sexuality of the adolescent may trigger anxiety in the parent. A few parents may be attracted to their opposite-sex offspring and then deal with the subsequent anxiety in maladaptive ways, such as getting angry (reaction formation).

References

Adelson J B: The mystique of adolescence. In *Childhood Psychopathology*, S I Harrison and J F McDermott, editors, p. 214. International Universities Press, New York, 1972.

Blos P: *On Adolescence: A Psychoanalytic Interpretation*. Free Press, New York, 1962.

Freud A: *Adolescence*. Psychoanal Study Child, *13:* 255, 1958.

Group for the Advancement of Psychiatry: *Normal Adolescence*, no. 68. Group for the Advancement of Psychiatry, New York, 1968.

Lidz T: *The Person: His and Her Development Throughout the Life Cycle*. Basic Books, New York, 1976.

Looney J G, Oldham D G: Normal adolescent development. In *Comprehensive Textbook of Psychiatry*, ed 5, H I Kaplan and B J Sadock, editors, p 1710. Williams & Wilkins, Baltimore, 1989.

Mussen, P H, Conger J J, Kagan, J, et al.: Adolescence. In *Essentials of Child Development and Personality*. Harper & Row, New York, 1984.

Newcomb, M D: *Life Change Events among Adolescents*. J Nerv Ment Dis *175:* 280, 1986.

Offer D, Ostrov E, Howard K I: *The Mental Health Professional Concept of Normal Adolescents*. Arch Gen Psychiatry *38:* 149, 1981.

Sarnoff C A: *Latency*. Aronson, New York, 1976.

Vaughan V C, Litt I F: *Child and Adolescent Development*. Saunders, Philadelphia, 1990.

2.5 / Adulthood

The onset of adulthood varies from person to person, and the successful passage into adulthood depends on the satisfactory resolution of childhood and adolescent crises. Adulthood is the time during which a person reaches full maturity and the potential for personal fulfillment is at its peak. The person should be capable of adapting to the ever-changing demands that this longest part of the life cycle requires.

Adulthood may be divided into three major periods: young or early adulthood, middle adulthood, and late adulthood or old age. Much of psychiatry is concerned with phenomena that occur during adulthood—marriage, child rearing, work, divorce, illness, and other stresses. Adulthood is a time of great change, which is sometimes dramatic, at other times subtle, but always continuous.

EARLY ADULTHOOD (END OF ADOLESCENCE TO 40 YEARS)

Early adulthood is characterized by the peaking of biological development, the assumption of major social roles, and the evolution of an adult self and life structure. During late adolescence, the young person leaves home and begins to function more independently. Relationships with the opposite sex become serious, and the quest for intimacy begins. This transitional period into early adulthood involves a variety of important events: high school graduation, starting a job or entry into college, and leaving home. The 20s are spent, for the most part, exploring options for occupation, marriage, or alternative relationships and making commitments in various areas. The choices made in the late teens and early 20s, however, are tentative at best; the young adult may make several false starts before a lasting commitment is reached.

Erikson's Stage of Intimacy versus Self-Absorption or Isolation (20 to 40 Years)

Classical psychoanalysis, with its emphasis on the early years of human development, was not overly concerned with this period, which extends from late adolescence through early middle age. Erik Erikson pointed out that an important psychosocial conflict can arise during this stage and that, as in previous stages, success or failure depends on how well the groundwork has been laid in earlier periods and on how the young adult interacts with the environment. The intimacy of sexual relations, friendships, and all deep associations are not frightening to the person with a resolved identity crisis. In contrast, the person who reaches the adult years in a state of continued role confusion is unable to become involved in intense and long-term relationships. Without a friend or a partner in marriage, a person may become self-absorbed and self-indulgent; as a result, a sense of isolation may grow to dangerous proportions.

In true intimacy there is mutuality. This word is reminiscent of the first stage of life. If a child achieves initiative in genitality, the sensual pleasure of childhood merges with the idea of genital orgasm, and the young adult is able to make and share love with another person. Through the crisis of intimacy versus isolation, a person transcends the exclusivity of earlier dependencies and establishes a mutuality with an extended and more diverse social group.

Developmental Tasks

During this phase of adulthood, options for occupation and marriage (or other intimate relationships) are explored. For most young adults, selecting a mate and starting a family are of paramount importance.

Carl Jung described the additional task of *individuation,* in which the adult learns to accept himself or herself as a unique person distinct from, as well as a part of, society. According to Jung, the failure to individuate leads to overconformity and uncritical acceptance of social norms.

Persons in their late 30s also become increasingly concerned with achieving greater authority, independence, and self-sufficiency. The primary goal of early adulthood is to become more autonomous and less dependent on the persons and institutions in one's life.

At about age 30 young adults are likely to feel a need to take life more seriously. Many young adults ask themselves at this time whether the life they have is the one they really want. This period of reappraisal is called the "age 30 transition" by Daniel Levinson. Some young people who feel their lives are going well reaffirm their commitments and experience a smooth transition at this time. Others, however, may experience a major crisis, manifested by marital problems, job changes, and psychiatric symptoms, such as anxiety and depression.

Roger Gould reported a similar process among persons in their late 20s and early 30s who discover new talents, wishes, tendencies, and interests not previously appreciated or acknowledged. This awareness may bring out either disillusionment and depression or a new sense of self with a more realistic appraisal of one's strengths and weaknesses.

Occupation. Social class, gender, and race affect the pursuit and development of a particular occupational choice. Blue-collar workers generally enter the work force directly from high school; white-collar workers and professionals usually enter the work force after college or professional school.

Women often exhibit one of two patterns in their 20s: Work for pay is the central component of their life structure, and family is absent or secondary; or marriage and family are primary, and career is absent or secondary. Housewives and mothers face particular problems if they decide to work. These women are expected to continue to take care of child rearing and housework, maintain the marital relationship, and at the same time deal with the demands of a career. In general, men are still not expected to juggle the roles of husband, father, and worker. Some changes are occurring in these gender expectations, but they are not sufficient to upset the stereotype of the working woman having to be Supermom and Superwife at the same time.

Ninety percent of all women have to work to support themselves. Economic necessity and personal desire now prompt the homemaker to enter the labor force, something that may not have been a consideration in the past. Dual-career families, in which both the husband and the wife have jobs, constitute more than 50 percent of all families. Employers who do not recognize family-oriented needs—such as flexible working hours, negotiable leaves, and shared or part-time jobs—contribute to family stress.

Members of racial minorities are frequently burdened with lower-class status, which limits their opportunities for rewarding and satisfying work. They frequently begin their 20s with hopes of becoming successful but are often disappointed in this endeavor later in life.

A healthy adaptation to work provides an outlet for creativity, satisfactory relationships with colleagues, pride in accomplishment, and increased self-esteem. Job satisfaction is not wholly dependent on money. In contrast, maladaptation can lead to dissatisfaction with oneself and the job, insecurity, decreased self-esteem, anger, and resentment at having to work. Symptoms of job dissatisfaction are a high rate of job changes, absenteeism, mistakes at work, accident proneness, and even sabotage.

Unemployment. The effects of unemployment transcend those of loss of income; the psychological and physical tolls are enormous. The incidence of alcoholism, homicide, violence, suicide, and mental illness rises with unemployment. The person's core identity, which is often tied to occupation and work, is seriously damaged when a job is lost, whether it is through firing, attrition, or early or regular retirement.

Marriage. Most Americans marry in their mid-20s; however, the marriage rate is going down, and an increasing number of marriages in the United States end in divorce. Most of these divorced persons marry again—in most cases more successfully than the first time—which indicates that the marital unit still provides the means for sustained intimacy, perpetuating the culture, and gratifying interpersonal needs.

Marital problems. Although marriage tends to be regarded as a permanent tie, unsuccessful unions may be terminated, as indeed they are, in most societies. In spite of this, many marriages that do not end in separation or divorce are disturbed.

In considering marital problems, the clinician is concerned not only with the persons involved but also with the marital unit itself. How any marriage works out relates to the partners selected, the personality organization or disorganization of each, the interaction between them, and the original reasons for the union. People marry for a variety of reasons—emotional, social, economic, and political, among others. One person may look to the spouse to meet unfulfilled childhood needs for good parenting. Another sees the spouse as someone to be saved from an otherwise unhappy life. Neurotic expectations between spouses increase the risk of marital problems.

Marital therapy. When families consist of grandparents, parents, children, and other relatives living under the same roof, assistance for marital problems can sometimes be obtained from a member of the extended family with whom one or both partners have rapport. However, with the contraction of the extended family in recent times, this source of informal help is no longer as accessible as it once was. Similarly, religion once played a more important role than it does now in the maintenance of family stability. Wise religious leaders are available to provide counseling; but they are not sought out to the extent that they once were, a reflection of the decline of religious influence for large segments of the population. Formerly, both the extended family and religion not only provided guidance for the couple in distress but also prevented dissolution of the marriage by virtue of the social pressure that each exerted on the couple to stay together. As family, religious, and societal pressures relaxed, legal procedures for relatively easy separation and divorce expanded. Concurrently, the need for formalized marriage counseling services developed.

Marital therapy is a form of psychotherapy for married people who are in conflict with each other. A trained person establishes a professional contract with the patient-couple and, through definite types of communication, attempts to alleviate the disturbance, reverse or change maladaptive patterns of behavior, and encourage personality growth and development.

In *marriage counseling,* only a particular conflict related to the immediate concerns of the family is discussed; it is conducted in a much more superficial manner than marital therapy by persons with less training in psychotherapy. In marriage therapy, there is a greater emphasis on restructuring the interaction between the couple, including, at times, an exploration of the psychodynamics of each of the partners. Both therapy and counseling place emphasis on helping the marital partners cope more effectively with their problems.

Parenthood. By age 30, most persons have established families and have to deal with a variety of parent-child problems. In addition to the economic burden of raising a child (estimated to be over $100,000 for a middle-class family whose child goes to college), there are emotional costs as well. The child may reawaken conflicts in parents that they themselves had as children, or the child may have a chronic illness that challenges the emotional resources of the family. In general, men are more concerned with their work and advancement in their occupation than with child rearing. Women are more concerned about their role as mothers; however, this emphasis is changing dramatically for both sexes as more women enter the job market. At about age 35, women may dramatically change the course of their lives. As their children get older, they reenter the work force to resume their careers or to start a career for the first time.

Single-parent families. There are over 30 million families with one or more children under the age of 18, and of these, 20 percent are single-parent homes in which the woman is the sole head of the household. Although the majority of these children are left in the care of their mothers, who are awarded custody by the courts in the divorce proceedings, others are abandoned by their fathers. Among black families with one or more children under 18, almost 48 percent are headed by women with no spouse present.

Children in one-parent families are characterized by a higher incidence of academic underachievement and emotional problems. When mothers are forced to work following divorce or abandonment, their children are at further risk for emotional problems because these mothers cannot devote sufficient time to the care of the children. A small number of children in single-parent homes are precocious, their maturity fostered by having to take on increased responsibilities at a young age.

MIDDLE ADULTHOOD (40 TO 65 YEARS)

The ages used to define this period vary among different theorists. Typically, this period is known as middle age. Jung referred to age 40 as the noon of life. The task of terminating early adulthood involves a process of reviewing the past, considering how one's life has gone, and deciding what the future will be like. With regard to occupation, many persons may begin to experience the gap between early aspirations and current achievements. They may wonder if the life-style and commitments they chose in early adulthood are worth continuing. They may feel that they would like to live the remaining years in a different, more satisfying way, without knowing exactly how. As children grow up and leave home, the parental roles change; at this time, people redefine their roles as husbands and wives as well.

There are important gender changes at this time. Many women, no longer needing to nurture young children, develop attitudes that have been considered masculine (e.g., becoming independent, competitive, and aggressive). Alternatively, men may develop qualities that have traditionally been considered feminine (e.g., expressiveness, dependency, and emotionalism). The new balance of the masculine and the feminine in the self may be valuable in that it enables a person to relate more effectively to someone of the opposite sex.

Erikson's Stage of Generativity versus Stagnation (40 to 65 Years)

During the decades that span the middle years of life, the adult chooses between generativity and stagnation. Generativity not only refers to a person's having or raising children but also includes a vital interest outside the home in establishing and guiding the oncoming generation or in improving society. The childless can be generative if they develop a sense of altruism and creativity. But most persons, if able, want to continue their personalities and energies in the production and care of common offspring. Wanting or having children, however, does not ensure generativity. The parents need to have achieved successful identities themselves to be truly generative.

The adult who has no interest in guiding or establishing the oncoming generation is likely to look obsessively for intimacy that is not truly intimate. Such people may marry and even produce children but all within a cocoon of self-concern and isolation. Those persons pamper themselves as if they were the children and become preoccupied with themselves. Indeed, parents who do not truly believe that life in a given society is worthwhile may find that their children absorb that message only too well, the result being a lack of grandchildren.

Developmental Tasks

Robert Butler described a number of critical underlying themes in middle adulthood that appear to be present regardless of marital and family status, gender, or economic level. They are presented in Table 2.5-1.

Table 2.5-1
Features Salient to Middle Life

Issues	Positive Features	Negative Features
Prime of life	Responsible use of power; maturity; productivity	Winner-loser view; competitiveness
Stock taking: What to do with rest of one's life	Possibility; alternatives; organization of commitments; redirection	Closure; fatalism
Fidelity and commitments	Commitment to self, others, career, society; filial maturity	Hypocrisy, self-deception
Growth-death (to grow is to die); juvenescence and rejuvenation fantasies	Naturality regarding body, time	Obscene or frenetic efforts (e.g., to be youthful); hostility and envy of youth and progeny; longing
Communication and socialization	Matters understood; continuity: picking up where left off; large social network; rootedness of relationships, places, and ideas	Repetitiveness; boredom; impatience; isolation; conservatism; confusion; rigidity

Data from Robert N. Butler, M.D.

In his longitudinal study of 173 men who have been interviewed at five-year intervals since they graduated from Harvard, George Vaillant found a strong correlation between physical health and emotional health in middle age. In addition, those persons who had the poorest psychological adjustment during college years had a high incidence of physical illness in middle age. There was no single factor in childhood to account for adult mental health; however, an overall sense of stability in the parental home was predictive of a well-adjusted adulthood. An interesting finding was that a close sibling relationship during the college years was correlated with emotional and physical well-being in middle age. In another study he found that childhood work habits correlated with adult work habits and that adult mental health and good interpersonal relationships were associated with the capacity to work in childhood.

Sexuality

Sexuality in general is a major issue in midlife. Although William Masters and Virginia Johnson report, as have Alfred Kinsey and others, that enjoyable sexual activity (including coitus) may continue well into old age, a decline in sexual functioning may occur. For some persons, however, the erroneous belief that vigorous sexual activity is the prerogative of youth is sufficient to interfere with their normal physiological sexual responses.

Fears and the reality of impotence are a common problem in middle-aged men. The most common cause of impotence in the middle years is not aging but excessive alcohol intake, drugs (such as tranquilizers and antidepressants), and stress with fatigue and anxiety; 90 percent of the cases of chronic impotence in middle adulthood are due to psychological, rather than organic, causes.

Middle-aged women also may experience a decline in sexual functioning that is more related to psychological than to physical causes. Women do not reach their sexual prime until their mid-30s; consequently, they have a greater capacity for orgasm in middle adulthood than in young adulthood. Women, however, are more vulnerable than men to narcissistic blows to their self-esteem as they lose their youthful appearance, which is overvalued in today's society. During this time, they may feel less sexually desirable and, therefore, feel less entitled to an adequate sex life.

An inability to deal with changes in body image prompts many women and men to undergo cosmetic surgery in an effort to maintain their youthful appearance.

Male and Female Climacterium

Middle adulthood is the time of the male and female climacterium, that period in life characterized by a decrease in biological and physiological functioning.

For women, the menopausal period is considered to be the climacterium and may start anywhere from the 40s to the early 50s. Bernice Neugarten studied this period and found that over 50 percent of the women described the menopause as an unpleasant experience; however, a significant portion of women believed that their lives had not changed in any significant way, and many women experienced no adverse effects. Because they no longer had to worry about becoming pregnant, several women reported feeling freer after the menopause than they had felt before its onset. Generally, the female climacterium has been stereotyped as a sudden or radical psychophysiological experience. However, it is more often a gradual experience as estrogen secretion decreases with changes in the flow, timing, and eventual cessation of the menses. Vasomotor instability (hot flashes) may occur, and the menopause may extend over a period of several years. Some women experience anxiety and depression, but usually one's premenopausal personality structure predisposes the person to the menopausal syndrome.

For men, the climacterium has no clear demarcation, such as the menopause. Male hormones stay fairly constant through the 40s and 50s. Nevertheless, men must adapt to a decline in biological functioning and overall physical vigor. The crisis can be mild or severe, characterized by a sudden drastic change in work or marital relationship, severe depression, increased use of alcohol or drugs, or a shift to an alternate life-style.

There are normal turning points during middle age that are mastered without distress. It is only when life events are so severe or so unexpected—such as the death of a spouse, the loss of a job, or a serious illness—that the person experiences an emotional disorder of such proportion to warrant the term "midlife crisis." Men and women who are most prone to midlife crisis tend to come from families characterized by one or more of the following during their adolescence: parental discord, withdrawal by the same-sex parent, anxious parents, and impulsive parents with a low level of sense of responsibility.

Empty-nest syndrome. Another phenomenon described at this time has been called the empty-nest syndrome, a depression that occurs in men and women when their youngest child is about to leave home. Most parents however, perceive the departure of the youngest child as a relief, rather than a stress. If no compensating activities have been developed, particularly by the mother, some of these parents become depressed.

Other Tasks of Middle Adulthood

As persons approach the age of 50, they more clearly define what they want from work, family, and leisure. Those men who have reached their highest level of advancement in work may experience disillusionment or frustration when they realize they can no longer anticipate new work challenges. For the woman who has invested herself completely in the mothering role, this period of life leaves her with no suitable identity after the children leave home. Sometimes social rules become rigidly established; less freedom in life-style and a sense of entrapment may lead to depression and a loss of confidence at this time. There may also be unique financial burdens in middle age, resulting from pressures to care for aged parents, at one end of the spectrum, and one's own young children at the other.

Levinson describes a transitional period between the ages of 50 and 55, during which a developmental crisis may occur if the person feels incapable of changing an intolerable life structure. Although no single event characterizes this transition, the physiological changes that begin to appear may have a dramatic impact on the person's sense of self. There is, for example, a decrease in cardiovascular efficiency that accompanies aging; but chronological age and physical infirmity are not linear. Those who exercise regularly, do not smoke, and eat and drink in moderation are able to maintain their physical health and emotional well-being.

Middle adulthood is the period when one frequently feels overwhelmed by too many obligations and duties, but it is also a time of great satisfaction for most persons. People have developed a wide array of acquaintances, friendships, and relationships. The satisfaction a person expresses about his or her network of friends is predictive of positive mental health. Some social ties, however, may be a source of stress if demands are made on the person that cannot be met or that assault the person's self-esteem. Power, leadership, wisdom, and understanding are most generally possessed by the middle-aged, and if one's health and vitality remain intact, it is truly the prime of life.

DIVORCE

Divorce is a major crisis of adult life. Persons often grow, develop, and change at different rates. One spouse may discover that the other is not the same as when they first married. In truth, both partners have changed and evolved—not necessarily in complementary directions. Frequently, one spouse blames a third person for alienation of affections and refuses to examine his or her own role in marital problems. Certain aspects of marital deterioration and divorce seem related to specific qualities of middle life—the need for change, the weariness with acting responsibly, the fear of facing up to oneself. The following cases by Robert W. Butler are informative.

A 43-year-old woman was divorced after 21 years of marriage. She had brought up four children. She felt she had contributed to the material success of her husband, who received all the credit. She was bitter and hurt over his failure to appreciate her but saw this failure as his problem alone. She was dismayed when he pressed for a divorce. Neither wanted marital counseling. The end came very quickly. They no longer even talked to each other. Neither of them could quite believe they were divorced.

Some men and women begin to seek a last fling or a last chance to experience something they feel they have missed. This phenomenon is not confined to heterosexual relationships.

Mary and Joan had lived together for 23 years. Their homosexuality was only part of their rich relationship together. They had lived through many painful public remarks. They had developed good relations with their neighbors. Mary had always struggled with the possibility of trying a heterosexual relationship. At 44, she felt she had little time. An opportunity arose, and she seized the chance for a heterosexual affair. Joan was deeply hurt. Despite the long-standing success of their life together, they were not certain it would survive this development. They jointly sought therapeutic help.

Types of Separation That Accompany Divorce

Paul Bohannan, an anthropologist with expertise in marriage and divorce, described types of separation that take place at the time of divorce.

Psychic divorce. In psychic divorce the love object is given up, and a grief reaction about the death of the relationship occurs. Sometimes a period of anticipatory mourning sets in before the divorce actually occurs. Separating from a spouse forces the person to become autonomous, to change from a position of dependence. This separation may be difficult to achieve, especially if both persons are used to being dependent on each other (as normally happens in marriage) or if one was so dependent as to be afraid or incapable of becoming more independent. Most persons report feelings such as depression, ambivalence, and mood swings at the time of divorce. Studies indicate that the process of recovery from divorce takes about two years. At this time, the ex-spouse may be viewed neutrally, and each spouse accepts his or her new identity as a single person.

Legal divorce. This process involves going through the courts so that each of the parties is remarriageable. Seventy-five percent of divorced women and 80 percent of divorced men remarry within three years of divorce. No-fault divorce, in which neither person is judged to be the guilty party in the divorce, has become the most widely used legal mechanism for divorce.

Economic divorce. The division of the couple's property between them and economic support for the wife are major concerns. Many men who are ordered by the courts to pay alimony or child support flout the law, creating a major social problem.

Community divorce. The social network of the divorced couple changes markedly. A few relatives and friends are retained from the community, and new ones are added. The task of meeting new friends is often difficult for divorced persons, who may realize how dependent they were on the spouse for social exchange.

Coparental divorce. This refers to separation of a parent from the child's other parent. Being a single parent is very different from being a married parent.

Custody

The parental-right doctrine is a concept in law that awards custody to the more fit natural parent and attempts to ensure that the best interest of the child is served. Most often, custody is awarded to the mother, but in about 5 percent of cases, custody is awarded to the father.

Types of custody include (1) joint custody, in which the child spends equal time with the two parents, which is becoming increasingly common; (2) split custody, in which siblings are separated and each parent has custody of one or more of the children; and (3) single custody, in which the child lives solely with one parent, the other parent having rights of visitation that may be limited in some ways by the court.

Problems may surface in the parent-child relationship with the custodial parent or the noncustodial parent. The presence of the custodial parent in the home represents the reality of the divorce, and this parent may become the target of the child's anger. The parent under such stress may not be able to deal with the child's increased needs and anger at this time.

The noncustodial parent must cope with limits placed on time spent with the child. This parent loses the day-to-day gratification and the responsibilities involved with parenting. Emotional distress is common in both the parent and the child. Joint custody offers a solution with some advantages; however, it requires a high degree of maturity on the part of the parents and can present some problems. Parents must separate their child-rearing practices from their postdivorce resentments, and they must develop a spirit of cooperation regarding the rearing of the child. They must also have the ability to tolerate frequent communication with an ex-spouse.

Reasons for Divorce

Divorce tends to run in families and is highest in couples who marry as teenagers or come from different socioeconomic backgrounds. Every marriage is psychologically unique, and so is each divorce. If a person's parents were divorced, he or she may choose to resolve a marital problem in the same way—through divorce. Expectations of the spouse may be unrealistic. One partner may expect the other to act as an all-giving mother or as a magically protective father. The parenting experience places the greatest strain on a marriage. In surveys of couples with and without children, those without children report getting more pleasure from the spouse than those couples with children. Illness in the child creates the greatest strain of all, and in marriages in which a child has died through illness or accident, over 50 percent end in divorce.

Other causes of marital distress are problems concerning sex and money. Both areas may be used as a means of control, and withholding sex or money is a means of expressing aggression. There is also less social pressure to remain married. As previously discussed, the easing of divorce laws and the declining influence of religion and the extended family make divorce a more acceptable course of action today.

Extramarital intercourse. Adultery is defined as voluntary sexual intercourse between a married person and someone other than his or her spouse. Studies report that, by middle age, 60 percent of men and 40 percent of women have had at least one extramarital affair. For men, the first extramarital affair is often associated with the wife's pregnancy, during which time coitus may be interdicted. Most of these incidents are kept secret from the spouse and, if known, rarely account for divorce. This event, however, may serve as the catalyst for basic dissatisfactions in the marriage to surface, which then may lead to its dissolution. Adultery may decline as potentially fatal sexually transmitted diseases, such as acquired immune deficiency syndrome (AIDS), begin to serve as sobering deterrents.

References

Arnstein R L: Overview of normal transition to young adulthood. Adolesc Psychiatry *16*: 127, 1989.

Arthur M B, Bailyn L, Levinson D J: *Working with Cancers.* Center for Research in Career Development, Columbia University, New York, 1984.

Colarusso C A, Nemiroff R A: *Adult Development: A New Dimension in Psychodynamic Theory and Practice.* Plenum, New York, 1981.

Gould R L: Adulthood. In *Comprehensive Textbook of Psychiatry,* ed 5, H I Kaplan and B J Sadock, editors, p 1998. Williams & Wilkins, Baltimore, 1989.

Hornstein G A: The structuring of identity among midlife women as a function of their degree of involvement in employment. J Pers *54*: 551, 1986.

Howe M L, Brainerd C J: *Cognitive Development in Adulthood: Progress in Cognitive Development Research.* Springer, New York, 1988.

Kimmel D C: *Adulthood and Aging: An Interdisciplinary Developmental View.* Wiley, New York, 1974.

Krause N: Stress and sex differences in depressive symptoms among older adults. J Gerontol *41*: 727, 1986.

Levinson, D J: A conception of adult development. Am Psychol *41*: 3, 1986.

Levinson, D J, Damow, C N, Klein E B, Levinson M H, McKeeb A: *The Seasons of a Man's Life.* Knopf, New York, 1978.

Lusski W, et al.: Effective elderly adjustment. J Am Geriatr Soc *34*: 764, 1986.

Matthews K A, Wing R R, Kuller L H, Meilahn E N, Kelsey S F, Costello E J, Caggiula A W: Influences of natural menopause on psychological characteristics and symptoms of middle-aged healthy women. J Consult Clin Psychol *58*: 345, 1990.

Nemiroff R A, Colarusso C A: Frontiers of adult development in theory and practice. J Geriatr Psychiatry *21*: 7, 1988.

Neugarten B L: *Personality in Middle and Late Life.* Atherton, New York, 1964.

Roberts P, Newton P M: Levinsonian studies of women's adult development. Psychol Aging *2*: 154, 1987.

Vaillant G E: *Adaptation to Life.* Little, Brown, Boston, 1977.

Vaillant G E, Vaillant C O: Natural history of male psychological health: 12. A 45-year study of predictors of successful aging at age 65. Am J Psychiatry *147*: 31, 1990.

Van Gennep A: *The Rites of Passage.* University of Chicago Press, Chicago, 1960.

Whitbourne S K: Personality development in adulthood and old age: Relationships among identity style, health, and well-being. Ann Rev Gerontol Geriatr *7*: 189, 1987.

2.6 / Late Adulthood and Old Age

Late adulthood, also known as old age, usually refers to the phase of the life cycle beginning at age 65. The elderly population is the fastest growing age group in America; more people are living longer now, a phenomenon that Robert N. Butler has called a triumph of survivorship, rather than a cause for despair. Gerontology—the study of aging—has become a new field of specialization. Gerontologists divide the aged into two groups: the young-old, age 65 to 74, and the old-old, age 75 and older. In addition, there are the well-old, who are healthy and do not suffer from any illness, and the sick-old, who have an infirmity that interferes with functioning and that requires medical or psychiatric attention. The health needs of these old adults have become enormous, and the role of the geriatric physician and psychiatrist has never been more important.

DEMOGRAPHICS

There are now about 30 million elderly in the United States, approximately 12 percent of the population. According to the U.S. Census Bureau, 15 percent of the population, 51 million persons, will be over the age of 65 by the year 2020. This number represents the aging of the so-called baby boom generation—those born between the years 1946 and 1964. Table 2.6-1 lists demographic characteristics of the aged population.

Table 2.6-1
Characteristics of the Aged Population

Item	Comments
Number of old persons (U.S. Census Bureau)	1980: 25.5 million persons or 11.3% of population. 2000: 35 million persons or 13.1% of population. 2020: 51 million persons or 15% of population. There are 3 million persons over age 85 and 30,000 over age 100.
Life expectancy	Women live longer than men: Men who became 65 in 1980 live another 14 years; women who became 65 in 1980 live another 18 years. Average life expectancy is 75 years.
Race	Whites live longer than blacks. Over 90% of the aged in U.S. are white; 8% are black; 2% are Hispanic.
Geographic location	25% of all aged persons in U.S. reside in California, New York, and Florida.
Death rate for those over 65	White: 5.3 per 1,000 Black: 7.9 per 1,000 Highest death rate is in Northeast, followed by Midwest and South. Lowest rate is in West. Black men have highest death rate.
Marital status	80% of men age 65 to 74 are married, only 49% of women. Over age 75, 70% of men are married, only 30% of women. There are five times as many widows as widowers, and widowers remarry seven times more frequently than widows.
Institutional care	5% of all the aged live in institutions. After age 85, 20% live in nursing homes, 25% live alone, 45% live with family members.
Education	Only 6.5% are college graduates, but this number is increasing.
Work	20% of men over 65 work, less than 10% of women.

BIOLOGY OF AGING

The aging process is called senescence (from Latin *senescere*, meaning to grow old) and is characterized by a gradual decline in functioning of all systems of the body—cardiovascular, respiratory, genitourinary, endocrine, and immune, among others. The belief that old age is invariably associated with profound intellectual and physical infirmity, however, is a myth. Most aged persons retain their cognitive ability and physical capacity to a remarkable degree.

An overview of the biological changes that accompany old age is given in Table 2.6-2. The various decrements listed do not occur in a linear fashion in all systems. Not all organ systems deteriorate at the same rate, nor do they follow a similar pattern of decline for all persons. Each person is genetically endowed with one or more vulnerable systems, or a system may become vulnerable because of environmental stressors or intentional misuse (e.g., excessive ultraviolet exposure, smoking, alcohol). Moreover, not all organ systems deteriorate at the same time; a person does not disintegrate like the one-horse shay in Oliver Wendell Holmes's poem, *The Deacon's Masterpiece*, which "went to pieces all at once." Rather, any one of a number of organ systems begins to deteriorate, which then leads to illness or death.

In general, the aging of a person is the aging of cells. The most commonly held theory is that each cell has a genetically determined life span during which it can replicate itself a limited number of times before it dies. Structural changes in cells occur with age. In the central nervous system, for example, age-related cell changes occur in neurons, which show signs of degeneration. In senility (characterized by severe memory loss and a loss of intellectual functioning), signs of degeneration are much more severe and are known as neurofibrillary degeneration, seen most commonly in Alzheimer's disease.

Changes in the structure of deoxyribonucleic acid (DNA) and ribonucleic acid (RNA) are also found in aging cells; the cause has been attributed to genotypic programming, X-rays, chemicals, and food products, among others. There is probably no single cause of aging. All areas of the body are affected to some degree.

Genetic factors have been implicated in disorders that commonly occur in the aged, such as hypertension, coronary artery disease, arteriosclerosis, and neoplastic disease. Family studies indicate inheritance factors for breast and stomach cancer, colon polyps, and certain mental disorders of old age. Huntington's chorea shows an autosomal dominant mode of inheritance with complete penetrance. The average age of onset is between 35 and 40, but cases have occurred as late as 70 years of age.

Longevity

Longevity has been studied since the beginning of recorded history and has remained a topic of immense interest. The research about longevity reveals that a family history of longevity is the best indicator of a long life: Almost half of the fathers of persons who live past 80 also have lived past 80. However, many of the conditions leading to a shortened life can be prevented, ameliorated, or delayed with effective intervention. Heredity is but one factor—one that is beyond the person's control. Predictors

Table 2.6-2
Biological Changes Associated with Aging

Cellular level Change in cellular DNA and RNA structures; intracellular organelle degeneration Neuronal degeneration in central nervous system, primarily in superior temporal, precentral, and inferior temporal gyri; no loss in brain stem nuclei Receptor sites and sensitivity altered Decreased anabolism and catabolism of cellular transmitter substances Intercellular collagen and elastin increase	*Neuropsychiatric* *Learning* Takes longer to learn new material, but complete learning still occurs Intelligence quotient (I.Q.) remains stable until age 80 Verbal ability maintained with age Psychomotor speed declines
Immune system Impaired T-cell response to antigen Increase in function of autoimmune bodies Increased susceptibility to infection and neoplasia Leukocytes unchanged, T-lymphocytes reduced Increased erythrocyte sedimentation (nonspecific)	*Memory* Tasks requiring shifting attentions performed with difficulty Encoding ability diminishes (transfer of short-term to long-term memory and vice versa) Recognition of right answer on multiple-choice tests remains intact Simple recall declines
Musculoskeletal Decrease in height because of shortening of spinal column (two-inch loss in both men and women from the second to the seventh decade) Reduction in lean muscle mass and muscle strength; deepening of thoracic cage Increase in body fat Elongation of nose and ears Loss of bone matrix, leading to osteoporosis Degeneration of joint surfaces may produce osteoarthritis Risk of hip fracture is 10%–25% by age 90 Continual closing of cranial sutures (parietomastoid suture does not attain complete closure until age 80) Men gain weight until about age 60, then lose; women gain weight until age 70, then lose.	*Neurotransmitters* Norepinephrine decreases in central nervous system Increased monoamine oxidase and serotonin in brain *Brain* Decrease in gross brain weight, about 17% by age 80 in both sexes Widened sulci, smaller convolutions, gyral atrophy Ventricles enlarge Increased transport across blood-brain barrier Decreased cerebral blood flow and oxygenation *Cardiovascular* Increase in size and weight of heart (contains lipofuscin pigment derived from lipids) Decreased elasticity of heart valves Increased collagen in blood vessels Increased susceptibility to arrhythmias Altered homeostasis of blood pressure Cardiac output maintained in absence of coronary heart disease
Integument Graying of hair results from decreased melanin production in hair follicles (by age 50, 50% of all persons male and female are at least 50% gray; pubic hair is last to turn gray) General wrinkling of skin Less active sweat glands Decrease in melanin Loss of subcutaneous fat Nail growth slowed	*Gastrointestinal (GI) system* At risk for atrophic gastritis, hiatal hernia, diverticulosis Decreased blood flow to gut, liver Diminished saliva flow Altered absorption from GI tract (at risk for malabsorption syndrome and avitaminosis) Constipation
Genitourinary and reproductive Decreased glomerular filtration rate and renal blood flow Decreased hardness of erection, diminished ejaculatory spurt Decreased vaginal lubrication Enlargement of prostate Incontinence	*Endocrine* Estrogen levels decrease in women Adrenal androgen decreases Testosterone production declines in men Increase in follicle stimulating hormone (FSH) and luteinizing hormone (LH) in postmenopausal women Serum thyroxine (T_4) and thyroid stimulating hormone (TSH) normal, triiodothyronine (T_3) reduced Glucose tolerance test result decreases
Special senses Thickening of optic lens, reduced peripheral vision Inability to accommodate (presbyopia) High-frequency sound hearing loss (presbyacusis)—25% show loss by age 60, 65% by age 80 Yellowing of optic lens Reduced acuity of taste, smell, and touch Decreased light-dark adaptation	*Respiratory* Decreased vital capacity Diminished cough reflex Decreased bronchial epithelium ciliary action

of longevity that are within one's control include regular medical check-ups, minimal or no caffeine or alcohol consumption, work gratification, and a perceived sense of the self as being socially useful in an altruistic role, such as spouse, teacher, mentor, parent, or grandparent. Diet and exercise are also associated with health and longevity.

Life Expectancy

In the United States the average life expectancy has increased in every decade—from 48 years in 1900 to 75 years in 1980. Changes in morbidity and mortality have also occurred. Over the past 30 years, for example, there has been a 60 percent decline in mortality from stroke and a 30 percent decline in mortality from coronary artery disease. In contrast, mortality from cancer, which has a steep rise with age, has increased, especially from cancer of the lung, colon, stomach, skin, and prostate.

Prediction of mortality is important to actuaries and insurance companies, among others. All mortality formulas have flaws, but the one that has been most accepted is the law of human mortality. Proposed in 1825 by Benjamin Gompertz, this formula holds that mortality in a given population rises exponentially with the passage of time, and, after age 30, the mortality rate doubles approximately every 8.5 years. The death rate in the United States for all ages is 816 deaths a year per 100,000 population from all causes. In age group 65 to 74, it is 2,070 per 100,000; 74 to 85, it is 5,102 per 100,000; and 85 and over, it is 14,377 per 100,000.

Accidents rank among the top seven causes of death in persons over age 65. Most fatal accidents are caused by falls, pedestrian fatalities, and burns. Neurological and sensory defects are the major causes of accidents. Most falls result from cardiac arrhythmias and hypotensive episodes.

Some gerontologists consider death in very old persons (over 85) to be the result of an aging syndrome characterized by diminished elastic-mechanical properties of the heart, arteries, lungs, and other organs. Death results from trivial tissue injuries that would not be fatal to a younger person; accordingly, senescence is viewed as the cause of death.

Diet, Exercise, and Health

Diet and exercise play a role in a variety of chronic diseases of the elderly, such as arteriosclerosis and hypertension.

Hyperlipemia correlates with coronary artery disease and can be controlled by reducing body weight, decreasing the intake of saturated fat, and limiting the intake of cholesterol. Increasing the daily intake of dietary fiber can also help decrease serum lipoprotein levels.

Reduced salt intake (under 3 g a day) is associated with a lower risk of developing hypertension. Hypertensive geriatric patients can often correct their condition by moderate exercise and decreased salt intake without the addition of drugs.

A regimen of daily moderate exercise (walking for 30 minutes a day) has been associated with a reduction in cardiovascular disease, a decreased incidence of osteoporosis, improved respiratory function, the maintenance of ideal weight, and a general sense of well-being. In many cases a disease process has been reversed and even cured by diet and exercise, without additional medical or surgical intervention.

Table 2.6-3 lists the biological changes associated with diet and exercise. A comparison with Table 2.6-2 reveals that almost every biological change associated with aging is positively affected by these two factors.

Table 2.6-3
Positive and Healthy Physiological Effects of Exercise and Nutrition

Increases
Strength of bones, ligaments, and muscles
Muscle mass and body density
Articular cartilage thickness
Skeletal muscle ATP, CrP, K+, and myoglobin
Skeletal muscle oxidative enzyme content and mitochondria
Skeletal muscle arterial collaterals and capillary density
Heart volume and weight
Blood volume and total circulating hemoglobin
Cardiac stroke volume
Myocardial contractility
Maximal $C(a\text{-}v)O_2$
Maximal blood lactate concentration
Maximal pulmonary ventilation
Maximal respiratory work
Maximal oxygen diffusing capacity
Maximal exercise capacity as measured by the maximal oxygen intake, exercise time, and distance
Serum high-density lipoprotein concentration
Anaerobic threshold
Plasma insulin concentration with submaximal exercise

Decreases
Heart rate at rest and during submaximal exercise
Blood lactate concentration during submaximal exercise
Pulmonary ventilation during submaximal work
Respiratory quotient during submaximal work
Serum triglyceride concentration
Body fatness
Serum low-density lipoprotein concentration
Systolic blood pressure
Core temperature threshold for initiation of sweating
Sweat sodium and chloride content
Plasma epinephrine and norepinephrine with submaximal exercise
Plasma glucagon and growth hormone concentrations with submaximal exercise
Relative hemoconcentration with submaximal exercise in the heat

Table by E R Buskirk. From *Diet and Exercise: Synergism in Health Maintenance,* P L White and T Monderka, editors. American Medical Association, Chicago, 1982, with permission.

DEVELOPMENTAL TASKS

Erikson's Stage of Integrity versus Despair and Isolation (Over 65 Years)

Old age is Erik Erikson's eighth stage of the life cycle, described as the conflict that exists between integrity (the sense of satisfaction one feels in reflecting on a life productively lived) and despair (the sense that life has had little purpose or meaning). Late adulthood can be a period of contentment—a time to enjoy grandchildren, to contemplate one's major efforts, and perhaps to see the fruits of one's labor being put to good use by younger generations. Integrity allows for an acceptance of one's place in the life cycle and of the knowledge that one's life is one's own responsibility.

In regard to one's parents, there is an acceptance of who they are or were and an understanding of how they lived their lives.

However, there is no peace or contentment in old age unless one has achieved intimacy and generativity. Without generativity, there is no sense of purpose and no conviction that one's life has been purposeful. Without that conviction, there is fear of death and a sense of despair or disgust. Misanthropes and others who are contemptuous of people are in a state of despair.

Maintenance of Self-Esteem

Heinz Kohut's theory of self-psychology has special application to the elderly because of its emphasis on narcissism. Old persons must continually cope with narcissistic injury as they attempt to adapt to the biological, psychological, and social losses associated with the aging process. Self-esteem and self-sufficiency are continually at risk, particularly if the elderly person loses external sources of support.

The maintenance of self-esteem is a major task of old age. Self-esteem can be promoted by several factors: (1) economic security, which allows the person to secure the basic necessities of life; (2) supportive persons, who protect against isolation and allow dependency needs to be gratified; (3) psychological health, which allows mature coping and defense mechanisms to function; and (4) physical health, which enables the person to pursue productive or pleasurable activities. When all or any of these factors are affected adversely, the aged person is unable to maintain self-esteem; tension, anxiety, frustration, anger, and depression can result. In addition, the perceived changes in physical and psychological functioning cause the aging person to question his or her continued adequacy.

Other Tasks of Old Age

Bernice Neugarten described the major conflicts of old age as related to having to give up one's position of authority and evaluating one's former competence, achievements, and pleasures. For both sexes there is, as Neugarten described,

> the yielding of a position of authority and the questioning of one's former competence; the reconciliations with significant others and with one's achievements and failures; the resolution of grief over the death of others and of the approaching death of self; the maintenance of a sense of integrity in terms of what one has been, rather than what one is; and concern over legacy and how to leave traces of oneself.

Daniel Levinson described a transitional period into old age between the ages of 60 and 65, which he termed the "late adult transition." The physiological changes that accompany aging create feelings of physical decline and mortality. These feelings are escalated by the increased incidence of illness and death among loved ones and friends. If a person is narcissistic and too heavily invested in the image and appearance of the body, he or she is liable to become overly preoccupied with death. Creative mental activity is a normal and healthy substitute for reduced physical activity.

According to Freudian theory, as the person matures, there is increasing control of the ego and the id, resulting in increased autonomy. A movement in the opposite direction (i.e., a loss of autonomy or regression) permits more primitive modes of function to emerge. Such regressions are associated with the aging process and account for such phenomena as the inability to distinguish external sensory perceptions from internal fantasies or the emergence of primitive aggressive or sexual drives. Regression of superego functions also occurs and can be manifested either by excessive guilt or, conversely, by the absence of guilt related to various conflicts or situations.

George Vaillant followed a group of Harvard freshmen into old age and found that emotional health at age 65 was related to the following factors: (1) Having been close to one's brothers and sisters at college correlated with emotional well-being; (2) early traumatic life experiences, such as death of a parent or parental divorce, did not correlate with poor adaptation in old age; (3) being depressed at some point between ages 21 and 50, however, was predictive of emotional problems at age 65; and (4) two personality traits—pragmatism and dependability—when present in the young adult, were associated with a sense of well-being at age 65.

PSYCHOSOCIAL ASPECTS OF AGING

Social Activity

Healthy old persons usually maintain a level of social activity that is only slightly changed from that of earlier years. For many, old age is a period of continued intellectual, emotional, and psychological growth. In some cases, however, physical illness or the death of friends or relatives may preclude continued social interaction. Moreover, as persons experience an increased sense of isolation, they may become vulnerable to depression. There is growing evidence that maintaining social activities is valuable for physical and emotional well-being. Contact with younger persons is also important because old persons can pass on cultural values and can provide care services to the younger generation and thereby maintain a sense of usefulness that contributes to self-esteem.

Ageism

Ageism, a term coined by Robert N. Butler, refers to the discrimination toward old persons and the negative stereotypes about old age that are held by younger adults. Old persons may themselves resent and fear other old people and discriminate against them. In this scheme, old age is universally associated with loneliness, poor health, senility, and general weakness or infirmity. The experience of aged persons, however, does not consistently support these attitudes. For example, although 50 percent of young adults expect poor health to be a problem for those over 65, only 20 percent of those over 65 report health as a problem. Similarly, although 65 percent of young adults expect loneliness to be a problem for the aged, only 13 percent of old persons actually experience loneliness.

Countertransference

The feelings and attitudes that the physician has toward old persons stems from a variety of sources: countertransference, societal attitudes, and the attitudes projected by the patient about being old. Countertransference feelings about aging are determined by the physician's needs and past experiences and function on both a conscious and an unconscious level. Physicians may have fears about their own old age or may have had conflicts about the aging or death of parents or grandparents. It is important that they be aware of these feelings, especially if negative views of aging exist. Some aged persons may act out the poor expectations held for them by the physician. Consequently, they may lose confidence in their abilities and appear to be what, in fact, they are not.

Psychodynamics

Adaptation to aging also depends on the defense mechanisms used throughout adult life. The healthiest or most mature defenses include suppression, anticipation of reality, altruism, and humor. If acquired during early and middle adulthood, these defenses enable the aged person to cope with the vicissitudes of life in the most effective manner.

Mature defenses are the normal adaptive mechanisms that are found in psychologically and physically healthy adults. Suppression is the conscious or semiconscious decision not to think about an impulse or conflict. It is normally coupled with anticipation of reality, which permits the person to plan realistically for future events (its antithesis is denial). Altruism is the provision of service to others and is related to Erikson's concept of generativity, which is characterized by the conviction that one's life has been purposeful. Humor is characterized by the ability to stand outside oneself and observe and comment on events and their incongruities and inconsistencies. Humor may also be expressed as playfulness.

In contrast to these mature defenses, a group of coping mechanisms seen in the aged are not as adaptive. They include the following:

(1) denial, in which external reality is negated; (2) regression, in which the person returns to an earlier level of functioning; (3) counterphobia, in which the person attempts to deny a fear by engaging in a dangerous or fearful activity; (4) rigidity, in which the person maintains habits or traits that are no longer useful or adaptive; (5) exclusion of stimuli, in which the person blocks out stimuli that may be upsetting or that require a response the old person is no longer capable of giving; (6) selective memory, in which the person remembers past events that may be more satisfying and full of accomplishment than current events; (7) projection, in which incompatible thoughts or feelings are externalized or directed toward the self from another person, which may cause paranoid ideation in severe cases; and (8) reaction formation, in which the unacceptable thought or impulse is expressed in opposite ways, which leads to prejudice and bias.

Defense mechanisms are not static. They are learned and can be unlearned; adaptive mature defenses can replace immature or neurotic defenses, even in old age. The tendency of old persons to reminisce has been postulated to be part of a normal life-review process brought about by the realization of approaching death. It is characterized by a progressive return to consciousness of past experiences and, in particular, by the resurgence of unresolved conflicts that can be worked through and reintegrated.

Socioeconomics

The economics of old age is of paramount importance to the aged themselves and to the society at large. In the United States about 75 percent of the aged have incomes below $10,000, and only about 10 percent have incomes above $20,000. About 3.5 million persons over age 65 live below the poverty level of $6,872 for a two-person household and $5,447 for a one-person household.

Women make up the largest single group of the elderly poor and are twice as likely as men to be poor. Black elderly women over 65 are five times more likely to be poor than are white elderly women.

The poor economic conditions of many aged persons have a direct impact on both their psychological and their physical health. For many aged persons, worrying about money can become an obsessive preoccupation that interferes with their enjoyment of life. Obtaining proper medical care may be especially difficult if personal funds are not available or sufficient.

Medicare (Title 18) provides both hospital and medical insurance for those over age 65. About 150 million bills are reimbursed under the Medicare program each year; but only about 40 percent of all medical expenses incurred by the aged person are covered under Medicare. The rest is paid by private insurance, state insurance, or personal funds. Some services—such as outpatient psychiatric treatment, skilled nursing care, physical rehabilitation, and preventive physical exams—are covered minimally or not at all.

In addition to Medicare, the Social Security program pays benefits to persons over age 65 (over age 66 in the year 2009 and age 67 in 2027). Average monthly benefits payable to retired workers average about $500 a month. To qualify for benefits, the person must have worked long enough to become insured. In 1991 a worker will have to have worked for 10 years to be eligible for benefits. Benefits are also paid to the spouse of a worker who is receiving Social Security benefits and to widows or widowers if the person receiving benefits dies (survivor benefits).

Retirement

For many old persons, retirement is a time for the pursuit of leisure and freedom from the responsibility of previous working commitments. For others, it is a time of stress, especially if retirement results in economic problems or a loss of self-esteem. Ideally, employment after age 65 should be a matter of choice. With the passage of the Age Discrimination in Employment Act of 1967 and its amendments, forced retirement at age 70 has been virtually eliminated in the private sector, and it is not legal in federal employment.

Of those persons who voluntarily retire, a majority reenter the work force within two years. They do this for a variety of reasons—negative reactions to being retired, feelings of being unproductive, economic hardship, and loneliness.

Sexual Activity

It is estimated that approximately 70 percent of men and 20 percent of women over age 60 are sexually active. Sexual activity is usually limited by the absence of an available partner. Longitudinal studies have demonstrated that the sex drive does not decrease as men and women get older; in fact, some report an increase in sex drive. William Masters and Virginia Johnson reported sexual functioning of persons in their 80s. Expected physiological changes in men include a longer time period for erection to occur, decreased penile turgidity, and ejaculatory seepage; in women, decreased vaginal lubrication and vaginal atrophy are associated with lower estrogen levels. Medications can also adversely affect sexual behavior. A significant finding was that the more active one's sex life was in early adulthood, the more likely it was to be active in old age.

Institutionalization

Many aged patients who are infirm require institutional care. Although only 5 percent of the aged are institutionalized in nursing homes at any one time, about 35 percent of the aged require care in a long-term facility at some time during their lives. Elderly nursing-home residents are mainly widowed women, and about 50 percent are over age 85.

Nursing-home care costs are not covered by Medicare and range from $20,000 to $40,000 a year. There are about 20,000 long-term nursing-care institutions in the United States—not enough to meet the need. Those elderly persons who do not require skilled nursing care can be managed in other types of health-related facilities, such as a center they attend during the daytime hours. However, the need for care far exceeds the availability of such centers.

Outside the institution, care for the aged is provided by their children, primarily their daughters or daughters-in-law. Over 50 percent of these women also work in jobs outside the home, and about 40 percent care for their own children as well. In general, women end up as caretakers more often than men because of cultural and societal expectations. According to the American Association of Retired Persons, those daughters with jobs spend an average of 12 hours a week providing care and currently spend an average $117 a month for travel, telephone calls, special foods, and medication for the elderly.

EMOTIONAL PROBLEMS OF THE AGED

Loss is the predominant theme that characterizes the emotional experiences of the aged. An elderly person must deal with the grief of multiple losses (death of spouse, friends, family, and colleagues), change of work status and prestige, and decline of physical abilities and health. They expend enormous amounts of emotional and physical energy in grieving, resolving grief, and adapting to the changes that result from loss. Depression is a maladaptive response to loss that in the elderly may mimic senile dementia. In addition to the classic signs of depression—such as appetite and sleep disturbances, loss of interest in outside events, self-deprecatory remarks, and thoughts that life is no longer worth living—the person may show memory impairment, difficulty in concentrating, poor judgment, and irritability.

There is a high incidence of suicide in the aged (80 per 100,000 population). The suicide of aged persons is perceived differently by surviving friends and family members, depending on gender: Men are thought to have been physically ill, and women are thought to have been mentally ill.

For a more complete discussion of psychiatric disorders of the aged, see Chapter 45, "Geriatric Psychiatry."

References

Anderson J E, ed: *Psychological Aspects of Aging.* American Psychological Association, Washington, DC, 1956.

Andrews G R: Cross-cultural studies: An important development in aging research. J Am Geriatr Soc *37:* 483, 1989.

Blair K A: Aging: Physiological aspects and clinical implications. Nurse Pract *15:* 14, 1990.

Bromley D B: The idea of ageing: An historical and psychological analysis. Compr Gerontol *2:* 30, 1988.

Busse E W, Pfeiffer E, eds: *Behavior and Adaptation in Late Life.* Little, Brown, Boston, 1969.

Butler R N: *Why Survive? Being Old in America.* Harper & Row, New York, 1975.

Butler R N, Lewis M I: *Aging and Mental Health: Positive Psychosocial and Biomedical Approaches,* ed 3. Mosby, St. Louis, 1982.

Cunningham W R, Brookbank J W: *Gerontology: The Psychology, Biology, and Sociology of Aging.* Harper & Row, New York, 1988.

Eisdorfer C, Lawbon, M P: *The Psychology of Adult Development and Aging.* American Psychological Association, Washington, DC, 1973.

Gutmann D: Psychoanalysis and aging: A development view. In *The Course of Life: Psychoanalytic Contributions toward Understanding Personality Development,* vol. 3, G H Pollock, S I Greenspan, editors. US Department of Health and Human Services, Mental Health Study Center, Adelphi, MD, 1981.

Kenney R A: *Physiology of Aging: A Synopsis,* ed 2. Year Book Medical Publishers, Chicago, 1989.

Nemiroff R A, Colarusso C A: *The Race Against Time: Psychotherapy and Psychoanalysis in the Second Half of Life.* Plenum, New York, 1985.

Pollock G M: Aging or aged: Development or pathology? In *The Course of Life: Psychoanalytic Contributions toward Understanding Personality Development,* vol 3, S I Greenspan and G M Pollock, editors: US Department of Health and Human Services, Mental Health Study Center, Adelphi, MD, 1981.

Rinn W E: Mental decline in normal aging: A review. J Geriatr Psychiatry Neurol *1:* 144, 1988.

Sahey B J, Birkner K: Stress and aging, Int J Psychosom *35:* 49, 1988.

Schiavi R C, Schreiner-Engel P, Mandeli J, Schanzer H, Cohen E: Healthy aging and male sexual function. Am J Psychiatry *147:* 766, 1990.

2.7 / Thanatology: Death and Bereavement

Thanatology is the study of the phenomenon of death and the emotional and psychological processes involved in the reaction to death, including grief, bereavement, and mourning. To work most effectively with patients, physicians must understand the nature of people's reactions to death (both those who are dying and those who are grieving). They must also understand their own feelings and attitudes, which can affect the doctor-patient relationship in this very emotional situation.

MEANING OF DEATH

The reaction to death, in part, depends on the context. For instance, death may be experienced as timely or untimely. *Timely death* implies that one's expected survival and actual life span are approximately equal; essentially, one dies when one is expected to, and those left to grieve are not surprised by the death. In Erik Erikson's scheme of the life cycle, the last phase of life involves the conflict between integrity and despair. According to Erikson, a positive developmental resolution of this conflict in the face of inevitable death involves a sense of fulfillment, peace, and integrity, rather than a sense of failure, horror, and despair. This positive resolution is predicated, in Erikson's theory, on having successfully resolved the conflicts of the preceding adult developmental phases.

Untimely death implies an unexpected or premature death, and those left to grieve are in shock. Untimely death may refer to (1) the death of a young person, (2) sudden death, or (3) catastrophic death associated with violence or accident and utter meaninglessness.

Death has also been described as intentional (suicide), unintentional (trauma or disease), and subintentional (substance abuse, alcoholism, cigarette smoking). Death may have multiple psychological meanings, both for the person who is dying and for society in general. In Susan Sontag's formulation, death may even take on the power of metaphor. For example, some persons view death as deserved punishment for what are perceived as immoral or sinful life-styles.

SUDDEN DEATH OF PSYCHOGENIC ORIGIN

Emotional factors alone may be sufficient to trigger sudden death in certain persons not otherwise at risk. For instance, heart attacks may follow sudden psychic stress. Voodoo death or death secondary to hexes occurs when a person who is thought to have the power to cause death psychically puts a curse on someone who believes in this person's power. In such instances it is theorized that the hypothalamic-pituitary-adrenal axis and the autonomic nervous system become dysfunctional from emotional stress, which causes the cessation of vital functions. Unless a folk healer removes the curse, a person under such a spell or hex may die.

LEGAL ASPECTS OF DEATH

According to law, the physician must sign a death certificate that attests to the cause of death (e.g., congestive heart failure, pneumonia). The physician must also classify death as being from natural, accidental, suicidal, homicidal, or unknown causes. Anyone who dies unattended by a physician must be examined by the appointed medical examiner, coroner, or pathologist, and an autopsy must be performed to determine the cause of death. In some cases, a psychological autopsy is performed, in which the person's sociocultural and psychological background is examined retrospectively by interviewing friends, relatives, and doctors to determine whether a mental illness, such as depression, was present. A determination can be made that a patient died because he was pushed (murder) or because he jumped (suicide) from a high building. Each situation has clear medical and legal implications.

REACTIONS TO IMPENDING DEATH

A number of researchers have studied reactions to death. One of the earliest and most useful organizations of reactions to impending death came from the psychiatrist and thanatologist Elisabeth Kübler-Ross. Seldom does any dying patient follow a regular series of responses that can be clearly identified; no established sequence is applicable to all patients. The following five stages proposed by Kübler-Ross are widely encountered.

Stage 1—Shock and Denial

On being told that he or she is dying, a patient has an initial reaction of shock. The patient may appear dazed at first and then may refuse to believe the diagnosis or deny that anything is wrong. Some patients never pass beyond this stage and may go from doctor to doctor until they find one who supports their position. The degree to which denial is adaptive or maladaptive appears to involve whether the patient continues to obtain treatment even while experiencing some denial. In such cases, the physician must communicate to the patient and the patient's family, in a respectful and direct way, basic information about the illness, its prognosis, and the options for treatment. Inherent in effective communication is allowing for the patient's emotional response and reassuring the patient that he or she will not be abandoned.

Stage 2—Anger

Patients become frustrated, irritable, and angry that they are ill. A common response is, "Why me?" They may become angry at God, their fate, a friend, or a family member; they may even blame themselves. The anger may be displaced onto the hospital staff and the doctor, who are blamed for the illness. Patients in this stage are difficult to manage. The doctor who has difficulty understanding that this anger is a predictable reaction and really one of displacement may withdraw from the patient or transfer the patient to another doctor's care. Management of angry patients involves the understanding that the anger being expressed cannot be taken personally. An empathic, nondefensive response can help defuse the patient's anger and can help the patient refocus on the deeper feelings (e.g., grief, fear, loneliness) that underlie the anger. Also, the physician should recognize that anger may represent the patient's desire for greater control in a situation in which he or she feels completely out of control.

Stage 3—Bargaining

The patient may attempt to negotiate with physicians, friends, or even God: In return for a cure, the person will fulfill one or many promises, such as giving to charity and attending church regularly. Another aspect of bargaining is that patients believe that, by their being good (compliant, nonquestioning, cheerful), the doctor will make them better. The management of such patients involves making it clear that they will be taken care of to the best of the doctor's abilities and that everything that can be done will be done, regardless of any action or behavior on their part. The patient must also be encouraged to participate as a partner in the case and to understand that being a good patient means being as honest and straightforward as possible.

Stage 4—Depression

In this stage the patient shows clinical signs of depression—withdrawal, psychomotor retardation, sleep disturbances, hopelessness, and, possibly, suicidal ideation. The depression may be a reaction to the effects of the illness on his or her life (e.g., loss of a job, economic hardship, helplessness, hopelessness, isolation from friends and family), or it may be in anticipation of the actual loss of life that will eventually occur. If a true major depression with vegetative signs and suicidal ideation develops, treatment with antidepressant medication or electroconvulsive therapy (ECT) may be indicated. All persons feel some degree of sadness at the prospect of their own deaths, and normal sadness does not require biological intervention. Major depression and active suicidal ideation, however, can be alleviated and should not be accepted as just a normal reaction to impending death. A person who suffers from a major depression may be unable to sustain hope. Hope may also alter longevity, and it is likely to enhance the dignity and the quality of the patient's life.

Stage 5—Acceptance

The patient realizes that death is inevitable and accepts the universality of the experience. Feelings may range from a mood that is neutral to one that is euphoric. Under ideal circumstances, the patient resolves his or her feelings about the inevitability of death and is able to talk about death in the face of the unknown. Those persons who have strong religious beliefs and are convinced of a life after death can find comfort in those beliefs and in the ecclesiasticism: Fear not death; remember those who have gone before you and those who will come after.

CARING FOR THE DYING PATIENT

Physicians' ability to care compassionately and effectively for dying patients depends, in large part, on their awareness of their own attitudes toward death and dying. Some physicians have dysfunctional attitudes toward death and the dying patient that may be reinforced by their medical training. When training focuses almost entirely on the control and eradication of disease, at the expense of the care and comfort of the person with disease, death, as well as the dying patient, becomes the enemy. In other words, death and the dying patient may become equated with failure and may thus reflect the doctor's inadequacy and limitations. When this occurs, it is no surprise that the dying patient is avoided or is experienced as a source of irritation, impatience, and fear.

Because of their extensive knowledge of the human body and their technical expertise in controlling many disease states, physicians may begin unconsciously to feel omnipotent (i.e., all-powerful) with regard to preventing death. When these physicians confront death, they may feel threatened and defensive; their image of themselves has been badly injured. These physicians, too, view dying patients as painful reminders of their own fallibility. Some physicians enter the practice of medicine because of their own unconscious fears of death. These doctors unconsciously hope that, through the study and the mastery of medicine, they may actually achieve some degree of control over their own mortality. Although these doctors must deal with dying patients, they may feel an inordinate amount of anxiety, coupled with a strong need to avoid the patient. These physicians may attempt to deal with their underlying fear of death through extensive intellectualization; for instance, they may provide the patient with minute and often unnecessary details about the day-to-day vicissitudes of the illness while sidestepping any real discussion of the patient's fears, concerns, and feelings.

The major task of the physician caring for the dying patient is to provide compassionate concern and continuing support. The hallmarks of appropriate care are visiting with the patient regularly, maintaining eye contact, touching appropriately, listening to what the patient has to say, and being willing to answer all questions in as respectful a way as possible. What is most important is to be tactfully honest. Most patients want their doctors to be truthful with them; for example, they prefer to know that they have cancer. Honesty, however, does not preclude hope. If 85 percent of patients with a particular disease die within five years, then 15 percent are still alive after that time. Still, some patients do not want to know the facts of their illness. The doctor may ask a patient how much he or she wants to know about the illness and should respond to the patient's wishes.

The patient, the family, and the hospital staff vary in the extent of their knowledge of the patient's illness. In one classification, four patterns of awareness may exist: *open awareness,* in which staff, family, and patient are completely aware of the diagnosis, treatment, and prognosis of the illness; *mutual pretense awareness,* in which these same persons know but pretend not to know; *suspected awareness,* in which everyone knows except the patient, who suspects that such is the case; and *closed awareness,* in which everyone except the patient knows. There is a trend in hospitals toward open awareness when it can be tolerated by all concerned; but some terminally ill patients may choose not to know their condition, and that wish should be respected. However, every attempt should be made, gently and respectfully, to encourage a dying patient and the family to speak openly with one another. Many times, what initially appeared to be a reluctance to talk about the impending death may, in fact, have been fear of isolation, rejection, or perceived lack of courage.

Other factors need to be considered in caring for the dying patient. Pain management should be vigorous in the terminally ill. It is important for a dying patient to function as effectively as possible, given the illness. This is made easier when the patient is relatively free of pain. The physician should use narcotics as liberally as needed and tolerated, so that the patient can attend to any business with a minimum of discomfort. In addition, physicians should not take personally the complaints of a patient who may be in the anger phase of dying and should help the members of the dying patient's family deal with their feelings about the patient's illness. For many patients, family members are the main source of emotional support, and they are far more available to and knowledgeable about the patient than is the doctor on the case.

Family Interventions

The first step in working with the family of a dying patient is to develop an alliance with them. This can be accomplished by allowing the family to talk about their own lives and stresses and offering some understanding. The physician should try to assess to what degree the family wants direction or help and to what degree they prefer a sense of autonomy. At times of great external stress, such as the impending death of a family member, family conflicts may intensify. A physician can help the family to refocus attention on confronting the external stress, rather than on mutual blame and argument. Opening communication channels among family members can be extremely helpful. Family members may be reluctant to talk to the dying patient about the impending death for fear of being too upset themselves or upsetting the patient. Conversely, the dying patient may be reluctant to talk about his or her own impending death for fear of burdening the family. In this situation a physician can let each party know what the others are feeling and can encourage discussion or even raise the topic when all parties are present.

DEATH CRITERIA, DNR, AND LIVING WILLS

The Uniform Determination of Death Act states that "an individual who has sustained either (a) irreversible cessation of circulatory and respiratory functions, or (b) cessation of function of the entire brain, including the brain stem, is dead. A determination of death must be made in accordance with acceptable medical standards."

It is necessary to anticipate the wishes of the patient and his or her family regarding the use of life-sustaining procedures. Moreover, it is ideal to discuss the patient's wishes with the family and the patient while the patient is still competent. A patient may ask that his life not be prolonged by artificial means (e.g., "Do not resuscitate [DNR] if in extremis").

Living wills are legal documents in which patients give instructions to their physicians about withholding life-support measures. But physicians must use their best judgment, even in the absence of a living will. If major questions arise with regard to any of these decisions, the physician should consult the hospital administrator or lawyer.

The American Medical Association states that doctors can withhold all means of life-prolonging medical treatment, including food and water, from patients in irreversible comas, provided there are adequate safeguards to confirm the accuracy of the diagnosis. The decision is made in conjunction with the patient's family or legal guardians. In these cases, the physician lets a terminally ill patient die; the physician does not intentionally cause death. A person is brain-dead when he or she suffers irreversible cessation of the functions of the entire brain, including the brain stem, even if the heart and lungs continue to function.

EUTHANASIA

Physicians often walk a fine line between their responsibility to relieve suffering and their obligation to preserve life. The ethical and legal issues surrounding the active or passive deprivation of life in severely ill patients are controversial. *Euthanasia,* the act of killing a hopelessly ill or injured person for reasons of mercy, may take one of two forms, either direct (active) or indirect (passive). Either form may be voluntary or nonvoluntary. It seems likely that in the context of technological advances that prolong life, coupled with limitations on resources required to sustain human life of acceptable quality, society will move increasingly in the direction of designing a legal framework within which euthanasia can be clarified.

ATTITUDES TOWARD DEATH ACROSS THE LIFE CYCLE

The stages of emotional and cognitive development of children play a significant role in their perception, interpretation, and understanding of death. The ability of children to understand death reflects their ability to understand any abstract concept. Preschool children under age 5 (Piaget's preoperational phase) are animistic (they believe everything, even an inanimate object, is alive) and are aware of death but only in the sense that it is a separation similar to sleep. Between the ages of 5 and 10 years (concrete operations), there is a developing sense of inevitable human mortality; children fear that their parents may die and that they will be abandoned. At about age 9 or 10, death is conceptualized as something that can happen to the child, as well as to the parent. Usually by puberty, children are able to conceptualize death as universal, irreversible, and inevitable, as do adults.

In contrast to parents from other parts of the world, middle-class parents in the United States tend to shield children from a knowledge of death. The air of mystery surrounding death in such instances may create irrational fears in children, which is just the opposite of what is intended.

Adolescents may be preoccupied with issues related to body image and control of the environment; thus, they may appear to focus on what adults perceive to be concerns more trivial than that of death itself. Treating dying adolescents may be difficult because of their intense need at given times for independence and control. Young adults, in Erikson's stage of intimacy versus isolation, are in the process of developing new and deeper relationships. They may focus on the issues of never having the chance to marry or to have children and, therefore, may feel threatened by the potential isolation. Young adult parents fear that their untimely deaths will result in their children's growing up alone. They also fear that they will not experience the role of grandparent. Middle-age adults, in Erikson's stage of generativity versus stagnation, may feel frustrated in their hopes to become involved with the next generation and in their plans to enjoy hard-earned pleasures. Elderly persons, facing the Eriksonian conflict between integrity and despair, must confront the increasing reality of their own mortality through the deaths of family and friends.

Children with fatal illnesses create major emotional stresses on their caregivers, be they parents, relatives, hospital staff, or physicians. A consistent, trusted person is essential in providing optimal care for the dying child. The separation of the child from its mother is as traumatic an event for the hospitalized child as the illness itself, perhaps even more so. As John Bowlby pointed out, the mother (or an equally valued and familiar caregiver) rooming in with the hospitalized child can help alleviate the child's anxiety and facilitate necessary medical care.

GRIEF, MOURNING, AND BEREAVEMENT

These terms apply to the psychological reactions of persons who survive a significant loss. *Grief* refers to the subjective feelings that are precipitated by the death of a loved one. The term is used synonymously with *mourning*, although, in the strictest sense, mourning refers to the processes by which grief is resolved; it is the societal expression of postbereavement behavior and practices. *Bereavement* literally means to be deprived of someone by death and refers to being in the state of mourning. Regardless of the fine points that may differentiate these terms, there are sufficient similarities in the experience of grief and bereavement to warrant its characterization as a syndrome that has signs, symptoms, a demonstrable course, and an expected resolution.

Grief can occur as the result of a variety of losses in addition to the loss of a loved person. These include loss of status, loss of a national figure, and loss of a pet. The expression of grief encompasses a wide range of emotions, depending on the cultural norms and expectations (e.g., some cultures encourage or demand an intense display of emotions, whereas others expect just the opposite) and on the circumstances of the loss (e.g., a sudden unexpected death versus one that is clearly anticipated). *Grief work* is a complex psychological process of withdrawal of attachment and working through the pain of bereavement.

Characteristics of Normal Grief

Uncomplicated grief is viewed as a normal response in view of the predictability of its symptoms and its course. Initial grief is often manifested as a state of shock that may be expressed as a feeling of numbness and a sense of bewilderment. This apparent inability to comprehend what has happened may be short-lived. It is followed by such expressions of suffering and distress as sighing and crying, although in Western culture this expected feature of grief is less common among men than among women. Other physical expressions of grief may include the following: feelings of weakness, decreased appetite, weight loss, and difficulty in concentrating, breathing, and talking. Sleep disturbances may include difficulty in falling asleep, waking up during the night, and awakening early. Dreams of the deceased often occur, after which the dreamer awakens with a sense of disappointment in finding that the experience was only a dream.

Self-reproach is not unusual, although it is less common and less intense in normal grief than in pathological grief. These thoughts usually center on some relatively minor act of omission or commission toward the deceased. A phenomenon known as *survivor guilt* occurs in persons who are relieved that the death is someone else's and not their own. The survivor sometimes believes that he or she should have been the person who died and may (if the guilt persists) have difficulty in establishing new intimate relationships out of fear of betraying the deceased. Forms of denial occur throughout the entire period of bereavement; often, the bereaved person inadvertently thinks or acts as if the loss had not occurred. Efforts to perpetuate the lost relationship are evidenced by an investment in objects that were treasured by the deceased or that remind the grief-stricken person of the deceased (linkage objects).

A sense of the deceased's presence may be so intense as to constitute an illusion or a hallucination (e.g., hearing the deceased person's voice or feeling his or her presence). In normal grief, however, the person realizes that this perception is not real. As part of what has been labeled *identification phenomena,* the person may take on the qualities, mannerisms, or characteristics of the deceased person, as if to perpetuate that person in some concrete way. This maneuver can reach potentially pathological expression with the development of physical symptoms similar to those experienced by the deceased or to ones suggestive of the illness from which the deceased died.

John Bowlby hypothesized four states of bereavement: *Stage 1* is an early phase of acute despair characterized by numbness and protest. Denial may be immediate, and outbursts of anger and distress are common. This stage may last moments to days and may be periodically revisited by the grieving person throughout the mourning process. *Stage 2* is a phase of intense yearning and searching for the deceased, characterized by a physical restlessness and an all-consuming preoccupation with the deceased. This phase may last several months or even years in a more attenuated form. In *Stage 3,* which has been described as a phase of disorganization and despair, the reality of the loss begins to sink in. A sense of going through the motions is dominant, and the grieving person appears withdrawn, apathetic, and listless. Insomnia and weight loss often occur, as well as a feeling that life has lost meaning. There is also a constant reliving of memories of the deceased and an associated, inevitable feeling of disappointment when the bereaved recognizes that they are just memories. *Stage 4* is defined as a phase of reorganization, during which the acutely painful aspects of grief begin to recede and the grieving person begins to feel like returning to life. The deceased is now remembered with a sense of joy, as well as sadness, and the image of the lost person becomes internalized.

C. M. Parkes described five stages of bereavement. (1) *Alarm*—a stressful state manifested by physiological changes, such as a rise in blood pressure and heart rate—is somewhat similar to Bowlby's first stage of protest, fear, and anger. (2) *Numbness* is a state in which the person appears to be superficially unaffected by the loss but is, in reality, protecting himself or herself from feeling the acute distress produced by the loss. (3) In *pining* or searching the person looks for or is constantly reminded of the lost person. The illusions or hallucinations of the deceased mentioned above (sometimes called pseudoillusions or pseudohallucinations because the person immediately recognizes them as such) may occur during this phase. This phase resembles Bowlby's second stage of yearning and searching for the lost figure. (4) In *depression* the bereaved feels hopeless about the future, cannot go on living, and tends to withdraw from family and friends. (5) In the final stage, *recovery and reorganization,* the person recognizes that his or her life will continue with new adjustments and different goals.

Length of Grief

Because there are great variations among persons, the various signs, symptoms, and phases of mourning and bereavement are not as discrete as their characterizations may imply. Nevertheless, the diverse manifestations of grief usually tend to subside over time. Traditionally, grief lasts about one year, as the person has the opportunity to experience the entire calendar year at least once without the lost person. It has become increasingly apparent that some signs and symptoms of grief may persist much longer than one or two years and that a person may have various grief-related feelings, symptoms, and behavior through life. Eventually, however, normal grief resolves, and people return to a state of productivity and relative well-being.

Delayed, Inhibited, or Denied Grief

Delayed, inhibited, or denied grief refers to the absence of the expression of grief at the time of the loss, when it ordinarily would be expected. In some instances, grieving is simply delayed until it can no longer be avoided.

Persons vary greatly in their need to hide their grief. Familial and cultural influences affect how the mourner behaves in public. The stiff upper lip admired by one group contrasts dramatically with the weeping, wailing, and fainting accepted by another group as the norm. Hence, it may be difficult to gauge the extent of another's grief from outward appearances unless one has some understanding of the person's background.

Grief that is inhibited or denied expression is potentially pathogenic because the person avoids dealing with the reality of the loss. A false euphoria may prevail, suggesting that bereavement is on a pathological course. Inhibited or denied grief reactions contain the seeds of such unfortunate consequences as experiencing persistent physical symptoms similar to those of the deceased and unaccountable reactions on the anniversary of the loss or on occasions of significance to the deceased. Denied or inhibited grief may also reach expression by being displaced to some other loss that, although seemingly insignificant in its own right, may symbolize the original loss. Overreaction to another person's trouble may be one manifestation of displacement.

Finally, it must be recognized that some relationships, regardless of their public appearance, are sufficiently negative to render reduced or absent grief a totally normal and appropriate response. In these cases, the consequences of the death of a spouse or a parent may be decidedly positive for the survivor.

Anticipatory Grief

The concept of anticipatory grief applies to grief expressed in advance of a loss that is perceived as inevitable, as distinguished from grief that occurs at or after the loss. By definition, anticipatory grief ends with the occurrence of the anticipated loss, regardless of what reactions follow. Unlike conventional grief, which diminishes in intensity with the passage of time, anticipatory grief may increase in intensity as the expected loss becomes more imminent. In some instances, particularly when the occurrence of the loss is delayed, anticipatory grief may be expended, and the bereaved shows few manifestations of acute grief when the actual loss occurs. Once anticipatory grief has been expended, it may be difficult for the bereaved to reestablish the prior relationship; this phenomenon is experienced with the return of persons long gone (e.g., in combat or concentration camps) and of persons thought to have been dead.

Grief versus Depression

Both grief and depression may be manifested by sadness, crying, and tension expressed as either psychomotor retardation or psychomotor agitation. Deceased appetite, weight loss, insomnia, diminished sexual interest, and withdrawal from outside activities are also common to both conditions. As the loss becomes more remote, however, the grief-stricken person shows shifts of mood from sadness to a more normal state and finds increasing enjoyment in life's experiences. Self-blame generally centers on what was done or not done in relation to the lost person, whereas the self-accusation of depressed persons is more likely to involve being bad, worthless, or even evil. The general demeanor of a grief-stricken person intuitively elicits sympathy, support, and consolation from others, to which the person shows some responsiveness and appreciation. In contrast, the complaints and laments of the depressed person may irritate and annoy the listener. In normal grief, the response is accepted as appropriate and normal by both the grieving person and others; in depression, the response readily conveys the notion that something is not right about what is going on. People who have experienced previous depressions are more likely to experience depression, rather than normal grief, at the time of a major loss; the person's clinical history, therefore, may be helpful in judging a current reaction. Depressed persons threaten suicide more often than grieving persons, who, except in unusual instances—for example, physically dependent and aged persons—do not seriously wish to die, even if they claim that life is unbearable. Marked feelings of worthlessness, extended functional impairment, and psychomotor retardation argue more for a major depression than for uncomplicated bereavement. Frank psychotic symptoms, such as true hallucinations or delusions, may be part of the clinical picture of major depression but not of normal grief. It is incumbent on the physician to be able to determine when grief has become pathological and, in essence, has evolved into a major depression. Grief is a normal, albeit intensely painful, state that is responsive to support, empathy, and the passage of time. Major depression is potentially a medical emergency requiring immediate intervention to forestall a complication, such as suicide. Intervention may involve hospitalization or the use of antidepressant medication.

Bereavement in Children

Bowlby also studied the bereavement process in children. It is similar to that of adults, especially once the child is able to understand the irrevocability of death. The mourning process resembles that of separation in that there are three phases: protest, despair, and detachment. In the *protest* phase, the child has a strong desire for the mother or other caregiver who died and cries for her return; in the *despair* phase, the child begins to feel hopeless about her return, crying is intermittent, and withdrawal and apathy set in. In the *detachment* phase, the child begins to relinquish some of the emotional attachment to the parent and to show a reawakening of interest in the surroundings. In dealing with the bereaved child, the physician should recognize the child's need to find a person who will substitute for the parent. The child may transfer his or her need for a parent to several adults, rather than to one. If no consistent person is available, severe psychological damage to the child may result, so that the child no longer looks for or expects intimacy in any relationship. The importance of managing grief reactions in children is highlighted by the increased evidence that depressive disorders and suicide attempts occur more frequently in adults who in early childhood experienced the death of a parent.

Grief in Parents

Parents react to a child's death or the birth of a malformed infant in stages similar to those described in terminal illness by Kübler-Ross: shock, denial, anger, bargaining, depression, and acceptance. The death of a child is often a more intense emotional experience than the death of an adult. Parental feelings of guilt and helplessness may be overwhelming; they may believe that somehow they did not protect their children and have unnaturally outlived them. Lost hopes, wishes, and fulfillments associated with a new generation cause additional pain. Manifestations of this grief may well last a lifetime.

A sudden death is often more traumatic than a prolonged death, because anticipatory grief can occur in the latter case. In these instances a parent may become overprotective toward the child or shower the child with gifts that were previously denied. The stress of dealing with the child's death may cause a marriage that has had conflicts to disintegrate. One parent may blame the other for the child's fatal illness, especially if there is some hereditary basis for the disease. The physician should be alert to these patterns of dissension. Some studies indicate that up to 50 percent of marriages in which a child dies or is malformed end in divorce.

Psychodynamics

In 1917 Freud wrote in *Mourning and Melancholia* that normal grief (mourning) resulted from the withdrawal of the libido from its attachment to the lost object. In normal mourning the loss is clearly and unambivalently perceived, and the deceased person is eventually, through the grief work, internalized as a loving and loved object. In abnormal grief (melancholia) the lost object is not really given up but incorporated within the psyche as an object infused with negative feelings. These negative feelings toward the deceased are now experienced as part of the self, and the person becomes depressed, develops low self-esteem, feels worthless, and becomes self-accusatory, with possible delusional expectations of punishment. Freud's distinction between mourning and melancholia is still considered valid; that is, an exaggerated loss of self-esteem is not part of normal grieving. Other psychoanalytic theorists have stressed the role of unconscious dynamics in grief reactions. The greater the role of unconscious and ambivalent factors (e.g., anger toward the deceased), the greater the likelihood of an abnormal grief reaction. Karl Abraham described the introjection of an ambivalently loved lost object and the subsequent direction of anger toward the introjected object.

Grief and Medical Illness

Compelling evidence suggests that, during bereavement, the person is in a vulnerable physical state of biological disequilibrium. Clinical evidence and research findings support the hypothesis that bereavement may be a factor in the development of a wide range of physical and emotional disorders, including fatal illness. Comparisons of close relatives of deceased persons with relatives of living persons (matched for age, sex, and marital status) indicate that bereaved relatives have a much higher mortality rate during the first year of bereavement, the greatest risk being for widowed people. During bereavement, widows have a much higher consultation rate for all causes than before the loss of their spouses. Aged persons, in particular, tend to express their reactions in terms of somatic symptoms.

The physician's role in the grieving process. The physician has an important role in dealing with bereaved spouses, relatives, and friends. First, the physician may have to prepare the family for the possibility that a loved one will die. In the event of the person's death, the physician should encourage the ventilation of feelings. If this emotional expression is inhibited, in all likelihood these feelings will be expressed in a more intense manner at a later date. Outcomes of bereavement are most favorable if the grief-stricken person can interact with others who share or empathize with their feelings of loss. Persons in normal grief seldom seek psychiatric help because they accept their reactions and behavior as appropriate. Accordingly, the attending physician should not routinely recommend that the bereaved see a psychiatrist unless a markedly divergent reaction to the loss is noted. For example, under usual circumstances the bereaved will not make a suicide attempt. Should that occur, psychiatric intervention is indicated. When professional assistance is sought, it usually involves a request for sleeping medication from the family physician. A mild sedative to induce sleep may be useful in these situations; but there is rarely an indication for antidepressant medication or antianxiety agents in normal grief. It can be argued that the bereaved must go through the mourning process, however painful it may be, for successful resolution to occur. To narcotize the patient with drugs interferes with a normal process that ultimately can lead to a favorable outcome.

Grief Management and Therapy

Because grief reactions may develop into depressive reactions or pathological mourning, specific counseling sessions for the bereaved are often valuable. Grief therapy is becoming an increasingly important skill. In regularly scheduled sessions, the person is encouraged to talk about feelings of loss and about the deceased. Many bereaved persons have difficulty recognizing and expressing angry or ambivalent feelings toward the deceased, and it is important that they be reassured that these feelings are normal.

During grief therapy, an attachment to the therapist usually occurs; that attachment provides the bereaved with temporary support until a new sense of confidence about the future develops. The therapist gradually encourages the patient to take on new responsibilities and to develop a sense of autonomy. To do grief therapy, the therapist must be comfortable dealing with the issues of death and dying and able to handle such intense emotional reactions on the patient's part as sadness, anger, guilt, and self-denigration. In addition, grief therapy requires that the therapist be active and participate in the decision-making process with the patient, especially in decisions that guide the patient toward greater independence.

Grief therapy need not be conducted only on a one-to-one basis; group counseling can also be effective. Self-help groups have value in certain cases. About 30 percent of widows and widowers report that they become isolated from friends, withdraw from social life, and thus experience feelings of isolation and loneliness. Self-help groups offer companionship, social contacts, and emotional support; they eventually enable their members to reenter society in a meaningful way.

Bereavement care and grief therapy have been most effective with widows and widowers. The necessity for this type of therapy stems, in part, from the contraction of the family unit. Previously, extended family members were able to provide the needed emotional support and guidance during the mourning period.

HOSPICE MOVEMENT

A *hospice* is a domicile in which care is provided for dying patients; its primary emphasis is on the physical and psychological comfort of the terminally ill. Such care may also be provided in an institution or at home. The central concept of the hospice is the humanization of terminal care by helping dying patients and their families to carry out final choices with dignity and control.

The hospice movement began in the early 1960s, when Dame Cicely Saunders established a small residential unit to care for the terminally ill. At present, there are about 1,700 such units in the United States. Most hospices are sponsored by hospitals or are affiliated with home health care agencies; some are approved by Medicare, which reimburses patients for hospice care with certain restrictions. Round-the-clock coverage is provided by a multidisciplinary team composed of physicians, psychiatrists, social workers, and trained volunteers.

There are many positive features of a hospice program. A supervised organized routine provides intensive care for both the patient and the family; control of pain is a primary goal, and narcotics are given without the fear of addiction; and group support is provided for the patients, who are not as isolated as they are in general hospitals.

Because the bereavement process is a major focus, hospice care also helps prevent pathological grief reactions from occurring in surviving family members. Several studies have indicated that hospice care has a more favorable effect than standard hospital care on families' abilities to cope and adapt. The *burn-out syndrome,* in which health care providers become uninterested and irritable with the terminally ill patient who requires almost constant attention, is rarely seen. If the patient is in home hospice care, visiting nurses provide important relief for overburdened family members.

Medicare pays for hospice care if the patient's doctor states that the patient has a life expectancy of six months or less. In one study by C. M. Parkes, however, it was shown that predictions concerning the length of survival for patients referred to a hospice did not correlate with actual length of survival. Doctors were able to state only that patients with incurable cancer would die within a relatively short period of time and could not be more precise. Unfortunately, current federal regulations do not provide for financing hospital care once federally sponsored hospice care has begun; thus, a patient who utilizes a hospice's care system will not be insured on reentry to a hospital if the need should arise.

The hospice movement is in its ascendancy, especially because it costs more to keep a terminally ill patient in a general hospital than it does to provide hospice benefits. It is also a more compassionate and humane method for managing preterminal and terminal patients.

Acquired Immune Deficiency Syndrome (AIDS) Patients and the Hospice Concept

AIDS patients provide a special case example of the need for greatly increased hospicelike care centers for terminally ill patients. The AIDS epidemic poses profound challenges to the medical care system, to the mental health care system, and to social service agencies, as well as to patients and their families. AIDS has a devastating effect on most areas of human functioning, with patients often severely debilitated for long periods of time before death. Many patients' needs rapidly overwhelm the capabilities of their own social network, just as the needs of AIDS patients are overwhelming the capacities of the existing traditional health care facilities. Furthermore, the incidence of the burn-out or chronic professional stress syndrome in caretakers of AIDS patients is very high and presents a major challenge to the development and maintenance of an adequate care system for these patients.

References

Bowlby J: Process of mourning. Int J Psychoanal *42*: 317, 1961.

Freud S: Mourning and melancholia (1917). In *Standard Edition of the Complete Psychological Works of Sigmund Freud,* vol. 14. Hogarth Press, London, 1957.

Gonda T A: Death, dying, and bereavement. In *Comprehensive Textbook of Psychiatry*, ed 5, H I Kaplan and B J Sadock, editors, p 1339. Williams & Wilkins, Baltimore, 1989.

Jeret J S: Discussing dying: Changing attitudes among patients, physicians, and medical students. Pharos *52*: 15, 1989.

Kübler-Ross E: *On Death and Dying.* Macmillan, New York, 1969.

Kutscher A, Carr A, Kutscher L, eds: *Principles of Thanatology.* Columbia University Press, New York, 1987.

Leming M R, Dickinson, G E: *Understanding Dying, Death and Bereavement.* Holt, Rinehart and Winston, New York, 1985.

Lindemann E: Symptomatology and management of acute grief. Am J Psychiatry *101*: 141, 1945.

Ness D E, Pfeffer C R: Sequelae of bereavement resulting from suicide. Am J Psychiatry *147*: 279, 1990.

Osterweis M, Solomon F, Green M, eds: *Bereavement: Reaction Consequences and Care.* National Academy Press, Washington, DC, 1984.

Parkes C M, Weiss R S: *Recovery from Bereavement.* Basic Books, New York, 1983.

Roberts G, Owen J. The near-death experience. Br J Psychiatry *153*: 607, 1988.

Saunders C M, Baines M: *Living with Dying: The Management of Terminal Disease,* ed 2. Oxford University Press, Oxford, 1989.

Warren W G: *Death Education and Research: Critical Perspectives.* Haworth Press, New York, 1989.

Weiss L, Frischer L, Richman J: Parental adjustment to intrapartum and delivery room loss: The role of hospital-based support program. Clin Perinatol *16*: 1009, 1989.

Zisook S, DeVaul R: Unresolved grief. Am J Psychoanal *45*: 370, 1985.

3

The Brain and Behavior

3.1 / Neuroanatomy and Neuropsychiatry

An understanding of the biology of the brain is central to a complete appreciation of human behavior. Although most diseases that involve a specific area of the brain (e.g., strokes) are treated by neurologists, many patients with these diseases also demonstrate psychiatric symptoms. The study of psychiatric symptoms associated with classical neurological conditions (e.g., depression associated with Parkinson's disease) and the study of neurological symptoms associated with classical psychiatric conditions (e.g., abnormal eye tracking associated with schizophrenia) are two major aspects of the field of *neuropsychiatry*. An appreciation of these areas of overlap between psychiatry and neurology helps in the understanding of the brain and its functioning. A knowledge of the neurological syndromes aids in the correct diagnosis of neurological conditions that may initially present with psychiatric symptoms alone. An understanding of the interface between psychiatry and neurology helps clarify the process by which discrete disorders of the brain can result in the complex symptoms seen in psychiatric disorders.

GROSS ANATOMY

The *central nervous system* (CNS) consists of the brain and the spinal cord. The adult human brain weighs approximately 1,350 g and contains approximately 10^{11} neurons. Each of these 10^{11} neurons has 10^3 to 10^4 synaptic connections on its cell surface from as many as 10^3 different neurons. The *peripheral nervous system* (PNS) consists of the cranial nerves, spinal nerves, and peripheral ganglia. The PNS brings sensory information to the CNS and conducts motor information from the CNS. The autonomic nervous system (ANS) innervates the internal organs. Sensory receptors in these peripheral organs also relay information back to the CNS, either directly by afferent nerves or indirectly by released hormones (e.g., atriopeptin from the heart).

In the CNS, gray matter contains the neuronal cell bodies, whereas white matter consists mainly of myelinated neuronal axons. The three areas of gray matter are the cerebral cortex, the cerebellar cortex, and the subcortical cerebral and cerebellar nuclei. The right and left cerebral hemispheres are connected by the corpus callosum and other smaller commissural tracts. The cerebral cortex itself is heavily folded with gyri (convolutions) and fissures (sulci or grooves). The medulla oblongata, pons, and mesencephalon together make up the brain stem.

Ventricular System

Within each cerebral hemisphere, there is a lateral ventricle that is divided into the anterior horn, the central part, the posterior horn, and the temporal horn. Both lateral ventricles are continuous with the third ventricle through the interventricular foramina of Monro. The third ventricle is connected to the fourth ventricle through the cerebral aqueduct.

Cerebrospinal Fluid

The ventricular system is filled with cerebrospinal fluid (CSF). CSF is produced by the choroid plexi in the lateral ventricles and within the brain parenchyma itself. The CSF leaves the ventricular system by the median aperture of Magendie and the two lateral apertures of Luschka; it is then absorbed into the venous system through the arachnoid villi. The CSF has a volume of approximately 125 mL in the normal adult; approximately 500 mL is made each day. The total volume of CSF, therefore, is replaced approximately four times each day. *Hydrocephalus* results from a disorder of CSF drainage, which causes CSF pressure to increase. On computed tomographic (CT) scans, dilated ventricles can indicate its presence.

Because it reflects neurochemical activity in the brain, the CSF is a source of research information in psychiatry. However, metabolites from the spinal cord may significantly contribute to the CSF, and neurotransmitter metabolites from deep brain structures may not reach the CSF efficiently.

Normal-Pressure Hydrocephalus

Normal-pressure hydrocephalus is a treatable type of dementia in patients with enlarged ventricles and normal cerebrospinal fluid pressure. The disorder is relatively uncommon, and only rare cases of dementia are caused by this disorder. The clinical features are a progressive dementia, a gait disturbance, and urinary incontinence. When the disorder is diagnosed, the treatment of choice is shunting the CSF from the ventricular space to either the atrium or the peritoneal space. Reversal of dementia and associated signs is sometimes dramatic after treatment.

Meninges

The brain and the spinal cord are covered by the meninges. The dura mater, attached to the inside of the skull, is the strongest of the coverings. Beneath the dura mater are the arachnoid and pia mater, the latter of which is attached to the brain's surface. Between the arachnoid and pia mater is the subarachnoid space which is filled with CSF. A *subdural hematoma* usually results from trauma that tears a vein and causes relatively slow accumulation of blood beneath the dura mater. An *epidural hematoma* usually results from trauma tearing an artery, resulting in a rapid and life-threatening accumulation of blood between the dura mater and the skull. *Meningitis* is an infection and inflammation of one or more of the meningeal layers.

NEURONS AND GLIA

Neurons

The *neuron*, or nerve cell, is the basic functional unit of the nervous system. A large diversity of neuronal types vary in size, shape, number of incoming and outgoing synapses, and chemistry.

The neuronal cell body is also called the soma or perikaryon. Classically, the two projections from the cell body are the axon and the dendrite. The axon arises from the cell body or from the base of one of the main dendrites. The initial axon segment, the axon hillock, is the actual site of initiation for the action potential in many neurons. The axon hillock is unmyelinated, even if the remainder of the axon is myelinated. The myelin sheath is interrupted over the course of the axon at the nodes of Ranvier. The myelination stops at the distal end of the axon, where the axon may branch and enlarge at its tips. These terminal enlargements are called the axon terminals or boutons and are the sites of presynaptic neurotransmitter release. Within the axon terminals are the synaptic vesicles, which contain neurotransmitter substances. There are different types of synaptic vesicles, varying in size and other characteristics. These different types of vesicles contain different neurotransmitters and, conceivably, differentially respond to the stimulation of the axon terminal.

There may be none, one, or many unmyelinated dendrites emerging from the cell body. Most dendrites receive neurotransmitter messages from an axon. The dendrites are usually profusely branched and studded with small spikes, called dendritic spines, which are the sites of synaptic connection.

Glia

Glia, glial cells, and neuroglia are synonymous terms for a class of nonneuronal cells in the nervous system. There are four types of glial cells in the CNS (astrocytes, oligodendrocytes, ependyma, and microglia) and two types in the PNS (Schwann and satellite cells). The astrocytes provide structural support to neurons and are the major cell type in glial scar tissue in the CNS. The astrocytes may also serve an important role in isolating the receptive surfaces of neurons. The oligodendrocytes, the myelin-forming cells of the CNS, may perform a nurturing role for neurons. Both astrocytes and oligodendrocytes are involved in phagocytosis. The ependyma line the brain ventricles and the central canal of the spinal cord. Its surface is covered with cilia whose beating facilitates the movement of CSF. In addition to their functional support of neurons, glial cells may have a direct and critical role in neuronal activity.

Blood-brain barrier. Glia contribute to the blood-brain permeability barrier. This semipermeable barrier between the blood vessels and the brain is so constructed that many chemical compounds are unable to pass from the blood into the brain. The ability of a chemical to pass into the brain is based on its molecular size, electrical charge, and solubility and on the presence in the blood-brain barrier of specific transport systems for the compound. The blood-brain permeability barrier also affects the ability of compounds to leave the CNS.

CEREBRAL CORTEX

The cerebral cortex contains approximately 70 percent of the neurons in the CNS. The cerebral cortex is also the area of the brain that is more developed in humans than in any other animal. The cerebral cortex, therefore, has been a major focus of psychiatric research. Characteristic neuropsychiatric symptoms are seen with injury to specific cortical regions (Table 3.1-1).

Divisions

The cerebral cortex can be divided according to a variety of characteristics, including anatomy, cytoarchitecture, and modality.

Anatomy. The cerebral cortex is divided anatomically into four lobes—frontal, temporal, parietal, and occipital (Figures 3.1-1 and 3.1-2). The longitudinal cerebral fissure separates the right and left cerebral hemispheres at the midline. The central sulcus (Rolando's fissure) separates the frontal lobe from the parietal lobe. The lateral cerebral sulcus (fissure of Sylvius) marks the superior border of the temporal lobe, demarcating the temporal and frontal lobes. The occipital lobe, located at the posterior end of the brain, is separated from the parietal lobe by an imaginary line running down from the parietal-occipital sulcus.

Cytoarchitecture. Cytoarchitecture refers to the differential arrangement of neuron layers within the cortex. There are six classically defined layers in the cerebral cortex. The presence or absence and the relative thickness of each of these layers distinguish different cytoarchitectural areas of the cerebral cortex. In 1909, Korbinian Brodmann described 47 areas of the cortex on the basis of cerebral cytoarchitecture (Figure 3.1-3).

Whereas Brodmann divided the cerebral cortex into areas according to the individual cytoarchitectural characteristics of each area, other neuroanatomists have divided the cerebral cortex on the basis of shared cytoarchitectural characteristics. Specifically, one system divides the cerebral cortex into five categories on the basis of increasing structural complexity (number and differentiation of cortical cell layers). The corticoid areas are structurally the simplest, followed by the allocortical, the paralimbic, and the homotypical association isocortex. The most complex cortical architecture is found in the idiotypic cortex. The corticoid and allocortical areas are closely associated with the hypothalamus and are involved in the regulation of the person's internal state, such as memory, learning, modulation of drives, affective coloring of experiences, hormonal regulation, and autonomic functioning. The paralimbic cortex includes many limbic areas and is conceptualized as a functional bridge between the allocortex and the isocortex. The homotypical association isocortex and the idiotypic cortex are involved in interpreting the external envi-

Table 3.1-1
Major Behavioral and Psychological Symptoms of Cortical Injury

Lobe	Functions	Dysfunctions*
Frontal	Reciprocally connected with motor, sensory, and emotional brain areas Controls contralateral movement Produces speech (dominant hemisphere) Critical to personality, abstract thinking, memory, concentration, judgment, and other higher mental functions	Frontal lobe syndrome that may include inappropriate or uninhibited behavior, irritability and labile affect, depression and flat affect, lack of motivation, difficulty with attention, memory, and other cognitive deficits Peculiar facetious sense of humor (*witzelsucht*) Broca's aphasia Aprosody (nondominant) Contralateral motor weakness and slowing Contralateral apraxia
Temporal	Memory (especially hippocampus) Sexual and aggressive behavior Comprehension of language Interpretation of gustatory and olfactory sensations Major component of limbic system	Memory impairment (bilateral) Language comprehension Control of sexual and aggressive drives Wernicke's aphasia (dominant hemisphere) Klüver-Bucy syndrome Aprosody (nondominant hemisphere)
Parietal	Receives and identifies sensory information from tactile receptors Processes visual and auditory sensations Praxes	Either or both hemispheres: right-left disorientation, finger agnosia, astereognosis Dominant: alexia, agraphia, anomia, idiokinetic and kinesthetic apraxias, dyscalculia Nondominant: impaired spatial abilities; denial of illness (anosognosia); inability to recognize body parts (autopagnosia); dressing, constructional, and kinesthetic apraxias; left spatial neglect
Occipital	Interpretation of visual images Visual memory	Disturbed spatial orientation (metamorphopsia) Visual illusions Visual hallucinations Blindness Symptoms may simulate hysteria

*The actual dysfunction is related to the specific area of the lobe that is lesioned.

ronment. The homotypical association isocortex is synonymous with the association cortex, and the idiotypic cortex is synonymous with the primary motor and sensory areas discussed below. The cytoarchitecture of the primary sensorimotor cortex is more complex than the cytoarchitecture of the sensorimotor association cortex.

Modality. Dividing the cerebral cortex by modality results in two major categories: the primary motor and sensory areas and the motor and sensory association areas. The primary motor cortex is anterior to the central sulcus in the precentral gyrus (Brodmann's area 4). The primary sensory cortex is modality-specific; that is, it receives afferent pathways from a single sensory modality (visual, auditory, or somatosensory). The visual primary cortex is located in the occipital poles and along the calcarine fisure in the occipital lobes (Brodmann's area 17). The auditory primary cortex is located in Heschl's gyrus in the temporal lobes (Brodmann's areas 41 and 42). The somatosensory primary cortex is in the postcentral gyrus of the parietal lobes (Brodmann's areas 1, 2, and 3). Association areas of cortex can be either unimodal or heteromodal. Unimodal motor association areas are involved in the planning of motor activity and project to the primary motor cortex; unimodal sensory association areas are involved in the interpretation of primary sensory input and receive afferent pathways from the primary sensory cortex. The unimodal motor association cortex is located in Brodmann's area 6; the unimodal visual association cortex is located in Brodmann's areas 18, 19, 20, 21, and 37; the unimodal auditory association cortex is located in Brodmann's area 22 (also known as Wernicke's area); and the unimodal somatosensory association cortex is located in Brodmann's area 5. Heteromodal association areas receive afferent input from unimodal association areas and are involved in the process of organizing the totality of the sensory and motor information that the brain is receiving. There are three major areas of the heteromodal association cortex: parietal-temporal-occipital (probably involved in sensory evaluation and language); prefrontal (probably involved in cognitive planning and motor activity); and limbic (probably involved in memory and emotion).

Interhemispheric Connectivity and Laterality

The most obvious gross features of the brain are the two cerebral hemispheres. They are connected by the myelinated axons that run through the corpus callosum, the anterior commissure, the hippocampal commissure, the posterior commissure, and the habenular commissure.

The dominant hemisphere is the one organized to express language. The left hemisphere is dominant in 97 percent of the population, including 99 percent of right-handed persons and 60 to 70 percent of left-handed persons. Language dominance is not completely synonymous with hand dominance, and a few persons have mixed dominance for language.

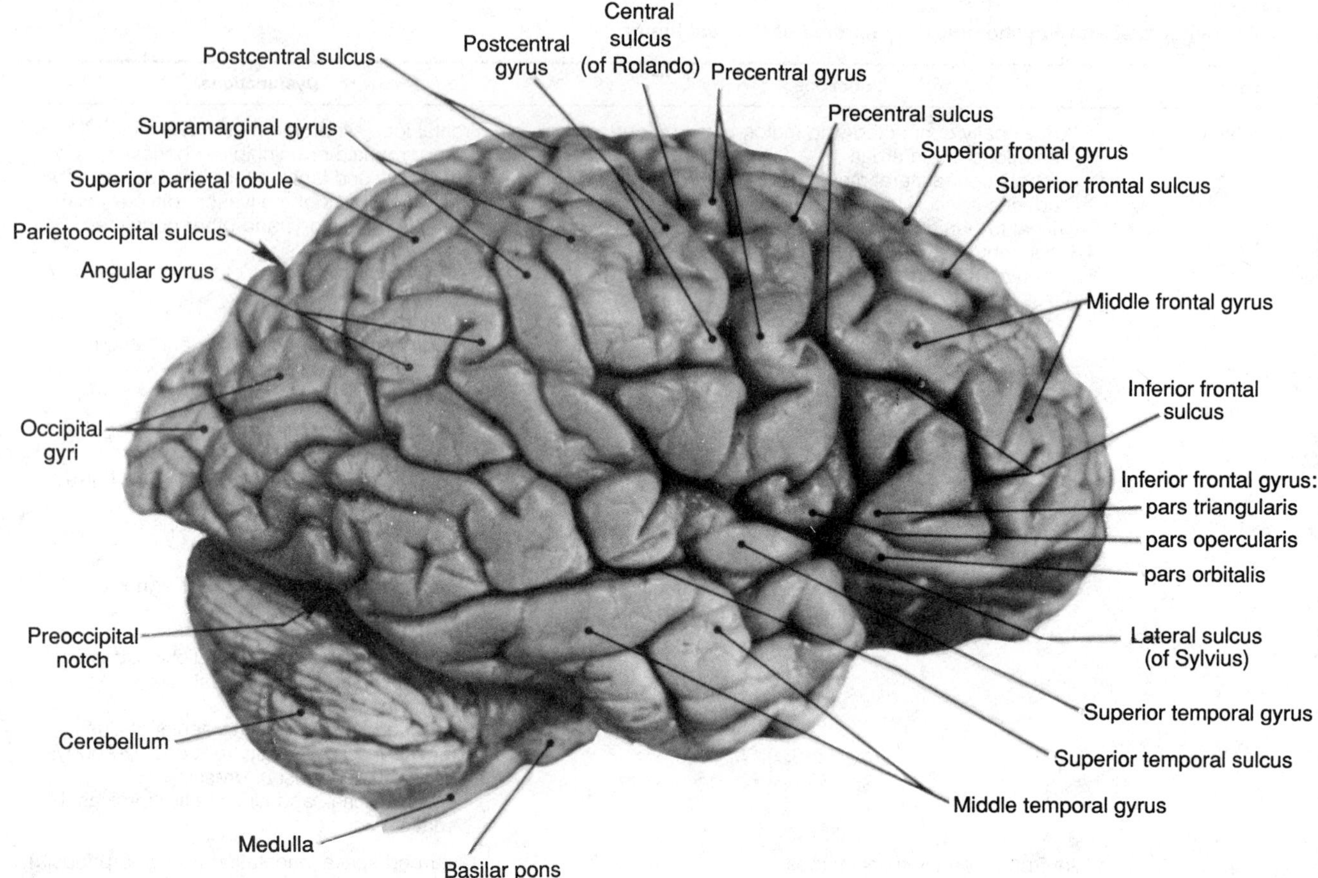

Figure 3.1-1. Lateral view of the right cerebral hemisphere, showing principal gyri and sulci. (From D E Haines: *Neuroanatomy: An Atlas of Structures, Sections, and Systems*, ed 2, p 16. Urban & Schwarzenberg, Baltimore-Munich, 1987, with permission.)

Psychological studies of persons with unilateral brain trauma or epileptic lesions have led to many theories about hemispheric functions. In addition to regulating language ability, the left hemisphere has been described as being the rational half of the brain, the one concerned with analytical, sequencing, abstracting, and logistical abilities. Damage to the left hemisphere, as in strokes, is thought to result in clinical depression more often than is damage to the right hemisphere. The right hemisphere is more involved with perceptual, visual-spatial, artistic, musical, and synthetic cortical activity. It is involved with both the perception and the expression of affective content, including the perception of social cues. Damage to the right hemisphere is often characterized by apathy and indifference, except for occasional exaggerated but short-lived emotional responses under some circumstances.

Corpus callosum syndromes. Lesions of the posterior portion of the corpus callosum prevent written language, seen by the right hemisphere, from getting to the left-hemisphere language centers and results in *alexia*. Lesions of the anterior portion of the corpus callosum prevent the right motor and sensory cortices from communicating with the language and praxis areas of the left hemisphere. This results in an inability to write with the left hand, an inability to name unseen objects placed in the left hand, and a generalized *apraxia* of the left hand. Complete transection of the corpus callosum has been performed surgically in some patients in an attempt to prevent the spread of seizure activity. Essentially, the procedure produces two independent hemispheres. The patients have been tested by presenting information to only one hemisphere at a time. Those who have a severed corpus callosum still have a sense of themselves as a unitary being, even though both hemispheres of their brains function independently. One model of the brain hypothesizes that the left hemisphere contains an interpreter for both internal and external experiences. This interpretive function is hypothesized to be a major contributor to one's sense of unitary being.

Frontal Cortex

The frontal lobes can be divided anatomically into the superior, middle, and inferior frontal gyri (Figure 3.1-1). Functionally, the frontal lobes can be divided into the motor cortex, the premotor cortex, and the prefrontal associational cortex. On the medial aspect of the frontal cortex (Figure 3.1-2), the cingulate gyrus wraps around the corpus callosum. The frontal cortex receives afferents from the sensory association cortex and projects to the midbrain and to the supplementary motor and basal ganglia and the limbic system.

The functions of the cortical areas have been deduced primarily from the study of animals and humans with lesions of specific cortical areas. In general, the frontal cortex is involved in motor behavior, expressive language, ability to concentrate and attend, reasoning and thinking, and orientation to time, place, and person. The prefrontal cortex also has a complex involvement in the evaluation of sensory information. Although it is possible to localize functions to a somewhat specific area of the cortex, this localization does not mean that a spec-

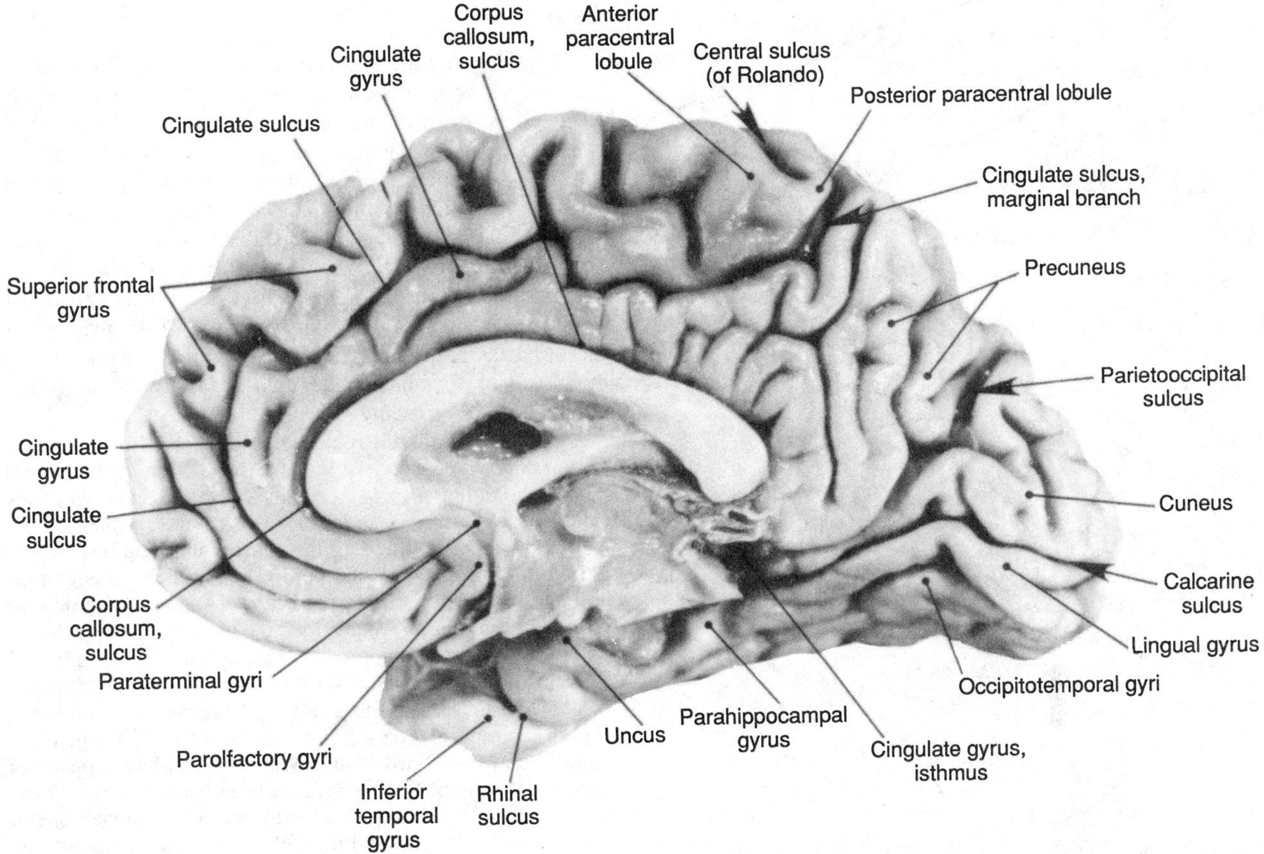

Figure 3.1-2. Mid-sagittal view of the right cerebral hemisphere and diencephalon, with brain stem removed, showing the principal gyri and sulci. (From D E Haines: *Neuroanatomy: An Atlas of Structures, Sections, and Systems*, ed 2, p 24. Urban & Schwarzenberg, Baltimore-Munich, 1987, with permission.)

ified area of the cortex is the only one associated with the function or that it is not involved in other processes within the cerebral cortex. The localization of functions within the cerebral cortex means only that a specific area has a particularly important role in that process.

Two general patterns of symptoms have been related to two different frontal lesions—a *dorsolateral convexity syndrome* and an *orbitomedial syndrome*. The dorsolateral cortex has diverse connections to other cortical and subcortical areas. Afferents are received from sensory association areas of the inferior parietal and temporal cortex and from the dorsomedial nucleus of the thalamus. Efferents are reciprocal to afferents and project to the hypothalamus, the hippocampus, and the basal ganglia. Lesions of the dorsolateral prefrontal cortex are associated with apathy, decreased drive, poor grooming, psychomotor retardation, decreased attention, and, if the dominant hemisphere is affected, Broca's aphasia. Other symptoms include indifference, motor perseveration, difficulty in changing mental sets, and poor ability to abstract. This syndrome is somewhat similar to so-called negative-symptom schizophrenia, and, indeed, evidence from brain imaging techniques has suggested that this area of the cortex is a potential lesion site in a subgroup of patients with schizophrenia.

The orbitomedial frontal cortex is closely linked to the limbic system and is reciprocally innervated by the dorsomedial nucleus of the thalamus and the amygdala. Efferents also project to the rostral brain stem. Lesions of this area of the cortex result in withdrawal, fearfulness, lability of mood, explosiveness, loss of inhibitions, and occasional violent outbursts.

Temporal Cortex

The lateral aspect of the temporal lobe has three gyri—superior, middle, and inferior (Figure 3.1-1). The primary functions of the temporal cortex include language, memory, and emotion. Because lesions of the temporal cortex can lead to symptoms resembling those of psychiatric conditions (e.g., hallucinations, delusions, and mood disturbances), this area has received particular attention in psychiatric research. The most common causes of temporal lobe lesions are stroke, trauma, and tumor. CNS infections with herpes virus show a particular predilection toward the temporal lobes. Bilateral lesions of the temporal lobes lead to dementia. Lesions of the dominant temporal lobe are associated with euphoria, auditory hallucinations, delusions, thought disorders, decreased ability to learn new material, and poor verbal comprehension. Lesions of the nondominant temporal lobe are associated with dysphoria, irritability, and cognitive deficits, including decreased visual and musical ability.

Parietal Cortex

The parietal lobe includes the postcentral gyrus, the superior parietal lobule, and the inferior parietal lobule (Figures 3.1-1 and 3.1-2). The inferior parietal lobule includes the supramarginal gyrus and the angular gyrus. The parietal lobes contain the associational cortices for visual, tactile, and auditory input and, therefore, are involved in the intellectual processing of sensory information. The left parietal lobe has

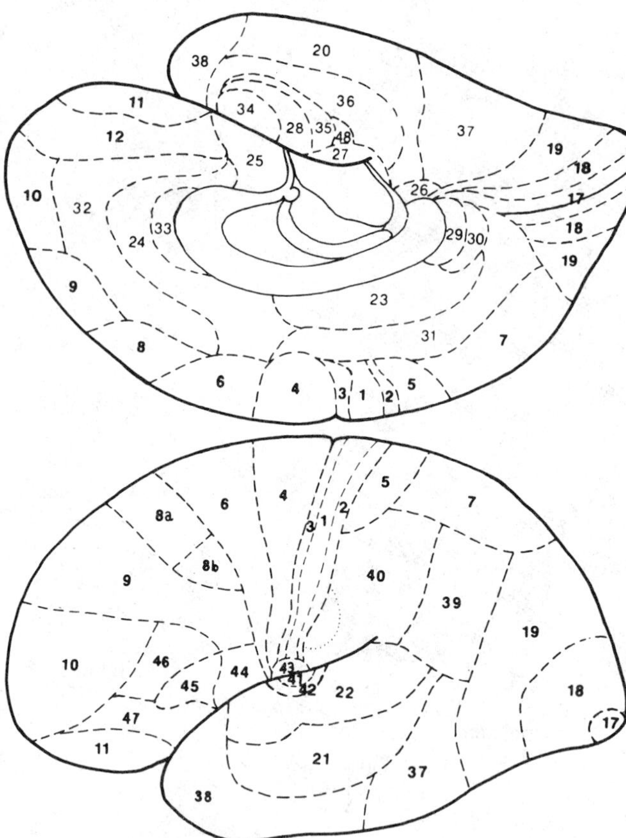

Figure 3.1-3. Brodmann's areas. (From C Romero-Sierra: *Neuroanatomy: A Conceptual Approach*. Churchill Livingstone, New York, 1986, with permission.)

a preferential role in verbal processing; the right parietal lobe has a greater role in visual-spatial processing. *Gerstmann syndrome* has been attributed to lesions of the dominant parietal lobe; it includes agraphia, calculation difficulties (acalculia), right-left disorientation, and finger agnosia. Two symptoms of nondominant parietal lesions are denial of illness (known as anosognosia) and neglect of the left side. Classically, persons with a right-sided parietal stroke may deny that they have a paralyzed left arm and may completely ignore the left side of the body (e.g., not washing it).

Occipital Cortex

The occipital lobe includes the superior and inferior occipital gyri and the cuneus and lingual gyri (Figure 3.1-2). The occipital lobes are the primary sensory cortex for visual input, and the major sign of a lesion in one lobe is impairment on visual field testing. Total destruction of the occipital cortex results in cortical blindness. More subtle dysfunction, however, can result in distortion of images, persistent afterimages, and loss of depth perception. Some of these symptoms may be similar to those seen in psychiatric conditions and may cause the clinician to miss the diagnosis of a neurological disorder of the occipital lobes. *Anton's syndrome* is associated with bilateral occlusion of the posterior cerebral arteries, resulting in cortical blindness and denial of blindness. The occurrence of visual hallucinations in patients with occipital epileptic foci has also been reported. The anatomy of the visual system is diagramed in Figure 3.1-4.

Aphasias

Frontal, parietal, and temporal lobes are involved in the reception and production of language. An *aphasia* is an acquired disorder of language (comprehension, word choice, expression, syntax) that is not due to a dysarthria—that is, a dysfunction of the muscles necessary for speech production (Table 3.1-2). Aphasias not only are of classical neurological interest vis-à-vis localization of cortical function but also provide some insight into the thought disorders of psychiatric patients, who often present with disorganized speech as a major symptom. A knowledge of the aphasias helps prevent the clinician from mistakenly diagnosing a psychiatric illness when a treatable neurological disorder is present.

Broca's aphasia. Broca's area is involved in the motor production of speech. Lesions of Broca's area in the frontal lobe (Brodmann's area 44) result in an aphasia that is variously called Broca's aphasia, anterior aphasia, motor aphasia, and expressive aphasia. Such lesions leave comprehension unimpaired but produce an aphasia in which speech is telegraphic and agrammatical. Broca's aphasia is associated with depressive symptoms in the majority of patients; however, some patients experience inappropriate elation and irritability.

Wernicke's aphasia. Wernicke's area is involved in the comprehension of speech. Lesions of Wernicke's area in the superior temporal gyrus (Brodmann's area 22) result in an aphasia that is variously called Wernicke's aphasia, posterior aphasia, fluent aphasia, and receptive aphasia. Lesions of this area result in fluent but incoherent speech because patients are unable to comprehend their own language or that of others. Because Wernicke's aphasia can present without other major neurological symptoms, it is possible to misdiagnose a patient with Wernicke's aphasia as having a thought disorder associated with a psychotic disorder. There are differences, however, between these two language disorders. Although the examination of a psychotic patient may not always reveal it, such a patient almost always retains normal comprehension of spoken and written language and the ability to repeat phrases. These abilities are lost in a patient with Wernicke's aphasia, who may use neologisms frequently in a random and changeable manner. In contrast, schizophrenic patients tend to use neologisms infrequently but consistently because the neologisms have a systemized and delusional significance. Psychiatric symptoms that can be seen in patients with Wernicke's aphasia include delusions, paranoia, agitation, and occasional euphoria or indifference.

Other aphasias. Broca's area and Wernicke's area are connected by the arcuate fasciculus. Lesions of the arcuate

Table 3.1-2
Aphasias

Type	Fluency	Comprehension	Repetition	Naming
Broca's	No*	Yes†	No	No
Wernicke's	Yes	No	No	No
Conduction	Yes	Yes	No	No
Motor transcortical	No	Yes	Yes	No
Sensory transcortical	Yes	No	Yes	No
Mixed transcortical	No	No	Yes	No
Global	No	No	No	No
Anomic	Yes	Yes	Yes	No
Thalamic	Yes	Variable	Yes	No

*No = Impaired.
†Yes = Relatively spared.

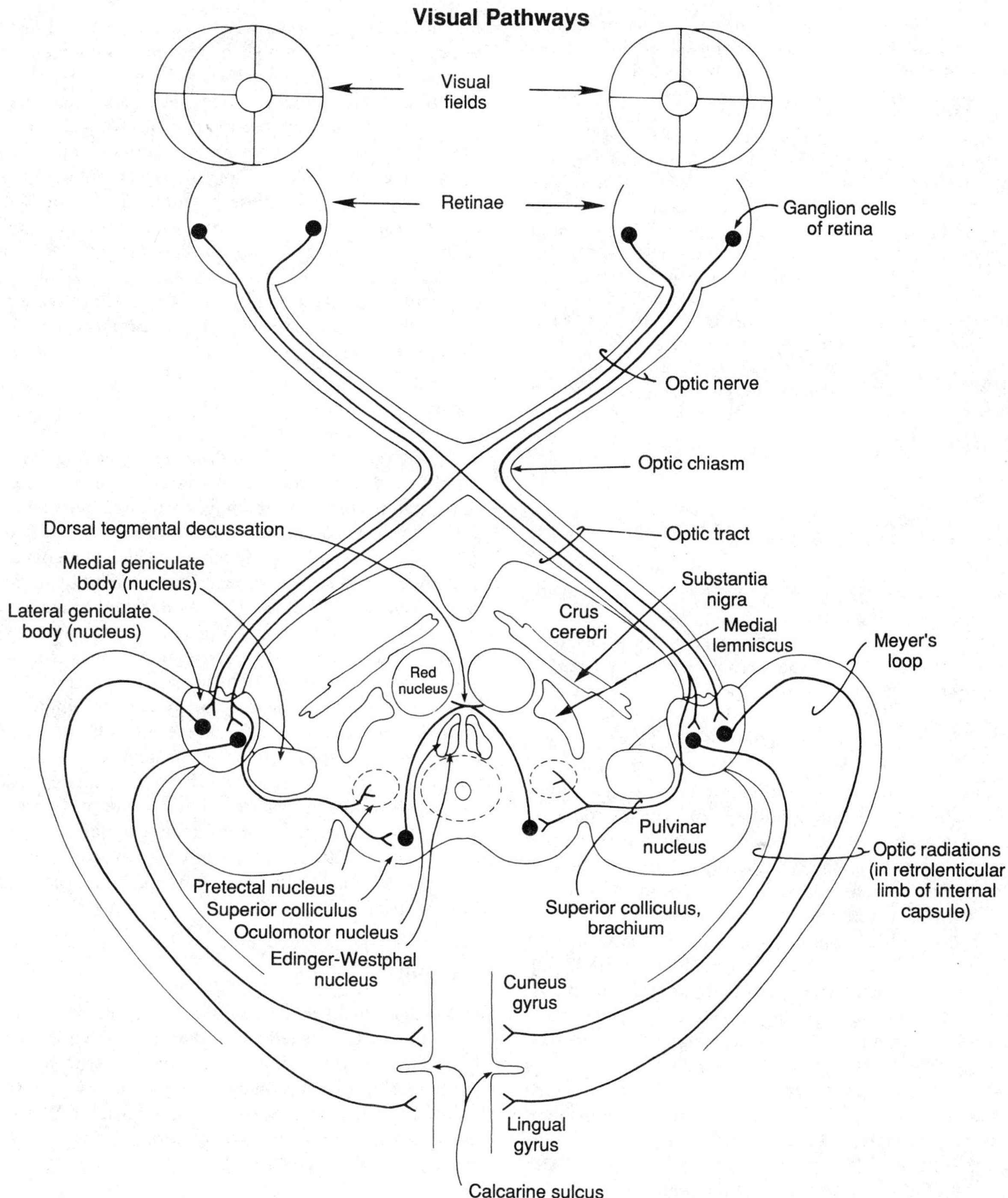

Figure 3.1-4. The origin, course, and distribution pattern of fibers constituting the visual pathway. Retinogeniculate and geniculocalcarine pathways are retinotopically organized. (From D E Haines: *Neuroanatomy: An Atlas of Structures, Sections, and Systems*, ed 2, p 200. Urban & Schwarzenberg, Baltimore-Munich, 1987, with permission.)

fasciculus result in a *conduction aphasia*, with symptoms resulting from the disconnection of the center of language production from the center of language comprehension. Comprehension and speech production are not severely impaired. An inability to repeat phrases is the most profound symptom of this aphasia. Broca's, Wernicke's, and conduction aphasias affect regions surrounding the fissure of Sylvius. *Transcortical aphasias* can be caused by lesions in the medial aspect of the frontal lobe, the basal ganglia, or the pulvinar thalamus. Patients with transcortical aphasias are able to repeat phrases normally, and, in fact, echolalia can be seen in some patients with severe transcortical aphasias. Transcortical aphasias can result in impaired comprehension or speech production or both. *Global aphasia* usually results from an infarction of the entire region of the left hemisphere that receives its blood supply from the middle cerebral artery. The patients almost invariably have a right hemiparesis and hemisensory defect. All language functions are lost, although some patients still spontaneously say such overlearned words as "good-bye" and "no." Although anomia is present in all aphasias, patients with an *anomic aphasia* have an isolated defect in naming. The speech of these patients is characterized by frequent pauses while the person searches for words and by frequent use of such vague words as "it" and "thing." Anomic aphasia is caused by a lesion localized to the dominant angular gyrus. The previously discussed aphasias all involve the cerebral cortex; however, it is also possible for a lesion of the dominant thalamus to produce a *thalamic aphasia*, with symptoms similar to those of a sensory transcortical aphasia.

Aprosodies. Although most attention has been focused on the dominant hemisphere in speech production, regional cerebral blood flow studies have shown increased blood flow to the nondominant hemisphere during speech. The nondominant hemisphere has a parallel role in the *prosody* of language, the emotional inflections in speech as it is received and produced. Patients with frontal nondominant lesions are not able to inflect their speech with affect, and patients with posterior nondominant lesions are not able to comprehend the prosody of another person's speech.

Apraxias

An *apraxia* is the loss of the ability to carry out or to learn specific movements (e.g., blowing out a candle) in response to stimuli that usually would have elicited the movement (e.g., the verbal request of the examiner) in a person who has normal strength, coordination, sensation, comprehension, and attention. A patient with an *ideomotor apraxia* is unable to execute a request on command. For example, when an examiner asks a patient to perform acts such as flipping a coin or brushing his or her teeth, the patient may, for example, merely drop the coin on the floor or just move the toothbrush between his or her hands. Nevertheless, the patient is able to perform the identical act automatically without a mistake. Lesions are most often either dominant or bilateral in the supramarginal gyrus or the motor association cortex or in the conduction fibers between these two areas. A patient with an *ideational apraxia* is unable to mime a sequence of tasks, such as licking an envelope closed and putting a stamp on it. Lesions are most often in the dominant parietal lobe or the corpus callosum. Ideational apraxias are also seen in patients with dementia and acute delirium. *Constructional apraxia* refers to an inability to complete tasks, such as drawing figures supplied by the examiner or arranging blocks. Lesions are most often in the right hemisphere. *Dressing apraxias* are also seen with right-sided lesions. Patients seem unable to orient themselves correctly with articles of clothing—for example, they may try to put on a shirt as if it were a pair of pants.

Agnosias

The word "gnosis" means to know. In order to know something, a person has to compare present sensory information with past sensory information. The key symptom of an agnosia is the failure to recognize sensory stimuli in the absence of intellectual or primary sensory mechanism impairment. Patients with *visual agnosias* are unable to identify an object they see unless they are able to touch it with their hands. The classic lesion for visual agnosias is bilateral damage to Brodmann's areas 18 and 19 in the occipital lobes. Patients with a particular visual agnosia, *prosopagnosia*, are unable to recognize familiar faces in person or in magazines. Such patients can immediately identify relatives, however, once they speak. Patients with *tactile agnosias* are unable to recognize objects that they touch. Lesions are most often contralateral lesions of Brodmann's areas 1, 2, 3, or 5 or the supramarginal gyrus of the parietal lobe. The patients often have an inability to recognize particular body parts on themselves or on the examiner (e.g., finger agnosia). Patients with *auditory agnosias* are unable to recognize nonverbal sounds (e.g., paper rustling, car horns) or music. Lesions are located bilaterally in the posterior superior temporal convolution (Brodmann's area 22).

Alexias

An *alexia* is an acquired disorder in reading ability. It should be distinguished from dyslexia, which is a developmental problem in reading. Although an alexia can occur alone, it is often associated with an aphasia. Reading comprehension and reading out loud can be independently impaired. Alexia is sometimes accompanied by agraphia, which is described below. The usual lesion for alexia without agraphia involves the left occipital cortex and the posterior corpus callosum. A right homonymous hemianopsia (the inability to see the right visual field) results from an occipital lesion. An inability to transfer the intact visual image from the left visual field (received by the right occipital cortex) to the left posterior hemisphere language-comprehension centers results from a corpus callosal lesion. As a result, the patient cannot see in one visual field and cannot decode the written information seen in the other. Alexia with agraphia can be a symptom in patients with Gerstmann's syndrome, Wernicke's aphasia, or Broca's aphasia.

Agraphias

An *agraphia* is an acquired inability to write. Agraphia should be distinguished from illiteracy, which is a lack of knowledge and training about how to write and read. Agraphias always accompany the aphasias. In Broca's aphasia, writing is sparse and agrammatical; in Wernicke's aphasia, writing appears grossly normal but contains nonsense words and neologisms.

AMYGDALA, HIPPOCAMPUS, AND LIMBIC SYSTEM

The amygdala and the hippocampus are groups of neurons within the temporal lobe. They are major components of the limbic system and have been implicated in the production of memory, emotions, and violent behavior.

Anatomy

Amygdala. The amygdaloid complex is in the dorsomedial portion of the temporal lobe, just anterior to the inferior horn of the lateral venticle (Figure 3.1-5). The amygdala is a heterogeneous structure with a large basolateral group of nuclei and a smaller corticomedial nuclear group. The basolateral group is connected to the cerebral cortex and the striatum. Parts of the corticomedial nuclear group are continuous with the olfactory cortex, whereas other parts are connected to the hypothalamus and the brain stem. Reciprocal cortical input to the amygdala comes from frontal and temporal sensory association areas and from the olfactory bulb and the cortex. The principal connections between the amygdala and the hypothalamus are the stria terminalis and the ventral amygdaloid fugal projection. The amygdala also connects with the corpus striatum, thereby allowing the limbic system direct access to the motor system. There are projections from the amygdala to the thalamus and also afferent projections from the dopaminergic, noradrenergic, and serotonergic nuclei located in the brain stem.

Hippocampal formation. The hippocampus lies along the floor and the medial wall of the temporal horn of the lateral ventricle. The hippocampal formation consists of the hippocampus, the dentate gyrus, and the subiculum, a region of the temporal cortex. The hippocampus is reciprocally connected to cortical sensory areas by the entorhinal cortex of the parahippocampal gyrus. The hippocampus also sends efferent projections to the septum, the anterior thalamus, and the hypothalamus.

Limbic system. In 1939 James Papez proposed a reverberating circuit as the CNS localization for emotions; he called this area the limbic system (also known as the Papez circuit). The original circuit included the hippocampus, which transmits information by the fornices to the mammillary bodies, which, in turn, transmit information by the mammillothalamic tracts to the anterior nucleus of the thalamus. The anterior nucleus of the thalamus then transmits information by the internal capsule to the cingulate gyrus, which transmits information back to the hippocampus. Subsequent investigators have added the orbitofrontal cortex, the temporal pole, the insula, the amygdala, the septal nuclei, and the dorsomedial thalamus to the limbic system. The nucleus accumbens is occasionally considered part of the limbic system as well.

Clinical Considerations

Klüver-Bucy syndrome. The Klüver-Bucy syndrome was first described in monkeys that had undergone bilateral anterior temporal lobectomies; a similar syndrome can be seen in humans. The symptoms include placidity, apathy, bulimia, hypersexuality, and visual and auditory agnosias. Amnesia, aphasia, dementia, and seizures are also seen in humans with this type of lesion. The syndrome can be caused by tumors, trauma, herpes encephalitis, Alzheimer's disease, and bitemporal lobe surgery.

Korsakoff's syndrome. Korsakoff's syndrome is an amnestic syndrome caused by chronic thiamine deficiency and associated with alcoholism. Although many brain regions are affected, the amnesia is the result of neuronal

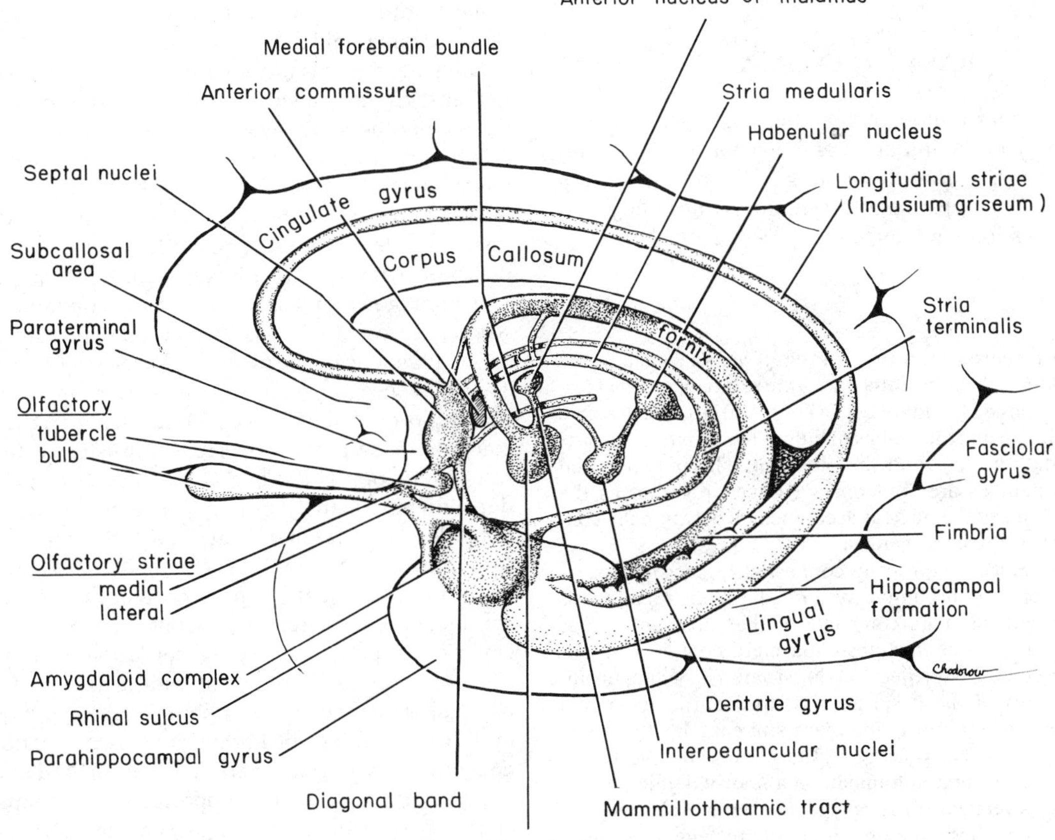

Figure 3.1-5. Semischematic drawing showing the anatomical relationships of amygdala, hippocampus, other components of the limbic system, and part of the olfactory pathway. (From M B Carpenter, J Sutin: *Core Text of Neuroanatomy*, ed 3, p 329. Williams & Wilkins, Baltimore, 1985.)

damage in the mammillary bodies and the thalamus. Patients have difficulty in learning new information (*anterograde amnesia*) and are often amnestic for past memories as well (*retrograde amnesia*). Once the neurons are damaged, treatment with thiamine is not effective in restoring memory abilities. Other causes of thiamine deficiency include intestinal malabsorption, gastric carcinoma, and prolonged intravenous (IV) hyperalimentation. Damage to other parts of the limbic system, especially the hippocampus, also results in various amnestic syndromes.

Violence. An association between violence and the limbic system is suggested by the docility of animals with a lesion of the amygdala and by animal experiments that have shown rage reactions to amygdala stimulation. Lesions of the amygdala and the anterior temporal lobes have been clinically correlated with a variety of behaviors in humans, including symptoms similar to schizophrenia, depression, and mania. In summarizing the vast literature on animal studies, one may conclude that the cerebral cortex, the limbic system, and the brain stem are involved in the production of rage and violence in humans. Lesions of the posterior hypothalamus, not considered a part of the limbic system, can result in sham rage, a syndrome of excessive rage to trivial stimuli, as first described in cats by Walter Cannon. A history of brain trauma and the presence of abnormal electroencephalograms (EEGs) are very common in populations of violent children and prisoners.

BASAL GANGLIA

It was formerly thought that the basal ganglia were involved only in the initiation and control of movement. It now seems clear that the basal ganglia are involved in a number of neuropsychiatric symptoms, including psychosis, depression, and dementia.

Anatomy

For most neuroanatomists, the basal ganglia include the corpus striatum, the substantia nigra, the subthalamic nucleus, and the substantia innominata. The corpus striatum is divisible into the striatum and the globus pallidus. The striatum consists of the caudate nucleus and the putamen. The putamen and the globus pallidus are sometimes grouped together as the lentiform nucleus. The nucleus accumbens is occasionally considered part of the basal ganglia.

The striatum is reciprocally connected to sensory association areas and to the limbic system; the globus pallidus is continuous with the pars compacta of the substantia nigra. The pars compacta of the substantia nigra contains the dopaminergic cells that project to the striatum. Although not considered part of the basal ganglia, the ventral tegmental area is medial to the substantia nigra and contains the dopaminergic neurons that project to the cortex and the limbic system. The substantia innominata is a poorly defined group of cells that is related to the amygdala, the lateral hypothalamus, and the globus pallidus. The basal nucleus of Meynert is sometimes considered part of the substantia innominata. This nucleus contains a group of cholinergic neurons that project to the cortex. It has been suggested that these neurons degenerate in some forms of dementia (e.g., Alzheimer's disease, Parkinson's disease, Down's syndrome). The subthalamic nucleus is caudal to the substantia nigra, and lesions to this nucleus result in hemiballism.

Clinical Considerations

The major clinical observation regarding disorders of the basal ganglia is that, in addition to disorders of movement, disorders of thought processes, affect, and cognition are very common. The psychiatric symptoms are as much a result of the organic lesion as are the neurological symptoms. Basal ganglia disorders are the neurological disorders most associated with symptoms of psychosis. Untreated schizophrenic patients show many subtle movement disorders (extreme openings and closings of the eyes, flaring of the nares, grimacing and pouting with the mouth, protrusion of the tongue, and shaking of the head) that imply an involvement of the basal ganglia.

Parkinson's disease. Parkinson's disease is a progressive disorder that generally begins in late adult life. The annual prevalence in the Western hemisphere has been reported to be about 200 per 100,000 persons. In most cases the cause is unknown. There is a loss of cells in the substantia nigra, a decrease in dopamine, and a degeneration of dopaminergic tracts. Often, the first characteristic sign is a loss of associated movements, with a peculiar immobility of the patient. Tremor may become apparent later. The tremor is a characteristic pill-rolling tremor that is most prominent at rest or on assuming a posture. As in most extrapyramidal disorders, the tremor becomes more prominent with tension and disappears with sleep. In some patients, tremor never becomes an important part of the illness; in others, it may be the most prominent symptom.

Physical examination reveals an impairment of fine movements and a peculiar cogwheel kind of rigidity that is most apparent in the neck and in the upper extremities. Sucking reflexes, positive Babinski's signs, and other evidence of pyramidal tract involvement are also present.

Depression and dementia are more common in Parkinson's disease patients than would be expected by chance or is explainable by the psychosocial factors of the disorder. The incidence of depression in Parkinson's disease has been reported to be between 50 and 90 percent and is more common in men than in women. Consistent with this clinical observation is the hypothesis that there is decreased dopaminergic activity in unipolar depression and that L-dopa (levodopa [Dopar, Larodopa]), the major treatment for Parkinson's disease, has been reported to elevate mood in normal volunteers. Up to 60 percent of patients on chronic, long-term treatment with L-dopa have serious psychiatric symptoms, including confusion and psychoses. This observation is consistent with a theory of hyperdopaminergic activity in schizophrenia. Dementia is present in 30 to 80 percent of Parkinson's disease patients. This dementia may be similar to that seen in Alzheimer's disease, a correlation that is supported by the common presence of basal ganglia–related movement disorders in many patients with Alzheimer's disease.

The cause of Parkinson's disease can be idiopathic (most common), encephalitic, toxic (carbon monoxide), or traumatic. Parkinson's disease can also be caused by ingesting a contaminant of an illicitly made synthetic heroin, N-methyl-4-phenyl-1,2,3,6 tetrahydropyridine (MPTP). The mechanism for the neurotoxic effect is as follows: MPTP is converted into MPP^+ by the enzyme monoamine oxidase (MAO) and then is taken up by the dopaminergic neurons. Because MPP^+ binds to melanin in substantia nigra neurons, MPP^+ is concentrated in these neurons and eventually kills the cells. Positron emission tomographic (PET) studies of persons who ingested MPTP but who remained asymptomatic have shown a decrease in the number of dopamine-binding sites in the substantia nigra. The demonstration of MPTP-induced parkinsonism has raised the possibility that some forms of idiopathic Parkinson's disease may actually be environmentally induced. Two recent studies have shown that the administration of deprenyl (a specific MAO type-B inhibitor) may stop the progression of Parkinson's disease and result in clinical improvement.

Classically, because dopamine does not cross the blood-brain barrier, the treatment of Parkinson's disease is L-dopa, a metabolic precursor of dopamine. L-dopa is often combined with carbidopa, a dopa-decarboxylase inhibitor that aids L-dopa in reaching the brain. Amantadine (Symmetrel) has also proved useful; it acts synergistically with L-dopa. One experimental treatment for Parkinson's disease involves the transplantation of adrenal medullary tissue or fetal substantia nigra tissue into the brain of the patient with Parkinson's disease. These tissues produce dopamine and release it directly into the brain. Although controversial, this procedure may have helped some patients.

Huntington's chorea. In 1872 George Huntington described an autosomal-dominant disorder with complete penetrance, characterized by choreiform movements and dementia that began in adult life. Huntington's chorea is rare; it is estimated that there are about 6 cases per 100,000 persons in the Western hemisphere. The neuropathology involves atrophy of the caudate nuclei, which can be visualized by computed tomography (CT) in many patients.

The onset is usually insidious; it is often heralded by a personality change that interferes with the patient's ability to adapt to his or her environment. The disease may begin at any age but is most common in late middle life. The two sexes are affected in equal numbers. When choreiform movements are first noted, they are frequently misinterpreted as inconsequential habit spasms or tics. As a result, the disease is frequently not recognized for several years, especially if the family history is not known. The diagnosis depends on recognition of the progressive choreiform movements and dementia in a patient with a family history of the disorder. Eventually, the choreiform movements or the dementia makes chronic hospitalization necessary. The clinical course is one of gradual progression, with death occurring 15 to 20 years after the onset of the disease. The only satisfactory treatment at present is prevention of the transmission of the responsible gene. Some symptomatic relief of the movement disorder and the psychotic symptoms may be achieved by an antipsychotic, such as haloperidol (Haldol).

Dementia is the presenting symptom in about 10 percent of cases, and at least 90 percent of patients develop dementia during their illness. Depression is the major psychiatric symptom in Huntington's chorea (approximately 40 percent of patients), and suicide is a major complication of this disorder. Psychosis is reported in approximately 20 percent of cases, but many other psychiatric disorders have been described.

The application of restriction fragment length polymorphism (RFLP) studies to Huntington's chorea has identified the short arm of human chromosome 4 as the site of the genetic abnormality in this disease. These studies utilized large affected pedigrees from Venezuela and North America. The specific gene and gene product involved in Huntington's chorea is yet to be determined. The identification of a specific genetic marker for Huntington's chorea, however, greatly facilitates accurate genetic counseling.

Wilson's disease. Wilson's disease, or hepatolenticular degeneration, is an autosomal-recessive disorder resulting in diminished levels of ceruloplasmin, a copper-binding enzyme, and the subsequent deposition of copper in both the liver and the lenticular nuclei. Clinically, this disease results in liver dysfunction and CNS signs, including irritability, depression, psychosis, and dementia. Other clinical signs include jaundice, Kayser-Fleischer rings in the cornea, blue moons on the fingernails, and a wide flapping tremor of the arms. In addition, the patients often experience rigidity, dysarthria, and dysphagia.

Fahr's syndrome. Fahr's syndrome, also called idiopathic calcification of the basal ganglia, is a rare hereditary disorder that presents with a parkinsonian movement disorder, neuropsychiatric symptoms, and calcification of the basal ganglia on CT. There is a bimodal curve for age of onset, with patients about age 30 presenting with psychosis that progresses to dementia and patients about age 50 presenting with dementia. This syndrome has a close clinical resemblance to negative-symptom schizophrenia and is important in both differential diagnosis and theoretical formulations.

Subcortical dementia. This concept relates to the presence of dementia in the aforementioned movement disorders. Previously, dementia had been thought to be pathognomonic for cerebral cortical injury. It is now appreciated that lesions of the basal ganglia often present with dementia that is accompanied by abnormal movements, psychomotor retardation, apathy, and an absence of other cortical signs (e.g., aphasias). In addition to the diseases discussed above, progressive supranuclear palsy and spinocerebellar degeneration may present with subcortical dementia.

HYPOTHALAMUS, PITUITARY, AND PINEAL BODY

The hypothalamus and the pituitary constitute the master endocrine gland, thereby functioning as a major integrating and output system for the entire CNS. In addition to its role in endocrine regulation, the hypothalamus is often considered part of the limbic system and is involved in appetite and sexual regulation. Because clinical observations indicate that many endocrine disorders have psychiatric symptoms and that many psychiatric disorders have endocrine dysregulations, psychiatrists have been carefully examining the anatomy of this region. The hypothalamus also appears to have a major role in the control of biological rhythms and immune system regulation.

The pineal body develops from the epithalamus, which, with the hypothalamus and the thalamus, constitutes the diencephalon. The major function of the pineal gland is the excretion of melatonin.

Anatomy

The hypothalamus is located beneath the thalamus and on either side of the third ventricle. Although the hypothalamus contains many nuclear groups, four of these nuclei are of particular relevance to mental functioning—the mamillary bodies of the middle hypothalamic nuclei and the suprachiasmatic, supraoptic, and paraventricular nuclei of the anterior hypothalamic nuclei. For psychiatry, the most important pathways are the fornix, connecting the hippocampal formation with the mamillary bodies, and the stria terminalis and ventral amygdalofugal pathway, connecting the amygdala with the hypothalamus. The mamillothalamic tract connects the mamillary bodies to the anterior thalamus. The mesolimbic dopamine pathway and the ascending noradrenergic, serotonergic, and cholinergic pathways from the brain stem (the medial forebrain bundle) have terminations in the hypothalamus.

The pituitary (hypophysis) consists of the anterior pituitary (adenohypophysis) and posterior pituitary (neurohypophysis) (Figure 3.1-6). The supraopticohypophyseal tract contains axons from the supraoptic and paraventricular nuclei that project to the posterior pituitary, where they release vasopressin and oxytocin into the venous drainage of the posterior pituitary. The ventromedial and infundibular nuclei of the medial hypothalamic nuclei, as well as other basomedial hypothalamic nuclei, project their axons into the pituitary stalk, where they terminate on the capillaries of the hypophyseal portal veins. These nuclei release inhibiting and releasing hormones that control the emission of trophic hormones from the anterior pituitary.

The pineal body is a single midline structure located on the roof of the third ventricle.

Clinical Considerations

The hypothalamus and the pituitary are involved in the regulation of the endocrine and autonomic nervous systems and the control of eating behavior, sexual activity, body temperature, and the sleep-wake cycle. Various nuclei of the hypothalamus project sympathetic and parasympathetic nuclei to the brain stem and regulate and coordinate the autonomic nervous system (ANS). This hypothalamic involvement in the ANS implicates it in psychosomatic disorders. There is extensive synaptic input into the hypothalamus from the amygdala, the hippocampus, and the brain stem. The hypothalamic regulation of

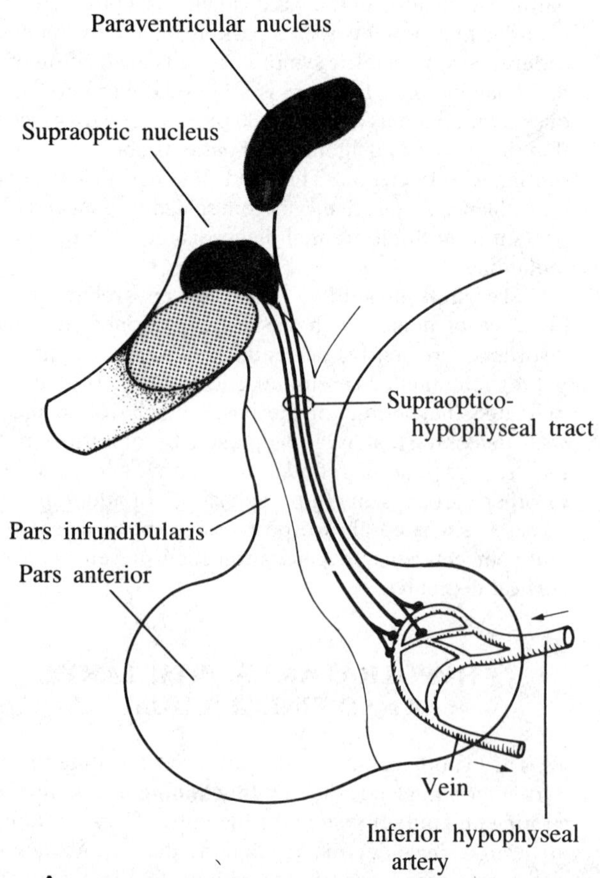

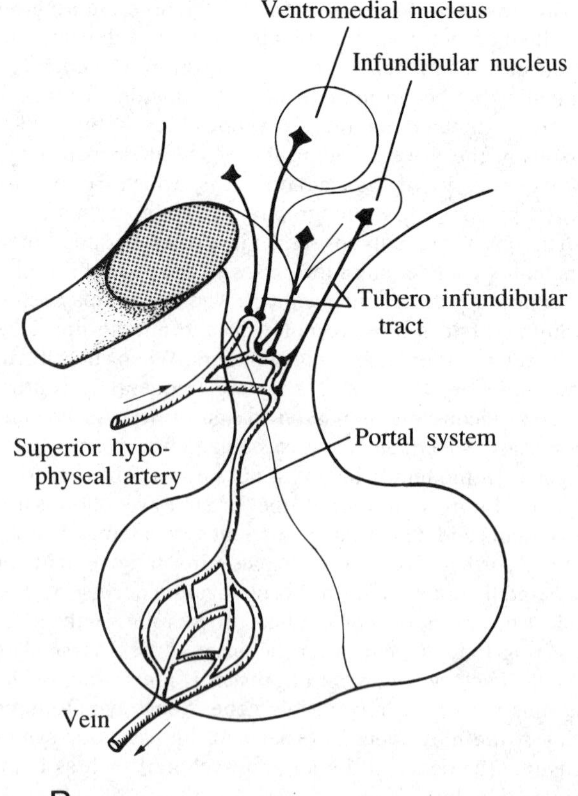

Figure 3.1-6. Hypothalamohypophyseal pathways. *A.* Supraopticohypophyseal tract. *B.* Tuberoinfundibular tract and the hypophyseal portal system. (From L Heimer: *The Human Brain and Spinal Cord.* Springer, New York, 1983, with permission.)

temperature may be the anatomic focus of pathology in neuroleptic malignant syndrome, a life-threatening complication of antipsychotics involving autonomic dysregulation and hyperthermia.

Control of eating behavior. Many studies of animals have shown that destruction of the ventromedial hypothalamus results in hyperphagia and obesity and that destruction of the lateral hypothalamus results in anorexia and starvation. These areas of the hypothalamus have been called the satiety center and the appetitive center, respectively, and represent relatively high concentrations of pathways relevant to the particular behavior. The limbic system and the prefrontal cortex are also involved in eating behavior.

THALAMUS

The thalamus develops with and is intimately and reciprocally connected to the cerebral cortex and the limbic system. Although once described as merely a relay station for sensory information, the thalamus clearly integrates and processes information at a very sophisticated level.

Anatomy

The thalamus is located above the hypothalamus and consists of many nuclei that project to diverse areas. The anterior nucleus receives input through the mamillothalamic tract and projects to the cingulate cortex, thereby being an integral part of the limbic system. The dorsomedial group is reciprocally innervated by the prefrontal cortex and receives input from other thalamic nuclei and the amygdala. The lateral and medial geniculate bodies receive input from visual and auditory pathways, respectively. The ventral nuclei receive input from the basal ganglia and the cerebellum and project to the motor cortex. The output of these ventral areas is also affected by converging input from limbic and cerebral cortical structures.

Clinical Considerations

The thalamus is critical in the perception of pain. Pain receptors (nociceptors) in the periphery project to the spinal cord, where they synapse in the dorsal horn and ascend in spinothalamic and spinoreticulothalamic tracts. The ventroposterolateral and ventroposteromedial nuclei serve as focal points for the transmission of this information into the somatosensory cortex (Brodmann's areas 1, 2, and 3) in the parietal cortex. Tumors or vascular lesions of the thalamus can produce severe pain syndromes. Other areas are involved in the control of pain sensation. The periaqueductal region of the midbrain and the nucleus raphe magnus of the medulla project onto the dorsal horn ascending neurons and can inhibit the transmission of pain sensation to the thalamus. These regions have high concentrations of opiate receptors, and it is likely that the endogenous opioids (e.g., enkephalins, endorphins) are involved as neurotransmitters in this region for the control of pain. Some studies have suggested that release of endorphins in this area is the molecular basis for the therapeutic effects of placebos and acupuncture.

CEREBELLUM

The cerebellum consists of the cerebellar cortex, the midline cerebellar vermis, and deep cerebellar (dentate, emboliform, globose, and fastigial) nuclei. The cerebellum is involved in the control of movements and postural adjustment. The cerebellum projects reciprocally to the cerebral cortex, the limbic system, the brain stem, and the spinal cord. It is, therefore, possible that the cerebellum is involved in higher mental functions as well. Animal studies have shown that parts of the cerebellum are necessary for the acquisition of particular conditioned responses. There are also case reports in which cerebellar tumors and vascular events present as psychiatric disorders.

BRAIN STEM

The brain stem is composed of the mesencephalon, the pons, and the medulla oblongata. The most basic functions of this area concern respiration, cardiovascular activity, sleep, and consciousness. This area, however, is also the site of the neuronal cell bodies for the ascending biogenic amine (dopamine, noradrenalin, serotonin) pathways to higher brain areas. These ascending biogenic amine pathways have been called the medial forebrain bundle.

RETICULAR ACTIVATING SYSTEM

The reticular system is a loosely organized network of neurons coursing up the midline of the brain stem. These neurons receive input from ascending sensory neurons, the cerebellum, the basal ganglia, the hypothalamus, and the cerebral cortex and send projections to the hypothalamus, the thalamus, and the spinal cord. Stimulation of this area activates the cortex into a state of alert wakefulness. Psychiatric disorders in which motivation and level of arousal are impaired may involve pathology in this region.

References

Cummings J L: *Clinical Neuropsychiatry*. Grune & Stratton, Orlando, 1985.
Fuster J M: *The Prefrontal Cortex*, ed 2. Raven, New York, 1988.
Gazzaniga M S: Organization of the human brain. Science *245*: 947, 1989.
Markowitsch H J: Diencephalic amnesia: A reorientation towards tracts. Brain Res Rev *13*: 351, 1988.
McNaughton B L, Morris R G M: Hippocampal synaptic enhancement and information storage within a distributed memory system. TINS 10: 408, 1987.
Mesulam M-M: *Principles of Behavioral Neurology*. Davis, Philadelphia, 1985.
Mueller J, ed: *Neurology and Psychiatry*, Karger, Basel, 1989.
Roberts J K A: *Differential Diagnosis in Neuropsychiatry*. Wiley, New York, 1984.
Robinson R G, Starkstein S E: Current research in affective disorders following stroke. J Neuropsychiatry *2*: 1, 1990.
Signer S, Cummings J L, Benson D F: Delusions and mood disorders in patients with chronic aphasia. J Neuropsychiatry *1*: 40, 1989.
Strub R L, Black F W: *Neurobehavioral Disorders: A Clinical Approach*. Davis, Philadelphia, 1988.
Van Hoesen G W, Alheid G F, Heimer L: Major brain structures. In *Comprehensive Textbook of Psychiatry*, ed 5, H I Kaplan and B J Sadock, editors, p. 5. Williams & Wilkins, Baltimore, 1989.

3.2 / Brain Imaging

A variety of techniques are now available that can image the living human brain. Some of these techniques (e.g., computed tomography [CT]) assess only the structure of the brain, whereas other techniques (e.g., positron emission tomography [PET]) assess both the structure and some aspect of brain function (e.g., blood flow). Of the brain-imaging techniques, five are widely utilized in clinical settings—electroencephalography (EEG), evoked potentials (EPs), polysomnography, CT, and magnetic resonance imaging (MRI). A sixth brain-imaging technique, computed topographic EEGs and EPs, is used in some clinical settings. The remaining brain-imaging techniques—magnetoencephalography (MEG), PET, and single photon emission tomography (SPECT)—are currently used only in research settings. The research data from studies using these brain-imaging techniques have already had both direct and indirect effects on clinical practice. Eventually, all the brain-imaging techniques described in this section may prove to have direct clinical utility in the diagnosis, assessment, and treatment of psychiatric disorders. The reader should refer to the chapter on a specific clinical disorder for information about brain-imaging abnormalities for that disorder.

ELECTROENCEPHALOGRAPHY

Developed by Hans Berger in 1929, the EEG utilizes electrodes placed on the scalp to measure the electrical activity of the brain. The electrical activity of the neurons in the uppermost cortical layers is the major determinant of the EEG. The electrodes themselves are most often placed on the scalp in positions according to the International 10-20 System (Figure 3.2-1). The recordings from each electrode are placed in different arrangements, called montages, on the recording paper (Figure 3.2-2).

Visual inspection of the EEG involves the assessment of the frequency, amplitude, and distribution of the wave forms and an inspection for any paroxysmal events, such as spikes and wave bursts, which may indicate epileptic activity. Other EEG abnormalities include the presence of abnormal slow wave activity, the suppression of EEG amplitude, and abnormal asymmetries. EEG frequencies are divided as follows: delta activity (< 4 cycles per second [Hz]), theta activity (4–8 Hz), alpha activity (8–13 Hz), and beta activity (> 13 Hz). Alpha activity is present in the normal awake adult whose eyes are closed. Alpha activity is replaced by beta activity when the person is stimulated or opens his or her eyes. Delta and theta activity is normally present only in sleep. There are many potential sources of artifact in an EEG recording. The two most common sources are scalp muscle activity, which may be confused with fast beta activity, and eye movements, which may be confused with slow delta activity over the frontal poles. The EEG changes with age. The same EEG recording

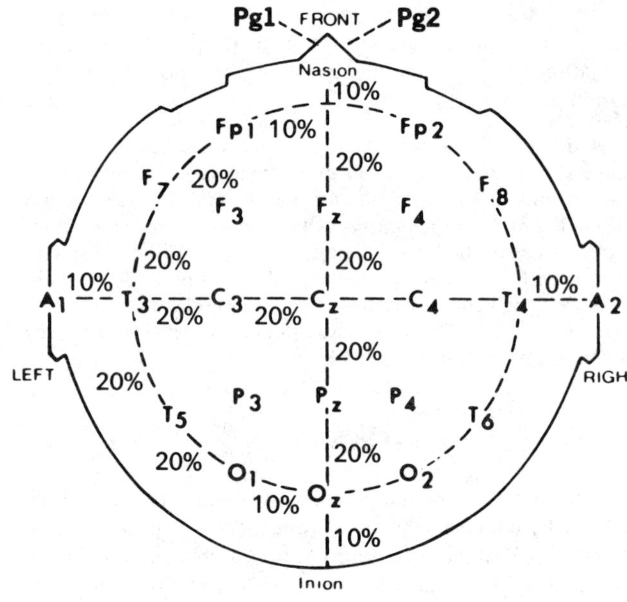

Figure 3.2-1. The International 10-20 System for specifying EEG electrode placement. The system is based on meaurements made from the nasion (depression at the bridge of the nose) to the inion (raised portion of the skull at the back of the head) and from the left to right auricular depressions (slight valleys just in front of and above the earlobes). Electrodes are placed at either 10 or 20 percent of these distances on the scalp, as indicated in the figure. Frontal (*F*); central (*C*); parietal (*P*); occipital (*O*); midline (*Z*); nasopharyngeal lead (*Pg*). Odd-numbered subscripts are found on the left side of the head; even-numbered subscripts are on the right side of the head. (*Note:* O_z is a placement location not always associated with the conventional International 10-20 System, but it has been included here because this electrode location, which is based on the 10-20 system, is frequently utilized.) (From R B Rosse, D L Warden, J M Morihisa: Applied electrophysiology. In *Comprehensive Textbook of Psychiatry,* ed 5, H I Kaplan and B J Sadock, editors, p 74. Williams & Wilkins, Baltimore, 1989.)

that is normal for a 10-year-old child may be abnormal for an 80-year-old adult.

Clinical Indications

The major clinical indication for an EEG is in the evaluation of epilepsy, although an EEG is also obtained in the evaluation of dementia and delirium. The EEG of an epileptic person contains various types of paroxysmal wave activities, which are the hallmark of epileptic activity. Sleep deprivation of a person for one night can increase the likelihood of detecting paroxysmal events during the EEG recording the next morning. The use of nasopharyngeal electrodes may or may not increase the likelihood of detecting paroxysmal activity in the temporal cortex. EEG abnormalities may be either focal (i.e., localized to a specific region of the cortex) or generalized. In addition to focal epileptic loci, focal abnormalities include decreases in beta amplitude because of a subdural hematoma or a focal cortical injury. Generalized increases in beta activity are most commonly associated with drug ingestion. A major advantage of the EEG technique is that it does not require the patient to receive any radiation or chemical exposure. Another advantage is that brain events of very short duration can be recorded. This is not true for other measures of brain activity, such as PET, SPECT, and regional cerebral blood flow (rCBF). Disadvantages of the EEG are that only

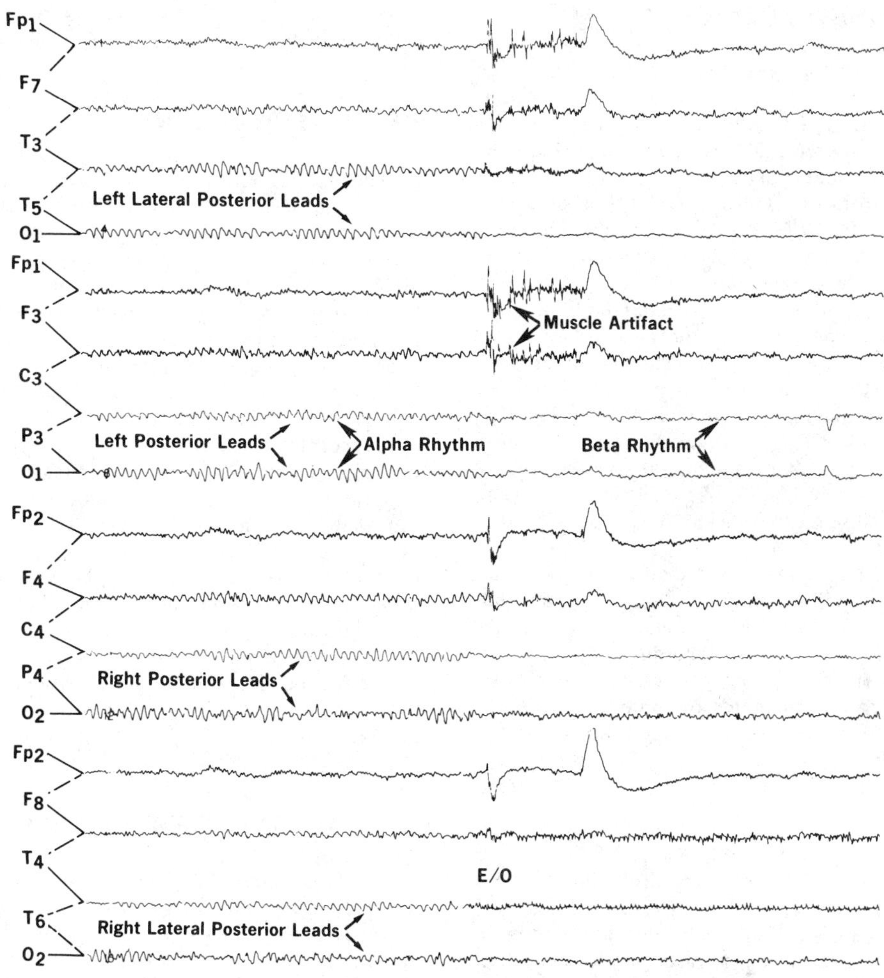

Figure 3.2-2. A normal EEG tracing demonstrating well-formed posterior dominant alpha of 9–10 Hz. The α-rhythm attenuates with eye opening (*E/O*) and is replaced by lower amplitude, higher frequency (24- to 28-Hz) β-rhythm. Muscle artifact is identified during eye opening. The montage is indicated on the left of the figure. (Courtesy of Charlotte McCutchen, M.D., Veterans Administration Medical Center, Washington, DC.)

cortical activity is detected and that spatial resolution of the EEG is limited by the number of electrodes used.

In the initial workup of a psychiatric patient, the clinician can obtain a sleep-deprived EEG to attempt to rule out the presence of an epileptic disorder. Unfortunately, an EEG may be normal even when an epileptic disorder is present. Repeat EEGs and 24-hour telemetric recordings are options to be considered in some cases. Another indication for obtaining an EEG recording is a history of brain injury (e.g., accidents, infections, and birth complications).

EEG recordings have been used in many research investigations of psychiatric patients. Much of this research has assessed relative amounts of slow or fast activity, abnormalities in the normal EEG asymmetries, and decreased reactivity to various conditions (e.g., changing from eyes closed to eyes open).

POLYSOMNOGRAPHY

Polysomnography is an EEG recording that is performed on a person who is asleep. Polysomnography is often used in conjunction with an electrocardiogram (ECG), an electromyogram (EMG), and sometimes a recording of penile tumescence. In research settings, polysomnography can be accompanied with recordings of blood oxygen saturation, body movement, body temperature, galvanic skin response, and gastric acid secretion. Polysomnography is most often used in the evaluation of sleep-related disorders, such as insomnia, nocturnal myoclonus, sleep apnea, functional enuresis, and somnambulism. Polysomnography has also been used extensively to study the sleep architecture of psychiatric patients. Such research has been directed toward describing abnormalities in sleep architecture, which may serve as markers of specific psychiatric disorders, particularly depression. Measures of sleep assessed in such research include amount of time spent in rapid eye movement (REM) sleep, how soon after falling asleep the first REM episode appears (REM latency), and the number of REM episodes in a night.

Sleep can be grossly divided into two phases—REM sleep and non-REM sleep. Non-REM sleep is further divided into four stages. Stage 1 represents the lightest sleep, and stage 4 the deepest. Alpha activity is present when adults lie down in bed and close their eyes. In stage 1 sleep, the alpha activity gradually disappears. In stages 2 through 4, slow delta activity becomes increasingly prevalent. In REM sleep, the high amplitude slow waves are replaced by betalike activity resembling that of an awake, alert person.

EVOKED POTENTIALS

EPs are a measure of how the cortex responds to particular sensory stimuli. EPs utilize the same electrode and recording arrangements as an EEG. The different types of EPs include somatosensory evoked potentials (SEPs), auditory evoked potentials (AEPs), and visual evoked potentials (VEPs). In EP testing, a stimulus from one sensory modality is presented multiple times while the EEG recording is made. The brain electrical activity on the EEG that follows each repeated stimulus is then averaged by a computer to reduce nonstimulus-related activity. The result is a smooth curve (the EP), which includes various peaks and valleys (Figure 3.2-3). Downward deflections on an EP recording are often called positive waves, and upward deflections are called negative waves. Waves are further identified by the number of milliseconds that they occur after the stimulus. The P300 wave, therefore, is a downward (positive) deflection that occurs approximately 300 ms after the stimulus. The evaluation of an EP involves an assessment of the timing and the magnitude of the individual waves within an EP.

The waves of an EP have been divided into early (occurring < 50 ms after the stimulus), middle (50–250 ms), and late (> 250 ms) components. Early EP components represent specific anatomical relays of sensory information as it passes from sensory organ (e.g., eyes) to primary sensory cortex to association cortex. Later EP components are thought to represent increasingly complex cognitive or psychological processing of sensory information.

Clinical Indications

EPs are most commonly used in the evaluation of a demyelinating disorder, such as multiple sclerosis. Unless such a disorder is suspected, an EP is probably not indicated in the routine workup of a psychiatric patient. EPs have been used extensively, however, in psychiatric research. Many of these studies have found that specific groups of psychiatric patients have larger or smaller waves that occur either earlier or later than in nonpsychiatrically ill persons. EP recordings are especially subject to contamination by various artifacts in addition to those affecting EEG recordings. Attention, compliance, fatigue, coffee and cigarette consumption, and the age of the person, as well as diurnal variations in EPs, have all been reported to affect the data from EP recordings.

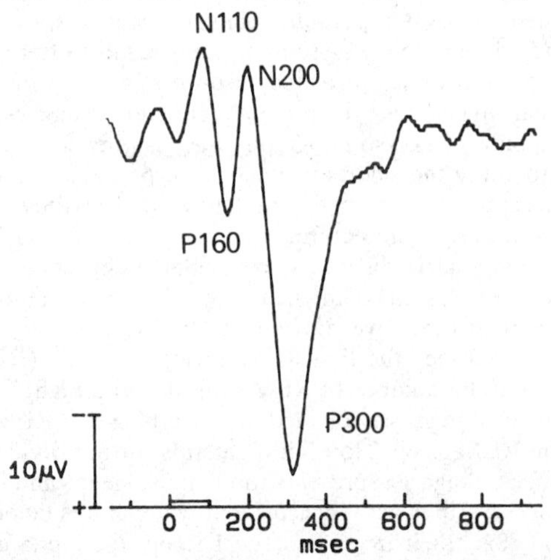

Figure 3.2-3. An auditory evoked potential (AEP) elicited by a 50-dB SL tone pip. (Courtesy of Connie C. Duncan, Ph.D., Unit on Psychophysiology, Laboratory of Psychology and Psychopathology. National Institute of Mental Health, Bethesda, MD.)

COMPUTED TOPOGRAPHIC EEGs AND EPs

The amount of raw data contained in EEG and EP recordings is staggering. Although the visual inspection of EEGs and EPs by trained electroencephalographers results in much useful information, it is reasonable to hypothesize that much more information about brain function is included in those records. Various computer programs have now been designed to translate EEG and EP recordings into graphic and understandable images of the brain (Figure 3.2-4) (see color plate).

Computer analysis of EEG data quantitates the amount of voltage present in alpha, beta, theta, and delta activity for each recording electrode. The results of these calculations are then represented on topographic maps of the brain and utilize either a gray scale or a color scale to indicate which parts of the brain have more or less activity of a specific frequency range (Figure 2.3-4). Although some psychiatric researchers believe that computed topographic EEGs and EPs already have clinical relevance for psychiatry, other psychiatrists believe that this technique is best used only in research settings. In such settings, the computer analysis of the data can combine the EEGs and EPs from groups of patients; thus, comparisons can be made between groups of psychiatric and nonpsychiatric patients.

MAGNETOENCEPHALOGRAPHY

MEG is a brain-imaging technique that is still under development and that is currently utilized only in research settings. The electrical activity of neurons results in minute magnetic fields, which can be detected by MEG. MEG involves the computer analysis of these magnetic fields. In contrast to the EEG and EP, MEG is able to provide information about both cortical and subcortical brain structures. Like the EEG and EP, MEG does not expose the patient to any radiation or chemical substances and, therefore, may eventually be particularly useful in the clinical setting.

COMPUTED TOMOGRAPHY

CT is based on X-ray technology. X-ray photons are emitted from a source, pass through the tissue being studied, and are then detected (Figure 3.2-5). The X-ray tube and detector are rotated around the head and are also moved in parallel in a rostral-caudal direction. The resulting data are entered into a computer, which is able to process the information into a three-dimensional reconstruction of the brain. This reconstruction can then be viewed as slices of the brain in sagittal, coronal, and transverse images (Figure 3.2-6). The more a tissue absorbs the X radiation, the lighter it appears in the image; the less it absorbs, the darker it appears. CT is particularly good at examining bony structures and calcified regions of brain tissue. CT is not able to discriminate gray brain matter from white brain matter, as is the MRI technique.

Clinical Indications

CT is most often used in the evaluation of patients for strokes, traumas, and tumors (Figures 3.2-7 through 3.2-13). Most lesions larger than 0.5 cm on cross-section can

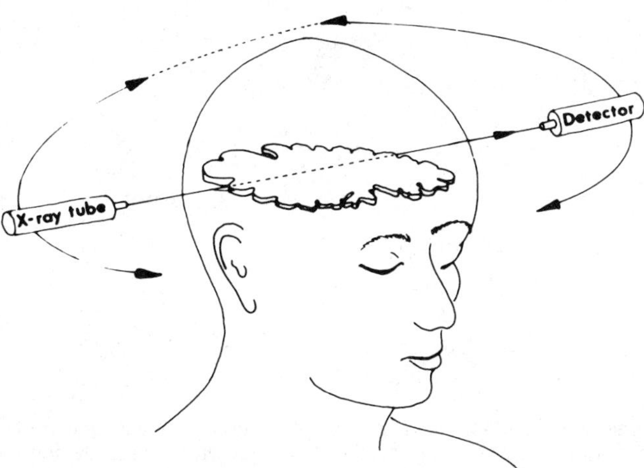

Figure 3.2-5. Principles of computed tomography. (From G Sedvall: Brain imaging. In *Comprehensive Textbook of Psychiatry,* ed 5, H I Kaplan and B J Sadock, editors, p 92. Williams & Wilkins, Baltimore, 1989.)

be visualized by CT. In some instances, a lesion may not be demonstrated by CT, either because the defect is too small or because the density of the lesion is not distinguishable from the density of healthy brain tissue. The CT is inferior to MRI in its ability to image lesions in the posterior fossa, the brain stem, and the temporal and apical areas of the brain, where the presence of bone can distort the CT image. CT may be of value in the workup of psychiatric patients who present with confusion or dementia of unknown cause, a first episode of psychosis, a movement disorder of unknown cause, an aphasialike speech disorder, a diagnosis of anorexia nervosa, prolonged catatonia, a first episode of depression or mania after age 50, new psychiatric symptoms in a person with a history of alcohol abuse, or a history of trauma or seizures. In psychiatric research, studies have focused on enlargement of the ventricles, cortical atrophy, cerebellar atrophy, and the reversal of normal brain asymmetries.

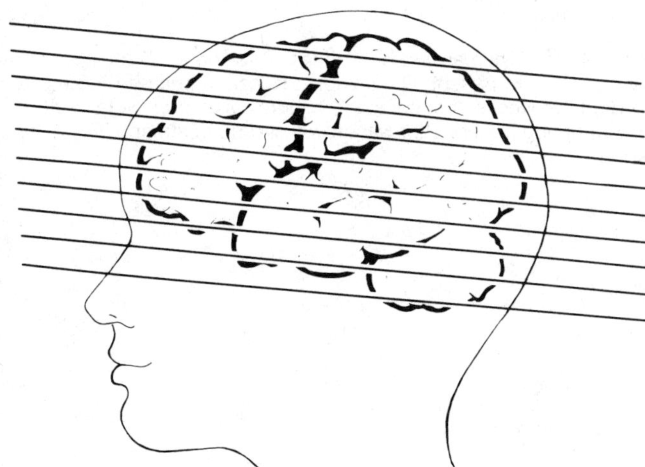

Figure 3.2-6. Cross-section through the head illustrating the planes of 10 CT scans parallel with the canto-meatal line. (From G Sedvall: Brain imaging. In *Comprehensive Textbook of Psychiatry,* ed 5, H I Kaplan and B J Sadock, editors, p 92. Williams & Wilkins, Baltimore, 1989.)

MAGNETIC RESONANCE IMAGING

When a strong magnetic field is applied to the brain, the hydrogen nuclei become aligned in such a way that the nuclei have a precessional motion about the magnetic field direction. These nuclei emit characteristic electromagnetic energy patterns when exposed to pulses of electromagnetic energy. These patterns of released energy are analyzed by a computer to produce the final image. The MRI image is remarkable for its ability to delineate gray and white matter more clearly than does CT (Figure 3.2-14). The MRI technique is also superior at detecting demyelinating lesions but is inferior at detecting bony lesions or calcifications. The indications for obtaining an MRI scan in psychiatric patients are identical to those for obtaining a CT scan. Either CT or MRI but usually not both should be used in these cases. MRI avoids exposing the patient to radiation. MRI is contraindicated in patients with steel surgical clips, metal skull plates, and cardiac pacemakers.

Research applications of MRI have utilized the improved spatial resolution of MRI to look at smaller brain structures than is possible with CT. Development of MRI instruments that can image elements other than hydrogen is underway. Such machines can already image the phosphorous nuclei, which may allow the MRI technique to be applied to molecules of functional and metabolic significance.

REGIONAL CEREBRAL BLOOD FLOW

Regional CBF imaging, PET, and SPECT all provide information about the functioning of the brain. The amount of blood flowing to a region of the cortex is positively correlated to the metabolic activity of that region. Xenon^{133} is an inert, γ-emitting gas that, when inhaled, distributes itself to the blood. When γ-ray detectors are placed in an ordered array over the patient's scalp, it is possible to measure how much blood is flowing to different parts of the brain. Regional CBF has the advantages of exposing the patient to less radiation and being less expensive than PET. The technical procedures of rCBF testing can be combined with psychological testing during the measurement of blood flow. This allows investigators to assess the effects of cognitive activation procedures on blood flow in specific regions of the cortex (Figure 3.2-15) (see color plate). The rCBF technique measures blood flow to the cerebral cortex and not to deep brain structures. In contrast, both PET and SPECT are able to image deep brain structures. The technique of rCBF is currently confined to research settings and does not have clinical utility at this time.

POSITRON EMISSION TOMOGRAPHY

PET allows for the assessment of cortical and subcortical brain function. For PET studies various organic compounds that have been labeled with positron-emitting isotopes (e.g., F^{18}, C^{14}) are administered to the subjects. Once these compounds have reached the brain, they emit positrons which then collide with electrons in the brain, thereby emitting γ-rays that are detected by the probes of the PET camera. This information is analyzed by a computer, which generates topographic maps of the brain (Figure 3.2-16 and 3.2-17) (see color plate). A variety of organic compounds are used in PET studies. An analogue of glucose—2-deoxyglucose—is used to measure glucose metabolism in the brain. The amount of glucose that a neuron takes up is proportional to its metabolic activity. Although 2-deoxyglucose is taken up by neurons as if it were glucose, it cannot be metabolized further along the glucose

Figure 3.2-4. Example of a computed topographic (CT) map of brain electrical activity. This example is from an investigation of schizophrenic patients that correlated electrophysiological differences with structural abnormalities. Such figures are read by comparing the values along the color scale (lower right) with the colors in particular regions of the map of the head. When looking at color-coded maps, particularly when comparing different color-coded maps, the investigator should always check the color scale because there is no standardization of these scales. (Courtesy of John M. Morihisa, M.D., Department of Psychiatry, Georgetown University School of Medicine, and Frank H. Duffy, M.D., Harvard University Medical School.)

Figure 3.2-15. From a study of patients with schizophrenia using regional cerebral blood flow (rCBF). The study compared rCBF under two conditions for each patient: (1) while performing the Wisconsin Card-Sorting Test (WCS), which is believed to be a fairly specific test for dorsolateral prefrontal cortex functioning, and (2) while performing a numbers task (NUM) that controlled for nonspecific test-taking factors. The figure shows rCBF maps for both left and right hemispheres for both the normal and the schizophrenic groups. The map depicts the percentage change between the two tasks, calculated by dividing WCS blood flow by NUM blood flow. The color scale to the right depicts the colors assigned to a range of percentage changes from 96.1 to 112.1 percent. The schizophrenic group had essentially no increase in blood flow during the WCS test, as compared with the NUM test in either hemisphere. This contrasts with the control group, which did increase blood flow to both hemispheres (particularly the frontal cortex) during the WCS test, as compared with the NUM test. (Courtesy of Daniel R. Weinberger, M.D.; Karen F. Berman, M.D.; and Ronald F. Zec, Ph.D: Physiologic dysfunction in dorsolateral prefrontal cortex in schizophrenia: I. Regional cerebral blood flow evidence. Arch Gen Psychiatry *43*: 114, 1986.)

Figure 3.2-16. PET scan images of midbrain sections of healthy volunteers after administration of four different neuroreceptor ligands. (*A*) ^{11}C SCH 23390; (*B*) ^{11}C-raclopride; (*C*) ^{11}C-piquindone; (*D*) ^{11}C-Ro 15-1788. (*A*): Illustration of high density of D_1 dopamine receptors (as indicated by dark areas) in the major basal ganglia. The PET scan image also reflects the low but significant density of D_1 and 5-HT-2 receptors in the neocortex. (Gray areas around the edge represent the frontal cortex and the parietal cortex.) (*B*): Illustration of the high density of D_2 dopamine receptors in the basal ganglia. The figure also illustrates the relative lack of D_2 dopamine receptors in all other areas of the brain. (*C*): Distribution of D_2 dopamine receptors in the basal ganglia. The fairly high degree of accumulation of this ligand in nonstriatal tissues presumably reflects a fairly high nonspecific binding of this ligand. (*D*): Illustration of the high density of benzodiazepine receptors in the occipital and parietal cortical areas of the brain. Because this is a black-and-white reproduction of a color image, the ventricular system also appears as black in this figure. (Courtesy of Göran Sedvall, M.D., Ph.D., Karolinska Institute, Stockholm, Sweden.)

Figure 3.2-17. ^{11}C-labeled raclopride (100 mBq to each subject) binding in human brain. *A*: healthy volunteer; *B*: haloperidol (Haldol)-treated (8 mg a day) patient; *C*: fluphenthixol-treated (100 mg a week) patient; *D*: clozapine (Clozaril)-treated (600 mg a day) patient; *E*: sulpiride-treated (1,600 mg a day) patient; *F*: same patient two weeks after complete withdrawal of drug. Note marked reduction of specific raclopride ^{11}C binding in basal ganglia (dark areas) during but not after withdrawal of drug treatment. (Courtesy of Göran Sedvall, M.D., Ph.D., Karolinska Institute, Stockholm, Sweden.)

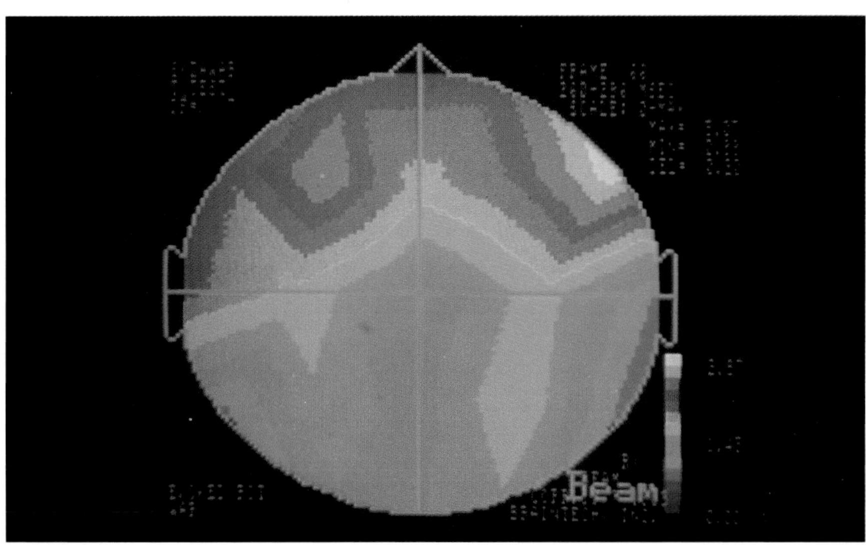

Figure 3.2-4

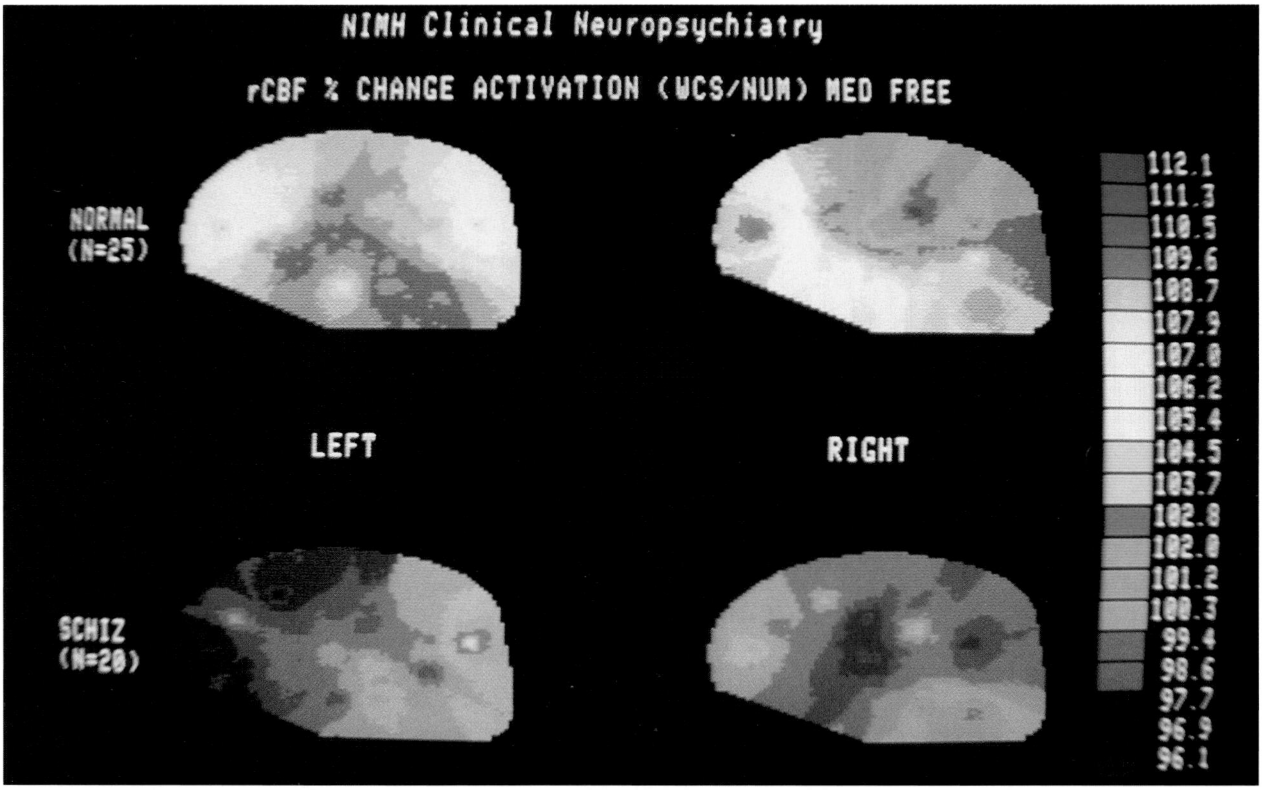

NIMH Clinical Neuropsychiatry

rCBF % CHANGE ACTIVATION (WCS/NUM) MED FREE

NORMAL (N=25)

LEFT

RIGHT

SCHIZ (N=20)

112.1
111.3
110.5
109.6
108.7
107.9
107.0
106.2
105.4
104.5
103.7
102.8
102.0
101.2
100.3
99.4
98.6
97.7
96.9
96.1

Figure 3.2-15

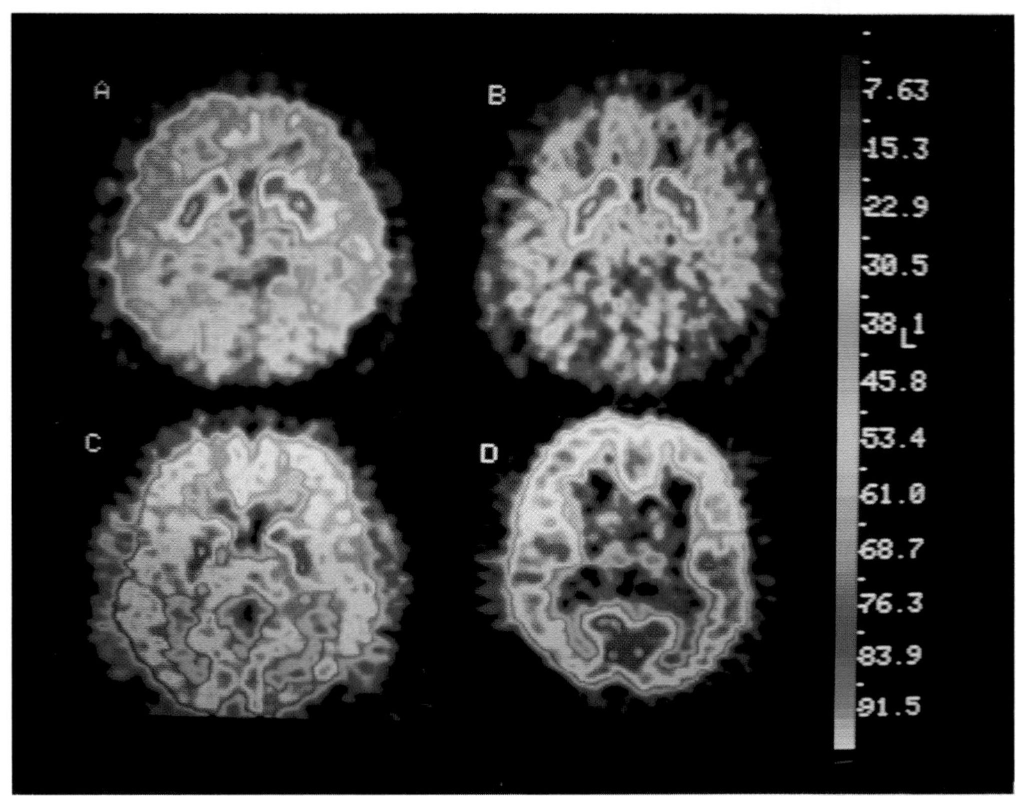

Figure 3.2-16

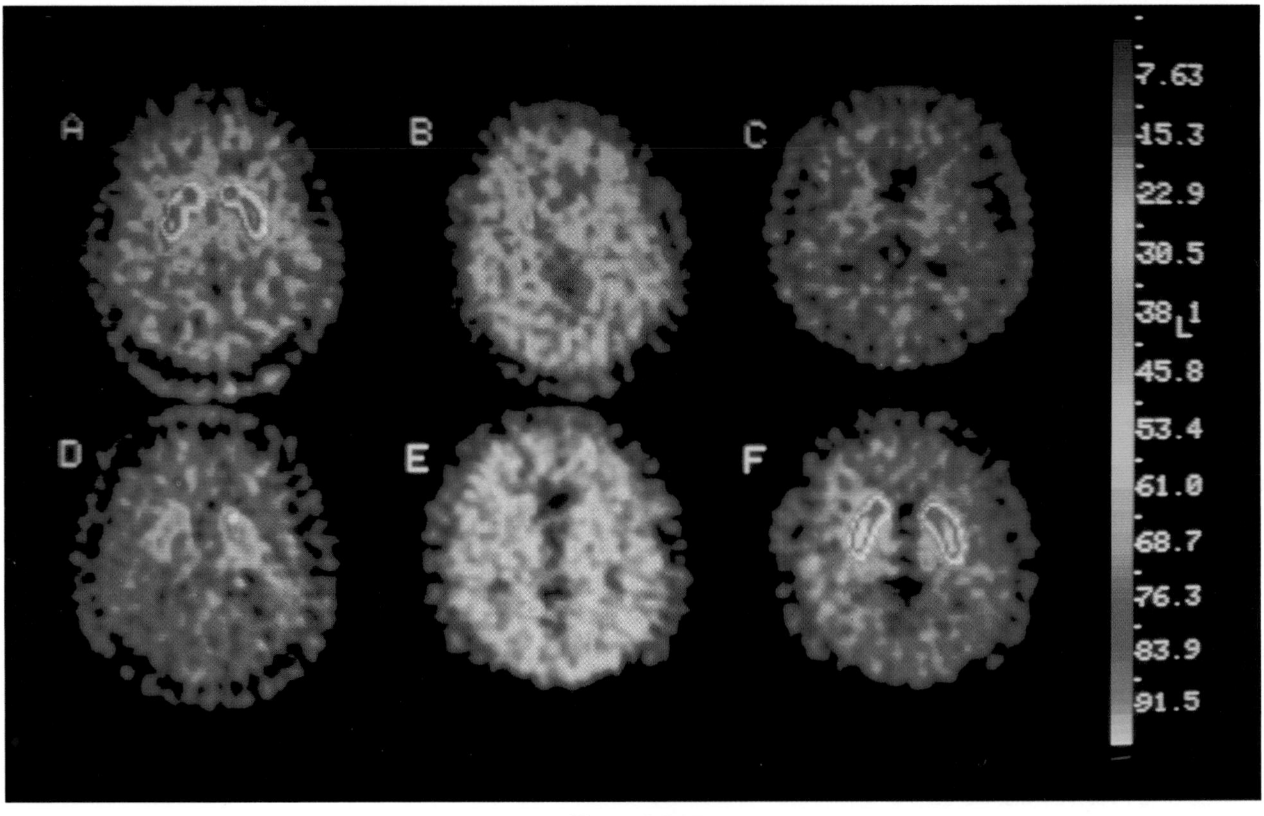

Figure 3.2-17

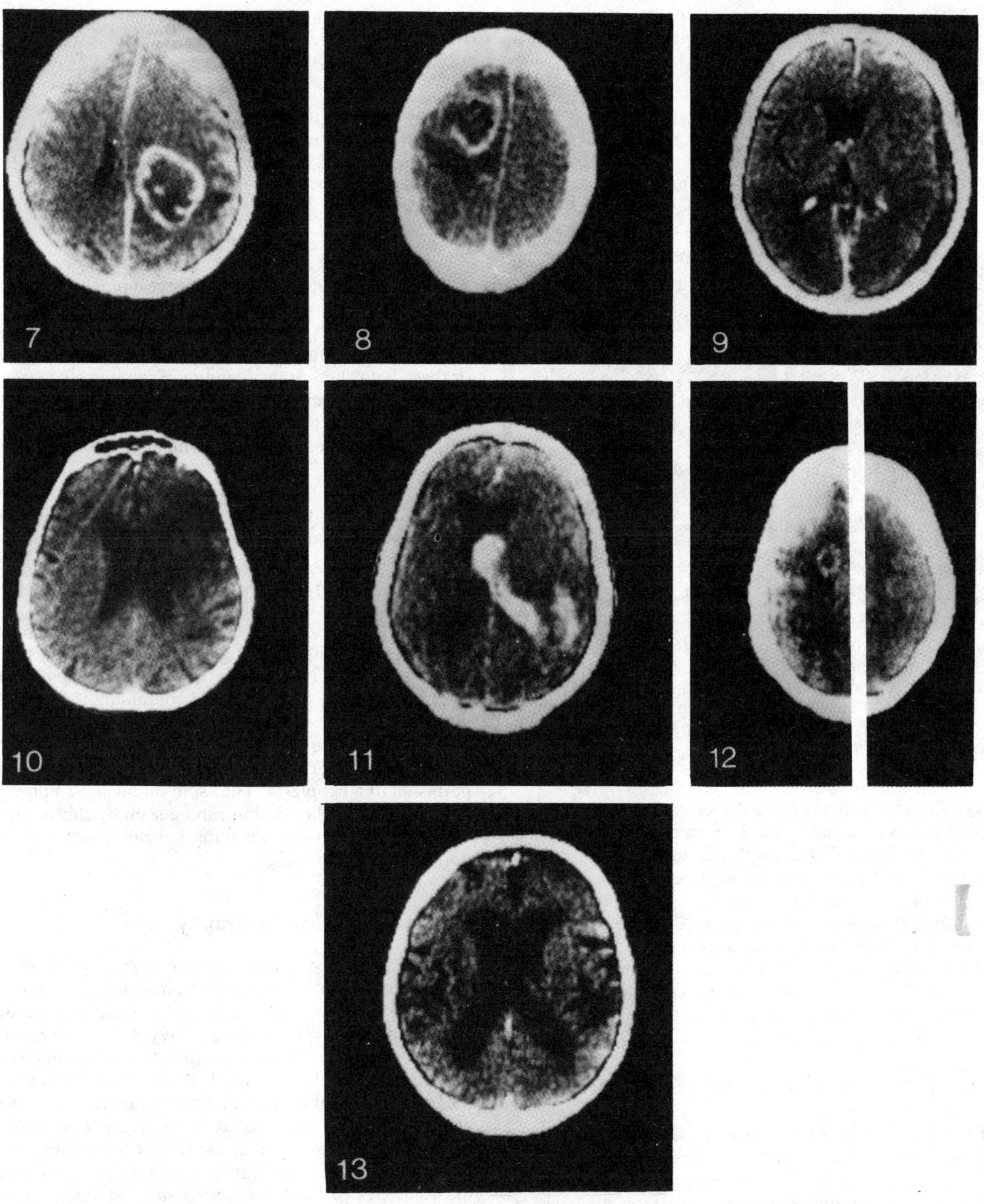

Figures 3.2-7 through 3.2-13. Computed tomograms of the head are presented as if looking down on a coronal cross-section, with the frontal area at the top and the occipital area at the bottom of the picture; the left and right sides are the same as the viewer's right and left. In the pictures, the least dense substances, such as air and cerebrospinal fluid, are the darkest; the densest areas, such as the skull and blood clots, are the lightest. Although air and clear fluid may appear equally dark and bone and blood clot may appear equally light, the great differences in the densities of these materials can be determined with the aid of the computer. (Courtesy of Norman Leeds, M.D., Montefiore Medical Center, New York, NY.)

Figure 3.2-7. Cerebral neoplasm. A large mass, glioblastoma multiforme, is present within the right hemisphere. Circumferential density is enhanced by intravenous contrast, and there is adjacent edema, as manifested by rarefaction.

Figure 3.2-8. Cerebral abscess. A large left frontal abscess is enclosed by a hypervascular capsule (density enhanced by intravenous contrast) and surrounded by a zone of edema (decreased density). The tiny markedly lucent zones within the lesion represent gas produced by bacteria and indicate that this mass is an abscess, rather than a neoplasm.

Figure 3.2-9. Subdural hematoma. A chronic subdural hematoma over the right convexity has caused a ventricular shift from right to left. A small rim of increased density between the surface of the brain and the hematoma represents the membrane enclosing the hematoma. The hematoma has, for the most part, changed from dense blood clot to a less dense fluid.

Figure 3.2-10. Cerebral infarct. An old right frontal infarct is manifested by a zone of decreased density. The adjacent right lateral ventricle is, if anything, larger than the left lateral ventricle.

Figure legends continued

Figure 3.2-11. Cerebral hemorrhage. A right parietal hemorrhage has broken into the posterior horn of the right lateral ventricle. There is swelling of the right hemisphere and a shift of the ventricles from right to left.

Figure 3.2-12. *A* and *B*, acute multiple sclerosis. With intravenous contrast, multiple circular densities are seen on both the right and the left sides at slightly different levels in a patient with acute multiple sclerosis. These lesions might be mistaken for metastases were it not for the absence of mass effect. This picture is not an invariable finding in multiple sclerosis, but the lesions here are even more prominent than are those seen on sectioning of the brain at autopsy.

Figure 3.2-13. Cerebral atrophy. Cerebral atrophy is manifested in this case by both ventricular dilation and widened cortical sulci. (From S Solomon: Neurological evaluation. In *Comprehensive Textbook of Psychiatry,* ed 4, H I Kaplan and B J Sadock, editors, p 102. Williams & Wilkins, Baltimore, 1985.)

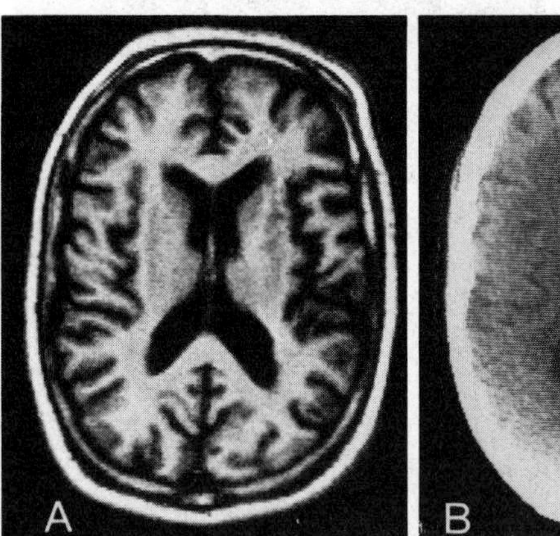

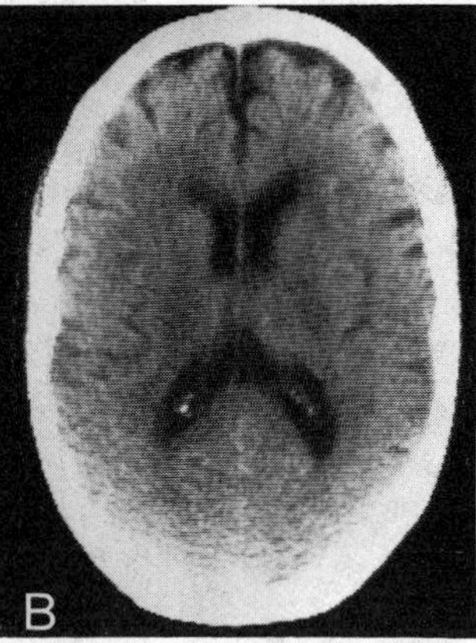

Figure 3.2-14. (*A*) MRI scan through the canto-meatal line of a 33-year-old healthy man. (*B*) CT scan through the canto-meatal line of the same 33-year-old healthy man. Note that details of the brain structure cannot be distinguished, as in the MRI scan shown in *A*. (From G Sedvall: Brain imaging. In *Comprehensive Textbook of Psychiatry,* ed 5, H I Kaplan and B J Sadock, editors, p 92. Williams & Wilkins, Baltimore, 1989.)

pathway. The radioactively labeled 2-deoxyglucose builds up in neurons and is detected by the PET camera. Brain oxygen metabolism can be studied using the isotope of oxygen O^{15}. It is also possible to use radioligands labeled with positron-emitting isotopes to measure the number and the affinity of neurotransmitter receptors in the brain (Figure 3.2-16). Virtually any drug class that is used in psychiatry can now be labeled and used in PET studies to assess the state of those receptors. PET is currently used only in research settings and does not have clinical applications at this time.

SINGLE PHOTON EMISSION TOMOGRAPHY

SPECT is similar to PET in that it uses radioactive substances introduced into the body to visualize functional aspects of both cortical and subcortical areas. In contrast to PET, SPECT uses single-photon-emitting isotopes (e.g., I^{123}), which are then incorporated into organic compounds administered to the patient. Because of the longer half-lives of the isotopes used, SPECT is able to image the brain over a longer period of time than PET. The spatial resolution of brain structures imaged with SPECT, however, is currently inferior to those imaged with PET. As with PET, either CBF or specific CNS receptors can be visualized, depending on the compound used for the study. SPECT is currently used only in research settings.

RADIOISOTOPE BRAIN SCANNING

In contrast to normal brain tissue, abnormal brain tissue may retain radioisotope compounds. This retention is due to the breakdown of the blood-brain barrier associated with organic disease. By means of scanning equipment, the γ energies emitted by the radioisotope retained in a lesion can be recorded on X-ray film. The radioisotope labeled with technetium (Tc^{99}) is intravenously injected from 30 minutes to two or three hours before the scanning. Scanning equipment projects signals to an image read-out oscilloscope, and the image, in turn, may be photographed. The isotope gallium (Ga^{67}) tends to be picked up in inflammatory and lymphomatous lesions.

A cerebral infarct picks up the radioactive isotope only one to four days after the onset; the zone of infarction often has a wedge-shaped appearance. Brain scans are frequently negative when the lesion is small (less than 2 cm in diameter), avascular (such as a cyst), or obscured by muscle mass or a confluence of blood vessels.

Dynamic brain scanning is an additional technique. From 9 to 12 seconds after the intravenous injection of the radioactive isotope, serial pictures are taken in rapid sequence. Asymmetry in the flow of blood containing the radioisotope may be indicative of stenosis or occlusion of a carotid artery or ischemia within the cerebral zone of the artery. There is usually delayed perfusion in the area of ischemia and increased perfusion of a neoplasm. The rapid filling and emptying of an arteriovenous malformation can be seen by this method.

Radioisotope brain scanning is seldom used in contemporary clinical neurology.

Radioisotope Cisternography

The radioisotope cisternography test helps to determine the rate of absorption of cerebrospinal fluid (CSF) in normal pressure hydrocephalus and is used to trace leakage of CSF. When indium (In^{111}) is injected through a lumbar puncture, the isotope diffuses through the spinal canal and into the basal cisterns in two to four hours. It is seen over the convexity of the brain in 24 hours, is predominantly parasagittal in 48 hours, and is minimally detectable at 72 hours. In patients with normal pressure hydrocephalus caused by a chronic defect impairing absorption of CSF, the radioactive isotope diffuses into the ventricles of the brain and is still seen in the ventricles after 24 hours.

References

Andreasen N C: Brain imaging: Applications in psychiatry. Science *239*: 1381, 1988.

Andreason N C: Evaluation of brain imaging techniques in mental illness. Annu Rev Med *39*: 335, 1988.

Cohen B M, Buonanno F, Keck P E, Finklestein S P, Benes F M: Comparison of MRI and CT scans in a group of psychiatric patients. Am J Psychiatry *145*: 1084, 1988.

Garber H J, Weilburg J B, Buonanno F S, Manschreck T C, New P F J: Use of magnetic resonance imaging in psychiatry. Am J Psychiatry *145*: 164, 1988.

Gur D, Yonas H, Good W F: Local cerebral blood flow by Xenon-enhanced CT: Current status, potential improvements, and future directions. Cerebro Brain Metabol Rev *1*: 68, 1989.

Gur R C, Gur R E, Obrist W D, Skolnick B E, Reivich M: Age and regional cerebral blood flow at rest and during cognitive activity. Arch Gen Psychiatry *44*: 617, 1987.

Henriques J B, Davidson R J: Regional brain electrical asymmetries discriminate between previously depressed and healthy control subjects. J Abnorm Psychol *99*: 22, 1990.

Jacobson H G, ed: Positron emission tomography: A new approach to brain chemistry. JAMA *260*: 2704, 1988.

John E R: The role of quantitative EEG topographic mapping or "neurometrics" in the diagnosis of psychiatric and neurological disorders: The pros. Electroencephalogr Clin Neurophysiol *73*: 2, 1989.

Journal of Neuropsychiatry and Clinical Neurosciences: PET and SPECT. J Neuropsychiatry Clin Neurosci *1* (Supp 1): 1989.

Maurer K, Dierks T: Functional imaging of the brain in psychiatry: Mapping of EEG and evoked potentials. Neurosurg Rev *10*: 275, 1987.

Moonen C T W, van Zijl P C M, Frank J A, LeBihan D, Becker E D: Functional magnetic resonance imaging in medicine and physiology. Science *250*: 53, 1990.

Morihisa J M: Brain imaging approaches in psychiatry: Early developmental considerations. J Clin Psychiatry *51*: 44, 1990.

Petersen S E, Fox P T, Posner M I, Mintun M, Raichle M E: Positron emission tomographic studies of the cortical anatomy of single-word processing. Nature *331*: 585, 1988.

Rosse R B, Warden D L, Morihisa J M: Applied electrophysiology. In *Comprehensive Textbook of Psychiatry,* ed 5, H I Kaplan and B J Sadock, editors, p 74. Williams & Wilkins, Baltimore, 1989.

Sedvall G: Brain imaging. In *Comprehensive Textbook of Psychiatry,* ed 5, H I Kaplan and B J Sadock, editors, p 92. Williams & Wilkins, Baltimore, 1989.

Wagner H N Jr, Weinberger D R, Kleinman J E, Casanova M F, Gibbs C J Jr, Gur R E, Hornykiewicz O, Kuhar M J, Pettegrew J W, Seeman P: Neuroimaging and neuropathology. Schizophr Bull *14*: 383, 1988.

Weinberger D R: Brain disease and psychiatric illness: When should a psychiatrist order a CAT scan? Am J Psychiatry *141*: 1521, 1984.

Weinberger D R, Salzman C: Brain imaging techniques and their usefulness in psychiatry. Hosp Community Psychiatry *35*: 325, 1984.

Williamson P C, Kaye H: EEG mapping applications in psychiatric disorders. Can J Psychiatry *34*: 680, 1989.

3.3 / Neurochemistry and Neurophysiology

Two major foci of contemporary research in psychiatry are the processes of chemical neurotransmission and signal transduction. *Chemical neurotransmission* refers to the release of a neurotransmitter by the presynaptic neuron and the detection of this neurotransmitter by receptor proteins. *Signal transduction* refers to the general process by which an electrical signal (the nerve impulse) is converted into a chemical signal (neurotransmitter release) by the presynaptic neuron and the process by which the chemical signal is converted back into an electrical signal by the postsynaptic neuron.

The first step in neurotransmission involves transport of the necessary molecules down the axon to the axon terminal (Figure 3.3-1). Once primed, the axon terminal waits until it is signaled by an *action potential* carried down the axonal membrane. An action potential is a self-propagating transmembrane current that occurs when the intraneuronal electrical potential reaches its threshold. The resulting depolarization of the axon terminal causes calcium ions to enter the nerve terminal through calcium channels. The rise in intraneuronal calcium initiates a series of molecular events causing synaptic vesicles that contain neurotransmitters to migrate toward the neuronal membrane, fuse with the membrane, and release their contents into the synaptic cleft. Once released,

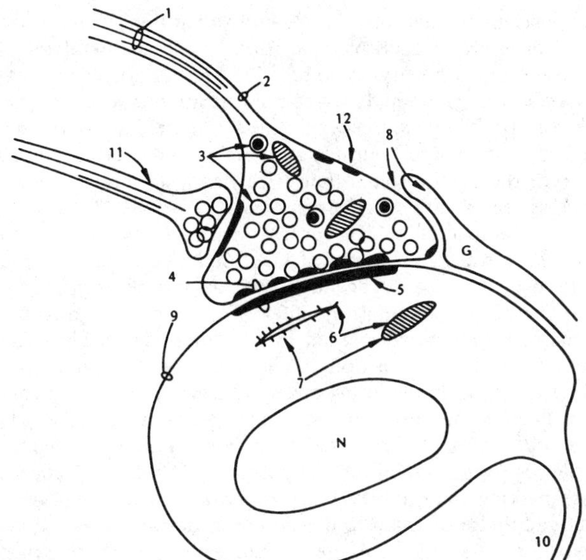

Figure 3.3-1. Twelve steps in the synaptic transmission process are indicated in this idealized synaptic connection. Step 1 is transport down the axon along microtubules. Step 2 involves the electrically excitable membrane of the axon. Step 3 involves the synthesis and storing of the neurotransmitter. Step 4 includes the actual release and reuptake of the neurotransmitter. Step 5 is the postsynaptic receptor that triggers the response of the postsynaptic cell to the transmitter. Step 6 shows the organelles within the postsynaptic cells that respond to the receptor trigger. Step 7 is the interaction between genetic expression of the postsynaptic nerve cell and the cytoplasmic organelles that respond to neurotransmitter action. Step 8 includes the enzymes present in the extracellular space and within glia for catabolizing excess neurotransmitter released from the nerve terminals. Step 9 includes the electrical portion of the nerve cell membrane that, in response to various neurotransmitters, is able to integrate the postsynaptic potentials. Step 10 is the continuation of the information transmission by which the postsynaptic cell sends information to its cell body. Step 11 indicates that the release of neurotransmitter is subjected to modification by a presynaptic (axoaxonic) synapse. Step 12 indicates presynaptic autoreceptors that respond to the neurotransmitter released by the neuron itself. (Modified from J R Cooper, F E Bloom, R H Roth: *The Biochemical Basis of Neuropharmacology,* ed 5, p 42. Oxford University Press, New York, 1986.)

the neurotransmitter molecules diffuse across the synaptic cleft and bind to a postsynaptic receptor. The released neurotransmitter substance is inactivated by diffusing away from the synapse into the extracellular fluid or by active reuptake into the neuron (or a glial cell), followed by degradation by enzymes.

SYNAPSES

There is not just one type of synapse. A synapse can be chemical (also called humoral) or electrical. Chemical synapses use a neurotransmitter as the message, whereas electrical synapses (more commonly called gap junctions) use electric current (i.e., a flow of charged ions). Some synapses, called conjoint synapses, use both messages.

The most conventional types of synapses are the axodendritic and axosomatic synapses, in which the axon of the presynaptic neuron synapses with a dendrite or the cell body of the postsynaptic neuron. In axoaxonic synapses, the presynaptic axon synapses with the axon hillock or axon terminal of the postsynaptic neuron. Two recently identified synapses are dendrodritic and dendroaxonic. Both types are involved in local modulation of synaptic function and do not elicit postsynaptic action potentials. To complicate matters, nonsynaptic neurons probably exist as well. These neurons have axon terminals that release neurotransmitters into the extracellular fluid or the cerebrospinal fluid (CSF) and, therefore, do not have synapses with specific neurons.

Each individual neuron receives many synaptic inputs. In the resting state, the interior of a neuron is negatively charged with respect to the extracellular space. For a neuron to generate an action potential, the interior of the neuron must become less negatively charged, until it reaches an electrical potential at which an action potential is generated. *Inhibitory* synapses result in the influx of negative ions into the neuron, thus making the intraneuronal compartment more negatively charged and less able to develop an action potential. *Excitatory* synapses result in the influx of positive ions into the neuron, thus making the intraneuronal compartment less negatively charged and more able to develop an action potential. Each neuron must integrate all the inhibitory and excitatory inputs it receives.

Neuronal Membrane

The neuronal cell membrane is a complex regulatory mechanism for the functions of the cell. The membrane is a sea of phospholipids, organized as a bilayer with the hydrophobic ends of the molecules pointing toward each other. Within this lipid bilayer are cholesterol and protein molecules. Some proteins are embedded in the external or internal surface of the membrane. Other proteins, such as ion channels, extend the entire width of the membrane. Cholesterol molecules within the membrane tend to keep the lipid molecules relatively fixed and orderly.

NEUROMESSENGERS

"Neuromessenger" is a generic term for neurotransmitters, neuromodulators, and neurohormones. *Neurotransmitters* are the classic neuromessengers that are released rapidly by the presynaptic neuron, diffuse across the synaptic cleft, and have either an excitatory or an inhibitory effect on a postsynaptic neuron. *Neuromodulators* also bind to specific receptors but are conceptualized as tuning or grading the response of the postsynaptic cell to the neurotransmitter. *Neurohormones* are chemical messengers released by neurons into the bloodstream.

There are three classes of neurotransmitters—biogenic amines, amino acids, and peptides (Figure 3.3-2). The biogenic amines (monoamines) consist of three catecholamines (dopamine, norepinephrine, and epinephrine), an indoleamine (serotonin), a quaternary amine (acetylcholine), and an ethylamine (histamine). The biogenic amines account only for 5 to 10 percent of the synapses of the human brain, whereas the amino acid neurotransmitters account for up to 60 percent of the synapses.

Dale's law states that the same neurotransmitter is released by all processes of a single neuron. This law now includes the fact that a single neuron can contain more than one neurotransmitter. This observation is referred to as the *coexistence of neurotransmitters*. For example, a

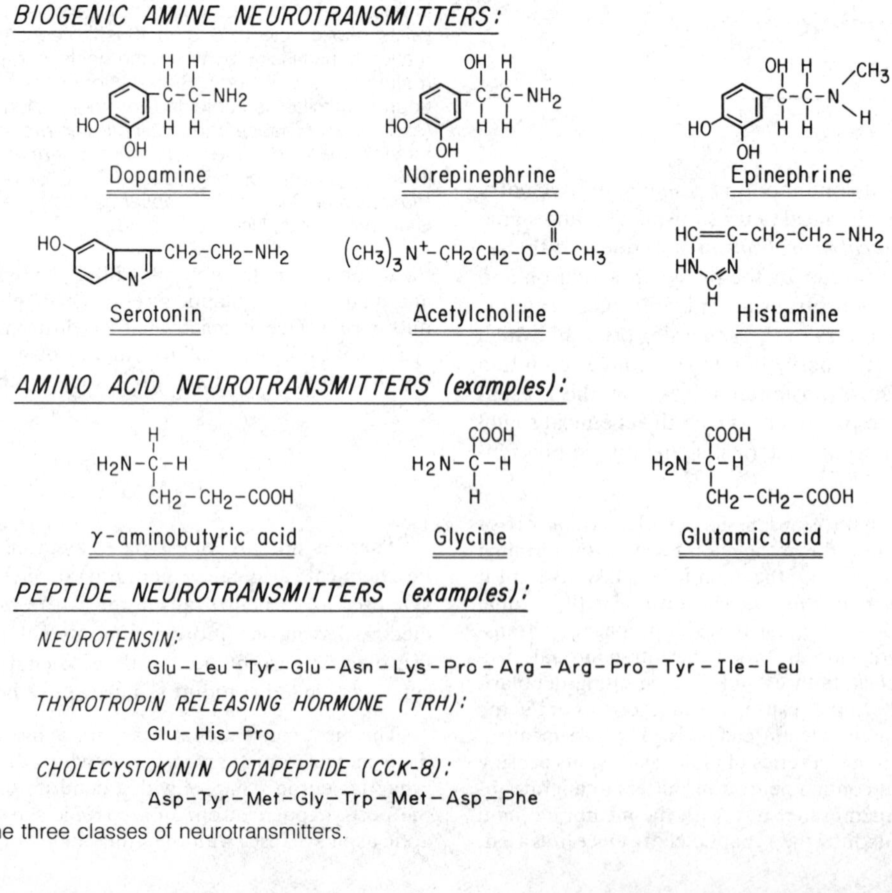

BIOGENIC AMINE NEUROTRANSMITTERS:

Dopamine

Norepinephrine

Epinephrine

Serotonin

$(CH_3)_3N^+-CH_2CH_2-O-C(=O)-CH_3$

Acetylcholine

Histamine

AMINO ACID NEUROTRANSMITTERS (examples):

$H_2N-CH(H)-CH_2-CH_2-COOH$

γ-aminobutyric acid

$H_2N-CH(COOH)-H$

Glycine

$H_2N-CH(COOH)-CH_2-CH_2-COOH$

Glutamic acid

PEPTIDE NEUROTRANSMITTERS (examples):

NEUROTENSIN:

Glu-Leu-Tyr-Glu-Asn-Lys-Pro-Arg-Arg-Pro-Tyr-Ile-Leu

THYROTROPIN RELEASING HORMONE (TRH):

Glu-His-Pro

CHOLECYSTOKININ OCTAPEPTIDE (CCK-8):

Asp-Tyr-Met-Gly-Trp-Met-Asp-Phe

Figure 3.3-2. The three classes of neurotransmitters.

neuron may contain a biogenic amine neurotransmitter and a peptide neurotransmitter.

Receptors

Receptors are proteins in the neuronal membrane that are, in part, exposed to the extracellular fluid and specifically recognize neuromessengers. Receptors may be postsynaptic or presynaptic. In an axodendritic synapse, for example, the receptors on the receiving dendrite are postsynaptic. The receptors on the axon itself are presynaptic. They are called presynaptic autoreceptors if they bind a neurotransmitter that their parent neuron released; they are called presynaptic heteroreceptors if they bind a neurotransmitter released by some other neuron.

The concepts of supersensitivity and subsensitivity are applied to receptors. These properties signify that a specific neuron is more or less sensitive, respectively, to a constant amount of neurotransmitter. Such regulation of a synaptic response could involve three receptor-related changes. First, the number of receptors available for neurotransmitter binding could increase or decrease. Second, the affinity of the receptor could increase or decrease. Third, the mechanism by which the receptor translates its message into the neuron could be more or less efficient. These three changes are all examples of neuronal plasticity.

The evolution of the receptor message into an intraneuronal biological response involves translating the first message (e.g., the neuromessenger, hormone, or nerve impulse) into a second message (e.g., cyclic adenosine monophosphate [cAMP], cyclic guanosine monophosphate [cGMP], calcium ion). As part of the receptor protein or as a second protein in the membrane, there is an effector component to the receptor complex. This effector is either an enzyme or an ion channel. When a receptor is stimulated, it can then, for example, activate adenylate cyclase to produce cAMP or open chloride channels to change the neuronal electric potential. In many receptor complexes, a modulator component (e.g., G protein) is intercalated between the receptor and the effector components. The modulator component may bind a neuromodulator or other molecule that affects its functioning.

Molecular structure of receptors. A number of neurotransmitter receptors have been isolated and purified. Using the techniques of molecular genetics, investigators have determined the specific amino acid sequences of these proteins. Two general types of receptor proteins have been described.

One type—which includes the α_2-adrenergic, β_2-adrenergic, D_2-dopaminergic, and M_1-muscarinic receptors—consists of a polypeptide chain that crosses back and forth through the neuronal membrane seven times. The N-terminal of the protein is on the extracellular side of the membrane, and the C-terminal of the protein is on the cytoplasmic side. The seven transmembrane domains result in three cytoplasmic loops. The third of these loops is the longest and may be the part of the receptor that interacts with the G proteins. As described below, the β-adrenergic receptor has been shown to be phosphorylated, and its state of phosphorylation has been shown to regulate its ability to activate its associated G protein.

The second basic type of neurotransmitter receptor is exemplified by the nicotinic acetylcholine receptor. This receptor consists of five different proteins that are aggregated to form the receptor complex. The proteins are arranged such that an ion channel transverses the membrane. The neurotransmitter, acetylcholine, binds directly to the receptor complex, which results in the opening of the ion channel.

Interneuronal Neurotransmitter Molecular Biochemistry

First messenger signals (e.g., dopamine) are variously translated into five different intracellular *second messengers*—cAMP, cGMP, calcium, diacylglycerol, and inositol trisphosphate (Figure 3.3-3).

Two receptors are linked to the functioning of adenylate cyclase, one excitatory and the other inhibitory (Figure 3.3-3). For example, dopamine type-1 receptors stimulate adenylate cyclase, whereas one function of dopamine type-2 receptors is to inhibit this enzyme. Both of the dopamine receptor proteins are linked to an appropriate G protein, either G_s for stimulation or G_i for inhibition. (The G protein is so named because it requires guanosine triphosphate [GTP] for its actions. G proteins are sometimes referred to as the N proteins, for nucleotide-binding regulatory protein.) The G proteins affect the activity of adenylate cyclase, which, when active, converts adenosine triphosphate (ATP) into cAMP. The deactivation of cAMP into AMP is catalyzed by the enzyme phosphodiesterase.

The second major transducing system is referred to as the phosphatidylinositol system (Figure 3.3-3). This system is currently known to have only a stimulatory receptor. The receptor acts through a G protein to stimulate an enzyme (phospholipase C) that converts a membrane lipid, phosphatidylinositol, 4,5-bisphosphate (PIP_2) into diacylgylcerol(DG) and inositol trisphosphate (IP_3). IP_3 causes an increase in the concentration of calcium ions within the neuron by inducing the release of Ca^{2+} from intraneuronal compartments. Both DG and IP_3 are metabolized quickly within the neuron. IP_3 is converted back into PIP_2 through a series of enzymatic steps, the last of which involves the enzyme inositol-1-phosphatase; this enzyme is inhibited by lithium, thereby limiting the amount of PIP_2 available for signal transduction.

Many proteins in the neuron exist in two states—active and inactive. Research suggests that a major mechanism for switching proteins on and off is protein phosphorylation. Two classes of enzymes, protein kinases and phosphates, respectively, put on and take off a phosphate group from a protein molecule. The protein kinases themselves are activated by second messengers.

Research Approaches to Neurotransmission in Neuropsychiatry

Assessing neurotransmission in disease states. The most common approach to assessing neurotransmission status in disease states is to measure one of the following variables: neurotransmitter synthesizing enzymes, neurotransmitters, and neurotransmitter metabolites. These substances can be measured in patients by collecting blood, urine, or CSF. A variation of this same research methodology is to measure neurotransmitter receptor number and affinity in patients' nonneuronal tissue, such as platelets or white blood cells. These measures provide a first approximation of neurotransmitter status in the central nervous system (CNS). It is also possible to measure neurotransmitter and receptor characteristics in brain tissue postmortem.

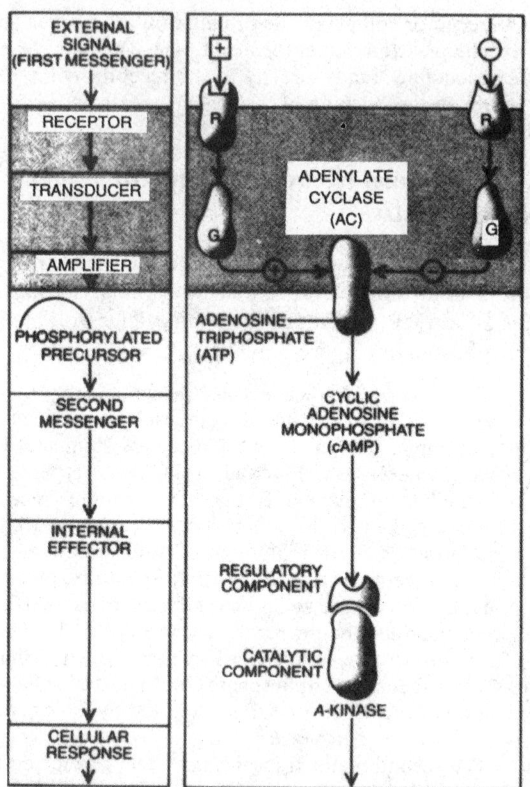

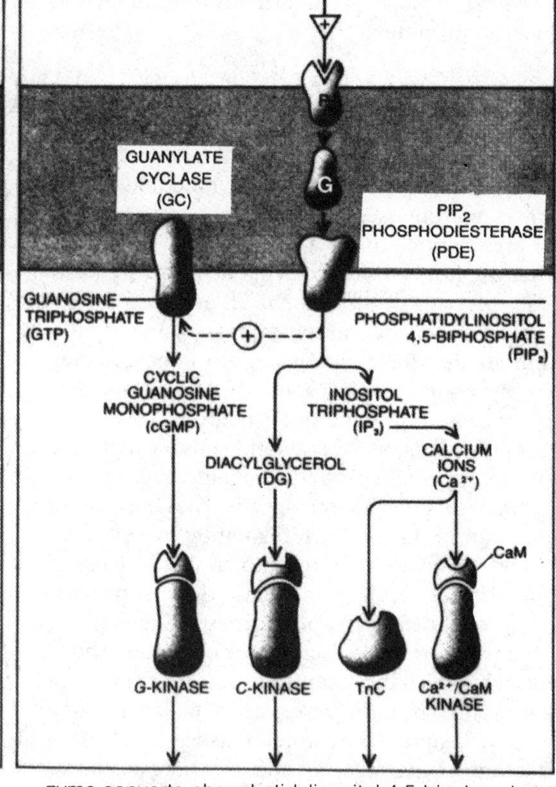

Figure 3.3-3. Known signal pathways in cells are few in number. In functional terms they share a sequence of events (*left*). External messengers arriving at receptror molecules in the plasma membrane (*gray*) activate a closely related family of transducer molecules, which carry signals through the membrane, and amplifier enzymes, which activate internal signals carried by second messengers. The pathway employing the second messenger cAMP (middle) has stimulatory (R_s) and inhibitory receptors (R_i), which both communicate with the amplifier adenylate cyclase (AC) by way of stimulatory or inhibitory transducers called G proteins because they require guanosine triphosphate (GTP) to function. Adenylate cyclase converts ATP into cAMP The other major pathway (right) is not known to recognize inhibitory external signals. It employs a stimulatory G protein to activiate its amplifier, a phosphodiesterase (PDE) enzyme. The enzyme converts phosphatidylinositol 4,5-bisphosphate (PIP_2) into a pair of second messengers, diacylglycerol (DG) and inositol trisphosphate (IP_3). In turn, IP_3 induces the cell to mobilize still another messenger, calcium ions (Ca^{2+}). Moreover, the pathway somehow induces the amplifier guanylate cyclase (GC) to convert GTP into the second messenger cyclic guanosine monophosphate (cGMP). In general, the second messengers bind to the regulatory component of a protein kinase, a class of enzymes that activate a cellular response by adding phosphate (PO_4) groups to particular proteins. Calcium binds to a family of proteins including calmodulin (CaM) and troponin C (TnC). In turn, CaM activates a protein kinase; TnC stimulates muscle contraction directly. (From M J Berridge: The molecular basis of communication within cells. Sci Am *253*: 142, 1985.)

Challenge strategies. The concept of challenge strategies is germane to many areas of biological research in psychiatry. Challenge strategies contrast baseline measures. The measurement of morning cortisol levels is an example of a baseline measure. The measurement of cortisol levels in response to dexamethasone is an example of a challenge strategy. For another example, one can measure resting cerebral blood flow, or one can ask the patient to do a psychological test as a challenge while measuring the patient's cerebral blood flow.

Basic neurochemical research. The complexity of the nervous system makes it impossible to predict which avenues of research may eventually result in major clinical gains in understanding and treating mental illness. Many researchers use animal models of behavior, such as the motor activity of rodents. Other researchers use less complex animals in an attempt to understand how a simple nervous system may work. The best known example of this strategy in psychiatric research involves the study of the biological basis of learning.

The major experimental models for studying the biology of learning and memory are (1) identified neuronal pathways controlling specific behaviors in invertebrates (e.g., *Hermissenda* and *Aplysia californica*), (2) cerebellar neuronal pathways controlling the rabbit nictating membrane and eyelid response, and (3) hippocampal neurons involved in long-term potentiation of behavioral sequences in vertebrates. Research conducted by Eric Kandel and his colleagues at Columbia University with *Aplysia californica* has been particularly well covered in the psychiatric literature. The details of this work are discussed below; however, the summary point is that it is now clear that there is a *reciprocal* interaction between CNS biological processes and environmental influences, resulting in the development and modification of behaviors.

Aplysia californica. The *Aplysia*, a sea mollusk, is a useful animal to study because of the simplicity of its nervous system as compared with that of humans. The *Aplysia* contains approximately 20,000 neurons, and many of these are quite large and readily identifiable during repeated experiments. The specific behavior studied is a defensive reflex involving the withdrawal of the siphon of the snail when the animal is tactually stimulated. If the snail is touched repeatedly, it learns not to withdraw its siphon and gill, a process called habituation. If the snail receives a strong stimulus (e.g., an electric shock), it will become sensitized, such that even a previously subthreshold tactile stimulation will cause the animal to withdraw its gill and siphon. Furthermore, it is possible to condition the snail classically in such a way that it withdraws its siphon and gill to a conditioned stimulus. Habituation, sensitization, and classical conditioning of this reflex in the snail can be considered forms of learning and memory. Parallels have been drawn between classical conditioning and phobias and between a hypothetical lack of habituation and generalized anxiety.

The neuronal, anatomical, and chemical bases for these learning processes have been well established in this animal model. Sensory neurons receiving tactile information form excitatory synapses with the gill and siphon motor neurons that cause the withdrawal activity. Habituation, sensitization, and classical conditioning all involve neurochemical changes in the sensory neuron, resulting in alterations in the amount of excitatory neurotransmitter released. The neurochemical basis of habituation is that, on repeated stimulation of the sensory neuron (e.g., from repeated tactile stimulation), less calcium enters the presynaptic nerve terminal, resulting in the release of less neurotransmitter and, thus, less activity of the motor neurons. Sensitization requires the presence of additional neurons, called facilitator interneurons, which synapse onto the sensory neurons. The sensitizing stimulus (e.g., an electric shock) causes the facilitator interneuron to release serotonin, which binds to serotonin receptors on the sensory neuron. Activation of the serotonin receptors activates adenylate cyclase, producing cAMP, thereby activating a cAMP-dependent protein kinase, which, in turn, phosphorylates an S-type potassium channel. Phosphorylation of this potassium channel results in increased calcium influx during the action potential and increased neurotransmitter release. Although it is known that classical conditioning also results in the release of an increased amount of neurotransmitter by the sensory neuron, the neurochemical basis is less well understood at this time but may involve additional protein kinases.

Experimental work with young *Aplysia* has shown that the processes of habituation and sensitization develop at different times, habituation before sensitization. This finding suggests that it may be possible to identify the separate biological processes that give rise to both these important learning phenomena.

BIOGENIC AMINES

The biogenic amine neurotransmitters are well known to most psychiatrists because they were the first neurotransmitters discovered and, therefore, have been the subject of research studies for the longest amount of time. Most of the standard psychiatric drugs have one or more of the biogenic amine neurotransmitters as their initial site of action.

The biogenic amine neurotransmitters are synthesized in the nerve terminals, where they are released. This is in contrast to the peptide neurotransmitters, which are synthesized in the cell body and transported down the axon to the nerve terminal. These observations have led researchers to hypothesize that the biogenic amines are particularly important in chemical synapses, which require the rapid release of large or sustained amounts of neurotransmitter.

Dopamine

CNS dopaminergic tracts. There are three dopaminergic tracts of relevance to neuropsychiatry (Figure 3.3-4). The neurons of the nigrostriatal tract have their cell bodies in the pars compacta of the substantia nigra and project their axons to the corpus striatum. This tract is involved in the initiation and coordination of movement; in Parkinson's disease, this tract degenerates. Parkinsonian side effects of antipsychotics are caused by a blockade of postsynaptic dopamine receptors receiving input from this tract.

The tuberoinfundibular tract has its cell bodies in the arcuate nucleus and periventricular area of the hypothalamus and projects to the infundibulum and anterior pituitary. Dopamine acts as a release-inhibiting factor in this tract by inhibiting the release of prolactin from the anterior pituitary. Patients who take antipsychotic drugs have elevated prolactin levels because the blockade of dopamine receptors eliminates these inhibitory effects of dopamine.

The mesolimbic-mesocortical tract has its cell bodies in the ventral tegmental area and projects its axons widely to the neocortex and the limbic system. It is tempting to assign a role in emotional expression to this tract because of its projection to the neocortex and the limbic system, brain areas thought to be involved in complex behavior.

Dopaminergic synapse. The dopaminergic terminal requires tyrosine for the production of dopamine. Tyrosine is converted to 3,4-dihydroxyphenylalanine (DOPA) by tyrosine hydroxylase. Tyrosine hydroxylase is the rate-limiting enzyme for the synthesis of dopamine and is under regulatory control by protein kinases. DOPA is converted into dopamine by an aromatic amino acid decarboxylase. Dopamine is then taken up and stored in vesicles. Reserpine interferes with the uptake and storage of dopamine in synaptic vesicles. On stimulation, the dopaminergic neuron releases dopamine into the synaptic cleft.

Once in the synaptic cleft, dopamine interacts with presynaptic and postsynaptic dopamine receptors. Dopamine dissociates from the receptor and is actively taken back up into the presynaptic neuron. Free dopamine in the presynaptic neuron is metabolized by monoamine oxidase (MAO), which is located in the mitochondria. (There are two types of MAO in the CNS—MAO_A, which selectively metabolizes norepinephrine and serotonin, and MAO_B, which metabolizes dopamine more selectively.) MAO metabolism of dopamine produces DOPAC, which is further metabolized by catechol-o-methyltransferase (COMT) to produce homovanillic acid (HVA). Dopamine also may be metabolized, in reverse order, by COMT and MAO in the synaptic cleft. HVA is the dopamine metabolite that is most often measured in psychiatric research.

Dopamine receptors. There are two types of dopamine receptors. Dopamine D_1 receptors stimulate adenylate cyclase. Dopamine D_2 receptors inhibit adenylate cyclase, although some D_2 receptors may also be involved in the regulation of calcium and potassium channels. Both D_1 and D_2 receptors are located on postsynaptic neurons; D_2 receptors are also located on presynaptic neurons. Dopamine receptors are linked to adenylate cyclase through G proteins. The D_1 receptor is linked by the stimulatory G protein, G_S; the D_2 receptor is linked by the inhibitory G protein, G_i. The clinical potency of antipsychotic drugs is most closely associated with their binding affinity to the D_2 receptor.

The D_2 receptor has recently been cloned and sequenced. In fact, there are two D_2 receptors in the human brain—one 415 amino acids long and the other 444 amino acids long. Both D_2 receptors seem to have a structure similar to other identified receptors, such as the β-adrenergic and muscarinic receptors. Specifically, the receptor protein is thought to have seven transmembrane domains; the long third cytoplasmic loop is the putative site of interaction with G proteins. The

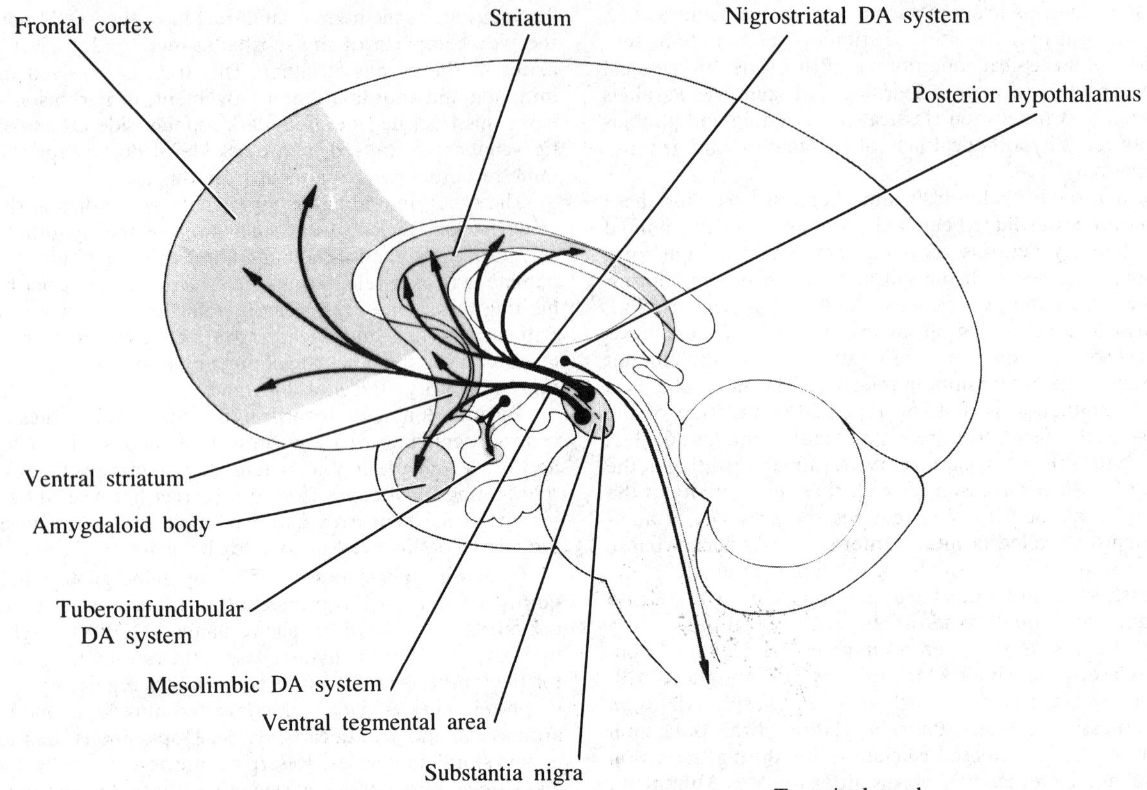

Figure 3.3-4. Dopaminergic (DA) pathways. The nigrostriatal DA system originates in the substantia nigra and terminates in the main dorsal part of the striatum. The ventral tegmental area gives rise to the mesolimbic DA system, which terminates in the ventral striatum, amygdaloid body, frontal lobe, and some other basal forebrain areas. The tuberoinfundibular system innvervates the median eminence and the posterior and intermediate lobes of the pituitary, and dopamine neurons in the posterior hypothalamus project to the spinal cord. (From L Heimer: *The Human Brain and Spinal Cord.* Springer, New York, 1983 with permission.)

dopamine D_1 receptor has also been recently cloned and sequenced. The D_1 receptor sequence indicates that it has the standard structure of a G-protein-linked receptor. Most recently, the existence of a D_3 receptor has been reported. This receptor is not linked to adenylyl cyclase, and some investigators have proposed that it may be of special relevance to schizophrenia.

Dopamine and antipsychotics. Both the clinical effects and the adverse effects of antipsychotics result from the blockade of dopaminergic receptors. The parkinsonian and other adverse motor system effects of antipsychotics relate to their blockade of dopaminergic neurotransmission, presumably in the nigrostriatal tract. Tardive dyskinesia has been hypothesized to result from a compensatory development of supersensitive postsynaptic dopamine receptors following chronic blockade.

Dopamine and psychopathology

Dopamine hypothesis of schizophrenia. The dopamine hypothesis of schizophrenia states that the symptoms of schizophrenia are caused by hyperactivity of the dopaminergic system. The major evidence for this hypothesis is the clinical efficacy of dopamine blocking agents, such as the phenothiazines, in the treatment of schizophrenia. The two main problems with this hypothesis are that (1) antipsychotics are clinically effective in treating almost all agitated and psychotic states, regardless of whether they are related to schizophrenia, and (2) other biochemical evidence supporting a dopaminergic overactivity in schizophrenia (e.g., measurement of dopamine metabolites or receptors) has not consistently supported the hypothesis.

Dopamine and mood disorders. It has been hypothesized that some patients with mania have dopaminergic overactivity and that some patients with depression have dopaminergic hypoactivity. This hypothesis is supported by some clinical observations. Parkinson's patients receiving L-dopa (levodopa [Dopar, Larodopa]), a precursor of dopamine, have been reported to become hypomanic, and, in fact, L-dopa has been reported to be useful in treating retarded depressions. There have also been reports of state-related tardive dyskinesia that worsens when a patient is depressed (presumably with low dopamine) and improves during mania (presumably with high dopamine). Biochemical evidence has demonstrated that dopamine metabolites are elevated in some manic patients and decreased in some depressed patients.

Norepinephrine and Epinephrine

Central nervous system noradrenergic tracts. The largest population of noradrenergic neurons in a single identified location is the locus ceruleus in the pons (Figure 3.3-5). The axons of these neurons, along with the axons of more loosely scattered noradrenergic neurons in the brain stem, ascend in the medial forebrain bundle to the cerebral cortex, the limbic system, the thalamus, and the hypothalamus. Noradrenergic pathways also descend in the spinal cord from these neurons.

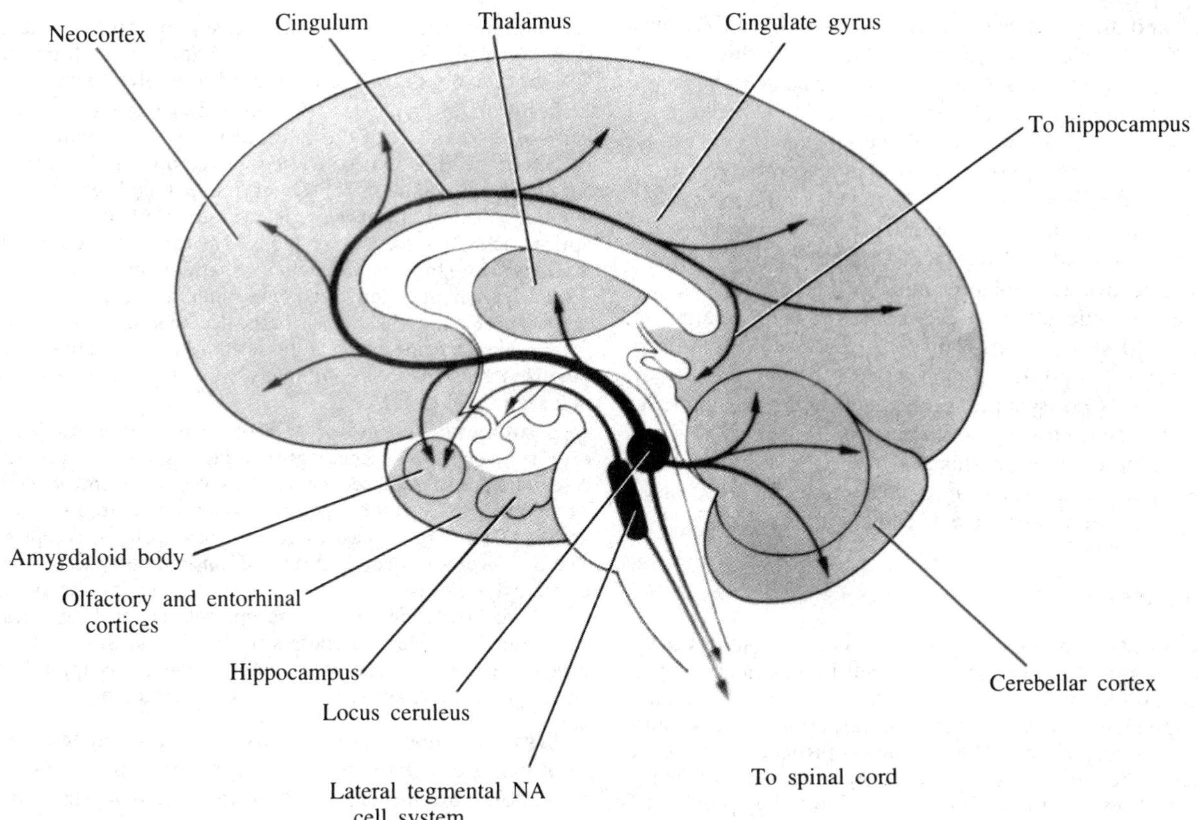

Figure 3.3-5. Noradrenergic pathways. The locus ceruleus, which is located immediately underneath the floor of the fourth ventricle in the rostrolateral part of pons, is the most important noradrenergic nucleus in the brain. Its projections reach many areas in the forebrain, the cerebellum, and the spinal cord. Noradrenergic neurons in the lateral brain stem tegmentum innervate several structures in the basal forebrain including the hypothalamus and the amygdaloid body. (From L Heimer: *The Human Brain and Spinal Cord*. Springer, New York, 1983, with permission.)

Adrenergic (epinephrine-containing) neurons are much rarer and less well studied than noradrenergic neurons.

Noradrenergic (adrenergic) synapse. The noradrenergic terminal uses the same enzymes to make dopamine as the dopaminergic neuron. The noradrenergic neuron, however, contains dopamine-β-carboxylase, which converts dopamine into norepinephrine. Norepinephrine is converted to epinephrine by phenylethanolamine-N-methyltransferase (PNMT) in adrenergic neurons. Norepinephrine is taken up and stored in synpatic vesicles, a process that is blocked by reserpine. Norepinephrine is released when the synaptic vesicle fuses with the presynpatic membrane. Once in the synaptic cleft, norepinephrine interacts with noradrenergic receptors. The metabolic steps for norepinephrine are similar to those for dopamine; the most significant metabolic product from CNS norepinephrine is 3-methoxy-4-hydroxyphenylglycol (MHPG).

Noradrenergic receptors. The two classes of noradrenergic receptors are α and β. Alpha$_1$ receptors are postsynaptic, and α_2 receptors are both postsynaptic and presynaptic. It is clinically useful to know that presynaptic α_2 receptors are more sensitive than postsynaptic α_1 receptors to α-adrenergic agonists. At least three subtypes each of both the α_1 and α_2 receptors have been described. β_1 and β_2 receptors are located postsynaptically. It is currently believed that β receptors are the primary receptors for locus ceruleus input. A β-subtype has recently been reported in the basic neuroscience literature.

Norepinephrine and psychotropics. Both the tricylcic antidepressants (TCAs) and the monoamine oxidase inhibitors (MAOIs) affect the noradrenergic system. The acute effect of TCAs is to block reuptake of norepinephrine and serotonin; the acute effect of MAOIs is to block the metabolism of norepinephrine and serotonin. Thus, both antidepressants acutely increase the concentrations of these biogenic amines in the synaptic cleft. The acute effects of both antidepressants (but especially the tertiary TCAs—doxepin [Sinequan], amitriptyline [Elavil], and imipramine [Tofranil]) and many antipsychotics include the blockade of α_1 receptors, causing sedation and postural hypotension. A unique side effect of MAOIs occurs when a patient being treated with these drugs eats tyramine-rich food, thereby promoting an adrenergic surge that can result in a life-threatening hypertensive crisis.

Two other drugs of interest are clonidine (Catapres) and propranolol (Inderal). Clonidine is an alpha-agonist, which selectively stimulates presynaptic α_2 receptors. Clonidine has been used with partial success in a variety of neuropsychiatric disorders, including opiate withdrawal. Propranolol is one of a class of β-blocking drugs; in addition to being antihypertensive, these drugs have been reported to be clinically useful in treating lithium-induced tremor, social phobias, and akathisia.

Norepinephrine and mood disorders. The major hypothesis regarding norepinephrine is the monoamine hypothesis of mood disorders, which states that depression is the result of too little noradrenergic or serotonergic activity and that this activity is increased by TCAs and MAOIs. There are three major problems with this original hypothesis: (1) there is a three- to four-week delay between the acute biochemical effects of increasing synaptic norepinephrine and serotonin and the clinical effects of reduced depression; (2) some drugs that are potent reuptake blockers (e.g., cocaine) are not effective antidepressants; and (3) newly developed antidepressants that have no reuptake blockade activity or MAOI-like activity are clinically effective as antidepressants. A recent theory is that the therapeutic effect of all antidepressant treatments (TCAs, MAOIs, electroconvulsive therapy [ECT], sleep deprivation) is produced by a decrease in the number or sensitivity of postsynaptic β receptors and presynaptic α_2 receptors and, possibly, an increase in sensitivity to serotonin. These receptor changes are seen approximately three weeks after initiation of treatment, thereby correlating with the time course of clinical improvement.

Serotonin

Central nervous system serotonergic tracts. Serotonergic neurons have their cell bodies in the upper pons and the midbrain—specifically, the median and dorsal raphe nuclei, caudal locus ceruleus, area postrema, and interpeduncular area. These neurons project to the basal ganglia, the limbic system, and the cerebral cortex (Figure 3.3-6). These neurons also project down the spinal cord and modulate the transmission of sensory pain input. These spinal cord tracts may be the site of action for serotonergic antidepressants that have been used to control pain.

Serotonergic synapse. The serotonergic terminal is similar to the terminals of the catecholamines. The amino acid precursor tryptophan is converted into serotonin (also called 5-hydroxytryptamine [5-HT]) by tryptophan hydroxylase and an amino acid decarboxylase. The serotonin is stored in synaptic vesicles, a process that is blocked by reserpine. Serotonin is released into the synaptic cleft on synaptic stimulation. Once inside the synaptic cleft, serotonin binds to serotonergic receptors. The major mechanism of the deactivation of serotonin is reuptake into the presynaptic terminals. Serotonin is metabolized by MAO (preferentially type A) to 5-hydroxyindoleacetic acid (5-HIAA).

Serotonergic receptors. The delineation of serotonin receptors has become exceedingly complex as a result of recent research, and a finalized system has yet to be introduced. There are at least three types of serotonin receptors—S_1, S_2, and S_3. There are at least three subtypes of the S_1 receptor. The S_{1A} receptor is coupled through an inhibitory G protein to adenylyl cyclase and is the site of action for the novel anxiolytic buspirone. The S_2 receptor is coupled to phosphoinositol turnover. In contrast to the S_1 and S_2 receptors, which are G-linked receptor proteins, the S_3 receptor is a ligand-gated ion channel for positively charged ions (cations).

Serotonin and psychotropics. Catecholamines and serotonin are interrelated. Antidepressants, for example, affect both noradrenergic and serotonergic synapses. Most

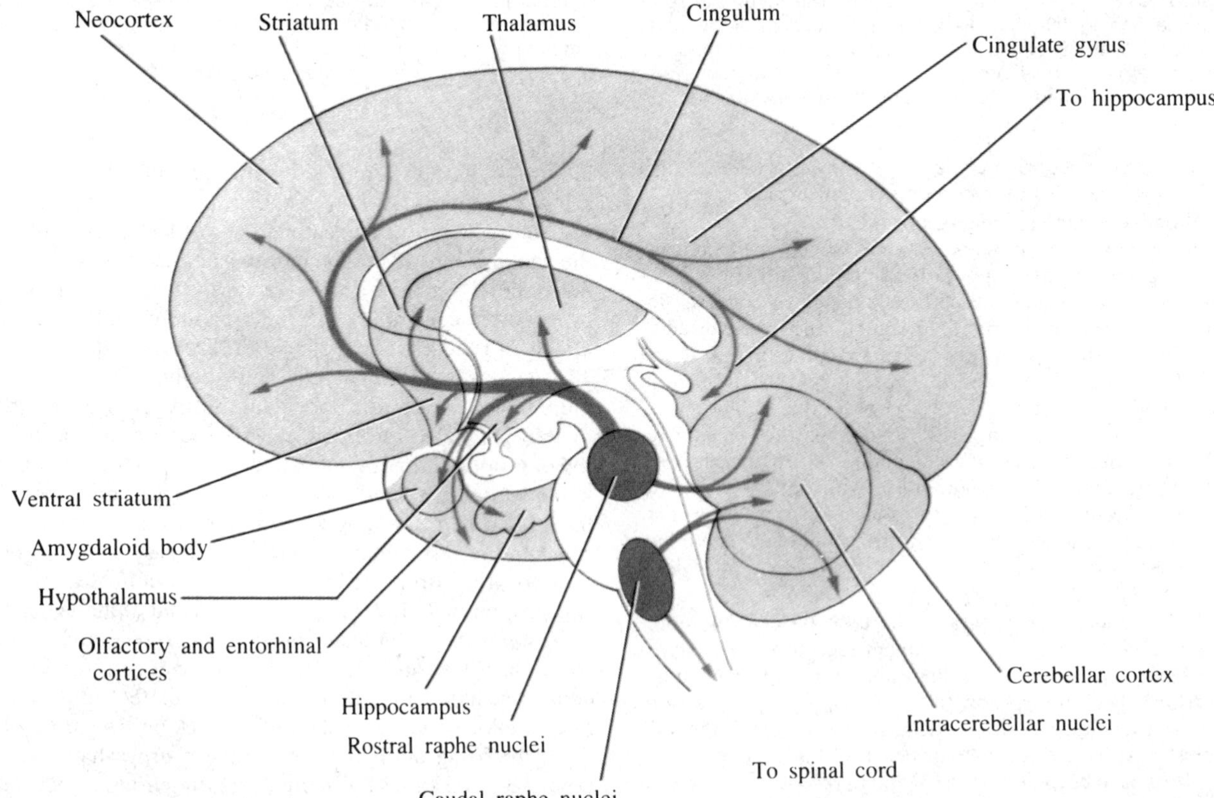

Figure 3.3-6. Serotonergic pathways. The raphe nuclei form a more or less continuous collection of cell groups close to the midline throughout the brain stem, but, for the sake of simplicity, they have been subdivided into a rostral group and a caudal group in the drawing. The rostral raphe nuclei project to a large number of forebrain structures. The fibers that project laterally through the internal and external capsules to widespread areas of the neocortex are not indicated in this highly schematic drawing. (From L Heimer: *The Human Brain and Spinal Cord*. Springer, New York, 1983, with permission.)

nine. Other excitatory amino acids include aspartic acid and probably cysteine and homocysteine acid.

γ-Aminobutyric Acid (GABA)

The two identified long GABA-ergic tracts are the neurons that project from the corpus striatum to the substantia nigra and the cerebellar Purkinje cells that project out of the cerebellum. Local GABA-ergic interneurons exist in the cerebral and cerebellar cortices and in the hypothalamus, where they may play a regulatory role in the neuroendocrine system.

In the GABA-ergic synapse, GABA is synthesized by the actions of glutamic acid decarboxylase (GAD) and degraded by GABA-transaminase (GABA-T). There are two types of GABA receptors—$GABA_A$ and $GABA_B$. $GABA_A$ receptors seem to be limited to a postsynaptic distribution on dendrites and cell bodies. The $GABA_A$ receptor complex consists of a GABA recognition site, a benzodiazepine-binding site, and a chloride ion channel. The binding of GABA to the receptor causes the ion channel to open, thus allowing negatively charged chloride ions to flow into the neuron. The binding of a benzodiazepine to a benzodiazepine-binding site increases the affinity of the GABA-binding site for GABA. Endogenous ligands may exist for the benzodiazepine-binding site. Theoretically, there could be endogenous benzodiazepine agonists (e.g., diazepam-binding inhibitor [DBI]) that reduce anxiety and endogenous benzodiazepine antagonists (e.g., GABA-modulin) that create anxiety. Barbiturates also act through the $GABA_A$ receptor by prolonging the length of time the chloride channel is open. A third drug that is used to treat epilepsy, valproic acid (Depakene), increases GABA-ergic activity by inhibiting the actions of GABA-T. The $GABA_B$ receptor is linked by a G protein to a potassium ion channel.

GABA and psychopathology. The clinical efficacy of benzodiazepines in treating anxiety has led to the hypothesis that too little GABA activity is the molecular pathophysiological basis for anxiety. In addition, decreased GABA activity may be involved in the pathophysiology of epilepsy, because a number of anticonvulsants increase GABA activity. GABA-ergic neuronal loss has been reported in Huntington's chorea and Parkinson's disease; and tardive dyskinesia may involve the GABA-ergic system. Finally, it has been hypothesized that schizophrenia can result from an underactivity of GABA-ergic inhibition on dopaminergic and nonadrenergic neurons.

Glutamate

Glutamate and aspartate are the two primary excitatory amino acid neurotransmitters in the mammalian brain. Glutamate is currently the better understood of the two. It is hypothesized that drugs designed to inhibit glutamate activity function similarly to drugs that enhance GABA activity (e.g., benzodiazepines) and thereby are drugs with the potential for treating anxiety, insomnia, and epilepsy.

Three glutamate receptors have been identified: the N-methyl-D-aspartate (NMDA) receptor, the quisqualate receptor, and the kainate receptor. All three receptor types appear to be linked to ion channels that allow the passage of cations into the neuron. The NMDA receptor is linked to an ion channel that preferentially allows the calcium ion to enter the neuron. As part of the NMDA receptor-calcium channel complex, a region binds glycine, another amino acid. The binding of glycine increases the affinity of the glutamate receptor for glutamate. It is of clinical interest that the specific binding site for phencyclidine (PCP) is within the calcium channel associated with the glutamate receptor. The binding of PCP within this channel prevents the entrance of calcium into the neuron.

PEPTIDES

Over 100 neuroactive peptides have been identified (Table 3.3-1), and some investigators have suggested that as many as 300 different neuroactive peptides may exist. A peptide is a short protein consisting of fewer than 100 amino acids. Peptides are made in the neuronal cell body by the transcription and translation of a genetic message coded on deoxyribonucleic acid (DNA) (Figure 3.3-7). This contrasts with the biogenic amines and amino acids, which are synthesized in the nerve terminals by the actions of enzymes on appropriate substrates. Once synthesized, the peptide neurotransmitters are transported down the neuronal axons and stored in synaptic vesicles within the nerve terminals. The peptide neurotransmitters are released by a calcium-dependent mechanism and bind to peptide-specific receptors. These peptide receptors function in a manner very similar to biogenic amine receptors.

Table 3.3-1
Selected CNS Neuroactive Peptides

Adrenocorticotropic hormone
Androgens
Angiotensin I, II, and III
Bombesin
Bradykinin
Calcitonin
Cardioexcitatory peptide
Carnosine
Cholecystokinin
Corticotropin-releasing hormone
Cortisol
Endogenous opioids
Estrogens
Follicle-stimulating hormone
Gastrin
Gastrin-inhibiting peptide
Glucagon
Gonadotropin-releasing hormone
Growth hormone
Growth hormone-releasing factor
Insulin
Luteinizing hormone
Melanocyte-inhibiting factor
Melanocyte-stimulating hormone
Melatonin
Motilin
Neural growth factor
Neuronal polypeptide
Neuropeptide Y
Neurotensin
Oxytocin
Progesterone
Prolactin
Secretin
Sleep-inducing peptide
Somatostatin
Substance K
Substance P
Thyroid hormones
Thyroid-stimulating hormone
Thyrotropin-releasing hormone
Vasoactive intestinal peptide
Vasopressin

tricyclic antidepressants (except desipramine [Norpramin]) acutely block serotonin reuptake. L-Tryptophan affects the serotonergic system by supplying more of the amino acid precursor, thereby pushing the pathway to synthesize more serotonin. L-Tryptophan has been used both as a hypnotic and as an antidepressant.

The Food and Drug Administration (FDA) has requested all manufacturers of the dietary supplement L-tryptophan to remove these products from the marketplace voluntarily because of a strong link between the consumption of L-tryptophan and eosinophilia-myalgia syndrome, a rare blood disease. Evidence suggests that the syndrome is caused by a chemical constituent introduced in the manufacturing process.

Two new drugs—fluoxetine (Prozac) and clozapine (Clozaril)—are thought to have their major effects on serotonergic systems. Fluoxetine is an effective antidepressant that specifically blocks serotonin reuptake. Clozapine is an effective antipsychotic that has unique clinical properties of not causing extrapyramidal symptoms and probably not causing tardive dyskinesia. Clozapine is an extremely weak dopamine D_2 receptor antagonist and is only a very weak dopamine D_1 receptor antagonist. Although its mechanism of action is not definitely known, one hypothesis is that clozapine acts as an antagonist of a serotonin receptor.

Serotonin and psychopathology. Serotonin has been implicated in mood disorders, anxiety disorders (including obsessive-compulsive disorder), violence, and schizophrenia. The acute effects of TCAs and MAOIs to increase the availability of serotonin (and norepinephrine) in the synaptic cleft led to the inclusion of serotonin in the monoamine hypothesis of mood disorders. Imipramine-binding sites (a neurochemical label of serotonin reuptake sites) in platelets have been reported to be decreased in depressed patients and in the postmortem brains of patients who committed suicide. The involvement of serotonin in violence is supported by findings of decreased concentrations of CSF 5-HIAA in patients with anxiety disorders and suicide attempts. The major reason to suspect dysregulation of serotonin in schizophrenia was data that suggested that the serotonergic synapse was the primary site of action for lysergic acid diethylamide (LSD). Both the complexity of the biochemical actions of LSD and the dissimilarity between LSD-induced and schizophrenic symptoms argue against this hypothesis.

Acetylcholine

Central nervous system cholinergic tracts. In humans, there is a group of cholinergic neurons in the nucleus basalis of Meynert that project to the cerebral cortex and the limbic system. These neurons degenerate in some patients with dementing conditions, including Alzheimer's disease, Down's syndrome, and Parkinson's disease. There is also a group of cholinergic neurons in the reticular system that project to the cerebral cortex, the limbic system, the hypothalamus, and the thalamus.

Cholinergic synapse. The cholinergic terminal synthesizes acetylcholine from acetylcoenzme A (acetyl-CoA) and choline by the enzyme acetyltransferase. Once acetylcholine is released, it interacts with its receptors and is then degraded to choline and acetate by acetylcholinesterase. The choline is taken back up into the presynaptic nerve terminal, where it can be resynthesized into acetylcholine.

Cholinergic receptors. The two types of cholinergic receptors are nicotinic and muscarinic, which have a selective preference for nicotinic and muscarinic drugs, respectively. Muscarinic receptors are antagonized by atropine, and nicotinic receptors are antagonized by *d*-tubocurarine.

Acetylcholine and psychotropics. Anticholinergic drugs are used to treat the parkinsonian side effects of antipsychotics. Many psychotropics (especially low-potency antipsychotics and TCAs) block muscarinic receptors, thereby causing the side effects of blurred vision, dry mouth, constipation, and difficulty in initiating urination. Excessive blockade of CNS cholinergic receptors causes confusion and delirium. This condition is seen when patients take illicit drugs laced with scopolamine or when a patient is treated simultaneously with too many drugs with anticholinergic effects (e.g., thioridazine [Mellaril], amitriptyline, and benztropine [Cogentin]).

Acetylcholine and psychopathology. Cholinergic pathophysiology has been implicated in movement disorders (e.g., Parkinson's disease, Huntington's chorea, and tardive dyskinesia) because of the effectiveness of cholinergic agents in treating some of these conditions. The degeneration of cholinergic neurons in the nucleus basalis of Meynert has prompted the hypothesis that such degeneration is a specific pathology for dementia. Acetylcholine has been implicated in the pathophysiology of mood and sleep disorders, with an overactivity of cholinergic pathways suggested to be involved in depression.

Histamine

Histaminergic cells are found in the hypothalamus and project to the cerebral cortex, the limbic system, and the thalamus. Histamine receptors have been divided into two classes; however, an H_3 receptor has recently been discovered. H_1 receptors act through adenylate cyclase, guanylate cyclase, and phosphatidylinositol. H_1 receptor blockade is the mechanism of action for allergy medications and also contributes to the psychotropic-induced side effects of sedation, weight gain, and hypotension. H_2 receptors activate adenylate cyclase. Doxepin, a tricyclic antidepressant, is a powerful blocker of histamine receptors and has been used, like cimetidine (Tagamet), to treat peptic ulcer disease.

AMINO ACIDS

In addition to being the structural building blocks of proteins, amino acids have many roles in intraneuronal metabolism. Amino acids function as neurotransmitters similar to the function of biogenic amines. An amino acid is involved as a neurotransmitter in 60 to 70 percent of the synapses in the brain. The best-studied amino acid neurotransmitters are γ-aminobutyric acid (GABA), an inhibitory amino acid neurotransmitter, and glutamate, an excitatory amino acid neurotransmitter. Other inhibitory amino acids are glycine and probably taurine and β-ala-

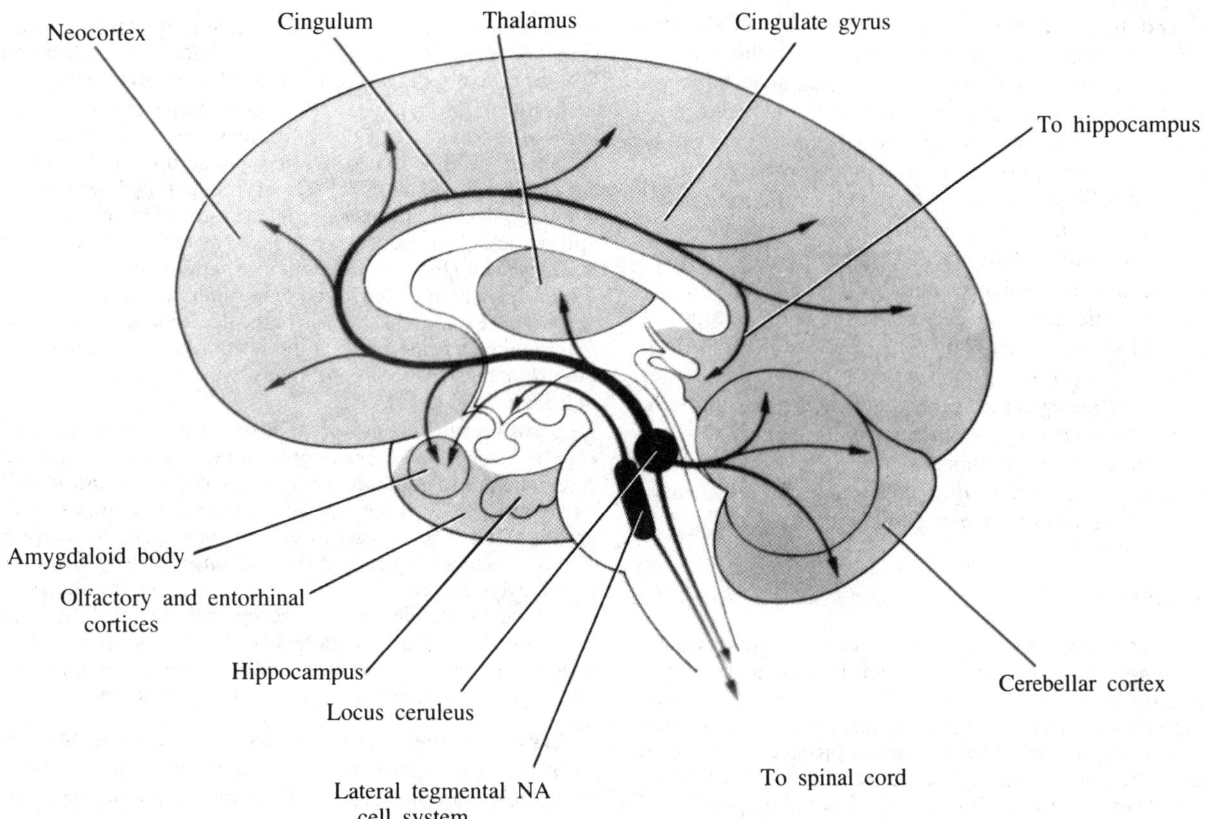

Figure 3.3-5. Noradrenergic pathways. The locus ceruleus, which is located immediately underneath the floor of the fourth ventricle in the rostrolateral part of pons, is the most important noradrenergic nucleus in the brain. Its projections reach many areas in the forebrain, the cerebellum, and the spinal cord. Noradrenergic neurons in the lateral brain stem tegmentum innervate several structures in the basal forebrain including the hypothalamus and the amygdaloid body. (From L Heimer: *The Human Brain and Spinal Cord.* Springer, New York, 1983, with permission.)

Adrenergic (epinephrine-containing) neurons are much rarer and less well studied than noradrenergic neurons.

Noradrenergic (adrenergic) synapse. The noradrenergic terminal uses the same enzymes to make dopamine as the dopaminergic neuron. The noradrenergic neuron, however, contains dopamine-β-carboxylase, which converts dopamine into norepinephrine. Norepinephrine is converted to epinephrine by phenylethanolamine-N-methyltransferase (PNMT) in adrenergic neurons. Norepinephrine is taken up and stored in synpatic vesicles, a process that is blocked by reserpine. Norepinephrine is released when the synaptic vesicle fuses with the presynpatic membrane. Once in the synaptic cleft, norepinephrine interacts with noradrenergic receptors. The metabolic steps for norepinephrine are similar to those for dopamine; the most significant metabolic product from CNS norepinephrine is 3-methoxy-4-hydroxyphenylglycol (MHPG).

Noradrenergic receptors. The two classes of noradrenergic receptors are α and β. Alpha$_1$ receptors are postsynaptic, and α_2 receptors are both postsynaptic and presynaptic. It is clinically useful to know that presynaptic α_2 receptors are more sensitive than postsynaptic α_1 receptors to α-adrenergic agonists. At least three subtypes each of both the α_1 and α_2 receptors have been described. β_1 and β_2 receptors are located postsynaptically. It is currently believed that β receptors are the primary receptors for locus ceruleus input. A β-subtype has recently been reported in the basic neuroscience literature.

Norepinephrine and psychotropics. Both the tricylcic antidepressants (TCAs) and the monoamine oxidase inhibitors (MAOIs) affect the noradrenergic system. The acute effect of TCAs is to block reuptake of norepinephrine and serotonin; the acute effect of MAOIs is to block the metabolism of norepinephrine and serotonin. Thus, both antidepressants acutely increase the concentrations of these biogenic amines in the synaptic cleft. The acute effects of both antidepressants (but especially the tertiary TCAs—doxepin [Sinequan], amitriptyline [Elavil], and imipramine [Tofranil]) and many antipsychotics include the blockade of α_1 receptors, causing sedation and postural hypotension. A unique side effect of MAOIs occurs when a patient being treated with these drugs eats tyramine-rich food, thereby promoting an adrenergic surge that can result in a life-threatening hypertensive crisis.

Two other drugs of interest are clonidine (Catapres) and propranolol (Inderal). Clonidine is an alpha-agonist, which selectively stimulates presynaptic α_2 receptors. Clonidine has been used with partial success in a variety of neuropsychiatric disorders, including opiate withdrawal. Propranolol is one of a class of β-blocking drugs; in addition to being antihypertensive, these drugs have been reported to be clinically useful in treating lithium-induced tremor, social phobias, and akathisia.

Norepinephrine and mood disorders. The major hypothesis regarding norepinephrine is the monoamine hypothesis of mood disorders, which states that depression is the result of too little noradrenergic or serotonergic activity and that this activity is increased by TCAs and MAOIs. There are three major problems with this original hypothesis: (1) there is a three- to four-week delay between the acute biochemical effects of increasing synaptic norepinephrine and serotonin and the clinical effects of reduced depression; (2) some drugs that are potent reuptake blockers (e.g., cocaine) are not effective antidepressants; and (3) newly developed antidepressants that have no reuptake blockade activity or MAOI-like activity are clinically effective as antidepressants. A recent theory is that the therapeutic effect of all antidepressant treatments (TCAs, MAOIs, electroconvulsive therapy [ECT], sleep deprivation) is produced by a decrease in the number or sensitivity of postsynaptic β receptors and presynaptic α_2 receptors and, possibly, an increase in sensitivity to serotonin. These receptor changes are seen approximately three weeks after initiation of treatment, thereby correlating with the time course of clinical improvement.

Serotonin

Central nervous system serotonergic tracts. Serotonergic neurons have their cell bodies in the upper pons and the midbrain—specifically, the median and dorsal raphe nuclei, caudal locus ceruleus, area postrema, and interpeduncular area. These neurons project to the basal ganglia, the limbic system, and the cerebral cortex (Figure 3.3-6). These neurons also project down the spinal cord and modulate the transmission of sensory pain input. These spinal cord tracts may be the site of action for serotonergic antidepressants that have been used to control pain.

Serotonergic synapse. The serotonergic terminal is similar to the terminals of the catecholamines. The amino acid precursor tryptophan is converted into serotonin (also called 5-hydroxytryptamine [5-HT]) by tryptophan hydroxylase and an amino acid decarboxylase. The serotonin is stored in synaptic vesicles, a process that is blocked by reserpine. Serotonin is released into the synaptic cleft on synaptic stimulation. Once inside the synaptic cleft, serotonin binds to serotonergic receptors. The major mechanism of the deactivation of serotonin is reuptake into the presynaptic terminals. Serotonin is metabolized by MAO (preferentially type A) to 5-hydroxyindoleacetic acid (5-HIAA).

Serotonergic receptors. The delineation of serotonin receptors has become exceedingly complex as a result of recent research, and a finalized system has yet to be introduced. There are at least three types of serotonin receptors—S_1, S_2, and S_3. There are at least three subtypes of the S_1 receptor. The S_{1A} receptor is coupled through an inhibitory G protein to adenylyl cyclase and is the site of action for the novel anxiolytic buspirone. The S_2 receptor is coupled to phosphoinositol turnover. In contrast to the S_1 and S_2 receptors, which are G-linked receptor proteins, the S_3 receptor is a ligand-gated ion channel for positively charged ions (cations).

Serotonin and psychotropics. Catecholamines and serotonin are interrelated. Antidepressants, for example, affect both noradrenergic and serotonergic synapses. Most

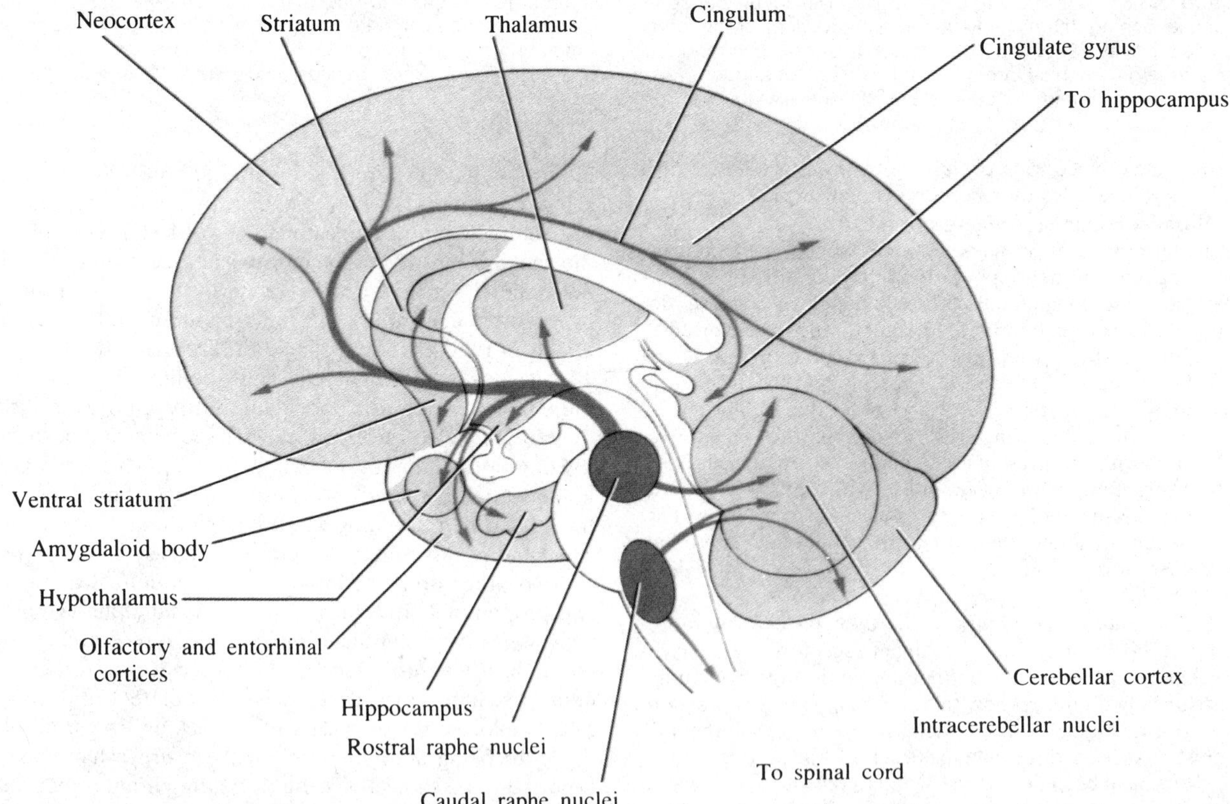

Figure 3.3-6. Serotonergic pathways. The raphe nuclei form a more or less continuous collection of cell groups close to the midline throughout the brain stem, but, for the sake of simplicity, they have been subdivided into a rostral group and a caudal group in the drawing. The rostral raphe nuclei project to a large number of forebrain structures. The fibers that project laterally through the internal and external capsules to widespread areas of the neocortex are not indicated in this highly schematic drawing. (From L Heimer: *The Human Brain and Spinal Cord.* Springer, New York, 1983, with permission.)

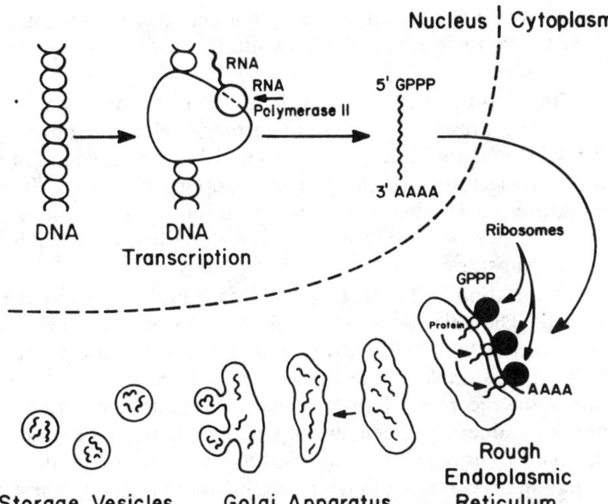

Figure 3.3-7. Sequence of neuropeptide synthesis. Within the nucleus, the gene for the precursor neuropeptide is transcribed into mRNA. The mRNA is transported from the nucleus into the cytoplasm, where it binds to ribosomes. The mRNA is then translated by protein synthesis on the ribosomes in the rough endoplasmic reticulum. Within the Golgi apparatus, the precursor peptide is enzymatically modified to yield the neuropeptide, which is packaged in storage vesicles for axoplasmic transport to the nerve terminal. (From J T Coyle: Neuroscience and psychiatry. In *The American Psychiatric Press Textbook of Psychiatry,* J A Talbott, R E Hales, and S C Yudofsky, editors, p 9. American Psychiatric Press, Washington DC, 1988, with permission.)

For example, the receptor for one peptide—substance K—has been shown to have the same basic structure as the β-adrenergic receptor and to be coupled to a G protein. Once peptides are released, their action is terminated by degradative peptidases in the synaptic cleft.

There are several regulatory points in the synthesis of peptide neurotransmitters. Both the transcription of the DNA message for a peptide into a ribonucleic acid (RNA) message and the translation of the RNA message into a protein are regulated. *Differential RNA processing* of the RNA first transcribed from the DNA (heterogeneous nuclear RNA [hnRNA]) can result in different messenger RNA (mRNA) species, which are then translated into different proteins. For example, because of differential RNA processing, expression of the same preprotachykinin gene results in the synthesis of substance K in some neurons and substance P in others. Research has demonstrated other mechanisms by which one gene can code from more than one peptide. Specifically, the first protein translated from the mRNA is often a *preprohormone,* which is then broken down by proteases into a *prohormone,* which is further modified by proteases or glycosylases to become the final form of one or more hormones or peptides.

Peptide neurotransmitters often coexist in a neuron with biogenic amine neurotransmitters. It has yet to be demonstrated whether there is a differential regulation of the release of such coexisting neurotransmitters.

Selected Peptide Neurotransmitters

Endogenous opioids. The endogenous opioids are a large family of peptide neurotransmitters. There are three subgroups of opioid peptides, which are derived from three different precursor prohormones. Proenkephalin is the precursor hormone for metenkephalin, leuenkephalin, and other opioids. Proopiomelanocortin is the precursor hormone for endorphins and for several nonopioid peptides, adrenocorticotrophic hormone (ACTH), and several melanocyte stimulating hormones (MSHs). Prodynorphoin is the precursor hormone for the dynorphins and neoendorphins. Once released into the synaptic cleft, the endogenous opioids are metabolized by a family of enkephalinases. There are at lease five receptor subtypes for the endogenous opioids—delta (δ), kappa (κ), xi (ξ), epsilon (ϵ) and mu (μ). Endogenous opioids are involved in the regulation of stress and pain. There is some evidence that the opioids are also involved in the normal homeostatic regulation of mood.

Hypothalamic hormones. Many hypothalamic hormones (e.g., ACTH, thyrotropin-releasing hormone [TRH], and gonadotropin-releasing hormone [GnRH]) are found in neurons outside the hypothalamus. In these extrahypothalamic neurons, the peptides act as neurotransmitters. There are two lessons to be learned from these observations. First, peptides are usually named for the function for which they are first identified. These same peptides may exist elsewhere in the nervous system, where they are involved in the regulation of a completely different function. For example, ACTH that exists in extrahypothalamic neurons may have nothing to do with the regulation of the cortisol axis. Second, the same peptide may function as a hormone in one setting and as a neurotransmitter in another. For example, vasopressin is a hormone when secreted by the hypothalamus and the pituitary, but it also functions as a classical neurotransmitter when released from other neurons.

Cholecystokinin (CCK). CCK has been reported to coexist with GABA and dopamine, thereby implying a potential pathophysiological role in schizophrenia. CCK has also been implicated in eating and movement disorders.

Neurotensin. This peptide coexists with dopamine and norepinephrine and may be a modulator of dopaminergic neurotransmission. It has been postulated, therefore, that neurotensin is involved in the pathophysiology of schizophrenia.

Somatostatin. Somatostatin has been strongly implicated by postmortem studies in the pathophysiology of Huntington's chorea and Alzheimer's disease. Clinical studies have also suggested a role for somatostatin in mood disorders.

Substance P. Substance P coexists with acetylcholine and serotonin; it appears to be the primary neurotransmitter in many primary afferent sensory neurons and in the striatonigral pathway. Substance P neurotransmission, therefore, has been suggested as a possible pathological mechanism underlying pain syndromes, movement disorders (particularly Huntington's chorea), and mood disorders.

Vasopressin. Vasopressin may modulate the effects of norepinephrine and potentially may be involved in mood disorders. Parallel to ACTH and corticotropin-releasing hormone (CRH), vasopressin has an independent role as a neurotransmitter in addition to its role in the hypothalmic-posterior pituitary axis.

PSYCHOENDOCRINOLOGY, PSYCHOIMMUNOLOGY, AND CHRONOBIOLOGY

Three systems in the body are designed so that different parts of each system can mutually communicate with other parts—the nervous, endocrine, and immune systems. All three systems change in both predictable and unpredictable fashions with the passage of time and are responsive to changes in the environment. The study of the periodic variation of biological functions of the body is known as chronobiology.

The actions of the endocrine and immune systems are relevant to psychiatry. Both endocrine disorders (e.g., Cushing's disease) and immune disorders (e.g., systemic lupus erythematosus) can have neuropsychiatric symptoms—even as the presenting symptoms. Conversely, endocrine and immunological abnormalities are seen in psychiatric disorders.

Psychoendocrinology

Psychoendocrinology studies the interactions between the nervous system and the endocrine system. The neuroendocrine axes can be conceptualized as starting in the hypothalamus, where they receive input from the cerebral cortex and the limbic system. Various types of hormonal messengers (e.g., CRH) are relayed from the hypothalamus to the pituitary. Many of these hormones then stimulate or inhibit the secretion of additional types of hormones (e.g., ACTH from specific pituitary cells). These pituitary hormones can then circulate in the peripheral circulation, from which they can then stimulate peripheral organs to secrete yet other hormones (e.g., cortisol). The hormones from each level of this axis can feed back onto any of the higher levels, which usually results in the inhibition of the axis.

Anterior pituitary. The hypothalamus transmits releasing factors and release-inhibiting factors to the anterior pituitary. Some axes have only releasing hormones, some have only release-inhibiting hormones, and some have both. CRH stimulates the release of ACTH from pituitary corticotrophs; ACTH stimulates the release of cortisol from the adrenal gland. TRH stimulates the release of thyrotropin or thyroid-stimulating hormone (TSH) from the pituitary thyrotrophs; TSH stimulates the release of thyroid hormones from the thyroid glands. Luteinizing hormone—follicle-stimulating-hormone-releasing hormone (LH—FSH-RH) stimulates the release of luteinizing hormone (LH) and follicle-stimulating hormone (FSH) from the pituitary gonadotrophs. LH and FSH are involved in the stimulation and maintenance of the gonads and in the regulation of estrogen and testosterone secretion. Prolactin release-inhibiting hormone is actually dopamine and inhibits the release of prolactin from the pituitary lactotrophs. One adverse effect of antipsychotic drugs is abnormal lactation associated with high prolactin levels. This is caused by the blockade of the pituitary dopamine receptors, which results in no inhibition of prolactin release. Two other axes in the anterior pituitary are the growth hormone (GH) and MSH axes, which are regulated by both releasing and release-inhibiting hormones.

Posterior pituitary. Vasopressin (also called antidiuretic hormone) and oxytocin are synthesized in both the supraoptic and paraventricular nuclei. Vasopressin is involved with the control of blood pressure and fluid and electrolyte balance. Its release is stimulated by pain, stress, morphine, and barbiturates and is inhibited by alcohol. Oxytocin, released in the female by suckling, stimulates glandular contraction in the breast. Oxytocin also stimulates uterine contractions during delivery.

Pineal body. The pineal body contains many peptides (e.g., vasopressin, luteinizing hormone-releasing hormone [LHRH]) in addition to its principal hormone, melatonin, which is secreted in the dark and suppressed in the light. Melatonin is synthesized from serotonin by the actions of two enzymes: serotonin-N-acetylase and 5-hydroxyindole-O-methyltransferase.

Regulation and testing of neuroendocrine interactions. The release of hypothalamic and pituitary peptides and hormones is affected by biogenic amine neurotransmitters; one example is the interaction between estrogens and dopamine receptors. Estrogens have mixed dopaminergic and antidopaminergic effects in the CNS. Although estrogens do not bind to dopamine receptors, they increase the number of dopamine receptors and decrease the amount of dopamine in the nigrostriatal, mesolimbic, and tuberoinfundibular pathways. The coadministration of antipsychotics and estrogens has an additive effect on the increase in dopamine receptor number. These interactions are reflected clinically. Tardive dyskinesia is more frequent in women than in men, with a higher prevalence in postmenopausal women. The concomitant use of estrogen-containing birth control pills and antipsychotics increases the incidence of antipsychotic-induced motor system symptoms. In female parkinsonian patients, L-dopa–induced dyskinesias improve with estrogens, and chorea has been reported as a complication of both pregnancy and birth control pills.

Endocrine assessment. There are two basic approaches to assessing neuroendocrine function: to measure baseline or resting values of various peptides and hormones and to challenge the axis with some stimulus. Each level of the axis can be challenged, and, when the assays are available, the response of different levels of the axis can be measured. Psychological stress (e.g., taking an examination) can challenge the suprahypothalamic areas. Insulin-induced hypoglycemia is believed to represent a fairly pure hypothalamic challenge. The pituitary can be challenged by the administration of exogenous releasing and inhibiting peptides, and the peripheral glands can be challenged by the administration of exogenous trophic hormones. Many factors can affect the results of these tests, including alcohol withdrawal, administration of other drugs (including some psychotropics), malnutrition (as is seen in anorexia nervosa), and especially pharmacokinetic differences among persons regarding the metabolism of the administered hormones.

Psychiatric abnormalities in endocrine disorders. Classic psychiatric symptoms are observed in many endocrine syndromes. Cushing's syndrome (hyperadrenalism) involves psychiatric symptoms in 40 to 90 percent of patients. The most commonly seen symptom is depression, and suicide attempts occur in approximately 10 percent of patients. The administration of endogenous steroids (e.g., ACTH for multiple sclerosis) also causes depression and is associated with hypomania, emotional lability, and even psychosis. Addison's disease (hypoadrenalism) involves depression in approximately 40 percent of patients; apathy, fatigue, and occasionally psychosis characterize its symptoms. Although anxiety is the hallmark of hyperthyroidism, apathetic hyperthyroidism, characterized by depression, can be seen in elderly patients. Hypothyroidism is most commonly associated with depression and some anxiety. Some female patients with autoimmune thyroiditis may present with only symptoms of depression. Both hyperparathyroidism and hypoglycemia are associated with anxiety and depression.

Endocrine dysregulation in psychiatric syndromes. Third ventricle enlargement has been noted in some schizophrenic patients and suggests lesions in the surrounding hypothalamus may be involved in the pathophysiology of schizophrenia. Such lesions cause endocrine dysregulation, and research data indicate a dysregulation of the gonadal, growth hormone, and adrenal axes in these patients. Some patients with mood disorders show dysregulation in the adrenal, thyroid, and growth hormone axes. There is an interesting conceptual continuum between endocrine disorders and mood disorders. As an example of this continuum, both Cushing's syndrome and depression have dysregulations of the adrenal axis. Whether a disease process is diagnosed as a psychiatric disorder or an endocrine disorder, for example, may depend more on whether a particular person has more marked behavioral or more hormonal abnormalities than on any fundamental differences in the disease processes.

Psychoimmunology

The basic function of the immune system is to remove pathogens from the body without damaging the body itself. The erythema, swelling, and pain around an infection are examples of how the immune system, on the verge of damaging the body, eliminates an infecting organism. In more serious dysregulations of the immune system, overactivity can result in autoimmune diseases (e.g., myasthenia gravis, systemic lupus erythematosus), allergies, and anaphylaxis; underactivity (e.g., acquired immune deficiency syndrome [AIDS]) can result in cancer or serious infections. The immune system reciprocally interacts with the nervous and endocrine systems. Psychiatric conditions are associated with abnormalities in the immune system, but it is not known whether immunological dysfunction in psychiatric conditions is the result or is involved in the causality of the psychiatric disorder. The immune system can be involved in the pathogenesis of psychiatric disorders by allowing a neurotoxic virus to infect the brain, by interfering with normal endocrine function either by damaging endocrine tissue or by releasing chemical messengers, or by damaging brain tissue itself (e.g., an autoimmune reaction against a certain class of receptors).

Neural regulation of immunity. Animal studies have shown that lesions of the hypothalamus, the hippocampus, and the pituitary all result in fairly specific dysfunctions of the immune system. The principal neurochemical messengers for this regulation are thought to be norepinephrine, β-endorphin, metenkephalin, and cortisol. Increased immune function has been correlated with a decrease in norepinephrine in the hypothalamus (presumably functioning as an inhibitory neurotransmitter) and an increase in cell firing (measured by implanted electrodes). The lymphocytes can communicate back to the brain through the release of chemical messengers, including ACTH, β-endorphin, and unique lymphyocyte-secreted chemicals.

Stress. Studies of animals in experimentally designed stressful situations demonstrate a decrease in lymphocyte number, a decreased proliferation in response to stimulation, and a reduction in the production of antibodies. Although true for animals in experimental paradigms of inescapable stress (e.g., foot shock without anywhere to go), these immune responses are not found in animals that have a way to stop the stressful stimulus. It has also been found that infant monkeys taken away from their mothers exhibit similar immune system dysfunction.

Conditioning. A series of experiments with different animal models have demonstrated that immunosuppression can be conditioned, so that, on receiving a nonbiologically relevant stimulus (e.g., bell ringing), the animal's immune response is suppressed. One of these experiments paired a conditioned stimulus (a sweet drinking solution) with an unconditioned stimulus (an immunosuppressive drug). Once conditioned, the animal, when exposed to a previously stimulating antigen in the presence of the conditioned stimulus, exhibited a blunted immune response. Therefore, the possibility exists that patients with autoimmune disorders can learn to suppress their immune response through conditioning or behavior modification. Another series of animal experiments have suggested that the left side of the brain is involved in the stimulation of the immune response and that the role of the right hemisphere is to inhibit the left hemisphere. These data may be consistent with observations that left-handed persons are more prone to autoimmune disorders than are right-handed persons.

Psychiatric abnormalities in immune disorders. The classic immune disorder that presents with psychiatric manifestations is systemic lupus erythematosus (SLE). Between 5 and 50 percent of SLE patients have psychiatric symptoms at initial presentation, and approximately 50 percent of patients eventually develop neuropsychiatric manifestations. The major symptoms are depression, insomnia, emotional lability, nervousness, and confusion. Treatment with steroids commonly induces further psychiatric complications, including mania and psychosis. The pathophysiological mechanism by which SLE causes neuropsychiatric symptoms is not known.

Immunological abnormalities in psychiatric patients. At least two studies have investigated T-cell proliferation in bereaved spouses and have reported a decreased proliferation around one to two months following the death of the spouse. Stress in college students has been reported to correspond to a decrease in natural killer cell activity. Those students who have poor coping skills or who complain of loneliness are most likely to show the abnormality. Patients with major depression also have been reported to have decreased T-cell proliferation and an overall decrease in the number of lymphocytes. Although cortisol hypersecretion could explain these findings, there is evidence that the endocrine, immune, and nervous systems are mutually interactive and that it is not possible to draw a one-way, cause-and-effect arrow between hypercortisolemia and impaired immune function.

Schizophrenia may also be associated with immunological abnormalities, perhaps supporting a viral hypothesis of schizophrenia. Various reports have found abnormal-looking lymphocytes, decreased numbers of natural killer cells, variations in T- and B-cell function and number, and high and low levels of immunoglobulins. It is possible either that an infection results in an abnormal immune response or that an abnormal immune system allows an infection to develop. Other schizophrenia researchers have investigated the hypothesis that the disorder represents an autoimmune phenomenon caused by antibrain antibodies. This research is supported by increased skin reactivity to intradermal test antigens and by reports of antibodies to brain proteins in the CSF from some patients with schizophrenia.

Chronobiology

Chronobiology objectively explores and quantifies mechanisms of time structure in biological systems; it is the study of biological rhythms. There are rhythms in endocrine secretion, neurotransmitter synthesis, receptor number, enzyme levels and affinities, brain electrical activity, weights of body organs, duration of cell cycle times, and ultrastructural components of cellular organelles. These rhythms can have different cycle lengths—less than a day (infradian), approximately 24 hours (circadian), more than one day (ultradian), approximately one week (circaseptan), approximately one month, and approximately one year (circannual).

There are multiple biological rhythms in a living organism. In a human, for example, these rhythms include the sleep-wake cycle, hormone levels, body temperature, and the menstrual cycle. When all these rhythms are in correct or normal relationship to one another, the rhythms of the organism are said to be in phase. In disease states, however, one or more rhythms may be out of phase. A biological rhythm may have an abnormal *phase advance,* in which it begins earlier than usual, or a *phase delay,* in which it begins later than usual. Under experimental conditions, a phase-response curve for a biological rhythm may show whether a particular stimulation (e.g., light) causes either a phase advance or a phase delay when it is delivered at different times in the cycle (e.g., sleep-wake cycle).

Zeitgebers (time givers, time clues, synchronizers) entrain or set the biological rhythms. The principal *endogenous* zeitgeber is believed to be the suprachiasmatic nuclei of the hypothalamus. Examples of *exogenous* zeitgebers include the light-dark cycle, patterned mealtimes, and the nine-to-five work day. In the absence of exogenous clues, the period of human circadian rhythms is a bit longer than a day—24.5 hours. The implications of these rhythms include the likelihood that the response to drugs varies with time of day, that the response to environmental stress varies with time, and that biological measures themselves vary with time. Information about chronobiology could guide such decisions as when it is best to perform surgery and when it is best to give psychotropic or pain medications.

Chronobiological considerations in psychiatry. The most common and normal perturbation of chronobiology is the phenomenon of jet lag, usually presenting with fatigue and dysphoric mood. When people travel from east to west, they experience a phase delay, not a large problem because the body actually wants a slightly longer (24.5 hours) day. Traveling west to east, however, presents a phase advance that opposes the natural tendency and particularly disrupts biological rhythms. The subjective discomfort of a phase advance may be further influenced by variations in the time taken by different biological rhythms to adjust to the new schedule of exogenous clues. Shift work, including the difficult hours of interns and residents, also disrupts biological rhythms.

One theory of depression is that it represents a phase-advance disorder, as evidenced by early morning awakening, decreased latency of rapid eye movement (REM) sleep, and neuroendocrine perturbations. One hypothesis is that depression occurs in some persons when the sleep-sensitive phase of the circadian system advances from the first hours of awakening to the last hours of sleep. There is also a group of patients who appear to have a seasonal affective disorder (SAD), also called seasonal mood disorder, with the occurrence of fatigue, oversleeping, overeating, and depression during winter. These patients are often women and relatively young (in their 20s), but this disorder may also appear in some children presenting with school problems. There is research evidence that alterations in the light-dark cycle for these patients, either by prolonged exposure to artificial light or by changing the patients' sleep-wake cycles, can relieve the symptoms. The observation that lithium and many of the TCAs and MAOIs delay rhythms in experimental animal models supports the hypothesis that depression is a phase-advance disorder.

GENETICS

Two aims of investigations in population genetics are to demonstrate the existence and relative contribution of hereditary influences on a disorder and to determine the mode of inheritance of these influences. See Table 3.3-2 for a listing of commonly used terms in genetics.

Family Risk Studies

Family risk studies compare the prevalence of a psychiatric condition among relatives of the affected persons with its prevalence in the general population. Affected persons in the original group of patients are called index cases or probands. For a genetic illness, first-degree relatives (mother, father, siblings) are more likely to have the disorder of the proband than are more distant relatives.

Twin Studies

Monozygotic (MZ) twins develop from a single ovum, whereas dizygotic (DZ) twins develop from two different ova and share, on the average, no more genetic information than nontwin siblings. Twin studies are useful for separating genetic and environmental influences and for looking at protective and precipitating factors. A genetic disorder should occur (e.g., be concordant) in MZ twins more often than in DZ twins. The DZ concordance rate, moreover, should be quite similar to that for nontwin siblings. Futhermore, for a genetic illness, first-degree relatives should be more likely to have the disorder of the proband than more distant relatives.

Adoption Studies

Adoption studies attempt to assess what effect the environment has on the expression of genes. In studies using the *adoptees family method,* the biological and adoptive parents of affected adopted probands are compared with the biological and adoptive parents of unaffected adopted control subjects. If adoptive parents of affected probands have a higher rate of the disorder under study than the adoptive parents of unaffected controls, then the family environment is implicated in the development of the disorder. If biological parents of af-

Table 3.3-2
Glossary of Genetic Terms

Age correction procedure: A statistical procedure used in genetic studies of families that takes into account the fact that different psychiatric diagnoses have different ages of onset.

Allele (allelomorph): Alternative form of a gene. There may be many alleles for a given gene, but each person possesses only two alleles for each gene, receiving one of each pair of alleles from each parent. A person with a pair of similar alleles is a homozygote; one with a dissimilar pair is a heterozygote.

Amniography: Opacification of amniotic fluid by injecting radiopaque material in order to visualize the fetal skeleton and soft tissues more clearly.

Aneuploidy: An irregular number of chromosomes (e.g., 45, 47, or 48 chromosomes in a human being), caused by the loss or addition of one or more chromosomes or parts of chromosomes.

Autoradiography: The process by which a radioactive label is used to identify a specific biological process or material by overlaying with X-ray film and observing exposed areas that usually appear as dots or bands.

Autosomal: Located on or transmitted by an autosome.

Autosome: A chromosome that is not a sex chromosome. A human being has 22 pairs of autosomes.

Barr body: The sex chromatin mass in somatic cells of the female (see Sex chromatin).

Carrier: One who carries a recessive gene, either autosomal or sex-linked, together with its normal allele, but who does not show any clinically detectable effect of the gene (i.e., a heterozygote for a recessive gene).

Centimorgan: The genetic distance in which the probability of a recombination occurring is one percent.

Centromere: The constricted portion of the chromosome, which is the point of attachment to the equatorial plane of the mitotic or meiotic spindle.

Chromatid: A chromosome at prophase and metaphase consists of two strands attached to the centromere. Each strand is a chromatid (see Mitosis).

Chromatin: The substance in cell nuclei and chromosomes that stains intensely with basic dyes and that is composed of DNA combined with proteins. In the fixed intermitotic nucleus, chromatin usually takes the form of an irregular network of long coiled threads, which are gradually condensed into individual chromosomes as the cell undergoes division.

Chromatin-negative: Refers to nuclei that lack the sex chromatin mass, or Barr body. Characteristic of the normal human male.

Chromatin-positive: Refers to nuclei containing the distinctive sex chromatin mass. Characteristic of the normal human female.

Chromosomal aberration (or **abnormality):** A deviation from the normal morphology of chromosomes.

Chromosome: One of a number of small bodies, occurring in pairs, into which the chromatin material of a cell nucleus resolves itself prior to cell division. Chromosomes are visible only during cell division. Homologous chromosomes are the two members of one pair, one of maternal and one of paternal origin. Chromosomes bear the vehicles of hereditary traits, the genes. The morphologic characteristics of the individual chromosomes and their total number are constant for all the somatic cells of a given species. Major chemical components are DNA, RNA, histones, and nonhistone proteins.

Chromosome number: The number of chromosomes found in the somatic cells of an individual or of a species; normally, 46 in a human being.

Clone: A colony of cells that originated from a single cell.

Concordance rate: A measure of the similarity of the presence or absence of a disease or specific trait in pairs of twins.

Congenital: Present at birth; not necessarily genetic.

Consanguinity: Relationship by descent from a common ancestor.

Crossing-over: The exchange of corresponding segments between maternal and paternal homologous chromosomes, occurring when maternal and paternal homologous chromosomes are paired during prophase of the first meiotic division.

Cytogenetics: A branch of genetics dealing with the cytological basis of heredity (i.e., with the study of the chromosomes).

Deoxyribonucleic acid (DNA): The primary storage molecule for genetic information. DNA consists of a long chain of nucleotides, each of which is made up of a deoxyribose (a five-carbon sugar) molecule, a phosphate group, and one of four organic bases—adenine (A), guanine (G), thymine (T), or cytosine (C). The genetic code is contained in the linear array of these organic bases. Each arrangement of three bases (e.g., ACA, GCG) specifies the incorporation of a specific amino acid into a protein molecule.

Diploid: The normal complement of chromosomes (in humans, 22 pairs of homologous chromosomes and the sex chromosomes).

Dizygotic (or **dizygous) twins:** Twins resulting from the simultaneous fertilization of two ova by two spermatozoa. Recurrence in families is common. (*Synonym:* Fraternal twins.)

Dominant gene: A gene that expresses its effect even when it is present on only one chromosome.

Empiric risk: The prediction of the probability that a genetic or congenital abnormality will occur in a family.

Exon: A segment of a gene that is represented in the mature messenger RNA and that codes for a portion of the structure of a protein.

Expressivity: The extent to which a trait is manifested. The kind or degree of phenotypic expression may be slight or pronounced.

Family risk study: Study of the occurrence of a specific disorder in the family members of an identified person, the proband, who has the specific disorder.

Gamete: A male or female reproductive cell; a spermatozoon or ovum.

Gene: A segment of DNA that contains the coding information for a single protein molecule or a limited set of protein molecules.

Gene frequency: Refers to the relative proportion of each of two or more alleles of a particular gene in a given population. The gene frequency may be expressed as a percentage (0 to 100 percent) or as a probability (0 to 1).

Gene marker: Identified chromosomal locus for which the genomic position is known. Gene markers are used in RFLP studies.

Genetic code: The sequential order of the bases of DNA, which carry the genetic information.

Genocopy: Refers to one who shares a trait with another because they have the same gene or genes.

Genome: All the genes found in a diploid set of chromosomes.

Genotype: The full set of genes carried by an individual. The term is sometimes used in a more limited way to refer to the alleles present at one or more loci.

Table 3.3-2
Continued

Haploid: The number of chromosomes in a normal gamete, which contains only one member of each chromosome pair; in a human being, the haploid number is 23.

Hemizygous: Since males have only one X chromosome, they are said to be hemizygous with respect to X-linked genes.

Heritability: A measure of the relative importance of genetic information in the determination of a particular observable feature.

Hermaphrodite: One with both male and female gonadal tissue (not necessarily functional).

Heterologous: Refers to chromosomes or chromosomal segments that are nonhomologous (see Homologous) or nonidentical.

Heterozygote: One possessing differing alleles at a given locus on a pair of homologous chromosomes. (*Adjective:* Heterozygous.)

Homologous: Refers to chromosomes or chromosomal segments that are identical with respect to genetic loci and visible structure; e.g., two normal chromosome 15s. (*Noun:* Homologues.)

Homozygote: One possessing a pair of identical alleles at a given locus on a pair of homologous chromosomes. (*Adjective:* Homozygous).

Inborn error of metabolism: A genetically determined biochemical disorder in which a specific enzyme defect produces a metabolic block that may have pathological consequences.

Incidence: The number of infants born with a condition divided by the number of live births in a given population. (Compare with Prevalence.)

Intron: A segment of a gene that is initially transcribed but then spliced out of the messenger RNA: It is an intervening segment of DNA between two exons.

Isochromosome: A chromosome in which the arms on either side of the centromere are identical.

Karyotype: The full complement of chromosomes; the term covers the number, relative sizes, and morphology of the chromosomes.

Linkage: Genes that have their loci on the same chromosome are said to be linked. Also used to describe traits transmitted by a gene of known locus on a specific chromosome (e.g., see X-linkage).

Locus: The precise location of a gene on a chromosome. Different forms of the gene (alleles)are always found at the same locus on the chromosome.

LOD score: A measure of the probability of genetic linkage between a genetic trait and a polymorphism within a particular pedigree or series of pedigrees. The LOD score ranges from 0.0 to 0.5, with 0.5 representing no linkage.

Meiosis: Nuclear division that occurs during the formation of gametes. Two consecutive cell divisions (the first and second meiotic divisions) occur, but only one division of the chromosomes occurs. Thus, the number of chromosomes is reduced from the diploid (46) to the haploid (23) number. During meiosis, pairing of homologous chromosomes takes place, followed by chromosomal breakage and crossing-over. The end result of meiosis is four cells, each with half the number of chromosomes possessed by the original cell.

Mendelian: Refers to the genetic principles of Gregor Mendel, which included the descriptions of the heritability of dominant and recessive traits.

Metaphase: That stage of cell division (mitosis or meiosis) during which the chromosomes line up on the spindle equatorial plate.

Mitosis: A form of nuclear division in which each chromosome splits lengthwise (**replicates** itself); one chromatid of each chromosome passes to one daughter cell and the other chromatid to the second daughter cell. Thus, each daughter cell receives the full complement of 46 chromosomes. This type of cell division is characteristic of somatic cells and of germ cells before the onset of meiosis.

Mode of inheritance: The pattern of inheritance (e.g., dominant or recessive) of a particular allele.

Monozygotic (or **monozygous) twins:** Twins resulting from the division into two embryos of a single zygote, following fertilization of a single ovum by a single spermatozoon. Recurrence within families is rare. (*Synonym:* Identical or one-egg twins.)

Mosaic: One with two or more cell lines differing in genotype.

Multifactorial inheritance: Inheritance of a trait governed by many genes or multiple factors. Each gene may act independently with cumulative total effect. Height, weight, and other body dimensions are determined by multifactorial inheritance.

Mutation: A permanent heritable change in the genetic material. Mutations are an important source of hereditary diversity.

Mutation rate: The frequency of detectable mutations for a genetic locus in a generation.

Northern hybridization: A research technique involving the hybridization (i.e., annealing) of cDNA probes to mRNA molecules that have been separated by gel electrophoresis and then transferred onto specialized materials (e.g., nitrocellulose membranes).

Oncogene: A gene that encodes a protein that is involved in tumor formation.

Pedigree study: A study of a family that usually includes multiple members of multiple generations. The heritability or lack of heritability of a particular trait can then be studied from one generation to the next and among members of the same generation.

Penetrance: The frequency of phenotypic expression of a dominant gene or a homozygous recessive gene. When a dominant gene produces no detectable phenotypic expression, it shows **lack of penetrance**.

Phenocopy: One with all the hallmarks of a particular genetic disorder but with no hereditary cause apparent in the pedigree or genome.

Phenotype: The total of all observable features of a person (including anatomical, physiological, biochemical, and psychological makeup and disease reactions, potential or actual). The phenotype is the result of interaction between the genotype and the environment. The term may also apply to the trait produced by a single gene or several genes.

Population genetics: The study of mutant genes in populations, rather than in individuals.

Prediction study: A type of family genetic study based on the prospective study of persons who are at high risk (e.g., child of two affected parents) for the development of a specific psychiatric disorder.

Prevalence: The number with a specific condition in a given population.

Proband: The person with an abnormality whose relatives are studied to determine the hereditary or genetic aspects of the trait. (*Synonyms:* Propositus [male]; proposita [female]; index case.)

Probe: A radioactive DNA or RNA sequence used to detect the presence of a complementary sequence by molecular hybridizaiton.

Table 3.3-2
Continued

Prophase: The first stage of cell division, during which the chromosomes become visible as discrete structures.

Recessive: A **trait** or **gene** is recessive if it is expressed only in those who are homozygous (or hemizygous) for the gene concerned.

Recombination: The process by which a pair of homologous chromosomes physically exchange sections, which yields a new combination of genes.

Restriction endonucleases: A family of bacterial enzymes, each of which breaks DNA or RNA at specific base sequences. In bacteria, these enzymes restrict the entry of foreign genetic material (e.g., viruses) that would be harmful.

Restriction fragment length polymorphism (RFLP): Different-length fragments of DNA containing the same site or locus in a chromosome as revealed by exposure of the DNA to restriction endonucleases.

Ribonucleic acid (RNA): A long chain of nucleotides that differ in two ways from the nucleotides of DNA; ribose is the sugar instead of deoxyribose, and uracil is substituted for thymine. Several subtypes of RNA molecules are involved in the process by which the genetic information in DNA is transformed into a specific protein molecule.

Ring chromosome: A circular chromosome resulting from breakage in both arms of a chromatid followed by fusion of the broken ends to form a ring. Varying amounts of chromosomal material are lost or deleted from both arms.

Segregation: The separation of the two alleles of a pair of allelic genes during meiosis, so that they pass to different gametes.

Sex chromatin: A chromatin mass in the nucleus of interphase cells of females. It represents a single X chromosome, which is inactive in the metabolism of the cell. Normal females have sex chromatin, thus are **chromatin-positive;** normal males lack it, hence are **chromatin-negative.** (*Synonym:* Barr body.)

Sex chromosomes: Chromosomes responsible for sex determination (XX in females; XY in males).

Sex-limited: Affecting one sex only.

Sex-linkage: Inheritance by genes on the sex chromosomes, especially on the X chromosomes.

Somatic cell: A nonreproductive cell. Somatic cells are diploid; germ cells are haploid.

Southern blot: A technique for transferring DNA fragments separated by gel electrophoresis onto nitrocellulose paper for molecular hybridization to labeled probes.

State-dependent: Refers to measures that vary with the person's particular clinical status. For example, intoxicated behavior is state-dependent on a person's being intoxicated.

Teratogen: Any agent that causes a physical defect or defects in a developing embryo or fetus.

Trait-dependent: Refers to measures that do not vary with the person's particular clinical status. For example, the genetic marker for Huntington's chorea is present in an affected person both before and after the person has the symptoms of Huntington's chorea.

Transcription: The molecular process by which the genetic code contained in a DNA molecule is used as a template to make a corresponding molecule of RNA.

Translation: The molecular process by which the genetic code contained in an RNA molecule is used as a template to construct a specific protein molecule.

Translocation: A change in location of genetic material, either within a chromosome or from one chromosome to another.

Trisomy: The presence of three, rather than two, chromosomes in a particular set; humans with three sex chromosomes—XXX, XXY, or XYY—are trisomic for the sex chromosomes.

X chromosome: A sex chromosome that occurs singly in the normal male, in duplicate in the normal female.

X-linkage: Transmission of a trait by a gene on the X chromosome.

Y chromosome: A sex chromosome that occurs singly in the normal male but is absent in the normal female.

Table adapted from R Berkow ed: *Merck Manual,* ed 15, p 2161, Merck Sharp & Dohme Research Laboratories, Rahway, NJ, 1987.

fected probands have a higher rate of the disorder under study than the biological parents of unaffected controls, then genetic factors are implicated in the development of the disorder. In the *adoptees study method,* adopted children who had affected parents are studied for the development of the disorder under study. If adopted children develop the disorder more often than a control group, in spite of having adoptive parents, then a genetic factor from the biological parents is implicated. The most powerful version of this study involves MZ twins who are reared apart in different environments—for example, one with adoptive parents and one with biological parents. In the *cross-fostering method,* adopted children of affected biological parents and unaffected adoptive parents are compared with children of unaffected biological parents and affected adoptive parents.

Molecular Genetics

From DNA to proteins. The organism's complete set of genes is referred to as its genome. The human genome consists of 23 pairs of chromosomes; one member of each pair is inherited from each parent. There are 22 pairs of somatic chromosomes and one pair of sex chromosomes (XX for females, XY for males). The chromosomes consist of DNA tightly packed in an organized fashion. In addition, chromosomes contain proteins (histones and nonhistone proteins) that are believed to be involved in the folding and organization of the DNA within the chromosome. The complete set of chromosomes defines the genotype not only of an individual cell but also of every cell in that organism. Each cell, however, expresses only a portion of that genotype to produce its unique characteristics, called its phenotype. A cerebellar Purkinje neuron and a thalamic neuron from a given person, for example, have the same genotype but differ in their phenotypic expressions.

The gene is the unit of functional information on the chromosome. It is easiest to conceptualize a gene as a unit containing the information necessary to produce a functional protein or proteins. The only exception to this concept is that some genes produce either rRNA (ribosomal RNA) or tRNA transfer RNA, both involved in the synthesis of proteins. *Alleles* is the term applied to the multiple alternative states in which a particular gene can exist. For example, the genes for hair color exist in different alleles for brown, blonde, and red.

Application to psychiatric research. The development of recombinant DNA technology, which is synonymous with the concept of genetic engineering, has generated a great deal of excitement in the field of genetics. Both phrases refer to the ability to modify DNA and RNA so that both the messages and the expression of the messages can be manipulated experimentally.

Restriction fragment length polymorphisms (RFLPs). Studies utilizing RFLPs have been successful in identifying chromosome 4 as the site for the genetic defect in Huntington's chorea. Other RFLP studies have suggested chromosome 21 as a site for the genetic defect in Alzheimer's disease, the X chromosome and chromosome 11 in bipolar disorder, and chromosome 5 in schizophrenia. These studies have met with few replications for two possible reasons. First, disorders such as schizophrenia and bipolar disorder may be quite heterogeneous, and the cause of the syndrome in one family may be different from the cause in another family. Second, complex psychiatric disorders may involve polygenic mechanisms involving genes with incomplete penetrance, thus making genetic analysis exceedingly complex. Nevertheless, the use of the RFLP technique continues to be a useful research tool in psychiatry.

RFLP studies begin with the identification of large pedigree families that contain affected and nonaffected members. Each member of the family is first carefully diagnosed. DNA is then extracted from the lymphocytes of blood samples collected from each member of the family. The DNA is then subjected to partial digestion by one of a class of enzymes called the *restriction endonucleases* (Figure 3.3-8). Each restriction endonuclease cuts DNA molecules between specific base pairs, resulting in several smaller pieces of DNA from each chromosome. The pattern with which a restriction endonuclease cuts a person's DNA is constant, but the patterns between persons differ. Hence, there are various (i.e., polymorphous) lengths of DNA fragments seen when different samples of DNA are cut with the same restriction endonucleases. These different lengths of DNA are separated using the biochemical technique of gel electrophoresis. The DNA is visualized by the use of a *genetic probe*. This genetic probe is radioactively labeled, single-stranded DNA that binds (*hybridizes*) to a specific complementary region of the restriction fragments that have been separated. It is then the task of the researcher to evaluate whether a particular pattern of RFLPs is associated with the presence of a particular disease within the family and among different families.

Once a fragment of DNA that is associated with a disease is isolated, it is possible to use this DNA marker in the diagnosis of the disease, including prenatal and presymptomatic diagnosis. Through the use of genetic markers, it may be possible to identify and localize the genes involved in a disease process, thereby allowing the molecular and cellular pathophysiology of the disease to be understood, potentially treated, and perhaps prevented.

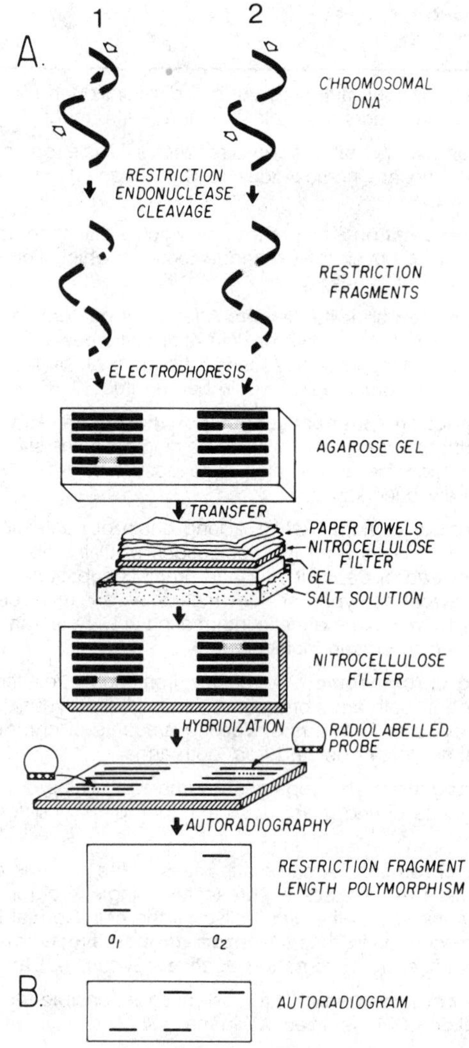

Figure 3.3-8. Restriction fragment length polymorphisms (RFLPs). (A) Depicted are two homologous chromosomes, 1 and 2, that differ in the presence or absence of a polymorphic restriction endonuclease cleavage site (closed arrowhead) in the vicinity of a unique marker locus (hatched region). Endonuclease cleavage (arrowheads) results, on average, in tens of thousands of restriction fragments. The aformentioned variable sites result in different-sized fragments from each chromosome. Restriction fragments are separated by size using agarose gel electrophoresis and are transferred by capillary action to a nitrocellulose filter. The filter is then hybridized to a radiolabelled probe contraining the complementary base sequence to the maker locus. Following autoradiography, individual bands corresponding to restriction fragments from each chromosome are visualized. This combination of restriction endonuclease and probe permits the detection of allelic variations (a1 and a2) in DNA sequence around the marker locus. (B) Autoradiographic patterns for each of three possible genotypes (pairs of alleles) are shown. (From R O Reider, C A Kaufmann: Genetics. In *The American Psychiatric Press Textbook of Psychiatry,* J A Talbott, R E Hales, and S C Yudofsky, editors, p 44. American Psychiatric Press, Washington DC, 1988, with permission.)

BRAIN MODELS

The neuroanatomical, neurophysiological, neurochemical, and brain-imaging research has led to the development of many new, biologically based models of brain function. The development of these models can be seen as similar to the development of models based on psychological observations and theories. In fact, many of these biologically based models combine data from psychology and biology. One particular brain model has focused on two basic concepts—*neural networks* and *neural selection.* Gerald Edelman's model of neural Darwinism and its related computer modeling programs are examples of this type of model. The concept of the neural network refers to the observation that neither single neurons nor single neuronal pathways are likely to be as important as larger networks of neurons in complex human mental functions. The neural system involved in the generation and perception of speech may be considered a type of neural network. Neural selection refers to the process by which different neurons or groups of neurons within a neural network may become more or less significant as a result of experience. The physical bases for this change in significance could include changes in the number of synapses, the shape or efficiency of the synapse, the types of proteins expressed in the synapse, and the amount of neurotransmitter released.

References

Agras W S: Learning theory. In *Comprehensive Textbook of Psychiatry,* ed 5, H I Kaplan and B J Sadock, editors, p 262. Williams & Wilkins, Baltimore, 1989.

Alheid G F, VanHoesen G W, Heimer L: Functional neuroanatomy. In *Comprehensive Textbook of Psychiatry,* ed 5, H I Kaplan and B J Sadock, editors, p 26. Williams & Wilkins, Baltimore, 1989.

Baraban J M, Worley P F, Nyder S H: Second messenger systems and psychoactive drug action: Focus on the phosphoinositide system and lithium. Am J Psychiatry *146*: 1251, 1989.

Belongia E: An investigation of the cause of the eosinophilia-myalgia syndrome associated with tryptophan use. N Engl J Med *323*: 357, 1990.

Choi D W: Glutamate neurotoxicity and diseases of the nervous system. Neuron *1*: 623, 1988

Journal of Clinical Psychiatry: Interrelations between depression, the immune system, and the endocrine system. J Clin Psychiatry 50 (Supp): 2, 1989.

Kandel E R: Genes, nerve cells, and the remembrance of things past. J Neuropsychiatry Clin Neurosci *1*: 103, 1989.

Klein W L, Sullivan J, Skorupa A, Aguilar J S: Plasticity of neuronal receptors. FASEB J *3*: 2132, 1989.

Pardes H J, Kaufman C A, Pincus H A, West A: Genetics and psychiatry: Past discoveries, current dilemmas, and future directions. Am J Psychiatry *146*: 435, 1989.

Ross E M: Signal sorting and amplification through G protein-coupled receptors. Neuron *3*: 141, 1989.

Schmidt A W, Peroutka S J: 5-hydroxytryptamine receptor "families." FASEB J *3*: 2242, 1989.

Schofield P R, Shivers B D, Seeburg P: The role of receptor subtype diversity in the central nervous system. TINS *13*: 8, 1990.

Snyder S H, Largent B L: Receptor mechanisms in antipsychotic drug action: Focus on sigma receptors. J Neuropsychiatry Clin Neurosci *1*: 7, 1989.

Vaughn J E: Review: Fine structure of synaptogenesis in the vertebrate central nervous system. Synapse *3*: 255, 1989.

4

Contributions of the Psychosocial Sciences to Human Behavior

4.1 / Jean Piaget

The Swiss psychologist Jean Piaget (1896–1980) (Figure 4.1-1) formulated a theory describing how children and adolescents think and acquire knowledge. His theory of cognitive or intellectual development, called *genetic epistemology,* is the study of the acquisition, modification, and growth of abstract ideas and abilities based on an inherited or biological substrate. What is innate is an intelligent functioning that makes the growth of abstract thought possible. Piaget derived his theories from direct observations of children (including his own) and by questioning children about their thinking. He was less interested in whether children answered incorrectly than in how they arrived at their incorrect answers.

Piaget viewed intelligence as being an extension of biological adaptation and as having a logical structure. Central to Piaget's theory is the concept of *epigenesis,* which holds that growth and development occur in a series of stages, each of which is built on the successful mastery of the one that comes before. Every stage occurs at a certain age, and the child demonstrates a higher level of thought organization during each successive stage of development.

THE PROCESS OF ADAPTATION

Adaptation is the ability of the person to adjust to the environment through two complementary processes: *assimilation* and *accommodation*. Assimilation is a subjective process that involves the filtering of the world through one's own system of knowledge—a taking in of new experience through the person's established mental structure. Accommodation involves the adjustment of one's knowledge to the reality demands of the environment by reorganizing or modifying the existing cognitive structure, or *scheme*. (In general, the term "scheme" is used to refer to early structures, and the term "operations" is used to refer to schemes of higher intelligence.) Taken together, they enable the infant or child to adapt to the outside world and react with increasingly complex patterns of awareness and behavior called *organization*.

Organization is both biological and psychological, and all species inherit the ability to organize, which is different for different species: Birds organize flying, and babies organize crawling.

Organization varies among individuals, but its function is constant. For instance, every baby crawls in his or her own way, but crawling is constant.

STAGES IN THE DEVELOPMENT OF INTELLIGENCE

Piaget described four major stages leading to the capacity for adult thought. Each stage is a prerequisite for the one that follows. The rate at which different children move through different stages, however, varies with their native endowment and environmental circumstances. The four stages are: (1) sensorimotor stage, (2) stage of preoperational thought, (3) stage of concrete operations, and (4) stage of formal operations.

Sensorimotor Stage (Birth to 2 Years)

Piaget used the term "sensorimotor" to describe this stage because infants first begin to learn through sensory

Figure 4.1-1. Jean Piaget. (By permission of the Jean Piaget Society, Temple University, Philadelphia.)

observation and gain control of their motor functions through activity, exploration, and manipulation of the environment. Piaget divided this stage into six substages, which are discussed in Section 2.3, "Infancy and Childhood." From the outset, biology and experience blend to produce learned behavior. For example, infants are born with a sucking reflex. A type of learning occurs when an infant alters the shape of the mouth and discovers the location of the nipple. A stimulus is received, and a response results, accompanied by a sense of awareness called a *schema* or elementary concept. As the infant becomes more mobile, one scheme is built on another, and new and more complex *schemata* are developed. The spatial, visual, and tactile world of the infant expands during this period, and the child actively interacts with the environment, using previously learned behavior patterns. For example, having learned to use a rattle, infants shake a new toy like the rattle they have already learned to use. Infants also use the rattle in new ways.

The critical achievement of this period is the development of *object permanence.* This term defines the child's ability to understand that objects have an existence independent of his or her involvement with them. Infants learn to differentiate themselves from the world and are able to maintain a mental image of an object, even though it is not present and visible.

Also, at about this age (approximately 18 months), infants begin to develop mental symbols and use words, a process known as *symbolization.* Infants are able to create a visual image of a ball or a mental symbol of the word "ball" to stand for or signify the real object. Such mental representations allow children to operate on new conceptual levels. The attainment of object permanance marks the transition from the sensorimotor stage to the preoperational stage of development.

Stage of Preoperational Thought (Intuitional Stage; 2 to 7 Years)

During this stage the child uses symbols and language more extensively than in the sensorimotor stage. Thinking and reasoning is on an intuitive level in that the child learns without the use of reasoning. Children are unable to think logically or deductively, and concepts are primitive; they can name objects but not classes. Preoperational thought is midway between socialized adult thought and the completely autistic Freudian unconscious. Events are linked not by logic but by juxtaposition. Early in this stage, if the child drops a glass and it breaks, there is no sense of cause and effect. The child believes the glass was ready to break, not that he or she broke it. Also, the child is unable to grasp the sameness of an object in different circumstances; the same doll in a carriage, a crib, or a chair is perceived to be three different objects. During this time things are represented in terms of their function. For example, a child defines a bike as "to ride" and a hole as "to dig."

In this phase children begin to use language and drawings in more elaborate ways. From one-word utterances, two-word phrases made up of either noun plus verb or noun plus objective develop. A child may say, "Bobby up" or "Bobby eat."

Children in the preoperational phase are unable to deal with moral dilemmas, although they have a sense of what is good and what is bad. For example, when asked, "Who is more guilty: the person who breaks one dish on purpose or the person who breaks 10 dishes by accident?" the young child usually answers that the latter is more guilty because he broke more dishes.

During this period children are described as being *egocentric.* They see themselves as the center of the universe, have a limited point of view, and are unable to take the role of the other person. The child is unable to modify behavior for someone else. For example, children are not being negativistic when they do not listen to commands to be quiet because their brother has to study. Instead, egocentric thinking prevents an understanding of their brother's point of view.

During this stage children also employ a type of magical thinking, called *phenomenalistic causality,* in which events that occur together are thought to cause one another (e.g., thunder causes lightning, bad thoughts cause accidents). In addition, children demonstrate *animistic thinking,* which is the tendency to endow physical events and objects with psychological attributes, such as feelings or intentions.

Semiotic function. The semiotic function occurs during the preoperational period. With this new ability, a child can represent something—such as an object, event, or conceptual scheme—with a *signifier,* which serves a representative function (e.g., language, mental image, symbolic gesture). During this period, the child is able to utilize a symbol or a sign to stand for something else.

Stage of Concrete Operations (Operational Stage; 7 to 11 Years)

This stage is so named because in this period the child operates and acts on the concrete, real, and perceivable world of objects and events. Egocentric thought is replaced by *operational thought,* which involves attending to and dealing with a wide array of information outside the child. Therefore, a child can now see things from someone else's perspective. Children in this stage begin to use limited *logical thought processes* and are able to serialize, order, and group things in classes based on common characteristics. Syllogistic reasoning, in which a logical conclusion is formed from two premises, occurs during this period; for example, all horses are mammals (premise); all mammals are warm-blooded (premise); therefore, all horses are warm-blooded (conclusion). Children are able to reason and follow rules and regulations. They are able to regulate themselves and begin to develop a moral sense and a code of values.

Children who become overly invested in rules may show obsessive-compulsive behavior; children who resist a code of values often seem willful and inactive. The most desirable developmental outcome for this period is for the child to attain a healthy respect for rules and to understand that there are legitimate exceptions to rules.

Conservation is the ability to recognize that, even though the shape and form of objects may change, the objects still maintain or conserve other characteristics that enable them to be recognized as the same. For example, if a ball of clay is rolled into a long and thin sausage shape, the child recognizes that there is the same amount of clay in the two forms. An inability to conserve (which is characteristic of the preoperational stage) is observed when the child declares that there is more clay in the sausage-shaped form because it is longer. The child in this stage realizes that the act of reshaping the clay into a ball reverses the act of stretching it—a concept known as reversibility.

The task of the 7- to 11-year-old is to organize and order occurrences in the real world. Dealing with the future and its possibilities occurs in the formal operational stage.

Stage of Formal Operations (11 Through the End of Adolescence)

This period of cognitive development is characterized by the young person's ability to think abstractly, to reason deductively, and to define concepts (hypotheticodeductive thinking). This stage is so named because the person's thinking operates in a formal, highly logical, systematic, and symbolic manner. This stage is also characterized by skills in dealing with permutations and combinations; the young person can grasp the concept of probabilities. The adolescent attempts to deal with all possible relations and hypotheses to explain data and events. During this stage, language use is complex, follows formal rules of logic, and is grammatically correct. *Abstract thinking* is demonstrated by the adolescent's interest in a variety of issues: philosphy, religion, ethics, and politics.

Because young people can reflect on their own and other people's thinking, they are prone to self-conscious behavior. As the adolescent attempts to master new cognitive tasks, there may be a return of egocentric thought but on a higher level. For example, adolescents may think that they can accomplish everything or change events by thought alone.

Not all adolescents enter the stage of formal operations at the same time or to the same degree. Depending on individual capacity, some may not reach the stage of formal operational thought at all and may remain in the concrete operational mode throughout life.

APPLICATIONS TO PSYCHIATRY

Piaget's theories have psychiatric implications. The hospitalized child who is in the sensorimotor stage has achieved object permanency and, so, suffers from separation anxiety. Such children are best off if the mother is allowed to stay in the room with them overnight. The preoperational child, unable to deal with concepts or abstractions, benefits more from role-playing proposed medical procedures or situations than by having them described verbally in detail. For example, if the child is to receive intravenous therapy, it may be useful to act out the procedure, using a toy intravenous set and dolls. Also, since the preoperational child does not understand cause and effect, physical illness may be interpreted as punishment for bad thoughts or deeds. Because the child has not yet mastered the capacity to conserve and does not understand the concept of reversibility (which normally occurs during the concrete operational stage), he or she cannot understand that a broken bone can mend or that blood lost in an accident can be replaced.

The clinician must also be aware that the thinking of the adolescent during formal operations may appear to be overly abstract when it is, in fact, a normal developmental stage. A picture of adolescent turmoil may not herald a psychotic process; it may well be the result of the normal adolescent coming to grips with his or her newly acquired abilities to deal with the unlimited possibilities of the surrounding world.

Finally, it is important to remember that adults under stress can regress cognitively, as well as emotionally. Their thinking can become preoperational, egocentric, and sometimes animistic.

References

Chapman M: *Constructive Evolution: Origins and Development of Piaget's Thought.* Cambridge University Press, Cambridge, 1988.

Chapman M: Piaget, attentional capacity, and the functional implications of formal structure. Adv Child Dev Behav *20*: 289, 1987.

Ginsburg H, Brant S O: *Piaget's Theory of Intellectual Development,* ed 3. Prentice-Hall, Englewood Cliffs, 1988.

Greenspan S I, Curry J F: Piaget's approach to intellectual functioning. In *Comprehensive Textbook of Psychiatry,* ed 5, H I Kaplan and B J Sadock, editors, p 256. Williams & Wilkins, Baltimore, 1989.

Kitchener R F: *Piaget's Theory of Knowledge: Genetic Epistemology and Scientific Reason.* Yale University Press, New Haven, 1986.

Lane R O, Schwartz G E: Levels of emotional awareness: A cognitive developmental theory and its application to psychopathology. Am J Psychol *144*: 133, 1987.

Moses N, Klein H B, Altman E: An approach to assessing and facilitating causal language in adults with learning disabilities based on Piagetian theory. J Learn Disabil *23*: 220, 1990.

Parkins E J: Piaget's genetic epistemology. Genet Soc Gen Psychol Monogr *114*: 77, 1988.

Piaget J: *Genetic Epistemology.* Columbia University Press, New York, 1973.

Piaget J: *The Grasp of Consciousness.* Harvard University Press, Cambridge, MA, 1976.

Piaget J: *Judgement and Reasoning in the Child.* Harcourt, New York, 1926.

Piaget J: *The Language and Thought of the Child.* Routledge and Kegnan Paul, London, 1926.

Piaget J: *Logic and Psychology.* Basic Books, New York, 1957.

Piaget J: *The Moral Judgement of the Child.* Harcourt, New York, 1932.

Piaget J: *The Origins of Intelligence in Children.* International Universities Press, New York, 1952.

Piaget J: *Play, Dreams, and Imitation in Childhood.* Norton, New York, 1951.

Piaget J, Inhelder B: *Memory and Intelligence.* Basic Books, New York, 1973.

Piaget J, Inhelder B: *The Psychology of the Child.* Basic Books, New York, 1969.

4.2 / John Bowlby and Attachment Theory

The British psychoanalyst John Bowlby (1907–1990) formulated a theory that attachment is crucial to healthy development. *Attachment* is the emotional tone that exists between the developing child and the outer-provider or caretaker and that is characterized by the infant's seeking out, clinging to, and wanting to be near that person. By the second half of the first year, with some individual variation, infants develop specific attachments to certain people in their lives. Proper attachments in infancy play an important part in the person's ability to form relationships later in life. The process of attachment occurs in every human social group and in subhuman primates and many other animals.

ATTACHMENT PROCESS

According to Bowlby, attachment occurs when there is a "warm, intimate and continuous relationship with the mother in which both find satisfaction and enjoyment." Infants tend to attach to one person—they are *monotropic*—but multiple attachments may also occur, and attachment may be directed toward the father or a surrogate. Attachment is a gradually developing phenomenon; it results in one person's wanting to be with a preferred person, who is perceived as stronger, wiser, and able to reduce anxiety or distress.

Attachment occurs during the first year of life and has a reciprocal quality in that the infant and the mother attach to each other. The term *bonding* is sometimes used synonymously with attachment, but they are actually different phenomena. Bonding refers to the mother's feelings for her infant and differs from attachment because a mother does not normally rely on her infant as a source of security—a requirement of attachment behavior. There has been a great deal of research on the bonding of mother to infant, which occurs when there is skin-to-skin contact between the two or when other types of contact are made, such as voice or eye contact. Some workers have concluded that a mother who has skin-to-skin contact with her baby immediately after birth shows a stronger bonding pattern and may provide more attentive care than the mother who does not have this experience. Some researchers have even proposed a critical period immediately after birth, during which such skin-to-skin contact must occur if bonding is to take place. This is a much disputed concept because many mothers are clearly bonded to their infants and display excellent maternal care, even though they did not have this contact immediately postpartum. Humans are also able to develop so-called representational models of their babies in utero or even before conception. This type of representational thinking may be as important to the bonding process as skin, voice, or eye contact.

Attachment behavior is reinforced by signs of distress, or signal indicators, which elicit a behavioral response in the mother. Crying is the primary signal, and, although the infant cries most often from hunger, the mother generalizes the crying stimulus to represent distress from pain, frustration, or anger, Other signal indicators that reinforce attachment are smiling, cooing, and looking.

As the developing child becomes attached to the caretaker or mother, he or she cries when the mother goes away. The meaning of the separation depends on the child's developmental level and the current phase of attachment.

Attachment Phases

In the first phase, sometimes called the *preattachment stage* (birth to 8 to 12 weeks), the baby orients to the mother, follows her with its eyes over a 180-degree range, and turns toward and moves rhythmically with her voice. In the second phase, sometimes called *attachment-in-the-making* (8 to 12 weeks to 6 months), the infant becomes attached to one or more persons in the environment. Separation from a particular person is not a problem for infants in either of these stages, provided their needs are satisfied. In the next phase, sometimes called *clear-cut attachment* (6 months through 24 months), the infant cries and shows other signs of distress when separated from the caretaker or mother (this may occur as early as 3 months in some infants). On being returned to the mother, the infant stops crying and clings, as if to gain further assurance of the mother's return. Sometimes, seeing the mother after separation is sufficient for crying to stop. In the fourth phase (24 months and beyond), the mother figure is seen as independent, and a more complex relationship between mother and child develops. (See also Table 2.1-1 in Section 2.1, "Overview of the Life Cycle and Normality.")

Theory of Anxiety

Bowlby's theory of *anxiety* holds that the child's sense of distress during separation is perceived and experienced as anxiety. Any stimuli that alarm the child and cause fear (such as loud noises, falling, and cold blasts of air) mobilize signal indicators (such as crying), which cause the mother to respond in a caring way by cuddling and reassuring the baby. The ability of the mother to relieve the infant's anxiety or fear is fundamental to the increasing attachment in the infant or child. *Security*—the opposite of anxiety—occurs when the mother is close to the child and the child experiences no fear.

A syndrome known as maternal deprivation (also called *hospitalism* and *anaclitic depression* by René Spitz) occurs in some children under 2 years old who are placed in institutions and separated from their mothers for long periods of time (over three months).

Bowlby described a predictable set and sequence of behavior patterns in these children: (1) *protest*, in which the child protests against the separation by crying, calling out, and searching for the lost person; (2) *despair*, in which the child appears hopeless that the mother will ever return; and (3) *detachment*, in which the child emotionally separates self from mother. Bowlby believed this sequence involves ambivalent feelings toward the mother; the child both wants her and is angry at her for her desertion.

The child in the detachment stage responds in an indifferent manner when the mother returns; the mother has not been forgotten, but the child is angry at her having gone away in the first place and fears that it may happen again. Some children develop affectionless personalities, characterized by emotional withdrawal, little or no feeling, and a limited ability to form affectionate relationships.

Bowlby's theories have had an immense impact on understanding normal and abnormal child development. Failure-to-thrive syndromes, psychosocial dwarfism, depression, delinquency, academic problems, and borderline intelligence have been traced to negative attachment experiences. When maternal care was deficient because the mother was mentally ill, the child was institutionalized for a long period of time, or the primary object of attachment died, emotional damage to the child occurred. Bowlby originally thought that the damage was permanent and invariable; but he revised his theories to take into account the time at which separation took place, the type and degree of the separation, and the level of security the child had experienced prior to the separation.

Ethological Studies

Bowlby suggested a Darwinian evolutionary basis for attachment behavior; it ensures that adults protect their young. Ethological studies show that subhuman primates and other animals show attachment behavior patterns that are presumed to be instinctual and governed by inborn tendencies. An instinctual attachment system is seen in *imprinting*, in which certain stimuli are capable of eliciting innate behavior patterns during a critical period of the animal's behavioral development; thus, the infant offspring becomes attached to its mother at a critical period early in its development. The presence of imprinting behavior in humans is highly controversial. However, bonding and attachment behavior during the first year of life closely approximate it.

Harry Harlow. Harlow's work in monkeys is relevant to attachment theory (see Section 4.5, "Ethology, Experimental Disorders, and Sociobiology"). Harlow demonstrated the emotional and behavioral effects in monkeys who were isolated from birth and were thereby prevented from forming attachments. The isolates were withdrawn, unable to relate to peers, unable to mate, and incapable of caring for their offspring.

RECENT ADVANCES IN ATTACHMENT RESEARCH

Mary Ainsworth

A great deal of research has been done by followers of Bowlby that supports and expands on his observations, particularly the theory that there is an evolutionary, genetic basis for human infants to become attached to their principal caretakers. Mary Ainsworth has shown that the interaction between the mother and her baby during the attachment period significantly influences the baby's current and future behavior. Patterns of attachment also vary among babies; for example, some babies signal or cry less than others. Sensitive responsiveness to infant signals, such as cuddling the baby when he or she cries, causes infants to cry less in later months, rather than reinforcing crying behavior. Close bodily contact by the mother when the baby signals for her also is associated with the growth of self-reliance, rather than a clinging dependence, as the baby grows older. Less responsive mothers produce more anxious babies, and these mothers are characterized as having lower intelligence quotients (I.Q.s) and as being emotionally immature and younger than more responsive mothers.

Ainsworth also found that attachment serves the purpose of anxiety reduction, which she called the *secure base effect* that enables a child to move away from the presence of the attachment figure and to explore the environment. Inanimate objects, such as a teddy bear and a blanket (called the *transitional object* by Donald Winnicot), also serve as a secure base, one that often accompanies children as they investigate the world.

Attachments Throughout Life

Attachment behavior persists throughout life—from the cradle to the grave—as Bowlby hypothesized. Clinical studies have demonstrated attachment behavior in middle childhood, adolescence, and adulthood. College students, away from home for the first time, make good social adjustments if their early attachments to caretakers were secure. Low self-esteem, poor social relatedness, and emotional vulnerability to stress are associated with less secure attachments during the first year of life.

Humans continue to be attached to their parents, regardless of whether their early attachments were optimal. Attachments also occur at various stages in life to various other persons, such as teachers, relatives, coaches, and older siblings—especially when attachments to the parent were poor or inadequate. Such attachment figures are cast in the parental role and may be mentors or even therapists. By inspiring trust, these figures provide a secure base from which persons gain confidence in themselves and in their ability to deal with the outside world. Thus, the new attachment figure promotes a corrective emotional experience.

Affectional bonds that later develop between persons have attachment components in them. The sharing of experience is important in a variety of attachment bonds between persons other than parent-child, such as siblings, friends, relatives, and marital pairs. What makes the adult attachment bond unique is that it provides a sense of security, a sense of being needed, and a sense of being able to give. The absence of the attachment figure makes the person feel lonely or anxious.

Severing attachments. Bowlby reported that reactions to the death of a parent or spouse can be traced to the nature of the person's past and present attachment to the lost figure. When a lack of demonstrable grief occurs, it may be due to real experiences of rejection and lack of closeness in the relationship. The person may even consciously offer an idealized picture of the deceased. This person usually tries to present himself or herself as an independent type, for whom closeness and attachment mean little.

The severing of attachments, however, can be quite traumatic. The death of a parent or spouse can precipitate a depressive disorder and the possibility of suicide in some persons. Similarly, the death of a spouse increases the chance that the surviving spouse will develop a physical or mental disorder during the following year. The onset of depression and other dysphoric states often involves having been rejected by a significant person in one's life. George Vaillant's finding that early close sibling relationships are related to later adult mental health points to the importance of maintaining attachments.

Child Abuse

Abused children often maintain their attachment to the abusive parent. Animal studies in dogs have shown that severe punishment and maltreatment actually increase attachment behavior. If children are hungry, sick, or in pain, they show clinging attachment behavior. Similarly, if children are rejected by or are afraid of their parent, their attachment may increase. These findings account for the phenomenon of some children's wanting to remain with an abusive parent. Nevertheless, if a choice must be made between a punishing figure and a nonpunishing one, the latter will be chosen, especially if that person is sensitive to the needs of the child.

References

Ainsworth M D S: Attachments across the life span. Bull NY Acad Med *61*: 792, 1985.

Bowlby J: *Attachment and Loss*, vols 1, 2, 3. Basic Books, New York, 1969, 1973, 1980.

Bowlby J: *Maternal Care and Mental Health.* World Health Organization, Geneva, 1951.
Bowlby J: The nature of the child's tie to his mother. Int J Psychoanal *39*: 350, 1958.
Klaus M H, Kennell J H: *Bonding: The Beginnings of Parent-Infant Attachment.* Mosby, St. Louis, 1983.
Klaus M H, Kennell J H: *Parent-Infant Bonding*, ed 2. Mosby, St. Louis, 1982.
Morris D: Bowlby's 80th birthday (editorial). Br Med J *295*: 157, 1987.
Osofsky J D, ed: *Handbook of Infant Development.* Wiley, New York, 1979.
Papovsek K H, Papovsek M: The Evolution of parent-infant attachment: New psychobiological perspectives. In *Frontiers of Infant Psychiatry*, J D Can, editor, vol 2, p 276. Saunders, Philadelphia, 1984.
Sroufe L A: Bowlby's contribution to psychoanalytic theory and developmental psychology: Attachment, separation, loss. J Child Psychol Psychiatry *27*: 841, 1986.
Tavecchio L W C, Van Ijzendoorn M H, eds: *Attachment in Social Networks: Contributions to the Bowlby-Ainsworth Attachment Theory.* Elsevier, New York, 1987.

4.3 / Learning Theory

Learning is defined as the change in a person's behavior to a given situation brought about by repeated experiences in that situation, provided that the behavior cannot be explained on the basis of native response tendencies, maturation, or temporary states of the person.

To assess learning, one must measure some aspect of performance, such as the accuracy of a motor skill or the ability to recognize and repeat words. Learning and performance are related; but it is important not to confuse the two concepts. Performance can be adversely affected by insufficient motivation or anxiety, so that learning may have occurred but is not demonstrable. State-dependent learning is another case in which performance may be impaired. If a behavior is acquired under the influence of a pharmacological agent and tests for learning are carried out in the absence of the drug, there may be little or no evidence of acquisition. However, if the learning test is carried out under the influence of the drug, performance may change, and learning may then be demonstrated.

Among the building blocks of learning theory are classical and operant conditioning. In *classical conditioning*, learning is thought to take place as a result of the contiguity of environmental events. When events occur closely together in time, it is likely that persons will come to associate the two. In the case of *operant conditioning*, learning is thought to occur as a result of the consequences of one's actions and the resultant effect on the environment. As B.F. Skinner put it, "A person does not act upon the world, the world acts upon him." Skinner, in his definition of the sphere of interest of psychology, specifically eschewed the role of intervening variables, such as thoughts. *Social learning theory* incorporates both the classical and the operant models of learning but considers a reciprocal interaction between the person and the environment. Cognitive processes are viewed as important factors in modulating the person's responses to environmental events.

Psychoanalytic theory and practice developed concurrently with learning theory. A number of attempts have been made over the past half century to integrate these two theoretical approaches. For example, in 1950 John Dollard and Neal Miller reformulated many psychoanalytic concepts in terms of learning theory. But such attempts have not had a lasting influence on psychoanalytic thought or therapy.

More recently, there has been much interest in the neurophysiological and biochemical components of learning. For example, research with simple organisms, such as the *Aplysia*, a sea mollusk, has revealed that the learning of avoidance behavior alters the chemical structure of cells in the nervous system and that, when the avoidance is unlearned, these chemical changes are reversed. Thus, the foundation for understanding the neurochemistry of learning has been laid, and it is now clear that there is a reciprocal interaction between ongoing biological processes in the central nervous system and behavior changes resulting from environmental influences.

MODELS OF CONDITIONING

Two types of conditioning have been described: classical and operant.

Classical Conditioning

Classical conditioning (also known as respondent conditioning) results from the repeated pairing of a neutral (conditioned) stimulus with one that evokes a response (unconditioned stimulus) such that the neutral stimulus eventually comes to evoke the response. The time relationship between the presentation of the conditioned and unconditioned stimuli is important, varying for optimal learning from a fraction of a second to several seconds.

Ivan Pavlov (1849–1936), the Russian physiologist and Nobel prize winner, observed in his work on gastric secretion that a dog salivated not only when food was placed in its mouth but also at the sound of the footsteps of the person coming to feed the dog, even though the dog could not see or smell the food. He analyzed these events and called the flow of saliva that occurred with the sound of footsteps a *conditioned response* (CR)—that is, a response that could be elicited under certain conditions by a particular stimulus. In a typical Pavlovian experiment, a *stimulus* (S) that had no capacity to evoke a particular type of response before training does so after consistent association with another stimulus. For example, under normal circumstances, a dog will not salivate when a bell is sounded. If bell sounds are always followed by the presentation of food, however, the dog ultimately pairs the bell and food. Eventually, the bell sound alone elicits salivation (CR). Because the food naturally produces salivation, it is referred to as an *unconditioned stimulus* (UCS). Salivation, a response that is reliably elicited by food (UCS), is referred to as an *unconditioned response* (UCR). The bell, which was originally unable to evoke salivation but came to do so when paired with food, is referred to as a *conditioned stimulus* (CS). Classical conditioning is most often applied to responses mediated by the autonomic nervous system.

Classical conditioning is diagramed as follows:

Before Conditioning

Food (UCS) ⟶ Salivation (UCR)
Bell (CS) paired with food (UCS) ⟶ Salivation (UCR)

After Conditioning

Bell (CS) ⟶ Salivation (CR)

Extinction. Extinction occurs when the conditioned stimulus is constantly repeated without the unconditioned stimulus until the response evoked by the conditioned stimulus gradually weakens and eventually disappears. In the above example, extinction occurs if the bell (CS) is presented repeatedly without being paired with food (UCS). Eventually, salivation (CR) will not occur when the bell sounds, and extinction will take place. However, extinction is not a complete destruction of the conditioned response. If an animal is rested after extinction, the conditioned response returns but is less strong than before; this phenomenon is known as *partial recovery*.

The American psychologist John B. Watson (1878–1958) used Pavlov's theory of classical conditioning to explain certain aspects of human behavior. In 1920 Watson described how he produced a phobia in an 11-month-old boy called Little Albert. At the same time that the boy was shown a white rat that he initially did not fear, a loud frightening noise was sounded. After several such pairings, Albert became fearful of the white rat, even though no loud noise was present. Watson and his colleagues obtained the same results using a white rabbit, and eventually, the response was generalized to any furry object. Many theorists believe that this process accounts for the development of childhood phobias in general; that is, they are learned responses based on classical conditioning.

Stimulus generalization. Stimulus generalization refers to the process whereby a conditioned response is transferred from one stimulus to another. Animals respond to stimuli that are similar to the original conditioned stimulus. A dog conditioned to respond to a bell will also respond to the sound of a tuning fork. Stimulus generalization is one theory used to explain higher learning because it enables one to learn similarities. For example, a street sign will be recognized whether or not it is on a pole, building, or curb. There is sufficient stimulus similarity for generalization to occur.

Discrimination. Discrimination is the process of recognizing and responding to the differences between similar stimuli. If the two stimuli are sufficiently different, the animal can be taught to respond to one and not to the other; for example, an animal can learn to respond differentially to similar bells. In higher learning, a child learns to discriminate four-legged animals (the common stimulus) into dogs, cats, cows, and other quadrupeds.

Learning can be viewed as a balance of generalization and discrimination. Some disorders of thinking may stem from difficulties with these two processes. For example, a person may have had a traumatic experience as a child involving a person with a moustache. The transfer of those negative feelings to all men with moustaches is an example of both faulty discrimination and stimulus generalization.

Operant Conditioning

B. F. Skinner (1904–1990) proposed a theory of learning and behavior known as operant or instrumental conditioning. In classical conditioning, the animal is passive or restrained. In operant conditioning, however, the animal is active and behaves in a way that produces a reward—that is, learning occurs as a consequence of action. For example, a rat receives the reinforcing stimulus (food) only if it gives the response of pressing a lever. In addition to food, approval, praise, good grades, or any other response that satisfies a need in the animal or person can serve as a reward. In operant conditioning, in contrast, behavior is reinforced by the experimenter.

Operant conditioning is related to trial-and-error learning, as described by the American psychologist Edward L. Thorndike (1874–1949). In trial-and-error learning, one attempts to solve a problem by trying out a variety of actions until one proves successful—a freely moving organism behaves in a way that is *instrumental* in producing a reward. For example, a cat in a Thorndike puzzle box must learn to lift a latch in order to escape from the box. Operant conditioning is sometimes called instrumental conditioning for that reason. Thorndike's law of effect states that certain responses are reinforced by reward, and the organism learns from these experiences.

Four kinds of instrumental or operant conditioning are described in Table 4.3-1: primary reward conditioning, escape conditioning, avoidance conditioning, and secondary reward conditioning.

Respondent and operative behavior. Skinner described two types of behavior: (1) *respondent behavior*, behavior that results from known stimuli (e.g., the knee jerk reflex to patellar stimulation or the pupillary constriction to light); and (2) *operant behavior*, which is independent of a stimulus (e.g., the random movements of an infant or the aimless movements of a laboratory rat in a cage). Skinner took advantage of operant behavior by placing one of those rats in a Skinner box (named after him, its developer). The rat was deprived of food and randomly pressed a bar. At some point in the experiment, food was released by the experimen-

Table 4.3-1
Four Kinds of Operant or Instrumental Conditioning

1. Primary reward conditioning	The simplest kind of conditioning. The learned response is instrumental in obtaining a biologically significant reward, such as a pellet of food or a drink of water.
2. Escape conditioning	The organism learns a response that is instrumental in getting out of some place he or she prefers not to be.
3. Avoidance conditioning	The kind of learning in which a response to a cue is instrumental in avoiding a painful experience. A rat on a grid, for example, may avoid a shock if it quickly pushes a lever when a light signal goes on.
4. Secondary reward conditioning	The kind of learning in which there is instrumental behavior to get at a stimulus that has no biological utility itself but that has in the past been associated with a biologically significant stimulus. For example, chimpanzees will learn to press a lever to obtain poker chips, which they insert into a slot to secure grapes. Later they will work to accumulate poker chips even when they are not interested in grapes.

ter when the bar was pressed. The food reinforced the bar pressing, which increased or decreased in rate depending on the level of reinforcement given by the experimenter. A *reinforcer* is anything that maintains a response or increases its strength. It is used synonymously with the term *reward*; however, some workers make this distinction: Responses are reinforced; individuals are rewarded.

Reinforcement schedule (programming). Reinforcers are described as *primary* when they are independent of previous learning (e.g., the need for food or water) or *secondary* when based on previous learning that has led to rewards (e.g., money, grades). In operant conditioning, it is possible to vary the schedule of reward or reinforcement given to a behavioral pattern—a process known as programming. The intervals between reinforcements may be *fixed* (e.g., every third response rewarded) or *variable* (e.g., sometimes the third response is rewarded; other times, the sixth). A *continuous reinforcement* (also known as contingency reinforcement or management) schedule, in which every response is reinforced, leads to the most rapid acquisition of a behavior. When the response is reinforced only a fraction of the time the behavior occurs, it is called *partial reinforcement*. Partial or intermittent reinforcement is very effective in maintaining behavior and is resistant to extinction. For example, a person's use of a gambling slot machine is more frequent when the reward is partially reinforced—that is, when money is won at variable times. That procedure keeps the gambler guessing or trying to anticipate when a payoff will occur. The strength of operant learning is reflected in how often an animal responds. A high response frequency indicates strong operant learning. A decrease in frequency indicates that extinction is occurring. Table 4.3-2 illustrates the effects of various reinforcement schedules on behavior.

In operant conditioning, *positive reinforcement* refers to the process by which certain consequences of a response increase the probability that the response will occur again. Food, water, praise, and money are positive reinforcers. It should be noted, however, that events viewed as aversive by some might be reinforcing for others. For example, the behavior of some children will be reinforced by scolding, which, after all, is a form of attention. Many drugs also appear to be positive reinforcers, including opium, cocaine, nicotine, and barbiturates.

Negative reinforcement describes the process by which a response that leads to the removal of an aversive event increases that response. For example, a teenager mows the lawn in order to avoid his parents' complaints, or an animal jumps off a grid in order to escape a painful shock. Any behavior that enables one to avoid or escape a punishing consequence will be strengthened.

Negative reinforcement is not punishment. *Punishment* is an aversive stimuli (e.g., a slap) that is presented specifically to weaken or suppress an undesired response. Punishment reduces the probability that a response will recur. It is important to distinguish between the usual use of the term "punishment" and the technical use of the term. In learning theory, the punishing event delivered is always contingent on performance and demonstrably reduces the frequency of the behavior being punished. This is different from the use of the term to denote imprisonment, for example, because the prison sentence follows long after the crime has been committed and may not affect future criminal behavior.

Aversive control. In aversive control or conditioning, the organism changes its behavior to avoid a painful, noxious, or aversive stimulus. Electric shocks are common aversive stimuli used in laboratory experiments. Any behavior that avoids an aversive stimulus is reinforced as a result.

Escape learning and avoidance learning. Negative reinforcement is related to two types of learning, *escape learning* and *avoidance learning*. In escape learning, the animal learns a response to get out of some place where it does not want to be (e.g., an animal jumps off an electric grid whenever it is charged). Avoidance learning requires an additional response. The same rat on the grid learns to avoid a shock if it quickly pushes a lever when a light signal goes on. To move from escape learning to avoidance learning, the animal must make an *anticipatory response* to prevent the punishment from occurring. Escape learning and avoidance learning are two forms of aversive control. Behavior that terminates the source of aversive stimuli is strengthened and maintained.

Shaping behavior. Shaping involves changing behavior in a deliberate and predetermined way. By reinforcing those responses that are in the desired direction, the experimenter shapes the animal's behavior. If the experimenter wants to train a seal to ring a bell with its nose, he or she can give a food reinforcement as the animal's random behavior brings its nose nearer to the bell. To teach a mute schizophrenic patient to talk, the therapist may first reward the patient for simply looking at him or her. This would be followed by the reinforcement of any vocalizations and then by the reinforce-

Table 4.3-2
Reinforcement Schedules in Operant Conditioning

Reinforcement Schedule	Example	Behavioral Effect
Fixed ratio (FR) schedule	Reinforcement occurs after every 10 responses (10:1 ratio); 10 bar presses release a food pellet; workers are paid for every 10 items they make.	Rapid rate of response to obtain greatest number of rewards. Animal knows that next reinforcement depends on certain number of responses being made.
Variable ratio (VR) schedule	Variable reinforcement occurs (e.g., after the third, sixth, then second response, and so on).	Generates fairly constant rate of response because probability of reinforcement at any given time remains relatively stable.
Fixed interval (FI) schedule	Reinforcement occurs at regular intervals (e.g., every 10 minutes or every third hour).	Animal keeps track of time. Rate of responding drops to near 0 after reinforcement and then increases at about expected time of reward.
Variable interval (VI) schedule	Reinforcement occurs after variable intervals (e.g., every 3, 6, and then 2 hours) similar to VR.	Response rate does not change between reinforcement. Animal responds at steady rate in order to get reward when it is available; common in trout fisherman, use of slot machines, checking mailbox.

ment of simple speech. The closer the time of the reinforcement to the operant behavior, the better the learning. Shaping is also called *successive approximation*.

Adventitious reinforcement. Responses that are reinforced accidentally by coincidental pairing of response and reinforcement are adventitious. Such events may have clinical implications in the development of phobias or other neurotic behavior.

Premack's principle. The concept developed by David Premack states that a behavior engaged in at a higher frequency can be used to reinforce a lower-frequency behavior. In one experiment, Premack observed that children spent more time playing with a pinball machine than eating candy when both were freely available. When he made playing with the pinball machine contingent on eating a certain amount of candy, the children increased the amount of candy they ate. In a therapeutic application of this principle, schizophrenic patients were observed to spend more time sitting down doing nothing than working at a simple task in a rehabilitation center. When five minutes of sitting down was made contingent on a certain amount of work, then work output was considerably increased, as was skill acquisition. This principle is also known as "Grandma's rule" (e.g., "If you eat your spinach, you can have dessert.").

Application of Conditioning Theory to Psychiatry

In 1950 Joseph Wolpe defined anxious behavior as persistent habits of learned or conditioned responses acquired in anxiety-generating situations. If a response inhibitory to anxiety can occur in the presence of anxiety-evoking stimuli, then it will weaken the connection between these stimuli and the anxiety response. Wolpe referred to this process as *reciprocal inhibition*. Relaxation, for example, is considered to be incompatible with anxiety and, therefore, is inhibitory to it.

Anxiety hierarchy. In Wolpe's method of therapy, known as *systematic desensitization*, the goal is to eliminate maladaptive anxiety and behavior. To accomplish this goal, Wolpe asked his patient to imagine the least disturbing item on a list of potentially anxiety-evoking stimuli and then to proceed up the list to the most disturbing stimuli. For example, a patient with a fear of heights would rank the sight of a tall building lower in the anxiety hierarchy than standing on a high ledge; being on the 10th floor of a building would fall somewhere in between. In the relaxed state (usually induced by hypnosis, but sometimes induced by drugs), the patient was instructed to visualize the least anxiety-producing situation; if that visualization did not produce anxiety, the person moved up the hierarchy. Eventually, the patient was desensitized to the source of anxiety.

Tension-reduction theory. John Dollard and Neal Miller attempted to reconcile behavioral theory and Freudian psychodynamics by stressing the commonalities between the two. Subscribing to the *tension-reduction* theory of behavior, they saw behavior as motivated by the organism's attempt to reduce tension produced by unsatisfied or unconscious drives. Freud's pleasure principle is a tension-reducing force and, consequently, is a strong motivator. If repressed, fear is learned and is transformed into anxiety. In either case, it acts as an acquired drive; thus, a person's behavior may be motivated by an attempt to reduce fear. Early childhood events may be traumatic—that is, may cause anxiety. If such events are repressed, the adult may avoid situations that are likely to stimulate anxiety but may be completely unaware of those avoidance patterns. Therapy, in part, is an unlearning process. The organism learns that certain behaviors can reduce anxiety, and avoidance patterns are replaced by approach patterns.

For a comparison of the behavioral and psychoanalytic models, see Table 4.3-3.

Learned helplessness model of depression. A laboratory animal may be classically conditioned to accept a painful stimulus when restrained. Such restraint eventually teaches the animal that there is no way to avoid the aversive stimulus. A condition known as *learned helplessness* develops when an organism learns that there is no behavioral pattern that can influence the environment. The learned helplessness paradigm has been used to explain depression in humans who feel helpless, without options, and unable to control events.

Brain stimulation and reinforcement. When certain areas of the hypothalamus are electrically stimulated, intense pleasure is experienced by both animals and humans. Nonhuman primates were provided with a method by which they could stimulate pleasure centers in their brains. The animals preferred stimulating themselves to eating or drinking. In human beings, similar phenomena occur, and in one case, a patient stimulated his brain 1,000 times in a six-hour period until he was forced to stop.

Table 4.3-3
Behavioral and Psychoanalytic Models

Behavioral Model	Psychoanalytic Model
1. Behavior is determined by current contingencies, reinforcement history, and genetic endowment.	Behavior is determined by intrapsychic processes.
2. Problem behavior is the focus of study and treatment.	Behavior is but a symbol of intrapsychic processes and a symptom of unconscious conflict. The underlying conflict is the focus of treatment.
3. Contemporary variables, such as contingencies of reinforcement, are the focus of the analysis.	Historical variables, such as childhood experiences, are the focus of the analysis.
4. Treatment entails application of principles of operant or classical conditioning.	Treatment consists of bringing unconscious conflicts into consciousness.
5. Objective observation, measurement, and experimentation are the methods employed. The focus is on observable behavior and environmental events (antecedents and consequences).	Subjective methods of interpretation of behavior and inference regarding unobservable events (e.g., intrapsychic processes) are employed.
6. Theory is based on experimentation.	Theory is predominantly based on case histories.
7. Tenets can be formulated into testable hypotheses and evaluated through experimentation.	Many tenets cannot be formulated into testable hypotheses to be evaluated through experimentation.

Table from P G Dorsett: Behavioral and social learning psychology. In *Human Behavior: An Introduction for Medical Students*, A Stoudemire, editor, p 105. Lippincott, Philadelphia, 1990, with permission.

COGNITIVE LEARNING THEORY

Cognition is defined as the process of obtaining, organizing, and utilizing intellectual knowledge. Cognitive learning theories focus on the role of understanding. Mental operations are performed by the person, and bits of information are stored in memory to be retrieved at some later time. Cognition implies an understanding of the connection between cause and effect, between action and the consequences of that action. *Cognitive strategies* are mental plans used by a person to understand self and environment.

Depressed patients have a cognitive strategy that focuses on what is wrong, rather than what is right. A form of cognitive therapy developed by Aaron Beck for the treatment of depression teaches patients to recognize and value their assets and alerts them to the cognitive pattern that causes their depression. Beck described the cognitive triad that exists in depression as consisting of a person's (1) negative view of self, (2) negative interpretation of experience, and (3) negative expectation of the future.

Many theorists, such as Jean Piaget, define a series of stages in cognitive growth. Another approach toward cognition is termed *information processing*, which refers to a sequence of mental operations involving input, storage, and output of information. Cognition involves calling up and processing relevant information from stored memory.

Behavior can change through techniques in which persons learn by listening to or by reading instructions. Therapeutic instructions modify both outcome and efficacy expectations of patients. For example, patients told that their blood pressure readings would drop if they followed certain relaxation procedures did show a decline in blood pressure. To learn new patterns of behavior, patients can monitor their behavior by charting events, such as when they eat or smoke. Self-monitoring has also been shown to reduce the rate of relapse. If the therapist helps patients to define and set realistic and well-specified goals, they have a greater likelihood of achieving them than if goals are poorly defined or unrealistic. Goal attainment enhances self-efficacy, which in turn positively affects future performance.

ATTRIBUTION THEORY

Attribution theory is a cognitive approach; it is concerned with how people perceive the causes of behavior. According to attribution theory, (1) persons are more likely to attribute their own behavior to situational causes but are more likely to attribute others' behavior to stable internal dispositions (personality traits) and (2) the particular cause that a person attributes to a given event influences subsequent feelings and behavior. In psychiatry, attribution theory may help to explain why some persons attribute a change in behavior to an external event (situation) or to a change in one's internal state (disposition or ability). Similarly, behavioral change may be attributed to the results of a drug or to the results of interpersonal events. Research on drug effects by attribution theorists have shown that it may be unwise to describe a drug as very strong or as very effective because, if it does have the desired effect, patients may believe that is the only reason they got better.

SOCIAL LEARNING THEORY

Social learning theory relies on role modeling, identification, and human interactions. A person can learn by imitating the behavior of another person, but personal factors are involved. If the role model is not someone the person likes, imitative behavior is not likely to occur. Social learning theorists combine operant and classical conditioning theories. For example, although observation of models may be a major factor in the learning process, imitation of the model must be reinforced or rewarded if the behaviors are to become part of the person's repertoire.

Albert Bandura is a major proponent of the social learning school. Behavior occurs as a result of the interplay between cognitive and environmental factors, a concept known as *reciprocal determinism*. Persons learn by observing others, intentionally or accidentally; this process is known as *modeling* or learning through imitation. The person's choice of a model is influenced by a variety of factors, such as age, sex, status, and similarity to oneself. If the chosen model reflects healthy norms and values, the person develops *self-efficacy*, the capacity to adapt to normal everyday life and to threatening situations. It is possible to eliminate negative behavior patterns by having a person learn alternate techniques from other role models. For example, fearful children become less fearful when they watch other children acting fearless in the same situation. Similarly, demonstrating a fearless approach to a phobic situation may be useful to motivate a patient's approach to the feared object or situation.

Modeling has also been used in weight reduction and smoking cessation programs. It is an important component of group treatment plans in which members of the group learn from one another.

NEUROPHYSIOLOGY OF LEARNING

One of the first theorists to approach the neurophysiological aspects of learning was Clark L. Hull (1884–1952), who developed a drive-reduction theory of learning. Hull postulated that neurophysiological connections are established in the central nervous system that reduce the level of a drive (e.g., obtaining food reduces hunger). An external stimulus stimulates an efferent system and elicits a motor impulse. The critical connection is between the stimulus and the motor response, which is a neurophysiological reaction that leads to what Hull called a habit. Habits are strengthened when a response leads to a further reduction in the drive associated with the aroused need.

By exploring the human brain, researchers such as Broca and Wernicke identified specific areas of the brain involved in the development and retention of speech and language. Electrical stimulation of certain brain sites evoked vivid mental imagery in patients. Also, lesions of the amygdaloid nucleus in animals have been demonstrated to interfere with learning. Learning produces changes in the structure and function of nerve cells. In one study, monkeys that were trained to use a particular finger to obtain food showed hypertrophy of the area of the brain responsible for finger control.

Habituation and Sensitization

In the study of the snail *Aplysia*, Eric Kandel demonstrated how simple forms of learning—habituation and sensitization—can occur. The specific behavior studied is a defensive reflex involving the withdrawal of the siphon of the snail when the animal is tactually stimulated. If the snail is touched repeatedly, it is subject to habituation and learns not to withdraw its syphon and gill. Habituation causes the organism to stop responding reflexively as a result of the repeated stimulus.

Aplysia can also be sensitized; that is, a reflex response can be made more sensitive, so that a subthreshold stimulus elicits a response. Thus, if the snail receives a strong stimulus (e.g., an electric shock), it will become sensitized such that even a previously subthreshold stimulation will cause the animal to withdraw its gill and siphon. Experimental work with *Aplysia* has also shown that the processes of habituation and sensitization develop at different times, habituation before sensitization.

Memory Formation and Storage

The neurobiological basis of learning is located in the structures of the brain involved in forming and storing information. These structures include the hippocampus, the cortex, and the cerebellum. One hundred billion neurons in the brain are involved in forming memories, including a layer of 4.6 million cells in the hippocampus.

Learning begins with the senses taking in an environmental stimulus that is eventually transformed into a memory trace or memory link. An electrical or chemical impulse passes through the neuron when the brain receives information, which triggers the formation of connections between synapses. Animal experiments have demonstrated an increase in synaptic connections when learning occurs.

Long-term memories are retained longer than short-term memories because of the increased time such memories have had to link up with a number of locations in the cortex. The more connections, the better the chance of contacting a neural pathway leading to the memory. Repeated reliving of a memory enhances its permanence.

Storage is the key to a good memory. Relating material to something that is already known creates more pathways and increases the storage power. Processing information at a semantic level involves more of the mind than rote memorization. This information decays at a slower rate than information memorized on a superficial level, without meaning and comprehension.

Memory is divided into short-term and long-term memory. Long-term memory is also known as recent memory, recent past memory, remote memory, and secondary memory. Short-term memory—also called immediate memory, working memory, primary memory and buffer memory—is adversely affected by chronic emotional stress and lack of effort due to psychological exhaustion or too much input. Short-term memory and long-term memory differ in the amount of information that can be stored. The capacity of short-term memory is limited (five to nine bits of information).

Smell and emotion may underlie long-term memories. Scent conveys information through the olfactory nerve to the hippocampus, which plays a role in the control of emotions. Learning and memory are affected by stress. The increase in adrenaline resulting from stress can enhance learning, but if stress is too great, learning is inhibited. A person's mood affects the learning and recall of material; that is, learning material while in a happy mood enhances memory, and the person recalls material better while in a happy mood. Some childhood memories survive. They are usually those associated with the period when the child learned to speak, between the ages of 3 and 5 years. Before that time, only memories associated with traumatic events or with smell are likely to be remembered.

MOTIVATION

Motivation is a state of being that produces a tendency toward some type of action. That state may be a state of deprivation (e.g., hunger), a value system, or a strongly held belief (e.g., religion). In the mediation of learning and perception, biological mechanisms play an important role in motivating behavior. The organism tries to maintain homeostasis or internal balance against any disturbance of equilibrium (e.g., the thirsty animal is motivated to find water and drink). Social motives, such as the need for recognition and achievement, also account for behavioral patterns (e.g., studying hard to get good grades). However, the intensity of motivation to achieve at any task in any particular situation is determined by at least two factors: the achievement motive (desire to achieve) and the likelihood of success.

There are marked individual differences in the values placed on objects and goals. Some students strive for A's; others depreciate the importance of grades, placing higher value on intellectual satisfactions or on extracurricular activities. The expectancy factor refers to the subjective probability that, with the expenditure of sufficient effort, the object may be acquired or the goal reached.

Cognitive dissonance. Cognitive dissonance means incongruity or disharmony among one's beliefs, knowledge, and behavior. When dissonance becomes too great, the person changes ways of thinking or behaving so that there is less disharmony. An example of cognitive dissonance is the unwillingness of a person to believe that a car for which he or she paid a great deal of money or which is considered to be a status symbol could have anything wrong with it or be defective in any way; another example is believing more strongly in a decision after it has been made. In general, dissonance occurs when there is a palpable disparity between two experimental or behavioral elements. It is postulated that cognitive dissonance produces an uncomfortable tension state (like hunger) that one is motivated to change.

References

Agras W S: Learning theory. In *Comprehensive Textbook of Psychiatry*, ed 5, H I Kaplan and B J Sadock, editors, p 262. Williams & Wilkins, Baltimore, 1989.

Bandura A, Walters R H: *Social Learning and Personality Development*. Holt, Rinehart and Winston, New York, 1963.

Cattell R B: *Psychotherapy by Structured Learning Theory*. Springer, New York, 1987.

Dollard J, Miller N E: *Personality and Psychotherapy*. McGraw-Hill, New York, 1950.

Dunn A J: Neurochemistry of learning and memory: An evaluation of recent data. Annu Rev Psychol *33*: 343, 1982.

Ettenberg A : Dopamine, neuroleptics, and reinforced behavior. Neurosci Biobehav Rev *13*: 105, 1989.

Hilgard E R, Bower G H: *Theories of Learning*, ed 3. Appleton-Century-Crofts, New York, 1966.

Hull C L: *Principles of Behavior: An Introduction to Behavior Therapy*. Appleton-Century-Crofts, New York, 1943.

Lovibond PF: Animal learning theory and the future of human Pavlovian conditioning. Biol Psychol *27*: 199, 1988.

Mowrer O H: *Learning Theory and Behavior*. Wiley, New York, 1960.

Pavlov I P: *Conditioned Reflexes*. Oxford University Press, London, 1927.

Rescorla R A, Holland P C: Behavioral studies of associative learning in animals. Annu Rev Psychol *33*: 265, 1982.

Skinner B F: *Science and Human Behavior*. Macmillan, New York, 1953.

Slangen J L, Earley B, Jaffard R, Richelle M, Olton D S: Behavioral models of memory and amnesia. Pharmacopsychiatry *23*: 81, 1990.

Walker S: *Learning Theory and Behavior Modification*. Methuen, London, 1984.
Wolpe J: The genesis of neurosis. S Afr Med J *24*: 613, 1950.
Zolten A J: Constructive integration of learning theory and phenomenological approaches to biofeedback training. Biofeedback Self Regul *14*: 89, 1989.

4.4 / Aggression: Violence, Homicide, Injuries, and Accidents

AGGRESSION

Aggression is any form of behavior directed toward the goal of harming or injuring another person who is motivated to avoid such treatment. Aggression also implies intent to do harm, which must be inferred from events that precede or follow acts of aggression. In some cases, establishing the presence of an intention to harm others is difficult; however, aggressors often admit their desire to harm their victims and express disappointment if the attempt fails. Aggression may also be directed toward the self, many times unconsciously, taking the form of accidents or injuries.

Incidence of Aggression

According to the Federal Bureau of Investigation (FBI) Uniform Crime Reports, there were 1,566,220 violent crimes (murder, rape, forcible robbery, and aggravated assault) in the United States in 1988. Of this number, 92,490 cases were rape, and 20,680 cases were homicide. In 1988 violent crime increased 16 percent from previous years. These data suggest that people are behaving more aggressively.

Homicides are most prevalent among people who know each other, and over 50 percent are accomplished with handguns. Much lower rates of homicide have been reported in such countries as England, Sweden, and Japan, all of which have strict handgun control laws. Homicide is most prevalent in the low socioeconomic groups and is more commonly carried out by men than by women.

Some Characteristics of Aggression

The majority of adults with and without psychiatric disorders who commit aggressive acts are more likely to do so against familiar persons, usually family members. This fact suggests that aggression is not indiscriminately directed. A possible exception to the familiar-person generalization is reported among adolescent males, who often aggress against casual acquaintances or persons who are unknown to them.

Generally, the probability of aggressive behavior increases as persons become more psychologically decompensated and perhaps also if the onset of a psychiatric disorder is rapid. Otherwise, very little is known about the relationship between the course of illness and aggression. Episodic decompensation may occur in persons who ingest large quantities of alcohol: more than 50 percent of persons who commit criminal homicides and who engage in assaultive behavior are reported to have imbibed significant amounts of alcohol immediately prior to aggressing.

With the exception of antisocial personality disorder, efforts to identify specific personality disorders for aggressive patients have been unsuccessful. Aggressive patients comprise a heterogenous group of personality types.

Recently, there has been an increasing interest in sex differences in the predisposition for and frequency of aggression. For aggression classified as homicide, battery, assault with a weapon, or rape, the frequency among males clearly exceeds that of females. For domestic violence, in which one marital partner acts to hurt another, the frequency among males and females is about equal. Studies of persons who are hospitalized in psychiatric facilities over long periods of time indicate that the prevalence of male and female aggression is approximately equal.

Theoretical Perspectives

Aggression as instinctive behavior

Freud's view. In his early writings Sigmund Freud held that all human behavior stems either directly or indirectly from *eros*—the life instinct—whose energy, or libido, is directed toward the enhancement or reproduction of life. In this framework, aggression was viewed simply as a reaction to the blocking or thwarting of libidinal impulses. As such, it was neither an automatic nor an inevitable part of life.

After the tragic events of World War I, Freud gradually came to adopt a somewhat gloomier position regarding the nature of human aggression. He proposed the existence of a second major instinct—*thanatos*, the death force—the energy of which is directed toward the destruction or termination of life. According to Freud, all human behavior stems from the complex interplay of this instinct with eros and the constant tension between them.

Because the death instinct, if unrestrained, soon results in self-destruction, it was hypothesized that through other mechanisms, such as displacement, the energy of thanatos is redirected outward, so that it serves as the basis for aggression against others. In Freud's view, aggression stems primarily from the redirection of the self-destructive death instinct away from the self and toward others.

Lorenz's view. According to Konrad Lorenz, aggression that causes physical harm to others springs from a fighting instinct that humans share with other organisms. The energy associated with this instinct is spontaneously produced in organisms at a more or less constant rate. The probability of aggression increases as a function of the amount of stored energy and the presence and strength of aggression-releasing stimuli. Aggression is inevitable, and, at times, spontaneous eruptions occur.

Aggression as learned social behavior. This perspective regards aggression primarily as a learned form of social behavior—one that is acquired and maintained in much the same manner as other forms of activity. According to Albert Bandura, neither innate urges toward violence nor aggressive drives aroused by frustration are the roots of human aggression. Rather, persons engage in assaults against others because (1) they acquired aggressive responses through past experience, (2) they receive or anticipate various forms of reward for performing such actions, or (3) they are directly instigated to aggression by specific social or environmental conditions. In contrast to both instinct and drive theories, the social learning perspective does not attribute aggression to one or a few potential causes. It suggests that the roots of such behavior are quite varied in scope, involving aggressors' past experience and learning, as well as a wide range of external, situational factors. For example, soldiers receive medals for killing enemy troops during times of war, and professional athletes attain widespread admiration and large financial rewards by competing aggressively (Table 4.4-1).

Aggression as neuroanatomical damage. Increasingly, a number of investigators are hypothesizing that, for a certain group of chronically aggressive individuals, the root of the aggressive behavior is actual organic brain damage. This perspective is an elaboration of the theory that aggression is a learned social behavior, in that individuals who have been the victims of severe physical abuse themselves may suffer neurological sequelae secondary to the abuse, which predispose them biologically to violent behavior. In 1986 Dorothy Lewis reported that every death-row inmate studied by her team of researchers had a history of head injury, often inflicted by abusive parents. This study concluded "that death row inmates comprise an especially neuropsychiatrically impaired prison population." Researchers investigating the association between head injury and violent behavior have been careful to point out that the linkage of physical abuse, head injury, and violence is uncertain, although most studies do show an association between early physical abuse and later aggressive behavior. Some researchers speculate that the combination of brain injury plus a history of undergoing and observing chronic severe abuse is a particularly lethal one.

Determinants of Aggression

Social determinants

Frustration. The single most potent means of inciting human beings to aggress is frustration. Widespread acceptance of this view stems mainly from John Dollard's frustration-aggression hypothesis. In its original form this hypothesis suggested that (1) frustration always leads to some form of aggression and (2) aggression always stems from frustration.

Frustrated persons, however, do not always respond with aggressive thoughts, words, or deeds. They may actually show a wide variety of reactions, ranging from resignation, depression, and despair to attempts to overcome the source of their frustration. It is also apparent that not all aggression results from frustration. People (e.g., boxers, football players) act aggressively for many reasons and in response to many different stimuli.

A careful examination of existing evidence suggests that whether frustration increases or fails to enhance overt aggression depends largely on two factors. First, it appears that frustration increases aggression only when the frustration is quite intense. When it is mild or moderate, aggression may fail to be enhanced. Second, growing evidence suggests that frustration is more likely to facilitate aggression when it is perceived as arbitrary or illegitimate rather than when it is viewed as deserved or legitimate.

Direct provocation from others. Existing evidence suggests that physical abuse or verbal taunts from others often serve as powerful elicitors of aggressive actions. Once aggression begins, it often shows an unsettling pattern of escalation; as a result, even mild verbal slurs or glancing blows may initiate a process in which stronger and stronger provocations are exchanged.

Exposure to aggressive models. A link between aggression and exposure to televised violence has been noted. The more televised violence children watch, the greater their level of aggression against others. The strength of this relationship appears to increase over time, pointing to the cumulative impact of media violence. The processes that account for the effects of filmed or televised violence on the behavior of children are outlined in Table 4.4-2.

Environmental determinants

Effects of air pollution. It has been reported that exposure to noxious odors, such as the ones produced by chemical plants and other industries, may increase personal irritability and, therefore, aggression. This effect appears to be true only up to a point. If the odors in question are truly foul, aggression appears to decrease—perhaps because escaping from the unpleasant environment becomes a dominant goal for the persons involved.

Effects of noise. Several studies have reported that individuals who are exposed to loud and irritating noise direct stronger assaults against others than persons who are not exposed to such environmental conditions.

Effects of crowding. Some studies suggest that overcrowding may produce elevated levels of aggression; other investigations have failed to obtain evidence for such a link. Crowding may enhance the likelihood of aggressive outbursts when typical reactions are negative (e.g., annoyance, irritation, frustration).

Situational determinants

Heightened physiological arousal. Some research indicates that heightened arousal stemming from such diverse sources as participation in competitive activities, vigorous ex-

Table 4.4-1
Three Contrasting Theoretical Perspectives on Human Aggression

Theory/Perspective	Assumed Source of Human Aggression	Possibility of Preventing or Controlling Such Behavior
Instinct theory	Innate tendencies or instincts	Low: aggressive impulses constantly generated; impossible to avoid
Drive theory	Externally elicited aggressive drive	Low: external sources of aggressive drive very common (e.g., frustration) and impossible to eliminate
Social learning theory	Present social or environmental conditions plus past social learning	Moderate to high: appropriate changes in current social and environmental conditions or in reinforcement contingencies can reduce or prevent overt aggressive actions

Table from R A Baron: Aggression. In *Comprehensive Textbook of Psychiatry*, ed 4, H I Kaplan, B J Sadock, editors, p 216. Williams & Wilkins, Baltimore, 1985.

Table 4.4-2
Mechanisms Underlying the Impact of Televised or Filmed Violence on the Behavior of Viewers

Mechanism	Description of Effects
Observational learning	Viewers acquire new means of harming others not previously present in their behavior repertoires.
Disinhibition	Viewers' restraints or inhibitions against performing aggressive actions are weakened as a result of observing others engaging in such behavior.
Densensitization	Viewers' emotional responsivity to aggressive actions and their consequences—signs of suffering on the part of victims—is reduced. As a result, they demonstrate little, if any, emotional arousal in response to such stimuli.

Table from R A Baron: Aggression. In *Comprehensive Textbook of Psychiatry*, ed 4, H I Kaplan, B J Sadock, editors, p 219. Williams & Wilkins, Baltimore, 1985.

ercise, and exposure to provocative films enhances overt aggression.

Sexual arousal and aggression. Recent investigations suggest that the impact of sexual arousal on aggression strongly depends on the type of erotic materials employed to induce such reactions and on the precise nature of the reactions themselves. When the erotica viewed by subjects is mild in nature, such as photos of attractive nudes, aggression is reduced. When they are more explicit, such as films of couples engaged in various acts of lovemaking, aggression is enhanced.

Pain as an elicitor. Physical pain may serve to arouse an aggressive drive—the motive to harm or injure others. That drive, in turn, may find expression against any available target, including ones not in any way responsible for the aggressor's discomfort. This hypothesis may explain, in part, why persons exposed to aggression act aggressively toward others.

Hormones, drugs, and aggressive behavior. Aggression has been linked in animals with testosterone, progesterone, luteinizing hormone, renin, beta-endorphin, prolactin, melatonin, norepinephrine, dopamine, epinephrine, acetylcholine, serotonin, 5-hydroxyindoleacetic acid (5-HIAA), and phenylacetic acid, among others.

Some studies have related the level of aggression to androgen levels. These studies point to the androgen insensitivity syndrome (in which there is defective binding of androgens to proteins, resulting in male offspring who have a feminine appearance and a decreased propensity for rough-and-tumble play) and to the adrenogenital syndrome (in which the mother's adrenal cortex exposes the fetus to elevated adrenal androgens, resulting in masculinization, as evidenced in part by an increase in rough-and-tumble play in masculinized girls).

In regard to drugs and chemicals, the following generalizations appear to hold: Small doses of alcohol inhibit aggression and large doses facilitate it; barbituate effects are similar to those of alcohol; aerosols and commercial solvent effects also resemble alcohol's effects; anxiolytics generally inhibit aggression, although paradoxical aggression is sometimes observed; opiate dependence (but not opiate intoxication) is associated with increased aggression, as is the use of stimulants, cocaine, hallucinogens, and, in some cases, variable doses of marijuana.

Neurotransmitters. Generally, cholinergic and catecholaminergic mechanisms seem to be involved in the induction and enhancement of predatory aggression, whereas serotonergic systems and γ-aminobutyric acid (GABA) seem to inhibit this type of behavior. Affective aggression is evidently modulated by both the catecholaminergic and serotonergic systems. Dopamine seems to facilitate aggression, whereas norepinephrine and serotonin appear to inhibit it. Recently, serotonin has again gained attention as a potentially important mediating factor in aggression. It is well known that rapid declines in serotonin levels or function are associated with increased irritability and, in nonhuman primates, with increased aggression. Some human studies have suggested that cerebrospinal fluid of 5-HIAA levels inversely correlate with the frequency of aggression, particularly among persons who commit suicide.

Genetic data and aggressive behavior

Twin studies. Research of monozygotic twins suggests that there is a hereditary component to aggressive behavior. Thus far, most studies have focused on nonpsychiatric populations. In these studies, concordance rates for monozygotic twins exceed those for dizygotic twins.

Pedigree studies. A number of studies show that persons from families with histories of psychiatric disorders are more prone to develop psychiatric disorders and engage in aggressive behavior than persons without such histories. Persons with low intelligence quotient (I.Q.) scores appear to have a higher frequency of deliquency and aggression than persons with normal I.Q. scores. Observed correlations between aggressive behavior and other atypical behaviors suggest that genetic predispositions for atypical behavior, including behaviors associated with psychiatric disorders, are associated with atypical physiological function, one consequence of which is an increase in the probability of aggression.

Chromosome influences. Behavior research involving the influence of chromosomes has concentrated primarily on abnormalities in X and Y chromosomes, particularly the 47-XYY syndrome. Early studies suggested that persons with this syndrome could be characterized as tall, of below-average intelligence, and more likely to be apprehended and in prison for engaging in criminal behavior. Subsequent studies suggest that, at most, the 47-XYY syndrome contributes to aggressive behavior in only a small percentage of the cases. Studies of the androgen and gonadotropin characteristics of 47-XYY persons also have been inconclusive and have not established that such persons are biochemically atypical.

Certain inborn metabolic disorders, genetic in origin, that diffusely involve the nervous system have been reported to be associated with aggressive personalities. Examples include Sanfilippo's syndrome (increased mucopolysaccharide storage), Spielmeyer-Vogt syndrome (a diffuse neuronal storage disorder with increased ganglioside storage), and phenylketonuria.

PREVENTION AND CONTROL OF AGGRESSION

The prevention of death and disability that result from aggressive, violent, or homicidal behavior begins for the physician at the individual level. For instance, violence within a family (e.g. sexual and physical abuse of children, wife-beating, self-destructive behavior) is often revealed through sensitive questioning and a high index of suspicion on the part of the physician. Preventive interventions include psychiatric referral, notification of the proper legal or other authorities (mandatory in such cases as child abuse and specific threats of harm to persons), and skilled coun-

Table 4.4-3
Assessing the Risk of Committing a Homicide

Clinical Characteristics	Low	Medium	High
Hostility indicators (past history):			
Family life	Wanted child, good loving family	Some family disruption, loss of a parent or one-parent family	Early violence, battered child, poor parent model
Significant others	Several reliable family members or friends available	Few or one available	None available
Daily functioning	Good in most activities	Moderately good in some activities	Not good in any activities
Life-style	Stable	Moderately stable	Unstable
Socioeconomic	Upper	Middle	Lower
Employment	Employed	Employment history fairly stable	Unemployed
Education	High school graduate or more (university or technical training)	High school dropout, can read and write	School dropout, semiliterate to illiterate
Housing	Lives in adequate housing, clean environment and space	Fair housing, some overcrowding	Poor housing, crowded, slums
Isolation or withdrawal	Able to relate well to others, outgoing	Mild, some withdrawal and feelings of hopelessness	Long history of being a loner, antisocial, withdrawn, hopeless, helpless feelings
Alcohol or drug use	Nondrinker, occasional social use	Social drinker or user to occasional abuse	Chronic abuse
Psychological help	No history of need for or use of psychiatric hospitalization	Some outpatient psychiatric help, moderately satisfied with self	History of psychiatric hospitalization, negative view of help
Personal history	No history of violence or impulsive behavior	Occasional history of violence or impulsive behavior	Frequent history of violence or impulsive behavior

Perturbation (negative emotional states):			
Anxiety	Low, good emotional control	Occasional feelings of anxiety	Easily aroused to anxiety, high or panic state
Depression	Low	Occasional depression	Severe, chronically moody
Self-esteem	Good, has reinforcements from others	Usually good	Chronically poor self-image
Hostility	Low	Some	Marked, aggressive
Impulse control	Controlled	Some impulsive acting out not physically violent	Feels need for violence
Constriction (narrowing of vision):			
Coping strategies and devices being utilized	Able to cope with stress and outside irritating influences; well-developed defense mechanisms	Usually can cope under most pressures; sometimes becomes constrictive in thinking and acts out	Becomes constrictive under most stress; acts out in destructive, socially unacceptable ways
Disorientation and disorganization	None, is in good contact with what is happening	Little to moderate	Marked, losing contact with reality
Resources	Able to make good use of resources available	Some use, aware of most resources	Unable either to use resources available or to recognize that there is help available
Cessation (stop the person causing the problem):			
Previous arrests	None	Has been arrested, has not served time	Multiple arrest history, served time in prison, would murder to avoid going back to prison
Previous homicide	None	Has exhibited aggressive behavior; been in fights but no attempt to kill another	Yes, looks at the killing of another as a feasible act
Homicide plan	None	Has held fleeting thoughts of killing another, no definite plan	Frequent or constant thoughts with a specific plan
Weapon available	None that person thinks of	Yes, person aware of weapons in immediate environment but not seriously considering use	Yes, and planning on use (a loaded gun should be considered as highly lethal)

This table lists clinical characteristics of persons who are potential homicidal risks and relates characteristics to low-, medium-, and high-risk persons. No one clinical characteristic predicts homicide. However, the greater the number of clinical characteristics that are present in the medium and high categories, the greater the risk. Adapted from N Allen: *Homicide: Perspectives on Prevention*. Human Sciences Press, New York, 1979, with permission.

seling by appropriately trained people. Table 4.4-3 lists in detail risk factors for committing a homicide.

Punishment as a Deterrent

Punishment is sometimes effective as a deterrent to overt aggression. Research findings suggest that the frequency or intensity of such behavior can be reduced by even mild forms of punishment, such as social disapproval; but there appear to be strong grounds for doubting that punishment always, or even usually, produces such effects.

The recipients of punishment often interpret it as an attack against them. To the extent that this is so, individuals may respond even more aggressively. Strong punishment is more likely to provoke desires for revenge or retribution than to instill lasting restraints against violence in the subject. Persons who administer punishment may serve as aggressive models for those on the receiving end of such discipline, and, as noted earlier, exposure to such models may potentiate violent acts. There is some indication that punishment, because of the conditions under which it is usually administered (a long while after the aggression is committed) only temporarily reduces the strength or frequency of aggressive behavior. Once punishment is discontinued, aggressive acts quickly reappear. For these reasons, it seems likely that certain types of punishment often backfire and actually enhance, rather than inhibit, the dangerous actions they are designed to prevent.

Catharsis

For many years it has been widely believed that providing angry persons with an opportunity to engage in expressive but noninjurious behaviors reduces their tension or arousal and weakens their tendency to engage in overt and potentially dangerous acts of aggression. These effects embody the catharsis hypothesis. Although Sigmund Freud accepted the existence of such catharsis, he was relatively pessimistic about its usefullness in preventing overt aggression. At present the benefits of catharsis are thought to be mixed. It may help some people to discharge aggression, while others may become more aggressive as a result.

Training in Social Skills

A major reason why many persons become involved in repeated aggressive encounters is that they lack basic social skills. They do not know how to communicate effectively and, so, adopt an abrasive style of self-expression. Their ineptness in performing such basic tasks as making requests, engaging in negotiations, and lodging complaints often irritates friends, acquaintances, and strangers. These severe social deficits seem to ensure that they will experience repeated frustration and that they will frequently anger those with whom they have direct contact. One technique for reducing the frequency of such behavior may involve providing such persons with the social skills that they so sorely lack. Social skills training has been applied to diverse groups of persons, including highly aggressive teenagers, police, and even child-abusing parents. In many cases, dramatic changes in the targeted behaviors have been produced (e.g., enhanced interpersonal communication, improved ability to handle rejection and stress), and reductions in aggressive behavior related to these shifts have frequently been observed. These results are encouraging and suggest that training in appropriate social skills can offer a promising approach to the reduction of human violence.

Induction of Incompatible Responses

Empathy. When aggressors attack other persons in face-to-face confrontations, they may block out, ignore, or deny signs of pain and suffering on the part of their victims. If the aggressor is exposed to such feedback, one reaction may be the arousal of empathy and a subsequent reduction in further aggression. In several experiments, exposure to signs of pain or discomfort on the part of the victim has been found to inhibit further aggression.

Humor. Informal observation suggests that anger can often be reduced through exposure to humorous material, and some laboratory studies support this proposal. It appears that several types of humor, presented in several different formats, may induce reactions or emotions incompatible with aggression among the persons who observe them.

Other incompatible responses. Many other reactions may also prove to be incompatible with anger or overt aggression. As noted above, mild sexual arousal sometimes operates in this fashion. Similarly, feelings of guilt concerning the performance of aggressive actions may often reduce such behavior. There is also some indication that participation in absorbing cognitive tasks, such as solving mathematics problems, may induce reactions incompatible with anger or aggressive actions.

Drug Treatment

Current reports suggest that different types of drugs, as well as different types of clinical monitoring (e.g., blood pressure and electroencephalogram [EEG]), are essential for optimal treatment of specific aggressive persons. The current findings may be summarized as follows: Lithium appears to be a drug of major promise for some populations of violent patients, especially delinquent adolescent boys; anticonvulsants occasionally reduce seizure-induced forms of aggression, and they may have the same effect on nonepileptics; antipsychotic medications appear to reduce aggression in both psychotic and nonpsychotic violent patients; antidepressants may be effective in reducing violence in some depressed patients; antianxiety agents appear to have a limited role in reducing aggression; and antiandrogen agents may be effective in the treatment of the aggressive sex offender. Beta-blockers and stimulants may be effective in aggressive children. And electroconvulsive therapy may be effective in a small group of selected patients.

VICTIMS OF AGGRESSION

It has been estimated that 18 million Americans have suffered psychiatric disturbance at some point as a result of crime and that, at any given moment, up to 5 million Americans suffer from crime-related symptoms. The National Institute of Justice estimates that a 12-year-old American has an 80 percent chance of being the victim of a serious crime at some point in his or her life. Recent research suggests that many victims of violent crimes are at increased risk for developing major psychiatric problems. Long-term depression and phobias are two of the psychiatric disorders reported to occur more frequently among victims of crime. Many researchers believe that there are distinct and characteristic emotional effects associated with being the victim of a crime and that these effects are related to the fact that victims are the targets of another person's intentional aggression. Table 4.4-4 lists the main emotional aftereffects of crime.

ACCIDENTS AND INJURIES

An accident is an event that occurs by chance or unexpectedly, without any cause or any conscious planning. Careful study of these occurrences shows that causes can sometimes be determined and possibly corrected. However, causes are often multiple and require a many-faceted approach to the problem. For instance, both behavioral and psychological characteristics can be related to the occurrence of accidents. These characteristics include anxiety, boredom, fatigue, and the ingestion of substances that alter concentration and motor coordination. In 1988, according to the National Safety Council, a total of 96,000 deaths and 9 million disabling injuries resulted from accidents.

Injuries are the most common cause of death in the United States for persons under age 44. Accidents are the fourth most common cause of death overall in the United States. The most recent national data on the cost of injuries reported that for the noninstitutionalized population intentional and unintentional injuries were the second leading cause of direct medical costs (second only to heart disease and exceeding cancer) and also accounted for major indirect costs, such as work loss and disability.

Vehicular accidents, industrial accidents, and home accidents were the most frequent types of injury. One third of all injury deaths are secondary to automobile accidents, and one third to other accidents. The remaining third is evenly divided between suicide and homicide. After motor vehicle accidents, the most common causes of accidental death are falls, followed by fire, drowning, and poisoning.

Table 4.4-4
Aftermath of Crime: Main Emotional Effects

Sense of helplessness. The world seems unsafe; victims lack confidence in their judgment and competence to deal with the world.

Rage at being a victim. Intense anger is usually expressed toward family members and those who try to help; conversely, sometimes there is an inability to express any anger at anything.

Sense of being permanently damaged. Rape victims, for example, may feel they'll never be attractive again.

Inability to trust or to be intimate with others. This can include a loss of faith in institutions like the police and the courts.

Persistent preoccupation with the crime. Excessive concern with the crime and its details may reach the point of obsession.

Loss of belief that the world is just. This may include self-blame and a sense of having done something to deserve being a victim.

Table courtesy of Stuart Kleinman, M.D.

Psychophysiological Considerations

The victim's psychophysiological state must be considered in all injuries and accidents. A physical condition, such as fatigue, may lead either to distraction or to an inability to respond quickly enough to avoid an accident. More important is the role of such toxic factors as barbiturates, antihistamines, marijuana, and particularly alcohol. About half of the automobile accidents reported occur in conjunction with alcohol intake. Persons with diabetes, epilepsy, cardiovascular disease, and psychiatric illness have been reported to be involved in more than twice the number of accidents per 1,000 miles of driving than are persons who do not have these illnesses.

Age-related impairments, both motor and cerebral function deficits, may lead to potentially impaired judgment, which contributes to fatal accidents among persons age 65 and older.

Motivations

From a motivational point of view, the first writings dealing with the subject of an accident-prone personality date back to *The Psychopathology of Everyday Life* (1904), in which Freud wrote:

> Many apparently accidental injuries that happen to such patients are really instances of self-injury. What happens is an impulse to self-punishment, which is constantly on the watch and which normally finds expression in self-reproach or contributes to the formation of a symptom, takes ingenious advantage of an external situation that chance happens to offer, or lends *assistance* [italics added] to that situation until the desired injurious effect is brought about.

A number of retrospective studies have looked at the personality characteristics of people who have had severe or frequent accidents. These studies have speculated that individuals repeatedly involved in accidents may have an underlying self-destructive tendency suggestive of the existence of depression, poor control over hostility, a tendency to be more action-oriented and less reflective than the general population, and a propensity for intrapsychic or interpersonal difficulties at least partially resolved by the occurrence of the accident. The concept of an unconscious sense of guilt and a need to atone or to be punished for such guilt feelings may provide the motivation of many unintended accidents. Motivations other than an unconscious sense of guilt may be found by examining the life situations of people involved in accidents. An unconscious wish to escape or avoid something is often apparent. This desire to escape may be related to external situations in which an accident provides a convenient way of avoiding a possibly humiliating experience. One such example is the man who has an accident on his way to a job interview, thereby avoiding the possible humiliation of not obtaining the position he was seeking. Accidents help a person to avoid new responsibilities by providing a convenient and acceptable rationale for not entering into the new situation without losing self-esteem or the esteem of others.

References

Alessi N E, Wittekindt J: Childhood aggressive behavior. Pediatr Ann *18*: 94, 1989.
Archer J, Browne K, eds: *Human Aggression: Naturalistic Approaches*. Routledge, London, 1989.
Bandura A: *Aggression: A Social Learning Analysis*. Prentice-Hall, Englewood Cliffs, NJ, 1973.
Baron R A: *Human Aggression*. Plenum, New York, 1977.
Berkowitz L: On the formation and regulation of anger and aggression: A cognitive-neoassociationistic analysis. Am Psychol *45*: 494, 1990.
Berkowitz L, Cochran S T, Embree M C: Physical pain and the goal of aversity stimulated aggression. J Pers Soc Psychol *40*: 587, 1981.
Coccaro E F: Central serotonin and impulsive aggression. Br J Psychiatry Suppl *8*: 52, 1989.
Danforth J S, Drabman R S: Aggressive and disruptive behavior. Monogr Am Assoc Ment Retard *12*: 111, 1989.
Dollard J, Doob L, Miller N, Mowrer O H, Sears R R: *Frustration and Aggression*. Yale University Press, New Haven, CT, 1939.
Eichelman B: Toward a rational pharmacotherapy for aggressive and violent behavior. Hosp Community Psychiatry *39*: 31, 1988.
Eichelman B S: Neurochemical and psychopharmacologic aspects of aggressive behavior. Annu Rev Med *41*: 149, 1990.
Fonberg E: Dominance and aggression. Int J Neurosci *41*: 201, 1988.
Goldstein A P, Carr E G, Davidson W S, Wehr P: *In Response to Aggression*. Pergamon, New York, 1981.
Liebert R M, Sprafkin J N, Davidson E S: *The Early Window: Effects of Television on Children and Youth*, ed 2. Pergamon, New York, 1982.
Lorenz K: *On Aggression*. Bantam, New York, 1966.
McGuire M T, Troisi A: Aggression. In *Comprehensive Textbook of Psychiatry*, ed 5, H I Kaplan and B J Sadock, editors, p 271. Williams & Wilkins, Baltimore, 1989.
Miczek K A, Mos J, Oliver B: Brain 5-HT and inhibition of aggressive behavior in animals: 5-HIAA and receptor subtypes. Psychopharmacol Bull *25*: 399, 1989.
Neuman G G, ed: *Origins of Human Aggression: Dynamics and Etiology*. Human Sciences Press, New York, 1987.
Prentky R A, Quinsey V L, eds: *Human Sexual Aggression: Current Perspectives*. New York Academy of Sciences, New York, 1988.
Toch H: *Violent Men*. Schenkman, Cambridge, MA, 1980.
Weiger W A, Bear D M: An approach to the neurology of aggression. J Psychiatr Res *22*: 85, 1988.

4.5 / Ethology, Experimental Disorders, and Sociobiology

Ethologists are concerned with the study of animal behavior and the origins of such behavior. The direct observation of animals in their natural environments has been the basic technique of behavioral measurement. However, ethologists have increasingly used other techniques, from introducing experimental factors into a natural environment to actually conducting laboratory investigations. Ethology is particularly relevant for psychiatry because findings of animal studies can shed light on the understanding of human behavior. In 1973 the Nobel prize in medicine was awarded to three ethologists: Konrad Lorenz, Nikolaas Tinbergen, and Karl von Frisch, whose work is described below.

KONRAD LORENZ

Born in Austria, Konrad Lorenz (1903–1988) is best known for his studies of *imprinting*. Imprinting implies that, during a certain short period of development, a young animal is highly sensitive to a certain type of stimulus that then, but not at other times, provokes a specific behavior pattern. Lorenz described how newly hatched goslings are programmed to follow a moving object, whereupon they rapidly become imprinted to follow this and possibly similar objects. Typically, the mother is the first moving object the young sees, but should it see something else first, the gosling will follow it. For instance, a gosling imprinted by Lorenz followed him and refused to follow a goose (Figure 4.5-1). Imprinting is an important concept for psychiatrists to understand in their effort to link early developmental experiences with later behaviors.

Lorenz also studied the forms of behavior that function as sign stimuli—that is, as social releasers—in communications between individuals of the same species. Many of the signals have the character of fixed motor patterns in that they appear automatically and the reaction of other members of the species is equally automatic.

Lorenz is also well known for his study of aggression. He has written about the practical function of aggression, such as the defense of their territory by fish and birds. Aggression among members of the same species is common, but Lorenz has pointed out that, in normal conditions, it seldom leads to killing or even to serious injury. Although the animals attack

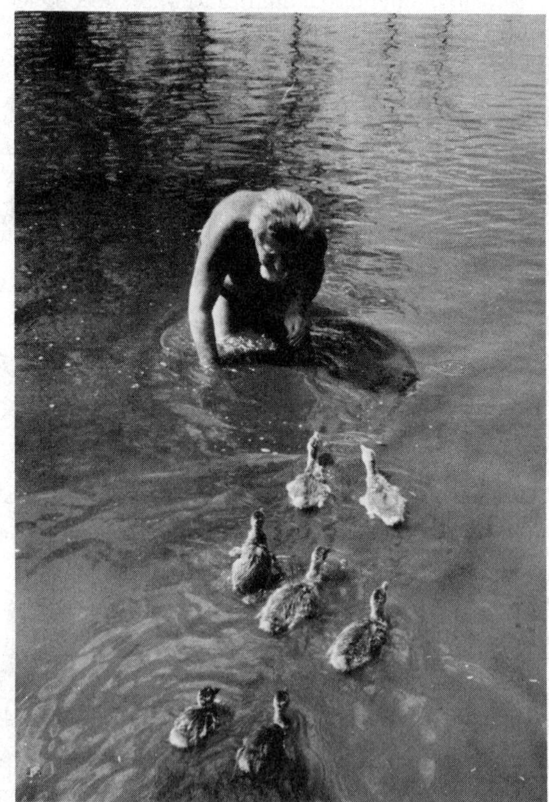

Figure 4.5-1. In a famous experiment, Lorenz demonstrated that goslings would respond to him as if he were the natural mother. (From E H Hess: Imprinting: An effect of early experience. Science *130*: 133, 1959, with permission.)

one another, a certain balance appears between tendencies to fight and flight, with the tendency to fight being strongest in the center of the territory and the tendency to flight strongest at a distance from the center.

In many of his works, Lorenz has tried to draw conclusions from his ethological studies of animals that can also be applied to human problems. The postulation of a primary need for aggression in humans, cultivated by the pressure of selection, is a primary example. This need might have served a practical purpose at an earlier time when human beings lived in small groups that had to defend themselves from other groups. Competition with neighboring groups became the most important factor of selection. However, Lorenz has pointed out how this need has survived the advent of weapons that can be used not merely to kill individuals but to wipe out all human beings.

NIKOLAAS TINBERGEN

Born in 1907 in the Netherlands, Nikolaas Tinbergen, a British zoologist, conducted a series of experiments to analyze various aspects of animal behavior. He also was successful in quantifying behavior and in obtaining measures of the power or strength of different stimuli in eliciting specific behavior. Tinbergen described "displacement activities," which have been studied mainly in birds. For example, in a conflict situation, when the need for fight and the need for flight are of roughly equal strength, birds sometimes do neither. Rather, they display behavior that appears to be irrelevant to the situation (e.g., a herring gull defending its territory can start to pick grass). Displacement activities of this kind will vary according to the situation and the species concerned. It is well known that human beings can engage in displacement activities when under stress.

Lorenz and Tinbergen described *innate releasing mechanisms*, animal responses triggered by releasers, which are specific environmental stimuli. Releasers (including shapes, colors, and sounds) evoke sexual, aggressive, or other responses. For example, big eyes in human infants evoke more caretaking behavior than small eyes do.

In his later work Tinbergen, along with his wife, studied early childhood autism. They began by observing the behavior of autistic and normal children when they meet strangers, which is analogous to the techniques used in observing animal behavior. In particular, they observed in animals the conflict that arises between fear and the need for contact, and noted that it can lead to behavior that is similar to that of autistic children. They hypothesized that in certain specially predisposed children, fear can greatly predominate and can also be provoked by stimuli that normally have a positive social value for most children. This innovative approach to studying infantile autism has opened up new avenues of inquiry. Although their conclusions regarding preventive measures and treatment must be considered tentative, the methodology illustrates another way in which ethology and clinical psychiatry can relate to each other.

KARL VON FRISCH

Born in Austria, Karl von Frisch (1886–1982) conducted studies on changes of color in fish and demonstrated that fish could learn to distinguish among several colors and that their sense of a color was fairly congruent with that of human beings. He later went on to study the color vision and behavior of bees and is most widely known for his analysis of how they communicate with one another—that is, their language or what is known as their dances. His description of this exceedingly complex behavior of bees has prompted an investigation of information systems of other animal species.

ANIMAL MODELS OF PSYCHOPATHOLOGY

Pharmacological Experimentation

With the emergence of biological psychiatry, many researchers have utilized pharmacological means to produce syndrome analogues in animal subjects. Two classic examples are the reserpine model of unipolar depression and the amphetamine psychosis model of paranoid schizophrenia. In the depression studies, animals given the norepinephrine-depleting drug reserpine exhibited behavioral abnormalities analogous to those of major depression in humans. The behavioral abnormalities produced were generally reversed by antidepressant drugs. These studies tended to corroborate the theory that unipolar depression in humans is, in part, the result of diminished levels of norepinephrine. Similarly, animals given amphetamines acted in a stereotyped, inappropriately aggressive, and apparently frightened manner that was similar to paranoid psychotic symptoms in humans. Both of these models are currently thought to be too simplistic in their concepts of etiology, but they remain as early paradigms for this type of research.

Studies were done on the effects of catecholamine-depleting drugs on monkeys during separation and reunion periods. These studies showed that catecholamine-depletion and social separation can interact in a highly synergistic fashion, yielding depressive symptoms in subjects for whom mere separation or low-dose treatment by itself is not sufficient to produce depression.

Environmental Experimentation

A number of researchers, including Ivan Pavlov in Russia and W. Horsley Gantt and H. S. Liddell in America, studied the effects of stressful environments on animals, such as dogs and sheep. Pavlov produced a phenomenon in dogs which he labeled *experimental neurosis*, by use of a conditioning technique that led to symptoms of extreme and persistent agitation. The technique involved teaching dogs to discriminate between a circle and an ellipse and then progressively diminishing the difference between the two. Gantt used the term *behavior disorders* to describe the reactions he elicited from dogs forced into similar conflictual learning situations. Liddell described the stress response he obtained in sheep, goats, and dogs as *experimental neurasthenia*, which was obtained in some cases by merely doubling the number of daily test trials in an unscheduled manner.

Learned helplessness. The *learned helplessness model* of depression, developed by Martin Seligman, is a good example of an experimental disorder. Dogs were exposed to electric shocks from which they could not escape. The dogs eventually "gave up," making no attempt to escape new shocks. This apparent giving up generalized to other situations, and eventually the dogs always appeared to be helpless and apathetic. Because the cognitive, motivational, and affective deficits displayed by these dogs resembled symptoms common to human depressive disorders, learned helplessness, although controversial, was proposed as an animal model of human depression. Research on subjects with learned helplessness and the expectation of inescapable punishment has discovered brain release of endogenous opiates, destructive effects on the immune system, and elevation of the pain threshold.

A social application of this concept involves school children who have learned that they fail in school no matter what they do—they view themselves as helpless losers, and this self-concept causes them to stop trying. Teaching them to persist may reverse this process with excellent results in self-respect and school performance.

Chronic stress. Rats subjected to chronic unpredictable stress (crowding, shocks, irregular feeding, and interrupted sleep time) show decreased movement and exploratory behavior, which demonstrates the role that unpredictability and not having any control over the environment has in producing stress. These behavioral changes can be reversed by antidepressant medication. Animals under experimental stress (Figure 4.5-2) become tense, restless, hyperirritable, or inhibited in certain conflict situations.

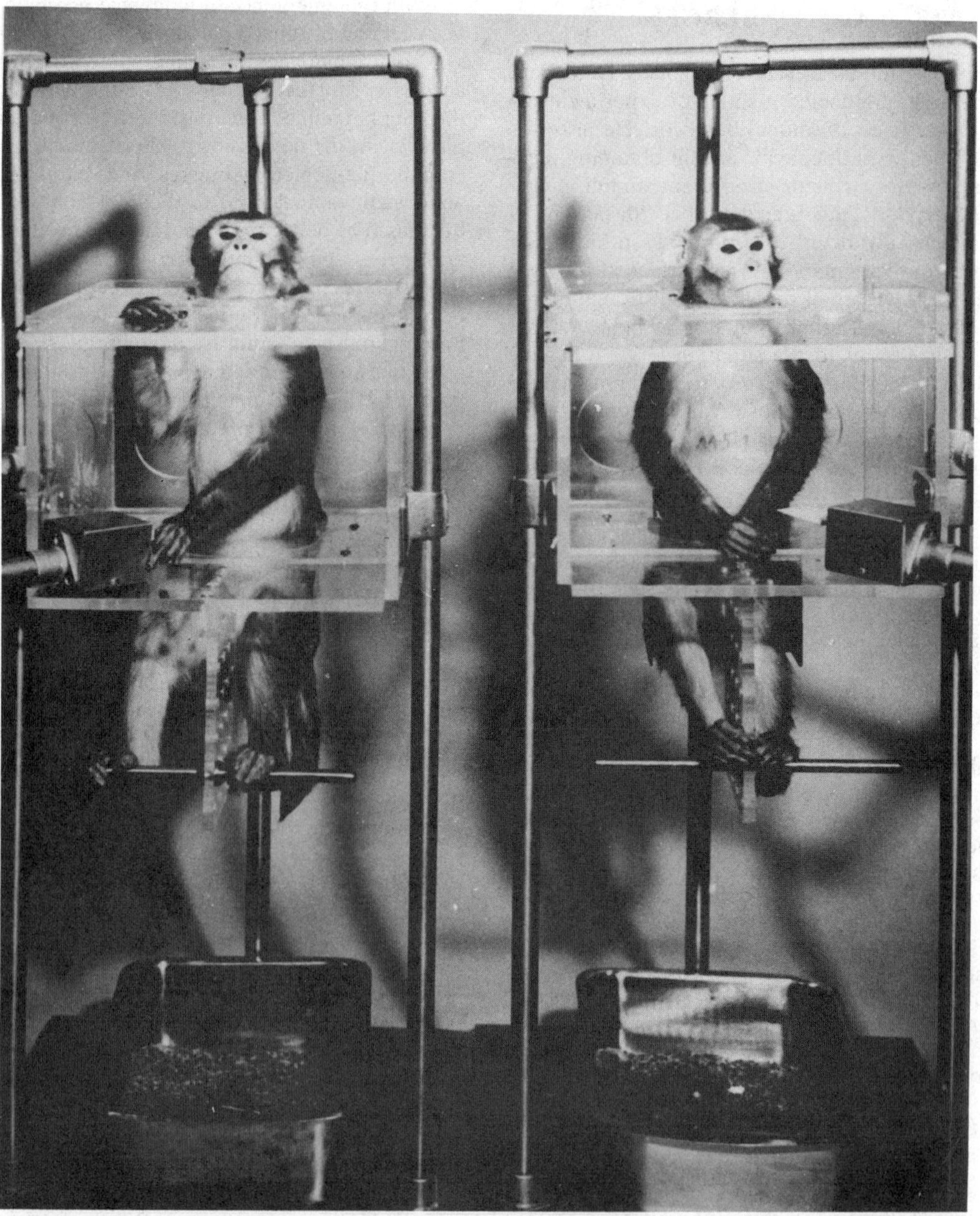

Figure 4.5-2. The monkey on the left, known as the executive monkey, controls whether or not both will receive an electric shock. The decision-making task produces a state of chronic tension. Note the more relaxed attitude of the monkey on the right. (From United States Army Photographs.)

Dominance hierarchy. Animals in a dominant position in a hierarchy have certain advantages (e.g., mating and feeding). Being more dominant than one's peers is associated with elation, and a fall in one's position in the hierarchy is associated with depression. When persons lose jobs, are replaced in organizations, or otherwise have their dominance or hierarchical status changed, they can develop a depression.

Genetics and temperament. Temperament mediated by genetics plays a role in behavior. For example, one group of pointer dogs was bred for fearfulness and a lack of friendliness toward people, and another group was bred for the opposite characteristics. The phobic line of dogs was extremely timid and fearful and showed decreased exploratory capacity, increased startle response, and cardiac arrhythmias. Benzodiazepines diminished these fearful, anxious responses. Amphetamines and cocaine aggravated the responses of genetically nervous dogs to a greater extent than the stable dogs.

Intracranial stimulation. Pleasurable sensations have been produced in both humans and animals through self-stimulation of certain brain areas, such as the medial forebrain bundle, the septal area, and lateral hypothalamus. Rats engaged in repeated self-stimulation (2,000 stimulations per hour) in order to gain rewards. Catecholamine production increases with self-stimulation of these brain areas, and drugs that decrease catecholamines decrease the process.

STUDIES OF DEVELOPMENTAL PROCESSES IN NONHUMAN PRIMATES

An area of animal research that has important relevance to human behavior and psychopathology is longitudinal study of nonhuman primates. Monkeys have been followed from birth to maturity, not only in their natural habitats and laboratory facsimiles but also in laboratory settings that involve differing degrees of social deprivation early in life. Social deprivation has been produced through two predominant conditions: *social isolation* and *separation*. *Socially isolated* monkeys are raised in varying degrees of isolation and are not permitted to develop normal attachment bonds. Monkeys that are *separated* are taken from their primary caretaker and thereby experience a disruption in an already developed bond. Social isolation techniques illustrate the impact of an infant's early social environment on subsequent development (Figure 4.5-3), while separation techniques illustrate the effects of loss of a significant attachment figure. The name most associated with the isolation and separation studies is Harry Harlow. A summary of Harlow's work is presented in Table 4.5-1.

In a series of experiments, Harlow separated rhesus monkeys from their mothers during their first weeks of life. During this time, the monkey infant is dependent on its mother for nourishment and protection, as well as for physical warmth and emotional security—"contact comfort," as Harlow first termed it in 1958. Harlow substituted a surrogate mother made from wire or cloth for the real mother. The infants preferred the cloth-covered surrogate mother that provided contact comfort to the wire-covered surrogate that provided food but no contact comfort.

Rehabilitation of Abnormal Behavior in Primates

In 1972 Stephen Suomi demonstrated that isolates could be rehabilitated if they were exposed to monkeys that would

Figure 4.5-3. Social isolate upon removal of isolation screen.

promote physical contact without threatening the isolates with aggression or overly complex play interactions. These monkeys were called therapist monkeys. To fill such a therapeutic role, young normal monkeys were chosen that would play gently with the isolates and approach and cling to them. Within two weeks, the isolates were reciprocating the social contact, and their incidence of abnormal self-directed behaviors began to decline significantly. By the end of the six-month therapy period, the isolates were actively initiating play bouts with both the therapists and each other, and most of their self-directed behaviors had disappeared. These isolates were observed closely for the following two years, and it was found that their improved behavioral repertoires did not regress over time. The results of this and subsequent monkey therapist studies have underscored the potential reversibility of early cognitive and social deficits at the human level. These studies also have served as a model for developing therapeutic treatments for socially retarded or withdrawn children.

Several investigators have argued that social separation manipulations with nonhuman primates provide a compelling basis for developing animal models of depression and anxiety. Some monkeys react to separations with behavioral and physiological symptoms very similar to those seen in depressed human patients; both electroconvulsive therapy (ECT) and tricyclic antidepressant drugs are effective in reversing the symptoms in monkeys. It is also true that not all separations produce depressive reactions in monkeys, just as separation does not always precipitate depression in humans, young or old.

Individual Differences in Reactions to Social Situations

Recent research has revealed that some rhesus monkey infants consistently display fearfulness and anxiety in situations when similarly reared peers demonstrate normal exploratory behavior and play. These situations generally involve exposure to some kind of novel object or situation. Once the object or situation has become familiar, any behavioral differences between these anxiety-prone or timid infants and their more outgoing peers disappear. These individual differences, however, appear to be quite stable during development.

Table 4.5-1
Social Deprivation in Nonhuman Primates*

Type of Social Deprivation	Effect
Total isolation (not allowed to develop caretaker or peer bond)	Self-orality, self-clasping, very fearful when placed with peers, unable to copulate (Figure 4.5-3). If impregnated, female is unable to nurture young (motherless mothers). If isolation goes beyond six months, no recovery is possible.
Mother-only reared	Fails to leave mother and explore. Terrified when finally exposed to peers. Unable to play or to copulate.
Peer-only-reared	Engages in self-orality, grasps others in clinging manner, easily frightened, reluctant to explore, timid as adult, play is minimal (Figure 4.5-4).
Partial isolation (can see, hear, and smell other monkeys)	Stares vacantly into space, engages in self-mutilation, stereotyped behavior patterns.
Separation (taken from caretaker after bond has developed)	Initial protest stage changing to despair 48 hours after separation; refuses to play. Rapid reattachment when returned to mother.

*Table adaped from work of Harry Harlow, M.D.

Infant monkeys at 3 to 6 months of age that are at high risk for fearful or anxious reactions tend to remain at high risk for such reactions, at least until adolescence.

Long-term follow-up study of the above monkey subjects has revealed some interesting behavioral differences between fearful and nonfearful females when they become adults and have their first infants. Fearful female monkeys that grow up in socially benign and stable environments typically become fine mothers; however, fearful females who have reacted to frequent social separations during childhood with depression are at high risk for maternal dysfunction; more than 80 percent of these mothers either neglect or abuse their first offspring. Yet, nonfearful females who encounter the same number of social separations but do not react to any of these separations with depression subsequently turn out to be good mothers.

SENSORY DEPRIVATION

The history of sensory deprivation and its potentially deleterious effects evolved from instances of aberrant mental behavior in explorers, shipwrecked sailors, and prisoners in solitary confinement. Toward the end of World War II, startling confessions, induced by brainwashing prisoners of war, caused a rise of interest in this psychological phenomenon brought about by the deliberate diminution of sensory input.

To test the hypothesis that an important element in brainwashing is prolonged exposure to sensory isolation, Hebb and his coworkers brought solitary confinement into the laboratory and demonstrated that volunteer subjects—under conditions of visual, auditory, and tactile deprivation for periods of up to seven days—reacted with increased suggestibility. Some of the subjects also showed

Figure 4.5-4. Choo-choo phenomenon in peer-only-reared infant rhesus monkeys.

characteristic symptoms of the sensory deprivation state: anxiety, tension, inability to concentrate or organize one's thoughts, increased suggestibility, body illusions, somatic complaints, intense subjective emotional distress, and vivid sensory imagery—usually visual, sometimes reaching the proportions of hallucinations with delusionary quality.

Theories of Sensory Deprivation

Psychological theories. Anticipating psychological explanations, Freud wrote: "It is interesting to speculate what could happen to ego function if the excitations or stimuli from the external world were either drastically diminished or repetitive. Would there be an alteration in the unconscious mental processes and an effect upon the conceptualization of time?"

Indeed, under conditions of sensory deprivation, the abrogation of such ego functions as perceptual contact with reality and logical thinking brings about confusion, irrationality, fantasy formation, hallucinatory activity, and wish-dominated mental reactions. In the sensory deprivation situation, the subject becomes even more dependent on the experimenter and must trust him for the satisfaction of such basic needs as feeding, toileting, and physical safety. It has been suggested that a patient undergoing psychoanalysis is in a kind of sensory deprivation room (e.g., soundproofed, dim lights, couch) in which primary-process mental activity is encouraged through free association.

Physiological theories. The maintenance of optimal conscious awareness and accurate reality testing depends on a necessary state of alertness. This alert state, in turn, depends on a constant stream of changing stimuli from the external world, mediated through the ascending reticular activating system in the brain stem. In the absence or impairment of such a stream, as occurs in sensory deprivation, alertness falls away, direct contact with the outside world diminishes, and impulses from the inner body and the central nervous system may gain prominence. For example, idioretinal phenomena, inner ear noise, and somatic illusions may take on a hallucinatory character.

Other theories

Personality. Personality theories attempt to explain not the phenomena of sensory deprivation but, rather, the variation in these phenomena from subject to subject. For example, why do some volunteers in experiments quit sooner than others? Different approaches are offered by different investigators—introversion-extroversion, body-field orientation, and optimal stimulation level.

Expectation. These hypotheses involve social influences, including the important role played by the experimenter. Modern researchers place great emphasis on anticipation, instructional set, and the demand characteristics of the experimental situation (tacit and overt suggestion).

Cognitive. These theories stress that the organism is an information-processing machine, the purpose of which is optimal adaptation to the perceived environment. Lacking sufficient information, the machine is unable to form a cognitive map, against which current experience is matched. Disorganization and maladaptation are the result. In order to monitor one's own behavior and attain optimal responsiveness, the organism must receive continuous feedback. Without this feedback, the person is forced to project outward idiosyncratic themes that have little relationship to reality. This situation is similar to that of many psychotics.

SOCIOBIOLOGY

Sociobiology is the study of the biological basis of social behavior. It is a relatively new discipline that integrates principles of evolution, genetics, ecology, and ethology. Sociobiologists see many similarities in animal and human behavior, such as competition, territoriality, aggression, reproduction, mate selection, male-female differences, parenting, and altruism. A sociobiological postulate is that human behavior has evolved to achieve maximum fitness and adaptation. *Fitness* is defined as the highest measure of evolutionary success in that the best genes are passed on from one generation to the next. *Inclusive fitness* is the sum of the individual's personal fitness and that of his or her relatives compared with the rest of the population.

Role of evolution. Evolution is any change in the genetic makeup of a population. It occurs through natural (Darwinian) selection, which is the reproduction of those genes produced by mutation that account for the most successful individual. Lamarckian evolution occurs through the inheritance of acquired characteristics and explains the evolution of culture.

Competition. Individuals vie with one another for resources or territory. *Territory* is an area that is defended for the exclusive use of the animal and ensures access to food and reproduction. The ability of one animal to defend a disputed territory or resource is called *resource holding potential*, and the greater that potential, the more successful the animal.

Aggression. Aggression serves both to increase territory and to eliminate competitors. Defeated individuals can emigrate, disperse, or remain in the social group as subordinate animals. A dominance hierarchy in which individuals are associated with one another in subtle but well-defined ways is part of every social pattern.

Reproductive strategies. Because behavior is influenced by heredity, those behaviors that promote reproduction and survival of the species are among the most important. The usual pattern is for males to compete with other males for the females and to produce the most fit offspring. Male-male competition can take various forms. For example, sperm can be thought of as competing for access to the ovum. Females compete with females but in more subtle ways, primarily in terms of dominance, nest-building ability, and breeding potential. Different behavioral patterns between males and females, called *sexual dimorphism*, evolve to ensure the maintenance of resources and reproduction.

Altruism. Altruistic behavior benefits another individual and appears to enhance his or her success, with no benefit derived to the altruistic individual. Altruism is explained by sociobiology as a way of maintaining the gene pool at its highest level. It is a selfish act but selfishness at the level of the gene, rather than the individual. The classic case of altruism is in the female worker classes of certain wasps, bees, and ants. These insects are sterile and do not reproduce; rather, they labor altruistically for the reproductive success of the queen.

There is another possible mechanism for the evolution of altruism: group selection. If groups containing altruists are more successful than those composed entirely of selfish members, these altruistic groups succeed at the expense of the selfish ones, and altruism evolves. However, there is a serious problem. Within each group, altruists are at a severe disadvantage relative to selfish individuals, however well the group as a whole is able to do.

References

Alcock J: *Animal Behavior: An Evolutionary Approach*. Sinauer Associates, Sunderland, MA, 1989.

Barabasz A F: Restricted environmental stimulation and the enhancement of hypnotizability: Pain, EEG alpha, skin conductance and temperature responses. Int Clin Exp Hypn *30*: 147, 1982.

Barash D P: *Sociobiology and Behavior*, ed 2, Elsevier, New York, 1982.

Borrie R A, Suedfeld P: Restricted environmental stimulation therapy in a weight reduction program. J Behav Med *3*: 147, 1980.

Dixon A K, Fisch H U, Huber C, Walser A: Ethological studies in animals and man: Their use in psychiatry. Pharmacopsychiatry *22*: 44, 1989.

Fine T H, Turner J W Jr: The effect of brief restricted environmental stimulation therapy in the treatment of essential hypertension. Behav Res Ther *20*: 567, 1982.

Harlow H F: The nature of love. Am Psychol *13*: 673, 1958.

Lister R G: Ethologically based animal models of anxiety disorders. Pharmacol Ther *46*: 321, 1990.

Lorenz K Z: *The Foundations of Ethology*. Springer, New York, 1981.

McKinney W T: Interdisciplinary animal research and its relevance to psychiatry. In *Comprehensive Textbook of Psychiatry*, ed 5, H I Kaplan and B J Sadock, editors, p 326. Williams & Wilkins, Baltimore, 1989.

Pavlov I P: *Conditioned Reflexes* (G V Arrep, trans.). Oxford University Press, London, 1927.

Pitman R K, Kolb B, Orv S P, Singh M: Ethological study of facial behavior in non-paranoid and paranoid schizophrenic patients. Am J Psychiatry *144*: 99, 1987.

Spear N E, Miller J S, Jagielo J A: Animal memory and learning. Annu Rev Psychol *41*: 169, 1990.

Suedfeld P, Ballard E J, Murphy M: Water immersion and flotation: From stress experiment to stress treatment. J Environ Psychol *3*: 147, 1983.

Suomi S J: Social development in rhesus monkeys: Consideration of individual difference. In *The Behaviour of Human Infants*, A Oilverio, M Zappella, editors. Plenum, New York, 1983.

Suomi S J, Harlow H F: Social rehabilitation of isolate-reared monkeys. Dev Psychol *6*: 487, 1972.

Tinbergen N: *The Study of Instinct*. Clarendon, Oxford, 1989.

4.6 / Anthropology and Psychiatry

Anthropology and psychiatry are both concerned with the understanding of human behavior. Anthropology is the study of culture, which is the external expression of individual mental life as represented by manners, customs, skills, language, parent-child interactions, beliefs, and social life. Cultures differ in their definitions of health, illness, and healing and also vary greatly in child-rearing patterns, social models and expectations, role opportunities, and other variables. Anthropology also includes cross-cultural studies, which are used in the field of *comparative psychiatry* to describe and analyze cross-cultural variations in the incidence and prevalence of syndromes and symptoms. Disorders are compared from one culture to another to see if there are universal characteristics that transcend cultural differences.

Culture is traditional in that social practices are passed from generation to generation. Culture also encompasses the notion of a group of persons sharing a system of action and beliefs capable of persisting longer than the life span of any one individual, a group whose adherents come from the sexual reproduction of the group members. In that sense, every culture is *historical* and *genetic*. A culture also possesses a value system of good, bad, desirable, and undesirable behavioral patterns and can be examined from both a *psychological* and a *normative* viewpoint in terms of how the majority adapt to stresses unique to a particular culture.

PSYCHOANALYTICAL ANTHROPOLOGY

Beginning with *Sigmund Freud*, psychoanalysts have applied their insight to cultural data. In 1913 in *Totem and Taboo*, Freud described earliest humans as a group of brothers who killed and devoured their violent primal father. That criminal act and the so-called totem meal made the brothers feel guilty. Consequently, they set up rules formulated so that similar acts would never occur again; these rules were the beginning of social organization. *Carl Jung*'s writings include many anthropological references, especially to archeology and mythology. In *Symbols and Transformations*, written in 1912, Jung traced patients' fantasies back to earliest human artifacts. Neither Freud nor Jung had field experience, but *Erik Erikson*, for one example, did. Erikson is best known for his psychocultural biographies of Gandhi and Martin Luther and for the 1950 book *Childhood and Society*, in which he attempted to integrate individual psychosexual development with cultural influences. Many of his conclusions were based on his experiences with the Pine Ridge Indians in the Dakotas and the Yurok Indians in Oregon.

George Devereux studied American Plains Indians and provided insights into the problems that arise in dealing with patients from diverse ethnic backgrounds. In the 1930s and 1940s *Abram Kardiner* worked with the concept of *national character* and suggested that each culture is associated with a common (or at least widely shared) personality structure. Kardiner believed that the adult Russian personality, for example, was characterized by depressive and manic traits. Other such generalities about national character were set forth by various workers, but those descriptions were often used to foster political, ideological, or discriminatory attitudes and, so, have fallen out of favor. The current consensus is that a clinically meaningful prediction about one's personality cannot be made on the basis of nationality alone. But as *Ruth Benedict* wrote in *Patterns of Culture*, personality types may reflect a culture's configuration because people are malleable and they assume a society's expected behavior pattern.

Bronislaw Malinowski and *Margaret Mead* were among the group of anthropologists who examined the psychoanalytic concept that adult personality and mental functioning are largely determined during childhood. Malinowski examined childhood and adult sexuality in the Trobriand Islanders and claimed that he found no evidence of the Oedipus complex, which at the time was believed to be universal. Margaret Mead examined gender and sex-role behavior. She observed three tribes in New Guinea and found different patterns of sex-role behavior for men and women in each tribe. According to Mead, behavior is relative, and a society can create deviancy by either condoning or condemning certain behavior patterns. Mead believed the Oedipus complex to be a useful concept in its widest meaning, which is that in all societies adults are involved in the growing child's sexual attitudes, especially toward the parent of the opposite sex.

Child-Rearing Practices

The effects of early life experience on adult mental health and what accounts for deviance or maladaptive behavior are still controversial issues. Psychodynamic psychiatrists and theorists rely on historical data about adverse experiences to explain later behavior; but new work shows that few experiences are irreversible. Some affection-deprived children described by Bowlby are able to grow up capable of forming attachments if other experiences later in life are favorable. Similarly, many successful adults come from deprived or otherwise toxic homes and appear to be or are invulnerable to those stressors. Nevertheless, studies of child-rearing practices among different cultures have included the following: (1) Indulgence and care in early infancy are important determinants of adult mental health; (2) the nurture of the child by various caretakers, in addition to the mother, is not harmful; (3) a wide variety of child-rearing practices are found in different cultures; and (4) the major influences on personality development revolve around love-hate and dependence-independence issues, rather than the control of sexual behavior. The basic relationship, however, between child-rearing patterns and subsequent adult personality in complex societies, such as the United States, has not yet been elucidated. In this country there are cycles of permissiveness and constraint, reward and punishment, and a general tendency to focus on bowel and bladder training as important child-rearing practices.

Some universals observed among children of different cultures are as follows: (1) Smiling is a social greeting exhibited by all normal members of every known society; (2) there is a taboo againts incest and homicide; (3) there are gender differences in roles that go beyond reproduction; (4) males are more aggressive than females; and (5) strong attachments and fear of separation and of strangers appear in the second half of the first year of life.

Anthropologists place humans in the same group as other old-world higher primates, which include monkeys and apes. These primates all share the following characteristics: (1) single birth, (2) frequent nursing, (3) late weaning, (4) high mother-infant proximity, (5) gradual transition to peer play in groups, and (6) variable but low direct involvement by adult males in child rearing.

CROSS-CULTURAL STUDIES

Cross-cultural studies examine and compare different cultures along a number of parameters: attitudes, beliefs, expectations, memories, opinions, roles, stereotypes, prejudices, and values. Usually, the cultures studied use different languages and have different political organizations. Cross-cultural studies are subject to extreme bias because of problems in translation. Questions have to be asked in ways that are clearly understood by the group under study. One of the best known cross-cultural studies, *Psychiatric Disorder among the Yoruba* by Alexander Leighton, was his attempt to replicate in Nigeria the Stirling County study he had conducted in Canada. The study was criticized because not only did it fail to distinguish psychophysiological symptoms from those associated with infections, parasites, and nutritional diseases but it assumed that the same indicators for sociocultural disintegration in Stirling County could be used among the Yoruba. Other studies have confirmed that psycholinguistics—the study of language and its communicative functions—must be taken into account if cross-cultural approaches are to be valid. All cultures are relative; that is, each must be examined within the context of its own language, customs, and beliefs. Various cultures assign different roles depending on status. Research has shown that there is a high incidence of depression among adult women in Kikuyu society, where women are subject to heavy role demands. There is also a high prevalence of schizophrenia among last-born sons in rural Ireland because of the stresses linked to that role.

Diagnoses of mental disorders have been conducted among various cultures by the World Health Organization. The International Pilot Study of Schizophrenia confirmed that schizophrenia exists among all groups studied (e.g., Nigerians, Danes, Laotians, Celts, Croatians, Hutterites, South Pacific Tongans, and Taiwanese) and is constant across cultures. Outcome studies of patients with schizophrenia, however, are not reliable because some societies (in contrast to the United States) do not stigmatize persons with mental illness, who are quickly reintegrated into the society. A major difficulty in cross-cultural diagnosis is the bias arising from the researcher's cultural background. That bias can be reduced if careful attention is given to translation and to the attitude of the examiner. Nevertheless, some generalizations can be made about cross-cultural or comparative psychiatry. Certain symptoms exist in all societies: anxiety, mania, depression, suicidal ideation, somatization, paranoia (persecutory delusions), and thought disorder. Although different labels may be applied in different cultures, recognition of deviant behavior and agreement that conditions are treatable (whether by the psychiatrist in one culture or the shaman in another) are universal.

ETHNOGRAPHY

Ethnography (from Greek *ethnos*, meaning race or people) is an inductive method of describing cultural forms through the examination of a series of cases. Ethnographers document phenomena by various methods, such as the examination of written records, folk tales, and myths; linguistic analysis; interviews with key informants; collections of life histories; questionnaire surveys; psychological tests; and, most important, participant observation.

United States Culture

The United States is a multiethnic country, but the values of the white middle class predominate. The numerous subgroups that represent waves of immigration over the years have influenced our culture but not to such an extent that these groups have lost their identity. They have been partially *acculturated*; that is, they have assumed characteristics of the larger or more advanced society. But they have not been *assimilated*; that is, their unique cultural traits have not been absorbed totally. Recognized minority subcultures in this country include Hispanics (Mexican Americans, Puerto Ricans, Cuban Americans), Asian Americans (Chinese, Japanese, Korean, Pacific Islanders), African Americans, and Native Americans (American Indians, Eskimos).

As of the 1980 census, the resident population in the United States by race and national origin was as follows:

white, 188 million; African American, 26 million; American Indian (including Eskimo), 1.4 million; Chinese, 806,000; Filipino, 775,000; Japanese, 701,000; Asian Indian, 361,000; Korean, 354,000; Vietnamese, 262,000; Americans of Spanish origin, 14.5 million. The 1990 census shows that the Asian population grew by 65 percent between 1980 and 1990, and the number of Hispanics grew by 44 percent. Asians, however, are still a small part of the population—just 3 percent in 1990. Hispanics are now 8 percent of Americans, up from 6 percent in 1980. African Americans hold a steady 12 percent share of the population, and the white share has fallen slightly, to 84 percent from 86 percent.

It is hazardous to attempt to describe ethnic characteristics of a culture. The risk of stereotyping is great, and, as mentioned above, the concept of national character is controversial among contemporary anthropologists. Nevertheless, U.S. society has been described as having certain characteristics against which the ethnic groups in this country are compared. Table 4.6-1 lists the characteristics attributed to the national character of the United States.

Some subcultures approximate the U.S. national character more than others, and some characteristics are more highly valued and prevalent within a particular ethnic group than in the culture as a whole. Hispanics, for example, value the nuclear family and place great emphasis on having more, rather than fewer, children. Asian Americans place an extremely high value on education; although they make up about 3 percent of the general population, they represent about 15 to 20 percent of college students. Another example is that of filial piety, a strong value among Chinese Americans; Chinese-American parents expect their children to care for them in their old age.

The nuclear family of mother, father, and children is a universal unit in all cultures. The extended family—in which grandparents, parents, children, and other relatives all live under the same roof—is no longer common in the United States, but it is still prevalent in less industrialized cultures. Functions of the extended family, such as caring for the sick and elderly, have been taken over by institutions.

In the United States, over 85 percent of men and women between the ages 35 and 45 are husband or wife in a nuclear family. Even though close to one out of two marriages ends in divorce, a majority of persons remarry and create new nuclear units. In fact, serial monogamy, in which persons remarry after divorce but remain faithful to the spouse during the course of the marriage, is a noticeable trend. Other family configurations are outlined in Table 4.6-2.

Table 4.6-1
American Cultural Characteristics*

1. Nuclear family unit valued highly with few children; financially independent by age 18
2. Bowel and bladder training important in child rearing
3. Personal hygiene emphasized, neatness valued
4. Self-reliance and rugged individualism valued
5. Avoidance of dependency role, especially after age 65; unwillingness to be cared for by children
6. Ambivalence about overt expressions of sexuality
7. Ownership of own home desirable
8. Belief that hard work will be rewarded
9. Collective approach to solving common problems
10. Upward social mobility desirable

*The concept of national character is controversial among contemporary anthropologists, many of whom would not agree with this list.

Table 4.6-2
Family Systems

Types	Characteristics
Monandry	Woman has one husband.
Polyandry	Woman has multiple husbands at once; biological father generally unknown, all males in family take paternal responsibility.
Polygamy	Husband has multiple wives at once; woman's status inferior to man's; pecking order among wives exists in some form, one claiming more rights than others.
Patrimony	Property is inherited from the father.
Patronymic	Bride takes the groom's name; son takes the name of the father.
Patrilocal	Fathers arrange marriages of sons and daughters by making contracts with other fathers; wife resides with the family or tribe of her husband.
Patrilineal	Kinship or descent is through the father.
Matrilineal	Kinship or descent is through the mother.
Bigamy	The crime of marrying while one has a wife or husband still living from whom one is not divorced.
Monogamy	Marriage with only one person at a time.
Matrilocal	Married couple lives in home of bride.
Neolocal	Married couple sets up new home independent of mother and father.
Bilineal	Both male and female parents are considered equal in regard to descent.

Urbanization. Urbanization is a major social, cultural, and ecological process in 20th-century America. By the year 2000, more than 90 percent of the population will live in urban areas. City life has altered the factors that cause illness and has affected the incidence and prevalence of many diseases. Accordingly, urbanization has influenced many approaches used in the diagnosis and treatment of somatic illness and the methods used in the delivery of health services.

The U.S. Bureau of the Census uses operational definitions that recognize degrees of urbanization. The basic urban unit, according to the Census Bureau, is the standard metropolitan statistical area. That unit represents an integrated economic and social region with a recognized urban population nucleus of substantial size. In formulating the boundaries of an urban unit, the Census Bureau also takes into account such features as population density, nonagricultural employment, and community ties. The population living outside metropolitan areas is subdivided into farm population and nonfarm population.

The trend of people's migrating and populating urban areas continues. The country's top 25 metropolitan areas are home to one in three Americans. Of these, six are in the Northeast, five are in the Midwest, seven are in the South, and seven are in the West.

The major metropolitan areas in the South and the West are rapidly growing. Riverside-San Bernadino, California, grew faster than any other large metropolitan area in the 1980s, up by 45 percent. It jumped to 17th place, up from 24th place in 1980. In contrast, Pittsburgh lost 6 percent of its population and now ranks 20th among large metropolitan areas. In 1980 it was 11th.

Nearly 1 in 10 Americans lives alone, accounting for 24 percent of households. Since 1980 single-person households have grown by almost 5 million. Most people who live alone are women, primarily old widows. But an increasing number of Americans live alone at all ages, as people postpone marriage into their late 20s and divorce in middle age.

Redefining the family. There has been a slight decline in the number of family units in this country over the past decade. Of the country's 94 million households (minimum of three people), 71 percent are families, down from 74 percent in 1980. The definition of a family is two or more related people living together. The number of traditional or nuclear families, defined as married couples with children under age 18 in the home, fell by 5 percent between 1980 and 1990. Married couples with children in the home are now 26 percent of households, down from 31 percent in 1980. By contrast, the number of couples without dependent children at home grew by 17 percent during the 1980s.

The number of people living with nonrelatives has been growing faster than any other household type, up by 46 percent in the 1980s. These households include unmarried male-female couples, homosexual couples, and nonromantic partners—for example, friends sharing an apartment. People living with nonrelatives, however, are not a large segment of households, accounting for just 5 percent of the total, up from 4 percent in 1980.

A modern ethnographic approach in Western subcultures is demonstrated by the 1971 study of a predominantly African American ghetto in a large northern U.S. city. The researchers studied the community by living in it and by experiencing ghetto life directly. They progressed from being observer-participants to active participants in community life, becoming partisans who openly identified with the population under study. The scientific motivation for their study was to examine the patterns usually ascribed to persons living in a culture of poverty. They found that 83 percent of African American families were conventional male-headed households and that the social structure beyond the family level consisted of a multiplicity of local institutions, such as churches, social clubs, and political organizations. Since then, a radical change has occurred: In 1983 only 42 percent of African American families were made up of two parents with a male head of household, and that figure has continued to decline.

Culture Change

Persons respond to culture change either by moving into a different culture or by staying put while the culture changes around them. When change is acute and sweeping, the adaptive mechanisms of individuals and of their social support may be overwhelmed. *Culture shock* is characterized by anxiety or depression, a sense of isolation, derealization, and depersonalization. Culture shock is minimized if persons are part of an intact family unit and if they are prepared for the new culture in advance. It is minimal if refugees, for example, are clustered in a few central locations, rather than dispersed throughout the nation.

Studies have demonstrated a higher rate of psychiatric hospitalization in the United States for immigrants, especially young men, than for the native-born. There also appears to be a higher incidence of paranoid symptoms among immigrant groups, which may be related to their differences (color, language, habit) from the larger society. Acute psychotic episodes that occur among third-world immigrants in this country usually have clear-cut precipitating factors, are recurrent, and have a good prognosis.

MEDICAL ANTHROPOLOGY

Medical anthropology focuses on the practice of medicine and the cultural aspects of providing and receiving health care. The study of culture, attitudes, and beliefs has a special importance for psychiatry and medicine. For example, an effective prevention program for alcoholism involves changing attitudes and values about drinking. Similarly, the success of antismoking campaigns depends on altering attitudes about tobacco. Cultural aspects of health care are best understood within the context of the particular culture under study.

Culture of the Mental Hospital

The physical and sociocultural environment of mental hospitals was studied in terms of its effects on patients. When disagreements concerning a patient's management occurred among staff members, patients did not do as well as when staff consensus existed. The environment of the hospital is as much a therapeutic agent as the medication a patient receives. A psychiatric hospital, as described by Alfred Staunton, is a small society with established hierarchical categories. Dissension or confusion about staff roles or expectations may be transmitted to patients, whose symptoms may be exacerbated as a result. The English psychiatrist Maxwell Jones attempted to organize the psychiatric hospital as a *therapeutic community*. Jones's primary goal was the elimination of the divisions between various mental health professions, for he believed divisions to be artificial and harmful to the patient.

Cultural Aspects of Disease

Class status and ethnic identity influence the experience of illness. It is important, however, to avoid generalizations. The patient must be understood in terms of the specific culture or ethnic group to which he or she belongs. Mexican Americans and Puerto Rican Americans, for example, share as many group cultural differences as they do commonalities. Different cultures—Haitians, West Indians, Puerto Ricans, and Christian faith healers—incorporate shamans, persons who follow a divine call to healing. The clinician must find out how acculturated the patient is to the cultural mainstream of life. The influence of culture on the reporting and presentation of symptoms must be considered. A reluctance to discuss certain topics may stem from the patient's individual psychology or from adherence to the customs and etiquette of the social group.

Hispanic Americans. Mexican Americans make up the largest group (10 million) of Americans of Spanish origin and are referred to as Chicanos, particularly in the southwestern United States, where most Mexican Americans live. They frequently receive health care from folk healers (*curanderos*), who prescribe herbs or dietary change or use magic.

Puerto Rican Americans are the second largest Hispanic group (2 million). Most live in the northeastern states. In a study of Puerto Rican households in New York City, a significant number of adults visited folk healers or spiritists (*espiritismos*) during times of emotional crisis. Spiritism is practiced in small neighborhood centers (*centros*) where a medium performs magical procedures, such as drawing off evil spirits that may have entered into the patient, a therapeutic process known as *trabajando la causa* (working the cause).

Asian Americans. The two largest groups of Asian Americans, Chinese and Japanese, have shown different degrees of acculturation in the United States. During World War II, internment of second-generation West Coast Japanese (Nisei) in concentration camps was imposed by the United States government. Over 100,000 people were forcibly detained; when they regained their freedom in 1945, they were filled with fear and resentment. Chinese immigration preceded that of the Japanese, and they, too, were subject to discriminatory legislation. Prejudice tends to reinforce ethnic identity and retard assimilation. Since the 1960s civil rights movement, greater assimilation of Asian Americans has occurred. Nevertheless, the clinician must be aware of unique cultural behavior patterns. For example, a Japanese patient may say yes (*hai*) as a sign of polite participation in a conversation, rather than as a sign of agreement; Hawaiian patients may avoid eye con-

Table 4.6-3
Culture-Bound Syndromes

Diagnosis	Country or Culture	Characteristics
Amok	Southeast Asia, Malaysia	Sudden rampage, usually including homicide and suicide; occurs in males; ends in exhaustion and amnesia
Boufée délirante	France	Transient psychosis with elements of trance or dream states
Brain fog	Sub-Saharan Africa	Headache, agnosia, chronic fatigue, visual difficulties, anxiety; seen in male students
Bulimia	North America	Food binges, self-induced vomiting; may occur with depression, anorexia, or substance abuse
Colera	Mayan Indians (Guatemala)	Temper tantrums, violent outbursts, gasping, stuporousness, hallucinations, delusions
Empacho	Mexican and Cuban American	Inability to digest and excrete recently ingested food
Grisi siknis	Miskito of Nicaragua	Headache, anxiety, anger, aimless running
Hi-Wa itck	Mohave American Indian	Anorexia, insommia, depression, suicide associated with unwanted separation from loved one
Involutional paraphrenia	Spain, Germany	Paranoid disorder occurring in midlife; distinct from schizophrenia but may have elements of both schizophrenia and paranoia
Koro	Asia	Fear that the penis will withdraw into the abdomen, causing death
Latah	Southeast Asia, Malaysia, Bantu of Africa, Ainu of Japan	Automatic obedience reaction with echopraxia and echolaia precipitated by a sudden minimal stimulus; occurs in females; also called a startle reaction.
Nervios	Costa Rica and Latin America	Headache, insomnia, anorexia, fears, anger, diarrhea, despair
Piblokto (Arctic hysteria)	Eskimos of northern Greenland	Mixed anxiety and depression, confusion, depersonalization, derealization; occurs mainly in females; ends in stuporous sleep and amnesia
Reactive psychosis	Scandinavia	Psychosis precipitated by psychosocial stress; acute onset with good prognosis, premorbid personality fairly intact; in DSM-II-R known as schizophreniform disorder
Shinkeishitsu	Japan	Syndrome marked by obsessions, perfectionism, ambivalence, social withdrawal, neurasthenia, and hypochondriais
Susto	Latin America	Severe anxiety, restlessness, fear of black magic and of evil eye
Taijin-kyofusho	Japan	Anxiety, fear of rejection, easy blushing, fear of eye contact, concern about body odor
Windigo	Native American Indians (Algonkian)	Fear of being turned into a cannibal through possession by supernatural monster, the windigo

tact if they were taught that eye contact is a sign of aggression; Chinese patients may smile or laugh when they are embarrassed or sad; and Pacific Islanders may miss medical sessions because it is socially acceptable to be casual about fixed dates and appointments.

American Indians. Native Americans are among the most widely studied groups and have the best known ethnographies. They are the only ethnic group in America to have a separate medical care program administered by the federal government, the Indian Health Service. There is a long tradition of healing rituals among Native Americans, who make no distinction between mental and physical illness. Illness is thought to result from a disharmony among a person's natural, supernatural, and human environments caused by culturally unacceptable behavior or by witchcraft. High rates of alcoholism and suicide are found in Native Americans and Eskimos.

African Americans. The 26 million African Americans constitute a heterogeneous group; however, most belong to the lower and lower-middle socioeconomic classes. Only 20 percent hold white-collar jobs, compared with 40 percent of white workers, and the median income of African American families is only about 55 percent that of white families.

Unique to certain African American subgroups, such as those from Haiti, is root work or voodoo. Rites, hexes, prayers, curses, and other practices are used by shamans and witch doctors to influence health or illness. Persons undergoing healing experiences often enter trance states, during which they are vulnerable to shamanistic suggestions. Shamans give objective reality to popular and emotionally accepted beliefs of the cultural group.

Certain generalizations about the health of African Americans can be made. They have a shorter life expectancy than whites, a higher incidence of hypertensive disease, a higher suicide rate (among young African American men compared with young white men; other age cohorts have the same rates), and a higher homicide rate. Some of these differences are related to the low socioeconomic level of most African Americans; in general, the poor do not utilize health care facilities as readily as the more affluent.

Christian beliefs. The past two decades have seen a growing interest in Christian faith healing directed toward what is called sickness of the spirit, the emotions, and the body. According to certain fundamentalist groups, any form of sickness may have a demonic origin, and some cases call for prayer and exorcism in order for recovery to occur. The role of the physician is to heal through divine intervention. Some faith healers are willing to work with physicians. Others, however, believe that participation in a close-knit Christian community, participation in a bible-study group, and prayer are sufficient.

Culture-Bound Syndromes

Some disorders are found only in certain cultures or among certain groups. They often occur with little warning, their course is usually short, and their prognosis is generally favorable.

The notion of culture-bound syndromes is conceptually simple but operationally complex. Because culture is the matrix in which all biological, psychological, and social functioning operates, it follows that all psychiatric syndromes are, to some extent, culture-bound. Western psychiatrists, for example, tend to view mental syndromes in Western societies as culture-free; but bulimia is as shaped by Western culture as koro is by Oriental culture. If African healers with limited Western contact were transplanted briefly to this country, they would be equally surprised by the odd symptoms of the patients here.

Conversion disorder is seen much less frequently in America today compared with 19th-century European society. The symptoms of anorexia nervosa are related to the cultural expectations of weight and body image in modern Western industrial society. Table 4.6-3 briefly outlines some culture-bound syndromes. See Section 15.2 for additional information on culture-bound syndromes.

References

Andreasen N C: The American concept of schizophrenia. Schizophr Bull *15*: 519, 1989.

Andrews G R: Cross cultural studies: An important development in aging research. J Am Geriatr Soc *37*: 483, 1989.

Benedict R: *Patterns of Culture*. Houghton Mifflin, Boston, 1934.

Cole M: *Comparative Studies of How People Think: An Introduction*. Harvard University Press, Cambridge, 1981.

Erikson E: *Childhood and Society*. Norton, New York, 1950.

Fabrega H Jr: An ethnomedical perspective of Anglo-American psychiatry. Am J Psychiatry *146*: 588, 1989.

Fabrega H Jr: On the significance of an anthropological approach to schizophrenia. Psychiatry *52*: 45, 1989.

Favazza A, Faheem A: *Themes in Cultural Psychiatry*. University of Missouri Press, Columbia, 1982.

Freud S: *Totem and Taboo*. Norton, New York, 1950.

Jung C: *Symbols and Transformations*, ed 2. Princeton University Press, Princeton, 1967.

Kardiner A, Linton R, DuBois C: *The Psychological Frontiers of Society*. Columbia University Press, New York, 1945.

Kirmayer L J: Cultural variations in the response to psychiatric disorders and emotional distress. Soc Sci Med *29*: 327, 1989.

Kleinman A, Eisenberg L, Good B: Culture, illness, and care. Ann Intern Med, *88*: 251, 1978.

Konner M: Anthropology and psychiatry. In *Comprehensive Textbook of Psychiatry*, ed 5, H I Kaplan and B J Sadock, editors, p 283. Williams & Wilkins, Baltimore, 1989.

Leff J: *Psychiatry around the Globe: A Transcultural View*. Marcel Dekker, New York, 1981.

Malinowski B: *Sex and Repression in Savage Society*. Harcourt, New York, 1927.

Mezzich J E: International diagnostic systems and Latin-American contributions and issues. Br J Psychiatry Suppl *4*: 84, 1989.

Mollica R, Wyshak G, de Marneffe D, Khwon F, Lavelle J: Indochinese versions of the Hopkins symptom checheirt-25: A screening instrument for the psychiatric care of refugees. Am J Psychiatry *144*(4): 497, 1987.

Westermeyer J: Psychiatric diagnosis across cultural boundaries. Am J Psychiatry *142*: 7, 1985.

Wohl J: Integration of cultural awareness into psychotherapy. Am J Psychother *43*: 343, 1989.

4.7 / Epidemiology, Biostatistics, and Social Psychiatry

Epidemiology, biostatistics, and social psychiatry rely on methods that observe, describe, and record events. This process, called the *scientific method*, is based on strict adherence to honesty, accuracy, and controlled experimentation. An *experiment* is a test designed to validate a hypothesis or to determine the probability of a theory. It relies on two types of reasoning—inductive and deductive. *Inductive reasoning* is the process of reasoning from the particular to the general or making a hypothesis from observing events. It is the complement to *deductive reasoning*, which is reasoning from the general to the particular or making a new hypothesis from already known principles.

The scientific method stems from several different philosophical schools. The first system relevant to psychology and psychiatry is that of *empiricism*, which is the doctrine that all knowledge is derived from experience. Most empiricists recognize that the mind and inner experience affect one's perceptions of the outer world. This position is contrary to the school of *rationalism*, which holds that by reason alone, unaided by experience, one can arrive at basic truths regarding the world.

The school of *determinism* is also relevant to psychiatry because of its tenet that the individual is a product of and controlled by his or her history and personal experience. The scientific method as applied to the behavioral sciences relies on the theory of *parsimony*, which holds that there should be one explanation, rather than many. In medicine the theory of parsimony is expressed in the adage that two diagnoses should not be made when one diagnosis can account for all the signs and symptoms. In view of the complexities of human behavior and experience, however, a parsimonious approach is often not possible.

EPIDEMIOLOGY

Epidemiology is the study of the distribution, incidence, prevalence, and duration of disease. In psychiatry epidemiological methods contribute to an understanding of the causes, treatment, and prevention of mental illness. Such methods also help define and evaluate strategies to prevent and control disease and disability. In addition, epidemiological studies help in the overall planning and evaluating of mental health programs on both a local and a national level.

Epidemiological surveys reveal that about one-third of all Americans have had or will have a psychiatric disorder at some time in their lives. The most common mental disorder is anxiety, and the next most common are depression and alcohol or other substance abuse. In addition, surveys have demonstrated that about 15 percent of all patients seen for a medical or surgical problem by nonpsychiatric physicians have an associated emotional disorder, most often depression or alcohol abuse or both.

Epidemiology advances psychiatric research by correlating clinical findings with sociodemographic variables such as age, gender, and socioeconomic status. For example, higher rates of almost every emotional disorder are found in persons under age 45 than in those over 45. In general, women have significantly higher rates than men for all disorders, particularly depression and anxiety. Men, however, have significantly higher rates of substance use disorder and antisocial personality disorder. Schizophrenia, which affects about 1 percent of the population, shows similar rates for both men and women.

Epidemiological studies are also used to compare the incidence and the prevalence of diseases internationally and cross-culturally. In general, the prevalence of emotional disorder appears to be fairly constant, regardless of nationality or cultural background; however, schizophrenia has a better prognosis and outcome in less-developed third-world countries than it does in better-developed societies, such as the United States and the United Kingdom.

Types of Clinical and Epidemiological Studies

Clinical and epidemiological studies in psychiatry attempt to answer questions relating to the causes, treatment, course, prognosis, and prevention of various disorders. There are two main types: (1) observational, in which the natural course of an illness is followed without any intervention, and (2) experimental, in which some or all factors under study are controlled by the investigator. Most studies are experimental in design; however, because of the many variables involved in psychiatric disorders, it is difficult to design well-controlled experimental studies. The most common types of experimental designs used in psychiatry are described below.

Cohort study. A cohort is a group chosen from a well-defined population that is studied over a long period of time. These are also known as longitudinal studies. An example is the study by Stella Chess and Alexander Thomas of temperamental characteristics of the same group of infants at ages 3 months, 2 years, 5 years, and 20 years. They were able to discern a relationship between the initial characteristics of the infant and a subgroup of children who eventually had clinical psychiatric problems. In this study the cohort is the group born and studied in the year the study began.

Cohort studies provide direct estimates of risk associated with a suspected causal factor. They are more time-consuming and expensive to perform than case history studies, which are usually quick and inexpensive. Cohort studies are usually conducted when there is ample evidence from case history studies that a relationship exists between a risk factor and a disorder. For example, in the relationship between lung cancer and smoking, many case history studies had been published before the first cohort study.

Retrospective and prospective study. Prospective studies, also called longitudinal studies, are based on observing events as they occur. A major problem in psychiatric longitudinal studies is that some persons are lost to follow-up over time. Retrospective studies are based on past data or past events.

Cross-sectional study. These studies provide information about the prevalence of disease in a representative study population at a *particular point in time*. For this reason, they are also known as prevalence studies.

Case-history study. This is a retrospective study that examines persons with a particular disease.

Case-control study. This is a retrospective study that examines persons without a particular disease.

Clinical trial. Specially selected patients receive a course of treatment, and another group does not in a clinical trial. Eligible patients are assigned to the treatment group or to the control group on a random basis, and the goal of the study is to determine the effects of a given treatment.

Double-blind study. This type of study helps eliminate bias because neither the patient nor the persons involved in the study know which, if any, treatment is being given to the patient. In drug studies, a control group of patients may receive a *placebo*, an inert substance prepared to resemble the active drug being tested in the experiment. A response to the placebo may represent the psychological effect of taking a pill, a response not due to any psychopharmacological property (so-called *placebo effect*). In addition, the doctor does not know the treatment given because drugs are identified by special codes unknown to him or her. Assessment of outcome may also be made by persons other than those administering the treatment—the so-called blind evaluators. Control subjects may also receive an alternative comparison treatment, rather than just a placebo.

Crossover study. This type of study is a variation of the double-blind study. The treatment group and the control or placebo group change at some point, so that the placebo group gets the treatment and the initial treatment group gets the placebo. This procedure eliminates bias because, if the treatment group improves in each instance and the placebo group does not, one can conclude that the makeup of both groups is truly random. Each group serves as the control for the other in both trials.

Psychiatric case register. A case register maintains a longitudinal record of psychiatric contacts for each person receiving care in a geographically defined community. Not all areas lend themselves to a register because persons may leave the area for treatment or the population may be highly mobile. A well-maintained register is of great value in reporting accurate treated-incidence rates, lifetime- or period-treated-prevalence rates, comparative rates for different time periods for the same population, information regarding utilization of services over time, and identification of high-risk groups for further study.

Major Epidemiological Studies

Major psychiatric epidemiological research studies have been conducted over the years. The goal of each study was to determine the prevalence of psychopathology in a defined community. Persons in a particular community were interviewed directly (usually using a structured interview protocol) to determine the presence or absence of psychological symptoms. The major studies are described below.

Chicago area. A team under the direction of R. Faris and H. Dunham examined about 35,000 admissions to mental hospitals in Chicago between 1922 and 1934. The survey reported that first hospital admissions for schizophrenia were highest among persons from the central sections of Chicago, members of the city's lowest socioeconomic group. It was also reported that rates of admission decreased as one moved away from the central areas and into more affluent communities. Faris and Dunham postulated a *drift hypothesis*, which holds that impaired persons slide down the social scale because of their illness. By contrast, a *segregation hypothesis* holds that, instead of helplessly drifting downward, schizophrenic persons actively seek city areas where anonymity and isolation protect them from the demands that more organized societies make on them. This study helped conceptualize two additional hypotheses about mental illness: (1) the *social causation* theory, which holds that being a member of a low socioeconomic group is etiologically significant in causing illness, and (2) the *social selection* theory, which holds that having a mental illness leads one to become a member of the lower socioeconomic group as a secondary phenomenon. In other words, the illness is caused by genetic or psychological factors, and the drift downward occurs as a result.

Monroe County, New York. The Monroe County, New York, psychiatric case register is an epidemiological data file maintained by the University of Rochester School of Medicine since 1960. The case register contains information on all county residents who utilize psychiatric services. The data found that 3 percent of the county received care in mental health care facilities in the region, including the offices of private practitioners. The so-called newly-treated incidence rate was less than 1 percent.

Midtown Manhattan study. In 1954 a team directed by Thomas Rennie and Leo Srole designed and conducted a survey involving 1,660 adults sampled from a specific section of New York City. The objectives of the study were to determine the effects of demographic, social, and personal factors on mental health and illness, using a structured interview conducted by nonpsychiatrists. Mental illness was rated not present, mild, moderate, or marked. The main objective was to test the association between life stress and psychological symptoms. Some of the findings follow: There was a rise in mental disorders as age increased; 81 percent of persons from 20 to 59 years of age had symptoms that were mild to severely incapacitating, and 23.4 percent of persons in this age group were substantially impaired. Socioeconomic status was the single most significant variable affecting mental illness, persons in the lower socioeconomic group having six times as many symptoms as those in the higher groups.

New Haven study. In 1950 A. B. Hollingshead and F. C. Redlich studied the relation of social class to the prevalence of treated mental illness in New Haven, Connecticut. Their studies included a census of psychiatric patients, a survey of the population at large, a study of psychiatrists, and a controlled case study. Analysis of the data revealed a definite relationship between social class and mental illness. Neurosis was more prevalent among persons in the higher socioeconomic groups; psychosis was more prevalent among persons in the lower socioeconomic groups. The poor were more often seen in mental health clinics than by private psychiatrists. In addition, low socioeconomic status, occupational instability, and downward mobility were associated with the highest frequency of psychiatric disability. Hollingshead and Redlich devised a subgrouping of class structure in this county based on a particular level of education, occupation, and income. Their class distinctions, described in Table 4.7-1, are used widely by sociologists and epidemiologists. A more recent New Haven study used a structured diagnostic interview to make specific diagnoses. A major finding of that study was that 15.1 percent of the adult population over age 26 showed evidence of a mental disorder, and a probable mental disorder was present in an additional 2.7 percent.

Stirling County study. In 1952 Alexander H. Leighton conducted a psychiatric epidemiological study of Stirling County, a Nova Scotian county of 20,000 persons. Information was recorded using structured interviews by nonclinician interviewers that was later rated by a psychiatrist. Unlike the New Haven and Midtown Manhattan surveys, subjects of the Stirling County study lived in rural areas, with persons from small villages, one small town, and many isolated farms. Male and female household heads were interviewed. The major findings were that 57 percent of persons could be identified as having a lifetime prevalence of some mental disorder, 24 percent having notable impairment, and 20 percent being in need of psychiatric attention. Women showed considerably more psychiatric disorders than did men, and psychiatric disorders were found to increase with age and degree of poverty.

The NIMH Epidemiologic Catchment Area Program (NIMH-ECA)

The NIMH-ECA project evolved from the report of the 1977 *President's Commission on Mental Health*, which highlighted the need to identify who are the mentally ill,

Table 4.7-1
Class Status and Cultural Characteristics of Subjects in the New Haven Study

Class	Class Status and Cultural Characteristics
I	Class I, containing the community's business and professional leaders, has two segments: a long-established core group of interrelated families and a smaller upwardly mobile group of new people. Members of the core group usually inherit money, along with group values that stress tradition, stability, and social responsibility. Those in the newer group are highly educated, self-made, able, and aggressive. Their family relations often are not cohesive or stable. Socially, they are rejected by the core group, to whom they are, however, a threat by the vigor of their leadership in community affairs.
II	Class II is marked by at least some education beyond high school and occupations as managers or in the lower-ranking professions. Four of five are upwardly mobile. They are joiners at all ages and tend to have stable families, but they have usually gone apart from parental families and often from their home communities. Tensions arise generally from striving for educational, economic, and social success.
III	Class III men for the most part are in salaried administrative and clerical jobs (51 percent) or own small businesses (24 percent); many of the women also have jobs. Typically, they are high school graduates. They usually have economic security but little opportunity for advancement. Families tend to be somewhat less stable than in class II. Family members of all ages tend to join organizations and to be active in them. There is less satisfaction with present living conditions and less optimism than in class II.
IV	In class IV, 53 percent say they belong to the working class. Seven of 10 show no generational mobility. Most are content and make no sacrifices to get ahead. Most of the men are semiskilled (53 percent) or skilled (35 percent) manual employees. Practically all the women who are able to hold jobs do so. Education usually stops shortly after graduation from grammar school for both parents and children. Families are much different from those in class III. Families are larger, and they are more likely to include three generations. Households are more likely to include boarders and roomers. Homes are more likely to be broken.
V	Class V adults usually have not completed elementary school. Most are semiskilled factory workers or unskilled laborers. They are concentrated in tenement and cold-water-flat areas of New Haven or in suburban slums. There are generally brittle family ties. Very few participate in organized community institutions. Leisure activities in the household and on the street are informal and spontaneous. Adolescent boys frequently have contact with the law in their search for adventure. There is a struggle for existence. There is much resentment, expressed freely in primary groups, about how they are treated by those in authority. There is much acting out of hostility.

how they are treated, and by whom. Darrel Regier and his associates at the Division of Biometry and Epidemiology of the NIMH sought to identify the percentage of the population with mental disorders. The objective was to determine what percentage of the population with mental disorders was receiving treatment in mental health settings (such as psychiatric clinics), private psychiatrists' offices, and in such nonpsychiatric settings as general medical treatment centers and internists' offices. In 1978 provisional estimates indicated that at least 15 percent of the population of the United States was affected by mental disorders in one year, and only one-fifth of these persons received care from mental health specialists. Three-fifths of persons with identified mental disorders were treated by primary care physicians.

A major goal of the NIMH-ECA study is to determine more specifically the prevalence of mental disorders as defined by the third edition of *Diagnostic and Statistical Manual of Mental Disorders* (DSM-III) and its revision (DSM-III-R) and to establish longitudinal data on the course of various mental disorders.

Various sites around the country are being studied to assess mental disorder prevalence, incidence, and service use from geographically defined community populations of at least 200,000 residents. Random samples are drawn to obtain completed interviews on at least 20,000 community and institutional residents. The Diagnostic Interview Schedule (DIS)—which assesses the presence, duration, and severity of symptoms—is the major instrument that the trained lay interviewer used to interview each subject.

Compared with all previous studies, the NIMH-ECA study utilizes better diagnostic tools and more specific critieria to make a reliable diagnosis. These include careful clinical description and follow-up studies. Much larger samples are used than in the previously described studies.

In general, early findings of the ECA program show the following: Rates of depression are twice as high for females as for males; males are more likely than females to have alcoholism; and drug abuse is more common in persons under age 30 than in older persons.

The most current epidemiological findings of prevalence rates for specific mental disorders in the five ECA sites are listed in Table 4.7-2. More specific data about each disorder are found in the chapter that discusses the disorder in depth.

Assessment Instruments

The major obstacle to identification of cases has been the lack of an explicit set of criteria for diagnostic classification. Over the years a variety of diagnostic procedures and assessment instruments have been developed.

Information about a subject can be collected in several ways. Medical records are often used for patients in clinical settings. Records in central data banks called *case registers* can be used. In Scandinavian countries, particularly Sweden, control data banks are extensive. An important source of information about a subject is the *direct interview*, which is a person-to-person interaction. *Indirect surveys* using a structured self-report form may be used, but they lack the clinical judgment of an experienced practitioner that may be necessary in some instances.

The most common assessment approach is an interview format, which may be *structured* (the same questions asked of all subjects) or *unstructured* (interviewers choose their questions based on their own clinical judgment). Several structured instruments with acceptable interrater reliability are outlined in Table 4.7-3.

An effective assessment instrument must be reliable, valid, and free of bias. *Reliability* refers to whether or not the find-

Table 4.7-2
Comparison of Standardized One-Month, Six-Month, and Lifetime Prevalence Rates of DIS/*DSM-III* Disorders per 100 Persons 18 Years and Older: All Sites Combined*

	Rate, % (Standard Error)		
Disorders	**1 mo**	**6 mo**	**Lifetime**
Any DIS disorder covered	15.4 (0.4)	19.1 (0.4)	32.2 (0.5)
Any DIS disorder except cognitive impairment, substance use disorder, and antisocial personality	11.2 (0.3)	13.1 (0.4)	19.6 (0.4)
Any DIS disorder except phobia	11.2 (0.3)	14.0 (0.4)	25.2 (0.5)
Any DIS disorder except substance use disorders	12.6 (0.3)	14.8 (0.4)	22.1 (0.4)
Any DIS disorder except substance use or phobia	8.3 (0.3)	9.4 (0.3)	13.8 (0.4)
Substance use disorders	3.8 (0.2)	6.0 (0.3)	16.4 (0.4)
Alcohol abuse/dependence	2.8 (0.2)	4.7 (0.2)	13.3 (0.4)
Drug abuse/dependence	1.3 (0.1)	2.0 (0.1)	5.9 (0.2)
Schizophrenic/ schizophreniform disorders	0.7 (0.1)	0.9 (0.1)	1.5 (0.1)
Schizophrenia	0.6 (0.1)	0.8 (0.1)	1.3 (0.1)
Schizophreniform disorder	0.1 (0.0)	0.1 (0.0)	0.1 (0.0)
Affective [mood] disorders	5.1 (0.2)	5.8 (0.3)	8.3 (0.3)
Manic episode	0.4 (0.1)	0.5 (0.1)	0.8 (0.1)
Major depressive episode	2.2 (0.2)	3.0 (0.2)	5.8 (0.3)
Dysthymia†	3.3 (0.2)	3.3 (0.2)	3.3 (0.2)
Anxiety disorders	7.3 (0.3)	8.9 (0.3)	14.6 (0.4)
Phobia	6.2 (0.2)	7.7 (0.3)	12.5 (0.3)
Panic	0.5 (0.1)	0.8 (0.1)	1.6 (0.1)
Obsessive-compulsive	1.3 (0.1)	1.5 (0.1)	2.5 (0.2)
Somatization disorder	0.1 (0.0)	0.1 (0.0)	0.1 (0.0)
Personality disorder, antisocial personality	0.5 (0.1)	0.8 (0.1)	2.5 (0.2)
Cognitive impairment (severe)†	1.3 (0.1)	1.3 (0.1)	1.3 (0.1)

Data from Darrell Regier and associates, Arch Gen Psychiatry *45*: 981, 1988, with persmission.
*The rates are standardized to the age, sex, and race distribution of the 1980 noninstitutionalized population of the United States age 18 years and older. DIS indicates Diagnostic Interview Schedule.
†Dysthymia and cognitive impairment have no recency information; thus, the rates are the same for all three time periods.

ings of the assessment instrument or diagnostic procedure are reproducible and can be replicated when the instrument is used by different examiners (*interrater reliability*) or on different occasions (*test-retest reliability*). For example, are various clinicians referring to the same thing when they diagnose schizophrenia? *Validity* refers to whether the test measures what it is supposed to measure. Does the assessment instrument identify cases that it is designed to identify?

Validity can be broken down further into the following categories: *Criterion validity*, in which results from one test instrument are compared with the results of another test whose validity has already been established; *face validity*, which refers to the test's making sense to the investigator using it; *content validity*, which refers to the test's covering specific types of information that can be interpreted or scored at a later date; *concurrent validity*, which refers to the results' corresponding to the results of another test with the same variable; and *construct validity*, which refers to the test instrument's being constructed so that it measures what it is designed to measure. The two properties of validity and reliability are extremely important in psychiatric epidemiology, especially if one is attempting to identify a specific disorder or syndrome.

Analytic studies can also be flawed by *bias*, an error in construction that favors one outcome over another. Bias can occur if examiners know something about the status of the case that influences their judgment (e.g., they know that one group is receiving medication). These potential flaws can affect the validity of a study's findings. To eliminate this kind of bias, researchers developed the *double-blind method*. Bias is also diminished by *randomization* of the sample, in which each member of the total group studied has an equal chance of being selected; for example, each person may be assigned a number from a table of random numbers.

Assessment instruments must be *sensitive*; that is, they must be able to detect the thing being evaluated (e.g., to diagnose a disorder when it is present). If an instrument detects a disorder in a person who does not have the disorder, the result is called a *false-positive*, rather than a *true-positive*. Tests must also be *specific*; that is, they must not detect things not being evaluated. For example, tests must be able to diagnose the absence of a disorder in a person who does not have the disorder, which is called *true-negative*. If a disorder is diagnosed as absent in a person when it is present, it is called a *false-negative result*. Assessment instruments should also have good *predictive value*, which is the proportion of true-positive or true-negative tests. Predictive values indicate what percentage of test outcomes are expected to coincide with assigned diagnoses. Table 4.7-4 summarizes the interpretation of the concepts of sensitivity, specificity, and predictive value.

BIOSTATISTICS

Biostatistics is the mathematical science of describing, organizing, and interpreting data related to medicine. Epidemiology relies on statistics to enable investigators to examine possible causes of disease and to determine which, if any, are relevant. Similarly, treatment strategies can be tested for specific disorders with analytical epidemiological studies using statistics.

The principles of statistics are beyond the scope of this book; however, a glossary of statistical terms that can be found in most elementary textbooks of statistics is presented below. A knowledge of such terms is necessary not only for understanding epidemiological concepts but also for accurately assessing statistical methods that appear in scientific publications.

Statistical Overview

There are two major types of statistics: descriptive and inferential. *Descriptive statistics* are methods for summarizing, organizing, and describing observations (e.g., the average number of symptoms associated with anxiety disorder). Examples include the mean, standard deviation, and variance. *Inferential statistics* are methods used to draw general conclusions about probabilities on the basis of a sample (e.g., the influences of drug A versus drug B in the treatment of a group

Table 4.7-3
Commonly Used Assessment Instruments

Instrument	Condition	Interviewer	Comments
Present State Examination (PSE)	Psychotic conditions, schizophrenia	Psychiatrists	Limited to 1-month period prior to interview; can be used with computer program CATEGO
Schedule for Affective Disorders and Schizophrenia (SADS)	Schizophrenia and affective disorders	Psychiatrists or specially trained interviewer	Variations: SADS-C measures current disorder, and SADS-L measures lifetime disorders
General Health Questionnaire (GHQ)	Medical patients with psychiatric symptoms of anxiety or depression	Self-report	Does not identify specific mental disorders
Diagnostic Interview Schedule (DIS)	Covers over 30 mental disorders, including schizophrenia, affective disorders, anxiety, substance abuse, organic mental disorders	Self-report combined with specially trained interviewers	Correlates with range of DSM-III diagnostic classification; assesses symptoms over lifetime; used in the NIMH-ECA program
Iowa Structured Psychiatric Interview (ISPI)	Major psychiatric disorders	Trained interviewer	Provides detailed psychosocial and family history; covers lifetime prevalence

Table 4.7-4
Definitions and Calculations for Interpreting Performance of Diagnostic Tests

Term	Definition	Calculation
True positive (TP)	Diseased person with abnormal test results	
True negative (TN)	Nondiseased person with normal test results	
False positive (FP)	Nondiseased person with abnormal test results	
False negative (FN)	Diseased person with normal test results	
Referent value	A value to which laboratory results can be referred and from which the probability of disease or predictive value can be calculated	
Sensitivity	True positive rate	$\frac{TP}{TP + FN} \times 100$
Specificity	True negative rate	$\frac{TN}{TN + FP} \times 100$
Predictive value of abnormal test results (PV +)	Proportion of abnormal test results that are true positive	$\frac{TP}{TP + FP} \times 100$
Predictive value of normal test results (PV −)	Proportion of normal test results that are true negative	$\frac{TN}{TN + FN} \times 100$
Efficiency	Percentage of all results that are true results, whether positive or negative	$\frac{TP + TN}{\text{Grand Total}} \times 100$

Table by John F. Greden, M.D.

of depressed patients). Examples include the *t*-test, chi-square, and analysis of variance.

Data refer to factual information derived from a population or a sample. A *population* is the entire collection of a set of objects, people, or events in a particular context (e.g., all schizophrenic patients in a particular hospital). A *sample* is a subset selected from that population (e.g., one-half of the schizophrenic patients in a particular hospital). Data can be nominal (organized into categories), ordinal (ranked in order), or organized into interval ratios (measured on a scale, graph, or table).

Glossary of Statistical Terms

Analysis of variance (ANOVA). A set of statistical procedures designed to compare two or more groups of observations. It determines whether the differences between groups are due to experimental influence or to chance alone.

Canonical correlation. A multivariate technique for simultaneously finding the relationship of linear combinations of two or more predictors and two or more outcomes.

Chi-square. A nonparametric test used to evaluate the relative frequency or proportion of events in a population that fall into well-defined categories.

Coefficient of correlation. The relationship between two sets of paired measurements. Correlation coefficients—which may be positive, negative, or curvilinear, depending on whether the variations are in the same direction, the opposite direction, or both directions—can be computed in a variety of ways (see Scatter diagram). The most common is the product moment correlation referred to as Pearson's *r* or simply *r*. Correlation coefficients are intended to show degree of relation and not that one variable causes the other. The maximum value of a correlation coefficient is 1; the minimum value of 0 indicates that no relationship exists between two variables.

Confidence interval. An interval that is likely to capture the population mean with a specified level of confidence. For the 95 percent confidence interval, the changes are estimated to be 95 in 100 that the true mean falls within that interval.

Control group. A group that does not receive treatment and is used as a standard of comparison.

Critical ratio. In a statistical study involving 30 or more subjects, the system used to determine whether differences found between two items are larger than could be expected from chance. The term "T-ratio" is used in studies involving fewer than 30 subjects to determine whether differences are related to chance.

Discriminant analysis. A multivariate method for finding the relationship between a single discrete outcome and a linear combination of two or more predictors.

Distribution. A series or range of values that can be organized according to their frequency of occurrence (*frequency distribution*). A symmetrical, bell-shaped frequency distribution of scores is called a *normal distribution* (the bell curve).

Factor analysis. A data reduction technique used to reduce a large number of variables to a smaller number of linear combinations of variables.

Incidence. The number of new cases occurring over a specified period of time. The most common time period used is one year, producing an annual incidence calculated as follows:

$$\text{Incidence} = \frac{\text{Number of new persons developing a disease (over a one-year period)}}{\text{Total number of persons at risk (over a one-year period)}}$$

A study of incidence is more difficult to do than a study of prevalence cases because one has to exclude from the incidence numerator those persons who already have the disease; they cannot be considered new cases. Since persons who have had the disease are no longer at risk for it, they must also be excluded from the denominator. A broader concept of total incidence includes those persons with a new episode of illness, regardless of whether there were previous episodes.

Lifetime expectancy is the total probability of a person's developing a disorder during a lifetime. Prevalence and incidence vary for sex and age; thus, *sex-specific* rates and *age-specific* rates are used to express the relative frequency of cases in each category.

McCall's T. A specialized standard score with a mean of 50 and a standard deviation of 10.

Mean deviation. A measure of variation determined by dividing the sum of deviations in a set of variables by the number of cases involved.

Measure of central tendency. A central value in a distribution around which other values are distributed. Three measures of central tendency are the mean, the median, and the mode.

Mean. A statistical measurement derived from adding a set of scores and then dividing by the number of scores. The mean is the average score.

Median. The value in the middle of a set of measurements. For example, in the series 2, 3, 5, 11, 21, the number "5" is the median value.

Mode. The value that appears most frequently in a set of measurements.

Multiple regression. A form of multivariate analysis in which a scaled variable is correlated with a linear combination of independent or predictor variables.

Multivariate analysis. Methods for considering the relationship of three or more variables. Multivariate methods include multiple regression, discriminant analysis, canonical correlation, and factor analysis.

Multivariate analysis of variance (MANOVA). A multivariate technique that uses an ANOVA design but includes multiple dependent variables.

Nonparametric. Statistical methods that do not require restrictive assumptions about population distributions.

Null hypothesis. The assumption that there is no significant difference between two random samples of population. When the null hypothesis is rejected, observed differences between groups are deemed to be improbable by chance alone.

Percentile rank. The percentage of scores in a distribution exceeded by any particular score. For example, a percentile rank of 80 means that 20 percent of the scores exceed a score of 80.

Population. The entire collection of a set having the same definition.

Power. The probability of rejecting the null hypothesis when, in the real world, it should have been rejected. Power is the probability of identifying a true difference.

Predictive value. Ability of a test to predict a condition. *Positive predictive value* is the number of true positives divided by the sum of the number of true positives and false positives; it is the probability that a patient with a positive test result does, in fact, have the condition in question. *Negative predictive value* is the number of true negatives divided by the sum of the number of true negatives and false negatives; it is the probability that a patient with a negative test result is, in fact, free of the condition in question.

Prevalence. The number of cases of a disorder that exist. There are several types of prevalence.

Point prevalence. The number of persons who have a disorder at a specified point in time. The point can be a certain calendar day (e.g., April 1, 1986) or any day during a particular study (e.g., the fourth day of the study), regardless of the calendar day. It is calculated as follows:

$$\text{Point prevalence} = \frac{\text{Number of persons with a disorder at a specified point in time}}{\text{Total population at specified point in time}}$$

Period prevalence. The number of people who have a disorder at any time during a specified time period (longer than a calendar day or point in time). It is calculated as follows:

$$\text{Period prevalence} = \frac{\text{Number of persons with a disorder during a time period}}{\text{Total population during time period}}$$

The numerator includes any existing cases at the start of the time period and any new cases that develop during the period. Period prevalence may be used to determine the number of persons with a disorder, the number of persons in treatment, and the duration of an illness.

Lifetime prevalence. A measure at a point in time of the number of persons who had the disorder at some time during their lives. A potential problem with lifetime prevalence is that it is almost always based on subject recall, which can be inaccurate.

Treated prevalence. The number of persons being treated for a disorder, arrived at by counting all the persons in a defined geographic area who are receiving treatment. One may measure treated point prevalence (e.g., the number of patients being treated for a disorder in a clinic on a certain day) or treated period prevalence (e.g., the number of patients being treated for a disorder at a clinic over the past year).

Cross-sectional prevalence. A single assessment of prevalence at a particular point in time. It differs from a longitudinal study, in which a population is studied over a long period of time.

Probability. A quantitative statement of the likelihood that an event will occur. A probability of 0 means that the event is certain not to occur; a probability of 1.0 means that the event will occur with certainty.

P value. The probability of obtaining a result by chance alone. A *p* value of .01 means that the probability of obtaining a result by chance alone is less than 1 in 100; a value of .05 means that the result will occur above 5 times out of every 100 times by chance alone.

Random assignment. The nonsystematic selection of subjects into a group to ensure that there are differences in group composition.

Randomization. The process that allows each patient in a clinical trial to have an equal chance to be assigned to a control or experimental treatment group. It protects against selection bias and guarantees the validity of statistical tests of significance.

Random variable. A variable for which the variation is determined by chance.

Regression analysis. Obtaining a prediction from observed data in order to predict the value of one variable (x) in relation to the value of another variable (y).

Relative frequency. The number of persons in a specific group (e.g., sex or age) who have a disorder. Measures of disease frequency involve two major concepts, prevalence and incidence.

Risk factor. Something associated with a disorder that may support a causal connection. A risk may be *factor-specific* (e.g., it occurs only in one sex) or *factor-related* (e.g., it is more likely to occur in a certain environment). A causal connection between a risk factor and a disorder is shown by (1) temporality—a factor precedes the disorder being studied; (2) the repeated appearance of the same risk factor in multiple studies; (3) specificity—a risk factor is associated with one disorder only; and (4) finding that the experimental intervention that eliminates the risk factor also eliminates the disorder. Determining what factor or factors account for increased risk of a disorder is one of the challenges of psychiatric epidemiology.

Relative risk. Relative risk is the ratio of the incidence of the disease among persons exposed to the risk factor to the incidence among those not exposed. For example, the relative risk of lung cancer is much greater for heavy smokers than for nonsmokers.

Attributable risk. Attributable risk is the absolute incidence of the disease in exposed persons that can be attributed to the exposure. This measure is derived by subtracting the incidence of the disease in question among unexposed persons from its total incidence among exposed persons. For example, the lung cancer death rate for nonsmokers may be subtracted from the total community lung cancer death rate. The results are the attributable community risk of lung cancer. Attributable risk is a useful concept because it tells what may be expected if the risk is removed. For example, on the basis of available data, the attributable risk of deaths from lung cancer could be avoided if smoking were eliminated.

Sample. A subset of observations selected from a population.

Scatter diagram. A visual means of determining the relationship between two variables. It may be linear (positive relationship), curvilinear (negative relationship), or nonlinear (no relationship).

Sensitivity. The number of true positives divided by the sum of the number of true positives and false negatives. It is the proportion of patients with the condition in question that the test is able to detect.

Specificity. The number of true negatives divided by the sum of the number of true negatives and false positives. It is the proportion of patients that do not have the condition that the test will call negative.

Standard deviation (SD). A measure of variation derived by squaring each deviation in a set of scores, taking the average of these squares, and then taking the square root of the result. The standard deviation is represented by the Greek letter sigma (Σ). In a normal distribution, ± 1 SD includes 68 percent of the population; ± 2 SD includes 95 percent of the population; and ± 3 SD includes 99 perent of the population.

Standard error (SE). A measure of how much variation in test results is due to chance and error and how much is due to experimental influences.

Standardized or Z-score. The deviation of a score from its group mean expressed in standard deviation units.

Time-series design. The type of experiment in which there are repeated observations of the same subject over a specific time period.

T-test. A statistical procedure designed to compare two sets of observations. *T*-tests can be compared using an advanced statistical concept called the *Bonferroni procedure* that reduces errors between experiments.

Type I error. The error that occurs when the null hypothesis is rejected when it should have been retained or the false claim of a true difference because the observed difference is due entirely to chance.

Type II error. The error that occurs when the null hypothesis is retained when it should have been rejected or the false acceptance of the null hypothesis when, in fact, there is a true difference but the difference is so small that it falls within the acceptance region of the null hypothesis.

Variable. A characteristic that can assume different values in different experimental situations. In research methodology, *independent variables* are those qualities that the experimenter systematically varies (e.g., time, age, sex, type of drug) in the experiment. *Dependent variables* are those qualities that measure the influence of the independent variable or the outcome of the experiment (e.g., measurement of a person's specific physiological reactions to a drug).

Variance. A measure arrived at by squaring all the deviations in a set of measures, summing them, and then dividing them by the number of measures. Variance is helpful in analyzing how much variation is due to experimental influence and how much is due to chance or error influence.

Variation. A term referring to different results obtained in measuring the same phenomenon. Variation may be associated with known variables within the data or with variables that result from error or chance.

Z-score. The difference between the score and the mean, divided by the standard deviation. It is a transformation into standardized units that are easier to interpret.

SOCIAL PSYCHIATRY

Social psychiatry is the behavioral science concerned with the social and cultural determinants of behavior, both normal and abnormal. It deals with the distribution of disorders and in that sense relates to the field of epidemiology. It also addresses the social and cultural responses to health and illness and to that extent relates to cross-cultural psychiatry. In addition, the field is concerned with the prevention and maintenance of physical and mental health (salutogenesis) and with the role of the environment and life-style factors as contributory determinants of illness.

Social psychiatry is part of the broader field of *medical sociology*, which has been by described by David Mechanic as covering the following areas: social groups and organizations and their role in health delivery services; demographics of illness; cultural and social attitudes about illness; mortality and morbidity and the accommodation of medical institutions to changing patterns of disease and health; and the sociology of medical practice, community health care, and hospital practice.

Sociocultural Determinants of Mental Illness

The concept of social class has been variously formulated in terms of economic power, social prestige, political identification, and patterns of association. In American society class position is most frequently characterized by occupation and education. White-collar occupations, which are usually coupled with a college education, tend to place one in the middle class; blue-collar occupations, which are coupled with a high-school education at most, tend to place one in the working class. Studies by social psychologists have shown that life-styles, aspirations, and, to a degree, cognition and modes of personality, coping, and defense tend to differ by class. However, a major problem with social class studies is the tendency toward broad generalization that may promote stereotypical thinking. For example, statements that characterize working-class persons as impulsive and unable to delay gratification have little validity. Many studies that compare traits among class groups are related, on careful examination, more to income than to other factors. Similarly, feelings of personal efficacy—of being in control of one's destiny and not subject to external controls—are more characteristic of the middle class than of the working class. But a sense of autonomy and one's level of income are not unrelated. Nevertheless, behavioral science research has established that chronic life stresses occur more often in the working class than in the middle class. Moreover, working-class members are more vulnerable to stressors than are members of the middle class. The preponderance of evidence suggests that both treated mental disorders and the symptoms of psychological discomfort are found more frequently in (1) the lower socioeconomic class, (2) among persons without meaningful social ties, (3) among those who do not have useful social roles, and (4) among those who have suffered traumatic loss of significant social ties.

Social Network and Social Support

The term "social network" refers to the network of persons to whom someone relates, and the term "social support" refers to the mechanism by which interpersonal relationships protect people from the deleterious effects of stress. In general, when there is a strong social support system, the vulnerability to mental illness is low and the chance for recovery, should a disorder develop, is high. Research comparing the social networks of psychiatric patients and normals have shown that schizophrenic patients have a much smaller social network than controls and that neurotic patients have a loose or sparse network. Similarly, a stable support system can ameliorate the effects of physical illness on the person. For example, patients with low social support are more likely to die after myocardial infarct than are patients with a larger and more supportive social network. A similar correlation was found in obstetrical and asthmatic patients: Those with low social support had an increased incidence of complications.

Expressed emotion (EE). The sociologist George Brown and his colleagues in London isolated a pattern of EE characterized by hostile feelings and intrusiveness on the part of families of schizophrenic patients. EE is strongly associated with poor prognosis after discharge. If EE can be diminished through family therapy, the relapse of first-episode schizophrenia has been shown to be reduced.

Life Events and Illness

A number of studies of life events and life crises suggest a correlation between physical and mental illness. Studies of schizophrenic patients, for example, suggest that specific life changes in the weeks immediately preceding breakdown frequently serve as precipitants of the onset of schizophrenia. In one study it was found that in the three weeks before onset of a schizophrenic episode, 60 percent of schizophrenic patients experienced objectively confirmable events that impinged directly on themselves or on close relatives. The comparable figure for a control group was only 19 percent. Other investigators have shown that life changes are associated with symptoms and with a number of physical ailments.

In the Midtown Manhattan study mentioned above, life stress was taken into account in the following categories: economic deprivation, single-parent homes, medical illness, social isolation, concern about work. A correlation between psychiatric symptoms and life stresses was found.

In a well-known study by T. H. Holmes and B. Rahe, point values were assigned to various life changes that required the person to change or adapt. This is known as the *social readjustment rating scale.* If a critical number of events happened to a person during a one-year period, he or she was at risk for some type of medical or psychiatric illness. Of those people who accumulated 300 points in one year, 80 percent were at risk of illness in the near future.

Recent work, however, indicates that external events may not, in and of themselves, be sufficient to cause mental illness. Rather, a combination of genetic and experiential factors have to exist in order for illness to occur. This *vulnerability theory* presumes that the occurrence of illness depends on such factors as child-rearing practices, physical disorders, psychological stressors, genetics, and adverse social stressors. Each person has a personal threshold of vulnerability and innate ability to tolerate stress. It had been thought that any response could be conditioned to any stimulus. It is now known that conditioning associations occur on the basis of the *principle of preparedness*—that is, organisms are biologically prepared to make some associations more easily than others. This factor is important in conditioned states of sickness, such as reactions to radiation therapy (i.e., some patients are more likely than others to become ill from this treatment).

Hans Selye, who developed the major theories of stress and illness, did not view stress as always being a negative factor in a person's life. Only when stress overwhelms the person and produces distress did he consider it to be damaging. Similarly, Holmes and Rahe's work has been reviewed in terms of whether the life change was viewed as pleasant or unpleasant, wanted or unwanted, and expected or unexpected. The quality of the stress and the effect of change on the person's life is as important as the nature of the life event itself.

The effects of stress and psychosomatic disorders are discussed further in Chapter 25, "Behavioral Medicine and Psychological Factors Affecting Physical Condition."

Effects of crises. Studies of specific life crises have focused on how people react to crises and how these reactions change over time.

Careful comparative studies have demonstrated that people who experience a crisis such as bereavement, rape, or a life-threatening illness have higher rates of psychopathology than people who have not been subjected to such an event. Furthermore, there is evidence that between 20 and 40 percent of the people who experience a major life crisis do not recover emotionally with the passage of time. Among the bereaved, for example, one study found 30 percent to have a bad outcome on a combined assessment of psychological distress, social functioning, and physical health measured two to four years after the loss.

Psychiatric Help Seeking

Needs-assessment surveys show that most people with serious emotional problems do not seek professional help. This practice is changing, however, as people increasingly accept the view that emotional problems should be treated by a mental health professional. Nonetheless, informal helpers are still sought most often in times of emotional turmoil. Furthermore, a person seeking professional help is more likely to turn to a primary care physician than to a psychiatrist. This choice is partly a result of the lack of psychiatrists in some areas of the country, but other variables are also involved.

Sociologists have been particularly interested in structural determinants, the strongest and most consistent of which is social class. A positive correlation between social class and help seeking has persisted, even though community mental health centers and other inexpensive treatment facilities have reduced the financial barriers to care. In the most recent surveys, education has emerged as a stronger predictor of help seeking than income, which suggests that some cultural facilitating factors are more important than financial resources in accounting for the influence of social class.

Women are much more likely than men to seek mental health care, even given the higher prevalence of disorder among women. Sociological research over the past few years has made considerable progress in understanding this sex difference by showing that women are more likely to recognize their problems than are men and that this recognition of a problem is the main point in the decision-making process that distinguishes men and women. Once either men or women recognize that they have a problem, they do not differ in the likelihood that they will obtain professional help.

Community Responses to the Mentally Ill

Attitudes about the mentally ill have been charted in public opinion surveys since the 1950s. Dislike and fear have remained high among the attitudes surveyed. Negative attitudes are particularly pronounced among poorly educated and elderly people. Men consistently report more negative attitudes than women.

The core concerns about persons who are mentally ill revolve around their presumed unpredictability and dangerousness. These concerns have some basis in reality, as patients released from state psychiatric hospitals have demonstrated comparatively high arrest rates. However, most crimes committed by released patients are property crimes that do not involve violence.

Fortunately, most people have feelings that can be modified on the basis of experience, and, as they become more knowledgeable, they can learn to make finer distinctions about kinds of mental illness and treatment. Visits to a psychotherapist, for example, have much less stigma attached than hospitalization for a mental illness. Private hospitalization seems to be less stigmatizing than public hospitalization.

References

Bland R C: Psychiatric epidemiology. Can J Psychiatry *33*: 618, 1988.

Breslau M, Davis G C: Chronic stress and major depression. Arch Gen Psychiatry *43*: 309, 1986.

Cooper B: Epidemiology and prevention in the mental health field. Soc Psychiatry Psychiatr Epidemiol *25*: 9, 1990.

Costello E J: Developments in child psychiatric epidemiology. J Am Acad Child Adolesc Psychiatry *28*: 836, 1989.

Duncan R, Knapp R, Miller M C: *Introductory Biostatistics for the Health Sciences*, ed 2. Wiley, New York, 1983.

Fenton W S, Robinowitz C B, Leaf P J: Male and female psychiatrists and their patients. Am J Psychiatry *144*: 358, 1987.

Friedman G D: *Primer of Epidemiology*. McGraw-Hill, New York, 1987.

Grant I, Kaplan R M: Statistics and experimental design. In *Comprehensive Textbook of Psychiatry*, ed 5, H I Kaplan and B J Sadock, editors, p 340. Williams & Wilkins, Baltimore, 1989.

Johnson E H: Psychiatric morbidity and health problems among black Americans: A national survey. J Natl Med Assoc *81*: 1217, 1989.

Kessler R C: Sociology and psychiatry. In *Comprehensive Textbook of Psychiatry*, ed 5, H I Kaplan and B J Sadock, editors, p 299. Williams & Wilkins, Baltimore, 1989.

Klerman G L: Paradigm shifts in USA psychiatric epidemiology since World War II. Soc Psychiatry Psychiatr Epidemiol *25*: 27, 1990.

Regier D A, Burke J D: Epidemiology. In *Comprehensive Textbook of Psychiatry*, ed 5, H I Kaplan and B J Sadock, editors, p 308. Williams & Wilkins, Baltimore, 1989.

Regier D A, Goldberg I D, Taube C A: The de facto U.S. mental health services system: A public health perspective. Arch Gen Psychiatry *35*: 685, 1978.

Robins L N: Epidemiology: Reflection on testing the validity of psychiatric interviews. Arch Gen Psychiatry *42*: 918, 1985.

Robins L N, Helzer J E, Croughan J, Ratcliff K S: National Institute of Mental Health diagnostic interview schedule: Its history, characteristics, and validity. Arch Gen Psychiatry *38*: 381, 1981.

Srole L, Langner T S, Michael S T, Opler M K, Rennie T A C: *Mental Health in the Metropolis: The Midtown Manhattan Study*. McGraw-Hill, New York, 1962.

Weissman M M, Klerman G L: Epidemiology of mental disorders: Emerging trends in the United States. Arch Gen Psychiatry *35*: 705, 1978.

Westermeyer J: National differences in psychiatric morbidity: Methodological issues, scientific interpretations, and social implications. Acta Psychiatr Scand Suppl *344*: 23, 1988.

4.8 / Community Psychiatry

Community psychiatry is concerned with the prevention and treatment of mental disorders and with the rehabilitation of former psychiatric patients through the use of organized community programs. It approaches individual patients through the resources of the community. Other terms used for community psychiatry are community mental health, preventive psychiatry, outreach psychiatry, and public health psychiatry. It has been called the "third psychiatry revolution." (The first was the age of enlightenment following the Middle Ages, during which it was decided that mental illness was not the result of witchcraft, and the second was the development of psychoanalysis by Sigmund Freud.)

DEVELOPMENT OF COMMUNITY PSYCHIATRY

In 1963 Congress passed the Community Mental Health Centers Act, which provided funds for the construction of community mental health centers (CMHC) with specified catchment areas (geographic regions with a population of 75,000 to 200,000). Each CMHC must provide five basic psychiatric services: inpatient care, emergency services (on a 24-hour basis), community consultation, day care (including partial hospitalization programs, halfway houses, aftercare services, and a broad range of outpatient services), and research and education. By the early 1980s the CMHC movement had made a major impact on mental health services and on the practice of psychiatry and the other mental health professions. At that time there were about 800 such centers in operation, with over half in urban areas. Currently, because of severe financial constraints, the CMHC function is severely limited and is considered by many to be an ineffective program.

In 1981 a block grant program was created to provide federal funds to states for drug abuse, alcohol abuse, and other mental health programs. Several states established community support systems to help furnish needed mental health services; these programs are currently available nationwide. In spite of these efforts, state mental hospitals still utilize the majority of state-allocated mental health dollars. Financial limitations have interfered with the block grant programs and state programs.

CHARACTERISTICS OF A COMMUNITY MENTAL HEALTH CENTER

Commitment

Commitment to a population implies a responsibility for planning. Commitment suggests (1) that the plan should identify all the mental health needs of the population, inventory the resources available to meet these needs, and organize a system of care; (2) a responsibility for involving the citizens and political figures in the planning process; (3) that prevention is at least as important as direct treatment; and (4) that the responsibility is to all persons in the population, including children, the aged, minorities, the chronically ill, the acutely ill, and those who live in geographically remote areas.

The requirement that mental health services be located close to the patient's residence or place of work makes it easy for people to get to a treatment site. Furthermore, this proximity enables illness to be identified early, making it likely that hospitalization, when required, will be brief.

Services

The community mental health movement views community mental health as a total system, rather than a single service. It has proposed a number of services suited to the needs of those served. The original legislation called for five required services—emergency services, outpatient services, partial hospitalization, inpatient services, and consultation-education services. Public Law 94-63 required the addition of services for children, services for the aged, screening before hospitalization, follow-up services for those who had been hospitalized, transitional housing services, alcoholism services, and drug abuse services.

The community mental health team includes psychiatrists (including child psychiatrists), clinical psychologists, psychiatric social workers, psychiatric nurses, necessary administrative help and clerical staff, and occupational and recreational therapists for inpatient and partial hospitalization programs. Links to welfare workers, clergy, family agencies, schools, and other human services groups are also maintained.

Long-Term Care

Stemming from concerns about fragmentation of care and the tendency to keep patients hospitalized or unnecessarily restricted to one type of service, community mental health programs encourage continuity of care. This continuity of care enables a single clinician to follow a given patient through emergency services, hospitalization, partial hospitalization as a transition to the community, and outpatient treatment as follow-up. It also provides an exchange of information and team responsibility for the patient when different therapists, for reasons of convenience or economy, treat the patient in several different settings. A free exchange of clinical information between centers and a liaison between different agencies are also part of the total system of care.

Community Participation

The community should participate in decisions about its mental health care needs and programs, instead of having them defined solely by professionals. Mental health services are sensitive to the needs of those served if the public is actively involved. The expectation is that mental health services are apt to be used when knowledgeable persons interpret and educate the community about their availability.

Consultation

Consultation ranges from attention to or even treatment of the emotional problems of an individual patient to using knowledge about human behavior to help the organization achieve its professional goals with the program and its patients. With a focus on the total system or program, the consultant offers assistance to the mental health professional who works in an outpatient center or agency. The consultant may also provide direct educational activities, liaison with consumer and advocacy groups, and administrative services.

Evaluation and Research

Evaluation refers to the process of obtaining information about the total community mental health program and its effect on persons, institutions, and communities. Program evaluation should also provide feedback to the planners and decision makers, so that the operating programs can be modified and new ones planned. It is a required activity on which federally funded centers have to spend at least 2 percent of their budgets. Research may focus specifically on key issues, rather than on the total program. The problem addressed may be a particular disorder or treatment method.

PREVENTION IN PSYCHIATRY

Preventive psychiatry is part of community psychiatry. The goal of prevention is to decrease the onset (incidence), duration (prevalence), and residual disability of mental disorders. The prevention of mental disorders is based on public health principles and is divided into primary, secondary, and tertiary prevention.

Primary Prevention

The goal of primary prevention is to prevent the onset of a disease or disorder, thereby reducing its incidence (number of new cases occurring in a specific period of time). This goal is accomplished by eliminating causative agents, reducing risk factors, enhancing host resistance, or interfering with the mode of disease transmission. For some physical disorders the identification and modification of one or more of these factors has revolutionized the health care of the population. These successes are best exemplified by the virtual elimination of many infectious diseases and vitamin deficiency states and by the reduction of certain forms of cancer, heart disease, and lung disease.

Examples of primary prevention to help someone cope include mental health education programs (e.g., parent training in child development and alcohol and drug education programs); efforts at competence building (e.g., Head Start and other enriched day care programs for disadvantaged children, Outward Bound); development and utilization of social support systems to reduce the effects of stress on persons at high risk (e.g., widow-to-widow programs); anticipatory guidance programs to assist people in preparing for expected stressful situations (e.g., counseling of Peace Corp volunteers); and crisis intervention following the occurrence of stressful life events, such as bereavement, marital separation and divorce, individual traumas, and group disasters. The hostage-release program, in which American hostages released from captivity are prepared for reentry into their culture, is another example of primary prevention.

Primary prevention also aims at eradicating stressful agents and reducing stress. Such programs include prenatal and perinatal care to decrease the incidence of mental retardation and organic mental disorders in children (e.g., improved nutrition and abstinence from alcohol and drugs during pregnancy, improved obstetrical practices, specific dietary modification for neonates vulnerable to phenylketonuria); stricter lead-elimination laws to reduce the incidence of lead encepahlopathy; modification of divorce, adoption, and child abuse laws to provide a healthy environment for child development; enrichment or replacement of institutional settings for infants, children, and the elderly; modification of certain risk factors for mental disorders that appear to be associated with low socioeconomic status; and genetic counseling for parents at a high risk for chromosomal abnormalities to prevent the unwitting conception of compromised infants; and efforts to reduce the spread of certain sexually transmitted diseases (e.g., acquired immune deficiency syndrome [AIDS], syphilis), among the sequelae of which are mental disorders.

Secondary Prevention

Secondary prevention is defined as early identification and prompt treatment of an illness or disorder, with the goal of reducing the prevalence (total number of existing cases) of the condition by shortening its duration.

The experiences in military psychiatry in World War II and the Korean War renewed interest in secondary prevention. Military personnel observed that treatment duration could be considerably reduced and treatment effectiveness increased by treating soldiers with combat-induced mental disorders promptly, near the front. This procedure enabled soldiers to maintain ties to the social support of their military units, with the expectation that they would recover quickly. It became clear that these three principles—immediacy, proximity, and expectancy—could be applied in a civilian context. Thus, by providing rapid treatment of emerging mental disorders in the social milieu of the patient's home community, with the expectation that the patient can improve, a clinician can facilitate a patient's recovery.

Tertiary Prevention

The goal of tertiary prevention is to reduce the prevalence of residual defect or disability caused by illness or disorder. In the case of psychiatric conditions, tertiary prevention involves rehabilitative efforts to enable those who have a chronic mental illness to reach the highest level of functioning feasible.

The disabilities associated with chronic mental illness represent major social, economic, and public health problems. In the United States they afflict more than 3 million people, are extremely costly, and create immense suffering for the affected persons, their families, and society. Although the term "chronic mental illness" has traditionally been associated with old patients who have a long history of mental hospitalization, it has recently been broadened to include young adults with a variety of mental disorders who have grown up in the era of deinstitutionalization. Many of them have never been hospitalized, but their ability to lead productive controlled lives in the community is severely impaired.

DEINSTITUTIONALIZATION

The discharging of large numbers of patients from public psychiatric hospitals back into the community to receive care in outpatient facilities is the process known as deinstitutionalization. This policy, which began in the late 1950s, resulted in a decrease in the state psychiatric hospital population from over 560,000 beds at that time to fewer than 130,000 beds today. Many of these patients were released into various aftercare clinics, where they continued to receive psychiatric treatment and rehabilitative services. Others were placed in new types of institutions, such as halfway houses, board and care facilities, and public housing units. Many had to be rehospitalized, and a revolving-door policy emerged, with up to 80 percent of patients being readmitted within two years of discharge. Some call the phenomenon of transferring the state hospital patient to these other facilities transinstitutionalization and believe that one set of problems has been exchanged for another, without solving the problem of the chronically mentally ill.

Several studies have clearly demonstrated that without an active, multifaceted treatment system that is willing to assume ongoing responsibility for all facets of the patient's care these chronic mental patients will regress in the community as they did in the state hospital. One of the major problems faced by chronic patients is that their illnesses interfere with their coping skills, rendering them particularly likely to drift downward into even more stressful, impoverished environments. The end result is an increase in homeless persons in urban areas.

The deinstitutionalized patient needs extensive social support, such as vocational and recreational counseling, comprehensive psychiatric treatment, a paying job, and affordable housing. That support has not been given to the extent that the planners and supporters of deinstitutionalization would like, primarily because of the lack of adequate funding on the federal, state, and local levels. In fact, funding for aftercare community services for the mentally ill continues to decline; unless this trend is reversed, deinstitutionalization will remain a failed public policy. It has been suggested that the limited funds available be channeled into improving existing state hospitals, so that chronic mental patients and the homeless mentally ill can be referred to the system and receive appropriate care.

Homelessness

A growing body of literature acknowledges the scope and special problems of persons who are both chronically mentally ill and homeless. These persons may be in psychiatric inpatient facilities, in prisons, in temporary shelters, or on the streets. In one survey of psychiatric inpatients in Kansas public mental hospitals, nearly 40 percent had no home to go to, were rejected by their families and unable to return to their previous homes, or did not wish to return to their previous homes.

As with the larger population of chronically mentally ill, the homeless mentally ill represent a heterogeneous population, with no uniformity in diagnosis, demographics, functional performance, or residential history. One categorization divides this population into street people, the episodic homeless, and the situationally homeless. Street people usually have a diagnosis of schizophrenia or substance abuse or both, a history of psychiatric hospitalization, and a variety of health problems. The episodic homeless are usually younger than street people and are likely to be regarded as difficult patients, with a diagnosis of personality disorder, substance abuse, or mood disorder. They sporadically use a wide variety of mental health services. The situationally homeless have problems in regard to a situational stress more than to their psychopathology.

The characteristics of this population vary according to geographic location—urban ghetto, urban park, suburb, rural area—and to their mobility. Some remain fairly fixed within geographic limits, whereas others travel from one part of the country to another. Because demography, epidemiology, history, and treatment needs vary, there is no single method of providing mental health services to these patients. In addition to the full range of traditional services—evaluation, crisis intervention, medication review, psychosocial skill training, and so on—and beyond housing, these patients may require less traditional services, such as a mailbox where welfare checks can be delivered, bathing facilities, and delousing.

Traditional mental health service systems may present barriers to access by homeless mentally ill persons. Sometimes these barriers are simply the result of a lack of services to meet the special needs of this population or the result of geographic or functional limitations. Housing programs for chronically mentally ill persons are often limited to high-functioning patients, thereby screening out the poorly functioning street people. Effective service programs include provisions for shelter and food, drop-in centers, outreach contact, and a cooperative endeavor between mental health and non-mental health agencies in the community (e.g., Salvation Army, church-affiliated organizations).

Psychogeriatric Long-Term Care

The trend to empty out state mental hospitals has been particularly hard on the geriatric population, which make up about 20 percent of all state hospital patients. Aftercare facilities for these patients are inadequate, and nursing homes are not in a position to function as a quasi-mental hospital because of a lack of psychiatric, social work, and other services that exist in the better state hospitals. In fact, many nursing homes will not take patients with organic mental disorders, cognitive impairment, or disturbed behavior—conditions that are present in many of these patients. Despite these factors, current policies continue to favor deinstitutionalization. The practice of trying to avoid state hospital placement for psychogeriatric patients has led to exclusion at the gate, which bans admission to geriatric patients, with the stated aim of maintaining them in the community. But the pressure for placement in nursing homes and home care programs has been too great for them to handle the load; much of the burden of elderly long-term care falls on the family.

References

Angermeyer M C, Glink B, Majcher-Angermeyer A: Stigma perceived by patients attending modern treatment settings: Some unanticipated effects of community psychiatry. J Nerv Ment Dis *175*: 4, 1987.

Avison W R, Nixon Speechley K: The discharged psychiatric patient: A review of social, social-psychological and psychiatric correlates of outcome. Am J Psychiatry *144*: 10, 1987.

Bachrach L L, Lamb H R: Public psychiatry in an era of deinstitutionalization. New Dir Ment Health Serv *42*: 9, 1989.

Barrett J, Rose R M: *Mental Disorders in the Community*. Guilford, New York, 1986.

Beiser M, Shore J H, Peters R: Does community care for the mentally ill make a difference? Am J Psychiatry *142*: 1047, 1985.

Berlin R M, Kales J D, Humphrey F J, Kales A: The patient care crisis in community mental health centers: A need for more psychiatric involvement. Am J Psychiatry *138*: 450, 1981.

Borus J F: Strangers bearing gifts: A retrospective look at the early years of community mental health center consultation. Am J Psychiatry *141*: 868, 1984.

Caplan G: *Population-Oriented Psychiatry*. Human Sciences Press, New York, 1989.

Caplan G: *Principles of Preventive Psychiatry*. Basic Books, New York, 1964.
Chacko R C, ed: *The Chronic Mental Patient in a Community Context*. American Psychiatric Press, Washington, DC, 1985.
Friedman M J, West A N: Current need versus treatment history: Predictors of use of outpatient psychiatric care. Am J Psychiatry *144*: 355, 1987.
Hess R, Morgan J, eds: *Prevention in Community Mental Health Centers*. Haworth Press, New York, 1990.
Jones M: *The Therapeutic Community*. Basic Books, New York, 1953.
Katz S E: Hospitalization and the mental health service system. In *Comprehensive Textbook of Psychiatry*, ed 5, H I Kaplan and B J Sadock, editors, p 2083. Williams & Wilkins, Baltimore, 1989.
Marmor T R, Gill K C: The political and economic context of mental health care in the United States. J Health Polit Policy Law *14*: 459, 1989.
Menninger W W: The chronically mentally ill. In *Comprehensive Textbook of Psychiatry*, ed 5, H I Kaplan and B J Sadock, editors, p 2090. Williams & Wilkins, Baltimore, 1989.
Okin R L, Borus J F: Primary, secondary, and tertiary prevention of mental disorders. In *Comprehensive Textbook of Psychiatry*, ed 5, H I Kaplan and B J Sadock, editors, p 2067. Williams & Wilkins, Baltimore, 1989.
Okin R L, Dolnick J A, Pearsall D T: Patients' perspectives on community alternatives to hospitalization: A follow-up study. Am J Psychiatry *140*: 460, 1983.
Shore J H: Community psychiatry. In *Comprehensive Textbook of Psychiatry*, ed 5, H I Kaplan and B J Sadock, editors, p 2063. Williams & Wilkins, Baltimore, 1989.
Strayhorn J M, Jr.: Control groups for psychosocial intervention outcome studies. Am J Psychiatry *144*: 275, 1987.

4.9 / Socioeconomic Aspects of Health Care

Social and economic factors significantly affect the nation's health status and the delivery of health services. Knowing the qualities of a population that influence its health, illness, and death is invaluable when assessing current health care requirements, designing future facilities and programs, and allocating dollars to optimize the provision of adequate services.

The World Health Organization (WHO) defines health as the state of complete physical, mental, and social well-being and not merely the absence of disease. In its effort to promote health, the American health care delivery system attempts to provide and maintain high-quality medical care for all of its citizens while advancing medical research and technology. The current emphasis in health care is on prevention and health promotion, as well as treatment and diagnosis of medical disorders. Increasing health care costs have become significant obstacles in fulfilling these objectives. The focus on efforts to control these costs affects the distribution of health care funds, delivery of health care services, and reimbursement mechanisms for these services.

SOCIAL FACTORS

Life-Style

Life-style and personal habits are major factors in the causes of illness and death in the United States, accounting for about 70 percent of all illness, both mental and physical. Obesity, for example, is related to heart disease and diabetes, and a person's weight bears a direct relation to habit patterns of eating and exercise.

Many cancer deaths have been related to both poor dietary habits and the chewing and smoking of tobacco. Over the past five years cigarette smoking has continued to decline steadily. The age-adjusted percentage of men 20 years of age and over who smoke cigarettes declined, from 35 percent in 1983 to 32 percent in 1987; smoking among women decreased from 30 percent in 1983 to 27 percent in 1987. In 1990, however, the number of female smokers was greater than the number of male smokers. For women 55 to 70 years of age, lung cancer is the primary cause of cancer deaths.

Regular physical activity has a positive effect on stress reduction. It is also useful in treating and preventing such mental problems as anxiety and depression and such physical problems as obesity, heart disease, diabetes, and high blood pressure. A trend in this country over the past two decades indicates that, although the number of adults involved in a daily exercise regimen is rising, less than half of all school-age children are exercising on a daily basis.

Accident prevention also would avoid many premature deaths. Education about safe driving habits, especially the need to abstain from alcohol when driving, would save over 100,000 lives each year, especially among young adults.

Table 4.9-1 lists personal health practices related to life-style.

Age

The incidence of illness is affected by age. Eighty-six percent of persons over 65 years of age have one or more chronic conditions. The three leading chronic conditions of old age are arthritis, hypertension, and heart disease. Hearing impairments, diabetes, cataracts, and varicose veins also are common chronic problems. Mental health problems increase with age as well. Although chronicity is a factor among the elderly, young persons are more predisposed to acute illnesses. The three most common acute medical problems, across age groups, are upper respiratory conditions, influenza, and injuries.

Age influences the utilization of all health care services. Both young persons (age 20 to 30) and persons over 65 tend to have more illnesses and health care needs than persons in middle adulthood. Young children's health care habits are often modeled after those of their parents. Prior experiences with health care influence future attitudes and behavior.

Education about accidents in the home would save about 28,000 lives each year, especially among the elderly, who account for two-thirds of all accidents that occur at home.

Socioeconomic Status (SES)

A person's SES is not based solely on income but includes such factors as education, occupation, and life-style. The incidence of physical illness is affected by SES. Persons in low SES groups are likely to be afflicted with hypertension, arthritis, upper respiratory illness, speech difficulties, and eye diseases. There is a reduced life expectancy for low SES persons, as longevity is positively correlated to SES level.

There is a positive correlation between SES and mental health; consequently, high SES persons have better mental health than persons of low SES. With regard to the incidence of psychopathology, some studies have found a slightly higher percentage of bipolar disease among high SES persons and a greater number of schizophrenic persons in low SES groups.

Table 4.9-1
Personal Health Practices
[For persons 18 years of age and over. Based on National Health Interview Survey.]

Characteristic	Sleeps 6 Hours or Less (%)	Never Eats Breakfast (%)	Snacks Every Day (%)	Less Physically Active Than Contemporaries (%)	Had 5 or More Drinks on Any One Day (%)	Current Smoker (%)	30% or More above Desirable Weight† (%)
All persons‡	22.0	24.3	39.0	16.4	37.5	30.1	13.0
Age							
18–29 years old	19.8	30.4	42.2	17.1	54.4	31.9	7.5
30–44 years old	24.3	30.1	41.4	18.3	39.0	34.5	13.6
45–64 years old	22.7	21.4	37.9	15.3	24.6	31.6	18.1
65 years old and over	20.4	7.5	30.7	13.5	12.2	16.0	13.2
65–74 years old	19.7	9.0	32.4	15.8	NA	19.7	14.9
75 years old and over	21.5	5.1	27.8	9.8	NA	10.0	10.3
Sex							
Male	22.7	25.2	40.7	16.5	49.3	32.6	12.1
Female	21.4	23.6	37.5	16.3	23.3	27.8	13.7
Race							
White	21.3	24.5	39.4	16.7	38.3	29.6	12.4
All other	26.6	23.2	36.3	14.3	29.9	33.1	16.4
Black	27.8	23.6	37.2	13.9	29.3	34.9	18.7
Other	21.4	21.5	32.6	16.5	33.3	24.8	6.7
Education Level							
Less than 12 years	23.3	22.6	37.8	12.3	35.9	35.4	17.5
12 years	21.9	26.5	39.6	16.5	38.9	33.4	13.4
More than 12 years	21.2	23.3	39.2	19.1	36.8	23.1	9.4
Family Income							
Less than $7,000	24.4	22.4	37.0	13.5	NA	31.1	16.1
$7,000 to $14,999	21.6	22.9	37.4	14.7	NA	33.4	15.3
$15,000 to $24,999	21.2	24.9	40.3	16.8	NA	32.2	13.4
$25,000 to $39,999	22.4	26.1	41.2	17.2	NA	30.0	12.1
$40,000 or more	21.8	25.4	39.9	19.4	NA	25.2	9.4

Table from U.S. National Center for Health Statistics, *Health Promotion and Disease Prevention, United States 1985*, series 10, No. 163 and unpublished data.
NA = not available.
†Based on 1960 Metropolitan Life Insurance Company standards. Data are self-reported.
‡Excludes persons whose health practices are unknown.

Poverty

Poverty is associated with many long-term problems, such as poor health and increased mortality, mental illness, school failure, crime, and drug use. Approximately 13.5 percent of all Americans fall below the poverty level, which is set by the federal government at about $9,500 a year for a three-person household of two adults and one child. Women are more likely to be poor than men, and children are the poorest age group, with one child in five living below the poverty line. Poverty is also associated with ethnicity, with about 85 percent of the poor being black or Hispanic.

Sex

Regardless of age, women seek health care and are hospitalized more often than men. Women are most frequently hospitalized for childbirth, heart disease, and cancer, whereas men are hospitalized for heart disease, cancer, and fractures. The three leading chronic conditions that can limit activity for men are heart conditions, arthritis, and impairment of the back or spine; for women, they are arthritis, heart conditions, and hypertension.

Race

Race affects the utilization of health care facilities. In 1984 approximately 10 times as many visits were made to physicians' offices by white persons as by blacks. The rates of such chronic conditions as obesity, diabetes, heart disease, hypertension, and arthritis are higher among blacks than among whites.

Environment

The environment contributes to approximately one-quarter of today's health problems. The exposure to such environmental risks as toxic waste, natural disasters, lead, asbestos, and dioxins is a major source of disease and death in humans. Water-borne diseases, especially those that occur in shellfish from polluted waters, are a major cause of morbidity and mortality.

Approximately 75 percent of all carcinogens come from the environment. One of the highest incidences of bladder cancer is in certain industrial sites in New Jersey, where 25 percent of all workers are employed in the chemical industry. Nearly 67 percent of the men who die from coal workers' pneumoconiosis live in Pennsylvania.

Between 1985 and 1986, lead emissions declined by almost 60 percent, from 21,000 to 9,000 metric tons a year, in large part because of Environmental Protection Agency (EPA) rules requiring petroleum refineries to lower the lead content of gasoline.

With regard to mental health, there is a general rise in mental disorders among people as their environments change from the suburban community to the inner city.

MORTALITY AND MORBIDITY TRENDS

The health status and health needs of a population can be assessed by examining general health trends, including death rates, causes of death, and longevity. The existence of certain medical disorders influences the need for particular health care delivery systems, programs, and personnel. A population's general health status determines the overall need for services and dollars.

In 1989 the death rate across all age groups in the United States was 524.1 per 100,000, according to the U.S. National Center for Health Statistics. This is the lowest level ever recorded. The rate fell about 10.5 percent in the 1980s. In 1989 HIV became the 11th leading cause of death (up from the 15th leading cause of death in 1988). The causes of death have varied through the years. Pneumonia, tuberculosis, and gastrointestinal disease were the three leading causes of death at the beginning of the 20th century. In 1989 the three leading causes of death were heart disease, cancer, and stroke, in decreasing order. Although psychiatric illness does not play a major role in the mortality rate, it is probably the major factor in the morbidity rate and is also a major cause of days lost from work.

Mortality rates differ considerably by race and sex. Females have lower mortality rates than males in all age groups, but the difference has been decreasing in recent years. Racial minorities within a given population have higher death rates than the majority population.

The primary cause of death for each of the different sex and race groups is heart disease. The mortality rate for heart disease, cancer, and stroke is greatest among black males and is higher for males than for females.

The most common cause of death among adolescents and young adults (age 15 to 24) is accidents; approximately three-fourths of these fatalities occur in automobiles. Homicide and suicide are the second and third leading causes of death, respectively, in this age group. For children under age 14, the leading causes are accidents, cancer, and congenital anomalies, in that order.

Men are more likely to die from heart attacks, but women have a higher rate of strokes. Cancer accounted for 22.5 percent of all deaths. Cancer deaths increased among women while dropping for men, pointing to increased smoking by women beginning in the 1960s as a likely factor in that change. Cigarette smoking poses a higher risk for women than for men: a 55-year-old woman who smokes has a higher risk of hypertension, high cholesterol, and heart attack than a 55-year-old man who smokes.

Infant Mortality

Infant mortality in the United States is high compared with other countries. The rate is 10.4 deaths per 1,000 live births as of 1989, which ranks this country behind 21 other nations. The mortality rate for black infants (18.0) is twice as high as for white infants (8.9). Good prenatal care contributes to a low infant mortality rate; although about 80 percent of white women receive prenatal care, only about 65 percent of black women, 60 percent of Native Americans, and 75 percent of Asian Americans receive such care. In addition, a growing number of blacks are being diagnosed with acquired immune deficiency syndrome (AIDS), which contributes to neonatal mortality. In 1990 blacks made up 55 percent of all AIDS cases among children under 13 years of age, and Hispanic Americans accounted for 21 percent.

The three leading causes of infant death are congenital anomalies, respiratory distress syndrome, and sudden infant death syndrome, in descending order of frequency.

Life Expectancy

According to the U.S. National Center for Health Statistics, in the United States life expectancy of all age, sex, and race groups has been steadily increasing since the turn of the century. The increase in Americans' longevity in the past two decades is due in part to the dramatic decline in deaths from heart disease, down 33 percent, and from stroke, down 50 percent from 1970 to 1987. In 1988 the average life expectancy from birth was 74.8 years. Black males have the shortest life expectancy from birth (65.4 years). White males (72.1 years), black females (73.8 years), and white females (78.8 years) all live longer than black males. Although life expectancy of females is greater than that of males (78.3 years versus 71.1 years), this difference has been diminishing in recent years. The differential attributable to race has lessened as well. The reduction is more significant for black females than for black males.

HEALTH CARE PROVIDERS

Health care providers include a broad array of persons from a variety of professions who care for the sick. In addition to physicians, health care personnel include nurses, dentists, psychologists, social workers, podiatrists, speech therapists, and vocational therapists. Over 3 million people are employed in health-related occupations.

Physician Supply

In 1990 there were about 595,000 physicians, 130,000 dentists, and 1.5 million nurses practicing in the United States. About 21 percent of M.D.s were educated outside the United States or Canada, a figure that has remained fairly constant since 1980. Psychiatrists number about 35,000. Although the number of physicians is adequate, there is a problem in their distribution. High physician-patient ratios exist in the Northeast and in California; but low concentrations are the norm in the South and in the mountain states. Psychiatrists tend to be concentrated in major urban areas.

Primary care physicians number about 35 percent of all doctors and are usually defined as general practitioners, family practitioners, internists, and pediatricians. Primary care has been defined as a type of medical care delivery that emphasizes first-contact care and assumes ongoing responsibility for the patient in both health maintenance and therapy of illness. Many believe that psychiatry also should be classified as a primary care specialty. This is not currently the case.

Projections through the 1990s show shortages, balances, and surpluses in the overall distribution of physicians in various specialties. By the year 2000, there will be over 650,000 physicians in the United States. There will be an oversupply of physicians in certain specialties, such as surgery, ophthalmology, internal medicine, obstetrics and gynecology, and neurosurgery. Fields in which supply will equal demand are dermatology, family practice, otolaryngology, and pediatrics. The only fields in which a shortage is expected are psychiatry, emergency medicine, and preventive medicine.

In 1990 the average physician had gross earnings of about $200,000 a year; neurosurgery, orthopedic surgery, and plastic surgery are the highest-paid specialties (over $350,000 a year); family practice, pediatrics, and psychiatry are the lowest paid (under $150,000 a year). Physicians work an average of 60 to 70 hours a week.

Private Practice

Most physicians in America are in traditional autonomous office-based practices, and the majority of patients receive health care in the physician's private office. Physicians utilize their own facilities and equipment to provide a variety of health care services.

Private practices are organized in one of three ways: independent, partnership, and group. Independent or solo practitioners constitute a significant part of the health care delivery system today. Physicians in independent private practices work for themselves and provide personalized service to patients.

In a partnership the overhead (office, personnel, equipment expenses) is shared by two or more physicians. The patients, in contrast, may or may not be shared by the doctors; the practice may remain independent in this respect.

Group practice is gaining popularity in the United States. The American Medical Association defines group practice as the delivery of medical services by three or more physicians who are formally organized to provide care, consultation, diagnosis, and treatment. The group shares the use of equipment and personnel, and income from the medical practice is distributed among the members of the group.

Group practices may concentrate on a single specialty or may be multidisciplinary in nature, delivering a great variety of services to patients. As with the partnership, the group practice offers the physician economic benefits and fewer working hours than in a solo practice. The group practice also enables the physician to maintain a more regular work schedule. The ability to form ongoing doctor-patient relationships diminishes, however, as the number of patients increases. Recently, private practitioners have been inclined to move away from independent practice and to participate in group practices and, to a smaller extent, partnerships.

In private practice, patients pay for services directly or through third-party payers—that is, insurance companies. As economic conditions change, however, office-based physicians are joining, at an increasing rate, prospective (prepayment) reimbursement systems.

Liability Insurance

One of the most expensive components of physician practices is liability insurance. From 1982 to 1986 average premiums increased at an annual rate of 21.9 percent, from $5,800 to $12,800. The high premiums result from increased incidence of malpractice claims and high jury awards. More than one-third of all physicians have been sued at least once during their medical careers. The average award is about $500,000 in liability cases. In 1990, for the first time in a decade, liability insurance rates began to level off because of increased diligence and quality assurance by physicians and because of tort reform, limiting monetary awards in various states.

Patient Visits

Physician services tend to be underutilized. Twenty-five percent of the population do not see a physician at all in a given year. Of the 75 percent who do, most are very young or old or are women, and they average about five visits a year. Physician visits may take place in the doctor's office (56 percent); hospital outpatient departments, including the emergency room (15 percent); and over the telephone (16 percent). As family income rises, the rates of office and phone consultations increase, and the rate of hospital outpatient visits decreases. The five leading reasons for office visits are general examination, prenatal examination, throat problems, hypertension, and postoperative visits, in descending order of frequency.

Americans do not utilize physician services as much as persons in other countries do. The average number of visits a year to their doctors by Germans is 14, by French 7, and by Americans 5. Americans give as their reason for not seeking care the cost of an office visit. Both Germany and France have national health systems that cover the bulk of medical care.

Women visit their doctors more often than men, and whites more often than blacks. Most visits are to family physicians, followed by pediatricians. The average American visits a dentist twice a year.

HEALTH CARE COSTS

The provision of adequate cost-effective services to the American public is a critical concern. Spending for all types of health care, including the care of the mentally ill, continues to escalate. The growth rate of health care expenditures continues to outdistance the pace of growth of the economy. Health care has become increasingly expensive as a result of inflation, population growth, and advanced technology.

In 1989 approximately $600 billion, 11 percent of the gross national product (GNP), was spent for health care. By 2000 it will reach $1.5 trillion, 15 percent of the GNP. This compares with 9 percent in Sweden, 8.5 percent in Canada and France, 8 percent in Germany, 7 percent in Japan, and 6 percent in the United Kingdom. The health share of the GNP remains fairly stable in most industrialized countries but increases by about one-fifth each year in the United States, thereby widening the gap between the health care expenditures of the United States and those of other countries.

Mental illness accounts for a large proportion of health care expenditures. The cost of mental illness is approximately $2.5 billion a year.

Government spending for health care is on the rise. In part because of Medicare and Medicaid, the federal government's monetary contribution to health care has grown from about 10 percent in 1965 to about 30 percent in 1985. Overall, the government pays approximately 40 percent (30 percent federal, 10 percent state) of personal health care expenditures. Private funds account for the other 60 percent through direct payments (28 percent), private health insurance (31 percent), and industry and philanthropy (1 percent).

Representing approximately 41 percent of expenditures, hospitals utilize the largest proportion of health care dollars. Physicians' fees are about 20 percent of costs, followed by nursing homes, drugs, and dental services. In general, hospital costs and general medical care services have risen at a far greater rate than physicians' fees.

As many as 85 percent of Americans have some form of health insurance, which covers approximately 80 percent of hospital costs and 60 percent of physicians' services, except in the case of psychiatry. Twenty-five percent of hospital costs to the patient represent laboratory tests and imaging, and the remaining costs are for administration, nursing, drugs, and other support services.

HEALTH CARE DELIVERY

Hospitals

The hospital is the institutional provider of general medical and surgical services in the United States health care system. There are currently over 6,000 hospitals of all types in the United States, with about 1 million beds. Approximately 65 percent of beds are occupied at any one time. According to the WHO, hospitals must have physician staff, offer continuous medical and nursing care to patients, and maintain inpatient facilities. Because hospitals consume the biggest percentage of health dollars, their utilization is the focus of current cost-containment strategies.

In the past decade 75 percent of adults have been in a hospital at least once, women more often than men. Rates of hospitalization for all illnesses increase with age. The average general hospital stay across specialties is 6.3 days, which represents a reduction over the past decade from 7.1 days in 1980. A slight increase in hospital use, however, has been reported for children and elderly persons. At present, there is a 10 percent oversupply of hospital beds in this country, particularly in urban areas; the expense of maintaining the beds continues even if they are empty. The health care staff is the largest component of hospital costs.

The classification of hospitals may be based on ownership, length of stay, or nature of service. See Table 4.9-2 for an overview of important aspects of hospital organization.

Nursing Homes

In 1987 there were approximately 25,000 nursing homes in the United States, with approximately 1,500,000 beds. Nursing homes are classified by the intensity of care they offer: (1) *Nursing care homes*, which employ one or more full-time registered or licensed practical nurses and provide nursing care to at least half the residents. (2) *Personal care homes with nursing*, which employ one or more registered or licensed practical nurses and provide medications and treatments in accordance with physicians' orders. (3) *Personal care homes without nursing*. (4) *Domiciliary care homes*, which primarily provide supervisory care but also provide one or two personal services. (5) *Skilled nursing facilities*, which provide the most intensive nursing care available outside a hospital, such as application of dressings or bandages, bowel and bladder care, catheterization, enema, intramuscular or intravenous injection, irrigation, nasal feeding, and oxygen therapy. (6) *Intermediate care facilities*, which are certified by the Medicaid program to provide health-related services on a regular basis to Medicaid eligibles who do not require hospital or skilled nursing facility care but who do require institutional care above the level of room and board.

Psychiatric Care Delivery

Psychiatric care is provided by a variety of mental health organizations in addition to the private practitioner. These include the following: (1) psychiatric hospitals, including Veteran Administration psychiatric hospitals, state and county mental hospitals, and private mental hospitals; (2) psychiatric units of general hospitals; (3) residential treatment centers for emotionally disturbed children; (4) federally funded community mental health centers; and (5) free-standing psychiatric outpatient clinics, where a psychiatrist has medical responsibility for all patients in the program.

Most patients are seen in one of these organizations; fewer than 5 percent of all psychiatric patients are seen by psychiatrists in private practice.

Health Maintenance Organization (HMO)

An HMO is an organized system providing comprehensive (both inpatient and outpatient) health care in all specialties, including psychiatry. Members voluntarily enroll in the plan and pay a prepayment or capitation fee to cover all health care services for a fixed period of time (a month or a year). There are currently about 600 HMOs in the United States (up from 300 in 1988), with an enrollment of approximately 33 million people.

By employing a capitation or prospective payment method, the HMO is assuming a more dominant role in U.S. health care. The primary reason for the popularity of the HMO is that it decreases health care costs by limiting the number of new hospitalizations and by discharging patients from the hospital earlier. The emphasis on prevention and health promotion and on performing as much diagnosis and therapy as possible on an outpatient basis also helps control expenses.

There are three types of HMOs. (1) In the Staff Model, physicians receive a salary to provide services in the HMO's own facility. (2) In the Group Model, health care is furnished by one or more groups of doctors; payment is received on a contractual basis at a predetermined rate. Physicians in Staff and Group Models often own stock in their HMO. (3) The Individual Practice Association (IPA) is also referred to as the Network Model. The HMO negotiates with individual physicians to receive a capitation fee for providing services to each IPA member seen in their private offices. Physicians

Table 4.9-2
Aspects of Hospital Organization

Criteria	Voluntary Hospital	Investor-Owned Hospitals	State Mental Hospital System	Municipal Hospital System	Federal Hospital System	Special Hospital
Patient population	All illnesses	All illnesses, although hospital may specialize	Mental illness	All illnesses	All illnesses	70 percent of facility must be for single diagnosis
Number of hospitals	5,843	834	285 (119,000 beds nationally)	Variable by city	342	150
Profit orientation	Nonprofit	For profit	Nonprofit	Nonprofit	Nonprofit	For profit or nonprofit
Ownership	Private management board	Private corporation; may be owned by MDs	State	City government	Federal government	Private or public
Affiliation	1200 church-affiliated; remainder are privately owned or university-sponsored	May be owned by large chains such as Humana Corporation	Free-standing or affiliated with various medical schools	Voluntary teaching hospitals and medical schools	Department of Defense (190); Public Health Service, Coast Guard, Prison, Merchant Marine, Indian Health Service; Veterans Administration (139)	Optional affiliation with medical schools
Other	Provide bulk of care in U.S.	Increasing in importance nationally	Deinstitutionalization—number of patients has been reduced	Most physicians at municipal hospitals are employed by their affiliated medical school	V.A. hospitals usually have affiliations with medical schools	Less regulated than other types of hospitals (see note 5)

Notes: (1) To be designated a teaching hospital, a hospital must offer at least four types of approved residencies, clinical experiences for medical students, and an affiliation with a medical school. (2) As of 1982, there were 364 state-operated facilities and approximately 14,600 private facilities for the mentally retarded. (3) In 1989 there were 751 investor-owned for-profit hospitals for psychiatric patients in the United States. (4) Short-term hospitals have an average patient stay of less than 30 days; long-term, an average of longer duration. (5) Special hospitals include obstetrics and gynecology; eye, ear, nose, and throat. They do not include psychiatric hospitals or substance abuse hospitals.

retain their office-based private practices when they join an IPA. The percentage of IPAs in HMOs has increased from 7 percent in 1976 to 41 percent in 1987.

Preferred Provider Organization (PPO)

Like the HMO, this type of alternative delivery organization employs a prospective payment system. In the PPO, however, a corporation or insurance company makes an agreement with a particular group of community hospitals and doctors to supply health services to PPO members at a previously determined rate lower than their usual rates. Patients who enroll in a PPO select their physicians from among the list of participating doctors, which includes both specialists and primary care physicians. Inpatient care is received at one of the designated hospitals, which the patient chooses. There are about 200 PPOs in the United States at this time.

BASIC CONCEPTS OF HEALTH CARE ORGANIZATION

Regulation of Hospital Standards and Performance

A group of agencies, such as the Joint Commission on Accreditation of Healthcare Organizations (JCAHO) (previously called the Joint Commission on Accreditation of Hospitals [JCAH]) and the Liaison Committee on Medical Education (LCME), influence the standards of hospital care and performance. In addition, hospitals must comply with governmental regulations (city and state health rules). The JCAHO inspects hospitals every two years. The JCAHO is also responsible for determining the requirements for hospital accreditation. Hospital reimbursements from Medicare and Medicaid are contingent on meeting these standards. This accreditation, however, is done on a voluntary basis. The LCME and the Liaison Committee on Graduate Education are charged with accrediting medical schools and residency training programs, respectively. The two accrediting committees review education and training programs every four years; this procedure is voluntary.

Currently, there is a trend toward monitoring all the hospitals in a community as a single health entity and community resource. That means that each unit does not have the prerogative to develop new facilities without concern for the services offered by the other hospitals in the area.

Utilization review. This in-house evaluation process was created to ensure that institutions provide efficient, quality health care that meets patients' needs. The members of the utilization review committee consist of hospital administrators, doctors, and nurses. The committee reviews each patient's chart within a specified number of days of admission. The appropriateness of admission, treatment strategies, and length of hospital stay are reviewed to facilitate the patient's discharge. Through this process the utilization review committee determines whether a particular admission was really indicated and whether the hospital stay was longer than necessary. A hospital must conduct utilization reviews to be eligible for JCAH accreditation.

Professional Standards Review Organization (PSRO). The PSRO was set up by the federal government to review and to monitor care received by patients whose care is paid for with government funds. PSROs have been established by local medical associations and serve several functions. They attempt to ensure high-quality care, control costs, determine maximum lengths of stay by patients in hospitals, conduct utilization reviews, and censure physicians who do not adhere to established guidelines. The PSRO may conduct a medical audit to evaluate the quality of care retrospectively by carefully examining charts. The PSRO is made up of doctors elected by local medical societies.

Peer Review Organization (PRO). In the early 1980s the PRO replaced the PSRO as the federal review organization for hospitals receiving Medicare funds. In order to promote compliance with federal guidelines for health and hospital care, the PRO conducts independent utilization reviews and quality-of-care studies, validates Diagnosis Related Group (DRG) assignments, and reviews hospital admissions and readmissions.

Federally mandated and funded, the PROs have greater authority than the PSROs. PROs can impose sanctions on hospitals for inadequate care. They can even recommend the termination of federal funding to hospitals that consistently violate federal standards. In addition, PROs can adjust or refuse payment for health services that they consider unnecessary.

The PRO operates on a statewide level and can be either for profit or nonprofit in nature. In order to reduce costs, a PRO is chosen through a competitive bidding process from among qualified, physician-sponsored organizations.

Health Systems Agency (HSA). These nonprofit organizations are mandated by the federal government and set up on a statewide basis. HSAs promote or limit the development of health services and facilities, depending on the needs of a particular locality or state. They are made up of consumers and have considerable power in medicine. For example, before one can build a new hospital or conduct extensive renovations on an existing one, the HSA must approve a Certificate of Need (CON). In order to receive a CON, the necessity for a new facility in a specified locale must be established. HSAs control capital expenditures and, therefore, the availability of health resources. In each state, HSAs develop both long- and short-term goals and plans, approve health care proposals requesting federal funding, review existing facilities and services, and suggest future construction and renovation projects on the basis of their findings.

Reimbursement Programs

Medicare (Title 18). Set up by the Federal Social Security Act of 1965, Medicare is a federally funded health insurance program. It provides both hospital and medical insurance for persons 65 years or older and for persons with certain disabilities (e.g., blindness, renal disease). Medicare consists of two parts. Part A covers inpatient hospital care, home health services, dialysis, and nursing home care after hospitalization. Funding is derived from a federal trust fund, which, in turn, receives its funds from Social Security contributions. Part B is optional medical insurance that can be purchased by the patient to cover such services as physicians' fees, medical supplies, home health care, outpatient hospital care, and therapy services. Benefits and eligibility standards of Medicare are uniform throughout the United States. More than 33 million persons are covered by Medicare. Table 4.9-3 shows the dramatic increase in Medicare expenditures between 1980 and 1989.

Medicaid (Title 19). Mandated by the federal government in 1965, Medicaid is an assistance program for certain needy and low-income persons. It is financed by both federal and state governments, but each state defines its requirements for eligibility and is responsible for its administration. Although benefits vary from state to state, federal provisions require that Medicaid cover inpatient and outpatient hospital care (including psychiatric care), physician's services, laboratory tests, diagnostic imaging, home health care services, and nursing home care. Additional services may be provided at the state's option. Increasingly tight eligibility requirements have left many low-income people without coverage and unable to pay. Currently, about 24 million people are covered by Medicaid.

Blue Cross Association (BCA). This association of more than 80 independent insurance plans around the country pays primarily for inpatient hospital service. Blue Shield pays for physician services during the patient's hospital stay. In contrast to commercial insurance carriers, BCA is a nonprofit organization. Its premiums cover administrative expenses and benefits and provide a reserve to cover financial losses. It is regulated by state insurance departments. Benefits for psychiatric services are severely limited compared with those for other medical illnesses, though inpatient psychiatric care is less limited than outpatient care.

Self-pay. Persons contract with commercial insurance companies to cover both inpatient and outpatient costs, including physicians' fees, diagnostic procedures, and laboratory tests. For this type of insurance, self-pay patients pay a pre-

Table 4.9-3
Medicare Expenses

	1980	1989
Total Medicare expenditures	$33.9 billion	$95.8 billion
Physician services	$ 7.2 billion	$26 billion
Physician services as percentage of total	21%	27%
Part B premium	$ 9.60	$27.90

Data from Health Care Financing Administration.
Note: Based on federal fiscal years; 1989 is an estimate.

mium that may be based on (1) an experience rating determined by one's risk or prior record for reimbursement on insurance claims or (2) a community rating system in which each participant pays the same premium because the plan's cost is divided equally among group members.

As a result of increased claim costs of private insurance companies, cost control strategies are being employed to reduce financial risk and increase profits. By utilizing such procedures as benefit maximums for a given year, deductibles, and copayments, health insurance companies can limit increases in premium rates while still covering most of the costs incurred by the patient.

Cost Containment

As protection against soaring health care expenditures, government and commercial insurance programs have enacted measures to limit spending. Several such mechanisms are described below.

Diagnosis Related Group (DRG). A DRG is a classification system consisting of 470 disease categories. In the 1970s DRGs were developed at Yale University as a way to help health care personnel determine the appropriate length of hospitalization for any given patient. The assignment of a patient to a DRG category is based on principal diagnosis, treatment procedures, personal attributes (e.g., age, sex), complications, and discharge status.

In 1983 the federal Health Care Financing Administration adopted DRGs as the method for repaying hospitals for Medicare services. Most states now use this prospective payment system, whereby a hospital is reimbursed for patient care on the basis of a predetermined rate for each diagnostic category. An advantage of a prospective price system is that hospitals and physicians must deliver health services with greater than usual efficiency in order to conserve resources and funds. The hospital knows in advance the dollar amount it will be reimbursed for each DRG, and it will make money if the actual cost of treatment is less than this designated amount. The institution assumes a monetary loss, however, if the costs of hospitalization exceed this amount.

Criticisms of the DRG system include the concern that necessary but cost-ineffective medical services and programs will be eliminated. It is also feared that, if the service provider anticipates that adequate treatment will cost more than the assigned rate, patients will be either prematurely released or refused care.

Resource-Based Relative Value Scale (RBRVS). This is a newly devised method by which reimbursement to physicians by third-party payers can be determined. Developed at Harvard University, the RBRVS is based on several factors, including the number of years and the cost of training to become a specialist, the cost of running an office, other overhead costs, and the amount of time spent with the patient either in discussion (cognitive skills) or in performing a procedure. Some specialists, such as surgeons, will be reimbursed a smaller than usual amount, and some, such as family physicians, will be reimbursed a greater than usual amount. The RBRVS plan will be phased in over a five-year period beginning in 1992.

Claims review. This method of peer review consists of the examination of claims for the reimbursement of treatment after it has been rendered. It has the disadvantage of being a decision to pay or not to pay after the treatment has been given. Insurance companies and governments have been doing claims reviews for many years. Traditionally, it has consisted of the examination of a claim by a clerk, with determination of eligibility by nonprofessionals. For example, when a claim for psychiatric treatment payment is turned down and appealed or when a claim is for a large amount, in the past the claim was reviewed by a single psychiatric consultant, who was an employee of the insurance company concerned. That system resulted in idiosyncratic decisions that may or may not have reflected local practice quality. In many instances, guidelines for insurance companies were developed without any input from practicing psychiatrists.

The first level of claims review generally consists of a clerical examination to determine whether the bill shows the necessary administrative information and whether the claimant is, indeed, insured. There is no determination of appropriateness of care. The second level of claims review is generally done by trained personnel, often nurses. Here the claims reviewer compares the treatment rendered with previously established criteria of treatment that have been established as appropriate for the condition. The second-level reviewer may approve payment for the claim. If the second-level reviewer has questions or if the treatment is considered inappropriate according to the criteria, the claim is reviewed by a third-level group or a true peer review committee. Here a professional determination is made as to the appropriateness of care. The peer review committee—one or more psychiatrists review each claim—may approve or disapprove. There are levels of appeal for the practitioner who is dissatisfied with the committee determination. The appeals process often goes to a special committee of the county or state medical society.

Managed care. Managed care is a method of cost containment; its goal is to eliminate unnecessary medical procedures and to obtain discounted services from doctors and hospitals. Business and insurance companies have advocated managed care in an effort to cut their medical costs for employees and insurance beneficiaries. In some cases payment may be denied to patients who are not members of a health maintenance organization (HMO) or a similar network of health care providers who have agreed to certain fees and certain guidelines before a service is rendered. In other cases a second opinion is mandatory before payment of benefits. If the patient objects to obtaining a second opinion, the insurance company can withhold payment. Half of all Blue Cross enrollees are now part of a managed care system that requires (1) that mandatory second opinions be obtained for surgical procedures and (2) that precertification of need be obtained before a patient is admitted to a hospital. Many large insurance companies and other groups have developed benefit-consulting services, also known as utilization review companies, which evaluate all medical claims in an effort to cut medical costs. Some of these companies receive a percentage of the amount of money saved as payment for their service, which has led to charges of conflict of interest.

Most physicians acknowledge the need for accountability but view utilization review procedures as cumbersome and inequitable. A doctor may have to deal with 10 to 20 different review organizations, each of which has its own criteria as to what constitutes a necessary medical procedure for which it is willing to allow payment. A troubling aspect of managed care is that denial of payment occurs for some treatments that are called experimental by utilization review companies but that are considered accepted treatment by medical experts. Payment denials of this sort are on the increase and threaten to interfere with both innovative medical treatment and traditional medical care. Another particularly troubling issue resulting from these overseeing activities has been the breaching of confidentiality in the doctor-patient relationship. Moreover, denials of payment, demands to justify clinical decisions, and requirements for prior approval of procedures undermine professional decision making and contribute to a growing sense of frustration among physicians in all specialties.

References

Bennett M J: The greening of the HMO: Implications for prepaid psychiatry. Am J Psychiatry *145*: 1544, 1988.

Center for Health Policy Research (American Medical Association): *Socioeconomic Characteristics of Medical Practice, 1987*. Center for Health Policy Research, Chicago, 1987.

Chang R S, ed.: *Preventive Health Care*. G K Hall, Boston, 1981.

Chollet D: *Uninsured in the United States: The Nonelderly Population Without Health Insurance*. Employee Benefit Research Institute, Washington, DC, 1987.

Dallek G, Hurwit C, Golde M: *Insuring the Uninsured: Options for State Action*. Americans for Health, Inc., and Citizen Action, Washington, DC, 1987.

Enthoven A, Kronick R: A consumer-choice health plan for the 1990s: Universal health insurance in a system designed to promote quality and economy. N Engl J Med *320*: 29, 1989.

Freiman M P, Mitchell J B, Rosenbach M L: An analysis of DRG-based reimbursement for psychiatric admissions to general hospitals. Am J Psychiatry *144*: 603, 1987.

Freis J R: Aging, natural death, and the compression of morbidity. N Engl J Med *303*: 130, 1980.

Haddon W, Barker S P: Injury control. In *Preventive and Community Medicare*. D Clark and B MacMahon, editors. Little, Brown, Boston, 1981.

Health Insurance Institute: *Source Book of Health Insurance Data*. Health Insurance Institute, New York, 1989.

Himmelstein D U, Woolhandler S: A national health program for the United States: A physicians' proposal. N Engl J Med *320*: 102, 1989.

Iglehart J K: The new era of prospective payment for hospitals. N Engl J Med *307*: 1288, 1982.

Institute of Medicine: *Assessing Medical Technologies*. National Academy Press, Washington, DC, 1985.

Johnston J B, Reinhardt U E: Addressing the health of a nation: Two views. Health Affect *8*: 5, 1989.

Lamb H R: Will we save the homeless mentally ill? Am J Psychiatry *147*: 649, 1990.

Mitchell J B, Dickey B, Liptzin B, Sederer L I: Bringing psychiatric patients into the medicare prospective payment system: Alternatives to DRGs. Am J Psychiatry *144*: 610, 1987.

National Data Book and Guide to Sources: Statistical Abstracts of the United States, ed 106. U S Department of Commerce, U S Bureau of the Census, Washington, DC, 1986.

Relman A S: The new medical-industrial complex. N Engl J Med *303*: 963, 1980.

Steven R S, Epstein A M: Institutional responses to prospective payment based on diagnostic-related groups. N Engl J Med *312*: 621, 1985.

Wennberg J E, McPherson K, Caper P: Will payment based on diagnostic-related groups control hospital costs? N Engl J Med *311*: 295, 1984.

Psychology and Psychiatry: Psychometric and Neuropsychological Testing

5.1 / Psychological Testing of Intelligence and Personality

Formal psychological testing of intelligence and personality play an integral role in clinical practice. Personality assessment provides information on patients' strengths and weaknesses, on how and why they are in their current situation, and on their prognosis. Valuable information regarding diagnosis may result from a thorough personality evaluation. It may also help in assessing the progress patients make over the course of psychotherapy or other treatment programs.

Most of the commonly used assessment instruments are standardized against normal controls, who are required to respond to the same stimuli or set of questions. The responses are tabulated into a normal distribution pattern against which new subjects are compared. When responses are limited—that is, when the subject is required to answer in some fixed response pattern (e.g., yes or no, true or false)—standardization is used to ensure that any variability that occurs is in the subject and not in the test.

Standardization refers to the tendency for test administration and scoring to be invariant across time and examiners. Related to the standardization of any test are the available data that presumably demonstrate whether the test is valid and reliable. Reliability refers to the reproducibility of results; validity refers to the concept of whether the test measures what it purports to measure.

CLASSIFICATION OF TESTS

Tests are classified in various ways as follows:

Objective tests. Objective tests are typically pencil-and-paper tests based on specific items and questions. They yield numerical scores and profiles easily subjected to mathematical or statistical analysis. An example is the Minnesota Multiphasic Personality Inventory (MMPI).

Projective tests. These tests present stimuli whose meaning is not immediately obvious; that is, some degree of ambiguity forces the person to project his or her own needs into the test situation. The projective tests presumably have no right or wrong answers. The person being tested must give meaning to the stimulus in accordance with his or her own inner needs, drives, abilities, and defenses. Examples include the Thematic Apperception Test (TAT), the Draw-a-Person test, the Rorschach test, and the Sentence Completion Test.

Individual or group tests. Tests may be administered individually or given simultaneously to a group. Individual testing has the advantage of providing an opportunity for the examiner to evaluate rapport and motivational factors and to observe and record the patient's behavior during testing. Careful timing of responses is also possible. Group tests, on the other hand, are usually more easily administered and scored.

Battery tests. A number of individual tests used together make up a psychological or neuropsychological battery. The test battery can give more information about different areas of function than an individual test and can increase the level of confidence if there is a positive correlation between them. The Halstead-Reitan is an example of a test battery.

INTELLIGENCE TESTING

Intelligence can be defined as a person's ability to assimilate factual knowledge, to recall either recent or remote events, to reason logically, to manipulate concepts (either numbers or words), to translate the abstract to the literal and the literal to the abstract, to analyze and synthesize forms, and to deal meaningfully and accurately with problems and priorities deemed important in a particular setting. There are tremendous individual differences in intelligence.

In 1905 Alfred Binet introduced the concept of the mental age (M.A.), which is the average intellectual level of a particular age. The intelligence quotient (I.Q.) is the ratio of M.A. over C.A. (chronological age) multiplied by 100 to do away with the decimal point; it is represented by the following equation:

$$\text{I.Q.} = \frac{\text{M.A.}}{\text{C.A.}} \times 100$$

When chronological and mental ages are equal, the I.Q. is 100—that is, average. Since it is impossible to measure increments of intellectual power past the age of 15 by available intelligence tests, the highest divisor in the I.Q. formula is 15. One way of expressing the relative standing of a person within a group is by percentile. The higher the percentile, the higher one's rank within a group. An I.Q. of 100 corresponds to the 50th percentile in intellectual ability for the general population.

As measured by most intelligence tests, I.Q. is an interpretation or classification of a total test score in relation to norms established by a group. I.Q. is a measure of present functioning ability, not necessarily of future potential. Although under ordinary circumstances the I.Q. is stable throughout life, there is no absolute certainty about its predictive properties. A person's I.Q. must be examined in the light of past experiences and future opportunities.

The I.Q. itself is no indicator of the origins of its reflected capacities, genetic (innate) or environmental. The most useful intelligence test must measure a variety of skills and abilities, including verbal and performance, early learned and recently learned, timed and untimed, culture-free and culture-bound. No intelligence test is totally culture-free, although tests do differ significantly in degree.

Wechsler Adult Intelligence Scale (WAIS)

The WAIS is the best standardized and most widely used intelligence test in clinical practice today. It was constructed by David Wechsler at New York University Medical Center and Bellevue Psychiatric Hospital.

Designed in 1939, the original WAIS has gone through several revisions. A scale for children ages 5 through 15 years has been devised (the WISC— Wechsler Intelligence Scale for Children) and a scale for children ages 4 to 6½ years (WPPSI—Wechsler Preschool and Primary Scale of Intelligence). In practice, the WAIS, WISC, or WPPSI is used as part of a battery of psychological tests. A revised version of the WAIS (WAIS-R) was constructed in 1981, and it has been translated for use with Spanish-speaking persons. A revised version of the WISC (WISC-R) has been constructed as well.

The WAIS comprises 11 subtests made up of six verbal subtests and five performance subtests, yielding a verbal I.Q., a performance I.Q., and a combined or full-scale I.Q. Intelligence levels are based on the assumption that intellectual abilities are normally distributed (in a bell-shaped curve) throughout the population (see Table 5.1-1 for a classification of intelligence scores). Verbal and performance I.Q.s and the full-scale I.Q. are determined by the use of separate tables for each of the seven age groups (from 16 to 64 years) on which the test was standardized. Variability in functioning is revealed through discrepancies between verbal and performance I.Q.s and by the scatter pattern between subtests.

Construction of the test. The following subtests are described in the order in which they are presented to the subject:

Table 5.1-1
Classification of Intelligence by I.Q. Range

Classification	I.Q. Range
Profound mental retardation (MR)*	Below 20 or 25
Severe MR*	20–25 to 35–40
Moderate MR*	35–40 to 50–55
Mild MR*	50–55 to approx 70
Borderline	70–79
Dull normal	80 to 90
Normal	90 to 110
Bright normal	110 to 120
Superior	120 to 130
Very superior	130 and above

*According to the revised third edition of the *Diagnostic and Statistical Manual of Mental Disorders* (DSM-III-R).

Verbal:

Information. This subtest covers general information and general knowledge and is subject to cultural variables. Persons from low socioeconomic groups with little schooling do not perform as well as those from high socioeconomic groups with more schooling.

Comprehension. This subtest measures the subject's ability to adhere to social conventions and to understand social judgment by asking about proverbs and how one ought to behave under certain circumstances.

Arithmetic. Ability to do arithmetic and other simple calculations is reflected on this subtest, which is adversely influenced by anxiety and poor attention and concentration.

Similarities. This subtest covers the ability to abstract by asking subjects to explain the similarity between two things. It is a sensitive indicator of intelligence.

Digit span. Immediate retention is measured in this subtest. The subject is asked to learn a series of two to nine digits, which are immediately recalled both forward and backward. Anxiety, poor attention span, and brain dysfunction interfere with recall.

Vocabulary. The subject is asked to define 35 vocabulary words of increasing difficulty. Intelligence has a high correlation with vocabulary, which is related to level of education. Idiosyncratic definitions of words may give clues to personality structure.

Performance:

Picture completion. This subtest initiates the performance part of the WAIS and consists of completing a picture that is missing a part. Visuoperceptive defects become evident when mistakes are made.

Block design. This subtest requires the subject to match colored blocks and visual designs. Brain dysfunction involving impairment of left-right dominance interferes with performance.

Picture arrangement. The subject is required to arrange a series of pictures in a sequence that tells a story (e.g., a person committing a crime). In addition to testing performance, this subtest provides data about the subject's cognitive style.

Object assembly. The subject has to assemble objects, such as the figure of a woman or an animal, in their proper order and organization. Visuoperception, somatoperception, and manual dexterity are tested.

Digit symbol. In this final subtest of the WAIS, the subject is given a code that pairs symbols with digits. The test consists of matching a series of digits to their corresponding symbols in as little time as possible.

Distribution of I.Q. scores. The average or normal range of I.Q. is 90 to 110; I.Q. scores of at least 120 are considered superior (Figure 5.1-1). According to the American Association of Mental Deficiency (AAMD), mental retardation is defined as an I.Q. of less than 70, which corresponds to the lowest 2.2 percent of the population. Consequently, 2 out of every 100 persons have I.Q. scores consistent with mental deficiency, which can range from mild to profound (Table 5.1-1).

Interpretation of I.Q. scores. The reliability of the WAIS is very high. Retesting of persons 18 years and older rarely reveals changes in I.Q. scores.

The verbal scale of the I.Q. measures retention of previously acquired factual information, and the performance scale measures visuospatial capacity and visuomotor speed in problem-solving tasks. The performance scale is more

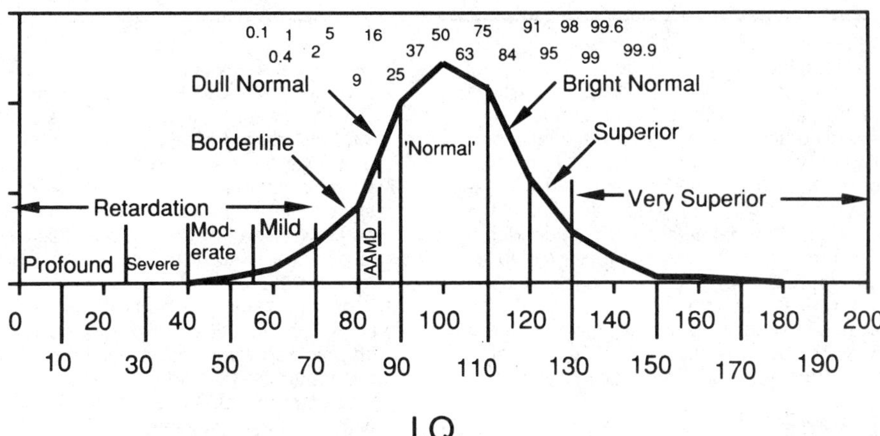

Figure 5.1-1. The distribution of Wechsler Adult Intelligence Scale I.Q. categories. (Adapted from J D Matarazzo: *Wechsler's Measurement and Appraisal of Adult Intelligence, ed 5, p 124.* New York, Oxford University Press, 1972, with permission.)

sensitive to normal aging than is the verbal scale, which is more sensitive to education. Arithmetic and memory for digits is adversely affected by anxiety. A disparity between the verbal test and the performance test (usually greater than 15 points) may be indicative of psychopathology and requires further testing.

Stanford-Binet Test

Lewis Terman at Stanford University devised the Stanford-Binet Test in 1916. It is a comprehensive intelligence test that is used in psychiatry and education. The WAIS, however, is more widely used than the Stanford-Binet.

ADULT PERSONALITY ASSESSMENT

Objective Personality Assessment

The objective orientation to personality assessment is characterized by the reliance on structured, standardized measurement devices, which are typically of a self-report nature. *Structured* refers to the tendency toward straightforward test stimuli, such as direct questions regarding the persons' opinions of themselves, and unambiguous instructions regarding completion of the test.

Response sets refer to attitudes or styles in responding to personality questionnaires. For the most part, these sets appear to be problematic with objective inventories; however, they are also potential error sources with projective and behavioral assessment. A socially desirable response set is indicative of persons who attempt to present themselves in a favorable light. Conversely, "faking bad" refers to an opposite response set; that is, persons attempt to present a more dismal outlook than is the case. Some of the well-constructed objective personality measures, such as the Minnesota Multiphasic Personality Inventory (MMPI) and the California Personality Inventory (CPI), have built-in scales designed to detect the presence of these types of response sets.

Minnesota Multiphasic Personality Inventory (MMPI). The MMPI is a self-report inventory that is the most widely used and most thoroughly researched of the objective personality assessment instruments. It was developed in 1937 by Starke Hathaway, a psychologist, and J. Charnley McKinley, a psychiatrist. The test consists of 550 statements—such as, "I worry about sex matters," "I sometimes tease animals," "I believe I am being plotted against"—to which the subject must respond with "true," "false," or "cannot say." The test may be used in card or booklet form, and several programs exist to process the responses by computer.

The MMPI gives scores on 10 standard clinical scales, each of which was derived empirically (that is, homogeneous criterion groups of psychiatric patients were used in developing the scales). The items for each scale were selected for their ability to separate medical and psychiatric patients from normal controls.

Clinical scales. The clinical scales are numbered and are often referred to by number, rather than by name, particularly in coding deviantly high scores. A high score on a particular scale does not mean that the person has that illness. For example, an elevated 8 (Sc) score does not indicate that the patient is necessarily schizophrenic. An accurate interpretation requires great experience with the test and some understanding of the social, educational, and socioeconomic background from which the patient comes. Recent evidence suggests that religion and race are both potential variables in MMPI responses. The scales are listed in Table 5.1-2.

Interpretation. Although the MMPI was initially viewed as a diagnostic aid (i.e., a patient with a major depressive disorder would show an elevation on the depression scale), the advantages of a configural approach to interpretation quickly became apparent. The configural approach, which involves interpretations based on the patterning of the entire profile, has become the preferred method and has increased the effectiveness of the MMPI as a personality measurement device. Various researchers have identified numerous personality correlates of different MMPI scale configurations, frequently using the two highest scales as the basis for core interpretive statements. Actuarial research of this nature has also served as the basis for computerized interpretative services. These services, though not a substitute for a comprehensive personality evaluation, can assist the clinician in hypothesis formulation. Computerized services are especially useful when the MMPI is to be interpreted by a person knowl-

Table 5.1-2
MMPI Validity and Clinical Scales

Validity

L: Lie Scale A nonempirically derived social desirability scale. Items tend to reflect behaviors that are considered socially desirable, but rarely practiced. The score can suggest defensiveness, illiteracy, psychosis, or personality processes, depending on various factors.

F: Infrequency Scale Measures a tendency to endorse selected items that are statistically rare responses (less than 10 percent of the original normal sample). Useful in identifying illiteracy, malingering, panic, confusion, psychosis, and personality processes.

K: Suppressor Scale It is used to adjust mathematically certain clinical scales in order to decrease false positives and false negatives. The scale is also useful in determining overall test-taking attitude and is an indication of personality variables.

Clinical

1: Hypochondriasis This scale reflects somatic concerns and preoccupation with bodily functioning. Interpretation needs to take into account factors such as age and actual health status. As with all MMPI scales, interpretation is furthered by looking at its relationship with other scales.

2: Depression Scores on this scale tend to be reflective of depression as a mood disorder or neurotic depression. The fact that the scale is quite sensitive to situational variables suggests that it may be a good index of state personality status.

3: Hysteria Items on this scale involve the identification of classical histrionic symptoms, including the presence of physical symptoms coupled with indifference, denial, repression, and inhibition. The scale does not necessarily measure other more popularly conceived traits, such as lability and melodramatic attitude.

4: Psychopathic Deviance This scale was developed to assess the amorality and asociality aspects of psychopathy, rather than the criminal or antisocial. Its meaning is very dependent on other scale configurations. The scale provides good information on the quality of interpersonal relationships.

5: Masculinity-Femininity Although it was originally developed to identify homosexuality, the scale is rarely used for that purpose, although it does provide information on gender identity. The scale reflects a variety of personality and interest areas, such as dependency, sensitivity, intellectuality, and tendencies toward introspection.

6: Paranoia Developed by the empirical identification of classic paranoids, the scale thus assesses vigilance, sensitivity, delusional thought, distrust, and suspicion. Except for the paranoid areas, the members of the original criterion group were considered functional in their lives.

7: Psychasthenia A very diverse scale designed to measure anxiety and obsessive-compulsive traits. Endorsed items can reflect fear, obsessive-compulsive symptomatology, interpersonal hostility, tension, specific phobias, and impaired concentration.

8: Schizophrenia Reflects the more acute positive symptoms of psychotic breaks with reality, rather than the more chronic negative symptoms. The scale also assesses alienation, impaired self-identity, and isolation.

9: Hypomania Measures the rather classic symptomatology of mania, including elated and unstable mood, psychomotor excitement, and flight of ideas. It also appears to reflect narcissistic personality traits. In general, the scale provides information on the degree of drivenness of the person's personality characteristics. It has a strong age component.

10: Social Introversion Provides information on social withdrawal, shyness, leadership, talkativeness, levels of gregariousness, and, to a smaller degree, self-concept and neurotic tendencies. It is, perhaps, more two-dimensional and bipolar (introversion versus extroversion) than the other scales.

Special

A: Anxiety The first general factor extracted from factor analytic studies on the MMPI. It is thought to reflect generalized endorsement of psychopathology.

R: Repression The second factor that is found on factor analytic studies of the MMPI. It can be conceptualized as measuring the tendency to engage in denial.

ES: Ego Strength Provides an index of how functional the patient may be in terms of work and other social areas, regardless of level of psychopathology.

MAC: McAndrews Alcoholism Scale Estimates degree of addiction proneness, especially with alcohol and opiates. Especially sensitive to daily substance abuse, rather than episodic abuse.

Table produced by Robert W. Butler, Ph.D., and Paul Satz, Ph.D. with the assistance of Alex Caldwell, Ph.D.

edgeable in all aspects of the MMPI and the nature of the development of the computerized program. Blind use of these services by professionals not trained in the use of the MMPI is clearly inappropriate and, perhaps, even unethical.

The fact that the MMPI is the most widely used and researched psychological personality measurement device is undoubtedly one of its major strengths. Several hundred research papers on the MMPI appear in the literature each year, and it has been utilized extensively in cross-cultural clinical and research applications. The huge body of literature generated has resulted in a catalog of MMPI correlates on a wide variety of clinical cases, providing descriptive, predictive, diagnostic, and prognostic information. Another strength of the MMPI is its atheoretical nature, a characteristic that probably increases its usefulness over a broad spectrum. The presence of validity scales designed to assess test-taking attitude, in addition to clinical and personality information, is a distinct advantage that the MMPI maintains over many personality assessment tools. The MMPI has been restandardized on the basis of a contemporary sample of normal people. Questions and language are being updated to reflect current cultural views.

Millon Clinical Multiaxial Inventory (MCMI). The MCMI is a 175-item, true-false, paper-and-pencil personality inventory, developed by Theodore Millon and co-workers in the late 1970s. The test allows for scoring and interpretation on 11 scales, which represent personality disorders from the third edition of the American Psychiatric Association's *Diagnostic and Statistical Manual of Mental Disorders* (DSM-III). The test also contains a brief validity scale and nine scales designed to assess reactive symptom disorders, which the test authors claim are of a less enduring nature than the personality scales. The scales are described in detail in Table 5.1-3.

Type A-type B behavior. Two cardiologists, Meyer Friedman and Ray Rosenman, developed the concept that a specific behavior pattern, type A, set into motion the pathophysiology necessary for the production of coronary artery disease. They further hypothesized that the type A behavior pattern is a major risk factor (along with cholesterol, hypertension, smoking, and positive family history) for this disease.

Table 5.1-3
MCMI Clinical Scales

Personality Disorders (Axis II)

Scale 1: Schizoid Assesses the probability (as do the other scales of the MCMI) that a person meets DSM-III diagnostic criteria for schizoid personality disorders. Symptoms include indifference, insensitivity, affect deficit, and apathy.

Scale 2: Avoidant Includes the measurement of characteristics of dysphoria, alienation, aversion to interpersonal behavior, and hypersensitivity.

Scale 3: Dependent Assesses trait characteristics of docility, submissiveness, initiation difficulties, poor self-image, and naivete.

Scale 4: Histrionic Assesses lability of affect, sociability, seductiveness, immaturity, inability to delay immediate need gratification, and a dissociative cognitive style.

Scale 5: Narcissistic Measures the presence of inflated self-image, exploitiveness, expansive thinking, imperturbability, and deficits in social conscience.

Scale 6: Antisocial (Aggressive) High scores suggest hostile affect, vindictiveness, power-oriented life-style, malevolence, poor impulse control, and an inability to benefit from punishment.

Scale 7: Compulsive Key trait characteristics of a high score include restrained affect, conscientiousness, adherence to social conventions, conforming, cognitive constriction, and behavioral rigidity.

Scale 8: Passive-Aggressive Prominent personality traits include labile affect, contrariness, disillusionment, interpersonal ambivalence, and a discontented self-image.

Scale S: Schizotypal Assesses for the presence of social detachment, eccentricity, nondelusional autistic thinking, depersonalization, emptiness, emotional flatness, and anxious wariness.

Scale C: Borderline The salient characteristics of those scoring high on this scale are intense moodiness, dysregulated activation, self-destructive behavior, dependency anxiety, and ambivalence between thought-affect and action.

Scale P: Paranoid This scale measures the enduring traits of vigilant mistrust, distorted thought, criticalness and provocative interpersonal behavior.

Clinical Syndromes (Axis I)

Scale A: Anxiety A high score suggests apprehension, phobias, tension, indecision, and psychophysiological symptoms.

Scale H: Somatoform Assesses the degree to which psychological conflict is likely to be channeled physically and overall preoccupation with health.

Scale N: Hypomanic Measures the presence of unstable mood, restlessness, overactivity, pressured speech, impulsiveness, irritability, and other manic-type behavior.

Scale D: Dysthymia An elevation on this scale is likely to suggest despondency, guilt, discouragement, futility, and other symptoms of depression. The scale does not necessarily reflect extreme severity and, instead, implies preserved ego strength.

Scale B: Alcohol Abuse This scale provides a probability index for the presence or history of alcoholism.

Scale T: Drug Abuse This scale extends Scale B to include substance abuse, in general, and also implies poor impulse control and unconventionality.

Scale SS: Psychotic Thinking A high score on this scale suggests disorganized-regressed behavior, hallucinatory experiences, delusions, and inappropriate affect.

Scale CC: Psychotic Depression A high score suggests the presence of severe depression that is usually of incapacitating proportions.

Scale PP: Psychotic Delusions Elevations indicate that the person is suffering from delusions, usually persecutory or grandiose in nature. Accompanying belligerency is common.

Table produced by Robert W. Butler, Ph.D., and Paul Satz, Ph.D, with the assistance and permission of Theodore Millon, Ph.D.

According to Friedman, the most important aspects of the type A behavior pattern are excesses of time urgency and competitive hostility (Table 5.1-4). Persons designated as type B display obverse qualities of behavior. They are relaxed, less aggressive, unhurried, and less apt to strive vigorously to achieve a goal. Although one might expect type A persons to be more successful than type B persons, that is not the case. In fact, some data suggest that type A persons are less successful than type B persons, despite the ardent desire of type A persons to achieve.

Eysenck Personality Inventory. Developed by H. Eysenck, this self-assessment personality scale measures emotionality versus stability, extroversion versus introversion, tough-mindedness, sociability, and a tendency by some subjects to fake good answers (comparably to the Lie Scale on the MMPI). Eysenck introduced the concept of psychotocism, which is an underlying personality trait present in varying degrees in all persons. If present in marked degree, it predisposes a person to the development of a psychiatric disorder.

A listing of popular objective tests is given in Table 5.1-5.

Projective Personality Assessment

The projective approach to personality assessment is defined by the use of unstructured, often ambiguous test stimuli. A basic assumption is that, when confronted with a vague stimulus and required to respond to it in some manner, persons cannot help but reveal information about themselves—not only in the way in which or process by which the ambiguity is confronted but also in the content of their responses.

The projective approach is essentially idiographic in nature, and most commonly the tests are not interpreted by comparing a person's responses with a set of criterion-referenced normative data. More typically, interpretation is based on a theory of human behavior and personality, and it is assumed that persons bring certain needs, characteristics, defenses, and other qualities that become apparent through the testing process.

A number of semistructured situations and projective-type stimuli have been developed, including perceiving inkblots, drawing pictures, and telling stories on the basis of presented pictures. Brief descriptions of some of the more popular projective techniques follow.

Rorschach test. With the possible exception of the WAIS, the Rorschach test is the most frequently used individual test in clinical settings throughout the United States. The Rorschach was devised by Hermann Rorschach, a Swiss psychiatrist, who began around 1910 to experiment with ambiguous inkblots. A standard set of 10 inkblots serves as stimuli for associations, one of which is shown in Figure 5.1-2. In the standard series, the blots are reproduced on cards 7 by 9½ inches and are numbered from I to X. Five of the blots are

Table 5.1-4
Diagnostic Indicators of Type A Behavior

Time Urgency	Excessive Competitiveness and Hostility
Psychomotor manifestations Characteristic facial tautness expressing tension Rapid horizontal eyeball movements during ordinary conversation Rapid eye blinking (over 40 blinks a min) Knee jiggling or rapid vigorous tapping of fingers Rapid, frequently dysrhythmic speech involving elimination of terminal words of sentences Lip clicking during ordinary speaking Rapid ticlike eyebrow lifting Head nodding when speaking Sucking in of air during speech Humming (tuneless) Speech hurrying Tense posture Motorization accompanying responses Expiratory sighing Rapid body movements Direct behavior tests The interviewer, in posing a question whose answer is already clear from its contents, hesitates, becomes laboriously tedious or repetitive, and then stammers. The subject interrupts the stammering with his answer. Physiological indicators Periorbital pigmentation Excessive forehead and upper lip perspiration Significant biographical content Self-awareness of presence of type A behavior Polyphasic activities, e.g. reads while driving, reads while using electric shaver, and thinks of other matters during conversation with others Walks fast, eats fast, and does not dawdle at table Subject makes fetish of always being on time under all circumstances	Has been told by spouse to slow down in working and living habits Difficulty in sitting and doing nothing Subject habitually substitutes numerals for metaphors in his speech Psychomotor manifestations Characteristic facial set exhibiting aggression and hostility (eye and jaw muscles) Characteristic ticlike drawing back of corner of lips, almost exposing teeth Hostile, jarring laugh Use of clenched fist and table pounding or excessively forceful use of hands and fingers Explosive, staccato, frequently unpleasant voice Frequent use of obscenity Subject exhibits irritation and rage when asked about some past event in which he or she became angered Direct behavior tests The interviewer directly challenges the validity of some comment or behavior that the subject has reported. The subject reacts in a hostile or unpleasant manner. The interviewer questions the subject about his or her views on politics, races, women or men, or competitors. The subject responds with absolute, almost angry generalizations. Significant biographical content The subject reports that he or she is irritated if kept waiting for any reason or if driving behind a car moving too slowly in his or her view. The subject expresses general distrust of other people's motives, e.g. distrust of altruism. The subject reports that he or she almost always plays any type of game to win (even with young children).

Table from M Friedman, C E Thoresen, J J Gill, D Ulmer, L Thompson, L Powell, V Price, S R Elek, D D Rabin, W S Breall, G Piaget, T Dixon, E Bourge, R A Levy, D L Tasto: Feasibility of altering type A behavior pattern after myocardial infarction: Recurrent Coronary Prevention Project Study: Methods, baseline results, and preliminary findings. Circulation *66*: 83, 1982, with permission.

in black and white; the remainder include colors. The cards are shown to the patient in a particular order. A record is kept of the patient's verbatim responses, along with initial reaction times and total time spent on each card. After completion of what is called the free-association phase, an inquiry phase is conducted by the examiner to determine important aspects of each response that will be crucial to its scoring. Table 5.1-6 contains examples of responses to Rorschach stimuli.

Scoring of responses converts the important aspects of each response into a symbol system related to location areas, determinants, content areas, and popularity.

Location. Location is scored in terms of which portion of the blot was used as the basis for a response (e.g., the whole blot, a common detail of the blot, an unusual detail of the blot, or an area of white space). Attention to the whole blot with accurate form perception reflects good organizational ability and high intelligence. Overattention to detail is common in obsessive and paranoid subjects.

Determinants. The determinants of each response reflect the features of the blot that made it look the way the patient thought it looked (e.g., form, shading, color, movement of either humans or animals, inanimate movements, or combinations of these determinants with varying emphasis). Overemphasis on form suggests rigidity and constriction of the personality. Color responses relate to the emotional reactions of the person to the environment and to the control of affect.

Content. Responses are scored in terms of the content they reflect—human, animal, anatomy, sex, food, nature, and so on. In general, content areas reflect breadth and range of interests.

Popularity. Certain responses to the different cards are more popular than others.

Interpretation. The Rorschach is particularly useful as an aid in diagnosis. The thinking and association patterns of the subject are brought more clearly into focus because the ambiguity of the stimulus provides relatively few cues about what are conventional, standard, or normal responses. Proper interpretation, however, requires a great deal of experience. There is a high reliability among experienced clinicians who administer the test. In proper hands, it is extremely useful, especially in eliciting psychodynamic formulations, defense mechanisms, and subtle disorders of thinking.

The Rorschach elicits data that can aid in differential diagnosis, particularly in evaluating whether or not a thought disorder exists. For example, patients with schizotypal and borderline personality disorders are characterized by idiosyncratic thought, peculiarities of language, and unconventional thinking.

Thematic Apperception Test (TAT). The TAT was designed by Henry Murray and Christiana Morgan as part of the normal personality study conducted at the Harvard Psychological Clinic in 1943. It consists of a series of 30 pictures and one blank card. Not all the pictures are used. The choice

Table 5.1-5
Objective Measures of Personality

Name	Description	Strengths	Weaknesses
Minnesota Multiphasic Personality Inventory (MMPI)	566 items, true-false; self-report format; 17 scales (numerous special scales)	Provides wide range of data on numerous personality variables; strong research base	Tends to emphasize major psychopathology. In need of revision with current normative data
Millon Clinical Multiaxial Inventory (MCMI)	175 items, true-false; self-report format; 20 scales	Brief administration time; corresponds well with DSM-III-R diagnostic classifications	In need of more validation research. No information on disorder severity
16 Personality Factor Questionnaire (16 PF)	True-false; self-report format; 16 personality dimensions	Sophisticated psychometric instrument with considerable research conducted on nonclinical population	Limited usefulness with clinical populations
California Personality Inventory (CPI)	True-false; self-report format; 17 scales	Well-accepted method of assessing patients who do not present with major psychopathology	Limited usefulness with clinical populations
Jackson Personality Inventory (JPI)	True-false; self-report format; 15 personality scales	Constructed in accord with sophisticated psychometric techniques; controls for response sets	Unproved usefulness in clinical settings
Edwards Personal Preference Schedule (EPPS)	Forced choice; self-report format	Follows Murray's theory of personology; accounts for social desirability	Not widely used clinically because of restricted nature of information obtained
Beck Depression Inventory (BDI)	Self-report on Likert-type format; measures depression	Follows Beck's theory of depression quite well; widely used	Assesses mood and thought well but inadequate on neurovegetative symptoms
State-Trait Anxiety Inventory (STAI)	Self-report on Likert-type format; measures anxiety	Allows for differentiation of state and trait anxiety; well researched	STAI items are quite transparent
Psychological Screening Inventory (PSI)	130 items, true-false; self-report format	Produces 4 scores, which can be used as screening measures on the possibility of a need for psychological help	The scales are short and have correspondingly low reliability
Eysenck Personality Questionnaire (EPQ) or Inventory (EPI)	True-false; self-report format	Useful as a screening device; test has a theoretical basis with research support	Scales are short, and items are quite transparent as to purpose; not recommended for other than a screening device
Adjective Checklist (ACL)	True-false; self-report or informant report	Can be used for self or other rating	Scores rarely correlate highly with more conventional personality inventories
Comrey Personality Scales (CPS)	True-false; self-report format; 8 scales	Factor analytic techniques used with a high degree of sophistication in test construction	Not widely used; factor analytic interpretation problems
Tennessee Self-Concept Scale (TSCS)	100 items, true-false; self-report format; 14 scales	Brief administration time yields considerable information	Brevity is also a disadvantage, lowering reliability and validity; useful as a screening device only

Table by Robert W. Butler, Ph.D., and Paul Satz, Ph.D.

depends on what conflict area one wishes to clarify with a patient. Examples of TAT pictures are a young woman seated on a couch looking up at an older man, a man standing beside a nude woman in a bed, and a gray-haired man looking at a younger man.

Although most of the pictures depict people and all are representational (making the test stimuli more structured than the inkblots of the Rorschach test), there is ambiguity in each picture. Unlike the Rorschach blots, to which the patient is asked to associate, the TAT requires that the patient construct or create a story.

As the test was originally conceived, an important aspect of each story was the figure (the hero) with whom subjects seemed to identify and to whom they were presumably at-

Figure 5.1-2. Plate I of the Rorschach test. (From Hans Huber Medical Publisher, Berne, with permission.)

tributing their own wishes, strivings, and conflicts. The characteristics of people other than the hero were considered to represent the subject's views of other people in his or her environment. It is assumed that all the figures in a TAT story are equally representative of the subject, with the more accepted and conscious traits and motives attributed to figures closest to the subject in age, sex, and appearance and the more unacceptable and unconscious traits and motives attributed to figures most unlike the subject.

The stories must be considered from the standpoint of unusualness of theme or plot. Whether patients are dealing with a common or an uncommon theme, however, their story reflects their own idiosyncratic approach to organization, sequence, vocabulary, style, preconceptions, assumptions, and outcome. TAT cards have different stimulus values and can be assumed to elicit data pertaining to different areas of functioning. Generally, the TAT is more useful as a technique for inferring motivational aspects of behavior than as a basis for making a diagnosis.

Sentence Completion Test (SCT). The SCT is designed to tap the patient's conscious associations to areas of functioning in which the clinician may be interested. It is composed of a series (usually 75 to 100) of sentence stems—such as, "I like . . ." "Sometimes I wish . . ."—that the patient is asked to complete in his or her own words.

Most frequently, some time pressure is applied, and the patient is instructed to write down the first thing that comes to mind. In other instances, the text is administered verbally by the examiner, as in the word-association technique. Sentence stems vary in their ambiguity; hence, some items serve more as a projective test stimulus ("Sometimes I . . ."). Others more closely resemble direct-response questionnaires ("My greatest fear is . . .").

With the individual protocol, most clinicians use an inspection technique, noting particularly those responses that are expressive of strong affects, that tend to be given repeti-

Table 5.1-6
Responses to Rorschach Card I by Five Male Patients

	Free Association	Inquiry
Patient A:	A bug with two witches attached to it.	This whole thing in the middle, just the way it looks. [Points] Just the wings here. Looks like a witch.
	Also a halloween mask. About all I can see.	That—the whole thing. The eyes, the mouth [White space] [?] Nothing else about it.
Patient B:	A bat, a bug.	Bat. [Whole] The blackness and the wings. Bug—that was just a pure reference to the color. I just see it as unpleasant.
	One of the furies. A headless woman with black wings, grasping hands, claws, whatever. Bottom part of her torso is compressed, held in, like she's reaching forward.	Furies. [Whole] The central portion could represent legs pressed together. She represents a figure of death launching forward, and the head gets lost. Sort of snakelike, and the outer parts are reaching forth at the shadow of the earth.
Patient C:	It looks like a monster bat. It has pincers. And an ass over here.	The whole thing. It has wings. It's kind of ragged, that's all. [Top center] Arches. Just shaped that way. Feel uptight, knowing I'm taking a test[?] Shape, two mounds.
	And a butterfly.	Whole object. The wings, the shape. I just feel I want to get out of here.
Patient D:	Two dancers and two children in between them like they're dancing around them.	[Whole] Head, cape, clothing, legs. Matching heads. A pair of children or a pair of dancers, since it's symmetrical, one on one side and one on the other.
Patient E:	Looks like a bat? That's all I can make of it.	Whole blot. The middle makes it look like a body. And it looks like he has a tail and two short feet.

Table by Arthur C. Carr, Ph.D.
This table gives the Rorschach responses, both free associations and inquiries, given to Card I by five male patients. These extracted test responses are reported primarily to illustrate the range given by different patients to the same stimulus. As such, these responses may not themselves always delineate the varying DSM-III-R diagnosis represented.

Patient A: 26 years old, multiple psychiatric hospitalizations within past four years. Unable to care for himself, believing himself controlled by a force that makes him act inappropriately. Suffers from chronic delusions, obsessional thinking, and social withdrawal. Schizophrenia.

Patient B: 23 years old, long history of social isolation, repetitive self-destructive behavior, depression, and inability to function academically. Has shown depersonalization and derealization phenomena but no admitted delusions or hallucinations. Schizotypal personality disorder.

Patient C: 28 years old, complaints of chronic and overwhelming anxiety, feelings of loneliness, and ambivalence about homosexual identification. History of excessive use of psychotropic medication. Borderline personality disorder.

Patient D: 20 years old, presently hospitalized for manic episode, with history of two clear-cut manic and depressive episodes, followed by remissions. Bipolar mood disorder.

Patient E: 33 years old, hospitalized on neurology service for organic mental disorder assumed to be related to occupational hazard: mercury poisoning. Prior history of behavior difficulties.

tively, or that are unusual or particularly informative in any way. Areas in which denial operates are often revealed through omissions, bland expressions, or factual reports ("My mother is a woman"). Humor may also reflect an attempt to deny anxiety about a particular issue, person, or event. Important historical material is sometimes revealed directly ("I feel guilty about the way my sister was drowned").

Word-association technique. The word-association technique was devised by Carl Jung, who presented stimulus words to patients and had them respond with the first word that came to mind. After the initial administration of the list, some clinicians repeat the list, asking the patient to respond with the same words that he or she used previously; discrepancies between the two administrations may reveal associational difficulties. Complex indicators include long reaction times, blocking difficulties in making responses, unusual responses, repetition of the stimulus word, apparent misunderstanding of the word, clang associations, perseveration of earlier responses, and ideas or unusual mannerisms or movements accompanying the response. Because it is easily quantified, the test has continued to be used as a research instrument, although its popularity has diminished greatly over the years.

Draw-a-Person test. The Draw-a-Person test was first used as a measure of intelligence in children. Detail was correlated with intelligence and developmental level. It has since become more useful as an adult test. The test is easily administered, usually with the instructions, "I'd like you to draw a picture of a person; draw the best person you can." After the completion of the first drawing, the patient is asked to draw a picture of a person of the sex opposite to that of the first drawing. Some clinicians use an interrogation procedure in which the patient is questioned about his or her drawings. ("What is he doing?" "What are her best qualities?") Modifications include asking for a drawing of a house and a tree (House-Tree-Person test), of one's family, and of an animal.

A general assumption is that the drawing of a person represents the expression of the self or of the body in the environment. Interpretive principles rest largely on the assumed functional significance of each body part. Most clinicians use drawings primarily as a screening technique, particularly for the detection of brain damage.

INTEGRATION OF TEST FINDINGS

The integration of test findings into a comprehensive, meaningful report is probably the most difficult aspect of psychological evaluation. Inferences from different tests must be related to one another in terms of the confidence the clinician holds about them and the presumed level of the patient's awareness or consciousness being tapped.

Most clinicians follow some general outline in preparing a psychological report, such as test behavior, intellectual functioning, personality functioning (reality-testing ability, impulse control, manifest depression and guilt, manifestations of major dysfunction, major defenses, overt symptoms, interpersonal conflicts, self-concept, affects), inferred diagnosis, degree of present overt disturbance, prognosis for social recovery, motivation for personality change, primary assets and weaknesses, recommendations, and summary.

References

American Psychological Association: *Standards for Educational and Psychological Tests and Manuals.* American Psychological Association, Washington, DC, 1974.

Anastasi A: *Psychological Testing*. ed 5. Macmillan, New York, 1968.

Barlow D, ed: *Behavioral Assessment of Adult Disorders*. Guilford, New York, 1981.

Buros O K, ed: *The Eighth Mental Measurements Yearbook.* University of Nebraska Press, Buros Institute of Mental Measurements, Lincoln, 1978.

Butcher J N, Keller L S: Objective personality assessment. In *Handbook of Psychological Assessment.* G Goldstein and M Hersen, editors, p 307. Pergamon, New York, 1984.

Butler R W, Satz P: Psychological assessment of personality of adults and children. In *Comprehensive Textbook of Psychiatry,* ed 5, H I Kaplan and B J Sadock, editors, p 475. Williams & Wilkins, Baltimore, 1989.

Caligan R C, Offord K P: Revitalizing the MMPI: The development of contemporary norms. Psychiatr Ann *15*: 558, 1985.

Cronbach L: *Essentials of Psychological Testing.* Harper & Row, New York, 1960.

Dahlstrom W G, Welsh G, Dahlstrom L: *An MMPI Handbook*: vol. 1. *Clinical Interpretation*. University of Minnesota Press, Minneapolis, 1972.

Exner J E: *The Rorschach: A Comprehensive System,* vols 1, 2, and 3. Wiley, New York, 1982.

Hackett T P, Rosenbaum J F, Cassem N H: Cardiovascular disorders. In *Comprehensive Textbook of Psychiatry,* ed 5, H I Kaplan and B J Sadock, editors, Williams & Wilkins, Baltimore, 1989.

Halstead W: *Brain and Intelligence: A Quantitative Study of the Frontal Lobes.* University of Chicago Press, Chicago, 1947.

Holt R R: *Assessing Personality.* Harcourt Brace Jovanovich, Orlando, FL, 1971.

Kleinmuntz B: *Personality and Psychological Assessment.* St. Martin's Press, New York, 1982.

Lezak M D: *Neuropsychological Assessment,* ed 2. Oxford, New York, 1983.

Matarazzo J D: *Wechsler's Measurement and Appraisal of Adult Intelligence.* ed 5. Oxford, New York, 1972.

Millon T: *Millon Clinical Multiaxial Inventory Manuals,* ed 5. Interpretive Scoring Systems, Minneapolis, 1983.

Rorschach H; *Psychodiagnostik.* Bircher, Bern, 1921.

Terman L M, Merrill M A: *Stanford-Binet: Manual for the Third Revision.* Houghton Mifflin, Boston, 1960.

Wechsler D: *WAIS-R Manual.* Psychological Corporation, New York, 1981.

Wolman B, ed: *Handbook of Clinical Diagnosis of Mental Disorders.* Plenum, New York, 1978.

Zimmerman I, Woo-Sam J: *Clinical Interpretation of the Wechsler Adult Scale.* Grune & Stratton, New York, 1973.

Zubin J, Eron L, Schumer B J, eds: *An Experimental Approach to Projective Techniques.* Wiley, New York, 1965.

5.2 / Neuropsychological Assessment of Adults

Neuropsychological assessment applies the methods of experimental and clinical psychology to the analysis of the cognitive and behavioral disturbances produced by injury, disease, or abnormal development of the brain. These procedures, which are employed both in clinical evaluation and in research, may be viewed as constituting a refinement and extension of certain aspects of the neurological examination. The same behavioral and mental capacities (e.g., orientation, memory, language functions) that are evaluated in the neurological examination are also evaluated in a more precise and objective manner by neuropsychological assessment. Neuropsychological tests are standardized techniques that yield quantifiable and reproducible results that are referable to the scores of normal persons of an age and demographic background similar to those of the person being tested.

PURPOSES AND GOALS

The purposes and indications for assessment are as follows: (1) to identify cognitive defects, (2) differential diagnosis of incipient depression from dementia, (3) to determine the course of the illness, (4) to assess neurotoxic effects (e.g., memory impairment by substance abuse), (5) to evaluate the effects of treatment (e.g., surgery for epilepsy, pharmacotherapy), and (6) to evaluate developmental disorders and learning disabilities.

GENERAL INTELLIGENCE AND DEMENTIA

Patients with cerebral disease may show an overall behavioral inefficiency and be unable to meet the diverse intellectual demands associated with the responsibilities of daily life. Dementia implies an overall impairment in mental capacity, with a consequent decline in social and economic competence. There are clinically distinguishable types of dementia—for example, an aphasic type, an amnesic type, a type showing prominent visuoperceptual and somatoperceptual defects, and a relatively pure type manifesting impairment in abstract reasoning and problem solving within a setting of fairly intact linguistic and perceptual capacity.

In this country the Wechsler Adult Intelligence Scale (WAIS) is by far the most widely used test battery to assess general intelligence in adult subjects. In its clinical application a number of procedures have been used to evaluate the possibility of a decline in general intelligence that may be attributable to the presence of cerebral disease. The most direct approach is to compare the patient's obtained age-corrected intelligence quotient (I.Q.) score with the age-corrected I.Q. score that might be expected in view of his or her educational background, cultural level, and occupational history. An obtained I.Q. below the expected I.Q. may raise the question of the presence of cerebral disease. However, many patients with unquestionable cerebral disease do not show an overall decline in general intelligence of sufficient severity to be reflected in a significant lowering of their WAIS I.Q. score. Consequently, this procedure may be expected to yield a fair proportion of false-negative results.

REASONING, CONCEPT FORMATION, AND PROBLEM SOLVING

The patient with cerebral disease is likely to show cognitive impairment of a general nature, which Kurt Goldstein designated the "loss of the abstract attitude." He characterized the deficit as a loss of the capacity to reason abstractly and lack of flexibility in problem solving or in adapting to changed situations. Frontal lobe disease is often associated with impaired abstract reasoning, although other areas of the brain may also be involved.

A number of tests are used to assess the capacity for concept formation.

Wisconsin Card-Sorting Test (WCST)

Stimulus cards differing in color, form, and number are presented to the patient for sorting into groups according to a principle reestablished by the examiner. The number of trials required to achieve 10 consecutive correct responses is recorded. The procedure is repeated a number of times, and measures of the capacity for abstract thinking (i.e., the number of trials required to achieve a solution) and of flexibility in problem solving (i.e., perseverative errors on successive sorting) are derived from the patient's performance.

Patients who have undergone frontal lobe excisions for amelioration of epilepsy exhibit a greater deficit on the WCST when compared with patients with posterior surgical lesions. Chronic schizophrenic patients have also been demonstrated to show impaired performance on the WCST in relation to reduced cerebral blood flow in their frontal lobes.

Shipley Abstraction Test

This test requires the patient to complete logical sequences; it assesses the capacity to abstract. Because performance on a test of this type is related to educational background, an accompanying vocabulary test is also given to the patient, and a comparison is made between performances on the two tests. A low abstraction score in relation to vocabulary level is interpreted as reflecting impairment in conceptual thinking.

MEMORY

Impairment of various types of memory, most notably short-term and recent memory, is a prominent behavioral deficit in brain-damaged patients, and it is often the first sign of cerebral disease and of aging. Memory is a comprehensive term that covers the retention of all types of material over different periods of time and involves diverse forms of response. Consequently, the neuropsychological examiner is more inclined to give specific memory tests and evaluate them separately than to use an omnibus battery that provides a brief assessment of a large variety of performances and yields a single score.

Immediate (or *short-term*) *memory* may be defined as the reproduction, recognition, or recall of perceived material within a period of up to 30 seconds after presentation. It is most often assessed by digit repetition and reversal (auditory) and memory-for-designs (visual) tests. Both an auditory-verbal task, such as digit span or memory for words or sentences, and a nonverbal visual task, such as memory for designs or for objects or faces, should be given to assess the patient's immediate memory. Patients can also be asked to listen to a standardized story and to repeat the story as closely as possible to what they heard. Patients with lesions of the right hemisphere are likely to show more severe defects on visual nonverbal tasks than on auditory verbal tasks. Conversely, patients with left hemisphere disease, including those who are not aphasic, are likely to show more severe deficits on the auditory verbal tests, with variable performance on the visual nonverbal tasks.

Recent memory refers to events over the past few hours or days and can be tested by asking patients what they had for breakfast and who visited with them in the hospital. *Recent past memory* refers to the retention of information over the past few months. The patient can be asked questions about current events.

Remote memory is the ability to remember events in the distant past. It is commonly believed that remote memory is well preserved in patients who show pronounced defects in recent memory. However, the remote memory of senile and amnesic patients is usually significantly inferior to that of normal persons of comparable age and education. Even patients who appear to be able to recount their past fairly accurately show, on close examination, gaps and inconsistency in their recitals. Recent memory, recent past memory, and remote memory are also known as *long-term memory*.

Memory theorists have described three other types of memory: (1) episodic, for specific events (e.g., a telephone message); (2) semantic, for knowledge and facts (e.g., the first president of the United States); and (3) implicit, for automatic skills (e.g., speaking grammatically or driving a car). Semantic and implicit memory do not decline with age, and persons continue to accumulate information over a lifetime. There is a minimal decline in episodic memory with aging that may relate to impaired frontal lobe functioning.

Testing Memory

Wechsler Memory Scale (WMS). The WMS is the most widely used memory test battery for adults. It is a composite of verbal paired associate and paragraph retention, visual memory for designs, orientation, digit span, rote recall of the alphabet, and counting backward. This scale yields a memory quotient (M.Q.), which is corrected for age and generally approximates the Wechsler Adult Intelligence Scale intelligence quotient (WAIS I.Q.); amnesic conditions, such as the alcoholic Korsakoff's syndrome, are characterized by a disproportionately low M.Q. but a relatively preserved I.Q.

Benton Visual Retention Test. This test is sensitive to short-term memory loss (Figure 5.2-1).

ORIENTATION

Orientation for person or place is rarely disturbed in the brain-damaged patient who is not psychotic or severely demented; but defects in temporal orientation, which can be considered to reflect the integrity of recent memory, are common. These defects are often missed by the clinical examiner because of the tendency to regard as inconsequential slight inaccuracy in giving the day of the week or the date of the month. However, about 25 percent of nonpsychotic patients with hemispheric cerebral disease are likely to show significant decreased performance with respect to precision of temporal orientation. A simple test for orientation is outlined in Table 5.2-1.

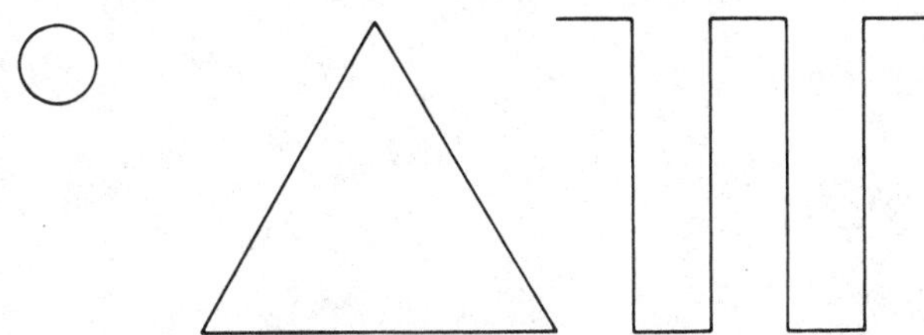

Figure 5.2-1. Test item from the Benton Visual Retention Test. The most frequently employed testing condition involves presentation of each geometric figure for 10 seconds, after which the patient attempts to draw them from memory. (From A L Benton: *The Revised Visual Retention Test: Clinical and Experimental Applications*, ed 4. Psychological Corporation, New York, 1974, with permission.)

PERCEPTUAL AND PERCEPTUOMOTOR PERFORMANCE

Many patients with brain disease show impaired ability to analyze complex stimulus constellations or inability to translate their perception into appropriate motor action. Unless the impairment is of a gross nature, as in visual object agnosia or dressing apraxia, or interferes with a specific occupation skill, these deficits are not likely to be the subject of spontaneous complaint. However, appropriate testing discloses a remarkably high incidence of impaired performance on visuoanalytic, visuospatial, and visuoconstructive tasks in brain-damaged patients, particularly in those persons with disease involving the right hemisphere. This type of impairment also extends to tactile and auditory perceptual task performances.

Visuoperceptive and visuoconstructive capacity and somatoperceptual defects can be assessed by tests. Double simultaneous stimulation (DSS) is tested by lightly touching one of the patient's cheeks with one hand and simultaneously touching the back of the patient's hand with the other. A patient with brain dysfunction is unable to recognize one or both of the stimuli. The DSS is a general test of defective capacity for perceptual integration.

Table 5.2-1
Temporal Orientation Schedule

Administration
What is today's date? (The patient is required to give month, day, and year.)
What day of the week is it?
What time is it now? (Examiner makes sure that the patient cannot look at a watch or clock.)
Scoring
Day of week: 1 error point for each day removed from the correct day to a maximum of 3 points
Day of month: 1 error point for each day removed from the correct day to a maximum of 15 points
Month: 5 error points for each month removed from the correct month with the qualification that, if the stated date is within 15 days of the correct date, no points are scored for the incorrect month (for example, May 29 for June 2 = 4 points off)
Year: 10 error points for each year removed from the correct year to a maximum of 60 points with the qualification that, if the stated date is within 15 days of the correct date, no points are scored for the incorrect year (for example, December 26, 1982 for January 2, 1983 = 7 points off)
Time of day: 1 error point for each 30 minutes removed from the correct time to a maximum of 5 points

Table from A L Benton: Psychological testing for brain damage. In *Comprehensive Textbook of Psychiatry, ed 4, H I Kaplan, B J Sadock, editors, p 539. Williams & Wilkins, Baltimore, 1985.*

Perceptuomotor tests often help localize the cerebral lesion. A significant portion of patients with lesions of the right hemisphere who do not show obvious impairment in language functions perform poorly on perceptual tests.

Bender Visual Motor Gestalt Test

The Bender-Gestalt test is a test of visuomotor coordination, useful for both children and adults. It was designed in 1938 by Lauretta Bender, New York University Medical Center and Bellevue Psychiatric Hospital, who used it to evaluate maturational levels in children. Developmentally, a child under 3 years of age is generally unable to reproduce any of the test's designs meaningfully. Around 4 years of age, the child may be able to copy several designs but poorly. At about age 6, the child should produce some recognizable, though still uneven, representations of all the designs. By age 10 and certainly by age 12, the child's copies should be reasonably accurate and well organized. Bender also presented studies of adults with organic brain defects, mental retardation, aphasias, psychoses, neuroses, and malingering.

The test material consists of nine separate designs, adapted from those used by Wertheimer in his studies in Gestalt psychology. Each design is printed against a white background on a separate card (Figure 5.2-2). Presented with unlined paper, patients are asked to copy each design with the card in front of them. There is no time limit. This phase of the test is highly structured and does not investigate memory function, because the cards remain in front of patients while they copy them. Many clinicians include a subsequent recall phase, in which (after an interval of 45 to 60 seconds) patients are asked to reproduce as many of the designs as they can from memory. This phase not only investigates visual memory but also presents a less structured situation, since patients must now rely essentially on their own resources. It is often particularly helpful to compare the patient's functioning under the two conditions.

Probably, the Bender-Gestalt test is used most frequently with adults as a screening device for signs of organic dysfunction. Evaluation of the protocol depends on the form of the reproduced figures and on their relationship to one another and to the whole spatial background (Figures 5.2-3 and 5.2-4).

Complex Visual Discrimination

Although the inability to recognize familiar faces (prosopagnosia) is an uncommon disorder, defective discrimination of unfamiliar faces is a common finding in patients with right-hemisphere or bilateral lesions. The *Facial Recognition Test,* in which the patient is required to identify a photograph of a face presented in a front view when it is included in various displays (e.g, side view or front view with shadows) produces a high frequency of failure in patients with posterior right-hemisphere lesions. Performance is generally intact in patients with left-hemisphere lesions (provided that receptive language is not seriously limited) and patients with schizophrenia.

Visual Matrices

Raven's Progressive Matrices requires the patient to select from a multiple-choice pictorial display the stimulus that completes a design in which a part is omitted. The difficulty of the discrimination increases over trials in this lengthy test. A briefer, less difficult version (Color Matrices) is especially useful for patients who are unable to complete the standard test, which can require 30 to 45 minutes. Impaired performance is associated with poor visuoconstructive ability and with posterior lesions of either hemisphere, but receptive language

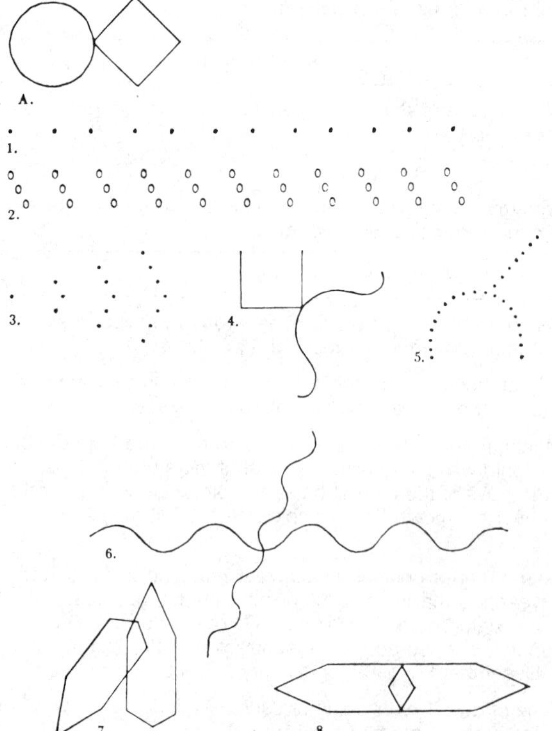

Figure 5.2-2. Test figures from the Bender Visual Motor Gestalt Test, adopted from Wertheimer. (From L Bender: *A Visual Motor Gestalt Test and Its Clinical Use.* Research Monograph, no. 3, American Orthopsychiatric Association, New York, 1938).

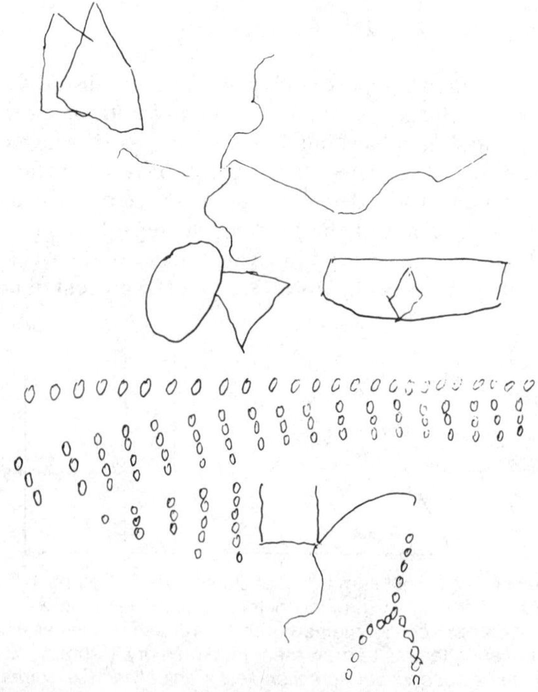

Figure 5.2-3. Bender-Gestalt drawing of a 57-year-old brain-damaged female patient.

Figure 5.2-4. Bender-Gestalt recall of the 57-year-old brain damaged female patient in Figure 5.2-3.

deficit may be contributory in patients with dominant-hemisphere damage.

LANGUAGE FUNCTIONS

Relatively minor defects in the use of language may be valid indicators of the presence of brain disease. The dominant hemisphere controls language function. The affective part of speech that conveys mood is called prosody and is controlled by the nondominant hemisphere. Fluency is tested by asking patients to give all the words they can think of beginning with a given letter of the alphabet. Aphasic patients with left-hemisphere disease fail this task. Variables influencing language tests are educational background, sex, and age. Reading and writing are also associated with the dominant hemisphere and are tested by asking patients to read aloud from prepared material and to write their names or a brief passage. Dyslexia and dysgraphia are suspected if difficulties in performing those tasks are found.

The *Boston Diagnostic Aphasia Examination* includes a speech rating scale that is useful for comparing with test scores and a brief schedule of items for assessing ideomotor praxis—that is, symbolic buccofacial and limb movements to exhibit gestures and to demonstrate the use of imagined or real objects.

ATTENTION AND CONCENTRATION

The capacity to sustain a maximal level of attention over a period of time is sometimes impaired in brain-damaged patients, and this impairment is reflected in oscillation in performance level on a continuous or repeated activity. There is some evidence that this instability in performance is related to electroencephalographic abnormality and that inexplicable decline in performance is related temporally to the occurrence of certain types of abnormal electrical activity. Simple reaction time provides a convenient measure of the variability and speed of simple responses.

The reaction time needed to respond to a stimulus is impaired in 40 to 45 percent of brain-damaged patients and is a sensitive indicator of overall cerebral integrity. Comparison of the reaction times of the right and left hands often provides an indication of the site of the lesion in a patient and of unilateral cerebral disease.

Behavioral flexibility is also reduced in brain-damaged patients who are unable to modify their approach to a problem in accordance with changing requirements. This was described by Kurt Goldstein as part of the catastrophic reaction first noted in brain-injured soldiers.

Attention and information processing can be evaluated by a number of widely employed clinical procedures—for example, the Arithmetic, Digit School (coding), and Digit Span subtests to the WAIS, the Wechsler Intelligence Scale for Children (WISC), the Mental Control section of the Wechsler Memory Scale, the Reitan Trail Making Test, and cancellation tests in which the patient marks only designated letters (targets) interspersed with other letters (nontarget or distractor items) in lengthy sequences.

The Continuous Performance Test (CPT), an experimental task that involves rapid identification of a target and withholding response to distractor stimuli, permits analysis of both the accuracy and the latency of response. The CPT, which is one of the few tests designed to assess attention, has been widely employed in psychopharmacological research and in studies of attentional deficit in schizophrenic patients. In an adjustive version of the CPT, a microcomputer changes the rate of presentation according to the patient's performance. The shortest interstimulus interval at which responding is still accurate is the primary performance measure.

BEHAVIORAL INDICES OF BRAIN DAMAGE IN CHILDREN

If present, the behavioral consequences of early brain damage may take many forms, of which the hyperkinetic (or attention-deficit hyperactivity) disorder is only one. Early brain damage may result in little or no behavioral deficit, and, when such a deficit does appear, it is usually less severe than that caused by a comparable lesion in adults. Thus, there is reason to believe that many brain-damaged children are not identified by current methods of behavioral assessment.

General Intelligence

The most frequently used batteries are the WISC, the Stanford-Binet, and the Wechsler Preschool and Primary Scale of Intelligence (WPPSI). A relatively low level of general intelligence is probably the most constant behavioral result of brain damage in children.

Perceptual and Perceptuomotor Performances

Many brain-damaged children with adequate verbal skills show strikingly defective visuoperceptive and visuomotor performance. The test most frequently used is copying of designs, either from a model or from memory. About 25 percent of brain-damaged schoolchildren of adequate verbal intelligence perform defectively. The task helps discriminate between brain-damaged children and those suffering from presumably psychogenic emotional disturbances.

Language Functions

There is considerable evidence that children who show gross maldevelopment of oral language abilities, as compared with general mental level, suffer from brain damage. Perinatal brain injury may be a causative factor in at least some cases of developmental dyslexia or more generalized

Table 5.2-2
Mental Status Cognitive Tasks

Task	Dysfunction	Abnormal Response	Suggested Localization
Spell "earth" backward	Concentration	Any improper letter sequence	Frontal lobes
Serial sevens	Concentration	One or more errors or longer than 90 seconds	Frontal lobes
Name the day of the week, month, year, location	Global disorientation	Any error	Frontal lobes (if memory intact)
Repeat: "No ifs, ands, or buts," "The president lives in Washington," "Methodist Episcopal," "Massachusetts"	Expressive language	Missed words or syllables; repetition of internal syllables; dropping of word endings	Dominant frontal lobe
Name common objects (e.g., key, watch, button)	Anomia	Cannot name; word approximations; describes functions, rather than word	Dominant temporal lobe, angular gyrus
Conversation during examination	Receptive language	Word approximations, neologisms, word salad, stock words, tangential speech	Dominant temporal lobe
a. Repeat four words or items (e.g., blue, chair, swim, glove)	Immediate recall	One or more errors	Temporal lobes and frontal lobes (hippocampus)
b. Remember them after 10 minutes with interposed tasks	Recent memory	One or more errors	Temporal lobes (hippocampus, thalamus, fornix, mamillothalamic tract)
c. Provide accurate detail and sequence of past events	Long-term memory	Significant loss of detail; confused sequence	Temporal lobes (hippocampus)
Copy examiner's hand and arm movements (each hand and arm)	Dyspraxia	Any error, mirror movements	Contralateral parietal lobe

learning disability. The finding of a relatively high incidence of electroencephalographic abnormality in children with learning disabilities points to the same conclusion.

Motor Performances

Motor awkwardness and inability to carry out movement sequences on command or by imitation are commonly seen in brain-damaged children. A variety of tests are available for the assessment of manual dexterity (e.g., manipulations with tweezers, paper cutting, and peg placing).

Motor impersistence—an inability to sustain an action initiated on command, such as keeping the eyes closed—is seen in a relatively small proportion of adult patients with cerebral disease. However, it is shown with remarkably high frequency by nondefective brain-damaged children. Many children with mental defects also show excessive motor impersistence, particularly those with brain damage.

COMPREHENSIVE TESTING

A number of test batteries have been developed to help in the neuropsychological and neuropsychiatric evaluation. Among these are the Luria-Nebraska and Halstead-Reitan neuropsychological test batteries.

Luria-Nebraska Neuropsychological Battery (LNNB)

Based on the work of the Russian neuropsychologist A. R. Luria, the LNNB was developed at the University of Nebraska. The test assesses a wide range of cognitive functions: memory; motor functions; rhythm; tactile, auditory, and visual functions; receptive and expressive speech; writing; spelling; reading; and arithmetic. The test is designed for persons at least 15 years of age, and a children's version for use with 8- to 12-year-olds is being developed. The LNNB is extremely sensitive for identifying specific types of problems (e.g., dyslexia, dyscalculia), rather than being limited to global impressions of brain dysfunction. It also helps localize the various cortical zones that are involved in a particular function and is useful in establishing left or right cerebral dominance.

Halstead-Reitan Battery (HRB) of Neuropsychological Tests

In the early 1940s, Ward Halstead at Chicago and his student, Ralph Reitan, developed a battery of tests that were

Table 5.2-2
Continued

Task	Dysfunction	Abnormal Response	Suggested Localization
Demonstrate use of key, hammer, flipping a coin	Ideomotorapraxia	Use of hand as object; failure to use fine hand and wrist movements; verbal overflow	Dominant parietal lobe, disconnected dominant from nondominant frontal lobe
a. Left hand only plus some expressive language difficulty			Dominant frontal lobe or anterior corpus callosum
b. Both hands			Dominant parietal lobe, arcuate fasciculus
Name fingers	Finger agnosia	Two or more errors; cannot identify after examiner numbers each	Dominant parietal lobe
Calculations	Dyscalculia	Errors in borrowing or carrying over when concentration is intact	Dominant parietal lobe
Write a sentence	Dysgraphia	No longer able to write cursive; loss of word structure; abnormally formed letters	Dominant parietal lobe
In individual steps, copy sentence, read it, and do what it says ("Put the paper in your pocket")	Dysgraphia, dyslexia, comprehension	No longer able to write cursively; loss of sentence structure; loss of word structure; abnormally formed letters	Dominant temporoparietal lobe
Place left hand to right ear, right elbow, right knee; same for right hand	Right-left disorientation	Two or more errors or two or more seven-second delays in carrying out tasks	Dominant parietal lobe
Copy the outline of simple objects (e.g., Greek cross, key)	Construction apraxia	Loss of gestalt, loss of symmetry, distortion of figures	Nondominant parietal lobe
Camouflaged object(s)	Visual-perception deficit	Cannot name when camouflaged, can name when clear	Occipital lobes

Table from M A Taylor et al: Cognitive tasks in the mental status examination. J Nerv Ment Dis *168:* 168, 1980.

used to determine the location and effects of specific brain lesions. The battery is composed of the following 10 tests:

1. Category test. The patient must discover the common element in a set of pictures; it measures concept function, abstraction, and visual acuity.

2. Tactual performance test. The patient places shapes in a form board while blindfolded and then must recall the arrangement of the board; it tests dexterity, spatial memory, and tactual discrimination.

3. Rhythm test. The patient identifies 30 pairs of rhythmic beats as either the same or different; it tests auditory perception, attention, and concentration.

4. Finger-oscillation test. The patient taps the index finger of each hand in a measured 10-second period; it measures dexterity and motor speed.

5. Speech-sounds perception test. The patient matches 60 nonsense syllables that he or she hears with several printed alternatives; it measures auditory discrimination and phonetic skills.

6. Trail-making test. The patient first connects 25 numbered circles in order and then connects 25 lettered and numbered circles in order, alternating between numbered and alphabetical circles; it tests visuomotor perception and motor speed.

7. Critical flicker frequency. The patient notes when a flickering light becomes steady; it tests visual perception.

8. Time sense test. The patient judges, without looking, the time it takes for the second hand of a watch to make several revolutions; it tests memory and spatial perception.

9. Aphasia screening test. The patient must name objects, read, write, calculate, draw shapes, identify body parts, perform acts, differentiate between left and right; it tests a wide range of verbal and nonverbal brain functions.

10. Sensory-perceptual tests. The patient performs a number of tasks with eyes closed—such as identifying where he or she is touched when touched on the hand and face simultaneously (simultaneous sensory stimulation test), which finger is touched (finger localization), what coins are placed in the hand (stereognosis), and what numbers are written on the skin (tactile perception).

The HRB has the advantage of providing a uniform profile of scores that must be weighed against the considerable time required for administration. The test is able to differentiate brain-damaged from neurologically intact persons. Schizophrenic patients tend to perform above the level of subacutely brain-damaged patients but not differently from chronic brain-damaged groups. Moreover, the pattern of deficits on the HRB is similar in brain-damaged and schizophrenic patients.

INTERPRETATION

In any neuropsychiatric examination the clinician must be careful that a deviation from normal is not due to factors unrelated to neuropathology. Anxiety and depression are two major causes of cognitive dysfunction, and a careful assessment of the patient's mental state should be carried out to rule out these conditions as sources of poor performance. Other sources of error result from the patient's not understanding the directions given by the examiner, problems with language, and general uncooperativeness. A summary of the many mental status cognitive tasks discussed in this section and other tasks that can be used to test and localize various dysfunctions is presented in Table 5.2-2.

References

Bender L: *A Visual Motor Gestalt Test and Its Clinical Use.* American Orthopsychiatric Association, New York, 1938.

Benton A L, Hamsher K deS, Varney N R: *Contributions to Neuropsychological Assessments.* Oxford University Press, New York, 1983.

Benton A L, Hamsher K deS, Varney N R, Spreen O: *Contributions to Neuropsychological Assessment: A Clinical Manual.* Oxford University Press, New York, 1983.

Christensen A-L: *Luria's Neuropsychological Investigation.* ed 2. Ejnar Munksgaards, Copenhagen, 1979.

Filskov S B, Boll T J: *Handbook of Clinical Neuropsychology.* Wiley, New York, 1981.

Gazzaniga M S: Right hemisphere language following brain bisection: A 20-year perspective. Am Psychol *38:* 525, 1983.

Gilandas A, Touyz S, Bermont P J V, Greenberg H P: *Handbook of Neuropsychological Assessment.* Grune & Stratton, Orlando, FL, 1984.

Grant I, Adams K M: *Neuropsychological Assessment of Neuropsychiatric Disorders.* Oxford University Press, New York, 1986.

Heaton R K, Baade L E, Johnson K L: Neuropsychological test results associated with psychiatric disorders in adults. Psychol Bull *85:* 141, 1978.

Heilman K M, Bowers D, Valenstein E, Watson R T: The right hemisphere: Neuropsychological functions. J Neurosurg *64:* 693, 1986.

Incagnoli T, Goldstein G, Golden C J: *Clinical Application of Neuropsychological Test Batteries,* Plenum, New York, 1986.

Levin H S, Benton A L, Fletcher J M, Satz P: Neuropsychological and intellectual assessment of adults. In *Comprehensive Textbook of Psychiatry,* ed 5, H I Kaplan and B J Sadock, editors, p 496. Williams & Wilkins, Baltimore, 1989.

Lezak, M D: *Neuropsychological Assessment,* ed 2. Oxford University Press, New York, 1983.

Matarazzo J D: Computerized clinical psychological test interpretations. Am Psychol *41:* 14, 1986.

Mesulam M M: A cortical network for directed attention and unilateral neglect. Ann Neurol *10:* 309, 1981.

Milner B: Effects of different brain lesions on card sorting. Arch Neurol *9:* 90, 1963.

Moses J A: Relationship of the profile evaluation and impairment scales of the Luria-Nebraska Neuropsychological Battery to neuropsychological examination outcome. Int J Clin Neuropsychol *7:* 4, 1985.

Reitan R M: Theoretical and methodological bases of the Halstead-Reitan Neuropsychological Test Battery. In *Neuropsychological Assessment of Neuropsychiatric Disorders.* I Grant and K M Adams, editors, p 3. Oxford University Press, New York, 1986.

Reitan R M, Davison L A: *Clinical Neuropsychology: Current Status and Applications.* Wiley, New York, 1974.

Sperry R W: Lateral specialization in the surgical separated hemispheres. In *Hemispheric Specialization and Interaction,* B Milner, editor. MIT Press, Cambridge, MA, 1975.

Wexler B E: Cerebral laterality and psychiatry: A review of the literature. Am J Psychiatry *137:* 3, 1980.

Wishaw I Q, Kolb B: *Fundamentals of Human Neuropsychology.* Freeman, New York, 1985.

Theories of Personality and Psychopathology

6.1 / Sigmund Freud: Founder of Classical Psychoanalysis

Psychoanalysis, founded by Sigmund Freud, seeks to understand the basis of all human behavior. Formidable advances have been made in biological and social psychiatry, but psychoanalytic theory remains a cornerstone of modern psychiatry. Freud elucidated two fundamental concepts of psychoanalytic theory—the existence of an unconscious mind and the concept of psychic determinism, or causality. Unconscious mental processes occur with great frequency and are present in both normal and abnormal mental functioning. Examples of unconscious phenomena may be found in dreams, selective forgetting, errors in everyday life, and posthypnotic events. According to the concept of psychic determinism, nothing happens by chance. Essentially every psychic event is determined by previous ones. Discontinuity does not exist in mental life. These two concepts are intimately related, and it is not possible to consider one without the other.

Freud then evolved a third concept central to psychoanalytic theory—the mechanism of repression, or the unconscious selective forgetting of events or things that are too painful or objectionable for the conscious mind to acknowledge. Freud developed the concept of repression in connection with his studies of psychopathology, believing that the repression of sexuality was connected with the development of neuroses. But greater and more complex theoretical considerations were to build on this conclusion. Freud observed the development of infantile sexuality, and, calling on his knowledge of perversions, he hypothesized that the sexual instinct must follow a complicated developmental sequence that can be subject to fixations and distortions.

A profound thinker, Freud conceptualized a model of mental structure and the economics of mental functioning, as well as its dynamics. Initially, he divided the mind into three regional or topographic areas: the unconscious, the preconscious, and the conscious. Later, dissatisfied with this model, he evolved the structural, or tripartite, model of the ego, the id, and the superego. Currently, psychoanalysis has a threefold aspect: It is a method of investigation, it is a therapeutic technique, and it is a body of scientific knowledge based on theoretical constructs.

LIFE OF FREUD

Sigmund Freud was born of Jewish parents on May 6, 1856, in Freiburg, a small town in Moravia, which has since become part of Czechoslovakia. When he was 4 years old, his father, a wool merchant, took the family to Vienna, where Freud lived most of his life. Freud attended medical school in Vienna from 1873 to 1881. At first, he specialized in neurology, and in 1885 he studied with Jean-Martin Charcot in Paris. He also studied hypnosis with Ambroise-Auguste Liebault and Hippolyte-Marie Bernheim in France and on his return to Vienna began his work with emotionally disturbed patients. From 1887 to 1897, the period in which Freud seriously began to study the disturbances of his hysterical patients, psychoanalysis can be said to have taken root. See Figures 6.1-1 through 6.1-9 for highlights in the life of Freud.

BEGINNINGS OF PSYCHOANALYSIS

Case of Anna O.

Josef Breuer was a prominent Viennese physician who formed a close friendship with Freud. Breuer's treatment of "Anna O."—specifically, his communication to Freud of the details of the case—was one of the factors that led to the development of psychoanalysis.

Breuer treated Anna O. (Bertha Pappenheim) from December 1880 to June 1882. The patient was an intelligent girl of 21 who had developed a number of hysterical symptoms in association with the illness of her father, of whom she was passionately fond. These symptoms included paralysis of the limbs, contractures, anesthesias, disturbances of sight and speech, anorexia, and a distressing nervous cough. Her illness was further characterized by two distinct phases of consciousness. During one, she was normal; during the second, she took on another, more pathological, personality. The transition between these states of consciousness was influenced by autohypnosis, which Breuer subsequently supplemented with artificial hypnosis. Anna had shared with her mother the duties of nursing her father until his death. During her altered states of consciousness, called hypnoid states, Anna was able to relate the vivid fantasies and intense emotions that she had experienced while tending to her father. To the great amazement of Anna—and Breuer—the patient's symptoms could disappear if she could recall, with an accompanying expression

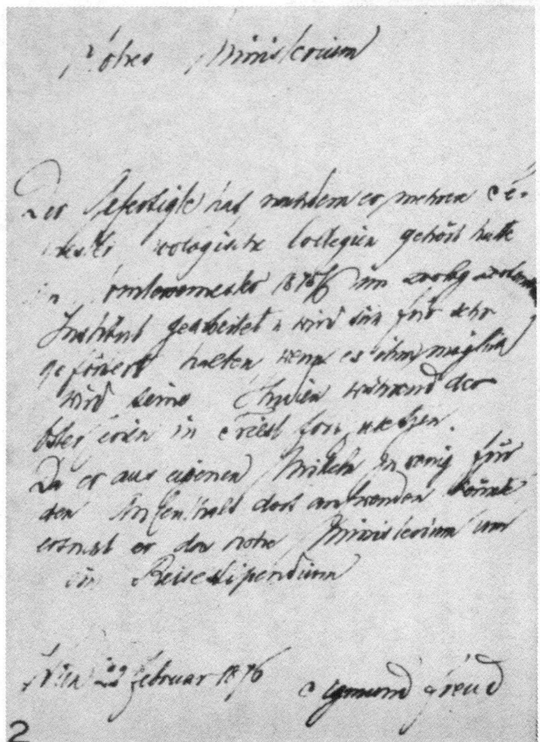

Hohes Ministerium

[illegible]

Wien 22 Februar 1876 Sigmund Freud

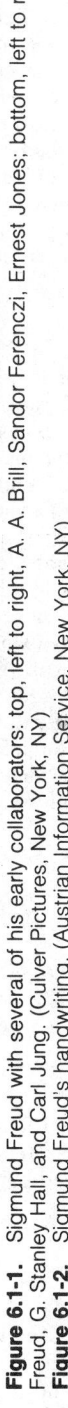

Figure 6.1-1. Sigmund Freud with several of his early collaborators: top, left to right, A. A. Brill, Sandor Ferenczi, Ernest Jones; bottom, left to right, Freud, G. Stanley Hall, and Carl Jung. (Culver Pictures, New York, NY)
Figure 6.1-2. Sigmund Freud's handwriting. (Austrian Information Service, New York, NY)
Figure 6.1-3. Sigmund Freud as a young man. (Austrian Information Service, New York, NY)
Figure 6.1-4. Berggasse 19, the building in which Freud had his offices and that now houses the Freud Museum. (Austrian Information Service, New York, NY)
Figure 6.1-5. Sigmund Freud and his father. (Austrian Information Service, New York, NY)
Figure 6.1-6. Sigmund Freud and his mother in 1872. (Austrian Information Service, New York, NY)
Figure 6.1-7. Sigmund Freud's office in Vienna. (Austrian Information Service, New York, NY)
Figure 6.1-8. Sigmund Freud at his desk in his Vienna office. (Austrian Information Service, New York, NY)
Figure 6.1-9. Mrs. Paula Fichtl, Freud's last maid, with some personal items: hat, cane. (Austrian Information Service, New York, NY)

of affect, the circumstances under which her emotions had arisen. Once she had become aware of the value of this "talking cure," or "chimney sweeping," Anna proceeded to eliminate each of her manifold symptoms, one after another.

In the course of treatment Breuer had become increasingly preoccupied with this unusual patient, and his wife had grown increasingly jealous and resentful. When he realized this, Breuer abruptly terminated treatment. Only a few hours had elapsed, however, before he was recalled to Anna's bedside. He found the patient, whom he had believed to be greatly improved, in a state of acute excitement. Anna, who had never alluded to the forbidden topic of sex during the course of treatment, was then experiencing a hysterical childbirth (pseudocyesis), a logical termination of the phantom pregnancy that she had developed in response to Breuer's therapeutic efforts, a development of which he had been quite unaware. Breuer managed to calm her through hypnosis. However, the experience unnerved him and served to restrict his further participation in Freud's investigations into the unknown and, therefore, unpredictable and dangerous sphere of the mind.

Freud's Use of Hypnosis

Late in 1887 Freud began to use hypnosis intensively in his own practice. Partly as a result of his interest in Breuer's treatment of Anna, Freud was eager to learn what lay behind his hysterical patients' symptoms and to investigate them in depth. As a result, in 1889 Freud turned to the cathartic method in conjunction with hypnosis in order to trace the cause of the psychoneuroses, which had hitherto been attributed to heredity, to unfavorable childhood experiences.

Freud discovered early in his practice that his patients were often unwilling or unable to recount memories that later proved to be significant. He defined this reluctance as resistance. Later he found that, in the majority of his patients, resistance was due to active forces in the mind (of which the patients themselves were often unaware) that led to the exclusion from consciousness of painful or distressing material. Freud described this active force as repression. In a broad sense, Freud considered repression to be at the core of symptom formation.

THEORY OF THE INSTINCTS

Freud used the term "libido" to refer to "that force by which the sexual instinct is represented in the mind." He recognized that the sexual instinct does not originate in finished form. Rather, it undergoes a complex process of development, during which it has many manifestations apart from the simple aim of genital union. The libido theory referred to the investigation of all these manifestations and the complicated paths they may follow in the course of development.

Infantile Sexuality

Of all Freud's theories, the concepts that he advanced with regard to the erotic life of infants and young children undoubtedly aroused the most adamant and continued opposition.

Freud noted that infants were capable of erotic activity from birth, and he described the various stages of sexual development during the first four years of life. The fifth year marks the beginning of the latency period, at which point sexual development comes to a halt until children reach puberty, when they are approximately 11 years old. At puberty there is renewed growth of the genital organs and a resurgence of the sexual drive, and children begin their final preparations for their adult sexual roles.

The earliest manifestations of sexuality arise in relation to bodily functions that are basically nonsexual, such as feeding and the development of bowel and bladder control. During the oral phase, which extends into the second year of life, erotic activity centers on the mouth and lips and is manifested in sucking, biting, and chewing. During the anal phase, when the child is increasingly preoccupied with bowel function and control from ages 2 to 4, the dominant erotic activity shifts from the oral to the anal and rectal regions. The phallic phase of sexual development begins during the third year of life and continues until approximately the end of the fifth year. Erotic activity at this time is linked both psychologically and physiologically with the activities and sensations associated with urination.

Freud described the erotic impulses that arise from the pregenital zones as component or part instincts. Ordinarily, in the course of development, these component instincts undergo repression or retain a restricted role in sexual foreplay. The failure to achieve genital primacy may result in various forms of pathology. The persistent attachment of the sexual instinct at a particular phase of pregenital development was termed a fixation.

Freud further discovered that in the psychoneuroses only a limited number of the sexual impulses that had undergone repression and were responsible for creating and maintaining the neurotic symptoms were of a normal kind. For the most part, these were the same impulses that were given overt expression in the perversions. The neuroses, then, were the negative of perversions.

Development of Object Relationships

Throughout his description of the libidinal phases of development, Freud made constant reference to the significance of the child's relationships with crucial figures in his or her environment. Freud postulated that the choice of a love object in later life, the love relationship itself, and object relationships in other spheres of activity depend largely on the nature and quality of the child's object relationships during the earliest years of life.

At birth, infants have no awareness of the external world of objects. At most, they are capable of an undifferentiated sensitivity to pain and pleasure. Hunger, cold, and pain give rise to tension and to a corresponding need to seek relief from these painful stimuli in sleep. At the same time, human infants cannot survive unless they are cared for, and they cannot achieve relief from painful stimuli without help from outside. Object relationships of a primitive kind are established when infants begin to grasp this fact. Because they are aware only of their own tension and relaxation and are unaware of the external world, longing for the object exists only as long as disturbing stimuli persist and the object is absent. Once the object appears and the infants' needs are gratified, the longing disappears.

A summary of the stages of psychosexual development and object relationships associated with each stage is presented in Table 6.1-1.

Concept of Narcissism

Prior to the psychoanalytic application of the concept of self-love, the term "narcissism" was applied in a restricted sense to designate a sexual perversion of the type demonstrated by the Greek youth Narcissus, who fell in love with his own reflection. In 1908 Freud observed that, in cases of dementia praecox (schizophrenia), libido appeared to have been withdrawn from other persons or objects, and he concluded that this may account for the loss of contact with reality that was typical of such patients. He then speculated as to where this libido had been invested instead. The megalomanic

Table 6.1-1
Stages of Psychosexual Development

	Oral Stage		
Definition	The earliest stage of development, in which the infant's needs, perceptions, and modes of expression are primarily centered in the mouth, lips, tongue, and other organs related to the oral zone.	Objectives	To establish a trusting dependence on nursing and sustaining objects, to establish comfortable expression and gratification of oral libidinal needs without excessive conflict or ambivalence from oral sadistic wishes.
Description	The oral zone maintains its dominant role in the organization of the psyche through approximately the first 18 months of life. Oral sensations include thirst, hunger, pleasurable tactile stimulations evoked by the nipple or its substitute, sensations related to swallowing and satiation. Oral drives consist of two separate components: libidinal and aggressive. States of oral tension lead to a seeking for oral gratification, typified by quiescence at the end of nursing. The oral triad consists of the wish to eat, to sleep, and to reach the relaxation that occurs at the end of sucking just before the onset of sleep. Libidinal needs (oral erotism) are thought to predominate in the early parts of the oral phase, whereas they are mixed with more aggressive components later (oral sadism). Oral aggression may express itself in biting, chewing, spitting, or crying. Oral aggression is connected with primitive wishes and fantasies of biting, devouring, and destroying.	Pathological traits	Excessive oral gratifications or deprivation can result in libidinal fixations that contribute to pathological traits. Such traits can include excessive optimism, narcissism, pessimism (often seen in depressive states), and demandingness. Oral characters are often excessively dependent and require others to give to them and to look after them. Such persons want to be fed but may be exceptionally giving to elicit a return of being given to. Oral characters are often extremely dependent on objects for the maintenance of their self-esteem. Envy and jealousy are often associated with oral traits.
		Character traits	Successful resolution of the oral phase provides a basis in character structure for capacities to give to and receive from others without excessive dependence or envy. A capacity to rely on others with a sense of trust and with a sense of self-reliance and self-trust.
	Anal Stage		
Definition	The stage of psychosexual development that is prompted by maturation of neuromuscular control over sphincters, particularly the anal sphincters, thus permitting more voluntary control over retention or expulsion of feces.	Objectives	The anal period is essentially a period of striving for independence and separation from the dependence on and control of the parent. The objectives of sphincter control without overcontrol (fecal retention) or loss of control (messing) are matched by the child's attempts to achieve autonomy and independence without excessive shame or self-doubt from loss of control.
Description	This period, which extends roughly from 1 to 3 years of age, is marked by a recognizable intensification of aggressive drives mixed with libidinal components in sadistic impulses. Acquisition of voluntary sphincter control is associated with an increasing shift from passivity to activity. The conflicts over anal control and the struggle with the parent over retaining or expelling feces in toilet training give rise to increased ambivalence, together with a struggle over separation, individuation, and independence. Anal erotism refers to the sexual pleasure in anal functioning, both in retaining the precious feces and in presenting them as a precious gift to the parent. Anal sadism refers to the expression of aggressive wishes connected with discharging feces as powerful and destructive weapons. These wishes are often displayed in such children's fantasies as bombing or explosions.	Pathological traits	Maladaptive character traits, often apparently inconsistent, are derived from anal erotism and the defenses against it. Orderliness, obstinancy, stubbornness, willfulness, frugality, and parsimony are features of the anal character derived from a fixation on anal functions. When defenses against anal traits are less effective, the anal character reveals traits of heightened ambivalence, lack of tidiness, messiness, defiance, rage, and sadomasochistic tendencies. Anal characteristics and defenses are most typically seen in obsessive-compulsive neuroses.
		Character traits	Successful resolution of the anal phase provides the basis for the development of personal autonomy, a capacity for independence and personal initiative without guilt, a capacity for self-determining behavior without a sense of shame or self-doubt, a lack of ambivalence, and a capacity for willing cooperation without either excessive willfulness or sense of self-diminution or defeat.

Table 6.1-1
Continued

Urethral Stage			
Definition	This stage was not explicitly treated by Freud but is envisioned as a transitional stage between the anal and the phallic stages of development. It shares some of the characteristics of the preceding anal phase and some from the subsequent phallic phase.	Objectives	Issues of control and urethral performance and loss of control. It is not clear whether or to what extent the objectives of urethral functioning differ from those of the anal period.
Description	The characteristics of the urethral phase are often subsumed under those of the phallic phase. Urethral erotism, however, is used to refer to the pleasure in urination and the pleasure in urethral retention analogous to anal retention. Similar issues of performance and control are related to urethral functioning. Urethral functioning may also be invested with a sadistic quality, often reflecting the persistence of anal sadistic urges. Loss of urethral control, as in enuresis, may frequently have regressive significance that reactivates anal conflicts.	Pathological traits	The predominant urethral trait is that of competitiveness and ambition, probably related to the compensation for shame caused by loss of urethral control. In control this may be the start for development of penis envy, related to the feminine sense of shame and inadequacy in being unable to match the male urethral performance. This is also related to issues of control and shaming.
		Character traits	Besides the healthy effects analogous to those from the anal period, urethral competence provides a sense of pride and self-competence derived from performance. Urethral performance is an area in which the small boy can imitate and match his father's adult performance. The resolution of urethral conflicts sets the stage for budding gender identity and subsequent identifications.
Phallic Stage			
Definition	The phallic stage of sexual development begins sometime during the third year of life and continues until approximately the end of the fifth year.	Pathological traits	The derivation of pathological traits from the phallic-oedipal involvement are sufficiently complex and subject to such a variety of modifications that it encompasses nearly the whole of neurotic development. The issues, however, focus on castration in males and on penis envy in females. The other important focus of developmental distortions in this period derives from the patterns of identification that are developed out of the resolution of the oedipal complex. The influence of castration anxiety and penis envy, the defenses against both of these, and the patterns of identification that emerge from the phallic phase are the primary determinants of the development of human character. They also subsume and integrate the residues of previous psychosexual stages, so that fixations or conflicts that derive from any of the preceding stages can contaminate and modify the oedipal resolution.
Description	The phallic phase is characterized by a primary focus of sexual interests, stimulation, and excitement in the genital area. The penis becomes the organ of principal interest to children of both sexes, with the lack of a penis in the girl being considered evidence of castration. The phallic phase is associated with an increase in genital masturbation, accompanied by predominantly unconscious fantasies of sexual involvement with the opposite-sex parent. The threat of castration and its related castration anxiety arise in connection with guilt over masturbation and oedipal wishes. During this phase the oedipal involvement and conflict are established and consolidated.		
Objectives	The objective of this phase is to focus erotic interest in the genital area and genital functions. This focusing lays the foundation for gender identity and serves to integrate the residues of previous stages of psychosexual development into a predominantly genital-sexual orientation. The establishing of the oedipal situation is essential for the furtherance of subsequent identifications that will serve as the basis for important and enduring dimensions of character organization.	Character traits	The phallic stage provides the foundations for an emerging sense of sexual identity, a sense of curiosity without embarrassment and of initiative without guilt, and a sense of mastery not only over objects and persons in the environment but also over internal processes and impulses. The resolution of the oedipal conflict at the end of the phallic period gives rise to powerful internal resources for the regulation of drive impulses and their direction to constructive ends. This internal source of regulation is the superego, and it is based on identifications derived primarily from parental figures.

Table 6.1-1
Continued

	Latency Stage		
Definition	The stage of relative quiescence or inactivity of the sexual drive during the period from the resolution of the Oedipus complex until pubescence (from about 5–6 years until about 11–13 years).	Pathological traits	The danger in the latency period can arise either from a lack of development of inner controls or an excess of them. The lack of control can lead to a failure of the child to sufficiently sublimate energies in the interests of learning and development of skills; an excess of inner control, however, can lead to premature closure of personality development and the precocious elaboration of obsessive character traits.
Description	The institution of the superego at the close of the oedipal period and the further maturation of ego functions allow for a considerably greater degree of control of instinctual impulses. Sexual interests during this period are generally thought to be quiescent. This is a period of primarily homosexual affiliations for both boys and girls and of a sublimation of libidinal and aggressive energies into energetic learning and play activities, exploring the environment, and becoming more proficient in dealing with the world of things and persons around them. It is a period for the development of important skills. The relative strength of regulatory elements often gives rise to patterns of behavior that are somewhat obsessive and hypercontrolling.	Character traits	The latency period has frequently been regarded as a period of relatively unimportant inactivity in the developmental scheme. More recently, greater respect has been gained for the developmental processes that take place in this period. Important consolidations and additions are made to the basic postoedipal identifications. It is a period of integrating and consolidating previous attainments in psychosexual development and an establishment of decisive patterns of adaptive functioning. The child can develop a sense of industry and a capacity for mastery of objects and concepts that allow autonomous function with a sense of initiative without running the risk of failure or defeat or a sense of inferiority. These are all important attainments that need to be further integrated, ultimately as the essential basis for a mature adult life of satisfaction in work and love.
Objectives	The primary objective in this period is the further integration of oedipal identifications and a consolidation of sex-role identity and sex roles. The relative quiescence and control of instinctual impulses allow for the development of ego apparatuses and mastery skills. Further identificatory components may be added to the oedipal ones on the basis of broadening contacts with other significant figures outside the family, e.g., teachers, coaches, and other adult figures.		
	Genital Stage		
Definition	The genital or adolescent phase of psychosexual development extends from the onset of puberty from ages 11 to 12 until the person reaches young adulthood. There is a tendency to subdivide this stage in current thinking into preadolescent, early adolescent, middle adolescent, late adolescent, and even postadolescent periods.	Pathological traits	The pathological deviations caused by a failure to achieve successful resolution of this stage of development are multiple and complex. Defects can arise from the whole spectrum of psychosexual residues, because the developmental task of the adolescent period is in a sense a partial reopening and reworking and reintegrating of all these aspects of development. Previous unsuccessful resolutions and fixations in various phases or aspects of psychosexual development produce pathological defects in the emerging adult personality. A more specific defect from a failure to resolve adolescent issues has been described by Erikson as "identity diffusion."
Description	The physiological maturation of systems of genital (sexual) functioning and attendant hormonal systems leads to an intensification of drives, particularly libidinal drives. This produces a regression in personality organization, which reopens conflicts of previous stages of psychosexual development and provides the opportunity for a reresolution of these conflicts in the context of achieving a mature sexual and adult identity.	Character traits	The successful resolution and reintegration of previous psychosexual stages in the adolescent, fully genital phase sets the stage normally for a fully mature personality with a capacity for full and satisfying genital potency and a self-integrated and consistent sense of identity. Such a person has reached a satisfying capacity for self-realization and meaningful participation in areas of work and love and in the creative and productive application to satisfying and meaningful goals and values. Only in the past few years has the presumed relationship between psychosexual genitality and maturity of personality functioning been put in question.
Objectives	The primary objectives of this period are the ultimate separation from dependence on and attachment to the parents and the establishment of mature, nonincestuous, heterosexual object relations. Related to this are the achievement of a mature sense of personal identity and acceptance and integration of a set of adult roles and functions that permit new adaptive integrations with social expectations and cultural values.		

Table by William W. Meissner, S.J., M.D.

delusions of these patients appeared to indicate that the libido they had withdrawn from external objects was then invested in themselves, in their own egos. Freud also became aware of the fact that the phenomenon of narcissism was not limited to the psychoses: it might occur in neurotic and normal persons as well under certain conditions, such as physical illness and sleep.

Freud's observations of the narcissistic behavior of young children provided incontrovertible evidence of the role of narcissism in development and led him to incorporate such considerations into his libido theory. Freud postulated that a state of primary narcissism exists at birth; that is, neonates are entirely narcissistic; their libidinal energies are devoted entirely to the satisfaction of their needs and the preservation of their well-being. Later , as infants gradually begin to recognize the person immediately responsible for their care as a source of tension relief or pleasure, libido is released for investment in that person, usually the mother. Thus, the development of object relations parallels this shift from primary narcissism to object attachment. However, some narcissistic libido is normally present throughout adult life; this is considered healthy narcissism and finds expression in the person's sense of well-being. Moreover, Freud observed that in a variety of traumatic situations—such as injury or the threat of injury, object loss, and excessive frustration—libido is withdrawn from objects and reinvested in the self.

Narcissism differs from autoeroticism in that autoeroticism refers to eroticism in relation to the person's own body or its parts; narcissism refers to the love of something more abstract, either the self or the person's ego.

Love objects may be chosen in adult life because they resemble the person's idealized self-image or fantasied self-image or because they resemble those who took care of the person during the early years of life. Persons who have an intense degree of self-love, especially certain beautiful women, have, according to Freud, an appeal over and above their esthetic attraction. Such women supply for their lovers the lost narcissism that was painfully renounced in the process of turning toward object love. A homosexual object relationship represents still another example of a narcissistic object choice. In this case the person's choice of an object is predicated on sexual resemblance.

Instincts

According to Freud, an instinct has four principal characteristics: source, impetus, aim, and object. In general, the source of an instinct refers to the part of the body from which it arises, the site of its inception. The impetus refers to the amount of force or demand for work made by the instinct. The aim is any action directed toward satisfaction or tension release, such as the infant's activity in seeking the nipple. The object is the person or thing that is the target for this action.

Ego instincts. Until 1910 Freud's predominant interest was in the sexual basis of the neuroses, so he rather neglected the self-preservative or ego instincts. However, his increasing interest in the phenomenon of self-love or narcissism led, in turn, to greater emphasis on the ego instincts.

Aggression. Freud's discovery and early formulations regarding the ego instincts led him in 1915 to reconsider the nature and role of aggression. Previously, Freud had considered aggression largely in terms of sadism, which he had defined as one of the sexual part or component instincts that were manifest at every level of psychosexual development. But he clearly differentiated between aggression and hate, which he assigned to the ego instincts, and the libidinal aspects of sadism, which were assigned to the sexual instinct. But this classification gave rise to still another problem. In many instances aggression or aggressive impulses were not self-preservative; therefore, they could not be properly assigned to the ego instincts. Thus, when Freud set forth his new structural theory of the mind in the 1920s, he gave aggression separate status as an instinct whose source was largely in the skeletal muscles and whose aim was destruction.

Life and death instincts. Freud introduced his theory of the dual life and death instincts, Eros and Thanatos, in 1920. This classification of the instincts is more abstract and had broader applications than his previous concept of libidinal and aggressive drives. The life and death instincts were thought to represent the forces that underlie the sexual and aggressive instincts. Although Freud conceded that the death instinct was not clinically verifiable, he felt that the validity of the concept was substantiated by observable phenomena. He pointed in particular to the tendency of persons to repeat past behavior (a phenomenon he described as the repetition compulsion), even if such behavior had proved to be ill-advised.

Freud defined the death instinct or Thanatos as the tendency of organisms and their cells to return to an inanimate state. In contrast, the life instinct or Eros refers to the tendency of particles to reunite, of parts to bind to one another to form greater unities, as in sexual reproduction. Inasmuch as the ultimate destiny of all biological matter, with the exception of the germ cells, is to return to an inanimate state, the death instinct was thought to be the dominant force.

Pleasure and Reality Principles

The pleasure principle, which Freud considered to be largely inborn, refers to the tendency of the organism to avoid pain and to seek pleasure through tension discharge. In essence, the pleasure principle persists throughout life, but it must be modified by the reality principle. The demands of external reality, called the reality principle, necessitate the postponement of immediate pleasure, with the aim of achieving perhaps even greater pleasure in the long run. The reality principle is largely a learned function; therefore, it is closely related to the maturation of ego functions, and it may be impaired in a variety of mental disorders that are the result of impeded ego development.

PSYCHIC APPARATUS AND EGO PSYCHOLOGY

Topographical Theory of the Mind

The topographical theory, as set forth in *The Interpretation of Dreams* in 1900, represented an attempt to divide the mind into three regions—the unconscious, the preconscious, and the conscious—which were distinguished from one another by their relationship to consciousness.

Unconscious. The unconscious contains repressed ideas and affects and is characterized as follows:

1. Ordinarily, its elements are inaccessible to consciousness and can become conscious only through the preconscious, which excludes them by means of censorship or repression. Repressed ideas may reach consciousness when the censor is overpowered (as in psychoneurotic symptom formation), relaxes (as in dream states), or is fooled (as in jokes).

2. The unconscious is associated with the particular form of mental activity that Freud called the primary process or primary process thinking. The primary process has as its principal aim the facilitation of wish fulfillment and instinctual discharge; thus, it is intimately associated with the pleasure principle. Primary process thinking disregards logical connections, permits contradictions to coexist, knows no negatives, has no conception of time, and represents wishes as already fulfilled; it is primitive, prelogical thought. Primary process thinking is characteristic of very young children, who are dedicated to the immediate gratification of their desires.

3. Memories in the unconscious have lost their connection with verbal expression. However, when words are reapplied to the forgotten memory trace, it can reach consciousness once more.

4. The content of the unconscious is limited to wishes seeking fulfillment. These wishes provide the motive force for dream and neurotic symptom formation.

5. The unconscious is closely related to the instincts. It contains the mental representatives and derivatives of the instinctual drives, especially the derivatives of the sexual instinct.

Preconscious. This region of the mind is not present at birth but develops in childhood. The preconscious is accessible to both the unconscious and the conscious. Elements of the unconscious can gain access to consciousness only by first becoming linked with words and reaching the preconscious. However, one of the functions of the preconscious is to maintain repression or censorship of wishes and desires. The type of mental activity associated with the preconscious is called secondary process or secondary process thinking. Such thinking is aimed at avoiding unpleasure, delaying instinctual discharge, and binding mental energy in accordance with the demands of external reality and the person's moral precepts or values. It respects logical connections and tolerates inconsistencies less well than does the primary process. Thus, the secondary process is closely allied with the reality principle, which governs its activities for the most part.

Conscious. Freud regarded the conscious as a kind of sense organ of attention that operated in close association with the preconscious. Through attention, the person can become conscious of perceptual stimuli from the outside world. Within the organism, however, only elements in the preconscious enter consciousness; the rest of the mind is outside of awareness.

Significance of the topographical theory. The topographical theory's main deficiencies lay in its inability to account for two important characteristics of mental conflict. First, many of the defense mechanisms that patients employed to avoid pain or unpleasure were themselves not initially accessible to consciousness. Clearly, then, the agency of repression could not be identical with the preconscious, inasmuch as this region of the mind was by definition accessible to consciousness. Second, patients frequently demonstrated an unconscious need for punishment. However, according to the topographical theory, the moral agency making this demand was allied with the antiinstinctual forces available to awareness in the preconscious.

These criticisms were among the important considerations that led Freud to discard the topographical theory insofar as it was concerned with the assignment of specific processes to specific regions of the mind. He came to realize that what is more important is whether these processes belong to the primary or the secondary system. The concepts included in Freud's topographical theory that have retained their usefulness refer to the characteristics of primary and secondary thought processes, the essential importance of wish fulfilment, the tendency toward regression under conditions of frustration, and the existence of a dynamic unconscious.

Theory of Dreams

Freud first became aware of the significance of dreams in therapy when he realized that, in the process of free association, his patients frequently described their dreams of the night before or of years past. He then discovered that these dreams had a definite meaning, although it was disguised. And he found that encouraging his patients to free-associate to dream fragments was more productive than their associations to real-life events insofar as it facilitated the disclosure of unconscious memories and fantasies.

In *The Interpretation of Dreams* Freud concluded that a dream, like a psychoneurotic symptom, is the conscious expression of an unconscious fantasy or wish that is not readily accessible in waking life. Although dreams were considered one of the normal manifestations of unconscious activity, they were shown later to bear some resemblance to the pathological thoughts of psychotic patients in the waking state. The dream images represent unconscious wishes or thoughts disguised through symbolization and other distorting mechanisms.

The analysis of dreams elicits material that has been repressed or otherwise excluded from consciousness. The dream as it is consciously recalled is but the end result of the unconscious mental activity that occurs during sleep and that, because of its intensity, threatens to interfere with sleep itself. But instead of waking, the sleeper dreams. The unconscious thoughts and wishes that threaten to waken the sleeper may be categorized as nocturnal sensory stimuli (sensory impressions such as pain, hunger, thirst, urinary urgency), the day's residue (thoughts and ideas that are connected with the activities and the preoccupations of the dreamer's current waking life), and repressed id impulses (one or several impulses from the repressed part of the id—that is, from wishes that have their origin in the oedipal and preoedipal phases of development). Nocturnal sensations and the day's residue play only indirect roles in initiating a dream. However intense, they must be associated with one or more repressed wishes to give rise to a dream.

Throughout *The Interpretation of Dreams,* Freud maintains that every dream represents a wish fulfillment, the gratification of an id impulse in fantasy. Since motility is blocked by the sleep state, the dream enables partial but safer gratification of the repressed impulse.

The unconscious wishes and impulses that press for discharge have been repressed because of their unacceptable nature. Because there is continued resistance to their discharge, these wishes and impulses must attach themselves to more neutral or innocent images to pass the scrutiny of the dream censor. This is achieved by the selection of apparently trivial or unimportant images from the dreamer's current psychological experience, images that are linked or associated dynamically with latent images that they resemble in some respect.

Symbolism. For certain body parts or other highly cathected objects, the dreamer substitutes innocent images that resemble the original part in one or more essential features. For example, the snake is a familiar symbol for the penis; a house may symbolize the female genitalia or womb. "Cathexis" is a term used to describe psychic energy invested in an object.

Displacement. The mechanism of displacement refers to the transference of emotions from the original object to which such emotions are attached to a substitute or symbolic representation of that object in the dream. Whereas symbolism refers to the substitution of one object for another, displacement facilitates the distortion of unconscious wishes through the transference of affect from one object to another. For example, the mother may be represented visually in the dream by an unknown woman or one who has less emotional significance for the dreamer.

Projection. Through the process of projection, the dreamer's unacceptable impulses or wishes are perceived in the dream as emanating from another person. Moreover, the person to whom these unacceptable impulses are ascribed is often the one toward whom the dreamer's own unconscious impulses are directed. For example, a man who has a strong but repressed wish to be unfaithful to his wife or sweetheart may dream that she has been unfaithful to him.

Condensation. Condensation is the mechanism by which several unconscious wishes, impulses, or attitudes are combined and expressed in a single image. In a child's dream an attacking monster may represent not only the dreamer's father but also some aspects of his or her mother, and the monster may stand for his or her own primitive impulses as well.

Affects in dreams. Repressed emotions may not appear in the dream at all, or they may be experienced in somewhat altered form. For example, repressed rage toward another person may take the form of a mild dislike. Or a repressed longing may be represented by a manifest repugnance.

Secondary revision. Secondary revision is the mechanism through which the absurd, illogical, and bizarre characteristics of the dream—the distorted effects of symbolism, displacement, and condensation—acquire the coherence and rationality required by the dreamer. Secondary revision employs intellectual processes resembling the thought processes that govern states of consciousness.

Anxiety dreams. Symbolism, displacement, condensation, projection, and secondary revision serve a dual purpose: They facilitate the discharge of latent impulses, and they prevent the direct discharge of instinctual drives, thereby protecting the dreamer from the excessive anxiety and pain that would accompany such discharge. Of course, these mechanisms may fail. Then the ego reacts to the direct expression of repressed impulses with severe anxiety.

Punishment dreams. In the punishment dream the ego anticipates superego condemnation if repressed impulses find direct expression in the dream. In anticipation of the terrible consequences of the loss of the ego's control over the instincts in sleep, the demands of the superego are satisfied by giving expression to punishment fantasies.

Structural Theory of the Mind

From a structural viewpoint, the psychic apparatus is divided into three provinces—id, ego, and superego—which are distinguished by their different functions.

Id. Freud postulated that the infant is endowed at birth with an id—that is, with instinctual drives that seek gratification. The infant does not, however, have the capacity to delay, control, or modify these drives. And in the matter of coping with the external world, the infant is completely dependent on the egos of other persons in the environment.

Ego. Freud believed that the modification of the id occurs as a result of the impact of the external world on the drives. The pressures of external reality enable the ego to appropriate the energies of the id to do its work. In the process of formation, the ego seeks to bring the influences of the external world to bear on the id, to substitute the reality principle for the pleasure principle; it thereby contributes to its own further development. Freud emphasized the role of the instincts in ego development, particularly the role of conflict. At first, this conflict is between the id and the outside world; later, it is between the id and the ego itself.

At first, infants are unable to differentiate their own bodies from the rest of the world. The ego begins with the child's ability to perceive his or her body as distinct from the external world.

Gratification and frustration of drives and needs in the early months of life affect the future fate of the ego. Adequate satisfaction of the infant's libidinal needs by the mother or mother surrogate is crucially important. And, although it is less clearly understood and appreciated, a certain amount of drive frustration in infancy and early childhood is equally important for the development of a healthy ego. Maternal deprivation at significant stages of development leads to the impairment of ego functions to varying degrees. However, overindulgence of the child's instinctual needs interferes with the development of the ego's capacity to tolerate frustration and, consequently, with its ability to regulate the demands of the id in relation to the outside world.

The loss of the loved object or of a particularly gratifying relationship with the object is a painful experience at any stage of life, but it is particularly traumatic in infancy and early childhood, when the ego is not yet strong enough to compensate for the loss. Yet in the early years of life, the child is constantly subjected to such deprivation. In the normal course of events, young children do not suffer the actual loss of their parents, but they must endure constant alterations in their relationship with them. Moreover, at each stage in their development, they must endure the loss of the kind of gratification that was appropriate to the previous phase of their maturation but that must then be given up.

The child attempts to retain the gratifications derived from these earlier relationships, at least in fantasy, through the process of identification. By this mechanism, the aspects or qualities of the person who was once the center of the gratifying relationship are internalized and reestablished as part of the developing ego. The psychological mechanism of symbolic incorporation—that is, the taking in of another person or of his or her qualities—is called introjection, and this mechanism continues to influence character development long after the oral period.

Identification with the aggressor is a defense maneuver based on the child's need to protect himself or herself from severe anxiety experienced in relation to the object. The child identifies with and incorporates the characteristics of the feared person, who is perceived as the attacker and on whom the child is dependent. The child wishes to become allied with the aggressor, rather than to be his or her victim; thus, the child may share in the other's power rather than be powerless before the aggressor.

Superego. The superego comes into being with the resolution of the Oedipus complex, which leads to a rapid acceleration of the identification process with the parent of the same sex. This identification forms a kind of precipitate within the ego, which then confronts the other contents of the ego as a superego. The identification is based on the child's struggles to repress instinctual aims, and this effort of renunciation gives the superego its prohibiting character.

Throughout the latency period and thereafter, persons continue to build on their early identifications through contact with teachers, heroic figures, and admired persons, who form their moral standards, values, and ultimate aspirations and ideals. The standards, restrictions, commands, and punishments that were imposed by the parents from without are internalized in the superego, which then judges and guides a person's behavior from within, even in the absence of the parents.

MODERN EGO PSYCHOLOGY

Many advances have been made in studying the ego, and this study of the ego makes up the important field of ego psychology.

Relation to Reality

The ego's capacity for maintaining a relationship to the external world is among its principal functions. The character of its relationship to the external world may be divided into three components: (1) the sense of reality, (2) reality testing, and (3) the adaptation to reality.

1. Sense of reality. The sense of reality originates simultaneously with the development of the ego. Infants first become aware of the reality of their own body dimensions. Only gradually do they develop the capacity to distinguish a reality outside their bodies.

2. Reality testing. The ego's capacity for objective evaluation and judgment of the external world depends on the primary autonomous functions of the ego, such as memory and perception. Because of the fundamental importance of reality testing for negotiating with the outside world, its impairment may be associated with severe mental disorder.

3. Adaptation to reality. The capacity of the ego to use the person's resources to form adequate solutions is based on previously tested judgments of reality. Adaptation is closely allied to the concept of mastery in respect to both external tasks and the instincts. It should be distinguished from adjustment, which may entail accommodation to reality at the expense of certain resources or potentialities of the person. The function of adaptation to reality is closely related to the defensive functions of the ego.

Control and Regulation of Instinctual Drives

The development of a capacity to delay immediate discharge of urgent wishes and impulses is essential if the ego is to assure the integrity of the person and fulfill its role as mediator between the id and the outside world.

Synthetic Function

The synthetic function—the ego's integrative capacities; its tendency to bind, unite, coordinate, and create; and its tendency to simplify or generalize—is concerned with the overall organization and functioning of the ego. It must enlist the cooperation of other ego functions in the course of its operation.

Primary Autonomous Functions

Primary autonomous ego functions are based on rudimentary apparatuses that are present at birth; they develop outside the conflict with the id. Heinz Hartmann (1894–1970) included perception, intuition, comprehension, thinking, language, certain phases of motor development, learning, and intelligence among the functions in this conflict-free sphere. However, each of these functions may become involved in conflict secondarily in the course of development. For example, if aggressive, competitive impulses intrude on the impetus to learn, they may evoke inhibitory reactions on the part of the ego.

Object Relations Theory

Object relations theory deals with the capacity to make mutually satisfying object relationships, which is a fundamental function of the ego. The term "object" refers to the relationship of the infant to another person. This process may be disturbed by retarded development or regression or, conceivably, by inherent—that is, genetic—defects or limitations in the capacity to develop object relationships. The evolution in the child's capacity for relationships with others, which progresses from narcissism to social relationships within the family and then within the group, has been described by Anna Freud (1895–1982) and Dorothy Burlingham. Ronald Fairbairn (1889–1964), along with such workers as Michael Balint (1986–1970), discussed the early stages in the relationship of the infant with need-satisfying objects and the gradual development of a sense of separateness from the mother. Donald W. Winnicott (1897–1971) described the *transitional object* (e.g., blanket, teddy bear) as the link between developing children and their mothers. The child develops feelings of security from the object, which symbolizes the good breast and reduces anxiety.

The stages of human development and object relations theory are summarized in Figure 6.1-10.

Defense Mechanisms

A systematic and comprehensive study of the defenses employed by the ego was presented for the first time by Anna Freud, Sigmund Freud's daughter. In her classic contribution *The Ego and the Mechanisms of Defense,* she maintained that everyone, normal or neurotic, employs a

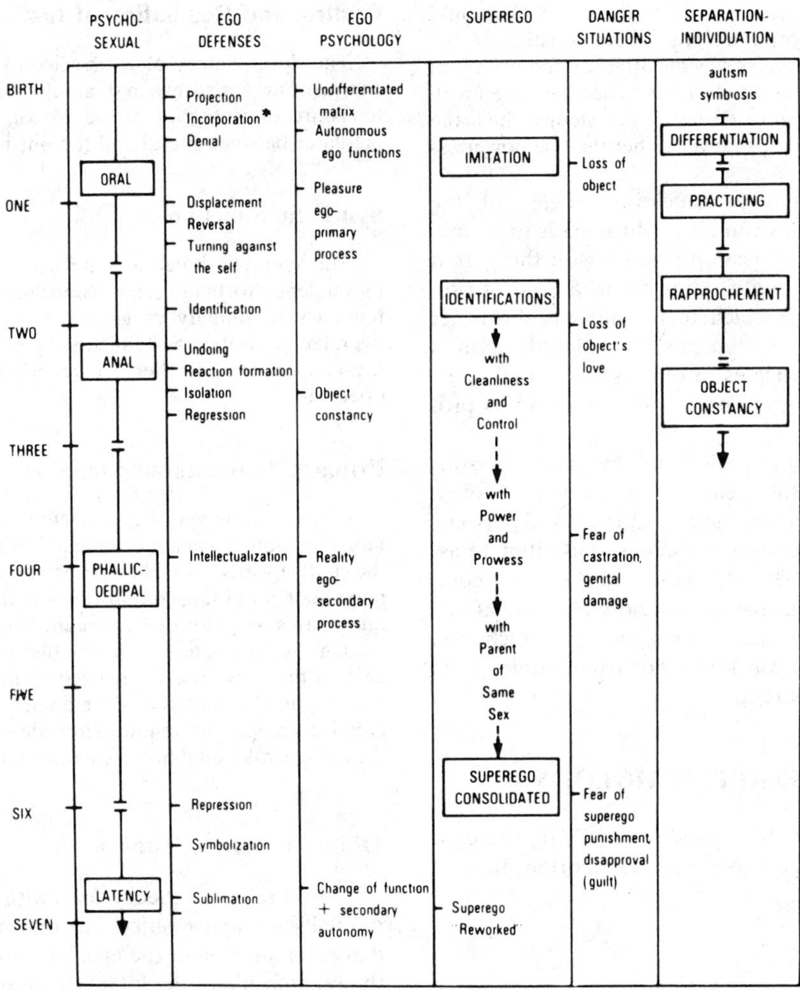

Figure 6.1-10. Parallel lines of human development. *Also introjection. (From L B Inderbitzin, C M Luke, M E James: Psychoanalytic psychotherapy. In *Human Behavior: An Introduction for Medical Students,* A Stoudemire, editor, p 74. Lippincott, Philadelphia, 1990, with permission.)

characteristic repertoire of defense mechanisms to varying degrees.

At each phase of libidinal development, associated drive components evoke characteristic ego defenses. For example, introjection, denial, and projection are defense mechanisms associated with oral sadistic impulses, whereas reaction formations, such as shame and disgust, develop in relation to anal impulses and pleasures. Defense mechanisms from earlier phases of development persist side by side with those of later periods. When defenses associated with pregenital phases of development tend to become predominant in adult life over more mature mechanisms, such as sublimation and repression, the personality retains an infantile cast.

Recent developments in defense mechanisms. George Vaillant has further classified defenses into four types, according to the level of adaptation and use. (1) Narcissistic defenses are used by children and psychotics. (2) Immature defenses are used by adolescents and are seen in depression, obsessions, and compulsions. (3) Neurotic defenses are seen in adults under stress and are encountered in obsessive-compulsive and hysteric persons. (4) Mature defenses are normal adult adaptive mechanisms. These defenses are encountered in psychologically and physically healthy adults with good marriages, successful and satisfying careers, and gratifying recreational outlets. Some overlapping of defenses may exist among these groups—for example, mature sublimation may be used by a psychotic, or narcissistic defenses may be used by a mature adult. Table 6.1-2 lists the defense mechanisms and Vaillant's classification of the four types of defenses.

Theory of Anxiety

According to Freud both real anxiety and neurotic anxiety are a signal—the response of the organism to danger. In real anxiety, the threat emanates from a known danger outside the person; neurotic anxiety is precipitated by an unknown or repressed danger.

Freud distinguished two kinds of anxiety-provoking situations. In the first, for which the phenomenon of birth is the prototype, anxiety occurs as a result of excessive instinctual stimulation that the organism is unable to bind or handle. In the second, more common situation, which occurs after the defensive system has matured, anxiety arises in anticipation of danger rather than as the result of

Table 6.1-2
Classification of Defense Mechanisms

Narcissistic Defenses

Denial. Psychotic denial of external reality, unlike repression, affects the perception of external reality more than the perception of internal reality. Seeing but refusing to acknowledge what one sees and hearing but negating what is actually heard are examples of denial and exemplify the close relationship of denial to sensory experience. Not all denial, however, is necessarily psychotic. Like projection, denial may function in the service of more neurotic or even adaptive objectives. Denial avoids becoming aware of some painful aspects of reality. At the psychotic level, the denied reality may be replaced by a fantasy or delusion.

Distortion. Grossly reshaping external reality to suit inner needs—including unrealistic megalomanic beliefs, hallucinations, wish-fulfilling delusions—and employing sustained feelings of delusional superiority or entitlement.

Primitive idealization. Through this mechanism, external objects that are viewed as either "all good" or "all bad" are unrealistically endowed with great power. Most commonly, the "all good" object is seen as omnipotent, or ideal, while the badness in the "all bad" object is greatly inflated.

Projection. Perceiving and reacting to unacceptable inner impulses and their derivatives as though they were outside the self. On a psychotic level, this takes the form of frank delusions about external reality, usually persecutory, and includes both perception of one's own feelings in another and subsequent acting on the perception (psychotic paranoid delusions). The impulses may derive from the id or the superego (hallucinated recriminations) but may undergo transformation in the process. Thus, according to Freud's analysis of paranoid projections, homosexual libidinal impulses are transformed into hatred and then projected onto the object of the unacceptable homosexual impulse.

Projective identification. Unwanted aspects of the self are deposited into another person such that the person projecting feels at one with the object of the projection. The extruded aspects are modified by and recovered from the recipient. This defense allows one to distance and make oneself understood by exerting pressure on another person to experience feelings similar to one's own.

Splitting. External objects are divided into "all good" and "all bad" accompanied by the abrupt shifting of an object from one extreme category to the other. Sudden and complete reversal of feelings and conceptualizations about a person may occur. The extreme repetitive oscillation between contradictory self-concepts is another manifestation of this mechanism.

Immature Defenses

Acting out. The direct expression of an unconscious wish or impulse in action to avoid being conscious of the accompanying affect. The unconscious fantasy, involving objects, is lived out impulsively in behavior, thus gratifying the impulse more than the prohibition against it. On a chronic level, acting out involves giving in to impulses to avoid the tension that would result from postponement of expression.

Blocking. An inhibition, usually temporary in nature, of affects especially but possibly also thinking and impulses. It is close to repression in its effects but has a component of tension arising from the inhibition of the impulse, affect, or thought.

Hypochondriasis. The transformation of reproach toward others—arising from bereavement, loneliness, or unacceptable aggressive impulses—into self-reproach and complaints of pain, somatic illness, and neurasthenia. Existent illness may also be overemphasized or exaggerated for its evasive and regressive possibilities. Thus, responsibility may be avoided, guilt may be circumvented, instinctual impulses may be warded off.

Identification. Identification, which plays a crucial role in ego development, may also be used as a defense mechanism under certain circumstances. Identification with the loved object may serve as a defense against the anxiety or pain that accompanies separation from or loss of the object, whether real or threatened. If identification occurs out of guilt, the person identifies for self-punitive purposes with a quality or symptom of the person who is the source of the guilt feelings. The mechanism of *identification with the aggressor*, first described by Anna Freud, may also be enlisted as a defense mechanism.

Introjection. In addition to the developmental functions of the process of introjection, it also serves specific defensive functions. The introjection of a loved object involves the internalization of characteristics of the object with the goal of establishing closeness to and constant presence of the object. Anxiety consequent to separation or tension arising out of ambivalence toward the object is thus diminished. If the object is a lost object, introjection nullifies or negates the loss by taking on characteristics of the object, thus in a sense internally preserving the object. Even if the object is not lost, the internalization usually involves a shift of cathexis, reflecting a significant alteration in the object relationships.

Introjection of a feared object serves to avoid anxiety through internalizing the aggressive characteristic of the object, thereby putting the aggression under one's own control. The aggression is no longer felt as coming from outside but is taken within and utilized defensively, thus turning the subject's weak, passive position into an active, strong one. The classic example is identification with the aggressor. Introjection can also be out of a sense of guilt in which the self-punishing introject is attributable to the hostile-destructive component of an ambivalent tie to an object. Thus, the self-punitive qualities of the object are taken over and established within one's self as a symptom or character trait, which effectively represents both the destruction and the preservation of the object. This is also called identification with the victim.

Passive-aggressive behavior. Aggression toward an object expressed indirectly and ineffectively through passivity, masochism, and turning against the self.

Projection. Attributing one's own unacknowledged feelings to others; it includes severe prejudice, rejection of intimacy through suspiciousness, hypervigilance to external danger, and injustice collecting. Projection operates correlatively to introjection, such that the material of the projection is derived from the internalized configuration of the introjects. At higher levels of function, projection may take the form of misattributing or misinterpreting motives, attitudes, feelings, or intentions of others.

Regression. A return to a previous stage of development or functioning to avoid the anxieties or hostilities involved in later stages. A return to earlier points of fixation embodying modes of behavior previously given up. This is often the result of a disruption of equilibrium at a later phase of development. This reflects a basic tendency to achieve instinctual gratification or to escape instinctual tension by returning to earlier modes and levels of gratification when later and more differentiated modes fail.

Schizoid fantasy. The tendency to use fantasy and to indulge in autistic retreat for the purpose of conflict resolution and gratification.

Somatization. The defensive conversion of psychic derivatives into bodily symptoms; tendency to react with somatic, rather than psychic, manifestations. Infantile somatic responses are re-

Table 6.1-2
Continued

Immature Defenses

placed by thought and affect during development (desomatization); regression to earlier somatic forms of response (resomatization) may result from unresolved conflicts and may play an important role in psychological reactions.

Turning against the self. Changing an unacceptable impulse that is aimed at others by redirecting it against oneself.

Neurotic Defenses

Controlling. The excessive attempt to manage or regulate events or objects in the environment in the interest of minimizing anxiety and solving internal conflicts.

Displacement. Involves a purposeful, unconscious shifting from one object to another in the interest of solving a conflict. Although the object is changed, the instinctual nature of the impulse and its aim remain unchanged.

Dissociation. A temporary but drastic modification of character or sense of personal identity to avoid emotional distress; it includes fugue states and hysterical conversion reactions.

Externalization. A general term, correlative to internalization, referring to the tendency to perceive in the external world and in external objects components of one's own personality, including instinctual impulses, conflicts, moods, attitudes, and styles of thinking. It is a more general term than projection, which is defined by its derivation from and correlation with specific introjects.

Inhibition. The unconsciously determined limitation or renunciation of specific ego functions, singly or in combination, to avoid anxiety arising out of conflict with instinctual impulses, superego, or environmental forces or figures.

Intellectualization. The control of affects and impulses by way of thinking about them, instead of experiencing them. It is a systematic excess of thinking, deprived of its affect, to defend against anxiety caused by unacceptable impulses.

Isolation. The intrapsychic splitting or separation of affect from content, resulting in repression of either idea or affect or the displacement of affect to a different or substitute content.

Rationalization. A justification of attitudes, beliefs, or behavior that may otherwise be unacceptable by an incorrect application of justifying reasons or the invention of a convincing fallacy.

Reaction formation. The management of unacceptable impulses by permitting expression of the impulse in antithetical form. This is equivalently an expression of the impulse in the negative. Where instinctual conflict is persistent, reaction formation can become a character trait on a permanent basis, usually as an aspect of obsessional character.

Repression. Consists of the expelling and withholding from conscious awareness of an idea or feeling. It may operate by excluding from awareness what was once experienced on a conscious level (secondary repression), or it may curb ideas and feelings before they have reached consciousness (primary repression). The "forgetting" in repression is unique in that it is often accompanied by highly symbolic behavior, which suggests that the repressed is not really forgotten. The role of repression in the development of psychoanalytic theory is central, particularly the important discrimination between repression and the more general concept of defense.

Sexualization. The endowing of an object or function with sexual significance that it did not previously have or possesses to a smaller degree, to ward off anxieties connected with prohibitive impulses.

Undoing. A person symbolically acts out in reverse something unacceptable that has already been done; a form of magical expiatory action.

Mature Defenses

Altruism. Vicarious but constructive and instinctually gratifying service to others. This must be distinguished from altruistic surrender, which involves a surrender of direct gratification or of instinctual needs in favor of fulfilling the needs of others to the detriment of the self, with vicarious satisfaction only being gained through introjection.

Anticipation. The realistic anticipation of or planning for future inner discomfort; implies overly concerned planning, worrying, and anticipation of dire and dreadful possible outcomes.

Asceticism. The elimination of directly pleasurable affects attributable to an experience. The moral element is implicit in setting values on specific pleasures. Asceticism is directed against all "base" pleasures perceived consciously, and gratification is derived from the renunciation.

Humor. The overt expression of feelings without personal discomfort or immobilization and without unpleasant effects on others. Humor allows one to bear and yet focus on what is too terrible to be borne, in contrast to wit, which always involves distraction or displacement away from the affective issue.

Sublimation. The gratification of an impulse whose goal is retained but whose aim or object is changed from a socially objectionable one to a socially valued one. Libidinal sublimation involves a desexualization of drive impulses and the placing of a value judgment that substitutes what is valued by the superego or society. Sublimation of aggressive impulses takes place through pleasurable games and sports. Unlike neurotic defenses, sublimation allows instincts to be channeled, rather than be dammed-up or diverted. Thus, in sublimation, feelings are acknowledged, modified, and directed toward a relatively significant person or goal so that modest instinctual satisfaction results.

Suppression. The conscious or semiconscious decision to postpone attention to a conscious impulse or conflict.

Compiled and adapted from Elvin Semrad, G. L. Bibring and associates, and George Vaillant by William W. Meissner, S.J., M.D.

it, although the affect may be experienced as if the danger has already occurred. In these situations, the anxiety may arise because the person has learned to recognize, at a preconscious or unconscious level, aspects of a situation that were once traumatic. Anxiety serves as a signal to mobilize protective measures that avert the danger and prevent a traumatic situation from taking place. The person may use avoidance mechanisms to escape from a real or imagined danger from without, or the ego may use psychological defenses from within to guard against or reduce the quantity of instinctual excitation.

Character

In 1913 Freud made an important distinction between neurotic symptoms and character or personality traits. Neurotic symptoms come into being as a result of the failure of repression; character traits owe their existence to the success of repression or, more accurately, to the defense system that achieves its aim through a persistent pattern of reaction formation and sublimation. In 1923 Freud observed that the replacement of object attachments by identification (introjection), in which the ego internalized the lost object, also made a significant contribution to character formation. In 1932 Freud emphasized the particular importance of identification with the parents for the construction of character, particularly with reference to superego formation.

Psychoanalysis has come to regard character as the pattern of adaptation to instinctual and environmental forces that is typical or habitual for a given person. Character is distinguished from the ego in that it largely refers to styles of defense and directly observable behavior rather than to thinking and feeling.

Innate biological predisposition, the interaction of id forces with early ego defenses and environmental influences, and various early identifications and imitations of other human beings leave their lasting stamp upon character. The degree to which the ego has developed a capacity to tolerate delay in drive discharge and to neutralize instinctual energy determines the degree to which such character traits will emerge in later life.

The exaggerated development of certain character traits at the expense of others may lead to character disorders or produce a vulnerability or predisposition to the psychoses.

Classic Psychoanalytic Theory of Neurosis

Neuroses develop under the following conditions: (1) There is an inner conflict between drives and fears that prevents drive discharge. (2) Sexual drives are involved in this conflict. (3) The conflict has not been worked through to a realistic solution. Instead, the drives that seek discharge have been expelled from consciousness through repression or another defense mechanism. (4) The repression has merely rendered the drives unconscious; it has not deprived them of their power and made them innocuous. Consequently, the repressed tendencies—disguised neurotic symptoms—have fought their way back into consciousness. (5) A rudimentary neurosis based on the same type of conflict existed in early childhood.

Maternal deprivation in the first few months of life may impair ego development. Failure to make the necessary identifications, either because of overindulgence or because of excessive frustration, interferes with the ego's task of mediating between the instincts and the environment. Lack of capacity for equitable expression of drives, especially aggressive ones, may lead children to turn them onto themselves and to become overtly self-destructive. Inconsistency, excessive harshness, or undue permissiveness on the part of the parents may result in the disordered functioning of the superego. Instinctual conflict may impair the ego's capacity for sublimation, resulting in excessive inhibition of its autonomous functions. Severe conflict that cannot be dealt with through symptom formation may lead to severe restrictions in ego functioning and to the impairment of the capacity to learn and develop new skills.

When the ego has been weakened, a shock or traumatic event that seems to threaten survival may break through the ego defenses. A large amount of libido is then required to master the resultant excitation. But the libido thus mobilized is withdrawn from the supply normally applied to external objects and from the ego itself, and this withdrawal further diminishes the strength of the ego and produces a sense of inadequacy. Disappointments or frustrations of adult strivings can revive infantile longings that may be dealt with through symptom formation or further regression.

Secondary gains of neurosis. The reduction of tension and conflict through neurotic illness is the primary purpose or gain of the disorder. The ego, however, may try to gain advantages from the external world by provoking pity in order to get attention and sympathy, by manipulating others, or even by receiving monetary compensation. These are the secondary gains of the illness.

Each disorder has its characteristic form of secondary gain. In phobias there is a regression to childhood, when one was still protected. Gaining attention through dramatic acting out and, at times, deriving material advantages are characteristic of conversion hysteria. In obsessive-compulsive disorder, there is frequently a narcissistic gain through pride in illness.

Treatment and Technique

Psychoanalysis as a treatment method devised by Freud depends on the patients' ability to understand the emotional significance of an experience and to develop and retain insights about past events. The patients try to bring repressed material back to consciousness, and, on the basis of a greater understanding of their needs and motives, they may find a realistic solution to current conflicts. This type of psychoanalysis is known as Freudian, classical, traditional, or orthodox psychoanalysis.

The cornerstone of the psychoanalytic technique is *free association* (i.e., the patient relates freely everything that passes through his or her mind). The primary function of free association, besides providing content for the analysis, is to induce the necessary regression and passive dependence that are connected with establishing and working through the transference neurosis. Although it remains the basic technique that guides the patient's participation in the analysis, the use of free association in the analytical process is a relative matter. The *fundamental rule* of psychoanalysis is that the patient agrees to be completely honest with the analyst.

The analysis becomes a recurring conflict among *transference, transference neurosis,* and *resistance.* Manifested by involuntary inhibitions of the patient's effort to free-associate, this conflict is a repetition of the sexuality-guilt conflict that produced the neurosis itself. The analysis of resistance is the analyst's prime function, and interpretation is the chief tool. The patient displaces the feelings that were originally directed toward the participants in these early events onto the analyst. The analyst alternately becomes a friend or an enemy and is, correspondingly, loved or hated. To an increasing extent, the patient's feelings toward the analyst replicate his or her feelings toward the specific people talked about. This object displacement, which is an inevitable concomitant of psychoanalytic treatment, is called *transference.* As unresolved childhood attitudes emerge during transference, patients begin to see themselves as they really are, with all their unfulfilled and contradictory needs exposed. Psychoanalysis and other techniques devised from it are discussed in great detail in Section 29.1, "Psychoanalysis and Psychoanalytic Psychotherapy."

References

Buckley P: Fifty years after Freud: Dora, the Rat Man, and the Wolf-Man. Am J Psychiatry *146:* 1394, 1989.

Compton A: Freud: Objects and structure. J Am Psychoanal Assoc *34:* 561, 1986.

Davidson A I: How to do the history of psychoanalysis: A reading of Freud's three essays on the theory of sexuality. Crit Inq *13:* 252, 1987.

Dilman I: *Freud, Insight, and Change.* Basil Blackwell, Oxford, 1988.

Gay P, ed.: *The Freud Reader.* Norton, New York, 1989.

Fenichel O: *The Psychoanalytic Theory of Neurosis.* Norton, New York, 1945.

Freud A: *The Ego and the Mechanisms of Defense.* International Universities Press, New York, 1946.

Freud S: *Beyond the Pleasure Principle.* Norton, New York, 1961.

Freud S: *The Ego and the Id.* Norton, New York, 1960.

Freud S: *An Outline of Psycho-Analysis.* Norton, New York, 1969.

Freud S: *The Standard Edition of the Complete Psychological Works of Sigmund Freud.* vols 1–24, Hogarth Press, London, 1953–1966.

Gelfand T: "Mon cher Docteur Freud": Charcot's unpublished correspondence to Freud, 1888–1893. Bull Hist Med *62:* 563, 1988.

Holt R R: *Freud Reappraised: A Fresh Look at Psychoanalytic Theory.* Guilford, New York, 1989.

Jones E: *The Life and Work of Sigmund Freud,* 3 vols. Basic Books, New York, 1953–1957.

Kiell N: *Freud Without Hindsight: Reviews of His Work, 1893–1939.* International Universities Press, Madison CT, 1988.

Manson W C: *The Psychodynamics of Culture: Abram Kardiner and Neo-Freudian Anthropology.* Greenwood Press, New York, 1988.

Meltzer F, ed.: *The Trial(s) of Psychoanalysis.* University of Chicago Press, Chicago, 1988.

Olsen O A, Koppe S: *Freud's Theory of Psychoanalysis.* New York, New York University Press, 1988.

Wong N: Classical psychoanalysis. In *Comprehensive Textbook of Psychiatry,* ed 5, H I Kaplan and B J Sadock, editors, p 356. Williams & Wilkins, Baltimore, 1989.

Zetzel E R: *The Capacity for Emotional Growth.* International Universities Press, New York, 1970.

Zetzel E R, Meissner W W: *Basic Concepts of Psychoanalytic Psychiatry.* Basic Books, New York, 1973.

6.2 / Schools Derived from Psychoanalysis and Psychology

KARL ABRAHAM (1877–1925)

Karl Abraham was one of Sigmund Freud's earliest followers and the first psychoanalyst in Germany. He elaborated on Freud's stages of psychosexual development and separated the oral period into a sucking phase and a biting phase, divided the anal period into a destructive-expulsive (anal-sadistic) phase and a mastering-retentive (anal-erotic) phase, and divided the phallic period into an early phase of partial genital love (true phallic phase) and a later mature genital phase. He focused on adult character development and concluded that depression is a result of fixation at the oral stage of development and that obsessional neurosis is the result of fixation at the anal-sadistic phase.

ALFRED ADLER (1870–1937)

Alfred Adler expanded on Freud's theories to such an extent that the two men eventually were estranged. Adler turned away from the sexual theory of neurosis and focused on the instinct of aggression. His theories are collectively known as *individual psychology.*

Aggression expresses itself as a striving for power, which Adler believed to be a masculine trait. He introduced the term *masculine protest* to depict the tendency to move from a passive and feminine role to a masculine and active role.

The child's development of self-esteem is hindered by any defect in his or her bodily structure, which Adler called *organ inferiority.* He expanded on that concept and introduced the term *inferiority complex* to refer to a sense of weakness and inadequacy that everyone is born with and must overcome. That sense of inferiority is tied to the child's oedipal strivings that can never be gratified.

According to Adler, children's *birth order* in the family affects their life-styles. The firstborn reacts against the birth of siblings and is angry about having to give up the powerful position of being the only child. The second-born child wants to equal and wrest power from the first; the child born last can never be displaced and will always be the youngest.

Encouragement was Adler's main therapeutic approach to help patients overcome their feelings of inferiority. As a result of consistent human relatedness, patients become more hopeful, feel less isolated, and feel more a part of society. Adler placed even greater emphasis on the patients' needs to realize their strengths and abilities and to develop a belief in their own dignity and worth.

FRANZ ALEXANDER (1891–1964)

Franz Alexander moved from his native Germany to the United States, where he founded the Chicago Institute for Psychoanalysis. He developed the concept of the *corrective emotional experience,* in which patients modify the results of traumatic events of their past lives in the analytic situation.

Because of the positive emotional involvement with a therapist, who is supportive and trustworthy, the patients are able to master past traumas and grow from the experience. Alexander also influenced the field of psychosomatic medicine with his *specificity hypothesis* that certain organic diseases are associated with specific personality constellations.

GORDON ALLPORT (1897–1967)

Gordon Allport taught the first course in psychology of personality to be offered in an American college—Harvard. He represents the *humanistic school* of psychology, which holds that there is an inherent potential for growth and autonomous function in every person.

A sense of self is a person's only real guarantee of personal existence. Selfhood develops in stages—the early self of the infant proceeds through the awareness of the body to self-identity. For the self that is known, Allport used the term *propriem;* propriate strivings are related to the maintenance of self-esteem and self-identity. In Allport's system *traits* are the chief units of personality structure. A trait has actual existence, and some are common to people in the same culture. Individual traits, known as *personal dispositions,* represent the essence of the personality that is unique to the individual. *Maturity* is characterized by a greatly extended sense of self and a capacity to relate warmly and intimately to others. Mature persons have zest, enthusiasm, humor, insight, and security. Psychotherapy directs the person to realize these characteristics.

ERIC BERNE (1910–1970)

Eric Berne received training in classical psychoanalysis but set aside the analytic technique to develop *transactional analysis.* A *transaction* is a stimulus from one person that produces a corresponding response in another person. If the transaction is stereotyped and predictable, it is referred to as a psychological *game,* which people learn in childhood and play throughout their lives. *Strokes* are the basic motivating factors of human behavior and consist of rewards, such as love, approval, and other positive reinforcements. Berne defined three ego states that exist within each person: (1) the *child,* which represents archaic elements that become fixed in early childhood; (2) the *adult,* which is the part of the personality capable of objectively appraising reality; and (3) the *parent,* which is an introject of the person's actual parents' values. The therapeutic process involves helping patients understand whether they are functioning in the adult, child, or parent mode as they interact with others. They learn to recognize the games they play. The ultimate goal is for persons to function in the adult mode as much as possible as they relate to others.

RAYMOND CATTELL (b. 1905)

Raymond Cattell obtained his Ph.D. in England before moving to the United States. He introduced the use of *multivariate analysis* and *factor analysis*—statistical procedures that simultaneously examine the relationship among multiple variables and factors—to the study of personality. By objectively examining the person's life record, using personal interviewing and questionnaire data, Cattell described a variety of traits that represent the building blocks of personality.

Traits are both biologically based and environmentally determined or learned. Biological traits include sex, gregariousness, aggression, and parental protectiveness. Environmentally learned traits include cultural ideas such as work, religion, intimacy, romance, and identity. An important concept is the *law of coercion to the biosocial mean,* which holds that society exerts pressure on genetically different persons to conform to social norms. Thus, for example, a person with a strong genetic tendency toward dominance is likely to receive social encouragement for restraint, whereas the naturally submissive person will be encouraged toward self-assertion.

SANDOR FERENCZI (1873–1933)

Sandor Ferenczi, a close associate of Freud, was a Hungarian psychiatrist who studied early childhood thinking. Infants start out with a sense of magic hallucinatory omnipotence. They then move toward the use of words and finally to acceptance of reality, in which not all needs can be gratified. The therapeutic process, known as *active therapy,* helps the patient develop an awareness of reality through active confrontations by the therapist. Ferenczi tried to shorten analysis, and he was once cautioned by Freud about the need to keep aloof from patients, especially in the sexual area.

ERICH FROMM (1900–1980)

Erich Fromm came to the United States in 1933 from Germany, where he received his Ph.D. He helped found the William Alanson White Institute for Psychiatry in the United States. Fromm identified five character types that are common to and determined by Western culture; each person may possess qualities from one or more types. They are (1) the *receptive personality,* who is passive; (2) the *exploitative personality,* who is manipulative; (3) the *marketing personality,* who is opportunistic and changeable; (4) the *hoarding personality,* who saves and stores; and (5) the *productive personality,* who is mature and enjoys love and work. The therapeutic process involves strengthening the person's sense of ethical behavior toward others and developing *productive love,* characterized by care, responsibility, and respect for other persons.

KURT GOLDSTEIN (1878–1965)

Kurt Goldstein was born in Germany and received his M.D. from the University of Breslau; he was influenced by Gestalt psychology and existentialism. Every organism has dynamic properties, which are energy supplies that are relatively constant and evenly distributed. When states of tension-disequilibrium occur, the organism automatically attempts to return to its normal state. What happens in one part of the organism affects every other part, a phenomenon known as *holocoenosis.*

A major concept used by Goldstein is *self-actualization*—the genuinely creative powers inherent in each person that lead one to fulfill one's potentialities. Each person has different innate potentialities; therefore, people strive for self-actualization along different paths.

To function reasonably well, the organism must come to terms with the environment, which can produce imbalances in the system but can also act as one's source of supply. As persons' coping methods improve, their chances of self-actualization increase. When sickness occurs, self-actualization is severely disrupted. An organism's whole integrity is threatened, and responses may be rigid and compulsive. A regression to primitive levels of behavior may occur. Under major stress (e.g., damage to the brain), a *catastrophic reaction* may occur in which the person becomes agitated and fearful and refuses to perform even the simplest task because of fear of possible failure. As health returns and the person masters illness, self-actualization resumes.

KAREN HORNEY (1885–1952)

Karen Horney was an American psychiatrist who believed that a person's current personality attributes are the result of the interaction between the person and the environment and are not based on infantile libidinal strivings carried over from childhood. Her theory, known as *holistic psychology,* maintains that a person needs to be seen as a unitary whole who influences and is influenced by the environment. She challenged the concept of the Oedipus complex and attributed excessive concern with the genitals to parental attitudes, such as maternal overconcern or rigidity regarding sexuality.

There are three concepts of the self: (1) The *actual self* consists of the sum total of experience; (2) the *real self* is the harmonious healthy person; and (3) the *idealized self* is a neurotic expectation or glorified image of what the person feels he or she should be. The *pride system* alienates the person from the real self because it overemphasizes prestige, intellect, power, strength, appearance, and sexual prowess. It can lead to self-hatred, self-contempt, and self-effacement. Horney also introduced the concepts of *basic anxiety* and *basic trust.* The therapeutic process emphasizes *self-realization,* which removes distorting influences on the personality that prevent growth from occurring.

EDITH JACOBSON (1897–1978)

Edith Jacobson was an object relations theorist who viewed the infant's experience of pleasure or unpleasure as the core of the relationship with the mother. Inadequate responses from the mother to the infant's needs frustrate and disappoint the infant, which results in the discharge of aggressive drive energies. A fixation may occur, and, later, objects are perceived as noxious and disappointing. An excess of gratification in infancy may lead to idealization and a desire to merge with future objects, thus preventing mature object relationships from taking place.

CARL GUSTAV JUNG (1875–1961)

Carl Jung's psychoanalytic school, known as *analytical psychology,* includes basic ideas related to but going beyond Freud's theories. He expanded on Freud's concept of the unconscious by describing the *collective unconscious* as consisting of all humankind's common and shared mythological and symbolic past.

The collective unconscious includes *archetypes*—representational images and configurations that have universal symbolic meanings. Archetypal figures exist for the mother, father, child, and hero, among others. Archetypes contribute to *complexes,* which are feeling-toned ideas that develop as a result of personal experience interacting with archetypal imagery. Thus, a mother complex is determined not only by the mother-child interaction but also by the conflict between archetypal expectation and actual experience with the real woman who functions in a motherly role.

Jung noted that there are two types of personality organization: introversion and extroversion. *Introverts* focus on their inner world of thoughts, intuitions, emotions, and sensations; *extroverts* are more oriented toward the outer world, other people, and material goods. Each person has a mixture of both components. The *persona* is the mask covering the personality that the person presents to the outside world. The persona may become fixed, so that the real person is hidden from himself or herself. *Anima* and *animus* are unconscious traits possessed by men and women, respectively, and are contrasted with the persona. Anima refers to a man's undeveloped femininity, whereas animus refers to a women's undeveloped masculinity.

The aim of Jungian treatment is to bring about an adequate adaptation to reality, which involves fulfilling one's creative potentialities. The ultimate goal is to achieve *individuation,* a process that continues throughout life in which persons develop a unique sense of their own identity. This developmental process may lead persons down new paths that may differ from their previous directions in life.

OTTO KERNBERG (b. 1928)

For Otto Kernberg, the object means the human object, who is social by nature. He has studied transference reactions extensively and has described several defense mechanisms responsible for rapid alterations of transference, particularly among disturbed patients. Among these defense mechanisms are splitting and projective identification. Splitting occurs from a contradictory state of mind, in which experience is organized according to "good" or "bad," which remains separated because of ego weakness. Kernberg's analytic treatment strives to address this splitting and contradictory state of mind to allow the patient to integrate split-off images to form a more unified version of the self and others. Projective identification is the attribution to another person of an introjected part of the self that is repressed. Persons who use this defense do not have a mature level of ego identity and are unable to form object relationships.

Kernberg proposed the term "borderline personality organization" for a broad spectrum of patients characterized by a lack of an integrated sense of identity, ego weakness, absence of superego integration, and primary process thinking. He suggested a special type of psychoanalytic psychotherapy for such patients in which transference issues are discussed with a greater emphasis on current reality than there is in traditional psychoanalysis.

SØREN KIERKEGAARD (1813–1855)

Søren Kierkegaard was one of the major developers of existentialism, a philosophical theory on which the teachings of such men as Martin Heidegger (1889–1976), Jean-Paul Sartre (1905–1980), and Martin Buber (1878–1965) are based. Existentialism questions methodologies that view persons as objects or theories that explain behavior on the basis of responses to stimuli. It goes beyond observable behavior and questions the purpose and nature of existence itself. Existentialism deals with what it means to be human and, in doing so, denies entirely the question of heredity versus environment as behavioral determinants. Instead, it deals with the issue of *existential anxiety,* which is one's awareness of being and nonbeing, the latter suggesting an awareness of one's own death. To compensate for that knowledge, one must strive for *authenticity,* the ability to live one's life with dignity and self-respect. Buber made a distinction between *I-thou* and *I-it* relationships; the former is authentic in that it is subjective, whereas the latter is inauthentic because it is detached.

Existentialism has not evolved into a clear-cut therapeutic approach; however, it has influenced therapists to explore what is experienced by patients and in what manner mental phenomena present themselves to consciousness—a school known as *phenomenology*.

MELANIE KLEIN (1882–1960)

Although still close to traditional psychoanalysis, Melanie Klein modified psychoanalytic theory and techniques in various ways, particularly in its application to infants and very young children. The libido is experienced at birth as pleasurable contacts with gratifying objects, primarily the good breast. Gratifying experiences reinforce basic trust, but, if experience is frustrating—especially in the first year of life—the person develops a paranoid-schizoid position characterized by isolation and persecutory fears. Oedipal strivings are experienced during the first year of life, and a longing for the good breast is displaced onto a longing for the father's penis by both sexes. Klein stressed that envy of the opposite sex occurs in both sexes; she assumed that the infant possesses an inborn knowledge of the genitals. *Splitting,* a major defense mechanism used in development, occurs when good and bad objects exist with a splitting of love and aggression between them. In the first year of life, a primitive superego exists, and, if too severe, it may lead to a depressive position later in life. Klein developed an analytical play technique with children in which play was treated in a symbolic fashion, much as dreams are used in adult therapy.

HEINZ KOHUT (1913–1981)

Heinz Kohut, an important innovator in psychoanalysis, expanded Freud's concept of narcissism. Originally, the infant's energies are devoted entirely to the satisfaction of his or her own needs and well-being, a state known as *primary,* or *primitive,* narcissism. Primary narcissism can be divided into two basic archaic configurations—the grandiose self and the idealized parent image. Eventually, narcissism must be modified to accommodate frustration and disappointment; otherwise, people remain unable to relate to others unless those relationships serve to gratify narcissistic needs.

Initially, the infant develops an idealized self-image in which it fuses with the object; eventually, a separate line of development must occur if a mature identity is to emerge. Otherwise, the person retains an unhealthy narcissistic orientation. Kohut used the term *mirroring* to refer to the mother's empathic response to the infant by which she gratifies healthy narcissistic needs. Overindulgence causes a retention of primary narcissism and leads to the development of the narcissistic personality disorder, characterized by grandiosity, egocentric behavior, and the inability to empathize with others. In the technique of *mirroring the transference,* the therapist reflects back to the patient the irrational aspects of the therapeutic relationship.

Kohut's theories are known as *self-psychology,* and the therapeutic process requires that patients become aware of their excessive needs for approval and self-gratification.

JACQUES LACAN (1901–1981)

Born in Paris and trained as a psychiatrist, Jacques Lacan founded his own institute, the Freudian School of Paris. He attempted to integrate the intrapsychic concepts of Freud with concepts related to linguistics and semiotics, the latter being the study of language and symbols. Whereas Freud saw the unconscious as a seething cauldron of needs, wishes, and instincts, Lacan saw it as a sort of language that helps to structure the world. Two of his principal concepts are that the unconscious is structured like a language and that the unconscious is a discourse. Primary process thoughts are actually uncontrolled free-flowing sequences of meaning. Symptoms are signs or symbols of underlying processes. The role of the therapist is to interpret the semiotic text of the personality structure. Lacan's most basic phase is the mirror stage; it is here that infants learn to recognize themselves by taking the perspective of others. In this sense, the ego is not a part of the self but something outside of and viewed by the self. The ego comes to represent parents and society, more than it represents the actual self of the person.

Lacan's therapeutic approach involves the need to become less alienated from the self and more involved with others. Relationships are often fantasized, which distorts reality and which must be corrected. Among his most controversial beliefs was that the resistance to understanding the real relationship can be reduced by shortening the length of the therapy session and that psychoanalytic sessions need be standardized not to time but, rather, to content and process.

KURT LEWIN (1890–1947)

Kurt Lewin received his Ph.D. in Berlin. In the 1930s Lewin came to the United States and taught at Cornell, Harvard, and the Massachusetts Institute of Technology (MIT). He adapted the field approach from physics into a concept called *field theory.* A field is the totality of coexisting parts that are mutually interdependent. Behavior becomes a function of the person and his or her environment, which together make up the *life space.* The life space represents a field in constant flux that has *valences* or needs that require satisfaction. A hungry person is more aware of restaurants than someone who has just eaten, and a person who wants to mail a letter is aware of mailboxes.

Lewin applied field theory to groups. *Group dynamics* refers to the interaction among members of a group, each of whom is dependent on the others. The group is capable of exerting pressure on a person to change behavior, but the person also influences the group when change occurs.

ABRAHAM MASLOW (1908–1970)

Abraham Maslow was born in Brooklyn, New York, and completed both his undergraduate and graduate work at the University of Wisconsin. Maslow, along with Kurt Goldstein, believed in the self-actualization theory—the need to understand the totality of a person. He was also a major worker in the field of humanism.

A hierarchical organization of needs is present in each person. Among the most powerful of these needs are survival-oriented needs, such as hunger and thirst. As they are fulfilled, other less powerful needs (e.g., needs for shelter, affection, and self-esteem) become effective motivators in their turn. Self-actualization is the highest need.

A *peak experience,* frequently occurring to self-actualizers, is an episodic, brief occurrence in which a person suddenly experiences a powerful transcendental state of consciousness. During this state, a person experiences a sense of heightened understanding, an intense euphoria, an integrated nature and unity with the universe, and an altered perception of time and space. This powerful experience tends to occur most often in the psychologically healthy and may produce long-lasting beneficial effects.

ADOLPH MEYER (1866–1950)

Adolph Meyer came to the United States from Switzerland in 1892 and eventually become director of the psychiatric Henry Phipps Clinic of Johns Hopkins Medical School. Although he did not entirely reject Freud's theoretical emphasis of mental functioning, Meyer preferred to examine the verifiable and objective aspects of a person's life. His theory of *psychobiology* explained disordered behavior as reactions to genetic, physical, psychological, environmental, and social stresses. Meyer introduced the concept of *common sense psychiatry,* focusing on ways in which the patient's current life situation can be realistically improved. He coined the concept of *ergasia,* which stands for the action of the total organism. The goal of therapy is to aid patients' adjustment by helping them modify unhealthy adaptations. One of Meyer's tools was an autobiographical life chart constructed by the patient during therapy.

GARDNER MURPHY (1895–1979)

Gardner Murphy was born in Ohio and received his Ph.D. at Columbia University. He was among the first to publish a comprehensive history of psychology and made major contributions to social, general, and educational psychology.

According to Murphy, three essential stages of personality development are (1) the stage of undifferentiated wholeness, (2) the stage of differentiation, and (3) the stage of integration. This development is frequently uneven, with the occurrence of both regression and progression along the way.

There are four inborn human needs: visceral, motor, sensory, and emergency-related. These needs become increasingly specific in time as they are molded by a person's experiences in various social and environmental contexts. *Canalization* brings about those changes by establishing a connection between a need and a specific way of satisfying that need.

Murphy was interested in parapsychology. Certain phenomena, such as clairvoyance and mental telepathy, may be more normal than paranormal. States such as sleep, drowsiness, certain drug and toxic conditions, hypnosis, and delirium tend to be favorable to paranormal experiences. Impediments to paranormal awareness include various intrapsychic barriers, conditions in the general social environment, and a heavy investment in the ordinary types of sensory experience.

HENRY MURRAY (1893–1988)

Henry Murray was born in New York City, attended medical school there, and was a founder of the Boston Psychoanalytic Institute. He proposed the term *personology* to describe the study of human behavior. He focused on motivation, which is a need that is aroused by internal or external stimulation; once aroused, it produces continued activity until it is reduced or satisfied. He developed the *Thematic Apperception Test* (TAT), a projective technique used to reveal both unconscious and conscious mental processes and problem areas.

FREDERICK S. PERLS (1893–1970)

Gestalt theory developed in Germany under the influence of several men: Max Westheimer (1880–1943), Wolfgang Kohler (1887–1967), and Kurt Lewin (1890–1947).

Frederick "Fritz" Perls applied Gestalt theory to a type of therapy that emphasizes the current experiences of the patient in the here and now, as contrasted to the there and then of the psychoanalytic schools. In terms of motivation, the patients learn to recognize what their needs are at any given time and how the drive to satisfy those needs may influence their current behavior. According to the Gestalt point of view, behavior represents more than the sum of its parts. A *gestalt,* or a whole, both includes and goes beyond the sum of smaller, independent events. It deals with essential characteristics of actual experience, such as value, meaning, and form.

SANDOR RADO (1890–1972)

Sandor Rado came to the United States from Hungary in 1945 and founded the Columbia Psychoanalytic Institute in New York. His theories of *adaptational dynamics* hold that the organism is a biological system operating under hedonic control, which is somewhat similar to Freud's pleasure principle. Cultural factors often cause excessive hedonic control and disordered behavior by interfering with the organism's ability for *self-regulation.* In therapy, the patient needs to relearn how to experience pleasurable feelings.

OTTO RANK (1884–1939)

In his 1924 publication, *The Trauma of the Birth,* Otto Rank broke with Freud and developed a new theory, which he called *birth trauma.* Anxiety is correlated with separation from the mother—specifically, with separation from the womb, the source of effortless gratification. This painful experience results in *primal anxiety.* Sleep and dreams symbolize the return to the womb.

The personality is divided into impulses, emotions, and will. The child's impulses seek immediate discharge and gratification. As impulses are mastered, as in toilet training, the child begins the process of will development. If will is carried too far, pathological traits—such as stubbornness, disobedience, and inhibitions—may develop.

WILHELM REICH (1897–1957)

Wilhelm Reich's major contributions to psychoanalysis were in the area of character formation and character types. *Character armor* is a term that refers to the defenses built up by the personality that serve as a resistance to self-understanding and change. There are four major character types: (1) The *hysterical character* is sexually seductive, anxious, and fixated at the phallic phase of libido development. (2) The *compulsive character* is controlled, distrustful, indecisive, and fixated at the anal phase. (3) The *narcissistic character* is confident, arrogant, aggressive, and fixated at the phallic stage of development; if male, there is a contempt for women. (4) The *masochistic character* is long-suffering, complaining, and self-deprecatory, with an excessive demand for love.

The therapeutic process—called *will therapy*—emphasizes the relationship between patient and therapist; the goal of treatment is to help patients accept their separateness. A definite date is used for termination of therapy to protect against excessive dependence on the therapist.

CARL ROGERS (1902–1987)

Carl Rogers received a Ph.D. in psychology at Columbia University. After attending Union Theological Seminary in New York, Rogers studied for the ministry. His name is most clearly associated with the *person-centered theory* of personality and psychotherapy. In this view major emphasis rests on the concepts of self-actualization and self-direction. Specifically, people are born with a capacity to direct themselves in the healthiest way, toward a level of completeness called *self-actualization.* From his person-centered approach, Rogers viewed personality not as a static entity composed of traits and patterns but as a dynamic phenomenon involving ever-changing communications, relationships, and self-concepts.

Rogers developed a treatment program called *client-centered psychotherapy*. The therapist attempts to produce an atmosphere in which clients can reconstruct their strivings for self-actualization. The therapist holds the client in *unconditional positive regard,* which is the total nonjudgmental acceptance of clients as they are. Other therapeutic practices include attention to the present, focus on the feelings of the client, emphasis on process, trust in the potential and self-responsibility of the client, and a philosophy grounded in a positive attitude toward others, rather than a preconceived structure of treatment.

B. F. SKINNER (1904–1990)

B. F. Skinner received his Ph.D. in psychology from Harvard University, where he taught for many years. It was Skinner's seminal work in *operant learning* that laid much of the groundwork for many of the current methods of behavior modification, programmed instruction, and general education. His global beliefs about the nature of behavior have been applied more widely, it can be argued, than those of any other theorist except, perhaps, Freud. His impact has been impressive in scope and magnitude.

Skinner's approach to personality was more a derivation of his basic beliefs about behavior than a specific theory of personality per se. To Skinner, personality was not different from other behaviors or sets of behaviors; it is acquired, maintained, and strengthened or weakened according to the same rules of reward and punishment that alter any other form of behavior. *Behaviorism,* as Skinner's basic theory is most commonly known, is concerned only with observable, measurable, and operationalizable behavior. Many of the abstract and mentalistic hallmarks of other dominant personality theories have little place in Skinner's framework: concepts such as self, ideas, and ego are considered unnecessary for the understanding of behavior and are shunned. There is no mind as such, only a learning brain affected by stimuli in the internal and external environment. Through the process of operant conditioning and the application of basic principles of learning, people are believed to develop sets of behavior that characterize their responses to the world of stimuli that they face in their lives. This set of responses is called personality.

HARRY STACK SULLIVAN (1892–1949)

Harry Stack Sullivan received his training in psychiatry in the 1930s, during the early years of Freud's profound influence on American psychiatry; but, like Adolf Meyer, under whom he studied, Sullivan insisted on formulating his concepts on observable data.

There are three modes of experiencing and thinking about the world: (1) The *prototaxic mode* is undifferentiated thought that is unable to separate the whole into parts or to use symbols. It occurs normally in infancy and is also seen in patients with schizophrenia. (2) The *parataxic mode* sees events as causally related because of temporal or serial connections. Logical relationships, however, are not perceived. (3) The *syntaxic mode* is the logical, rational, and most mature type of cognitive functioning of which a person is capable. These three types of thinking and experiencing occur side by side in all persons; it is the rare person who functions in the syntaxic mode exclusively.

The total configuration of personality traits is known as the *self-system,* which develops in various stages and is the outgrowth of interpersonal experiences, rather than the unfolding of intrapsychic forces. During *infancy*, anxiety occurs for the first time as a result of the infant's failure to achieve satisfaction of his or her primary needs. During *childhood,* from age 2 to 5 years, the child's main tasks are to become educated as to the requirements of the culture and to learn how to deal with powerful adults. As a *juvenile,* ranging from 5 to 8 years, the child has a need for and must learn how to deal with peers. In *preadolescence,* ranging from 8 to 12 years, the development of the capacity for love and collaboration with another person of the same sex develops. This so-called chum period is the prototype for a sense of intimacy; in the history of schizophrenic patients, this experience of chums is often missing. During *adolescence,* major tasks include the separation from one's family, the development of standards and values, and the transition to heterosexuality.

The process of therapy requires the active participation of the therapist, who is known as a *participant observer.* Modes of experience, particularly the parataxic, need to be clarified, and new patterns of behavior need to be implemented. Ultimately, persons need to see themselves as they really are, instead of what they think they are or what they want others to think they are.

References

Adler A: *The Individual Psychology of Alfred Adler: A Systematic Presentation in Selections from His Writings,* H L Ansbacher and R R Ansbacher, editors. Basic Books, New York, 1956.

Baker H S, Baker M N: Heinz Kohot's self psychology: An overview. Am J Psychiatry *144:* 1, 1987.

Blum G S: *Psychodynamics: The Science of Unconscious Mental Forces,* Brooks/Cole, Belmont, CA, 1966.

Bromberg W: *The Mind of Man.* Harper, New York, 1959.

Duke M P, Nowicki S Jr: Theories of personality and psychopathology: Approaches derived from psychology and philosophy. In *Comprehensive Textbook of Psychiatry,* ed 5, H I Kaplan and B J Sadock, editors, p 432. Williams & Wilkins, Baltimore, 1989.

Harris R J: Lacan and Klein: Towards a dialogue. J Melanie Klein Soc *6:* 58, 1988.

Horney K: *The Neurotic Personality of Our Time.* Norton, New York, 1937

Jung C G: *Memories, Dreams, Reflections.* Random House, New York, 1961.

Lawrence L: The covert seduction theory: Filling the gap between the seduction theory and the Oedipus complex. Am J Psychoanal *48:* 247, 1988.

Millon T: *Theories of Psychopathology* (part 2). Saunders, Philadelphia. 1967.

Munroe R L: *Schools of Psychoanalytic Thought: An Exposition, Critique, and Attempt at Integration.* Dryden, New York, 1955.

Perry H S: *Psychiatrist of America: The Life of Harry Stack Sullivan*. Belknap Press, Harvard University Press, Cambridge, MA, 1982.

Segal H: *Melanie Klein*. Viking Press, New York, 1980.

Smith S: *Ideas of the Great Psychologists*. Harper & Row, Philadelphia, 1983.

Weiner M F: Theories of personality and psychopathology: Other psychodynamic schools. In *Comprehensive Textbook of Psychiatry*, ed 5, H I Kaplan and B J Sadock, editors, p 411. Williams & Wilkins, Baltimore, 1989.

Wyss D: *Psychoanalytic Schools: From the Beginning to the Present*. Jason Aronson, New York, 1973.

Clinical Examination of the Psychiatric Patient

7.1 / Psychiatric Interview, History, and Mental Status Examination

PSYCHIATRIC INTERVIEW

A psychiatric interview is a purposeful encounter between physician and patient. The purposes are many, but they can be subsumed under two major headings: gathering necessary information to assess the patient's condition and establishing a therapeutic doctor-patient relationship.

In the psychiatric interview the patient usually reveals intimate, private, and potentially painful aspects of his or her life to the doctor. Patients may be highly motivated to reveal themselves in order to gain relief from suffering; but they may also be both consciously and unconsciously motivated to conceal innermost feelings that they perceive to be shameful or threatening. Patients may be unwilling to disclose such material until they feel certain that they will not jeopardize their doctor's respect. The psychiatric interview may also be complicated by the fact that not all psychiatric patients have voluntarily sought the doctor's help (e.g., they may have been taken to the doctor by police or family members), and their willingness or ability to cooperate may be impaired for this reason. The psychiatrist's relationship with the patient strongly influences what the patient does and does not say; therefore, a large portion of a psychiatrist's training involves the specific and sophisticated techniques of listening, observation, and interpretation that are necessary to make an accurate diagnosis and to provide effective treatment.

Management of Time

The initial consultation lasts for 30 minutes to one hour, depending on the circumstances. Interviews with psychotic or medically ill patients are brief because the patient may find the interview stressful. Longer interviews may be required in the emergency room. Second visits and ongoing therapeutic interviews also vary in length. The American Board of Psychiatry and Neurology in its clinical oral examination in psychiatry allows 30 minutes for a psychiatric examination.

Patients' management of appointment times reveals important aspects of personality and coping. Most often, patients arrive a few minutes before their appointments. An anxious patient may arrive as much as a half hour early. If the patient arrives very early, the doctor may want to explore the reasons. The patient who arrives significantly late for an appointment poses another set of potential questions. The first time it occurs, the interviewer may listen to the explanation offered and respond sympathetically if the lateness is due to circumstances beyond the patient's control. If the patient states, "I forgot all about the appointment," this is a clue that something about going to the doctor is making the patient anxious or uncomfortable, and that needs to be explored further. The psychiatrist may ask directly, "Did you feel reluctant to come in today?" If the answer is, "Yes," the doctor can begin to explore the possible reasons for the patient's reluctance. If the answer is, "No," it is probably best to drop the direct questioning about the lateness and just listen to the patient. By listening carefully, the psychiatrist can usually detect themes that the patient may not be aware of. Those themes can then be explored by both the patient and the doctor in an attempt to understand better what the patient is experiencing.

The psychiatrist's handling of time is also an important factor in the interview. Carelessness regarding time indicates a lack of concern for the patient. If the psychiatrist is unavoidably detained for an interview, it is appropriate to express regret to have kept the patient waiting.

Seating Arrangements

The way chairs are arranged in the doctor's office affects the interview. Both chairs should be of approximately equal heights so that neither person looks down on the other. Most psychiatrists think that it is desirable to place the chairs without any furniture between the doctor and the patient. If the room contains several chairs, the doctor indicates his or her own chair and then allows the patient to choose the chair in which he or she will feel most comfortable.

Doctor's Office

A psychiatrist can never remain entirely unknown to the patient. The physician's office can tell the patient a good deal about the personality of the doctor. The color of the office, paintings and diplomas on the wall, furniture, plants, books, and personal photographs—all describe the doctor in ways that are not directly verbalized. Patients often have reactions to their doctors' offices that may or may not be distortions, and carefully listening to any comments can help the doctor better understand patients. Studies have shown that patients respond more positively to male physicians who wear jackets and ties than to those who do not. No studies have been done on the dress of female physicians, but by extrapolation, a positive response would probably be elicited by professional attire.

Note Taking

For legal and medical reasons an adequate written record of each patient's treatment must be maintained. The patient's record also aids the psychiatrist's memory. Each interviewer must establish a system of record keeping and decide which information to record. Many psychiatrists make fairly complete notes during the first few sessions while eliciting historical data. After this time most psychiatrists record only new historical information, important events in the patient's life, medications prescribed, dreams, and general comments about the patient's progress. Some psychiatrists maintain detailed process notes (verbatim record of a session) on specific patients, writing out immediately after a session as much of the session as they can remember. Process notes make it much easier to determine trends in the treatment (with regard to transference and countertransference issues) and to go back over the session to pick up ideas that may have been missed. Process notes are also helpful if the psychiatrist is working with a supervisor or consultant who needs an accurate presentation of a particular session.

Most psychiatrists do not recommend taking extensive notes during a session, as writing can cut down on the ability to listen. Some patients, however, may express resentment if the psychiatrist does not write notes during an interview; they may fear that their comments were not important enough to record or that the psychiatrist was not interested in them. Since, presumably, not taking notes during a session has no relationship to the doctor's actual listening, this type of feeling on a patient's part can be further explored in order to understand better the fear of not being taken seriously.

Subsequent Interviews

Interviews subsequent to the initial one allow the patient to correct any misinformation provided in the first meeting. It is often helpful to start the second interview by asking the patient whether he or she has thought about the first interview and for any reactions to that experience. Another variation of this technique is to say, "Frequently, people think of additional things they wanted to discuss after they leave. What thoughts have you had?"

Psychiatrists often learn something of value when they ask patients if they have discussed the interview with anyone else. If the patient has done so, the details of that conversation and with whom the patient spoke are enlightening. There are no set rules concerning which topics are best deferred until the second interview. In general, as patients' comfort and familiarity with the doctor increase, they become more able to reveal the intimate details of their lives.

Specific Interviewing Situations: Differences Linked to Diagnosis

The manner in which an interview is conducted—the specific techniques and structure—vary depending on the setting in which the interview takes place, the interview's purpose, and the particular patient's strengths, weaknesses, and diagnosis. Psychiatrists are trained to be flexible in modifying their interview style to fit the existing situation. Patients who carry different psychiatric diagnoses differ in their capacities to participate in an interview and differ in the challenges they present to the interviewing doctor. Certain consistent themes are often observed in interviews with patients who have the same diagnosis, although it is important to remember that, even with the same diagnosis, patients may require subtly different interview strategies.

Depressed and potentially suicidal patient. Depressed patients are often unable to provide spontaneously an adequate account of their illness because of such factors as psychomotor retardation and hopelessness. The doctor must be prepared to ask a depressed person very specifically about history and symptoms related to depression, including questions about suicidal ideation, which the patient may not initially volunteer. Another reason for being specific in questioning a depressed patient is that the patient may not realize that such symptoms as waking during the night or increased somatic complaints are related to depressive disorders.

One of the most difficult aspects of dealing with depressed patients is experiencing their hopelessness. Many severely depressed patients believe that their current feeling will continue indefinitely and that there is no hope. The psychiatrist must be careful not to reassure such patients prematurely that everything is going to be fine, as the patients most likely will experience this as an indication that the psychiatrist does not understand the degree of pain that they are feeling. A reasonable approach is for the doctor to indicate that he or she is aware how bad patients are feeling, that help is certainly possible, and that it is understandable at this point for patients not to believe that they can be helped. Furthermore, the doctor must also make it clear that he or she is committed to helping patients feel better, that all specific and effective pharmacological and psychological tools will be used, and that patients will not be abandoned during what may be a somewhat lengthy period of recovery. Up to this point, everything patients have done to relieve their distress has not worked, and, by the time the psychiatrist interviews them, they may be desperate. It can be a relief to depressed patients when the psychiatrist truthfully tells them that their depression can be treated but that it may take a little work and time for the psychiatrist to find the method that will most effectively treat their specific depressive disorder. This message conveys not a false sense of reassurance, which could make depressed patients feel even more depressed, but a sense that the doctor is committed to understanding who this particular patient is and what treatment will work most quickly and effectively for him or her. Every depressed person wishes, consciously or unconsciously, that the psychiatrist will magically and immediately produce a cure, but most people are willing to proceed along a therapeutic path, even when a part of them believes there is no hope. The interviewing psychiatrist must be careful not to make promises about specific treatments' being the answer. If those treatments turn out not to work for the patient, the disappointment may eliminate the patient's last hope.

Suicide. Of special concern when interviewing depressed patients is the potential for suicide. Being mindful of the possibility of suicide is imperative when interviewing any depressed patient, even if there is no apparent suicidal risk. The interviewer must inquire in some detail about the presence of suicidal thoughts. The psychiatrist should ask specifically, "Are you suicidal now, or do you have plans to take your own life?" A suicide note, a family history of suicide, or previous suicidal behavior on the part of the patient increases the risk for suicide. Evidence of impulsivity or of pervasive pessimism about the future also places patients at risk. If the psychiatrist decides that the patient is in imminent risk for suicidal behavior, the patient must be hospitalized or otherwise protected. A more difficult situation arises when there does not seem to be an immediate risk but the potential for suicide is present as long as the patient remains depressed. If the decision is made not to hospitalize the patient immediately, the doctor should insist that the patient promise to call at any time suicidal pressure mounts. It is common in such situations for the patient to have a crisis after midnight and to call the doctor, who should assure the patient that he or she is reachable at all times. Having determined that the doctor is, in fact, available, the patient is often reassured and can thus better control the impulses and utilize regularly scheduled sessions for exploration of the suicidal feelings.

Violent patient. Potentially violent patients should be approached with some of the same attitudes and techniques used with suicidal patients. For example, indicating that one is capable of dealing with the patient's capacity for violence is important. It conveys that one is accustomed to the unpleasant, as well as the pleasant, in life and that part of one's job is to help the patient stay in control and to make sure that neither the patient nor anyone else is going to get hurt.

Frequently, the psychiatrist encounters a violent patient in the hospital setting. For example, when the police bring a patient into the emergency room, the patient is often in some type of physical restraint (e.g., handcuffs). The psychiatrist must establish whether effective verbal contact can be made with the patient or whether the patient's sense of reality is so impaired that effective interviewing is impossible. If impaired reality testing is an issue, it may be necessary to medicate the patient before any attempts at interviewing can begin. If reality testing is not severely impaired, however, one of the first questions to be addressed is whether it is safe to remove the physical restraints from the patient. This question can be addressed in a straightforward manner, expressing concern for the safety of the patient and other persons in the surrounding area. Many psychiatrists may opt to leave restraints on the patient until at least some history has been obtained and some rapport established. Should a decision be made to undo the restraints, the psychiatrist must carefully monitor what is happening to the patient as the restraints are loosened. If the patient remains calm and seems to be relieved, the process of removing the restraints can continue. If the patient does or says anything that indicates that the removal of restraints is leading to increased agitation, the decision to remove them should be reassessed immediately.

With or without restraints, the interview of a violent patient should not be done alone; there should always be at least one other person present, and in some situations this other person should be a security guard or a police officer. Other precautions include leaving the interview room's door open and sitting between the patient and the door, so that the interviewer has unrestricted access to an exit should it become necessary. The interviewer must make it clear, in a firm but nonangry manner, that the patient may say or feel anything but is not free to act in a violent way. This statement must be backed up by a unified, calm, consistent staff presence that the patient understands is there to lend support in efforts to maintain control, including the ability to subdue the patient physically if necessary.

Confrontation with a violent patient is to be assiduously avoided, as is any behavior that could be construed as demeaning or disrespectful of the patient. Within the limits of safety, the interviewer should respect as much as possible the patient's need for space.

Specific questions that need to be asked of violent patients include those pertaining to their previous acts of violence and to violence experienced as a child. The interviewer should determine under what specific conditions the patient resorts to violence, and corroboration as to critical aspects of the patient's history must be obtained from friends and family members. Table 7.1-1 summarizes the dos and don'ts of managing the violent patient.

Delusional patient. A patient's delusion should never be directly challenged. Delusions may be thought of as a patient's defensive and self-protective, albeit maladaptive, strategy against overwhelming anxiety, lowered self-esteem, and confusion. Challenging a delusion by insisting that it is not true or possible only increases the patient's anxiety and often leads the threatened patient to defend the belief ever more desperately. It is inadvisable, however, to pretend that one believes the patient's delusion. Often, the more helpful approach is to indicate that the interviewer understands that the patient believes the delusion to be true but that the interviewer does not hold the same belief. It is probably most productive to focus on the feelings, fears, and hopes that underlie the delusional belief to understand better what particular function the delusion holds for this patient. The more that patients feel the psychiatrist respects, understands, and listens to them, the more likely they are to talk about themselves, not about the delusion.

Interviewing relatives. Interviews with family members of a patient can be both valuable and fraught with difficulties. For example, a spouse may be so closely identified with the patient that anxiety overwhelms the ability to provide coherent information. Family members may not realize that certain kinds of information are best provided by an observer and that other kinds of information may be obtained only from the patient; for example, family members may be better able to describe the social activity of the patient, but only the patient can describe what he or she is thinking and feeling. It is crucial for the interviewer to be highly sensitive to discussions with family members; if these discussions are not properly handled by the interviewer, the relationship between the patient and the doctor may break down.

Interviews with family members can be viewed from a variety of perspectives. If one's goal is to diagnose a disease, then the more facts at one's disposal, the easier it will be to formulate a diagnosis, prognosis, and treatment. From the dynamic or analytical viewpoint, however, if one sees patients' problems as largely influenced by interactions with the important figures in their lives, then the external reality is somewhat less important than the patients' own perceptions. In general, the more acutely serious a patient's presenting situation (e.g., major depression, suicidal ideation, or psychosis), the more likely and perhaps the more appropriate it is for the interviewer to deal with family members.

Table 7.1-1
Dos and Don'ts of Treating Violent Patients

Do	Don't
Anticipate possible violence from hostile, threatening, agitated, restless, abusive patients or from those who lack control for any reason.	Don't ignore your gut feeling that a patient may be dangerous.
Heed your gut feeling. If you feel frightened or uneasy, discontinue the interview and get help.	Don't see angry, threatening, restless persons right away.
Summon as many security guards or orderlies as possible at the first sign of violence. Patients who see that you take them seriously often will not act out further. If they do, you will be prepared.	Don't compromise your ability to escape a dangerous situation. Don't sit behind a desk.
Ask if the patient is carrying a weapon. These must be surrendered to security personnel. Never see an armed patient.	Don't antagonize the patient by responding angrily or being patronizing.
Offer help, food, medication. Bolster the patient by commenting on his or her strength and self-control.	Don't touch or startle the patient or approach quickly without warning.
If restraint becomes necessary, assign one team member each to the patient's head and to each extremity. Be humane but firm, and do not bargain. Search the patient for drugs and weapons.	Don't try to restrain a patient without sufficient backup.
If the patient refuses oral medication, offer an injection after a few moments. Be prepared to administer it if the patient continues to refuse.	Don't neglect looking for organic causes of violence.
Keep a close eye on patients who are sedated or restrained. Restrained patients should never be left alone.	Don't bargain with a violent person about the need for restraints, medication, or psychiatric admission.
Hospitalize patients who state their intention to harm anyone, refuse to answer questions about their intent to harm, are abusing alcohol or drugs, are psychotic, have an organic mental syndrome, or refuse to cooperate with treatment.	Don't forget medicolegal concerns, such as full documentation of all interventions and the duty to warn and protect. If the patient is transferred, tell the admitting physician about any specific threats and victims.
Warn potential victims of threatened violence, and notify the appropriate protection agencies.	Don't overlook family and friends as important sources of information.
Follow up on any violent person, and document this in the chart.	

Table from B Dwyer, M Weissberg: Treating violent patients. *Psychiatric Times* p 11, December 1988, with permission.

One of the most important aspects related to talking with family members has to do with confidentiality. Ultimately, the physician must learn to elicit information and to offer hope to family members without revealing information concerning the patient that the patient does not want revealed. Betraying a confidence can make treatment of the patient impossible. If the issues concern acute suicidal or homicidal ideation, however, the patient must understand that this information cannot remain entirely confidential, for the protection of the patient and others.

PSYCHIATRIC HISTORY

The psychiatric history is the record of the patient's life that allows the psychiatrist to understand who the patient is, where the patient has come from, and where the patient is likely to go in the future. The history is the patient's life story told to the doctor in the patient's own words from his or her own point of view. Many times the history also includes information about the patient obtained from other sources, such as a parent or a spouse. Obtaining a careful and comprehensive history from a patient and, if necessary, from informed sources is essential to making a correct diagnosis and formulating a specific and effective treatment plan. The psychiatric history differs slightly from histories taken in medicine or surgery. In addition to gathering the concrete and factual data related to the chronology of symptom formation and to past psychiatric and medical history, the doctor strives to derive from the psychiatric history the more elusive picture of patients' individual personality characteristics, including both their strengths and their weaknesses. The psychiatric history provides insight into the nature of relationships with those closest to them and includes all the important people in their past and present lives. A reasonably comprehensive picture of the patients' development, from the earliest formative years until the present, can usually be elicited.

The most important technique in obtaining the psychiatric history is to allow patients to tell their own stories in their own words in the order that they feel is most important. Skillful interviewers recognize the points, as patients relate their stories, at which they can introduce relevant questions concerning the areas described in the outline of the history and mental status examination.

The structure presented in this section is not intended as a rigid plan for interviewing a patient; it is intended as a guide to organizing the patient's history when it is written up. There are a number of acceptable and standard formats for the psychiatric history. One such format is presented in Table 7.1-2.

Identifying Data

This information provides a succinct demographic summary of the patient by name, age, marital status, sex, occupation, language if other than English, ethnic back-

Table 7.1-2
Outline of Psychiatric History

I. Identifying data
II. Chief complaint
III. History of present illness
IV. Previous illnesses
   A. Psychiatric
   B. Medical
V. Past personal history (anamnesis)
   A. Prenatal and perinatal
   B. Early childhood (through age 3)
   C. Middle childhood (ages 3–11)
   D. Late childhood (puberty through adolescence)
   E. Adulthood
      1. Occupational history
      2. Marital and relationship history
      3. Military history
      4. Educational history
      5. Religion
      6. Social activity
      7. Current living situation
   F. Psychosexual history
   G. Family history
   H. Dreams, fantasies, and values

ground and religion insofar as they are pertinent, and current circumstances of living. The information can also include in what place or situation the current interview took place, the sources of this information, and whether this is the first episode of this type for the patient. The identifying data are meant to provide a thumbnail sketch of potentially important patient characteristics that may affect diagnosis, prognosis, treatment, and compliance.

An example of this part of the interview is as follows:

John Jones is a 25-year-old white single Catholic man, currently unemployed and homeless, living in public shelters and on the street. The current interview occurred in the emergency room (ER) with the patient in four-point restraints in the presence of two clinical staff members and one police officer. This was approximately the 10th such visit to the ER for Mr. Jones in the past year. The sources of information on Mr. Jones included the patient himself and the police officer who brought the patient to the ER.

Chief Complaint (CC)

The chief complaint, in the patient's own words, states why he or she has come or been brought in for help. It should be recorded even if the patient is unable to speak, and a description of the person who provided the information should be included. The patient's explanation, regardless of how bizarre or irrelevant it is, should be recorded verbatim in the section on the chief complaint. The others present as sources of information can then give their versions of the presenting events in the section on the history of the present illness.

Examples of chief complaints follow:

"I was feeling very depressed and thinking about killing myself." "Every car outside my house has a license plate number that is sending me hidden messages concerning a plot to kill the president." "There's nothing wrong with me; it's her that's crazy."

History of Present Illness (HPI)

This part of the psychiatric history provides a comprehensive and chronological picture of the events leading up to the current moment in the patient's life. An understanding of the history of the present illness helps answer the question, "Why now?" Why did the patient come to the doctor at this time? What immediate precipitating events triggered the current episode? What were the patient's life circumstances at the onset of the symptoms or behavioral changes, and how did they affect the patient so that the presenting illness became manifest? Knowing what the personality was of the previously well patient also helps give perspective on the currently ill patient. What less immediate precipitating events were part of the chain leading up to the more immediate ones? In what ways has the patient's illness affected his or her life activities (e.g., work, important relationships)? What is the nature of the dysfunction (e.g., details about changes in such factors as personality, memory, speech)? Are there psychophysiological symptoms? If so, they should be described in terms of location, intensity, and fluctuation. If there is a relationship between physical and psychological symptoms, it should be noted. Evidence of secondary gain—the extent to which illness serves some additional purpose—should also be noted. A description of the patient's current anxieties, whether they are generalized and nonspecific (free-floating) or are specifically related to particular situations, is helpful. How does the patient handle these anxieties? Frequently, a relatively open-ended question, such as, "How did this all begin?" leads to an adequate unfolding of the history of the present illness. A well-organized patient is generally able to present a chronological account of the history. However, a disorganized patient is more difficult to interview, as the chronology of events is less evident and more confused.

Previous Illnesses (Past Psychiatric and Medical History)

This section of the psychiatric history is a transition between the story of the present illness and the patient's past personal history (anamnesis). Past episodes of both psychiatric and medical illnesses are described. Ideally, at this point a detailed account of the patient's preexisting and underlying psychological and biological substrates is given, and important clues and evidence of vulnerable areas in the patient's functioning are provided. The patient's symptoms, extent of incapacity, type of treatment received, names of hospitals, length of each illness, effects of prior treatments, and degree of compliance should all be explored and recorded chronologically. Particular attention should be paid to the first episode that signaled the onset of illness, as first episodes can often provide crucial data about precipitating events, diagnostic possibilities, and coping capabilities.

With regard to past medical history, the physician should obtain a medical review of symptoms and note any major medical or surgical illness and major traumas, particularly those requiring hospitalization, experienced by the patient. Episodes of craniocerebral trauma, neurological illness, tumors, and seizure disorders are especially relevant to psychiatric histories and so is a history of having tested positive for the human immunodeficiency virus (HIV) or of having acquired immune deficiency syndrome (AIDS). Specific questions need to be asked about the presence of a seizure disorder, episodes of loss of consciousness, changes in usual headache patterns, changes in vision, and episodes of confusion and disorientation. A history of infection with syphilis is critical and relevant.

The cause, complications, and treatment of any illness and the effects of the illness on the patient should be noted. Specific questions about psychosomatic disorders should be asked and noted. Included in this category are hay fever, rheumatoid arthritis, ulcerative colitis, asthma, hyperthyroidism, gastrointestinal upsets, recurrent colds, and skin conditions. All patients must be asked about alcohol and drug use, including details about the quality and the frequency of use. It is often advisable to frame one's questions in the form of an assumption of use, such as, "How much alcohol would you say you drink in a day?" rather than "Do you drink?" The latter question may put the patient on the defensive, concerned about what the physician will think if the answer is yes. If the physician assumes that drinking is a fact, the patient may be more likely to feel comfortable admitting use.

Past Personal History (Anamnesis)

In addition to studying the patient's present illness and current life situation, the psychiatrist needs a thorough understanding of the patient's past life and its relationship to the present emotional problem. The anamnesis or past personal history is usually divided into the major developmental periods of prenatal and perinatal, early childhood, middle childhood, late childhood, and adulthood. The predominant emotions associated with the different life periods (e.g., painful, stressful, conflictual) should be noted. Depending on time and situation, the psychiatrist may go into more or less detail with regard to each of these areas.

Prenatal and perinatal history. The psychiatrist considers the nature of the home situation into which the patient was born and whether the patient was planned and wanted. Were there any problems with the mother's pregnancy and delivery? Was there any evidence of defect or injury at birth? What was the mother's emotional and physical state at the time of the patient's birth? Were there any maternal health problems during pregnancy? Was the mother abusing alcohol or drugs during her pregnancy?

Early childhood (birth through age 3 years). The early childhood period consists of the first three years of the patient's life. The quality of the mother-child interaction during feeding and toilet training is important. It is frequently possible to learn whether the child presented problems in these areas. Early disturbances in sleep patterns and signs of unmet needs, such as head banging and body rocking, provide clues about possible maternal deprivation. In addition, it is important to obtain a history of human constancy during the first three years. Was there psychiatric or medical illness present in the parents that may have interfered with parent-child interactions? Did persons other than the mother care for the patient? Did the patient exhibit excessive problems at an early period with stranger anxiety or separation anxiety? The patient's siblings and the details of his or her relationship to them should be explored. The emerging personality of the child is also a topic of crucial importance. Was the child shy, restless, overactive, withdrawn, studious, outgoing, timid, athletic, friendly? The clinician should seek data concerning the child's increasing ability to concentrate, to tolerate frustration, and to postpone gratification. The child's preference for active or passive roles in physical play should also be noted. What were the child's favorite games or toys? Did the child prefer to play alone, with others, or not at all? What is the patient's earliest memory? Were there any recurrent dreams or fantasies during this period? A summary of the important areas to be covered in this age group follows:

Feeding habits. Breast-fed or bottle-fed, eating problems

Early development. Walking, talking, teething, language development, motor development, signs of unmet needs, sleep pattern, object constancy, stranger anxiety, maternal deprivation, separation anxiety, other caretakers in the home

Toilet training. Age, attitude of parents, feelings about it

Symptoms of behavior problems. Thumb sucking, temper tantrums, tics, head bumping, rocking, night terrors, fears, bed wetting or bed soiling, nail biting, excessive masturbation

Personality as a child. Shy, restless, overactive, withdrawn, persistent, outgoing, timid, athletic, friendly; patterns of play

Early or recurrent dreams or fantasies.

Middle childhood (ages 3 to 11 years). In this section the psychiatrist can address such important subjects as gender identification, punishments used in the home, and who provided the discipline and influenced early conscience formation. The psychiatrist must inquire about the patient's early school experiences, especially how the patient first tolerated being separated from his or her mother. Data about the patient's earliest friendships and personal relations are valuable. The psychiatrist should identify and define the number and closeness of the patient's friends, describe whether the patient took the role of a leader or a follower, and describe the patient's social popularity and participation in group or gang activities. Was the child able to cooperate with peers, to be fair, to understand and comply with rules, and to develop an early conscience? Early patterns of assertion, impulsiveness, aggression, passivity, anxiety, or antisocial behavior emerge in the context of school relationships. A history of the patient's learning to read and the development of other intellectual and motor skills are important. A history of learning disabilities, their management, and their impact on the child are of particular significance. The presence of nightmares, phobias, bed wetting, fire setting, cruelty to animals, and excessive masturbation should also be explored.

Late childhood (prepuberty through adolescence). During late childhood, people begin to develop independence from their parents through relationships with peers and in group activities. The psychiatrist should attempt to define the values of the patient's social groups and determine who were the patient's idealized figures. This information provides useful clues concerning the patient's emerging idealized self-image.

Further exploration is indicated of the patient's school history, relationships with teachers, and favorite studies and interests, both in school and in the extracurricular area. The psychiatrist should ask about the patient's participation in sports and hobbies and inquire about any emotional or physical problems that may have first appeared during this phase. Examples of the types of questions that are commonly asked include the following: What was the patient's sense of personal identity? How extensive was the use of alcohol and drugs? Was the patient sexually active, and what was the quality of the sexual relationships? Was the patient interactive and involved with school and peers, or was he or she isolated, withdrawn, perceived as odd by others? Did the patient have a generally intact sense of self-esteem, or was there evidence of excessive self-loathing? What was the patient's body image? Were there suicidal episodes? Were there problems in school, including excessive truancy? How did the patient use private time? What was the relationship with the parents? What were the feelings about the development of secondary sex characteristics? What was the response to menarche? What were the attitudes about dating, petting, crushes, parties, and sex games? One way to organize this diverse and large amount of information is to break late childhood into different subsets of behavior (e.g., social relationships, school history, cognitive and motor development, emotional and physical problems, and sexuality), as described below.

Social relationships. Attitudes toward sibling(s) and playmates, number and closeness of friends, leader or follower, social popularity, participation in group or gang activities, idealized figures, patterns of aggression, passivity, anxiety, antisocial behavior

School history. How far the patient progressed, adjustment to school, relationships with teachers—teacher's pet versus rebel—favorite studies or interests, particular abilities or assets, extracurricular activities, sports, hobbies, relationships of problems or symptoms to any social period

Cognitive and motor development. Learning to read and other intellectual and motor skills, minimal cerebral dysfunctions, learning disabilities—their management and effects on the child

Adolescent emotional or physical problems. Nightmares, phobias, masturbation, bed wetting, running away, delinquency, smoking, drug or alcohol use, anorexia, bulimia, weight problems, feelings of inferiority

Sexuality

a. Early curiosity, infantile masturbation, sex play
b. Acquisition of sexual knowledge, attitude of parents toward sex, sexual abuse
c. Onset of puberty, feelings about it, kind of preparation, feelings about menstruation, development of secondary sexual characteristics
d. Adolescent sexual activity: crushes, parties, dating, petting, masturbation, nocturnal emissions and attitudes toward them
e. Attitudes toward opposite sex: timid, shy, aggressive, need to impress, seductive, sexual conquests, anxiety
f. Sexual practices: sexual problems, paraphilias, promiscuity, sexual orientation, homosexual experiences in both heterosexual and homosexual adolescents

Adulthood

Occupational history. The psychiatrist should describe the patient's choice of occupation, the requisite training and preparation, any work-related conflicts, and the long-term ambitions and goals. The interviewer should also explore the patient's feelings about his or her current job and relationships at work (with authorities, peers, and, if applicable, subordinates) and describe the job history (e.g., number and duration of jobs, reasons for job changes, and changes in job status). What would the patient do for work if he or she could freely choose?

Marital and relationship history. In this section the interviewer describes the history of each marriage, legal or common law. Significant relationships with persons with whom the patient has lived for a protracted period of time are also included. The story of the marriage or long-term relationship should give a description of the evolution of the relationship, including the age of the patient at the beginning of the marriage or the long-term relationship. The areas of agreement and disagreement—including the management of money, housing difficulties, the roles of the in-laws, and attitudes toward raising children—should be described. Other questions include: Is the patient currently in a long-term relationship? How long is the longest relationship that the patient has had? What is the quality of the patient's sexual relationship (e.g., is the patient's sexual life experienced as satisfactory or inadequate)? What does the patient look for in a partner? Is the patient able to initiate a relationship or to approach someone he or she feels attracted to or compatible with? How does the patient describe the current relationship in terms of its positive and negative qualities? How does the patient perceive failures of past relationships in terms of understanding what went wrong and who was or was not to blame?

Military history. The psychiatrist should inquire about patients' general adjustment to the military, whether they saw combat or sustained an injury, and the nature of their discharge. Were they ever referred for psychiatric consultation, and did they suffer any disciplinary action during their periods of service?

Educational history. The psychiatrist needs to have a clear picture of the patient's educational background. This information can provide clues as to the patient's social and cultural background, intelligence, motivation, and any obstacles to achievement. For instance, a patient from a very economically deprived background who never had the opportunity to attend the best schools and whose parents never graduated from high school demonstrates strength of character, intelligence, and tremendous motivation by graduating from college. A patient who dropped out of high school because of violence and drugs displays creativity and determination by going to school at night to obtain a high school diploma while working during the day as a drug counselor. How far did the patient go in school? What was the highest grade or graduate level attained? What did the patient like to study, and what was the level of academic performance? How far did the other members of the patient's family go in school, and how does that compare with the patient's progress? What is the patient's attitude toward academic achievement?

Religion. The psychiatrist should describe the religious background of both parents and the details of the patient's religious instruction. Was the family's attitude toward religion strict or permissive, and were there any conflicts between the two parents over the religious education of the child? The psychiatrist should trace the evolution of the patient's adolescent religious practices to present beliefs and activities. Does the patient have a strong religious affiliation, and, if so, how does this affect the patient's life? What does the patient's religion say about treatment of psychiatric or medical illness? What is the religious attitude toward suicide?

Social activity. The psychiatric should describe the patient's social life and the nature of friendships, with an emphasis on the depth, duration, and quality of human relations. What type of social, intellectual, and physical interests does the patient share with friends? What types of relationships does the patient have with people of the same sex and the opposite sex? Is the patient essentially isolated and asocial? Does the patient prefer isolation, or is the patient isolated because of anxieties and fears about other people? Who visits the patient in the hospital and how frequently?

Current living situation. The psychiatrist should ask the patient to describe where he or she lives in terms of the neighborhood and the residence. He or she should include the number of rooms, the number of family members living in the home, and the sleeping arrangements. The psychiatrist should inquire as to how issues of privacy are handled, with particular emphasis on parental and sibling nudity and bathroom arrangements. He or she should ask about the sources of family income and any financial hardships. If applicable, the psychiatrist may inquire about public assistance and the patient's feelings about it. If the patient has been hospitalized, have provisions been made so that he or she will not lose a job or an apartment? The psychiatrist should ask who is caring for the children at home, who visits the patient in the hospital, and how frequently.

Psychosexual history. Much of the history of infantile sexuality is not recoverable, although many patients are able to recall curiosities and sexual games played from the ages of 3 to 6 years. The interviewer should ask how patients learned about sex and what they felt their parents' attitudes were about their sexual development. The interviewer can also inquire if the patient was sexually abused during childhood. Some of the material discussed in this section may also be covered in the section on adolescent sexuality. It is not important where in the history it is covered, as long as it is included.

The onset of puberty and the patient's feelings about that milestone are important. The adolescent masturbatory history, including the nature of the patient's fantasies and feelings about them, is of significance. Attitudes toward sex should be described in detail. Is the patient shy, timid, aggressive? Or does the patient need to impress others and boast of sexual conquests? Did the patient experience anxiety in the sexual setting? Was there promiscuity?

The sexual history should include any sexual symptoms—such as anorgasmia, vaginismus, impotence, premature or retarded ejaculation, lack of sexual desire, and paraphilias (e.g., sadism, fetishism, voyeurism). Attitudes toward fellatio, cunnilingus, and coital techniques may be discussed. The topic of sexual adjustment should include a description of how sexual activity is usually initiated, the frequency of sexual relations, and sexual preferences, variations, and techniques. It is usually appropriate to inquire if the patient has engaged in extramarital relationships and, if so, under what circumstances and whether the spouse knew of the affair. If the spouse did learn of the affair, it is important to describe what happened. The reasons underlying an extramarital affair are just as important as an understanding of its effect on the marriage. Attitudes toward contraception and family planning are important. What form of contraception does the patient use?

Are there questions about sexual functioning and sexuality that the patient would like to ask? Is the patient aware of the issues involved in safe sex? Does the patient have a sexually transmitted disease, such as herpes or AIDS? Does the patient worry about being HIV positive?

Family history. A brief statement about any psychiatric illnesses, hospitalizations, and treatments of the patient's immediate family members should be placed in this part of the report. Is there a family history of alcohol and drug abuse or of antisocial behavior? In addition, the family history should provide a description of the personalities and intelligence of the various people living in the patient's home from childhood to the present and descriptions of the different households lived in. The psychiatrist should also define the role each person has played in the patient's upbringing and the current relationship with the patient. What have been the ethnic, national, and religious traditions of the family? Informants other than the patient may be available to contribute to the family history, and the source should be cited in the written record. Often, different members of the family give different descriptions of the same people and events. The psychiatrist should determine the family's attitude toward and insight into the patient's illness. Does the patient feel that they are supportive, indifferent, destructive? What is the role of illness in the family?

Other questions that provide useful information in this section include: What are the patient's attitudes toward his or her parents and siblings? Ask the patient to describe each family member. Whom does the patient mention first? Whom does the patient leave out? What does each of the parents do for a living? What do the siblings do? How does this compare with what the patient is currently doing, and how does the patient feel about this? Whom does the patient feel he or she is most like in the family and why?

Dreams, fantasies, and values. Sigmund Freud stated that the dream is the royal road to the unconscious. Repetitive dreams are of particular value. If the patient has nightmares, what are their repetitive themes? Some of the most common themes of dreams are food, examinations, sex, helplessness, and impotence. Can the patient describe a recent dream and discuss its possible meanings? Fantasies and daydreams are another valuable source of unconscious material. As with dreams, the psychiatrist can explore and record all manifest details and attendant feelings.

What are the patient's fantasies about the future? If the patient could make any change in his or her life, what would it be? What are the patient's most common or favorite current fantasies? Does the patient experience daydreams? Are the patient's fantasies grounded in reality, or is the patient unable to tell the difference between fantasy and reality?

Finally, the psychiatrist may inquire about the patient's system of values—both social and moral—including values that concern work, money, play, children, parents, friends, sex, community concerns, and cultural issues. For instance, are children seen as a burden or a joy? Is work experienced as a necessary evil, an avoidable chore, or an opportunity? What is the patient's concept of right and wrong?

MENTAL STATUS EXAMINATION (MSE)

The MSE is the part of the clinical assessment that describes the sum total of the examiner's observations and impressions of the psychiatric patient at the time of the interview. Whereas the patient's history remains stable, the patient's mental status can change from day to day or hour to hour. The MSE is the description of the patient's appearance, speech, actions, and thoughts during the interview. Even when a patient is mute or incoherent or refuses to answer questions, one can obtain a wealth of information through careful observation. Although practitioners' organizational formats for writing up the MSE vary slightly, formats must contain certain categories of information. One such format is outlined in Table 7.1-3.

Table 7.1-3
Outline of the Mental Status Examination

I. General description
   A. Appearance
   B. Behavior and psychomotor activity
   C. Attitude toward examiner
II. Mood and affect
   A. Mood
   B. Affect
   C. Appropriateness
III. Speech
IV. Perceptual disturbances
V. Thought
   A. Process or form of thought
   B. Content of thought
VI. Sensorium and cognition
   A. Alertness and level of consciousness
   B. Orientation
   C. Memory
   D. Concentration
   E. Abstract thinking
   F. Fund of information and intelligence
VII. Impulse control
VIII. Judgment and insight
IX. Reliability

General Description

Appearance. This is a description of the patient's appearance and overall physical impression conveyed to the interviewer, as reflected by posture, poise, clothing, and grooming.

Examples of items in the appearance category include body type, posture, poise, clothes, grooming, hair, and nails. Common terms used to describe appearance are healthy, sickly, ill at ease, poised, old-looking, young-looking, disheveled, childlike, and bizarre. Signs of anxiety are noted: moist hands, perspiring forehead, tense posture, wide eyes.

Behavior and psychomotor activity. This category refers to both the quantitative and the qualitative aspects of the patient's motor behavior. These include mannerisms, tics, gestures, twitches, stereotyped behavior, echopraxia, hyperactivity, agitation, combativeness, flexibility, rigidity, gait, and agility. Restlessness, wringing of hands, pacing, and other physical manifestations are described. Psychomotor retardation or generalized slowing down of body movements should be noted. Any aimless, purposeless activity should be described.

Attitude toward examiner. The patient's attitude toward the examiner can be described as cooperative, friendly, attentive, interested, frank, seductive, defensive, contemptuous, perplexed, apathetic, hostile, playful, ingratiating, evasive, or guarded; any number of other adjectives can be used. The level of rapport established should be recorded.

Mood and Affect

Mood. Mood is defined as a pervasive and sustained emotion that colors the person's perception of the world. The psychiatrist is interested in whether the patient remarks voluntarily about feelings or whether it is necessary to ask the patient how he or she feels. Statements about the patient's mood should include depth, intensity, duration, and fluctuations. Common adjectives used to describe mood include depressed, despairing, irritable, anxious, angry, expansive, euphoric, empty, guilty, awed, futile, self-contemptuous, frightened, and perplexed. Mood may be labile, meaning that it fluctuates or alternates rapidly between extremes (e.g., laughing loudly and expansive one moment, tearful and despairing the next).

Affect. Affect may be defined as the patient's external expression of emotional responsiveness. Affect is what the examiner observes as the patient's facial expression, including the amount and the range of expressive behavior. Affect may or may not be congruent with mood. Affect is described as being within normal range, constricted, blunted, or flat. In the normal range of affect, there is a variation in facial expression, tone of voice, use of hands, and body movements. When affect is constricted, there is a clear reduction in the range and intensity of expression. Similarly, in blunted affect, emotional expression is further reduced. To diagnose flat affect, one should find virtually no signs of affective expression, the patient's voice should be monotonous, and the face should be immobile. Blunted, flat, and constricted are terms used to refer to the apparent depth of emotion; depressed, proud, angry, fearful, anxious, guilty, euphoric, and expansive are terms used to refer to particular moods. It is also important to note the patient's difficulty in initiating, sustaining, or terminating an emotional response.

Appropriateness. The appropriateness of the patient's emotional responses can be considered in the context of the subject matter the patient is discussing. Paranoid patients who are describing a delusion of persecution should be angry or frightened about the experiences they believe are happening to them. Anger or fear in this context is not an inappropriate expression of mood. Some psychiatrists have reserved the term inappropriateness of affect for a quality of response found in some schizophrenic patients, in which the patient's affect is incongruent with what the patient is saying (e.g., flattened affect when speaking about murderous impulses).

Speech

This part of the report describes the physical characteristics of speech. Speech can be described in terms of its quantity, rate of production, and quality. The patient may be described as talkative, garrulous, voluble, taciturn, unspontaneous, or normally responsive to cues from the interviewer. Speech may be rapid or slow, pressured, hesitant, emotional, dramatic, monotonous, loud, whispered, slurred, staccato, or mumbled. Impairments of speech, such as stuttering, are included in this section. Unusual rhythms (termed dysprosody) and any accent that may be present should be noted.

Perceptual Disturbances

Perceptual disturbances, such as hallucinations and illusions, may be experienced in reference to the self or the environment. The sensory system involved (e.g., auditory, visual, olfactory, tactile) and the content of the hallucinatory experience should be described. The circumstances of the occurrence of any hallucinatory experience are important, because hypnagogic hallucinations (occurring as a person falls asleep) and hypnopompic hallucinations (occurring as a person awakens) are of much less serious significance than other types of hallucinations. Hallucinations may also occur in particular times of stress for individual patients. Feelings of depersonalization and derealization (extreme feelings of detachment from one's self or the environment) are other examples of perceptual disturbance. Formication, the feeling of bugs crawling on or under the skin, is seen in cocainism.

Thought

Thought is divided into process (or form) and content. Process refers to the way in which a person puts together ideas and associations, the form in which a person thinks. Process or form of thought may be logical and coherent or completely illogical and even incomprehensible. Content refers to what a person is actually thinking about: ideas, beliefs, preoccupations, obsessions. Table 7.1-4 lists common disorders of thought, divided into process and content. Each of these disorders is briefly discussed below.

Thought process (form of thinking). The patient may have either an overabundance or a poverty of ideas. There may be rapid thinking, which, if carried to the extreme, is called a flight of ideas. A patient may exhibit slow or hesitant thinking. Thought may be vague or empty. Do the patient's replies really answer the questions asked, and does the patient have the capacity for goal-directed thinking? Are the responses relevant or irrelevant? Is there a clear cause-and-effect relationship in the patient's explanations? Does the patient have loose associations (e.g., the ideas expressed appear to be unrelated and idiosyncratically connected)? Disturbances of the continuity of thought include statements that are tangential, circumstantial, rambling, evasive, or perseverative. Blocking is an interruption of the train of thought before an idea has been completed; the patient may indicate an inability to recall what was being said or intended to be said. Circumstantiality indicates the loss of capacity for goal-directed thinking; in the process of explaining an idea, the patient brings in many irrelevant details and parenthetical comments but eventually does get back to the original point. Tangentiality is a disturbance in which the patient loses the thread of the conversation and pursues tangential thoughts stimulated by various external or internal irrelevant stimuli and never returns to the original point. Thought process impairments may be reflected by incoherent or incomprehensible connections of thoughts (word salad), clang associations (association by rhyming), punning (association by double meaning), and neologisms (new words created by the patient through the combination or condensation of other words).

Table 7.1-4
Examples of Disorders of Thought

Process (or Form) of Thought
Loosening of associations (LOA) or derailment
Flight of ideas (FOI)
Racing thoughts
Tangentiality
Circumstantiality
Word salad or incoherence
Neologisms
Clang associations
Punning
Thought blocking
Vague thought
Content of Thought
Delusions
Paranoia
Preoccupations
Obsessions and compulsions
Phobias
Suicidal or homicidal ideas
Ideas of reference and influence
Poverty of content

Content of thought. Disturbances in content of thought include delusions, preoccupations (which may involve the patient's illness), obsessions, compulsions, phobias, plans, intentions, recurrent ideas about suicide or homicide, hypochondriacal symptoms, and specific antisocial urges. Specific questions should always be asked about suicidal ideation. Does the patient have thoughts of doing harm to himself or herself? Is there a plan? A major category of disturbances of thought content involves delusions. Delusions may be mood-congruent (in keeping with a depressed or elated mood) or mood-incongruent. Delusions are fixed, false beliefs out of keeping with the patient's cultural background. The content of any delusional system should be described, and the psychiatrist should attempt to evaluate its organization and the patient's conviction as to its validity. The manner in which it affects the patient's life is appropriately described in the history of the present illness. Delusions may be bizarre and may involve beliefs about external control. Delusions may have themes that are persecutory or paranoid, grandiose, somatic, guilty, nihilistic, or erotic. Ideas of reference and ideas of influence should also be described. Examples of ideas of reference include beliefs that one's television or radio is speaking to or about one. Examples of ideas of influence are beliefs involving another person or force controlling some aspect of one's behavior.

Sensorium and Cognition

This portion of the mental status examination seeks to assess organic brain function and the patient's intelligence, capacity for abstract thought, and level of insight and judgment.

Alertness and level of consciousness. Disturbances of consciousness usually indicate organic brain impairment. The term "clouding of consciousness" describes an overall reduced awareness of the environment. A patient may be unable to sustain attention to environmental stimuli or to sustain goal-directed thinking or behavior. Clouding or obtunding of consciousness is frequently not a fixed mental state. The typical patient manifests fluctuations in the level of awareness of the surrounding environment. The patient who has an altered state of consciousness often shows some impairment of orientation as well, although the reverse is not necessarily true. Some terms used to describe the patient's level of consciousness are clouding, somnolence, stupor, coma, lethargy, alertness, and fugue state.

Orientation. Disorders of orientation are traditionally separated according to time, place, and person. Any impairment usually appears in this order (i.e., sense of time is impaired before sense of place); similarly, as the patient improves, the impairment clears in the reverse order. It is necessary to determine whether patients can give the approximate date and time of day. In addition, if patients are in a hospital, do they know how long they have been there? Do the patients behave as though they are oriented to the present? In questions about the patients' orientation to place, it is not sufficient that they be able to *state* the name and the location of the hospital correctly; they should also *behave* as though they know where they are. In assessing orientation for person, the interviewer asks patients whether they know the names of the people around them and whether they understand their roles in relationship to them. Do they know who the examiner is? It is only in the most severe instances that patients do not know who they themselves are.

Memory. Memory functions have traditionally been divided into four areas: remote memory, recent past memory, recent memory, and immediate retention and recall. Recent memory may be checked by asking patients about their appetite and then inquiring what they had for breakfast or for dinner the previous evening. Patients may be asked at this point if they recall the interviewer's name. Asking patients to repeat six digits forward and then backward is a test for immediate retention. Remote memory can be tested by asking patients for information about their childhoods that can be later verified. Asking patients to recall important news events from the past few months checks recent past memory. Often in organic mental syndromes, recent or short-term memory is impaired first, and remote or long-term memory is impaired later. If there is impairment, what are the efforts made to cope with or to conceal impairment? Is denial, confabulation, catastrophic reaction, or circumstantiality used to conceal a deficit? Reactions to the loss of memory can give important clues as to underlying diagnoses and coping mechanisms. For instance, a patient who appears to have memory impairment but, in fact, is depressed is more likely to be very concerned about memory loss than someone with memory loss secondary to dementia. Confabulation (unconsciously making up false answers when memory is impaired) is most closely associated with organic mental syndromes. See Table 7.1-5 for a summary of memory tests.

Concentration. A patient's concentration may be impaired for a variety of reasons. For instance, organic brain disease, anxiety, depression, and internal stimuli, such as auditory hallucinations—all may contribute to impaired concentration. Subtracting serial 7s from 100 is a simple task that requires both concentration and cognitive capacities to be intact. The test is performed by asking the patient to subtract 7 from 100 and keep subtracting 7s. If the patient cannot subtract 7s, try subtracting 3s. Can easier tasks be accomplished—4 × 9, 5 × 4? The examiner must always assess whether anxiety, some disturbance of mood or consciousness, or learning deficit is responsible for the difficulty.

Table 7.1-5
Summary of Memory Tests

It is important to try to assess whether the process of registration, retention, or recollection of material is involved.
Remote memory: childhood data, important events known to have occurred when the patient was younger or free of illness, personal matters, neutral material
Recent past memory: the past few months
Recent memory: the past few days, what the patient did yesterday, the day before; what the patient had for breakfast, lunch, dinner
Immediate retention and recall: digit-span measures: ability to repeat six figures after examiner dictates them—first forward, then backward (patients with unimpaired memory can usually repeat six digits backward).

Abstract thinking. This is the ability of patients to deal with concepts. Patients present with disturbances in the manner in which they conceptualize or handle ideas. Can patients explain similarities, such as those between an apple and a pear or those between truth and beauty? Are the meanings of simple proverbs, such as, "A rolling stone gathers no moss," understood? Answers may be concrete (giving specific examples to illustrate the meaning) or overly abstract (giving too generalized an explanation). Appropriateness of answers and the manner in which answers are given should be noted. In the catastrophic reaction, brain-damaged patients become extremely emotional and cannot think abstractly.

Fund of information and intelligence. If a possible organic mental impairment is suspected, the physician can inquire as to whether the patient has trouble with mental tasks, such as counting the change from $10 after a purchase of $6.37. If this task is too difficult, easier problems (such as how many nickels are in $1.35) may be substituted. The patient's intelligence is related to vocabulary and general fund of knowledge (e.g., the distance from New York to Paris, presidents of the United States). The patient's educational level (both formal and self-education) and socioeconomic status must be taken into account. A patient's handling of difficult or sophisticated concepts can be reflective of intelligence, even in the absence of formal education or an extensive fund of information. Ultimately, the examiner attempts to estimate the patient's intellectual capability and whether the patient is capable of functioning at the level of basic endowment. Questions should have relevance to the patient's educational and cultural background so that an accurate picture of the patient's intelligence can be obtained.

Impulse Control

Is the patient capable of controlling sexual, aggressive, and other impulses? Assessment of impulse control is critical to ascertaining the patient's awareness of socially appropriate behavior and is a measure of the patient's potential danger to self and others. Some patients may be unable to control impulses secondary to organic mental disease, others secondary to psychosis, and others as the result of chronic characterological defects, as observed in the personality disorders. Impulse control can be estimated from information in the patient's recent history and from behavior observed during the interview.

Judgment and Insight

Judgment. During the course of the history taking, the examiner should be able to assess many aspects of the patient's capability for social judgment. Does the patient understand the likely outcome of his or her behavior, and is he or she influenced by that understanding? An example of test judgment involves the patient's prediction of what he or she would do in imaginary situations. For instance, a patient may be asked, "What would you do if you smelled smoke in a crowded movie theater?"

Insight. Insight refers to the patients' degree of awareness and understanding that they are ill. Patients may exhibit a complete denial of their illness or may show some awareness that they are ill but place the blame on others, on external factors, or even on organic factors. They may acknowledge that they have an illness but ascribe it to something unknown or mysterious in themselves.

Intellectual insight is present when patients can admit that they are ill and acknowledge that their failures to adapt are, in part, due to their own irrational feelings. However, the major limitation to intellectual insight is that patients are unable to apply the knowledge to alter future experiences. True emotional insight is present when patients' awareness of their own motives and deep feelings leads to a change in their personality or behavior patterns.

A summary of levels of insight follows:

1. Complete denial of illness
2. Slight awareness of being sick and needing help but denying it at the same time
3. Awareness of being sick but blaming it on others, on external factors, or on organic factors
4. Awareness that illness is due to something unknown in the patient
5. *Intellectual insight:* admission that the patient is ill and that symptoms or failures in social adjustment are due to the patient's own particular irrational feelings or disturbances without applying that knowledge to future experiences
6. *True emotional insight:* emotional awareness of the motives and feelings within the patient and the important people in his or her life, which can lead to basic changes in behavior.

Reliability

The mental status part of the report concludes with the examiner's impressions of the patient's reliability and capacity to report his or her situation accurately. This includes an estimate of the examiner's impression of the patient's truthfulness or veracity. For instance, if the patient is open about significant active substance abuse or about circumstances that the patient knows may reflect badly (e.g., trouble with the law), the examiner may estimate the patient's reliability to be good.

PSYCHIATRIC REPORT

When the examiner has completed a comprehensive psychiatric history and MSE, the information obtained is written up and organized into the psychiatric report. The report follows the outline of the standard psychiatric history and MSE. In the psychiatric report the examiner (1) addresses the critical questions of further diagnostic studies that must be performed, (2) adds a summary of both positive and negative findings, (3) makes a tentative multiaxial diagnosis, (4) gives a prognosis, (5) gives a psychodynamic formulation, and (6) gives a set of management recommendations. A summary of this section of the psychiatric report follows:

Further Diagnostic Studies

A. Physical examination

B. Additional psychiatric diagnostic interviews

C. Interviews with family members, friends, or neighbors by social worker

D. Psychological, neurological, or laboratory tests as indicated: electroencephalogram, computed tomography scan, positron emission tomography, tests of other medical conditions, reading comprehension and writing tests, tests for aphasia, projective psychological tests, dexamethasone-suppression test

Summary of Positive and Negative Findings

Mental symptoms, historical data (e.g. family history), medical and laboratory findings, and psychological and neurological test results, if available, are noted.

Diagnosis

Diagnostic classification is made according to the revised third edition of the American Psychiatric Association's *Diagnostic and Statistical Manual of Mental Disorders* (DSM-III-R). DSM-III-R uses a multiaxial classification scheme consisting of five axes, each of which should be covered in the diagnosis.

A. Axis I. This consists of all clinical syndromes (e.g., mood disorders, schizophrenia, generalized anxiety disorder).

B. Axis II. This consists of personality disorders and specific developmental disorders.

C. Axis III. This consists of any existing medical or physical illness (e.g., epilepsy, cardiovascular disease, gastrointestinal disease).

D. Axis IV. This refers to psychosocial stressors (e.g., divorce, injury, death of a loved one) relevant to the illness; a rating scale with a continuum from 1 (no stressors) to 6 (catastrophic stressors) is used.

E. Axis V. This relates to the highest level of functioning exhibited by the patient during the previous year (e.g., social, occupational, and psychological functioning); a rating scale with a continuum from 90 (superior functioning) to 1 (grossly impaired functioning) is used.

Prognosis

This is an opinion as to the probable immediate and future course, extent, and outcome of the illness. The good and bad prognostic factors, as known, are listed.

Psychodynamic Formulation

This is a summary of proposed psychological influences on or causes of the patient's disturbance, influences in the patient's life that contributed to the present illness; environmental and personality factors relevant to determining the patient's symptoms and how these influences have interacted with the patient's genetic, temperamental, and biological makeup; primary and secondary gains. An outline of the major defense mechanisms used by the patient should be listed.

Recommendations

In formulating the treatment plan, the clinician should note whether the patient requires psychiatric treatment at this time and, if so, at which problems and target symptoms the treatment is aimed, what kind of treatment or combination of treatments the patient should receive, and what treatment setting seems most appropriate. For instance, the examiner evaluates the role of medication, inpatient or outpatient treatment, frequency of sessions, probable duration of therapy, and type of psychotherapy (individual, group, or family therapy). Specific goals of therapy are noted. If hospitalization is recommended, the clinician should specify the reasons for hospitalization, the type of hospitalization indicated, the urgency with which the patient has to be hospitalized, and the anticipated duration of inpatient care. The clinician should also estimate the length of treatment.

If either the patient or the family are unwilling to accept the recommendations for treatment and the clinician thinks that the refusal of the recommendations may have serious consequences, the patient (or parent or guardian) should sign a statement that the recommended treatment was refused.

References

American Psychiatric Association: *Diagnostic and Statistical Manual of Mental Disorders,* ed 3, revised. American Psychiatric Association, Washington, DC, 1987.

Baker N J, Berry S L, Adler L E: Family diagnoses missed on a clinical inpatient service. Am J Psychiatry *144:* 630, 1987.

Keller M B, Manschreck T C: The bedside mental status examination: Reliability and validity. Compr Psychiatry *22:* 500, 1981.

Kerns L L: Falsifications in the psychiatric history: A differential diagnosis. Psychiatry *49:* 13, 1986.

Leon R L, Bowden C L, Faber R A: The psychiatric interview, history, and mental status examination. In *Comprehensive Textbook of Psychiatry,* ed 5, H I Kaplan and B J Sadock, editors, p 449. Williams & Wilkins, Baltimore, 1989.

Lewis N D C: *Outlines for Psychiatric Examinations,* ed 3. New York State Department of Mental Hygiene, Albany, 1943.

MacKinnon R A, Michels R: *The Psychiatric Interview in Clinical Practice.* Saunders, New York, 1971.

Ryback R: *The Problem-Oriented Record in Psychiatry and Mental Health Care.* Grune & Stratton, New York, 1974.

Shea S C, Mezzich J E: Contemporary psychiatric interviewing: New directions for training. Psychiatry *51:* 385, 1988.

Stevenson I: *The Psychiatric Examination.* Little, Brown, Boston, 1969.

Strub R L, Black F W: *The Mental Status Examination in Neurology,* ed 2. Davis, Philadelphia, 1985.

Westermeyer J, Wahmenholm K: Assessing the victimized psychiatric patient. Hosp Community Psychiatry *40:* 245, 1989.

Wittchen H U, Burke J D, Semler G, Pfister H, VonCranach M, Zaudig M: Recall and dating of psychiatric symptoms: Test-retest reliability of time-related symptom questions in a standardized psychiatric interview. Arch Gen Psychiatry *46:* 437, 1989.

7.2 / Laboratory Tests in Psychiatry

Laboratory tests have come to play a more important role in psychiatry than ever before. They are of help in a variety of ways, such as screening for medical illness, improving diagnostic reliability, monitoring treatment (especially through measurement of the blood levels of psychoactive drugs), and continuing research into psychiatric illness. In this section, an overview and outline of laboratory tests used in psychiatry are presented. However, psychiatric diagnoses cannot be made on the basis of any of these tests alone, given the present state of knowledge.

Brain-imaging techniques are discussed in Section 3.2.

BASIC SCREENING TESTS

Before initiating psychiatric treatment, a clinician should undertake a routine medical evaluation for the purposes of screening for concurrent disease, ruling out organicity, and establishing baseline values of functions to be monitored. Such an evaluation includes a medical history and routine medical laboratory tests, such as a complete blood count (CBC); hematocrit and hemoglobin; renal, liver, and thyroid function; electrolytes; and blood sugar.

Thyroid disease and other endocrinopathies may present as a mood disorder or psychosis; cancer or infectious disease may present as depression; infection and connective tissue diseases may present as acute changes in mental status. In addition, a range of organic mental or neurological conditions may present initially to the psychiatrist. These conditions include multiple sclerosis, Parkinson's disease, Alzheimer's disease, Huntington's chorea, acquired immune deficiency syndrome (AIDS) dementia, and temporal lobe epilepsy. Any suspected medical or neurological condition should be thoroughly evaluated with appropriate laboratory tests and consultation.

NEUROENDOCRINE TESTS

Thyroid-Function Tests

Several thyroid-function tests are available, including tests for thyroxine (T_4) by competitive protein binding (T_4 [D]) and by radioimmunoassay (T_4 [RIA]) involving a specific antigen-antibody reaction. Over 90 percent of T_4 is bound to serum protein and is responsible for thyroid-stimulating hormone (TSH) secretion and cellular metabolism. Other thyroid measures include the free T_4 index (FT_4I), triiodothyronine uptake, and total serum triiodothyronine measured by radioimmunoassay (T_3 [RIA]). These tests are used to rule out hypothyroidism, which can present with symptoms of depression. In some studies, up to 10 percent of patients complaining of depression and associated fatigue had incipient hypothyroid disease. Lithium can cause hypothyroidism and more rarely hyperthyroidism. Neonatal hypothyroidism results in mental retardation and is preventable if the diagnosis is made at birth.

Thyrotropin-releasing hormone stimulation test. The thyrotropin-releasing hormone (TRH) stimulation test is indicated in patients who have marginally abnormal thyroid test results with suspected subclinical hypothyroidism, which may account for clinical depression. It is also used in patients with possible lithium-induced hypothyroidism. The procedure entails an intravenous (IV) injection of 500 mg of TRH, which produces a sharp rise in serum TSH when measured at 15, 30, 60, and 90 minutes. An increase in serum TSH of from 5 to 25 μIU/mL above the baseline is normal. An increase of less than 7μIU/mL is considered a blunted response, which may correlate with a diagnosis of depression. Eight percent of all patients with depression have some thyroid illness.

Dexamethasone-Suppression Test

Dexamethasone is a long-acting synthetic glucocorticoid with a long half-life. Approximately 1 mg of dexamethasone is equivalent to 25 mg of cortisol. The dexamethasone-suppression test (DST) is used to help confirm a diagnostic impression of major depression with melancholia (revised third edition of the *Diagnostic and Statistical Manual of Mental Disorders* [DSM-III-R] classification) or endogenous depression (Research Diagnostic Criteria [RDC] classification).

Procedure. The patient is given 1 mg of dexamethasone by mouth at 11 P.M., and plasma cortisol is measured at 8 A.M., 4 P.M., and 11 P.M. Plasma cortisol above 5 μg/dL (known as nonsuppression) is considered abnormal (i.e., positive). Suppression of cortisol indicates that the hypothalamic-adrenal-pituitary axis is functioning properly. Since the 1930s, dysfunction of that axis has been known to be associated with stress.

The DST can be used to follow the response of a depressed person to treatment. Normalization of the DST, however, is not an indication to stop antidepressant treatment, because the DST may normalize before the depression resolves.

There is some evidence that patients with a positive DST (especially 10 μg/dL) will have a good response to somatic treatment, such as electroconvulsive therapy (ECT) or cyclic antidepressant therapy. The problems associated with the DST include varying reports of sensitivity and specificity. False-positive and false-negative results are common and are listed in Table 7.2-1. The sensitivity of the DST is considered to be 45 percent in major depression and 70 percent in psychotic mood disorders. The specificity is 90 percent compared with controls and 77 percent compared with other psychiatric diagnoses.

Other Endocrine Tests

A variety of other hormones affect behavior. Exogenous hormonal administration has been shown to affect behavior, and known endocrine diseases have associated psychiatric disorders.

In addition to thyroid hormones, these include the anterior pituitary hormone prolactin, growth hormone, somastatin, gonadotrophin-releasing hormone (GnRH), and the sex steroids—luteinizing hormone (LH), follicle-stimulating hormone (FSH), testosterone, and estrogen. Melatonin from the pineal gland has been implicated in seasonal affective disorder.

Table 7.2-1
Medical Conditions and Pharmacological Agents That May Interfere with Results of the Dexamethasone-Suppression Test

False-positive results are associated with
- Phenytoin
- Barbiturates
- Meprobamate
- Glutethimide
- Methyprylon
- Methaqualone
- Carbamazepine
- Cardiac failure
- Hypertension
- Renal failure
- Disseminated cancer and serious infections
- Recent major trauma or surgery
- Fever
- Nausea
- Dehydration
- Temporal lobe disease
- High-dosage estrogen treatment
- Pregnancy
- Cushing's disease
- Unstable diabetes mellitus
- Extreme weight loss (malnutrition, anorexia nervosa)
- Alcohol abuse
- Benzodiazepine withdrawal
- Tricyclic antidepressant withdrawal
- Dementia
- Bulimia nervosa
- Acute psychosis
- Advanced age

False-negative results are associated with
- Hypopituitarism
- Addison's disease
- Long-term synthetic steroid therapy
- Indomethacin
- High-dosage cyproheptadine treatment
- High-dosage benzodiazepine treatment

From M Young, J Stanford: The dexamethasone suppression test for the detection, diagnosis, and management of depression. Arch Intern Med *100:* 309, 1984, with permission.

Symptoms of anxiety or depression may be explained in some patients on the basis of unspecified changes in endocrine function or homeostasis.

Catecholamines

The serotonin metabolite 5-hydroxyindoleacetic acid (5-HIAA) is elevated in the urine of patients with carcinoid tumors and at times in patients who take phenothiazine medication or in persons who eat foods high in serotonin (e.g., walnuts, bananas, avocados). The amount of 5-HIAA in cerebrospinal fluid is low in some persons who are in a suicidal depression and in those who have committed suicide in particularly violent ways. Low cerebrospinal fluid 5-HIAA is associated with violence in general. Norepinephrine and its metabolic products—metanephrine, normetanephrine, and vanillylmandelic acid (VMA)—can be measured in the urine, blood, and plasma. Plasma catecholamines are markedly elevated in pheochromocytoma, which is associated with anxiety, agitation, and hypertension. Some cases of chronic anxiety may share elevated blood norepinephrine and epinephrine levels. Some depressed patients have a lower urinary norepinephrine to epinephrine ratio (NE:E).

High levels of urinary norepinephrine and epinephrine have been found in some patients with post-traumatic stress disorder. The norepinephrine metabolite, 3-methoxy-4-hydroxyphenylglycol (MHPG) level is decreased in patients with severe depressive disorders, especially in those patients who attempt suicide.

Renal-Function Tests

Creatinine clearance detects early kidney damage and can be serially monitored to follow the course of renal disease. Blood urea nitrogen (BUN) is also elevated in renal disease. Lithium may cause renal damage, and the serum BUN and creatinine are followed in patients taking lithium. If the serum BUN or creatinine is abnormal, the patient's two-hour creatinine clearance and ultimately the 24-hour creatinine clearance are tested.

Liver-Function Tests

Total bilirubin and direct bilirubin are elevated in hepatocellular injury and intrahepatic bile stasis that can occur with phenothiazine or tricyclic medication and with alcohol and drug abuse. Certain drugs (e.g., phenobarbital) may decrease serum bilirubin. Liver damage or disease, which is reflected by abnormal findings in liver-function tests (LFTs), may present with signs and symptoms of an organic mental syndrome, including disorientation and delirium. Impaired hepatic function may increase the elimination half-lives of certain drugs, including some of the benzodiazepines, so that the drug may stay in the system longer than it would under normal circumstances.

BLOOD TESTS FOR SEXUALLY TRANSMITTED DISEASES

The Venereal Disease Research Laboratory (VDRL) test is used as a screening test for syphilis. If positive, the result is confirmed by using the more specific fluorescent treponemal antibody-absorption test (FTA-ABS test), which uses the spirochete *Treponema pallidum* as the antigen. Central nervous system VDRL is measured in patients with suspected neurosyphilis. A positive human immunodeficiency virus (HIV) test result indicates that the person has been exposed to infection with the virus that causes AIDS. See Chapter 11 for the psychiatric effects of HIV seropositivity and of AIDS.

PLASMA LEVELS OF AND OTHER LABORATORY TESTS RELATED TO PSYCHOTROPIC DRUGS

There is a trend in caring for patients receiving psychotropic medication to have regular measurements taken of their plasma levels of the prescribed drug. For some types of drugs, such as lithium, it is essential; but for other types of drugs, such as antipsychotics, it is mainly of academic or research interest. The clinician need not practice defensive medicine by insisting that all patients receiving psychotropic drugs have blood levels taken for medicolegal purposes. In the discussion that follows, the major classes of drugs and the suggested guidelines are outlined. The current status of psychopharmacological treatment is such that the psychiatrist's clinical judgment and experience, except in very rare instances, is a better indication of a drug's therapeutic efficacy than is a plasma-level determination. Moreover, the reliance on plasma levels cannot replace clinical skills and the need to maintain humanitarian aspects of patient care.

Benzodiazepines

No special tests are needed for patients taking benzodiazepines. Among those metabolized in the liver by oxidation, impaired hepatic function will increase the half-life. Baseline LFTs are indicated in patients with suspected liver damage. Urine testing for benzodiazepines is used routinely in cases of substance abuse.

Antipsychotics

Antipsychotics can cause leukocytosis, leukopenia, mild anemia, and, in rare cases, angranulocytosis. A baseline may be desirable; but, because bone marrow side effects can occur abruptly even when the dosage of a drug has remained constant, a baseline normal CBC will not be conclusive. Antipsychotics are metabolized in the liver, so LFTs may be useful. Antipsychotic plasma levels do not correlate with clinical response; however, there is a possible correlation between high plasma levels and toxic side effects (especially with chlorpromazine [Thorazine] and haloperidol [Haldol]). There is no known relationship between antipsychotic levels and tardive dyskinesia. Plasma levels are currently of clinical use only to detect noncompliance or nonabsorption and thus may be useful in identifying the nonresponder.

Clozapine. Because of the risk of agranulocytosis (1 to 2 percent), patients who are being treated with clozapine (Clozaril) must have a baseline white blood cell (WBC) and differential count before initiation of treatment, a WBC count every week throughout treatment, and a WBC count for four weeks after the discontinuation of clozapine. Clozapine is available only through the Clozaril patient management system (CPMS), which is administered by Sandoz Pharmaceutical Corporation.

Cyclic Antidepressants

An electrocardiogram (ECG) should be given before starting cyclic antidepressants to assess for conduction delays, which may lead to heart block at therapeutic levels. Some clinicians believe that all patients receiving prolonged cyclic antidepressant therapy should have an annual ECG. At therapeutic levels, these drugs suppress arrhythmias through a quinidinelike effect. Trazodone (Desyrel), an antidepressant unrelated to cyclic antidepressants, has been reported to cause ventricular arrhythmias and priapism, mild leukopenia, and neutropenia.

Blood levels should be tested routinely when using imipramine (Tofranil), desipramine (Norpramin), or nortriptyline (Pamelor) in the treatment of depression. Taking blood levels may also be of use in patients in whom there is a poor response at normal dose ranges and in high-risk patients for whom there is an urgent need to know whether a therapeutic or toxic plasma level of drug has been reached. Blood level tests should also include measurement of active metabolites (e.g., imipramine is converted to desipramine, amitryptiline [Elavil] to nortriptyline). Some characteristics of tricyclic drug plasma levels are as follows:

1. *Imipramine.* The percentage of favorable responses correlates with plasma levels in a linear manner between 200 and 250 ng/mL, but some patients may respond at a lower level. At levels over 250 ng/mL, there is no improved favorable response, and side effects increase.
2. *Nortriptyline.* The *therapeutic window* (the range within which a drug is most effective) is between 50 and 150 ng/mL. There is a decreased response rate at levels over 150 ng/mL.
3. *Desipramine.* Levels greater than 125 ng/mL correlate with a higher percentage of favorable responses.
4. *Amitriptyline.* Different studies have produced conflicting results with regard to blood levels.

Procedure. The procedure for taking blood levels is as follows: Draw the blood specimen 10 to 14 hours after the last dose, usually in the morning after a bedtime dose. Patients must be on a stable daily dose for at least five days for the test to be valid. Some patients are unusually poor metabolizers of cyclic antidepressants and may have levels as high as 2,000 ng/mL while taking normal doses and before showing a favorable clinical response. Such patients must be monitored very closely for cardiac side effects. Patients with levels greater than 1,000 ng/mL are generally at risk for cardiotoxicity.

Monoamine Oxidase Inhibitors

Patients taking monoamine oxidase inhibitors (MAOIs) are instructed to avoid tyramine-containing foods because of the danger of a potential hypertensive crisis. A baseline normal blood pressure (BP) must be recorded, and the BP must be followed during treatment. MAOIs may also cause orthostatic hypotension as a direct drug side effect unrelated to diet. Other than their potential for causing elevated BP when taken with certain foods, MAOIs are relatively free of other side effects. There are no clinical blood level values available for MAOIs, although a research test involves correlating therapeutic response with the degree of platelet monoamine oxidase inhibition.

Lithium

Patients receiving lithium should have baseline thyroid-function tests, electrolytes, a white blood cell count (WBC), and renal-function tests (specific gravity, BUN, and creatinine), and a baseline ECG. The rationale for these tests is that lithium can cause renal concentrating defects, hypothyroidism, and leukocytosis; sodium depletion can cause toxic lithium levels; and approximately 95 percent of lithium is excreted in the urine. Lithium has also been shown to cause ECG changes, including various conduction defects.

Lithium is most clearly indicated in the prophylactic treatment of mania (direct antimanic effect may take up to two weeks) and is commonly coupled with antipsychotics for the treatment of acute mania. Lithium itself may have antipsychotic activity as well. The maintenance level is 0.6 to 1.2 mEq per L, although acutely manic patients can tolerate up to 1.5 to 1.8 mEq per L. Some patients may respond at lower levels, whereas others may require higher levels. A response below 0.4 mEq per L is probably placebo. Toxic reactions may occur with levels over 2.0 mEq per L. Regular lithium monitoring is essential, since there is a narrow therapeutic range beyond which cardiac problems and central nervous system (CNS) effects can occur.

Lithium levels are drawn 8 to 12 hours after the last dose, usually in the morning after the bedtime dose. The level should be measured at least twice a week while stabilizing the patient and may be drawn monthly thereafter.

Carbamazepine (Tegretol)

A pretreatment CBC including platelet count should be done. Reticulocyte count and serum iron are also desirable. These tests should be repeated weekly during the first three months of treatment and monthly thereafter. Carbamazepine can cause aplastic anemia, agranulocytosis, thrombocytopenia, and leukopenia. Because of the minor risk of hepatotoxicity, LFTs should be done every three to six months. The medication should be discontinued if there are any signs of bone marrow suppression as measured with periodic CBCs. The therapeutic level of carbamazepine is 8 to 12 ng/mL, with toxicity most often reached at levels of 15 ng/mL. Most clinicians report that levels as high as 12 ng/mL are hard to achieve.

PROVOCATION OF PANIC ATTACKS WITH SODIUM LACTATE

Up to 72 percent of patients with panic disorder will have a panic attack when administered an IV injection of sodium lactate. Thus, lactate provocation is used to confirm a diagnosis of panic disorder. Lactate provocation has also been used to trigger flashbacks in patients with posttraumatic stress disorder. Hyperventilation, another known trigger of panic attacks in predisposed persons, is not as sensitive as lactate provocation in inducing panic attacks. CO_2 inhalation also precipitates panic attacks in those so predisposed. Panic attacks triggered by sodium lactate are not inhibited by peripherally acting beta-blockers but are inhibited by alprazolam (Xanax) and tricyclic antidepressants.

Table 7.2-2
Drugs of Abuse That Can Be Tested in Urine

Drug	Length of Time Detected in Urine
Alcohol	7–12 hours
Amphetamine	48 hours
Barbiturate	24 hours (short-acting) 3 weeks (long-acting)
Benzodiazepine	3 days
Cocaine	6–8 hours (metabolites 2–4 days)
Codeine	48 hours
Heroin	36–72 hours
Marijuana (THC)	3 days to 4 weeks (depending on use)
Methadone	3 days
Methaqualone	7 days
Morphine	48–72 hours
Phencyclidine (PCP)	8 days
Propoxyphene	6–48 hours

AMYTAL INTERVIEW

Amobarbital (Amytal) interviews have both diagnostic and therapeutic indications. Diagnostically, the interviews are helpful in differentiating nonorganic and organic conditions, particularly in patients who present with symptoms of catatonia, stupor, and muteness. Organic conditions tend to worsen with infusions of amobarbital, but nonorganic or psychogenic conditions tend to get better because of disinhibition, decreased anxiety, or increased relaxation. Therapeutically, Amytal interviews are useful in disorders of repression and dissociation—for example, in the recovery of memory in psychogenic amnesia and fugue, in the recovery of function in conversion disorder, and in the facilitation of emotional expression in posttraumatic stress disorder.

URINE TESTING FOR DRUGS OF ABUSE

A number of drugs may be detected in a patient's urine if the urine is tested within a specific (and variable) period of time after ingestion. Knowledge of urine drug testing is becoming crucial for practicing physicians as the controversial issue of mandatory or random drug testing becomes prevalent. Table 7.2-2 provides a summary of drugs of abuse that can be tested in urine.

OTHER LABORATORY TESTS

Laboratory tests not discussed above are covered in Table 7.2-3 in terms of indications and significance in medical conditions that affect behavior.

Table 7.2-3
Other Laboratory Tests

Test	Major Psychiatric Indications	Comments
Acid phosphatase	Organic mental syndrome (OMS) workup	Increased in prostate cancer, benign prostatic hypertrophy, excessive platelet destruction, bone disease
Adrenocorticotropic hormone (ACTH)	OMS workup	Increased in steroid abuse; may be increased in seizures, psychoses, or Cushing's disease or in response to stress. Decreased in Addison's disease
Alanine aminotransferase (ALT) (formerly called serum glutamic-pyruvic transaminase [SGPT])	OMS workup	Increased in hepatitis, cirrhosis, liver metastases Decreased in pyridoxine (vitamin B_6) deficiency
Albumin	OMS workup	Increased in dehydration Decreased in malnutrition, hepatic failure, burns, multiple myeloma, carcinomas
Aldolase	Eating disorders Schizophrenia	Increased in patients who abuse ipecac (e.g., bulimic patients), schizophrenia (60–80%)
Alkaline phosphatase	OMS workup Use of psychotropic medications	Increased in Paget's disease, hyperparathyroidism, hepatic disease, hepatic metastases, heart failure, phenothiazine use Decreased in pernicious anemia (Vitamin B_{12} deficiency)
Amylase, serum	Eating disorders	May be increased in bulimia nervosa

Table 7.2-3
Continued

Test	Major Psychiatric Indications	Comments
Aspartate aminotransferase (AST) (formerly SGOT)	OMS workup	Increased in heart failure, hepatic disease, pancreatitis, eclampsia, cerebral damage, alcoholism Decreased in pyridoxine (vitamin B_6) deficiency or terminal stages of liver disease
Bicarbonate, serum	Panic disorder Eating disorders	Decreased in hyperventilation syndrome, panic disorder, and anabolic steroid abuse May be elevated in patients with bulimia nervosa, in laxative abuse, and in psychogenic vomiting
Bilirubun	OMS workup	Increased in hepatic disease
Blood urea nitrogen (BUN)	Delirium Use of psychotropic medications	Elevations associated with lethargy, delirium If elevated, can increase toxic potential of psychiatric medications, especially lithium and amantadine (Symmetrel)
Bromide, serum	Dementia Psychosis	Bromide intoxication can cause psychosis, hallucinations, delirium Part of dementia workup, especially when serum chloride is elevated
Caffeine level, serum	Anxiety	Evaluation of patients with suspected caffeinism
Calcium (Ca), serum	OMS workup Mood disorders Psychosis Eating disorders	Increased in hyperparathyroidism, bone metastases Increase associated with delirium, depression, psychosis Decreased in hypoparathyroidism, renal failure Decrease associated with depression, irritability, delirium, chronic laxative abuse
Carotid ultrasound	Dementia	Occasionally included in dementia workup, especially to rule out multi-infarct dementia Primary value is in search for possible infarct causes
Cerebrospinal fluid (CSF)	OMS workup	Increased protein and cells in infection, positive VDRL in neurosyphilis, bloody CSF in hemorrhagic conditions
Ceruloplasmin, serum; copper, serum	OMS workup	Low in Wilson's disease (hepatolenticular disease)
Chloride (Cl), serum	Eating disorders Panic disorder	Decreased in patients with bulimia and psychogenic vomiting Mild elevation in hyperventilation syndrome and panic disorder
Cholecystokinin (CCK)	Eating disorders	Compared with controls, blunted in bulimic patients after eating meal (may normalize after treatment with antidepressants)
CO_2 inhalation; sodium bicarbonate infusion	Anxiety	Panic attacks produced in subgroup of patients
Coombs' test, direct and indirect	Hemolytic anemias secondary to psychotropic medications	Evaluation of drug-induced hemolytic anemias, such as those secondary to chlorpromazine, phenytoin, levodopa, and methyldopa
Copper, urine	OMS workup	Elevated in Wilson's disease
Cortisol (hydrocortisone)	OMS workup Mood disorders	Excessive level may indicate Cushing's disease associated with anxiety, depression, and a variety of other conditions
Creatine phosphokinase (CPK)	Use of antipsychotics Use of restraints Substance abuse	Increased in neuroleptic malignant syndrome, intramuscular injection, rhabdomyolysis (secondary to substance abuse) patients in restraints, patients experiencing dystonic reactions; asymptomatic elevations seen with use of antipsychotics
Dopamine (DA) (L-dopa stimulation of dopamine)	Depression	Inhibits prolactin Test used to assess functional integrity of dopaminergic system, which is impaired in Parkinson's disease, depression
Doppler ultrasound	Impotence OMS workup	Carotid occlusion in organic mental syndrome (OMS), transient ischemic attack (TIA), reduced penile blood flow in impotence
Echocardiogram	Panic disorder	10–40% of patients with panic disorder show mitral valve prolapse
Electroencephalogram (EEG)	OMS workup	Seizures, brain death, lesions; shortened REM latency in depression High-voltage activity in stupor; low-voltage fast activity in excitement; in functional nonorganic cases (e.g., dissociative states), alpha activity is present in the background, which responds to auditory and visual stimuli

Table 7.2-3
Continued

Test	Major Psychiatric Indications	Comments
		Biphasic or triphasic slow bursts seen in dementia of Creutzfeldt-Jakob disease
Epstein-Barr virus (EBV); cytomeglovirus (CMV)	OMS workup Chronic fatigue Mood disorders	Part of herpes virus group EBV is causative agent for infectious mononucleosis, which can present with depression and personality change CMV can produce anxiety, confusion, mood disorders EBV associated with chronic mononucleosislike syndrome associated with chronic depression and fatigue. May be association between EBV and major depression
Erythrocyte sedimentation rate (ESR)	OMS workup	An increase in ESR represents a nonspecific test of infectious, inflammatory, autoimmune, or malignant disease
Estrogen	Mood disorder	Decreased in menopausal depression and premenstrual syndrome; variable changes in anxiety
Ferritin, serum	OMS workup	Most sensitive test for iron deficiency
Folate (folic acid), serum	Alcohol abuse Use of specific medications	Usually measured with vitamin B_{12} deficiencies associated with psychosis, paranoia, fatigue, agitation, dementia, and delirium Associated with alcoholism, use of phenytoin, oral contraceptives, and estrogen
Follicle-stimulating hormone (FSH)	Depression	High normal in anorexia nervosa, higher values in postmenopausal women; low levels in patients with panhypopituitarism
Glucose, fasting blood (FBS)	Panic attacks Anxiety Delirium Depression	Very high FBS associated with delirium Very low FBS associated with delirium, agitation, panic attacks, anxiety, depression
Glutamyl transaminase, serum	Alcohol abuse OMS workup	Increase in alcohol abuse, cirrhosis, liver disease
Gonadotrophic-releasing hormone (GnRH)	Depression Anxiety Schizophrenia	Decrease in schizophrenia; increase in anorexia; variable in depression, anxiety
Growth hormone (GH)	Depression Schizophrenia	Blunted GH responses to insulin-induced hypoglycemia in depressed patients; increased GH responses to dopamine agonist challenge in schizophrenic patients; increased in some cases of anorexia
Hematocrit (Hct); hemoglobin (Hb)	OMS workup	Assessment of anemia (anemia may be associated with depression and psychosis)
Hepatitis A viral antigen (HAAg)	Mood disorders OMS workup	Less severe, better prognosis than hepatitis B; may present with anorexia, depression
Hepatitis B surface antigen (HBsAg); hepatitis Bc antigen (HBcAg)	Mood disorders OMS workup	Active hepatitis B infection indicates greater degree of infectivity and of progression to chronic liver disease May present with depression
Holter monitor	Panic disorder	Evaluation of panic disordered patients with palpitations and other cardiac symptoms
Human immunodeficiency virus (HIV)	OMS workup	CNS involvement: AIDS dementia, organic personality disorder, organic mood disorder, acute psychosis
17-Hydroxycorticosteroid	Depression	Deviations detect hyperadrenocorticalism, which can be associated with major depression Increased in steroid abuse
5-Hydroxyindoleacetic acid (5-HIAA)	Depression Suicide Violence	Decrease in CSF in aggressive or violent patients with suicidal or homicidal impulses May be indicator of decreased impulse control and predictor of suicide
Iron, serum	OMS workup	Iron-deficiency anemia
Lactate dehydrogenase (LDH)	OMS workup	Increased in myocardial infarction, pulmonary infarction, hepatic disease, renal infarction, seizures, cerebral damage, megaloblastic (pernicious) anemia, factitious elevations secondary to rough handling of blood specimen tube

Table 7.2-3
Continued

Test	Major Psychiatric Indications	Comments
Lupus anticoagulant (LA)	Use of phenothiazines	An antiphospholipid antibody, which has been described in some patients using phenothiazines, especially chlorpromazine
Lupus erythematosus (LE) test	Depression Psychosis Delirium Dementia	Positive test associated with systemic LE, which may present with various psychiatric disturbances, such as psychosis, depression, delirium, and dementia; also tested for with antinuclear antibody (ANA) and antiDNA antibody tests
Luteinizing hormone (LH)	Depression	Low in patients with panhypopituitarism; decrease associated with depression
Magnesium, serum	Alcohol abuse OMS workup	Decreased in alcoholism; low levels associated with agitation, delirium, seizures
MAO, platelet	Depression	Low in depression
MCV (mean corpuscular volume) (average volume of a red blood cell)	Alcohol abuse	Elevated in alcoholism and vitamin B_{12} and folate deficiency
Melatonin	Seasonal affective disorder	Produced by light and pineal gland and decrease in seasonal affective disorder
Metal (heavy) intoxication (serum or urinary)	OMS workup	Lead—apathy, irritability, anorexia, confusion Mercury—psychosis, fatigue, apathy, decreased memory, emotional lability, "mad hatter" Manganese—manganese madness, Parkinson-like syndrome Aluminum—dementia Arsenic—fatigue, blackouts, hair loss
3-Methoxy-4-hydroxyphenyglycol (MHPG)	Depression Anxiety	Most useful in research; decreases in urine may indicate decreases centrally
Myoglobin, urine	Phenothiazine use Substance abuse Use of restraints	Increased in neuroleptic malignant syndrome; in PCP, cocaine, or lysergic acid diethylamide (LSD) intoxication; and in patients in restraints
Nicotine	Anxiety Nicotine addiction	Anxiety, smoking
Nocturnal penile tumescence (NPT)	Impotence	Quantification of penile circumference changes, penile rigidity, frequency of penile tumescence Evaluation of erectile function during sleep Erections associated with rapid eye movement (REM) sleep Helpful in differentiation between organic and functional causes of impotence
Parathyroid (parathormon) hormone	Anxiety OMS workup	Low level causes hypocalcemia and anxiety Dysregulation associated with wide variety of organic mental disorders
Phosphorous, serum	OMS workup Panic disorder	Increased in renal failure, diabetic acidosis, hypoparathyroidism, hypervitamin D; decreased in cirrhosis, hypokalemia, hyperparathyroidism, panic attack, hyperventilation syndrome
Platelet count	Use of psychotropic medications	Decreased by certain psychotropic medications (carbamazepine, clozapine, phenothiazines)
Porphobilinogen (PBG)	OMS workup	Increased in acute porphyria
Porphyria synthesizing enzyme	Psychosis OMS workup	Acute panic attack or OMS can occur in acute porphyria attack, which may be precipitated by barbiturates, imipramine
Potassium (K), serum	OMS workup Eating disorders	Increased in hyperkalemic acidosis; increase is associated with anxiety in cardiac arrhythymia Decreased in cirrhosis, metabolic alkalosis, laxative abuse, diuretic abuse; decrease is common in bulimic patients and in psychogenic vomiting, anabolic steroid abuse
Prolactin, serum	Use of antipsychotic medications Cocaine use Pseudoseizures	Antipsychotics, by decreasing dopamine, increase prolactin synthesis and release, especially in women Elevated prolactin levels may be seen secondary to cocaine withdrawal Lack of prolactin rise after seizure suggests pseudoseizure

Table 7.2-3
Continued

Test	Major Psychiatric Indications	Comments
Protein, total serum	OMS workup Use of psychotropic medications	Increased in multiple myeloma, myxedema, lupus Decreased in cirrhosis, malnutrition, overhydration Low serum protein can result in greater sensitivity to conventional doses of protein-bound medications (lithium is not protein-bound)
Prothrombin time (PT)	OMS workup	Elevated in significant liver damage (cirrhosis)
Reticulocyte count (estimate of red blood cell production in bone marrow)	OMS workup Use of carbamazepine	Low in megaloblastic or iron deficiency anemia and anemia of chronic disease Must be monitored in patient taking carbamazepine
Salicylate, serum	Organic hallucinosis Suicide attempts	Toxic levels may be seen in suicide attempts and may cause organic hallucinosis
Sodium (NA^+), serum	OMS workup Use of lithium	Increased with excessive salt ingestion; decreased with excessive diaphoresis Decreased in hypoadrenalism, myxedema, congestive heart failure, diarrhea, polydipsia, use of carbamazepine, anabolic steroid Low levels associated with greater sensitivity to conventional dose of lithium
Testosterone, serum	Impotence Inhibited sexual desire	Increase in anabolic steroid abuse May be decreased in organic workup of impotence Decrease may be seen with inhibited sexual desire
Urinalysis	OMS workup Pretreatment workup of lithium Drug screening	Provides clues to cause of various OMSs (assessing general appearance, pH, specific gravity, bilirubin, glucose, blood, ketones, protein, etc.); specific gravity may be affected by lithium
Urinary creatinine	OMS workup Substance abuse Lithium use	Increased in renal failure, dehydration Part of pretreatment workup for lithium
Venereal Disease Research Laboratory (VDRL)	Syphilis	Positive (high titers) in secondary syphilis (may be positive or negative in primary syphilis) Low titers (or negative) in tertiary syphilis
Vitamin A, serum	Depression Delirium	Hypervitaminosis A is associated with a variety of mental status changes
Vitamin B_{12}, serum	OMS workup Dementia	Part of workup of megaloblastic anemia and dementia B_{12} deficiency associated with psychosis, paranoia, fatigue, agitation, dementia, delirium Often associated with chronic alcohol abuse
White blood cell (WBC)	Use of psychotropic medications	Leukopenia and agranulocytosis associated with certain psychotropic medications, such as phenothiazines and carbamazepine, clozapine Leukocytosis associated with lithium and neuroleptic malignant syndrome

References

Arana G W, Baldessarini R J, Ornsteen M: The dexamethasone suppression test for diagnosis and prognosis in psychiatry. Arch Gen Psychiatry *42:* 1193, 1985.

Carroll B J: Dexamethasone suppression test: A review of contemporary confusion. J Clin Psychiatry *46:* 13, 1985.

Evans L: Some biological aspects of panic disorder. Int J Clin Pharmacol Res *9:* 139, 1989.

Galen R S, Gambino S R: *Beyond Normality: The Predictive Value and Efficiency of Medical Diagnoses*. Wiley, New York, 1975.

Garattini S, Tognoni G, eds: Biological markers in mental disorders (symposium). J Psychiatr Res *18:* 327, 1984.

Gold M S, Pottash A L C: *Diagnostic and Laboratory Testing in Psychiatry*, Plenum, New York, 1986.

Griner P F, Glaser R J: Misuse of laboratory tests and diagnostic procedures. N Engl J Med *307:* 1336, 1982.

Hall R C W, Beresford T P, eds: *Handbook of Psychiatric Diagnostic Procedures*, vols 1, 2. SP Medical and Scientific Books, New York, 1984, 1985.

Kirch D G: Medical assessment and laboratory testing in psychiatry. In *Comprehensive Textbook of Psychiatry*, ed 5, H I Kaplan and B J Sadock, editors, p 525. Williams & Wilkins, Baltimore, 1989.

Koranyi E K: Morbidity and rate of undiagnosed physical illnesses in a psychiatric clinic population. Arch Gen Psychiatry *36:* 414, 1979.

Lake C R, Ziegler M G, eds: *The Catecholamines in Psychiatric and Neurologic Disorders*. Butterworth, Boston, 1985.

Martin R L, Preskorn S H: Use of the laboratory in psychiatry. In *The Medical Basis of Psychiatry*, G Winokur and P Clayton, editors, p 522. Saunders, Philadelphia, 1986.

Norman T R, Burrows G D, Judd F K, McIntyre I M: Serotonin and panic disorders: A review of clinical studies. Int J Clin Pharmacol Res *9:* 151, 1989.

Perry J C, Jacobs, D: Overview: Clinical applications of the Amytal interview in psychiatric emergency settings. Am J Psychiatry *139:* 552, 1982.

Usdin E, Hanin I, eds: *Biological Markers in Psychiatry and Neurology*. Pergamon, New York, 1982.

Weinberger D R: Brain disease and psychiatric illness: When should a psychiatrist order a CAT scan? Am J Psychiatry *141:* 1521, 1984.

Typical Signs and Symptoms of Psychiatric Illness Defined

The terms "signs" and "symptoms" refer to specific events: *Signs* are objective findings observed by the clinician (e.g., tachycardia and motor hyperactivity); *symptoms* are subjective complaints listed by the patient (e.g., palpitations and anxiety). A *syndrome* is a group of signs and symptoms that occur together and constitute a recognizable condition; the term "syndrome" is less specific than "disorder" or "disease." Most psychiatric disorders are, in reality, syndromes.

In the outline that follows, a comprehensive list of various signs and symptoms is given, each with a precise definition or description. The student of human behavior needs to be familiar with each sign and symptom, some of which are traced from their roots in essentially normal behavior.

Table 8-1 lists in alphabetical order the signs and symptoms of psychiatric illness discussed in this chapter. The numbers and letters in the right-hand column refer to the place in the outline where each term is defined.

I. Consciousness: state of awareness

Apperception: perception modified by one's own emotions and thoughts. Sensorium: state of functioning of the special senses (sometimes used as a synonym for consciousness). Disturbances of consciousness are most often associated with organic pathology.

A. Disturbances of consciousness

1. Disorientation: disturbance of orientation in time, place, or person
2. Clouding of consciousness: incomplete clearmindedness with disturbance in perception and attitudes
3. Stupor: lack of reaction to and unawareness of surroundings
4. Delirium: bewildered, restless, confused, disoriented reaction associated with fear and hallucinations
5. Coma: profound degree of unconsciousness
6. Coma vigil: coma in which the patient appears to be asleep but ready to be aroused (also known as akinetic mutism)
7. Twilight state: disturbed consciousness with hallucinations
8. Dreamlike state: often used as synonym for complex partial seizure or psychomotor epilepsy
9. Somnolence: abnormal drowsiness seen most often in organic processes

B. Disturbances of attention: attention is the amount of effort exerted in focusing on certain portions of an experience; ability to sustain a focus on one activity; ability to concentrate

1. Distractibility: inability to concentrate attention; attention drawn to unimportant or irrelevant external stimuli
2. Selective inattention: blocking out only those things that generate anxiety
3. Hypervigilance: excessive attention and focus on all internal and external stimuli secondary to paranoid stance.

C. Disturbances in suggestibility: compliant and uncritical response to an idea or influence

1. *Folie à deux* (or *folie à trois*): communicated emotional illness between two (or three) persons
2. Hypnosis: artificially induced modification of consciousness characterized by a heightened suggestibility

II. Emotion: a complex feeling state with psychic, somatic, and behavioral components that is related to affect and mood

A. Affect: the expression of emotion as observed by others. Affect has outward manifestations that can be observed. Affect can vary over time, in response to changing emotional states.

1. Appropriate affect: the normal condition in which emotional tone is in harmony with the accompanying idea, thought, or speech; also further described as broad or full affect, in which a full range of emotions is appropriately expressed
2. Inappropriate affect: disharmony between the emotional feeling tone and the idea, thought, or speech accompanying it
3. Blunted affect: a disturbance in affect manifested by a severe reduction in the intensity of externalized feeling tone
4. Restricted or constricted affect: reduction in intensity of feeling tone less severe than blunted affect but clearly reduced
5. Flat affect: absence or near absence of any signs of affective expression; voice monotonous, face immobile
6. Labile affect: rapid and abrupt changes in emotional feeling tone, unrelated to external stimuli

B. Mood: a pervasive and sustained emotion, subjectively experienced and reported by the patient, as well as

Table 8-1
Index to Signs and Symptoms of Psychiatric Illness. (This table lists in alphabetical order the signs and symptoms of psychiatric illness discussed in this chapter. The numbers and letters in the right-hand column refer to the place in the outline where each item is defined.)

Acrophobia	IV, C, 11c
Acting out	III, 14
Affect	II, A
Aggression	III, 13
Agitation	II, C, 4
Agnosia	VI, B
Agoraphobia	IV, C, 11d
Akathisia	III, 11e
Akinetic mutism	I, A, 6
Alexithymia	II, B, 12
Algophobia	IV, C, 10e
Ambivalence	II, C, 8
Amnesia	VII, A, 1
Anhedonia	II, B, 10
Anomia	V, B, 3
Anorexia	II, D, 1
Anosognosia	VI, B, 1
Anxiety	II, C, 1
Apathy	II, C, 7
Aphasic disturbances	V, B
Apperception	I
Appropriate affect	II, A, 1
Apraxia	VI, B, 6
Astereognosia	VI, B, 4
Attention	I, B
Auditory hallucination	VI, A, 1c
Autistic thinking	IV, A, 7
Automatic judgment	X, B
Automatic obedience	III, 8
Automatism	III, 7
Autotopagnosia	VI, B, 2
Bizarre delusion	IV, C, 3a
Blocking	IV, B, 15
Blunted affect	II, A, 3
Broca's aphasia,	V, B, 1
Catalepsy	III, 2a
Cataplexy	III, 4
Catatonia	III, 2
Catatonic excitement	III, 2b
Catatonic posturing	III, 2e
Catatonic rigidity	III, 2d
Catatonic stupor	III, 2c
Cenesthesic hallucination	VI, A, 1, h
Cerea flexibilitas (waxy flexibility)	III, 2f
Circumstantiality	IV, B, 3
Clang association	IV, B, 14
Claustrophobia	IV, C, 11f
Clérembault's syndrome	III, C, 3l
Clouding of consciousness	I, A, 2
Cluttering	V, A, 10
Coma	I, A, 5
Coma vigil	I, A, 6
Command automatism	III, 8
Compulsion	IV, C, 9
Conation	III
Concrete thinking	VIII, D
Condensation	IV, B, 9
Confabulation	VII, A, 2c
Consciousness	I
Constipation	II, D, 7
Constricted affect	II, A, 4
Conversion symptom	VI, C
Coprolalia	IV, C, 10
Déjà entendu	VII, A, 2e
Déjà pensé	VII, A, 2f
Déjà vu	VII, A, 2d
Delirium	I, A, 4
Delusion	IV, C, 3
Delusional jealousy	IV, C, 3k
Delusion of control	IV, C, 3j
Delusion of grandeur	IV, C, 3h, ii
Delusion of infidelity	IV, C, 3k
Delusion of persecution	IV, C, 3h, i
Delusion of poverty	IV, C, 3f
Delusion of reference	IV, C, 3h, iii
Delusion of self-accusation	IV, C, 3i
Dementia	VIII, B
Depersonalization	VI, C, 4
Depression	II, B, 9
Derailment	IV, B, 12
Derealization	VI, C, 5
Dereism	IV, A, 6
Diminished libido	II, D, 6
Dipsomania	III, 10f, i
Disorientation	I, A, 1
Distractibility	I, B, 1
Disturbances associated with conversion and dissociative phenomena	VI, C
Disturbances associated with organic mental disease	VI, B
Disturbances in content of thought	IV, C
Disturbances in form of thinking	IV, A
Disturbances in speech	V, A
Disturbances in suggestibility	I, C
Disturbances of attention	I, B
Disturbances of consciousness	I, A
Disturbances of memory	VII, A
Diurnal variation	II, D, 5
Dreamlike state	I, A, 8
Dysarthria	V, A, 7
Dyscalculia	VIII, B, 1
Dysgraphia	VIII, B, 2
Dysphoric mood	II, B, 1
Dysprosody	V, A, 6
Echolalia	IV, B, 8
Echopraxia	III, 1
Ecstacy	II, B, 8
Egomania	IV, C, 5
Eidetic image	VII, A, 4
Elevated mood	II, B, 6
Emotion	II
Erotomania	IV, C, 3
Euphoria	II, B, 7
Euthymic mood	II, B, 2
Excessively loud or soft speech	V, A, 8
Expansive mood	II, B, 3
Expressive aphasia	V, B, 1
Fausse reconnaissance	VII, A, 2a
Fear	II, C, 3l
Flat affect	II, A, 5
Flight of ideas	IV, B, 13
Fluent aphasia	V, B, 2
Folie à deux (folie à trois)	I, C, 1
Formal thought disorder	IV, A, 4
Formication	VI, A, 1g
Free-floating anxiety	II, C, 2
Freudian slip	IV
Fugue	VI, C, 6
Global aphasia	V, B, 6
Glossolalia	IV, B, 16
Grief	II, B, 11
Gustatory hallucination	VI, A, 1f

Table 8-1
Continued

Hallucination	VI, A, 1	Obsession	IV, C, 8
Hallucinosis	VI, A, 1l	Olfactory hallucination	VI, A, 1e
Haptic hallucination	VI, A, 1g	Overactivity	III, 10
Hyperactivity (hyperkinesis)	III, 10b	Overvalued idea	IV, C, 2
Hypermnesia	VII, A, 3	Panic	II, C, 6
Hyperphasia	II, D, 2	Paramnesia	VII, A, 2
Hypersomnia	II, D, 4	Paranoid delusions	IV, C, 3h
Hypervigilance	I, B, 3	Paranoid ideation	IV, C, 3h
Hypnagogic hallucination	VI, A, 1a	Parapraxis	IV
Hypnopompic hallucination	VI, A, 1b	Pathological jealousy	IV, C, 3k
Hypnosis	I, C, 2	Perception	VI
Hypoactivity (hypokinesis)	III, 11	Persecutory delusion	IV, C, 3h, i
Hypochondria	IV, C, 7	Perseveration	IV, B, 6
Hysterical anesthesia	VI, C, 1	Phantom limb	VI, A, 1g
Idea of reference	IV, C, 3b, iii	Phobia	IV, C, 11
Illogical thinking	IV, A, 5	Physiological disturbances associated with mood	II, D
Illusion	VI, A, 2	Posturing	III, 2e
Immediate memory	VII, B, 1	Poverty of content of speech	V, A, 5
Impaired insight	IX, C	Poverty of speech	V, A, 3
Impaired judgment	X, C	Preoccupation of thought	IV, C, 4
Inappropriate affect	II, A, 2	Pressure of speech	V, A, 1
Incoherence	IV, B, 5	Primary process thinking	IV, A, 9
Increased libido	II, D, 6	Prosopagnosia	VI, B, 5
Initial insomnia	II, D, 3a	Pseudodementia	VIII, C
Insight	IX	Pseudologia fantastica	IV, C, 3m
Insomnia	II, D, 3	Psychomotor agitation	III, 10a
Intellectual insight	IX, A	Psychosis	IV, A, 2
Intelligence	VIII	Reality testing	IV, A, 3
Irrelevant answer	IV, B, 10	Recent memory	VII, B, 2
Irritable mood	II, B, 4	Recent past memory	VII, B, 3
Jamais vu	VII, A, 2g	Receptive aphasia	V, B, 2
Jargon aphasia	V, B, 5	Remote memory	VII, B, 4
Kleptomania	III, 10f, ii	Restricted affect	II, A, 4
Labile affect	II, A, 6	Retrospective falsification	VII, A, 2b
Labile mood	II, B, 5	Rigidity	III, 2d
Lilliputian hallucination	VI, A, 1i	Ritual	III, 10f, vi
Logorrhea	V, A, 2	Rumination	IV, C, 8
Loosening of associations	IV, B, 11	Satyriasis	III, 10f, iv
Macropsia	VI, C, 2	Selective inattention	I, B, 2
Magical thinking	IV, A, 8	Sensorium	I
Mannerism	III, 6	Sensory aphasia	V, B, 2
Memory	VII	Simple phobia	IV, C, 11a
Mental disorder	IV, A, 1	Sleepwalking	III, 10d
Mental retardation	VIII, A	Social phobia	IV, C, 11b
Micropsia	VI, C, 3	Somatic delusion	IV, C, 3g
Middle insomnia	II, D, 3b	Somatic hallucination	VI, A, 1h
Mimicry	III, 12	Somnambulism	III, 10d
Monomania	IV, C, 6	Somnolence	I, A, 9
Mood	II, B	Speaking in tongues	IV, B, 16
Mood-congruent delusion	IV, C, 3c	Specific disturbances in form of thought	IV, B
Mood-congruent hallucination	VI, A, 1j	Stereotypy	III, 5
Mood-incongruent delusion	IV, C, 3d	Stupor	I, A, 3; III, 2c
Mood-incongruent hallucination	VI, A, 1k	Stuttering	V, A, 9
Mood swings	II, B, 5	Synesthesia	VI, A, 1m
Motor aphasia	V, B, 1	Syntactical aphasia	V, B, 4
Motor behavior (conation)	III	Systematized delusion	IV, C, 3b
Mourning	II, B, 11	Tactile (haptic) hallucination	VI, A, 1g
Multiple personality	VI, C, 7	Tangentiality	IV, B, 4
Mutism	III, 9	Tension	II, C, 5
Negativism	III, 3	Terminal insomnia	II, D, 3c
Neologism	IV, B, 1	Thinking	IV
Neurosis	IV, A, 2	Thought broadcasting	IV, C, 3j, iii
Nihilistic delusion	IV, C, 3e	Thought control	IV, C, 3j, iv
Noesis	IV, C, 12	Though deprivation	IV, B, 15
Nominal aphasia	V, B, 3	Thought insertion	IV, C, 3j, ii
Nonfluent aphasia	V, B, 1	Thought withdrawal	IV, C, 3j, i
Nymphomania	III, 10f, iii		

Table 8-1
Continued

Tic	III, 10c	Visual agnosia	VI, B, 3
Trailing phenomenon	VI, A, 1n	Visual hallucination	VI, A, 1d
Trend of thought	IV, C, 4	Volubility	V, A, 2
Trichotillomania	III, 10, f, v	Waxy flexibility	III, 2f
True insight	IX, B	Wernicke's aphasia	V, B, 2
Twilight state	I, A, 7	Word salad	IV, B, 2
Unio mystica	IV, C, 13	Xenophobia	IV, C, 11g
Vegetative signs	II, D	Zoophobia	IV, C, 11h
Verbigeration	IV, B, 7		

observed by others; examples include depression, elation, anger

1. Dysphoric mood: an unpleasant mood
2. Euthymic mood: normal range of mood, implying absence of depressed or elevated mood
3. Expansive mood: expression of one's feelings without restraint, frequently with an overestimation of one's significance or importance
4. Irritable mood: easily annoyed and provoked to anger
5. Mood swings (labile mood): oscillations between euphoria and depression or anxiety
6. Elevated mood: air of confidence and enjoyment; a mood more cheerful than normal but not necessarily pathological
7. Euphoria: intense elation with feelings of grandeur
8. Ecstasy: feeling of intense rapture
9. Depression: psychopathological feeling of sadness
10. Anhedonia: loss of interest in and withdrawal from all regular and pleasurable activities, often associated with depression
11. Grief or mourning: sadness appropriate to a real loss
12. Alexithymia: inability or difficulty in describing or being aware of one's emotions or moods

C. Other emotions

1. Anxiety: feeling of apprehension caused by anticipation of danger, which may be internal or external
2. Free-floating anxiety: pervasive, unfocused fear not attached to any idea
3. Fear: anxiety caused by consciously recognized and realistic danger
4. Agitation: severe anxiety associated with motor restlessness
5. Tension: increased motor and psychological activity that is unpleasant
6. Panic: acute, episodic, intense attack of anxiety associated with overwhelming feelings of dread and autonomic discharge
7. Apathy: dulled emotional tone associated with detachment or indifference
8. Ambivalence: coexistence of two opposing impulses toward the same thing in the same person at the same time

D. Physiological disturbances associated with mood: signs that refer to somatic (usually autonomic) dysfunction of the person, most often associated with depression (also called vegetative signs)

1. Anorexia: loss of or decrease in appetite
2. Hyperphagia: increase in appetite and intake of food
3. Insomnia: lack of or diminished ability to sleep
   a. Initial: difficulty in falling asleep
   b. Middle: difficulty in sleeping through the night without waking up and difficulty in going back to sleep
   c. Terminal: early-morning awakening
4. Hypersomnia: excessive sleeping
5. Diurnal variation: mood is regularly worst in morning, immediately after awakening, and improves as day progresses
6. Diminished libido: decreased sexual interest, drive, and performance (increased libido is associated with manic states)
7. Constipation: inability or difficulty in defecating

III. Motor behavior (conation): the aspect of the psyche that includes impulses, motivations, wishes, drives, instincts, and cravings, as expressed by a person's behavior or motor activity

1. Echopraxia: pathological imitation of movements of one person by another
2. Catatonia: motor anomalies in nonorganic disorders (as opposed to disturbances of consciousness and motor activity secondary to organic pathology).
   a. Catalepsy: general term for an immobile position that is constantly maintained
   b. Catatonic excitement: agitated, purposeless motor activity, uninfluenced by external stimuli
   c. Catatonic stupor: markedly slowed motor activity, often to a point of immobility and seeming unawareness of surroundings
   d. Catatonic rigidity: voluntary assumption of a rigid posture, held against all efforts to be moved
   e. Catatonic posturing: voluntary assumption of an inappropriate or bizarre posture, generally maintained for long periods of time
   f. *Cerea flexibilitas* (waxy flexibility): the person can be molded into a position that is then maintained; when the examiner moves the person's limb, the limb feels as if it were made of wax
3. Negativism: motiveless resistance to all attempts to be moved or to all instructions

4. Cataplexy: temporary loss of muscle tone and weakness precipitated by a variety of emotional states
5. Stereotypy: repetitive fixed pattern of physical action or speech
6. Mannerism: ingrained, habitual involuntary movement
7. Automatism: automatic performance of an act or acts generally representative of unconscious symbolic activity
8. Command automatism: automatic following of suggestions (also called automatic obedience)
9. Mutism: voicelessness without structural abnormalities
10. Overactivity
    a. Psychomotor agitation: excessive motor and cognitive overactivity, usually nonproductive and in response to inner tension
    b. Hyperactivity (hyperkinesis): restless, aggressive, destructive activity, often associated with some underlying organic pathology
    c. Tic: involuntary, spasmodic motor movement
    d. Sleepwalking (somnambulism): motor activity during sleep
    e. Akathisia: subjective feeling of muscular tension secondary to antipsychotic or other medication, which can cause restlessness, pacing, repeated sitting and standing; can be mistaken for psychotic agitation
    f. Compulsion: uncontrollable impulse to perform an act repetitively
        i. Dipsomania: compulsion to drink alcohol
        ii. Kleptomania: compulsion to steal
        iii. Nymphomania: excessive and compulsive need for coitus in a woman
        iv. Satyriasis: excessive and compulsive need for coitus in a man
        v. Trichotillomania: compulsion to pull out one's hair
        vi. Ritual: automatic activity compulsive in nature, anxiety-reducing in origin
11. Hypoactivity (hypokinesis): decreased motor and cognitive activity, as in psychomotor retardation; visible slowing of thought, speech, movements
12. Mimicry: simple, imitative motor activity of childhood
13. Aggression: forceful goal-directed action that may be verbal or physical; the motor counterpart of the affect of rage, anger, or hostility
14. Acting out: direct expression of an unconscious wish or impulse in action; unconscious fantasy is lived out impulsively in behavior

IV. Thinking: goal-directed flow of ideas, symbols, and associations initiated by a problem or task and leading toward a reality-oriented conclusion; when a logical sequence occurs, thinking is normal; parapraxis (unconsciously motivated lapse from logic is also called "Freudian slip") considered part of normal thinking

A. General disturbances in form or process of thinking

1. Mental disorder: clinically significant behavioral or psychological syndrome, associated with distress or disability, not just an expected response to a particular event
2. Psychosis: inability to distinguish reality from fantasy; impaired reality testing, with creation of a new reality (as opposed to neurosis: mental disorder in which reality testing is intact, behavior does not violate gross social norms, relatively enduring or recurrent without treatment; disorder not in form of thought but, rather, with how one thinks about different aspects of oneself and one's life)
3. Reality testing: the objective evaluation and judgment of the world outside the self
4. Formal thought disorder: disturbance in the form of thought instead of the content of thought; thinking characterized by loosened associations, neologisms, and illogical constructs; thought process is disordered, and the person is defined as psychotic
5. Illogical thinking: thinking containing erroneous conclusions or internal contradictions; is psychopathological only when it is marked and when not caused by cultural values or intellectual deficit
6. Dereism: mental activity not concordant with logic or experience
7. Autistic thinking: thinking that gratifies unfulfilled desires but has no regard for reality; preoccupation with inner, private world; term used somewhat synonymously with dereism
8. Magical thinking: a form of dereistic thought; thinking that is similar to that of the preoperational phase in children (Piaget), in which thoughts, words, or actions assume power (for example, they can cause or prevent events)
9. Primary process thinking: general term for thinking that is dereistic, illogical, magical; normally found in dreams, abnormally in psychosis

B. Specific disturbances in form of thought

1. Neologism: new word created by the patient, often from combining syllables of other words, for idiosyncratic psychological reasons
2. Word salad: incoherent mixture of words and phrases
3. Circumstantiality: indirect speech that is delayed in reaching the point but eventually gets from original point to desired goal; characterized by an overinclusion of detail and parenthetical remarks
4. Tangentiality: inability to have goal-directed associations of thought; patient never gets from desired point to desired goal
5. Incoherence: thought that, generally, is not understandable; running together of thoughts or words with no logical or grammatical connection, resulting in disorganization
6. Perseveration: persisting response to a prior stimulus after a new stimulus has been presented, often associated with organic mental disease
7. Verbigeration: meaningless repetition of specific words or phrases
8. Echolalia: psychopathological repeating of words or phrases of one person by another; tends to be repetitive and persistent, may be spoken with mocking or staccato intonation

9. Condensation: fusion of various concepts into one
10. Irrelevant answer: answer that is not in harmony with question asked (appears to ignore or not attend to question)
11. Loosening of associations: flow of thought in which ideas shift from one subject to another in a completely unrelated way; when severe, speech may be incoherent
12. Derailment: gradual or sudden deviation in train of thought without blocking; sometimes used synonymously with loosening of associations
13. Flight of ideas: rapid, continuous verbalizations or plays on words produce constant shifting from one idea to another; the ideas tend to be connected and in the less severe form may be followed by a listener
14. Clang association: association of words similar in sound but not in meaning; words have no logical connection, may include rhyming and punning
15. Blocking: abrupt interruption in train of thinking before a thought or idea is finished; after brief pause, person indicates no recall of what was being said or was going to be said (also known as thought deprivation)
16. Glossolalia: the expression of a revelatory message through unintelligible words (also known as speaking in tongues); not considered a disturbance in thought if associated with practices of specific Pentecostal religion

C. Specific disturbances in content of thought

1. Poverty of content: thought that gives little information because of vagueness, empty repetitions, or obscure phrases
2. Overvalued idea: unreasonable, sustained false belief maintained less firmly than delusion
3. Delusion: false belief, based on incorrect inference about external reality, not consistent with patient's intelligence and cultural background, that cannot be corrected by reasoning
   a. Bizarre delusion: an absurd, totally implausible, very strange false belief (e.g., invaders from space have implanted electrodes in the patient's brain)
   b. Systematized delusion: false belief or beliefs united by a single event or theme (e.g., patient is being persecuted by the CIA, FBI, Mafia, or the boss)
   c. Mood-congruent delusion: delusion with mood-appropriate content (e.g., a depressed patient who believes he or she is responsible for the destruction of the world)
   d. Mood-incongruent delusion: delusion with content that has no association to mood or is mood-neutral (e.g., a depressed patient who has delusions of thought control or thought broadcasting)
   e. Nihilistic delusion: false feeling that self, others, or the world is nonexistent or ending
   f. Delusion of poverty: false belief that one is bereft or will be of all material possessions
   g. Somatic delusion: false belief involving functioning of one's body (e.g., belief that one's brain is rotting or melting)
   h. Paranoid delusions: includes persecutory delusions and delusions of reference, control, and grandeur (this is to be distinguished from paranoid ideation, which is suspiciousness of less than delusional proportions)
      i. Delusion of persecution: false belief that one is being harassed, cheated, or persecuted; often found in litigious patients who have a pathological tendency to take legal action because of imagined mistreatment
      ii. Delusion of grandeur: exaggerated conception of one's importance, power, or identity
      iii. Delusion of reference: false belief that the behavior of others refers to oneself; that events, objects, or other people have a particular and unusual significance, usually of a negative nature; derived from idea of reference, in which one falsely feels one is being talked about by others (e.g., belief that people on television or radio are talking to or about the patient); this differs from an idea of reference, in which the false belief is not as firmly held as a delusion
   i. Delusion of self-accusation: false feeling of remorse and guilt
   j. Delusion of control: false feeling that one's will, thoughts, or feelings are being controlled by external forces
      i. Thought withdrawal: delusion that one's thoughts are being removed from one's mind by other people or forces
      ii. Thought insertion: delusion that thoughts are being implanted in one's mind by other people or forces
      iii. Thought broadcasting: delusion that one's thoughts can be heard by others, as though they were being broadcast into the air
      iv. Thought control: delusion that one's thoughts are being controlled by other people or forces
   k. Delusion of infidelity (delusional jealousy): false belief derived from pathological jealousy that one's lover is unfaithful
   l. Erotomania: delusional belief, more common in women, that a man is deeply in love with them (also known as Clérembault's syndrome)
   m. Pseudologia fantastica: a type of lying, in which the person appears to believe in the reality of his or her fantasies and acts on them
4. Trend or preoccupation of thought: centering of thought content on a particular idea, associated with a strong affective tone, such as a paranoid trend or a suicidal or homicidal preoccupation
5. Egomania: pathological self-preoccupation
6. Monomania: preoccupation with a single object
7. Hypochondria: exaggerated concern over one's health that is based not on real organic pathology but, rather, on unrealistic interpretation of physical signs or sensations as abnormal
8. Obsession: pathological persistence of an irresistible thought or feeling that cannot be eliminated from consciousness by logical effort, which is associated with anxiety (also termed rumination)
9. Compulsion: pathological need to act on an impulse

that, if resisted, produces anxiety; repetitive behavior in response to an obsession or performed according to certain rules, with no true end in itself other than to prevent something from occurring in the future

10. Coprolalia: compulsive utterance of obscene words
11. Phobia: persistent, irrational, exaggerated, and invariably pathological dread of some specific type of stimulus or situation; results in a compelling desire to avoid the feared stimulus
    a. Simple phobia: circumscribed dread of a discrete object or situation (e.g., dread of spiders or snakes)
    b. Social phobia: dread of public humiliation, as in fear of public speaking, performing, or eating in public
    c. Acrophobia: dread of high places
    d. Agoraphobia: dread of open places
    e. Algophobia: dread of pain
    f. Claustrophobia: dread of closed places
    g. Xenophobia: dread of strangers
    h. Zoophobia: dread of animals
12. Noesis: a revelation in which immense illumination occurs in association with a sense that one has been chosen to lead and command
13. *Unio mystica*: an oceanic feeling, one of mystic unity with an infinite power; not considered a disturbance in thought content if congruent with patient's religious or cultural milieu

V. Speech: ideas, thoughts, feelings as expressed through language; communication through the use of words and language

A. Disturbances in speech

1. Pressure of speech: rapid speech that is increased in amount and difficult to interrupt
2. Volubility (logorrhea): copious, coherent, logical speech
3. Poverty of speech: restriction in the amount of speech used; replies may be monosyllabic
4. Nonspontaneous speech: verbal responses given only when asked or spoken to directly; no self-initiation of speech
5. Poverty of content of speech: speech that is adequate in amount but conveys little information because of vagueness, emptiness, or stereotyped phrases
6. Dysprosody: loss of normal speech melody (called prosody)
7. Dysarthria: difficulty in articulation, not in word finding or in grammar
8. Excessively loud or soft speech: loss of modulation of normal speech volume; may reflect a variety of pathological conditions ranging from psychosis to depression to deafness
9. Stuttering: frequent repetition or prolongation of a sound or syllable, leading to markedly impaired speech fluency
10. Cluttering: erratic and dysrhythmic speech, consisting of rapid and jerky spurts

B. Aphasic disturbances (disturbances in language output)

1. Motor aphasia: disturbance of speech caused by an organic mental disorder in which understanding remains but ability to speak is grossly impaired; speech is halting, laborious, and inaccurate (also known as Broca's, nonfluent, or expressive aphasia)
2. Sensory aphasia: organic loss of ability to comprehend the meaning of words; speech is fluid and spontaneous, but incoherent and nonsensical (also known as Wernicke's, fluent, or receptive aphasia)
3. Nominal aphasia: difficulty in finding correct name for an object (also termed anomia)
4. Syntactical aphasia: inability to arrange words in proper sequence
5. Jargon aphasia: words produced are totally neologistic; nonsense words repeated with various intonations and inflections
6. Global aphasia: combination of a grossly nonfluent aphasia and a severe fluent aphasia

VI. Perception: process of transferring physical stimulation into psychological information; mental process by which sensory stimuli are brought to awareness

A. Disturbances of perception

1. Hallucination: false sensory perception not associated with real external stimuli; there may or may not be a delusional interpretation of the hallucinatory experience; hallucinations indicate a psychotic disturbance only when associated with impairment in reality testing
    a. Hypnagogic hallucination: false sensory perception occurring while falling asleep; generally considered nonpathological phenomenon
    b. Hypnopompic hallucination: false perception occurring while awakening from sleep; generally considered nonpathological
    c. Auditory hallucination: false perception of sound, usually voices but also other noises, such as music; most common hallucination in psychiatric disorders
    d. Visual hallucination: false perception involving sight consisting of both formed images (e.g., people) and unformed images (e.g., flashes of light); most common in organically determined disorders
    e. Olfactory hallucination: false perception in smell; most common in organic disorders
    f. Gustatory hallucination: false perception of taste, such as unpleasant taste caused by an uncinate seizure; most common in organic disorders
    g. Tactile (haptic) hallucination: false perception of touch or surface sensation, as from an amputated limb (phantom limb), crawling sensation on or under the skin (formication)
    h. Somatic hallucination: false sensation of things occurring in or to the body, most often visceral in origin (also known as cenesthetsic hallucination)
    i. Lilliputian hallucination: false perception in which objects are seen as reduced in size (also termed micropsia)

j. Mood-congruent hallucination: hallucination the content of which is consistent with either a depressed or a manic mood (e.g., a depressed patient hears voices saying that the patient is a bad person; a manic patient hears voices saying that the patient is of inflated worth, power, knowledge, etc.)
k. Mood-incongruent hallucination: hallucination whose content is not consistent with either depressed or manic mood (e.g., in depression, hallucinations not involving such themes as guilt, deserved punishment, or inadequacy; in mania, hallucinations not involving such themes as inflated worth or power)
l. Hallucinosis: hallucinations, most often auditory, that are associated with chronic alcohol abuse and that occur within a clear sensorium (as opposed to DTs, which occur in the context of a clouded sensorium)
m. Synesthesia: sensation or hallucination caused by another sensation (e.g., an auditory sensation is accompanied by or triggers a visual sensation; a sound is experienced as being seen, or a visual experience is heard)
n. Trailing phenomenon: perceptual abnormality associated with hallucinogenic drugs in which moving objects are seen as a series of discrete and discontinuous images

2. Illusion: misperception or misinterpretation of real external sensory stimuli

B. Disturbances associated with organic mental disorder: agnosia—an inability to recognize and interpret the significance of sensory impressions

1. Anosognosia: inability to recognize illness as occurring to oneself
2. Autotopagnosia: inability to recognize a body part as one's own
3. Visual agnosia: inability to recognize objects or persons
4. Astereognosia: inability to recognize objects by touch
5. Prosopagnosia: inability to recognize faces
6. Apraxia: inability to carry out specific tasks

C. Disturbances associated with conversion and dissociative phenomena: somatization of repressed material or the development of physical symptoms and distortions involving the voluntary muscles or special sense organs; not under voluntary control and not explained by any physical disorder

1. Hysterical anesthesia: loss of sensory modalities resulting from emotional conflicts
2. Macropsia: state in which objects seem larger than they are
3. Micropsia: state in which objects seem smaller than they are (both macropsia and micropsia can also be associated with clear organic conditions, such as complex partial seizures)
4. Depersonalization: a subjective sense of being unreal, strange, or unfamiliar to oneself
5. Derealization: a subjective sense that the environment is strange or unreal; a feeling of changed reality
6. Fugue: taking on a new identity with amnesia for the old identity; often involves travel or wandering to new environments
7. Multiple personality: one person who appears at different times to be in possession of an entirely different personality and character

VII. Memory: function by which information stored in the brain is later recalled to consciousness

A. Disturbances of memory

1. Amnesia: partial or total inability to recall past experiences, may be organic or emotional in origin
2. Paramnesia: falsification of memory by distortion of recall
   a. *Fausse reconnaissance:* false recognition
   b. Retrospective falsification: memory becomes unintentionally (unconsciously) distorted by being filtered through patient's present emotional, cognitive, and experiential state
   c. Confabulation: unconscious filling of gaps in memory by imagined or untrue experiences that patient believes but that have no basis in fact; most often associated with organic pathology
   d. *Déjà vu:* illusion of visual recognition in which a new situation is incorrectly regarded as a repetition of a previous memory
   e. *Déjà entendu:* illusion of auditory recognition
   f. *Déjà pensé:* illusion that a new thought is recognized as a thought previously felt or expressed
   g. *Jamais vu:* false feeling of unfamiliarity with a real situation one has experienced
3. Hypermnesia: exaggerated degree of retention and recall
4. Eidetic image: visual memory of almost hallucinatory vividness

B. Levels of memory

1. Immediate: reproduction or recall of perceived material within seconds to minutes
2. Recent: recall of events over past few days
3. Recent past: recall of events over past few months
4. Remote: recall of events in distant past

VIII. Intelligence: the ability to understand, recall, mobilize, and constructively integrate previous learning in meeting new situations

A. Mental retardation: lack of intelligence to a degree in which there is interference with social and vocational performance: mild (I.Q. of 50 or 55 to approximately 70), moderate (I.Q. of 35 or 40 to 50 or 55), severe (I.Q. of 20 or 25 to 35 or 40), or profound (I.Q. below 20 or 25); obsolete terms are "idiot" (mental age less than 3 years), "imbecile" (mental age of 3 to 7 years), and "moron" (mental age of about 8)

B. Dementia: organic and global deterioration of intellectual functioning without clouding of consciousness

1. Dyscalculia: loss of ability to do calculations not caused by anxiety or impairment in concentration.
2. Dysgraphia: loss of ability to write in cursive style; loss of word structure

C. Pseudodementia: clinical features resembling a dementia not caused by an organic mental dysfunction; most often caused by depression

D. Concrete thinking: literal thinking; limited use of metaphor without understanding of nuances of meaning; one-dimensional thought

E. Abstract thinking: ability to appreciate nuances of meaning; multidimensional thinking with ability to use metaphors and hypotheses appropriately

IX. Insight: ability of the patient to understand the true cause and meaning of a situation (such as a set of symptoms)

A. Intellectual insight: understanding of the objective reality of a set of circumstances without the ability to apply the understanding in any useful way to master the situation

B. True insight: understanding of the objective reality of a situation, coupled with the motivation and the emotional impetus to master the situation

C. Impaired insight: diminished ability to understand the objective reality of a situation

X. Judgment: ability to assess a situation correctly and act appropriately within that situation

A. Critical judgment: ability to assess, discern, and choose among different options in a situation

B. Automatic judgment: reflex performance of an action

C. Impaired judgment: diminished ability to understand a situation correctly and to act appropriately

References

Andreasen N C: The clinical assessment of thought, language, and communication disorders: I. The definition of terms and evaluation of their reliability. Arch Gen Psychiatry *36*: 1315, 1979.

Bender M D: *Disorders of Perception*. Charles C Thomas, Springfield, IL, 1952.

Bensen D F, Blumer D, eds: *Psychiatric Aspects of Neurological Disease*, vol 2. Grune & Stratton, Orlando, FL, 1982.

Bleuler E: *Dementia Praecox: The Group of Schizophrenias*. International Universities Press, New York, 1950.

Campbell R J: *Psychiatric Dictionary*, ed 6. Oxford University Press, New York, 1989.

Cassano G B, Perugi G, Musetti L, Akiskal H S: The nature of depression presenting concomitantly with panic disorder. Compr Psychiatry *30*: 473, 1989.

Cavenar J O, Brodie, H K M: *Signs and Symptoms in Psychiatry*. Lippincott, Philadelphia, 1983.

Fenichel O: *Psychoanalytic Theory of Neuroses*, Norton, New York, 1945.

Frances A J, Hales R E: *Annual Review*, vol 5. American Psychiatric Press, Washington, DC, 1986.

Geschwind N: Aphasia. N Engl J Med *284*: 654, 1971.

Hellerstein D, Frosch W, Koenigsberg H W: The clinical significance of command hallucinations. Am J Psychiatry *144*: 219, 1987.

Kaplan H I, Sadock B J: Typical signs and symptoms of psychiatric illness. In *Comprehensive Textbook of Psychiatry*, ed 5, H I Kaplan and B J Sadock, eds, p 468. Williams & Wilkins, Baltimore, 1989.

Spitzer R L, Skodol A E, Williams J B W: *Case Book: Diagnostic and Statistical Manual of Mental Disorders*. American Psychiatric Association, Washington, DC, 1988.

Classification in Psychiatry and Psychiatric Rating Scales

DSM-III-R

Diagnostic and Statistical Manual of Mental Disorders (DSM), which is published by the American Psychiatric Association (APA), lists specific criteria that enable the clinician to establish a diagnosis. The first edition (DSM-I) was published in 1952, and there have been three editions since that time: DSM-II, published in 1968; DSM-III, published in 1980; and a revised third edition, DSM-III-R, published in 1987, which is the one currently in use. All the terminology used in this textbook conforms to the official DSM-III-R nomenclature. An entirely new edition (DSM-IV) will be published in 1993.

Basic Features

Descriptive approach. The approach in DSM-III-R is atheoretical with regard to etiology. Thus, DSM-III-R attempts to describe comprehensively what the manifestations of mental disorders are and only rarely attempts to account for how the disturbances come about. The general approach is descriptive in that the definitions of these disorders consist, by and large, of descriptions of the clinical features.

Diagnostic criteria. Specified diagnostic criteria are provided for each specific mental disorder. These criteria include a list of essential features that must be present for the diagnosis to be made. Such criteria have been shown to increase the reliability of the diagnostic process between and among clinicians.

Systematic description. DSM-III-R systematically describes each disorder in terms of its essential features and associated features, with brief comments about such factors as age at onset, course, impairment, complications, predisposing factors, prevalence, sex ratio, familial pattern, and differential diagnosis. DSM-III-R does not purport to be a textbook. No mention is made of theories of etiology, management, or treatment, nor are the controversial issues surrounding a particular diagnostic category discussed.

Diagnostic uncertainties. An important feature of DSM-III-R is the provision of explicit rules to be used in situations in which the information is insufficient (diagnosis to be deferred or provisional) or the patient's clinical presentation and history do not meet the full criteria of a prototypical category (an atypical, residual, or not otherwise specified [NOS] subclass within the general category).

Guidelines

The American Psychiatric Association has issued a cautionary statement concerning the proper use and interpretation of the diagnostic categories in DSM-III-R. It reads as follows:

> The specified diagnostic criteria for each mental disorder are offered as guidelines for making diagnoses, since it has been demonstrated that the use of such criteria enhances diagnostic agreement among clinicians and investigators. The proper use of these criteria requires specialized clinical training that provides both a body of knowledge and clinical skills.
>
> Those diagnostic criteria reflect a consensus of current formulations of evolving knowledge in our field but do not encompass all the conditions which may legitimately be the subject of treatment or research efforts.
>
> The purpose of DSM-III-R is to provide clear descriptions of diagnostic categories in order to enable clinicians and investigators to diagnose, communicate about, study, and treat various mental disorders. It is to be understood that inclusion here, for clinical and research purposes, of a diagnostic category such as pathological gambling or pedophilia does not imply that the condition meets legal or other nonmedical criteria for what constitutes mental disease, mental disorder, or mental disability. The clinical and scientific considerations involved in the categorization of these conditions as mental disorders may not be wholly relevant to legal judgments, for example, that take into account such issues as individual responsibility, disability determination, and competency.

Multiaxial Evaluation

DSM-III-R is a multiaxial system that evaluates the patient along several variables and contains the following five axes:

Axis I. Clinical syndromes, plus conditions not attributable to a mental disorder

Axis II. Developmental disorders (includes mental retardation, specific developmental disorders, and pervasive developmental disorders) and personality disorders

Axis I and Axis II constitute the entire classification of mental disorders, which includes 18 major classifications and more than 200 specific disorders (Table 9-1). In many instances there is a disorder on both axes. For example, an adult may have major depression noted on Axis I and obsessive-compulsive personality disorder on Axis II, or a child may have conduct disorder noted on Axis I and developmental language disorder on Axis II.

Axis III. Axis III lists any physical disorder or con-

Table 9-1
Classes or Groups of Conditions in DSM-III-R

1. Disorders usually first evident in infancy, childhood, or adolescence (includes DSM-III-R category of developmental disorders)
2. Organic mental disorders
3. Psychoactive substance use disorders
4. Schizophrenia
5. Delusional (paranoid) disorder
6. Psychotic disorders not elsewhere classified
7. Mood disorders (previously known in DSM-III as affective disorders)
8. Anxiety disorders (or anxiety and phobic neuroses)
9. Somatoform disorders
10. Dissociative disorders (or hysterical neuroses, dissociative type)
11. Sexual disorders
12. Sleep disorders
13. Factitious disorders
14. Impulse control disorders not elsewhere classified
15. Adjustment disorder
16. Psychological factors affecting physical condition
17. Personality disorders
18. Conditions not attributable to a mental disorder that are a focus of attention or treatment

dition that may be present in addition to a mental disorder. The physical condition may be causative (e.g., kidney failure causing delirium), the result of the mental disorder (e.g., alcohol gastritis secondary to alcohol dependence), or unrelated to the mental disorder.

Axis IV. Axis IV provides a six-point rating scale for coding the psychosocial stressors that significantly contribute to the development or exacerbation of the current disorder. There are examples for adults (Table 9-2) and for children and adolescents (Table 9-3).

DSM-III-R has defined the stressors as predominantly acute events, with a duration less than six months (e.g., death of a spouse), or predominantly enduring circumstances, with a duration greater than six months (e.g., chronic marital discord). A score of 6 represents catastrophic stress (e.g., multiple family deaths), and a score of 1 represents no apparent stress. The stressors are organized for adults and for children and adolescents.

The severity-of-stress rating is based on the clinician's assessment of the stress that an average person with similar sociocultural values and circumstances would experience from the psychosocial stressors. This judgment considers the amount of change in the person's life due to the stressor, the degree to which the event is desired and under the person's control, and the number of stressors. In addition, in certain settings it may be useful to note the specific psychosocial stressors. This information may be important in formulating a treatment plan that includes attempts to remove the psychosocial stressors or to help the person cope with them. Table 9-4 lists various stressors in different areas of life, such as work, illness, and marriage.

Axis V. Axis V is a global assessment of functioning (GAF) scale in which the clinician judges the person's highest level of functioning during the past year. Functioning is conceptualized as a composite of three major areas: social relations, occupational functioning, and psychological functioning. The scale, based on a continuum of mental health and mental illness, is a 90-point scale, 90 representing the highest level of functioning in all areas (Table 9-5).

Persons who had a high level of functioning before an episode of illness generally have a better prognosis than those who had a low level of functioning. Ratings are made both for current functioning (at the time of evaluation) and for the highest level of functioning shown by the patient for at least a few months during the year preceding the current evaluation.

Table 9-2
Axis IV: Severity of Psychosocial Stressors Scale: Adults

Code	Term	Examples of Stressors: Acute Events	Examples of Stressors: Enduring Circumstances
1	None	No acute events that may be relevant to the disorder	No enduring circumstances that may be relevant to the disorder
2	Mild	Broke up with boyfriend or girlfriend; started or graduated from school; child left home	Family arguments; job dissatisfaction; residence in high-crime neighborhood
3	Moderate	Marriage; marital separation; loss of job; retirement; miscarriage	Marital discord; serious financial problems; trouble with boss; being a single parent
4	Severe	Divorce; birth of first child	Unemployment; poverty
5	Extreme	Death of spouse; serious physical illness diagnosed; victim of rape	Serious chronic illness in self or child; ongoing physical or sexual abuse
6	Catastrophic	Death of child; suicide of spouse; devastating natural disaster	Captivity as hostage; concentration camp experience
0	Inadequate information, or no change in condition		

Table from DSM-III-R, *Diagnostic and Statistical Manual of Mental Disorders*, ed 3, revised. Copyright American Psychiatric Association, Washington, DC, 1987, with permission.

Table 9-3
Axis IV: Severity of Psychosocial Stressors Scale: Children and Adolescents

Code	Term	Examples of Stressors: Acute Events	Examples of Stressors: Enduring Circumstances
1	None	No acute events that may be relevant to the disorder	No enduring circumstances that may be relevant to the disorder
2	Mild	Broke up with boyfriend or girlfriend; change of school	Overcrowded living quarters; family arguments
3	Moderate	Expelled from school; birth of sibling	Chronic disabling illness in parent; chronic parental discord
4	Severe	Divorce of parents; unwanted pregnancy; arrest	Harsh or rejecting parents; chronic life-threatening illness in parent; multiple foster home placements
5	Extreme	Sexual or physical abuse; death of a parent	Recurrent sexual or physical abuse
6	Catastrophic	Death of both parents	Chronic life-threatening illness
0	Inadequate information, or no change in condition		

Table from DSM-III-R, *Diagnostic and Statistical Manual of Mental Disorders*, ed 3, revised. Copyright American Psychiatric Association, Washington, DC, 1987, with permission.

Table 9-4
Types of Psychosocial Stressors

To ascertain etiologically significant psychosocial stressors, the following areas may be considered:
Conjugal (marital and nonmarital): e.g., engagement, marriage, discord, separation, death of spouse.
Parenting: e.g., becoming a parent, friction with child, illness of child.
Other interpersonal: problems with one's friends, neighbors, associates, or nonconjugal family members, e.g., illness of best friend, discordant relationship with boss.
Occupational: includes work, school, homemaking, e.g., unemployment, retirement, school problems.
Living circumstances: e.g., change in residence, threat to personal safety, immigration.
Financial: e.g., inadequate finances, change in financial status.
Legal: e.g., arrest, imprisonment, lawsuit, or trial.
Developmental: phases of the life cycle, e.g., puberty, transition to adult status, menopause, "becoming 50."
Physical illness or injury: e.g., illness, accident, surgery, abortion. (Note: A physical disorder is listed on Axis III whenever it is related to the development or management of an Axis I or II disorder. A physical disorder can also be a psychosocial stressor if its impact is due to its meaning to the individual, in which case it would be listed on both Axis III and Axis IV.)
Other psychosocial stressors: e.g., natural or manmade disaster, persecution, unwanted pregnancy, out-of-wedlock birth, rape.
Family factors (children and adolescents): In addition to the above, for children and adolescents the following stressors may be considered: cold, hostile, intrusive, abusive, conflictual, or confusingly inconsistent relationship between parents or toward child; physical or mental illness in a family member; lack of parental guidance or excessively harsh or inconsistent parental control; insufficient, excessive, or confusing social or cognitive stimulation; anomalous family situation, e.g., complex or inconsistent parental custody and visitation arrangements; foster family; institutional rearing; loss of nuclear family members.

Table from DSM-III-R, *Diagnostic and Statistical Manual of Mental Disorders*, ed 3, revised. Copyright American Psychiatric Association, Washington, DC, 1987, with permission.

Use of the multiaxial system. The multiaxial scheme of DSM-III-R assists clinicians in separating developmental and personality disorders (Axis II), social stressors (Axis IV), and degree of adaptive functioning (Axis V) from the underlying form of the disorder, which is represented by the descriptive and syndromal diagnosis (Axis I). The clinician is also expected to assess any relevant physical disease (Axis III) that may cause, contribute to, precipitate, maintain, or modify the expression of the Axis I disorder or interact with its treatment.

Each axis is used to document the presence or absence of findings. The clinician should be able to infer a great deal of information about the patient by scanning the multiaxial tree, including the presence or absence of a specific psychiatric syndrome (Axis I); whether a concomitant premorbid personality disorder is present (Axis II); the presence of a physical condition that may influence the management or prognosis of the psychiatric illness (Axis III); the life events that may be relevant to understanding precipitating factors or problems in management (Axis IV); and, finally, a global assessment of the patient's highest level of functioning during the past year before the onset of the illness, which provides a baseline from which to gauge severity of the illness and the prognosis (Axis V).

Severity of disorder. Depending on the clinical picture, the presence or absence of signs and symptoms, and their intensity, the severity of a disorder may be mild, moderate, or severe and in partial remission or in full remission. The following guidelines are used according to DSM-III-R.

Table 9-5
Axis V: Global Assessment of Functioning Scale (GAF Scale)

Consider psychological, social, and occupational functioning on a hypothetical continuum of mental health-illness. Do not include impairment in functioning due to physical (or environmental) limitations.

Note: Use intermediate codes when appropriate, e.g., 45, 68, 72.

Code	
90–81	**Absent or minimal symptoms** (e.g., mild anxiety before an exam), **good functioning in all areas, interested and involved in a wide range of activities, socially effective, generally satisfied with life, no more than everyday problems or concerns** (e.g., an occasional argument with family members)
80–71	**If symptoms are present, they are transient and expectable reactions to psychosocial stressors** (e.g., difficulty concentrating after family argument); **no more than slight impairment in social, occupational, or school functioning** (e.g., temporarily falling behind in school work)
70–61	**Some mild symptoms** (e.g., depressed mood and mild insomnia) **OR some difficulty in social, occupational, or school functioning** (e.g., occasional truancy, or theft within the household), **but generally functioning pretty well, has some meaningful interpersonal relationships**
60–51	**Moderate symptoms** (e.g., flat affect and circumstantial speech, occasional panic attacks) **OR moderate difficulty in social, occupational, or school functioning** (e.g., few friends, conflicts with co-workers)
50–41	**Serious symptoms** (e.g., suicidal ideation, severe obsessional rituals, frequent shoplifting) **OR any serious impairment in social, occupational, or school functioning** (e.g., no friends, unable to keep a job)
40–31	**Some impairment in reality testing or communication** (e.g., speech is at times illogical, obscure, or irrelevant) **OR major impairment in several areas, such as work or school, family relations, judgment, thinking, or mood** (e.g., depressed man avoids friends, neglects family, and is unable to work; child frequently beats up younger children, is defiant at home, and is failing at school)
30–21	**Behavior is considerably influenced by delusions or hallucinations OR serious impairment in communication or judgment** (e.g., sometimes incoherent, acts grossly inappropriately, suicidal preoccupation) **OR inability to function in almost all areas** (e.g., stays in bed all day; no job, home, or friends)
20–11	**Some danger of hurting self or others** (e.g., suicide attempts without clear expectation of death, frequently violent, manic excitement) **OR occasionally fails to maintain minimal personal hygiene** (e.g., smears feces) **OR gross impairment in communication** (e.g., largely incoherent or mute)
10–1	**Persistent danger of severely hurting self or others** (e.g., recurrent violence) **OR persistent inability to maintain minimal personal hygiene OR serious suicidal act with clear expectation of death**

Table from DSM-III-R, *Diagnostic and Statistical Manual of Mental Disorders*, ed 3, revised. Copyright American Psychiatric Association, Washington, DC, 1987, with permission.

Mild: Few, if any, symptoms in excess of those required to make the diagnosis and symptoms result in only minor impairment in occupational functioning or in usual social activities or relationships with others.

Moderate. Symptoms or functional impairment between "mild" and "severe."

Severe: Several symptoms in excess of those required to make the diagnosis and symptoms markedly interfere with occupational functioning or with usual social activities or relationships with others.

In partial remission or residual state: The full criteria for the disorder were previously met, but currently only some of the symptoms or signs of the illness are present. *In partial remission* should be used when there is the expectation that the person will completely recover (or have a complete remission) within the next few years, as, for example, in the case of a major depressive episode. *Residual state* should be used when there is little expectation of a complete remission or recovery within the next few years, as, for example, in the case of autistic disorder or attention-deficit hyperactivity disorder. (*Residual state* should not be used with schizophrenia, since by tradition there is a specific residual type of schizophrenia.) In some cases the distinction between *in partial remission* and *residual state* will be difficult to make.

In full remission: There are no longer any symptoms or signs of the disorder. The differentiation of *in full remission* from recovered (no current mental disorder) requires consideration of the length of time since the last period of disturbance, the total duration of the disturbance, and the need for continued evaluation or prophylactic treatment.

Example. An example of a multiaxial diagnostic schema follows:

Axis I	Delusional (paranoid) disorder; moderate (3)
Axis II	Paranoid personality; moderate
Axis III	Hypertension
Axis IV	Psychosocial stressor: extreme (6) (death of spouse)
Axis V	Global assessment of functioning: major impairment in work (40) (patient avoids close relationships; is suspicious of coworkers; high absenteeism because of frequent headaches)

INTERNATIONAL CLASSIFICATION OF DISEASES

The ninth revision of the *International Classification of Diseases* (ICD-9), published by the World Health Organization, is the official classification system used in Europe and Great Britain. All DSM-III-R categories are found in ICD-9, but not all ICD-9 categories are in DSM-III-R. A clinical modification of ICD-9, known as ICD-9-CM (for clinical modification), was published in 1979 in an effort to make the two systems as compatible as possible. However, many ICD-9-CM terms are not included in the DSM-III-R classification.

Unlike DSM-III-R, ICD-9 is not multiaxial and limits itself to the more formal diagnostic categories that DSM-III-R lists on Axes I and II. ICD-9 also lists certain categories preferred by one national school or another (e.g., *bouffée délirante*, which in France is used in lieu of the Scandinavian schizophreniform or reactive psychosis and overlaps to some extent with the categories of brief reactive and atypical psychoses in the American classification). The tenth revision of ICD (ICD-10) is now in preparation and is expected to be published in 1993. The goal is to have ICD-10 and the new DSM-IV published at the same time and to be similar in content.

CLASSIFICATION OF MENTAL DISORDERS

Table 9-6 presents the DSM-III-R classification of mental disorders (Axis I and II). Table 9-7 presents the ICD-9 classification of mental disorders. The reader is referred to the specific section of this textbook where each disorder is discussed separately and in depth.

Psychosis and Neurosis

Psychosis. Although the traditional meaning of the term "psychotic" emphasized loss of reality testing and impairment of mental functioning—manifested by delusions, hallucinations, confusion, and impaired memory—two other meanings have evolved during the past 50 years. In the most common psychiatric use of the term, psychotic became synonymous with severe impairment of social and personal functioning characterized by social withdrawal and inability to perform the usual household and occupational roles. The other use of the term specifies degree of ego regression as the criterion for psychotic illness. As a consequence of those multiple meanings, the term has lost its precision in current clinical and research practice.

According to the glossary of the American Psychiatric Association, the term "psychotic" refers to gross impairment in reality testing. It may be used to describe the behavior of a person at a given time or a mental disorder in which at some time during its course all persons with the disorder have grossly impaired reality testing. When there is gross impairment in reality testing, the person incorrectly evaluates the accuracy of his or her perceptions and thoughts and makes incorrect inferences about external reality, even in the face of contrary evidence. The term "psychotic" does not apply to minor distortions of reality that involve matters of relative judgment. For example, a depressed person who underestimates his or her achievements is not described as psychotic, whereas one who believes he or she caused a natural catastrophe is so described.

Direct evidence of psychotic behavior is the presence of either delusions or hallucinations without insight into their pathological nature. The term "psychotic" is sometimes appropriate when behavior is so grossly disorganized that a reasonable inference can be made that reality testing is disturbed. Examples include markedly incoherent speech without apparent awareness by the person that the speech is not understandable, and the agitated, inattentive, and disoriented behavior seen in alcohol withdrawal delirium. It should also be noted that a person with a nonpsychotic mental disorder may exhibit psychotic behavior, though rarely. For example, a person with obsessive-compulsive disorder may at times come to believe in the reality of the danger of being contaminated by shaking hands with strangers. In DSM-III-R the psychotic disorders include pervasive developmental disorders, schizophrenia, delusional (paranoid) disorders, psychotic disorders not elsewhere classified, some organic mental disorders, and some mood (affective) disorders.

Neurosis. A neurosis is a chronic or recurrent nonpsychotic disorder that is characterized mainly by anxiety, which is experienced or expressed directly or altered through defense mechanisms; it appears as a symptom, such as obsession, compulsion, phobia, or sexual dysfunction. According to DSM-III, a neurotic disorder is defined as follows:

> A mental disorder in which the predominant disturbance is a symptom or group of symptoms that is distressing to the individual and is recognized by him or her as unacceptable and alien (ego-dystonic); reality testing is grossly intact. Behavior does not actively violate gross social norms (though it may be quite disabling). The disturbance is relatively enduring or recurrent without treatment, and is not limited to a transitory reaction to stressors. There is no demonstrable organic etiology or factor.

In DSM-III-R no overall diagnostic class is called "neuroses"; however, the following DSM-III-R diagnostic categories are considered neuroses by many clinicians, and the reader will note that DSM-III-R uses the term "neurosis" in parentheses for some of these conditions.

Anxiety disorders (or anxiety and phobic neuroses). These include agoraphobia without history of panic disorder, social phobia, and simple phobia; panic disorder (with or without agoraphobia), generalized anxiety disorder, and obsessive-compulsive disorder (or obsessive-compulsive neurosis); and posttraumatic stress disorder.

Somatoform disorders. These disorders include somatization disorder, conversion disorder (or hysterical neurosis, conversion type), somatoform pain disorder, hypochondriasis (or hypochondriacal neurosis), body dysmorphic disorder, and undifferentiated somatoform disorder.

Dissociative disorders (or hysterical neuroses, dissociative type). These disorders include psychogenic amnesia, psychogenic fugue, multiple personality disorder, and depersonalization disorder (or depersonalization neurosis).

Sexual disorders. This broad category includes paraphilias and sexual dysfunctions. In common use, the categories have been considered neurotic disorders.

Dysthymia (or depressive neurosis). This disorder is now classified in DSM-III-R as a type of mood disorder.

In summary, the term "neuroses" encompasses a broad range of disorders of different signs and symptoms. As such, it has lost any degree of precision except to signify

Table 9-6
DSM-III-R Classification: Axes I and II Categories and Codes

All official DSM-III-R codes are included in ICD-9-CM. Codes followed by a * are used for more than one DSM-III-R diagnosis or subtype in order to maintain compatibility with ICD-9-CM.

A long dash following a diagnostic term indicates the need for a fifth digit subtype or other qualifying term.

The term *specify* following the name of some diagnostic categories indicates qualifying terms that clinicians may wish to add in parentheses after the name of the disorder.

NOS = not otherwise specified

The current severity of a disorder may be specified after the diagnosis as:

mild / moderate / severe — currently meets diagnostic criteria

in partial remission (or residual state)
in complete remission

DISORDERS USUALLY FIRST EVIDENT IN INFANCY, CHILDHOOD, OR ADOLESCENCE

DEVELOPMENTAL DISORDERS
Note: These are coded on Axis II.

Mental Retardation
317.00 Mild mental retardation
318.00 Moderate mental retardation
318.10 Severe mental retardation
318.20 Profound mental retardation
319.00 Unspecified mental retardation

Pervasive Developmental Disorders
299.00 Autistic disorder
Specify if childhood onset
299.80 Pervasive developmental disorder NOS

Specific Developmental Disorders
Academic skills disorders
315.10 Developmental arithmetic disorder
315.80 Developmental expressive writing disorder
315.00 Developmental reading disorder

Language and speech disorders
315.39 Developmental articulation disorder
315.31* Developmental expressive language disorder
315.31* Developmental receptive language disorder

Motor skills disorder
315.40 Developmental coordination disorder
315.90* Specific developmental disorder NOS

Other Developmental Disorders
315.90* Developmental disorder NOS

Disruptive Behavior Disorders
314.01 Attention-deficit hyperactivity disorder
Conduct disorder
312.20 group type
312.00 solitary aggressive type
312.90 undifferentiated type
313.81 Oppositional defiant disorder

Anxiety Disorders of Childhood or Adolescence
309.21 Separation anxiety disorder
313.21 Avoidant disorder of childhood or adolescence
313.00 Overanxious disorder

Eating Disorders
307.10 Anorexia nervosa
307.51 Bulimia nervosa
307.52 Pica
307.53 Rumination disorder of infancy
307.50 Eating disorder NOS

Gender Identity Disorders
302.60 Gender identity disorder of childhood
302.50 Transsexualism
Specify sexual history: asexual, homosexual, heterosexual, unspecified
302.85* Gender identity disorder of adolescence or adulthood, nontranssexual type
Specify sexual history: asexual, homosexual, heterosexual, unspecified
302.85* Gender identity disorder NOS

Tic Disorders
307.23 Tourette's disorder
307.22 Chronic motor or vocal tic disorder
307.21 Transient tic disorder
Specify: single episode or recurrent
307.20 Tic disorder NOS

Elimination Disorders
307.70 Functional encopresis
Specify: primary or secondary type
307.60 Functional enuresis
Specify: primary or secondary type
Specify: nocturnal only, diurnal only, nocturnal and diurnal

Speech Disorders Not Elsewhere Classified
307.00* Cluttering
307.00* Stuttering

Other Disorders of Infancy, Childhood, or Adolescence
313.23 Elective mutism
313.82 Identity disorder
313.89 Reactive attachment disorder of infancy or early childhood
307.30 Stereotypy/habit disorder
314.00 Undifferentiated attention-deficit disorder

ORGANIC MENTAL DISORDERS

Dementias Arising in the Senium and Presenium
Primary degenerative dementia of the Alzheimer type, senile onset
290.30 with delirium
290.20 with delusions
290.21 with depression
290.00* uncomplicated
(Note: code 331.00 Alzheimer's disease on Axis III)

Code in fifth digit:
1 = with delirium, 2 = with delusions, 3 = with depression, 0* = uncomplicated

Table 9-6
Continued

290.1x	Primary degenerative dementia of the Alzheimer type, presenile onset, ____
	(Note: code 331.00 Alzheimer's disease on Axis III)
290.4x	Multi-infarct dementia, ____
290.00*	Senile dementia NOS
	Specify etiology on Axis III if known
290.10*	Presenile dementia NOS
	Specify etiology on Axis III if known (e.g., Pick's disease, Jakob-Creutzfeldt disease)

Psychoactive Substance-Induced Organic Mental Disorders

	Alcohol
303.00	intoxication
291.40	idiosyncratic intoxication
291.80	Uncomplicated alcohol withdrawal
291.00	withdrawal delirium
291.30	hallucinosis
291.10	amnestic disorder
291.20	Dementia associated with alcoholism
	Amphetamine or similarly acting sympathomimetic
305.70*	intoxication
292.00*	withdrawal
292.81*	delirium
292.11*	delusional disorder
	Caffeine
305.90*	intoxication
	Cannabis
305.20*	intoxication
292.11*	delusional disorder
	Cocaine
305.60*	intoxication
292.00*	withdrawal
292.81*	delirium
292.11*	delusional disorder
	Hallucinogen
305.30*	hallucinosis
292.11*	delusional disorder
292.84*	mood disorder
292.89*	Posthallucinogen perception disorder
	Inhalant
305.90*	intoxication
	Nicotine
292.00*	withdrawal
	Opioid
305.50*	intoxication
292.00*	withdrawal
	Phencyclidine (PCP) or similarly acting arylcyclohexylamine
305.90*	intoxication
292.81*	delirium
292.11*	delusional disorder
292.84*	mood disorder
292.90*	organic mental disorder NOS
	Sedative, hypnotic, or anxiolytic
305.40*	intoxication
292.00*	Uncomplicated sedative, hypnotic, or anxiolytic withdrawal
292.00*	withdrawal delirium
292.83*	amnestic disorder
	Other or unspecified psychoactive substance
305.90*	intoxication
292.00*	withdrawal
292.81*	delirium
292.82*	dementia
292.83*	amnestic disorder
292.11*	delusional disorder
292.12	hallucinosis
292.84*	mood disorder
292.89*	anxiety disorder
292.89*	personality disorder
292.90*	organic mental disorder NOS

Organic Mental Disorders associated with Axis III physical disorders or conditions, or whose etiology is unknown

293.00	Delirium
294.10	Dementia
294.00	Amnestic disorder
293.81	Organic delusional disorder
293.82	Organic hallucinosis
293.83	Organic mood disorder
	Specify: manic, depressed, mixed
294.80*	Organic anxiety disorder
310.10	Organic personality disorder
	Specify if explosive type
294.80*	Organic mental disorder NOS

PSYCHOACTIVE SUBSTANCE USE DISORDERS

	Alcohol
303.90	dependence
305.00	abuse
	Amphetamine or similarly acting sympathomimetic
304.40	dependence
305.70*	abuse
	Cannabis
304.30	dependence
305.20*	abuse
	Cocaine
304.20	dependence
305.60*	abuse
	Hallucinogen
304.50*	dependence
305.30*	abuse
	Inhalant
304.60	dependence
305.90*	abuse
	Nicotine
305.10	dependence
	Opioid
304.00	dependence
305.50*	abuse
	Phencyclidine (PCP) or similarly acting arylcyclohexylamine
304.50*	dependence
305.90*	abuse
	Sedative, hypnotic, or anxiolytic
304.10	dependence
305.40*	abuse
304.90*	Polysubstance dependence
304.90*	Psychoactive substance dependence NOS
305.90*	Psychoactive substance abuse NOS

Table 9-6
Continued

SCHIZOPHRENIA

Code in fifth digit: 1 = subchronic, 2 = chronic, 3 = subchronic with acute exacerbation, 4 = chronic with acute exacerbation, 5 = in remission, 0 = unspecified

	Schizophrenia
295.2x	catatonic, ___
295.1x	disorganized, ___
295.3x	paranoid, ___
	Specify if stable type
295.9x	undifferentiaed, ___
295.6x	residual, ___
	Specify if late onset

DELUSIONAL (PARANOID) DISORDER

297.10	Delusional (Paranoid) disorder
	Specify type: erotomanic, grandiose, jealous, persecutory, somatic, unspecified

PSYCHOTIC DISORDERS NOT ELSEWHERE CLASSIFIED

298.80	Brief reactive psychosis
295.40	Schizophreniform disorder
	Specify: without good prognostic features or with good prognostic features
295.70	Schizoaffective disorder
	Specify: bipolar type or depressive type
297.30	Induced psychotic disorder
298.90	Psychotic disorder NOS (Atypical psychosis)

MOOD DISORDERS

Code current state of Major Depression and Bipolar Disorder in fifth digit:

1 = mild
2 = moderate
3 = severe, without psychotic features
4 = with psychotic features (*specify* mood-congruent or mood-incongruent)
5 = in partial remission
6 = in full remission
0 = unspecified

For major depressive episodes, *specify* if chronic and *specify* if melancholic type.

For Bipolar Disorder, Bipolar Disorder NOS, Recurrent Major Depression and Depressive Disorder NOS, *specify* if seasonal pattern.

Bipolar Disorders

	Bipolar disorder
296.6x	mixed, ___
296.4x	manic, ___
296.5x	depressed, ___
301.13	Cyclothymia
296.70	Bipolar disorder NOS

Depressive Disorders

	Major Depression
296.2x	single episode, ___
296.3x	recurrent, ___
300.40	Dysthymia (or Depressive neurosis)
	Specify: primary or secondary type
	Specify: early or late onset
311.00	Depressive disorder NOS

ANXIETY DISORDERS (or Anxiety and Phobic Neuroses)

	Panic disorder
300.21	with agoraphobia
	Specify current severity of agoraphobic avoidance
	Specify current severity of panic attacks
300.01	without agoraphobia
	Specify current severity of panic attacks
300.22	Agoraphobia without history of panic disorder
	Specify with or without limited symptom attacks
300.23	Social phobia
	Specify if generalized type
300.29	Simple phobia
300.30	Obsessive compulsive disorder (or Obsessive compulsive neurosis)
309.89	Post-traumatic stress disorder
	Specify if delayed onset
300.02	Generalized anxiety disorder
300.00	Anxiety disorder NOS

SOMATOFORM DISORDERS

300.70*	Body dysmorphic disorder
300.11	Conversion disorder (or Hysterical neurosis, conversion type)
	Specify: single episode or recurrent
300.70*	Hypochondriasis (or Hypochondriacal neurosis)
300.81	Somatization disorder
307.80	Somatoform pain disorder
300.70*	Undifferentiated somatoform pain disorder
300.70*	Somatoform disorder NOS

DISSOCIATIVE DISORDERS (or Hysterical Neuroses, Dissociative Type)

300.14	Multiple personality disorder
300.13	Psychogenic fugue
300.12	Psychogenic amnesia
300.60	Depersonalization disorder (or Depersonalization neurosis)
300.15	Dissociative disorder NOS

SEXUAL DISORDERS

Paraphilias

302.40	Exhibitionism
302.81	Fetishism
302.89	Frotteurism
302.20	Pedophilia
	Specify: same sex, opposite sex, same and opposite sex
	Specify if limited to incest
	Specify: exclusive type or nonexclusive type
302.83	Sexual masochism
302.84	Sexual sadism
302.30	Transvestic fetishism
302.82	Voyeurism
302.90*	Paraphilia NOS

Table 9-6
Continued

Sexual Dysfunctions
Specify: psychogenic only, or psychogenic and biogenic
(Note: If biogenic only, code on Axis III)
Specify: lifelong or acquired
Specify: generalized or situational

	Sexual desire disorders
302.71	Hypoactive sexual desire disorder
302.79	Sexual aversion disorder
	Sexual arousal disorders
302.72*	Female sexual arousal disorder
302.72*	Male erectile disorder
	Orgasm disorders
302.73	Inhibited female orgasm
302.74	Inhibited male orgasm
302.75	Premature ejaculation
	Sexual pain disorders
302.76	Dyspareunia
306.51	Vaginismus
302.70	Sexual dysfunction NOS

Other Sexual Disorders

302.90*	Sexual disorder NOS

SLEEP DISORDERS

Dyssomnias

	Insomnia disorder
307.42*	related to another mental disorder (nonorganic)
780.50*	related to known organic factor
307.42*	Primary insomnia
	Hypersomnia disorder
307.44	related to another mental disorder (nonorganic)
780.50*	related to known organic factor
780.54*	Primary hypersomnia
307.45	Sleep-wake schedule disorder
	Specify: advanced or delayed phase type, disorganized type, frequently changing type
	Other dyssomnias
307.40*	Dyssomnia NOS

Parasomnias

307.47	Dream anxiety disorder (Nightmare disorder)
307.46*	Sleep terror disorder
307.46*	Sleepwalking disorder
307.40*	Parasomnia NOS

FACTITIOUS DISORDERS

	Factitious disorder
301.51	with physical symptoms
300.16	with psychological symptoms
300.19	Factitious disorder NOS

IMPULSE CONTROL DISORDERS NOT ELSEWHERE CLASSIFIED

312.34	Intermittent explosive disorder
312.32	Kleptomania
312.31	Pathological gambling
312.33	Pyromania
312.39*	Trichotillomania
312.39*	Impulse control disorder NOS

ADJUSTMENT DISORDER

	Adjustment disorder
309.24	with anxious mood
309.00	with depressed mood
309.30	with disturbance of conduct
309.40	with mixed disturbance of emotions and conduct
309.28	with mixed emotional features
309.82	with physical conditions
309.83	with withdrawal
309.23	with work (or academic) inhibition
309.90	Adjustment disorder NOS

PSYCHOLOGICAL FACTORS AFFECTING PHYSICAL CONDITION

316.00	Psychological factors affecting physical condition
	Specify physical condition on Axis III

PERSONALITY DISORDERS
Note: These are coded on Axis II.

Cluster A

301.00	Paranoid
301.20	Schizoid
301.22	Schizotypal

Cluster B

301.70	Antisocial
301.83	Borderline
301.50	Histrionic
301.81	Narcissistic

Cluster C

301.82	Avoidant
301.60	Dependent
301.40	Obsessive compulsive
301.84	Passive aggressive
301.90	Personality disorder NOS

V CODES FOR CONDITIONS NOT ATTRIBUTABLE TO A MENTAL DISORDER THAT ARE A FOCUS OF ATTENTION OR TREATMENT

V62.30	Academic problem
V71.01	Adult antisocial behavior
V40.00	Borderline intellectual functioning (Note: This is coded on Axis II.)
V71.02	Childhood or adolescent antisocial behavior
V65.20	Malingering
V61.10	Marital problem
V15.81	Noncompliance with medical treatment
V62.20	Occupational problem
V61.20	Parent-child problem
V62.81	Other interpersonal problem
V61.80	Other specified family circumstances
V62.89	Phase of life problem or other life circumstance problem
V62.82	Uncomplicated bereavement

Table 9-6
Continued

ADDITIONAL CODES

300.90	Unspecified mental disorder (nonpsychotic)
V71.09*	No diagnosis or condition on Axis I
799.90*	Diagnosis or condition deferred on Axis I
V71.09*	No diagnosis or condition on Axis II
799.90*	Diagnosis or condition deferred on Axis II

Table from DSM-III-R, *Diagnostic and Statistical Manual of Mental Disorders*, ed 3, revised. Copyright American Psychiatric Association, Washington, DC, 1987, with permission.

Table 9-7
ICD-9 Classification of Mental Disorders

ORGANIC PSYCHOTIC CONDITIONS
Senile and pre-senile organic psychotic conditions
290.0 Senile dementia, simple type
290.1 Pre-senile dementia
290.2 Senile dementia, depressed or paranoid type
290.3 Senile dementia with acute confusional state
290.4 Arteriosclerotic dementia
290.8 Other
290.9 Unspecified

Alcoholic psychoses
291.0 Delirium tremens
291.1 Korsakov's psychosis, alcoholic
291.2 Other alcoholic dementia
291.3 Other alcoholic hallucinosis
291.4 Pathological drunkenness
291.5 Alcoholic jealousy
291.8 Other
291.9 Unspecified

Drug psychoses
292.0 Drug withdrawal syndrome
292.1 Paranoid and/or hallucinatory states induced by drugs
292.2 Pathological drug intoxication
292.8 Other
292.9 Unspecified

Transient organic psychotic conditions
293.0 Acute confusional state
293.1 Subacute confusional state
293.8 Other
293.9 Unspecified

Other organic psychotic conditions (chronic)
294.0 Korsakov's psychosis (non-alcoholic)
294.1 Dementia in conditions classified elsewhere
294.8 Other
294.9 Unspecified

OTHER PSYCHOSES
Schizophrenic psychoses
295.0 Simple type
295.1 Hebephrenic type
295.2 Catatonic type
295.3 Paranoid type
295.4 Acute schizophrenic episode
295.5 Latent schizophrenia
295.6 Residual schizophrenia
295.7 Schizo-affective type
295.8 Other
295.9 Unspecified

Affective psychoses
296.0 Manic-depressive psychosis, manic type
296.1 Manic-depressive psychosis, depressed type
296.2 Manic-depressive psychosis, circular type but currently manic
296.3 Manic-depressive psychosis, circular type but currently depressed
296.4 Manic-depressive psychosis, circular type, mixed
296.5 Manic-depressive psychosis, circular type, current condition not specified
296.6 Manic-depressive psychosis, other and unspecified
296.8 Other
296.9 Unspecified

Paranoid states
297.0 Paranoid state, simple
297.1 Paranoia
297.2 Paraphrenia
297.3 Induced psychosis
297.8 Other
297.9 Unspecified

Other nonorganic psychoses
298.0 Depressive type
298.1 Excitative type
298.2 Reactive confusion
298.3 Acute paranoid reaction
298.4 Psychogenic paranoid psychosis
298.8 Other and unspecified reactive psychosis
298.9 Unspecified psychosis

Psychoses with origin specific to childhood
299.0 Infantile autism
299.1 Disintegrative psychosis
299.8 Other
299.9 Unspecified

NEUROTIC DISORDERS, PERSONALITY DISORDERS, AND OTHER NONPSYCHOTIC MENTAL DISORDERS
Neurotic disorders
300.0 Anxiety states
300.1 Hysteria
300.2 Phobic state
300.3 Obsessive-compulsive disorders
300.4 Neurotic depression
300.5 Neurasthenia
300.6 Depersonalization syndrome
300.7 Hypochondriasis
300.8 Other neurotic disorders
300.9 Unspecified

Personality disorders
301.0 Paranoid personality disorder
301.1 Affective personality disorder
301.2 Schizoid personality disorder
301.3 Explosive personality disorder
301.4 Anankastic personality disorder
301.5 Hysterical personality disorder
301.6 Asthenic personality disorder
301.7 Personality disorder with predominantly sociopathic or asocial manifestation
301.8 Other personality disorders
301.9 Unspecified

Table 9-7
Continued

Sexual deviations and disorders
302.0 Homosexuality
302.1 Bestiality
302.2 Paedophilia
302.3 Transvestism
302.4 Exhibitionism
302.5 Transsexualism
302.6 Disorders of psychosexual identity
302.7 Frigidity and impotence
302.8 Other
302.9 Unspecified

303. Alcohol dependence syndrome

Drug dependence
304.0 Morphine type
304.1 Barbiturate type
304.2 Cocaine
304.3 Cannabis
304.4 Amphetamine type and other psychostimulants
304.5 Hallucinogens
304.6 Other
304.7 Combinations of morphine type drug with any other
304.8 Combinations excluding morphine type drug
304.9 Unspecified

Nondependent abuse of drugs
305.0 Alcohol
305.1 Tobacco
305.2 Cannabis
305.3 Hallucinogens
305.4 Barbiturates and tranquilizers
305.5 Morphine type
305.6 Cocaine type
305.7 Amphetamine type
305.8 Antidepressants
305.9 Other, mixed or unspecified

Physiological malfunction arising from mental factors
306.0 Musculoskeletal
306.1 Respiratory
306.2 Cardiovascular
306.3 Skin
306.4 Gastrointestinal
306.5 Genitourinary
306.6 Endocrine
306.7 Organs of special sense
306.8 Other
306.9 Unspecified

Special symptoms or syndromes not elsewhere classified
307.0 Stammering and stuttering
307.1 Anorexia nervosa
307.2 Tics
307.3 Stereotyped repetitive movements
307.4 Specific disorders of sleep
307.5 Other and unspecified disorders of eating
307.6 Enuresis
307.7 Encopresis
307.8 Psychalgia
307.9 Other and unspecified

Acute reaction to stress
308.0 Predominant disturbance of emotions
308.1 Predominant disturbance of consciousness
308.2 Predominant psychomotor disturbance
308.3 Other
308.4 Mixed
308.9 Unspecified

Adjustment reaction
309.0 Brief depressive reaction
309.1 Prolonged depressive reaction
309.2 With predominant disturbance of other emotions
309.3 With predominant disturbance of conduct
309.4 With mixed disturbance of emotions and conduct
309.8 Other
309.9 Unspecified

Specific nonpsychotic mental disorders following organic brain damage
310.0 Frontal lobe syndrome
310.1 Cognitive or personality change of other type
310.2 Postconcussional syndrome
310.8 Other
310.9 Unspecified

311. Depressive disorders, not elsewhere classified

Disturbance of conduct not elsewhere classified
312.0 Unsocialized disturbance of conduct
312.1 Socialized disturbance of conduct
312.2 Compulsive conduct disorder
312.3 Mixed disturbance of conduct and emotions
312.8 Other
312.9 Unspecified

Disturbance of emotions specific to childhood and adolescence
313.0 With anxiety and fearfulness
313.1 With misery and unhappiness
313.2 With sensitivity, shyness and social withdrawal
313.3 Relationship problems
313.8 Other or mixed
313.9 Unspecified

Hyperkinetic syndrome of childhood
314.0 Simple disturbance of activity and attention
314.1 Hyperkinesis with developmental delay
314.2 Hyperkinetic conduct disorder
314.8 Other
314.9 Unspecified

Specific delays in development
315.0 Specific reading retardation
315.1 Specific arithmetical retardation
315.2 Other specific learning difficulties
315.3 Developmental speech or language disorder
315.4 Specific motor retardation
315.5 Mixed development disorder
315.8 Other
315.9 Unspecified

316. Psychic factors associated with diseases classified elsewhere

317. Mild mental retardation

Other specific mental retardation
318.0 Moderate mental retardation
318.1 Severe mental retardation
318.2 Profound mental retardation

319. Unspecified mental retardation

From World Health Organization: *Manual of the International Classification of Diseases, Injuries, and Causes of Death,* ed 9, revised. World Health Organization, Geneva, 1978, with permission.

that the person's gross reality testing and personality organization are intact. A neurosis, however, can be and usually is sufficient to impair the person's functioning in a variety of areas.

FUTURE PERSPECTIVES

New and Controversial Categories

DSM-III-R contains three new categories (discussed below) that are considered to be controversial for a variety of reasons. Not all psychiatrists agree that they exist as discrete psychological disorders; for those who believe that they exist, there is lack of consensus as to what are the essential diagnostic features of each of the disorders. In addition, certain groups argue that the new categories reflect lingering antifeminist cultural biases that may be promulgated by assigning diagnostic labels with a high potential for misapplication and abuse. DSM-III-R will probably undergo revision as data regarding the diagnostic validity and reliability of these three disorders accumulate.

Late luteal phase dysphoric disorder (LLPDD). This condition occurs in women and is associated with the luteal phase of the menstrual cycle that occurs in the week before the onset of menses. Essential features include affective lability, irritability, anger, and signs and symptoms of depression (e.g., feelings of worthlessness, loss of energy, appetite change, and sleep disorders). Some women may develop suicidal ideation. Physical symptoms (e.g., headache, musculoskeletal pain, and edema) may occur premenstrually. The prevalence of the disorder is unknown. It has been reported to occur at any age after menarche but most frequently in women over 30. See Chapter 25, which discusses psychological factors affecting physical condition, for a further discussion of this syndrome.

Self-defeating personality disorder. In this condition persons deliberately place themselves in situations in which they will suffer, be hurt, be disappointed, or be mistreated and subsequently feel humiliated or guilty.

Sadistic personality disorder. In this condition the person behaves in a cruel and aggressive way (including the use of physical violence) toward others. The person takes pleasure in being sadistic and is often fascinated by violence and methods of torture.

DSM-IV

A fourth edition of *Diagnostic and Statistical Manual of Mental Disorders* (DSM-IV) is scheduled for publication in 1993. Although many psychiatrists have been critical of the many versions of DSM to appear within the past decade, DSM-III-R is the law of the land. It is used by mental health professionals of all disciplines and is cited for insurance reimbursement, disability deliberations, and forensic matters. The major reason for another revision is the scheduled publication of the World Health Organization's ICD-10 in 1993. Diagnostic systems used in the United States must be compatible with ICD to ensure uniform reporting of national and international health statistics. In addition, Medicare requires that billing codes used for reimbursement follow ICD. Currently, a task force of the APA headed by Allen Frances, M.D., is preparing DSM-IV, and a variety of literature reviews, data analyses, and field trials are underway to clarify and codify the new diagnostic categories. Some issues include adding or deleting certain diagnostic categories or subtypes, problems or inconsistencies in selected diagnostic criteria, and placement of categories within the diagnostic rubric. Some of the specific questions that are being addressed are how best to distinguish between abuse and dependence across a variety of substances, altering the duration criteria of active symptoms of schizophrenia (such as hallucinations and delusions) to be compatible with duration criteria in ICD-10, adding postpartum onset as a modifier to mood and other relevant disorders, evaluating the best placement for posttraumatic stress disorder, instructing how to use the multiaxial system to designate better the course and severity of disorders, and adding a new category of mixed anxiety and depression. In the interim the current edition of DSM-III-R is and will continue to be the official nomenclature of mental disorders.

PSYCHIATRIC RATING SCALES

Psychiatric rating scales, also called rating instruments, provide a method of quantifying aspects of a patient's psyche, behavior, and relationships with individuals and society. The measurement of pathology in these areas of a person's life may initially seem much less straightforward than the measurement of pathology—hypertension, for example—seen by other medical specialists. Nevertheless, many psychiatric rating scales have been developed that are able to measure carefully chosen features of well-formulated concepts. Moreover, without using these rating scales, psychiatrists are left with only their clinical impressions, which are difficult to record in a manner that allows for reliable comparison and communication in the future. Without psychiatric rating scales, quantitative data in psychiatry are quite crude (e.g., length of hospitalization or other treatment, discharge and readmission to hospital, length of relationships or employment, the presence of legal troubles).

Characteristics of Rating Scales

Rating scales can be specific or comprehensive, and they can measure both internally experienced (e.g., mood) and externally observable (e.g., behavior) variables. Specific scales measure discrete thoughts, moods, or behaviors, such as obsessive thoughts and temper tantrums; comprehensive scales measure broader abstractions, such as depression and anxiety. The broadest type of rating scale measures the overall severity of illness, such as the Global Assessment of Functioning Scale (GAF Scale) (Table 9-5). This scale comprises Axis V in DSM-III-R.

Signs and symptoms. Classic items from the mental status examination are the most frequently assessed items on rating scales. These items include thought disorders, mood disturbances, and gross behaviors. Another type of information covered by rating scales is the assessment of adverse effects from psychotherapeutic drugs. Social adjustment (e.g., occupational success, quality of relationships) and psychoanalytic concepts (e.g., ego strength, defense mechanisms) are also measured by some rating scales, although the reliability and the validity of such scales are lowered by the absence of agreed-on norms, the high level of inference required on some items, and the lack of independence between measures.

Other characteristics. Other characteristics of rating scales include the time period covered, the level of judgment required, and the method of recording the answers. It is absolutely critical that the time period covered by a rating scale be specified and that the rater adhere to this time period. For example, a particular rating scale may rate a five-minute observation period, a week-long period of time, or the entire life of the patient.

The most reliable rating scales require a limited amount of judgment or inference on the part of the rater. Whatever the level of judgment required, clear definitions of the answer scale, preferably with clinical examples, should be provided by the developer of the scale and be read by the rater.

The actual answer may be recorded as either a dichotomous (e.g., true or false, present or absent) or a continuous variable. Continuous items may ask the rater to choose a term to describe severity (absent, slight, mild, moderate, severe, extreme) or frequency (never, rarely, occasionally, often, very often, always). Although many psychiatric symptoms are thought of as existing in dichotomous states—for example, the presence or absence of delusions—most experienced clinicians know that the world is not so simple.

A comprehensive outline of the many available rating scales is beyond the scope of this textbook. Some commonly used instruments are found in Tables 9-8 through 9-10. The interested reader is referred to Table 9-11 for a list of the different rating scales and the initial reference source.

ALGORITHMS FOR DIFFERENTIAL DIAGNOSIS

Algorithms, also known as decision trees, are diagrammatic tracks that organize the clinician's thinking so that all differential diagnoses are considered and ruled in or out, resulting in a presumptive diagnosis. Beginning with

Table 9-8
Brief Psychiatric Rating Scale

DIRECTIONS: Place an X in the appropriate box to represent level of severity of each symptom.

PATIENT ______________________

RATER ______________________

NO. ______________________

DATE ______________________

	Not Present = 0	Very Mild = 1	Mild = 2	Moderate = 3	Mod. Severe = 4	Severe = 5	Extremely Severe = 6
	0	1	2	3	4	5	6
1. Somatic concern—preoccupation with physical health, fear of physical illness, hypochondriases.	☐	☐	☐	☐	☐	☐	☐
2. Anxiety—worry, fear, overconcern for present or future.	☐	☐	☐	☐	☐	☐	☐
3. Emotional withdrawal—lack of spontaneous interaction, isolation, deficiency in relating to others.	☐	☐	☐	☐	☐	☐	☐
4. Conceptual disorganization—thought processes confused, disconnected, disorganized, disrupted.	☐	☐	☐	☐	☐	☐	☐
5. Guilt feelings—self-blame, shame, remorse for past behavior.	☐	☐	☐	☐	☐	☐	☐
6. Tension—physical and motor manifestations or nervousness, overactivation, tension.	☐	☐	☐	☐	☐	☐	☐
7. Mannerisms and posturing—peculiar, bizarre unnatural motor behavior (not including tic).	☐	☐	☐	☐	☐	☐	☐
8. Grandiosity—exaggerated self-opinion, arrogance, conviction of unusual power or abilities.	☐	☐	☐	☐	☐	☐	☐
9. Depressive mood—sorrow, sadness, despondency, pessimism.	☐	☐	☐	☐	☐	☐	☐
10. Hostility—animosity, contempt, beligerence, disdain for others.	☐	☐	☐	☐	☐	☐	☐
11. Suspiciousness—mistrust, belief that others harbor malicious or discriminatory intent.	☐	☐	☐	☐	☐	☐	☐
12. Hallucinatory behavior—perceptions without normal external stimulus correspondence.	☐	☐	☐	☐	☐	☐	☐
13. Motor retardation—slowed weakened movements or speech, reduced body tone.	☐	☐	☐	☐	☐	☐	☐
14. Uncooperativeness—resistance, guardedness, rejection of authority.	☐	☐	☐	☐	☐	☐	☐
15. Unusual thought content—unusual, odd, strange, bizarre thought content.	☐	☐	☐	☐	☐	☐	☐
16. Blunted affect—reduced emotional tone, reduction in normal intensity of feelings, flatness.	☐	☐	☐	☐	☐	☐	☐
17. Excitement—heightened emotional tone, agitation, increased reactivity.	☐	☐	☐	☐	☐	☐	☐
18. Disorientation—confusion or lack of proper association for person, place, or time.	☐	☐	☐	☐	☐	☐	☐

Table 9-9
Hamilton Anxiety Rating Scale

Instructions: This checklist is to assist the physician or psychiatrist in evaluating each patient as to his degree of anxiety and pathological condition. Please fill in the appropriate rating:

NONE = 0 MILD = 1 MODERATE = 2 SEVERE = 3 SEVERE, GROSSLY DISABLING = 4

Item		Rating	Item		Rating
Anxious mood	Worries, anticipation of the worst, fearful anticipation, irritability	______	Somatic (sensory)	Tinnitus, blurring of vision, hot and cold flushes, feelings of weakness, picking sensation	______
Tension	Feelings of tension, fatigability, startle response, moved to tears easily, trembling, feelings of restlessness, inability to relax	______	Cardiovascular symptoms	Tachycardia, palpitations, pain in chest, throbbing of vessels, fainting feelings, missing beat	______
Fears	Of dark, of strangers, of being left alone, of animals, of traffic, of crowds	______	Respiratory symptoms	Pressure or constriction in chest, choking feelings, sighing, dyspnea	______
Insomnia	Difficulty in falling asleep, broken sleep, unsatisfying sleep and fatigue on waking, dreams, nightmares, night-terrors	______	Gastrointestinal symptoms	Difficulty in swallowing, wind, abdominal pain, burning sensations, abdominal fullness, nausea, vomiting, borborygmi, looseness of bowels, loss of weight, constipation	______
Intellectual (cognitive)	Difficulty in concentration, poor memory	______	Genitourinary symptoms	Frequency of micturition, urgency of micturition, amenorrhea, menorrhagia, development of frigidity, premature ejaculation, loss of libido, impotence	______
Depressed mood	Loss of interest, lack of pleasure in hobbies, depression, early waking, diurnal swing	______	Autonomic symptoms	Dry mouth, flushing, pallor, tendency to sweat, giddiness, tension headache, raising of hair	______
Somatic (muscular)	Pains and aches, twitching, stiffness, myoclonic jerks, grinding of teeth, unsteady voice, increased muscular tone	______	Behavior at interview	Fidgeting, restlessness or pacing, tremor of hands, furrowed brow, strained face, sighing or rapid respiration, facial pallor, swallowing, belching, brisk tendon jerks, dilated pupils, exophthalmos	______

ADDITIONAL COMMENTS ______

Investigator's signature:

Table from M Hamilton: The assessment of anxiety states by rating. Br J Med Psychiatry *32:* 50, 1959, with permission.

Table 9-10
Hamilton Depression Rating Scale

Clinic No. ____________ Date ____________ Rating No. ____________ Code Number ____________
Sex ____________ Age ____________ Patient's Name ____________
Patient's Address ____________ Tel ____________

Item	Range	Score
1. Depressed mood	0–4	
2. Guilt	0–4	
3. Suicide	0–4	
4. Insomnia initial	0–2	
5. Insomnia middle	0–2	
6. Insomnia delayed	0–2	
7. Work and interest	0–4	
8. Retardation		
9. Agitation	0-n4	
10. Anxiety (psychic)	0–4	
11. Anxiety (somatic)	0–4	
12. Somatic gastrointestinal	0–2	
13. Somatic general	0–2	
14. Genital	0–2	
15. Hypochondriasis	0–2	
16. Insight	0–4	
17. Loss of weight	0–2	
	Total Score	
Diurnal variation (morning, afternoon, evening)	0–2	
Depersonalization	0–4	
Paranoid symptoms	0–4	
Obsessional symptoms	0–4	

Table from M Hamilton: Personal communication to the editors, Feb. 1988.

The scale is designed to measure the severity of illness of patients already classified as suffering from depressive illness. It is obviously not a diagnostic instrument because that requires much more information (e.g., previous history, family history, precipitating factors).

As far as possible, the scale should be used in the manner of a clinical interview. The first time, the interview should be conducted in a relaxed, free, and easy manner, giving the patients time to unburden themselves and giving them the opportunity to speak of their problems and ask whatever questions they wish. It may then be necessary to obtain further information by asking them questions. At subsequent assessments, the interview can be briefer and more to the point.

An observer rating scale is not a checklist in which each item is strictly defined. The raters must have sufficient clinical experience and judgment to be able to interpret the patients' statements and reticences about some symptoms and to compare them with other patients. They should use all sources of information (e.g., from relatives and nurses).

The scale consists of 17 items, the scores on which are summed to give a total score. There are four other items, one of which (diurnal variation) is excluded on the grounds that it is not an additional burden on the patient. The last three are excluded from the total score because they occur infrequently, although information on them may be useful for other purposes.

The method of assessment is simple. For some symptoms it is difficult to elicit such information as will permit of full quantification. If present, score 2; if absent, score 0; and if doubtful or trivial, score 1. For those symptoms for which more detailed information can be obtained, the score of 2 is expanded into 2 for mild, 3 for moderate, and 4 for severe. In case of difficulty, the raters should use their judgment as clinicians.

Table 9-11
Psychiatric Rating Scales

Scale	Source
Rating Scales Used for Schizophrenia and Psychosis	
Brief Psychiatric Rating Scale	Psychological Reports *10:* 799,1962
Schedule for Affective Disorders and Schizophrenia (SADS)	Archives of General Psychiatry *35:* 837, 1978
Scale for the Assessment of Negative Symptoms (SANS)	The University of Iowa Press, 1983
Scale for the Assessment of Thought, Language, and Communication (TLC)	The University of Iowa Press, 1978
Thought Disorder Index (TDI)	Archives of General Psychiatry *40:* 1281, 1983
Quality of Life Scale (QLS)	Schizophrenia Bulletin *10:* 383, 1984
Chestnut Lodge Prognostic Scale for Chronic Schizophrenia	Schizophrenia Bulletin *13:* 277, 1987
Rating Scales Used for Mood Disorders	
Beck Depression Inventory	Archives of General Psychiatry *4:* 561, 1961
Standard Assessment of Depressive Disorders (SADD)	Psychological Medicine *10:* 743, 1979
Zung Self-Rating Scale for Depression	Archives of General Psychiatry *12:* 63, 1965
Carroll Rating Scale for Depression	British Journal of Psychiatry *138:* 194, 1981
Montgomery-Asberg Scale	British Journal of Psychiatry *134:* 382, 1979
Raskin Depression Rating Scale	Journal of Nervous and Mental Disease *148:* 87, 1969
Inventory to Diagnose Depression	Archives of General Psychiatry *43:* 1976, 1986
Mania Rating Scale	Journal of Clinical Psychiatry *44:* 98, 1983
Manic State Rating Scale	Archives of General Psychiatry *25:* 256, 1971
Rating Scales Used for Anxiety Disorders	
Brief Outpatient Psychopathology Scale	Journal of Clinical Pharmacology *9:* 187, 1969
Physicians Questionnaire	Psychopharmacologia *17:* 338, 1970
Covi Anxiety Scale	Psychopharmacology Bulletin *18:* 69, 1982
Anxiety States Inventory	Psychosomatics *12:* 371, 1971
Fear Questionnaire	Behavioral Research and Therapeutics *17:* 263, 1979
Mobility Inventory for Agoraphobia	Behavioral Research and Therapeutics *23:* 35, 1985
Social Avoidance and Distress Scale	Journal of Consulting and Clinical Psychology *33:* 448, 1969
Acute Panic Inventory	Archives of General Psychiatry *41:* 764, 1984
Leyton Obsessional Inventory	Psychological Medicine *1:* 48, 1970
Maudsley Obsessional-Compulsive Inventory	Behavioral Research and Therapeutics *15:* 389, 1977
Fear Thermometer	Journal of Consulting and Clinical Psychiatry *15:* 488, 1983
Impact of Events Scale	Psychosomatic Medicine *41:* 209, 1979
Other Rating Scales	
Child and adolescent patients	
General reference for adult scales that have been modified for children	Psychopharmacology Bulletin *21:* entire issue, 1985
Adverse effects of drugs	
Systematic Assessment for Treatment of Emergent Events (SAFTEE):	Psychopharmacology Bulletin *22:* 343, 1986
General Inquiry (GI)	
Systematic Inquiry (SI)	
Quality of life	
Patterns of Individual Change Scale (PICS)	Archives of General Psychiatry *42:* 703, 1985

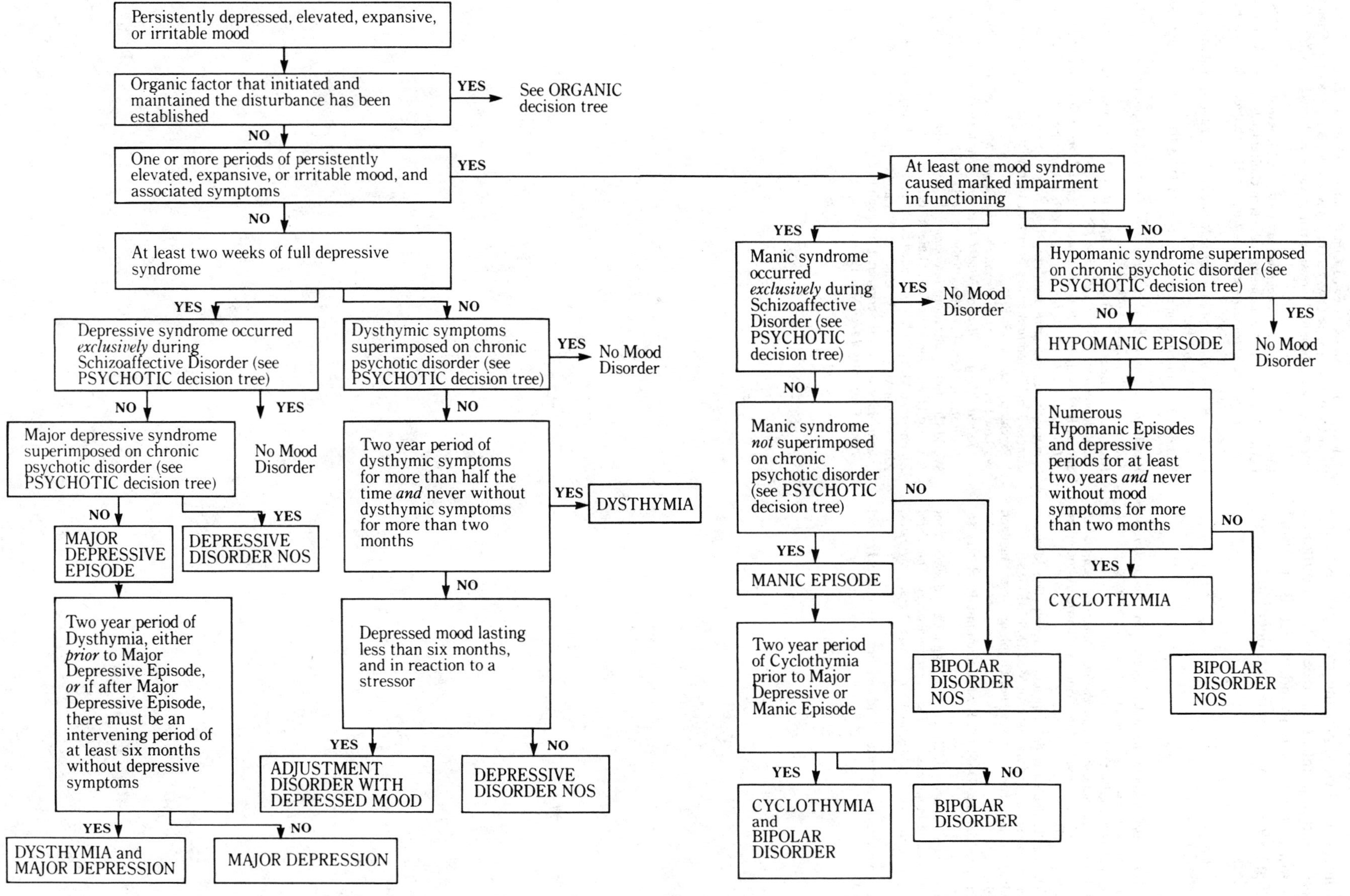

Figure 9-1. Differential diagnosis of mood disturbances. (From DSM-III-R, *Diagnostic and Statistical Manual of Mental Disorders*, ed 3, revised. Copyright American Psychiatric Association, Washington, DC, 1987, with permission.)

specific signs or symptoms, the psychiatrist follows the positive or negative track down the tree (by answering "yes" or "no") until a point in the tree with no outgoing branches (known as a leaf) is found, which is the final diagnosis. Figure 9-1 is an example of a decision tree for mood disorders.

References

Akiskal H S: The classification of mental disorders. In *Comprehensive Textbook of Psychiatry*, ed 5, H I Kaplan and B J Sadock, editors, p 583. Williams & Wilkins, Baltimore, 1989.

American Psychiatric Association: *Diagnostic and Statistical Manual of Mental Disorders*, ed 3, revised. American Psychiatric Association, Washington, DC, 1987.

Berrios G E, Hauser R: The early development of Kraepelin's ideas on classification: A conceptual history. Psychol Med *18*: 813, 1988.

Buros O K, ed: *Personality Tests and Reviews*. Gryphon Press, Highland Park, NJ, 1970.

Frances A: An introduction to DSM-IV. Hosp Community Psychiatry *41*: 493, 1990.

Fyer A J, Mannuzza S, Endicott J: Differential diagnosis and assessment of anxiety: Recent developments. In *Psychopharmacology: The Third Generation of Progress*, H Y Meltzer, editor. Raven Press, New York, 1987.

Goldberg L R: Objective diagnostic tests and measures. Annu Rev Psychol *25*: 102, 1974.

Hughes J R, O'Hara M W, Rehm L P: Measurement of depression in clinical trials: An overview. J Clin Psychiatry *43*: 85, 1982.

Kearns N P, Cruikshank C A, McGuigan K J, Riley S A, Shaw S P, Snaith R P: A comparison of depression rating scales. Br J Psychiatry *141*: 45, 1982.

Kendell R E: *The Role of Diagnosis in Psychiatry*. Blackwell, Oxford, 1975.

Levine J, Ban T A: Assessment methods in clinical trials. In *Psychopharmacology: The Third Generation of Progress*, H Y Meltzer, editor. Raven Press, New York, 1987.

Lyerly S B: *Handbook of Psychiatric Rating Scales*, ed 2. National Institute of Mental Health, Bethesda, MD, 1973.

Mezzich J E: International experience with DSM-III. J. Nerv Ment Dis *173*: 12, 1985.

Raskin A, Jarvik L S: *Psychiatric Symptoms and Cognitive Loss in the Elderly*. Wiley, New York, 1979.

Riskind J H, Beck A T, Brown G, Steer R A: Taking measure of anxiety and depression. J Nerv Ment Dis *175*: 474, 1987.

Spitzer R L, Williams J B W: *Instruction Manual for the Structured Clinical Interview for DSM-III (SCID) New York*. Biometrics Research Department, State Psychiatric Institute, New York, 1985.

Strauss J S: A comprehensive approach to psychiatric diagnosis. Am J Psychiatry *132*: 1193, 1975.

Waskow I G, Parloff M B: *Psychotherapy Change Measures: Report on the Clinical Research Branch-NIMH Outcome Measures Project*. National Institute of Mental Health, Bethesda, MD, 1975.

World Health Organization: *International Classification of Diseases*, rev 9. World Health Organization, Geneva, 1977.

Zimmerman M: Is DSM-IV needed at all? Am J Psychiatry *147*: 974, 1990.

Zimmerman M, Coryell W, Black D: Variability in the application of contemporary diagnostic criteria: Endogenous depression as an example. Am J Psychiatry *147*: 1173, 1990.

10

Organic Mental Syndromes and Disorders

The division in the revised third edition of *Diagnostic and Statistical Manual of Mental Disorders* (DSM-III-R) between the organic diagnoses and the nonorganic or functional diagnoses is maintained more for historical reasons than for strictly scientific or data-based reasons. The original gross distinction between organic and functional mental disorders was based on the reports of 19th-century neuropathologists. Some patients had mental disorders that were caused by gross, easily identifiable lesions, such as brain tumors, and were classified as having organic disorders; other patients had mental disorders, such as schizophrenia, for which a brain lesion could not be found by 19th-century neuroanatomical techniques. The application of this approach throughout the 19th and 20th centuries has led to the current, somewhat confusing, differentiation in DSM-III-R.

Nevertheless, the organic mental syndromes and disorders are defined in DSM-III-R as being caused directly by abnormalities of brain structure, neurochemistry, or neurophysiology. The underlying disease may be primary (e.g., originating in the brain) or secondary (caused by some systemic disease). The symptoms include cognitive, emotional, and motivational impairments. Cognitive impairment is generally considered the hallmark of organic mental syndromes and disorders. Deficits in orientation, memory, language comprehension, calculation, and judgment are common. Cognitive impairment may be accompanied by anxiety, depression, irritability, and shame. Paranoia, euphoria, apathy, and decreased control over sexual and aggressive impulses may also accompany cognitive loss.

CLASSIFICATION

In DSM-III-R the term "organic mental syndrome" refers to a specific set of psychological or behavioral signs or symptoms without reference to cause. The term "organic mental disorder" is used when an organic mental syndrome is associated with a specific, identified or presumed organic cause, which is then coded as an Axis III diagnosis. For example, an organic delusional syndrome may be diagnosed in a person with prominent delusions if the physician suspects but has not demonstrated a specific organic pathology, such as a brain tumor. If the physician then finds abnormal reflexes consistent with a brain tumor, the diagnosis can be changed to organic delusional disorder with an Axis III notation of "abnormal reflexes consistent with a brain tumor." If, however, the computed tomography (CT) scan turns out to be normal and the physician can find no identifiable organic cause, the diagnosis is changed to delusional disorder.

Syndromes

The organic mental syndromes are delirium, dementia, amnestic syndrome, organic hallucinosis, organic delusional syndrome, organic mood syndrome, organic personality syndrome, organic anxiety syndrome, intoxication, withdrawal, and organic mental syndrome not otherwise specified (NOS, a residual category). A diagnosis of organic mental syndrome requires that specific diagnostic criteria be met and that an organic cause be suspected. When an organic mental syndrome is diagnosed, the clinician indicates that, although an organic cause is suspected, no clinical data are yet available to validate the suspicion.

Disorders

Each of the organic mental syndromes can also be a disorder when there is an identified or strongly suspected organic cause, which should be recorded as an Axis III diagnosis. The organic mental disorders include dementias arising in the senium and presenium, psychoactive substance-induced organic mental disorders, and specific organic mental disorders, such as organic delusional disorder and organic personality disorder. An Axis III diagnosis must be included with the diagnosis of an organic mental disorder. DSM-III-R is not consistent and allows for the diagnosis of an organic mental disorder with unknown cause; however, even DSM-III-R states that "strictly speaking, in such a case it would be more correct to use *syndrome*." Some of this confusion in DSM-III-R may be clarified in the forthcoming edition (DSM-IV).

DELIRIUM

Delirium can be diagnosed as either an organic mental syndrome when the specific organic cause is completely unknown or as an organic mental disorder when the specific organic cause is suspected or known. Delirium can also be a symptom of several substance abuse disorders. Delirium is usally characterized by the acute onset of impaired cognitive functioning resulting from diffuse brain dysfunction. The course is usually fluctuating and brief. Delirium is most often a reversible condition.

Epidemiology

About 10 percent of all hospital inpatients manifest some degree of delirium. The incidence varies in different studies and on different hospital services. For example, delirium occurs in 30 percent of patients in surgical intensive care and in coronary intensive care units. About 20 percent of severely burned patients become delirious. Delirium most commonly occurs in the aged and in children, and preexisting brain damage or a history of delirium seems to increase the risk of the syndrome.

Etiology

The etiology of delirium is multifactorial—a combination of individual, situational, and pharmacological variables. Table 10-1 outlines many of the causes of delirium. Certain nonpsychoactive drugs—such as the frequently used antiulcer agent cimetidine (Tagamet)—can produce delirium.

Patients with organic brain lesions are especially liable to have delirium, as are patients with alcohol or drug addictions. Patients who have had a prior episode of delirium are likely to have a recurrent episode under the same conditions. The causes of *postoperative delirium* include the stress of surgery, postoperative pain, insomnia, pain medication, electrolyte imbalances, infection, fever, and blood loss. *Black-patch delirium*, a particular type of delirium after cataract surgery, results from the disorientation caused by covering the eyes. A pinhole in the patch that allows light to enter reduces the syndrome markedly.

Psychiatric patients being treated with psychotropic agents are at risk of delirium because of overmedication (such as an anticholinergic delirium), as are the elderly, who are susceptible to drug side effects. According to some studies, patients who are most fearful of medical and surgical procedures are more likely to become delirious than patients who are less frightened.

Table 10-1
Causes of Delirium

- Intracranial causes
  - Epilepsy and postictal states
  - Brain trauma (especially concussion)
  - Infections
    - Meningitis
    - Encephalitis
  - Neoplasms
  - Vascular disorders
- Extracranial causes
  - Drugs (ingestion or withdrawal) and poisons
    - Sedatives (including alcohol) and hypnotics
    - Tranquilizers
    - Other drugs
      - Anticholinergic agents
      - Anticonvulsants
      - Antihypertensive agents
      - Antiparkinsonian agents
      - Cardiac glycosides
      - Cimetidine
      - Disulfiram
      - Insulin
      - Opiates
      - Phencyclidine
      - Salicylates
      - Steroids
    - Poisons
      - Carbon monoxide
      - Heavy metals and other industrial poisons
  - Endocrine dysfunction (hypo- or hyperfunction)
    - Pituitary
    - Pancreas
    - Adrenal
    - Parathyroid
    - Thyroid
  - Diseases of nonendocrine organs
    - Liver
      - Hepatic encephalopathy
    - Kidney and urinary tract
      - Uremic encephalopathy
    - Lung
      - Carbon dioxide narcosis
      - Hypoxia
    - Cardiovascular system
      - Cardiac failure
      - Arrhythmias
      - Hypotension
  - Deficiency diseases
    - Thiamin deficiency
  - Systemic infections with fever and sepsis
  - Electrolyte imbalance of any cause
  - Postoperative states

Table by Charles E. Wells, M.D.

Clinical Features

Although the onset of delirium is usually acute, prodromal symptoms (such as daytime restlessness, anxiety, fearfulness, and hypersensitivity to light or sounds) may occur. The patient is usually confused and disoriented and has impaired reality testing. The patient is unable to distinguish among dreams, illusions, and true hallucinations or between sleep and wakefulness, thus contributing to a disturbance of the sleep-wake cycle. The patient is easily distracted by irrelevant stimuli. The ability to think coherently is reduced, and thought processes often become slowed, disorganized, and more concrete. Reasoning and problem solving may become difficult or impossible. Recall of what transpires during a delirium once it is over is characteristically spotty, and the patient may refer to it as a bad dream or a nightmare that is remembered only vaguely.

As a rule, orientation to time and place is impaired. According to DSM-III-R, disorientation to time may be the first symptom to appear in mild delirium. Except for the most severe cases, orientation to person is intact; that is, the patient is aware of his or her own identity. Attempts to compensate for basic cognitive deficits may cause the patient to misidentify persons in the environment. Perceptual disturbances are common, including illusions and hallucinations. These disturbances are most often visual, but they may occur in all sensory modalities. Accompanying the disturbances is often a belief of delusional proportion in the reality of the experience. The emotional and behavioral response is usually appropriate to the content of the disturbance.

Cognitive impairment in delirium tends to fluctuate unpredictably. Diurnal variability is a clinical sign of delirium. Delirium is predictably more severe and incapacitating during the night and early morning hours, an observation that has led to delirious patients' being called *sundowners*. Some patients, in fact, may appear delirious only at night and regain lucidity during the day. So-called lucid intervals—during which patients are more attentive, more rational, and in better contact with their surroundings—may appear at any time and last for minutes to hours.

Psychomotor behavior is usually abnormal. The patient is either hypoactive and lethargic or hyperactive to the point of exhaustion and may unexpectedly and abruptly shift from a relatively quiet state to a state of agitation and vice versa. Autonomic dysfunction may also occur. Autonomic symptoms include pallor, flushing, sweating, cardiac irregularities, nausea, vomiting, and hyperthermia. The most commonly observed emotions are fear and anxiety. If fear is intense and is the result of frightening illusions and hallucinations, the patient may attempt to escape possible injury to himself or herself or to others. A deeply depressed patient may attempt suicide, but a delirious patient is much more likely to sustain an injury as a result of an accident. A clinical case example follows:

An internist requested consultation on a 59-year-old antique dealer admitted to the hospital for workup of severe hypertension. On the third hospital day the patient appeared depressed. The consultant found him dozing in bed; it was apparent that the patient had spilled some of his lunch on the sheets. The patient was difficult to arouse; he responded to his name and looked at the consultant but did not appear to understand simple questions, such as where he was or what the date was. He mumbled incoherently and, when tested, had obvious weakness in his right arm and right leg. A neurological consultation confirmed the diagnosis of a stroke.

Discussion. Reduced ability to maintain attention (the patient did not appear to understand simple questions), disorganized thinking (incoherent speech), reduced level of consciousness (he dozed in bed and was difficult to arouse), and disorganized thinking (his speech was incoherent) in the presence of evidence of an organic cause (right-sided weakness) indicate the organic mental syndrome delirium. Although in the past the term "delirium" had the connotation of an agitated or excited confusional state, more recently the essence of the syndrome is thought to be a disturbance in attention and goal-directed thinking. Other common symptoms of delirium, which this patient did not display, include perceptual disturbances (misinterpretations, illusions, or hallucinations), increased psychomotor activity, and memory impairment.

Although neurologists would generally agree that, technically, this patient had a delirium when he was seen by the psychiatric consultant, they would probably not note it in their own diagnostic formulation, as they would focus diagnostically on the causative process, the cerebrovascular accident (stroke).

In DSM-III-R, delirium is coded from the section of the organic mental disorders associated with Axis III physical disorders or conditions or the cause of which is unknown, since the cause (cerebrovascular accident) is outside the mental disorders section of the ICD-9-CM classification. The physical disorder (cause) is noted on Axis III.

DSM-III-R Diagnosis:
Axis I: Delirium
Axis III: Cerebrovascular accident

Course and Prognosis

Delirium is reversible if the underlying cause is diagnosed and treated in a timely manner. Untreated delirium may clear spontaneously, or it may progress to dementia or to another organic mental syndrome. Delirium characteristically lasts less than a week; however, delirium may linger if it takes time to resolve the underlying cause. In general, the older the patient and the longer he or she has been delirious, the longer it takes for the delirium to resolve. Because of the seriousness of many of the causes of delirium, about 10 to 30 percent of delirious patients progress to coma and death.

Diagnosis

Delirium is usually diagnosed at the bedside and is characterized by the sudden onset of symptoms. The physical examination often reveals clues to the cause (Table 10-2). Diurnal fluctuations are characteristic. The presence of a known physical illness or a history of head trauma, alcoholism, or drug addiction increases the likelihood of the diagnosis. Multiple cognitive deficits in the mental status examination and clouding of consciousness are characteristic. The DSM-III-R diagnostic criteria for delirium are presented in Table 10-3.

Differential Diagnosis

Delirium must be distinguished from other organic mental syndromes, especially dementia. Dementia usually has an insidious onset. Although both conditions include cognitive impairment, the changes in dementia are more fixed. A patient with dementia is alert. Delirium usually lasts a few days to a month; dementia usually lasts much longer. The sleep-wake cycle is almost always disrupted in delirium, whereas it is most often intact in dementia. Occasionally, delirium occurs in a patient suffering from dementia, a condition known as *beclouded dementia.* According to DSM-III-R, dementia cannot be diagnosed in the presence of significant delirium because the symptoms of delirium interfere with the proper assessment of dementia. Both diagnoses are given only when there is a definite history of preexisting dementia. When the diagnosis of delirium is in question, a provisional diagnosis of delirium should be made, so that a rigorous therapeutic approach can be taken.

Delirium must also be differentiated from functional disorders. Patients with factitious disorder may attempt to simulate the symptoms of delirium; however, they usually reveal the factitious nature of their symptoms by inconsistencies on their mental status examinations. An electroencephalogram (EEG) can distinguish between these conditions because delirium is associated with a diffuse slowing of background activity on the EEG. Schizophrenia is characterized by hallucinations or delusions that are more constant and better organized than are those of delirium. Schizophrenic patients usually experience no change in their level of consciousness or orientation. Brief reactive psychosis and schizophreniform disorder include

Table 10-2
Physical Examination of the Delirious Patient

Parameter	Finding	Clinical Implication
1. Pulse	Bradycardia	Hypothyroidism Stokes-Adams syndrome Increased intracranial pressure
	Tachycardia	Hyperthyroidism Infection Heart failure
2. Temperature	Fever	Sepsis Thyroid storm Vasculitis
3. Blood pressure	Hypotension	Shock Hypothyroidism Addison's disease
	Hypertension	Encephalopathy Intracranial mass
4. Respiration	Tachypnea	Diabetes Pneumonia Cardiac failure Fever Acidosis (metabolic)
	Shallow	Drug or alcohol intoxication
5. Carotid vessels	Bruits or decreased pulse	Transient cerebral ischemia
6. Scalp and face	Evidence of trauma	
7. Neck	Evidence of nuchal rigidity	Meningitis Subarachnoid hemorrhage
8. Eyes	Papilledema	Tumor Hypertensive encephalopathy
	Pupillary dilatation	Anxiety Autonomic overactivity (e.g., delirium tremens)
9. Mouth	Tongue or cheek lacerations	Evidence of generalized tonic-clonic seizures
10. Thyroid	Enlarged	Hyperthyroidism
11. Heart	Arrhythmia	Inadequate cardiac output, possibility of emboli
	Cardiomegaly	Heart failure Hypertensive disease
12. Lungs	Congestion	Primary pulmonary failure Pulmonary edema Pneumonia
13. Breath	Alcohol	
	Ketones	Diabetes
14. Liver	Enlargement	Cirrhosis Liver failure
15. Nervous system		
a. Reflexes-muscle stretch	Asymmetry with Babinski's signs	Mass lesion Stroke Preexisting dementia
	Snout	Frontal mass Bilateral posterior cerebral artery occlusion
b. Abducent nerve (sixth cranial nerve)	Weakness in lateral gaze	Increased intracranial pressure
c. Limb strength	Asymmetrical	Mass lesion Stroke
d. Autonomic	Hyperactivity	Anxiety Delirium

Table from R L Strub, F W Black: *Neurobehavioral Disorders: A Clinical Approach*, p 120. Davis, Philadelphia, 1981, with permission.

Table 10-3
Diagnostic Criteria for Delirium

A. Reduced ability to maintain attention to external stimuli (e.g., questions must be repeated because attention wanders) and to appropriately shift attention to new external stimuli (e.g., perseverates answer to a previous question)
B. Disorganized thinking, as indicated by rambling, irrelevant, or incoherent speech
C. At least two of the following:
   (1) reduced level of consciousness (e.g., difficulty keeping awake during examination)
   (2) perceptual disturbances: misinterpretations, illusions, or hallucinations
   (3) disturbance of sleep-wake cycle with insomnia or daytime sleepiness
   (4) increased or decreased psychomotor activity
   (5) disorientation to time, place, or person
   (6) memory impairment (e.g., inability to learn new material, such as the names of several unrelated objects after five minutes, or to remember past events, such as history of current episode of illness)
D. Clinical features develop over a short period of time (usually hours to days) and tend to fluctuate over the course of a day.
E. Either (1) or (2):
   (1) evidence from the history, physical examination, or laboratory tests of a specific organic factor (or factors) judged to be etiologically related to the disturbance
   (2) in the absence of such evidence, an etiologic organic factor can be presumed if the disturbance cannot be accounted for by any nonorganic mental disorder (e.g., manic episode accounting for agitation and sleep disturbance)

Table from DSM-III-R, *Diagnostic and Statistical Manual of Mental Disorders*, ed 3, revised. Copyright American Psychiatric Association, Washington, DC, 1987, with permission.

symptoms of disorganized speech and loosening of associations, but the global cognitive impairment of delirium is absent. Patients with dissociative disorders may appear disoriented and show purposeless wandering. However, such episodes and the associated memory disturbances are usually self-limited.

Treatment

A cardinal rule in the treatment of delirium is to identify the cause and to apply appropriate medical or surgical therapeutic techniques. Laboratory tests should be obtained as indicated. In addition to treating the underlying cause, the physician manages the delirium with general and symptomatic measures aimed at the relief of distress and the prevention of complications, such as accidents and trauma. Proper nutritional, electrolyte, and fluid balance must be maintained.

Optimal sensory, social, and nursing environment should be provided. If sensory isolation is playing a role in the delirium, the patient will benefit from a dimmed light at night, frequent visits by the staff and his or her family, and explanations and reassurances about the procedures being performed. Placing a television set in a patient's room and addressing the patient by name may help the patient maintain orientation.

An agitated, restless, fearful, or belligerent patient needs to be sedated to prevent complications and accidents. No single psychotropic drug is recommended for all cases of delirium. As a general rule, haloperidol (Haldol) is the drug of choice. Depending on the patient's age, weight, and physical condition, the initial dose may range from 2 to 10 mg intramuscularly, repeated in an hour if the patient remains agitated. As soon as the patient is calm, oral medication in liquid concentrate or tablet form sould begin. Two daily oral doses should suffice, two-thirds of the dose being given at bedtime. To achieve the same therapeutic effect, the oral dose should be about 1.5 times higher than the parenteral dose. The effective total daily dose of haloperidol may range from 5 to 50 mg for the majority of delirious patients. The patient's insomnia is best treated with small doses of a short-acting benzodiazepine, such as triazolam (Halcion).

DEMENTIA

DSM-III-R indicates that dementia can be either an organic mental syndrome or an organic mental disorder. DSM-III-R describes two types of dementia disorders—primary degenerative dementia of the Alzheimer type (DAT) and multi-infarct dementia. DAT is further specified as having a senile onset (after age 65) or a presenile onset. DAT or multi-infarct dementia can be further subtyped as being uncomplicated or complicated with delirium, delusions, or depression. DSM-III-R also allows for the diagnosis of presenile or senile dementia not otherwise specified (NOS) for dementias associated with other causes, which should be specified as Axis III diagnoses.

Dementia is characterized by a loss of cognitive and intellectual abilities severe enough to impair social or occupational performance. The full clinical picture consists of the impairment of memory, abstract thinking, and judgment and some degree of personality change. The disorder may be progressive or static, permanent or reversible. An underlying organic cause is always assumed, although in rare cases it is impossible to determine a specific organic factor. The reversibility of a dementia is related to the underlying pathology and to the availability and the application of effective treatment.

Dementia Syndrome

Epidemiology. Dementia occurs most often in old age. One million Americans over age 65 (5 percent of the aged population) have a significant degree of dementia and are unable to care for themselves. Another 2 million (10 percent of the aged) have mild dementia, and about 60 percent of persons in nursing homes have some dementia. The prevalence of dementia increases with age; it is five times more common in persons 80 years of age and older than in those 70 and younger. By the year 2030 an estimated 20 percent of the population will be over age 65. Thus, the current annual cost of $15 billion for caring for patients with dementia is likely to increase.

Etiology. The most common cause of dementia is primary degenerative dementia of the Alzheimer type (about 65 percent of all cases). The next most common causative factor is multi-infarct dementia (10 percent of all cases).

The alarming increase in acquired immune deficiency syndrome (AIDS) has led to the recognition of an increasing number of dementias related to human immunodeficiency virus (HIV). About 15 percent of all dementia cases are reversible if the physician initiates timely treatment, before irreversible damage has taken place. Table 10-4 lists the various causes of dementia and indicates the most treatable causes. Dementia is a common symptom in diseases that affect the basal ganglia, such as Huntington's chorea and Parkinson's disease (see Section 3.1).

Clinical features. Defects in orientation, memory, perception, intellectual function, reasoning, and judgment are characteristic features of dementia. Affective and behavioral changes, such as defective control of impulses and lability of mood, are frequent, as are accentuations and alterations of premorbid personality traits.

In mild or early cases of dementia there is difficulty in sustaining mental performance, along with an early appearance of fatigue and a tendency for the patient to fail when a task is novel or complex or requires a shift in problem-solving strategy. As the disorder progresses, an inability to perform tasks becomes increasingly more frequent and spreads to simple everyday tasks, so that the patient is rendered incapable of taking care of basic needs.

Table 10-4
Diseases That Cause Dementia

Parenchymatous diseases of the central nervous system
- Alzheimer's disease (primary degenerative dementia)
- Pick's disease (primary degenerative dementia)
- Huntington's disease
- Parkinson's disease*
- Multiple sclerosis

Systemic disorders
- Endocrine and metabolic disorders
  - Thyroid disease*
  - Parathyroid disease*
  - Pituitary-adrenal disorders*
  - Posthypoglycemic states
- Liver disease
  - Chronic progressive hepatic encephalopathy*
- Urinary tract disease
  - Chronic uremic encephalopathy*
  - Progressive uremic encephalopathy (dialysis dementia)*
- Cardiovascular disease
  - Cerebral hypoxia or anoxia*
  - Multi-infarct dementia*
  - Cardiac arrhythmias*
  - Inflammatory diseases of blood vessels*
- Pulmonary disease
  - Respiratory encephalopathy*

Deficiency states
- Cyanocobalamin deficiency*
- Folic acid deficiency*

Drugs and toxins*

Intracranial tumors* and brain trauma*

Infectious processes
- Creutzfeldt-Jakob disease
- Cryptococcal meningitis*
- Neurosyphilis*
- TB and fungal meningitis*
  - Viral encephalitis
  - Human immunodeficiency virus (HIV)-related disorders (e.g. AIDS and AIDS-related complex [ARC])

Miscellaneous disorders
- Hepatolenticular degeneration*
- Hydrocephalic dementia*
- Sarcoidosis*
- Normal pressure hydrocephalus*

Adapted from C E Wells: Organic syndromes: dementia. In *Comprehensive Textbook of Psychiatry*, ed 4, H I Kaplan and B J Sadock, editors, p 855. Williams & Wilkins, Baltimore, 1985.
*Conditions calling for specific therapeutic intervention.

Memory impairment. Memory disturbance is formally detected by demonstrating difficulty in learning new information (short-term memory loss) and in recalling personal data or commonly known facts (long-term memory loss). Memory impairment is typically an early and prominent feature. According to DSM-III-R (Table 10-5), in mild dementia there is moderate memory loss, more marked for recent events, such as forgetting telephone numbers, conversations, and events of the day. In more severe cases only highly learned material is retained, and new information is rapidly forgotten. In the most advanced stages patients may forget the names of close relatives, their own occupations, or even their own names. Memory impairment is partly responsible for faulty orientation in space and time. The patient with advanced dementia who displays spatial disorientation tends to get lost in familiar surroundings. Impaired orientation for time may appear early and always precedes disorientation for place and person. Level of consciousness, however, remains stable.

Language impairment. Language may be affected by some dementias. DSM-III-R states that language may be vague, stereotyped, imprecise, and circumstantial. There may be evidence of aphasia, such as difficulty in naming objects. Severely demented people may actually be mute. DSM-III-R describes a disturbance in so-called constructional ability, which can be tested by having the person copy three-dimensional figures, assemble blocks, or arrange sticks in specific designs. Agnosias and apraxias may also be present.

Other impairments. The patient also exhibits a reduced ability to apply what Kurt Goldstein called the abstract attitude. The patient has difficulty in generalizing from a single instance, in forming concepts, and in grasping similarities and differences among concepts. Further, the ability to solve problems, to reason logically, and to make sound judgments is compromised. Goldstein also described a catastrophic reaction, which is marked by agitation secondary to the subjective awareness of one's intellectual deficits under stressful circumstances. Patients usually attempt to compensate for defects by using strategies to avoid demonstrating failures in intellectual performance, such as changing the subject, making jokes, or otherwise diverting the interviewer. Lack of judgment and poor impulse control are commonly found, particularly in dementias that primarily affect the frontal lobes. Examples given in DSM-III-R of these impairments include coarse language, inappropriate jokes, neglect of personal appearance and hygiene, and a general disregard for the conventional rules of social conduct.

Sundowner syndrome. This syndrome is characterized by drowsiness, confusion, ataxia, and accidental falls. It occurs in the aged who are overly sedated and in demented patients who react adversely to even a small dose of a psychoactive drug. The syndrome also occurs in demented persons when external stimuli, such as light and interpersonal orienting cues, are diminished.

Table 10-5
Diagnostic Criteria for Dementia

A. Demonstrable evidence of impairment in short- and long-term memory. Impairment in short-term memory (inability to learn new information) may be indicated by inability to remember three objects after five minutes. Long-term memory impairment (inability to remember information that was known in the past) may be indicated by inability to remember past personal information (e.g., what happened yesterday, birthplace, occupation) or facts of common knowledge (e.g., past Presidents, well-known dates).
B. At least one of the following:
  (1) impairment in abstract thinking, as indicated by inability to find similarities and differences between related words, difficulty in defining words and concepts, and other similar tasks
  (2) impaired judgment, as indicated by inability to make reasonable plans to deal with interpersonal, family, and job-related problems and issues
  (3) other disturbances of higher cortical function, such as aphasia (disorder of language), apraxia (inability to carry out motor activities despite intact comprehension and motor function), agnosia (failure to recognize or identify objects despite intact sensory function), and "constructional difficulty" (e.g., inability to copy three-dimensional figures, assemble blocks, or arrange sticks in specific designs)
  (4) personality change (i.e., alteration or accentuation of premorbid traits)
C. The disturbance in A and B significantly interferes with work or usual social activities or relationships with others.
D. Not occurring exclusively during the course of delirium.
E. Either (1) or (2):
  (1) there is evidence from the history, physical examination, or laboratory tests of a specific organic factor (or factors judged to be etiologically related to the disturbance
  (2) in the absence of such evidence, an etiologic organic factor can be presumed if the disturbance cannot be accounted for by any nonorganic mental disorder (e.g., major depression accounting for cognitive impairment)

Criteria for severity of Dementia:

Mild: Although work or social activities are significantly impaired, the capacity for independent living remains, with adequate personal hygiene and relatively intact judgment.

Moderate: Independent living is hazardous, and some degree of supervision is necessary.

Severe: Activities of daily living are so impaired that continual supervision is required (e.g., unable to maintain minimal personal hygiene; largely incoherent or mute).

Table from DSM-III-R, *Diagnostic and Statistical Manual of Mental Disorders*, ed 3, revised. Copyright American Psychiatric Association, Washington DC, 1987, with permission.

Course and prognosis. Once dementia has been diagnosed on clinical grounds (with or without the aid of neuropsychological tests), a determination of its cause and the possibility of treatment should be made. About 10 percent of dementias are treatable. Most cases, however, are progressive and incurable.

The onset of dementia may be sudden, resulting from head trauma, cardiac arrest with cerebral hypoxia, or encephalitis. More often, however, the onset is insidious, as in primary degenerative dementia of the Alzheimer type, cerebrovascular disease, and hypothyroidism. Dementia resulting from brain tumors, subdural hematomas, and metabolic disorders may also have an insidious onset.

The syndrome may gradually recede over a period of weeks, months, or even years in response to treatment or as a result of natural healing processes when the underlying disorder can be treated. Dementia secondary to hypothyroidism, subdural hematoma, normal pressure hydrocephalus, or tertiary neurosyphilis has the potential to be reversed. The dementia syndrome may progress relentlessly and steadily (e.g., primary degenerative dementia of the Alzheimer type) or incrementally (as in multi-infarct dementia), or the syndrome may remain relatively stationary after a single acute insult (as in head trauma). The variability of the onset, course, and prognosis of dementia must be emphasized, since the term "dementia" no longer connotes progressive and irreversible intellectual deterioration.

Psychosocial factors influence the degree and the severity of dementia in many cases. For example, the greater the premorbid intelligence and education, the better the patient's ability to compensate for intellectual deficits. Patients who have a rapid onset of dementia use fewer defenses than patients who experience an insidious onset. Anxiety and depression may intensify and aggravate the symptoms. As described below, a condition known as *pseudodementia* occurs in depressed patients who complain of impaired memory but are, in fact, suffering from a depressive disorder. When the depression is treated, the cognitive defects disappear.

The earliest symptoms of dementia are manifold and subtle and may escape the attention of people in the patient's environment. Alcohol is poorly tolerated by demented persons and may precipitate grossly disinhibited behavior. As dementia progresses or is temporarily severe, the symptoms tend to become more conspicuous, and new ones may appear. At this stage, the family or the employer is liable to become alarmed, but patients are likely to be oblivious to their deterioration. Patients may display insomnia with agitated and psychotic behavior. They may get lost in familiar surroundings and be picked up wandering helplessly in the streets. In the end, patients become empty shells of their former selves—profoundly disoriented, incoherent, amnesic, and incontinent of urine and feces.

Diagnosis. Clinical diagnosis of dementia is based on the history derived from the patient and available informants and on the mental status examination. Evidence of changes in the patient's accustomed performance and behavior at home or in the workplace is sought. Behavioral or personality changes in a person known to suffer from some form of cerebral pathology or even in one not known to be physically ill should raise the question of dementia, especially if the patient is more than 40 years old and lacks a positive psychiatric history.

Complaints by the patient about intellectual impairment and forgetfulness should be noted, as should any evidence of evasion, denial, or rationalization aimed at concealing cognitive deficits. Excessive orderliness, social withdrawal, or a tendency to relate events in minute detail can be characteristic. Sudden outbursts of anger or sarcasm may occur. The patient's appearance and behavior should be noted. A dull, apathetic, or vacuous facial expression and manner; a lability of emotions; sloppy grooming; uninhibited remarks; or silly jokes suggest the presence of dementia, especially when coupled with memory impairment. According to DSM-III-R, paranoid ideation may at times be very marked and result in false accusations and verbal or physical attacks. These accusations can lead a person whom DSM-III-R calls "habitually jealous" to develop a delusion of spousal infidelity when demented and to actually assault the spouse. The clinical diagnosis of dementia depends on whether the patient fulfills the criteria specified in DSM-III-R (Table 10-5).

According to DSM-III-R, the diagnosis of dementia may be made at any time after the intelligence quotient (I.Q.) is fairly stable, usually by the age of 3 or 4. Thus, according to DSM-III-R, a child of age 4 or above who develops a chronic neurological disorder that significantly interferes with already acquired intellectual and adaptive functions would be diagnosed as both mentally retarded and demented.

A comprehensive workup of both delirium and dementia is given in Table 10-6.

Table 10-6
Comprehensive Workup of Dementia and Delirium

Physical exam, including thorough neurological exam
Vital signs
Mental status examination
Mini-Mental State Exam (MMSE)
Review of medications and drug levels
Blood and urine screens for alcohol, drugs, and heavy metals*
Physiological workup
- Serum electrolytes/glucose/Ca^{++}, Mg^{+}
- Liver, renal function tests
- SMA-12 or equivalent serum chemistry profile
- Urinalysis
- Complete blood cell count with differential cell type count
- Thyroid function tests (including TSH level)
- RPR (serum screen)
- FTA-ABS (if CNS disease suspected)
- Serum B_{12}
- Folate levels
- Urine corticosteroids*
- Erythrocyte sedimentation rate (Westergren)
- Antinuclear antibody* (ANA), C_3C_4, Anti-DS DNA*
- Arterial blood gases*
- HIV screen*†
- Urine porphobilinogens*

Chest X-ray
Electrocardiogram
Neurological workup
- CT or MRI scan of head*
- SPECT**
- Lumbar puncture*
- EEG*

Neuropsychological testing§

Adapted from A Stoudemire, T L Thompson: Recognizing and treating dementia. Geriatrics *36*: 112, 1981, with permission.
*If indicated by history and physical examination
†Requires special consent and counseling
**May detect cerebral blood flow perfusion deficits
§May be useful in differentiating dementia from other neuropsychiatric syndromes if this cannot be done clinically

Differential diagnosis. Dementia must be distinguished from other organic mental syndromes and disorders and from nonorganic mental disorders.

Delirium. The distinction between delirium and dementia may be difficult or, at times, impossible to make. Delirium is distinguished by rapid onset, brief duration, fluctuation of cognitive impairment during the course of the day, nocturnal exacerbation of symptoms, marked disturbance of the sleep-wake cycle, and prominent disturbances of attention and perception. Hallucinations, especially visual ones, and transient delusions are more common in delirium than in dementia. An organic mental disorder lasting longer than a few months is more likely to represent dementia than delirium.

Mood disorders. A major diagnostic problem concerns the differentiation of dementia from a mood disorder, especially depression. A depressive disorder frequently accompanies dementia and may be one of its presenting features. *Pseudodementia* or, as DSM-III-R also refers to it, the dementia syndrome of depression, refers to a major depressive disorder featuring cognitive dysfunction that resembles dementia (Table 10-7).

According to DSM-III-R, abnormalities of mood in dementia are less frequent and, when present, less pervasive than in depression. Cognitive defects in depression usually occur at about the same time as the depression itself, and the patient expresses concern about the memory defect. Symptoms usually progress more rapidly than in true dementia. In dementia, however, depression usually follows the patient's intellectual deterioration, which the patient then rationalizes or denies. In addition, in pseudodementia there may be a history of a previous episode of mood disorder. DSM-III-R states that in the dementia syndrome of depression, the depression unmasks an underlying structural abnormality in the central nervous system, resulting in the clinical features of dementia. DSM-III-R also states that, in the absence of a specific organic causative factor, if the symptoms of depression are at least as prominent as those suggesting dementia, it is best to diagnose a major depressive episode and to assume that the symptoms suggesting dementia are secondary to the depression.

Factitious disorder. Rarely, persons who attempt to simulate memory loss, as in factitious disorder, do so in an erratic and inconsistent manner. In dementia, memory for time and place is lost before memory for person, and recent memory is lost before remote memory.

Schizophrenia. Schizophrenia is an illness associated with a clear sensorium. Schizophrenia, especially when chronic, may be associated with some degree of intellectual deterioration. DSM-III-R states that the absence of identifiable brain pathology helps rule out the additional diagnosis of dementia.

Table 10-7
Major Clinical Features Differentiating Pseudodementia from Dementia

Pseudodementia	Dementia
Clinical course and history	
Family always aware of dysfunction and its severity	Family often unaware of dysfunction and its severity
Onset can be dated with some precision	Onset can be dated only within broad limits
Symptoms of short duration before medical help is sought	Symptoms usually of long duration before medical help is sought
Rapid progression of symptoms after onset	Slow progression of symptoms throughout course
History of previous psychiatric dysfunction common	History of previous psychiatric dysfunction unusual
Complaints and clinical behavior	
Patients usually complain much of cognitive loss	Patients usually complain little of cognitive loss
Patients' complaints of cognitive dysfunction usually detailed	Patients' complaints of cognitive dysfunction usually vague
Patients emphasize disability	Patients conceal disability
Patients highlight failures	Patients delight in accomplishments, however trivial
Patients make little effort to perform even simple tasks	Patients struggle to perform tasks
	Patients rely on notes, calendars, etc., to keep up
Patients usually communicate strong sense of distress	Patients often appear unconcerned
Affective change often pervasive	Affect labile and shallow
Loss of social skills often early and prominent	Social skills often retained
Behavior often incongruent with severity of cognitive dysfunction	Behavior usually compatible with severity of cognitive dysfunction
Nocturnal accentuation of dysfunction uncommon	Nocturnal accentuation of dysfunction common
Clinical features related to memory, cognitive, and intellectual dysfunctions	
Attention and concentration often well preserved	Attention and concentration usually faulty
"Don't know" answers typical	Near-miss answers frequent
On tests of orientation, patients often give "don't know" answers	On tests of orientation, patients often mistake unusual for usual
Memory loss for recent and remote events usually severe	Memory loss for recent events usually more severe than for remote events
Memory gaps for specific periods or events common	Memory gaps for specific periods unusual*
Marked variability in performance on tasks of similar difficulty	Consistently poor performance on tasks of similar difficulty

Table from C. E. Wells: Am J Psychiatry, *136*: 898, 1979, with permission.
*Except when caused by delirium, trauma, seizures, etc.

Normal aging. Normal aging is accompanied by a reduction in the speed of mental processes and by some difficulty in committing new material to memory. However, such changes do not interfere with the person's ordinary social or occupational life, as they do in dementia.

Treatment. Dementia is regarded as a treatable syndrome because in some cases the dysfunctional brain tissue retains the capacity for recovery if treatment is timely. A complete medical history, physical examination, and laboratory tests, including appropriate brain imaging, should be undertaken as soon as the diagnosis is suspected (Table 10-6). If the patient is suffering from a treatable cause of dementia, therapy is directed toward treating the underlying disorder. For example, the dementia that accompanies hypothyroidism can be treated with thyroid replacement; but if hormone replacement is delayed too long, recovery may be incomplete.

Symptomatic or general treatment of dementia is used in conjunction with disease-specific treatment. Such symptomatic treatment measures include the maintenance of a nutritious diet, proper exercise, recreational and activity therapy, attention to visual and auditory problems, and the treatment of associated medical problems, such as urinary tract infection, decubitus ulcers, and cardiopulmonary dysfunction.

Psychosocial treatment involves giving support and advice to the patient and the family. Demented patients do best in quiet, familiar surroundings with adequate but familiar distractions. New and complex situations are often disruptive.

Pharmacotherapy of dementia is indicated for the symptoms of agitation, impulsiveness, aggression, anxiety, depression, paranoid ideation, insomnia, and night wandering. Anxiety is best treated with small doses of a benzodiazepine. For depression, tricyclics may be used, especially those with few anticholinergic side effects, to which the aged are susceptible. A therapeutic trial with an antidepressant or electroconvulsive therapy (ECT) may help to distinguish pseudodementia from true dementia. If the disorder is, in fact, a major depressive episode, the cognitive impairments usually resolve as mood improves. The antipsychotic agents are generally used to treat paranoid and other psychotic symptoms and to control potentially harmful behavior, such as hyperactivity and assaultiveness. For insomnia, a shorter-acting benzodiazepine, such as triazolam, is of use. Patients with dementia are liable to develop delirium from any of the psychotropic agents, so the clinician should be alert for an idiosyncratic drug reaction, such as the exacerbation of symptoms.

Primary Degenerative Dementia of the Alzheimer Type

Primary degenerative dementia of the Alzheimer type (DAT) is a progressive clinical disorder that can have either a senile or a presenile onset; it is characterized by a severe loss of intellectual functioning. DSM-III-R distinguishes Alzheimer's disease itself as a physical disorder coded on Axis III, whereas DAT is coded on Axis I. Practically speaking, since the diagnosis of Alzheimer's disease is based on neuropathological examination, most patients are diagnosed as having DAT, rather than Alzheimer's disease itself.

Epidemiology. About 5 percent of persons over age 65 have dementia; of this group, about 65 percent of all patients are thought to have DAT. Prevalence increases with age. DAT occurs slightly more frequently in women than in men.

Etiology. The cause of Alzheimer's disease remains unknown. Genetic factors are presumed to play a role. In one study 40 percent of patients had a family history of the disease. A high concordance rate has been found in twins. Several families have been reported with apparent autosomal dominant transmission.

Other causative theories have been proposed. Aluminum toxicity or metabolism has been hypothesized to be a causative factor, since high levels of aluminum have been found in the brains of some patients who died from the disease. Other studies have reported specific degeneration of the cholinergic neurons located in the nucleus basalis of Meynert. A viral cause has been postulated because some degenerative brain diseases, such as Creutzfeldt-Jakob disease, are virally transmitted; however, no direct evidence supports a viral cause for Alzheimer's disease.

Pathology. Pathological findings in Alzheimer's disease include diffuse atrophy (Figure 10-1) of the brain with flattened cortical sulci and enlarged cerebral ventricles. Microscopically, senile plaques (Figure 10-2), neurofibrillary tangles (Figure 10-3), and granulovacuolar degeneration of the neurons are present. Neurofibrillary tangles are found inside neurons. Neurofibrillary tangles are not specifically associated with Alzheimer's disease; they are also found in progressive supranuclear palsy, Hallervorden-Spatz disease, Guam-Parkinson-dementia complex, and dementia pugilistica (punch-drunk).

In contrast to neurofibrillary tangles, plaques are found outside of neurons and around cerebral blood vessels. Plaques are found only in Alzheimer's disease, Down's syndrome (trisomy 21), and, to a smaller extent, normal aging. The appearance of some plaques in normal aging suggests that Alzheimer's disease and Down's syndrome represent an acceleration of a normal process. The appearance of plaques in Down's syndrome is particularly interesting because the gene for the primary protein component of plaques, beta amyloid protein, is located on chromosome 21. Persons with Down's syndrome, therefore, have three genes, rather than two, for this protein. The presence of an extra gene for the beta amyloid protein may result in an overproduction of the protein. The vast majority of Alzheimer cases cannot, however, be explained by the presence of an extra gene for the beta amyloid protein. Nevertheless, the relative specificity of beta amyloid accumulation in Alzheimer's disease does suggest the possibility that Alzheimer's disease is a specific type of protein storage disease and that the excessive accumulation of amyloid protein may be either the cause or the result of the disease process. The beta amyloid protein itself has been cloned and sequenced. Its primary structure suggests that the protein is a transmembrane protein that may function as some type of receptor, but its actual function is unknown.

Clinical features, course, and prognosis. DAT may begin at any age, but it is most common late in life. Fifty percent of DAT patients are stricken between the ages of 65 and 70. The symptoms appear insidiously with impaired memory or subtle personality changes, which are usually first noticed by the family, rather than the patient. The

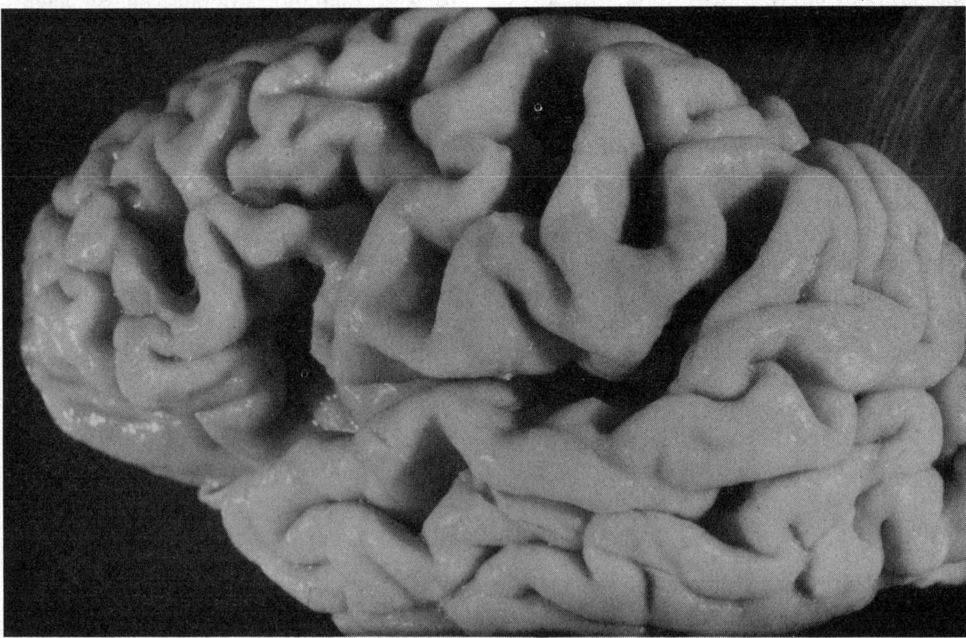

Figure 10-1. Gross external appearance of the brain of a patient who had primary degenerative dementia of the Alzheimer type, senile onset. The leptomeninges have been removed so that the generalized atrophy may be fully appreciated. (Courtesy of Daniel P. Perl, M.D.)

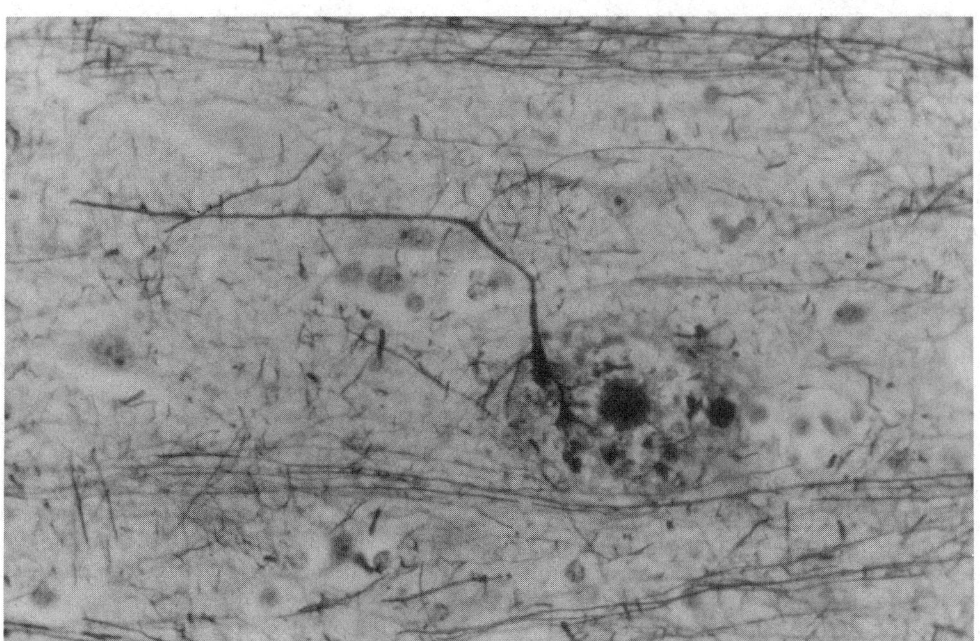

Figure 10-2. Microscopic appearance of a senile (neuritic) plaque in the neocortex. Notice the silver-staining neuronal process (neurite) entering the periphery of the plaque (modified Bielschowsky's stain, original magnification × 420. (Courtesy of Daniel P. Perl, M.D.)

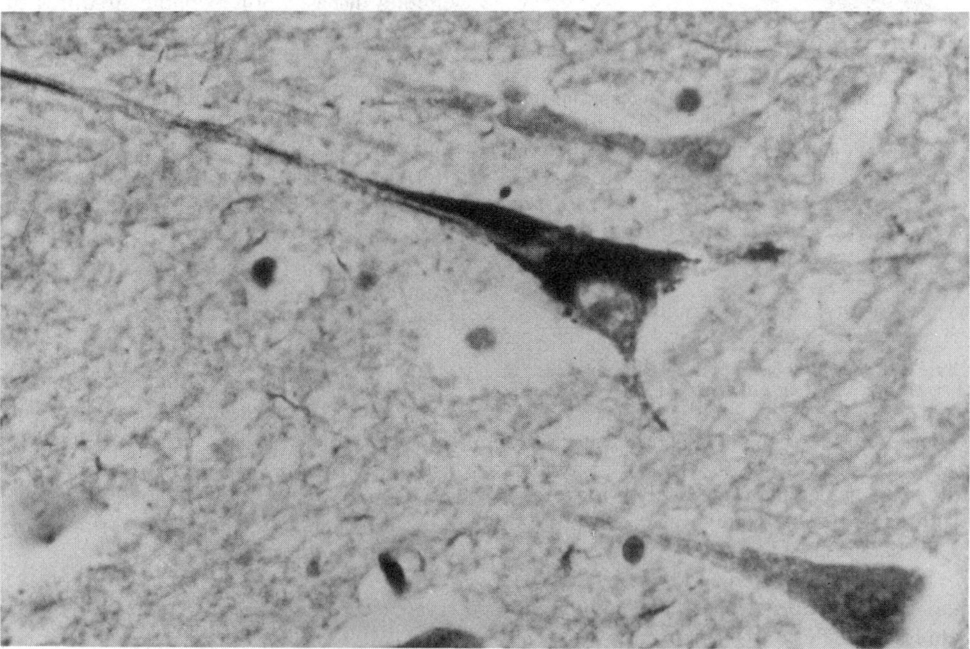

Figure 10-3. Microscopic appearance of a neuron containing a neurofibrillary tangle. Notice the dark-staining fibers within the neuronal cytoplasm (modified Bielschowsky's stain, original magnification × 420. (Courtesy of Daniel P. Perl, M.D.)

classical features of dementia—such as disturbances of orientation, memory, calculation, and judgment—eventually appear.

Psychiatric symptoms are commonly seen in patients with DAT. Mild symptoms of depression and anxiety are present in almost half of all DAT cases. Suspiciousness, paranoia, delusions, and visual hallucinations may be present in one-quarter to one-third of all patients. Previous personality traits become accentuated or exaggerated, and patients may become paranoid or withdrawn. Obsessive thoughts and compulsive rituals are usual. Defects in judgment may account for inappropriate behavior, such as exhibitionism.

The disorder eventually progresses to severe dementia. With senile onset, death intervenes from two to five years after the diagnosis has been made. A clinical case example follows:

A 65-year-old architectural draftsman began to have difficulty remembering details necessary for performing his job. At home he was having problems keeping accurate financial records and, on several occasions, forgot to pay bills. It became increasingly difficult for him to function properly at work, and eventually he was forced to retire. Intellectual deterioration continued, and behavioral problems appeared. He became extremely stubborn and, when thwarted, was verbally and physically abusive.

When seen by a neurological consultant five years after the problem began, the patient was fully alert and cooperative but obviously anxious and fidgety. He thought he was at his place of employment and the year was "1960 or something" (it was actually 1982). He could not remember any one of six objects after an interval of 10 minutes, even when prompted by multiple-choice answers. He knew his birthplace and high school but not the names of his parents or siblings. He said he had two children, whereas in fact he had only one. Although he insisted he was still working, he could not describe his job. He did not know the current president and could not explain the resignation of President Nixon or remember the assassination of President Kennedy. His speech was well articulated but vague and circuitous, with many empty, meaningless phrases. He had difficulty in naming common objects and repeating sentences. He could not do the simplest arithmetic calculations. He could not write a proper sentence, copy a two- or three-dimensional figure, or draw a house. He interpreted proverbs concretely and had difficulty in finding similarities between related objects.

An elementary neurological examination revealed nothing abnormal. All laboratory studies were normal, including B_{12}, folate, T_4 levels, and serology; but a computed tomography (CT) scan showed marked cortical atrophy.

Discussion. The difficulties with short- and long-term memory, abstract thinking (difficulty in finding similarities between related objects), and other higher cortical functions (e.g., inability to name common objects, to do arithmetic calculations, or to copy a figure)—all severe enough to interfere with social and occupational functioning, occurring in a clear state of consciousness, and not accounted for by a nonorganic mental disorder (such as major depression)—indicate a dementia.

The insidious onset with a generally progressive deteriorating course, the absence of focal neurological signs, the absence of a history of trauma or a stroke, the normal blood tests, and the cortical atrophy evident from the CT scan add up to the diagnosis of primary degenerative dementia of the Alzheimer type. Because there were no psychotic features or mood disturbances, the diagnosis was noted to be uncomplicated. The severity of the dementia was noted to be moderate because the patient required some supervision.

Diagnosis. The diagnosis of DAT is specified in DSM-III-R (Table 10-8). DSM-III-R recommends specifying the age of onset and the presence of specific complicating symptoms of depression, delusions, or delirium.

Table 10-8
Diagnostic Criteria for Primary Degenerative Dementia of the Alzheimer Type

A. Dementia

B. Insidious onset with a generally progressive deteriorating course

C. Exclusion of all other specific causes of dementia by history, physical examination, and laboratory tests

Table from DSM-III-R, *Diagnostic and Statistical Manual of Mental Disorders*, ed 3, revised. Copyright American Psychiatric Association, Washington, DC, 1987, with permission.

Differential diagnosis. DAT is distinguished from normal aging by clear evidence of progressive and significant deterioration in intellectual, social, or occupational functioning. Specific and potentially reversible causes of dementia—such as subdural hematoma, cerebral neoplasm, vitamin B_{12} deficiency, and hypothyroidism—need to be ruled out by history, physical examination, and laboratory tests. Multi-infarct dementia is distinguished from DAT by its more variable and classically stepwise deteriorating course and by the presence of focal neurological signs and symptoms of vascular disease. Old people with a major depressive episode may have pseudodementia, which is discussed in the subsection on the differential diagnosis of the dementia syndrome.

Pick's disease. Pick's disease is a progressive dementing condition with the same general age of onset and course as Alzheimer's disease. Pick's disease is similar to Alzheimer's disease, and distinguishing between the two diseases clinically is often impossible. Nonetheless, subtle clinical differences between the two conditions have been reported. Patients with Pick's disease present with less impairment of memory, calculation, and visuospatial abilities than do patients with Alzheimer's disease. The personalities of patients with Pick's disease, however, are much more affected than those of patients with Alzheimer's disease. For example, features of Klüver-Bucy syndrome (e.g., hypersexuality, placidity, hyperorality) are much more common in Pick's disease than in Alzheimer's disease. The EEG of a Pick's disease patient may show marked slowing over the frontal lobes. Neuropathologically, the cortical atrophy is limited to the frontal and anterior temporal lobes. A particular bloated type of neuron, *Pick's bodies*, are seen in some postmortem specimens but are not necessary for the diagnosis.

Treatment. There is no specific treatment for DAT. Experimental drugs have been tried with mixed results. Ultimately, all patients require institutionalization or 24-hour custodial care because of the severe psychological and physical deterioration that accompanies the disorder. Maintenance of physical health, supportive environment, and symptomatic psychopharmacological treatment are indicated. Particular attention must be provided to caretakers and family members who must deal with frustration, grief, and psychological burnout as they care for the patient over a long period of time.

Multi-Infarct Dementia

Multi-infarct dementia (MID) is characterized by a decremental or patchy deterioration in cognitive functioning because of significant cerebrovascular disease.

Epidemiology. The disorder is most prevalent between ages 60 and 70, although it may begin in middle age; it generally appears earlier than DAT. MID occurs more frequently in men than in women. Hypertension predisposes a person to the disease. MID accounts for about 15 percent of all cases of dementia in the elderly.

Etiology. Vascular disease is assumed to be present and responsible for the dementia and the focal neurological signs. The disorder affects small- and medium-size cerebral vessels, which undergo infarction and produce multiple parenchymal lesions spread over wide areas of the brain (Figure 10-4). Cerebral infarcts may result from damage in situ of a particular vessel or by thromboemboli originating in the heart or the other vessels outside the brain. Carotid bruits, funduscopic abnormalities, or an enlarged heart may be present. Hypertension is commonly associated with MID and may indicate a genetic contribution to the disorder.

Clinical features and diagnosis. A variety of symptoms occur in MID: headaches, dizziness, faintness, weakness, focal neurological symptoms, memory impairment, sleep disturbance, and personality changes, such as emotional lability and hypochondriasis. Pseudobulbar palsy, dysarthria, and dysphagia are common. The DSM-III-R diagnostic criteria for MID are listed in Table 10-9.

Course and prognosis. The onset of MID is usually sudden, and the course is progressive, although the clinical picture may appear to stabilize for a period of time before worsening again. There is decremental and fluctuating deterioration in cognitive functioning that, early in the course, leaves some functions unaffected. Seizures occur in about 20 percent of patients.

Differential diagnosis. MID must be differentiated from a single stroke, from transient ischemic attacks (TIA), and from DAT. A single stroke in general does not cause dementia. MID is due to multiple strokes that occur over a period of time.

TIAs are brief episodes of focal neurological dysfunction lasting less than 24 hours (usually 5 to 15 minutes). Although a variety of mechanisms may be responsible, these episodes are frequently the result of microembolization from a proximal extracranial arterial lesion that produces transient brain ischemia and resolve without significant pathological alteration of the parenchymal tissue.

The clinican should distinguish episodes involving the vertebrobasilar system from those involving the carotid arterial system. In general, symptoms of vertebrobasilar disease reflect a transient functional disturbance in either the brain stem or the occipital lobe; carotid distribution symptoms reflect unilateral retinal or hemispheric abnormality. Anticoagulant therapy, antiplatelet agglutinating drugs such as acetylsalicylic acid (aspirin), and extra- and intracranial reconstructive vascular surgery have been reported to be effective in reducing the risk of infarction in patients with TIAs.

Table 10-9
Diagnostic Criteria for Multi-Infarct Dementia

A. Dementia

B. Stepwise deteriorating course with "patchy" distribution of deficits (i.e., affecting some functions, but not others) early in the course

C. Focal neurological signs and symptoms (e.g., exaggeration of deep tendon reflexes, extensor plantar response, pseudobulbar palsy, gait abnormalities, weakness of an extremity, etc.)

D. Evidence from history, physical examination, or laboratory tests of significant cerebrovascular disease (recorded on Axis III) that is judged to be etiologically related to the disturbance

Table from DSM-III-R, *Diagnostic and Statistical Manual of Mental Disorders*, ed 3, revised. Copyright American Psychiatric Association, Washington, DC, 1987, with permission.

About one-third of untreated patients with transient ischemic attacks later develop a brain infarction. Since nearly half of the patients with TIAs who later develop an infarction do so within a few weeks after the transient episodes, prompt recognition and treatment are crucial to the prevention of a major cerebrovascular accident.

MID is distinguished from DAT by the typical decremental deterioration of the patient (as opposed to the continuous progression observed in DAT). Patients with MID are also more likely to show focal neurological signs and symptoms, presumably as a result of ischemic areas of the

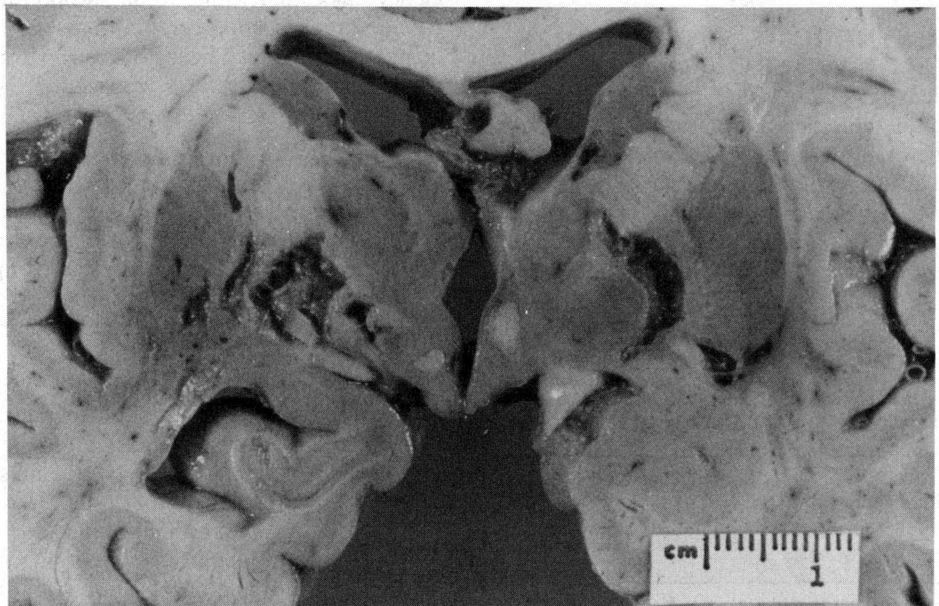

Figure 10-4. Gross appearance of the cerebral cortex on coronal section from a case of multi-infarct dementia. Notice the multiple bilateral lacunar infarcts involving the thalamus, internal capsule, and globus pallidus. (Courtesy of Daniel P. Perl, M.D.)

brain. Hypertension and evidence of cerebrovascular disease are also more common in MID than in DAT. It is possible for MID and DAT to coexist. If clinical features of both are present, both diagnoses should be made.

Treatment. Once the diagnosis of MID is made, contributing risk factors should be identified and treated as early as possible to prevent further progression. These factors include hypertension, hyperlipidemia, heart disease, diabetes, and alcoholism. Control of hypertension prevents stroke in these patients. Cessation of smoking improves their cerebral perfusion and cognitive functioning.

The general principles of management of dementia apply: maintenance of overall physical health, stable supportive environment, and drug therapy for symptoms. The clinician may prescribe benzodiazepines for insomnia and anxiety, antidepressants for depression, and antipsychotic drugs for delusions and hallucinations; however, the clinician should be aware of possible idiosyncratic drug effects in the elderly (such as paradoxical excitement, confusion, and increased sedation).

Other Dementias

A variety of other disorders have dementia as a presenting symptom or associated feature of the disease. These are dementias associated with an organic factor that arise before (presenile) or after (senile) the age of 65 and that cannot be classified as a specific dementia. Some disorders have known causes, such as infarction and disorders of inborn errors of metabolism; others are idiopathic. At times, delirium or mental confusion is the only sign present, and it may progress to irreversible dementia if the underlying condition is not diagnosed and treated. According to DSM-III-R, these conditions are classified as either presenile dementia not otherwise specified (NOS) or senile dementia NOS (Tables 10-10 and 10-11).

AMNESTIC SYNDROME AND DISORDER

An impairment of memory is the single or predominant cognitive defect in amnestic syndrome and amnestic disorder. Amnestic disorder is diagnosed when an Axis III disorder is implicated in the cause. Psychologists hypothesize the existence of two kinds of memory—short-term (also known as primary or immediate memory) and long-term (also known as secondary, recent, recent past, or remote memory). Short-term memory usually includes the first few seconds or minutes of memory; long-term memory covers all memories after that time period.

Table 10-10
Diagnostic Criteria for Presenile Dementia Not Otherwise Specified

Dementias associated with an organic factor and arising before age 65 that cannot be classified as a specific dementia (e.g., primary degenerative dementia of the Alzheimer type, presenile onset)

Table from DSM-III-R, *Diagnostic and Statistical Manual of Mental Disorders*, ed 3, revised. Copyright American Psychiatric Association, Washington, DC, 1987, with permission.

Table 10-11
Diagnostic Criteria for Senile Dementia Not Otherwise Specified

Dementias associated with an organic factor and arising after age 65 that cannot be classified as a specific dementia (e.g., as primary degenerative dementia of the Alzheimer type, senile onset, or dementia associated with alcoholism)

Table from DSM-III-R, *Diagnostic and Statistical Manual of Mental Disorders*, ed 3, revised. Copyright American Psychiatric Association, Washington, DC, 1987, with permission.

There are three basic types of amnesia. Retrograde amnesia refers to memory loss of events that occurred before the amnesia-producing event. Posttraumatic amnesia refers to memory loss of events for a restricted period of time after the amnesia-producing event. Anterograde amnesia refers to an impairment in acquiring new memories.

Epidemiology

There are no adequate studies on the incidence or the prevalence of this syndrome. Amnestic syndrome is most often encountered in persons with chronic alcoholism.

Etiology

A number of organic pathological factors and conditions can give rise to the amnestic syndrome, which results from any pathological process that causes bilateral damage to such diencephalic and medial temporal structures as the mamillary bodies, hippocampal complex, and fornix. It has been hypothesized that frontal dysfunction may be present when confabulation is a major feature of the syndrome. The most common cause in this country is thiamin deficiency associated with chronic alcoholism. Other causes include brain trauma, cerebral hypoxia, tumors, and degenerative diseases. The factors known to cause the amnestic syndrome and disorder are listed in Table 10-12.

Clinical Features and Types

The core feature of the amnestic syndrome is the impairment of memory. Short-term memory and recent memory (a few minutes to a few days) are impaired. Patients cannot remember what they had for breakfast or lunch, the name of the hospital, or their doctor. The deficit in recent memory accounts for the anterograde amnesia. Memory for overlearned information or events from the remote past, such as childhood experiences, is good; but memory for events from the less remote past (over the past decade) is impaired, which accounts for retrograde amnesia. Immediate memory (tested by asking the patient to repeat six numbers) remains intact.

The patient frequently lacks insight into memory deficits and tends to minimize, rationalize, or even explicitly deny them. Minor deficits in perception and concept formation may be found in alcoholic patients, but generally

Table 10-12
Causes of Amnestic Syndrome and Disorder

Thiamin deficiency (Korsakoff's syndrome)
Alcoholic blackouts
Electroconvulsive therapy
Head injury
Cerebral neoplasm
Cerebrovascular accidents (especially hippocampal)
Transient global amnesia
Epilepsy
Cerebral anoxia (e.g., carbon monoxide poisoning, unsuccessful hanging attempts)
Herpes simplex encephalitis

the sensorium is relatively clear. A significant degree of amnesia, however, can result in disorientation. Lack of initiative, emotional blandness, and apathy are common, although the patient is responsive to the environment. Because immediate memory is intact, patients are able to recognize surroundings or communications addressed to them, but they soon forget these because of their impaired forward memory span. Confabulation, in which the patient fills in memory gaps with false information, is a common characteristic. Confabulation tends to disappear with time.

Korsakoff's syndrome. Korsakoff's syndrome is the persistent amnestic syndrome associated with alcoholism. Recent memory tends to be affected more than remote memory; however, this feature is variable. Confabulation is often a prominent symptom in the syndrome. Korsakoff's syndrome should be differentiated from Wernicke's encephalopathy; however, signs of Wernicke's encephalopathy (confusion, ataxia, nystagmus) often precede the development of Korsakoff's syndrome.

Alcoholic blackouts. Alcoholic blackouts occur in alcoholics with particularly heavy drinking patterns. In classic cases the alcoholic patient awakens in the morning with a conscious awareness of being unable to remember a period of time the night before while intoxicated. Sometimes specific behaviors (hiding money in a secret place, provoking fights) are associated with a particular person's blackouts.

Electroconvulsive therapy. ECT is associated with retrograde and anterograde amnesia, which usually resolves almost completely by six months after treatment, although the patient is often left with an amnesia for events immediately around the time of the convulsions.

Head injury. Head injury is often associated with a brief period of retrograde amnesia and a bit longer period of posttraumatic amnesia. The severity of the brain injury is somewhat correlated with the duration and the severity of the amnestic syndrome.

Transient global amnesia. Patients with transient global amnesia abruptly lose their ability to recall recent events or to record new memories. Events of the distant past are readily recalled. Although patients are often aware of some disturbance in function during the episodes, they may still perform highly complex mental and physical acts. Episodes last from 6 to 24 hours. Recovery is usually complete, with few recurrences. The disorder is thought to result from a temporary physiological alteration of the brain. Transient global amnesia is most likely caused by ischemia involving midline limbic structures, but it may also be an epileptiform phenomenon.

Course and Prognosis

The course and the prognosis of the amnestic syndrome depend on the cause of the case in question. The onset in most cases tends to be relatively sudden. The syndrome may be transient or persistent, and its outcome may be a complete or partial recovery of memory function or an irreversible or even progressive memory defect. Generally, the course is chronic. Transient amnestic syndrome with full recovery is common in temporal lobe epilepsy, vascular insufficiency, ECT, intake of such drugs as benzodiazepines and barbiturates, and cardiac arrest. Permanent amnestic syndrome may follow head trauma, carbon monoxide poisoning, subarachnoid hemorrhage, cerebral infarction, and herpes simplex encephalitis.

Diagnosis

The diagnosis of amnestic syndrome rests on finding its essential features, particularly short- and long-term memory impairment. The DSM-III-R diagnostic criteria for amnestic syndrome are listed in Table 10-13.

Differential Diagnosis

The amnestic syndrome associated with chronic alcoholism (Korsakoff's syndrome) should be differentiated from Wernicke's syndrome, an encephalopathy that develops acutely in patients with a history of many years of alcohol abuse. Wernicke's syndrome is marked by delirium, ataxia of gait, nystagmus, and ophthalmoplegia. Brain autopsies show characteristic lesions of the mamillary bodies. Although the delirium clears up within a month or so, the amnestic syndrome either accompanies

Table 10-13
Diagnostic Criteria for Amnestic Syndrome

A. Demonstrable evidence of impairment in both short- and long-term memory; with regard to long-term memory, very remote events are remembered better than more recent events. Impairment in short-term memory (inability to learn new information) may be indicated by inability to remember three objects after five minutes. Long-term memory impairment (inability to remember information that was known in the past) may be indicated by inability to remember past personal information (e.g., what happened yesterday, birthplace, occupation) or facts of common knowledge (e.g., past presidents, well-known dates).

B. Not occurring exclusively during the course of delirium, and does not meet the criteria for dementia (i.e., no impairment in abstract thinking or judgment, no other disturbances of higher cortical function, and no personality change).

C. There is evidence from the history, physical examination, or laboratory tests of a specific organic factor (or factors) judged to be etiologically related to the disturbance.

Table from DSM-III-R, *Diagnostic and Statistical Manual of Mental Disorders*, ed 3, revised. Copyright American Psychiatric Association, Washington, DC, 1987, with permission.

or follows untreated Wernicke's syndrome in about 85 percent of all cases.

In dementia and delirium, amnesia is only one component of global intellectual and cognitive dysfunction. The development of a slowly progressive amnestic syndrome should suggest a brain tumor, Alzheimer's disease, or another dementia.

Psychogenic amnesia is characterized by the sudden onset of retrograde amnesia for personally significant memories; it is usually accompanied by a loss of the sense of personal identity, of which the patient may or may not be aware. There is usually evidence of a subjectively stressful or conflict-arousing precipitating event. Anterograde amnesia is rarely psychogenic. Psychogenic amnesia may be precipitated by head trauma, an epileptic seizure, or acute alcohol intoxication. In the psychogenic memory disorders, however, the patient's responses are typically inconsistent, and there is usually an intact memory for personally neutral information. A sodium amobarbital (Amytal) interview may help distinguish amnestic syndrome from psychogenic amnesia by revealing the motivation for the psychogenic amnesia. The patient who has a factitious disorder with psychological symptoms gets inconsistent results on memory testing and has no organic problem. These findings, coupled with evidence of primary or secondary gain on the part of the patient, should suggest a factitious disorder.

Treatment

Treatment of the amnestic syndrome must first be directed at its underlying cause, such as a brain tumor. It is particularly important to try to prevent the development of Wernicke's encephalopathy in the alcoholic patient by giving high doses of thiamin and other vitamins. Once encephalopathy has developed, it must be treated vigorously to prevent or minimize the amnestic syndrome that is likely to follow. In addition, the patient should receive other B-complex vitamins. Once the amnestic syndrome has become fixed, supportive measures, such as a structured environment and pharmacotherapy for anxiety or agitation, are helpful.

ORGANIC HALLUCINOSIS

Organic hallucinosis is defined in DSM-III-R as both a syndrome (when the cause is completely unknown) and a disorder (when there is an Axis III diagnosis causing the syndrome). Organic hallucinosis is characterized by prominent recurrent or persistent hallucinations in a state of full wakefulness. The causative factor is either known to be or assumed to be organic.

Epidemiology

Relevant epidemiological data about organic hallucinosis are lacking. The syndrome and the disorder are most often encountered in patients who abuse alcohol or other drugs on a chronic basis.

Etiology

Psychoactive drug abuse is the most common cause of organic hallucinosis. The most commonly involved drugs are alcohol, indole hallucinogens (such as lysergic acid diethylamide [LSD]), amphetamine, cocaine, mescaline, phencyclidine (PCP), and ketamine. Many other drugs, including steroids and thyroxin, can be associated with organic hallucinosis. Physical conditions—such as cerebral neoplasms, particularly of the occipital or temporal areas—should be considered. Sensory deprivation, as occurs in blind and deaf persons, can also cause the syndrome. Other physical causes of organic hallucinosis are listed in Table 10-14.

Clinical Features

Hallucinations may occur in one or more sensory modalities. Tactile or haptic hallucinations (such as bugs crawling on the skin) are characteristic of cocainism; auditory hallucinations are common in alcoholic hallucinosis; visual hallucinations are usually associated with psychoactive substance abuse; and olfactory hallucinations occur in temporal lobe epilepsy. Auditory hallucinations may occur in deaf people; visual hallucinations may occur in people who are blind from cataracts. Hallucinations are either recurrent or persistent. They are experienced in a state of full wakefulness and alertness, and the patient shows no significant change in cognitive functions. Visual hallucinosis often takes the form of scenes involving diminutive (Lilliputian) human figures or various small animals. Rare musical hallucinosis typically features religious songs. A patient with hallucinosis may act on the hallucinations. In alcoholic hallucinosis there are typically threatening, critical, or insulting voices of people speaking about the patient in the third person. They may tell patients to harm either themselves or others; such patients are dangerous and are at significant risk for suicide or homicide. The patient may or may not believe that the hallucinations are real. Delusional conviction of their reality, however, is not the major feature of this syndrome.

Diagnosis

Hallucinosis is diagnosed on the basis of the patient's history and the presence of persistent or recurrent hallu-

Table 10-14
Organic Causes of Hallucinosis

Visual
Opthalmological disorders
Optic nerve disease
Occipital lobe neoplasms
Auditory
Middle and inner ear disorders
Auditory nerve disease
Any sensory modality
Cerebral neoplasms
Epilepsy
Migraine headaches
Toxic or drug-related
Cerebrovascular accidents
Temporal arteritis

cinations. The sensorium is clear. When a patient has hallucinations, an organic cause should be sought. The DSM-III-R diagnostic criteria for this syndrome are presented in Table 10-15.

Course and Prognosis

The course and the prognosis depend on the underlying pathology. The onset is usually acute, and the average duration is days or weeks or, as in the case of ingested hallucinogens, only a few hours. In some patients hallucinosis becomes chronic, as with untreated cataracts or deafness secondary to otosclerosis. Some patients with acute hallucinosis progress to delirium.

Differential Diagnosis

Organic hallucinosis needs to be distinguished from delirium, in which there is a clouded sensorium, and from dementia, in which there are major intellectual deficits. Delusions that occur in organic hallucinosis are related to the hallucinations and are not prominent. In organic delusional syndrome the delusions are predominant and are usually well systematized. If prominent delusions and prominent hallucinations coexist, DSM-III-R states that both organic delusional syndrome and organic hallucinosis may be diagnosed. It may be difficult at times to differentiate hallucinations from confabulations, but memory impairment is absent in hallucinosis and present in confabulatory states. Hypnagogic and hypnopompic hallucinations occur only on falling asleep or on awakening.

Epilepsy, especially the temporal lobe type, may be accompanied by either auditory or visual hallucinations. Such hallucinations are usually part of an ictus (attack), are accompanied by other ictal phenomena, are paroxysmal, and occur in a setting of reduced awareness. Alcoholic hallucinosis is differentiated from delirium tremens (DTs) by the presence of a clear sensorium in hallucinosis. The hallucinations of DTs are usually visual, rather than auditory, and are usually most prominent at night. Schizophrenia and mood disorders may present with hallucinations but within the context of the clear overriding diagnosis and with no specific organic factor demonstrated.

Treatment

Treatment depends on the underlying condition. If the cause is temporary, the anxious or agitated patient responds to the reassurance that he or she is suffering from what is likely to be a temporary mental disorder. It is best to hospitalize a markedly fearful and delusional patient. Antipsychotic medication (such as haloperidol) often relieves hallucinatory phenomena, and antianxiety agents (such as diazepam [Valium]) are useful for agitation.

Table 10-15
Diagnostic Criteria for Organic Hallucinosis

A. Prominent persistent or recurrent hallucinations.

B. There is evidence from the history, physical examination, or laboratory tests of a specific organic factor (or factors) judged to be etiologically related to the disturbance.

C. Not occurring exclusively during the course of delirium.

Table from DSM-III-R, *Diagnostic and Statistical Manual of Mental Disorders*, ed 3, revised. Copyright American Psychiatric Association, Washington, DC, 1987, with permission.

ORGANIC DELUSIONAL SYNDROME AND DISORDER

Organic delusional syndrome and disorder are characterized by the presence of prominent delusions in a state of full wakefulness and alertness. The delusions can be attributed to some clearly defined or presumed organic factor.

Epidemiology

There are few epidemiological studies of incidence or prevalence of the disorder. The delusional syndrome that accompanies complex partial seizures is more common in women than in men.

Etiology

Drugs are the most common cause of the disorder. A variety of chemical substances—especially amphetamine, cannabis, hallucinogens, and cocaine—may induce the syndrome. The syndrome often (but not always) lifts after the toxic agent has been withdrawn or the physical illness has subsided. Lesions involving the temporal lobe and other cerebral regions, especially of the right hemisphere and the parietal lobe, are associated with delusions. According to DSM-III-R, some people with temporal lobe epilepsy have an interictal organic delusional syndrome that can look like schizophrenia. DSM-III-R also describes a paranoid organic delusional syndrome that has been reported in some cases of Huntington's chorea.

Clinical Features and Diagnosis

The essential feature of the organic delusional syndrome is the presence of delusions in a state of full wakefulness. There is no change in the level of consciousness, although mild cognitive impairment may be observed. The delusions may be systematized or fragmentary, and their content may vary. Persecutory delusions are the most common. A diagnosis of the syndrome involves finding evidence of an organic factor that antedates the onset of the syndrome and is judged to be etiologically significant. The person may appear confused, disheveled, or eccentric. Speech may be tangential or even incoherent; hyperactivity and apathy may be observed. An associated dysphoric mood is thought to be common. The diagnostic criteria are listed in Table 10-16.

Course and Prognosis

The course and the prognosis depend to some extent on the underlying cause. Amphetamine psychosis is usually self-limited, with delusions abating after 7 to 10 days. Flashbacks may be triggered by the use of even small amounts of amphetamines. Epileptic patients may have

Table 10-16
Diagnostic Criteria for Organic Delusional Syndrome

A. Prominent delusions.

B. There is evidence from the history, physical examination, or laboratory tests of a specific organic factor (or factors) judged to be etiologically related to the disturbance.

C. Not occurring exclusively during the course of delirium.

Table from DSM-III-R, *Diagnostic and Statistical Manual of Mental Disorders*, ed 3, revised. Copyright American Psychiatric Association, Washington, DC, 1987, with permission.

delusional experiences for many years. Their delusions, however, may be phasic and may paradoxically vary inversely with seizure frequency; that is, the greater the frequency of seizures, the fewer the number of delusional experiences.

Differential Diagnosis

The major differential diagnosis is between organic delusional syndrome and paranoid schizophrenia. For example, amphetamine abuse may lead to a highly systematized paranoid delusional condition that appears to be identical to the active phase of schizophrenia. In contrast to paranoid schizophrenia, however, hallucinations in organic delusional syndrome are more often visual than auditory. The affect is also more appropriate, and the thought processes are better preserved. A history of a specific organic factor known to produce delusional psychoses also helps in distinguishing the organic delusional syndrome from the nonorganic psychotic disorders. According to DSM-III-R, the first appearance of a delusion occurring after the age of 35, when there is no history of schizophrenia or delusional disorder, necessitates a workup for organic delusional syndrome. Clearly, if there is concern about a possible organic factor in a person with a history of a nonorganic psychosis, the workup must still be done.

Delirium is associated with a change in the level of consciousness. Dementia shows significant impairment of intellectual capacities. Organic hallucinosis shows persistent and prominent hallucinations. Organic anxiety shows neither hallucinations nor delusions. Organic mood disorder shows predominant symptoms of a mood disorder, and any delusions or hallucinations present are related in content to the mood disturbance.

Treatment

Management of the syndrome depends on its underlying cause, which should be identified and treated. Otherwise, symptomatic treatment follows the general guidelines applicable to schizophrenia and delusional disorders—antipsychotics, supportive environment or hospitalization, and psychotherapy.

ORGANIC MOOD SYNDROME AND DISORDER

Previously called organic affective syndrome, organic mood syndrome and disorder are characterized by either a depressive or a manic mood that is attributed to a clearly defined organic factor.

Etiology

Medications, especially antihypertensives, are probably the most frequent cause. Drugs such as reserpine and methyldopa (both antihypertensive agents) can precipitate a depression by depleting serotonin in more than 10 percent of persons who take these drugs. A number of somatic disorders have been implicated in the causes of mood changes: endocrine disorders, especially Cushing's syndrome, and cerebral disorders of various causes, such as brain tumors, encephalitis, epilepsy. Structural damage to the brain, similar to what occurs with hemispheric strokes, is a common cause of the syndrome and disorder. Conditions associated with organic depressive or manic features are listed in Tables 10-17, 10-18, and 10-19.

Clinical Features and Diagnosis

Disturbances of mood resembling those observed in depressive or manic states are the predominant and essential clinical features. To make the diagnosis, the physician must find an organic cause that antedates the onset of symptoms and is known to be associated with the disorder. The syndrome may vary in severity from mild to severe or psychotic and may be indistinguishable from manic and depressive episodes that are not attributable to a specific organic factor. Delusions, hallucinations, and other associated features of bipolar disorder may also be present in an organic mood disorder; mild cognitive impairment may be observed. Table 10-20 lists the criteria for organic mood disorder.

Course and Prognosis

The onset may be acute or insidious, and the course varies, depending on the underlying cause. The removal of the cause does not necessarily result in the patient's prompt recovery from the mood disorder. The syndrome may persist for weeks or months after the successful treatment of the underlying physical condition or the withdrawal of the implicated toxic agent. It has been reported that 10 percent of patients with depressed mood secondary to Cushing's syndrome attempt suicide.

Differential Diagnosis

The major differential diagnosis is between organic mood disorder and nonorganic (functional) mood disorder. Functional illness is usually accompanied by a family history of depression or mania, recurrent cycles of depression or mania, and the absence of a specific organic causative factor. Drugs may trigger an underlying mood disorder in a patient who is biologically vulnerable; according to DSM-III-R, this would not be an organic mood disorder. For instance, antidepressants may trigger manic episodes in patients with underlying bipolar disorder. A history of previous mood disorder in the patient or in relatives suggests that the psychoactive substance merely triggered an existing underlying disorder; the absence of such a history suggests a true organic mood syndrome.

Table 10-17
Principal Neurological and Systemic Disorders Producing Depression

Neurological disorders
- Extrapyramidal diseases
  - Parkinson's disease
  - Huntington's disease
  - Progressive supranuclear palsy
- Cerebrovascular disease (especially anterior hemispheric lesions)
- Cerebral neoplasms
- Cerebral trauma
- CNS infections
- Multiple sclerosis
- Epilepsy
- Narcolepsy
- Hydrocephalus

Systemic disorders
- Infections
  - Viral
  - Bacterial

Endocrine disorders
- Hyperthyroidism
- Hypothyroidism
- Hyperparathyroidism
- Hypoparathyroidism
- Cushing's syndrome (steroid excess)
- Addison's disease (steroid insufficiency)
- Hyperaldosteronism
- Premenstrual depression

Inflammatory disorders
- Systemic lupus erythematosus
- Rheumatoid arthritis
- Temporal arteritis
- Sjögren's syndrome

Vitamin deficiencies
- Folate
- Vitamin B_{12}
- Niacin
- Vitamin C

Miscellaneous systemic disorders
- Cardiopulmonary disease
- Renal disease and uremia
- Systemic neoplasms
- Porphyria
- Klinefelter's syndrome
- Acquired immune deficiency syndrome (AIDS)
- Postpartum mood disorders
- Postoperative mood disorders

Table from J L Cummings: *Clinical Neuropsychiatry*, p 187. Grune & Stratton, Orlando, FL, 1985, with permission.

Table 10-18
Drugs Implicated in Producing Depression Syndromes

Cardiac and antihypertensive drugs	
Bethanidine	Digitalis
Clonidine	Prazosin
Guanethidine	Procainamide
Hydralazine	Veratrum
Methyldopa	Lidocaine
Propranolol	Oxprenolol
Reserpine	Methoserpidine
Sedatives and hypnotics	
Barbiturates	Benzodiazepines
Chloral hydrate	Chlormethiazole
Ethanol	Chlorazepate
Steroids and hormones	
Corticosteroids	Triamcinalone
Oral contraceptives	Norethisterone
Prednisone	Danazol
Stimulants and appetite suppressants	
Amphetamine	Diethylpropion
Fenfluramine	Phenmetrazine
Psychotropic drugs	
Butyrophenones	Phenothiazines
Neurological agents	
Amantadine	Baclofen
Bromocriptine	Carbamazepine
Levodopa	Methosuximide
Tetrabenazine	Phenytoin
Analgesics and anti-inflammatory drugs	
Fenoprofen	Phenacetin
Ibuprofen	Phenylbutazone
Indomethacin	Pentazocine
Opiates	Benzydamine
Antibacterial and antifungal drugs	
Ampicillin	Griseofulvin
Sulfamethoxazole	Metronidazole
Clotrimazole	Nitrofurantoin
Cycloserine	Nalidixic acid
Dapsone	Sulfonamides
Ethionamide	Streptomycin
Tetracycline	Thiocarbanilide
Antineoplastic drugs	
Azathioprine	6-Azauridine
C-Asparaginase	Bleomycin
Mithramycin	Trimethoprim
Vincristine	
Miscellaneous drugs	
Acetazolamide	Anticholinesterases
Choline	Cimetidine
Cyproheptadine	Diphenoxylate
Disulfiram	Lysergide
Methysergide	Mebeverine
Meclizine	Metaclopramide
Pizotifen	Salbutamol

Table from J L Cummings: *Clinical Neuropsychiatry*, p 187. Grune & Stratton, Orlando, FL, 1985, with permission.

Treatment

Management of the syndrome involves determining the cause and treating the underlying disorder. Psychopharmacological treatment may be indicated and should follow the guidelines applicable to the treatment of depression or mania, with due regard for the coexisting physical condition. Psychotherapy is used as an adjunct to the other treatments.

ORGANIC PERSONALITY SYNDROME AND DISORDER

Organic personality syndrome and disorder are characterized by a marked change in personality style and traits from a previous level of functioning. There must be evidence of a causative organic factor antedating the onset of the personality change.

Etiology

Structural damage to the brain is usually the cause of the sydrome. Head trauma is probably the most common

Table 10-19
Causes of Secondary Mania

Neurological disorders
Extrapyramidal disease
Huntington's disease
Postencephalitic Parkinson's disease
Wilson's disease
CNS infections
General paresis
Viral encephalitis
Miscellaneous conditions
Cerebral neoplasms
Cerebral trauma
Thalamotomy
Cerebrovascular accidents
Multiple sclerosis
Temporal lobe epilepsy
Pick's disease
Kleine-Levin syndrome
Klinefelter's syndrome
Systemic disorders
Uremia and hemodialysis
Dialysis dementia
Hyperthyroidism
Pellagra
Carcinoid syndrome
Vitamin B_{12} deficiency
Postpartum mania
Drugs
Levodopa
Bromocriptine
Sympathomimetics
Isoniazid
Procarbazine
Bromide
Cocaine
Amphetamines
Procyclidine
Hydralazine
Cyclobenzaprine
Phencyclidine (PCP)
Cimetidine
Yohimbine
Baclofen
Metrizamide (following myelography)

Table from J L Cummings: *Clinical Neuropsychiatry*, p 187. Grune & Stratton, Orlando, FL, 1985, with permission.

cause. Cerebral neoplasms and vascular accidents, particularly of the temporal and frontal lobes, are also common causes. As described below, steroid abuse by young athletes is an increasingly common cause of organic personality disorder. The conditions most often associated with this syndrome or disorder are listed in Table 10-21.

Clinical Features and Diagnosis

A change in personality from previous patterns of behavior or an exacerbation of previous personality characteristics is notable. Impaired control of the expression of emotions and impulses is a cardinal feature. Emotions are characteristically labile and shallow, although euphoria or apathy may be prominent. The euphoria may mimic hypomania, but true elation is absent, and the patient may admit to not really feeling happy. There is a hollow and silly ring to the patient's excitement and facile jocularity, particularly if the frontal lobes are involved. Also associated with damage to the frontal lobes, the so-called frontal lobe syndrome, is prominent indifference and apathy, characterized by a lack of concern for events in the immediate environment. Temper outbursts with little or no provocation may occur, especially after alcohol ingestion, and may result in violent behavior. The expression of impulses may be manifested by inappropriate jokes, a coarse manner, improper sexual advances, and antisocial conduct resulting in conflicts with the law, such as assaults on others, sexual misdemeanors, and shoplifting. Foresight and the ability to anticipate the social or legal consequences of one's actions are typically diminished. People with temporal lobe epilepsy characteristically demonstrate humorlessness, hypergraphia, hyperreligiosity, and marked aggressiveness during seizures.

Table 10-20
Diagnostic Criteria for Organic Mood Syndrome

A. Prominent and persistent depressed, elevated, or expansive mood.

B. There is evidence from the history, physical examination, or laboratory tests of a specific organic factor (or factors) judged to be etiologically related to the disturbance.

C. Not occurring exclusively during the course of delirium.

Specify: manic, depressed, or **mixed.**

Table from DSM-III-R, *Diagnostic and Statistical Manual of Mental Disorders*, ed 3, revised. Copyright American Psychiatric Association, Washington, DC, 1987, with permission.

Table 10-21
Conditions Associated with Organic Personality Syndrome

Head trauma
Cerebrovascular accidents
Cerebral tumors
Epilepsy (particularly complex partial epilepsy)
Huntington's chorea
Multiple sclerosis
Endocrine disorders
Heavy metal poisoning (manganese, mercury)
Drugs (cannabis, LSD, steroids, etc.)
Neurosyphilis

Patients with organic personality syndrome have a clear sensorium. Mild disorders of cognitive function often coexist but do not amount to intellectual deterioration. Patients tend to be inattentive, which may account for disorders of recent memory. With some prodding, however, patients are likely to recall what they claim to have forgotten. The diagnosis of organic personality syndrome should be suspected in patients who show marked changes in behavior or personality involving emotional lability and impaired impulse control, who have no history of psychiatric illness, and whose personality changes occur abruptly or over a relatively brief period of time. See Table 10-22 for the DSM-III-R diagnostic criteria.

Anabolic steroids. An increasing number of high school and college athletes and other persons involved with weight lifting are using anabolic steroids as a shortcut to maximize their physical development. Anabolic steroids include such drugs as methandrostenolone (Dianabol), ox-

Table 10-22
Diagnostic Criteria for Organic Personality Syndrome

A. A persistent personality disturbance, either lifelong or representing a change or accentuation of a previously characteristic trait, involving at least one of the following:
   (1) affective instability (e.g., marked shifts from normal mood to depression, irritability, or anxiety)
   (2) recurrent outbursts of aggression or rage that are grossly out of proportion to any precipitating psychosocial stressors
   (3) markedly impaired social judgment (e.g., sexual indiscretions)
   (4) marked apathy and indifference
   (5) suspiciousness or paranoid ideation
B. There is evidence from the history, physical examination, or laboratory tests of a specific organic factor (or factors) judged to be etiologically related to the disturbance.
C. This diagnosis is not given to a child or adolescent if the clinical picture is limited to the features that characterize attention-deficit hyperactivity disorder.
D. Not occurring exclusively during the course of delirium, and does not meet the criteria for dementia.

Specify explosive type if outbursts of aggression or rage are the predominant feature.

Table from DSM-III-R, *Diagnostic and Statistical Manual of Mental Disorders*, ed 3, revised. Copyright American Psychiatric Association, Washington, DC, 1987, with permission.

androlone (Anavar), oxymetholone (Anadrol), somatropin (Humatrope), stanozolol (Winstrol), and testosterone cypionate (DEPO-Testosterone). For further discussion, see Section 12.10, "Inhalants and Anabolic Steroids."

Course and Prognosis

Both the course and the prognosis of organic personality syndrome depend on its cause. If organic personality syndrome is the result of structural damage to the brain, then the syndrome tends to persist. The syndrome may follow a period of coma and delirium in cases of head trauma or vascular accident and may be permanent. Organic personality syndrome may evolve into dementia in cases of brain tumor, multiple sclerosis, and Huntington's chorea. Personality changes produced by chronic intoxication, medical illness, or drug therapy (such as levodopa [Larodopa] for parkinsonism) may be reversed if the underlying cause is treated. Some patients require custodial care or, at least, close supervision to meet their basic needs, avoid repeated conflicts with the law, and protect them and their families from the hostility of others and destitution resulting from impulsive and ill-considered actions.

Differential Diagnosis

Dementia involves global deterioration in intellectual and behavioral capacities, of which personality change is just one category. A personality change may herald an organic mental syndrome that will eventually evolve into dementia. In these cases, as the deterioration begins to encompass significant memory and cognitive deficits, the diagnosis is changed from organic personality syndrome to dementia. In differentiating the specific syndrome from other disorders in which personality change may occur—such as schizophrenia, delusional disorders, mood disorders, and impulse control disorders—the physician must consider the most important factor, the presence in organic personality syndrome of a specific organic causative factor.

Treatment

Management of the organic personality syndrome involves treatment of the underlying organic condition, if the condition is indeed treatable. Psychopharmacological treatment of specific symptoms may be indicated in some cases, such as imipramine (Tofranil) for depression.

The patient may need counseling to help avoid difficulties at work or to prevent social embarrassment. As a rule, the patient's family needs emotional support and concrete advice on how to help minimize the patient's undesirable conduct. Alcohol should be avoided. Social engagements should be curtailed if the patient has a tendency to act in a grossly offensive manner.

ORGANIC ANXIETY SYNDROME AND DISORDER

Organic anxiety syndrome and disorder are characterized by prominent, recurrent panic attacks or by generalized anxiety attributable to some clearly defined organic factor. As a secondary phenomenon, cognitive functioning may be adversely affected.

Etiology

A variety of general central nervous system stimulants can cause massive anxiety. A broad class of sympathomimetic drugs— such as epinephrine, norepinephrine, amphetamine, caffeine, and cocaine—are included in this group. Other drugs, such as atropine and scopolamine, can cause excitement because of idiosyncrasy. Hyperthyroidism, hypothyroidism, hypoparathyroidism, and vitamin B_{12} deficiency are other causes of organic anxiety syndrome. A pheochromocytoma produces epinephrine, which can cause paroxysmal anxiety attacks. Certain lesions of the brain and postencephalitic states have produced obsessive-compulsive symptoms as sequelae. Some medical conditions, such as cardiac arrhythmia, can produce physiological symptoms of panic. Hypoglycemia can also mimic anxiety. Autonomic nervous system imbalance and mitral value prolapse have been associated with anxiety. A list of disorders associated with anxiety is found in Table 10-23.

Clinical Features and Diagnosis

In general, according to DSM-III-R, the clinical features of this syndrome are similar to those of panic disorder and generalized anxiety disorder. The presence of chronic or paroxysmal anxiety associated with physical disease known to produce anxiety should lead the clinician to suspect an organic cause. Paroxysmal bouts of hypertension suggest a pheochromocytoma; in such cases, elevated uri-

Table 10-23
Disorders Associated with Anxiety

Neurological disorders	Miscellaneous conditions
Cerebral neoplasms	Hypoglycemia
Cerebral trauma and postconcussive syndromes	Carcinoid syndrome
Cerebrovascular disease	Systemic malignancies
Subarachnoid hemorrhage	Premenstrual syndrome
Migraine	Febrile illnesses and chronic infections
Encephalitis	Porphyria
Cerebral syphilis	Infectious mononucleosis
Multiple sclerosis	Posthepatitis syndrome
Wilson's disease	Uremia
Huntington's disease	Toxic conditions
Epilepsy	Alcohol and drug withdrawal
Systemic conditions	Amphetamines
Hypoxia	Sympathomimetic agents
Cardiovascular disease	Vasopressor agents
Cardiac arrhythmias	Caffeine and caffeine withdrawal
Pulmonary insufficiency	Penicillin
Anemia	Sulfonamides
Endocrine disturbances	Cannabis
Pituitary dysfunction	Mercury
Thyroid dysfunction	Arsenic
Parathyroid dysfunction	Phosphorus
Adrenal dysfunction	Organophosphates
Pheochromocytoma	Carbon disulfide
Virilization disorders of females	Benzene
Inflammatory disorders	Aspirin intolerance
Lupus erythematosus	Idiopathic psychiatric disorders
Rheumatoid arthritis	Depression
Polyarteritis nodosa	Mania
Temporal arteritis	Schizophrenia
Deficiency states	Anxiety disorders
Vitamin B_{12} deficiency	Generalized anxiety
Pellagra	Panic attacks
	Phobic disorders
	Posttraumatic stress disorder

Table from J L Cummings: *Clinical Neuropsychiatry*, p 214. Grune & Stratton, Orlando, FL, 1985, with permission.

nary catecholamines are found. A history of chronic low-level drug use, especially of sympathomimetics, may produce chronic anxiety and aid in the diagnosis. As a result of anxiety, the patient may perform poorly on cognitive tests of comprehension, calculation, and memory. Such changes are reversible if the anxiety is diminished. A general medical workup may reveal diabetes, adrenal tumor, thyroid disease, or neurological conditions that may be accompanied by or present with anxiety as a sign or symptom (Table 10-24). Some patients with complex partial seizures have extreme episodes of anxiety or fear as the only manifestation. There have also been reports of compulsive behavior after prolonged use of phenmetrazine (Preludin), cocaine, and amphetamines.

Course and Prognosis

The unremitting experience of anxiety can be extremely disabling, interfering with every aspect of functioning—social, occupational, and psychological. A sudden change in behavior may prompt the person to seek medical or psychiatric help more quickly than when the onset is insidious. The treatment and removal of the cause should help diminish the anxiety in most cases (e.g., cessation of the intake of sympathomimetics). In some cases the cause of the anxiety may not abate after the illness is cured, as in postencephalitic anxiety. In those instances attempts to manage the symptoms through medication, environmental modification, and social support systems are necessary. The prognosis for reversing cognitive changes is excellent if the offending anxiety symptoms are removed. The least favorable prognosis is for conditions with associated obsessive-compulsive features. Even though the causative agent is removed, a pattern of obsessive-compulsive behavior may be fixed in the personality. In such cases, specific interventions, such as behavior modification techniques, may be desirable. Some patients medicate themselves with antianxiety agents or alcohol, thus producing a secondary drug dependence.

Table 10-24
Diagnostic Criteria for Organic Anxiety Syndrome

A. Prominent, recurrent, panic attacks.
B. There is evidence from the history, physical examination, or laboratory tests of a specific organic factor (or factors) judged to be etiologically related to the disturbance.
C. Not occurring exclusively during the course of delirium.

Table from DSM-III-R, *Diagnostic and Statistical Manual of Mental Disorders*, ed 3, revised. Copyright American Psychiatric Association, Washington, DC, 1987, with permission.

Differential Diagnosis

Anxiety as a symptom is associated with many psychiatric disorders. To diagnose organic anxiety syndrome, the physician must note the presence of both predominant anxiety and a specific causative organic factor. To ascertain the degree to which an organic factor is truly causative, the physician must know how closely related the organic factor and the anxiety are, the age of onset (for most anxiety disorders, before age 35), and the family history of organic factors (such as hyperthyroidism) that cause organic anxiety syndrome.

Treatment

Management of the organic anxiety syndrome requires treatment of the underlying organic condition. Specific symptoms—such as phobias, panic, and generalized anxiety—can be treated with the appropriate psychopharmacological agent. Obsessive-compulsive symptoms have been treated successfully with antidepressants in some cases. The patient who has become alcohol dependent must be treated accordingly. In some cases of severe disabilities (such as postencephalitic obsessive-compulsive states) that have not responded to other treatments, psychosurgery has been used successfully.

OTHER ORGANIC MENTAL DISORDERS

Epilepsy

Psychiatric problems are common in patients with epilepsy. The prevalence of epilepsy in the general population is approximately 1 percent, making it the most common chronic neurological disease. Thirty to fifty percent of all epileptic persons have significant psychiatric difficulties. Although the incidence of psychosis is high in epilepsy, personality disturbances are the most frequently encountered psychiatric problems.

Definition. The term "epilepsy" refers to a chronic condition of recurrent or repeated seizures. A *seizure* is a transient, paroxysmal, pathophysiological disturbance of cerebral function caused by a spontaneous, excessive discharge of cortical neurons. The clinical manifestations of a seizure depend on the site of origin and on the pattern and spread of the discharge in the brain. A seizure may cause abnormal movements or an arrest of movement, a disorder of sensation or perception, a disturbance of behavior, or an impairment of consciousness.

Classification. Seizures are broadly characterized as partial seizures, which involve a localized brain region, and generalized seizures, which involve an entire brain region. See Table 10-25 for an outline of the various types of seizures.

Clinical features. Changes in mental function after generalized tonic-clonic convulsions (Figure 10-5) seldom present diagnostic problems when the convulsion itself has been witnessed. The postictal state is manifested by a slow, gradual recovery of consciousness and cognition from the level of coma that usually characterizes the immediate postictal condition. The period required for full recovery varies from a few minutes to many hours. The clinical picture is that of a gradually clearing delirium.

Far less frequent and less well recognized are the transient episodes of psychiatric dysfunction that occur with petit mal epilepsy and with focal seizures that arise in a limited area of the brain, especially in the temporal lobes. The epileptic nature of these episodes may go unrecognized, because the characteristic motor or sensory manifestations of epilepsy may be absent or so slight that they do not arouse the physician's suspicion. A functional psychiatric disorder is especially likely to be suspected when the patient suffers from what has been called subclinical status epilepticus—that is, when the epileptic discharge persists for long periods, even many hours, without producing the characteristic movements of epilepsy.

Table 10-25
Outline of the International Classification of Epileptic Seizures

- I. Partial seizures (seizures beginning locally)
  - A. Partial seizures with elementary symptoms (generally without impairment of consciousness)
    1. With motor symptoms
    2. With sensory symptoms
    3. With autonomic symptoms
    4. Compound forms
  - B. Partial seizures with complex symptoms (generally with impairment of consciousness; temporal lobe or psychomotor seizures)
    1. With impairment of consciousness only
    2. With cognitive symptoms
    3. With affective symptoms
    4. With psychosensory symptoms
    5. With psychosensory symptoms (automatisms)
    6. Compound forms
  - C. Partial seizures secondarily generalized
- II. Generalized seizures (bilaterally symmetrical and without local onset)
  - A. Absences (petit mal)
  - B. Myoclonus
  - C. Infantile spasms
  - D. Clonic seizures
  - E. Tonic seizures
  - F. Tonic-clonic seizures (grand mal)
  - G. Atonic seizures
  - H. Akinetic seizures
- III. Unilateral seizures
- IV. Unclassified seizures (because of incomplete data)

Table modified from H Gastaut: Clinical and electroencephalographical classification of epileptic seizures. Epilepsia *11*: 102, 1970.

Petit mal epilepsy. Petit mal (or absence) epilepsy usually begins in childhood between the ages of 5 and 7 and ceases by puberty. Absence seizures produce brief disruptions of consciousness, during which the patient suddenly loses contact with the environment, without true loss of consciousness or convulsive movements. The EEG produces a characteristic pattern of three-per-second spike-and-wave activity (Figure 10-6). Petit mal epilepsy may have a different clinical picture when the onset is in adulthood. The classic absence pattern may not appear; in its place may be sudden, recurrent psychotic episodes or deliriums that appear and disappear abruptly. The EEG pattern of three-per-second spike-and-wave activity is present. In the adult pattern a history of falling or fainting spells may be elicited.

Complex partial epilepsy. There are some notable parallels between complex partial epilepsy (and other epilepsies) and psychiatric conditions. Primary complex partial epilepsy is an idiopathic condition, often without demonstrable anatomical or biochemical pathophysiology. The onset is during childhood and early adolescence, and there is a genetic predisposition to its development. Approximately 1 percent of the population have epilepsy, and the disorder has significant psychosocial consequences. Seizure activity is usually not constant, and anticonvulsant medication helps control seizure activity but may have adverse side effects that affect behavior and cognition.

Complex partial epilepsy is the most common form of epilepsy in adults, affecting about 3 in 1,000 persons. A discussion of the phenomenology of complex partial epilepsy can be divided into preictal, ictal, postictal, and interictal events. Preictal events (auras) include autonomic sensations (e.g., fullness in stomach, blushing, changes in respiration), cognitive sensations (e.g., *déjà vu, jamais vu*, forced thinking, dreamy states), affective states (e.g., fear, panic, depression, elation), and, classically, automatisms (e.g., lip smacking, rubbing, chewing). The ictal event is characterized by brief, disorganized, and uninhibited behavior. Violence is rare during a complex partial epileptic attack. Patients are amnestic for behavior during the seizure. After the ictus, there is a postictal period of confusion. In patients with complex partial epilepsy, a seizure focus can be found on an EEG in approximately 50 percent of all patients. Performing the EEG with sleep deprivation and, possibly, sphenoidal or nasopharyngeal leads may increase the percentage slightly.

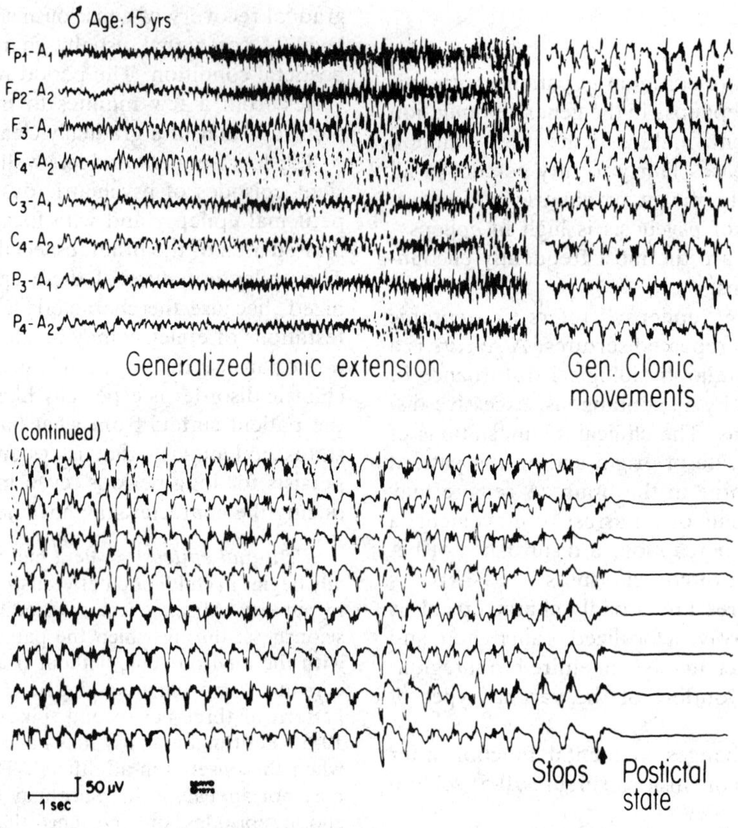

Figure 10-5. EEG recording during generalized tonic-clonic seizure, showing rhythmic sharp waves and muscle artifact during tonic phase, spike-and-wave discharges during clonic phase, and attenuation of activity during postictal state. (Courtesy of Barbara F. Westmoreland, M.D.)

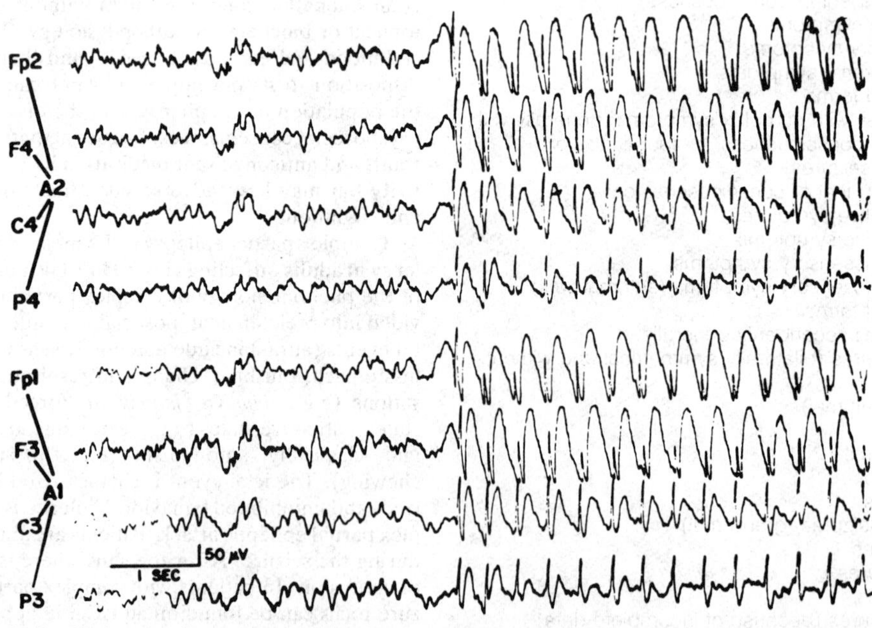

Figure 10-6. Petit mal epilepsy characterized by bilaterally synchronous, 3-Hz spike-and-slow-wave activity.

Interictal manifestations

Psychoses. Interictal psychotic states are encountered more often than ictal psychoses but less often than interictal personality disturbances. Psychoses that resemble schizophrenia have been described, and evidence has accumulated that the psychoses are more frequent in patients with epilepsy of temporal lobe origin than in patients with epilepsy that is nonfocal in origin or that arises from foci outside the temporal lobe. The prevalence of schizophreniclike psychosis in complex partial epilepsy is 10 to 30 percent. Risk factors for psychosis associated with complex partial epilepsy include female gender, left-handedness, the onset of seizures during puberty, and a left-sided lesion.

These chronic schizophreniform psychoses may come on acutely, subacutely, or insidiously. They usually occur only after the patients have suffered from complex partial seizures of temporal lobe origin for many years, so the duration of the epilepsy has come to be regarded as an important factor in the causation. Personality changes often precede the appearance of psychosis.

These psychoses are manifested most prominently by paranoid delusions and hallucinations (especially auditory hallucinations) in the presence of a clear consciousness. Affective flattening may occur, but patients are often described as remaining warm and appropriate in affect. Although thought disorders of a schizophrenic variety are commonly reported, thought disorders of an organic type, such as poor conceptualization or circumstantiality, are more frequent. The relationship between these psychoses and seizure frequency is unclear. In some patients worsening of the psychosis has been observed when good seizure control has been achieved, but this deterioration is not inevitable. Response to treatment with antipsychotic medications is variable and unpredictable.

In most patients these psychoses differ from classic schizophrenia in several important respects. Affect and personality are often less disturbed than in many chronic schizophrenic patients, and the prevalence of schizophrenia in family members is considerably lower than in the families of patients with true schizophrenia. Several observations point to the overriding importance of organic factors in the causation of these psychoses. They generally appear only after the patient has suffered from epilepsy for many years. They are much more common in epilepsy that originates in the dominant temporal lobe, especially when the epileptic foci involve the deep mesial temporal structures of the dominant hemisphere. When these patients are followed over time, they come to resemble patients with chronic organic mental disorders much more than patients with chronic schizophrenia; that is, cognitive losses overshadow abnormalities in thought processes.

Mood disorders such as depression, mania, and bipolar disorder are seen less often than the schizophreniform psychoses. Mood disorders that do occur tend to be episodic and to occur more often when the epileptic foci affect the temporal lobe of the nondominant cerebral hemisphere. The importance of the mood disorders in epilepsy may be attested to by the increased incidence of attempted suicide in persons with epilepsy.

PERSONALITY DISTURBANCES. Personality disturbances are the most frequent psychiatric abnormalities reported in epileptic patients and are especially likely to occur in patients with epilepsy of temporal lobe origin. Although the homogeneity and the specificity of these personality changes in people with complex partial seizures of temporal lobe origin (temporal lobe epilepsy) remain debatable, the specific features reported to make up this syndrome generally include changes in sexual behavior, a quality usually called viscosity, religiosity, and a heightened experience of emotions.

Changes in sexual behavior may be manifested by hypersexuality; deviations in sexual interest, such as fetishism or transvestism; and, most commonly, hyposexuality. Hyposexuality is manifested both by a lack of interest in sexual matters and by reduced sexual arousal. Patients whose complex partial seizures begin before puberty may fail to develop normal levels of sexuality, a circumstance that may not greatly distress the affected person. For patients whose complex partial seizures lead to hyposexuality after they have developed a normal level of sexuality, however, the problem may be severely troubling.

Perhaps the most difficult of these personality changes to describe is viscosity (stickiness). This change is apt to be most noticeable in the patient's conversation, which is likely to be slow, serious, ponderous, pedantic, overly replete with nonessential details, and often circumstantial. The listener grows bored, wonders if the speaker will ever reach the point, and wants to escape, but the speaker offers no opportunity for courteous and successful disengagement. These tendencies in speech are mirrored in writing, a feature called hypergraphia, which is considered by some clinicians to be a cardinal manifestation of this syndrome. Some patients are able, with much effort, to improve their style of communication when these difficulties are pointed out to them by a sympathetic counselor, but many cannot accept the criticism or do not perceive it as a problem. Religiosity may be striking and may be manifested not only by increased participation in overtly religious activities but also by unusual concern for moral and ethical issues, preoccupation with right and wrong, and heightened interest in global and philosophical concerns.

The syndrome in its complete form is relatively rare, even in those with complex partial seizures of temporal lobe origin. Many patients are not affected by personality disturbances; others suffer from a variety of disturbances that differ strikingly from the syndrome delineated above.

Diagnosis. Difficult diagnostic problems arise in distinguishing an organic mental disorder of epileptic origin from a functional psychiatric disorder when the clinical manifestations of epilepsy are more floridly emotional or psychotic and when changes in level of consciousness and cognition are not so readily apparent. In these instances, the episodes may not even be recognized as organic in origin, much less as epileptic, for they may be manifested by hallucinations, delusions, severe agitation and hyperactivity, profound depression, transient aphasia or muteness, and catatonic states, effectively mimicking many functional psychiatric disorders. Such episodes are called pseudoseizures and must be differentiated from true seizures (Table 10-26).

Episodic psychiatric dysfunction should always be suspected to be epileptic in origin when it occurs in patients in whom epilepsy has been diagnosed previously. The diagnosis is confirmed if the EEG during the episode reveals continuous or nearly continuous epileptic discharges. However, it is often impossible to obtain an EEG during the episode. The diagnosis is substantially confirmed if the episodes disappear or are greatly reduced in number and severity with careful regulation of anticonvulsant medications.

The diagnosis is clearly much more difficult in patients who are not known to have epilepsy. In these cases four clinical features should suggest to the physician the possibility of epilepsy: the abrupt onset of psychosis in a person previously regarded as psychologically healthy, the

Table 10-26
Differentiating Features of Pseudoseizures and Epileptic Seizures

Feature	Epileptic Seizure	Pseudoseizure
Clinical features		
Nocturnal seizure	Common	Uncommon
Stereotyped aura	Usually	None
Cyanotic skin changes during seizures	Common	None
Self-injury	Common	Rare
Incontinence	Common	Rare
Postictal confusion	Present	None
Body movements	Tonic or clonic or both	Nonstereotyped and asynchronous
Affected by suggestion	No	Yes
EEG features		
Spike and waveforms	Present	Absent
Postictal showing	Present	Absent
Interictal abnormalities	Variable	Variable

Table from J M Stevenson, J H King: Neuropsychiatric aspects of epilepsy and epileptic seizures. In *American Psychiatric Press Textbook of Neuropsychiatry*. R E Hales and S C Yudofsky, editors, p 220. American Psychiatric Press, Washington, DC, 1987, with permission.

abrupt onset of delirium that cannot be accounted for by more common causes, a history of similar episodes with abrupt and spontaneous onset and remission, and a history of previous falling or fainting spells that were unexplained. Correct diagnosis is especially important, because treatment with appropriate anticonvulsant medications may prevent the individual episodes.

Episodic violence has been a problem in some patients with epilepsy, especially epilepsy of temporal lobe origin. The question has arisen, whether this violence is a manifestation of the seizure itself (an epileptic automatism) or of interictal psychopathology. To date, most of the evidence points to the extreme rarity of violence as an ictal phenomenon. Only in very rare cases should violence of an epileptic patient be attributed to the seizure itself.

Treatment. The most commonly used anticonvulsant agents are phenobarbital, phenytoin (Dilantin), carbamazepine (Tegretol), primidone (Mysoline), ethosuximide (Zarontin), trimethadione (Tridione), diazepam, clonazepam (Klonopin), and, most recently, valproic acid (Depakene). The drugs of choice for the various types of seizures are listed in Table 10-27.

Table 10-27
Drugs of Choice for Various Types of Seizures

Generalized tonic-clonic (grand mal) seizures
- Phenobarbital
- Phenytoin (Dilantin)
- Carbamazepine (Tegretol)

Absence (petit mal) seizures
- Ethosuximide (Zarontin)
- Valproic acid (Depakene)
- Trimethadione (Tridione)

Simple partial (focal) seizures
- Phenobarbital
- Phenytoin (Dilantin)

Complex partial (temporal lobe) seizures
- Phenytoin (Dilantin)
- Carbamazepine (Tegretol)

Myoclonic, atonic, akinetic, and atypical absence seizures
- Clonazepam (Klonopin)
- Diazepam (Valium)

Infantile spasms
- Adrenocorticotropic hormone
- Corticosteroids

Satus epilepticus
- Diazepam (Valium)
- Phenobarbital
- Amobarbital (Amytal)
- Phenytoin (Dilatin)
- Paraldehyde
- Anesthetic agent

The personality disturbances associated with temporal lobe epilepsy sometimes respond well to psychotherapy or anticonvulsant medication or a combination of both. Carbamazepine is often helpful in controlling the symptoms of irritability and the outbursts of aggression, as are the antipsychotic drugs.

Side effects of anticonvulsant medications. Many psychiatric patients also have epileptic disorders and are treated with both psychotropic drugs and anticonvulsants. The epileptogenesis of psychotropic drugs has been overstated in the past, although reasonable caution is still advised. The neuropsychiatric effects of anticonvulsants, however, have been underemphasized, and most of these drugs are associated with measurable cognitive deficits and lethargy at therapeutic doses.

Intracranial Neoplasms

Psychiatric symptoms are often the earliest and, occasionally, the only symptoms of an intracranial tumor. The symptoms may be those of dementia or of a particular organic mental syndrome. The symptoms may precede the more obvious motor or sensory manifestations of the brain tumor by weeks or months. The mental symptoms of patients who have brain tumors vary not only among patients but in the same patient from hour to hour. The earliest psychiatric symptom is often irritability. Later, the patient may become anxious and depressed. Eventually, some patients completely deny their cerebral impairments. Computed tomography and magnetic resonance imaging are the major diagnostic approaches indicated in these patients.

Clinical features, course, and prognosis. The patient with a brain tumor suffers a relentless progression of symptoms. The classic neurological symptoms are headache and impaired motor or sensory function. Even when these disturbances are present, they may be initially obscured by the patient's mental symptoms and may be detected only after a careful interview and examination. Certain focal brain lesions produce specific intellectual deficits, although most patients with brain tumors have simultaneous evidence of more generally impaired intellectual function.

Cognition. Impaired intellectual function often accompanies the presence of a brain tumor, regardless of its type or location.

Language skills. Disorders of language function may be severe, particularly if tumor growth is rapid. In fact, defects of language function often obscure all other mental symptoms.

Memory. Loss of memory is a frequent symptom of brain tumors. Patients with brain tumors may present with Korsakoff's syndrome, retaining no memory of events that occurred since the illness began. Events of the immediate past, even painful ones, are lost. Old memories, however, are retained, and patients are unaware of their loss of recent memory.

Perception. Prominent perceptual defects are often associated with behavioral disorders, especially when the patient needs to integrate tactile, auditory, and visual perceptions.

Awareness. Alterations of consciousness are common late symptoms of increased intracranial pressure caused by a brain tumor. Tumors arising in the upper part of the brain stem may produce a unique symptom called akinetic mutism or vigilant coma. The patient is immobile and mute, yet alert.

Metabolic Disorders

Metabolic encephalopathy is a common cause of organic brain dysfunction and is capable of producing alterations in mental processes, behavior, and neurological function. This diagnosis should be considered whenever recent and rapid changes in behavior, thinking, and consciousness have occurred. The earliest signals are likely to be impairment of memory, particularly recent memory, and orientation. Some patients become agitated, anxious, and hyperactive; others become quiet, withdrawn, and inactive. As metabolic encephalopathies progress, confusion or delirium gives way to decreased responsiveness, to stupor, and, eventually, to coma.

Hepatic encephalopathy. This brain dysfunction results from the severe impairment of liver function from acute or chronic liver disease or the shunting of portal vein blood into the systemic circulation. Hepatic encephalopathy may present with disturbances of consciousness, mental changes, asterixis, hyperventilation, and electroencephalographic abnormalities. Disturbances of consciousness can vary from apathy and drowsiness to coma. The changes in memory, intellect, and personality are nonspecific. Death is likely in severe cases.

Uremic encephalopathy. Acute or chronic failure of normal renal function leads to serious systemic metabolic changes. Neurological dysfunction—particularly alterations in memory, orientation, and consciousness—is a common accompaniment. Restlessness, crawling sensations of the limbs, twitching of muscles singly or in groups, and persistent hiccups can be distressing and exhausting to the patient. In severe uremia generalized convulsions can occur, at times in rapid succession, increasing the risk of death. Intravenously administered diazepam may be an effective treatment, but the use of barbiturates or even anesthetics may be required for seizure control. When episodes of uremia are short-lived, especially in young patients, the organic mental syndrome is more likely to be reversible, but older people with recurrent and chronic uremia often develop irreversible damage. During rapid renal dialysis in the presence of very high blood urea levels, a dialysis dysequilibrium syndrome has been seen, with headache, confusion, alterations in consciousness, and convulsions.

Hypoglycemic encephalopathy. Excessive or inappropriate administration of insulin and hyperinsulinism caused by a functioning benign adenoma of islet cells of the pancreas are the most likely causes of hypoglycemic encephalopathy. Hypoglycemic episodes are likely to occur in the early morning hours or after exercise. Premonitory symptoms, which do not occur in every patient, include nausea, sweating, tachycardia, and feelings of hunger, apprehension, and restlessness. With progressive impairment, disorientation, confusion, hallucinations, pallor, and extreme restlessness or agitation develop. Diplopia, grand mal or focal seizures, myoclonic jerks, and hyperreflexia with clonus and Babinski's responses can be other features. Stupor and then coma may follow quickly. Prolonged coma can be followed by a residual and persistent dementia. An occasional patient has no signs or symptoms preceding convulsions.

Diabetic ketoacidosis. The condition begins with feelings of weakness, early fatigability and listlessness, and increasing polyuria and polydipsia. Headache and sometimes nausea and vomiting appear. Depending on the severity of the diabetes and the presence of infection, the situation worsens in a matter of hours to several days. Patients with diabetes mellitus have an increased likelihood of developing a chronic dementia associated with general arteriosclerosis.

Diabetic coma is a medical emergency. In any unconscious patient who is known or suspected to be diabetic, the differential diagnosis of hypoglycemic coma and diabetic coma must be made. Hypoglycemia as a cause of the coma can be virtually excluded if the patient does not regain consciousness within a few minutes after the intravenous administration of 25 ml of a 50 percent glucose solution.

Diabetic coma without ketoacidosis (nonketotic hyperglycemic coma) may occur, particularly in old persons with adult-onset diabetes mellitus, and it may be the first manifestation of that disease. The principles of treatment include adequate fluid and electrolyte replacement, insulin, and the management of any associated infection or underlying disease.

Acute intermittent porphyria. This disorder is inherited as an autosomal dominant trait, and its symptoms are most apt to begin after puberty or in the third or fourth decade of life. Women are affected more often than men. An inborn error of metabolism exists in the regulation of the liver enzyme δ-aminolevulinic acid synthetase, which is important to pyrrole metabolism. Barbiturates precipitate or aggravate the attacks of acute porphyria. The use of barbiturates for any reason is absolutely contraindicated in a person with acute intermittent porphyria and in anyone who has a relative with the disease.

Symptoms of nervousness and emotional instability are frequently present for a long while. Recurrent abdominal pains, often colicky in nature, are common and sometimes lead to an unnecessary abdominal operation before an accurate diagnosis is made. Neurological symptoms are also common and may become so severe that death results. Peripheral neuropathy involving one or all of the limbs and cranial nerve signs—such as optic atrophy, facial palsy, ophthalmoplegia, and dysphagia—may be seen. Confusion, delirium, convulsions, and coma can develop during acute attacks.

As yet, there is no satisfactory or specific treatment for acute intermittent porphyria. During acute episodes only careful symptomatic measures can be used. Antipsychotic medications may be safely used and can provide significant relief from psychiatric symptoms.

Endocrine Disorders

Changes in personality, mental functions, and memory, as well as neurological abnormalities, frequently occur in endocrine disorders and may become prominent in some instances. Correction of the underlying endocrine problem usually reverses these changes.

Thyroid disorders. Thyroid disorders produce hyperthyroidism or hypothyroidism. A sensation of easy fatigability and generalized weakness is felt by most hyperthyroid patients. Insomnia, weight loss in spite of increased appetite, tremulousness, palpitations, and increased perspiration are all common changes. Prominent mental disturbances can include impairment of memory, orientation, and judgment; manic excitement; delusions; and hallucinations.

Treatment of hyperthyroidism in most adults consists of the administration of radioactive iodine. Antithyroid agents and surgical thyroidectomy are useful in certain patients. Mental symptoms can be expected to improve with adequate treatment of the hyperthyroidism, but, for the occasional patient with severe mental symptoms, hospitalization is necessary.

Hypothyroidism (myxedema) arises because of a deficiency of thyroid hormone. Easy fatigability, feelings of weakness and sleepiness, increased sensitivity to cold, reduced sweating with dryness and thickening of the skin, brittle and thinning hair, and puffy facies are all common manifestations of myxedema. There is evidence of hypochromic anemia, diffuse slowing on the EEG, and reduced or absent T waves on a low-voltage electrocardiogram (ECG). In some patients, changes in personality, memory, and intellectual function are prominent, which may simulate major psychiatric or organic brain disease. Cerebellar gait ataxia is a feature of some cases. Congenital hypothyroidism produces mental retardation (cretinism) and is potentially treatable if discovered and managed promptly.

Parathyroid disorders. Parathyroid dysfunction results in derangements of calcium metabolism. Excessive secretion of parathyroid hormone from a parathyroid adenoma or hyperplasia causes hypercalcemia. Common complaints are lassitude, weakness, increased irritability, and anxiety. Some patients display frank disorders of personality and mental function, such as agitation, paranoid thinking, depression, psychotic reactions, confusion, and stupor. Neuromuscular excitability, which depends on a proper calcium ion concentration, is reduced, and muscle weakness may appear.

Lowered serum calcium levels in hypoparathyroidism lead to increased neuromuscular excitability, with transient paresthesias, muscle cramping and twitching, overt tetany with spontaneous carpopedal muscle spasms, and convulsive seizures. Such mental symptoms as confusion, agitation, drowsiness, hallucinations, and depression may also develop.

Adrenal disorders. Adrenal disorders cause changes in the normal secretion of hormones from the adrenal cortex and produce significant neurological and psychological changes. Patients with chronic adrenocortical insufficiency (Addison's disease), which is most frequently the result of adrenocortical atrophy or granulomatous invasion caused by tuberculous or fungal infection, exhibit mild mental symptoms such as apathy, easy fatigability, irritability, and depression. Occasionally, psychotic reaction or confusion develops. Cortisone or one of its synthetic derivatives is effective in correcting such abnormalities.

Excessive quantities of cortisol produced endogenously by an adrenocortical tumor or hyperplasia (Cushing's syndrome) lead to an organic mood disorder of agitated depression with risk of suicide. Decreased concentration and memory defects may also be present. Psychotic reactions, with schizophreniform symptoms, are seen in a small number of patients. The administration of high doses of exogenous corticosteroids, on the other hand, more typically leads to an organic mood disorder similar to mania. Severe depression may follow the sudden termination of steroid therapy.

Nutritional Disorders

Beriberi. Thiamin (vitamin B_1) is required in the formation of the coenzyme thiamin pyrophosphate, which is essential in the intermediary metabolism of carbohydrate. Thiamin deficiency leads to beriberi, characterized chiefly by cardiovascular and neurological changes, and also Wernicke-Korsakoff's syndrome, which is most often associated with chronic alcoholism.

Beriberi occurs primarily in Asia and in areas of famine or poverty; historically it was a prevalent disease in prisoner-of-war camps in Asia during World War II. Subacute or chronic onset is most common, but it occasionally runs a more rapid, acute course. Such mental disturbances as apathy, depression, irritability, nervousness, and poor concentration are frequently seen. However, Wernicke-Korsakoff syndrome is difficult to exclude when more severe changes in memory and intellectual functions occur.

Pellagra. Dietary insufficiency of niacin (nicotinic acid) and its precursor, tryptophan, is associated with pellagra, a nutritional deficiency disease of global importance. Nervous system involvement includes headaches, insomnia, apathy, confusional states, delusions, and, eventually, dementia. Cerebellar ataxia can be seen, as well as skin and gastrointestinal involvement. Peripheral neuropathy is also a frequent feature, but it is probably a manifestation of other associated vitamin deficiencies, particularly thiamin deficiency. Traditionally pellagra was described by five words beginning with the letter D—dermatitis, diarrhea, delirium, dementia, and death.

The response of the pellagra patient to treatment with nicotinic acid is rapid; significant improvements in confusion, abdominal symptoms, and painful swollen tongue are evident in the first 24 hours. However, dementia from prolonged illness may improve slowly and incompletely. If a peripheral neuropathy is present, administration of supplemental thiamin is important.

Vitamin B_{12} deficiency. This state arises because of the failure of the gastric mucosal cells to secrete a specific substance, intrinsic factor, required for the normal absorption of dietary vitamin B_{12} from the ileum. The deficiency state is characterized by the development of a chronic macrocytic megaloblastic anemia (pernicious anemia) and neurological manifestations resulting from degenerative changes in the peripheral nerves, the spinal cord, and the brain. Neurological changes are seen in about 80 percent of all patients. These changes are commonly associated with the megaloblastic anemia, but they occasionally precede the onset of hematological abnormalities.

Mental changes such as apathy, depression, irritability, and moodiness are common. In a few patients encephalopathy and its associated confusion, delusions, hallucinations, dementia, and sometimes paranoid features are prominent manifestations and have been called megaloblastic madness. Presumably, they are related to cerebral involvement with patchy areas of demyelination and degeneration. The neurological manifestations of vitamin B_{12} deficiency can be completely and rapidly arrested by the early and continued administration of parenteral vitamin B_{12} therapy.

Infectious and Degenerative Disorders

Creutzfeldt-Jakob disease. Creutzfeldt-Jakob disease is a rare degenerative brain disease caused by a slow virus infection. A progressive dementia occurs, accompanied by ataxia, extrapyramidal signs, choreoathetosis, and dysarthria. The disease is most common in adults in their 50s, and death occurs usually within one year after the diagnosis is made. Men and women are affected equally. No treatment is known. CT scans show cerebellar and cortical atrophy, and specific EEG changes occur in the later stages.

Kuru. Kuru is a progressive dementia accompanied by extrapyramidal signs. It is found among the natives of New Guinea who practice cannibalistic rites. In eating the brains of infected persons, the natives take in the slow virus that produces this fatal disease.

General paresis. This disorder is a chronic dementia and psychosis caused by the tertiary form of syphilis that affects the brain. Symptoms include dementia, a manic syndrome with euphoria and grandiose delusions, and neurological signs, such as Argyll-Robertson pupil. Depression and delusions of persecution may also occur. There are prominent abnormalities in the cerebrospinal fluid, and there is generally a positive Wassermann reaction. The disease appears 10 to 15 years after the primary *Treponema* infection and affects approximately 5 percent of patients who have neurosyphilis. Since the advent of penicillin, general paresis has rarely been seen.

Multiple sclerosis. Multiple sclerosis is characterized by diffuse multifocal lesions in the white matter of the central nervous system and a course characterized by exacerbations and remissions. The cause is unknown, but studies have been focused on slow viral infections and disturbances in the immune system.

The estimated prevalence of multiple sclerosis in the Western hemisphere is 50 patients per 100,000 people. The disease is much more frequent in cold and temperate climates than in the tropics and subtropics. It is more common in women than in men and is predominantly a disease of young adults. The onset in the vast majority of patients is between the ages of 20 and 40 years. Initially, neurological symptoms often include weakness, ataxia, diffuse sensory and motor abnormalities, and vision changes. Early stages of the illness may mimic a conversion disorder. In some patients there is a change in emotional tone, which is usually reported as being euphoric, although mood instability is noted just as often. Less often, signs and symptoms of an acute psychosis may be associated with the neurological symptoms. Impairment of cognition can occur as the disease progresses, and this impairment may lead to dementia or an amnestic syndrome in some cases. CT scans show patchy degenerative areas of cerebral white matter. Cerebrospinal fluid findings, especially the elevation of γ-globulins, help to confirm the diagnosis.

Amyotrophic lateral sclerosis. Amyotrophic lateral sclerosis (ALS) is a progressive, noninherited, asymmetrical muscle atrophy. It begins in adult life and progresses over months or years to involve all the striated muscles except the cardiac and ocular muscles. In addition to muscle atrophy, patients have signs of pyramidal tract involvement. The illness is rare, occurring in about 1.6 persons per 100,000 a year. A few of these patients have concomitant dementia. The disease progresses rapidly, and death generally occurs within four years of onset.

References

Bear D, Hermann B, Fogel B: Interictal behavior in epilepsy: The views of three experts. J Neuropsychiatry Clin Neurosci *1*: 308, 1989.

Cummings J L: Dementia and depression: An evolving enigma. J Neuropsychiatry Clin Neurosci *1*: 236, 1989.

Dickson L R, Ranseen J D: An update on selected organic mental syndromes. Hosp Community Psychiatry *41*: 290, 1990.

Goate A M, Hardy J A, Owen M J, Haynes A, James L, Farrall M, Mullan M J, Roques P, Rossor M N: Genetics of Alzheimer's disease. Adv Neurol *51*: 197, 1990.

Graves A B, White E, Koepsell T D, Reifler B V, van Belle G, Larson E B, Raskind M: The association between head trauma and Alzheimer's disease. Am J Epidemiol *13*: 491, 1990.

Herman B P, Whitman S, Wyler A R, et al: Psychological predictors of psychopathology in epilepsy. Br J Psychiatry *156*: 98, 1990.

Horvath T B, Siever L J, Mohs R C, Davis K L: Organic mental syndromes and disorders. In *Comprehensive Textbook of Psychiatry*, ed 5, H I Kaplan and B J Sadock, editors, p 599. Williams & Wilkins, Baltimore, 1989.

Journal of Clinical Psychiatry: Faces of dementia: Current concepts. J Clin Psychiatry *49* (5, Suppl): 2, 1988.

Kopelman M D: Amnesia: Organic and psychogenic. Br J Psychiatry *150*: 428, 1987.

Levin R, Banks S, Berg B: Psychological dimensions of epilepsy: A review of the literature. Epilepsia *29*: 805, 1988.

Lewis D O, Pincus J H: Epilepsy and violence: Evidence for a neuropsychotic-aggressive syndrome. J Neuropsychiatry Clin Neurosci *1*: 413, 1989.

Mayeux R: Therapeutic strategies in Alzheimer's disease. Neurology *40*: 175, 1990.

Ramsdell J W, Rothrock J F, Ward H W, Volk D M: Evaluation of cognitive impairment in the elderly. J Gen Intern Med *5*: 55, 1990.

Rundell J R, Wise M G: Causes of organic mood disorder. J Neuropsychiatry Clin Neurosci *1*: 398, 1989.

Selkoe D J: Molecular pathology of amyloidogenic proteins and the role of vascular amyloidosis in Alzheimer's disease. Neurobiol Aging *10*: 387, 1989.

Solomon S, Masdeu J C: Neuropsychiatry and behavioral neurology. In *Comprehensive Textbook of Psychiatry*, ed 5, H I Kaplan and B J Sadock, editors, p 217. Williams & Wilkins, Baltimore, 1989.

Stoudemire A, Hill C, Gulley L R, et al: Neuropsychological and biomedical assessment of depression-dementia syndromes. J Neuropsychiatry Clin Neurosci *1*: 362, 1989.

Thal L J, Grundman M G, Klauber M R: Dementia: Characteristics of a referral population and factors associated with progression. Neurology *38*: 1083, 1988.

11

Psychiatric Aspects of Acquired Immune Deficiency Syndrome (AIDS)

The first case of acquired immune deficiency syndrome (AIDS) in the United States was reported in 1981, although it is now known that there were cases much earlier. The causative agent of AIDS is the human immunodeficiency virus (HIV), which was isolated and identified as a ribonucleic acid (RNA)-containing retrovirus in 1983. HIV is lymphotropic and neurotropic; that is, the virus infects both lymphatic and neural cells. HIV replicates in these cells, eventually causing cell death. Specifically, HIV infects helper T4 lymphocytes, resulting in decreased stimulation of macrophages, natural killer cells, killer lymphocytes, and B lymphocytes. This impairment of immunological function allows opportunistic infections and specific neoplasms to develop in HIV-infected persons. HIV infection of the central nervous system (CNS) can give rise to various organic mental syndromes. Glial cells, particularly astrocytes, are the targets of HIV infection. Whether neurons themselves can be infected is currently unknown. CNS functions of HIV-infected persons can also be impaired by opportunistic infections and cerebral neoplasms.

The Centers for Disease Control (CDC) has defined AIDS as "a disease, at least moderately predictive of a defect in cell-mediated immunity, occurring in a person with no known cause for diminished resistance to that disease. Such diseases include Kaposi's sarcoma (KS), *Pneumocystis carinii* pneumonia (PCP), and other serious opportunistic infections." Other conditions considered indicative of AIDS are HIV encephalopathy (also called AIDS dementia complex), HIV wasting syndrome, recurrent salmonella septicemia, lymphoid interstitial pneumonia, extrapulmonary tuberculosis, and multiple or recurrent pyogenic infections in children. The CDC has further classified AIDS into four groups: group I, acute infection; group II, asymptomatic infection; group III, persistent generalized lymphadenopathy (also called lymphadenopathy syndrome [LAS]); and group IV, constitutional disease, neurological disease, secondary infectious diseases, secondary cancers, and other diseases. AIDS-related complex (ARC) is a term used to describe HIV-infected persons who have some symptoms of AIDS but have not yet had a major complication of AIDS. These patients have usually had persistent generalized lymphadenopathy, oral candidiasis, herpes zoster skin infections, hairy leukoplakia, or persistent unexplained fevers or diarrhea.

EPIDEMIOLOGY AND TRANSMISSION

HIV infection has been reported worldwide. An estimated 1 to 1.5 million HIV-infected persons are in the United States, approximately a half million in Europe, and perhaps as many as 10 million in Africa. After infection with HIV, the mean length of time to the development of AIDS is eight years. What percentage of HIV-infected persons will eventually have ARC or AIDS is unknown. After the diagnosis of AIDS, the mean length of survival is 18 months, although this figure is steadily increasing with the use of various antiviral treatments. As of December 1988 a total of approximately 82,000 cases of AIDS had been reported in the United States, and approximately 56 percent of these patients had died. Homosexual and bisexual men constitute 62 percent of all cases; intravenous (IV) drug abusers, 27 percent; non-IV drug-abusing women and heterosexuals, 4 percent. Approximately 20 to 25 percent of all homosexual men (higher in some areas) and 50 to 65 percent of all IV-drug-abusing persons may be affected.

In infected persons, HIV is present in blood, semen, cervical and vaginal secretions, and, to a lesser extent, saliva, tears, breast milk, and cerebrospinal fluid. Transmission of HIV most often occurs through sexual intercourse or the transfer of contaminated blood between persons. Unprotected anal, vaginal, and oral sex are the sexual activities most likely to transmit the virus. Health providers should be aware of the guidelines for safe sexual practices and should advise their patients (Table 11-1). Although male-to-male transmission has been the most common route of sexual transmission, male-to-female and female-to-male transmissions have also been documented. Transmission by contaminated blood most often occurs when IV drug addicts share hypodermic needles without proper sterilization techniques. Transmission of HIV through blood transfusions, organ transplantation, and artificial insemination is no longer a problem because of the testing of donors for HIV infection. Unfortunately, transfusions of blood products did infect many persons with hemophilia before HIV was identified as the causative agent. Children can be infected in utero or through breast feeding when their mothers are HIV-positive. Health workers are theoretically at risk because of potential contact with bodily fluids from HIV-infected patients. In practice, however, only a very few cases of infection of health workers have been reported, and these have all occurred through accidental needle punctures with contaminated hypodermic needles. No evidence has been found that HIV can be contracted through casual contact, such as sharing a living space or classroom with an HIV-infected person, although direct or indirect contact with an infected person's body fluids should be avoided (Table 11-2). One case of a patient being infected by an HIV-positive dentist has been re-

Table 11-1
AIDS Safe Sex Guidelines

Remember: ANY activity that allows for exchange of body fluids of one person and the mouth, anus, vagina, bloodstream, cuts, or sores of another person is considered UNSAFE at this time.

Safe-Sex Practices

Massage, hugging, body-to-body rubbing
Dry social kissing
Masturbation
Acting out sexual fantasies (that do not include any unsafe sex practices)
Using vibrators or other instruments (provided they are not shared)

Low-Risk Sex Practices

These activities are not considered completely safe.
French (wet) kissing (without mouth sores)
Mutual masturbation
Vaginal and anal intercourse using a condom
Oral sex, male (fellatio), using a condom
Oral sex, female (cunnilingus), with barrier
External contact with semen or urine, provided there are no breaks in the skin

Unsafe-Sex Practices

Vaginal or anal intercourse without a condom
Semen, urine, or feces in the mouth or vagina
Unprotected oral sex (fellatio or cunnilingus)
Blood contact of any kind
Sharing sex instruments or needles

Table from B Moffatt, J Spiegel, S Parrish, M Helquist: *AIDS: A Self-Care Manual*. IBS Press, Santa Monica, CA, 1987, p 125, with permission.

Table 11-2
CDC Guidelines for Prevention of HIV Transmission from Infected to Uninfected Persons

Infected persons should be counseled to prevent the further transmission of HIV by:

1. Informing prospective sex partners of his or her infection with HIV, so they can take appropriate precautions. Clearly, abstention from sexual activity with another person is one option that would eliminate any risk of sexually transmitted HIV infection.
2. Protecting a partner during any sexual activity by taking appropriate precautions to prevent that individual from coming into contact with the infected person's blood, semen, urine, feces, saliva, cervical secretions, or vaginal secretions. Although the efficacy of using condoms to prevent infections with HIV is still under study, consistent use of condoms should reduce transmission of HIV by preventing exposure to semen and infected lymphocytes.
3. Informing previous sex partners and any persons with whom needles were shared of their potential exposure to HIV and encouraging them to seek counseling and testing.
4. For IV drug abusers, enrolling or continuing in programs to eliminate abuse of IV substances. Needles, other apparatus, and drugs must never be shared.
5. Not sharing toothbrushes, razors, or other items that could become contaminated with blood.
6. Refraining from donating blood, plasma, body organs, other tissue, or semen.
7. Avoiding pregnancy until more is known about the risks of transmitting HIV from mother to fetus or newborn.
8. Cleaning and disinfecting surfaces on which blood or other body fluids have spilled, in accordance with previous recommendations.
9. Informing physicians, dentists, and other appropriate health professionals of his or her antibody status when seeking medical care so that the patient can be appropriately evaluated.

Table from Morbidity and Mortality Weekly Report *35*: 152, 1986, with permission.

ported. In the United States and western Europe, homosexual and bisexual men and IV drug abusers are the two most affected groups, accounting for approximately 90 percent of all cases. Although the rate of new cases among homosexual and bisexual men is decreasing because of changing sexual practices in these groups, the rate of new cases among IV drug abusers is increasing. In the United States and western Europe, the ratio of infected men to infected women is 14 to 1. In contrast, the ratio of infected men to infected women in Africa is approximately 1 to 1 because transmission is primarily through heterosexual and perinatal contact. Approximately 7 percent of AIDS patients in the United States are women, and 1.5 percent are children, mainly children with HIV-infected parents.

Geographic distribution is heavily skewed toward large urban centers, with the cities of New York, Los Angeles, and San Francisco representing almost 50 percent of all cases in the United States. In the United States Caucasians represent 61 percent of all cases, African-Americans 24 percent, and Hispanics 14 percent (Table 11-3).

SERUM TESTING

After infection with HIV, antibodies to the virus develop in most persons in 6 to 12 weeks, although seroconversion can take 6 to 12 months. The antibodies produced by the immune system can be detected by two serum tests: enzyme linked immunosorbent assay (ELISA) and immunoblotting. The ELISA is used as the first screening procedure, and a single positive result on ELISA should be followed with a second ELISA. If both results are positive, an immunoblot is then conducted for final confirmation of HIV seroconversion. Health care workers and patients must understand that the presence of HIV antibodies indicates infection and does not indicate immunity to infection.

Counseling

Counseling should be conducted in person, not over the telephone, before and after the testing. Pretest counseling

Table 11-3
Possible indications for Human Immunodeficiency Virus (HIV) Testing

1. Patients who belong to a high-risk group: (1) men who have had sex with another man since 1977; (2) intravenous drug abusers since 1977; (3) hemophiliacs or other patients who have received since 1977 blood or blood product transfusions not screened for HIV; (4) sexual partners of people from any of these groups; (5) sexual partners of people with known HIV exposure—people with cuts, wounds, sores, or needlesticks whose lesions have had direct contact with HIV-infected blood.
2. Patients who request testing. Note that not all patients will admit to the presence of risk factors (e.g., because of shame, fear).
3. Patients with symptoms of AIDS or ARC.
4. Women belonging to a high-risk group who are planning pregnancy or who are pregnant.
5. Blood, semen, or organ donors.
6. Patients with dementia in a high-risk group.

Table from R B Rosse, A A Giese, S I Deutsch, J M Morihisa: *Laboratory and Diagnostic Testing in Psychiatry*, p 54. American Psychiatric Press, Washington, DC, 1989, with permission.

should review the person's past practices that may have put him or her at risk for HIV infection and should also include education about safe sexual practices (Table 11-4). The meaning of a positive or negative test result should be explained. Specifically, a negative test result means that the person either has not been exposed to HIV or has not yet developed antibodies to HIV if the potential exposure was less than one year before the test. A negative test finding should suggest to the person that continued safe sexual behavior is recommended to remain free of HIV infection. A positive test result indicates that the person has been infected with HIV and is at risk of both spreading the infection and having AIDS develop. A person with a positive test result must receive counseling regarding safe practices and potential treatment options (Table 11-5).

A person may react to a positive HIV test finding with a syndrome similar to that of posttraumatic stress disorder. Concern about minor physical symptoms, insomnia, and dependence on health care workers are commonly seen. The clinician should watch for depression, anxiety, and even suicidal ideation. The clinical interactions with the patient should emphasize the meaning of a positive test result and should encourage the reestablishment of emotional and functional stability. It is often appropriate to refer AIDS and ARC patients to one of the support organizations that have been established in many areas of the country.

Table 11-4
Pretest HIV Counseling

1. Discuss meaning of a positive result and clarify distortions (e.g., the test detects exposure to the AIDS virus; it is not a test for AIDS).
2. Discuss the meaning of a negative result (e.g., seroconversion requires time, recent high-risk behavior might require follow-up testing).
3. Be available to discuss the patient's fears and concerns (unrealistic fears might require appropriate psychological intervention).
4. Discuss why the test is necessary. (Remember, not all patients will admit to high-risk behaviors.)
5. Explore the patient's potential reactions to a positive result (e.g., "I'll kill myself if I'm positive.") Take appropriate necessary steps to intervene in a potentially catastrophic reaction.
6. Explore past reactions to severe stresses.
7. Discuss the confidentiality issues relevant to the testing situation (e.g., is it an anonymous or nonanonymous setting?). Inform the patient of other possible testing options where the counseling and testing can be done completely anonymously (e.g., where the result would not be made a permanent part of a hospital chart). Discuss who might have access to the test results.
8. Discuss with the patient how being seropositive can potentially affect social status (e.g., health and life insurance coverage, employment, housing).
9. Explore high-risk behaviors and recommend risk-reducing interventions.
10. Document discussions in chart.
11. Allow the patient time to ask questions.

Table from R B Rosse, A A Giese, S I Deutsch, J M Morihisa: *Laboratory and Diagnostic Testing in Psychiatry*, p 55. American Psychiatric Press, Washington, DC, 1989, with permission.

Table 11-5
Posttest HIV Counseling

1. Interpretation of test result:
   Clarify distortion (e.g., "a negative test still means you could contract the virus at a future time—it does not mean you are immune from AIDS").
   Ask questions of the patient about his or her understanding and emotional reaction to test result.
2. Recommendations for prevention of transmission (careful discussion of high-risk behaviors and guidelines for prevention of transmission).
3. Recommendations on the follow-up of sexual partners and/or needle contacts.
4. If test is positive, recommendations against donating blood, sperm, or organs and against sharing razors, toothbrushes, or anything else that might have blood on it.
5. Referral for appropriate psychological support:
   HIV-positive individuals often need access to a mental health team (assess need for inpatient versus outpatient care; consider individual or group supportive therapy). Common themes include shock of diagnosis, fear of death and social consequences, grief over potential losses, and dashed hope for good news. Also look for depression, hopelessness, anger, frustration, guilt, and obsessional themes.
   Activate supports available to patient (e.g., family, friends, community services).

Table from R B Rosse, A A Giese, S I Deutsch, J M Morihisa: *Laboratory and Diagnostic Testing in Psychiatry*, p 58. American Psychiatric Press, Washington, DC, 1989, with permission.

Confidentiality

Confidentiality is a key issue in serum testing. No person should be given an AIDS test without his or her knowledge and consent. Although the results of an HIV serum test can be shared with other members of the treatment team, this information should not be shared with anyone else except in the special circumstances described below. The patient should also be counseled regarding the advisability of informing people unnecessarily about a positive test finding, because this information may result in discrimination in employment, housing, and insurance.

The specific exceptions to maintaining the confidentiality of a positive HIV test result include notifying potential sexual or IV drug partners. The majority of patients act responsibly. If, however, the treating physician knows that an HIV-infected patient is putting another person at risk of becoming infected, the physician may try to either involuntarily hospitalize the infected patient to prevent danger to others or to notify the potential victim. Another potential exception to the rule of confidentiality can occur on inpatient psychiatric wards in which sexual contact among patients is a possibility. If an HIV-infected patient is incapable of maintaining responsible behavior on an inpatient ward, notifying other patients regarding the infected patient's HIV status may be justified.

SIGNS AND SYMPTOMS

Nonneurological

Some persons infected with HIV have a two- to three-week-long, flulike syndrome—with fever, malaise, gastrointestinal symptoms, and myalgias—three to six weeks after exposure to the virus. This flulike syndrome is sometimes accompanied by lymphadenopathy, splenomegaly, or a maculopapular rash. Some persons infected with HIV, however, do not experience any symptoms in the first few weeks after infection.

Most HIV-infected persons are asymptomatic, although they are still capable of spreading the infection. On hematological testing, these patients may show defects in immunological or hematological state and function, such as leukopenia, anemia, decreased T-helper cell lymphocytes, and cutaneous anergy. These patients may also occasionally suffer nonspecific symptoms—such as malaise, fatigue, and fevers—that may not be severe enough to warrant a diagnosis of ARC.

Symptomatic AIDS most commonly presents as either a specific neoplastic process (Kaposi's sarcoma or lymphoma) or an opportunistic infection involving protozoa (*Pneumocystis carnii*, *Toxoplasma gondii*), fungi (*Cryptococcus neoformans, Candida albicans*), bacteria (*Mycobacterium avium-intracellulare*), or viruses (cytomegalovirus [CMV], herpes simplex). Most patients have only opportunistic infections, not neoplasms. *Pneumocystis carnii* pneumonia is the most common presenting complication of AIDS, occurring in approximately 60 percent of patients. The pneumonia presents with a nonproductive cough, low-grade fever, exertional dyspnea, and generalized chest pain. These major complications are often accompanied with chronic diarrhea, weight loss, malaise, fatigue, fevers, and night sweats.

Neurological

A wide variety of neurological conditions can develop in persons with AIDS (Table 11-6). A psychiatrist who is asked to consult on a patient with AIDS must be sure that the medical team has adequately assessed the presence or absence of these conditions.

Opportunistic infections. The treating physician must be aware of the possibility of an opportunistic infection of the CNS and must follow up CNS symptoms with appropriate neurodiagnostic measures. Meningeal infection with *Cryptococcus neoformans* often presents with meningeal signs, fever, headache, and an altered mental status. Examination of the cerebrospinal fluid for the fungus is diagnostic. CNS infection with *Toxoplasma gondii* often results in focal lesions associated with impaired consciousness, focal neurological signs, headache, and seizures. Magnetic resonance imaging (MRI) and computed tomography (CT) scans, along with biopsy, are the indicated neurodiagnostic procedures. CNS infection with CMV can result in meningitis and cerebritis and can quickly lead to death even with treatment. CMV infection can also lead to blindness.

Central nervous system HIV infection. HIV can infect the brain directly and cause two general syndromes—asep-

Table 11-6
Anatomical Location of Neurological Disease States and Their Clinical Manifestations in Patients with AIDS and ARC

Disease Process	Clinical Manifestations
Cerebrum	
Acute meningitis Acute encephalitis Acute meningoencephalitis Cerebrovascular accident	Headache, nausea, vomiting, fever, lethargy, delirium, meningeal irritation, expressive language dysfunction, focal neurological deficits, seizures
Chronic meningitis Chronic meningoencephalitis Chronic encephalitis	As above, plus cortical atrophy, dementia, organic [mood] affective and personality syndromes
Mass lesions (infections, neoplasms)	Seizures, hydrocephalus, movement disorders, focal neurological deficits, increased intracranial pressure
Brain stem Meningitis Infections Neoplasms	Long-tract dysfunction (motor, sensory)
Cerebellum Infections, neoplasms	Gait disorders, incoordination
Spinal cord Posterolateral column Lateral column (ALS) Viral myelitis Landry Guillain-Barré	Sensation impairment, motor weakness (flaccid, spastic), incontinence
Neuropathies, myopathy Cranial and peripheral mononeuropathies and polyneuropathies, radiculitis, myopathy, polymositis	Sensory and motor dysfunction (e.g., distal symmetrical, Bell's palsy, dermatomal pain, muscle pain, tenderness, and wasting)

Table from D L Wolcott: Neuropsychiatric syndromes in AIDS and AIDS-related illnesses. In *What to Do about AIDS: Physicians and Mental Health Professionals Discuss the Issues*, L McKusick, editor, p 33. University of California Press, Berkeley, CA, 1987, with permission.

tic meningitis and subacute encephalitis (also called AIDS encephalopathy or AIDS dementia complex). Aseptic meningitis occurs in 5 to 10 percent of all patients and presents with fever, headache, meningeal signs, and cranial nerve involvement. Examination of the cerebrospinal fluid shows mononuclear pleocytosis and increased protein concentrations.

Subacute encephalitis (AIDS dementia complex). Subacute encephalitis caused by HIV can result in the symptoms seen in AIDS dementia complex (Table 11-7), involving progressive cognitive impairment and affecting as many as 65 to 70 percent of all AIDS patients. Later symptoms of subacute HIV encephalitis can include ataxia, hypertonia, weakness, tremor, incontinence, frontal release signs, myoclonus, and seizures. A laboratory workup may show a mild mononuclear pleocytosis in the cerebrospinal fluid in 20 percent of patients, an increased cerebrospinal fluid protein in 60 percent of patients, white matter lesions on MRI, cortical atrophy on CT or MRI, and diffuse electroencephalogram (EEG) slowing. A neuropathological examination may reveal gliosis, small foci of necrosis, microglial nodules, demyelination, and perivascular inflammation (Figure 11-1). Although all areas of brain can be involved, the white matter and the basal ganglia seem to be most affected.

Whether AIDS dementia complex can be present before the symptoms of ARC or AIDS develop in HIV-infected persons has been the subject of much research. The current conclusion is that no evidence exists for clinically significant cognitive impairment in these persons, although research has demonstrated subtle early cognitive changes. Patients may complain of or show mental slowing, forgetfulness, apathy, lethargy, and social isolation. The patient's condition may be mistakenly diagnosed as functional depression. Research studies using neuropsychological testing have shown impairment in verbal measures, fine motor speed, and mental flexibility.

The treatment of AIDS dementia complex should focus on resolving as many coexisting medical problems as possible, limiting the number and dosage of medications that may affect mental functioning, and supporting the patient mentally and socially. Frequent contact with the patient and the presence of organizing sensory inputs—such as calendars, clocks, and television sets—can help comfort and orient the patient.

Table 11-7
Clinical Manifestations of AIDS Dementia Complex

Common manifestations
Decreased memory
Inability to concentrate
Apathy
Social withdrawal
Psychomotor retardation
Abulia (loss of will)
Mild headache
Occasional manifestations
Motor deficits
Seizures
Psychiatric problems
Uncommon manifestations
Decreased level of consciousness
Aphasia
Apraxia

Table from D E Bredesen: Clinical features: The acquired immunodeficiency syndrome (AIDS) dementia complex. Ann Intern Med *111*: 401, 1989, with permission.

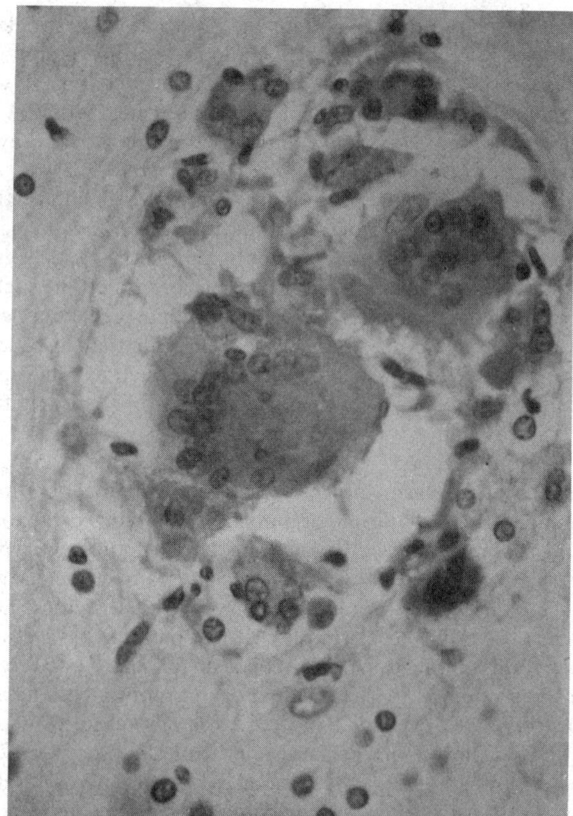

Figure 11-1. Abnormal cell masses contain the AIDS virus. Multinucleated giant cells are seen in brain tissue from an AIDS patient. These fused clumps of cells contain the AIDS retrovirus (courtesy of Anthony Fauci). (From D M Barnes: AIDS-related brain damage unexplained. Science *232*: 1092, 1986, with permission.)

Other neurological signs and symptoms

Neoplasms. Kaposi's sarcoma or lymphoma lesions may occur in the CNS of AIDS patients. The presenting signs of CNS lymphomas include altered mental status, lethargy, confusion, dysarthria, and motor abnormalities. CT or MRI examinations of the head usually reveal a well-defined lesion.

Peripheral nervous system manifestations. Because of the neurotropic character of HIV, the peripheral nerves can also be affected. The two major peripheral syndromes are vacuolar myelopathy and peripheral neuropathy. Vacuolar myelopathy affects the lateral and posterior columns of the spinal cord and occurs in 10 to 20 percent of all patients, most commonly in patients already exhibiting symptoms of dementia. The lesions result in progressive spastic paraparesis, gait ataxia, leg weakness, and incontinence. Peripheral neuropathy often causes painful dysesthesias, numbness, paresthesias, weakness, and autonomic dysfunctions.

Encephalitis in children. Children infected in utero with HIV have a variety of symptoms, including microcephaly, severe cognitive defects, weakness, failure to reach developmental milestones, pseudobulbar palsy, extrapyramidal rigidity, and seizures. Afflicted children may require special schooling. Children with AIDS who come from single-parent homes or who have parents who are unable to provide care may require foster care placement. HIV-infected children who are not severely neurologically impaired can attend regular schools without putting fellow classmates at risk for infection as long as reasonable guidelines are followed (Table 11-2).

Psychiatric

According to the revised third edition of the *Diagnostic and Statistical Manual of Mental Disorders* (DSM-III-R), it is theoretically possible for a functional disorder to develop in a patient with AIDS, given the involvement of the CNS with HIV infection, but it seems more logical to consider psychiatric signs and symptoms as belonging to the organic mental disorder classification. Therefore, a patient with depression and AIDS usually receives a diagnosis of organic mood disorder on Axis I and HIV infection on Axis III. The full range of psychiatric symptoms can be seen in patients with AIDS—depression, mania, psychosis, generalized anxiety symptoms, and obsessive-compulsive symptoms, among others. Impairment in occupational functioning is commonly seen in patients with ARC and AIDS. As many as 50 to 75 percent of ARC and AIDS patients are unable to remain employed.

Some anxiety is a normal response to having AIDS as a diagnosis. The specific symptoms of anxiety may include agitation, panic attacks, phobic disorders, anorexia, tachycardia, and insomnia. Chronic anxiety, coupled with constant attention to every detail of medical treatment, can sometimes complicate the adjustment of an AIDS patient. Stress management, hypnosis, and relaxation techniques may be helpful with some patients.

Dysthymia and adjustment disorders with depressive symptoms are common diagnoses in patients with AIDS and ARC. Anticipatory grief and actual grief are topics for supportive and insight-oriented psychotherapy for AIDS and ARC patients. Treatment strategies include allowing the patient to take control of some aspects of medical decision making or care.

Suicide. Suicidal ideation, as well as suicide, is not rare in patients with ARC or AIDS. Risk factors include having friends who died from AIDS, recent notification of HIV seropositivity, relapses of symptoms, difficult social issues relating to homosexuality, inadequate social and financial support, and the presence of an organic mental disorder.

Worried well population. A subgroup of patients termed the worried well consists of persons in high-risk groups who, although they are seronegative and disease-free, are anxious or have an obsession about contracting the virus or AIDS. Some of these patients are reassured by repeated negative serum tests. Others, however, obsess about the possible long incubation period and cannot be reassured. Supportive or insight-oriented psychotherapy is indicated in these cases. Symptoms can include generalized anxiety, panic attacks, obsessive-compulsive disorder, and hypochondriasis. Some concern among healthy HIV-noninfected members of high-risk groups is warranted, but, when this concern evolves into psychological symptoms that impair functioning, psychiatric attention is warranted.

TREATMENT

The primary treatment of AIDS and its neuropsychiatric symptoms is directed against HIV itself and at the opportunistic infections and neoplastic disorders. A variety of treatments, including azidothymidine (AZT), are currently being used, and many more are in various stages of research and clinical testing.

Medical Treatment

The medical treatment of AIDS is complex. Specific opportunistic infections are treated with the appropriate antibacterial agents, and precautions are taken to prevent further infections. The ultimate goal of treatment is to restore immunocompetence and to clear the body of opportunistic infections. Currently, drugs that block reverse transcriptase, such as AZT, have improved longevity and the quality of life of many AIDS victims. Since these drugs only block the production of new viruses, however, their long-term efficacy is doubtful. Other tested drugs include suramin, ribavirin, ansamycin, and interferon. Vaccines, although under development, are not expected to be available for at least a decade. Chemotherapy and radiotherapy administered for Kaposi's sarcoma do not affect the basic pathology of immunosuppression. During the late stages of AIDS, the patient may be delirious or demented, and the major issues of treatment should be support and patient comfort.

Psychotherapy

It is advisable to view AIDS in the context of other chronic, debilitating, and potentially fatal diseases. Once the diagnosis has been made, most AIDS patients react with overwhelming anxiety, especially when they become aware of the fatal outcome. If a sense of hopelessness develops, patients are likely to go into a suicidal depression; however, if patients can be reassured that they will not be abandoned by their families and friends and that every effort will be made to deal with their medical and psychiatric complications, including pain relief, a sense of despair can be converted into one of acceptance or even hope. Some patients use denial as a defense. That can be healthy, provided it does not interfere with obtaining proper medical treatment.

The role of psychotherapy, both individual and group, is important. The psychiatrist can help patients deal with feelings of guilt regarding behaviors that contributed to the development of AIDS. Some AIDS patients feel that they are being punished for a deviant life-style. Difficult health care decisions, such as whether to participate in an experimental drug trial, and terminal care and life-support systems should be explored. In addition, all infected patients must be educated concerning safe sexual practices, such as the use of condoms. Treatment of homosexuals and bisexuals with AIDS often involves helping the patients come out to their families and deal with the possible issues of rejection, guilt, shame, and anger.

Treatment of IV drug users involves discussing the patient's continued use of IV drugs. The possible ill effects of drug abuse on a patient's health need to be weighed against the effect of adding drug withdrawal to an AIDS patient's existing problems. Educating patients about the danger of sharing contaminated needles is of utmost importance.

Involvement of significant others. Involvement in therapy or counseling of the patient's family, lover, and close friends can often aid both the patient and the others. The patient's spouse or lover may have guilt feelings about possibly having infected the patient or may experience anger at the patient for possibly infecting him or her. Early involvement of significant others can strengthen the patient's support system if cognitive symptoms develop and further impair the patient's functioning. It is also useful to discuss issues of finances and companionship as the disease progresses, two issues about which the patient may be quite concerned.

Legal matters. Mental health care workers are often enlisted in helping the patient deal with legal matters, such as making a will and taking care of hospital and other medical expenses. The resolution of such matters is of such practical importance that it is often well worth the time of the mental health care workers to make sure these matters are addressed satisfactorily.

Pharmacotherapy

When the patient has CNS involvement, especially symptoms of an organic mental disorder—such as anxiety, psychosis, and depression—appropriate psychotropic medications are indicated. Antipsychotics in small doses may be useful in controlling agitation. Some clinicians have suggested using high-potency agents because of their lower possibility of aggravating cognitive impairment with anticholinergic effects. Other clinicians have used small doses of low-potency antipsychotics because of an increased incidence of extrapyramidal adverse effects from high-potency antipsychotics in AIDS patients. Carbamazepine (Tegretol) may be useful in controlling episodic dyscontrol in patients with AIDS whose EEGs show paroxysmal activity.

Depression associated with AIDS can be treated best with a tricyclic antidepressant or an atypical antidepressant. Nortriptyline (Pamelor, Aventyl) may be the best choice of the standard tricyclics because of its relatively low anticholinergic profile and low incidence of orthostatic hypotension. AIDS patients often respond to low dosage of tricyclics in the range of 100 mg a day. Although experience is limited, the absence of severe adverse effects (except for one case of suicide from overdose) of fluoxetine (Prozac) may make it an effective antidepressant, and the drug of first choice, for these patients.

Another alternative treatment of depression are the sympathomimetics, such as amphetamine. Clinicians' concerns about the addictive potential of these drugs is generally unwarranted in AIDS patients. Monoamine oxidase inhibitors (MAOIs) are generally contraindicated in AIDS patients because the dietary restrictions may further complicate meeting patients' nutritional needs and there may be unpredictable interactions with other drug treatments. Lithium should probably be administered only if the patient was receiving it before the onset of AIDS. The monitoring of lithium blood levels can be greatly complicated by many of the medical problems, such as diarrhea, that accompany AIDS.

Anxiety can usually be effectively treated with benzodiazepines. Short-acting benzodiazepines may be less associated with cognitive impairment than long-acting benzodiazepines. There has been too little experience with buspirone (BuSpar) to make firm recommendations, but it may be a good anxiolytic choice in patients who are intolerant of benzodiazepines but who need pharmacotherapy for chronic anxiety. In general, beta-adrenergic antagonists, such as propranolol (Inderal), should be avoided in AIDS patients because of an increased incidence of hypotension.

Institutional Treatment

AIDS patients in hospitals must deal with staff members whose attitudes about the illness range from acceptance to prejudicial rejection. A significant number of medical and nonmedical staff members still have a high degree of concern about contracting AIDS from patients under their care, in spite of the fact that AIDS cannot be spread by casual contact. These professionals must be identified and allowed to withdraw from caring for AIDS patients if they cannot master their anxiety about working with homosexual or bisexual men, IV drug abusers, and HIV-infected patients. Staff members who deal with AIDS patients also require support services, such as education in grief therapy, if they are to maintain their effectiveness and avoid professional burnout, which is common among those who work with chronically and terminally ill patients.

AIDS IN CHILDREN

Mothers can transmit the virus to fetuses. AIDS has been diagnosed in several hundred children, although the actual number of children who are seropositive may be much larger nationwide. Like adults, children are subject to opportunistic infections; they usually die by the age of 2, although some children live longer.

Fetal transmission usually occurs in the first trimester. Newborn infants with AIDS are reported to have characteristic AIDS facies. A seropositive mother-to-be may elect to have an abortion, rather than risk having a baby with AIDS.

Afflicted children may require special schooling, especially if they are neurologically impaired. Others may be treated in pediatric units during the day and permitted to return to their parental homes at night. The majority of children with AIDS come from single-parent homes or have inadequate mothers, so foster care placement and day care centers are necessary. AIDS is apparently not transmitted among family members, so AIDS children need not be segregated. Able children should be permitted to attend school without fear of their transmitting the disease to others. However, non-AIDS-infected children may pose a threat if they have contagious diseases that may be transmitted to an AIDS child with a compromised immune system.

References

Baer J W: Study of 60 patients with AIDS or AIDS-related complex requiring psychiatric hospitalization. Am J Psychiatry *146*: 1285, 1989.

Faulstich M E: Psychiatric aspects of AIDS. Am J Psychiatry *144*: 551, 1987.

Fenton T W: AIDS-related psychiatric disorder. Br J Psychiatry *151*: 579, 1987.

Gabuzda D H, Hirsch M S: Neurologic manifestations of infection with human immunodeficiency virus. Ann Intern Med *107*: 383, 1987.

Goldfinger S M, Robinowitz C B, eds: AIDS and HIV infections. In *American Psychiatric Press Review of Psychiatry*, vol 9, A Tasman, S M Goldfinger, and C Kaufmann, editors: American Psychiatric Press, Washington, DC, 1990.

Grant I, Atkinson J H, Hesselink J R: Evidence for early central nervous system involvement in the acquired immunodeficiency syndrome (AIDS) and other human immunodeficiency virus (HIV) infections. Ann Intern Med *107*: 828, 1987.

Lomax G L, Sandler J: Psychotherapy and consultation with persons with AIDS. Psychiatr Ann *18*: 253, 1988.

Marotta R, Perry S: Early neuropsychological dysfunction caused by human immunodeficiency virus. J Neuropsychiatry Clin Neurosci *1*: 225, 1989.

Ostrow D G, Monjan A, Joseph J: HIV-related symptoms and psychological functioning in a cohort of homosexual men. Am J Psychiatry *146*: 737, 1989.

Poutiainen E, Iivanainen M, Elovaara I: Cognitive changes as early signs of HIV infection. Acta Neurol Scand *78*: 49, 1988.

Simon R I, ed: Ethical treatment of patients with AIDS. Psychiatr Ann *18*: 559, 1988.

Psychoactive Substance-Induced Organic Mental Disorders and Psychoactive Substance Use Disorders

12.1 / Overview

The revised third edition of the *Diagnostic and Statistical Manual of Mental Disorders* (DSM-III-R) divides the diagnosis of substance-related disorders into two broad categories. The *psychoactive substance-induced organic mental disorders* are classified under the organic mental disorders discussed in Chapter 10. The substance-induced organic mental disorders define the specific symptom patterns, such as hallucinosis and anxiety disorder, that result from the acute and chronic effects of psychoactive substances on the central nervous system (CNS). The *psychoactive substance use disorders* are classified separately from the organic mental disorders. The psychoactive substance use disorders define the specific patterns of maladaptive behavior related to regular drug abuse.

PSYCHOACTIVE SUBSTANCE-INDUCED ORGANIC MENTAL DISORDERS

The substance-induced organic mental disorders include all the organic mental disorders described in Chapter 10—delirium, dementia, amnestic disorder, delusional disorder, hallucinosis, mood disorder, anxiety disorder, and personality disorder. Additional substance-induced organic mental disorders are intoxication (Table 12.1-1) and withdrawal (Table 12.1-2). There is a controversy about whether these syndromes are specific to a particular substance. For example, there is little reason to believe that the delirium caused by alcohol withdrawal or barbiturate withdrawal can be distinguished with any certainty on clinical grounds alone. From both a conceptual and a nosological standpoint, it is best for the clinician to aim first for syndrome recognition and second for identification of the specific cause of the syndrome. Only in this way can a reasonable and serviceable differential diagnosis be constructed.

There are three substance-induced organic mental disorders that occur with specific substances: idiosyncratic intoxication (with alcohol), withdrawal delirium (with alcohol, sedatives, hypnotics, and anxiolytics), and posthallucinogen perception disorder. These three disorders are discussed in the sections on the specific substances. When a psychoactive substance-induced organic mental disorder is diagnosed, the organic mental disorder diagnosis is listed as an Axis I diagnosis, and the substance or substances are listed as an Axis III diagnosis. The substance-induced organic mental disorders seen with various psychoactive substances are listed in Tables 12.1-3 and 12.1-4.

PSYCHOACTIVE SUBSTANCE USE DISORDERS

The psychoactive substance use disorders define the patterns of maladaptive behavior related to the procurement and ingestion of substances of abuse, as well as the behavioral and social consequences of these patterns of behavior. In DSM-III-R the psychoactive substance use disorders are divided into *psychoactive substance dependence* (Table 12.1-5) and *psychoactive substance abuse* (Table 12.1-6). Substance abuse is the classification for those persons whose pathological pattern of drug use does not meet all the criteria for drug dependence. According to DSM-III-R, the diagnosis of an abuse disorder is most likely in persons who have just recently started using psychoactive substances. Moreover, the psychoactive substance abuse disorders are more likely to involve substances such as cannabis and hallucinogens, which are less associated with marked withdrawal symptoms.

Dependence may vary from person to person or from time to time in one person. It can be classified as mild, moderate, or severe and as being in full or partial remission (Table 12.1-7). Some persons use several categories of drugs and are clearly drug-dependent. However, it is sometimes not possible to know if they are dependent on any one specific class of drugs. In DSM-III-R this condition is called *polysubstance dependence* (Table 12.1-8).

DSM-III-R also describes two additional substance dependence-related diagnoses: psychoactive substance dependence not otherwise specified and psychoactive substance abuse not otherwise specified. These are residual categories for disorders in which there is dependence or abuse, respectively, on a psychoactive substance that cannot be classified in any of the previous categories (e.g., anticholinergics) or for use as an initial diagnosis in cases of dependence or abuse in which the specific substance is not yet known.

Table 12.1-1
Diagnostic Criteria for Intoxication

A. Development of a substance-specific syndrome due to recent ingestion of a psychoactive substance. (**Note:** More than one substance may produce similar or identical syndromes.)

B. Maladaptive behavior during the waking state due to the effect of the substance on the central nervous system (e.g., belligerence, impaired judgment, impaired social or occupational functioning).

C. The clinical picture does not correspond to any of the other specific organic mental syndromes, such as delirium, organic delusional syndrome, organic hallucinosis, organic mood syndrome, or organic anxiety syndrome.

Table from DSM-III-R, *Diagnostic and Statistical Manual of Mental Disorders,* ed 3, revised. Copyright American Psychiatric Association, Washington, DC, 1987, with permission.

Table 12.1-2
Diagnostic Criteria for Withdrawal

A. Development of a substance-specific syndrome that follows the cessation of, or reduction in, intake of a psychoactive substance that the person previously used regularly.

B. The clinical picture does not correspond to any of the other specific organic mental syndromes, such as delirium, organic delusional syndrome, organic hallucinosis, organic mood syndrome, or organic anxiety syndrome.

Table from DSM-III-R, *Diagnostic and Statistical Manual of Mental Disorders,* ed 3, revised. Copyright American Psychiatric Association, Washington, DC, 1987, with permission.

DEFINITIONS OF TERMS

In 1964 the World Health Organization concluded that the term "addiction" was no longer a scientific term and recommended substituting the term "drug dependence." In spite of that, the word "addiction" continues to appear in both the medical and lay literature and is used to refer to (1) psychological dependence on a substance that produces drug-seeking behavior, (2) an inability to stop using the drug because of a physical dependence on the drug and tolerance to its effects, and (3) deterioration of physical and mental health as a result of continued substance abuse. In DSM-III-R the term "psychoactive substance use disorder" involves two major areas:

A. Pattern of pathological use: inability to reduce or stop use; intoxication throughout the day; use of the offending substance nearly every day for at least a month; episodes of overdose or intoxication so that mental functioning is impaired.

B. Impairment in physical, social, or occupational functioning due to use of the substance (e.g., fights, loss of friends, absence from work, loss of job, or legal difficulties).

Tolerance is defined as the need for markedly increased amounts of the substance to achieve the desired effect that results from repeated use of a drug. Tolerance that develops to one drug as a result of exposure to another drug is called *cross-tolerance. Dispositional tolerance,* sometimes known as metabolic tolerance, refers to the drug's being metabolized more quickly than it is ingested; therefore, a constant intake does not produce the desired (euphoric) response. People vary widely in the amount of substance—in particular, alcohol—they can tolerate independent of their experience with the substance. Some people cannot drink more than a small amount without distressing symptoms, whereas others seem to be able to drink large amounts with few bad effects. This capacity appears to be inborn, not one developed from exposure. Difference in tolerance for alcohol also applies to certain racial groups. Many Asians develop uncomfortable symptoms after taking only small amounts of alcohol. Women tolerate alcohol less well than men.

Dependence on a drug may be physical or psychological or both. *Psychological dependence,* also referred to as habituation, is characterized by a continuous or intermittent craving for the substance in order to avoid a dysphoric state. *Physical dependence* is characterized by a need to take the substance to prevent the occurrence of a withdrawal or abstinence syndrome.

Drug abuse and drug misuse are defined differently. *Abuse* usually refers to the person's illicit use of a substance, whereas *misuse* usually refers to a physician's prescribing a drug in a medically unacceptable way.

Table 12.1-3
Psychoactive Substance-Induced Organic Mental Disorders*

	Withdrawal	Withdrawal Delirium	Delirium	Delusional Disorder	Mood Disorder	Other Syndromes†
Alcohol	X	X				1
Sedative-anxiolytics	X	X				2
Amphetamines	X		X	X		
Cocaine	X		X	X		
Opioids	X					
PCP	—			X	X	3
Hallucinogens	—		X	X	X	4
Cannabis	—			X		
Caffeine	X					
Nicotine	X					
Inhalants	—	—	?	—	?	

Table modified by Jerome H. Jaffe, M.D., from DSM-III-R, *Diagnostic and Statistical Manual of Mental Disorders,* ed 3, revised. Copyright American Psychiatric Association, Washington, DC, 1987, with permission.

*DSM-III-R recognizes an intoxication syndrome for all drug categories but nicotine (to which tolerance develops rapidly).

†Keys:

1. Hallucinosis, amnestic disorder, dementia, idiosyncratic intoxication.
2. Sedative-anxiolytic amnestic disorder.
3. Flashback (posthallucinogen perception disorder).
4. PCP: mental disorder NOS.

PSYCHOACTIVE SUBSTANCES

A great variety of psychoactive substances can induce organic mental disorders and behavioral patterns of substance dependence or abuse. These include sedatives, hypnotics, alcohol, anxiolytics, opioids, cocaine, amphetamines and similarly acting sympathomimetics, phencyclidine (PCP) and similarly acting arylcyclohexylamines, hallucinogens, cannabis, caffeine, nicotine, and inhalants with psychoactive properties. A *psychoactive substance* is defined as one that, when taken into the body, can alter consciousness or state of mind. Such compounds in the form of therapeutic drugs, liquids, potions, and plants have been used since antiquity. In the United States such substances are (1) legal, although controlled or taxed by the government (e.g., alcohol, tobacco), (2) legal and prescribed by physicians (e.g., diazepam [Valium], barbiturates), or (3) illegal (e.g., PCP, heroin). Some drugs may be prescribed in certain states only on special governmental forms (e.g., state triplicate prescriptions for amphetamines). All psychoactive substances are subject to abuse, misuse, and psychological or physical dependence.

Table 12.1-4
Psychoactive Drugs Associated with Organic Mental Disorders

Drug	Behavioral Effects	Physical Effects	Laboratory Findings	Treatment
Opioids: opium, morphine, heroin, meperidine (Demerol), methadone, pentazocine (Talwin)	Euphoria, drowsiness, anorexia, decreased sex drive, hypoactivity, change in personality	Miosis, pruritus, nausea, bradycardia, constipation, needle tracks in arms, legs, groin	Detected in blood up to 24 hours after last dose	For gradual withdrawal: methadone 5–10 mg every 6 hours for 24 hours, then decrease dose for 10 days For overdose: naloxone (Narcan) 0.4 mg IM every 20 minutes for 3 doses, keep airway open; give O_2
Amphetamine and other sympathomimetics, including cocaine	Alertness, loquaciousness, euphoria, hyperactivity, irritability, aggressiveness, agitation, paranoid trends, impotence, visual and tactile hallucinations	Mydriasis, tremor, halitosis, dry mouth, tachycardia, hypertension, weight loss, arrhythmias, fever, convulsions, perforated nasal septum (with cocaine)	Detected in blood and urine	For agitation: diazepam (Valium) IM or PO 5–10 mg every 3 hours; for tachyarrhythmias: propranolol (Inderal) 10–20 mg PO q every 4 hours; vitamin C 0.5/g qid PO may increase urinary excretion by acidifying urine
Central nervous system depressants: barbiturates, methaqualone (illegal to make in U.S.), meprobamate (Equanil), benzodiazepines, glutethimide (Doriden)	Drowsiness, confusion, inattentiveness	Diaphoresis, ataxis hypotension, seizures, delirium, miosis	Detected in blood	For barbiturates: Substitute 30 mg liquid phenobarbital for every 100 mg barbiturates abused and give in divided doses every 6 hours and then decrease by 20% every other day; may also substitute diazepam (Valium) for barbiturate abused. Give 10 mg every 2–4 hours for 24 hours and then reduce dose; for benzodiazepines; gradual reduction of diazepam every other day over 10-day period
Other inhalants: nitrous oxide	Euphoria, drowsiness, ataxia, confusion	Analgesia, respiratory depression, hypotension	None	Hypoxia is treated with O_2 inhalation
Alcohol	Poor judgment, loquaciousness, mood change, aggression, impaired attention, amnesia	Nystagmus, flushed face, ataxia, slurred speech	Blood level between 100 and 200 mg/dL	For delirium: diazepam (Valium) 5–10 mg IM or PO every 3 hours, IM vitamin B complex, hydration; for hallucinosis: haloperidol (Haldol) 1–4 mg every 6 hours IM or PO

Table 12.1-4
Continued

Drug	Behavioral Effects	Physical Effects	Laboratory Findings	Treatment
Hallucinogens: LSD (lysergic acid diethylamide), psilocybin (mushrooms), mescaline (peyote), DET (diethyltryptamine), DMT (dimethyltryptamine), DOM or STP (dimethoxymethylamphetamine), MDA (methylene dioxyamphetamine)	8–12-hour duration with flashback after abstinence, visual hallucinations, paranoid ideation, false sense of achievement and strength, suicidal or homicidal tendencies, depersonalization, derealization	Mydriasis, ataxia, hyperemic conjunctiva, tachycardia, hypertension	None	Emotional support (talking down); for mild agitation: diazepam (Valium) 10 mg IM or PO every 2 hours for 4 doses; for severe agitation: haloperidol (Haldol) 1–5 mg IM and repeat every 6 hours prn. May have to continue haloperidol 1–2 mg a day PO for weeks to prevent flashback syndrome. Phenothiazines may be used only with LSD. Caution: phenothiazines can produce *fatal* results if used with other hallucinogens (DET, DMT, etc.), especially if they are adulterated with strychnine or belladonna alkaloids.
Phencyclidine (PCP)	8–12-hour duration, hallucinations, paranoid ideation, labile mood, loose associations (may mimic schizophrenia), catatonia, violent behavior, convulsions	Nystagmus, mydriasis, ataxia, tachycardia, hypertension	Detected in urine up to 5 days after ingestion	Phenothiazines contraindicated for first week after ingestion; for violent delusions: haloperidol (Haldol) 1–4 mg IM or PO every 2–4 hours until patient is calm
Volatile hydrocarbons and petroleum derivatives: glue, benzene, gasoline, varnish thinner, lighter fluid, aerosols	Euphoria, clouded sensorium, slurred speech, ataxia, hallucinations in 50% of cases, psychoses, permanent brain damage if used daily over 6 months	Odor on breath, tachycardia with possible ventricular fibrillation, possible damage of brain, liver, kidneys, myocardium	Relevant to determine tissue damage (SGOT)	For agitation: haloperidol (Haldol) 1–5 mg every 6 hours until calm; avoid epinephrine because of myocardial sensitization
Belladonna alkaloids (found in over-the-counter medications and morning glory seeds): stramonium, homatropine, atropine, scopolamine, hyoscyamine	Hot skin, erythema, weakness, thirst, blurred vision, confusion, excitement, delirium, stupor, coma (anticholinergic delirium)	Dry mouth and throat, mydriasis, twitching, dysphagia, light sensitivity, pyrexia, hypertension followed by shock, urinary retention	None	Antidote is physostigmine (Antilirium) 2 mg IV every 20 minutes; IV should be controlled at no more than 1 mg a minute; watch for copious salivary secretion because of anticholinesterase activity. Propranolol (Inderal) for tachyarrhythmias

Modified from *Desk Reference on Drug Misuse and Abuse,* New York State Medical Society, New York, 1984, with permission.

About 1.4 billion prescriptions for more than 10,000 different chemical substances are written in the United States each year. About 20 percent of them are for psychoactive or mood altering drugs, such as tranquilizers, sedatives, stimulants, sleeping pills, and analgesics. Fifty percent of all patients who suffer from chronic pain take between one and five pain relievers, and 25 percent of this group become physically dependent on one of these drugs.

EPIDEMIOLOGY

Substance-related mental disorders are a common diagnosis. The lifetime prevalence of alcohol abuse or dependence is 13.3 percent; the one-year incidence is 1.7 percent. The lifetime prevalence of nonalcohol drug abuse or dependence is 5.9 percent; the one-year incidence is approximately 1 percent. Alcohol abuse or dependence is

Table 12.1-5
Diagnostic Criteria for Psychoactive Substance Dependence

A. At least three of the following:
 (1) substance often taken in larger amounts or over a longer period than the person intended
 (2) persistent desire or one or more unsuccessful efforts to cut down or control substance use
 (3) a great deal of time spent in activities necessary to get the substance (e.g., theft), taking the substance (e.g., chain smoking), or recovering from its effects
 (4) frequent intoxication or withdrawal symptoms when expected to fulfill major role obligations at work, school, or home (e.g., does not go to work because hung over, goes to school or work "high," intoxicated while taking care of his or her children), or when substance use is physically hazardous (e.g., drives when intoxicated)
 (5) important social, occupational, or recreational activities given up or reduced because of substance use
 (6) continued substance use despite knowledge of having a persistent or recurrent social, psychological, or physical problem that is caused or exacerbated by the use of the substance (e.g., keeps using heroin despite family arguments about it, cocaine-induced depression, or having an ulcer made worse by drinking)
 (7) marked tolerance: need for markedly increased amounts of the substance (i.e., at least a 50% increase) in order to achieve intoxication or desired effect, or markedly diminished effect with continued use of the same amount
 Note: The following items may not apply to cannabis, hallucinogens, or phencyclidine (PCP):
 (8) characteristic withdrawal symptoms (see specific withdrawal syndromes under psychoactive substance-induced organic mental disorders)
 (9) substance often taken to relieve or avoid withdrawal symptoms

(B). Some symptoms of the disturbance have persisted for at least one month, or have occurred repeatedly over a longer period of time.

Table from DSM-III-R, *Diagnostic and Statistical Manual of Mental Disorders,* ed 3, revised. Copyright American Psychiatric Association, Washington, DC, 1987, with permission.

approximately five to six times more common in men than in women, and nonalcohol drug abuse or dependence is approximately two to three times more common in men than in women. Alcohol-related diagnoses are most common among members of low socioeconomic groups. Alcohol-related diagnoses are more common in rural than in urban settings; nonalcohol-related drug abuse diagnoses are more common in urban than in rural settings.

According to the National Institute on Drug Abuse (NIDA) (July 1989): (1) Current use (past month) of illicit drugs continued a decreasing trend, which began in 1979 and accelerated between 1985 and 1988. Current prevalence rates for any illicit drug use decreased from 23 million (12 percent) of the population aged 12 and over in 1985 to 14.5 million (7 percent) in 1988. (2) Between 1985 and 1988, current drug use declined significantly (37 percent) in all age categories among both men and women and for blacks, whites, and Hispanics. The decline was also seen in all regions of the United States and for all levels of educational attainment. (3) Alcohol and cigarette use also declined from 1985 to 1988. There were 105.8 million current drinkers of alcohol in 1988, compared with 113.1 million in 1985. This represents a decrease in the

Table 12.1-6
Diagnostic Criteria for Psychoactive Substance Abuse

A. A maladaptive pattern of psychoactive substance use indicated by at least one of the following:
 (1) continued use despite knowledge of having a persistent or recurrent social, occupational, psychological, or physical problem that is caused or exacerbated by use of the psychoactive substance
 (2) recurrent use in situations in which use is physically hazardous (e.g., driving while intoxicated)

B. Some symptoms of the disturbance have persisted for at least one month, or have occurred repeatedly over a longer period of time.

C. Never met the criteria for psychoactive substance dependence for this substance.

Table from DSM-III-R, *Diagnostic and Statistical Manual of Mental Disorders,* ed 3, revised. Copyright American Psychiatric Association, Washington, DC, 1987, with permission.

Table 12.1-7
Diagnostic Criteria for Severity of Psychoactive Substance Dependence

Mild: Few, if any, symptoms in excess of those required to make the diagnosis, and the symptoms result in no more than mild impairment in occupational functioning or in usual social activities or relationships with others.

Moderate: Symptoms or functional impairment between "mild" and "severe."

Severe: Many symptoms in excess of those required to make the diagnosis, and the symptoms markedly interfere with occupational functioning or with usual social activities or relationships with others.*

In Partial Remission: During the past six months, some use of the substance and some symptoms of dependence.

In Full Remission: During the past six months, either no use of the substance, or use of the substance and no symptoms of dependence.

Table from DSM-III-R, *Diagnostic and Statistical Manual of Mental Disorders,* ed 3, revised. Copyright American Psychiatric Association, Washington, DC, 1987, with permission.
*Because of the availability of cigarettes and other nicotine-containing substances and the absence of a clinically significant nicotine intoxication syndrome, impairment in occupational or social functioning is not necessary for a rating of severe nicotine dependence.

Table 12.1-8
Diagnostic Criteria for Polysubstance Dependence

This category should be used when, for a period of at least six months, the person has repeatedly used at least three categories of psychoactive substances (not including nicotine and caffeine), but no single psychoactive substance has predominated. During this period the criteria have been met for dependence on psychoactive substances as a group, but not for any specific substance.

Table from DSM-III-R, *Diagnostic and Statistical Manual of Mental Disorders,* ed 3, revised. Copyright American Psychiatric Association, Washington, DC, 1987, with permission.

Table 12.1-9
Extent of Nonmedical Drug Use: 1988*

Age Range: Estimated Population:	12–17 21,640,000		18–25 32,490,000		26+ 136,660,000		Total† 190,790,000	
	Ever Used‡	**Current User‡**	**Ever Used**	**Current User**	**Ever Used**	**Current User**	**Ever Used**	**Current User**
Marijuana or hashish	17%	6%	56%	16%	31%	4%	33%	6%
Hallucinogens	3	1	14	2	7	—§	7	—
Inhalants	9	2	12	2	4	—	6	1
Cocaine	3	1	20	5	10	1	11	2
Crack	1	—	3	1	—	—	1	—
Heroin	1	—	—	—	1	—	1	—
Stimulants	4	1	11	2	7	1	7	1
Sedatives	2	1	6	1	3	—	4	—
Tranquilizers	2	—	8	1	5	1	5	1
Analgesics	4	1	9	1	5	—	5	1
Alcohol	50	25	90	65	89	55	85	53
Cigarettes	42	12	75	35	80	30	75	29
Smokeless tobacco	15	4	24	6	13	3	15	4

Table by Jerome H. Jaffe, M.D.
*Estimates of the percentage of people 12 years of age and older who have used drugs nonmedically were developed from the National Household Survey on Drug Abuse, 1988, for the National Institute on Drug Abuse. Drugs used under a physician's care are not included.
†Totals may not equal the sum of the three age groups because of rounding.
‡Ever used: used at least once in a person's lifetime.
Current user: used at least once in the 30 days prior to the survey.
§Amounts of less than 0.5% are not listed.

rate from 59 to 53 percent for those aged 12 and over. Current cigarette use in this period dropped from 32 to 29 percent. This is a decrease of 3.2 million in the number of cigarette smokers. (4) Overall, 72.4 million Americans age 12 or older (37 percent of the population) had tried marijuana, cocaine, or other illicit drugs at least once in their lifetime (Table 12.1-9). (5) In 1988, 28 million Americans (14 percent) had used marijuana, cocaine, or other illicit drugs at least once in the past year, compared with 37 million in 1985—a decrease of almost 25 percent. (6) Among youth (ages 12 to 17), 17 percent used an illicit drug in the past year, and 9 percent used an illicit drug at least once in the past month. Comparable rates for young adults (aged 18 to 25) are 32 percent and 18 percent, respectively; for mid-adults (aged 26 to 34), 23 percent and 13 percent, respectively; and for older adults (aged 35+) 6 percent and 2 percent. (7) While the overall current prevalence of (any) illicit drug use was 7 percent, the rate for males (9 percent) was higher than the rate for females (6 percent). Other demographic subgroups with elevated current rates were those in large metropolitan areas (9 percent), those living in the West (10 percent), those employed part-time (9 percent), and the unemployed (18 percent). (8) Over 5 million (9 percent) of the nearly 60 million women 15 to 44 years of age (the childbearing years) have used an illicit drug in the past month. Almost 1 million (2 percent) have used cocaine, and 3.8 million (6 percent) have used marijuana in the past month. (9) Among 20-to-40-year-old full-time employed Americans, 22 percent used an illicit drug in the past year, and 12 percent used an illicit drug in the past month. Ten percent used marijuana, and 3 percent used cocaine in the past month. These figures may change as the population ages.

COMORBIDITY WITH OTHER PSYCHIATRIC DIAGNOSES

Symptoms of anxiety and depression are often present in persons with substance use–related diagnoses. Some research data suggest that persons with substance-related disorders are attempting to self-medicate underlying anxiety and mood disorders; however, other research data suggest just the opposite—that substance use can lead to symptoms of anxiety and depression. It seems quite likely that either of these scenarios may be present in an individual patient. Furthermore, substance abuse and either an anxiety or a mood disorder may be mutually interactive in an individual patient, so that each exacerbates the other. The relationships between specific substances of abuse and mood and anxiety symptoms are discussed in the sections on the specific substances.

Another DSM-III-R diagnosis that is often thought to be associated with substance-related disorders is antisocial personality disorder. Some research data suggest an association between antisocial personality disorder and the substance-related disorders. A family history of antisocial personality disorder may predispose a person to a substance-related disorder, and a family history of alcohol dependence or abuse may predispose a person to an antisocial personality disorder. The psychosocial environment of a person is also of critical importance in the development of substance-related disorders.

References

Cadoret R J, Troughton E, O'Gorman T W, Heywood E: An adoption study of genetic and environmental factors in drug abuse. Arch Gen Psychiatry *43*: 1131, 1986.

Dilsaver S C: The pathophysiologies of substance abuse and affective disorders: An integrative model? J Clin Psychopharmacol *7*:, 1987.

Grove W M, Eckert E D, Heston L, Bouchard T J, Segal N, Lykken D T: Heritability of substance abuse and antisocial behavior: A study of monozygotic twins reared apart. Biol Psychiatry *27*: 1293, 1990.

Kandel D B, Raveis V H: Cessation of illicit drug use in young adulthood. Arch Gen Psychiatry *46*: 109, 1989.

Kofoed L, Kania J, Walsh T, Atkinson R M: Outpatient treatment of patients with substance abuse and coexisting psychiatric disorders. Am J Psychiatry *143*: 867, 1986.

Koob G F, Bloom F E: Cellular and molecular mechanisms of drug dependence. Science *242*: 715, 1988.

Kranzler H R, Liebowitz N R: Anxiety and depression in substance abuse: Clinical implications. Med Clin North Am *72*: 867, 1988.

Millman R B, ed: Drug abuse and drug dependence. In *Psychiatry Update*, vol 5, A J Frances and R E Hales, p 120. American Psychiatric Association, Washington, DC, 1986.
Mirin S M, ed: Substance abuse. Psychiatr Clin North Am *9*: entire issue, 1986.
National Institute on Drug Abuse: 1988 National Household Survey on Drug Abuse, 1989.
Nicholi A M: The nontherapeutic use of psychoactive drugs. N Engl J Med *308*: 925, 1983.
Roth M: Anxiety disorders and the use and abuse of drugs. J Clin Psychiatry *50* (Suppl): 30, 1989.
U S Department of Health and Human Services: H H S News, July 1989.

12.2 / Alcoholism

"Alcoholism" is the commonly used term for a disorder marked by the chronic, excessive use of alcohol, resulting in psychological, interpersonal, and medical problems. The term "alcoholism" is not used in the revised third edition of the *Diagnostic and Statistical Manual of Mental Disorders* (DSM-III-R). DSM-III-R classifies the central nervous system (CNS)-related symptoms of alcohol abuse under the psychoactive substance-induced organic mental disorders and the maladaptive behavioral patterns of alcohol abuse under the psychoactive substance use disorders.

ALCOHOL DEPENDENCE

According to DSM-III-R, alcohol dependence is characterized by any one of three major patterns of pathological alcohol use: (1) the need for daily use of large amounts of alcohol for adequate functioning, (2) regular heavy drinking limited to weekends, and (3) long periods of sobriety interspersed with binges of heavy alcohol intake lasting for weeks or months. These patterns are associated with such behaviors as (1) the inability to cut down or stop drinking; (2) repeated efforts to control or reduce excessive drinking by going on the wagon (periods of temporary abstinence) or restricting drinking to certain times of the day; (3) binges (remaining intoxicated throughout the day for at least two days); (4) the occasional consumption of a fifth of spirits (or its equivalent in wine or beer); (5) amnestic periods for events occurring while intoxicated (blackouts); (6) the continuation of drinking despite a serious physical disorder that the person knows is exacerbated by alcohol use; and (7) the drinking of nonbeverage alcohol, such as fuel and commercial products containing alcohol. In addition, alcoholic persons show impaired social or occupational functioning due to alcohol use, such as violence while intoxicated, absence from work, loss of job, legal difficulties (e.g., arrest for intoxicated behavior, traffic accidents while intoxicated), and arguments or difficulties with family or friends because of excessive alcohol use.

Subtypes

According to DSM-III-R, some researchers have divided alcoholism into different patterns of drinking, which they call "species." One example of this is the species called "gamma alcoholism," which is thought to be common in the United States and is representative of the alcoholism seen in persons who are active Alcoholics Anonymous (AA) members. Gamma alcoholism refers to control problems; such alcoholic persons are unable to stop drinking once they start. If the drinking ends as a result of ill health or lack of money, they are capable of abstaining for varying periods of time. In another species of alcoholism, more common in Europe, the alcoholic person must drink a certain amount each day but is unaware of a lack of control. The alcoholism may not be discovered until the person must stop drinking and develops withdrawal symptoms.

EPIDEMIOLOGY

Alcohol is the major psychoactive drug used worldwide. In the United States, an estimated 13 million people are classified as alcoholics. DSM-III-R reports that, according to one community study, approximately 13 percent of all adults had alcohol abuse or dependence at some point in their lives. After heart disease and cancer, alcoholism is the third largest health problem in the United States today. According to the National Institute on Drug Abuse (NIDA) (July 1989): (1) Fifty percent of the youth (aged 12 to 17) have tried an alcoholic beverage at some time in their lives. Use in the past year (45 percent) is almost as high; and 25 percent have had at least one drink during the past month. These rates are all significantly lower than comparable rates for youth in 1985 (56 percent, 52 percent, and 31 percent, respectively). (2) For young adults (aged 18 to 25), the prevalence of drinking (alcohol) is substantially higher than for youth: 90 percent have tried alcohol, 82 percent had used alcohol in the preceding year, and 65 percent had used alcohol during the preceding month. The 1988 rates for drinking among young adults in both the last year and last month, however, are significantly lower than those for the 1985 (87 percent and 71 percent, respectively). (3) The number of current drinkers of alcohol declined from 113 million in 1985 to 106 million in 1988. Of the 135 million people who drank (alcohol) in the past year (68 percent), more than one-third, or 47 million, drank once a week or more often.

Age and Sex

Drinking patterns vary by age and by sex. For both men and women, the prevalence of drinking is highest and abstention is lowest in the 21-to-34-year age range. Young white men drink more than any other group in this country. Among persons 65 years and older, abstainers exceed drinkers in both sexes, and only 7 percent of men and 2 percent of women in this age group are considered heavy drinkers (defined as one who drinks almost every day and becomes intoxicated several times a month). More men use alcohol (20 percent) than women (8 percent). The lifelong expectancy rate for alcoholism among men is 3 to 5 percent; the rate for women is about 1 percent.

Men and women tend to have differing courses of alcoholism. Alcoholism usually has an onset in men their late teens or 20s. Alcoholism often has an insidious course and is not recognized as alcohol dependence until a person is in his or her 30s. In men symptoms of alcohol dependence rarely occur for the first time after age 45. If symptoms do appear for the first time after age 45, DSM-III-R suggests that mood disorders and organic mental disorders be considered as possible diagnoses. Studies of alcoholic women indicate that the course is more varied in women than in men. The onset of alcoholism is generally later in women than in men.

Race and Locale

In the United States blacks in urban ghettos appear to have a particularly high rate of alcohol-related problems. It is not known whether the risk among rural blacks is comparable. American Indians and Eskimos have high rates of alcoholism. Consumption varies markedly in different geographic areas. In the United States consumption is greatest in the Northeast and lowest in the South.

Expectancy rates for alcoholism are about the same as the United States (3 to 5 percent) in Germany, Sweden, Denmark, and England. Expectancy rates are higher in Portugal, Spain, Italy, France, and the Soviet Union.

Psychosocial Factors

Alcohol-related problems are correlated with a history of school difficulty. High school dropouts and persons with a record of frequent truancy and delinquency appear to be at particularly high risk for alcoholism.

Alcoholism is associated with at least 50 percent of traffic fatalities, 50 percent of homicides, and 25 percent of suicides. Alcoholism reduces life expectancy by about 10 years. Alcohol leads all other drugs in drug-related deaths.

Comorbidity with Other Psychiatric Disorders

Alcoholism is particularly likely to coexist with a mood disorder diagnosis in an individual patient. Various studies have estimated the lifetime prevalence of depression in alcoholic persons as ranging from 10 to 50 percent. Depression is more common in alcoholic women than in alcoholic men. It is sometimes recommended that depressive symptoms that remain after two to three weeks of sobriety be treated with antidepressant drugs. Bipolar patients are thought to be at great risk for the development of alcoholism because they use alcohol to self-medicate their manic episodes. The elevation of mood associated with acute alcohol intake by both alcoholic and nonalcoholic persons is followed by increased anxiety and depression in alcoholic persons than in nonalcoholic persons.

Anxiety disorders can also be seen in alcoholic persons. In some alcoholic men a history of panic disorder precedes the development of alcoholism. In some alcoholic women a history of phobias precedes the development of alcoholism.

A relationship between antisocial personality disorder and alcoholism has also been frequently reported. Some studies have suggested that antisocial personality disorder is particularly common in alcoholic men and can precede the development of alcoholism. Other studies have suggested that antisocial personality disorder and alcoholism are completely distinct entities that are not causatively related.

ETIOLOGY

There is a strong genetic factor in the development of alcoholism. Children of alcoholic parents become alcoholic about four times more often than children of nonalcoholic parents. Sons of alcoholic parents are more likely to become alcoholic than are daughters. In a 30-year longitudinal Swedish study of adopted male children who eventually became alcoholic, about 25 percent had biological fathers who were alcoholic. Another Swedish study found that monozygotic twins had about twice the concordance rate for alcoholism as dizygotic twins of the same sex. Some studies report a higher concordance rate for alcoholism among dizygotic twins than among nontwin siblings.

Childhood History

A childhood history of attention-deficit hyperactivity disorder or conduct disorder or both increases a child's risk of becoming alcoholic, particularly if there is alcoholism in the family. Personality disorders, particularly antisocial personality disorder, predispose to the development of alcoholism.

Psychoanalytic Factors

Alcohol is extremely effective in alleviating anxiety, and many persons use alcohol for this reason. Psychoanalytic theory posits that persons with harsh superegos who are self-punitive turn to alcohol as a way of diminishing their unconscious stress. A common psychoanalytic aphorism is that the superego is soluble in alcohol. It is hypothesized that some alcoholic persons are fixated at the oral stage of development and relieve frustration by taking in substances by mouth. The alcoholic personality is described as shy, isolated, impatient, irritable, anxious, hypersensitive, and sexually repressed. Alcoholic persons may have an enhanced need for power but feel inadequate to achieve their goals. Alcohol may give such persons a sense of release and of power and feelings of achievement.

Cultural Factors

Some cultures are more restrained than others about alcohol consumption. For example, Jewish, Asian, and conservative Protestant persons use alcohol less frequently than do liberal Protestant and Catholic persons. Social and cultural factors need to be taken into account when evaluating a person's risk for alcoholism.

Learning Theory

Learning theory suggests that alcohol results in a temporary reduction of fear and conflict, which strengthens the drive to drink. The release of anxiety arising from the first drinking experience is the source of reinforcement in alcoholism.

Biological Factors

Previously it was theorized that the ethanol in alcohol is a lipid solvent that can change the properties of neuronal membranes. This theory was consistent with the observation that—compared with other drugs of abuse, such as lysergic acid diethylamide (LSD)—ethanol is a very low potency drug and, possibly, does not have a specific receptorlike site of action. This theory was also consistent with the observation that ethanol seems to have diverse effects on the nervous system. More recently, however, it has been demonstrated that ethanol may have much more specific effects on selected neurotransmitter systems, particularly the γ-aminobutyric acid (GABA) system. This finding helps to explain the cross-tolerance and additive effects that can occur when alcohol is used in combination with barbiturates and benzodiazepines, both of which also act on the GABA system. Ethanol also has been demonstrated to have relatively specific effects on noradrenergic neurons in the locus ceruleus and on dopaminergic neurons of the ventral tegmental area.

PHYSIOLOGICAL EFFECTS OF ALCOHOL

Ingested alcohol first gets into the bloodstream in very small amounts through the oral mucous membranes and the lungs. It is then absorbed from the alimentary tract and carried by the blood to the brain and other organs. The speed with which alcohol enters the bloodstream depends on many factors: the amount and type of food in the stomach, the type of beverage consumed and its alcohol concentration, the circumstances under which it is being drunk, and the drinker's constitutional state.

Absorption

Foods in the stomach, especially mixed meals, slow alcohol absorption. Drinking water or carbonated beverages with alcohol increases absorption: champagne and highballs cause rapid and heightened effects.

The body has certain protective devices against being inundated by alcohol. For example, unlike other foodstuffs, alcohol can be absorbed into the bloodstream directly from the stomach. If the concentration of alcohol becomes too high in the stomach, mucus is then secreted, and the pyloric valve closes. This action slows absorption and prevents the alcohol from passing into the small intestine, where no significant restraints to absorption exist. Thus, a large amount of alcohol can remain unabsorbed for hours. Further, the pylorospasm often results in nausea and vomiting.

Once alcohol is absorbed into the bloodstream, it is distributed to all the tissues of the body. Because alcohol is uniformly dissolved in the water of the body, tissues containing a high proportion of water receive a high concentration of alcohol. The intoxicating effects are greater when the blood alcohol concentration is rising than when it is falling (the Mellanby effect). For this reason the rate of absorption has a direct bearing on the intoxicating responses.

Metabolism

Immediately after absorption, destruction and elimination begin. The kidneys and lungs excrete about one-tenth of the total alcohol ingested unchanged; the remaining alcohol undergoes oxidation. The rate of oxidation of alcohol is fairly constant and is independent of the body's energy requirements. The average person oxidizes three-fourths of an ounce of 40 percent alcohol (80 proof) in an hour. If the person sips alcohol at this rate, he or she does not accumulate alcohol in the body or become intoxicated.

Alcohol is metabolized by two enzymes: alcohol dehydrogenase (ADH) and aldehyde dehydrogenase (AldDH). Alcohol is metabolized primarily by the liver, which has the highest ADH content in the body. ADH catalyzes the conversion of alcohol into acetaldehyde, which is a very toxic compound. AldDH catalyzes the conversion of acetaldehyde into acetic acid. AldDH is inhibited by disulfiram (Antabuse), which is often used in the treatment of alcoholism. Some studies have shown women to have a lower ADH content, which accounts for their getting intoxicated more easily than men.

The oxidation of alcohol produces energy; however, because excessive drinkers receive so many calories from their alcohol intake, they tend to neglect other food sources and may ignore nutritional needs. Vitamin-deficiency diseases and other nutritional disorders (e.g., pellagra, beriberi) may result.

Effects on the Brain

Alcohol is a CNS depressant, similar to other anesthetics. At a level of 0.05 percent alcohol in the blood, thought, judgment, and restraint are loosened and sometimes disrupted. At a concentration of 0.10 percent, voluntary motor actions usually become perceptibly clumsy. In most states legal intoxication ranges from 0.10 to 0.15 percent blood alcohol level. At 0.20 percent, the function of the entire motor area of the brain is measurably depressed; the parts of the brain that control emotional behavior may be affected. At 0.30 percent, a person is commonly confused or may become stuporous. At 0.40 to 0.50 percent, a person is in a coma. At higher levels, the primitive centers of the brain, which control breathing and heart rate, are affected, and death ensues. Death is secondary to direct respiratory depression or by aspiration of vomitus.

Blackouts. Alcohol can produce anterograde amnesia (blackouts). These periods of amnesia can be particularly distressing because people may fear that they have unknowingly harmed someone or behaved imprudently while intoxicated. During a blackout people have relatively intact remote memory. However, people experience a specific short-term memory deficit in which they are unable to recall events that happened in the previous 5 or 10 minutes. Because their other intellectual faculties are well preserved, they can perform complicated tasks and appear normal to the casual observer. Present evidence suggests that alcoholic blackouts represent an impaired consolidation of new information.

A variety of biological theories have been suggested to explain blackouts. Some studies have reported that plasma levels of tryptophan, the amino acid precursor of serotonin, are lower in persons who have alcohol-related blackouts. Consistent with this finding are reports that drugs that inhibit serotonin reuptake may improve memory in intoxicated persons. Another neurotransmitter implicated in blackouts is glutamate, an excitatory amino acid neurotransmitter, which has been implicated in the biochemical basis of learning and memory.

Other Physiological Effects

Alcohol affects the liver, the main site for alcohol catabolism. A reversible fatty infiltration of the liver occurs with heavy consumption of alcohol. What relation, if any, this infiltration plays in the production of liver cirrhosis is not yet known. Acute intoxication may be associated with hypoglycemia, which, when unrecognized, may be responsible for some of the sudden deaths of intoxicated persons.

Chronic heavy drinking is associated with gastritis, achlorhydria, and gastric ulcers. Occasionally, maladies of the small intestine, pancreatitis, and pancreatic insufficiency are associated with alcoholism. Heavy alcohol intake may interfere with the normal processes of food digestion and absorption. As a result, the food that is consumed is inadequately digested. Alcohol abuse also appears to inhibit the capacity of the intestine to absorb various nutrients, including vitamins and amino acids. Muscle weakness is a side effect of alcoholism. Alcohol has been shown to affect the hearts of even nonalcoholic persons, increasing the resting cardiac output, heart rate, and myocardial oxygen consumption. Chronic excessive use can cause cardiomyopathy.

Drug Interactions

The interaction between alcohol and other drugs can be dangerous, even fatal. Certain drugs, such as alcohol and phenobarbital, are metabolized by the liver; the prolonged use of these drugs may lead to an acceleration of their metabolism. When the alcoholic person is sober, this accelerated metabolism makes him or her unusually tolerant to many other drugs, such as sedatives and tranquilizers, but, when the alcoholic person is intoxicated, these other drugs compete with the alcohol for the same detoxification mechanism, and potentially toxic blood levels can accumulate.

The effects of alcohol and other CNS depressants are usually synergistic. Sedatives, hypnotics, and drugs that relieve pain, motion sickness, head cold, and allergy symptoms must be used with caution by alcoholic persons. Narcotics depress the sensory areas of the cerebral cortex, resulting in pain relief, sedation, apathy, drowsiness, and sleep. High doses can result in respiratory failure and death. Increasing doses of sedative-hypnotic drugs, such as chloral hydrate and benzodiazepines, especially when combined with alcohol, produce a range of effects from sedation to motor and intellectual impairment, progressing to stupor, coma, and death. Since tranquilizers and other psychotropics can potentiate the effects of alcohol, patients should be instructed about the dangers of combining CNS depressants and alcohol, particularly when driving or operating machinery.

ALCOHOL-INDUCED ORGANIC MENTAL DISORDERS

Alcohol Intoxication

Intoxication is characterized by maladaptive behavior after the ingestion of alcohol (Table 12.2-1). Ataxia, nystagmus, and impaired attention are among the signs of intoxication. The severity of the symptoms correlates roughly with the blood concentration of alcohol, which reflects the alcohol concentration in the brain. It is thought that the initial effects of alcohol are secondary to preferential involvement of the polysynaptic pathways in the reticular formation, cerebral cortex, and cerebellum. Some persons become talkative and gregarious; some become withdrawn and sullen; others become belligerent. In some there is a lability of mood with intermittent episodes of laughing and crying. A short-term tolerance to alcohol may occur, so that a person seems less intoxicated after many hours of drinking than after only a few hours.

Table 12.2-1
Diagnostic Criteria for Alcohol Intoxication

A. Recent ingestion of alcohol (with no evidence suggesting that the amount was insufficient to cause intoxication in most people)

B. Maladaptive behavior changes (e.g., disinhibition of sexual or aggressive impulses, mood lability, impaired judgment, impaired social or occupational functioning)

C. At least one of the following signs:
(1) slurred speech
(2) incoordination
(3) unsteady gait
(4) nystagmus
(5) flushed face

D. Not due to any physical or other mental disorder

Table from DSM-III-R, *Diagnostic and Statistical Manual of Mental Disorders*, ed 3, revised. Copyright American Psychiatric Association, Washington, DC, 1987, with permission.

Medical complications of intoxication include those that result from falls, such as subdural hematomas and fractures. A telltale sign of chronic bouts of intoxication are facial hematomas, particularly about the eyes, a result of falls or fights while drunk. In cold climates hypothermia and death may occur because the intoxicated person is exposed to the elements. A person with alcohol intoxication may also be predisposed to infections, secondary to a suppression of the immune system.

Alcohol Idiosyncratic Intoxication

This condition, also known as pathological intoxication, is characterized by the sudden onset of marked behavioral changes after the consumption of a small amount of alcohol (Table 12.2-2). The person is confused and disoriented and may experience illusions, transitory delusions, and visual hallucinations. There is greatly increased psychomotor activity. The person may display impulsive, aggressive behavior and be dangerous to others. The person may also exhibit suicidal ideation and attempts. The disorder, which usually lasts for a few hours, terminates in a prolonged period of sleep; the person is unable to recall the episode. The cause of the condition is unknown but is most common in persons with high levels of anxiety. The alcohol may cause sufficient disorganization and loss of control to release aggressive impulses. It has also been suggested that brain damage, particularly encephalitic or traumatic, predisposes people to intolerance for alcohol, which may lead to abnormal behavior after taking a small amount. Other

Table 12.2-2
Diagnostic Criteria for Alcohol Idiosyncratic Intoxication

A. Maladaptive behavioral changes (e.g., aggressive or assaultive behavior, occurring within minutes of ingesting an amount of alcohol insufficient to induce intoxication in most people)

B. The behavior is atypical of the person when not drinking

C. Not due to any physical or other mental disorder

predisposing factors include advancing age, taking sedative-hypnotic drugs, and feeling fatigued. The behavior tends to be atypical of the person when not under the influence; for example, a quiet, shy person after one weak drink becomes belligerent and aggressive.

Treatment involves protecting patients from harming themselves and others. Physical restraint may be necessary but is difficult because of the abrupt onset of the condition. Once the patient has been restrained, an injection of an antipsychotic, such as haloperidol (Haldol), is useful in controlling assaultiveness.

The condition must be differentiated from other causes of abrupt behavior change, such as temporal lobe seizures. In fact, several persons with this disorder have been reported to show temporal lobe spiking on an electroencephalogram (EEG) after ingesting small amounts of alcohol.

Uncomplicated Alcohol Withdrawal

Alcohol withdrawal is a syndrome that follows the cessation of or reduction in prolonged or heavy drinking. Within hours, a variety of signs and symptoms develop, including tremors, hyperreflexia, tachycardia, hypertension, general malaise, and nausea or vomiting. Major motor seizures may occur, particularly in people with a preexisting history of seizure disorder. Patients may have transient, poorly formed hallucinations and illusions or vivid nightmares, and sleep is usually disturbed (Table 12.2-3). Conditions that may predispose to or aggravate the syndrome include fatigue, malnutrition, physical illness, and depression. Treatment is symptomatic, with bed rest and hydration. A cross-dependent drug, such as a benzodiazepine, can be valuable in controlling the overactivity of the sympathetic nervous system and is used until symptoms subside. Other drugs used to treat alcohol withdrawal include clonidine (Catapres), propranolol (Inderal), and carbamazepine (Tegretol), but they are not generally as effective as benzodiazepines. Nevertheless, the ability of adrenergic drugs to affect withdrawal syndromes suggests that epinephrine and norepinephrine neuronal systems are involved in the production of withdrawal symptoms.

Alcohol Withdrawal Delirium

Patients with uncomplicated alcohol withdrawal should be carefully monitored to prevent progression to alcohol withdrawal delirium, the most severe form of the withdrawal syndrome, also known as delirium tremens (DTs) (Table 12.2-4). The essential feature of this syndrome is delirium that occurs within one week after the person stops drinking actively or reduces his or her intake. Additional features include (1) autonomic hyperactivity, such as tachycardia, sweating, and elevated blood pressure; (2) a severe disturbance in sensorium manifested by disorientation and clouding of consciousness; (3) perceptual distortions, which are most frequently visual or tactile hallucinations; and (4) fluctuating levels of psychomotor activity ranging from hyperexcitability to lethargy. Delusions and agitated behavior are commonly present. Fever is common. Grand mal seizures are common occurrences in withdrawal, although they usually precede the onset of the delirium. Withdrawal seizures may be caused by the increased number of calcium channels and the resultant increased calcium influx that has been observed in various experimental models of alcoholism.

Table 12.2-3
Diagnostic Criteria for Uncomplicated Alcohol Withdrawal

A. Cessation of prolonged (several days or longer) heavy ingestion of alcohol or reduction in the amount of alcohol ingested, followed within several hours by coarse tremor of hands, tongue, or eyelids, and at least one of the following:
(1) nausea or vomiting
(2) malaise or weakness
(3) autonomic hyperactivity (e.g., tachycardia, sweating, elevated blood pressure)
(4) anxiety
(5) depressed mood or irritability
(6) transient hallucinations or illusions
(7) headache
(8) insomnia

B. Not due to any physical or other mental disorder, such as alcohol withdrawal delirium

The delirious patient is a danger to self and to others because of the unpredictability of behavior. The patient may be assaultive or suicidal or may be acting on the hallucinations or delusional thoughts as if they were genuine dangers. Untreated, DTs has a mortality rate of 20 percent, usually as a result of intercurrent medical illness, such as pneumonia, renal disease, hepatic insufficiency, and heart failure.

Approximately 5 percent of all alcoholics who are hospitalized develop DTs. Since the syndrome most commonly develops on the third hospital day, a patient admitted for an unrelated condition may unexpectedly go into an episode of delirium, which is the first sign of previously undiagnosed alcoholism. Episodes of DTs usually begin in the patient's 30s or 40s after 5 to 15 years of heavy drinking, typically of the binge type. Physical illness predisposes to this syndrome; a person in good physical health rarely develops DTs during alcohol withdrawal. A clinical case example follows:

A 43-year-old divorced carpenter was examined in the hospital emergency observation ward. The patient's sister was available to provide some information. She reported that the

Table 12.2-4
Diagnostic Criteria for Alcohol Withdrawal Delirium

A. Delirium developing after cessation of heavy alcohol ingestion or a reduction in the amount of alcohol ingested (usually within one week)

B. Marked autonomic hyperactivity (e.g., tachycardia, sweating)

C. Not due to any physical or other mental disorder

Table from DSM-III-R, *Diagnostic and Statistical Manual of Mental Disorders,* ed 3, revised. Copyright American Psychiatric Association, Washington, DC, 1987, with permission.

patient had consumed large quantities of cheap wine daily for over five years. He had had a reasonably stable home life and job record until his wife left him for another man five years previously. The sister indicated that the patient had been consuming more than a fifth of wine a day since his divorce. He often had had blackouts from drinking and had missed work; consequently, he had been fired from several jobs. Fortunately for him, carpenters are in great demand, and he had been able to provide marginally for himself during these years. However, three days ago he had run out of money and wine and had to beg on the street to buy a meal. The patient had been poorly nourished, eating perhaps one meal a day and evidently relying on wine for nourishment.

The morning after his last day of drinking (three days earlier), he felt increasingly tremulous, his hands shaking so grossly that it was difficult for him to light a cigarette. Accompanying this was an increasing sense of inner panic, which had made him virtually unable to sleep. A neighbor became concerned about the patient when he seemed not to be making sense and was clearly unable to take care of himself. The neighbor contacted the sister, who brought him to the hospital.

On examination, the patient alternated between apprehension and chatty, superficial warmth. He was quite keyed up and talked almost constantly in a rambling and unfocused manner. At times he recognized the doctor, but at other times he got confused and thought the doctor was his older brother. Twice during the examination he called the doctor by his older brother's name and asked when he arrived, evidently having lost track entirely of the interview up to that point. He had a gross hand tremor at rest, and there were periods when he picked at "bugs" he saw on the bed sheets. He was disoriented for a time and thought that he was in a supermarket parking lot, rather than in a hospital. He indicated that he felt he was fighting against a terrifying sense that the world was ending in a holocaust. He was startled every few minutes by sounds and scenes of fiery car crashes (evidently provoked by the sound of rolling carts in the hall). Efforts at testing memory and calculation failed because his attention shifted too rapidly. An electroencephalogram indicated a pattern of diffuse encephalopathy.

DSM-III-R diagnosis: Axis I: alcohol withdrawal delirium and alcohol dependence, severe.

Treatment. The best way to deal with DTs is to prevent it. Patients withdrawing from alcohol who exhibit any withdrawal phenomena should receive a benzodiazepine, such as 25 to 50 mg of chlordiazepoxide (Librium) every two to four hours, until they seem to be out of danger. Once the delirium appears, however, doses of 50 to 100 mg of chlordiazepoxide should be given every four hours orally (PO) (or intramuscularly [IM] if the patient cannot retain oral medication). A high-calorie, high-carbohydrate diet supplemented by multivitamins is important. Patients with DTs should never be physically restrained, as they may fight the restraints to exhaustion. When patients are disorderly and uncontrollable, a seclusion room can be used. Dehydration can be corrected with fluids by mouth or intravenously (IV). Anorexia, vomiting, and diarrhea often occur during withdrawal. Diaphoresis and fever may also contribute to volume depletion. Phenothiazines should be avoided because they tend to reduce seizure thresholds.

The need for warm, supportive psychotherapy in the treatment of DTs must be emphasized. Patients are often bewildered, frightened, and anxious because of their tumultuous symptoms. Skillful verbal support is imperative.

The emergence of focal neurological symptoms, lateralizing seizures, increased intracranial pressure, skull fracture, or other indications of CNS pathology calls for further neurological investigation and treatment. It is now generally believed that anticonvulsant medication is not useful in preventing or treating alcohol withdrawal convulsions; the use of chlordiazepoxide or diazepam (Valium) is generally effective.

Alcohol Hallucinosis

The essential feature of alcohol hallucinosis is an organic hallucinosis, either visual or auditory, usually beginning within 48 hours after cessation of drinking and persisting after a person has recovered from the symptoms of alcohol withdrawal (Table 12.2-5). The hallucinations are not part of alcohol withdrawal delirium. For most people they are unpleasant, perhaps taking the form of voices or unformed sounds, such as buzzing. The disorder can occur at any age; however, the person must have been drinking to excess long enough to become alcohol-dependent. In some cases, the hallucinations last for several weeks; in other cases, for several months; and in still other cases, they seem to be permanent. The condition is considered rare.

The typical case of alcohol hallucinosis differs from schizophrenia in its temporal relation to alcohol withdrawal, its short-lived course, and the absence of a history of schizophrenia. The disorder is four times as common in men as in women. Alcohol hallucinosis is usually described as a condition manifested primarily by auditory hallucinations, sometimes accompanied by delusions, in the absence of symptoms of a mood disorder or organic mental

Table 12.2-5
Diagnostic Criteria for Alcohol Hallucinosis

A. Organic hallucinosis with vivid and persistent hallucinations (auditory or visual) developing shortly (usually within 48 hours) after cessation of or reduction in heavy ingestion of alcohol in a person who apparently has alcohol dependence

B. No delirium as in alcohol withdrawal delirium

C. Not due to any physical or other mental disorder

Table from DSM-III-R, *Diagnostic and Statistical Manual of Mental Disorders,* ed 3, revised. Copyright American Psychiatric Association, Washington, DC, 1987, with permission.

disorder. Alcoholic hallucinosis is differentiated from DTs by the absence of a clear sensorium in DTs.

The treatment of alcohol hallucinosis is much like that of DTs—benzodiazepines, adequate nutrition, and fluids if necessary. When that regimen fails and in chronic cases, antipsychotics may be used. A clinical case example follows:

A 44-year-old unemployed man who lived alone in a single-room-occupancy hotel was brought to the emergency room by police, to whom he had gone for help, complaining that he was frightened by hearing voices of men in the street below his window talking about him and threatening him with harm. When he looked out the window, the men had always "disappeared."

The patient had a 20-year history of almost daily alcohol use, was commonly drunk each day, and often had experienced the shakes on awakening. On the previous day he had reduced his intake to one pint of vodka because of gastrointestinal distress. He was fully alert and oriented on the mental status examination.

DSM-III-R diagnosis: Axis I: alcohol hallucinosis and alcohol dependence, severe.

Alcohol Amnestic Disorder (Korsakoff's Syndrome) and Alcoholic Encephalopathy (Wernicke's Syndrome)

The essential feature of alcohol amnestic disorder is a disturbance in short-term memory because of the prolonged heavy use of alcohol. Other complications of alcoholism—such as cerebellar signs, peripheral neuropathy, and cirrhosis—may be present. Since the disorder usually occurs in persons who have been drinking heavily for many years, it rarely occurs before the age of 35 years (Table 12.2-6).

The irreversible memory deficit known as Korsakoff's syndrome or alcohol amnestic disorder often follows an acute episode of Wernicke's syndrome, also called alcoholic encephalopathy or Wernicke's encephalopathy, a neurological disease manifested by ataxia, ophthalmoplegia (particularly involving the sixth cranial nerve), nystagmus, and confusion. Alcoholic encephalopathy may clear spontaneously in a few days or weeks. It can also progress into the alcohol amnestic disorder, in which the patient has an irreversible short-term memory impairment in the presence of a clear sensorium. The early acute stage of Wernicke's syndrome responds rapidly to large doses of parenteral thiamine, which is believed to be effective in preventing the progression into the alcohol amnestic disorder. However, once the disorder is established, the course is chronic, and impairment is always severe. Lifelong custodial care is often required.

Table 12.2-6
Diagnostic Criteria for Alcohol Amnestic Disorder

A. Amnestic syndrome following prolonged, heavy ingestion of alcohol

B. Not due to any physical or other mental disorder

Table from DSM-III-R, *Diagnostic and Statistical Manual of Mental Disorders*, ed 3, revised. Copyright American Psychiatric Association, Washington, DC, 1987, with permission.

Wernicke's encephalopathy and alcohol amnestic disorder—the two are sometimes combined in the term "Wernicke-Korsakoff's syndrome"—are believed to be caused by thiamine deficiency. Therefore, malnutrition can be considered a predisposing factor. Heavy alcohol ingestion produces a malabsorption syndrome. The prevalence is unknown, but the condition is apparently rare and may have become more rare in recent years because of the almost routine administration of thiamine during detoxification. Although the syndrome is usually irreversible, various degrees of recovery have been reported with a daily regimen of 50 to 100 mg of thiamine hydrochloride.

The pathophysiological connection between thiamine deficiency and the brain lesions of Wernicke's encephalopathy and Korsakoff's syndrome is unclear. Thiamine is a cofactor for several important enzymes, and it may also be involved in the conduction of the axon potential along the axon and in synaptic transmission. The neuropathological lesions include atrophy of the mamillary bodies. A clinical case example follows:

A 46-year-old house painter was admitted to the hospital with a history of 30 years of heavy drinking. He had had two previous admissions for detoxification, but his family stated that he had not had a drink in several weeks, and he showed no signs of alcohol withdrawal. He looked malnourished, however, and on examination was found to be ataxic and to have a bilateral sixth-cranial-nerve palsy. He appeared confused and mistook one of his physicians for a dead uncle.

Within a week the patient walked normally, and there was no longer any sign of a sixth-nerve palsy. He seemed less confused and could now find his way to the bathroom without direction. He remembered the names and birthdays of his siblings but had difficulty naming the past five U.S. presidents. More strikingly, he had great difficulty in retaining information for longer than a few minutes. He could repeat a list of numbers immediately after he had heard them but a few minutes later did not recall being asked to perform the task. Shown three objects (keys, comb, ring), he could not recall them three minutes later. He did not seem worried about this. Asked if he could recall the name of his doctor, he replied, "Certainly," and proceeded to call the doctor "Dr. Masters" (not his name), whom he claimed he had first met during the Korean War. He told a long untrue story about how he and "Dr. Masters" had served as fellow soldiers.

The patient was calm, alert, and friendly. Because of his intact immediate memory and spotty but sometimes adequate remote memory, one could be with him for a short period and not realize he had a severe memory impairment. His amnesia, in short, was largely anterograde. Although treated with high doses of thiamine, the short-term memory deficit persisted and appeared to be irreversible.

DSM-III-R diagnosis: Axis I: alcohol amnestic disorder, severe, and alcohol dependence, severe; Axis III: Wernicke's encephalopathy.

Dementia Associated with Alcoholism

The essential feature of dementia associated with alcoholism is a dementia that persists at least three weeks after cessation of prolonged alcohol use and for which all other causes of dementia have been ruled out. Other complications of alcoholism—such as cerebellar signs, peripheral neuropathy, and cirrhosis—may be present. Since the disorder occurs in persons who have been drinking heavily for many years, the disorder rarely occurs before the age of 35 years (Table 12.2-7).

By definition, there is always some impairment in social or occupational functioning. In mild cases cognitive deficits may be demonstrable only by neuropsychological testing. More rarely, when impairment is severe, the patient becomes totally oblivious to his or her surroundings and requires constant care. It is not yet known whether dementia associated with alcoholism is the primary effect of alcohol or its metabolites on the brain or an indirect consequence of the malnutrition, frequent head injury, and liver disease that occur with chronic alcoholism.

FETAL ALCOHOL SYNDROME

Studies of infants with neonatal abnormalities revealed that many of the mothers had alcoholism. Mental retardation, growth deficiencies, craniofacial and midline defects, limb malformations, cardiac defects, and delayed motor development are some of the disabling consequences of fetal alcohol syndrome.

The risk of an alcoholic woman's having a defective child is as high as 35 percent. Although the precise mechanism of the damage to the fetus is unknown, the damage seems to be the result of exposure in utero to ethanol or its metabolites. Alcohol may also cause hormone imbalances that increase the risk of abnormalities.

TREATMENT

A major issue in the treatment of alcoholism is the question of abstinence: Must the person never again have alcohol, or can the drinking be controlled? In general, controlled drinking, such as one drink on a weekend, carries a high risk of relapse. Groups such as Alcoholics Anonymous (AA) and most experts are proponents of the abstinence approach and believe that there is no such condition as a recovered alcoholic.

Most alcoholic patients come to treatment as a result of pressure from a spouse or employer or fear that continued drinking will have a fatal outcome. Those patients who are persuaded, encouraged, or even coerced into treatment by persons who are meaningful to them, such as their spouses and children, are more apt to remain in treatment and have a better prognosis than those who are not so pressured. The best prognosis is for those persons who come to a psychiatrist voluntarily because they conclude that they are alcoholic and need help.

Table 12.2-7
Diagnostic Criteria for Dementia Associated with Alcoholism

A. Dementia following prolonged, heavy ingestion of alcohol and persisting at least three weeks after cessation of alcohol ingestion

B. Exclusion, by history, physical examination, and laboratory tests, of all causes of dementia other than prolonged heavy use of alcohol

Table from DSM-III-R, *Diagnostic and Statistical Manual of Mental Disorders,* ed 3, revised. Copyright American Psychiatric Association, Washington, DC, 1987, with permission.

Psychotherapy

Psychotherapy is useful when it focuses on the reasons for the alcoholic person's desire to be intoxicated, such as higher tolerance for frustration and reduction of anxiety. The drinking itself and its past, present, and future consequences must be given firm emphasis. Involving an interested and cooperative spouse in conjoint therapy is often beneficial to the psychotherapeutic process.

The initial contact with an alcoholic person is crucial to successful treatment. In the early encounter the therapist needs to be active and supportive, because patients with alcohol problems anticipate rejection and interpret the passive role of a therapist as rejecting. The therapist must also deal with alcohol as a psychological defense; the removal of the emotional and intellectual barriers between patient and therapist should be an early goal. The therapist must be prepared to have the therapeutic bond tested again and again, and he or she cannot hide behind the screen of the patient's lack of motivation when relapses become threatening to the therapist. Depressions can be countered by the active, supportive role of the therapist and at times by the addition of antidepressant drug medication.

Sophisticated therapists view the problem of alcoholism not in terms of an isolated patient but in terms of the dynamics of a person who is part of a social system.

Medication

Two groups of drugs are useful in the treatment of alcoholism: the deterrent drug disulfiram and psychotropic drugs.

Disulfiram. Disulfiram (Antabuse) competitively inhibits the enzyme aldehyde dehydrogenase, so that even a single drink usually causes a toxic reaction because of acetaldehyde accumulation in the blood. Administration of the drug should not begin until 24 hours have elapsed since the patient's last drink. The patient must be in good health, highly motivated, and cooperative. The physician must warn the patient about the consequences of ingesting alcohol while on the drug or for as long as two weeks thereafter. Those who drink while taking the 250 mg daily dose of disulfiram experience flushing and feelings of heat in the face, sclera, upper limbs, and chest. They may become pale, hypotensive, and nauseated and experience serious malaise. There may also be dizziness, blurred vision, palpitations, air hunger, and numbness of the extremities. The most serious potential consequence is severe hypotension. Patients may also have a response to alcohol ingested in such substances as sauces and vinegars or even to inhaled alcohol vapors from after-shave lotions. The syndrome, once elicited, typically lasts some 30 to 60 minutes but can persist longer. With doses above 250 mg, toxic psychoses can occur, with memory impairment and confusion. The drug can also exacerbate psychotic symptoms in some schizophrenic patients.

Psychotropics. Antianxiety agents and antidepressants are useful during various stages of treatment. In the initial stage of abstinence, anxiety, restlessness, and insomnia may be prominent features; they can be controlled by one of the antianxiety agents, such as diazepam or chlordiazepoxide, which may have to be prescribed for weeks or even months. Under controlled conditions the risk of the alcoholic person's becoming addicted to an antianxiety agent is remote. Antidepressants are useful for those patients who are clinically depressed while abstinent. Lithium has also been used with some success. An experimental drug known as Ro 15-451B blocks the effects of alcohol and is currently being tested at the National Institute of Mental Health (NIMH). Rats given the drug do not become intoxicated or, if previously intoxicated, become sober within three minutes of ingesting the compound.

Behavior Therapy

Behavior therapy teaches the alcoholic person other ways to reduce anxiety. Relaxation training, assertiveness training, self-control skills, and new strategies to master the environment are emphasized. A number of operant conditioning programs have been described that condition alcoholic persons to modify their drinking behavior or to stop. The reinforcers have included monetary rewards, an opportunity to live in an enriched inpatient environment, and access to pleasurable social interactions. Trials of aversive conditioning—apomorphine and emetine to induce vomiting, electrical stimulation to produce pain—were consistently successful only in very highly motivated persons and are no longer widely used in the treatment of alcoholism.

Alcoholics Anonymous (AA)

AA is a voluntary, supportive fellowship of hundreds of thousands of alcoholic persons that was founded in 1935 by two alcoholic persons, a stockbroker and a surgeon. Physicians should refer an alcoholic patient to AA as part of a multiple-treatment approach. Frequently, patients who object when AA is initially suggested later derive much benefit from the organization and become enthusiastic participants. Its members make a public admission of their alcoholism, and abstinence is the rule.

Al-Anon. This organization for the spouses of alcoholic persons is structured along the same lines as AA. The aims of Al-Anon are through group support to assist the efforts of the spouses to regain self-esteem, to refrain from feeling responsible for the spouse's drinking, and to develop a rewarding life for themselves and their families. Alateen is directed to children of alcoholics, so that they may better understand their parents' alcoholism.

Halfway Houses

The discharge of an alcoholic patient from the hospital often poses serious placement problems. Home or other familiar environments may be counterproductive, unsupportive, or too unstructured. The halfway house is an important treatment resource that provides emotional support, counseling, and progressive entry into society.

References

Berglund M: Suicide in alcoholism: A prospective study of 88 suicides: I. The multidimensional diagnosis at first admission. Arch Gen Psychiatry *41*: 888, 1984.

Brandt J, Butters N, Ryan C, Bayog R: Cognitive loss and recovery in long-term alcohol abusers. Arch Gen Psychiatry *40*: 435, 1983.

Castaneda R, Cushman P: Alcohol withdrawal: A review of clinical management. J Clin Psychiatry *50*: 278, 1989.

Charness M E, Simon R P, Greenberg D A: Ethanol and the nervous system. N Engl J Med *321*: 442, 1989.

Devor E J, Cloninger C R: Genetics of alcoholism. Annu Rev Genet *23*: 19, 1989.

Gurnack A M, Thomas J L: Behavioral factors related to elderly alcohol abuse: Research and policy issues. Int J Addict *24*: 641, 1989.

Holt S: Identification and intervention for alcohol abuse. J S C Med Assoc *85*: 554, 1989.

Mendelson J H, Babor T F, Mello N K, Pratt H: Alcoholism and prevalence of medical and psychiatric disorders. J Stud Alcohol *47*: 361, 1986.

Meyer R E: Prospects for a rational pharmacotherapy of alcoholism. J Clin Psychiatry *50*: 403, 1989.

Meyer R E, ed: Alcoholism. In *American Psychiatric Press Review of Psychiatry*, vol 8, A Tasman, R E Hales, and A J Frances, editors, p 267. American Psychiatric Press, Washington, DC, 1989.

Mirin S M, ed: Alcohol abuse. Psychiatr Ann *19*(5): entire issue, 1989.

Monteiro M G, Schuckit M A: Populations at high alcoholism risk: Recent findings. J Clin Psychiatry *49* (9, Suppl): 3, 1988.

National Institute on Drug Abuse: 1988 National Household Survey on Drug Abuse, 1989.

Schulsinger F, Knop J, Goodwin D W, Teasdale T W, Mikkelsen U: A prospective study of young men at high risk for alcoholism. Arch Gen Psychiatry *43*: 755, 1986.

U S Department of Health and Human Services: H H S News, July 1989.

Waterson E J, Murray-Lyon I M: Preventing alcohol related birth damage: A review. Soc Sci Med *30*: 349, 1990.

12.3 / Sedatives, Hypnotics, and Anxiolytics

This class of substances includes the barbiturates, various barbituratelike drugs (e.g., methaqualone, meprobamate [Equanil], glutethimide [Doriden]), and the benzodiazepines. Sedative drugs induce mental calmness; hypnotic drugs induce sleep; anxiolytic drugs reduce anxiety. Sedative and anxiolytic drugs can induce sleep if used in high enough doses, and hypnotic drugs can induce calmness, rather than sleep, if used in low doses. These three classes of drugs are sometimes grouped together as minor tranquilizers.

Sedative-hypnotics and anxiolytics are also used to raise the convulsive threshold, to increase muscle relaxation, and to induce general anesthesia (although they possess no analgesic qualities themselves). All sedative-hypnotics and anxiolytics are cross-tolerant with one another and with alcohol. All are capable of producing both physical and psychological dependence and typical withdrawal syndromes. Addicted persons can die from withdrawal. Overdose can be fatal.

DSM-III-R CLASSIFICATION

The revised third edition of *Diagnostic and Statistical Manual of Mental Disorders* (DSM-III-R) contains diagnostic classifications for psychoactive substance use disorders and psychoactive substance-induced organic mental disorders related to the sedative-hypnotic and anxiolytic drugs. This class of drugs can be associated with two psychoactive substance use disorders—dependence and abuse—and with four psychoactive substance-induced organic mental disorders—intoxication, uncomplicated withdrawal, withdrawal delirium, and amnestic disorder.

EPIDEMIOLOGY

Approximately one-third of drug-related visits to the emergency room involve sedative-hypnotic or anxiolytic drugs. In this group women are represented two to three times more commonly than men, and whites are two to three times more common than blacks. Approximately 70 percent of the prescriptions for benzodiazepines are written by nonpsychiatric medical doctors. Patients commonly mix drugs of this class with alcohol, creating a particularly dangerous combination that can result in death because of the additive sedative properties. Opiate addicts sometimes use sedative-hypnotics and anxiolytics, particularly benzodiazepines, to add a euphoric effect to methadone.

BARBITURATES

The first barbiturate, barbital (Veronal), was introduced in 1903. Barbital and phenobarbital, which was introduced shortly thereafter, are long-acting drugs with half-lives of 12 to 24 hours. Amobarbital (Amytal) is an intermediate-acting barbiturate with a half-life of 6 to 12 hours. Pentobarbital (Nembutal) and secobarbital (Seconal) are short-acting barbiturates with half-lives of three to six hours. Barbiturates are used as sedatives, hypnotics, and anticonvulsants, although the introduction of other drugs that are less lethal and less prone to cause addiction has led to a reduction in their use.

Because they are legitimately manufactured in large quantities and are readily available in numerous forms, barbiturates are the target of illicit activity. The black market meets its needs by diverting shipments from manufacturers and by robbing drug warehouses; the drugs are then often cut with sugar and other substances. The three major barbiturates common on the black market are secobarbital (reds, red devils, seggys, downers), pentobarbital (yellow jackets, yellows, nembies), and a combination of secobarbital and amobarbital (reds and blues, rainbows, double-trouble, tooies). Pentobarbital, secobarbital, and amobarbital are now under the same federal legal controls as morphine. Both legal and illegal use of barbiturates seems to be declining.

Mechanism of Action

Barbiturates act primarily on the γ-aminobutyric acid ($GABA_A$) receptor complex. This receptor complex includes a binding site for the inhibitory amino acid neurotransmitter GABA, a regulatory site that binds benzodiazepines, and a chloride ion channel. Binding of the barbiturates to this receptor complex results in the facilitation of chloride ion influx into the neuron, thus making the neuron more negatively charged and less likely to be stimulated.

Patterns of Abuse

Oral use. Barbiturates can be taken orally either occasionally for a high or chronically for a constant calmness. These two patterns of abuse generally involve two different groups of persons. Generally, teenagers and young adults are most likely to take an occasional barbiturate to produce a transient sense of euphoria or well-being. The user's personality, the expectations of the drug's effects, and the setting in which the drug is taken also affect the drug experience.

Chronic intoxication occurs mainly in middle-aged, middle-class people who obtain the drug from the family physician as a prescription for insomnia or anxiety. Now that the number of refills is limited by law, these abusers may visit many physicians, obtaining a prescription from each. Their drug dependence may go unnoticed for months or even years or until their work begins to suffer or they show physical signs, such as slurred speech.

Intravenous use. The most dangerous pattern is intravenous barbiturate use. Users are mainly young adults intimately involved in illegal drugs. Typically, their drug experience has been extensive. They often use barbiturates because the habit is less expensive to maintain than a heroin habit. The rush is described as a pleasant, warm, drowsy feeling. Like amphetamine abusers (speed freaks), these barbiturate abusers tend to be irresponsible, violent, and disruptive. The physical dangers of injection include acquired immune deficiency syndrome (AIDS) through the sharing of needles, cellulitis, vascular complications from accidental injection into an artery, infections, and allergic reactions to contaminants. Barbiturates are also used by heroin addicts to boost the effects of weak heroin, by alcoholics to enhance the intoxication or relieve the symptoms of alcohol withdrawal, and by speed freaks as a sedative to help avoid paranoia and agitation.

Adverse Effects

Mild barbiturate intoxication, acute or chronic, resembles alcohol intoxication (Table 12.3-1). Symptoms include sluggishness, incoordination, difficulty in thinking, poor memory, slowness of speech and comprehension, faulty judgment, disinhibition of sexual or aggressive impulses, narrowed range of attention, emotional lability, and exaggeration of basic personality traits. The sluggishness usually wears off after a few hours, but impaired judgment, distorted mood, and impaired motor skills may remain for as long as 10 to 22 hours. Other symptoms are hostility, quarrelsomeness, moroseness, and, occasionally, paranoid ideation and suicidal tendencies. Neurological effects include nystagmus, diplopia, strabismus, ataxic gait, positive Romberg's sign, hypotonia, dysmetria, and decreased su-

Table 12.3-1
Diagnostic Criteria for Sedative, Hypnotic, or Anxiolytic Intoxication

A. Recent use of a sedative, hypnotic, or anxiolytic

B. Maladaptive behavioral changes (e.g., disinhibition of sexual or aggressive impulses, mood lability, impaired judgment, impaired social or occupational functioning)

C. At least one of the following signs:
 (1) slurred speech
 (2) incoordination
 (3) unsteady gait
 (4) impairment in attention or memory

D. Not due to any physical or other mental disorder

Note: When the differential diagnosis must be made without a clear-cut history or toxicologic analysis of body fluids, it may be qualified as "provisional."

perficial reflexes. The diagnosis of barbiturate intoxication, based on these signs and symptoms, may be confirmed by blood tests for barbiturates.

All patterns of use present dangers to health. Acute intoxication can produce death from suicide, accident, or unintentional overdose. Barbiturates in home medicine cabinets are second only to aspirin as a cause of fatal drug overdose in children. Barbiturates are a common cause of lethal accidents and are commonly taken with suicidal intent. The effects of alcohol and barbiturates are additive, and the combination is especially dangerous. Barbiturate-induced death follows a sequence of deep coma, respiratory arrest, and cardiovascular failure. The lethal dose varies with the route of administration, excitability of the central nervous system (CNS), and acquired tolerance. For the most commonly abused barbiturates the ratio of lethal to effective dose can be as low as 3 to 1 or as high as 50 to 1.

Treatment of Overdose

Barbiturate overdose patients who are awake should be kept from slipping into unconsciousness. Vomiting should be induced and activated charcoal administered to delay gastric absorption. The airway should be kept clear and vital signs monitored until there is no danger of coma. If the patient is comatose, a life-threatening emergency exists. It is then necessary to establish an intravenous fluid system, monitor vital signs, insert an endotracheal tube to maintain an airway, and perform gastric lavage with fluid containing activated charcoal. Nursing care in an intensive care unit should follow.

Tolerance and Withdrawal

Like many other drugs, barbiturates produce pharmacodynamic or CNS tolerance. They also produce metabolic tolerance and reduce the effectiveness of a number of other drugs, especially anticoagulants and tricyclic antidepressants. There is cross-tolerance with alcohol.

Withdrawal. A withdrawal reaction occurs when barbiturates are discontinued. This usually requires at least several weeks or more at doses well above the recommended therapeutic level. The barbiturate withdrawal reaction ranges from mild symptoms—such as anxiety, weakness, sweating, and insomnia—to seizures, delirium, and cardiovascular collapse leading to death (Tables 12.3-2 and 12.3-3). At its worst, it is the most severe of the drug abstinence syndromes. Pentobarbital or secobarbital users with 400-mg-a-day habits show only mild withdrawal symptoms. Users taking 800 mg a day experience orthostatic hypotension, weakness, tremor, anxiety, and considerable discomfort; about 75 percent have convulsions. Users of even higher doses may suffer from anorexia, confusion, delirium, hallucinations, psychoses, and convulsions resembling grand mal epilepsy. The psychosis is clinically indistinguishable from that of alcoholic delirium tremens. Its main features are agitation, delusions, and hallucinations that are usually visual but sometimes tactile or auditory. Fever may be present. Most of the symptoms appear in the first three days of abstinence, and seizures generally occur on the second or third day, when the symptoms are worst. If seizures do occur, they always precede the development of delirium. The syndrome rarely occurs more than a week after stopping the drug. Psychosis, if it develops, starts on the third to eighth day. The various symptoms generally run their course within two to three days but may last as long as two weeks. The first episode of the syndrome usually occurs after 5 to 15 years of heavy drug use.

Amnestic syndrome. An amnestic syndrome may occur as the result of sedative, hypnotic, or anxiolytic abuse. DSM-III-R states that the onset appears to be in the 20s, and the course is variable, having the potential for full recovery (Table 12.3-4).

Table 12.3-2
Diagnostic Criteria for Uncomplicated Sedative, Hypnotic, or Anxiolytic Withdrawal

A. Cessation of prolonged (several weeks or more) moderate or heavy use of a sedative, hypnotic, or anxiolytic, or reduction in the amount of substance used, followed by at least three of the following:
 (1) nausea or vomiting
 (2) malaise or weakness
 (3) autonomic hyperactivity (e.g., tachycardia, sweating)
 (4) anxiety or irritability
 (5) orthostatic hypotension
 (6) coarse tremor of hands, tongue, and eyelids
 (7) marked insomnia
 (8) grand mal seizures

B. Not due to any physical or other mental disorder, such as sedative, hypnotic, or anxiolytic withdrawal delirium

Note: When the differential diagnosis must be made without a clear-cut history or toxicologic analysis of body fluids, it may be qualified as "provisional."

Table 12.3-3
Diagnostic Criteria for Sedative, Hypnotic, or Anxiolytic Withdrawal Delirium

A. Delirium developing after the cessation of heavy use of a sedative, hypnotic, or anxiolytic, or a reduction in the amount of substance used (usually within one week)

B. Autonomic hyperactivity (e.g., tachycardia, sweating)

C. Not due to any physical or other mental disorder

Note: When the differential diagnosis must be made without a clear-cut history or toxicologic analysis of body fluids, it may be qualified as "provisional."

Table from DSM-III-R, *Diagnostic and Statistical Manual of Mental Disorders,* ed 3, revised. Copyright American Psychiatric Association, Washington, DC, 1987, with permission.

Table 12.3-4
Diagnostic Criteria for Sedative, Hypnotic, or Anxiolytic Amnestic Disorder

A. Amnestic syndrome following prolonged heavy use of a sedative, hypnotic, or anxiolytic

B. Not due to any physical or other mental disorder

Note: When the differential diagnosis must be made without a clear-cut history or toxicologic analysis of body fluids, it may be qualified as "provisional."

Table from DSM-III-R, *Diagnostic and Statistical Manual of Mental Disorders,* ed 3, revised. Copyright American Psychiatric Association, Washington, DC, 1987, with permission.

Lethal overdose. Dependent users often take an average daily dose of 1.5 g of a short-acting barbiturate, and some have been reported to take as much as 2.5 g a day for months. The lethal dose is not much greater for the chronic abuser than it is for the neophyte. Tolerance develops quickly to the point at which withdrawal in a hospital becomes necessary to prevent accidental death from overdose.

Treatment of withdrawal. To avoid sudden death during the withdrawal process, the clinician must use conservative treatment. First, barbiturates must be withheld from a comatose or grossly intoxicated patient until these symptoms clear. Meanwhile, the size of the habitual dose must be determined. Because the patient is not a reliable source for this information, often underestimating the dosage, family and pharmacists should be consulted for confirmation. The dose level must then be clinically verified; for example, a test dose of 200 mg pentobarbital may be given by mouth on an empty stomach and repeated every hour while the withdrawal syndrome is still evident. When a level has been attained at which mild intoxication and sedation occur, the patient should be stabilized on that dosage for one or two days. Then the dose can be gradually reduced (by no more than 10 percent a day). During this process the patient may begin to exhibit withdrawal symptoms; in that case the daily decrement should be halved.

Phenobarbital may be substituted in the withdrawal procedure for the more commonly abused short-acting barbiturates. The effects of phenobarbital last longer, and, because there is less fluctuation of barbiturate blood levels, this drug does not produce observable toxic signs or a serious overdose. An adequate dose is 30 mg of phenobarbital for every 100 mg of the short-acting substance. The user should be maintained for at least two days at this level before the dosage is reduced further. The regimen is somewhat analogous to the substitution of methadone for heroin.

After withdrawal is complete, the patient must overcome the desire to start taking the drug again. Although it has been suggested that nonbarbiturate sedative-hypnotics be substituted for barbiturates as a preventive therapeutic measure, this too often results in replacing one drug dependence with another. If a user is to remain drug-free, follow-up treatment, usually with psychiatric help and community support, is vital. Otherwise, the patient will almost certainly return to barbiturates or to a drug with similar hazards.

METHAQUALONE

Methaqualone (Quaalude) is a nonbarbiturate sedative-hypnotic used mostly by young people who believe that it heightens the sexual experience. There is no accepted medical use, and it is no longer manufactured in the United States. Most methaqualone is now manufactured here in illicit laboratories or smuggled into the United States. Users take one or two standard tablets (300 to 600 mg) to get high. Street names include "mandrakes" (from the British preparation Mandrax) and "soapers" (from the brand name Sopor). "Luding out" means taking methaqualone with alcohol, usually wine.

Adverse Effects

Undesirable effects are dryness of the mouth, headache, urticaria, dizziness, diarrhea, chills, tremors, hangover, paresthesia, menstrual disturbance, epistaxis, and depersonalization. Overdose may result in restlessness, delirium, hypertonia, muscle spasms, convulsions, and death. Unlike barbiturates, methaqualone rarely causes severe cardiovascular and respiratory depression, and most fatalities result from combining methaqualone with alcohol. Treatment consists mainly of supportive measures to maintain vital functions. If a patient who is still conscious recently ingested the drug, gastric lavage is indicated.

BENZODIAZEPINES

The benzodiazepines include about 20 drugs, such as diazepam (Valium), flurazepam (Dalmane), oxazepam (Serax), and chlordiazepoxide (Librium). They are used mainly to treat anxiety but are also used as sedatives, muscle relaxants, anticonvulsants, and anesthetics and in the treatment of alcohol withdrawal. Introduced in the 1960s, benzodiazepines soon became some of the most popular prescription drugs in the United States. About 15 percent of persons in this country have had a benzodiazepine prescribed by a physician; however, a recent substantial decline in medical use suggests that physicians are becoming more cautious about them. All benzodiazepines are classified in category IV of controlled substances by Drug Enforcement Agency (DEA) regulations. Diazepam is frequently taken by cocaine addicts to minimize the withdrawal reaction following cocaine intoxication and is taken by opioid addicts to enhance euphoria. The abuse incidence is unknown.

Mechanism of Action

The benzodiazepines exert their effects on the $GABA_A$ receptor complex. This complex includes a binding site for benzodiazepinelike drugs. When benzodiazepines bind to this site, the effects of GABA are enhanced, so that more chloride ions flow through the associated ion channel into the neuron. This results in inhibition of the neuron. A benzodiazepine antagonist, flumazenil, reverses the effects of benzodiazepines. It is useful in overdosage but may cause a withdrawal syndrome. Flumazenil is not yet available in the United States.

Adverse Effects

Unlike barbiturates, benzodiazepines do not cause microsomal enzyme induction or rapid eye movement (REM) sleep suppression, and they have a high margin of safety. Benzodiazepines produce little respiratory depression, and the ratio of lethal to effective dose is very high, approximately 200 to 1 or more. Very large amounts (more than 2 g) taken in suicide attempts produce drowsiness, lethargy, ataxia, some confusion, and mild depression of vital signs. The adverse effects of lower doses include drowsiness, unsteadiness, and weakness.

Some benzodiazepines have a disinhibiting effect, which may cause hostile or aggressive behavior in people susceptible to frustration. Benzodiazepines produce less euphoria than other tranquilizing drugs, so the risk of dependence and abuse is relatively low. But both tolerance and withdrawal symptoms can develop. The withdrawal reaction—for example, from diazepam—is most likely to occur at cessation of dosages in the 40-mg-a-day range, but it can occur at therapeutic dosages (as low as 10 or 20 mg a day) if the drug has been used for a month or more. The onset of withdrawal usually occurs within two or three days after cessation of use, but with longer-acting drugs, such as diazepam, the latency before onset may be five or six days. Symptoms include anxiety, numbness in the extremities, dysphoria, intolerance for bright lights and loud noises, nausea, sweating, muscle twitching, and sometimes convulsions (generally at dosages of 100 mg a day or more). Because benzodiazepines are eliminated from the body slowly, symptoms may continue to develop for several weeks. To prevent seizures and other problems, the clinician should reduce the dosage gradually.

LEGAL ISSUES

Attempts have been made by state and federal agencies to further restrict the distribution of benzodiazepines by requiring special reporting forms. For example, through the use of New York State triplicate prescription forms, the names of doctors and patients are kept on file in a data bank. Such measures have been taken to stem the tide of abuse. But most abuse is the result of the illicit manufacture, sale, and diversion of these drugs, particularly to cocaine and opioid addicts, and not from physicians' prescriptions or legitimate pharmaceutical companies. To attempt to curtail the use of these drugs, which have unquestionable and invaluable therapeutic benefits, is an example of increasing governmental interference in the practice of medicine and in the confidential relationship between doctor and patient. Such restrictions will do little to curb cocaine, opioid, or benzodiazepine abuse.

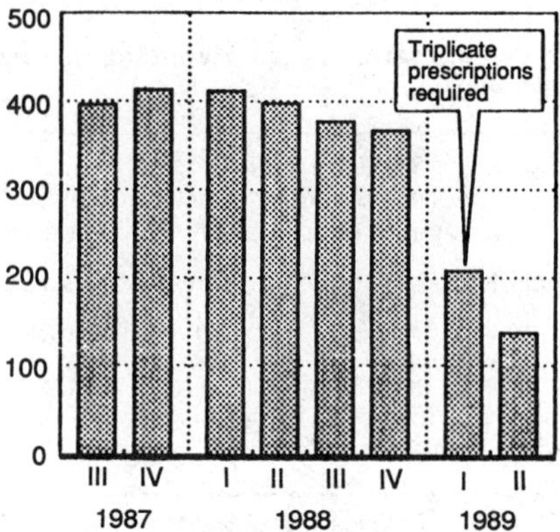

Figure 12.3-1. Number (in thousands) of prescriptions paid for by New York State Medicaid for benzodiazepines, including diazepam (Valium) and alprazolam (Xanax). (Source: New York State Department of Health. Courtesy of *The Wall Street Journal,* Jan. 30, 1990.)

Although the number of benzodiazepine prescriptions has decreased in New York State (Figure 12.3-1), whether this is due to improved medical prescribing standards of practice or to the intimidation of physicians is open to question.

References

Busto U E, Sykora K, Sellers E M: A clinical scale to assess benzodiazepine withdrawal. J Clin Psychopharmacol *9*: 412, 1989.

Dominguez R A, Goldstein B J: 25 years of benzodiazepine experience: Clinical commentary on use, abuse, and withdrawal. Hosp Formul *20*: 1000, 1985.

Fialip J, Aumaitre O, Eschalier A, Maradeix B, Dordain G, Lavarenne J: Benzodiazepine withdrawal seizures: Analysis of 48 case reports. Clin Neuropharmacol *6*: 538, 1987.

Martin I L: The benzodiazepines and their receptors: 25 years of progress. Neuropharmacology *26*: 957, 1987.

Noyes R, Garvey M J, Cook B L, Perry P J: Benzodiazepine withdrawal: A review of the evidence. J Clin Psychiatry *49*: 382, 1988.

O'Brien C P, Woody G E: Sedative-hypnotics and antianxiety agents. In *Psychiatry Update,* vol 5, A J Frances and R E Hales, editors. American Psychiatric Press, Washington, DC, 1986.

Rickels K, Schweizer E, Case G, Greenblatt D J: Long-term therapeutic use of benzodiazepines: I. Effects of abrupt discontinuation. Arch Gen Psychiatry *47*: 899, 1990.

Roth M: Anxiety disorders and the use and abuse of drugs. J Clin Psychiatry *50* (11, Suppl): 30, 1989.

Roy-Byrne P P, Homer D: Benzodiazepine withdrawal: Overview and implications for the treatment of anxiety. Am J Med *84*: 1041, 1988.

Uhlenhuth R H, DeWit H, Balter M B, Johanson C E, Mellinger G D: Risks and benefits of long-term benzodiazepine use. J Clin Psychopharmacol *8*: 161, 1988.

Woods J H, Katz J L, Winger G: Use and abuse of benzodiazepines. JAMA *260*: 3476, 1988.

12.4 / Opioid-Related Disorders

Opium is obtained from the juice of the opium poppy, *Papaver somniferum*. About 20 distinct opioid alkaloids are derived from opium, the best-known of which is morphine. Other opioid alkaloids occur naturally or can be synthesized from morphine, including heroin (diacetylmorphine), codeine, and hydromorphine (Dilaudid). Synthetic opioids made only in the laboratory include meperidine (Demerol), methadone, and propoxyphene (Darvon). Opioid antagonists, synthetic compounds that block the action of opium, include naloxone (Narcan), naltrexone (Trexan), nalorphine, levallorphan, and apomorphine. Mixed agents with both agonist and antagonist properties include pentazocine (Talwin), butorphanol (Stadol), and buprenorphine (Buprenex).

DSM-III-R CLASSIFICATION

Within the psychoactive substance use disorders, there are diagnoses for both opioid dependence and opioid abuse. Opioid intoxication and opioid withdrawal are diagnoses within the psychoactive substance-induced organic mental disorders.

EPIDEMIOLOGY

Heroin is the most widely abused opiate. Epidemics of heroin abuse occurred in the United States during the mid-1960s, the mid-1970s, and the early 1980s. Psychiatric epidemiological studies conducted from 1981 to 1983 found that 0.7 percent of the adult population had met the third edition of *Diagnostic and Statistical Manual of Mental Disorders* (DSM-III) diagnostic criteria for opioid abuse or dependence at some time in their lives. Heroin is smuggled into the United States primarily from the Middle and Far East, where the opium poppy is a major cash crop. There are an estimated 400,000 to 600,000 heroin addicts in this country. It has been estimated that almost half of all opioid addicts in the United States live in New York City. Male addicts outnumber female addicts by a ratio of 3 to 1. Most heroin addicts are in their early to mid-30s and started using drugs in their late teens or early 20s. Heroin addicts may spend $200 or more a day to support their habit, most of that money being obtained by criminal activity.

A variety of risk factors have been associated with heroin abuse. Intravenous drug abuse contributes to hepatitis B viral infection and more recently to acquired immune deficiency syndrome (AIDS). Intravenous drug abusers make up a major group at risk for AIDS and are a source of contamination to the general population through coital transmission. There is no permissible medical use for heroin in the United States.

MECHANISM OF ACTION

Opioids exert their effect by binding to specific sites in the brain that have been identified as opioid receptors. Antagonists, such as naltrexone, block opioid binding sites and reverse or block opioid effects. In 1974 enkephalin, an endogenous pentapeptide with opiatelike actions, was identified. This led to the identification of three classes of endogenous opiates within the brain, including the endorphins and enkephalins.

Endorphins are involved in neural transmission and serve to suppress pain. They are released naturally in the body when a person is physically hurt and account in part for the absence of pain during acute injury states. Heroin is more potent and more lipid-soluble than morphine; it crosses the blood-brain barrier in less time and produces a more rapid onset of action than morphine. Codeine, 3-methoxymorphine, occurs naturally (0.5 percent) in opium. After absorption, it is transformed to some degree into morphine and binds to the same neuroanatomical sites. Synthetic opioids—such as methadone, meperidine, and pentazocine—also bind to opioid receptors.

A recent positron emission tomographic (PET) study with [F^{18}]fluorodeoxyglucose of polydrug abusers reported that morphine reduced brain glucose utilization approximately 10 percent (Figure 12.4-1). This effect was most pronounced in particular cerebral and cerebellar cortical regions.

TOLERANCE AND DEPENDENCE

Changes in the number or sensitivity of opioid receptors may occur as the result of continuous exposure to opioids

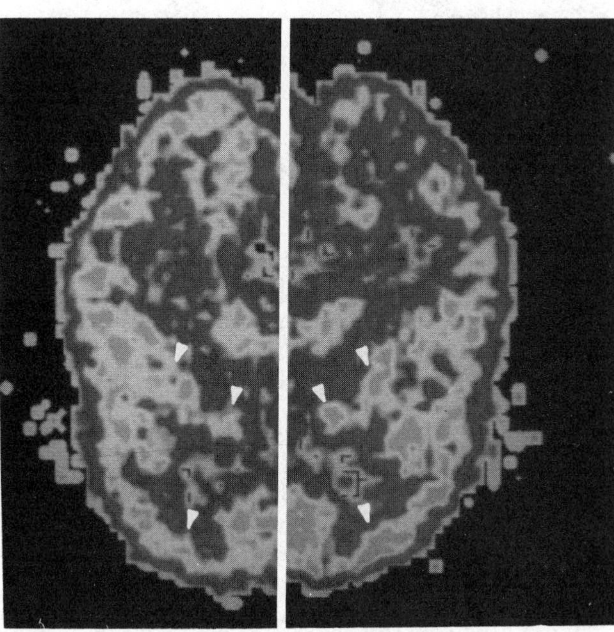

Figure 12.4-1. Glucose utilization, as revealed by positron emission tomography, in the brain of a heroin addict. High rates are pictured as light areas. On the left, the addict was given placebo. On the right, the addict was given 30 mg of morphine intramuscularly. (Courtesy of E. D. London, Ph.D.)

and can produce dependence on the drug. Intracellular changes in calcium, cyclic adenosine monophosphate (AMP), and adenyl nucleotides also result from chronic exposure. When the drug is displaced from its receptor (by an antagonist) or is unavailable (as in abstinence), a withdrawal syndrome occurs. Some tolerance probably develops in humans within the first four doses, but a longer period of continuous receptor occupancy by an opioid agonist is necessary before a withdrawal syndrome will develop when the drug is stopped. Withdrawal responses are more intense and more readily detectable when the opioid is rapidly removed from its receptor, as by an opioid antagonist. Chronic use may also induce supersensitivity of the dopaminergic, cholinergic, and serotonergic systems. The activity of adrenergic neurons in the locus ceruleus decreases. Rebound hyperactivity of those systems occurs with abstinence. Clonidine (Catapres), an adrenergic alpha-2 agonist, inhibits the activity of neurons in the locus ceruleus, which may explain its ability to block the withdrawal syndrome. A clinical case example follows:

A 42-year-old executive in a public relations firm was referred for psychiatric consultation by his surgeon, who discovered him sneaking large quantities of a codeine-containing cough medicine into the hospital. The patient had been a heavy cigarette smoker for 20 years and had a chronic, hacking cough. He had come to the hospital for a hernia repair and found the pain from the incision unbearable when he coughed.

An operation on his back five years ago had led his doctor to prescribe codeine to help relieve the incisional pain. Over the intervening five years, however, the patient had continued to use codeine-containing tablets and had increased his intake to 60 to 90 5-mg tablets daily. He stated that he often "just took them by the handful—not to feel good, you understand, just to get by." He had spent considerable time and effort developing a circle of physicians and pharmacists to whom he would make the rounds at least three times a week to obtain new supplies of pills. He had tried several times to stop using codeine but had failed. During this period he lost two jobs because of lax work habits and was divorced by his wife of 11 years.

ETIOLOGY

Psychosocial Factors

In psychoanalytic literature, the behavior of narcotic addicts was described in terms of libidinal fixation, with regression to pregenital, oral, or even more archaic levels of psychosexual development. Most notably, the oral state was emphasized. The need to explain the relationship of drug abuse, defense, impulse control, affective disturbances, and adaptive mechanisms led to the recent shift in dynamic formulations, emphasizing ego psychology.

Serious ego pathology is often thought to be associated with drug abuse and is considered to be indicative of profound developmental disturbances. Problems of the relationship between the ego and affects emerge as a key area of difficulty; the problems include affective experiencing, control, intensity, and ambivalence.

There are possible but not definitive warning signs among children who may turn to drugs in later years. These high-risk signs include early health problems, behavioral problems at mealtimes and in school, mild conduct disorders, and a lack of self-confidence. High-risk children also reflect a self-centered philosophy of life, coupled with antiauthoritarian views.

It seems that the parents themselves are often deeply involved in using prescribed or nonprescribed drugs or alcohol. By and large, the symptom of drug taking by the child is derivative or a reflection of the whole family's attitude of inconsistency and self-centeredness.

Environmental Factors

In recent years the steady increase in the number of middle-class addicts from privileged homes has cast doubt on any exclusive relationship between addiction and socioeconomic status.

Concomitant with the spread of heroin addiction from the minorities to the white population was a drop in the average age of heroin users. The initiation of heroin use reaches a peak at age 16 to 17. Social situation is most important in initiating drug experimentation and use. The age of initiation has been dropping steadily. Some 10- and 11-year-old children are now experimenting with opioids.

Certain consistent behavior patterns seem especially pronounced in adolescent addicts. These patterns have been called the heroin behavior syndrome: underlying depression, often of an agitated type and frequently accompanied by anxiety symptoms; impulsiveness expressed by a passive-aggressive orientation; fear of failure; use of heroin as an antianxiety agent to mask feelings of low self-esteem, hopelessness, and aggression; limited coping strategies and low frustration tolerance, accompanied by the need for immediate gratification; sensitivity to drug contingencies, with a keen awareness of the relation between good feelings and the act of drug taking; feelings of behavioral impotence counteracted by momentary control over the life situation by means of drugs; disturbances in social and interpersonal relations with peers maintained by mutual drug experiences.

With authentic engagement not attractive or feasible for many, drug abuse becomes, for a small but growing minority, a form of identification and engagement.

More than 50 percent of urban heroin users belong to single-parent or divorced families; alcoholism and drug abuse are common among the families of drug abusers. Neonatal addiction is a significant problem; approximately three-fourths of infants born to addicted mothers experience the withdrawal syndrome. Close to 90 percent of opioid addicts have a diagnosed psychiatric disorder, most often depression. Alcoholism, antisocial personality, and anxiety are the next most common disorders. Suicidal ideation is frequent; in one study, 13 percent of heroin addicts had made at least one suicide attempt.

CLINICAL EFFECTS

The clinical effects of morphine may be used as the model for all opioids. Analgesia, drowsiness, mood changes, and mental clouding follow ingestion of small amounts of the drug (5 to 10 mg). The analgesic effects peak about 20 minutes after intravenous injection or one hour after subcutaneous injection and last four to six hours, depending on the type of opioid, the dose, and the drug-taking history. Other manifestations are a feeling of warmth, heaviness of the extremities, and dry mouth. The face, particularly the nose, may itch and become flushed (this effect may occur from a release of histamine). Some patients experience euphoria, which may last 10 to 30 minutes. For many people the effect of taking an opioid for the first time is dysphoric, rather than euphoric, and nausea and vomiting may result. Among the intravenous users, an immediate high, described as being akin to an orgasm (called a rush) is reported when the drug reaches the brain a few minutes after injection. That is followed by sedation (known as nodding off). Morphine analgesia does not involve the sensitivity of the nerve ending to noxious stimuli or the conduction of nerve impulses. Rather, perception of pain is altered, so that the patient becomes indifferent to it.

Morphine is a respiratory depressant because of its direct effect on the brain stem respiratory center; in humans death from overdose is nearly always due to respiratory arrest. Changes in blood pressure, heart rate, and cerebral circulation may also occur but are not as prominent. Idiosyncratic responses such as allergic reactions, anaphylactic shock, and pulmonary edema account for cases of sudden death. The depressant effects of morphine and other opioids may be enhanced by phenothiazines and monoamine oxidase inhibitors (MAOIs). Fatalities have been reported in patients receiving antidepressants, especially MAOIs, who were also given meperidine. Other effects of morphine include pupillary constriction, smooth muscle contraction (including ureters and bile ducts), and constipation.

Heroin, pharmacologically similar to morphine, induces analgesia, drowsiness, and changes in mood. The pleasurable and euphoric actions of heroin are about twice as potent as those of morphine. Although the manufacture, sale, and possession of heroin are illegal in the United States, attempts have been made to make heroin available to pain-ridden terminal cancer patients because of its excellent analgesic and euphoric effects. Many people, including legislators, favor a change in the law, but such legislation has been repeatedly voted down by the U.S. Congress.

Tolerance to opioids develops in terminally ill patients, who may require 200 to 300 mg of morphine a day to manage pain. Tolerance to the respiratory depressant effects does not develop, however, which places such patients at risk if their needs for opiates are met. Many patients suffer unnecessary pain before they die because physicians are unwilling to prescribe such large doses or because of restrictive legislation.

INTOXICATION AND OVERDOSE

Opioid intoxication occurs after the recurrent use of an opioid and is characterized by altered mood, psychomotor retardation, drowsiness, slurred speech, and impaired memory or attention (Table 12.4-1). An overdose is life-threatening and is characterized by marked unresponsiveness, coma, slow respiration, hypothermia, hypotension, shock, and bradycardia. Death is usually from respiratory arrest. Needle tracks in the arms, legs, ankles, groin, or even the dorsal vein of the penis of an unconscious patient should alert the physician to the possibility of narcotic overdose (Figures 12.4-2 and 12.4-3). The triad of coma, pinpoint pupils, and respiratory depression suggests opioid overdose.

Table 12.4-1
Diagnostic Criteria for Opioid Intoxication

A. Recent use of an opioid

B. Maladaptive behavioral changes (e.g., initial euphoria followed by apathy, dysphoria, psychomotor retardation, impaired judgment, impaired social or occupational functioning)

C. Pupillary constriction (or pupillary dilation due to anoxia from severe overdose) and at least one of the following signs:
(1) drowsiness
(2) slurred speech
(3) impairment in attention or memory

D. Not due to any physical or other mental disorder

Note: When the differential diagnosis must be made without a clear-cut history, testing with an opioid antagonist, or toxicologic analysis of body fluids, it may be qualified as "provisional."

Table from DSM-III-R, *Diagnostic and Statistical Manual of Mental Disorders*, ed 3, revised. Copyright American Psychiatric Association, Washington, DC, 1987, with permission.

MPTP-Induced Parkinsonism

In 1976, after ingesting a synthetic opioid contaminated with MPTP (N-methyl-4-phenyl-1,2,3,6 tetrahydropyridine), a number of persons developed a syndrome of irreversible parkinsonism. The mechanism for the neurotoxic effect is as follows: MPTP is converted into 1-methyl-4-phenylpyridinium (MPP^+) by the enzyme monoamine oxidase and then is taken up by dopaminergic neurons. Because MPP^+ binds to melanin in substantia nigra neurons, MPP^+ is concentrated in these neurons and eventually kills the cells. Positron emission tomographic (PET) studies of persons who ingested MPTP but who remained asymptomatic have actually shown a decrease in the number of dopamine binding sites in the substantia nigra.

Treatment of Overdose

Opioid overdose is a medical emergency. The patient's respiration is severely depressed, and he or she may be semicomatose or comatose or in shock. The first task is to ensure that there is an open airway and that vital signs are maintained. An opioid antagonist, naloxone, is administered, 0.4 mg intravenously; that dose can be repeated four to five times within the first 30 to 45 minutes. The patient generally becomes more responsive, but, because naloxone has a short duration of action, the patient may relapse into a semicomatose state in four or five hours; therefore, careful observation is imperative. Grand mal seizures occur with meperidine overdose and are prevented by naloxone. Antagonists must be used carefully because they can precipitate a severe withdrawal reaction. Other narcotic antagonists include nalorphine and levallorphan.

Figure 12.4-2. A heroin user puffs her cheeks to force blood into the jugular vein. (Courtesy of Steve Raymer, Copyright National Geographic Society, 1985.)

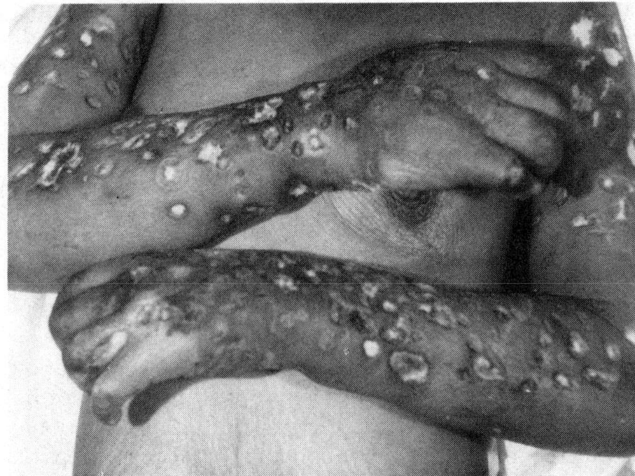

Figure 12.4-3. Skin-popper: Circular depressed scars, often with underlying chronic abscesses, can result from skin-popping. (Courtesy of Michael Baden, M.D.)

Table 12.4-2
Opioid Withdrawal Symptoms

Behavioral	Physical
Anxiety	Sweating
Craving for opioids	Fever
Insomnia	Rhinorrhea
Anorexia	Mydriasis
Agitation	Piloerection
Possible violence	Nausea and vomiting
	Cardiovascular instability: hypertension, tachycardia
	Abdominal cramping
	Grand mal seizures with meperidine

WITHDRAWAL

Morphine and heroin addicts may take hundreds of milligrams of heroin; as much as 5,000 mg of morphine has been taken by tolerant addicts. In nontolerant persons death from overdose may occur with 60 mg of morphine. The morphine and heroin withdrawal syndrome begins in six to eight hours after the last dose, usually after a one- to two-week period of continuous use or the administration of a narcotic antagonist. The withdrawal syndrome reaches its peak intensity during the second or third day and subsides during the next 7 to 10 days. However, some symptoms may persist for six months or longer (Table 12.4-2). The withdrawal syndrome from meperidine begins more quickly, reaches a peak in 8 to 12 hours, and is complete in four to five days. Methadone withdrawal usually begins one to three days after the last dose and is complete in 10 to 14 days. The general rule is that substances with short durations of action tend to produce short, intense withdrawal syndromes, and substances that have long durations of action produce prolonged but mild withdrawal syndromes. An exception to the rule, narcotic antagonist-precipitated withdrawal after long-acting substance addiction, can be very severe.

The withdrawal syndrome consists of severe muscle cramps and bone aches, profuse diarrhea, abdominal cramps, rhinorrhea, lacrimination, piloerection or gooseflesh (from which comes the name "cold turkey" for the abstinence syndrome), yawning, fever, pupillary dilation, hypertension, tachycardia, and temperature dysregulation, including fever (Table 12.4-3). An addict seldom dies from withdrawal, unless there is a severe preexisting physical illness, such as cardiac disease. Residual effects of insomnia, bradycardia, changes in temperature, and a craving for opioids may persist for months after withdrawal. At any time during the abstinence syndrome, a single injection of morphine or heroin eliminates all symptoms. Associated features include restlessness, irritability, depression, tremor, weakness, nausea, and vomiting. All the symptoms described resemble the clinical picture of influenza. An abstinence syndrome may be precipitated by the administration of an antagonist. The symptoms may begin within 60 seconds after such an intravenous injection and peak in about one hour. It is relatively uncommon for opioid craving to occur in the context of analgesic administration for pain from physical disorders or associated with surgery. The full withdrawal syndrome, including intense craving for opioids, usually occurs only secondary to an abrupt cessation of use in opioid-dependent persons.

Table 12.4-3
Diagnostic Criteria for Opioid Withdrawal

A. Cessation of prolonged (several weeks or more) moderate or heavy use of an opioid, or reduction in the amount of opioid used (or administration of an opioid antagonist after a brief period of use), followed by at least three of the following:
(1) craving for an opioid
(2) nausea or vomiting
(3) muscle aches
(4) lacrimation or rhinorrhea
(5) pupillary dilation, piloerection, or sweating
(6) diarrhea
(7) yawning
(8) fever
(9) insomnia

B. Not due to any physical or other mental disorder

Table from DSM-III-R, *Diagnostic and Statistical Manual of Mental Disorders*, ed 3, revised. Copyright American Psychiatric Association, Washington, DC, 1987, with permission.

Treatment of Withdrawal

Methadone. Methadone is a synthetic opioid that substitutes for heroin and can be taken orally. It is given to addicts in place of their usual drug of abuse and suppresses withdrawal symptoms. The action of methadone is such that 20 to 80 mg a day (although doses up to 120 mg a day have been used) is sufficient to stabilize the patient. It has a duration of action exceeding 24 hours. Methadone maintenance is continued until the patient can be withdrawn from methadone, which is itself addicting. Patients are detoxified from methadone more easily than from heroin, although a similar abstinence syndrome occurs with methadone. Usually clonidine (0.1 to 0.3 mg, three to four times a day) is given during the detoxification period.

Levo-α-acetylmethadol (LAMM) is a longer-acting opioid than methadone. In contrast to the daily methadone treatment, LAMM can be administered in dosages of 30 to 80 mg three times a week.

Methadone maintenance has several advantages: It frees the addict from dependence on injectable heroin (invariably taken with contaminated needles); it is legal; it causes minimal euphoria and rarely causes drowsiness or depression when taken chronically; and it allows the person to engage in gainful employment, instead of criminal activity. The disadvantage is that the patient remains addicted to a narcotic.

Pregnant addict. Although opioid withdrawal is almost never fatal for the otherwise healthy adult, opioid withdrawal is hazardous to the fetus and can lead to miscarriage or fetal death. Maintaining the pregnant addict on low dosages of methadone (10 to 40 mg a day) may be the least hazardous course to follow. At this dosage, neonatal withdrawal is usually mild and can be managed with low doses of paregoric. If the pregnancy begins while the patient is on a high dosage of methadone, the dosage should be reduced slowly (e.g., 1 mg every three days), and fetal movements should be monitored. If withdrawal is necessary or desired, it is accomplished with least hazard during the second trimester.

The other major risk for the fetus of an opioid-addicted woman is AIDS. Pregnant women can pass the causative agent of AIDS, the human immunodeficiency virus (HIV), to the fetus through placental circulation. The HIV-infected mother can also pass HIV to the infant through breast feeding.

Opioid antagonists. Opioid antagonists block or antagonize the effects of opioids, preventing them from acting. Unlike methadone, they do not in themselves exert narcotic effects, nor are they addicting. The antagonists include the following drugs: naloxone, which is used in the treatment of opioid overdose because it reverses the effects of narcotics, and naltrexone, which is the longest-acting (72 hours) antagonist. The theory behind the use of antagonists for opioid addiction is that the blocking of drug effects, particularly euphoria, discourages addicts from drug-seeking behavior and thus deconditions them to opioids. The major weakness of the antagonist model is the lack of any mechanism compelling addicts to continue to take the antagonist.

Therapeutic community. The therapeutic community is a residence composed of members who all have the same problem of drug abuse. Abstinence is the rule, and, in order to be admitted to such a community, the person requires a high level of motivation. The goals are to effect a complete change of life-style, including abstinence from drugs; the development of personal honesty, responsibility, and useful social skills; and the elimination of antisocial attitudes and criminal behavior.

The staff of most therapeutic communities is made up of former addicts, who often put the prospective candidate through a rigorous screening process to test motivation. Self-help through the use of confrontational groups and isolation from the outside world and from friends associated with the drug life are emphasized. The prototypical community for addicts is Phoenix House, where patients live for long periods (usually 12 to 18 months) while receiving treatment. They are allowed to return to their old environments only when they have demonstrated their ability to handle increased responsibility in the center. Therapeutic communities are effective, but they require large staffs and extensive facilities. Moreover, dropout rates are high; as many as 75 percent of those who enter therapeutic communities leave within the first month.

References

Harding G: Patterns of heroin use: What do we know? Br J Addict *83*: 1247, 1988.

Herridge P, Gold M S: Pharmacological adjuncts in the treatment of opioid and cocaine addicts. J Psychoactive Drugs *20*: 233, 1988.

Jaffe J H: Drug dependence: Opioids, nonnarcotics, nicotine (tobacco), and caffeine. In *Comprehensive Textbook of Psychiatry*, ed 5, H I Kaplan and B J Sadock, editors, p 642. Williams & Wilkins, Baltimore, 1989.

Jasinski D R, Johnson R E, Kocher T R: Clonidine in morphine withdrawal. Arch Gen Psychiatry *42*: 1063, 1985.

Khantzian E J, Treece C: DSM-III psychiatric diagnosis of narcotic addicts: Recent findings. Arch Gen Psychiatry *42*: 1067, 1985.

Kleber H D, Weissman M M, Rounsaville B J, Wilber C H, Prusoff B A, Riordan C E: Imipramine as treatment for depression in addicts. Arch Gen Psychiatry *40*: 649, 1983.

Kosten T R, Rounsaville B J, Kleber H D: A 25-year follow-up of depression, life crises, and effects on abstinence among opioid addicts. Arch Gen Psychiatry *43*: 733, 1986.

Kreek M J: Opiate-ethanol interactions: Implications for the biological basis and treatment of combined addictive diseases. NIDA Res Monogr *81*: 428, 1988.

London E D, Broussolle E P M, Links J M, Wong D F, Cascella N G, Dannals R F, Sano M, Herning R, Snyder F R, Rippetoe L R, Toung

T J K, Jaffe J H, Wagner H W: Morphine-induced metabolic changes in human brain. Arch Gen Psychiatry *47*: 73, 1990.
Mansour A, Khachaturian H, Lewis M E, Akil H, Watson S J: Anatomy of CNS opioid receptors. TINS *11*: 308, 1988.
Milby J B: Methadone maintenance to abstinence: How many make it? J Nerv Ment Dis *176*: 409, 1988.
Rounsaville B J, Kleber H D: Untreated opiate addicts: How do they differ from those seeking treatment? Arch Gen Psychiatry *42*: 1072, 1985.
Rounsaville B J, Kosten T R, Weissman M M, Kleber H D: Prognostic significance of psychopathology in treated opiate addicts. A 25-year follow-up study. Arch Gen Psychiatry *43*: 739, 1986.
Woody G E, McLellan A T, Luborsky L, O'Brien C: Twelve-month follow-up of psychotherapy for opiate dependence. Am J Psychiatry *144*: 590, 1987.
Woody G E, O'Brien C P, McLellan A T: Treatments for opiate dependence. Psychiatr Ann *14*: 257, 1984.

12.5 / Cocaine

The addictive properties of cocaine and the serious consequences of its use are more fully appreciated today than they were in the 1960s and 1970s, when cocaine was erroneously considered a largely innocuous drug. In the 1980s the general population, as well as the medical profession, became aware of an increasing number of cocaine-related deaths and more cocaine-related psychosocial pathology. The introduction of crack, an especially addictive form of cocaine, further highlighted cocaine abuse as a very serious medical and neuropsychiatric problem.

Cocaine (snow, coke, girl, lady) is an alkaloid derived from the shrub *Erythroxylon coca,* a plant indigenous to Bolivia and Peru, where its leaves are chewed by peasants for their stimulating effect. Cocaine was isolated in 1860, and after 1884 it became the first effective local anesthetic, the only purpose for which it is still used in medicine. In the 1880s and 1890s cocaine was used therapeutically in a variety of ways. In 1914 cocaine was placed under the same laws as morphine and heroin and was legally classified as a narcotic.

DSM-III-R CLASSIFICATION

In the revised third edition of *Diagnostic and Statistical Manual of Mental Disorders* (DSM-III-R), diagnoses related to cocaine are included within the psychoactive substance-induced organic mental disorders and within the psychoactive substance use disorders. Within the psychoactive substance use disorders, both cocaine abuse and cocaine dependence are diagnoses. Cocaine intoxication, withdrawal, delirium, and delusional disorder are diagnoses within the psychoactive substance-induced organic mental disorders.

EPIDEMIOLOGY

According to the National Institute on Drug Abuse (NIDA) (July 1989): (1) The number of current cocaine users decreased significantly (50 percent) from 5.8 million in 1985 to 2.9 million in 1988. The rate decreased from 3 percent of the household population aged 12 and older in 1985 to 1.5 percent in 1988. (2) Among the 8.2 million people who used cocaine in the past year, 11 percent used the drug once a week or more, and 4 percent used the drug daily or almost daily. Although this represents a decrease in past-year users from 12.2 million in 1985, only 5 percent of the 1985 users were weekly users, and 2 percent were daily or almost daily users. (3) Rates of use of cocaine in the past year declined for youth (aged 12 to 17) from 4 to 3 percent; for young adults (aged 18 to 25) from 16 to 12 percent; and for older adults (aged 26+) from 4 to 3 percent. (4) Over half (53 percent) of youth in 1988 believed that trying cocaine poses a great risk, compared with only 31 percent of youth in 1985. A similar increase in awareness of the danger of cocaine use occurred in young and older adults. (5) The rate of current (past month) cocaine use was 1.5 percent overall. The demographic subgroups for which the rates of current cocaine use were the highest were the unemployed (4.6 percent) and those aged 18 to 25 (4.5 percent). The rate of current cocaine use for males (2 percent) was twice as high as that for females (1 percent). (6) While lifetime prevalence of cocaine use remained stable for whites and blacks, a significant increase occurred among Hispanics between 1985 and 1988, from 7 to 11 percent. The Hispanic population also did not experience a decrease in current cocaine use during the period. (7) Approximately 1.9 million (8 percent) lifetime cocaine users have used cocaine intravenously at some time in their lives, and 2 percent have done so during the past year. Thirty-one percent of past-year users smoked cocaine during the past year. (8) Approximately 1.3 percent of the population aged 12 and over have used crack (a form of freebase cocaine) at some time in their lives, and one-half of one percent used in the past year. This translates to about 1 million past-year crack users. Past-year crack use is highest among 18 to 25 year olds (2 percent). There are almost half a million current crack users. (Crack is marketed at approximately $5 to $10 for a 65- to 100-mg dose [in contrast to approximately $100 for 1 g of pure cocaine powder].) (9) There were approximately 900 cocaine-related deaths in 1988.

PHARMACOLOGY

The main pharmacological effect of cocaine is the blockade of reuptake of serotonin and the catecholamine neurotransmitters, particularly dopamine. The euphoria produced by cocaine is intense, and cocaine may, in fact, be the most addictive drug available to drug users. Psychological dependence may occur after a single dose of this drug. The effects of cocaine are much shorter than those of amphetamine, usually lasting 30 minutes to an hour after intravenous or intranasal use; however, some research data suggest that active metabolites of cocaine may remain in the brain for as long as 10 days. There is often a period of depression following the acute drug effect. This depression can include suicidal ideation, particularly after periods of extensive cocaine use (e.g., an entire day).

METHODS OF USE

Street cocaine varies greatly in purity. It is usually cut with sugar, procaine, amphetamine, or other substances. It is rarely taken by mouth, because the effect is regarded as too mild to warrant the expense. There are three widespread methods of ingestion: inhaling (snorting), subcutaneous or intravenous injection, and freebasing (smoking). Inhalation is the most common and least dangerous method, but it does not provide the ecstatic sensation of smoking or injection. Freebasers mix street cocaine and chemically extracted pure cocaine alkaloid (the free base) to produce a strong effect when smoked. Both smoking and injection are frequently associated with cocaine-induced cardiac arrest.

Crack

Crack, an extremely potent freebase form of cocaine, is sold in small, ready-to-smoke amounts. Its existence has increased the number of persons with cocaine addiction. Crack cocaine is so addictive, in fact, that persons have been known to literally sell their children into prostitution to obtain money for the drug. Many urban emergency rooms and police departments report extremes of violent behavior in crack-addicted persons.

Chronic Use

Chronic use is associated with a runny or clogged nose, which is often self-treated with nasal decongestant sprays. Noses may also become inflamed, swollen, or ulcerated; heavy users occasionally have perforated septa. Freebasing may damage the surface of the lungs, and injection involves the usual dangers of infection and embolism as well as an increased risk of contracting acquired immune deficiency syndrome (AIDS) through the practice of sharing needles.

COCAINE USE DISORDERS

Cocaine abuse is common among middle-class and upper-socioeconomic-status persons. In such persons cocaine abuse can be associated with severe disruption in job performance and family life. Even infrequent cocaine abuse can lead to accidental overdose resulting in death.

Cocaine abuse can also lead to cocaine dependence, even in persons who thought they were not at risk for becoming dependent. In fact, the treatment of cocaine abuse and dependence has become a large percentage of clinical practice in public and private inpatient psychiatric hospitals.

COCAINE-INDUCED ORGANIC MENTAL DISORDERS

The central nervous system (CNS) effects of cocaine are similar to those of amphetamine—elation, euphoria, heightened self-esteem, and improved performance of mental and physical tasks. The peripheral sympathomimetic effect of vasoconstriction and the analgesic effect account for its being the anesthetic of choice for many surgical procedures of the eye, ear, nose, and throat.

Cocaine Intoxication

Cocaine intoxication is characterized by extreme agitation, irritability, impaired judgment, impulsive sexual behavior, aggression, increased psychomotor activity, and manic excitement (Table 12.5-1). Tachycardia, hypertension, and mydriasis occur. The course of cocaine intoxication is usually self-limited, full recovery occurring within 48 hours. As the drug's effects wear off, the person experiences marked dysphoria and agitation, which can be relieved by taking more cocaine. The dysphoric mood (or crash) is associated with anxiety, irritability, and fatigue. When the crash extends beyond 24 hours after the last use of cocaine, it becomes cocaine withdrawal. As an alternative, the person may use alcohol, sedatives, or antianxiety agents, such as diazepam (Valium), to alleviate these symptoms.

Adverse effects. Although cocaine is often used as an aphrodisiac and as a method to delay orgasm, both acute use and chronic use often lead to impotence. Common neurological effects include focal neurological signs and symptoms, such as numbness and weakness; persistent headache; and loss of consciousness. Life-threatening neurological conditions associated with cocaine abuse include seizures and strokes. These neurological complications may be related to the cortical atrophy that has been noted on computed tomography (CT) examination of cocaine abusers in some research studies.

Cocaine-related deaths. In high doses cocaine can induce seizures and depression of the medullary centers of respiration, resulting in death from cardiac or respiratory arrest. Often, periods of syncope or chest pain that are warning signs that the cocaine abuser ignores precede death. In fact, studies show that laboratory animals self-administer cocaine until they die. Death can also come from a combination of opioids and cocaine taken together intravenously (a speedball).

Table 12.5-1
Diagnostic Criteria for Cocaine Intoxication

A. Recent use of cocaine

B. Maladaptive behavioral changes (e.g., euphoria, fighting, grandiosity, hypervigilance, psychomotor agitation, impaired judgment, impaired social or occupational functioning)

C. At least two of the following signs within one hour of using cocaine:
(1) tachycardia
(2) pupillary dilation
(3) elevated blood pressure
(4) perspiration or chills
(5) nausea or vomiting
(6) visual or tactile hallucinations

D. Not due to any physical or other mental disorder

Table from DSM-III-R, *Diagnostic and Statistical Manual of Mental Disorders*, ed 3, revised. Copyright American Psychiatric Association, Washington, D.C., 1987, with permission.

Cocaine Withdrawal

DSM-III-R describes cocaine withdrawal as consisting of symptoms that reach a peak in two to four days but with depression and irritability potentially persisting for weeks (Table 12.5-2). Abrupt cocaine withdrawal by a chronic user may produce a severe craving for the drug and drug-seeking behavior. Some persons become hypersomnolent and complain of fatigue, anhedonia, depression, suicidal ideas, and general malaise. These symptoms usually resolve within a few weeks or months. An underlying emotional disorder may then surface, which may include a dependence on alcohol or benzodiazepines if those substances were used to manage the crash after each bout of cocaine abuse. DSM-III-R states that a coexisting depressive disorder should be considered if a depressive syndrome persists for several weeks.

Cocaine-Induced Delirium and Delusional Disorder

Symptoms of psychosis are common in habitual intravenous abusers and freebasers; cocaine psychosis is apparently qualitatively similar to amphetamine psychosis. Cocaine intoxication with high doses may lead to transient ideas of reference, paranoid ideation, increased libido, and bizarre behavior. Perceptual disturbances and persecutory trends with overt paranoid delusions (commonly delusions of jealousy) are associated with prolonged use and classified as cocaine delusional disorder (Table 12.5-3). Homicidal impulses may be carried out. Tactile or haptic hallucinations have been described, in which the person believes that bugs are crawling just beneath the skin (also known as formication). Delirium with disorientation and violent behavior may also occur (Table 12.5-4).

Table 12.5-2
Diagnostic Criteria for Cocaine Withdrawal

A. Cessation of prolonged (several days or longer) heavy use of cocaine, or reduction in the amount of cocaine used, followed by dysphoric mood (e.g., depression, irritability, anxiety) and at least one of the following, persisting more than 24 hours after cessation of substance use:
(1) fatigue
(2) insomnia or hypersomnia
(3) psychomotor agitation

B. Not due to any physical or other mental disorder, such as cocaine delusional disorder.

Table 12.5-3
Diagnostic Criteria for Cocaine Delusional Disorder

A. Organic delusional syndrome developing shortly after use of cocaine

B. Rapidly developing persecutory delusions are the predominant clinical feature

C. Not due to any physical or other mental disorder

Table 12.5-4
Diagnostic Criteria for Cocaine Delirium

A. Delirium developing within 24 hours of use of cocaine

B. Not due to any physical or other mental disorder

DIAGNOSIS

Cocaine abuse should be suspected if a person shows a change in personality characterized by irritability, disturbed concentration, compulsive behavior, perceptual changes, severe insomnia, and weight loss. Increased debt (to support the expensive cocaine habit) should also arouse suspicion. Cocaine users often excuse themselves from social situations frequently (every 30 minutes) to snort or inject the drug privately.

TREATMENT

The treatment of cocaine abuse requires the coordination of social, psychological, and biological strategies. The most critical social intervention is removing persons from their drug source. In fact, hospitalization is often necessary to accomplish this separation. Urine testing for toxilogical analysis should always be a part of the treatment program to make sure patients are staying abstinent. Psychological intervention should be directed toward the underlying causes for the pattern of abuse. The use of family and group therapy and support groups (such as Narcotics Anonymous) is often indicated in the treatment of cocaine abuse. Biological intervention includes the use of two drugs that have been reported to be most useful in the treatment of cocaine abuse: bromocriptine (Parlodel), a dopamine agonist, and desipramine (Norpramin), a tricyclic antidepressant that is selective for the noradrenergic system. Doxepin (Sinequan) has also been used.

References

Baker F M: Cocaine psychosis. J Natl Med Assoc *81*: 987, 1989.
Doering P L, Davidson C L, LaFauce L, Williams C A: Effects of cocaine on the human fetus: A review of clinical studies. DICP *23*: 639, 1989.
Ettinger N A, Albin R J: A review of the respiratory effects of smoking cocaine. Am J Med *87*: 664, 1989.
Farrar H C, Kearns G L: Cocaine: Clinical pharmacology and toxicology. J Pediatr *115*: 665, 1989.
Frishman W H, Karpenos A, Molloy T J: Cocaine-induced coronary artery disease: Recognition and treatment. Med Clin North Am *73*: 475, 1989.
Gawin F H, Allen D, Humblestone B: Outpatient treatment of "crack" cocaine smoking with flupenthixol decanoate. Arch Gen Psychiatry *46*: 322, 1989.
Gold M S: Cocaine update. Psychiatr Ann *18* (9): entire issue, 1988.
Griffin M L, Weiss R D, Mirin S M, Lange U: A comparison of male and female cocaine abusers. Arch Gen Psychiatry *46*: 122, 1989.
Hall W C, Talbert R L, Ereshefsky L: Cocaine abuse and its treatment. Pharmacotherapy *10*: 47, 1990.
Howard J: Cocaine and its effects on the newborn. Dev Med Child Neurol *31*: 255, 1989.

Johanson C E, Fischman M W: The pharmacology of cocaine related to its abuse. Pharmacol Rev *41*: 3, 1989.
Journal of Clinical Psychiatry: Cocaine abuse and its treatment. J Clin Psychiatry *49* (2, Suppl): 2, 1988.
Kalivas P W, Duffy P, DuMars L A, Skinner C: Behavioral and neurochemical effects of acute and daily cocaine administration in rats. J Pharmacol Exp Ther *245*: 485, 1988.
Kosten T R: Pharmacotherapeutic interventions for cocaine abuse: Matching patients to treatments. J Nerv Ment Dis *177*: 379, 1989.
Kosten T R, Rounsaville B J, Kleber H D: A 2.5-year follow-up of cocaine use among treated opioid addicts. Arch Gen Psychiatry *44*: 281, 1987.
Lowenstein D H, Massa S M, Rowbotham M C, Collins S D, McKinney H E, Simon R P: Acute neurologic and psychiatric complications associated with cocaine abuse. Am J Med *83*: 841, 1987.
Mangiardi J R, Daras M, Geller M E, Weitzner I, Tuchman A J: Cocaine-related intracranial hemorrhage: Report of nine cases and review. Acta Neurol Scand *77*: 177, 1988.
Miller N S, Gold M S, Millman R B: Cocaine: General characteristics, abuse, and addiction. N Y State J Med *89*: 390, 1989.
National Institute on Drug Ause: 1988 National Household Survey on Drug Abuse, 1989.
Sherer M A: Intravenous cocaine: Psychiatric effects, biological mechanisms. Biol Psychiatry *24*: 865, 1988.
Sherer M A, Kumor K M, Cone E J, Jaffe J H: Suspiciousness induced by four-hour intravenous infusions of cocaine. Arch Gen Psychiatry *45*: 673, 1988.
U S Department of Health and Human Services: HHS News, July 1989.
VanDette J M, Cornish L A: Medical complications of illicit cocaine use. Clin Pharm *8*: 401, 1989.
Weddington W W, Brown B S, Haertzen C A, Cone E J, Dax E M, Herning R I, Michaelson B J: Changes in mood, craving, and sleep during short-term abstinence reported by male cocaine addicts: A controlled residential study. Arch Gen Psychiatry *47*: 861, 1990.

12.6 / Central Nervous System Stimulants

Amphetamine and amphetaminelike drugs are used by members of all socioeconomic groups. Some persons use amphetamines to increase performance—for example, students preparing for examinations, long-distance truck drivers, businesspeople with important deadlines, and athletes. Amphetamine is a very addictive drug, although not as addictive as cocaine. Its occasional use often leads to a chronic pattern of abuse, eventually resulting in serious physical and psychosocial morbidity.

Amphetamines and amphetamine congeners comprise a large group of central stimulant drugs. Among the best known are dextroamphetamine (Dexedrine), methamphetamine (Methedrine), and methylphenidate (Ritalin). Racemic amphetamine sulfate (Benzedrine) was first synthesized in 1887, but it was not introduced as a pharmaceutical until 1932. At that time, the Benzedrine inhaler became available as a nonprescription, over-the-counter drug for the treatment of nasal congestion and asthma. In late 1937 the new drug was introduced in tablet form to treat narcolepsy and postencephalitic parkinsonism. It was also recommended to treat depression and to heighten energy. Soon amphetamine was receiving much sensational publicity, with numerous references to brain, pep, and superman pills. Amphetamine abuse reached epidemic proportions in the 1970s. By then the annual legal U.S. production reached more than 10 billion 5-mg tablets. There was also considerable growth in both illicit laboratory synthesis of amphetamines and black market diversion of legitimately produced drugs.

DSM-III-R CLASSIFICATION

The revised third edition of *Diagnostic and Statistical Manual of Mental Disorders* (DSM-III-R) includes a drug classification of amphetamine or similarly acting sympathomimetics. Sympathomimetic refers to the class of drugs that causes the release of catecholamine neurotransmitters. DSM-III-R specifies both dependence and abuse as patterns of use for these drugs. Amphetamine, like cocaine, is associated with the psychoactive substance-induced organic mental disorders of intoxication, withdrawal, delirium, and delusional disorder.

CLINICAL FEATURES

Amphetamine is readily absorbed orally and has a rapid onset of action. Abusers often use the drug intravenously. It acts mainly by releasing catecholamines (dopamine and norepinephrine) from presynaptic terminals. In the average person, a dose of 5 mg produces an increased sense of well-being; improves performance on written, verbal, and performance tasks; decreases fatigue; induces anorexia; and elevates the pain threshold. These effects account for its therapeutic use in conditions such as attention-deficit hyperactivity disorder of children and adults, narcolepsy, obesity, and mild depression and for augmentation of tricyclic antidepressants and analgesics. Only the first three disorders mentioned above are currently listed as recommended indications by the Food and Drug Administration (FDA). However, there are reports in the literature about the positive effects of these drugs when used judiciously in other selected cases. In medically ill depressed patients, for example, amphetamine in dosages of 2.5 to 30 mg a day can be effective in alleviating depressive symptoms.

Many psychiatrists believe that amphetamine use has been overly regulated by governmental authorities. Amphetamines and narcotics are listed as schedule II drugs by the U.S. Drug Enforcement Agency. In addition, in New York State, for example, physicians must use triplicate prescriptions for such drugs, one copy of which is filed with a state government agency. Such mandates worry both patients and doctors about breaches in confidentiality; and doctors are concerned that their prescribing practices may be misinterpreted by official agencies. Consequently, some doctors may withhold amphetamines, even from a patient who may benefit from the medication.

The outstanding psychopharmacologist Donald Klein and associates in their 1980 book *Diagnosis and Drug Treatment of Psychiatric Disorders* (and reaffirmed in a personal communication [1990]) summarized the use of stimulant medication in the practice of psychiatry as follows:

> The use of stimulant medication, e.g., dextroamphetamine, methylphenidate, and magnesium pemoline, has been en-

ergetically discouraged in our present social climate, the reason being that such drugs may be abused, in common with cocaine, their illegal relative. In addition, there is the frightening possibility that prolonged use of stimulants in high doses may result in a paranoid psychosis or the exacerbation of a schizophrenic disorder. In view of these two considerations, it is not surprising that the prescription of these agents is attended by considerable anxiety and that many doctors simply refuse to use them. In certain jurisdictions, e.g., Sweden, they are outlawed.

. . . Short-term use of stimulant medication is often of marked value in helping demoralized people to get going by overcoming their hampering appetitive inhibition. A daily dose of dextroamphetamine (5 to 15 mg) may enable a patient to start constructive activity, such as searching for a job or becoming socially active. . . .

A much more difficult question is whether chronic administration of stimulant medication is ever justified, in view of the risks of addiction and psychosis.

We have treated a number of patients who seem in chronically "low gear," have difficulty mustering energy and initiative, have a variety of neurasthenic complaints and, despite high intelligence, are underachievers, with chronic small doses of dextroamphetamine (5 to 15 mg) daily. The potential development of tolerance and dependence and the conceivable psychotogenic effects are thoroughly discussed with these patients, and the utilization of the medication is closely monitored. Strikingly, some have been able to maintain the use of amphetamines, at a level that has never exceeded 15 mg daily, for years. During this period their mood has remained consistently improved and their ability to muster energy and function effectively has been clearly benefited. They have been able to cease taking the medication on numerous occasions, such as during vacations, when a high level of focused attention was not necessary and the circumstances were rewarding, so that the mood-elevating effects were superfluous. Several of these patients have been switched from dextroamphetamine to a MAOI with good results.

Ice

Ice has been called the drug of the 90s. Ice is a very pure form of methamphetamine that can be either inhaled or injected intravenously by abusers of this substance. The psychological effects of ice last for hours and are described as being particularly potent. Unlike crack cocaine, which has to be imported, ice is a synthetic drug that can be manufactured in domestic illicit laboratories. Some law enforcement agencies and urban emergency room physicians think that ice may become the major drug of abuse in the next several years.

Adverse Effects

Physical effects. Both the physical and the psychological effects of amphetamine use begin within one hour after administration and may occur within a few seconds when the drug is administered intravenously. There are numerous adverse physical effects of both acute amphetamine intoxication and chronic use (Table 12.6-1). As the dose of amphetamine increases as a result of abuse or misuse, adverse effects eventually occur. Tolerance develops, and some abusers may take 1 g of amphetamine a day. In persons not used to the drug, death may occur with doses of 120 mg. The physical signs and symptoms include flushing, pallor, cyanosis, fever, headache, tachycardia and palpitations, markedly elevated blood pressure, nausea, vomiting, bruxism (teeth grinding), difficulty in breathing, tremor, ataxia, and loss of sensory abilities.

Table 12.6-1
Diagnostic Criteria for Amphetamine or Similarly Acting Sympathomimetic Intoxication

A. Recent use of amphetamine or a similarly acting sympathomimetic

B. Maladaptive behavioral changes (e.g., fighting, grandiosity, hypervigilance, psychomotor agitation, impaired judgment, impaired social or occupational functioning)

C. At least two of the following signs within one hour of use:

(1) tachycardia
(2) pupillary dilation
(3) elevated blood pressure
(4) perspiration or chills
(5) nausea or vomiting

D. Not due to any physical or other mental disorder

Table from DSM-III-R, *Diagnostic and Statistical Manual of Mental Disorders*, ed 3, revised. Copyright American Psychiatric Association, Washington, D.C., 1987, with permission.

Life-threatening adverse effects include cardiac arrest, stroke, and a neurological progression from twitching to tetany to convulsions, coma, and death. Death from overdose is usually associated with hyperpyrexia, convulsions, and cardiovascular shock. Intravenous abuse is associated with a risk for human immunodeficiency virus (HIV) infection and produces other serious physical reactions, including serum hepatitis, lung abscess, endocarditis, and necrotizing angiitis.

Psychological effects. The psychological effects of amphetamine use include restlessness, dysphoria, logorrhea, insomnia, irritability, hostility, confusion, anxiety, and panic. When amphetamine is taken intravenously, there is a characteristic rush of well-being and euphoria. Intoxication with high doses can lead to transient ideas of reference, paranoid ideation, increased libido, and formication (tactile sensation of bugs crawling on the skin). Stereotyped movements can occur.

The course of the intoxication is usually self-limited, with full recovery within 48 hours. A letdown or crash occurs when the immediate effects of high doses have diminished. A debilitating cycle of runs (heavy use for several days to a week) and crashes is a common pattern of amphetamine abuse. The physical and psychological symptoms of the crash include anxiety, tremulousness, dysphoric mood, lethargy, fatigue, nightmares (from greatly increased rapid eye movement [REM] sleep), headache, profuse sweating, muscle cramps, stomach cramps, and insatiable hunger. Loss of self-control may lead to violent acting out of aggressive impulses. According to DSM-III-R, when the crash extends beyond 24 hours after the last use of the substance, the condition is reclassified as amphetamine or similarly acting sympathomimetic withdrawal (Table 12.6-2). Withdrawal symptoms peak usually in two to four days. The most characteristic and dangerous symptom is a depression, suicidal at times, that peaks 48

Table 12.6-2
Diagnostic Criteria for Amphetamine or Similarly Acting Sympathomimetic Withdrawal

A. Cessation of prolonged (several days or longer) heavy use of amphetamine or a similarly acting sympathomimetic, or reduction in the amount of substance used, followed by dysphoric mood (e.g., depression, irritability, anxiety) and at least one of the following, persisting more than 24 hours after cessation of substance use:
   (1) fatigue
   (2) insomnia or hypersomnia
   (3) psychomotor agitation
B. Not due to any physical or other mental disorder, such as amphetamine or similarly acting sympathomimetic delusional disorder

Table from DSM-III-R, *Diagnostic and Statistical Manual of Mental Disorders*, ed 3, revised. Copyright American Psychiatric Association, Washington, D.C., 1987, with permission.

to 72 hours after the last dose of amphetamine but that may persist for several weeks.

Amphetamine or similarly acting sympathomimetic delirium and delusional disorder. A syndrome of amphetamine-induced delirium can be seen in some persons (Table 12.6-3). A psychotic syndrome with prominent delusions is also associated with amphetamine abuse (Table 12.6-4). The symptoms of amphetamine delusional disorder may resemble those of paranoid schizophrenia, with predominately and rapidly developing persecutory delusions; however, the predominance of visual hallucinations, appropriate affect, at times confusion and incoherence, hyperactivity, hypersexuality, or absence of thought disorder helps to distinguish amphetamine psychosis from schizophrenia. Distortions of body image and misperceptions of people's faces may occur with amphetamines. At times, a strictly clinical differentiation is all but impossible.

DIAGNOSIS

The most reliable methods of diagnosis are specific laboratory tests that detect amphetamine in urine; however, these tests are ineffective if more than 48 hours have elapsed since the last dose of amphetamine. In the absence of a reliable history, urinalysis, or obvious physical signs, amphetamine delusional disorder is often recognized only in retrospect, when the symptoms disappear—generally within days or, at most, weeks after the drug has been withdrawn. However, delusions, suspiciousness, tendencies toward misinterpretation, and ideas of reference may persist for months.

Table 12.6-3
Diagnostic Criteria for Amphetamine or Similarly Acting Sympathomimetic Delirium

A. Delirium developing within 24 hours of use of amphetamine or a similarly acting sympathomimetic
B. Not due to any physical or other mental disorder

Table from DSM-III-R, *Diagnostic and Statistical Manual of Mental Disorders*, ed 3, revised. Copyright American Psychiatric Association, Washington, D.C., 1987, with permission.

Table 12.6-4
Diagnostic Criteria for Amphetamine or Similarly Acting Sympathomimetic Delusional Disorder

A. Organic delusional syndrome developing shortly after use of amphetamine or a similarly acting sympathomimetic
B. Rapidly developing persecutory delusions are the predominant clinical feature
C. Not due to any physical or other mental disorder

Table from DSM-III-R, *Diagnostic and Statistical Manual of Mental Disorders*, ed 3, revised. Copyright American Psychiatric Association, Washington, D.C., 1987, with permission.

TREATMENT

Because amphetamine intoxication and delusional disorder are generally self-limiting, treatment usually requires supportive measures. Antipsychotics, either a phenothiazine or haloperidol (Haldol), may be prescribed for the first few days. In the absence of psychosis, diazepam (Valium) is useful for agitation and hyperactivity. The physician should establish a therapeutic alliance to deal with the underlying depression or personality disorder or both; however, because many of these patients are heavily dependent on the drug, psychotherapy may be especially difficult.

AMPHETAMINELIKE DRUGS

Amphetaminelike drugs include three stimulant drugs—caffeine, ephedrine, and propanolamine (PPA)—which, until recently, were sold legally over the counter in the form of tablets designed to resemble, but not duplicate, the appearance of prescription amphetamines. Ephedrine and PPA are still marketed as nasal decongestants and PPA as an appetite suppressant. Either drug can be dangerous to people suffering from high blood pressure or diabetes and may cause a toxic psychosis after long-term use at high doses. PPA has a relatively narrow safety margin: as little as three or four times the amount in an average tablet can produce a hypertensive crisis.

References

American Medical Association Council on Scientific Affairs: Clinical aspects of amphetamine abuse. JAMA *240*: 2317, 1978.
Angrist B, Sothananthan G, Wilk S, Geshon S: Amphetamine psychosis: Behavioral and biochemical aspects. J Psychiatr Res *11*: 13, 1974.
Chiarello R J, Cole J O: The use of psychostimulants in general psychiatry. Arch Gen Psychiatry *44*: 286, 1987.
Cho A K: Ice: A new dosage form of an old drug. Science *249*: 631, 1990.
Dougan D, Wade D, Duffield P: How metabolites may augment some psychostimulant actions of amphetamine. Trends Pharmacol Sci *8*: 277, 1987.
Fishman M W: Cocaine and the amphetamines. In *Psychopharmacology: The Third Generation of Progress,* H Y Meltzer, editor, p 1543. Raven Press, New York, 1987.
Grinspoon L, Hedblom P: *The Speed Culture: Amphetamine Use and Abuse in America.* Harvard University Press, Cambridge, MA, 1975.
Harvey J A: Behavioral pharmacology of central nervous system stimulants. Neuropharmacology *26*: 887, 1987.

Miller N S, Millman R B, Gold M S: Amphetamines: Pharmacology, abuse and addiction. Adv Alcohol Subst Abuse *8*: 53, 1989.
Morgan J P: Amphetamine. In *Substance Abuse: Clinical Problems and Perspectives,* J H Lowinson and P Ruiz, editors, p 167. Williams & Wilkins, Baltimore, 1981.
Piazza P V, Deminiere J-M, Le Moal M, Simon H: Factors that predict individual vulnerability to amphetamine self-administration. Science *245*: 1511, 1989.
Seiden L S, Kleven M S: Methamphetamine and related drugs: Toxicity and resulting behavioral changes in response to pharmacological probes. NIDA Res Monogr *94*: 146, 1989.
Woods S W, Tesar G E, Murray G B, Cassem N H: Psychostimulant treatment of depressive disorders secondary to medical illness. J Clin Psychiatry *47*: 12, 1986.

12.7 / Hallucinogens and Arylcyclohexylamines

Hallucinogens are an ill-defined category of over 100 natural and synthetic drugs. The two best-known natural hallucinogens are psilocybin, which is found in a particular type of mushroom, and mescaline, which is found in the peyote cactus. The prototypical synthetic hallucinogen is lysergic acid diethylamide (LSD). The revised third edition of *Diagnostic and Statistical Manual of Mental Disorders* (DSM-III-R) puts another class of drugs, the arylcyclohexylamines, in the same category with the hallucinogens in terms of abuse and dependence. However, hallucinogens and arylcyclohexylamines have slightly different substance-induced organic mental disorders associated with them. The prototypical arylcyclohexylamine is phencyclidine (PCP). Pharmacologically, the arylcyclohexylamines are categorized as dissociative anesthetics, but their clinical effects may be indistinguishable from those of the hallucinogens.

Hallucinogens and arylcyclohexylamines (also called psychedelics and psychotomimetics) produce psychosis-like symptoms, including hallucinations, loss of contact with reality, and other dramatic changes in thinking and feeling. Psychedelic drugs are said by some to expand or heighten consciousness.

EPIDEMIOLOGY

According to the National Institute for Drug Abuse (NIDA) (July 1989), prevalence rates for hallucinogens did not change significantly for any age group between 1985 and 1988. Lifetime prevalence is highest among 26-to-34-year-olds (18 percent).

DSM-III-R CLASSIFICATION

Within the psychoactive substance use disorders, DSM-III-R allows for the diagnosis of hallucinogen and phencyclidine (PCP) or similarly acting arylcyclohexylamine abuse and dependence. DSM-III-R specifies the following psychoactive substance-induced organic mental disorders for hallucinogens: hallucinosis, delusional disorder, mood disorder, and posthallucinogen perception disorder. There is no classification for hallucinogen intoxication per se, and there is no recognized withdrawal syndrome from hallucinogens. DSM-III-R specifies the following psychoactive substance-induced organic mental disorders for PCP or similarly acting arylcyclohexylamines: intoxication, delirium, delusional disorder, mood disorder, and organic mental disorder not otherwise specified (NOS).

PHARMACOLOGY

Hallucinogens produce sympathomimetic effects, such as tremors, tachycardia, hypertension, sweating, blurring of vision, tremors, and mydriasis. They affect the catecholamines, acetylcholine, serotonin, and γ-aminobutyric acid (GABA). LSD has an inhibitory effect on the serotonin-producing neurons of the dorsal raphe, which may account for its effects. Specific receptor sites for PCP are located in the calcium ion channel that is associated with the NMDA subtype of the receptor for the excitatory amino acid glutamate. The major pharmacological effect of 3, 4-methylenedioxymethamphetamine (MDMA [also known as ecstasy]) may be to stimulate the release of serotonin.

Humans develop tolerance for the effects of LSD. After three or four days of use, psychedelic effects are no longer produced; however, they return if the drug is taken again after two to three days of abstinence. Tolerance to PCP does not occur. Physical dependency to psychedelics has not been reported, but many persons become psychologically dependent and use the drugs repeatedly for their "mind-expanding experiences."

LSD

The synthetic drug lysergic acid diethylamide (LSD) is related to psychoactive alkaloids found in morning glory seeds, known as lysergic acid amides. LSD's effects are typical of those of all hallucinogens. Other psychedelic drugs include the natural substances harmine, harmaline, ibogaine, dimethyltryptamine (DMT) and a large number of synthetic drugs with a tryptamine or methoxylated amphetamine structure. Examples of these drugs are diethyltryptamine (DET), dipropyltryptamine (DPT), 5-methoxy-3,4-methylenedioxyamphetamine (MMDA), and 2, 5-dimethoxy-4-methylamphetamine (DOM, also known as STP). The average effective dose varies considerably: 75 μg of LSD, 3 μg of DOM, 6 μg of psilocybin, 50 μg of DMT, 100 μg of MDA, and 200 μg of mescaline.

Clinical Features

There are some differences in quality and duration of the subjective effects of these drugs, but LSD produces the widest range of effects and can be taken as a prototype. The onset of effects is usually within an hour of ingestion. For LSD, the effects last from 8 to 12 hours. Physical symptoms include mydriasis, tachycardia, palpitations, diaphoresis, blurred vision, and tremors.

Psychological effects. Psychological reactions to LSD vary among persons and among separate ingestions for a single person. Nevertheless, LSD invariably produces alterations in perception, mood, and thinking (Table 12.7-1). Usually, the user realizes that the perceptual alterations are caused by the drug. At other times, the person is convinced that he or she is going crazy and fears never regaining sanity. When the user develops a delusional conviction that the disturbed perceptions correspond to reality, DSM-III-R classifies this as hallucinogen delusional disorder (Table 12.7-2). Perceptions become unusually brilliant and intense: Colors and textures seem richer, contours sharpened, music more emotionally profound, and smells and tastes heightened. Synesthesia is common; colors may be heard or sounds seen. Changes in body image and alterations of time and space perception also occur. Hallucinations are usually visual, often of geometric forms and figures, but auditory and tactile hallucinations are sometimes experienced. Emotions become unusually intense and may change abruptly and often; two seemingly incompatible feelings may be experienced at one time. Suggestibility is greatly heightened, and sensitivity to nonverbal cues is increased. Exaggerated empathy with or detachment from other people may arise. Other features that often appear are seeming awareness of internal organs, recovery of lost early memories, release of unconscious material in symbolic form, and regression and apparent reliving of past events, including birth. Introspective reflection and feelings of religious and philosophical insight are common. The sense of self is greatly changed, sometimes to the point of depersonalization, merging with the external world, separation of self from body, or total dissolution of the ego in mystical ecstasy. Some drugs, such as MDMA, cause less disorientation and perceptual distortion than LSD.

Long-term hallucinogen use is not very common. There is no physical addiction, and although psychological dependence occurs, it is rare, partly because each LSD experience is different and there is no reliable euphoria. Tolerance to these drugs develops quickly but also disappears rapidly after two or three days. There is no clear evidence of drastic personality change or chronic psychosis produced by long-term LSD use in moderate users not otherwise predisposed to these conditions. It is likely, however, that some heavy users of hallucinogens may suffer from chronic anxiety or depression and may benefit from a psychological or pharmacological approach that addresses the underlying problem.

Table 12.7-1
Diagnostic Criteria for Hallucinogen Hallucinosis

A. Recent use of a hallucinogen

B. Maladaptive behavioral changes (e.g., marked anxiety or depression, ideas of reference, fear of losing one's mind, paranoid ideation, impaired judgment, impaired social or occupational functioning)

C. Perceptual changes occurring in a state of full wakefulness and alertness (e.g., subjective intensification of perceptions, depersonalization, derealization, illusions, hallucinations, synesthesias)

D. At least two of the following signs:
(1) pupillary dilation
(2) tachycardia
(3) sweating
(4) palpitations
(5) blurring of vision
(6) tremors
(7) incoordination

E. Not due to any physical or other mental disorder

Table from DSM-III-R, *Diagnostic and Statistical Manual of Mental Disorders*, ed 3, revised. Copyright American Psychiatric Association, Washington, D.C., 1987, with permission.

Table 12.7-2
Diagnostic Criteria for Hallucinogen Delusional Disorder

A. Organic delusional syndrome developing shortly after hallucinogen use

B. Not due to any physical or other mental disorder, such as schizophrenia

Table from DSM-III-R, *Diagnostic and Statistical Manual of Mental Disorders*, ed 3, revised. Copyright American Psychiatric Association, Washington, D.C., 1987, with permission.

Many persons maintain that a single experience with LSD has given them increased creative capacity, new psychological insight, relief from neurotic or psychosomatic symptoms, or a desirable change in personality. Psychiatrists in the 1950s and 1960s showed great interest in LSD and related drugs both as a potential model for functional psychoses and as possible pharmacotherapeutic agents. The availability of these compounds to researchers in the basic neurosciences has led to many scientific advances. Although none of these drugs are currently available for any clinical application, there continues to be some interest in studying some of them—for example, MDMA—as possible adjuvants to psychotherapy. Large doses of MDMA can produce amphetaminelike stimulant effects.

Bad trip. The most common adverse effect of LSD and related drugs is a bad trip, which resembles the acute panic reaction to cannabis but can be more severe and occasionally produces true psychotic symptoms. The bad trip generally ends when the immediate effects of the drug wear off—in the case of LSD, generally within 8 to 12 hours. However, the course of a bad trip is variable, and occasionally a protracted psychotic episode that is difficult to distinguish from a nonorganic psychotic disorder may ensue. Whether a chronic psychosis following a drug ingestion in a particular person is the result of the drug ingestion, unrelated to the drug ingestion, or a combination of both the drug ingestion and predisposing factors is currently an unanswerable question.

The best treatment for a person who is having a severely unpleasant experience under the influence of LSD is protection, companionship, and reassurance, although occasionally tranquilizers may be required—diazepam (Valium), chloral hydrate, or haloperidol (Haldol) in extreme cases. The use of phenothiazine antipsychotics is not recommended, owing to the possible synergistic anticholinergic and central nervous system (CNS)-depressant effects.

Flashback. Another common effect of hallucinogenic drugs is the flashback, a spontaneous transitory recurrence of drug-induced experience that occurs even though the person has not taken the drug recently. Most flashbacks are episodes of visual distortion, geometric hallucinations, hallucinations of sounds or voices, false perceptions of movement in peripheral fields, flashes of color, trails of images from moving objects, positive afterimages and halos, macropsia and micropsia, time expansion, physical symptoms, or relived intense emotion lasting usually a few seconds to a few minutes but sometimes longer. More rarely, paresthesias and echos occur. The flashback is sometimes triggered by emerging from a dark room or by the use of cannabis. Sometimes the person can bring flashbacks on voluntarily. Probably about a quarter of all psychedelic drug users have experienced some form of flashback. In DSM-III-R the diagnosis of posthallucinogen perception disorder (Table 12.7-3) is made if these flashback symptoms cause marked distress. Most often, even in the presence of distinct perceptual disturbance, the person has insight into the pathological nature of the disturbance. Approximately 50 percent of those with this perception disorder experience a remission within months; others continue to have symptoms for years. Suicidal behavior, major depression, and panic disorder are potential complications. There are no significant personality differences on objective tests between those persons who have flashbacks and those who do not. Flashbacks are more likely to occur in people who are under stress or at a time of diminished ego control, such as when fatigued or ill. Most people can be reassured that the experience will pass, but in cases of extreme agitation or panic, an antipsychotic or an anxiolytic may be necessary. Flashbacks have lasted 24 to 48 hours, and some persist even longer.

Hallucinogen-induced flashbacks must be distinguished from the flashbacks associated with posttraumatic stress disorder (PTSD). PTSD is associated with a severe, identifiable stressor, such as war or a serious accident. There is no relationship between flashbacks in PTSD and the presence or absence of a history of hallucinogen abuse.

Prolonged reactions. Prolonged reactions to LSD present the same variety of symptoms as bad trips and flashbacks. They have been classified as mood disorders (Table 12.7-4) and delusional disorders (Table 12.7-2); often they resemble prolonged and more or less attenuated bad trips. Most of these adverse reactions end after 24 to 48 hours, but they sometimes last weeks or even months. Psychedelic drugs are capable of magnifying and bringing into consciousness almost any internal conflict, so there is no typical prolonged adverse reaction to LSD, as there is a typical amphetamine delusional disorder.

Table 12.7-3
Diagnostic Criteria for Posthallucinogen Perception Disorder

A. The reexperiencing, following cessation of use of a hallucinogen, of one or more of the perceptual symptoms that were experienced while intoxicated with the hallucinogen (e.g., geometric hallucinations, false perceptions of movement in the peripheral visual fields, flashes of color, intensified colors, trails of images from moving objects, positive afterimages, halos around objects, macropsia, and micropsia).

B. The disturbance in A causes marked distress.

C. Other causes of the symptoms, such as anatomic lesions and infections of the brain, delirium, dementia, sensory (visual) epilepsies, schizophrenia, entoptic imagery, and hypnopompic hallucinations, have been ruled out.

Table from DSM-III-R, *Diagnostic and Statistical Manual of Mental Disorders*, ed 3, revised. Copyright American Psychiatric Association, Washington, D.C., 1987, with permission.

Table 12.7-4
Diagnostic Criteria for Hallucinogen Mood Disorder

A. Organic mood syndrome developing shortly after hallucinogen use (usually within one or two weeks), and persisting more than 24 hours after cessation of such use

B. Not due to any physical or other mental disorder

Table from DSM-III-R, *Diagnostic and Statistical Manual of Mental Disorders*, ed 3, revised. Copyright American Psychiatric Association, Washington, D.C., 1987, with permission.

Instead, many different mood, neurotic, and psychotic symptoms may appear, depending on individual forms of vulnerability. This lack of specificity makes it difficult to distinguish between LSD reactions and unrelated pathological processes, especially when some time passes between the drug trip and the onset of the disturbance.

The most likely candidates for prolonged reactions are persons with schizoid and prepsychotic personalities, an unstable ego balance, and a great deal of anxiety. Such persons cannot cope with the perceptual changes, body-image distortions, and symbolic unconscious material produced by the drug trip. There is a very high rate of previous mental instability in persons hospitalized for LSD reactions. In the late 1960s a number of adverse reactions occurred because LSD was being promoted as a self-prescribed psychotherapy for emotional crises in the lives of seriously disturbed people. Because that is happening less today, prolonged adverse reactions are much less commonly seen now.

The treatment for prolonged reactions to psychedelic drugs is the same as the treatment for similar symptoms not produced by drugs: an appropriate form of support and psychotherapy and, if necessary, anxiolytics or antidepressants. Antipsychotics carry a greater risk and are recommended only when the hallucinogen-induced episode is protracted, suggesting that a nonorganic psychosis may be present.

PHENCYCLIDINE (PCP)

Phencyclidine, 1-(1-phenylcyclohexy-l)piperidine, was first investigated for its properties as an intravenous surgical anesthetic and as a general preoperative and postoperative analgesic. Because of a severe syndrome characterized by disorientation, agitation, and delirium in patients emerging from the anesthesia, the drug is now available for veterinary use only. PCP first appeared in San Francisco in 1967 as a street drug known as the peace pill. Widespread use began in the 1970s and continues today. Although it may be taken orally, intravenously, or by sniffing, it is usually sprinkled onto a parsley or marijuana cigarette and smoked, as this is the best means of self-titration. Street names include angel dust, crystal, peace, peace weed, super grass, super weed, hog, rocket fuel, and horse tranq's.

Phencyclidine is relatively inexpensive and easy to synthesize in an illegal laboratory. This provides a powerful incentive for street chemists, whose illicit products are not always pure PCP. One very common contaminant is 1-piperidinocyclo-hexanecarbonitrile (PCC), a by-product of illicit synthesis that on decomposition releases hydrogen cyanide in small amounts. Another of its degradation products, piperidine, has a strong fishy odor. There are about

30 chemical analogues of PCP, some of which have appeared on the illicit market. Another related drug is ketamine (Ketalar), a clinically used, short-acting anesthetic with psychoactive properties similar to those of phencyclidine.

Clinical Features

Psychological effects. There is great variation in the amount of PCP from cigarette to cigarette; 1 g may be used to make as few as four or as many as several dozen cigarettes. This variability in dose, together with the extreme uncertainty of PCP content in street samples, makes it difficult to predict the effect, which also depends on the setting and the user's previous experience. The onset of effects may occur within five minutes. Less than 5 mg of phencyclidine is considered a low dose, and doses above 10 mg are considered high. Convulsions, coma, and possible death are associated generally with doses of 20 mg or more. Experienced users report that the effects of 2 to 3 mg of smoked PCP are felt within five minutes and plateau within half an hour. Users are frequently uncommunicative, appear oblivious, and report active fantasy production (Table 12.7-5). They experience speedy feelings, euphoria, bodily warmth, tingling, peaceful floating sensations, and occasionally feelings of depersonalization, isolation, and estrangement. Sometimes there are auditory and visual hallucinations. There are often striking alterations of body image, distortions of space and time perception, and delusions. There may be intensification of dependency feelings, confusion, and disorganization of thought. The user may be sympathetic, sociable, and talkative at one moment, hostile and negative at another. Anxiety is also sometimes reported; it is often the most prominent presenting symptom in an adverse reaction. Sometimes observed are head-rolling movements, stroking, grimacing, muscle rigidity on stimulation, repeated episodes of vomiting, and repetitive chanting speech. The high lasts three to six hours and sometimes gives way to a mild depression in which the user may become irritable, somewhat paranoid, and occasionally belligerent, irrationally assaultive, suicidal, or homicidal. Effects can last for several days. Users sometimes find that it takes 24 to 48 hours to recover completely from the high; laboratory tests show that PCP may remain in the blood and urine for more than a week.

Table 12.7-5
Diagnostic Criteria for Phencyclidine (PCP) or Similarly Acting Arylcyclohexylamine Intoxication

A. Recent use of phencyclidine or a similarly acting arylcyclohexylamine

B. Maladaptive behavioral changes (e.g., belligerence, assaultiveness, impulsiveness, unpredictability, psychomotor agitation, impaired judgment, impaired social or occupational functioning)

C. Within an hour (less when smoked, insufflated ["snorted"], or used intravenously), at least two of the following signs:
   (1) vertical or horizontal nystagmus
   (2) increased blood pressure or heart rate
   (3) numbness or diminished responsiveness to pain
   (4) ataxia
   (5) dysarthria
   (6) muscle rigidity
   (7) seizures
   (8) hyperacusis

D. Not due to any physical or other mental disorder (e.g., phencyclidine [PCP] or similarly acting arylcyclohexylamine delirium)

Table from DSM-III-R, *Diagnostic and Statistical Manual of Mental Disorders*, ed 3, revised. Copyright American Psychiatric Association, Washington, D.C., 1987, with permission.

Patients with mild cases of adverse PCP reaction or overdose usually do not come to medical attention. When they do, they are often treated in the outpatient department. Low-dose symptoms are quite variable and may range from mild euphoria and restlessness to increasing levels of anxiety, fear, confusion, and agitation. Patients may exhibit difficulty in communication and have a blank, staring expression, disordered thinking, depression, and occasionally violent, self-destructive behavior. If the symptoms are not severe and if one can be certain that enough time has elapsed so that all PCP has been absorbed, the patient may be monitored in the outpatient department and, if the symptoms improve, released to family or friends. Even at low doses, however, symptoms may worsen, requiring that the person be hospitalized.

As with the other effects of phencyclidine intoxication, neurological and physiological symptoms are dose-related. Among the common symptoms seen in emergency rooms are hypertension, increased pulse rate, and nystagmus (horizontal or vertical or both). At low doses, there may be dysarthria, gross ataxia, and muscle rigidity, particularly of the face and neck. Increased deep tendon reflexes and diminished response to pain are commonly observed. Higher doses may lead to massive heat production and fatal hyperthermia, agitated and repetitive movement, athetosis or clonic jerking of the extremities, and occasionally opisthotonic posturing. Involuntary isometric muscle activity can lead to acute rhabdomyolysis, myoglobinuria, and kidney failure. With even larger doses patients may be drowsy, stuporous with eyes open, comatose, and, in some instances, responsive only to noxious stimuli. Clonic movements and muscle rigidity may sometimes precede generalized seizure activity, and status epilepticus has been reported. Cheyne-Stokes breathing has also been observed; respiratory arrest can occur and can be fatal. Vomiting, probably of central origin, may occur; hypersalivation and diaphoresis are occasional symptoms, and ptosis, usually bilateral, has been observed.

Although some patients may be brought to psychiatric attention within hours of ingesting PCP, it is not at all uncommon for two to three days to elapse before psychiatric help is sought. The long interval between drug ingestion and appearance at a clinic usually reflects the attempts of friends to deal with the psychosis through talking down; persons who lose consciousness are brought for help earlier than those who remain conscious. Although most recover completely within a day or two, some remain psychotic for as long as two weeks. Patients who are first seen in coma often manifest disorientation, hallucinations, confusion, and difficulty in communication on regaining consciousness. These symptoms may also be seen in noncomatose patients, but their symptoms appear to be less severe. A PCP psychotic patient also commonly manifests the following symptoms: staring into space, echolalia, posturing, sleep disturbance, paranoid ideation, depression, and a behavior disorder. Sometimes, the behavioral disturbance is quite severe; it may include public masturbation, stripping off clothes, violence, urinary incontinence, crying, and inappropriate laughing. Frequently, there is amnesia for the entire period of the psychosis.

In addition to the effects of PCP intoxication, a syndrome of PCP-induced delirium is not uncommon (Table 12.7-6). This syndrome is characterized by the presence of the symptoms of an organic delirium. The presence of a delirium in a person who has taken PCP puts the person at risk of accidental physical injury because of the confusion and impaired orientation.

Extended PCP-related syndromes. PCP has been associated with a myriad of symptoms lasting several weeks after the PCP ingestion. It has been hypothesized that this may be due to the intermittent release of PCP that has been sequestered in adipose tissue. The two most common syndromes are PCP-induced delusional disorder (Table 12.7-7) and mood disorder (Table 12.7-8).

For syndromes that contain an admixture of symptoms, there is a residual diagnostic category (Table 12.7-9). The street term "crystallized" is sometimes applied to chronic PCP users who seem to suffer from dulled thinking and reflexes, loss of memory and impulse control, depression, lethargy, and difficulty in concentrating. There is no clear evidence of permanent brain damage, but neurological and cognitive dysfunction has been reported in chronic users even after two to three weeks of abstinence. Tolerance and a withdrawal reaction consisting of lethargy, depression, and craving have been reported.

Table 12.7-6
Diagnostic Criteria for Phencyclidine (PCP) or Similarly Acting Arylcyclohexylamine Delirium

A. Delirium developing shortly after use of phencyclidine or a similarly acting arylcyclohexylamine

B. Not due to any physical or other mental disorder

Table 12.7-7
Diagnostic Criteria for Phencyclidine (PCP) or Similarly Acting Arylcyclohexylamine Delusional Disorder

A. Organic delusional syndrome developing shortly after use of phencyclidine or a similarly acting arylcyclohexylamine, or emerging up to a week after an overdose

B. Not due to any physical or other mental disorder, such as schizophrenia

Table 12.7-8
Diagnostic Criteria for Phencyclidine (PCP) or Similarly Acting Arylcyclohexylamine Mood Disorder

A. Organic mood syndrome developing shortly after use of phencyclidine or a similarly acting arylcyclohexylamine (usually within one or two weeks) and persisting more than 24 hours after cessation of substance use

B. Not due to any physical or other mental disorder

Table 12.7-9
Diagnostic Criteria for Phencyclidine (PCP) or Similarly Acting Arylcyclohexylamine Organic Mental Disorder Not Otherwise Specified

A. Recent use of phencyclidine or a similarly acting arylcyclohexylamine

B. The resulting illness involves features of several organic mental syndromes or a progression from one organic mental syndrome to another (e.g., initially there is delirium, followed by an organic delusional syndrome)

C. Not due to any physical or other mental disorder.

Diagnosis and Treatment

Depending on the patient's status at the time of admission, the differential diagnosis may include sedative or narcotic overdose, psychosis as a consequence of the use of psychedelic drugs, and brief reactive psychosis. Laboratory analysis may be helpful in establishing the diagnosis, particularly in the many cases in which the drug history is unreliable or unattainable.

Acute PCP intoxication can have potentially severe complications and often must be considered a psychiatric emergency. Unconscious patients must be carefully monitored, particularly those who are toxic with PCP, because the excessive secretions may interfere with already compromised respiration. In an alert patient who has recently taken PCP, gastric lavage presents a risk of inducing laryngeal spasm and aspiration of emesis. Muscle spasm and seizures are best treated with diazepam. The environment should afford minimal sensory stimulation; reassurance or talking down is generally useless. Ideally, one person stays with the patient in a quiet, dark room. Four-point restraint is dangerous, because it may lead to rhabdomyolysis; total body immobilization may occasionally be necessary. Diazepam is often effective in reducing agitation, but a patient with severe behavioral disturbance may require short-term antipsychotic medication; some clinicians recommend haloperidol, rather than a phenothiazine, because PCP is somewhat anticholinergic and because illegal drugs are often contaminated with belladonna alkaloids. A hypotensive drug, such as phentolamine (Regitine), may occasionally be needed. Ammonium chloride at the acute stage and ascorbic acid or cranberry juice later on are used to acidify the urine and promote elimination of the drug.

PCP intoxication can lead to death due to hyperpyrexia and other autonomic instability. Intravenous benzodiazepines are an effective treatment.

References

Abraham H D, Wolfe E: Visual function in past users of LSD: Psychophysical findings. J Abnorm Psychol *97*: 443, 1988.
Becher M, Wang B-W, Wong H, Morgan J P: Phencyclidine and violence: Clinical and legal issues. Psychopharmacology *8*: 397, 1988.
Cohen S: Lysergic acid diethylamide: Side effects and complications. J Nerv Ment Dis *130*: 30, 1960.
Graeven D B, Sharp J G, Glatt S: Acute effects of phencylidine (PCP) on chronic and recreational users. Am J Drug Alcohol Abuse *8*: 39, 1981.
Grinspoon L, Bakalar J B: *Psychedelic Drugs Reconsidered.* Basic Books, New York, 1979.
Luisada P V: Phencyclidine. In *Substance Abuse: Clinical Problems and Perspectives*, J M Lowinson and R Ruiz, editors, p 209. Williams & Wilkins, Baltimore, 1981.
National Institute on Drug Abuse: 1988 National Household Survey on Drug Abuse, 1989.
Peroutka S J, Newman H, Harris H: Subjective effects of 3,4-methylenedioxymethamphetamine in recreational users. Neuropsychopharmacology *1*: 273, 1988.
Pradhan S N: Phencyclidine (PCP): Some human studies. Neurosci Biobehav Rev *8*: 493, 1984.
Schwartz R H, Comerci G D, Meeks J E: LSD: Patterns of use by chemically dependent adolescents. J Pediatr *111*: 936, 1987.
Stillman R C, Willette R E, eds: *The Pharmacology of Hallucinogens.* Pergamon Press, New York, 1978.
Strassman R J: Adverse reactions to psychedelic drugs: A review of the literature. J Nerv Ment Dis *172*: 577, 1984.
U S Department of Health and Human Services: HHS News, July 1989.
Vardy M, Kay S: LSD psychosis or LSD-induced schizophrenia? Arch Gen Psychiatry *40*: 877, 1983.
Willetts J, Balster R L, Leander J D: The behavioral pharmacology of NMDA receptor antagonists. Trends Pharmacol Sci *11*: 423, 1990.

12.8 / Marijuana

Known for thousands of years as a medicine and intoxicant, marijuana was widely used in the 19th century as an analgesic, anticonvulsant, and hypnotic. Recently, interest has developed in using it to treat glaucoma and the nausea produced by cancer chemotherapy. One of marijuana's nonpsychoactive constituents, cannabidiol, may also prove useful as an anticonvulsant; yet marijuana has been valued throughout history mainly as a euphoriant.

EPIDEMIOLOGY

According to the National Institute on Drug Abuse (NIDA) (July 1989): (1) Marijuana remains the most commonly used illicit drug in the United States. Almost 66 million Americans (33 percent) have tried marijuana at least once in their lives. Four million youth, 17 million young adults, and over 45 million adults aged 26 and older have tried marijuana. (2) In 1988 the lifetime rate of marijuana use for youth (aged 12 to 17) was 17 percent; the rate for young adults (aged 18 to 25) was 56 percent. These rates have been steadily decreasing since 1979, when they were 31 percent and 68 percent, respectively. The lifetime rate among adults 26 and older was 31 percent in 1988 and has been steadily increasing since 1972. The increase in this age group is largely explained by the aging of persons who began using drugs in previous years. (3) Current use of marijuana continued to decrease, as it has since 1979, for all age groups. The number of current users declined from 18 million (9 percent) in 1985 to 12 million (6 percent) in 1988. Prevalence rates for youth and young adults were the lowest measured since the survey was first done in 1972. (4) Of the 21 million people who used marijuana (at least once) in the past year, almost one-third, or 6.6 million, used the drug once a week or more.

PREPARATIONS

Marijuana is the common name for the hemp plant *Cannabis sativa*, the resin of which contains the psychoactive constituents. In the United States the drug is most commonly smoked either in a pipe or in a cigarette called a joint. The drug can also be ingested in drinks or in foods, such as brownies. The dose of active drug a person receives varies considerably because of the variability in potency of preparations from the hemp plant.

Preparations of the drug come in three grades, identified by Indian names. The cheapest and least potent grade, called *bhang*, is derived from the cut tops of uncultivated plants and has a low resin content. Much of the marijuana smoked in the United States is of this grade. *Ganja*, the second grade, is obtained from the flowering tops and leaves of carefully selected cultivated plants, and it has a higher quality and quantity of resin than bhang. More cannabis of this strength is now available in the United States. The third and highest grade, called *charas* in India, is made largely from the resin itself, obtained from the tops of mature plants; only this version is properly called hashish. Indoor growing operations on the West Coast of the United States produce superior quality, high Δ-9-tetrahydrocannabinol (THC)-content marijuana for sale in this country. Marijuana is also known as grass, pot, Mary Jane, tea, and weed.

Many derivatives of cannabinol have been prepared. The active constituents of the resin are various isomers of tetrahydrocannabinol; the most important as an intoxicant is THC. The metabolite 11-hydroxy THC is more active than the parent compound.

Recently, a specific receptor for the cannabinoids has been identified, and its gene has been cloned. The receptor is a G protein-coupled receptor that appears to have its effects by inhibiting adenylyl cyclase.

DSM-III-R CLASSIFICATION

The revised third edition of *Diagnostic and Statistical Manual of Mental Disorders* (DSM-III-R) classifies both abuse and dependence patterns of cannabis use within the psychoactive substance use disorders. The DSM-III-R psychoactive substance-induced organic mental disorders for cannabis are intoxication and delusional disorder.

CLINICAL FEATURES

The psychological effects of cannabis include euphoria, oneiroid states, calmness, and drowsiness. DSM-III-R classifies this disorder as cannabis intoxication (Table 12.8-1). Intoxication occurs almost immediately after smoking marijuana, peaks within 30 minutes, and lasts for two to four hours. The effects from ingestion continue for 5 to 12 hours. The intoxication heightens sensitivity to external stimuli, reveals details that would ordinarily be overlooked, makes colors seem brighter and richer, and subjectively enhances the appreciation of art and music. Time seems to slow down, and more seems to happen in each moment. There is an increase in appetite, conjunctival injection, tachycardia, and dry mouth.

Curiously, there is often a splitting of consciousness; while smokers are experiencing the high, they are objective observers of their own intoxication. They may have paranoid thoughts and, at the same time, laugh at them. Depersonalization and derealization may occur.

If very high blood levels of the active ingredients of marijuana are attained, the person may experience some of the hallucinogenic effects of drugs such as lysergic acid diethylamide (LSD). These effects can include distorted perception of body parts, spatial and temporal distortions, increased sensitivity to sound, synesthesia, heightened suggestibility, and a deep sense of awareness. Although marijuana can also cause anxiety and paranoid reactions, the extremely unpleasant reactions that even the experienced LSD user may endure are rarely seen in a person who has taken marijuana. It is doubtful whether the average doses of marijuana used in this country produce true hallucinations. Cannabis tends to sedate, whereas LSD and the LSD–type drugs often induce wakefulness and even restlessness.

Cannabis Dependence

There are some indications of tolerance and a mild withdrawal reaction after frequent use of high doses. However, there is no clinical evidence that withdrawal symptoms or a need to increase the dose presents any serious problem to users. Craving or difficulty in withdrawal can occur as part of a pattern of pathological use. An abstinence syndrome of sleep disturbances, nausea, vomiting, tremors, and sweating has been observed.

Table 12.8-1
Diagnostic Criteria for Cannabis Intoxication

A. Recent use of cannabis.

B. Maladaptive behavioral changes (e.g., euphoria, anxiety, suspiciousness or paranoid ideation, sensation of slowed time, impaired judgment, social withdrawal)

C. At least two of the following signs developing within two hours of cannabis use:
(1) conjunctival injection
(2) increased appetite
(3) dry mouth
(4) tachycardia

D. Not due to any physical or other mental disorder

Table from DSM-III-R, *Diagnostic and Statistical Manual of Mental Disorders*, ed 3, revised. Copyright American Psychiatric Association, Washington, D.C., 1987, with permission.

Chronic Use

Chronic heavy use has been said to cause an *amotivational syndrome* characterized by the person's unwillingness to persist at a task, be it school, work, or any activity that requires prolonged attention or tenacity. The person becomes apathetic and anergic, usually gains weight, and has been described as slothful. Reports by many investigators, particularly in Egypt and in parts of the Orient, indicate that long-term users of the potent versions of cannabis are passive, unproductive, and lacking in ambition. This finding suggests that chronic use of the drug in its strong forms may have debilitating effects, as does prolonged heavy drinking.

Chronic marijuana use may cause various syndromes, which are described below.

Psychosis. Hemp insanity or cannabis psychosis has been reported mainly in India, Egypt, and Morocco—more often in the late 19th and early 20th centuries than today. It is described as a prolonged psychosis caused mainly by chronic heavy use of the drug. This phenomenon, however, has not been reported among marijuana smokers in the United States. Several studies of large sample populations of marijuana users have found no evidence of a cannabis psychosis produced *de novo* in well-integrated, stable persons.

In DSM-III-R there is a classification of an organic delusional syndrome called cannabis delusional disorder (Table 12.8-2), which is characterized by persecutory delusions developing shortly after use. Associated features are listed as marked anxiety, emotional lability, depersonalization, and possible amnesia for the episode. The delusional disorder is rare and remits within a day but may persist for a few days.

Delirium. Although not recognized in DSM-III-R, a syndrome of delirium can result when marijuana is taken in large enough doses. The delirium is characterized by clouding of consciousness, restlessness, confusion, disorientation, apprehension, illusions, and hallucinations. Cannabis-induced delirium is rare in the United States, although it may be becoming more common with the availability of increasingly potent forms of the drug. It is also possible that some cases of cannabis-induced delirium are actually caused by the smoking of marijuana tainted with phencyclidine (PCP).

Anxiety. Cannabis users may also suffer short-lived, acute anxiety states, sometimes accompanied by paranoid thoughts. The anxiety may become so intense as to be called panic. Although uncommon, panic is probably the most frequent adverse reaction to the moderate use of smoked marijuana. The sufferer may believe that body-image distortions mean illness or possible death or may interpret psychological changes induced by the drug as an indication of loss of sanity. Rarely does the panic become incapacitating; when it does, it usually lasts for a relatively short time. The likelihood of panic varies directly with the dose and inversely with the user's

Table 12.8-2
Diagnostic Criteria for Cannabis Delusional Disorder

A. Organic delusional syndrome developing shortly after cannabis use

B. Not due to any physical or other mental disorder

Table from DSM-III-R, *Diagnostic and Statistical Manual of Mental Disorders*, ed 3, revised. Copyright American Psychiatric Association, Washington, D.C., 1987, with permission.

experience; thus, the most vulnerable persons are the inexperienced users who inadvertently, because they lack familiarity with the drug, take a large dose that produces perceptual and somatic changes for which they are unprepared. Simple reassurance is the best treatment.

Flashback. One rather rare reaction to cannabis is the flashback, a spontaneous recurrence of drug symptoms when not intoxicated. Some reports suggest that this effect may occur in marijuana users even without prior use of any other drug. In general, however, flashbacks seem to arise only when people use more powerful hallucinogenic or psychedelic drugs and then smoke marijuana at a later time. When the flashbacks follow a history of hallucinogen use, they are classified as posthallucinogen perception disorder.

Physical effects. The main physical effects are reddening of the conjunctiva and a dose-related increase in heart rate. The ratio of lethal to effective dose is estimated to be in the range of 20,000 to 1 to 40,000 to 1. There is no adequately documented case of a fatality in a human being.

Chronic marijuana use has adverse effects on the lungs, partly because it contains the same carcinogenic hydrocarbons as tobacco smoke does. Chronic users are at increased risk of chronic respiratory disease and lung cancer. Other adverse physical effects of marijuana, however, are much less well documented.

There have been studies of cerebral atrophy, seizure susceptibility, chromosome damage and birth defects, impairment of immune response, and effects on testosterone and the menstrual cycle. Results generally have been contradictory and inconclusive. Nevertheless, irregular menstrual cycles and decreased testosterone have been reported with chronic use. Clinical observation of marijuana users, including recent studies of long-term users in the Caribbean and Greece, shows no evidence of disease or organic pathology attributable to any of these causes.

TREATMENT

There is no specific treatment for cannabis abuse. Treatment programs should include education; behavioral modification; individual, family, and group psychotherapy; and, if appropriate, pharmacological interventions. If the person uses the substance for anxiety reduction or for the alleviation of depression, an antianxiety agent or an antidepressant should be considered as substitution therapy. For an acute anxiety reaction to the drug, diazepam (Valium) is useful. Accidental ingestion by children is treated with gastric emptying and activated charcoal.

Educating people about the amotivational syndrome and the possible complications may dissuade some from using the drug in the first place. There is a strong movement to legalize marijuana in this country, but this movement has met with limited success.

References

American Medical Association Council on Scientific Affairs: Marijuana: Its health hazards and therapeutic potentials. JAMA *246*: 1823, 1981.

Bloodworth R C: Medical problems associated with marijuana abuse. Psychiatr Med *3*: 173, 1985.

Gold M, ed.: Marijuana update. Psychiatr Ann *16*: 203, 1986.

Grinspoon L: Effects of marijuana. Hosp Community Psychiatry *34*: 307, 1983.

Grinspoon L: Marijuana. Sci Am *221*: 17, 1969.

Hollister L E: Health aspects of cannabis. Pharmacol Rev *38*: 1, 1986.

Hollister L E: Marijuana and immunity. J Psychoactive Drugs *20*: 3, 1988.

Husain S, Khan I: An update on cannabis research. Bull Narc *37*: 3, 1985.

Mancall A C, DiGregorio J, Brill C B, Ruch E: The effect of delta-9-tetrahydrocannabinol on rat cerebrospinal fluid. Arch Neurol *42*: 1069, 1985.

Matsuda L A, Lolait S J, Brownstein M J, Young A C, Bonner T I: Structure of a cannabinoid receptor and functional expression of the cloned cDNA. Nature *346*: 561, 1990.

Miller N S, Gold M S, Pottash A C: A 12-step treatment approach for marijuana (Cannabis) dependence. J Subst Abuse Treat *6*: 241, 1989.

Moyer T P, Palmen M A, Johnson P: Marijuana testing: How good is it? Mayo Clin Proc *62*: 413, 1987.

National Institute on Drug Abuse: 1988 National Household Survey on Drug Abuse, 1989.

Schwartz R H: Marijuana: An overview. Pediatr Clin North Am *34*: 305, 1987.

Schwartz R H, Hawks R L: Toward optimal laboratory use: Laboratory detection of marijuana use. JAMA *254*: 788, 1985.

Seithi B B, Trivedi J K, Kumar P, Gulati A, Agarwal A K, Sethi N: Antianxiety effect of cannabis: Involvement of central benzodiazepine receptors. Biol Psychiatry *21*: 3, 1986.

U S Department of Health and Human Services: HHS News, July 1989.

Weller R A, Halikas J A: Change in effects from marijuana: A five-to-six-year study. J Clin Psychiatry *43*: 362, 1983.

Wert R C, Raulin M L: The chronic cerebral effects of cannabis use: I. Methodological issues and neurological findings. Int J Addict *21*: 605, 1986.

12.9 / Caffeine and Nicotine (Tobacco) Dependence

CAFFEINE

Caffeine, in the form of coffee, is consumed regularly by over 80 percent of North American adults. Caffeine is also present in tea, cola drinks, cocoa, chocolate, and many over-the-counter (OTC) cold preparations (Table 12.9-1).

The revised third edition of *Diagnostic and Statistical Manual of Mental Disorders* (DSM-III-R) does not include caffeine as one of the psychoactive substances of abuse or dependence. The only DSM-III-R category regarding caffeine is caffeine intoxication.

Clinical Features

A rough guide to calculating caffeine intake is as follows: 100 to 150 mg of caffeine in a cup of coffee; tea is about half as strong; a glass of cola is about one-third as strong. Most prescription drugs and OTC medications containing caffeine are one-third to one-half the strength of a cup of coffee. Two exceptions to this are migraine medications and OTC stimulants that contain 100 mg in a tablet. The clinical effects of an acute dose of caffeine (50 to 100 mg) include increased alertness, a sense of well-being, and improved verbal and motor performance. It is because of these effects that persons become psychologically dependent on caffeine. In addition, caffeine produces diuresis, cardiac muscle stimulation, increased peristalsis, gastric acid secretion, and blood pressure elevation.

Tolerance. Chronic users develop tolerance to the effects of caffeine. The average adult American consumes more than 500 mg of caffeine a day but usually in the markedly diluted form of brewed coffee. The plasma half-life varies from

Table 12.9-1
Some Common Sources of Caffeine and Representative Decaffeinated Products

Source	Approximate Amounts of Caffeine per Unit
Beverages and foods	5–6 oz
Fresh drip coffee, brewed coffee	90–140 mg
Instant coffee	66–100 mg
Tea (leaf or bagged)	30–100 mg
Cocoa	5–50 mg
Decaffeinated coffee	2–4 mg
Chocolate bar or ounce of baking chocolate	25–35 mg
Selected soft drinks	8–12 oz
Pepsi, Coke, Tab, Royal Crown, Pepsi Light, Dr. Pepper, Mountain Dew	25–50 mg
Canada Dry Ginger Ale, Caffeine Free Coke, Like, Pepsi Free, 7-Up, Sprite, Squirt, Caffeine Free Tab	0 mg
Prescription medications (1 tablet)	
Cafergot, Migralam	100 mg
Anoquan, Aspir-code, BAC, Darvon, Fiorinal	32–50 mg
Over-the-counter analgesics and cold preparations	
Excedrin	60 mg
Aspirin compound, Anacin, B-C powder, Capron, Cope, Dolor, Midol, Nilain, Norgesic, PAC, Trigesic, Vanquish	30–32.5 mg
Advil, Aspirin, Empirin, Midol 200, Nuprin, Pamprin	0 mg
Over-the-counter stimulants and appetite suppressants	
Caffin-TD, Caffedrine	250 mg
Vivarin, Ver capsules	200 mg
Quick-Pep	140–150 mg
Amostat, Anorexin, Appedrine, Nodoz, Wakoz	100 mg

Table by Jerome H. Jaffe, M.D.

3 to 10 hours; peak plasma concentrations occur at about 30 to 60 minutes after absorption. Caffeine intake over 500 mg increases the risk of developing intoxication; however, some persons can consume 2 to 3 g a day without complaints.

Neuropharmacology. The leading theory regarding the mechanism of action for caffeine involves antagonism of adenosine receptors. Adenosine is a nucleoside that appears to function as a neuromodulator and possibly a neurotransmitter in the human brain. Caffeine may also affect dopaminergic systems, and withdrawal symptoms from caffeine may involve adrenergic neurons.

Caffeine Intoxication

Signs of caffeine intoxication include anxiety, psychomotor agitation and restlessness, irritability, and psychophysiological complaints, such as muscle twitching, flushed face, nausea, diuresis, gastrointestinal complaints, and insomnia (Table 12.9-2). Intoxication can occur with daily doses of as little as 250 mg of caffeine, but most people require much larger doses. At levels of more than 1 g per day, there may be rambling flow of thought and speech, cardiac arrhythmia, inexhaustibility, and agitation. Tinnitus and flashes of light have been reported. With doses of 10 g or higher, grand mal seizures and respiratory failure can lead to death.

Table 12.9-2
Diagnostic Criteria for Caffeine Intoxication

A. Recent consumption of caffeine, usually in excess of 250 mg

B. At least five of the following signs:

(1) restlessness
(2) nervousness
(3) excitement
(4) insomnia
(5) flushed face
(6) diuresis
(7) gastrointestinal disturbance
(8) muscle twitching
(9) rambling flow of thought and speech
(10) tachycardia or cardiac arrhythmia
(11) periods of inexhaustibility
(12) psychomotor agitation

C. Not due to any physical or other mental disorder, such as an anxiety disorder

Table from DSM-III-R, *Diagnostic and Statistical Manual of Mental Disorders*, ed 3, revised. Copyright American Psychiatric Association, Washington, D.C., 1987, with permission.

Caffeine Withdrawal

Various studies have reported that from 25 to 100 percent of caffeine users experience symptoms of withdrawal on discontinuation of the drug. Withdrawal symptoms usually have their onset in 12 to 24 hours, peak in 20 to 48 hours, and last approximately one week. The major symptoms of caffeine withdrawal are headache and fatigue. Other symptoms include anxiety, impaired psychomotor performance, nausea and vomiting, and craving for caffeine. Anhedonia, irritability, and depression can occur in some persons, especially those with a long history of relatively high caffeine intake.

Chronic Use

Chronic caffeine use stimulates gastric hyperacidity, which can aggravate ulcer disease and can lead to the development of cardiac arrhythmias, especially in persons with preexisting cardiac disease. Some studies have demonstrated that the elimination of caffeine produces clinical improvement in women with fibrocystic disease. Users of excessive amounts of caffeine have been misdiagnosed as suffering from generalized anxiety disorder and have been treated unnecessarily with antianxiety agents.

Diagnosis and Treatment

Caffeine intoxication or withdrawal is diagnosed on the basis of a detailed history to confirm significant caffeine intake. The patient's report should include caffeine sources other than coffee in addition to signs and symptoms of anxiety in the case of intoxication and headache or lethargy in the case of withdrawal. The clinician needs to rule out general anxiety disorders, mood disorder, sleep disorder, and thyroid disease, all of which may coexist.

Treatment consists of abstinence, which can be accomplished if the person is highly motivated. Anxiolytics are not indicated except in rare cases, and simple analgesics, such as aspirin, may be used to treat headache. Water and decaffeinated coffee and soft drinks can be substituted for caffeinated beverages. Withdrawal usually takes four to five days.

NICOTINE

Nicotine is used worldwide and is consumed by about 30 percent of the American population in the form of cigarettes. Although the overall percentage of smoking adults has decreased, the percentage of female, teenage, and black smokers is rising. Cigarette smoking has been implicated in a variety of illnesses, primarily lung cancer, emphysema, cardiovascular disease, and stroke. There has been an increase in the use of chewing tobacco and snuff among some segments of the population, primarily teenagers, and both have been implicated in oropharyngeal cancer. There is no doubt that cigarettes and cigarette smoke inflict physical damage on the nicotine addict.

The intake of nicotine is particularly high among psychiatric patients. Several studies have estimated that approximately 50 percent of psychiatric outpatients, in contrast with 30 percent of the general population, smoke cigarettes. Patients with severe psychiatric illnesses tend to smoke more than other psychiatric patients. One study found that 88 percent of schizophrenic outpatients and 70 percent of bipolar outpatients smoked cigarettes.

DSM-III-R includes nicotine as a psychoactive substance on which a person can become dependent, although there is no classification for nicotine abuse in DSM-III-R. DSM-III-R also includes a syndrome of nicotine withdrawal within the psychoactive substance-induced organic mental disorders.

Epidemiology

According to the National Institute on Drug Abuse (NIDA) (July 1989): (1) Three-quarters of the American population (75 percent) have tried cigarettes, and between a quarter and a third (29 percent) are current smokers. Current use of cigarettes among youth (aged 12 to 17) is 12 percent; among young adults (aged 18 to 25), it is 35 percent; and among adults 26 and older, it is 30 percent. The number of current cigarette users declined from 60 million in 1985 to 57 million in 1988. There were significant decreases in the current prevalence rates for smoking among youth and older adults between 1985 and 1988, but this was not true for young adults. (2) Seven percent of youth and 9 percent of young adults used smokeless tobacco during the past year. Among youth, more males (13 percent) than females (1 percent) used smokeless tobacco in the past year. Comparable figures for young adults are 17 percent for males and less than one half a percent for females.

Pharmacology

Nicotine is believed to exert its effects on the central nervous system through the nicotinic receptors, which are one subclass of the acetylcholine receptors. The nicotinic receptor is a receptor-gated ion channel.

Nicotine is highly toxic, and an overdose of 60 mg is fatal. The average cigarette contains 0.5 mg of nicotine. The physiological effects of nicotine include vasoconstriction of peripheral blood vessels, increased peristalsis, increased catecholamine output with norepinephrine and epinephrine release, stimulation of the hypothalamic pleasure center (which may account for the habitual use of the drug), decreased metabolic rate, rapid eye movement (REM) sleep changes, and tremor. Women who smoke are reported to have low-birth-weight babies more frequently than women who do not smoke. An occasional case of nicotine poisoning may be seen, consisting of excessive salivation, abdominal pain, vomiting, tachycardia, mental confusion, and headache.

Nicotine Dependence

Dependence on nicotine develops quickly. The average smoker uses 20 to 30 cigarettes a day. Dependence is also reinforced by psychosocial factors. For example, among adolescent girls, smoking is associated with being rebellious or with peer group pressure to smoke. For adults, smoking is often associated with pleasurable events, such as parties, dinners, and sex. Other reinforcers include smoking paraphernalia and advertising.

Nicotine Withdrawal

The nicotine withdrawal syndrome develops in 90 to 120 minutes after the last cigarette smoked and peaks within the first 24 hours after cessation (Table 12.9-3). It lasts for several weeks or months in some persons. The major symptom is an intense craving for a cigarette associated with tension and irritability. The person feels generally frustrated or angry, restless, and anxious; has difficulty concentrating; and is drowsy but has difficulty in sleeping. Decreased heart rate and blood pressure, reduced motor performance, increased muscle contractions, and slow electroencephalogram (EEG) rhythms also occur. Increased appetite and weight gain occur in most persons after they stop smoking. Some former smokers report that their craving for a cigarette remains intense even after 10 to 20 years, although they have no other signs of the withdrawal syndrome. Mild symptoms of withdrawal may occur after switching to low-tar or low-nicotine cigarettes and after stopping the use of chewing tobacco or nicotine gum.

Table 12.9-3
Diagnostic Criteria for Nicotine Withdrawal

A. Daily use of nicotine for at least several weeks

B. Abrupt cessation of nicotine use, or reduction in the amount of nicotine used, followed within 24 hours by at least four of the following signs:

(1) craving for nicotine
(2) irritability, frustration, or anger
(3) anxiety
(4) difficulty concentrating
(5) restlessness
(6) decreased heart rate
(7) increased appetite or weight gain

Table from DSM-III-R, *Diagnostic and Statistical Manual of Mental Disorders*, ed 3, revised. Copyright American Psychiatric Association, Washington, D.C., 1987, with permission.

Health Benefits of Smoking Cessation

In a report of the Surgeon General in 1990 on the health benefits of smoking cessation, the following five major conclusions were reached: (1) Smoking cessation has major and immediate health benefits for persons of all ages and provides benefits for persons with and without smoking-related diseases. (2) Former smokers live longer than continuing smokers. (3) Smoking cessation decreases the risk for lung and other cancers, heart attack, stroke, and chronic lung diseases. (4) Women who stop smoking before pregnancy or during the first three to four months of pregnancy reduce their risk for having a low-birth-weight infant to that of women who never smoked. (5) The health benefits of smoking cessation substantially exceed any risks from the average 5-pound (2.3-kg) weight gain or any adverse psychological effects after quitting.

Treatment

The relapse rate for smokers who attempt to stop is as high as 80 percent within the first two years of abstinence. Most smoking-cessation programs report a success rate of only 20 percent. Treatment includes the use of drugs (e.g., doxepin [Sinequan], clonidine [Catapres]), hypnosis, aversive therapy, acupuncture, lobeline (a congener of nicotine) chewing gum, and nicotine nasal sprays. Persons who successfully discontinue smoking are likely to have been encouraged by someone close to them (such as a spouse or children), to have been fearful of the ill effects of smoking, and to have joined a support group of ex-smokers. Encouragement from a nonsmoking physician is also highly correlated with abstinence.

References

Aaronson L S, Macnee C L: Tobacco, alcohol, and caffeine use during pregnancy. J Obstet Gynecol Neonatal Nurs *18*: 279, 1989.
Berger A: Effects of caffeine consumption on pregnancy outcome: A review. J Reprod Med *33*: 945, 1988.
Ghoneim M M, Hinrichs J V, Chiang C-K, Loke W H: Pharmacokinetic and pharmacodynamic interactions between caffeine and diazepam. J Clin Psychopharmacol *6*: 75, 1986.
Griffiths R R, Woodson P P: Caffeine physical dependence: A review of human and laboratory animal studies. Psychopharmacology *94*: 437, 1988.
Griffiths R R, Woodson P P: Reinforcing properties of caffeine: Studies in humans and laboratory animals. Pharmacol Biochem Behav *29*: 419, 1988.
Hughes J R, Gust S W, Pechacek T F: Prevalence of tobacco dependence and withdrawal. Am J Psychiatry *144*: 205, 1987.
Hughes J R, Hatsukami D: Signs and symptoms of tobacco withdrawal. Arch Gen Psychiatry *43*: 289, 1986.
Hughes J R, Hatsukami D K, Mitchell J E, Dahlgren L A: Prevalence of smoking among psychiatric outpatients. Am J Psychiatry *143*: 993, 1986.
Jaffe J H: Drug dependence: Opioids, nonnarcotics, nicotine (tobacco), and caffeine. In *Comprehensive Textbook of Psychiatry*, ed 5, H I Kaplan and B J Sadock, editors, p 642. Williams & Wilkins, Baltimore, 1989.
Lieberman H R, Wurtman R J, Emde G G, Coviella I L G: The effects of caffeine and aspirin on mood and performance. J Clin Psychopharmacol *7*: 315, 1987.
Murphy J K, Edwards N B, Downs A D, Ackerman B J, Rosenthal T L: Effects of doxepin on withdrawal symptoms in smoking cessation. Am J Psychiatry *147*: 1353, 1990.
National Institute on Drug Abuse: 1988 National Household Survey on Drug Abuse, 1989.
Shiffman S, Fischer L B, Zettler-Segal M, Benowitz N L: Nicotine exposure among nondependent smokers. Arch Gen Psychiatry *47*: 333, 1990.
Somani S M, Gupta P: Caffeine: A new look at an age-old drug. Int J Clin Pharmacol Ther Toxicol *26*: 521, 1988.
Stoner G R, Skirboll L R, Werkman S, Hommer D W: Preferential effects of caffeine on limbic and cortical dopamine systems. Biol Psychiatry *23*: 761, 1988.
U S Department of Health and Human Services: HHS News, July 1989.

12.10 / Inhalants and Anabolic Steroids

INHALANTS

The revised third edition of *Diagnostic and Statistical Manual of Mental Disorders* (DSM-III-R) specifies inhalants as a class of psychoactive substances subject to abuse and dependence. DSM-III-R specifies inhalant intoxication as the only psychoactive substance-induced organic mental disorder associated with the use of these solvents.

Epidemiology

According to the National Institute on Drug Abuse (NIDA) (July 1989), while too many youth (aged 12 to 17) (9 percent) have experimented with inhalants, current use is rare: only 2 percent of youth and young adults (aged 18 to 25) and less than one-half of 1 percent of older adults (aged 26+) used an inhalant in the past month.

Clinical Features

Among abused volatile solvents (i.e., inhalants) are gasoline, varnish remover, lighter fluid, airplane glue, rubber cement, cleaning fluid, and aerosols (especially spray paints). The active ingredients include toluene, acetone, benzene, trichloroethane, perchloroethylene, trichloroethylene, 1,2-dichloropropane, and halogenated hydrocarbons. Because these substances are legal, cheap, and accessible, they are used mostly by the young (ages 6 to 16 years) and the poor, who inhale them from a tube, a can, a plastic bag, or a rag held over the nose. Intoxication often comes on within five minutes and usually lasts 15 to 30 minutes. Volatile solvents cannot be detected in urine. Solvents produce a central nervous system depressant effect (the initial effects being disinhibitory and the later effects inhibitory) characterized by euphoria, excitement, a floating sensation, dizziness, slurred speech, ataxia, and a sense of heightened power.

Solvents can cause inhalant intoxication (Table 12.10-1), consisting of apathy, diminished social and occupational function, and impaired judgment leading to impulsive and aggressive behavior; there may also be amnesia for the period of intoxication. Other acute effects are nausea, anorexia, nystagmus, depressed reflexes, diplopia, and, with high doses, stupor and even unconsciousness. Death may be caused by central respiratory depression, cardiac arrhythmias, asphyxiation, or accident. Inhalants often leave visible external evidence, such as a rash around the nose and mouth, breath odors, and residue on the face, hands, and clothing. Irritation of the eyes, throat, lungs, and nose is common.

Table 12.10-1
Diagnostic Criteria for Inhalant Intoxication

A. Recent use of an inhalant

B. Maladaptive behavioral changes (e.g., belligerence, assaultiveness, apathy, impaired judgment, impaired social or occupational functioning)

C. At least two of the following signs:
   (1) dizziness
   (2) nystagmus
   (3) incoordination
   (4) slurred speech
   (5) unsteady gait
   (6) lethargy
   (7) depressed reflexes
   (8) psychomotor retardation
   (9) tremor
   (10) generalized muscle weakness
   (11) blurred vision or diplopia
   (12) stupor or coma
   (13) euphoria

D. Not due to any physical or other mental disorder

Table from DSM-III-R, *Diagnostic and Statistical Manual of Mental Disorders*, ed 3, revised. Copyright American Psychiatric Association, Washington, D.C., 1987, with permission.

Other clinical features. It is not yet clear whether there is a withdrawal reaction, but substantial tolerance develops after repeated sniffing. A serious risk is irreversible damage to the liver, kidney, and other organs from benzene and halogenated hydrocarbons. Peripheral neuritis has also been reported. Permanent neuromuscular and brain damage must be considered a possibility, particularly because inhalants often contain high concentrations of copper, zinc, and heavy metals. There are reports of brain atrophy, renal tubular acidosis, and chronic motor impairment in toluene users.

According to DSM-III-R, excluded from the official classification of inhalant intoxication are anesthetic gases (e.g., nitrous oxide, ether) and short-acting vasodilators, such as the amylnitrites and butylnitrites. These substances are excluded because the intoxication associated with them is sometimes different clinically from inhalant intoxication, and they are generally used by a population who may be different from those who abuse inhalants. Use of these or other substances is classified in DSM-III-R under other or unspecified psychoactive substance-induced organic mental disorder. The distinction, however, is mainly one of classification, because these substances are also volatile inhalants and there is much overlap in signs and symptoms.

ANABOLIC STEROIDS

Beginning in 1988, reports of athletes abusing anabolic or androgenic steroids began to appear in the psychiatric literature. These substances are used to enhance stamina or strength. They may produce adverse behavioral effects, such as confusion, poor judgment, impulsiveness, delusions, mania, and violence. About one-third of abusers develop psychotic symptoms. Extreme aggression is called "roid rage," and some cases of homicide have been reported. Abusers may use dosages 10 to 100 times greater than that prescribed by physicians for legitimate therapeutic purposes.

Withdrawal symptoms characterized by severe major depression occur for up to three months after discontinuance of the drug. No specific treatment is available. In DSM-III-R this condition is classified as unspecified psychiatric substance-induced organic mood disorder. In New York State anabolic steroids have been classified as controlled substances requiring a triplicate prescription in an effort to stop abuse.

References

Anderson H R, Macnair R S, Ramsey J D: Deaths from abuse of volatile substances: A national epidemiological study. Br Med J *290*: 304, 1985.

Barnes G E, Vulcano B A: Bibliography of the solvent abuse literature. Int J Addict *14*: 403, 1979.

Golding A S, Stewart H M: Organic lead encephalopathy: Behavioral change and movement disorder following gasoline inhalation. J Clin Psychiatry *43*: 70, 1982.

National Institute on Drug Abuse: 1988 Household Survey on Drug Abuse, 1989.

Pollard T G: Relative addiction potential of major centrally active drugs and drug classes: Inhalants and anesthetics. Adv Alcohol Subst Abuse *9*: 149, 1990.

Ron M A: Volatile substance abuse: A review of possible long-term neurological, intellectual, and psychiatric sequelae. Br J Psychiatry *148*: 235, 1986.

U S Department of Health and Human Services: HHS News, July 1989.

Westermeyer J: The psychiatrist and solvent-inhalant abuse: Recognition, assessment, and treatment. Am J Psychiatry *144*: 903, 1987.

13

Schizophrenia

Schizophrenia is sometimes considered the most devastating of the mental illnesses because its onset is early in a patient's life and its symptoms can be destructive to the patient and to the patient's family and friends. Although schizophrenia is discussed as if it were a single disease, this diagnostic category can include a variety of disorders that present with somewhat similar behavioral symptoms. Schizophrenia probably comprises a group of disorders with heterogeneous causes and definitely includes patients whose clinical presentations, treatment responses, and courses of illness are varied.

HISTORY

The two key people in the history of schizophrenia were Emil Kraepelin (German, 1856–1926) and Eugen Bleuler (Swiss, 1857–1939). At least three important figures preceded Kraepelin and Bleuler. Benedict Morel (1809–1873), a French psychiatrist, used the term *démence précoce* for deteriorated patients whose illness began in adolescence; Karl Kahlbaum (German, 1828–1899) described the symptoms of catatonia; and Ewold Hecker (German, 1843–1909) wrote about the extremely bizarre behavior of hebephrenia.

Emil Kraepelin

Kraepelin (Figure 13-1) organized the seriously mentally ill patients into three diagnostic groups: dementia precox, manic-depressive psychosis, and paranoia. Kraepelin's description of dementia precox emphasized a chronic deteriorating course and such clinical phenomena as hallucinations and delusions. Kraepelin reported that approximately 4 percent of his patients had complete recoveries and 13 percent had significant remissions. The term "manic-depressive psychosis" identified patients who experienced episodes of illness separated by virtually complete remissions. Patients classified as having paranoia had as their major symptom persistent persecutory delusions.

Eugen Bleuler

Bleuler (Figure 13-2) coined the term "schizophrenia," which means split mindedness, in reference to a theoretical schism between thought, emotion, and behavior. Unfortunately, this term has caused confusion with split personality (now called multiple personality disorder), a completely different disorder from schizophrenia. Bleuler's definition of schizophrenia differed from Kraepelin's dementia precox in that Bleuler did not believe that deterioration was a necessary symptom of the disorder.

Figure 13-1. Emil Kraepelin. (From G C Davison, J M Neale: *Abnormal Psychology: An Experimental Clinical Approach.* Wiley, New York, 1974, with permission.)

The four A's. Bleuler also divided the symptoms into fundamental (primary) and accessory (secondary) symptoms. The most important fundamental symptom was a thought disorder characterized by associational disturbances, particularly looseness. The other fundamental symptoms were affective disturbances, autism, and ambivalence. (Bleuler's so-called four A's consist of associations, affect, autism, and ambivalence.) Accessory symptoms included hallucinations and delusions.

Other Theorists

Four modern psychiatrists who theorized about schizophrenia were Adolf Meyer, Harry Stack Sullivan, Gabriel Langfeldt, and Kurt Schneider. Meyer, the founder of psychobiology, believed that schizophrenia and other mental disorders were reactions to a variety of life stresses, so he called the syndrome a "schizophrenic reaction." Sullivan, the founder of the interpersonal psychoanalytic school, emphasized social isolation as both a cause and a symptom of schizophrenia.

Gabriel Langfeldt. Gabriel Langfeldt, unlike Bleuler, derived his criteria from empirical experience, rather than a theoretical formulation. Langfeldt divided the disorder into

Figure 13-2. Eugen Bleuler, (From G C Davison, J M Neale: *Abnormal Psychology: An Experimental Clinical Approach*. Wiley, New York, 1974, with permission.)

true schizophrenia and schizophreniform psychosis (see Section 15.2). The diagnosis of true schizophrenia rests on the findings of depersonalization, autism, emotional blunting, insidious onset, and feelings of derealization and unreality. True schizophrenia is often referred to as nuclear schizophrenia, process schizophrenia, or nonremitting schizophrenia.

Kurt Schneider and first-rank symptoms. Kurt Schneider described a number of so-called first-rank symptoms of schizophrenia that he considered in no way specific for the disease but of great pragmatic value in making a diagnosis (Table 13-1). Schizophrenia, Schneider pointed out, can also be diagnosed exclusively on the basis of second-rank symptoms, along with an otherwise typical clinical appearance. Schneider did not mean these symptoms to be applied rigidly. He warned the clinician that the diagnosis should be made in certain patients, even though they failed to show first-rank symptoms. Unfortunately, this warning is frequently ignored, and the absence of such symptoms in a single interview is taken as evidence that the person is free of schizophrenia.

EPIDEMIOLOGY

The incidence of schizophrenia in the United States and Europe is between 0.3 and 0.6 per 1,000 persons. In the United States the lifetime prevalence is about 1.5 percent. Approximately 0.025 to 0.05 percent of the total population are treated for schizophrenia in any one year; two-thirds of these patients require hospitalization. Some geographical regions have an unusually high prevalence of schizophrenia, which has led to some claims of an infectious (e.g., viral) cause of schizophrenia.

Age and Sex

The peak age of onset for men is between age 15 and 25 and for women between 25 and 35. Onset of schizophrenia before age 10 or after age 50 is extremely rare. Approximately 90 percent of patients in treatment for schizophrenia are between 15 and 54 years old. There is no difference in the prevalence of schizophrenia between males and females.

Reproduction Rates, Suicide, and Risk of Death

Marriage and fertility rates have increased among schizophrenic persons. This increase is due to many factors, including the use of psychotherapeutic drugs, the open-door policies in hospitals, the deinstitutionalization in the state hospitals, the emphasis on rehabilitation, and the community-based care for patients with schizophrenia. Because of these factors, the number of children born to schizophrenic parents doubled from 1935 to 1955; the fertility rate is now believed to be quite close to that of the general population.

Approximately 50 percent of all patients with schizophrenia attempt suicide, and 10 percent succeed sometime during a 20-year follow-up period. Schizophrenic persons also have a high mortality rate from accidents and natural causes, a phenomenon not explained by institution-related or treatment-related variables.

Cultural and Socioeconomic Considerations

Schizophrenia has been described in all cultures and socioeconomic status (SES) groups studied. In industrialized nations a disproportionate number of schizophrenic patients are in the lower SES groups. This observation has been explained by the downward drift hypothesis, suggesting that affected persons either move into a lower SES group or fail to rise out of a low SES group because of the illness. An alternative explanation, less supported by research, is the social causation hypothesis, proposing that stresses experienced by members of low SES groups contribute to the development of or even cause schizophrenia.

The prevalence of schizophrenia has been correlated with local population density in cities with populations over 1 million. But the correlation is weaker in cities of 100,000 to 500,000 people and nonexistent in cities with fewer than 10,000 people. This effect of population density is consistent with the observation that the incidence of schizophrenia in children of either one or two schizophrenic parents is twice as high in cities as in rural communities, suggesting that social stressors may affect the development of schizophrenia in persons at risk. The problem of the homeless in large cities may be related to the deinstitutionalization of schizophrenic patients who were not adequately engaged in follow-up care. Although the exact percentage of homeless persons who are, in fact, schizophrenic is difficult to obtain, an estimated one-third to two-thirds of the homeless have schizophrenia.

It has been hypothesized that immigration and industrialization contribute to the cause of schizophrenia. Because some studies report a higher prevalence of schizophrenia among recent immigrants, this finding has implicated abrupt cultural change as a stressor involved in the cause of this disorder. The prevalence of schizophrenia

Table 13-1
Essential Features* of Various Diagnostic Criteria for Schizophrenia

KURT SCHNEIDER

1. First-rank symptoms
   a. Audible thoughts
   b. Voices arguing or discussing or both
   c. Voices commenting
   d. Somatic passivity experiences
   e. Thought withdrawal and other experiences of influenced thought
   f. Thought broadcasting
   g. Delusional perceptions
   h. All other experiences involving volition, made affects, and made impulses
2. Second-rank symptoms
   a. Other disorders of perception
   b. Sudden delusional ideas
   c. Perplexity
   d. Depressive and euphoric mood changes
   e. Feelings of emotional impoverishment
   f. ". . . and several others as well"

GABRIEL LANGFELDT

1. Symptom criteria
   Significant clues to a diagnosis of schizophrenia are (if no sign of organic mental disorder, infection, or intoxication can be demonstrated):
   a. Changes in personality, which manifest themselves as a special type of emotional blunting followed by lack of initiative, and altered, frequently peculiar behavior. (In hebephrenia, especially, these changes are quite characteristic and are a principal clue to the diagnosis.)
   b. In catatonic types, the history and the typical signs in periods of restlessness and stupor (with negativism, oily facies, catalepsy, special vegetative symptoms, etc.)
   c. In paranoid psychoses, essential symptoms of split personality (or depersonalization symptoms) and a loss or reality feeling (derealization symptoms) or primary delusions
   d. Chronic hallucinations
2. Course criterion
   A final decision about diagnosis cannot be made before a follow-up period of at least five years has shown a chronic course of disease.

NEW HAVEN SCHIZOPHRENIA INDEX

1. a. Delusions: not specified or other-than-depressive: 2 points	
b. Auditory hallucinations	any one: 2 points
c. Visual hallucinations	
d. Other hallucinations	
2. a. Bizarre thoughts	any one: 2 points
b. Autism or grossly unrealistic private thoughts	
c. Looseness of associations, illogical thinking, overinclusion	
d. Blocking	either: 2 points
e. Concreteness	
f. Derealization	each: 1 point
g. Depersonalization	
3. Inappropriate affect: 1 point	
4. Confusion: 1 point	
5. Paranoid ideation (self-referential thinking, suspiciousness): 1 point	
6. Catatonic behavior	any one: 1 point
a. Excitement	
b. Stupor	
c. Waxy flexibility	
d. Negativism	
e. Mutism	
f. Echolalia	
g. Stereotyped motor activity	

Scoring: To be considered part of the schizophrenic group, the patient must score on Item 1 or Item 2a, 2b, or 2c, and must receive a total score of at least 4 points.

Table 13-1
Continued

FLEXIBLE SYSTEM

Minimum number of symptoms required can be four to eight, depending on investigator's choice.
1. Restricted affect
2. Poor insight
3. Thoughts aloud
4. Poor rapport
5. Widespread delusions
6. Incoherent speech
7. Unreliable information
8. Bizarre delusions
9. Nihilistic delusions
10. Absence of early awakening (one to three hours)
11. Absence of depressed facies
12. Absence of elation

RESEARCH DIAGNOSTIC CRITERIA

Criteria 1 through 3 required for diagnosis.
1. At least two of the following for definite illness, and one for probable (not counting those occurring during period of drug or alcohol abuse or withdrawal):
   a. Thought broadcasting, insertion, or withdrawal
   b. Delusions of being controlled or influenced, other bizarre delusions, or multiple delusions
   c. Delusions other than persecution or jealousy lasting at least one month
   d. Delusions of any type if accompanied by hallucinations of any type for at least one week
   e. Auditory hallucinations in which either a voice keeps up a running commentary on subject's behaviors or thoughts as they occur or two or more voices converse with each other
   f. Nonaffective verbal hallucinations spoken to subject
   g. Hallucinations of any type throughout day for several days or intermittently for at least one month
   h. Definite instances of marked formal thought disorders accompanied by blunted or inappropriate affect, delusions or hallucinations of any type, or grossly disorganized behavior
2. One of the following:
   a. Current period of illness lasted at least two weeks from onset of noticeable change in subject's usual condition
   b. Subject has had previous period of illness lasting at least two weeks, during which he or she met criteria, and residual signs of illness have remained (e.g., extreme social withdrawal, blunted or inappropriate affect, formal thought disorder, or unusual thoughts or perceptual experiences)
3. At no time during active period of illness being considered did subject meet criteria for probable or definite manic or depressive syndrome to the degree that it was a prominent part of illness

ST. LOUIS CRITERIA

1. Both necessary:
   a. Chronic illness with at least six months of symptoms before index evaluation, without return to premorbid level of psychosocial adjustment
   b. Absence of period of depressive or manic symptoms sufficient to qualify for mood (affective) disorder or probable mood (affective) disorder
2. At least one of the following:
   a. Delusions or hallucinations without significant perplexity or disorientation
   b. Verbal production that makes communication difficult owing to lack of logical or understandable organization (in presence of muteness, diagnostic decision must be deferred)
3. At least three for definite, two for probable, illness:
   a. Never married
   b. Poor premorbid social adjustment or work history
   c. Family history of schizophrenia
   d. Absence of alcoholism or drug abuse within one year of onset
   e. Onset before age 40

TAYLOR AND ABRAMS' CRITERIA

All criteria must be met for diagnosis.
1. Duration of episode greater than six months
2. Clear consciousness
3. Presence of delusions, hallucinations, or formal thought disorder (verbigeration, non sequiturs, word approximations, neologisms, blocking, and derailment)
4. Absence of broad affect
5. Absence of signs and symptoms sufficient to make diagnosis of affective disease
6. No alcoholism or drug abuse within one year of index episode
7. Absence of focal signs and symptoms of coarse brain disease or major medical illness known to produce significant behavioral changes

Table 13-1
Continued

PRESENT STATE EXAMINATION

The following 12 items from the Present State Examination correspond to a 12-point diagnostic system for schizophrenia, with varying levels of certainty of diagnosis based on the cut-off score determined by the examiner. Nine of the symptoms are scored 1 point each when present (+), and three are scored 1 point each when absent (−).

1. Restricted affect (+)
2. Poor insight (+)
3. Thoughts aloud (+)
4. Awaking early (−)
5. Poor rapport (+)
6. Depressed facies (−)
7. Elation (−)
8. Widespread delusions (+)
9. Incoherent speech (+)
10. Unreliable information (+)
11. Bizarre delusions (+)
12. Nihilistic delusions (+)

The criteria of Schneider and Langfeldt from World Psychiatric Association: *Diagnostic Criteria for Schizophrenic and Affective Psychoses*. American Psychiatric Press, Washington, DC, 1983, with permission. The criteria of St. Louis, RDC, NHSI, Flexible, and Taylor and Abrams from J Endicott, J Nee, L Fleiss, J Cohen, J B W Williams, R Simon: Diagnostic criteria for schizophrenia. Arch Gen Psychiatry *39*: 884, 1982, with permission.
*Only the essential features of the criteria are listed here. Investigators who plan to use any of these systems should refer to the original sources. (See body of chapter for Bleulerian, Kraepelinian, and DSM-III-R diagnostic criteria for schizophrenia.)

appears to rise among third-world populations as contact with technologically advanced cultures increases. Finally, it has been argued that cultures may be more or less schizophrenogenic, depending on how mental illness is perceived, the nature of the patient role, the system of social supports, and the complexity of social communication. Schizophrenia is prognostically more benign in less developed nations where patients are reintegrated into their communities and families more completely than they are in more highly civilized Western societies.

Seasonality of Birth

In the northern hemisphere, including the United States, most schizophrenic patients are born in the months from January to April. In the southern hemisphere, most schizophrenic patients are born in the months from July to September. This seasonality of birth has suggested to some researchers the possibility that schizophrenia is related to in utero or perinatal viral infections, which are most common during the winter months.

Mental Hospital Beds and Financial Cost to Society

Patterns of hospitalization for schizophrenic patients have changed over the past three decades. The duration of hospitalizations has decreased, and the number of admissions has increased. The probability of readmission within a two-year period after discharge from the first hospitalization is about 40 to 60 percent. Schizophrenic patients occupy approximately 50 percent of all mental hospital beds and account for approximately 16 percent of all psychiatric patients who receive any type of treatment.

Schizophrenia is the most expensive of all mental disorders in direct treatment costs, loss of productivity, and expenditures for public assistance. The annual cost of schizophrenia in the United States is estimated to be about 2 percent of the gross national product. The direct delivery of psychiatric care accounts for only 20 percent of this figure; the remaining costs reflect the loss in productive capacity and costs of hospitalization.

ETIOLOGY

The cause of schizophrenia is not known. Schizophrenia is quite likely a heterogeneous disorder, and very few of the etiological factors discussed here are exclusionary. The major model for integrating these putative causative factors is the stress-diathesis model. It postulates that a person may have a specific vulnerability (diathesis) that, when acted on by some stressful environmental influence, allows the symptoms of schizophrenia to develop. In the most general stress-diathesis model, the diathesis or the stress can be biological or environmental or both. The environmental component can be either biological (e.g., an infection) or psychological (e.g., a stressful family situation, death of a close relative). The biological basis of a diathesis can be further shaped by epigenetic influences, such as drug abuse, psychosocial stress, and trauma. Until a specific causative factor for schizophrenia is identified, the stress-diathesis model is the most concise way to conceptualize the available data and theories.

Biological Factors

Since the discovery of the effectiveness of antipsychotic drugs in the treatment of schizophrenia, many studies have compared specific, objective biological features of schizophrenic patients with those of nonschizophrenic psychiatric patients and those of normal controls. There are two major caveats in interpreting biological abnormalities reported in schizophrenia. First, one must consider what a biological abnormality signifies. Such an abnormality is, at most, a correlation and rarely, if ever, can be seen as causal. Second, it is difficult to determine whether the abnormality is related to the disease process itself or to treatment, especially antipsychotic medications.

Two other observations about the nature of the brain need to be considered. First, the fact that pathology has been identified in one area does not mean that the primary area of pathology has been defined. For example, the hypoactive frontal lobe function in schizophrenia can be caused by hyperactive inhibitory input from some other region of the brain. Second, a single pathological process in the brain can cause a wide range of phenomena in different patients. For example, patients with Huntington's chorea can present with the entire range of diagnoses in the revised third edition of *Diagnostic and Statistical Manual of Mental Disorders* (DSM-III-R) diagnoses, including no mental disorder. Conversely, a single specific abnormality in the brain can have many different causes. Parkinson's disease, for example, can have idiopathic, infectious, traumatic, or toxic causes.

Dopamine hypothesis. The simplest version of the dopamine hypothesis, the major neurotransmitter hypothesis for schizophrenia, states that there is a hyperactivity of dopaminergic systems in schizophrenia. The major support for this hypothesis is that virtually all effective antipsychotic drugs are dopamine receptor antagonists. Specifically, the clinical potency of antipsychotic drugs is closely correlated with their binding affinity to dopamine (D_2) receptors, the dopamine receptor subtype that does not stimulate adenylate cyclase. The observation that administration of two dopaminergic agonists—amphetamine and levodopa (L-dopa [Dopar, Larodopa])—exacerbates the symptoms of many schizophrenic patients lends additional support to this hypothesis.

A significant role for dopamine in the pathophysiology of schizophrenia is consistent with recent reports that have measured plasma concentrations of the major dopamine metabolite, homovanillic acid (HVA). Some of these studies report a positive correlation between high pretreatment concentrations of HVA and two factors—severity of psychotic symptoms and treatment response to antipsychotic drugs. Studies of plasma HVA have also reported that, after a transient increase in plasma HVA concentrations, there is a steady decline in HVA concentration, which is correlated with symptom improvement in some patients.

There are at least two major problems with the dopamine hypothesis. First, dopamine antagonists are effective in treating virtually all psychotic and agitated patients, regardless of diagnosis. Response to dopaminergic antagonists, therefore, is not uniquely associated with schizophrenia. Second, some electrophysiological data suggest that dopaminergic neurons may increase their firing rate in reponse to chronic exposure to antipsychotic drugs. These data imply that the initial abnormality in schizophrenia may involve a hypodopaminergic state. The precise role of dopamine in the pathophysiology of schizophrenia remains unclear.

Of the dopaminergic tracts in the central nervous system (CNS), the mesocortical and the mesolimbic tracts have received the most attention in schizophrenia research. Both of these tracts have their cell bodies in the substantia nigra and the ventral tegmental area. One objection to focusing on these tracts is that D_2 receptors are much less common than D_1 receptors on the target neurons of these tracts. For this reason, some investigators have focused on the nigrostriatal tract and on the basal ganglia in general because this is the brain area richest in D_2 receptors.

A recent advance in neuroscience has been the cloning and sequencing of two forms of the human D_2 receptor—a short form (415 amino acids) and a long form (444 amino acids). The long form is thought to be the predominant one in most brain regions. The receptor is related to the β-adrenergic receptor and has seven putative transmembrane domains and a large third cytoplasmic loop, which may be involved in the regulation of interactions between the receptor and G-proteins. Most recently, dopamine receptors that are neither D_1 nor D_2 (e.g., D_3, D_4) have been identified by using the techniques of molecular biology. The role of these receptors in the pathophysiology and the treatment of schizophrenia is an active area of research.

Other neurotransmitters. Just as the dopamine hypothesis arose from the clinical efficacy of drugs that blocked the D_2 receptor, new hypotheses of schizophrenia are beginning to emerge from two new drugs with antipsychotic activity—clozapine (Clozaril) and the sigma receptor antagonists. The receptor that mediates the antipsychotic effects of clozapine has not yet been conclusively identified. The sigma receptor is the subject of active neuroscience research.

Virtually every known neurotransmitter has been studied in schizophrenia. There is some evidence that norepinephrine activity is increased in schizophrenia. This idea is supported by increased cerebrospinal fluid (CSF) 3-methoxy-4-hydroxyphenylglycol (MHPG) in some schizophrenic patients and the fact that amphetamine, which can produce a paranoid schizophrenialike clinical picture, acts on both dopaminergic and noradrenergic neurons. Because of its function as an inhibitory neurotransmitter, γ-aminobutyric acid (GABA) may play a role in schizophrenia. Presumably, decreased GABA activity could result in hyperactivity of dopaminergic neurons. Some neurochemical evidence supports this hypothesis, and a small number of patients with schizophrenia improve with benzodiazepine treatment.

Neuropathology. Two main types of neuropathological studies of schizophrenia have been reported. Neurochemical studies have measured neurotransmitter concentrations and receptor properties in specific areas of postmortem human brain specimens. Morphometric studies have examined postmortem human brain tissue for areas of cell loss or abnormal histology. Many postmortem neurochemical studies have reported an increased number of D_2 receptors in the basal ganglia and the limbic system (particularly the amygdala, nucleus accumbens, and hippocampus). These studies have been unable to distinguish changes in dopamine receptors related to schizophrenia from the increase in dopamine receptors related to antipsychotic drug treatment. Morphometric studies in schizophrenia have historically reported diverse findings. Several recent postmortem studies, however, have provided evidence for a pattern of degeneration of the limbic system (the medial temporal lobe, cingulate gyrus, nucleus accumbens, amygdala, and hippocampus) and the basal ganglia (especially the medial pallidus). These studies have reported increased gliosis, decreased numbers of neurons, and decreased volume.

Brain imaging. The majority of computed tomographic (CT) studies of the brains of schizophrenic patients have reported enlargement of the lateral and third ventricles in 10 to 50 percent of patients and cortical atrophy in 10 to 35 percent (Figure 13-3). Most of the available data support the interpretation that these findings are not the result of treatment. The majority of the studies also support the conclusions that the ventricular enlargement and cortical atrophy are present at the time of diagnosis and that the lesions are neither progressive nor reversible. Recent studies using siblings (including discordant monozygotic twins) as the control group have found that virtually all schizophrenic persons have larger ventricles

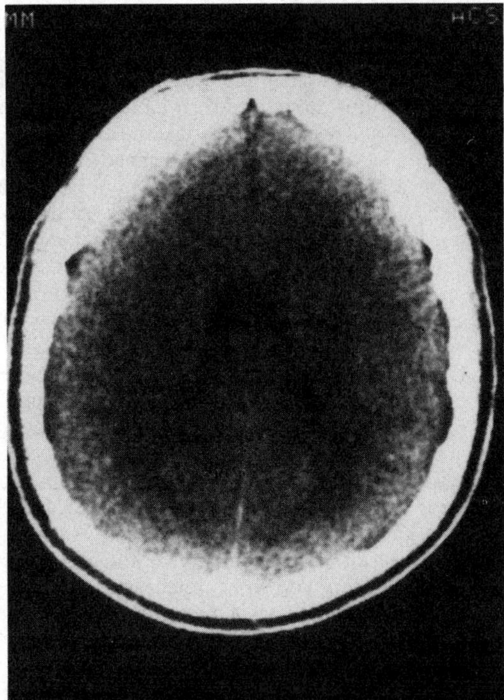

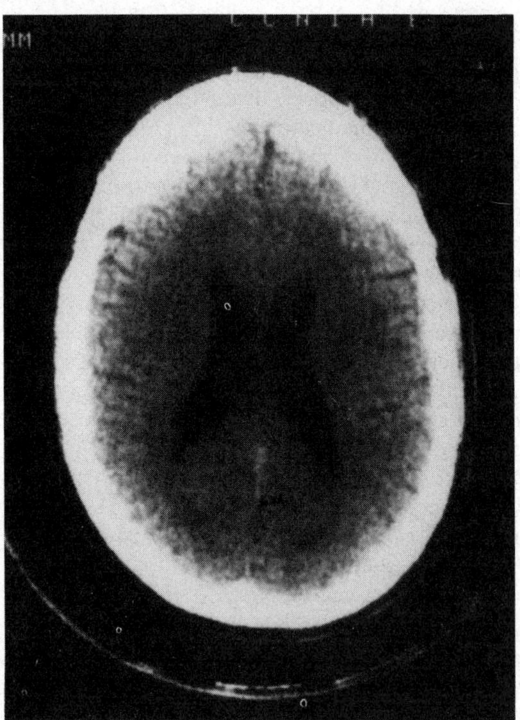

Figure 13-3. CT scans showing the lateral ventricles. The scan on the right shows enlarged lateral ventricles (Courtesy of Karen Berman, M.D., and Daniel Weinberger, M.D.)

than their control siblings. These data suggest that perhaps most cases of schizophrenia are associated with a decreased amount of brain tissue. Whether this decreased amount of brain tissue is caused by abnormal development or a degenerative process is unknown. The application of magnetic resonance imaging (MRI) to this type of research has provided evidence that the temporal lobe is particularly implicated as the site of neuronal loss in schizophrenia (Figure 13-4). Other studies have correlated the presence of CT scan abnormalities with the presence of negative or deficit symptoms, neuropsychiatric impairment, increased neurological signs, more frequent extrapyramidal symptoms from antipsychotics, poorer premorbid adjustment, increased delta activity on the electroencephalogram (EEG), and more suicide attempts.

Metabolic brain imaging studies of schizophrenic patients have been performed with regional cerebral blood flow (rCBF) and positron emission tomography (PET). Many PET studies have reported decreased blood flow or glucose utilization in the frontal lobes of schizophrenic patients who were supposedly in a resting state, although other studies have not corroborated this finding. Several PET studies have investigated the number of D_2 receptors in the basal ganglia of drug-free schizophrenic patients. Although one study reported an increased number of D_2 receptors, two studies have reported no difference between schizophrenic patients and healthy controls. Recent rCBF studies have used psychological activation procedures and have demonstrated an inability of schizophrenic patients to turn on their frontal lobes when performing a psychological task (see Figure 3.2-15 in Section 3.2, "Brain Imaging").

Electrophysiology. EEG studies of schizophrenic patients indicate a higher number of patients with abnormal records, increased sensitivity (e.g., more frequent spike activity) to activation procedures (e.g., sleep deprivation), decreased alpha activity, increased theta and delta activity, possibly more epileptiform activity, and possibly more left-sided abnormalities. Evoked potential studies have generally shown increased amplitude of early components and decreased amplitude of late components. This difference has been interpreted as an indication that, although schizophrenic patients are more sensitive to sensory stimulation, they compensate for this increased sensitivity by blunting the processing of information at higher cortical levels.

Psychoimmunology. Data suggesting an infectious cause in some cases of schizophrenia include increased numbers of physical anomalies at birth, increased rate of pregnancy and birth complications, seasonality of birth consistent with viral infections, geographical clusters of adult cases, seasonality of hospitalizations, neuropathological changes consistent with past infections, and a variety of immunological abnormalities, such as atypical lymphocytes. Other data supporting the hypothesis of an infectious cause, such as transmission in an animal model and identification of an infectious particle, are lacking. The positive data have been interpreted in several ways: An infectious agent may directly produce both the psychiatric symptoms and the immune dysfunction; an infectious agent may induce an autoimmunity against specific brain regions; or a primary immune disorder may produce an autoimmune disorder of the brain.

Psychoendocrinology. Psychoendocrine dysregulation has been reported in schizophrenia. Some data suggest decreased levels of luteinizing hormone (LH)–follicle-stimulating hormone (FSH), perhaps correlated with the age of onset and the length of illness. Two additional reported abnormalities are a blunted release of prolactin and growth hormone to gonadotropin-releasing hormone (GnRH) or thyrotropin-releasing hormone (TRH) stimulation and a blunted release of growth hormone to apomorphine stimulation that may be correlated with the presence of negative symptoms.

Integration of biological theories. Neuropsychiatric approaches to schizophrenia attempt to use biological data to locate the site of a lesion, much as neurologists use the neu-

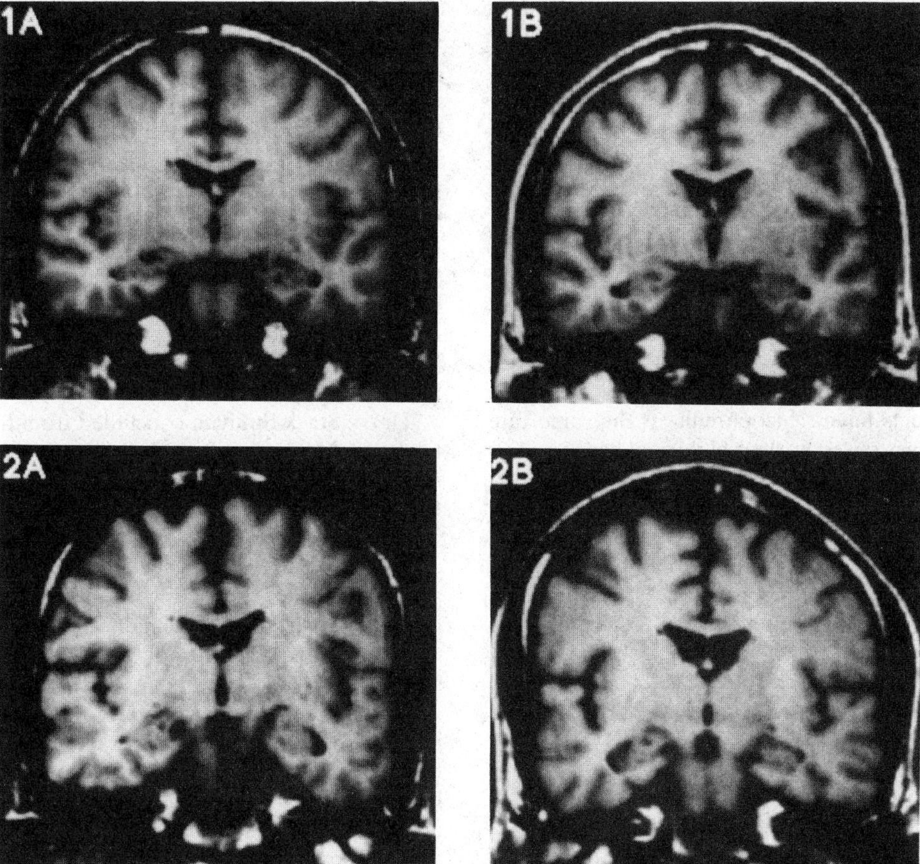

Figure 13-4. Magnetic resonance images (MRI). MRI coronal views from two sets of monozygotic twins discordant for schizophrenia showing subtle enlargement of the lateral ventricles in the affected twins (panels 1B and 2B) as compared with the unaffected twins (panels 1A and 2A), even when the affected twin had small ventricles. (Figure from R L Suddath, G W Christison, E F Torrey, M F Casanova, D R Weinberger: Anatomical abnormalities in the brains of monozygotic twins discordant for schizophrenia. N Engl J Med *322*: 789, 1990, with permission.)

rological examination to locate a lesion. The three major areas of interest are the frontal lobes, the limbic system, and the basal ganglia. Brain imaging studies, electrophysiological studies, and neuropsychological data all support involvement of the frontal lobes. Neuropathological data support limbic involvement. Both the common occurrence of psychosis in movement disorders and neuropathological data implicate the basal ganglia. The variety of possible sites for a lesion is consistent with a heterogeneous model of the cause of schizophrenia.

Electrophysiological theorists have focused on the processing of sensory information and abnormalities in laterality. Some electrophysiological data suggest deficits in attention and sensory filtering, leading to theories of hypervigilance in schizophrenia. The increased incidence of psychosis in temporal lobe epileptics with left-sided foci, the abnormalities in language seen in schizophrenia, and the reported increase of left-handedness in schizophrenic populations all support theories of left-hemisphere dysfunction.

The nature of the presumed lesion is unknown. The neurochemical hypothesis suggests some relatively specific abnormality, such as in the structure of some protein. The evidence of neuropathological damage would support an infectious, degenerative, traumatic, or developmental insult. The increased incidence of prenatal (e.g., bleeding), perinatal (e.g., long labor), and neonatal (e.g., convulsions) complications in patients who later become schizophrenic supports trauma as a causative factor.

Genetics

Investigations into the population genetics of schizophrenia have produced data consistent with the hypothesis that there is a genetic basis for schizophrenia—that is, that the genes of affected persons confer a vulnerability for schizophrenia. It is possible, however, that environmental forces (both psychological and biological) affect the expression of these genes and provide a stress that precipitates the syndrome of schizophrenia. Current approaches in genetics are directed toward identifying large pedigrees of affected persons and investigating the families for restriction fragment length polymorphisms (RFLPs). In fact, two studies reported a linkage between markers on chromosome 5 and schizophrenia in several families. Other investigators, however, have been unable to replicate this association in additional families. Possible reasons for this lack of replicability are genetic heterogeneity and incomplete penetrance.

The risks among members of various groups for schizophrenia support a genetic hypothesis of schizophrenia (Table 13-2). The closer the genetic relationship of any person to an affected proband, the more likely he or she is to have schizophrenia. Monozygotic twins (who share the same genetic information) have the highest concordance rate. (Very few genetic illnesses have a 100-percent

Table 13-2
Prevalence of Schizophrenia in Specific Populations

Population	Prevalence (%)
General population	1.0
Nontwin sibling of a schizophrenic patient	8.0
Child with one schizophrenic parent	12.0
Dizygotic twin of a schizophrenic patient	12.0
Child of two schizophrenic parents	40.0
Monozygotic twin of a schizophrenic patient	47.0

concordance rate in monozygotic twins.) The studies of adopted monozygotic twins demonstrate that twins reared by adoptive parents have schizophrenia at the same rate as their twin siblings raised by their biological parents. This finding suggests that the genetic influence outweighs that of the environment. In further support of the genetic basis is the observation that the more severe the schizophrenia, the more likely the twins are to be concordant for the disorder. One study that supports the stress-diathesis model showed that adopted monozygotic twins who later had schizophrenia had been adopted by psychologically disordered families.

Psychosocial Factors

Patients with schizophrenia seem to have a significant, albeit unidentified, biologically based vulnerability. Nevertheless, psychosocial factors are considered significant and are a major area of research and study that affects the development, expression, and course of the disorder.

Theories regarding the individual

Psychoanalytic theories. According to psychoanalytic theory, a crucial defect in schizophrenia is a disturbance in ego organization, which affects the interpretation of reality and the control of inner drives, such as sex and aggression. The disturbances occur as a consequence of distortions in the reciprocal relationship between the infant and the mother. As described by Margaret Mahler, the child is unable to separate and progress beyond the closeness and complete dependence that characterizes the mother-child relationship in the oral phase of development. The schizophrenic person never achieves object constancy, which is characterized by a sense of secure identity and which results from a close attachment to the mother during infancy. Paul Federn concluded that the fundamental disturbance in schizophrenia is the patient's early inability to achieve self-object differentiation. Some psychoanalysts hypothesize that the defect in rudimentary ego functions permits intense hostility and aggression to distort the mother-infant relationship, leading to a personality organization that is vulnerable to stress. The onset of symptoms during adolescence occurs at a time when the person requires a strong ego to deal with the need to function independently, separation, identity tasks, increased internal drives, and intense external stimulation.

Sigmund Freud believed that schizophrenic patients regress to a phase of primary narcissism and ego disintegration. The concept of ego disintegration refers to a return to the time when the ego was not yet established or had just begun to be established. The person is unable to develop a mature ego capable of interpreting reality.

Current psychoanalytic theory postulates that the various symptoms of schizophrenia have symbolic meaning for the individual patient. For example, fantasies of the world coming to an end indicate a perception that the person's internal world has broken down; feelings of grandeur reflect reactivated narcissism, in which the person believes that he or she is omnipotent; hallucinations are substitutes for the patient's inability to deal with objective reality and represent his or her inner wishes or fears; and delusions, similar to hallucinations, are regressive, restitutive attempts to create a new reality or to express hidden fears or impulses.

Harry Stack Sullivan concluded from his clinical investigations that some schizophrenic patients had been made anxious as infants by their anxious mothers, which caused the disintegration of ego function seen in the disorder.

Learning theory. According to learning theorists, as children, patients with schizophrenia learn irrational reactions and ways of thinking by imitating parents who may have their own significant emotional problems. Deficiency in social skills accounts for poor interpersonal relationships.

Theories regarding the family. No controlled evidence indicates that a specific family pattern plays a causative role in the development of schizophrenia; however, there have been at least three major theories in the past 35 years. (1) Gregory Bateson described a family situation called the double bind, in which a child is put into a situation in which he or she has to make a choice between two alternatives, both of which produce confusion and are unbearable. (2) Theodore Lidz described two abnormal patterns of family behavior. In one type of family, there is a prominent "schism" between the parents (one parent gets overly close to the child of the opposite sex), and in the other, there is a "skewed" relationship with one parent (a power struggle in which one parent is dominant). (3) Lyman Wynne described families in which emotional expression is suppressed by the consistent use of a "pseudomutual" or "pseudohostile" verbal communication and all members relate to one another in a characteristic way unique to that family.

Social theories. Some theorists have suggested that industrialization and urbanization are involved in the etiology of schizophrenia. Although some data have supported such theories, these stresses are now thought to have their major effects on the development and course of the illness.

CLINICAL FEATURES

There are three key issues regarding the clinical signs and symptoms of schizophrenia. First, no clinical sign or symptom is pathognomonic for schizophrenia; every sign or symptom seen in schizophrenia can be seen in other psychiatric and neurological disorders. This observation is contrary to the often heard clinical opinion that certain symptoms are diagnostic of schizophrenia. Therefore, it is not possible to diagnose schizophrenia simply by a mental status examination; past history is essential for the diagnosis of schizophrenia. Second, the symptoms of an individual patient change with time. For example, a patient may have intermittent hallucinations and a varying ability to perform adequately in social situations. Third, it is absolutely necessary to take into account the educational level, intellectual ability, and cultural and subcultural membership of the patient. An impaired ability to understand abstract concepts, for example, may reflect the patient's education or intelligence. Various religious organizations and cults may have customs that seem strange to those outside that organization but are considered perfectly normal to those within the cultural setting.

Premorbid Symptoms

An arbitrary line for each patient divides the premorbid or prepsychotic personality from the prodromal phase of the illness. The typical but not invariable history is that of a schizoid or schizotypal personality—quiet, passive, with few friends as a child, daydreaming, introverted, and shut in as an adolescent and adult. The child is often reported to have been especially obedient and never in any mischief. The preschizophrenic adolescent may have no close friends and few dates. The adolescent may avoid competitive sports but enjoy watching movies and television and listening to music, to the exclusion of more social activities.

Although the onset of illness is often defined at either the time of diagnosis or first hospitalization, symptoms of the illness often develop slowly over months or years. The person may begin complaining of somatic symptoms, such as headache, back and muscle pain, weakness, and digestive problems. The initial diagnosis may be malingering or a somatization disorder. Family and friends may eventually notice that the person has changed and is no longer functioning well in occupational, social, and personal activities. During this stage the patient may begin to feel anxious or perplexed and may develop an interest in abstract ideas, philosophy, the occult, or religious matters. DSM-III-R includes markedly peculiar behavior, abnormal affect, unusual speech, bizarre ideas, and strange perceptual experiences among the prodromal signs.

Mental Status Examination

General description. The patient may be quite talkative and may exhibit bizarre postures, and behavior may be quite agitated or violent and apparently in response to hallucinations. Catatonic excitement is the term used to describe a state of particularly intense but disorganized activity. This behavior contrasts dramatically with catatonic stupor, often referred to merely as catatonia, in which the patient seems completely lifeless and may exhibit symptoms such as muteness, negativism, and automatic obedience. Waxy flexibility used to be a common symptom in catatonia, but now it is quite rare (Figure 13-5). Many patients have a less extreme presentation of marked social withdrawal and egocentricity, lack of spontaneous speech or movement, and an absence of goal-directed behavior. Other obvious behaviors may include an odd clumsiness

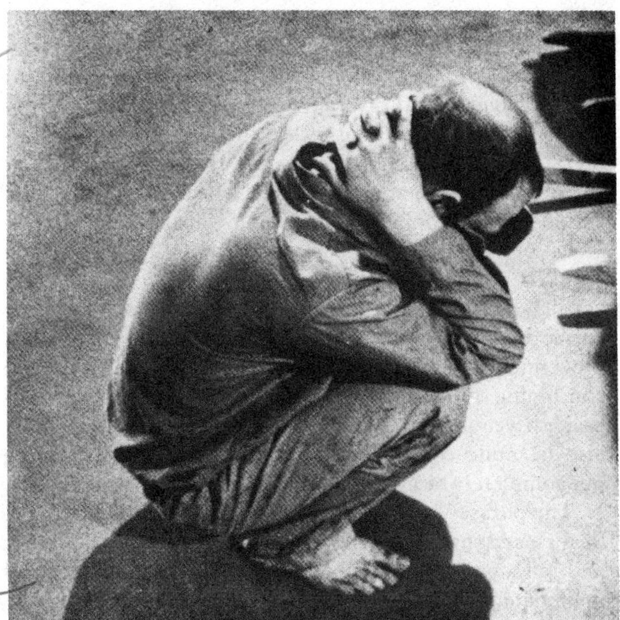

Figure 13-5. A patient exhibiting catatonic posturing. (From G C Davison, J M Neale: *Abnormal Psychology: An Experimental Clinical Approach.* Wiley, New York, 1974, with permission.)

or stiffness in body movements, deterioration of social habits (e.g., very poor grooming, obvious failure to bathe, smearing of feces), odd tics, stereotypies or mannerisms, and, in some cases, echopraxia.

Some clinicians report a "precox feeling" that describes an intuitive experience of their inability to establish an emotional rapport with the patient. Although this experience is common for clinicians to experience, no data indicate that it is a valid or reliable criterion in the diagnosis of schizophrenia.

Mood, feelings, and affect. The two most common affective presentations of schizophrenia are reduced emotional responsiveness or even anhedonia and overly active and inappropriate emotions of extreme rage, happiness, or anxiety. The presentation of a flat or blunted affect can represent either symptoms of the illness itself or the parkinsonian side effects of antipsychotic medications. The patient may describe exultant feelings of omnipotence, religious ecstasy, terror at the disintegration of his or her soul, or paralyzing anxiety about the destruction of the universe. Other feeling tones include perplexity, terror, a sense of isolation and overwhelming ambivalence.

Perceptual disturbances. Hallucinations may occur in any of the five sensory modalities. Auditory hallucinations are the most common in schizophrenic patients; they may complain of hearing one or more voices, which may be threatening, obscene, accusatory, or insulting. Visual hallucinations occur less frequently, but they are not rare. Tactile, olfactory, and gustatory hallucinations do occur, but their presence should cause the clinician to investigate carefully and rule out organic causes. Schizophrenic patients may experience cenesthetic hallucinations (sensations of altered states in body organs without plausible explanation, such as a burning sensation in the brain, a pushing sensation in the blood vessels, or a cutting sensation in the bone marrow). Illusions may also occur in schizophrenia, and the differentiation between hallucinations and illusions is often quite difficult.

Thought process. Nonperceptual disorders of thought may be divided into disorders of content, form, and process. Disorders of content reflect ideas, beliefs, and interpretations of stimuli. Delusions are the most obvious example of a disorder of content. Delusions can be quite varied in schizophrenia—persecutory, grandiose, religious, or somatic. Patients may believe that some outside entity is controlling their thoughts or behavior or, conversely, that they are controlling outside events in some extraordinary fashion (e.g., causing the sun to rise and set, preventing earthquakes). Patients may have an intense and consuming preoccupation with esoteric, abstract, symbolic, psychological, or philosophical ideas. Patients may also be quite concerned about allegedly life-threatening but completely bizarre and implausible somatic conditions.

The phrase "loss of ego boundaries" describes the lack of a clear sense of where the patient's own body, mind, and influence end and where those of other animate and inanimate objects begin. For example, the patient may think that other people, the television, or the newspapers are making reference to him or her. Other symptoms include the sense that the patient has fused with outside objects (e.g., a tree, another person) or that the patient has disintegrated. Given this state of mind, some schizophrenic patients may have doubts as to what sex they are or what their sexual orientation is. These symptoms, however, should not be confused with transvestism, transsexuality, or homosexuality.

Disorders of the form of thought are objectively observable in the spoken and written language and in the drawings (Figure 13-6) of the patient. These disorders include looseness of associations, derailment, incoherence, tangentiality, circumstantiality, neologisms, echolalia, verbigeration, word salad, and mutism. Although looseness of associations was once described as pathognomonic for schizophrenia, this symptom is seen frequently in mania. Distinguishing between looseness of associations and tangentiality can be difficult for even the most experienced clinician.

Disorders in process of thought concern how ideas and language are formulated. The examiner infers a disorder from what and how the patient speaks, writes, or draws. It may also be possible to assess the patient's thought process by observing the patient's behavior, especially in carrying out discrete tasks that the clinician may see in occupational therapy. Disorders of thought process include flight of ideas, thought blocking, impaired attention, poverty of thought and content of speech, poor memory, poor abstraction abilities, perseveration, idiosyncratic association (e.g., identical predicates, clang associations), overinclusion, illogical ideas, vagueness, and circumstantiality.

Impulse control, suicide, and homicide. Patients with schizophrenia may be quite agitated and have little impulse control when acutely ill. They may also have decreased social sensitivity, appearing impulsive when, for example, they grab another patient's cigarettes, change television channels abruptly, or throw food on the floor. Some of the apparently impulsive behavior, including suicide or homicide attempts, may be in response to hallucinations commanding the patient to act.

As previously stated, 50 percent of all schizophrenic patients attempt suicide, and 10 percent succeed. Suicide may be precipitated by feelings of absolute emptiness, depression, a need to escape from the mental torture, or auditory hallucinations that command the patient to kill himself or herself. Risk factors for suicide are as follows: the patient's awareness of his or her illness, a college education, a young male, a large number of exacerbations and remissions, a change in the course of the disease, an improvement from a relapse, depression, dependence on the hospital, overly high ambitions, prior suicide attempts early in the course of the illness, and living alone.

It is currently believed that homicide is no more common in schizophrenic patients than it is in the general population. A schizophrenic patient is often driven to homicide for unpredictable and bizarre reasons based on hallucinations or delusions. Furthermore, some schizophrenic patients display dangerous behavior in the hospital, such as violence toward others. These problems are related to the severity of the psychosis, a history of prior violence, and inadequate or low serum concentrations of antipsychotic drugs.

Orientation. Schizophrenic patients are usually oriented to person, time, and place. Lack of such orientation should prompt an investigation for an organic brain disorder. Some schizophrenic patients, however, may give incorrect or bizarre answers to such questions—for example, "I am Christ; this is heaven; and it is 35 A.D."

Memory. Memory, as tested in the mental status examination, is usually intact. It may be impossible, however, to get a patient to attend closely enough to the memory tests for this ability to be assessed adequately.

Judgment and insight. Classically, schizophrenic patients have little insight into their illness, at least as evidenced by their ability to talk about the disease process or their emotional reactions to it. The judgment of the patient is variable in schizophrenia and is best assessed from both the patient's behavior in the interview and outside sources of information.

Reliability. Although a particular schizophrenic patient may be a completely reliable historian, the nature of the illness requires that the examiner verify important information through additional sources.

Neurological Findings

The neurological findings in schizophrenia are subtle. Some research has shown that the presence of neurological signs and symptoms correlates with increased severity of illness, affective blunting, and a poor prognosis. Minor neurological symptoms, also called soft signs, are nonlocalizing neurological findings that include agraphesthesia, glabellar reflex, grasp reflex, and dysdiadochokinesia. They are seen in groups of schizophrenic patients more often than in normal persons or in patients with other psychiatric disorders. Schizophrenic patients also have disorders of motor behavior, as evidenced by tics and stereotypies, grimacing, impaired fine motor skills, and abnormal motor tone.

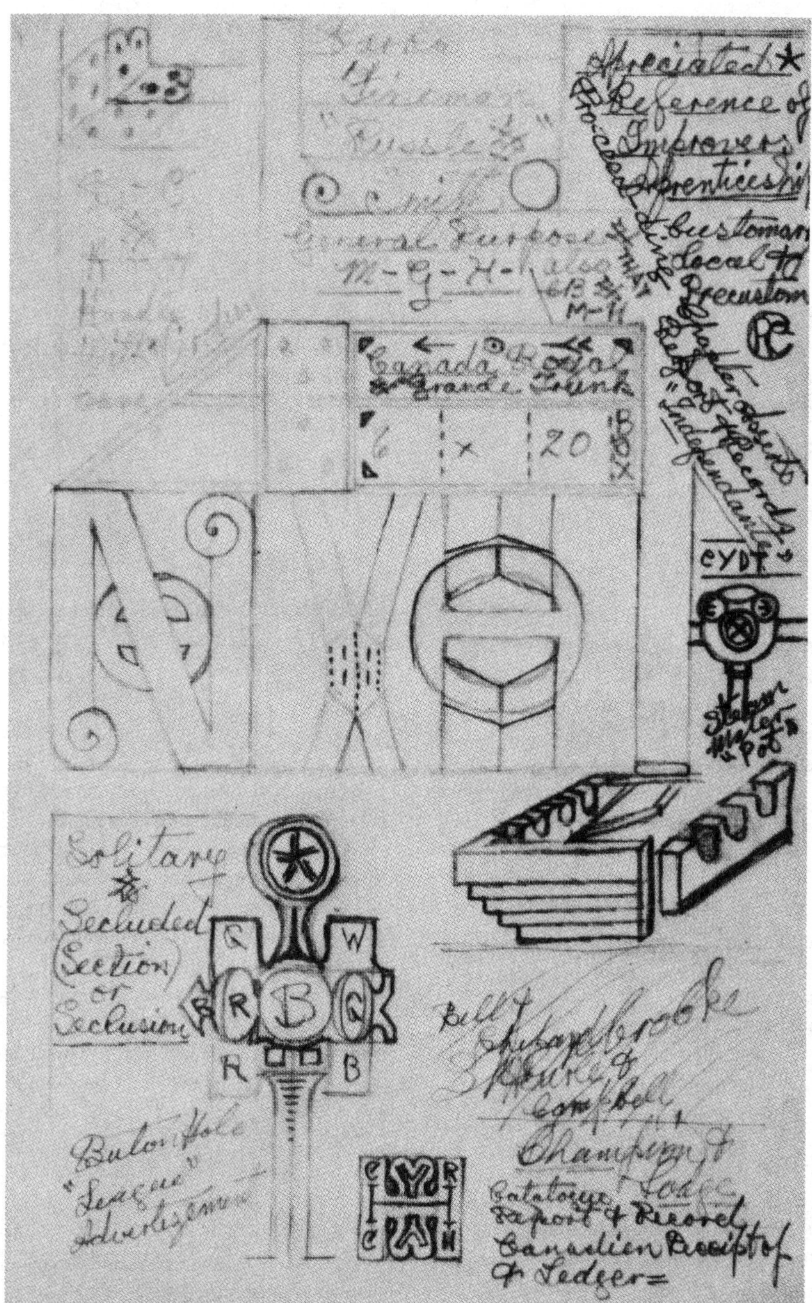

Figure 13-6. This drawing, carefully executed by a schizophrenic woman, expresses graphically her incoherent thinking and her tendency to perseveration of ideas, combined with an ability to accomplish quite complex drafting. Similar drawings may be produced when normal people doodle while their attention is not focused on what they are doing.

Eye examination reveals two major abnormalities in schizophrenic patients. First, they have an increased rate of blinking, thought to reflect hyperdopaminergic CNS activity. Second, they have abnormal rapid eye movement, saccadic movement. Approximately 50 to 80 percent of patients are unable to follow an object through space with smooth eye movements. Although seen in only 8 percent of normal persons, saccadic movement is seen in 40 percent of first-degree relatives of schizophrenic patients and may be a neurophysiological marker of a vulnerability for schizophrenia.

Some investigators consider the disorders of form of thought a *forme fruste* of an aphasia in schizophrenia, perhaps implicating the dominant parietal lobe. The inability of schizophrenic patients to perceive the prosody of speech or to inflect their own speech can be seen as a neurological symptom of the nondominant parietal lobe. Other parietallike symptoms in schizophrenia include the inability to carry out tasks (apraxias, which may also implicate the frontal lobes), right-left disorientation, and lack of concern about the illness.

Psychological Tests

Projective tests (e.g., the Rorschach, Thematic Apperception Test [TAT]) may indicate bizarre ideation. Personality inventories (e.g., the Minnesota Multiphasic Personality Inventory [MMPI]) often give abnormal findings in schizophrenia, but their contribution to diagnosis or treatment planning is minimal. Objective measures of neuropsychological performance, such as the Halstead-Reitan battery and the Luria-Nebraska battery, may also give abnormal findings, but they may indicate specific cognitive deficits that can be addressed in practical ways in the treatment program. These test results are consistent with bilateral frontal and temporal lobe dysfunction, including impaired attention, retention time, problem-solving ability, and intelligence. Low intelligence is often present at the onset, and intelligence may continue to deteriorate with the progress of the illness. In general, the findings are comparable to those in organic mental disorders.

COURSE AND PROGNOSIS

Course

The course of schizophrenia often begins with the prodromal symptoms described in the previous subsection. The onset of more pronounced symptoms may be acute (days) or gradual (a few months). The onset is usually in adolescence, and there may be an identified precipitating event, such as moving away to college, an experience with an hallucinogenic drug, or the death of a relative. The prodromal symptoms may be present for a year before a diagnosis is made.

The classic course of schizophrenia is one of exacerbations and relative remissions. The major distinction between schizophrenia and the mood disorders is the failure to return to baseline functioning after each relapse in schizophrenia. Sometimes a clinically observable postpsychotic depression follows an acute episode, and a vulnerability to stress is often lifelong. Deterioration progresses for an average of five years, at which point most patients reach a plateau. Positive symptoms tend to become less severe with time, but the socially debilitating negative symptoms may increase. The patient's life is characterized by aimlessness, inactivity, frequent hospitalizations, and, in urban settings, homelessness and poverty.

Prognosis

Schizophrenia does not always run a deteriorating course. A variety of factors are associated with good and poor prognoses (Table 13-3). The range of recovery rates in the literature is 10 to 60 percent, and a reasonable estimate is that 20 to 30 percent are able to lead somewhat normal lives. Approximately 20 to 30 percent of patients continue to experience moderate symptoms, and 40 to 60 percent of patients remain significantly impaired by their illness for their entire lives. It is clear that schizophrenic patients do much less well than patients with mood disorders, although approximately 20 to 25 percent of mood disorder patients are also severely disturbed at long-term follow-up.

DIAGNOSIS AND TYPES

DSM-III-R contains the official diagnostic guidelines for schizophrenia of the American Psychiatric Association (Table 13-4). The criteria for other diagnostic systems are given in Table 13-1.

DSM-III-R Types

Many efforts have been made to type schizophrenia, the major clinical value of which is to identify patients with good prognoses. This differentiation, however, can be done most pragmatically by following the guidelines described in Table 13-3. Although some typing schemes have had prognostic differences in mind, others have paid more attention to differences in clinical presentation. DSM-III-R has based its types mostly on clinical distinctions. There are five types—disorganized (previously called hebephrenic), catatonic, paranoid, undifferentiated, and residual—which are discussed below. The DSM-III-R diagnostic criteria for the types of schizophrenia are listed in Table 13-5.

Disorganized type (hebephrenic). The disorganized or hebephrenic type is characterized by a marked regression to primitive, disinhibited, and unorganized behavior. The onset is usually early, before age 25. Disorganized

Table 13-3
Features Weighting Toward Good or Poor Prognosis in Schizophrenia

Good Prognosis	Poor Prognosis
Late onset	Young onset
Obvious precipitating factors	No precipitating factors
Acute onset	Insidious onset
Good premorbid social, sexual, and work history	Poor premorbid social, sexual, and work history
Affective symptoms (especially depression)	Withdrawn, autistic behavior
Married	Single, divorced, or widowed
Family history of mood disorders	Family history of schizophrenia
Good support systems	Poor support systems
Positive symptoms	Negative symptoms
	Neurological signs and symptoms
	History of perinatal trauma
	No remissions in three years
	Many relapses
	History of assaultiveness

Table 13-4
Diagnostic Criteria for Schizophrenia

A. Presence of characteristic psychotic symptoms in the active phase: either (1), (2), or (3) for at least one week (unless the symptoms are successfully treated):
   (1) two of the following:
      (*a*) delusions
      (*b*) prominent hallucinations (throughout the day for several days or several times a week for several weeks, each hallucinatory experience not being limited to a few brief moments)
      (*c*) incoherence or marked loosening of associations
      (*d*) catatonic behavior
      (*e*) flat or grossly inappropriate affect
   (2) bizarre delusions involving a phenomenon that the person's culture would regard as totally implausible (e.g., thought broadcasting, being controlled by a dead person)
   (3) prominent hallucinations [as defined in (1)(*b*) above] of a voice with content having no apparent relation to depression or elation, or a voice keeping up a running commentary on the person's behavior or thoughts, or two or more voices conversing with each other

B. During the course of the disturbance, functioning in such areas as work, social relations, and self-care is markedly below the highest level achieved before onset of the disturbance (or, when the onset is in childhood or adolescence, failure to achieve expected level of social development).

C. Schizoaffective disorder and mood disorder with psychotic features have been ruled out, i.e., if a major depressive or manic syndrome has ever been present during an active phase of the disturbance, the total duration of all episodes of a mood syndrome has been brief relative to the total duration of the active and residual phases of the disturbance.

D. Continuous signs of the disturbance for at least six months. The six-month period must include an active phase (of at least one week, or less if symptoms have been successfully treated) during which there were psychotic symptoms characteristic of schizophrenia (symptoms in A), with or without a prodromal or residual phase, as defined below.

   Prodromal phase: A clear deterioration in functioning before the active phase of the disturbance that is not due to a disturbance in mood or to a psychoactive substance use disorder and that involves at least two of the symptoms listed below.

   Residual phase: Following the active phase of the disturbance, persistence of at least two of the symptoms noted below, these not being due to a disturbance in mood or to a psychoactive substance use disorder.

   Prodromal or residual symptoms:
   (1) marked social isolation or withdrawal
   (2) marked impairment in role functioning as wage-earner, student, or homemaker
   (3) markedly peculiar behavior (e.g., collecting garbage, talking to self in public, hoarding food)
   (4) marked impairment in personal hygiene and grooming
   (5) blunted or inappropriate affect
   (6) digressive, vague, overelaborate, or circumstantial speech, or poverty of speech, or poverty of content of speech
   (7) odd beliefs or magical thinking, influencing behavior and inconsistent with cultural norms (e.g., superstitiousness, belief in clairvoyance, telepathy, "sixth sense," "others can feel my feelings," overvalued ideas, ideas of reference)
   (8) unusual perceptual experiences (e.g., recurrent illusions, sensing the presence of a force or person not actually present)
   (9) marked lack of initiative, interests, or energy

   Examples: Six months of prodromal symptoms with one week of symptoms from A; no prodromal symptoms with six months of symptoms from A; no prodromal symptoms with one week of symptoms from A and six months of residual symptoms.

E. It cannot be established that an organic factor initiated and maintained the disturbance.

F. If there is a history of autistic disorder, the additional diagnosis of schizophrenia is made only if prominent delusions or hallucinations are also present.

Classification of course. The course of the disturbance is coded in the fifth digit:

1-Subchronic. The time from the beginning of the disturbance, when the person first began to show signs of the disturbance (including prodromal, active, and residual phases) more or less continuously, is less than two years but at least six months.

2-Chronic. Same as above, but more than two years.

3-Subchronic with acute exacerbation. Reemergence of prominent psychotic symptoms in a person with a subchronic course who has been in the residual phase of the disturbance.

4-Chronic with acute exacerbation. Reemergence of prominent psychotic symptoms in a person with a chronic course who has been in the residual phase of the disturbance.

5-In remission. When a person with a history of schizophrenia is free of all signs of the disturbance (whether or not on medication), "in remission" should be coded. Differentiating schizophrenia in remission from no mental disorder requires consideration of overall level of functioning, length of time since the last episode of disturbance, total duration of the disturbance, and whether prophylactic treatment is being given.

0-Unspecified.

Specify late onset if the disturbance (including the prodromal phase) develops after age 45.

Table 13-5
Diagnostic Criteria for the Types of Schizophrenia

Paranoid type
A type of schizophrenia in which there are:
A. Preoccupation with one or more systematized delusions or with frequent auditory hallucinations related to a single theme

B. *None* of the following: incoherence, marked loosening of associations, flat or grossly inappropriate affect, catatonic behavior, grossly disorganized behavior

Specify stable type if criteria A and B have been met during all past and present active phases of the illness.

Catatonic type
A type of schizophrenia in which the clinical picture is dominated by any of the following:
(1) catatonic stupor (marked decrease in reactivity to the environment and/or reduction in spontaneous movements and activity) or mutism
(2) catatonic negativism (an apparently motiveless resistance to all instructions or attempts to be moved)
(3) catatonic rigidity (maintenance of a rigid posture against efforts to be moved)
(4) catatonic excitement (excited motor activity, apparently purposeless and not influenced by external stimuli)
(5) catatonic posturing (voluntary assumption of inappropriate or bizarre postures)

Disorganized type
A type of schizophrenia in which the following criteria are met:
A. Incoherence, marked loosening of associations, or grossly disorganized behavior

B. Flat or grossly inappropriate affect

C. Does not meet the criteria for catatonic type

Undifferentiated type
A type of schizophrenia in which there are:
A. Prominent delusions, hallucinations, incoherence, or grossly disorganized behavior

B. Does not meet the criteria of paranoid, catatonic, or disorganized type

Residual type
A type of schizophrenia in which there are:
A. Absence of prominent delusions, hallucinations, incoherence, or grossly disorganized behavior

B. Continuing evidence of the disturbance, as indicated by two or more of the residual symptoms listed in criterion D of schizophrenia

Table from DSM-III-R, *Diagnostic and Statistical Manual of Mental Disorders*, ed 3, revised. Copyright American Psychiatric Association, Washington, DC, 1987, with permission.

patients are usually active but in an aimless, nonconstructive manner. Their thought disorder is pronounced, and their contact with reality is extremely poor. Their personal appearance and their social behavior are dilapidated. Their emotional responses are inappropriate, and they often burst out laughing without any apparent reason. Incongruous grinning and grimacing are common in this type of patient, whose behavior is best described as silly or fatuous. A clinical case example of the disorganized type of schizophrenia follows:

The patient was a 40-year-old man who looked 30. He was brought in for his 12th hospitalization by his mother because she was afraid of him. He was dressed in a ragged overcoat, bedroom slippers, and a baseball cap and wore several medals around his neck. His affect ranged from anger at his mother—"She feeds me shit . . . what comes out of other people's rectums"—to a giggling, obsequious seductiveness toward the interviewer. His speech and manner had a childlike quality, and he walked with a mincing step and exaggerated hip movements. His mother reported that he stopped taking his medication about a month before, and had since begun to hear voices and to look and act more bizarre. When asked what he had been doing, he said, "eating wires and lighting fires." His spontaneous speech was often incoherent and marked by frequent rhyming and clang associations.

The patient's first hospitalization occurred after he dropped out of school at age 16. Since that time he had never been able to attend school or hold a job. He lived with his elderly mother but sometimes disappeared for several months at a time and was eventually picked up by the police as he wandered the streets. There was no known history of drug or alcohol abuse.

Discussion. The combination of a chronic illness with marked incoherence, inappropriate affect, auditory hallucinations, and bizarre behavior leaves little doubt that the diagnosis is chronic schizophrenia with an acute exacerbation. The presence of marked loosening of associations and grossly inappropriate affect and the absence of prominent catatonic symptoms indicate the disorganized type.

Catatonic type. DSM-III-R states that the essential feature of this type is marked psychomotor disturbance, which may involve stupor, negativism, rigidity, excitement, or posturing. Sometimes there is rapid alternation between the extremes of excitement and stupor. Associated features include stereotypies, mannerisms, and waxy flexibility. Mutism is particularly common.

During catatonic stupor or excitement, schizophrenic patients need careful supervision to avoid hurting themselves or others. Medical care may be needed because of malnutrition, exhaustion, hyperpyrexia, or self-inflicted injury.

Although this type was very common several decades ago, it is now rare in Europe and North America.

Paranoid type. The paranoid type of schizophrenia is characterized mainly by the presence of delusions of persecution or grandeur. Paranoid schizophrenic patients are usually older than catatonic or disorganized schizophrenic patients when they break down; that is, they are usually in their late 20s or in their 30s. Patients who have been well up to that age have usually established a place and an identity for themselves in the community. Their ego resources are greater than those of catatonic and disorganized patients. Paranoid schizophrenic patients show less regression of mental faculties, emotional response, and behavior than do the other types of schizophrenic patients.

Typical paranoid schizophrenic patients are tense, suspicious, guarded, and reserved. They are often hostile and aggressive. Paranoid schizophrenic patients usually conduct themselves quite well socially. Their intelligence in areas not invaded by their delusions may remain high. A clinical case example of the paranoid type of schizophrenia follows:

A 44-year-old single unemployed man was brought into an emergency room by the police for striking an elderly woman in his apartment building. He complained that the woman he struck was a bitch and that she and the "others" deserved more than that for what they put him through.

The patient had been continuously ill since the age of 22. During his first year of law school, he gradually became more and more convinced that his classmates were making fun of him. He noticed that they would snort and sneeze whenever he entered the classroom. When a girl he was dating broke off the relationship with him, he believed that she had been replaced by a look-alike. He called the police and asked for their help in solving the "kidnapping." His academic performance in school declined dramatically, and he was asked to leave and seek psychiatric care.

The patient got a job as an investment counselor at a bank, which he held for seven months. However, he was getting an increasing number of distracting "signals" from coworkers, and he became more and more suspicious and withdrawn. At this time he first reported hearing voices. He was eventually fired and soon thereafter was hospitalized for the first time, at age 24. He had not worked since.

The patient had been hospitalized 12 times, the longest stay for eight months. However, in the past five years he had been hospitalized only once, for three weeks. During the hospitalizations he had received various antipsychotic drugs. Although outpatient medication had been prescribed, he usually stopped taking it shortly after leaving the hospital. Aside from twice-yearly lunch meetings with his uncle and his contacts with mental health workers, he was totally isolated socially. He lived on his own and managed his own financial affairs, including a modest inheritance. He read the *Wall Street Journal* daily. He cooked and cleaned for himself.

The patient maintained that his apartment was the center of a large communication system that involved all three major television networks, his neighbors, and apparently hundreds of "actors" in his neighborhood. There were secret cameras in his apartment that carefully monitored all his activities. When he was watching television, many of his minor actions (e.g., getting up to go to the bathroom) were soon directly commented on by the announcer. Whenever he went outside, the "actors" had all been warned to keep him under surveillance: everyone on the street watched him. His neighbors operated two different "machines"; one was responsible for all his voices, except the "joker." He was not certain who controlled this voice, which visited him only occasionally and was very funny. The other voices, which he heard many times each day, were generated by this machine, which he sometimes thought was directly run by the neighbor whom he attacked. For example, when he was going over his investments, these "harassing" voices constantly told him which stocks to buy. The other machine he called "the dream machine." This machine put erotic dreams into his head, usually of black women.

The patient described other unusual experiences. For example, he recently went to a shoe store 30 miles from his home in the hope of getting some shoes that would not be "altered." However, he soon found out that, like the rest of the shoes he bought, special nails had been put into the bottom of the shoes to annoy him. He was amazed that his decision about which shoe store to go to must have been known to his "harassers" before he himself knew it, so that they had time to get the altered shoes made up especially for him. He realized that great effort and "millions of dollars" were involved in keeping him under surveillance. He sometimes thought this was all part of a large experiment to discover the secret of his superior intelligence.

At the interview, the patient was well-groomed, and his speech was coherent and goal-directed. His affect was, at most, only mildly blunted. He was initially very angry at being brought in by the police. After several weeks of treatment with an antipsychotic drug failed to control his psychotic symptoms, he was transferred to a long-stay facility with the plan to arrange a structured living situation for him.

Discussion. The patient's long illness apparently began with delusions of reference (his classmates making fun of him by snorting and sneezing when he entered the classroom). Over the years his delusions had become increasingly complex and bizarre (his neighbors were actually actors; his thoughts were monitored; a machine put erotic dreams into his head). In addition, he had prominent hallucinations of different voices that harassed him.

Bizarre delusions and prominent hallucinations are the characteristic psychotic symptoms of schizophrenia. The diagnosis was confirmed by the marked disturbance in his work and social functioning and the absence of a sustained mood disturbance and of any known organic factor that could account for the disturbance.

All the patient's delusions and hallucinations seemed to involve the single theme of a conspiracy to harass him. This systematized persecutory delusion—in the absence of incoherence, marked loosening of associations, flat or grossly inappropriate affect, or catatonic or grossly disorganized behavior—indicates the paranoid type. Schizophrenia, paranoid type, is further specified as stable type if, as in this case, all past and present active phases of the illness have been the paranoid type. The prognosis for the stable paranoid type is better than the prognosis for the disorganized and undifferentiated types. The patient did, in fact, do remarkably well in spite of a chronic psychotic illness; over the past five years he had been able to take care of himself.

Undifferentiated type. Frequently, patients who are clearly schizophrenic cannot be easily fitted into one of the other types, usually because they meet the criteria for more than one type. Some acute, excited schizophrenic patients—classified in the ninth revision of the International Classification of Diseases (ICD-9) as suffering from acute schizophrenic episode—and some inert, chronic patients fall into this category, for which DSM-III-R provides the designation undifferentiated. A clinical case example of the undifferentiated type of schizophrenia follows:

A 15-year-old girl was seen at the request of her school district authorities for advice on placement. She had recently moved into the area with her family and, after a brief period in a regular class, was placed in a class for the emotionally disturbed. She proved very difficult, had a poor understanding of schoolwork, and functioned at about the fifth-grade level despite an apparently good vocabulary. She disturbed the class by making animal noises and telling fantastic stories, causing other students to laugh at her.

At home the patient was aggressive, biting or hitting her parents or brother when frustrated. She was often bored, had no friends, and found it difficult to occupy herself. She spent a lot of time drawing pictures of robots, spaceships, and fantastic or futuristic inventions. Sometimes she said she would like to die, but she never made any attempt at suicide and apparently had not thought of killing herself. Her mother said that from birth she had been different and that the onset of her current behavior had been so gradual that no definite date could be assigned to it.

The patient's prenatal and parental history were unremarkable. Her milestones were delayed, and she did not use single words until 4 or 5 years of age. Ever since she entered school, there had been concern about her ability. Repeated evaluations had suggested an intelligence quotient (I.Q.) in the low 70s, but her achievement was somewhat behind what was expected at that level of ability. Because her father was in the military service, there had been many moves, and the results of her earlier evaluations were not available.

The parents reported that the patient had always been difficult and restless. Several doctors had said that she was not just mentally retarded but that she also suffered from a serious mental disorder. The results of an evaluation done at the age of 12, because of difficulties in school, showed evidence of bizarre thought processes and fragmented ego structure. At that time she was sleeping well at night and was not getting up with nightmares or bizarre requests, although this apparently had been a feature of her earlier behavior. At this time, however, she was reported to sleep very poorly, disturbing the household nightly by getting up and wandering around. Her mother emphasized the patient's unpredictability, the funny stories that she told, and the way in which she talked to herself in "funny voices." Her mother regarded the stories the patient told as childish make-believe and preoccupation and paid little attention to them. She said that, since the patient went to see the movie *Star Wars,* she was obsessed with ideas about space, spaceships, and the future.

Her parents were in their early 40s. Her father, having retired from military service, worked as an engineer. The patient's mother had many unusual beliefs about herself. She was loquacious and very circumstantial in her history giving. She dwelled a great deal on her strange childhood experiences. She claimed to have grown up in India and to have had a very bizarre early childhood, full of dramatic and violent episodes. Many of these episodes sounded highly improbable. Her husband, in contrast, refused to let her talk about her past in his presence and tried to play down this material and the patient's problems. The parents appeared to have a rather restricted relationship. The father played the role of a taciturn, masterful head of household, and the mother bore the brunt of everyday family duties.

In the interview the patient presented as a tall, overweight, pasty-looking child, dressed untidily and with a somewhat disheveled appearance. She complained vociferously of her insomnia, although it was difficult to elicit details of the sleep disturbance. She talked at length about her interests and occupations. She said she had made a robot in the basement that ran amok and was about to cause a great deal of damage when she was finally able to stop it by remote control. She claimed to have built the robot from spare computer parts, which she acquired from the local museum.

When pressed for details of how the robot worked, the patient became increasingly vague. When asked to draw a picture of one of her inventions, she drew a picture of an overhead railway and went into what appeared to be complex mathematical calculations to substantiate the structural details but that, in fact, consisted of meaningless repetitions of symbols (e.g., plus, minus, divide, multiply). When the interviewer expressed some gentle incredulity, she blandly replied that many people did not believe that she was a supergenius. She also talked about her unusual ability to hear things other people cannot hear and said she was in communication with some sort of creature. She thought she might be haunted, or perhaps the creature was a being from another planet. She could hear his voice talking to her and asking her questions, but he did not attempt to tell her what to do. The voice was outside her own head and was inaudible to others. She did not regard the questions being asked as upsetting; they did not make her angry or frightened.

Her teacher commented that, although the patient's reading was apparently at the fifth-grade level, her comprehension was much lower. She read what was not there and sometimes changed the meaning of the paragraph. Her spelling was at about the third-grade level, and her mathematics was a little below that. She worked hard at school, although very slowly. If pressure was placed on her, she became upset, and her work deteriorated.

Discussion. At that time the patient exhibited several psychotic symptoms. She was apparently delusional in that she believed she had made a complicated invention and that she was in communication with "some sort of creature." She had auditory hallucinations of voices talking to her and asking her questions. The presence of delusions and hallucinations, in the absence of a specific organic factor that initiated and maintained the disturbance or of a full mood syndrome, raised the question of schizophrenia.

The DSM-III-R criteria for schizophrenia require that "During the course of the disturbance, functioning in such areas as work, social relations, and self-care is markedly below the highest level achieved before the onset of the disturbance (or, when the onset is in childhood or adolescence, failure to achieve expected level of social development)." Certainly, the onset of the patient's illness was in childhood, and she had failed to achieve the expected level of social development for someone her age. Therefore, the diagnosis of the patient's condition was schizophrenia, chronic. Because her delusions had many different themes, they were not systematized, ruling out the paranoid type; the absence of prominent catatonic features ruled out catatonic type; and the absence of flat or grossly inappropriate affect ruled out the disorganized type. That left the undifferentiated type.

The patient's I.Q. level above 70 spared her from the additional diagnosis of mild mental retardation. One could argue for the Axis V code borderline intellectual functioning. However, it was not the patient's limited intellectual capacity but, rather, her bizarre behavior that was creating difficulties at school.

Residual type. According to DSM-III-R, this category should be used when there has been at least one episode of schizophrenia but the clinical picture that occasioned the evaluation or admission to clinical care is without prominent psychotic symptoms, although signs of the illness persist. Emotional blunting, social withdrawal, eccentric behavior, illogical thinking, and mild loosening of associations are common. If delusions or hallucinations are present, they are not prominent and are not accompanied by strong affect. The course of this type is either chronic or subchronic.

Some ICD-9 Types

Three types in ICD-9 are not included in DSM-III-R: paraphrenia, simple, and latent.

Paraphrenia. This term is used as a synonym for paranoid schizophrenia in ICD-9. In other systems it is used to describe a chronic downhill course with well-systematized delusions but with a well-preserved personality. Its multiple meanings render the term of little use for the communication of information.

Simple. ICD-9 includes schizophrenia, simple type, which is characterized by a gradual, insidious loss of drive and ambition. The patient is usually not hallucinating or delusional, and, if these symptoms do occur, they do not persist. The patient withdraws from contact with other people and often stops working. Clinicians are advised to exercise caution in making this diagnosis because this condition is not particularly responsive to medication, and the diagnostic label of schizophrenia, even if warranted, can do more harm than good to the patients.

Latent. Latent schizophrenia is diagnosed in those patients who may have marked schizoid personalities and who show occasional behavioral peculiarities or thought disorders, without consistently manifesting any clearly psychotic pathology. The syndrome was termed borderline schizophrenia in the past. It most closely resembles the DSM-III-R diagnosis of schizotypal personality disorder. Again, the clinician is wise to make a diagnosis of schizophrenia only with more significant pathology.

Type I and Type II

In 1980 T. J. Crow proposed a classification of schizophrenic patients into type I and type II. This system is based on the presence of positive or negative symptoms, sometimes referred to as productive or deficit symptoms, respectively. The *negative symptoms* include affective flattening or blunting, poverty of speech or speech content, blocking, poor grooming, lack of motivation, anhedonia, social withdrawal, cognitive defects, and attention deficits. The *positive symptoms* include loose associations, hallucinations, bizarre behavior, and increased speech. Type I patients have mostly positive symptoms, normal brain structures, and relatively good responses to treatment; type II patients have mostly negative symptoms, structural brain abnormalities seen on CT scans, and poor responses to treatment (Table 13-6).

Other Types

There are a variety of other types, mostly of historical or theoretical interest. Some types have obvious definitions—late-onset, childhood, and process. Late-onset schizophrenia begins after age 45 and is now included in the DSM-III-R criteria for schizophrenia. Schizophrenia with childhood onset is simply called schizophrenia in DSM-III-R. Process schizophrenia is synonymous with poor-prognosis, deteriorating schizophrenia.

***Bouffée délirante* (acute delusional psychosis).** This diagnostic category is used in France and is considered to be a diagnostic category in its own right, not a type of schizophrenia. The criteria are similar to those for DSM-III-R schizophrenia, but the symptoms must be present for less than three months, thereby approximating the DSM-III-R diagnosis of schizophreniform disorder. French psychiatrists report that about 40 percent of patients with this diagnosis are later classified as having schizophrenia.

Oneiroid. In the oneiroid state, patients feel and behave as though in a dream. They may be deeply perplexed and not fully oriented in time and place. The oneiroid schizophrenic patient acknowledges everyday realities but gives priority to the world of hallucinatory experiences. Oneiroid states are usually limited in duration and may be classified as psychotic disorder not otherwise specified in DSM-III-R. The clinician should be careful to examine the patient for an organic cause in the presence of these symptoms.

Pseudoneurotic. Patients with this type present predominantly with neurotic symptoms but on closer examination reveal schizophrenic abnormalities in thinking and emotional reaction. These patients are characterized by pananxiety, panphobia, panambivalence, and chaotic sexuality. Unlike patients suffering from anxiety disorders, these patients have anxiety that is free-floating and hardly ever subsides. They rarely become overtly psychotic.

DIFFERENTIAL DIAGNOSIS

There are three principal guidelines in the differential diagnosis of schizophrenia. First, the clinician should aggressively investigate the possibility of an identifiable organic cause, especially if there are unusual or rare symptoms. Second, there should be a complete evaluation of each exacerbation of psychotic symptoms in a schizophrenic patient. The clinician should have an open mind about the possibility of a superimposed organic cause, especially when the patient has been in remission for a long time or if there is a change in the quality of symptoms. Third, the clinician should carefully elicit and consider a family history of psychiatric and neurological disease.

A large number of neurological and medical diseases can have symptoms identical to those of schizophrenia (Table 13-7). The psychiatric manifestations of these disorders often come early in the course, before the development of other symptoms. It is generally true that patients with neurological disorders have more insight into and more distress from their symptoms than patients with schizophrenia. The fact that so many disorders can mimic schizophrenia is consistent with the notion that schizophrenia is a heterogeneous disorder.

The psychiatric differential diagnosis for schizophrenia-like symptoms is also quite lengthy.

Malingering and Factitious Disorder with Psychological Symptoms

It is possible to fake the symptoms of schizophrenia because the diagnosis depends so much on the patient's report. Patients who do, in fact, have schizophrenia may sometimes falsely complain of symptoms for secondary gain, such as increased assistance benefits or admission to a hospital.

Autistic Disorder

Autistic disorder is diagnosed when the onset is after 30 months of age but before 12 years. Delusions, hallucinations, and looseness of associations are absent.

Table 13-6
Percentage of Patients with Negative and Positive Symptoms (111 Consecutively Admitted Schizophrenic Patients)

Symptoms	Mild or Moderate	Severe or Extreme
Negative symptoms		
Affective flattening		
Unchanging facial expression	54	33
Decreased spontaneous movements	37	14
Paucity of expressive gestures	34	24
Poor eye contact	39	16
Affective nonresponsivity	18	18
Inappropriate affect	29	22
Lack of vocal inflections	40	9
Alogia		
Poverty of speech	20	20
Poverty of content of speech	33	6
Blocking	12	3
Increased response latency	17	6
Avolition-apathy		
Grooming and hygiene	33	41
Impersistence at work or school	13	74
Physical anergia	36	31
Anhedonia-asociality		
Recreational interests, activities	38	41
Sexual interest, activity	11	23
Intimacy, closeness	24	35
Relationship with friends, peers	25	63
Attention		
Social inattentiveness	25	32
Inattentiveness during testing	33	19
Positive symptoms		
Hallucinations		
Auditory	19	51
Voices commenting	22	12
Voices conversing	27	12
Somatic-tactile	10	6
Olfactory	5	1
Visual	16	15
Delusions		
Persecutory	19	47
Jealousy	2	1
Guilt, sin	16	2
Grandiose	15	15
Religious	12	11
Somatic	11	11
Delusions of reference	13	21
Delusions of being controlled	25	12
Delusions of mind reading	19	14
Thought broadcasting	11	2
Thought insertion	15	4
Thought withdrawal	11	6
Bizarre behavior		
Clothing, appearance	8	4
Social, sexual behavior	17	7
Aggressive-agitated behavior	14	6
Repetitive-stereotyped behavior	7	4
Positive formal thought disorder		
Derailment	30	4
Tangentiality	28	4
Incoherence	9	1
Illogicality	10	1
Circumstantiality	14	0
Pressure of speech	14	0
Distractible speech	12	1
Clanging	1	0

Table adapted from N C Andreasen: The diagnosis of schizophrenia. Schizophr Bull *13*: 9, 1987, with permission.

Table 13-7
Differential Diagnosis of Schizophrenialike Symptoms

Medical and Neurological:

Drug-induced—amphetamine, hallucinogens, belladonna alkaloids, alcohol hallucinosis, barbiturate withdrawal, cocaine, phencyclidine (PCP)
Epilepsy—especially temporal lobe epilepsy
Neoplasm, stroke, or trauma—especially frontal or limbic
Other conditions—acquired immune deficiency syndrome (AIDS)
acute intermittent porphyria
B_{12} deficiency
carbon monoxide poisoning
cerebral lipoidosis
Creutzfeldt-Jakob disease
Fabry's disease
Fahr's disease
Hallervorden-Spatz disease
heavy metal poisoning
herpes encephalitis
homocystinuria
Huntington's chorea
metachromatic leukodystrophy
neurosyphilis
normal pressure hydrocephalus
pellagra
systemic lupus erythematosus
Wernicke-Korsakoff syndrome
Wilson's disease

Psychiatric:

atypical psychosis
brief reactive psychosis
factitious disorder with psychological symptoms
infantile autism
malingering
mood disorders
normal adolescence
obsessive-compulsive disorder
paranoid disorder
personality disorders—schizotypal, schizoid, borderline, paranoid
schizoaffective disorder
schizophrenia
schizophreniform disorder

Mood Disorders

The differential diagnosis of schizophrenia and mood disorders can be quite difficult, but it is particularly important because of the availability of specific and effective treatments for mania and depression. DSM-III-R specifies that affective or mood symptoms in schizophrenia must be brief relative to the duration of the primary symptoms. In the absence of information other than a single mental status examination, it is usually prudent to delay a final diagnosis or to assume the presence of a mood disorder, rather than to diagnose schizophrenia prematurely.

Schizoaffective Disorder

This diagnosis is made when a manic or depressive syndrome develops concurrently with the major symptoms of schizophrenia. In addition, delusions or hallucinations must be present for at least two weeks in the absence of prominent affective symptoms during some phase of the illness.

Schizophreniform Disorder and Brief Reactive Psychosis

Schizophreniform disorder is diagnosed when all the criteria for schizophrenia have been met but symptoms have been present for less than six months. Brief reactive psychosis is diagnosed when those symptoms have been present for less than one month and there is either a clear precipitating stressor or a series of stressors.

Delusional Disorder

A diagnosis of delusional disorder is warranted if nonbizarre delusions have been present for at least six months in the absence of the other symptoms of schizophrenia or a mood disorder.

Personality Disorder

A variety of personality disorders may present with some features of schizophrenia. Personality disorders are longstanding patterns of behavior; their date of onset is less identifiable than that of schizophrenia.

TREATMENT

Hospitalization

The primary indications for hospitalization are for diagnostic purposes, stabilization on medications, patient safety because of suicidal or homicidal ideation, and grossly disorganized or inappropriate behavior, including the inability to take care of basic needs, such as food, clothing, and shelter. A primary goal of hospitalization should be to establish an effective link between the patient and community support systems. Introduced in the early 1950s, antipsychotic medications have revolutionized the treatment of schizophrenia. Approximately two to four times as many patients relapse when treated with a placebo rather than antipsychotics. Antipsychotics, however, treat the symptoms of the illness and are not a cure for schizophrenia. Other aspects of clinical management flow logically from a medical model of disease. Rehabilitation and adjustment imply that the specific handicaps of the patient are taken into account when planning treatment strategies. The physician must also educate the patient and the patient's caretakers and family about schizophrenia.

Hospitalization decreases stress on a patient and helps him or her structure daily activities. The length of hospitalization depends on the severity of the patient's illness and the availability of outpatient treatment facilities. Research has shown that short hospitalizations are just as effective as long-term hospitalizations and that active treatment programs with behavioral approaches are more effective than custodial institutions and insight-oriented therapeutic communities. The hospitalization treatment plan should have a practical orientation toward issues of living situation, self-care, quality of life, employment, and social relationships. Hospitalization should be directed toward aligning the patient with aftercare facilities, including his or her family home, a foster family, board and care homes, and halfway houses. Day care centers and home visits can sometimes help a patient remain out of the hospital for long periods of time and can improve the quality of the patient's daily life.

Somatic Treatments

Antipsychotics. The antipsychotics (also called neuroleptics and major tranquilizers) include the dopamine receptor antagonists (see Section 30.2.13) and clozapine (Clozaril) (see Section 30.2.14). There are five major guidelines for the use of antipsychotics in schizophrenia. First, the clinician should carefully define the target symptoms to be treated. Second, an antipsychotic that has worked in the past for the patient should be used again. In the absence of such information, it is important to realize that no antipsychotic has been shown to be more effective than any other, although an individual patient may respond to one and not to another. The choice of an antipsychotic is usually based on its side-effect profile. Although high-potency antipsychotics are associated with more neurological adverse effects, current clinical practice greatly favors their use because of their lower incidence of other adverse effects (e.g., cardiac, hypotensive, epileptogenic, sexual, and allergic). Third, the minimum length of an antipsychotic trial is four to six weeks at adequate dosages. If the trial is unsuccessful, an antipsychotic from another class should be tried. Fourth, polypharmacy, especially using more than one antipsychotic at a time, should be avoided. Fifth, maintenance dosages of antipsychotics can usually be lower than the dosages necessary for acute episodes.

A clinical observation that is supported by some research is that an unpleasant experience by the patient to the first dose of an antipsychotic correlates highly with future poor response and noncompliance. Such experiences include a subjective negative feeling, oversedation, and acute dystonia. If a patient reports such a reaction, the clinician may be well advised to switch to a different antipsychotic.

Antipsychotic drugs are remarkably safe, and, if necessary, a clinician can administer these drugs without conducting a physical or laboratory examination of the patient. The major contraindications to antipsychotics are (1) a history of a serious allergic response; (2) the possibility that the patient has ingested a drug that will interact with the antipsychotic to induce CNS depression (e.g., alcohol, opioids, barbiturates, benzodiazepines) or anticholinergic delirium (e.g., scopolamine, possibly phencyclidine); (3) the presence of a severe cardiac abnormality; (4) a high risk of seizures from organic or idiopathic causes; and (5) the presence of narrow-angle glaucoma if an anticholinergic antipsychotic is to be used. In the usual assessment, however, it is best to obtain a complete blood count (CBC) with white blood cell indices, liver function tests, and an electrocardiogram (ECG), especially in women over 40 and men over 30.

Compliance. Noncompliance with antipsychotics is a major reason for relapse. Although several studies have failed to demonstrate a difference between oral and long-acting injectable regimens, a trial of a long-acting injectable antipsychotic is warranted when noncompliance is a problem.

Failure of a drug trial. In the acute state, virtually all patients respond eventually to repeated doses of an antipsychotic (every one to two hours with intramuscular (IM) administration or every two to three hours by mouth), sometimes with a benzodiazepine. The failure of a patient to respond in the acute situation should cause the clinician to seriously consider the possibility of an organic lesion.

A major reason for a failed drug trial is insufficient length of the trial. It is generally a mistake to increase the dosage or change antipsychotic medications in the first two weeks of treatment. If a patient is improving on the current regimen at the end of this time, continued treatment with the same regimen will likely result in steady clinical improvement. If, however, a patient has shown little or no improvement in two weeks, the possible reasons for a drug failure, including noncompliance, should be considered (see Section 30.1). In a noncompliant patient, the use of liquid preparations or depot forms of fluphenazine (Prolixin) or haloperidol (Haldol) may be indicated. Because of the great diversity in the metabolism of these drugs, it is reasonable to obtain plasma levels if this laboratory capability is available. Plasma levels of antipsychotics provide a gross measure of compliance and absorption. There are no clearly defined therapeutic blood level ranges for antipsychotics similar to those for tricyclic antidepressants.

Having eliminated other possible reasons for an antipsychotic's therapeutic failure, the clinician may try a second antipsychotic with a structure different from that of the first one. Additional strategies include adding or removing coadministered anticholinergic drugs; supplementing the antipsychotic with lithium, carbamazepine (Tegretol), or a benzodiazepine; and using megadose therapy. Megadose therapy is the use of high doses of antipsychotics (in the range of 100 to 200 mg a day of haloperidol). If this strategy is used, a specified time (approximately one month) should be set for the drug trial. If no improvement is seen, the high doses should be discontinued.

Combinations of antipsychotics. It has not been experimentally demonstrated that combining two antipsychotics produces a treatment superior to comparable amounts of a single antipsychotic alone; however, it also has not been demonstrated that this practice is harmful. The only reasonable indication for this practice is the use of a nonsedating, high-potency antipsychotic during the day and a sedating, low-potency antipsychotic at bedtime. This drug regimen is rarely indicated, as the single bedtime dose almost always results in antipsychotic activity throughout the following day.

Clozapine. Although it is appropriate to use drugs from the dopamine receptor antagonist group as first-line drugs in the treatment of schizophrenia, clozapine is a clear second-line drug for those patients who either do not respond to these drugs or develop severe tardive dyskinesia. Clozapine is not a D_2 receptor antagonist and has not been associated with extrapyramidal adverse effects, such as tardive dyskinesia. Some evidence indicates that clozapine is more effective than the traditional antipsychotics in the treatment of the negative symptoms of schizophrenia. Although clozapine may be a weak D_1 antagonist, it is currently hypothesized that clozapine makes its therapeutic effects by blocking serotonin receptors. Clozapine is not a first-line drug because it is associated with a 1 to 2 percent incidence of agranulocytosis, an adverse effect that necessitates the weekly monitoring of blood indices. In addition, clozapine is extremely expensive, which is a limiting factor in its use.

Other drugs. If antipsychotic dopamine receptor antagonists are unsuccessful in the treatment of a patient, clozapine is a reasonable alternative. Additional pharmacological alternatives are lithium, carbamazepine, and the benzodiazepines. These three drugs are usually used as adjuvants to treatment with traditional antipsychotic agents.

Lithium. Lithium (see Section 30.2.16) may be effective in further reducing psychotic symptoms in up to 50 percent of patients with schizophrenia. Lithium may also be a reasonable drug to use if patients are unable to take antipsychotics.

Carbamazepine. Carbamazepine (see Section 30.2.10) may be used alone or in combination with lithium. Carbamazepine has not been shown to be effective in treating the psychosis of schizophrenia; however, this drug may reduce the episodic violence associated with some cases of schizophrenia.

Benzodiazepines. There is increasing interest in the possibility of coadministering alprazolam (Xanax) and antipsychotics to patients who do not respond to an antipsychotic alone. There are also reports of schizophrenic patients' responding to high doses of diazepam (Valium) alone. The clinician should be aware, however, of reports that the severity of the psychosis may be exacerbated after the withdrawal of a benzodiazepine (see Section 30.2.5).

Other somatic treatments. Although much less effective than antipsychotics, electroconvulsive treatment (ECT) may be indicated for catatonic patients and for patients who for some reason cannot take antipsychotics. Patients who have been ill less than one year are most likely to respond.

Historical treatments for schizophrenia include insulin-induced and barbiturate-induced coma. These treatments are no longer used because of the associated hazards. Psychosurgery, particularly frontal lobotomies, were used from 1935 to 1955 for the treatment of schizophrenia. Although more sophisticated approaches to psychosurgery for schizophrenia may eventually be developed, psychosurgery is no longer considered an appropriate treatment for schizophrenia, but it is being used on a very limited experimental basis.

Psychosocial Treatments

Although antipsychotic medications are the mainstay of treatment for schizophrenia, research has demonstrated that psychosocial interventions can augment the clinical improvement. Psychosocial modalities should be carefully integrated into the drug treatment regimen and should support it. Most schizophrenic patients benefit from the combined use of antipsychotics and psychosocial treatment.

Behavior therapy. Treatment planning for schizophrenia should address both the abilities and the deficits of the patient. Behavioral techniques use token economies and social skills training to increase social abilities, self-sufficiency, practical skills, and interpersonal communication. Adaptive behaviors are reinforced by praise or tokens that can be redeemed for desired items, such as more hospital privileges and passes. Consequently, the frequency of maladaptive or deviant behavior—such as talking loudly, talking to oneself in public, and bizarre posturing—is reduced.

Family therapy. Families tend to blame themselves for any illness or accident that happens to a family member. The problem is magnified with schizophrenia, since at one time many psychiatrists counted family pathology as a causative factor. It may, therefore, be difficult to enlist the aid of families in the treatment program. Nevertheless, it has been demonstrated that specific approaches to family therapy can reduce the relapse rates of some schizophrenic patients. Families with so-called high expressed emotion can have hostile, critical, emotionally overinvolved, or intrusive interactions with the schizophrenic patient. If these behaviors are directly modified, the relapse rate for the patients may be dramatically reduced. The psychiatrist should also educate the family, support them in their difficult situation, and introduce them to family support groups for parents of schizophrenic children.

Group therapy. Group therapy with schizophrenia generally focuses on real-life plans, problems, and relationships. Groups may be behaviorally oriented, psychodynamically or insight-oriented, or supportive. There is some doubt whether dynamic interpretation and insight therapy are valuable for the typical schizophrenic patient. But group therapy is particularly effective in reducing social isolation, increasing the sense of cohesiveness, and improving reality testing for patients with schizophrenia. Groups led in a supportive manner, rather than an interpretive one, appear to be most helpful for schizophrenic patients.

Social skills training. This process is a highly structured form of group therapy for schizophrenic patients (Table 13-8). Social skills can be defined as those interpersonal behaviors required to attain instrumental goals necessary for community survival and independence and to establish, maintain, and deepen supportive and socially rewarding relationships. Applying behavior analysis principles to identify and remedy deficits in social behaviors, the clinician uses a variety of techniques, such as focused instructions, role modeling, feedback, and social reinforcement.

Individual psychotherapy. Schizophrenic patients can be helped by individual psychotherapy that provides a positive treatment relationship and therapeutic alliance. The relationship between the clinician and the patient is different from that encountered in the treatment of neurosis. In general, orthodox formal psychoanalysis has no place in the treatment of schizophrenia. Supportive psychotherapy is the type most often employed. Establishing a relationship is often a particularly difficult matter; the schizophrenic patient is desperately lonely yet defends against closeness and trust and is likely to become suspicious, anxious, hostile, or regressed when someone attempts to draw close. The scrupulous observance of distance and privacy, simple directness, patience, sincerity, and sensitivity to social conventions are preferable to premature informality and the condescending use of first names. Exaggerated warmth or professions of friendship are out of place and are likely to be perceived as attempts at bribery, manipulation, or exploitation.

In the context of a professional relationship, however, flexibility may be essential in establishing a working alli-

Table 13-8
Goals and Targeted Behaviors for Social Skills Training

Phase	Goals	Target Behaviors
Stabilization and assessment	Establish therapeutic alliance Assess social performance and perception skills Assess behaviors that provoke expressed emotion	Empathy and rapport Verbal and nonverbal communication
Social performance within family	Express positive feelings within family Teach effective strategies for coping with conflict	Compliments, appreciation, interest in others Avoidance response to criticism, stating preferences and refusals
Social perception in the family	Correctly identify content, context, and meaning of messages	Reading a message Labeling an idea Summarizing other's intent
Extrafamilial relationships	Enhance socialization skills Enhance prevocational and vocational skills	Conversational skills Dating Recreational activities Job interviewing, work habits
Maintenance	Generalize skills to new situations	

Table adapted from G E Hogarty, C M Anderson, D J Reiss, S J Kornblith, D P Greenwald, C D Javna, M J Madonia: Family psychoeducation, social skills training and maintenance chemotherapy: I. One-year effects of a controlled study on relapse and expressed emotion. Arch Gen Psychiatry *43*: 633, 1986, with permission.

ance with the patient. At those times, the therapist may have meals with the patient, sit on the floor, go for a walk, eat at a restaurant, accept and give gifts, play table tennis, remember the patient's birthday, allow the patient to telephone the therapist at any hour, or just sit silently with the patient. The major aim is to convey that the therapist can be trusted, wants to understand the patient and will try to do so, and has faith in the patient's potential as a human being, no matter how disturbed, hostile, or bizarre the patient may be at the moment. Manfred Bleuler stated that the correct therapeutic attitude toward schizophrenic patients is to accept them, rather than watch them as persons who have become unintelligible and different from the therapist.

References

Andreasen N C: Positive and negative symptoms in schizophrenia: A critical reappraisal. Arch Gen Psychiatry *47*: 615, 1990.

Casanova M F, Kleinman J E: The neuropathology of schizophrenia: A critical assessment of research methodologies. Biol Psychiatry *27*: 353, 1990.

Ciompi L: Learning from outcome studies: Toward a comprehensive biological-psychosocial understanding of schizophrenia. Schizophr Res *1*: 373, 1988.

Falkai P, Bogerts B, Rozumek M: Limbic pathology in schizophrenia: The entorhinal region: A morphometric study. Biol Psychiatry *24*: 515, 1988.

Goldberg T E, Weinberger D R: Probing prefrontal function in schizophrenia with neuropsychological paradigms. Schizophr Bull *14*: 179, 1988.

Heinrichs D W, Buchanan R W: Significance and meaning of neurological signs in schizophrenia. Am J Psychiatry *145*: 11, 1988.

Johnstone E C: The assessment of negative and positive features in schizophrenia. Br J Psychiatry (Suppl): 41, November 1989.

Kay S R, Singh M M: The positive-negative distinction in drug-free schizophrenic patients: Stability, response to neuroleptics, and prognostic significance. Arch Gen Psychiatry *46*: 11, 1989.

Lohr J B, Bracha H S: Can schizophrenia be related to prenatal exposure to alcohol? Some speculations. Schizophr Bull *15*: 595, 1989.

Martinot J L, Peron Magnan P, Huret J-D: Striatal D_2 dopaminergic receptors assessed with positron emission tomography and [^{76}Br]Bromospiperone in untreated schizophrenic patients. Am J Psychiatry *147*: 44, 1990.

Meltzer H Y, Zureick J: Negative symptoms in schizophrenia: A target for new drug development. Psychopharmacol Ser *7*: 68, 1989.

Parker G, Johnston P, Hayward L: Parental "expressed emotion" as a predictor of schizophrenic relapse. Arch Gen Psychiatry *45*: 806, 1988.

Saugstad L F: Social class, marriage, and fertility in schizophrenia. Schizophr Bull *15*: 9, 1989.

Suddath R L, Casanova M F, Goldberg T E: Temporal lobe pathology in schizophrenia: A quantitative magnetic resonance imaging study. Am J Psychiatry *146*: 464, 1989.

Suddath R L, Christison G W, Torrey E F, Casanova M F, Weinberger D R: Anatomical abnormalities in the brains of monozygotic twins discordant for schizophrenia. N Engl J Med *322*: 789, 1990.

Weinberger D R, Berman K F, Illowsky B P: Physiological dysfunction of dorsolateral prefrontal cortex in schizophrenia: III. A new cohort and evidence for a monoaminergic mechanism. Arch Gen Psychiatry *45*: 609, 1988.

14

Delusional Disorder

Although delusional disorders are called paranoid disorders in some diagnostic nomenclatures, the term "delusional" is used in the revised third edition of *Diagnostic and Statistical Manual of Mental Disorders* (DSM-III-R) to indicate that the content of the delusion can be of any type, not just paranoid (i.e., persecutory). Furthermore, DSM-III-R uses the term "delusional disorder" to highlight that the delusion or the delusional system is the primary symptom in this syndrome. Patients with delusional disorders have no identifiable organic basis for their delusions.

Patients with delusional disorder do not have affective symptoms of a major mood disorder, and their affect is appropriate to the content of the delusion. The delusions of these patients lack the bizarre quality that is often seen in the delusions of schizophrenic patients, and their thought processes and personalities remain intact.

HISTORY

In 1818 Johann Christian Heinroth introduced the basic concept of paranoia when he described disorders of the intellect under the term *Verrücktheit.* In 1838 the French psychiatrist Jean Etienne Dominique Esquirol coined the term "monomania" to characterize delusions with no associated defect in logical reasoning or general behavior. Karl Ludwig Kahlbaum in 1863 used the term "paranoia" and characterized the illness as uncommon but distinct. Emil Kraepelin in 1921 described paraphrenia as an illness with an insidious onset and chronic course but differentiated it from schizophrenia by the absence of hallucinations and other psychotic symptoms and by the lack of deterioration in personality.

EPIDEMIOLOGY

The prevalence of delusional disorders in the United States is currently estimated to be 0.03 percent. This number is much lower than the prevalence of 1 percent for schizophrenia and 5 percent for mood disorders. The annual incidence of delusional disorders is from 1 to 3 new cases per 100,000 population. This number represents approximately 4 percent of all first admissions to psychiatric hospitals for nonorganic psychoses. There may be an underreporting of delusional disorders because delusional patients rarely seek psychiatric help unless forced to do so by their families or the courts.

The mean age of onset is approximately 40 years, but the age range is from 25 to the 90s. There is a slight preponderance of female patients. Many patients are married and employed, and there may be some association with recent immigration or low socioeconomic status.

ETIOLOGY

The cause of delusional disorder is not known. Although one possibility is that delusional disorders are a subtype of schizophrenia or the mood disorders, family studies suggest that delusional disorders are a distinct clinical entity. These studies report an increased prevalence of delusional disorder and related personality traits in the relatives of delusional disorder probands. Family studies have also reported that there is neither an increased incidence of schizophrenia and mood disorders in the families of delusional disorder probands nor an increased incidence of delusional disorders in the families of schizophrenic probands. Long-term follow-up of patients with delusional disorders found that their diagnoses rarely changed to schizophrenia or to a mood disorder, suggesting that delusional disorders are not merely an early stage of these other disorders. Delusional disorders are also differentiated from schizophrenia and the mood disorders by their later age of onset.

Biological Factors

The neuropsychiatric approach to delusional disorders derives from the observation that delusions are a common symptom in many neurological conditions, particularly those involving the limbic system and the basal ganglia. Patients who have delusions caused by neurological diseases in the absence of intellectual impairment tend to have complex delusions quite similar to those seen in patients with delusional disorders. Conversely, neurological patients with intellectual impairments more often have simple delusions that are unlike those seen in patients with delusional disorders.

The limbic system and basal ganglia have significant reciprocal innervations and are thought to be involved in mood and motivation. Discrete anatomical or molecular lesions of these regions, in the presence of otherwise intact cognitive functions, may provide the biological basis for delusions and delusional disorders.

Psychodynamic Factors

Practitioners have a strong clinical impression that many patients with delusional disorders are socially isolated and have attained less than expected levels of achievement. More specific psychodynamic theories regarding the cause and evolution of delusional symptoms involve suppositions regarding hypersensitive persons and specific ego mechanisms: reaction formation, projection, and denial.

Freud's contributions. Sigmund Freud believed that delusions, rather than being symptoms of the illness, were part of a healing process. In 1896 he described projection as the main defense mechanism in paranoia. Later, Freud read *Memoirs of My Nervous Illness*, an autobiographical account by the gifted jurist Daniel Paul Schreber. Although he never personally met Schreber, Freud theorized from his review of the autobiography how unconscious homosexual tendencies were defended against by denial and projection. Because homosexuality is consciously inadmissible to some paranoid patients, the feeling of "I love him" is denied and changed by reaction formation into "I do not love him; I hate him." This feeling is further transformed through projection into "It is not I who hate him; it is he who hates me." In a full-blown paranoid state this feeling is elaborated into "I am persecuted by him." The patient is then able to rationalize his anger by consciously hating those he perceives to hate him. Instead of being aware of passive homosexual impulses, the patient rejects the love of anyone except himself. In erotomanic delusions the male patient changes "I love him" to "I love her," and this feeling, through projection, becomes "She loves me."

Freud also believed that unconscious homosexuality is the cause of delusions of jealousy. In an attempt to ward off threatening impulses, the patient becomes preoccupied by jealous thoughts; thus, the patient asserts, "I do not love him; she loves him." Freud believed that the man the paranoid patient suspects his wife of loving is a man to whom the patient feels sexually attracted. According to classic psychoanalytic theory, the dynamics underlying the formation of delusions for a female patient are the same as for a male patient.

Clinical evidence has not supported Freud's thesis. A significant number of delusional patients do not have demonstrable homosexual inclinations, and the majority of homosexual men do not have symptoms of paranoia or delusions.

Paranoid pseudocommunity. Norman Cameron described at least seven situations that favor the development of delusional disorders: (1) an increased expectation of receiving sadistic treatment, (2) situations that increase distrust and suspicion, (3) social isolation, (4) situations that increase envy and jealousy, (5) situations that lower self-esteem, (6) situations that cause persons to see their own defects in others, and (7) situations that increase the potential for rumination over probable meanings and motivations. When frustration from any combination of these conditions exceeds the limits that the persons can tolerate, they become withdrawn and anxious; they realize that something is wrong and seek an explanation for the problem. The crystallization of a delusional system offers a solution. Elaboration of the delusion to include imagined persons and the attribution of malevolent motivations to both real and imagined people result in the organization of the pseudocommunity—that is, a perceived community of plotters. This delusional entity hypothetically binds together projected fears and wishes to justify the patient's aggression and to provide a tangible target.

Other psychodynamic factors. Clinical observations indicate that some paranoid patients experience a lack of trust in relationships. This distrust has been hypothesized to be related to a consistently hostile family environment, often with an overcontrolling mother and a distant or sadistic father.

Patients with delusional disorders primarily use the defense mechanisms of reaction formation, denial, and projection. Reaction formation is used as a defense against aggression, dependency needs, and feelings of affection. The need for dependency is transformed into staunch independence. Denial is used to avoid awareness of painful reality. Consumed with anger and hostility and unable to face responsibility for this rage, the patients project their resentment and anger onto others. Projection is used to protect patients from recognizing unacceptable impulses in themselves.

Hypersensitivity and feelings of inferiority have been hypothesized to lead, through reaction formation and projection, to delusions of superiority and grandiosity. Delusions of erotic ideas have been suggested as replacements for feelings of rejection. Some clinicians have noted that children who are expected to perform impeccably and are undeservedly punished when they fail to do so may develop elaborate fantasies as a way of enhancing their injured self-esteem. These secret thoughts may eventually evolve into delusions. Critical and frightening delusions are often described as projections of superego criticism.

The delusions of female paranoid patients often involve accusations of prostitution. As a child, the female paranoiac turned to her father for the maternal love that she was unable to receive from her mother. Incestuous desires developed. Later heterosexual encounters are an unconscious reminder of the incestuous desires of childhood; these desires are defended against by superego projection, accusing the female paranoiac of prostitution.

Somatic delusions can be psychodynamically explained as a regression to the infantile narcissistic state in which patients withdraw emotional involvement from other people and fixate on their physical selves. In erotic delusions the love can be conceptualized as projected narcissistic love used as a defense against low self-esteem and severe narcissistic injury. Delusions of grandeur may represent a regression to the omnipotent feelings of childhood, in which feelings of undenied and undiminished powers predominated.

CLINICAL FEATURES AND MENTAL STATUS EXAMINATION

General Description

The patient is usually well groomed and well dressed without evidence of gross disintegration of personality or daily activities. The patient may seem suspicious, eccentric, or hostile. The patient is sometimes quite litigious and may make this inclination quite clear to the examiner. If the patient attempts to engage the clinician as an ally in the delusion, the clinician should not pretend to accept the delusion, since doing so merely further confounds reality and also sets the stage for eventual therapeutic distrust.

Mood, Feelings, and Affect

The patient's mood is consistent with the delusion. A patient with grandiose delusions is euphoric; a patient with persecutory delusions is suspicious. Whatever the nature of the delusional system, the examiner may sense some mild depressive qualities.

Perceptual Disturbances

Delusional disorder patients do not have prominent or sustained hallucinations. However, a few delusional patients have rare hallucinatory experiences, virtually always auditory in nature.

Thought Content

This area of the mental status examination contains the key pathology of the disorder—the delusion itself. In contrast to many of the delusions reported in patients with schizophrenia, the delusions in delusional disorder are defined as being possible, albeit highly improbable. The delusion may be persecutory, jealous, erotomanic, somatic, grandiose, or some mixture of these and other themes. The delusional system may be quite complex or rather simple. The patient usually lacks other signs of thought disorder, although some patients may seem verbose, circumstantial, or idiosyncratic in their speech when they talk about their delusions.

Impulse Control

It is important to evaluate patients with delusional disorders for ideation or plans to act on their delusional material by suicide, homicide, or other violence. The incidence of these behaviors in delusional disorder patients is not known. The therapist should not hesitate to ask patients about their suicidal, homicidal, or sexual plans and preparations for their completion. Destructive aggression is most common in patients with a history of violence. If aggressive feelings existed in the past, patients should be asked how they managed them. If the patients are unable to control their impulses, hospitalization is probably necessary. The therapist can sometimes help foster the therapeutic alliance by openly discussing how hospitalization can help the patient gain additional control of his or her impulses.

Orientation

There is usually no abnormality in orientation in patients with delusional disorder unless there is a specific delusion concerning person, place, or time.

Memory

Memory and other cognitive processes are intact in patients with delusional disorder.

Judgment and Insight

Judgment can best be assessed by evaluating the patient's past and present behavior. Patients with delusional disorder most often have virtually no insight into their condition and are almost always brought to the hospital by the police, family members, friends, or employers.

Reliability

Patients are usually quite reliable in their information, except when it impinges on their delusional system.

COURSE AND PROGNOSIS

At the outset of the illness, there is often an identifiable event or social situation about which a modest level of suspicion is warranted. An acute onset of symptoms is thought to be more common than an insidious onset. The initial suspicions become more elaborate and eventually delusional. Approximately 50 percent of patients are recovered at long-term follow-up; another 20 percent may have a decrease in symptoms; the final 30 percent have had no change in their symptoms.

The following factors correlate with a good prognosis: high levels of occupational, social, and functional adjustment; female sex; onset before age 30; acute onset; short duration of illness; and the presence of precipitating factors. Patients with persecutory, somatic, and erotic delusions have a better prognosis than do patients with grandiose and jealous delusions.

DIAGNOSIS AND TYPES

The diagnostic guidelines for delusional disorders are listed in Table 14-1. Patients who have delusions because of their relationship with another delusional person, patients who have had delusional symptoms for less than one month, and patients who have atypical delusional features are classified in DSM-III-R under psychotic disorders not elsewhere classified.

The ninth revision of the *International Classification of Diseases* (ICD-9) groups together the *paranoid states. Simple paranoid states* are characterized by the presence of either an acute or a chronic delusional system. *Paranoia* defines the gradual onset of chronic systematized delusions without hallucinations. The presence of hallucinations defines *paraphrenia*, and ICD-9 includes *shared paranoid disorder*.

Types

DSM-III-R defines six types of delusional disorder based on the content of the delusions—erotomanic, grandiose, jealous, persecutory, somatic, and unspecified. Persecutory and jealous types are the most common; grandiose delusions are not quite as common; erotomanic and somatic types are the most unusual.

Table 14-1
Diagnostic Criteria for Delusional Disorder

A. Nonbizarre delusion(s) (i.e., involving situations that occur in real life, such as being followed, poisoned, infected, loved at a distance, having a disease, being deceived by one's spouse or lover) of at least one month's duration
B. Auditory or visual hallucinations, if present, are not prominent [as defined in schizophrenia, A(1)(*b*)]
C. Apart from the delusion(s) or its ramifications, behavior is not obviously odd or bizarre
D. If a major depressive or manic syndrome has been present during the delusional disturbance, the total duration of all episodes of the mood syndrome has been brief relative to the total duration of the delusional disturbance
E. Has never met criterion A for schizophrenia, and it cannot be established that an organic factor initiated and maintained the disturbance

Specify type: The following types are based on the predominant delusional theme. If no single delusional theme predominates, specify as **Unspecified Type**

Erotomanic Type
Delusional disorder in which the predominant theme of the delusion(s) is that a person, usually of higher status, is in love with the subject

Grandiose Type
Delusional disorder in which the predominant theme of the delusion(s) is one of inflated worth, power, knowledge, identity, or special relationship to a deity or famous person

Jealous Type
Delusional disorder in which the predominant theme of the delusion(s) is that one's sexual partner is unfaithful

Persecutory Type
Delusional disorder in which the predominant theme of the delusion(s) is that one (or someone to whom one is close) is being malevolently treated in some way. People with this type of delusional disorder may repeatedly take their complaints of being mistreated to legal authorities

Somatic Type
Delusional disorder in which the predominant theme of the delusion(s) is that the person has some physical defect, disorder, or disease

Unspecified Type
Delusional disorder that does not fit any of the previous categories, e.g., persecutory and grandiose themes without a predominance of either; delusions of reference without malevolent content

Erotomanic. The central theme of an erotic delusion is that one is loved by another. The delusion usually concerns idealized romantic love and spiritual union, rather than sexual attraction. The person about whom this conviction is held is usually of higher status, such as a famous person or a superior at work, and may even be a complete stranger. Efforts to contact the object of the delusion—through telephone calls, letters, gifts, visits, and even surveillance and stalking—are common, although occasionally the person keeps the delusion secret.

Whereas in clinical samples most of the patients are female, in forensic samples most are male. Some people with this disorder, particularly men, come into conflict with the law in their efforts to pursue the objects of their delusions or in misguided efforts to rescue them from some imagined dangers. Erotic delusions are significant sources of harassment to public figures. The erotomanic type has also been called *Clérambault's syndrome*.

Grandiose. Grandiose delusions usually take the form of being convinced that one possesses some great but unrecognized talent or insight or has made some important discovery, which one may take to various governmental agencies, such as the Federal Bureau of Investigation and the U.S. Patent Office. Less common is the delusion that one has a special relationship with a prominent person, in which case the actual person, if alive, is regarded as an imposter. Grandiose delusions may have a religious content, and persons with these delusions can become leaders of religious cults.

Jealous. When delusions of jealousy are present, a person is convinced, without due cause, that his or her spouse or lover is unfaithful. Bits of "evidence," such as disarrayed clothing and spots on the sheets, may be collected and used to justify the delusion. Almost invariably the person with the delusion confronts his or her spouse or lover and may take extraordinary steps to intervene in the imagined infidelity. These attempts may include restricting the autonomy of the spouse or lover by insisting that he or she never leave the house unaccompanied, secretly following the spouse or lover, and investigating the other "lover." The person with the delusion may physically attack the spouse or lover and, more rarely, the other "lover." When the delusions concern the fidelity of the spouse, these patients have been said to have conjugal paranoia or *Othello syndrome*. The jealous type is illustrated by the following case:

A beautiful, successful 34-year-old interior designer was brought to a clinic by her 37-year-old husband, a prominent attorney. The husband lamented that for the past three years his wife had made increasingly shrill accusations that he was unfaithful to her. He declared that he had done everything in his power to convince her of his innocence, but there was no shaking her conviction. A careful examination of the facts revealed no evidence that the man had been unfaithful. When his wife was asked what her evidence was, she became vague and mysterious, declaring that she could tell such things by a faraway look in his eye.

She was absolutely sure that she was right and felt highly insulted by the suggestion that she was imagining the disloyalty. Her husband reported that for the past year she had been increasingly bitter, creating a cold-war atmosphere in the household. Militantly entrenched against her husband, she refused to show him any affection except at social gatherings. She seemed intent on giving the impression socially that they had a good relationship; but when they were alone, the coldness reentered the picture. She had physically assaulted her husband on occasion, but her account obscured the fact that she initiated the assaults; her description of the tussles actually began at the point at which the husband attempted to interrupt her assault by holding her arms. She declared that she would never forgive him for holding her down and squeezing her arms, and her account made it appear that she was unfairly restrained.

The patient experienced no hallucinations; her speech was well organized; she interpreted proverbs with no difficulty; she seemed to have a good command of current events and generally displayed no difficulty in thinking, aside from her conviction of the infidelity. She described herself as having a generally full life, with a few close friends and no problems except those centering on her experiences of unhappiness in the marriage. The husband reported that his wife was respected for her skills but that she had had difficulties for most of her life in close relationships with friends. She had lost a number of friends because of her apparent intolerance of differences in opinion. The patient reported that she did not want to leave the marriage, nor did she want her husband to leave her; instead, she was furious about the "injustice" and demanded that it be confessed and redeemed.

Discussion. Not all complaints of infidelity are unfounded, but in this case the evidence supported the notion that the wife's jealousy was delusional. Delusional jealousy may be seen in schizophrenia; but in the absence of the characteristic psychotic symptoms of schizophrenia—such as bizarre delusions, hallucinations, and disorganized speech—it is a symptom of a delusional disorder. As is commonly the case in delusional disorder, this woman's impairment because of her delusion did not involve her daily functioning apart from her relationship with her husband.

Persecutory. This is the most common type of delusional disorder. The persecutory delusion may be simple or elaborate, and it usually involves a single theme or series of connected themes, such as being conspired against, cheated, spied on, followed, poisoned or drugged, maliciously maligned, harassed, or obstructed in the pursuit of long-term goals. Small slights may be exaggerated and become the focus of a delusional system. In certain cases the focus of the delusion is some injustice that must be remedied by legal action (querulous paranoia), and the affected person often engages in repeated attempts to obtain satisfaction by appeal to the courts and other government agencies. Persons with persecutory delusions are often resentful and angry, and they may resort to violence against those they believe are hurting them. The persecutory type is illustrated by the following case:

A 42-year-old married black postal worker, the father of two, was brought to the emergency room by his wife because he had been insisting, "There is a contract out on my life."

According to the patient, his problems began four months before, when his supervisor at work accused him of tampering with a package. The patient denied that he had and, because his job was in jeopardy, filed a protest. At a formal hearing he was exonerated and, according to him, "This made my boss furious. He felt he had been publicly humiliated."

About two weeks later the patient noticed that his coworkers were avoiding him. "When I'd walk toward them, they'd just turn away like they didn't want to see me." Shortly thereafter, he began to feel that they were talking about him at work. He never could make out clearly what they were saying, but he gradually became convinced that they were avoiding him because his boss had taken out a contract on his life.

This state of affairs was stable for about two months, until the patient began noticing several "large white cars," new to his neighborhood, driving up and down the street on which he lived. He became increasingly frightened and was convinced that the "hit men" were in these cars. He refused to go out of his apartment without an escort. Several times, when he saw the white cars, he would panic and run home. After one such incident, his wife finally insisted that he accompany her to the emergency room.

The patient was described by his wife and his brother as a basically well adjusted, outgoing man who enjoyed being with his family. He had served with distinction in Vietnam. He saw little combat there but was pulled from a burning truck by a buddy seconds before the truck blew up.

When interviewed, the patient was obviously frightened. Aside from his belief that he was in danger of being killed, his speech, behavior, and demeanor were in no way odd or strange. His predominant mood was anxious. He denied having hallucinations and all other psychotic symptoms except those noted above. He claimed not to be depressed; although he noted that he had recently had some difficulty in falling asleep, he said there had been no change in his appetite, sex drive, energy level, or concentration.

Discussion. The patient's anxiety stemmed from his belief that his boss had a contract out on his life. There was no reason to believe this; thus, psychiatrists concluded that he had a delusion. Since contract killers *are* sometimes hired in real life, the delusion was nonbizarre. The patient had no auditory or visual hallucinations, no manic or depressive syndrome, and no evidence of an organic factor that initiated and maintained the disturbance. His behavior, apart from the delusion and its ramifications, was not odd or bizarre. These are the characteristics of delusional disorder. Since the content of his delusion involved the theme of being malevolently treated in some way, the disorder is specified as persecutory type.

Often, people with the persecutory type of delusional disorder are reluctant to seek help. The patient, however, was apparently frightened enough to be persuaded to seek help.

Somatic. Somatic delusions occur in several forms. Most common are convictions that the persons emit foul odors from the skin, mouth, rectum, or vagina; that they have infestations of insects on or in the skin; that they have internal parasites; that certain parts of their bodies are, contrary to all evidence, misshapen and ugly; or that certain parts of their bodies, such as the large intestine, are not functioning. Persons with somatic delusions usually consult nonpsychiatric physicians for treatment of their perceived somatic conditions. The somatic type is illustrated by the following case:

A fit-looking man of 70 consulted a dermatologist, complaining of being infested with fleas for about a year. The dermatologist found no evidence of infestation and referred him for psychiatric consultation. Although angry about the referral, the patient followed through and gave the following history.

About a year previously, he had bought a canary and soon noticed that it had fleas. He applied an insecticide, but the fleas "attacked" him and "invaded" his house. He washed his clothes repeatedly, applied many lotions, and saw a number of physicians, but nothing helped. He insisted he could see the fleas. He was distressed and too ashamed to see his friends, so he had become almost completely isolated.

The patient had enjoyed good health until two years before, when he had had a severe myocardial infarction. He had made a good recovery and kept himself active. He had given up heavy pipe smoking at that time. He had always been a moderate drinker. There was no personal or family history of emotional problems. He had married as a young man, but his wife had deserted him, and he had lived alone for many years.

When interviewed, the patient looked considerably younger than his stated age and was alert and friendly, although he became angry when talking about the "incompetent" doctors who had failed to cure him and he bristled when asked if the infestation could possibly be due to his imagination. His sensorium and cognitive functions were normal; his mood was essentially normal except for some anxiety and, at times, anger. His basic personality appeared to be stable. His conviction about the infestation was unshakable, but there was no evidence of other false beliefs.

Discussion. It was unclear whether the insects the patient "saw" were the result of delusional misinterpretations of normal visual stimuli or visual hallucinations with a delusional explanation. In any case, his primary symptom was a somatic delusion. Since it is actually possible to be infested with fleas, the delusion was not bizarre. The persistence of nonbizarre somatic delusions in the absence of other psychotic symptoms such as prominent hallucinations and incoherence, a mood syndrome, or a known organic cause indicates delusional disorder, somatic type.

Other recognized specific delusions. Other delusions have been given specific names in the literature. In the absence of an organic explanation, patients with these delusions may be classified according to DSM-III-R either as delusional disorder (unspecified type) or as psychotic disorder not elsewhere classified. *Capgras's syndrome* is the delusion that familiar people have been replaced by identical impostors. *Fregoli's phenomenon* is the delusion that a persecutor is taking on a variety of faces, as if he or she were an actor. *Lycanthropy* is the delusion of being a werewolf, and *heutoscopy* is the false belief that one has a double. *Cotard's syndrome* was originally called *délire de négation*. Persons with this syndrome may believe that they have lost everything—possessions, strength, even bodily organs, such as the heart.

Table 14-2
Some Neurological and Medical Conditions That Can Present with Delusions

Basal ganglia disorders—Parkinson's disease, Huntington's chorea
Deficiency states—B_{12}, folate, thiamine, niacin
Delirium
Dementia—Alzheimer's disease, Pick's disease
Drug-induced—amphetamines, anticholinergics, antidepressants, antihypertensives, antituberculosis drugs, antiparkinsonism, cimetidine, disulfiram (Antabuse), hallucinogens
Endocrinopathies—adrenal, thyroid, parathyroid
Limbic system pathology—epilepsy, strokes, tumors
Systemic—hepatic encephalopathy, hypercalcemia, hypoglycemia, porphyria, uremia

DIFFERENTIAL DIAGNOSIS

Many medical and neurological illnesses can present with delusions (Table 14-2). As mentioned previously, the most common sites for lesions are the basal ganglia and the limbic system. The medical evaluation should include toxicology screening and routine admission laboratory work. Neuropsychological testing (such as the Bender-Gestalt and the Wechsler Memory Scale) and an electroencephalogram (EEG) or a computed tomography (CT) scan may be indicated at the time of the initial presentation, especially if other signs or symptoms suggest cognitive impairment or electrophysiological or structural lesions. Delirium can be differentiated by the presence of a fluctuating level of consciousness or impaired cognitive abilities. Delusions early in the course of a dementing illness, as in Alzheimer's disease, may give the appearance of a delusional disorder; however, neuropsychological testing usually detects cognitive impairment. Although alcohol abuse is an associated feature for patients with delusional disorders, delusional disorders should be distinguished from alcoholic hallucinosis. Intoxication with sympathomimetics (including amphetamine), marijuana, or L-dopa is particularly likely to result in delusional symptoms.

The psychiatric differential diagnosis for delusional disorders includes malingering and factitious disorder with psychological features (Table 14-3). The nonfactitious disorders in the differential diagnosis are schizophrenia, mood disorders, psychotic disorders not elsewhere classified, and paranoid personality disorder. Delusional disorders are distinguished from schizophrenia by the absence of other schizophrenic symptoms and by the nonbizarre quality of the delusions. Persecutory and jealous types of delusional disorder, however, may be difficult to distinguish from some presentations of schizophrenia. The grandiose and erotomanic types may resemble mania in clinical presentation; the somatic type may resemble depression. The absence of other signs and symptoms of mood disorders help the clinician make the appropriate diagnosis. If the symptoms do not meet the guidelines for a delusional disorder, schizophrenia, or mood disorder, then one of the diagnoses in psychotic disorders not elsewhere classified may be appropriate. Separating paranoid personality disorder from a delusional disorder requires the sometimes difficult clinical distinction between extreme suspiciousness and a frank delusion. In general, if the clinician doubts whether the symptom is a delusion, the diagnosis of a delusional disorder should not be made.

TREATMENT

Hospitalization

The initial clinical consideration is whether the patient requires hospitalization. The possibility of suicide or homicide, severe impairment in occupational or social functioning, and the need for a diagnostic workup are strong indications for hospitalization. If the physician is convinced that the patient is best treated in a hospital, an attempt should be made to persuade the patient to accept hospitalization; failing that, legal commitment may be indicated. Often, if the physician convinces the patient that hospitalization is inevitable, the patient voluntarily enters a hospital to avoid legal commitment.

Pharmacotherapy

In an emergency, severely agitated patients should be given a tranquilizing drug intramuscularly. For chronic

Table 14-3
Differential Diagnosis for Delusional Disorder

Paranoid personality disorder	Pervasive and long-standing suspiciousness of other people
Schizophrenia	One symptom from the following: Delusions of being controlled Thought broadcasting Thought insertion Thought withdrawal Fantastic or implausible delusions Other delusions without persecutory or jealous content Auditory hallucination in which a noise keeps up a running commentary on the patient's thoughts or behavior Auditory hallucination not associated with depression or elation or limited to two words Delusions of any type accompanied by hallucination of any type Loosening of association combined with inappropriate affect
Manic episode	Elevated, expansive, or irritable mood with pressured speech and hyperactivity
Depressive episode	Pervasive loss of interest or pleasure combined with at least four of the following: Change in weight when not dieting Sleep difficulty Psychomotor agitation or retardation Loss of energy Decrease in sex drive Feelings of self-reproach or excessive guilt, either of which may be delusional Indecisiveness Suicidal thoughts
Organic mental disorder	Disordered memory and orientation Impairment in judgment and impulse control Perceptual disturbance—simple misinterpretations, illusions and hallucinations Clinical features that may fluctuate rapidly

Table adapted from DSM-III, *Diagnostic and Statistical Manual of Mental Disorders*, ed 3. American Psychiatric Association, Washington, DC, 1980, with permission.

treatment, antipsychotic drugs are currently considered the drugs of choice, although adequate proof of their efficacy is lacking. Delusional disorder patients are likely to refuse medication, because they can easily incorporate the administration of drugs into their delusional system. It may be prudent for the physician not to insist on medication immediately after hospitalization but, rather, to spend a few days establishing rapport with the patient. The physician should explain potential side effects to the patient, so that the patient does not later suspect that the physician lied to him or her.

The prior history of medication response is the best guide to choosing a drug. It is often wise to start with low doses—for example, 2 mg haloperidol (Haldol)—and to increase the dosage slowly. If a patient fails to respond to a drug at a reasonable dosage in a six-week trial, antipsychotics from other classes should be given clinical trials. A common cause of drug failure is noncompliance, and this possibility should be carefully evaluated.

If the patient receives no benefit from antipsychotic medication, the drug should be discontinued. In patients who do respond to antipsychotics, maintenance doses can often be quite low. Essentially no data suggest whether antidepressants, lithium, or carbamazepine (Tegretol) are effective in treating delusional disorders. Clinical trials of these medications may be warranted in patients with features suggestive of mood disorders or family histories positive for such illnesses.

Psychotherapy

The essential element in effective psychotherapy is establishing a relationship in which the patient begins to trust the therapist. Individual therapy seems to be more effective than group therapy. Initially, the therapist should neither agree with nor challenge the patient's delusions. The physician may stimulate the patient's motivation to receive help by emphasizing a willingness to help the patient with his or her anxiety or irritability, without suggesting that the delusions be treated. The examiner, however, should not actively support the notion that the delusions represent reality.

The unwavering reliability of the therapist is essential. The therapist should be on time and make appointments as regularly as possible, the goal being to develop a solid and trusting relationship with the patient. Overgratification may actually increase the patient's hostility and suspiciousness because of the core realization that all demands cannot be met. The therapist can avoid overgratification by not extending the designated appointment period, not giving extra appointments unless absolutely necessary, and not being lenient about the fee.

Therapists should not make disparaging remarks about patients' delusions or ideas but can sympathetically indicate to patients that their preoccupation with their delusions both distresses themselves and interferes with a constructive life. When patients begin to waver in their delusional beliefs, the therapist may increase reality testing by asking patients to clarify their concerns.

When family members are available, the clinician may decide to involve them in the treatment plan. Although the clinician has to avoid being delusionally seen as "siding with the enemy," he or she should attempt to enlist the family as allies in the treatment process. Consequently, both the patient and the family need to understand that physician-patient confidentiality will be maintained by the therapist and that communications from relatives will be discussed at some point with the patient. The family may benefit from the support of the doctor and, in turn, may be more supportive of the patient.

Outcome of therapy. Psychodynamic theories hypothesize that, through a relationship with the therapist, patients begin to neutralize their drives and to strengthen the ego. Trust develops, defenses are reinforced, and the presenting conflict begins to resolve. Patients can learn to adjust to the delusions that remain intact. They can be taught to recognize those situations that produce and increase delusional behavior, and alternative responses to stress can be encouraged.

A good therapeutic outcome depends on the psychiatrist's ability to respond to the patient's mistrust of others and the resulting interpersonal conflicts, frustrations, and failures. The mark of successful treatment may be a satisfactory social adjustment, rather than an abatement of the patient's delusions.

References

Akiskal H S, Arana G W, Baldessarini R J: A clinical report of thymoleptic-responsive atypical paranoid psychoses. Am J Psychiatry *140*: 1187, 1983.

Cummings J L: Organic delusions: Phenomenology, anatomical correlations, and review. Br J Psychiatry *146*: 184, 1985.

Kamanitz J R, el-Mallakh R S, Tasman A: Delusional misidentification involving the self. J Nerv Ment Dis *177*: 658, 1989.

Kendler K S: Demography of paranoid psychosis (delusional disorder): A review and comparison with schizophrenia and affective illness. Arch Gen Psychiatry *39*: 890, 1982.

Kendler K S: The nosologic validity of paranoia (simple delusional disorder): A review. Arch Gen Psychiatry *37*: 699, 1980.

Kendler K S, Masteson C, Davis K: Psychiatric illness in first-degree relatives of patients with paranoid psychosis, schizophrenia, and medical illness. Br J Psychiatry *147*: 524, 1985.

Kulick A R, Pope H G Jr, Keck P E Jr: Lycanthropy and self-identification. J Nerv Ment Dis *178*: 134, 1990.

Lantos V: On the "organicity" of paranoid syndromes. Psychiatr J Univ Ottawa *13*: 32, 1988.

Manschreck T C: Delusional (paranoid) disorders. In *Comprehensive Textbook of Psychiatry*, ed 5, H I Kaplan and B J Sadock, editors, p 816. Williams & Wilkins, Baltimore, 1989.

Meissner W W: *Psychotherapy and the Paranoid Process*. Jason Aronson, Northvale, NJ, 1986.

Munro A: Delusional (paranoid) disorders: Etiologic and taxonomic considerations: I. The possible significance of organic brain factors in etiology of delusional disorders. Can J Psychiatry *3*: 171, 1988.

Opjordsmoen S: Long-term course and outcome in delusional disorder. Acta Psychiatr Scand *78*: 627, 1988.

Rudden M, Sweeney J, Frances A: Diagnosis and clinical course of erotomanic and other delusional patients. Am J Psychiatry *147*: 625, 1990.

Sacks M H: Folie a deux. Compr Psychiatry *29*: 270, 1988.

Segal J H: Erotomania revisited: From Kraepelin to DSM-III-R. Am J Psychiatry *146*: 1261, 1989.

Winokur G: Delusional disorder (paranoia). Compr Psychiatry *18*: 511, 1977.

Winokur G: Familial psychopathology in delusional disorder. Compr Psychiatry *26*: 241, 1985.

15

Psychotic Disorders Not Elsewhere Classified

15.1 / Schizoaffective Disorder

Some psychiatric patients have symptoms of both schizophrenia and a mood disorder. It is not possible to classify these patients as having just one of the two disorders without distorting some aspect of their clinical presentation. The traditional diagnostic term for these patients has been "schizoaffective." The specific diagnostic criteria for schizoaffective disorder have been modified by different generations of psychiatrists, mostly as a reflection of changes in the diagnostic criteria for schizophrenia and the mood disorders.

HISTORY

In 1913 G. H. Kirby and in 1921 A. Hoch both described patients with mixed features of schizophrenia and affective (mood) disorders. Because their patients did not demonstrate the deteriorating course of dementia precox, Kirby and Hoch classified them in Emil Kraepelin's manic-depressive psychosis group.

In 1933 Jacob Kasanin described a group of patients with concurrent schizophrenic and affective symptoms, a history of a precipitating stressor, an acute onset, and a family history of mood disorder in some cases. Although these patients recovered from their symptoms, Kasanin classified them as having a type of schizophrenia. By this time the diagnostic importance of schizophrenic symptoms, as emphasized by Eugen Bleuler, had eclipsed Kraepelin's emphasis on the course of the illness for differentiating schizophrenia from affective conditions. From 1933 to approximately 1970, patients whose symptoms were similar to those of Kasanin's were variously classified as having schizoaffective disorder, atypical schizophrenia, good-prognosis schizophrenia, remitting schizophrenia, or cycloid psychosis—terms that emphasized a relation to schizophrenia.

Around 1970 two sets of data caused the shift from viewing schizoaffective disorder as a schizophrenic illness to viewing it as a mood disorder. First, lithium carbonate was demonstrated to be an effective and specific treatment for both bipolar and some schizoaffective disorders. Second, the United States–United Kingdom study, published in 1968 by J. Cooper and his colleagues, demonstrated that the variation in the number of patients classified as schizophrenic in the United States and the United Kingdom was the result of an overemphasis in the United States on the presence of psychotic symptoms as a diagnostic criterion for schizophrenia.

EPIDEMIOLOGY

The epidemiology of schizoaffective disorder, as currently defined, is not well explored because the frequent changes in diagnostic criteria have rendered information from earlier studies difficult to interpret. Based on available data, however, the lifetime prevalence is less than 1 percent, possibly in the range of 0.5 to 0.8 percent. In clinical practice a preliminary diagnosis of schizoaffective disorder is frequently used when the clinician is uncertain of the diagnosis. There does not appear to be a difference between men and women in the prevalence of schizoaffective disorder.

ETIOLOGY

Although the cause of schizoaffective disorder is unknown, there are four conceptual models: (1) It may be a type of either schizophrenia or a mood disorder. (2) It may represent a combination of both schizophrenia and a mood disorder. (3) It may be completely distinct from either schizophrenia or a mood disorder. (4) Perhaps most likely, it may comprise a heterogeneous group representing the first three possibilities.

Studies designed to explore these possibilities have examined family histories, biological markers, short-term treatment responses, and long-term outcomes. Most of these studies have considered schizoaffective disorder as a homogeneous group. More recent studies have examined the bipolar and depressive types of schizoaffective disorder separately.

One reasonable conclusion from available data is that patients with schizoaffective disorder are a heterogeneous group, some having schizophrenia with prominent affective symptoms and others having a mood disorder with prominent schizophrenic symptoms. As a group, schizoaffective patients have a better prognosis than patients with schizophrenia and a worse prognosis than patients with mood disorders. Depending somewhat on the type of schizoaffective disorder studied, an increased prevalence of schizophrenia or mood disorders may be found in the relatives of the schizoaffective probands.

The idea that schizoaffective disorder is a type of schizophrenia is not supported by research; an increased prevalence of schizophrenia is not found among relatives of schizoaffective disorder, bipolar type, probands. Other investigations have demonstrated that schizoaffective patients, as a group, do not have schizophrenialike deficits in smooth pursuit eye movements, neurological soft signs, or attentional abilities. The possibility that schizoaffective disorder is a type of mood disorder is not supported by the increased prevalence of schizophrenia in relatives of probands with schizoaffective disorder, depressive type. However, a similarity between patients with schizoaffective disorder and patients with mood disorders is suggested by the higher prevalence of mood disorders in relatives of schizoaffective probands than in relatives of schizophrenic probands. It has also been reported that, as a group, schizoaffective patients respond to lithium and tend to have a nondeteriorating course. The view that schizoaffective disorder represents a completely different disorder is not supported by the observation that only a very small percentage of relatives of schizoaffective probands have schizoaffective disorder. Finally, the hypothesis that schizoaffective patients have both schizophrenia and a mood disorder is untenable because the calculated co-occurrence of these two disorders is much lower than the incidence of schizoaffective disorder.

CLINICAL FEATURES

The clinical signs and symptoms of schizoaffective disorder include all the signs and symptoms of schizophrenia, mania, and depression. The schizophrenic and affective symptoms can present together or in an alternating fashion. The course can vary from one of exacerbations and remissions to one of a chronic deteriorating course. The incidence of suicide among patients with schizoaffective disorder is thought to be at least 10 percent. A clinical case example follows:

A 44-year-old mother of three teenagers was hospitalized for treatment of depression. She gave the following history: One year previously, after breaking up with her lover, she became acutely psychotic. She was frightened that people were going to kill her and heard voices of friends and strangers sometimes talking to one another, talking about killing her. She heard her own thoughts broadcast aloud and was afraid that others could also hear what she was thinking. Over a three-week period she stayed in her apartment, had new locks put on the doors, kept the shades down, and avoided everyone but her immediate family. She was unable to sleep at night because the voices kept her awake and unable to eat because of a constant "lump" in her throat. In retrospect, she could not say whether she was depressed. She denied being elated or overactive and remembered only that she was terrified of what would happen to her. The family persuaded her to enter a hospital, where, after six weeks of treatment with chlorpromazine (Thorazine), the voices stopped. She remembered feeling "back to normal" for a week or two, but then she seemed to lose her energy and motivation to do anything. She became increasingly depressed, lost her appetite, and woke at 4 or 5 every morning and was unable to get back to sleep. She could no longer read a newspaper or watch TV because she could not concentrate.

The patient's condition had persisted for nine months. She had done very little except sit in her apartment and stare at the walls. Her children had managed most of the cooking, shopping, and bill paying. She had continued in outpatient treatment and was maintained on chlorpromazine until four months before admission. There had been no recurrence of the psychotic symptoms since the medication was discontinued; but her depression, with all the accompanying symptoms, had persisted.

The patient was rather guarded when discussing her past history. There was, however, no evidence of a diagnosable illness before the previous year. She was apparently a shy, emotionally constricted person who "had never broken any rules." She had been separated from her husband for 10 years but in that time had had two enduring relationships with boyfriends. In addition to rearing three apparently healthy and very likable children, she cared for a succession of foster children full-time in the four years before her illness. She enjoyed this and was highly valued by the agency she worked for. She had maintained close relationships with a few girlfriends and with her extended family.

Discussion. During her initial period of illness, this patient demonstrated such characteristic schizophrenic symptoms as bizarre delusions (people could hear what she was thinking) and auditory hallucinations (voices of friends and strangers talking to each other). There was deterioration in functioning to the point that she was unable to take care of her house. With treatment, after about nine weeks, the psychotic symptoms remitted, but she remembered being "back to normal" for only about a week. She then had the characteristic symptoms of a major depressive episode with depressed mood, poor appetite, insomnia, lack of energy, loss of interest, and poor concentration. The depressive period had lasted about nine months.

This case seemed to be an instance in which it is impossible to make a differential diagnosis with any degree of certainty between a mood disorder and schizophrenia or schizophreniform disorder; hence, a diagnosis of schizoaffective disorder seemed appropriate. This diagnosis conveyed the lack of certainty and the prominence of both affective and schizophreniclike features.

COURSE AND PROGNOSIS

The course and the prognosis of schizoaffective disorder are variable. As a group, patients with schizoaffective disorder have a prognosis intermediate between those of patients with schizophrenia and of patients with mood disorders. Data suggest that patients with schizoaffective disorder, bipolar type, have a prognosis similar to that for patients with bipolar disorder and that patients with schizoaffective disorder, depressive type, have a prognosis similar to that for patients with schizophrenia. Regardless of the type, the following variables weigh toward a poor prognosis: poor premorbid history; insidious onset; no precipitating factor; a predominance of psychotic symptoms, especially negative (i.e., deficit) symptoms; early onset; unremitting course; and a positive family history of schizophrenia. The opposite of each of these characteristics weighs toward a better outcome. The presence or absence of Schneiderian first-rank symptoms does not seem to predict the course.

DIAGNOSIS AND TYPES

The revised third edition of *Diagnostic and Statistical Manual of Mental Disorders* (DSM-III-R) diagnostic criteria for schizoaffective disorder consist of two inclusion criteria and one exclusion criterion (Table 15.1-1). The two types are bipolar type (history of a manic episode) and depressive type (no history of a manic episode). The delineation of the types may be particularly important in determining the prognosis of this disorder. The Research Diagnostic Criteria (RDC), the ninth revision of the *International Classification of Diseases* (ICD-9), and other recent diagnostic systems vary somewhat in their diagnostic criteria; however, most require the occurrence of full schizophrenic, depressive, and manic syndromes, together or in alternating fashion.

DIFFERENTIAL DIAGNOSIS

All the organic conditions listed in the differential diagnoses for schizophrenia and mood disorders need to be considered in the differential diagnosis of schizoaffective disorder. Patients treated with steroids, amphetamine and phencyclidine (PCP) abusers, and some patients with temporal lobe epilepsy are particularly likely to present with concurrent schizophrenic and affective symptoms.

The psychiatric differential diagnosis also includes all the possibilities usually considered for schizophrenia and mood disorders. In clinical practice, psychosis at the time of presentation may hinder the detection of current or past mood disorder symptoms. Therefore, one may wish to delay making a final psychiatric diagnosis until the most acute symptoms of psychosis have been controlled.

TREATMENT

The major treatment modalities for schizoaffective disorder are hospitalization, medication, and psychosocial interventions. The basic principles underlying pharmacotherapy for schizoaffective disorders are that antidepressant and antimanic protocols should be followed if at all possible and that antipsychotics should be used only as needed for acute control. If thymoleptic protocols are not effective in controlling the symptoms on an ongoing basis, antipsychotics may be indicated. Patients with schizoaffective disorder, bipolar type, should receive trials of lithium or carbamazepine (Tegretol) or a combination of the two. Patients with schizoaffective disorder, depressive type, should be given trials of antidepressants and electroconvulsive therapy (ECT) before they are determined to be unresponsive to antidepressant treatment.

Table 15.1-1
Diagnostic Criteria for Schizoaffective Disorder

A. A disturbance during which, at some time, there is either a major depressive or a manic syndrome concurrent with symptoms that meet the A criterion of schizophrenia.

B. During an episode of the disturbance, there have been delusions or hallucinations for at least two weeks, but no prominent mood symptoms.

C. Schizophrenia has been ruled out (i.e., the duration of all episodes of a mood syndrome has not been brief relative to the total duration of the psychotic disturbance).

D. It cannot be established that an organic factor initiated and maintained the disturbance.

Specify: **bipolar type** (current or previous manic syndrome) or **depressive type** (no current or previous manic syndrome)

Table from DSM-III-R, *Diagnostic and Statistical Manual of Mental Disorders*, ed 3, revised. Copyright American Psychiatric Association, Washington, DC, 1987, with permission.

References

Clayton P J: Schizoaffective disorders. J. Nerv Ment Dis *170*: 646, 1982.
Levinson D F, Levitt M E M: Schizoaffective mania reconsidered. Am J Psychiatry *144*: 415, 1987.
Levitt J J, Tsuang M T: The heterogeneity of schizoaffective disorder: Implications for treatment. Am J Psychiatry *145*: 926, 1988.
Maj M: Evolution of the American concept of schizoaffective psychosis. Neuropsychobiology *11*: 7, 1984.
Marneros A, Rohde A, Deister A: Unipolar and bipolar schizoaffective disorders: A comparative study. Eur Arch Psychiatry Neurol Sci *239*: 164, 1989.
McGlashan T H, Bardenstein K K: Gender differences in affective, schizoaffective, and schizophrenic disorders. Schizophr Bull *16*: 319, 1990.
McGlashan T H, Williams P V: Schizoaffective psychosis: II. Manic, bipolar, and depressive subtypes. Arch Gen Psychiatry *44*: 128, 1987.
Miller F T, Libman H: Lithium carbonate in the treatment of schizophrenia and schizoaffective disorder: Review and hypothesis. Biol Psychiatry *14*: 705, 1979.
Pope H G, Lipinski J F, Cohen B M: Schizo-affective disorder: An invalid diagnosis? A comparison of schizo-affective disorder, schizophrenia, and affective disorder. Am J Psychiatry *137*: 921, 1980.
Procci W R: Schizoaffective disorder, schizophreniform disorder, and brief reactive psychosis. In *Comprehensive Textbook of Psychiatry*, ed 5, H I Kaplan and B J Sadock, editors, p 830. Williams & Wilkins, Baltimore, 1989.
Samson J A, Simpson J C, Tsuang M T: Outcome studies of schizoaffective disorders. Schizophr Bull *14*: 543, 1988.
Shenton M E, Solovay M R, Holzman P: Comparative studies of thought disorders: II. Schizoaffective disorder. Arch Gen Psychiatry *44*: 21, 1987.
Williams P V, McGlashan T H: Schizoaffective psychosis: I. Comparative long-term outcome. Arch Gen Psychiatry *44*: 130, 1987.
Yasamy M T: Schizoaffective disorder: A dimensional approach. Acta Psychiatr Scand *76*: 609, 1987.

15.2 / Other Psychotic Disorders

This section contains the diagnostic criteria for schizophreniform disorder, brief reactive psychosis, induced psychotic disorder, and psychotic disorder not otherwise specified (NOS). Psychotic disorder NOS is called atypical psychosis in several diagnostic systems. This diagnosis is used for patients with psychotic symptoms who do not meet the diagnostic criteria for any other psychotic disorder. The DSM-III-R description of this classification includes such examples as postpartum psychosis (Table 15.2-1).

Table 15.2-1
Diagnostic Criteria for Psychotic Disorder Not Otherwise Specified (Atypical Psychosis)

Disorders in which there are psychotic symptoms (delusions, hallucinations, incoherence, marked loosening of associations, catatonic excitement or stupor, or grossly disorganized behavior) that do not meet the criteria for any other nonorganic psychotic disorder. This category should also be used for psychoses about which there is inadequate information to make a specific diagnosis. (This is preferable to "diagnosis deferred," and can be changed if more information becomes available.) This diagnosis is made only when it cannot be established that an organic factor initiated and maintained the disturbance.

Examples:

(1) psychoses with unusual features (e.g., persistent auditory hallucinations as the only disturbance)
(2) postpartum psychoses that do not meet the criteria for an organic mental disorder, psychotic mood disorder, or any other psychotic disorder
(3) psychoses with confusing clinical features that make a more specific diagnosis impossible

Table from DSM-III-R, *Diagnostic and Statistical Manual of Mental Disorders*, ed 3, revised. Copyright American Psychiatric Association, Washington, D.C., 1987, with permission.

SCHIZOPHRENIFORM DISORDER

As defined in the revised third edition of *Diagnostic and Statistical Manual of Mental Disorders* (DSM-III-R), schizophreniform disorder is identical to schizophrenia with the following exceptions: schizophreniform symptoms resolve, and there is a return to normal functioning within six months. Symptoms must be present for longer than six months to make a diagnosis of schizophrenia.

This definition of schizophreniform disorder is distinctly different from previous meanings attached to this diagnosis. In 1939 Gabriel Langfeldt devised the term "schizophreniform" to separate patients with this disorder from those with so-called true schizophrenia. Patients with schizophreniform disorder had good premorbid histories, abrupt onset of symptoms often related to a specific stressor, and good prognoses. The patients with true schizophrenia, however, had more classic chronic and deteriorating courses. The DSM-III-R criteria for schizophreniform disorder define a group of patients with schizophrenialike symptoms who have better prognoses than patients with schizophrenia. The basis for this diagnostic distinction is strictly the duration of symptoms.

Epidemiology

The incidence, prevalence, and sex ratio of DSM-III-R schizophreniform disorder have not yet been reported in the literature. Some clinicians have the impression that the disorder is most common in adolescents and young adults, and most investigators believe that the disorder is less than half as common as schizophrenia.

Etiology

The cause of schizophreniform disorder is not known. The few available studies strongly suggest that a heterogeneous group of patients have this diagnosis. Some have an illness similar to schizophrenia, whereas others have an illness similar to the mood disorders. Several studies have shown that schizophreniform patients, as a group, have more affective symptoms (especially mania) and a better outcome than do schizophrenic patients. Also, relatives of schizophreniform patients have schizophrenia less frequently than the relatives of schizophrenic patients but more frequently than the relatives of mood disorder patients. One study reports a similar enlargement of cerebral ventricles in schizophreniform and schizophrenic patients, supporting the notion that some schizophreniform patients have an illness resembling schizophrenia. The biological data are consistent with the hypothesis that the current diagnostic category defines a group of patients who have illnesses similar to schizophrenia or the mood disorders.

Clinical Features

The clinical signs and symptoms and the mental status examination are identical to those in schizophrenia. It is important, however, to note the patient's affect, because the presence of affective symptoms may predict a favorable course. A clinical case example follows:

The patient was a 19-year-old man who, until admission, was working in a mailroom while waiting to apply to college. The onset of his illness was not clear. According to the patient, he had not been the same since his mother died of a cerebral hemorrhage nine months before his admission. According to his father, however, the patient exhibited a normal mourning response to his mother's death, and the change took place six months after the mother died.

At that time, shortly after his girlfriend had rejected him for another man, the patient began to think that male coworkers were making homosexual advances toward him. He began to fear that he was homosexual and that his friends believed he was homosexual. He finally developed the conviction that he had a disorder of the reproductive system—that he had one normal testicle that produced sperm and one testicle that was actually an ovary and produced eggs. He thought that this was evidence that a "woman's body resides inside my man's body." He began to gamble and was convinced that he had won $400,000 and was not paid by his bookie and that he was sought after by talk-show hosts to be a guest on their shows and tell his unusual story (all not true). He claimed that he had a heightened awareness, an "extra sense," and that sounds were unusually loud. He had difficulty sleeping at night but no appetite disturbance.

On admission, the patient's speech was somewhat rapid, and he jumped from topic to topic. His affect was not irritable, euphoric, or expansive. He said he was seeking treatment because "there is a war between my testicles, and I prefer to be male."

When the patient was 10, his pediatrician became concerned that he had an undersized penis. This led to a complete endocrine workup and examinations of his genitals every four months for the next four years. At that time it was concluded that there were no significant abnormalities.

During high school the patient had been a poor student with poor attendance. He claimed to have had many friends throughout his life. He had never received psychiatric treatment. He admitted to occasional marijuana and phencyclidine use in the past but denied any use of hallucinogens.

The patient was the oldest child in a family of six children.

His parents met when they were both patients in a psychiatric hospital.

Discussion. The significant features of the patient's illness include bizarre somatic delusions, grandiose delusions, and disorganization in his speech (he jumped from topic to topic). Although the grandiose delusions and pressured speech suggested the possibility of a manic episode, this was ruled out by the absence of an elevated, expansive, or irritable mood.

When did his illness begin? Although he said he had not been the same since his mother died nine months ago, he did not describe any change in himself that was out of keeping with normal bereavement. Furthermore, his father claimed that his abnormal behavior began only three months ago. Giving the patient the benefit of the doubt, the interviewer dated the onset of the illness three months before admission. The presence of the characteristic symptoms of schizophrenia in an illness of less than six months' duration indicated schizophreniform disorder. His affect was not blunted or flat. However, because it was unclear whether the onset of the illness was rapid (he and his father gave different accounts), the disorder could not be typed as to with or without good prognostic features.

Course and Prognosis

By definition, this disorder resolves within six months with a return to baseline mental functioning. The prognosis of this disorder also involves the likelihood of further schizophreniform episodes and the possible development of schizophrenia or a mood disorder. Studies have indicated that the requirement for six months of symptoms in schizophrenia weighs heavily toward a poor prognosis; therefore, schizophreniform patients have a better prognosis than most schizophrenic patients. In addition to the indicators of good prognosis listed in DSM-III-R (Table 15.2-2), acute onset and short periods of illness weigh toward a good prognosis. There is a risk of suicide during the symptomatic period and also during the period of depression that often follows the psychosis.

Table 15.2-2
Diagnostic Criteria for Schizophreniform Disorder

A. Meets criteria A and C of schizophrenia.

B. An episode of the disturbance (including prodromal, active, and residual phases) lasts less than six months. (When the diagnosis must be made without waiting for recovery, it should be qualified as "provisional.")

C. Does not meet the criteria for brief reactive psychosis, and it cannot be established that an organic factor initiated and maintained the disturbance.

Specify: without good prognostic features or **with good prognostic features** (i.e., with at least two of the following):

(1) onset of prominent psychotic symptoms within four weeks of first noticeable change in usual behavior or functioning
(2) confusion, disorientation, or perplexity at the height of the psychotic episode
(3) good premorbid social and occupational functioning
(4) absence of blunted or flat affect

Diagnosis and Types

DSM-III-R contains specific diagnostic criteria for schizophreniform disorder and two types—with and without good prognostic features (Table 15.2-2). The period of illness must include all prodromal, active, and residual symptoms. The diagnosis of provisional schizophreniform disorder can be made while waiting for the symptoms to resolve. The diagnosis of schizophreniform disorder is more accurate than a diagnosis of schizophrenia when the clinician is unable to obtain a reliable history from a psychotic patient regarding the duration of his or her symptoms. However, a patient's anamnesis for prodromal symptoms may mislead the physician away from a correct diagnosis of schizophrenia, and a patient's anamnesis for affective symptoms may cause the physician to miss a diagnosis of mood disorder.

Differential Diagnosis

The differential diagnosis for schizophreniform disorder is identical to that for schizophrenia. Factitious disorder with psychological symptoms and organic disorders must be ruled out. Temporal lobe epilepsy, central nervous system (CNS) tumors, strokes, infections, and drug ingestion (e.g., steroids, hallucinogens) may be associated with a relatively short-lived psychosis.

Treatment

Hospitalization is often necessary in the treatment of patients with schizophreniform disorder. Hospitalization allows for effective assessment, treatment, and supervision of the patient's behavior. The psychotic symptoms can usually be treated by a three- to six-month course of antipsychotic drugs. Electroconvulsive therapy (ECT) may be indicated for some patients, especially those with marked catatonic or depressed features. A trial of lithium or carbamazepine (Tegretol) or both may be warranted for treatment and prophylaxis if a patient has a recurrent episode. Psychotherapy is usually necessary to help the patients integrate their psychotic experiences as part of their lives.

BRIEF REACTIVE PSYCHOSIS

The hallmarks of brief reactive psychosis are that it follows a significant stressor in the patient's life and that symptoms last less than one month. Brief reactive psychosis is one of the few DSM-III-R diagnoses for which a specific causative factor (i.e., a psychosocial stressor) is identified. Patients with similar disorders have previously been labeled as having reactive, hysterical, stress, and psychogenic psychoses. The entity in French psychiatry *bouffée délirante* is quite similar to these disorders. The DSM-III-R classification of brief reactive psychosis, however, differs from those prior terms. Reactive psychosis was often used as a synonym for good-prognosis schizophrenia; brief reactive psychosis does not imply a relationship to schizophrenia. Hysterical psychosis required the absence of any evidence of premorbid thought disorder.

Epidemiology

The incidence, prevalence, and sex ratio of DSM-III-R brief reactive psychosis have not yet been definitively studied. Many clinicians believe it to be a rare disorder that occurs most often in adolescence and early adulthood. It may be most common in persons in low socioeconomic groups and in patients with previously existing personality disorders (most commonly, histrionic, narcissistic, paranoid, schizotypal, and borderline). Persons who have experienced disasters or major cultural changes may also be at high risk.

Etiology

By definition, a significant psychosocial stressor is a causative factor for this disorder. However, many patients with the disorder have preexisting personality disorders, which may have both biological and psychological bases. Although schizophrenia has not been found to be more common in the relatives of persons with brief reactive psychosis, mood disorders may be more common among them. Psychodynamic formulations highlight inadequate coping mechanisms and the possibility of secondary gain in these patients. It has been hypothesized that the psychosis represents a defense, wish fulfillment, or escape related to the specific stressor.

Clinical Features

The clinical signs and symptoms are similar to those seen in other psychotic disorders, such as schizophrenia and psychotic mood disorders. Affective symptoms may be more common than classic schizophrenic symptoms. Emotional volatility, outlandish dress or behavior, screaming and muteness, disorientation, and impaired recent memory may be present. The patient may be unable initially to relate the details of the precipitating event but later may be able to relate the details in a histrionic fashion. The signs and symptoms of a preexisting personality disorder may be observable during the mental status examination. A clinical case example follows:

A 17-year-old high school junior was brought to the emergency room by her distraught mother, who was at a loss to understand her daughter's behavior. Two days earlier the patient's father had been buried; he had died of a sudden myocardial infarction earlier in the week. The patient had become wildly agitated at the cemetery, screaming uncontrollably and needing to be restrained by relatives. She was inconsolable at home, sat rocking in a corner, and talked about a devil that had come to claim her soul. Before her father's death, she had been a "typical teenager, popular, and a very good student but sometimes prone to overreacting." There was no previous psychiatric history.

Discussion. Grief is an expected reaction to the loss of a loved one. This young woman's reaction, however, not only was more severe than would be expected (wildly agitated, screaming uncontrollably) but also involved psychotic symptoms (the belief that a devil had come to claim her soul). The sudden onset of a florid psychotic episode immediately after a marked psychosocial stressor, in the absence of prodromal signs of schizophrenia or a schizotypal personality disorder preceding the onset of the disturbance, indicated the Axis I diagnosis of brief reactive psychosis. Typically, the psychotic symptoms last for more than a few hours but less than one month. The diagnosis can be made before the one-month period—the maximum duration of symptoms consistent with the diagnosis—has elapsed, but it should be qualified as provisional. In this case it was anticipated that the symptoms would subside and that the patient would return to her usual level of good functioning. If the symptoms persist beyond that time, the diagnosis would be changed to another psychotic disorder, such as schizophreniform disorder.

Axis II indicates the absence of a personality disorder but the presence of the histrionic traits the patient's mother described as "overreacting."

Axis III notes the absence of any physical disorder or condition.

Axis IV rates the severity of the father's death as an extreme psychosocial stressor.

Axis V: Because of the recent development of severe psychotic symptoms and the inability to function ("sat rocking in a corner"), the patient's current functioning was rated 20; on the basis of the limited information that she was a "typical teenager, popular, and a very good student but sometimes prone to overreacting," the highest level of functioning during the year was rated 80.

DSM-III-R Diagnosis:

Axis I: Brief reactive psychosis (provisional)
Axis II: Histrionic traits
Axis III: None
Axis IV: Psychosocial stressor: death of father
Severity: 5 - Extreme (acute event)
Axis V: Current GAF: 20
Highest GAF past year: 80

Course and Prognosis

There are no prodromal symptoms before the precipitating stressor. The onset of symptoms is usually abrupt, following the stressor by as little as a few hours. The length of the acute and residual symptoms is often just a few hours or days and is always less than one month. Occasionally, depressive symptoms follow the resolution of the psychotic symptoms. Suicide is a concern during both the psychotic and the postpsychotic depressive phases. There are several indicators of good prognosis (Table 15.2-3). Patients with these features are not likely to have subsequent episodes and less likely to develop schizophrenia or a mood disorder.

Table 15.2-3
Good Prognostic Features for Brief Reactive Psychosis

Good Prognostic Features
Good premorbid adjustment
Few premorbid schizoid traits
Severe precipitating stressor
Acute onset of symptoms
Affective symptoms
Confusion and perplexity during psychosis
Little affective blunting
Short duration of symptoms
Absence of schizophrenic relatives

Diagnosis

The diagnostic criteria for brief reactive psychosis are listed in DSM-III-R (Table 15.2-4). The psychosocial stressor can be either a single event or a series of events but must be of sufficient severity to cause significant stress to any person in the same socioeconomic and cultural group. It is often necessary to obtain the history of the psychosocial stressor from a family member when the patient initially presents with the psychotic symptoms.

Differential Diagnosis

The clinician must not assume that the correct diagnosis of a briefly psychotic patient is brief reactive psychosis, even when a clear precipitating factor is evident. Such a stressor could be merely coincidental or involved in another organic or psychiatric condition. Factitious disorder with psychological symptoms, malingering, and organic causes must be considered in the differential diagnosis. Drug intoxication and withdrawal can mimic brief reactive psychosis, and the patients may be unwilling to admit the use of illegal drugs. Epilepsy and organic delirium can also present with brief psychotic periods. In addition to schizophrenia, mood disorders, and delusional disorders, other psychiatric diagnoses to be considered are multiple personality disorder and psychotic episodes associated with borderline or schizotypal personality disorders.

Treatment

Hospitalization may be necessary for the diagnosis and treatment of the psychosis. The support of the hospital environment may be enough to help the patient recover. Low doses of antipsychotics may be necessary in the first week of treatment but should be withdrawn as early as possible. Individual, family, and group psychotherapy should address the significance of the specific stress and bolster established coping mechanisms and encourage new ones. Therapy should help the patient cope with the loss of self-esteem and confidence. Hypnotic medications may be useful during the first two to three weeks of the disorder.

Table 15.2-4
Diagnostic Criteria for Brief Reactive Psychosis

A. Presence of at least one of the following symptoms indicating impaired reality testing (not culturally sanctioned):
   (1) incoherence or marked loosening of associations
   (2) delusions
   (3) hallucinations
   (4) catatonic or disorganized behavior

B. Emotional turmoil (i.e., rapid shifts from one intense affect to another, or overwhelming perplexity or confusion).

C. Appearance of the symptoms in A and B shortly after, and apparently in response to, one or more events that, singly or together, would be markedly stressful to almost anyone in similar circumstances in the person's culture.

D. Absence of the prodromal symptoms of schizophrenia, and failure to meet the criteria for schizotypal personality disorder before onset of the disturbance.

E. Duration of an episode of the disturbance of from a few hours to one month, with eventual full return to premorbid level of functioning. (When the diagnosis must be made without waiting for the expected recovery, it should be qualified as "provisional.")

F. Not due to a psychotic mood disorder (i.e., no full mood syndrome is present), and it cannot be established that an organic factor initiated and maintained the disturbance.

Table from DSM-III-R, *Diagnostic and Statistical Manual of Mental Disorders*, ed 3, revised. Copyright American Psychiatric Association, Washington, D.C., 1987, with permission.

INDUCED PSYCHOTIC DISORDER

If a patient's delusional system has developed out of a close relationship with another person who had a previously established and similar delusional system, the new patient is classified as having an induced psychotic disorder. This disorder has previously been called *folie à deux.* Induced psychotic disorder is rare, and most commonly involves only two persons. Cases involving more than two persons have been called *folie à trois, à quatre, à cinq,* and so on. One case involving an entire family (*folie à famille*) involved 12 persons (*folie à douze*).

Induced psychotic disorder was first described in 1877 by the French psychiatrists Lasègue and Falret, who called it *folie à deux.* (Other names for this disorder are double insanity and psychosis of association.) These psychiatrists described three clinical types—*folie simultanèe,* in which the patients had the same delusions at the same time coincidentally; *folie communiquée,* in which two persons shared aspects of their delusions with each other; and *folie imposée,* in which there was one dominant delusional person and a second, more submissive person who absorbed the more dominant person's delusions. *Folie imposée* is the type that is currently characterized in DSM-III-R as induced psychotic disorder.

Epidemiology

Induced psychotic disorder is very rare. It is more common in women than in men. It may also be more common in low than in high socioeconomic groups. Patients with physical disabilities, such as stroke and deafness, may also be at increased risk because of the dependency relationships that can exist for such people. Over 95 percent of cases involve two members of the same family. Approximately one-third of the cases involve two sisters; another one-third involve husband and wife or mother and child. Two brothers, a brother and a sister, and a father and a child have been reported less frequently.

Etiology

The cause of this disorder is defined as having a psychosocial basis. The key ingredients include a dyad of a dominant person and a submissive person, a relationship that is closely knit and relatively isolated from the outside world, and mutual gain for both persons. The dominant person has an already established mental disorder with delusions as a symptom. It is hypothesized that the dominant person maintains some contact with the real world through the submissive one, who then has induced psychotic disorder. The submissive person, in turn, gains the acceptance of the dominant person, whom the submissive person may admire. This admiration for the dominant person may lead to a hatred for that person as well. Such hatred may be turned inward by the submissive person, producing depression and even suicide.

The recipient or passive partner in this psychotic relationship has much in common with the dominant partner because of many shared life experiences, common needs and hopes, and, most important, a deep emotional rapport with the partner.

There are almost no biological investigations of patients with this disorder. One interpretation of the observation that this disorder affects family members is that there is a genetic basis. A modest amount of data suggest that there is an increased family history of schizophrenia in the relatives of affected persons.

Clinical Features

The key symptom is the unquestioning acceptance of the delusions of another person. The delusions themselves are often somewhat in the realm of possibility and usually not as bizarre as in schizophrenia. The content of the delusions is often persecutory or hypochondriacal. Symptoms of a coexisting personality disorder may be present, but signs and symptoms that meet the diagnostic criteria for schizophrenia, mood disorders, or delusional disorders are absent. There may be ideation about suicide or homicide pacts, information that must be carefully elicited. A clinical case example follows:

A 43-year-old housewife entered the hospital with a chief complaint of being concerned about her "sex problem"; she stated that she needed hypnotism to find out what was wrong with her sexual drive. Her husband supplied the history: he complained that she had had many extramarital affairs, with many different men, all through their married life. He insisted that in one two-week period she had had as many as a hundred sexual experiences with men outside the marriage. The patient herself agreed with this assessment of her behavior but would not speak of the experiences, saying that she "blocked" the memories out. She denied any particular interest in sexuality but said that apparently she felt a compulsive drive to go out and seek sexual activity, despite her lack of interest.

The patient had been married to her husband for over 20 years. He was clearly the dominant partner in the marriage. The patient was fearful of his frequent jealous rages, and apparently it was he who suggested that she enter the hospital to receive hypnosis. The patient maintained that she could not explain why she sought out other men, that she really did not want to do this. Her husband stated that on occasion he had tracked her down, and, when he found her, she acted as if she did not know him. She confirmed this and believed it was because the episodes of her sexual promiscuity were blotted out by "amnesia."

When the physician indicated that he questioned the reality of the wife's sexual adventures, the husband became furious and accused the doctor and a ward attendant of having sexual relations with her.

Neither an amobarbital (Amytal) interview nor considerable psychotherapy with the woman was able to clear the "blocked out" memory of periods of sexual activities. The patient did admit to a memory of having had two extramarital relationships in the past: one, 20 years before the time of admission, and the other just a year before admission. She stated that the last one had actually been planned by her husband and that he was in the same house at the time. She continued to believe that she had actually had countless extramarital sexual experiences, although she remembered only two of them.

Discussion. The first impression was that an amnestic syndrome, either psychogenic or organic, should be considered. However, evidence accumulated that the husband, the chief informant, had delusional jealousy, believing that his wife was repeatedly unfaithful to him. Apparently, under his influence, his wife had accepted this delusional belief, explaining her lack of memory of the events by believing that she had amnesia. It seemed that she had adopted his delusional system and did not really have any kind of amnesia. Before the onset of her delusion, there was no indication that she had a preexisting psychotic disorder or that she had any of the prodromal symptoms of schizophrenia. Because her delusional system developed as a result of a close relationship with another person who had an already established delusion (i.e., her husband) and because her delusions were similar in content to his delusions, the diagnosis was induced psychotic disorder, formerly called *folie à deux*. An interesting twist to this case was that it was the patient who, by virtue of her alleged extramarital activity, was the source of the husband's distress. It is more common in an induced psychotic disorder for the person who has adopted the other's delusional system to believe that he or she is also being harmed.

Course and Prognosis

Conventional wisdom is that the separation of the passive partner with induced psychotic disorder from the dominant one usually results in a rapid and dramatic reduction of symptoms. Clinical reports vary, however, and several papers have reported recovery rates as low as 10 percent. If symptoms continue after separation, the patient may eventually meet the diagnostic criteria for delusional disorder or schizophrenia.

Diagnosis

The diagnostic criteria for induced psychotic disorder (Table 15.2-5) include the presence of induced delusions that are similar in content to the delusions of the dominant

Table 15.2-5
Diagnostic Criteria for Induced Psychotic Disorder

A. A delusion develops (in a second person) in the context of a close relationship with another person, or persons, with an already established delusion (the primary case).

B. The delusion in the second person is similar in content to that in the primary case.

C. Immediately before onset of the induced delusion, the second person did not have a psychotic disorder or the prodromal symptoms of schizophrenia.

Table from DSM-III-R, *Diagnostic and Statistical Manual of Mental Disorders*, ed 3, revised. Copyright American Psychiatric Association, Washington, D.C., 1987, with permission.

person. The affected person must not have had a psychotic disorder before the inducement of the delusional system.

Differential Diagnosis

Malingering, factitious disorder with psychological symptoms, and organic disorders need to be considered in the differential diagnosis of this condition. There may be a personality disorder in the affected person. The boundary between induced psychotic disorder and group madness, such as the Jonestown massacre in Guyana, is unclear.

Treatment

The initial step in treatment is the separation of the affected person from the source of the delusions, the dominant partner. Significant support may be needed by the patient to compensate for the loss of this person. The person with induced psychotic disorder should be observed for remission of the delusional symptoms. Antipsychotic drugs can be used if the delusional symptoms have not abated in one or two weeks. Psychotherapy with nondelusional members of the patient's family should be undertaken, and psychotherapy with both the patient with induced psychotic disorder and the dominant partner may be indicated later in the course of treatment. In addition, the mental disorder of the dominant partner should be treated.

ATYPICAL PSYCHOSES

The category of atypical psychosis subsumes a diverse group of syndromes that have such psychotic features as delusions, hallucinations, incoherence, loosening of associations, cataplexy, and other signs of disorganized behavior that cannot be classified clearly as schizophrenia or another well-delineated psychotic condition.

In general, the atypical psychoses include the rare, the exotic, and the unusual mental disorders. The classification of this group of disorders includes the following: (1) psychoses with unusual features such as a persistent auditory hallucination; (2) syndromes that occur only at a particular time, such as during the menses or postpartum; (3) syndromes that are restricted to a specific cultural setting (culture-bound syndromes) or part of the world; (4) syndromes that seem to belong to a well-known diagnostic entity but that show some features that cannot be reconciled with the generally accepted typical characteristics of that diagnostic category; and (5) psychoses about which there is inadequate information to make a more specific diagnosis.

An attempt should be made to place each of the disorders described below in one of the conventional categories of mood disorders or schizophrenia if possible. Treatment is directed toward the predominant symptoms.

Postpartum Psychosis

A postpartum psychosis is a clinical syndrome that occurs after childbirth and is characterized by delusions and severe depression. Thoughts of wanting to harm the newborn infant or oneself may occur and represent a real danger.

Epidemiology. Postpartum psychosis occurs in 1 to 2 per 1,000 deliveries. The disorder is fundamentally a disease affecting women, although exceedingly rare cases of postpartum psychosis have been reported in fathers. The risk of a postpartum psychosis is increased if the patient or her mother had a previous postpartum psychiatric illness or if there is a history of a mood disorder in the patient or her family.

Etiology. Most patients with this disorder have an underlying mental illness, most commonly a bipolar disorder and less commonly schizophrenia. A few cases result from an organic mental syndrome associated with perinatal events (e.g., infection, drug intoxication—particularly scopoloamine and meperdine [Demerol] used together in obstetrics and known as twilight sleep—toxemia, and blood loss). The sudden fall in estrogen and progesterone levels immediately after pregnancy may contribute to the disorder, but treatment with those hormones has not been successful.

Psychodynamic studies of postpartum mental illness point to conflicting feelings of the mother about her mothering experience. Some women may not have wanted to become pregnant; others may feel trapped in an unhappy marriage by motherhood. Marital discord during pregnancy is associated with an increased incidence of illness. In the rare cases of postpartum disorders in fathers, the husband feels displaced by the child and competitive for the mother's love and attention.

Clinical features. The symptoms usually occur about the third postpartum day. The patient begins to complain of insomnia, restlessness, and feelings of fatigue and shows lability of mood with bouts of tearfulness. Later symptoms include suspiciousness, evidence of confusion, incoherence, irrational statements, and obsessive concerns about the baby's health or welfare. There may be feelings of not wanting to care for the baby, of not loving the baby, and, in some cases, of wanting to do harm to the baby, to self, or both. Delusional material may involve the idea that the baby is dead or defective. The birth may be denied, and thoughts of being unmarried, virginal, persecuted, influenced, or perverse may be expressed. Hallucinations may occur with similar content and may involve voices telling the patient to kill her baby.

Course and prognosis. The onset of florid psychotic symptoms is usually preceded by prodromal signs, such as insomnia, restlessness, agitation, lability of mood, and mild cognitive defects. Once the full-blown psychosis occurs, the patient may be a danger to herself or to her newborn, depending on the content of her delusional system and degree of agitation. In one study, 5 percent of patients killed themselves, and 4 percent killed the baby. A favorable outcome is associated with a good premorbid adaptation, the absence of depression or schizophrenia, and a supportive family network. Subsequent pregnancies are associated with an increased risk of having another episode; however, most episodes occur to primiparas.

Diagnosis. The main diagnostic feature of this disorder is the association with the postpartum period. Most cases begin within 30 days of giving birth. Symptoms of cognitive impairment associated with mood changes—particularly depression, delusions, and hallucinations with content related to the infant or mothering—are characteristic. A premorbid history of the patient's attitudes about pregnancy and conception, whether the baby was planned, attitudes of the father toward the birth, marital problems, and anticipated life-style changes may be helpful. In addition to a routine clinical psychiatric examination, a thorough neurological and medical examination is necessary to rule out an organic cause of the disorder.

Differential diagnosis. Those women with prior histories of schizophrenia or mood disorders should be classified as having recurrences of those disorders, rather than atypical psychoses. In the absence of those disorders, a diagnosis of postpartum psychosis may be made related to the stresses of pregnancy. Because of its clinical similarity to postpartum depression, hypothyroidism should always be considered. Cushing's syndrome, which may occur after a pregnancy, is frequently associated with a depressive state. Drug-induced depression is common, especially in those receiving antihypertensive or other drugs with known central nervous system depressant properties. Pentazocine (Talwin), a drug with psychotomimetic properties, is sometimes used in the postpartum period and has been reported to produce bizarre mental phenomena. Those patients with prominent organic mental symptoms should receive careful evaluation for infections, toxemia, and neoplasms.

Postpartum psychosis should not be confused with the so-called postpartum blues, a normal condition that occurs in up to 50 percent of women after childbirth. That syndrome is self-limited, lasts only a few days, and is characterized by tearfulness, fatigue, anxiety, and irritability that begins shortly after childbirth and lessens in severity each day postpartum.

Treatment. Postpartum psychosis is a psychiatric emergency. Antidepressants are the treatment of choice for depressed postpartum patients. Suicidal patients may require transfer to a psychiatric unit to help prevent a suicide attempt. For patients who suffer manic illnesses, lithium therapy, alone or in combination with an antipsychotic agent during the first seven days, is the treatment of choice. For patients with schizophrenic psychoses, phenothiazines or other antipsychotic agents are indicated. No pharmacological agents are recommended for use by mothers who are breast feeding.

It is usually advantageous for the mother to have contact with her baby if she so desires. But these visits must be closely supervised, especially if the mother is preoccupied with doing harm to the infant.

Psychotherapy is indicated after the period of acute psychosis is past. Therapy is usually directed at the conflictual areas that have become evident during the period of evaluation. Therapy may involve helping the patient to accept the mothering role or to accept her angry, jealous feelings toward the child as they relate to her thwarted need to depend on her own mother. Changes in environmental factors may also be indicated. Increased support from the husband and other persons in the environment may help to reduce stress. Most studies report high rates of recovery from the acute phase of illness.

Culture-Bound Syndromes

Amok. The Malayan word *amok* means to engage furiously in battle. The amok syndrome consists of a sudden, unprovoked outburst of wild rage that causes affected persons, armed with knives, to run madly about (today frequently with a firearm or grenade) and to attack and maim or kill indiscriminately any persons and animals in their way until they are overpowered or kill themselves. This savage homicidal attack is generally preceded by a period of preoccupation, brooding, and mild depression. After the attack, the person feels exhausted, has no memory of the attack, and often commits suicide. The Malayan natives also refer to the attack as *mata elap* (darkened eye).

Epidemiology. The condition used to be associated almost exclusively with Malayan men, but it has also been reported occasionally in African and other tropical cultures.

Etiology. It has been theorized that a culture that imposes heavy restrictions on adolescents and adults but allows children free rein to express their aggression may be especially prone to psychopathological reactions of the amok type. The belief in magical possession by demons and evil spirits may be another cultural factor that contributes to the development of the amok syndrome in the Malayan people. Shame and loss of face have been proposed as determining factors.

Prognosis and treatment. The only immediate treatment consists of overpowering amok persons and gaining complete physical control over them. The attack is usually over within a few hours. Afterward, the patient may require treatment for a chronic psychotic condition, which may have been the underlying cause.

Koro. This acute anxiety reaction is characterized by the patient's desperate fear that his penis is shrinking and may disappear into his abdomen and that he may die.

Epidemiology. The koro syndrome occurs among the people of Southeast Asia and in some areas of China, where it is known as *suk-yeong*. A corresponding disorder of women involves complaints of shrinkage of the vulva, labia, and breasts. Occasional cases of a koro syndrome among people belonging to a Western culture have been reported.

Etiology. Koro is a psychogenic disorder resulting from the interaction of cultural, social, and psychodynamic factors in especially predisposed personalities. Culturally elaborated fears about nocturnal emission, masturbation, and sexual overindulgence seem to give rise to the condition.

Prognosis and treatment. Patients have been treated with psychotherapy, antipsychotic drugs, and, in a few cases, electroconvulsive therapy. As with other psychiatric disorders, the prognosis is related to the premorbid personality adjustment and the associated pathology. Some cultures prescribe fellatio as a cure.

Piblokto. Occurring among the Eskimos and sometimes referred to as Arctic hysteria (Figure 15.2-1), piblokto is characterized by attacks lasting from one to two hours, during which the patient (usually a woman) begins to scream and to tear off and destroy her clothing. While imitating the cry of some animal or bird, she may then throw herself on the snow or run wildly about on the ice, although the temperature may be well below zero. After the attack, the person appears quite normal and usually has no memory of it. The Eskimos are reluctant to touch any afflicted person during the attack because they think that it involves evil spirits. Piblokto is almost certainly a hysterical state of dissociation. It has become much less frequent than it used to be among the Eskimos.

Wihtigo. Wihtigo or windigo psychosis is a psychiatric illness confined to the Cree, Ojibwa, and Salteaux Indians of

Figure 15.2-1. Eskimo woman exhibiting piblokto or Arctic hysteria. (Courtesy of The American Museum of Natural History.)

North America. Affected persons believe that they may be transformed into a wihtigo, a giant monster that eats human flesh. During times of starvation, persons may have the delusion that they have been transformed into a wihtigo, and they may feel and express a craving for human flesh. Because of the belief in witchcraft and in the possibility of such a transformation, symptoms concerning the alimentary tract, such as loss of appetite and nausea from trivial causes, may sometimes cause the patient to become greatly excited for fear of being transformed into a wihtigo. For further information about cross-cultural syndromes, see Section 4.6, "Anthropology and Psychiatry."

Other Atypical Psychoses

These syndromes consist of one or more psychotic symptoms, usually a recurrent hallucination or single delusion (previously called monomania). Except for the particular symptom, the rest of the personality appears entirely intact.

Autoscopic psychosis. This syndrome consists of hallucinatory experiences in which all or part of the person's own body (called a phantom) is perceived as if appearing in a mirror. This specter is usually colorless and transparent, but it is seen clearly, appears suddenly and without warning, and imitates the person's movements.

The phantom usually appears for only a few seconds, usually at dusk. In addition to the visual perception, hallucinations in auditory and other modalities may be present. The person usually retains a certain detached insight into the unreality of the experience and reacts with bewilderment and often with sadness.

Epidemiology. Autoscopy is a rare phenomenon. Sex, age, heredity, and intelligence do not seem to be significantly related to its occurrence. Some persons have this experience once in a lifetime, but a few persons seem to be always close to it.

Etiology. The cause of the autoscopic phenomenon is not known. An irritating neurological lesion must always be ruled out as a cause. One theory holds that the phenomenon reflects an irritation of areas in the temporoparietal lobes. Occasionally, but certainly not often, the phenomenon is symptomatic of schizophrenia or depression. Some normal persons with well-developed imaginations, visualizer-type personality structures, and narcissistic character traits may occasionally have these experiences under conditions of emotional stress.

Prognosis and treatment. There is rarely any need for special treatment of this condition, as in most cases it is neither incapacitating nor progressive. Treatment of any accompanying neurological condition is indicated.

Capgras's syndrome. This psychiatric syndrome was described by the French psychiatrist Jean Marie Joseph Capgras in 1923 as *illusion des sosies.* Its main characteristic is the delusional conviction that other persons in the patient's environment are not their real selves but are, instead, their own doubles who, like impostors, assume the roles of the persons they impersonate and behave like them.

Epidemiology. This rare syndrome occurs somewhat more frequently in women than in men. The condition is sometimes classified as one of the delusional disorders and may be a manifestation of schizophrenia.

Etiology. A necessary condition for the occurrence of this syndrome is the impairment of reality testing that develops as a result of a psychotic process. Capgras explained the particular nature of this illusion as a result of feelings of strangeness combined with a paranoid tendency to distrust. The uncoupling of normally fused components of perception and recognition may have a neurophysiological cause related to parietal lobe dysfunction.

Capgras's syndrome may, on the other hand, be determined psychodynamically. What the patient really feels about the person with whom he or she is confronted (e.g., anger, fear) is displaced to the double, who is an impostor and, therefore, may be safely and righteously rejected.

Prognosis and treatment. The outcome of this condition depends on the success in treating the psychosis with which it is associated. Like other psychotic manifestations, it often responds to pharmacotherapy, at least temporarily.

Cotard's syndrome. In the 19th century, the French psychiatrist Jules Cotard described several patients who suffered from a syndrome he referred to as *délire de négation*. Patients exhibiting this syndrome may complain of having lost not only possessions, status, and strength but also the heart, blood, and intestines. The world beyond them may be reduced to nothingness. The full-blown syndrome may be characterized by a delusion of immortality, which may occur in combination with other megalomanic ideas.

Epidemiology. The syndrome is usually seen as a precursor to an acute schizophrenic or depressive episode. It is relatively rare and, with the advent of psychopharmacotherapy, is seen less frequently.

Etiology. In its pure form the syndrome is seen in patients suffering from depression, schizophrenia, and certain organic mental syndromes, particularly of the senile and presenile types. The cause is unknown. It has been classified as a nihilistic delusional disorder.

Prognosis and treatment. The syndrome usually lasts only a few days or weeks and responds to treatment that influences the basic disorder of which it is a part. Chronic forms of the full syndrome are today almost exclusively associated with organic mental syndromes, such as Alzheimer's disease.

Atypical cycloid psychoses. This group of disorders shows some features of bipolar disorders but cannot meet the generally accepted characteristics of that diagnostic category. Three types have been described: motility psychosis (hyperkinetic or akinetic), confusional psychosis, and anxiety-blissfulness psychosis.

Motility psychosis. In its hyperkinetic form, motility psychosis may resemble manic or catatonic excitement. A hyperkinetic motility psychosis may be distinguished from a manic state by the presence of many abrupt gestures and expressive movements that seem to be the result of autonomous mechanisms and are apparently not responses to environmental stimuli or expressions of the patient's mood. The disorder may be differentiated from catatonic excitement by the absence of stereotyped and bizarre movements.

The akinetic form of motility psychosis seems to be identical with the typical picture of a catatonic stupor. This state is separated from typical schizophrenia mainly on the basis of the rapid and favorable course, which does not lead to any personality deterioration.

Confusional psychosis. The excited confusional psychosis must be distinguished from some confused manic states. The difference is mainly in the patient's emotional state, which may be characterized by prevailing anxiety, rather than euphoria. The patients are not likely to be as distracted as manic patients are. The incoherence of their speech seems to be independent of a flight of ideas.

Anxiety-blissfulness psychosis. The anxiety-blissfulness psychosis may resemble the clinical picture of what is generally known as agitated depression, but it may also be characterized by so much inhibition that the patient can hardly move. Periodic states of overwhelming anxiety and paranoid ideas of reference are characteristic of this condition, but self-accusation, hypochondriacal preoccupation, other depressive symptoms, and hallucinations may accompany it.

The blissful phase manifests itself most frequently in expansive behavior and grandiose ideas, which are concerned less with self-aggrandizement than with the mission of making others happy and of saving the world. In women the dominant emotion is usually passive ecstasy, often the result of fantastic religious delusions.

Atypical schizophrenia. A particular form of schizophrenia was described by R. Gjessing and called periodic catatonia. Patients affected with this disease have periodic bouts of stuporous or excited catatonia, which Gjessing believed were related to metabolic shifts in nitrogen balance. The syndrome is rarely seen, responds well to standard antipsychotic agents, and is prevented by maintenance medication.

References

Anis-Ur-Rehman, St. Clair D, Platz C: Puerperal insanity in the 19th and 20th centuries. Br J Psychiatry *156*: 861, 1990.

Beiser M, Fleming J A E, Iacono W G, Lin T-yL: Refining the diagnosis of schizophreniform disorder. Am J Psychiatry *145*: 695, 1988.

Coryell W H, Tsuang M T: DSM-III schizophreniform disorder: Comparisons with schizophrenia and affective disorder. Arch Gen Psychiatry *39*: 66, 1982.

Coryell W, Tsuang M T: Outcome after 40 years in DSM-III schizophreniform disorder. Arch Gen Psychiatry *43*: 324, 1986.

Fogelson D L, Cohen B M, Pope H G: A study of DSM-III schizophreniform disorder. Am J Psychiatry *139*: 1281, 1982.

Frank E, Kupfer D J, Jacob M, Blumenthal S J, Jarrett D B: Pregnancy-related affective episodes among women with recurrent depression. Am J Psychiatry *144*: 288, 1987.

Harding J J: Postpartum psychiatric disorders: A review. Compr Psychiatry *30*: 109, 1989.

Inwood D G: Postpartum psychotic disorders. In *Comprehensive Textbook of Psychiatry*, ed 5, H I Kaplan and B J Sadock, editors, p 852. Williams & Wilkins, Baltimore, 1989.

Lazarus A: Folie à deux: Psychosis by association or genetic determinism. Compr Psychiatry *26*: 129, 1985.

Munoz R A, Amado H, Hyatt S: Brief reactive psychosis. J Clin Psychiatry *48*: 324, 1987.

Neppe V M, Tucker G J: Atypical, unusual, and cultural psychoses. In *Comprehensive Textbook of Psychiatry*, ed 5, H I Kaplan and B J Sadock, editors, p 842. Williams & Wilkins, Baltimore, 1989.

Nurnberg H G: An overview of somatic treatment of psychosis during pregnancy and postpartum. Gen Hosp Psychiatry *11*: 328, 1989.

Procci W R: Schizoaffective disorder, schizophreniform disorder, and brief reactive psychosis. In *Comprehensive Textbook of Psychiatry*, ed 5, H I Kaplan and B J Sadock, editors, p 830. Williams & Wilkins, Baltimore, 1989.

Refsum H E, Astrup C: Hysteric reactive psychoses: A follow-up. Neuropsychobiology *8*: 172, 1982.

Stephens J H, Shaffer J W, Carpenter W T: Reactive psychoses. J Nerv Ment Dis *170*: 657, 1982.

Taylor M A, Abrams R: Mania and DSM-III schizophreniform disorder. J Affective Disord *6*: 19, 1984.

Weinberger D R, DeLisi L E, Perman G D: Computed tomography and schizophreniform disorder and other acute psychiatric disorders. Arch Gen Psychiatry *39*: 778, 1982.

16 Mood Disorders

16.1 / Depressive and Bipolar Disorders

Depression and mania are the most serious of the mood disorders that are described in the revised third edition of *Diagnostic and Statistical Manual of Mental Disorders* (DSM-III-R). Depression and mania are often referred to as affective disorders; however, the critical pathology in these disorders is one of *mood,* the internal emotional state of a person, and not of *affect,* the external expression of emotional content.

Mood may be normal, elevated, or depressed. Normal persons experience a wide range of moods and have an equally large repertoire of affective expressions; they feel in control of their moods and affects. Mood disorders are a group of clinical conditions characterized by a loss of that sense of control and a subjective experience of great distress. Patients with elevated mood demonstrate expansiveness, flight of ideas, decreased sleep, heightened self-esteem, and grandiose ideas. Patients with depressed mood have a loss of energy and interest, feelings of guilt, difficulty in concentrating, loss of appetite, and thoughts of death or suicide. Other signs and symptoms of mood disorders include changes in activity level, cognitive abilities, speech, and vegetative functions (such as sleep, appetite, sexual activity, and other biological rhythms). These disorders virtually always result in impaired interpersonal, social, and occupational functioning.

It is tempting to consider disorders of mood on a continuum with normal variations in mood. Patients with mood disorders, however, often report an ineffable but distinct quality to their pathological state. The concept of a continuum, therefore, may represent the clinician's over-identification with the pathology, thus possibly distorting his or her approach to mood disorder patients.

Patients who are afflicted with only major depressive episodes are said to have major depressive disorder or unipolar depression. Patients with both manic and depressive episodes or patients with manic episodes alone are said to have bipolar disorder. The terms "unipolar mania" and "pure mania" are sometimes used for bipolar patients who do not have depressive episodes.

Three additional categories of mood disorders are hypomania, cyclothymia, and dysthymia. Hypomania is an episode of manic symptoms that does not meet the full DSM-III-R criteria for a manic episode. Cyclothymia and dysthymia are DSM-III-R–defined disorders that represent less severe forms of bipolar disorder and major depression, respectively.

There are at least three major theories regarding the relationship between unipolar depression and bipolar disorder. The most accepted hypothesis, which is supported by several types of genetic and biochemical studies, is that unipolar depression and bipolar disorder represent two different disorders. Recently, some investigators have suggested that bipolar disorder may be a more severe expression of the same pathophysiological process as that seen in unipolar depression. The third hypothesis is that depression and mania are two ends of a continuum of emotional experience. This conceptualization is not supported by the common clinical observation that many patients have mixed states with both depressed and manic features.

HISTORY

Depression has been recorded since antiquity, and descriptions of what are now called the mood disorders can be found in many ancient documents. The Old Testament story of King Saul describes a depressive syndrome, as does the story of Ajax's suicide in Homer's *Iliad.* About 400 B.C. Hippocrates used the terms "mania" and "melancholia" to describe mental disturbances. About A.D. 30 Aulus Cornelius Celsus described melancholia in his work *De re medicina* as a depression caused by black bile. The term continued to be used by other medical authors, including Arataeus (A.D. 120–180), Galen (A.D. 129–199), and Alexander of Tralles in the sixth century. The 12th-century Jewish physician Maimonides considered melancholia a discrete disease entity. In 1686 Bonet described a mental illness that he called *maniaco-melancholicus.*

In 1854 Jules Falret described a condition called *folie circulaire* in which the patient experienced alternating moods of depression and mania. About the same time another French psychiatrist, Jules Baillarger, described the condition *folie á double forme,* in which the patient became deeply depressed and fell into a stuporous state from which he would eventually recover. In 1882 the German psychiatrist Karl Kahlbaum, using the term "cyclothymia," described mania and depression as stages of the same illness.

Emil Kraepelin, in 1899, building on the knowledge of previous French and German psychiatrists, described a concept of manic-depressive psychosis that contained most of the criteria that psychiatrists now use to establish the diagnosis. The absence of a dementing and deteriorating course in manic-depressive psychosis differentiated it from dementia precox (schizophrenia). Kraepelin also described a type of depression that began after menopause in women and during late adulthood in men that came to be known as involutional melancholia and has since come to be viewed as a variant form of the mood disorders.

EPIDEMIOLOGY

Unipolar depression is among the most common psychiatric disorders of adults. The lifetime prevalence for unipolar depression is approximately 6 percent; the lifetime prevalence for bipolar disorder is approximately 1 percent. Although most patients with bipolar disorder are eventually seen by a physician, it is estimated that only 50 percent of those who meet the criteria for major depression receive treatment.

Sex

An almost universal observation, independent of country, is the approximately twofold greater prevalence of unipolar depression in women than in men. Although the reasons for the difference are unknown, it is not because of socially biased diagnostic practices. The reasons may include varying stresses, childbirth, learned helplessness, and hormonal effects. In bipolar disorder the prevalence is equal for men and women.

Age

The onset of unipolar depression can occur from childhood through senescence, but 50 percent of all patients have an onset between ages 20 and 50, the mean age being about 40. Bipolar disorder begins somewhat earlier, the range being from childhood to 50 years, with a mean age of 30.

Race

The prevalence of mood disorders does not differ from race to race. However, there is a tendency for examiners to underdiagnose mood disorders and overdiagnose schizophrenia in patients who have racial or cultural backgrounds different from their own. White psychiatrists, for example, tend to underdiagnose mood disorders in blacks and Hispanics.

Marital Status

In general, unipolar depression occurs most often in persons who have no close interpersonal relationships or who are divorced or separated. Bipolar disorder may be more common in divorced and single persons than among married persons, but this difference may reflect the early onset and the resulting marital discord that are characteristic of the disorder.

Socioeconomic and Cultural Considerations

There is no correlation between socioeconomic status and unipolar depression; there appears to be a higher than average incidence of bipolar disorder among the upper socioeconomic groups, possibly because of biased diagnostic practices. Depression may be more common in rural areas than in urban areas. Bipolar disorder is more common in persons who did not graduate from college than in college graduates, probably reflecting the relatively early age of onset for this disorder.

ETIOLOGY

The causes of the mood disorders are unknown. As with other psychiatric disorders, the groups of patients defined by DSM-III-R as having a mood disorder undoubtedly constitute a heterogeneous population of patients.

Biological Factors

Biogenic amines. Norepinephrine and serotonin are the two neurotransmitters most implicated in the pathophysiology of mood disorders. In animal models all effective somatic antidepressant treatments that have been tested are associated with a decrease in the sensitivity of postsynaptic β-adrenergic and 5–hydroxtryptamine (5HT) type 2 receptors after chronic treatment. These receptor changes in animal models correlate with the one- to three-week delay in clinical improvement usually seen in patients. It is perhaps consistent with the decrease in serotonin receptors after chronic exposure that a decrease in the number of serotonin reuptake sites (assessed by measuring the binding of tritium [^{3}H]-imipramine) and an increased concentration of serotonin have been found at postmortem in the brains of suicide victims. It has also been reported that there is decreased ^{3}H-imipramine binding to blood platelets from some depressed persons. Data indicate that dopaminergic activity may be reduced in depression and increased in mania. There is also evidence for a dysregulation of acetylcholine in mood disorders. One recent study reported an increased number of muscarinic receptors on cultured skin fibroblasts from bipolar disorder patients. An enormous number of studies have reported various abnormalities in biogenic amine metabolites (such as 5-hydroxyindoleacetic acid [5-HIAA], homovanillic acid [HVA], 3-methoxy-4-hydroxyphenylglycol [MHPG]) in blood, urine, and cerebrospinal fluid (CSF) from mood disorder patients. The data reported are most consistent with the hypothesis that mood disorders are associated with heterogeneous dysregulations of the biogenic amine system.

Other neurochemical considerations. Although the data are not conclusive at this point, amino acid neurotransmitters (particularly γ-aminobutyric acid [GABA]) and neuroactive peptides (particularly vasopressin and the endogenous opioids) have been implicated in the pathophysiology of some mood disorders. Some investigators have suggested that second messenger systems—such as adenylate cyclase, phosphatidylinositol, and calcium regulation—may also be of etiological relevance.

Neuroendocrine regulation. A variety of neuroendocrine dysregulations have been reported in patients with mood disorders. Although it is theoretically possible for a particular dysregulation of a neuroendocrine axis (e.g., thyroid axis, adrenal axis) to be involved in the cause of a mood disorder, the dysregulations are more likely reflections of a more fundamental underlying brain disorder. The hypothalamus is central to the regulation of the neuroendocrine axes and itself receives multiple neuronal inputs that use biogenic amine neurotransmitters. It is possible, therefore, that the abnormal regulation of neuroendocrine axes is a result of abnormal functioning of biogenic amine-containing neurons.

Abnormalities of the limbic-hypothalamic-pituitary-adrenal (LHPA) axis are the most consistently reported neuroendocrine dysregulations. The finding that hypersecretion of cortisol is present in some depressed patients has been used in the dexamethasone-suppression test (DST). (Dexamethasone is an exogenous steroid that suppresses the blood level of cortisol.) The DST is abnormal in approximately 50 percent of depressed patients, indicating a hyperactivity of the LHPA axis. The DST is not specific for depression, however, and may be abnormal in patients with obsessive-compulsive disorder, eating disorders, organic mental disorders (e.g., Alzheimer's disease), and other medical conditions. Some patients with mania or schizophrenia also demonstrate nonsuppression on the DST. Several recent studies have demonstrated that a significant amount of variation among persons in the DST may lie in the differential metabolism of the dexamethasone and not in the differential response to the dexamethasone. The differential metabolism of dexamethasone itself may be relevant in the pathophysiology of the mood disorders; nevertheless, the use of the DST is still not indicated in the routine evaluation of mood disorder patients.

Other neuroendocrine markers of depression include a blunted (diminished) release of thyroid-stimulating hormone (TSH) on administration of thyrotropin-releasing hormone (TRH), a decreased release of growth hormone to noradrenergic stimulation with clonidine (Catapres), decreased nocturnal secretion of melatonin, decreased prolactin release to tryptophan administration, decreased basal levels of follicle-stimulating hormone (FSH) and luteinizing hormone (LH), and decreased testosterone levels in males. A blunted response of TSH to TRH administration has been reported in mania as well.

Sleep abnormalities. Abnormalities of sleep architecture are among the most robust biological markers of depression. The major abnormalities are a decreased rapid eye movement (REM) latency (the time between falling asleep and the first REM period), which is seen in two-thirds of depressed patients; an increased length of the first REM period; and an increased density of REM in the first part of sleep. There is also early morning awakening and increased discontinuity of sleep, with multiple awakenings during the night.

Kindling. Kindling is the electrophysiological process in which repeated subthreshold stimulation of a neuron eventually generates an action potential. At the organ level repeated subthreshold stimulation of an area of the brain results in the generation of a seizure. The clinical observation that anticonvulsants (e.g., carbamazepine [Tegretol], valproic acid [Depakene]) are sometimes useful in the treatment of mood disorders, particularly bipolar disorder, has given rise to the theory that the pathophysiology of mood disorders may involve kindling in the temporal lobes.

Other biological data. The abnormalities of sleep architecture in depression and the transient clinical improvement in depression associated with sleep deprivation have led to theories that depression reflects an abnormal regulation of circadian rhythms. Some experimental studies with animals suggest that many of the standard antidepressant treatments are effective in changing the settings of internal biological clocks (i.e., endogenous *zeitgebers*).

Still other researchers have reported immunological abnormalities in depressed persons and also in persons who are grieving the loss of a relative. It is possible that the dysregulation of the cortisol axis affects the immune status. It is also possible that there is abnormal hypothalamic regulation of the immune system. A less likely possibility is that in some patients a primary pathophysiological process involving the immune system also leads to the psychiatric symptoms of mood disorders.

Brain imaging. Brain imaging studies using computed tomography (CT) scans and magnetic resonance imaging (MRI) have not been consistent in their findings. The data suggest, however, that a subgroup of seriously affected depressed and manic patients have enlarged lateral ventricles, although this enlargement is generally not as significant as that seen in schizophrenic patients. Some studies have noted a correlation between particularly enlarged lateral ventricles and a late age of onset, the presence of delusions and hallucinations, low intelligence quotient (I.Q.), increased number of hospitalizations, and frequent unemployment. Positron emission tomographic (PET) and regional cerebral blood flow (rCBF) studies have also not been entirely consistent in their findings as yet. Several studies, however, have reported decreased blood flow and glucose metabolism in the frontal brain regions and in the left hemispheres of depressed patients.

Consolidation of biological data. Both the symptoms of the mood disorders and biological research findings support the hypothesis that mood disorders involve pathology of the limbic system, the basal ganglia, and the hypothalamus. It has been noted that neurological disorders of the basal ganglia and the limbic system (especially excitatory lesions of the nondominant hemisphere) are likely to present with depressive symptoms. The limbic system and the basal ganglia are quite intimately connected, and a major role in the production of emotions is hypothesized for the limbic system. Dysfunction of the hypothalamus is suggested by the alterations in sleep, appetite, and sexual behavior and by the biological changes in endocrine, immunological, and chronobiological measures. The stooped posture, motor slowness, and minor cognitive impairment seen in depression are quite similar to disorders of the basal ganglia, such as Parkinson's disease and other subcortical dementias.

Genetic Factors

The fact that both bipolar disorders and unipolar depression run in families is also consistent with a biological cause for mood disorders. The evidence for the heritability of bipolar disorder is stronger than that for unipolar depression. Approximately 50 percent of all bipolar patients have at least one parent with a mood disorder, most often unipolar depression. If one parent has bipolar disorder, there is a 27 percent chance that any child will have a mood disorder; if both parents have bipolar disorder, there is a 50 to 75 percent chance that a child will have a mood disorder. Adoption studies have shown that the biological parents of adopted mood-disordered children have a prevalence of mood disorder similar to that of the parents of nonadopted mood-disordered children. The prevalence of mood disorders in the adoptive parents is similar to the baseline prevalence of mood disorders in the general population. Twin studies have shown a concordance rate of 0.67 for bipolar disorder in monozygotic twins and 0.20 for bipolar disorder in dizygotic twins. The concordance for bipolar disorder is higher than that reported for unipolar depression. The genetic data, therefore, are consistent with the concept of a genetic basis for mood disorders.

Linkage studies. Several investigators have reported the presence of restriction (fragment) length polymorphisms (RFLPs) associated with bipolar disorder in various family pedigrees. One set of studies reported that bipolar disorder is linked to the X chromosome, and another set of studies reported that bipolar disorder is linked to a site on chromosome 11. Although the X chromosome finding has been replicated in other pedigrees, investigators have been unable to replicate the chromosome 11 finding. These data suggest that in some families an important gene for the development of bipolar disorder may be located on the X chromosome. These data also suggest that it is unlikely that the site identified on chromosome 11 is involved in the pathogenesis of bipolar disorder in a significant number of families.

Psychosocial Factors

Life events and environmental stress. Some clinicians believe that life events play the primary or principal role in depression; other clinicians are more conservative, suggesting that life events have only a limited role in the onset and timing of depression. The most compelling data indicate that the life event most associated with the later development of depression is loss of a parent before age 11. The environmental stressor most associated with the onset of an episode of depression is the loss of a spouse. Although reasonable data suggest a significant relationship between life events and the onset of depression, almost no data support a significant relationship between life events and the onset of manic episodes.

Premorbid personality factors. No single personality trait or type has been established as being uniquely predisposing to depression. All humans, of whatever personality pattern, can and do become depressed under appropriate circumstances; however, certain personality types—oral-dependent, obsessive-compulsive, hysterical—may be at greater risk for depression than antisocial, paranoid, and other personality types who use projection and other externalizing defense mechanisms. No evidence suggests that any particular personality disorder is associated with the later development of bipolar disorder. There is an association, however, between dysthymia and cyclothymia and the later development of bipolar disorder.

Psychoanalytic factors. Karl Abraham hypothesized that episodes of depression are precipitated by the loss of a libidinal object, resulting in a regressive process in which the ego retreats from its mature functioning state to one in which the infantile trauma of the oral-sadistic stage of libidinal development dominates because of a fixation process in earliest childhood.

In Sigmund Freud's structural theory the ambivalent introjection of the lost object into the ego leads to the typical depressive symptoms diagnostic of a lack of energy available to the ego. The superego, unable to retaliate against the lost object externally, flails out at the psychic representation of the lost object, now internalized in the ego as an introject. When the ego overcomes or merges with the superego, there is a release of energy that was previously bound in the depressive symptoms, and, as a result of denial, a mania supervenes with the typical symptoms of excess. Later analytic writers have elaborated the basic Abraham-Freud conceptualization in various ways.

Heinz Kohut made significant contributions to the psychology of the self and the treatment of narcissistic personality disorder. Narcissistic personality disorder is one of the frequent differential diagnostic considerations in manic-depressive patients because patients with narcissistic personality disorder frequently demonstrate transient periods of elation and depression, often with grandiosity and euphoria in one phase of self-depreciation in a succeeding phase, just as is seen in classic manic-depressive disorder.

Learned helplessness. In experiments in which animals were repeatedly exposed to electric shocks from which they could not escape, the animals eventually gave up and made no attempt at all to escape future shocks. They learned that they were helpless. In humans who are depressed, one can find a similar state of helplessness. According to learned helplessness theory, depression can improve if the clinician instills in a depressed patient a sense of control and mastery of the environment. Behavioral techniques of reward and positive reinforcement are employed in such efforts.

Cognitive theory. According to this theory, common cognitive misinterpretations involve negative distortions of life experience, negative self-evaluation, pessimism, and hopelessness. These learned negative views then lead to the feeling of depression. A cognitive therapy approach attempts to identify and modify negative cognitions by using behavioral tasks, such as recording and consciously modifying thoughts.

CLINICAL FEATURES

There are two basic symptom patterns in the mood disorders, one for depression and one for mania. The depressive episodes in bipolar disorder are identical to the depressive disorders in unipolar depression. Some patients with bipolar disorder, however, have mixed states with manic and depressive features. Also, some bipolar patients experience very brief—minutes to a few hours—episodes of depression during a manic episode.

Depressive Episodes

A depressed mood and a loss of interest or pleasure are the key symptoms of depression. Patients may say that they feel blue, hopeless, in the dumps, or worthless. For the patient, the depressed mood often has a distinct quality that differentiates it from the completely normal emotion of sadness. Patients often describe the symptom of depression as one of agonizing emotional pain. DSM-III-R lists these and other symptoms of depression under the diagnostic criteria for major depressive episode (Table 16.1-1) and its melancholic type (Table 16.1-2), a particular set of vegetative depressive symptoms.

Approximately two-thirds of depressed patients contemplate suicide, and 10 to 15 percent commit suicide. Depressed patients sometimes complain about being unable to cry, a symptom that resolves as they improve. Depressed patients, however, sometimes appear unaware of their depression and do not complain of a mood disturbance, even though they may exhibit withdrawal from family, friends, and activities that previously interested them.

Almost all depressed patients (97 percent) complain about reduced energy resulting in difficulty finishing tasks,

Table 16.1-1
Diagnostic Criteria for Major Depressive Episode

Note: A major depressive syndrome is defined as criterion A below.

A. At least five of the following symptoms have been present during the same two-week period and represent a change from previous functioning; at least one of the symptoms is either (1) depressed mood, or (2) loss of interest or pleasure. (Do not include symptoms that are clearly due to a physical condition, mood-incongruent delusions or hallucinations, incoherence, or marked loosening of associations.)

(1) depressed mood (or can be irritable mood in children and adolescents) most of the day, nearly every day, as indicated either by subjective account or observation by others
(2) markedly diminished interest or pleasure in all, or almost all, activities most of the day, nearly every day (as indicated either by subjective account or observation by others of apathy most of the time)
(3) significant weight loss or weight gain when not dieting (e.g., more than 5 percent of body weight in a month), or decrease or increase in appetite nearly every day (in children, consider failure to make expected weight gains)
(4) insomnia or hypersomnia nearly every day
(5) psychomotor agitation or retardation nearly every day (observable by others, not merely subjective feelings of restlessness or being slowed down)
(6) fatigue or loss of energy nearly every day
(7) feelings of worthlessness or excessive or inappropriate guilt (which may be delusional) nearly every day (not merely self-reproach or guilt about being sick)
(8) diminished ability to think or concentrate, or indecisiveness, nearly every day (either by subjective account or as observed by others)
(9) recurrent thoughts of death (not just fear of dying), recurrent suicidal ideation without a specific plan, or a suicide attempt or a specific plan for committing suicide

B. (1) It cannot be established that an organic factor initiated and maintained the disturbance.
(2) The disturbance is not a normal reaction to the death of a loved one (uncomplicated bereavement)

Note: Morbid preoccupation with worthlessness, suicidal ideation, marked functional impairment or psychomotor retardation, or prolonged duration suggest bereavement complicated by major depression.

C. At no time during the disturbance have there been delusions or hallucinations for as long as two weeks in the absence of prominent mood symptoms (i.e., before the mood symptoms developed or after they have remitted).

D. Not superimposed on schizophrenia, schizophreniform disorder, delusional disorder, or psychotic disorder NOS.

Table from DSM-III-R, *Diagnostic and Statistical Manual of Mental Disorders,* ed 3, revised. Copyright American Psychiatric Association, Washington, DC, 1987, with permission.

school and work impairment, and decreased motivation in undertaking new projects. Approximately 80 percent of patients complain of trouble sleeping, especially early morning awakening (i.e., terminal insomnia) and multiple awakenings at night, during which they ruminate about their problems.

Many patients have decreased appetite and weight loss. Some patients, however, have increased appetite, weight gain, and increased sleep. The latter patients, especially when their symptoms are accompanied by marked anxiety, are sometimes referred to as having an atypical depression, but this term has acquired too many different meanings to be of much practical use. Anxiety, in fact, is a common symptom of depression, affecting as many as 90 percent of depressed patients. The various changes in food intake and rest can aggravate coexisting medical illnesses, such as diabetes, hypertension, chronic obstructive lung disease, and heart disease. Other vegetative symptoms include abnormal menses and decreased interest and performance in sexual activities. Sexual problems can sometimes lead to inappropriate referrals, such as marital counseling or sex therapy, if the clinician fails to recognize the underlying depressive disorder.

Table 16.1-2
Diagnostic Criteria for Melancholic Type

The presence of at least five of the following:

(1) loss of interest or pleasure in all, or almost all, activities
(2) lack of reactivity to usually pleasurable stimuli (does much better, even temporarily, when something good happens)
(3) depression regularly worse in the morning
(4) early morning awakening (at least two hours before usual time of awakening)
(5) psychomotor retardation or agitation (not merely subjective complaints)
(6) significant anorexia or weight loss (e.g., more than 5 percent of body weight in a month)
(7) no significant personality disturbance before first major depressive episode
(8) one or more previous major depressive episodes followed by complete, or nearly complete, recovery
(9) previous good response to specific and adequate somatic antidepressant therapy (e.g., tricyclics, ECT, MAOI, lithium)

Table from DSM-III-R, *Diagnostic and Statistical Manual of Mental Disorders,* ed 3, revised. Copyright American Psychiatric Association, Washington, DC, 1987, with permission.

Anxiety (including panic attacks), alcohol abuse, and somatic complaints (such as constipation and headaches) often complicate the treatment of depression. Approximately 50 percent of all patients describe a diurnal variation in their symptoms, with an increased severity in the morning and a lessening of symptoms by evening. Cognitive symptoms include subjective reports of an inability to concentrate (84 percent of all patients) and impairments in thinking (67 percent). The diagnosis of major depressive disorder, melancholic type, is illustrated by the following case:

A 79-year-old retired Army colonel and lawyer was first treated at a psychiatric clinic in 1968. None of his parents, siblings, or near relatives had had any psychiatric illness, nor had the patient in the past. He attended college and received an officer's commission. During World War I he sustained a machine gun injury to his right elbow. After the war the patient received a law degree and practiced law in his hometown until World War II, in which he served. After World War II he retired from the Army on full disability because of emphysema.

In 1966 he developed memory impairment and completely retired from his law practice. He was referred to the psychiatric service because of recent memory loss, insomnia, loss of appetite, periodic agitation, and persistent verbal preoccupation with having failed to report his income tax correctly; he maintained that he had been picked up by the Internal Revenue Service and jailed for his crime. Recent memory and new learning seemed impaired. His emphysema required supervision by a chest specialist. Phenothiazines soon controlled his delusions of guilt, need for punishment, and associated anxious-depressive-apprehensive state.

In March 1969 he was again seen for agitation and epigastric symptoms of several weeks' duration. No physical reason for his discomfort was detected. No delusions were verbalized, and he was discharged after nine days on prior medication. He was readmitted in 1973 with gradual worsening of his cardiorespiratory status and progressive debility. He was forgetful of most things but constantly reiterated the belief that he had signed away his veteran's benefits, had no means of livelihood, and someone was coming to take him to "he knew not where." He was almost completely bedridden; he conversed in a normal manner if he was not questioned; his delusions persisted in spite of various psychotropic drugs. It became apparent that denial was a strong factor and that his memory functions were not impaired to the degree first suspected, for his grooming and gentlemanly demeanor were unaltered. He was too ill physically to chance somatic therapy.

Discussion. This case of melancholia reveals the exaggerated delusions of guilt and need for punishment early in its course, followed later by ideas of poverty and fear of punishment. The patient illustrates the concept of masked depression, whereby hypochondriasis masks depressive symptoms, as does moderate organic brain disease.

Depression in Children and Adolescents

Excessive clinging to parents and school phobia may be symptoms of depression in children. Poor academic performance, drug abuse, antisocial behavior, sexual promiscuity, truancy, and running away may be symptoms of depression in adolescent children. See Section 43.1 for further discussion of this area of child psychiatry.

Manic Episodes

The features of a manic episode are defined in DSM-III-R (Table 16.1-3). Elevated, expansive, or irritable mood is the hallmark. The elevated mood is euphoric and often infectious in nature, sometimes causing a countertransferential denial of illness by an inexperienced clinician. Although uninvolved people may not recognize the unusual nature of the patient's mood, those who know the patient recognize it as abnormal for that person. Alternatively, the mood may be irritable, especially when the patient's overly ambitious plans are thwarted. Often, a patient exhibits a change of predominant mood from euphoria early in the course of the illness to irritability later in the process.

In addition to the criteria listed in DSM-III-R, manic patients often exhibit other symptoms. The treatment of manic patients on an inpatient ward can be complicated by their testing the limits of ward rules, a tendency to shift responsibility for their acts onto others, exploitation of the weaknesses of others, and a tendency to divide ward staffs. Manic patients often drink alcohol excessively, perhaps in an attempt to self-medicate. The disinhibited nature of these patients is reflected in excessive use of the telephone, especially long distance calls during the early hours of the morning. Pathological gambling, a tendency to disrobe in public places, clothing and jewelry of bright colors in unusual combinations, and an inattention to small details (such as forgetting to hang up the phone) are also symptomatic of this disorder. The impulsive nature of many of the patient's acts is coupled with a sense of conviction and purpose. The patient is often preoccupied by religious, political, financial, sexual, or persecutory ideas that can evolve into complex delusional systems. Occasionally, manic patients become quite regressed and play with their urine and feces. The diagnosis of bipolar disorder, manic, with psychotic features is illustrated by the following case:

A 24-year-old man, when brought to the emergency room, was mute and rigid. The friends who brought him stated that he was playing basketball with them at the student athletic building when he suddenly put his head down on the floor, made sounds as if he were praying, and became "catatonic." When interviewed an hour later, the patient would only say, "I am communicating directly with God."

According to his friends, the patient had been getting

Table 16.1-3
Diagnostic Criteria for Manic Episode

Note: A manic syndrome is defined as including criteria A, B, and C below. A hypomanic syndrome is defined as including criteria A and B, but not C (i.e., no marked impairment).

A. A distinct period of abnormally and persistently elevated, expansive, or irritable mood.

B. During the period of mood disturbance, at least three of the following symptoms have persisted (four if the mood is only irritable) and have been present to a significant degree:
   (1) inflated self-esteem or grandiosity
   (2) decreased need for sleep (e.g., feels rested after only three hours of sleep)
   (3) more talkative than usual or pressure to keep talking
   (4) flight of ideas or subjective experience that thoughts are racing
   (5) distractibility (i.e., attention too easily drawn to unimportant or irrelevant external stimuli)
   (6) increase in goal-directed activity (either socially, at work or school, or sexually) or psychomotor agitation
   (7) excessive involvement in pleasurable activities which have a high potential for painful consequences (e.g., the person engages in unrestrained buying sprees, sexual indiscretions, or foolish business investments)

C. Mood disturbance sufficiently severe to cause marked impairment in occupational functioning or in usual social activities or relationships with others, or to necessitate hospitalization to prevent harm to self or others.

D. At no time during the disturbance have there been delusions or hallucinations for as long as two weeks in the absence of prominent mood symptoms (i.e., before the mood symptoms developed or after they have remitted).

E. Not superimposed on schizophrenia, schizophreniform disorder, delusional disorder, or psychotic disorder NOS.

F. It cannot be established that an organic factor initiated and maintained the disturbance. **Note:** Somatic antidepressant treatment (e.g., drugs, ECT) that apparently precipitates a mood disturbance should not be considered an etiologic organic factor.

Table from DSM-III-R, *Diagnostic and Statistical Manual of Mental Disorders*, ed 3, revised. Copyright American Psychiatric Association, Washington, DC, 1987, with permission.

"hyper" recently, but they emphatically denied that he used either drugs or alcohol to excess. A call to his girlfriend, whose name and number were provided by his friends, revealed the following.

The patient had been doing well, with no evidence of unusual behavior, up until one week before admission. He had been living with his girlfriend, going to school, and working at a part-time job. One week before admission he began to say odd things, usually of a religious nature. He also stopped sleeping at night and became sexually demanding of his girlfriend. He had begun working out even more than usual at the gym in order to "burn off excess energy." His girlfriend said that he had similar symptoms when he was hospitalized the year before. At that time he left the hospital against medical advice and became increasingly depressed for about three months. He did not seek professional help. He withdrew from social activities at school and slept up to 14 hours a day. Just when his girlfriend decided to break up with him, he spontaneously returned to his normal self. She described him as a friendly, outgoing, energetic young man, interested in school and athletics, who performed well both academically and at work.

Toxicology findings in the emergency room were negative, as were other medical findings. Physical examination revealed an extremely healthy, athletic young man who was largely mute and held his body in a rigid posture. The hospital chart noted one previous psychiatric admission a year before. The diagnosis was "atypical psychosis, rule out some kind of organic or drug psychosis." The patient had previously been in the hospital only four days, during which time he was observed to have auditory hallucinations and a delusion that he was communicating directly with God.

During the first few days of the current hospitalization, the patient was observed to alternate between rigid posturing and mild hyperactivity. He would spontaneously become unstuck and begin pacing actively around the unit, talking about his newfound faith in religion to "anyone he could corral."

Discussion. The bizarre behavior (becoming mute and rigid) that was the reason for the patient's admission to the hospital is a catatonic symptom. Traditionally, catatonic symptoms have been understood to be evidence of either schizophrenia or unusual forms of a central nervous system disorder. Now it is recognized that catatonic symptoms are also seen in manic episodes of bipolar disorder.

The patient continued to have catatonic symptoms (rigid posturing) when he was in the hospital, but at other times he had the classic symptoms of a manic episode: his mood was expansive (that is what was meant by his friends' describing him as "hyper," "talking to anyone he could corral" about his religious ideas, and his girlfriend's description of him as sexually demanding); he was grandiose (communicated with God), hyperactive (paced), and did not sleep. In addition, there was a history of what seemed to be a major depressive episode: he was extremely depressed, socially withdrawn, and slept 14 hours a day.

Also characteristic of bipolar disorder is the rapid development of the manic episode and the full return to usual functioning between episodes of mood disturbance. The patient's delusion of communicating with God was a typical mood-congruent grandiose delusion. Therefore, the diagnosis was bipolar disorder, manic, with mood-congruent psychotic features.

Mania in adolescents. Mania in adolescents is often misdiagnosed as sociopathy or schizophrenia. Symptoms of mania in adolescents may include psychosis, alcohol or drug abuse, suicide attempts, academic problems, philosophical brooding, obsessive-compulsive symptoms, multiple somatic complaints, marked irritability resulting in fights, and other antisocial behaviors. Although many of these symptoms can be seen in normal adolescence, severe or persistent symptoms should cause the clinician to consider bipolar disorder in the differential diagnosis.

MENTAL STATUS EXAMINATION

Depressive Episodes

General description. Generalized psychomotor retardation is the most common symptom, although psychomotor agitation is also seen, especially in elderly patients. Hand wringing and hair pulling are the most common symptoms of agitation. The classic presentation of a depressed patient is that of a person with stooped posture, no spontaneous movements, and a downcast, averted gaze (Figures 16.1-1 and 16.2-2). Depressed patients exhibiting gross symptoms of psychomotor retardation may appear identical on clinical examination to patients with catatonic schizophrenia.

Mood, affect, and feelings. Depression is the key symptom in this disorder, although approximately one-half of patients may deny depressive feelings and may not appear to the examiner as particularly depressed. These patients are often brought in by family members or employers for social withdrawal and generally decreased activity.

Perceptual disturbances. Depressed patients with delusions or hallucinations are said to have a psychotic depression; the term is also used by some clinicians to describe grossly regressed depressed patients—mute, not bathing, soiling—even in the absence of delusions or hallucinations. Delusions and hallucinations that are consistent with a depressed mood are said to be mood-congruent. Mood-congruent delusions include those of guilt, sinfulness, worthlessness, poverty, failure, persecution, and terminal somatic illnesses (e.g., cancer, "rotting" brain). The content of the mood-incongruent delusions or hallucinations is not consistent with the depressed mood. Mood-incongruent delusions in a depressed person involve grandiose themes of exaggerated power, knowledge, and worth—for example, the belief that one is the Messiah. Hallucinations occur in psychotic depression but are relatively rare.

Thought content and process. Depressed patients customarily have a negative view of the world and of themselves. Thought content often involves nondelusional ruminations about loss, guilt, suicide, and death. Many patients evidence a decreased rate and volume in speech, responding to questions with single words and exhibiting delayed responses to questions. The examiner may literally have to wait two or three minutes for a response to a question. Approximately 10 percent of all depressed patients have marked symptoms of a thought disorder, usually thought blocking, profound poverty of content or speech, or gross circumstantiality.

Impulsiveness, suicide, and homicide. Approximately 10 to 15 percent of all depressed patients complete suicide, and about two-thirds have suicidal ideation. A patient with

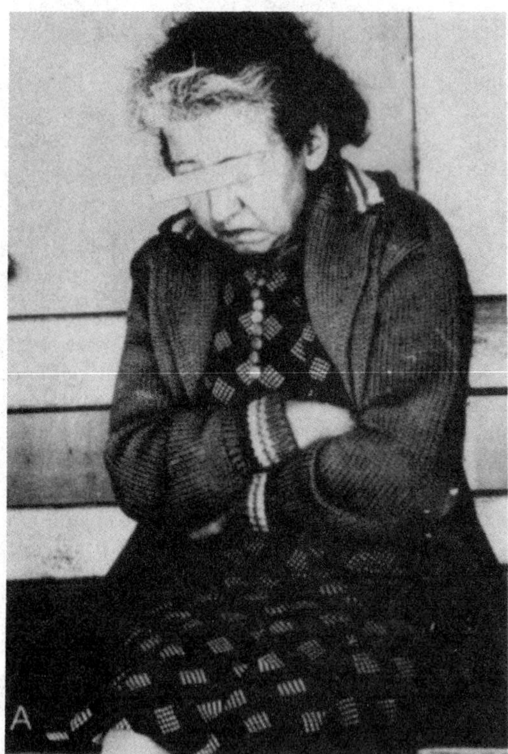

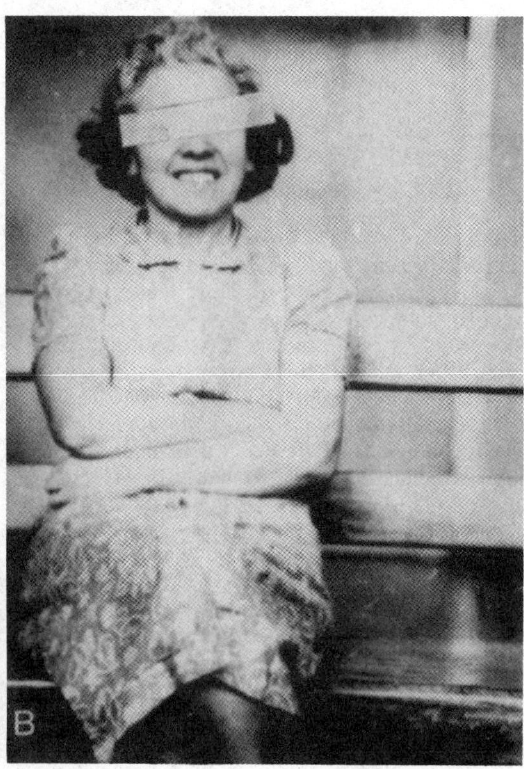

Figure 16.1-1. A 38-year-old woman during a state of deep retarded depression (A) and two months later, after recovery (B). Note the turned-down corners of the mouth, the stooped posture, the drab clothing, and the hairdo during the depressed episode. (Courtesy of Heinz E Lehmann.)

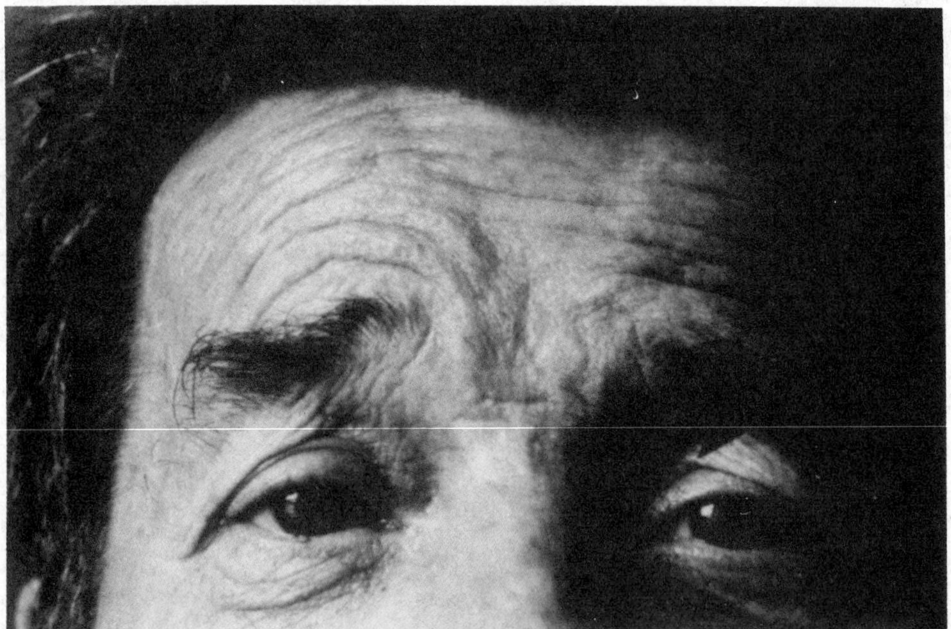

Figure 16.1-2. The Swiss neuropsychiatrist Otto Veraguth has described a peculiar triangle-shaped fold in the nasal corner of the upper eyelid. This fold is often associated with depression and referred to as Veraguth's fold. The photograph illustrates this physiognomic feature in a 50-year-old man during a major depressive episode. Veraguth's fold may also be seen in persons who are not clinically depressed, usually while they are harboring a mild depressive affect. Electromyographically, it has been shown that distinct changes in the tone of the corrugator and zygomatic facial muscles accompany depression. (Courtesy of Heinz E Lehmann.)

psychotic depression may occasionally consider killing a person involved in his or her delusional system. However, the most severely depressed patients often lack the motivation or energy to act in an impulsive or violent way. Patients with depression are at increased risk of suicide as they begin to improve and regain the energy needed to plan and carry out a suicide (paradoxical suicide). It is a clinical mistake to give a depressed patient a large prescription for antidepressants, especially tricyclic antidepressants, on discharge from the hospital.

Orientation. Most depressed patients are oriented to person, place, and time, although some may not have enough energy or interest to answer questions during an interview.

Memory. Approximately 50 to 75 percent of all depressed patients have cognitive impairment, sometimes referred to as depressive pseudodementia. Such patients commonly complain of impaired concentration and forgetfulness.

Judgment and insight. Patients' judgment is best assessed by reviewing their actions in the recent past and their behavior during the interview. Depressed patients' insight into their illness is often excessive in that they overly emphasize their symptoms, their disease, and their life problems. It is difficult to convince such patients that improvement is possible.

Reliability. All information obtained from a depressed patient overemphasizes the bad and minimizes the good. A common clinical mistake is to believe unquestioningly a depressed patient who states that a previous trial of antidepressant medications did not work. Such statements may be false and require confirmation from another source. The psychiatrist should not view the patient's misinformation as an intentional fabrication, since the admission of any hopeful information may be literally impossible for a person in a depressed state of mind.

Objective rating scales of depression. Objective rating scales of depression can be useful in clinical practice for the documentation of clinical state in depressed patients.

Zung scale. The Zung Self-Rating Depression Scale is a 20-item report scale. A normal score is 34 or less, and depressed, 50 or above. This scale provides a global index of the intensity of depressive symptoms, including the affective expression of depression.

Raskin scale. The Raskin Depression Scale is a clinician-rated scale measuring severity of depression, as reported by the patient and as observed by the physician on a five-point scale of three dimensions: verbal report, behavior displayed, and secondary symptom. It has a range of 3 to 13; normal is 3; depressed, 7 or above.

Hamilton scale. The Hamilton Rating Scale for Depression is a widely used depression scale with 24 items, each of which is rated 0 to 4 or 0 to 2, with a maximum total range of 0 to 76. The ratings are derived from a clinical interview with the patient. Answers to questions about feelings of guilt, suicide, sleep habits, and other symptoms of depression are evaluated by the clinician.

Manic Episodes

General appearance. Manic patients are excited, talkative, sometimes amusing, and frequently hyperactive. At times they are grossly psychotic and disorganized, requiring physical restraints and intramuscular tranquilizers.

Mood, affect, and feelings. Manic patients are classically euphoric but can also be quite irritable, especially when the mania has been present for some time. They also have a low frustration tolerance, which may lead to feelings of anger and hostility. Manic patients may be emotionally labile, switching from laughter to irritability to depression in minutes or hours with little control.

Perceptual disturbances. Delusions are present in 75 percent of manic patients. Mood-congruent manic delusions often involve great wealth, abilities, or power. Delusions and hallucinations that are bizarre and not mood-congruent are also seen in mania.

Thought process. Thought content includes themes of self-confidence and self-aggrandizement. Manic patients cannot be interrupted while they are speaking, and they are often intrusive nuisances to those around them. Manic patients are often quite easily distracted. The cognitive functioning of the manic state is characterized by an unrestrained and accelerated flow of ideas in which speech is often disturbed. As the mania gets more intense, speech becomes louder, more rapid, and difficult to interpret. As the activated state increases, speech becomes full of puns, jokes, rhymes, plays on words, and irrelevancies. As the activity level increases still more, associations become loosened. The ability to concentrate fades, leading to flight of ideas, word salad, and neologisms. In acute manic excitement, speech may be totally incoherent and indistinguishable from that of a schizophrenic person.

Impulsiveness, suicide, and homicide. Approximately 75 percent of all manic patients are assaultive or threatening. Manic patients do attempt suicide and homicide, but the incidences of these behaviors are not known. There is some indication that patients who threaten particularly important people (such as the president of the United States) more often have bipolar disease than schizophrenia.

Orientation and memory. Orientation and memory are usually intact, although some manic patients may be so euphoric that they answer incorrectly. This symptom was called delirious mania by Kraepelin.

Judgment and insight. Impaired judgment is a hallmark of manic patients. They may break laws regarding credit cards, sexual activities, and finances, sometimes involving their families in financial ruin. Manic patients also have little insight into their illness.

Reliability. Manic patients are notoriously unreliable in their information. Lying and deceit are common in this disorder, often causing inexperienced clinicians to treat such patients with inappropriate disdain.

COURSE AND PROGNOSIS

Depressive Disorders

Course. Patients with depressive disorders usually have not had a premorbid personality disorder. Approximately 50 percent have their first episode of depression before age 40. A later onset is associated with the absence of a family history for mood disorder, sociopathy, and alcoholism. An untreated episode of depression lasts 6 to 13 months; most treated episodes last approximately three months. The withdrawal of antidepressants before three months has elapsed almost always results in the return of the symptoms. As patients become older, they tend to have more frequent episodes that last longer. Over a 20-year period the mean number of episodes is five or six.

Approximately 5 to 10 percent of patients with an initial diagnosis of major depression have a manic episode 6 to 10 years after the first depressive episode. The mean age for this switch is 32 years, and it often occurs after two to four depressive episodes. The depression of patients who are later classified as bipolar disorder patients is often characterized by hypersomnia, psychomotor retardation, psychotic symptoms, a history of postpartum episodes, a family history of bipolar disorder, and a history of antidepressant-induced hypomania.

Prognosis. Major depression is fundamentally a cyclic disorder with periods of illness separated by periods of mental health. Approximately 50 to 85 percent of all patients have a second depressive episode, often in the next four to six months. The risk of recurrence is increased by coexisting dysthymia, alcohol and drug abuse, anxiety symptoms, and a history of more than one previous depressive episode. Approximately half of all patients are mentally healthy at long-term follow-up; about 30 percent have moderate impairment; and 20 percent have significant impairment. Men are more likely than women to experience a chronically impaired course.

Bipolar Disorders

Course. The natural history of bipolar disorders is such that it is often useful to make a graph of the patient's illness and to keep the graph up to date as treatment proceeds (Figure 16.1-3). Although cyclothymia is sometimes diagnosed retrospectively in bipolar disorder patients, no identified personality traits are specifically associated with this disorder. Bipolar disorder most often starts with depression (75 percent of the time in females, 67 percent in males) and is a recurring illness. Most patients experience both depression and mania, although approximately 10 to 20 percent experience only manic episodes. The manic episodes typically have a rapid onset (hours or days), but they may evolve over a few weeks. An untreated manic episode lasts about three months; therefore, it is unwise to discontinue drugs before that time. As the illness progresses, there is often a decrease in the amount of time between episodes. After approximately five episodes, however, the interepisode interval often stabilizes at about six to nine months. Some bipolar disorder patients have rapidly cycling episodes. Rapid cycling is much more common in women than in men, although it is not related temporally to the menstrual cycle. Rapid cycling may be

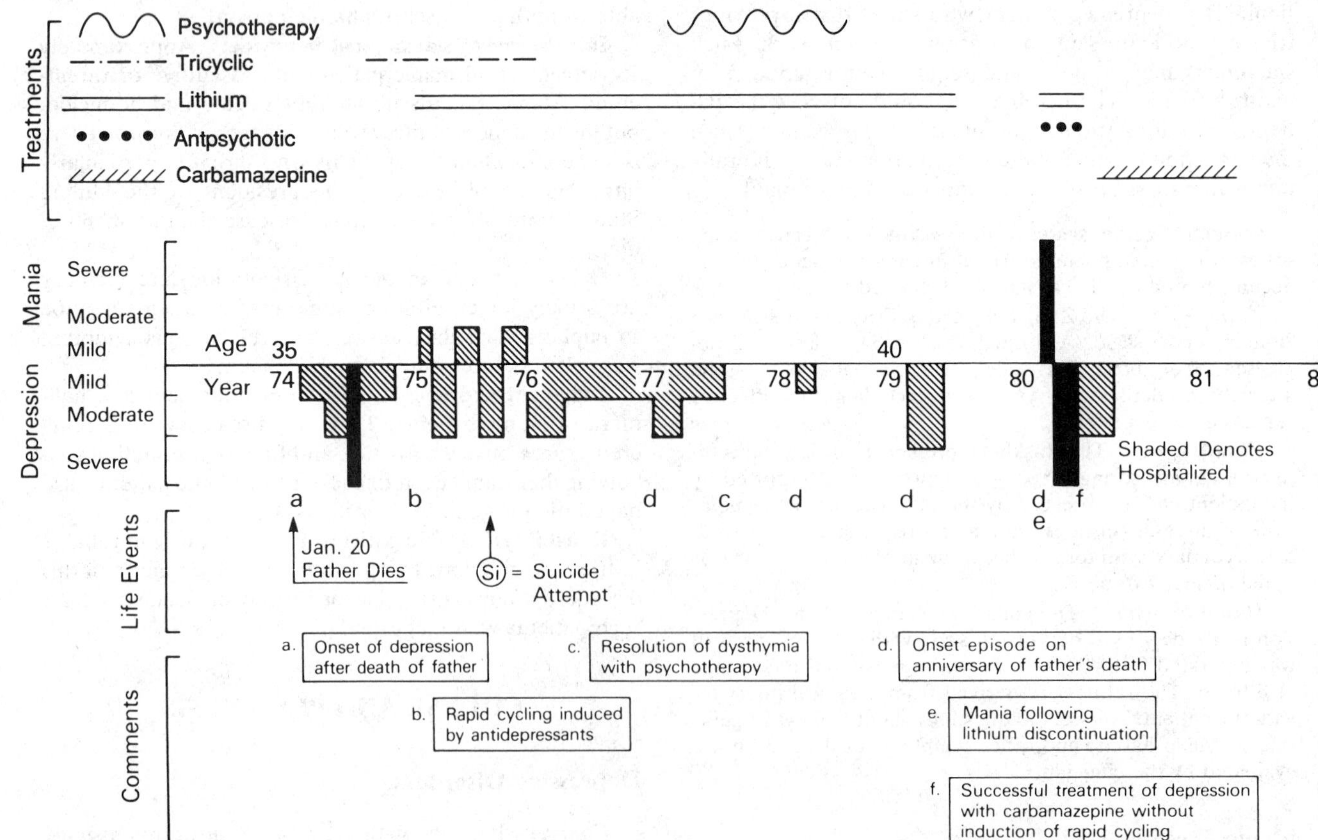

Figure 16.1-3. Graphing the course of mood disorder: Prototype of a life chart. (Figure by Robert M. Post, M.D., with permission.)

associated with treatment with tricyclic antidepressants, and patients often respond to combination therapies of lithium and monoamine oxidase inhibitors (MAOIs).

Prognosis. Bipolar disorders have a worse prognosis than depressive disorders. Patients with pure manic symptoms do better than patients with depressed or mixed symptoms. The presence of psychotic symptoms during manic episodes, however, does not imply a poor prognosis. Short duration of manic episodes, older age of onset, few suicidal thoughts, and few coexisting psychiatric or medical problems weigh toward a good prognosis.

Approximately 7 percent of all bipolar disorder patients do not have a recurrence of symptoms, 45 percent have more than one episode, and 40 percent have a chronic illness. Patients may have from 2 to 30 episodes of mania (mean, nine episodes); 40 percent have more than 10. On long-term follow-up, 15 percent of all bipolar disorder patients are well, 45 percent are well but have had multiple relapses, 30 percent are in partial remission, and 10 percent are chronically ill. One-third of all bipolar disorder patients have chronic symptoms and evidence of social decline.

DIAGNOSIS AND TYPES

Depressive Disorders

Diagnosis. For the diagnosis of major depression, DSM-III-R requires the presence of one or more major depressive episodes (Table 16.1-1) and the absence of either a manic episode or an unequivocal hypomanic episode. DSM-III-R also specifies types—single episode (Table 16.1-4), recurrent (Table 16.1-5), and seasonal pattern (Table 16.1-6). In addition, DSM-III-R specifies the severity of illness—mild, moderate, severe without psychotic features, with psychotic features (indicating mood-congruent or mood-incongruent delusions or hallucinations), in partial remission, in full remission, chronic, and unspecified (Table 16.1-7). A diagnosis of depressive disorder not otherwise specified (NOS) is used for disorders with depressive features that do not meet the criteria for any specific mood disorder or adjustment disorder with depressed mood. Intermittent dysthymic episodes is an example of such a disorder (Table 16.1-8).

Types. A variety of types have been suggested to divide depressive patients into more homogeneous groups. DSM-III-R distinguishes a type of depression based on the presence of symptoms of melancholia (Table 16.1-2). Several investigators suggest that melancholic patients are particularly likely to respond to antidepressant medications.

Seasonal affective disorder (SAD). DSM-III-R contains specific diagnostic criteria for a seasonal pattern of major depressive episodes (Table 16.1-6). SAD, also known as seasonal mood disorder, is most frequently characterized by depression, psychomotor slowing, hypersomnia, and hyperphagia that appear in autumn or winter and improve in spring and summer. Recently, a seasonal pattern in which the depression appears in the spring and summer and resolves in the autumn and winter has been recognized in some patients. These depressive episodes may be related to abnormal regulation of melatonin se-

Table 16.1-4
Diagnostic Criteria for Major Depression, Single Episode

For fifth digit, use the major depressive episode codes to describe current state.

A. A single major depressive episode

B. Has never had a manic episode or an unequivocal hypomanic episode

Specify if **seasonal pattern.**

Refer to Table 16.1-1 for depressive criteria.

Table from DSM-III-R, *Diagnostic and Statistical Manual of Mental Disorders,* ed 3, revised. Copyright American Psychiatric Association, Washington, DC, 1987, with permission.

Table 16.1-5
Diagnostic Criteria for Major Depression, Recurrent

For fifth digit, use the major depressive episode codes to describe current state.

A. Two or more major depressive episodes, each separated by at least two months of return to more or less usual functioning. (If there has been a previous major depressive episode, the current episode of depression need not meet the full criteria for a major depressive episode.)

B. Has never had a manic episode or an unequivocal hypomanic episode.

Specify if **seasonal pattern.**

Refer to Table 16.1-1 for depressive criteria.

Table from DSM-III-R, *Diagnostic and Statistical Manual of Mental Disorders,* ed 3, revised. Copyright American Psychiatric Association, Washington, DC, 1987, with permission.

Table 16.1-6
Diagnostic Criteria for Seasonal Pattern

A. There has been a regular temporal relationship between the onset of an episode of bipolar disorder (including bipolar disorder NOS) or recurrent major depression (including depressive disorder NOS) and a particular 60-day period of the year (e.g., regular appearance of depression between the beginning of October and the end of November).

Note: Do not include cases in which there is an obvious effect of seasonally related psychosocial stressors (e.g., regularly being unemployed every winter).

B. Full remissions (or a change from depression to mania or hypomania) also occurred within a particular 60-day period of the year (e.g., depression disappears from mid-February to mid-April).

C. There have been at least three episodes of mood disturbance in three separate years that demonstrated the temporal seasonal relationship defined in A and B; at least two of the years were consecutive.

D. Seasonal episodes of mood disturbance, as described above, outnumbered any nonseasonal episodes of such disturbance that may have occurred by more than three to one.

Table from DSM-III-R, *Diagnostic and Statistical Manual of Mental Disorders,* ed 3, revised. Copyright American Psychiatric Association, Washington, DC, 1987, with permission.

Table 16.1-7
Diagnostic Criteria for Major Depressive Episode Codes

Fifth-digit code numbers and criteria for severity of current state of bipolar disorder, depressed, or major depression

1-Mild: Few, if any, symptoms in excess of those required to make the diagnosis, **and** symptoms result in only minor impairment in occupational functioning or in usual social activities or relationships with others.

2-Moderate: Symptoms or functional impairment between "mild" and "severe."

3-Severe, without psychotic features: Several symptoms in excess of those required to make the diagnosis, **and** symptoms markedly interfere with occupational functioning or with usual social activities or relationships with others.

4-With psychotic features: Delusions or hallucinations. If possible, **specify** whether the psychotic features are *mood-congruent or mood-incongruent.*

Mood-congruent psychotic features: Delusions or hallucinations whose content is entirely consistent with the typical depressive themes of personal inadequacy, guilt, disease, death, nihilism, or deserved punishment.

Mood-incongruent psychotic features: Delusions or hallucinations whose content does *not* involve typical depressive themes of personal inadequacy, guilt, disease, death, nihilism, or deserved punishment. Included here are such symptoms as persecutory delusions (not directly related to depressive themes), thought insertion, thought broadcasting, and delusions of control.

5-In partial remission: Intermediate between "in full remission" and "mild," **and** no previous dysthymia. (If major depressive episode was superimposed on dysthymia, the diagnosis of dysthymia alone is given once the full criteria for a major depressive episode are no longer met.)

6-In full remission: During the past six months no significant signs or symptoms of the disturbance.

0-Unspecified.

Specify chronic if current episode has lasted two consecutive years without a period of two months or longer during which there were no significant depressive symptoms.

Specify if current episode is **melancholic type.**

Table 16.1-8
Diagnostic Criteria for Depressive Disorder Not Otherwise Specified

Disorders with depressive features that do not meet the criteria for any specific mood disorder or adjustment disorder with depressed mood.

Examples:

(1) a major depressive episode superimposed on residual schizophrenia
(2) a recurrent, mild, depressive disturbance that does not meet the criteria for dysthymia
(3) non-stress-related depressive episodes that do not meet the criteria for a major depressive episode

Specify if **seasonal pattern.**

Refer to Table 16.1-1 for depressive criteria.

cretion from the pineal gland. This type of depression seems particularly amenable to treatment with sleep deprivation or, for a more enduring remission, with light therapy, also known as phototherapy. Treatment with light involves extending the photoperiod of a patient's day by exposing the patient to bright light for usually two hours in the morning or evening.

Hysteroid dysphoria. Hysteroid dysphoria and atypical depression are terms sometimes used to describe depressed patients with so-called reversed vegetative symptoms and marked anxiety symptoms. Reversed vegetative symptoms are increased appetite, rather than decreased appetite; increased sleep, rather than decreased sleep; weight gain, rather than weight loss; and sometimes hyperactivity. Although anxiety is a frequent symptom in all depressed persons, persons with hysteroid dysphoria have such marked symptoms of anxiety that they are at risk of being classified as having an anxiety disorder, instead of a depressive disorder. Research data support the conclusion that these patients are more likely to respond to treatment with MAOIs than with tricyclic antidepressants.

Other types. Other systems have been devised to identify patients with good and poor prognoses. These differentiations have included endogenous-reactive, psychotic-neurotic, and primary-secondary schemes. The endogenous-reactive continuum is a controversial division because it implies that endogenous depressions are biological and reactive depressions are psychological, based primarily on the presence or absence of an identifiable precipitating stress. Other symptoms of endogenous depression include diurnal variation, delusions, psychomotor retardation, early morning awakening, and feelings of guilt; thus, endogenous depression is somewhat similar to the DSM-III-R diagnosis of major depressive episode with psychotic features, melancholic type. Symptoms of reactive depression include initial insomnia, anxiety, emotional lability, and multiple somatic complaints. The psychotic-neurotic division separates more severely ill from less severely ill patients. Primary depressions are what DSM-III-R calls the mood disorders, and secondary depression is a depression that is a component of some other psychiatric or medical condition. Double depression is the condition in which major depression is superimposed on dysthymia. A depressive equivalent is a symptom or syndrome that may be a *forme fruste* of a depressive episode. For example, the triad of truancy, alcohol abuse, and sexual promiscuity in a formerly well-behaved adolescent may constitute a depressive equivalent.

Bipolar Disorders

Diagnosis. DSM-III-R requires the presence of a manic episode (Table 16.1-3) for the diagnosis of bipolar disorder, manic type (Table 16.1-9). If there has been a previous complete manic episode, however, the current episode need not meet the full criteria for a manic episode. The diagnosis of a bipolar disorder, depressed type (Table 16.1-10), requires a past history of one or more manic episodes (Table 16.1-3) and the presence of a depressive episode. If there has been a previous major depressive episode, however, the current episode does not need to

Table 16.1-9
Diagnostic Criteria for Bipolar Disorder, Manic

For fifth digit, use the manic episode codes to describe current state.

Currently (or most recently) in a manic episode (If there has been a previous manic episode, the current episode need not meet the full criteria for a manic episode.)

Specify if **seasonal pattern.**

Refer to Table 16.1-3 for manic criteria.

Table 16.1-10
Diagnostic Criteria for Bipolar Disorder, Depressed

For fifth digit, use the major depressive episode codes to describe current state.

A. Has had one or more manic episodes

B. Currently (or most recently) in a major depressive episode. (If there has been a previous major depressive episode, the current episode need not meet the full criteria for a major depressive episode.)

Specify if **seasonal pattern.**

Refer to Table 16.1-1 for depressive criteria.

meet the full criteria for a major depressive episode (Table 16.1-1). The diagnosis of bipolar disorder, mixed type (Table 16.1-11), requires the presence of both complete manic and depressive episodes (lasting at least a full day) or the rapid alternation of these syndromes every few days.

The severity of a manic episode is also specified in DSM-III-R: mild, moderate, severe without psychotic features, with psychotic features (indicate mood-congruent or mood-incongruent), partial remission, full remission, and unspecified (Table 16.1-12). Bipolar disorder not otherwise specified (NOS) is a residual category for manic and hypomanic episodes that are not classified elsewhere in DSM-III-R (Table 16.1-13).

Table 16.1-11
Diagnostic Criteria for Bipolar Disorder, Mixed

For fifth digit, use the manic episode codes to describe current state.

A. Current (or most recent) episode involves the full symptomatic picture of both manic and major depressive episodes (except for the duration requirement of two weeks for depressive symptoms), intermixed or rapidly alternating every few days.

B. Prominent depressive symptoms lasting at least a full day.

Specify if **seasonal pattern.**

Refer to Table 16.1-1 for depressive criteria and to Table 16.1-3 for manic criteria

Table 16.1-12
Diagnostic Criteria for Manic Episode Codes

Fifth-digit code numbers and criteria for severity of current state of bipolar disorder, manic or mixed

1-Mild: Meets minimum symptom criteria for a manic episode (or almost meets symptom criteria if there has been a previous manic episode).

2-Moderate: Extreme increase in activity or impairment in judgment.

3-Severe, without psychotic features: Almost continual supervision requried in order to prevent physical harm to self or others.

4-With psychotic features: Delusions, hallucinations, or catatonic symptoms. If possible, **specify** whether the psychotic features are *mood-congruent* or *mood-incongruent.*

Mood-congruent psychotic features: Delusions or hallucinations whose content is entirely consistent with the typical manic themes of inflated worth, power, knowledge, identity, or special relationship to a deity or a famous person.

Mood-incongruent psychotic features: Either (*a*) or (*b*):

(*a*) Delusions or hallucinations whose content does *not* involve the typical manic themes of inflated worth, power, knowledge, identity, or special relationship to a deity or famous person. Included are such sympotms as persecutory delusions (not directly related to grandiose ideas or themes), thought insertion, and delusions of being controlled.

(*b*) Catatonic symptoms (e.g., stupor, mutism, negativism, posturing).

5-In partial remission: Full criteria were previously, but are not currently, met; some signs or syumptoms of the disturbance have persisted.

6-In full remission: Full criteria were previously met, but there have been no significant signs or symptoms of the disturbance for at least six months.

0-Unspecified.

Types. The major types of bipolar disorder are depressed, manic, and mixed. One other division involves the concepts of bipolar I and bipolar II. Bipolar I is synonymous with the DSM-III-R criteria for bipolar disorder. Bipolar II is used for patients who have major depressive episodes with only hypomanic episodes. According to DSM-III-R, if such patients do not meet the criteria for cyclothymia, they are classified as having bipolar disorder NOS. Bipolar II has been reported in the families of unipolar, bipolar, and bipolar II probands. It has been suggested that bipolar II patients may represent a personality disorder superimposed on a unipolar depressive disorder.

DIFFERENTIAL DIAGNOSIS

Depressive Disorders

Medical disorders. Many neurological and medical disorders and pharmacological agents can produce symptoms of

Table 16.1-13
Diagnostic Criteria for Bipolar Disorder Not Otherwise Specified

Disorders with manic or hypomanic features that do not meet the criteria for any specific bipolar disorder.

Examples:

(1) at least one hypomanic episode and at least one major depressive episode, but never either a manic episode or cyclothymia. Such cases have been referred to as bipolar II

(2) one or more hypomanic episodes, but without cyclothymia or a history of either a manic or a major depressive episode

(3) a manic episode superimposed on delusional disorder, residual schizophrenia, or psychotic disorder NOS

Specify if **seasonal pattern.**

Table from DSM-III-R, *Diagnostic and Statistical Manual of Mental Disorders,* ed 3, revised. Copyright American Psychiatric Association, Washington, DC, 1987, with permission.

depression (Table 16.1-14). Many patients with depression first go to their general practitioners with somatic complaints. Most organic causes of depression can be detected with a comprehensive medical history, a complete physical and neurological examination, and routine blood and urine tests. The workup should include tests for thyroid and adrenal functions because disorders of both of these endocrine systems can present as depression.

The most common neurological problems that manifest depressive symptoms are Parkinson's disease, dementing illnesses (including Alzheimer's disease), epilepsy, strokes, and tumors. Approximately 50 to 75 percent of all patients with Parkinson's disease have marked symptoms of depression that are not correlated with the degree of physical disability, age, or duration of illness but are correlated with the presence of abnormalities on neuropsychological tests. These symptoms of depression may be masked by the almost identical motor symptoms of Parkinson's disease. Depressive symptoms often respond to antidepressant drugs or electroconvulsive therapy (ECT).

It is usually possible to differentiate the pseudodementia of depression from the dementia of a disease, such as Alzheimer's disease, on clinical grounds. The cognitive symptoms in depression have a more acute onset, and other symptoms of depression, such as self-reproach, are present. A diurnal variation to the cognitive problems that is not seen in the primary dementias may be present. Depressed patients with cognitive difficulties often do not try to answer questions ("I don't know"), whereas demented patients may confabulate. In depressed patients recent and remote memory are equally affected; in demented patients recent memory is more affected than remote memory. Finally, depressed patients sometimes can be coached and encouraged during an interview into having better memory, an ability demented patients lack.

The interictal changes associated with temporal lobe epilepsy can mimic a depressive disorder, especially if the epileptic focus is on the right side. Depression is a common complicating feature of strokes, particularly in the two years after the episode. Depression is more common after anterior (than posterior) strokes and with left-sided lesions. Poststroke depression often responds to antidepressant medications. Tumors of the diencephalic and temporal regions are particularly likely to be associated with depressive symptoms.

Failure to take a good clinical history or to consider the context of the patient's current life situation may lead to diagnostic errors. Adolescents with depression should be tested for mononucleosis. Women and men who are markedly overweight or underweight should be tested for adrenal and thyroid dysfunctions. Homosexual and bisexual men and intravenous drug users should be tested for acquired immune deficiency syndrome (AIDS). Elderly patients should be evaluated for viral pneumonia.

The list of drugs associated with depression is also long (Table 16.1-14). A good rule of thumb is that any drug a depressed patient is taking should be considered a potential factor in the mood disorder. Cardiac drugs, antihypertensives, sedatives, hypnotics, antipsychotics, antiepileptics, antiparkinsons, analgesics, antibacterials, and antineoplastics are all commonly associated with depressive symptoms.

Psychiatric disorders. Depression can be a feature of virtually any mental disorder listed in DSM-III-R, but the psychiatric disorders listed in Table 16.1-15 should be particularly considered in the differential diagnosis. The differentiation of syndromes is best done by following the DSM-III-R guidelines for each disorder. Perhaps the most difficult differential is between anxiety disorders (with depression) and depressive disorders (with marked anxiety). An abnormal DST, the presence of shortened REM latency on a sleep electroencephalogram (EEG), and a negative lactate infusion test result support a diagnosis of depression. Uncomplicated bereavement is not considered a mental disorder, even though approximately one-third of bereaved spouses meet the criteria for depressive disorder for a time. Some patients with uncomplicated bereavement do go on to major depression. However, the diagnosis is not made unless a resolution of grief does not occur; the differentiation is based on the severity and the length of the symptoms. Symptoms commonly seen in a depressive disorder that evolves from unresolved bereavement are a morbid preoccupation with worthlessness, suicidal ideation, marked functional impairment, psychomotor retardation, feeling that he or she committed an act (not just an omission) that caused the death, mummification (keeping the deceased's belongings exactly as they were), and a particularly severe anniversary reaction, which sometimes includes a suicide attempt.

Bipolar Disorder (Manic Episodes)

Medical disorders. Many of the potential neurological and medical causes of depressive symptoms can also cause manic symptoms (see asterisked items in Table 16.1-14). Many pharmacological agents may precipitate mania (Table 16.1-16), as can antidepressant treatment or withdrawal.

Psychiatric disorders. The major psychiatric differential diagnosis for manic symptoms includes disorders that may present with depression (Table 16.1-15). Of special consideration for manic symptoms, however, are the borderline, narcissistic, histrionic, and antisocial personality disorders.

A great deal has been written recently about the clinical difficulty of separating a manic episode from a schizophrenic episode. Although difficult, a differential diagnosis is possible with a few clinical guidelines. Merriment, elation, and infectiousness of mood are much more common in mania than in schizophrenia. The combination of a manic mood, rapid or pressured speech, and hyperactivity weighs heavily toward a diagnosis of mania. The onset in mania is often rapid, being a marked change from previous behavior. One-half of bipolar patients have a family history of a mood disorder. Catatonia may be a depressive phase in a bipolar disorder. When evaluating catatonic patients, the clinician should carefully look for a past history of manic or depressive episodes, as well as

Table 16.1-14
Neurological, Medical, and Pharmacological Causes of Depressive Symptoms

Neurological
Dementias (including Alzheimer's disease)
Epilepsy*
Fahr's disease*
Huntington's chorea*
Hydrocephalus
Infections (including HIV and neurosyphilis)*
Migraines*
Multiple sclerosis*
Narcolepsy
Neoplasms*
Parkinson's disease
Progressive supranuclear palsy
Sleep apnea
Strokes*
Trauma*
Wilson's disease*

Endocrine
Adrenal (Cushing's*, Addison's diseases)
Hyperaldosteronism
Menses-related*
Parathyroid disorders (hyper- and hypo-)
Postpartum*
Thyroid disorders (hypothyroidism and apathetic hyperthyroidism)*

Infectious and Inflammatory
Acquired immune deficiency syndrome (AIDS)*
Chronic fatigue syndrome
Mononucleosis
Pneumonia—viral and bacterial
Rheumatoid arthritis
Sjogren's arteritis
Systemic lupus erythematosus*
Temporal arteritis
Tuberculosis

Miscellaneous Medical
Cancer (especially pancreatic and other GI)
Cardiopulmonary disease
Porphyria
Uremia (and other renal diseases)*
Vitamin deficiencies (B_{12}, C, folate, niacin, thiamin)*

Pharmacological (representative drugs)
Analgesics and anti-inflammatory
- Ibuprofen
- Indomethacin
- Opiates
- Phenacetin

Antibacterials and antifungals
- Ampicillin
- Clycloserine
- Ethionamide
- Griseofulvin
- Metronidazole
- Nalidixic acid
- Nitrofurantoin

Pharmacological (continued)
- Streptomycin
- Sulfamethoxazole
- Sulfonamides
- Tetracycline

Antihypertensives and cardiac drugs
- Alphamethyldopa
- Bethtanidine
- β-Blockers (propranolol)
- Clonidine
- Digitalis
- Guanethidine
- Hydralazine
- Lidocaine
- Prazosin
- Procainamide
- Quanabenzacetate
- Rescinnamine
- Reserpine
- Veratrum

Antineoplastics
- C-Asparaginase
- Azathioprine (AZT)
- 6-Azauridine
- Bleomycin
- Trimethoprim
- Vincristine

Neurological and Psychiatric
- Amantadine
- Antipsychotics (butyrophenones, phenothiazines, oxyindoles)
- Baclofen
- Bromocriptine
- Carbamazepine
- Levodopa
- Phenytoin
- Sedatives and hypnotics (barbiturates, benzodiazepines, chloral hydrate)
- Tetrabenazine

Steroids and hormones
- Corticosteroids (including ACTH)
- Danazol
- Oral contraceptives
- Prednisone
- Triamcinolone

Miscellaneous
- Acetazolamide
- Choline
- Cimetidine
- Cyproheptadine
- Diphenoxylate
- Disulfiram
- Methysergide
- Stimulants (amphetamines, fenfluramine.)

*These conditions are also associated with manic symptoms.

Table 16.1-15
Psychiatric Disorders That Commonly Have Depressive Features

Adjustment disorder with depressed mood
Alcohol abuse
Anorexia nervosa
Anxiety disorders
Bipolar disorders
Bulimia nervosa
Cyclothymia
Dysthymia
Major depression
Psychoactive substance abuse
Schizoaffective disorder
Schizophrenia
Schizophreniform disorder
Somatization disorder

Table 16.1-16
Drugs Associated with Manic Symptoms

Amphetamines
Baclofen
Bromide
Bromocriptine
Captopril
Cimetidine
Cocaine
Corticosteroids (including ACTH)
Cyclosporine
Disulfiram
Hallucinogens (intoxication and flashbacks)
Hydralazine
Isoniazid
Levodopa
Methylphenidate
Metrizamide (following myelography)
Opiates
Procarbazine
Procyclidine
Yohimbine

a family history of mood disorders. Manic symptoms in minorities (particularly blacks and Hispanics) are often misdiagnosed as schizophrenic symptoms.

TREATMENT

The treatment of mood disorders is rewarding for the psychiatrist; specific treatments are now available for both manic and depressive episodes. Because the prognosis for each episode is good, optimism is always warranted and welcomed by both the patient and the family, even if initial treatment results are not promising.

Hospitalization

The first and most critical decision the physician must make is whether to hospitalize the patient or to attempt outpatient treatment. Clear indications for hospitalization are the need for diagnostic procedures, risk of suicide or homicide, and grossly reduced ability to care for food, shelter, and clothing. A history of rapidly progressing symptoms and rupture of the usual support systems are also indications for hospitalization.

Mild depression or hypomania may be safely treated in the office if the physician evaluates the patient frequently. Clinical signs of impaired judgment, weight loss, or insomnia should be minimal. The patient's support system should be strong, neither overinvolved with nor withdrawing from the patient. Any adverse changes in symptoms, external behavior, and attitude of the support system are sufficient to warrant hospitalization.

Patients with mood disorders are often unwilling to come into a hospital voluntarily, so they may have to be committed. Depressive disorder patients are often incapable of making a decision because of their slowed thinking, negative *Weltanschauung* (worldview), and hopelessness. Manic patients often have such a complete lack of insight into their illness that hospitalization seems absolutely absurd to them.

Psychosocial Therapies

Most studies have demonstrated that a combination of psychotherapy and pharmacotherapy is the most efficacious therapy. The majority of these studies, however, have been conducted with hospitalized patients with serious depressive illnesses. Some recent studies, which have compared the various treatment modalities in outpatients with milder depressive illnesses, have demonstrated that cognitive therapy or interpersonal therapy may be virtually as effective as pharmacotherapy. The relative long-term benefits of the various modalities in preventing relapses are the subject of ongoing research efforts.

Interpersonal and cognitive therapies have developed approaches specifically for the treatment of depression. Insight-oriented psychoanalytically based psychotherapy, behavior therapy, and family therapy can also be used in the treatment of depression. The selection of the appropriate therapy depends on patient variables (Table 16.1-17) and the clinician's experience.

Interpersonal therapy. Interpersonal therapy (IPT) is a short-term psychotherapy, normally consisting of 12 to 16 weekly sessions. It was developed specifically for the treatment of unipolar, nonpsychotic, ambulatory depressed patients. It is characterized by an active therapeutic approach and an emphasis on the patient's current issues and social functioning. Intrapsychic phenomena, such as defense mechanisms and internal conflicts, are not addressed in therapy. Discrete behaviors—such as lack of assertiveness, social skills, and distorted thinking—may be addressed but only in the context of their meaning or effect on interpersonal relationships.

Cognitive therapy. The cognitive theory of depression posits that cognitive dysfunctions are the core of depression; the signs and symptoms of depression are hypothesized to be consequences of the cognitive dysfunctions. For example, apathy and low energy are results of the patient's expectation of failure in all areas. The goal of cognitive therapy is to alleviate depression and to prevent its recurrence by helping the patient to identify and test negative cognitions; to develop alternative, more flexible and pos-

Table 16.1-17
Nonselective and Selective Patient Variables for Psychotherapy of Depression

Nonselective Patient Variables	Selective Patient Variables: Psychodynamic Therapy	Selective Patient Variables: Cognitive Therapy	Selective Patient Variables: Interpersonal Therapy
Feelings of hopelessness and helplessness Apathy, decreased enjoyment, diminished desire or gratification Too high ego ideals and expectations Oversleeping, morbid dreams or nightmares Feelings of restlessness or being slowed down Lack of motivation or will Low self-esteem, inappropriate or excessive guilt and self-reproach Distractibility, sluggish thinking or decision making Wish or intention to be dead Social withdrawal, fear of rejection or failure Psychosomatic complaints, hypochondriasis	Chronic sense of emptiness and underestimation of self-worth Loss or long separation in childhood Conflicts in past relationships (e.g., with parent, sexual partner) Capacity for insight Ability to modulate regression Access to dreams and fantasy Little need for direction and guidance Stable environment	Obvious distorted thoughts about self, world, and future Pragmatic (logical) thinking Real inadequacies (including poor response to other psychotherapies) Moderate to high need for direction and guidance Responsiveness to behavioral training and self-help (high degree of self-control)	Recent, focused dispute with spouse or significant other Social or communication problems Recent role transition or life change Abnormal grief reaction Modest to moderate need for direction and guidance Responsiveness to environmental manipulation (available support network)

Table from T B Karasu: Toward a clinical model of psychotherapy for depression: II. An integrative and selective treatment approach. Am J. Psychiatry *147*: 269, 1990, with permission.

itive ways of thinking; and to rehearse new cognitive and behavioral responses.

Psychoanalytically oriented therapy. The psychoanalytic approach to mood disorders is based on the psychoanalytic theories for depression and mania. In general, the goal of psychoanalytic psychotherapy is to effect a change in the personality structure or character, not simply to alleviate symptoms. Improvement in interpersonal trust, intimacy, coping mechanisms, the capacity to grieve, and the ability to experience a wide range of emotions are some of the aims of psychoanalytic therapy. Treatment may often require the patient to experience heightened anxiety and distress during the course of therapy, which may continue for several years.

Behavior therapy. Several behavior therapies have been developed for the treatment of depression. Although they vary in terms of specific techniques and foci, they have certain assumptions and strategies in common. The treatment program is highly structured and generally short-term. The principle of reinforcement is seen as the key element in depression. Changing behavior is considered the most effective way to alleviate depression. Finally, the focus is on the articulation and attainment of specific goals.

Family therapy. Family therapy is not generally viewed as a primary therapy for the treatment of depression, but it is indicated for cases in which (1) the depression appears to be seriously jeopardizing that patient's marriage and family functioning or (2) a patient's depression appears to be promoted and maintained by marital and family interaction patterns. Family therapy examines the role of the depressed member in the overall psychological well-being of the whole family; it also examines the role of the entire family in the maintenance of the depression. Patients with mood disorders have a very high rate of divorce, and approximately 50 percent of spouses report they would not have married the patient or had children had they known that the patient was going to have a mood disorder. Family therapy, therefore, can be a crucial and effective modality in the treatment of mood disorders.

Pharmacotherapy

Drugs that treat mood disorders (thymoleptics) are the mainstay of the treatment regimen. It is imperative that the physician integrate pharmacotherapy with psychotherapeutic interventions. If physicians view mood disorders as fundamentally evolving from psychodynamic issues, their ambivalence about the use of drugs may result in poor response, noncompliance, and probably inadequate does for too short a treatment period. Alternatively, if physicians ignore the psychosocial needs of the patient, the outcome of pharmacotherapy may be compromised. Several studies have demonstrated an additive treatment effect for combining optimally administered pharmacotherapy with appropriately conducted psychotherapeutic interventions.

The risk of suicide in mood disorder patients must always be borne in mind by the physician when writing prescriptions. Most antidepressants are particularly lethal if taken in large amounts. It is unwise to give most mood disorder patients large prescriptions when they are discharged from the hospital unless another person will monitor administration.

Depressive Disorders

Acute depression is a treatable condition in 70 to 80 percent of patients. The major somatic treatment modality is pharmacotherapy. *Electroconvulsive therapy* (ECT) (see Section 30.3) is generally used in the following situations: (1) The patient is unresponsive to pharmacotherapy; (2) the patient cannot tolerate pharmacotherapy; and (3) the clinical situation is so severe as to require the more rapid clinical improvement seen with ECT. Although the application of ECT is often limited to these three situations, it is an effective antidepressant treatment and can reasonably be considered as the treatment of choice in some patients, such as elderly depressed persons. *Phototherapy* (see Section 30.4) is a novel therapy that has been used in the treatment of patients with seasonal affective disorder (SAD). It is reasonable practice to use phototherapy alone for patients with less severe SAD or in combination with pharmacotherapy for more severely ill patients, although studies of the efficacy of this combination have not been conducted as yet.

When introducing the topic of a drug trial to the patient, the physician should emphasize that depression is a combination of biological and psychological factors, both of which benefit from drug therapy. The physician should also stress that the patient will not become addicted to antidepressants, because these drugs do not give immediate gratification. The doctor should tell the patient that it may take three to four weeks for the effects of the antidepressant to be felt; and even if there is no improvement at that time, there are other medications to try. It is almost always good practice to explain expected side effects in detail but to emphasize that they are signs that the drug is working. Finally, it may be useful to tell the patient that sleep and appetite will improve first, followed by a sense of returned energy; the feeling of depression, unfortunately, will be the last symptom to change.

The drugs referred to as antidepressants include tricyclic and tetracyclic antidepressants (see Section 30.2.22), monoamine oxidase inhibitors (MAOIs) (see Section 30.2.18), several atypical antidepressants (e.g., fluoxetine [Prozac] [see Section 30.2.15], bupropion [Wellbutrin] [see Section 30.2.7], trazodone [Desyrel] [see Section 30.2.21], alprazolam [Xanax] [see Section 30.2.5]), and sympathomimetics (e.g., amphetamines) (see Section 30.2.19). The nomenclature for the "-cyclic" drugs has become somewhat confusing, since antidepressants have been developed that are monocyclics (or unicyclics), dicyclics (or bicyclics), tricyclics, and tetracyclics. Sometimes these drugs have been grouped together as the heterocyclics. Because the tricyclic and tetracyclic antidepressants are most easily understood when presented together, this textbook combines the presentation of these drugs. In common use the acronym TCA refers to the tricyclic antidepressants, but, for the purpose of this section, TCA here refers to both tricyclic and tetracyclic antidepressants.

The TCAs and the MAOIs are considered the classical antidepressant drugs; however, they all have a two- to three-week onset of action and are associated with various unpleasant adverse effects. The development of new antidepressants has been directed toward finding quicker-acting drugs with fewer adverse effects. Three of these new compounds—fluoxetine, trazodone, and bupropion—are associated with fewer adverse effects in patients, although their onset of action remains the same as the older compounds.

The principal indication for antidepressants is a major depressive episode. As previously mentioned, the first symptoms to improve are poor sleep and appetite patterns. Then agitation, anxiety, depression, and hopelessness are reduced. Other target symptoms include low energy, poor concentration, helplessness, and decreased libido. The use of these drugs as antidepressants approximately doubles the chance that a depressed patient will recover within one month. Recent indications for antidepressant medications (such as eating disorders and anxiety) make the grouping of these drugs under a single label of antidepressants somewhat confusing.

The antidepressant drugs do not markedly influence the brain of a mentally healthy human but, rather, correct an abnormal condition. The TCAs, MAOIs, and atypical antidepressants are antidepressants for depressed persons but have relatively little or no effect as general euphoriants or stimulants in most mentally healthy persons. In contrast, sympathomimetic antidepressants are euphoriants in such persons.

Choice of drug. In the treatment of all mental disorders, the best reason for choosing a particular drug is a past history of response to that agent in the patient or a family member. If such information is not available, the choice of drug is based principally on the side-effect profile of the drug and secondarily on the clinical type of the depressive episode. Specifically, some clinicians preferentially use MAOIs for the treatment of patients with atypical depression.

When choosing an antidepressant drug based on side-effect profiles, the clinician may choose among the TCAs, MAOIs, atypical antidepressants, and sympathomimetics. Tyramine-induced hypertensive crises are associated with the use of MAOIs when foods containing tyramine or certain drugs are ingested by persons taking MAOIs. Although this adverse interaction can be avoided by following fairly simple dietary guidelines, the potentially life-threatening nature of a hypertensive crisis causes most clinicians to avoid MAOIs as first-line drugs in the treatment of depression. Although the sympathomimetics can be effective antidepressant drugs, they are associated with a high abuse potential and are, therefore, rarely indicated as a first-choice drug in the treatment of depression. This leaves the clinician to choose among the 20 or so different tricyclic, tetracyclic, and atypical antidepressant drugs (Table 16.1-18).

Depressed bipolar disorder patients. Lithium can be considered a first-line pharmacological agent in treating depression in bipolar disorder patients and in some depressed patients with marked periodicity to their illness. Bipolar disorder patients who are being treated with conventional antidepressant agents must be observed carefully for the emergence of manic symptoms.

Psychotically depressed patients. Patients with psychotic depression virtually always require an antipsychotic medication in addition to their antidepressant regimen. The antipsychotic medication can be tapered and stopped when the psychosis has subsided. Some clinicians recommend the use of amoxapine (Asendin), a TCA with antipsychotic activity, alone.

General clinical guidelines. The most common clinical mistake leading to an unsuccessful trial of an antidepressant drug is the use of too low a dosage for too short a time. Unless adverse effects prevent it, the dosage of an antidepressant should be raised to the maximum recommended levels and maintained at those levels for at least four weeks before a drug trial is considered unsuccessful. Alternatively, if a patient is improving clinically on a low dosage of the drug, then the

Table 16.1-18
Relative Side Effects of Tricyclic, Tetracyclic, and Atypical Antidepressants

Drug	Sedation	Hypotension	Anticholinergic‡	Relative Action† NE/5HT	Other Effects
TERTIARY AMINE TRICYCLICS					
Amitriptyline	+ + +	+ + +	+ + +	±/+ + +	H.O.D.
Imipramine	+ +	+ + +	+ + +	+ +/+ + +	H.O.D.
Doxepin	+ + +	+ +	+ +	+ +/+ +	C.T. and H.O.D. Useful blockage of H_2 receptors; will not reverse guanethidine effects.
Trimipramine	+ + +	+ + +	+ +	+/+	H.O.D.
Clomipramine	+ + +	+	+ +	+/+ +	H.O.D., seizures
SECONDARY AMINE TRICYCLICS					
Nortriptyline	+ +	+	+ +	+ + +/+ +	H.O.D.; possible inverted "U" relationship of blood levels to clinical response.
Protriptyline	±	+ +?	+ + +	+ + +/+	H.O.D.
Desipramine	+	+ + +	+	+ + +/0	H.O.D.; ? Less weight gain.
TETRACYCLICS					
Maprotiline	+ +	+ +	+ +	+ + +/0	*Seizures;* long half-life; C.T. and H.O.D.
Amoxapine	+ +	+	+ +	+ + +/±	Extrapyramidal effects and tardive dyskinesia; ? Rapid onset, L.O.D.
ATYPICAL					
Bupropion	0	0	0	?	Seizures in high doses
Trazodone	+ +	+ + +	0	0/+ +	Priapism; no prolongation of cardiac conduction but possible arrhythmogenic; L.O.D.
Fluoxetine	±	0	0	0/+ + +	No weight gain; possible insomnia, rash
Alprazolam	+ + +	±?	?	?/?	? Tolerance, dependence

Adapted from table by Robert M. Post, M.D., with permission.
+ + + = marked; + + = moderate; + = mild; ± = equivocal; 0 = absent
†Reuptake blockage of norepinephrine (NE) or serotonin (5-HT)
‡Effects include dry mouth, blurred vision, constipation, tachycardia, and urinary hesitancy and retention.
C.T.: as cardiotoxic as tricyclics.
H.O.D.: potentially lethal in overdose.
L.O.D.: low cardiotoxicity in overdose.

dosage should not be raised unless clinical improvement stops before maximal benefit is obtained. If a patient does not respond to appropriate dosages of a drug after one to two weeks, a clinician may decide to obtain a plasma concentration of the drug if the test is available for the particular drug being used. This test may indicate either noncompliance or particularly unusual pharmacokinetic disposition of the drug, thereby suggesting an alteration of the dosage.

It is important for the clinician to communicate to the patient at the start of treatment that, if the first drug is not effective, other drugs can be tried. Current clinical practice is to switch among the three major classes: TCAs, MAOIs, and atypical antidepressants. That is, if the patient has been on a TCA, the next drug trial should be with either an MAOI or an atypical antidepressant. If the patient has been on an atypical antidepressant, the next drug trial should be with either a TCA or an MAOI. Until recently, it had been general clinical practice almost always to use a TCA as the first drug and then to switch to a second TCA if the first one did not work before trying the patient on either an MAOI or an atypical antidepressant. Some clinicians, in fact, still follow this reasonable practice. The change in clinical practice has taken place because experience with the atypical antidepressants, such as fluoxetine (Prozac), has shown that they are as efficacious as the TCAs.

Antidepressant treatment should be maintained for at least six months or the length of a previous episode, whichever is greater. Chronic treatment may be indicated as prophylaxis against depression in patients with a history of recurrent serious depression. Antidepressants should be tapered gradually over a minimum of two weeks, or up to two months in cases with which care is particularly warranted. Although discontinuation is less critical for lithium, it is best to taper this agent over at least a week.

Failure of drug trial. If an antidepressant has been used for four weeks at maximal dosages without a therapeutic effect, the clinician should obtain a plasma level and adjust the dosage accordingly. If plasma levels are adequate, supplementation with lithium (see Section 30.2.16) or liothyronine (T_3 or L-triiodothyronine) (Cytomel) (see Section 30.2.20) should be considered.

Lithium. Lithium (900 to 1,200 mg a day, serum level between 0.6 and 0.8 mEq per liter) can be added to the antidepressant dosage for 7 to 14 days. This approach converts a significant number of antidepressant nonresponders into responders. The mechanism of action is not known, although it has been hypothesized that the lithium potentiates the serotonergic neuronal system. Some data indicate that the pretreatment with antidepressants is necessary for this effect and that starting the treatment with both drugs is not as effective.

Liothyronine. The addition of 25 to 50 μg a day of T_3 to an antidepressant regimen for 7 to 14 days also may convert antidepressant nonresponders into responders. The adverse effects of T_3 are minor but may include a headache and feeling warm. The mechanism of action for T_3 augmentation is not known, although the modulation of β-adrenergic receptors and the presence of undetectable thyroid axis abnormalities have been suggested. If T_3 augmentation is successful, the T_3 should be continued for two months and then tapered at the rate of 12.5 μg a day every three to seven days.

L-Tryptophan. L-Tryptophan, the amino acid precursor to serotonin, has been used as an adjuvant to both antidepressant drugs and lithium treatment of bipolar disorder. L-Tryptophan has also been used alone as an antidepressant and a hypnotic. Recently, L-tryptophan and L-tryptophan-containing products have been recalled in the United States because of an outbreak of eosinophilia-myalgia syndrome (EMS) associated with the use of L-tryptophan. The symptoms of EMS include fatigue, myalgia, shortness of breath, rashes, and swelling of the extremities. Congestive heart failure and death can also occur. Although several studies had showed that L-tryptophan has been an efficacious adjuvant in the treatment of mood disorders, this drug should not be used for any purpose until the problem with EMS is resolved. It appears possible that the EMS was related to a contaminant in a single manufacturing plant, but this has yet to be proved definitively.

TCA and MAOI combinations. The combination of a TCA and an MAOI is sometimes used in patients who have not been responsive to several other pharmacological treatments. This is not a treatment of first or second choice because of the high incidence of adverse effects. It is best to initiate treatment with these two drugs simultaneously at very low dosages for each and to raise the dosage slowly. Imipramine (Tofranil) or trimipramine (Surmontil) and an MAOI should not be used in combination because of the particularly high incidence of toxic effects, including restlessness, dizziness, tremulousness, muscle twitching, sweating, convulsions, hyperpyrexia, and sometimes death.

If a patient has been on a TCA, the dosage of the TCA should be quartered for five to seven days, and then the MAOI can slowly be added to the regimen. If the patient has been on an MAOI, the drug should be stopped for two weeks, and both drugs started together at that point. The reason for this latter strategy is that MAOIs irreversibly inhibit monoamine oxidase and it takes approximately two weeks for normal MAO activity levels to be achieved.

Bipolar Disorders

A variety of drugs are now available to treat bipolar disorders. Lithium-containing salts, such as lithium carbonate and citrate (see Section 30.2.16), are the major pharmacological treatments for bipolar disorders. In the past five years, anticonvulsants (carbamazepine [see Section 31.2.10] and valproic acid [see Section 30.2.24]) have also been used to treat these disorders. Levothyroxine (T_4 or thyroxine) (Levothroid) (see Section 30.2.20) is sometimes used to augment the clinical response to these drugs in patients with rapid cycling. Finally, several studies and case reports have reported calcium channel inhibitors (e.g., verapamil [Isoptin, Calan]) (see Section 30.2.9), a benzodiazepine anticonvulsant (clonazepam [Klonopin]) (see Section 30.2.5), and an α2-adrenergic agonist (clonidine) (see Section 30.2.12) to be effective treatments.

Lithium is the standard drug for the treatment of manic episodes. Most manic patients, however, require antipsychotics (or, in some instances, an antianxiety agent, such as intramuscular lorazepam [Ativan]) at the initiation of treatment to control agitation. Noncompliance with drug regimens is a major problem in the treatment of manic patients, and the clinician should always be aware of this potential reason for the lack of a therapeutic response to drug treatment.

The second-line drug in the treatment of mania is carbamazepine. Some clinicians may use carbamazepine to avoid certain side effects associated with lithium. Also, the combination of lithium and carbamazepine may be indicated for patients who do not respond to either drug alone.

Rapid cycling. One type of treatment failure is the rapid cycling of manic and depressive episodes (more than three or four a year) that are not adequately controlled by lithium treatment. Rapid cycling may respond to the addition of T_4 0.3 to 0.5 mg a day. The mechanism for this response is not known. The substitution or addition of carbamazepine for lithium may also be effective in reducing the frequency of episodes. Clorgyline, a selective MAO-A inhibitor that is not available in the United States, may be particularly effective in the treatment of rapid cycling.

Maintenance. The decision to maintain a patient on lithium prophylaxis is based on the severity of the patient's illness, the risk of adverse effects from lithium, and the quality of the patient's support systems. Maintenance serum levels of lithium can be lower than those needed for acute treatment. Such levels are usually kept between 0.6 and 0.8 mEq a liter. In addition to periodic measurements of lithium levels, serum creatinine and TSH levels should be monitored every three to six months.

References

Elkin I, Shea T, Watkins J T, Imber S D, Sotsky S M, Collins J F, Glass D R, Pilkonis P A, Leber W R, Docherty J P, Fiester S J, Parloff M B: National Institute of Mental Health treatment of depression collaborative research program: General effectiveness of treatments. Arch Gen Psychiatry *46:* 971, 1989.

Georgotas A, Cancro R, eds.: *Depression and Mania*. Elsevier, New York, 1988.

Gold M S, Herridge, P, Hapworth W E: Depression and "symptomless" autoimmune thyroiditis. Psychiatr Ann *17:* 750, 1987.

Goodwin F K, Jamison K R: *Manic-Depressive Illness*. Oxford University Press, New York, 1990.

Gurguis G N M, Meador-Woodruff J H, Haskett R F, Greden J F: Multiplicity of depressive episodes: Phenomenological and neuroendocrine correlates. Biol Psychiatry *27:* 1156, 1990.

Jeste D V, Lohr J B, Goodwin F K: Neuroanatomical studies of major affective disorders: A review and suggestions for further research. Br J Psychiatry *153:* 444, 1988.

Karasu T B: Toward a clinical model of psychotherapy for depression: II. An integrative and selective treatment approach. Am J Psychiatry *147:* 269, 1990.

Larson E W, Richelson E: Organic causes of mania. Mayo Clin Proc *63:* 906, 1988.

McGuffin P, Katz R: The genetics of depression and manic-depressive disorder. Br J Psychiatry *155:* 294, 1989.

Merikangas K R, Spence A, Kupfer D J: Linkage studies of bipolar disorder: Methodologic and analytic issues. Arch Gen Psychiatry *46:* 1137, 1989.

Nasrallah H A, Coffman J A, Olson S C: Structural brain-imaging findings in affective disorders: An overview. J Neuropsychiatry *1:* 21, 1989.

Post R M: Mood disorders: Somatic treatment. In *Comprehensive Textbook of Psychiatry,* ed 5, H I Kaplan and B J Sadock, editors, p 913. Williams & Wilkins, Baltimore, 1989.

Prien R F, Gelenberg A J: Alternatives to lithium for preventive treatment of bipolar disorder. Am J Psychiatry *146:* 840, 1989.

Rosenbaum J F, ed: Mania: Important new findings. J Clin Psychiatry *50* (12, Suppl): 2, 1989.

Sackheim H A, Prohovnik I, Moeller J R, Brown R P, Apter S, Prudic J, Devanand D P, Mukherjee S: Regional cerebral blood flow in mood disorders: I. Comparison of major depressives and normal controls at rest. Arch Gen Psychiatry *47:* 60, 1990.

Shamoian C A, ed: Depression in the elderly. Psychiatr Ann *20:* 62, 1990.

Wehr T A, Rosenthal N E: Seasonality and affective illness. Am J Psychiatry *146:* 829, 1989.

Wehr T A, Sack D A, Rosenthal N E, Cowdry R W: Rapid cycling affective disorder: Contributing factors and treatment responses in 51 patients. Am J Psychiatry *145:* 179, 1988.

Zimmerman M, Spitzer R L: Melancholia: From DSM-III to DSM-III-R. Am J Psychiatry *146:* 20, 1989.

16.2 / Dysthymia and Cyclothymia

Dysthymia and cyclothymia are sometimes referred to as subaffective disorders, a name that conveys the conceptualization of dysthymia as a less severe form of major depression and of cyclothymia as a less severe form of bipolar disorder. The revised third edition of *Diagnostic and Statistical Manual of Mental Disorders* (DSM-III-R) classifies dysthymia and cyclothymia as Axis I mood disorders.

The inclusion of dysthymia and cyclothymia within the mood disorders implies that their causes, genetic bases, prognoses, and treatment responses are similar to those of major depression and bipolar disorders. This implied similarity, however, is controversial. Some psychodynamically oriented psychiatrists believe that dysthymia and cyclothymia are more accurately conceptualized as primarily the result of incompletely resolved issues in a person's psychodynamic development.

DYSTHYMIA

Dysthymia is characterized by chronic, nonpsychotic signs and symptoms of depression that do not meet the diagnostic criteria for a major depressive episode. Dysthymia means "ill-humored," and patients with the disorder are often introverted, morose, and self-deprecating. Dysthymia does not include patients who have episodic, rather than chronic, periods of mild depression. Such syndromes of episodic dysthymia are classified as depressive disorder not otherwise specified (NOS) in DSM-III-R.

The diagnosis of dysthymia has gone by a variety of names in the past. Although each of the terms has its own history and connotations, they describe overlapping groups of patients. Dysthymia implies a temperamental dysphoria—that is, an inborn tendency to experience a depressed mood. In contrast, *neurotic depression* (also called *depressive neurosis*), implies a maladaptive, repetitive pattern of thinking and behavior resulting in depression. Patients described as having a depressive neurosis are often anxious, obsessive, and prone to somatization. *Characterological depression* implies a dysphoric mood that is integral to a person's character. *Hypochondriacal depression* refers to a condition characterized by multiple somatic complaints. Such patients may more appropriately be classified as having either somatization disorder or dysthymia.

Epidemiology

Both clinical impressions and research data suggest that dysthymia is relatively common. The prevalence is estimated to be about 3 percent of all adults, with a lifetime prevalence ranging from 2.9 to 5.4 percent in various studies. The prevalence of dysthymia in psychiatric outpatients may be as high as 25 to 30 percent. The disorder is approximately two times more common in women than in men. Additional associated epidemiological features include being unmarried and being young with a low income.

Etiology

Biological factors. Some patients with dysthymia have decreased rapid eye movement (REM) latency, a positive therapeutic response to antidepressants, and a family history of mood disorders. These clinical features suggest that at least some dysthymic patients truly have a subaffective syndrome that shares a genetic and pathophysiological basis with major depression.

Psychosocial factors. In contrast to the theories that suggest that early-onset dysthymia represents the expression of an inborn temperament, psychodynamic theories suggest that dysthymia results from faulty personality and ego development, culminating in difficulty adapting to adolescence and young adulthood. Karl Abraham, for example, suggested that the conflicts of depression center on oral- and anal-sadistic traits. Anal traits include excessive orderliness, guilt, and concern for others; anal traits are postulated to be a defense against preoccupation with anal matters and with disorganization, hostility, and self-preoccupation. A major defense used is reaction formation. Low self-esteem, anhedonia, and introversion are often associated with the depressive character.

In *Mourning and Melancholia* Sigmund Freud asserted that a vulnerability to depression could be caused by an interpersonal disappointment very early in life, which leads to ambivalent love relationships as an adult, and that real or threatened losses in adult life then trigger depression. Persons prone to depression are orally dependent and require constant narcissistic gratification. If deprived of such love, affection, and care, they become clinically depressed. When these persons experience a real loss, they internalize or introject the lost object and turn their anger on it and thus on themselves.

The cognitive theory of depression holds that a disparity between actual and fantasized situations leads to diminished self-esteem and a sense of helplessness. One study of dysthymic persons reported increased neurotic features, both extra- and intrapunitive tendencies, and decreased self-esteem.

Clinical Features

The clinical signs and symptoms are specified in DSM-III-R (Table 16.2-1). The specifics of the mental status examination are similar to those for major depression. Dysthymic persons may have symptoms of depression almost as severe as those for major depression, although the duration of these symptoms may be insufficient to warrant a diagnosis of a major depressive episode. Dysthymia is conceptualized as a chronic disorder, not an episodic disorder with extended asymptomatic periods. Nevertheless, dysthymic persons can have temporal variations in the severity of their symptoms. The major symptom is a depressed mood, characterized by feeling sad, blue, down in the dumps, or low and by a lack of interest in usual activ-

Table 16.2-1
Diagnostic Criteria for Dysthymia

A. Depressed mood (or can be irritable mood in children and adolescents) for most of the day, more days than not, as indicated either by subjective account or observation by others, for at least two years (one year for children and adolescents).

B. Presence, while depressed, of at least two of the following:
(1) poor appetite or overeating
(2) insomnia or hypersomnia
(3) low energy or fatigue
(4) low self-esteem
(5) poor concentration or difficulty making decisions
(6) feelings of hopelessness

C. During a two-year period (one-year for children and adolescents) of the disturbance, never without the symptoms in A for more than two months at a time.

D. No evidence of an unequivocal major depressive episode during the first two years (one year for children and adolescents) of the disturbance.

Note: There may have been a previous major depressive episode, provided there was a full remission (no significant signs or symptoms for six months) before development of the dysthymia. In addition, after these two years (one year in children or adolescents) of dysthymia, there may be superimposed episodes of major depression, in which case both diagnoses are given.

E. Has never had a manic episode or an unequivocal hypomanic episode.

F. Not superimposed on a chronic psychotic disorder, such as schizophrenia or delusional disorder.

G. It cannot be established that an organic factor initiated and maintained the disturbance (e.g., prolonged administration of an antihypertensive medication).

Specify primary or **secondary type:**

Primary type: the mood disturbance is not related to a preexisting, chronic, nonmood, Axis I or Axis III disorder (e.g., anorexia nervosa, somatization disorder, a psychoactive substance dependence disorder, an anxiety disorder, or rheumatoid arthritis).

Secondary type: the mood disturbance is apparently related to a preexisting, chronic, nonmood, Axis I or Axis III disorder.

Specify early onset or **late onset:**

Early onset: onset of the disturbance before age 21

Late onset: onset of the disturbance at age 21 or later

Table from DSM-III-R, *Diagnostic and Statistical Manual of Mental Disorders,* ed 3, revised. Copyright American Psychiatric Association, Washington, DC, 1987, with permission.

ities. Patients with dysthymia can often be sarcastic, nihilistic, brooding, demanding, and complaining. They can be tense and rigid and resistant to therapeutic interventions, even though they may come regularly to appointments. As a result, the clinician may feel angry toward the patient and may even disregard the patient's complaints. By definition, dysthymic patients do not have any psychotic symptoms.

Associated symptoms include changes in appetite and sleep patterns, low self-esteem, loss of energy, psychomotor retardation, decreased sexual drive, and obsessive preoccupation with health matters. Patients may complain that they have difficulty concentrating and may report that their school or work performance is suffering. Pessimism, hopelessness, and helplessness may cause dysthymic patients to be seen as masochistic. If the pessimism is directed outward, however, the patients may rant against the world and complain that they have been poorly treated by relatives, children, parents, colleagues, and the "system."

Impairment in social functioning is sometimes the reason the patient seeks psychiatric help. Dysthymic patients may have marital problems resulting from an inability to sustain emotional intimacy or from sexual dysfunction (e.g., impotence). Because of social withdrawal and difficulty concentrating, patients' performance at work may suffer. They may miss many workdays and social occasions as a result of physical illness. Consequently, divorce, unemployment, and school failure are common problems for these patients.

Alcohol and drug abuse. Alcohol and drug abuse can present a diagnostic dilemma to the clinician. Not only can dysthymia result in alcohol and drug abuse, but alcohol and drug abuse can result in symptoms that are indistinguishable from those of dysthymia. Treatment of a primary dysthymia may result in the disappearance of the drug dependency syndrome.

Course and Prognosis

Most commonly, dysthymia has an insidious onset, starting before age 25 in more than 50 percent of all patients. Patients have often had symptoms for more than 10 years before they first seek psychiatric help. Approximately 25 percent of all dysthymic patients never attain a complete recovery. The course of dysthymia, however, does vary with the specific type. The course of secondary dysthymia depends on the response to treatment of the primary disorder, although symptoms of dysthymia occasionally remain even after the primary disorder has been cured.

Early-onset dysthymia may be so chronic that patients accept the symptoms as part of their natures. Early-onset dysthymia, especially with a positive family history for mood disorder, may eventually evolve into a major mood disorder. Studies of patients classified as having depressive neurosis indicate that approximately 20 percent go on to major depression, 15 percent go on to major depressive episodes with hypomanic episodes (bipolar II), and less than 5 percent go on to bipolar disorder. In addition to a family history of mood disorder, a positive therapeutic response to antidepressants increases the possibility that a major mood disorder will develop in the future. Late-onset dysthymia has a variable onset, prognosis, and course. All patients with dysthymia are at an increased risk for anxiety disorders, psychoactive substance use disorders, and major depression.

Diagnosis and Types

The diagnosis of dysthymia is made on the basis of specific inclusion and exclusion criteria in DSM-III-R

(Table 16.2-1). The symptoms of criterion A must be present for at least two years (one year in children and adolescents) without an asymptomatic period of longer than two months. Although a major depressive episode may not be present during the first two years of dysthymic symptoms, dysthymia can be diagnosed if a prior major depressive episode has been in full remission for six months before the development of dysthymic symptoms. If a major depressive episode follows two years or more of dysthymic symptoms, then the patient is given both diagnoses. The concurrent appearance of dysthymia and major depression has been called double depression by some clinicians. The patients are likely to have more frequent and severe depressive episodes than are major depression patients who do not have a diagnosis of dysthymia. Exclusion criteria include a past history of a manic or hypomanic episode, psychotic symptoms, and the presence of residual schizophrenia. If the dysthymic symptoms are sustained by a specific organic factor or drug, a diagnosis of dysthymia is excluded. Primary and secondary types and early and late onset are also specifically defined.

Differential Diagnosis

Symptoms identical to those of dysthymia may be present in several organic and idiopathic disorders. When a patient presents with a dysthymic symptom pattern, especially if the symptoms have not been present for two years, all the diagnoses listed in Table 16.2-2 should be considered.

Treatment

Individual insight-oriented psychotherapy. Individual insight-oriented psychotherapy is the most common treatment modality for dysthymia, and many clinicians believe this to be the treatment of choice; however, psychotherapy is sometimes combined with medication. This psychotherapeutic approach attempts to relate the development and maintenance of depressive symptoms and maladaptive personality features to unresolved conflicts from early childhood. Insight into depressive equivalents (such as substance abuse) or into childhood disappointments as antecedents to adult depression can be gained through treatment. Ambivalent current relationships with parents, friends, and others in the patients' current life are examined. The patients' understanding of how they try to gratify an excessive need for outside approval to counter low self-esteem and a harsh superego is an important goal in such insight-oriented therapies.

Interpersonal therapy for depression. In interpersonal therapy for depression (IPT) the patient's current interpersonal experiences and ways of coping with stress are examined with the goal of reducing depressive symptoms and improving self-esteem. IPT consists of about 12 to 16 weekly sessions and can be combined with antidepressant medication.

Behavior therapy. Behavior therapy for depression is based on the theory that depression is caused by a loss of positive reinforcement as a result of separation, death, or sudden environmental change. The various treatment methods focus on specific goals to increase activity, to provide pleasant experiences, and to teach patients how to relax. The alteration of personal behavior in depressed patients is believed to be the most effective way to change the associated depressed thoughts and feelings. Behavior therapy is often used to treat the learned helplessness of some patients, who seem to meet every life challenge with a sense of impotence.

Cognitive therapy. Cognitive therapy is a technique in which patients are taught new ways of thinking and behaving to replace faulty negative attitudes about themselves, the world, and the future. It is a short-term therapy program oriented toward current problems and their resolution. See Section 29.8 for an expanded discussion of this approach.

Family and group therapies. Family therapy may help both the patient and the family deal with the symptoms of this disorder, especially when a biologically based subaffective syndrome seems to be present. Group therapy may help withdrawn patients learn new ways to overcome their interpersonal problems in social situations.

Hospitalization. Hospitalization is usually not indicated for dysthymic patients; however, the presence of particularly severe symptoms, marked social or professional incapacitation, and suicidal ideation are all indications for hospitalization.

Pharmacotherapy. Many clinicians believe that dysthymia is not responsive to psychopharmacological treatment. However, a history of unsuccessful treatment by psychotherapy alone, the presence of severe symptoms that interfere with work and social functioning, a family history of mood disorder, decreased REM latency on a sleep electroencephalogram (EEG), and, possibly, abnormal findings on neuroendocrine tests (e.g., dexamethasone-suppression test [DST]) should encourage the clinician to attempt a trial of drug therapy as an adjuvant to psychotherapy.

Antidepressants (possibly with lithium or liothyronine [T_3 or L-triiodothyronine] [Cytomel] supplementation) have been the drugs of choice. Fluoxetine (Prozac), how-

Table 16.2-2
Differential Diagnosis for Dysthymic Symptoms

- Organic causes
  - Medical illness (e.g., cancer, cardiac disorder, chronic fatigue syndrome)
  - Prescription drug treatment
  - Drug dependency syndrome
- Major depression
- Bipolar disorder, depressed or mixed type
- Cyclothymia
- Generalized anxiety disorder
- Anorexia nervosa
- Bulimia nervosa
- Obsessive-compulsive disorder
- Ego-dystonic homosexuality
- Personality disorders
  - Borderline
  - Dependent
  - Histrionic
- Somatization disorder

ever, is increasingly being used as the drug of first choice because of its ease of administration and relative lack of serious or disturbing adverse effects. Monoamine oxidase inhibitors (MAOIs) may be the drugs of first choice in the presence of hypersomnia, hyperphagia, marked anxiety, and multiple somatic complaints—a syndrome sometimes referred to as atypical depression or hysteroid dysphoria.

CYCLOTHYMIA

Cyclothymia is generally considered to be a mild form of bipolar disorder. The conceptualization of cyclothymia as a disorder of inborn temperament with a strong biological basis is somewhat less controversial than the parallel view for dysthymia. Some psychiatrists, however, see certain cyclothymic patients as having a disorder resulting primarily from chaotic object relations early in life.

The history of cyclothymia is based to some extent on the observations of Emil Kraepelin and later Kurt Schneider that one-third to two-thirds of patients with mood disorders exhibited personality disorders. The four types of personality disorders described by Kraepelin were depressive (i.e., gloomy) manic (i.e., cheerful and uninhibited), irritable (i.e., labile and explosive), and cyclothymic. Kraepelin described the irritable personality as the simultaneous presence of the depressive and manic personalities and the cyclothymic personality as the alternation of the manic and depressive personalities.

Epidemiology

The lifetime prevalence of cyclothymia has been reported as less than 1 percent. This figure, however, is likely to be an underestimation because of the tendency for cyclothymic persons not to come to the attention of psychiatrists. Other estimates are that cyclothymia represents 3 to 10 percent of all psychiatric outpatients, including many patients with interpersonal or marital difficulties. The female-to-male ratio is approximately 3 to 2, and approximately 50 to 75 percent of all cases have an onset between ages 15 and 25.

Etiology

Biological factors. Considerable research data support the hypothesis that cyclothymia is a subaffective disorder related to bipolar disorder. Approximately 30 percent of all cyclothymic patients have positive family histories for bipolar disorder; this rate is similar to that for patients with bipolar disorder. Moreover, the pedigrees of families with bipolar disorder often contain generations of bipolar disorder linked by a generation with cyclothymia. Conversely, the prevalence of cyclothymia in the relatives of bipolar disorder patients is much higher than the prevalence of cyclothymia either in relatives of patients with other psychiatric disorders or in mentally healthy persons. The observations that approximately one-third of patients with cyclothymia subsequently have major mood disorders, that they are particularly sensitive to antidepressant-induced hypomania, and that approximately 60 percent respond clinically to lithium add further support to the conceptualization of cyclothymia as a mild or attenuated form of bipolar disorder.

Psychosocial factors. Most psychodynamic theories postulate that the development of cyclothymia lies in traumas and fixations during the oral stage of infant development. Freud hypothesized that the cyclothymic state was an attempt by the ego to overcome a harsh and punitive superego. Hypomania is explained psychodynamically as occurring when a depressed person throws off the burden of an overly harsh superego, resulting in a lack of self-criticism and an absence of inhibitions. The major defense mechanism in hypomania is denial, by which the patient avoids external problems and internal feelings of depression.

Clinical Features

Patients with cyclothymia can present with all the symptoms of bipolar disorder in depressed, manic, and mixed states (Table 16.2-3). The details of the mental status examination are similar to those described for depressive and manic episodes in the previous section. The symptoms can often be almost as severe as in bipolar disorder but may not be of sufficient duration to meet the criteria for that disorder.

Approximately one-half of all cyclothymic patients have depression as their major symptom, and these patients are most likely to seek psychiatric help while depressed. Some cyclothymic patients have primarily hypomanic symptoms and are less likely to consult a psychiatrist than the primarily depressed patients. Rarely, patients suffer from equally long periods of mania and depression. Almost all

Table 16.2-3
Diagnostic Criteria for Cyclothymia

A. For at least two years (one year for children and adolescents), presence of numerous hypomanic episodes (all of the criteria for a manic episode, except criterion C that indicates marked impairment) and numerous periods with depressed mood or loss of interest or pleasure that did not meet criterion A of major depressive episode.

B. During a two-year period (one year in children and adolescents) of the disturbance, never without hypomanic or depressive symptoms for more than two months at a time.

C. No clear evidence of a major depressive episode or manic episode during the first two years of the disturbance (or one year in children and adolescents).

Note: After this minimum period of cyclothymia, there may be superimposed manic or major depressive episodes, in which case the additional diagnosis of bipolar disorder or bipolar disorder NOS should be given.

D. Not superimposed on a chronic psychotic disorder, such as schizophrenia or delusional disorder.

E. It cannot be established that an organic factor initiated and maintained the disturbance (e.g., repeated intoxication from drugs or alcohol).

Table from DSM-III-R, *Diagnostic and Statistical Manual of Mental Disorders,* ed 3 revised. Copyright American Psychiatric Association, Washington, DC, 1987, with permission.

cyclothymic patients have periods of mixed symptoms with marked irritability.

Most cyclothymic patients seen by psychiatrists have not succeeded in their professional and social lives because of this disorder. A few cyclothymic patients, however, have become high achievers who have worked especially long hours and have required little sleep. The ability of some persons to successfully control the symptoms of this disorder depends on multiple individual, social, and cultural differences.

The lives of most cyclothymic patients are very difficult. The cycles of cyclothymia tend to be much shorter than those in bipolar disorder. The changes in mood are irregular and abrupt, sometimes occurring within hours. Occasional periods of normal mood and the unpredictable nature of the mood changes cause the patients a great deal of stress. Patients often feel out of control of their moods. In irritable, mixed periods, they may become involved in unprovoked disagreements with friends, family, and coworkers.

Although many patients seek psychiatric help for depression, their problems are often related to the chaos that their manic episodes have caused. The clinician must consider a diagnosis of cyclothymia when a patient presents with what may seem to be sociopathic behavioral problems. Marital difficulties and instability of relationships are common complaints because cyclothymic patients are often promiscuous and irritable while in manic and mixed states. Although there are anecdotal reports of increased productivity and creativity while patients are hypomanic, most clinicians report that their patients become disorganized and ineffective in work and school during these periods. Alcohol and drug abuse are common in cyclothymic patients, who use these agents either to self-medicate (with alcohol, benzodiazepines, and marijuana) or to achieve even further stimulation (with cocaine, amphetamines, and hallucinogens) when they are manic. Approximately 5 to 10 percent of all cyclothymic patients have drug dependency disorders. Cyclothymic persons often have a history of multiple geographic moves, past involvements in different religious cults, and dilettantism. The following is a case example of cyclothymia:

A 29-year-old car salesman was referred by his current girlfriend, a psychiatric nurse, who suspected that he had a mood disorder, even though the patient was reluctant to admit that he was a moody person. According to him, since the age of 14 he had experienced repeated alternating cycles that he termed "good times and bad times." During a "bad" period, usually lasting four to seven days, he slept 10 to 14 hours daily and lacked energy, confidence, and motivation—"just vegetating," as he put it. Often he abruptly shifted, characteristically on waking up in the morning, to a three- to four-day stretch of overconfidence, heightened social awareness, promiscuity, and sharpened thinking—"things would flash in my mind." At such times he indulged in alcohol to enhance the experience but also to help him sleep. Occasionally the "good" periods lasted 7 to 10 days but culminated in irritable and hostile outbursts, which often heralded the transition back to another period of bad days. He admitted to frequent use of marijuana, which he claimed helped him "adjust" to daily routines.

In school, As and Bs had alternated with Cs and Ds, with the result that the patient was considered a bright student whose performance was mediocre overall because of unstable motivation. As a car salesman, he had shown uneven performance, with good days canceling out the bad days; yet even during his good days he was sometimes perilously argumentative with customers and lost sales that appeared sure. Although considered a charming man in many social circles, he alienated friends when he was hostile and irritable. He typically accumulated social obligations during the bad days and took care of them all at once on the first day of a good period.

Discussion. This patient had had numerous periods during the preceding two years in which he had had some symptoms characteristic of both the depressive and the manic syndromes. Characteristic of the good days were overconfidence, heightened social awareness, promiscuity, and sharpened thinking. Although those periods came close to meeting the criteria for a manic episode, they were not sufficiently severe to justify a diagnosis of bipolar disorder. Similarly, the bad days—characterized by oversleeping and lack of energy, confidence, and motivation—were not of sufficient severity and duration to meet the criteria for a major depressive episode. Moreover, the brief cycles followed each other with intermittent irregularity on a chronic basis. Therefore, the appropriate diagnosis was cyclothymia.

Course and Prognosis

Cyclothymia most often has an insidious onset in the late teens and early 20s. Retrospectively, cyclothymic patients are often described as having been sensitive, hyperactive, or moody as young children. The presence of cyclothymia during late adolescence and early adulthood may cause disruptive relationships with family and friends and may result in poor performance in school and work. The reactions of patients to such a disorder in life vary; patients with adaptive coping strategies or ego defenses have better outcomes than patients with poor coping strategies. Approximately 40 to 50 percent of all cyclothymic patients treated with antidepressants experience hypomanic or manic episodes. About one-third of all cyclothymic patients go on to a major mood disorder, usually bipolar II—that is, major depressive episodes with hypomanic periods.

Diagnosis

DSM-III-R contains specific inclusion and exclusion criteria for cyclothymia (Table 16.2-3). A two-year period of numerous episodes of abnormally elevated, expansive, or irritable mood and numerous periods of depressed mood are required, with no asymptomatic period lasting longer than two months. The symptoms must not meet the criteria for either a major depressive episode or manic episode. By definition, no psychotic features are present. Nor may the symptoms be sustained by a specific organic factor or substance.

Differential Diagnosis

Organic mental disorders (e.g., seizures) and drug abuse (e.g., cocaine, amphetamines, steroids) need to be ruled out as causes of a cyclothymic presentation. Borderline, antisocial, histrionic, and narcissistic personality disorders should also be considered in the differential diagnosis. A pattern of chaotic behavior and unstable relationships, which may appear to meet the criteria for borderline personality disorder, may actually be a case of cyclothymia, which would respond to lithium treatment. Attention-deficit hyperactivity disorder can be hard to differentiate from cyclothymia in children and adolescents. A trial of stimulants helps most patients with attention-deficit hyperactivity disorder and exacerbates the symptoms of most patients with cyclothymia.

Treatment

Lithium is the mainstay of treatment of cyclothymia. Approximately 60 percent of all cyclothymic patients respond with lithium serum levels in the 0.7 to 1.0 mEq a liter range. Treatment of depressed cyclothymic patients with antidepressants should be done with caution because of their increased susceptibility to antidepressant-induced hypomanic or manic episodes.

Although individual psychotherapy alone is generally not considered adequate treatment for cyclothymia, it is often useful in helping patients to be more aware of their mood swings and the consequences of their acts on others. Because of the chronic nature of their mental disorder, patients often require lifelong treatment. Family and group therapy may be supportive, educational, and therapeutic for these patients and those in their support systems.

References

Akiskal H S, Khani M K, Scott-Strauss A: Cyclothymic temperamental disorders. Psychiatr Clin North Am *2:* 527, 1979.

Alnaes R, Torsensen S: Personality and personality disorders among patients with major depression in combination with dysthymic or cyclothymic disorders. Acta Psychiatr Scand *79:* 363, 1989.

Chodoff P: The depressive personality: A critical review. Arch Gen Psychiatry *27:* 666, 1972.

Fichtner C G, Grossman L S, Harrow M, Goldberg J F, Klein D N: Cyclothymic mood swings in the course of affective disorders and schizophrenia. Am J Psychiatry *146:* 1149, 1989.

Frances A, Kocsis J, Marin D, Manning D, Markowitz J, Mason B, Widiser T: Diagnostic criteria for dysthymic disorder. Psychopharmacol Bull *25:* 325, 1989.

Hickie I, Lloyd A, Wakefield D, Parker G: The psychiatric status of patients with chronic fatigue syndrome. Br J Psychiatry *156:* 534, 1990.

Keller M B, Lavori P W, Endicott J: "Double depression:" Two-year follow-up. Am J Psychiatry *140:* 689, 1983.

Klein D N, Depue R A, Slater J F: Cyclothymia in the adolescent offspring of parents with bipolar affective disorder. J Abnorm Psychol *94:* 115, 1985.

Klein D N, Depue R A, Slater J F: Inventory identification of cyclothymia: IX. Validation in offspring of bipolar I patients. Arch Gen Psychiatry *43:* 441, 1986.

Kocsis J H, Frances A J: A critical discussion of DSM-III dysthymic disorder. Am J Psychiatry *144:* 1524, 1987.

Peselow E D, Dunner D L, Fieve R R, Lautin A: Lithium prophylaxis of depression in unipolar, bipolar II, and cyclothymic patients. Am J Psychiatry *139:* 747, 1982.

Weissman M M, Leaf P J, Bruce M L, Florio L: The epidemiology of dysthymia in five communities: Rates, risks, comorbidity, and treatment. Am J Psychiatry *145:* 815, 1988.

Yerevanian B I, Akiskal H S: "Neurotic," characterological, and dysthymic depressions. Psychiatr Clin North Am *2:* 595, 1979.

Anxiety Disorders (or Anxiety and Phobic Neuroses)

17.1 / Normal and Pathological Anxiety

The current complexity of civilization, the rapidity of change, and the loss of some traditional religious and familial values are creating new conflicts and anxieties for individuals and society. Attention is now being paid to the amount, type, and effect of anxiety, as reflected in current medical practice. Indeed, anxiety is integral to psychosomatic medicine and psychiatric theory and practice. Even in patients with structural damage, anxiety caused by feelings of incompetence, inadequacy, and helplessness is a prominent feature of the disturbance.

When evaluating a patient with anxiety, the clinician must distinguish between normal and pathological types and levels of anxiety. On a practical level, pathological anxiety is differentiated from normal anxiety by the belief of patients, their families, their friends, and the clinician that pathological anxiety is, in fact, present. Such an assessment is based on the patients' reported internal state, their behavior, and their ability to function. A patient with pathological anxiety requires a complete neuropsychiatric evaluation and an individually tailored treatment plan. The clinician must be aware that anxiety can be a component of many medical conditions and other psychiatric disorders, especially depression.

NORMAL ANXIETY

Anxiety is a diffuse, highly unpleasant, often vague feeling of apprehension, accompanied by one or more bodily sensations—for example, an empty feeling in the pit of the stomach, tightness in the chest, a pounding heart, perspiration, headache, or the sudden urge to void. Restlessness and a desire to move around are also common.

Fear and Anxiety

Anxiety is an alerting signal; it warns of impending danger and enables the person to take measures to deal with a threat. Fear, a similar alerting signal, is differentiated from anxiety as follows: Fear is in response to a threat that is known, external, definite, or nonconflictual in origin; anxiety is in response to a threat that is unknown, internal, vague, or conflictual in origin.

The distinction between fear and anxiety arose by accident. The early translators of Sigmund Freud mistranslated *angst,* the German word for fear, as anxiety. Freud himself generally ignored the distinction that associates anxiety with a repressed, unconscious object and fear with a known, external object. The distinction may be difficult to make because fear may also be due to an unconscious, repressed, internal object displaced to another object in the external world. For example, a boy may be afraid of dogs because he is actually afraid of his father and unconsciously associates his father with dogs. As another example, a boy may be vaguely apprehensive about leaving his home because he has experienced sexual excitement while witnessing dogs mating in the street and now unconsciously links dogs with his guilt-laden sexual feelings.

According to psychoanalytic formulations, the separation of fear and anxiety is psychologically justifiable. The emotion caused by a rapidly approaching car as one crosses a street differs from the vague discomfort one may experience when one meets new people in a strange setting. The main psychological difference between the two emotional responses is in the acuteness of fear and the chronicity of anxiety. Charles Darwin pointed out that the word "fear" is derived from words meaning what is sudden and dangerous. Duration also seems to be vital in the neurophysiological phenomena of anxiety and fear. In 1896 Darwin gave the following psychophysiological description of acute fear merging into terror.

> Fear is often preceded by astonishment, and is so far akin to it, that both lead to the senses of sight and learning being instantly aroused. In both cases the eyes and mouth are widely opened, and the eyebrows raised. The frightened man at the first stands like a statue motionless and breathless, or crouches down as if instinctively to escape observation. The heart beats quickly and violently, so that it palpitates or knocks against the ribs; but it is very doubtful whether it then works more efficiently than usual, so as to send a greater supply of blood to all parts of the body; for the skin instantly becomes pale, as during incipient faintness. This paleness of the surface, however, is probably in large part, or exclusively, due to the vasomotor centre being affected in such a manner as to cause the contraction of the small arteries of the skin. That the skin is much affected under the sense of great fear, we see in the

marvelous and inexplicable manner in which perspiration immediately exudes from it. This exudation is all the more remarkable, as the surface is then cold, and hence the term a cold sweat; whereas, the sudorific glands are properly excited into action when the surface is heated. The hairs also on the skin stand erect; and the superficial muscles shiver. In connection with the disturbed action of the heart, the breathing is hurried. The salivary glands act imperfectly; the mouth becomes dry, and is often opened and shut. I have also noticed that under slight fear there is a strong tendency to yawn. One of the best-marked symptoms is the trembling of all the muscles of the body; and this is often first seen in the lips. From this cause, and from the dryness of the mouth, the voice becomes husky or indistinct, or may altogether fail. . . .

As fear increases into an agony of terror, we behold, as under all violent emotions, diversified results. The heart beats wildly or may fail to act and faintness ensues; there is a deathlike pallor; the breathing is labored; the wings of the nostrils are widely dilated; there is a gasping and convulsive motion of the lips, a tremor on the hollow cheek, a gulping and catching of the throat; the uncovered and protruding eyeballs are fixed on the object of terror; or they may roll restlessly from side to side. The pupils are said to be enormously dilated. All the muscles of the body may become rigid, or may be thrown into convulsive movements. The hands are alternately clenched and opened, often with a twitching movement. The arms may be protruded, as if to avert some dreadful danger, or may be thrown wildly over the head. . . . In other cases there is a sudden and uncontrollable tendency to headlong flight; and so strong is this, that the boldest soldiers may be seized with a sudden panic.

Individual patterns of anxiety vary widely. Some patients have cardiovascular symptoms, such as palpitation and sweating; some have gastrointestinal symptoms, such as nausea, vomiting, feeling of emptiness, butterflies in the stomach, gas pains, and even diarrhea; some have urinary frequency; and some have shallow breathing and tightness in the chest. All the above are visceral reactions. However, in some patients muscle tension prevails, and they complain of muscle tightness or of spasm, headache, and wry neck.

Stress, Conflict, and Anxiety

Whether an event is perceived as stressful depends on the nature of the event and on the resources, the defenses, and the coping mechanisms of the person. These all involve the ego, a collective abstraction that refers to the processes by which a person perceives, thinks, and acts on external events or internal drives. A person whose ego is functioning properly is in adaptive balance with both external and internal worlds; if it is not functioning properly and the imbalance continues long enough, the person has chronic anxiety. The time required to establish a psychoneurosis varies widely among human beings.

Whether the imbalance is external, between the pressures of the outside world and the patient's ego, or internal, between the patient's impulses (e.g., aggressive, sexual, or dependent) and conscience, the imbalance produces a conflict. Conflicts caused by external events are usually termed *interpersonal*, whereas those caused by internal events are called *intrapsychic* or *intrapersonal*. A combination of the two is possible, as in the case of the underling who has an excessively demanding or critical boss and who must control his impulse to hit the boss on the head for fear of losing his job. Interpersonal and intrapsychic conflicts are, in fact, usually combined because human beings are social animals and their main conflicts are with other people.

Conflict seems to be another essential ingredient of anxiety; but its absence is not a requisite for fear, as conflict is present in a special type of fear called phobia. In the genesis of experimental neurosis, conflict is a necessity. Conflict also exists when sexual arousal is prevented or interfered with, so that a strong excitation cannot be discharged, or when an attack of rage is not executed because of an inhibition of movement.

The cause of chronic anxiety can be summarized in the following way. Repeated attacks of fear—or a single attack in exceptional cases, as in persons with posttraumatic stress disorder or in those with certain phobias—provide the chronic stress to produce intense and long-lasting autonomic neuroendocrine reactivity, accompanied at the psychological level by conflict. This pattern results in chronic anxiety.

Psychological and Cognitive Symptoms of Anxiety

The experience of anxiety has two components: (1) the awareness of the physiological sensations (such as palpitation, sweating, butterflies in the stomach, tightness in the chest, shaking knees, and quavering voice) and (2) the awareness of being nervous or frightened. The anxiety may be increased by a feeling of shame—"Others will recognize that I am frightened." Many persons are astonished to find that others are not cognizant of their anxiety or, if they are, do not appreciate its intensity.

In addition to the motor and visceral effects of anxiety, its effects on thinking, perception, and learning should not be overlooked. Anxiety tends to produce confusion and distortions of perception, not only of time and space but of people and the meaning of events. These distortions can interfere with learning by lowering concentration, reducing recall, and impairing the ability to relate one item to another (association).

An important aspect of emotions is their selectivity. Anxious persons are apt to select certain items in their environment and overlook others in their effort to prove that they are justified in considering the situation frightening and in responding accordingly. If they falsely justify their fear, their anxieties are augmented by the selective response, setting up a vicious circle of anxiety, distorted perception, and increased anxiety. If, alternatively, they falsely reassure themselves by selective thinking, appropriate anxieties may be reduced, and they may then fail to take the necessary precautions.

Adaptive Functions of Anxiety

As an alerting signal, anxiety can be considered to be basically the same emotion as fear. It warns of an external or internal threat; it has lifesaving qualities. At a lower level, anxiety warns of threats of bodily damage, pain, helplessness, possible punishment, or frustration of social or bodily needs; of separation from loved ones; of a menace to one's success or status; and ultimately of threats to one's unity or wholeness. In this way it prompts the organism to take the necessary steps to prevent the threat or at least to lessen its consequences. A few examples of warding off threats in daily life include getting down to the hard work of preparing for an examination, dodging a ball thrown at one's head, sneaking into the dormitory after curfew to prevent punishment, and running to catch the last commuter train. Anxiety prevents damage by alerting the person to carry out certain acts that forestall the danger.

Because it is clearly to one's advantage to respond with anxiety in certain threatening situations, one can speak of normal anxiety in contrast to abnormal or pathological anxiety. Anxiety is normal for the infant who is threatened by separation from parents or by loss of love, for children on their first day in school, for adolescents on their first date, for adults when they contemplate old age and death, and for anyone who is faced with illness. Anxiety is a normal accompaniment of growth, of change, of experiencing something new and untried, and of finding one's own identity and meaning in life. Pathological anxiety, by contrast, is an inappropriate response to a given stimulus by virtue of either its intensity or its duration.

Anxiety usually leads to action designed to remove or reduce a threat. This action may be constructive, in which case a person uses coping mechanisms if the action is mainly conscious or deliberate (such as studying for an examination) or defense mechanisms if behavior is largely determined by unconscious forces (such as repressing or pushing out of awareness a threatening impulse or idea).

A defense mechanism can be adaptive or nonadaptive, depending on the consequences. Repression is used many times in the course of a person's life to achieve harmony with environment and self. Only if symptoms of pathological behavior result can repression or any other defense mechanism be considered abnormal. For a summary of common defense mechanisms, see Table 6.1-2 in Section 6.1, "Sigmund Freud: Founder of Classical Psychoanalysis."

PATHOLOGICAL ANXIETY

DSM-III-R Anxiety Disorders

Pathological anxiety can be a symptom of an organic anxiety disorder, an adjustment disorder with anxious mood, or an anxiety disorder. The revised third edition of *Diagnostic and Statistical Manual of Mental Disorders* (DSM-III-R) anxiety disorders include panic disorder, phobias (agoraphobia, social, and simple), obsessive-compulsive disorder, posttraumatic stress disorder, and generalized anxiety disorder. There is also a diagnosis of anxiety disorder not otherwise specified (NOS) for disorders involving prominent anxiety or phobic avoidance that are not classifiable as a specific anxiety disorder or as an adjustment disorder with anxious mood. The lifetime prevalence of the anxiety disorders in the United States is estimated to be between 10 and 15 percent. This group of disorders is classified together because anxiety is theorized to be the fundamental symptom in all those syndromes. However, the fact that these disorders respond differentially to pharmacotherapy suggests that the DSM-III-R anxiety disorders represent a heterogeneous group of diseases.

Etiology

Three major schools of psychological theory—psychoanalytic, behavioral, and existential—have contributed theories regarding the causes of anxiety. Each of these theories has both conceptual and practical utility in the treatment of patients with anxiety disorders.

Psychoanalytic theories. The evolution of the theories of Sigmund Freud regarding anxiety can be traced from his 1895 paper *Obsessions and Phobias* to a later paper, *Studies in Hysteria,* and finally to his 1926 paper *Inhibitions, Symptoms, and Anxiety*. In this last paper, Freud proposes that anxiety is a signal to the ego that an unacceptable drive is pressing for conscious representation and discharge. As a signal, anxiety arouses the ego to take defensive action against the pressures from within. If anxiety rises above the low level of intensity characteristic of its function as a signal, it may emerge with all the fury of a panic attack. Ideally, the use of repression alone should result in a restoration of psychological equilibrium without symptom formation, because effective repression completely contains the drives and their associated affects and fantasies by rendering them unconscious. If repression is unsuccessful as a defense, other defense mechanisms (such as conversion, displacement, and regression) may result in symptom formation, thus producing the picture of a classic neurotic disorder (such as hysteria, phobia, and obsessive-compulsive neurosis). The classification in DSM-III-R of the psychoanalytically defined neurotic disorders attempts to maintain an atheoretical stance (Table 17.1-1). Thus, rather than classifying all the classic neurotic disorders as anxiety disorders, as might be suggested by the psychoanalytic model, DSM-III-R classifies each disorder according to its primary symptoms.

Within psychoanalytic theory, anxiety is seen as falling into four major categories, depending on the nature of the feared consequences: superego anxiety, castration anxiety, separation anxiety, and id or impulse anxiety. These varieties of anxiety are believed to develop at various points along the continuum of early growth and development. *Id* or *impulse anxiety* is seen as being related to the primitive, diffuse discomforts of infants when they feel overwhelmed with needs and stimuli over which their helpless state provides no control. *Separation anxiety* refers back to the stage of somewhat older but still preoedipal children, who fear the loss of love or even abandonment by their parents if they fail to control and direct

Table 17.1-1
Comparison of Psychoanalytic Neuroses with Classification of Neuroses in DSM-III-R

Neurosis (Classical)	DSM-III-R Classification
Anxiety	Generalized anxiety disorder
Phobic	Agoraphobia, simple and social phobias
Obsessive-compulsive	Obsessive-compulsive disorder
Depressive	Dysthymia
Hysterical (conversion)	Conversion disorder
Hysterical (dissociative)	Depersonalization disorder
Hypochondriacal	Hypochondriasis
Paraphilic	Sexual disorders

their impulses in conformity with their parents' standards and demands. The fantasies of castration that characterize the oedipal child, particularly in relation to the child's developing sexual impulses, are reflected in the *castration anxiety* of the adult. *Superego anxiety* is the direct result of the final development of the superego that marks the passing of the Oedipus complex and the advent of the prepubertal period of latency.

There are differences of opinion in psychoanalysis about the sources and nature of anxiety. Otto Rank, for example, traced the genesis of all anxiety back to the processes associated with the trauma of birth. Harry Stack Sullivan placed emphasis on the early relationship between mother and child and on the importance of the transmission of the mother's anxiety to her infant. Regardless of the particular school of psychoanalysis, however, treatment of anxiety disorders within this model usually involves long-term, insight-oriented psychotherapy or psychoanalysis directed toward the formation of a transference that then allows the reworking of the developmental problem and the resolution of the neurotic symptoms.

Behavioral theories. The behavioral or learning theories of anxiety have spawned some of the most effective treatments for anxiety disorders. Behavioral theories suggest that anxiety is a conditioned response to specific environmental stimuli. In a model of classical conditioning, a person who does not have any food allergies may, for example, become sick after eating contaminated shellfish at a restaurant. Subsequent exposures to shellfish may cause that person to feel sick. Conceivably, through generalization, such a person may come to distrust all food prepared by others. As an alternative etiological possibility, persons may learn to have an internal response of anxiety by imitating the anxiety responses of their parents (social learning theory). In either case, treatment is usually with some form of desensitization by repeated exposure to the anxiogenic stimulus, coupled with cognitive psychotherapeutic approaches.

In recent years proponents of behavioral theories have shown increasing interest in cognitive approaches to conceptualizing and treating anxiety disorders, and cognitive theorists have proposed potentially more helpful alternatives to traditional learning-theory etiological models of anxiety. Cognitive conceptualizations of nonphobic anxiety states suggest that faulty, distorted, or counterproductive thinking patterns accompany or precede maladaptive behaviors and emotional disorders. According to one model, patients suffering from anxiety disorders tend to overestimate the degree of danger and the probability of harm in a given situation and to underestimate their abilities to cope with perceived threats to their physical or psychological well-being. This model asserts that panic-disordered patients often have thoughts of loss of control and fears of dying that follow inexplicable physiological sensations (such as palpitations, tachycardia, and light-headedness) but precede and then accompany panic attacks. Patients with generalized anxiety disorders are viewed as holding distorted, disabling thoughts with regard to events perceived as threatening to their physical or social well-being.

Cognitive-behavioral treatment strategies, designed to modify maladaptive thought patterns that putatively underlie pathological affective reactions, have emerged as alternatives to exposure-based treatment procedures. Systematic research is required to determine the overall and relative efficacy of these new cognitive-behavioral approaches in the treatment of panic and generalized anxiety disorders.

Existential theories. Existential theories of anxiety provide excellent models for generalized anxiety disorder in which there is no specifically identifiable stimulus for a chronically anxious feeling. The central concept of existential theory is that persons become aware of a profound nothingness in their lives, feelings that may be even more profoundly discomforting than an acceptance of their inevitable death. Anxiety is the person's response to this vast void of existence and meaning. It has been suggested that existential concerns have increased since the development of nuclear weapons.

Biological theories. As with all mental functions, anxiety—both normal and pathological—is represented within the brain as a biological entity. Some combination of neurochemicals and neurohormones affects an array of brain regions whenever a person experiences anxiety. Biological theories are partially based on objective measures that compare brain function in patients with anxiety disorders with that of normal persons. Whether the biological measures are primary or secondary to the anxious affect is currently an unanswerable question. It is also not known whether biological changes in patients with anxiety disorders represent overstimulation of an otherwise normal system or whether they represent a uniquely pathological function. It is possible that certain persons are more susceptible to the development of an anxiety disorder on the basis of a biologically based sensitivity to the development of this affect.

Autonomic nervous system. Stimulation of the autonomic nervous system (ANS) causes certain cardiovascular, muscular, gastrointestinal, and respiratory symptoms (Table 17.1-2). These peripheral manifestations of anxiety are neither peculiar to anxiety states nor necessarily correlated with the subjective experience of anxiety. In the first third of the 20th century, Walter Cannon demonstrated that cats exposed to barking dogs exhibited behavioral and physiological signs of fear that were associated with the adrenal release of epinephrine. The James-Lange theory hypothesized that subjective

Table 17.1-2
Peripheral Manifestations of Anxiety

Diarrhea
Dizziness, light-headedness
Hyperhidrosis
Hyperreflexia
Hypertension
Palpitations
Pupillary mydriasis
Restlessness (e.g., pacing)
Syncope
Tachycardia
Tingling in the extremities
Tremors
Upset stomach ("butterflies")
Urinary frequency, hesitancy, urgency

anxiety was a response to these peripheral phenomena. It is now generally thought that central nervous system (CNS) anxiety precedes the peripheral manifestations of anxiety, except when there is a specific peripheral cause, such as pheochromocytoma. Some anxiety disorder patients, especially those with panic disorders, have an ANS that exhibits increased sympathetic tone, adapts more slowly to repeated stimuli, and responds excessively to moderate stimuli.

Neurotransmitters. Much of the basic neuroscience information about anxiety comes from animal experiments involving behavioral paradigms and psychoactive agents. One such animal model of anxiety is the conflict test in which the animal is simultaneously presented with positive (e.g., food) and negative (e.g., electric shock) stimuli. Anxiolytic drugs (e.g, benzodiazepines) tend to facilitate the adaptation of the animal to this situation, whereas other drugs (e.g., amphetamines) further disrupt the behavioral responses of the animal. The three major neurotransmitters associated with anxiety on the basis of such studies are norepinephrine, γ-aminobutyric acid (GABA), and serotonin.

Norepinephrine. The locus ceruleus in the rostral pons contains the cell bodies for most of the noradrenergic neurons in the brain. These neurons project to the cerebral cortex, limbic system, brain stem, and spinal cord. The locus ceruleus receives sensory input regarding pain and potentially dangerous situations and projects to all the brain areas that may be activated during escape from such situations. In experiments with monkeys, stimulation of the locus ceruleus produced a fear response, and ablation of it decreased this response.

Data defining a pathological role for norepinephrine in human anxiety are inconsistent. Drugs affecting norepinephrine (e.g., tricyclics and monoamine oxidase inhibitors [MAOIs]) are effective in treating several of the anxiety disorders. Some studies have reported increased norepinephrine metabolites (e.g., 3-methoxy-4-hydroxyphenylglycol [MHPG]) in urine; others have not. It is clear, however, that the administration of isoproterenol (a β-adrenergic agonist) and yohimbine (an α2-adrenergic antagonist) causes anxiety in humans, and that clonidine (Catapres) (an α2-adrenergic agonist) can reduce anxiety in some situations. Research is currently under way to identify unique β-adrenergic and α2-adrenergic receptor pathology in specific anxiety disorders.

GABA. GABA is the principal inhibitory neurotransmitter in the CNS. The $GABA_A$ receptor complex consists of a GABA binding site, a site that binds benzodiazepines, and a chloride ion channel. Stimulation of the $GABA_A$ receptor causes chloride ions to flow into the neuron, thereby hyperpolarizing and inhibiting that neuron. When a benzodiazepine binds to the $GABA_A$ complex, the affinity of the GABA binding site for GABA is increased. This results in increased binding of GABA to the receptor complex and a greater influx of chloride ions into the neuron.

The efficacy of benzodiazepines in treating anxiety implicates GABA in the pathophysiology of this disorder. Benzodiazepine binding sites are found throughout the brain but are particularly concentrated in the hippocampal formation, prefrontal cortex, amygdala, hypothalamus, and thalamus.

Other anxiolytic substances may affect the $GABA_A$ receptor complex. The anxiolytic effects of barbiturates are thought to result from their binding to the chloride channel and increasing the amount of time the ion channel is open. Ethanol, phenytoin (Dilantin), and valproic acid (Depakene) also may act on the $GABA_A$ receptor complex. It has been hypothesized that there are endogenous ligands for the benzodiazepine binding site that may either increase or decrease anxiety. β-Carboline-3-carboxy acid ethyl ester (β-CCE) has been identified in human urine and rat brain. This molecule binds to the benzodiazepine binding site and has been called an active antagonist because it actually causes anxiety and seizures. Ro-15-1788 is a benzodiazepine receptor antagonist that blocks the effects of benzodiazepines but does not itself cause effects opposite to those of benzodiazepines. Other possible endogenous ligands include purines, nicotinamide, tryptophan, and endogenous peptides (such as GABA-modulin and diazepam [Valium]-binding inhibitor [DBI]).

Serotonin. The serotonergic neurons of the raphe nuclei in the rostral brain stem project to the cerebral cortex, the limbic system (especially the amygdala and the hippocampus), and the hypothalamus. Administration of serotonin to animals is associated with signs suggestive of anxiety. The data are much less compelling in human studies, although the efficacy of antidepressant treatment in panic disorders may be associated with serotonergic effects. The reduced number of imipramine (Tofranil) binding sites (which label serotonin reuptake sites) seen in the postmortem brain tissue of suicides may suggest a role in anxiety and depression for serotonin.

Other neurotransmitters. Increased dopaminergic activity may be associated with anxiety, but it appears not to be specifically related to anxiety disorders. Psychotropic drugs that block dopamine receptors are not effective in treating anxiety disorders, although they do reduce the anxiety associated with psychosis. It has been suggested that the endogenous opioids may interact with α2-adrenergic binding sites and thus may be involved in anxiety. The efficacy of treating anxiety disorder patients with opioid agonists and antagonists has not yet been demonstrated. The anxietylike withdrawal symptoms of heroin addicts, however, are reduced by clonidine, an α2-adrenergic agonist. Other neurotransmitters implicated in anxiety include histamine, acetylcholine, and adenosine. Adenosine receptors, in fact, may be the site of action for the anxiogenic effects of caffeine.

Aplysia. A neurotransmitter model for anxiety has been proposed based on the study of aplysia, a sea snail that reacts to danger by moving away, withdrawing into its shell, and decreasing its feeding behavior. These behaviors can be classically conditioned so that the snail responds to a neutral stimulus as if it were a dangerous stimulus. The snail can also be sensitized by random shocks so that it exhibits a flight response in the absence of real danger. Parallels have been drawn between the classically conditioned model and human phobic anxiety. The classically conditioned aplysia demonstrates measurable changes in presynaptic facilitation, resulting in the release of increased amounts of neurotransmitter. Although the sea snail is a simple animal, this work illustrates an experimental approach to complex neurochemical processes potentially involved in anxiety.

Neuroanatomical considerations. The locus ceruleus and the raphe nuclei were mentioned above in discussions of norepinephrine and serotonin, respectively, and both brain areas are potential sites of pathology in anxiety disorders.

Limbic system. The limbic system receives input from the locus ceruleus and the raphe nuclei. It also contains a very high concentration of benzodiazepine binding sites. Ablation of the limbic system and temporal cortex results in reduced levels of fear and aggression; stimulation of this area results in the expression of these behaviors. Two areas of the limbic system have received special attention in the literature. It has been hypothesized that the septohippocampal pathway takes a dominant role in physiological functioning in anxiety states; increased activity in this pathway leads to anxiety. The cingulate gyrus has been implicated by a variety of research evidence in obsessive-compulsive disorder.

Cerebral cortex. The frontal cerebral cortex is connected

with the parahippocampal region, the cingulate gyrus, and the hypothalamus; therefore, it may be important in the production of anxiety. The temporal cerebral cortex has been implicated as a pathophysiological site in anxiety. This association is based on the similarity in clinical presentation and electrophysiology between some patients with temporal lobe epilepsy and patients with obsessive-compulsive disorder.

References

Cameron O G, Thyer B A, Neese R M: Symptom profiles of patients with DSM-III anxiety disorders. Am J Psychiatry *142:* 1132, 1986.

Curtis G C, Thyer B A, Rainey J M, eds.: Anxiety disorders. Psychiatr Clin North Am *8:* 1, 1985.

Freud S: Inhibitions, symptoms, and anxiety. In *Standard Edition of the Complete Psychological Works of Sigmund Freud,* vol. 20. Hogarth Press, London, 1959.

Freud S: *The Problem of Anxiety*. Norton, New York, 1936.

Gray J A: *The Neuropsychology of Anxiety*. Oxford, New York, 1982.

Hoehn-Saric R: Neurotransmitters of anxiety. Arch Gen Psychiatry *39:* 735, 1982.

Kahn R S, van Praag H M, Wetzler S, Asnis G M, Barr G: Serotonin and anxiety revisted. Biol Psychiatry *23:* 189, 1988.

Kandel E R: From metapsychology to molecular biology: Explorations into the nature of anxiety. Am J Psychiatry *140:* 1277, 1983.

Kuhar M J: Neuroanatomical substrates of anxiety: A brief survey. TINS, July, 307, 1986.

Mathew R J, Wilson W H: Anxiety and cerebral blood flow. Am J Psychiatry *147*: 838, 1990.

Teicher M H: Biology of anxiety. Med Clin North Am *72:* 791, 1988.

Uhde T W, Nemiah J C: Panic and generalized anxiety disorders. In *Comprehensive Textbook of Psychiatry,* ed 5, H I Kaplan and B J Sadock, editors, p 952. Williams & Wilkins, Baltimore, 1989.

17.2 / Panic Disorder and Agoraphobia

The hallmark symptoms of panic disorder are spontaneous, episodic, and intense periods of anxiety, usually lasting less an than hour. These panic attacks usually occur approximately two times a week, although they can be much more or less frequent. Patients with panic disorder may also have agoraphobia, the fear of being alone in public places, especially in situations in which a rapid exit would be difficult. It has been estimated that at least two-thirds of patients with agoraphobia also have panic attacks, and some clinicians believe that panic attacks are a causative factor in virtually all agoraphobic patients. Agoraphobia can be the most disabling of the phobic disorders. The revised third edition of *Diagnostic and Statistical Manual of Mental Disorders* (DSM-III-R) contains diagnostic criteria for panic disorder with agoraphobia, panic disorder without agoraphobia, and agoraphobia without history of panic disorder.

HISTORY

The term "agoraphobia" was coined in 1871 for the condition in which patients seem afraid to venture into public places unaccompanied by friends or relatives. The word is derived from Greek and means "fear of the marketplace." The concurrence of agoraphobia and panic attacks was noted by Sigmund Freud in 1885. The importance of this observation was rediscovered when it was demonstrated that tricyclic antidepressant treatment of many patients with panic attacks and agoraphobia often resulted in amelioration of both symptom complexes. It is now hypothesized that many patients have agoraphobia as a result of classical conditioning after experiencing a panic attack in a public place (such as a crowded supermarket).

EPIDEMIOLOGY

The epidemiological data on panic disorder and agoraphobia are somewhat confusing because many studies have not adequately defined whether they were investigating patients with one or both of these disorders. Nevertheless, panic disorder is thought to have a lifetime prevalence of approximately 1.5 to 2 percent of the population. The female to male ratio for panic disorder with agoraphobia is approximately 2 to 1. Panic disorder most commonly develops in young adulthood, the mean age of presentation being about 25, but both panic disorder and agoraphobia can develop at virtually any age.

Agoraphobia is estimated to have a lifetime prevalence of 0.6 percent. At least two-thirds of agoraphobic patients actually have panic disorder with agoraphobia. The onset of agoraphobia is in the middle to late 20s; agoraphobia is more common among women than among men. In many cases the onset of agoraphobia is reported to follow a traumatic event.

ETIOLOGY

Biological Factors

The search for biological factors in the etiology of panic disorder was encouraged by the finding that this disorder can be treated successfully by tricyclic antidepressants and monoamine oxidase inhibitors (MAOIs). The three major areas of biological interest in panic disorder have been the lactate infusion test, brain-imaging studies, and the coexistence of panic disorder and mitral valve prolapse that has been observed in many patients. In addition, the autonomic nervous system of some panic disorder patients has been reported to exhibit increased sympathetic tone, to adapt more slowly to repeated stimuli, and to respond excessively to moderate stimuli. Studies of the neuroendocrine status of panic disorder patients have described several abnormalities, although the studies have been inconsistent in these findings. The totality of the biological data has focused research attention on the brain stem (particularly the noradrenergic locus ceruleus), the limbic system (possibly responsible for the generation of anticipatory anxiety), and the prefrontal cortex (possibly responsible for the generation of phobic avoidance).

Lactate infusions. Some patients with anxiety disorder have poor exercise tolerance and produce more lactic acid than is normal, sometimes resulting in postexercise panic attacks. Research now indicates that infusions of sodium lactate bring on panic attacks in 70 percent of panic disorder patients and in only 5 percent of normal persons. Although increased serum concentrations of lactate or decreased concentrations of calcium were initially thought to be the chemical basis of this response, it now seems that lactate infusions induce an abnormal increase of norepinephrine in susceptible persons. One study found that panic disorder patients with high pretest plasma concentrations of 3-methoxy-4-hydroxyphenylglycol (MHPG), the metabolite of norepinephrine, were more likely to have a lactate-induced panic attack. Inhalation of carbon dioxide (CO_2) by susceptible persons may also bring on anxiety, panic, and mitral valve prolapse. Although the mechanisms for this response are not known, it has been shown that CO_2 inhalation increases the firing rate of neurons in the locus ceruleus.

Brain-imaging studies of cerebral blood flow using either the regional cerebral blood flow (rCBF) or positron emission tomography (PET) technique have been inconclusive about what brain regions may have abnormal blood flow during a lactate-induced panic attack and also about whether there is an increase or a decrease in blood flow. At present, the lactate infusion test remains an interesting research tool but is not yet appropriate for general clinical application.

Brain imaging. One magnetic resonance (MR) study has reported abnormalities, particularly cortical atrophy, in the right temporal lobe of panic disorder patients. This study is consistent with the hypothesis that limbic system pathology is involved in panic disorder, as are the following PET studies.

One cerebral blood flow study demonstrated increased blood flow in the right (nondominant) parahippocampal area of panic disorder patients who had positive findings on lactate infusion tests. These patients also had increased whole brain metabolism. These results were not present in panic disorder patients with negative findings after lactate infusions or in normal persons. These data are consistent with the neuroanatomical and neurochemical data in that the parahippocampal region contains both the input (entorhinal cortex) and output (subiculum) tracts of the hippocampus. The laterality difference is supported by one cerebral blood flow study of normal persons infused with a benzodiazepine. They showed decreased blood flow only on the right side following lactate infusion, particularly in the frontal area. One PET study in normal persons has shown that a small degree of anxiety results in increased frontal metabolic activity but that increases in anxiety result in decreased metabolic activity. This finding may eventually prove to be a remarkable physiological correlate to the U-shaped anxiety-performance curve.

Mitral valve prolapse. Mitral valve prolapse is a heterogeneous syndrome consisting of prolapse of one of the mitral valve leaflets, resulting in a midsystolic click on cardiac auscultation. Mitral valve prolapse is commonly seen in connective tissue diseases, such as Marfan's and Ehlers-Danlos syndromes. It is present in as many as 50 percent of all patients with panic disorder but in only 5 percent of the general population. Although mitral valve prolapse is asymptomatic in approximately 20 percent of all patients, the cardiac and respiratory symptoms that are usually associated with it are quite similar to those seen in panic disorder. Mitral valve prolapse and panic disorder seem to have a genetic component, and both are more common in women than in men. The presence of a midsystolic click on physical examination of a patient with panic disorder should prompt the psychiatrist to order an electrocardiogram (ECG), and perhaps a phonocardiogram and an echocardiogram. Such validation requires close cooperation with an internist because most psychiatrists do not perform physical examinations in an outpatient or office practice. Because thyrotoxicosis is associated with both mitral valve prolapse and panic disorder, the presence of these two disorders should prompt the clinician to assess the patient's thyroid status. Mitral valve prolapse or the occasionally coexisting ventricular ectopic foci seen on an ECG are not contraindications to treatment with antidepressants. Imipramine (Tofranil), in fact, may be of benefit in treating such cardiac disorders. Nevertheless, consultation with a cardiologist and more frequent ECGs are indicated when treating a mitral valve prolapse patient with antidepressants. The basis and the significance of the association between mitral valve prolapse and panic disorder are unknown. The following case illustrates this association:

A 38-year-old professional man began to experience sudden attacks of rapid heartbeat and pounding chest that were transiently disabling, lasting for seconds to minutes. He was forced to interrupt business meetings, often abruptly leaving the conference room. Episodes increased in frequency to several times a day. After each episode, he felt washed out and jittery for the interval between attacks. The distress began to occur in traffic as well, and he found himself avoiding bridges, tunnels, and traffic bottlenecks, at great inconvenience.

He sought consultation from his internist, who identified on cardiac auscultation a midsystolic click and a systolic murmur. Two-dimensional echocardiography confirmed the presence of mitral valve prolapse. Therapy was initiated with propranolol (Inderal), which was increased to 160 mg a day. The patient noted that he was slightly less jittery and suffered less from the symptoms; nevertheless, the attacks persisted. He began to feel demoralized and, for the first time in his career, was absent from work. Furthermore, he found that the medication was unpleasant because it impaired his energy level and alertness. He discontinued the drug. After reading about agoraphobia in a newsletter, he attended a psychopharmacology unit evaluation, where the diagnosis of panic disorder was proposed. Medication treatment with imipramine—25 mg given just before sleep—was initiated, but he was unable to tolerate the imipramine because of jitteriness, sweating, and grogginess. He was switched to phenelzine (Nardil) 15 mg twice a day.

In two weeks, the patient reported complete remission of all his symptoms. Eight months later, he discontinued treatment without relapse.

Genetics

There is very strong evidence for a genetic basis to panic disorder. Approximately 15 to 17 percent of first-degree relatives of patients with panic disorder are affected. The concordance rate for monozygotic twins is 80 to 90 percent, as compared with 10 to 15 percent for dizygotic twins. The genetic basis for agoraphobia is less certain, although several reports suggest that as many as 20 percent of first-degree relatives of agoraphobic patients may have agoraphobia.

Psychosocial Factors

Psychoanalytic theories conceptualize panic attacks as resulting from an unsuccessful defense against anxiety-provoking impulses. What was previously a less severe signal anxiety becomes an overwhelming feeling of apprehension, complete with somatic symptoms. Regarding agoraphobia, psychoanalytic theories emphasize the loss of a parent in childhood and a history of separation anxiety. The phobia of being alone in public places symbolizes this childhood anxiety about being abandoned. Defense mechanisms used are repression, displacement, avoidance, and symbolization, among others. Perhaps traumatic separations during childhood affect the child's developing nervous system in such a manner that the child becomes more susceptible to such anxieties in adulthood.

Behavioral theorists postulate that anxiety is a learned response either from modeling parental behavior or through the process of classical conditioning. According to behavioral theories, panic attacks and agoraphobia develop simultaneously, or agoraphobia may even precede the development of panic attacks; however, this sequence contrasts with what most clinicians have observed.

CLINICAL FEATURES

The first panic attack is often completely spontaneous, although panic attacks occasionally follow excitement, physical exertion, sexual activity, or moderate emotional trauma. The clinician should attempt to ascertain any habit or situation that commonly precedes a patient's panic attack. Such activities may include the ingestion of caffeine, alcohol, nicotine, or other drugs; unusual patterns of sleeping or eating; and specific environmental settings, such as harsh lighting at work.

The onset of the attack often begins with a 10-minute period of rapidly increasing symptoms. The major mental symptoms are extreme fear and a sense of impending death and doom, and patients may not be able to name the source of their fear. They may feel quite confused and have trouble concentrating. Physical signs often include tachycardia, palpitations, dyspnea, and sweating. Patients often try to leave whatever situation they are in to seek help. The attack generally lasts 20 to 30 minutes and rarely more than an hour. A formal mental status examination during a panic attack may also demonstrate rumination, difficulty speaking (e.g., stammering), and impaired memory. Patients may also experience depression or depersonalization during an attack. The symptoms may disappear quickly or gradually. Between attacks patients may have anticipatory anxiety about having another attack. The differentiation between anticipatory anxiety and generalized anxiety disorder can be somewhat difficult, although panic disorder patients with anticipatory anxiety should be able to name the focus of their anxiety.

Somatic concerns regarding death from a cardiac or respiratory problem may be the major focus of patients' attention during panic attacks. Patients may believe that the palpitations and pain in the chest indicate that they are about to die from a heart attack. As many as 20 percent of these patients actually have syncopal episodes during a panic attack. Such patients may present to emergency rooms as young (20s), physically healthy persons who nevertheless insist that they are about to die from a heart attack. Rather than immediately considering such patients hypochondriacs, the emergency room physician should consider a diagnosis of panic disorder. Hyperventilation may produce respiratory alkalosis and additional symptoms. The age-old treatment of breathing into a paper bag sometimes helps in this situation.

Agoraphobic patients rigidly avoid situations in which it would be difficult to obtain help. They prefer to be accompanied by a friend or family member in such places as busy streets, crowded stores, closed-in spaces (such as tunnels, bridges, elevators), and closed-in vehicles (such as subways, buses, airplanes). These patients may begin to insist that they be accompanied every time they leave the house. This behavior may result in marital discord, which may be misdiagnosed as the primary problem. More severely affected patients may simply refuse to leave the house. Patients with panic disorder and agoraphobia, particularly before a correct diagnosis is made, may be terrified that they are going crazy.

Recent research and clinical experience have indicated that the psychopathology of panic disorder and agoraphobia, along with related social consequences, can be as disabling to patients as mood disorders. Depressive symptoms are often present, and in some panic disorder patients a depressive disorder coexists with the anxiety disorder. (That there may be commonalities between the mood and anxiety disorders is suggested by some research data on sleep abnormalities, neuroendocrine dysregulations, and treatment responses.) Studies have found that the lifetime rates of suicide attempts in persons with uncomplicated panic disorder were consistently higher than those for persons with no psychiatric disorder. The psychiatrist should be alert to the increased suicide risk in such patients. In addition to agoraphobia, other phobias and obsessive-compulsive disorder can coexist with panic disorder in a patient. Psychosocial consequences of this disorder, in addition to marital discord mentioned above, can include time lost from work, financial difficulties related to loss of work, and alcohol and drug abuse. The following clinical case example describes a patient with panic disorder with agoraphobia.

A 30-year-old accountant was referred by his internist to a psychiatric consultant because of a six-month history of recurrent bouts of extreme fear of sudden onset, accompanied by sweating, shortness of breath, palpitations, chest pain, dizziness, numbness in his fingers and toes, and the thought that he was going to die. His internist had given him a complete physical, an ECG, and glucose tolerance and other blood tests and had found no abnormalities.

The patient had been married for five years; he had no children. He went to night school, while working, to get a master's degree in business administration and was quite successful and well liked at his firm. He and his wife, a teacher, generally got along well and had several couples with whom they enjoyed going out.

Because of the attacks, which occurred unexpectedly and in a variety of situations several times a week, the patient started to avoid driving his car and going into department stores, lest he have an attack in these situations. He began to coax his wife to accompany him on errands; and during the previous month he had felt comfortable only at home with his wife. Finally, he could not face the prospect of leaving home to go to work and took a medical leave of absence. When at home, he experienced only twinges of chest pain and slight numbness in his fingers but no full-blown attacks.

When asked about circumstances surrounding the onset of his attacks, the patient said that he and his wife had been discussing buying a house and moving from their apartment. He admitted that the responsibilities of home ownership intimidated him and related the significance of the move to similar concerns his mother had had that prevented his parents from ever buying a house.

Discussion. Recurrent, unexpected bouts of extreme fear of sudden onset, with sweating, shortness of breath, palpitations, chest pain, dizziness, numbness, and thoughts of being about to die, in the absence of an organic cause, indicate panic disorder.

As is often the case, agoraphobia developed as the patient increasingly constricted his normal activities (he could not face the prospect of leaving home to go to work) because of a fear of being in situations from which escape might be difficult or embarrassing or in which help might not be available in the event of a panic attack (he avoided driving his car or going into department stores).

In panic disorder with agoraphobia, the current severity of the agoraphobic avoidance and of the panic attacks can be specified. In this case the agoraphobia was severe because the patient became virtually housebound. The panic attacks were noted as mild because the patient had experienced only limited symptom attacks (fewer than four characteristic symptoms) since developing agoraphobia.

COURSE AND PROGNOSIS

Panic Disorder

Although most research suggests that panic disorder usually appears without any preceding psychosocial provocation, some data argue that the number of stressful life events increases in the month preceding the onset of the disorder.

After the first one or two panic attacks, patients may be relatively unconcerned about their condition; however, the symptoms soon become a major concern. Patients may attempt to keep the panic attacks secret, thereby causing their families and friends concern about unexplained changes in their behavior. The frequency and the severity of panic attacks may fluctuate. The frequency of such attacks is often as many as one to two a week (though they can happen several times a day or just once a year). Excessive intake of caffeine may exacerbate the symptoms. Approximately 50 percent of all patients with panic disorder have recovered at long-term follow-up; approximately 20 percent remain unchanged. Depression may complicate the symptom picture in as many as 70 percent of patients. Although these patients do not tend to talk about suicidal ideation, they are at increased risk of committing suicide. Alcohol and other drug dependence occurs in approximately one-fifth of patients, and obsessive-compulsive disorder may also develop. Performance in school and at work and family interactions may suffer. Patients with good premorbid function and a briefer duration of symptoms tend to have a better prognosis.

Agoraphobia

Most cases of agoraphobia are thought to be due to panic disorder. If the panic disorder is treated, the agoraphobia often improves with time. For a more rapid and more complete reduction of agoraphobia, behavioral therapy is sometimes indicated. Agoraphobia without panic attacks can often be quite incapacitating and chronic. Depression and alcoholism often complicate the symptom picture.

DIAGNOSIS AND TYPES

Panic Disorder

DSM-III-R contains the specific diagnostic criteria for panic disorder (Table 17.2-1) and two major types—with and without agoraphobia (Tables 17.2-2 and 17.2-3). The diagnosis of panic disorder requires that a specific organic cause be ruled out; however, the presence of mitral valve prolapse does not exclude the diagnosis of panic disorder. The severity of the panic attacks and of the agoraphobic avoidance must be specified. There are no exclusion criteria for other psychiatric disorders; therefore, a patient may have a diagnosis of both panic disorder and another Axis I disorder, such as depression or schizophrenia.

Agoraphobia

The DSM-III-R criteria for agoraphobia specify two types (Table 17.2-4). One type is agoraphobia without lim-

Table 17.2-1
Diagnostic Criteria for Panic Disorder

A. At some time during the disturbance, one or more panic attacks (discrete periods of intense fear or discomfort) have occurred that were (1) unexpected (i.e., did not occur immediately before or on exposure to a situation that almost always caused anxiety) and (2) not triggered by situations in which the person was the focus of others' attention.

B. Either four attacks, as defined in criterion A, have occurred within a four-week period, or one or more attacks have been followed by a period of at least a month of persistent fear of having another attack.

C. At least four of the following symptoms developed during at least one of the attacks:
   (1) shortness of breath (dyspnea) or smothering sensations
   (2) dizziness, unsteady feelings, or faintness
   (3) palpitations or accelerated heart rate (tachycardia)
   (4) trembling or shaking
   (5) sweating
   (6) choking
   (7) nausea or abdominal distress
   (8) depersonalization or derealization
   (9) numbness or tingling sensations (paresthesias)
   (10) flushes (hot flashes) or chills
   (11) chest pain or discomfort
   (12) fear of dying
   (13) fear of going crazy or of doing something uncontrolled

   Note: Attacks involving four or more symptoms are panic attacks; attacks involving fewer than four symptoms are limited symptom attacks (see agoraphobia without history of panic disorder).

D. During at least some of the attacks, at least four of the C symptoms developed suddenly and increased in intensity within 10 minutes of the beginning of the first C symptom noticed in the attack.

E. It cannot be established that an organic factor initiated and maintained the disturbance (e.g., amphetamine or caffeine intoxication, hyperthyroidism).

Note: Mitral valve prolapse may be an associated condition, but does not preclude a diagnosis of panic disorder.

Table 17.2-2
Diagnostic Criteria for Panic Disorder with Agoraphobia

A. Meets the criteria for panic disorder.

B. Agoraphobia: Fear of being in places or situations form which escape might be difficult (or embarrassing) or in which help might not be available in the event of a panic attack. (Include cases in which persistent avoidance behavior originated during an active phase of panic disorder, even if the person does not attribute the avoidance behavior to fear of having a panic attack.) As a result of this fear, the person either restricts travel or needs a companion when away from home, or else endures agoraphobic situations in spite of intense anxiety. Common agoraphobic situations include being outside the home alone; being in a crowd or standing in a line; being on a bridge; and traveling in a bus, train, or car.

Specify current severity of agoraphobic avoidance:

Mild: Some avoidance (or endurance with distress), but relatively normal life-style (e.g., travels unaccompanied when necessary, such as to work or to shop; otherwise avoids traveling alone).

Moderate: Avoidance results in constricted life-style (e.g., the person is able to leave the house alone, but not to go more than a few miles unaccompanied).

Severe: Avoidance results in being nearly or completely housebound or unable to leave the house unaccompanied.

In partial remission: No current agoraphobic avoidance, but some agoraphobic avoidance during the past six months.

In full remission: No current agoraphobic avoidance and none during the past six months.

Specify current severity of panic attacks:

Mild: During the past month, either all attacks have been limited symptom attacks (i.e., fewer than four symptoms), or there has been no more than one panic attack.

Moderate: During the past month attacks have been intermediate between "mild" and "severe."

Severe: During the past month, there have been at least eight panic attacks.

In partial remission: The condition has been intermediate between "in full remission" and "mild."

In full remission: During the past six months, there have been no panic or limited symptom attacks.

Table from DSM-III-R, *Diagnostic and Statistical Manual of Mental Disorders,* ed 3, revised. Copyright American Psychiatric Association, Washington, DC, 1987, with permission.

Table 17.2-3
Diagnostic Criteria for Panic Disorder Without Agoraphobia

A. Meets the criteria for panic disorder.

B. Absence of agoraphobia, as defined above.

Specify current severity of panic attacks, as defined above.

Table from DSM-III-R, *Diagnostic and Statistical Manual of Mental Disorders,* ed 3, revised. Copyright American Psychiatric Association, Washington, DC, 1987, with permission.

Table 17.2-4
Diagnostic Criteria for Agoraphobia Without History of Panic Disorder

A. Agoraphobia: Fear of being in places or situations from which escape might be difficult (or embarrassing) or in which help might not be available in the event of suddenly developing a symptom(s) that could be incapacitating or extremely embarrassing. Examples include: dizziness or falling, depersonalization or derealization, loss of bladder or bowel control, vomiting, or cardiac distress. As a result of this fear, the person either restricts travel or needs a companion when away from home, or else endures agoraphobic situations despite intense anxiety. Common agoraphobic situations include being outside the home alone, being in a crowd or standing in a line, being on a bridge, and traveling in a bus, train, or car.

B. Has never met the criteria for panic disorder.

Specify with or **without limited symptom attacks**

Table from DSM-III-R, *Diagnostic and Statistical Manual of Mental Disorders,* ed 3, revised. Copyright American psychiatric Association, Washington, DC, 1987, with permission.

ited symptom attacks, and the other is agoraphobia with limited symptom attacks that are not thought to be causatively related to the agoraphobia.

DIFFERENTIAL DIAGNOSIS

The organic differential diagnosis for panic disorder, as for other anxiety disorders, is lengthy (Table 17.2-5). The clinician should consider hyperthyroidism, hypoglycemia, pheochromocytoma, and temporal lobe epilepsy, among other organic conditions. The psychiatric differential diagnosis includes malingering, factitious disorder, hypochondriasis, depersonalization, social and simple phobias, posttraumatic stress disorder, depression, and schizophrenia.

The organic differential diagnosis for agoraphobia without panic attacks includes all the disorders that may cause anxiety or depression. The psychiatric differential diagnosis includes major depression, schizophrenia, paranoid personality disorder, avoidant personality disorder, and dependent personality disorder.

TREATMENT

Pharmacotherapy

The first drugs reported to be useful in the treatment of panic disorder were the tricyclic antidepressants and the MAOIs. Imipramine has been the most frequently used drug, although several studies report that desipramine (Norpramin) is as effective and has fewer side effects. Many studies also report that phenelzine, an MAOI, is effective. There are a few initial reports that fluoxetine (Prozac), an atypical antidepressant, is effective in the treatment of panic disorder.

Table 17.2-5
Organic Differential Diagnosis for Anxiety Disorders

Cardiovascular
- Anemia
- Angina
- Congestive heart failure
- Hyperactive β-adrenergic state
- Hypertension
- Mitral valve prolapse
- Myocardial infarction
- Paradoxical atrial tachycardia

Pulmonary
- Asthma
- Hyperventilation
- Pulmonary embolus

Neurological
- Cerebrovascular accident
- Epilepsy
- Huntington's chorea
- Infection
- Ménière's disease
- Migraine
- Multiple sclerosis
- Transient ischemic attack
- Tumor
- Wilson's disease

Endocrine
- Addison's disease
- Carcinoid
- Cushing's syndrome
- Diabetes
- Hyperthyroid
- Hypoglycemia
- Hypoparathyroid
- Menopausal
- Pheochromocytoma
- Premenstrual

Drug intoxications
- Amphetamine
- Amyl nitrite
- Anticholinergics
- Cocaine
- Hallucinogens
- Marijuana
- Nicotine
- Theophylline

Drug withdrawal
- Alcohol
- Antihypertensives
- Opiates
- Sedative hypnotics

Other
- Anaphylaxis
- B_{12} deficiency
- Electrolyte disturbances
- Heavy metal poisoning
- Systemic infections
- Systemic lupus erythematosus
- Temporal arteritis
- Uremia

Tricyclics and MAOIs should be used in the same manner in which they are used for treating depression. It may be advisable, though, to increase the dose about half as quickly in these anxiety disorder patients because of a high incidence of adverse effects. The full maximum dose may be required to obtain relief from the panic symptoms. It may take two to four weeks for panic attacks to decrease with treatment. The clinician should obtain blood levels of antidepressants if the patient is not responsive to maximal doses. After recovery, patients should be maintained on the drug for 6 to 12 months; then an attempt may be made to taper the drug dosage slowly. If symptoms return, the drug treatment should be reinstituted. No conclusive data are available on whether antidepressant treatment is effective in agoraphobia without panic attacks. If the agoraphobia is particularly disabling, however, a trial of drug therapy in coordination with behavioral approaches would seem warranted.

Benzodiazepines, particularly alprazolam (Xanax) and clonazepam (Klonopin), have also been demonstrated to be effective in the treatment of panic disorder. It is likely that all benzodiazepines would be effective, although not all have been studied in research settings. Buspirone (BuSpar), the nonbenzodiazepine anxiolytic, is not effective in the treatment of panic disorder. Alprazolam is usually given in four daily doses with a total daily dosage of 4 to 6 mg. Clonazepam may be preferable to alprazolam because it can be given twice daily, usually in a total dose of 0.50 mg a day. Benzodiazepine treatment, particularly with alprazolam, must be tapered slowly and not discontinued abruptly.

Behavior Therapy

Even if panic attacks disappear with pharmacological treatment, the patient may continue to have agoraphobic symptoms or anticipatory anxiety. These symptoms are often most responsive to behavioral desensitization involving increased exposure to the real or imagined phobic situation. When a patient is committed to improvement of symptoms, this repeated exposure to the phobic stimulus frequently results in a desensitization to the stimulus. Behavioral approaches often also involve cognitive exercises to deal with the anxiety and formal muscle relaxation or mediation exercises.

Family Therapy

The family of a patient with panic disorder and agoraphobia may have become quite disrupted during the course of the illness. Family therapy directed toward education and support are often quite beneficial.

Insight-Oriented Psychotherapy

Insight-oriented psychotherapy can be of benefit in the treatment of panic disorder or agoraphobia. Treatment focuses on helping the patient understand the unconscious meaning of the anxiety, the symbolism of the avoided situation, the need to repress impulses, and the secondary gain of the symptoms. A resolution of early infantile and oedipal conflicts correlates with the resolution of current stresses.

References

Cowley D S, Arana G W: The diagnostic utility of lactate sensitivity in panic disorder. Arch Gen Psychiatry *47:* 277, 1990.

Dager S R, Cowley D C, Dunner D L: Biological markers in panic states: Lactate-induced panic and mitral valve prolapse. Biol Psychiatry *22:* 339, 1987.

Gorman J M, Liebowitz M R, Fyer A J, Stein J: A neuroanatomical hypothesis for panic disorder. Am J Psychiatry *146:* 148, 1989.

Grunhaus L: Clinical and psychobiological characteristics of simultaneous panic disorder and major depression. Am J Psychiatry *145:* 1214, 1988.

Johnson J, Weissman M M, Klerman G L: Panic disorder, comorbidity, and suicide attempts. Arch Gen Psychiatry *47:* 805, 1990.

Katon W, Roy-Byrne P P: Panic disorder in the medically ill. J Clin Psychiatry *50:* 299, 1989.

Klerman G L: Overview of the cross-national collaborative panic study. Arch Gen Psychiatry *45:* 407, 1989.

Markowitz J S, Weissman M M, Ouellette R, Lish J D, Klerman G L: Quality of life in panic disorder. Arch Gen Psychiatry *46:* 984, 1989.

Pollard C A, Lewis L M: Managing panic attacks in emergency patients. J Emerg Med *7:* 547, 1989.

Raj A, Sheehan D V: Medical evaluation of panic attacks. J Clin Psychiatry *48:* 309, 1987.

Reiman E M, Fusselman M J, Fox P T, Raichle M E: Neuroanatomical correlates of anticipatory anxiety. Science *243:* 1071, 1989.

Reiman E M, Raichle M E, Robins E, Mintun M A, Fusselman M J, Fox P T, Price J L, Hackman K A: Neuroanatomical correlates of a lactate-induced anxiety attack. Arch Gen Psychiatry *46:* 493, 1989.

Roth W T, Telch M J, Taylor C B, Agras W S: Autonomic changes after treatment of agoraphobia with panic attacks. Psychiatry Res *24:* 95, 1988.

Roy-Byrne P P, ed.: Panic disorder. Psychiatr Ann *18*(8): entire issue, 1988.

Stewart R S, Devous M D, Rush, A J, Lane L, Bonte F J: Cerebral blood flow changes during sodium-lactate-induced panic attacks. Am J Psychiatry *145:* 442, 1988.

17.3 / Social and Simple Phobias

A phobia is an irrational fear resulting in a conscious avoidance of the specific feared object, activity, or situation. The patient consciously realizes that the fear is unfounded and experiences the fear as ego-dystonic.

The revised third edition of *Diagnostic and Statistical Manual of Mental Disorders* (DSM-III-R) defines social phobia as the fear of humiliation or embarrassment in public places. It differs from agoraphobia in that patients with agoraphobia are not overly concerned with the reaction of other people to their behavior. Social phobias include phobias about eating in restaurants, urinating in public rest rooms, public speaking, and public musical performances.

Simple phobia is a residual category that includes specific phobias not covered in agoraphobia or social phobia. A classic example of a simple phobia is an irrational and overly intense belief about the danger of spiders.

EPIDEMIOLOGY

Social phobia is less common than simple phobia. Social phobias affect 3 to 5 percent of the population. Males and females are represented about equally. The onset of social phobia is usually in the early to late teens, although it can begin at any age.

For simple phobia the six-month prevalence varies from 5 to 12 percent in different studies. Women are more often affected than men. The feared objects and situations in simple phobia (listed in descending frequency of appearance) are animals, storms, heights, illness, injury, and death.

ETIOLOGY

Psychoanalytic Factors

Sigmund Freud presented a formulation of phobic neurosis, which in essence has remained the analytic explanation of social and simple phobias. Freud hypothesized that the major function of anxiety is to signal the ego that a forbidden unconscious drive is pushing for conscious expression, thus alerting the ego to strengthen and marshal its defenses against the threatening instinctual force. Freud viewed the phobic disorder—or "anxiety hysteria," as he continued to call it—as a result of conflicts centered on an unresolved childhood oedipal situation. Because the sex drive continues to have a strong incestuous coloring in the adult, sexual arousal tends to kindle anxiety that is characteristically a fear of castration. When repression fails to be entirely successful, it is necessary for the ego to call on auxiliary defenses. In phobic patients the defense involves primarily the use of displacement; that is, the sexual conflict is displaced from the person who evokes the conflict to a seemingly unimportant, irrelevant object or situation, which then has the power to arouse the entire constellation of affects, including signal anxiety. It can be plausibly suggested that the phobic object or situation has a direct associative connection with the primary source of the conflict and thus has come to symbolize it (the defense mechanism of symbolization). Furthermore, the situation or object is usually such that the patient is able to keep out of its way and, by this additional defense mechanism of avoidance, escape suffering from serious anxiety. Freud first discussed this theoretical formulation of phobia formation, which attributes the phobia to the use of the ego defense mechanisms of displacement and avoidance against incestuous oedipal genital drives and castration anxiety, in his famous case history of Little Hans, a 5-year-old boy who had a fear of horses.

Although it was originally thought that phobias resulted from castration anxiety, more recent psychoanalytic theorists have suggested that other types of anxiety may be involved. In agoraphobia, for example, separation anxiety clearly plays a leading role, and in erythrophobia (a fear of red that can be manifested as a fear of blushing), the element of shame implies the involvement of superego anxiety. It is perhaps closer to clinical observation to view the anxiety associated with phobias as having a variety of sources and colorings.

Counterphobic attitude. Otto Fenichel called attention to the fact that phobic anxiety can be hidden behind attitudes and behavior patterns that represent a denial, either that the dreaded object or situation is dangerous or that one is afraid of it. Basic to this phenomenon is a reversal of the situation in which one is the passive victim of external circumstances to a position of attempting actively to confront and master what one fears. The counterphobic person seeks out situations of danger and rushes enthusiastically toward them. The devotee of dangerous sports, such as parachute jumping and rock climbing, may be exhibiting counterphobic behavior. Such patterns may be secondary to neurotic phobic anxieties or may be used as a normal means of dealing with a realistically dangerous situation. The play of children may contain counterphobic elements, as when children play doctor and give to a doll the shot they received earlier in the day in the pediatrician's office. This pattern of behavior may involve the related defense mechanism of identification with the aggressor.

Behavioral Factors

In 1920 John B. Watson wrote an article called "Conditioned Emotional Reactions," in which he recounted his experiences with Little Albert, an infant with a phobia of rats and rabbits. Unlike Freud's Little Hans, who developed symptoms in the natural course of his maturation, Little Albert's difficulties were the direct result of the scientific experiments of two psychologists who used techniques that had successfully induced conditioned responses in laboratory animals.

Watson's formulation invokes the traditional Pavlovian stimulus-response model of the conditioned reflex to account for the initial creation of the phobia. That is, anxiety is aroused by a naturally frightening stimulus that occurs in contiguity with a second inherently neutral stimulus. As a result of the contiguity, especially when the two stimuli are aired on several successive occasions, the originally neutral stimulus takes on the capacity to arouse anxiety by itself. The neutral stimulus, therefore, becomes a conditioned stimulus for anxiety production.

In the classical stimulus-response theory, the conditioned stimulus is seen as gradually losing its potency to arouse a response if it is not reinforced by a periodic repetition of the unconditioned stimulus. In the phobic symptom, this attenuation of the response to the phobic—that is, conditioned—stimulus does not occur, yet the symptom may last for years without any apparent external reinforcement. In the more recently formulated operant conditioning theory, however, a model is provided for explaining that phenomenon. In the newer theory, anxiety is viewed as a drive that motivates the organism to do what it can to obviate the painful affect. In the course of its random behavior, the animal soon learns that certain actions enable it to avoid the stimulus for anxiety. These avoidance patterns remain stable for long periods of time as a result of the reinforcement they receive from their capacity to diminish anxiety. This model is readily applicable to phobias in that avoidance of the anxiety-provoking object or situation plays a central part. Such avoidance behavior becomes fixed as a stable symptom because of its effectiveness in protecting the patient from the phobic anxiety.

Learning theory has a particular relevance to phobic disorders and provides simple and intelligible explanations for many aspects of phobic symptoms. Critics contend, however, that it deals mostly with surface mechanisms of symptom formation and is perhaps less useful than psychoanalytic theories in providing an understanding of some of the complex underlying psychic processes involved.

Biological Factors

There have been relatively few biological investigations of phobic disorders other than agoraphobia (see Section 17.2). Some biological theorists have proposed that phobic patients have a specific inability to habituate to certain situations. At least two controlled studies have demonstrated that the first-degree relatives of patients with simple phobias are much more likely to have simple phobias than are first-degree relatives of control persons without simple phobias. The relatives of the phobic patients were not, however, more likely than controls to have any other mental disorder. These data are consistent with the notion that simple phobia is a familial disorder with a genetic component. In the absence of adoption studies, however, it could also be argued that these data demonstrate how the family environment can transfer specific phobic attitudes and behaviors. One positron emission tomography (PET) study of phobic patients who were afraid of animals was unable to demonstrate a difference in either global or regional cerebral blood flow between phobic and nonphobic persons exposed to the phobic stimulus.

CLINICAL FEATURES

Phobias are characterized by the arousal of severe anxiety when the patient is exposed to a specific phobic situation or object. Both mental and somatic symptoms of anxiety are present. The somatic symptom of blushing is said to be common in social phobias. In an attempt to prevent the development of anxiety, patients do everything in their power to avoid the situation that stimulates their phobic response. The patient's daily activities may be hindered to some degree, depending on how easy it is to avoid the phobic situation. Alcohol and drug dependence and major depressive disorder can be complicating associated features in phobic disorder.

The major finding on the mental status examination is the presence of an irrational and ego-dystonic fear of a specific situation, activity, or object. Patients are also able to describe how they avoid contact with the phobic situation. Depression is commonly observable on the mental status examination and may be present in as many as one-third of phobic patients. A case example of social phobia follows:

The patient was a 33-year-old man who lived in Seattle with his wife. He had been employed as a salesperson for an insurance company since graduating from college, where he had majored in mathematics. He had gone to a private psychiatrist, recommended by a friend, complaining of "anxiety at work."

The patient described himself as having been outgoing and popular throughout his adolescence and young adulthood, with no serious problems until his third year of college. He then began to become extremely tense and nervous when studying for tests and writing papers. His heart would pound; his hands would sweat and tremble. Consequently, he often did not write the required papers and, when he did, would submit them after the date due. He could not understand why he was so nervous about doing papers and taking tests when he had always done well in these tasks in the past. As a result of his failure to submit certain papers and his late submission of others, his college grades were seriously affected.

Soon after graduation, the patient was employed as a salesperson for an insurance firm. His initial training (attending lectures, completing reading assignments) proceeded smoothly, but as soon as he began to take on clients, his anxiety returned. He became extremely nervous when anticipating phone calls from clients. When his business phone rang, he would begin to tremble and sometimes would not answer. Eventually, he avoided becoming anxious by not scheduling appointments and by not contacting clients whom he was expected to see.

When asked what is was about these situations that made him nervous, he said that he was concerned about what the client would think of him. "The client might sense that I am nervous and might ask me questions that I don't know the answers to, and I would feel foolish." As a result, he would repeatedly rewrite and reword sales scripts for telephone conversations because he was "so concerned about saying the right thing. I quess I'm just very concerned about being judged."

Although never unemployed, the patient estimated that he had been functioning at only 20 percent of his work capacity, which his employer tolerated because a salesperson is paid only on a commission basis. For the previous several years, he had had to borrow large sums of money to make ends meet.

Although financial constraints were a burden, the patient and his wife entertained guests at their home regularly and enjoyed socializing with friends at picnics, parties, and formal affairs. The patient lamented, "It's just when I'm expected to do something. Then, it's like I'm on stage, all alone, with everyone watching me."

COURSE AND PROGNOSIS

Most patients are able to live relatively normal lives in spite of their phobic disorder because the phobic object or situation is easily avoidable. For example, the fear of horses is not a problem for a city dweller. The onset of social phobias is often gradual and occasionally follows a precipitating psychosocial stressor. Social phobias may have a chronic course, although some evidence indicates that they decrease after middle age. Simple phobias that begin in childhood usually remit spontaneously; however, some simple phobias may be chronic. Rigorous studies of the outcome of phobic disorders are not available.

DIAGNOSIS

The DSM-III-R diagnostic criteria for social phobia (Table 17.3-1) require that the primary fear not be related to another Axis I or Axis III disorder and that the condition interfere with the life of the patient. The generalized type of social phobia describes a patient who is phobic about most social situations.

The DSM-III-R diagnostic criteria for simple phobia (Table 17.3-2) define a residual category that covers phobias not included in agoraphobia or social phobia. The diagnostic guidelines also indicate that the phobic stimulus cannot be related to the obsessional component of obsessive-compulsive disorder. Impairment in occupational or social functioning is required.

Table 17.3-1
Diagnostic Criteria for Social Phobia

A. A persistent fear of one or more situations (the social phobic situations) in which the person is exposed to possible scrutiny by others and fears that he or she may do something or act in a way that will be humiliating or embarrassing. Examples include: being unable to continue talking while speaking in public, choking on food when eating in front of others, being unable to urinate in a public lavatory, hand-trembling when writing in the presence of others, and saying foolish things or not being able to answer questions in social situations.

B. If an Axis III or another Axis I disorder is present, the fear in A is unrelated to it (e.g., the fear is not of having a panic attack [panic disorder], stuttering [stuttering], trembling [Parkinson's disease], or exhibiting abnormal eating behavior [anorexia nervosa or bulimia nervosa]).

C. During some phase of the disturbance, exposure to the specific phobic stimulus (or stimuli) almost invariably provokes an immediate anxiety response.

D. The phobic situation is avoided, or is endured with intense anxiety.

E. The avoidant behavior interferes with occupational functioning or with usual social activities or relationships with others, or there is marked distress about having the fear.

F. The person recognizes that his or her fear is excessive or unreasonable.

G. If the person is under 18, the disturbance does not meet the criteria for avoidant disorder of childhood or adolescence.

Specify generalized type if the phobic situation includes most social situations, and also consider the additional diagnosis of avoidant personality disorder.

Table from DSM-III-R, *Diagnostic and Statistical Manual of Mental Disorders,* ed 3, revised. Copyright American Psychiatric Association, Washington, DC, 1987, with permission.

DIFFERENTIAL DIAGNOSIS

The most common organic differential diagnosis of phobic disorder is intoxication with hallucinogens, sympathomimetics, and other abused drugs. Most organic disorders do not cause isolated symptoms of phobia in the absence of other psychiatric or neurological symptoms. Nevertheless, it is possible for a small cerebral tumor or cerebrovascular accident to produce such a symptom complex. The clinician should be especially careful to consider unusual organic causes whenever atypical symptoms are present.

The psychiatric differential diagnosis of social phobia includes depression, schizophrenia, and schizoid and avoidant personality disorders. Social phobia and alcohol dependence may coexist more often than has been appreciated; therefore, phobic disorder should also be considered in the differential diagnosis of alcohol abuse. The psychiatric differential diagnosis of simple phobia should include schizophrenia, major depression, obsessive-compulsive disorder, paranoid personality disorder, and avoidant personality disorder.

Schizophrenia. The differentiation of a phobia from a delusion of schizophrenia is based primarily on three clinical observations. First, phobic patients are very aware of the irrational nature of their feelings and avoidant behavior. Second, the phobia lacks the bizarre quality that can be seen in schizophrenic patients who may have phobias. Third, the other symptoms of schizophrenia are not present in phobic patients.

Obsessive-compulsive disorder. The differentiation of a phobia from obsessive-compulsive disorder can sometimes be difficult. For example, the common phobia of knives or other dangerous objects often rests on the patient's fantasy of actively hurting someone else. The patient

Table 17.3-2
Diagnostic Criteria for Simple Phobia

A. A persistent fear of a circumscribed stimulus (object or situation) other than fear of having a panic attack (as in panic disorder) or of humiliation or embarrassment in certain social situations (as in social phobia).

Note: Do not include fears that are part of panic disorder with agoraphobia or agoraphobia without history of panic disorder.

B. During some phase of the disturbance, exposure to the specific phobic stimulus (or stimuli) almost invariably provokes an immediate anxiety response.

C. The object or situation is avoided, or endured with intense anxiety.

D. The fear or the avoidant behavior significantly interferes with the person's normal routine or with usual social activities or relationships with others, or there is marked distress about having the fear.

E. The person recognizes that his or her fear is excessive or unreasonable.

F. The phobic stimulus is unrelated to the content of the obsessions of obsessive-compulsive disorder or the trauma of post-traumatic stress disorder.

Table from DSM-III-R, *Diagnostic and Statistical Manual of Mental Disorders,* ed 3, revised. Copyright American Psychiatric Association, Washington DC, 1987, with permission.

is able to control the anxiety by avoiding such objects. The differentiation between these two conditions, however, is of less clinical relevance at this time, since the treatments for the two disorders are similar.

TREATMENT

Pharmacotherapy

Pharmacotherapy is indicated as an adjuvant to behavior therapy or for patients for whom behavior therapy has been ineffective. For such patients pharmacotherapy may be used in combination with insight-oriented psychotherapy.

Social phobia. The most solid research data support the use of monoamine oxidase inhibitors (MAOIs), particularly phenelzine (Nardil) and tranylcypromine (Parnate), in the treatment of social phobia. Standard antidepressant doses are used; improvement may take three to four weeks, and symptoms often reappear when the drug is discontinued. Other antidepressants, particularly the tricyclic and tetracyclic antidepressants, may also be effective in the treatment of social phobia. One study reported the usefulness of alprazolam (Xanax) in the treatment of social phobia. The social phobia of stage fright in musicians and other performers has been particularly effectively treated with β-adrenergic antagonists, such as propranolol (Inderal).

Simple phobia. There are very few studies regarding the pharmacotherapy for simple phobias. Nevertheless, therapeutic drug trials with the same drugs that are used for social phobia may be warranted in the treatment of simple phobia.

Behavior Therapy

The most studied and most effective treatment for phobias is probably behavior therapy. The key aspects of successful treatment are (1) the patient's commitment to treatment, (2) clearly identified problems and objectives, and (3) available alternative strategies for coping with the feelings. A variety of behavioral treatment techniques have been employed, the most common being systematic desensitization, a method pioneered by Joseph Wolpe. In this method, the patient is exposed serially to a predetermined list of anxiety-provoking stimuli graded in a hierarchy from the least to the most frightening. Through the use of tranquilizing drugs, hypnosis, and instruction in muscle relaxation, patients are taught how to induce in themselves both mental and physical repose. Once they have mastered the techniques, patients are instructed to employ them to induce relaxation in the face of each anxiety-provoking stimulus. As they become desensitized to each stimulus in the scale, the patients move up to the next stimulus until, ultimately, what previously produced the most anxiety is no longer capable of eliciting the painful affect.

Other behavioral techniques that have more recently been employed involve intensive exposure to the phobic stimulus through either imagery or desensitization in vivo. In imaginal flooding, patients are exposed to the phobic stimulus for as long as they can tolerate the fear until they reach a point at which they can no longer feel it. Flooding (also known as implosion) in vivo requires patients to experience similar anxiety through exposure to the actual phobic stimulus.

Insight-Oriented Psychotherapy

Early in the development of psychoanalysis and the dynamically oriented psychotherapies, it was believed that these methods were the treatment of choice for phobic neurosis, which was then thought to stem from oedipal-genital conflicts. Soon, however, therapists recognized that, in spite of progress in uncovering and analyzing unconscious conflicts, patients frequently failed to lose their phobic symptoms. Moreover, by continuing to avoid the phobic situation, patients excluded a significant degree of anxiety and its related associations from the analytic process. Both Freud and his pupil Sandor Ferenczi had recognized that, if progress in analyzing the symptoms was to be made, therapists had to go beyond their analytic roles and actively urge phobic patients to seek out the phobic situation and experience the anxiety and resultant insight. Since then, psychiatrists have generally agreed that a measure of activity on the part of the therapist is often required to treat phobic anxiety successfully. The decision to apply the techniques of psychodynamic insight-oriented therapy should be based not on the presence of the phobic symptom alone but on positive indications from the patient's ego structure and life patterns for the use of this method of treatment. Insight-oriented therapy enables the patient to understand the origin of the phobia, the phenomenon of secondary gain, and the role of resistance and enables the patient to seek healthy ways of dealing with anxiety-provoking stimuli.

Other Therapeutic Modalities

Hypnosis, supportive therapy, and family therapy may be useful in the treatment of phobic disorders. Hypnosis is used to enhance the therapist's suggestion that the phobic objection is not dangerous, and self-hypnosis can be taught to the patient as a method of relaxation when confronted with the phobic object. Supportive psychotherapy and family therapy are often useful in helping the patient actively confront the phobic object during treatment. Not only can family therapy enlist the aid of the family in treating the patient, but it may help the family understand the nature of the patient's problem.

References

Aimes P L, Gelder M G, Shaw P M: Social phobia: A comparative clinical study. Br J Psychiatry *142:* 174, 1983.

Freud S: Analysis of a phobia of a five-year-old boy. In *Standard Edition of the Complete Psychological Works of Sigmund Freud,* vol 10, p 5. Hogarth Press, London, 1955.

Fyer A J, Mannuzza S, Gallops M S, Martin L Y, Aaronson C, Gorman J M, Liebowitz M R, Klein D F: Familial transmission of simple phobias and fears. Arch Gen Psychiatry *47:* 252, 1990.

Liebowitz M R, Fyer A J, Gorman J M: Social phobia: Review of a neglected anxiety disorder. Arch Gen Psychiatry *42:* 729, 1985.

Liebowitz M R, Gorman J M, Fyer A J, Campeas R, Levin A P, Sandberg D, Hollander E, Papp L, Goetz D: Pharmacotherapy of social phobia: An interim report of a placebo-controlled comparison of phenelzine and atenolol. J Clin Psychiatry *49:* 252, 1988.

Mountz J M, Modell J G, Wilson M W, Curtis G C, Lee M A, Schmaltz S, Kuhl D E: Positron emission tomographic evaluation of cerebral blood flow during state anxiety in simple phobia. Arch Gen Psychiatry *46:* 501, 1989.

Nemiah J: A psychoanalytic view of phobias. Am J Psychoanal *41:* 115, 1981.

Reich J, Noyes R, Yates W: Alprazolam treatment of avoidant personality traits in social phobic patients. J Clin Psychiatry *50:* 91, 1989.

Stein M B, Tancer M E, Gelernter C S, Vittone B J, Uhde T W: Major depression in patients with social phobia, Am J Psychiatry *147:* 637, 1990.

Versiani M, Munsim F D, Nardi A E, Liebowitz M R: Tranylcypromine in social phobia. J Clin Psychopharmacol *8:* 279, 1988.

17.4 / Obsessive-Compulsive Disorder

According to the revised third edition of *Diagnostic and Statistical Manual of Mental Disorders* (DSM-III-R), the essential feature of obsessive-compulsive disorder is the symptom of recurrent obsessions or compulsions sufficiently severe to cause marked distress to the person. The obsessions or compulsions are time-consuming and interfere significantly with the person's normal routine, occupational functioning, usual social activities, or relationships. A patient with obsessive-compulsive disorder may have an obsession or a compulsion or both.

An *obsession* is a recurrent and intrusive thought, feeling, idea, or sensation. In contrast to an obsession, which is a mental event, a compulsion is a behavior. Specifically, a *compulsion* is a conscious, standardized, recurrent behavior, such as counting, checking, or avoiding. A patient with obsessive-compulsive disorder realizes the irrationality of the obsession and experiences both the obsession and the compulsion as ego-dystonic.

Although the compulsive act may be carried out in an attempt to reduce the anxiety associated with the obsession, it does not always succeed in doing so. The completion of the compulsive act may not affect the anxiety, and it may even increase the anxiety.

EPIDEMIOLOGY

The prevalence of obsessive-compulsive disorder is now recognized as being much higher than previously appreciated. Perhaps the secretive nature of affected patients contributed to an underestimation of its occurrence. The lifetime prevalence of obsessive-compulsive disorder is approximately 2.0 to 2.4 percent; the one-year prevalence is approximately 0.7 percent. The disorder begins most often in adolescence and early adulthood (ages 18 to 24) and may occur in childhood. It affects males and females equally. The prevalence of obsessive-compulsive disorder is highest among persons who are divorced, separated, unemployed, or members of low socioeconomic groups. The prevalence among blacks is somewhat lower than that among whites.

ETIOLOGY

Biological Factors

There are two major themes in research reports regarding a biological cause for obsessive-compulsive disorder. First, a body of data suggest similarities between obsessive-compulsive disorder and depressive disorder. Second, data suggest that the prefrontal cortex, the basal ganglia, and regions of the limbic system are possible sites of pathophysiology.

Electrophysiological studies, sleep electroencephalogram (EEG) studies, and neuroendocrine studies have contributed data that suggest some commonality between depression and obsessive-compulsive disorder. There is a higher than usual incidence of nonspecific EEG abnormalities in obsessive-compulsive patients. It has been hypothesized that these abnormalities are often located in the left hemisphere, a hypothesis that is supported by the observation that there is a higher than usual occurrence of left-handedness in these patients. Sleep EEG studies have demonstrated abnormalities similar to those seen in depression, such as decreased rapid eye movement (REM) latency. Neuroendocrine studies have also found some similarities to depression, such as nonsuppression on the dexamethasone-suppression test in about one-third of these patients and decreased growth hormone secretion with clonidine (Catapres) infusions.

Brain-imaging studies of obsessive-compulsive disorder patients have used computed tomography (CT), regional cerebral blood flow (rCBF), and positron emission tomography (PET). Several CT studies have found that severely affected obsessive-compulsive patients may have enlarged cerebral ventricles and possibly a decreased volume of the caudates. Although still somewhat controversial, the data from several rCBF and PET studies suggest abnormalities in the caudate nuclei and prefrontal cortex. The frontal abnormalities found in brain-imaging studies may be consistent with the observation in one study that the presence of soft neurological signs (such as impaired fine motor coordination) is correlated with the severity of the obsessive-compulsive symptoms.

Genetics

The genetic studies of obsessive-compulsive disorder patients have been few in number. However, there does seem to be a heritable basis for at least some cases. There is a prevalence of 3 to 7 percent of the disorder in first-degree relatives, compared with only 0.5 percent in relatives of patients with other anxiety disorders.

Psychosocial Factors

Personality factors. Obsessive-compulsive disorder is not a severe form of obsessive-compulsive personality disorder. The majority of obsessive-compulsive disorder patients do not have premorbid compulsive symptoms; therefore, such traits are neither necessary nor sufficient for the development of the obsessive-compulsive disorder. Approximately 15 to 35 percent of patients have had premorbid obsessional traits, as compared with 50 percent of psychiatric patients without obsessive-compulsive disorder who have such traits.

Psychodynamic factors. Sigmund Freud described three major psychological defense mechanisms that determine the form and the quality of obsessive-compulsive symptoms and character traits: isolation, undoing, and reaction formation.

Isolation. Isolation is a defense mechanism that protects a person from anxiety-provoking affects and impulses. Under ordinary circumstances a person experiences in consciousness both the affect and the imagery of an emotion-laden idea, whether it be a fantasy or the memory of an event. When isolation occurs, the affect and the impulse of which it is a derivative are separated from the ideational component and pushed out of consciousness. If isolation is completely successful, the impulse and its associated affect are totally repressed, and the patient is consciously aware only of the affectless idea that is related to it.

Undoing. Because of the constant threat that the impulse may escape the primary defense of isolation and break free, further secondary defensive operations are required to combat it and to quiet the anxiety that the imminent eruption of the impulse into consciousness arouses.

The compulsive act constitutes the surface manifestation of a defensive operation aimed at reducing anxiety and at controlling the underlying impulse that has not been sufficiently contained by isolation. A particularly important secondary defensive operation of this sort is the mechanism of undoing. As the word suggests, it refers to a compulsive act that is performed in an attempt to prevent or undo the consequences that the patient irrationally anticipates from a frightening obsessional thought or impulse.

Reaction formation. Both isolation and undoing are defensive maneuvers that are intimately involved in the production of clinical symptoms. Reaction formation results in the formation of character traits, rather than symptoms. As the term implies, reaction formation involves manifest patterns of behavior and consciously experienced attitudes that are exactly the opposite of the underlying impulses. Often, these patterns seem to an observer to be highly exaggerated and at times quite inappropriate.

Other psychogenic factors. One of the striking features of patients with obsessive-compulsive disorder is the degree to which they are preoccupied with aggression or cleanliness, either overtly in the content of their symptoms or in the associations that lie behind them. This and other observations have led to the proposition that the psychogenesis of the obsessive-compulsive disorder lies in disturbances in normal growth and development related to the anal-sadistic phase.

Ambivalence. Ambivalence is the direct result of a change in the characteristics of the impulse life. It is an important feature of the normal child during the anal-sadistic developmental phase; that is, the child feels both love and murderous hate toward the same object, sometimes seemingly simultaneously. One finds the obsessive-compulsive patient often consciously experiencing both love and hate toward an object. This conflict of opposing emotions may be seen in the doing-undoing patterns of behavior and in the paralyzing doubt in the face of choices that are frequently found in persons with this emotional disorder.

Magical thinking. In the phenomenon of magical thinking, the regression uncovers earlier modes of thought, rather than impulses; that is, ego functions, as well as id functions, are affected by regression. Inherent in magical thinking is the phenomenon of the omnipotence of thought. Persons feel that, merely by thinking about an event in the external world, they can cause that event to occur without intermediate physical actions. This feeling makes having an aggressive thought frightening to obsessive-compulsive patients.

Behavioral factors. According to learning theory, obsessions represent a conditioned stimulus to anxiety. A relatively neutral stimulus becomes associated with fear or anxiety through a process of respondent conditioning by becoming paired with events that are by nature noxious or anxiety producing. Thus, previously neutral objects and thoughts become conditioned stimuli capable of provoking anxiety or discomfort.

The compulsion is established in a different way. The person discovers that a certain action reduces the anxiety attached to the obsessional thought. Thus, active avoidance strategies in the form of compulsions or ritualistic behaviors are developed to control anxiety. Gradually, because of their efficacy in reducing a painful secondary drive (the anxiety), the avoidance strategies become fixed as learned patterns of compulsive behaviors. Learning theory provides useful concepts for explaining certain aspects of the obsessive-compulsive phenomena—for example, the anxiety-provoking capacity of ideas that are not necessarily frightening in themselves and the establishment of compulsive patterns of behavior.

CLINICAL FEATURES

Obsessions and compulsions have certain features in common: (1) An idea or an impulse intrudes itself insistently and persistently into the person's conscious awareness. (2) A feeling of anxious dread accompanies the central manifestation and frequently leads the person to take countermeasures against the initial idea or impulse. (3) The obsession or compulsion is ego-alien; that is, it is experienced as being foreign to the person's experience of himself or herself as a psychological being. (4) No matter how vivid and compelling the obsession or compulsion, the person recognizes it as absurd and irrational. (5) The person suffering from obsessions and compulsions feels a strong desire to resist them. However, approximately one-half of all patients offer little resistance to the compulsion. Approximately 80 percent of all patients believe that the compulsion is irrational and silly. The relative proportion of patients with specific obsessions and compulsions was reported in one study of 70 child and adolescent patients (Table 17.4-1). Examples of the types of symptoms that may bring an obsessive-compulsive person to the attention of a nonpsychiatric physician are given in Table 17.4-2.

There are four major symptom patterns in obsessive-compulsive disorder. The most common is an obsession of contamination followed by washing. The feared object is often hard to avoid (such as feces and urine), and the compulsion involves washing and cleansing. Patients may literally rub the skin off their hands from excessive hand washing.

The second most common pattern is an obsession of doubt followed by a compulsion of checking. The obsession often implies some danger of violence (such as forgetting to turn off the stove). The checking may involve multiple trips back into the house to check the stove. The patients have an obsessional self-doubt, as if they always felt guilty for having forgotten or committed something. Other descriptive terms for various compulsions are avoiding, repeating, completeness, and meticulousness. Patients with both obsessions and compulsions constitute 75 percent of the total.

A less common form of obsessive-compulsive disorder is one with merely intrusive obsessional thoughts without a compulsion. Such obsessions are usually repetitious thoughts of some sexual or aggressive act that is reprehensible to the patient.

Finally, there is obsessional slowness, in which the obsession and the compulsion seem to be united into the slow carrying out of daily behaviors. Patients can take literally hours to eat a meal or shave their faces. Although it is possible to delineate somewhat separate clinical pictures, the symptoms of an individual patient may overlap and change in character with time.

The other major finding on mental status examination of obsessive-compulsive disorder patients is depression or symptoms of dysthymia. Such symptoms are present in approximately 50 percent of all patients. Some obsessive-compulsive patients have character traits suggestive of obsessive-compulsive personality disorder, but most do not. These patients, especially the men, have a higher than average celibacy rate. There is also a greater than usual amount of marital discord. A clinical case example follows:

Table 17.4-1
Reported Obsessions and Compulsions for 70 Consecutive Child and Adolescent Patients

Major Presenting Symptom	No. (%) Reporting Symptom at Initial Interview*
Obsession	
Concern or disgust with bodily wastes or secretions (urine, stool, saliva), dirt, germs, environmental toxins, etc.	30 (43)
Fear something terrible might happen (fire, death or illness of loved one, self, or others)	18 (24)
Concern or need for symmetry, order, or exactness	12 (17)
Scrupulosity (excessive praying or religious concerns out of keeping with patient's background)	9 (13)
Lucky and unlucky numbers	6 (8)
Forbidden or perverse sexual thoughts, images, or impulses	3 (4)
Intrusive nonsense sounds, words, or music	1 (1)
Compulsion	
Excessive or ritualized hand washing, showering, bathing, toothbrushing, or grooming	60 (85)
Repeating rituals (going in and out of door, up and down from chair, etc)	36 (51)
Checking doors, locks, stove, appliances, car brakes, etc	32 (46)
Cleaning and other rituals to remove contact with contaminants	16 (23)
Touching	14 (20)
Ordering and arranging	12 (17)
Measures to prevent harm to self or others (e.g., hanging clothes a certain way)	11 (16)
Counting	13 (18)
Hoarding and collecting	8 (11)
Miscellaneous rituals (e.g., licking, spitting, special dress pattern)	18 (26)

Table from J L Rapoport: The neurobiology of obsessive-compulsive disorder. JAMA *260*: 2889, 1988, with permission.
*Multiple symptoms recorded, so total exceeds 70.

A 20-year-old junior at a Midwestern college complained to his internist that he was having difficulty studying because, over the previous six months, he had become increasingly preoccupied with thoughts that he could not dispel. He spent hours each night rehashing the day's events, especially interactions with friends and teachers, endlessly making right in his mind any and all regrets. He likened the process to playing a videotape of each event over and over again in his mind,

Table 17.4-2
Nonpsychiatric Clinical Specialists Likely to See Obsessive-Compulsive Patients

Specialist	Presenting Problem
Dermatologist	Chapped hands, eczematoid appearance
Family practitioner	Family member washing excessively, may mention counting or checking compulsions
Oncologist, infectious disease internist	Insistent belief that person has acquired immune deficiency syndrome (AIDS)
Neurologist	Obsessive-compulsive disorder associated with Tourette's disorder, head injury, epilepsy, choreas, other basal ganglia lesions or disorders
Neurosurgeon	Severe, intractable obsessive-compulsive disorder
Obstetrician	Postpartum obsessive-compulsive disorder
Pediatrician	Parents' concern about child's behavior, usually excessive washing
Pediatric cardiologist	Obsessive-compulsive disorder secondary to Sydenham's chorea
Plastic surgeon	Repeated consultations for "abnormal" features
Dentist	Gum lesions from excessive teeth cleaning

Table from J L Rapoport: The neurobiology of obsessive-compulsive disorder. JAMA *260*: 2889, 1988, with permission.

asking himself if he had behaved properly and telling himself that he had done his best or had said the right thing every step of the way. He would do this while sitting at his desk, supposedly studying; and it was not unusual for him to look at the clock after such a period of rumination and note that, to his surprise, two or three hours had elapsed. His declining grades worried him.

The patient admitted, on further questioning, that he had a two-hour grooming ritual when getting ready to go out with friends. Here again, shaving, showering, combing his hair, and putting on his clothes all demanded perfection. In addition, for several years he had been bothered by certain superstitions that, it turned out, dominated his daily life. These included avoiding certain buildings while walking on campus, always sitting in the third seat in the fifth row in his classrooms, and lining up his books and pencils in a certain configuration on his desk before studying.

Discussion. Obsessions are recurrent ideas that are experienced not as voluntarily produced ideas but, rather, as thoughts that invade consciousness and are experienced as senseless (ego-dystonic). Certainly, this patient did not experience his rumination about the day's events as under his voluntary control. It is less evident that he regarded the *content* of these thoughts as senseless, although he clearly attempted to ignore or suppress them. This ambiguity about whether such thoughts represent true obsessions or merely obsessional brooding could be of diagnostic importance in distinguishing obsessive-compulsive disorder from obsessive-compulsive personality disorder or generalized anxiety disorder, in which rumination is often present. In this case, however, the patient showed clear signs of compulsions—repetitive behavior performed according to certain rules or in a stereotyped fashion that served no useful function, was not pleasurable in itself, and was generally experienced as senseless (the patient's grooming rituals and superstitions).

COURSE AND PROGNOSIS

Over 50 percent of these patients experience the onset of symptoms before 24 years of age, and over 80 percent before age 35. The mean age of onset is 20 years. Approximately 50 to 70 percent of patients have the onset of symptoms after a stressful event, such as a pregnancy, a sexual problem, or the death of a relative. There is an acute onset in over half the cases. Because many patients manage to keep their symptoms secret, there is often a delay of 5 to 10 years before the patients come to psychiatric attention, and the mean age of first hospitalization is 30 years. The course is usually chronic. Symptoms fluctuate in some patients and remain quite constant in others.

It has been reported that approximately 20 to 30 percent of the patients have significant improvement in their symptoms, and 40 to 50 percent have moderate improvement. It has been variously reported that 20 to 40 percent of patients either remain ill or even have a worsening of their symptoms. Approximately one-third of these patients develop major depression, and suicide is a risk for all these patients. Various reports suggest that they are at a minimally increased risk of developing schizophrenia. A poor prognosis is suggested by yielding to (rather than resisting) compulsions, childhood onset, bizarre compulsions, and the need for hospitalization. A better prognosis is suggested by good social and occupational adjustment, the absence of compulsions in the presence of obsessions, the presence of a precipitating event, and an episodic nature to the symptoms. The actual obsessional content does not seem to be related to prognosis.

DIAGNOSIS AND DIFFERENTIAL DIAGNOSIS

The DSM-III-R diagnostic criteria for obsessive-compulsive disorder require the presence of either obsessions or compulsions (Table 17.4-3). The criteria also require that the symptoms cause distress and interfere with social and occupational functioning.

The DSM-III-R diagnostic requirement of personal distress and functional impairment differentiates obsessive-compulsive disorder from ordinary or mildly excessive thoughts and habits. The major neurological disorders to consider in the differential diagnosis are Tourette's disorder, other tic disorders, and temporal lobe epilepsy. The major psychiatric considerations are schizophrenia, depression (with obsessive thoughts), phobic disorders, and obsessive-compulsive personality disorder. Obsessive-compulsive disorder can usually be distinguished from schizophrenia by the absence of other schizophrenic symptoms, the less bizarre nature of the symptoms, and the patient's insight into his or her disorder. Depression with

Table 17.4-3
Diagnostic Criteria for Obsessive-Compulsive Disorder

A. Either obsessions or compulsions:

Obsessions: (1), (2), (3), and (4):

(1) recurrent and persistent ideas, thoughts, impulses, or images that are experienced, at least initially, as intrusive and senseless (e.g., a parent's having repeated impulses to kill a loved child, a religious person's having recurrent blasphemous thoughts)
(2) the person attempts to ignore or suppress such thoughts or impulses or to neutralize them with some other thought or action
(3) the person recognizes that the obsessions are the product of his or her own mind, not imposed from without (as in thought insertion)
(4) if another Axis I disorder is present, the content of the obsession is unrelated to it (e.g., the ideas, thoughts, impulses, or images are not about food in the presence of an eating disorder, about drugs in the presence of a psychoactive substance use disorder, or guilty thoughts in the presence of a major depression)

Compulsions: (1), (2), and (3):

(1) repetitive, purposeful, and intentional behaviors that are performed in response to an obsession, or according to certain rules or in a stereotyped fashion
(2) the behavior is designed to neutralize or to prevent discomfort or some dreaded event or situation; however, either the activity is not connected in a realistic way with what it is designed to neutralize or prevent, or it is clearly excessive
(3) the person recognizes that the behavior is excessive or unreasonable (this may not be true for young children; it may no longer be true for people whose obsessions have evolved into overvalued ideas)

B. The obsessions or compulsions cause marked distress, are time-consuming (take more than an hour a day), or significantly interfere with the person's normal routine, occupational functioning, or usual social activities or relationships with others.

Table from DSM-III-R, *Diagnostic and Statistical Manual of Mental Disorders*, ed 3, revised. Copyright American Psychiatric Association, Washington, DC, 1987, with permission.

obsessive thoughts is distinguished by the presence of depressive symptoms that meet the DSM-III-R criteria for major depression. Phobias can be somewhat difficult to distinguish from obsessive-compulsive disorder; however, obsessive-compulsive disorder patients are usually much less successful at avoiding the feared object than are phobic patients.

TREATMENT

Pharmacotherapy

Pharmacotherapy is used by some clinicians as a first-line approach to the treatment of obsessive-compulsive disorder. Other clinicians use pharmacotherapy as an adjuvant to insight-oriented psychotherapy or behavior therapy or only for those patients for whom psychotherapy or behavior therapy alone has been ineffective. Clomipramine (Anafranil) has become the standard drug for use in the treatment of obsessive-compulsive disorder. Clomipramine is classified as a tricyclic antidepressant drug, and it has the usual adverse effects of those drugs—hypotension, anticholinergic effects, and sedation. Clomipramine is a potent inhibitor of serotonin reuptake.

Recent pharmacological research and basic research have suggested that other agents that act on the serotonergic system may also be effective in the treatment of obsessive-compulsive disorder. Such drugs include trazodone (Desyrel) and fluoxetine (Prozac), two atypical antidepressants that are potent inhibitors of serotonin reuptake. The monoamine oxidase inhibitors (MAOIs), especially phenelzine (Nardil) and tranylcypromine (Parnate), have also been shown to be effective drugs in several studies. Less well studied pharmacological agents for the treatment of unresponsive patients include benzodiazepines (especially alprazolam [Xanax] and clonazepam [Klonopin]) and, possibly, fenfluramine (Pondimin).

The therapeutic effects of any of the above drugs may be delayed for as long as two months. In general, pharmacotherapy may be more effective in treating the compulsions than the obsessions. Treatment should continue for 6 to 12 months before an attempt is made to taper the medication. Many patients relapse when medication is discontinued.

Behavior Therapy

Many clinicians consider behavior therapy to be the treatment of choice for obsessive-compulsive disorder. Behavior therapy can be conducted in both outpatient and inpatient settings. Behavior therapy is successful in 60 to 75 percent of all patients. Desensitization, thought stopping, flooding, implosion therapy, and aversive conditioning have all been used in these patients. It is important that the patient be truly committed to improvement. Some behavioral therapists use response prevention, in which the patient is sometimes forcibly prevented from carrying out the compulsion.

Psychotherapy

Obsessive-compulsive patients do respond to the psychotherapeutic maneuvers of the psychiatrist. However, in the absence of adequate studies of psychotherapy in obsessive-compulsive disorder, it is hard to make any valid generalizations about its effectiveness. Individual analysts have seen striking and lasting changes for the better in patients with obsessional personality disorders, especially when they are able to come to terms with the aggressive impulses lying behind the patients' character traits. Likewise, analysts and dynamically oriented psychiatrists have observed marked symptomatic improvement in their patients in the course of analysis or prolonged insight psychotherapy.

Supportive psychotherapy undoubtedly has its place, especially for that group of obsessive-compulsive patients who, despite symptoms of varying degrees of severity, are able to work and make a social adjustment. The continuous and regular contact with an interested, sympathetic, and encouraging professional person may make it possible for patients to continue to function by virtue of that help, without which they would become completely incapacitated by their symptoms. Occasionally, when obsessional rituals and anxiety reach an intolerable intensity, it is necessary to hospitalize the patient until the shelter of an institution and the removal from external environmental stresses bring about a lessening of the symptoms to a more tolerable level. Nor must it be forgotten that the patient's family is often driven to the verge of despair by the patient's behavior. Any psychotherapeutic endeavors must include attention to family members through the provision of emotional support, reassurance, explanation, and advice on how to manage and respond to the patient.

Other Therapies

Family therapy is often very useful in supporting the family, helping reduce marital discord resulting from the disorder, and building a treatment alliance with the family members for the good of the patient. Finally, for the most seriously impaired patients who have not responded to any other treatment modality, bimedial leukotomies that produce lesions in the thalamofrontal connections have been reported to be effective.

References

Baxter L R, Schwartz J M, Guze B H, Bergman K, Szuba M P: PET imaging in obsessive compulsive disorder with and without depression. J Clin Psychiatry *51*(4, Suppl): 61, 1990.

Dysken M W, Davis J M, eds.: Obsessive compulsive disorder. Psychiatr Ann *19*(2): entire issue, 1989.

Goodman W K, Price L H, Rasmussen S A, Mazure C, Fleischmann R L, Hill C L, Heninger G R, Charney D S: The Yale-Brown obsessive compulsive scale: I. Development, use, and reliability. Arch Gen Psychiatry *46*: 1006, 1989.

Karno M, Golding J M, Sorenson S B, Burnam M A: The epidemiology of obsessive-compulsive disorder in five US communities. Arch Gen Psychiatry *45*: 1094, 1988.

Kim S W, Dysken M W: A review of serotonin reuptake inhibitors in obsessive-compulsive disorder. Psychiatr Ann *18*: 373, 1988.

Insel T R, ed.: Obsessive compulsive disorder: New perspectives. J Clin Psychiatry *51*(2, Suppl): 2, 1990.

Jenike M A: Approaches to the patient with treatment-refractory obsessive compulsive disorder. J Clin Psychiatry *51*(2, Suppl): 15, 1990.

Modell J G, Mountz J M, Curtis G C, Greden J F: Neurophysiologic dysfunction in basal ganglia-limbic striatal and thalamocortical circuits as a pathogenetic mechanism of obsessive-compulsive disorder. J Neuropsychiatry *1*: 27, 1989.

Nemiah J C, Uhde T W: Obsessive-compulsive disorder. In *Comprehensive Textbook of Psychiatry,* ed 5, H I Kaplan and B J Sadock, editors, p 984. Williams & Wilkins, Baltimore, 1989.

Perse R: Obsessive-compulsive disorder: A treatment review. J Clin Psychiatry *49*: 48, 1988.

Rapoport J L: The biology of obsessions and compulsions. Sci Am 83, March 1989.

Rapoport J L: The neurobiology of obsessive-compulsive disorder. JAMA *260*: 2888, 1988.

Rasmussen S A, Eisen J L: Epidemiology of obsessive compulsive disorder. J Clin Psychiatry *51*(2, Suppl): 10, 1990.

Swedo S E, Rapoport J L, Leonard H, Lenane M, Chelsow D: Obsessive-compulsive disorder in children and adolescents. Arch Gen Psychiatry *46*: 335, 1989.

Zohar J, Insel T R: Obsessive-compulsive disorder: Psychobiological approaches to diagnosis, treatment, and pathophysiology. Biol Psychiatry *22*: 667, 1987.

17.5 / Posttraumatic Stress Disorder

The three major features of posttraumatic stress disorder are (1) the reexperiencing of the trauma through dreams and waking thoughts, (2) emotional numbing to other life experiences and relationships, and (3) symptoms of autonomic instability, depression, and cognitive difficulties (such as poor concentration). Posttraumatic stress disorder develops in persons who have experienced emotional or physical stress that was of a magnitude that would be extremely traumatic for virtually anyone. Examples of such traumas include combat experience, natural catastrophes, assault, rape, and serious accidents (e.g., automobile accidents, building fires).

HISTORY

A syndrome very similar to what is now called posttraumatic stress disorder was noted in soldiers during the American Civil War. It was then called soldier's heart because of the presence of autonomic cardiac symptoms. Jacob DaCosta's 1871 paper, *On Irritable Heart,* described such soldiers. In World War I the syndrome was called shell shock and was hypothesized to result from brain trauma from the explosion of shells. Posttraumatic stress disorder was seen in World War II in the survivors of Nazi concentration camps and in the survivors of the atomic bombings of Japan. In 1941 the survivors of a fire in a crowded nightclub in Boston, the Coconut Grove, showed increased nervousness, fatigue, and nightmares. In all these situations the appearance of the syndrome was correlated with the severity of the stressor—the most severe stresses (e.g., concentration camp) resulted in the appearance of the syndrome in over 75 percent of the victims.

EPIDEMIOLOGY

The epidemiology of posttraumatic stress disorder varies with the occurrence of disasters and traumatic situations affecting large numbers of people. After a devastating disaster 50 to 80 percent of the survivors may have the syndrome. The prevalence of posttraumatic stress disorder in the general population is 0.5 percent for men and 1.2 percent for women; children can also have the disorder. The trauma for men is usually combat experience, and the severity of the syndrome is related to the degree of the trauma. The trauma for women is most often assault or rape. Though posttraumatic stress disorder can appear at any age, it is most prevalent in young adults, owing to the nature of the precipitating situations.

ETIOLOGY

The likelihood of posttraumatic stress disorder developing in persons after a disaster or trauma is positively correlated with the severity of the stressor. The more severe the stressor, the more people have the syndrome and the more severe the disorder is. When the trauma is comparatively mild—for example, an auto accident without fatalities—fewer of those involved later have posttraumatic stress disorder. Being part of a group who live through a disaster sometimes enables a person to deal better with the trauma because others share the experience. However, survivor guilt sometimes complicates the management of posttraumatic stress.

In general, the very young and the very old have more difficulty coping with traumatic events than do those in midlife. For example, about 80 percent of young children who sustain a burn injury show symptoms of posttraumatic stress disorder one or two years after the initial injury. Alternatively, only 30 percent of adults who suffer such an injury have a posttraumatic stress disorder after one year. Presumably, young children do not yet have adequate coping mechanisms to deal with the physical and emotional insults of the trauma. Likewise, old people, when compared with younger adults, are likely to have more rigid coping mechanisms and to be less able to muster a flexible approach to dealing with the effects of the trauma. Furthermore, the effects of the trauma may be exacerbated by physical disabilities characteristic of late life, particularly disabilities of the nervous and cardiovascular systems, such as reduced cerebral blood flow, failing vision, palpitations, and arrhythmias. Preexisting psychiatric disability, whether a personality disorder or a more serious condition, also increases the effects of particular stressors.

The availability of social supports may also influence the development, severity, and duration of posttraumatic stress disorder. In general, patients who have a good network of social supports are less likely to have the disorder or to experience it in its most severe forms. The disorder is most likely to occur in those who are single, divorced, widowed, economically handicapped, or socially deprived.

Biological Factors

Biologically oriented theorists have proposed that patients with posttraumatic stress disorder were premorbidly prone to excessive autonomic reactions to stress. Considerable data indicate a state of hyperarousal in persons who are affected with posttraumatic stress disorder. Patients with this disorder tend to have increased sympathetic nervous system baseline activity and reactivity to stimulation. This increased sympathetic tone is evidenced by increased electroencephalogram (EEG) alpha activity, heart rate, respiratory rate, and muscle tension. Some research reports have also found an increased urinary excretion of norepinephrine. A related hypothesis is that, when a patient reexperiences the trauma, endogenous opioids are released. The intervening symptoms of the disorder are the result of a withdrawal from the release of endogenous opioids.

Some research reports have suggested a similarity between posttraumatic stress disorder and two other psychiatric disorders, depressive disorder and panic disorder. Patients with posttraumatic stress disorder show an increase in rapid eye movement (REM) latency and decreases in REM amount, stage 4 sleep, and sleep efficiency. They also have an increased occurrence of nightmares in both REM and non–REM sleep. The abnormality in sleep architecture is somewhat reminiscent of that in depression and panic disorder, but there are abnormalities specific to posttraumatic stress disorder. Nevertheless, there may be some biological overlap among these diagnostic groups.

Psychodynamic Factors

The psychoanalytic view of posttraumatic stress disorder is that the trauma reactivates unresolved conflicts from early childhood, including emotional traumas of childhood that had been unconscious. The revival of the childhood trauma results in regression and the use of the defense mechanisms of repression, denial, and undoing. There is a repetition by the ego to relive and thereby master and reduce anxiety. The victim also receives secondary gain from the external world, common forms being monetary compensation, increased attention or sympathy, and the satisfaction of dependency needs. These serve to reinforce the disorder and its persistence. A cognitive view of posttraumatic stress disorder suggests that the brain is trying to process the massive amount of information that the trauma provoked by alternating periods of acknowledging and blocking the event.

CLINICAL FEATURES

The specific clinical signs and symptoms of the episodes of reexperiencing and numbing are described in the revised third edition of *Diagnostic and Statistical Manual of Mental Disorders* (DSM-III-R) (Table 17.5-1). The mental status examination often reveals feelings of guilt, rejection, and humiliation. The patient may also describe dissociative states and panic attacks. Illusions and hallucinations may be present. Cognitive testing may reveal that the patient has impairments of memory and attention. Associated symptoms are aggression, violence, poor impulse control, and alcohol and drug dependence. The patients have elevated Sc, D, F, and Ps scores on the Minnesota Multiphasic Personality Inventory (MMPI), and the Rorschach findings often include aggressive and violent material. A clinical case example follows:

A 23-year-old Vietnam veteran was admitted to the hospital one year after the end of the Vietnam War at the request of his wife after he began to experience depression, insomnia, and flashbacks of his wartime experiences. He had been honorably discharged two years previously, having spent nearly a year in combat. He had had only minimal difficulties in returning to civilian life, resuming his college studies, and then marrying within six months of his return. His wife had noticed that he was always reluctant to talk about his military experience, but she wrote it off as a natural reaction to unpleasant memories.

The patient's current symptoms had begun at about the time of the fall of Saigon. He had become preoccupied with watching television news stories about it. He then began to have difficulty sleeping and at times would awaken at night in the midst of a nightmare in which he was reliving his past experiences. His wife became particularly concerned one day when he had a flashback experience while out in the backyard: As a plane flew overhead, flying somewhat lower than usual, the patient threw himself to the ground, seeking cover, thinking it was an attacking helicopter. The more he watched the

Table 17.5-1
Diagnostic Criteria for Posttraumatic Stress Disorder

A. The person has experienced an event that is outside the range of usual human experience and that would be markedly distressing to almost anyone (e.g., serious threat to one's life or physical integrity; serious threat or harm to one's children, spouse, or other close relatives and friends; sudden destruction of one's home or community; or seeing another person who has recently been, or is being, seriously injured or killed as the result of an accident or physical violence).

B. The traumatic event is persistently reexperienced in at least one of the following ways:
(1) recurrent and intrusive distressing recollections of the event (in young children, repetitive play in which themes or aspects of the trauma are expressed)
(2) recurrent distressing dreams of the event
(3) sudden acting or feeling as if the traumatic event were recurring (includes a sense of reliving the experience, illusions, hallucinations, and dissociative [flashback] episodes, even those that occur upon awakening or when intoxicated)
(4) intense psychological distress at exposure to events that symbolize or resemble an aspect of the traumatic event, including anniversaries of the trauma

C. Persistent avoidance of stimuli associated with the trauma or numbing of general responsiveness (not present before the trauma), as indicated by at least three of the following:
(1) efforts to avoid thoughts or feelings associated with the trauma
(2) efforts to avoid activities or situations that arouse recollections of the trauma
(3) inability to recall an important aspect of the trauma (psychogenic amnesia)
(4) markedly diminished interest in significant activities (in young children, loss of recently acquired developmental skills such as toilet training or language skills)
(5) feeling of detachment or estrangement from others
(6) restricted range of affect (e.g., unable to have loving feelings)
(7) sense of a foreshortened future (e.g., does not expect to have a career, marriage, children, or a long life)

D. Persistent symptoms of increased arousal (not present before the trauma), as indicated by at least two of the following:
(1) difficulty falling or staying asleep
(2) irritability or outbursts of anger
(3) difficulty concentrating
(4) hypervigilance
(5) exaggerated startle response
(6) physiologic reactivity upon exposure to events that symbolize or resemble an aspect of the traumatic event (e.g., a woman who was raped in an elevator breaks out in a sweat when entering any elevator)

E. Duration of the disturbance (symptoms in B, C, and D) of at least one month

Specify delayed onset if the onset of symptoms was at least six months after the trauma.

Table from DSM-III-R, *Diagnostic and Statistical Manual of Mental Disorders,* ed 3, revised. Copyright American Psychiatric Association, Washington, DC, 1987, with permission.

news on television, the more agitated and morose he became. Stories began to spill out about atrocities that he had seen and experienced, and he began to feel guilty that he had survived while many of his friends had not. At times he also seemed angry and bitter, feeling that the sacrifices he and others had made were all wasted.

The veteran's wife expressed concern that his preoccupation with Vietnam had become so intense that he seemed uninterested in anything else and was emotionally distant from her. When she suggested that they try to plan their future, including having a family, he responded as if his life consisted completely of the world of events experienced two years earlier, as if he had no future.

COURSE AND PROGNOSIS

The full syndrome of posttraumatic stress usually develops some time after the trauma. The delay can be as little as one week or as long as 30 years. Symptoms can fluctuate over time and may be most intense during periods of stress. Approximately 30 percent of patients recover, 40 percent have mild symptoms, 20 percent have moderate symptoms, and 10 percent remain unchanged or become worse. A good prognosis is predicted by a rapid onset of symptoms, short duration of symptoms (less than six months), good premorbid functioning, strong social supports, and the absence of any other psychiatric or medical problems.

DIAGNOSIS AND DIFFERENTIAL DIAGNOSIS

The specific criteria for diagnosis are included in DSM-III-R (Table 17.5-1). Delayed onset is specified if the onset of symptoms occurs more than six months after the traumatic event.

A major consideration in the diagnosis of posttraumatic stress disorder is the possibility that the patient also incurred a head injury during the trauma. Other organic considerations that can both cause and exacerbate the symptoms are alcohol and drug dependencies. The psychiatric differential diagnosis includes factitious disorder, malingering, adjustment reaction, borderline personality disorder, schizophrenia, depression, panic disorder, and generalized anxiety disorder. Posttraumatic stress disorder is commonly misdiagnosed as one of these other syndromes, resulting in the inappropriate treatment of the condition. It is particularly important to consider posttraumatic stress disorder in patients who have pain disorders, substance abuse, other anxiety disorders, or mood disorders.

TREATMENT

Pharmacotherapy

Imipramine (Tofranil), a tricyclic antidepressant, and phenelzine (Nardil), a monoamine oxidase inhibitor (MAOI), are the two drugs that have been most often reported to be useful in the treatment of posttraumatic stress disorder. Recently, however, several well-controlled studies have called into question the design of earlier studies and have not been able to demonstrate a dramatic reduction in symptoms with those treatments. A trial of drug treatment is, however, still indicated in patients who are seriously affected and have not responded to other therapeutic interventions. Other drugs that have been reported to be effective in preliminary studies of posttraumatic stress disorder include clonidine (Catapres), propranolol (Inderal), benzodiazepines, lithium, and carbamazepine (Tegretol). With posttraumatic stress disorder patients who are abusing drugs or alcohol, it is probably reasonable not to use phenelzine or benzodiazepines.

Psychotherapy

Psychotherapeutic interventions for posttraumatic stress disorder include behavior therapy, cognitive therapy, and hypnosis. Many clinicians advocate time-limited psychotherapy for the victims of trauma. Such therapy usually takes a cognitive approach and also provides support and security. The short-term nature of the psychotherapy minimizes the risk of dependency and chronicity. Issues of suspicion, paranoia, and trust, however, often adversely affect compliance. In this disorder the therapist should overcome patients' denial of the traumatic event, encourage them to relax, and remove them from the source of the stress. The patient should be encouraged to sleep, using medication if necessary. Support from the environment (such as friends and relatives) should be provided. The patient should be encouraged to review and abreact emotional feelings associated with the traumatic event and plan for future recovery.

Group therapy and family therapy have been reported to be effective in treating posttraumatic stress disorder patients. Group therapy has been particularly successful with Vietnam veterans. Family therapy often helps sustain a marriage through periods of exacerbated symptoms. Hospitalization may be necessary when symptoms are particularly severe or there is a risk of suicide or other violence.

References

Brett E A, Spitzer R L, Williams J B W: DSM-III-R criteria for posttraumatic stress disorder. Am J Psychiatry *145*: 1232, 1988.

Davidson J, Kudler H, Smith R, Mahorney S L, Lipper S, Hammett E, Saunders W B, Cavenar J O: Treatment of posttraumatic stress disorder with amitriptyline and placebo. Arch Gen Psychiatry *47*: 259, 1990.

Epstein R S: Posttraumatic stress disorder: A review of diagnostic and treatment issues. Psychiatr Ann *19*: 556, 1989.

Friedman M J: Toward rational pharmacotherapy for posttraumatic stress disorder: An interim report. Am J Psychiatry *145*: 281, 1988.

Horowitz M J: Stress response syndromes: Character style and brief psychotherapy. Arch Gen Psychiatry *31*: 768, 1974.

Kolb L C: A neuropsychological hypothesis explaining post-traumatic stress disorders. Am J Psychiatry *144*: 8, 1987.

Krupnock J L, Horowitz M J: Stress response syndromes. Arch Gen Psychiatry *38*: 428, 1981.

Kulka R A: *The National Vietnam Veterans Readjustment Study: Tables of Findings and Technical Appendices.* Brunner/Mazel, New York, 1990.

Paige S R, Reid G M, Allen M G, Newton J E O: Psychophysiological correlates of posttraumatic stress disorder in Vietnam veterans. Biol Psychiatry *27*: 419, 1990.

Ross R J, Ball W A, Sullivan K A, Caroff S N: Sleep disturbance as the hallmark of posttraumatic stress disorder. Am J Psychiatry *146*: 697, 1989.

Watson I P B, Hoffman L, Wilson G V: The neuropsychiatry of posttraumatic stress disorder. Br J Psychiatry *152*: 164, 1988.

17.6 / Generalized Anxiety Disorder

Persons who seem to be pathologically anxious about everything are likely to be classified by the revised third edition of *Diagnostic and Statistical Manual of Mental Disorders* (DSM-III-R) criteria as having generalized anxiety disorder. DSM-III-R defines generalized anxiety disorder as a chronic disorder (lasting longer than six months) characterized by unrealistic or excessive worry about two or more life circumstances.

EPIDEMIOLOGY

The prevalence of generalized anxiety disorder has been estimated by some studies to be 2 to 5 percent. Other studies have suggested that this disorder is much less common and that many patients classified as having generalized anxiety disorder actually have other anxiety disorders (such as panic disorder), anxiety associated with depression, or anxiety associated with personality disorders.

The ratio of women to men is approximately 2 to 1; however, the ratio of women to men receiving inpatient treatment for this disorder is closer to 1 to 1. The disorder most often develops in the 20s, although persons of any age can be affected. Only one-third of patients who have generalized anxiety disorder actually seek psychiatric treatment. Many go to their general practitioners, cardiologists, or pulmonary specialists.

ETIOLOGY

It is hypothesized that noradrenergic, γ-aminobutyric acid (GABA)-ergic, and serotonergic neuronal systems in the frontal lobe and limbic system are involved in the pathophysiology of this disorder. Many studies have demonstrated that the patients tend to have increased sympathetic tone with a greater than usual response and slower adaptation to stressful stimuli. At least one recent study, however, reported that patients with generalized anxiety disorder have a decreased autonomic response to stressful stimuli. A variety of electroencephalogram (EEG) abnormalities have been noted in alpha rhythm and evoked potentials. Sleep EEG studies have reported increased sleep discontinuity, decreased delta sleep, decreased stage 1 sleep, and reduced rapid eye movement (REM) sleep—changes that are different from those seen in depression. Although many studies were used to support the separation of generalized anxiety disorder from panic disorder in DSM-III-R, a few studies suggest that a subset of patients with generalized anxiety disorder may have some biological similarities to patients with panic disorder.

Genetic evidence indicates that some aspects of this disorder may be inherited. Approximately 25 percent of first-degree relatives are affected, women more often than men. Male relatives are more likely to have an alcohol-related disorder. Although they are controversial, some twin studies report a concordance rate of 50 percent in monozygotic twins and 15 percent in dizygotic twins.

The psychosocial theories involve the principles discussed previously about the genesis of anxiety in a person. (For a more complete overview of this topic, see Section 17.1, "Normal and Pathological Anxiety.")

CLINICAL FEATURES

The clinical signs and symptoms of generalized anxiety disorder are listed in DSM-III-R (Table 17.6-1). It has been reported that the cardiac and respiratory symptoms are fewer and less severe in generalized anxiety disorder than in panic disorder but that the gastrointestinal and muscular symptoms are similar in intensity. Depression is a common feature. It is important to elicit the cause or focus of a patient's anxiety because such information is necessary for the differential diagnosis.

COURSE AND PROGNOSIS

Some data suggest that life events are associated with the onset of generalized anxiety disorder. The data suggest that the occurrence of several negative life events greatly increases the likelihood that this disorder will develop in a person. By definition, generalized anxiety disorder is a chronic condition that may well be lifelong. As many as 25 percent of the patients go on to panic disorder. DSM-III-R notes that generalized anxiety disorder occasionally develops following a major depressive episode.

DIAGNOSIS

The diagnosis is made according to the criteria listed in DSM-III-R (Table 17.6-1). The focus of the anxiety cannot be a single item, and it cannot be related to the anticipatory anxiety seen in panic disorder or the obsession in obsessive-compulsive disorder. If a patient has a mood disorder, in order for the diagnosis of generalized anxiety disorder to be made, the symptoms of anxiety must be present in the absence of active mood disorder symptoms.

The differential diagnosis of generalized anxiety disorder includes all medical disorders that may cause anxiety (see Table 17.2-5 in Section 17.2, "Panic Disorder and Agoraphobia"). It is particularly important to rule out caffeine intoxication, stimulant abuse, alcohol withdrawal, and sedative or hypnotic withdrawal. The mental status examination and history should carefully explore the diagnostic possibilities of panic disorder, phobias, and obsessive-compulsive disorder. Other diagnostic possibilities to be considered are adjustment disorder with anxious mood, depression, dysthymia, schizophrenia, somatization

Table 17.6-1
Diagnostic Criteria for Generalized Anxiety Disorder

A. Unrealistic or excessive anxiety and worry (apprehensive expectation) about two or more life circumstances (e.g., worry about possible misfortune to one's child who is in no danger and worry about finances for no good reason), for a period of six months or longer, during which the person has been bothered more days than not by these concerns. In children and adolescents, this may take the form of anxiety and worry about academic, athletic, and social performance.

B. If another Axis I disorder is present, the focus of the anxiety and worry in A is unrelated to it, e.g., the anxiety or worry is not about having a panic attack (as in panic disorder), being embarassed in public (as in social phobia), being contaminated (as in obsessive-compulsive disorder), or gaining weight (as in anorexia nervosa).

C. The disturbance does not occur only during the course of a mood disorder or a psychotic disorder.

D. At least 6 of the following 18 symptoms are often present when anxious (do not include symptoms present only during panic attacks):

Motor tension

(1) trembling, twitching, or feeling shaky
(2) muscle tension, aches, or soreness
(3) restlessness
(4) easy fatigability

Autonomic hyperactivity

(5) shortness of breath or smothering sensations
(6) palpitations or accelerated heart rate (tachycardia)
(7) sweating, or cold clammy hands
(8) dry mouth
(9) dizziness or light-headedness
(10) nausea, diarrhea, or other abdominal distress
(11) flushes (hot flashes) or chills
(12) frequent urination
(13) trouble swallowing or "lump in throat"

Vigilance and scanning

(14) feeling keyed up or on edge
(15) exaggerated startle response
(16) difficulty concentrating or "mind going blank" because of anxiety
(17) trouble falling or staying asleep
(18) irritability

E. It cannot be established that an organic factor initiated and maintained the disturbance (e.g., hyperthyroidism, caffeine intoxication).

disorder, and depersonalization disorder. The following illustrates a case of generalized anxiety disorder:

A 27-year-old married electrician complained of dizziness, sweating palms, heart palpitations, and ringing in the ears of more than 18 months' duration. He also experienced dry throat, periods of uncontrollable shaking, and a constant edgy and watchful feeling that often interfered with his ability to concentrate. These feelings had been present most of the time over the previous two years; they had not been limited to discrete periods.

Because of these symptoms he had seen a family practitioner, a neurologist, a neurosurgeon, a chiropractor, and an ear, nose, and throat specialist. He had been given a hypoglycemic diet, received physiotherapy for a pinched nerve, and told he might have an inner ear problem.

For the past two years he had had few social contacts because of his nervous symptoms. Although he sometimes had to leave work when the symptoms became intolerable, he continued to work for the same company for which he had worked since his apprenticeship after high school graduation. He tended to hide his symptoms from his wife and children, to whom he wanted to appear perfect, and he reported few problems with them as a result of his nervousness.

Discussion. Symptoms of motor tension (uncontrollable shaking), autonomic hyperactivity (dizziness, sweating palms, heart palpitations), and vigilance and scanning (a constant edgy and watchful feeling) suggested an anxiety disorder. Because the symptoms were not limited to discrete periods, as in panic disorder, and were not focused on a discrete stimulus, as in a phobic disorder, the diagnosis was generalized anxiety disorder.

Although the patient had consulted numerous physicians for his symptoms, the absence of preoccupation with fears of having a specific physical disease precluded a diagnosis of hypochondriasis.

TREATMENT

Psychotherapy

Psychotherapy is the treatment of choice and can be combined with antianxiety medication if indicated. Once the suitability of the patient for such therapy has been determined, the method of approach depends on the nature of the problem underlying the anxiety. As a general rule, neurotic difficulties that involve characterological difficulties require insight-oriented, long-term psychotherapy. If the psychological problem is circumscribed and is related to specific external circumstances, brief forms of uncovering therapy may be quite effective in freeing patients from their conflicts and relieving them of their symptoms.

Most patients experience a marked lessening of anxiety when given the opportunity to discuss their difficulties with a concerned and sympathetic physician. Frequently, after the initial hidden precipitants have been determined in the course of a few interviews, the specific supportive technique to be used becomes clear. Reassurance about unrealistic fears, encouragement to face anxiety-provoking situations, and the continued opportunity to talk regularly to the psychiatrist about their problems are all helpful to patients, even if these techniques are not definitively curative. If doctors discover external situations that are anxiety provoking, they may be able themselves or with the help of the patients and their families to change the environment and thus reduce the stressful pressures. A reduction in symptoms may often allow the patients to function more effectively in their daily work and relationships, which provides new rewards and gratifications that are in themselves therapeutic.

Behavioral approaches to generalized anxiety disorder involve emphasis on cognitive coping strategies, relaxation, meditation, and biofeedback.

Pharmacotherapy

The decision to prescribe an anxiolytic drug to patients with generalized anxiety disorder should rarely be made on the first visit. Because of the chronic nature of this disorder, a treatment plan must be carefully thought out. The two major drugs to be considered for the treatment of generalized anxiety disorder are the benzodiazepines and buspirone (BuSpar). Other drugs that may be useful are the tricyclic antidepressants, the β-adrenergic antagonists, and the antihistamines. There is virtually never a reason to justify the use of the older anxiolytic agents, such as the barbiturates, carbamates (such as meprobamate [Equanil, Miltown]), or piperidinediones (such as glutethimide [Doriden]).

Benzodiazepines. Benzodiazepines have been the drugs of choice for this disorder. In generalized anxiety disorder, these drugs can be prescribed on an as-needed basis, so that patients take a rapidly acting benzodiazepine when they feel particularly anxious. The alternative approach is to prescribe a standing dose of benzodiazepines for a limited period, during which psychosocial therapeutic approaches are implemented. Several problems are associated with the use of benzodiazepines in this disorder. Approximately 25 to 30 percent of all patients fail to respond, and tolerance and dependence may occur. Some patients also experience impaired alertness while taking these drugs and are, therefore, at risk for accidents involving automobiles or machinery.

The clinical decision to initiate treatment with a benzodiazepine should be a considered and specific one. The patient's diagnosis, the specific target symptoms, and the duration of treatment—all should be defined, and this information should be shared with the patient. Treatment for most anxiety conditions lasts for two to six weeks, followed by one or two weeks of tapering the drug before it is discontinued. The most common clinical mistake with benzodiazepine treatment is to decide passively to continue treatment indefinitely.

For the treatment of anxiety, it is usual to begin a drug at the low end of its therapeutic range (Table 17.6-2) and to increase the dose to achieve a therapeutic response. The use of a benzodiazepine with an intermediate half-life (8 to 15 hours) is likely to avoid some of the adverse effects associated with the use of benzodiazepines with long half-lives. The use of divided doses prevents the development of adverse effects associated with high peak plasma levels. The improvement produced by benzodiazepines may go beyond a simple antianxiety effect. For example, these drugs may cause the patient to regard various occurrences in a positive light. The drugs may also have a mild disinhibiting action, similar to that observed after modest amounts of alcohol.

Buspirone. Buspirone (BuSpar), a nonbenzodiazepine anxiolytic, is a useful drug for patients with generalized anxiety disorder. Although its onset of action may be delayed, buspirone lacks many of the problems of sedation and the potential for abuse of the benzodiazepines. Buspirone should be started at a dosage of 5 mg twice daily and increased to 15 to 60 mg daily in divided doses. The antianxiety effects of buspirone may take one to three weeks to appear, thereby paralleling the delayed therapeutic effects of antipsychotic and antidepressant medications. Some clinicians suggest that buspirone may be the drug of first choice for the treatment of anxiety in patients who have not received benzodiazepines in the past. Patients who have previously received benzodiazepines often complain that buspirone is not as effective. This

Table 17.6-2
Benzodiazepine and Triazolobenzodiazepine Drugs

Generic Name	Trade Name	Half-Life (hour)	Dosage (mg a day)
Long-acting			
Diazepam	Valium	60	2–60
Chlordiazepoxide	Librium	24–48	15–100
Clorazepate	Tranxene	100	7.5–60
Halazepam	Paxipam	50	60–160
Prazepam	Centrax	100	20–60
Clonazepam*	Klonopin	34	1.5–20
Flurazepam†	Dalmane	100	15–30
Quazepam†	Doral	40–60	7.5–15
Short-acting			
Oxazepam	Serax	8	30–120
Lorazepam	Ativan	15	2–6
Alprazolam‡	Xanax	12	0.5–6
Temazepam†	Restoril	11	15–30
Triazolam†,‡	Halcion	2	0.125–0.5
Midazolam§	Versed	2	2–4

Table by Jack M. Gorman, M.D., and John M. Davis, M.D.
*Marketed as an anticonvulsant.
†Marketed as a hypnotic.
‡Triazolobenzodiazepine.
§Only manufactured in parenteral form.

response may be due to the absence, with buspirone treatment, of some of the nonanxiolytic effects of benzodiazepines (such as muscle relaxation and the additional sense of well-being). Buspirone is not an effective treatment for benzodiazepine withdrawal.

Other drugs. It was thought previously that tricyclic antidepressants were ineffective in treating generalized anxiety disorder. More recent studies, however, demonstrate that tricyclic antidepressants can be effective in treating this disorder. The onset of effects is delayed two to three weeks, but some data suggest that the tricyclic drugs may be more effective than the benzodiazepines in treating the psychic component of anxiety. Conversely, the benzodiazepines may be more effective in treating the somatic components of anxiety. β-Adrenergic blocking drugs, such as propranolol (Inderal), have been used to treat the peripheral symptoms of anxiety, and antihistamines have been used in patients whose abuse potential for benzodiazepine treatment was particularly high.

References

Anderson D J, Noyes R Jr, Crowe R R: A comparison of panic disorder and generalized anxiety disorder. Am J Psychiatry *141*: 572, 1984.

Barlow D H, Blanchard E B, Vermilyea J A: Generalized anxiety and generalized anxiety disorder: Description and reconceptualization. Am J Psychiatry *143*: 40, 1986.

Blazer D, Hughes D, George L K: Stressful life events and the onset of a generalized anxiety syndrome. Am J Psychiatry *144*: 1178, 1987.

Buchsbaum M S, Hazlett E, Sicotte N: Topographic EEG changes with benzodiazepine administration in generalized anxiety disorder. Biol Psychiatry *20*: 832, 1985.

Cowley D S, Dager S R, McClellan J, Roy-Byrne P P, Dunner D L: Response to lactate infusion in generalized anxiety disorder. Biol Psychiatry *24*: 409, 1988.

Dubovsky S L: Generalized anxiety disorder: New concepts and psychopharmacologic therapies. J Clin Psychiatry *51*(1, Suppl): 3, 1990.

Gorman J M, Papp L A: Chronic anxiety: Deciding the length of treatment. J Clin Psychiatry *51*(1, Suppl): 11, 1990.

Hoehn-Saric R, McLeod D R, Zimmerli W D: Differential effects of alprazolam and imipramine in generalized anxiety disorder: Somatic versus psychic symptoms. J Clin Psychiatry *49*: 293, 1988.

Hoehn-Saric R, McLeod D R, Zimmerli W D: Somatic manifestations in women with generalized anxiety disorder. Arch Gen Psychiatry *46*: 1113, 1989.

Hoehn-Saric R, McLeod D R, Zimmerli W D: Symptoms and treatment responses of generalized anxiety disorder patients with high versus low levels of cardiovascular complaints. Am J Psychiatry *146*: 854, 1989.

Kahn R J, McNair D M, Lipman R S: Imipramine and chlordiazepoxide in depressive and anxiety disorders. Arch Gen Psychiatry *43*: 79, 1986.

Prusoff B, Klerman G L: Differentiating depressed from anxious neurotic outpatients. Arch Gen Psychiatry *30*: 302, 1974.

Riskind J H, Beck A T, Berchick R J, Brown G, Steer R A: Reliability of DSM-III diagnoses for major depression and generalized anxiety disorder using the structured clinical interview for DSM-III. Arch Gen Psychiatry *44*: 817, 1987.

18

Somatoform Disorders

The somatoform disorders have in common the presence of one or more physical complaints for which an adequate physical explanation cannot be found. There is usually an absence of findings or only minor findings on physical or laboratory examination. The complaints of the patient may seem greatly exaggerated in comparison with the minor physical or laboratory abnormalities that are identified.

The nomenclature for the somatoform disorders has been quite confused over the years. The terms "hysteria" and "hypochondriasis" have been used with many different meanings by different writers. The revised third edition of *Diagnostic and Statistical Manual of Mental Disorders* (DSM-III-R) has divided the somatoform disorders into seven categories based on the number of somatic complaints, the type of physical complaint, and the cognitive or delusional state of the patient. The first six types of somatoform disorders are (1) somatization disorder, (2) conversion disorder, (3) somatoform pain disorder, (4) hypochondriasis, (5) body dysmorphic disorder, and (6) undifferentiated somatoform disorder. DSM-III-R includes a seventh category, somatoform disorder not otherwise specified (NOS), for disorders that cannot be classified as any of the previous categories.

SOMATIZATION DISORDER

Somatization disorder is a chronic syndrome of multiple somatic symptoms that cannot be explained medically and is associated with psychosocial distress and medical help-seeking. The DSM-III-R diagnosis (Table 18-1) requires a history of several years' duration, beginning before the age of 30. The somatic symptoms must not be caused by medical disease or by medication, drugs, or alcohol; and they must be troublesome enough to cause patients to take a medication other than aspirin, to visit a physician, or to alter their life-styles. These diagnostic symptoms must come from among a list of symptoms, which are clustered into six groups. There is no requirement regarding the distribution of the symptoms among the groups.

Somatization disorder was first known as hysteria, a term first used in the 1850s to describe the syndrome as it appears today. It was also called Briquet's syndrome, after Paul Briquet, the French physician who identified patients with medical symptoms but no demonstrable medical disease.

Epidemiology

Estimates of the lifetime prevalence of somatization disorder range from 0.2 to 0.4 percent. Because of an approximately twentyfold greater prevalence in women than in men, the point prevalence in women is estimated to be 1 to 2 percent. For outpatient primary care patients, the point prevalence may be as high as 10 percent. Somatization disorder is inversely related to social position, occurring most often among the little-educated, the poor, and those of low occupational status. Somatization disorder is defined as beginning before age 30; it most often begins during a person's teens.

Somatization disorder tends to run in families, occurring in 10 to 20 percent of the first-degree female relatives of somatization disorder patients. Within these families first-degree male relatives are prone to alcoholism, drug abuse, and antisocial personality disorder. One study also reported a concordance rate of 29 percent in monozygotic twins and 10 percent in dizygotic twins.

Etiology

The cause of somatization disorder is unknown, although its familial aggregation suggests genetic or environmental factors. Social, cultural, and ethnic factors that foster somatization in general may have a causative role in the disorder or at least contribute to its expression. Parental teaching, parental example, and cultural and ethnic mores teach some children to somatize. In addition, many patients with the disorder come from unstable homes and have been physically abused.

Some studies suggest a neuropsychological basis for somatization disorder. They propose that the patients have characteristic attentional and cognitive impairments that result in the faulty perception and assessment of somatosensory input. The reported impairments include excessive distractibility, inability to habituate to repetitive stimuli, the grouping of cognitive constructs on an impressionistic basis, and partial and circumstantial associations.

Clinical Features

Patients with somatization disorder have a multitude of somatic complaints and long, complicated medical histories. Nausea and vomiting (other than during pregnancy), difficulty swallowing, pain in the arms and legs, shortness of breath unrelated to exertion, amnesia, and complica-

Table 18-1
Diagnostic Criteria for Somatization Disorder

A. A history of many physical complaints or a belief that one is sickly, beginning before the age of 30 and persisting for several years.

B. At least 13 symptoms from the list below. To count a symptom as significant, the following criteria must be met:
(1) no organic pathology or pathophysiological mechanism (e.g., a physical disorder or the effects of injury, medication, drugs, or alcohol) to account for the symptom or, when there is related organic pathology, the complaint or resulting social or occupational impairment is grossly in excess of what would be expected from the physical findings
(2) has not occurred only during a panic attack
(3) has caused the person to take medicine (other than over-the-counter pain medication), see a doctor, or alter life-style

Symptom list:

Gastrointestinal symptoms:

(1) **vomiting (other than during pregnancy)**
(2) abdominal pain (other than when menstruating)
(3) nausea (other than motion sickness)
(4) bloating (gassy)
(5) diarrhea
(6) intolerance of (gets sick from) several different foods

Pain symptoms:

(7) **pain in extremities**
(8) back pain
(9) joint pain
(10) pain during urination
(11) other pain (excluding headaches)

Cardiopulmonary symptoms:

(12) **shortness of breath when not exerting oneself**
(13) palpitations
(14) chest pain
(15) dizziness

Conversion or pseudoneurological symptoms:

(16) **amnesia**
(17) **difficulty swallowing**
(18) loss of voice
(19) deafness
(20) double vision
(21) blurred vision
(22) blindness
(23) fainting or loss of consciousness
(24) seizure or convulsion
(25) trouble walking
(26) paralysis or muscle weakness
(27) urinary retention or difficulty urinating

Sexual symptoms for the major part of the person's life after opportunities for sexual activity:

(28) **burning sensation in sexual organs or rectum (other than during intercourse)**
(29) sexual indifference
(30) pain during intercourse
(31) impotence

Female reproductive symptoms judged by the person to occur more frequently or severely than in most women:

(32) **painful menstruation**
(33) irregular menstrual periods
(34) excessive menstrual bleeding
(35) vomiting throughout pregnancy

Note: The seven items in boldface may be used to screen for the disorder. The presence of two or more of these items suggests a high likelihood of the disorder.

tions of pregnancy and menstruation are among the most common symptoms. The belief that one has been sickly most of one's life is also common.

Psychological distress and interpersonal problems are prominent, with anxiety and depression being the most prevalent psychiatric conditions. Suicide threats are frequent, but actual suicide is rare. If suicide does occur, it is usually associated with substance abuse. The patients' medical histories are circumstantial, vague, imprecise, inconsistent, and disorganized. They describe their complaints in a dramatic, emotional, and exaggerated fashion, with vivid and colorful language. Such patients confuse temporal sequences and cannot clearly distinguish current symptoms from past history. They are often dressed in an exhibitionistic manner and may be coy or seductive. They are described as dependent, self-centered, hungry for admiration and praise, and manipulative.

Somatization disorder is commonly associated with other psychiatric diagnoses, most often with antisocial and histrionic personality disorders and substance abuse (both alcohol and other drugs). These associated disorders and the symptoms of somatization disorder can, not surprisingly, lead to an increased incidence of marital, occupational, and social problems. There is increasing appreciation for an association between somatization disorder and both depression and anxiety disorders. A clinical case example reported by Arthur J. Barsky, M.D., follows:

A 29-year-old mother of two requested medical clearance for impending surgery for cysts in her breasts. She described the cysts as rapidly enlarging and unbearably painful. While drawing attention to her breasts, she noted, "They are so large and so tender to the touch. And I just can't have relations—forget that."

She also had disabling back pain that spread up and down her spine and made her "legs give out" on her suddenly, causing her to fall. When discussing this, she winced visibly, adding: "Oh, there it goes—my back keeps clicking. The pain is so severe it affects me with my kids. Pain like that will make anyone into a beast." (She had previously been suspected of child abuse.) She also complained of dyspnea and a dry cough that prevented her from walking uphill.

Her medical history began at menarche with dysmenorrhea and menorrhagia. At 18 she had exploratory surgery for a possible ovarian cyst and was subsequently reoperated on for suspected abdominal adhesions. She also had a history of recurrent urinary tract symptoms, although no organisms were ever clearly documented, and she had a normal workup for "an enlarged thyroid." At various times she had received the diagnoses of spastic colon, migraine, and endometriosis.

Two marriages, both to alcoholic and abusive men who refused to pay child support, had ended in divorce. She had lost several clerical jobs because of excessive absences. During the periods when she felt worst, she spent most of the day at home in a bathrobe while her relatives cared for her children. She had a history of narcotic addiction and claimed that she began using analgesics for her back pain and then, "I overdid it."

The physical examination at the time of her visit revealed inconsistencies of the breast tissue but no frank masses, and mammography findings were normal.

Differential Diagnosis

The clinician must always rule out organic causes for the patient's symptoms. Medical disorders that present with nonspecific, transient abnormalities pose the greatest diagnostic difficulty: these include multiple sclerosis, systemic lupus erythematosus, acquired immune deficiency syndrome (AIDS), acute intermittent porphyria, hyperparathyroidism, and chronic systemic infections. Moreover, the onset of many somatic symptoms late in life must be presumed to be caused by a medical illness until testing rules it out.

The psychiatric differential diagnosis includes depression, anxiety disorders, and schizophrenia. Although the symptoms of anxiety or panic attacks generally supersede the somatic complaints in anxiety disorder patients, patients with anxiety disorders often complain about the somatic symptoms before they mention the subjective anxiety. The initial stages of both depression and schizophrenia can begin with a patient's complaints about somatic problems. Eventually, the characteristic symptoms of these disorders evidence themselves and make the correct diagnosis more straightforward.

Conversion symptoms form one of the six groups of symptoms in somatization disorder; therefore, multiple recurrent conversion reactions beginning before age 30 should be diagnosed as somatization disorder. The symptoms of somatization disorder are not, however, restricted to sensorimotor and neurological complaints; they cover a far broader range.

Hypochondriasis is distinguished from somatization disorder in that it includes the conviction and fear of disease, as well as bodily preoccupation, and it usually begins in young adulthood. Somatoform pain patients have symptoms limited to pain but in other ways may be quite similar to patients with somatization disorder.

Course and Prognosis

Somatization disorder is a chronic condition that runs a fluctuating course, but patients are rarely entirely asymptomatic. It is unusual for them to go for more than a year without some medical attention. But they do not appear to have a significantly higher mortality rate than the general population.

Treatment

Somatization patients need a long-term, empathic relationship with a single physician, as the more physicians are involved, the more opportunities such patients have for manipulation and for unnecessary medical interventions.

Psychotherapy is helpful to patients with somatization disorder and has been shown to decrease somatization disorder patients' personal health care expenditures by 50 percent, largely by decreasing their rates of hospitalization but without lowering their functional status or satisfaction with medical care. In psychotherapy, patients are helped to cope with their symptoms and possibly to eliminate them.

In treating somatization disorder patients, clinicians should avoid psychotropic medications and prescription analgesics, although some clinicians think that antianxiety agents and antidepressants are helpful when anxiety or depression is prominent. In any case, medications must be carefully monitored because somatization disorder patients tend to use them erratically and unreliably.

CONVERSION DISORDER

DSM-III-R specifically includes the presence of an etiologically relevant psychological conflict in the diagnostic criteria of conversion disorder, a disorder involving a loss of or change in bodily functioning that cannot be explained by any known medical disorder or pathophysiological process (Table 18-2). The psychological conflict is in the patient's unconscious, and the physical symptom is not under voluntary control.

Epidemiology

The incidence and the prevalence of conversion disorders are unclear. In some surveys the lifetime prevalence of conversion symptoms is as high as 33 percent. The prevalence among general hospital inpatients receiving psy-

Table 18-2
Diagnostic Criteria for Conversion Disorder

A. A loss of, or alteration in, physical functioning suggesting a physical disorder.

B. Psychological factors are judged to be etiologically related to the symptom because of a temporal relationship between a psychosocial stressor that is apparently related to a psychological conflict or need and initiation or exacerbation of the symptom.

C. The person is not conscious of intentionally producing the symptom.

D. The symptom is not a culturally sanctioned response pattern and cannot, after appropriate investigation, be explained by a known physical disorder.

E. The symptom is not limited to pain or to a disturbance in sexual functioning.

Specify: single episode or **recurrent.**

Table from DSM-III-R, *Diagnostic and Statistical Manual of Mental Disorders,* ed 3, revised. Copyright American Psychiatric Association, Washington, DC, 1987, with permission.

chiatric consultations has been reported to be between 5 and 16 percent. In contrast, the prevalence of conversion reactions among patients in ongoing psychiatric treatment appears to be considerably lower. The annual incidence of conversion disorders in patients seen by general psychiatrists has been reported to be 0.01 to 0.02 percent.

Conversion disorder is from two to five times more common in women than in men. Men with conversion disorder have often been involved in an industrial, other occupational, or military accident. Conversion disorder can occur in persons of any age, although it is most common in adolescents and young adults. A high incidence of conversion disorder appears among low socioeconomic groups, rural populations, and persons with little education. Some evidence suggests a familial aggregation and a tendency for a conversion disorder patient to be the youngest child in the family.

Etiology

According to psychoanalytic theory, conversion is caused by the repression of unconscious intrapsychic conflict and the conversion of the anxiety into a physical symptom. The conflict occurs between an instinctual impulse (e.g., aggressive or sexual) and the prohibitions against its expression. The symptoms allow partial expression of the forbidden wish or urge but disguise it sufficiently that the patients need not consciously confront their unacceptable impulses. That is, the conversion symptom has a symbolic relationship to the unconscious conflict. The conversion symptoms also enable the patients to communicate that they need special consideration and special treatment. Such symptoms may thus function as a nonverbal means of controlling or manipulating others.

Some clinicians believe that conversion disorder has a neuropsychological basis, as some conversion disorder patients appear to have a disturbance in their central nervous system arousal. It has been theorized that their symptoms are caused by an excessive cortical arousal that sets off negative feedback loops between the cerebral cortex and the brain stem's reticular formation. Elevated levels of corticofugal output, in turn, inhibit afferent sensorimotor impulses, thus diminishing the awareness of bodily sensation that in some conversion disorder patients could explain the observed sensory deficits. In some conversion disorder patients, neuropsychological tests reveal subtle cerebral impairments in verbal communication and memory, vigilance, and attention; affective incongruity; and suggestibility. Some follow-up studies indicate that 50 to 70 percent of conversion disorder patients have some diagnosable neurological disorder three to four years after the diagnosis of conversion disorder.

Clinical Features

Paralysis, blindness, and mutism have been reported to be the most common conversion disorder symptoms. It has been reported that conversion disorder is often associated with passive-aggressive, dependent, antisocial, or histrionic personality disorder. Depressive symptoms can accompany conversion disorder, and patients with conversion disorder are also at risk for suicide.

Sensory symptoms. In conversion disorder, anesthesia and paresthesia are common, especially of the extremities. All sensory modalities can be involved, and the distribution of the disturbance is inconsistent with that of either central or peripheral neurological disease. Thus, one may see the characteristic stocking-and-glove anesthesia of the hands or feet or the hemianesthesia of the body beginning precisely along the midline.

Conversion symptoms may involve the organs of special sense, producing deafness, blindness, and tunnel vision. These symptoms may be unilateral or bilateral. Neurological evaluation, however, reveals intact sensory pathways. In conversion blindness, for example, patients walk around without collisions or self-injury; their pupils react to light; and their cortical evoked potentials are normal. Anosmia, vomiting, and pseudocyesis (false pregnancy) are other conversion symptoms.

Motor symptoms. Motor symptoms include abnormal movements, gait disturbance, weaknesses, and paralyses. Gross rhythmical tremors, choreiform tics, and jerks may be present. These movements generally worsen when attention is called to them. A common gait disturbance is a wildly ataxic, staggering gait accompanied by gross, irregular, jerky truncal movements and thrashing and waving arms (known as astasia-abasia). Patients with these symptoms rarely fall, and, if they do, they are generally not injured. Convulsive movements are also sometimes seen.

Other common motor disturbances are paralysis and paresis, involving one, two, or all four limbs, although the distribution of the involved muscles does not conform to neural pathways. Reflexes remain normal; there are no fasciculations or muscle atrophy (except after long-standing conversion paralysis); and electromyography findings are normal.

Other associated features. The absence of a medical cause is necessary but not sufficient for the diagnosis of conversion disorder. A psychological cause should also be established. DSM-III-R requires the identification of a psychological cause, as evidenced by a temporal relationship between the symptom and a significant psychosocial stressor or by the presence of secondary gain.

Primary gain. Patients achieve primary gain by keeping internal conflicts outside their awareness. The symptom then has symbolic value in that it represents the unconscious psychological conflict.

Secondary gain. Secondary gain refers to the tangible advantages and benefits that accrue to people as a result of their becoming sick, such as being excused from obligations and difficult life situations, receiving support and assistance that might not otherwise be forthcoming, and controlling other people's behavior.

La belle indifférence. *La belle indifférence* refers to the patient's inappropriately cavalier attitude toward a serious symptom. That is, the patient seems unconcerned about what appears to be a major impairment. This bland indifference, however, may be lacking in some conversion disorder patients and is also seen in some seriously ill medical patients who develop a stoic attitude.

Identification. Conversion patients may unconsciously model their symptoms on those of someone important to them. For example, a parent or a person who has recently died may serve as a model for the conversion disorder. It is common during the bereaved's pathological grief reaction to have the symptoms of the deceased.

A clinical case example follows:

A 46-year-old housewife was referred by her husband's psychiatrist for consultation. In the course of discussing certain marital conflicts that he was having with his wife, the husband had described attacks of dizziness that his wife experienced that left her incapacitated.

In consultation the wife described being overcome with feelings of extreme dizziness, accompanied by slight nausea, four or five nights a week. During these attacks, the room around her would take on a "shimmering" appearance, and she would have the feeling that she was floating and unable to keep her balance. Inexplicably, the attacks almost always occurred at about 4 P.M. She usually had to lie down on a couch and often did not feel better until 7 or 8 P.M. After recovering, she generally spent the rest of the evening watching television; more often than not, she would fall asleep in the living room, not going to bed in the bedroom until 2 or 3 A.M.

The patient had been pronounced physically fit by her internist, a neurologist, and an ear, nose, and throat specialist on more than one occasion. Hypoglycemia had been ruled out by glucose tolerance tests.

When asked about her marriage, the patient described her husband as a tyrant, frequently demanding and verbally abusive of her and their four children. She admitted that she dreaded his arrival home from work each day, knowing that he would comment that the house was a mess and the dinner, if prepared, not to his liking. Since the onset of her attacks, when she was unable to make dinner, he and the four children would go to McDonald's or the local pizza parlor. After that he would settle in to watch a ball game on television in the bedroom, and their conversation was minimal. In spite of their troubles, the patient claimed that she loved and needed her husband very much.

Differential Diagnosis

One of the major problems in diagnosing conversion disorder is the difficulty in definitively ruling out a medical disorder. Concomitant organic disease is common in hospitalized patients with conversion disorder, and evidence of a current or prior neurological disorder or of a systemic disease affecting the brain has been reported in from 18 to 64 percent of such patients.

Neurological disorders (such as dementia and other degenerative diseases), brain tumors, and basal ganglia disease must be ruled out. For instance, weakness may be confused with myasthenia gravis, polymyositis, acquired myopathies, or multiple sclerosis. Optic neuritis may be misdiagnosed as conversion blindness. Signs and symptoms that are inconsistent with anatomical distributions and known pathophysiological mechanisms or that vary from one examination to another are more likely to be caused by conversion disorder than by medical disease. A thorough medical and neurological workup is, thus, essential to all cases. If the symptoms can be resolved by suggestion, hypnosis, or intravenous amobarbital (Amytal), the symptoms are probably psychogenic.

Conversion symptoms occur in schizophrenia and in depressive disorder. Schizophrenia, with its dissolution of reality testing and illogical thinking, generally can be distinguished. Depression can usually be separated from conversion disorder because it is more pervasive and lasts longer.

Sensorimotor symptoms occur in somatization disorder as well. But somatization disorder is a more chronic illness, beginning early in life and including symptoms in many other organ systems. In hypochondriasis there is no actual loss or distortion of function. The somatic complaints are more chronic and are not limited to neurological symptoms, and the characteristic hypochondriacal attitudes and beliefs are present. If the patient's symptoms are limited to pain, then somatoform pain disorder can be diagnosed. The patient whose complaints are limited to sexual function is classified as having a sexual dysfunction, rather than a conversion disorder.

In both malingering and factitious disorders, the symptoms are under conscious, voluntary control. The malingerer's history is usually more inconsistent and contradictory than is the conversion patient's history, and the malingerer's fraudulent behavior is clearly goal-directed.

Course and Prognosis

Individual conversion symptoms are generally of short duration, starting and stopping abruptly. About 25 percent of all patients develop another conversion symptom during the succeeding one to six years. There is generally only one symptom during a single conversion episode. Subsequent episodes may involve either the same or a different symptom. Patients with long histories of conversion symptoms and those with many secondary gains do poorly.

Treatment

A thorough medical workup is essential for diagnosis and is a cornerstone for the initiation of treatment. If no medical causes are found, the patients can be reassured that the symptom will eventually subside. It can be suggested to the patients that a psychological approach to managing the problem should be tried and that the therapy will focus on issues of stress and coping. Telling such patients that their symptoms are imaginary often makes things worse, rather than better. Psychodynamic approaches include psychoanalysis and insight-oriented psychotherapy, in which patients explore intrapsychic conflicts and the symbolism of the conversion symptom. Hypnosis, anxiolytics (for those patients who are unusually anxious), and behavioral relaxation exercises are effective in some cases. An amobarbital (Amytal) interview may be necessary to obtain more history, especially when there has been a specific traumatic event, to help the patient reexperience the traumatic event and to suggest that the symptom will disappear. Brief and direct forms of short-term psychotherapy have also been used to treat conversion disorder. The longer that such patients have been in the sick role and the more that they have regressed, the more difficult the treatment is.

SOMATOFORM PAIN DISORDER

The predominant symptom in somatoform pain disorder is severe and prolonged pain for which there is no medical explanation. DSM-III-R includes specific diagnostic criteria for this disorder (Table 18-3), which had previously been called psychogenic pain disorder and idiopathic pain disorder.

Somatoform pain disorder patients do not constitute a uniform or internally cohesive group but, instead, are a collection of heterogeneous patients with pain, such as low back pain, headache, atypical facial pain, and chronic pelvic pain. The patients' pain may be posttraumatic, neuropathic, neurological, iatrogenic, or musculoskeletal. Some patients have another psychiatric disorder (especially depression, an anxiety disorder, or a somatoform disorder), whereas others do not.

The causes of somatoform pain disorder are presumed to be psychological, even though evidence for them may not be readily apparent in each case. DSM-III-R requires that there be six months of preoccupation with pain and either that there be no organic pathology to account for the pain or that the pain grossly exceed whatever demonstrable pathology is present.

Table 18-3
Diagnostic Criteria for Somatoform Pain Disorder

A. Preoccupation with pain for at least six months.

B. Either (1) or (2):
  (1) appropriate evaluation uncovers no organic pathology or pathophysiological mechanism (e.g., a physical disorder or the effects of injury) to account for the pain.
  (2) when there is related organic pathology, the complaint of pain or resulting social or occupational impairment is grossly in excess of what would be expected from the physical findings.

Table from DSM-III-R, *Diagnostic and Statistical Manual of Mental Disorders*, ed 3, revised. Copyright American Psychiatric Association, Washington, DC, 1987, with permission.

Epidemiology

The symptom of pain is perhaps the most frequent complaint in medical practice. Intractable pain syndromes are also common. In 1980 more than $10 billion was spent on disability payments to patients with chronic pain problems. Low back pain alone has disabled an estimated 7 million Americans and accounts for more than 8 million physician office visits yearly.

Somatoform pain disorder is diagnosed twice as frequently in women as in men. The peak age of onset is in the fourth and five decades, as the tolerance for pain declines with age. It is also most common among people in blue-collar occupations. There is an increased likelihood for first-degree relatives of somatoform pain disorder patients to have the same disorder. Depression and alcohol abuse are also more common than usual in the families of these patients.

Etiology

Psychodynamic factors. Pain has unconscious meanings, which originate in infantile and childhood experiences. Pain can function as a method of obtaining love, a punishment for wrongdoing, and a way of expiating guilt and of atoning for an innate sense of badness. Among the defense mechanisms used are displacement, substitution, and repression. Identification plays a role when the patient takes on the role of an ambivalent love object who also had pain, such as a parent. The defense of symbolization is used when the pain represents a nonarticulated affective equivalent.

Behavioral factors. Pain behaviors are reinforced when rewarded and are inhibited when ignored or punished. For example, pain symptoms may become more intense when followed by the solicitous and attentive behavior of others, monetary gain, or the successful avoidance of distasteful activities.

Interpersonal factors. Intractable pain has been conceptualized as a means for manipulation and gaining advantage in interpersonal relationships—for example, to ensure the devotion of a family member or to stabilize a fragile marriage. Such secondary gain is most important to patients with somatoform pain disorder.

Neurological factors. The cerebral cortex can inhibit the firing of afferent pain fibers. Serotonin is probably the main neurotransmitter in the descending inhibitory pathways, and endorphins also probably play a role in the central modulation of pain. Endorphin deficiency seems to correlate with the augmentation of incoming sensory stimuli. Particular patients may develop somatoform pain disorder, rather than other psychiatric disorders, because of sensory and limbic structural or chemical abnormalities that predispose them to experience pain.

Clinical Features

The predominant feature of somatoform pain disorder is a preoccupation with severe and continuous pain of at least six months' duration that has no adequate medical explanation. The pain is often inconsistent with the anatomical distribution of the nervous system, but it may sometimes closely mimic the pain distribution of a known disease.

Somatoform pain disorder patients often have long histories of medical and surgical care, visiting many doctors and requesting many medications. They may be especially insistent in their desire for surgery. Indeed, they are completely preoccupied with their pain, citing it as the source of all their misery. Such patients often deny any emotional dysphoria and maintain that their lives are blissful except for the pain. They frequently have a history of drug abuse or alcoholism.

Major depression is present in about 25 to 50 percent of all somatoform pain disorder patients, and dysthymia or depressive symptoms are reported in 60 to 100 percent of these patients. Some investigators believe that chronic pain is almost always a variant of depressive disorder, that it is a masked or somatized form of depression. The most prominent depressive symptoms in such pain patients are anergia, anhedonia, decreased libido, insomnia, and irritability. Diurnal variation, weight loss, and psychomotor retardation appear to be less common.

Differential Diagnosis

Organic pain can be difficult to distinguish from psychogenic pain, especially because they are not mutually exclusive. Organic pain fluctuates in intensity and is highly sensitive to emotional, cognitive, attentional, and situational influences. Pain that does not vary and is insensitive to any of those factors is more likely to be psychogenic. If the pain does not wax and wane and is not even temporarily relieved by distraction or analgesics, the clinician can suspect an important psychogenic component.

Pain is among the symptoms of somatization disorder, and both somatization disorder and somatoform pain disorder may be diagnosed if the patient meets the criteria for both disorders. Somatization disorder, however, includes many other physical symptoms, begins before the age of 30, and is rare in men. Hypochondriacal patients may complain of pain, and their bodily preoccupation and disease conviction are present in somatoform pain disorder patients as well. Hypochondriacal patients, however, have many symptoms, and the clinical picture fluctuates over time. Conversion disorder is generally short-lived, whereas somatoform pain disorder is chronic; moreover, pain is not, by definition, a conversion disorder symptom. Malingering patients consciously provide a false symptom report, and their complaints are connected to clearly recognizable goals. The differential diagnosis can be difficult because chronic pain disorder patients often receive disability compensation or a litigation award. They are not, however, pretending to be in pain. For example, muscle contraction (tension) headaches have a pathophysiological mechanism to account for the pain and so are not diagnosed as a somatoform pain disorder.

Course and Prognosis

By definition, somatoform pain disorder lasts for at least six months. The pain generally begins abruptly and increases in severity over the next few weeks or months. The prognoses of the various somatoform pain syndromes are not clear, but, in general, they are chronic, very disturbing, and disabling. Psychogenic pain may sometimes subside with treatment, after the elimination of external reinforcement, or after the successful therapy of associated psychopathology. But more often, it persists for years. The patients with the poorest prognoses, with or without treatment, have preexisting characterological problems, especially pronounced passivity; are involved in litigation or receive financial compensation; use addictive drugs; or have long histories of pain.

Treatment

Treatment aims to rehabilitate the patient, rather than to cure the pain. It may be useful to discuss the issue of psychological causes with the patients early in treatment, telling them frankly that psychological factors are important to the cause and consequence of both organic and psychogenic pain. The therapist may also explain how various brain circuits (such as the limbic system) may influence the sensory pain pathways. An example is that hitting one's head while happy and at a party can seem to hurt less than hitting one's head while angry and at work. However, the therapist must fully understand that the patient's pain is real.

Medical interventions. Analgesic medications are not helpful for most chronic psychogenic pain. In addition, drug abuse and addiction are often major problems for somatoform pain disorder patients.

Sedatives and antianxiety agents are not especially beneficial and often become problems in themselves because of their frequent abuse, misuse, and side effects. Antidepressants—such as amitriptyline (Elavil), imipramine (Tofranil), and doxepin (Sinequan)—are more useful. Whether antidepressants reduce pain through their antidepressant action or exert an independent, direct analgesic effect (possibly by stimulating the efferent inhibitory pain pathways) remains controversial. Although few data are available now, it is possible that the selective serotonergic antidepressants (such as clomipramine [Anafranil] and fluoxetine [Prozac]) are especially effective in treating chronic pain syndromes.

Biofeedback can be helpful, particularly in migraine, myofascial pain, and muscle tension states, such as tension headaches. Hypnosis, transcutaneous nerve stimulation, and dorsal column stimulation have also been used. Nerve blocks and surgical ablative procedures are ineffective for most patients, with pain returning after 6 to 18 months.

Pain control programs. It may sometimes be necessary to remove the patients from their usual settings and place them in a comprehensive, inpatient pain control program. These multidisciplinary pain units use many different modalities, such as cognitive, behavioral, and group therapies. They provide extensive patient education, teach relaxation techniques, emphasize improved physical conditioning through physical therapy and exercise, and offer vocational evaluation and rehabilitation. Concurrent psychiatric disorders are diagnosed and treated, and patients addicted to analgesics and hypnotics are detoxified. Inpatient treatment programs generally report encouraging results.

HYPOCHONDRIASIS

Hypochondriasis is an excessive concern about disease and a preoccupation with one's health. Hypochondriasis is an unrealistic interpretation of physical symptoms and sensations, leading to a preoccupation with the fear or belief that one has a serious disease, even though no medical disease accounts for the physical signs or sensations. This fear or conviction of disease is disabling and persists despite appropriate reassurance (Table 18-4).

Epidemiology

In general medical practice, hypochondriasis is present in 3 to 14 percent of all patients. The prevalence in the

Table 18-4
Diagnostic Criteria for Hypochondriasis

A. Preoccupation with the fear of having, or the belief that one has, a serious disease, based on the person's interpretation of physical signs or sensations as evidence of physical illness.

B. Appropriate physical evaluation does not support the diagnosis of any physical disorder that can account for the physical signs or sensations or the person's unwarranted interpretation of them, **and** the symptoms in A are not just symptoms of panic attacks.

C. The fear of having, or belief that one has, a disease persists despite medical reassurance.

D. Duration of the disturbance is at least six months.

E. The belief in A is not of delusional intensity, as in delusional disorder, somatic type (i.e., the person can acknowledge the possibility that his or her fear of having, or belief that he or she has, a serious disease is unfounded).

Table from DSM-III-R, *Diagnostic and Statistical Manual of Mental Disorders,* ed 3, revised. Copyright American Psychiatric Association, Washington, DC, 1987, with permission.

general population is unknown. Hypochondriasis is found approximately equally in men and women but perhaps somewhat more often in men. The peak incidence is thought to occur during the fourth or fifth decade; however, all age groups are affected, particularly adolescents and those over age 60. Some evidence shows an increased prevalence of hypochondriasis among identical twins and other first-degree relatives of probands with hypochondriasis.

Etiology

Hypochondriasis is believed by most clinicians to have a psychodynamic origin: aggressive and hostile wishes toward others are transferred (repression and displacement) into physical complaints. The anger of hypochondriacal patients originates in past disappointments, rejections, and losses, but they express it in the present by soliciting the help and concern of other people and then rejecting them as ineffective. Hypochondriasis has also been viewed as a defense against guilt, a sense of innate badness, an expression of low self-esteem, and a sign of excessive self-concern. Pain and somatic suffering thus become a means of atonement and expiation (undoing) and can be experienced as deserved punishment for past wrongdoing (either real or imaginary) and the sense that one is wicked and sinful.

Hypochondriasis may have a sociocultural origin. It has been viewed as a request for admission to the sick role made by a person who is facing seemingly insurmountable and insolvable problems. The sick role offers a way out because the sick patient is allowed to avoid noxious obligations and to postpone unwelcome challenges and is excused from onerous duties.

Some evidence suggests that hypochondriacal persons augment and amplify somatic sensations, in that they have lower thresholds for and a lower tolerance of physical discomfort. For example, what a normal person perceives as abdominal pressure, the hypochondriacal person experiences as abdominal pain. There may also be a faulty cognitive scheme in which the hypochondriacal person focuses on bodily sensations, misinterprets them, and becomes alarmed by them.

A medical disorder can predispose a patient to develop hypochondriasis in two ways. First, transient hypochondriacal reactions often follow a severe or life-threatening illness (such as during recuperation after a myocardial infarction). Second, patients with primary hypochondriasis seem to have had more childhood medical illnesses and more extensive medical histories than did those without primary hypochondriasis.

Clinical Features

Hypochondriacal patients complain of many symptoms involving multiple organ systems and many anatomical locations. The most common complaints are pain and symptoms regarding the gastrointestinal and cardiovascular systems.

Hypochondriacal patients also believe that they have a serious disease that has not yet been detected, and they cannot be persuaded to the contrary. This conviction persists despite negative laboratory results, a benign course over time, and appropriate reassurance from physicians. But this belief is not so fixed that it is a delusion, nor is it culturally unacceptable.

Transient hypochondriacal reactions occur after major stresses, most commonly the death or serious illness of someone important to the patient or a serious and perhaps life-threatening illness that has been resolved but leaves the patient temporarily hypochondriacal in its wake. Such hypochondriacal states lasting less than six months should be diagnosed as somatoform disorder not otherwise specified. Transient hypochondriacal responses to external stress generally remit when the stress is resolved, but they can become chronic if reinforced by people in the patient's social system or by health professionals.

Hypochondriasis is often accompanied by symptoms of depression and anxiety. Depressive disorder can coexist with hypochondriasis, and the treatment of the depression may alleviate the hypochondriasis. Patients with panic disorder may initially complain that they are affected by some disease, and careful questioning during the medical history is necessary to uncover the classic symptoms of a panic attack.

Differential Diagnosis

Like all somatoform disorders, hypochondriasis must be differentiated from organic diseases, especially disorders that can present with symptoms in many organ systems. Such disorders include AIDS, endocrinopathies, myasthenia gravis, multiple sclerosis, degenerative diseases of the nervous system, systemic lupus erythematosus, and occult neoplastic disorders.

Depression is diagnosed if the hypochondriacal symptoms have an episodic course similar to that of recurrent depression or if they appear for the first time in elderly patients who were never before hypochondriacal. Other depressive symptoms—such as hopelessness, suicidal ideas, and low self-esteem—are also present.

Hypochondriacal symptoms are also common in generalized anxiety disorder and panic disorder. According to DSM-III-R, hypochondriasis cannot be diagnosed if the symptoms occur only during panic attacks. Indeed, anxiety disorder patients are often alarmed about their health, have prominent somatic symptoms, and manifest extreme bodily vigilance and disease fears. But for such patients the hypochondriasis is not the predominant disturbance; it is, rather, a feature of a more pervasive disorder.

Hypochondriacal concerns and frank somatic delusions occur in schizophrenia, other psychotic states, and organic mental syndromes. The disease conviction is not delusional, and patients with those disorders can entertain, if only briefly, the possibility that they do not have the particular disease they dread. In contrast, somatic delusions are static and unchanging, whereas hypochondriacal symptoms fluctuate over time. In addition, schizophrenic patients' somatic delusions tend to be bizarre, idiosyncratic, and out of keeping with their cultural milieus.

Some obsessions and phobias may resemble hypochondriasis, but in those cases the patients know that their symptoms are irrational, excessive, or unrealistic.

The relationship of hypochondriasis to the other somatoform disorders is somewhat unclear. It is possible to diagnose hypochondriasis along with any other somatoform disorder. Somatization disorder does not include disease conviction, disease fear, or bodily preoccupation, and it begins before age 30. The somatization disorder patient is usually female and is likely to have a hysterical cognitive and interpersonal style, as compared with the more obsessional hypochondriacal patient. These two conditions may, however, overlap significantly. Conversion disorder is acute and transient, involving a single neurological symptom at a time, whereas hypochondriasis is chronic and involves several symptoms in multiple sites and organ systems. If *la belle indifférence* is present in conversion disorder, it contrasts markedly with the anguish of the hypochondriacal patient. Somatoform pain disorder is chronic, as is hypochondriasis, but the symptoms are limited to pain. Body dysmorphic disorder patients wish to appear normal but believe that others notice that they are not, whereas hypochondriacal patients wish to draw attention to themselves and proclaim loudly that they are not normal.

Hypochondriasis is distinguished from factitious disorder with physical symptoms and from malingering in that hypochondriacal patients actually experience and do not simulate the symptoms they report.

Course and Prognosis

On long-term follow-up, one-quarter of all hypochondriacal patients do poorly, and about two-thirds run chronic, fluctuating courses. Most hypochondriacal children, however, recover by late adolescence or early adulthood. Treatment helps a significant proportion of patients. Favorable prognostic features include the concurrent presence of anxiety or depression, acute onset, the absence of personality disorder, high socioeconomic status, young age, and the absence of organic disease.

Treatment

Hypochondriacal patients are usually resistant to psychiatric treatment. Some hypochondriacal patients accept psychiatric treatment if it takes place in a medical setting and focuses on stress reduction and education in coping with chronic illness. Among such patients, group psychotherapy has been reported to be the modality of choice, in part because it provides the social support and social interaction that these patients need. Individual insight-oriented traditional psychotherapy for primary hypochondriasis is generally not successful.

Frequent, regularly scheduled physical examinations are useful to reassure the patients that they are not being abandoned by their doctors and that their complaints are being taken seriously. Invasive diagnostic and therapeutic procedures, however, should be undertaken only on the basis of objective evidence. When possible, it is best to refrain from treating equivocal or incidental findings.

Pharmacotherapy alleviates hypochondriacal symptoms only when there is an underlying drug-sensitive condition, such as an anxiety disorder or a major depression. When hypochondriasis is secondary to some other primary psychiatric disorder, that entity must be treated in its own right. When hypochondriasis is a transient situational reaction, clinicians must help patients cope with the stress without reinforcing their illness behavior and their use of the sick role as solutions to the problem.

BODY DYSMORPHIC DISORDER

The strongly held but nondelusional belief that a body part is misshapen or defective in some way is the key symptom in body dysmorphic disorder. This disorder is also known as dysmorphophobia, the fear of a deformed body part. In spite of the patient's stated fear, the particular body part about which there is concern is objectively unremarkable. According to DSM-III-R, body dysmorphic disorder can be diagnosed as long as anorexia nervosa and transsexualism are absent (Table 18-5).

Epidemiology

The average age of patients with body dysmorphic disorder is 30 years. The sex distribution is unknown.

Etiology

The cause of body dysmorphic disorder is unknown. Some patients' beliefs are based on another more pervasive psychiatric disorder, such as schizophrenia, mood disorder, or severe personality disorder. Psychodynamically, some persons invest a particular body part with a high level of unconscious meaning that can be traced to an event during an earlier stage of psychosexual development. Important

Table 18-5
Diagnostic Criteria for Body Dysmorphic Disorder

A. Preoccupation with some imagined defect in appearance in a normal-appearing person. If a slight physical anomaly is present, the person's concern is grossly excessive.

B. The belief in the defect is not of delusional intensity, as in delusional disorder, somatic type (i.e., the person can acknowledge the possibility that he or she may be exaggerating the extent of the defect or that there may be no defect at all).

C. Occurrence not exclusively during the course of anorexia nervosa or transsexualism.

Table from DSM-III-R, *Diagnostic and Statistical Manual of Mental Disorders,* ed 3, revised. Copyright American Psychiatric Association, Washington, DC, 1987, with permission.

defense mechanisms are repression, dissociation, distortion, symbolization, and projection.

Clinical Features

Body dysmorphic disorder patients imagine some defect in their appearance, most commonly in regard to the face, nose, hair, breasts, or genitals. The patients' anguish is intensified in social situations. Secondary symptoms include depression, insomnia, and severe anxiety. Such persons are normal in appearance, and, if they do have a slight physical anomaly, their concern is excessive. A clinical case example follows:

The patient was a happily married 23-year-old investment counselor who had reluctantly agreed to see a psychiatrist, an old friend of her husband's. She told the psychiatrist that she did not think she needed to see a psychiatrist, because her problem was "these ugly lines on my forehead." The psychiatrist asked, "What lines?" The patient pointed to the frown lines above her nose, which to the psychiatrist seemed no more pronounced than they are on the foreheads of most people her age.

The patient continued: "It's horrible, isn't it? I mean, I don't have to be the most gorgeous girl on earth, but I also don't want to be disfigured."

The psychiatrist asked, "What makes you think it looks so awful? Everyone has those lines."

"C'mon. I appreciate your trying to make me feel better, but I can see what I look like."

"What *do* you look like?"

"It's horrible. Everybody notices. They make me look so old. I'm sure my husband is turned off. I don't know what I would ever do if he left me. I have started to wear all this heavy makeup to hide them, but try to hide something like this."

"Let me ask you this. Most of us are sensitive about our appearance, and sometimes we exaggerate some minor imperfection. Do you think you may be doing that?"

The patient sighed. "My husband has been saying the same thing. I think about that, and sometimes I can convince myself that I am too concerned about something that is really very minor. But then I go to the mirror, and there it is. Can't you help me convince my husband that I should see if a plastic surgeon can do something about it?"

"Before we get into that, how long have you been bothered by the lines?"

"I'm not sure, but I didn't pay any attention to it until a few months ago. A friend at work mentioned that she had seen a doctor for a bad sunburn and told me I had better be careful because my skin was so fair. I began looking in the mirror and kept noticing the lines."

The psychiatrist asked about other problems in the patient's life and learned that her concern with her appearance was not affecting her ability to work but that she had started to avoid social situations because she did not want people looking at her blemish. The patient acknowledged being upset and unhappy about her problem but denied having a persistently depressed mood or any associated symptoms of depression.

Differential Diagnosis

Another underlying primary psychiatric disorder—most commonly schizophrenia, a mood disorder, or an organic mental syndrome (such as that accompanying temporal lobe epilepsy)—must be ruled out. Distortions of body image occur in anorexia nervosa, transsexualism, and some specific types of brain damage, and body dysmorphic disorder should not be diagnosed if these conditions are present.

Table 18-6
Diagnostic Criteria for Undifferentiated Somatoform Disorder

A. One or more physical complaints (e.g., fatigue, loss of appetite, gastrointestinal or urinary complaints).

B. Either (1) or (2):
   (1) appropriate evaluation uncovers no organic pathology or pathophysiologic mechanism (e.g., a physical disorder or the effects of injury, medication, drugs, or alcohol) to account for the physical complaints.
   (2) when there is related organic pathology, the physical complaints or resulting social or occupational impairment is grossly in excess of what would be expected from the physical findings.

C. Duration of the disturbance is at least six months.

D. Occurrence not exclusively during the course of another somatoform disorder, a sexual dysfunction, a mood disorder, an anxiety disorder, a sleep disorder, or a psychotic disorder.

Table from DSM-III-R, *Diagnostic and Statistical Manual of Mental Disorders,* ed 3, revised. Copyright American Psychiatric Association, Washington, DC, 1987, with permission.

Table 18-7
Diagnostic Criteria for Somatoform Disorder Not Otherwise Specified

Disorders with somatoform symptoms that do not meet the criteria for any specific somatoform disorder or adjustment disorder with physical complaints

Examples:
   (1) an illness involving nonpsychotic hypochondriacal symptoms of less than six months' duration
   (2) an illness involving non-stress-related physical complaints of less than six months' duration

Table from DSM-III-R, *Diagnostic and Statistical Manual of Mental Disorders,* ed 3, revised. Copyright American Psychiatric Association, Washington, DC, 1987, with permission.

Table 18-8
A Summary of the Clinical Features of Somatoform Disorders

Diagnostic Subtype	Clinical Presentation	Demographic and Epidemiological Features	Diagnostic Features	Management Strategy	Prognostic Outlook	Associated Disturbances	Primary Differential Presentation	Psychological Processes Contributing to Symptoms	Motivation for Symptom Production
Somatization disorder	Polysymptomatic Recurrent and chronic "Sickly" by history	Younger age Female predominance 20 to 1 Familial pattern 5–10% incidence in primary care populations	Review of systems (ROS) profusely positive Multiple clinical contacts Polysurgical	•Therapeutic alliance •Regular appointments •Crisis intervention	Poor to fair	Histrionic personality Sociopathy Substance and alcohol use Many life problems Conversion	Physical disease Depression	Unconscious Cultural and developmental	Unconscious psychological factors
Conversion disorder	Monosymptomatic Mostly acute Simulates disease	Highly prevalent Female predominance Younger age Rural and lower social class Less educated and psychologically unsophisticated	Simulation incompatible with known physiological mechanisms or anatomy	•Suggestion and persuasion •Multiple techniques	Excellent except chronic conversion	Drug and alcohol dependence Sociopathy Somatization disorder Histrionic personality	Depression Schizophrenia Neurological disease	Unconscious Psychological stress or conflict may be present	Unconscious psychological factors
Somatoform pain disorder	Pain syndrome simulated	Female predominance 2 to 1 Older: 4th or 5th decade Familial pattern Up to 40% of pain populations	Simulation or intensity incompatible with known physiological mechanisms or anatomy	•Therapeutic alliance •Redefine goals of treatment •Antidepressant medications	Guarded, variable	Depression Substance and alcohol use Dependent or histrionic personality	Depression Psychophysiological Physical disease Malingering and disability syndrome	Unconscious Acute stressor and developmental Physical trauma may predispose	Unconscious psychological factors
Hypochondriasis	Disease concern or preoccupation	Previous physical disease Middle or older age Male-female ratio equal	Disease conviction amplifies symptoms Obsessional	•Document symptoms •Psychosocial review •Psychotherapeutic	Fair to good Waxes and wanes	Obsessional neurosis Depression-anxiety	Depression Physical disease Personality disorder Delusional disorder	Unconscious Stress—bereavement Developmental factors	Unconscious psychological factors
Body dysmorphic disorder	Subjective feelings of ugliness or concern with body defect	Adolescence or young adult ? Female predominance Largely unknown	Pervasive bodily concerns	•Therapeutic alliance •Stress management •Psychotherapies •Antidepressant medications	Unknown	Anorexia nervosa Psychosocial distress Avoidant or obsessive-compulsive personality disorder	Delusional psychosis Depression Somatization disorder	Unconscious Self-esteem factors	Unconscious psychological factors

Table from D G Folks, C V Ford, C A Houck: Somatoform disorders, factitious disorders, and malingering. In *Clinical Psychiatry for Medical Students,* A Stoudemire, editor. Lippincott, Philadelphia, 1990, with permission.

Course and Prognosis

The onset of body dysmorphic disorder is insidious; the concern about one's appearance develops gradually. Indeed, patients often brood about their imagined defect for several years before consulting a physician.

Treatment

In spite of intense suffering, patients with body dysmorphic disorder tend to refuse psychiatric treatment outright. If another underlying psychiatric disorder is present, that condition should be treated first. Some persons persist in seeking plastic surgery to correct what they perceive as deformities, and so an essential part of a surgeon's diagnostic task—often with the help of a psychiatric consultant—is to identify those with legitimate indications.

Several old studies reported effectiveness in treating body dysmorphic disorder with pimozide (Orap), an antipsychotic, and with standard antidepressants and monoamine oxidase inhibitors. It was shown that most patients retain some concern about their problem, but its intensity is blunted enough to allow them to lead more normal lives. Long-term treatment is necessary, as relapses after discontinuing medication are common. More recent reports have documented successful treatment with serotonin reuptake specific drugs, such as fluoxetine and clomipramine. Controlled clinical trials will be necessary to evaluate the effectiveness of these treatments.

UNDIFFERENTIATED SOMATOFORM DISORDER

The diagnosis of undifferentiated somatoform disorder requires six months of multiple physical symptoms without an adequate medical explanation. The symptoms must occur outside the course of any other major psychiatric disorder. The classification of undifferentiated somatoform disorder was created because of the common finding that, although cases meeting the full criteria for somatization disorder are relatively rare, many cases of chronic multiple functional symptoms are otherwise similar to somatization disorder and do not meet the criteria for any other somatoform disorder (Table 18-6). These symptoms include general fatigue, anorexia, and vague gastrointestinal or urinary symptoms.

SOMATOFORM DISORDER NOT OTHERWISE SPECIFIED

Somatoform disorder not otherwise specified is a residual category for hypochondriacal symptoms of less than six months' duration and for an illness with a single complaint (such as malaise and emitting a bad smell). (See Table 18-7 for the DSM-III-R criteria for this disorder.) For example, patients who fear that they have a symptom of AIDS, although they had no exposure to a putative carrier, can be classified as being in this category.

A summary of the clinical features of somatization disorder, conversion disorder, somatoform pain disorder, hypochondriasis, and body dysmorphic disorder are presented in Table 18-8.

References

Barsky A J: Somatoform disorders. In *Comprehensive Textbook of Psychiatry,* ed 5, H I Kaplan and B J Sadock, editors, p 1009. Williams & Wilkins, Baltimore, 1989.

Barsky A J, Wyshak G, Klerman G L: Hypochondriasis: An evaluation of the DSM-III criteria in medical outpatients. Arch Gen Psychiatry *43*: 493, 1986.

Cloninger C R, Martin R L, Guze S B, Clayton P J: A prospective follow-up and family study of somatization in men and women. Am J Psychiatry *143*: 873, 1986.

Dworkin S F, von Korff M, LeResche L: Multiple pains and psychiatric disturbance: An epidemiologic investigation. Arch Gen Psychiatry *47*: 239, 1990.

Escobar J I, Burnam M A, Karno M, Forsythe A, Golding J M: Somatization in the community. Arch Gen Psychiatry *44*: 713, 1987.

Hollander E, Liebowitz M R, Winchel R, Klumker A, Klein D F: Treatment of body dysmorphic disorder with serotonin reuptake blockers. Am J Psychiatry *146*: 768, 1989.

Kellner R: Hypochondriasis and somatization. JAMA *258*: 2718, 1987.

Kellner R: Somatization: Theories and research. J Nerv Ment Dis *178*: 150, 1990.

Kellner R, Wiggins R G, Pathak D: Hypochondriacal fears and beliefs in medical and law students. Arch Gen Psychiatry *43*: 487, 1986.

Lipowski Z J: Somatization: The concept and its clinical applications. Am J Psychiatry *145*: 1358, 1988.

Othmer E, ed.: Somatization disorder. Psychiatr Ann *18*(6): entire issue, 1988.

Smith G R, Monson R A: Patients with multiple unexplained symptoms: Their characteristics, functional health, and health care utilization. Arch Intern Med *146*: 69, 1986.

Smith G R, Monson R A, Ray D C: Psychiatric consultation in somatization disorder: A randomized controlled study. N Engl J Med *314*: 1407, 1986.

Torgersen S: Genetics of somatoform disorders. Arch Gen Psychiatry *43*: 502, 1986.

19

Dissociative Disorders

The revised third edition of *Diagnostic and Statistical Manual of Mental Disorders* (DSM-III-R) defines five dissociative disorders: psychogenic amnesia, psychogenic fugue, multiple personality disorder, depersonalization disorder, and dissociative disorder not otherwise specified (NOS). In the past these disorders were known as hysterical neuroses of the dissociative type. Although the prevalences of the specific dissociative disorders are not well established, it is thought that psychogenic amnesia is the most common. Multiple personality disorder is generally considered the most severe and chronic of the dissociative disorders.

The hallmark symptom of these disorders is a sudden, usually temporary alteration in the normally integrated functions of consciousness, identity, and motor behavior, such that one or two of these functions cease to perform in concert with the others. For example, a person may be alert, conscious, and behaving normally but not be able to remember his or her name, address, or occupation. If organic mental disorders are ruled out, such a person is classified as having a dissociative disorder—specifically, psychogenic amnesia.

PSYCHOGENIC AMNESIA

Psychogenic amnesia is characterized by the sudden inability of persons to recall information that has already been stored in their memories. This inability cannot be explained by ordinary forgetfulness, and there is no evidence of an underlying brain disorder. The capacity to learn new information is retained in patients with psychogenic amnesia.

Except for their amnesia, these patients appear completely intact and function coherently. This contrasts with most organically induced amnesias (such as postictal and toxic amnesias), in which the patient may be confused and have disorganized behavior. Other organically induced amnesias (such as transient global amnesia and postconcussion amnesia) are associated with an ongoing anterograde amnesia, which does not occur in psychogenic amnesia patients.

Epidemiology

Psychogenic amnesia is the most common type of dissociative disorder. It is most common during periods of war and natural disasters. The disorder occurs most often in adolescents and young adults and is more common in women than in men.

Etiology

Although some episodes of amnesia occur spontaneously, a careful history usually reveals some precipitating emotional trauma charged with painful emotions and psychological conflict—for example, natural disasters in which patients witnessed severe injuries or feared for their lives. Fantasized or actual expression of an impulse (sexual or aggressive) with which the patient is unable to deal may also act as a precipitant. Amnesia may follow an extramarital affair that the patient finds morally reprehensible. At times amnesia follows a physical head trauma that is so slight that it does not seem severe enough to have physiological significance.

Clinical Features and Diagnosis

The disorder usually begins abruptly, and the patients are usually aware that they have lost their memory. Some patients are upset about the memory loss, but others appear to be unconcerned or indifferent. Amnestic patients are usually alert before and after the amnesia occurs. A few patients, however, report a slight clouding of consciousness during the period immediately surrounding the amnestic period. Depression is a common predisposing factor and a coexisting finding on the mental status examination.

The amnesia may take one of several forms: (1) *localized amnesia,* the most common type, characterized by a loss of memory for the events of a short period of time (a few hours to a few days); (2) *generalized amnesia,* the loss of memory for a whole lifetime of experience; (3) *selective* (also known as *systematized*) *amnesia,* failure to recall some but not all events during a short period of time; and (4) *continuous amnesia,* characterized by forgetting each successive event as it occurs, although the patient is clearly alert and aware of what is happening in the environment at the time.

Amnesia may have a primary or secondary gain. The woman who is amnestic for the birth of a dead baby achieves primary gain by protecting herself from painful emotions. An example of secondary gain is a soldier who develops sudden amnesia and is removed from combat areas as a result. The DSM-III-R diagnostic criteria for psychogenic amnesia are presented in Table 19-1. A clinical case example follows:

Psychiatric consultation was requested by an emergency room physician on an 18-year-old man who had been brought into the hospital by the police. The youth appeared exhausted and showed evidence of prolonged exposure to the sun. He identified the current date incorrectly, giving it as September 27, instead of October 1. It was difficult to get him to focus on specific questions, but with encouragement he supplied a number of facts. He recalled sailing with friends, apparently about September 25, on a weekend cruise off the Florida coast, when bad weather was encountered. He was unable to recall any subsequent events and did not know what became of his companions. He had to be reminded several times that he was in a hospital, since he expressed uncertainty as to his whereabouts. Each time he was told, he seemed surprised.

There was no evidence of head injury or dehydration. Electrolytes and cranial nerve examination were unremarkable. Because of the patient's apparent exhaustion, he was permitted to sleep for six hours. On awakening, he was much more attentive but was still unable to recall events after September 25, including how he came to the hospital. There was no longer any doubt in his mind that he was in the hospital, however, and he was able to recall the contents of the previous interview and the fact that he had fallen asleep. He was able to remember that he was a student at a Southern college, maintained a B average, had a small group of close friends, and had a good relationship with his family. He denied any previous psychiatric history and said he had never abused drugs or alcohol.

Because of the patient's apparently sound physical condition, a sodium amobarbital (Amytal) interview was performed. During this interview he related that neither he nor his companions were particularly experienced sailors or capable of coping with the ferocity of the storm they encountered. Although he had taken the precaution of securing himself to the boat with a life jacket and tie line, his companions had failed to do this and were washed overboard in the heavy seas. He completely lost control of the boat and felt he was saved only by virtue of good luck and his lifeline. Over a three-day period he was able to consume a small supply of food that was stowed away in the cabin. He never saw either of his sailing companions again. He was picked up on October 1 by a Coast Guard cutter and brought to shore, and subsequently the police brought him to the hospital.

Discussion. The differential diagnosis of acute memory loss begins with a consideration of an organic mental disorder—such as delirium, dementia, or amnestic syndrome—that may be due to head trauma, cerebrovascular accident, or drug use. The normal findings on the physical and neurological examinations and the absence of a history of drug use ruled out these possibilities in this patient. With the amobarbital interview it became clear that the amnestic period developed after a particularly traumatic and life-threatening experience. Amnesia (an episode of sudden inability to recall important personal information that is too extensive to be considered forgetfulness) that was not due to an organic mental disorder justified the diagnosis of psychogenic amnesia. In this case the circumscribed nature of the amnesia and the patient's perplexity and disorientation during the amnestic period, all following a traumatic event, were quite characteristic of the diagnosed disorder.

Table 19-1
Diagnostic Criteria for Psychogenic Amnesia

A. The predominant disturbance is an episode of sudden inability to recall important personal information that is too extensive to be explained by ordinary forgetfulness.

B. The disturbance is not due to multiple personality disorder or to an organic mental disorder (e.g., blackouts during alcohol intoxication).

Table from DSM-III-R, *Diagnostic and Statistical Manual of Mental Disorders,* ed 3, revised. Copyright American Psychiatric Association, Washington, DC, 1987, with permission.

Defense mechanisms. The major defense mechanism in this disorder is dissociation: the person alters consciousness as a way of dealing with an emotional conflict or an external stressor. Secondary defenses include repression (disturbing impulses are blocked from consciousness) and denial (some aspect of external reality is ignored by the conscious mind). Similar defenses are used in the other dissociative disorders.

Differential Diagnosis

The organic differential diagnostic considerations for amnesia are listed in Table 19-2. A careful medical history, physical examination, and laboratory workup should be conducted with these disorders in mind.

Transient global amnesia. Transient global amnesia (TGA) is an acute and transient period of retrograde amnesia affecting recent memories more than remote memories. Although patients are usually aware of the amnesia, they may still perform highly complex mental and physical acts during the 6 to 24 hours the TGA episodes usually last. Recovery from TGA is usually complete. TGA is most often caused by transient ischemic attacks (TIAs) affecting limbic midline brain structures. TGA can also be associated with migraine headaches, seizures, and intoxication with sedative-hypnotic drugs.

TGA can be differentiated from psychogenic amnesia in several ways. TGA is associated with an anterograde amnesia during the episode; psychogenic amnesia is not. Patients with TGA tend to be more upset and concerned about the symptoms than are patients with psychogenic amnesia. The personal identity of the patient with psychogenic amnesia is lost; that of the patient with TGA is retained. The memory loss of a patient with psychogenic amnesia may be selective for certain areas and usually does

Table 19-2
Differential Diagnostic Considerations in Patients with Amnesia

Anoxic amnesia
Cerebral infections (e.g., herpes simplex affecting temporal lobes)
Cerebral neoplasms (especially limbic and frontal)
Cerebrovascular accidents (especially limbic and frontal)
Drug-induced (e.g., barbiturates, benzodiazepines, phencyclidine, LSD, steroids) disorders
Electroconvulsive therapy
Epilepsy
Metabolic (e.g., uremia, hypoglycemia, hypertensive encephalopathy, porphyria) disorders
Postconcussion amnesia
Sleep-related amnesia (e.g., somnambulism)
Transient global amnesia
Wernicke-Korsakoff syndrome

not show a temporal gradient. The memory loss of a patient with TGA is generalized, and remote events are remembered better than recent events. Finally, because of the association of TGA with vascular problems, TGA is most common in patients in their 60s and 70s, whereas psychogenic amnesia is most common in patients in their 20s to 40s, a period associated with the common types of psychological stressors seen in these patients.

Other conditions. In postconcussion amnesia, the memory disturbance follows head trauma and is often retrograde (as opposed to the anterograde disturbance of psychogenic amnesia) and usually does not extend beyond one week. Hypnosis or an amobarbital interview can often be used to distinguish between the retrograde and anterograde disturbances. Prompt return of memory strongly suggests a psychological cause. Epilepsy leads to sudden memory impairment associated with motor and electroencephalogram (EEG) abnormalities. A history of an aura, head trauma, or incontinence assists in the diagnosis. Malingering, in this case a deliberate attempt to mimic amnesia, may be difficult to confirm. Any possible secondary gain should increase suspicion; information may be gained by questioning the patient while he or she is under hypnosis or during an amobarbital interview.

Course and Prognosis

Amnesia usually terminates very abruptly, and recovery is generally complete with few recurrences. In some cases, especially if there is secondary gain, the condition may last a long time. It is important to restore the lost memories to consciousness as soon as possible; otherwise, the repressed memory may form a nucleus in the unconscious mind for the production of future amnestic episodes.

Treatment

Psychotherapy should be performed with the amnestic patient. Careful interviewing may give the examiner clues to the psychologically traumatic precipitant. Intermediate and short-acting barbiturates, such as thiopental (Pentothal) and sodium amobarbital given intravenously, may be used to help patients recover their memories. Hypnosis can be used primarily as a means of relaxing the patient enough to recall what has been forgotten. The patient is placed in a somnolent state, at which point mental inhibitions are diminished, and the repressed material emerges into consciousness and is then recalled. Once the lost memories have been retrieved, psychotherapy is generally recommended to help the patient deal with the associated emotions.

PSYCHOGENIC FUGUE

The behavior of patients with psychogenic fugue is more purposefully integrated with their amnesia than is that of patients with psychogenic amnesia. Patients with psychogenic fugue have physically traveled away from their customary homes or work situations and fail to remember important aspects of their previous identities (name, family, occupation, etc.). These patients often take on an entirely new identity and occupation, although this identity is usually less complete than are the alternate personalities seen in multiple personality disorder. Also, in psychogenic fugue, the old and new identities do not alternate, as they do in multiple personality disorder.

Epidemiology

The disorder is rare and, like psychogenic amnesia, occurs most often during wartime, after natural disasters, and as a result of personal crises with intense conflict.

Etiology

Although it is believed that heavy alcohol abuse may predispose a person to the disorder, the cause is thought to be basically psychological. The essential motivating factor appears to be a desire to withdraw from emotionally painful experiences. Patients with mood disorders and certain personality disorders (such as borderline, histrionic, and schizoid) are predisposed to psychogenic fugue.

A variety of stressors and personal factors have been identified as being predisposing to the development of psychogenic fugue. The psychosocial stressors include marital, financial, occupational, and war-related factors. Other associated predisposing features include depression, suicide attempt, other organic disorders (especially epilepsy), and a history of substance abuse. A past history of head trauma also predisposes a person to this disorder.

Clinical Features and Diagnosis

There are several typical features of psychogenic fugue. Patients wander in a purposeful way, usually far from home and often for days at a time. During this period they have complete amnesia for their past lives and associations but, unlike patients with psychogenic amnesia, they are unaware that they have forgotten anything. Only when they suddenly return to their former selves do they recall the time antedating the onset of the fugue, but then they remain amnesic for the period of the fugue itself. Patients in a psychogenic fugue do not seem to others to be behaving in extraordinary ways, nor do they give evidence of acting out any specific memory of a traumatic event. On the contrary, fugue patients lead quiet, prosaic, somewhat reclusive existences; work at simple occupations; live modestly; and in general do nothing to draw attention to themselves. The DSM-III-R criteria for psychogenic fugue are listed in Table 19-3. A clinical case example follows:

The patient was a 42-year-old man who was brought to the emergency room by the police. He was involved in an argument and fight at the diner where he is employed. When the police arrived and began to question the patient, he gave his name as Burt Tate but had no identification. He had drifted into town several weeks earlier and begun working as a short-order cook at the diner. He could not recall where he had worked or lived before his arrival in town. There were no charges against him, but the police convinced him to come to the emergency room for an examination.

When questioned in the emergency room, the patient knew

Table 19-3
Diagnostic Criteria for Psychogenic Fugue

A. The predominant disturbance is sudden, unexpected travel away from home or one's customary place of work, with inability to recall one's past.

B. Assumption of a new identity (partial or complete).

C. The disturbance is not due to multiple personality disorder or to an organic mental disorder (e.g., partial complex seizures in temporal lobe epilepsy).

Table from DSM-III-R, *Diagnostic and Statistical Manual of Mental Disorders,* ed 3, revised. Copyright American Psychiatric Association, Washington, DC, 1987, with permission.

what town he was in and the current date. He admitted that it was somewhat unusual that he could not recall the details of his past life, but he did not appear very upset about that. There was no evidence of alcohol or drug abuse, and a physical examination revealed no head trauma or any other physical abnormalities. He was kept overnight for observation.

When the police ran a description check on the patient, they found that he fit the description of a missing person, Gene Saunders, who had disappeared a month before from a city 200 miles away. A visit by Mrs. Saunders confirmed the identity of the patient as Gene Saunders. Mrs. Saunders explained that, for 18 months before his disappearance, her husband, who was a middle-level manager at a large manufacturing company, had been having considerable difficulty at work. He had been passed over for a promotion, and his supervisor had been very critical of his work. Several of his staff had left the company for other jobs, and the patient found it impossible to meet production goals. Work stress made him difficult to live with at home. Previously an easygoing, gregarious person, he became withdrawn and critical of his wife and children. Immediately preceding his disappearance, he had had a violent argument with his 18-year-old son. The son had called him a failure and stormed out of the house to live with some friends who had an apartment. It was two days after this argument that the patient disappeared.

When brought into the room where his wife was waiting, the patient stated that he did not recognize her. He appeared noticeably anxious.

Discussion. The police brought this man to the emergency room because of his amnesia concerning where he had previously lived and worked. Although this impairment in memory suggested an organic mental disorder, ordinarily in such a disorder the disturbance in memory would be more marked for recent events than for remote events. The lack of any disturbance in attention or orientation also weighed against the presence of an organic mental disorder.

The critical role of psychological factors in the patient's amnesia became more apparent when it was learned that, just before the development of his symptoms, on top of increasing difficulties at work, he had a violent argument with his son. The additional features of sudden, unexpected travel away from his home and the assumption of a new identity justified the diagnosis of psychogenic fugue.

Differential Diagnosis

Differential diagnosis includes organic mental disorder, although the wandering that occurs in organic conditions is usually not the same complex or socially adaptive type seen in psychogenic fugue. Temporal lobe epilepsy may involve episodes of travel, but a new identity is not assumed, and the episodes are generally not precipitated by psychological stress. Psychogenic amnesia presents with a loss of memory as the result of psychological stress, but there are no episodes of purposeful travel or of a new identity. Malingering may be very difficult to distinguish from psychogenic fugue. Any evidence of clear secondary gain should raise suspicions. Hypnosis and amobarbital interviews are often useful in clarifying the picture.

Course and Prognosis

A fugue is usually brief—hours to days. Less commonly, a fugue lasts many months and involves extensive travel covering thousands of miles. Generally, recovery is spontaneous and rapid. Recurrences are rare.

Treatment

Outside of supportive care, no treatment is usually required. If the fugue is particularly prolonged, psychotherapy may facilitate recall of the past identity; techniques such as hypnosis and amobarbital interviews may be useful.

MULTIPLE PERSONALITY DISORDER

Persons with multiple personality disorder (MPD) have two or more distinct and separate personalities, each of which determines their behavior and attitudes during any period when it is the dominant personality. Multiple personality disorder used to be considered the most serious of the dissociative disorders. In recent years, however, the diagnosis of MPD has been increasingly recognized as appropriate for a wider range of patients, including some less severely ill than the more classic cases described in the literature, such as *The Three Faces of Eve* and *Sybil.*

Epidemiology

Recent reports suggest that this disorder is not nearly as rare as it was thought to be. It is most common in late adolescence and young adult life and is much more frequent in women than in men. Several studies have demonstrated that the disorder is more common in first-degree biological relatives of people with the disorder than in the general population. There has been a great deal of interest in MPD, and its incidence is being reappraised.

Etiology

It is believed that severe sexual, physical, or psychological abuse in childhood predisposes a person to this condition. In some studies a history of sexual abuse was reported in 70 to 90 percent of patients. Epilepsy was found in 25 percent of cases in another study. One study of regional cerebral blood flow revealed temporal hyperperfusion in one of the subpersonalities but not in the main personality. Several studies have found remarkable differences in EEG activity, pain sensitivity, and galvanic skin response among different personalities within a single person. These data need to be replicated in additional studies; however, they suggest that the brain can parse itself into different personalities.

Clinical Features and Diagnosis

Patients with MPD are probably often thought to have a personality disorder or schizophrenia. Clinicians must be aware of this diagnostic category and listen for specific suggestive features of MPD in the clinical interview (Table 19-4). The relative frequency of specific symptoms was reported in one recent study of 102 MPD patients (Table 19-5).

The transition from one personality to another is sudden, often dramatic. There is generally amnesia during each personality state for the existence of the others and for the events that took place when another personality was dominant. Sometimes, however, one personality state is not bound by such amnesia and retains complete awareness of the existence, qualities, and activities of the other personalities. At other times, personalities are aware of all or some of the others to varying degrees and may experience the others as friends, companions, or adversaries. In classic cases each personality has a fully integrated, highly complex set of associated memories with characteristic attitudes, personal relationships, and behavior patterns. Most often, the personalities have proper names; occasionally, one or more is given the name of its function—for example, "the Protector." On examination, patients generally show nothing unusual in their mental status, other than a possible amnesia for periods of varying duration; other people are unable to tell from a single, casual encounter that the patient at times leads other lives. Only prolonged contact that affords the opportunity to observe the sudden discontinuities in mental functioning and personality presentation provides this information. See Table 19-6 for the DSM-III-R diagnostic criteria for this disorder.

Table 19-4
Signs of Multiplicity

1. Reports of time distortions, lapses, and discontinuities
2. Being told of behavioral episodes by others that are not remembered by the patient
3. Being recognized by others or called by another name by people whom the patient does not recognize
4. Notable changes in the patient's behavior reported by a reliable observer; the patient may call himself or herself by a different name or refer to himself or herself in the third person
5. Other personalities are elicited under hypnosis or during amobarbital interviews
6. Use of the word "we" in the course of an interview
7. Discovery of writings, drawings, or other productions or objects (identification cards, clothing, etc.) among the patient's personal belongings that are not recognized or cannot be accounted for
8. Headaches
9. Hearing voices originating from within and not identified as separate
10. History of severe emotional or physical trauma as a child (usually before the age of 5 years)

Table from J L Cummings: Dissociative states, depersonalization, multiple personality, episodic memory lapses. In *Clinical Neuropsychiatry*, p. 122. Grune & Stratton, Orlando, FL, 1985, with permission.

Table 19-5
Frequency of 16 Secondary Features of Multiple Personality Disorder in 102 Patients

Item	Patients No.	%
Another person existing inside	92	90.2
Voices talking	89	87.3
Voices coming from inside	84	82.4
Another person taking control	83	81.4
Amnesia for childhood	83	81.4
Referring to self as "we" or "us"	75	73.5
Person inside has a different name	72	70.6
Blank spells	69	67.7
Flashbacks	68	66.7
Being told by others of unremembered events	64	62.8
Feelings of unreality	58	56.9
Strangers know the patient	45	44.1
Noticing that objects are missing	43	42.2
Coming out of blank spell in a strange place	37	36.3
Objects are present that cannot be accounted for	32	31.4
Different handwriting styles	28	27.5

Table from C A Ross, S D Miller, P Reagor, L Bjornson, G A Fraser, G Anderson: Structured interview data from 102 cases of multiple personality disorder from four centers. Am J Psychiatry *147*: 596, 1990, with permission.

The first appearance of the secondary personality or personalities may be spontaneous, or it may emerge in relation to what seems to be a precipitant (including hypnosis or an amobarbital interview). The personalities may be of the opposite sex, of different races and ages, and from a family different from the family of origin. The most common subordinate personality is childlike. Often the different personalities are quite disparate and may even be opposites. In the same person, one of the personalities may be very extroverted, even sexually promiscuous, while others may be introverted, withdrawn, and sexually inhibited. According to DSM-III-R, studies have indicated that different personalities may have different physiological characteristics (such as different eyeglass prescriptions) and different responses on psychological testing (such as different I.Q.s).

Differential Diagnosis

The differential diagnosis of multiple personality disorder includes psychogenic fugue and psychogenic amne-

Table 19-6
Diagnostic Criteria for Multiple Personality Disorder

A. The existence within the person of two or more distinct personalities or personality states (each with its own relatively enduring pattern of perceiving, relating to, and thinking about the environment and self).

B. At least two of these personalities or personality states recurrently take full control of the person's behavior.

Table from DSM-III-R, *Diagnostic and Statistical Manual of Mental Disorders*, ed 3, revised. Copyright American Psychiatric Association, Washington, DC, 1987, with permission.

sia. Both of these dissociative disorders, however, lack the shifts in identity and the awareness of the original identity that are seen in multiple personality disorder. Schizophrenia may be confused with multiple personality disorder only because schizophrenic persons may be delusional and believe they have many separate identities or report hearing other personalities' voices. In schizophrenia, a formal thought disorder, chronic social deterioration, and other signs are present. Malingering presents a particularly difficult diagnostic problem. Clear secondary gain raises suspicion; amobarbital interviews and hypnosis are useful in resolving the diagnosis. Borderline personality disorder may coexist with multiple personality disorder, but often the alteration of personalities is mistakenly interpreted as nothing more than the irritability of mood and self-image that are characteristic of borderline personality disorder patients.

Course and Prognosis

The earlier the onset of multiple personality disorder, the worse the prognosis. One or more of the different personalities may function relatively well, while others function quite marginally. The level of impairment ranges from moderate to severe, the determining variables being the number, type, and chronicity of the various subpersonalities. This disorder is considered the most severe and chronic of the dissociative disorders, and recovery is generally incomplete. To compound the diagnostic challenge, individual personalities may have their own separate mental disorders, of which mood, personality, and other dissociative disorders are the most common.

Treatment

The two most efficacious therapeutic interventions are hypnotherapy and psychotherapy. Hypnotherapy can be useful in obtaining additional history, identifying previously unrecognized personalities, and fostering abreaction. A psychotherapeutic treatment plan should begin by confirming the diagnosis by identifying and characterizing the several separate and distinct personalities. If any of the personalities are inclined toward self-destructive or otherwise violent behavior, the therapist should engage the patient and appropriate personalities in treatment contracts regarding these dangerous behaviors. Hospitalization may be necessary in some cases.

The next phase of psychotherapy should begin to foster communication between different personalities, so as to begin some form of reintegration of the patient. Communication among personalities also helps patients control their overall behavior. An attempt must be made to identify the personalities that remember the traumatic childhood events that are almost invariably associated with this disorder.

The use of antipsychotic medications in these patients is almost never indicated. Some data indicate that antidepressant and antianxiety medications may be useful as adjuvants to psychotherapy. A few uncontrolled studies report that antiepileptic medications, especially carbamazepine (Tegretol), help selected patients.

DEPERSONALIZATION DISORDER

DSM-III-R characterizes depersonalization disorder as a persistent or recurrent alteration in the perception of the self to the extent that the sense of one's own reality is temporarily lost. Patients with depersonalization disorder may feel that they are mechanical, in a dream, or detached from their bodies. The episodes are ego-dystonic, and the patients realize the unreality of these symptoms.

Some clinicians distinguish between depersonalization and derealization. *Depersonalization* is the feeling that one's body or one's personal self is strange and unreal; *derealization* is the perception of objects in the external world as being strange and unreal. The distinction provides a more accurate description of each phenomenon than would be achieved by grouping them together under the rubric of depersonalization.

Epidemiology

As an occasional isolated experience in the life of any person, depersonalization is a common phenomenon and is not necessarily pathological. Studies indicate that transient depersonalization may occur in as much as 70 percent of a given population, with no significant difference between men and women. It is a frequent event in children as they develop the capacity for self-awareness, and adults often undergo a temporary sense of unreality when they travel to new and strange places.

Information about the epidemiology of depersonalization of pathological proportions is scanty. In a few recent studies depersonalization was found to occur in women at least twice as frequently as in men; it is rarely found in persons over 40 years of age.

Etiology

Depersonalization disorder may be caused by psychological, neurological, or systemic disease. Experiences of depersonalization have been associated with epilepsy, brain tumors, sensory deprivation, and emotional trauma. Depersonalization disorder is associated with an array of drugs, including alcohol, barbiturates, benzodiazepines, scopolamine (Donnatal), clioquinol (Vioform), β-adrenergic antagonists, marijuana, and virtually any phencyclidinelike or lysergic acid diethylamide (LSD)-like psychotomimetic. Depersonalization phenomena have been caused by electrical stimulation of the cortex of the temporal lobes during neurosurgery. Systemic causes include endocrine disorders of the thyroid and the pancreas. Anxiety and depression are predisposing factors, as is severe stress, such as what one experiences in combat or in an auto accident. Depersonalization is frequently a symptom in association with anxiety, depression, and schizophrenia; it is apparently rare as a pure disorder.

Clinical Features and Diagnosis

The central characteristic of depersonalization is the quality of unreality and estrangement that is attached to conscious experience. Inner mental processes and external events seem to go on exactly as before, but they feel different and no longer seem to have any relation or significance to the person. Parts of the body or the entire physical being may seem foreign, as may mental operations and accustomed behavior. Hemidepersonalization, the patient's feeling that half of the body is unreal or does not exist, may be related to contralateral parietal lobe disease. Anxiety often accompanies the disorder, and many patients complain of distortions in their senses of time and space. Particularly common is the sensation of a change in the patient's body; for instance, patients may feel that their extremities are bigger or smaller than usual.

An occasional and particularly curious phenomenon is that of doubling; patients feel that the point of conscious "I-ness" is outside their bodies, often a few feet overhead, from where they actually observe themselves, as if they were totally separate persons. Sometimes patients believe they are in two different places at the same time, a condition known as *reduplicative paramnesia* or *double orientation.* Most patients are aware of the disturbances in their sense of reality, which is considered one of the salient characteristics of the syndrome. Psychodynamically, there seems to be a heightening of the psychic energy invested in the self-observing ego, the mental function on which the capacity for insight rests. The DSM-III-R diagnostic criteria are presented in Table 19-7. A clinical case example follows:

A 20-year-old male college student sought psychiatric consultation because he was worried that he might be going insane. For the past two years he had experienced increasingly frequent episodes of feeling outside himself. These episodes were accompanied by a sense of deadness in his body. In addition, during these periods he was uncertain of his balance and frequently stumbled into furniture; this was more apt to occur in public, especially if he was somewhat anxious. During these episodes he felt a lack of easy, natural control of his body; his thoughts seemed foggy as well, in a way that reminded him of receiving intravenous anesthetic agents for an appendectomy some five years previously.

The patient's subjective sense of lack of control was especially troublesome, and he would fight it by shaking his head and saying "stop" to himself. This would momentarily clear his mind and restore his sense of autonomy but only temporarily, as the feelings of deadness and of being outside himself would return. Gradually, over a period of several hours, the unpleasant experiences would fade. The patient was anxious, however, about their return, since he found them increasing in both frequency and duration.

At the time the patient came for treatment, he was experiencing these symptoms about twice a week, and each incident lasted from three to four hours. On several occasions the episodes had occurred while he was driving his car and was alone; worried that he might have an accident, he had stopped driving unless someone accompanied him. Increasingly, he had begun to discuss this problem with his girlfriend, and eventually she had become less affectionate toward him, complaining that he had lost his sense of humor and was totally self-preoccupied. She threatened to break off with him unless he changed, and she began to date other men.

The patient's college grades remained unimpaired—they had, in fact, improved over the past six months because the patient was spending more time studying than had previously been the case. Although discouraged by his symptoms, the patient slept well at night, had noted no change in appetite, and had experienced no impairment in concentration. He was neither fatigued nor physically edgy because of his worry.

Because a cousin had been hospitalized for many years with severe mental illness, the patient had begun to wonder if a similar fate would befall him, and he sought direct reassurance on the matter.

Discussion. Depersonalization—that is, alteration in the perception or experience of the self, so that the usual sense of one's own reality is lost—can be a symptom of a variety of mental disorders, such as schizophrenia and anxiety, mood, personality, and organic mental disorders. Mild depersonalization, without functional impairment, occurs at some time in a large proportion of young adults and does not by itself warrant diagnosis as a mental disorder. When, as in this case, the symptom of depersonalization occurs in the absence of a more pervasive disorder and is sufficiently severe and persistent to cause marked distress, the diagnosis of depersonalization disorder is made.

Table 19-7
Diagnostic Criteria for Depersonalization Disorder

A. Persistent or recurrent experiences of depersonalization as indicated by either (1) or (2):
   (1) an experience of feeling detached from, and as if one is an outside observer of, one's mental processes or body
   (2) an experience of feeling like an automation or as if in a dream

B. During the depersonalization experience, reality testing remains intact.

C. The depersonalization is sufficiently severe and persistent to cause marked distress.

D. The depersonalization experience is the predominant disturbance and is not a symptom of another disorder, such as schizophrenia, panic disorder, or agoraphobia without history of panic disorder but with limited symptom attacks of depersonalization, or temporal lobe epilepsy.

Table from DSM-III-R, *Diagnostic and Statistical Manual of Mental Disorders,* ed 3, revised. Copyright American Psychiatric Association, Washington, DC, 1987, with permission.

Differential Diagnosis

Depersonalization may occur as a symptom in numerous other psychiatric disorders (Table 19-8). The common occurrence of depersonalization in patients with depression and schizophrenia should alert the clinician to the possibility that the patient who initially complains of feelings of unreality and estrangement is actually suffering from one of those more common disorders. A carefully taken history and the mental status examination should in most cases disclose the characteristic features of these two illnesses. Because psychotomimetic drugs often induce long-lasting changes in the experience of the reality of self and environment, it is important to inquire about the use of these substances. The presence of other clinical phenomena in patients complaining of unreality should usually take precedence in determining the diagnosis; in general, the label "depersonalization disorder" is reserved for those conditions in which depersonalization constitutes the main and predominating symptom.

The fact that depersonalization phenomena may result from gross disturbances in brain function underlines the

Table 19-8
Causes of Depersonalization

Neurological disorders Epilepsy Migraine Brain tumors Cerebrovascular disease Cerebral trauma Encephalitis General paresis Alzheimer's disease Huntington's disease Spinocerebellar degeneration	Idiopathic psychiatric disorders Schizophrenia Depression Mania Hysteria Anxiety Obsessive–compulsive disorders Personality disorders Phobic–anxiety depersonalization syndrome
Toxic and metabolic disorders Hypoglycemia Hypoparathyroidism Carbon monoxide poisoning Mescalin intoxication Botulism Hyperventilation Hypothyroidism	"Normal" persons Exhaustion Boredom; sensory deprivation Emotional shock Hemidepersonalization Lateralized (usually right parietal) focal brain lesion

Table by J L Cummings: Dissociative states, depersonalization, multiple personality, episodic memory lapses. In *Clinical Neuropsychiatry,* p 123. Grune & Stratton, Orlando, FL, 1985, with permission.

necessity for a careful neurological evaluation, especially when the depersonalization is not accompanied by more common and obvious psychiatric symptoms. In particular, the possibility of a brain tumor or epilepsy should be considered. The experience of depersonalization may be the earliest presenting symptom of a neurological disorder; therefore, patients complaining of a depersonalization phenomena should be observed carefully.

Course and Prognosis

In the large majority of patients, the symptoms first appear suddenly; only a few patients report a gradual onset. The disorder starts most often between the ages of 15 and 30 years, but it has been seen in patients as young as 10 years of age; it occurs less frequently after age 30 and almost never in the later decades of life. A few follow-up studies indicate that, in more than half the cases, depersonalization tends to be a long-lasting, chronic condition. In many patients the symptoms run a steady course without significant fluctuation of intensity; but they may occur episodically, interspersed with symptom-free intervals. Little is known about precipitating factors, although the disorder has been observed to begin during a period of relaxation after a person has experienced fatiguing psychological stress. The disorder is sometimes ushered in by an attack of acute anxiety that is frequently accompanied by hyperventilation.

Treatment

Little attention has been given to the treatment of patients with depersonalization disorder. At this time there are not sufficient data on which a specific pharmacological regimen may be based. However, the anxiety usually responds to an antianxiety agent. Any underlying disorder (e.g., schizophrenia) can also be treated pharmacologically. Psychotherapeutic approaches are equally untested. As with all patients with neurotic symptoms, the decision to use psychoanalysis or insight-oriented psychotherapy is determined not by the presence of the symptom itself but by a variety of positive indications derived from an assessment of the patient's personality, human relationships, and life situation.

DISSOCIATIVE DISORDER NOT OTHERWISE SPECIFIED

This is a residual category for disorders in which the predominant feature is a dissociative symptom that does not meet the criteria for one of the specific dissociative disorders described above (Table 19-9). According to DSM-III-R, it includes derealization in the absence of depersonalization.

Ganser's Syndrome

Ganser's syndrome is the voluntary production of severe psychiatric symptoms, sometimes described as the giving of approximate answers or talking past the point (e.g., when asked to multiply 4 times 5, the patient answers "21"). This syndrome may occur in persons with other

Table 19-9
Diagnostic Criteria for Dissociative Disorder Not Otherwise Specified

Disorders in which the predominant feature is a dissociative symptom (i.e, a disturbance or alteration in the normally integrative functions of identity, memory, or consciousness) that does not meet the criteria for a specific dissociative disorder

Examples:

(1) Ganser's syndrome: the giving of "approximate answers" to questions, commonly associated with other symptoms such as amnesia, disorientation, perceptual disturbances, fugue, and conversion symptoms

(2) cases in which there is more than one personality state capable of assuming executive control of the individual, but not more than one personality state is sufficiently distinct to meet the full criteria for multiple personality disorder, or cases in which a second personality never assumes complete executive control

(3) trance states (i.e., altered states of consciousness with markedly diminished or selectively focused responsiveness to environmental stimuli). In children this may occur following physical abuse or trauma

(4) derealization unaccompanied by depersonalization

(5) dissociated states that may occur in people who have been subjected to periods of prolonged and intense coercive persuasion (e.g., brainwashing, thought reform, or indoctrination while the captive of terrorists or cultists)

(6) cases in which sudden, unexpected travel and organized, purposeful behavior with inability to recall one's past are not accompanied by the assumption of a new identity, partial or complete.

Table from DSM-III-R, *Diagnostic and Statistical Manual of Mental Disorders,* ed 3, revised. Copyright American Psychiatric Association, Washington, DC, 1987, with permission.

mental disorders, such as schizophrenia, depression, toxic states, paresis, alcoholism, and factitious disorder. The psychological symptoms generally represent the patient's sense of mental illness, rather than any recognized diagnostic category. The syndrome is commonly associated with such dissociative phenomena as amnesia, fugue, perceptual disturbances, and conversion symptoms. Ganser's syndrome is apparently most common in men and in prisoners, although prevalence data and familial patterns are not established. A major predisposing factor is the existence of a severe personality disorder. Differential diagnosis may be extremely difficult. Unless the patient is able to admit the factitious nature of the presenting symptoms or unless there is conclusive evidence from objective psychological tests that the symptoms are false, it may be impossible to determine whether the patient has a true disorder. The disorder may be recognized by its pansymptomatic nature or by the fact that symptoms are often worse when patients believe that they are being watched. Recovery from the syndrome is sudden; patients claim amnesia for the events. Ganser's syndrome was previously classified as a factitious disorder.

Variants of Multiple Personality Disorder

Variants do occur; an example is a case in which there is more than one entity capable of assuming executive control of the person but only one entity sufficiently complex and integrated to meet the full criteria for multiple personality disorder. Another example is a case in which a second personality never assumes complete executive control.

Trance States

Trance states are altered states of consciousness with diminished responsivity to environmental stimuli. Children may exhibit repeated amnestic periods or trancelike states after physical abuse or trauma. Possession and trace states are curious and imperfectly understood forms of dissociation. A common example of a trance state is the medium who presides over a spiritual seance. Typically, mediums enter a dissociative state, during which a person from the so-called spirit world takes over much of their conscious awareness and influences their thoughts and speech.

Automatic writing and crystal gazing are curious but less common manifestations of possession or trance states. In automatic writing the dissociation affects only the arm and hand that write the message, which often discloses mental contents of which the writer is unaware. Crystal gazing, however, results in a trance state in which visual hallucinations are prominent.

Phenomena related to trance states include highway hypnosis and the similar mental states experienced by airplane pilots. In both the monotony of moving at high speeds through environments that provide little in the way of distractions to the operator of the vehicle leads to a fixation on a single object—for example, a dial on the instrument panel or the never-ending horizon of a road running straight ahead for miles. A trancelike state of consciousness results in which visual hallucinations may occur and in which the danger of a serious accident is always present. Possibly in the same order of phenomena are the hallucinations and dissociated mental states in patients who have been confined to respirators for long periods without adequate environmental distractions.

In the religions of many cultures, it has been recognized that the practice of concentration may lead to a variety of dissociative phenomena, such as hallucinations, paralyses, and other sensory disturbances. On occasion, hypnosis may precipitate a self-limited but sometimes prolonged trance state.

Dissociated States

Certain degrees of dissociation may occur in persons who have been subjected to periods of prolonged and intense coercive persuasion (such as brainwashing, thought reform, and indoctrination while being held captive by terrorists or cultists). Whether these are truly dissociative states is open to question, since some evidence, especially in victims of Nazi concentration camps, indicates that such persons are often alexithymic, which results from massive regression, rather than from dissociation.

Patients suffering from somnambulism behave in a strange manner that resembles the behavior of someone in a dissociative state. In somnambulism patients exhibit an altered state of conscious awareness of their surroundings; they often have vivid hallucinatory recollections of an emotionally traumatic event in the past of which there is no memory during the usual waking state. Such patients are out of contact with the environment, appear preoccupied with a private world, and stare into space if their eyes are open. They may appear emotionally upset, speak excitedly in words and sentences that are frequently hard to understand, or engage in a pattern of seemingly meaningful activities that is repeated every time an episode occurs. There is amnesia for the somnambulistic episode once it has ended.

Although amnesia for a period of immediate past experience is found in patients with somnambulism and with localized or general amnesia, the state of consciousness during the period for which they are amnestic differs in character. Somnambulistic patients seem out of touch with the environment and appear to be dreaming. Amnestic patients, by contrast, usually give no indication to observers that there is anything amiss and seem entirely alert both before and after the amnesia occurs.

In DSM-III-R somnambulism is classified as a sleep disorder and is termed sleepwalking disorder, one of the parasomnias.

References

Coons P M, Bowman E S, Milstein V: Multiple personality disorder: A clinical investigation of 50 cases. J Nerv Ment Dis *176*: 519, 1988.

Dysken M W: Clinical usefulness of sodium amobarbital interviewing. Arch Gen Psychiatry *36*: 789, 1979.

Fahy T A: The diagnosis of multiple personality disorder: A critical review. Br J Psychiatry *153*: 597, 1988.

Fahy T A, Abas M, Brown J C: Multiple personality: A symptom of psychiatric disorder. Br J Psychiatry *154*: 99, 1989.

or noncoital, and something less than every aspect of behavior directed toward attaining pleasure.

Sexual Identity and Gender Identity

Gender identity refers to a person's sense of maleness or femaleness. *Sexual identity* refers to biological sexual characteristics: chromosomes, external genitalia, internal genitalia, hormonal composition, gonads, and secondary sex characteristics. In normal development, they form a cohesive pattern, so that a person has no doubt about his or her sex.

Modern embryologic studies have shown that all mammalian embryos—the genetically male and the genetically female—are anatomically female during the early stages of fetal life. Differentiation of the male from the female results from the action of fetal androgen; the action begins about the sixth week of embryonic life and is completed by the end of the third month. The fetus is also vulnerable to exogenously administered androgen during this period. For instance, if the pregnant mother receives sufficient exogenous androgen, a female fetus possessing ovaries can develop external genitalia resembling those of a male (Table 20.1-1).

By the age of 2 or 3 years, almost everyone has a firm conviction that "I am male" or "I am female." Yet even if maleness and femaleness develop normally, the person still has the adaptive task of developing a sense of masculinity or femininity.

Gender identity, according to Robert Stoller, "connotes psychological aspects of behavior related to masculinity and femininity." He considers gender social and sex biological: "Most often the two are relatively congruent, that is, males tend to be manly and females womanly." But sex and gender may develop in conflicting or even opposite ways. Gender identity results from an almost infinite series of cues derived from experiences with family members, teachers, friends, and coworkers and from cultural phenomena. Physical characteristics derived from one's biological sex—such as general physique, body shape, and physical dimensions—interrelate with an intricate system of stimuli, including rewards and punishment and parental gender labels, to establish gender identity.

The formation of gender identity is based on parental and cultural attitudes, the infant's external genitalia, and a genetic influence, which is physiologically active by the sixth week of fetal life. Even though family, cultural, and biological influences may complicate the establishment of a sense of masculinity or femininity, the standard and healthy outcome is a relatively secure sense of identification with one's biological sex—a stable gender identity.

Gender role. Related to and in part derived from gender identity is gender role behavior. This is described, in the words of John Money, as "all those things that a person says or does to disclose himself or herself as having the status of boy or man, girl or woman, respectively. . . . A gender role is not established at birth but is built up cumulatively through experiences encountered and transacted through casual and unplanned learning, through explicit instruction and inculcation, and through spontaneously putting two and two together to make sometimes four and sometimes, erroneously, five." The standard and healthy outcome is a congruence of gender identity and gender role. Although biological attributes are significant, the major factor in attaining the role appropriate to one's sex is learning.

Research on sex differences in behavior in children reveals more psychological similarities than differences. However, girls are found to be less prone to tantrums after the age of 18 months than boys, and boys generally are more aggressive than girls—both physically and verbally—from age 2 onward. Little girls and boys are similarly active, but the boys are more easily stimulated to sudden

Table 20.1-1
Classification of Intersexual Disorders*

Syndrome	Description
Virilizing adrenal hyperplasia (andrenogenital syndrome)	Results from excess androgens in fetus with XX genotype; most common female intersex disorder; associated with enlarged clitoris, fused labia, hirsutism in adolescence
Turner's syndrome	Results from absence of second female sex chromosome (XO); associated with web neck, dwarfism, cubitus valgus; no sex hormones produced; infertile; usually assigned as females because of female-looking genitals
Klinefelter's syndrome	Genotype is XXY; male habitus present with small penis and rudimentary testes because of low androgen production; weak libido; usually assigned as male
Androgen insensitivity syndrome (testicular-feminizing syndrome)	Congenital X-linked recessive disorder that results in inability of tissues to respond to androgens; external genitals look female and cryptorchid testes present; assigned as females, even though they have XY genotype; in extreme form patient has breasts, normal external genitals, short blind vagina, and absence of pubic and axillary hair
Enzymatic defects in XY genotype (e.g., 5-α-reductase deficiency, 17-hydroxysteroid deficiency)	Congenital interruption in production of testosterone that produces ambiguous genitals and female habitus; usually assigned as female because of female-looking genitalia
Hermaphroditism	True hermaphrodite is rare and characterized by both testes and ovaries in same person (may be 46 XX or 46 XY)
Pseudohermaphroditism	Usually the result of endocrine or enzymatic defect (e.g., adrenal hyperplasia) in persons with normal chromosomes; female pseudohermaphrodites have masculine-looking genitals but are XX; male pseudohermaphrodites have rudimentary testes and external genitals and are XY; assigned as males or females, depending on morphology of genitals

*Intersexual disorders include a variety of syndromes that produce persons with gross anatomical or physiological aspects of the opposite sex. For further discussion of intersexual disorders, see p. 754.

bursts of activity when they are in groups. Some researchers speculate that, although aggression is a learned behavior, male hormones may have sensitized boys' neural organizations to absorb those lessons better than girls.

Gender role can appear to be in opposition to gender identity. Persons may identify with their own sex and yet adopt the dress, hairstyle, or other characteristics of the opposite sex. Or they may identify with the opposite sex yet for expediency adopt much of the behavior characteristic of their own sex.

Sexual Behavior

Masturbation. Masturbation is usually a normal precursor of object-related sexual behavior. It has been said that no other form of sexual activity has been more frequently discussed, more roundly condemned, and more universally practiced than masturbation. Research by Alfred Kinsey into the prevalence of masturbation indicated that nearly all men and three-fourths of all women masturbate sometime during their lives.

Longitudinal studies of development show that sexual self-stimulation is very common in infancy and childhood. Just as infants learn to explore the functions of their fingers and mouths, they do the same with their genitalia. At about 15 to 19 months of age, both sexes begin genital self-stimulation. Pleasurable sensations result from any gentle touch to the genital region. These sensations, coupled with the ordinary desire for exploration of one's body, produce a normal interest in masturbatory pleasure at this time. Children also develop an increased interest in the genitalia of others—parents, children, and even animals. As youngsters acquire playmates, this curiosity about their own and others' genitalia motivates episodes of exhibitionism or genital exploration. Such experiences, unless blocked by guilty fear, contribute to continued pleasure from sexual stimulation.

With the approach of puberty, the upsurge of sex hormones, and the development of secondary sex characteristics, sexual curiosity is intensified, and masturbation increases. Adolescents are physically capable of coitus and orgasm but are usually inhibited by social restraints. They are under the dual and often conflicting pressures of establishing their sexual identities and controlling their sexual impulses. The result is a great deal of physiological sexual tension that demands release, and masturbation is a normal way of reducing sexual tensions. An important emotional difference between the pubescent child and the youngster of earlier years is the presence of coital fantasies during masturbation in the adolescent. These fantasies are an important adjunct to the development of sexual identity, for in the comparative safety of the imagination, the adolescent learns to perform the adult sex role. This autoerotic activity is usually maintained into the young adult years, when it is normally replaced by coitus.

It is incorrect to assume that couples in a sexual relationship abandon masturbation entirely. When coitus is unsatisfactory or is unavailable because of illness or absence of the partner, self-stimulation often serves an adaptive purpose, combining sensual pleasure and tension release.

Kinsey found that, when women masturbate, most prefer clitoral stimulation to any other. William Masters and Virginia Johnson reported that women prefer the shaft of the clitoris to the glans because the glans is hypersensitive to intense stimulation.

Moral taboos against masturbation have generated myths that masturbation causes mental illness or a decrease in sexual potency. No scientific evidence supports such claims. Masturbation is a psychopathological symptom only when it becomes a compulsion beyond the willful control of the person. It is then a symptom of emotional disturbance—not because it is sexual but because it is compulsive. Masturbation is almost a universal and inevitable aspect of psychosexual development, and in most cases it is adaptive.

Physiological responses. Normal men and women experience a sequence of physiological responses to sexual stimulation. In the first detailed description of these responses, Masters and Johnson observed that the physiological process involves increasing levels of vasocongestion and myotonia (*tumescence*) and the subsequent release of the vascular activity and muscle tone as a result of orgasm (*detumescence*). Tables 20.1-2 and 20.1-3 describe the male and female sexual response cycles, respectively. The revised third edition of *Diagnostic and Statistical Manual of Mental Disorders* (DSM-III-R) defines a four-phase response cycle: phase 1, appetitive; phase 2, excitement; phase 3, orgasm; phase 4, resolution.

Phase 1: appetitive. This phase is distinct from any phase identified solely through physiology, and it reflects the psychiatrist's fundamental concern with motivations, drives, and personality. This phase is characterized by sexual fantasies and the desire to have sexual activity.

Phase 2: excitement. This phase is brought on by psychological stimulation (fantasy or the presence of a love object) or physiological stimulation (stroking or kissing) or a combination of the two. It consists of a subjective sense of pleasure. The excitement phase is characterized by penile tumescence leading to erection in the man and by vaginal lubrication in the woman. The nipples of both sexes become erect, although nipple erection is more common in women than in men. The woman's clitoris becomes hard and turgid, and her labia minora become thicker as a result of venous engorgement. Initial excitement may last several minutes to several hours. With continued stimulation, the man's testes increase in size 50 percent and elevate. The woman's vaginal barrel shows a characteristic constriction along the outer third, known as the orgasmic platform. The clitoris elevates and retracts behind the symphysis pubis. As a result, the clitoris is not easily accessible. As the area is stimulated, however, traction on the labia minora and the prepuce occurs, and there is intrapreputial movement of the clitoral shaft. Breast size in the woman increases 25 percent. Continued engorgement of the penis and the vagina produces specific color changes, particularly in the labia minora, which become bright or deep red. Voluntary contractions of large muscle groups occur, the rate of heartbeat and respiration increases, and blood pressure rises. Heightened excitement lasts 30 seconds to several minutes.

Phase 3: orgasm. This phase consists of a peaking of sexual pleasure, with release of sexual tension and rhythmic contraction of the perineal muscles and pelvic reproductive organs. A subjective sense of ejaculatory inevitably triggers the man's orgasm. The forceful emission of semen follows. The male orgasm is also associated with four to five rhythmic spasms of the prostate, seminal vesicles, vas, and urethra. In the woman, orgasm is characterized by 3 to 15 involuntary contractions of the lower third of the vagina and by strong pectations and neurotic themes such as these probably exist in all personalities and in all matings. When they predominate and the couple act mainly to exchange patterns of exploitation or when interlocking complementary needs fail to bring sufficient security or happiness, discomfort and anxiety occur, and a breakdown in the relationship is possible.

References

Farber M: *Human Sexuality*. Macmillan, New York, 1985.

Freud S: General theory of the neuroses (1917). In *Standard Edition of the Complete Psychological Works of Sigmund Freud*, vol 16, p 241, Hogarth Press, London, 1953–1966.

Harlow H F: The nature of love. Am Psychol *13*: 673, 1958.

Kinsey A C, Pomeroy W B, Martin C E: *Sexual Behavior in the Human Male*. Saunders, Philadelphia, 1948.

Kinsey A C, Pomeroy W B, Martin C E, Gebbard P H: *Sexual Behavior in the Human Female*. Saunders, Philadelphia, 1953.

Kirkpatrick M: *Women's Sexual Development*. Plenum, New York, 1980.

Maccoby E, Jacklen C: *The Psychology of Sex Differences*. Stanford University Press, Palo Alto, CA, 1974.

May R: *Love and Will*. Norton, New York, 1969.

Masters W H, Johnson V E: *Human Sexual Response*. Little, Brown, Boston, 1966.

Money J, Ehrhardt A A: *Man and Woman/Boy and Girl*. Johns Hopkins University Press, Baltimore, 1972.

Sherfey M J: *The Nature and Evolution of Female Sexuality*. Random House, New York, 1972.

Stoller R J: *Sex and Gender*. Science House, New York, 1968.

20.2 / Paraphilias

Paraphilias are sexual disorders characterized by specialized sexual fantasies and intense sexual urges and practices that are usually repetitive in nature and distressing to the person. The special fantasy, with its unconscious and conscious components, is the pathognomonic element, sexual arousal and orgasm being associated phenomena. The influence of the fantasy and its behavioral manifestations extend beyond the sexual sphere to pervade the person's life. The major functions of sexual behavior for human beings are to assist in bonding, to express and enhance love between persons, and for procreation. Paraphilias are divergent behavior in that they are concealed by their participants, appear to exclude or harm others, and disrupt the potential for bonding between persons. Paraphilic arousal may be transient in some persons who act out their impulses only during periods of stress or conflict.

DSM-III-R CLASSIFICATION

The major categories of paraphilias included in the revised third edition of *Diagnostic and Statistical Manual of Mental Disorders* (DSM-III-R) are pedophilia, exhibitionism, sexual sadism, sexual masochism, voyeurism, fetishism, transvestic fetishism, frotteurism, and a separate category for other paraphilias not otherwise specified (e.g., zoophilia). A given person may have multiple paraphilic disorders.

EPIDEMIOLOGY

Paraphilias are practiced by a small percentage of the population. However, the insistent, repetitive nature of this disorder results in the high frequency of the commission of paraphilic acts; thus, a large proportion of the population have been victimized by persons with paraphilias.

Among legally identified cases of paraphilias, pedophilia is far more common than the others. Ten to 20 percent of all children have been molested by age 18. Because a child is the object, the act is taken more seriously, and greater effort is spent tracking down the culprit than in other paraphilias. Exhibitionists, who publicly display themselves to young children, are also commonly apprehended. Voyeurs may be apprehended, but their risk is not great. Twenty percent of adult females have been the targets of exhibitionists and voyeurs. Sexual masochism and sadism are underrepresented in any prevalence estimates. Sexual sadism usually comes to attention only in sensational cases of rape, brutality, or lust murder. The excretory perversions are scarcely reported, since any activity usually takes place between consenting adults or between prostitute and client. Fetishists ordinarily do not become entangled in the legal system. Transvestites may be arrested occasionally on disturbing-the-peace or other misdemeanor charges if they are obviously men dressed in women's clothes, but arrest is more common among the gender identity disorders. Zoophilia as a true paraphilia is rare.

As usually defined, the sexual perversions seem to be largely male conditions. In the gender identity disorders, the ratio of clinically active men to women is about 2 to 1. Fetishism almost always occurs in men.

Over 50 percent of all paraphilias have their onset prior to age 18. Paraphiliacs frequently have three to five different paraphilias, either concomitantly or at different times in their lives. This is especially the case with exhibitionism, fetishism, masochism, sadism, transvestic fetishism, voyeurism, and zoophilia.

The occurrence of paraphilic behavior peaks between ages 15 and 25 and gradually declines; in men of 50, paraphilic acts are rare, except for those that occur in isolation or with a cooperative partner (Table 20.2-1).

ETIOLOGY

Psychosocial Factors

In the psychoanalytic model, a paraphiliac is a person who has failed to complete the normal developmental process toward heterosexual adjustment. What distinguishes one paraphilia from another is the method chosen by the person (usually male) to cope with the anxiety caused by the threat of (1) castration by the father and (2) separation from the mother. However bizarre its manifestation, the resulting perversion

Table 20.2-1
Frequency of Paraphilic Acts Committed by Paraphiliacs Seeking Outpatient Treatment

Diagnostic Category	Approximate Percentage of All Paraphiliacs Seeking Outpatient Treatment	Median Number of Paraphilic Acts per Paraphiliac
Pedophilia	45	5
Exhibitionism	25	50
Sexual sadism	3	3
Sexual masochism	3	36
Voyeurism	12	17
Fetishism	2	3
Transvestic fetishism	3	25
Frotteurism	6	30
Zoophilia	1	2

Table by Gene Abel, M.D.

provides an outlet for the sexual and aggressive drives that would otherwise have been channeled into proper gender behavior.

Failure to resolve the oedipal crisis by identifying with the father-aggressor (for boys) or mother-aggressor (for girls) results either in improper identification with the opposite-gender parent or in an improper choice of object for libido cathexis. Regardless of current DSM-III-R classifications, psychoanalytic theory holds that homosexuality, transsexualism, and transvestic fetishism are all perversions because each demonstrates identification with the opposite-gender parent, instead of the same-gender parent. For instance, a man dressing in women's clothes is believed to identify with his mother. Exhibitionism and voyeurism are also seen as expressions of feminine identification, since the paraphiliacs must constantly examine their own or others' genitals to calm their anxiety about castration. Fetishism is an attempt to avoid anxiety by displacing libidinal impulses to inappropriate objects. The shoe fetishist unconsciously denies that women have lost their penises through castration by attaching libido to a phallic object, the shoe, that symbolizes the female penis. Both pedophiles and sexual sadists have a need to dominate and control their victims, as though to compensate for their feelings of powerlessness during the oedipal crisis. Some theorists believe the pedophile's choice of a child as love object is a narcissistic one. Sexual masochists overcome their fear of injury and sense of powerlessness by demonstrating that they are impervious to harm. Although recent developments in psychoanalysis place more emphasis on treating defense mechanisms than oedipal traumas, the course of psychoanalytic therapy for the paraphiliac remains consistent with Sigmund Freud's theory.

Other theories attribute the development of paraphilia to early experiences that condition or socialize the child into committing a paraphilic act. The first shared sexual experience can be important in this regard. Molestation as a child can predispose the person toward being the recipient of continued abuse as an adult or, conversely, toward becoming an abuser of others. The onset of paraphilic acts can result from modeling the behavior of others who have carried out paraphilic acts, mimicking sexual behavior depicted in the media, or recalling emotionally laden events from one's past, such as one's own molestation. Learning theory suggests that, because fantasizing of paraphilic interests begins at such an early age and because personal fantasies and thoughts are not shared with others (who could block or discourage such ideas), the use and misuse of paraphilic fantasies and urges continues uninhibited until late in life. Only then does the person begin to realize that such paraphilic interests and urges are inconsistent with societal norms. Unfortunately, by that time the repetitive use of such fantasies has become chronic; the person's sexual thoughts and behaviors have become associated with or conditioned to paraphilic fantasies.

Organic Factors

A number of studies have begun to identify abnormal organic findings in paraphiliacs. None has used random samples of paraphiliacs; the studies are, instead, extensive investigations of paraphiliacs who have been referred to large medical centers. Of those paraphiliacs evaluated at referral centers who had positive organic findings, 74 percent had abnormal hormone levels, 27 percent had hard or soft neurological signs, 24 percent had chromosomal abnormalities, 9 percent had seizures, 9 percent had dyslexia, 4 percent had abnormal electroencephalograms (EEGs) (without seizures), 4 percent had major psychiatric disorders, and 4 percent were mentally retarded. The remaining question, however, is whether these abnormalities are causatively related to paraphilic interests or are incidental findings that bear no relevance to the development of paraphilic interests.

Psychophysiological tests have been developed to measure penile volumetric size in response to paraphilic and nonparaphilic stimuli. The procedure may be of use in diagnosis and treatment but is of questionable diagnostic validity because some men are successfully able to suppress their erectile response.

PEDOPHILIA

Pedophilia involves recurrent intense sexual urges toward or arousal by children 13 years of age or younger that have persisted over a minimum of six months. The person classified as a pedophile should be at least 16 years of age and at least five years older than the victim (Table 20.2-2). When the paraphiliac is younger than 16, clinical judgment should determine whether the diagnosis is warranted (given the maturity of the perpetrator and the victim).

The vast majority of child molestations involve genital fondling or oral sex. Vaginal or anal penetration of the child is an infrequent occurrence except in cases of incest. Although the majority of child victims coming to public

Table 20.2-2
Diagnostic Criteria for Pedophilia

A. Over a period of at least six months, recurrent intense sexual urges and sexually arousing fantasies involving sexual activity with a prepubescent child or children (generally age 13 or younger).

B. The person has acted on these urges, or is markedly distressed by them.

C. The person is at least 16 years old and at least five years older than the child or children in A.

Note: Do not include a late adolescent involved in an ongoing sexual relationship with a 12- or 13-year-old.

Table from DSM-III-R, *Diagnostic and Statistical Manual of Mental Disorders*, ed 3, revised. Copyright American Psychiatric Association, Washington, DC, 1987, with permission.

attention are female, this finding appears to be a product of the referral process. Offenders report that, when they actually touch the child, the majority (60 percent) of victims are male. This figure is in sharp contrast to that for nontouching victimization of children, such as window peeping or exhibitionism, which in 99 percent of cases is perpetrated against female children. Moreover, 95 percent of pedophiles are heterosexual, and 50 percent have consumed alcohol to excess at the time of the incident. In addition to their pedophilia, a significant number of pedophiles are concomitantly or have previously been involved in exhibitionism, voyeurism, or rape.

Although not classifiable as a perversion in the true sense, incest is superficially related to pedophilia by the frequent selection of an immature child as a sex object, the subtle or overt element of coercion, and, occasionally, the preferential nature of the adult-child liaison.

EXHIBITIONISM

Exhibitionism is the recurrent urge and desire to expose the genitals to a stranger or an unsuspecting person (Table 20.2-3). Sexual excitement occurs in anticipation of the exposure, and orgasm is brought about by masturbation during or after the event. In almost 100 percent of cases, exhibitionists are males exposing themselves to females.

The dynamic of the exhibitionist is to assert his masculinity by showing his penis and by watching the reaction of the victim—fright, surprise, disgust. Unconsciously, the man feels castrated and impotent. Wives of exhibitionists often substitute for the mother to whom the men were excessively attached during childhood.

In other related perversions, the central themes involve derivatives of looking or showing. For example, in obscene phone calling, tension and arousal begin in anticipation of phoning, an unsuspecting partner is involved, the recipient of the call listens while the telephoner verbally exposes his preoccupations or induces her to talk about her sexual activity, and the conversation is accompanied by masturbation, which is often completed after the contact is interrupted.

SEXUAL SADISM

The DSM-III-R diagnostic criteria for sexual sadism are presented in Table 20.2-4. The onset is usually before the age of 18 years, and most sadists are men. According to psychoanalytic theory, sadism is a defense against fears of castration—sadists do to others what they fear will happen to them. Pleasure is derived from expressing the aggressive instinct. The disorder was named after the Marquis de Sade, an 18th-century French author, who was repeatedly imprisoned for his violent sexual acts against women. Sexual sadism is related to rape, although rape is more aptly considered a form of aggression. Some sadistic rapists, however, kill their victims after having sex (so-called lust murders). In many cases, these persons have underlying schizophrenia. John Money believes lust murderers have the dissociative disorder of multiple personality and may have had a history of head trauma. He lists five contributory causes of sexual sadism: hereditary predisposition, hormonal malfunctioning, pathological relationships, a history of sexual abuse, and the presence of other psychiatric syndromes.

Table 20.2-3
Diagnostic Criteria for Exhibitionism

A. Over a period of at least six months, recurrent intense sexual urges and sexually arousing fantasies involving the exposure of one's genitals to an unsuspecting stranger.

B. The person has acted on these urges, or is markedly distressed by them.

Table from DSM-III-R, *Diagnostic and Statistical Manual of Mental Disorders*, ed 3, revised. Copyright American Psychiatric Association, Washington, DC, 1987, with permission.

Table 20.2-4
Diagnostic Criteria for Sexual Sadism

A. Over a period of at least six months, recurrent intense sexual urges and sexually arousing fantasies involving acts (real, not simulated) in which the psychological or physical suffering (including humiliation) of the victim is sexually exciting to the person.

B. The person has acted on these urges, or is markedly distressed by them.

Table from DSM-III-R, *Diagnostic and Statistical Manual of Mental Disorders*, ed 3, revised. Copyright American Psychiatric Association, Washington, DC, 1987, with permission.

SEXUAL MASOCHISM

Masochism takes its name from the activities of Leopold von Sacher-Masoch, a 19th-century Austrian novelist whose characters derived sexual pleasure from being abused and dominated by women. According to DSM-III-R, persons with this disorder have a recurrent preoccupation with sexual urges or fantasies of being humiliated, beaten, bound, or otherwise made to suffer (Table 20.2-5). Masochistic practices are more common among men than among women. Freud believed masochism to result from destructive fantasies turned against the self. In some cases, persons can allow themselves to experience sexual feelings only if punishment for them follows. Masochists may have had childhood experiences that convinced them that pain is a prerequisite for sexual pleasure. About 30 percent of masochists also have sadistic fantasies and are

Table 20.2-5
Diagnostic Criteria for Sexual Masochism

A. Over a period of at least six months, recurrent intense sexual urges and sexually arousing fantasies involving the act (real, not simulated) of being humiliated, beaten, bound, or otherwise made to suffer.

B. The person has acted on these urges, or is markedly distressed by them.

Table from DSM-III-R, *Diagnostic and Statistical Manual of Mental Disorders*, ed 3, revised. Copyright American Psychiatric Association, Washington, DC, 1987, with permission.

known as sadomasochists. Moral masochism involves a need to suffer but is not accompanied by sexual fantasies; it is a controversial category called self-defeating personality in DSM-III-R.

VOYEURISM

Voyeurism is the recurrent preoccupation with fantasies or acts that involve seeking out or observing people who are naked or are engaged in grooming or in sexual activity (Table 20.2-6). It is also known as scopophilia. Masturbation to orgasm usually occurs during or after the event. The first voyeuristic act usually occurs during childhood and is most common in males. When voyeurs are apprehended, it is usually for loitering. Telephone scatologia, more commonly known as obscene phone calls, is related to voyeurism in that the person attempts to demonstrate his masculinity to a stranger.

FETISHISM

In fetishism the sexual focus is on objects (such as shoes, gloves, pantyhose, and stockings) that are intimately associated with the human body (Table 20.2-7). The particular fetish is linked to someone closely involved with the patient during childhood and has some quality associated with this loved, needed, or even traumatizing person. Usually, the disorder begins by adolescence, although the fetish may have been established in childhood. Once established, this disorder tends to be chronic.

Table 20.2-6
Diagnostic Criteria for Voyeurism

A. Over a period of at least six months, recurrent intense sexual urges and sexually arousing fantasies involving the act of observing an unsuspecting person who is naked, in the process of disrobing, or engaging in sexual activity.

B. The person has acted on these urges or is markedly distressed by them.

Table from DSM-III-R, *Diagnostic and Statistical Manual of Mental Disorders*, ed 3, revised. Copyright American Psychiatric Association, Washington, DC, 1987, with permission.

Table 20.2-7
Diagnostic Criteria for Fetishism

A. Over a period of at least six months, recurrent intense sexual urges and sexually arousing fantasies involving the use of nonliving objects by themselves (e.g., female undergarments).

Note: The person may at other times use the nonliving object with a sexual partner.

B. The person has acted on these urges, or is markedly distressed by them.

C. The fetishes are not only articles of female clothing used in cross-dressing (transvestic fetishism) or devices designed for the purpose of tactile genital stimulation (e.g., vibrator).

Table from DSM-III-R, *Diagnostic and Statistical Manual of Mental Disorders*, ed 3, revised. Copyright American Psychiatric Association, Washington, DC, 1987, with permission.

Sexual activity may be directed toward the fetish itself (e.g., masturbation with or into a shoe), or the fetish may be incorporated in sexual intercourse (e.g., with the demand that high-heeled shoes be worn). The disorder is almost exclusively male. According to Freud, the fetish serves as a symbol of the phallus because the fetishist has unconscious castration fears. Learning theorists believe that the object was associated with sexual stimulation at an early age. In females, kleptomania (compulsive stealing) may produce sexual excitement. The kleptomaniac's act of stealing symbolizes forbidden sexual pleasures, such as masturbation.

TRANSVESTIC FETISHISM

Transvestic fetishism or transvestism is marked by fantasized or actual dressing by heterosexual men in female clothes for purposes of arousal and as an adjunct to masturbation or coitus (Table 20.2-8). Transvestism typically begins in childhood or early adolescence. As years pass, some men with transvestism want to dress and live permanently as women. Usually, more than one article of clothing is involved; frequently, an entire wardrobe is involved. When a transvestite is cross-dressed, the appearance of femininity may be quite striking, although usually not to the degree found in transsexualism. When not dressed in women's clothes, transvestite men may be hypermasculine in appearance and occupation. Cross-dressing exists on a gradient from solitary, depressed, guilt-ridden dressing to ego-syntonic, sociable membership in a transvestite subculture.

The overt clinical syndrome of transvestism may begin in latency, but it is more often seen around pubescence or in adolescence. Frank dressing in women's clothes usually does not begin until mobility and relative independence from parents are fairly well established.

FROTTEURISM

This disorder is characterized by the male's rubbing his penis against the buttocks or body of a fully clothed woman to achieve orgasm (Table 20.2-9). At other times, he may use his hands to rub an unsuspecting victim. These acts usually occur in crowded places, particularly subways and buses. The frotteur is extremely passive and isolated, and frottage is often his only source of sexual gratification.

Table 20.2-8
Diagnostic Criteria for Transvestic Fetishism

A. Over a period of at least six months, in a heterosexual male, recurrent intense sexual urges and sexually arousing fantasies involving cross-dressing.

B. The person has acted on these urges, or is markedly distressed by them.

C. Does not meet the criteria for gender identity disorder of adolescence or adulthood, nontranssexual type, or transsexualism.

Table from DSM-III-R, *Diagnostic and Statistical Manual of Mental Disorders*, ed 3, revised. Copyright American Psychiatric Association, Washington, DC, 1987, with permission.

Table 20.2-9
Diagnostic Criteria for Frotteurism

A. Over a period of at least six months, recurrent intense sexual urges and sexually arousing fantasies involving touching and rubbing against a nonconsenting person. It is the touching, not the coercive nature of the act, that is sexually exciting.

B. The person has acted on these urges, or is markedly distressed by them.

PARAPHILIAS NOT OTHERWISE SPECIFIED

This group of atypical paraphilias is extremely varied and does not meet the criteria for any of the aforementioned categories.

Zoophilia

In zoophilia, animals—which may be trained to participate—are preferentially incorporated into arousal fantasies or sexual activities, including intercourse, masturbation, and oral-genital contact. Zoophilia as an organized perversion is rare. For a number of people, animals are the major source of relatedness, so it is not surprising that a broad variety of domestic animals are sensually or sexually used.

Sexual relations with animals may occasionally be an outgrowth of availability or convenience, especially in parts of the world where rigid convention precludes premarital sexuality or in situations of enforced isolation. However, because masturbation is also available in such situations, it is reasonable to suspect that some predilection for animal contact is present in opportunistic zoophilia.

Coprophilia

This is sexual pleasure associated with the desire to defecate on a partner, to be defecated on, or to eat feces (coprophagia). A variant is the compulsive utterance of obscene words (coprolalia). These paraphilias are associated with fixation at the anal stage of psychosexual development. Similarly, the use of enemas as part of sexual stimulation (klismaphilia) is related to anal fixation.

Urophilia

Also known as urolagnia, urophilia is sexual pleasure associated with the desire to urinate on a partner or to be urinated on; it is a form of urethral eroticism. It may be associated with masturbatory techniques involving the insertion of foreign objects into the urethra for sexual stimulation in both men and women.

Oralism

Mouth-genital contact—such as cunnilingus (oral contact with the external female genitals), fellatio (oral contact with the penis), and analingus (oral contact with the anus)—is an activity normally associated with foreplay. Freud recognized the mucosal surfaces of the body as being erotogenic and capable of producing pleasurable sensation. But when a person uses these activities as the sole source of sexual gratification and cannot or refuses to have coitus, a paraphilia exists. It is also known as *partialism*, focusing on one part of the body to the exclusion of all other parts.

Necrophilia

Necrophilia is the act of obtaining sexual gratification from cadavers. Most necrophiles find corpses for their exploitation from morgues. Some have been known to rob graves. At times, persons murder in order to satisfy their perversion. In the few cases studied, the necrophiles believed that they were inflicting the greatest conceivable humiliation on their lifeless victims. According to Richard Krafft-Ebing, the diagnosis of psychosis is, under all circumstances, justified.

Masturbation

Masturbation is a normal activity that is common in all stages of life from infancy to old age. It was not always thought to be so. Freud believed neurasthenia to be caused by excessive masturbation. In the early 1900s, "masturbatory insanity" was a common diagnosis in hospitals for the criminally insane in the United States. It can be defined as achieving sexual pleasure—usually resulting in orgasm—by oneself (autoeroticism). Alfred Kinsey found it to be more prevalent in males than in females, but this discrepancy may no longer exist. The frequency of masturbation varies from three to four times a week in adolescence to one to two times a week in adulthood. It is common among married people; Kinsey reported that it occurred on the average of once a month.

Techniques of masturbation vary in both sexes and among persons. Most common is direct stimulation of the clitoris or penis with the hand or fingers. Indirect stimulation may also be used, such as rubbing against a pillow or squeezing the thighs. Kinsey found that 2 percent of women are capable of achieving orgasm through fantasy alone. Men and women have been known to insert objects into the urethra to achieve orgasm. Recently, the hand vibrator has been used as a masturbatory device by both sexes.

Masturbation is abnormal when it is the only type of sexual activity performed, when it is done with such frequency as to indicate a compulsion or sexual dysfunction, or when it is consistently preferred to sex with a partner.

Hypoxyphilia

Newly classified in DSM-III-R, hypoxyphilia is the desire to achieve an altered state of consciousness secondary to hypoxia while experiencing orgasm. In this disorder, the person may use a drug (such as a volatile nitrite or nitrous oxide) that produces hypoxia. Autoerotic asphyxiation is also associated with hypoxic states but should be classified as a form of sexual masochism. For further discussion of autoerotic asphyxiation, see Section 20.3, "Sexual Dysfunctions and Other Sexual Disorders."

DIAGNOSIS

In DSM-III-R the diagnostic criteria for paraphilia include the presence of the pathognomonic fantasy and its behavioral elaboration. The fantasy contains unusual sexual material that is relatively fixed and shows only minor variations. The achievement of arousal and orgasm depends on mental elaboration or behavioral playing out of the fantasy. Sexual activity is ritualized or stereotyped and makes use of degraded, reduced, or dehumanized objects.

The clinician needs to differentiate paraphilia from experimentation in which the act is done for its novel effect and not recurrently or compulsively. This activity is most likely to occur during adolescence. Some paraphilias (especially the more bizarre) are part of another disorder, such as schizophrenia. Organic mental syndromes may release perverse impulses.

PROGNOSIS

Poor prognosis for paraphilias is associated with early age of onset, high frequency of acts, no guilt or shame about the act, and alcoholism or drug abuse. The prognosis is better when there is a history of coitus in addition to the paraphilia, when there is high motivation for change, and when the patient is self-referred, rather than referred by a legal agency.

TREATMENT

Insight-oriented psychotherapy is the most common approach to treating the paraphilias. Patients have the opportunity to understand their dynamics and the events that caused the paraphilia to develop. In particular, they become aware of the daily events that cause them to act on their impulses (e.g., after a real or fantasized rejection). Psychotherapy also allows these patients to regain self-esteem and to improve interpersonal skills and find acceptable methods for sexual gratification. Group therapy is also of use in this regard.

Sex therapy is an appropriate adjunct to treatment with patients who suffer from specific sexual dysfunctions when they attempt nondeviant sexual activities with partners.

Behavior therapy is used to disrupt the learned paraphilic pattern. Noxious stimuli, such as electric shocks and bad odors, have been paired with the impulse, which then diminishes. The stimuli can be self-administered and used by patients whenever they feel they will act on the impulse.

Drug therapy, including antipsychotic or antidepressant medication, is indicated for the treatment of schizophrenia or depression if the paraphilia is associated with those disorders. Antiandrogens, such as cyproterone acetate in Europe and medroxyprogesterone acetate (Depo-Provera) in the United States, have been used experimentally in hypersexual perversions. In some carefully selected cases, there have been reports of decreases in the hypersexual behavior. Medroxyprogesterone acetate seems to benefit those patients whose driven hypersexuality (e.g., virtually constant masturbation, sexual contact at every opportunity, compulsively assaultive sexuality) is out of control or dangerous.

References

Abel G G: Paraphilias. In *Comprehensive Textbook of Psychiatry*, ed 5, H I Kaplan and B J Sadock, editors, p 1069. Williams & Wilkins, Baltimore, 1989.

Abel G G, Blanchard E B: The role of fantasy in the treatment of sexual deviation. Arch Gen Psychiatry *30*: 467, 1974.

Berlin F S, Meinecke C F: Treatment of sex offenders with antiandrogenic medication: Conceptualization, review of treatment modalities, and preliminary findings. Am J Psychiatry *3*: 237, 1981.

Blair C D, Lanyon R I: Exhibitionism: Etiology and treatment. Psychol Bull *89*: 439, 1981.

Cook M, Howells K: *Adult Sexual Interest in Children.* Academic Press, New York, 1981.

Freud S: Three essays on the theory of sexuality. In *Standard Edition of the Complete Psychological Works of Sigmund Freud.* Hogarth Press, London, 1953–1966.

Gange P: Treatment of sex offenders with medroxyprogesterone acetate. Am J Psychiatry *138*: 644, 1981.

Kinsey A, Pomeroy W, Martin C E: *Sexual Behavior in the Human Male.* Saunders, Philadelphia, 1948.

Krafft-Ebing R: *Psychopathia Sexualis.* Stein and Day, New York, 1965.

Leif H, ed: *Sex Problems in Medical Practice.* American Medical Association, Chicago, 1981.

Levine S M, Stava L: Personality characteristics of sex offenders: A review. Arch Sex Behav *16*: 57, 1987.

Money J: Forensic sexology: Paraphilic serial rape (biastophilia) and lust murder (erotophonophilia). Am J Psychother *44*: 26, 1990.

Slag, M F: Impotence in medical clinic outpatients. JAMA *249*: 1736, 1983.

20.3 / Sexual Dysfunctions and Other Sexual Disorders

Six major categories of sexual dysfunction are listed in the revised third edition of *Diagnostic and Statistical Manual of Mental Disorders* (DSM-III-R): (1) sexual desire disorders, (2) sexual arousal disorders, (3) orgasm disorders, (4) sexual pain disorders, (5) sexual dysfunction not otherwise specified, and (6) other sexual disorders, a residual category for a miscellaneous group of disorders that are not classifiable in any of the previous categories.

It is useful to think of the dysfunctions as disorders related to a particular phase of the sexual response cycle. Thus, sexual drive disorders are associated with the first phase of the response cycle, known as the appetitive phase. Table 20.3-1 lists each of the DSM-III-R phases of the sexual response cycle and the sexual dysfunctions usually associated with it.

Sexual dysfunctions can be symptomatic of biological problems (biogenic) or intrapsychic or interpersonal conflicts (psychogenic) or a combination of these factors. Sexual function can be adversely affected by stress of any kind, by emotional disorders, or by ignorance of sexual function and physiology. The dysfunctions may be lifelong or develop after a period of normal functioning. The dysfunction may be generalized or situational—that is, limited to a specific partner or a certain situation—and it may be total or partial.

In considering each of the disorders, the clinician needs to rule out a physical disorder that could account for or contribute to the dysfunction. If the disorder is biogenic, it is coded on Axis III in DSM-III-R; if psychogenic, it is coded on Axis I. If both psychogenic and biogenic factors are involved—for example, a sexual arousal disorder secondary to both diabetes and intrapsychic conflict—both codes may be used. In some cases, a patient may suffer

Table 20.3-1
The DSM-III-R Phases of the Sexual Response Cycle and Associated Sexual Dysfunctions*

Phases	Characteristics	Dysfunction
1. Appetitive	This phase is distinct from any identified solely through physiology and reflects the patient's motivations, drives, and personality. The phase is characterized by sexual fantasies and the desire to have sex.	Hypoactive sexual desire disorder; sexual aversion disorder.
2. Excitement	This phase consists of a subjective sense of sexual pleasure and accompanying physiological changes. All the physiological responses noted in Masters and Johnson's excitement and plateau phases are combined and occur under this phase.	Female sexual arousal disorder; male erectile disorder (may also occur in stage 3 and stage 4)
3. Orgasm	This phase consists of a peaking of sexual pleasure, with release of sexual tension and rhythmic contraction of the perineal muscles and pelvic reproductive organs.	Inhibited female orgasm (anorgasmia); inhibited male orgasm (retarded ejaculation); premature ejaculation
4. Resolution	This phase entails a sense of general relaxation, well-being, and muscle relaxation. During this phase men are refractory to orgasm for a period of time that increases with age, whereas women are capable of having multiple orgasms without a refractory period.	Postcoital dysphoria; postcoital headache

*DSM-III-R consolidates the Masters and Johnson excitement and plateau phases into a single excitement phase, which is preceded by the appetitive phase. The orgasm and resolution phases remain the same as originally described by Masters and Johnson.

from more than one dysfunction—for example, premature ejaculation and erectile dysfunction.

SEXUAL DESIRE DISORDERS

Sexual desire disorders (previously called inhibited sexual desire) are divided into two classes: hypoactive sexual desire disorder, characterized by deficiency or absence of sexual fantasies and desire for sexual activity (Table 20.3-2), and sexual aversion disorder, characterized by an aversion to and avoidance of genital sexual contact with a sexual partner (Table 20.3-3). The former condition is more common than the latter. An estimated 20 percent of the total population have hypoactive sexual desire disorder. The complaint is more common among women than among men.

A variety of causative factors are associated with sexual desire disorders. Patients with desire problems often use inhibition of desire in a defensive way to protect against unconscious fears about sex. Unacceptable homosexual impulses can also suppress libido or cause an aversion to heterosexual contact. Sigmund Freud conceptualized low sexual desire as the result of inhibition during the phallic psychosexual phase

Table 20.3-2
Diagnostic Criteria for Hypoactive Sexual Desire Disorder

A. Persistently or recurrently deficient or absent sexual fantasies and desire for sexual activity. The judgment of deficiency or absence is made by the clinician, taking into account factors that affect sexual functioning, such as age, sex, and the context of the person's life

B. Occurrence not exclusively during the course of another Axis I disorder (other than a sexual dysfunction), such as major depression.

Table from DSM-III-R, *Diagnostic and Statistical Manual of Mental Disorders*, ed 3, revised. Copyright American Psychiatric Association, Washington, DC, 1987, with permission.

Table 20.3-3
Diagnostic Criteria for Sexual Aversion Disorder

A. Persistent or recurrent extreme aversion to, and avoidance of, all or almost all genital sexual contact with a sexual partner

B. Occurrence not exclusively during the course of another Axis I disorder (other than a sexual dysfunction), such as obsessive-compulsive disorder or major depression.

Table from DSM-III-R, *Diagnostic and Statistical Manual of Mental Disorders*, ed 3, revised. Copyright American Psychiatric Association, Washington, DC, 1987, with permission.

and unresolved oedipal conflicts. Some men, fixated at the phallic stage of development, are fearful of the vagina, believing they will be castrated if they approach it, a concept Freud called *vagina dentata*, because they believe unconsciously that the vagina has teeth. Hence, they avoid contact with the female genitalia entirely. Lack of desire can also be the result of chronic stress, anxiety, or depression. In some cases biochemical correlates are associated with hypoactive desire (Table 20.3-4). A recent study found markedly decreased levels of serum testosterone in men complaining of low desire when they were compared with normal controls in a sleep-laboratory situation. Drugs that depress the central nervous system (CNS) or decrease testosterone production can decrease desire. Abstinence from sex for a prolonged period sometimes results in suppression of the sexual impulse. Desire commonly decreases after major illness or surgery, particularly when the body image is affected after such procedures as mastectomy, ileostomy, hysterectomy, and prostatectomy. Loss of desire may also be an expression of hostility or the sign of a deteriorating relationship.

In one study of young married couples who ceased having sexual relations for a period of two months, marital discord was the reason most frequently given for the cessation or inhibition of sexual activity.

The presence of desire depends on several factors: biological drive, adequate self-esteem, previous good experiences with sex, the availability of an appropriate partner, and a good relationship in nonsexual areas with one's partner. Damage to any of these factors may result in diminished desire.

Table 20.3-4
Neurophysiology of Sexual Dysfunction

	DA	5HT	NE	ACh	Clinical Correlation
Erection	↑	0	$\alpha_1\beta$ ↓ ↑	M	Neruoleptics may lead to erectile dysfunction (DA block); DA agonists may lead to enhanced erection and libido; priapism with trazodone (α_1 block); β-blockers may lead to impotence.
Ejaculation and orgasm	0	± ↓	α_1 ↑	M	α_1-Blockers (TCAs, MAOIs, thioridazine) may lead to imparied ejaculation; 5HT agents may inhibit orgasm.

↑ = facilitates ↓ = inhibits or decreases M = modulates O = minimal ± = some
DA = dopamine 5HT = serotonin NE = norepinephrine ACh = acetylcholine

Table from R Segraves, *Psychiatric Times,* 1990.

In making the diagnosis, the clinician must evaluate the age, general health, and life stresses of the patient. An attempt should be made to establish a baseline of sexual interest before the disorder began. The need for sexual contact and satisfaction varies among persons and over time in any given person. In a group of 100 couples with stable marriages, 8 percent reported having intercourse less than once a month. In another group of couples, one-third reported episodic lack of sexual relations for periods averaging eight weeks. Finally, the diagnosis should not be made unless the lack of desire is a source of distress to the patient.

SEXUAL AROUSAL DISORDERS

These disorders, previously called inhibited sexual excitement, are divided by DSM-III-R into (1) male erectile disorder, characterized by the recurrent and persistent partial or complete failure to attain or maintain an erection until the completion of the sex act, and (2) female sexual arousal disorder, characterized by the persistent or recurrent partial or complete failure to attain or maintain the lubrication-swelling response of sexual excitement until the completion of the sexual act. The diagnosis takes into account the focus, intensity, and duration of the sexual activity in which the patient engages (Tables 20.3-5 and 20.3-6). If sexual stimulation is inadequate in focus, intensity, or duration, the diagnosis should not be made.

Table 20.3-5
Diagnostic Criteria for Male Erectile Disorder

A. Either (1) or (2):
  (1) persistent or recurrent partial or complete failure in a male to attain or maintain erection until completion of the sexual activity
  (2) persistent or recurrent lack of a subjective sense of sexual excitement and pleasure in a male during sexual activity
B. Occurrence not exclusively during the course of another Axis I disorder (other than a sexual dysfunction), such as major depression

Table from DSM-III-R, *Diagnostic and Statistical Manual of Mental Disorders,* ed 3, revised. Copyright American Psychiatric Association, Washington, DC, 1987, with permission.

Table 20.3-6
Diagnostic Criteria for Female Sexual Arousal Disorder

A. Either (1) or (2):
  (1) persistent or recurrent partial or complete failure to attain or maintain the lubrication-swelling response of sexual excitement until completion of the sexual activity
  (2) persistent or recurrent lack of a subjective sense of sexual excitement and pleasure in a female during sexual activity
B. Occurrence not exclusively during the course of another Axis I disorder (other than a sexual dysfunction), such as major depression

Table from DMS-III-R, *Diagnostic and Statistical Manual of Mental Disorders,* ed 3, revised. Copyright American Psychiatric Association, Washington, DC, 1987, with permission.

Female Sexual Arousal Disorder

The prevalence of female sexual arousal disorder is generally underestimated. Women who have excitement phase dysfunction often have orgasm problems as well. In one study of relatively happily married couples, 33 percent of the women described difficulty in maintaining sexual excitement.

Many psychological factors are associated with female sexual inhibition. These conflicts may be expressed through inhibition of excitement or orgasm and are discussed under orgasmic phase dysfunctions. In some women, excitement phase disorders are associated with dyspareunia or with lack of desire.

Physiological studies of dysfunction suggest that a hormonal pattern may contribute to responsiveness in women who have excitement phase dysfunction. William Masters and Virginia Johnson found normally responsive women to be particularly desirous of sex before the onset of the menses. However, some women report that they feel the greatest sexual excitement immediately after the menses or at the time of ovulation. Alterations in testosterone, estrogen, prolactin, and thyroxin levels have been implicated in excitement disorder in women. Also, medications with antihistaminic or anticholinergic properties cause a decrease in vaginal lubrication. There is some evidence that dysfunctional women are less aware of the physiological responses of their bodies, such as vasocongestion, during arousal.

Male Erectile Disorder

Male erectile disorder is also called erectile dysfunction or impotence. In primary impotence the man has never been able to obtain an erection sufficient for vaginal insertion. In secondary impotence the man has successfully achieved vaginal penetration at some time in his sexual life but is later unable to do so. In selective impotence the man is able to have coitus in certain circumstances but not in others; for example, a man may function effectively with a prostitute but be impotent with his wife.

Secondary impotence has been reported in 10 to 20 percent of all men. Freud declared it to be a very common complaint among his patients. Among all men treated for sexual disorders, more than 50 percent have impotence as the chief complaint. Primary impotence is a rare disorder, occurring in about 1 percent of men under age 35. The incidence of impotence increases with age. Among young adults it has been reported in about 8 percent of the population. Alfred Kinsey reported that over 75 percent of all men were impotent at age 80. Masters and Johnson report a fear of impotence in all men over 40, which the researchers believe reflects the masculine fear of loss of virility with advancing age. As it happens, however, impotence is not universal in aging men; having an available sex partner is more closely related to continuing potency than is age.

The cause of impotence may be organic or psychological or a combination of both. The incidence of psychological as opposed to organic impotence has been the focus of many studies. Statistics indicate that 20 to 50 percent of men with erectile dysfunction have an organic basis for their disorder. The organic causes of impotence are listed in Table 20.3-7. Side effects of medication may impair sexual functioning in a variety of ways in both men and women (Table 20.3-8). Castration (removal of the ovaries or the testes) does not always lead to sexual dysfunction, depending on the person. Erection may still occur after castration. A reflex arc, fired when the inner thigh is stimulated, passes through the sacral cord erectile center to account for the phenomenon.

Freud described one type of impotence as caused by an inability to reconcile feelings of affection toward a woman with feelings of desire for her. Such men can function only

Table 20.3-7
Diseases Implicated in Erectile Dysfunction

Infectious and parasitic diseases
- Elephantiasis
- Mumps

Cardiovascular diseases*
- Atherosclerotic disease
- Aortic aneurysm
- Leriche's syndrome
- Cardiac failure

Renal and urological disorders
- Peyronie's disease
- Chronic renal failure
- Hydrocele and varicocele

Hepatic disorders
- Cirrhosis (usually associated with alcoholism)

Pulmonary disorders
- Respiratory failure

Genetics
- Klinefelter's syndrome
- Congenital penile vascular and structural abnormalities

Nutritional disorders
- Malnutrition
- Vitamin deficiencies

Endocrine disorders*
- Diabetes mellitus
- Dysfunction of the pituitary-ardrenal-testis axis
- Acromegaly
- Addison's disease
- Chromophobe adenoma
- Adrenal neoplasia
- Myxedema
- Hyperthyroidism

Neurological disorders
- Multiple sclerosis
- Transverse myelitis
- Parkinson's disease
- Temporal lobe epilepsy
- Traumatic and neoplastic spinal cord diseases*
- Central nervous system tumor
- Amyotrophic lateral sclerosis
- Peripheral neuropathy
- General paresis
- Tabes dorsalis

Pharmacological contributants
- Alcohol and other addictive drugs (heroin, methadone, morphine, cocaine, amphetamines, and barbituates)
- Prescribed drugs (psychotropic drugs, antihypertensive drugs, estrogens, and antiandrogens)

Poisoning
- Lead (plumbism)
- Herbicides

Surgical procedures*
- Perineal prostatectomy
- Abdominal-perineal colon resection
- Sympathectomy (frequently interferes with ejaculation)
- Aortoiliac surgery
- Radical cystectomy
- Retropertioneal lymphadenectomy

Miscellaneous
- Radiation therapy
- Pelvic fracture
- Any severe systemic disease or debilitating condition

Table by Virginia Sadock, M.D.
*In the United States it is estimated that 2 million men are impotent because they suffer from diabetes mellitus; an additional 300,000 are impotent because of other endocrine diseases; 1.5 million are impotent as a result of vascular disease; 180,000 because of multiple sclerosis; 400,000 because of traumas and fractures leading to pelvic fractures or spinal cord injuries; and another 650,000 are impotent as a result of radical surgery, including prostatectomies, colostomies, and cystectomies.

Table 20.3-8
Pharmacological Agents Implicated in Male Sexual Dysfunction

Drug	Impairs Erection	Impairs Ejaculation
Psychiatric Drugs		
Cyclic antidepressants*		
Imipramine (Tofranil)	+	+
Protriptyline (Vivactil)	+	+
Desipramine (Pertofrane)	+	+
Clomipramine (Anafranil)	+	+
Amitriptyline (Elavil)	+	+
Trazodone (Desyrel)†	–	–
Monoamine oxidase inhibitors		
Tranylcypromine (Parnate)	+	
Phenelzine (Nardil)	+	+
Pargyline (Eutonyl)	–	+
Isocarboxazid (Marplan)	–	+
Other mood-active drugs		
Lithium	+	
Amphetamines	+	+
Fluoxetine (Prozac)	–	+
Major tranquilizers‡		
Fluphenazine (Prolixin)	+	
Thioridazine (Mellaril)	+	+
Chlorprothiexene (Taractan)	–	+
Mesoridazine (Serentil)	–	+
Perphenazine (Trilafon)	–	+
Trifluoperazine (Stelazine)	–	+
Reserpine (Serpasil)	+	+
Haloperidol (Haldol)	–	+
Minor tranquilizers§		
Chlordiazepoxide (Librium)	–	+
Antihypertensive Drugs		
Clonidine (Catapres)	+	
Methyldopa (Aldomet)	+	+
Spironolactone (Aldactone)	+	–
Hydrochlorothiazide (Apresoline)	+	–
Guanethidine (Ismelin)	+	+
Commonly Abused Drugs		
Alcohol	+	+
Barbiturates	+	+
Cannabis	+	–
Cocaine	+	+
Heroin	+	+
Methadone	+	–
Morphine	+	+
Miscellaneous Drugs		
Antiparkinsonian agents	+	+
Clofibrate (Atromid-S)	+	–
Digoxin	+	–
Glutethimide (Doriden)	+	+
Indomethacin (Indocin)	+	–
Phentolamine (Regitine)	–	+
Propranolol (Inderal)	+	–

Table by Virginia Sadock, M.D.

*The incidence of erectile dysfunction associated with the use of tricyclic antidepressants is low.

†Trazodone has been causative in some cases of priapism.

‡Impairment of sexual function is not a common complication of the use of major tranquilizers. Priapism has occasionally occurred in association with the use of major tranquilizers.

§Benzodiazepines have been reported to decrease libido, but in some patients the diminution of anxiety caused by those drugs enhances sexual function.

with women whom they see as degraded. Other factors that have been cited as contributing to impotence include a punitive superego, an inability to trust, and feelings of inadequacy or a sense of being undesirable as a partner. There may be an inability to express the sexual impulse because of fear, anxiety, anger, or moral prohibition. In an ongoing relationship, impotence may reflect difficulties between the partners, particularly if the man cannot communicate his needs or his anger in a direct and constructive way. In addition, episodes of impotence are reinforcing, with the man becoming increasingly anxious before each sexual encounter.

A good history is of primary importance in determining the cause of the dysfunction. If a man reports having spontaneous erections at times when he does not plan to have intercourse, having morning erections, or having good erections with masturbation or with partners other than his usual one, the organic causes of his impotence can be considered negligible, and costly diagnostic procedures can be avoided.

A number of procedures, benign and invasive, are used to help differentiate organically caused impotence from functional impotence. These procedures include monitoring nocturnal penile tumescence (erections that occur during sleep), normally associated with rapid eye movement; monitoring tumescence with a strain gauge; measuring blood pressure in the penis with a penile plethysmograph or an ultrasound (Doppler) flow meter, both of which assess blood flow in the internal pudendal artery; and measuring pudendal nerve latency time. Other diagnostic tests that delineate organic bases for impotence include glucose tolerance tests, plasma hormone assays, liver and thyroid function tests, prolactin and follicle stimulating hormone (FSH) determinations, and cystometric examinations. Invasive diagnostic studies include penile arteriography, infusion cavernosography, and radioactive xenon penography. Invasive procedures require expert interpretation and are used only for patients who are candidates for vascular reconstructive procedures.

ORGASM DISORDERS

Inhibited Female Orgasm (Anorgasmia)

Inhibited female orgasm is defined as the recurrent and persistent inhibition of the female orgasm, as manifested by the absence of orgasm after a normal sexual excitement phase that the clinician judges to be adequate in focus, intensity, and duration. It is the inability of the woman to achieve orgasm by masturbation or coitus. Women who can achieve orgasm with one of these methods are not necessarily categorized as anorgasmic, although some degree of sexual inhibition may be postulated (Table 20.3-9).

Research on the physiology of the female sexual response has demonstrated that orgasms caused by clitoral stimulation and those caused by vaginal stimulation are physiologically identical. Freud's theory that women must give up clitoral sensitivity for vaginal sensitivity in order to achieve sexual

Table 20.3-9
Diagnostic Criteria for Inhibited Female Orgasm

A. Persistent or recurrent delay in, or absence of, orgasm in a female following a normal sexual excitement phase during sexual activity that the clinician judges to be adequate in focus, intensity, and duration. Some females are able to experience orgasm during noncoital clitoral stimulation, but are unable to experience it during coitus in the absence of manual clitoral stimulation. In most of the these females, this represents a normal variation of the female sexual response and does not justify the diagnosis of inhibited female orgasm. However, in some of these females, this does represent a psychological inhibition that justifies the diagnosis. This difficult judgment is assisted by a thorough sexual evaluation, which may even require a trial of treatment.

B. Occurrence not exclusively during the course of another Axis I disorder (other than a sexual dysfunction), such as major depression.

Table from DSM-III-R, *Diagnostic and Statistical Manual of Mental Disorders,* ed 3, revised. Copyright American Psychiatric Association, Washington, DC, 1987, with permission.

Table 20.3-10
Psychiatric Drugs Implicated in Inhibited Female Orgasm*

Antidepressants
- Amoxapine (Asendin)†
- Fluoxetine (Prozac)

Cyclic antidepressants
- Imipramine (Tofranil)
- Clomipramine (Anafranil)‡
- Nortriptyline (Aventyl)§

Monomamine oxidase inhibitors (MAOIs)**
- Tranylcypromine (Parnate)
- Phenelzine (Nardil)
- Isocarboxazid (Marplan)

Major tranquilizers
- Thioridazine (Mellaril)
- Trifluoperazine (Stelazine)

Table by Virginia Sadock, M.D.

*The interrelationship between female sexual dysfunction and pharmacological agents has been less extensively evaluated than have male reactions. Oral contraceptives are reported to decrease libido in some women, and some drugs with anticholinergic side effects may impair arousal and orgasm. Benzodiazepines have been reported to decrease libido, but in some patients the diminution of anxiety caused by those drugs enhances sexual function.

Both increase and decrease in libido have been reported with psychoactive agents. It is difficult to separate those effects from the underlying condition or from improvement of the condition. Sexual dysfunction associated with the use of a drug disappears when the drug is discontinued.

†Bethanechol (Urecholine) can reverse the effects of amoxapine-induced anorgasmia.

‡Clomipramine is also reported to increase arousal and orgasmic potential.

§Cyproheptadine (Periactin) reverses fluoxetine- and nortriptyline-induced anorgasmia.

**MAO-induced anorgasmia may be a temporary reaction to the medication that disappears even though administration of the drug is continued.

maturity is now considered misleading; however, some women say that they gain a special sense of satisfaction from an orgasm precipitated by coitus. Some workers attribute that to the psychological feeling of closeness engendered by the act of coitus, but others maintain that the coital orgasm is a physiologically different experience. Many women achieve orgasm during coitus by a combination of manual clitoral stimulation and penile vaginal stimulation.

Primary nonorgasmic dysfunction exists when the woman has never experienced orgasm by any kind of stimulation. Secondary orgasmic dysfunction exists if the woman has previously experienced at least one orgasm, regardless of the circumstances or means of stimulation, whether by masturbation or during sleep while dreaming. Kinsey found that the proportion of married women over 35 years of age who had never achieved orgasm by any means was only 5 percent. The incidence of orgasm increases with age. According to Kinsey, the first orgasm occurs during adolescence in about 50 percent of women; the rest usually experience orgasm as they get older. Primary anorgasmia is more common among unmarried women than among married women. Increased orgasmic potential in women over 35 has been explained on the basis of less psychological inhibition or greater sexual experience or both.

Secondary orgasmic dysfunction is a common complaint in clinical populations. One clinical treatment facility reported having about four times as may nonorgasmic women in its practice as patients with all other sexual disorders. In another study 46 percent of the women complained of difficulty in reaching orgasm, and 15 percent described inability to have orgasm. The true prevalence of problems in maintaining excitement is not known, but inhibition of excitement and orgasmic problems often occur together. Overall prevalence of inhibited female orgasm from all causes is given as 30 percent in DSM-III-R.

Some medical conditions—specifically, endocrine diseases such as hypothyroidism, diabetes mellitus, and primary hyperprolactinemia—can affect a woman's ability to have orgasms. Also, a number of drugs affect some women's capacity to have orgasms (Table 20.3-10). Antihypertensive medications, CNS stimulants, tricyclic antidepressants, fluoxetine (Prozac), and, frequently, monoamine oxidase (MAO) inhibitors have interfered with female orgasmic capacity. However, one study of women taking MAO inhibitors found that, after 16 to 18 weeks of pharmacotherapy, this side effect of the medication disappeared, and the women were able to reexperience orgasms, although they continued on an undiminished dosage of the drug.

Numerous psychological factors are associated with inhibited female orgasm. They include fears of impregnation, rejection by the sex partner, or damage to the vagina; hostility toward men; and feelings of guilt regarding sexual impulses. For some women, orgasm is equated with loss of control or with aggressive, destructive, or violent behavior; their fear of these impulses may be expressed through inhibition of excitement or orgasm. Cultural expectations and societal restrictions on women are also relevant. Nonorgasmic women may be otherwise symptom-free or may experience frustration in a variety of ways, including such pelvic complaints as lower abdominal pain, itching, and vaginal discharge, as well as increased tension, irritability, and fatigue.

Inhibited Male Orgasm

In inhibited male orgasm, also called retarded ejaculation, the man achieves ejaculation during coitus with great difficulty, if at all. A man suffers from primary retarded ejaculation if he has never been able to ejaculate during coitus. The disorder is diagnosed as secondary if it develops after previous normal functioning (Table 20.3-11).

Some workers suggest that a differentiation should be made between orgasm and ejaculation. Certainly, inhibited orgasm

Table 20.3-11
Diagnostic Criteria for Inhibited Male Orgasm

A. Persistent or recurrent delay in, or absence of, orgasm in a male following a normal sexual excitement phase during sexual activity that the clinician, taking into account the person's age, judges to be adequate in focus, intensity, and duration. This failure to achieve orgasm is usually restricted to an inability to reach orgasm in the vagina, with orgasm possible with other types of stimulation, such as masturbation.

B. Occurrence not exclusively during the course of another Axis I disorder (other than a sexual dysfunction), such as major depression.

Table from DSM-III-R, *Diagnostic and Statistical Manual of Mental Disorders*, ed 3, revised. Copyright American Psychiatric Association, Washington, DC, 1987, with permission.

must be differentiated from retrograde ejaculation, in which ejaculation occurs but the seminal fluid passes backward into the bladder. The latter condition always has an organic cause. Retrograde ejaculation can develop after genitourinary surgery and is also associated with medications that have anticholinergic side effects, such as the phenothiazines. Some men ejaculate but complain of a decreased or absent subjective sense of pleasure during the orgasmic experience (orgasmic anhedonia).

The incidence of inhibited male orgasm is much lower than that of premature ejaculation or impotence. Masters and Johnson reported only 3.8 percent in one group of 447 sexual dysfunction cases. A general prevalence of 5 percent has been reported.

Inhibited male orgasm may have physiological causes and can occur after surgery of the genitourinary tract, such as prostatectomy. It may also be associated with Parkinson's disease and other neurological disorders involving the lumbar or sacral sections of the spinal cord. The antihypertensive drug guanethidine monosulfate (Ismelin), methyldopa (Aldomet), the phenothiazines, the tricyclic antidepressants, and fluoxetine, among others (Table 20.3-8), have been implicated in retarded ejaculation.

Primary inhibited male orgasm is indicative of more severe psychopathology. The man often comes from a rigid, puritanical background; he may perceive sex as sinful and the genitals as dirty; and he may have conscious or unconscious incest wishes and guilt. There are usually difficulties with closeness that extend beyond the area of sexual relations.

In an ongoing relationship, secondary ejaculatory inhibition frequently reflects interpersonal difficulties. The disorder may be the man's way of coping with real or fantasized changes in the relationship. These changes may include plans for pregnancy about which the man is ambivalent, the loss of sexual attraction to the partner, or demands by the partner for greater commitment as expressed by sexual performance. In some men the inability to ejaculate reflects unexpressed hostility toward the woman. This problem is more common among men with obsessive-compulsive disorders than among others.

Premature Ejaculation

In premature ejaculation the man recurrently achieves orgasm and ejaculation before he wishes to. There is no definite time frame within which to define the dysfunction. The diagnosis is made when the man regularly ejaculates before or immediately after entering the vagina. The clinician needs to consider factors that affect duration of the excitement phase, such as age, novelty of the sex partner, and frequency and duration of coitus (Table 20.3-12). Masters and Johnson conceptualize the disorder in terms of the couple and consider a man a premature ejaculator if he cannot control ejaculation for a sufficient length of time during intravaginal containment to satisfy his partner in at least one-half of their episodes of coitus. This definition assumes that the female partner is capable of an orgasmic response. Like the other dysfunctions, this disturbance is not caused exclusively by organic factors and is not symptomatic of any other clinical psychiatric syndrome.

There is an absence of data on female premature orgasm; no separate category of premature orgasm for women is included in DSM-III-R. The authors have seen a case of multiple spontaneous orgasms occurring in a woman without sexual stimulation that was caused by an epileptogenic focus in the temporal lobe.

Premature ejaculation is more common today among college-educated men than among men with less education and is thought to be related to their concern for partner satisfaction; however, the true incidence of this disorder has not been determined. About 35 to 40 percent of men treated for sexual disorders have premature ejaculation as the chief complaint. Difficulty in ejaculatory control may be associated with anxiety regarding the sex act or with unconscious fears about the vagina. It may also result from negative cultural conditioning. The man who has most of his early sexual contacts with prostitutes who demand that the sex act proceed quickly or in situations in which discovery would be embarrassing (such as in the back seat of a car or in the parental home) may become conditioned to achieve orgasm rapidly. In ongoing relationships the partner has been found to have great influence on the premature ejaculator. A stressful marriage exacerbates the disorder. The developmental background and psychodynamics found in this disorder and in impotence are similar.

SEXUAL PAIN DISORDERS

Dyspareunia

Dyspareunia is recurrent and persistent pain occurring before, during, or after intercourse in either the man or the woman. Much more common in women, it is related to and often coincides with vaginismus. Repeated episodes of vaginismus may lead to dyspareunia and vice versa, but in either case, somatic causes must be ruled out. Dyspareunia should not be diagnosed when an organic basis for the pain is found or when, in a woman, it is caused exclusively by vaginismus or by a lack of lubrication (Table 20.3-13). The true incidence of dyspareunia is unknown, but it has been estimated that 30 percent of surgical procedures

Table 20.3-12
Diagnostic Criteria for Premature Ejaculation

Persistent or recurrent ejaculation with minimal sexual stimulation or before, upon, or shortly after penetration and before the person wishes it. The clinician must take into account factors that affect duration of the excitement phase, such as age, novelty of the sexual partner or situation, and frequency of sexual activity.

Table from DSM-III-R, *Diagnostic and Statistical Manual of Mental Disorders*, ed 3, revised. Copyright American Psychiatric Association, Washington, DC, 1987, with permission.

Table 20.3-13
Diagnostic Criteria for Dyspareunia

A. Recurrent or persistent genital pain in either a male or a female before, during, or after sexual intercourse.

B. The disturbance is not caused exclusively by lack of lubrication or by vaginismus.

Table 20.3-14
Diagnostic Criteria for Vaginismus

A. Recurrent or persistent involuntary spasm of the musculature of the outer third of the vagina that interferes with coitus.

B. The disturbance is not caused exclusively by a physical disorder, and is not due to another Axis I disorder

on the female genital area result in temporary dyspareunia. In addition, of women with this complaint who are seen in sex therapy clinics, 30 to 40 percent have pelvic pathology. Chronic pelvic pain is a common complaint in women with a history of rape or childhood sexual abuse.

Organic abnormalities leading to dyspareunia and vaginismus include irritated or infected hymenal remnants, episiotomy scars, Bartholin's gland infection, various forms of vaginitis and cervicitis, and endometriosis. Postcoital pain has been reported by women with myomata and endometriosis and is attributed to the uterine contractions during orgasm. The postmenopausal woman may have dyspareunia resulting from thinning of the vaginal mucosa and reduced lubrication. In the majority of cases, however, dynamic factors are considered causative. Painful coitus may result from tension and anxiety about the sex act that cause the woman to involuntarily contract her vaginal muscles. The pain is real and makes intercourse unpleasant or unbearable. The anticipation of further pain may cause the woman to avoid coitus altogether. If the partner proceeds with intercourse regardless of the woman's state of readiness, the condition is aggravated. Dyspareunia can also occur in men, but it is uncommon and is usually associated with an organic condition, such as Peyronie's disease, which consists of sclerotic plaques on the penis that cause penile curvature.

Vaginismus

Vaginismus is an involuntary muscle constriction of the outer one-third of the vagina that prevents penile insertion and intercourse. This response may occur during a gynecological examination when involuntary vaginal constriction prevents the introduction of the speculum into the vagina. The diagnosis is not made if the dysfunction is caused exclusively by organic factors or if it is symptomatic of another Axis I psychiatric syndrome (Table 20.3-14). Vaginismus is less prevalent than anorgasmia. It most often afflicts highly educated women and those in the high socioeconomic groups. The woman suffering from vaginismus may consciously wish to have coitus but unconsciously prevent the penis from entering her body. A sexual trauma such as rape may result in vaginismus. Women with psychosexual conflicts may perceive the penis as a weapon. In some women pain or the anticipation of pain at the first coital experience causes vaginismus. A strict religious upbringing that associates sex with sin is frequently noted in these cases. For others there are problems in the dyadic relationship; if the woman feels emotionally abused by her partner, she may protest in this nonverbal fashion.

SEXUAL DYSFUNCTIONS NOT OTHERWISE SPECIFIED

This category is for psychosexual dysfunctions that cannot be classified under the categories described above. Examples include persons who experience the physiological components of sexual excitement and orgasm but report no erotic sensation or even anesthesia (orgasmic anhedonia). Women with conditions analogous to premature ejaculation in the man are classified here. The orgasmic woman who desires but has not experienced multiple orgasms can be classified under this heading as well. Also, disorders of excessive rather than inhibited dysfunction, such as compulsive masturbation, may be diagnosed here, as is genital pain occurring during masturbation. Other unspecified disorders are found in persons who have one or more sexual fantasies about which they feel guilty or otherwise dysphoric. However, the range of common sexual fantasies is broad.

Postcoital Headache

This phenomenon is characterized by headache immediately after coitus and may last for several hours. It is usually described as throbbing in nature and is localized in the occipital or frontal area. The cause is unknown. There may be vascular, muscle contraction (tension), or psychogenic causes. Coitus may precipitate migraine or cluster headaches in predisposed persons.

Orgasmic Anhedonia

Orgasmic anhedonia is a condition in which there is no physical sensation of orgasm, even though the physiological component (i.e., ejaculation) remains intact. Organic causes such as sacral and cephalic lesions that interfere with afferent pathways from the genitalia to the cortex must be ruled out. Psychic causes usually relate to extreme guilt about experiencing sexual pleasure. These feelings produce a type of dissociative response that isolates the affective component of the orgasmic experience from consciousness.

Masturbatory Pain

In some cases persons may experience pain during masturbation. Organic causes should always be ruled out. A small vaginal tear or early Peyronie's disease may produce a painful sensation. This condition should be differentiated from compulsive masturbation. People may masturbate to the extent that they do physical damage to their genitals and eventually experience pain during subsequent masturbatory acts. Such cases constitute a separate sexual disorder and should be so classified.

Certain masturbatory practices have resulted in what has been called *autoerotic asphyxiation.* These practices may involve masturbating while hanging oneself by the neck to heighten erotic sensations and the intensity of orgasm through the mechanism of mild hypoxia. Although the persons intend to release themselves from the noose after orgasm, an estimated 500 to 1,000 persons a year accidentally kill themselves by hanging. Most who indulge in this practice are male; transvestism is often associated with the habit, and the majority of deaths occur among adolescents. Such masochistic practices are usually associated with severe mental disorders, such as schizophrenia and major mood disorders.

OTHER SEXUAL DISORDERS

Many sexual disorders are not classifiable in any of the previous categories of sexual disorders (e.g., paraphilia and sexual dysfunction). They are either rare, poorly documented, not easily classified, or not specifically described in DSM-III-R (Table 20.3-15).

Postcoital Dysphoria

Postcoital dysphoria is not currently listed in DSM-III-R. It occurs during the resolution phase, when the person normally experiences a sense of general well-being and muscular and psychological relaxation. Some persons, however, experience a postcoital dysphoria. After an otherwise satisfactory sexual experience, they become depressed, tense, anxious, and irritable and show psychomotor agitation. They often want to get away from the partner and may become verbally or even physically abusive. The incidence of the disorder is unknown, but it is more common in men than in women. The causes are several and relate to the attitude of the person toward sex in general and toward the partner in particular. It may occur in adulterous sex and with prostitutes. Recently, the fear of acquired immune deficiency syndrome (AIDS) has caused some persons to experience this phenomenon postcoitally. Treatment requires insight-oriented psychotherapy to help patients understand the unconscious antecedents to their behavior and attitudes.

Table 20.3-15
Diagnostic Criteria for Sexual Disorder Not Otherwise Specified

Sexual disorders that are not classifiable in any of the previous categories. In rare instances, this category may be used concurrently with one of the specific diagnoses when both are necessary to explain or describe the clinical disturbance.

Examples:

(1) marked feelings of inadequacy concerning body habitus, size and shape of sex organs, sexual performance, or other traits related to self-imposed standards of masculinity or femininity

(2) distress about a pattern of repeated sexual conquests or other forms of nonparaphilic sexual addition, involving a succession of people who exist only as things to be used

(3) persistent and marked distress about one's sexual orientation

Table from DSM-III-R, *Diagnostic and Statistical Manual of Mental Disorders,* ed 3, revised. Copyright American Psychiatric Association, Washington, DC, 1987, with permission.

Couple Problems

At times, a complaint must be viewed in terms of the spousal unit or the couple, rather than as an individual dysfunction. An example is a couple in which one prefers morning sex while the other functions more readily at night; another example is a couple with unequal frequencies of desire.

Unconsummated Marriage

The couple involved in an unconsummated marriage have never had coitus and are typically uninformed and inhibited about sexuality. Their feelings of guilt, shame, or inadequacy are increased by their problem, and they experience conflict between their need to seek help and their need to conceal their difficulty. Couples present with the problem after having been married several months or several years. Masters and Johnson reported an unconsummated marriage of 17 years' duration.

Frequently, the couple do not seek help directly, but the woman may reveal the problem to her gynecologist on a visit ostensibly concerned with vague vaginal or somatic complaints. On examining her, the gynecologist may find an intact hymen. In some cases though, the wife may have undergone a hymenectomy to resolve the problem. This surgical procedure is another stress and often increases the feelings of inadequacy in the couple. The wife may feel put on, abused, or mutilated, and the husband's concern about his manliness may increase. The hymenectomy usually aggravates the situation without solving the basic problem. The inquiry of a physician who is comfortable in dealing with sexual problems may be the first opening to frank discussion of the couple's distress. Often, the pretext of the medical visit is a discussion of contraceptive methods or—even more ironically—a request for an infertility workup. Once presented, the complaint can often be successfully treated. The duration of the problem does not significantly affect the prognosis or the outcome of the case.

The causes are varied: lack of sex education, sexual prohibitions overly stressed by parents or society, neurotic problems of an oedipal nature, immaturity in both partners, overdependence on primary families, and problems in sexual identification. Religious orthodoxy, with severe control of sexual and social development or the equation of sexuality with sin or uncleanliness, has also been cited as a dominant cause. Many women involved in an unconsummated marriage have distorted concepts about their vaginas. There can be a fear of being too small or too soft or a confusion of the vagina with the rectum, leading to feelings of being unclean. The man may share in these distortions of the vagina and, in addition, perceive it as dangerous to himself. Similarly, both partners may have distortions about the man's penis, perceiving it as a weapon, as too large, or as too small. Many patients can be helped by simple education about genital anatomy and physiology, by suggestions for self-exploration, and by correct information from a physician. The problem of the unconsummated marriage is best treated by seeing both members of the couple. Dual-sex therapy (discussed below) involving a male-female cotherapist team has been markedly effective. However, other forms of conjoint therapy, marital counseling, traditional psychotherapy on a one-to-one basis, and counseling from a sensitive family physician, gynecologist, or urologist are all helpful.

Body Image Problems

Persons who are ashamed of their bodies and who experience feelings of inadequacy related to self-imposed standards of masculinity or femininity may have this sexual disorder. They may insist on sex only during total darkness, not allow certain body parts to be seen or touched, or seek unnecessary operative procedures to deal with their imagined inadequacies. Body dysmorphic disorder should be ruled out.

Don Juanism

Some men who appear to be hypersexual, as manifested by their need to have many sexual encounters or conquests, use their sexual activities to mask deep feelings of inferiority. Some have unconscious homosexual impulses, which they deny by compulsive sexual contacts with women. After having sex, most Don Juans are no longer interested in the woman. The condition is sometimes referred to as satyriasis.

Nymphomania

Nymphomania is a descriptive term that signifies excessive or pathological desire for coitus in a woman. There have been few scientific studies of the condition. Those patients who have been studied usually have had one or more sexual disorders, usually including anorgasmia. There is often an intense fear of loss of love. The woman attempts to satisfy her dependency needs, rather than to gratify sexual impulses through her actions.

Sexual Orientation Distress

Persistent and marked distress about one's sexual orientation is listed as an example of a sexual disorder in DSM-III-R. Previously known in the third edition of DSM (DSM-III) as ego-dystonic homosexuality, it was defined as a desire to acquire or increase heterosexual arousal so that a heterosexual relationship could be initiated. The person with the disorder explicitly states that homosexual arousal and behavior are unwanted and a source of distress, hence the term "ego-dystonic." The category was eliminated in the revised third edition for several reasons. As stated in DSM-III-R:

> It suggested to some that homosexuality was itself considered a disorder. In the United States, almost all individuals who are homosexual first go through a phase in which their homosexuality is ego-dystonic. Furthermore, the diagnosis of ego-dystonic homosexuality has rarely been used clinically, and there have been only a few articles in the scientific literature that use the concept. Finally, the treatment programs that attempt to help bisexual men become heterosexual have not used this diagnosis. In DSM-III-R, an example of sexual disorder not otherwise specified are cases that in DSM-III would have met the criteria for ego-dystonic homosexuality.

Homosexuality was eliminated as a mental diagnosis by the American Psychiatric Association's Board of Directors in 1973. It has been maintained as a diagnosis by the World Health Organization's ninth revision of the *International Classification of Diseases* (ICD-9), published in 1980.

According to DSM-III-R, persons with an exclusive or predominant preference for same-sex partners constitute a substantial minority of the adult and adolescent population. Kinsey reported that 4 percent of adult men were exclusively homosexual throughout their lives and that another 13 percent were predominantly homosexual for at least three years between the ages of 16 and 55. More than one in three men had experienced a sexual interaction leading to orgasm with another male during the postpubertal years. For women, the reported rates were approximately half those for men. Data indicate that approximately 2 to 4 percent of adult women are exclusively or preferentially homosexual.

Overview of homosexuality

Psychological causes. The causes of homosexual behavior are enigmatic. Freud viewed homosexuality as an arrest of psychosexual development. Castration fears for the male and fears of maternal engulfment in the preoedipal phase of psychosexual development are mentioned. According to psychodynamic theory, early-life situations that can result in male homosexual behavior include a strong fixation on the mother, lack of effective fathering, inhibition of masculine development by the parents, fixation or regression at the narcissistic stage of development, and losing competition with brothers and sisters. Freud's views on the causes of female homosexuality included a lack of resolution of penis envy in association with unresolved oedipal conflicts.

Homosexual females, as compared with heterosexual females, have been reported to have fathers who were close and intimate, the converse of that found for male homosexuals. However, the descriptions given of the mothers of female homosexuals were not different from the descriptions given of the mothers of the heterosexuals.

Biological causes. There is evidence from recent studies that genetic and biological components may contribute to homosexual orientation. There are reports that homosexual men exhibit lower levels of circulatory androgen than do heterosexual men. There have also been reports of atypical estrogen feedback patterns among homosexual males. Such males show abnormal rebound increases in luteinizing hormone (LH) levels after estrogen injections. But neither of these results has been replicated in similar studies. Prenatal hormones appear to play a role in the organization of the central nervous system. The effective presence of androgens in prenatal life is purported to contribute to a sexual orientation toward females, and a deficiency of prenatal androgens (or a tissue insensitivity to them) may lead to a sexual orientation toward males. Preadolescent girls exposed to large amounts of androgens before birth are unusually aggressive and unfeminine, and boys exposed to excessive female hormones in utero are less athletic, less assertive, and less aggressive than other boys. Women with hyperadrenocorticalism become bisexual or homosexual in greater proportion than expected in the general population.

Genetic studies demonstrate a higher incidence of homosexual concordance among monozygotic twins than among dizygotic twins, which suggests a hidden genetic predisposition; but chromosome studies have been unable to differentiate homosexuals from heterosexuals. Male homosexuals also show a familial distribution; homosexual men have more brothers who are homosexual than do heterosexual men.

Sexual behavior patterns. The behavioral features of male and female homosexuals are as varied as those of male and female heterosexuals. Sexual practices engaged in by homosexuals are the same as for heterosexuals, with the obvious limitations imposed by anatomical differences.

A variety of ongoing relationship patterns exist among homosexuals, as they do among heterosexuals. Some homosexual dyads live in a common household in either a monogamous or a primary relationship for decades, and other homosexual persons typically have only fleeting sexual contacts. Although more stable male-male relationships exist than were previously thought, it appears that male-male relationships are less stable and more fleeting than female-female relationships. Many fleeting male relationships are initiated in gay baths and bars, with a smaller number initiated in public restrooms and parks. Comparable female institutions are practically nonexistent. The amount of male homosexual promiscuity is anecdotally reported to have diminished since the onset of AIDS and its rapid spread in the homosexual community through sexual contact. However, no research data demonstrate this reduction.

Homosexual male couples are subjected to civil and social discrimination and do not have the legal social support system of marriage or the biological capacity for childbearing that bonds some otherwise incompatible heterosexual couples together. Female-female couples experience less social stigmatization and appear to have more enduring monogamous or primary relationships.

Psychopathology. The range of psychopathology that may be found among distressed homosexuals parallels that found among heterosexuals. Distress about one's sexual orientation is characterized by a dissatisfaction with homosexual arousal patterns, a desire to increase heterosexual arousal, and strong negative feelings about being homosexual.

Occasionally statements to the effect that life would be easier if the person were not homosexual do not constitute the syndrome of sexual orientation distress. Also, distress resulting only from conflict between the homosexual and the societal value structure is not classifiable as a disorder. If the distress is sufficiently severe to warrant a diagnosis, an adjustment disorder or a depressive disorder is to be considered. Some homosexuals suffering from major depression may experience guilt and self-hatred that becomes directed toward their sexual orientation; then the desire for sexual reorientation is only a symptom of the depressive disorder.

Course and treatment. Some homosexuals, particularly males, report being aware of same-sex romantic attractions before puberty. According to Kinsey's data, about half of all prepubertal males have some genital experience with a same-sex partner. However, this experience is often of an exploratory nature, particularly if shared with a peer, not an adult, and typically lacks a strong affective component. Most male homosexuals recall the onset of romantic and erotic attractions to same-sex partners during early adolescence. For females the onset of romantic feelings toward same-sex partners may also be in preadolescence. However, the clear recognition of a same-sex partner preference typically occurs in middle to late adolescence or not until young adulthood. More homosexual women than homosexual men appear to have heterosexual experiences during their primary homosexual careers. In one study 56 percent of a lesbian sample had heterosexual intercourse before their first genital homosexual experience, compared with 19 percent of a male homosexual sample who had heterosexual intercourse first. Nearly 40 percent of the lesbians had had heterosexual intercourse during the year preceding the survey.

Treatment of sexual orientation distress is controversial. It has been reported that, with a minimum of 350 hours of psychoanalytic therapy, approximately one-third of about 100 bisexual and homosexual males achieved a heterosexual reorientation at a five-year follow-up; but this study has been challenged. Behavior therapy and avoidance conditioning techniques have also been used, but a basic problem with behavioral techniques is that the behavior may be changed in the laboratory setting but not outside the laboratory. Prognostic factors weighing in favor of heterosexual reorientation for men include being under 35 years of age, some experience of heterosexual arousal, and high motivation for reorientation.

An alternative style of intervention is directed at enabling the person with sexual orientation distress to live more comfortably as a homosexual without shame, guilt, anxiety, or depression. Gay counseling centers are engaged with patients in such treatment programs. At present, outcome studies of such centers have not been reported in detail. As for the treatment of women with sexual orientation distress, there are few data, and those are primarily single-case studies with variable outcomes.

TREATMENT

Before 1970 the most common treatment of psychosexual dysfunction was individual psychotherapy. Classic psychodynamic theory holds that sexual inadequacy has its roots in early developmental conflicts, and the sexual disorder is treated as part of a more pervasive emotional disturbance. Treatment focuses on the exploration of unconscious conflicts, motivation, fantasy, and various interpersonal difficulties. One of the assumptions of therapy is that the removal of the conflicts will allow the sexual impulse to become structurally acceptable to the patient's ego and thereby find appropriate means of satisfaction in the environment. Unfortunately, the symptoms of sexual dysfunction frequently become secondarily autonomous and continue to persist, even when other problems evolving from the patient's pathology have been resolved. The addition of behavioral techniques is often necessary to cure the sexual problem.

Dual-Sex Therapy

The theoretical basis of the dual-sex therapy approach is the concept of the marital unit or dyad as the object of therapy; this approach represents the major advance in the diagnosis and treatment of sexual disorders in this century. The methodology was originated and developed by William Masters and Virginia Johnson. In dual-sex therapy, there is no acceptance of the idea of a sick half of a patient couple. Both are involved in a relationship in which there is sexual distress, and both must, therefore, participate in the therapy program.

The sexual problem often reflects other areas of disharmony or misunderstanding in the marriage. The marital relationship as a whole is treated, with emphasis on sexual functioning as a part of that relationship. Psychological and physiological aspects of sexual functioning are discussed, and an educative attitude is used. Suggestions are made for specific sexual activities, and those suggestions are followed in the privacy of the couple's home. The keystone of the program is the roundtable session in which a male and female therapy team clarifies, discusses, and works through the problems with the couple. These four-way sessions require active participation on the part of the patients. The aim of the therapy is to establish or reestablish communication within the marital unit. Sex is emphasized as a natural function that flourishes in the appropriate domestic climate, and improved communication is encouraged toward that end.

Treatment is short-term and is behaviorally oriented. The therapists attempt to reflect the situation as they see it, rather than interpret underlying dynamics. An undistorted picture of the relationship presented by the psychiatrist often corrects the myopic, narrow view held by each marriage partner. The new perspective can interrupt the couple's vicious circle of relating, and improved, more effective communication can be encouraged.

Specific exercises are prescribed for the couple to help them with their particular problem. Sexual inadequacy often involves lack of information, misinformation, and performance fear. Therefore, the couples are specifically prohibited from any sexual play other than that prescribed by the therapists. Beginning exercises usually focus on heightening sensory awareness to touch, sight, sound, and smell. Initially, intercourse is interdicted, and couples learn to give and receive bodily pleasure without the pressure of performance. At the same time, they learn how to communicate nonverbally in a mutually satisfactory way and learn that sexual foreplay is as important as intercourse and orgasm.

During these *sensate focus* exercises, the couple receive much reinforcement to reduce their anxiety. They are urged to use fantasies to distract them from obsessive concerns about performance (spectatoring). The needs of both the dysfunctional partner and the nondysfunctional partner are considered. If either partner becomes sexually excited by the exercises, the other is encouraged to bring him or her to orgasm by manual or oral means. Open communication between the partners is urged, and the expression of mutual needs is encouraged. Resistances, such as claims of fatigue or not enough time to complete the exercises, are common and must be dealt with by the therapist. Genital stimulation is eventually added to general body stimulation. The couple are instructed sequentially to try various positions for intercourse, without necessarily completing the act, and to use varieties of stimulating techniques before they are instructed to proceed with intercourse.

Roundtable sessions follow each new exercise period, and problems and satisfactions, both sexual and in other areas of the couple's lives, are discussed. Specific instructions and the introduction of new exercises geared to the individual couple's progress are reviewed in each session. Gradually, the couple gain confidence and learn to communicate, verbally and sexually. Dual-sex therapy is most effective when the sexual dysfunction exists apart from other psychopathology.

Specific techniques and exercises. Different techniques are used to treat the various dysfunctions. In cases of vaginismus, the woman is advised to dilate her vaginal opening with her fingers or with dilators.

In cases of premature ejaculation, an exercise known as the *squeeze technique* is used to raise the threshold of penile excitability. In that exercise the man or the woman stimulates the erect penis until the earliest sensations of impending ejaculation are felt. At that point, the woman forcefully squeezes the coronal ridge of the glans, the erection is diminished, and ejaculation is inhibited. The exercise program eventually raises the threshold of the sensation of ejaculatory inevitability and allows the man to become more aware of his sexual sensations and confident about his sexual performance. A variant of the exercise is the stop-start technique developed by J. H. Semans, in which the woman stops all stimulation of the penis when the man first senses an impending ejaculation. No squeeze is used. Research has shown that the presence or absence of circumcision has no bearing on a man's ejaculatory control; the glans is equally sensitive in the two states. Sex therapy has been most successful in the treatment of premature ejaculation.

A man with inhibited desire or inhibited excitement is sometimes told to masturbate to demonstrate that full erection and ejaculation are possible. In cases of primary anorgasmia, the woman is directed to masturbate, sometimes using a vibrator. The shaft of the clitoris is the masturbatory site most preferred by women, and orgasm depends on adequate clitoral stimulation. An area on the anterior wall of the vagina has been identified in some women as a site of sexual excitation known as the G-spot; however, reports of an ejaculatory phenomenon at orgasm in women have not been satisfactorily verified. Men masturbate by stroking the shaft and glans of the penis.

Retarded ejaculation is managed by extravaginal ejaculation initially and gradual vaginal entry after stimulation to the point of near ejaculation.

Hypnotherapy

Hypnotherapists focus specifically on the anxiety-producing symptom—that is, the particular sexual dysfunction. The successful use of hypnosis enables the patient to gain control over the symptom that has been lowering self-esteem and disrupting psychological homeostasis. The cooperation of the patient is first obtained and encouraged during a series of nonhypnotic sessions with the therapist. These discussions permit the development of a secure doctor-patient relationship, a sense of physical and psychological comfort on the part of the patient, and the establishment of mutually desired treatment goals. During this time, the therapist assesses the patient's capacity for the trance experience. The nonhypnotic sessions also permit the clinician to take a careful psychiatric history and do a mental status examination before beginning hypnotherapy. The focus of treatment is on symptom removal and attitude alteration. The patient is instructed in developing alternative means of dealing with the anxiety-provoking situation, the sexual encounter.

Patients are also taught relaxation techniques to use on themselves before sexual relations. With those methods to alleviate anxiety, the physiological responses to sexual stimulation can more readily result in pleasurable excitation and discharge. Psychological impediments to vaginal lubrication, erection, and orgasm are removed, and normal sexual functioning ensues. Hypnosis may be added to a basic individual psychotherapy program to accelerate the impact of psychotherapeutic intervention.

Behavior Therapy

Behavior therapists assume that sexual dysfunction is learned maladaptive behavior. Behavioral approaches were initially designed for the treatment of phobias. In cases of sexual dysfunction, the therapist sees the patient as being fearful of sexual interaction. Using traditional techniques, the therapist sets up a hierarchy of anxiety-provoking situations for the patient, ranging from the least threatening to the most threatening situation. Mild anxiety may be experienced at the thought of kissing, and massive anxiety may be felt when imagining penile penetration. The behavior therapist enables the patient to master the anxiety through a standard program of systematic desensitization. The program is designed to inhibit the learned anxious response by encouraging behaviors antithetical to anxiety. The patient first deals with the least anxiety-producing situation in fantasy and progresses by steps to the most anxiety-producing situation. Medication, hypnosis, or special training in deep muscle relaxation is sometimes used to help with the initial mastery of anxiety.

Assertiveness training is helpful in teaching the patient to express sexual needs openly and without fear. Exercises in assertiveness are given in conjunction with sex therapy; the patient is encouraged to make sexual requests and to refuse to comply with requests perceived as unreasonable. Sexual exercises may be prescribed for the patient to perform at home, and a hierarchy may be established, starting with those activities that have proved most pleasurable and successful in the past.

One treatment variation involves the participation of the patient's sexual partner in the desensitization program. The partner, rather than the therapist, presents items of increasing stimulation value to the patient. In such situations a cooperative partner is necessary to help the patient carry gains made during treatment sessions to sexual activity at home.

Group Therapy

Methods of group therapy have been used to examine both intrapsychic and interpersonal problems in patients with sexual disorders. The therapy group provides a strong support system for a patient who feels ashamed, anxious, or guilty about a particular sexual problem. It is a useful forum in which to counteract sexual myths, correct misconceptions, and provide accurate information regarding sexual anatomy, physiology, and varieties of behavior.

Groups for the treatment of sexual disorders can be organized in several ways. Members may all share the same problem, such as premature ejaculation; members may all be of the same sex with different sexual problems; or groups may be composed of both men and women who are experiencing different sexual problems. Group therapy may be an adjunct to other forms of therapy or the prime mode of treatment. Groups organized to cure a particular dysfunction are usually behavioral in approach.

Groups composed of sexually dysfunctional married couples have also been effective. The group provides the opportunity to gather accurate information, provides consensual validation of individual preferences, and enhances self-esteem and self-acceptance. Techniques such as role playing and psychodrama may be used in treatment. Such groups are not indicated for couples when one partner is uncooperative, when a patient is suffering from a severe depression or psychosis, when there is a strong repugnance for explicit sexual audiovisual material, or when there is a strong fear of groups.

Analytically Oriented Sex Therapy

One of the most effective treatment modalities is the use of sex therapy integrated with psychodynamic and psychoanalytically oriented psychotherapy. The sex therapy is conducted over a longer than usual time period, and the extended schedule of treatment allows for the learning or relearning of sexual satisfaction under the realities of the patients' day-to-day lives. The addition of psychodynamic conceptualizations to the behavioral techniques used to treat sexual dysfunctions allows for the treatment of patients with sex disorders associated with other psychopathology.

The themes and dynamics that emerge in patients in analytically oriented sex therapy are the same as those seen in psychoanalytic therapy, such as relevant dreams, fear of punishment, aggressive feelings, difficulty with trusting the partner, fear of intimacy, oedipal feelings, and fear of genital mutilation.

The combined approach of analytically oriented sex therapy is used by the general psychiatrist, who carefully judges the optimal timing of sex therapy and the ability of patients to tolerate the directive approach that focuses on their sexual difficulties.

Biological Treatments

Biological forms of treatment have limited application, but more attention than in the past is being given to this approach. Intravenous methohexital sodium (Brevital) has been used in desensitization therapy. Antianxiety agents may have application in very tense patients, although these drugs can also interfere with sexual response. Sometimes the side effects of such drugs as thioridazine (Mellaril) and the tricyclic antidepressants are used to prolong the sexual response in such conditions as premature ejaculation. The use of tricyclics has also been advocated in the treatment of patients who are phobic about sex.

Pharmacological approaches also involve treating any underlying psychiatric disorder that may be contributing to the sexual dysfunction. For example, patients whose sexual functioning is impaired as a result of depression usually show improved performance as their depression responds to antidepressant medication.

Specific medications to deal with the dysfunctions are not generally successful. Testosterone, which affects libido, is beneficial to those patients who have a demonstrated low testosterone level. In women, however, testosterone leads to masculinization—such as deep voice, enlarged clitoris, and hirsutism—which may not be reversible on discontinuing the medication. Testosterone is contraindicated when fertility needs to be maintained. There are case reports that cyproheptadine (Periactin) can reverse drug-induced anorgasmia in women and in men taking fluoxetine. Clomipramine (Anafranil) has been reported to both induce spontaneous orgasms and inhibit orgasms in women. There are no known aphrodisiacs. Although recent studies report improvement in erectile responses in men ingesting yohimbine (Yocon), these findings remain controversial. Also controversial is the use of gonadotropin-releasing hormone as an inhalant. Such substances as powdered rhinoceros horn, used in Asia for their alleged stimulant effects, are of benefit only through the power of suggestion in a particular culture.

Surgical treatment is even more rarely advocated, but improved penile prosthetic devices are available for men with inadequate erectile responses who are resistant to other treatment methods or who have deficiencies of organic origin. Placement of a penile prosthesis in a man who has lost the ability to ejaculate or have an orgasm through organic causes will not enable him to recover those functions. Men with prosthetic devices have generally reported satisfaction with their subsequent sexual functioning. Their wives, however, report much less satisfaction than do the men. Presurgical counseling is strongly recommended so that the couple have a realistic expectation of what the prosthesis can do for their sex lives. Some physicians are attempting revascularization of the penis as a direct approach to treating erectile dysfunction caused by vascular disorders. In patients with corporal shunts that allow normally entrapped blood to leak from the corporal spaces leading to inadequate erections (steal phenomenon), such surgical procedures may be indicated. There are limited reports of prolonged success with this technique. Endarterectomy can be of benefit if aortoiliac occlusive disease is responsible for erectile dysfunction.

Surgical approaches to female dysfunctions include hymenectomy in the case of dyspareunia in an unconsummated marriage, vaginoplasty in multiparous women who complain of reduced vaginal sensations, and release of clitoral adhesions in women with inhibited excitement. Such surgical treatments have not been carefully studied and should be considered with great caution.

Injections of papaverine into the corporal bodies of the penis produce erections for several hours; however, repeated use may cause vascular damage, and this treatment cannot be recommended on a long-term basis. In addition, patients quickly become resistant to injecting themselves.

Results

The reported effectiveness of various treatment methods for problems of sexual dysfunction varies from study to study. Demonstrating the effectiveness of traditional outpatient psychotherapy is just as difficult when therapy is oriented to sexual problems as it is in general. In some cases the patient improves in all areas except the sexual area. Unfortunately, the more severe the psychopathology associated with a problem of long duration, the more adverse the outcome is likely to be.

The difficult treatment cases involve couples with severe marital discord. Cases with problems of fear of intimacy, excessive dependency, or excessive hostility are also complex. Other challenges are posed by patients with lack of desire, impulse disorders, unresolved homosexual conflicts, and fetishistic defenses. Patients phobic of sex also present treatment difficulties.

When behavioral approaches are used, empirical criteria that are supposed to predict outcome are more easily isolated than in other treatment methods. Using these criteria, for instance, it appears that couples who regularly practice assigned exercises have a much greater likelihood of successful outcome than do more resistant couples or couples whose interaction involves sadomasochistic or depressive features or mechanisms of blame and projection. Flexibility of attitude is also a positive prognostic factor. Overall, young couples tend to complete sex therapy more often than do older couples. Those couples whose interactional difficulties center on their sex problems—such as inhibition, frustration, fear of failure, and fear of performance—are also likely to respond well to therapy.

Masters and Johnson have reported high positive results for their dual-sex therapy approach. They have studied the failure rates of their patients; failure is defined as the failure to initiate reversal of the basic symptom of the presenting dysfunction. They compared initial failure rates with five-year follow-up findings for the same couples. Although some have criticized their definition of the percentage of presumed successes, other studies have confirmed the effectiveness of their approach. A single therapist, however, seems to be nearly as effective as a dual-sex therapy team.

In general, methods that have proved effective singly or in combination include training in behavioral-sexual skills, systematic desensitization, directive marital counseling, traditional psychodynamic approaches, and group therapy. Although treating a couple for sexual dysfunction is the mode preferred by most workers, treatment of individual patients has also been successful.

References

Dawkins S, Taylor R: Non-consummation of marriage. Lancet *2*: 1029, 1961.

Fordney D S: Dyspareunia and vaginismus. Clin Obstet Gynecol *21*: 205, 1978.

Frank E: Frequency of sexual dysfunction in "normal" couples. N Engl J Med *299*: 111, 1978.

Freud S: Three essays on the theory of sexuality. In *Standard Edition of the Complete Psychological Works of Sigmund Freud*, vol 7, p 125. Hogarth Press, London, 1953.

Furlow W L, ed.: Male sexual dysfunction. Urol Clin North Am *8*: 1, 1981.

Herman J, Lo Piccolo J: Clinical outcome of sex therapy. Arch Gen Psychiatry *40*: 443, 1983.

Person E, Ovesy L: Homosexual cross-dressers. J Am Acad Psychoanal *12*: 167, 1984.

Marmor J, ed.: *Homosexual Behavior.* Basic Books, New York, 1980.

Masters W H, Johnson V E: *Human Sexual Inadequacy.* Little, Brown, Boston, 1970.

Sadock B J, Kaplan H I, Freedman A M, eds.: *The Sexual Experience.* Williams & Wilkins, Baltimore, 1976.

Segraves R T: Effects of psychotropic drugs on human erection and ejaculation. Arch Gen Psychiatry *46*: 782, 1989.

Semans J H: Premature ejaculation: A new approach. South Med J *49*: 353, 1956.

Zorgniotto A W, Leflueck R S: Autoinjection of corpus cavernosum with vasoactive drug combination with vasculogenic impotence. J Urol *133*: 39, 1985.

20.4 / Rape, Incest, and Special Areas of Interest

RAPE

The problem of rape is most appropriately discussed under the heading of aggression. Rape is an act of violence and humiliation that happens to be expressed through sexual means. Rape is used to express power or anger. There are rarely rapes in which sex is the dominant issue; sexuality is usually used in the service of nonsexual needs.

A legal definition of rape in the United States is: "The perpetration of an act of sexual intercourse with a female, not one's wife, against her will and consent, whether her will is overcome by force or fear resulting from the threat of force or by drugs or intoxicants; or when because of mental deficiency she is incapable of exercising rational judgment, or when she is below an arbitrary age of consent."

The crime of rape requires slight penile penetration of the victim's outer vulva. Full erection and ejaculation are not necessary. Forced acts of fellatio and anal penetration, although they frequently accompany rape, are legally considered sodomy.

Rape of Women

Recent research has categorized male rapists into separate groups: sexual sadists, who are aroused by the pain of their victims; exploitative predators, who use their victims as objects for their gratification in an impulsive way; inadequate men, who believe no woman would voluntarily sleep with them and who are obsessed with fantasies about sex; and men for whom rape is a displaced expression of anger and rage. Some workers believe that the anger was originally directed toward a wife or mother. Feminist theory, however, proposes that the woman serves as an object for the displacement of aggression that the rapist cannot express directly toward other men. The woman is considered the property or vulnerable possession of men and is the rapist's instrument for revenge against other men.

Rape often occurs as an accompaniment to another crime. The rapist always threatens his victim with fists, a gun, or a knife and frequently harms her in nonsexual ways, as well as in sexual ways. The victim may be beaten, wounded, and sometimes killed.

Statistics show that most men who commit rapes are between 25 and 44 years of age; 51 percent are white and tend to rape white victims, 47 percent are black and tend to rape black victims, and the remaining 2 percent come from all other races. Alcohol is involved in 34 percent of all forcible rapes. A composite characterization of the archetypical rapist drawn from police statistics portrays a single, 19-year-old man from the low socioeconomic groups who has a police record of acquisitive offenses.

Rape is a highly underreported crime. It is estimated that only 1 out of 4 to 1 out of 10 rapes is reported. If the lower estimated figure is used, the reported incidence of 60,000 rapes in 1986 increases to over 200,000 rapes a year. The underreporting is attributed to feelings of shame on the part of the victim and to the belief that there is no recourse through the legal system.

Victims of rape can be of any age. Cases have been reported in which the victims were as young as 15 months and as old as 82 years. The greatest danger exists for women age 10 to 29. Rape most commonly occurs in a woman's own neighborhood, frequently inside her own home. Most rapes are premeditated. About half are committed by strangers and half by men known, to varying degrees, by the victims; 7 percent of all rapes are perpetrated by close relatives of the victim. Twenty percent of rapes involve more than one attacker.

The woman being raped is frequently in a life-threatening situation. During the rape she experiences shock and fright approaching panic. Her prime motivation is to stay alive. In most cases rapists choose victims slightly smaller than themselves. The rapist may urinate or defecate on his victim, ejaculate into her face and hair, force anal intercourse, and insert foreign objects into her vagina and rectum.

After the rape the woman may experience shame, humiliation, confusion, fear, and rage. The type and the duration of the reaction are variable, but women report effects lasting for a year or longer. Many women experience the symptoms of posttraumatic stress disorder. Some women are able to resume sexual relations with men, particularly if they have always felt sexually adequate. Others become phobic of sexual interaction or have such symptoms as vaginismus. Few women emerge from the assault completely unscathed. The manifestations and the degree of damage depend on the violence of the attack itself, the vulnerability of the woman, and the support systems available to her immediately after the attack.

The victim fares best when she receives immediate support and is able to ventilate her fear and rage to loving family members and to sympathetic physicians and law enforcement officials. She is helped when she knows that she has socially acceptable means of recourse, such as the arrest and conviction of the rapist. Therapy is usually supportive in approach unless there is a severe underlying disorder. It focuses on restoring the victim's sense of adequacy and control over her life and relieving the feelings of helplessness, dependency, and obsession with the assault that frequently follow rape. Group therapy with homogeneous groups composed of rape victims is a particularly effective form of treatment.

The rape victim experiences a physical and psychological trauma when she is assaulted. Until recently, she also faced frequent skepticism from those to whom she reported the crime (if she had sufficient strength to do so) or accusations of having provoked or desired the assault. In reality, the National Commission on the Causes and Prevention of Violence found discernible victim precipitation of rape in only 4.4 percent of cases. This statistic is lower than in any other crime of violence. The education of police officers and the assignment of policewomen to deal with rape victims have helped increase the reporting of the crime. Rape crisis centers and telephone hot lines are available for immediate aid and information for victims. Volunteer groups work in emergency rooms in hospitals and with physician education programs to assist the treatment of victims.

Legally, women no longer have to prove that they actively struggled against the rapist when they appear in court. Testimony regarding the prior sexual history of the victim has recently been declared inadmissible as evidence in a number of states. Also, penalties for first-time rapists have been reduced, making juries more likely to consider a conviction. In some states wives can now prosecute husbands for rape.

Date rape. Date or acquaintance rape is a term applied to rapes in which the rapist is known to the victim. The assault can occur on a first date or after the man and the woman have known each other for many months. Considerable data on this type of rape have been gathered from college populations. In one study 38 percent of male students said they would commit rape if they thought they could get away with it, and 11 percent stated they had committed rape; 16 percent of the female students said they had been raped by men they knew or were dating.

In addition to suffering the symptoms of all rape survivors, victims of date rape berate themselves for exercising poor judgment in their choice of male friends and are more likely to blame themselves for provoking the rapist than are other victims. Many schools have set up programs for rape prevention and for counseling those who have been assaulted.

Rape of Men

In some states the definition of rape is being changed to substitute the word "person" for "female." In most states male rape is legally defined as sodomy. Homosexual rape is much more frequent among men than among women, and it occurs primarily in closed institutions, such as prisons and maximum-security hospitals. The dynamics are identical to those of heterosexual rape. The crime enables the rapist to discharge aggression and to aggrandize himself. The victim is usually smaller than the rapist, is always perceived as passive and unmanly (weaker), and is used as an object. The rapist selecting a male victim may be heterosexual, bisexual, or homosexual. The most common act is anal penetration of the victim; the second most common act is fellatio.

Homosexual-rape victims often feel, as do raped women, that they have been ruined. In addition, some fear they will become homosexual because of the attack.

Statutory Rape

Intercourse is unlawful between a male over 16 years of age and a female under the age of consent, which varies from 14 to 21 years, depending on the jurisdiction. Thus, a man of 18 and a girl of 15 may have consensual intercourse, yet the man may be held for statutory rape. This type of rape may vary dramatically from the crimes described above in being nonassaultive and sexual, not a violent act. Nor is it a deviant act, unless the age discrepancy is sufficient for the man to be defined as a pedophile—that is, when the girl is less than 13 years old. Charges of statutory rape are rarely pressed by the consenting girl; they are brought by her parents.

INCEST

Incest is defined as the occurrence of sexual relations between close blood relatives. A broader definition describes incest as intercourse between participants who are related to one another by some formal or informal bond of kinship that is culturally regarded as a bar to sexual relations. For example, sexual relations between stepparents and stepchildren or among stepsiblings are usually considered incestuous, even though no blood relationship exists.

The strongest and most universal taboo exists against mother-son incest. It occurs much less frequently than any other form of incest. Such behavior is usually indicative of more severe psychopathology in the participants than is father-daughter or sibling incest.

Sociologists have underlined the role of incest prohibitions as socialization factors. Biological factors also support the taboo. Groups that inbreed risk the unmasking of lethal or detrimental recessive genes, and the progeny of inbreeding groups are generally less fit than other progeny. Anthropologists have observed that the particular form of the incest taboo is culturally determined. In *Totem and Taboo,* Sigmund Freud developed the concept of primal horde, in which the young men collectively murdered the group's patriarch, who had kept all the women of the tribe to himself. The incest taboo arose both out of guilt after the murder and to prevent a repetition of the act, further rivalry after the murder, and subsequent disintegration of the horde.

Accurate figures on the incidence of incest are difficult to obtain because of the general shame and embarrassment of the entire family. Females are victims more often than males. About 15 million women in the United States have been the object of incestuous attention, and one-third of sexually abused persons have been molested before the age of 9.

Incestuous behavior is reported much more frequently among families of low socioeconomic status than among other families. This difference may be due to greater contact with reporting officials—such as welfare workers, public health personnel, and law enforcement agents—and is not a true reflection of higher incidence in that demographic group. Incest is more easily hidden by economically stable families than by the poor.

Social, cultural, physiological, and psychological factors all contribute to the breakdown of the incest taboo. Incestuous behavior has been associated with alcoholism, overcrowding, increased physical proximity, and rural isolation that prevents adequate extrafamilial contacts. Some communities may be more tolerant of incestuous behavior than is society in general. Major mental illnesses and intellectual deficiencies have been described in some cases of clinical incest. Some family therapists view incest as a defense designed to maintain a dysfunctional family unit. The older and stronger participant in incestuous behavior is usually male. Thus, incest may be viewed as a form of child abuse, as a pedophilia, or as a variant of rape.

About 75 percent of reported cases involve father-daughter incest. However, there are many cases of sibling incest that are denied by parents or that involve nearly normal interaction if the activity is prepubertal sexual play and exploration.

The daughter in father-daughter incest has frequently had a close relationship with her father throughout her childhood and may be pleased at first when he approaches her sexually. The onset of incestuous behavior usually occurs when the daughter is 10 years old. As the behavior continues, however, the abused daughter becomes bewildered, confused, and frightened. As she nears adolescence, she undergoes physiological changes that add to her confusion. She never knows whether her father will be parental or sexual. Her mother may be alternately caring and competitive; she often refuses to believe her daughter's reports or to confront her husband with her suspicions. The daughter's relationships with her siblings are also affected as they sense her special position with her father and treat her as an outsider. The father, fearful that his daughter may expose their relationship and often jealously possessive of her, interferes with her development of normal peer relationships.

The physician must be aware of the possibility of intrafamilial sexual abuse as the cause of a wide variety of emotional and physical symptoms, including abdominal pain, genital irritations, separation anxiety, phobias, nightmares, and school problems. When incest is suspected, it is essential to interview the child apart from the rest of the family.

Homosexual Incest

In father-son incest, two cultural sanctions are violated: the taboo against incestuous behavior and that against homosexual behavior.

The family in which such behavior occurs is usually highly disturbed, with a violent, alcoholic, or psychopathic father; a dependent or disabled mother who is unable to protect her children; and an absence of the usual family roles and individual identities. Father-son and mother-daughter incest are rarely reported. The son in father-son incest is frequently the eldest child, and, if he has a sister, she is often sexually abused by the father as well. The father does not necessarily have any other history of homosexual behavior. The sons in this situation may experience homicidal or suicidal ideation and may first present to a psychiatrist with self-destructive behavior.

Treatment

The first step in the treatment of incestuous behavior is its disclosure. Once a breakthrough of the denial and collusion or fear by the family members has been achieved, incest is less likely to recur. When the participants suffer from severe psychopathology, treatment must be directed toward the underlying illness. Family therapy is useful to reestablish the group as a functioning unit and to develop healthier role definitions for each member. While the participants are learning to develop internal restraints and more appropriate methods of gratifying their needs, the external control provided by therapy helps prevent further incestuous behavior. At times, legal agencies are involved to help enforce external controls.

SPOUSE ABUSE

Spouse abuse is estimated to occur in 2 million to 12 million families in the United States. This aspect of domestic violence has been recognized as a severe problem, largely as a result of recent cultural emphasis on civil rights and the work of feminist groups. However, the problem itself is one of long standing.

The major problem in spouse abuse is wife abuse. One study estimates that there are 1.8 million battered wives in the United States, excluding divorced women and girls battered on dates. Some beatings of husbands are also reported. In these cases the husbands complain of fear of ridicule if they expose the problem, fear of charges of counterassault, and inability to leave the situation because of financial difficulties. Husband abuse has also been reported when a frail elderly man is married to a much younger woman.

Wife beating occurs in families of every racial and religious background and in all socioeconomic strata. It is most frequent in families with problems of drug abuse, particularly when there is alcoholism or use of crack.

Behavioral, cultural, intrapsychic, and interpersonal factors all contribute to the development of the problem. Abusive men are likely to have come from violent homes where they witnessed wife beating or were abused themselves as children. The act itself is reinforcing; once a man has beaten his wife, he is likely to do so again. Abusive husbands tend to be immature, dependent, and nonassertive and to suffer from strong feelings of inadequacy.

Their aggression is bullying behavior, designed to humiliate their wives to build up their own low self-esteem. The abuse is most likely to occur when the man feels threatened or frustrated at home, at work, or with peers. The Surgeon General's office has identified pregnancy as a high risk period for battering. Impatient and impulsive, abusive husbands physically displace aggression provoked by others onto their wives. The dynamics include identification with an aggressor (father, boss), testing behavior (Will she stay with me no matter how I treat her?), distorted desires to express manhood, and dehumanization of the woman. As in rape, aggression is "permissible" when the woman is perceived as property. Approximately 50 percent of battered wives grew up in violent homes. The trait most commonly found in abused wives is dependency.

Recently, hot lines, emergency shelters for women, and other organizations (such as Respond) have been developed to aid battered wives and to educate the public. A presidential commission was established to investigate spouse abuse. A major problem for abused women has been where to find a place to go when they leave home, frequently in fear of their lives. Battering is often severe, involving broken limbs, broken ribs, internal bleeding, and brain damage. When an abused wife tries to leave her husband, he often becomes doubly intimidating and threatens, "I'll get you." If the woman has small children to care for, her problem is compounded. The abusive husband wages a conscious campaign to isolate his wife and to make her feel worthless.

Some men feel remorse and guilt after an episode of violent behavior and become particularly loving. This behavior gives the wife hope, and she remains until the next cycle of violence, which inevitably occurs.

Change is initiated when the man is convinced that the woman will not tolerate the situation and when she begins to exert control over his behavior. She can do so by leaving for a prolonged period—if she is physically and economically able to do so—with therapy for the man as a condition of return. Family therapy is effective in treating the problem, usually in conjunction with social and legal agencies. With relatively less impulsive men, external controls, such as calling the neighbors or the police, may be sufficient to stop the behavior.

INFERTILITY

It is not one factor or one mate but a combination of several factors in each that contribute to infertility in 80 percent of all cases. A couple is considered infertile if they have had coitus without contraception for a period of one year and pregnancy has not occurred. In the United States 12 percent of all marriages are estimated to be involuntarily childless. Various clinics report that 20 to 50 percent of couples presently facing infertility can be helped.

Until recently, the onus for the failure to conceive was on the woman, and feelings of guilt, depression, and inadequacy frequently accompanied her perception of being barren. Current practice encourages simultaneous investigation of factors preventing conception in both the man and the woman. However, it is still frequently the woman who first presents for an infertility workup.

A thorough sexual history of the couple—including such factors as frequency of contact, erectile or ejaculatory dysfunction, and coital position—must be obtained. Frequently, conception is less likely simply because the woman rises to void, wash, or even douche immediately after coitus. Preference for coitus with the woman in the superior position is also not conducive to conception because of the lessened retention of semen.

A psychiatric evaluation of the couple may be advisable. Marital disharmony or emotional conflicts around intimacy, sexual relations, or parenting roles can directly affect endocrine function and such physiological processes as erection, ejaculation, and ovulation. There is no evidence for any simple, causal relationship between stress and infertility.

The stress of infertility itself in a couple who want children can lead to emotional disturbance. When a preexisting conflict gives rise to problems of identity, self-esteem, and neurotic guilt, the disturbance may be severe. It may manifest itself through regression; extreme dependency on the physician, the mate, or a parent; diffuse anger; impulsive behavior; or depression. The problem is further complicated if hormone therapy is being used to treat the infertility, because the therapy may temporarily increase depression in some patients.

People who have difficulty conceiving experience shock, disbelief, and a general sense of helplessness, and they develop an understandable preoccupation with the problem. Involvement in the infertility workup and the development of expertise about infertility can be a constructive defense against feelings of inadequacy and the humiliating, sometimes painful aspects of the workup itself. Worries about attractiveness and sexual desirability are common. Partners may feel ugly or impotent, and episodes of sexual dysfunction and loss of desire are reported. These problems are aggravated if a couple is scheduling their sexual relations according to temperature charts.

In addition, they are dealing with a narcissistic blow to their senses of femininity and masculinity. An infertile partner may fear abandonment or feel that the spouse is remaining in the relationship resentfully. Single people who are aware of their own infertility may shy away from relationships for fear of being rejected once their "defect" is known. Infertile people may have particular difficulty in their adult relationships with their own parents. The identification and the equality that come from sharing the experience of parenthood must be replaced by internal reserves and other generative aspects of their lives.

Professional intervention may be necessary to help infertile couples ventilate their feelings and go through the process of mourning their lost biological functions and the children they cannot have. Couples who remain infertile must cope with an actual loss. Couples who decide not to pursue parenthood may develop a renewed sense of love, dedication, and identity as a pair. Others may need help in exploring the options of husband or donor insemination, laboratory implantation, and adoption.

STERILIZATION

Sterilization is a procedure that prevents a man or a woman from producing offspring. In a woman the procedure is usually salpingectomy, litigation of the fallopian tubes. It is a hospital procedure with low morbidity and low mortality. A man is usually sterilized by vasectomy, ligation of the vas deferens. It is a simpler procedure than a salpingectomy and is performed in the physician's office. Voluntary sterilization, especially vasectomy, has become the most popular form of birth control in couples married for more than 10 years.

A small proportion of patients who elect sterilization may suffer a neurotic poststerilization syndrome. It may manifest itself through hypochondriasis, pain, loss of libido, sexual unresponsiveness, depression, and concerns about masculinity or femininity. One study of a group of women who regretted sterilization found they had chosen the procedure while in poor relationships, frequently with abusing husbands. Cases of regret are most prevalent when a new relationship has formed and the sterilized person wishes to bear a child with a new partner.

Psychiatric consultation can frequently separate patients seeking sterilization for psychotic or neurotic reasons from those who have made the decision after some time or thought.

Involuntary sterilization procedures have been performed to prevent the reproduction of traits considered genetically undesirable. There have been statutes allowing for the sterilization of hereditary criminals, sex offenders, syphilitics, the mentally retarded, and epileptics. Some of these statutes have been declared unconstitutional. In recent years human rights and civil liberties groups have been challenging the legality and ethical standing of such sterilization procedures with increasing vigor.

References

Becker J V, Skinner L J, Abel G G, Treacy E C: Incidence and types of sexual dysfunctions in rape and incest victims. J Sex Marital Ther *8*: 65, 1982.

Brownmiller S: *Against Our Will: Men, Women and Rape*. Simon & Schuster, New York, 1975.

Burgess A W, Holmstrom L L: Rape trauma syndrome. Am J Psychiatry *131*: 981, 1974.

Ellenberg J J, Koren Z: Infertility and depression. Int J Fertil *27*: 219, 1982.

Freud S: *Totem and Taboo*. Norton, New York, 1950.

Henderson D J: Incest. In *The Sexual Experience*, B J Sadock, H I Kaplan, and A M Freedman, editors, p 415. Williams & Wilkins, Baltimore, 1976.

Herman J L, Gartrell N, Olarte S, Feldstein M, Cocalio R: Psychiatrist-patient sexual contact: Results of a national survey: II. Psychiatrist's attitudes. Am J Psychiatry *144*: 164, 1987.

Herman J L, Hirschman L: Families at risk for father-daughter incest. Am J Psychiatry *138*: 967, 1981.

Hilberman E: "Wife-beater's wife" reconsidered. Am J Psychiatry *137*: 11, 1980.

Johnson R L, Shrier D: Past sexual victimization by females of male patients in an adolescent medicine clinic population. Am J Psychiatry *144*: 650, 1987.

Sarrel P M, Masters W H: Sexual molestation of men by women. Arch Sex Behav *11*: 117, 1982.

Stewart B D, Hughes C, Frank E, Andersen B, Kendall K, West D: The aftermath of rape: Profiles of immediate and delayed treatment seekers. J Nerv Ment Dis *175*: 90, 1987.

Vessey M, Higgins G, Lawless M, McPherson K, Yeates D: Tubal sterilization: Findings in a large prospective study. Br J Obstet Gynaecol *90*: 203, 1983.

Normal Sleep and Sleep Disorders

21.1 / Normal Sleep

The scientific study of sleep has progressed more in the past 35 years—beginning with the discovery of rapid eye movement (REM) sleep and its association with dreaming—than in the previous two centuries. The greatest gains have ensued from the development of new technology, a multidisciplinary approach to evaluating sleep complaints, and a better understanding of the chemistry of the brain. Despite such significant accomplishments, the basic phenomenon of sleep remains enshrouded in mystery to sleeper and investigator alike. Researchers and clinicians are still perplexed by many unanswered questions. Why do organisms sleep? What biological need does this cyclical process fulfill? What is the purpose of dreaming? Why is disordered sleep often a forerunner or prominent symptom of mental or medical illness? The exploration of these enigmas has led current sleep research away from its former emphasis on the description of sleep and its stages, phenomenology, and ontology, to two main areas: (1) basic sleep mechanisms and sleep physiology and (2) sleep problems in clinical medicine.

Sleep is a regular, recurrent, easily reversible state of the organism that is characterized by relative quiescence and by a great increase in the threshold of response to external stimuli relative to the waking state. Close monitoring of sleep is an important part of clinical practice, since sleep disturbance is often an early symptom of impending mental illness. Recent advances in sleep research have demonstrated that some mental disorders are associated with characteristic changes in sleep physiology. These changes can provide insight into the underlying pathophysiology of mental disorders and help determine diagnoses in complex clinical presentations.

NORMAL SLEEP PATTERNS

As persons fall asleep, their brain waves go through certain characteristic changes, classified as stages 1, 2, 3, and 4 (Figure 21.1-1). The waking electroencephalogram (EEG) is characterized by alpha waves of 8 to 12 cycles a second and low-voltage activity of mixed frequency. As the person falls asleep, alpha activity begins to disappear. Stage 1, considered the lightest stage of sleep, is characterized by low-voltage, regular activity at 3 to 7 cycles a second. After a few seconds or minutes, this stage gives way to stage 2, a pattern showing frequent spindle-shaped tracings at 12 to 14 cycles a second (sleep spindles) and slow, triphasic waves known as K complexes. Soon thereafter, delta waves—high-voltage activity at 0.5 to 2.5 cycles a second—make their appearance and occupy less than 50 percent of the tracing (stage 3). Eventually, in stage 4, delta waves occupy more than 50 percent of the record. It is common practice to describe stages 3 and 4 as delta sleep or slow-wave sleep (SWS) because of their characteristic appearance on the EEG record.

POLYSOMNOGRAM REM FINDINGS

Nonrapid eye movement (NREM) sleep is composed of stages 1 through 4. As compared with wakefulness, most physiological functions are markedly reduced during NREM sleep. REM sleep is a qualitatively different kind of sleep characterized by a highly active brain and physiological activity levels similar to those in wakefulness. About 90 minutes after sleep onset, NREM yields to the first REM episode of the night. This REM latency of 90 minutes is a consistent finding in normal adults. A shortening of REM latency frequently occurs with disorders such as depression and narcolepsy. The EEG records the rapid conjugate eye movements that are the identifying feature of this sleep state (there are no or few rapid eye movements in NREM sleep); the EEG pattern consists of low-voltage, random fast activity with sawtooth waves; the electromyograph (EMG) shows marked reduction in muscle tone.

In normal persons NREM sleep is a peaceful state relative to waking. Pulse rate is typically slowed 5 or 10 beats a minute below the level of restful waking and is very regular. Respiration behaves in the same way. Blood pressure also tends to be low, with few minute-to-minute variations. Resting muscle potential of body musculature is lower in REM sleep than in a waking state. Episodic, involuntary body movement is present in NREM sleep. There are few rapid eye movements, if any, and seldom any penile erections. Blood flow through most tissues, including cerebral blood flow, is also slightly reduced.

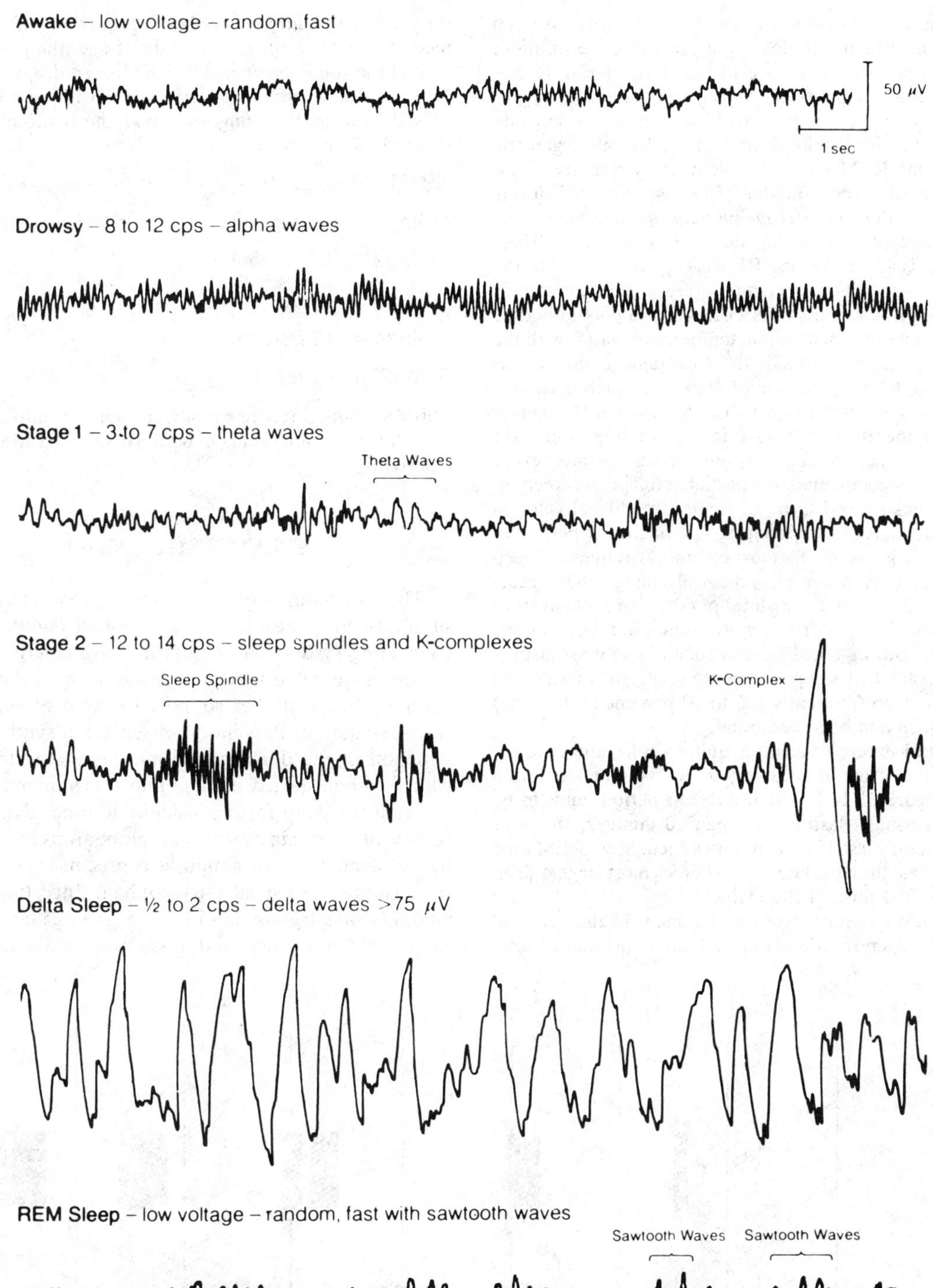

Figure 21.1-1. Human sleep stages. (From P Hauri: *The Sleep Disorders,* p 7. Current Concepts, Upjohn, Michigan, 1982, with permission.)

The deepest portions of NREM sleep—stages 3 and 4—are sometimes associated with unusual arousal characteristics. When persons are aroused a half hour to one hour after sleep onset—usually in SWS—they are disoriented, and their thinking is disorganized. Brief arousals from SWS are also associated with amnesia for events that occur during the arousal. The disorganization during arousal from stage 3 or stage 4 may result in specific problems, including enuresis, somnambulism, and stage 4 nightmares or night terrors.

Polygraphic measures during REM sleep show irregular patterns, sometimes close to aroused waking patterns. Indeed, if one was not aware of the behavioral stage of the person and one happened to be recording a variety of physiological measures (but not muscle tone) during REM periods, one would undoubtedly conclude that the person or animal was in an active waking state. Because of this observation, REM sleep has also been termed paradoxical sleep. Pulse, respiration, and blood pressure in humans are all high during REM sleep—much higher than during NREM sleep and quite often higher than during waking. Even more striking than the level or rate is the variability from minute to minute. Brain oxygen use increases during REM sleep. The ventilatory response to increased levels of carbon dioxide (CO_2) is depressed during REM sleep, so that there is no increase in tidal volume as partial pressure of carbon dioxide (pCO_2) increases. Thermoregulation is altered during REM sleep. In contrast to the homeothermic condition of temperature regulation that is present during wakefulness or NREM sleep, a poikilothermic condition (a state in which animal temperature varies with the changes in the temperature of the surrounding medium) is present during REM sleep. Poikilothermia, which is characteristic of reptiles, results in a failure to respond to changes in ambient temperature with shivering or sweating, whichever is appropriate to maintaining body temperature. Almost every REM period is accompanied by a partial or full penile erection. This finding has proved to be of significant clinical value in evaluating the cause of impotence. The nocturnal penile tumescence study is one of the most commonly requested sleep laboratory tests. Another physiological change that occurs during REM sleep is the near total paralysis of skeletal (postural) muscles. Because of this motor inhibition, body movement is absent during REM sleep. Probably the most distinctive feature of REM sleep is dreaming. Persons awakened during REM sleep frequently (60 to 90 percent of the time) report that they had been dreaming.

The cyclical nature of sleep is quite regular and reliable; a REM period occurs about every 90 to 100 minutes during the night (Figure 21.1-2). The first REM period tends to be the shortest, usually lasting less than 10 minutes; the later REM periods may last 15 to 40 minutes each. Most REM time occurs in the last third of the night, whereas most stage 4 sleep occurs in the first third of the night.

Sleep patterns change over the life span. In the neonatal period, REM sleep represents more than 50 percent of total sleep time. In addition, newborns pass from wakefulness directly to REM sleep. By 4 months of age, the pattern shifts, so that the total percentage of REM sleep drops to less than 40 percent and entry into sleep occurs with an initial period of NREM sleep. By young adulthood, the distribution of sleep stages is as follows:

NREM (75 percent)

- Stage 1: 5 percent
- Stage 2: 45 percent
- Stage 3: 12 percent
- Stage 4: 13 percent

REM (25 percent)

This distribution remains relatively constant into old age, although a reduction occurs in both SWS and REM sleep in the elderly.

SLEEP REGULATION

The prevailing view at present is that there is not a simple sleep control center but a small number of interconnecting systems or centers that are chiefly located in the brain stem and that mutually activate and inhibit one another. Many studies support the role of serotonin in sleep regulation. Prevention of serotonin synthesis or destruction of the dorsal raphe nucleus of the brain stem, which contains nearly all the brain's serotonergic cell bodies, reduces sleep for a considerable time. Synthesis and release of serotonin by serotonergic neurons are influenced by the availability of amino acid precursors of that neurotransmitter, such as L-tryptophan. Ingestion of large amounts of L-tryptophan (1 to 15 g) has been shown to reduce sleep latency and nocturnal awakenings. Con-

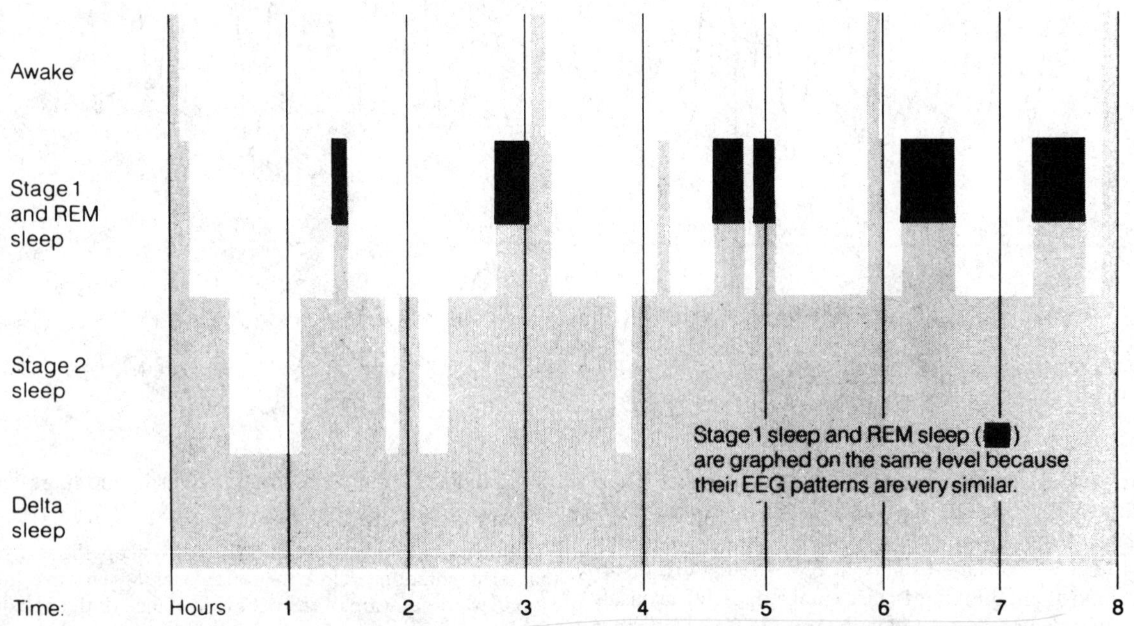

Figure 21.1-2. Typical sleep pattern of a young human adult. (From P Hauri: *The Sleep Disorders*, p 8. Current Concepts, Upjohn, Michigan, 1982, with permission.)

versely, L-tryptophan deficiency is associated with less time spent in REM sleep.

Norepinephrine-containing neurons with cell bodies located in the locus ceruleus play an important role in controlling normal sleep patterns. Drugs and manipulations that increase firing of these noradrenergic neurons produce a marked reduction in REM sleep (REM-off neurons) and an increase in wakefulness. Electrical stimulation of the locus ceruleus in humans with chronically implanted electrodes (for control of spasticity) profoundly disrupts all sleep parameters.

Brain acetylcholine is also involved in sleep, particularly in the production of REM sleep. In animal studies injection of cholinergic-muscarinic agonists into pontine reticular formation neurons (REM-on neurons) results in a shift from wakefulness to REM sleep. Disturbances in central cholinergic activity are associated with the sleep changes observed in major depression. As compared with healthy persons and nondepressed psychiatric controls, depressed patients have marked disruption of REM sleep patterns. These include shortened REM latency (60 minutes or less), greater percentage of REM sleep, and a shift in REM distribution from the last half to the first half of the night. Administration of a muscarinic agonist, such as arecoline, to depressed patients during the first or second NREM period results in a rapid onset of REM sleep. It is postulated that depression is associated with an underlying supersensitivity to acetylcholine.

Another intriguing observation suggests a link between acetylcholine and depression. Drugs that reduce REM sleep, such as antidepressants, produce beneficial effects in depression. Indeed, about half of the patients with major depression experience temporary improvement when deprived or restricted from sleep. Conversely, reserpine, which is one of the few drugs that increases REM sleep, also produces depression.

Patients with Alzheimer's disease have sleep disturbances characterized by reduced REM and SWS. Loss of cholinergic neurons in the basal forebrain has been implicated as the cause of these changes. Melatonin secretion from the pineal gland is inhibited by bright light, so that the lowest serum melatonin concentrations occur during the day. The suprachiasmatic nucleus of the hypothalamus may act as the anatomical site of a circadian pacemaker that regulates melatonin secretion and the entrainment of the brain to a 24-hour sleep-wake cycle.

Evidence shows that dopamine has an alerting effect. Drugs that increase brain dopamine tend to produce arousal and wakefulness. In contrast, dopamine blockers, such as pimozide (Orap) and the phenothiazines, tend to increase sleep time.

FUNCTIONS OF SLEEP

The function of sleep has been examined in a variety of ways; most investigators conclude that sleep serves a restorative, homeostatic function. Sleep appears to be crucial for normal thermoregulation and energy conservation.

Sleep Deprivation

Prolonged periods of sleep deprivation sometimes lead to ego disorganization, hallucinations, and delusions. Depriving persons of REM sleep by awakening them at the beginning of REM cycles produces an increase in the number of REM periods and in the amount of REM sleep (rebound increase) when they are allowed to sleep without interruption. REM-deprived patients may exhibit irritability and lethargy.

In studies with rats, sleep deprivation has been shown to produce a syndrome that includes debilitated appearance, skin lesions, increased food intake, weight loss, increased energy expenditure, decreased body temperature, and death. Neuroendocrine changes include increased plasma norepinephrine and decreased plasma thyroxine.

Sleep Requirements

Some persons are normally short sleepers who require less than six hours each night and function adequately. Long sleepers are those who sleep more than nine hours each night in order to function adequately. Long sleepers have more REM periods and more rapid eye movements within each period (known as REM density) than do short sleepers. These movements are sometimes considered a measure of the intensity of REM sleep and are related to the vividness of dreaming. Short sleepers are generally efficient, ambitious, socially adept, and content. Long sleepers tend to be mildly depressed, anxious, and socially withdrawn. Increased sleep needs occur with physical work, exercise, illness, pregnancy, general mental stress, and increased mental activity. REM periods increase after strong psychological stimuli, such as difficult learning situations and stress, and after the use of chemicals or drugs that decrease brain catecholamines.

SLEEP-WAKE RHYTHM

Sleep is influenced by biological rhythms. Within a 24-hour period, adults sleep once, sometimes twice. This rhythm is not present at birth but develops over the first two years of life.

In some women, sleep patterns change during the phases of the menstrual cycle. It has also been demonstrated that naps taken at different times of the day differ greatly in their content of REM and NREM sleep. In a normal nighttime sleeper, a nap taken in the morning or at noon contains a great deal of REM sleep, whereas a nap taken in the afternoon or the early evening contains much less. There is apparently a circadian cycle affecting the tendency to have REM sleep.

Sleep patterns are not physiologically the same when one sleeps in the daytime or during the time when one's body is accustomed to being awake; the psychological and behavioral effects of sleep differ as well. In a world of industry and communications that often functions on a 24-hour-day basis, these interactions are becoming increasingly significant.

Even in persons who do not work at night, the interference with the various rhythms can produce problems. The best-known example is jet lag, in which, after flying east to west, one tries to convince one's body to go to sleep at a time that is out of phase with some of the body cycles. Most bodies adapt within a few days, but some require more time. These conditions are more serious and apparently involve long-term cycle disruption and interference.

References

Akerstedt T: Review article: Sleepiness as a consequence of shift work. Sleep *11*: 17, 1988.

Cespuglio R, Faradji H, Gomez M E, et al: Single unit recordings in the nuclei raphe dorsalis and magnus during the sleep waking cycle of semichronic prepared cats. Neurosci Lett *24*: 133, 1981.

Czeisler C A, Weitzman E D, Moore-Ede M C, Zimmerman J C, Knaner R S: Human sleep: Its duration and organization depend on its circadian phase. Science *210*: 1264, 1980.
Dement W, Kleitman N: Cyclic variations in EEG during sleep and their relation to eye movements, body motility, and dreaming. Electroencephalogr Clin Neurophysiol *9*: 673, 1975.
Drucker-Colin R, Sckurovich M, Sterman B M, eds.: *The Functions of Sleep*. Academic Press, Orlando, FL, 1979.
Hartmann E: *The Functions of Sleep*. Yale University Press, New Haven, CT, 1973.
Hobson A J: Sleep and dreaming. J Neurosci *10*: 371, 1990.
Inoue S T, Kawamura H: Persistence of circadian rhythmicity in a mammalian hypothalamic "island" containing the suprachiasmatic nucleus. Proc Natl Acad Sci U S A *26*: 5962, 1971.
Karacan I, Goodenough D R, Shapiro A, Starker S: Erection cycle during sleep in relation to dream anxiety. Arch Gen Psychiatry *15*: 183, 1966.
Koella W P, ed.: *Sleep 1982: Sixth European Congress of Sleep Research*. Karger, Basel, 1983.
McGuinty D J, Drucker-Colin R: Sleep mechanisms: Biology and control of REM sleep. Int Rev Neurobiol *23*: 391, 1982.
Monnier M, Gaillard J M: Biochemical regulation of sleep. Experientia *36*: 21, 1980.
Moore C A, Karacan I, Williams R L: Basic science of sleep. In *Comprehensive Textbook of Psychiatry*, ed 5, H I Kaplan and B J Sadock, editors, p 86. Williams & Wilkins, Baltimore, 1989.
Orr W C, Robinson M G, Johnson L F: Acid clearing during sleep in the pathogenesis of reflux esophagitis. Dig Dis Sci *26*: 423, 1981.
Parmeggiani P: Integrative aspects of hypothalamic influences on respiratory brain stem mechanisms during wakefulness and sleep. In *Central Control Mechanisms in Breathing*, C von Euler and H Lagercrantz, editors, p 53. Pergamon, New York, 1979.
Passonneau J V, Hawkins R A, Lust W D, Welsh F A: *Cerebral Metabolism and Neurologic Function*. Williams & Wilkins, Baltimore, 1980.
Rechtschaffen A, Kales A: *The Manual of Standardized Terminology, Techniques, and Scoring System for Sleep Stages of Human Subjects*, NIH Publication No 204. National Institutes of Health, Bethesda, MD, 1968.
Suda M, Hayaishi O, Nakagawa H, eds.: *Biological Rhythms and Their Central Control Mechanism*. Elsevier, New York, 1979.
Sullivan C, Lizar L, Murphy E, Phillipson E: Primary role of respiratory afferents in sustaining breathing rhythm. J Appl Physiol *45*: 11, 1978.
Townsend R E, Prinz P N, Obrist W D: Human cerebral blood flow during sleep and waking. J Appl Physiol *35*: 620, 1973.
Wauquier A, Monti J M, Gaillard J M, Radulovacki M R: *Sleep Neurotransmitters and Neuromodulators*. Raven Press, New York, 1985.
Webb W B, ed.: *Biological Rhythms, Sleep, and Performance*. Wiley, New York, 1982.
Wheatley D, ed.: *Psychopharmacology of Sleep*. Raven Press, New York, 1981.
Williams R L, Karacan I, Hursch C J: *Electroencephalography (EEG) of Human Sleep: Clinical Applications*. Wiley, New York, 1974.
Zales M R, ed.: *Eating, Sleeping, and Sexuality: Treatment of Disorders in Basic Life Functions*. Brunner/Mazel, New York, 1982.

21.2 / Sleep Disorders

Sleep disorders are major psychiatric disorders that affect many persons. For instance, in the course of a year, up to 30 percent of the population suffer from insomnia and seek help for it. In many sleep disorders a careful diagnostic workup reveals a specific cause of the insomnia, and a specific treatment aimed at the cause may be used.

There are two major categories of sleep disorders in the revised third edition of *Diagnostic and Statistical Manual of Mental Disorders* (DSM-III-R): the dyssomnias and the parasomnias. The dyssomnias are insomnia, difficulty in falling asleep; hypersomnia, excessive amounts of sleep or complaints about excessive daytime somnolence; and sleep-wake schedule disorder. The parasomnias are a heterogeneous group of disorders in which episodic nocturnal events occur during sleep or at the threshold between wakefulness and sleep.

DYSSOMNIAS

Insomnia Disorders

Insomnia is a disorder of initiating or of maintaining sleep (DIMS). It is the most common sleep complaint. Insomnia may be transient or persistent. In the latter case, according to DSM-III-R, the disturbance occurs at least three times a week for at least one month and results in significant daytime fatigue or impaired social or occupational functioning (Table 21.2-1). A causal classification of insomnia is presented in Table 21.2-2.

A brief period of insomnia is most often associated with anxiety, either as a sequela to an anxious experience or in anticipation of an anxiety-provoking experience (e.g., an examination or an impending job interview). In some persons transient insomnia of this kind may be related to grief reaction, reaction to loss, or almost any life change. This condition is not likely to be serious, although it should be kept in mind that a psychotic episode or a severe depression may sometimes begin with an acute insomnia. Specific treatment for this condition is usually not required. When treatment with hypnotic medication is indicated, the physician and the patient should both be clear that the treatment is of short duration and that some symptoms, including brief recurrence of the insomnia, may be expected when the medication is discontinued.

Persistent insomnia is a fairly common type. It consists of a group of conditions in which the problem is most often difficulty falling asleep, rather than remaining asleep, and involves two sometimes separable but often intertwined problems: somatized tension and anxiety and a conditioned associative response. The patients often have no clear complaint other than insomnia. They may not experience anxiety per se but discharge it through physiological channels. They may complain chiefly of apprehensive feelings or ruminative thoughts that appear to keep them from falling asleep. Sometimes but not always, a patient describes how the condition is exacerbated at times of stress at work or at home and remits during vacations.

Table 21.2-1
Diagnostic Criteria for Insomnia Disorders

A. The predominant complaint is of difficulty in initiating or maintaining sleep, or of nonrestorative sleep (sleep that is apparently adequate in amount, but leaves the person feeling unrested).

B. The disturbance in A occurs at least three times a week for at least one month and is sufficiently severe to result in either a complaint of significant daytime fatigue or the observation by others of some symptom that is attributable to the sleep disturbance (e.g., irritability or impaired daytime functioning).

C. Occurrence not exclusively during the course of sleep-wake schedule disorder or a parasomnia.

Table from DSM-III-R, *Diagnostic and Statistical Manual of Mental Disorders*, ed 3, revised.

Table 21.2-2
Causes of Insomnia

Symptom	Insomnias Secondary to Medical Conditions	Insomnias Secondary to Psychiatric or Environmental Conditions
Difficulty in falling asleep	Any painful or uncomfortable condition CNS lesions Conditions listed below, at times	Anxiety, common Anxiety, chronic neurotic Anxiety, prepsychotic Tension anxiety, muscular Environmental changes Conditioned (habit) insomnia Sleep-wake schedule disorder
Difficulty in remaining asleep	Sleep apnea syndromes Nocturnal myoclonus and restless legs syndrome Dietary factors (probably) Episodic events (parasomnias) Direct drug effects (including alcohol) Drug withdrawal effects (including alcohol) Drug interactions Endocrine or metabolic diseases Infectious, neoplastic, or other diseases Painful or uncomfortable conditions Brain stem or hypothalamic lesions or diseases Aging	Depression, especially primary depression Environmental changes Sleep-wake schedule disorder Dream interruption insomnia

Table by Ernest L. Hartmann, M.D.

Treatment of this condition is among the most difficult problems in sleep disorders. In pure cases in which the conditioned component is prominent, a deconditioning technique may be useful. The patients are asked to use the bed for sleeping and for nothing else; if they are not asleep after five minutes in bed, they are instructed to simply get up and do something else. Sometimes actually changing to another bed or to another room is useful. In some cases in which the somatized tension or muscle tension is prominent, relaxation tapes, transcendental meditation, and practicing the relaxation response and biofeedback are occasionally helpful. Psychotherapy has not been very useful in the treatment of this sort of insomnia.

Insomnia is commonly treated with benzodiazepine hypnotics, chloral hydrate (Noctec), and other sedatives. Hypnotic drugs should be used with care. Various nonspecific measures—so-called sleep hygiene—can be helpful in improving sleep (Table 21.2-3).

Table 21.2-3
Nonspecific Measures to Induce Sleep (Sleep Hygiene)

1. Arise the same time daily.
2. Limit daily in-bed time to usual amount present prior to sleep disturbance.
3. Discontinue CNS-acting drugs (caffeine, nicotine, alcohol, stimulants).
4. Avoid daytime naps (except where sleep chart shows they induce better night sleep).
5. Establish physical fitness by means of graded program of vigorous exercise early in the day.
6. Avoid evening stimulation; substitute radio or relaxed reading for television.
7. Try very hot, 20-minute, body temperature–raising bath soaks near bedtime.
8. Eat at regular times daily; avoid large meals near bedtime.
9. Practice evening relaxation routines, such as progressive muscle relaxation or meditation.
10. Maintain comfortable sleeping conditions.

Table from Q R Regestein: Sleep disorders. In *Clinical Psychiatry for Medical Students,* A Stoudemire, editor, p 578. Lippincott, Philadelphia, 1990, with permission.

Insomnia related to another mental disorder (nonorganic). Insomnia that is clearly related to the psychological and behavioral symptoms of the clinically well-known psychiatric disorders are classified here (Table 21.2-4). This category consists of a heterogeneous group of conditions. In these cases the sleep problem is usually but not always difficulty in falling asleep and is secondary to anxiety that is part of any of the various psychiatric illnesses and conditions listed. Nonorganic insomnia is more common in females than in males. In clear-cut cases in which the anxiety has psychological roots, psychiatric treatment of the cause of the anxiety (e.g., individual psychotherapy, group psychotherapy, and family therapy) often relieves the insomnia.

The insomnia associated with major depression involves relatively normal sleep onset but repeated awakenings during the second half of the night and premature morning awakening, usually with a very uncomfortable mood in the morning. (Morning is the worst time of day for patients with major depression.) Polysomnography shows reduced stages 3 and 4 sleep, often a short rapid eye movement (REM) latency, and a long first REM period.

Bipolar disorder and less severe depression may involve some of the sleep maintenance insomnia described above, but they are also frequently associated with hypersomnia. Depression secondary to another illness often causes sleep maintenance insomnia; the patient awakens during the night but does not display reduced REM latency.

Manic and hypomanic patients appear to be extreme cases of short sleepers. They sometimes appear to have difficulty falling asleep but most often do not complain of any sleep problem. They awaken refreshed after two to four hours of sleep and appear to have a true reduction in need for sleep during the course of the manic episode.

Treatment involves treatment of the underlying mania and depression, rather than of the sleep problem. If possible, patients with this disorder should not be given sleeping medication in addition to their antidepressants.

Table 21.2-4
Diagnostic Criteria for Insomnia Related to Another Mental Disorder (Nonorganic)

Insomnia disorder, as defined by criteria A, B, and C in Table 21.2-1, that is related to another Axis I or Axis II mental disorder, such as major depression, generalized anxiety disorder, adjustment disorder with anxious mood, or obsessive compulsive personality disorder. This category is not used if the insomnia disorder is related to an Axis I disorder involving a known organic factor, such as a psychoactive substance use disorder (e.g., amphetamine dependence).

Insomnia related to a known organic factor. The essential feature of this disorder is insomnia caused by a known physical condition, medication, or drugs (Table 21.2-5).

Physical condition. Almost any medical condition associated with pain and discomfort (e.g., arthritis, angina) can produce insomnia. Some conditions are associated with insomnia even when pain and discomfort are not specifically present. These include neoplasms, vascular lesions, infections, and degenerative and traumatic conditions. Other conditions, especially endocrine and metabolic diseases, frequently involve some sleep disturbance.

Awareness of the possibility of such conditions and obtaining a good medical history usually lead to a correct diagnosis; the treatment, whenever possible, is treatment of the underlying medical condition.

Medication. Insomnia is associated with tolerance to or withdrawal from central nervous system (CNS) depressants. With sustained use of such agents—usually undertaken to treat insomnia arising from a different source—tolerance increases, and the depressants lose their sleep-inducing effects; then patients often increase the dosage. On sudden discontinuation of the drug, severe sleeplessness supervenes, often accompanied by the general features of a drug withdrawal syndrome.

Chronic use (over 30 days) of a hypnotic agent is well tolerated by some patients, but others begin to complain of sleep disturbance, most often multiple brief awakenings during the night. Recordings show disruption of sleep architecture, reduced stages 3 and 4 REM sleep, increases of stage 1 and 2, and fragmentation of sleep throughout the night.

The clinician should be aware of CNS stimulants as a possible cause of insomnia and remember that various medications for weight reduction, beverages containing caffeine, and occasionally adrenergic drugs taken by asthmatics may all produce this sort of insomnia. Alcohol may help induce sleep but frequently results in nocturnal awakening. Alcohol use during the cocktail hour can produce difficulty in falling asleep later in the evening.

Table 21.2-5
Diagnostic Criteria for Insomnia Related to a Known Organic Factor

Insomnia disorder, as defined by criteria A, B, and C in Table 21.2-1, that is related to a known organic factor, such as a physical disorder (e.g., sleep apnea, arthritis), a psychoactive substance use disorder (e.g., amphetamine dependence), or a medication (e.g., prolonged use of decongestants).

The known organic factor should be listed on Axis III (if a physical disorder or use of a medication that does not meet the criteria for a psychoactive substance use disorder) or Axis I (if a psychoactive substance use disorder).

For reasons that are not always clear, a wide variety of drugs occasionally produce sleep problems as a side effect. These drugs include antimetabolites and other cancer chemotherapeutic agents, thyroid preparations, anticonvulsant agents, antidepressant drugs, adrenocorticotropic hormone (ACTH)-like drugs, oral contraceptives, α-methyldopa, and β-blocking drugs.

Another group of agents do not produce sleep disturbance while they are being used but may after withdrawal. Almost any drug with sedating or tranquilizing agents can have this effect, including at times the benzodiazepines, the phenothiazines, the sedating tricyclics, and various street drugs, including marijuana and the opiates.

Alcohol is a CNS depressant and produces the serious problems of other CNS depressants, both during administration—perhaps related to the development of tolerance—and after withdrawal. The insomnia after long-term alcohol consumption is sometimes extremely severe and lasts for weeks or longer. It is inadvisable to give a patient who has just recovered from an addiction another potentially addicting medication; thus, sleeping medication, if possible, should be avoided.

Primary insomnia. Primary insomnia, a new category in DSM-III-R, is an insomnia disorder not due to any of the causes mentioned above (e.g., psychiatric illness, medical illness, and drug use). The term "primary" indicates that the insomnia occurs independently of any known physical or mental condition (Table 21.2-6). Some persons who complain of insomnia may be malingerers; others, who have a hypochondriacal condition, may choose sleep as the problem on which to concentrate. Aging persons complain because they do not sleep as much as they used to, although they actually have normal sleep for their age. So-called variable sleepers have not yet become accustomed to their need for less sleep. They are distinguished from short sleepers who have no complaints, although they may on occasion want to sleep longer. In general, patients with this disorder are preoccupied with getting enough sleep, which may be a lifelong pattern.

Repeated REM sleep interruptions. REM–interruption insomnia, originally called dream-interruption insomnia, is quite rare. It has been related to psychological difficulties and periods of nightmares or other disturbing dreams. In these cases it may represent a conditioned avoidance response in which the patient's CNS senses the beginnings of a dream period (REM period), associates it with an oncoming unpleas-

Table 21.2-6
Diagnostic Criteria for Primary Insomnia

Insomnia disorder, as defined by criteria A, B, and C in Table 21.2-1, that apparently is not maintained by any other mental disorder or any known organic factor, such as a physical disorder, a psychoactive substance use disorder, or a medication.

Table 21.2-7
Diagnostic Criteria for Hypersomnia Disorders

A. The predominant complaint is either (1) or (2):
   (1) excessive daytime sleepiness or sleep attacks not accounted for by an inadequate amount of sleep
   (2) prolonged transition to the fully awake state on awakening (sleep drunkenness)

B. The disturbance in A occurs nearly every day for at least one month, or episodically for longer periods of time, and is sufficiently severe to result in impaired occupational functioning or impairment in usual social activities or relationships with others.

C. Occurrence not exclusively during the course of sleep-wake schedule disorder.

Table from DSM-III-R, *Diagnostic and Statistical Manual of Mental Disorders*, ed 3, revised. Copyright American Psychiatric Association, Washington, DC, 1987, with permission.

ant dream or nightmare, and produces an immediate arousal response.

Atypical polysomnographic features. Atypical polysomnographic features is a condition in which sleep is frequently interrupted and nonrestorative and in which the sleep stage structure is marked by abnormal physiological features.

The diagnosis can be made on the basis of sleep recordings, preferably multiple sleep recordings. Most commonly, the patient describes the quality of sleep as poor, light, or unrestful.

Hypersomnia Disorders

Hypersomnia disorders have two groups of symptoms: complaints about excessive amounts of sleep and complaints about excessive daytime sleepiness (somnolence). In some situations both groups of symptoms are present. The DSM-III-R diagnostic criteria for hypersomnia disorders are presented in Table 21.2-7. These disorders are also known as disorders of excessive somnolence (DOES). The term "somnolence" should be reserved for patients who complain of sleepiness and have a clear demonstrable tendency to fall asleep suddenly in the waking state, who have sleep attacks, and who cannot remain awake; it should not be used for persons who are simply physically tired or weary. The distinction, however, is not always clear. The complaints of hypersomnolence are much less frequent than are the complaints of insomnia, but they are by no means rare if the clinician is alert to them. It has been estimated that there are more than 100,000 narcoleptics in the United States, and narcolepsy is just one well-known condition clearly producing hypersomnolence. If one includes drug-related and alcohol-related conditions, it turns out that hypersomnolence is quite a common symptom.

Table 21.2-8 presents a causal classification of hypersomnolence. As with the symptom of insomnia, there are borderline conditions, situations that are hard to classify, and idiopathic cases.

According to a recent survey, the most common conditions responsible for hypersomnolence severe enough to be evaluated by all-night recordings at a sleep disorders center were sleep apnea and narcolepsy. It is worth keeping in mind that sleep requirements vary. Many people are long sleepers and require 9 to 10 hours of sleep a night; but, like short sleepers, they do not have any problem.

Transient and situational hypersomnia consists of a disruption of the normal sleep-wake pattern marked by excessive difficulty in remaining awake and a tendency to remain in bed for unusually long periods or to return to bed frequently during the day to nap. This pattern is experienced suddenly in response to an identifiable recent life change, conflict, or loss. It is much less common than insomnia. It is seldom marked by definite sleep attacks or unavoidable sleep but, rather, is marked by tiredness or falling asleep sooner than usual and by difficulty in arising in the morning.

Hypersomnia related to another mental disorder (nonorganic). Hypersomnia associated with a mental disorder is found in a variety of conditions, including mood disorders. Excessive daytime sleepiness may be reported in the initial stages of many mild depressive disorders and characteristically in the depressed phase of bipolar disorder. It is sometimes associated for a few weeks with uncomplicated grief. Other

Table 21.2-8
Causes of Hypersomnolence

Symptom	Chiefly Medical	Chiefly Psychiatric or Environmental
Excessive sleep (hypersomnia)	Kleine-Levin syndrome Menstrual-associated somnolence Metabolic or toxic conditions Encephalitic conditions Alcohol and other depressant medications Withdrawal from stimulants	Depression (some) Avoidance reactions
Excessive daytime sleepiness	Narcolepsy and narcolepsylike syndromes Sleep apneas Hypoventilation syndrome Hyperthyroidism and other metabolic and toxic conditions Alcohol and other depressant medications Withdrawal from stimulants Sleep deprivation or insufficient sleep Any condition producing serious insomnia	Depression (some) Avoidance reactions Sleep-wake schedule disorder

Table by Ernest Hartmann, M.D.

mental disorders—such as personality disorders, dissociative disorders, somatoform disorders, psychogenic fugue, and amnesia—can produce hypersomnia (Table 21.2-9).

Hypersomnia related to a known organic factor. The essential feature is hypersomnia caused by a physical condition, medication, or substance abuse. This condition makes up 85 percent of all hypersomnias (Table 21.2-10).

Medications. Somnolence related to tolerance or withdrawal from a CNS stimulant is very common in persons withdrawing from amphetamines, cocaine, caffeine, and related drugs. It may be associated with severe depression, which occasionally reaches suicidal proportions.

The sustained use of CNS depressants, such as alcohol, can cause somnolence. Heavy alcohol use in the evening produces sleepiness and difficulty in arising the next day. This reaction may present a diagnostic problem if the patient does not admit to alcohol abuse.

Respiratory disorders. Breathing disturbances that may occur during sleep include apneas, hypopneas, and oxygen desaturations. These disturbances invariably cause hypersomnia. Two disorders of the respiratory system that can produce hypersomnia are the sleep apnea syndrome and the alveolar hypoventilation syndrome. Both of these syndromes can also cause insomnia; however, hypersomnolence is more common.

SLEEP APNEA SYNDROME. Many persons—elderly persons and obese persons, even those who do not have clinical symptoms—are likely to have apneic periods and, in general, more respiratory problems in sleep than when awake.

Sleep apnea refers to the cessation of air flow at the nose or mouth. By convention an apneic period is one that last 10 seconds or more. Sleep apnea can be of several distinct types. In pure central sleep apnea, both air flow and respiratory effort (abdomen and chest) cease during the apneic episodes and begin again during arousals. In pure obstructive sleep apnea, air flow ceases, but respiratory effort increases during apneic periods, indicating an obstruction in the airway and increasing efforts by the abdominal and thoracic muscles to force air past the obstruction. Again, the episode ceases with an arousal. The mixed types involve elements of both obstructive and central sleep apnea.

Usually, sleep apnea is considered pathological if there are at least five apneic episodes an hour or 30 apneic episodes during the night. In severe cases of obstructive sleep apnea, there may be as many as 300 apneic episodes, each followed by an arousal, so that almost no normal sleep occurs, even though the patients have been in bed and often assume that they have been sleeping for the entire night.

Sleep apnea can be a dangerous condition. It is thought to account for a certain number of unexplained deaths and crib deaths of children and infants. It is probably also responsible for a large number of pulmonary and cardiovascular deaths in adults and in the elderly. Episodes of sleep apnea can produce cardiovascular changes, including arrhythmias, and transient alterations in blood pressure for each apneic episode. Long-standing sleep apnea is associated with an increase in pulmonary blood pressure and eventually an increase in systemic blood pressure as well. These cardiovascular changes in sleep apnea may account for a considerable number of cases in which the diagnosis is essential hypertension.

The prevalence of sleep apnea in the population has not been established, but increasing numbers of cases are discovered as growing awareness of its existence develops. In a recent survey of patients with DOES whose disorder was serious enough for them to be evaluated polygraphically at a sleep disorders center, 42 percent were found to be suffering from one of the variants of sleep apnea.

A tentative diagnosis of sleep apnea can be made even without polysomnographic recordings. The most characteristic picture is that of middle-aged or older men who report tiredness and inability to stay awake in the daytime, sometimes associated with depression, mood changes, and daytime sleep attacks. They may or may not complain of anything unusual during sleep. If a history is obtained from a spouse or bed partner, however, it includes reports of loud, intermittent snoring, at times accompanied by gasping. Sometimes, observers recall apneic periods when patients appeared to be trying to breathe but were unable to do so. Such patients almost certainly have obstructive sleep apnea. With central or mixed apnea, the complaints are of repeated awakenings during the night, with no difficulty in falling asleep, associated with morning headaches and mood changes. At onset there may be no complaints at all by patients, although bed partners or roommates report heavy snoring and very restless sleep. Obese patients with this disorder are said to have *Pickwickian syndrome*.

Patients suspected of having sleep apnea should undergo laboratory recordings. The usual all-night sleep recordings—including electroencephalogram (EEG), electromyogram (EMG), electrocardiogram (ECG), and respiratory tracings of various kinds, are useful. Recording air flow and respiratory effort is usually necessary to make a diagnosis. The severity of apneic episodes is determined by using oximetry to measure oxygen saturation during the night. Twenty-four-hour ECG monitoring is sometimes useful to monitor cardiac changes.

Nasal continuous positive airway pressure (nCPAP) is the treatment of choice for obstructive sleep apnea. Other procedures include weight loss, nasal surgery, tracheostomy, and uvulopalatoplasty. No medications have been shown to be consistently effective in normalizing sleep in apneic patients. When sleep apnea is established or suspected, it is very important for the patient to avoid the use of sedative medication, including alcohol, because it can considerably exacerbate the condition, which may then become life-threatening.

ALVEOLAR HYPOVENTILATION SYNDROME. The alveolar hypoventilation syndrome consists of several conditions

Table 21.2-9
Diagnostic Criteria for Hypersomnia Related to Another Mental Disorder (Nonorganic)

Hypersomnia, as defined by criteria A, B, and C in Table 21.2-7, that is related to another Axis I or II mental disorder, such as major depression or dysthymia.

Table from DSM-III-R, *Diagnostic and Statistical Manual of Mental Disorders,* ed 3, revised. Copyright American Psychiatric Association, Washington, DC, 1987, with permission.

Table 21.2-10
Diagnostic Criteria for Hypersomnia Related to a Known Organic Factor

Hypersomnia disorder, as defined by criteria A, B, and C in Table 21.2-7, that is related to a known organic factor, such as a physical disorder (e.g., sleep apnea), a psychoactive substance use disorder (e.g., cannabis dependence), or a medication (e.g., prolonged use of sedatives or antihypertensives).

The known organic factor should be listed on Axis III (if a physical disorder or use of a medication that does not meet the criteria for a psychoactive substance use disorder) or Axis I (if a psychoactive substance use disorder).

Table from DSM-III-R, *Diagnostic and Statistical Manual of Mental Disorders,* ed 3, revised. Copyright American Psychiatric Association, Washington, DC, 1987, with permission.

marked by impaired ventilation, in which the respiratory abnormality appears or greatly worsens only during sleep and in which significant apneic pauses are not present. The ventilatory dysfunction is characterized by inadequate tidal volume or respiratory rate during sleep. Death may occur during sleep (Ondine's curse).

Narcolepsy. Narcolepsy is a syndrome consisting of excessive daytime sleepiness and abnormal manifestations of REM sleep. The latter includes hypnagogic hallucinations, cataplexy, and sleep paralysis. The appearance of REM sleep within 10 minutes of sleep-onset REM periods (SOREMPs) is also considered evidence of narcolepsy.

Narcolepsy is not as rare as was once thought. It is estimated to occur at a rate of at least 4 cases per 10,000 and shows some familial incidence. Twenty-five percent of hypersomnia related to a known organic factor is caused by narcolepsy. Narcolepsy is neither a type of epilepsy nor a psychogenic disturbance. It is an abnormality of the sleep mechanisms—specifically, REM–inhibiting mechanisms—and it has been demonstrated and studied in dogs and humans.

The most common symptom is sleep attacks: The patient cannot avoid falling asleep. Often associated with this problem (close to 50 percent of long-standing cases) is cataplexy—a sudden loss of muscle tension, such as jaw drop, head drop, weakness of the knees, or paralysis of all skeletal muscles with collapse. The patient often remains awake during brief cataplectic episodes; the long episodes usually merge with sleep and show the EEG of REM sleep. The rare symptoms include hypnagogic hallucinations: vivid perceptual experiences, either auditory or visual, occurring at sleep onset or on awakening. The patient is often momentarily frightened but within a minute or two returns to an entirely normal frame of mind and is quite aware that nothing was actually there.

Another less common symptom is sleep paralysis, most often occurring on awakening in the morning; during the episode the patient is apparently awake and conscious but unable to move a muscle. If this symptom persists for more than a few seconds, as it often does in narcoleptics, it can become extremely uncomfortable. (Note that isolated brief episodes of sleep paralysis occur in many nonnarcoleptic persons.) Narcoleptics report falling asleep quickly at night but often experience broken sleep.

Narcolepsy can occur at any age, but it most frequently begins in adolescence or young adulthood, in most instances before the age of 30. The disorder either progresses very slowly or reaches a plateau that is maintained throughout life. Narcolepsy can be dangerous because it can lead to automobile and industrial accidents.

When the diagnosis is not clear clinically, a nighttime polysomnographic recording reveals a characteristic SOREMP. A daytime multiple sleep latency test (several recorded naps at two-hour intervals) shows very rapid sleep onset and usually one or more SOREMPs. A type of human lymphocyte antigen called HLA-DR2 is found in over 99 percent of narcoleptic patients and only 30 percent of unaffected persons.

Occasionally, a regimen of forced naps at a regular time of day can help, and in some cases it can almost cure the patient without medication. When medication is required, stimulants (e.g., amphetamine and methylphenidate [Ritalin]) are most useful, sometimes combined with antidepressants (e.g., protriptyline [Vivactil]) when cataplexy is prominent. Treatment should be conducted very cautiously, avoiding excessive medication, because the medications used have many associated problems.

Idiopathic CNS hypersomnolence (non–REM [NREM] narcolepsy). Idiopathic CNS hypersomnolence is characterized by recurrent daytime sleepiness, but sleep attacks do not occur, because the sleepiness is not as irresistible as in narcolepsy. Naps are lengthy, not refreshing, and preceded by long periods of drowsiness. If actual sleep is resisted, automatic behaviors occur because of microsleeps. There is a familial type and an isolated type of this condition. This is not a well-understood condition.

Other conditions producing hypersomnolence or disorders of excessive somnolence

Kleine-Levin syndrome. Kleine-Levin syndrome is a relatively rare condition consisting of recurrent periods of exceedingly prolonged sleep (from which the patient may be aroused) with intervening periods of normal sleep and alert waking. During the hypersomnic episodes, wakeful periods are usually marked by withdrawal from social contacts and a return to bed at the first opportunity; however, the patient may also display apathy, irritability, confusion, voracious eating, loss of sexual inhibitions, delusions and hallucinations, frank disorientation, memory impairment, incoherent speech, excitation or depression, and truculence. Unexplained fevers have occurred in a few patients.

Kleine-Levin syndrome is relatively uncommon. Almost 100 cases with features suggesting the diagnosis have been reported. In most cases several periods of hypersomnia, each lasting for one or several weeks, are experienced by the patient in a year. With few exceptions the first attack occurs between the ages of 10 and 21 years. Rare instances of onset in the fourth and fifth decades of life have been reported. The disorder appears almost invariably self-limited, enduring remission occurring spontaneously before age 40 in early-onset cases. In one instance narcolepsy was reported to develop as a sequel to periodic hypersomnia. No residual abnormalities have been noted in other cases.

Menstrual-associated syndrome. Some women experience intermittent, marked hypersomnolence; altered behavioral patterns; and voracious eating at or shortly before the onset of their menses. Nonspecific EEG abnormalities similar to the ones associated with Kleine-Levin syndrome have been documented in several instances. Endocrine factors are probably involved, but specific abnormalities in laboratory endocrine measures have not been reported. Increased cerebrospinal fluid (CSF) turnover of 5-hydroxytryptamine (5HT) was identified in one case.

Somnolence associated with insufficient sleep. Insufficient sleep is defined as an earnest complaint of DOES and associated waking symptoms by a person who persistently fails to obtain sufficient daily sleep needed to support alert wakefulness. The person is voluntarily, but often unwittingly, chronically sleep-deprived.

This diagnosis can usually be made on the basis of a careful history, including a sleep log. Some persons, especially students and shift workers, who want to maintain an active daytime life and perform their nighttime jobs may seriously deprive themselves of sleep, producing somnolence during waking hours.

Sleep drunkenness. Sleep drunkenness is an abnormal form of awakening in which the lack of a clear sensorium in the transition from sleep to full wakefulness is prolonged and exaggerated. A confusion state develops that often leads to individual or social inconvenience and sometimes to criminal acts. Essential to the diagnosis is the absence of sleep deprivation. It is a rare condition, and there may be a familial tendency. Before making this diagnosis, the clinician should examine the patient's sleep carefully and rule out such conditions as apnea, myoclonus, narcolepsy, and an excessive use of drugs and alcohol.

Primary hypersomnia. Primary hypersomnia is diagnosed when no other cause for excessive somnolence can be found. Some persons are long sleepers who, like short sleepers, show a normal variation. The sleep, although long, is normal in architecture and physiology. Sleep efficiency and the sleep-wake schedule are normal. This pattern is without complaints about quality of sleep, daytime sleepiness, or difficulties with awake mood, motivation, and performance.

Long sleep may be a lifetime pattern, and it appears to have a familial incidence. Many persons are variable sleepers and may become long sleepers at certain times in their lives.

Some persons have subjective complaints of feeling sleepy without objective findings. They do not have a tendency to fall asleep more often than normal or have any objective signs. One should try to rule out more clear-cut causes of excessive somnolence (Table 21.2-11).

Sleep-Wake Schedule Disorder

Sleep-wake schedule disorder has only recently been studied in detail. Classification is still tentative, although DSM-III-R has three types listed: (1) frequently changing, (2) advanced or delayed, and (3) disorganized (Table 21.2-12). The common symptom is that patients cannot sleep when they wish to sleep, although they are able to sleep at other times. Correspondingly, they cannot be fully awake when they want to be fully awake, but they are able to be awake at other times. In this sense this sleep disorder does not produce precisely insomnia or somnolence. In practice the initial complaint is often either insomnia or somnolence only, and the above inabilities are elicited only on careful questioning.

Table 21.2-11
Diagnostic Criteria for Primary Hypersomnia

Hypersomnia, as defined by criteria A, B, and C in Table 21.2-7, that is apparently not maintained by any other mental disorder or any known organic factor, such as a physical disorder, a psychoactive substance use disorder, or a medication.

Table 21.2-12
Diagnostic Criteria for Sleep-Wake Schedule Disorder

Mismatch between the normal sleep-wake schedule for a person's environment and his or her circadian sleep-wake pattern, resulting in a complaint of either insomnia (criteria A and B of insomnia disorders in Table 21.2-1) or hypersomnia (criteria A and B of hypersomnia disorders in Table 21.2-7).

Specify type:

Advanced or delayed type: Sleep-wake schedule disorder with onset and offset of sleep considerably advanced or delayed (if sleep-wake schedule is not interfered with by medication or environmental demands) in relation to what the person desires (usually the conventional societal sleep-wake schedule).

Disorganized type: Sleep-wake schedule disorder apparently due to disorganized and variable sleep and waking times, resulting in absence of a daily major sleep period.

Frequently changing type: Sleep-wake schedule disorder apparently due to frequently changing sleep and waking times, such as recurrent changes in work shifts or time zones.

The types of sleep-wake schedule disorder listed below can all be considered misalignments between sleep and wake behaviors.

Frequently changing sleep-wake schedule. The condition of a frequently changing sleep-wake schedule, increasingly prevalent in recent years, occurs in persons who frequently fly east to west, such as flight crews and frequent overseas travelers; in persons who repeatedly and rapidly change their work schedules; and occasionally with self-imposed chaotic sleep schedules. The most frequent symptom found is a period of mixed insomnia and somnolence; however, many other symptoms and somatic problems, including peptic ulcer, may be associated with this pattern after some time. Some adolescents and young adults appear to withstand changes of this kind remarkably well with few symptoms, but older persons and persons with sensitivity to change are clearly affected.

Jet lag syndrome usually disappears spontaneously in two to seven days, depending on the length of the east-to-west trip and individual sensitivity, and no specific treatment is required. Some people find they can prevent the symptoms by altering their mealtimes and sleep times in an appropriate direction before traveling. Others find that what appear to be symptoms of jet lag (tiredness and so on) are actually associated with sleep deprivation and that simply obtaining enough sleep helps.

Symptoms of work shift change are generally worst the first few days after shifting to a new schedule, but in some persons the disrupted sleep-wake patterns persist for a long time. Many persons never adapt completely to unusual shift schedules because they maintain the altered pattern only five days a week, returning to the prevailing pattern of the rest of the population on days off and on vacations.

Shift work schedules are an extremely important area that has not received sufficient study, since a large proportion of the population now work unusual shifts and sometimes in changing shift schedules. People's sensitivities to shifting schedules vary widely, and there are a fair number of persons whose bodies simply do not adapt to shift work and who, therefore, should not be assigned to it. Temperamentally, some people are "owls," who like to stay up at night and sleep during the day, and others are "larks," who rise early and retire early.

A particular problem occurs in the training of physicians, who are often required to work 36 to 48 hours without sleeping. That condition is dangerous to doctors and their patients. It behooves medical educators to develop more shifts for doctors in training.

Advanced or delayed type sleep-wake schedule

Delayed sleep phase syndrome. Delayed sleep phase syndrome is marked by sleep onsets and wake times that are intractably later than desired, actual sleep times at virtually the same daily clock hour, no reported difficulty in maintaining sleep once begun, and inability to advance the sleep phase by enforcing conventional sleep and wake times. The syndrome often presents with the major complaint of difficulty in falling asleep at a desired conventional time and may appear to be similar to a sleep-onset DIMS. Daytime DOES symptoms commence secondary to sleep loss.

Advanced sleep phase syndrome. Advanced sleep phase syndrome is characterized by sleep onsets and wake times that are intractably earlier than desired, actual sleep times at virtually the same daily clock hour, no reported difficulty in maintaining sleep once begun, and inability to delay the sleep phase by enforcing conventional sleep and wake times. Unlike delayed sleep phase syndrome, this condition does not interfere with the work or school day. The major presenting complaint is the inability to stay awake in the evening and to sleep in the morning until desired conventional times.

Disorganized type. Disorganized sleep-wake pattern is defined as irregular and variable sleep and waking behavior that disrupts the regular sleep-wake pattern. This condition is associated with frequent daytime naps at irregular times and excessive bed rest. Sleep at night is not of adequate length, and the condition may present as a DIMS, although the total amount of sleep in 24 hours is normal for the patient's age.

Dyssomnias Not Otherwise Specified

According to DSM-III-R, dyssomnias not otherwise specified are insomnias, hypersomnias, and sleep-wake schedule disturbances that cannot be classified in the above categories.

PARASOMNIAS

Parasomnias are a group of clinical conditions that are not basically disorders of sleeping and waking but are unusual or undesirable phenomena that appear suddenly during sleep or that occur at the threshold between waking and sleeping. Most of the parasomnias occur in stages 3 and 4 and are thus associated with poor recall of the disturbance.

Sleepwalking Disorder

Sleepwalking, also known as somnambulism, consists of a sequence of complex behaviors that are initiated in the first third of the night during deep NREM (stages 3 and 4) sleep and frequently, although not always, progress—without full consciousness or later memory of the episode—to leaving bed and walking about (Table 21.2-13).

Table 21.2-13
Diagnostic Criteria for Sleepwalking Disorder

A. Repeated episodes of arising from bed during sleep and walking about, usually occurring during the first third of the major sleep period.

B. While sleepwalking, the person has a blank, staring face, is relatively unresponsive to the efforts of others to influence the sleepwalking or to communicate with him or her, and can be awakened only with great difficulty.

C. On awakening (either from the sleepwalking episode or the next morning), the person has amnesia for the episode.

D. Within several minutes after awakening from the sleepwalking episode, there is no impairment of mental activity or behavior (although there may initially be a short period of confusion or disorientation).

E. It cannot be established that an organic factor initiated and maintained the disturbance (e.g., epilepsy).

The patient sits up and sometimes performs perseverative motor acts, such as walking, dressing, going to the bathroom, talking, screaming, and even driving. The behavior occasionally terminates in an awakening with several minutes of confusion; more frequently, the person returns to sleep and has no recollection of the sleepwalking event. An artificially induced arousal from stage 4 sleep can sometimes produce the condition. For instance, in children, especially children with a history of sleepwalking, an attack can sometimes be provoked by standing them on their feet and thus producing a partial arousal during stage 4 sleep.

Sleepwalking usually begins between ages 6 and 12 but is still seen in adolescents and young adults. The disorder is more common in males than in females, and about 15 percent of children have an occasional episode. It tends to run in families. A minor neurological abnormality probably underlies this condition; the episodes should not be considered purely psychogenic, although stressful periods are associated with an increase in sleepwalking in affected persons. Extreme tiredness or prior sleep deprivation exacerbates attacks. This is occasionally a dangerous condition because of the possibility of accidental injury.

Sleeptalking (Somniloquy)

Sleeptalking is quite common in children and adults. It has been studied extensively in the sleep laboratory and is found to occur in all stages of sleep. The talking usually involves a few words that are difficult to distinguish. Long episodes of talking involve the sleeper's life and concerns, but sleeptalkers do not relate their dreams during sleep, nor do they often reveal deep secrets. Episodes of sleeptalking sometimes accompany night terrors and somnambulism. Sleeptalking alone requires no treatment.

Sleep Terror Disorder (Pavor Nocturnus)

A sleep terror is an arousal in the first third of the night during deep NREM (stages 3 and 4) sleep. It is almost invariably inaugurated by a piercing scream or cry and accompanied by behavioral manifestations of intense anxiety bordering on panic (Table 21.2-14).

Table 21.2-14
Diagnostic Criteria for Sleep Terror Disorder

A. A predominant disturbance of recurrent episodes of abrupt awakening (lasting 1 to 10 minutes) from sleep, usually occurring during the first third of the major sleep period and beginning with a panicky scream.

B. Intense anxiety and signs of autonomic arousal during each episode, such as tachycardia, rapid breathing, and sweating, but no detailed dream is recalled.

C. Relative unresponsiveness to efforts of others to comfort the person during the episode and, almost invariably, at least several minutes of confusion, disorientation, and perseverative motor movements (e.g., picking at pillow).

D. It cannot be established that an organic factor initiated and maintained the disturbance (e.g., brain tumor).

Typically, patients sit up in bed with a frightened expression, scream loudly, and sometimes awaken immediately with a sense of intense terror. Sometimes patients remain awake in a disoriented state. More often, patients fall asleep, and, as with sleepwalking, they forget the episodes. Frequently, a night terror episode after the original scream develops into a sleepwalking episode. Polygraphic recordings of night terrors are somewhat like those of sleepwalking. In fact, the two conditions appear to be closely related. Night terrors, as isolated episodes, are especially frequent in children. About 1 to 4 percent of children have the disorder, which is more common in males than in females and tends to run in families. It is possible that night terrors represent a minor neurological abnormality, perhaps in the temporal lobe or underlying structures, because, when night terrors begin in adolescence and young adulthood, they turn out to be the first symptom of temporal lobe epilepsy. In a typical case of night terrors, however, no signs of temporal lobe epilepsy or other seizure disorders are seen either clinically or on EEG recordings.

Night terrors are closely related to sleepwalking and are occasionally related to enuresis but are quite different from nightmares. Night terrors are associated with simply awakening in terror. There is generally no dream recall, but occasionally there is recall of a single frightening image.

Specific treatment for night terror or sleepwalking episodes is seldom required. Investigation of stressful family situations may be important, and individual or family therapy is sometimes useful. In the rare cases in which medication is required, diazepam (Valium) in small doses at bedtime improves the condition and sometimes completely eliminates the attacks.

Dream Anxiety Disorder

A dream anxiety disorder or nightmare (incubus) is characterized by a long, frightening dream from which one awakens frightened (Table 21.2-15). As with other dreams, nightmares almost always occur during REM sleep. They usually occur after a long REM period late in the night. Some persons have frequent nightmares as a lifelong condition; others experience them predominantly at times of stress and illness. According to George Vaillant, persons with frequent nightmares as a lifelong condition appear to have a certain vulnerability to schizophrenia, but they are also artistic, creative persons. About 5 percent of the general population report dream anxiety disorders at some time in their lives.

Table 21.2-15
Diagnostic Criteria for Dream Anxiety Disorder

A. Repeated awakenings from the major sleep period or naps with detailed recall of extended and extremely frightening dreams, usually involving threats to survival, security, or self-esteem. The awakenings generally occur during the second half of the sleep period.

B. On awakening from the frightening dreams, the person rapidly becomes oriented and alert (in contrast to the confusion and disorientation seen in sleep terror disorder and some forms of epilepsy).

C. The dream experience or the sleep disturbance resulting from the awakenings causes significant distress.

D. It cannot be established that an organic factor initiated and maintained the disturbance (e.g., certain medications).

Table from DSM-III-R, *Diagnostic and Statistical Manual of Mental Disorders*, ed 3, revised. Copyright American Psychiatric Association, Washington, DC, 1987, with permission.

REM Sleep Behavior Disorder

REM sleep behavior disorder is a chronic and progressive condition found mainly in old men. It is characterized by loss of atonia during REM sleep and subsequent emergence of violent and complex behaviors. In essence, patients with this disorder are acting out their dreams. Serious injury to the patient or the bed partner is a major risk. REM sleep behavior disorder is treated with clonazepam (Klonopin), 0.5 to 2.0 mg a day.

Parasomnias Not Otherwise Specified

Sleep-related epileptic seizures. The relationship of sleep and epilepsy is complex. Almost every form of epilepsy either improves or becomes worse at various times in the sleep cycle. When seizures occur almost exclusively during sleep, the condition is called sleep epilepsy.

Sleep-related bruxism. Bruxism, tooth grinding, occurs throughout the night, most prominently in stage 2 sleep. According to dentists, 5 to 10 percent of the population suffer from bruxism severe enough to produce noticeable damage to teeth. The condition often goes unnoticed by the sleeper, except for an occasional feeling of jaw ache in the morning; however, bed partners and roommates are consistently awakened by the sound.

Sleep-related (nocturnal) myoclonus syndrome. Sleep-related (nocturnal) myoclonus syndrome consists of highly stereotyped abrupt contractions of certain leg muscles during sleep. It is also known as restless legs syndrome because the person feels deep sensations of creeping inside the calves whenever sitting or lying down. These dysesthesias are rarely painful, but they are agonizingly relentless and cause an almost irresistible urge to move the legs, thus interfering with sleep. The diagnosis is made by polygraphic recordings with surface electrodes placed over the tibial muscles and occasionally on other muscles as well.

There is no established treatment. Very careful medical and drug histories are indicated, because sometimes changing a patient's current medication schedule is helpful. Because metabolic and perhaps electrolyte changes may be involved, changes of diet may also make a difference, particularly if foods high in L-tryptophan are added. When pharmacotherapy is required, the benzodiazepine clonazepam is the only drug that has shown some clear positive results; but the effects have been variable, and it cannot be considered a firmly established treatment. Restless legs syndrome may be helped by regular moderate exercise.

Sleep-related head banging (jactatio capitis nocturna). Sleep-related head banging is the term for a sleep behavior consisting chiefly of rhythmic to-and-fro head rocking, less commonly of total body rocking, occurring just before or during sleep. Usually, it is observed in the immediate presleep period and is sustained into light sleep. It uncommonly persists into or occurs in deep NREM sleep.

Familial sleep paralysis. Familial sleep paralysis is characterized by a sudden inability to execute voluntary movements either just at the onset of sleep or on awakening during the night or in the morning.

Sleep-related cluster headaches and chronic paroxysmal hemicrania. Sleep-related cluster headaches are agonizingly severe unilateral headaches that appear often during sleep and are marked by an on-off pattern of attacks. Chronic paroxysmal hemicrania is a similar unilateral headache that occurs every day with more frequent but short-lived onsets that are without a preponderant sleep distribution. Both types of vascular headache are examples of sleep-exacerbated conditions and appear in association with REM sleep periods, paroxysmal hemicrania being virtually REM sleep-locked.

Sleep-related abnormal swallowing syndrome. Abnormal swallowing syndrome is a condition during sleep in which inadequate swallowing results in aspiration of saliva, coughing, and choking. It is intermittently associated with brief arousals or awakenings.

Sleep-related asthma. Asthma is exacerbated by sleep in some persons and may result in significant sleep disturbances.

Sleep-related cardiovascular symptoms. Sleep-related cardiovascular symptoms derive from disorders of cardiac rhythm, myocardial incompetence, coronary artery insufficiency, and blood pressure variability, which may be induced or exacerbated by sleep-altered or sleep-stage-modified cardiovascular physiology.

Sleep-related gastroesophageal reflux. Sleep-related gastroesophageal reflux is a disorder in which the patient awakens from sleep with burning, substernal pain or a feeling of general pain or tightness in the chest or a sour taste in the mouth. Coughing, choking, and vague respiratory discomfort may also occur repeatedly.

Sleep-related hemolysis (paroxysmal nocturnal hemoglobinuria). Paroxysmal nocturnal hemoglobinuria is a rare, acquired, chronic hemolytic anemia in which intravascular hemolysis results in hemoglobinemia and hemoglobinuria. The hemolysis and consequent hemoglobinuria are accelerated during sleep, coloring the morning urine a brownish red. Hemolysis is linked to the sleep period, even if the period is acutely shifted.

References

Aserinsky E, Kleitman N: Regularly occurring periods of eye motility and concomitant phenomena during sleep. Science *118*: 273, 1953.

Association of Sleep Disorders Centers: Diagnostic classification of sleep and arousal disorders. Sleep *2*: 1, 1979.

Coleman R M, Pollak C P, Weitzman E D: Periodic movements in sleep (nocturnal myoclonus): A case series analysis. Ann Neurol *4*: 416, 1980.

Czeisler C A, Allan J S, Strogatz S H, Ronda J M, Sanchez R, Rios C, Frietag W O, Richardson G S, Kronauer R E: Bright light resets the human circadian pacemaker independent of the timing of the sleep-wake cycle. Science *233*: 667, 1986.

Dement W: Dream recall and eye movements during sleep in schizophrenics and normals. J Nerv Ment Dis *122*: 263, 1955.

Guilleminault C, ed.: *Sleeping and Waking Disorders: Indications and Techniques.* Addison-Wesley, Menlo Park, CA, 1982.

Guilleminault C, Lugaresi E, eds.: *Sleep-Wake Disorders: Natural History, Epidemiology, and Long-Term Evolution.* Raven Press, New York, 1983.

Karacan I, ed.: *Psychophysiological Aspects of Sleep.* Noyes Medical, Park Ridge, NJ, 1981.

Karacan I, Williams R L, Moore C A: Sleep disorders. In *Comprehensive Textbook of Psychiatry,* ed 5, H I Kaplan and B J Sadock, editors, p 1105. Williams & Wilkins, Baltimore, 1989.

Moran M G, Thompson T L, Nies A S: Sleep disorders in the elderly. Am J Psychiatry *145*: 1369, 1988.

Reich L, Weiss B L, Coble P, McPartland R, Kupfer D J: Sleep disturbance in schizophrenia: A revisit. Arch Gen Psychiatry *32*: 51, 1975.

Roffwarg H, Erman M: Evaluation and diagnosis of the sleep disorders: Implications for psychiatry and other clinical specialties. In *Annual Review,* vol 4, R E Hales and A J Frances, editors, p 294. American Psychiatric Association, Washington, DC, 1985.

Schroeder J S, Motta J, Guilleminault C: Hemodynamic studies in sleep apnea. In *Sleep Apena Syndromes,* C Guilleminault and W C Dement, editors, p 177. Alan Liss, New York, 1978.

Weitzman E D: Sleep and its disorders. Ann Rev Neurosci *4*: 381, 1981.

Williams R L, Karacan I, Hursch C J: *EEG of Human Sleep: Clinical Applications.* Wiley, New York, 1974.

Williams R L, Karacan I, Moore C, eds.: *Sleep Disorders: Diagnosis and Treatment,* ed 2. Wiley, New York, 1988.

Zales M R, ed.: *Eating, Sleeping, and Sexuality: Treatment of Disorders of Basic Life Functions.* Brunner/Mazel, New York, 1982.

Factitious Disorders

Factitious disorders are characterized by physical or psychological symptoms that are intentionally produced or feigned. The person simulates a physical or mental illness with the sole objective of assuming the role of a patient. For many of these persons, hospitalization itself is a primary objective and often a way of life. There is a compulsive quality to these disorders, but the behaviors are considered voluntary in that they are deliberate and purposeful, even if they cannot be controlled.

EPIDEMIOLOGY

The prevalence of factitious disorders is unknown, although some believe that they are more common than acknowledged. They appear to occur most frequently in men and among hospital and health care workers. One study reported a 9 percent rate of factitious illness among all patients admitted to a hospital; another study found factitious fever in 3 percent of all patients. A data bank of persons who feign illness is being established to alert hospitals about these patients, many of whom travel from place to place, seeking admission under different names or simulating different illnesses.

ETIOLOGY

Such patients frequently have a personal history of early deprivation, or of serious illness or disability from which they recovered and in which they found a series of caretakers (such as doctors, nurses, and hospital workers) loving and caring. In contrast, these patients' families of origin usually contain a rejecting mother or an absent father. The usual history reveals that the patient perceives one or both parents as rejecting figures who are unable to form close relationships. The facsimile of genuine illness, therefore, is used to re-create the desired positive parent-child bond. The disorder is a form of repetition compulsion—repeating the basic conflict of needing and seeking acceptance and love while expecting that they will not be forthcoming. Hence, the patient transforms the physician and staff into rejecting parents.

Patients who seek out painful procedures, such as surgical operations and invasive diagnostic tests, may have a masochistic personality makeup in which pain serves as punishment for past sins, imagined or real. Some patients may attempt to master the past and early trauma of serious medical illness or hospitalization by assuming the role of the patient and reliving the painful and frightening experience over and over again through multiple hospitalizations.

Patients who feign psychiatric illness may have had a relative who was hospitalized with the illness they are simulating. Through identification these patients hope to reunite with the relative in a magical way.

Many of these patients have the poor identity formation and disturbed self-image characteristic of the borderline personality. Some are as-if personalities who have assumed the identify of those around them. If these patients are health professionals, they are often unable to differentiate themselves from the patients with whom they come in contact.

The cooperation or encouragement of persons other than the patient in simulating a factitious illness occurs in a rare variant of the disorder, suggesting another possible causative factor. Although the majority of such patients act alone, friends or relatives participate in fabricating the illness in some instances.

Significant defense mechanisms are repression, identification, identification with the aggressor, regression, and symbolization.

DIAGNOSIS AND CLINICAL FEATURES

Factitious Disorder with Physical Symptoms

Factitious disorder with physical symptoms has been designated by a variety of labels, the best known being Munchausen syndrome, named after the German Baron von Münchausen, who lived in the 18th century and wrote many travel and adventure stories. The disorder has also been called hospital addiction, polysurgical addiction, and professional patient syndrome, among other names.

The essential feature of patients with this disorder is their ability to present physical symptoms so well that they are able to gain admission to and stay in a hospital (Table 22-1). To support their history, these patients may feign symptoms suggestive of a disorder that may involve any organ system. They are familiar with the diagnoses of most disorders that usually require hospital admission or medication and can give excellent histories capable of deceiving even the most experienced clinician. Clinical presentations are myriad and include hematoma, hemoptysis, abdominal pain, fever, hypoglycemia, lupuslike syndromes, nausea, vomiting, dizziness, and seizures. Urine

Table 22-1
Diagnostic Criteria for Factitious Disorder with Physical Symptoms

A. Intentional production or feigning of physical (but not psychological) symptoms

B. A psychological need to assume the sick role, as evidenced by the absence of external incentives for the behavior, such as economic gain, better care, or physical well-being

C. Occurrence not exclusively during the course of another Axis I disorder, such as schizophrenia

is contaminated with blood or feces; anticoagulants are taken to simulate bleeding disorders; insulin is used to produce hypoglycemia; and so on. Such patients often insist on surgery, claiming adhesions from previous surgical procedures. These people may acquire a gridiron abdomen from multiple procedures. Complaints of pain, especially that simulating renal colic, are common, with the patients wanting narcotics. In about half the reported cases, the patients demand treatment with specific medications, usually analgesics. Once in the hospital, they continue to be demanding and difficult. As each test is returned with a negative result, they may accuse the doctor of incompetence, threaten litigation, and become generally abusive. Some may sign out abruptly shortly before they believe they are going to be confronted with their factitious behavior. They then go to another hospital in the same or another city and begin the cycle again. According to the revised third edition of *Diagnostic and Statistical Manual of Mental Disorders* (DSM-III-R), specific predisposing factors are true physical disorders during childhood leading to extensive medical treatment, a grudge against the medical profession, employment as a medical paraprofessional, and an important relationship with a physician in the past. A clinical case example follows:

A 29-year-old female laboratory technician was admitted to the medical service through the emergency room because of bloody urine. The patient said she was being treated for lupus erythematosus by a physician in a different city. She also mentioned that she had had von Willebrand's disease (a rare hereditary blood disorder) as a child. On the third day of her hospitalization, a medical student mentioned to the resident that she had seen the patient several weeks before at a different hospital in the area, where the patient had been admitted for the same problem. A search of the patient's belongings revealed a cache of anticoagulant medication. When confronted with this information, she refused to discuss the matter and hurriedly signed out of the hospital against medical advice.

Discussion. The circumstances (bloody urine, possession of anticoagulants, history of repeated hospitalizations, leaving the hospital when confronted) strongly suggest that this patient's symptoms were intentionally produced and were not genuine symptoms of a physical order.

The differential diagnosis of simulated illness was between factitious disorder and malingering. From what is known of this case, it appeared that there were no external incentives for the behavior and that the woman's goal was only to assume the patient role. Therefore, the diagnosis was factitious disorder with physical symptoms.

If the facts had suggested, for example, that her goal was primarily to get disability payments, that would have indicated malingering (coded in section V, codes for conditions not attributable to a mental disorder that are a focus of attention or treatment), rather than a mental disorder.

Factitious Disorder with Psychological Symptoms

Some patients present with psychiatric symptoms that are judged to be feigned. This determination can be extremely difficult and is often made only after a prolonged investigation (Table 22-2). Feigned symptoms often include depression, hallucinations, dissociative and conversion symptoms, and bizarre behavior. Because there is no response to routine therapeutic measures, patients with this disorder may receive large doses of psychoactive drugs and may undergo electroconvulsive therapy.

Factitious psychological symptoms resemble the phenomenon of pseudomalingering, conceptualized as satisfying the need to maintain an intact self-image, which would be marred by admitting psychological problems that are beyond the person's capacity to master through conscious effort. In that case, deception is a transient ego-supporting device.

Recent findings suggest that factitious psychotic symptoms are more common than was previously suspected. The presence of simulated psychosis as a feature of other disorders, such as mood disorders, indicates a poor overall prognosis.

Psychotic inpatients found to have definite factitious illness with psychological symptoms—that is, exclusively simulated psychotic symptoms—generally have a concurrent diagnosis of borderline personality disorder. In these cases, the outcome appears to be worse than that of manic or schizoaffective disorder.

Patients may present as being depressed, offering as the reason a false history of the recent death of a significant friend or relative. Elements of the history that could suggest factitious bereavement include a violent or bloody death, a death under dramatic circumstances, and the dead person's being a child or young adult. Other patients may present with both recent and remote memory loss or with both auditory and visual hallucinations.

Other symptoms, which also appear in the physical type, include pseudologia fantastica and impostorship. In pseudologia fantastica, limited factual material is mixed with extensive and colorful fantasies. The listener's interest

Table 22-2
Diagnostic Criteria for Factitious Disorder with Psychological Symptoms

A. Intentional production or feigning of psychological (but not physical) symptoms

B. A psychological need to assume the sick role, as evidenced by the absence of external incentives for the behavior, such as economic gain, better care, or physical well-being

C. Occurrence not exclusively during the course of another Axis I disorder, such as schizophrenia pleases the patient and, thus, reinforces the symptom. This distortion of truth is not limited, however, to the history of an illness's symptoms; the patients often give false and conflicting accounts about other areas of their lives (such as claiming the death of a parent, so as to play on the sympathy of others). Impostorship is commonly related to lying in these cases. Many patients assume the identity of a prestigious person. Men, for example, report being war heroes, attributing their surgical scars to wounds received during battle or other dramatic and dangerous exploits. Similarly, they may represent themselves as having ties with an accomplished or renowned figure. A clinical case example follows:

A muscular 24-year-old man presented himself to the admitting office of a state hospital. He told the admitting physician that he had taken thirty 200-mg tablets of chlorpromazine (Thorazine) in the bus on the way over to the hospital. After receiving medical treatment for the "suicide attempt," he was transferred to the inpatient ward.

On mental status examination the patient told a fantastic story about his father, a famous surgeon, who had a woman he was operating on die in surgery and who was then killed by the husband of the woman. The patient then stalked his father's murderer several thousand miles across the United States and, when he found him, was prevented from killing him, at the last moment, by the timely arrival of the man's 94-year-old grandmother. He also related several other intriguing stories involving his $64,000 sports car, which had a 12-cylinder diesel engine, and about his children, two sets of identical triplets. All these stories had a grandiose tinge, and none of them could be confirmed. The patient claimed that he was hearing voices, as on television or in a dream. He answered affirmatively to questions about thought control, thought broadcasting, and other Schneiderian first-rank symptoms; he also claimed depression. He was oriented and alert and had a good range of information except that he kept insisting that it was the Germans (not the Russians) who had invaded Afghanistan. There was no evidence of any associated features of mania or depression, and the patient did not seem elated, depressed, or irritable when he related the stories.

On the ward the patient bullied the other patients and took food and cigarettes from them. He was very reluctant to be discharged, and, whenever the subject of his discharge was brought up, he renewed his complaints about "suicidal thoughts" and "hearing voices." It was the opinion of the ward staff that the patient was not truly psychotic but merely feigned his symptoms whenever the subject of further disposition of his case came up. They thought that he wanted to remain in the hospital primarily so that he could bully the other patients and be a "big man" on the ward.

Discussion. Although this patient would have the ward staff believe that he was psychotic, his story, almost from the start, seemed to conform to no recognizable psychotic syndrome. That his symptoms were not genuine was confirmed by the observation of the ward staff that he seemed to feign his symptoms whenever the subject of discharge was brought up.

Why did he try so hard to act crazy? His motivation was not to achieve some external incentive, such as avoiding the draft, as would be the case in malingering; his goal of remaining a patient was understandable only with knowledge of his individual psychology (the suggestion that he derived satisfaction from being the "big man" on the ward). The diagnosis was, therefore, factitious disorder with psychological symptoms.

Factitious Disorder Not Otherwise Specified

Factitious disorder not otherwise specified is a combination of the characteristics described for each of the single disorders. Many clinicians believe that the pure form of either the physical or the psychological disorder is less common than the combined form (Table 22-3).

COURSE AND PROGNOSIS

Factitious illness typically begins in early adult life, although it may appear during childhood or adolescence. The actual onset of this disorder or of discrete episodes of treatment seeking may follow a real illness, loss, rejection, or abandonment. Usually, there was a hospitalization in childhood or early adolescence for a genuine physical illness of the patient or a close relative. Thereafter, a long pattern of successive hospitalizations unfolds, which is insidious in its beginning. If this is the case, the onset was actually earlier than generally reported. As the disorder progresses, the patient becomes knowledgeable about medicine and hospitals.

Factitious disorder is extremely incapacitating to the patient, often producing severe trauma or untoward reactions related to treatment. As may seem obvious, a course of chronic hospitalization is incompatible with meaningful vocational work and sustained interpersonal relationships. The prognosis in most cases is poor. A few patients occasionally spend time in jail, usually for minor crimes, such as burglary, vagrancy, and disorderly conduct. There may also be intermittent psychiatric hospitalization.

Although no adequate data are available about the ultimate outcome for these patients, it is likely that a few of them die as a result of needless medication, instrumentation, or surgery. In view of these patients' often expert simulation and the risks that they take, it is possible that some die without this disorder's being suspected. Possible features that indicate a favorable prognosis are (1) the presence of a depressive-masochistic character; (2) functioning at a borderline, not a continuously psychotic, level; and (3) the presence of minimal psychopathic antisocial personality attributes.

DIAGNOSIS

The psychiatric examination should emphasize securing information from any available friend, relative, or other informant, because interviews with reliable outside sources often reveal the false nature of the patient's illness. Al-

Table 22-3
Diagnostic Criteria for Factitious Disorder Not Otherwise Specified

Factitious disorders that cannot be classified in any of the previous specific categories (e.g., a disorder with both factitious physical and factitious psychological symptoms)

Table from DSM-III-R, *Diagnostic and Statistical Manual of Mental Disorders*, ed 3, revised. Copyright American Psychiatric Association, Washington, DC, 1987, with permission.

though time-consuming and tedious, verifying all the facts presented by the patient concerning prior hospitalizations and medical care is essential.

Psychiatric evaluation is requested on a consultation basis in about 50 percent of the cases, usually after the presence of a simulated illness is suspected. The psychiatrist is often asked to confirm the diagnosis of factitious disorder. Under these circumstances it is necessary to avoid pointed or accusatory questioning that may provoke truculence, evasion, or flight from the hospital. There may be a danger of provoking frank psychosis if vigorous confrontation is used, because in some instances the feigned illness serves an adaptive function and represents a desperate attempt to ward off further disintegration.

DIFFERENTIAL DIAGNOSIS

Any disorder in which physical symptoms are prominent should be considered in the differential diagnosis, and the possibility of authentic or concomitant physical illness must always be explored.

Somatoform Disorders

A factitious disorder is differentiated from somatization disorder (Briquet's syndrome) by the voluntary production of factitious symptoms, the extreme course of multiple hospitalizations, and the patient's seeming willingness to undergo an extraordinary number of mutilating procedures. Patients with a conversion disorder are not usually conversant with medical terminology and hospital routines, and their symptoms have a direct temporal relation or symbolic reference to specific emotional conflicts.

Hypochondriasis differs from factitious illness in that the hypochondriacal patient does not voluntarily initiate the production of symptoms, and hypochondriasis typically has a later age of onset. As is the case with somatization disorder, patients with hypochondriasis do not usually submit to potentially mutilating procedures.

Personality Disorders

Because of their pathological lying, lack of close relationships with others, hostile and manipulative manner, and associated drug and criminal history, factitious disorder patients are often classified as having an antisocial personality disorder; however, antisocial persons do not usually volunteer for invasive procedures or resort to a way of life marked by chronic hospitalization.

Because of attention seeking and a flair for the dramatic, factitious disorder patients may be classified as having a histrionic (hysterical) personality disorder. But not all factitious disorder patients have this dramatic flair; many are withdrawn and bland.

Consideration of the patient's chaotic life-style, past history of disturbed interpersonal relations, identity crisis, drug abuse, self-damaging acts, and manipulative tactics may lead to the diagnosis of borderline personality disorder.

Schizophrenia

The diagnosis of schizophrenia is often based on patients' admittedly bizarre life-styles, but factitious disorder patients do not usually meet the specified criteria of schizophrenia unless they have the fixed delusion that they are actually ill and act on that belief by seeking chronic hospitalization. This practice seems to be the exception, for few patients with a factitious disorder show evidence of a severe thought disorder or bizarre delusions.

Factitious disorder persons usually do not have the eccentricities of dress, thought, or communication that characterize schizotypal personality disorder patients.

Malingering

Factitious disorder must be distinguished from malingering. Malingerers have an obvious, recognizable environmental goal in producing symptoms. They may seek hospitalization in order to secure financial compensation, evade the police, avoid work, or merely obtain free bed and board for the night; but they always have some apparent end for their behavior. Moreover, they can usually stop producing their symptoms when the symptoms are no longer considered profitable or when the stakes rise too high and the patients risk life and limb.

Malingering is further discussed in Chapter 27, "Conditions Not Attributable to a Mental Disorder."

Drug Abuse

Although patients with a factitious disorder may have a complicating history of drug abuse, they should be considered not merely as drug addicts but, rather, as having coexisting diagnoses.

Ganser's Syndrome

Ganser's syndrome, a controversial condition most typically associated with prison inmates, is characterized by the use of approximate answers. Persons with the syndrome respond to simple questions with astonishingly incorrect answers. For example, when asked about the color of a blue car, the person answers "red." Ganser's syndrome may be a variant of malingering, in that the patients avoid punishment or responsibility for their actions. Ganser's syndrome is classified in DSM-III-R as an atypical dissociative disorder and is further discussed in Chapter 19.

Psychological Tests

Psychological testing may reveal specific underlying pathology in individual patients. Features that are overrepresented in factitious disorder patients include normal or above-average intelligence quotient (I.Q.); absence of a formal thought disorder; poor sense of identity, including confusion over sexual identity; poor sexual adjustment; poor frustration tolerance; strong dependency needs; and narcissism.

TREATMENT

No specific psychiatric therapy has been effective in treating factitious disorders. It is a clinical paradox that patients with the disorder simulate serious illness, seeking and submitting to unnecessary treatment, while denying to themselves and others their true illness. Ultimately, these patients elude meaningful therapy by abruptly leaving the hospital or failing to keep follow-up appointments.

Treatment, thus, is best focused on management, rather than on cure. Perhaps the single most important factor in successful management is a physician's early recognition of the disorder. The physician can then forestall the patient's undergoing a multitude of painful and potentially dangerous diagnostic procedures.

Legal intervention has been obtained in several instances, particularly with children. An obstacle to successful court action is the senselessness of the disorder and the denial of false action by parents, thereby often making conclusive proof unobtainable. In such cases the child welfare services should be notified and arrangements made for the ongoing monitoring of these children's health.

The personal reactions of physicians and staff members are of great significance in treating and establishing a working alliance with the patients, who invariably evoke feelings of futility, bewilderment, betrayal, hostility, and even contempt. In essence, staff members are forced to abandon a basic element of their relationship with patients: acceptance of the truthfullness of the patient's statements.

Physicians should try not to feel resentment when patients humiliate their diagnostic prowess, and they should avoid any unmasking ceremony that sets up these patients as adversaries and precipitates their flight from the hospital.

References

Asher R: Munchausen's syndrome. Lancet *1:* 339, 1951.

Black D: The extended Munchausen syndrome: A family case. Br J Psychiatry *138:* 466, 1981.

Bursten D: On Munchausen's syndrome. Arch Gen Psychiatry *13:* 261, 1965.

Eisendrath S J: Factitious illness: A clarification. Psychosomatics *25:* 100, 1984.

Fairbank J A, McCaffrey R J, Keane T M: Psychometric detection of fabricated symptoms of posttraumatic stress disorder. Am J Psychiatry *142:* 142, 1985.

Hyler S E, Sussman N: Chronic factitious disorder with physical symptoms (the Munchausen syndrome). Psychiatr Clin North Am *4:* 365, 1981.

Ireland P, Sapira J D, Templeton B: Munchausen's syndrome. Am J Med *43:* 579, 1967.

Lipsit D R: The factitious patient who sues (letter to the editor). Am J Psychiatry *143:* 1482, 1986.

London M, Ghaffari K: Munchausen syndrome and drug dependence. Br J Psychiatry *149:* 651, 1986.

Meadow R: Management of Munchausen syndrome by proxy. Arch Dis Child *60:* 385, 1985.

Phillips M R, Ward N G, Ries R K: Factitious mourning: Painless parenthood. Am J Psychiatry *140:* 420, 1983.

Raspe R E: *The Singular Travels, Campaigns, and Adventures of Baron Munchausen.* Cresset Press, London, 1948.

Reich P, Gottfried L A: Factitious disorders in a teaching hospital. Ann Intern Med *99:* 240, 1983.

Sinanan K, Haughton H: Evolution of variants of the Munchausen syndrome. Br J Psychiatry *148:* 465, 1986.

Sparr L, Pankrantz L D: Factitious posttraumatic stress disorder. Am J Psychiatry *140:* 1016, 1983.

Sussman N: Factitious disorders. In *Comprehensive Textbook of Psychiatry,* ed 5, H I Kaplan and B J Sadock, editors, p 1136. Williams & Wilkins, Baltimore, 1989.

Sussman N, Borod J, Cancelmo J, Braun D: Single case study: Munchausen's syndrome: A reconceptualization of the disorder. J Nerv Ment Dis *175:* 692, 1987.

Impulse Control Disorders Not Elsewhere Classified

Six categories of impulse control disorders are listed in the revised third edition of *Diagnostic and Statistical Manual of Mental Disorders* (DSM-III-R): intermittent explosive disorder, kleptomania, pathological gambling, pyromania, trichotillomania, and impulse control disorder not otherwise specified for disorders of impulse control that do not meet the criteria for any of the specific disorders.

Patients with disorders of impulse control share the following features: (1) They fail to resist an impulse, drive, or temptation to perform some action that is harmful to themselves or others. They may or may not consciously resist the impulse and may or may not plan the act. (2) Before committing the act, they feel an increasing sense of tension or arousal. (3) While committing the act, they feel pleasure, gratification, or release. The act is ego-syntonic in that it is consonant with the patients' immediate conscious wishes. Immediately after the act, the patients may or may not feel genuine regret, self-reproach, or guilt.

ETIOLOGY

The causes of impulse disorders are unknown, but it is believed that psychodynamic, biological, and psychosocial factors interact to cause these disorders.

Psychodynamic Factors

An impulse is a disposition to act so as to decrease the heightened tension caused by the welling up of instinctual drives or by the diminished ego defenses against them. An impulse often has the qualities of hastiness, lack of deliberation, and impetuosity. The disorders of impulse control share a similar source of tension—that is, the libidinal and aggressive instinctual drives—and a similar episodic lapse in the ego's defenses against them. Sigmund Freud conceptualized the impulse disorders in terms of the pleasure principle and the reality principle.

Usually, there is a compromise in the drive gratification that includes punishment. For example, the kleptomaniac or pyromaniac is caught; the aggressive person is arrested or beaten up; and the pathological gambler is disgraced or gets into legal trouble because of bad debts. In effect, these patients are free to act on their impulses because their superegos will have their eventual moment in court, often literally. With the explosive breakthrough of murderous impulses, one can often see the aggressor's suicidal impulse. As demonstrated in repeated episodic impulses, the knowledge of past guilt and pain can often reinforce the behavior. In fact, in some cases the need for punishment is antecedent to the impulse.

The psychodynamics of persons designated as having impulse disorders are varied even when the symptoms are similar. Otto Fenichel believed that impulsive actions defend against danger, including depression, and produce a distorted sexual or aggressive satisfaction. Such actions are directed less toward achieving a goal than toward getting rid of tension; that is, the acquisition of pleasure is less significant than is the discontinuance of pain. Several therapists have stressed the patients' fixation at the oral stage of development. The patients attempt to master anxiety, guilt, depression, and other painful affects by means of action, but such actions aimed at obtaining relief seldom succeed even temporarily.

Biological Factors

Many investigators have focused on a possible organic involvement in the impulse disorders, especially regarding those patients presenting with overtly violent behavior. Experiments have shown that specific brain regions, such as the limbic system, are associated with impulsive and violent activity and that others are associated with the inhibition of such behaviors. Certain hormones, especially testosterone, have been associated with violent and aggressive behavior. Some reports have described a relationship between temporal lobe epilepsy and certain impulsive violent behaviors, an association of aggressive behavior with patients with histories of head trauma, increased numbers of emergency room visits, and other potential organic antecedents. It has been suggested that there is a high incidence of mixed cerebral dominance in some violent populations. Recent work has suggested the continuance of impulse disorder symptoms into adulthood in persons who were classified as suffering from childhood minimal brain dysfunction syndrome. Lifelong or acquired mental deficiency, epilepsy, and even reversible brain syndromes have long been implicated in lapses of impulse control. An excess of 5-hydroxyindoleacetic acid (5-HIAA) has been found in the cerebrospinal fluid (CSF) of some impulsive (especially violent or suicidal) patients.

The capacity of temporary organic states produced by alcohol and other drugs to undermine ego defenses is well known. Stealing and setting fires for the fun of it, gambling, and physical fighting are common antisocial acts caused by intoxicants.

In some disorders of impulse control, the ego defenses are overwhelmed without actual nervous system pathology. Fatigue, incessant stimulation, and psychic trauma can lower resistance and temporarily suspend the ego's control.

Psychosocial Factors

Some workers have stressed the disorder's psychosocial aspects, such as early life events, as being important. Improper models for identification and parental figures who themselves have difficulty in controlling impulses have also been implicated. In addition, such parental factors as violence in the home, alcohol abuse, promiscuity, and antisocial tendencies have been thought to be significant.

INTERMITTENT EXPLOSIVE DISORDER

Intermittent explosive disorder is found in persons who have discrete episodes of losing control of aggressive impulses, resulting in serious assault or the destruction of property. The degree of aggressiveness expressed is grossly out of proportion to any stressors that may have helped elicit the episodes. The symptoms, which the patient may describe as spells or attacks, appear within minutes or hours and, regardless of duration, remit spontaneously and quickly. Each episode is usually followed by genuine regret or self-reproach. Signs of generalized impulsivity or aggressiveness are absent between episodes. The diagnosis of intermittent explosive disorder should not be made if the loss of control can be accounted for by schizophrenia, antisocial or borderline personality disorder, conduct disorder, or intoxication with a psychoactive substance (Table 23-1).

The term "epileptoid personality" has been used to convey the seizurelike quality of its characteristic outbursts, which are not typical of the patient, and to convey the suspicion of an organic disease process. A number of associated features suggest the possibility of an epileptoid state: There may be an aura; postictallike changes in the sensorium, including partial or spotty amnesia; or hypersensitivity to photic, aural, or auditory stimuli. Persons with the disorder have a high incidence of hyperactivity, soft neurological signs, nonspecific electroencephalogram (EEG) findings, and accident proneness.

Table 23-1
Diagnostic Criteria for Intermittent Explosive Disorder

A. Several discrete episodes of loss of control of aggressive impulses resulting in serious assaultive acts or destruction of property.

B. The degree of aggressiveness expressed during the episodes is grossly out of proportion to any precipitating psychosocial stressors.

C. There are no signs of generalized impulsiveness or aggressiveness between the episodes.

D. The episodes of loss of control do not occur during the course of a psychotic disorder, organic personality syndrome, antisocial or borderline personality disorder, conduct disorder, or intoxication with a psychoactive substance.

Epidemiology

Intermittent explosive disorder is underreported. It appears to be more common in males than in females. The males are more likely to be found in a correctional institution and the females in a psychiatric facility. In one study about 2 percent of all admissions to a university hospital psychiatric service were diagnosed with intermittent explosive disorder; 80 percent were men.

There is evidence that intermittent explosive disorder is more common in first-degree biological relatives of persons with the disorder than in the general population. A variety of factors, other than a simple genetic explanation, could be responsible.

Etiology

Some investigators suggest that disordered brain physiology, particularly in the limbic system, is involved in most cases of episodic violence. It is generally believed, however, that an unfavorable environment in childhood is the major determinant. Predisposing factors in childhood are thought to include perinatal trauma, infantile seizures, head trauma, encephalitis, minimal brain dysfunction, and hyperactivity. The patients' childhood environments are often filled with alcoholism, beatings, threats to life, and promiscuity.

Those workers who have concentrated on psychogenesis in the etiology of episodic explosiveness have stressed identification with assaultive parental figures or the symbolism of the target of the violence. Early frustration, oppression, and hostility have been noted as predisposing factors. Situations that are directly or symbolically reminiscent of those early deprivations (e.g., persons who directly or indirectly evoke the image of the frustrating parent) become targets for destructive hostility.

Typical patients have been described as physically large but dependent men whose sense of masculine identity is poor. A sense of being useless and impotent or of being unable to change the environment often precedes the episode of physical violence.

Clinical Features

The diagnosis of intermittent explosive disorder should be the result of careful history taking that reveals several episodes of loss of control associated with aggressive outbursts; a single discrete episode does not justify the diagnosis. This latter condition was referred to in the past as a catathymic crisis. The history is typically of a childhood in the midst of alcoholism, violence, and emotional instability. The patients' work histories are poor. The patients report job losses, marital difficulties, and trouble with the law. Most have sought psychiatric help in the past but to no avail. A high level of anxiety, guilt, and depression is usually present after an episode. Neurological examination sometimes reveals soft neurological signs, such as left-right ambivalence and perceptual reversal. EEG findings are frequently normal or show nonspecific changes. Psychological test findings for organicity are frequently normal.

Course and Prognosis

According to DSM-III-R, intermittent explosive disorder may begin at any stage of life but usually begins in the second or third decade. In most cases the disorder decreases in severity with the onset of middle age. Heightened organic impairment, however, can lead to more frequent and severe episodes.

Differential Diagnosis

The diagnosis of intermittent explosive disorder can be made only after other disorders associated with the occasional loss of control of aggressive impulses have been ruled out. These other disorders include psychotic disorders, organic personality syndrome, antisocial or borderline personality disorder, conduct disorder, and intoxication with a psychoactive substance.

One can differentiate intermittent explosive disorder from the antisocial and borderline personality disorders because, in the personality disorders, aggressiveness and impulsivity are part of the patient's character and are present between outbursts. In paranoid or catatonic schizophrenia, there may be violent behavior in response to delusions and hallucinations, and there is gross impairment in reality testing. Hostile manic patients may be impulsively aggressive, but their underlying diagnosis is generally clear from their mental status and clinical presentation. Organic disorders—such as epilepsy, brain tumors, degenerative diseases, and endocrine disorders—must be considered and ruled out, as must acute intoxications with such psychoactive substances as alcohol, barbiturates, hallucinogens, and amphetamines. Conduct disorder is ruled out by a repetitive and resistant pattern of behavior, as opposed to an episodic pattern.

Treatment

A combined pharmacological and psychotherapeutic approach has the best chance of success. Psychotherapy with these patients is difficult, dangerous, and often unrewarding, as the therapist may have difficulties with countertransference and limit setting. Group psychotherapy may be of some help, as may family therapy, particularly when the explosive patient is an adolescent or a young adult.

Anticonvulsants have long been used in treating explosive patients, with mixed results. Phenothiazines and antidepressants have been effective in some cases, but then one must wonder whether schizophrenia or mood disorder is the true diagnosis. When there is a likelihood of subcortical seizurelike activity, these medications can aggravate the situation. Benzodiazepines have been reported to produce a paradoxical reaction of dyscontrol in some cases. Lithium has been reported to be useful in generally lessening aggressive behavior, and carbamepazine (Tegretol) and phenytoin (Dilantin) have also been reported to be helpful. Propranolol (Inderal) has also been effective in some cases.

Operative treatments for intractable violence and aggression have been performed by some neurosurgeons; there is no evidence that such treatment is effective.

KLEPTOMANIA

The essential feature of kleptomania is a recurrent failure to resist impulses to steal objects not needed for personal use or their monetary value. According to DSM-III-R, the objects taken are given away, returned surreptitiously, or kept and hidden (Table 23-2).

Kleptomaniacs usually have the money to pay for the objects they impulsively steal. Like other impulse disorders, kleptomania is characterized by mounting tension before the act, followed by gratification and less tension with or without guilt, remorse, or depression. The stealing is not planned and does not involve others. Although the thefts do not occur when immediate arrest is probable, kleptomaniacs do not always consider the chances of their apprehension. Kleptomaniacs may feel guilt and anxiety after the theft, but they do not feel anger or vengeance. Furthermore, when the object stolen is the goal, the diagnosis is not kleptomania, for in kleptomania the act of stealing itself is the goal.

Epidemiology

Kleptomania is quite rare. According to DSM-III-R, fewer than 5 percent of arrested shoplifters give a history consistent with the disorder, and, in some of these cases, the history may have been fabricated to conform to the stereotype of the disorder. The sex ratio is unknown, but because shoplifting is more common among females than among males, kleptomania-related shoplifting is also probably more common in females than in males.

Etiology

Psychodynamic factors. Some psychoanalytic writers have stressed the expression of the aggressive impulses in kleptomania; others have discerned a libidinal aspect. Those who focus on symbolism see meaning in the act itself, the object

Table 23-2
Diagnostic Criteria for Kleptomania

A. Recurrent failure to resist impulses to steal objects not needed for personal use or their monetary value.

B. Increasing sense of tension immediately before committing the theft.

C. Pleasure or relief at the time of committing the theft.

D. The stealing is not committed to express anger or vengeance.

E. The stealing is not due to conduct disorder or antisocial personality disorder.

Table from DSM-III-R, *Diagnostic and Statistical Manual of Mental Disorders*, ed 3, revised. Copyright American Psychiatric Association, Washington, DC, 1987, with permission.

stolen, and the victim of the theft. Kleptomania is often associated with other psychological disturbances, such as chronic depression, anorexia nervosa, bulimia nervosa, and pyromania (in females). The symptoms of kleptomania tend to appear in times of significant stress—for example, losses, separations, and the ending of important relationships.

Analytic writers have focused on stealing by children and adolescents. Anna Freud pointed out that the first thefts from the mother's purse indicate the degree to which all stealing is rooted in the initial oneness between mother and child. Karl Abraham wrote of the central feeling of being neglected, injured, or unwanted. One theoretician established seven categories of stealing in chronically acting-out children: (1) as a means of restoring the lost mother-child relationship, (2) as an aggressive act, (3) as a defense against fears of being damaged (perhaps a search by females for a penis or a protection against castration anxiety in males), (4) as a means of seeking punishment, (5) as a means of restoring or adding to self-esteem, (6) in connection with and as a reaction to a family secret, and (7) as excitement (*lust Angst*) and a substitute for a sexual act. One or more of these categories can also apply to adult kleptomania.

Biological factors. Brain diseases and mental retardation have been associated with kleptomania, as they have with other disorders of impulse control. Focal neurological signs, cortical atrophy, and enlarged lateral ventricles have been found in some cases. Disturbances in catecholamine metabolism have been postulated.

Clinical Features

In addition to the essential feature of kleptomania noted in DSM-III-R of a recurrent failure to resist impulses to steal unneeded objects, several associated features are often present. Kleptomaniacs may be distressed about the possibility or actuality of their being apprehended and so manifest signs of depression, anxiety, and guilt. They often have serious problems with interpersonal relationships and often, but not invariably, show signs of personality disturbance.

Course and Prognosis

Kleptomania may begin in childhood, although most children and adolescents who steal do not become kleptomaniacs in adulthood. The course of the disease waxes and wanes, but the disease tends to be chronic. The spontaneous recovery rate is unknown. Serious impairment and complications are usually secondary to being caught, particularly when linked to being arrested. Many persons seem never to have consciously considered the possibility of having to face the consequences of their acts, a feature in line with some descriptions of kleptomaniacs as people who feel wronged and, therefore, entitled to steal. Some persons have bouts of being unable to resist the impulse to steal, followed by free periods that last for weeks or months. The prognosis with treatment can be good, but few patients come for help of their own accord. Often, the disease in no way impairs the person's social or work functioning. In quiescent cases new bouts of the illness may be precipitated by loss or disappointment.

Differential Diagnosis

Because most kleptomaniacs are referred for examination in connection with legal proceedings after apprehension, the clinical picture may be clouded by subsequent symptoms of depression and anxiety. The major differentiation is between kleptomania and other forms of stealing. For a diagnosis of kleptomania, the stealing must always follow a failure to resist the impulse and be a solitary act, and the stolen articles must be without immediate usefulness or monetary gain. In ordinary stealing the act is usually planned, and the objects are stolen for their use or financial value. Malingerers may try to simulate the disorder to avoid prosecution. Stealing that occurs in association with conduct disorder, antisocial personality disorder, and manic episodes is clearly related to the pervasive, underlying disorder. Schizophrenic patients may steal in response to hallucinations and delusions, and patients with organic mental disorders may be accused of stealing because of their forgetting to pay for objects.

Treatment

Because true kleptomania is rare, reports of treatment tend to be individual case descriptions or a short series of cases. Insight-oriented psychotherapy and psychoanalysis have been successful but depend on the patient's motivation. Persons who feel guilt and shame are perhaps most helped by insight-oriented psychotherapy, because of their increased motivation to change the behavior.

Behavior therapy—including systematic desensitization, aversive conditioning, and a combination of aversive conditioning and altered social contingencies—have been reported to be successful, even when motivation was lacking. These reports cite follow-up studies of up to two years.

PATHOLOGICAL GAMBLING

As currently defined by DSM-III-R, the essential features of pathological gambling are a chronic and progressive failure to resist impulses to gamble and gambling behavior that compromises, disrupts, or damages personal, family, or vocational pursuits. The gambling preoccupation, urge, and activity increase during periods of stress. Problems that arise as a result of the gambling intensify the gambling behavior. Characteristic problems include extensive indebtedness and consequent default on debts and other financial responsibilities, disrupted family relationships, inattention to work, and financially motivated illegal activities to pay for the gambling (Table 23-3).

Epidemiology

Estimates place the number of pathological gamblers at 2 to 3 percent of the adult U.S. population. The disorder is more common in men than in women. Both the fathers of males and the mothers of females with the disorder are more likely to have the disorder than are the population at large. Women with the disorder are more likely than

Table 23-3
Diagnostic Criteria for Pathological Gambling

Maladaptive gambling behavior, as indicated by at least four of the following:

(1) frequent preoccupation with gambling or with obtaining money to gamble
(2) frequent gambling of larger amounts of money or over a longer period of time than intended
(3) a need to increase the size or frequency of bets to achieve the desired excitement
(4) restlessness or irritability if unable to gamble
(5) repeated loss of money by gambling and returning another day to win back losses ("chasing")
(6) repeated efforts to reduce or stop gambling
(7) frequent gambling when expected to meet social or occupational obligations
(8) sacrifice of some important social, occupational, or recreational activity in order to gamble
(9) continuation of gambling despite inability to pay mounting debts, or despite other significant social, occupational, or legal problems that the person knows to be exacerbated by gambling

Table from DSM-III-R, *Diagnostic and Statistical Manual of Mental Disorders*, ed 3, revised. Copyright American Psychiatric Association, Washington, DC, 1987, with permission.

are those not so affected to be married to alcoholics who are usually absent from the home. Alcohol dependence in general is more common among the parents of pathological gamblers than among the overall population.

Etiology

The following may be predisposing factors for the development of the disorder: loss of a parent by death, separation, divorce, or desertion before the child is 15 years of age; inappropriate parental discipline (absence, inconsistency, or harshness); exposure to and availability of gambling activities for the adolescent; a family emphasis on material and financial symbols; and a lack of family emphasis on saving, planning, and budgeting.

There is an association between pathological gambling and major mood disorder, especially depression. Other associated disorders include panic disorder, obsessive-compulsive disorder, and agoraphobia. Disorders of catecholamine metabolism have been suggested, with the gambler seeking to experience the activating effects of norepinephrine that accompany the tension associated with gambling.

Clinical Features

In addition to the features described above, pathological gamblers most often appear overconfident, somewhat abrasive, very energetic, and free spending when there are obvious signs of personal stress, anxiety, and depression. These persons commonly have the attitude that money is both the cause of and the solution to all their problems. As their gambling increases, they are usually forced to lie to obtain money and to continue gambling while hiding the extent of their gambling behavior. They make no serious attempt to budget or save money. When their borrowing resources are strained, they are likely to engage in antisocial behavior to obtain money for gambling. Their criminal behavior is typically nonviolent, such as forgery, embezzlement, or fraud. The conscious intent is to return or repay the money.

Complications include alienation from family and acquaintances, loss of one's life accomplishments, suicide attempts, and association with fringe and illegal groups. Arrest for nonviolent crimes may lead to imprisonment. A clinical case example follows:

A 48-year-old male attorney was interviewed while he was being detained awaiting trial. He had been arrested for taking funds from his firm, which he stated he had fully intended to return after he had a big win at gambling. He appeared deeply humiliated and remorseful about his behavior, although he had a previous history of near arrests for defrauding his company of funds. His father had provided funds to extricate him from those past financial difficulties but refused to assist him this time. The patient had to resign his job under pressure from his firm. That seemed to distress him greatly, since he had worked diligently and effectively at his job, although he had been spending more and more time away from work to pursue gambling.

The patient had gambled on horse racing for many years. He spent several hours each day studying the results of the previous day's races in the newspaper. Recently, he had been losing heavily and had resorted to illegal borrowing to increase his bets and win back his losses (called "chasing" in gambling circles). He was being pressured by loan sharks for payment. He stated that he embezzled the money to pay off the illegal debts because the threats of the loan sharks were so frightening to him that he could not concentrate or sleep. He admitted to problems with his friends and wife since he had borrowed from them. They were now alienated and giving him little emotional support, since they no longer had any faith in his repeated promises to limit his gambling. His wife had decided to leave him and live with her parents.

During the interview the patient was tense and restless, at times having to stand up and pace. He said he was having a flare-up of a duodenal ulcer. He was somewhat tearful throughout the interview and said that, although he realized his problems stemmed from his gambling, he still had a strong urge to gamble.

Discussion. This man was preoccupied with gambling, which had led to his being arrested for embezzlement and defaulting on debts and to the disruption of his marriage. This was clearly beyond the bounds of recreational gambling and, in conjunction with the man's inability to limit his gambling behavior, indicated a disturbance in impulse control—pathological gambling. The essential features of this disorder parallel the features of dependence on a psychoactive substance. In both cases the person who is addicted has impaired control over the behavior and continues it despite severe adverse consequences.

Although this patient had engaged in antisocial behavior, a diagnosis of antisocial personality disorder was not appropriate because the antisocial behavior was limited to attempts to obtain money to pay off gambling debts and there was neither a childhood history of antisocial behavior nor evidence of impaired occupational and interpersonal functioning other than that associated with his gambling.

A complete diagnostic assessment would also make note of the duodenal ulcer (recorded on Axis III), which was apparently being exacerbated by the stress associated with his out-of-control gambling (recorded on Axis I as psychological factors affecting physical condition).

DSM-III-R Diagnosis:
Axis I: Pathological gambling
Psychological factors affecting physical condition
Axis III: Duodenal ulcer

Course and Prognosis

Pathological gambling usually begins in adolescence in males and late in life for females. Its course waxes and wanes and tends to be chronic. There are three phases in pathological gambling: (1) the winning phase, ending with a big win, equal to approximately a year's salary, which hooks the patient; (2) the progressive-loss stage, in which patients structure their lives around gambling; they move from being excellent gamblers to being stupid ones—taking considerable risks, cashing in securities, owing money, missing work, and losing jobs; and (3) the desperate stage, with the patients gambling in a frenzy with larger amounts of money, not paying debts, becoming involved with loan sharks, writing bad checks, and possibly embezzling. It may take up to 15 years to reach the third phase, but then, within a year or two, the patients are totally deteriorated.

Differential Diagnosis

Social gambling is distinguished from pathological gambling in that the former is associated with gambling with friends, on special occasions, and with predetermined acceptable and tolerable losses.

Gambling that is symptomatic of a manic episode can usually be distinguished from pathological gambling by the history of a marked mood change and loss of judgment preceding the gambling. Maniclike mood changes are common in pathological gambling but always follow winning and are usually followed by depressive episodes because of subsequent losses.

Persons with antisocial personality disorder may have problems with gambling, and DSM-III-R suggests that, in cases in which both disorders are present, both should be diagnosed.

Treatment

Gamblers seldom come forward voluntarily for treatment. Legal difficulties, family pressures, or other psychiatric complaints are what bring the gamblers into treatment. Gamblers Anonymous (GA) was founded in Los Angeles in 1957 and modeled on Alcoholics Anonymous (AA); it is accessible—at least in large cities—and is probably the most effective treatment for gambling. It is a method of inspirational group therapy, which involves public confession, peer pressure, and the presence of reformed gamblers available (as are sponsors in AA) to help members resist the impulse to gamble.

It may be helpful in some cases to hospitalize the patients so as to remove them from their environments and not to work to achieve insight until the patients have been away from gambling for three months. At this point pathological gamblers may become excellent candidates for insight-oriented psychotherapy.

If gambling is associated with depression, mania, anxiety, or other psychiatric disorders, pharmacotherapy with antidepressants, lithium, or antianxiety agents is useful.

PYROMANIA

As defined by DSM-III-R, the essential features of pyromania are deliberate and purposeful fire setting on more than one occasion; tension or affective arousal before setting the fires; and intense pleasure, gratification, or relief when setting the fires or seeing fires burn (Table 23-4). There is also a general fascination with and interest in every aspect of fires. Although the fire setting results from the failure to resist an impulse, there may be considerable advance preparation to start the fire.

According to DSM-III-R, a diagnosis of pyromania should not be made when fires are set to make money, to express a sociopolitical ideology, to conceal criminal activity, to express anger or vengeance, to improve one's living circumstances, or to respond to a delusion or hallucination.

Epidemiology

No information is available on the prevalence of pyromania, only that a small percentage of those adults who set fires can be classified as having pyromania. The disorder is found far more often in males than in females, and people who set fires are more likely to be mildly retarded than are the general population. Some studies have noted an increased incidence of alcohol abuse in people who set fires. Fire setters also tend to have a history of antisocial traits, such as truancy, running away from home, and delinquency. Enuresis has been considered a common finding in the history of fire setters, although controlled studies have failed to confirm these findings. However, studies have suggested an association between cruelty to animals and fire setting.

Table 23-4
Diagnostic Criteria for Pyromania

A. Deliberate and purposeful fire-setting on more than one occasion.

B. Tension or affective arousal before the act.

C. Fascination with, interest in, curosity about, or attraction to fire and its situational context or associated characteristics (e.g., paraphernalia, uses, consequences, exposure to fires).

D. Intense pleasure, gratification, or relief when setting fires, or when witnessing or participating in their aftermath.

E. The fire-setting is not done for monetary gain, as an expression of sociopolitical ideology, to conceal criminal activity, to express anger or vengeance, to improve one's living circumstances, or in response to a delusion or hallucination.

Etiology

Freud gave unconscious meaning to fire, seeing it as a symbol of sexuality. The warmth that is radiated by fire evokes the same sensation that accompanies a state of sexual excitation, and the shape and movements of a flame suggest a phallus in activity. Other therapists have associated pyromania with an abnormal craving for power and social prestige. Some pyromaniacs are volunteer fire fighters who set fires to prove themselves brave, to force other fire fighters into action, or to demonstrate their power to extinguish a blaze. The incendiary act is a way to vent accumulated rage over the frustration caused by a sense of social, physical, or sexual inferiority. A number of studies have noted that the fathers of pyromanic patients were absent from the home. Thus, one explanation of fire setting is that it represents a wish for the absent father to return home as a rescuer, to put out the fire, and to save the child from a difficult existence.

It has been found that female fire setters, in addition to being much fewer in number than male fire setters, do not start fires to put fire fighters into action, as men frequently do. Rather, promiscuity without pleasure and petty stealing, often approaching kleptomania, have been frequently noted to be delinquent trends in female fire setters. Significantly low CSF levels of 5-HIAA and 3-methoxy-4-hydroxyphenylglycol (MHPG) were found in one group of male fire setters.

Clinical Features

In addition to the essential features described above, DSM-III-R lists the following: Persons with the disorder are often regular watchers at fires in their neighborhoods, frequently set off false alarms, and show interest in fire-fighting paraphernalia. They may be indifferent to the consequences of the fire for life or property, or they may gain satisfaction from the resulting destruction. Frequently, they leave obvious clues. Common associated features include alcohol intoxication, psychosexual dysfunctions, lower-than-average intelligence quotient (I.Q.), chronic personal frustrations, and resentment toward authority figures. In some cases, the fire setter becomes sexually aroused by the fire.

Course and Prognosis

Pyromania usually begins in childhood. When the onset is in adolescence or adulthood, the fire setting tends to be more deliberately destructive. The prognosis for treated children is good, and complete remission is a realistic goal. The prognosis for adults is much more guarded, owing to their frequent use of denial and refusal to take responsibility and their possible concurrent alcoholism and lack of insight.

Differential Diagnosis

In discussing the differential diagnosis of pyromania, DSM-III-R notes that there should be little trouble distinguishing between pyromania and the fascination of many young children with matches, lighters, and fire as part of the normal investigation of their environments. Pyromania must also be separated from incendiary acts of sabotage carried out by dissident political extremists or paid torches, which are termed arson in the legal system.

When fire setting occurs in conduct disorders and antisocial personality disorders, it is a deliberate act, rather than the failure to resist an impulse. Fires may be set for profit, sabotage, or retaliation. Patients with schizophrenia may set fires in response to delusions or hallucinations. And patients with organic mental disorders may set fires because of failure to appreciate the consequences of the act.

Treatment

Little has been written about the treatment of pyromania. The treatment of fire setters has been difficult because of their lack of motivation. Incarceration may be necessary as the only method available to prevent a recurrence. Behavior therapy can then be administered in the institution.

Fire setting in children must be treated with the utmost seriousness. Intensive interventions should be undertaken when possible but as therapeutic and preventive measures, rather than as punishment. Because of the recurrent nature of pyromania, any treatment program should include careful supervision of the patient to prevent a repeated episode of fire setting.

TRICHOTILLOMANIA

According to DSM-III-R, the essential feature of trichotillomania is the recurrent failure to resist impulses to pull out one's own hair. The diagnosis should not be made when hair pulling is associated with a preexisting inflammation of the skin or is in response to a delusion or hallucination (Table 23-5).

Epidemiology

According to DSM-III-R, trichotillomania is apparently more common in females than in males. There is no information on the familial pattern, but one study reported

Table 23-5
Diagnostic Criteria for Trichotillomania

A. Recurrent failure to resist impulses to pull out one's own hair, resulting in noticeable hair loss

B. Increasing sense of tension immediately before pulling out the hair

C. Gratification or a sense of relief when pulling out the hair

D. No association with a preexisting inflammation of the skin, and not a response to a delusion or hallucination

Table from DSM-III-R, *Diagnostic and Statistical Manual of Mental Disorders*, ed 3, revised. Copyright American Psychiatric Association, Washington, DC, 1987, with permission.

that 5 of 19 children had family histories of some form of alopecia. Prevalence data are unavailable, but trichotillomania may be more common than is now believed. It has been reported that mainly oldest or only children have the disorder. The disorder usually begins in childhood but can occur at any age. It is often associated with obsessive-compulsive disorder or personality disorder, borderline personality disorder, and depression.

Etiology

DSM-III-R states that, although trichotillomania is regarded as multidetermined, its onset has been linked to stressful situations in more than one-quarter of all cases. Disturbances in mother-child relationships, fear of being left alone, and recent object loss are often cited as critical factors contributing to the condition. Psychoactive substance abuse may encourage the development of this disorder. Depressive dynamics are often cited as predisposing factors. Some see self-stimulation as the primary goal of hair pulling.

Clinical Features

According to DSM-III-R, before engaging in the behavior, trichotillomaniacs experience an increasing sense of tension and achieve a sense of release or gratification from pulling out their hair. All areas of the body may be affected. The most common site is the scalp. Other areas involved are the eyebrows, eyelashes, and beard; less commonly, the trunk, armpits, and pubic area are involved. Such a hair loss is often characterized by short, broken strands appearing together with long, normal hairs in the affected areas. No abnormalities of the skin on the scalp are present.

Trichophagy, mouthing of the hair, may follow the hair plucking. Hair pulling is not reported to be painful, although pruritus and tingling in the involved areas may be present.

Characteristic histopathological changes in the hair follicle, known as trichomalacia, are demonstrated by biopsy and help distinguish trichotillomania from other causes of alopecia. Patients usually deny the behavior and often try to hide the resultant alopecia. Head banging, nail biting, scratching, gnawing, excoriation, and other acts of self-mutilation may be present. A clinical case example follows:

A 25-year-old single woman came to the dermatology clinic of a university hospital with the complaint of increasing baldness of the crown of her scalp. Because no dermatological disease could be identified, she was referred to the psychiatry department. She reported to the psychiatrist that, since childhood, she had pulled out single hairs from the top of her head after twirling the strand of hair on a finger. The behavior was described as usually occurring when she was alone, tired, unoccupied, and ruminating over some unpleasant, stressful interaction. After plucking out the hair, she commonly inspected it and ran it across her lips. This pattern of hair pulling was often repeated for several minutes at a time; she did not find it painful—in fact, it often produced a sense of relief. By wearing her hair up, the patient had always managed to hide the bald area, but this had now become almost impossible. She indicated that seeing a woman with a wig at work had prompted her to seek medical attention; she feared her problem would soon require that she wear a wig.

The patient complained of long-standing problems with her temper, drinking too much, and a series of unsatisfying relationships. She had had no previous psychiatric treatment and had never been hospitalized for any physical reason. She traced the hair pulling to her childhood and associated it with absences of her mother from the home.

Further sessions revealed that the patient had sustained a series of traumatic events in her first decade, foremost among them being the death of her father from a malignancy. In spite of her young age at the time of his death, she had a series of vivid recollections of him, especially memories associated with his illness. Only after many sessions did she mention to the psychiatrist that her father had been a barber.

The patient regarded herself as a clean, orderly person and denied cleaning or compulsive rituals. She smoked a pack of cigarettes a day and had tried speed and marijuana but found that they each made her "paranoid." She had been working long hours in a family business and was considering changing jobs.

Discussion. Stroking and fiddling with the hair are common parts of the repertoire of social primates. In this patient's case, however, hair pulling had escalated to the point of marked alopecia. She was unable to control the impulse to pull out her own hair and achieved a sense of release by engaging in the behavior. This behavior met the requirements for the diagnosis of trichotillomania.

This diagnosis is characterized by specific histopathological changes of the hair follicle, which can be demonstrated by biopsy and distinguished from other causes of alopecia. The disorder usually begins in childhood and is commonly associated with mental retardation and possibly with schizophrenia, although not in this case.

Course and Prognosis

Trichotillomania is generally a disorder of childhood, but onsets have been reported much later in adulthood. Some believe that an adult onset is strongly associated with the presence of a psychotic disorder. According to DSM-III-R, the course of the disorder is not well known. In some cases it has been known to persist for more than two decades. Of people presenting for treatment, approximately one-third report a duration of one year or less. Frequent exacerbations and remissions are common.

Differential Diagnosis

According to DSM-III-R, stroking and playing with one's hair are common and normal activities. In obsessive-compulsive disorder, the behavior has particular meaning and is designed to prevent or produce some future event or situation. Patients with factitious disorder with physical symptoms actively seek medical attention and the patient role and deliberately simulate illness toward those ends. Patients with stereotypy or habit disorder have stereotypical and rhythmic movements, and they usually do not seem distressed by their behavior. This condition may be difficult to distinguish from alopecia areata.

Treatment

There appears to be no consensus on the best treatment modality for trichotillomania. Treatment usually involves psychiatrists and dermatologists in a joint endeavor. Psychopharmacological methods that have been used to treat psychodermatological disorders include hydroxyzine hydrochloride, an anxiolytic with both anxiolytic and antihistamine properties; antidepressants; serotonergic agents; and antipsychotics. Many psychotropic agents have been used to treat dermatological manifestations, and their use testifies to the wide belief that emotional factors underlie their causes. When depression is present, antidepressant agents may lead to dermatological improvement. Obsessive-compulsive components may respond to clomipramine (Anafranil) and fluoxetine (Prozac). Successful behavioral treatments, such as biofeedback, have been reported; however, most of these reports have been about individual cases or small series of studies with relatively short follow-up periods. Further controlled study of these techniques is warranted.

Hypnotherapy has been mentioned as a potentially effective modality in the treatment of dermatological disorders in which psychological factors are clearly involved. There have been repeated demonstrations of the skin's susceptibility to hypnotic suggestion. Most of this work has been research-oriented with little effect yet on clinical management.

Finally, many reports detail treatment outcomes with individual, group, and family psychotherapy approaches to psychophysiological skin disorders. Generally, supportive and insight-oriented psychotherapies are effective.

References

Allcock C C: Pathological gambling. Aust N Z J Psychiatry *20*: 259, 1986.

Custer R L: Profile of the pathological gambler. J Clin Psychiatry *45*: 35, 1984.

Elliott F A: The neurology of explosive rage: The dyscontrol syndrome. Practitioner *217*: 51, 1976.

Fenichel O: *The Psychoanalytic Theory of Neurosis*. Norton, New York, 1945.

Friman P C, Finney J W, Christophersen E R: Behavioral treatment of trichotillomania: An evaluative review. Behav Res Ther *15*: 249, 1984.

Frosch J: The relation between acting out and disorders of impulse control. Psychiatry *40*: 295, 1977.

Geller J L, Bertsch G: Fire-setting behavior in the histories of a state hospital population. Am J Psychiatry *142*: 465, 1985.

Greenberg H R, Sarner C A: Trichotillomania: Symptom and syndrome. Arch Gen Psychiatry *12*: 482, 1965.

Hood T W, Siegfried J, Wieser H G: The role of stereotactic amygdalotomy in the treatment of temporal lobe epilepsy associated with behavioral disorders. Proc Am Soc Stereotact Func Neurosurg Appl Neurophysiol *46*: 19, 1983.

Jenkins S C, Maruta T: Therapeutic use of propranolol for intermittent explosive disorder. Mayo Clin Proc *62*: 204, 1987.

Kammerer T, Singer L, Michel D: The incendiaries: Criminological, clinical and psychological study of 72 cases. Ann Med Psychol *1*: 687, 1967.

Khan K, Martin I C: Kleptomania as a presenting feature of cortical atrophy. Acta Psychiatr Scand *56*: 168, 1977.

Linden R D, Pope H G, Jonas J M: Pathological gambling and major affective disorder: Preliminary findings. J Clin Psychiatry *47*: 201, 1986

Monopolis S, Lion J R: Problems in the diagnosis of intermittent explosive disorder. Am J Psychiatry *140*: 1200, 1983.

Popkin M K: Impulse control disorders not elsewhere classified. In *Comprehensive Textbook of Psychiatry*, ed 5, H I Kaplan and B J Sadock, editors, p 1145. Williams & Wilkins, Baltimore, 1989.

Raichlin S, Halpern A L, Portnow S L: The volitional rule, personality disorders and the insanity defense. Psychiatr Ann *14*: 139, 1984.

Sticher M, Abramovits W, Newcomer V D: Trichotillomania in adults. Cutis *26*: 97, 1980.

Vikkunen M, Nuutila A, Goodwin F K, Linnoila M: Cerebrospinal fluid monoamine metabolite levels in male arsonists. Arch Gen Psychiatry *44*: 241, 1987.

Yassa R, Ananth J: Hair loss in the course of lithium treatment: A report of two cases. Can J Psychiatry *28*: 132, 1983.

24

Adjustment Disorder

An adjustment disorder is a short-term maladaptive reaction to a clearly identifiable life stress that occurs within three months of the stressor's onset. It is a pathological response to what a layperson may call a personal misfortune or to what a psychiatrist calls a psychosocial stressor. It is not an exacerbation of an already existing psychiatric disorder. The adjustment disorder is expected to remit soon after the stressor ceases or, if the stressor persists, a new level of adaptation is achieved. The response is maladaptive because of an impairment in social or occupational functioning or because of symptoms or behaviors that are beyond the normal, usual, or expected response to such a stressor.

EPIDEMIOLOGY

Adjustment disorders are quite common. In one study 5 percent of hospital admissions over a three-year period were diagnosed as adjustment disorders. They are most frequently diagnosed in adolescents but may occur at any age.

Single women are overly represented as being most at risk. Among adolescents of either sex, common types of precipitating stresses are school problems, parental rejection, parental divorce, and drug use. Among adults, common precipitating stresses are marital problems, divorce, moving to a new environment, and financial problems.

ETIOLOGY

Adjustment disorders are precipitated by one or more stressors. The severity of the stressor or stressors is not always predictive of the severity of the adjustment disorder; the stressor severity is a complex function of degree, quantity, duration, reversibility, environment, and personal context. For example, the loss of a parent is quite different for a 10-year-old and a 40-year-old. Personality organization and cultural or group norms and values contribute to the disproportionate responses to stressors.

Stressors may be single, such as a divorce or the loss of a job, or multiple, such as the death of an important person occurring at the same time as one's own physical illness and loss of a job. Stressors may be recurrent, such as seasonal business difficulties, or continuous, such as chronic illness or living in poverty. A discordant intrafamilial relationship may produce adjustment disorders that affect the whole family system. Or the disorder may be limited to the patient, as when the patient is the victim of a crime or has a physical illness. Sometimes adjustment disorders occur in a group or community setting, and the stressor affects several people, as in a natural disaster or in racial, social, or religious persecution. Specific developmental stages—such as beginning school, leaving home, getting married, becoming a parent, failing to achieve occupational goals, having one's last child leave home, and retiring—are often associated with adjustment disorders.

Several psychoanalytic researchers have discussed the capacity of the same stress to produce a range of responses in different normal human beings. Throughout his life Sigmund Freud remained interested in why the stresses of ordinary life produced illness in some and not in others, why an illness took a particular form, and why some experiences and not others predisposed a person to psychopathology. He gave considerable weight to constitutional factors and viewed them as interacting with a person's life experiences to produce fixation.

Psychoanalytic research has emphasized the role of the mother and the rearing environment in a person's later capacity to respond to stress. Particularly important was D. W. Winnicott's concept of the good-enough mother, a person who adapts to the infant's needs and provides enough support to enable the growing child to tolerate the frustrations in life.

A concurrent personality disorder or organic impairment may make a person more vulnerable to an adjustment disorder. Vulnerability is also associated with the loss of a parent during infancy.

COURSE AND PROGNOSIS

The overall prognosis of adjustment disorders is generally favorable with appropriate treatment. Most patients return to their previous level of functioning within three months. Adolescents usually require a longer time to recover than do adults. Some persons (particularly adolescents) who receive a diagnosis of an adjustment disorder later have mood disorders or psychoactive substance use disorders.

DIAGNOSIS AND TYPES

Although by definition an adjustment disorder follows a stressor, the symptoms do not necessarily begin immediately, nor do they always subside as soon as the stressor ceases. If the stressor continues, the disorder may be lifelong. The disorder may occur at any age. Its symptoms vary considerably, with depressive, anxious, and mixed features the most common in adults.

Physical symptoms are most common in children and the elderly but may occur in any age group. Manifestations may also include assaultive behavior and reckless driving, excessive drinking, defaulting on legal responsibilities, and withdrawal. See Table 24-1 for the revised third edition of *Diagnostic and Statistical Manual of Mental Disorders* (DSM-III-R) diagnostic criteria for adjustment disorder.

The clinical presentations of adjustment disorder can vary widely. DSM-III-R lists nine types.

Adjustment Disorder with Depressed Mood

In adjustment disorder with depressed mood, the predominant manifestations are depressed mood, tearfulness, and hopelessness. This type must be distinguished from a major depressive disorder or uncomplicated bereavement. A clinical case example follows:

A 39-year-old divorced woman was referred for psychiatric evaluation after a brief hospitalization for complaints of intermittent numbness in her arms and the right side of her face. Extensive neurological and neurosurgical evaluation revealed stenosis of the outlets of several cervical vertebrae; intermittently compromised nerve roots were thought to account for the physical symptoms. The patient, an artist who composed large structures from various work materials, was advised by her physicians to stop for the next several months all lifting, reaching, raising her arms, and other strenuous activities requisite to her work. She had felt despondent for more than two months, with episodes of tearfulness, anxiety, and increased irritability. She continued to supervise her assistants but was increasingly disinterested in work. She had no sleep or appetite change, but her libido was diminished. She was still able to enjoy music. The patient had no prior personal or familial history of mood disorder.

The identified stressors in her case were the physical illness and the directive to minimize for an indefinite interval the use of her arms. The net result was to preclude the patient's ability to continue her artistic endeavors, which were crucial to her sense of self. In response, she experienced the emergence of a depressive constellation with less than a full vegetative set of symptoms. The clinician diagnosed adjustment disorder with depressed mood. Intervention was directed to (1) clarification with the neurosurgeon of the likely course and necessary treatment of the outlet problem and (2) several sessions with the patient to explore her responses to and perceptions of the changes in her life imposed by the neurological problem.

Table 24-1
Diagnostic Criteria for Adjustment Disorder

A. A reaction to an identifiable psychosocial stressor (or multiple stressors) that occurs within three months of onset of the stressor(s).

B. The maladaptive nature of the reaction is indicated by either of the following:
   (1) impairment in occupational (including school) functioning or in usual social activities or relationships with others
   (2) symptoms that are in excess of a normal and expectable reaction to the stressor(s)

C. The disturbance is not merely one instance of a pattern of overreaction to stress or an exacerbation of one of the mental disorders previously described.

D. The maladaptive reaction has persisted for no longer than six months.

E. The disturbance does not meet the criteria for any specific mental disorder and does not represent uncomplicated bereavement.

Table from DSM-III-R, *Diagnostic and Statistical Manual of Mental Disorders*, ed 3, revised. Copyright American Psychiatric Association, Washington, DC, 1987, with permission.

Adjustment Disorder with Anxious Mood

Symptoms of anxiety—such as palpitations, jitteriness, and agitation—are present in adjustment disorder with anxious mood, which must be differentiated from anxiety disorders.

Adjustment Disorder with Mixed Emotional Features

In adjustment disorder with mixed emotional features, the predominant symptoms are combinations of anxiety and depression or other emotions. This type of adjustment disorder must be differentiated from depressive and anxiety disorders.

Adjustment Disorder with Disturbance of Conduct

In adjustment disorder with disturbance of conduct, the predominant manifestation involves conduct in which the rights of others are violated or age-appropriate societal norms and rules are disregarded. Examples of behavior in this category are truancy, vandalism, reckless driving, and fighting. This category must be differentiated from conduct disorders and antisocial personality disorder. A clinical case example follows:

An 18-year-old male high school senior was referred by his father for evaluation after an episode in which he was arrested for the second time for shoplifting merchandise worth several hundred dollars from a major department store. In the final three months of his senior year, the patient, a B student without prior legal problems, had displayed a sudden shift in behavior. He was twice ticketed for driving violations, failed several school tests, and became increasingly irritable and uncommunicative. He was given to angry outbursts. Initially uncooperative with his psychiatrist, the patient was more forthcoming when his attorney told him that his participation would be viewed favorably by the court. After several sessions with the therapist, the patient admitted that he was overwhelmed by the prospect of moving in the fall from his home to a college 2,000 miles away. This stressor had prompted his abuse of alcohol, marijuana, and frequent risk-taking behaviors, each of which was ineptly executed. With several months of weekly psychotherapy, the patient completed his first year of college without incident.

Adjustment Disorder with Mixed Disturbance of Emotions and Conduct

This combination of the above two disturbances sometimes occurs. Clinicians are encouraged to try to make one or the other diagnosis in the interest of parsimony.

Adjustment Disorder with Withdrawal

Adjustment disorder with withdrawal is the category for cases of social withdrawal without significant depressed or anxious mood. A clinical case example follows:

A 33-year-old man, the father of an 8-year-old girl, was referred for psychiatric evaluation by his primary care physician. The patient's wife had left him and filed for divorce. The patient perceived her decision as based on his physical and interpersonal inadequacies and responded by restricting his activities to work and visits with his daughter. He would occasionally spend time with his sister but consciously withdrew from all other social intercourse for several months. At the time of his initial evaluation, the patient seemed not to recognize the temporal relationship of his wife's actions to his ensuing withdrawal from nearly all social engagements. With short-term therapy the patient cautiously resumed a more regular pattern of activities.

Adjustment Disorder with Physical Complaints

Adjustment disorder with physical complaints is manifested in such symptoms as headache, backache, fatigue, and other bodily complaints.

Adjustment Disorder with Work (or Academic) Inhibition

Adjustment disorder with work or academic inhibition is applicable to an inhibition of work or academic functioning in a person who has previously functioned adequately in this area. Frequently, there is anxiety and depression, and so the condition must be differentiated from depressive disorder and phobic disorder.

Adjustment Disorder Not Otherwise Specified

Adjustment disorder not otherwise specified is a residual category for atypical maladaptive reactions to stress. Examples include inappropriate responses to the diagnosis of physical illness, such as massive denial and severe noncompliance with treatment.

DIFFERENTIAL DIAGNOSIS

Adjustment disorders must be differentiated from conditions not attributable to a mental disorder. According to DSM-III-R, patients with conditions not attributable to a mental disorder do not have impairment in social or occupational functioning or symptoms beyond the normal and expectable reaction to the stressor. Because no absolute criteria aid in distinguishing between an adjustment disorder and a condition not attributable to a mental disorder, clinical judgment is necessary.

Although uncomplicated bereavement often includes temporarily impaired social and occupational functioning, the person's dysfunctioning remains within the expectable bounds of a reaction to the loss of a loved one and, thus, is not considered an adjustment disorder.

Other disorders from which an adjustment disorder must be differentiated include major depressive disorder, chronic depressive disorder, brief reactive psychosis, generalized anxiety disorder, somatization disorder, various substance use disorders, conduct disorders, specific academic or work inhibition, identity disorder, and posttraumatic stress disorder. These diagnoses should be given precedence in all cases that meet their criteria, even in the presence of a stressor or group of stressors that served as a precipitant. However, some patients meet the criteria for both an adjustment disorder and a personality disorder.

Posttraumatic stress disorder. In posttraumatic stress disorder (PTSD), the symptoms develop after a psychologically traumatizing event or events outside the range of normal human experience. That is, the stressors producing such a syndrome are expected to do so in the average human being. They may be experienced alone, as in rape or assault, or in groups, as in military combat. A variety of mass catastrophes—such as floods, airplane crashes, atomic bombings, and death camps—have also been identified as stressors. The stressor always contains a psychological component and frequently a concomitant physical component that directly damages the nervous system. Clinicians believe that the disorder is more severe and lasts longer when the stressor is of human origin, as in rape, than when it is not, as in floods.

TREATMENT

Psychotherapy

Because a stressor can be clearly delineated in adjustment disorders, it is often believed that psychotherapy is not indicated and that the disorder will remit spontaneously. But such thinking fails to consider that many persons exposed to the same stressor do not develop similar symptoms and that the response is pathological. Psychotherapy can help the person adapt to the stressor if it is not reversible or time-limited and can serve as a preventive intervention if the stressor does remit.

Psychotherapy remains the treatment of choice for adjustment disorders. Group therapy can be particularly useful for patients who have undergone similar stresses—for example, a group of retired persons or renal dialysis patients. Individual psychotherapy offers the opportunity to explore the meaning of the stressor to the patient, so that earlier traumas can be worked through. After successful therapy, patients sometimes emerge from an adjustment disorder stronger than in the premorbid period, although no pathology was evident during that period.

The psychiatrist treating an adjustment disorder must be particularly mindful of problems of secondary gain. The illness role may be rewarding to some normal persons who have had little experience with its capacity to free one from responsibility. Thus, the therapist's attention, empathy, and understanding—which are necessary for success— can become rewarding in their own right, thereby reinforcing the symptoms. Such considerations must be weighed before intensive psychotherapy is begun. When a secondary gain has already been established, therapy is more difficult.

Patients whose adjustment disorder includes a conduct disturbance may have difficulties with the law, authorities, or school. It is not advisable for psychiatrists to attempt to rescue such patients from the consequences of their actions. Too often, such kindness only reinforces socially unacceptable means of tension reduction and hinders the acquisition of insight and subsequent emotional growth. In those cases family therapy can help.

Crisis intervention. A brief type of therapy, crisis intervention is aimed at helping the person with an adjustment disorder resolve the situation quickly by supportive techniques, suggestion, reassurance, environmental modification, and even hospitalization, if necessary. The frequency and the length of visits for crisis support vary according to the patient's needs; daily sessions may be necessary, sometimes two or three times each day. Flexibility is essential in this approach.

Pharmacotherapy

The judicious use of medications can help patients with an adjustment disorder, but they should be prescribed for brief periods. A patient may respond to an antianxiety agent or to an antidepressant, depending on the type of adjustment disorder. Patients with severe anxiety bordering on panic or decompensation can benefit from small doses of antipsychotic medications. Patients in withdrawn or inhibited states may benefit from a short course of psychostimulant medication. Few, if any, adjustment disorders can be adequately treated by medication alone. In most cases psychotherapy should be added to the treatment regimen.

References

Andreasen N, Hoenk P: The predictive value of adjustment disorders: A follow-up study. Am J Psychiatry *139*: 584, 1982.

Andreasen N, Wasek P: Adjustment disorders in adolescents and adults. Arch Gen Psychiatry *37*: 1166, 1980.

Elliot C, Eisdorfer C: *Stress and Human Health*. Springer, New York, 1982.

Fard F, Hudgens R W, Welner A: Undiagnosed psychiatric illness in adolescents: A prospective and seven-year follow-up. Arch Gen Psychiatry *35*: 279, 1979.

Garmezy N, Rutter M: *Stress, Coping, and Development in Children*. McGraw-Hill, New York, 1983.

Holmes J, Raphe R: The social readjustment rating scale. J Psychosom Res *11*: 213, 1967.

Horowitz M J: *Stress Response Syndromes*. Jason Aronson, New York, 1976.

Klerman G L, Weissman M M: Affective response to stressful life events. Presented at the NIMH Conference on Prevention of Stress-Related Psychiatric Disorders. University of California, San Francisco, December 1981.

Lewis D: *Vulnerability to Delinquency*. Spectrum, New York, 1981.

Popkin M K: Adjustment disorder. In *Comprehensive Textbook of Psychiatry*, ed 5, H I Kaplan and B J Sadock, editors, p 1141. Williams & Wilkins, Baltimore, 1989.

Popkin M K, Mackenzie T B, Callies A L: Psychiatric consultation to geriatric medically ill inpatients in a university hospital. Arch Gen Psychiatry *41*: 703, 1984.

Regier D A, Meyers J K, Kramer M, Robins L N, Blazer D G, Hough R L, Eaton W W, Locke B Z: The NIMH epidemiologic catchment area program. Arch Gen Psychiatry *41*: 934, 1984.

Winnicott D W: Translational objects and transitional phenomena. Int J Psychoanal *34*: 89, 1953.

Behavioral Medicine and Psychological Factors Affecting Physical Condition (Psychosomatic Disorders)

25.1 / Overview

Psychosomatic medicine emphasizes the unity of and interaction between mind and body. In general, the conviction is that psychological factors are important in the development of all disease. Whether that role is in the initiation, progression, aggravation, or exacerbation of a disease or in the predisposition or reaction to a disease has been open to debate and varies from disorder to disorder. The term "psychosomatic" has now become part of the larger concept of behavioral medicine, which was defined in 1978 by the National Academy of Science as "the interdisciplinary field concerned with the development and integration of behavioral and biomedical science knowledge and techniques relevant to health and illness and the application of this knowledge and these techniques to prevention, diagnosis, and rehabilitation." Behavioral medicine, thus, is a more inclusive term for the field of psychosomatic medicine.

In the third and revised third editions of *Diagnostic and Statistical Manual of Mental Disorders* (DSM-III and DSM-III-R), the term "psychosomatic" was replaced with the diagnostic category "psychological factors affecting physical condition."

DSM-III-R CLASSIFICATION

The DSM-III-R diagnostic criteria for psychological factors affecting physical condition (i.e., psychosomatic disorders) specify that psychologically meaningful environmental stimuli are temporally related to the initiation or the exacerbation of a specific physical condition or disorder. The physical condition involves either demonstrable organic pathology, such as rheumatoid arthritis, or a known pathophysiological process, such as migraine headache. Many believe that the DSM-III-R deletion of the nosological term "psychophysiological" (a synonym for psychosomatic) de-emphasized the interaction of mind (psyche) and body (soma), a concept that emphasizes a unitary causative or holistic approach to medicine, since all disease is influenced by psychological factors. The DSM-III-R diagnostic criteria for psychological factors affecting physical condition are presented in Table 25.1-1.

Specifically excluded from this DSM-III-R classification are (1) classical psychiatric disorders presenting with physical symptoms as part of the disorder (e.g., conversion disorder in which a physical symptom is produced by psychological conflict); (2) somatization disorders, in which the physical symptoms are not based on organic pathology; (3) hypochondriasis, in which patients have an exaggerated concern with their health; (4) physical complaints that are frequently associated with psychological disorders (e.g., dysthymia, which usually has such somatic accompaniments as muscle weakness, asthenia, fatigue, and exhaustion); and (5) physical complaints associated with habit disorders (e.g., coughing associated with nicotine dependence). Table 25.1-2 lists some psychosomatic disorders.

HISTORY

The history of psychosomatic medicine parallels the history of humankind. A historical summary of the psyche–soma interaction is presented in Table 25.1-3.

Exactly where and how do the psyche and the soma interact? Representatives from both psychiatry and medicine have agreed for more than 100 years that, in some disorders, emotional and somatic activities overlap. These disorders were first called psychosomatic by Johann Christian Heinroth in 1818, when he used the term in regard to insomnia. The word was later popularized by Maximilian Jacobi, a German psychiatrist. The number of disorders identified as pyschosomatic grew to include ulcerative colitis, peptic ulcer, migraine headache, bronchial asthma, and rheumatoid arthritis.

ETIOLOGY

Investigators have questioned the validity of the concept of psychophysiological medicine. Some have suggested that it is too vague a term; others say that it is too

Table 25.1-1
Diagnostic Criteria for Psychological Factors Affecting Physical Condition

A. Psychologically meaningful environmental stimuli are temporally related to the initiation or exacerbation of a specific physical condition or disorder (recorded on Axis III).
B. The physical condition involves either demonstrable organic pathology (e.g., rheumatoid arthritis) or a known pathophysiological process (e.g., migraine headache).
C. The condition does not meet the criteria for a somatoform disorder.

Table from DSM-III-R, *Diagnostic and Statistical Manual of Mental Disorders*, ed 3, revised. Copyright American Psychiatric Association, Washington, DC, 1987, with permission.

narrow. But most agree that chronic, severe, and perceived stress plays some causative role in the development of many somatic diseases. The character of the stress, the general underlying psychophysiological factors, the genetic and organ vulnerability, the nature of the emotional conflicts (whether they are specific or nonspecific), and the way they interact to produce disease—all are still controversial and are summarized in Figure 25.1-1.

General Stress

A stressful traumatic life event or situation generates challenges to which the organism cannot adequately respond. Particular life traumas are listed in Holmes and Rahe's social readjustment rating scale of 43 life events associated with varying amounts of disruption and stress in the average person's life—for example, death of a spouse, 100 units; divorce, 73 units; marital separation, 65 units; and death of a close family member, 63 units (Table

Table 25.1-2
Some Psychosomatic Disorders

Acne	Migraine headache
Allergic reactions	Mucous colitis
Angina pectoris	Nausea
Angioneurotic edema	Neurodermatitis
Arrhythmia	Obesity
Asthmatic wheezing	Painful menstruation
Bronchial asthma	Pruritus ani
Cardiospasm	Pylorospasm
Chronic pain syndromes	Regional enteritis
Coronary heart disease	Rheumatoid arthritis
Diabetes mellitus	Sacroiliac pain
Duodenal ulcer	Skin diseases, such as psoriasis
Essential hypertension	Spastic colitis
Gastric ulcer	Tachycardia
Headache	Tension headache
Herpes	Tuberculosis
Hyperinsulinism	Ulcerative colitis
Hyperthyroidism	Urticaria
Hypoglycemia	Vomiting
Immune diseases	Warts
Irritable colon	

Table 25.1-3
History of Psychosomatic Medicine

Date	Historical Period	Psychosomatic Orientation
10,000 B.C.	Primitive society	Disease is caused by spiritual powers and must be fought by spiritual means; the evil spirit that enters and affects the total being must be liberated through exorcism, trepanation, and so on.
2500–500 B.C.	Babylonian-Assyrian civilization	Medicine is dominated by religion, and suggestion is the major tool of treatment. Sigerist: "Mesopotamian medicine was psychosomatic in all its aspects."
400 B.C.	Greek civilization	Socrates: "As it is not proper to cure the eyes without the head, nor the head without the body, so neither is it proper to cure the body without the soul." Hippocrates: "In order to cure the human body, it is necessary to have a knowledge of the whole of things."
100 B.C.–A.D. 400	Late Greek–early Roman civilization	Galen's humoral theory postulates that disease is caused by disturbances in the fluids of the body. Medicine adopts a holistic approach to disease.
500–1450	Middle Ages	Mysticism and religion dominate medicine. Sinning is the cause of mental and somatic illness.
1500–1700	Renaissance	Renewed interest in the natural sciences and their application to medicine; advances in anatomy (Vesalius), autopsy (Morgagni), microscopy (Leeuwenhoek). Psychic influences on the soma are rejected as unscientific; the study of the mind is relegated to religion and philosophy.
1800–1900	19th century	Modern laboratory-based medicine of Pasteur and Virchow. Virchow: "Disease has its origin in disease of the cell." Psychosomatic approach discarded, as all disease must be associated with structural cell change. The disease is treated, not the patient.
1900–present	20th century	Freud's psychoanalytic formulations emphasize the role of psychic determinism in somatic conversion reactions (Dora case). Early concepts are limited to major hysterical conversions; subsequently, Alexander differentiates conversion reactions from psychosomatic disorders and studies psychological factors in a series of diseases.

25.1-4). The scale was constructed by querying hundreds of persons with different backgrounds in order to rank the relative degree of adjustment necessitated by changing life events. It was found that an accumulation of 200 or more life-change units in a single year increased the incidence of psychosomatic disorders.

More recent studies have demonstrated that persons who face these general stresses optimistically, rather than pessimistically, are less apt to develop a psychosomatic disorder and, if they do, are apt to recover from it more easily.

Specific versus Nonspecific Stress

In addition to general stresses, such as a divorce and the death of a spouse, various investigators have suggested that specific personalities and conflicts are associated with different psychosomatic diseases. But others believe that nonspecific generalized anxiety from any type of conflict may lead to a number of different diseases.

Specific psychic stress may be defined as a specific personality or unconscious conflict causing a homeostatic disequilibrium that contributes to the development of a psychosomatic disorder.

Specific personality types were first identified in regard to the coronary personality (a hard-driving, aggressive person who tends to develop myocardial occlusion). For example, the so-called type A personality (similar to the coronary personality) was singled out as one that predisposes to coronary disease. Type A and type B personalities were first defined by Meyer Friedman and Ray Rosenman. See Section 5.1, "Psychological Testing of Intelligence and Personality," for further discussion of type A and type B personalities.

That specific unconscious conflicts are associated with various psychosomatic disorders (e.g., unconscious dependency conflict predisposes to peptic ulcer) was hypothesized by Franz Alexander. Alexander's multifactorial theories were later confirmed by Arthur Mirsky and Herbert Weiner. Both the specific personality type and the unconscious conflicts fall under the rubric of specific causative theories of psychosomatic diseases. See Table 25.1-5 for some psychological correlates of psychophysiological disorders.

Alternatively, chronic nonspecific stress, usually with the intervening variable of anxiety, has been suggested as having physiological correlates that, combined with genetic organ vulnerability, predispose certain persons to a psychosomatic disorder. Alexithymic persons are unable to read their own emotions. They have poor fantasy lives and are not conscious of their emotional conflicts; psychosomatic disorders may serve as an outlet for their accumulated tension. Nonspecific theories of etiology are supported by experimental evidence that, under chronic stress, animals have psychosomatic disorders (such as peptic ulcer); clearly, animals do not have the specific personality or unconscious psychological conflicts that people do.

Physiological Variables

The mediator between stress and disease may be hormonal, as can be seen in the general adaptation syndrome (GAS) of Hans Selye, in which hydrocortisone is the mediator. Or there may be changes in the functioning of the anterior pituitary-hypothalamic-adrenal axis with autonomic effects, adrenal enlargement, and lymphoid shrinkage. Alexander pointed to the autonomic nervous system—for example, the parasympathetic nervous system in peptic ulcer and the sympathetic nervous system in hy-

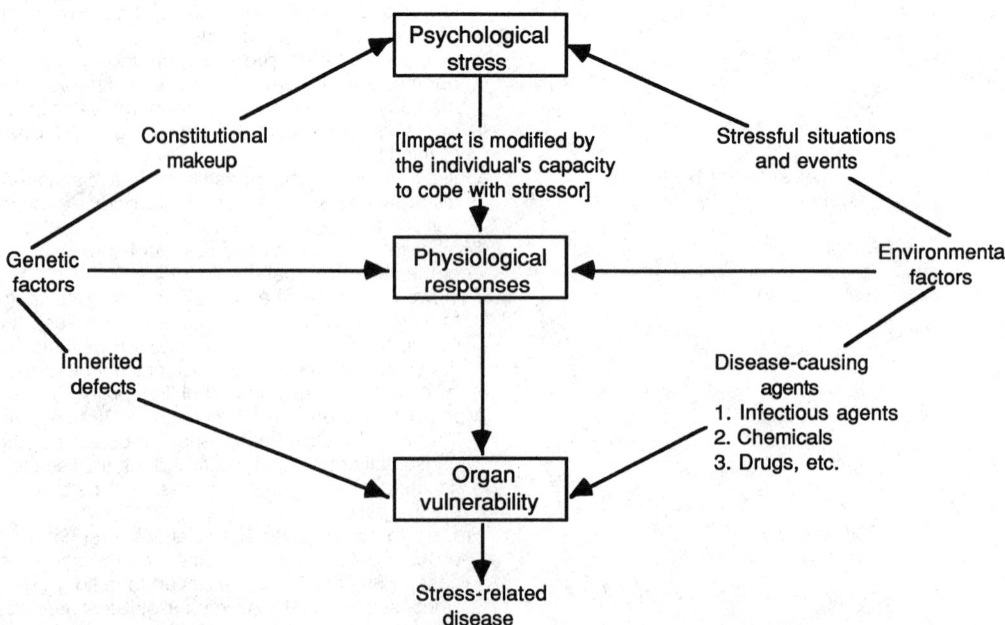

Figure 25.1-1. Scheme for the etiology of stress-related diseases. (Figure from J J Braunstein, R P Toister, eds.: *Medical Applications of the Behavioral Sciences*, p 168. Year Book Medical Publishers, Chicago, 1981, with permission.)

Table 25.1-4
Social Readjustment Rating Scale

Life Event	Mean Value
1. Death of spouse	100
2. Divorce	73
3. Marital separation from mate	65
4. Detention in jail or other institution	63
5. Death of a close family member	63
6. Major personal injury or illness	53
7. Marriage	50
8. Being fired at work	47
9. Marital reconciliation with mate	45
10. Retirement from work	45
11. Major change in the health or behavior of a family member	44
12. Pregnancy	40
13. Sexual difficulties	39
14. Gaining a new family member (through birth, adoption, oldster moving in, etc.)	39
15. Major business readjustment (merger, reorganization, bankruptcy, etc.)	39
16. Major change in financial state (a lot worse off or a lot better off than usual)	38
17. Death of a close friend	37
18. Changing to a different line of work	36
19. Major change in the number of arguments with spouse (either a lot more or a lot less than usual regarding child rearing, personal habits, etc.)	35
20. Taking on a mortgage greater than $10,000 (purchasing a home, business, etc.)*	31
21. Foreclosure on a mortgage or loan	30
22. Major change in responsibilities at work (promotion, demotion, lateral transfer)	29
23. Son or daughter leaving home (marriage, attending college, etc.)	29
24. In-law troubles	29
25. Outstanding personal achievement	28
26. Wife beginning or ceasing work outside the home	26
27. Beginning or ceasing formal schooling	26
28. Major change in living conditions (building a new home, remodeling, deterioration of home or neighborhood)	25
29. Revision of personal habits (dress, manners, associations, etc.)	24
30. Troubles with the boss	23
31. Major change in working hours or conditions	20
32. Change in residence	20
33. Changing to a new school	20
34. Major change in usual type or amount of recreation	19
35. Major change in church activities (a lot more or a lot less than usual)	19
36. Major change in social activities (clubs, dancing, movies, visiting, etc.)	18
37. Taking on a mortgage or loan less than $10,000 (purchasing a car, TV, freezer, etc.)	17
38. Major change in sleeping habits (a lot more or a lot less sleep or change in part of day when asleep)	16
39. Major change in number of family get-togethers (a lot more or a lot less than usual)	15
40. Major change in eating habits (a lot more or a lot less food intake or very different meal hours or surroundings)	15
41. Vacation	15
42. Christmas	12
43. Minor violations of the law (traffic tickets, jaywalking, disturbing the peace, etc.)	11

Table from T Holmes: Life situations, emotions, and disease. Psychosom Med *19*: 747, 1978, with permission.
*This figure no longer has any relevance in the light of inflation; what is significant is the total amount of debt from all sources-Ed.

pertension—as the mechanism linking chronic stress and psychosomatic disorders.

Another intervening variable may be the action of the monocytes of the immune system. The monocytes are shaped in such a way that they interact with brain neuropeptides, which serve as messengers between brain cells. Thus, immunity may influence psychic state and mood. Herbert Benson, in explaining the effects of relaxation therapy on certain psychosomatic disorders, postulated that relaxation decreases the activity of cerebral adrenergic catecholamines and that these substances affect the limbic system—the Papez circuit—which is important in psychosomatic and psychiatric etiology. A summary of the major theories of psychosomatic medicine is presented in Table 25.1-6.

RELATIONSHIP OF PSYCHOSOMATIC MEDICINE TO BEHAVIORAL MEDICINE

Both psychosomatic medicine and behavioral medicine are concerned with the interaction of the psyche and the soma. Traditionally, psychoanalysis and psychotherapy have been used to treat psychosomatic disorders. Within the past two decades, a great deal of interest has developed in the use of behavior modification (learning theory) techniques to treat these disorders. Among the therapeutic techniques emphasized in behavior modification are muscle relaxation therapy, biofeedback, hypnosis, controlled breathing, yoga, and massage. The goal of both the behavioral techniques and the usual psychotherapeutic modalities is to improve the psychosomatic equation.

Table 25.1-5
Some Hypothesized Psychological Correlates of Psychophysiological Disorders

Disorder	Psychogenic Causes, Personality Characteristics, and Coping Aims
Peptic ulcer	Feels deprived of dependency needs; is resentful; represses anger; cannot vent hostility or actively seek dependency security; characterizes self-sufficient and responsible "go-getter" types who are compensating for dependency desires; has strong regressive wish to be nurtured and fed; revengeful feelings are repressed and kept unconscious
Colitis	Was intimidated in childhood into dependency and conformity; feels conflict over resentment and desire to please; anger restrained for fear of retaliation; is fretful, brooding, and depressive or passive, sweet and bland; seeks to camouflage hostility by symbolic gesture of giving
Essential hypertension	Was forced in childhood to restrain resentments; inhibited rage; is threatened by and guilt-ridden over hostile impulses which may erupt; is a controlled, conforming, and "mature" personality; is hard-driving and conscientious; is guarded and tense; needs to control and direct anger into acceptable channels; desires to gain approval from authority
Migraine	Is unable to fulfill excessive self-demands; feels intense resentment and envy toward intellectually or financially more successful competitors; has meticulous, scrupulous, perfectionistic, and ambitious personality; failure to attain perfectionist ambitions results in self-punishment
Bronchial asthma	Feels separation anxiety; was given inconsistent maternal affection; has fear and guilt that hostile impulses will be expressed toward loved persons; is demanding, sickly, and "cranky" or clinging and dependent; symptom expresses suppressed cry for help and protection
Neurodermatitis	Has overprotective but ungiving parents; has craving for affection; has conflict regarding hostility and dependence; demonstrates guilt and self-punishment for inadequacies; is a superficially friendly and oversensitive personality with depressive features and low self-image; symptoms are atonement for inadequacy and guilt by self-excoriation; displays oblique expression of hostility and exhibitionism in need for attention and soothing

Table from T Millon, R Millon: Psychophysiologic disorders. In *Medical Behavioral Science*, T Millon, editor, p 211. Saunders, Philadelphia, 1975, with permission. Also from J J Braunstein, R B Toister: *Medical Application of the Behavioral Sciences*. Year Book Medical Publishers, Chicago, 1981, with permission.

Table 25.1-6
Modern Concepts of Psychosomatic Medicine

Psychological Factors

Freud (1900) Somatic involvement occurs in conversion hysteria, which is psychogenic in origin—for example, paralysis of an extremity. Conversion hysteria always has a primary psychic cause and meaning; that is, it represents the symbolic substitutive expression of an unconscious conflict. It involves organs innervated only by the voluntary neuromuscular or sensory-motor nervous system. Psychic energy that is dammed up is discharged through physiological outlets.

↓

Jelliffe; Groddeck (1910) Clearly organic disorders, such as fever and hemorrhage, were held to have primary psychic meanings; that is, they were interpreted as conversion symptoms, which therefore represented the expression of unconscious fantasies.

↓

Ferenczi (1910) Concept of conversion hysteria applied to organs innervated by the autonomic nervous system; for example, the bleeding of ulcerative colitis may be described as representing a specific psychic fantasy. (Diseases such as colitis are known today as psychosomatic diseases that occur only in organs innervated by the autonomic nervous system.) Ferenczi's interpretation of psychosomatic symptoms as being conversion reactions was the first application of this concept to diseases such as colitis.

↓

Garma (1950) Peptic ulcer has a specific psychological meaning. This is an extension of Freud's conversion concept to an organ innervated by the autonomic nervous system. Similar to Ferenczi's concept.

Cannon (1927) Cannon demonstrated the physiological concomitants of certain emotions and the important role of the autonomic nervous system in producing those reactions and causing fight or flight: fight (adrenergic sympathetic) mobilization or flight (cholinergic parasympathetic) inhibition.

Dunbar (1936) Suggested a specific conscious personality picture and behavioral pattern associated with specific psychosomatic diseases. Similar to type A coronary type, Friedman and Rosenman (1959)

Somatic Factors

Deutsch (1939) and Greenacre (1949) believed trauma during birth, infancy, and childhood predisposed to adult psychosomatic disease.

Genetic and other somatic studies.

Selye (1945) demonstrated that under stress a general adaptation syndrome develops. Adrenal cortical hormones are responsible for this physiological reaction. Rogers (1979) studied role of immune response. Dimsdale (1987).

→

Alexander (1934) (1968) Psychosomatic symptoms occur only in organs innervated by the autonomic nervous system and have no specific psychic meaning (as does conversion hysteria) but are end results or prolonged physiological states, which are the physiological accompaniments of certain specific unconscious repressed conflicts. There are also certain constitutional organic genetic (multifactorial) predisposing factors in addition to the psychic factors involved in which repressed psychic energy is discharged physiologically. Alexander's observations supported by Weiner's and Mirsky's (1957) study of pepsinogen hypersecretion. Schmale (1970): "giving up-given up" concept and Engel (1968) using Selye's conservation-withdrawal versus Cannon's fight or flight.

Cultural Factors

Ruesch (1958) emphasized the importance of the interaction between persons; that is, communication between the patient and the environment. Disturbance in communication results in psychosomatic illness, which is a regressive type of communication.

Horney (1939), Halliday (1948), and Mead (1947) emphasized the influence of the culture in the development of psychosomatic illness. They felt that influence acted on the mother, who, in turn, affected the child in her relationship with the child—for example, nursing, child rearing, anxiety transmission.

Laboratory Factors

Wolff (1943) attempted to correlate life stress (conscious) to physiological protective human response, using objective laboratory tests. Physiological change, if prolonged, may lead to structural change. Margolin (1951) recommended the correlation of unconscious conflicts and physiological response.

↓

Mahl (1949) questioned whether any specific conflict is associated with ulcer. He believed that what is important is chronic anxiety, which may result from any conflict, conscious or unconscious, external or internal. Mahl was influenced by animal experimenters, such as Gantt (1944) and Masserman (1943). Later workers were Brady (1958) (executive monkey), Ader (1971), and Seligman's learned helplessness (1972).

↓

Engel (1968) and Lipowski (1970) thought a total approach to psychosomatic disease was necessary. External (ecological, infectious, cultural, environmental), internal (emotional), genetic, somatic, and constitutional factors and past and present history are important and should be studied by multiple investigators, each working in the frame of reference in which he or she is trained (e.g., Engel's biopsychosocial model). DSM-III-R (1987) de-emphasizes psychosomatic holism in nosology.

References

Alexander F: *Psychosomatic Medicine*. Norton, New York, 1950.
Alexander F, French T M, Pollack G H: *Psychosomatic Specificity: Experimental Study and Results*. University of Chicago Press, Chicago, 1968.
Angell M: Disease as a reflection of the psyche. N Engl J Med *312*: 1570, 1985.
Barefoot J C, Dahlstrom W G, William R B Jr: Hostility CHD incidence, and total mortality: 25-year follow-up study of 255 physicians. Psychosom Med *45*: 59, 1983.
Engel G H, Reichsman F, Siegel H L: A study of an infant with a gastric fistula. Psychosom Med *18*: 374, 1956.
Feifel H, Strack S, Nagy V T: Degree of life-threat and differential use of coping modes. J Psychol Res *31*: 91, 1987.
Schwartz G E, Weiss S M: Behavioral medicine revisited: An amended definition. J Behav Med *1*: 249, 1978.
Wolf S, Wolff H G: *Human Gastric Function*. Oxford University Press, New York, 1943.

25.2 / Specific Disorders

CARDIOVASCULAR SYSTEM

Coronary Artery Disease

Coronary artery disease causes myocardial ischemia and is characterized by episodic precordial pain, discomfort, or pressure; it is usually precipitated by exertion or stress.

Personality type. Flanders Dunbar first described coronary disease patients as aggressive-compulsive personalities with a tendency to work long hours and to seize authority. Later, Meyer Friedman and Ray Rosenman defined type A and type B personalities, type A being more strongly associated with the development of coronary heart disease. Type A personalities are action-oriented persons who struggle to achieve poorly defined goals by means of competitive hostility. Type B personalities are the opposite—they are relaxed and less aggressive and tend to strive less vigorously to achieve their goals. Type A personalities have increased amounts of low-density lipoprotein, serum cholesterol, triglycerides, and 17-hydroxycorticosteroids, and they tend to have coronary heart disease.

Treatment. When coronary occlusion occurs, various medications for the patient's cardiac status are used. To alleviate the psychic distress associated with the disease, clinicians use psychotropics (e.g., diazepam [Valium]). Pain is treated with analgesics (e.g., morphine). Medical treatment should be supportive and reassuring, with some psychological emphasis on the alleviation of psychic stress, compulsivity, and tension.

Essential Hypertension

Hypertension is a disease characterized by a blood pressure of 160/95 mm Hg or greater. Twenty percent of the adult population in the United States are hypertensive.

Personality type. Hypertensive persons appear to be outwardly congenial, compliant, and compulsive; although their anger is not expressed openly, they have much inhibited rage. There appears to be a familial genetic predisposition to hypertension; that is, when chronic stress occurs in a genetically predisposed compulsive personality who has repressed and suppressed rage, hypertension may result.

Treatment. Supportive psychotherapy and behavioral techniques (e.g., biofeedback, meditation, and relaxation therapy) have been reported to be useful in treating hypertension. Medically, there must be good compliance in taking antihypertensive medication.

Congestive Heart Failure

Congestive heart failure is a disorder in which the heart fails to move the blood forward normally, causing congestion in the lungs and systemic circulation and decreased tissue blood flow with diminished cardiac output. Psychological factors, such as nonspecific emotional stress and conflict, are frequently significant in the initiation or exacerbation of this disorder. Thus, supportive psychotherapy is important in its treatment.

Vasomotor (Vasodepressor) Syncope

Vasomotor (vasodepressor) syncope is characterized by a sudden loss of consciousness (fainting) caused by a vasovagal attack. Sympathetic autonomic activity is inhibited, and parasympathetic vagal nerve activity is augmented, resulting in decreased cardiac output, decreased vascular peripheral resistance, vasodilation, and bradycardia. According to Franz Alexander, acute fear or fright inhibits the impulse to fight or flee, thereby pooling the blood in the lower extremities, from the vasodilation of the blood vessels in the extremities. This reaction results in decreased ventricular filling, a drop in the blood supply to the brain, and consequent brain hypoxia and loss of consciousness.

Treatment. Because patients with vasomotor syncope normally put themselves or fall into a prone position, the decreased cardiac output is corrected. Raising their legs also helps correct the physiological imbalance. Psychotherapy should be used to determine the cause of the fright or trauma associated with syncope. When syncope is related to orthostatic hypotension, the patient should be advised to shift slowly from a sitting to a standing position.

Cardiac Arrhythmias

Life-threatening arrhythmias, such as ventricular tachycardia and ventricular fibrillation, sometimes occur in conjunction with an emotional upset. Also associated with emotional trauma are sinus tachycardia, ST- and T-wave changes, ventricular ectopy, increased plasma catecholamines, and free fatty-acid concentrations. Emotional stress is nonspecific, as is the personality description associated with these disorders.

Treatment. Psychotherapy and β-blocking drugs, such as propranolol (Inderal), help protect against these emotionally induced arrhythmias.

Psychogenic Cardiac Nondisease

A different problem is presented by patients who are free of heart disease and yet complain of symptoms suggestive of cardiac disease. They often exhibit a morbid concern about their hearts and exaggerated fears of heart disease. Their fear may range from an anxious concern, manifested by a severe phobia or hypochondriasis, to a delusional conviction about cardiac disease. Many of these patients suffer from an ill-defined syndrome often referred to as neurocirculatory asthenia.

Neurocirculatory asthenia was first described in 1871 by Jacob DaCosta, who named it irritable heart. It has some 20 names, including effort syndrome, DaCosta's syndrome, cardiac neurosis, vasoregulatory asthenia, hyperkinetic heart syndrome, and hyperdynamic-adrenergic circulatory state. Psychiatrists tend to view it as a clinical variant of anxiety disorder, although it does not appear in the official revised third edition of *Diagnostic and Statistical Manual of Mental Disorders* (DSM-III-R) nomenclature.

Diagnosis. The diagnostic criteria for neurocirculatory asthenia are (1) respiratory complaints, such as sighing respiration, inability to take a deep breath, smothering and choking, and dyspnea; (2) palpitations, chest pain, or discomfort; (3) nervousness, dizziness, faintness, or discomfort in crowds; (4) undue fatigue or limitation of activities; and (5) excessive sweating, insomnia, and irritability. The symptoms usually start in adolescence or the early 20s but may begin in middle age. Such symptoms are twice as common in women as in men and tend to be chronic, with recurrent acute exacerbations.

Treatment. The management of neurocirculatory asthenia may be difficult, and the prognosis is guarded if the condition is chronic. Phobic elements are prominent, and patients often derive primary or secondary gains from this disability. Psychotherapy aimed at uncovering psychodynamic factors—often relating to hostility, unacceptable sexual impulses, dependence, guilt, and death anxiety—may be effective in some cases, but most patients with the condition tend to shun psychiatric help. Other behavioral techniques may be useful. Physical training programs aimed at correcting faulty breathing habits and gradually increasing the patient's effort tolerance may be helpful, especially if the programs are combined with group psychotherapy. Psychopharmacological treatment focuses on the predominant symptoms. The use of propranolol may interrupt the vicious circle of cardiac symptoms and have a positive reinforcement feedback effect on anxiety, which aggravates the symptoms. Antianxiety agents (e.g., diazepam) can be used for major anxiety symptoms. If fatigue, lassitude, and weakness are the major complaints, the judicious use of amphetamines or methylphenidate (Ritalin) may be helpful.

RESPIRATORY SYSTEM

Bronchial Asthma

Bronchial asthma is a chronic recurrent obstructive disease of the bronchial airways, which tend to respond to various stimuli by bronchial constriction, edema, and excessive secretion. Genetic factors, allergic factors, infections, and acute and chronic stress all combine to produce the disease. Whereas the rate and depth of a healthy person's breathing can be changed voluntarily to correlate with different emotional states, in a person with asthma, such changes are aggravated and prolonged.

Psychological factors. Although asthmatics are characterized as having excessive dependency needs, no specific personality type has been identified. Alexander pointed to psychodynamic conflictual factors, as he found in many asthmatic patients a strong unconscious wish for protection and for envelopment by the mother or surrogate mother. These mother figures tend to be overprotective and oversolicitous, perfectionistic, dominating, and helpful. When protection is sought but is not received, an asthmatic attack occurs.

Treatment. Some asthmatic children improve by being separated from the mother (so-called parentectomy). All standard psychotherapies are used: individual, group, behavioral, and hypnotic. Asthmatics should be treated jointly by internists, allergists, and psychiatrists.

Hay Fever

Strong psychological factors combine with allergic elements to produce hay fever. One factor may dominate over the others, and they may alternate in importance.

Treatment. Psychiatric, medical, and allergic factors must be considered in treating hay fever.

Hyperventilation Syndrome

Normal persons can voluntarily change the rate, depth, and regularity of their breathing, which can also be correlated with different emotional states. Hyperventilative patients breathe rapidly and deeply for several minutes, feel light-headed, and then faint because of cerebral vasoconstriction and a respiratory alkalosis. Other symptoms, such as paresthesias and carpopedal spasm, may be present. Specific medical differentials for the syndrome are epilepsy, hysteria, vasovagal or hypoglycemic attacks, myocardial attacks, bronchial asthma, acute porphyria, Ménière's disease, and pheochromocytoma. Psychiatric differentials include anxiety attacks, panic attacks, schizophrenia, borderline or histrionic personality disorder, and phobic or obsessive complaints.

Treatment. Instruction or retraining regarding particular symptoms and how they are evoked by hyperventilation should be provided, so that patients can consciously avoid precipitating symptoms. Breathing into a paper bag can abort the attack.

GASTROINTESTINAL SYSTEM

Peptic Ulcer

Peptic ulcer is a circumscribed ulceration of the mucous membrane of the stomach or duodenum, penetrating to the muscularis mucosae and occurring in areas exposed to gastric acid and pepsin.

Etiology

Specific theory. Alexander hypothesized that chronic frustration of intense dependency needs results in a characteristic unconscious conflict. This unconscious conflict pertains to intense dependent oral-receptive longings to be cared for and loved, which causes a chronic regressive unconscious hunger and anger. This reaction is manifested physiologically by persistent vagal hyperactivity leading to gastric acid hypersecretion, which is particularly ominous in a genetically predisposed hypersecretor of acid. With the aforementioned equation, ulcer formation may result. Genetic factors and preexisting organ damage or disease (e.g., gastritis) are etiologically important. Such gastritis may result from excessive caffeine, nicotine, or alcohol.

Nonspecific theories. Stress and anxiety caused by varied nonspecific conflicts may produce gastric hyperacidity and hypersecretion of pepsin, resulting in an ulcer. Because various traumatic occurrences in animals (e.g., electric shock in dogs), may produce ulcers, such experimental data support a nonspecific approach. Peptic ulcers have been diagnosed in all personality types.

Treatment. Psychotherapy is directed toward the patient's dependency conflicts. Biofeedback and relaxation therapy may be useful. Medical treatment with cimetidine (Tagamet) or ranitidine (Zantac) antacid medications and dietary control (e.g., no alcohol) are indicated in ulcer management.

Ulcerative Colitis

Ulcerative colitis is a chronic inflammatory ulcerative disease of the colon and is usually associated with a bloody diarrhea. Familial incidence and genetic factors are significant. Related diseases include regional ileitis and irritable bowel syndrome.

Personality type. Most studies show a predominance of compulsive personality traits. Patients with ulcerative colitis are neat, orderly, clean, punctual, hyperintellectual, timid, and inhibited in expressing their anger.

Etiology

Specific theory. Alexander described a typical specific conflictual constellation in ulcerative colitis. The key issue is an inability to fulfill an obligation (usually of accomplishment) to a key dependency figure. Essentially frustrated dependency stimulates oral-aggressive feelings, producing guilt and anxiety and resulting in restitution through the "gifting" of diarrhea. In regard to colitis, George Engel described a pathological mother-child relationship, resulting in feelings of hopelessness-helplessness and a giving up–given up complex.

Nonspecific theory. Nonspecific stress of many types may aggravate ulcerative colitis.

Treatment. Supportive psychotherapy is indicated during the acute phase of ulcerative colitis, with more interpretative psychotherapy during the chronic quiescent periods. Medical treatment consists of nonspecific supportive medical measures, such as anticholinergics and antidiarrheal agents. Prednisone therapy is useful in severe cases. Bismuth-containing medications (e.g., Pepto-Bismol) are very useful in managing diarrhea.

OBESITY

Obesity is a condition characterized by the excessive accumulation of fat (when the body weight exceeds by 20 percent the standard weight listed in the usual height-weight tables).

Psychosomatic Considerations

There is a familial genetic predisposition to obesity, and early developmental factors are seen in childhood obesity. Those factors suggest that obese children increase their fat-cell number (hyperplastic obesity), which predisposes them to adult obesity. When obesity occurs first in adult life, it is usually hypertrophic obesity (an increase in fat-cell size), rather than an increase in the number of fat cells. Obesity also tends to limit physical activity, which further aggravates the condition. Psychological factors are important in hyperphagic obesity (overeating). Among the psychodynamic factors suggested are oral fixation, oral regression, and overvaluation of food. Bulimia—usually associated with binge eating—may be present. In addition, there is often a past history of body-image disparagement and poor early conditioning to food intake.

Treatment

Obesity must be controlled through dietary limitation and the reduction of calorie intake. Emotional support and behavior modification are helpful for the anxiety and depression associated with overeating and dieting. Gastric reduction surgery and similar techniques are of limited value.

ANOREXIA NERVOSA

Anorexia nervosa is characterized by behavior directed toward losing weight, peculiar patterns of handling food, weight loss, intense fear of gaining weight, disturbance of body image, and, in women, amenorrhea. It is one of the few psychiatric illnesses that may have a course unremitting until death. Anorexia nervosa is discussed in Section 37.3.

MUSCULOSKELETAL SYSTEM

Rheumatoid Arthritis

Rheumatoid arthritis is a disease characterized by chronic musculoskeletal pain caused by inflammatory disease of the joints. This disorder has significant hereditary, allergic, immunological, and psychological causative factors. It has been suggested that psychological stress predisposes patients to rheumatoid arthritis and other autoimmune diseases. The arthritic person feels restrained, tied down, and confined. Because many arthritic persons have a past history of being very active physically (e.g., dancers), they often have repressed rage about the inhibition of their muscle function, which aggravates their stiffness and immobility.

Treatment. Treatment should include psychotherapy, which is usually supportive during the acute attack and interpretative during the chronic phase. Rest and exercise should be structured, and patients should be encouraged not to become bed-bound and to return to their former activities. The rest and exercise program should be coordinated with the medical treatment for pain and inflammation of the joints.

Low Back Pain

Low back pain is felt in the lower lumbar, lumbosacral, and sacroiliac regions. It is often accompanied by sciatica, with pain radiating down one or both buttocks or following the distribution of the sciatic nerve. Although low back pain may be caused by a ruptured intervertebral disk, a fracture of the back, congenital defects of the lower spine, or a ligamentous muscle strain, many cases are psychosomatic in origin. Some reports indicate that 95 percent of cases are psychological in origin.

The examining physician should be particularly alert to a patient who gives a history of minor back trauma followed by severe disabling pain. Very often the patient with low back pain reports that the pain was initiated at a time of psychological trauma or stress. In addition, the patient's reaction to the pain is disproportionately emotional, with excessive anxiety and depression. Furthermore, the distribution of the pain rarely follows a normal neuroanatomical distribution (e.g., of sciatica).

Treatment. Treatment should be conservative. Aspirin—up to a total of 4 g daily—is a useful analgesic. Diazepam, 5 to 10 mg every four to six hours, acts as both a muscle relaxant and an anxiolytic. A careful exercise and physical therapy regimen, supportive psychotherapy regarding the precipitating emotional trauma, relaxation therapy, and biofeedback are helpful. Patients should be encouraged to return to their usual activities as soon as possible. Surgical intervention is rarely indicated.

HEADACHES

Headaches are the most common neurological symptom and one of the most common medical complaints. Every year about 80 percent of the population are estimated to suffer from at least one headache, and 10 to 20 percent of the population present to physicians with headache as their primary complaint. Headaches are also a major cause of absenteeism from work and avoidance of social and personal activities.

The majority of headaches are not associated with significant organic disease. Many persons are susceptible to headaches at times of emotional stress. Moreover, many psychiatric disorders, including anxiety and depressive disorders, frequently have headaches as a prominent symptom. Patients with headaches are often referred to psychiatrists by primary care physicians and neurologists after extensive biomedical workups, which often include a computed tomography (CT) scan of the head. The overwhelming majority of such workups for common headache complaints have negative findings, and such results may be frustrating for both patient and physician. The psychologically unsophisticated physician may attempt to reassure such patients by telling them that there is no disease. But that reassurance may have the opposite effect, increasing the patients' anxiety and even escalating into a disagreement about whether the pain is real or imagined.

Psychological stresses usually exacerbate headaches, whether their primary underlying cause is physical or psychological. Psychosomatic headaches are sometimes differentiated from psychogenic (e.g., anxiety, depression, hypochondriacal, delusional) headaches. For example, headaches may be a conversion symptom of inpatients with hysterical or other types of personality traits. In those patients the headache symbolizes unconscious psychological conflicts, and the symptoms are mediated through the voluntary sensorimotor nervous system. In contrast, psychosomatic headaches are defined as autonomic responses to conscious or unconscious conflicts and are not symbolic in nature. This distinction is important for psychiatrists to make so as to reach the proper diagnosis, which then allows the most specific treatment to be recommended.

Migraine (Vascular) Headaches

Migraine (vascular) headaches are a paroxysmal disorder characterized by recurrent headaches, with or without related visual and gastrointestinal disturbances. They are probably caused by a functional disturbance in the cranial circulation.

Personality type. Two-thirds of all patients with migraine headaches have family histories of similar disorders. Obsessional personalities who are overly controlled and perfectionistic, suppress anger, and are genetically predisposed to migraines may have such headaches under severe nonspecific emotional conflict or stress.

Treatment. Migraines are best treated during the prodromal period with ergotamine tartrate and analgesics. The prophylactic administration of propranolol or phenytoin (Dilantin) is useful if the headaches are frequent. Psychotherapy to diminish the effect of conflict and stress and certain behavioral techniques (e.g., biofeedback) have been reported as useful.

Tension (Muscle Contraction) Headaches

Emotional stress is often associated with the prolonged contraction of head and neck muscles, which over several hours may constrict the blood vessels and result in ischemia. A dull, aching pain often begins suboccipitally and may spread over the head, sometimes feeling like a tightening band. The scalp may be tender to the touch, and, in contrast to a migraine, the headache is usually bilateral and not associated with prodromata, nausea, and vomiting. The onset is often toward the end of the workday or in early evening, possibly after the person has been removed from stressful job pressures, has tried to relax, and has focused more on somatic sensations. But if family or personal pressures are equal to or greater than those at work, the headaches may be worse later in the evening, on weekends, or during vacations.

Tension headaches may occur to some degree in about 80 percent of the population during periods of emotional stress. Anxiety and depression are frequently associated with these headaches. Tense, high-strung, competitive, type A personalities are especially prone to this disorder. They may be treated in the acute stage with antianxiety agents, muscle relaxants, and massage or heat application to the head and neck. If an underlying depression is present, antidepressants may be prescribed. However, psychotherapy is usually the treatment of choice for patients chronically afflicted by tension headaches. Learning to avoid or better cope with tension is the most effective long-term management approach. Electromyogram (EMG) feedback from the frontal or temporal muscles may help some tension-headache patients. Relaxation associated with practice periods, meditation, or other changes in a pressured life-style may provide symptomatic relief for some patients.

ENDOCRINE SYSTEM

Hyperthyroidism

Hyperthyroidism (thyrotoxicosis) is a syndrome characterized by biochemical and psychological changes that occur as a result of a chronic endogenous or exogenous excess of thyroid hormone.

Psychosomatic considerations. In a genetically predisposed person, stress is often associated with the onset of hyperthyroidism. According to psychoanalytic theory, during childhood, hyperthyroid patients have an unusual attachment to and dependence on a parent, usually the mother, and so they find intolerable any threat to their mother's approval. As children, such patients often have inadequate support because of economic stress, divorce, death, or multiple siblings. This persistent threat to security in early life leads to premature and unsuccessful attempts to identify with an adult object. It also causes early stress and overuse of the endocrine system and further frustration of childhood dependency cravings. Because of this failure, the patients continuously strive toward premature self-sufficiency and tend to dominate others with smothering attention and affection. They need to build defenses against a repetition of the unbearable feelings of rejection and isolation that occurred in childhood. Should these mechanisms break down, requiring a premature stimulation of the body's psychophysiological defense in a genetically predisposed patient, thyrotoxicosis may result.

Treatment. Antithyroid medication, tranquilizers, and supportive psychotherapy are useful. Crisis intervention may be helpful at the acute onset of the disease.

Diabetes Mellitus

Diabetes mellitus is a disorder of metabolism and the vascular system manifested by a disturbance of the body's handling of glucose, lipid, and protein.

Etiology. Heredity and family history are extremely important in the onset of diabetes. An acute onset is often associated with emotional stress, which disturbs the homeostatic balance in a predisposed patient. Psychological factors that seem significant are those provoking feelings of frustration, loneliness, and dejection. Diabetic patients must usually maintain some sort of dietary control of their diabetes. When they are depressed and dejected, they often overeat or overdrink self-destructively, causing their diabetes to get out of control. This is especially common in juvenile diabetics. In addition, terms such as oral, dependent, seeking maternal attention, and excessive passivity have been applied to diabetics.

Treatment. Supportive psychotherapy is necessary in order to achieve cooperation in the medical management of this complex disease. Therapy should encourage diabetics to lead as normal a life as possible, with the recognition that they have a chronic but manageable disease.

Female Endocrine Disorders

Premenstrual syndrome. The premenstrual syndrome (PMS) is characterized by cyclical subjective changes in mood and general sense of physical and psychological well-being correlated with the menstrual cycle. The symptoms usually begin soon after ovulation, increase gradually, and reach a maximum of intensity about five days before the menstrual period. Psychological, social, and biological factors have been implicated in the syndrome's pathogenesis. In particular, changes in estrogen, progesterone, androgen, and prolactin levels have been hypothesized to be important to the cause. Recently, it has been proposed that excessive exposure to and subsequent abrupt withdrawal from endogenous opiate peptides, which fluctuate under the influence of gonadal steroids, may contribute to PMS. An increase in prostaglandins secreted by the uterine musculature has been implicated in the pain associated with the syndrome. PMS also occurs in women past the menarche and after hysterectomy, provided the ovaries remain intact. Seventy to 90 percent of all women of childbearing age report at least some symptoms.

Late luteal phase dysphoric disorder. A new and controversial diagnostic category called late luteal phase dysphoric disorder (LLPDD) was suggested to be added to DSM-III-R. The signs and symptoms of LLPDD are more severe and create more distress than those of PMS, and they are more likely to occur in women over 30. LLPDD is considered controversial in that many clinicians do not think that the menstrual cycle should be associated with a diagnosable mental disorder. Also, there are no data regarding LLPDD's prevalence, predisposing factors, course, or specific treatment. DSM-III-R cautiously states that the category has a high potential for misapplication and misinterpretation and encourages its further study. Because of this controversy over LLPDD, this classification was placed in an appendix to DSM-III-R and not in DSM-III-R proper.

According to DSM-III-R, LLPDD is characterized by a pattern of significant emotional and behavioral symptoms that are sufficiently severe to cause a marked impairment in social or occupational functioning. The symptoms occur during the last week of the luteal phase of the menstrual cycle (hence the term "late luteal") and remit within a few days after the onset of the follicular phase. Among the most commonly experienced symptoms that DSM-III-R lists are affective lability; feelings of depression, which may be accompanied by suicidal ideation; decreased energy and greater fatigue; loss of appetite or craving for certain foods, such as carbohydrates; sleep disturbances; and physical complaints, such as joint or muscle pain, weight gain, headaches, breast tenderness, and a feeling of being bloated. Similar symptoms are seen in PMS but to a much smaller degree. (DSM-III-R's diagnostic criteria for LLPDD are listed in Table 25.2-1.) The differential diagnosis of this disorder is listed in DSM-III-R as follows: dysmenorrhea, depressive disorder, and panic disorder. According to DSM-III-R, dysmenorrhea (painful menses) is characterized by symptoms that occur with the menses, whereas in LLPDD the onset of the symptoms is premenstrual. The diagnosis of LLPDD should not be made if the symptoms preceding the menses are limited to pain and physical discomfort. Other disorders that are symptomatically similar to LLPDD, such as depressive disorders and panic disorder, do not remit regularly with the onset of menses.

Treatment. The symptoms of PMS and LLPDD are treated symptomatically. Water retention—which accounts for the bloated feeling—weight gain, and edema may be relieved by antidiuretic medication and salt restriction. Pain,

Table 25.2-1
Diagnostic Criteria for Late Luteal Phase Dysphoric Disorder

A. In most menstrual cycles during the past year, symptoms in B occurred during the last week of the luteal phase and remitted within a few days after onset of the follicular phase. In menstruating females, these phases correspond to the week before, and a few days after, the onset of menses. (In nonmenstruating females who have had a hysterectomy, the timing of luteal and follicular phases may require measurement of circulating reproductive hormones.)
B. At least five of the following symptoms have been present for most of the time during each symptomatic late luteal phase, at least one of the symptoms being either (1), (2), (3), or (4):
   (1) marked affective lability (e.g., feeling suddenly sad, tearful, irritable, or angry)
   (2) persistent and marked anger or irritability
   (3) marked anxiety, tension, feelings of being "keyed up," or "on edge"
   (4) markedly depressed mood, feelings of hopelessness, or self-deprecating thoughts
   (5) decreased interest in usual activities (e.g., work, friends, hobbies)
   (6) easy fatigability or marked lack of energy
   (7) subjective sense of difficulty in concentrating
   (8) marked change in appetite, overeating, or specific food cravings
   (9) hypersomnia or insomnia
   (10) other physical symptoms, such as breast tenderness or swelling, headaches, joint or muscle pain, a sensation of "bloating," weight gain
C. The disturbance seriously interferes with work or with usual social activities or relationships with others.
D. The disturbance is not merely an exacerbation of the symptoms of another disorder, such as major depression, panic disorder, dysthymia, or a personality disorder (although it may be superimposed on any of these disorders).
E. Criteria A, B, C, and D are confirmed by prospective daily self-ratings during at least two symptomatic cycles. (The diagnosis may be made provisionally prior to this confirmation.)

Table from DSM-III-R, *Diagnostic and Statistical Manual of Mental Disorders*, ed 3, revised. Copyright American Psychiatric Association, Washington, DC, 1987, with permission.

such as headaches and particularly dysmenorrhea, responds to analgesics. Acetaminophen is preferable to aspirin because it does not interfere with clotting mechanisms. Mental manifestations (e.g., fatigue, lassitude, and general malaise) respond to small doses of amphetamine, which also appears to act synergistically with analgesics for the relief of associated pain. Antiprostaglandins help some women whose dysmenorrhea is the result of uterine prostaglandin release; however, for the medication to be effective, it should be started before the onset of pain. Other drugs—including progesterone, lithium, antidepressants, and antianxiety agents—have been tried with uncertain success. It is helpful to many women to be made aware that premenstrual symptoms represent a recurring syndrome that can be anticipated. Psychotherapy may be helpful in individual cases. In very rare cases, psychotic symptoms have been described that occur exclusively in the latter part of the luteal phase of the menstrual cycle and that respond to antipsychotic medication.

Menopausal distress. Menopause is a natural physiological event. It is usually dated as having occurred after an absence of menstrual periods for one year. Usually, the menses taper off during a two- to five-year span, most often between the ages of 48 and 55; the median age is 51.4 years. Menopause also occurs immediately after the surgical removal of the ovaries. The term "involutional period" refers to advancing age, and "climacteric" refers to involution of the ovaries.

Clinical features. Many psychological symptoms have been attributed to the menopause, including anxiety, fatigue, tension, emotional lability, irritability, depression, dizziness, and insomnia. There is no general agreement on the relative contribution of those complaints or of the physiological changes to the psychological and social meanings of menopause and this developmental era in a woman's life.

Physical signs and symptoms include night sweats, flushes, and hot flashes. A hot flash is a sudden perception of heat within or on the body that may be accompanied by sweating or color change. The cause of the hot flash is unknown; it may be linked to pulsatile luteinizing hormone (LH) secretion. Estrogen-dependent functions are sequentially lost, and there may be atrophic changes in mucosal surfaces, accompanied by vaginitis, pruritus, dyspareunia, and stenosis. There are changes in calcium and lipid metabolism, probably as secondary effects of the lower levels of estrogen, and these changes may be associated with a number of medical problems occurring in the postmenopausal era, such as osteoporosis and coronary atherosclerosis. The physical changes may begin as much as four to eight years before the last menstrual period. During this time women may have irregular menstrual periods with variations in the menstrual intervals and the quantity of the menstrual flow.

Hormonal changes. Blood levels of ovarian hormones decline gradually during the climacteric period, usually over a period of several years. For many years decreasing estrogen levels were thought to be of primary importance in relation to the clinical manifestations of menopause. Both estrogen and progesterone bind directly to brain tissue and were thought to act directly on brain function. More recently, however, it has been thought that other hormones, such as androgens and LH, are also involved. The effects of estrogen on mood may be indirectly moderated through its influence on androgen production. In any case the significance of hormonal changes is evidenced by the severe physical and psychological symptoms that follow abrupt (surgical) depletion of ovarian hormones. One difficulty in those studies that have attempted to assess the relationships of changing hormonal levels in normal women is that the date of the last menstrual period is often difficult to establish, as is the menarche, for they merely mark a point on a curve of changing hormonal function. That is, the presence or absence of menstrual bleeding is not an exact measure of hormonal status.

The severity of the symptoms at the menopause seems to be related to the rate of hormone withdrawal; the amount of hormone depletion; a woman's constitutional ability to withstand the overall aging process, including her overall health and level of activity; and the psychological meaning of aging for her.

Psychological and psychosocial factors. Clinically significant psychiatric difficulties may develop during the life cycle's involutional phase. Women who have previously experienced psychological difficulties, such as low self-esteem and low life satisfaction, are likely to be vulnerable to difficulties during menopause. A woman's response to menopause has been noted to parallel her response to other crucial developmental events in her life, such as puberty and pregnancy. Attempts to link the severity of menopausal distress with the premenstrual tension syndrome have been inconclusive.

Women who have invested heavily in childbearing and child-rearing activities are most likely to suffer distress during the postmenopausal years. Concerns about aging, loss of child-bearing capacity, and changes in appearance—all may be focused on the social and symbolic significance attached to the physical changes of the menopause.

Although in the past it was assumed that the incidence of mental illness and depression would increase during the menopause, epidemiological evidence casts some doubt on this assumption as an all-inclusive and complete explanation. Epidemiological studies of mental illness showed no increase in symptoms of mental illness or in depression during the menopausal years, and studies of psychological complaints found no greater frequency in menopausal women than in younger women.

Treatment. Treatment programs must be individualized. Postclimacteric women may be asymptomatic for estrogen deprivation or may manifest estrogen excess (dysfunctional uterine bleeding).

The use of estrogen replacement treatment is still controversial. For women with signs of estrogen depletion, recent studies have been more encouraging in regard to the use of long-term combined estrogen and progesterone replacement therapy, both in estrogen depletion syndrome and to prevent osteoporesis. Topical estrogen cream used to treat mucosal atrophy is readily absorbed systemically. The increased risk of cancer, particularly endometrial cancer, has been implicated in the use of exogenous estrogen, but the addition of a progestational agent to the replacement estrogen regime is thought to reduce this increased risk.

Exercise, diet, and symptomatic treatment are all helpful in reducing physical discomfort. Psychological distress should be evaluated and treated primarily by appropriate psychotherapeutic and sociotherapeutic measures. Psychotherapy should include an exploration of the life stage and the meaning of aging and reproduction to the patient. The patient should be encouraged to accept the menopause as a natural life event and to develop new activities, interests, and gratifications. Psychotherapy should also attend to family dynamics and enlist family and other social support systems when necessary.

Idiopathic amenorrhea. The cessation of normal menstrual cycles in nonpregnant, premenopausal women with no demonstrable structural abnormalities in the brain, pituitary, or ovaries is termed idiopathic amenorrhea.

The diagnosis is made first by exclusion and then, if possible, by identifying the primary psychogenic cause. Amenorrhea may occur as one feature of complex clinical psychiatric syndromes, such as anorexia nervosa and pseudocyesis. Other conditions associated with amenorrhea include massive obesity, diseases of the pituitary and hypothalamus, and, in some cases, excessive amounts of running or jogging. Drugs such as reserpine and chlorpromazine (Thorazine) can block ovulation and so delay the menses. Drug-induced amenorrhea is almost always accompanied by galactorrhea and elevated levels of prolactin.

The patterns of hormone defect that result in psychogenic amenorrhea are not well understood. Disturbed menstrual function with delayed or precipitate menses is a well-known response by healthy women to stress. The stress can be as minor as going away to college or as catastrophic as being put into a concentration camp.

In most women menstrual cycling returns without medical intervention, sometimes even in continuing stressful conditions. Psychotherapy should be undertaken for psychological reasons, not just in response to the symptom of amenorrhea and to determine its cause. However, if the amenorrhea has been protracted and refractory, psychotherapy may be helpful in restoring regular menses.

CHRONIC PAIN

Persistent pain is the most frequent complaint of patients, yet it is one of the most difficult symptoms to treat because of differing causes and individual responses to pain.

Pain is affected by a myriad of subjective, unmeasurable factors, including level of attention, emotional state, personality, and past experiences. Pain may simultaneously serve as a symptom of and as a defense against psychological stress. Psychological factors may cause a person to become somatically preoccupied and magnify even normal sensations to chronic pain. Patients may be excessively responsive to pain for personal, social, or financial secondary gain. Chronic pain may be a way of justifying failure in establishing relationships with others. Cultural, ethnic, or religious affiliations may influence the degree and manner in which persons express pain and the way in which their families react to the symptoms. Therefore, in evaluating and treating persistent pain, the physician should realize that pain is not a simple stimulus-response phenomenon. Rather, the perception of a reaction to pain is multifactorial, combining many biopsychosocial variables.

Pain Threshold and Perception

Peripheral sensations are transmitted through the pain pathways (e.g., lateral spinothalamic tract, posterior thalamus of the diencephalon) to cortical somatosensory regions of the central nervous system (CNS) for conscious perception. The parietal cortex both localizes pain and perceives intensity. However, psychogenic pain may be entirely of central origin. Complex reactions to pain involve other areas of the cortex responsible for memory and conscious and unconscious elements of a person's personality.

The threshold for perception of pain is the same for most people but may be heightened by about 40 percent by biofeedback, a positive emotional state, relaxation exercises, physical therapy or other physical activity, meditation, guided imagery, suggestion, hypnosis, placebos, or analgesics. The beneficial response to placebos is sometimes falsely thought to differentiate organic from functional causes. In fact, about one-third of normal persons, those with organic causes of pain, have at least a transient positive response to a placebo.

Variations in the effectiveness and responsiveness of persons' endorphin or other neurotransmitter systems may modulate pain perception and tolerance. A gate-control theory has been proposed, which suggests that large peripheral afferent nerve fibers modulate sensory input by inhibiting hypothetical sensory transmitting neurons (gateway cells) in the substantia gelatinosa of the spinal cord. Relief of pain by transcutaneous or dorsal column electrical stimulators may result from this system's activation.

Classification

DSM-III-R classifies chronic pain patients under somatoform disorders (see Chapter 18). If patients have multiple recurrent pains of at least several years' duration that began before age 30, they are considered to have a somatization disorder. If the patients' pain suggests a physical illness but may be attributed to psychological factors alone, the diagnosis is conversion disorder or somatoform pain disorder (if pain is the only symptom). Patients with somatization disorder, depressive disorder, or schizophrenia complain of various aches and pains, but pain is not the major complaint. In conversion disorders, the distribution and referral of pain are inconsistent.

Treatment

Psychotherapy with pain patients is summarized in Table 25.2-2.

Patients with pain are often undermedicated with analgesics because of a lack of knowledge of the pharmacology of analgesics, an unrealistic fear of causing addiction (even in terminal patients), and the ethical judgment that only bad physicians prescribe large doses of narcotics. In this regard it is critical to separate patients with chronic benign pain (who tend to do much better with psychotherapy and psychotropic drugs) from those with chronic pain caused by cancer or other chronic medical disorders. The former often respond to the combination of an antidepressant and a phenothiazine. The latter usually respond better to analgesics or nerve blocks. Many cancer patients may be kept relatively active, alert, and comfortable with the judicious use of morphine, avoiding costly and incompletely effective surgical procedures, such as peripheral nerve section, cordotomy, and stereotaxic thalamic ablations.

A behavior modification, deconditioning program may also be useful. Analgesics should be prescribed at regular intervals, rather than only as needed. Otherwise, patients must suffer before receiving relief, which only increases their anxiety and sensitivity to pain. Standing orders dissociate experiencing pain from receiving medication. The deconditioning of needed care from experiencing increased pain should also extend to patients' interpersonal relationships. Patients should receive as much or more attention for displaying active and healthy behavior as they receive for passive, dependent, pain-related behaviors. Their spouses, bosses, friends, physicians, and health care or social agencies should not reinforce chronic pain and penalize patients (including threatening to discontinue disability payments) if the patients begin to relinquish the sick role. Patients should be assured of regular and supportive appointments that are not contingent on pain. Hospitalization should be avoided, if possible, to prevent further regression.

Table 25.2-2
Psychotherapy with Pain Patients

Explain the nature of the pain signal.
Explain realistic expectations about the degree and course of the pain.
Explain realistic expectations of analgesic and, as much as possible, reframe side effects positively.
Maximize placebo effect by making the initial doses large rather than small, by supporting belief in efficacy, and by using suggestion through the attitude of the physician and the staff administering the analgesic.
Relieve concomitant anxiety, if necessary.
Chronic pain requires special arrangements:
- Eliminate doubts about availability of medication.
- Do not make medication availability contingent on proof of need, leading to subjective struggles.
- Focus therapeutic encounters on healthy material; do not reinforce obsession with pain.
- Do not make contact with the care system contingent on pain; remove this contingency.

Table by Barry Blackwell, M.D.

Pain clinics with a multispecialty staff evaluate and treat patients with complex pain disorders. These clinics include the early involvement of psychiatrists, rather than only after the real causes of pain have been ruled out and the patient and physicians are frustrated. The patients are managed without addictive drugs, although many patients commence treatment already addicted. Exploratory or neurodestructive surgery is not encouraged, especially if the patient has a hysterical personality or a history of multiple surgical procedures. Pain clinics also recognize that most chronic pain patients experience a vicious circle of biological and psychosocial factors, so that the most effective treatment involves a systems approach that addresses each biopsychosocial component relevant to the patient.

IMMUNE DISORDERS

There is considerable evidence of a relationship among psychosocial factors, immune function, and health and illness. It seems that psychosocial processes, including a range of the person's life experiences and state and trait characteristics, influence the CNS, thereby encouraging the suppression of immune activity.

In 1968 George Solomon suggested that emotional stress affects the immune system, especially through a decrease in T lymphocytes. S. Keller later demonstrated that there was a decrease in lymphocytes in rats that were helpless to escape or to stop electric shocks. In 1975 Robert Ader further demonstrated a conditioned suppression of the immune response in rats.

Transposing the research to humans, other investigators demonstrated a decrease in lymphocytic response in bereavement, in medical students during final exams, in women who were separated or divorced, in the elderly who had a lack of social support, and in the unemployed. A decrease in lymphatic activity parallels a decrease in immunity and an increased incidence of infections and malignancy, which is probably correlated with increased psychic stress.

Most of the aforementioned studies show the negative effects of psychic stress on psychoimmunity and lymphatic activity and related diseases. A recent study by D. Phillips and D. Smith suggests that positive psychological events may have beneficial effects on certain persons in certain areas. They found that important symbolic events have a positive significant short-time effect on mortality and potentially on health in general. Symbolic events that they studied—such as Passover for Jewish men and the Chinese harvest moon festival for Chinese women—often prolong the lives of patients dying from malignant neoplasms or cerebrovascular diseases. This demonstrates an additional parameter, not previously considered, that should be evaluated in the psychosomatic equation.

Recent investigations have revealed that the interaction between neuroendocrines and the CNS is reciprocal (i.e., immune responses are affected by the CNS and vice versa). It has been demonstrated, for example, that a monokene released by macrophages and monocytes, interleukin-1 (IL-1), activates the hypothalamus-pituitary-adrenal axis (HPA) at the hypothalamus and pituitary level and stimulates the release of the potent adrenocorticotropic hormone (ACTH). Lymphocytes also synthesize peptides, such as ACTH and endorphins, which have numerous behavioral effects. It has also been demonstrated recently that regulation of the immune system can be learned and conditioned, further demonstrating the potential effect of the immune system in the brain.

Infectious Diseases

Clinical studies have reported that psychological variables influence the rate of recovery from infectious mononucleosis and influenza and the susceptibility to rhinovirus-induced common cold symptoms and tularemia. Recurrent herpes simplex and genital herpes lesions have been shown to occur most frequently in patients who have a clinical depression or who experience unusual stress. Stressful life events and a poor psychological state have been found to decrease resistance to tuberculosis and to influence the course of the illness. Social supports have also been shown to play a role in recovery from tuberculosis. Life experiences that induce anger have been noted to alter the intestine's bacterial composition. College students who respond to upsetting events with maladaptive aggression or affective changes were found to have a high incidence of subsequent upper respiratory infections. In these studies the primary immune response was cell-mediated. In acquired immune deficiency syndrome (AIDS), transmitted by the human immunodeficiency virus (HIV), psychiatric symptoms are common, and many think that the progress of the disease is influenced by the person's psychological state. See Chapter 11 for further discussion of the psychiatric aspects of AIDS.

Allergic Disorders

Considerable clinical evidence suggests that psychological factors are related to the precipitation of many allergic disorders. Bronchial asthma is a prime example of a pathological process involving immediate hypersensitivity that is associated with psychosocial processes. Emotional reactions to life experience, personality patterns, and conditioning have been reported to contribute to the onset and course of asthma.

Organ Transplantation

Psychosocial factors seem to play a role in organ transplantation. A number of clinical studies have reported that stressful life events, anxiety, and depression precede some cases of graft rejection. Psychosocial effects on the immune system may contribute to the mechanisms involved in such rejections.

Autoimmune Diseases

A prime function of the immune system is to distinguish between self and nonself and to reject foreign antigens (nonself). Occasionally, for reasons that are unclear at the present time, a cell-mediated or humoral immune response develops against a person's own cells. This reaction results in a variety of pathological effects that are known clinically as autoimmune diseases. Disorders in which an autoimmune component has been implicated include Graves' disease, Hashimoto's disease, rheumatoid arthritis, ulcerative colitis, regional ileitis, systemic lupus erythematosus, psoriasis, myasthenia gravis, and pernicious anemia.

Psychiatric Disorders

Although a number of investigators have found evidence suggesting altered immunity and autoimmunity in patients with schizophrenia, the specific findings have been difficult to replicate. Whether the immune abnormalities are involved in the pathogenesis of some or all types of schizophrenia or whether such abnormalities are related to a wide range of factors, including chronic institutionalization and antipsychotic agents, remains to be determined.

Immune phenomena in psychiatric disorders other than schizophrenia have been less extensively studied. Work indicates that psychiatric patients manifest increased immunoglobulin M (IgM) and immunoglobulin A (IgA) levels. These findings indicate the need for further study. The notion that patients with depression have an increased incidence of autoimmune antibodies has sparked some controversy. In some studies the frequency of antinuclear antibodies, commonly found in patients with autoimmune disorders, such as systemic lupus erythematosus, has been reported as increased in patients with depression.

CANCER

Because improved treatment has changed cancer from an incurable to a frequently chronic and often curable disease, the psychiatric aspects of cancer—the reaction to both the diagnosis and the treatment—are of increasing importance. At least one-half of the 1 million patients who contracted cancer in the United States in 1988 will be alive five years later. Currently, an estimated 3 million cancer survivors have no evidence of the disease.

Patient Problems

When patients learn they have cancer, their psychological reactions include fear of death, disfigurement, and disability; fear of abandonment and loss of independence; fear of disruption in relationships, role functioning, and financial standing; and denial, anxiety, anger, and guilt.

About one-half of cancer patients have psychiatric disorders. The largest group have adjustment disorders (68 percent), with major depression (13 percent) and delirium (8 percent) being the next most common diagnoses. Most of these disorders are thought to be reactive to the knowledge of having cancer. The psychiatric, medical, and environmental factors that should be explored in the cancer patient are listed in Table 25.2-3. Some of the most common causes of organic mood syndromes in cancer patients

Table 25.2-3
Areas of Assessment in Cancer Patients

Psychiatric
- Past history
- Current mental state
- Understanding of the illness
- Meaning of the illness

Medical
- Cancer
- Cancer treatment
- Associated medical conditions and treatments

Environmental
- Interface with the family
- Interface with the medical team
- Other social supports
- Financial issues

Table by Marguerite Lederberg, M.D., and Jimmie Holland, M.D.

are listed in Table 25.2-4, and some of the medical conditions associated with delirium in cancer patients are listed in Table 25.2-5.

Suicide. Although suicidal thoughts and wishes are frequent in cancer patients, the incidence of actual suicide is only 1.4 to 1.9 times that of the general population. Factors that signal a vulnerability to suicide in cancer patients are listed in Table 25.2-6.

Treatment-Related Problems

The most common medical treatments used with cancer are radiation and drugs (chemotherapy). Drugs are toxic when given in tumoricidal dosages. Patients undergoing long courses of treatment may become much sicker symptomatically from the treatment than from their disease.

Radiation therapy. The side effects of radiation therapy include encephalopathy associated with increased intracranial pressure (nausea, vomiting, dizziness), headache, somnolence, personality changes, cognitive disturbances, and reactive psychic symptoms of fear and depression.

Chemotherapy. The most common side effects of chemotherapy are nausea and vomiting. In Table 25.2-7 the emetogenic problems with various chemotherapeutic agents are summarized. Antiemetic treatments for these complications

Table 25.2-4
Causes of Organic Mood Syndromes Common in Cancer Patients

Drugs
- Chemotherapeutic agents such as prednisone, dexamethasone, procarbazine, vincristine, vinblastine, L-asparaginase, tamoxifen, interferon
- Additive effect of narcotics and many other drugs known to cause depression, such as antihypertensives, benzodiazepines, antiparkinson agents, and β-blockers

Tumor effects
- Hormone secreting tumors
- Central nervous system tumors

Associated medical conditions
- Uremia
- Viral encephalopathies
- Electrolyte imbalances

Table by Marguerite Lederberg, M.D., and Jimmie Holland, M.D.

Table 25.2-5
Medical Conditions Associated with Delirium in Cancer Patients

- Metabolic encephalopathy
- Vital organ failure
- Electrolyte inbalance (such as hypercalcemia in patients with bony metastases or those receiving tamoxifen, diethylstilbestrol, or chlorotrianisene)
- Hypoxia, especially in patients with pulmonary involvement or severe anemia
- Nutritional deficiencies, such as thiamin, folic acid, or B_{12}
- Infections, especially in immunosuppressed hosts
- Vascular disorders, especially in patients with coagulopathies
- Endocrine and hormonal abnormalities

Table by Marguerite Lederberg, M.D., and Jimmie Holland, M.D.

Table 25.2-6
Suicide Vulnerability Factors in Cancer Patients

- Depression and hopelessness
- Poorly controlled pain
- Mild delirium (disinhibition)
- Feeling of loss of control
- Exhaustion
- Anxiety
- Preexisting psychopathology (substance abuse, character pathology, major psychiatric disorder)
- Acute family problems
- Threats, history of prior attempts of suicide
- Positive family history of suicide
- Other usually described risk factors in psychiatric patients

Table adapted from W Breitbart: Suicide in cancer patients. Oncology *1*: 49, 1987, with permission.

Table 25.2-7
Emetogenic Potential of Some Commonly Used Anticancer Agents

Highly emetogenic	Cisplatin Dacarbazine Streptozocin Actinomycin Nitrogen mustard
Moderately emetogenic	Doxorubicin Daunorubicin Cyclophosphamide Nitrosoureas Mitomycin-C Procarbazine
Minimally emetogenic	Vincristine Vinblastine 5-Fluorouracil Bleomycin

Table by Marguerite Lederberg, M.D., and Jimmie Holland, M.D.

are summarized in Table 25.2-8. Other complications of chemotherapy are the neurological complications listed in Table 25.2-9 and the mood and psychotic symptoms listed in Table 25.2-10.

Pain. Pain in cancer patients should not be underestimated or undermedicated. Because cancer patients with pain have a significantly higher incidence of depression and anxiety than those without pain, proper and adequate treatment is essential for their psychological well-being. Cancer patients with acute pain respond well to treatment

Table 25.2-8
Antiemetic Regimens

For a highly emetic drug:	
Metoclopramide* (Reglan), 2–3 mg/kg IV	given 30 minutes before the IV infusion and repeated every two hours for two times
Dexamethasone (Decadron)	(as above)
Lorazepam (Ativan), 1–3 mg IV	(as above)
For a moderately emetic drug:	
Prochlorperazine (Compazine), 10–20 mg IV	
Chlorpromazine (Thorazine), 25 mg IV	
THC (Dronabinol) (Marinol), 2.5–10 mg PO	

Table by Marguerite Lederberg, M.D., and Jimmie Holland, M.D.
*Haloperidol (Haldol), 2–4 mg IV, may be substituted.

Table 25.2-9
Neurological Complications of Chemotherapy

Encephalopathy	Myelopathy
Methotrexate w/radiotherapy	Intrathecal methotrexate
Hexamethylmelamine	Intrathecal cytarabine
5-Fluorouracil	Intrathecal thiotepa
Procarbazine	Neuropathy
Carmustine (BCNU) (intracarotid)	Vinca alkaloids*
Cisplatin (intracarotid)	Cisplatin*
Cyclophosphamide	Procarbazine
5-Azacytidine	5-Azacytidine
Spirogermanium	Vasopressin 16
Misonidazole	VM-26
Cytarabine (high dose)	Misonidazole
L-Asparaginase	Methyl-G
	Cytarabine
Acute cerebellar syndrome, ataxia	Ototoxicity
5-Fluorouracil	Cisplatin
Cytarabine	Misonidazole
Procarbazine	
Hexamethylmelamine	

Table by Marguerite Lederberg, M.D., and Jimmie Holland, M.D.
Table adapted from R A Patchell, J B Posner: Neurologic complications of systemic cancer. In *Symposium on Neuro-oncology Neurologic Clinics*, N A Vick and D D Bigner, editors, vol 3, p 729. Saunders, Philadelphia, 1985, with permission.
*Also involve cranial nerves.

with antipain medications, such as opiates, but their tolerance levels rise, and they require more medication if the pain lasts more than a few days. This is often inappropriately viewed as addiction, for studies have shown that these patients easily and voluntarily wean themselves when pain eases. Cancer patients with acute pain require sympathetic and supportive treatment from medical personnel, as do those with chronic pain, whose addictive problems are more common and who nevertheless may require additional medication. As tolerance levels rise, as they always do, patients require higher doses of narcotics, and there appears to be no ceiling to the dosage required. In cancer patients, however, tolerance to opiates does not imply addiction. Adjuvants to opiate medications, which potentiate their effects, are antidepressants, anticonvulsants, phenothiazines, and butyrophenones. One should be cautious about drug-drug interactions, such as meperidine (Demerol) and monoamine oxidase inhibitors (MAOIs), which can be fatal.

Table 25.2-10
Chemotherapy Agents with Mood and Psychotic Symptoms

Dacarbazine: depression and suicide reported, especially when used with hexamethylamine.
Vinblastine: frequent reversible depression.
Vincristine: 5 percent incidence of hallucinations; depression noted.
L-Asparaginase: reversible depression noted.
Procarbazine: MAOI; concurrent tricyclics are contraindicated; associated with mania and depression; potentiates alcohol, barbiturates, phenothiazines.
Hydroxyurea: hallucinations reported.
Interferon: anxiety, depression with suicidal ideation common at doses above 40 million units.
Steroids: frequent alterations of mental state ranging from emotional lability through mania or severe, suicidal depression to frank psychosis.

Table by Marguerite Lederberg, M.D., and Jimmie Holland, M.D.

Palliative care. For the medical staff, palliation should be an active and involved process, with no hint of withdrawal or abandonment.

Ethical issues. Included among the ethical issues are questions of informed consent for both traditional and experimental treatments and third-party consent (e.g., insurance companies), which may not pay for such treatments in certain cases.

Staff Problems

The care of cancer patients causes special stresses for caretakers. For a summary of these stresses, see Table 25.2-11.

Family Problems

Because cancer strikes not only the patient but also the family, caretakers in the family must provide care for the patient and also respond to the increased demands of other family members. Anxiety and depression of family members require active intervention. The family problems re-

Table 25.2-11
Staff Stresses Common to Special Care Settings

High morbidity, high mortality
Complex technology used under high pressure
High frequency of life-death decisions
Terminal care issues
Third-party conflicts
Interstaff conflicts
Response to severe debilitation and disfigurement
Response to difficult patients (excessive dependency, anger, uncooperativeness)
Response to suicidal ideation
Issue of inflicting pain as part of treatment

Table by Marguerite Lederberg, M.D., and Jimmie Holland, M.D.

quiring treatment are preexisting intrafamily conflicts, family abandonment, and family exhaustion.

Cancer in Children

Fewer children than adults have cancer. Of approximately 7,000 new cases of cancer in children in the United States in 1986, more than 60 percent had leukemia, lymphoma, and CNS tumors, and they received a combination of chemotherapy and radiation therapy. Five-year survival rates for children with fibrosarcomas, retinoblastomas, Hodgkin's disease, and gonadal and germ cell tumors have passed the 80 percent mark, and the survival rate for most other childhood cancers is between 40 and 60 percent.

SKIN DISORDERS

Psychosomatic skin disorders include a great variety of abnormal skin sensations. Emotional factors are important in every aspect of skin disorders: manifestations, aggravations, responses, causes, and prognoses.

Generalized Pruritus

Itch, tickle, and pain are all conveyed by the same afferent fibers and are differentiated only by the frequency of electrical impulse.

The itching dermatoses include scabies, pediculosis, bites of insects, urticaria, atopic dermatitis, contact dermatitis, lichen ruber planus, and miliaria. Internal disorders that frequently cause itching are diabetes mellitus, nephritis, diseases of the liver, gout, diseases of the thyroid gland, food allergies, Hodgkin's disease, leukemia, and cancer. Itching can also occur during pregnancy and senility.

The term "generalized psychogenic pruritis" denotes that no organic cause for the itching exists or, at least, no longer exists and that, on psychiatric examination, emotional conflicts have been established that convincingly account for its occurrence.

The emotions that most frequently lead to generalized psychogenic pruritus are repressed anger and repressed anxiety. Whenever persons consciously or preconsciously experience anger or anxiety, they scratch themselves, often violently. An inordinate need for affection is a common characteristic of these patients. Frustrations of this need elicit aggressiveness that is inhibited. The rubbing of the skin provides a substitute gratification of the frustrated need, and the scratching represents aggression turned against the self.

Localized Pruritus

Pruritus ani. The investigation of pruritus ani commonly yields a history of local irritation (e.g., thread worms, irritant discharge, fungal infection) or general systemic factors (e.g., nutritional deficiencies, drug intoxication). However, after running a conventional course, pruritus ani often fails to respond to therapeutic measures and acquires a life of its own, apparently perpetuated by scratching and superimposed inflammation. It is a distressing complaint that often interferes with work and social activity. Careful investigation of large numbers of patients with the disorder has revealed that personality deviations often precede this condition and that emotional disturbances often precipitate and maintain it.

Pruritus vulvae. As in pruritus ani, specific physical causes, either localized or generalized, may be demonstrable in pruritus vulvae, and the presence of glaring psychopathology in no way lessens the need for adequate medical investigation. In some patients, pleasure derived from rubbing and scratching is quite conscious—they realize that it is a symbolic form of masturbation—but more often than not the pleasure element is repressed. Most of the patients studied gave a long history of sexual frustration, which was frequently intensified at the time of the onset of pruritus.

Hyperhidrosis

States of fear, rage, and tension can induce an increase of sweat secretion. It has been demonstrated that perspiration in the human has two distinct forms: thermal and emotional. Emotional sweating appears primarily on the palms, soles, and axillae; thermal sweating is most evident on the forehead, neck, trunk, and dorsum of the hands and forearms. The sensitivity of the emotional sweating response serves as the basis for the measurement of sweat by the galvanic skin response (an important tool of psychosomatic research), biofeedback, and the polygraph (lie detector test).

Under conditions of prolonged emotional stress, excessive sweating (hyperhidrosis) may lead to secondary skin changes, rashes, blisters, and infections; therefore, hyperhidrosis may underlie a number of other dermatological conditions that are not primarily related to emotions. Basically, hyperhidrosis may be viewed as an anxiety phenomenon mediated by the autonomic nervous system; it must be differentiated from drug-induced states of hyperhidrosis.

References

Ader R, Cohen N, Felten D: Brain, behavior, and immunity. Brain Behav Immun *1*: 1, 1987.

Blackwell B: Chronic pain. In *Comprehensive Textbook of Psychiatry*, ed 5, H I Kaplan and B J Sadock, editors, p 1264. Williams & Wilkins, Baltimore, 1989.

Breitbart W: Psychiatric management of cancer pain. Cancer *63* (11, Suppl): 2336, 1989.

Byrne D G: Personality, life events and cardiovascular disease. J Psychosom Res *31*: 661, 1987.

Case R B, Heller S S, Case N B: Type A behavior and survival after acute myocardial infarction. N Engl J Med *312*: 737, 1984.

Cassileth B R, Lusk E J, Miller D S, Brown L L, Miller R: Psychosocial correlates of survival in advanced malignant disease. N Engl J Med *312*: 1551, 1985.

Dimsdale J E, Young D, Moore L, Strauss H W: Do plasma norepinephrine levels reflect behavioral stress? Psychosom Med *49*: 375, 1987.

Drossman D A, Powell D W, Sessions J T Jr: The irritable bowel syndrome. Gastroenterology *73*: 811, 1977.

Dunn A J: Nervous system-immune system interactions: An overview. J Recept Res *8*: 589, 1988.

Dworkin R H, Caligor E: Psychiatric diagnosis and chronic pain: DSM-III-R and beyond. J Pain Symp Manag *3*: 87, 1988.

Engel G L: *Psychological Development in Health and Disease.* Saunders, Philadelphia, 1962.

Engel G L: Studies of ulcerative colitis: III. The nature of the psychological processes. Am J Med *19*: 231, 1955.

Fernandez E, Turk D C: The utility of cognitive coping strategies for altering pain perception: A meta-analysis. Pain *38*: 123, 1989.

Kiecolt-Glaser J K, Glaser R: Psychological influences on immunity: Making sense of the relationship between stressful life events and health. Adv Exp Med Biol *245*: 237, 1988.

Kusnecov A, King M G, Husband A J: Immunomodulation by behavioural conditioning. Biol Psychol *28*: 25, 1989.

Lederberg M F, Holland J C: Psycho-oncology. In *Comprehensive Textbook of Psychiatry*, ed 5, H I Kaplan and B J Sadock, editors, p 1249. Williams & Wilkins, Baltimore, 1989.

Melnechuck T: Emotions, brain, immunity, and health: A review. In *Emotions and Psychopathology*, M Clynes and J Panksepp, editors. Plenum, New York, 1988.

Merskey H: Psychiatry and chronic pain. Can J Psychiatry *34*: 329, 1989.

Miller T W: Advances in understanding the impact of stressful life events on health. Hosp Community Psychiatry *39*: 615, 1988.
Norton C S, Clouse R E, Spitznagel E L, Alpers D H: The relation of ulcerative colitis to psychiatric factors: A review of findings and methods. Am J Psychiatry *147*: 974, 1990.
Nunes E V, Frank K A, Kornfeld D S: Psychologic treatment for the type A behavior pattern and for coronary heart disease: A metanalysis of the literature. Psychosom Med *49*: 159, 1987.
Paykel E S: Methodology of life events research. Adv Psychosom Med *17*: 13, 1987.
Phillips D P, King E W: Death takes a holiday: Mortality surrounding major social occasions. Lancet *2*: 728, 1988.
Phillips D P, Smith D G: Postponement of death until symbolically meaningful occasions. JAMA *263*: 1947, 1990.
Price D D: *Psychological and Neural Mechanisms of Pain*. Raven Press, New York, 1988.
Shekelle R B, Gale M, Ostfeld A M, Paul O: Hostility, risk of coronary heart disease and mortality: Psychosom Med *45*: 109, 1983.
Siegel L J, Smith K E: Children's strategies for coping with pain. Pediatrician *16*: 110, 1989.
Siegmann A W, Feldstein S, Tomasso C T, Ringel N, Lating B A: Expressive vocal behavior and the severity of coronary artery disease. Psychosom Med *49*: 545, 1987.
Solomon G F: Psychoneuroimmunology: Interactions between central nervous system and immune system. J Neurosci Res *18*: 1, 1987.
Stoler M H, Eskin T A, Benn R C, Argerer R C, Argerer L M: Human T-cell lymphotropic virus type III infection of the central nervous system: A preliminary in situ analysis. JAMA *256*: 2360, 1986.
Yager J, Kurtzman F, Landsverk J, Wiesmeier E: Behaviors and attitudes related to eating disorders in homosexual male college students. Am J Psychiatry *145*: 4, 1988.

25.3 / Consultation–Liaison Psychiatry

In consultation–liaison (C–L) psychiatry, the psychiatrist serves as a consultant to a medical colleague (either another psychiatrist or, more commonly, a nonpsychiatric physician) or another mental health professional (psychologist, social worker, or psychiatric nurse). In addition, the C–L psychiatrist consults in regard to patients in medical or surgical settings and provides follow-up psychiatric treatment as needed. In general, C–L psychiatry is associated with all the diagnostic, therapeutic, research, and teaching services that the psychiatrist performs in the general hospital and serves as a bridge between psychiatry and other specialties.

DIAGNOSIS

Knowledge of psychiatric diagnosis is essential to the C–L psychiatrist. Both dementia and delirium frequently complicate organic medical illness, especially among hospital patients. Psychoses and neuroses often complicate the treatment of medical illness. And deviant illness behavior, such as suicide, is a common problem in organically ill patients. The C–L psychiatrist must be aware of the many medical illnesses that can present with psychiatric symptoms. (A list of such medical problems is presented in Table 25.3-1.) The tools that the C–L psychiatrist has for diagnosis are the interview and serial clinical observations. The purposes of the diagnosis are to identify psychiatric disorders and psychological responses to the physical illness, to identify the patient's personality features, and to identify the patient's characteristic coping techniques in order to recommend the therapeutic intervention that is most appropriate to the patient's needs.

PATIENT MANAGEMENT

The C–L psychiatrist's principal contribution to medical management is a comprehensive analysis of the patient's response to illness, psychological and social resources, coping style, and psychiatric illness, if any.

This assessment is the basis of the plan for patient management. In discussing that plan, the C–L psychiatrist makes known his or her assessment of the patient to nonpsychiatric health professionals. The psychiatrist's recommendations should be clear, concrete guidelines for action. The C–L psychiatrist may recommend a specific therapy, suggest areas for further medical inquiry, inform doctors and nurses of their roles in the patient's psychosocial care, recommend a transfer to a psychiatric facility for long-term psychiatric treatment, or suggest or undertake with the patient brief psychotherapy on the medical ward.

The range of problems with which the C–L psychiatrist must deal is very broad. Studies show that up to 65 percent of medical inpatients have psychiatric disorders, the most common symptoms being anxiety, depression, and disorientation. Management problems account for 50 percent of the consultation requests made of psychiatrists. (Table 25.3-2 covers the most common C–L problems with which the psychiatrist must deal.)

SPECIAL SETTINGS

Intensive Care Units

The central psychological aspect of patients in intensive care units (ICUs) is that they are suffering life-threatening illnesses with psychological responses that are predictable and that, if untreated, could threaten life or recovery. Coronary and medical ICU staffs see patients' reactions to acute unexpected illnesses. At first there is fear and anxiety, followed by the psychological behaviors associated with denial, such as acting out, signing out, hostility, and excessive dependency. Staff working in burn units encounter patients going through the problems of acute unexpected illness and, later, depression, grief, and disassociation related to pain and disfigurement. Staff in surgical ICUs see patients recovering from major surgery with the expected disorientation of delirium, depression, and adjustment reactions to surgery.

Treatment of the psychological problems in the ICU requires close attention to diagnostic possibilities and details of the environment, as well as careful team communication. Clinicians clearly are helped by familiarity with the patient's premorbid character, because the reactions to disease and illness are influenced by prior conditioning. The most common initial reactions to acute medical di-

Table 25.3-1
Medical Problems That Present with Psychiatric Symptoms

Disease	Sex and Age Prevalence	Common Medical Symptoms	Psychiatric Symptoms and Complaints	Impaired Performance and Behavior	Diagnostic Problems
Acquired immune deficiency syndrome (AIDS)	Males>females; IV drug abusers, homosexuals, female sex partners of bisexual men	Lymphadenopathy, fatigue, opportunistic infections, Kaposi's sarcoma	Depression, anxiety, disorientation	Dementia with global impairment	Seropositive HIV virus is diagnostic when clinical signs are present
Hyperthyroidism (thyrotoxicosis)	Females 3:1, 20 to 50	Tremor, sweating, loss of weight and strength, heat intolerance	Anxiety, depression	Occasional hyperactive or grandiose behavior	Long lead time; rapid onset resembles anxiety attack
Hypothyroidism (myxedema)	Females 5:1, 30 to 50	Puffy face, dry skin, cold intolerance	Lethargy anxiety with irritability, thought disorder, somatic delusions, hallucinations	Myxedema madness; delusional, paranoid, belligerent behavior	Madness may mimic schizophrenia; mental status is clear, even during most disturbed behavior
Hyperparathyroidism	Females 3:1, 40 to 60	Weakness, anorexia, fractures, calculi, peptic ulcers	Either state may cause anxiety, hyperactivity, and irritability or depression, apathy, and withdrawal	Either state may proceed to a toxic psychosis: confusion, disorientation, and clouded sensorium	Anorexia and fatigue of slow-growing adenoma resemble involutional depression
Hypoparathyroidism	Females, 40 to 60	Hyperreflexia, spasms, tetany			None; rare condition except after surgery
Hyperadrenalism (Cushing's disease)	Adults, both sexes	Weight gain, fat alteration, easy fatigability	Varied; depression, anxiety, thought disorder with somatic delusions	Rarely produces aberrant behavior	Bizarre somatic delusions caused by bodily changes resemble schizophrenia
Adrenal cortical insufficiency (Addison's disease)	Adults, both sexes	Weight loss, hypotension, skin pigmentation	Depression—negativism, apathy; thought disorder—suspiciousness	Toxic psychosis with confusion and agitation	Long lead time; weight loss, apathy, despondency resemble involutional depression
Porphyria—acute intermittent type	Females, 20 to 40	Abdominal crises, paresthesias, weakness	Anxiety—sudden onset, severe; mood swings	Extremes of excitement or withdrawal; emotional or angry outbursts	Patients often have truly neurotic life-styles; crises resemble conversion reactions or anxiety attacks
Pernicious anemia (Addisonian anemia)	Females, 40 to 60	Weight loss, weakness, glossitis, extremity neuritis	Depression—feelings of guilt and worthlessness	Eventual brain damage with confusion and memory loss	Long lead time, sometimes many months; easily mistaken for involutional depression; normal early blood studies may give false reassurance
Hepatolenticular degeneration (Wilson's disease)	Males 2:1, adolescence	Liver and extrapyramidal symptoms	Mood swings—sudden and changeable; anger—explosive	Eventual brain damage with memory and I.Q. loss; combativeness	In late teens, may resemble adolescent storm, incorrigibility, or schizophrenia

(Continued)

Table 25.3-1
Continued

Disease	Sex and Age Prevalence	Common Medical Symptoms	Psychiatric Symptoms and Complaints	Impaired Performance and Behavior	Diagnostic Problems
Hypoglycemia (islet cell adenoma)	Adults, both sexes	Tremor, sweating, hunger, fatigue, dizziness	Anxiety—fear and dread, depression with fatigue	Agitation, confusion; eventual brain damage	Can mimic anxiety attack or acute alcoholism; bizarre behavior may draw attention away from somatic symptoms
Intracranial tumors	Adults, both sexes	None early; headache, vomiting, papilledema later	Varied; depression, anxiety, personality changes	Loss of memory, judgment, self-criticism; clouding of consciousness	Tumor location may not determine early symptoms
Pancreatic carcinoma	Males 3:1, 50 to 70	Weight loss, abdominal pain, weakness, jaundice	Depression, sense of imminent doom but without severe guilt	Loss of drive and motivation	Long lead time; exact age and symptoms of involutional depression
Pheochromocytoma	Adults, both sexes	Headache, sweating during elevated blood pressure	Anxiety, panic, fear, apprehension, trembling	Inability to function during an attack	Classic symptoms of anxiety attack, intermittently normal blood pressures may discourage further studies
Multiple sclerosis	Females, 20 to 40	Motor and sensory losses, scanning speech, nystagmus	Varied; personality changes, mood swings, depression; bland euphoria uncommon	Inappropriate behavior caused by personality changes	Long lead time; early neurological symptoms mimic hysteria or conversion disorders
Systemic lupus erythematosus	Females 8:1, 20 to 40	Multiple symptoms of cardiovascular, genitourinary, gastrointestinal, other systems	Varied; thought disorder, depression, confusion	Toxic psychosis unrelated to steroid treatment	Long lead time, perhaps many years; psychiatric picture variable over time; thought disorder resembles schizophrenia, steroid psychosis

Adapted from table prepared by Maurice J. Martin, M.D.

sasters include shock, fear, and anxiety. In many patients these reactions respond to treatment by the care team, especially succinct, authoritative, and consistent reassurance. When these are insufficient, benzodiazepines—preferably the short-acting forms—should be considered and used cautiously. When fear leads to panic or psychotic loss of control, fast-acting major tranquilizers (e.g., haloperidol [Haldol]) should be used.

Denial and associated behaviors of acting out, hostility, dependency, and demanding behavior must be dealt with individually, on the basis of knowledge of the patient and the reasons for these reactions. Several general points are pertinent. Direct communication with the patient, which allows but does not force a discussion of feelings, often eliminates disruptive behaviors without dealing with them directly. Allowing patients as much mastery as they want and can handle is the most reassuring approach. Permitting patients to make small choices restores some sense of control over the self and the future and calms them far beyond the meaning of the specific choices. They feel a symbolic sense of progress. For example, allowing patients to control pain medications, the lighting level, or where they sit reassures and relaxes them. Whether the disruptive behavior is hostility, dependency, or panic, allowing some to be shown while setting limits on their extremes reassures patients. Thus, the independent patient can be allowed to move around but not too far; the dependent patient can be allowed a limited number of interactions, such as use of the call button; and the hostile patient can be permitted some disagreement and ventilation but be limited in disruptive acts.

All ICUs deal mainly with anxiety, depression, and delirium. ICUs also impose extraordinarily high stress, both on the staff and on the patients, related to the intensity of the problems. Patients and staff alike frequently observe cardiac arrests, deaths, and medical disasters, which leave all autonomically aroused and psychologically defensive. ICU nurses and their patients experience particularly high levels of anxiety, depression, turnover, and burnout.

Attention is often given, especially in the nursing literature, to the problem of stress in the ICU staff. Much

Table 25.3-2
Common Consultation–Liaison Problems

Reason for Consultation	Comments
Suicide attempt or threat	High-risk factors are men over 45, no social support, alcoholism, previous attempt, incapacitating medical illness with pain, and suicidal ideation. If risk is present, transfer to psychiatric unit or start 24-hour nursing care.
Depression	Suicidal risks must be assessed in every depressed patient (see above); presence of cognitive defects in depression may cause diagnostic dilemma with dementia (pseudodementia); check for history of substance abuse or depressant drugs (e.g., reserpine, propranolol); use antidepressants cautiously in cardiac patients because of conduction side effects, orthostatic hypotension.
Agitation	Often related to organic mental disorder, withdrawal from drugs, (e.g., opioids, alcohol, sedative-hypnotics); haloperidol most useful drug for excessive agitation; use physical restraints with great caution; examine for command hallucinations or paranoid ideation to which patient is responding in agitated manner; rule out toxic reaction to medication (e.g., cortisol paranoia, anticholinergic delirium).
Hallucinations	Most common cause in hospital is delirium tremens; onset three to four days after hospitalization. In intensive care units, check for sensory isolation; rule out brief reactive psychosis, schizophrenia, organic mental disorder. Treat with antipsychotic medication.
Sleep disorder	Common cause is pain; early morning awakening associated with depression; difficulty falling asleep associated with anxiety. Use antianxiety or antidepressant agent, depending on cause. These drugs have no analgesic effect, so prescribe adequate painkillers. Rule out early drug withdrawal reaction.
No organic basis for symptoms	Rule out conversion disorder, somatization disorder, factitious disorder, and malingering; glove and stocking anesthesia with autonomic nervous system symptoms seen in conversion; multiple body complaints seen in somatization; wish to be hospitalized seen in factitious disorder; obvious secondary gain in malingering (e.g., compensation case).
Disorientation	Delirium versus dementia; review metabolic status, neurological findings, drug history. Prescribe small dose of antipsychotics for major agitation; benzodiazepines may worsen condition and cause sundowner syndrome (ataxia, confusion); modify environment so patient does not experience sensory deprivation.
Noncompliance or refusal to consent to procedure	Explore relationship of patient and treating doctor; negative transference is most common cause of noncompliance; fears of medication or procedure require education and reassurance. Refusal to give consent is issue of judgment; if impaired, patient can be declared incompetent but only by a judge; organic mental disorder is main cause of impaired judgment in hospitalized patients.

less attention is given to the house staff, especially on the surgical services. All persons in ICUs need to be able to deal directly with their feelings about the extraordinary experiences they are having and the difficult emotional and physical circumstances they are experiencing. Regular support groups in which these persons are able to discuss how they are feeling are important to the ICU staff and the house staff. Such groups are needed to protect the staff from the otherwise predictable psychiatric morbidity that some experience and also to protect their patients from the loss of concentration, the decreased energy, and the psychomotor-retarded communications that some staff otherwise exhibit.

Hemodialysis Units

Hemodialysis units represent a paradigm of complex modern medical treatment settings. Patients are coping with lifelong, debilitating, and limiting disease; they are totally dependent on a multiplex group of care providers for access to a machine controlling their well-being. Dialysis is scheduled three times a week and takes four to six hours, thereby disrupting their previous living routines.

In this context, such patients' major struggle is with the disease. Invariably, however, they also have to come to terms with a level of dependency on others, a dependency they probably have not experienced since childhood. Predictably, patients entering dialysis struggle for their independence; regress to childhood states; show denial by acting out against doctor's orders, by breaking their diet, or by missing sessions; show anger directed against staff; bargain and plead or become infantilized and obsequious; but most often are accepting and courageous. The determinants of the patients' responses to entering dialysis include personality styles and their prior experiences with this or another chronic illness. Patients who have had time to react and adapt to their chronic renal failure face less new psychological work of adaptation than do those to whom renal failure and machine dependency are new. Although little has been written about social factors, the effect of cultural factors in reaction to dialysis and the management of the dialysis unit are known to be important. Units that are run with a firm hand, are consistent in dealing with patients, have clear contingencies for behavioral failures, and have adequate psychological support for staff tend to do the best. Complications of dialysis treatment can include psychiatric problems, such as depression, and suicide is not rare. Sexual problems can be neurogenic, psychogenic, or related to gonadal dysfunction and testicular atrophy.

Table 25.3-3
Transplantation and Surgical Problems

Organ	Biological Factors	Psychological Factors
Kidney	50 to 90 percent success rate. May not be done if patient over age 55. Increasing use of cadaver kidneys, rather than those from living donors.	Living donors must be emotionally stable; parents are best donors, siblings may be ambivalent; donors are subject to depression. Patients who panic before surgery may have poor prognoses; altered body image with fear of organ rejection is common. Group therapy for patients is helpful.
Bone marrow	Used in aplastic anemias and immune system disease.	Patients are usually very ill and must deal with death and dying; compliance is important. Commonly done in children who present problems of prolonged dependency; siblings are often donors who may be angry or ambivalent about procedure.
Heart	End-stage coronary artery disease and cardiomyopathy.	Donor is legally dead; relatives of deceased may refuse permission or be ambivalent. No fall-back position if organ is rejected; kidney rejection patient can go on hemodialysis. Some patients seek transplant hoping to die. Postcardiotomy delirium in 25 percent of patients.
Breast	Radical mastectomy versus lumpectomy.	Reconstruction of breast at time of surgery leads to better postoperative adaptation; veteran patients used to counsel new patients; lumpectomy patients are more open about surgery and sex than are mastectomy patients; group support helpful.
Uterus	Hysterectomy performed on 10 percent of women over 20.	Fear of loss of sexual attractiveness with sexual dysfunction may occur in small percentage of women; loss of childbearing capacity upsetting.
Brain	Anatomical location of lesion determines behavioral change.	Environmental dependency syndrome in frontal lobe tumors characterized by inability to show initiative; memory disturbances involved in periventricular surgery; hallucinations in parieto-occipital area.
Prostate	Cancer surgery has more negative psychobiological effects and is more technically difficult than is surgery for benign hypertrophy.	Sexual dysfunction common except in transurethral prostatectomy (TUP). Perineal prostatectomy produces absence of emission, ejaculation, and erection; penile implant may be of use.
Colon and rectum	Colostomy and ostomy are common outcomes, especially for cancer.	One-third of patients with colostomies feel worse about themselves than before bowel surgery; shame and self-consciousness about stoma can be alleviated by self-help groups that deal with those issues.
Limbs	Amputation performed for massive injury, diabetes, or cancer.	Phantom-limb phenomenon occurs in 98 percent of cases; experience may last for years; sometimes sensation is painful, and neuroma at stump should be ruled out; no known cause or treatment; may stop spontaneously.

Dialysis dementia is a rare condition that consists of loss of memory, disorientation, dystonias, and seizures. It occurs in patients who have been on dialysis for many years. The cause is unknown.

The psychological treatment of dialysis patients falls into two areas. First, careful preparation before dialysis, including the work of adaptation to chronic illness, is important, especially in dealing with denial and unrealistic expectations. All predialysis patients should have a psychosocial evaluation. Second, once in a dialysis program, the patient needs periodic specific inquiries about adaptation, which does not encourage dependence or the sick role. The staff should be sensitive to the likelihood of depression and sexual problems. Group sessions function well for support, and patient self-help groups serve to restore a useful social network, self-esteem, and self-mastery. When needed, tricyclic antidepressants or phenothiazines can be used for dialysis patients. Psychiatric care is best if brief and problem-oriented.

The use of home dialysis units has been of great help. The home-treated patients, compared with hospital-treated patients, are better able to integrate the treatment into their daily lives and feel more autonomous and less dependent on others for their care.

Surgical Units

Some surgeons believe that patients who expect to die during surgery will do so. This belief now seems less superstitious than it did earlier. Kimball and others have studied the premorbid psychological adjustment of patients headed for surgery and have shown that those who show evident depression or anxiety and deny it have a higher risk for morbidity and mortality than do those who, given similar depression or anxiety, are able to express it. Even better is to have a positive attitude toward impending surgery. The factors that contribute to an improved outcome for surgery are informed consent, the education of patients so that they know what to expect concerning what they will feel, where they will be (e.g., it is useful to show patients the recovery room), what loss of function to expect, what tubes and gadgets will be in place, and how to cope with the anticipated pain. In cases in which the patients will not be able to talk or see, it is extremely helpful to explain before the surgery what they can do to compensate for these losses. If postoperative states such as confusion, delirium, and pain can be predicted, they should be discussed with the patients in advance to avoid their experiencing them as unwarranted or as signs of danger. The presence of constructive family support members is helpful both before and after the surgery. Table 25.3-3 lists various surgical conditions with which the C–L psychiatrist must deal.

References

Burns B S, Scott J, Burke J, Kessler L: Mental health training of primary care residents: A review of recent literature (1974–1984). Gen Hosp Psychiatry *5*: 157, 1983.

Cohen-Cole S A, Pincus H A, Stoudemire A, Fiester S, Houpt J L: Recent research developments in consultation–liaison psychiatry. Gen Hos Psychiatry *8*: 316, 1986.

Engle G L: The need for a new medical model: A challenge for biomedical science. Science *196*: 129, 1977.

Feifel H, Strack S, Nagy V T: Coping strategies and associated features of medically ill patients. Psychosom Med *49*: 545, 1987.

Fulop G, Strain J, Hammer J S, Lyons J S: Psychiatric and medical comorbidity: Length of stay. Am J Psychiatry *144*: 878, 1987.

Greenhill M B: The development of liaison programs. In *Psychiatric Medicine*, G Usdin, editor. Brunner/Mazel, New York, 1977.

Hammer J S, Lyons J, Strain J J: Microcomputers and consultation psychiatry in the general hospital. Gen Psychiatry *7*: 119, 1985.

Houpt J L, Brodie H K H, eds.: Consultation–liaison psychiatry and behavioral medicine. In *Psychiatry*, R Michael, J O Cavenar, A M Cooper, et al., editors, p 76. Lippincott, Philadelphia, 1987.

Jacobs J, Bernhard M R, Delgado A, Strain J: Screening for organic mental syndrome in the medically ill. Ann Intern Med *86*: 40, 1977.

Levenson J L, Mishra A, Hamer R, Hastillo A: Denial and medical outcome in unstable angina. Psychosom Med *51*: 27, 1989.

Levitan S, Kornfeld D: Clinical and cost benefits of liaison psychiatry. Am J Psychiatry *138*: 790, 1981.

Lipowski Z J: Consultation–liaison psychiatry: The first half century. Gen Hosp Psychiatry *8*: 305, 1986.

Lipowski Z J: *Psychosomatic Medicine and Liaison Psychiatry: Selected Papers*. Plenum, New York, 1985.

Mumford E, Schlesinger H J, Glass G V, Patrick C, Cuerdon T: A new look at evidence about reduced cost of medical utilization following mental health treatment. Am J Psychiatry *141*: 1145, 1984.

Pincus H A: Linking general health and mental health systems of care: Conceptual models of implementation. Am J Psychiatry *137*: 315, 1980.

Popkin M, MacKenzie T, Callies A: Consultation liaison outcome evaluation system. Arch Gen Psychiatry *40*: 215, 1983.

Regier D A, Myers J K, Kramer M, Robins L N, Blazer D G, Hough R L, Eaton W W, Locke B Z: The NIMH epidemiologic catchment area (ECA) program: Historical context, major objectives, and study population characteristics. Arch Gen Psychiatry *41*: 934, 1984.

Schwab J J: Consultation–liaison psychiatry: A historical overview. Psychosomatics *30*: 245, 1989.

Strain J: Diagnostic considerations in the medical setting. In *The Medically Ill Patient*, J Strain, editor. Clin North Am *4*: 287, 1981.

Strain J: *Psychological Interventions in Medical Practice*. Appleton-Century-Crofts, New York, 1978.

Strain J, Pincus H A, Houpt J L, Gise L H, Taintor Z: Models of mental health training for primary care physicians. Psychosom Med *47*: 95, 1985.

Strain J J, Taintor Z: Consultation–liaison psychiatry. In *Comprehensive Textbook of Psychiatry*, ed 5, H I Kaplan and B J Sadock, editors, p 1272. William & Wilkins, Baltimore, 1989.

Uhlenhuth E H, Balter M B, Mellinger G D, et al: Symptom checklist syndromes in the general population: Correlations with psychotherapeutic drug use. Arch Gen Psychiatry *40*: 1167, 1983.

Wallen J, Pincus H A, Goldman H A, Marcus S E: Psychiatric consultations in short-term general hospitals. Arch Gen Psychiatry *44*: 163, 1987.

Weiner H: *Psychobiology of Health and Disease*. Elsevier, New York, 1977.

25.4 / Treatment

The concept of psychomedical treatment—that is, the approach that emphasizes the interrelation of mind and body in the genesis of symptom and disorder—calls for a greatly expanded sharing of responsibility among various professions. If one views disease from a multicausal point of view, every disease can be considered psychosomatic, since every disorder is affected in some fashion by emotional factors.

Hostility, depression, and anxiety, in varying proportions, are at the root of most psychosomatic disorders. Psychosomatic medicine is principally concerned with those illnesses that present primarily somatic manifestations. The presenting complaint is usually physical; patients rarely complain of their anxiety or depression or tension but, rather, of their vomiting or diarrhea or anorexia.

TYPES OF PATIENTS

A special evaluation of the psychological and somatic factors of three major groups of medical patients is required.

Psychosomatic Illness Group

Patients in this group suffer from such classic psychosomatic disorders as peptic ulcer and ulcerative colitis. In these disease processes one cannot posit a strictly psychogenic explanation, since the particular set of emotional factors found, for example, in the typical ulcer case may also appear in the patient with no history of ulcer.

Psychiatric Group

Patients in this group suffer from physical disturbances caused by psychological illness, rather than physical illness. Their somatic disabilities may be real (objective) or unreal. When real, the disability involves the voluntary nervous system and is termed a conversion disorder, previously called a conversion hysteria. Among the unreal disabilities are hypochondriasis and delusional preoccupation with physical functioning, which is often seen in schizophrenic patients. Patients in this group suffer primarily from a psychological disturbance that requires psychiatric treatment, but auxiliary medical therapy may be necessary.

Reactive Group

Patients in this group do have actual organic disorders, but they also suffer from an associated psychological disturbance. For example, a patient with heart disease or renal disease requiring dialysis may have a reactive anxiety and depression regarding this life-threatening condition. This anxiety, in turn, may produce physical manifestations that complicate the somatic situation.

COMBINED PSYCHOMEDICAL TREATMENT APPROACH

The combined treatment approach, in which the psychiatrist handles the psychiatric aspects of the case and the internist or other specialist treats the somatic aspects, requires the closest collaboration between the two physicians. The purpose of the medical therapy is to build up the patient's physical state so that the patient can successfully participate in psychotherapy for total cure.

Disorders such as bronchial asthma, in which psychosocial processes play a distinct role in the development and the course, may respond well to the combined treatment approach. Although the asthmatic attacks themselves may be treated successfully by the physician, psychiatric treatment can be useful in the short run by helping to alleviate the anxiety associated with the attacks and in the long run by helping to uncover the causes of the interdependency involved in the disorder.

In the acute phase of a somatic illness, such as an acute attack of ulcerative colitis, medical therapy is the primary form of treatment; psychotherapy, with its long-range goals, consists at that stage of reassurance and support. As the pendulum of disease activity shifts and the illness progresses to a chronic state, psychotherapy assumes the primary role and medical therapy the less active position.

Sometimes reassurance is all that is needed in the treatment of psychosomatic syndromes.

Patients must participate in the process of improving their life situations. The symptoms themselves must be treated by the internist, but the psychiatrist can help patients focus on their feelings about the symptoms and gain understanding of the unconscious processes involved.

If patients are handled insensitively or if their illness is regarded unsympathetically, the results can be grave.

Indications for Combined Treatment

If during an initial attack of a psychosomatic disorder the patient responds to active medical therapy in association with the superficial support, ventilation, reassurance, and environmental manipulation provided by the internist, additional psychotherapy by a psychiatrist may not be required. Psychosomatic illness that does not respond to medical treatment or that is in a chronic phase should receive psychosomatic evaluation by a psychiatrist and combined therapy as indicated.

Goal of Combined Therapy

It is useful to set up a tentative, elastic spectrum of therapeutic goals in the treatment of psychosomatic disorders. The end desired is cure, which means resolution of the structural impairment and reorganization of the personality, so that needs and tensions no longer produce pathophysiological results. Treatment should aim at a more mature general life adjustment, increased capacity for physical and occupational activity, amelioration of the progression of the disease, reversal of the pathology, avoidance of complications of the basic disease process, decreased use of secondary gain associated with the illness, and increased capacity to adjust to the presence of the disease.

PSYCHIATRIC ASPECTS

Treatment of psychosomatic disorders from the psychiatric viewpoint is a difficult task. The purpose of therapy should be to understand the motivations and mechanisms of disturbed function and to help patients understand the nature of their illness and the implications of their costly adaptive patterns. This insight should result in changed and healthier patterns of behavior.

Psychotherapy based on analytic principles is effective in treating psychosomatic disorders mainly in terms of the patients' experiences in the treatment, particularly regarding their relationships with the therapist. These patients are usually even more reluctant to deal with their emotional problems than are patients with other psychiatric problems. Psychosomatic patients try to avoid responsibility for their illness by isolating the diseased organ and presenting it to the doctor for diagnosis and cure. The patients, thus, may be satisfying an infantile need to be cared for passively, at the same time denying that they are adults, with all the attendant stresses and conflicts.

Resistance to Entering Psychotherapy

When psychosomatic patients first become ill, they are usually convinced that the illness is purely organic in origin. They reject psychotherapy as treatment for their sickness, and, in fact, the very idea of emotional illness may be repugnant because of personal prejudices concerning psychiatry.

In the initial phase, physical treatment and psychotherapeutic procedures must be combined subtly. A good arrangement in the early stage is treatment by a psychologically oriented physician, one who is sensitive to unconscious and transference phenomena and who is perhaps working with a psychotherapist.

Development of Relationship and Transference

Psychotherapy with the psychosomatic patient must often proceed more slowly and cautiously than with other psychiatric patients. Positive transference should be developed gradually. The psychiatrist must be supportive and reassuring during the acute phase of the illness. As the disorder enters a chronic stage, the psychiatrist may make exploratory interpretations, but a strong patient-physician relationship is essential for any such exploration. The psychosomatic patient is very dependent, and this characteristic may be used supportively and interpretatively at crucial periods in the treatment. During therapy, a great deal of hostility appears—first in the form of overt ventilation and then in the framework of the transference. Free and appropriate expression of the patient's hostility is to be encouraged.

Interpretation

The therapist must pay particular attention to current problems in the patient's immediate life situation and deal with the patient's reaction to the therapist and to treatment. There should be increased emphasis on evaluation of the patient's characterological difficulties and habitual reactions, particularly reactions to himself or herself (self-esteem, guilt) and reactions to his or her environment (dependency, submission, need for affection). The psychiatrist should also analyze the patient's anxieties and coping mechanisms for stress situations, such as asking for complete care, always having to be right, refraining from self-assertion, and suppressing all forbidden impulses.

Some psychoanalytic investigators have reported dramatic results when unconscious material was interpreted as a drastic measure during an acute phase. Although most Freudian psychoanalysts seem to think that genetic material must eventually be interpreted for a complete cure, newer approaches have demonstrated that adequate results can be obtained when psychotherapy is limited to the analysis of characterological and ego defenses associated with disturbed interpersonal relations.

Psychosomatic patients are often involved in a repetitious pattern involving stress in their interpersonal relations. Because such patients are usually unaware of this pattern, it is helpful to show them that the pattern is not accidental but is determined by factors of which they are unaware, and it is essential to show them how they may change this disturbing pattern and act in a new and healthier manner.

Psychosomatic patients tend to drive toward psychologically regressed mental and physical behavior. Usually, their regression is to a traumatic or highly conflictual period. By reenacting certain specific attitudes of childhood or infancy, they are attempting to master the anxiety and illness first manifested during those earlier stages.

In the treatment of psychosomatic disorders, the key concept is flexibility in technique. Because of the patient's poor motivation and poor physical condition, it may be necessary to make frequent changes in the psychotherapeutic approach.

Resistance During Therapy

Since psychosomatic patients frequently have a great deal of resistance to entering psychotherapy, it is not surprising that the resistance often continues unabated during therapy. In many patients the motivation for entering treatment is so poor that they frequently drop out of therapy for minor reasons.

Interruption of Psychotherapy for a Medical Emergency

During a course of psychotherapy, a patient with a psychosomatic disorder may require medical or surgical treatment for the organic disorder. The psychiatrist should cooperate closely with the surgeon or medical personnel and should maintain contact with the patient—in person or by telephone—during the emergency. Such interest offers valuable emotional support in a time of crisis.

If a patient is hospitalized, the psychiatrist should help other hospital personnel recognize and learn to tolerate the frequently difficult and provocative behavior of certain psychosomatic patients. The preparation can be of use to such patients as well; if they see their demands being met considerately, they may be less inclined to view their world as hostile and formidable.

Danger of Psychosis

There are no simple relationships between psychosomatic disorders and psychoses. Some people in whom physiological and psychological processes are poorly integrated manifest both psychosomatic disorders and psychoses. In others, the ego integration is such that stress produces a breakdown of bodily function, rather than a psychotic maladjustment. Some nonpsychotic psychosomatic patients can become psychotic or exhibit symptoms as a result of too active an interpretation and the removal of defensive elements in the personality structure.

MEDICAL ASPECTS

The internist's treatment of psychosomatic disorders should follow the established rules for their medical management. Generally, the internist should spend as much time as possible with the patient and listen sympathetically to the many complaints. The internist must be reassuring and supportive. Before performing a physically manipulative procedure—particularly if it is painful, such as a colonoscopy—the internist should explain to the patient just what will happen. The explanation allays the patient's anxiety, makes the patient more cooperative, and actually facilitates the examination.

The patient's attitude toward taking drugs may also affect the outcome of the psychosomatic treatment. For example, patients suffering from diabetes who do not accept their illness and who have self-destructive impulses of which they are unaware, may purposely not control their diet and, as a result, end up in a hyperglycemic coma. In the case of cardiac patients, some refuse to curtail their physical activity after a myocardial infarction because of a reluctance to admit weakness or because of a fear that they will somehow be considered less successful. Others use their illness as a welcome punishment for guilt or as a way of avoiding responsibility. Therapy in such cases must strive to help patients to minimize their fears and to focus on self-care and the reestablishment of a healthy body image.

ACCEPTANCE OF PSYCHOMEDICAL TREATMENT

The advantages of the collaborative approach are that the patient receives the benefit of the efforts of specialists trained in various medical disciplines, each working in the area in which he or she is best equipped to function. However, some physicians have resisted the psychiatric approach because of inadequate training in psychiatry in medical school, unfamiliarity with the specialized language of psychiatry, and a general prejudice based on the high cost of psychotherapy and the alleged unscientific and subjective aspects of psychiatry.

OTHER TYPES OF THERAPY FOR PSYCHOSOMATIC DISORDERS

Other types of treatment have been introduced for psychosomatic disorders, some of which are described below. The first category includes psychotherapies based on psychological insight and change, such as group and family psychotherapy; the second category is composed of behavior therapies based on Pavlovian principles of learning new behavior, such as biofeedback and relaxation therapy.

Group Psychotherapy and Family Therapy

Because of the psychopathological significance of the mother-child relationship in the development of psychosomatic reactions, modification of this relationship has been suggested as a likely focus of emphasis in the psychotherapy of psychosomatic disorders. T. B. Karasu suggested that the group approach should also offer greater interpersonal contact, providing increased ego support for the weak egos of psychosomatic patients who fear the threat of isolation and parental separation. Family therapy offers hope of a change in the relationship between the family and the child. Both therapies have had excellent initial clinical results.

The long-term evaluation of results of the various psychotherapies, individual and group, of psychosomatic disorders remains to be carried out. Karasu concluded after an exhaustive study of psychosomatic psychotherapeutic treatment that "some patients with medical disorders may respond positively to psychological treatment, either physically or psychologically. Some medical disorders appear to be more amenable to psychotherapy than other disorders. Some therapeutic modalities appear to be more effective than others. Some persons appear to be more responsive to psychotherapy than others, especially in relation to the nature of their psychopathology, rather than their physical pathology."

Behavior Therapies

Biofeedback. The application of biofeedback treatment techniques to patients with hypertension, cardiac arrhythmias, epilepsy, and tension headaches has provided encouraging but inconclusive therapeutic results.

Relaxation treatment. The treatment of hypertension may be accomplished through the use of the relaxation response. Positive results have been published about alcoholism and drug abuse treatment's using the relaxation response through the practice of transcendental meditation. Workers have also used meditation in the therapy for headaches. See Section 29.6 for further discussion of the various types of behavior therapies.

References

Alexander F: *Psychosomatic Medicine*. Norton, New York, 1950.

Book H E: Empathy: Misconceptions and misuses in psychotherapy. Am J Psychiatry *145*: 4, 1988.

Gilbert M M: Reactive depression as a model psychosomatic disease. Psychosomatics *11*: 426, 1970.

Karasu T B: Psychotherapy of the medically ill. Am J. Psychiatry *136*: 1, 1979.

Karush A, Daniels G E, Flood C, O'Connor J F: *Psychotherapy in Chronic Ulcerative Colitis*. Saunders, Philadelphia. 1977.

Kyle J: *Crohn's Disease*. Heinemann, London, 1972.

Lipowski Z J: Psychosomatic medicine: Past and present. Can J Psychiatry *31*: 2, 1986.

Miller L: The mind and the body. Int J Psychiatry *7*: 518, 1967.

Vitaliano P P, Maivro R D, Russo J, et al: A biopsychosocial model of medical student distress. J Behav Med *11*: 311, 1988.

26

Personality Disorders

Personality can be defined as the totality of emotional and behavioral traits that characterize the person in day-to-day living under ordinary conditions; it is relatively stable and predictable. A personality disorder is a variant of those character traits that goes beyond the range found in most people. According to the revised third edition of *Diagnostic and Statistical Manual of Mental Disorders* (DSM-III-R), it is only when personality traits are inflexible and maladaptive and cause either significant functional impairment or subjective distress that they constitute a class of personality disorder. Patients with personality disorders show deeply ingrained, inflexible, and maladaptive patterns of relating to and perceiving both the environment and themselves.

These patients are far more likely to refuse psychiatric help and to deny their problems than are patients with anxiety, depression, or obsessive-compulsive disorder. The personality disorder symptoms are alloplastic (i.e., capable of adapting and altering the external environment) and ego-syntonic (i.e., acceptable to the ego); patients with a personality disorder do not feel anxiety about their maladaptive behavior. Because such patients do not routinely acknowledge pain from what society perceives as their symptoms, they are often regarded as unmotivated for treatment and impervious to recovery.

CLASSIFICATION

DSM-III-R groups the personality disorders into three clusters. The first cluster (A) includes the paranoid, schizoid, and schizotypal personality disorders. Persons with these disorders often appear odd and eccentric. The second cluster (B) includes the histrionic, narcissistic, antisocial, and borderline personality disorders. Persons with these disorders often appear dramatic, emotional, and erratic. The third cluster (C) includes the avoidant, dependent, obsessive-compulsive, and passive-aggressive personality disorders. Persons with these disorders often appear anxious or fearful.

According to DSM-III-R, many people exhibit traits that are not limited to a single personality disorder, and, if a patient meets the criteria for more than one disorder, each one should be diagnosed. Personality disorders are coded on Axis II of DSM-III-R.

ETIOLOGY

Genetic Factors

The best evidence that genetic factors contribute to the genesis of personality disorders comes from the investigations of psychiatric disorders in 15,000 pairs of twins in the United States. Among monozygotic twins, the concordance for personality disorders was several times higher than that among dizygotic twins. Moreover, according to one recent study, on multiple measures of personality and temperament, occupational and leisure-time interests, and social attitudes, monozygotic twins reared apart are about as similar as are monozygotic twins reared together.

Cluster A illnesses (paranoid, schizoid, and schizotypal) are more common in the biological relatives of schizophrenics than among control groups. Significantly more relatives with schizotypal personality disorder are found in the family histories of persons with schizophrenia than among control groups. There is less correlation between paranoid and schizoid personality disorders and schizophrenia.

Cluster B illnesses (histrionic, narcissistic, antisocial, and borderline) demonstrate a genetic predisposition for antisocial personality disorder, which is also associated with alcoholism. Depression is more common in the family backgrounds of borderline personality disorder patients. There is also a strong association between histrionic personality disorder and somatization disorder (Briquet's syndrome), in that patients with each disorder show an overlap of symptoms. Borderline personality disorder patients have more relatives with mood disorders than do control groups, and borderline personality disorder and mood disorder often coexist.

Cluster C disorders (obsessive-compulsive, passive-aggressive, dependent, and avoidant) may also have a genetic base. Obsessive-compulsive traits are more common in monozygotic twins than in dizygotic twins, and obsessive-compulsive personality disorder patients show some signs associated with depression (e.g., shortened rapid eye movement [REM] latency period, abnormal dexamethasone-suppression test [DST] results). The avoidant personality disorder patient often has a high anxiety level.

Temperamental Factors

Temperamental factors have been identified in childhood that may be associated with personality disorders in adulthood. For example, children who are temperamentally fearful may develop avoidant personality disorders.

Central nervous system dysfunctions in childhood associated with soft neurological signs are most common in antisocial and borderline personality disorders. Children with minimal brain damage are at risk for personality disorders, particularly the antisocial types.

Certain personality disorders may arise from poor parental fit—that is, a poor match between temperament and child-rearing practices. For example, an anxious child reared by an equally anxious mother is more vulnerable to a personality disorder than would be the same child raised by a tranquil mother. Stella Chess and Alexander Thomas referred to this as goodness of fit. Cultures that encourage aggression may unwittingly reinforce and thereby contribute to paranoid and antisocial personality disorders. The physical environment may also play a role. For example, an active young child may appear hyperactive if kept in a small closed apartment but may appear normal in a large middle-class house with a fenced-in yard.

Biological Factors

Hormones. Persons who show impulsive traits often also show increased levels of testosterone, 17-estradiol, and estrone. In nonhuman primates, androgens increase the likelihood of aggression and sexual behavior; however, the role of testosterone in human aggression is not clear. DST results are abnormal in some borderline personality disorder patients with depressive symptoms.

Platelet monoamine oxidase. Low platelet monoamine oxidase (MAO) has been associated with activity and sociability in monkeys. College students with low platelet MAO report spending more time in social activities than do students with high platelet MAO. Low platelet MAO has also been noted in some schizotypal patients.

Smooth pursuit eye movements. Smooth pursuit eye movements (SPEM) are abnormal in persons with the traits of introversion, low self-esteem, and withdrawal and in patients with schizotypal personality disorder. Movements in those persons are saccadic (i.e., jerky). These findings have no clinical application, but they do indicate the role of inheritance.

Neurotransmitters. Endorphins have effects similar to those of exogenous morphine, including analgesia and suppression of arousal. High endogenous endorphins may be associated with a phlegmatic passive person. Studies of personality traits and the dopaminergic and serotonergic systems indicate an arousal-activating function for these neurotransmitters. Levels of 5-hydroxyindoleacetic acid (5-HIAA), a metabolite of serotonin, are low in persons who attempt suicide and in patients who are impulsive and aggressive.

Electrophysiology. Changes in electrical conductance on the electroencephalogram (EEG) have been found in some patients with personality disorders, most commonly in the antisocial and borderline types, in which slow-wave activity is seen.

Psychoanalytic Theory

Sigmund Freud believed that personality traits resulted from a fixation at one of the psychosocial stages of development and from the interplay between impulses and persons in the environment (known as object choices). He used the term "character" to describe the organization of the personality and identified several character types: (1) oral characters, who are passive and dependent and who take in food or other substances excessively; (2) anal characters, who are precise, parsimonious, punctual (the three Ps of the anal triad), and stubborn; (3) obsessional characters, who are rigid and dominated by a harsh superego; and (4) narcissistic characters, who are aggressive and self-serving.

Wilhelm Reich used the term "character armor" to describe defensive mechanisms that protect people from internal impulses and that must be analyzed if psychotherapy is to be successful. Carl Jung used the term "introvert" to describe solitary, introspective types and "extrovert" to describe outgoing, sensation-seeking types. Erik Erikson believed that the inability to establish basic trust led to paranoid disorders and that the failure to become autonomous led to dependent characters.

Defense mechanisms. To help patients with personality disorders, the psychiatrist needs to appreciate their underlying defenses. Defenses are unconscious mental processes that the ego uses to resolve conflicts among the four lodestars of the inner life—instinct (wish or need), reality, important people, and conscience. When defenses are most effective, especially in personality disorders, they can abolish anxiety and depression. Thus, a major reason that patients with personality disorders are so reluctant to alter their behavior is that to abandon a defense is to increase conscious anxiety and depression.

Although patients with personality disorders may be characterized by their most dominant or most rigid mechanism, each patient uses several defenses. Therefore, the management of the defense mechanisms used by patients with personality disorders is discussed here as a general topic, rather than under the specific disorders. Many of the formulations presented here in the language of psychoanalytic psychiatry can be translated into principles consistent with cognitive and behavioral approaches.

Fantasy. Many persons—especially eccentric, lonely, frightened persons who are often labeled schizoid—make extensive use of the defense of fantasy. They seek solace and satisfaction within themselves by creating imaginary lives, especially imaginary friends, within their minds. Often, such persons seem strikingly aloof. One needs to understand the unsociability of such persons as resting on a fear of intimacy, rather than to criticize them or feel rebuffed by their rejection. The therapist should maintain a quiet, reassuring, and considerable interest in them without insisting on reciprocal responses. Recognition of their fear of closeness and respect for their eccentric ways are useful.

Dissociation. Dissociation or neurotic denial consists of a Pollyannalike replacement of unpleasant affects with pleasant ones. Frequent users of dissociation are often seen as dramatizing and as emotionally shallow; they may be labeled histrionic personalities. Their behavior is reminiscent of the stunts of anxious adolescents who, to erase anxiety, carelessly expose themselves to exciting dangers. Accepting such patients as exuberant and seductive is to miss their anxiety; but confronting them with their vulnerabilities and defects is to make them still more defensive. Because they seek appreciation of their attractiveness and courage, the therapist should not be too reserved. While remaining calm and firm, the therapist should realize that these patients are often inadvertent liars. Patients who use dissociation benefit from having a chance to ventilate their own anxieties; in the process they may "remember" what they "forgot." Often, dissociation and denial are best dealt with by the therapist's using displacement. Thus, the clinician may talk with patients about the same affective issue but in a context of a less threatening circumstance. The clinician's empathizing with the denied affect of such patients without directly confronting them with the facts may allow the patients to raise the original topic themselves.

Isolation. Isolation is characteristic of the orderly, controlled person, often labeled an obsessive-compulsive personality, who, unlike the histrionic personality, remembers the truth in fine detail but without affect. In a crisis there may be an intensification of self-restraint, overformal social behavior, and obstinacy. The patient's quest for control may be annoying or boring to the clinician. Often, such patients respond well to precise, systematic, and rational explanations. They value efficiency, cleanliness, and punctuality as much as they do the clinician's affective responsiveness. Whenever possible, clinicians should allow such patients to control their own care, rather than engage in a battle of wills.

Projection. In projection the patients attribute their own unacknowledged feelings to others. Excessive fault finding and sensitivity to criticism may seem to be prejudiced, hypervigilant injustice collecting but should not be met by defensiveness and argument. Instead, even minor mistakes on the part of the examiner and the possibility of future difficulties should be frankly acknowledged. Strict honesty, concern for the patient's rights, and maintaining the same formal, concerned distance as with a patient using fantasy are helpful. Confrontation guarantees a lasting enemy and an early termination of the interview. The therapist need not agree with the patient's injustice collecting, though, but should ask if they can agree to disagree.

The technique of counterprojection is especially helpful. In that technique the clinician acknowledges and gives paranoid patients full credit for their feelings and for their perceptions. Further, the clinician neither disputes the patient's complaints nor reinforces them but acknowledges that the world the paranoid patient describes can be imagined. The interviewer can then talk about the real motives and feelings, even though they are misattributed to someone else, and begin to cement an alliance with the patient.

Splitting. In splitting the patient divides ambivalently regarded people, both past and present, into good people and bad people. For example, in an inpatient setting, some staff members are idealized, and others are uniformly disparaged. The effect of that defensive behavior on a hospital ward can be highly disruptive; it ultimately provokes the staff to turn against the patient. Splitting is best mastered if the staff members anticipate the process, discuss it at staff meetings, and gently confront the patient with the fact that no one is all good or all bad.

Passive aggression. In passive-aggressive defenses the anger is turned against the self. In military psychiatry and DSM-III-R, such behavior is called passive-aggressive or self-defeating; in psychoanalytic terminology it is most often described as masochism. It includes failure, procrastinations, silly or provocative behavior, self-demeaning clowning, and frankly self-destructive behavior. The hostility in such behavior is never entirely concealed; indeed, the mechanism, as in the case of wrist cutting, engenders such anger in others that they feel they themselves have been assaulted and view the patient as a sadist, not a masochist. Passive aggression is best dealt with by trying to get the patients to ventilate their anger.

Acting out. In acting out there is direct expression through action of an unconscious wish or conflict to avoid being conscious of either the idea or the affect that accompanies it. Tantrums, apparently motiveless assaults, child abuse, and pleasureless promiscuity are common examples. Because the behavior occurs outside reflective awareness, acting out often appears to the observer to be unaccompanied by guilt. Once acting out is not possible, the conflict behind the defense may be accessible. Faced with acting out, either aggressive or sexual, in an interview situation, the clinician must recognize (1) that the patient has lost control, (2) that anything the interviewer says will probably be misheard, and (3) that getting the patient's attention is of paramount importance. Depending on the circumstances, the clinician's response may be, "How can I help you if you keep screaming?" Or, if the patient's loss of control seems to be escalating, "If you continue screaming, I'll leave." The interviewer who feels genuinely frightened of the patient can simply leave and ask for help, if necessary, from the police.

INDIVIDUAL PERSONALITY DISORDERS

Paranoid Personality Disorder

Definition. Persons with paranoid personality disorder are characterized by long-standing suspiciousness and mistrust of people in general. They refuse responsibility for their own feelings and assign responsibility to others. They are often hostile, irritable, and angry. The bigot, the injustice collector, the pathologically jealous spouse, and the litigious crank often have paranoid personality disorder.

Epidemiology. The prevalence of this disorder is not known. Persons with paranoid personality disorder rarely seek treatment themselves; when referred to treatment by a spouse or an employer, they can often pull themselves together and not appear distressed. Relatives of schizophrenic patients show a higher incidence of paranoid personality disorder than do controls. The disorder is more common in men than in women, and it does not appear to have a familial pattern. There is no higher than usual incidence among homosexuals, as was once thought, but it is believed to be more common among minority groups, immigrants, and the deaf than in the general population.

Clinical features. According to DSM-III-R, the essential feature of this disorder is a pervasive and unwarranted tendency—beginning by early adulthood and present in a variety of contexts—to interpret other people's actions as deliberately demeaning or threatening. Almost invariably, persons with this disorder expect to be exploited or harmed by others in some way. Frequently, they question, without justification, the loyalty or trustworthiness of friends or associates. Often, such persons are pathologically jealous, questioning without justification the fidelity of their spouses or sexual partners.

These patients externalize their own emotions and use the defense of projection—that is, they attribute to others impulses and thoughts that they are unable to accept in themselves. Ideas of reference and logically defended illusions are common.

Patients with this disorder are affectively restricted and appear unemotional. They pride themselves on being rational and objective, but such is not the case. Such patients lack warmth and are impressed with and pay close attention to power and rank, expressing disdain for those who are seen as weak, sickly, impaired, or defective in some way. In social situations persons with paranoid personality disorder may appear businesslike and efficient, but they often generate fear or conflict in others.

Course and prognosis. There are no adequate and systematic long-term studies of paranoid personality disorder. In some persons the paranoid personality disorder is lifelong. In others it is a harbinger of schizophrenia. In still others, as they mature or as stress diminishes, paranoid traits give way to reaction formation, appropriate concern with morality, and altruistic concerns. In general, however, patients with this disorder have lifelong problems working and living with others. Occupational and marital problems are common.

Diagnosis. On psychiatric examination, patients with paranoid personality disorder may appear quite formal and baffled at having been required to seek psychiatric help. Muscular tension, an inability to relax, and a need to scan the environment for clues may be evident. Their affect is often humorless and serious. Although some of the premises of their arguments may be false, their speech is goal-directed and logical. Their thought content shows evidence of projection, prejudice, and occasional ideas of reference. The DSM-III-R diagnostic criteria are listed in Table 26-1.

Differential diagnosis. Paranoid personality disorder can usually be differentiated from delusional disorder because fixed delusions are absent in paranoid personality disorder. It can be differentiated from paranoid schizophrenia because hallucinations and formal thought disorder are absent in the personality disorders. Paranoid personality disorder can be distinguished from borderline personality disorder because the paranoid patient is rarely as capable as the borderline patient is of overinvolved, tumultuous relations with others. Paranoid patients lack the antisocial character's long history of antisocial behavior. Persons with schizoid personality disorder are withdrawn and aloof and do not have paranoid ideation.

Table 26-1
Diagnostic Criteria for Paranoid Personality Disorder

A. A pervasive and unwarranted tendency, beginning by early adulthood and present in a variety of contexts, to interpret the actions of people as deliberately demeaning or threatening, as indicated by at least *four* of the following:
   (1) expects, without sufficient basis, to be exploited or harmed by others
   (2) questions, without justification, the loyalty or trustworthiness of friends or associates
   (3) reads hidden demeaning or threatening meanings into benign remarks or events (e.g., suspects that a neighbor put out trash early to annoy him)
   (4) bears grudges or is unforgiving of insults or slights
   (5) is reluctant to confide in others because of unwarranted fear that the information will be used against him or her
   (6) is easily slighted and quick to react with anger or to counterattack
   (7) questions, without justification, fidelity of spouse or sexual partner

B. Occurrence not exclusively during the course of schizophrenia or a delusional disorder

Table from DSM-III-R, *Diagnostic and Statistical Manual of Mental Disorders,* ed 3, revised. Copyright American Psychiatric Association, Washington, DC, 1987, with permission.

Treatment

Psychotherapy. Psychotherapy is the treatment of choice. Therapists should be straightforward in all their dealings with the patient. If a therapist is accused of some inconsistency or fault, such as lateness for an appointment, honesty and an apology are better than a defensive explanation. Therapists must remember that trust and toleration of intimacy are troubled areas for patients with this disorder. Individual psychotherapy thus requires a professional and not overly warm style from the therapist. Paranoid patients do not do well in group psychotherapy, nor are they likely to tolerate the intrusiveness of the behavior therapies. Too zealous a use of interpretation—especially interpretation concerning deep feelings of dependency, sexual concerns, and wishes for intimacy—significantly increases the patient's mistrust.

At times, the behavior of patients with paranoid personality disorder becomes so threatening that it is important to control it or set limits on it. Delusional accusations must be dealt with realistically but gently and without humiliating the patient. It is profoundly frightening for paranoid patients to feel that those trying to help them are weak and helpless; therefore, therapists should never threaten to take over control unless they are both willing and able to do so.

Behavior therapy has been used to improve social skills and to diminish suspiciousness through role playing.

Pharmacotherapy. Pharmacotherapy is useful in dealing with agitation or anxiety. In most cases an antianxiety agent such as diazepam (Valium) is sufficient. But it may be necessary to use an antipsychotic, such as thioridazine (Mellaril) or haloperidol (Haldol), in small doses and for brief periods of time to manage severe agitation or quasidelusional thinking.

The antipsychotic drug pimozide (Orap) has been successful in reducing paranoid ideation in some patients.

Schizoid Personality Disorder

Definition. Schizoid personality disorder is diagnosed in patients who display a lifelong pattern of social withdrawal. Their discomfort with human interaction, their introversion, and their bland, constricted affect are noteworthy. Persons with schizoid personality disorder are often seen by others as eccentric, isolated, or lonely.

Epidemiology. The prevalence of schizoid personality disorder is not clearly established. Schizoid personality disorder may affect 7.5 percent of the general population. The sex ratio of the disorder is unknown, although some studies report a 2-to-1 male-to-female ratio. Persons with the disorder tend to gravitate toward solitary jobs that involve little or no contact with others. Many prefer night work to day work, so that they do not have to deal with many people.

Clinical features. Persons with schizoid personality disorder give an impression of being cold and aloof and display a remote reserve and a lack of involvement with everyday events and the concerns of others. They appear quiet, distant, seclusive, and unsociable. They may pursue their own lives with remarkably little need or longing for emotional ties with others. They are the last to catch on to changes in popular fashion.

The life histories of such persons reflect solitary interests and success at noncompetitive, lonely jobs that others find difficult to tolerate. Their sexual lives may exist exclusively in fantasy, and they may postpone mature sexuality indefinitely. Men may not marry because they are unable to achieve intimacy; women may passively agree to marry an aggressive man who wants the marriage. Usually, persons with schizoid personality disorder reveal a lifelong inability to express anger directly. They are able to invest enormous affective energy in nonhuman interests, such as mathematics and astronomy, and they may be very attached to animals. They are often engrossed in dietary and health fads, philosophical movements, and social improvement schemes, especially those that require no personal involvement.

Although persons with schizoid personality disorder appear self-absorbed and engaged in excessive daydreaming, they show no loss of capacity to recognize reality. Because aggressive acts are rarely included in their repertoire of usual responses, most threats, real or imagined, are dealt with by fantasied omnipotence or resignation. They are often seen as aloof; yet, at times, such persons are able to conceive, develop, and give to the world genuinely original, creative ideas.

Course and prognosis. The onset of schizoid personality disorder is usually in early childhood. Like all personality disorders, a schizoid personality disorder is long-lasting but not necessarily lifelong. The proportion of patients who go on to schizophrenia is unknown.

Diagnosis. On initial psychiatric examination, patients with schizoid personality disorder may appear ill at ease. They rarely tolerate eye contact. The interviewer may surmise that such patients are eager for the interview to end. Their affect may be constricted, aloof, or inappropriately serious. But underneath the aloofness, the sensitive clinician may recognize fear. These patients find it difficult to act lightheartedly: Their efforts at humor may seem adolescent and off the mark. The patients' speech is goal-directed, but they are likely to give short answers to questions and avoid spontaneous conversation. Occasionally, they may use an unusual figure of speech, such as an odd metaphor. Their mental content may reveal an unwarranted sense of intimacy with people they do not know well or whom they have not seen for a long time. They may be fascinated with an overvaluation of inanimate objects or metaphysical constructs. The patients' sensorium is intact; their memory functions well; and their proverb interpretations are abstract. The DSM-III-R diagnostic criteria are listed in Table 26-2.

Table 26-2
Diagnostic Criteria for Schizoid Personality Disorder

A. A pervasive pattern of indifference to social relationships and a restricted range of emotional experience and expression, beginning by early adulthood and present in a variety of contexts, as indicated by at least *four* of the following:
   (1) neither desires nor enjoys close relationships, including being part of a family
   (2) almost always chooses solitary activities
   (3) rarely, if ever, claims or appears to experience strong emotions, such as anger and joy
   (4) indicates little if any desire to have sexual experiences with another person (age being taken into account)
   (5) is indifferent to the praise and criticism of others
   (6) has no close friends or confidants (or only one) other than first-degree relatives
   (7) displays constricted affect (e.g., is aloof, cold, rarely reciprocates gestures or facial expressions, such as smiles or nods)

B. Occurrence not exclusively during the course of schizophrenia or a delusional disorder

Table from DSM-III-R, *Diagnostic and Statistical Manual of Mental Disorders,* ed 3, revised.

Differential diagnosis. In contrast to patients with schizophrenia or schizotypal personality disorder, patients with schizoid personality disorder do not have schizophrenic relatives, and they may have very successful, if isolated, work histories. Schizophrenic patients also differ by exhibiting thought disorder or delusional thinking. Although they share many traits with the schizoid personality disorder patients, those with paranoid personality disorder exhibit more social engagement, a history of aggressive verbal behavior, and a greater tendency to project their feelings onto others. If just as emotionally constricted, the obsessive-compulsive and avoidant personality disorder patients experience loneliness as dysphoric, possess a richer history of past object relations, and do not engage as much in autistic reverie. Theoretically, the chief distinction between the schizotypal personality disorder patient and the schizoid personality disorder patient is that the schizotypal patient shows a greater similarity to the schizophrenic patient in oddities of perception, thought, behavior, and communication. Avoidant personality disorder patients are isolated but strongly wish to participate in activities, a characteristic absent in persons with schizoid personality disorder.

Treatment

Psychotherapy. The treatment of schizoid personality disorder patients is similar to that of those with paranoid personality disorder. However, schizoid patients' tendencies toward introspection are consistent with the psychotherapist's expectations, and schizoid patients may become devoted, if distant, patients. As trust develops, schizoid patients may, with great trepidation, reveal a plethora of fantasies, imaginary friends, and fears of unbearable dependency—even of merging with the therapist.

In group therapy settings, schizoid personality disorder patients may be silent for long periods of time; nonetheless, they do become involved. These patients should be protected against aggressive attack by group members in regard to their proclivity for silence. With time the group members become important to schizoid patients and may provide the only social contact in their otherwise isolated existence.

Pharmacotherapy. Pharmacotherapy with small doses of antipsychotics, antidepressants, and psychostimulants has been effective in some patients.

Schizotypal Personality Disorder

Definition. Persons with schizotypal personality disorder are strikingly odd or strange, even to laypersons. Magical thinking, peculiar ideas, ideas of reference, illusions, and derealization are part of their everyday world.

Epidemiology. The epidemiology, prevalence, and sex ratio of schizotypal personality disorders are unknown. There is a greater association of cases among the biological relatives of chronic schizophrenic patients than among controls and a higher incidence among monozygotic than among dizygotic twins (33 percent versus 4 percent in one study).

Clinical features. In schizotypal personality disorder, thinking and communicating are disturbed. Like schizophrenic patients, persons with schizotypal personality disorder may not know their own feelings; yet they are exquisitely sensitive to detecting the feelings of others, especially negative affects like anger. They may be superstitious or claim clairvoyance. Their inner world may be filled with vivid imaginary relationships and childlike fears and fantasies. They may believe that they have special powers of thought and insight. Although frank thought disorder is absent, their speech may often require interpretation. They may admit that they have perceptual illusions or macropsia or that people appear to them as wooden and alike.

The speech of persons with schizotypal personality disorder may be odd or peculiar and have meaning only to them. They show poor interpersonal relationships and may act inappropriately. As a result, they are isolated and have few, if any, friends. According to DSM-III-R, these patients may show features of borderline personality disorder, and, indeed, both diagnoses can be made. Under stress, schizotypal personality disorder patients may decompensate and have psychotic symptoms, but the symptoms are usually of brief duration. In severe cases anhedonia and severe depression may occur.

Course and prognosis. A long-term study by Thomas McGlashan reported that 10 percent of persons with schizotypal personality disorder eventually committed suicide. Retrospective studies have shown that many patients thought to have been suffering from schizophrenia actually had schizotypal personality disorder, and the current clinical thinking suggests the schizotype to be the premorbid personality of the schizophrenic patient. Many patients, however, maintain a stable schizotypal personality throughout their lives and marry and work in spite of their oddities.

Diagnosis. Schizotypal personality disorder is diagnosed on the basis of the patients' peculiarities of thinking, behavior, and appearance. History taking may be difficult because of the patients' unusual way of communicating. The DSM-III-R diagnostic criteria for schizotypal personality disorder are given in Table 26-3.

Differential diagnosis. Theoretically, those with schizotypal personality disorder can be distinguished from schizoid and avoidant personality disorder patients by the presence of oddities in their behavior, thinking, perception, and communication and perhaps by a clear family history of schizophrenia. Schizotypal personality disorder patients can be distinguished from schizophrenic patients by their absence of psychosis. If psychotic symptoms do appear, they are brief and fragmentary in nature. At present, some patients meet the criteria for both schizotypal personality disorder and borderline personality disorder. The paranoid personality disorder patient is characterized by suspiciousness but lacks the odd behavior of the schizotypal personality disorder patient.

Table 26-3
Diagnostic Criteria for Schizotypal Personality Disorder

A. A pervasive pattern of deficits in interpersonal relatedness and peculiarities of ideation, appearance, and behavior, beginning by early adulthood and present in a variety of contexts, as indicated by at least *five* of the following:
 (1) ideas of reference (excluding delusions of reference)
 (2) excessive social anxiety (e.g., extreme discomfort in social situations involving unfamiliar people)
 (3) odd beliefs or magical thinking, influencing behavior and inconsistent with subcultural norms (e.g., superstitiousness, belief in clairvoyance, telepathy, or "sixth sense," "others can feel my feelings") (in children and adolescents, bizarre fantasies or preoccupations)
 (4) unusual perceptual experiences (e.g., illusions, sensing the presence of a force or person not actually present [e.g., "I felt as if my dead mother were in the room with me"])
 (5) odd or eccentric behavior or appearance (e.g., unkempt, unusual mannerisms, talks to self)
 (6) no close friends or confidants (or only one) other than first-degree relatives
 (7) odd speech (without loosening of associations or incoherence) (e.g., speech that is impoverished, digressive, vague, or inappropriately abstract)
 (8) inappropriate or constricted affect (e.g., silly, aloof, rarely reciprocates gestures or facial expressions, such as smiles or nods)
 (9) suspiciousness or paranoid ideation

B. Occurrence not exclusively during the course of schizophrenia or a pervasive development disorder

Table from DSM-III-R, *Diagnostic and Statistical Manual of Mental Disorders,* ed 3, revised. Copyright American Psychiatric Association, Washington, DC, 1987, with permission.

Treatment

Psychotherapy. The principles of treatment of schizotypal personality disorder should be no different from those of schizoid personality disorder. However, the odd and peculiar thinking of schizotypal personality disorder patients must be handled carefully. Some patients are involved in cults, strange religious practices, and the occult. Therapists must not ridicule such activities or be judgmental about those beliefs or activities.

Pharmacotherapy. Antipsychotic medication may be useful in dealing with ideas of reference, illusions, and other symptoms of the disorder and can be used in conjunction with psychotherapy. Positive results have been reported with haloperidol. Antidepressants are of use when a depressive component of the personality is present.

Histrionic Personality Disorder

Definition. Histrionic personality disorder is characterized by colorful, dramatic, extroverted behavior in excitable, emotional persons. Accompanying their flamboyant presentations, however, is often an inability to maintain deep, long-lasting attachments. This is also known as hysterical personality.

Epidemiology. The exact prevalence of histrionic personality disorder is unknown. It is diagnosed more frequently in women than in men. Some studies have found an association with somatization disorder and alcoholism.

Clinical features. Patients with histrionic personality disorder show a high degree of attention-seeking behavior. They tend to exaggerate their thoughts and feelings, making everything sound more important than it really is. They display temper tantrums, tears, and accusations if they are not the center of attention or are not receiving praise or approval.

Seductive behavior is common in both sexes. Sexual fantasies about persons with whom the patients are involved are common, but they are inconsistent about verbalizing these fantasies and may be coy or flirtatious, rather than sexually aggressive. In fact, histrionic patients may have a psychosexual dysfunction: The women may be anorgasmic, and the men may be impotent. They may act on their sexual impulses to reassure themselves that they are attractive to the other sex. Their need for reassurance is endless. Their relationships tend to be superficial, however, and these persons can be vain, self-absorbed, and fickle. Their strong dependency needs make them overly trusting and gullible.

The major defenses of histrionic personality disorder patients are repression and dissociation. Accordingly, such patients are unaware of their true feelings and are unable to explain their motivations. Under stress, reality testing easily becomes impaired.

Course and prognosis. With age, patients with histrionic personality disorder tend to show fewer symptoms, but, because they lack the same energy they had when younger, that difference may be more apparent than real. These patients are sensation seekers and may get into trouble with the law, abuse drugs, and act promiscuously.

Diagnosis. In the interview histrionic personality disorder patients are generally cooperative and eager to give a detailed history. Gestures and dramatic punctuation in their conversation are common. They may make frequent slips of the tongue, and their language is colorful. Affective display is common, but, when pressed to acknowledge certain feelings (such as anger, sadness, and sexual wishes), they may respond with surprise, indignation, or denial. The results of the cognitive examination are usually normal, although a lack of perseverance may be shown on arithmetic or concentration tasks, and the patients' forgetfulness of affect-laden material may be astonishing. The DSM-III-R diagnostic criteria are listed in Table 26-4.

Differential diagnosis. The distinction between histrionic personality disorder and borderline personality disorder is difficult. In the latter, suicide attempts, identity diffusion, and brief psychotic episodes are more likely. Although DSM-III-R states that both conditions may be diagnosed in the same patient, it is preferable that the clinician separate the two. Somatization disorder (Briquet's syndrome) may occur in conjunction with histrionic personality disorder. Patients with brief reactive psychosis and dissociative disorders may warrant a coexisting diagnosis of histrionic personality disorder.

Treatment

Psychotherapy. Patients with histrionic personality disorder are often unaware of their own real feelings; therefore, clarification of their inner feelings is an important therapeutic process. Psychoanalytically oriented psychotherapy, whether group or individual, is probably the treatment of choice for this personality disorder.

Pharmacotherapy. Pharmacotherapy can be adjunctive when symptoms are targeted (such as antidepressants for depression and somatic complaints, antianxiety agents for anxiety, and antipsychotics for derealization or illusions).

Table 26-4
Diagnostic Criteria for Histrionic Personality Disorder

A pervasive pattern of excessive emotionality and attention-seeking, beginning by early adulthood and present in a variety of contexts, as indicated by at least *four* of the following:

(1) constantly seeks or demands reassurance, approval, or praise
(2) is inappropriately sexually seductive in appearance or behavior
(3) is overly concerned with physical attractiveness
(4) expresses emotion with inappropriate exaggeration (e.g., embraces casual acquaintances with excessive ardor, uncontrollable sobbing on minor sentimental occasions, has temper tantrums)
(5) is uncomfortable in situations in which he or she is not the center of attention
(6) displays rapidly shifting and shallow expression of emotions
(7) is self-centered, actions being directed toward obtaining immediate satisfaction; has no tolerance for the frustration of delayed gratification
(8) has a style of speech that is excessively impressionistic and lacking in detail (e.g., when asked to describe mother, can be no more specific than, "She was a beautiful person.")

Table from DSM-III-R, *Diagnostic and Statistical Manual of Mental Disorders,* ed 3, revised. Copyright American Psychiatric Association, Washington, DC, 1987, with permission.

Narcissistic Personality Disorder

Definition. Persons with narcissistic personality disorder are characterized by a heightened sense of self-importance and grandiose feelings that they are unique in some way.

Epidemiology. There are no data on the prevalence, sex ratio, and familial pattern of narcissistic personality disorder. There may be a higher than usual risk in the offspring of parents with this disorder who impart to them an unrealistic sense of omnipotence, grandiosity, beauty, and talent. The number of cases reported is increasing steadily.

Clinical features. According to DSM-III-R, persons with this disorder have a grandiose sense of self-importance. They consider themselves special people and expect special treatment. They handle criticism poorly and may become enraged that anyone would dare to criticize them, or they may appear to be completely indifferent to it. They want their own way and are frequently ambitious, desiring fame and fortune. Their sense of entitlement is striking. Their relationships are fragile, and they can make others furious because they refuse to obey the conventional rules of behavior. They are unable to show empathy, and they feign sympathy only to achieve their selfish ends. Interpersonal exploitiveness is commonplace. These patients have fragile self-esteem and are prone to depression. Interpersonal difficulties, rejection, loss, and occupational problems are among the stresses that narcissists commonly produce by their behavior—stresses they are least able to handle.

Course and prognosis. This disorder is chronic and difficult to treat. Patients with the disorder must constantly deal with blows to their narcissism resulting from their own behavior or from life experiences. Aging is handled poorly, as these patients value beauty, strength, and youthful attributes, to which they cling inappropriately. They may be more vulnerable, therefore, to mid-life crises than are other groups.

Diagnosis. See Table 26-5 for the DSM-III-R diagnostic features of narcissistic personality disorder.

Differential diagnosis. According to DSM-III-R, borderline, histrionic, and antisocial personality disorders are often present together with narcissistic personality disorder, which means that a differential diagnosis is difficult. Patients with narcissistic personality disorder have less anxiety than do patients with borderline personality disorder, and their lives tend to be less chaotic. Suicidal attempts are also more likely to be associated with borderline personality disorder patients than with narcissistic personality disorder patients. Antisocial personality disorder patients give a history of impulsive behavior, often associated with alcohol or drug abuse, that frequently gets them into trouble with the law. And histrionic personality disorder patients show features of exhibitionism and interpersonal manipulativeness that are similar to those of narcissistic personality disorder patients.

Treatment

Psychotherapy. The treatment of narcissistic personality disorder is extremely difficult, as the patients must renounce their narcissism if progress is to be made. Psychiatrists such as Otto Kernberg and Heinz Kohut advocate using psychoanalytic approaches to effect change; however, much research is required to validate the diagnosis and to determine the best treatment.

Pharmacotherapy. Lithium has been used with patients who have mood swings as part of the clinical picture. Because narcissistic personality disorder patients tolerate rejection

Table 26-5
Diagnostic Criteria for Narcissistic Personality Disorder

A pervasive pattern of grandiosity (in fantasy or behavior), lack of empathy, and hypersensitivity to the evaluation of others, beginning by early adulthood and present in a variety of contexts, as indicated by at least *five* of the following:

(1) reacts to criticism with feelings of rage, shame, or humiliation (even if not expressed)
(2) is interpersonally exploitative: takes advantage of others to achieve his or her own ends
(3) has a grandiose sense of self-importance (e.g., exaggerates achievements and talents, expects to be noticed as "special" without appropriate achievement)
(4) believes that his or her problems are unique and can be understood only by other special people
(5) is preoccupied with fantasies of unlimited success, power, brilliance, beauty, or ideal love
(6) has a sense of entitlement: unreasonable expectation of especially favorable treatment (e.g., assumes that he or she does not have to wait in line when others must do so)
(7) requires constant attention and admiration (e.g., keeps fishing for compliments)
(8) lack of empathy: inability to recognize and experience how others feel (e.g., annoyance and surprise when a friend who is seriously ill cancels a date)
(9) is preoccupied with feelings of envy

Table from DSM-III-R, *Diagnostic and Statistical Manual of Mental Disorders,* ed 3, revised. Copyright American Psychiatric Association, Washington, DC, 1987, with permission.

poorly and are prone to depression, antidepressants may also be of use.

Antisocial Personality Disorder

Definition. Antisocial personality disorder is characterized by continual antisocial or criminal acts, but it is not synonymous with criminality. Rather, it is an inability to conform to social norms that involves many aspects of the patient's adolescent and adult development.

Epidemiology. The prevalence of antisocial personality disorder is 3 percent in men and 1 percent in women. It is most common in poor urban areas and among mobile residents of those areas. Boys with the disorder come from larger families than do girls with the disorder. The onset of the disorder is before the age of 15. Girls usually have symptoms before puberty, and boys even earlier. In prison populations the prevalence of antisocial personality disorder may be as high as 75 percent. A familial pattern is present in that it is five times more common among first-degree relatives of males with the disorder than among controls.

Clinical features. Patients with antisocial personality disorder often present a normal and even a charming and ingratiating exterior. Their histories, however, reveal many areas of disordered life functioning. Lying, truancy, running away from home, thefts, fights, drug abuse, and illegal activities are typical experiences that the patients report as beginning in childhood. Often, antisocial personality disorder patients impress opposite-sex clinicians with the colorful, seductive aspects of their personalities, but same-sex clinicians may regard them as manipulative and demanding. Antisocial personality disorder patients demonstrate a lack of anxiety or depression that may seem grossly incongruous with their situations, and their own explanations of their antisocial behavior make it seem mindless. Suicide threats and somatic preoccupations may be common. Nevertheless, the patients' mental content reveals the complete absence of delusions and other signs of irrational thinking. In fact, they frequently demonstrate a heightened sense of reality testing. They often impress observers as having good verbal intelligence.

Antisocial personality disorder patients are highly represented by so-called con men. They are highly manipulative and are frequently able to talk others into participating in schemes that involve easy ways to make money or to achieve fame or notoriety, which may eventually lead the unwary to financial ruin or social embarrassment or both. Antisocial personality disorder patients do not tell the truth and cannot be trusted to carry out any task or adhere to any conventional standard of morality. Promiscuity, spouse abuse, child abuse, and drunk driving are common events in these patients' lives. A notable finding is a lack of remorse for those actions; that is, these patients appear to lack a conscience.

Diagnosis. As mentioned, the patients may appear composed and credible in the interview. However, beneath the veneer (or, to use Hervey Cleckley's term, the mask of sanity), there is tension, hostility, irritability, and rage. Stress interviews, in which patients are vigorously confronted with inconsistencies in their histories, may be necessary to reveal the pathology. Even the most experienced clinicians have been fooled by such patients.

A diagnostic workup should include a thorough neurological examination. Because the patients often show abnormal EEG results and soft neurological signs suggestive of minimal brain damage in childhood, these findings can be used to confirm the clinical impression. The DSM-III-R diagnostic criteria are listed in Table 26-6.

Once an antisocial personality disorder develops, it runs an unremitting course, with the height of antisocial behavior usually occurring in late adolescence. The prognosis is variable. There are reports that symptoms decrease as patients grow older. Many patients have somatization disorder and multiple physical complaints. Depression, alcoholism, and substance abuse are common.

Differential diagnosis. Antisocial personality disorder can be distinguished from illegal behavior in that antisocial personality disorder involves many areas of the person's life. If antisocial behavior is the only manifestation, the patients are put in the DSM-III-R category called conditions not attributable to a mental disorder. Dorothy Lewis has demonstrated, however, that many of these patients have a neurological or mental disorder that has been either overlooked or not diagnosed. More difficult is the differentiation of antisocial personality disorder from psychoactive substance abuse. When both substance abuse and antisocial behavior begin in childhood and continue into adult life, both disorders should be diagnosed. When, however, the antisocial behavior is clearly secondary to premorbid alcohol abuse or drug abuse, the diagnosis of antisocial personality disorder is not warranted.

In diagnosing antisocial personality disorder, the clinician must adjust for the distorting effects of socioeconomic status, cultural background, and sex on its manifestations. Furthermore, the diagnosis of antisocial personality disorder is not warranted if mental retardation, schizophrenia, or mania can explain the symptoms.

Treatment

Psychotherapy. If antisocial personality disorder patients are immobilized (e.g., placed in hospitals), they often become amenable to psychotherapy. When these patients feel that they are among peers, their lack of motivation for change

Table 26-6
Diagnostic Criteria for Antisocial Personality Disorder

A. Current age at least 18

B. Evidence of conduct disorder with onset before age 15, as indicated by a history of *three* or more of the following:
 (1) was often truant
 (2) ran away from home overnight at least twice while living in parental or parental surrogate home (or once without returning)
 (3) often initiated physical fights
 (4) used a weapon in more than one fight
 (5) forces someone into sexual activity with him or her
 (6) was physically cruel to animals
 (7) was physically cruel to other people
 (8) deliberately destroyed others' property (other than by fire-setting)
 (9) deliberately engaged in fire-setting
 (10) often lied (other than to avoid physical or sexual abuse)
 (11) has stolen without confrontation of a victim on more than one occasion (including forgery)
 (12) has stolen with confrontation of a victim (e.g., mugging, purse-snatching, extortion, armed robbery)

C. A pattern of irresponsible and antisocial behavior since the age of 15, as indicated by at least *four* of the following:
 (1) is unable to sustain consistent work behavior, as indicated by any of the following (including similar behavior in academic settings if the person is a student):
  (a) significant unemployment for six months or more within five years when expected to work and work was available
  (b) repeated absences from work unexplained by illness in self or family
  (c) abandonment of several jobs without realistic plans for others
 (2) fails to conform to social norms with respect to lawful behavior, as indicated by repeatedly performing antisocial acts that are grounds for arrest (whether arrested or not) (e.g., destroying property, harassing others, stealing, pursuing an illegal occupation)
 (3) is irritable and aggressive, as indicated by repeated physical fights or assaults (not required by one's job or to defend someone or oneself), including spouse- or child-beating
 (4) repeatedly fails to honor financial obligations, as indicated by defaulting on debts or failing to provide child support or support for other dependents on a regular basis
 (5) fails to plan ahead, or is impulsive, as indicated by one or both of the following:
  (a) traveling from place to place without a prearranged job or clear goal for the period of travel or clear idea about when the travel will terminate
  (b) lack of a fixed address for a month or more
 (6) has no regard for the truth, as indicated by repeated lying, use of aliases, or "conning" others for personal profit or pleasure
 (7) is reckless regarding his or her own or others' personal safety, as indicated by driving while intoxicated, or recurrent speeding
 (8) if a parent or guardian, lacks ability to function as a responsible parent, as indicated by one or more of the following:
  (a) malnutrition of child
  (b) child's illness resulting from lack of minimal hygiene
  (c) failure to obtain medical care for a seriously ill child
  (d) child's dependence on neighbors or nonresident relatives for food or shelter
  (e) failure to arrange for a caretaker for young child when parent is away from home
  (f) repeated squandering, on personal items, of money required for household necessities
 (9) has never sustained a totally monogamous relationship for more than one year
 (10) lacks remorse (feels justified in having hurt, mistreated, or stolen from another)

D. Occurrence of antisocial behavior not exclusively during the course of schizophrenia or manic episodes.

Table from DSM-III-R, *Diagnostic and Statistical Manual of Mental Disorders,* ed 3, revised. Copyright American Psychiatric Association, Washington, DC, 1987, with permission.

disappears. Perhaps that is why self-help groups have been more useful than jails in alleviating the disorder.

Before treatment can begin, firm limits are essential. The therapist must find some way of dealing with the patient's self-destructive behavior. And to overcome the antisocial personality disorder patient's fear of intimacy, the therapist must frustrate the patient's wish to run from honest human encounters. In doing so, the therapist faces the challenge of separating control from punishment and of separating help and confrontation from social isolation and retribution.

Pharmacotherapy. Pharmacotherapy is used to deal with incapacitating symptoms—such as anxiety, rage, and depression—but, because the patients are often substance abusers, drugs must be used judiciously. If there is evidence of attention-deficit hyperactivity disorder, residual type, psychostimulants, such as methylphenidate (Ritalin), may be of use. Attempts have been made to alter catecholamine metabolism with drugs and to control impulsive behavior with antiepileptic drugs, especially if abnormal wave forms are noted on an EEG.

Borderline Personality Disorder

Definition. Borderline personality disorder patients stand on the border between neurosis and psychosis and are characterized by extraordinarily unstable affect, mood, behavior, object relationships, and self-image. The disorder has also been called ambulatory schizophrenia, "as if" personality (a term coined by Helene Deutsch), pseudoneurotic schizophrenia (described by Paul Hoch and Phillip Politan), psychotic character (described by John Frosch), and emotionally unstable personality.

Epidemiology. No definitive prevalence studies are available, but this disorder is thought to be present in about

1 or 2 percent of the population and is twice as common in women as in men. There is an increased prevalence of major depression, alcoholism, and psychoactive substance abuse in first-degree relatives of persons with borderline personality disorder.

Clinical features. Borderline personality disorder patients almost always appear to be in a state of crisis. Mood swings are common. The patients can be argumentative at one moment and depressed at the next and then complain of having no feelings at another time.

There may be short-lived psychotic episodes (so-called micropsychotic episodes), rather than full-blown psychotic breaks, and the psychotic symptoms of borderline personality disorder patients are almost always circumscribed, fleeting, or in doubt. The behavior of borderline personality disorder patients is highly unpredictable; consequently, they rarely achieve up to the level of their abilities. The painful nature of their lives is reflected in repetitive self-destructive acts. Such patients may perform wrist slashing and other self-mutilations to elicit help from others, to express anger, or to numb themselves to overwhelming affect.

Because they feel both dependent and hostile, borderline personality disorder patients have tumultuous interpersonal relationships. They can be dependent on those to whom they are close, and they can express enormous anger at their intimate friends when frustrated. Borderline personality disorder patients cannot tolerate being alone, however, and prefer a frantic search for companionship, no matter how unsatisfactory, to sitting by themselves. To assuage loneliness, if only for brief periods, they accept a stranger as a friend or are promiscuous. They often complain about chronic feelings of emptiness and boredom and the lack of a consistent sense of identify (*identity diffusion*); when pressed, they often complain about how depressed they feel most of the time in spite of the flurry of other affects.

Most therapists agree that borderline personality disorder patients demonstrate ordinary reasoning abilities on structural tests, such as the Wechsler Adult Intelligence Scale, and demonstrate deviant processes only on unstructured projective tests, such as the Rorschach.

Functionally, adult borderline personality disorder patients distort their present relationships by putting every person into either an all-good or an all-bad category. They see people as either nurturant and attachment figures or hateful and sadistic persons who deprive them of security needs and threaten them with abandonment whenever they feel dependent. As a result of this splitting, the good person is idealized, and the bad person is devalued. Shifts of allegiance from one person or group to another are frequent.

Some clinicians use the concepts of panphobia, pananxiety, panambivalence, and chaotic sexuality to describe the borderline personality disorder patient's characteristics.

Course and prognosis. The disorder is fairly stable in that patients change little over time. Longitudinal studies do not show a progression toward schizophrenia, but there is a high incidence of major depressive episodes in these patients. The diagnosis is usually made before the age of 40, when these patients are attempting to make occupational, marital, and other choices and are unable to deal with these normal stages in the life cycle.

Diagnosis. According to DSM-III-R, the diagnosis of borderline personality disorder can be made by early adulthood when the patient shows at least five of the criteria listed in Table 26-7.

Biological studies may aid in the diagnosis, as some borderline patients show shortened rapid eye movement (REM) latency and sleep continuity disturbances, abnormal dexamethasone-suppression test results, and abnormal thyrotropin-releasing hormone test results. But these changes are also seen in some cases of depression.

Table 26-7
Diagnostic Criteria for Borderline Personality Disorder

A pervasive pattern of instability of mood, interpersonal relationships, and self-image, beginning by early adulthood and present in a variety of contexts, as indicated by at least *five* of the following:

(1) a pattern of unstable and intense interpersonal relationships characterized by alternating between extremes of overidealization and devaluation
(2) impulsiveness in at least two areas that are potentially self-damaging (e.g., spending, sex, substance use, shoplifting, reckless driving, binge eating) (Do not include suicidal or self-mutilating behavior covered in [5].)
(3) affective instability: marked shifts from baseline mood to depression, irritability, or anxiety, usually lasting a few hours and only rarely more than a few days
(4) inappropriate, intense anger or lack of control of anger (e.g., frequent displays of temper, constant anger, recurrent physical fights)
(5) recurrent suicidal threats, gestures, or behavior, or self-mutilating behavior
(6) marked and persistent identity disturbance manifested by uncertainty about at least two of the following: self-image, sexual orientation, long-term goals or career choice, type of friends desired, preferred values
(7) chronic feelings of emptiness or boredom
(8) frantic efforts to avoid real or imagined abandonment (Do not include suicidal or self-mutilating behavior covered in [5].)

Table from DSM-III-R, *Diagnostic and Statistical Manual of Mental Disorders,* ed 3, revised. Copyright American Psychiatric Association, Washington, DC, 1987, with permission.

Differential diagnosis. The differentiation from schizophrenia is made on the basis of there being no prolonged psychotic episodes, thought disorder, or other classic schizophrenic signs. Schizotypal personality disorder patients show marked peculiarities of thinking, strange ideation, and recurrent ideas of reference. Paranoid personality disorder patients are marked by extreme suspiciousness. Histrionic and antisocial personality disorder patients are difficult to distinguish from borderline personality disorder patients. In general, the borderline personality disorder patient shows chronic feelings of emptiness, impulsivity, self-mutilation, short-lived psychotic episodes, manipulative suicide attempts, and unusually demanding involvement in close relationships.

Treatment

Psychotherapy. Psychotherapy for borderline personality disorder patients is an area of intensive investigation and has been the treatment of choice. Recently, pharmacotherapy has been added to the treatment regimen.

Psychotherapy is difficult for patient and therapist alike. Regression occurs easily in borderline personality disorder patients, who act out their impulses and show labile or fixed negative or positive transferences, which are difficult to analyze. Splitting as a defense mechanism causes the patient to alternately love and hate the therapist and others in the environment. A reality-oriented approach is more effective than in-depth unconscious interpretations.

Behavior therapy has been used with borderline personality disorder patients to control impulses and angry outbursts and to reduce sensitivity to criticism and rejection. Social skills training, especially with videotape playback, is helpful to enable patients to see how their actions affect others and thereby to improve their interpersonal behavior.

Borderline personality disorder patients often do well in a hospital setting in which they receive intensive psychotherapy on both an individual basis and a group basis. They also interact with trained staff members from a variety of disciplines and are provided with occupational, recreational, and vocational therapy. Such programs are especially helpful if the home environment is detrimental to the patient's rehabilitation because of intrafamilial conflicts or other stresses, such as parental abuse. The borderline personality disorder patient who is excessively impulsive, self-destructive, or self-mutilating can be provided with limits and observation within the protected environment of the hospital. Under ideal circumstances, the patient remains in the hospital until there is marked improvement, which may take up to one year in some cases. At that time patients can be discharged to special support systems, such as day hospitals, night hospitals, and halfway houses.

Pharmacotherapy. Pharmacotherapy for borderline personality disorder is useful to deal with specific personality features that interfere with the patients' overall functioning. Antipsychotics have been used to control anger, hostility, and brief psychotic episodes. Antidepressants improve the depressed mood that is common in the patients. The monoamine oxidase inhibitors (MAOIs) have been effective in modulating impulsive behavior in some patients. Benzodiazepines, particularly alprazolam (Xanax), help anxiety and depression, but some patients show a disinhibition with this class of drugs. Anticonvulsants, such as carbamazepine (Tegretol), may improve global functioning in some patients. Serotonergic agents, such as fluoxetine (Prozac), have been helpful in some cases.

Avoidant Personality Disorder

Definition. Persons with avoidant personality disorder show an extreme sensitivity to rejection, which may lead to a socially withdrawn life. They are not asocial and show a great desire for companionship but are shy; they need unusually strong guarantees of uncritical acceptance. Such persons are commonly referred to as having an inferiority complex.

Epidemiology. The prevalence of avoidant personality disorder is unknown; as defined, it is common. No information is available on sex ratio or familial pattern. Infants classified as having a timid temperament may be more prone to the disorder than are those high on activity-approach scales.

Clinical features. Hypersensitivity to rejection by others is the central clinical feature of this disorder. Persons with the disorder desire the warmth and security of human companionship but justify their avoidance of forming relationships by their alleged fear of rejection. When talking with someone, they express uncertainty and a lack of self-confidence and may speak in a self-effacing manner. They are afraid to speak up in public or to make requests of others, because they are hypervigilant about rejection. They are apt to misinterpret other people's comments as derogatory or ridiculing. The refusal of any request leads them to withdraw from others and to feel hurt.

In the vocational sphere, avoidant personality disorder patients often take jobs on the sidelines. They rarely attain much personal advancement or exercise much authority. Instead, at work they may seem simply shy and eager to please.

According to DSM-III-R, persons with this disorder are generally unwilling to enter relationships unless they are given an unusually strong guarantee of uncritical acceptance. Consequently, they often have no close friends or confidants. In general, their main personality trait is timidity.

Course and prognosis. Many avoidant personality disorder patients are able to function, provided they are in a protected environment. Some marry, have children, and live their lives surrounded only by family. Should their support system fail, however, they are subject to depression, anxiety, and anger. Phobic avoidance is common, and avoidant personality disorder patients may give histories of social phobias or go on to such phobias during the course of their illness.

Diagnosis. In the clinical interview the most striking aspect is the patient's anxiety about talking with the interviewer. The patients' nervous and tense manner appears to wax and wane with their perception of whether the interviewer likes them. They seem vulnerable to the interviewer's comments and suggestions and may regard a clarification or an interpretation as a criticism. The DSM-III-R diagnostic criteria for avoidant personality disorder are listed in Table 26-8.

Differential diagnosis. Avoidant personality disorder patients desire social interaction, compared with schizoid personality disorder patients, who want to be alone. Avoidant personality disorder patients are not as demanding, irritable, or unpredictable as are borderline and histrionic personality disorder patients. The avoidant personality disorder and the dependent personality disorder are very similar. The dependent personality disorder patient is presumed to have a greater fear of being abandoned or not loved than does the avoidant personality disorder patient; however, the clinical picture may be indistinguishable. The term "avoidant personality disorder" originated with DSM-III; further study is required to distinguish this category from dependent personality disorder.

Treatment

Psychotherapy. Psychotherapeutic treatment depends on solidifying an alliance with the patient. As trust develops, the therapist conveys an accepting attitude toward the patient's fears, especially that of rejection. The therapist eventually encourages the patient to move out into the world to

Table 26-8
Diagnostic Criteria for Avoidant Personality Disorder

A pervasive pattern of social discomfort, fear of negative evaluation, and timidity, beginning by early adulthood and present in a variety of contexts, as indicated by at least *four* of the following:

(1) is easily hurt by criticism or disapproval
(2) has no close friends or confidants (or only one) other than first-degree relatives
(3) is unwilling to get involved with people unless certain of being liked
(4) avoids social or occupational activities that involve significant interpersonal contact (e.g., refuses a promotion that will increase social demands)
(5) is reticent in social situations because of a fear of saying something inappropriate or foolish, or of being unable to answer a question
(6) fears being embarrassed by blushing, crying, or showing signs of anxiety in front of other people
(7) exaggerates the potential difficulties, physical dangers, or risks involved in doing something ordinary but outside his or her usual routine (e.g., may cancel social plans because she anticipates being exhausted by the effort of getting there)

take what are perceived as great risks of humiliation, rejection, or failure. But the therapist should be cautious when giving assignments to exercise new social skills outside therapy, because failure may reinforce the patient's already poor self-esteem. Group therapy may help patients understand the effects that their sensitivity to rejection has on themselves and others. Assertiveness training is a form of behavior therapy that may teach patients to express their needs openly and improve their self-esteem.

Pharmacotherapy. Pharmacotherapy has been used to manage anxiety and depression when present as an associated feature. Some patients are helped by β-blockers, such as atenolol (Tenormin), to manage autonomic nervous system hyperactivity, which tends to be high in patients with this disorder, especially when they approach feared situations.

Dependent Personality Disorder

Definition. Persons with dependent personality disorder subordinate their own needs to those of others, get others to assume responsibility for major areas in their lives, lack self-confidence, and may experience intense discomfort when alone for more than a brief period of time. In the first edition of *Diagnostic and Statistical Manual of Mental Disorders* (DSM-I), this condition was called passive-dependent personality. Freud described an oral-dependent dimension to personality characterized by dependence, pessimism, fear of sexuality, self-doubt, passivity, suggestibility, and lack of perseverance, which is similar to the DSM-III-R categorization of dependent personality disorder.

Epidemiology. This disorder is more common in women than in men. One study diagnosed 2.5 percent of all personality disorders as falling into this category. It is more common in young children than in older children. Persons with chronic physical illness in childhood may be most prone to the disorder.

Clinical features. According to DSM-III-R, dependent personality disorder is characterized by a pervasive pattern of dependent and submissive behavior. Persons with the disorder are unable to make decisions without an excessive amount of advice and reassurance from others.

Dependent personality disorder patients avoid positions of responsibility and become anxious if asked to assume a leadership role. They prefer to be submissive. When on their own, they find it difficult to persevere at tasks but may find it easy to perform those tasks for someone else.

Persons with this disorder do not like to be alone. They seek out others on whom they can depend, and their relationships are thus distorted by their need to be attached to that other person. In *folie à deux* (shared delusional disorder), one member of the pair is usually suffering from dependent personality disorder, and the submissive partner takes on the delusional system of the more aggressive, assertive partner on whom he or she is dependent.

Pessimism, self-doubt, passivity, and fears of expressing sexual and aggressive feelings characterize the behavior of the dependent personality disorder patient. An abusive, unfaithful, or alcoholic spouse may be tolerated for long periods of time in order not to disturb the sense of attachment.

Course and prognosis. Little is known about the course of this disorder. There tends to be impaired occupational functioning, as there is an inability to act independently and without close supervision. Social relationships are limited to those on whom the persons can depend, and many suffer physical or mental abuse because they cannot assert themselves. They risk major depression if they sustain the loss of the person on whom they are dependent. The prognosis with treatment, however, is favorable.

Table 26-9
Diagnostic Criteria for Dependent Personality Disorder

A pervasive pattern of dependent and submissive behavior, beginning by early adulthood and present in a variety of contexts, as indicated by at least *five* of the following:

(1) is unable to make everyday decisions without an excessive amount of advice or reassurance from others
(2) allows others to make most of his or her important decisions, e.g., where to live, what job to take
(3) agrees with people even when he or she believes they are wrong, because of fear of being rejected
(4) has difficulty initiating projects or doing things on his or her own
(5) volunteers to do things that are unpleasant or demeaning in order to get other people to like him or her
(6) feels uncomfortable or helpless when alone, or goes to great lengths to avoid being alone
(7) feels devastated or helpless when close relationships end
(8) is frequently preoccupied with fears of being abandoned
(9) is easily hurt by criticism or disapproval

Table from DSM-III-R, *Diagnostic and Statistical Manual of Mental Disorders,* ed 3, revised. Copyright American Psychiatric Association, Washington, DC, 1987, with permission.

Diagnosis. In the interview the patients appear to be very compliant. They try to cooperate, welcome specific questions, and look for guidance. The DSM-III-R diagnostic criteria for dependent personality disorder are listed in Table 26-9.

Differential diagnosis. The traits of dependency are found in many psychiatric disorders, which makes the differential diagnosis difficult. Dependency is a prominent factor in histrionic and borderline personality disorder patients; however, dependent personality disorder patients usually have a long-standing relationship with one person on whom they are dependent, rather than on a series of persons, and they do not tend to be overtly manipulative. Schizoid and schizotypal personality disorder patients may be indistinguishable from avoidant personality disorder patients.

Dependent behavior may occur in patients with agoraphobia, but there tends to be a much higher level of overt anxiety or even panic in agoraphobic patients.

Treatment

Psychotherapy. The treatment of dependent personality disorder traits can often be successful. Insight-oriented therapies enable patients to understand the antecedents of their behavior, and, with the support of a therapist, the patients can become more independent, assertive, and self-reliant.

A pitfall in the treatment may occur when the therapist encourages the patient to change the dynamics of a pathological relationship (e.g., that a physically abused wife seek help from the police). At that point the patient may become too anxious, be unable to cooperate in therapy, and feel torn between complying with the therapist and losing a pathological external relationship. The therapist must show great respect for a dependent personality disorder patient's feelings of attachment, no matter how pathological those feelings may seem.

Behavior therapy, assertiveness training, family therapy, and group therapy have all been used, with successful outcomes in many cases.

Pharmacotherapy. Pharmacotherapy has been used to deal with such specific symptoms as anxiety and depression, which are common associated features of this disorder. Those patients who develop panic attacks or who have high levels of separation anxiety may be helped by imipramine (Tofranil). Benzodiazepines and serotonergic agents have also been useful. If the patients' depression or withdrawal symptoms respond to psychostimulants, they may be used.

Obsessive-Compulsive Personality Disorder

Definition. The obsessive-compulsive personality disorder is characterized by emotional constriction, orderliness, perseverence, stubbornness, and indecisiveness. According to DSM-III-R, the essential feature of this disorder is a pervasive pattern of perfectionism and inflexibility.

Epidemiology. The prevalence of the obsessive-compulsive personality disorder is unknown. It is more common in males than in females and is diagnosed most often in oldest children. The disorder also occurs more frequently in first-degree biological relatives of persons with the disorder than in the general population. Patients often have backgrounds characterized by harsh discipline. Freud hypothesized that the disorder is associated with difficulties in the anal stage of psychosexual development, generally around the age of 2. However, in various studies that theory has not been validated.

Clinical features. Persons with this disorder are preoccupied with rules, regulations, orderliness, neatness, details, and the achievement of perfection. These traits account for a general constriction of the entire personality. Such persons are formal and serious and often lack a sense of humor. They insist that rules be followed rigidly and are unable to tolerate what they perceive to be infractions. Accordingly, they lack flexibility and are intolerant. They are capable of prolonged work, provided it is routinized and does not require changes to which they cannot adapt.

Obsessive-compulsive personality disorder patients' interpersonal skills are extremely limited. They alienate people, are unable to compromise, and insist that others submit to their needs. They are, however, eager to please those whom they see as more powerful than themselves and carry out their wishes in an authoritarian manner. Because of their fear of making mistakes, they are indecisive and ruminate about making decisions. Although a stable marriage and occupational adequacy are common, obsessive-compulsive personality disorder patients have few friends.

Anything that threatens to upset the routine of these patients' lives or their perceived stability can precipitate a great deal of anxiety that is otherwise bound up in the rituals that they impose on their lives and try to impose on others.

Course and prognosis. The course of obsessive-compulsive personality disorder is variable and not predictable. From time to time, obsessions or compulsions may develop in the course of the personality disorder. Some adolescents with obsessive-compulsive personality disorder evolve into warm, open, and loving adults; but in others, these traits can be either the harbinger of schizophrenia or—decades later and exacerbated by the aging process—major depression and melancholia.

Persons with this disorder may do well in positions demanding methodical, deductive, or detailed work, but they are vulnerable to unexpected changes, and their personal lives may remain barren. Depressive disorders, especially those of late onset, are common.

Diagnosis. In the interview, obsessive-compulsive personality disorder patients may have a stiff, formal, and rigid demeanor. Their affect is not blunted or flat but can be described as constricted. They lack spontaneity. Their mood is usually serious. Such patients may be anxious about not being in control of the interview. Their answers to questions are unusually detailed. The defense mechanisms they use are rationalization, isolation, intellectualization, reaction formation, and undoing. The DSM-III-R diagnostic criteria for obsessive-compulsive personality disorder are listed in Table 26-10.

Differential diagnosis. When recurrent obsessions or compulsions are present, obsessive-compulsive disorder should be noted on Axis I. Perhaps the most difficult distinction is between the outpatient with some obsessive-compulsive traits and one with obsessive-compulsive personality disorder. The diagnosis of personality disorder is reserved for those patients with significant impairments in their occupational or social effectiveness. In some cases, schizoid and paranoid disorders coexist with the personality disorder, and, if they do, they should be noted.

Treatment

Psychotherapy. Unlike patients with the other personality disorders, obsessive-compulsive personality disorder patients often know that they are suffering, and they seek treatment on their own. Free association and nondirective therapy are highly valued by the overtrained, oversocialized obsessive-compulsive personality disorder patient. However, the treatment of these patients is often long and complex, and countertransference problems are common.

Group and behavior therapy occasionally offer certain advantages. In both contexts it is easy to interrupt the patients in the midst of their maladaptive interactions or explanations. Having the completion of their habitual behavior prevented raises patients' anxiety and leaves them susceptible to learning new coping strategies. Patients can also receive direct rewards

Table 26-10
Diagnostic Criteria for Obsessive-Compulsive Personality Disorder

A pervasive pattern of perfectionism and inflexibility, beginning by early adulthood and present in a variety of contexts, as indicated by at least *five* of the following:

(1) perfectionism that interferes with task completion, e.g., inability to complete a project because own overly strict standards are not met
(2) preoccupation with details, rules, lists, order, organization, or schedules to extent that the major point of the activity is lost
(3) unreasonable insistence that others submit to exactly his or her way of doing things, **or** unreasonable reluctance to allow others to do things because of the conviction that they will not do them correctly
(4) excessive devotion to work and productivity to the exclusion of leisure activities and friendships (not accounted for by obvious economic necessity)
(5) indecisiveness: decision making is either avoided, postponed, or protracted (e.g., the person cannot get assignments done on time because of ruminating about priorities) (do not include if indecisiveness is due to excessive need for advice or reassurance from others)
(6) overconscientiousness, scrupulousness, and inflexibility about matters of morality, ethics, or values (not accounted for by cultural or religious identification)
(7) restricted expression of affection
(8) lack of generosity in giving time, money, or gifts when no personal gain is likely to result
(9) inability to discard worn-out or worthless objects even when they have no sentimental value

for change in group therapy, something less often possible in individual psychotherapies.

Pharmacotherapy. Clonazepam (Klonopin) is a benzodiazepine with anticonvulsant use that has reduced symptoms in patients with severe obsessive-compulsive disorder. Whether it is of use in the personality disorder is not known. Clomipramine (Anafranil) and fluoxetine may be of use if obsessive-compulsive signs and symptoms break through.

Passive-Aggressive Personality Disorder

Definition. The person with passive-aggressive personality disorder is characterized by covert obstructionism, procrastination, stubbornness, and inefficiency. Such behavior is a manifestation of underlying aggression, which is expressed passively.

Epidemiology. No data are available about the epidemiology of this disorder. Sex ratio, familial patterns, and prevalence have not been adequately studied.

Clinical features. Passive-aggressive personality disorder patients characteristically procrastinate, resist demands for adequate performance, find excuses for delays, and find fault with those on whom they depend; yet they refuse to extricate themselves from the dependent relationship. They usually lack assertiveness and are not direct about their own needs and wishes. They fail to ask needed questions about what is expected of them and may become anxious when forced to succeed or when their usual defense of turning anger against themselves is removed.

In interpersonal relationships, passive-aggressive personality disorder patients attempt to manipulate themselves into a position of dependency, but their passive, self-detrimental behavior is often experienced by others as punitive and manipulative. Others must do their errands and carry out their routine responsibilities. Friends and clinicians may become enmeshed in trying to assuage the patients' many claims of unjust treatment. The close relationships of passive-aggressive personality disorder patients are rarely tranquil or happy. Because these patients are bound to their resentment more closely than to their satisfaction, they may never even formulate what they want for themselves in regard to enjoyment.

According to DSM-III-R, people with this disorder lack self-confidence and are typically pessimistic about the future.

Course and prognosis. In a follow-up study averaging 11 years of 100 passive-aggressive inpatients, Small demonstrated that passive-aggressive personality disorder was the primary diagnosis in 54 of them, 18 were also alcoholic, and 30 could be clinically labeled as depressed. Of the 73 former patients located, 58 (79 percent) had persistent psychiatric difficulties, and 9 (12 percent) were considered symptom-free. Most seemed irritable, anxious, and depressed; somatic complaints were numerous. Only 32 (44 percent) were employed full-time as workers or homemakers. Although neglect of responsibility and suicide attempts were common, only 1 patient had committed suicide in the interim. Although 28 (38 percent) were readmitted to a hospital, only 3 patients were called schizophrenic.

Diagnosis. The diagnostic criteria for passive-aggressive personality disorder are presented in Table 26-11.

Table 26-11
Diagnostic Criteria for Passive-Aggressive Personality Disorder

A pervasive pattern of passive resistance to demands for adequate social and occupational performance, beginning by early adulthood and present in a variety of contexts, as indicated by at least *five* of the following;

(1) procrastinates (i.e., puts off the things that need to be done so that deadlines are not met)
(2) becomes sulky, irritable, or argumentative when asked to do something he or she does not want to do
(3) seems to work deliberately slowly or to do a bad job on tasks that he or she really does not want to do
(4) protests, without justification, that others make unreasonable demands on him or her
(5) avoids obligations by claiming to have "forgotten"
(6) believes that he or she is doing a much better job than others think he or she is doing
(7) resents useful suggestions from others concerning how he or she could be more productive
(8) obstructs the efforts of others by failing to do his or her share of the work
(9) unreasonably criticizes or scorns people in positions of authority

Table from DSM-III-R, *Diagnostic and Statistical Manual of Mental Disorders,* ed 3, revised. Copyright American Psychiatric Association, Washington, DC, 1987, with permission.

Differential diagnosis. Passive-aggressive personality disorder needs to be differentiated from histrionic and borderline personality disorders; however, the passive-aggressive personality disorder patient is less flamboyant, dramatic, affective, and openly aggressive than are the histrionic and borderline personality disorder patients. Patients with oppositional defiant disorder are similar to patients with passive-aggressive personality disorder, but the former diagnosis is reserved, according to DSM-III-R, to persons under age 18.

Treatment

Psychotherapy. Passive-aggressive personality disorder patients who receive supportive psychotherapy have good outcomes. However, psychotherapy for patients with passive-aggressive personality disorder has many pitfalls: To fulfill their demands is often to support their pathology, but to refuse their demands is to reject them. The therapy session can thus become a battleground in which the patient expresses feelings of resentment against a therapist on whom the patient wishes to become dependent. In passive-aggressive personality disorder patients, it is important to treat suicide gestures as one would any covert expression of anger and not as one would treat object loss in major depression.

Pharmacotherapy. Antidepressants should be prescribed only when there are clinical indications of depression and the possibility of suicide exists. The therapist must point out the probable consequences of passive-aggressive behaviors as they occur. Such confrontations may be more helpful in changing the patient's behavior than is a correct interpretation. Some patients have responded to benzodiazepines and psychostimulants, depending on the clinical features.

Personality Disorder Not Otherwise Specified

Personality disorder not otherwise specified includes disorders of personality functioning that cannot be classified as a specific personality disorder. In the third edition of *Diagnostic and Statistical Manual of Mental Disorders* (DSM-III), this was called mixed personality disorder, a useful and frequently diagnosed personality disorder. A person may have features of more than one personality disorder that do not meet the full criteria for any one disorder yet cause significant impairment in social or occupational functioning or subjective distress (Table 26-12).

This category can also be used when the clinician judges that a specific personality disorder is not included in any of

Table 26-12
Diagnostic Criteria for Personality Disorder Not Otherwise Specified

Disorders of personality functioning that are not classifiable as a specific personality disorder. An example is features of more than one specific personalty disorder that do not meet the full criteria for any one, yet cause significant impairment in social or occupational functioning, or subjective distress. In DSM-III, this was called mixed personality disorder.

This category can also be used when the clinician judges that a specific personality disorder not included in this classification is appropriate, such as Impulsive personality disorder, immature personality disorder, self-defeating personality disorder, or sadistic personality disorder. In such instances the clinician should note the specific personality disorder in parentheses (e.g., personality disorder NOS [self-defeating personality disorder]).

Table from DSM-III-R, *Diagnostic and Statistical Manual of Mental Disorders,* ed 3, revised. Copyright American Psychiatric Association, Washington, DC, 1987, with permission.

Table 26-13
Diagnostic Criteria for Self-Defeating Personality Disorder

A. A pervasive pattern of self-defeating behavior, beginning by early adulthood and present in a variety of contexts. The person may often avoid or undermine pleasurable experiences, be drawn to situations or relationships in which he or she will suffer, and prevent others from helping him or her, as indicated by at least *five* of the following:
   (1) chooses people and situations that lead to disappointment, failure, or mistreatment even when better options are clearly available
   (2) rejects or renders ineffective the attempts of others to help him or her
   (3) following positive personal events (e.g., new achievement), responds with depression, guilt, or a behavior that produces pain (e.g., an accident)
   (4) incites angry or rejecting responses from others and then feels hurt, defeated, or humiliated (e.g., makes fun of spouse in public, provoking an angry retort, then feels devastated)
   (5) rejects opportunities for pleasure, or is reluctant to acknowledge enjoying himself or herself (despite having adequate social skills and the capacity for pleasure)
   (6) fails to accomplish tasks crucial to his or her personal objectives despite demonstrated ability to do so (e.g., helps fellow students write papers, but is unable to write his or her own)
   (7) is uninterested in or rejects people who consistently treat him or her well (e.g., is unattracted to caring sexual partners)
   (8) engages in excessive self-sacrifice that is unsolicited by the intended recipients of the sacrifice

B. The behaviors in A do not occur exclusively in response to, or in anticipation of, being physically, sexually, or psychologically abused.

C. The behaviors in A do not occur only when the person is depressed.

Table from DSM-III-R, *Diagnostic and Statistical Manual of Mental Disorders,* ed 3, revised. Copyright American Psychiatric Association, Washington, DC, 1987, with permission.

the preceding categories or, for that matter, is not part of the official DSM-III-R nomenclature.

Sadomasochistic personality disorder. Some personality types are characterized by elements of sadism or masochism or a combination of both. Sadomasochistic personality disorder is listed here because it is of major clinical and historical interest in psychiatry. It is not an official diagnostic category in DSM-III-R or its appendix but is classified as personality disorder not otherwise classified.

Sadism (named after the Marquis de Sade, who wrote about persons who experienced sexual pleasure while inflicting pain on others) is the desire to cause others pain by being either sexually abusive or physically or psychologically abusive in general. Freud believed that sadists ward off castration anxiety and are able to achieve sexual pleasure only when they are able to do to others what they fear will be done to them.

Masochism (named after Leopold von Sacher-Masoch, a 19th-century Austrian novelist) is the achievement of sexual gratification by inflicting pain on the self. More generally, the so-called moral masochist seeks humiliation and failure, rather than physical pain. Freud believed that masochists' ability to achieve orgasm is disturbed by anxiety and guilt feelings about sex that are alleviated by their own suffering and punishment.

Clinical observations indicate that elements of both sadistic and masochistic behavior are usually present in the same person. Treatment with insight-oriented psychotherapy, including psychoanalysis, has been effective in some cases. As a result of therapy, the patients become aware of the need for self-punishment secondary to excessive unconscious guilt and also come to recognize their repressed aggressive impulses, which originate in early childhood.

Self-defeating personality disorder. DSM-III-R includes the self-defeating personality disorder in its appendix for diagnostic categories requiring further study. It is not considered an official part of DSM-III-R because it is controver-

Table 26-14
Diagnostic Criteria for Sadistic Personality Disorder

A. A pervasive pattern of cruel, demeaning, and aggressive behavior, beginning by early adulthood, as indicated by the repeated occurrence of at least *four* of the following:
   (1) has used physical cruelty or violence for the purpose of establishing dominance in a relationship (not merely to achieve some noninterpersonal goal, such as striking someone in order to rob him or her)
   (2) humiliates or demeans people in the presence of others
   (3) has treated or disciplined someone under his or her control unusually harshly (e.g., a child, student, prisoner, or patient)
   (4) is amused by, or takes pleasure in, the psychological or physical suffering of others (including animals)
   (5) has lied for the purpose of harming or inflicting pain on others (not merely to achieve some other goal)
   (6) gets other people to do what he or she wants by frightening them (through intimidation or even terror)
   (7) restricts the autonomy of people with whom he or she has a close relationship (e.g., will not let spouse leave the house unaccompanied or permit teen-age daughter to attend social functions)
   (8) is fascinated by violence, weapons, martial arts, injury, or torture

B. The behavior in A has not been directed toward only one person (e.g., spouse, one child) and has not been solely for the purpose of sexual arousal (as in sexual sadism).

Table from DSM-III-R, *Diagnostic and Statistical Manual of Mental Disorders,* ed 3, revised. Copyright American Psychiatric Association, Washington, DC, 1987, with permission.

sial. To receive this diagnosis, a person must have a pervasive pattern of self-defeating behavior, beginning by early adulthood and present in a variety of contexts. Persons with this disorder often avoid or undermine pleasurable experiences and are drawn to situations or relationships in which they will suffer.

Persons with this disorder choose persons and situations that lead to disappointment, failure, or mistreatment, even when better options are clearly available to them. They reject the attempts of others to offer help. After positive personal events (e.g., new achievement), these persons respond with depression, guilt, or a behavior that produces pain (e.g., an accident). They also invite rejecting responses from others and then feel hurt, defeated, or humiliated (e.g., a man may make fun of his spouse in public, provoking an angry retort, and then feel devastated). In general, they engage in excessive self-sacrifice that is unsolicited and discouraged by others.

Self-defeating personality disorder persons do not derive any sexual pleasure from humiliation; those persons who do are classified as having a paraphilia. See Table 26-13 for the DSM-III-R diagnostic criteria for self-defeating personality disorder.

As mentioned above, the use of this diagnostic label is controversial, as there is concern that victims of abuse may

Table 26-15
Clinical Characteristics of DSM-III-R Personality Disorders

Personality Disorder	Personality Disorders with Overlapping Criteria	Other Major Differential Diagnoses	Distinguishing Features
Schizoid	Schizotypal Paranoid Avoidant Obsessive-compulsive	Schizophrenia	Social isolation without psychoticlike symptoms or excessive fear of rejection
Schizotypal	Schizoid Paranoid Avoidant Obsessive-compulsive	Borderline personality disorder Depersonalization disorder	1. Cognitive perceptual distortions 2. Social withdrawal
Paranoid	Schizoid Schizotypal Avoidant Obsessive-compulsive	Delusional disorder Antisocial personality disorder Schizophrenia, paranoid type	1. Pervasive hypervigilance 2. Suspiciousness
Borderline	Antisocial Histrionic Narcissistic	Depressive disorders Cyclothymia Bipolar II Attention-deficit hyperactivity disorder Brief reactive psychosis Psychoactive substance abuse	1. Intense unstable relationships 2. Impulsive behavior, particularly self-destructive 3. Unstable mood with rapid shifts
Antisocial	Borderline Histrionic	Attention-deficit hyperactivity disorder Mania Psychoactive substance abuse Adult antisocial behavior Depressive disorders	1. Consistent violation of the rights of others 2. Lack of loyalty in interpersonal relationships
Histrionic	Borderline Antisocial	Dysthymia Depressive disorders Somatization disorder Conversion disorder Brief reactive psychosis	1. Hyperemotional responses 2. Superficial charm but shallow relationships 3. Seductive behavior 4. Highly dependent relationships
Narcissistic	Obsessive-compulsive Histrionic Antisocial Borderline	Depressive disorders Dysthymia	1. Fragile self-esteem 2. Exaggerated self-importance 3. Constant seeking of admiration
Avoidant	Schizoid Schizotypal Dependent	Social phobia	Sensitivity to rejection
Dependent	Avoidant	Agoraphobia	1. Subordinates own needs 2. Avoids self-reliance
Obsessive-compulsive	Schizoid Schizotypal Paranoid	Obsessive-compulsive disorder	1. Perfectionism 2. Stubbornness
Passive-aggressive		Oppositional defiant disorder	Passive resistance to demands of others

Table adapted from *American Psychiatric Association Annual Review,* vol 5. A I Francis and R E Hales, editors, p 283. American Psychiatric Association, Washington, DC, 1986, with permission.

Table 26-16
Treatment Techniques for DSM-III-R Personality Disorders

Personality Disorder	Psychotherapy	Pharmacotherapy	Behavior Therapy
Paranoid	Honest, candid relationship Interpret tendency to oversimplify Acknowledge grain of truth in paranoid system Identification of activating stresses	Consider antipsychotics	Reduce hypersensitivity to criticism Improve social skills Cognitive approaches need more study
Schizotypal	Expand noninterpersonal pleasure capacity Understand patient's inner feelings and communicate this Importance of therapist's consistency and acceptance	Consider antipsychotics, tricyclics, MAOIs	Social skills training Strengthen cognitive process skills Anxiety management training for social phobia
Schizoid	Relatedness with therapist important Gradually encourage other interpersonal activities	Consider antipsychotics, β-blockers, MAOIs	Uncertain
Histrionic	Identify maladaptive patterns in choosing intimate partners with gradual interpretation of underlying dynamics Emphasize calm, reasonable, logical approaches to crises May require limit setting and attention to professional boundaries	MAOIs for hysteroid dysphoric patient and possibly others	Attempt to: Moderate emotional expression, use of attention-getting plays, and egocentric, manipulative, and inconsiderate acts Encourage warmth, genuineness, and empathy
Narcissistic	Mix confrontation and empathy Communicate awareness of patient's strengths and vulnerabilities	Consider lithium, MAOIs, tricyclics	Same as histrionic Impulse control training
Antisocial	Group therapy in institutional setting	Can treat associated conditions	Treat patient with respect and concern Assess patient's strengths and weaknesses Attempt to rechannel patient into more prosocial activities Aversive training, contingency contracting need more study
Borderline	Sympathic and understanding relationship Focus on fragile sense of identity, shifting and highly contradictory impressions of self and others, and highly conflicted and anxiety-provoking manner of existing in a love relationship Training in vocational and avocational pursuits	Consider antipsychotics, MAOIs, tricyclics, carbamazepine, lithium, stimulants	Impulse control training Systematic training in problem-solving skills Social skills training with video feedback of mood and attitude shifts
Avoidant	Gentle, careful building of trust in therapeutic relationship Facilitation of opportunities to enhance self-esteem	MAOIs, β-adrenergic blockers, stimulants	Systematic desensitization Social skills training Cognitive restructuring
Dependent	Interpretation of underlying dynamics Assessment of patient's overall capacity for more independent functioning	Tricyclics, MAOIs, alprazolam	Anxiety management program
Obsessive-compulsive	Dream analysis and other uses of conscious material Cognitive techniques Encourage loosening up, having fun Avoid overintellectualizing	Consider clomipramine, fluoxetine	Social skills training to focus on dealing appropriately with self and others' emotions Loosening up rational, logical, obstinate approach to life

Table 26-16
Continued

Personality Disorder	Psychotherapy	Pharmacotherapy	Behavior Therapy
Passive-aggressive	Avoid supportive advice giving, or rescuing Interpret hostility toward and noncompliance with demands of society, work, and family life Confront late payments, late arrivals, missed sessions, etc.	Consider benzodiazepines, MAOIs, stimulants	Uncertain

Table adapted from *American Psychiatric Association Annual Review,* vol 5. A I Francis and R E Hales, editors, p 364. American Psychiatric Association, Washington, DC, 1986, with permission.

be blamed for being abused when, in fact, they are true victims (i.e., blameless). There is also concern about whether a new diagnosis is necessary or whether the disorder could be subsumed under an existing classification.

J. Christopher Perry and George Vaillant believe that most patients classified as self-defeating concurrently meet the criteria for dependent or passive-aggressive personality disorder.

Sadistic personality disorder. Sadistic personality disorder is also a controversial addition to DSM-III-R. It is in the appendix of DSM-III-R. Persons with this personality disorder show a pervasive pattern of cruel, demeaning, and aggressive behavior, beginning in early adulthood, that is directed toward others. Physical cruelty or violence is used to inflict pain on others and not to achieve some other goal, such as mugging someone in order to steal. Persons with the disorder like to humiliate or demean people in front of others and usually have treated or disciplined someone unusually harshly, especially children. In general, sadistic personality disorder persons are fascinated by violence, weapons, injury, or torture. To be included in this category, such persons are not supposed to derive sexual arousal from their behavior; if they do, a paraphilia should be diagnosed. See Table 26-14 for the DSM-III-R diagnostic criteria for sadistic personality disorder.

Table 26-15 summarizes the clinical characteristics of the DSM-III-R personality disorders discussed in this chapter. Table 26-16 summarizes the treatment techniques for each of the personality disorders.

References

Akhtar S, Thompsan J A: Overview: Narcissistic personality disorder. Am J Psychiatry *139:* 12, 1982.

Baron M, Gruen R, Asnis L, Lord S: Familial transmissions of schizotypal and borderline personality disorders. Am J Psychiatry *142:* 927, 1985.

Bouchard T J Jr, Lykken D T, McGue M, Segal N L, Tellegen A: Sources of human psychological differences: The Minnesota study of twins reared apart. Science *250*: 223, 1990.

Gunderson J G: *Borderline Personality Disorder.* American Psychiatric Press, Washington, DC, 1984.

Kass F, MacKinnon R A, Spitzer R L: Masochistic personality: An empirical study. Am J Psychiatry *143:* 216, 1986.

Kendler K S, Masterson C C, Ungaro R, Davis K L: A family history study of schizophrenia-related personality disorders. Am J Psychiatry *143:* 424, 1984.

Kernberg O F: *Borderline Conditions and Pathological Narcissism.* Aronson, New York, 1975.

Kohut H, Wolff E S: The disorders of the self and their treatment: An outline. Int J Psychoanal *59:* 413, 1978.

Lazare A, Klerman G, Armor D: Oral, obsessive and hysterical personality patterns: An investigation of psychoanalytic concepts by means of factor analysis. Arch Gen Psychiatry *14:* 624, 1966.

Lion J R, ed.: *Personality Disorders: Diagnosis and Management,* ed 2. Williams & Wilkins, Baltimore, 1981.

McGlashan T H: Schizotypal personality disorder: Chestnut Lodge follow-up study: VI. Long-term follow-up perspectives. Arch Gen Psychiatry *43:* 329, 1986.

Millon T: *Disorders of Personality: DSM-III Axis II.* Wiley, New York, 1981.

Perry J C: Depression in borderline personality disorder: Lifetime prevalence at interview and longitudinal course of symptoms. Am J Psychiatry *142:* 15, 1985.

Perry J C, Cooper S H: A preliminary report on defense and conflicts associated with borderline personality disorder. J Am Psychoanal Assoc. *34*: 865, 1986.

Perry J C, Cooper S H: Psychodynamics, symptoms and outcome in borderline and antisocial personality disorders and bipolar type II affective disorder. In *The Borderline: Current Empirical Research,* T H McGlashan, editor. American Psychiatric Press, Washington, DC, 1985.

Perry J C, Vaillant G E: Personality disorders. In *Comprehensive Textbook of Psychiatry,* ed 5, H I Kaplan and B J Sadock, editors, p. 1352. Williams & Wilkins, Baltimore, 1989.

Robins L N: *Deviant Children Grown Up: A Sociological and Psychiatric Study of Sociopathic Personality.* Williams & Wilkins, Baltimore, 1966.

Rutter M: *Maternal Deprivation Reassessed,* ed 2. Penguin Books, London 1981.

Soloff P H, George A, Nathan S, Schulz P M, Ulrich R F, Perel J M: Progress in pharmacotherapy of borderline disorders: A double-blind study of amitriptyline, haloperidol and placebo. Arch Gen Psychiatry *43:* 691, 1986.

Thomas A, Chess S: *Temperament and Development.* Brunner/Mazel, New York, 1977.

Torgersen S: Genetic and nosologic aspects of schizotypal and borderline personality disorders: A twin study. Arch Gen Psychiatry *41:* 546, 1984.

Vaillant G E: *Adaptation to Life.* Little, Brown, Boston, 1977.

Vaillant G E: Sociopathy as a human process. Arch Gen Psychiatry *32:* 179, 1975.

Woody G E, McLellan A T, Luborsky L, O'Brien C P: Sociopathy and psychotherapy outcome. Arch Gen Psychiatry *42:* 1081, 1985.

27

Conditions Not Attributable to a Mental Disorder

There are 13 conditions listed in the revised third edition of *Diagnostic and Statistical Manual of Mental Disorders* (DSM-III-R) that make up the category of conditions not attributable to a mental disorder (CNAMD). They include the following, each of which is discussed in this chapter: marital problem, occupational problem, noncompliance with medical treatment, parent-child problem, other interpersonal problem, other specified family circumstances, phase of life problem or other life circumstance problem, academic problem, borderline intellectual functioning, malingering, adult antisocial behavior, childhood or adolescent antisocial behavior, and uncomplicated bereavement.

The CNAMDs are not true mental disorders and are not considered as such by DSM-III-R. Rather, they are conditions that have led to contact with the mental health care system. Once in the system, a person with a CNAMD should have a thorough neuropsychiatric evaluation, which may or may not uncover a mental disorder. The categories listed above are of clinical interest to psychiatrists because they may accompany mental illness or, in some cases, be early harbingers of underlying mental disorders. For recording purposes in DSM-III-R, CNAMDs are called Axis V codes.

According to DSM-III-R, even though a person may have a mental disorder, the focus of attention or treatment may be on a condition that is not due to the mental disorder. For example, the treatment of a person with social phobia who has a marital problem not directly related to the phobic disorder may focus on the marital problem. At times, however, the distinction is not clear-cut, and it behooves the clinician to attempt to do as thorough a workup as possible so as not to overlook a diagnosable mental disorder.

MARITAL PROBLEM

DSM-III-R states, "This category can be used when the focus of attention or treatment is a marital problem that is apparently not due to a mental disorder. An example is marital conflict related to estrangement or divorce."

When a person presents with marital problems, the psychiatrist must assess whether the patient's distress arises from the marital situation or whether it is part of a larger mental disorder. Studies have demonstrated that mental disorders are more common among single people—the never married, widowed, separated, and divorced—than among married people. The developmental, sexual, and occupational history, as well as the marital history, of the patients are necessary for purposes of diagnosis.

Demands of Marriage

Marriage demands a sustained level of adaptation from both partners. Areas to be explored in a troubled marriage include the extent of communication between partners, ways of solving disputes, attitudes toward childbearing and child rearing, relations with in-laws, attitudes toward social life, the handling of finances, and the couple's sexual interaction. Stressful periods in the relationship may be precipitated by the birth of a child, abortion or miscarriage, economic stresses, moves to new areas, episodes of illness, and any situations that involve a significant change in marital roles. Illness in a child exerts the greatest strain on a marriage, and marriages in which a child has died through illness or accident end in divorce more often than not. Complaints of primary anorgasmia or impotence by marital partners are usually indicative of deeper disturbances, although sexual dissatisfaction is involved in many cases of marital maladjustment.

Adjustment to marital roles can be a problem if partners are of different backgrounds and have been raised with different value systems. For example, members of low socioeconomic status (SES) groups perceive the wife as making most of the decisions regarding the family and accept physical punishment as a way to discipline children. Middle-class persons perceive the decision-making process as shared, the husband often being the final arbiter, and prefer to discipline by verbal chastisement.

Problems involving conflicts in values, adjustment to new roles, or poor communication are most effectively handled when the relationship between the two partners is examined, as in marital therapy. A clinical case example follows:

A 30-year-old male chemist was referred by his internist because he wanted to talk to someone about his shaky marriage. During five years of courtship and two years of marriage, there had been numerous separations, usually precipitated by his dissatisfaction. Although he and his wife shared many interests and, until recently, had had a satisfactory sexual relationship, he thought that his wife was basically a cold and self-centered person who had no real concern about his career or feelings. His dissatisfaction periodically built up to a point that led to fights, which often resulted in temporary separations. He then felt lonely and came "crawling back" to her. Their relationship currently was one of "icy separateness," and the patient seemed to be seeking support to make a permanent break. Although he was in extreme distress because of his marital situation, frequently choking back tears, there was no evidence that he had difficulties with his other interpersonal relationships. He had many good friends, functioned well in his job, and denied symptoms other than distress about his marital situation.

Divorce is discussed in Section 2.5, "Adulthood," and marital therapy is discussed in Section 29.4, "Family Therapy and Marital Therapy."

OCCUPATIONAL PROBLEM

Occupational or industrial psychiatry is that area of psychiatry specifically concerned with psychiatric aspects of problems at work and with vocational maladjustment. The practical symptoms of job dissatisfaction are mistakes at work, accident proneness, absenteeism, and sabotage. Psychiatric symptoms include insecurity, reduced self-esteem, and anger and resentment at having to work. DSM-III-R advises use of this diagnosis "when the focus of attention or treatment is an occupational problem that is apparently not due to a mental disorder." Examples include job dissatisfaction and uncertainty about career choices.

People are particularly vulnerable to occupational problems at several points in their working lives—on entry into the working world, at times of promotion or transfer, during periods of unemployment, and at retirement. Specific situations—such as having too much or too little to do, being subjected to conflicting demands, feeling distracted by family problems, having responsibility without authority, and working for demanding and unhelpful managers—also create occupational distress.

Career Choices and Changes

The choice of a career is a major life decision. A significant number of young people follow in their parents' footsteps, but many are unsure of what to do and try several jobs before settling on an occupation. Disadvantaged youngsters frequently have little choice about a career. When young adults have a poor education and lack training and skills, even overwhelming ambition rarely leads them out of poverty or into occupational satisfaction. When the disadvantaged are women or members of minority groups, they have even less chance of occupational success. In discussing career choices with a patient, a psychiatrist should explore special talents and interests, childhood goals, the patient's models, family influences, future expectations, work and academic histories, and motivation to work.

Distress about work is readily understood when an employee has been fired, demoted, or passed over for promotion. Those in low socioeconomic groups and minorities are particularly vulnerable to losing their jobs. In one recent five-year period, 11.5 million persons in the United States age 20 or over lost their jobs as a result of industrial plant closings and cutbacks. Some left the labor force altogether. Others moved to lower-paying, low-skill jobs with fewer benefits. Some worked intermittently. Demands for college graduates are three times greater than for all other workers, and college graduates also have the lowest rate of unemployment. Women are specifically at risk for stress when they leave outside employment for homemaking, a transition that researchers have found to be extremely stressful.

Some people have problems after receiving professional advancement. Nonneurotic reasons for this reaction include anxiety about assuming new responsibility and the fact that people are sometimes promoted to jobs that are beyond their capacities to perform.

Adjusting to retirement is most difficult for people who are unprepared for it. Adverse reactions occur when a person is forced to retire prematurely or because of illness. It is also a problem for the person whose identity is based primarily on occupational status and income. Women have been reported to be able to adjust faster to retirement than men. Some workers, however, feel that retirement poses a greater hardship for women, because they face a longer retirement period owing to their greater life expectancy, are more likely to be alone (widowed) during their retirement years, and are usually poorer and have lower retirement incomes than men.

Psychological Problems and the Work Place

Maladaptation at work may arise from psychodynamic conflicts. Those conflicts can be reflected in the person's inability to accept the authority of competent superiors or, conversely, in overdependency on authority figures to fulfill infantile needs. People with unresolved conflicts about their competitive and aggressive impulses may experience great difficulty in the work area. They may suffer from a pathological envy of the success of others or fear success for themselves because of their inability to tolerate envy from others. Those conflicts are manifest in other areas of the patient's life as well, and the maladaptation is not limited to occupation.

Career Problems of Women

A number of changes have occurred in the business world in the United States during the past two decades. A significant number of women have entered the work force; many corporations are now willing to employ a husband and wife in the same firm; and teenagers have entered the work force, on a part-time basis, on a large scale.

Ninety percent of all females alive today in the United States will have to work to support themselves and probably one or two other people. Economic necessity now prompts the homemaker to enter the labor force. Rejection by employers on the basis of age, lack of recent experience, or insufficient training can cause dysphoria and depression. That is particularly true for the recently divorced woman in her 40s or 50s who has spent most of her adult life in the occupations of wife and mother.

The younger woman has different stresses, primarily related to the conflicting demands of work and family responsibilities. Over 50 percent of all mothers in the work force have children 1 year old or younger. But women's organizations and other critics charge that very few corporations are removing barriers to women's advancement or are concerned about reducing the tension that arises when job and family demands conflict. Specific issues that need to be addressed are provisions for child care or for the care of elderly parents, the option of flexible work hours, and the availability of unpaid parental leaves. Studies reveal that, when those leaves are made available to both parents, fathers rarely take them; that managers are more sensitive to crises in men's lives than to those of female employees; and that managers respond to such major events as divorce and the death of a family member but ignore the stress placed on a worker by the illness of a child or a school closing because of a snow day. A few socially conscious corporations are holding workshops to address the changes arising from the influx of women into the work force and such issues as family responsibilities, sexual harrassment in the workplace, personal safety during business travel, and rape prevention.

Dual-career families (in which both the husband and the wife have jobs) now constitute more than 40 percent of all families. A problem arises if the employer wants one partner to make a geographic move to a new post. Even if the transfer is a promotion, it can result in lower total income for the family and the loss of job or the disruption of career for the spouse. Some corporations offer new jobs to both spouses when one is asked to relocate; however, such approaches are relatively rare. A more common advance is the acceptance of couples, married or unmarried, as employees of the same corporation. Formerly, the employment of a husband and wife by the same firm was considered taboo by many businesses. Couples employed by the same firm seem to suffer only if they are very competitive with each other. Those that fare best treat their spouses differently at the office than at home. Resentment from coworkers occurs if one spouse reports directly to the other. Otherwise, no adverse response from other employees has been noted.

NONCOMPLIANCE WITH MEDICAL TREATMENT

According to DSM-III-R, "this category can be used when the focus of attention or treatment is noncompliance with medical treatment that is apparently not due to a mental disorder. Examples include: irrationally motivated noncompliance due to denial of illness, noncompliance due to religious beliefs, and decisions based on personal value judgments about the advantages and disadvantages of the proposed treatment. The category should not be used if the noncompliance is due to a mental disorder, such as schizophrenia or a psychoactive substance use disorder."

A clinical case example follows:

The mother of an 18-year-old boy requested help from the Visiting Nurse Association. Her son, a recent high school graduate with no previous medical history, had suffered a myocardial infarction 16 days previously. After being released from the hospital, the patient was told to remain in bed, with only bathroom privileges, for one week, until his next appointment with the cardiologist. When seen at home by the visiting nurse two days after leaving the hospital, he was playing basketball in the backyard. He acknowledged that he had had a "heart attack" but said he now felt "fine" and, therefore, saw no need to further restrict his activities. He was planning to begin a full-time job in a local factory in two weeks and was unwilling to consider the possible effect of his physical condition on his plans.

The patient had been popular, a high school football hero, with many friends and a series of steady girlfriends. He had gotten average grades and had never been in any trouble. His use of alcohol had been moderate, and he had smoked marijuana only a few times. He was not interested in talking about plans beyond the next year but guessed he would probably go into the army at some point. His relationship with his family was distant but harmonious. The patient's mother had stopped trying to enforce the regimen prescribed by his doctor after her son had reassured her that he would go to bed if he felt any pain.

Discussion. By not following standard medical advice, this patient was in danger of killing himself. Why did he persist in acting as if he did not have a life-threatening illness? It was certainly not because he had rationally considered the pros and cons of the prescribed treatment, as might be the case, for example, with a patient with lung cancer who chose not to undergo postoperative chemotherapy recommended by a surgeon in view of the controversy surrounding the effectiveness of the treatment. One can only conclude that the patient was demonstrating massive denial, a smaller degree of which may have served him well up to that point. Apparently, it was only in this unusual situation that his denial could have caused him serious problems.

Although his noncompliance with medical treatment was maladaptive and represented psychopathology (broadly defined), it may not have been sufficient to make the diagnosis of a mental disorder. One therefore would note the V code noncompliance with medical treatment. The V codes are for conditions not attributable to a mental disorder that are nevertheless a focus of attention or treatment. Hence, using a V code to characterize this problem did not preclude offering treatment.

DSM-III-R Diagnosis:
Axis I: Noncomplicance with medical treatment
Axis III: Status postmyocardial infarction

A compliant patient follows the physician's recommendations regarding return visits, behavioral regimens (rest, exercise, diet, work), taking medication, and entering the hospital for procedures or prolonged care. This topic is discussed more extensively in Chapter 1, "The Doctor–Patient Relationship."

PARENT–CHILD PROBLEM

Parent–child problems apply to the parent or to the child or to both and often represent conflicts that fall within the range of normal developmental stages or crises of each.

Difficulties arise in a variety of situations that stress the usual parent–child interaction. For instance, in a family in which the parents are divorced, parent–child problems may arise in the relationship with either the custodial or the noncustodial parent. The remarriage of a divorced or widowed parent can also lead to a parent–child problem. The resentment of a stepparent and the favoring of a natural child are usual in the initial phases of adjustment of a new family.

Other situations that may cause a parent–child problem are the development of a fatal, crippling, or chronic illness in either the parent or the child, such as leukemia, epilepsy, sickle-cell anemia, spinal cord injury, or the birth of a child with congenital defects (e.g., cerebral palsy, blindness, deafness). Although these situations are not rare, they challenge the emotional resources of the people involved. The parents and the child have to face present and potential loss and adjust their day-to-day lives physically, economically, and emotionally. These situations can try the healthiest families and produce parent–child problems not just with the affected child but also with the unaffected siblings. These siblings may be resented, preferred, or neglected because the ill child requires so much time and attention.

OTHER INTERPERSONAL PROBLEM

This category covers interpersonal problems not attributable to a mental disorder and not covered under marital problem or parent–child problem. Problems causing sufficient strain to bring a person into contact with the mental health care system may arise in relations with romantic partners, coworkers, neighbors, teachers, students, friends, and social groups.

Racial and religious prejudices cause problems in interpersonal relationships. Some social scientists believe that racism and religious bigotry do not have a strong psychological base and choose to emphasize social and class factors as causative. Other investigators view prejudice as a learned attitude and consider it a cultural variant, but a number of psychiatrists believe that people are motivated to change their prejudices only if they see them as part of a mental disorder.

OTHER SPECIFIED FAMILY CIRCUMSTANCES

This category applies to conditions that produce family stress sufficient to necessitate contact with the mental health care system but that are not the outcome of a prior mental disorder and that are not covered under marital problem or parent–child problem. DSM-III-R cites interpersonal difficulties with an in-law and sibling rivalry as examples. Adults often assume the responsibility of caring for aging parents while they are still caring for their children. That dual obligation often creates stress. Also, caring for elderly parents involves adaptation of both parties to a reversal of former roles, facing the potential loss of the parent, and coping with evidence of one's own mortality.

A problem that is now receiving attention is abuse of the elderly by some caretaking children. This problem is most likely to occur when the abusing offspring have substance abuse problems, are under economic stress, and have no relief from their caretaking duties and when the elderly parent is bedridden or has a chronic illness that requires constant nursing attention. More elderly women are abused than are elderly men, and most abuse occurs in the elderly over age 75.

Problems arising from sibling rivalry can occur with the birth of a new child and can recur as the children grow up. Competition among children for the attention, affection, and esteem of their parents is a fact of family life. That rivalry can extend to others who are not siblings and remains a factor in normal and abnormal competitiveness throughout life. In good sibling relationships the pleasures of companionship and the bonds created by kinship and shared experiences outweigh feelings of rivalry.

PHASE OF LIFE PROBLEM OR OTHER LIFE CIRCUMSTANCE PROBLEM

According to DSM-III-R, this category can be used when the focus of attention or treatment is due to problems related to stresses in the life cycle.

External events are most likely to overwhelm a person's adaptive capacities if they are unexpected, if they are numerous—that is, a number of stresses occurring within a short time—if the strain is chronic and unremitting, or if one loss actually heralds a myriad of concomitant adjustments that strain a person's recuperative powers.

The strains most likely to produce anxiety and depression relate to major life-cycle changes: marriage, occupation, and parenthood. Those events affect both men and women, but women, the poor, and minority groups seem particularly vulnerable to adverse reactions. Again, the change creates significant strain when it is unexpected and when it involves not only adjustment to a loss (spouse or job) but also the need to adjust to a new status that entails further hardships and problems.

In general, people have demonstrated their ability to adjust to life changes if they have mature defense mechanisms, such as altruism, humor, and a capacity for sublimation. Flexibility, reliability, strong family ties, regular employment, adequate income, job satisfaction, a pattern of regular recreation and social participation, realistic goals, and a history of adequate performance—in short, a full and satisfying life—create resilience to deal with life changes.

Periods of cultural transition, with changing mores and fluidity of role definition, may increase a person's vulnerability to life strain. Extreme cultural transition can create a condition of severe distress. This problem, also called culture shock, occurs when a person is suddenly thrust into an alien culture or has divided loyalties to two different cultures. In a less extreme form, culture shock occurs when young men or women enter the army, when people change jobs, when families move or undergo a significant change in income, when children have their first day in school, and when black ghetto children are bused to white middle-class schools.

Brainwashing

First practiced by the Chinese communists on American prisoners in the Korean war, brainwashing is the deliberate creation of culture shock. A condition of isolation, alienation, and intimidation is developed for the express purpose of assaulting ego strengths and leaving the person to be brainwashed vulnerable to the imposition of alien ideas and behavior that would usually be rejected. Brainwashing relies on both mental and physical coercion. All people are vulnerable to brainwashing if they are exposed to it for a sufficient length of time, if they are alone and without support, and if they are without hope of escape from the situation. Help from the mental health care system is usually necessary to help brainwashed persons readjust to their usual environments after the brainwashing experience, a process known as deprogramming. Supportive therapy is offered, with emphasis on reeducation, restitution of ego strengths that existed before the trauma, and alleviation of the guilt and depression that are remnants of the frightening experience and the lost confidence and confusion in identity that results from it.

Cults

Cults are charismatic groups that can affect participants in adverse ways, which may eventually bring them into contact with the mental health care system. Cults are characterized by an intensely held belief system and ideology that are imposed on their members, by a high level of group cohesion that tries to prevent members' freedom of choice to leave the group, and by a profound influence on the members' behavior that may include frank psychiatric symptoms, including psychosis. Most potential cult members are in their adolescence or otherwise struggling with establishing their own identities.

They are drawn to the cult, which holds out the false promise of emotional well-being and purports to offer the sense of direction for which these persons are searching. Cult members are encouraged to proselytize and to draw new members into the group. They are often encouraged to break with family members and friends and to socialize only with other group members. Cults are invariably led by charismatic personalities, who are often ruthless in their quest for financial, sexual, and power gains and in their insistence on conformity to the cult's ideological belief system, which may have strong religious or quasireligious overtones. Exit therapy has been developed to guide cult members out of the group, provided that lingering emotional ties to persons outside the cult can be mobilized.

ACADEMIC PROBLEM

Academic problem is listed in DSM-III-R as a condition in which the focus of attention or treatment is an academic problem that is apparently not due to a mental disorder. An example is failing grades and underachievement in a person with adequate intellectual capacity and with no other mental disorder that would account for the problem.

Etiology

Academic problems may result from a variety of causes and may arise at any time in life, although they occur most often between the ages of 5 and 21, a span that includes the school years.

During this period, the school setting occupies a major portion of the person's time. School is an important social and educational instrument, being interconnected with the major developmental issues of childhood, adolescence, and young adulthood. Boys and girls must cope with the process of separation, adjustment to new environments, adaptation to social contacts, competition, assertion, intimacy, and a myriad of other issues. There is often a reciprocal relationship between how well these developmental tasks are mastered and the level of school performance.

Achievement-related anxiety represents a significant source of academic problems. In psychoanalytic terms, some students exhibit evidence of inner conflict believed to be connected with the Oedipus complex. Described by Sigmund Freud as "those wrecked by success," such persons fear the consequences that are imagined to accompany the attainment of success. Behaviorists may interpret the conflict as a learned disposition to fear success. An example is a woman whose motive to avoid success in school is linked to a fear of social rejection or loss of femininity or both, especially when success necessitates aggression and competition with men.

The loss of parents as substitute teachers and the diminished role of the parents themselves as a primary reference group may also undermine academic efforts. Studies reveal that boredom in school is often the result of identity diffusion. Lacking any real and stable sense of themselves and their goals, students become bored and unable to perform their student role.

The teachers' expectations concerning their students' performance influence that performance. Teachers serve as causal agents whose varying expectations can shape the differential development of students' skills and abilities. Such conditioning early in school, especially if negative, can disturb academic performance. Thus, a teacher's affective response to a child can prompt the appearance of academic problems. Most important is the teacher's humane approach to the student. This applies to all levels of education, including medical school.

Treatment

Although not considered a diagnosable psychiatric disorder, academic problems can best be alleviated by psychological means. Psychotherapeutic techniques can be used successfully for scholastic difficulties, including those related to poor motivation, poor self-concept, and underachievement.

Early efforts at relieving the problem should outweigh all other considerations, as sustained problems in learning and school performance are frequently compounded and precipitate more severe difficulties. Feelings of anger, frustration, shame, loss of self-respect, and helplessness—emotions that most often accompany school failures—emotionally and cognitively damage self-esteem, disabling future performance and clouding expectations for success.

Tutoring is an extremely effective technique in dealing with academic problems and should be considered in all cases. Tutoring is of proved value in preparing for objective multiple-choice examinations, such as the Scholastic Aptitude Test (SAT), Medical College Aptitude Test (MCAT), and national boards. Taking such examinations repetitively and using relaxation skills are two behavioral techniques of great value for diminishing anxiety.

Academic problems should be differentiated from adjustment disorder with academic inhibition, which is characterized by a change from previously adequate academic performance after a psychosocial stressor. That disorder is discussed in Chapter 24.

BORDERLINE INTELLECTUAL FUNCTIONING

As described in DSM-III-R, borderline intellectual functioning can be identified when the focus of attention or treatment is based on a deficit in functioning associated with borderline intellectual functioning, defined as an intelligence quotient (I.Q.) in the 71 to 84 range. The problem is often masked when a mental disorder is present, especially the residual type of schizophrenia.

Only about 6 to 7 percent of the population are found to have a borderline I.Q., as determined by the Stanford-Binet test or the Wechsler scales. The premise behind the inclusion of this category is that these persons may experience difficulties in their adaptive capacities, which may ultimately produce impaired social and vocational functioning. Thus, in the absence of specific intrapsychic conflicts, developmental traumas, biochemical abnormalities, and other factors linked to mental disorder, such persons may experience severe emotional distress. Frustration and embarrassment over their difficulties may shape their life choices and lead to circumstances warranting psychiatric intervention.

Once the underlying problem is known to the therapist, psychiatric treatment can be quite useful. Many persons with borderline intellectual functioning are able to function at a superior level in some areas while being markedly deficient in others. By directing such persons to appropriate areas of endeavor, by pointing out socially acceptable behavior, and by teaching them living skills, the therapist can help improve their self-esteem.

MALINGERING

Malingering is characterized by the voluntary production and presentation of false or grossly exaggerated physical or psychological symptoms. There is always an external motivation, which falls into one of three categories: (1) to avoid difficult or dangerous situations, responsibilities, or punishment; (2) to receive compensation, free hospital room and board, a source of drugs, or haven from the police; and (3) to retaliate when the victim feels guilt or suffers a financial loss, legal penalty, or job loss. The presence of a clearly definable goal is the main factor that differentiates malingering from a factitious illness.

Epidemiology

The incidence of malingering is unknown, but it is common. It occurs most frequently in settings in which there is a preponderance of men—the military, prisons, factories, and other industrial settings—although it also occurs in women.

Diagnosis

According to DSM-III-R, malingering should be strongly suspected if any combination of the following is noted: (1) medicolegal context of presentation (e.g., the person's being referred by his or her attorney to the physician for examination); (2) marked discrepancy between the person's claimed stress or disability and the objective findings; (3) lack of cooperation during the diagnostic evaluation and in complying with the prescribed treatment regimen; and (4) the presence of antisocial personality disorder.

Many malingerers express mostly subjective, vague, ill-defined symptoms—for example, headache; pains of the neck, lower back, chest, or abdomen; dizziness; vertigo; amnesia; anxiety; and depression— and symptoms often having a family history, in all likelihood not organically based but incredibly difficult to refute. Malingerers may complain bitterly, describing how much the symptoms impair their normal function and how much they are disliked. They may use the very best doctors, who are the most trusted (and perhaps most easily fooled), and promptly and willingly pay all their bills, even if excessive, to impress them with their integrity. To seem credible, malingerers must give the same report of symptoms but tell their physicians as little as possible. But often they complain of misery without objective signs or other symptoms congruent with recognized diseases or syndromes; if they do describe all symptoms, the symptoms are said to come and go. Malingerers are often preoccupied with cash, rather than cure, and have a knowledge of the law and precedents relative to their claims.

Objective tests—such as audiometry, brain stem audiometry, auditory and visually evoked potentials, galvanic skin response, electromyography, and nerve conduction studies—may be helpful in sorting out auditory, labyrinthine, ophthalmological, neurological, and other problems.

Differential Diagnosis

According to DSM-III-R, malingering differs from factitious disorders in that there are external incentives in malingering, whereas in factitious disorders there is an absence of external incentives. Rather, evidence of an intrapsychic need to maintain the sick role suggests a factitious disorder.

Conversion and somatoform disorders do not show intentionality; there are no obvious, external incentives. Moreover, the symptoms in malingering are less likely to be symbolically related to an underlying emotional conflict. Table 27-1 lists features that differentiate malingering from genuine illness.

Treatment

A patient suspected of malingering should be thoroughly and objectively evaluated, and the physician should refrain from demonstrating any suspicion. If the doctor becomes angry (a common response to malingerers), a confrontation may occur, with two consequences: (1) The doctor–patient relationship is disrupted, and no further positive intervention is possible. (2) The patient will be even more on guard, and proof of deception may become virtually impossible. If the patient is accepted and not discredited, subsequent observation, while hospitalized or an outpatient, may reveal the versatility of the symptoms, which are consistently present only when patients know they are being observed. Preserving the doctor–patient relationship is often essential to the diagnosis and long-term treatment of the patient. Careful evaluation usually reveals the relevant issue without the need for a confrontation. It is usually best to use an intensive treatment approach, as though the symptoms were real. The symptoms can then be given up in response to treatment, without the patient's losing face.

ADULT ANTISOCIAL BEHAVIOR AND CHILDHOOD OR ADOLESCENT ANTISOCIAL BEHAVIOR

Antisocial behavior is a behavioral pattern that usually begins in childhood and often persists throughout life. It is characterized by activities that are illegal or immoral or both and that violate the society's legal system. Examples include thievery, racketeering, drug dealing, and prostitution. According to DSM-III-R, the diagnosis of antiso-

Table 27-1
Features of Malingering Usually Not Found in Genuine Illness

Symptoms are vague, ill-defined, overdramatized, and not in conformity with known clinical conditions.
The patient seeks addicting drugs, financial gain, the avoidance of onerous (e.g., jail) or other unwanted conditions.
History, examination, and evaluative data do not elucidate complaints.
The patient is uncooperative and refuses to accept a clean bill of health or an encouraging prognosis.
The findings appear compatible with self-inflicted injuries.
History or records reveal multiple past episodes of injury or undiagnosed illness.
Records or test data appear to have been tampered with (e.g., erasures, unprescribed substances in urine).

Table by Arthur T. Meyerson, M.D.

cial behavior should not be made if the behavior is caused by a mental disorder (e.g., conduct disorder, antisocial personality disorder) or an impulse control disorder (e.g., kleptomania). In children and adolescents this condition is also known as juvenile delinquency.

The term "antisocial behavior" is sometimes confusing because it refers both to persons whose behavior is not due to a mental disorder and to persons who have never received an adequate neuropsychiatric workup to determine the presence or absence of a mental disorder. As Dorothy Lewis has noted, the term can apply to normal persons who "struggle to make a dishonest living."

Epidemiology

Estimates of the prevalence of antisocial behavior range from 5 to 15 percent of the population, depending on the criteria and sampling. Within the prison population, investigators report prevalence figures of between 20 and 80 percent. Males account for more antisocial behavior than do females.

Etiology

Antisocial behaviors in childhood and adulthood are characteristic of a variety of persons, ranging from those with no demonstrable psychopathology to those who are severely impaired, suffering from psychosis, organic mental syndromes, and retardation, among other conditions. A comprehensive neuropsychiatric assessment of antisocial persons usually reveals a myriad of potentially treatable psychiatric and neurological impairments that can easily be overshadowed by offensive behaviors and thus be overlooked. But, as DSM-III-R cautions, only in the absence of organic, psychotic, neurotic, or intellectual impairment should patients be categorized as displaying antisocial behavior.

Antisocial behavior may be influenced by genetic, environmental, or psychological factors.

Genetic factors. Data supporting the genetic transmission of antisocial behavior are based on studies that demonstrate a 60 percent concordance rate in monozygotic twins and about a 30 percent concordance rate in dizygotic twins. Adoption studies show a high rate of antisocial behavior in the biological relatives of adoptees identified with antisocial behavior and a high incidence of antisocial behavior in the adopted-away offspring of those with antisocial behavior.

There is a high incidence of abnormalities during the prenatal and perinatal periods in children who subsequently display antisocial behavior. There also is an association between attention-deficit hyperactivity disorder and antisocial behavior.

Environmental factors. Studies note that in neighborhoods in which low socioeconomic status (SES) families predominate, the sons of unskilled workers are more likely to commit more numerous and more serious criminal offenses than are the sons of middle-class or skilled workers, at least during adolescence and early adulthood. These data are not as clear for females, but the findings are generally similar in studies from many different countries. Areas of family training that have been particularly cited as differing by SES group are the use in middle-SES parents of love-oriented techniques in discipline, the withdrawal of affection versus physical punishment, negative parental attitudes toward aggressive behavior and attempts to curb it, and the verbal ability to communicate the various reasons for the values and proscriptions of behavior.

Delinquent children are likely to come from broken homes. Indeed, homes broken by divorce or separation seem to produce higher rates of delinquency than do homes disrupted by the death of a parent. Thus, the important factor seems to be family discord and disharmony, rather than parental absence.

Antisocial behavior is associated with the use and abuse of alcohol and drugs. Violent antisocial acts are also associated with the easy availability of handguns.

Psychological factors. If the parenting experience is poor, children experience emotional deprivation, which leads to low self-esteem and unconscious anger. They are not given any limits, and their consciences are deficient because they have not internalized parental prohibitions that account for superego formation. Therefore, they have so-called superego lacunae, which allow them to commit antisocial acts without guilt. At times, such children's antisocial behavior represents a vicarious source of pleasure and gratification for parents who act out through the children their own forbidden wishes and impulses. A consistent finding in persons with repeated acts of violent behavior is a history of physical abuse.

Clinical Features

Persons with antisocial behavior have difficulties in work, marriage, money matters, and conflicts with various authorities. The adult symptoms of antisocial (also known as sociopathic) behavior are summarized in Table 27-2.

The childhood behaviors most associated with antisocial behavior are theft, incorrigibility, truancy, running away, associating with undesirable persons, and staying out late at night. The greater the number of symptoms present in childhood is, the greater the probability of adult antisocial behavior; however, the presence of greater numbers of symptoms is also indicative of the development of other psychiatric illnesses in adult life.

Table 27-2
Adult Symptoms of Antisocial Behavior

Life Area	Antisocial Patients with Significant Problems in This Area (%)
Work problems	85
Marital problems	81
Financial dependency	79
Arrests	75
Alcohol abuse	72
School problems	71
Impulsiveness	67
Sexual behavior	64
Wild adolescence	62
Vagrancy	60
Belligerency	58
Social isolation	56
Military record (of those serving)	53
Lack of guilt	40
Somatic complaints	31
Use of aliases	29
Pathological lying	16
Drug abuse	15
Suicide attempts	11

Data from L Robins: *Deviant Children Grown Up: A Sociological and Psychiatric Study of Sociopathic Personality*. Williams & Wilkins, Baltimore, 1966, with permission.

Diagnosis

The diagnosis of antisocial behavior is one of exclusion. The intertwining of alcoholism and drug dependence in such behavior often makes it difficult to separate the antisocial behavior, related primarily to drug abuse or alcoholism, from disordered behaviors that occurred either before drug or alcohol use or during episodes unrelated to alcoholism or drug abuse.

During the manic phases of bipolar disorder, certain aspects of behavior can be similar to antisocial behavior, such as wanderlust, sexual promiscuity, and financial difficulty. Schizophrenia, especially in childhood, may often manifest itself as antisocial behavior. Adult schizophrenic patients may have episodes of antisocial behavior, but the symptom picture is usually clear, especially with regard to thought disorder, delusions, and hallucinations on the mental status examination.

Neurological conditions may cause antisocial behavior, and so electroencephalograms (EEGs), computed tomography (CT) scans, magnetic resonance imaging (MRIs), and a complete neurological examination should be done. Temporal lobe epilepsy is often considered in the differential diagnosis. When a clear-cut diagnosis of temporal lobe epilepsy or encephalitis can be made, that may account for the antisocial behavior. Abnormal EEG findings are prevalent among violent offenders. An estimated 50 percent of aggressive criminals have abnormal EEG findings.

Conduct disorder, which should be differentiated from antisocial behavior, is discussed in Section 35.1. Antisocial personality disorder is discussed in Chapter 26.

Treatment

In general, antisocial behavior provokes great therapeutic pessimism. That is, it is difficult for therapists to have much hope of changing a pattern of behavior that has been present almost continuously throughout the patient's life. Psychotherapy has not been effective, and there have been no major breakthroughs with biological treatments, including the use of medications.

There is more enthusiasm for the use of therapeutic communities and other forms of group treatment, even though the data provide little basis for enthusiasm. Many delinquents and adult criminals who are incarcerated and in institutional settings have shown some response to group therapy approaches. The history of violence, criminality, and antisocial behavior has shown that they seem to decrease after age 40. Recidivism in criminals, which can reach 90 percent in some studies, also decreases in middle age.

Prevention

Because antisocial behavior begins during childhood, one must focus on delinquency prevention. Any measures that improve the physical and mental health of socioeconomically disadvantaged children and their families are likely to reduce delinquency and violent crime. Since many recurrently violent persons have sustained a multiplicity of insults to the central nervous system (CNS), starting prenatally and continuing through childhood and adolescence, programs need to be developed to educate parents of the dangers to their children of CNS injury, including the effects of drugs and alcohol on the brain of the growing fetus. Public education regarding the releasing effect of alcohol on violent behaviors (not to mention its contribution to vehicular homicide) may also reduce crime.

In the Surgeon General's Report on Violence and Public Health of 1985, the committee on the prevention of assault and homicide emphasized the importance of discouraging corporal punishment in the home, forbidding it in the schools, and even abolishing capital punishment by the state, saying that all are models and sanctions of violence.

Although there is disagreement regarding the contribution of violence in the media to violent crime, there is universal recognition that the media have propaganda potential. The extent to which the media, such as television, could be used to transmit positive social values has not yet been realized.

The most successful preventive measures within the field of medicine have come from community-wide public health programs (such as the campaign against smoking) and from programs that detect individual vulnerabilities (such as individual monitoring of blood pressure). Studies of antisocial behavior reveal the contribution of broad cultural factors and constellations of individual biopsychosocial vulnerabilities. Prevention programs must recognize and address both kinds of factors.

UNCOMPLICATED BEREAVEMENT

Immediately after or within a few months of the loss of a loved one, a normal period of bereavement or grief begins. Feelings of sadness, preoccupation with thoughts about the deceased, tearfulness, irritability, insomnia, and difficulties in concentrating and carrying out one's daily activities are some of the signs and symptoms. A grief reaction is limited to a varying period of time based on one's cultural group (usually no longer than six months). Normal grief, however, may lead to a full depressive syndrome, which requires treatment. See Section 2.7 for a further discussion of grief, mourning, and bereavement.

References

Albert S, Fox H M, Kahn M W: Faking psychosis on the Rorschach: Can expert judges detect malingering? J Pers Assess *44:* 115, 1980.

Bash I Y, Alpert M: The determination of malingering. Ann NY Acad Sci *347:* 86, 1980

Blazer D, Hughes D, George L: Stressful life events and the onset of a generalized anxiety syndrome. Am J Psychiatry *144:* 1178, 1987.

Bow J N: A comparison of intellectually superior male reading achievers and underachievers from a neuropsychological perspective. J Learn Disabil *21:* 118, 1988.

Eiserman W D: Three types of peer tutoring: Effects on the attitudes of students with learning disabilities and their regular class peers. J Learn Disabil *21:* 249, 1988.

Holmes T: Life situations, emotions, and disease. J Acad Psychosom Med *19:* 747, 1978.

Keogh B K: Improving services for problem learners: Rethinking and restructuring. J Learn Disabil *21:* 19, 1988.

Lewis D O, ed.: *Vulnerabilities to Delinquency*. Spectrum, New York, 1981.

Lewis D O, Pincus J H, Feldman M, Jackson L, Bard B: Psychiatric, neurological, and psychoeducational characteristics of 15 death row inmates in the United States. Am J Psychiatry *143:* 7, 1986.

Lidz T: *The Person*. Basic Books, New York, 1968.

Martinson R, Palmer T, Adams S: *Rehabilitation, Recidivism, and Research*. National Council on Crime and Delinquency, Hackensack, NJ, 1976.

Meyerson A T: Malingering. In *Comprehensive Textbook of Psychiatry,* ed 5, H I Kaplan and B J Sadock, editors, p 1396. Williams & Wilkins, Baltimore, 1989.

Neugarten B L: Time, age and the life cycle. Am J Psychiatry *136:* 887, 1979.

Sadock V A: Other conditions not attributable to a mental disorder. In *Comprehensive Textbook of Psychiatry,* ed 5, H I Kaplan and B J Sadock, editors, p 1408. Williams & Wilkins, Baltimore, 1989.

Psychiatric Emergencies

28.1 / Suicide

Edwin Shneidman has defined suicide as "the conscious act of self-induced annihilation, best understood as a multidimensional malaise in a needful individual who defines an issue for which the act is perceived as the best solution." Suicide is not a random or pointless act. On the contrary, it is a way out of a problem or crisis that is invariably causing intense suffering. Suicide is associated with thwarted or unfulfilled needs, feelings of hopelessness and helplessness, ambivalent conflicts between survival and unbearable stress, a narrowing of perceived options, and a need for escape; the suicidal person sends out signals of distress.

EPIDEMIOLOGY

Incidence and Prevalence

Each year about 30,000 deaths are attributed to suicide in the United States. This figure represents successful suicides; the number of attempted suicides is estimated to be 8 to 10 times that number. Lost in the reporting are intentional misclassifications of cause of death, accident of undetermined cause, and the so-called chronic suicides—for example, deaths through alcoholism, drug abuse, and consciously poor adherence to medical regimens for diabetes, obesity, and hypertension.

Between 1970 and 1980 there were over 230,000 suicides in the United States—about one every 20 minutes, 75 suicides a day. The total suicide rate has remained fairly constant over the years. The rate in 1970 was 11.6 suicide deaths per 100,000; in 1980 it was 11.9 deaths per 100,000; and in 1985 it was 12.5 per 100,000 persons. In 1977 suicide was at a peak of 13.3 per 100,000. Since then there has been a slight decline. Currently, suicide is ranked as the eighth overall cause of death in this country, after heart disease, cancer, stroke, accidents, pneumonia, diabetes mellitus, and cirrhosis.

Suicide rates in the United States are at the midpoint of national rates reported to the United Nations by industrialized countries. Internationally, suicide rates range from highs of more than 25 per 100,000 people in Scandanavia, Switzerland, West Germany, Austria, the eastern European countries (the suicide belt), and Japan to fewer than 10 per 100,000 in Spain, Italy, Ireland, Egypt, and the Netherlands.

A state-by-state analysis of suicides from 1979 to 1981 among those aged 15 to 44 revealed that New Jersey had the nation's lowest suicide rates for both sexes. Nevada and New Mexico had the highest rates for men, and Nevada and Wyoming the highest rates for women. Women in Nevada killed themselves at a higher frequency than did men in New Jersey. The number one suicide site in the world is the Golden Gate Bridge in San Francisco, with more than 800 suicides since it opened.

Associated Factors

Sex. Men commit suicide more than three times as often as do women, a rate that is stable over all ages. Women, however, are four times as likely to attempt suicide as are men.

Methods. The higher rate of successful suicide for men is related to the methods they use. Men use firearms, hanging, or jumping from high places. Women are more likely to take an overdose of drugs or a poison, but they are beginning to use firearms more often than previously. The use of guns has decreased as a method of suicide in those states with gun control laws.

Age. Suicide rates increase with age. The significance of the mid-life crisis is underscored by suicide rates. Among men, suicides peak and continue to rise after age 45; among women, the greatest number of completed suicides occurs after age 55. Rates of 40 per 100,000 population are found in men aged 65 and older. The elderly attempt suicide less often than do younger people but are successful more often. The elderly account for 25 percent of the suicides, although they make up only 10 percent of the total population. The rate for those 75 or older is more than three times the rate of that among the young.

The suicide rate is rising most rapidly in young people. For males 15 to 24 years old, there was a 40 percent increase between 1970 and 1980, and the rate is still rising. The suicide rate for females in the same age group showed only a slight increase. Among men 25 to 34 years old, the suicide rate increased almost 30 percent. Suicide is the second leading cause of death in the 15- to 24-year-old group after accidents. Attempted suicides in this age group number between 1 million and 2 million annually. The majority of suicides now occur among those aged 15 to 44.

Race. The rate of suicide among whites is nearly twice that among nonwhites, but these figures are being questioned, as the suicide rate among blacks is increasing. Among ghetto youth and certain native American and Alaskan Indian groups, suicide rates have greatly exceeded the national rate. Suicide among immigrants is higher than in the native-born population. Two out of every three suicides are white males.

Religion. Historically, suicide rates among Catholic populations have been lower than rates among Protestants and Jews. It may be that a religion's degree of orthodoxy and integration is a more accurate measure of risk in this category than is simple institutional religious affiliation.

Marital status. Marriage reinforced by children seems to lessen significantly the risk of suicide. Among married persons the rate is 11 per 100,000. Single, never-married persons register an overall rate of nearly double the rate of married persons. However, previously married persons show sharply higher rates than do never-married persons: 24 per 100,000 among the widowed; 40 per 100,000 among divorced persons, with divorced men registering 69 suicides per 100,000, as compared with 18 per 100,000 for divorced women. Suicide is more common in persons who have a history of suicide (attempted or real) in the family and who are socially isolated. So-called anniversary suicides are suicides by persons who take their lives on the same day as did a member of their family.

Occupation. The higher a person's social status is, the greater is the suicide risk, but a fall in social status also increases the risk. Work, in general, protects against suicide.

Among occupational rankings, professionals, particularly physicians, have traditionally been considered to be at the greatest risk for suicide. However, the best recent studies have demonstrated that there is no increased suicide risk for male physicians in the United States. Their annual suicide rate is approximately 36 per 100,000, which is the same as that for white men over 25. Recent British and Scandinavian data, by contrast, show that the suicide rate for male physicians is two to three times the rate found in the general male population of the same age.

Studies agree that female physicians have a higher risk of suicide. In the United States, the annual suicide rate for female physicians is approximately 41 per 100,000, compared with the 12 per 100,000 among all white women over 25 years of age. Similarly, in England and Wales the suicide rate for unmarried female physicians is 2.5 times greater than the rate among unmarried women in the general population, although it is comparable to that found among other groups of professional women.

Studies show that the physician who commits suicide has a psychiatric disorder. The three most common psychiatric disorders found among physicians and among physician suicide victims are depression, drug dependence, and alcoholism. Often, the physician who commits suicide has experienced recent professional, personal, or family difficulties. Both male and female physicians commit suicide significantly more often by drug overdose and less often by firearms than do persons in the general population; thus, drug availability and knowledge about toxicity are important factors in physician suicide. There is some evidence that female physicians have an unusually high lifetime risk for mood disorders, which may be the major determinant of the elevated suicide risk.

Among physicians, psychiatrists are considered to be at greatest risk, followed by ophthalmologists and anesthesiologists, but the trend is toward an equalization among all specialties. Special at-risk populations are musicians, dentists, law enforcement officers, lawyers, and insurance agents. Suicide is higher among unemployed persons than among employed persons. During economic recessions, depressions, and times of high unemployment, the suicide rate increases. During times of high employment and during war, the rate decreases.

Climate. No seasonal correlation with suicide has been found. There is a slight increase in the spring and fall, but, contrary to popular belief, there is no increase in suicide during December or holiday periods.

Physical health. The relationship of physical health and illness to suicide is significant. Prior medical care appears to be a positively correlated risk indicator of suicide: 32 percent of suicides have had medical attention within six months of death. Postmortem studies show that a physical illness is present in some 25 to 75 percent of all suicide victims; a physical illness is estimated to be an important contributing factor in 11 to 51 percent of suicides. In each instance the percentage increases with age.

For example, 50 percent of men with cancer who commit suicide do so within a year of receiving the diagnosis. Cancer of the breast or genitals is found in 70 percent of women with cancer who commit suicide. There are seven diseases of the central nervous system (CNS) that increase the risk of suicide: epilepsy, multiple sclerosis, head injury, cardiovascular disease, Huntington's chorea, dementia, and acquired immune deficiency syndrome (AIDS). All are diseases in which an associated mood disorder is known to occur. Epileptics have available barbiturates and other medications with which to kill themselves.

Four endocrine conditions are associated with increased suicide risk: Cushing's disease, anorexia nervosa, Klinefelter's syndrome, and porphyria. Mood disorders also attend these disorders. The two gastrointestinal disorders with an increased suicide risk are peptic ulcer and cirrhosis, both physical disorders found among alcoholics. The two urogenital problems with an increased suicide risk are prostatic hypertrophy and renal disease treated with hemodialysis, both problems in which changes in mood occur.

Factors associated with illness and contributing to both suicides and suicide attempts are loss of mobility among persons to whom physical activity is occupationally or recreationally important; disfigurement, particularly among women; and chronic, intractable pain. In addition to the direct effects of illness, the secondary effects of illness—for example, disruption of relationships and loss of occupational status—are prognostic factors.

Certain drugs can produce depression, which may lead to suicide in some cases. Among these are reserpine, corticosteroids, antihypertensives (e.g., propranolol [Inderal]), and some anticancer agents.

Mental health. Highly significant psychiatric factors in suicide include alcoholism and other drug abuse, depression, schizophrenia, and other mental illnesses. Almost 95 percent of patients who commit or attempt suicide have a diagnosed mental illness. Depressive disorders account for 80 percent of that figure, schizophrenia accounts for 10 percent, and dementia or delirium for 5 percent. Patients who suffer from delusional depression are at the highest risk for suicide. The risk of suicide in patients with depressive disorder is about 15 percent. Twenty-five percent of all patients who have a history of impulsive behavior or violent acts are also at high risk for suicide. Previous psychiatric hospitalization for any reason increases the risk of suicide.

Among adult suicide victims, there are significant differences between the young and the old for both psychiatric diagnoses and antecedent stressors. A study in San Diego showed that diagnoses of drug use disorders and antisocial personality disorder were found more often among suicide victims under 30 years of age, and diagnoses of mood and organic disorders were found more among suicides aged 30 and over. Stressors associated with suicide in those under 30 were separation, rejection, unemployment, and legal troubles; illness stressors were found more often among suicide victims over 30.

Psychiatric patients. Psychiatric patients' risk of suicide is 3 to 12 times greater than that of nonpatients. The degree of risk varies according to age, sex, diagnosis, and inpatient or outpatient status. After adjustment for age, male and female psychiatric patients who have at some time been inpatients have 5 and 10 times higher suicide risks, respectively, than their counterparts in the general population. For male and female outpatients who have never been admitted, the suicide risks are three and four times greater, respectively, than those of their counterparts in the general population. The higher suicide risk for psychiatric patients who have been inpatients reflects the fact that patients with severe psychiatric disorders tend to be admitted—for example, depressive patients requiring electroconvulsive therapy (ECT). The psychiatric diagnosis that carries the greatest risk of suicide in both sexes is mood disorder.

Persons in the general population who commit suicide have tended to be middle-aged or elderly, though, increasingly, studies report that psychiatric patients who commit suicide tend to be relatively young. In one study the mean age of male suicide victims was 29.5 years and that of women 38.4 years. The relative youthfulness of these suicide victims was due partly to the fact that two early-onset, chronic psychiatric disorders—schizophrenia and recurrent mood disorder—accounted for just over half of all these suicides, reflecting an age and diagnostic pattern found in most studies of psychiatric patient suicides.

A small but significant percentage of psychiatric patients who commit suicide do so while they are inpatients. The majority of inpatients who commit suicide do not kill themselves in the psychiatric ward itself but do so on the hospital grounds, while on a pass or weekend leave, or when absent without leave.

The suicide risk is highest for both sexes in the first week of the psychiatric admission; after three to five weeks as inpatients, they have a risk no greater than the risk in the general population. Also, the inpatient rates of suicide do not rise uniformly with age, as they do in the general population. In fact, the rates for female psychiatric patients fall with advancing age. This difference is due mainly to the fact that suicidal elderly persons do not present themselves to the medical services. Times of staff rotation, particularly of the psychiatric residents, are periods associated with inpatient suicides. Epidemics of a few inpatient suicides tend to be associated with periods of ideological change on the ward, staff disorganization, and staff demoralization.

Among psychiatric outpatients the period after discharge is a period of increased suicide risk. A follow-up study of 5,000 patients discharged from an Iowa psychiatric hospital showed that, in the first three months after discharge, the rate of suicide for female patients was 275 times higher than that of all Iowa females, while that for male patients was 70 times higher than that of Iowa males.

Patients attending the emergency services, especially those with panic disorder, also have an increased suicide risk. A recent study reported that such patients have a suicide rate more than seven times the age- and sex-adjusted rate for the general population (but the rate is similar to that of other clinical psychiatric populations). There are two main risk groups: patients with depressive disorders, schizophrenia, and substance abuse and patients who make repeated visits to the emergency room. Thus, mental health professionals working in the emergency services must be well trained in the taking of the psychiatric history, the examination of the mental state, the assessment of the suicidal risk, and the making of appropriate dispositions and must be aware of the need to contact patients at risk who fail to keep follow-up appointments.

Depression. Mood disorder is the diagnosis most commonly associated with suicide. As the suicide risk in depression is raised mainly when the patient is depressed, it may be that the psychopharmacological advances of the last 20 years have reduced the suicide risk among depressed patients. Nevertheless, the age-adjusted suicide rates for patients suffering from either mood disorder or dysthymia have recently been estimated to be 400 and 190 per 100,000, respectively, for male patients and 180 and 70 per 100,000 for female patients.

More depressive disorder patients commit suicide early in the course of the illness; more males than females; and the chance of depressed persons killing themselves is increased by their being single, separated, divorced, widowed, or recently bereaved. Depressive disorder patients in the community who commit suicide tend to be middle-aged or elderly.

A few studies have investigated which mood disorder patients have an increased suicide risk. These studies suggest that, among depressed patients, social isolation enhances a suicidal tendency. This finding is in accord with the data from epidemiological studies showing that persons who commit suicide tend to be poorly integrated into society.

Suicide among depressed patients is more likely at the onset or the end of a depressive episode. As among other psychiatric patients, the months after discharge from a hospital are a time of high risk. Studies show that one-third or more of depressed patients who commit suicide do so within six months of leaving a hospital, presumably having relapsed.

Schizophrenia. The suicide risk is high among schizophrenic patients: up to 10 percent die by committing suicide. It is estimated that, in the United States, approximately 4,000 schizophrenic patients commit suicide each year. Since the age of onset of schizophrenia is typically in adolescence or early adulthood, most schizophrenic patients who commit suicide do so during the first few years of their illness; schizophrenic suicides tend to be relatively young.

About 75 percent of schizophrenic suicide victims are unmarried males. Approximately 50 percent have made a previous suicide attempt. Depressive symptoms are closely associated with their suicides. Hospital-based studies have reported that depressive symptoms were present during the last period of contact in at least two-thirds of schizophrenic patients who committed suicide; only a small percentage committed suicide because of hallucinated instructions or to escape persecutory delusions. Up to 50 percent of suicides among schizophrenic patients occur during the first few weeks and months after discharge from a hospital; only a minority commit suicide while inpatients.

Thus, the risk factors for suicide among schizophrenic patients are young age, male sex, single marital status, a previous suicide attempt, a vulnerability to depressive symptoms, and recent discharge from a hospital. It is likely that having three or four hospitalizations during their 20s undermines the social, occupational, and sexual adjustment of schizophrenic potential suicides. Consequently, the potential suicide is likely to be male, unmarried, unemployed, socially isolated, and living alone—perhaps in a room. After discharge from his last hospitalization, he may experience some new adversity or return to ongoing difficulties. Consequently, he becomes dejected, experiences feelings of helplessness and hopelessness, goes on to a depressed mood, and, in that state, has suicidal ideas that are eventually acted on.

Alcoholism. Up to 15 percent of alcoholics commit suicide. It is estimated that the suicide rate for alcoholics is about 270 per 100,000 a year and that, in the United States, there are between 7,000 and 13,000 alcoholic suicide victims each year.

About 80 percent of alcoholic suicide victims are male, largely reflecting the sex ratio for alcoholism. Alcoholic suicide victims tend to be white, middle-aged, unmarried, friendless, socially isolated, and currently drinking. Up to 40 percent have made a previous suicide attempt. Up to 40 percent of alcoholic suicides occur within a year of the patient's last hospitalization, elderly alcoholics being at particular risk during the postdischarge period.

Studies show that many alcoholics who eventually commit suicide are rated as being depressed during hospitalization and that up to two-thirds are assessed as having mood disorder symptoms during the period in which they commit suicide. As many as 50 percent of alcoholic suicide victims have experienced the loss of a close affectionate relationship during the previous year. It is likely that such interpersonal loss and other types of undesirable life events are brought about by the alcoholism and contribute to the development of the mood disorder symptoms, which are often present in the weeks and months before the suicide.

The largest group of male alcoholics are those with an associated antisocial personality disorder. Studies show that such alcoholics are particularly likely to attempt suicide; abuse other drugs; exhibit impulsive, aggressive, and criminal behaviors; and be found among alcoholic suicide victims.

Drug dependence. Studies in different countries have demonstrated that there is an increased suicide risk among drug abusers. The suicide rate for heroin addicts is about 20 times greater than that for the general population. Adolescent girls who use intravenous drugs also have a high suicide rate. The availability of a lethal amount of drugs, intravenous use, associated antisocial personality disorder, chaotic life-style, and impulsivity are some of the factors that predispose drug-dependent persons to suicidal behavior, particularly when they are dysphoric, depressed, or intoxicated.

Personality disorder. A high proportion of suicide victims have various associated personality difficulties or disorders. Having a personality disorder may be a determinant of suicidal behavior in several ways: by predisposing to major psychiatric disorders like depression or alcoholism, by leading to difficulties in relationships and social adjustment, by precipitating undesirable life events, by impairing the ability to cope with a psychiatric or physical disorder, and by drawing persons into conflicts with those around them, including family members, physicians, and hospital staff members.

An estimated 5 percent of patients with an antisocial personality disorder commit suicide. Suicide is three times more common among prisoners than among the general population. Over one-third of prisoner suicides have had past psychiatric treatment, and half have made a previous suicide threat or attempt, often in the previous six months.

Previous suicidal behavior. A past suicide attempt is perhaps the best indicator that a patient is at increased risk to commit suicide. Studies show that about 40 percent of depressed patients who commit suicide have made a previous attempt. The risk of a patient's making a second suicide attempt is highest within three months of the first attempt. The relationship between depression, completed suicide, and attempts at suicide is shown in Figure 28.1-1.

Depression is associated not only with completed suicide but also with serious attempts at suicide. Studies that relate the clinical characteristics of suicide attempters with various measures of the medical seriousness of the attempt or of the intent to die show that the clinical feature most often associated with the seriousness of the intent to die is a diagnosis of depression. Also, intent-to-die scores correlate significantly with both suicide risk scores and the number and severity of depressive symptoms. When attempters rated as having high suicide intent are compared with those with low intent, they are significantly more often male, older, single or separated, and living alone. The inference from these studies is that depressed patients who make a serious suicide attempt more closely resemble suicide victims than they do suicide attempters.

PREDICTION

It remains the clinician's task to assess an individual patient's risk of suicide on the basis of a careful clinical examination. The most predictive items associated with high suicide risk are listed in Table 28.1-1. Among the high-risk characteristics are age over 45, male sex, alcoholism (the suicide rate is 50 times higher in alcoholics than in nonalcoholics), violent behavior, prior suicidal behavior, and previous psychiatric hospitalization. Suicide is grouped into high risk–related and low risk–related factors (Table 28.1-2).

The clinician should always ask about suicide ideation as part of every mental status examination, especially if the patient is depressed. The patient should be asked directly, "Are you or have you ever been suicidal? Do you want to die?" Eight out of 10 persons who eventually kill themselves give warnings of their intent. Fifty percent say openly that they want to die. If the patient admits to a plan of action, that is a particularly dangerous sign. Also, if a patient who has been threatening suicide becomes quiet and less agitated, that may be an ominous sign. The clinician should be especially concerned with the factors listed in Table 28.1-3.

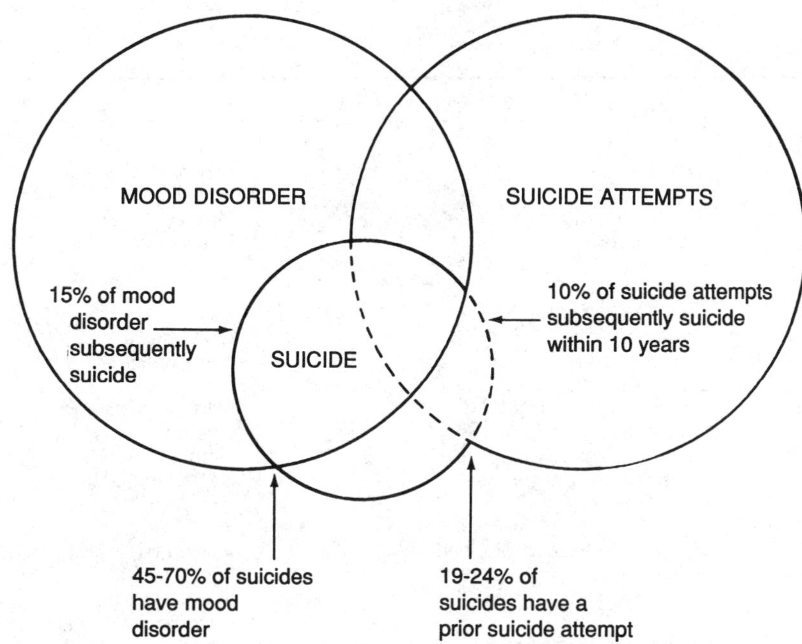

Figure 28.1-1 Venn diagram summarizing data concerning suicide and its relationship to mood disorder and suicide attempts. (Figure by Alec Roy, M.D.)

Table 28.1-1
Factors Associated with Suicide Risk

Variable in Rank Order	Content of Item
1	Age (45 and older)
2	Alcoholism
3	Irritation, rage, violence
4	Prior suicidal behavior
5	Sex (male)
6	Unwilling to accept help
7	Longer duration of current episode of depression
8	Prior inpatient psychiatric treatment
9	Recent loss or separation
10	Depression
11	Loss of physical health
12	Unemployed or retired
13	Single, widowed, divorced

Table modified from R E Litman, N L Faberow, C I Wold, T R Brown: Prediction models of suicidal behaviors. In *The Prediction of Suicide,* H Beck, L P Resnik, and D J Lettieri, editors, p 141. Charles Press, Bowie, MD, 1974, with permission.

THEORIES

Sociological Factors

Durkheim. The first major contribution to the study of the social and cultural influences on suicide was made at the end of the last century by the French sociologist Emile Durkheim. In an attempt to explain statistical patterns, Durkheim divided suicides into three social categories: egoistic, altruistic, and anomic. Egoistic suicide applies to those who are not strongly integrated into any social group. The lack of family integration can be used to explain why the unmarried are more vulnerable to suicide than are the married and why couples with children are the best protected group of all. Rural communities have more social integration than do urban areas and, thus, less suicide. Protestantism is a less-cohesive religion than Catholicism is, and so Protestants have a higher suicide rate than do Catholics.

Altruistic suicide applies to the group whose proneness to suicide stems from their excessive integration into a group, with suicide being the outgrowth of this integration—for example, the Japanese soldier who sacrifices his life in battle.

Anomic suicide applies to those persons whose integration into society is disturbed, thereby depriving them of the customary norms of behavior. Anomie can explain why those whose economic situation has changed drastically are more vulnerable than they were before their change in fortune. Anomie also refers to social instability, with a breakdown of society's standards and values.

Psychological Factors

Freud. The first important psychological insight into suicide came from Sigmund Freud. He described only one patient who actually made a suicide attempt, but he did see many depressed patients.

In his 1917 paper *Mourning and Melancholia,* Freud stated his belief that suicide represented aggression turned inward against an introjected, ambivalently cathected love object. Freud doubted that there would be a suicide without the earlier repressed desire to kill someone else.

Menninger. Building on Freud's concepts, Karl Menninger in *Man Against Himself* conceived of suicide as a retroflexed murder, inverted homicide as a result of the patient's anger toward another person, which is either turned inward or used as an excuse for punishment. He also described a self-

Table 28.1-2
Evaluation of Suicide Risk

Variable	High Risk	Low Risk
Demographic and social profile		
Age	Over 45 years	Below 45 years
Sex	Male	Female
Marital status	Divorced or widowed	Married
Employment	Unemployed	Employed
Interpersonal relationship	Conflictual	Stable
Family background	Chaotic or conflictual	Stable
Health		
Physical	Chronic illness	Good health
	Hypochondriac	Feels healthy
	Excessive drug intake	Low drug use
Mental	Severe depression	Mild depression
	Psychosis	Neurosis
	Severe personality disorder	Normal personality
	Alcoholism or drug abuse	Social drinker
	Hopelessness	Optimism
Suicidal activity		
Suicidal ideation	Frequent, intense, prolonged	Infrequent, low intensity, transient
Suicide attempt	Multiple attempts	First attempt
	Planned	Impulsive
	Rescue unlikely	Rescue inevitable
	Unambiguous wish to die	Primary wish for change
	Communication internalized (self-blame)	Communication externalized (anger)
	Method lethal and available	Method of low lethality or not readily available
Resources		
Personal	Poor achievement	Good achievement
	Poor insight	Insightful
	Affect unavailable or poorly controlled	Affect available and appropriately controlled
Social	Poor rapport	Good rapport
	Socially isolated	Socially integrated
	Unresponsive family	Concerned family

Table from K Adam: Attempted suicide. In *Self-Destructive Behavior*. Psychiatr Clin North Am *8:* 183, 1985, with permission.

Table 28.1-3
History, Signs, and Symptoms of Suicidal Risk

1. Previous attempt or fantasized suicide
2. Anxiety, depression, exhaustion
3. Availability of means of suicide
4. Concern for effect of suicide on family members
5. Verbalized suicidal ideation
6. Preparation of a will, resignation after agitated depression
7. Proximal life crisis, such as mourning or impending surgery
8. Family history of suicide

directed death instinct (Freud's concept of *Thanatos*). He described three components of hostility in suicide: the wish to kill, the wish to be killed, and the wish to die.

Recent theories. Contemporary suicidologists are not persuaded that there is a specific psychodynamic or personality structure associated with suicide. However, they have suggested that much can be learned about the psychodynamics of suicidal patients from their fantasies as to what would happen and what the consequences would be if they were to commit suicide. Such fantasies often include wishes for revenge, power, control, punishment; for atonement, sacrifice, or restitution; for escape or sleep; or for rescue, rebirth, reunion with the dead, or a new life. It is thought that the suicidal patients who are most likely to act out suicidal fantasies are those who have suffered the loss of a love object or narcissistic injury, who experience overwhelming affects like rage and guilt, or who identify with a suicide victim. Group dynamics underlie mass suicides like those at Masada and Jonestown.

Depressed persons may attempt suicide just as they appear to be recovering from their depression. And a suicide attempt can cause a long-standing depression to disappear, especially if it fulfills the patient's need for punishment. Of equal relevance, many suicide patients use a preoccupation with suicide as a way of fighting off intolerable depression and a sense of hopelessness. In fact, hopelessness was found, in a study by Aaron Beck, to be one of the most accurate indicators of long-term suicidal risks.

Physiological Factors

Genetics. A genetic factor in suicide has been suggested. Studies show that suicide tends to run in families. For example, at all stages of the life cycle, a family history of suicide has been noted to be present significantly more often among persons who have attempted suicide than among those who have not. In one major study it was found that the suicide risk of first-degree relatives of psychiatric patients was almost eight times greater than that of the relatives of controls. Furthermore, the suicide risk among the first-degree relatives of the psychiatric patients who had committed suicide was four times greater than that found among the relatives of patients who had not committed suicide. In some situations, particularly among adolescents, the family member who has committed suicide may serve as a role model with whom to identify when the option of committing suicide becomes one possible solution to intolerable psychological pain.

In one study, of 51 monozygotic twin pairs, there were nine cases of suicide, and no dizygotic twins were concordant for suicide. A longitudinal study of an Amish community found 26 suicides committed in just four families, all of whom exhibited heavy genetic loading for major depression, bipolar disorder, and other mood disorders.

There may be genetic factors in suicide, primarily those factors involved in the transmission of bipolar disorder, schizophrenia, and alcoholism—the psychiatric disorders most commonly associated with suicide. However, it has been suggested that there is a genetic factor for suicide independent of or in addition to the genetic transmission of psychiatric disorder. This may be a genetic factor for impulsivity, which may be related to an abnormality in the central serotonin system.

Neurochemistry. A serotonin deficiency, measured as a decrease in the metabolism of 5-hydroxyindoleacetic acid (5-HIAA), was found in a group of depressed patients who attempted suicide. Those patients who attempted suicide by violent means (e.g., guns, jumping) had a lower 5-HIAA level in the cerebrospinal fluid (CSF) than did those depressed patients who were not suicidal or who attempted suicide in a less violent manner (e.g., drug overdose).

Some animal and human studies have suggested an association between deficiency in the central serotonin system and poor impulse control. Some workers have viewed suicide as one type of impulsive behavior. Furthermore, a significant negative correlation between CSF 5-HIAA levels and lifetime aggression scores has been reported among personality disorder patients. Other patient groups thought to have problems with impulse control include violent offenders, arsonists, and alcoholics, groups who have also been noted to have lower CSF 5-HIAA levels than controls.

Possible peripheral markers of suicidal behavior have also been examined. High outputs of urinary free cortisol, nonsuppression of plasma cortisol after administration of dexamethasone, an exaggerated plasma cortisol response to infusion of 5-hydroxtryptophan, a blunted plasma thyroid-stimulating hormone (TSH) response to infusion of thyrotropin-releasing hormone (TRH), skin conductance abnormalities, altered urinary catechol ratios, decreases in platelet serotonin uptake or titrated imipramine binding number have all been reported to be associated with suicidal behavior among depressed patients.

A few studies have demonstrated ventricular enlargement and abnormal electroencephalograms (EEGs) in some suicidal patients.

Blood samples analyzed for platelet monoamine oxidase (MAO) from a group of normal volunteers revealed that those persons with the lowest level of this enzyme in their platelets had eight times the prevalence of suicide in their families, compared with persons with high levels of the enzyme. There is strong evidence for an alteration of platelet MAO activity in depressive disorders.

CHILD AND ADOLESCENT SUICIDE

In recent years the suicide rate among adolescents in the United States has risen dramatically, although in some other countries it has not. Between 1960 and 1981 the suicide rate for Americans 15 to 19 years of age increased from 5.6 to 13.6 per 100,000 for males and from 1.6 to 3.6 per 100,000 for females. More than 5,000 adolescents commit suicide each year in the United States, one every 90 minutes. The increased suicide rates are thought to reflect changes in the social environment, changing attitudes toward suicide, and the increasing availability of the means to commit suicide—for example, in the United States 66 percent of adolescent suicides are committed by firearms, compared with 6 percent in the United Kingdom.

The number of children under 15 who kill themselves each year increased from fewer than 40 in 1950 to 300 in 1985. However, suicide in children under the age of 12 is an exceedingly rare event. Suicidal thoughts (i.e., children's talk about wanting to harm themselves) or suicidal threats (i.e, children's statements that they want to jump in front of a car) are more common than is successful suicide. In the United States about 12,000 children are hospitalized each year because of suicidal threats or behavior. According to one study of a group of randomly selected normal children, about 13 percent had occasional ideas of suicide.

Among adolescents (ages 15 to 24) suicide is the second leading cause of death. Boys commit suicide three times more often than girls do, but girls attempt suicide three times more often than boys do.

Contributing Factors

The contributing factors in youth suicide include predisposing and precipitating factors. The main predisposing factors are a disturbed family background, a psychiatric disorder, a physical illness, and a previous suicide attempt. Up to one-half of adolescent suicide victims come from broken homes or have a parent who has a psychiatric disorder or has exhibited suicidal behavior. The most common psychiatric problems among adolescent suicide victims are drug and alcohol abuse, antisocial behavior, combined substance and alcohol abuse and antisocial behavior, mood disorder, and the combination of a depressed mood and antisocial behavior. About 40 percent of youthful suicides have had previous psychiatric treatment, and about 40 percent have made a previous suicide attempt. A child who has lost a parent by any means before the age of 13 has a high risk for mood disorders and suicide. The precipitating factors include disciplinary crises, loss of face with peers, arguments with parents, a broken romance, school difficulties, unemployment, bereavement, separation, and rejection.

Clusters of suicides among adolescents who know one another and go to the same school have been reported. Suicidal behavior may precipitate other such attempts within a peer group through identification—so-called copycat suicides. A 1986 study by David Shaffer indicated that there was an increase in adolescent suicide after television programs were shown whose main theme was the suicide of a teenager. In general, however, many other factors are involved, including a necessary substrate of psychopathology. In another recent study, two clusters of teenage suicide in Texas were investigated. Researchers found that indirect exposure to suicide through the media was not significantly associated with suicide. Factors that were associated included previous suicidal threats or attempts, self-injury, exposure to someone who had died violently, recent romantic breakups, high frequency of moves, school attended, and parental figures lived with.

The tendency of disturbed young persons to imitate

highly publicized suicides has been called the Werther syndrome, after the protagonist in Johann Wolfgang von Goethe's novel *The Sorrows of Young Werther*. The novel, in which the hero kills himself, was banned in some European countries after its publication nearly 200 years ago because of a rash of suicides by young men who had read it; some, when they killed themselves, dressed like Werther or left the book open to the passage describing his death.

TREATMENT

The great majority of suicides among psychiatric patients are preventable. There are occasional patients whose suffering is so great and intense or so chronic and unresponsive to treatment that their eventual suicide may be perceived as inevitable; fortunately, such patients are relatively uncommon. There are also patients who have severe personality disorders, who are highly impulsive, and who commit suicide apparently in an impulsive manner, often when dysphoric or intoxicated or both. The evidence that inadequacy of assessment or treatment is associated with suicide suggests that the great majority of suicides of psychiatric patients are probably preventable.

The evaluation for suicide potential involves a complete psychiatric history; a thorough examination of the mental state; and inquiry about depressive symptoms, suicidal thoughts, intents, plans, and attempts. Lack of future plans, giving away personal property, making a will, or having recently experienced a loss imply increased risk for suicide. The decision to hospitalize the patient depends on the diagnosis, the severity of the depression and suicidal ideation, the patient's and family's ability to cope, the living situation, the availability of social support, and the absence or presence of risk factors for suicide.

Inpatient versus Outpatient Treatment

Whether to hospitalize the patient with suicidal ideation is the most important clinical decision to be made. Not all such patients require hospitalization; some may be treated on an outpatient basis. But the absence of a strong social support system, a history of impulsive behavior, and a suicidal plan of action are indications for hospitalization. To determine whether outpatient treatment is feasible, the clinician should use a straightforward clinical approach—asking the patient considered suicidal to agree to call when reaching a point beyond which he or she is uncertain of controlling suicidal impulses. A patient who can make such an agreement reaffirms the belief that he or she has sufficient strength to control such impulses and seek help.

In return for the patient's commitment, the clinician should be available to the patient 24 hours a day. If a patient who is considered seriously suicidal cannot make this commitment, immediate emergency hospitalization is indicated, and both the patient and the patient's family should be so advised. If, however, the patient is to be treated on an outpatient basis, it is often useful for the therapist to note the patient's home and work telephone numbers for emergency reference; occasionally, a patient hangs up unexpectedly during a late night call or gives only a name to the answering service. If the patient refuses hospitalization, the family must take the responsibility to be with the patient 24 hours a day.

According to Schneidman, there are several practical preventive measures for dealing with a suicidal person: (1) reduce the psychological pain by modifying the patient's stressful environment, enlisting the aid of a spouse, employer, or friend; (2) build realistic support by recognizing that the patient may have a legitimate complaint; and (3) offer alternatives to suicide.

Many psychiatrists believe that any patient who has made a suicidal attempt, regardless of its lethality, should be hospitalized. Although most of these patients voluntarily enter the hospital, a danger to self is one of the few clear-cut indications currently acceptable in all states for involuntary hospitalization.

In the hospital the patient can receive antidepressant or antipsychotic medications as indicated; individual, group, and family therapy are available; and the patient receives the hospital's social support and sense of security. Other therapeutic measures depend on the patient's underlying diagnosis. For example, if alcoholism is an associated problem, treatment must be directed toward alleviating that condition.

Although patients classified as acutely suicidal may have favorable prognoses, chronically suicidal patients are difficult to treat, and they exhaust the caretakers. Constant observation by special nurses, seclusion, and restraints will not prevent a determined suicide. Electroconvulsive therapy (ECT) may be necessary for some severely depressed patients, who may require several treatment courses.

Useful measures for the treatment of the depressed suicidal inpatient include searching the patient's belongings and person on arrival on the ward for objects that may be used for suicide and repeating the search at times of exacerbation of suicidal ideation. Ideally, the suicidal depressed inpatient should be treated on a locked ward where the windows are shatter-proof, and the patient's room should be located near the nursing station to maximize observation by the nursing staff. The treating team has to assess how much to restrict the patient and whether there should be regular checks or continued direct observation. Vigorous treatment with antidepressant medication should be initiated.

Supportive psychotherapy by the psychiatrist demonstrates concern and may alleviate some of the patient's intense suffering. Some patients may be able to accept the idea that they are suffering from a recognized illness and that there is every hope that they will make a complete recovery. Patients should be dissuaded from making major life decisions while they are suicidally depressed, because such decisions are often morbidly determined and may be irrevocable. The consequences of such bad decisions can cause still more anguish and misery when the patient has recovered.

Patients recovering from a suicidal depression are at particular risk. As the depression lifts, patients become more energized and are thus able to put their suicidal plans into action. Sometimes depressed patients, with or without treatment, suddenly appear to be at peace with themselves, because they have reached a secret decision to commit suicide. The clinician should be especially suspicious of such a dramatic clinical change, which may portend a suicidal attempt.

Finally, a patient may commit suicide even when in the hospital. According to one survey, approximately 1 percent of suicides occurred in patients who were being treated in general medical-surgical or psychiatric hospitals; however, the annual suicide rate in psychiatric hospitals is only 0.003 percent.

LEGAL AND ETHICAL CONSIDERATIONS

Liability issues stemming from suicides in psychiatric hospitals frequently involve questions about the rate of deterioration of psychiatric status, the presence during hospitalization of clinical signs indicating risk, and the psychiatrist's and the staff's awareness of and response to these clinical signs.

In about half the cases in which suicide occurs while the patient is on a psychiatric unit, a lawsuit results. What the courts require is not that suicide never occur but that the patient be periodically evaluated for suicidal risk, that a treatment plan with a high level of security be formulated, and that the staff follow this treatment plan.

At present, suicide and attempted suicide are variously viewed as a felony and a misdemeanor; in some states the acts are considered not crimes but unlawful under common law and statutes. The role of an aider and abettor in suicide adds another dimension to the legal morass; some court decisions have held that, although neither suicide nor attempted suicide is punishable, anyone who assists in the act may be punished.

COMMUNITY ORGANIZATIONS

Community organizations seem to have fewer problems than do individual therapists with the ethics and legalities of helping suicidal people. Prevention centers, crisis listening posts, and so-called suicide telephone hot lines are clear attempts to intervene and diminish the isolation, withdrawal, and loneliness of the suicidal patient. Outreach programs enable highly motivated laypersons to respond to cries for help in a variety of ways. But it would be wrong to believe that such responses do more than just diminish an acute crisis; highly suicidal people place fewer than 10 percent of such calls. Two studies in the United States have failed to demonstrate that suicide prevention centers had an effect on suicide rates. Although it appears that suicide prevention centers are not effective in reducing the suicide rate, they do represent an important mental health resource for persons in distress.

SELF-INJURY

Studies show that about 4 percent of patients in psychiatric hospitals have cut themselves; the female-to-male ratio is almost 3 to 1. It is estimated that the incidence of self-injury in psychiatric patients is over 50 times greater than in the general population. Cutters presenting to psychiatrists tend to have cut chronically over several years. Self-injury is found in about 30 percent of abusers of oral drugs and 10 percent of intravenous users admitted to drug units.

The patients are usually in their 20s and may be single or married. Most cut delicately, not coarsely. Cutting is usually done in private with a razor blade, knife, broken glass, or mirror. The wrists, arms, thighs, and legs are the most common sites cut; the face, breasts, and abdomen are cut infrequently. Most cutters claim to experience no pain. The reasons given include anger at themselves or others, relief of tension, and the wish to die. The great majority of cutters are classified as personality disordered and are significantly more introverted, neurotic, and hostile than controls. Alcohol and drug abuse are common, and the majority of cutters have attempted suicide.

Self-mutilation has been viewed as localized self-destruction, with mishandling of aggressive impulses caused by an unconscious wish to punish either oneself or an introjected object. Some have referred to these persons as pseudosuicidal.

References

Barraclough B, Bunch J, Nelson B, Sainsbury P: A hundred cases of suicide. Br J Psychiatry *125:* 355, 1974.

Beskow J: Depression and suicide. Pharmacopsychiatry *23*: (Suppl 1): 3 1990.

Beskow J: Suicide and mental disorder in Swedish men. Acta Psychiatr Scand *277* (Suppl): 1, 1979.

Dorpat T, Ripley H: A study of suicide in the Seattle area. Compr Psychiatry *1:* 349, 1960.

Dublin L: *Suicide: A Sociological and Statistical Study*. Ronald Press, New York, 1963.

Durkheim E: *Suicide*. Free Press, Glencove, IL, 1951.

Farmer R, Hirsch S, eds.: *The Suicide Syndrome*. Croom Helm, London, 1980.

Griffith E E, Bell C C: Recent trends in suicide and homicide among blacks. JAMA. *262:* 2265, 1989.

Hawton K, Catalan J, eds.: *Attempted Suicide*. Oxford University Press, Oxford, 1982.

Kreitman N, ed.: *Parasuicide*. Wiley, New York, 1977.

Kreitman N: Suicide, age and marital status. Psychol Med *18:* 121, 1988.

Mann J, Stanley M, eds.: *Psychobiology of Suicidal Behavior,* Ann NY Acad Sci, New York, 1986.

Monk M: Epidemiology of suicide. Epidemiol Rev *9*: 51, 1987.

Perlin S, ed.: *A Handbook for the Study of Suicide*. Oxford University Press, Oxford, 1975.

Robins E: *The Final Months: A Study of the Lives of 134 Persons Who Committed Suicide*. Oxford University Press, New York, 1981.

Robins E, Murphy G, Wilkinson R, et al: Some clinical considerations based on a study of 134 successful suicides. Am J Public Health *49:* 888, 1959.

Roy A: Family history of suicide. Arch Gen Psychiatry *40*: 971, 1983.

Roy A: Risk factors for suicide in psychiatric patients. Arch Gen Psychiatry *39:* 1089, 1982.

Roy A, ed.: Self-destructive behavior. Psychiatr Clin North Am *8:* 215, 1985.

Roy A, ed.: *Suicide*. Williams & Wilkins, Baltimore, 1986.

Roy A: Suicide. In *Comprehensive Textbook of Psychiatry,* ed 5, H I Kaplan and B J Sadock, editors, p 1414. Williams & Wilkins, Baltimore, 1989.

Roy A: Suicide in chronic schizophrenia. Br J Psychiatry *141*: 171, 1982.

Roy A, Linnoila M: Alcoholism and suicide. Suicide Life Threat Behav *16*: 244, 1986.

Sainsbury P: *Suicide in London,* Chapman and Hall, London, 1955.

Shneidman E: *Definition of Suicide*. Wiley, New York, 1985.

28.2 / Other Psychiatric Emergencies

Emergency psychiatry is the treatment of disorders of mood, thought, and behavior in an emergency setting. Nowhere in mental health care is as much diagnostic skill and therapeutic expertise immediately demanded as in an emergency. The challenge to an emergency psychiatrist is to use the opportunity afforded by a crisis, no matter how induced, to facilitate growth and actualization that would not have been possible if the crisis had not occurred.

Most often, the patients themselves express the need for emergency psychiatric care. However, a state of psychiatric emergency may be declared by family members, teachers, or the public. This section discusses common conditions for which patients come or are brought to the psychiatric emergency room or admitting office.

EPIDEMIOLOGY

Psychiatric emergency rooms are used equally by men and women and more by single persons than by married persons. About 20 percent of patients are suicidal, and about 10 percent are violent. The most common diagnoses are mood disorder (including depression and mania), schizophrenia, and alcoholism. About 40 percent of all patients seen in psychiatric emergency rooms require hospitalization. Most visits occur during the night hours, but there is no utilization difference based on day of the week or month of the year. Contrary to popular belief, studies have not demonstrated a higher use of psychiatric emergency rooms during a full moon or during the Christmas season.

EMERGENCY PSYCHIATRIC INTERVIEW

The emergency room interview is similar to the standard psychiatric interview and mental status examination except for the time limitation imposed by the other patients waiting to be seen. In general, the psychiatrist focuses on the presenting complaint and the reasons that the patient with a chronic condition has come to the emergency room at that time. The time constraint requires that the clinician structure the interview, particularly with patients who suffer from chronic emotional disturbances and so may respond with long rambling accounts of their illness. If friends, relatives, or the police accompany the patient, a supplemental history should be obtained from them. That is especially necessary if the patient is negativistic, uncooperative, or otherwise unable to give a coherent history.

Sometimes the contact with the emergency room is by telephone. In such cases the psychiatrist should obtain the number from which the call is made and the exact address. These items are important in case the call is interrupted, and they allow the psychiatrist to direct help, depending on the circumstances. If the patient is alone, the police should be alerted. If possible, an assistant should call the police on another line while the psychiatrist keeps the patient engaged until help arrives. The patient should not be told to drive alone to the hospital. Rather, an emergency medical team should be dispatched to bring the patient to the hospital.

The greatest potential error of emergency room psychiatry is overlooking a physical illness as the cause of the emotional illness. Head trauma, drug abuse (including alcohol), stroke, metabolic abnormalities, and medication may all cause abnormal behavior, and a concise medical history concentrating on those areas should be taken. Studies have demonstrated that 5 to 30 percent of patients in psychiatric emergency rooms have medical disorders that account for all or most of their symptoms.

DIAGNOSIS

The emergency psychiatrist must consider a wide range of conditions that may account for the presenting signs or symptoms. The most common complaints fall within the categories of anxiety, depression, mania, and thought disorder. These conditions may overlap and have multiple causes.

The differential diagnoses of anxiety, depression, mania, and thought disorder are listed in Tables 28.2-1 through 28.2-4. Anxiety is different from depression, mania, and thought disorder in that a number of the illnesses that can cause it are life-threatening. Incipient heart attacks, pulmonary emboli, cardiac arrhythmias, and internal hemorrhage cause acute anxiety to the degree of panic. Untreated congestive heart failure secondary to a silent myocardial infarction or malignant cardiac arrhythmia may be fatal. Old people and those who have just suffered a loss may be perceived as having depressive or nihilistic ideation when, in fact, age or stress has propelled them into a life-threatening illness manifested by anxiety and a sense of impending doom. Persons who experience depression as a side effect of antihypertensive medication (e.g., propranolol [Inderal]) may perceive spouse, children, friends, or work in a negative light that changes on cessation of the medication.

Table 28.2-5 outlines features that should make the emergency room clinician consider an organic condition as the cause of the complaint.

Table 28.2-6 lists the central nervous system (CNS) disorders that require immediate treatment. Table 28.2-7 lists CNS disorders with behavioral features that may cause the patient to be brought to the psychiatric emergency room.

VIOLENCE AND ASSAULTIVE BEHAVIOR

The first task in evaluating violent behavior is to ascertain its cause. Cause directs treatment. Patients with thought disorders characterized by hallucinations com-

Table 28.2-1
Differential Diagnosis of Anxiety

Alcohol delirium and withdrawal
Amphetamine or similarly acting sympathomimetic intoxication and withdrawal disorders
Anxiety disorders
Bipolar disorder
Borderline personality disorder
Caffeine intoxication
Cerebral arteriosclerosis
Chronic schizophrenia
Cocaine intoxication
Encephalitis
Essential hypertension
Hyperthyroidism
Hyperventilation syndrome
Hypocalcemia
Hypoglycemia
Hypokalemia
Impending myocardial infarction
Internal hemorrhage
Major depression
Mitral valve prolapse
Normal anxiety
Other temporal lobe diseases
Panic disorder
Paroxysmal atrial tachycardia and other cardiac arrhythmias
Pheochromocytoma
Phobia
Postconcussion syndrome
Psychomotor epilepsy
Psychotic disorders
Pulmonary embolism
Sedative, hypnotic, or anxiolytic withdrawal and withdrawal delirium
Sexual disorders
Subacute bacterial endocarditis

Table by Andrew Edmund Slaby, M.D., Ph.D.

manding them to kill someone require psychiatric hospitalization and antipsychotic medication. If they are unwilling to accept treatment, certification is necessary to protect the intended victim and the patient. Those who take an extreme civil libertarian perspective fail to recognize that medical certification has evolved legally not only to protect society from the violent patient but also to protect patients from consequences of their uncontrollable behavior. Patients who, while psychotic, destroy families' and friends' property or threaten or actually commit violent assault destroy social supports that they need to help them function after the aberrant mood or delusional ideation is corrected.

The differential diagnosis of violent behavior includes psychoactive substance-induced organic mental disorder, antisocial personality disorder, catatonic schizophrenia, cerebral infection, cerebral neoplasm, decompensating obsessive-compulsive personality disorder, dissociative disorders, impulse control disorders, sexual disorders, alcohol idiosyncratic intoxication, delusional disorder, paranoid personality disorder, schizophrenia, social maladjustment without psychiatric disorder, temporal lobe epilepsy, bipolar disorder, and uncontrollable violence secondary to interpersonal stress.

Violence and assaultive behavior are difficult to predict. However, the fear with which some people regard all psychiatric patients is completely out of proportion to the small group representing an authentic danger to others. The best predictors of potential violent behavior are (1) excessive alcohol intake, (2) a history of violent acts with arrests or criminal activity, and (3) a history of childhood abuse. Although violent patients can arouse a realistic fear in the psychiatrist, they can also touch off irrational fears that impair clinical judgment and that may lead to the premature and excessive use of sedation or physical re-

Table 28.2-2
Differential Diagnosis of Depression

Adjustment disorder with depressed mood
Dysthymia
Schizoaffective disorder
Chronic schizophrenia
Major depression
Bipolar disorder
Borderline personality disorder
Hypokalemia
Brief reactive psychosis
Cyclothymia
Antihypertensive toxicity
Steroid psychosis
Hypothyroidism
Cerebral neoplasm
General paresis
Amphetamine or cocaine
Carcinoma of pancreas
Hepatitis
Postviral infection syndrome
Primary degenerative dementia of the Alzheimer type
Multi-infarct dementia
Senile dementia
Presenile dementia
Cirrhosis of the liver
Arteriosclerosis
Infectious mononucleosis
Hyperthyroidism
Occult malignancy
AIDS
Schizoid personality disorder
Schizotypal personality disorder

Table by Andrew Edmund Slaby, M.D., Ph.D.

Table 28.2-3
Differential Diagnosis of Mania

Bipolar disorder
Schizoaffective disorder
Alcohol intoxication
Catatonic schizophrenia
Delirium
Hyperthyroidism
Postencephalitic syndrome
Steroid-induced mania
Antidepressant-induced mania
Decongestant-induced mania
Amphetamine-induced mania
L-Dopa-induced mania
Bronchodilator-induced mania
Phencyclidine-induced mania
Cocaine-induced mania
AIDS
Atypical psychosis

Table by Andrew Edmund Slaby, M.D., Ph.D.

Table 28.2-4
Differential Diagnosis of Thought Disorder

Schizophrenia
Bipolar disorder
Major depression
Alcoholic hallucinosis
Presenile dementia
Frontal lobe neoplasm
Alcohol idiosyncratic intoxication
Adjustment disorders
Disassociative disorders
Delusional disorder
Drug-induced (e.g., PCP, amphetamine) psychoses
Steroid psychoses
Syphilis
Endocrine disease
Pernicious anemia
Temporal lobe epilepsy
Migraine equivalent
Cimetidine psychosis
AIDS
Brief reactive psychosis
Schizophreniform disorder
Induced psychotic disorder
Atypical psychosis
Primary degenerative dementia of the Alzheimer type
Multi-infarct dementia
Senile dementia

Table by Andrew Edmund Slaby, M.D., Ph.D.

Table 28.2-5
Features That Point to an Organic Cause of a Mental Disorder

a. Acute onset (within hours or minutes, with prevailing symptoms)
b. First episode
c. Geriatric age
d. Current medical illness or injury
e. Significant substance abuse
f. Nonauditory disturbances of perception
g. Neurological symptoms—loss of consciousness, seizures, head injury, change in headache pattern, change in vision
h. Classic mental status signs—diminished alertness, disorientation, memory impairment, impairment in concentration and attention, dyscalculia, concreteness
i. Other mental status signs—speech, movement, or gait disorders
j. Constructional apraxia—difficulties in drawing clock, cube, intersecting pentagons, Bender-Gestalt design.
k. Catatonic features—nudity, negativism, combativeness, rigidity, posturing, waxy flexibility, echopraxia, echolalia, grimacing, muteness

Table 28.2-6
Common Global Central Nervous System Disorders That Require Immediate Treatment

a. Hypoglycemia—dextrose 50% IV or juice orally, immediately; give to all diabetics.
b. Wernicke's encephalopathy—thiamine, 100 mg IV, immediately.
c. Opiate intoxication—nalaxone (Narcan), 4 mg IV, immediately.

Table 28.2-7
Common Focal Central Nervous System Disorders with Behavioral Features

a. Aphasias—fluent or receptive aphasia results in patients' not understanding spoken word, although they have fluent but incoherent speech
b. Frontal lobe syndromes—changes in motor behavior, ability to concentrate, reasoning, thinking, social judgment, and impulse control
c. Temporal lobe syndromes—psychosis, seizure, personality and Klüver-Bucy features
d. Parietal lobe syndromes—right lesion with denial and hypomania
e. Occipital lobe syndromes—Anton's syndrome (cortical blindness with denial)

straint. Violent patients are usually frightened by their own hostile impulses and desperately seek help to prevent loss of control. Nevertheless, restraints should be applied if there is a reasonable risk of violence.

Treatment

Patients in the grip of a violent episode pay no attention to the rational intercessions of others and probably do not even hear them. When armed, they are particularly dangerous and capable of murder. Such patients should be disarmed by trained law enforcement personnel without their harming the patients, if at all possible. If unarmed, such patients should be approached with sufficient help and with overwhelming strength, so that there is, in effect, no contest. In the emergency room, armed police should always remove bullets from their weapons. There have been numerous instances of disturbed patients grabbing a loaded gun and randomly killing others.

Patients must be placed in a safe setting. Some need to be transferred to a forensic unit because of the magnitude of their violent potential. Medication specific to a disorder is administered when indicated, unless a nonspecific measure is required to modify behavior until the cause is ascertained and more specific therapy can be initiated. Persons who are paranoid or in catatonic excitement require tranquilization. Episodic outbursts of violence respond to lithium, β-blockers, and carbamazepine (Tegretol). If the history is suggestive of a seizure disorder, clinical studies are performed to confirm the diagnosis, and an evaluation is performed to ascertain the cause. If findings are positive, anticonvulsants are commenced, or appropriate surgery is provided (e.g., in the instance of a cerebral mass). For intoxication from recreational drugs, conservative measures may be adequate. In some instances, drugs such as thiothixene (Navane) and haloperidol (Haldol), 5 to 10 mg every half hour to an hour, are needed until a patient is stabilized. Benzodiazepines are used instead of or in addition to antipsychotics (to reduce the antipsychotic dose). If a recreational drug has strong anticholinergic properties, benzodiazepines are more appropriate. Persons with allergic or aberrant responses to antipsychotics and benzodiazepines are treated with sodium amobarbital (Amytal) (e.g., 130 mg orally [PO] or intramuscularly [IM]), paraldehyde, or diphenhydramine (Benadryl, 50 to 100 mg PO or IM).

Violent, struggling patients are most effectively subdued with an appropriate sedative or antipsychotic. Diazepam (Valium), 5 to 10 mg, or lorazepam (Ativan), 2 to 4 mg, may be given slowly intravenously (IV) over two minutes. It is most important to give IV medication with great care so that respiratory arrest does not occur. Patients who require IM medication can be sedated with haloperidol, 5 to 10 mg IM, or with chlorpromazine (Thorazine), 25 mg IM. If the furor is due to alcohol or is part of a postseizure psychomotor disturbance, the sleep produced by a relatively small amount of IV medication may go on for hours. On awakening, the patients are often entirely alert and rational and typically have a complete amnesia for the violent episode.

If the furor is part of an ongoing psychotic process and returns as soon as the IV medication wears off, continuous medication may be given. It is sometimes better to use small IM or PO doses at half-hour to one-hour intervals—for example, haloperidol, 2 to 5 mg, or diazepam, 10 mg—until the patient is controlled than to use larger dosages initially and end up with an overmedicated patient. As the patient's disturbed behavior is brought under control, successively smaller and less frequent doses should be used. During the preliminary treatment, the patient's blood pressure and other vital signs should be carefully monitored. The use of medication is contraindicated in acutely agitated patients who have suffered head injury, because medication can confuse the clinical picture. In general, IM haloperidol is one of the most useful emergency treatments for violent psychotic patients. Electroconvulsive therapy (ECT) has also been used in emergencies to control psychotic violence. The administration of one or several ECT treatments within several hours usually ends an episode of psychotic violence.

For additional information, see Section 4.4, "Aggression: Violence, Homicide, Injuries, and Accidents."

PSYCHOTHERAPY

In an emergency psychiatric intervention, all attempts are made to help patients maintain self-esteem. Empathy is critical to healing in a psychiatric emergency. The acquired knowledge of how biogenetic, situational, developmental, and existential forces converge at one point in history to create a psychiatric emergency is tantamount to the maturation of skill in emergency psychiatry.

Adjustment disorders in all age groups may result in tantrumlike outbursts of rage. These outbursts are seen particularly in marital quarrels. Police are often summoned by neighbors distressed by the sounds of a violent altercation. Such family quarrels should be approached with great caution, because they may be complicated by the use of alcohol and the presence of dangerous weapons. The warring couple frequently turn their combined fury on the unwary outsider. Wounded self-esteem is a big issue. Therefore, patronizing or contemptuous attitudes must be avoided, and an effort must be made to communicate an attitude of respect and an authentic peacemaking concern.

In family violence the special vulnerability of selected close relatives should be noted. A wife or a husband may have a curious masochistic attachment to the spouse and provoke violence by taunting and otherwise undermining the partner's self-esteem. Such relationships often end in the murder of the provoking partner and sometimes in the suicide of the other partner, the dynamics behind most so-called suicide pacts.

As in the case of many suicidal patients, many violent patients require hospitalization and usually accept the offer of inpatient care with a sense of relief.

More than one psychotherapist or psychotherapy is frequently used in emergency therapy. For example, a 28-year-old man, depressed and suicidal after a colostomy for intractable colitis, whose wife was threatening to leave him because of his irritability and their constant altercations may be referred to a psychiatrist for supportive psychotherapy and antidepressants, to a marital therapist with his wife to improve marital functioning, and to a colostomy support group to learn ways of coping with a colostomy. Emergency psychiatric clinicians are pragmatic. They use every necessary mode of therapeutic intervention available to enhance the resolution of the crisis and to facilitate value exploration and growth. There is less concern than usual about the dilution of a therapeutic relationship. Emphasis is on how different psychiatric modalities act synergistically to enhance recovery.

No one word is appropriate for all people in similar situations. What does one say to a patient and family experiencing a psychiatric emergency, such as a suicide attempt or schizophrenic break? For some a genetic rationale helps. The information that an illness has a strong biological component relieves some people. For others it underlines lack of control and increases depression and anxiety; they feel helpless because neither the family nor the patient can alter behavior to minimize the likelihood of recurrence. Others may benefit from an explanation of family or individual dynamics. Still others only want someone to listen; in time, they will reach their own understanding.

In the emergency situation, as in any other psychiatric situation, when a clinician does not know what to say, the best approach is to listen. People in crisis reveal how much they need support, denial, ventilation, and words to conceptualize the meaning of their crisis and to discover paths to resolution.

EMERGENCY PSYCHOPHARMACOTHERAPY

The major indications for the use of psychotropic medication in the emergency room include violent or assaultive behavior, massive anxiety or panic, and extrapyramidal reactions, such as dystonia and akathisia as side effects of psychiatric drugs. A rare form of dystonia is laryngospasm, and the psychiatrist should be prepared to maintain an open airway with intubation if necessary.

Rapid Tranquilization

Antipsychotic medication can be given in a rapid manner at 30- to 60-minute intervals to achieve a therapeutic result as quickly as possible. This procedure is useful in extremely agitated patients and those in excited states. The drugs of choice for rapid tranquilization are haloperidol and other high-potency antipsychotics. In adults 5 to 10 mg of haloperidol can be given PO or IM and repeated in 20 to 30 minutes until the patient becomes calm. Some patients may develop mild extrapyramidal symptoms within the first 24 hours after rapid tranquilization, and, although these side effects are rare, the psychiatrist should not overlook them. In general, most patients respond before a total dose of 50 mg is given. The goal is not to produce sedation or somnolescence; rather, the patient should be able to cooperate in the assessment process and, ideally, be able to provide some explanation of the agitated behavior. Agitated or panic-stricken patients can be treated with small doses of lorazepam (Ativan), 2 to 4 mg IV or IM, which can be repeated if necessary in 20 to 30 minutes until the patient has quieted down.

The extrapyramidal emergencies respond to benztropine (Cogentin), 2 mg PO or IM, or diphenhydramine (Benadryl), 50 mg IM or IV. Some patients respond to diazepam (Valium), 5 to 10 mg PO or IV.

Table 28.2-8
Use of Restraints

1. Preferably five or a minimum of four persons should be used to restrain the patient. Leather restraints are the safest and surest type of restraints.
2. Explain to the patient why he or she is going into restraints.
3. A staff member should always be visible and reassuring the patient who is being restrained. This helps alleviate the patient's fear of helplessness, impotence, and loss of control.
4. Patients should be restrained with legs spread-eagled and one arm restrained to one side and the other arm restrained over the patient's head.
5. Restraints should be placed so that intravenous fluids can be given if necessary.
6. The patient's head is raised slightly to decrease the patient's feelings of vulnerability and to reduce the possibility of aspiration.
7. The restraints should be checked periodically for safety and comfort.
8. After the patient is in restraints, the clinician begins treatment, using verbal intervention.
9. Even in restraints, a majority of patients still take antipsychotic medication in concentrated form.
10. After the patient is under control, one restraint at a time should be removed at five-minute intervals until the patient has only two restraints on. Both of these remaining restraints should be removed at the same time, because it is inadvisable to keep a patient in only one restraint.
11. Always thoroughly document the reason for the restraints, the course of treatment, and the patient's response to treatment while in restraints.

Table data from W R Dubin, K J Weiss: Emergency psychiatry. In *Psychiatry,* vol 2, R Michaels, J O Cavenar, et al., editors. Lippincott, Philadelphia, 1987, with permission.

RESTRAINTS

Restraints are used when patients are so dangerous to themselves or others that they pose a severe threat that cannot be controlled in any other way. Patients may be restrained temporarily to receive medication or for longer periods if medication cannot be used. Most often, patients in restraints quiet down after some time has elapsed. On a psychodynamic level, such patients may even welcome the control of their impulses that restraints provide. Table 28.2-8 lists the guidelines for the use of restraints.

SPECIFIC PSYCHIATRIC EMERGENCIES

Table 28.2-9 outlines in alphabetical order common psychiatric emergencies. The reader is referred to the index and to specific chapters of this textbook for a more thorough discussion of each disorder.

Table 28.2-9
Common Psychiatric Emergencies

Syndrome	Emergency Manifestations	Treatment Issues
Acquired immune deficiency syndrome (AIDS)	Changes in behavior secondary to organic causes; changes in behavior secondary to fear and anxiety; suicidal behavior	Management of neurological illness; management of psychological concomitants; reinforcement of social support
Adolescent crises	Suicidal attempts and ideation; drug use, truancy, trouble with law, pregnancy, running away; eating disorders; psychosis	Evaluation of suicidal potential; extent of substance abuse; evaluation of family dynamics; crisis-oriented family and individual therapy; hospitalization if necessary; consultation with appropriate extrafamilial authorities
Agoraphobia	Panic; depression	Alprazolam (Xanax), 0.25 mg to 2 mg; propranolol (Inderal); antidepressant medication
Akathisia	Agitation, restlessness, muscle discomfort; dysphoria	Reduce antipsychotic dose; propranolol (30 to 120 mg a day); benzodiazepines; diphenhydramine (Benadryl) PO or IV; benztropine (Cogentin) IM
Alcohol-related emergencies		
Alcohol dementia	Rule out other causes for dementia	No effective treatment: hospitalization if necessary

Table 28.2-9
Continued

Syndrome	Emergency Manifestations	Treatment Issues
Alcohol hallucinosis	Vivid auditory (at times visual) hallucinations with affect appropriate to content (often feaful); clear sensorium	Haloperidol for psychotic symptoms
Alcohol idiosyncratic intoxication	Marked aggressive or assaultive behavior	Generally no treatment required other than protective environment
Alcohol intoxication	Disinhibited behavior, sedation at high doses	With time and protective environment, symptoms abate
Alcohol seizures	Grand mal seizures; rarely status epilepticus	Diazepam (Valium), phrenytoin (Dilantin); prevent by using chlordiazepoxide (Librium) during detoxification
Alcohol withdrawal	Irritability, nausea, vomiting, insomnia, malaise, autonomic hyperactivity, shakiness	Fluid and electrolytes maintained; sedation with benzodiazepines; restraints; monitoring of vital signs; 100 mg thiamin IM
Alcohol withdrawal delirium	Confusion, disorientation, fluctuating consciousness and perception, autonomic hyperactivity; may be fatal	Chlordiazepoxide; haloperidol (Haldol) for psychotic symptoms may be added if necessary
Amnesia	Confusion, loss of memory even for all personal identification data.	Hospitalization; hypnosis; amobarbital interview; rule out organic cause
Korsakoff's syndrome	Alcohol stigmata, amnesia, confabulation	No effective treatment; institutionalization often needed.
Wernicke's encephalopathy	Oculomotor disturbances, cerebellar ataxia; mental confusion	Thiamin, 100 mg IV or IM, with $MgSO_4$ given prior to glucose loading
Amphetamine intoxication or similarly acting sympathomimetic intoxication	Delusions, paranoia; violence; depression (from withdrawal); anxiety, delirium	Antipsychotics; restraints; hospitalization if necessary; no need for gradual withdrawal; antidepressants may be necessary
Anorexia nervosa	Loss of 25 percent of body weight of the norm for age and sex	Hospitalization; electrocardiogram (ECG), fluid and electrolytes; neuroendocrine evaluation
Anticholinergic intoxication	Psychotic symptoms, dry skin and mouth, hyperpyrexia, midriasis, tachycardia, restlessness, visual hallucinations	Discontinue drug, IV physostigmine (Antilirium), 0.5 to 2 mg, for severe agitation or fever, benzodiazepines; antipsychotics contraindicated
Anticonvulsant intoxication	Psychosis; delirium	Dose of anticonvulsant is reduced
Barbiturate and similarly acting sedative, hypnotic, or anxiolytic intoxication and withdrawal	Alterations in mood, behavior, thought—delirium; derealization and depersonalization; untreated, can be fatal; seizures	Naloxone (Narcan) to differentiate from opioid intoxication; slow withdrawal with phenobarinital or sodium thiopental or benzodiazepine; hospitalization
Borderline personality disorder	Suicidal ideation and gestures; homicidal ideations and gestures; drug abuse; micropsychotic episodes; burns, cut marks on body	Suicidal and homicidal evaluation (if great, hospitalization); small doses of antipsychotics; clear follow-up plan
Brief reactive psychosis	Emotional turmoil, extreme lability; acutely impaired reality testing after obvious psychosocial stress	Hospitalization often necessary; low dose of antipsychotics may be necessary, but often resolves spontaneously
Bromide intoxication	Delirium; mania; depression; psychosis	Serum levels obtained (>50 mg a day); bromide intake discontinued; large quantities of sodium chloride IV or PO; if agitation, paraldehyde or antipsychotic is used
Caffeine intoxication	Severe anxiety, resembling panic disorder; mania; delirium; agitated depression; sleep disturbance	Cessation of caffeine-containing substances; benzodiazepines
Cannabis intoxication	Delusions; panic; dysphoria; organic mental syndrome	Benzodiazepines, prn; antipsychotics, prn; evaluation of suicidal or homicidal risk; symptoms usually abate with time and reassurance
Catatonic schizophrenia	Marked psychomotor disturbance (either excitement or stupor); exhaustion, can be fatal	Rapid tranquilization with antipsychotics; monitor vital signs; amobarbital may release patient from catatonic mutism or stupor but can precipitate violent behavior
Chronic schizophrenia in exacerbation	Withdrawn; agitation; suicidal and homicidal risk	Suicide and homicide evaluation; screen for medical illness; restraints and rapid tranquili-

Table 28.2-9
Continued

Syndrome	Emergency Manifestations	Treatment Issues
		zation if necessary; hospitalization if necessary; reevaluation of medication regimen
Cimetidine psychosis	Delirium; delusions	Reduce dosage or discontinue drug
Clonidine withdrawal	Irritability; psychosis; violence; seizures	Symptoms abate with time, but antipsychotics may be necessary; gradual lowering of dosage
Cocaine intoxication and withdrawal	Paranoia and violence; severe anxiety; manic state; delirium; schizophreniform psychosis; tachycardia hypertension, myocardial infarction, stroke; depression and suicidal ideation	Antipsychotics and benzodiazepines; antidepressants or ECT for withdrawal depression if persistent; hospitalization
Delirium	Fluctuating sensorium; suicidal and homicidal risk; cognitive clouding; visual, tactile and auditory hallucinations; paranoia	Evaluate all potential contributing factors and treat each accordingly; reassurance, structure, clues to orientation; benzodiazepines and low-dose, high-potency antipsychotics must be used with extreme care because of their potential to act paradoxically and increase agitation
Delusional disorder	Most often brought in involuntarily; threats directed toward others	Antipsychotics if patient will comply (IM if necessary); intensive family intervention; hospitalization if necessary
Delusions with major depressions	Major depressive symptoms with delusions; agitation, severe guilt; ideas of reference; suicide and homicide risk	Antipsychotics plus antidepressants; evaluation of suicide and homicide risk; hospitalization and ECT if necessary
Dementia	Unable to care for self; violent outbursts; psychosis; depression and suicidal ideation; confusion	Small doses of high-potency antipsychotics; clues to orientation; organic evaluation, including medication use; family intervention
Depression	Suicidal ideation and attempts; self-neglect; substance abuse	Assessment of danger to self; hospitalization if necessary; nonpsychiatric causes of depression must be evaluated
L-Dopa intoxication	Mania; depression; schizophreniform psychosis; may induce rapid cycling in patients with bipolar disorder.	Lower dosage of drug or discontinue
Dystonia, acute	Intense involuntary spasm of muscles of neck, tongue, face, jaw, eyes, or trunk	Decrease dosage of antipsychotic; benztropine or diphenhydramine (Benadryl) IM
Explosive disorder, intermittent	Brief outbursts of violence; periodic episodes of suicide attempts	Benzodiazepines or antipsychotics acutely; long-term evaluation with computed tomography (CT) scan, sleep-deprived electroencephalogram (EEG), glucose tolerance curve
Grief and bereavement	Guilt feelings; irritability; insomnia; somatic complaints	Must be differentiated from major depression; antidepressants not indicated; benzodiazepines for sleep; encouragement of ventilation
Group hysteria	Groups of people exhibit extremes of grief or other disruptive behavior	Group is dispersed with help of other health care workers; ventilation, crisis-oriented therapy; if necessary, small doses of benzodiazepines
Hallucinogen hallucinosis	Symptom picture is result of interaction of type of drug, dose taken, duration of action, user's premorbid personality, setting; panic; agitation; atropine psychosis	Serum and urine screens; rule out underlying medical or psychiatric illness; benzodiazepines (2 to 20 mg) PO; reassurance and orientation; rapid tranquilization; often responds spontaneously
Homicidal and assaultive behavior	(Discussed in detail in first part of this chapter)	
Homosexual panic	Not seen with men or women who are comfortable with their sexual orientation; occurs in those who adamantly deny having any homoerotic impulses; impulses are aroused by talk, a physical overture, or play among same-sex friends, such as wrestling, sleeping together, or touching each other in a shower or hot tub; panicked person sees others as sexually interested in him or her and defends against them	Ventilation, environmental structuring, and, in some instances, medication for acute panic (e.g., alprazolam, 0.25 to 2 mg) or antipsychotics may be required; opposite-sex clinician should evaluate the patient, whenever possible, and the patient should not be touched save for the routine examination; patients have attacked physicians who were examining an abdomen or performing a rectal exam (e.g., on a man who harbors thinly veiled unintegrated homosexual impulses)

Table 28.2-9
Continued

Syndrome	Emergency Manifestations	Treatment Issues
Hypertensive crisis	Life-threatening hypertensive reaction secondary to ingestion of tyramine-containing foods in combination with MAOIs; headache, stiff neck, sweating, nausea, vomiting	α-Adrenergic blockers (e.g., pentolamine); chlorpromazine (thorazine); make sure symptoms are not secondary to hypotension (side effect of monoamine oxidase inhibitors [MAOIs] alone)
Hyperthermia	Extreme excitement or catatonic stupor or both; extremely elevated temperature; violent hyperagitation	Hydrate and cool; may be drug reaction, so discontinue any drug; rule out infection
Hyperventilation	Anxiety, terror; clouded consciousness; giddiness; faintness; bluring vision	Shift alkalosis by having patient breathe into paper bag; patient education; antianxiety agents
Hypothermia	Confusion; lethargy; combativeness; low body temperature and shivering; paradoxical feeling of warmth	IV fluids and rewarming; cardiac status must be carefully monitored; avoidance of alcohol
Incest	Suicidal behavior; adolescent crises; substance abuse	Corroboration of charge; protection of victim; contact social services; medical and psychiatric evaluation; crisis intervention
Insomnia	Depression and irritability; early morning agitation; frightening dreams; fatigue	Hypnotics only acutely, e.g., triazolam (Halcion), 0.25 to 0.5 mg, at bedtime; treat any underlying mental disorder; rules of sleep hygiene (see Table 21.2-3 in Section 21.2, "Sleep Disorders")
Jaundice	Uncommon complication of low-potency phenothiazine use (e.g., chlorpromazine)	Change drug to a low dose of a low-potency agent in a different class
Leukopenia and agranulocytosis	Side effects within the first two months of treatment with antipsychotics	Patient should call immediately for sore throat, fever, etc., and obtain immediate blood count; discontinue drug; hospitalize if necessary
Lithium toxicity	Vomiting; abdominal pain; profuse diarrhea; severe tremor, ataxia; coma; seizures; confusion; dysarthria; focal neurological signs	Lavage with wide-bore tube; osmotic diuresis; medical consultation; may require ICU treatment
Mania	Violent, impulsive behavior; indiscriminate sexual or spending behavior; psychosis; substance abuse	Hospitalization; restraints if necessary; rapid tranquilization with antipsychotics; restoration of lithium levels
Marital crises	Precipitant may be discovery of an extramarital affair, onset of serious illness, announcement of intent to divorce, or problems with children or work; one or both members of the couple may be in therapy or may be psychiatrically ill; one spouse may be seeking hospitalization for the other; each should be questioned alone regarding extramarital affairs, consultations with lawyers regarding divorce, and willingness to work in crisis-oriented or long-term therapy to resolve the problem	Sexual, financial, and psychiatric treatment histories from both, psychiatric evaluation at the time of presentation; may be precipitated by onset of untreated mood disorder or affective symptoms caused by medical illness or insidious-onset dementia; referral for management of the illness reduces immediate stress and enhances the healthier spouse's coping capacity; children may give insights available only to someone intimately involved in the social system
Mitral valve prolapse	Associated with panic disorder; dyspnea and palpitations; fear and anxiety	Echocardiogram; alprazolam or propranolol
Neuroleptic malignant syndrome	Hyperthermia; muscle rigidity; autonomic instability; parkinsonian symptoms; catatonic stupor; neurological signs; 10 to 30 percent fatality; elevated creatine phosphokinase monitor CPK levels	Discontinue antipsychotic; IV dantolene; PO bromocriptine; hydration and cooling; monitor CPK levels
Nitrous oxide toxicity	Euphoria and light-headedness	Symptoms abate without treatment within hours of use
Nutmeg intoxication	Agitation; hallucinations; severe headaches; numbness in extremities	Symptoms abate within hours of use without treatment
Opioid intoxication and withdrawal	Intoxication can lead to coma and death; withdrawal is not life-threatening	IV naloxone, narcotic antagonist; urine and serum screens; psychiatric and medical illness (e.g., AIDS) may complicate picture
Panic disorder	Panic, terror; acute onset	Must differentiate from other anxiety-producing disorders, both medical and psychiatric; electrocardiogram (ECG) to rule out mitral valve prolapse; propranolol (10 to 30 mg); alprazolam (0.25 to 2.0 mg); long-term management may include an antidepressant

Table 28.2-9
Continued

Syndrome	Emergency Manifestations	Treatment Issues
Paranoid schizophrenia	Command hallucinations; threat to others or themselves	Rapid tranquilization; hospitalization; long-acting depot medication; threatened persons must be notified
Parkinsonism	Stiffness, tremor, bradykinesia, flattened affect, shuffling gait, salivation, secondary to antipsychotic medication	Oral antiparkinsonian drug for four weeks to three months; decrease dosage of the antipsychotic
Perioral (rabbit) tremor	Perioral tremor (resembling rabbitlike facial grimacing) usually appearing after long-term therapy with antipsychotics	Decrease dosage or change to a medication in another class
Phencyclidine or similarly acting arylcyclohexylamine intoxication	Phencyclidine (PCP); paranoid psychosis; can lead to death; acute danger to self and others	Serum and urine assay; benzodiazepines may interfere with excretion; antipsychotics may worsen symptoms because of anticholinergic side effects; careful medical monitoring and hospitalization for severe intoxication
Phenelzine psychosis	Psychosis and mania in predisposed people	Reduce dosage or discontinue drug
Phenylpropanolamine toxicity	Psychosis; paranoia; insomnia; restlessness; nervousness; headache	Symptoms abate with dosage reduction or discontinuation (found in over-the-counter diet aids and oral and nasal decongestants)
Phobia	Panic, anxiety; fear	Treatment same as for panic disorders
Photosensitivity	Easy sunburning secondary to use of antipsychotic medication	Patient should avoid strong sunlight and use high-level sunscreens
Pigmentary retinopathy	Reported with dosages of thioridazine (Mellaril) equal to or greater than 800 mg a day	Remain below 800 mg a day of thioridazine
Posttraumatic stress disorder	Panic, terror; suicidal ideation; flashbacks	Reassurance; encouragement of return to responsibilities; avoid hospitalization if possible to prevent chronic invalidism; monitor suicidal ideation
Propranolol toxicity	Profound depression; confusional states	Reduce or discontinue drug; monitor suicidality
Psychotropic drug withdrawal	Abdominal pain; insomnia, drowsiness; delirium; seizures; symptoms of tardive dyskinesia may emerge; eruption of manic or schizophrenic symptoms	Symptoms of psychotropic drug withdrawal disappear with time and disappear with reinstitution of the drug; symptoms of antidepressant withdrawal can be successfully treated with anticholinergic agents, such as atropine; gradual withdrawal of psychotropic drugs over two to four weeks generally obviates development of symptoms
Puerperal or postpartum psychosis	Childbirth can precipitate schizophrenia, depression, reactive psychoses, mania, and depression; affective symptoms are most common; suicide risk is reduced during pregnancy but increased in the postpartum period	Danger to self and others (including infant) must be evaluated and proper precautions taken; medical illness presenting with behavioral aberrations is included in the differential diagnosis and must be sought and treated; care must be paid to the effects on father, infant, grandparents, and other children
Rape	Not all sexual violations are reported; silent rape reaction is characterized by loss of appetite, sleep disturbance, anxiety, and, sometimes, agoraphobia; long periods of silence, mounting anxiety, stuttering, blocking, and physical symptoms during the interview when the sexual history is taken; fear of violence and death and of contracting a sexually transmitted disease or being pregnant	Rape is a major psychiatric emergency; victim may have enduring patterns of sexual dysfunction; crisis-oriented therapy, social support, ventilation, reinforcement of healthy traits, and encouragement to return to the previous level of functioning as rapidly as possible; legal counsel; thorough medical examination and tests to identify the assailant (e.g., obtaining samples of pubic hairs with a pubic hair comb, vaginal smear to identify blood antigens in semen); if a woman, methoxyprogesterone or diethylstilbestrol PO for five days to prevent pregnancy; if menstruation does not commence within one week of cessation of the estrogen, all alternatives to pregnancy, including abortion, should be offered; if the victim has contracted venereal disease, appropriate antibiotics; witnessed written permission is required for the physician to examine, photo-

Table 28.2-9
Continued

Syndrome	Emergency Manifestations	Treatment Issues
		graph, collect specimens, and release information to the authorities; obtain consent, record the history in the patient's own words, obtain required tests, record the results of the examination, save all clothing, defer diagnosis, and provide protection against disease, psychic trauma, and pregnancy; men's and women's responses to rape affectively are reported similarly, although men are more hesitant to talk about the assault, particularly if it was homosexual, for fear they will be assumed to have consented
Reserpine intoxication	Major depression; suicidal ideation; nightmares	Evaluation of suicidal ideation; lower dosage or change drug; antidepressants or ECT may be indicated
Schizoaffective disorder	Severe depression; manic symptoms; paranoia	Evaluation of dangerousness to self or others; rapid tranquilizaiton if necessary; treatment of depression (antidepressants alone can enhance schizophrenic symptoms); use of antimanic agents
Schizophrenia	Extreme self-neglect; severe paranoia; suicidal ideation or assaultiveness; extreme psychotic symptoms	Evaluation of suicidal and homicidal potential; identification of any illness other than schizophrenia; rapid tranquilization
Seizure disorder	Confusion; anxiety; derealization and depersonalization; feelings of impending doom; gustatory or olfactory hallucinations; fuguelike state	Immediate electroencephalogram (EEG); admission and sleep-deprived and 24-hour EEG; rule out all organic substrates; rule out pseudoseizures (see Table 10-26 in Chapter 10, "Organic Mental Syndromes and Disorders"); anticonvulsants
Sudden death associated with antipsychotic medication	Seizures; asphyxiation; cardiovascular causes; postural hypotension; laryngeal-pharyngeal dystonia; suppression of gag reflex	Specific medical treatments
Sudden death of psychogenic origin	Heart attack after sudden psychic stress; voodoo and hexes; hopelessness, especially associated with serious physical illness	Specific medical treatments; folk healers
Suicide	(Covered extensively in Section 28.1)	
Sympathomimetic withdrawal	Paranoia; confessional states; depression	Most symptoms abate without treatment; antipsychotics; antidepressants if necessary
Tardive dyskinesia	Dyskinesias of mouth, tongue, face, neck, and trunk; choreoathetoid movements of extremities; usually but not always appearing after long-term treatment with antipsychotics, especially after a reduction in dosage; incidence highest in the elderly and brain-damaged; symptoms are intensified by antiparkinsonian drugs and masked but not cured by increased doses of antipsychotic	No effective treatment reported; may be prevented by prescribing the least amount of drug possible for as little time as is clinically feasible and using drug-free holidays for patients who need to continue taking the drug; decrease or discontinue drug at first sign of dyskinetic movements
Thyrotoxicosis	Tachycardia; gastrointestinal dysfunction; hyperthermia; panic, anxiety, agitation; mania; dementia; psychosis	Thyroid function tests (T_3, T_4, thyroid-stimulating hormone [TSH]); medical consultation
Toluene abuse	Anxiety; confusion; organic mental syndrome	Neurological damage is nonprogressive and reversible if toluene use is discontinued early
Vitamin B_{12} deficiency	Confusion; mood and behavior changes; ataxia	Treatment with vitamin B_{12}
Volatile nitrates	Alternations of mood and behavior; light-headedness; pulsating headache	Symptoms abate with cessation of use
Wernicke's encephalopathy	Ataxia; depression, anxiety; paralysis of external ocular muscles; disturbances of consciousness (see also Alcohol-related emergencies)	Serum thiamine level confirms diagnosis; 100 mg IM thiamine in ER; bed rest, alcohol withdrawal, high-calorie diet

References

Abrams R C, Alexopoulos G S: Substance abuse in the elderly: Alcohol and prescription drugs. Hosp Community Psychiatry *38*: 1288, 1987.

Barbee J G, Clark P D, Crapanzano M S, Heintz G C, Kehoe C E: Alcohol and substance abuse among schizophrenic patients presenting to an emergency psychiatric service. J Nerv Ment Dis *177*: 400, 1989.

Barton G M, Friedman R S, eds.: *Handbook of Emergency Psychiatry for Clinical Administrators.* Hayworth, New York, 1986.

Bassu K E C, Minden S, Apster R: Geriatric emergencies: Psychiatric or medical. Am J Psychiatry *140*: 539, 1983.

Beckett A, Summergrad P, Manschreck T, et al: Symptomatic HIV infection of the CNS in a patient without evidence of immune deficiency. Am J Psychiatry *144*: 1242, 1987.

Bellack L, Siegel H: *The Handbook of Intensive Brief and Emergency Psychiatry,* C.R.S., Larchmont, NY, 1983.

Boyer W F, Bakalar N H, Lake C R: Anticholinergic prophylaxis of acute haloperidol-induced acute dystonic reactions. J Clin Psychopharmacol *7*: 264, 1987.

Brown G L, Linnoila M I: CSF serotonin metabolite (5-HIAA) studies in depression, impulsivity, and violence. J Clin Psychiatry *51* (4, Suppl): 31, 1990.

Dubin W R, Stolberg R: *Emergency Psychiatry for the House Officer.* SP Medical & Scientific Books, New York, 1981.

Ellison J M, Blum N R, Barsky A J: Frequent repeaters in a psychiatric emergency service. Hosp Community Psychiatry *40*: 958, 1989.

Ellison J M, Hughes D H, White K A: An emergency psychiatry update. Hosp Community Psychiatry *40*: 250, 1989.

Emery R E: Family violence. Am Psychol *44*: 321, 1989.

Faulstick, M E: Psychiatric aspects of AIDS. Am J Psychiatry *144*: 551, 1987.

Fauman B J, Fauman M A: *Emergency Psychiatry for the House Officer.* Williams & Wilkins, Baltimore, 1981.

Frommer D A, Kulig K W, Mark J A, Rumack B: Tricyclic antidepressant overdose: A review. JAMA *257*: 521, 1987.

Hanke N: *Handbook of Emergency Psychiatry.* Health, Lexington, MA, 1984.

Johnson M C: Alcohol, street drugs and prescribed psychoactive medications: Seeking clarity in a "witches brew." Consult *1*: 2, 1987.

Marson D C, McGovern M P, Pomp H C: Psychiatric decision making in the emergency room: A research overview. Am J Psychiatry *145*: 918, 1988.

Monahan J, Shah S A: Dangerousness and commitment of the mentally disordered in the United States. Schizophr Bull *15*: 541, 1989.

Nicholi A M: The nontherapeutic use of psychoactive drugs. N Engl J Med *108*: 925, 1983.

Perry S W, Markowitz J: Psychiatric interventions for AIDS-spectrum disorders. Hosp Community Psychiatry *37*: 1001, 1986.

Saxena K: Glue sniffing and other deliriants. Top Emerg Med 7: 55, 1985.

Slaby A E: Other psychiatric emergencies. In *Comprehensive Textbook of Psychiatry,* ed 5, H I Kaplan and B J Sadock, editors, p 1427. Williams & Wilkins, Baltimore, 1989.

Walker J I: *Psychiatric Emergencies: Intervention and Resolution.* Lippincott, Philadelphia, 1983.

Weissman A: *Coping Capacity: On the Nature of Being Mortal.* Human Sciences Press, New York, 1984.

Psychotherapies

29.1 / Psychoanalysis and Psychoanalytic Psychotherapy

The problems that take people to psychiatrists for treatment are of two kinds: those that seem to have their origins largely in the remote past of patients' lives and those that seem to arise largely from current stresses and pressures that seem beyond the patients' conscious control. However, current external stresses may occur in combination with older problems, and some patients who have old but still active and unsolved problems may arrange their lives in such a way that they appear to be the victims of current life situations.

When a patient's problem stems mainly from the past with relatively little contribution from the present, psychoanalysis may well be the treatment of choice. During classic psychoanalysis, regressive patterns often appear in the patient's feelings and fantasies toward the psychoanalyst. These patterns provide the necessary ingress into the past.

Psychoanalytic therapy uses the theoretical framework provided by psychoanalysis, but its therapeutic goals are less extensive, and it uses some techniques that are not part of the analytic model. Current interpersonal and intrapsychic dynamics are likely to receive the greatest emphasis in psychoanalytic therapy, and there is less concern with detailed reconstructions of the patient's past life. The contrast, however, between the historical and the current loses its sharp outline in the treatment of the individual patient.

Tables 29.1-1 and 29.1-2 briefly outline the differences between classic psychoanalysis and psychoanalytically oriented psychotherapy. Each is discussed in greater detail below, and a more comprehensive comparison can be found in Table 29.1-4 at the end of this section.

PSYCHOANALYSIS

Psychoanalysis began with the treatment of patients by hypnosis. In 1881 Anna O, a neurotic young woman who suffered from multiple visual and motor disturbances and alterations of consciousness was treated by the Viennese internist Josef Breuer. He observed that the patient's symptoms disappeared when she expressed them verbally while hypnotized. Sigmund Freud used the technique with Breuer, and they reported their findings in 1895 in *Studies on Hysteria*. They explained hysteria (now called conversion disorder) as the result of a traumatic experience, which was usually sexual in nature and associated with a large quantity of affect, that was barred from consciousness and that expressed itself in a disguised form through various symptoms. Freud eventually gave up placing his patients in a hypnotic trance; instead, he urged them to recline on a couch and concentrate with their eyes closed on past memories related to their symptoms. This concentration method eventually became the technique of free association. Freud instructed his patients to say whatever came into their minds, without censoring any of their thoughts. This method is still used today and is one of the hallmarks of psychoanalysis, through which thoughts and feelings that are kept in the unconscious are brought into consciousness.

In *The Interpretation of Dreams* Freud described the topographical model of the mind as consisting of a conscious, preconscious, and unconscious. The conscious mind was conceptualized as awareness; the preconscious, as thoughts and feelings that are easily available to consciousness; and the unconscious, as thoughts and feelings that cannot be made conscious without overcoming strong resistances. The unconscious contains nonverbal forms of thought function and gives rise to dreams, parapraxes (slips of the tongue), and psychological symptoms. Psychoanalysis emphasizes the conflict between unconscious drives and moral judgments that patients may make about their impulses. That conflict accounts for the phenomenon of repression, which is regarded as pathological. Free association allows repressed memories to be recovered and thereby contributes to cure.

In 1923 Freud described his structural theory of the mind in *The Ego and the Id.* He saw the ego as a group of functions accessible to consciousness that mediate among the demands of the id, the superego, and the environment. He viewed anxiety as the ego's reaction to the threatened breakthrough of forbidden impulses.

Modern advances in psychoanalysis have focused on the increased understanding of the ego's functions (ego psychology), the role of early relationships (object relations), and the relationship between the analyst and the patient (transference and countertransference).

Goal

The chief requirement of psychoanalysis is the gradual integration of the previously repressed material into the total structure of the personality. It is a slow process, requiring the analyst to maintain a balance between the in-

Table 29.1-1
Psychoanalysis

Goal	Resolution of the childhood neurosis as it presents itself in the transference neurosis
Selection criteria	Primarily oedipal conflict Experiences internal conflict Obtains symptom relief through understanding Psychologically minded Able to experience and observe strong affects without acting out Supportive relationships available in both the present and the past
Duration	4 or 5 sessions a week 3 to 6 years, average duration
Techniques	Free association Therapeutic alliance Neutrality Abstinence Defense analysis Interpretation of transference

Table from R J Ursano, E K Silberman: Individual psychotherapies. In *The American Psychiatric Press Textbook of Psychiatry*, J A Talbott, R E Hales, and S C Yudofsky, editors, p 858. American Psychiatric Press, Washington DC, 1988, with permission.

Table 29.1-2
Intensive (Long-Term) Psychoanalytically Oriented Psychotherapy

Goal	Defense and transference analysis with limited reconstruction of the past
Selection criteria	When a narrower focus and less comprehensive outcome is acceptable, the same selection criteria as in psychoanalysis are used More seriously disturbed patients who can use understanding to resolve symptoms when some supportive elements are available in the treatment
Duration	2 or 3 sessions a week for 1 to 6 years on average
Techniques	Therapeutic alliance Face to face Free association Defense and transference interpretation More use of clarification, suggestion, and learning through experience than in psychoanalysis Medications

Table from R J Ursano, E K Silberman: Individual psychotherapies. In *The American Psychiatric Press Textbook of Psychiatry*, J A Talbott, R E Hales, and S C Yudofsky, editors, p 860. American Psychiatric Press, Washington DC, 1988, with permission.

tepretation of unconscious material and the patient's ability to deal with increased awareness. If the work proceeds too rapidly, the patient may experience the analysis as a new trauma. The work of analysis initially is preparing the patient to deal with the anxiety-producing material that has been uncovered. The patient is taught to be aware of innermost thoughts and feelings and to recognize the natural resistances to the mind's willingness or ability to deal directly with noxious psychic material. The patient and the analyst seldom follow a straight path to insight. Instead, the process of analysis is more like putting together the pieces of an immense and complicated jigsaw puzzle.

Analytic Setting

The usual analytic setting is for the patient to lie on a couch or sofa and the analyst to sit behind, partially or totally outside the patient's field of vision. The couch helps the analyst produce the controlled regression that favors the emergence of repressed material. The patient's reclining position in the presence of an attentive analyst also recreates symbolically the early parent-child situation, which varies from patient to patient. This position also helps the patient focus on inner thoughts, feelings, and fantasies, which can then become the focus of free associations. Moreover, the use of the couch introduces an element of sensory deprivation because the patient's visual stimuli are limited and the analyst's verbalizations are relatively few. That state promotes regression. There has been some disagreement, however, about the use of the couch as always characteristic of psychoanalysis. Otto Fenichel stated that whether the patient lies down or sits and whether certain rituals of procedure are used do not matter. The best condition is the one most appropriate to the analytic task.

Role of the Analyst

For the most part analysts' activity is limited to timely interpretation of the patient's associations. Ideally, analysts—who have undergone a personal psychoanalysis as part of their training—are able to maintain an attitude of benevolent objectivity or neutrality toward the patient, trying not to impose their own personalities or systems of values. Nevertheless, it is not possible or desirable for the analyst to be a so-called blank screen, *tabula rasa*, or analyst incognito. A real relationship underlies the analytic setting, and the handling of this real relationship may make the difference between success and failure in treatment.

Duration of Treatment

The patient and the psychoanalyst must be prepared to persevere in this process for an indefinite period. Psychoanalysis takes time—between three and six years, sometimes even longer. Sessions are usually held four or more times a week for 45 to 50 minutes each. Some analyses are conducted with less frequency and with the sessions varying from 20 to 30 minutes. The French psychoanalyst Jacques Lacan introduced sessions of variable length (3 to 45 minutes), which he believed to be equally effective.

Treatment Methods

Fundamental rule of psychoanalysis. The fundamental or basic rule is that the patient agrees to be completely honest with the analyst and "to tell everything" without selection. Freud referred to the technique that allowed for such honesty as free association.

Free association. Free association refers to patients' saying everything that comes to mind without any censoring, regardless of whether they believe the thought to be unacceptable, unimportant, or embarrassing. Associations are directed by three kinds of unconscious forces: the pathogenic conflicts of the neurosis, the wish to get well, and the wish to please the analyst. The interplay among these factors become very complex. For example, a thought or impulse that is unacceptable to patients and that is a part of their neuroses may conflict with their wishes to please the analyst, who, they assume, also finds the impulse unacceptable. But if patients follow the fundamental rule, they overcome the resistance.

Free-floating attention. The analysts' counterpart to patients' free association is a special way of listening called free-floating attention. Analysts allow the patients' associations to stimulate their own associations and are thereby able to discern a theme in the patients' free associations that may be reflected back to the patients then or at some later time. Analysts' careful attention to their own subjective experiences is an indispensable part of analysis.

Rule of abstinence. The rule of abstinence refers to the patient's being able to delay gratifying any instinctual wishes so as to talk about them in treatment. The tension thus engendered produces relevant associations that the analyst uses to increase the patient's awareness. The rule does not refer to sexual abstinence but, rather, to not allowing the treatment setting to gratify the patient's infantile longing for love and affection.

Analytic Process

Transference. A major criterion by which psychoanalysis can be differentiated in principle from other forms of psychotherapy is the management of the transference. Indeed, psychoanalysis has been defined as the analysis of transference to emphasize that point.

Transference was first described by Freud and refers to the patient's feelings and behavior toward the analyst that are based on infantile wishes the patient has toward parents or parental figures. These feelings are unconscious but are revealed in the transference neurosis, in which patients struggle to gratify their unconscious infantile wishes through the analyst. The transference may be positive, in which the analyst needs to be seen as a person of exceptional worth, ability, and character; or it may be negative, in which the analyst becomes the embodiment of what the patient experienced or feared from parental figures in the past. Negative transferences can be expressed and experienced in highly labile and volatile ways, especially in patients whose personalities are described as borderline or narcissistic. Both situations reflect the patient's need to repeat unresolved childhood conflicts.

The analyst's role is to help the patient gain true insight into the distortions of transference and, through insight, to increase the patient's capacity for gratifying relationships based on mature and realistic expectations, rather than on irrational, childhood-derived fantasies.

Interpretation. In psychoanalysis the analyst provides the patient with interpretations about psychological events that were neither previously understood by nor meaningful to the patient. The transference constitutes a major frame of reference for interpretation. A complete psychoanalytic interpretation includes meaningful statements of current conflicts and the historical factors that influenced them. However, complete interpretations of this kind constitute a relatively small part of the analysis. Most interpretations are limited in scope and deal with matters of immediate concern.

Interpretations must be well timed. The analyst may have a formulation in mind, but the patient may not be prepared to deal with it directly because of a variety of factors, such as anxiety level, negative transference, and external life stress. The analyst may decide to wait until the patient can fully understand the interpretation. The proper timing of interpretations requires great clinical skill.

Dream interpretation. In his classic work *The Interpretation of Dreams*, Freud referred to the dream as the "royal road to the unconscious." The *manifest content* of a dream is what the dreamer reports. The *latent content* represents the unconscious meaning of the dream after the condensations, substitutions, and symbols are analyzed. The dream arises from what Freud referred to as the *day's residue* (i.e., the events of the preceding day that stimulated the patient's unconscious mind). Dreams may serve as a wish-fulfillment mechanism and as a way of mastering anxiety about a life event.

Freud outlined several technical procedures to use in dream interpretation: (1) have the patient associate to elements of the dream in the order in which they occurred; (2) have the patient associate to a particular dream element that the patient or the therapist chooses; (3) disregard the content of the dream, and ask the patient what events of the previous day could be associated with the dream (the day's residue); and (4) avoid giving any instructions, and leave it to the dreamer to begin. The analyst uses the patient's associations to find a clue to the workings of the unconscious mind.

Countertransference. Just as the term "tranference" is used to encompass the patient's total range of feelings for and against the analyst, "countertransference" refers to a broad spectrum of the analyst's reactions to the patient. Countertransference has unconscious components based on conflicts of which the analyst is not aware. Ideally, the analyst ought to be aware of countertransference issues, which may interfere with his or her ability to remain detached and objective. The analyst should remove such impediments by either further analysis or self-analysis. For whatever reasons, however, there are some patients or groups of patients with whom a particular analyst does not work well, and the experienced clinician, recognizing this fact, refers such patients to a colleague.

Therapeutic alliance. In addition to transferential and countertransferential issues, a real relationship between the analyst and the patient represents two adults entering into a joint venture, referred to as the therapeutic or working alliance. Both commit themselves to exploring the patient's problems, to establishing mutual trust, and to cooperating with each other to achieve a realistic goal of cure or the amelioration of symptoms.

Resistance. Freud believed that unconscious ideas or impulses were repressed and prevented from reaching awareness because they were unacceptable to consciousness for some reason. He referred to that phenomenon as resistance, which had to be overcome if the analysis was to proceed. Resistance may sometimes be a conscious process manifested by withholding relevant information. Other examples of resistance are remaining silent for a long time, being late or missing appointments, and paying bills late or not at all. The signs of resistance are legion, and almost any feature of the analytic situation can be used to represent resistance. Freud once said that any treatment can be considered psychoanalysis that works by undoing resistance and interpreting transferences.

Indications for Treatment

The primary indications for psychoanalysis are long-standing psychological conflicts that have produced a symptom or disorder. The connection between the conflict and the symptom may be direct or indirect. Psychoanalysis is considered effective in treating certain anxiety disorders, such as phobia and obsessive-compulsive disorders, mild depressions (dysthymia), some personality disorders, and some impulse control and sexual disorders. More important than diagnosis, however, is the patient's ability to form an analytic pact and to maintain a commitment to a progressively deepening analytic process that brings about internal change through increasing self-awareness. Freud believed that the patient also had to be able to form a strong transference attachment to the analyst (termed *transference neurosis*), without which analysis was not possible. That excluded most psychotic patients because of the difficulty they have in forming the affective and realistic bonds that are essential to the development and resolution of the transference neurosis. The ego of a patient in analysis must be able to tolerate the frustrations of his or her impulses without responding with some serious form of acting out or by shifting from one pathological pattern to another. That excludes most drug-dependent patients, who are regarded as unsuitable because their egos are unable to tolerate the frustrations and the emotional demands of psychoanalysis.

Contraindications for Treatment

The various contraindications to psychoanalysis are relative, but each must be considered before embarking on a course of treatment.

Age. Traditionally, many analysts believed that most adults over age 40 lack sufficient flexibility for major personality changes. However, most analysts now believe that more important than age is the patient's individual capacity for thoughtful introspection and desire for change. The ideal candidates are generally young adults. Children are unable to follow the rule of free association, but, with modifications of technique (e.g., play therapy), they have been successfully analyzed.

Intelligence. Patients must be intelligent enough to be able to understand the procedure and to cooperate in the process.

Life circumstances. If the patient's life situations cannot be modified, analysis may only make it worse. For example, it can be hazardous to create goals for patients who are unable to fulfill them because of external limitations.

Time constraints. Unless the patient has time to participate and to wait for change, another type of therapy should be considered. This constraint applies especially to emergency symptoms and to those that the patient can no longer tolerate, including those that are dangerous (e.g., strong suicidal impulses).

Nature of the relationship. The analysis of friends, relatives, and acquaintances is contraindicated because it distorts the transference and the analyst's objectivity.

Other contraindications. Finally, some patients work better with some analysts than others. Sometimes this determination can be made after a single consultation, but often a trial analysis of several sessions may be necessary. This time may also allow patients to see whether they wish to continue. Experience has shown that it does not matter whether the analyst is a man or a woman, although some patients may initially prefer to see one or the other, a preference that is eventually understood as the analysis proceeds.

Dynamics of Therapeutic Results

The process of cure or improvement involves the release of repression safely and effectively. The structural apparatus of the mind—id, ego and superego—are modified. The ego is able to deal with repressed impulses and is finally in a position to accept or renounce them.

Analysis helps reduce the intensity of the conflicts and helps find more acceptable ways of handling impulses that cannot be reduced. Instead of a more acceptable method of channeling unmodified infantile strivings, the drives' primary-process quality itself is lessened, and they become better adapted to reality. The ultimate goal is the elimination of symptoms, thereby increasing the patient's capacity for work, enjoyment, and self-understanding.

There are few long-term outcome studies for psychoanalysis because of the complex patient-therapist variables. Nevertheless, psychoanalysis is thought to be effective under some circumstances for many disorders.

PSYCHOANALYTIC PSYCHOTHERAPY

Psychoanalytic therapy is psychotherapy based on psychoanalytic formulations that have been modified conceptually and technically. Unlike psychoanalysis, which has as its ultimate concern the uncovering and subsequent working through of infantile conflicts as they arise in the transference neurosis, psychoanalytic therapy takes as its focus the current conflicts and current dynamic patterns—that is, the analysis of the patients' problems with other persons and with themselves. Also unlike psychoanalysis, which has as its technique the use of free association and the analysis of the transference neurosis, psychoanalytic therapy is characterized by interviewing and discussion techniques that use free association much less frequently. And again unlike psychoanalysis, psychoanalytic therapy usually limits its work on transference to a discussion of the patient's reactions to the psychiatrist and others. The reaction to the psychiatrist is not interpreted to as great a degree as it is in psychoanalysis. Nevertheless, transference attitudes and responses to the therapist may arise from time to time and can be used productively. For example, spontaneous transferences in the therapeutic situation may give valuable clues to patients' behavior in extratherapeutic situations and, at times, to their childhood. These transferences may tell the therapist the probable focus for the patient at any given time, inside or outside the treatment relationship.

Treatment Techniques

One way in which psychoanalytic psychotherapy differs from classical psychoanalysis is that the former does not usually use a couch. The stimulation of temporary regressive patterns of feeling and thinking, which is valuable to psychoanalysis, is much less necessary in psychoanalytic therapy, with its greater focus on current dynamic patterns. In psychoanalytic therapy the patient and the therapist are usually in full view of each other, which may make the therapist seem more real and less a composite of projected fantasies. This type of therapy is much more flexible than psychoanalysis, and it may be used in conjunction with psychotropic medication more often than in psychoanalysis.

Psychoanalytic psychotherapy can range from a single supportive interview, centering on a current but pressing problem, to many years of treatment, with one to three interviews a week of varying length. In contrast to psychoanalysis, psychoanalytic psychotherapy treats most of the disorders in the field of psychopathology.

Types

There are two major types of psychoanalytic psychotherapy (1) insight-oriented or expressive and (2) supportive or relationship-oriented.

Insight-oriented psychotherapy. Insight is the patients' understanding of their psychological functioning and personalities. It is important to specify the area or level of understanding or experience into which the patient is to achieve insight. The psychiatrist's emphasis in insight-oriented therapy (also called expressive therapy and intensive psychoanalytic psychotherapy) is on the value to patients of gaining a number of new insights into the current dynamics of their feelings, responses, behavior, and, especially, current relations with other persons. To a smaller extent the emphasis is on the value of developing some insight into patients' responses to the therapist and responses in childhood.

Insight therapy is the treatment of choice for a patient who has fairly adequate ego strength but who, for one reason or another, should not or cannot undergo psychoanalysis.

The therapy's effectiveness does not depend solely on the insights developed or used. The patient's therapeutic response is also based on such factors as the ventilation of feelings in a nonjudgmental but limit-setting atmosphere, identification with the therapist, and other relationship factors. A therapeutic relationship does not, however, require an indiscriminate acceptance of all that a patient says and does. At times, the therapist must intervene on the side of a relatively weak ego by giving unmistakable evidence that the patient could try to achieve a better adjustment or by setting realistic limits to the patient's maladaptive behavior. In so doing, therapists try to be guided by their dynamic assessments of the situation and not by their countertransference responses.

Inevitably, the therapist's attitudes and responses to the patient are different from those of important figures in the patient's childhood. At times, the therapist discusses these differences. Patients may come to see that they have generalized their parents' attitudes as being universal and have generalized their own responses, so that they have become automatic responses to all parental or significant figures.

Insight-oriented psychotherapy is frequently complicated by spontaneous strong transferences to the therapist that at times threaten to disrupt the treatment. The insight therapist must decide, on the basis of an understanding of each individual patient, how to respond to these transference reactions. If the patient is highly introspective and psychologically minded, the therapist may choose to make relatively deep transference interpretations (e.g., relating the reactions to significant childhood fantasies). If the patient is more fragile and less capable of tolerating an interpretation that is perceived as emotionally threatening, the therapist may choose to remain more superficial in approach (e.g., relating the reactions to more current, reality-based feelings).

Supportive psychotherapy. Supportive psychotherapy (also called relationship-oriented psychotherapy) offers support by an authority figure during a period of illness, turmoil, or temporary decompensation. It also has the goal of restoring or strengthening the defenses and integrating capacities that have been impaired. It provides a period of acceptance and dependence for a patient who is in need of help in dealing with guilt, shame, and anxiety and in meeting the frustration or the external pressures that may be too great to handle.

Supportive therapy uses a number of methods, either singly or in combination, including (1) warm, friendly, strong leadership; (2) gratification of dependency needs; (3) support in the ultimate development of legitimate independence; (4) help in the development of pleasurable sublimations (e.g., hobbies); (5) adequate rest and diversion; (6) the removal of excessive external strain if possible; (7) hospitalization when indicated; (8) medication to alleviate symptoms; and (9) guidance and advice in dealing with current issues. It uses the techniques that help the patient feel more secure, accepted, protected, encouraged, and safe and less anxious.

One of the greatest dangers lies in the possibility of fostering too great a regression and too strong a dependency. From the beginning, the psychiatrist must plan to work persistently to enable the patient to assume a greater independence. But some patients require supportive therapy indefinitely, often with just the goal of maintaining a marginal adjustment that enables them to function in society.

The expression of emotion is an important part of supportive psychotherapy. The verbalization of unexpressed strong emotions may bring considerable relief. The goal of such talking out is not primarily to gain insight into the unconscious dynamic patterns that may be intensifying current responses. Rather, the reduction of inner tension and anxiety may result from the expression of emotion and its subsequent discussion and may lead to a greater insight into and objectivity in evaluating a current problem.

Corrective emotional experience. The relationship between the therapist and the patient gives the therapist an opportunity to display behavior different from the destructive or unproductive behavior of the patient's parents. At times, such experiences seem to neutralize or reverse some of the effects of the parents' mistakes. If the patient had overly authoritarian parents, the therapist's friendly, flexible, nonjudgmental, nonauthoritarian—but at times firm and limit-setting—attitude means that the patient has an opportunity to adjust to, be led by, and identify with a new type of parent figure. Franz Alexander called this process a corrective emotional experience.

Supportive psychotherapy is suitable for a variety of psychogenic illnesses. For example, it may be useful when a patient is very resistive to an expressive psychotherapy or is considered too emotionally disturbed for such a procedure. Supportive therapy may be chosen when the diagnostic assessment indicates that a gradual maturing process, based on the elaboration of new foci for identification, is the most promising path toward improvement. Table 29.1-3 summarizes important features of supportive psychotherapy. Table 29.1-4 outlines a comparison and description of the different types of therapies discussed in this section.

Table 29.1-3
Supportive Psychotherapy

Goal	Support reality testing Provide ego support Maintain or reestablish usual level of functioning
Selection criteria	Very healthy patient faced with overwhelming crises Patient with ego deficits
Duration	Days, months, or years—as needed
Technique	Therapist predictably available Interpretation used to strengthen defenses Therapist maintains working, reality-based relationship based on support, concern, and problem solving Suggestion, reenforcement, advice, reality testing, cognitive restructuring, and reassurance Psychodynamic life narrative Medication

Table from R J Ursano, E K Silberman: Individual psychotherapies. In *The American Psychiatric Press Textbook of Psychiatry*, J A Talbott, R E Hales, and S C Yudofsky, editors, p 878. American Psychiatric Press, Washington DC, 1988, with permission.

Table Table 29.1-4
Scope of Psychoanalytic Practice: A Clinical Continuum*

		Psychoanalytic Psychotherapy	
Feature	**Psychoanalysis**	**Expressive Mode**	**Supportive Mode**
Frequency	Regular four to five times a week: 50-minute hour	Regular one to three times a week: half to full hour	Flexible one time a week or less: or as needed, half to full hour
Duration	Long-term: usually three to five+ years	Short- or long-term: several sessions to months or years	Short- or intermittent long-term; single session to lifetime
Setting	Patient primarily on couch with analyst out of view	Patient and therapist face to face; occasional use of couch	Patient and therapist face to face; couch contraindicated
Modus operandi	Systematic analysis of all (positive and negative) transference and resistance; primary focus on analyst and intrasession events; transference neurosis facilitated; regression encouraged	Partial analysis of dynamics and defenses; focus on current interpersonal events and transference to others outside sessions; analysis of negative transference; positive transference left unexplored unless it impedes progress; limited regression encouraged	Formation of therapeutic alliance and real object relationship; analysis of transference contraindicated with rare exceptions: focus on conscious external events; regression discouraged
Analyst-therapist role	Absolute neutrality; frustration of patient; reflector-mirror role	Modified neutrality; implicit gratification of patient and greater activity	Neutrality suspended; limited explicit gratification, direction, and disclosure
Mutative change agents	Insight predominates within relatively deprived environment	Insight within more empathic environment; identification with benevolent object	Auxiliary or surrogate ego as temporary substitute; holding environment; insight to degree possible

Table 29.1-4
Continued

Feature	Psychoanalysis	Psychoanalytic Psychotherapy	
		Expressive Mode	**Supportive Mode**
Patient population	Neuroses; mild character psychopathology	Neuroses; mild to moderate character psychopathology, especially narcissitic and borderline personality disorders	Severe character disorders; latent or manifest psychoses; acute crises; physical illness
Patient requisites	High motivation; psychological-mindedness; good previous object relationships; ability to maintain transference neurosis; good frustration tolerance	High to moderate motivation and psychological-mindedness; ability to form therapeutic alliance; some frustration tolerance	Some degree of motivation and ability to form therapeutic alliance
Basic goals	Structural reorganization of personality; resolution of unconscious conflicts; insight into intrapsychic events; symptom relief an indirect result	Partial reorganization of personality and defenses; resolution of preconscious and conscious derivatives of conflicts; insight into current interpersonal events; improved object relations; symptom relief a goal or prelude to further exploration	Reintegration of self and ability to cope; stabilization or restoration of preexisting equilibrium; strengthening of defenses; better adjustment or acceptance of pathology; symptom relief and environmental restructuring as primary goals
Major techniques	Free association method predominates; full dynamic interpretation (including confrontation, clarification, and working through), with emphasis on genetic reconstruction	Limited free association; confrontation, clarification, and partial interpretation predominate, with emphasis on here and now interpretation and limited genetic interpretation	Free association method contraindicated; suggestion (advice) predominates; abreaction useful; confrontation, clarification, and interpretation in the here and now secondary; genetic interpretation contraindicated
Adjunct treatment	Primarily avoided; if applied, all negative and positive meanings and implications thoroughly analyzed	May be necessary (e.g., psychotropic drugs as temporary measure); if applied, negative implications explored and diffused	Often necessary (e.g., psychotropic drugs, family, rehabiitative therapy, or hospitalization); if applied, positive implications are emphasized

Table by Toksoz Byram Karasu, M.D.
*This division is not categorical: all practice resides on a clinical continuum.

References

Abend S M: Countertransference and psychoanalytic technique. Psychoanal Q *58*: 374, 1989.
Brenner C: *Psychoanalytic Technique and Psychic Conflict*. International Universities Press, New York, 1976.
Brewin C R: Cognitive change processes in psychotherapy. Psychol Rev *96*: 379, 1989.
Cameron P M: Psychodynamic psychotherapy for the depressive syndrome. Psychiatr J Univ Ottawa *14*: 397, 1989.
Fenichel O: *Problems of Psychoanalytic Technique*. Psychoanalytic Quarterly, Albany, NY, 1941.
Freud A: *The Ego and Mechanisms of Defense*. International Universities Press, New York, 1966.
Hartmann H: *Ego Psychology and the Problem of Adaptation*. International Universities Press, New York, 1959.
Havens L: *Approaches to the Mind*. Harvard University Press, Cambridge, MA, 1987.
Holinser P C: A developmental perspective on psychotherapy and psychoanalysis. Am J Psychiatry *146*: 1404, 1989.
Jones E: *The Life and Work of Sigmund Freud*, vols 1–3. Basic Books, New York, 1953–57.
Karasu T B: Psychoanalysis and psychoanalytic psychotherapy. In *Comprehensive Textbook of Psychiatry*, ed 5, H I Kaplan and B J Sadock, editors, p 1442. Williams & Wilkins, Baltimore, 1989.
Karasu T B: The specificity versus nonspecificity dilemma: Toward identifying therapeutic change agents. Am J Psychiatry *148*: 687, 1986.
Karasu T B: *Treatments of Psychiatric Disorders: A Task Force Report of the American Psychiatric Association*. American Psychiatric Press, Washington, DC, 1989.
Kernberg O: *Object Relations Therapy and Clinical Psychoanalysis*. Aronson, New York, 1976.
Klein M: *Contributions of Psychoanalysis, 1921–45*. Hogarth Press, London, 1948.
Kohut H H: *The Analysis of the Self*. International Universities Press, New York, 1984.
Mahler M: *On Human Symbiosis and the Vicissitudes of Individuation*. International Universities Press, New York, 1968.
May R, Angel E, Ellenberger H: *Existence: A New Dimension in Psychiatry and Psychology*. Basic Books, New York, 1958.
Reich W: *Character Analysis*. Touchstone Books, New York, 1974.
Schafer R: *A New Language for Psychoanalysis*. Yale University Press, New Haven, CT, 1976.
Sullivan H S: *Interpersonal Theory of Psychiatry*. Norton, New York, 1953.

29.2 / Brief Psychotherapy and Crisis Intervention

Because they are effective therapeutically and attractive economically, brief dynamic psychotherapy and crisis intervention have developed during the past decade into major additions to the psychotherapist's armamentarium. As a result, these interventions will soon become the most common forms of therapy for patients with circumscribed psychological difficulties in both Europe and North America.

Brief dynamic psychotherapy and crisis intervention are not simply short-term therapies but are primarily rooted in psychodynamic principles and utilize careful selection criteria for appropriate candidates. But because psychoanalytic and crisis theory constitute the basis of brief dynamic psychotherapy and crisis intervention, this discussion stresses the psychodynamic components of these types of short-term therapy, rather than the diagnostic categories of conditions for which they seem to be best suited.

HISTORY

Most of the basic characteristics of brief psychotherapy were identified by Franz Alexander and Thomas French in 1946. They described a therapeutic experience that puts the patient at ease, manipulates the transference, and uses trial interpretations in a flexible manner. The emphasis is aimed at developing a corrective emotional experience capable of repairing traumatic events of the past and convincing the patient that new ways of thinking, feeling, and behaving are possible.

At about the same time Eric Lindemann established a consultation service at the Massachusetts General Hospital for persons experiencing a crisis. New treatment methods were developed to deal with those situations and were eventually applied to persons who were not in crisis but who were experiencing emotional distress from a variety of sources.

SELECTION CRITERIA

The most valuable predictor of a successful outcome is the patients' motivation for treatment. In addition, patients must be able to deal with psychological concepts, to respond to interpretation, and to concentrate on and resolve the conflict around the central issue or focus that underlies their basic problem. Patients must also be able to develop a therapeutic alliance and work with the therapist toward achieving emotional health.

TYPES OF BRIEF PSYCHOTHERAPY

Brief Focal Psychotherapy (Tavistock–Malan)

Brief focal psychotherapy was originally developed by the Michael Balint team at the Tavistock Clinic in London in the 1950s. Daniel Malan, a member of that team, reported the results of the therapy. Malan's selection criteria for treatment are eliminating absolute contraindications; rejecting patients for whom certain dangers seem inevitable; clearly assessing the patient's psychopathology; and determining the patient's capacity to consider his or her problems in emotional terms and face disturbing material, respond to interpretations, and endure the stress of the treatment. Malan found that high motivation invariably correlated with successful outcome.

Contraindications to treatment are serious suicidal attempts, drug addiction, chronic alcoholism, incapacitating chronic obsessional symptoms, incapacitating chronic phobic symptoms, and gross destructive or self-destructive acting out.

Requirements and techniques. Malan emphasizes using the following routine: make the transference early and interpret it. Interpret also the negative transference. Link the transference to the patient's relation to his or her parents. Both patient and therapist must be willing to become deeply involved and to bear the ensuing tension. Successful dynamic interaction predominates. A circumscribed focus is formulated, and a termination date is set in advance. Grief and anger about termination are worked through.

About 20 sessions is suggested as an average length for this kind of therapy for an experienced therapist and about 30 sessions for a trainee. However, Malan does not go beyond 40 interviews.

Tables 29.2-1 and 29.2-2 summarize Malan's techniques and exclusion criteria.

Time-Limited Psychotherapy (Boston University–Mann)

A psychotherapeutic model of exactly 12 interviews focusing on a specified central issue was developed at Boston University by J. Mann and his colleagues in the early 1970s.

Table 29.2-1
Malan and the Tavistock Group: Brief Focal Psychotherapy

Goal	Clarify the nature of the defense, the anxiety, and the impulse Link the present, past, and transference
Selection criteria	Patient able to think in feeling terms High motivation Good response to trial interpretation
Duration	Up to one year Mean, 20 sessions
Focus	Internal conflict present since childhood
Termination	Set definite date at beginning of treatment

Table from R J Ursano, E K Silberman: Individual psychotherapies. In *The American Psychiatric Press Textbook of Psychiatry*, J A Talbott, R E Hales, and S C Yudofsky, editors, p 861. American Psychiatric Press, Washington DC, 1988, with permission.

Table 29.2-2
Malan and the Tavistock Group's Exclusion Criteria for Brief Focal Psychotherapy

1. Patient is unavailable to therapeutic contact.
2. Therapist anticipates that prolonged work will be needed.
   to generate motivation
   to penetrate rigid defenses
   to deal with complex or deep-seated issues
   to resolve unfavorable, intense transference, dependent or other, that may develop
3. Depressive or psychotic disturbance may intensify.

Table from R J Ursano, E K Silberman: Individual psychotherapies. In *The American Psychiatric Press Textbook of Psychiatry*, J A Talbott, R E Hales, and S C Yudofsky, editors, p 861. American Psychiatric Press, Washington DC, 1988, with permission.

In contrast with Malan's emphasis on clear-cut selection and rejection criteria, Mann has not been as explicit as to who is a good candidate to receive time-limited psychotherapy.

The main points that Mann considers important are the determination of a reasonably correct central conflict in the patient and, in young people, maturational crises with many psychological and somatic complaints.

Mann also mentioned a few exceptions, which are similar to Malan's rejection criteria. These exceptions are a major depression that interferes with the treatment agreement, an acute psychotic state, and a desperate patient who needs but is incapable of tolerating object relations.

Requirements and techniques. The following are Mann's technical requirements: strict limitation to 12 sessions; positive transference predominating early; specification and strict adherence to a central issue involving transference; positive identifications, making separation a maturational event for the patient; absolute prospect of termination, avoiding development of dependence; clarification of present and past experiences and resistances; an active therapist who supports and encourages the patient; and education of the patient through direct information, reeducation, and manipulation.

The conflicts likely to be encountered include independence versus dependence, activity versus passivity, unresolved or delayed grief, and adequate versus inadequate self-esteem. Table 29.2-3 summarizes features of Mann's time-limited psychotherapy.

Table 29.2-3
Mann: Time-Limited Psychotherapy

Goal	Resolution of the present and chronically endured pain and the patient's negative self-image
Selection criteria	High ego strength Able to engage and disengage Therapist quickly able to identify a central issue Excludes serious depression, acute psychosis, and borderline personality organization
Duration	12 treatment hours
Focus	Present and chronically endured pain Particular image of the self
Termination	Specific last session set at beginning of treatment Termination a major focus of the therapy work

Table from R J Ursano, E K Silberman: Individual psychotherapies. In *The American Psychiatric Press Textbook of Psychiatry*, J A Talbott, R E Hales, and S C Yudofsky, editors, p 864. American Psychiatric Press, Washington DC, 1988, with permission.

Short-Term Dynamic Psychotherapy (McGill University–Davanloo)

As conducted by Habib Davanloo at McGill University, short-term dynamic psychotherapy encompass all the varieties of brief psychotherapy and crisis intervention. Patients treated in Davanloo's series are classified as those whose psychological conflicts are predominantly oedipal, those whose conflicts are not oedipal, and those whose conflicts have more than one focus.

In addition, Davanloo devised a specific psychotherapeutic technique for patients suffering from severe, longstanding neurotic problems, specifically those suffering from incapacitating obsessive-compulsive and phobic disorders.

Davanloo's criteria emphasize the evaluation of those ego functions that are of primary importance to the psychotherapeutic work: the establishment of a psychotherapeutic focus; the psychodynamic formulation of the patient's psychological problem; the ability to get involved in emotional interaction with the evaluator; the history of a give-and-take relationship with a significant person in the patient's life; the extent to which the patient's emotional life is close to conscious awareness; the patient's ability to experience and tolerate anxiety, guilt, and depression; the patient's motivation for change; the patient's psychological-mindedness; and the patient's ability to respond to interpretation and to link the evaluator with people in the present and in the past.

Both Malan and Davanloo emphasize the patient's response to interpretation and consider it both an important selection criterion and a prognostic criterion.

Requirements and techniques. The highlights of this psychotherapeutic approach are flexibility (the therapist should adapt his or her technique to the patient's needs); control of the patient's regressive tendencies; active intervention, so as not to allow the development of overdependence on the therapist; and intellectual insight and emotional experiences by the patient in the transference. These emotional experiences become corrective as a result of the interpretation.

Table 29.2-4 summarizes features of Davanloo's short-term dynamic psychotherapy.

Short-Term Anxiety-Provoking Psychotherapy (Harvard University–Sifneos)

Short-term anxiety-provoking psychotherapy, STAPP, was first developed at the Massachusetts General Hospital by Peter Sifneos during the 1950s. The following criteria for selection are used: circumscribed chief complaint (this implies an ability to select one out of a variety of problems

Table 29.2-4
Davanloo: Short-Term Dynamic Psychotherapy

Goal	Resolution of oedipal conflict, loss focus, or multiple foci
Selection criteria	Psychological-mindedness
	At least one past meaningful relationship
	Able to tolerate affect
	Good response to trial transference interpretation
	High motivation
	Flexible defenses
	Lack of projection, splitting, and denial
Duration	5–40 sessions, usually 5–25
	Longer durations for more seriously ill
Termination	No specific termination date
	Patient is told that treatment will be short

Table from R J Ursano, E K Silberman: Individual psychotherapies. In *The American Psychiatric Press Textbook of Psychiatry*, J A Talbott, R E Hales, and S C Yudofsky, editors, p 865. American Psychiatric Press, Washington DC, 1988, with permission.

to which the patient assigns top priority and that he or she wants to resolve in the treatment); one meaningful or give-and-take relationship during early childhood; the ability to interact flexibly with the evaluator and to express feelings appropriately; above-average psychological sophistication (this implies not only an above-average intelligence but also an ability to respond to interpretations); a specific psychodynamic formulation (this usually means a set of psychological conflicts underlying the patient's difficulties and centering on an oedipal focus); a contract between the therapist and the patient to work on the specified focus and the formulation of minimal expectations of outcome; and good-to-excellent motivation for change and not just for symptom relief.

Requirements and techniques. The treatment can be divided into four major phases: patient–therapist encounter, early therapy, height of the treatment, and evidence of change and termination. The therapist uses the following techniques during these four phases:

Patient–therapist encounter. The therapist establishes a working alliance by using the quick rapport and the positive feelings for the therapist that appear in this phase. Judicious use of open-ended and forced-choice questions enables the therapist to outline and concentrate on a therapeutic focus. The therapist specifies the minimum expectations of outcome to be achieved by the therapy.

Early therapy. In transference, feelings for the therapist are clarified as soon as they appear, leading to the establishment of a true therapeutic alliance.

Height of the treatment. This phase emphasizes active concentration on the oedipal conflicts that have been chosen as the therapeutic focus for this kind of therapy; repeated use of anxiety-provoking questions and confrontations; avoidance of pregenital characterological issues, which the patient uses defensively to avoid dealing with the therapist's anxiety-provoking techniques; avoidance at all costs of a transference neurosis; repetitive demonstration to the patient of his or her neurotic ways or maladaptive patterns of behavior; concentration on the anxiety-laden material, even before the defense mechanisms have been clarified; repeated demonstrations of parent–transference links by the use of properly timed interpretations based on material given by the patient; establishment of a corrective emotional experience; encouragement and support of the patient, who becomes anxious while struggling to understand his or her conflicts; new learning and problem-solving patterns; and repeated presentations and recapitulations of the patient's psychodynamics until the defense mechanisms used in dealing with oedipal conflicts are understood.

Evidence of change and termination of psychotherapy. This phase emphasizes the tangible demonstration of change in the patient's behavior outside the therapy, evidence that more adaptive patterns of behavior are being used, and initiation of talk about terminating the treatment.

Table 29.2-5 summarizes features of the Sifneos short-term anxiety-provoking psychotherapy.

Outcome

The techniques that all these kinds of brief psychotherapy share far outdistance their differences. They include the therapeutic alliance or dynamic interaction between the therapist and the patient, the use of transference, the active interpretation of a therapeutic focus or central issue, the repetitive links between parental and transference issues, and the early termination of the therapy.

More than in any other form of psychotherapy, the outcomes of these brief treatments have been investigated extensively. Contrary to prevailing ideas that the therapeutic factors in psychotherapy are nonspecific, controlled studies and other assessment methods (e.g., interviews with unbiased evaluators, patients' self-evaluations) point to the importance of the specific techniques used. Malan summarized the results in five major generalizations: (1) The capacity for genuine recovery in certain patients is far greater than was thought. (2) A certain type of patient receiving brief psychotherapy can benefit greatly from a practical working through of his or her nuclear conflict in the transference. (3) Such patients can be recognized in advance through a process of dynamic interaction, because they are responsive and motivated and able to face disturbing feelings to live independently of therapy, and a circumscribed focus can be formulated for them. (4) The more radical the technique is in terms of transference, depth of interpretation, and the link to childhood, the more radical the therapeutic effects will be. (5) For some dis-

Table 29.2-5
Sifneos: Short-Term Anxiety-Provoking Psychotherapy

Goal	Resolution of oedipal conflict
Selection criteria	Above-average intelligence
	At least one past meaningful relationship
	High motivation
	Specific chief complaint
	Able to interact with evaluator
	Able to express feelings
	Flexible
Duration	A few months
	Average 12–16 sessions
Focus	Oedipal (triangular) conflict
Termination	No specific date given

Table from R J Ursano, E K Silberman: Individual psychotherapies. In *The American Psychiatric Press Textbook of Psychiatry*, J A Talbott, R E Hales, and S C Yudofsky, editors, p 863. American Psychiatric Press, Washington DC, 1988, with permission.

turbed patients a carefully chosen partial focus can be therapeutically effective.

Interpersonal Psychotherapy

A specific type of short-term psychotherapy called interpersonal psychotherapy (IPT), described by Myrna Weissman and Gerald Klerman, is used to treat depression. Therapy consists of 45- to 50-minute sessions held weekly over a three- to four-month period. It is called IPT because interpersonal behavior is emphasized as a cause of depression and as a method of cure. Patients are taught to evaluate realistically their interactions with others and to become aware of how they isolate themselves, which contributes to or aggravates the depression about which they complain. The therapist offers direct advice, aids the patient in making decisions, and helps clarify areas of conflict. Little or no attention is given to the transference. The therapist attempts to be consistently supportive, empathic, and flexible. Studies of IPT have shown that, in selected cases of depression, it compares favorably with drug therapy with antidepressant agents.

Table 29.2-6 summarizes features of IPT.

CRISIS THEORY

A crisis is a response to hazardous events and is experienced as a painful state. Consequently, it tends to mobilize powerful reactions to help the person alleviate the discomfort and return to the state of emotional equilibrium that existed before its onset. If this takes place, the crisis can be overcome, but, in addition, the person learns how to use adaptive reactions. Furthermore, it is possible that, by resolving the crisis, the patient may be in a better state of mind, superior to that before the onset of psychological difficulties. If, however, the patient uses maladaptive reactions, the painful state will intensify, the crisis will deepen, and a regressive deterioration will take place, producing psychiatric symptoms. These symptoms, in turn, may crystallize into a neurotic pattern of behavior that restricts the patient's ability to function freely. At times, however, the situation cannot be stabilized; new maladaptive reactions are introduced; and the consequences can be of catastrophic proportions, leading at times to death by suicide. It is in this sense that psychological crises are painful and may be viewed as turning points for better or for worse.

A crisis is self-limited and can last anywhere from a few hours to weeks. The crisis as such is characterized by an initial phase, in which anxiety and tension rise. This phase is followed by a phase in which problem-solving mechanisms are set in motion. These mechanisms may be successful, depending on whether they are adaptive or maladaptive.

Conservation of energy is another feature of a person in a state of crisis. All the available resources at one's disposal are used for only one purpose—namely, the resolution of the crisis and the diminution of its pain. Such a successful resolution has important mental health implications. The person who has been able to use resources efficiently, either alone or with the help of another person, not only has learned how to deal with the crisis by becoming acquainted with the ways in which to go about resolving it but has also discovered ways to anticipate future trouble and to avoid its recurrence. In this way the crisis resolution has also become a preventive intervention.

Patients during a period of turmoil are receptive to minimal help and obtain meaningful results. All sorts of services, therefore, have been devised for such purposes. Some are open-ended; others limit the time available or the number of sessions.

Crisis theory helps one understand healthy normal people and develop therapeutic tools aimed at preventing future psychological difficulties.

Table 29.2-6
Interpersonal Psychotherapy

Goal	Improvement in current interpersonal skills
Selection criteria	Outpatient, nonbipolar, nonpsychotic depression
Duration	12–16 weeks, usually once-weekly meetings
Technique	Reassurance Clarification of feeling states Improvement of interpersonal communication Testing perceptions Development of interpersonal skills Medication

Table from R J Ursano, E K Silberman: Individual psychotherapies. In *The American Psychiatric Press Textbook of Psychiatry*, J A Talbott, R E Hales, and S C Yudofsky, editors, p 868. American Psychiatric Press, Washington DC, 1988, with permission.

Crisis Intervention

Crisis intervention is offered to persons who are incapacitated or severely disturbed by a crisis.

Criteria for selection. The criteria used to select patients are a history of a specifc hazardous situation of recent origin that produced the anxiety, a precipitating event that intensified this anxiety, clear-cut evidence that the patient is in a state of psychological crisis as previously defined, high motivation to overcome the crisis, a potential for making a psychological adjustment equal or superior to the one that existed before the development of the crisis, and a certain degree of psychological sophistication—an ability to recognize psychological reasons for the present predicament.

Requirements and techniques. Crisis intervention deals with persons in the midst of a crisis in which rapidity is of the essence. Therapy is a joint understanding of the psychodynamics involved and an awareness of how they are responsible for the crisis. The participants work together, aiming at resolving the crisis. In addition, the patient, as well as the therapist, actively participates in the treatment.

Techniques include reassurance, suggestion, environmental manipulation, and psychotropic medications and may even be combined with brief hospitalization as part of the treatment plan. All these therapeutic maneuvers are aimed at decreasing the patient's anxiety. The length of crisis intervention varies from one or two sessions to several interviews over a period of one or two months. The technical requirements for crisis intervention involve rapidly establishing a rapport with the patient that is aimed at creating a therapeutic alliance; reviewing the steps that have led to the crisis; understanding the maladaptive reactions that the patient is using to deal with the crisis; focusing only on the crisis; learning to use different and more adaptive ways to deal with crises; avoiding the development of symptoms; using the predominating positive transference feelings for the therapist, so as to transform the work into a learning experience; teaching the patient how to avoid hazardous situations that are likely to produce future crises; and ending the intervention as soon as evidence indicates that the crisis has been resolved and that the patient clearly understands all the steps that led to its development and its resolution.

Outcome. The most striking result of crisis therapy pertains to the patient's ability to become better equipped to avoid or, if necessary, to deal with future hazards. In addition, on the basis of some patients' objective observations, this therapeutic experience has enabled them to attain a level of emotional functioning that is superior to that before the onset of the crisis. In this sense, therefore, one may view crisis intervention as being not only therapeutic but also preventive.

References

Brom D, Kleber R J, Defares P B: Brief psychotherapy for posttraumatic stress disorders. J Consult Clin Psychol *57*: 607, 1989.

Davanloo H: *Basic Principles and Technique of Short Term Dynamic Psychotherapy*. Spectrum, New York, 1978.

Flesenheimer W V, Pollack J: The time limit in brief psychotherapy. Bull Menninger Clin *53*: 44, 1989.

Gillieron E: Setting and motivation in brief psychotherapy. Psychother Psychosom *47*(2): 1987.

Hirschowitz R: Crisis theory: A formulation. Psychiatr Ann *3*: 33, 1973.

Horowitz M: *Personality Styles and Brief Psychotherapy*. Basic Books, New York, 1984.

MacKenzie K R: Recent developments in brief psychotherapy. Hosp Community Psychiatry *39*: 742, 1988.

Malan D: *The Frontier of Brief Psychotherapy*. Plenum, New York, 1976.

Malan D: *A Study of Brief Psychotherapy*. Plenum, New York, 1976.

Mann: *Time Limited Psychotherapy*. Harvard University Press, Cambridge, MA, 1973.

Maxim R E, Hunt D D: Appraisal and coping in the process of patient change during short-term psychotherapy. J Nerv Ment Dis *178*: 235, 1990.

Porter R: *The Role of Learning in Psychotherapy*. Churchill, London, 1968.

Schram P C, Burti, L: Crisis intervention techniques designed to prevent hospitalization. Bull Menninger Clin *50*: 194, 1986.

Sifneos P E: Brief dynamic and crisis therapy. In *Comprehensive Textbook of Psychiatry*, ed 5, H I Kaplan and B J Sadock, editors, p 1562. Williams & Wilkins, Baltimore, 1989.

Sifneos P E: The current status of individual short-term dynamic psychotherapy and its future. Am J Psychother *38*(4): 1984.

Sifneos P E: A historical account of preventive psychiatry in the greater Boston area, 1942–1979. Bibl Psychiatr *160*: 1981.

Sifneos P E: Learning to solve emotional problems: A controlled study of short-term anxiety provoking psychotherapy. In *The Role of Learning in Psychotherapy*, R Porter, editor. Churchill, London, 1968.

Sifneos P E: *Short-Term Dynamic Psychotherapy Evaluation and Technique*, ed 2. Plenum, New York, 1987.

Sifneos P E: *Short-Term Psychotherapy and Emotional-Crisis*. Harvard University Press, Cambridge, MA, 1972.

Sifneos P E, Greenberg W E: Patient management. In *The New Harvard Guide to Psychiatry*. Harvard University Press, Cambridge, MA, 1988.

Sloane R B: *Psychotherapy versus Behavior Therapy*. Harvard University Press, Cambridge, MA, 1975.

29.3 / Group Psychotherapy, Combined Individual and Group Psychotherapy, and Psychodrama

GROUP PSYCHOTHERAPY

Since the beginning of recorded history, the group has been the fundamental social unit. And such organization, cultural anthropologists suggest, may even go back to prehistoric times because it was found that groups were better able to ensure the survival of the species than was solitary man because groups worked for the preservation of the individual. As Sigmund Freud wrote: The group attempts to satisfy the great vital needs, and, in the development of mankind, love of one another in the group represents the beginning of altruism, which is the great civilizing factor. Therein lay its adaptive strength.

Group psychotherapy is a treatment in which carefully selected emotionally ill persons are placed into a group guided by a trained therapist to help one another effect personality change. By using a variety of technical maneuvers and theoretical constructs, the leader uses the group members' interactions to make that change.

Classification

At the present time there are many approaches to the group method of treatment. Many clinicians work within a psychoanalytic frame of reference. Other therapy techniques include transactional group therapy, which was devised by Eric Berne and emphasizes the "here-and-now" interactions among group members; behavioral group therapy, which relies on conditioning techniques based on learning theory; Gestalt group therapy, which was created from the theories of Frederick Perls and enables patients to get in touch with their feelings and express themselves openly and honestly; and client-centered group psychotherapy, which was developed by Carl Rogers and is based on the nonjudgmental expression of feelings among group members. Table 29.3-1 outlines the major group psychotherapy approaches.

Patient Selection

To determine a patient's suitability for group psychotherapy, the therapist needs a great deal of information, which is gathered in a screening interview. The psychiatrist should take a careful psychiatric history and perform a mental status examination to obtain certain dynamic, behavioral, and diagnostic information.

Authority anxiety. Those patients whose primary problem is their relationship to authority and who are extremely anxious in the presence of authority figures may or may not

Table 29.3-1
Comparison of Different Types of Group Psychotherapy

Parameters	Supportive Group Therapy	Analytically Oriented Group Therapy	Psychoanalysis of Groups	Transactional Group Therapy	Behavioral Group Therapy
Frequency	Once a week	1 to 3 times a week	1 to 5 times a week	1 to 3 times a week	1 to 3 times a week
Duration	Up to 6 months	1 to 3+ years	1 to 3+ years	1 to 3 years	Up to 6 months
Primary indications	Psychotic and anxiety disorders	Anxiety disorders, borderline states, personality disorders	Anxiety disorders, personality disorders	Anxiety and psychotic disorders	Phobias, passivity, sexual problems
Individual screening interview	Usually	Always	Always	Usually	Usually
Communication content	Primarily environmental factors	Present and past life situations, intragroup and extragroup relationships	Primarily past life experiences, intragroup relationships	Primarily intragroup relationships; rarely, past history, here and now stressed	Specific symptoms without focus on causality
Transference	Positive transference encouraged to promote improved functioning	Positive and negative transference evoked and analyzed	Transference neurosis evoked and analyzed	Positive relationships fostered, negative feelings analyzed	Positive relationships fostered, no examination of transference
Dreams	Not analyzed	Analyzed frequently	Always analyzed and encouraged	Analyzed rarely	Not used
Dependency	Intragroup dependency encouraged: members rely on leader to great extent	Intragroup dependency encouraged, dependency on leader variable	Intragroup dependency not encouraged, dependency on leader variable	Intragroup dependency encouraged, dependency on leader not encouraged	Intragroup dependency not encouraged; reliance on leader is high
Therapist activity	Strengthen existing defenses, active, give advice	Challenge defenses, active, give advice or personal response	Challenge defenses, passive, give no advice or personal response	Challenge defenses, active, give personal response, rather than advice	Create new defenses, active and directive
Interpretation	No interpretation of unconscious conflict	Interpretation of unconscious conflict	Interpretation of unconscious conflict extensive	Interpretation of current behavioral patterns in the here and now	Not used
Major group processes	Universalization, reality testing	Cohesion; transference, reality testing	Transference, ventilation, catharsis, reality testing	Abreaction, reality testing	Cohesion, reinforcement, conditioning
Socialization outside of group	Encouraged	Generally discouraged	Discouraged	Variable	Discouraged
Goals	Better adaptation to environment	Moderate reconstruction of personality dynamics	Extensive reconstruction of personality dynamics	Alteration of behavior through mechanism of conscious control	Relief of specific psychiatric symptoms

do well in group therapy. However, they often do better in a group setting than in a dyadic (one-to-one) setting because they are more comfortable in a group. Patients with a great deal of authority anxiety may be blocked, anxious, resistant, and unwilling to verbalize thoughts and feelings in an individual setting, generally for fear of censure or disapproval from the therapist. Thus, they may welcome the suggestion of group psychotherapy so as to avoid the scrutiny of the dyadic situation. Conversely, if the patient reacts negatively to the suggestion of group psychotherapy or is openly resistant to the idea, the therapist should consider the possibility of a high degree of peer anxiety.

Peer anxiety. Patients, such as those with borderline and schizoid personality disorders, who have destructive relationships with their peer groups or who have been extremely isolated from peer group contact generally react negatively or more anxiously when placed in a group setting. If such patients can work through their anxiety, however, group therapy can be very beneficial.

Diagnosis. The diagnosis of patients' disorders is important in determining the best therapeutic approach and in evaluating their motivations for treatment, capacities for change, and personality structures' strengths and weaknesses.

There are few contraindications to group therapy. Antisocial patients generally do poorly because they cannot adhere to group standards. Depressed patients do better after they have established a trusting relationship with the therapist. Manic patients are disruptive, but, once under pharmacological control, they do well in the group setting. Patients who are delusional and who may incorporate the group into their delusional system should be excluded, as should patients who pose a physical threat to other members because of uncontrollable aggressive outbursts.

Table 29.3-2 outlines general criteria for the selection of patients for group therapy.

Preparation

Patients who are prepared by the therapist for a group experience tend to continue in treatment longer and report less initial anxiety than do those who are not so prepared. This preparation consists of the therapist's explaining, before the first session, the procedure in as much detail as possible and answering any questions the patient may have.

Structural Organization

Size. Group therapy has been successful with as few as 3 members and as many as 15, but most therapists consider 8 to 10 members the optimal size. With fewer members there may not be enough interaction, unless they are especially verbal. But with a larger group the interaction may be too great for the members or the therapist to follow.

Frequency of sessions. Most group psychotherapists conduct group sessions once weekly. It is important to maintain continuity in sessions. When alternate sessions are used, the group meets twice a week, once with and once without the therapist.

Length of sessions. In general, group sessions last anywhere from one to two hours, but the time limit set should be constant.

Time-extended therapy (marathon group therapy) is a method in which the group meets continuously for 12 to 72 hours. Enforced interactional proximity and, during the longer time-extended sessions, sleep deprivation break down certain ego defenses, release affective processes, and promote more open communication. However, time-extended groups may be dangerous for patients with weak ego structures, such as schizophrenic or borderline personality disorder patients. Marathon groups were most popular in the 1970s but are much less often used today.

Homogenous versus heterogeneous groups. In general, most therapists believe that the group should be as heterogeneous as possible to ensure maximum interaction. Thus, the group should be composed of members from different diagnostic categories and with varied behavioral patterns; from all races, social levels, and educational backgrounds; and of varying ages and both sexes.

In general, patients between ages 20 and 65 can be effectively included in the same group. Age differences aid in the development of parent–child and brother–sister models. Moreover, patients have the opportunity to relive and rectify interpersonal difficulties that may have appeared insurmountable.

Both children and adolescents are best treated in groups composed mostly of patients of their own age group. Some adolescent patients are quite capable of assimilating the material of the adult group, regardless of content, but they should not be deprived of a constructive peer experience that they may otherwise not have.

Open versus closed groups. Some groups have a set number and composition of patients. If members leave, no new members are taken on; this is termed a closed group. An open group is one in which there is more fluidity of membership; new members are taken on whenever old members leave.

Table 29.3-3 summarizes some of the critical tasks that a group therapist must accomplish.

Table 29.3-2
General Membership Criteria for Group Therapy

Inclusion criteria

- ability to perform the group task
- problem areas compatible with goals of group
- motivation to change

Exclusion criteria

- marked incompatibility with group norms for acceptable behavior
- inability to tolerate group setting
- severe incompatibility with one or more of the other members
- tendency to assume deviant role

Table from S Vinogradov, I D Yalom: Group therapy. In *The American Psychiatric Press Textbook of Psychiatry,* J A Talbott, R E Hales, and S C Yudofsky, editors, p 956. American Psychiatric Press, Washington DC, 1988, with permission.

Table 29.3-3
Therapist's Basic Tasks in Group Therapy

1. The decision to establish a therapy group:
   (a) determine setting and size of the group
   (b) choose frequency and length of group sessions
   (c) decide on open versus closed group
   (d) select a cotherapist for the group
   (e) formulate policy on group therapy with other therapeutic modalities
2. The act of creating a therapy group:
   (a) formulate appropriate goals
   (b) select patients who can perform the group task
   (c) prepare patients for group therapy
3. The construction and maintenance of a therapeutic environment:
   (a) build the culture of the group explicitly and implicitly
   (b) identify and resolve common problems (membership turnover, subgrouping, conflict)

Table from S Vinogradov, I D Yalom: Group therapy. In *The American Psychiatric Press Textbook of Psychiatry,* J A Talbott, R E Hales, and S C Yudofsky, editors, p 964. American Psychiatric Press, Washington DC, 1988, with permission.

Mechanisms

Group formation. Each patient approaches the group differently, and in this sense the group is a microcosm. Patients use typical adaptive abilities, defense mechanisms, and ways of relating, which are ultimately reflected back to them by the group, thus allowing them to become introspective about their personality functioning. But a process inherent in group formation requires that the patients suspend their previous ways of coping. In entering the group, they allow their executive ego functions—reality testing, adaptation to and mastery of the environment, and perception—to be assumed to some degree by the collective assessment provided by the total membership, including the leader.

Therapeutic factors. Table 29.3-4 outlines 20 significant therapeutic factors that account for change in group psychotherapy. Table 29.3-5 summarizes the forces that shape learning and change secondary to the nature of the group as a social microcosm.

Role of the Therapist

Although opinions differ regarding how active or passive the therapist should be, it is generally agreed that the therapist's role is primarily a facilitative one. Ideally, the group members themselves are the primary source of cure and change.

The climate produced by the therapist's personality is a potent agent of change. The therapist is more than an expert applying techniques; the therapist exerts a personal influence that taps such variables as empathy, warmth, and respect.

Inpatient Group Psychotherapy

Group therapy is also an important part of the hospitalized patient's therapeutic experience. Groups may be organized on a ward in a variety of ways: An entire inpatient unit, known as a community meeting, can meet with all staff members (e.g., psychiatrists, psychologists, nurses); a group, called a team meeting, can consist of 15 to 20 patients and staff; and a regular or small group composed of 8 to 10 patients may meet with one or two therapists, as in traditional group therapy. Although the goals of each type of group vary, they all have a common purpose: (1) to increase the patients' awareness of themselves through their interactions with the other group members, who provide feedback about their behavior; (2) to provide patients with improved interpersonal and social skills; (3) to help the members adapt to the inpatient setting; and (4) to improve communication between the patients and the staff. In addition, there is a type of group meeting composed of only the inpatient hospital staff that is used to improve communication among the staff members and to provide mutual support and encouragement in their day-to-day work with the patients. The community meeting and the team group are more helpful in dealing with patient treatment problems than they are for providing insight-oriented therapy, which is more the province of the small group therapy meeting.

Tables 29.3-6 and 29.3-7 summarize the goals and techniques for acute inpatient therapy groups.

Group composition. Two key factors of the inpatient group, common to all short-term therapies, are the heterogeneity of its members and the rapid turnover of patients. Outside the hospital, however, the therapist has a larger caseload from which to select patients for group therapy. On the ward the therapist has a limited number of patients from which to draw and is restricted further to those patients who are both willing to participate in and suitable for a small group experience. In certain settings group participation may be mandatory (e.g., substance abuse and alcoholism units). But this is not usually true for a general psychiatry unit, and, in fact, most group experiences are better when the patients themselves choose to enter them.

More sessions are preferable to fewer sessions. During a patient's hospital stay, groups may meet daily, allowing for interactional continuity and the carryover of themes from one session to the next. A new member of the group can quickly be brought up to date, either by the therapist in an orientation meeting or by one of the members. It is not uncommon for a newly admitted patient to have learned many details about the small group program from another patient before actually attending the first session. The less frequently the group sessions are held, the greater is the need for the therapist to structure the group and be active.

Inpatient versus outpatient groups. Although the therapeutic factors that account for change in the small inpatient group are similar to those in the outpatient setting, there are qualitative differences. For example, the relatively high turnover of patients in the inpatient group complicates the process of cohesion. But the fact that all the members of the group are together in the hospital aids this cohesion, as do efforts by the therapist to foster this process, emphasizing other similarities. Sharing of information, universalization, and catharsis are the main therapeutic factors at work in inpatient groups. Although insight is more likely to occur in outpatient groups because of their long-term nature, it is possible within the confines of a single group session for some patients to obtain a new understanding of their psychological makeup. A unique quality of the inpatient group is the contact that patients have outside the regularly scheduled group meetings, which is extensive, as they live together on the same ward. If they verbalize their thoughts and feelings about such contacts in the therapy sessions, this will encourage interpersonal learning. In addition, conflicts between patients or between patients and staff can be anticipated and resolved. Table 29.3-8 lists the differences between inpatient and outpatient groups.

Self-Help Groups

Self-help groups are composed of persons who want to cope with a specific problem or life crisis. Usually organized with a particular task in mind, such groups do not attempt to explore individual psychodynamics in great depth or to change personality functioning significantly. But self-help groups have improved the emotional health and well-being of many people.

A distinguishing characteristic of the self-help group is its homogeneity. The members suffer from the same disorders, and they share their experiences—good and bad, successful and unsuccessful—with one another. By so doing, they educate one another, provide mutual support, and alleviate the sense of alienation that is usually felt by the person drawn to this type of group.

Self-help groups emphasize cohesion, which is excep-

Table 29.3-4
Twenty Therapeutic Factors in Group Psychotherapy

Factor	Definition
Abreaction	A process by which repressed material, particularly a painful experience or conflict, is brought back to consciousness. In the process, the person not only recalls but relives the material, which is accompanied by the appropriate emotional response; insight usually results from the experience.
Acceptance	The feeling of being accepted by other members of the group; differences of opinion are tolerated, and there is an absence of censure.
Altruism	The act of one member's being of help to another; putting another person's need before one's own and learning that there is value in giving to others. The term was originated by Auguste Comte (1798–1857), and Sigmund Freud believed it was a major factor in establishing group cohesion and community feeling.
Catharsis	The expression of ideas, thoughts, and suppressed material that is accompanied by an emotional response that produces a state of relief in the patient.
Cohesion	The sense that the group is working together toward a common goal; also referred to as a sense of "we-ness"; believed to be the most important factor related to positive therapeutic effects.
Consensual validation	Confirmation of reality by comparing one's own conceptualizations with those of other group members; interpersonal distortions are thereby corrected. The term was introduced by Harry Stack Sullivan; Trigant Burrow had used the phrase "consensual observation" to refer to the same phenomenon.
Contagion	The process in which the expression of emotion by one member stimulates the awareness of a similar emotion in another member.
Corrective familial experience	The group re-creates the family of origin for some members who can work through original conflicts psychologically through group interaction (e.g., sibling rivalry, anger toward parents).
Empathy	The capacity of a group member to put himself or herself into the psychological frame of reference of another group member and thereby understand his or her thinking, feeling, or behavior.
Identification	An unconscious defense mechanism in which the person incorporates the characteristics and qualities of another person or object into his or her ego system
Imitation	The conscious emulation or modeling of one's behavior after that of another (also called role modeling); also known as spectator therapy, as one patient learns from another.
Insight	Conscious awareness and understanding of one's own psychodynamics and symptoms of maladaptive behavior. Most therapists distinguish two types: (1) intellectual insight—knowledge and awareness without any changes in maladaptive behavior; (2) emotional insight—awareness and understanding leading to positive changes in personality and behavior.
Inspiration	The process of imparting a sense of optimism to group members; the ability to recognize that one has the capacity to overcome problems; also known as instillation of hope.
Interaction	The free and open exchange of ideas and feelings among group members; effective interaction is emotionally charged.
Interpretation	The process during which the group leader formulates the meaning or significance of a patient's resistance, defenses, and symbols; the result is that the patient has a cognitive framework within which to understand his or her behavior.
Learning	Patients acquire knowledge about new areas, such as social skills and sexual behavior; they receive advice, obtain guidance, and attempt to influence and are influenced by other group members.
Reality testing	Ability of the person to evaluate objectively the world outside the self; includes the capacity to perceive oneself and other group members accurately. See also Consensual validation.
Transference	Projection of feelings, thoughts, and wishes onto the therapist, who has come to represent an object from the patient's past. Such reactions, while perhaps appropriate for the condition prevailing in the patient's earlier life, are inappropriate and anachronistic when applied to the therapist in the present. Patients in the group may also direct such feelings toward one another, a process called multiple transferences.
Universalization	The awareness of the patient that he or she is not alone in having problems; others share similar complaints or difficulties in learning; the patient is not unique.
Ventilation	The expression of suppressed feelings, ideas, or events to other group members; the sharing of personal secrets that ameliorate a sense of sin or guilt (also referred to as self-disclosure).

Table by Benjamin J. Sadock, M.D.

Table 29.3-5
Learning from Behavioral Patterns in the Social Microcosm of the Therapy Group

Display of interpersonal pathology
↓
Feedback and self-observation
↓
Sharing reactions
↓
Examining the results of sharing reactions
↓
Understanding one's opinion of self
↓
Developing a sense of responsibility
↓
Realizing one's power to effect change
↓
High affect potentiates change

Table from S Vinogradov, I D Yalom: Group therapy. In *The American Psychiatric Press Textbook of Psychiatry,* J A Talbott, R E Hales, and S C Yudofsky, editors, p 962. American Psychiatric Press, Washington DC, 1988, with permission.

Table 29.3-6
Goals for Acute Inpatient Therapy Groups

1. Engaging patients in the therapeutic process
2. Teaching patients that talking helps
3. Problem spotting
4. Decreasing isolation
5. Allowing patients to be helpful
6. Alleviating hospital-related anxiety

Table from S Vinogradov, I D Yalom: Group therapy. In *The American Psychiatric Press Textbook of Psychiatry,* J A Talbott, R E Hales, and S C Yudofsky, editors, p 980. American Psychiatric Press, Washington DC, 1988, with permission.

Table 29.3-7
Techniques for Acute Inpatient Therapy Groups

1. Use a shortened time frame.
2. Show direct support.
3. Emphasize the here and now.
4. Provide structure.

Table from S Vinogradov, I D Yalom: Group therapy. In *The American Psychiatric Press Textbook of Psychiatry,* J A Talbott, R E Hales, and S C Yudofsky, editors, p 981. American Psychiatric Press, Washington DC, 1988, with permission.

tionally strong in these groups. Because of the group members' similar problems and symptoms, a strong emotional bond and the group's own characteristics develop, to which magical qualities of healing may be attributed. Examples of self-help groups are Alcoholics Anonymous (AA), Gamblers Anonymous (GA), and Overeaters Anonymous (OA).

The self-help group movement is in its ascendency. The groups meet their members' needs by providing acceptance, mutual support, and help in overcoming maladaptive patterns of behavior or states of feeling with which traditional mental health and medical professionals have not been generally successful. Self-help groups and therapy

Table 29.3-8
Differences Between Outpatient and Inpatient Groups

Outpatient Groups	Inpatient Groups
1. Stable composition	Rarely the same group for more than one or two meetings
2. Patients well selected and prepared	Patients admitted to the group with little prior selection or preparation
3. Group is homogeneous regarding ego function, although conflicts and issues differ	Heterogeneous level of ego functioning
4. Motivated, self-referred patients; growth-oriented	Ambivalent, often compulsory patients in crisis; relief-oriented
5. Treatment proceeds as long as required; 1 to 2 years; 50 to 100 meetings	Treatment limited to the hospitalization period; 1 to 3 weeks, with rapid patient turnover
6. Boundary of group well maintained with few external influences	Continuous boundary interface with the milieu
7. Group cohesion develops normally, given sufficient time in treatment	No time for cohesion to develop spontaneously; group development aborted at early phases
8. Therapy is private and unexposed	Exposed, open to observation and scrutiny by the milieu
9. Leader allows the process to unfold; there is ample time to set group norms	Group leader's structuring of the group is critical; passive analytic approaches lead to group disintegration
10. No extra group contact encouraged	Patients sleep, eat, and live together outside the group; extra group contact endorsed

Table from M Leszcz: Inpatient groups, Ann Rev Psychiatry 5: 729, 1986, with permission.

groups have begun to converge: The self-help groups have enabled their members to give up a pattern of unwanted behavior; the therapy groups also help their members understand why and how they got to be the way they were or are.

COMBINED INDIVIDUAL AND GROUP PSYCHOTHERAPY

In combined individual and group psychotherapy, patients are seen individually by the therapist and also take part in group sessions. The therapist for the group and the individual sessions is usually the same.

Groups can vary in size from 3 to 15 members, but the best size is 8 to 10. It is important that patients attend all group sessions. Attendance at individual sessions is also important, and the failure to attend either group or individual sessions should be examined as part of the therapeutic process.

Combined therapy is a particular treatment modality. It is not a system by which individual therapy is augmented by an occasional group session, nor does it mean that a participant in group therapy meets alone with the therapist from time to time. Rather, it is an ongoing plan in which the group experience interacts meaningfully with the individual sessions and in which there is reciprocal feedback that helps form an integrated therapeutic experience. Although the one-to-one doctor-patient relationship enables a deep examination of the transference reaction for some patients, it may not provide the corrective emotional experiences necessary for therapeutic change for others. The group gives patients a variety of persons with whom they can have transferential reactions. In the microcosm of the group, patients can relive and work through familial and other important influences.

Techniques

Various techniques based on different theoretical frameworks have been used in the combined therapy format. Some clinicians increase the frequency of the individual sessions to encourage the emergence of the transference neurosis. In the behavioral model, individual sessions are regularly scheduled but tend to be less frequent. Depending on the therapist's orientation, during the individual sessions the patient may use a couch or a chair. Techniques such as alternate meetings may be used in the group setting. Harold Kaplan and Benjamin Sadock developed a combined therapy approach called structured interactional group psychotherapy, in which a different member is the focus at each weekly group session and is discussed in some depth by the other members.

Results

Most workers in the field believe that combined therapy has the advantages of both the dyadic setting and the group setting, without sacrificing the qualities of either. Generally, the dropout rate in combined therapy is lower than that of group therapy alone. In many cases combined therapy appears to bring problems to the surface and to resolve them more quickly than may be possible with either method alone.

PSYCHODRAMA

Psychodrama is a method of group psychotherapy originated by the Viennese-born psychiatrist Jacob Moreno in which personality makeup, interpersonal relationships, conflicts, and emotional problems are explored by means of special dramatic methods. The therapeutic dramatization of emotional problems includes (1) the protagonist or patient, the person who acts out problems with the help of (2) auxiliary egos, persons who enact different aspects of the patient, and (3) the director, psychodramatist, or therapist, the person who guides those in the drama toward the acquisition of insight.

Roles

Director. The director is the leader or therapist and so must be active and participating. He or she encourages the members of the group to be spontaneous and so has a catalytic function. The director must also be available to meet the group's needs and not superimpose his or her values on it. Of all the group psychotherapies, psychodrama requires of the therapist the most participation and ability to lead.

Protagonist. The protagonist is the patient in conflict. The patient chooses the situation to portray in the dramatic scene, or the therapist may choose it if the patient so desires.

Auxiliary ego. An auxiliary ego is another group member who represents something or someone in the protagonist's experience. The auxiliary egos help account for the great range of therapeutic effects available in psychodrama.

Group. The members of the psychodrama and the audience make up the group. Some are participants, and others are observers, but all benefit from the experience to the extent that they can identify with the ongoing events. The concept of spontaneity in psychodrama refers to the ability of each member of the group, especially the protagonist, to experience the thoughts and feelings of the moment and to communicate emotion as authentically as possible.

Techniques

The psychodrama may focus on any special area of functioning (a dream, a family, or a community situation), a symbolic role, an unconscious attitude, or an imagined future situation. Such symptoms as delusions and hallucinations can also be acted out. Techniques to advance the therapeutic process, productivity, and creativity include the soliloquy (a recital of overt and hidden thoughts and feelings), role reversal (the exchange of the patient's role for the role of a significant person), the double (an auxiliary ego acting as the patient), the multiple double (several egos acting as the patient did on different occasions), and the mirror technique (an ego imitating the patient and speaking for him or her). Other modifying techniques include the use of hypnosis or psychoactive drugs to modify the acting behavior in various ways.

References

Amaranto E A, Bender S S: Individual psychotherapy as an adjunct to group psychotherapy. Int J Group Psychother *40*: 91, 1990.

American Psychiatric Association: *Task Force Report on Encounter Groups and Psychiatry*. American Psychiatric Association, Washington, DC, 1970.

Bloch S, Crouch E: *Therapeutic Factors in Group Psychotherapy*. Oxford University Press, New York, 1985.

Budman S H, Demby A, Feldstein M, Gold M: The effects of time-limited group psychotherapy: A controlled study. Int J Group Psychother *34*: 587, 1987.

Cartwright D, Zander A, eds.: *Group Dynamics and Research Theory*. Harper & Row, New York, 1960.

Dies R R: Clinical application of research instruments: Editor's introduction. Int J Group Psychother *37*: 31, 1987.

Erickson R C: *Inpatient Small Group Psychotherapy*. Charles C Thomas, Springfield, IL, 1984.

Freud S: *Group Psychology and Analysis of the Ego*. Hogarth Press, London, 1962.

Grotjohn M, Freedman C T H, eds.: *Handbook of Group Therapy*. Von Nostrand Reinhold, New York, 1983.

Hisli N: Effect of patient's evaluation of group behavior on therapy outcome. Int J Group Psychother *37*: 119, 1987.

Kaplan H I, Sadock B J, eds.: *Comprehensive Group Psychotherapy*, ed 2. Williams & Wilkins, Baltimore, 1983.

Klein R H, Brown S L: Large-group processes and the patient-staff community meeting. Int J Group Psychother *37*: 219, 1987.

Kofoed L, MacMillan J: Darwinian evolution of social behavior: Implications for group psychotherapy. Psychiatry *52*: 475, 1989.

Leszcz M: In inpatient groups. In *Psychiatry Update: Volume 5*, A J Frances and R E Aoles, editors, p 729. American Psychiatric Press, Washington, DC, 1986.
Lieberman M A: Effects of large group awareness training on participants' psychiatric status. Am J Psychiatry *144*: 460, 1987.
Lieberman M A, Berman L: *Self-Help Groups for Coping with Crisis: Origins, Members, Processes and Import*. Jossey-Bass, San Francisco, 1979.
Moreno J L: *Psychodrama*. Beacon Press, Beacon, NY, 1947.
O'Brien C P: Group therapy for schizophrenia: A practical approach. Schizophr Bull *13*: 119, 1975.
Olsen P A, Barth P A: New uses of psychodrama. Operational Psychiatry *14*: 95, 1983.
Ormont L: The leader's role in dealing with aggression in group. Int J Group Psychother *34*: 553, 1984.
Pilkonis P A, Imber S D, Lewis P, Rubinsky P: A comparative outcome study of individual, group and conjoint psychotherapy. Arch Gen Psychiatry *41*: 431, 1984.
Piper W E, Perrault E L: Pretherapy preparation for group members. Int J Group Psychother *39*: 17, 1989.
Rose S D: Coping skill training in groups. Int J Group Psychother *39*: 59, 1989.
Sadock B J: Group psychotherapy, combined individual and group psychotherapy, and psychodrama. In *Comprehensive Textbook of Psychiatry*, ed 5, H I Kaplan and B J Sadock, editors, p 1517. Williams & Wilkins, Baltimore, 1989.
Soldz S, Budman S, Demby A, Feldstein M: Patient activity and outcome in group psychotherapy: New findings. Int J Group Psychother *40*: 53, 1990.
Weiner M F: *Techniques of Group Psychotherapy*. American Psychiatric Press, Washington, DC, 1984.
Wolf A, Schwartz M: *Psychoanalysis in Groups*. Grune & Stratton, New York, 1962.
Yalom I: *The Theory and Practice of Group Psychotherapy*, ed 3, Basic Books, New York, 1985.

29.4 / Family Therapy and Marital Therapy

FAMILY THERAPY

Family therapy is often thought of as a therapeutic modality to be employed when overt conflict is recognized in members of the same family and requires psychotherapeutic intervention. This commonsense view of the scope of family therapy is too limited. For the general psychiatrist, family therapy is not just one among many types of treatment that can be conceptualized more or less on the same level but an approach to treatment derived from an overriding view of psychiatric disturbance in its interpersonal context that finds very general usage in psychiatric evaluation and treatment. Family workup and treatment are a major modality in the armamentarium of the general psychiatrist, one that should form part of the amalgam of specific treatment strategies for the vast majority of psychiatric patients.

Despite differences in specific models, what is unique to family therapy is its family orientation. All the members of the family are interrelated, and so one part of the family cannot be isolated from the rest. A family's structure and organization, therefore, must be viewed as a unit and are important in determining the behavior of the individual family members. Modern-day family therapy originated with the pioneering work of the American psychiatrist Nathan Ackerman.

Initial Consultation

Family therapy is well-enough known that families with a high level of conflict may request it specifically. When the initial complaint is about an individual family member, however, pretreatment work may be necessary. Typical fears underlying resistance to a family approach are fears (1) by parents that they will be blamed for their child's difficulties, (2) that the entire family will be pronounced sick, (3) that a spouse will object, and (4) that open discussion of one child's misbehavior will have a negative influence on younger siblings. Refusal by an adolescent or young adult patient to participate in family therapy is frequently a disguised collusion with the fears of one or both parents.

Interview Technique

The special quality of the family interview proceeds from two important facts: (1) The family comes to treatment with its history and dynamics firmly in place. To the family therapist, it is this established nature of the group, more than the symptoms, that constitutes the clinical problem. (2) Family members usually live together and, at some level, depend on one another for physical and emotional well-being. Whatever transpires in the therapy session is known to all. Central principles of technique derive from these facts. For example, the catharsis of anger by one family member toward another must be carefully channeled by the therapist. The person who is the object of the anger is present and will react to the attack, running the danger of escalation toward violence, fractured relationships, or withdrawal from therapy. Free association is likewise not appropriate because it would encourage one person to dominate the session. For these reasons the family interview must always be controlled and directed by the therapist.

Frequency and Length of Treatment

Unless an emergency arises, sessions are usually held no more than once a week. Each session, however, may require as much as two hours. Long sessions can include an intermission to give the therapist time to organize the material and plan a response. A flexible schedule is necessary when geography or personal circumstances make it physically difficult for the family to get together. The length of treatment depends not only on the nature of the problem but also on the therapeutic model. Therapists who use problem-solving models exclusively may accomplish their goals in a few sessions: therapists using growth-oriented models, however, may work with a family for years, with sessions at long intervals.

Models of Intervention

Psychodynamic-experiential models. Psychodynamic-experiential models emphasize individual maturation in the context of the family system, free from unconscious patterns of anxiety and projection rooted in the past. Therapists seek to establish an intimate bond with each family member, alternating between their exchanges with the members and the members' exchanges with one another. Clarity of communication and honestly admitted feelings are given high priority; toward this end, family members may be encouraged to change their seats, to touch one another, and to make direct eye contact. Their use of metaphor, body language, and parapraxes helps reveal the unconscious pattern of family relationships. The therapist may also use *family sculpting*, in which family members physically arrange one another in tableaus depicting their personal view of relationships, past or present. The therapist both interprets the sculpture and modifies it in a way to suggest new relationships. In addition, the therapist's subjective responses to the family are given great importance. At appropriate moments they are expressed to the family to form yet another feedback loop of self-observation and change.

Bowen model. Murray Bowen calls his model simply "family systems," but in the field it has rightfully been given the name of its originator. Its hallmark is personal differentiation from the family of origin, the ability to be one's true self in the face of the familial or other pressures that threaten the loss of love or social position. The problem family is assessed on two levels: (1) the degree of their enmeshment versus the degree of their ability to differentiate and (2) the analysis of emotional triangles in the presenting problem. An *emotional triangle* is defined as a three-party system (of which there can be many within a family) arranged so that the closeness of two members tends to exclude a third. The closeness may be expressed as either love or repetitive conflict. In either case, emotional cross-currents are activated when the excluded third party attempts to join with one of the others or when one of the involved parties shifts in the direction of the excluded one. The role of the therapist is, first, to stabilize or shift the hot triangle—the one that relates to the presenting symptoms—and, second, to work with the most psychologically available family members, individually if necessary, on achieving enough personal differentiation so that the hot triangle does not recur. To stay neutral in their triangles, the therapist minimizes emotional contact with family members. Bowen originated the *genogram*, which is a historical survey of the family going back several generations.

Structural model. In a structural model the family is viewed as a single interrelated system assessed along the following lines: (1) significant alliances and splits among family members, (2) hierarchy of power (i.e., the parents in charge of the children), (3) the clarity and firmness of boundaries between the generations, and (4) the family's tolerance of one another. The structural model uses concurrent individual and family therapy.

General systems model. Based on general systems theory, a general systems model holds that the family is a system and that every action in the family produces a reaction in one or more of its members. Every member is presumed to play a role (e.g., spokesperson, persecutor, victim, rescuer, symptom bearer, nurturer), which is relatively stable; however, the member who fills each role may change. Some families try to scapegoat one member by blaming him or her for the family's problems (identified patient). If the identified patient improves, another scapegoated family member may be found. The family is defined as having external boundaries and internal rules. The general systems model overlaps with some of the other models presented, particularly the Bowen and structural models.

An overview of family therapy models, techniques, and goals is given in Table 29.4-1.

Recent Modifications

Family group therapy. Family group therapy combines several families into a single group. Mutual problems are shared, and families compare their interactions with those of the other families in the group. Multiple family groups (MFGs) have been used quite effectively in the treatment of schizophrenia. Parents of disturbed children may also be gathered together to share their situations.

Social network therapy. Social network therapy gathers together the social community or network of a disturbed patient, all of whom meet in group sessions with the patient. The network includes those persons with whom the patient comes into contact in daily life, not only his or her immediate family but also relatives, friends, tradespeople, teachers, and coworkers.

Paradoxical therapy. This approach, which evolved from the work of Gregory Bateson, consists of suggesting that the patient intentionally engage in the unwanted behavior (called the paradoxical injunction), such as avoiding the phobic object or performing the compulsive ritual. Although paradoxical therapy and the use of paradoxical injunctions are relatively new, the therapy may create new insights for some patients. The danger of the approach is that it may be used in an arbitrary or routinized fashion.

Positive connotation. Positive connotation or reframing is a relabeling of all negatively expressed feelings or behavior as positive. The therapist attempts to get family members to view behavior from a new frame of reference—for example, "This child is impossible" becomes "This child is desperately trying to distract and protect you from what he or she perceives is an unhappy marriage."

Goals

The goals of treatment are (1) to resolve or reduce pathogenic conflict and anxiety within the matrix of interpersonal relationships, (2) to enhance the perception and fulfillment by family members of one another's emotional needs, (3) to promote more appropriate role relations between the sexes and between the generations, (4) to strengthen the capacity of individual members and the family as a whole to cope with destructive forces inside and outside the surrounding environment, and (5) to influence family identity and values so that members are oriented toward health and growth.

A final goal is to integrate the family into the larger systems in the society, which include not only the extended family but also society—as represented by such systems as schools, medical facilities, and social, recreational, and welfare agencies—so that the family is not isolated.

MARITAL THERAPY

Marital therapy is a form of psychotherapy designed to psychologically modify the interaction of two people who are in conflict with each other over one parameter or a variety of parameters—social, emotional, sexual, economic. In marital therapy a trained person establishes a therapeutic contract with the patient-couple and, through definite types of communication, attempts to alleviate the disturbance, to reverse or change maladaptive patterns of behavior, and to encourage personality growth and development.

Marriage counseling may be considered more limited in scope than marital therapy in that only a particular

Table 29.4-1
Major Models of Family Therapy: Normality, Dysfunction, and Therapeutic Goals

Model of Family Therapy	View of Normal Family Functioning	View of Dysfunction and Symptoms	Goals of Therapy
Structural Minuchin Montaivo Aponte	1. Boundaries clear and firm 2. Hierarchy with strong parental subsystem 3. Flexibility of system for (a) autonomy and interdependence (b) individual growth and system maintenance (c) continuity, and adaptive restructuring in response to changing internal (developmental) and external (environmental) demands	Symptoms result from current family structural imbalance: (a) malfunctioning hierarchical arrangement, boundaries (b) maladaptive reaction to changing requirements (developmental, environmental)	Reorganize family structure: (a) shift member's relative positions to disrupt malfunctioning pattern and strengthen parental hierarchy (b) create clear, flexible boundaries (c) mobilize more adaptive alternative patterns
Strategic Haley Milan team Palo Alto group	1. Flexibility 2. Large behavioral repertoire for (a) problem resolution (b) life-cycle passage 3. clear rules governing hierarchy (Haley)	Multiple origins of problems; symptoms maintained by family's (a) unsuccessful problem-solving attempts (b) inability to adjust to life-cycle transitions (Haley) (c) malfunctioning hierarchy: triangle or coalition across hierarchy (Haley) Symptom is a communicative act embedded in interaction pattern	Resolve presenting problem only: specific behaviorally defined objectives Interrupt rigid feedback cycle: change symptom-maintaining sequency to new outcome Define clearer hierarchy (Haley)
Behavioral-social exchange Liberman Patterson Alexander	1. Maladaptive behavior is not reinforced 2. Adaptive behavior is rewarded 3. Exchange of benefits outweighs costs 4. Long-term reciprocity	Maladaptive, symptomatic behavior reinforced by (a) family attention and reward (b) deficient reward exchanges (e.g., coercive) (c) communication deficit	Concrete, observable behavioral goals: change contingencies of social reinforcement (interpersonal consequences of behavior) (a) rewards for adaptive behavior (b) no rewards for maladaptive behavior
Psychodynamic Ackerman Boszormenyi–Nagy Framo Lidz Meissner Paul Stierlin	1. Parental personalities and relationships well differentiated 2. Relationship perceptions based on current realities, not projections from past Boszormenyi–Nagy: Relational equitability Lidz: Family task requisites: (a) parental coalition (b) generation boundaries (c) sex-linked parental roles	Symptoms caused by family projection process stemming from unresolved conflicts and losses in family of origin	1. Insight and resolution of family of origin conflict and losses 2. Family projection processes 3. Relationship reconstruction and reunion 4. Individual and family growth
Family systems therapy Bowen	Differentiation of self Intellectual–emotional balance	Functioning impaired by relationships with family of origin: (a) poor differentiation (b) anxiety (reactivity) (c) family projection process (d) triangulation	1. Differentiation 2. Cognitive functioning 3. Emotional reactivity 4. Modification of relationships in family system: (a) detriangulation (b) repair cutoffs

Table 29.4-1
Continued

Model of Family Therapy	View of Normal Family Functioning	View of Dysfunction and Symptoms	Goals of Therapy
Experiential Satir Whitaker	Satir: 1. Self-worth: high 2. Communication: clear, specific, honest 3. Family rules: flexible, human, appropriate 4. Linkage to society: open, hopeful Whitaker: Multiple aspects of family structure and shared experience	Symptoms are nonverbal messages in reaction to current communication dysfunction in system	1. Direct, clear communication 2. Individual and family growth through immediate shared experience

Table from F Walsh: Conceptualizations of normal family functioning. In *Normal Family Processes,* F Walsh, editor. Guilford, New York, 1982, with permission.

familial conflict is discussed. Marriage counseling may also be primarily task-oriented, geared to solving a specific problem, such as child rearing. Marriage therapy emphasizes restructuring the interaction between the couple, sometimes exploring the psychodynamics of each partner. Both therapy and counseling stress helping the marital partners cope more effectively with their problems. Most important is the definition of appropriate and realistic goals, which may involve extensive reconstruction of the union or problem-solving approaches or a combination of both.

Types of Therapy

Individual therapy. In individual therapy the marital partners may be seen by different therapists, who may not necessarily communicate with each other. Indeed, they may not even know each other. The goal of the treatment is to strengthen each partner's adaptive capacities. At times, only one of the partners is in treatment; in such cases, a visit by the spouse who is not in treatment with the therapist may be helpful. The visiting partner may give the therapist data about the patient that may otherwise be overlooked; overt or covert anxiety in the visiting partner as a result of change in the patient can be identified and dealt with; irrational beliefs about treatment events can be corrected; and conscious or unconscious attempts by the partner to sabotage the patient's treatment can be examined.

Individual marital therapy. In individual marital therapy each of the marriage partners is in therapy. When the same therapist conducts the treatment, it is called concurrent therapy; when the partners are seen by different therapists, it is called collaborative therapy.

Conjoint therapy. Conjoint therapy is the treatment of partners in joint sessions conducted by either one or two therapists; it is the treatment method most frequently used in marital therapy. Cotherapy with therapists of both sexes prevents a particular patient from feeling ganged up on when confronted by two members of the opposite sex.

Four-way session. In a four-way session each partner is seen by a different therapist, with regular joint sessions in which all four persons participate. A variation of the four-way session is the round-table interview, developed by William Masters and Virginia Johnson for the rapid treatment of sexually dysfunctional couples. Two patients and two opposite-sex therapists meet regularly. (See Section 20.3 for a discussion of dual-sex therapy.)

Group psychotherapy. Therapy for married couples placed in a group allows a variety of group dynamics to affect the couples. The group usually consists of three to four couples and one or two therapists. The couples identify with one another and recognize that others have similar problems; each gains support and empathy from fellow group members of the same or opposite sex; they explore sexual attitudes and have an opportunity to gain new information from their peer group; and each receives specific feedback about his or her behavior, either negative or positive, that may have more meaning and be better assimilated coming from a neutral nonspouse member.

When only one partner is in a therapy group, the spouse may occasionally visit the group, so as to allow the members to test reality more effectively. At times, a group may be so organized that only one married couple is part of the larger group.

Combined therapy. Combined therapy refers to all or any of the preceding techniques used concurrently or in combination. Thus, a particular patient-couple may begin treatment with one or both partners in individual psychotherapy, continue to conjoint therapy with the partner, and terminate therapy after a course of treatment in a married couples group. The rationale for combined therapy is that no single approach to marital problems has been shown to be superior to another. A familiarity with a variety of approaches thus allows the therapist a degree of flexibility that provides maximum benefit for the couple in distress.

Indications

Regardless of the specific therapeutic technique used, certain indications for initiating marital therapy have been agreed on: (1) when individual therapy has failed to resolve the marital difficulties, (2) when the onset of distress in one or both partners is clearly related to marital events, and (3) when marital therapy is requested by a couple in conflict. Problems in communication between partners are a prime indication for marital therapy. In such instances one spouse may be intimidated by the other, may become anxious when attempting to tell the other about thoughts or feelings, or may project unconscious expectations onto the other. The therapy is geared toward enabling each of the partners to see the other realistically.

Conflicts in one or several areas, such as the partners' sexual life, also are indications for treatment. Similarly, difficulty in establishing satisfactory social, economic, parental, or emotional roles is an indication for help. The clinician should evaluate all aspects of the marital relationship before attempting to treat only one problem, as it may be a symptom of a more pervasive marital disorder.

Contraindications

Contraindications for marital therapy include patients with severe forms of psychosis, particularly patients with paranoid elements and those in whom the marriage's homeostatic mechanism is a protection against psychosis; one or both of the partners really wants to divorce; or one spouse refuses to participate because of anxiety or fear.

Goals

Nathan Ackerman defined the aims of marital therapy as follows: The goals of therapy for marital disorders are to alleviate emotional distress and disability and to promote the levels of well-being of both partners together and each as an individual. In a general way, the therapist moves toward these goals by strengthening the shared resources for problem solving, by encouraging the substitution of more adequate controls and defenses for pathogenic ones, by enhancing both the immunity against the disintegrative effects of emotional upset and the complementarity of the relationship, and by promoting the growth of the relationship and each partner.

Part of the therapeutic task is to persuade each partner in the marriage to take responsibility in understanding the psychodynamic makeup of his or her personality. Accountability for the effects of behavior on one's own life, the life of the spouse, and the lives of others in the environment is emphasized, which often results in a deeper understanding of the problems that created the marital discord.

Marital therapy does not ensure the maintenance of any marriage. Indeed, in certain instances it may show the partners that they are in a nonviable union that should be dissolved. In those cases the couple may continue to meet with the therapist to work through the difficult process of separating and obtaining a divorce. This has been called divorce therapy. See Section 2.5, "Adulthood," for the stages of divorce and the issues that have to be addressed by the couple going through a divorce.

References

Berkowitz D: An overview of the psychodynamics of couples: Bridging concepts. In *Marriage and Divorce: A Contemporary Perspective*, C C Nadelson, D C Polonsky, editors. Guilford, New York, 1984.

Bowen M: *Family Theory in Clinical Practice*. Aronson, New York, 1978.

Brody S: Simultaneous psychotherapy of married couples in current psychiatric therapy. In *Current Psychiatric Therapy*, J Masserman, editor. Grune & Stratton, New York, 1961.

Brown G, Birley J L T, Wing J K: The influence of family life on the course of schizophrenic disorders: A replication. Br J Psychiatry *121*: 241, 1972.

Coyne J C: Strategic therapy with married depressed persons: Initial agenda, themes and interventions. J Mar Fam Ther *10*: 153, 1984.

Crago M A: Psychopathology in married couples. Psychol Bull *77*: 114, 1972.

Dicks H V: *Marital Tensions*. Basic Books, New York, 1967.

DiNicola V F: The child's predicament in families with a mood disorder: Research findings and family interventions. Psychiatr Clin North Am *12*: 933, 1989.

Framo J: Family of origin as a therapeutic response for adults in marital and family therapy: You can and should go home again. Fam Pract *15*: 193, 1976.

Goldstein M, ed.: *New Developments in Interventions with Families of Schizophrenics*. Jossey-Bass, San Francisco, 1981.

Green R J, Framo J L, eds.: *Family Therapy: Major Contributions*. International Universities Press, New York, 1981.

Greene B L, Broadhurst B P, Lustig N: Treatment of marital disharmony. In *Psychotherapy of Marital Disharmony*, B Greene, editor. Free Press, New York, 1965.

Guerin P J, Pendagast E: Evaluation of family systems and genogram. In *Family Therapy Theory and Practice*, P J Guerin, editor, p 450. Gardner Press, New York, 1976.

Houlihan M M, Jackson J, Rogers T R: Decision making of satisfied and dissatisfied married couples. J Soc Psychol *130*: 89, 1990.

Lansky M R: Family therapy. In *Comprehensive Textbook Psychiatry*, ed 5, H I Kaplan and B J Sadock, editors, p 1535. Williams & Wilkins, Baltimore, 1989.

Lansky M R, ed.: *Family Therapy and Major Psychopathology*. Grune & Stratton, New York, 1981.

Lidz T, Fleck S, Cornelison A: *Schizophrenia and the Family*. International Universities Press, New York, 1965.

Main T F: Mutual projection in marriage. Compr Psychiatry *7*: 432, 1966.

Minuchin S: *Families and Family Therapy*. Harvard University Press, Cambridge, MA, 1974.

Mittleman B: Complementary neurotic reactions in intimate relationships. Psychoanal Q *13*: 479, 1944.

Nadelson C, Bassuk E, Hopps C, Boutelle W: The use of videotape in couples therapy. Int J Group Psychother *27*: 241, 1977.

Nadelson C, Polonsky D C: Couples therapy. In *Comprehensive Textbook of Psychiatry*, ed. 5, H I Kaplan and B J Sadock, editors, p 1550. Williams & Wilkins, Baltimore, 1989.

Nadelson C C, Polonsky D C, Mathews M A: Marriage as a developmental process. In *Marriage and Divorce: A Contemporary Perspective*. C C Nadelson, D C Polonsky, editors. Guilford, New York, 1983.

O'Farrell T J: Marital and family therapy in alcoholism treatment. J Subst Abuse Treat *6*: 23, 1989.

O'Leary K D, Beach S R: Marital therapy: A viable treatment for depression and marital discord. Am J Psychiatry *147*: 183, 1990.

Paul N, Grosser G: Operational mourning and its role in conjoint family therapy. Community Ment Health J *1*: 339, 1965.

Pinsof W M: A conceptual framework and methodological criteria for family therapy process research. J Consult Clin Psychol *57*: 53, 1989.

Polonsky D, Nadelson C C: An integrative approach to couples therapy. In *New Clinical Concepts in Marital Therapy*. O J W Bjorksten, editor. American Psychiatric Press, Washington, DC, 1985.

Rioch J: The transference phenomenon in psychoanalytic therapy. Psychiatry *6*: 147, 1943.

Satir V: *Conjoint Family Therapy*. Science & Behavior Books, Palo Alto, CA, 1967.

Scharff D, Scharff J: *Object Relations Family Therapy*. Aronson, New York, 1987.

Snyder D K, Wills R M: Behavioral versus insight-oriented marital therapy: Effects on individual and interspousal functioning. J Consult Clin Psychol *57*: 39, 1989.

Tarrier N: Effect of treating the family to reduce relapse in schizophrenia: A review. J R Soc Med *82*: 423, 1989.

Weddige R L: The hidden psychotherapeutic dilemma: Spouse of the borderline. Am J Psychother *40*: 52, 1986.

Zinner J: The implication of projective identification for marital interaction. In *Contemporary Marriage*, H Grunebaum and J Christ, editors. Little, Brown, Boston, 1976.

29.5 / Biofeedback

Feedback is fundamental to biological adaptation, feedback not only from the environment but also from the body itself. Homeostasis is maintained and neurohumoral behavior is regulated also through feedback loops or servomechanism systems. Biofeedback is a special type of feedback that refers to information provided externally to a person about normal subthreshold biological or physiological processes.

BIOFEEDBACK THEORY

Neal Miller demonstrated the medical potential of biofeedback by showing that the normally involuntary autonomic nervous system can be operantly conditioned, using appropriate feedback. By means of instruments, the patient is given information about the status of certain involuntary biological functions, such as skin temperature and electrical conductivity, muscle tension, blood pressure, heart rate, and brain wave activity. The patient is then taught to regulate one or more of these biological states, which affect symptoms. For example, the ability to raise the temperature of one's hands may be used to reduce the frequency of migraine headaches, palpitations, or angina pectoris. A presumptive mechanism is a lowering of sympathetic activation and a voluntary self-regulation of arterial smooth muscle vasoconstrictive tendencies in predisposed persons.

BIOFEEDBACK METHODS

The type of feedback instrument used depends on the patient and the specific problem. The most effective instruments are the electromyogram (EMG), which measures the electrical potentials of muscle fibers; the electroencephalogram (EEG), which measures alpha waves that occur in relaxed states; the galvanic skin response gauge (GSR), which shows decreased skin conductivity during a relaxed state; and the thermister, which measures skin temperature, which drops during tension because of peripheral vasoconstriction. The patient is attached to one of the measuring instruments, which measures a physiological function and translates the impulse into an audible or visual signal that the patient uses to gauge his or her responses. For example, in the treatment of bruxism, an EMG is attached to the masseter muscle. The EMG emits a high tone when the muscle is contracted and a low tone when at rest. The patient can learn to alter the tone to indicate relaxation. He or she receives feedback about the masseter muscle; the tone reinforces the learning; and the condition ameliorates, all these events interacting synergistically.

Table 29.5-1 outlines some of the important clinical applications of biofeedback. As can be seen in the table, a wide variety of biofeedback modalities have been used to treat numerous conditions. Many less specific clinical applications—such as treating insomnia, dysmenorrhea, and speech problems; improving athletic performance; treating volitional disorders; achieving altered states of consciousness; managing stress; and using biofeedback as an adjunct to psychotherapy for anxiety associated with somatoform disorders—use a model in which frontalis muscle EMG biofeedback is combined with thermal biofeedback and verbal instructions in progressive relaxation.

Table 29.5-1
Biofeedback Applications

Condition	Effects
Asthma	Both frontal EMG and airway resistance biofeedback have been reported as producing relaxation from the panic associated with asthma, as well as improving air flow rate.
Cardiac arrhythmias	Specific biofeedback of the electrocardiogram has permitted patients to lower the frequency of premature ventricular contractions.
Fecal incontinence and enuresis	The timing sequence of internal and external anal sphincters has been measured, using triple lumen rectal catheters providing feedback to incontinent patients in order for them to reestablish normal bowel habits in a relatively small number of biofeedback sessions. An actual precursor of biofeedback dating to 1938 was the sounding of a buzzer for sleeping enuretic children at the first sign of moisture (the pad and bell).
Grand mal epilepsy	A number of EEG biofeedback procedures have been used experimentally to suppress seizure activity prophylactically in patients not responsive to anticonvulsant medication. The procedures permit patients to enhance the sensorimotor brain wave rhythm or to normalize brain activity as computed in real-time power spectrum displays.

Table 29.5-1
Continued

Condition	Effects
Hyperactivity	EEG biofeedback procedures have been used on children with attention-deficit hyperactivity disorder to train them to reduce their motor restlessness.
Idiopathic hypertension and orthostatic hypotension	A variety of specific (direct) and nonspecific biofeedback procedures—including blood pressure feedback, galvanic skin response, and foot-hand thermal feedback combined with relaxation procedures—have been used to teach patients to increase or decrease their blood pressure. Some follow-up data indicate that these changes may persist for years and often permit the reduction or elimination of antihypertensive medications.
Migraine headaches	The most common biofeedback strategy with classic or common vascular headaches has been thermal biofeedback from a digit accompanied by autogenic self-suggestive phrases encouraging hand warming and head cooling. The mechanism is thought to help prevent excessive cerebral artery vasoconstriction, often accompanied by an ischemic prodromal symptom, such as scintillating scotomata, followed by rebound engorgement of arteries and stretching of vessel wall pain receptors.
Myofacial and temporomandibular joint (TMJ) pain	Increased levels of EMG activity over the powerful muscles associated with bilateral temporomandibular joints have been decreased, using biofeedback in patients who are jaw clenchers or demonstrating bruxism.
Neuromuscular rehabilitation	Mechanical devices or an EMG measurement of muscle activity displayed to a patient increases the effectiveness of traditional therapies, as documented by relatively long clinical histories in peripheral nerve–muscle damage, spasmodic torticollis, selected cases of tardive dyskinesia, cerebral palsy, and upper motor neuron hemiplegias.
Raynaud's syndrome	Cold hands and cold feet are frequent concomitants of anxiety and also occur in Raynaud's syndrome, caused by vasospasm of arterial smooth muscle. A number of studies report that thermal feedback from the hand, an inexpensive and benign procedure compared with surgical sympathectomy, is effective in about 70 percent of cases of Raynaud's syndrome.
Tension headaches	Muscle contraction headaches are most frequently treated with two fairly large active electrodes spaced on the forehead to provide visual or auditory information about levels of muscle tension. This frontal electrode placement is sensitive to EMG activity regarding the frontalis and occipital muscles, which the patient learns to relax.

References

Basmajian J V, ed: *Biofeedback: Principles and Practice for Clinicians*. Williams & Wilkins, Baltimore, 1983.

Burgio K L, Engel B T: Biofeedback-assisted behavioral training for elderly men and women. J Am Geriatr Soc *38*: 338, 1990.

Butler F: *Biofeedback: A Survey of the Literature*. Plenum, New York, 1978.

Gaarder K R, Montgomery S: *Clinical Biofeedback: A Procedural Manual for Behavioral Medicine*. Williams & Wilkins, Baltimore, 1981.

Hatch J P, Fisher J G, Rugh J D, eds.: *Biofeedback: Studies in Clinical Efficacy*. Plenum, New York, 1987.

Lisspers J, Ost L G: BVP-biofeedback in the treatment of migraine: The effects of constriction and dilatation during different phases of the migraine attack. Behav Modif *14*: 200, 1990.

Olton D S, Noonberg A R: *Biofeedback: Clinical Applications in Behavioral Medicine*. Prentice-Hall, Englewood Cliffs, NJ, 1980.

Orne M T, ed: *Task Force Report No. 19: Biofeedback*. American Psychiatric Association, Washington, DC, 1980.

Peper E, Ancoli S, Quinn M, eds.: *Mind-Body Integration: Essential Readings in Biofeedback*. Plenum, New York, 1979.

Runck B: *Biofeedback: Issues and Treatment Assessment*. National Institute of Mental Health (DDHS Pub. No. ADM 80-1032), Rockville, MD, 1980.

Stroebel C F, ed: Biofeedback and behavioral medicine and biofeedback in clinical practice. Psychiatr Ann *11*: 1981.

29.6 / Behavior Therapy

The basic assumption of behavior therapy is that change of maladaptive behavior can occur without insight into its underlying causes. Behavioral symptoms are taken at face value and not as manifest symptoms of a deeper problem. The use of behavior therapy to treat mental disorders is of increasing importance. It is based on the principles of learning theory, using classical and operant conditioning techniques. Behavior therapy is directed at specific problems and works best when those problems are clearly delineated and the desired goals are clearly defined.

Clinicians who wish to embrace the behavioral approach must answer the four questions in Table 29.6-1 in conjunction with the patient, relatives, and other care-

Table 29.6-1
Behavior Analysis of Clinical Problems Requires Answers to These Questions

1. What are the problems and goals for therapy?
This question addresses the patient's assets, as well as deficits of adaptive behavior and excesses of maladaptive behavior. Often the patient's problems are related to inappropriate timing or context of behavioral responses. The assessment of problems and formulation of goals must consider the full range of objective, subjective, affective, social, and cognitive responses.
2. How can progress be measured and monitored?
Each problem and goal requires behavioral specification and ongoing monitoring in terms of frequency, duration, form, latency, or context of occurrence. Operationalizing the goals of therapy enables the therapist to determine whether selected interventions are effective and provides the empirical basis for behavior therapy.
3. What environmental contingencies are maintaining the problem?
A behavior analysis considers the functional relations between clinical problems and their environmental antecedents (precipitants or triggering stimuli) and consequences (reinforcers). Before formulating a treatment plan, the therapist must understand the current social and instrumental contingencies that may have to be modified for successful outcome.
4. Which interventions are likely to be effective?
This final question addresses the specific techniques that can be used in the treatment plan. Only after the first three questions are answered can a rational selection of interventions be made. Often, a combination of learning principles is packaged to maximize treatment effects.

Table by Robert Paul Liberman, M.D., and Jeffery Bedell, Ph.D.

takers. These questions are raised repeatedly throughout the course of treatment in recurring cycles—first tentatively and later more definitively as information accrues and progress occurs.

HISTORY

As early as the 1920s, scattered reports began to appear on the application of learning principles to the treatment of behavioral disorders. These reports, however, had little effect on the mainstream of psychiatry or clinical psychology. It was not until the 1960s that behavior therapy emerged as a systematic and comprehensive approach to psychiatric (behavioral) disorders. It is curious that these latter developments arose quite independently of one another and on three different continents. Joseph Wolpe and his colleagues in Johannesburg, South Africa, used largely Pavlovian techniques to produce and eliminate experimental neuroses in cats. From this research Wolpe developed systematic desensitization, the prototype of many current behavioral procedures for the treatment of maladaptive anxiety that is produced by identifiable stimuli in the environment. At about the same time a group at the Institute of Psychiatry of the University of London, particularly H. J. Eysenck and M. B. Shapiro, stressed the importance of an empirical, experimental approach to the understanding and treatment of the individual patient, using own-control, single-case experimental paradigms and modern learning theory. The third origin of behavior therapy was work inspired by the research of Harvard psychologist B. F. Skinner. Skinner's students began to apply his operant-conditioning technology, which was developed in animal-conditioning laboratories, to human beings in clinical settings.

SYSTEMATIC DESENSITIZATION

Systematic desensitization was developed by Joseph Wolpe and is based on the behavioral principle of counterconditioning, which states that a person can overcome maladaptive anxiety elicited by a situation or object by approaching the feared situation gradually and in a psychophysiological state that inhibits anxiety.

In systematic desensitization the patient attains a state of complete relaxation and is then exposed to the stimulus that elicits the anxiety response. The negative reaction of anxiety is then inhibited by the relaxed state, a process called *reciprocal inhibition.*

Rather than use actual situations or objects that elicit fear, the patient and the therapist prepare a graded list or hierarchy of anxiety-provoking scenes associated with the patient's fears. Finally, the learned relaxation state and the anxiety-provoking scenes are systematically paired in the treatment. Thus, systematic desensitization consists of three steps: relaxation training, hierarchy construction, and the desensitization of the stimulus.

Relaxation Training

Relaxation produces physiological effects that are opposite to those of anxiety—that is, slow heart rate, increased peripheral blood flow, and neuromuscular stability. A variety of relaxation methods have been developed, although some, such as yoga and Zen, have been known for centuries.

Most methods of achieving relaxation are based on a method called progressive relaxation. The patient relaxes major muscle groups in a fixed order, beginning with the small muscle groups of the feet and working cephalad or vice versa. Some clinicians use hypnosis to facilitate relaxation or use tape-recorded procedures to allow the patient to practice relaxation on his or her own.

Mental imagery is a relaxation method in which the patient is instructed to imagine himself or herself in a place associated with pleasant relaxed memories. Such images allow the patient to enter a relaxed state or experience or, as H. Benson termed it, the relaxation response.

Hierarchy Construction

When constructing the hierarchy, the clinician determines all the conditions that elicit anxiety and then has the patient create a list or hierarchy of 10 to 12 scenes in order of increasing anxiety. For example, the acrophobic hierarchy may begin with the patient's imagining standing near a window on the second floor and end with being on the roof of a 20-story building, leaning on a guard rail and looking straight down.

Desensitization of the Stimulus

The desensitization is done systematically by having the patient proceed through the list from the least anxiety-provoking scene to the most anxiety-provoking one while in a deeply relaxed state. The rate at which the patient progresses through the list is determined by his or her responses to the stimuli. When the patient can vividly imagine the most anxiety-provoking scene of the hierarchy with equanimity, he or she experiences little anxiety in the corresponding real-life situation.

Adjunctive Use of Drugs

Various drugs have been used to hasten desensitization. The widest experience is with the ultrarapidly acting barbiturate sodium methohexital (Brevital), which is given intranvenously in subanesthetic doses. Usually, up to 60 mg of the drug are given in divided doses in a session. Intranvenous diazepam (Valium) may also be used. If the procedural details are carefully followed, almost all patients find the procedure pleasant, with few unpleasant side effects. The advantages of pharmacological desensitization are that preliminary training in relaxation can be shortened, almost all patients are able to become adequately relaxed, and the treatment itself seems to proceed more rapidly.

Indications for Desensitization

This technique works best when there is a clearly identifiable anxiety-provoking stimulus. Phobias, obsessions, compulsions, and certain sexual disorders have been successfully treated with these techniques.

GRADED EXPOSURE

Graded exposure is similar to systematic desensitization except that relaxation training is not involved and treatment is usually carried out in a real-life context.

FLOODING

Flooding is based on the premise that escaping from an anxiety-provoking experience reinforces the anxiety through conditioning. Thus, by not allowing the person to escape, the clinician can extinguish the anxiety and prevent the conditioned avoidance behavior.

The technique is to encourage the patient to actually confront the feared situation. No relaxation exercises are used, as in systematic desensitization. The patient experiences fear, which gradually subsides after a time. The success of the procedure depends on the patient's remaining in the fear-generating situation until he or she is calm and feeling a sense of mastery. Prematurely withdrawing from the situation or prematurely terminating the fantasized scene is equivalent to an escape, and then both the conditioned anxiety and the avoidance behavior are reinforced, the opposite of what was intended. A variant of flooding is called *implosion*, in which the feared object or situation is confronted only in the imagination, rather than in real life. Many patients refuse flooding because of the psychological discomfort involved. It is also contraindicated in patients for whom intense anxiety would be hazardous (e.g., patients with heart disease or fragile psychological adaptation). These techniques work best with specific phobias.

PARTICIPANT MODELING

Participant modeling refers to having the patient learn by imitation. The patient learns a new behavior primarily by observation, without having to perform the behavior until the patient feels ready. Just as irrational fears may be acquired by learning, they can be unlearned by observing a fearless model confront the feared object. The technique has been useful with phobic children who are placed with other children of their own age and sex who approach the feared object or situation. With adults a therapist may describe the feared activity in a calm manner with which the patient can identify, or the therapist may act out with the patient the process of mastering the feared activity. Sometimes a hierarchy of activities is established, with the least anxiety-provoking activity being dealt with first. The participant-modeling technique has been used successfully with agoraphobia by having a therapist accompany the patient into the feared situation. A variant of this procedure is called *behavior rehearsal*, in which real-life problems are acted out under the therapist's observation or direction. The technique is useful for complex behavioral patterns, such as job interviews and shyness.

ASSERTIVENESS AND SOCIAL SKILLS TRAINING

To be assertive requires that persons have confidence in their judgment and sufficient self-esteem to express their opinions. Assertiveness and social skills training teaches people how to respond appropriately in social situations, to express their opinions in acceptable ways, and to achieve their goals. A variety of techniques—including role modeling, desensitization, and positive reinforcement (reward of desired behavior)—are used to increase assertiveness. Social skills training deals with assertiveness but also attends to a variety of real-life tasks, such as food shopping, looking for work, interacting with other people, and overcoming shyness.

AVERSION THERAPY

When a noxious stimulus (punishment) is presented immediately after a specific behavioral response, the response is eventually inhibited and extinguished. There are many types of noxious stimuli: electric shocks, substances that induce vomiting, corporal punishment, and social disapproval. The negative stimulus is paired with the behavior, which is thereby suppressed. The unwanted behavior

Table 29.6-2
Some Common Clinical Applications of Behavior Therapy

Specific Disorders	Comments
Agoraphobia	Graded exposure and flooding can reduce the fear of being in crowded places. About 60 percent of patients so treated are improved. In some cases, the spouse can serve as the therapist while accompanying the patient into the fear situation; however, there cannot be a secondary gain in which the patient attempts to keep the spouse nearby by displaying symptoms.
Alcoholism	Aversion therapy in which the alcoholic is made to vomit (by adding an emetic to the alcohol) every time a drink is ingested is effective in treating alcoholism. Disulfiram (Antabuse) can be given to alcoholics when they are alcohol-free. Such patients are warned of the severe physiological consequences of drinking (e.g., nausea, vomiting, hypotension, collapse) with disulfiram in the system.
Anorexia nervosa	Observe eating behavior; contingency management; record weight.
Bulimia nervosa	Record bulimic episodes; log of moods
Hyperventilation	Hyperventilation test; controlled breathing; direct observation.
Other phobias	Systematic desensitization has been effective in treating simple phobias, such as fears of heights, animals, and flying. Social skills training has also been used for shyness and fear of other people.
Paraphilias	Electric shocks or other noxious stimuli can be applied at the time of a paraphilic impulse, and eventually the impulse subsides. Shocks can be administered by either the therapist or the patient. The results are satisfactory but must be reinforced at regular intervals.
Schizophrenia	The token economy procedure, in which tokens are awarded for desirable behavior and can be used to buy ward privileges, has been useful in treating inpatient schizophrenic patients. Social skills training teaches schizophrenic patients how to interact with others in a socially acceptable way so that negative feedback is eliminated. In addition, the aggressive behavior of some schizophrenic patients can be diminished through these methods.
Sexual dysfunctions	Dual-sex therapy, developed by William Masters and Virginia Johnson, is a behavior therapy technique used for various sexual dysfunctions, especially impotence, anorgasmia, and premature ejaculation. It uses relaxation, desensitization, and graded exposure as the primary techniques. (See Section 20.3 for a further discussion of these therapies.)
Shy bladder	Inability to void in public bathroom; relaxation exercises.
Type A behavior	Physiological assessment; muscle relaxation, biofeedback (on EMG)

usually disappears after a series of such sequences. Aversion therapy has been used for alcoholism, paraphilias, and other behaviors with impulsive or compulsive qualities.

POSITIVE REINFORCEMENT

If a behavioral response is followed by a generally rewarding event—for example, food, avoidance of pain, or praise—it tends to be strengthened and to occur more frequently. That principle has been applied in a variety of situations. On inpatient hospital wards, mental patients have been rewarded for performing a desired behavior with tokens that they may use to purchase luxury items or certain privileges. The process has been successful in altering behavior and is known as a *token economy*. Some workers have suggestd that psychotherapy is effective, in part, because patients want to please the therapist and so change their behavior in order to receive the therapist's praise. Sigmund Freud stated that, in treating phobias, the doctor needs to encourage the patient to face the phobia at some point determined by the positive relationship between the doctor and the patient.

Table 29.6-2 lists some of the clinical applications of behavior therapy.

Table 29.6-3 summarizes a number of the specific tasks

Table 29.6-3
Social Skills Competency Checklist of Therapist-Trainer Behaviors

1. Actively helps the patient in setting and eliciting specific interpersonal goals.
2. Promotes favorable expectations, a therapeutic orientation, and motivation before role playing begins.
3. Assists the patient in building possible scenes in terms of: "What emotion or communication?" "Who is the interpersonal target?" "Where and when?"
4. Structures the role playing by setting the scene and assigning roles to patient and surrogates.
5. Engages the patient in behavioral rehearsal—getting the patient to role-play with others.
6. Uses self or other group members in modeling more appropriate alternatives for the patient.
7. Prompts and cues the patient during the role playing.
8. Uses an active style of training through coaching, shadowing, being physically out of a seat, and closely monitoring and supporting the patient.
9. Gives the patient positive feedback for specific verbal and nonverbal behavioral skills.
10. Identifies the patient's specific verbal and nonverbal behavioral deficits or excesses and suggests constructive alternatives.
11. Ignores or suppresses inappropriate and interfering behavior.
12. Shapes behavioral improvements in small, attainable increments.
13. Solicits from the patient or suggests an alternative behavior for a problem situation that can be used and practiced during the behavioral rehearsal or role playing.
14. Evaluates deficits in social perception and problem solving and remedies them.
15. Gives specific attainable and functional homework assignments.

Table by Robert Paul Liberman, M.D., and Jeffrey Bedell, Ph.D.

Table 29.6-4
Behavior Therapy

Goal	Modify learned maladaptive behavior patterns that lead to pathological symptoms
Selection criteria	Specific, well-delineated, circumscribed, easily identified maladaptive behaviors (e.g., phobias, overeating, sexual dysfunctions) Psychophysiological disorders in which manifestations of symptoms are affected by stress (e.g., asthma, pain, hypertension)
Duration	Generally time-limited, specific to specific behavior
Techniques	Based on learning theory principles (e.g., operant and classical conditioning) Relaxation training Reinforcements Aversive therapy Systematic desensitization Flooding Participant modeling Token economies

Table by Rebecca Jones, M.D.

a behavioral therapist addresses as part of a behavior rehearsal involving role playing.

RESULTS

Behavior therapy has been successful in a variety of disorders and can be easily taught. It requires less time than other therapies, such as psychoanalysis and psychoanalytic therapy, and is less expensive to administer. A limitation of the method is that it is useful for circumscribed symptoms, rather than for global areas of dysfunction (e.g., personality disorders). As with other forms of treatment, a careful evaluation of the patient's problems, motivation, and psychological strengths should be ascertained before instituting any of the behavior therapy approaches described.

See Table 29.6-4 for a summary of behavior therapy.

References

Agras W S, Kazdin A E, Wilson G T: *Behavior Therapy: Toward an Applied Clinical Science.* Freeman, San Francisco, 1979.

Antonuccio D O, Ward C H, Tearnan B H: The behavioral treatment of unipolar depression in adult outpatients. Prog Behav Modif *24*: 152, 1989.

Barlow D, ed.: *Clinical Handbook of Psychological Disorders.* Guilford, New York, 1985.

Baum M: Contributions of animal studies of response prevention (flooding) to human exposure therapy. Psychol Rep *63*: 421, 1988.

Becker R E, Heimberg R G, Bellack A S: *Social Skills Training Treatment for Depression.* Pergamon, New York, 1987.

Black J L, Bruce B K: Behavior therapy: A clinical update. Hosp Community Psychiatry *40*: 1152, 1989.

Ciminero A R, Calhoun K S, Adams H E, eds.: *Handbook of Behavioral Assessment,* ed 2. Wiley, New York, 1986.

Council on Scientific Affairs: Aversion therapy. JAMA *13*: 2562, 1987.

Frawley P J, Smith J W: Chemical aversion therapy in the treatment of cocaine dependence as part of a multimodal treatment program: Treatment outcome. J Subst Abuse Treat *7*: 21, 1990.

Grissby J P: The use of imagery in the treatment of posttraumatic stress disorder. J Nerv Ment Dis *175*: 55, 1987.

Hersen M, ed.: *Pharmacological and Behavioral Treatment: An Integrative Approach.* Wiley, New York, 1986.

Hersen M, Bellack A S, eds.: *Behavioral Assessment: A Practical Handbook.* Pergamon, New York, 1988.

Hersen M, Eisler R M, Miller P M, eds.: *Progress in Behavior Modification,* vols 1–19. Academic Press, New York, 1975–87.

Hogarty G E, Anderson C M: Family psychoeducation, social skills training, and maintenance chemotherapy in the aftercare treatment of schizophrenia. Arch Gen Psychiatry *43*: 633, 1987.

Kramer F M, Jeffrey R W, Forster J L, Snell M K: Long-term follow-up of behavioral treatment for obesity: Patterns of weight regain among men and women. Int J Obes *13*: 129, 1989.

Liberman R P: *A Guide to Behavioral Analysis and Therapy.* Pergamon, New York, 1972.

Liberman R P, Bedell J R: Behavior therapy. In *Comprehensive Textbook of Psychiatry,* ed 5, H L Kaplan and B J Sadock, editors, p 1462. Williams & Wilkins, Baltimore, 1989.

Liberman R P, Mueser K, DeRisi W J: *Social Skills Training for Psychiatric Disorders.* Pergamon, New York, 1988.

Marks, I M: *Fears, Phobias and Rituals.* Oxford University Press, New York, 1987.

Matson J L, Gorman-Smith D: A review of treatment research for aggressive and disruptive behavior in the mentally retarded. Appl Res Ment Retard *7*: 95, 1986.

McKee M G: Behavioral techniques in pain modification. Cleve Clin J Med *56*: 502, 1989.

Morrison R L, Bellack A S: Social functioning of schizophrenic patients. Schizophr Bull *13*: 715, 1987.

Sturgeon R S, Cooper L M, Howell R J: Pupil response: A psychophysiological measure of fear during analogue desensitization. Percept Mot Skills *69*: 1351, 1989.

29.7 / Hypnosis

Martin Orne defines hypnosis as that state or condition in which a person is able to respond to appropriate suggestions by experiencing alterations of perceptions, memory, or mood. The essential feature of hypnosis is the subjective experiential change.

Hypnosis is a complex mental phenomenon that has been defined as a state of heightened focal concentration and receptivity to the suggestions of another person. It has also been called an altered state of consciousness, a dissociated state, and a stage of repression. However, there is no known psychophysiological basis for hypnosis, as there is for sleep, in which characteristic electroencephalogram (EEG) changes appear.

HISTORY

Modern hypnosis originated with the Austrian physician Friedrich Anton Mesmer (1734–1815), who believed the phenomenon to be the result of animal magnetism or an invisible fluid that passes between the subject and the hypnotist, and was known as Mesmerism. The term "hypnosis" originated in the 1840s with a Scottish physician, James Braid (1795–1860), who believed the subject to be in a particular state of sleep (*hypnos* is the Greek word for sleep). In the late 19th century the French neurologist Jean Charcot (1825–1893) thought hypnotism to be a special physiological state, and his contemporary Hippolyte Bernheim (1840–1919) believed it to be a psychological state of heightened suggestibility.

Sigmund Freud, who studied with Charcot, used hypnosis early in his career to help patients recover repressed memories. He noted that patients would relive traumatic events while under hypnosis, a process known as abreaction. Freud later replaced hypnosis with the technique of free association.

Today, hypnosis is a method that is used as a form of therapy (hypnotherapy), a method of investigation to recover lost memories, and a research tool.

HYPNOTIC CAPACITY AND INDUCTION

The therapist can use a number of specific procedures to help the patient be hypnotized and respond to suggestion. These procedures involve capitalizing on some naturally occurring hypnosislike phenomena that very likely have occurred in the life experiences of most patients. However, these experiences are rarely talked about; consequently, patients find them fascinating. For example, when discussing what hypnosis is like with a patient, the therapist may say: "Have you ever had the experience of driving home while thinking about an issue that preoccupies you and suddenly realize that, although you have arrived safe and sound, you can't recall having driven past familiar landmarks? It's as if you had been asleep, and yet you stopped at all the red lights, and you avoided collisions. You were somehow traveling on automatic pilot." Most people resonate to this experience and are usually happy to describe similar personal experiences.

A discussion about experiences of that kind gives patients examples of hypnosislike experiences that they very likely have had; thus, it is made clear that the patients have the capacity to use the hypnotic mode, as it is merely an extension of that kind of experiences. Although they were not necessarily hypnotic states, the extent to which a person experiences them is correlated with hypnotizability. Virtually everyone has experienced some of those experiences in one form or another. Table 29.7-1 lists a variety of naturally occurring trancelike experiences that can be discussed with patients and that point to the capacity to be hypnotized.

Table 29.7-1
Naturally Occurring Hypnoticlike Experiences and the Percentage of Persons Indicating That They Have Had Such Experiences

Have you ever been in a room full of people, ostensibly taking part in the group yet mentally being far away from it?	90%
Have you ever been unsure whether you did something or just thought about having to do it (e.g., not knowing whether you either mailed a certain letter or just thought about mailing it)?	87%
Have you ever been able to block out sounds from your mind so that they were no longer important to you? Or so that they seemed very far away? Or so that you no longer understood them? Or so that you did not hear them at all?	87%
Have you ever been so lost in thought that you did not understand what people said to you, even when they were talking directly to you and even when you nodded token agreement?	84%
Have you ever been staring off into space, actually thinking of nothing and hardly been aware of the passage of time?	81%
Have you ever had the experience of recollecting a past experience in your life with such clarity and vitality that it was almost like living it again? Or so that it actually seemed identical with living it again?	78%
Have you ever been able to shut out your surroundings from your mind by concentrating very hard on something else?	77%
Have you ever had the experience of reading a novel (or watching a play) and, while doing so, actually forget yourself, your surroundings, and live the story with such great reality and vividness that it becomes temporarily almost reality for you? Or actually seemed to become reality for you?	75%
Have you ever been lulled into a groggy state or put to sleep by a lecture or concert, even though you were not otherwise fatigued or tired?	73%
Have you ever wandered off in your own thoughts while doing a routine task so that you actually forgot you were doing the task and then found, a few minutes later, that you had completed it without even being aware that you were doing it?	70%

Table by Martin Orne, M.D., Ph.D., and David Dinges, Ph.D.

The following is a typical induction protocol (courtesy of William Holt, M.D.) that is used to induce the trance state. There are many variations of such protocols, some less directive than this one. The one presented here is most likely to be effective in those persons with a high hypnotizability potential.

Take a long, deep, breath—inhale and exhale; now close your eyes and relax. Pay particular attention to the muscles in and about your eyes—relax them to the point that they just won't work. Are you trying to do that? Good. If you really have them relaxed, right at this very moment, no matter how hard you try, they just won't open. Test them. The harder you try, the faster they stick together, just as if they were glued together. That's fine!

Now you can open your eyes; that's good. When I tell you to and not before, open and close your eyes once more, and, when you close them this time, you will be 10 times as relaxed as you are right now. Go ahead, open and close, and feel that surge of relaxation go through your whole body, from the top of your head to the tip of your toes. Very good!

Now once again, open and close your eyes, and this time, when you close, you will double the relaxation that you now have. Fine.

If you have followed my suggestions, right at this very moment, when I lift your hand and let it drop into your lap, it will drop like a wet cloth, heavy and limp. That's very, very good.

You now have good physical relaxation, but medical relaxation consists of two phases: physical, which you now have, and mental, which I will now show you how to achieve.

When I ask you to and not before, I want you to start counting backward from 100. I know you can count; that is not what we're after. I just want you to relax mentally. As you say each number, pause momentarily, until you feel a wave of relaxation cover your whole body, from the top of your head to the tip of your toes. When you feel this wave of relaxation, then say the next number, and each time you say a number, you will double the relaxation you had before you said the number. If you do this properly, an interesting thing will happen—as you say the numbers and relax, the succeeding numbers will start to disappear and vanish from your mind. Command your mind to dispel these numbers. Now, aloud and slowly, start counting backward from 100.

Patient: One hundred.
Doctor: Very good.
Patient: Ninety-nine.
Doctor: Make them start to disappear now.
Patient: Ninety-eight.
Doctor: Now they're fading away, and after the next number they'll all be gone. Make them disappear. Let the numbers go.
Patient: Ninety-seven.
Doctor: And now they're all gone. Are they gone? Fine. If there are any numbers still lurking in your mind, when I lift your hand and drop it, they will all disappear.

TRANCE STATE

Persons under hypnosis are said to be in a trance state, which may be light, medium, or heavy (deep). In a light trance there are changes in motor activity such that the patient's muscles can feel relaxed, the hands can levitate, and paresthesia can be induced. A medium trance is characterized by diminished pain sensation and partial or complete amnesia. A deep trance is associated with induced visual or auditory experiences and deep anesthesia. Time distortion occurs at all trance levels but is most profound in the deep trance.

Posthypnotic suggestion is characterized by the patient's being instructed to perform a simple act or to experience a particular sensation after awakening from the trance state. It may be used to give a bad taste to cigarettes or a particular food, thus aiding in the treatment of nicotine dependence or obesity. Posthypnotic suggestions are associated with deep trance states.

HYPNOTHERAPY

The patient in a hypnotic trance can recall memories that are not available to consciousness in the nonhypnotic state. Such memories can be used in therapy to corroborate psychoanalytic hypotheses regarding the patient's dynamics or to enable the patient to use such memories as a catalyst for new associations. It is possible with some patients to induce age regression, during which they reexperience events that occurred at an earlier time in life. Whether the patient experiences the events as they actually occurred is controversial; however, the material elicited can be used to further the therapy. Patients in a trance state may describe an event with an intensity similar to that when it occurred (abreaction) and experience a sense of relief as a result. The trance state plays a role in the treatment of amnesia and fugue, although the clinician should be aware that it may be hazardous to bring the repressed memory into consciousness quickly, as the patient may be overwhelmed by anxiety.

INDICATIONS AND USES

Hypnosis has been used, with varying degrees of success, to control substance use disorders, alcoholism, smoking, and obesity. It has been used to induce anesthesia, and major surgery has been performed with no anesthetic except hypnosis. It has also been used to manage chronic pain conditions, asthma, warts, pruritis, aphonia, and a great variety of other conversion symptoms.

Relaxation can be achieved easily with hypnosis, so that patients may deal with phobic situations by controlling their anxiety. It has also been used to induce relaxation in systematic desensitization.

CONTRAINDICATIONS

Hypnotized patients are in a state of atypical dependency on the therapist, and so strong transference may develop, characterized by a positive attachment that must be respected and interpreted. In other instances a negative transference may erupt in patients who are fragile or who have difficulty testing reality. Patients who have difficulty with basic trust, such as paranoid patients, or who have problems giving up control, such as obsessive-compulsive patients, are not good candidates for hypnosis. A secure ethical value system is important to all therapy and particularly to hypnosis, in which patients (especially those in a deep trance) are extremely suggestible and malleable. There is controversy about whether patients will perform acts during a trance state that they otherwise find repugnant or that run contrary to their moral code.

References

Benson H: Hypnosis and the relaxation response. Gastroenterology *96*: 1609, 1989.

Bowers K: *Hypnosis for the Seriously Curious*. Norton, New York, 1976.

Crasilneck H, Hall J: *Clinical Hypnosis: Principles and Applications,* ed 2. Grune & Stratton, Orlando, FL, 1985.

Frankel F: *Hypnosis: Trance as a Coping Mechanism*. Plenum, New York, 1976.

Fromm E, Shor E: *Hypnosis: Developments in Research and New Perspectives: New and Revised Second Edition*. Aldine, New York, 1979.

Gabel S: The right hemisphere in imagery, hypnosis, rapid eye movement sleep and dreaming: Empirical studies and tentative conclusions. J Nerv Ment Dis *176*: 323, 1988.

Hilgard E: *The Experience of Hypnosis: A Shorter Version of Hypnotic Susceptibility*. Harcourt, Brace & World, New York, 1968.

Hilgard E, Hilgard J: *Hypnosis in the Relief of Pain*. Kaufmann, Los Altos, CA, 1983.

Kroger W: *Clinical and Experimental Hypnosis,* ed 2. Lippincott, Philadelphia, 1977.

Laurence J-R, Perry C: *Hypnosis, Will and Memory: A Psycho-Legal History*. Guilford, New York, 1988

MacHovec F: Hypnosis complications, risk factors, and prevention. Am J Clin Hypn *31*: 40, 1988.

Meares A: *A System of Medical Hypnosis*. Julian Press, New York, 1960.

Orne M: The construct of hypnosis: Implications of the definition for research and practice. Ann N Y Acad Sci *296*: 14, 1977.

Orne M, Dinges D: Hypnosis. In *Textbook of Pain,* P Wall, R Melzack, editors, p 806. Churchill Livingston, New York, 1984.

Orne M T, Dinges D F: Hypnosis. In *Comprehensive Textbook of Psychiatry,* ed 5, H I Kaplan and B J Sadock, editors, p 1501. Williams & Wilkins, Baltimore, 1989.

Pettinati H: *Hypnosis and Memory*. Guilford, New York, 1988.
Soskis D: *Teaching Self-Hypnosis: An Introductory Guide for Clinicians*. Norton, New York, 1986.
Spiegel D: Hypnosis in the treatment of victims of sexual abuse. Psychiatr Clin North Am *12*: 295, 1989.
Spiegel H, Spiegel D: *Trance and Treatment: Clinical Uses of Hypnosis*. Basic Books, New York, 1978.
Van Dyck R, Hoosduin K: Hypnosis and conversion disorders. Am J Psychother *43*: 430, 1989.
Wadden T, Anderton C: The clinical use of hypnosis. Psychol Bull *91*: 215, 1982.
Wolberg L: *Medical Hypnosis: The Practice of Hypnotherapy* vols. 1 and 2. Grune & Stratton, New York, 1948.

29.8 / Cognitive Therapy

Normal reactions are mediated by cognitive processes that enable persons to perceive reality accurately. In psychopathology this ability is impaired, and errors in cognition are made. Aaron Beck used the term "schemas" to describe stable cognitive patterns through which one interprets experiences. Cognitive errors produce negative schemas that persist despite contradictory evidence. Thus, depressogenic schemas may involve viewing experience as black or white, without shades of gray; as categorical imperatives that allow no options; or as expectations that people are either all good or all bad.

GENERAL CONSIDERATIONS

Cognitive therapy, developed by Aaron Beck, is a short-term structured therapy that uses active collaboration between the patient and the therapist to achieve the therapeutic goals. It is oriented toward current problems and their resolution. Therapy is usually conducted on an individual basis, although group methods are also used. Therapy may also be used in conjunction with drugs.

Cognitive therapy has been applied mainly to depression (with or without suicidal ideation); however, it is also used with other conditions, such as panic attacks, obsessive-compulsive disorders, paranoid disorders, and somatoform disorders. The treatment of depression can serve as a paradigm of the cognitive approach.

COGNITIVE THEORY OF DEPRESSION

The cognitive theory of depression holds that cognitive dysfunctions are the core of depression and that affective and physical changes and other associated features of depression are consequences of the cognitive dysfunctions. For example, apathy and low energy are results of a person's expectation of failure in all areas. Similarly, paralysis of will stems from a person's pessimism and feelings of hopelessness.

The cognitive trial of depression consists of (1) a negative self-percept that sees oneself as defective, inadequate, deprived, worthless, and undesirable; (2) a tendency to experience the world as a negative, demanding, and self-defeating place and to expect failure and punishment; and (3) the expectation of continued hardship, suffering, deprivation, and failure.

The goal of therapy is to alleviate depression and to prevent its recurrence by helping the patient (1) to identify and test negative cognitions, (2) to develop alternative and more flexible schemas, and (3) to rehearse both new cognitive responses and new behavioral responses. The goal is to change the way a person thinks and, subsequently, to alleviate the depressive syndrome.

STRATEGIES AND TECHNIQUES

Overall, therapy is relatively short, lasting up to about 25 weeks. If there is no response in that time, the diagnosis should be reevaluated. Maintenance therapy can be carried out over a period of years.

As with other psychotherapies, the therapists' attributes are important to successful therapy. The therapists must be able to exude warmth, understand the life experience of each patient, and be truly genuine and honest with themselves and with their patients. Therapists must be able to relate skillfully and interactively with their patients.

Cognitive therapy sets the agenda at the beginning of each session, assigns homework to be performed between sessions, and teaches new skills. The therapist and the patient actively collaborate (Table 29.8-1). Cognitive therapy has three components: didactic aspects, cognitive techniques, and behavioral techniques.

Didactic Aspects

The didactic aspects include explaining to the patient the cognitive triad, schemas, and faulty logic. The therapist

Table 29.8-1
Cognitive Psychotherapy

Goal	Identify and alter cognitive distortions that maintain symptoms
Selection criteria	Primarily used in dysthymia Nonendogenous depression Symptoms not sustained by pathological family
Duration	Time-limited, usually 15–25 weeks, once-weekly meetings
Techniques	Collaborative empiricism Structured and directive Assigned readings Homework and behavioral techniques Identification of irrational beliefs and automatic thoughts Identification of attitudes and assumptions underlying negatively biased thoughts

Table from R J Ursano, E K Silberman: Individual psychotherapies. In *The American Psychiatric Press Textbook of Psychiatry*, J A Talbott, R E Hales, and S C Yudofsky, editors, p 872. American Psychiatric Press, Washington, DC, 1988, with permission.

must tell the patient that they will formulate hypotheses together and test them over the course of the treatment. Cognitive therapy requires a full explanation of the relationship between depression and thinking, affect, and behavior, as well as the rationale for all aspects of the treatment. This explanation contrasts with the more psychoanalytically oriented therapies, which require very little explanation.

Cognitive Techniques

The cognitive approach includes four processes: (1) eliciting automatic thoughts, (2) testing automatic thoughts, (3) identifying maladaptive underlying assumptions, and (4) testing the validity of maladaptive assumptions.

Eliciting automatic thoughts. Automatic thoughts are cognitions that intervene between external events and the person's emotional reaction to the event. An example of an automatic thought is the belief that "everyone is going to laugh at me when they see how badly I bowl"—a thought that occurs to someone who has been asked to go bowling and responds negatively. Another example is a person's thought that "she doesn't like me" if someone passes the person in the hall without saying hello.

Automatic thoughts are also termed cognitive distortions. Every psychopathological disorder has its own specific cognitive profile of distorted thought, which, if known, provides a framework for specific cognitive interventions (Table 29.8-2).

Testing automatic thoughts. Acting as a teacher the therapist helps the patient test the validity of automatic thoughts. The goal is to encourage patients to reject inaccurate or exaggerated automatic thoughts after careful examination.

Patients often blame themselves for things that go wrong that may well have been outside their control. The therapist reviews with the patient the entire situation and helps reattribute more accurately the blame or cause of the unpleasant events. Generating alternative explanations for events is another way of undermining inaccurate and distorted automatic thoughts.

Table 29.8-2
Cognitive Profile of Psychiatric Disorders

Disorder	Specific Cognitive Content
Depression	Negative view of self, experience, and future
Hypomania	Inflated view of self, experience, and future
Anxiety disorder	Fear of physical or psychological danger
Panic disorder	Catastrophic misinterpretation of bodily and mental experiences
Phobia	Danger in specific, avoidable situations
Paranoid state	Negative bias, interference, and so forth by others
Hysteria	Concept of motor or sensory abnormality
Obsession	Repeated warning or doubting about safety
Compulsion	Repetitive acts to ward off threat
Suicidal behavior	Hopelessness and deficit in problem solving
Anorexia nervosa	Fear of being fat or unshapely
Hypochondriasis	Attribution of serious medical disorder

Table by Aaron Beck, M.D., and A. John Rush, M.D.

Identifying maladaptive assumptions. As the patient and the therapist continue to identify automatic thoughts, patterns usually become apparent, representing rules or maladaptive general assumptions that guide the patient's life. Samples of such rules are "In order to be happy, I must be perfect," or "If anyone doesn't like me, I'm not lovable." Such rules inevitably lead to disappointments and failure and then to depression.

Testing the validity of maladaptive assumptions. Similar to the testing of the validity of automatic thoughts is the testing of the accuracy of maladaptive assumptions. One particularly effective test is for the therapist to ask the patient to defend the validity of an assumption. For example, if a patient stated that he should always work up to his potential, the therapist might ask, "Why is that so important to you?"

Behavioral Techniques

Behavioral techniques go hand in hand with cognitive techniques: Behavioral techniques are used to test and change maladaptive or inaccurate cognitions. The overall purpose of such techniques is to help the patients understand the inaccuracy of their cognitive assumptions and learn new strategies and ways of dealing with issues.

Among the behavioral techniques used in therapy are scheduling activities, mastery and pleasure, graded task assignments, cognitive rehearsal, self-reliance training, role playing, and diversion techniques.

Among the first things done in therapy is to schedule activities on an hourly basis. A record of these activities is kept and reviewed with the therapist.

In addition to scheduling activities, patients are asked to rate the amount of mastery and pleasure their activities bring them. Patients are often surprised at how much more mastery and pleasure they get out of activities than they had otherwise believed.

To simplify the situation and allow for mini-accomplishments, therapists often break tasks down into subtasks, as in graded task assignments, to demonstrate to patients that they can succeed.

Cognitive rehearsal has the patient imagine the various steps in meeting and mastering a challenge and rehearse the various aspects of it.

Patients, especially inpatients, are encouraged to become self-reliant by doing such simple things as making their own beds, doing their own shopping, and preparing their own meals, rather than relying on other people. This is known as self-reliance training.

Role playing is a particularly powerful and useful technique to elicit automatic thoughts and to learn new behaviors.

Diversion techniques are useful in helping patients get through particularly difficult times and include physical activity, social contact, work, play, and visual imagery.

Imagery. Imagery is a phenomenon that affects behavior, as first discussed by Paul Schilder in his book *The Image and Appearance of the Human Body*, in which he described images as having physiological components. According to Schilder, visualizing oneself running activates subliminally the same muscles used in running, which can be measured with electromyography. This phenomenon is used in sports training, in which athletes visualize every conceivable event in a performance and develop a muscle memory for the activity. It can also be used to master anxiety or to deal with feared situations by combining behavioral and cognitive theories.

Impulsive or obsessive behavior has been treated with thought stoppage. For instance, patients imagine a stop sign with a police officer nearby or another image that evokes inhibition at the same time that they recognize an impulse or obsession that is alien to the ego. Similarly, obesity can be treated by having patients visualize themselves as thin, athletic, trim, and well muscled and then training them to evoke that image whenever they have an urge to eat. Such imagery can be enhanced with hypnosis or autogenic training. In a technique called guided imagery, patients are encouraged to have fantasies that can be interpreted as wish fulfillments or attempts to master disturbing affects or impulses.

EFFICACY

Cognitive therapy can be used alone in the treatment of mild to moderate depression or in conjunction with antidepressant medication for severe depression. Studies have clearly demonstrated that cognitive therapy is effective and in some cases is superior or equal to medication alone. It is one of the most useful psychotherapeutic interventions currently available for depression and shows promise in the treatment of other disorders.

Cognitive therapy has also been studied in relation to increasing compliance with lithium in bipolar disorder patients and as an adjunct in treating withdrawal from heroin.

Table 29.8-3 summarizes and contrasts major features of three of the most commonly used psychotherapeutic approaches to the treatment of depression, including the cognitive approach.

Table 29.8-3
Major Features of Three Psychotherapeutic Approaches to Depression

Feature	Psychodynamic Approach	Cognitive Approach	Interpersonal Approach
Major theorists	Freud, Abraham, Jacobson, Kohut	Plato, Adler, Beck, Rush	Meyer, Sullivan, Klerman, Weissman
Concepts of pathology and etiology	Ego regression: damaged self-esteem and unresolved conflict caused by childhood object loss and disappointment	Distorted thinking: dysphoria caused by learned negative views of self, others, and the world	Impaired interpersonal relations: absent or unsatisfactory significant social bonds
Major goals and mechanisms of change	To promote personality change through understanding of past conflicts; to achieve insight into defenses, ego distortions, and superego defects; to provide a role model; to permit cathartic release of aggression	To provide symptomatic relief through alteration of target thoughts; to identify self-destructive cognitions; to modify specific erroneous assumptions; to promote self-control over thinking patterns.	To provide symptomatic relief through solution of current interpersonal problems; to reduce stress involving family or work; to improve interpersonal communication skills
Primary techniques and practices	Expressive, empathic: fully or partially analyzing transference and resistance; confronting defenses; clarifying ego and superego distortions	Behavioral, cognitive: recording and monitoring cognitions; correcting distorted themes with logic and experimental testing; providing alternative thought content; homework	Communicative, environmental: clarifying and managing maladaptive relationships and learning new ones through communication and social skills training; providing information on illness
Therapist role, therapeutic relationship	Interpreter, reflector: establishment and exploration of transference; therapeutic alliance for benign dependency and empathic understanding	Educator, shaper: positive relationship instead of transference; collaborative empiricism as basis for joint scientific (logical) task	Explorer, prescriber: positive relationship, transference without interpretation; active therapist role for influence and advocacy
Marital, family role	Full individual confidentiality; exclusion of significant others except in life-threatening situations	Use of spouse as objective reporter; couples therapy for disturbed cognitions sustained in marital relationship	Integral role of spouse in treatment; examination of spouse's role in patient's predisposition to depression and effect of illness on marriage

Table from T B Karasu: Psychotherapy for depression. Am J Psychiatry *147*: 2, 1990, with permission.

References

Beck A T: *Cognitive Therapy and the Emotional Disorders.* International Universities Press, New York, 1976.

Beck A T: *Depression: Clinical, Experimental, and Theoretical Aspects.* Harper & Row, New York, 1970. (Reprinted as *Depression: Causes and Treatment.* University of Pennsylvania Press, Philadelphia, 1972.)

Beck A T, Emery G: *Anxiety Disorders and Phobias: A Cognitive Perspective.* Basic Books, New York, 1985.

Beck A T, Greenberg R L: Cognitive therapy of panic disorders. In *American Psychiatric Press Review of Psychiatry.* A J Frances and R E Hales, editors, vol. 7, p 571. American Psychiatric Press, Washington, DC, 1988.

Beck A T, Rush A J: Cognitive therapy. In *Comprehensive Textbook of Psychiatry*, ed 5, H I Kaplan and B J Sadock, editors, p 1541. Williams & Wilkins, Baltimore, 1989.

Beck A T, Rush A J, Shaw B F, Emery G: *Cognitive Therapy of Depression.* Guilford, New York, 1979.

Covi L, Primakoff L: Cognitive group therapy. In *American Psychiatric Press Review of Psychiatry*, A J Frances and R E Hales, editors, vol 7, p. 608. American Psychiatric Press, Washington, DC, 1988.

Hollon S D, Bedrosian R, eds: *New Directions in Cognitive Therapy: A Casebook.* Guilford, New York, 1981.

Hollon S D, Najavits L: Review of empirical studies on cognitive therapy. In *American Psychiatric Press Review of Psychiatry*, A J Frances and R E Hales, editors, vol 7, p 643. American Psychiatric Press, Washington, DC, 1988.

Jarrett R B, Rush A J: Psychotherapeutic approaches for depression. In *Psychiatry*, vol 1, chap 65. Lippincott, Philadelphia, and Basic Books, New York, 1985–86.

Mahoney M J: *Cognition and Behavior Modification.* Ballinger Press, Cambridge, MA, 1974.

Meichenbaum D H: *Cognitive Behavior Modification: An Integrative Approach.* Plenum, New York, 1977.

Rush A J: Cognitive therapy in combination with antidepressant medication. In *Combining Psychotherapy and Drug Therapy in Clinical Practice*, B D Beitman and G L Klerman, editors, p 121. Spectrum, New York, 1984.

Shaw B, Segal Z V: Introduction to cognitive theory and therapy. In *American Psychiatric Press Review of Psychiatry*, vol 7, A J Frances and R E Hales, editors, p 538. American Psychiatric Press, Washington, DC, 1988.

Trautman P D, Rotheram-Borum M J: Cognitive therapy with children and adolescents. In *American Psychiatric Press Review of Psychiatry*, vol 7, A J Frances and R E Hales, editors, p 584. American Psychiatric Press, Washington, DC, 1988.

30 Biological Therapies

30.1 / General Principles of Psychopharmacology

The numerous pharmacological agents used to treat psychiatric disorders are referred to by three general terms that are used interchangeably: psychotropic drugs, psychoactive drugs, and psychotherapeutic drugs. Traditionally, these agents were divided into four categories: (1) antipsychotic or neuroleptic drugs used to treat psychosis, (2) antidepressant drugs used to treat depression, (3) antimanic drugs used to treat bipolar disorder, and (4) antianxiety or anxiolytic drugs used to treat anxious states. This division, however, is less valid now than it was in the past for the following reasons: (1) Many antidepressant drugs are used to treat anxiety, and some antianxiety drugs are used adjunctively to treat psychosis. (2) Drugs from all four categories are used to treat other clinical disorders, such as eating disorders, panic disorders, and impulse control disorders. (3) Drugs such as clonidine (Catapres), propranolol (Inderal), and verapamil (Isoptin, Calan) can effectively treat a variety of psychiatric disorders and do not fit easily into the aforementioned classification of drugs. (4) Some descriptive psychopharmacological terms overlap in meaning. For example, anxiolytics decrease anxiety, sedatives produce a calming or relaxing effect, and hypnotics produce sleep. However, most anxiolytics function as sedatives and at high doses can be used as hypnotics, and all hypnotics at low doses can be used for daytime sedation.

For these reasons this section uses a classification in which each drug is discussed according to its pharmacological category. Each drug is described in terms of its pharmacological actions, including pharmacodynamics and pharmacokinetics. Indications, contraindications, drug-drug interactions, and adverse side effects are also discussed.

Table 30.1-1 lists the psychotherapeutic drugs according to the generic name, trade name, and section title and number in which it is discussed, and Table 30.1-2 lists the major drugs used in the various psychiatric disorders.

HISTORY

Organic therapies such as electroconvulsive therapy (ECT) (pioneered by Ugo Cerletti and Lucio Bini), insulin coma therapy (developed by Manfred Sakel), and psychosurgery (introduced by Egas Moniz) all began in the first third of the 20th century and heralded the biological revolution in psychiatry (Table 30.1-3). In 1917 Julius von Wagner-Jauregg introduced malaria toxin to treat syphilis and is the only psychiatrist to have won a Nobel prize.

In the second half of the 20th century, chemotherapy as a treatment for mental illness became a major field of research and practice. Almost immediately after the introduction of chlorpromazine (Thorazine) in the early 1950s, psychotherapeutic drugs became a mainstay of psychiatric treatment, particularly for the seriously mentally ill patients.

In 1949 the Australian psychiatrist John Cade described the treatment of manic excitement with lithium. While conducting animal experiments, Cade had somewhat incidentally noted that lithium carbonate made the animals lethargic, thus prompting him to administer this drug to several agitated psychiatric patients.

In 1950 Charpentier synthesized chlorpromazine (an aliphatic phenothiazine antipsychotic) in an attempt to develop an antihistaminergic drug that would serve as an adjuvant in anesthesia. Laborit reported the ability of this drug to induce an "artificial hibernation." Reports by Paraire and Sigwald, Delay and Deniker, and Lehmann and Hanrahan described the effectiveness of chlorpromazine in treating severe agitation and psychosis. Chlorpromazine was quickly introduced into American psychiatry, and many similarly effective drugs have since been synthesized, including haloperidol (Haldol) (a butyrophenone antipsychotic) in 1958 by Janssen.

Imipramine (Tofranil) (a tricyclic antidepressant) is structurally related to the phenothiazine antipsychotics. While carrying out clinical research on chlorpromazinelike drugs, Thomas Kuhn found that, although imipramine was not very effective in reducing agitation, it did seem to reduce depression in some patients. The introduction of monoamine oxidase inhibitors (MAOIs) to treat depression evolved from the observation that the antituberculosis agent iproniazid had mood-elevating effects in some patients. In 1958 Nathan Kline was one of the first investigators to report the efficacy of MAOI treatment in depressed psychiatric patients.

By 1960, with the introduction of chlordiazepoxide (Librium) (a benzodiazepine antianxiety agent synthesized by Sternbach at the Roche laboratories in the late 1950s), the psychiatric armamentarium of drugs included antipsychotics (e.g., chlorpromazine and haloperidol), tricyclic (e.g., imipramine) and MAOI (e.g., iproniazid [Marsalid]), antidepressants, an antimanic agent (lithium), and antianxiety agents

Table 30.1-1
Index to Section 30.2

Generic Name	Trade Name	Section Title	Section Number
Acetophenazine	Tindal	Dopamine Receptor Antagonists: Antipsychotics	30.2.13
Alprazolam	Xanax	Benzodiazepines	30.2.5
Amantadine	Symmetrel	Amantadine	30.2.1
Amitriptyline	Endep, Elavil	Tricyclics and Tetracyclics: Antidepressants	30.2.22
Amobarbital	Amytal	Barbiturates	30.2.4
Amoxapine	Asendin	Tricyclics and Tetracyclics: Antidepressants	30.2.22
Atenolol	Tenorectic, Tenorim	β-Adrenergic Receptor Antagonists	30.2.6
Benztropine	Cogentin	Anticholinergics	30.2.2
Biperiden	Akineton	Anticholinergics	30.2.2
Bupropion	Wellbutrin	Bupropion	30.2.7
Buspirone	BuSpar	Buspirone	30.2.8
Butabarbital	Butisol	Barbiturates	30.2.4
Butaperazine	Repoise	Dopamine Receptor Antagonists: Antipsychotics	30.2.13
Carbamazepine	Tegretol	Carbamazepine	30.2.10
Carisoprodol	Soma	Barbiturates	30.2.4
Carphenazine	Proketazine	Dopamine Receptor Antagonists: Antipsychotics	30.2.13
Chloral hydrate	Noctec	Chloral Hydrate	30.2.11
Chlordiazepoxide	Librium	Benzodiazepines	30.2.5
Chlorpromazine	Thorazine	Dopamine Receptor Antagonists: Antipsychotics	30.2.13
Chlorprothixene	Taractan	Dopamine Receptor Antagonists: Antipsychotics	30.2.13
Clomipramine	Anafranil	Tricyclics and Tetracyclics: Antidepressants	30.2.22
Clonazepam	Klonopin	Benzodiazepines	30.2.5
Clonidine	Catapres	Clonidine	30.2.12
Clozapine	Clozaril	Clozapine	30.2.14
Desipramine	Norpramin, Pertofrane	Tricyclics and Tetracyclics: Antidepressants	30.2.22
Dextroamphetamine	Dexedrine	Sympathomimetics	30.2.19
Diazepam	Valium	Benzodiazepines	30.2.5
Diltiazem	Cardizem	Calcium Channel Inhibitors	30.2.9
Diphenhydramine	Benadryl	Antihistamines	30.2.3
Doxepin	Adapin, Sinequan	Tricyclics and Tetracyclics: Antidepressants	30.2.22
Ethchlorvynol	Placidyl	Chloral Hydrate	30.2.11
Ethinamate	Valmid	Barbiturates	30.2.4
Ethopropazide	Paridol	Anticholinergics	30.2.2
Fluoxetine	Prozac	Fluoxetine	30.2.15
Fluphenazine	Permitil, Prolixin	Dopamine Receptor Antagonists: Antipsychotics	30.2.13
Flurazepam	Dalmane	Benzodiazepines	30.2.5
Glutethimide	Doriden	Barbiturates	30.2.4
Halazepam	Paxipam	Benzodiazepines	30.2.5
Haloperidol	Haldol	Dopamine Receptor Antagonists: Antipsychotics	30.2.13
Hydroxyzine	Atarax, Vistaril	Antihistamines	30.2.3
Imipramine	Tofranil	Tricyclics and Tetracyclics: Antidepressants	30.2.22
Isocarboxazid	Marplan	Monoamine Oxidase Inhibitors	30.2.18
Lithium	Eskalith, Lithobid	Lithium	30.2.16
Lorazepam	Ativan	Benzodiazepines	30.2.5
Loxapine	Loxitane	Dopamine Receptor Antagonists: Antipsychotics	30.2.13
Maprotiline	Ludiomil	Tricyclics and Tetracyclics: Antidepressants	30.2.22
Mephobarbital	Mebaral	Barbiturates	30.2.4
Meprobamate	Miltown, Equanil	Barbiturates	30.2.4
Mesoridazine	Serentil	Dopamine Receptor Antagonists: Antipsychotics	30.2.13
Methadone	Dolophine, Methadose	Methadone	30.2.17
Methylphenidate	Ritalin	Sympathomimetics	30.2.19
Methyprylon	Noludar	Barbiturates	30.2.4
Metoprolol	Lopressor	β-Adrenergic Receptor Antagonists	20.3.6
Molindone	Moban, Lidone	Dopamine Receptor Antagonists: Antipsychotics	30.2.13
Nadolol	Corzide, Corgard	β-Adrenergic Receptor Antagonists	30.2.6
Nifedipine	Procardia	Calcium Channel Inhibitors	30.2.9
Nortriptyline	Aventyl, Pamelor	Tricyclics and Tetracyclics: Antidepressants	30.2.22
Orphenadrine	Dispal, Norflex	Anticholinergics	30.2.2
Oxazepam	Serax	Benzodiazepines	30.2.5
Paraldehyde	No trade name	Barbiturates	30.2.4
Pemoline	Cylert	Sympathomimetics	30.2.19
Pentobarbital	Cafergot	Barbiturates	30.2.4
Perphenazine	Trilafon	Dopamine Receptor Antagonists: Antipsychotics	30.2.13
Phenelzine	Nardil	Monoamine Oxidase Inhibitors	30.2.18
Phenobarbital	Luminal	Barbiturates	30.2.4
Pimozide	Orap	Dopamine Receptor Antagonists: Antipsychotics	30.2.13
Piperacetazine	No trade name	Dopamine Receptor Antagonists: Antipsychotics	30.2.13
Prazepam	Centrax	Benzodiazepines	30.2.5

(Continued)

Table 30.1-1
Continued

Generic Name	Trade Name	Section Title	Section Number
Prochlorperazine	Compazine	Dopamine Receptor Antagonists: Antipsychotics	30.2.13
Procyclidine	Kemadrin	Anticholinergics	30.2.2
Propranolol	Inderal	β-Adrenergic Receptor Antagonists	30.2.6
Protriptyline	Vivactyl	Tricyclics and Tetracyclics: Antidepressants	30.2.22
Reserpine	Serpasil	Dopamine Receptor Antagonists: Antipsychotics	30.2.13
Quazepam	Doral	Benzodiazepines	30.2.5
Secobarbital	Seconal	Barbiturates	30.2.4
Sodium valproate	Depakene	Valproic Acid	30.2.24
Temazepam	Restoril	Benzodiazepines	30.2.5
Thioridazine	Mellaril	Dopamine Receptor Antagonists: Antipsychotics	30.2.13
Thiothixene	Navane	Dopamine Receptor Antagonists: Antipsychotics	30.2.13
Thyroxine	Levoxine, Levothoid, Synthroid	Thyroid Hormones	30.2.20
Tranylcypromine	Parnate	Monoamine Oxidase Inhibitors	30.2.18
Trazodone	Desyrel	Trazodone	30.2.21
Triazolam	Halcion	Benzodiazepines	30.2.5
Trifluoperazine	Stelazine	Dopamine Receptor Antagonists: Antipsychotics	30.2.13
Triflupromazine	Vesprin	Dopamine Receptor Antagonists: Antipsychotics	30.2.13
Trihexyphenidyl	Artane	Anticholinergics	30.2.2
L-Triiodothyronine	Cytomel	Thyroid Hormones	30.2.20
Trimipramine	Surmontil	Tricyclics and Tetracyclics: Antidepressants	30.2.22
L-Tryptophan	No trade name	L-Tryptophan	30.2.23
Valproic Acid	Depakene	Valproic Acid	30.2.24
Verapamil	Calan, Isoptin	Calcium Channel Inhibitors	30.2.9

Table 30.1-2
Drugs and Classes of Drugs Used in the Treatment of Major Psychiatric Disorders

Disorder / Drug	Section
Aggression (see Episodic dyscontrol disorder)	
Akathisia (see Drug-induced extrapyramidal movement disorders)	
Alcohol-related disorders	
β-Adrenergic receptor antagonists	30.2.6
Benzodiazepines	30.2.5
Carbamazepine	30.2.10
Lithium	30.2.16
Anorexia nervosa (see Eating disorders)	
Anxiety (also see specific anxiety disorder)	
Antihistamines	30.2.3
Barbiturates	30.2.4
Benzodiazepines	30.2.5
Bipolar disorder	
Benzodiazepines (especially clonazepam)	30.2.5
Calcium channel inhibitors	30.2.9
Carbamazepine	30.2.10
Dopamine receptor antagonists (antipsychotics)	30.2.13
Lithium	30.2.16
L-Tryptophan	30.2.23
Valproic acid	30.2.24
Bulimia nervosa (see Eating disorders)	
Cyclothymia (see Bipolar disorder)	
Depressive disorder	
Benzodiazepines (especially alprazolam)	30.2.5
Bupropion	30.2.7
Carbamazepine	30.2.10
Fluoxetine	30.2.15
Lithium	30.2.16
Monoamine oxidase inhibitors	30.2.18
Sympathomimetics	30.2.19
Thyroid hormones	30.2.20
Trazodone	30.2.21
Tricyclic and tetracyclic antidepressants	30.2.22
L-Tryptophan	30.2.23
Drug-induced extrapyramidal movement disorders	
β-Adrenergic receptor antagonists	30.2.6
Amantadine	30.2.1
Anticholinergics	30.2.2
Antihistamines	30.2.3
Benzodiazepines	30.2.5
Dysthymia (see Depressive disorder)	
Dystonias (see Drug-induced extrapyramidal movement disorders)	
Eating disorders	
Lithium	30.2.16
Monoamine oxidase inhibitors	30.2.18
Tricyclic and tetracyclic antidepressants	30.2.22
Episodic dyscontrol disorder	
β-Adrenergic receptor antagonists	30.2.6
Carbamazepine	30.2.10
Dopamine receptor antagonists (antipsychotics)	30.2.13
Lithium	30.2.16
Valproic acid	30.2.24
Generalized anxiety disorder	
β-Adrenergic receptor antagonists	30.2.6
Barbiturates	30.2.4
Benzodiazepines	30.2.5
Buspirone	30.2.8
Tricyclic and tetracyclic antidepressants	30.2.22
Obsessive-compulsive disorder	
Fluoxetine	30.2.15
Tricyclic and tetracyclic antidepressants (especially clomipramine)	30.2.22
Opiate-related disorders	
Clonidine	30.2.12
Methadone	30.2.17
Panic disorder (with and without agoraphobia)	
β-Adrenergic receptor antagonists	30.2.6

Table 30.1-2
Continued

Benzodiazepines (especially alprazolam and clonazepam)	30.2.5
Monoamine oxidase inhibitors	30.2.18
Tricyclic and tetracyclic antidepressants	30.2.22
Parkinsonism (see Drug-induced extrapyramidal movement disorders)	
Phobias (see also Panic disorder)	
β-Adrenergic receptor antagonists	30.2.6
Benzodiazepines	30.2.5
Post-traumatic stress disorder	
Monoamine oxidase inhibitors	30.2.18
Tricyclic and tetracyclic antidepressants	30.2.22
Psychosis (see Schizophrenia)	
Rabbit syndrome (see Drug-induced extrapyramidal movement disorders)	
Schizoaffective disorder (see Depressive disorder, Bipolar disorder, and Schizophrenia)	
Schizophrenia	
Benzodiazepines	30.2.5
Carbamazepine	30.2.10
Clozapine	30.2.14
Dopamine receptor antagonists (antipsychotics)	30.2.13
Lithium	30.2.16
Sleep disorders	
Antihistamines	30.2.3
Barbiturates	30.2.4
Benzodiazepines	30.2.5
Chloral hydrate	30.2.11
Sympathomimetics	30.2.19
L-Tryptophan	30.2.23
Violence (see Episodic dyscontrol disorder)	

(e.g., the benzodiazepines in addition to the older drugs, such as the barbiturates). The next 30 years were devoted primarily to clinical studies demonstrating the efficacy of these drugs and to the development of related compounds in each category. The efficacy of each of these classes of drugs for treating relatively specific psychiatric syndromes and for elucidating their pharmacodynamic effects provided the impetus to develop the various neurotransmitter hypotheses of mental disorders (e.g., the dopamine hypothesis of schizophrenia, the monoamine hypothesis of mood disorders).

Since 1960 the major additions to the psychotherapeutic drugs have been the anticonvulsants, particularly carbamazepine (Tegretol) and valproic acid (Depakene), which are effective in treating some patients with bipolar disorder. Buspirone (BuSpar), a nonbenzodiazepine anxiolytic, was introduced for clinical use in America in 1986. A number of new antidepressant drugs (fluoxetine [Prozac], bupropion [Wellbutrin], trazodone [Desyrel]) have also been marketed. It is expected that the burgeoning knowledge of basic neuroscience and neuropharmacology will lead to the development of many new psychotherapeutic drugs during the next decade.

Table 30.1-3
Some Historical Events in Psychopharmacology, 1845–1960

1845	Hashish intoxication proposed as a model of insanity (Moreau)
1869	Chloral hydrate introduced as a treatment for melancholia and mania
1875	Cocaine proposed as a treatment in psychiatry (Freud)
1882	Paraldehyde introduced
1892	Research with morphine, alochol, ether, and paraldehyde in normal persons (Kraepelin)
1903	Barbiturates introduced
1917	Psychosis of syphilis treated with malaria fever therapy (Julius von Wagner-Jauregg)
1922	Barbiturate-induced coma (Jacob Klaesi)
1927	Insulin shock for schizophrenia (Manfred Sakel)
1931	*Rauwolfia serpentina* (reserpine) introduced (Sen and Bose) (confirmed as a treatment for schizophrenia in 1953 by Nathan Kline)
1934	Pentylenetetrazol-induced convulsions (Laszlo von Meduna)
1936	Frontal lobotomies (Egas Moniz)
1938	Electroconvulsive therapy (Ugo Cerletti and Lucio Bini)
1940	Dilantin introduced as anticonvulsant (Tracy Putnam)
1943	Lysergic acid diethylamide (LSD) synthesized (Albert Hofmann)
1949	Lithium introduced
1952	Chlorpromazine introduced
1955–1958	Tricyclic antidepressants and monoamine oxidase inhibitors introduced
1960	Chlordiazepoxide introduced

PHARMACOLOGICAL ACTIONS

Pharmacokinetic interactions describe how the body handles a drug; pharmacodynamic interactions describe the effects of a drug on the body. In a parallel fashion pharmacokinetic drug interactions refer to plasma concentrations of drugs, and the pharmacodynamic drug interactions refer to receptor activities of drugs.

Pharmacokinetics

The principal divisions of pharmacokinetics are drug absorption, distribution, metabolism, and excretion.

Absorption. A psychotherapeutic drug must first reach the blood on its way to the brain, unless it is directly administered into the cerebrospinal fluid or the brain. Orally administered drugs must dissolve in the fluid of the gastrointestinal (GI) tract before the body can absorb them. Drug tablets can be designed to disintegrate either quickly or slowly, the absorption depending on the drug's concentration and lipid solubility and the GI tract's local pH, motility, and surface area. Depending on the drug's pK_a and the GI tract's pH, the drug may be present in an ionized form that limits its lipid solubility. If the pharmacokinetic absorption factors are favorable, the drug may reach therapeutic blood concentrations more quickly if it is administered intramuscularly. If a drug is coupled with an appropriate carrier molecule, intramuscular administration can sustain the drug's release over a long period of time. Some antipsychotic drugs are available in depot forms that allow the drug to be administered only once every one to four weeks. Even though intravenous administration is the quickest route to achieve therapeutic blood levels, it also carries the highest risk of sudden and life-threatening adverse effects.

Distribution. Drugs can be freely dissolved in the blood plasma, bound to dissolved plasma proteins (primarily albumin), or dissolved within the blood cells. If a drug is bound too tightly to plasma proteins, it may have to be metabolized and excreted before it can leave the bloodstream, thus greatly reducing the amount of active drug reaching the brain. The lithium ion is an example of a water-soluble drug that is not bound to plasma proteins. The distribution of a drug to the brain is determined by the blood-brain barrier, the brain's regional blood flow, and the drug's affinity with its receptors in the brain. Both high blood flow and affinity favor the distribution of the drug to the brain. Drugs may also reach the brain after passively diffusing into the cerebrospinal fluid from the bloodstream. The volume of distribution is a measure of the apparent space in the body available to contain the drug. The volume of distribution can also vary with the patient's age, sex, and disease state.

Metabolism and excretion. Metabolism is somewhat synonymous with the term "biotransformation." The four major metabolic routes for drugs are oxidation, reduction, hydrolysis, and conjugation. Although the usual result of metabolism is to produce inactive metabolites that are more readily excreted than is the parent compound, there are many examples of active metabolites produced from psychoactive drugs. The liver is the principal site of metabolism, and bile, feces, and urine are the major routes of excretion. Psychoactive drugs are also excreted in sweat, saliva, tears, and milk; therefore, mothers who are taking psychotherapeutic drugs should not breast feed their children. Disease states or coadministered drugs that affect the ability of the liver or the kidneys to metabolize and eliminate drugs can both raise and lower the blood concentrations of a psychoactive drug.

Four important concepts regarding metabolism and excretion are time of peak plasma level, half-life, first pass effect, and clearance. The time between the administration of a drug and the appearance of peak concentrations of the drug in plasma varies primarily according to the route of administration and absorption. A drug's half-life is defined as the amount of time it takes for one-half of a drug's peak plasma level to be metabolized and excreted from the body. A general guideline is that, if a drug is administered repeatedly in doses separated by time intervals shorter than its half-life, the drug will reach 97 percent of its steady-state plasma concentrations in a time equal to five times its half-life. The first pass effect refers to the extensive initial metabolism of some drugs within the portal circulation or liver, thereby reducing the amount of unmetabolized drug that reaches the systemic circulation. Clearance is a measure of the amount of drug excreted in each unit of time. If some disease process or other drug interferes with the clearance of a psychoactive drug, the drug may reach toxic levels.

Pharmacodynamics

The major pharmacodynamic considerations include receptor mechanism; the dose-response curve; the therapeutic index; and the development of tolerance, dependence, and withdrawal phenomena. The receptor for a drug can be defined generally as the cellular component that binds to the drug and initiates the drug's pharmacodynamic effects. A drug can be an agonist for its receptor, thereby stimulating a physiological effect; conversely, a drug can be an antagonist for the receptor, most often by blocking the receptor so that an endogenous agonist cannot affect the receptor. The receptor site for most psychotherapeutic drugs is also a receptor site for an endogenous neurotransmitter. For example, the primary receptor site for chlorpromazine is the dopamine receptor. However, for other psychotherapeutic drugs this may not be the case. The receptor for lithium may be the enzyme inositol-1-phosphatase, and the receptor for verapamil (a calcium channel inhibitor) is a calcium channel.

The dose-response curve plots the drug concentration against the effects of the drug (Figure 30.1-1). The potency of a drug refers to the relative dose required to achieve a certain effect. Haloperidol, for example, is more potent than is chlorpromazine because approximately 5 mg of haloperidol is required to achieve the same therapeutic effect as 100 mg of chlorpromazine. Both haloperidol and chlorpromazine, however, are equal in their clinical efficacy—that is, the maximum clinical response achievable by the administration of a drug.

The side effects of most drugs are often a direct result of their primary pharmacodynamic effects and are better conceptualized as adverse effects. The therapeutic index is a relative measure of a drug's toxicity or safety. It is defined as the ratio of the median toxic dose (TD_{50}) to the median effective dose (ED_{50}). The TD_{50} is the dose at which 50 percent of patients experience toxic effects, and the ED_{50} is the dose at which 50 percent of patients have a therapeutic effect. Haloperidol, for example, has a very high therapeutic index, as evidenced by the wide range of doses in which it is prescribed. Conversely, lithium has a very low therapeutic index, thereby requiring careful monitoring of serum lithium levels when prescribing this drug. There can be both inter- and intraindividual variation in the response to a specific drug. An individual patient may be hyporeactive, normally reactive, or hyperreactive to a particular drug. For example, some patients with schizophrenia require 1 mg a day of haloperidol, others require a more typical 10 mg a day, and still others require 100 mg a day to achieve a therapeutic response. Idiosyncratic drug responses occur when a person experiences a particularly unusual effect from a drug. For example, some patients become quite agitated when given benzodiazepines, such as diazepam (Valium).

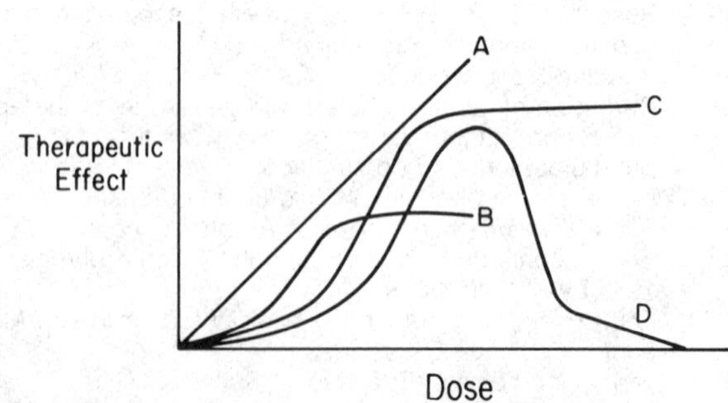

Figure 30.1-1. These dose-response curves plot the therapeutic effect as a function of increasing dose, often calculated as the log of the dose. Drug A has a linear dose response; drugs B and C have sigmoidal curves; and drug D has a curvilinear dose-response curve. Although smaller doses of drug B are more potent than are equal doses of drug C, drug C has a higher maximum efficacy than does drug B. Drug D has a therapeutic window, such that both low and high doses are less effective than are midrange doses.

A person may become less responsive to a particular drug as it is administered over time, which is referred to as tolerance. The development of tolerance is associated with the appearance of physical dependence, which may be defined as the necessity to continue administering the drug in order to prevent the appearance of withdrawal symptoms.

CLINICAL GUIDELINES

The practice of clinical psychopharmacology requires skill as both a diagnostician and a psychotherapist, knowledge of the available drugs, and the ability to plan a pharmacotherapeutic regimen. The selection and initiation of drug treatment should be based on the patient's past history, current clinical state, and the treatment plan. The psychiatrist should know the purpose or goal of a drug trial, the length of time that the drug needs to be administered in order to assess its efficacy, the approach to be taken to reduce any adverse effects that may occur, alternative drug strategies should the current one fail, and whether long-term maintenance of the patient on the drug is indicated. In almost all cases, the psychiatrist should explain the treatment plan to the patient and often to the family and other caretakers. The patient's reaction to and ideas about a proposed drug trial should be considered. However, if the psychiatrist believes that accommodating the patient's wishes would hinder treatment, this should be explained to the patient.

Choice of Drug

The first two steps in selecting drug treatment, the diagnosis and identification of target symptoms, should be carried out when the patient has been in a drug-free state for one to two weeks. The drug-free state should include the absence of medications for sleep, such as hypnotics, as the quality of sleep can be both an important diagnostic guide and a target symptom. If a patient is hospitalized, however, insurance guidelines may make a drug-free period difficult or even impossible to obtain. Psychiatrists often evaluate symptomatic patients who are already receiving one or more psychoactive medications, and so it is usually necessary to wean the patient from the current medications and then to make an assessment. An exception to this practice occurs when a patient presents to the psychiatrist on a suboptimal regimen of an otherwise appropriate drug. In such cases, the psychiatrist may decide to continue the drug at a higher dose to complete a full therapeutic trial.

From among the drugs appropriate to a particular diagnosis, the specific drug should be selected according to the patient's past history of drug response (compliance, therapeutic response, and adverse effects), the patient's family history of drug response, the profile of adverse effects for that drug with regard to a particular patient, and the psychiatrist's usual practice. If a drug has previously been effective in treating a patient or a family member, it should be used again unless there is some specific reason not to use the drug. A past history of severe adverse effects from a specific drug is a strong indicator that the patient would not be compliant with that drug regimen. It is unfortunate that patients and their families are often quite ignorant of what drugs have been used before, in what dosages, and for how long. This ignorance may reflect the tendency of psychiatrists not to explain drug trials to their patients, whereas psychiatrists should be encouraged to give their patients written records of drug trials for their personal medical records. A caveat to obtaining a past history of drug response from patients is that, because of their mental disorders, they may inaccurately report the effects of a previous drug trial. If possible, therefore, the patients' medical records should be obtained to confirm their reports. Most psychotherapeutic drugs of a single class have been demonstrated to be equally efficacious; however, these drugs do differ in their adverse effects on individual patients. A drug should be selected that minimally exacerbates any preexisting medical problems that a patient has.

Combination drugs. Some combination drugs (Table 30.1-4) may actually increase the patient's compliance by simplifying the drug regimen. A problem with combination drugs, however, is that the clinician has less flexibility in adjusting the dosage of one of the components. That is, the use of combination drugs may cause two drugs to be administered when only one continues to be effective.

Nonapproved dosages and uses. Under the federal Food, Drug, and Cosmetic (FDC) Act, the Food and Drug Administration (FDA) has authority to control the initial availability of a drug by approving only those new drugs that demonstrate both safety and effectiveness and then to ensure that the drug's proposed labeling is truthful and contains all pertinent information for the safe and effective use of that drug.

Before a new drug can be approved by the FDA, it must be studied in humans. For the drug ultimately to be approved for commercial use, the sponsor must justify the safety and effectiveness of the drug by submitting a New Drug Application (NDA) to the FDA. The NDA is approved or disapproved, depending on the clinical data accumulated. For approval, the FDA requires that adequate tests be conducted showing that the drug "is safe for use under the conditions prescribed, recommended, or suggested." There must also be "substantial evidence that the drug will have the effect it purports under the conditions of use prescribed, recommended, or suggested in the proposed labeling."

Use of FDA-approved drugs in private practice. According to the Medical Liability Mutual Insurance Company (MLMIC), once a drug is approved for commercial use, the physician may, as part of the practice of medicine, lawfully prescribe a different dosage for a patient or otherwise vary the conditions of use from what is approved in the package labeling without notifying or obtaining the FDA's approval. Specifically, the FDC Act does not limit the manner in which a physician may use an approved drug. However, although physicians may treat patients with an approved drug for unapproved purposes—that is, indications not included on the drug's official labeling—without violating the FDC Act, the patient's right to redress for possible medical malpractice still remains. This is a significant concern because the failure to follow the FDA-approved label may create an inference that the physician was varying from the prevailing standard of care. Although the failure to follow the contents of the drug label does not impose liability per se and should not preclude a

Table 30.1-4
Combination Drugs Used in Psychiatry

Ingredients	Preparation	Manufacturer	Amount of Each Ingredient	Recommended Dosage*	Indications	D.E.A.† Control
Perphenazine and amitriptyline	Triavil	Merck, Sharp & Dohme	Tablet—2:25, 4:25, 4:50, 2:10, 4:10	Initial therapy: tablet of 2:25 or 4:25 q.i.d.	Depression and associated anxiety	0
	Etrafon	Schering		Maintenance therapy: tablet 2:25 or 4:25 b.i.d. or q.i.d.		
Meprobamate and benactyzine	Deprol	Wallace	Tablet—400:1	Initial therapy: one tablet q.i.d. Maintenance therapy: initial dosage may be increased to six tablets a day, then gradually reduced to the lowest levels that provide relief	Depression and associated anxiety	IV
Dextroamphetamine and amphetamine	Biphetamine‡	Pennwalt	Sustained release capsule—6.25:6.25	One capsule in the morning	Exogenous obesity	II
Chlordiazepoxide and clinidium bromide	Librax	Roche	Capsule—5:25	One or two capsules t.i.d. or q.i.d. before meals and at bedtime	Peptic ulcer, gastritis, duodenitis, irritable bowel syndrome, spastic colitis, and mild ulcerative colitis	O
Chlordiazepoxide and amitriptyline	Limbitrol	Roche	Tablet—5:12.5, 10:25	Tablet of 5:12.5 t.i.d. or q.i.d. Tablet of 10:25 t.i.d. or q.i.d. initially, then may increase to six tablets daily as required	Depression and associated anxiety	IV

*t.i.d., q.i.d., and b.i.d.
†DEA, Drug Enforcement Administration.
‡The United States Food and Drug Administration recommends the use of amphetamine for weight reduction. However, various states (California, New York) allow these medications for short-term use as an appetite suppressant and in depression for a two- to three-day trial to gauge the effectiveness of certain tricyclics.

physician from using good clinical judgment in the interest of the patient, the physician should be aware that the drug label represents important information regarding safe and effective use (as determined by the scientific data submitted to the FDA).

In summary, the psychiatrist may prescribe medication for any reason that he or she believes to be medically indicated for the welfare of the patient. This clarification is important in view of the increasing regulation of physicians by federal, state, and local government agencies and the intimidation being experienced by many physicians in exercising their best medical judgment. A similar position was enunciated in an editorial by John D. Archer, M.D., in the *Journal of the American Medical Association* (*255:* 1055, 1984) as follows:

> Fortunately, the myth about the authoritarian status of the package insert is disappearing. An honorable and welcomed statement by the FDA has confirmed what I have said for two decades about "approved uses" of drugs: there is no such thing. The FDA statement even endorsed the same alternate and correct phrasing that I coined: An "unapproved use" should not connote a disapproved use, but merely an "unlabeled use." Uses *in* the labeling are merely that: "labeled uses."

The House of Delegates of the American Medical Association, at its 1982 Interim Meeting, adopted a report that quoted in full the FDA statement on this subject. The report called for the publisher of the *Physician's Desk Reference* (*PDR*) (Medical Economics Company, Oradell, NJ) to include this statement in future editions. Accordingly, in the 1983 and 1984 editions of the *PDR,* a summary of the FDA statement regarding the use of approved drugs for purposes not in the labeling appears in the FOREWORD.

If clinicians are in doubt about a drug treatment plan, they should consult with a colleague or suggest that the patient obtain a second opinion. The Drug Enforcement Agency (DEA) has classified drugs according to abuse potential (Table 30.1-5), and clinicians are advised to be cautious when prescribing any controlled substances.

Therapeutic trials. A drug's therapeutic trial should last for a previously determined length of time. Because behavioral symptoms are more difficult to assess than are other physiological symptoms, such as hypertension, it is particularly important for specific target symptoms to be identified at the initiation of a drug trial. The psychiatrist and the patient can then assess these target symptoms over the course of the drug trial to help determine whether the drug has been effective. A number of objective rating scales, such as the Brief Psychiatric Rating Scale (BPRS) and the Schedule for Affective Disorders and Schizophrenia (SADS), are available to help assess a patient's progress over the course of a drug trial. If a drug has not been effective in reducing target symptoms within the specified length of time and if other reasons for the lack of response can be eliminated, the drug should be tapered and stopped. The brain is not a group of on-and-off neurochemical switches; rather, it is an interactive network of neurons in a complex homeostasis. Thus, the abrupt discontinuation of virtually any psychoactive drug is likely to disrupt further the brain's functioning. Another common clinical mistake is the routine addition of medications without the discontinuation of a prior drug. Although this practice is indicated in specific circumstances, such as lithium potentiation of an unsuccessful trial of antidepressants, it often results in increased noncompliance and adverse effects and the clinician's not knowing whether it was the second drug alone or the combination of drugs that resulted in a therapeutic success.

Table 30.1-5
Characteristics of Drugs at Each DEA Level

DEA Control Level (Schedule)	Characteristics of Drug at Each Control Level	Examples of Drugs at Each Control Level
I	High abuse potential No accepted use in medical treatment in the United States at the present time and, therefore, not for prescription use Can be used for research	LSD, heroin, marijuana, peyote, PCP, mescaline, psilocybin, tetrahydrocannabinols, nicocodeine, nicomorphine
II	High abuse potential Severe physical dependence liability Severe psychological dependence liability No refills; no telephone prescriptions	Amphetamine, methamphetamine, opium, morphine, codeine, hydromorphine, phenmetrazine, cocaine, amobarbital, secobarbital, pentobarbital, methylphenidate
III	Abuse potential less than levels I and II Moderate or low physical dependence liability High psychological liability Prescriptions must be rewritten after six months or five refills	Glutethimide, methyprylon, nalorphine, sulfonmethane, benzphetamine, phendimetrazine, clortermine, mazindol, chlorphentermine; compounds containing codeine, morphine, opium, hydrocodone, dihydrocodeine, naltrexone, diethylpropion
IV	Low abuse potential Limited physical dependence liability Limited psychological dependence liability Prescriptions must be rewritten after six months or five refills	Phenobarbital, benzodiazepines,* chloral hydrate, ethchlorvynol, ethinamate, meprobamate, paraldehyde
V	Lowest abuse potential of all controlled substances	Narcotic preparations containing limited amounts of nonnarcotic active medicinal ingredients

*In New York State, benzodiazepines are treated as schedule II substances, which require a triplicate prescription for a maximum of one month's supply.

Therapeutic failures. The failure of a specific drug trial should prompt the clinician to consider a number of possibilities. First, was the original diagnosis correct? This reconsideration should include the possibility of an undiagnosed organic mental disorder, including illicit drug abuse. Second, are the observed remaining symptoms actually the drug's adverse effects and not related to the original disease? Antipsychotic drugs, for example, can produce akinesia, which resembles psychotic withdrawal, or akathisia and neuroleptic malignant syndrome, which resemble increased psychotic agitation. Third, was the drug administered in sufficient dosage for an appropriate period of time? Patients can have vastly different drug absorption and metabolic rates for the same drug, and plasma drug levels should be obtained to assess this variable. Fourth, was there a pharmacokinetic or pharmacodynamic interaction with another drug the patient was taking that reduced the efficacy of the psychotherapeutic drug? Fifth, did the patient actually take the drug as directed? Drug noncompliance is a very common clinical problem. Reasons for drug noncompliance are complicated drug regimens (more than one drug in more than one daily dose), adverse side effects (especially if unnoticed by the clinician), and poor patient education about the drug treatment plan.

Patient Education

As stated previously, patients should know their diagnosis, the target symptoms that the drug is supposed to reduce, the length of time they will be on the drug, both expected and unexpected adverse effects, and the treatment plan to be followed if the current drug is unsuccessful. Although some psychiatric disorders interfere with patients' ability to comprehend this information, the psychiatrist should relay as much of this information as possible. The clear presentation of this material is often less frightening than are patients' fantasies about drug treatment. It is important to tell patients how long it will take for them to receive benefits from the drug trial. This factor is perhaps most critical when patients have a mood disorder and may not observe therapeutic effects for three to four weeks.

Patient's attitudes toward drugs. Some patients' ambivalent attitudes toward drugs often reflect the confusion about drug treatment that exists in the field of psychiatry. Patients often feel that taking a psychotherapeutic drug means that they are "really sick" or not in control of their lives or that they may become addicted to the drug and have to take it forever. A simplified approach to these concerns is to describe the psychiatric disorder as a disease, analogous to diabetes, in which medication is necessary to maintain function. It is often helpful to draw pictures of neurons to demonstrate how the drug is working in the brain. Psychiatrists should explain the difference between drugs of abuse that affect the normal brain and psychiatric drugs that are used to treat emotional disorders. They should point out to patients that antipsychotics, antidepressants, and antimanic drugs are not addictive in the way that, for example, heroin is addictive. The psychiatrist's clear and honest explanation of how long the patient should take the drug will help the patient adjust to the idea of chronic maintenance medication if that is, indeed, the treatment plan. In some cases it is appropriate for the psychiatrist to give the patient increasing responsibility for adjusting the medications as the treatment progresses. This can often help the patient feel less controlled by the drug.

Informed consent. Informed consent is a legal term indicating that the patient has agreed to the suggested drug trial after having been advised of the potential benefits, the risks of the treatment, and alternative treatments. Some states require patients to sign a document stating that they have given informed consent, and some clinicians have adopted this practice in states that do not require a form. Clearly, the capacity of a psychiatric patient to understand this information is often difficult to assess. The problem represents an ethical dilemma that can best be met by psychiatrists' attempting to meet the letter and the spirit of the law to the best of their abilities. When in doubt about a patient's ability to make such a decision, the psychiatrist should consult the patient's family, friends, caretakers, or legal counsel.

Special Considerations

Children. Special care must be given when administering psychotherapeutic drugs to children. Although the small volume of distribution in children suggests the use of lower dosages than in adults, children's higher rate of metabolism suggests that higher ratios of milligrams of drug to kilograms of body weight should be used. In practice, it is best to begin with a small dose and to increase the dosage until clinical effects are observed. The clinician, however, should not hesitate to use adult dosages in children if the dosages are effective and there are no side effects.

Geriatric patients. The two major concerns when treating geriatric patients with psychotherapeutic drugs are that elderly persons may be more susceptible to adverse side effects (particularly adverse cardiac effects) and may metabolize drugs more slowly, thus requiring lower dosages of medication. Another concern is that geriatric patients are often taking other medications, thereby requiring psychiatrists to consider possible drug interactions carefully. In practice, psychiatrists should begin treating geriatric patients with a small dose, usually about one-half the usual dose. The dosage should be raised in small amounts more slowly than in middle-aged adults until either a clinical benefit is achieved or unacceptable adverse effects appear. Although many geriatric patients require a small dosage of medication, many others require the usual adult dosage.

Pregnant and nursing women. The basic rule is to avoid administering any drug to a woman who is pregnant (particularly during the first trimester) or who is breast feeding a child. This rule, however, occasionally needs to be broken when the mother's psychiatric disorder is severe. If psychotherapeutic medications need to be administered during a pregnancy, the possibility of therapeutic abortion should be discussed. The two most teratogenic drugs in the psychopharmacopeia are lithium and anticonvulsants. Lithium administration during pregnancy is associated with a high incidence of birth abnormalities, including Ebstein's malformation, a serious abnormality in cardiac development. Other psychoactive drugs (antidepressants, antipsychotics, and anxiolytics), although less clearly associated with birth defects, should also be avoided during pregnancy if at all possible. The most common clinical situation occurs when a pregnant women becomes psychotic. If a decision is made not to terminate the pregnancy, it is preferable to administer antipsychotics, rather than lithium.

The administration of psychotherapeutic drugs at or near delivery may cause the baby to be overly sedated at delivery, requiring a respirator, or to be physically dependent on the drug, requiring detoxification and treatment of a withdrawal syndrome. Virtually all psychotropic drugs are secreted in the milk of a nursing mother; therefore, mothers on these agents should be advised not to breast feed their children.

Medically ill patients. Considerations in administering psychotropic drugs to medically ill patients include a potentially increased sensitivity to side effects, either increased or decreased metabolism and excretion of the drug, and interactions with other medications. As with children and geriatric patients, the most reasonable clinical practice is to begin with a small dose, increase it slowly, and watch for both clinical and adverse effects. The testing of plasma drug levels may be particularly helpful in these patients.

ADVERSE EFFECTS

Most psychotherapeutic drugs do not affect a single neurotransmitter system, nor are their effects localized to the brain. The effects of psychotherapeutic drugs on neurotransmitter systems result in the wide range of adverse effects associated with their use. For example, some of the most common adverse effects of psychotherapeutic drugs are caused by the blockade of muscarinic acetylcholine receptors (Table 30.1-6). Many psychotherapeutic drugs antagonize dopaminergic, histaminergic, or adrenergic neurons, resulting in the adverse effects listed in Table 30.1-7. There are also several commonly observed adverse effects for which the neurotransmitters involved have not been specifically identified.

Patients generally have less trouble with adverse effects if they have previously been told to expect them. It is not unreasonable to explain the appearance of adverse effects as evidence that the drug is working. But clinicians should distinguish between probable or expected adverse effects and rare or unexpected adverse effects.

An extreme adverse effect of drug treatment is an attempt by a patient to kill himself or herself by overdosing on a psychotherapeutic drug. One psychodynamic theory of such behavior is that such patients are angry at their therapists for not having been able to help them. Whatever the motivation, psychiatrists should be aware of this risk and attempt to prescribe the safest possible drugs. It is good clinical practice to write nonrefillable prescriptions for small quantities of drugs when suicide is a consideration. In extreme cases, attempts should be made to verify that patients are actually taking the medication and not hoarding the pills for a later overdose attempt. It is a common clinical observation that patients may attempt suicide just as they are beginning to get better. Clinicians, therefore, should continue to be careful about prescribing large quantities of medication until the patient is almost completely recovered. Another consideration for psychiatrists is the possibility of accidental overdose, particularly by children in the household. Patients should be advised to keep psychotherapeutic medications in a safe place.

Table 30.1-6
Potential Adverse Effects Caused by Blockade of Muscarinic Acetylcholine Receptors

Blurred vision
Constipation
Decreased salivation
Decreased sweating
Delayed or retrograde ejaculation
Delirium
Exacerbation of asthma (through decreased bronchial secretions)
Hyperthermia (through decreased sweating)
Memory problems
Narrow-angle glaucoma
Photophobia
Sinus tachycardia
Urinary retention

Table 30.1-7
Potential Adverse Effects of Psychotherapeutic Drugs and Associated Neurotransmitter Systems

- Antidopaminergic
  - Endocrine dysfunction
    - Hyperprolactinemia
    - Menstrual dysfunction
    - Sexual dysfunction
  - Movement disorders
    - Akathisia
    - Dystonia
    - Parkinsonism
    - Tardive dyskinesia
- Antiadrenergic (primarily α_1)
  - Dizziness
  - Postural hypotension
  - Reflex tachycardia
- Antihistaminergic
  - Hypotension
  - Sedation
  - Weight gain
- Multiple neurotransmitter systems
  - Agranulocytosis (and other blood dyscrasias)
  - Allergic reactions
  - Anorexia
  - Cardiac conduction abnormalities
  - Nausea and vomiting
  - Seizures

Treatment of Common Adverse Effects

Many adverse effects are seen with a great number of different psychotherapeutic drugs. The management of these adverse effects is similar, regardless of which psychotherapeutic drug the patient is taking.

Dry mouth. Dry mouth is caused by the blockade of muscarinic acetylcholine receptors. When patients attempt to relieve the dry mouth by constantly sucking on sugar-containing hard candies, they increase their risk of dental caries. They can avoid this problem by chewing sugarless gum or sucking on sugarless hard candies. Some clinicians recommend the use of a 1 percent solution of pilocarpine, a cholinergic agonist, as a mouth wash three times daily. Other clinicians suggest bethanechol (Urecholine, Myotonachol) tablets, a cholinergic agonist, 10 to 30 mg, once to twice daily. It is best to start with 10 mg once a day and to increase the dosage slowly. Adverse effects of cholinomimetic drugs, such as bethanechol, include tremor, diarrhea, abdominal cramps, and excessive eye watering.

Blurred vision. The blockade of muscarinic acetylcholine receptors causes mydriasis (pupillary dilation) and cycloplegia (ciliary muscle paresis), resulting in presbyopia (blurred near vision). This symptom can be relieved by cholinomimetic eyedrops. A 1 percent solution of pilocarpine can be prescribed as one drop four times daily. Bethanechol can be used as for dry mouth as an alternative.

Urinary retention. The anticholinergic activity of many psychotropics can lead to urinary hesitation, dribbling, urinary retention, and increased urinary tract infections. Elderly patients with enlarged prostates are at increased risk for this adverse effect. Ten to thirty milligrams of bethanechol three to four times daily is usually effective in the treatment of this adverse effect.

Constipation. The anticholinergic activity of psychotropic drugs can result in the particularly disturbing adverse effect of constipation. The first line of treatment involves the prescribing of bulk laxatives, such as Metamucil and Fiberall. If this treatment fails, cathartic laxatives, such as milk of magnesia, can be tried. Prolonged use of cathartic laxatives can result in a loss of their effectiveness. Bethanechol, 10 to 30 mg three to four times daily, can also be used.

Orthostatic hypotension. Orthostatic hypotension is caused by the blockade of α_1-adrenergic receptors. It is absolutely necessary to warn patients of this possible adverse effect, particularly if the patient is elderly. The risk of hip fracture from falls is significantly elevated in patients who are taking psychotropic drugs. With patients at high risk of experiencing orthostatic hypotension, the clinician should choose a drug with low α_1-adrenergic activity. Most simply, the patient can be instructed to get up slowly and to sit down immediately if dizziness is experienced. The patient can also try support hose to help reduce venous pooling. Specific adjuvant medications have been recommended for specific pharmacotherapeutic agents.

Sexual dysfunction. Psychotropic drug use can be associated with sexual dysfunctions—decreased libido, impaired ejaculation and erection, and inhibition of female orgasm. Warning a patient about these adverse effects may increase the patient's concerns. Alternatively, patients are not likely to report adverse sexual effects to the physician. Also, some sexual dysfunctions may be related to the primary psychiatric disorder. Nevertheless, if sexual dysfunctions emerge after pharmacotherapy has begun, it may be worthwhile to attempt treatment of them. Neostigmine (Prostigmin), 7.5 to 15 mg orally 30 minutes before sexual intercourse, may help alleviate impaired ejaculation. Impaired erectile function may be helped with bethanechol given regularly. Cyproheptadine (Periactin), 4 mg every morning, can be used for the treatment of inhibited female orgasm or 4 to 8 mg orally one to two hours before anticipated sexual activity for the treatment of inhibited male orgasm secondary to serotonergic agents.

Weight gain. Weight gain accompanies the use of many psychotropic drugs. The weight gain can be the result of retained fluid, increased caloric intake, or decreased exercise. Edema can be treated by elevating the affected body parts or by administering a thiazide diuretic. If the patient is taking lithium or cardiac medications, drug levels, blood chemistries, and vital signs must be carefully monitored. The patient should also be instructed to minimize the intake of fats and carbohydrates and to exercise regularly. If the patient has not been exercising, however, the clinician should recommend that the patient start the exercise program at a very modest level of exertion.

Extrapyramidal side effects. Neurological side effects—such as dystonias, parkinsonian effects, rabbit syndrome, and tardive dyskinesia—are discussed in Section 30.2.13, "Dopamine Receptor Antagonists: Antipsychotics."

DRUG-DRUG INTERACTIONS

Drug-drug interactions may be either pharmacokinetic or pharmacodynamic and vary greatly in their potential to cause serious problems. An additional consideration is one of phantom drug-drug interactions. The patient may be taking only drug A and then later receive both A and B. The clinician may notice some effect and attribute it to the induction of metabolism. What may have gone on is that the patient was more compliant at one point in the observation period than in another, or there may have been some other effect of which the clinician was unaware. Thus, in the clinical literature, there are reports of phantom drug-drug interactions, but such interactions probably did not really take place.

There may be other interactions that are true but unproved, although reasonably plausible. Still other interactions have some modest effect and are well documented. There are also well-studied, well-proved, clinically important drug-drug interactions. However, it must be remembered that (1) animal pharmacokinetic data are not always readily generalizable to humans; (2) in vitro data do not necessarily replicate results obtained under in vivo conditions; (3) single case reports can contain misleading information; and (4) acute studies should not be uncritically regarded as relevant to investigations of chronic, steady-state conditions.

The informed clinician needs to keep these considerations in mind and to focus on the clinically important interactions, not on the ones that may be mild, unproved, or entirely phantom, and yet still maintain an open and receptive attitude toward drug-drug interactions.

PSYCHOPHARMACOLOGY AND PSYCHOTHERAPY

The goal of both clinical psychopharmacology and psychotherapy is to help patients. If either modality impedes the attainment of that goal, psychiatrists must try to remedy the situation. The integration of the nondirected approach of some psychotherapies and the doctor-directed approach of psychopharmacology requires the talents of a sophisticated clinician. Two unfortunate clinical mistakes are the avoidance of a time-limited drug trial, in order to maintain the purity of some types of psychotherapeutic relationships, and the psychiatrist's ambivalence about a drug trial, contributing to a therapeutic failure or the patient's noncompliance.

CONTINUING EDUCATION

The practice of psychopharmacology is continually changing, so psychiatrists must keep abreast of developments in the field and must evaluate research reports about the efficacy of new agents. Whenever psychiatrists try a new drug, they should review all the available current literature on the agent and possibly consult colleagues.

References

Beardsley R S, Gardocki G J, Larson D B, Hidalgo J: Prescribing of psychotropic medication by primary care physicians and psychiatrists. Arch Gen Psychiatry *45:* 1117, 1988.
Beers M, Avorn J, Sourmerai S B, Everitt D E, Sherman D S, Salem S: Psychoactive medication use in intermediate-care facility residents. JAMA *260:* 3016, 1988.
Cahn C, ed.: Pioneers in psychopharmacology. Psychiatr J Univ Ottawa *14:* 248, 1989.
Hollister L E: Psychopharmacology: The bridge between psychiatry and biology. Clin Pharmacol Ther *44:* 123, 1988.
Jacobsen E: The early history of psychotherapeutic drugs. Psychopharmacology *89:* 138, 1986.
Langer R: New methods for drug delivery. Science *249*: 1527, 1990.
Plaut E A: The ethics of informed consent: An overview. Psychiatr J Univ Ottawa *14:* 435, 1989.
Pollack M H, Rosenbaum J F: Management of antidepressant-induced side effects: A practical guide for the clinicians. J Clin Psychiatry *48:* 3, 1987.
Ray W A, Griffin M R, Schaffner W, Baugh D K, Melton L J: Psychotropic drug use and the risk of hip fracture. N Engl J Med *316:* 363, 1987.
Segraves R T: Effects of psychotropic drugs on human erection and ejaculation. Arch Gen Psychiatry *46:* 275, 1989.
Winer J A, Andriukaitis S M: Interpersonal aspects of initiating pharmacotherapy: How to avoid becoming the patient's feared negative other. Psychiatr Ann *19:* 318, 1989.

30.2 / Psychotherapeutic Drugs

30.2.1 / Amantadine

Amantadine (Symadine, Symmetrel) is a dopamine agonist that is used primarily for the treatment of drug-induced extrapyramidal disorders, such as parkinsonism.

PHARMACOLOGICAL ACTIONS

Pharmacokinetics

Amantadine is well absorbed from the gastrointestinal (GI) tract, reaches peak plasma levels in approximately two to three hours, has a half-life of about 24 hours, and attains steady-state plasma levels after approximately four to five days of therapy. Amantadine is excreted unmetabolized in the urine. Amantadine plasma concentrations can be as much as twice as high in elderly persons as in nonelderly adults. Patients with renal failure accumulate amantadine in their bodies.

Pharmacodynamics

Amantadine augments dopaminergic neurotransmission in the central nervous system (CNS); however, the precise mechanism for this effect is unknown. The mechanism may involve increasing release of dopamine from presynaptic vesicles, blocking reuptake of dopamine into presynaptic nerve terminals, or an agonist effect on postsynaptic dopamine receptors.

INDICATIONS

The primary indication for amantadine in psychiatry is for the treatment of extrapyramidal signs and symptoms, such as parkinsonism, akinesia, and rabbit syndrome (focal perioral tremor of the choreoathetotoid type) caused by the administration of antipsychotic drugs (e.g., haloperidol [Haldol]). Amantadine is as effective as the anticholinergics (e.g., benztropine [Cogentin, Tremin]) for these indications and results in improvement in approximately one-half of all patients. Amantadine is not, however, generally considered as effective as the anticholinergics for the treatment of acute dystonic reactions. It may be the drug of choice when the clinician does not want to add additional anticholinergic drugs to a patient's treatment regimen. This may be particularly true if a patient is taking an antipsychotic with high anticholinergic activity (e.g., chlorpromazine [Thorazine]) or is elderly; elderly patients are prone to anticholinergic adverse effects—both peripheral, such as urinary retention, and central, such as anticholinergic delirium. One study of patients being treated with antipsychotics reported that amantadine was associated with less memory impairment than the anticholinergics.

Amantadine is used in general medical practice for the treatment of parkinsonism with any cause, including idiopathic parkinsonism. It is also used for the prevention and symptomatic treatment of influenza type A infections.

CLINICAL GUIDELINES

Amantadine is available in 100 mg capsules and as a syrup (50 mg per mL). The usual starting dose of amantadine is 100 mg orally (PO) twice a day, although this dose can be cautiously increased up to 200 mg PO twice a day if indicated. Amantadine should be used in patients with renal impairment only in consultation with the physician treating the renal condition. If amantadine is successful in the treatment of the drug-induced extrapyramidal symptoms, it should be continued for four to six weeks and then discontinued to see if the patient has become tolerant to the neurological adverse effects of the antipsychotic medication. Amantadine should be tapered over one to two weeks once a decision has been made to discontinue the drug.

ADVERSE EFFECTS

The most common CNS effects are mild dizziness, insomnia, and impaired concentration, which occur in 5 to 10 percent of all patients. Irritability, depression, anxiety, and ataxia occur in 1 to 5 percent of patients. More severe CNS adverse effects, including seizures, have been reported. Nausea is the most common peripheral adverse effect of amantadine.

As stated above, amantadine is relatively contraindicated

in patients with renal disease or a seizure disorder. There is some evidence that amantadine is teratogenic and, therefore, should not be given to pregnant women. Because amantadine is excreted in milk, women who are breast feeding should not be given this drug.

Suicide attempts with amantadine overdoses are life-threatening. Symptoms can include toxic psychoses (confusion, hallucinations, aggressiveness) and cardiopulmonary arrest. Emergency treatment beginning with gastric lavage or induction of emesis is indicated.

DRUG-DRUG INTERACTIONS

There is one case report that amantadine coadministered with phenelzine (Nardil) resulted in a significant increase in resting blood pressure. Because of the dopaminergic activity of amantadine, this drug may augment the stimulatory effects of CNS stimulant drugs, such as cocaine and sympathomimetics (e.g., amphetamine).

References

Fayen M, Goldman M B, Moulthrop M A, Luchins D J: Differential memory function with dopaminergic versus anticholinergic treatment of drug-induced extrapyramidal symptoms. Am J Psychiatry *145*: 483, 1988.
Kelly J T, Abuzzahab F S: The antiparkinson properties of amantadine in drug-induced parkinsonism. J Clin Pharmacol *11*: 211, 1971.
McEvoy J P, McCue M, Spring B, et al: Effects of amantadine and trihexphenidyl on memory in elderly normal volunteers. Am J Psychiatry *144*: 573, 1987.
Snoey E R, Bessen H A: Acute psychosis after amantadine overdose. Ann Emerg Med *19*: 668, 1990.
Stenson R L, Donlon P T, Meyer J E: Comparison of benztropine mesylate and amantadine HCl in neuroleptic-induced extrapyramidal symptoms. Compr Psychiatry *17*: 763, 1976.

30.2.2 / Anticholinergics

Anticholinergic drugs are used in psychiatry for the treatment of drug-induced extrapyramidal symptoms, such as antipsychotic-induced parkinsonism. There are six anticholinergic drugs available in the United States for this indication (Table 30.2.2-1). The variations among these six drugs are of little significance except for local differences in price.

PHARMACOLOGICAL ACTIONS

The pharmacokinetics of the anticholinergic drugs are not well studied, although all are well absorbed from the gastrointestinal (GI) tract. Only three of the preparations are available in parenteral forms. Benztropine (Cogentin, Tremin) is probably the most often used parenteral anticholinergic. Benztropine is absorbed equally rapidly by intramuscular (IM) and intravenous (IV) administration; therefore, IM is preferred because of a lower risk of adverse effects. Although all six drugs have their primary effects through the blockade of muscarinic acetylcholine receptors, benztropine and ethopropazide (Parsidol) also have some antihistaminergic effects. Of the six drugs, benztropine tends to be least stimulating and trihexyphenidyl (Artane) tends to be most stimulating.

The major alternatives to the anticholinergic drugs are diphenhydramine (Benadryl) (an antihistamine) (Section 30.2.3) and amantadine (Symadine, Symmetrel) (Section 30.2.1). Amantadine has the advantage of not causing the adverse effects that are associated with the anticholinergics. Amantadine may also be associated with less memory impairment than the anticholinergics.

INDICATIONS

The anticholinergics are effective in the treatment of acute dystonic reactions, parkinsonism, akinesia, and rabbit syndrome. The anticholinergics are less effective for the treatment of akathisia, which is perhaps better treated with β-adrenergic receptor antagonists (e.g., propranolol [Inderal]) (Section 30.2.6) or a benzodiazepine (e.g., lorazepam [Ativan]) (Section 30.2.5).

CLINICAL GUIDELINES

For the treatment of acute dystonic reactions, benztropine, 1 to 2 mg, or its equivalent in another drug should be given IM. If this dose is not effective in 20 to 30 minutes, the drug should be administered again. If the patient still does not respond in another 20 to 30 minutes, a benzodiazepine (e.g., lorazepam, 1 mg IM or IV) should be given.

For the treatment of chronic drug-induced extrapyramidal symptoms, the equivalent of 1 to 4 mg benztropine given one to four times daily should be given. Patients usually respond to this dosage of benztropine in one to two days. The anticholinergic should be administered for four to eight weeks; then it should be discontinued to assess whether the patient still needs the drug. Anticholinergic drugs should be tapered over a one- to two-week period. If anticholinergics are not effective, diphenhydramine, amantadine, or a benzodiazepine can be tried.

Whether prophylaxis with anticholinergics is indicated when first giving a patient an antipsychotic has been debated. Clinicians in favor of prophylaxis argue that patient compliance is hindered if uncomfortable neurological adverse effects occur. Clinicians opposed to prophylactic treatment cite the increased risk of anticholinergic toxicity. Studies have shown that prophylactic treatment with anticholinergic drugs does reduce the incidence of acute dystonic reactions. A reasonable compromise is to use prophylactic treatment in patients at high risk of acute dystonic reactions, primarily young male patients.

ADVERSE EFFECTS

The adverse effects of the anticholinergics are those resulting from the blockade of muscarinic acetylcholine receptors (See Section 30.1 and Table 30.1-6). Anticholinergic drugs should be given very cautiously, if at all, to patients with prostatic hypertrophy, urinary retention, or narrow-arrow glaucoma, because the anticholinergic activity exacerbates-those medical problems. It has recently been recognized that the anticholinergics are occasionally used as drugs of abuse both on the street and by patients. Their abuse potential is related to their mild mood-elevating properties. The most se-

Table 30.2.2-1
Anticholinergic Drugs

Generic Name	Brand Name	Tablet Size	Injectable	Usual Daily PO Dose	Acute IM or IV
Benztropine mesylate	Cogentin, Tremin	0.5,1, 2 mg	1 mg per mL	1–4 mg one to three times	1–2 mg
Biperiden hydrochloride (tab) lactate (inj)	Akineton	2 mg	5 mg per mL	2 mg one to three times	2 mg
Ethopropazide hydrochloride	Parsidol	10, 50 mg		50–100 mg one to three times	
Orphenadrine citrate	Norflex, Dispal	100 mg	30 mg per mL	50–100 mg two to four times	60 mg IV given over 5 min
Procyclidine hydrochloride	Kemadrin	5 mg		2.5–5 mg three times	
Trihexyphenidyl hydrochloride	Artane, Trihexane, Trihexy-5	2, 5 mg elixer 2 mg per 5 mL		2–5 mg two to four times	

rious adverse effect associated with anticholinergic toxicity is anticholinergic intoxication.

Anticholinergic Intoxication

The symptoms of anticholinergic intoxication can include delirium, coma, seizures, extreme agitation, hallucinations, severe hypotension, supraventricular tachycardia, and the usual peripheral manifestations—flushing, mydriasis, dry skin, hyperthermia, and decreased bowel sounds. Treatment should begin with the immediate discontinuation of all anticholinergic drugs. The syndrome of anticholinergic intoxication can be diagnosed and treated with physostigmine (Antilirium, Eserine), an inhibitor of anticholinesterase, 1 to 2 mg IV (1 mg every two minutes) or IM every 30 or 60 minutes. Absorption of IM physostigmine can be erratic. The first dose should be repeated in 15 to 20 minutes if no response is seen. Benzodiazepines can be used to treat agitation. Treatment with physostigmine should be used only when emergency cardiac-monitoring and life-support services are available, because physostigmine can lead to severe hypotension and bronchial constriction. These effects of physostigmine can be reversed with rapid IV administration of atropine, 0.5 mg per each milligram of physostigmine administered. Physostigmine is also contraindicated in patients with unstable vital signs, asthma, or a history of cardiac abnormalities. In general, physostigmine should be used only to confirm a diagnosis of anticholinergic activity or to treat the most serious symptoms of anticholinergic intoxication—seizures, severe hypotension, delirium.

DRUG-DRUG INTERACTIONS

The most common drug-drug interactions with the anticholinergic drugs occur when they are coadministered with psychotropics that also produce high anticholinergic activity, such as most antipsychotics, tricyclic and tetracyclic antidepressants, and monoamine oxidase inhibitors [MAOIs]. Many over-the-counter cold preparations also produce significant anticholinergic activity. The coadministration of these drugs can result in a life-threatening anticholinergic intoxication syndrome.

References

Arana G W, Goff D C, Baldessarini R J, Keepers G A: Efficacy of anticholinergic prophylaxis for neuroleptic-induced acute dystonia. Am J Psychiatry *145*: 993, 1988.

Dilsaver S C: Antimuscarinic agents as substances of abuse: A review. J Clin Psychopharmacol *8*: 14, 1988.

Hidalgo H A, Mowers R M: Anticholinergic drug abuse. DICP *24*: 40, 1990.

Johnson A L, Hollister L E, Berger P A: The anticholinergic intoxication syndrome: Diagnosis and treatment. J Clin Psychiatry *42*: 313, 1981.

Keepers G A, Clappison V J, Casey D E: Initial anticholinergic prophylaxis for neuroleptic-induced extrapyramidal syndromes. Arch Gen Psychiatry *40*: 1113, 1983.

Modell J G, Tandon R, Beresford T P: Dopaminergic activity of the antimuscarinic antiparkinsonian agents. J Clin Psychopharmacol *9*: 347, 1989.

30.2.3 / Antihistamines

Antihistamines are used in psychiatry primarily for the treatment of drug-induced extrapyramidal symptoms and as mild hypnotics and sedatives. Diphenhydramine (Benadryl) is used for the treatment of extrapyramidal symptoms and sometimes as a hypnotic; hydroxyzine hydrochloride (Atarax) and hydroxyzine pamoate (Vistaril) are used as sedatives. Cyproheptadine (Periactin) has been used for the treatment of inhibited male and female orgasm caused by serotonergic agents, such as fluoxetine (Prozac).

PHARMACOLOGICAL ACTIONS

Both diphenhydramine and hydroxyzine are well absorbed from the gastrointestinal (GI) tract. Approximately 50 percent of diphenhydramine is metabolized in a first-pass effect by the liver, and the metabolites are excreted in urine. The antiextrapyramidal effects of intramuscular (IM) diphenhydramine have their onset in 15 to 30 minutes; the sedative effects of diphenhydramine peak in one to three hours. Hydroxyzine is also metabolized by the liver, but its metabolites are excreted in feces. The sedative effects begin 30 to 60 minutes after administration and last four to six hours. Because both drugs are metabolized in the liver, patients with hepatic disease, such as cirrhosis, may attain high plasma concentrations with chronic administration. Both drugs have their primary therapeutic effects through antihistaminergic activity; however, both drugs also possess some antimuscarinic cholinergic activity. Cyproheptadine has potent antihistaminic and serotonin antagonist properties. It is well absorbed following oral administration, and its metabolites are excreted in the urine.

INDICATIONS AND CLINICAL GUIDELINES

The use of antihistamines for drug-induced extrapyramidal disorders is a reasonable alternative to anticholinergics and amantadine (Symadine, Symmetrel), especially in patients who are particularly sensitive to anticholinergic effects but cannot tolerate amantadine. The antihistamines are relatively safe hypnotics, although they are not superior to benzodiazepines. The antihistamines have not been effective as chronic anxiolytic therapy for more than a few months. Either the benzodiazepines or buspirone (BuSpar) are preferable for such treatment.

Diphenhydramine is used in the acute and chronic treatment of drug-induced extrapyramidal symptoms and as a hypnotic. The drug is available in 25 and 50 mg tablets, 12.5 mg per 5 mL elixir, and 10 mg per mL and 50 mg per mL injectable forms. Injections given IM should be deep, since superficial injections can cause local irritation. Acute intravenous (IV) administration of 25 to 50 mg is an effective treatment for acute dystonic reactions. Treatment with 25 mg three times a day, up to 50 mg four times a day if necessary, can be used to treat drug-induced parkinsonism, akinesia, and rabbit syndrome. Diphenhydramine can be used as a hypnotic at a 50-mg dose. Doses of 100 mg have not been shown to be superior to doses of 50 mg.

Hydroxyzine is most commonly used as a sedative or short-term anxiolytic. Hydroxyzine is available in 10, 25, 50, and 100 mg tablets; 12.5 mg per 5 mL solution; and 10 mg per mL and 50 mg per mL injectable forms. Hydroxyzine should not be given IV, since it is irritating to the blood vessels. Doses of 50 to 100 mg orally (PO) four times a day for chronic treatment or 50 to 100 mg IM every four to six hours for acute treatment are usually effective.

The ability to achieve orgasm can be restored with 4 to 8 mg of cyproheptadine taken by mouth one to two hours before anticipated sexual activity. It is available in 4 mg tablets and 2 mg per 5 mL solution.

ADVERSE EFFECTS

Antihistamines are commonly associated with sedation, dizziness, and hypotension, all of which can be severe in elderly patients. Poor motor coordination can result in accidents; therefore, patients should be warned about driving or operating dangerous machinery. Other common adverse effects include epigastric distress, nausea, vomiting, diarrhea, and constipation. Because of the drugs' mild anticholinergic activity, dry mouth, urinary retention, blurred vision, and constipation can occur in some patients. Cyproheptadine has been associated with weight gain and has been used in anorexia nervosa to take advantage of that side effect.

DRUG-DRUG INTERACTIONS

The sedative property of antihistamines can be additive with central nervous system (CNS) depressants, including alcohol, other sedative-hypnotic drugs, and many psychotropic drugs. The anticholinergic activity of diphenhydramine and hydroxyzine can be additive with other drugs with producing anticholinergic activity, sometimes resulting in severe anticholinergic symptoms or intoxication. It has also been reported that coadministration of antihistamines with opioids can increase the rush experienced by addicts; therefore, some abuse potential is associated with these compounds. Finally, it has been reported that hydroxyzine can falsely elevate the values of urinary 17-hydroxycorticosteroids when assayed with either the Porter-Silber or the Glenn-Nelson method.

References

Carruthers S G, Shoeman D W, Hignite C E, Azarnoff D L: Correlation between plasma diphenhydramine level and sedative and antihistamine effects. Clin Pharmacol Ther *23*: 375, 1978.

Gengo F M, Gabos C, Mechtler L: Quantitative effects of diphenhydramine on mental performance measured using an automobile driving simulator. Ann Allergy *64*: 520, 1990.

30.2.4 / Barbiturates

The clinical use of barbiturates in psychiatry as sedative-hypnotics has been essentially eclipsed by the benzodiazepines. This change in clinical practice is based on the higher abuse potential and lower therapeutic index for barbiturates, compared with those for the benzodiazepines and buspirone (BuSpar).

PHARMACOLOGICAL ACTIONS

The barbiturates (Figure 30.2.4-1) are well absorbed after oral administration. The binding of barbiturates to plasma proteins is high, but lipid solubility varies. The individual barbiturates are differentially metabolized by the liver and excreted by the kidneys. The half-lives of specific barbiturates range from 1 hour to 120 hours. Barbiturates may also induce hepatic enzymes, thereby reducing the levels of both the barbiturate and any other concurrently administered drugs metabolized by the liver. The mechanism of action for the barbiturates involves the γ-aminobutyric acid (GABA) receptor-benzodiazepine receptor-chloride ion channel complex.

INDICATIONS

There are currently six indications for barbiturate administration. First, amobarbital (Amytal) (50 to 250 mg intra-

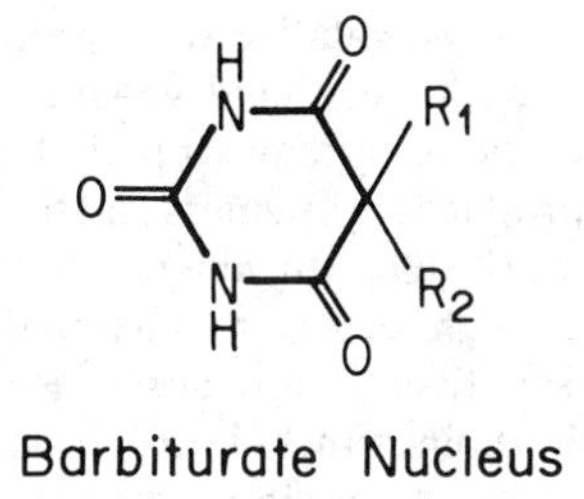

Barbiturate Nucleus

The different barbiturates are synthesized by substituting specific side chains at R_1 and R_2

Figure 30.2.4-1. Molecular structure of the barbiturate nucleus.

muscular [IM]) may be used in emergency settings to control agitation. The use of IM lorazepam (Ativan) or diazepam (Valium), however, seems to be replacing this application of amobarbital. Second, amobarbital interviews are sometimes used for diagnostic purposes. Several studies report that other sedative drugs, including the benzodiazepines, are as effective in this application. Third, there are several reports that barbiturates can activate some catatonic patients, although benzodiazepines may also have this effect. Fourth, barbiturates may be indicated for use in patients who have serious adverse effects from benzodiazepines or buspirone. Fifth, some patients who do not respond adequately to benzodiazepines or buspirone may respond to barbiturates. Sixth, some patients, particularly old persons, who have received barbiturates in the past may insist on taking barbiturates, rather than trying a benzodiazepine or buspirone.

CLINICAL GUIDELINES

The dosages for barbiturates vary (Table 30.2.4-1), and treatment should begin with low dosages that are increased to achieve a clinical effect. Barbiturates with half-lives in the 15- to 40-hour range are preferable, because longer-acting drugs build up in the body. The patient should be clearly instructed about the adverse effects and potential for dependence associated with barbiturate treatment.

ADVERSE EFFECTS

The adverse effects of barbiturates are similar to those for benzodiazepines, including paradoxical dysphoria, hyperactivity, and cognitive disorganization. The barbiturates differ from the benzodiazepines in their high abuse potential, marked development of tolerance, dependence, and low therapeutic index. The symptoms of barbiturate withdrawal are similar to but more marked than those for benzodiazepine withdrawal. Barbiturates are often lethal in overdoses because of respiratory depression, especially if combined with alcohol intake, as is often seen clinically.

DRUG-DRUG INTERACTIONS

Barbiturates interact with many other drugs, and the clinician should consult a reference text for the interactions when prescribing barbiturates. The two most important interactions are the additive effects of other sedatives and the increased metabolism of many cardiac-related drugs and heterocyclic antidepressants.

Because of respiratory suppression, barbiturates should be used cautiously in patients with respiratory illness. Barbiturates are absolutely contraindicated in patients with acute intermittent porphyria, because barbiturates cause the production of porphyrins. Patients with hepatic cirrhosis may have very high plasma barbiturate concentrations because of their impaired ability to metabolize the drug.

OTHER SEDATIVE-HYPNOTICS

Three other classes of drugs—carbamates, piperidinediones, and cyclic ethers—are still available for use as sedatives and hypnotics; however, these drugs are even more rarely used than the barbiturates because of their high abuse potential and potential toxic effects.

Carbamates

Meprobamate (Miltown, Equanil), ethinamate (Valmid), and carisoprodol (Soma) are carbamates that are effective as anxiolytics, sedatives, hypnotics, and muscle relaxants. These drugs have a lower therapeutic index and a higher abuse potential than benzodiazepines, and their use is indicated only if the previously described drugs are not an option. The carbamates may have even more abuse potential and may be more dependence-inducing than the barbiturates.

The usual dosage of meprobamate is 400 mg, three or four times daily. Drowsiness is a common adverse effect, and patients should be warned of the additive effects of sedative drugs. Sudden withdrawal may cause anxiety, restlessness, weakness, delirium, and convulsions. Adverse effects can include urticarial or erythematous rashes, anaphylactoid and

Table 30.2.4-1
Selected Barbiturates

				Sedative		Hypnotic
Generic Name	DEA Control Level	Trade Name	Half-Life (hrs)	Adult Dose Range (mg per day)	Adult Single Dose Range (mg)	Dose Range (mg)
Amobarbital	II	Amytal	8–42	65–400	65–100	100–200
Butabarbital	III	Butisol	34–42	15–120	15–30	50–100
Mephobarbital	IV	Mebaral	11–67	32–400	32–100	—
Pentobarbital	II	Nembutal	15–48	30–120	30–40	100–200
Phenobarbital	IV	Luminal	80–120	15–600	15–60	100–200
Secobarbital	II	Seconal	15–40	—	—	100–300

other allergic reactions, angioneurotic edema, dermatitis, blood dyscrasias, gastrointestinal upsets, and extraocular muscular paralysis. Fatal overdoses can occur with meprobamate in doses as low as 12 g (thirty 400 mg tablets) without the ingestion of any other sedatives.

Piperidinediones

Glutethimide (Doriden) and methyprylon (Noludar) are piperidinediones that are effective as hypnotics, sedatives, and anxiolytics but are even more subject to abuse and more lethal in overdoses than the barbiturates and carbamates. Glutethimide has a slow and unpredictable absorption after oral administration. Seizures, shock, and anticholinergic toxicity are more common in glutethimide overdoses than in barbiturate overdoses. It is a very rare patient for whom treatment with piperidinediones is indicated.

Cyclic Ethers

Paraldehyde was introduced in 1882 as an hypnotic. When 5 mL is given IM or 5 to 10 mL administered orally, it is an effective, albeit old-fashioned, treatment for alcohol withdrawal symptoms, anxiety, and insomnia. Paraldehyde is almost completely metabolized, but its excretion in unmetabolized form by the lungs limits its usefulness because of its offensive taste and ubiquitous odor.

References

Ator N A, Griffiths R R: Self-administration of barbiturates and benzodiazepines: A review. Pharmacol Biochem Behav *27*: 391, 1987.

Chierchetti S M: Beta-blockers and psychic stress: A double-blind, placebo-controlled study of bopindolol vs lorazepam and butalbital in surgical patients. Int J Clin Pharmacol Ther Toxicol *23*: 510, 1985.

Goodman R A, Mercy J A, Rosenberg M L: Drug use and interpersonal violence: Barbiturates detected in homicide victims. Am J Epidemiol *124*: 851, 1986.

Harris R A: Distinct actions of alcohols, barbiturates and benzodiazepines on GABA-activated chloride channels. Alcohol *7*: 273, 1990.

Jensen C F, Cowley D S, Walker R D: Drug preferences of alcoholic polydrug abusers with and without panic. J Clin Psychiatry *51*: 189, 1990.

Sullivan J T, Sellers E M: Treatment of the barbiturate abstinence syndrome. Med J Aust *145*: 456, 1986.

Taberber P V: The GABA system in functional tolerance and dependence following barbiturates, benzodiazepines, or ethanol: Correlation or causality? Compr Biochem Physiol *93*: 241, 1989.

Yu S, Ho I K: Effects of acute barbiturate administration, tolerance and dependence on brain GAMA system: Comparison to alcohol and benzodiazepines. Alcohol *7*: 261, 1990.

30.2.5 / Benzodiazepines

Benzodiazepines are variously referred to as antianxiety agents, anxiolytics, and minor tranquilizers. The term "minor tranquilizer" is misleading, because using it may cause confusion between this class of drug and the major tranquilizers, a faulty but commonly used term for the antipsychotic drugs. Benzodiazepines are also classified as sedative-hypnotics. A sedative drug reduces daytime activity, tempers excitement, and generally quiets the patient. An anxiolytic drug reduces pathological anxiety. A hypnotic drug produces drowsiness and facilitates the onset and maintenance of sleep. In general, benzodiazepines act as hypnotics in high doses, as anxiolytics in moderate doses, and as sedatives in low doses. Recent indications for the benzodiazepines include panic disorder, phobias, and bipolar disorder. In addition, the benzodiazepines are used as anesthetics, anticonvulsants, and muscle relaxants.

The benzodiazepines have become the sedative-hypnotic drugs of first choice, because they have a higher therapeutic index and significantly less abuse potential than many of the other sedative-hypnotics (e.g., barbiturates), with the exception of buspirone (BuSpar).

CLASSIFICATION

The benzodiazepine nucleus consists of a benzene ring fused to the seven-sided diazepine ring. All clinically important benzodiazepines also have a second benzene ring attached to the carbon at position 5 on the diazepine ring (Figure 30.2.5-1). The benzodiazepines can be classified as 2-keto, 3-hydroxy, or triazolo benzodiazepines (Table 30.2.5-1). The 2-keto benzodiazepines have a keto group off the carbon atom in position 2 on the diazepine ring. Although chlordiazepoxide (Librium)

Benzodiazepine Nucleus: *2-keto Benzodiazepine:* DIAZEPAM

3-hydroxy Benzodiazepine: OXAZEPAM *Triazolo Benzodiazepine:* ALPRAZOLAM

Figure 30.2.5-1. Representative benzodiazepine structures.

Table 30.2.5-1
Classification of Benzodiazepines

2-Keto	3-Hydroxy	Triazolo
Chlordiazepoxide	Oxazepam	Alprazolam
Diazepam	Lorazepam	Triazolam
Prazepam	Temazepam	
Clorazepate		
Halazepam		
Flurazepam		

has a different substitution (-$NHCH_3$) at this position, it is useful to classify it along with the 2-keto derivatives. Also, quazepam (Doral) substitutes a sulfur atom for the oxygen atom in the keto moeity. The 3-hydroxy benzodiazepines have a hydroxy group on the carbon at position 3 of the diazepine ring. The triazolo benzodiazepines have a triazolo ring fused to the nitrogen at position 1 and to the carbon at position 2 of the diazepine ring.

PHARMACOLOGICAL ACTIONS

Pharmacokinetics

With the exception of clorazepate (Tranxene), all the benzodiazepines are completely absorbed unchanged from the gastrointestinal (GI) tract. Clorazepate is converted to desmethyldiazapam in the GI tract and absorbed in that form. Absorption, attainment of peak levels, and onset of action are quickest for the following drugs in each class: 2-keto—diazepam (Valium); 3-hydroxy—lorazepam (Ativan); triazolo—both alprazolam (Xanax) and triazolam (Halcion) have rapid effects. The rapid onset of effects is important to patients who take a single dose of benzodiazepines to calm an episodic burst of anxiety. The rapid onset of effects for these drugs can be partly attributed to their high lipid solubility, a characteristic that varies fivefold among the different benzodiazepines. The range of time to peak plasma levels is one to three hours, although prazepam (Centrax) may take up to six hours. There may also be a secondary peak plasma level 6 to 12 hours after enterohepatic recirculation. Although several benzodiazepines are available in parenteral forms for intramuscular (IM) administration, only lorazepam has rapid and reliable absorption from this route. The use of IM lorazepam is beginning to replace the use of intravenous (IV) diazepam in psychiatric emergency settings, with the possible exception of the management of phencyclidine (PCP) intoxication.

The metabolism of benzodiazepines differs for the three classes. Chlordiazepoxide is metabolized to diazepam, then to desmethyldiazepam (nordiazepam), then to oxazepam, and finally to the glucuronide. Diazepam, clorazepate, prazepam, and halazepam (Paxipam) are metabolized first to desmethyldiazepam and then follow the same route as chlordiazepoxide does. The metabolism of flurazepam (Dalmane) and quazepam follows similar biochemical steps. As a result of the slow metabolism of desmethyldiazepam, all the 2-keto benzodiazepines have plasma half-lives of 30 to 100 hours and are, therefore, the longest-acting benzodiazepines. The plasma half-life can be as high as 200 hours in persons who are genetically slow metabolizers of these compounds. Because the attainment of steady plasma levels of these drugs can take up to two weeks, patients may develop toxicity after 7 to 10 days of treatment with a dosage that may have seemed therapeutic to the clinician. Patients with hepatic disease and elderly patients are particularly likely to have toxic effects from benzodiazepines that are administered in repeated or high doses.

The 3-hydroxy benzodiazepines have short half-lives (10 to 30 hours), because they are directly metabolized by glucuronidation and, thus, have no active metabolites. The triazolo benzodiazepines are hydroxylated before they undergo glucuronidation. Alprazolam has a half-life of 10 to 15 hours, and triazolam has the shortest half-life (two to three hours) of all the benzodiazepines.

Pharmacodynamics

The benzodiazepines bind to specific receptor sites that are associated with γ-aminobutyric acid (GABA) binding sites and chloride channels. Benzodiazepine binding increases the affinity of the GABA receptor for GABA, thereby increasing the flow of chloride ions into the neurons.

Recently, basic neuroscience research has found evidence for two types of central nervous system (CNS) benzodiazepine receptors—BZ_1 and BZ_2. BZ_1 receptors are believed to be involved in the mediation of sleep. BZ_2 receptors are believed to be involved in cognition, memory, and motor control. Theoretically, a benzodiazepine hypnotic that could affect only BZ_1 receptors might have fewer adverse cognitive effects. Both quazepam and halazepam are more specific for the BZ_1 receptor than the BZ_2 receptor and, therefore, may be expected to be associated with less amnesia and other cognitive impairments.

Tolerance, Dependence, and Withdrawal

When benzodiazepines are used for short periods of time (one to two weeks) in moderate doses, there is usually no evidence of tolerance, dependence, or withdrawal. The very short-acting benzodiazepines (e.g., triazolam) may be a slight exception to this rule, as some patients have reported increased anxiety the day after taking this drug. Some patients also report a tolerance to the anxiolytic effects of benzodiazepines and require increased doses to maintain clinical remission. There is also a cross-tolerance among most of the classes of antianxiety drugs, with the notable exception of buspirone.

The appearance of a withdrawal syndrome (Table 30.2.5-2) from benzodiazepines depends on the length of time a patient has taken the drug, the dosage the patient has been taking, the rate at which the drug is tapered, and the half-life of the particular compound. Serious symptoms may include depression, paranoia, delirium, and seizures. The incidence of this syndrome is controversial; however, some features of the syndrome may occur in as many as 50 percent of the patients treated with these drugs. The development of a severe

Table 30.2.5-2
Commonly Observed Withdrawal Symptoms (Benzodiazepine Withdrawal Syndrome)

Anxiety
Irritability
Insomnia
Fatigue
Headache
Muscle twitching or aching
Tremor, shakiness
Sweating
Dizziness
Concentration difficulties

*Nausea, loss of appetite
*Observable depression
*Depersonalization, derealization
*Increased sensory perception (smell, light, taste, touch)
*Abnormal perception or sensation of movement

Table from P P Roy-Byrne, D Hommer: Benzodiazepine withdrawal: Overview and implications for the treatment of anxiety. Am J Med *84*: 1041, 1988, with permission.

*Symptoms likely to represent true withdrawal, rather than an exacerbation or return of original anxiety.

withdrawal syndrome is seen only in patients who have taken high dosages for long periods. The appearance of the syndrome may be delayed for one to two weeks in patients who had been taking 2-keto benzodiazepines with very long half-lives. A number of clinicians have reported that alprazolam seems to be particularly associated with a withdrawal syndrome.

INDICATIONS

Anxiety

The major clinical application for these drugs in psychiatry is the treatment of anxiety—both idiopathic generalized anxiety disorder and anxiety associated with specific life events (e.g., adjustment disorder with anxious mood). Most patients should be treated for a specific and relatively brief period. Some patients, however, may have a disorder that requires maintenance on these drugs.

Insomnia

Flurazepam, temazepam (Restoril), quazepam, and triazolam are the four benzodiazepines approved for use as hypnotics. They differ principally in their half-lives, in that flurazepam has the longest and triazolam has the shortest half-life. Flurazepam may be associated with minor cognitive impairment on the day after its administration, and triazolam may be associated with mild rebound anxiety. Temazepam may represent a reasonable compromise between these two adverse effects for the usual adult patient. Because of its higher specificity for BZ_1 receptors, quazepam may be associated with fewer adverse cognitive effects; however, this hypothesis needs to be borne out with more extensive clinical experience.

Depression

In some studies, alprazolam has been demonstrated to have antidepressant effects equal to those of the tricyclic antidepressants. The starting dosage for this indication should be 1 to 1.5 mg a day and should be raised 0.5 mg a day every three to four days. The maximal dosage is usually 4 to 5 mg a day, although some investigators and clinicians have used dosages as high as 10 mg a day. There is some controversy about the use of high dosages because of the possibility of withdrawal symptoms. It is particularly important to taper, rather than abruptly stop, alprazolam, usually at the rate of 0.5 mg a day every three to four days.

Bipolar Disorder

Clonazepam (Klonopin) has been shown to be effective in the management of acute mania and also as an adjuvant to lithium therapy in lieu of antipsychotics. As an adjuvant to lithium, clonazepam may result in a longer time between cycles and fewer depressive episodes.

Panic Disorder and Social Phobia

In a number of studies, both alprazolam and clonazepam have been useful in treating panic disorder with and without agoraphobia and social phobia.

Akathisia

Standard anticholinergic drugs (e.g., benztropine [Cogentin, Tremin]) are often ineffective in treating drug-induced akathisia. The first-line drug for akathisia is most commonly a β-adrenergic antagonist (e.g., propranolol [Inderal]); however, several studies have found that benzodiazepines are also effective in treating some cases of akathisia.

Other Psychiatric Indications

Chloradiazepoxide is used to manage the symptoms of alcohol withdrawal. The benzodiazepines (especially IM lorazepam) are used to manage both drug-induced (except amphetamine) and psychotic agitation in the emergency room. There are a few reports of the use of high dosages of benzodiazepines in patients with schizophrenia who had not responded to antipsychotics or who were unable to take more traditional drugs because of adverse effects.

Medical Indications

Benzodiazepines are used as anticonvulsants, muscle relaxants, and adjuvants in anesthesia. Diazepam is also used for its minor analgesic properties.

CLINICAL GUIDELINES

The clinical decision to treat a patient for anxiety with a benzodiazepine should be carefully considered. Organic causes for anxiety—such as thyroid dysfunction, caffeinism, and medications—should be ruled out. The benzodiazepine should be started at a very low dosage, and the patient should be instructed regarding the sedative properties and abuse potential of the drug. An estimated length of therapy should be decided at the beginning of therapy, and the need for continued therapy should be reevaluated at least monthly because of the problem associated with long-term use. When the medication is to be discontinued, the drug must be tapered slowly (25 percent a week); otherwise, recurrence or rebound of symptoms is likely to occur. Monitoring of any withdrawal symptoms (possibly with a standardized rating scale) and support of the patient are helpful in the successful accomplishment of benzodiazepine discontinuation.

Benzodiazepine withdrawal syndrome. This syndrome occurs when patients discontinue benzodiazepines abruptly. Ninety percent of patients after long-term use experience this syndrome on withdrawal of the drug, even if tapered slowly (although only to a mild to moderate degree). Benzodiazepine withdrawal syndrome consists of anxiety, nervousness, diaphoresis, restlessness, irritability, fatigue, light-headedness, tremor, insomnia, and weakness. The higher the dose and the shorter the half-life, the worse the withdrawal syndrome is.

Duration of Treatment

Benzodiazepines can be used to treat illnesses other than anxiety disorders. In such cases the duration of treatment should generally be similar to that for the standard drugs used to treat those disorders. The use of benzodiazepines over a long period of time for the chronically anxious patient is often valuable although controversial. In his 1980 textbook on drug treatment in psychiatry, Donald Klein, M.D., stated: "There are many reports of patients maintained on benzodiazepines for years with apparent benefit and without the development of tolerance. Nonetheless, it is dubious practice to prescribe such medications indefinitely without accompanying psychotherapy."

The recent classification of benzodiazepines as controlled substances requiring a triplicate prescription form has created controversy, as illustrated by the article published in the *Area III Bulletin* (*32*: 7, May–June 1990) by the New York State Psychiatric Association entitled, "Researchers Question DOH [Department of Health] Claims on Triplicate Prescriptions." The article follows:

Controversy about triplicate use. Triplicate prescription forms for benzodiazepines were mandated in New York State in January, 1989. New York is the only state with such a regulation. When the regulation was first proposed by the Department of Health (DOH), it met with opposition from a significant part of the New York medical community. The State Medical Society obtained an injunction preventing its implementation, and the New York State psychiatric Association (APA's Area II executive council) filed a brief that focused on possible adverse effects on patient care and on the threat the regulation posed to confidentiality. Ultimately, however, the restraining order was overturned and the regulation was implemented.

DOH's Bureau of Controlled Substances gave several reasons for introducing the regulation: 1) despite educational efforts initiated in the 1970's it was alleged that the overall abuse associated with prescribing and dispensing benzodiazepines had not decreased; 2) more potent benzodiazepines were becoming available and were increasingly abused, to the extent that benzodiazepine abuse was threatening the health and welfare of the people of the state; 3) in the Medicaid program, benzodiazepine abuse was of such magnitude that it was draining the system of resources that should be used in areas of legitimate need.

Harold I. Schwartz, M.D., now Director of the Department of Psychiatry, Hartford Hospital, and Associate Professor and Associate Chairman, University of Connecticut School of Medicine, and Karen Blank, M.D., Adjunct Assistant Professor of Clinical Psychiatry at Mount Sinai School of Medicine, decided to study the consequences of the regulation in patients using a typical urban psychiatric emergency room and clinic. They were both on the staff of New York's Beth Israel Medical Center at the time, and they reviewed the psychiatric consultation notes of all emergency evaluations for a three month period, beginning two weeks after the triplicate prescription regulation went into effect. Their findings cast doubt on some of the premises accepted by DOH in framing the regulation, and they suggest that the final effect of the regulation may be to deprive patients of appropriate, legitimate, and efficacious treatments.

During the three-month period under study, 59 cases were identified in which use of benzodiazepines was a significant presenting problem. Of those, 41% were judged to be directly related to the new regulation. In all but one case, the patients' symptoms or concerns stemmed from refusal by a clinician to continue to prescribe a benzodiazepine in a previously established pattern. Typically, abrupt discontinuation led to a withdrawal syndrome or the unmasking of a previously treated anxiety disorder. Withdrawal symptoms typically included anxiety, irritability, fatigue, insomnia, muscle twitching or aching, tremor, sweating, dizziness, headache, and difficulty concentrating. More dangerous phenomena were convulsions and delirium, and in one case withdrawal appeared to trigger a psychotic episode. Several patients required hospitalization for supervised withdrawal.

According to Schwartz and Blank, negative attitudes towards benzodiazepines (as exemplified by the position statements of NYS-DOH) have led to a shift from overprescription in the 1970's to a situation in which patients who require these agents no longer receive them or they receive them improperly. This can follow from prescription of sub-therapeutic doses, precipitous termination of therapy, or reluctance to prescribe at all.

In a follow-up study six months after the regulation went into effect, DOH found a large reduction in benzodiazepine use in a group of individuals suspected of diverting drugs and a significant drop in benzodiazepine dispensing by pharmacies ("Medicaid mills") suspected of diversion. Nonetheless, in attempting to redress what are essentially criminal problems through the regulation of legitimate clinical practice, regulatory agencies may severely penalize patients who need benzodiazepines.

Choice of Drug

Clinicians need to choose among the array of benzodiazepines available (Table 30.2.5-3). The drugs primarily differ in their half-lives. Another difference is in the rate of onset of their anxiolytic effects. The three high-potency benzodiazepines—alprazolam, triazolam, and clonazepam—are the drugs indicated for the new applications, such as depression, bipolar disorder, panic disorder, and phobias. The advantages of the long half-life drugs include less frequent dosing, less variation in plasma concentration, and less severe withdrawal phenomena; disadvantages include drug accumulation and more daytime sedation. The advantages of short half-life drugs include no drug accumulation and less daytime sedation; disadvantages include more frequent dosing and earlier and more severe withdrawal syndromes. Rebound insomnia and anterograde amnesia (particularly with triazolam) are also more problematic with short half-life drugs.

DRUG COMBINATIONS

The most common drug combination is the use of benzodiazepines as hypnotics in patients who are also being treated with other drugs for schizophrenia or mood disorders. The combination of a benzodiazepine and an antidepressant may be indicated in the treatment of markedly anxious depressed patients. There are several reports that the combined use of alprazolam with antipsychotics may further reduce psychotic symptoms in patients who had not responded adequately to the antipsychotic alone.

ADVERSE EFFECTS

The most common adverse effect of benzodiazepines is drowsiness, occurring in approximately 10 percent of patients, and patients should be advised not to drive or use dangerous machinery while taking these drugs. Some patients also experience dizziness (less than 1 percent) and ataxia (less than 2 percent). The most serious adverse effects of benzodiazepines occur when other sedative drugs, such as alcohol, are taken concurrently. These combinations can result in marked drowsiness, disinhibition, or even respiratory depression.

Table 30.2.5-3
Benzodiazepine Trade Names and Dosage Ranges

Generic Name	Trade Name	Approximate Half-Life (Hour)′	Usual Adult Dosage Range (mg per day)	Adult Single Dose Range (mg)
Alprazolam	Xanax	12	0.5–6	0.25–1
Chlordiazepoxide*	Librium	24–48	15–100	5–25
Clonazepam	Klonopin	34	1.5–10	0.5–2
Clorazepate	Tranxene	100	7.5–60	3.25–22.5
Diazepam*	Valium	60	2–60	2–10
Flurazepam†	Dalmane	100	15–30	15–30
Halazepam	Paxipam	50	60–160	20–40
Lorazepam	Ativan	15	2–6	0.5–2
Oxazepam	Serax	8	30–120	10–30
Prazepam	Centrax	100	20–60	10–20
Quazepam†	Doral	50	7.5–30	7.5–30
Temazepam†	Restoril	11	15–30	15–30
Triazolam†	Halcion	2	0.125–0.5	0.125–0.5

*Also available for parenteral administration. Diazepam is available for IV administration in 5 mg per mL syringes. Lorazepam is available for IM administration in 2 and 4 mg per mL syringes.
†FDA-approved for use as a hypnotic.
′Over 30 hours = long half-life; under 30 hours = short half-life.

Other relatively rare adverse effects include weakness, nausea, vomiting, blurred vision, and epigastric distress. There have been several reports of mild cognitive deficits that could impair job performance in patients who are taking benzodiazepines. Anterograde amnesia has also been associated with benzodiazepines, particularly high-potency drugs. A rare, paradoxical increase in aggression has been reported in patients given a benzodiazepine. Allergic reactions to these drugs are also rare, but there are a few reports of maculopapular rashes and generalized itching.

Abuse and Dependence

Mentally healthy persons may take single doses of benzodiazepines for recreational purposes. Patients who take prescribed benzodiazepines may have both a physical dependence and a psychological dependence on these drugs and insist on taking them against the clinician's advice. As previously mentioned, withdrawal syndromes do occur, although much less often than with many other drugs in this class, such as barbiturates and carbamates.

Overdoses

Overdoses with benzodiazepines have a predictably favorable outcome unless other drugs—such as alcohol, antipsychotics, and antidepressants—have also been ingested. In these cases, respiratory depression, coma, seizures, and death are much more likely.

DRUG-DRUG INTERACTIONS

Cimetidine (Tagamet), disulfiram (Antabuse), isoniazid (Nydrazid), and estrogens increase the plasma levels of 2-keto benzodiazepines. Antacids and food may decrease the absorption of benzodiazepines, and smoking may increase the metabolism of benzodiazepines. The benzodiazepines may increase the plasma levels of phenytoin (Dilantin) and digoxin (Lanoxin). All benzodiazepines have additive central nervous system (CNS) depressant effects with other sedative drugs.

References

Ankier S I, Goa K L: Quazepam: A preliminary review of its pharmacodynamic and pharmacokinetic properties, and therapeutic efficacy in insomnia. Drugs *35*: 42, 1988.
Busto U E, Sykora K, Sellers E M: A clinical scale to assess benzodiazepine withdrawal. J Clin Psychopharmacol *9*: 412, 1989.
Dubin W R: Rapid tranquilization: Antipsychotics or benzodiazepines? J Clin Psychiatry *49(12*, Suppl): 5, 1988.
Gillin J C, Spinweber C L, Johnson L C: Rebound insomnia: A critical review. J Clin Psychopharmacol *9*: 161, 1989.
Greenblatt D J, Harmatz J S, Englehardt N, Shader R I: Pharmacokinetic determinants of dynamic differences among three benzodiazepine hypnotics. Arch Gen Psychiatry *46*: 326, 1989.
Noyes R, Garvey M J, Cook B L, Perry P J: Benzodiazepine withdrawal: A review of the evidence. J Clin Psychiatry *49*: 382, 1988.
Rickles K, Schweizer G, Case G, Greenblatt D J: Long-term therapeutic use of benzodiazepines. Arch Gen Psychiatry *47*: 899, 1990.
Rosenbaum J, ed.: High-potency benzodiazepines: Emerging uses in psychiatry. J Clin Psychiatry *51(5*, Suppl): 2, 1990.
Rosenbaum J, ed.: New uses for clonazepam in psychiatry. J Clin Psychiatry *48(10*, Suppl): 2, 1987.
Roth M: Anxiety disorders and the use and abuse of drugs. J Clin Psychiatry *50(11*, Suppl): 30, 1989.
Sachs G S, Rosenbaum J F, Jones L: Adjunctive clonazepam for maintenance treatment of bipolar affective disorder. J Clin Psychopharmacol *10*: 42, 1990.
Uhlenhuth E H, DeWit H, Balter M B, Johanson C E, Mellinger G D: Risks and benefits of long-term benzodiazepine use. J Clin Psychopharmacol *8*: 161, 1988.

30.2.6 / β-Adrenergic Receptor Antagonists

β-Adrenergic receptor antagonists (e.g., propranolol [Inderal]), also known as β-blockers and β-adrenergic drugs, are most useful in psychiatric practice in treating drug-induced akathisia, lithium-induced tremor, aggression, and somatic symptoms of anxiety. The β-adrenergic drugs have also been reported to be third- or fourth-line drugs for a wide range of other psychiatric disorders.

PHARMACOLOGICAL ACTIONS

Many β-adrenergic drugs are available in the United States. The β-adrenergic drugs that have been studied with regard to neuropsychiatric disorders are presented in Table 30.2.6-1. The drugs differ in terms of ability to dissolve in lipids, routes of metabolism, half-lives, and relative selectivity for β_1 or β_2 receptors. The β-adrenergic drugs are readily absorbed from the gastrointestinal (GI) tract and are either metabolized by the liver or excreted unchanged by the kidneys. The agents that are more soluble in lipids (i.e., lipophilic) are more likely to enter the brain; those that are less lipophilic (i.e., more water-soluble than lipid-soluble) are less likely to enter the brain. When central nervous system (CNS) effects are desired, a lipophilic drug may be preferred; when only peripheral effects are desired, a less lipophilic drug may be indicated.

Peripheral β_1-adrenergic receptors modulate chronotropic and inotropic cardiac functions; peripheral β_2-adrenergic receptors modulate bronchodilation and vasodilation. There are more β_1-adrenergic receptors than β_2-adrenergic receptors in the CNS. The so-called β_1-specific drugs still have some β_2 activity, and their use should be carefully monitored in patients with pulmonary disease or asthma; β_1-specific drugs are preferable for such patients.

INDICATIONS

Drug-Induced Akathisia

A large number of studies have now shown that β-adrenergic antagonists can be effective in the treatment of antipsychotic-induced akathisia, which can be particularly resistant to drug therapy. Other drugs used for the treatment of akathisia are the anticholinergics, benzodiazepines, and, perhaps, clonidine (Catapres). It is not yet possible to predict which patients will respond to a particular agent. The β-adrenergic antagonists are not effective at treating other antipsychotic-induced extrapyramidal symptoms, such as acute dystonia and parkinsonism. Propranolol is the drug that has been used most often in studies and seems to be the standard drug for this indication. Studies have not indicated whether peripheral-acting drugs are effective.

Lithium-Induced Tremor

Lithium can be associated with a tremor even when lithium concentrations are within normal therapeutic ranges. Propranolol (20 to 160 mg a day, two or three times a day) is effective treatment for this adverse effect. It is controversial whether nonlipophilic, peripherally acting β-adrenergic antagonists are as effective as propranolol.

Aggression and Violent Behavior

According to some studies, β-adrenergic antagonists are effective in treating the aggressiveness and violent behavior that can be associated with schizophrenia and organic mental diseases, such as trauma, tumor, anoxic injury, encephalitis, alcoholism, and Huntington's chorea. Most of the patients studied in these reports have been nonresponsive to antipsychotics, lithium, anticonvulsants, and benzodiazepines. Approximately 50 percent of the patients in the studies improved with β-adrenergic antagonist treatment. The range of propranolol dosages is from 50 to 960 mg a day. Two lipophilic, centrally acting drugs, pindolol (Visken) and metoprolol (Lopressor), have also been successfully used for this indication in case reports and open trials.

Social Phobias

Propranolol has been reported to be useful in reducing the peripheral manifestations of anxiety (e.g., tremor, tachycardia) associated with social phobia and the anxiety associated with performance (e.g., examinations, musical recitals). Propranolol (10 to 40 mg) taken 20 to 30 minutes before the performance is the usual dose.

Alcohol Withdrawal

Propranolol has been reported to be useful as an adjuvant to benzodiazepines but not as a sole agent in the treatment of alcohol withdrawal. One study used the following dose schedule: no propranolol for a pulse less than 50; 50 mg propranolol for a pulse between 50 and 79; 100 mg propranolol for a pulse equal to or greater than 80. The patients who also received propranolol had less severe withdrawal symptoms, more stable vital signs, and a shorter hospital stay than the patients who received only benzodiazepines.

Other Disorders

Various case reports found clinical uses for β-adrenergic antagonists in the treatment of mania, schizophrenia, and generalized anxiety disorder. The treatment of mania is promising; however, very high doses (1,000 mg a day) were required, and severe adverse effects were encountered. The data for schizophrenia are much more extensive and more contradictory. The β-adrenergic antagonists are useful, however, in controlling aggressive behavior in schizophrenia; a trial of propranolol may be warranted in schizophrenic patients who have not responded to other drugs.

Table 30.2.6-1
β-Adrenergic Drugs Used in Psychiatry

Generic Name	Trade Name	Lipophilic	Metabolism	Receptor Selectivity	Half Life (hrs)	Usual Starting Dose (mg)	Usual Maximal Dose (mg)
Atenolol	Tenormin	No	Renal	β_1	6–9	50 once a day	50–100 once a day
Metoprolol	Lopressor	Yes	Hepatic	β_1	3–4	50 twice a day	75–150 twice a day
Nadolol	Corgard	No	Renal	β_1-β_2	14–24	40 once a day	80–240 once a day
Propranolol	Inderal	Yes	Hepatic	β_1-β_2	3–6	10–20 two or three times a day	80–140 three times a day

CLINICAL GUIDELINES

For the treatment of chronic disorders, propranolol is usually initiated at 10 mg orally (PO) three times a day or 20 mg PO twice a day. The dosage can be raised by 20 to 30 mg a day until a therapeutic effect begins to emerge. The dosage should be leveled off at the appropriate range for the disorder under treatment. The treatment of aggressive behavior sometimes requires dosages up to 800 mg a day, and therapeutic effects may not be seen until the patient has been receiving the maximal dosage for four to eight weeks. The patient's pulse and blood pressure should be taken regularly, and the drug should be withheld if the pulse is less than 50 or the systolic blood pressure is less than 90. The drug should also be temporarily withheld if the patient has severe dizziness, ataxia, or wheezing. Treatment with β-adrenergic antagonists should never be discontinued abruptly. Propranolol should be tapered at 60 mg a day until a dosage of 60 mg a day is reached, after which the drug should be tapered by 20 mg a day every three or four days.

ADVERSE EFFECTS

The use of β-adrenergic antagonists is relatively contraindicated in patients with bronchial asthma, chronic obstructive pulmonary disease, diabetes, congestive heart failure, persistent angina, hyperthyroidism, and peripheral vascular disease. β-Adrenergic antagonists can worsen atrioventricular (AV) conduction defects and lead to complete AV heart block and death. β-Adrenergic drugs elevate blood glucose by inhibiting insulin release and are capable of masking the signs and symptoms of hypoglycemia (except hyperhidrosis).

The most common adverse effects of the β-adrenergic antagonists are hypotension and bradycardia. In patients at risk for these adverse effects, a test dose of 20 mg a day of propranolol can be given to assess the patient's reaction to the drug. Depression has been associated with lipophilic β-adrenergic antagonists, such as propranolol, but probably occurs in less than 2 percent of patients. Nausea, vomiting, diarrhea, and constipation may also be caused by treatment with these agents. More serious CNS adverse effects (agitation, confusion, and hallucinations) are rare.

DRUG-DRUG INTERACTIONS

Propranolol has been reported to increase dramatically the plasma concentrations of chlorpromazine (Thorazine), thioridazine (Mellaril), and theophylline. It is clinically indicated to monitor plasma concentrations of antipsychotics and anticonvulsants in patients who are taking β-adrenergic antagonists. Barbiturates increase the elimination of β-adrenergic antagonists that are metabolized in the liver. Several reports have associated hypertensive crises and bradycardia with the coadministration of β-adrenergic antagonists and monoamine oxidase inhibitors. Patients on these two drugs should be treated with lower dosages of both drugs and have their blood pressure and pulse rates monitored regularly.

References

Carney R M, Rich M W, Saini J, Clark K, Freedland K E: Prevalence of major depressive disorder in patients receiving β-blocker therapy versus other medications. Am J Med *83*: 223, 1987.

Dupuis B, Catteau J, Dumon J-P, Libert C, Petit H: Comparison of propranolol, sotalol, and βxolol in the treatment of neuroleptic-induced akathisia. Am J Psychiatry *144*: 802, 1987.

Fleischhacker W W, Roth S D, Kane J M: The pharmacologic treatment of neuroleptic-induced akathisia. J Clin Psychopharmacol *10*: 12, 1990.

Jenkins S C, Maruta T: Therapeutic use of propranolol for intermittent explosive disorder. Mayo Clin Proc *62*: 204, 1987.

Lipinski J F, Keck P E, McElroy S L: Beta-adrenergic antagonists in psychosis: Is improvement due to treatment of neuroleptic-induced akathisia? J Clin Psychopharmacol *8*: 409, 1988.

Tyrere P: Current status of β-adrenergic drugs in the treatment of anxiety disorders. Drugs *36*: 773, 1988.

30.2.7 / Bupropion

Bupropion (Wellbutrin) is a unicyclic antidepressant that is unrelated either to the tricyclic and tetracyclic antidepressants or to the monoamine oxidase inhibitors (Figure 30.2.7-1). The drug was introduced in the United States and then withdrawn because of the occurrence of seizures in some patients taking the drug. The drug has now been reintroduced with specific recommendations regarding dose ranges to limit the occurrence of seizures.

PHARMACOLOGICAL ACTIONS

Bupropion is well absorbed from the gastrointestinal (GI) tract and metabolized by the liver, with its metabolites excreted by the kidneys. Two metabolites of the drug, hydroxybupropion and threohydrobupropion, may be related to its clinical and adverse effects. One study found that plasma hydroxybupropion concentrations above 1,250 ng per mL were associated with a lack of clinical response. The mechanism of action for the antidepressant effects of bupropion is unknown. Although it was initially thought that bupropion may act through the blockade of dopamine reuptake, one study found an increase in homovanillic acid (a metabolite of dopamine) to be associated with a lack of clinical response. It is possible that bupropion has some as yet identified effect on noradrenergic neural transmission.

INDICATIONS

The primary indication for bupropion is the treatment of major depression. As an antidepressant, bupropion is as effective as standard antidepressant therapies and is associated with significantly fewer adverse effects, thus making bupropion a reasonable first-line drug for the treatment of depression.

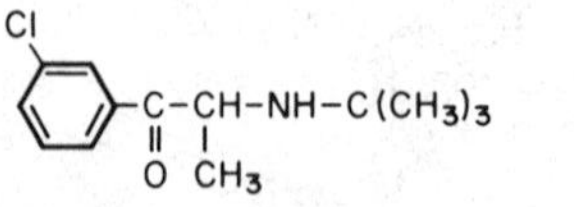

Cl
C-CH-NH-C(CH3)3
O CH3

Figure 30.2.7-1. Molecular structure of bupropion.

CLINICAL GUIDELINES

Bupropion is available in 75 and 100 mg tablets. Initiation of treatment in the average adult patient should be at 100 mg orally (PO) twice a day (bid). On the fourth day of treatment, the dosage can be raised to 100 mg PO three times a day (tid). Because 300 mg is the recommended dosage, it seems reasonable to maintain the patient on this dosage for several weeks before further increasing the dosage. Because of the risk of seizures, increases in dosage should never exceed 100 mg in a three-day period; a single dose of bupropion should never exceed 150 mg, and the total daily dose should not exceed 450 mg.

Bupropion should be given cautiously to patients with hepatic and renal diseases because of the potential accumulation of the drug in the body. Although bupropion is associated with minimal effects on cardiac conduction, the limited clinical experience makes it advisable to use the drug cautiously in patients with cardiac disease. Because of the increased incidence of seizures in patients with anorexia nervosa, bulimia nervosa, or a history of such disorders, bupropion is probably not the drug of choice for the treatment of depression in such patients. Bupropion is also contraindicated in patients with the following: seizure disorder; history of head trauma, central nervous system (CNS) tumor, or other organic brain disease; electroencephalogram (EEG) abnormalities; recent withdrawal from benzodiazepines or alcohol; and ingestion of other psychotropics that may affect seizure level, such as antipsychotics and lithium.

ADVERSE EFFECTS

Most notable about bupropion is the absence of significant drug-induced orthostatic hypotension, weight gain, daytime drowsiness, and anticholinergic effects; however, some patients may experience dry mouth or constipation. In fact, weight loss may occur in approximately 25 percent of patients. In one study (Table 30.2.7-1), the most common adverse effects were headache, insomnia, upper respiratory complaints,

Table 30.2.7-1
Adverse Events Associated with Treatment*

		Bupropion (No. = 110)		Placebo (No. = 109)	
Body System	**Adverse Event**	**No.**	**%**	**No.**	**%**
Cardiovascular					
	Palpitations	5	4.6	7	6.4
Gastrointestinal					
	Abdominal pain	6	5.5	3	2.8
	Anorexia	6	5.5	5	4.6
	Constipation	11	10.0	6	5.5
	Dyspepsia	7	6.4	8	7.3
	Nausea	14	12.7	11	10.1
Genitourinary					
	Dysmenorrhea†	3	4.2	6	8.5
	Impotence‡	2	5.1	0	0.0
Musculoskeletal					
	Back pain	9	8.2	8	7.3
	Muscle spasms	2	1.8	6	5.5
Neurological					
	Dizziness	16	14.6	6	5.5
	Headache	42	38.2	28	25.7
	Insomina	25	22.7	8	7.3
	Tremor	8	7.3	3	2.8
Psychiatric					
	Agitation	12	10.9	8	7.3
	Anxiety	10	9.1	5	4.6
	Irritability	6	5.5	6	5.5
Nonspecific					
	Fatigue	6	5.5	2	1.8
	Flulike symptoms	7	6.4	3	2.8
Oral complaints					
	Dry mouth	8	7.3	9	8.3
Respiratory					
	Upper respiratory complaints	21	19.1	36	33.0
Special senses					
	Blurred vision	6	5.5	1	0.9
	Tinnitus	7	6.4	2	1.8

Table from C G Lineberry, J A Johnston, R N Raymond, B Samara, J P Feighner, N E Harto, R P Granacher, R H Weisler, J S Carman, W F Boyer: A fixed-dose (300 mg) efficacy study of bupropion and placebo in depressed outpatients. J Clin Psychiatry *51*: 194, 1990.
*Those events reported at greater than a 5 percent incidence in either group.
†Percentages are based on number of female patients only (placebo, No. = 71; bupropion, No. = 71).
‡Percentages are based on number of male patients only (placebo, No. = 38, bupropion, No. = 39).

and nausea. Restlessness, agitation, and irritability may also occur. Although clinical experience is limited to fewer than 20 cases, overdoses of bupropion up to 4,200 mg when taken alone have not been fatal, thus suggesting that bupropion is significantly safer than conventional antidepressant drugs. At dosages less than 450 mg a day, the incidence of seizures is approximately 0.4 percent, which is fourfold that of standard antidepressants. The risk of seizures increases dramatically to about 4 percent in dosages from 450 to 600 mg a day.

DRUG-DRUG INTERACTIONS

Bupropion should not be coadministered with monoamine oxidase inhibitors (MAOIs); if bupropion treatment is indicated, MAOIs should be discontinued at least two weeks before. Although clinical experience is limited, care should be exercised when coadministering bupropion with other drugs metabolized by the liver, such as carbamazepine (Tegretol), cimetidine (Tagamet), barbiturates, and phenytoin (Dilantin).

References

Davidson J: Seizures and bupropion: A review. J Clin Psychiatry *50*: 256, 1989.

Golden R N, Rudorfer M V, Sherer M A, Linnoila M, Potter W Z: Bupropion in depression: I. Biochemical effects and clinical response. II. The role of metabolites in clinical outcome. Arch Gen Psychiatry *45*: 139, 145, 1988.

Journal of Clinical Psychiatry: New directions in the treatment of depression: Bupropion. J Clin Psychiatry *44* (5, Sec 2): 2, 1983.

Lineberry C G, Johnston J A, Raymond R N, Samara B, Feighner J P, Harto N E, Granacher R P, Weisler R H, Carman J S, Boyer W F: A fixed-dose (300 mg) efficacy study of bupropion and placebo in depressed outpatients. J Clin Psychiatry *51*: 194, 1990.

30.2.8 / Buspirone

Buspirone (BuSpar) is a novel azaspirodecanedione anxiolytic drug that offers a distinct and important alternative to treatment with benzodiazepines for anxiety. Buspirone is an exception to the general rule that anxiolytic drugs are also sedatives and hypnotics. In contrast to the benzodiazepines, buspirone carries a low potential for abuse and is not associated with withdrawal phenomena or sedation and cognitive impairment.

PHARMACOLOGICAL ACTIONS

Buspirone is well absorbed from the gastrointestinal (GI) tract, unaffected by food intake, and its metabolism involves both the liver and the kidneys. The drug reaches peak plasma levels 60 to 90 minutes after administration. The short half-life (2 to 11 hours) and the absence of active metabolites necessitate three-times-daily dosing.

In contrast to benzodiazepines and barbiturates, which act on the γ-aminobutyric acid (GABA)-associated chloride ion channel, buspirone has no effect on this receptor mechanism. Rather, buspirone acts as an agonist or partial agonist on serotonin type 1A receptors. Some reports have noted the influence of buspirone on dopaminergic neurons; however, it has not been shown that this is of any clinical significance in the production of anxiolytic or adverse effects. Figure 30.2.8-1 shows the molecular structure of buspirone.

INDICATIONS

The primary indication for buspirone treatment is anxiety, particularly generalized anxiety disorder. Although further research is required, at least one report has suggested that buspirone was effective in controlling anxiety and aggression in a small group of developmentally disabled persons. Most available data suggest that buspirone should not be used for the treatment of panic disorder. Because it does not act on the GABA-chloride channel complex, buspirone is not recommended for the treatment of withdrawal from benzodiazepines, alcohol, or other sedative drugs. Available data indicate that the use of buspirone in the elderly, in the same dosages as for nonelderly adults, is safe and effective.

There are advantages and disadvantages to both benzodiazepines and buspirone. The beneficial effects of the benzodiazepines are felt the same day they are started, and the full clinical response takes only days, whereas buspirone has no immediate effect, and the full clinical response may take two to four weeks. Sometimes the sedative effects of benzodiazepines, which are not found with buspirone, are desirable; however, these sedative effects are also associated with impaired motor performance and cognitive deficits, such as impaired memory. The major disadvantage of benzodiazepine treatment is its addictive potential and the development of withdrawal phenomena on discontinuation. Buspirone is not associated with any abuse potential, even in groups of patients who are at high risk for addictive behavior.

CLINICAL GUIDELINES

Buspirone is available in 5 and 10 mg tablets, and treatment is usually initiated with 5 mg orally (PO) three times a day. The dosage can be raised 5 mg every two to three days to the usual dosage range of 15 to 30 mg a day. The maximum dosage is 60 mg a day.

Buspirone is as useful as the benzodiazepines in the treatment of anxiety in patients who have not received benzodiazepines in the past. Buspirone does not achieve the same response, however, in patients who have received benzodiazepines in the past. The reason for this is probably the absence of the immediate mildly euphoric and sedative effects of the benzodiazepines. The most common clinical problem, therefore, is how to start giving buspirone to a patient who is currently taking benzodiazepines. The method least likely to work is to stop the benzodiazepine, allow a washout period, and then start buspirone treatment. There are two alterna-

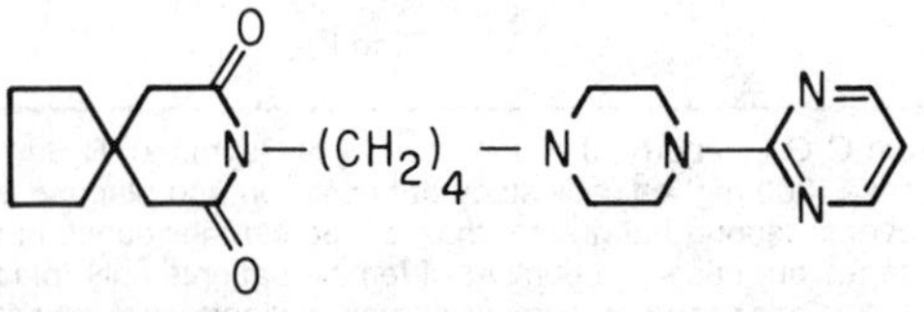

Figure 30.2.8-1. Molecular structure of buspirone.

tives. First, it is possible to start buspirone treatment gradually while the benzodiazepine is being withdrawn. Second, it is possible to start buspirone treatment and bring the patient up to a therapeutic dosage for two to three weeks while the patient is still receiving the regular dosage of benzodiazepine, at which point the benzodiazepine can be tapered. A few initial reports indicate that the coadministration of buspirone and benzodiazepines may be effective in the treatment of anxiety that has not responded to treatment with either drug alone.

ADVERSE EFFECTS

The most common adverse effects are headache, nausea, and dizziness. There is no sedation associated with buspirone; some patients report a minor feeling of restlessness, although this symptom may reflect incompletely treated anxiety. No deaths have been reported from overdoses of buspirone, and the median lethal dose (LD_{50}) is estimated to be 160 to 550 times the recommended daily dose. There is one report that coadministration of buspirone and haloperidol (Haldol) resulted in increased blood concentrations of haloperidol.

References

Lader M, Olajide D: A comparison of buspirone and placebo in relieving benzodiazepine withdrawal symptoms. J Clin Psychopharmacol 7: 11, 1987.

Robinson D, Napoliello M J, Schenk J: The safety and usefulness of buspirone as an anxiolytic drug in elderly verus young patients. Clin Ther *10*: 740, 1988.

Sheehan D V, Raj A B, Sheehan K H, Soto S: Is buspirone effective for panic disorder? J Clin Psychopharmacol *10*: 3, 1990.

Sussman N: Treatment of anxiety with buspirone. Psychopharmacol Update *17*: 114, 1987.

Taylor D P: Buspirone: A new approach to the treatment of anxiety. FASEB J *2*: 2445, 1988.

30.2.9 / Calcium Channel Inhibitors

Three calcium channel inhibitors have been used for neuropsychiatric disorders and are available in the United States: verapamil (Calan, Isoptin), diltiazem (Cardiazem), and nifedipine (Adalat, Procardia). The major medical indications for these drugs are angina and specific types of cardiac arrhythmias; the major psychiatric indication is bipolar disorder.

PHARMACOLOGICAL ACTIONS

The calcium ion is a major intracellular second messenger. Intraneuronal calcium has many functions, including the activation of calcium-dependent protein kinases. The calcium channel inhibitors inhibit the influx of calcium into neurons through one type of voltage-dependent calcium channel called the L-type calcium channel. The calcium channel inhibitors bind to the channel and inhibit its opening. Nifedipine (a dihydropyridine) binds to a different part of the channel from verapamil and diltiazem (both nondihydropyridines).

The calcium channel inhibitors are well absorbed from the gastrointestinal (GI) tract, but all three are substantially metabolized by the liver in a first-pass effect. There are considerable intraindividual and interindividual variations in the plasma concentrations of these drugs after a single dose. Verapamil is the most commonly used calcium channel inhibitor in psychiatry (Figure 30.2.9-1). The half-life of verapamil after the first dose is two to eight hours; the half-life increases to 5 to 12 hours after the first few days of therapy. According to some studies, verapamil does pass the blood-brain barrier and reaches the cerebrospinal fluid (CSF) in concentrations approximately 0.05 percent that of plasma.

INDICATIONS

Bipolar Disorder

The major indication for calcium channel inhibitors is in the acute and maintenance treatment of bipolar disorder, especially in patients who have not responded to or cannot tolerate lithium or carbamazepine (Tegretol). Verapamil is the calcium channel inhibitor that has been most studied in these cases, and a number of double-blind, placebo-controlled studies have shown it to be effective. Because of potential drug-drug interactions with lithium and carbamazepine, however, this drug should be coadministered with lithium and carbamazepine with caution.

Movement Disorders

Many reports have described improvement with calcium channel inhibitors in various movement disorders; however, these reports require verification by controlled studies. The movement disorders include tardive dyskinesia, Tourette's disorder, and Huntington's chorea.

Other Disorders

Most studies have not found a beneficial clinical effect of calcium channel inhibitors in the treatment of schizophrenia, although some data suggest that verapamil may reduce depressive or negative symptoms slightly. Calcium channel inhibitors have generally not been effective in the treatment of major depression. Other possible applications include premenstrual syndrome, primary degenerative dementia of the Alzheimer type, panic disorder, pain control, stuttering, and violent behavior.

CLINICAL GUIDELINES

Verapamil is available in 40, 80, and 120 mg tablets. The starting dosage is 40 mg orally (PO) three times a day and can

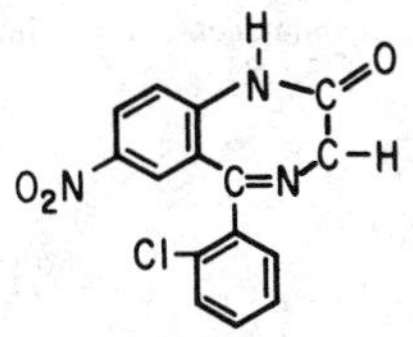

Figure 30.2.9-1. Molecular structure of verapamil.

be raised in increments every four to five days up to 80 to 120 mg three times a day. The patient's blood pressure, pulse, and electrocardiogram (ECG) (in patients over 40 years old or with a history of cardiac illness) should be followed routinely. Diltiazem is available in 30, 60, 90, and 120 mg tablets, should be started at 30 mg PO four times a day, and can be increased up to a maximum of 360 mg a day. Nifedipine is available in 10, 20, 30, 60, and 90 mg tablets. It should be started at 10 mg PO three or four times a day and can be increased up to a maximum dosage of 180 mg a day.

ADVERSE EFFECTS

The most common adverse effects associated with calcium channel inhibitors are hypotension and bradycardia, which sometimes necessitate discontinuing the drug. The calcium channel inhibitors interfere with atrioventricular (AV) conduction and can lead to AV heart block, especially in old patients. Common GI symptoms include constipation (9 percent), nausea (3 percent), and occasionally dry mouth, GI distress, or diarrhea. Adverse effects in the central nervous system (CNS) include dizziness (4 percent), headache (2 percent), and fatigue (2 percent). Rare adverse effects that have been reported include, with diltiazem, hyperactivity, akathisia, parkinsonism; with nifedipine, depression; and with verapamil, delirium, hyperprolactinemia, galactorrhea.

DRUG-DRUG INTERACTIONS

Calcium channel inhibitors should not be prescribed for patients taking β-adrenergic antagonists, hypotensives (e.g., diuretics, vasodilators, angiotensin-converting enzyme inhibitors), or antiarrhythmic drugs (e.g., quinidine, digoxin [Lanoxin]) without consultation with the patient's internist or cardiologist. Verapamil and diltiazem, but not nifedipine, have been reported to precipitate carbamazepine-induced neurotoxicity. Cimetidine (Tagamet) has been reported to increase plasma concentrations of nifedipine.

References

Deicken R F: Verapamil treatment of premenstrual syndrome. Biol Psychiatry *24*: 689, 1988.

Grebb J A, Shelton R C, Taylor E H, Bigelow L B: A negative, double-blind, placebo-controlled, clinical trial of verapamil in chronic schizophrenia. Biol Psychiatry *21*: 691, 1986.

Höschl C, Kožený J: Verapamil in affective disorders: A controlled, double-blind study. Biol Psychiatry *25*: 128, 1989.

Klein E, Uhde T W: Controlled study of verapamil for treatment of panic disorder. Am J Psychiatry *145*: 431, 1988.

Kushnir S L, Ratner J T: Calcium channel blockers for tardive dyskinesia in geriatric psychiatric patients. Am J Psychiatry *146*: 1218, 1989.

Pickar D, Wolkowitz O M, Doran A R, Labarca R, Roy A, Breier A, Narang P K: Clinical and biochemical effects of verapamil administration to schizophrenic patients. Arch Gen Psychiatry *44*: 113, 1987.

Pollack M H, Rosenbaum J F, Hyman S E: Calcium channel blockers in psychiatry. Psychosomatics *28*: 356, 1987.

Scriabine A, Schuurman T, Traber J: Pharmacological basis for the use of nimodipine in central nervous system disorders. FASEB J *3*: 1799, 1989.

Tollefson G D: Short-term effects of the calcium channel blocker nimodipine (Bay-e-9736) in the management of primary degenerative dementia. Biol Psychiatry *27*: 1133, 1990.

30.2.10 / Carbamazepine

Carbamazepine (Tegretol) is an iminodiabenzyl drug, structurally similar to imipramine (Tofranil), and approved for use in the United States for the treatment of temporal lobe epilepsy and trigeminal neuralgia (Figure 30.2.10-1). A large body of data support the use of carbamazepine for the treatment of acute mania and for the prophylactic treatment of bipolar disorder.

PHARMACOLOGICAL ACTIONS

Pharmacokinetics

Carbamazepine is absorbed slowly and erratically from the gastrointestinal (GI) tract, although absorption is enhanced when it is taken with meals. Peak plasma levels are reached two to eight hours after a single dose; steady-state levels are reached after two to four days on a steady dosage. The half-life of carbamazepine at the initiation of treatment has a wide range; during chronic administration the half-life ranges from 12 to 17 hours. Carbamazepine is metabolized in the liver and excreted by the kidneys. The 10-, 11-epoxide metabolite is active as an anticonvulsant, although its activity in the treatment of bipolar disorder is unknown.

Pharmacodynamics

The anticonvulsant effects of carbamazepine may be mediated through peripheral benzodiazepine receptors located in the brain, potentiation of α_2-adrenergic receptors, or stabilization of sodium channels on neurons. Central benzodiazepine receptors are more or less the same as the γ-aminobutyric acid (GABA) type A receptor and are acted on by benzodiazepines. These receptors are associated with the GABA binding site and chloride ion channel. Peripheral benzodiazepine receptors, which exist in both the periphery and the central nervous system (CNS), are thought to be regulators of calcium channel function. This potential effect of carbamazepine is interesting theoretically in the light of the increasing use of calcium channel inhibitors (Section 30.2.9) for the treatment of bipolar disorder.

Theoretically, another basis for the antimanic effect of carbamazepine involves the concept of kindling. Kindling is the electrophysiological process in which repeated subthreshold stimulations of a neuron eventually generate an action potential. It has been hypothesized that bipolar disorder represents

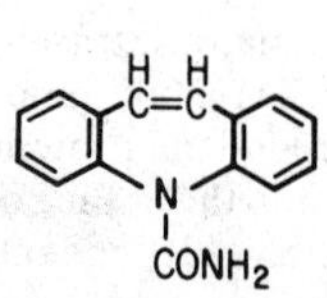

H H
C=C
N
CONH$_2$

Figure 30.2.10-1. Molecular structure of carbamazepine.

a covert form of limbic epilepsy, which is responsive to carbamazepine; however, electroencephalograms (EEGs) are normal in the majority of bipolar disorder patients who respond to carbamazepine.

INDICATIONS

Manic Episodes

Carbamazepine is as effective as lithium in the control of manic episodes. Nevertheless, lithium is still the drug of choice because of the absence of significant advantages of carbamazepine over lithium and the rare association of carbamazepine with severe adverse effects. Current clinical and research experience suggests, however, that carbamazepine may be more effective in the treatment of rapidly cycling bipolar disorder patients or patients with dysphoric manic episodes. Carbamazepine can be used alone or with an antipsychotic drug for the treatment of manic episodes, although carbamazepine-induced CNS adverse effects (drowsiness, dizziness, ataxia) with this combination are increasingly emerging. Patients who do not respond to lithium alone may respond when carbamazepine is added to the lithium treatment. If patients then respond, an attempt should be made to withdraw the lithium to see if the patient can be treated with carbamazepine alone. When lithium and carbamazepine are used together, the clinician should minimize or discontinue any antipsychotics, sedatives, or anticholinergic drugs the patient may be taking to reduce the increased risks of adverse effects associated with taking multiple drugs. The lithium and the carbamazepine should both be used at standard therapeutic plasma concentrations before a trial of combined therapy is considered to have been a therapeutic failure. Carbamazepine plasma concentrations from 8 to 12 μg per mL should be achieved for the treatment of manic episodes. A three-week trial of carbamazepine at therapeutic plasma concentrations is usually sufficient to determine whether the drug is effective.

Bipolar Disorder

Carbamazepine alone or in combination with lithium is an effective prophylactic treatment for bipolar disorder. It reduces the frequency of both manic and depressive episodes in 50 to 70 percent of patients.

Schizoaffective Disorder

Patients with schizoaffective disorder, as defined by the revised third edition of *Diagnostic and Statistical Manual of Mental Disorders* (DSM-III-R), probably constitute a particularly heterogeneous group of patients, some of whom may have a form of bipolar disorder. Both lithium and carbamazepine are usually effective treatments for these patients, although as yet there is no method for predicting the response of schizoaffective patients to these drugs.

Depression

The available data suggest that carbamazepine is an effective treatment for depression in some patients. Approximately 25 to 33 percent of depressed patients respond to carbamazepine; this percentage is significantly smaller than the 60 to 70 percent for standard antidepressants. Carbamazepine is an alternative for depressed patients who have not responded to conventional treatments, including electroconvulsive therapy (ECT).

Impulse Control Disorders

Several studies have reported carbamazepine to be effective in controlling impulsive, aggressive behavior in nonpsychotic patients. Other drugs for impulse control disorders, particularly episodic dyscontrol, include lithium, propranolol (Inderal), and antipsychotics. Because of the risk of serious adverse effects with carbamazepine, clinical trials with these other agents are warranted before a trial with carbamazepine.

Other Disorders

According to several studies, carbamazepine is as effective as the benzodiazepines in the control of symptoms associated with alcohol withdrawal. However, the lack of any advantage of carbamazepine over the benzodiazepines and the potential risk of adverse effects with carbamazepine limit the clinical usefulness of this application. Carbamazepine is also effective in controlling nonacute agitation and aggressive behavior in schizophrenic patients. Diagnoses to be ruled out before treatment with carbamazepine is begun include schizophrenic agitation, akathisia, and neuroleptic malignant syndrome. Lorazepam (Ativan) (1 to 2 mg every two to four hours) is more effective than carbamazepine for the control of acute agitation.

CLINICAL GUIDELINES

Pretreatment Medical Evaluation

The patient's medical history should include information about preexisting hematological, hepatic, and cardiac diseases, because all three can be relative contraindications to carbamazepine treatment. Patients with hepatic disease require only one-third to one-half the usual dose; the clinician should be cautious about raising the dose in such patients and should only do so slowly and gradually. Laboratory examination should include a complete blood count with platelet count, liver functions tests, serum electrolytes, and an electrocardiogram (ECG) in patients over 40 years of age or with preexisting cardiac disease. An EEG is not necessary before the initiation of treatment, but it may be helpful in documenting objective changes correlated with clinical improvement.

Initiation of Treatment and Plasma Levels

Carbamazepine is available in 100 and 200 mg tablets, and the usual starting dosage is 200 mg orally (PO) two times a day. Carbamazepine should be taken with meals, and the drug should be stored in a cool, dry place; carbamazepine stored in a bathroom medicine cabinet can lose up to one-third of its activity. In an inpatient setting with seriously ill patients, the dosage can be raised by not more than 200 mg a day until a dosage of 600 to 1000 mg a day is reached. Otherwise, in less ill patients and in outpatients, the dosage should be raised more slowly (200 mg every two to four days) to reduce the occurrence of minor adverse effects, such as nausea, vomiting, drowsiness, and dizziness. Plasma concentrations should be obtained when a patient has been receiving a steady dosage for at least five days. Blood for the determination of plasma levels is drawn in the morning before the first dose of carbamazepine is given. Although therapeutic concentrations for the treatment of epilepsy are 6 to 10 μg per mL, the therapeutic range for psychiatric indications is slightly higher, 8 to 12 μg per mL. Dosages required to achieve this level usually range from 400 to 1,600 mg a day in divided doses, with a mean around 1,000 mg a day. Some patients require doses as high as 2,200 mg a day to obtain therapeutic blood concentrations of carbamazepine.

Routine Laboratory Monitoring

The most serious potential adverse effects of carbamazepine are agranulocytosis and aplastic anemia. Patients should inform the physician immediately if fever, sore throat, infections, mouth ulcers, easy bruising, pallor, weakness, petechiae, or bleeding develop. The complete blood count (CBC), platelet count, electrolytes, and carbamazepine plasma concentration should be determined every two weeks for the first two months of treatment and quarterly thereafter. Liver and renal function tests should be conducted after the first month, then every three months for the first year, then annually. Transient leukopenias occur in approximately 10 percent of patients during the first few months and do not require discontinuation of treatment. Carbamazepine should be discontinued if laboratory values are lower than any of the following: total white blood cell count, 3,000 mm^3; neutrophils, 1,500 per mm^3; erythrocytes, 4.0×10^6 per mm^3; hematocrit, 32 percent; hemoglobin, 11 gm per 100 mL; platelet count, 100,000 per mm^3; reticulocyte count, 0.3 percent; serum iron level, 150 mg per 100 mL. A hematological consultation should be obtained if any such situation arises.

Table 30.2.10-1
Comparative and Differential Side Effects Profile of Lithium Carbonate and Carbamazepine

	Lithium Carbonate	Carbamazepine	Lithium and Carbamazepine Combination
Side effects			
White blood count	↑	↓	↑, —, Li*
Diabetes insipidus	↑	↓	↑, Li*
Thyroid hormones T_3, T_4	↓	↓	↓ ↓
TSH	↑	(—)	↑, Li*
Serum calcium	(↑)	↓	(↑), (Li*)
Weight gain	(↑)	(—)	
Tremor	(↑)	(—)	
Memory disturbances	(↑)	?	
Diarrhea	(↑)	—	
Teratogenic	(↑)	—	
Psoriasis	(↑)	(—)	
Pruritic rash (allergy)	—	↑	
Agranulocytosis	—	(↑)	
Hepatitis	—	(↑)	
Hyponatremia, water intoxication	—	(↑)	
Dizziness, ataxia, diplopia	—	↑	
Hypercortisolism, escape from dexamethasone suppression	—	↑	

Table adapted from Robert M. Post, M.D., with permission.

Side effects:
↑ : Increase
↓ : Decrease
( ): Inconsistent or rare
—: Absent
↓ ↓ : Potentiation
Li*: Effect of lithium predominates

ADVERSE EFFECTS

Although the benign hematological effects are not dose-related, most of the adverse effects of carbamazepine are correlated with plasma concentrations above 9 μg per mL. A comparison of the adverse effects for lithium and carbamazepine is given in Table 30.2.10-1. The most serious but rare adverse effects of carbamazepine are blood dyscrasias, hepatitis, and exfoliative dermatitis. Otherwise, carbamazepine is relatively well tolerated by patients except for mild GI and CNS effects that can be significantly reduced if the drug dosage is increased slowly and minimal effective plasma concentrations are maintained.

Blood Dyscrasias

Severe blood dyscrasias (aplastic anemia, agranulocytosis) occur in approximately 1 in 20,000 patients treated with carbamazepine. The early identification of these disorders through patient education about symptoms and with routine laboratory testing can reduce the likelihood of a serious outcome.

Hepatitis

Within the first few weeks of therapy, carbamazepine can cause both a hypersensitivity hepatitis associated with increases in liver enzymes and a cholestasis associated with elevated bilirubin and alkaline phosphatase. Hepatitis will recur if the drug is introduced and can be fatal.

Exfoliative Dermatitis

Stevens-Johnson syndrome of exfoliative dermatitis is a rare complication of carbamazepine requiring discontinuation of the drug. More common are urticaria and pruritic and erythematous rashes.

Gastrointestinal Adverse Effects

The most common adverse effects of carbamazepine are nausea, vomiting, gastric distress, constipation, diarrhea, and anorexia. The severity of these adverse effects is reduced if the dosage of carbamazepine is increased slowly.

Central Nervous System Adverse Effects

Acute confusional states can occur with carbamazepine alone but occur more often in combination with lithium or antipsychotic drugs. The symptoms include drowsiness, confusion, ataxia, hyperreflexia, clonus, and tremor. Elderly patients and patients with organic brain disease are at increased risk. The much more common CNS effects of dizziness, ataxia, clumsiness, and sedation are commonly associated with carbamazepine treatment, although they are reduced by a slower upward titration of the dosage.

Thyroid Adverse Effects

A decrease in L-triiodothyronine (T_3), thyroxine (T_4), and the free T_4 index can occur with carbamazepine treatment, although the development of hypothyroidism is rare. Patients who are taking both carbamazepine and lithium are at a greater risk of developing hypothyroidism than patients who are taking either drug alone.

Overdoses

No fatalities have been reported from overdoses of carbamazepine when taken alone. The symptoms of overdose include sinus tachycardia, atrioventricular (AV) conduction defects, seizures, coma, nystagmus, hyporeflexia or hyperreflexia, rigidity, orofacial dyskinesias, and mild respiratory depression.

Table 30.2.10-2
Clinically Important Interactions Between Carbamazepine and Other Drugs

Influences of Other Drugs on Carbamazepine	
Increased carbamazepine levels and toxicity produced by	*Increased carbamazepine levels not associated with marked toxicity*
Diltiazem (not nifedipine)	Cimetidine (mild acute increases; none after one week)
Erythromycin (and analogues)	Josamycin
Isoniazid (not tranylcypromine)	Nicotinamide
Nafimidone	Propoxyphene
Triacetyloleandomycin	Valproic acid (increases epoxide only)
Verapamil	
Viloxazine	
Decreased carbamazepine levels produced by	
Phenobarbital	
Phenytoin	
Primidone	
Theophylline	
Influences of Carbamazepine on Other Drugs	
Carbamazepine decreases levels or effects of	*Carbamazepine increases*
Clonazepam	Clomipramine
Dexamethasone	Desmethylclomipramine
Dicoumarol	Escape from dexamethasone suppression
Doxycycline	Phenytoin
Ethosuximide	
Haloperidol	
Pregnancy tests	
Theophylline	
Valproic acid	
Warfarin	

Table by Robert M. Post, M.D.

Other Adverse Effects

Although the teratogenicity of carbamazepine is unknown, its use in pregnancy should be undertaken only if absolutely necessary. Carbamazepine is secreted in breast milk; therefore, women taking carbamazepine should not breast feed their babies. Carbamazepine decreases cardiac conduction (although less than the tricyclic antidepressants do) and can, thus, exacerbate preexisting cardiac disease. Carbamazepine has been associated with the development of hyponatremia; therefore, if signs of neurotoxicity emerge, this condition should be considered.

DRUG-DRUG INTERACTIONS

Potential drug-drug interactions of carbamazepine are listed in Table 30.2.10-2. Coadministration with lithium, antipsychotic drugs, verapamil (Calan, Isoptin), or nifedipine (Adalat, Procardia) can precipitate carbamazepine-induced CNS adverse effects. Carbamazepine can decrease the blood concentrations of oral contraceptives, resulting in breakthrough bleeding and uncertain prophylaxis against pregnancy.

References

Adamec R E: Does kindling model anything clinically relevant? Biol Psychiatry *27*: 249, 1990.

Elphick M, Yang J-D, Cowen P J: Effects of carbamazepine on dopamine- and serotonin-mediated neuroendocrine responses. Arch Gen Psychiatry *47*: 135, 1990.

Gleason R P, Schenider L S: Carbamazepine treatment of agitation in Alzheimer's outpatients refractory to neuroleptics. J Clin Psychiatry *51*: 115, 1990.

Kessler A J, Barklage N E, Jefferson J W: Mood disorders in the psychoneurologic borderland: Three cases of responsiveness to carbamazepine. Am J Psychiatry *146*: 81, 1989.

Kramlinger K G. Post R M: The addition of lithium to carbamazepine: Antidepressant efficacy in treatment-resistant depression. Arch Gen Psychiatry *46*: 794, 1989.

Kramlinger K G, Post R M: Addition of lithium carbonate to carbamazepine: Hematological and thyroid effects. Am J Psychiatry *147*: 615, 1990.

Lerer B, Moore N, Meyendorff E, Cho S-R, Gershorn S: Carbamazepine versus lithium in mania: A double-blind study. J Clin Psychiatry *48*: 89, 1987.

Malcolm R, Ballenger J C, Sturgis E T, Anton R: Double-blind controlled trial comparing carbamazepine to oxazepam treatment of alcohol withdrawal. Am J Psychiatry *146*: 617, 1989.

Neppe W M, ed.: Carbamazepine use in neuropsychiatry. J Clin Psychiatry *49*(4, Suppl): 2, 1988.

Stuppaeck C, Barnas C, Miller C, Schwitzer J, Fleischhacker W W: Carbamazepine in the prophylaxis of mood disorders. J Clin Psychopharmacol *10*: 39, 1990.

30.2.11 / Chloral Hydrate

Chloral hydrate (Noctec) and a related compound (ethchlorvynol [Placidyl]) are among the oldest sedative-hypnotic drugs still in use, having been used since 1869. Because of the introduction of many compounds since that time, chloral hydrate is now used only as a very short-term (two- to three-day) hypnotic.

PHARMACOLOGICAL ACTIONS

Chloral hydrate is well absorbed from the gastrointestinal (GI) tract. The parent compound is metabolized within minutes by the kidneys, liver, and red blood cells. An active metabolite, trichloroethanol, has a half-life of approximately 8 to 11 hours. A dose of chloral hydrate induces sleep in 30 to 60 minutes and maintains sleep for four to eight hours. The pharmacodynamic basis for the hypnotic effect of chloral hydrate is not known.

INDICATIONS

The major indication for chloral hydrate is insomnia. Whether chloral hydrate affects rapid eye movement (REM) sleep is controversial; however, there is no REM rebound after discontinuation of chloral hydrate therapy. Chronic treatment with chloral hydrate is associated with an increased incidence and severity of adverse effects. Tolerance develops to the hypnotic effects of chloral hydrate after two weeks of treatment. Chloral hydrate is available in 250 and 500 mg tablets, 250 and 500 mg per 5 mL solutions, and 325, 500, and 650 mg rectal suppositories. The standard dose of chloral hydrate is 500 to 2,000 mg at bedtime.

In addition to the development of tolerance, dependence on chloral hydrate can occur with symptoms similar to those of alcohol dependence. The lethal dose of chloral hydrate is between 5,000 and 10,000 g, thus making chloral hydrate a particularly poor choice for potentially suicidal patients. The lethality of chloral hydrate is potentiated by other central nervous system (CNS) depressants, including alcohol.

ADVERSE EFFECTS

The most common GI adverse effects are nausea, vomiting, and diarrhea; however, these can be somewhat reduced by taking the drug with extra water. Patients should be warned that there may be residual daytime sedation and impaired motor coordination. With long-term use and with overdose, gastritis and gastric ulceration can develop. Hepatic and renal damage can follow overdose attempts, resulting in jaundice and albuminuria.

DRUG-DRUG INTERACTIONS

Patients who have received chloral hydrate less than 24 hours before receiving intravenous furosemide (Lasix) can have diaphoresis, flushes, and an unsteady blood pressure. Reports are somewhat controversial concerning the potentiation of warfarin (Coumadin) when coadministered with chloral hydrate.

References

Graham S R, Day R O, Lee R, Fulde G W: Overdose with chloral hydrate: A pharmacological and therapeutic review. Med J Aust *149*: 686, 1988.

Keeter S, Benator R M, Weinberg S M, Hartenburg M A: Sedation in pediatric CT: National survey of current practice. Radiology *175*: 745, 1990.

Rye L A: Clinical notes on therapeutics: Pharmacoanxiolytic therapy in dentistry: Barbiturates, chloral derivatives, and antihistamines. J Oral Med *41*: 66, 1986.

Schuler M E: Augmentation of chloral hydrate induced sleep by centrally acting hypertensive agents. Proc West Pharmacol Soc *25*: 347, 1982.

30.2.12 / Clonidine

Clonidine (Catapres) is an α_2-adrenergic receptor agonist used primarily as a hypotensive agent (Figure 30.2.12-1). Its major indications in psychiatry are the control of the withdrawal symptoms from opioids and the treatment of Tourette's disorder.

PHARMACOLOGICAL ACTIONS

Clonidine is well absorbed from the gastrointestinal (GI) tract and reaches peak plasma levels in one to three hours. Approximately 35 percent of the drug is metabolized by the liver, and 65 percent is excreted in both unchanged and metabolized forms by the kidneys. The half-life of the parent compound is 6 to 20 hours, and there are no active metabolites. The agonist effects on presynaptic α_2-adrenergic receptors result in a decrease in the amount of neurotransmitter released from the nerve terminal.

CLINICAL GUIDELINES AND INDICATIONS

Clonidine is available in 0.1, 0.2, and 0.3 mg tablets. The usual starting dosage is 0.1 mg orally (PO) twice a day and can be raised by 0.1 mg a day to an appropriate level. Clonidine must always be tapered when it is discontinued to avoid rebound hypertension, which occurs approximately 20 hours after the last clonidine dose.

Opioid Withdrawal

Clonidine is effective in reducing the autonomic symptoms of opiate withdrawal (hypertension, tachycardia, dilated pupils, sweating, lacrimation, rhinorrhea) but not the associated subjective sensations. Clonidine can be used either alone or, perhaps more effectively, as a method of withdrawing a patient from methadone. Usually, dosages of 0.15 mg twice a day are sufficient for this purpose. For clonidine to be effective for this indication, it is presumably affecting the activity of the locus ceruleus neurons.

Tourette's Disorder

Some clinicians now use clonidine as a first-line drug for the treatment of Tourette's disorder instead of the standard drugs, haloperidol (Haldol) and pimozide (Orap), because of

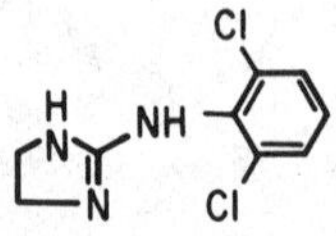

Cl H NH N Cl

Figure 30.2.12-1. Molecular structure of clonidine.

the serious adverse effects associated with those antipsychotics. The starting pediatric or child dosage is 0.05 mg a day, although it can be raised to 0.3 mg a day in divided doses. It takes up to three months to observe the beneficial effects of clonidine in this disorder.

Other Disorders

Other potential indications include the anxiety disorders (panic disorder, phobias, obsessive-compulsive disorder, post-traumatic stress disorder, generalized anxiety disorder), mania (possibly synergistic with lithium or carbamazepine [Tegretol]), and schizophrenia (in which it may help reduce tardive dyskinetic movements).

ADVERSE EFFECTS

The most common adverse effects associated with clonidine are dry mouth and eyes, fatigue, dizziness, nausea, hypotension, and constipation, which result in approximately 10 percent of patients' choosing to discontinue the drug. Uncommon central nervous system (CNS) adverse effects include insomnia, anxiety, and depression; rare CNS adverse effects include vivid dreams, nightmares, and hallucinations. Fluid retention associated with clonidine treatment can be treated with diuretics. Patients who overdose on clonidine can present with coma and constricted pupils, symptoms similar to an opioid overdose. Other symptoms of overdose are decreased blood pressure, pulse, and respiratory rates.

DRUG-DRUG INTERACTIONS

The most relevant drug-drug interaction is that the coadministration of clonidine with tricyclic antidepressants can inhibit the hypotensive effects of clonidine.

References

Charney D C, Heninger G R, Kleber H D: The combined use of clonidine and naltrexone as a rapid, safe, and effective treatment of abrupt withdrawal from methadone. Am J Psychiatry *143:* 831, 1986.

Giannini A J, Pascarzi G A, Loiselle R H, Price W A, Giannini M C: Comparison of clonidine and lithium in the treatment of mania. Am J Psychiatry *143:* 1608, 1986.

Hardy M-C, Lecrubier Y, Widlöcher D: Efficacy of clonidine in 24 patients with acute mania. Am J Psychiatry *143:* 1450, 1986.

Heidemann S M, Sarnaik A P: Clonidine poisoning in children. Crit Care Med *18:* 618, 1990.

Leckman J F, Ort S, Caruso K A, Anderson G M, Riddle M A, Cohen D J: Rebound phenomena in Tourette's syndrome after abrupt withdrawal of clonidine. Arch Gen Psychiatry *43:* 1168, 1986.

30.2.13 / Dopamine Receptor Antagonists: Antipsychotics

Dopamine receptor antagonists make up the largest group of drugs known as *antipsychotics*. The antipsychotics are a seemingly diverse group of drugs that have the single common pharmacodynamic property of antagonizing dopamine receptors (except for clozapine [Clozaril], which is discussed in the next subsection). These drugs have also been referred to as *neuroleptics* and *major tranquilizers*. The term "neuroleptic" refers more to the neurological or motor effects of these drugs. The term "major tranquilizer" inaccurately implies that the primary effect of these drugs is merely to sedate patients and also confounds these drugs with the so-called minor tranquilizers, such as the benzodiazepines. A common mistake is to use the term "phenothiazine" as synonymous with the term "antipsychotic"; the phenothiazine antipsychotics are only one class of antipsychotic drugs.

The major use of antipsychotics is to treat schizophrenia, although these drugs are also used to treat agitation and psychosis associated with other psychiatric and organic disorders. Antipsychotics have little or no abuse potential and thus are not classified as controlled substances. Although antipsychotics do not permanently cure schizophrenia, they greatly benefit many patients in a way that no treatment ever did before they were introduced. The clinical use of antipsychotics has reduced the population of inpatients in psychiatric hospitals from over 500,000 in 1950 to approximately 100,000 in 1985. This decline in the inpatient population is often referred to as deinstitutionalization. Nonetheless, although antipsychotics have allowed many patients to remain out of the hospital and to function in the community, these same drugs are also partly responsible for the problem of the homeless mentally ill. The antipsychotics have made these patients just barely well enough not to require hospitalization; yet the deinstitutionalization plan did not adequately provide for the outpatient treatment of many patients who are still impaired.

CLASSIFICATION

Seven classes of drugs can be grouped together as antipsychotic dopamine receptor antagonists (Figure 30.2.13-1).

Phenothiazines

All the phenothiazines have the same three-ring phenothiazine nucleus but differ in the side chains joined to the nitrogen atom of the middle ring. The phenothiazines are typed according to the aliphatic (e.g., chlorpromazine [Thorazine]), piperazine (e.g., fluphenazine [Prolixin, Permitil]), or piperidine (e.g., thioridazine [Mellaril]) nature of the side chain.

Thioxanthenes

The thioxanthene three-ring nucleus differs from the phenothiazine nucleus by the substitution of a carbon atom for the nitrogen atom in the middle ring. The two available thioxanthenes have either an aliphatic (chlorprothixene [Taractan]) or a piperazine (thiothixene [Navane]) side chain.

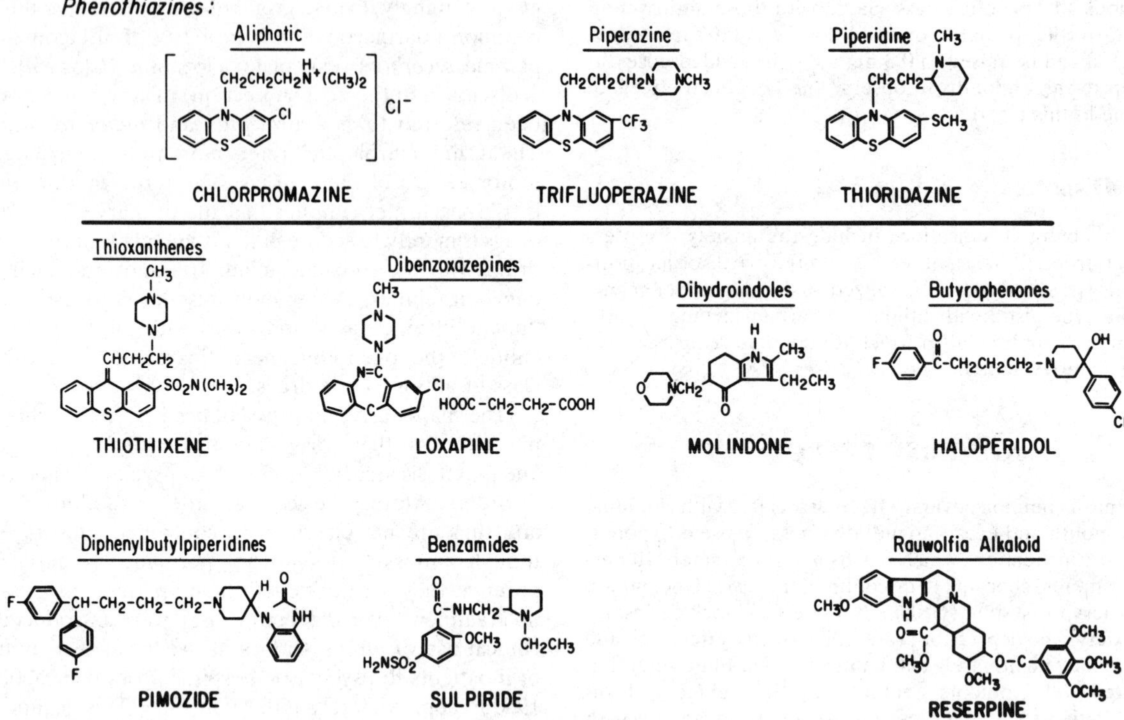

Figure 30.2.13-1. Molecular structure of representative antipsychotic dopamine receptor antagonists and reserpine.

Dibenzoxazepines

The dibenzoxazepines are based on another modification of the three-ring phenothiazine nucleus. The only dibenzoxazepine available in the United States is loxapine (Loxitane), which has a piperazine side chain.

Dihydroindoles

The only dihydroindole available in the United States, molindone (Moban, Lidone), has somewhat unusual properties, such as not inducing weight gain and perhaps being less epileptogenic than the phenothiazines.

Butyrophenones

Only two butyrophenones are available in the United States—haloperidol (Haldol) and droperidol (Inapsine). Haloperidol is perhaps the most widely used antipsychotic, and droperidol is used as an adjuvant in anesthesia. Some research groups, however, have been using droperidol as an intravenous (IV) antipsychotic drug in emergency settings. Spiroperidol is a butyrophenone compound widely used in research studies to label dopamine receptors.

Diphenylbutylpiperidines

Diphenylbutylpiperidines are somewhat similar structurally to the butyrophenones. Only one diphenylbutylpiperidine, pimozide (Orap), is available in the United States and is approved for treating Tourette's disorder. In Europe, however, pimozide has been shown to be an effective antipsychotic agent. A controversial clinical and research observation about pimozide is that it may be more effective than the other antipsychotics in reducing the deficit or negative symptoms of schizophrenia.

Benzamides

No benzamide derivatives are available in the United States; however, there is considerable evidence that sulpiride (Dogmatil) is an effective antipsychotic associated with significantly fewer neurological side effects than the other antipsychotics.

Reserpine

Although it is not a dopamine receptor antagonist, reserpine (Serpalan, Serpasil) does have antipsychotic effects. It is an indole alkaloid obtained from the root of *Rauwolfia serpentina*; it produces its antipsychotic effect by depleting the presynaptic stores of serotonin and catecholamines, rather than by the blockade of postsynaptic receptors. Reserpine is most commonly used as a hypotensive agent; it is rarely used as an antipsychotic. Its use is associated with the adverse side effect of depression.

PHARMACOLOGICAL ACTIONS

Pharmacokinetics

Although the pharmacokinetic details for the antipsychotics vary widely (e.g., half-lives ranging from 10 to 20 hours), the most important clinical generalization is that all the antipsychotics currently available in the United States can be given in one daily dose once the patient is in a stable condition and has adjusted to any adverse effects. Most antipsychotics are incompletely absorbed after oral administration. In addition, most have high binding to plasma proteins, volumes of distribution, and lipid solubilities. Antipsychotic drugs are metabolized in the liver and reach steady-state plasma levels in 5 to 10 days. There is some evidence that, after a few weeks of administration, chlorpromazine, thiothixene, and thioridazine induce metabolic enzymes, thereby decreasing the plasma concentrations. Chlorpromazine is notorious among psychopharmacologists for having over 150 metabolites, some of which are active. The nonaliphatic phenothiazines and the butyrophenones have very few metabolites, but the activity of these metabolites is still controversial. The potential presence of active metabolites complicates the interpretation of plasma drug levels that report the presence of only the parent compound.

Pharmacodynamics

The potency of antipsychotic drugs to reduce psychotic symptoms is most closely correlated with the affinity of these drugs with the dopamine type 2 (D_2) receptor (see Figure 3.2-17 in Section 3.2, "Brain Imaging"). The mechanism of therapeutic action for antipsychotic drugs is thought to be as D_2 receptor antagonists, preventing the binding of endogenous dopamine to this type of dopaminergic receptor. There are two caveats to this hypothesis. First, although the dopamine receptor blocking effect occurs immediately, the full antipsychotic effects may take weeks to develop. This observation suggests that some more slowly developing homeostatic change in the brain is the actual mechanism of action for the antipsychotic effects of these drugs. Second, although the correlation of dopamine blocking effects with the clinical potency has led to the dopamine hypothesis of schizophrenia, it is also true that these drugs reduce psychotic symptoms regardless of the diagnosis. The therapeutic effects of dopamine receptor blockade, therefore, are not unique to the pathophysiology of schizophrenia.

Most of the neurological and endocrinological adverse effects of antipsychotics can also be explained by the blockade of dopamine receptors. Various antipsychotics, however, also block noradrenergic, cholinergic, and histaminergic receptors, thus accounting for the variation in adverse effects profiles seen among these drugs.

Although the potency of the antipsychotics varies widely (Table 30.2.13-1), all available antipsychotics are equally efficacious in the treatment of schizophrenia. No type of schizophrenia or set of symptoms has been demonstrated conclusively to be more effectively treated by any single class of antipsychotics (with the controversial exception of pimozide for negative symptoms). The therapeutic index for antipsychotics is very favorable and has contributed to the unfortunate practice of routinely using high doses of these drugs. More recent investigations of the dose-response curve for antipsychotics indicate that the equivalent of 5 to 10 mg of haloperidol is usually efficacious for either the short-term or the long-term treatment of schizophrenia. Antipsychotics may have a bell-shaped dose-response curve. Overly high doses of antipsychotics may lead to neurological side effects, such as akinesia and akathisia, which are difficult to distinguish from an exacerbation of psychosis. Moreover, excessively high doses of some antipsychotics become less effective in reducing psychotic symptoms.

Although patients can build up a tolerance to most of the adverse effects caused by antipsychotics, patients do not build a tolerance to the antipsychotic effect. It is wise, nevertheless, to taper the dosage when the drugs are being discontinued, as there may be rebound effects from the other neurotransmitter systems that the drug blocked. Cholinergic rebound, for example, can produce a flulike syndrome in patients.

Table 30.2.13-1
Antipsychotic Drugs, Trade Names, and Potencies

Generic Name	Trade Name	Potency* (mg of drug equivalent to 100 mg chlorpromazine)
Phenothiazines		
Aliphatic		
Chlorpromazine	Thorazine	100
Triflupromazine	Vesprin	25–50
Piperazime		
Prochlorperazine	Compazine	15
Perphenazine	Trilafon	10
Trifluoperazine	Stelazine	3–5
Fluphenazine	Prolixin, Permitil	1.5–3
Acetophenazine	Tindal	25
Butaperazine	Repoise	10
Carphenazine	Proketazine	25
Piperidine		
Thioridazine	Mellaril	100
Mesoridazine	Serentil	50
Piperacetazine	Quide	10
Thioxanthenes		
Chlorprothixene	Taractan	50
Thiothixene	Navane	2–5
Dibenzoxazepine		
Loxapine	Loxitane	10–15
Dihydroindole		
Molindone	Moban, Lidone	6–10
Butyrophenone		
Haloperidol	Haldol	2–5
Diphenylbutyl-piperidine		
Pimozide	Orap	1

*Recommended adult dosages are 200 to 400 mg a day of chlorpromazine or an equivalent amount of another drug.

INDICATIONS

Idiopathic Psychosis

Idiopathic psychoses include schizophrenia, schizophreniform disorder, schizoaffective disorder, delusional disorder, brief reactive psychosis, manic episode, and major depressive episode with psychotic features. Antipsychotics are effective in both the short-term and the long-term management of these conditions; that is, antipsychotics both reduce acute symptoms and prevent future exacerbations. Antipsychotics are often used in combination with antimanic drugs to treat bipolar disorder and in combination with antidepressants to treat major depression. Because of the potential adverse effects of repeatedly administering antipsychotics, maintenance treatment with these drugs is indicated primarily for schizophrenia and in some cases of schizoaffective disorder.

Antipsychotics are superior to placebos in the treatment of acute and chronic schizophrenia and in the control of other agitated and psychotic behavior. Approximately 70 percent of patients improve significantly with antipsychotic treatment. The onset of sedation is rapid, often within one hour after intramuscular (IM) administration of these drugs. Antipsychotic activity has a slower onset, but most therapeutic gain occurs in the first six weeks of therapy. Patients may continue to improve, however, for up to six months. Antipsychotics are most effective against the positive symptoms of psychosis, such as agitation and hallucinations. Although the negative symptoms are less affected by antipsychotic treatment, with continued treatment many patients become less socially withdrawn.

Secondary Psychosis

Secondary psychoses are associated with an identified organic cause, such as a brain tumor or drug intoxication. The higher potency antipsychotics are usually safer to use in such patients because of their lower cardiogenic and epileptogenic potential. Antipsychotic drugs should not be used to treat drug intoxications or withdrawals when there is an increased risk of seizures. The drug of choice in such cases is usually a benzodiazepine. Psychosis secondary to amphetamine intoxication, however, is an indication for antipsychotic treatment if a pharmacological treatment is required.

Severe Agitation or Violent Behavior

The administration of antipsychotics calms most severely agitated or violent patients, although the use of a sedative drug (e.g., benzodiazepine or barbiturate) may be preferable in some cases. The agitation associated with delirium and dementia, most common in elderly patients, is an indication for antipsychotics. Small dosages of high-potency drugs (e.g., 0.5 to 1 mg a day of haloperidol) are usually the best choice. The repeated administration of antipsychotics to control disruptive behavior in mentally retarded children is a controversial indication.

Movement Disorders

Both the psychosis and the movement disorder of Huntington's chorea are often treated with antipsychotics. These drugs are also used to treat the motor and vocal tics of Tourette's disorder.

Other Psychiatric Indications

The use of thioridazine to treat depression with marked anxiety or agitation has been approved by the Food and Drug Administration (FDA). Some clinicians use small dosages of antipsychotics (0.5 mg of haloperidol or 25 mg of chlorpromazine two to three times a day) to treat severe anxiety. In addition, some investigators have reported using antipsychotics to control the behavioral turmoil in patients with borderline personality disorder. But because of the possible long-term adverse effects of antipsychotics, they should be used in these other psychiatric conditions only after more conventional drugs have been tried.

CLINICAL GUIDELINES

Antipsychotic drugs are remarkably safe in short-term use, and, if necessary, a clinician can administer these drugs without conducting a physical or laboratory examination of the patient. The major contraindications to antipsychotics are (1) a history of a serious allergic response; (2) the possibility that the patient has ingested a drug that will interact with the antipsychotic to induce central nervous system (CNS) depression (e.g., alcohol, opioids, barbiturates, benzodiazepines) or anticholinergic delirium (e.g., scopolamine, possibly phencyclidine [PCP]); (3) the presence of a severe cardiac abnormality; (4) a high risk of seizures from organic or idiopathic causes; (5) the presence of narrow-angle glaucoma if an anticholinergic antipsychotic is to be used; and (6) the presence of or a history of tardive dyskinesia. In the usual assessment, however, it is best to obtain a complete blood count (CBC) with white blood cell indices, liver function tests, and an electrocardiogram (ECG), especially in women over 40 and men over 30.

Choice of Drug

The general guidelines for choosing a particular psychotherapeutic drug should be followed (see Section 30.1). If no other rationale prevails, the choice should be based on adverse effect profiles, as described below, and the psychiatrist's preference. Although high-potency antipsychotics are associated with more neurological adverse effects, current clinical practice greatly favors using them because of the higher incidence of other adverse effects (e.g., cardiac, hypotensive, epileptogenic, sexual, and allergic) with the low-potency drugs. There is a myth in psychiatry that hyperexcitable patients respond best to chlorpromazine because it is more sedating, whereas withdrawn patients respond best to high-potency antipsychotics, such as fluphenazine. This hypothesis has never been proved; furthermore, if sedation is a desired goal, either the antipsychotic can be given in divided doses or a sedative drug (e.g., a benzodiazepine) can also be administered.

A clinical observation that is supported by some research is that an unpleasant reaction by the patient to the first dose of a antipsychotic correlates highly with future poor response and noncompliance. Such experiences include a subjective negative feeling, oversedation, and acute dystonia. If a patient reports such a reaction, the clinician may be well advised to switch the patient to a different antipsychotic.

Dosage and Schedule

Various patients may respond to widely different dosages of antipsychotics; therefore, there is no set dosage for any given antipsychotic drug. It is reasonable clinical practice to start each patient at a low dosage and increase it as necessary. It is important to remember that the maximal effects of a particular dosage may not be evident for four to six weeks.

Short-term treatment. The equivalent of 5 mg of haloperidol is a reasonable dose for an adult patient in an acute state. A geriatric patient may benefit from as little as 1 mg of haloperidol. The administration of more than 50 mg of chlorpromazine in one injection, however, may result in serious hypotension. The administration of the antipsychotic IM results in peak plasma levels in approximately 30 minutes, versus 90 minutes with the oral route. The patient should be observed for one hour; then most clinicians administer a second dose of the antipsychotic.

Rapid neuroleptization is the practice of administering hourly IM doses of antipsychotic medications until the desired clinical effect is achieved. Several research studies have shown, however, that merely waiting several more hours after one dose of an antipsychotic results in the same clinical improvement as that seen with repeated doses of antipsychotics. The clinician must be very careful to prevent patients from becoming violent while they are psychotic. Psychiatrists can do this by temporarily using physical restraints until the patients can control their behavior.

Because the administration of very high doses of high-potency antipsychotics is not associated with a higher incidence of adverse effects, the practice of giving very large cumulative antipsychotic doses in the emergency setting has become common. Physicians, therefore, may be pressured by their staff to use repeated administrations of antipsychotics. But hypotension can be a serious complication resulting from the repeated administration of low-potency antipsychotics.

Clinicians usually attempt to achieve sedation, in addition to the reduction of psychosis, with repeated administrations of antipsychotics. It may be reasonable, therefore, to use a sedative agent, rather than a antipsychotic, after one or two doses of the antipsychotic. Possible sedatives include lorazepam (Ativan) (2 mg IM) and amobarbital (Amytal) (50 to 250 mg IM).

Early treatment. The equivalent of 10 to 20 mg of haloperidol or 400 mg of chlorpromazine a day is adequate treatment for most patients with schizophrenia. Some research suggests that 5 mg of haloperidol or 200 mg of chlorpromazine may, in fact, be just as effective. It is wise to use divided doses when initiating the therapy. This practice reduces the incidence and the severity of adverse effects and may help sedate the patient. The sedative effects of antipsychotics last only a few hours, in contrast to the antipsychotic effects, which last for one to three days. After approximately one week of treatment, it is usually helpful to give the entire dose of the antipsychotic at bedtime. This practice usually helps the patient sleep and reduces the incidence of adverse effects. In old patients treated with low-potency antipsychotics, however, this practice may increase the risk of their falling if they get out of the bed during the night.

It is common clinical practice to order medications to be given as needed (PRN). Although this practice may be reasonable during the first few days that a patient is hospitalized, it has been shown that the time on antipsychotic drugs, rather than an increase in dosage, is what produces therapeutic improvement. Again, clinicians may feel pressured by their staff to write PRN antipsychotic orders. The orders for PRN medications should include the specific symptoms, how often the drugs should be given, and how many doses can be given each day. Clinicians may choose to use small doses for the PRNs (e.g., 2 mg of haloperidol) or may use a benzodiazepine (e.g., 2 mg lorazepam IM).

Maintenance treatment. A patient with schizophrenia should continue to receive an effective dosage of antipsychotics for at least six months after improvement. For a patient who has had only one or two psychotic episodes and has been in a stable clinical state for six months, it is reasonable to attempt to reduce the dosage by 50 percent gradually over three to six months. After the patient has had another six months in a stable clinical state, another 50 percent dosage reduction may be indicated. Some research data suggest that many patients with schizophrenia can be maintained with the equivalent of 5 mg of haloperidol a day. It is wise for the clinician to know enough about the patient's life to try to predict upcoming stressors, during which times the patient's antipsychotic dosage should perhaps be increased.

Patients who have had three or more exacerbations of schizophrenic symptoms should probably continue to receive antipsychotics indefinitely, although attempts to reduce the dosage may be warranted every four to five years if the patient has been clinically stable. Although antipsychotic drugs are effective, patients may report that they prefer being off the drugs, because they feel better without them. Normal persons who have taken antipsychotic drugs report a sense of dysphoria. The clinician must discuss maintenance medication with the patients and take into account the patients' wishes, the severity of their illness, and the quality of their support systems.

Alternative maintenance regimens. Alternative maintenance regimens have been designed to reduce both the risk of long-term adverse effects and any unpleasantness associated with taking antipsychotic medications. Intermittent medication is the use of antipsychotics only when patients require them. This arrangement requires that the patients or their caretakers be both willing and able to watch carefully for early signs of clinical exacerbations. At the earliest signs of such problems, antipsychotic medications should be reinstituted for a reasonable period, usually one to three months.

Drug holidays are regular two- to seven-day periods during which the patient is not given antipsychotic medications. There is currently no evidence that drug holidays reduce the risk of long-term adverse effects from antipsychotics, and it is possible that drug holidays increase the incidence of noncompliance.

Long-acting depot antipsychotics. Because some patients with schizophrenia do not reliably comply with oral antipsychotic regimens, it may be reasonable to treat them with long-acting depot preparations. These preparations are usually administered IM once every one to four weeks by a clinician. The clinician, therefore, immediately knows if a patient has missed a dose of medication. Depot antipsychotics may be associated with more adverse effects, including tardive dyskinesia. Although this concern is controversial, clinicians should probably refrain from using depot forms unless the patient is unable to comply with oral medications.

Two depot preparations (a decanoate and an enanthate) of fluphenazine and a decanoate preparation of haloperidol are available in the United States. These preparations are injected IM into an area of large muscle tissue, from where they are absorbed slowly into the blood. Decanoate preparations can be given less frequently than are enanthate preparations because they are absorbed more slowly. Although it is not absolutely necessary to stabilize a patient on the oral (PO) preparation of the specific drug before initiating the depot form, it is good practice to give at least one PO dose of the drug to assess the possibility of any adverse effect, such as an allergic reaction.

It is difficult to predict the correct dosage or time interval for depot preparations. It is reasonable to begin with 12.5 mg (0.5 cc) of either fluphenazine preparation or 25 mg (0.5 cc) of haloperidol decanoate. If symptoms emerge in the next two to four weeks, the patient can be treated temporarily with additional oral medications or with additional small depot injections. After three to four weeks the depot injection can be increased to include the supplemental doses given during this initial period.

A good reason to initiate depot treatment with low doses is that the absorption of these preparations may be faster at the onset of treatment, resulting in frightening episodes of dystonia that eventually discourage compliance with the medication. Some clinicians keep patients drug-free for three to seven days before initiating depot treatment and give very small doses of the depot preparations (3.125 mg fluphenazine or 6.25 mg haloperidol) every few days to avoid these initial problems. Because the major indication for depot medication is poor compliance with oral forms, it may be wise to go slowly with what is practically the last method of achieving compliance.

ADVERSE EFFECTS

Nonneurological Adverse Effects

One generalization about the adverse effects of antipsychotics is that low-potency drugs cause most nonneurological adverse effects and that high-potency drugs cause most neurological adverse effects (Table 30.2.13-2).

Orthostatic (postural) hypotension. Orthostatic (postural) hypotension is mediated by adrenergic blockade and is most common with chlorpromazine and thioridazine (Table 30.2.13-2). It occurs most frequently during the first few days of treatment, and patients readily have a tolerance to it. It is most apt to occur when high doses of intramuscular, low-potency antipsychotics are given. The chief dangers of this adverse effect are that the patients may faint, fall, and injure themselves, although such occurrences are uncommon. When using IM low-potency antipsychotics, the clinician should measure the patients' blood pressure (lying and standing) before and after the first dose and during the first few days of treatment. When appropriate, patients should be warned of the adverse effects and given the usual instructions—to rise from bed gradually, sit at first with their legs dangling, wait for a minute, and sit or lie down if they feel faint. Support hose may help with this symptom. If low-potency antipsychotics are used by patients with cardiac problems, the dosage should be increased very slowly.

If hypotension does occur in patients receiving these medications, the symptom can usually be managed by having the patients lie down with the feet higher than the head. On rare occasions, volume expansion or vasopressor agents, such as norepinephrine, may be indicated. Because hypotension is produced by α-adrenergic blockade, these drugs also block the α-adrenergic stimulating properties of epinephrine, leaving the β-adrenergic stimulating effects untouched. Therefore, administering epinephrine to these patients results in a paradoxical worsening of hypotension and so is contraindicated in cases of antipsychotic-induced hypotension. Pure α-adrenergic pressors such as metaraminol and norepinephrine (levarterenol) are the drugs of choice in the treatment of this disorder.

Peripheral anticholinergic effects. Peripheral anticholinergic effects are quite common and consist of dry mouth and nose, blurred vision, constipation, urinary retention, and mydriasis. Some patients also have nausea and vomiting. Chlorpromazine, thioridazine, mesoridazine (Serentil), and trifluoperazine (Stelazine) are potent anticholinergics (Table 30.2.13-2). Anticholinergic effects can be particularly severe if a low-potency antipsychotic is used with a tricyclic antidepressant and an anticholinergic drug; such a practice is seldom warranted.

Dry mouth can be quite a troubling symptom for patients. They should be advised to rinse out the mouth frequently with water and not to chew gum or candy containing sugar, as this can result in fungal infections of the mouth or an increased incidence of dental caries. Constipation should be treated with the usual laxative preparations, but this condition can progress to paralytic ileus. Pilocarpine may be used in such situations, although the relief is only transitory. A decrease in the antipsychotic or a change to another drug is warranted in such cases.

Endocrine effects. Blockade of the dopamine receptors in the tuberoinfundibular tract results in increased secretion of prolactin, which can result in breast enlargement, galactorrhea, impotence in men, and amenorrhea and inhibited orgasm in women. Both sexes may report decreased libido, and women may have a false pregnancy test result while taking some antipsychotics. Thioridazine is particularly associated with decreased libido and retrograde ejaculation in male patients. Psychiatrists may not find out about the disturbing sexual adverse effects of an antipsychotic if they do not ask about them specifically. Another adverse effect of antipsychotics is the inappropriate secretion of antidiuretic hormone. Some patients' glucose tolerance test results shift in a diabetic direction because of antipsychotic administration.

Skin effects. Allergic dermatitis and photosensitivity occur in a small percentage of patients, most commonly those taking low-potency drugs, particularly chlorpromazine. A variety of skin eruptions—urticarial, maculopapular, petechial, and edematous eruptions—have been reported. These eruptions occur early in treatment, generally in the first few weeks, and remit spontaneously. A photosensitivity reaction that resembles a severe sunburn also occurs in some patients taking chlorpromazine. Patients should be warned of this adverse effect, should spend no more than 30 to 60 minutes in the sun, and should use sun screens. Chlorpromazine is also associated with some cases of blue-gray discoloration of the skin over areas exposed to sunlight. The skin changes often begin with a tan or golden brown color and progress to such colors as slate gray, metallic blue, and purple.

Ophthalmological effects. Thioridazine is associated with irreversible pigmentation of the retina when given in dosages of more than 800 mg a day. This pigmentation is similar to that seen in retinitis pigmentosa, and it can progress even after the thioridazine is stopped and can result in blindness.

Chlorpromazine may induce whitish-brown granular deposits concentrated in the anterior lens and posterior cornea, visible only by slit-lens examination. They progress to opaque white and yellow-brown granules, often stellate in shape. Occasionally, the conjunctiva is discolored by a brown pigment. Retinal damage is not seen in these patients, and their vision is almost never impaired. The majority of patients who show

Table 30.2.13-2
Relative Adverse Effects of Antipsychotics

	Sedation	Anticholinergic	Hypotension	Extrapyramidal
Acetophenazine	Low	Low	Low	Medium
Chlorpromazine	High	High	High	Low
Chlorprothixene	High	High	High	Low
Fluphenazine	Medium	Low	Low	High
Haloperidol	Low	Low	Low	High
Loxapine	Medium	Medium	Medium	High
Mesoridazine	Medium	High	Medium	Medium
Molindone	Medium	Medium	Low	High
Perphenazine	Low	Low	Low	High
Pimozide	Low	Low	Low	High
Thioridazine	High	High	High	Low
Thiothixene	Low	Low	Low	High
Trifluoperazine	Medium	Low	Low	High
Triflupromazine	High	Medium	High	Medium

the deposits are those who have ingested 1 to 3 kg of chlorpromazine throughout their lives.

Cardiac effects. Low-potency antipsychotics are more cardiotoxic than are high-potency drugs. Chlorpromazine causes prolongation of the QT and PR intervals, blunting of T waves, and depression of the ST segment. Thioridazine, in particular, has marked effects on the T wave, and these unique cardiac effects may be why overdoses of the piperidine phenothiazines are the most lethal among the antipsychotics.

Sudden death. The cardiac effects of antipsychotics have been hypothesized to be related to sudden death in patients treated with these drugs. Careful evaluation of the literature, however, suggests that it is premature to attribute these sudden deaths to the antipsychotic drugs. Supporting this view is the observation that the introduction of antipsychotics had no effect on the incidence of sudden death in schizophrenic patients. In addition, both low-potency and high-potency drugs were involved in the cases. Furthermore, many reports were of patients with other medical problems, treated with other drugs.

Weight gain. A common adverse effect of treatment with antipsychotics is weight gain, which can be significant in some cases. Molindone and, perhaps, loxapine are not associated with this symptom and may be indicated in patients for whom weight gain is a serious health hazard or a reason for noncompliance.

Hematological effects. A leukopenia with a white blood count (WBC) around 3,500 is a common but not serious problem. A life-threatening hematological problem is agranulocytosis, occurring most often with chlorpromazine and thioridazine but seen with almost all antipsychotics. It occurs most frequently during the first three months and with an incidence of 1 in 500,000. Routine complete blood counts (CBCs) are not indicated; however, if a patient reports a sore throat and fever, a CBC should be done immediately to check for this possibility. If the blood indices are low, the antipsychotic should be stopped, and the patient should be transferred to a medical facility. The mortality rate for this complication may be as high as 30 percent. Thrombocytopenic or nonthrombocytopenic purpura, hemolytic anemias, and pancytopenia may occur rarely in patients treated with antipsychotics.

Jaundice. In the early days of chlorpromazine treatment, jaundice was not unusual, occurring in about 1 out of every 100 patients treated. More recently, for unexplained reasons, the incidence of chlorpromazine-induced jaundice has dropped considerably. Although accurate data are lacking, the incidence is probably in the range of 1 out of every 1,000 patients treated.

The jaundice occurs most often in the first five weeks of treatment and is generally preceded by a flulike syndrome. It is generally wise to discontinue chlorpromazine if patients have jaundice, although the value of this practice has never been proved. Indeed, patients have continued to receive chlorpromazine throughout the illness without adverse effects. Chlorpromazine-associated jaundice has also recurred in patients as long as 10 years later.

Jaundice has also been reported to occur with promazine (Sparine), thioridazine, mepazine (Pacalal), and prochlorperazine (Compazine) and very rarely with fluphenazine and trifluoperazine. No convincing evidence indicates that haloperidol or many of the other nonphenothiazine antipsychotics can produce jaundice. The majority of the cases reported in the literature are still associated with the use of chlorpromazine.

Overdoses of antipsychotics. With the exception of overdoses from thioridazine and mesoridazine, the outcome of antipsychotic overdose is favorable unless the patient has also ingested other CNS depressants, such as alcohol and benzodiazepines. The symptoms of overdose include drowsiness, which may progress to delirium, coma, dystonias, and seizures. The pupils are mydriatic; deep tendon reflexes are decreased; tachycardia and hypotension are present; and the electroencephalogram (EEG) shows diffuse slowing and low voltage. The piperazine phenothiazines can lead to heart block and ventricular fibrillation, resulting in death.

The treatment should include gastric lavage and activated charcoal followed by catharsis. Convulsions can be treated with IV diazepam (Valium) or diphenylhydantoin. Hypotension should be treated with either norepinephrine or dopamine, not epinephrine.

Neurological Adverse Effects

Epileptogenic effects. Antipsychotic administration is associated with a slowing and an increased synchronization of the EEG. This effect may be the mechanism by which some antipsychotics decrease the seizure threshold. Chlorpromazine, loxapine, and other low-potency antipsychotics are thought to be more epileptogenic than are high-potency drugs, especially molindone. The risk of inducing a seizure by drug administration warrants consideration when the patient already has a seizure disorder or an organic brain lesion.

Sedation. Sedation is primarily a result of the blockade of histamine type 1 receptors. Chlorpromazine is the most sedating antipsychotic; thioridazine, chlorprothixene, and loxapine are also very sedating; and the high-potency antipsychotics are much less sedating (Table 30.2.13-2). Patients should be warned about driving or operating machinery when first treated with antipsychotics. Giving the entire antipsychotic dose at bedtime usually eliminates any problems from sedation, and tolerance to this adverse effect often develops.

Central anticholinergic effects. The symptoms of central anticholinergic activity include severe agitation; disorientation to time, person, or place; hallucinations; seizures; high fever; and dilated pupils. Stupor and coma may ensue. The treatment consists of discontinuing the causal agent, close medical supervision, and physostigmine (Antilirium, Eserine) (2 mg by slow IV infusion, repeated within one hour as necessary). Too much physostigmine is dangerous, and symptoms of physostigmine toxicity include hypersalivation and sweating. Atropine sulfate (0.5 mg) can reverse these effects.

Dystonias. Approximately 10 percent of all patients experience dystonias as an adverse effect of antipsychotics, usually in the first few hours or days of treatment. Dystonic movements result from a slow, sustained muscular contraction or spasm that can result in an involuntary movement. Dystonias can involve the neck (spasmodic torticollis or retrocollis), jaw (forced opening resulting in a dislocation or trismus), tongue (protrusions, twisting), or the entire body (opisthotonos). Involvement of the eyes can result in an oculogyric crisis, characterized by their upward lateral movement. Unlike other dystonias, an oculogyric crisis may also occur late in treatment. Other dystonias include blepharospasm and glossopharyngeal dystonias, resulting in dysarthria, dysphagia, and even cyanosis. Children are particularly likely to evidence opisthotonos, scoliosis, lordosis, and writhing movements. Dystonias can be painful and frightening and often result in later noncompliance.

Dystonias are most common in young men (less than 40 years old) but can occur at any age in either sex. Although they are most common with IM doses of high-potency antipsychotics, dystonias can occur with any antipsychotic but are rare with thioridazine. The mechanism of action is thought to be the dopaminergic hyperactivity in the basal ganglia that occurs when the CNS levels of the antipsychotic begin to fall. Dystonias can fluctuate spontaneously, responding to reassurance and resulting in the clinician's false impression that the movement is hysterical. The differential diagnosis should include seizures and tardive dyskinesia. Prophylaxis with anticholinergics or related drugs (Table 30.2.13-3) usually prevents the development of dystonias. Treatment with IM anticholinergics or IV or IM diphenhydramine (Benadryl) (50 mg) almost always relieves the symptoms. Diazepam (10 mg IV), amobarbital, caffeine sodium benzoate, and hypnosis have also been reported to be effective. Although tolerance to this adverse effect usually develops, it is sometimes prudent to change the antipsychotic if the patient is particularly concerned about the reaction's recurrence.

Parkinsonian effects. Parkinsonian adverse effects occur in approximately 15 percent of patients, usually within 5 to 90 days of the treatment's initiation. Symptoms include muscle stiffness, cogwheel rigidity, shuffling gait, stooped posture, and drooling. The pill-rolling tremor of idiopathic parkinsonism is rare, but a regular, coarse tremor similar to essential tremor may be present. *Rabbit syndrome* is a focal, perioral tremor that resembles the other parkinsonian effects of antipsychotics but can occur late in treatment. The masklike facies, bradykinesia, and akinesia of this parkinsonian syndrome are often misdiagnosed as being part of the negative symptom picture of schizophrenia and are, therefore, not treated.

Women are affected about twice as often as men, and the syndrome can occur at all ages, although most frequently after age 40. All antipsychotics can cause the symptoms, especially high-potency drugs with low anticholinergic activity. Chlorpromazine and thioridazine are less likely to be involved. The blockade of dopaminergic transmission in the nigrostriatal tract is the cause of drug-induced parkinsonism. Because not all patients have this syndrome, those who do seem not to be able to compensate for the presence of antipsychotic blockade in the nigrostrital tract. The differential diagnosis should also include other causes of idiopathic parkinsonism, other organic causes of parkinsonism, and depression. The syndrome can be treated with anticholinergic agents, amantadine (Symadine, Symmetrel), or diphenhydramine. Although amantadine may have fewer side effects, it may be less effective at reducing muscular rigidity. Levodopa does not work in these cases, and it may exacerbate the psychosis. Anticholinergics should be withdrawn after four to six weeks to assess whether the patient has a tolerance to the parkinsonian effects; approximately 50 percent of patients need continued treatment. Even after the antipsychotics are withdrawn, parkinsonian symptoms may last for up to two weeks and even up to three months in elderly patients. In such patients it is reasonable to continue the anticholinergic drug after stopping the antipsychotic.

Akathisia. Akathisia is a subjective feeling of muscular discomfort that can cause the patient to be agitated, pace relentlessly, stand and sit continually, and feel quite dysphoric. The symptoms are primarily motor and cannot be controlled by the patient's will. Akathisia can appear at any time during treatment. It is probably underdiagnosed, because the symptoms are mistakenly attributed to psychosis, agitation, or lack of cooperation. The mechanism underlying akathisia is poorly understood, although it presumably involves dopamine receptor blockade. The antipsychotic dosage should be reduced and treatment with anticholinergics or amantadine attempted, although this latter approach is often not effective. Propranolol (Inderal) (30 to 120 mg a day), benzodiazepines, and clonidine (Catapres) have been shown to be effective in several research studies (Table 30.2.13-3). In some cases of akathisia, no treatment seems to be effective.

Tardive dyskinesia. Tardive dyskinesia is a delayed effect of antipsychotics, rarely occurring until after six months of treatment. The syndrome consists of abnormal, involuntary, irregular, choreoathetoid movements of muscles of the head, limbs, and trunk. The severity of these movements ranges from minimal—often missed by patients and their families—to grossly incapacitating. Perioral movements are the most

Table 30.2.13-3
Drug Treatment of Extrapyramidal Disorders

Generic Name	Trade Name	Usual Daily Dosage	Indications
Anticholinergic			
Benztropine	Cogentin, Tremin	PO 0.5–2 mg tid; IM or IV 1-2 mg	Acute dystonic reaction, parkinsonism, akinesia, akathisia, rabbit syndrome
Biperiden	Akineton	PO 2–6 mg tid; IM or IV 2 mg	
Procyclidine	Kemadrin	PO 2.5–5 mg bid-qid	
Trihexyphenidyl	Artane, Pipanol	PO 2–5 mg tid	
Ethopropazide	Parsidol	PO 50–100 mg bid-qid	
Orphenadrine	Norflex, Dispal	PO 50–100 mg bid-qid; IV 60 mg	
Antihistaminergic			
Diphenhydramine	Benadryl	PO 25 mg qid; IM or IV 25 mg	Acute dystonic reaction, parkinsonism, akinesia, rabbit syndrome
Dopamine agonists			
Amantadine	Symmetrel	PO 100–200 mg bid	Parkinsonism, akinesia, rabbit syndrome
β-Adrenergic antagonists			
Propranolol	Inderal	PO 20–40 mg tid	Akathisia
α-Adrenergic antagonists			
Clonidine	Catapres	PO 0.1 mg tid	Akathisia
Benzodiazepines			
Clonazepam	Klonopin	PO 1 mg bid	Akathisia, acute dystonic reactions
Lorazepam	Ativan	PO 1 mg tid	

common and include darting, twisting, and protruding movements of the tongue, chewing and lateral jaw movements, lip puckering, and facial grimacing. Finger movements and hand clenching are also quite common. Torticollis, retrocollis, trunk twisting, and pelvic thrusting are seen in severe cases. Respiratory dyskinesias have also been reported. Dyskinesias are exacerbated by stress and disappear during sleep. Other tardive or late-occurring syndromes may include tardive dystonias, tardive parkinsonism, and tardive behavioral syndromes, although the last of these is quite controversial.

All the antipsychotics have been associated with causing tardive dyskinesia, although some evidence indicates that thioridazine is less likely to be involved. The longer that patients are on antipsychotics, the more likely they are to have tardive dyskinesia. Women are more affected than men, and patients over 50 years of age, patients with brain damage, and patients with mood disorders also seem to be at high risk. The incidence increases by approximately 3 to 4 percent a year after four to five years of treatment. Approximately 50 to 60 percent of chronically institutionalized patients have the syndrome. It is an interesting observation that 1 to 5 percent of schizophrenic patients had similar abnormal movements before the introduction of antipsychotics in the early 1950s. Tardive dyskinesia is hypothesized to be caused by dopaminergic receptor supersensitivity in the basal ganglia resulting from chronic blockade of dopamine receptors by antipsychotics. This hypothesis, however, has not been proved.

The three basic approaches to tardive dyskinesia are prevention, diagnosis, and management. Prevention is best achieved by using antipsychotic medications only when clearly indicated and in the lowest effective dosages. Patients receiving antipsychotics should be checked regularly for the appearance of abnormal movements, preferably by using a standardized rating scale (Table 30.2.13-4). When abnormal movements are detected, a differential diagnosis should be considered (Table 30.2.13-5).

Once a diagnosis of tardive dyskinesia is made, it becomes imperative to complete regular objective ratings of the move-

Table 30.2.13-4
Abnormal Involuntary Movement Scale (AIMS) Examination Procedure

Patient Identification ____________________ Date ________

Rated by ____________________

Either before or after completing the examination procedure, observe the patient unobtrusively at rest (e.g., in waiting room).

The chair to be used in this examination should be a hard, firm one without arms.

After observing the patient, rate him or her on a scale of 0 (none), 1 (minimal), 2 (mild), 3 (moderate) and 4 (severe) according to the severity of symptoms.

Ask the patient whether there is anything in his or her mouth (i.e., gum, candy, etc.) and, if so, to remove it.

Ask the patient about the *current* condition of his or her teeth. Ask patient if he or she wears dentures. Do teeth or dentures bother patient *now*.

Ask patient whether he or she notices any movement in mouth, face, hands or feet. If yes, ask patient to describe and indicate to what extent they *currently* bother patient or interfere with his or her activities.

Rating	Procedure
0 1 2 3 4	Have patient sit in chair with hands on knees, legs slightly apart, and feet flat on floor. (Look at entire body for movements while in this position.)
0 1 2 3 4	Ask patient to sit with hands hanging unsupported. If male, between legs, if female and wearing a dress, hanging over knees. (Observe hands and other body areas.)
0 1 2 3 4	Ask patient to open mouth. (Observe tongue at rest within mouth.) Do this twice.
0 1 2 3 4	Ask patient to protrude tongue. (Observe abnormalities of tongue movement.) Do this twice.
0 1 2 3 4	Ask the patient to tap thumb, with each finger, as rapidly as possible for 10 to 15 seconds; separately with right hand, then with left hand. (Observe facial and leg movements.)
0 1 2 3 4	Flex and extend patient's left and right arms. (One at a time.)
0 1 2 3 4	Ask patient to stand up. (Observe in profile. Observe all body areas again, hips included.)
0 1 2 3 4	*Ask patient to extend both arms outstretched in front with palms down. (Observe trunk, legs and mouth.)
0 1 2 3 4	*Have patient walk a few paces, turn and walk back to chair. (Observe hands and gait.) Do this twice.

*Activated movements.

Table 30.2.13-5
Differential Diagnosis for Tardive Dyskinesialike Movements

Common—Schizophrenic mannerisms and stereotypies
Dental problems (e.g., ill-fitting dentures)
Meige's syndrome and other senile dyskinesias

Drug induced—Antidepressants
Antihistamines
Antimalarials
Antipsychotics
Diphenylhydantoin
Heavy metals
Levodopa
Sympathomimetics

CNS—Anoxia-induced
Hepatic failure
Huntington's chorea
Parathyroid hypoactivity
Postencephalitic
Pregnancy (chorea gravidarum)
Renal failure
Sydenham's chorea
Systemic lupus erythematosus
Thyroid hyperactivity
Torsion dystonia
Tumors
Wilson's disease

ment disorder. Although tardive dyskinesia often emerges while the patient is taking a steady dosage of medication, it is even more likely to emerge when the dosage is reduced. Some investigators have called the latter dyskinesias "withdrawal dyskinesias." Once tardive dyskinesia is recognized, consideration should be given to reducing or stopping the antipsychotic if at all possible. Consideration should also be given to treating the patient with clozapine (see Section 30.2.14). Between 5 and 40 percent of all tardive dyskinesias eventually remit, and between 50 and 90 percent of mild cases remit. It is not thought at this time that tardive dyskinesia is a progressive condition.

There is no single effective treatment for tardive dyskinesia. If the movement disorder is severe, an attempt should be made to decrease or stop the antipsychotic. Lithium, carbamazepine (Tegretol), or benzodiazepines may be effective in reducing both the psychotic symptoms and the movement disorder. Various studies have reported that cholinergic agonists and antagonists, dopaminergic agonists, and γ-aminobutyric acid (GABA)-ergic drugs (e.g., valproic acid [Depakene]) may be useful.

Neuroleptic malignant syndrome. Neuroleptic malignant syndrome (NMS) is a life-threatening complication of antipsychotic treatment, with a variable time of onset during treatment. Symptoms include muscular rigidity and dystonia, akinesia, mutism, obtundation, and agitation. Autonomic symptoms include hyperpyrexia (up to 107°F), sweating, and increased pulse and blood pressure. Laboratory findings include increased white blood cell count (WBC), blood creatinine phosphokinase, liver enzymes, and myoglobin in plasma resulting in renal shutdown. The symptoms usually evolve over 24 to 72 hours, and the untreated syndrome lasts 10 to 14 days. The diagnosis is often missed in the early stages, and the withdrawal or agitation may be mistakenly considered increased psychosis. Men are affected more frequently than women, and the mortality rate is between 15 and 25 percent. The pathophysiology of NMS is unknown, although it may be related to hyperthermic crises that were seen in psychotic patients before the advent of antipsychotic drugs.

The treatment is the immediate discontinuation of antipsychotic drugs, medical support to cool the patient, and the monitoring of vital signs and renal output. Dantrolene (Dantrium), a skeletal muscle relaxant (1 mg per kg PO four times a day, 1 to 5 mg per kg IV) may reduce the muscle spasms, and bromocriptine (Parlodel) (1.25 mg PO two times a day) has also been reported to be of some benefit in treating this syndrome.

Prevention and treatment of some neurological adverse effects. A variety of drugs (Table 30.2.13-3) may be used to prevent and treat extrapyramidal adverse effects caused by antipsychotics. These include anticholinergics (Section 30.2.2), amantadine (Section 30.2.1), antihistamines (Section 30.2.3), benzodiazepines (Section 30.2.5), β-adrenergic receptor antagonists (Section 30.2.6), and clonidine (Section 30.2.12). Most acute dystonias and parkinsonlike symptoms are effectively treated by these drugs, and akathisia may also respond in some cases. It is not known whether prophylactic treatment with these drugs is warranted when starting to give a patient an antipsychotic. The proponents of prophylactic treatment argue that the increased likelihood of avoiding adverse neurological effects is more humane to the patient and increases the possibility of future compliance. The opponents of this practice argue that the increased likelihood of anticholinergic adverse effects from these drugs offsets any possible gain. A reasonable compromise is to give these drugs to patients under age 45 who are more at risk of neurological adverse effects and not to use these drugs prophylactically in patients over 45 who are at increased risk for anticholinergic toxicity. If a patient does have dystonias, parkinsonlike symptoms, or akathisia, a trial of these drugs is warranted.

Once a patient has started taking these drugs, he or she should be treated for four to six weeks. Then the clinician should attempt to taper and stop the medication over one month. Many patients become tolerant to the neurological adverse effects and no longer require the drug. Some patients experience the return of neurological symptoms and have to start taking these drugs again. Other patients state that they feel less anxious or depressed while taking these medications, so it may be reasonable to give the medications again, even in the absence of neurological symptoms.

Most clinicians use one of the anticholinergic drugs or diphenhydramine to provide prophylaxis or treatment for neurological adverse effects. Of these drugs, diphenhydramine is the most sedating; biperiden (Akineton) is neutral; and trihexyphenidyl (Artane, Pipanol) may be slightly stimulating. In fact, trihexyphenidyl, benztropine (Cogentin, Tremin), and diphenhydramine can be abused, as some patients report obtaining a euphoria from these drugs. Amantadine is most often used when one of the anticholinergic drugs does not work. Although amantadine does not exacerbate the psychosis of schizophrenia, some patients become tolerant of its antiparkinsonian effects. Amantadine is also a sedating drug in some patients.

DRUG-DRUG INTERACTIONS

Antacids

Antacids and cimetidine (Tagamet), administered in intervals of one to two hours of antipsychotic administration, reduce the absorption of antipsychotic drugs.

Anticholinergics

Anticholinergics may decrease the absorption of antipsychotics. The additive anticholinergic activity of antipsychotics, anticholinergics, and tricyclic antidepressants may result in anticholinergic toxicity.

Anticonvulsants

Phenothiazines, especially thioridazine, may decrease the metabolism of diphenylhydantoin, resulting in toxic levels of the latter. Barbiturates may increase the metabolism of antipsychotics, and antipsychotics may lower the seizure threshold.

Antidepressants

Tricyclic antidepressants and antipsychotics may decrease each other's metabolism, resulting in increased plasma concentrations of both. The anticholinergic, sedative, and hypotensive effects of these drugs may also be additive.

Antihypertensives

Antipsychotics may inhibit the uptake of guanethidine (Esimil, Ismelin) into the synapse and may also inhibit the hypotensive effects of clonidine and α-methyldopa. Conversely, antipsychotics may have an additive effect on some hypotensives. Antipsychotics have a variable effect on clonidine.

CNS Depressants

Antipsychotics potentiate the CNS depressant effects of sedatives, antihistamines, opiates, and alcohol, particularly in patients with an impaired respiratory status.

Other Drugs

Cigarette smoking may decrease the plasma levels of antipsychotic drugs. Epinephrine has a paradoxical hypotensive effect in patients taking antipsychotics. The coadministration of lithium and antipsychotics may result in symptoms similar to those of lithium intoxication and neuroleptic malignant syndrome. There is no reason to believe that these two syndromes are more common with coadministration than when these agents are administered alone and that the interaction is no more common with one antipsychotic than another. Propranolol coadministration with antipsychotics increases the blood concentrations of both. Antipsychotics decrease the blood concentration of warfarin (Coumadin), resulting in decreased bleeding time.

References

Baldessarini R J, Cohen B M, Teicher M H: Significance of neuroleptic sode and plasma level in the pharmacological treatment of psychoses. Arch Gen Psychiatry *45*: 79, 1988.

Boyer P, Lecrubier Y, Puech A J: Treatment of positive and negative symptoms: Pharmacologic approaches. Mod Probl Pharmacopsychiatry *24*: 152, 1990.

Dixon L, Weiden P J, Frances A J, Rapkin B: Management of neuroleptic-induced movement disorders: Effects of physician training. Am J Psychiatry *146*: 104, 1989.

Feinberg S S, Kay S R, Elijovich L R, Fiszbein A, Opler L A: Pimozide treatment of the negative schizophrenic syndrome: An open trial. J Clin Psychiatry *49*: 235, 1988.

Jann M W, Lam Y W, Chang W H: Reversible metabolism of haloperidol and reduced haloperidol in Chinese schizophrenic patients. Psychopharmacology *101*: 107, 1990.

Kane J M: The current status of neuroleptic therapy. J Clin Psychiatry *50*: 322, 1989.

Keck P E, Cohen B M, Baldessarini R J, McElroy S L: Time course of antipsychotic effects of neuroleptic drugs. Am J Psychiatry *146*: 1289, 1989.

Keck P E, Pope H G, Cohen B M, McElroy S L, Nierenberg A A: Risk factors for neuroleptic malignant syndrome: A case-control study. Arch Gen Psychiatry *46*: 914, 1989.

Kellam A M P: The neuroleptic malignant syndrome, so-called: A survey of world literature. Br J Psychiatry *150*: 752, 1987.

Miller L G, Jankovic J: Neurologic approach to drug-induced movement disorders: A study of 125 patients. South Med J *83*: 525, 1990.

Owen R R, Cole J O: Molindone hydrochloride: A review of laboratory and clinical findings. J Clin Psychopharmacol *9*: 268, 1989.

Rearson G T, Rifkin A, Schwartz A, Myerson A, Siris S G: Changing patterns of neuroleptic dosage over a decade. Am J Psychiatry *146*: 726, 1989.

Rosebush P, Steward T: A prospective analysis of 24 episodes of neuroleptic malignant syndrome. Am J Psychiatry *146*: 717, 1989.

Schneider I S, Pollock V E, Lyness S A: A metaanalysis of controlled trials of neuroleptic treatment in dementia. J Am Geriatr Soc *38*: 553, 1990.

Yadalam K G, Simpson G M: Changing from oral to depot fluphenazine. J Clin Psychiatry *49*: 346, 1988.

30.2.14 / Clozapine

Clozapine (Clozaril) is a newly available alternative drug for the treatment of psychotic disorders, particularly schizophrenia (Figure 30.2.14-1). It is a dibenzodiazepine, not to be confused with the drug clonazepam (Klonopin), which is a benzodiazepine. Clozapine is unique among the antipsychotics in that its use is not associated with extrapyramidal adverse effects or with either tardive dyskinesia or neuroleptic malignant syndrome. The major disadvantage of clozapine is a 1 to 2 percent incidence of agranulocytosis in patients who take the drug.

PHARMACOLOGICAL ACTIONS

Clozapine is rapidly absorbed from the gastrointestinal (GI) tract, and peak plasma levels are reached in one to four hours. The drug is completely metabolized, with a half-life of approximately 16 hours. It is not known whether the metabolites are active. Clozapine differs from all other available antipsychotic drugs, which have their major effects as antagonists of dopamine receptors, particularly D_2 receptors. The antiserotonergic (5-hydroxytryptamine [$5HT_2$]), antiadrenergic (α_1 and α_2), anticholinergic (muscarinic), and anti-

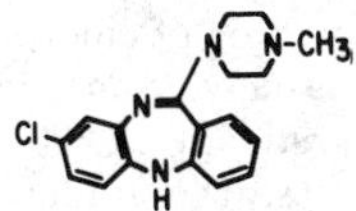

Figure 30.2.14-1. Molecular structure of clozapine.

histaminergic (H_1) activities are significantly more potent than the antidopaminergic activity of clozapine. Moreover, its D_1 antagonist activity is much greater than its D_2 antagonist activity. Clozapine is more effective in blocking dopaminergic activity in the cortical and limbic dopamine neurons than in the dopamine neurons in the basal ganglia; this observation may explain the lack of extrapyramidal adverse effects with clozapine. Some researchers have hypothesized that the combined antagonist activity of clozapine on multiple neurotransmitters results in its antipsychotic activity.

INDICATIONS

The sole indication for clozapine at this time is the treatment of psychotic patients, usually affected with schizophrenia, who have not responded to traditional antipsychotic drugs (Section 20.2.13) or who cannot tolerate the adverse effects associated with those drugs. Clozapine has been shown to be as effective as standard antipsychotics in both the short-term and the long-term management of psychosis. Lorazepam (Ativan) can be used when adjunctive drugs are necessary to control agitation. Clozapine has been reported to be more effective than standard drugs in reducing the negative symptoms of schizophrenia. Approximately 30 percent of patients who have not responded to standard antipsychotic treatments do respond to clozapine treatment.

CLINICAL GUIDELINES

The clinical guidelines are not standardized as to which patients warrant a trial of clozapine. A patient who has been unsuccessfully treated with three different antipsychotic drugs from different classes in sufficient doses (1,000 mg chlorpromazine equivalents), each for at least two months, is probably a candidate for treatment with clozapine. In such situations the clinician must confirm that the patient has been compliant with drug therapy and that no unusual pharmacokinetic factors have been operative. Some patients treated with standard antipsychotic drugs have intolerable adverse effects—such as parkinsonism, akathisia, and tardive dyskinesia—that cannot be controlled by other drugs. These patients are also candidates for treatment with clozapine.

The clinician must explain the risks and benefits of clozapine treatment to prospective patients and their families. The informed consent procedure should be documented in the patient's chart. In the United States it is necessary to register clozapine-treated patients in the Clozaril Patient Management System (CPMS), which has specific guidelines for hematological monitoring of the patients. However, other blood monitoring systems will be approved.

The patient's preadministration history should include information on blood disorders, epilepsy, and any hepatic or renal diseases. Blood disorders and epilepsy are contraindications to clozapine therapy. Hepatic and renal diseases make it imperative that clozapine be administered at low doses. Preadministration laboratory examination should include an electrocardiogram (ECG), several complete blood counts (CBCs) with white blood cell counts (WBCs), which can then be averaged, and liver and renal function tests. Clozapine is available in 25 and 100 mg tablets; 1 mg of clozapine is equivalent to approximately 2 mg of chlorpromazine (Thorazine). The initial dosage is usually 25 mg one or two times daily, which can be raised gradually to 300 mg a day divided into two or three daily doses. The gradual increase in dosage is necessitated by the development of hypotension and sedation, adverse effects to which patients have tolerance with continued treatment. The usual effective treatment range is 400 to 500 mg a day, although dosages up to 600 mg a day are not unusual. After the decision to terminate the drug, clozapine treatment should be tapered whenever possible to avoid cholinergic rebound systems of diaphoresis, flushing, diarrhea, and hyperactivity.

Laboratory Monitoring

The CPMS dictates the laboratory monitoring of clozapine-treated patients. Weekly WBCs are indicated to monitor the patient for the development of agranulocytosis. Although this careful monitoring is quite expensive, early identification of agranulocytosis can prevent a fatal outcome. If the WBC is less than 3,000 cells per mm^3 or the granulocyte count is less than 1,500 per mm^3, clozapine should be discontinued, and a hematological consultation should be obtained. If the WBC is less than 2,000 cells per mm^3, a bone marrow aspiration should be conducted to evaluate hematopoietic activity. Patients with agranulocytosis from clozapine should not be reexposed to the drug. The CPMS program is controversial because it contributes to the high cost of using the drug—several thousand dollars a year—which some critics believe is excessive.

ADVERSE EFFECTS

The feature of clozapine that distinguishes it from standard antipsychotics is the absence of extrapyramidal adverse effects. Clozapine does not cause acute dystonia, parkinsonism, akathisia, rabbit syndrome, or akinesia. It also appears that clozapine does not cause tardive dyskinesia or neuroleptic malignant syndrome. Because of its weak effects on D_2 receptors, clozapine does not affect prolactin secretion; thus, clozapine does not cause sexual or reproductive adverse effects or galactorrhea.

The two most serious adverse effects associated with clozapine use are agranulocytosis and seizures. Agranulocytosis is defined as a decrease in the number of white blood cells, with a specific decrease in the number of polymorphonuclear leukocytes, and a relative lymphopenia. The erythrocyte and platelet concentrations are unaffected. Agranulocytosis occurs in 1 to 2 percent of patients treated with clozapine; this contrasts with an incidence of 0.04 to 0.5 percent of patients treated with standard antipsychotics. Early studies showed that one-third of patients who developed agranulocytosis from clozapine died; careful clinical monitoring in the United States in recent years has prevented fatalities. The vast majority of patients recover from agranulocytosis if the condition is recognized early and clozapine is discontinued. Agranulocytosis can appear precipitously or gradually; it most often develops in the first six months of treatment, although it can appear much later. Clozapine is also associated with the development of benign cases of leukocytosis, leukopenia, eosinophilia, and elevated erythrocyte sedimentation rates.

Clozapine is also associated with the development of seizures. Approximately 14 percent of patients taking more than 600 mg a day of clozapine, 1.8 percent of patients taking 300 to 600 mg a day, and 0.6 percent of patients taking less than 300 mg a day have seizures. These percentages are higher than those of standard antipsychotics. If seizures develop in a patient, clozapine should be temporarily stopped. Phenobarbital treatment can be initiated, and clozapine can be restarted at approximately 50 percent of the previous dosage, then very gradually raised again. Carbamazepine (Tegretol) should not be used in combination with clozapine because of its association with agranulocytosis as well.

The most common adverse effects associated with clozapine treatment are sedation (21 percent of patients), tachycardia (17 percent), constipation (16 percent), dizziness (14 percent), hypotension (13 percent), hyperthermia (13 percent), and sialorrhea (13 percent). Weight gain, fainting spells, myoclonus, and periodic catalepsy have also been reported. The tachycardia is due to vagal inhibition and can be treated with peripherally acting β-adrenergic antagonists, such as atenolol (Tenormin, Tenoretic), although this treatment may aggravate the hypotensive effects of the clozapine. Hyperthermia of 1 to 2°F may develop, causing concern regarding the development of an infection because of agranulocytosis. Clozapine should be withheld, and, if the WBC is normal, clozapine can be reinstituted more slowly and at a lower dosage.

DRUG-DRUG INTERACTIONS

Clozapine should not be used with any other drug that is also associated with the development of agranulocytosis. Such drugs include carbamazepine, propylthiouracil, sulfonamides, and captopril (Capoten).

References

Cheng Y F, Lundberg T, Bondesson U, Lindström L, Gabrielsson J: Clinical pharmacokinetics of clozapine in chronic schizophrenic patients. Eur J Clin Pharmacol *34*: 445, 1988.

Claghorn J, Honigfeld G, Abuzzahab F S, Wang R, Steibook R, Tuason V, Klerman G: The risks and benefits of clozapine versus chlorpromazine. J Clin Psychopharmacol *7*: 377, 1987.

Green A I, Salzman C: Clozapine benefits and risks. Hosp Community Psychiatry *41*: 379, 1990.

Kane J, Honigfeld G, Singer J, Meltzer H: Clozaril Collaborative Study Group: Clozapine for the treatment-resistant schizophrenic. Arch Gen Psychiatry *45*: 789, 1988.

Lieberman J A, Johns C A, Kane J M, Rai K, Pisciotta A V, Saltz B L, Howard A: Clozapine-induced agranulocytosis: Non-cross-reactivity with other psychotropic drugs. J Clin Psychiatry *49*: 271, 1988.

Lieberman J A, Kane J M, Johns C A: Clozapine: Guidelines for clinical management. J Clin Psychiatry *50*: 329, 1989.

Marder S R, Van Putten T: Who should receive clozapine? Arch Gen Psychiatry *45*: 865, 1988.

Mattes J A: Clozapine for refractory schizophrenia: An open study of 14 patients treated up to 2 years. J Clin Psychiatry *50*: 389, 1989.

Small J G, Milstein V, Marhenke J D, Hall D D, Kellams J J: Treatment outcome with clozapine in tardive dyskinesia, neuroleptic sensitivity, and treatment-resistant psychosis. J Clin Psychiatry *48*: 263, 1987.

Wolters E C, Hurwitz T A, Mak E, Teal P, Peppard F R, Remick R, Caine S, Caine D B: Clozapine in the treatment of parkinsonian patients with dopaminomimetic psychosis. Neurology *40*: 832, 1990.

30.2.15 / Fluoxetine

Fluoxetine (Prozac) is a phenylpropylamine-derivative drug with antidepressant activity (Figure 30.2.15-1). It has the fewest adverse effects of any antidepressant drug currently available. This feature has made fluoxetine the largest-selling antidepressant in the United States. Despite its widespread clinical use, fluoxetine remains a new drug, and information about its clinical use, adverse effects, and drug-drug interactions is incomplete.

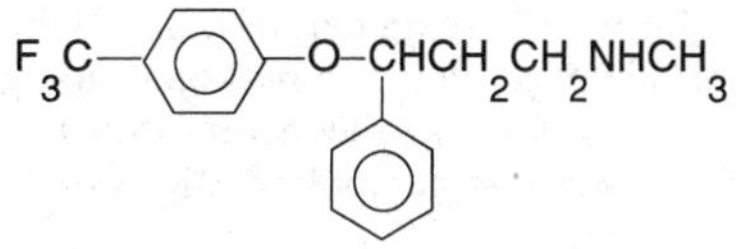

$F_3C-C_6H_4-O-CH(C_6H_5)CH_2CH_2NHCH_3$

Figure 30.2.15-1. Molecular structure of fluoxetine.

PHARMACOLOGICAL ACTIONS

Fluoxetine is well absorbed from the gastrointestinal (GI) tract and reaches peak plasma levels in approximately four to eight hours. Fluoxetine is metabolized in the liver to norfluoxetine, an active metabolite, which is eventually excreted by the kidneys. The half-life of fluoxetine is two to three days; the half-life of norfluoxetine is seven to nine days. Because of the very long half-life, steady state plasma levels are not attained until after two to three weeks at a steady dosage.

The therapeutic effects of fluoxetine result from a highly selective blockade of reuptake of serotonin into the presynaptic neurons. Fluoxetine has almost no effects on norepinephrine or dopamine neurotransmission. It also lacks anticholinergic, antihistaminergic, and anti-α_1-adrenergic activities; thus, it is associated with almost none of the adverse effects that are associated with the standard antidepressants—tricyclic and tetracyclic antidepressants and monoamine oxidase inhibitors (MAOIs).

INDICATIONS

Depression

Fluoxetine is as effective as the standard antidepressant drugs in the short-term treatment of major depression. Whether it can be used for the prevention of depressive episodes is being examined in long-term, controlled studies. Fluoxetine is regularly used as the drug of choice for the treatment of depression; however, many clinicians still prefer tricyclic or tetracyclic antidepressants for the treatment of depression. Fluoxetine is also effective for the treatment of depression associated with bipolar disorder.

Dysthymia

There are several reports that fluoxetine is useful in the treatment of mild depressive episodes and possibly of dysthymia. There are no data, however, regarding the long-term outcome of such treatments.

Other Disorders

As with most new drugs, there are many reports of its successful application in a wide range of disorders. It is known that serotonin is involved in the regulation of eating, and, in fact, fluoxetine very often has the effect of reducing appetite and weight. Fluoxetine has been reported to be useful in the treatment of obesity, anorexia nervosa, and bulimia nervosa. Serotonin is also implicated in the pathophysiology of anxiety disorders, and fluoxetine has been reported to be useful in the treatment of obsessive-compulsive disorder and panic disorder.

CLINICAL GUIDELINES

Fluoxetine is available in 20 mg capsules. The initial dosage is 20 mg orally (PO) a day, usually given in the morning, because insomnia is a potential adverse effect of the drug. The long half-life of the drug causes the drug to accumulate in the body over a period of two to three weeks. As with all available antidepressants, the antidepressant effects may be seen in the first one to three weeks, but it is much more reasonable to wait to evaluate antidepressant activity until the patient has been taking the drug for four to six weeks. Several studies have suggested that 20 mg a day is as effective as higher dosages. The maximum daily dosage recommended by the manufacturer is 80 mg a day. A reasonable strategy is to maintain a patient with 20 mg a day for three weeks; if there are no signs of clinical improvement, an increase to 20 mg PO two times a day may be warranted. The second dose is usually given at noon to avoid problems with insomnia. Occasionally, fluoxetine is associated with sedation, in which case the drug can be given in the evening. Any other antidepressant that a patient has been taking should be tapered and discontinued before initiating fluoxetine treatment. One week should elapse between the administration of tricyclic or tetracyclic antidepressants and fluoxetine, two weeks between MAOIs and fluoxetine.

ADVERSE EFFECTS

The most common adverse effects of fluoxetine involve the central nervous system (CNS) and the GI system (Table 30.2.15-1). Anorgasmia and delayed orgasm may affect approximately 5 percent of patients. This side effect may respond to cyproheptadine (Periactin), 4 to 8 mg PO taken one to two hours before sexual activity is planned. Various types of rashes may appear in 4 percent of patients. There have been rare reports of extrapyramidal side effects, and seizures have been reported in 0.2 percent of patients, approximately the incidence with standard antidepressants. Fluoxetine, like almost all antidepressants, suppresses rapid eye movement (REM) sleep, although it is arguable whether this is an adverse therapeutic effect of the drug. Most notable about fluoxetine is the absence of the anticholinergic adverse effects associated with standard antidepressants. Fluoxetine has no recognized adverse effects on the cardiovascular system, although it is associated with a decrease in heart rate of approximately three beats a minute. Because experience with fluoxetine is still limited, fluoxetine should be used with caution in patients with preexisting cardiac disorders.

Table 30.2.15-1
Common Adverse Effects of Fluoxetine

	Patients (%)
Central nervous system	
Headache	20
Nervousness	15
Insomnia	14
Drowsiness	12
Anxiety	9
Tremor	8
Dizziness	6
Gastrointestinal system	
Nausea	21
Diarrhea	12
Dry mouth	10
Anorexia	9
Stomach upset	6
Other	
Excessive sweating	8
Weight loss > 5% body weight	13
Increase in suicidal ideation or violent behavior (six cases reported)	

There has been only one report of a lethal overdose of fluoxetine taken by itself. This makes the drug very safe to give to suicidal patients compared with tricyclic and tetracyclic antidepressants, which are highly lethal in overdose and have a high suicide potential. There have been a number of reports of fatal overdoses of fluoxetine when taken with other psychotropic drugs. The symptoms of overdose include agitation, restlessness, insomnia, tremor, nausea, vomiting, tachycardia, and seizures. The clinician should try to ascertain whether other drugs were taken with the fluoxetine. The first steps in the treatment of overdose are gastric lavage and emesis.

In a few cases, patients who were taking fluoxetine had suicidal ideation, self-mutilation, and violent behavior, but the significance of these findings for fluoxetine use is questionable and unclear. The Food and Drug Administration (FDA) does not attribute these adverse effects to fluoxetine.

DRUG-DRUG INTERACTIONS

Experience with fluoxetine is still limited. The coadministration of fluoxetine with MAOIs, tricyclic and tetracyclic antidepressants, and L-tryptophan have resulted in the development of severe adverse effects; its coadministration with tricyclic antidepressants or benzodiazepines increases the plasma levels of the tricyclic antidepressants or the benzodiazepines. The coadministration of fluoxetine with buspirone (BuSpar) has been reported to decrease the therapeutic efficacy of the buspirone; however, in some cases, a positive synergistic effect occurred.

References

Byerley W F, Reimherr F W, Wood D R, Grosser B I: Fluoxetine, a selective serotonin uptake inhibitor, for the treatment of outpatients with major depression. J Clin Psychopharmacol *8*: 112, 1988.

Ciraulo D A, Shader R I: Fluoxetine drug-drug interactions: I. Antidepressants and antipsychotics. J Clin Psychopharmacol *10*: 48, 1990.

Herman J B, Brotman A W, Pollack M H, Falk W E, Biederman J, Rosenbaum J F: Fluoxetine-induced sexual dysfunction. J Clin Psychiatry *51*: 25, 1990.

Liebowitz M R, Hollander E, Schneier F, Campeas R, Hatterer J, Papp L, Fairbanks J, Sandberg D, Davies S, Stein M: Fluoxetine treatment of obsessive-compulsive disorder: An open clinical trial. J Clin Psychopharmacol *9*: 423, 1989.

Schweizer E, Rickels K, Amsterdam J D, Fox I, Puzzuoli G, Weise C: What constitutes an adequate antidepressant trial for fluoxetine? J Clin Psychiatry *51*: 8, 1990.

Teicher M H, Glod C, Cole J O: Emergence of intense suicidal preoccupation during fluoxetine treatment. Am J Psychiatry *147*: 207, 1990.

30.2.16 / Lithium

Lithium (Eskalith, Lithobid) is an element and is the lightest of the alkali metals (group IA of the periodic table), similar to sodium, potassium, magnesium, and calcium. Lithium is a monovalent ion and is available as a carbonate (Li_2CO_3) for oral use in both rapidly acting and slow-release tablets and capsules. Lithium citrate is available in a liquid form for oral administration.

PHARMACOLOGICAL ACTIONS

Pharmacokinetics

After ingestion, lithium is completely absorbed by the gastrointestinal tract. Serum levels peak in 0.5 to 2 hours for standard preparations and in 4 to 4.5 hours for the slow-release preparations. Lithium does not bind to plasma proteins and is distributed nonuniformly throughout body water. The half-life of lithium is about 20 hours, and equilibrium is reached after five to seven days of regular intake. Lithium is almost entirely eliminated by the kidneys. Renal clearance of lithium is decreased with renal insufficiency and in the puerperium and is increased during pregnancy. Lithium is excreted in breast milk and in insignificant amounts in feces and sweat.

Pharmacodynamics

The therapeutic mechanism of action for lithium remains uncertain. The most accepted current theory is that lithium works by blocking the enzyme inositol-1-phosphatase within neurons, thus reducing the reformation of phosphatidylinositolbisphosphate from inositoltriphosphate. This inhibition results in decreased cellular responses to neurotransmitters that are linked to the phosphatidylinositol second messenger system.

INDICATIONS

Bipolar Disorder

Lithium has been proved effective in both the short-term treatment and prophylaxis of bipolar disorder in approximately 70 to 80 percent of patients. Both manic and depressive episodes often respond to lithium treatment alone. However, because treatment with lithium alone can take a relatively long time, manic episodes are usually treated with both lithium and an antipsychotic, and depressive episodes are treated with a combination of lithium and an antidepressant. The clinician should be aware of the risk of inducing a manic episode with antidepressant treatment. Most studies have reported that lithium maintenance halves the number of recurrences and that the recurrences that do occur are less severe. The prophylactic effect of lithium, however, does not develop for several months. Consequently, a recurrence of symptoms before that time should not be taken as an indication that the lithium is not effective. In severe cases of cyclothymia, treatment with lithium may be indicated.

Schizoaffective Disorder

The use of lithium for schizoaffective disorder (bipolar type) is certainly indicated. If a patient's schizoaffective disorder (depressive type) demonstrates a particularly cyclic nature, a lithium trial may also be warranted.

Major Depression

The chief indication for lithium in depression is as an adjuvant treatment to tricyclics, tetracyclics, or monoamine oxidase inhibitors (MAOIs) to convert an antidepressant nonresponder into a responder. Lithium alone may also be an effective treatment for depressed patients who are actually bipolar disorder patients who have not yet had their first manic episode. Moreover, lithium has been reported to be effective in major depression patients whose illness has a marked cyclicity.

Schizophrenia

The symptoms of approximately one-fifth to one-half of schizophrenic patients are further reduced when lithium is coadministered with their antipsychotic drug. Some schizophrenic patients who cannot take antipsychotics may benefit from lithium treatment. Intermittent angry outbursts in schizophrenic patients may also be reduced by lithium.

Impulse Control Disorders

The impulse control disorders include episodic violence and rage. Patients whose episodes are not premeditated and are seemingly untriggered may respond to lithium. Episodic angry outbursts in patients with mental retardation may also be reduced with lithium.

Other Disorders

A few studies have reported that the episodic disorder characterizing the premenstrual syndrome, the intermittent behaviors seen in borderline personality disorder, bulimia nervosa, and episodes of binge drinking respond to lithium treatment.

CLINICAL GUIDELINES

Lithium is the drug of first choice to treat bipolar disorder unless there is a specific reason not to use lithium or a specific reason to use another drug.

Initial Medical Workup

Before starting to administer lithium, the clinician should conduct a routine laboratory and physical examination. The laboratory examination should include a serum creatinine level (or a 24-hour urine creatinine if there is any reason to be concerned about renal function), an electrolyte screen, thyroid functions tests (T_4, T_3RU, FT_4I, and thyroid stimulating hormone [TSH]), complete blood count (CBC), electrocardiogram (ECG), and a pregnancy test if there is any risk of the patient's being pregnant.

Dosage

A variety of lithium preparations are available (Table 30.2.16-1). Regular-release capsules or tablets are usually used first, and the syrup or slow-release preparations are used if noncompliance or nausea occurs. If a patient has previously been treated with lithium and the former dosage is known, it is reasonable to use that dosage in the current episode unless there have been changes in the patient's pharmacokinetic parameters for lithium clearance. For most adult patients, it is reasonable to start lithium at 300 mg three times daily. The starting dosage in patients who are elderly or who have renal impairment should be 300 mg once or twice daily. The usual eventual dosage range is between 900 and 2,100 mg a day. Serum concentrations of lithium can be obtained after five days, and the dosage can be adjusted to obtain a serum level between 0.8 and 1.2 mEq per L during the acute episode. Lithium levels should be obtained 12 hours after the last dose. Lithium levels in patients treated with slow-release preparations are approximately 30 percent higher than the levels obtained with other preparations. The use of divided doses (three to four doses a day) reduces gastric upset and avoids a single large peak in lithium levels. There is currently a debate over whether multiple small daily peaks are less likely than a single large daily peak to cause adverse effects. Single daily dosing, however, is not considered standard practice at this time. Slow-release lithium preparations can be given two to three times daily and result in lower peak levels of lithium, but this procedure has not yet been demonstrated to be of special value. A therapeutic trial of lithium should last a minimum of four to six weeks. If there is some response within that time, improvement may continue for another five months. If the lithium treatment has been successful, it should be continued for a minimum of six to nine months, then tapered over a month unless the patient is to receive maintenance on lithium prophylaxis.

Lithium Levels

The patient's lithium level should be monitored weekly for the first month and then biweekly for another two months. After six months it may be appropriate to check the patient's lithium level every two months. If a patient has been stable for a year, checking lithium levels three to four times a year may be sufficient.

Table 30.2.16-1
Lithium Carbonate Preparations

Regular-release capsules 150, 300, 600 mg
(Eskalith, Lithonate, generic)
Regular-release tablets 300 mg
(Eskalith, Lithane, Lithotabs)
Slow-release tablets 300, 450 mg
(Eskalith, Lithobid)
Syrup 8 mEq per 5 mL (lithium citrate)
(Cibalith-S, generic)

Patient Education

The patient should be advised that changes in the body's water and salt content can affect the amount of lithium excreted, resulting in either increases or decreases in lithium levels. Excessive intake of sodium (e.g., a dramatic dietary change) lowers lithium levels. Conversely, too little sodium (e.g., fad diets) can lead to potentially toxic levels of lithium. Decreases in body fluid (e.g., excessive sweating) can lead to dehydration and lithium intoxication.

Failure of Drug Treatment

If the drug produces no clinical response after four weeks at therapeutic levels, slightly higher serum levels (up to 1.4 mEq per L) may be tried if there are no severe adverse effects. If after two weeks at a higher serum concentration the drug is still ineffective, the patient should be tapered off the drug over one to two weeks. Other drugs should be given therapeutic trials at this point.

Maintenance

The decision to maintain a patient on lithium prophylaxis is based on the severity of the patient's illness, the risk of adverse effects from lithium, and the quality of the patient's support systems. Maintenance serum levels of lithium can be lower than those needed for short-term treatment. Such levels are usually kept between 0.6 and 0.8 mEq per L, although some researchers have reported successful prophylaxis with serum levels as low as 0.4 mEq per L. In addition to periodic measurements of lithium levels, serum creatinine and TSH levels should be monitored every three to six months.

ADVERSE EFFECTS

The most common adverse effects from lithium treatment are gastric distress, weight gain, tremor, fatigue, and mild cognitive impairment. Gastric distress may include nausea, vomiting, and diarrhea and can often be reduced by further dividing up the dosage, administering the lithium with food, or switching among the various lithium preparations. Weight gain and edema can be impossible to treat other than by encouraging the patient to eat less and to exercise moderately. The tremor affects mostly the fingers and sometimes can be worse at peak levels of the drug. It can be reduced by further dividing the dosage. Propranolol (Inderal) (30 to 160 mg a day in divided doses) reduces the tremor significantly in most patients. The fatigue and mild cognitive impairment may decrease with time. Rare neurological adverse effects include symptoms of mild parkinsonism, ataxia, and dysarthria. Leukocytosis is a common and not worrisome effect of lithium treatment.

Renal Effects

The most common adverse renal effect of lithium is polyuria with secondary polydipsia. This symptom is particularly problematic in 20 to 25 percent of treated patients. The polyuria is secondary to the decreased resorption of fluid from the distal tubules of the kidneys. When polyuria is a significant problem, the patient's renal function should be carefully evaluated and followed with 24-hour urine collections for creatinine clearance and with consultation with a nephrologist.

Lithium-induced nephrogenic diabetes insipidus is not responsive to vasopressin treatment and results in urine volumes up to 8 L a day and difficulty maintaining adequate lithium levels. This syndrome can be treated with chlorothiazide 500 mg a day, hydrochlorothiazide (50 mg a day), or amiloride (5 to 10 mg a day). The lithium dosage should be halved and the diuretic not started for five days, because the diuretic is likely to increase the retention of lithium.

The most serious renal adverse effects that were originally thought to be associated with lithium administration were minimal change glomerulopathy, interstitial nephritis, and renal failure. The original concern about these adverse effects was based on postmortem studies of kidneys from patients who had been treated with lithium. Although it is now generally thought that serious renal disorders are not associated with lithium administration, the clinician should vigorously explore any clinical changes in renal function.

Table 30.2.16-2
Signs and Symptoms of Lithium Toxicity

Mild to moderate intoxication
(lithium level, 1.5–2.0 mEq per L)

Gastrointestinal:
- Vomiting
- Abdominal pain
- Dryness of mouth

Neurological:
- Ataxia
- Dizziness
- Slurred speech
- Nystagmus
- Lethargy or excitement
- Muscle weakness

Moderate to severe intoxication
(lithium level, 2.0–2.5 mEq per L)

Gastrointestinal:
- Anorexia nervosa
- Persistent nausea and vomiting

Neurological:
- Blurred vision
- Muscle fasciculations
- Clonic limb movements
- Hyperactive deep tendon reflexes
- Choreoathetoid movements
- Convulsions
- Delirium
- Syncope
- Electroencephalographic changes
- Stupor
- Coma

Circulatory failure (lowered blood pressure, cardiac arrhythmias, and conduction abnormalities)

Severe intoxication
(lithium level, > 2.5 mEq per L)

Generalized convulsions
Oliguria and renal failure
Death

Table from Psychopharmacology and electroconvulsive therapy. In *The American Psychiatric Press Textbook of Psychiatry*, J A Talbott, R E Hales, and S C Yudofsky, editors, p 826. American Psychiatric Association Press, Washington, DC, 1988, with permission.

Thyroid Effects

Lithium also affects thyroid function, causing a generally benign and often transient diminution in the concentrations of circulating thyroid hormones. Reports have also attributed goiter (5 percent), benign reversible exophthalmos, and hypothyroidism (3 to 4 percent) to lithium treatment. About 50 percent of patients receiving long-term lithium treatment have an abnormal thyrotropin-releasing hormone (TRH) response, and approximately 30 percent have elevated levels of TSH. If laboratory values of thyroid hormone indicate dysfunction, thyroid supplementation can be administered safely. TSH levels should be measured and checked periodically. Hyperthyroidism has been reported rarely.

Cardiac Effects

The cardiac effects of lithium, which resemble those of hypokalemia on the ECG, are caused by displacement of intracellular potassium by the lithium ion. The most common changes on the ECG are T wave flattening or inversion. The changes are benign and disappear after the lithium is excreted from the body. Nevertheless, baseline ECGs are essential and should be repeated yearly.

Because lithium depresses the sinus node's pacemaking activity, lithium treatment is strongly contraindicated in patients with sick sinus syndrome. In rare cases, ventricular arrhythmias and congestive heart failure have been associated with lithium therapy.

Dermatological Effects

Several cutaneous adverse effects, which may be dose-dependent, have been associated with lithium treatment. The most prevalent effects include acneiform, follicular, and maculopapular eruptions; pretibial ulcerations; and worsening of psoriasis. Alopecia has also been reported. Many of these conditions respond to changing to another lithium preparation

Table 30.2.16-3
Management of Lithium Toxicity

1. The patient should immediately contact his or her personal physician or go to a hospital emergency room.
2. Lithium should be discontinued, and the patient instructed to ingest fluids, if possible.
3. Physical examination, including vital signs, and a neurological examination with complete formal mental status examination should be completed.
4. Lithium level, serum electrolytes, renal function tests, and electrocardiogram should be obtained as soon as possible.
5. For significant acute ingestions, residual gastric contents should be removed by induction of emesis, gastric lavage, and absorption with activated charcoal.
6. Vigorous hydration and maintenance of electrolyte balance is essential.
7. For any patient with a serum lithium level greater than 4.0 mEq per L within six hours of ingestion or for any patient with serious manifestations of lithium toxicity, hemodialysis should be initiated.
8. Repeat dialysis may be required every 6 to 10 hours, until the lithium level is within nontoxic range and the patient has no signs or symptoms of lithium toxicity.

Table from Psychopharmacology and electroconvulsive therapy. In *The American Psychiatric Press Textbook of Psychiatry*, J A Talbott, R E Hales, and S C Yudofsky, editors, p 827. American Psychiatric Association Press, Washington, DC, 1988, with permission.

or the usual dermatological measures. Lithium levels should be monitored if tetracycline is used because of several reports of its increasing the retention of lithium. Occasionally, the aggravated psoriasis or acneiform eruptions may force the discontinuation of lithium treatment.

Use in Pregnancy

Lithium should not be administered to pregnant women in the first trimester because of the increased incidence of birth defects, specifically Ebstein's anomaly, which occurs in 3 per-

Table 30.2.16-4
Drug Interactions with Lithium

Class and Generic Name	Effect on Plasma Lithium Concentration	Significance
Antibiotics		
Tetracycline	Possible increase	Case reports; possibly from nephrotoxic effect of antibiotics; tetracycline may be safe
Spectinomycin	Possible increase	
Tricyclic antidepressants	Unknown	May cause switch to mania; increase in tremors
Anti-inflammatory agents		
Ibuprofen	Increase	Case reports of piroxicam and diclofenac sodium increasing lithium concentrations; sulindac may have minimal effect
Indomethacin	Increase	
Naproxen	Increase	
Phenylbutazone	Increase	
Antipsychotics		
Chlorpromazine	Possibly increase red blood cell (RBC) lithium	All antipsychotics may increase lithium's neurotoxicity
Fluphenazine	Possibly increase RBC lithium	
Haloperidol	Possibly increase plasma lithium	
Perphenazine	Possibly increase RBC lithium	
Thioridazine	Possibly increase RBC lithium	
Cardiovascular drugs		
Digoxin	Unknown	Case report of CNS confusion and bradycardia
Methyldopa	Unknown	Case reports neurological toxicity
Diuretics		
Carbonic anhydrase inhibitors		
Acetazolamide	Decrease	Increase lithium excretion
Loop diuretics		
Furosemide	Unclear	May increase lithium concentrations
Ethacrynic acid	Unclear	
Distal tubule diuretics		
Thiazides	Increase	Well-documented interaction with increase in lithium concentrations
Metolazone	Increase	
Chlorthalidone	Increase	
Osmotic diuretics		
Mannitol	Decrease	Increase lithium excretion
Urea	Decrease	
Potassium-sparing diuretics		
Triamterene	Increase	May increase lithium concentrations
Spironolactone	Increase	
Amiloride	Unclear	May be used to treat lithium-induced polyuria
Xanthines		
Theophylline	Decrease	Increase lithium excretion
Caffeine	Decrease	
Neuromuscular blocking drugs		
Succinylcholine	Unknown	May prolong neuromuscular blockade
Pancuronium bromide	Unknown	
Miscellaneous		
Sodium chloride	Decrease	Increase lithium excretion
Sodium bicarbonate	Decrease	Alkalinization of urine increases lithium excretion
Metoclopramide	Unknown	Case report of extrapyramidal symptoms
Carbamazepine	Unknown	May have synergistic effect in treating mania and depression; case reports of neurotoxicity
Alcohol	Unknown	Increased lithium toxicity in animals; acute alcohol ingestion may increase peak lithium concentration
Phenytoin	Possible increase	Case reports of lithium toxicity and changes in phenytoin concentrations

Table from J L Kinney-Parker, M P Fankhauser: Bipolar disorder. In *Pharmacotherapy: A Pathophysiologic Approach*, J T DiPiro, R L Talbert, P E Hayes, G C Yee, and L M Posey, editors, p 741. Elsevier, New York, 1989, with permission.

cent of babies exposed to lithium in utero. Administration of lithium to the mother during the final months of pregnancy can result in babies who are lithium-toxic at birth. The syndrome consists of lethargy, cyanosis, abnormal reflexes, and sometimes hepatomegaly.

Lithium Toxicity

The symptoms of lithium toxicity are severe manifestations of the aforementioned pharmacodynamic organ interactions (Table 30.2.16-2). These include vomiting, abdominal pain, profuse diarrhea, severe tremor, ataxia, coma, and seizures. Initial neurological signs of mental confusion, hyperreflexia, focal neurological signs, and dysarthria can proceed to coma and death. Cardiac arrhythmias also may occur. Lithium toxicity requires immediate medical attention (Table 30.2.16-3).

Overdoses

Overdoses of lithium result in symptoms of severe lithium toxicity. Treatment should include lavage with a wide-bore tube because of the drug's clumping in the stomach. Activated charcoal does not help in this condition. Osmotic diuresis, intravenous sodium bicarbonate, and peritoneal or hemodialysis can also be used.

DRUG-DRUG INTERACTIONS

Most diuretics (e.g., thiazides, potassium-sparing, and loop) and prostaglandin synthetase inhibitors (e.g., indomethacin) can increase lithium levels to toxic levels. Osmotic diuretics, carbonic anhydrase inhibitors, and xanthines (including caffeine) may reduce lithium levels to below therapeutic levels.

When coadministered, antipsychotics and lithium may result in a synergistic increase in the symptoms of lithium-induced neurological adverse effects. This interaction is not, as initially thought, specifically associated with the coadministration of lithium and haloperidol (Haldol). The coadministration of lithium with anticonvulsants, including carbamazepine (Tegretol), may also aggravate neurological symptoms. Although it is reasonable practice to stop drug administration if serious symptoms of toxicity are noted, it is usually possible to restart both medications at lower dosages without the recurrence of the adverse effects.

A summary of drug interactions with lithium is given in Table 30.2.16-4.

References

Aagaard J, Vestergaard P: Predictors of outcome in prophylactic lithium treatment: A 2-year prospective study. J Affective Disord *18*: 259, 1990.

Aagaard J, Vestergaard P, Maarbjerg K: Adherence to lithium prophylaxis: II. Multivariate analysis of clinical, social, and psychosocial predictors of nonadherence. Pharmacopsychiatry *21*: 166, 1988.

Baraban J M, Worley P F, Snyder S H: Second messenger systems and psychoactive drug action: Focus on the phosphoinositide system and lithium. Am J Psychiatry *146*: 1251, 1989.

Berridge M J, Downses C P, Hanley M R: Neural and developmental actions of lithium: A unifying hypothesis. Cell *59*: 411, 1989.

Gitlin M J, Cochran S D, Jamison H R: Maintenance lithium treatment: Side effects and compliance. J Clin Psychiatry *50*: 127, 1989.

Jefferson J W: Lithium: A therapeutic magic wand. J Clin Psychiatry *50*: 81, 1989.

Maarbjerg K, Aagaard J, Vestergaard P: Adherence to lithium prophylaxis: I. Clinical predictors and patient's reasons for nonadherence. Pharmacopsychiatry *21*: 121, 1988.

Nierenberg A A, Price L H, Charney D S, Henlinger G R: After lithium augmentation: A retrospective follow-up of patients with antidepressant-refractory depression. J Affective Disord *18*: 167, 1990.

Phillips J D, Myers D H, King J R, Armond A D, Derham C, Puranik A, Corbett J A, Birch N J: Pharmacokinetics of lithium in patients treated with controlled release lithium formulations. Int Clin Psychopharmacol *5*: 65, 1990.

Schou M: Lithium prophylaxis: Myths and realities. Am J Psychiatry *146*: 573, 1989.

30.2.17 / Methadone

Methadone hydrochloride (Dolophine, Methadose) is a synthetic diphenylheptane-derivative opiate agonist. The primary use of methadone in psychiatry is the detoxification and maintenance therapy of persons addicted to opiates.

PHARMACOLOGICAL ACTIONS

Methadone is well absorbed from the gastrointestinal (GI) tract and has an initial duration of action of four to six hours. The duration of action increases to 22 to 48 hours with repeated administration and is elevated in persons who have been abusing opiate agonists. Methadone is metabolized by the liver and is excreted by the kidneys. Methadone is an agonist at mu, kappa, and, probably, delta opiate receptors.

INDICATIONS AND CLINICAL GUIDELINES

Methadone is used for the short-term detoxification (30 days), long-term detoxification (180 days), and maintenance of opiate addicts. Methadone is a schedule II drug, the administration of which is governed by specific federal laws and regulations. These regulations are currently in a state of flux because of the increase in efforts to place intravenous drug abusers in methadone programs. The aim of such efforts is to reduce the spread of acquired immune deficiency syndrome (AIDS), which can be contracted by the use of contaminated needles.

In maintenance programs, methadone is usually administered dissolved in water or fruit juices. For short-term detoxification, an initial dose of 15 to 20 mg usually suppresses withdrawal symptoms, and additional doses can be given if the initial dose is insufficient. A dosage of 40 mg a day in single or divided doses is usually sufficient to control withdrawal symptoms in most patients. After stabilization, the methadone dosage is tapered at a rate that is dependent on the type of program, on whether the patient is an inpatient or an outpatient, and on the patient's level of tolerance for withdrawal symptoms. If withdrawal takes more than 180 days, the treatment program is officially described as methadone maintenance. Maintenance should be at the lowest possible dosage of methadone, and, generally, the patient should eventually be withdrawn completely from methadone. The administration of methadone for both withdrawal and maintenance must follow the strict federal guidelines, generally requiring patients to receive the methadone in person to avoid its abuse by persons other than the patient.

Pregnancy

Methadone should be administered to pregnant women only if the potential benefits outweigh the possible risks. Detoxification is not recommended for pregnant women; maintenance methadone may be appropriate in some circumstances. Whether methadone treatment is harmful to the fetus is not known. Women should not breast feed their babies if they are taking methadone.

ADVERSE EFFECTS

An overdose of methadone can cause respiratory and circulatory depression, leading to respiratory arrest, cardiac arrest, and death. Methadone is also capable of inducing tolerance, psychological dependence, and physical dependence. Other adverse effects on the central nervous system (CNS) include dizziness, depression, sedation, euphoria, dysphoria, agitation, and seizures. Delirium and insomnia have also been reported in rare cases. Methadone has significant effects on the GI system, where it can cause biliary spasm or colic, nausea, vomiting, and constipation. It can also cause urinary retention and oliguria. Systemically, methadone is associated with sweating, flushing, pruritis, and urticaria.

Methadone Withdrawal

Abrupt cessation of methadone results in withdrawal symptoms in three to four days, with peak symptoms appearing at the sixth day. Withdrawal symptoms include weakness, anxiety, anorexia, insomnia, gastric distress, headache, sweating, and hot and cold flashes. The withdrawal symptoms usually resolve after two weeks.

DRUG-DRUG INTERACTIONS

Methadone can potentiate the CNS depressant effects of other opiate agonists, barbiturates, benzodiazepines, and alcohol. Antipsychotics, especially low-potency agents; tricyclic and tetracyclic antidepressants; and monoamine oxidase inhibitors (MAOIs) should be used very cautiously with methadone. Two other opiate agonists, meperidine (Demerol), and fentanyl, have been associated with fatal drug-drug interactions with the MAOIs.

References

Ball J C, Corty E: Basic issues pertaining to the effectiveness of methadone maintenance treatment. NIDA Res Monogr *86*: 178, 1988.

Cooper J R: Methadone treatment and acquired immunodeficiency syndrome. JAMA *262*: 1664, 1989.

Gold M, Sorensen J L, McCanlies N, Trier M, Dlugosch G: Tapering from methadone maintenance: Attitudes of clients and staff. J Subst Abuse Treat *5*: 37, 1988.

Grönbladh L, Gunne L: Methadone-assisted rehabilitation of Swedish heroin addicts. Drug Alcohol Depend *24*: 31, 1989.

Ladewig D: Opiate maintenance and abstinence: Attitudes, treatment modalities and outcome. Drug Alcohol Depend *25*: 245, 1990.

Liappas J A, Jenner F A, Vicente B: Literature on methadone maintenance clinics. Int J Addict *23*: 927, 1988.

Magura S, Shapiro J L, Grossman J L, Siddiqi Q, Lipton D S, Amann K R, Koger J, Gehan K: Reactions of methadone patients to HIV antibody testing. Adv Alcohol Subst Abuse *8*: 97, 1990.

Segest E, Mygind O, Bay H: The influence of prolonged stable methadone maintenance treatment on mortality and employment: An 8-year follow-up. Int J Addict *25*: 53, 1990.

30.2.18 / Monoamine Oxidase Inhibitors

The monoamine oxidase inhibitors (MAOIs) are probably as effective as the tricyclic antidepressants in treating depression. When MAOIs were first introduced into clinical practice, there was a lack of awareness of the risk of tyramine-induced hypertensive crises, leading to fatalities and the temporary withdrawal of these drugs from the market. It is now appreciated that these drugs are as safe as tricyclic antidepressants, provided reasonable dietary precautions are followed. Some clinicians believe that MAOIs are underused as effective antidepressant treatment.

CLASSIFICATION

Three MAOIs are available in the United States (Figure 30.2.18-1). Phenelzine (Nardil) and isocarboxazid (Marplan) are derivatives of hydrazine (-CNN is the hydrazine moiety), and tranylcypromine (Parnate) is a derivative of amphetamine. Clorgyline is a specific inhibitor of MAO_A (enzyme subtype more specific for norepinephrine and serotonin). Clorgyline may be particularly effective in treating depression in rapid cycling bipolar disorder patients, but it is not available for clinical use in the United States. Deprenyl is a specific inhibitor of MAO_B (enzyme subtype more specific for dopamine), but it is not available in the United States and does not appear to be an effective antidepressant.

PHARMACOLOGICAL ACTIONS

Pharmacokinetics

MAOIs are readily absorbed when administered orally. The hydrazine MAOIs are metabolized by acetylation. About one-half of North American and European persons and an even higher proportion of Asians are slow acetylators, which may explain why, when given these drugs, some patients have more adverse effects than do others.

Pharmacodynamics

MAOIs irreversibly inhibit monoamine oxidase (MAO), reaching maximum inhibition after 5 to 10 days. Antidepressant effects, however, take three to six weeks to develop. The measurement of MAO activity in platelets can be used as an indicator of MAO inhibition. Platelet MAO activity needs to be reduced 80 percent to achieve a therapeutic response. Because platelet MAO is of the B type, this measurement cannot be used if the effects of clorgyline are being studied. Because the MAO inhibition by MAOIs is irreversible, the body takes approximately two weeks after their discontinuation to synthesize enough new MAO to restore its baseline concentrations.

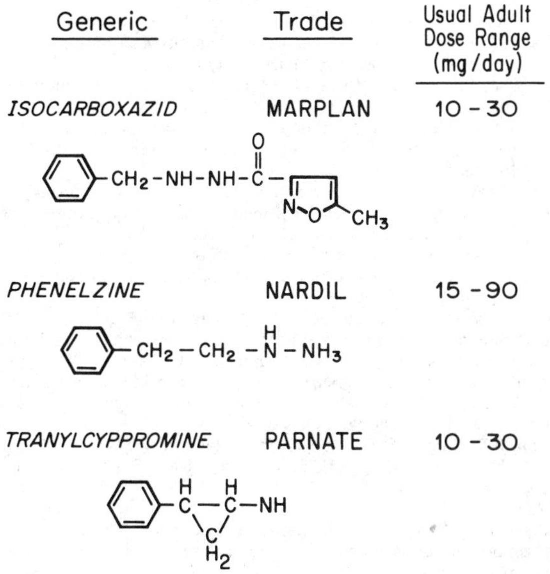

Generic	Trade	Usual Adult Dose Range (mg/day)
ISOCARBOXAZID	MARPLAN	10 - 30
PHENELZINE	NARDIL	15 - 90
TRANYLCYPPROMINE	PARNATE	10 - 30

Figure 30.2.18-1. Molecular structures of the monoamine oxidase inhibitors.

INDICATIONS

The indications for MAOIs are quite similar to those for tricyclic and tetracyclic antidepressants (see Section 30.2.22). MAOIs may be particularly effective in agoraphobia with panic attacks, posttraumatic stress disorder, eating disorders, and pain syndromes. Some investigators have reported that MAOIs may be preferable to tricyclic antidepressants in the treatment of atypical depression, characterized by hypersomnia, hyperphagia, anxiety, and the absence of vegetative symptoms. These depressions are often less severe than major depression, and the patients present with less functional impairment. A trial of MAOIs may be indicated for any depressed patient if a trial of a tricyclic antidepressant has been unsuccessful.

CLINICAL GUIDELINES

There is no definitive rationale for choosing one MAOI over another, except that tranylcypromine may be the most activating of the drugs. Phenelzine should be started with a test dose of 15 mg on the first day. On an outpatient basis, the dosage can be increased to 45 mg a day during the first week and increased by 15 mg a day each week thereafter until 90 mg a day is reached by the end of the fourth week. Tranylcypromine and isocarboxazid should begin with a test dose of 10 mg and may be increased to 30 mg a day by the end of the first week. Upper limits of 50 mg for isocarboxazid and 40 mg for tranylcypromine have been suggested by some researchers. If an MAOI trial is not successful after six weeks, lithium or L-triiodothyronine (T_3 or liothyronine) (Cytomel) augmentation is warranted. The combined treatment of MAOIs and tricyclic antidepressants is described in Section 30.2.22.

ADVERSE EFFECTS

The most frequent adverse effects of MAOIs are orthostatic hypotension, weight gain, edema, sexual dysfunction, and insomnia. The orthostatic hypotension, if severe, may respond to treatment with fludrocortisone (Florinef), a mineralocorticoid, 0.1 to 0.2 mg a day; support stockings; corsets; hydration; and increased salt intake. Weight gain, edema, and sexual dysfunction are often not responsive to any treatment and may warrant switching from a hydrazine to a nonhydrazine MAOI or vice versa. When switching from one MAOI to another, the clinician should taper and stop the first one for 10 to 14 days before beginning the second one. Insomnia and behavioral activation can be treated by dividing the dose, not giving medication after dinner, and using a benzodiazepine hypnotic if necessary. Insomnia may paradoxically be accompanied by sedation during the day. Myoclonus, muscle pains, and parathesias are also occasionally seen in patients treated with MAOIs. Occasionally, patients complain of feeling drunk or confused, perhaps indicating that the dosage should be reduced and then increased more gradually. There are uncommon reports that the hydrazine MAOIs are associated with hepatoxic effects. MAOIs are less cardiotoxic and less epileptogenic than tricyclic and tetracyclic antidepressants.

Tyramine-Induced Hypertensive Crisis

When patients taking MAOIs ingest foodstuffs rich in tyramine (Table 30.2.18-1), they may have a hypertensive reaction that can be life-threatening (e.g., cerebrovascular accident). Patients should also be warned that bee stings may cause a hypertensive crisis. The mechanism is MAO inhibition in the gastrointestinal (GI) tract, resulting in the increased absorption of tyramine, which then acts as a false neurotransmitter. Increased concentrations of noradrenaline in presynaptic endings is a result of MAO_A inhibition and may be an even more significant mechanism in producing this hypertensive effect.

Patients should be warned about the dangers of ingesting tyramine-rich foods while taking MAOIs, and they should be advised to continue the dietary restrictions for two weeks after

Table 30.2.18-1
Tyramine-Rich Foods To Be Avoided While Taking MAOIs

Very high tyramine content:

Alcohol (particularly beer and wines, especially Chianti; a small amount of scotch, gin, vodka, or sherry is permissible.)
Fava or broad beans
Aged cheese (e.g., Camembert, Liederkranz, Edam, and cheddar; cream cheese and cottage cheeses are permitted.)
Beef or chicken liver
Orange pulp
Pickled or smoked fish, poultry, or meats
Soups (packaged)
Yeast vitamin supplements
Meat extracts (e.g., Marmite, Bovril)
Summer (dry) sausage

Moderately high tyramine content (no more than one or two servings a day):

Soy sauce
Sour cream
Bananas (green bananas can be included only if cooked in their skins; ordinary peeled bananas are fine.)
Avocados
Eggplant
Plums
Raisins
Spinach
Tomatoes
Yogurt

Table 30.2.18-2
Drugs to Be Avoided during MAOI Treatment

Never use:

Anesthetic–never spinal anesthetic or local anesthetic containing epinephrine (Lidocaine and procaine are safe.)
Antiasthmatic medications
Antihypertensives (α-methyldopa, guanethidine, reserpine, pargyline)
L-Dopa, L-tryptophan
Narcotics (especially meperidine [Demerol]; morphine or codeine may be less dangerous.)
Over-the-counter cold, hay fever, and sinus medications, especially those containing dextromethorphan (aspirin, acetaminophen, and menthol lozenges are safe.)
Sympathomimetics (amphetamine, cocaine, methylphenidate, dopamine, metaraminol, epinephrine, norepinephrine, isoproterenol)

Use carefully:

Antihistamines
Hydralazine (Apresoline)
Propranolol (Inderal)
Terpin hydrate with codeine

they stop MAOI treatment in order to allow the body to resynthesize the enzyme. The prodromal symptoms of a hypertensive crisis may include headache, stiff neck, sweating, nausea, and vomiting. If these symptoms occur, a patient should seek immediate medical treatment. Treatment should include the administration of α-adrenergic blockers, such as phentolamine (Regitine). Chlorpromazine (Thorazine) may also be used, and some clinicians give their patients several 50 mg tablets of chlorpromazine to use in an emergency. A headache from the hypotensive effects of MAOIs may confuse the patient, however, and taking the chlorpromazine could result in more severe hypotension, fainting, and possibly injury.

Overdose Attempts

In general, intoxication caused by MAOIs is characterized by agitation that progresses to coma with hyperthermia, hypertension, tachypnea, tachycardia, dilated pupils, and hyperactive deep tendon reflexes. Involuntary movements may be present, particularly in the face and jaw.

There is often an asymptomatic period of one to six hours after the ingestion of the drugs before the occurrence of toxicity. Acidification of the urine markedly hastens the excretion of MAOIs, and dialysis may be of some use. Phentolamine and chlorpromazine may be useful if hypotension is a problem.

DRUG-DRUG INTERACTIONS

The inhibition of MAO can cause severe and even fatal interactions with various other drugs (Table 30.2.18-2). Patients should be instructed to tell any other physicians who are treating them that they are taking an MAOI.

References

Davidson J, Lipper S, Pelton S, Miller R D, Hammett E B, Majorney S, Varia I M: The response of depressed inpatients to isocarboxazid. J Clin Psychopharmacol *8*: 100, 1988.
Davidson J R T, Giller E L, Zisook S, Overall J E: An efficacy study of isocarboxazid and placebo in depression, and its relationship to depressive nosology. Arch Gen Psychiatry *45*: 120, 1988.
Davis J M, Janicak P G, Bruninga K: The efficacy of MAO inhibitors in depression: A metaanalysis. Psychiatr Ann *17*: 825, 1987.
Dilsaver S C: Heterocyclic antidepressant, monoamine oxidase inhibitor and neuroleptic withdrawal phenomena. Prog Neuropsychopharmacol Biol Psychiatry *14*: 137, 1990.
Georgotas A, McCue R E, Cooper T B: A placebo-controlled comparison of nortriptyline and phenelzine in maintenance therapy of elderly depressed patients. Arch Gen Psychiatry *46*: 783, 1989.
Kahn D, Silver J M, Opler L A: The safety of switching rapidly from tricyclic antidepressants to monoamine oxidase inhibitors. J Clin Psychopharmacol *9*: 198, 1989.
Keck P E, Vuckovic A, Pope H G, Nierenberg A A, Gribble G W, White K: Acute cardiovascular response to monoamine oxidase inhibitors: A prospective assessment. J Clin Psychopharmacol *9*: 203, 1989.
Kennedy S H, Piran N, Warsh J J, Prendergast P, Mainprize E, Whynot C, Garfinkel P E: A trial of isocarboxazid in the treatment of bulima nervosa. J Clin Psychopharmacol *8*: 391, 1989.
Quitkin F M, McGrath P J, Stewart J W, Harrison W, Wager S G, Nunes E, Rabikin J G, Tricamo E, Markowtiz J, Klein D F: Phenelzine and imipramine in mood reactive depressives. Arch Gen Psychiatry *46*: 787, 1989.
Shulman K I, Walker S E, MacKenzie S, Knowles S: Dietary restriction, tyramine, and the use of monoamine oxidase inhibitors. J Clin Psychopharmacol *9*: 397, 1989.

30.2.19 / Sympathomimetics

The sympathomimetic drugs used in psychiatry are dextroamphetamine (Dexedrine), methylphenidate (Ritalin), and pemoline (Cylert). These drugs are also known as psychostimulants and analeptics. The sympathomimetics are approved for use in narcolepsy and attention-deficit hyperactivity disorder (ADHD); these drugs are also sometimes used to treat depression. The chemical structure of methylphenidate is similar to that of amphetamine, whereas pemoline is unrelated to amphetamine (Figure 30.2.19-1).

PHARMACOLOGICAL ACTIONS

Dextroamphetamine is well absorbed from the gastrointestinal (GI) tract. Because it has a half-life of 8 to 12 hours, dextroamphetamine must be given two or three times a day. Dextroamphetamine is partially metabolized in the liver and partially excreted unchanged by the kidneys. Methylphenidate is well absorbed from the GI tract and reaches peak plasma levels in one to two hours. Because it has a short half-life of three to four hours, methylphenidate must be given three or four times a day. Methylphenidate is metabolized in the liver. Pemoline has the advantage of a long half-life and, therefore, can be given once daily.

The sympathomimetics are indirectly acting catecholamine stimulants. Amphetamine causes catecholamines, particularly dopamine, to be released from presynaptic neurons and also inhibits the reuptake of released catecholamines back into the presynaptic neurons. The net result is stimulation of several brain regions, particularly the ascending reticular activating system. Short-term use of the sympathomimetics induces a

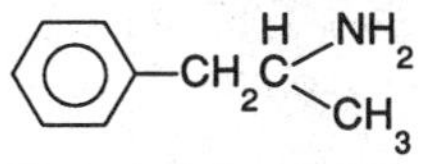

Dextroamphetamine

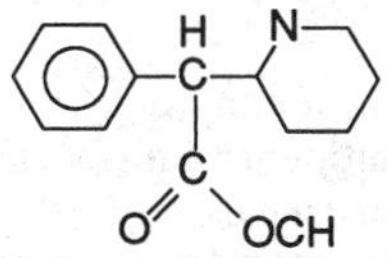

Methylphenidate

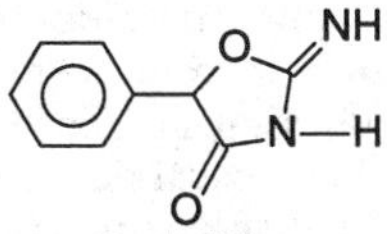

Pemoline

Figure 30.2.19-1. Molecular structures of sympathomimetics.

euphoric feeling; however, tolerance develops to both this euphoric feeling and the sympathomimetic activity. Tolerance does not develop to the therapeutic effects in ADHD.

INDICATIONS

The major indications for sympathomimetics are ADHD and narcolepsy. Sympathomimetics are an effective treatment in 70 to 80 percent of patients with ADHD. Although methylphenidate is the most commonly used drug for this indication, dextroamphetamine is equally effective. The data on the efficacy of pemoline are somewhat less robust; however, some clinicians prefer to use pemoline because of its lower abuse potential. The symptoms of narcolepsy include excessive daytime sleepiness and transient, irresistible attacks of daytime sleep. Unfortunately, patients with narcolepsy, unlike patients with ADHD, develop tolerance to the therapeutic effects of sympathomimetics.

Sympathomimetics may be used to treat depression. Possible indications for their use include treatment-resistant depressions; depression in the elderly, who are at increased risk for adverse effects from tricyclic and tetracyclic antidepressants and monoamine oxidase inhibitors (MAOIs); depression in medically ill patients (especially acquired immune deficiency syndrome [AIDS] patients); and clinical situations in which a rapid response is important but for which electroconvulsive therapy (ECT) is contraindicated. Sympathomimetics usually provide only short-term benefit (two to four weeks) for depression, because tolerance to the antidepressant effects of these drugs develops rapidly in most patients. Long-term treatment of chronic depression with sympathomimetics has been useful in carefully monitored situations, although this is controversial because of the abuse potential of these drugs. For further discussion of this issue, see Section 12.6.

Sympathomimetics were previously used in the treatment of obesity because of their anorexia-inducing effects. Because tolerance develops to the anorectic effects and because the drugs are associated with abuse, this treatment is no longer indicated.

CLINICAL GUIDELINES

Sympathomimetics are schedule II drugs and require triplicate prescriptions. Many clinicians initiate treatment with pemoline, because it is associated with somewhat less abuse potential than either amphetamine or methylphenidate. Pretreatment evaluation should include evaluation of cardiac function, with particular attention to the presence of hypertension or tachyarrhythmias. Patients should also be examined for the presence of movement disorders, such as tics and dyskinesias, because these can be exacerbated by the administration of sympathomimetics. Liver function and renal function should be assessed, and dosages of sympathomimetics should be reduced if their metabolism is impaired. There is virtually no justifiable indication for the use of sympathomimetics during pregnancy. The dose ranges for sympathomimetics are given in Table 30.2.19-1.

ADVERSE EFFECTS

The most common adverse effects associated with sympathomimetics are anxiety, irritability, insomnia, and dysphoria. Sympathomimetics cause a decreased appetite, although tolerance develops to this effect. They can also cause an increase in heart rate and blood pressure and may cause palpitations. Less common adverse effects include the induction of movement disorders, such as tics, Tourette's disorder-like symptoms, and dyskinesias. In children, sympathomimetics may cause a transient suppression of growth. The most limiting adverse effect of sympathomimetics is their association with psychological and physical dependence.

High doses of sympathomimetics can cause dry mouth, pupillary dilation, bruxism, formication, and emotional lability. Long-term use of high dosages can cause a delusional disorder that can be indistinguishable from paranoid schizophrenia. Overdoses of sympathomimetics present with hyper-

Table 30.2.19-1
Sympathomimetics

Generic Name	Trade Name	Preparations	Adult Starting Dose (mg a day)	Adult Average Daily Dose (mg)	Adult Maximum Daily Dose (mg)
Dextroamphetamine	Dexedrine	5 mg tablets 5 mg per 5 mL elixer 5, 10, 15 mg sustained-release tablets	2.5–10	10–20	40
Methylphenidate	Ritalin	5, 10, 20 mg tablets 20 mg sustained-release tablets	5–10	20–30	60–80
Pemoline	Cylert	18.75, 37.5, 75 mg tablets	18.75–37.5	56.25–75	112.5

tension, tachycardia, hyperthermia, toxic psychosis, delirium, and occasionally seizures. Overdoses of sympathomimetics can also result in death. Seizures can be treated with benzodiazepines, cardiac effects with propranolol (Inderal), fever with cooling blankets, and delirium with dopamine receptor antagonists.

DRUG-DRUG INTERACTIONS

The coadministration of sympathomimetics with tricyclic or tetracyclic antidepressants, warfarin (Coumadin), primidone (Mysoline), phenobarbital, phenytoin (Dilantin), or phenylbutazone (Butazolidin) decreases the metabolism of these compounds, resulting in increased plasma levels. Sympathomimetics decrease the therapeutic efficacy of many hypertensives, especially guanethidine (Esimil, Ismelin).

References

Angrist B, Corwin J, Bartlik B, Cooper T: Early pharmacokinetics and clinical effects of oral D-amphetamine in normal subjects. Biol Psychiatry *22*: 1357, 1987.

Cherek D R, Steinberg J L, Kelly T H, Robinson D E, Spiga R: Effects of acute administration of diazepam and d-amphetamine on aggressive and escape responding of normal male subjects. Psychopharmacology *100*: 173, 1990.

Chirarello R J, Cole J O: The use of psychostimulants in general psychiatry: A reconsideration. Arch Gen Psychiatry *44*: 286, 1987.

Harvey J A: Behavioral pharmacology of central nervous system stimulants. Neuropharmacology *26*: 887, 1987.

Lingam V R, Lazarus L W, Groves L, Oh S H: Methylphenidate in treating poststroke depression. J Clin Psychiatry *49*: 151, 1988.

Satel S L, Nelson J C: Stimulants in the treatment of depression: A critical overview. J Clin Psychiatry *50*: 241, 1989.

Shah K, Bradshaw C M, Szabadi E: Interaction between antidepressants and d-amphetamine on variable-interval performance. Psychopharmacology *100*: 548, 1990.

30.2.20 / Thyroid Hormones

Thyroid hormones are used in psychiatry as adjuvants to antidepressants, often in an attempt to convert an antidepressant-nonresponsive patient into an antidepressant-responsive patient. The most commonly used thyroid hormone is L-triiodothyronine (T_3 or liothyronine) (Cytomel); thyroxine (T_4 or levothyroxine) (Levoxine, Levothroid, Synthroid) is also sometimes used for the same purpose. Endogenous thyroxine and exogenous thyroxine are converted into triiodothyronine in the body.

PHARMACOLOGICAL ACTIONS

Thyroid hormones are administered orally, and their absorption from the gastrointestinal (GI) tract is variable. Absorption is increased if the drug is administered while the patient's stomach is empty. The half-life of thyroxine is six to seven days, and the half-life of triiodothyronine is one to two days. The mechanism of action for thyroid hormone effects on antidepressant efficacy is unknown, although interactions with the β-adrenergic receptors have been hypothesized.

INDICATIONS

The sole indication for thyroid hormones in psychiatry is as an adjuvant to antidepressants. There is no correlation between the laboratory measures of thyroid function and the response to thyroid hormone supplementation of antidepressants. If a patient has been nonresponsive to a six-week course of antidepressants at appropriate dosages, adjuvant therapy with either lithium or a thyroid hormone is an alternative. Most clinicians use adjuvant lithium before trying a thyroid hormone. The available clinical data suggest that triiodothyronine is more effective than thyroxine. Although several controlled trials have indicated that the use of triiodothyronine converts 33 to 75 percent of antidepressant nonresponders to responders, several other studies have failed to support this finding.

The dosage of triiodothyronine is 25 or 50 μg a day added to the patient's antidepressant regimen. Triiodothyronine has been used as an adjuvant for all the tricyclic and tetracyclic antidepressants, the monoamine oxidase inhibitors (MAOIs), and trazodone (Desyrel). Clinical data regarding its use with either bupropion (Wellbutrin) or fluoxetine (Prozac) are very limited. An adequate trial of triiodothyronine supplementation should last 7 to 14 days. If triiodothyronine supplementation is successful, it should be continued for two months, then tapered at the rate of 12.5 μg a day every three to seven days.

ADVERSE EFFECTS

Thyroid hormones should not be administered to patients with cardiac disease, angina, or hypertension. Thyroid hormones can be administered safely to pregnant women, because the thyroid hormones do not cross the placenta. The most common adverse effects associated with thyroid hormones are weight loss, palpitations, nervousness, diarrhea, abdominal cramps, sweating, tachycardia, increased pulse and blood pressure, tremors, headache, and insomnia. Overdoses can lead to cardiac failure and death.

DRUG-DRUG INTERACTIONS

Thyroid hormones can potentiate the effects of warfarin (Coumadin) and other anticoagulants by increasing the catabolism of clotting factors. Thyroid hormones may increase the insulin requirement for diabetic patients. Sympathomimetics and thyroid hormones should not be coadministered because of the risk of cardiac decompensation.

References

Bauer M S, Whybrow P C: Rapid cycling bipolar affective disorder: II. Treatment of refractory rapid cycling with high-dose levothyroxine: A preliminary study. Arch Gen Psychiatry *47*: 435, 1990.

Fudge J L, Perry P J, Garvey M J, Kelly M W: A comparison of the effect of fluoxetine and trazodone on the cognitive functioning of depressed outpatients. J Affective Disord *18*: 275, 1990.

Joffe R T: Triiodothyronine potentiation of the antidepressant effect of phenelzine. J Clin Psychiatry *49*: 409, 1988.

Moon C A, Chapman J P, Healey J C, Hannington J A: The treatment of mixed affective disorders in general practice: A comparison of trazodone and dothiepin. Curr Med Res Opin *12*: 34, 1990.

Stein D, Anvi A: Thyroid hormones in the treatment of affective disorders. Acta Psychiatr Scand *77*: 623, 1988.
Thase M E, Kupfer D K, Jarrett D B: Treatment of imipramine-resistant recurrent depression: I. An open clinical trial of adjunctive L-triiodothyronine. J Clin Psychiatry *50*: 385, 1989.

30.2.21 / Trazodone

Trazodone (Desyrel) is a triazolopyridine derivative that is used primarily for the treatment of depression (Figure 30.2.21-1). Trazodone shares the triazolo ring structure with alprazolam (Xanax), another atypical antidepressant drug. Trazodone is structurally unrelated to the tricyclic antidepressants, tetracyclic antidepressants, and monoamine oxidase inhibitors (MAOIs). It differs from these other antidepressants in having almost no anticholinergic adverse effects.

PHARMACOLOGICAL ACTIONS

Trazodone is readily absorbed from the gastrointestinal (GI) tract, reaches peak plasma levels in one to two hours, and has a half-life of 6 to 11 hours. Trazodone is metabolized in the liver, and 75 percent of its metabolites are excreted in urine.

Trazodone has its therapeutic effects as a specific inhibitor of serotonin reuptake. One active metabolite of trazodone, m-chlorophenyl-piperazine, also possesses some postsynaptic serotonin agonist activity. The adverse effects of trazodone are partially mediated by α_1-adrenergic antagonism and some antihistaminergic activity.

INDICATIONS

The primary indication for the use of trazodone is major depression. Trazodone is as effective as standard antidepressants in the short-term and long-term treatment of major depression. Trazodone is particularly effective at improving sleep quality. Trazodone increases total sleep time, decreases the number and the duration of nighttime awakenings, and decreases rapid eye movement (REM) sleep amount. Unlike tricyclic antidepressants, trazodone does not decrease stage 4 sleep.

There are a few case reports and uncontrolled trials of trazodone for the treatment of depression with marked anxiety symptoms and for panic disorder and agoraphobia. Final evaluation of the use of trazodone for these disorders requires further clinical research.

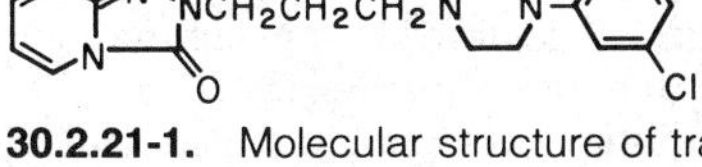

Figure 30.2.21-1. Molecular structure of trazodone.

CLINICAL GUIDELINES

Trazodone is available in tablets that can be divided into 50, 75, 100, 150, and 300 mg amounts. The usual starting dose is 50 mg orally (PO) the first day. This can be increased to 50 mg PO twice daily on the second day and possibly 50 mg PO three times daily on the third or fourth day if there are no problems with sedation or orthostatic hypotension. The therapeutic range for trazodone is 200 to 600 mg a day in divided doses. Some reports indicate that dosages of 400 to 600 mg a day are required for maximal therapeutic effects; other reports suggest that 300 to 400 mg a day is sufficient. The dosage may be titrated up to 300 mg a day and then evaluated for the need for further dosage increases on the basis of the presence or the absence of signs of clinical improvement.

ADVERSE EFFECTS

The most common adverse effects associated with trazodone are sedation, orthostatic hypotension, dizziness, headache, and nausea. As a result of α-adrenergic blockade, dry mouth is present in some patients. Trazodone is not associated with the usual anticholinergic adverse effects, such as urinary retention and constipation. There have been no reported fatalities from trazodone overdoses when the drug was taken alone; however, there have been fatalities when trazodone was taken with other drugs. Trazodone does not have the quinidinelike antiarrhythmic effects of imipramine (Tofranil). There have been a few case reports of an association between trazodone and arrhythmias in patients with preexisting premature ventricular contractions or mitral valve prolapse. The use of trazodone is contraindicated in pregnant and nursing women.

Trazodone is associated with the rare occurrence of priapism, the symptom of prolonged erection in the absence of sexual stimuli. Patients should be advised to report if erections are gradually becoming more frequent or prolonged; in such cases doctors should consider another antidepressant medication. Untreated priapism can lead to impotence. A male patient who has priapism while taking trazodone should stop taking the drug and consult a physician immediately. One effective treatment for priapism involves the intracavernosal injection of a 1 μg per mL solution of epinephrine (an α-adrenergic agonist).

DRUG-DRUG INTERACTIONS

Trazodone potentiates the central nervous system depressant effects of other centrally acting drugs. The combination of monoamine oxidase inhibitors and trazodone should be avoided.

References

Fabre L F, Feighner J P: Long-term therapy for depression with trazodone. J Clin Psychiatry *44*: 17, 1983.
Greenblatt D J, Friedman H, Burstein E S, Scavone J M, Blyden G T, Ochs H R, Miller L G, Harmatz J S, Shader R I: Trazodone kinetics: Effects of age, gender, and obesity. Clin Pharmacol Ther *42*: 193, 1987.
Hamik A, Peroutka S J: 1-(m-chlorophenyl)piperazine (mCPP) interactions with neurotransmitter receptors in the human brain. Biol Psychiatry *25*: 569, 1989.
Himmelhoch J M: Cardiovascular effects of trazodone in humans. J Clin Psychopharmacol *1* (6, Suppl): 76S, 1981.
Mouret J, Lemoine P, Minuit M P, Benkelfat C, Renardet M: Effects of trazodone on the sleep of depressed subjects: A polygraphic study. Psychopharmacology *95*: S37, 1988.

Newton R: The side effect profile of trazodone in comparison to an active control and placebo. J Clin Psychopharmacol *1* (6, Suppl): 89S, 1981.
Scharf M B (Guest ed): Insights in the use of trazodone in depressed patients. J Clin Psychiatry *51* (Suppl): 2, 1990.
Warner M D, Peabody C A, Whiteford H A, Hollister L E: Trazodone and priapism. J Clin Psychiatry *48*: 244, 1987.

30.2.22 / Tricyclics and Tetracyclics: Antidepressants

The tricyclic antidepressants (also known as the tricyclics) and the monoamine oxidase inhibitors (MAOIs) are often considered the classic antidepressant drugs. The indications for these drugs, however, have expanded beyond depression to include anxiety disorders, eating disorders, and chronic pain syndromes. The tricyclic antidepressants share many pharmacokinetic and pharmacodynamic properties and similar adverse effect profiles. Three tetracyclic drugs were initially introduced as being significantly different from the tricyclics. Further study and clinical use have demonstrated that the tetracyclic and tricyclic drugs can best be conceptualized as one family of drugs. The heterocyclic antidepressants generally include the monocyclic, dicyclic, tricyclic, and tetracyclic antidepressants. The term "heterocyclic antidepressant" is not used in this textbook because it is an overinclusive classification for a diverse group of drugs with no single side effect profile or therapeutic profile.

For the treatment of depression, the drugs available as alternatives to the tricyclics and tetracyclics include the MAOIs (Section 30.2.18), fluoxetine (Prozac) (Section 30.2.15), trazodone (Desyrel) (Section 30.2.21), bupropion (Wellbutrin) (Section 30.2.7), and the sympathomimetics (Section 30.2.19).

CLASSIFICATION

All tricyclics have a three-ring nucleus in their molecular structures (Figure 30.2.22-1). Imipramine (Tofranil), amitriptyline (Elavil), clomipramine (Anafranil), trimipramine (Surmontil), and doxepin (Adapin, Sinequan) are called *tertiary amines,* because there are two methyl groups on the nitrogen atom of the side chain. Desipramine (Norpramin, Pertofrane), nortriptyline (Pamelor, Aventyl), and protriptyline (Vivactil) are called *secondary amines,* because there is only one methyl group in this position. The tertiary amines are metabolized into their corresponding secondary amines in the body.

The classification of tetracyclic is somewhat arbitrarily based on a gross count of the number of rings in the molecular structure. Amoxapine (Asendin), actually a dibenzoxazepine, is a derivative of the antipsychotic drug loxapine (Loxitane) and has a cyclic side chain off the three-ring nucleus, for a total of four rings. Maprotiline (Ludiomil) is a tetracyclic with the same side chain as desipramine; its fourth ring actually bridges the center of the standard tricyclic nucleus. Mianserin is a tetracyclic drug whose side chain has been cyclicized to form a fourth ring; mianserin is not currently available for clinical use.

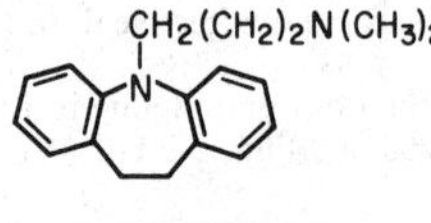

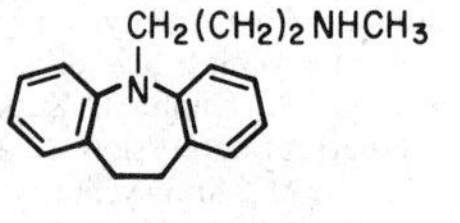

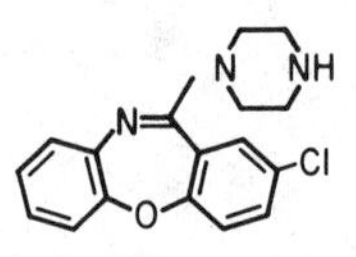

Figure 30.2.22-1. Molecular structures of representative tricyclic and tetracyclic antidepressants.

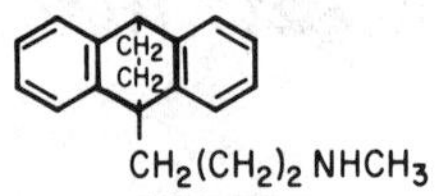

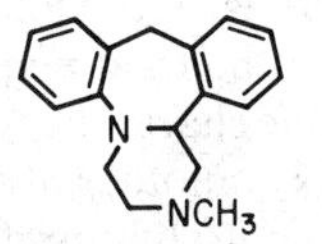

PHARMACOLOGICAL ACTIONS

Pharmacokinetics

Absorption from oral administration of most tricyclics and tetracyclics is incomplete, and there is a significant metabolism from the first-pass effect. Imipramine pamoate is a depot form of the drug for intramuscular (IM) administration; indications for the use of this preparation are limited. Protein binding is usually over 75 percent; the lipid solubility is quite high; and the volume of distribution ranges from 10 to 30 L per kg for tertiary amines to 20 to 60 L per kg for secondary amines. The tertiary amines are demethylated to form the related secondary amines. The ratio of methylated to demethylated forms varies widely from person to person. The tricyclic nucleus is oxidized in the liver, conjugated with glucuronic acid, and excreted. The 7-hydroxymetabolite of amoxapine has potent dopamine-blocking activity, thus causing the antipsychotic-like neurological and endocrinological adverse effects that are seen with this drug. The half-lives vary from 10 to 70 hours, although nortriptyline, maprotiline, and particularly proptriptyline can have longer half-lives. The long half-lives allow for all these compounds to be given once daily and means that five to seven days are needed to reach steady-state plasma levels.

Pharmacodynamics

The short-term effects of tricyclics and tetracyclics are to reduce the reuptake of norepinephrine and serotonin and to block muscarinic acetylcholine and histamine receptors. The different tricyclics and tetracyclics vary in their pharmacodynamic effects (Table 30.2.22-1). Amoxapine, nortriptyline, and maprotiline have the least anticholinergic activity, and doxepin has the most antihistaminergic activity. Clomipramine is the most serotonin-selective of the tricyclics and tetracyclics. The reuptake blockade of norepinephrine and serotonin by these drugs and the monoamine oxidase inhibition by the MAOIs led to the development of the monoamine hypothesis of mood disorders. Long-term administration of tricyclics and

Table 30.2.22-1
Neurotransmitter Effects of Tricyclic and Tetracyclic Antidepressants

	Reuptake Blockade		Receptor Blockade		
	NE	5HT	Muscarinic ACh	H_1	H_2
Imipramine	+	+	++	±	±
Desipramine	+++	±	±	−	−
Trimipramine	±	±	++	++	?
Amitriptyline	±	++	+++	++	++
Nortriptyline	++	±	+	±	±
Protriptyline	+++	±	+	+++	−
Amoxapine	++	±	+	±	?
Doxepin	+	±	++	+++	+
Maprotiline	+++	−	+	±	?
Clomipramine	±	++	+	?	?

tetracyclics results in a decrease in the number of β-adrenergic receptors and, perhaps, a similar decrease in the number of serotonin type 2 receptors. It is this downregulation of receptors after repeated administration that most closely correlates with the time that clinical effects appear in patients. This downregulation of β-adrenergic receptors occurs whether the initial effect is blocking noradrenergic or serotonin receptors. Research with animals has demonstrated, however, that intact noradrenergic and serotonergic systems are required for the downregulation to occur.

INDICATIONS

Major Depressive Episode

A major depressive episode in both major depression patients and bipolar disorder patients is the principal indication for using tricyclic and tetracyclic drugs. Symptoms of melancholia and prior episodes of depression increase the likelihood of a therapeutic response.

Secondary Depression

Depressions associated with organic syndromes may respond to tricyclic and tetracyclic drugs. These include depressions after cerebrovascular accidents and central nervous system (CNS) trauma and the depressive symptoms seen in some dementias and movement disorders, such as Parkinson's disease. Depression associated with acquired immune deficiency syndrome (AIDS) may also respond to these drugs.

Panic Disorder with Agoraphobia

Imipramine has been the tricyclic most studied for panic disorder with agoraphobia, although other tricyclics are also effective. Early reports suggested that small dosages of imipramine (50 mg a day) were often effective; however, recent studies indicate that the usual antidepressant dosages are usually required.

Generalized Anxiety Disorder

The use of doxepin for the treatment of anxiety is approved by the Food and Drug Administration (FDA). Some research data show that imipramine may also be useful, and some clinicians use a drug containing a combination of chlordiazepoxide and amitriptyline (marketed as Limbitrol) for mixed anxiety and depressive disorders.

Obsessive-Compulsive Disorder

Obsessive-compulsive disorder is classified under the anxiety disorders in the revised third edition of *Diagnostic and Statistical Manual of Mental Disorders* (DSM-III-R) and appears to respond somewhat specifically to clomipramine. It does not appear that any of the other tricyclics and tetracyclics are nearly as effective as clomipramine.

Eating Disorders

Both anorexia nervosa and bulimia nervosa have been successfully treated with imipramine and desipramine, although other tricyclics and tetracyclics may also be effective.

Pain

Chronic pain syndromes, including headaches (e.g., migraines), are often treated with tricyclics and tetracyclics.

Other Syndromes

Childhood enuresis is often treated with imipramine. Peptic ulcer disease, a psychosomatic condition, can be treated with doxepin, which has marked antihistaminergic effects. Other indications for tricyclics and tetracyclics are narcolepsy, nightmares, and posttraumatic stress disorder.

CLINICAL GUIDELINES

Choice of Drug

The specific choice of which tricyclic or tetracyclic to use should be based on the general guidelines outlined in Section 30.1. All available tricyclic and tetracyclic drugs have been demonstrated to be equally effective in the treatment of depression. In the case of an individual patient, however, one tricyclic or tetracyclic may be effective, whereas another one may be ineffective. The adverse effects of the tricyclic and tetracyclic drugs differ (Table 30.2.22-2). The tertiary amine tricyclics tend to produce more adverse effects—including sedation, orthostatic hypotension, and anticholinergic effects

Table 30.2.22-2
Side Effect Profile of Tricyclic and Tetracyclic Antidepressants

	Anticholinergic Effects	Sedation	Orthostatic Hypotension	Seizures	Conduction Abnormalities
Tertiary amines					
Amitriptyline	+ + + +	+ + + +	+ + +	+ + +	+ + + +
Doxepin	+ + +	+ + + +	+ +	+ + +	+ +
Imipramine	+ + +	+ + +	+ + + +	+ + +	+ + + +
Trimipramine	+ + + +	+ + + +	+ + +	+ + +	+ + + +
Secondary amines					
Desipramine	+ +	+ +	+ + +	+ +	+ + +
Nortriptyline	+ + +	+ + +	+	+ +	+ + +
Protriptyline	+ + +	+	+ +	+ +	+ + + +
Tetracyclic					
Amoxapine	+ + +	+ +	+	+ + +	+ +
Maprotiline	+ + +	+ + +	+ +	+ + + +	+ + +

+ + + +, high; + + +, moderate; + +, low; +, very low

(such as dry mouth)—whereas the secondary amines tend to produce fewer of these adverse effects. Clomipramine is an effective antidepressant that is also the first-line drug in the treatment of obsessive-compulsive disorder and, therefore, may be the drug of choice for depressed patients with marked obsessive features. Among the secondary amine tricyclics, nortriptyline is associated with the least orthostatic hypotension, and desipramine is associated with the least anticholinergic activity. Among the tetracyclic drugs, amoxapine is sometimes recommended for the treatment of major depression because of its antidopaminergic activity.

Researchers have demonstrated differences among the tricyclics and tetracyclics in their relative ability to block either serotonin reuptake or norepinephrine reuptake. No study has demonstrated that the serotonin-to-norepinephrine ratio for each of these drugs can be used to help choose a specific drug to treat a particular patient. It is perhaps reasonable to switch from a strongly serotonergic drug to a strongly noradrenergic drug or vice versa if the first drug is ineffective in relieving the patient's symptoms.

Initiation of Treatment

A routine physical and laboratory examination of a patient to be administered tricyclics or tetracyclics should be conducted. The routine laboratory tests include a complete blood count (CBC) with differential, a white blood cell count (WBC), and serum electrolytes (SMA-6) with liver function tests (SMA-12). An electrocardiogram (ECG) should probably be obtained for all patients, especially women over 40 and men over 30. The initial dose should be small and should be raised gradually. The clinician can raise the dosage for inpatients more quickly than for outpatients because of the inpatients' closer clinical supervision.

It should be explained to patients that, although sleep and appetite may improve in one to two weeks, tricyclics and tetracyclics usually take three to four weeks to have antidepressant effects, and a complete trial should last six weeks. It may be important to explain to some patients what the drug treatment plan will entail if there is no clinical response at that time.

Dosage

Imipramine, amitriptyline, doxepin, desipramine, clomipramine, and trimipramine can be started at 75 mg a day. Divided doses at first reduce the severity of the side effects, although most of the dose should be given at night to help induce sleep if a sedating drug, such as amitriptyline, is used. Eventually, the entire dose can be given at bedtime. Protriptyline and less-sedating drugs should be given not less than two to three hours before a patient goes to sleep. For outpatients the dosage can be raised to 150 mg a day the second week, 225 mg a day the third week, and 300 mg a day the fourth week. A common clinical mistake is to stop increasing the dosage when the patient is taking less than 250 mg a day and does not show clinical improvement. This can result in a further delay in obtaining a therapeutic response, disenchantment with the treatment, and even premature discontinuation of the drug. The clinician should routinely assess the patient's baseline pulse and postural hypotension while the dosage is being raised.

Other tricyclics and tetracyclics have different guidelines for dosage. Nortriptyline should be started at 50 mg a day and be raised to 150 mg a day over three or four weeks. Amoxapine should be started at 150 mg a day and be raised to 400 mg a day. Protriptyline should be started at 15 mg a day and be raised to 60 mg a day. Maprotiline has been associated with an increased incidence of seizures if the dosage is raised too quickly or is maintained at too high a level. Maprotiline should be started at 75 mg a day and be maintained at that level for two weeks. The dosage can be increased over four weeks to 225 mg a day but should be kept at that level for only six weeks and then reduced to 175 to 200 mg a day (Table 30.2.22-3).

Failure of Drug Trial

If a tricyclic or tetracyclic has been used for four weeks at maximal dosages without a therapeutic effect, the clinician should obtain a plasma level and adjust the dosage accordingly. If plasma levels are adequate, supplementation with lithium or L-triiodothyronine (T_3) (Cytomel) should be considered.

Lithium. Lithium (900 to 1,200 mg a day, serum level between 0.6 and 0.8 mEq per L) can be added to the tricyclic or tetracyclic dosage for 7 to 14 days. This approach converts a significant number of nonresponders into responders. The mechanism of action is not known, although it has been hypothesized that the lithium potentiates the serotonergic neuronal system. Some data indicate that pretreatment with tricyclics or tetracyclics is necessary for this effect and that starting the treatment with body drugs is not as effective.

L-Triiodothyronine. The addition of 25 to 50 μg a day of T_3 to the regimen for 7 to 14 days also may convert tricyclic and tetracyclic nonresponders into responders. The adverse effects of T_3 are minor but may include a headache and feeling warm. The mechanism of action for T_3 augmentation is not known, although the modulation of β-adrenergic receptors and the presence of undetectable thyroid axis abnormalities have been suggested. If T_3 augmentation is successful, the T_3 should be continued for two months and then tapered at the rate of 12.5 μg a day every three to seven days.

Maintenance

Tricyclics and tetracyclics should be continued at maximal dosage for three to four months after a successful therapeutic recovery. At that point it may be reasonable to reduce the dosage to three-fourths the maximal dosage for one month, then one-half the maximal dosage for another month. At this time, if no symptoms are present, the drug can be tapered by 25 mg (5 mg for protriptyline) every two to three days. This slow tapering process is indicated for most psychotherapeutic drugs, and, in the case of most tricyclics and tetracyclics, it avoids a cholinergic-rebound syndrome consisting of nausea, upset stomach, sweating, headache, neck pain, and vomiting. The appearance of this syndrome can be treated by reinstituting a small dosage of the drug and tapering more slowly. There are also several case reports of rebound mania or hypomania after the abrupt discontinuation of tricyclic and tetracyclic antidepressants. If a patient has been treated with lithium augmentation, it seems reasonable to taper and stop the lithium first and then the tricyclic or tetracyclic antidepressant. Clinical studies supporting this approach are lacking, however, and the guidelines may change as more physicians report their experience with this drug combination.

Tricyclics, tetracyclics, and lithium are useful in preventing the recurrence of depressive episodes. The decision to use a prophylactic treatment is based on the severity and the nature of the disorder in a particular patient. Some data suggest that the long-term use of antidepressants may induce a rapid cycling bipolar disorder. Lithium prophylaxis, therefore, may be an alternative treatment in a patient who has frequent, episodic, and serious depressive episodes.

Several investigators have suggested that neuroendocrine tests may be a guide for deciding when to maintain the use of tricyclics, tetracyclics, and other antidepressants. Specifically, the normalization of previously abnormal results in a dexamethasone suppression test or a thyrotropin-releasing hormone-stimulation test may indicate that a patient can safely discontinue drug treatment. This use of neuroendocrine monitoring is still being investigated.

Plasma Levels

Research has defined the dose-response curves for tricyclic and tetracyclic antidepressants. Clinical determinations of plasma levels should be conducted 8 to 12 hours after the last dose after five to seven days on the same dosage of medication. Because of variations in absorption and metabolism, there is a 30- to 50-fold difference in the plasma levels of humans given the same dose of a tricyclic or tetracyclic. The therapeutic ranges for plasma levels have been determined (Table 30.2.22-3). Nortriptyline is unique in its association with a therapeutic window; that is, plasma levels over 150 ng per mL may reduce its efficacy. Clinicians must follow the directions for collection from the testing laboratory and have confidence in the assay procedures used.

The use of plasma levels in clinical practice is still an evolving skill. Plasma levels may be useful in confirming compliance, assessing reasons for drug failures, and documenting effective plasma levels for future treatment. Clinicians should always treat the patient and never the plasma level. Some patients have adequate clinical responses with seemingly subtherapeutic plasma levels, and other patients have responses only at supratherapeutic plasma levels without experiencing adverse effects. The latter situation, however, should alert clinicians to carefully monitor the patient's condition (e.g., ECG).

ADVERSE EFFECTS

Psychiatric Effects

A major adverse effect of all tricyclic and tetracyclic antidepressants is the possibility of inducing a manic episode in both bipolar disorder patients and patients without a previous history of bipolar disorder. The clinician should watch carefully for this effect in bipolar disorder patients, especially if drug-induced mania has been a problem in the past. It is prudent to use very low doses of tricyclic and tetracyclic antidepressants in such patients.

Table 30.2.22-3
Clinical Information for the Tricyclic and Tetracyclic Antidepressants

Generic Name	Trade Name	Usual Adult Dose Range (mg a day)	Therapeutic Plasma Levels* (ng per ml)
Imipramine	Tofranil	150–300†	150–300
Desipramine	Norpramin, Pertofrane	150–300†	150–300
Trimipramine	Surmontil	150–300†	?
Amitriptyline	Elavil	150–300†	100–250†
Nortriptyline	Pamelor, Aventyl	50–150	50–150 (maximum)
Protriptyline	Vivactil	15–60	75–250
Amoxapine	Asendin	150–400	?
Doxepin	Adapin, Sinequan	150–300†	100–250
Maprotiline	Ludiomil	150–225	150–300
Clomipramine	Anafranil	150–250	?

*Exact range may vary among laboratories.
†Includes parent compound and desmethyl metabolite.

Anticholinergic Effects

Patients should be warned that anticholinergic effects are quite common but that they may have a tolerance to them with continued treatment. Amitriptyline, imipramine, trimipramine, and doxepin are the most anticholinergic; amoxapine, nortriptyline, and maprotiline are less anticholinergic; and desipramine may be the least anticholinergic. Anticholinergic effects include dry mouth, constipation, blurred vision, and urinary retention. Sugarless gum or candy or fluoride lozenges can alleviate the dry mouth. Bethanechol (Urecholine), 25 to 50 mg three or four times a day, may reduce urinary hesitancy and may be helpful for impotence when taken 30 minutes before sexual intercourse. Narrow-angle glaucoma can also be aggravated by anticholinergic drugs, and the precipitation of glaucoma requires emergency treatment with a miotic agent. Tricyclic and tetracyclic antidepressants can be used in patients with glaucoma, provided that pilocarpine eye drops are administered concurrently. More severe anticholinergic effects can lead to a CNS anticholinergic syndrome with confusion and delirium, especially if tricyclic and tetracyclic antidepressants are administered with antipsychotics and anticholinergics. Some clinicians have used IM or intravenous (IV) physostigmine (Antilirium, Eserine) as a diagnostic tool to confirm the presence of anticholinergic delirium.

Sedation

Sedation is a common effect of antidepressants and may be welcomed if sleeplessness has been a problem. The sedative effect of tricyclic and tetracyclic antidepressants is a result of serotonergic, cholinergic, and histaminergic (H_1) activity. Amitriptyline, trimipramine, doxepin, and trazodone are the most sedating agents; imipramine, amoxapine, nortriptyline, and maprotiline have some sedating effects; and desipramine and proptriptyline are the least sedating agents.

Autonomic Effects

The most common autonomic effect, partly because of α_1-adrenergic blockade, is orthostatic hypotension, which can result in falls and injuries in affected patients. Nortriptyline may be the drug least likely to cause this problem, and some patients respond to fludrocortisone (Florinef), 0.025 to 0.05 mg twice a day. Other possible autonomic effects are profuse sweating, palpitations, and increased blood pressure.

Cardiac Effects

When administered in their usual therapeutic doses, the tricyclic and tetracyclic antidepressants may cause tachycardia, flattened T waves, prolonged QT intervals, and depressed ST segments in the ECG. Imipramine has been shown to have a quinidinelike effect at therapeutic plasma levels and, indeed, may reduce the number of premature ventricular contractions. Because these drugs prolong conduction time, their use in patients with preexisting conduction defects is contraindicated. In patients with a cardiac history, tricyclic and tetracyclic antidepressants should be initiated at low doses, with gradual increases in dosage and careful monitoring of cardiac functions. At high plasma levels, as seen in overdoses, the drugs become arrhythmogenic.

Neurological Effects

In addition to the sedation induced by tricyclics and tetracyclics and the possibility of anticholinergic-induced delirium, two tricyclics—desipramine and protriptyline—are associated with psychomotor stimulation. Myoclonic twitches and tremors of the tongue and upper extremities are fairly common. Rarer effects include speech blockage, paresthesias, peroneal palsies, and ataxia.

Amoxapine is unique in causing parkinsonianlike symptoms, akathisia, and even dyskinesias because of the dopaminergic blocking activity of one of its metabolites. Maprotiline may cause seizures when the dosage is increased too quickly or is kept at high levels for too long. Amoxapine may also be a bit more epileptogenic than the other tricyclics and tetracyclics. All tricyclics and tetracyclics, however, may induce seizures in patients who have epilepsy or organic brain lesions. Although tricyclics and tetracyclics can still be used in such patients, the initial doses should be lower and be raised more slowly than in other patients.

Allergic Effects

Exanthematous skin rashes are seen in 4 to 5 percent of all patients treated with maprotiline. Jaundice is very rare. Agranulocytosis, leukocytosis, leukopenia, and eosinophilia are rare complications of tricyclic and tetracyclic treatment. However, a patient who has a sore throat or fever during the first few months of tricyclic or tetracyclic treatment should have a CBC done immediately.

Other Adverse Effects

Weight gain, primarily an effect of the blockade of histamine type 2 receptors, is common. If this is a major problem, changing to fluoxetine or trazodone may help. Impotence, an occasional problem, is perhaps most often associated with amoxapine because of its blockade of dopamine receptors in the tuberoinfundibular tract. Amoxapine can also cause hyperprolactinemia, galactorrhea, anorgasmia, and ejaculatory disturbances. Other tricyclic and tetracyclic antidepressants have also been associated with gynecomastia and amenorrhea. Inappropriate secretion of antidiuretic hormone has also been reported with tricyclic and tetracyclic antidepressants.

Overdose Attempts

Overdose attempts with tricyclic and tetracyclic antidepressants are very serious and can often be fatal. Prescriptions for tricyclic and tetracyclic antidepressants should be nonrefillable and for no longer than a week at a time. Amoxapine may be more likely than the other tricyclic and tetracyclic antidepressants to result in death when taken in an overdose attempt.

Symptoms of overdose include agitation, delirium, convulsions, hyperactive deep tendon reflexes, bowel and bladder paralysis, dysregulations of blood pressure and temperature, and mydriasis. The patient then progresses to coma and perhaps respiratory depression. Cardiac arrhythmias may not respond to treatment. Because of the long half-lives of tricyclic and tetracyclic antidepressants, the patients are at risk of cardiac arrhythmias for three to four days after the overdose attempt, and so they should be monitored carefully in an intensive care medical setting.

DRUG-DRUG INTERACTIONS

Antihypertensives

Tricyclic and tetracyclic antidepressants block the neuronal reuptake of guanethidine (Esimil, Ismelin), which is required for antihypertensive activity. The antihypertensive effects of propranolol (Inderal) and clonidine (Catapres) may also be blocked by tricyclic and tetracyclic antidepressants. Coadministration of tricyclic and tetracyclic antidepressants with α-methyldopa may cause behavioral agitation.

Antipsychotics

The plasma levels of tricyclic and tetracyclic antidepressants and antipsychotics are increased by their coadministration. Antipsychotics also add to the anticholinergic and sedative effects of the tricyclic and tetracyclic antidepressants.

CNS Depressants

Opioids, alcohol, anxiolytics, hypnotics, and over-the-counter cold medications have additive effects by causing CNS depression when coadministered with antidepressants.

Oral Contraceptives

Birth control pills may decrease tricyclic and tetracyclic plasma levels through the induction of hepatic enzymes.

Other Pharmacokinetic Interactions

Tricyclic and tetracyclic plasma levels may also be increased by acetazolamide, acetylsalicylic acid, thiazide diuretics, and sodium bicarbonate. Decreased plasma levels may be caused by ascorbic acid, ammonium chloride, barbiturates, cigarette smoking, chloral hydrate, lithium, and primidone (Mysoline).

References

Aronson T A, Shukla S: Long-term continuation antidepressant treatment: A comparison study. J Clin Psychiatry *50*: 285, 1989.

Balsessarini R J: Current status of antidepressants: Clinical pharmacology and therapy. J Clin Psychiatry *50*: 117, 1989.

Bourin M S, Kerguieris M F, Lapierre Y D: Therapeutic monitoring of treatment with antidepressants. Psychiatr J Univ Ottawa *14*: 460, 1989.

Cole J O: The drug treatment of anxiety and depression. Med Clin North Am *72*: 815, 1988.

Dietch J T, Fine M: The effect of nortriptyline in elderly patients with cardiac conduction disease. J Clin Psychiatry *51*: 65, 1990.

Roose S P, Glassman A H, Dalack G W: Depression, heart disease, and tricyclic antidepressants. J Clin Psychiatry *50* (7, Suppl): 12, 1989.

Wehr T A, Goodwin F K: Can antidepressant cause mania and worsen the course of affective illness? Am J Psychiatry *144*: 1403, 1987.

Wilens T E, Stern T A, O'Gara P T: Adverse cardiac effects of combined neuroleptic ingestion and tricyclic antidepressant overdose. J Clin Psychopharmacol *10*: 51, 1990.

30.2.23 / L-Tryptophan

L-Tryptophan, the amino acid precursor to serotonin, has been used as an adjuvant to antidepressant drugs and has also been used as a hypnotic. In 1989 L-tryptophan and L-tryptophan-containing products were recalled in the United States because of an outbreak of eosinophilia-myalgia syndrome (EMS) associated with these products. The symptoms of EMS include fatigue, myalgia, shortness of breath, rashes, and swelling of the extremities. Congestive heart failure and death can also occur. It appears possible that the EMS was related to a contaminant in a single manufacturing plant, but this epidemiological puzzle has not yet been solved. L-Tryptophan is described here because the drug is likely to be available again in the United States once the current problem is resolved.

PHARMACOLOGICAL ACTIONS

L-Tryptophan is somewhat erratically absorbed from the gastrointestinal (GI) tract. A significant portion of the drug is metabolized by the liver in a first-pass effect. Absorption of L-tryptophan can be enhanced by taking the drug with a low-protein, high-carbohydrate meal. The half-life of L-tryptophan may be as little as one to two hours; therefore, unless the drug is used as a hypnotic, four times daily dosing is necessary to maintain plasma levels. L-Tryptophan has its effects because a portion of the ingested dose crosses the blood-brain barrier, is taken up by serotonergic neurons, and is converted into serotonin, thus raising serotonin concentrations in the central nervous system (CNS).

INDICATIONS AND CLINICAL GUIDELINES

The most common indication for L-tryptophan is insomnia, although this indication does not have Food and Drug Administration (FDA) approval. Doses of 1 to 15 g taken at bedtime have a hypnotic effect in a significant number of persons. Whether the hypnotic effects of L-tryptophan persist with long-term treatment is not certain. L-Tryptophan is not associated with visuospatial, cognitive, or memory deficits the day after drug ingestion. Low doses of L-tryptophan are not associated with any change in the sleep electroencephalogram (EEG) other than earlier sleep onset; high doses of L-tryptophan are associated with increases in slow-wave sleep.

L-Tryptophan has been used as an adjuvant to tricyclic and tetracyclic antidepressants for depressed persons who did not respond to the tricyclic or tetracyclic antidepressant alone. The use of either lithium or L-triiodothyronine (T_3) (Cytomel) adjuvant therapy with antidepressant nonresponders is more often used than L-tryptophan supplementation. L-Tryptophan has also been used as an adjuvant to lithium treatment for bipolar disorder patients who had incomplete symptom remission with lithium alone.

ADVERSE EFFECTS

Other than EMS, mentioned above, moderate doses of L-tryptophan are well tolerated by most patients. The only significantly reported adverse effect is nausea, which is sometimes compared to the nausea of pregnancy.

DRUG-DRUG INTERACTIONS

Much more significant are drug interactions when L-tryptophan is taken with either fluoxetine (Prozac) or monoamine oxidase inhibitors (MAOIs). These combinations can cause diarrhea, insomnia, nausea, headaches, chills, agitation, and poor concentration. The symptoms are probably due to an excess serotonin concentration because of the additive effects of these compounds.

References

Brewerton T D, Reus V I: Lithium carbonate and L-tryptophan in the treatment of bipolar and schizoaffective disorders. Am J Psychiatry *140*: 757, 1983.

Flannery M T, Wallach P M, Espinoza L R, Dohrenwend M P, Moscisnski L C: A case of eosinophilia-myalgia syndrome associated with use of an L-tryptophan product. Ann Intern Med *112*: 300, 1990.

Hedaya R J: Pharmacokinetic factors in the clinical use of tryptophan. J Clin Psychopharmacol *4*: 347, 1984.

Schneider-Helmert D, Spinweber C L: Evaluation of L-tryptophan for treatment of insomnia: A review. Psychopharmacology *89*: 1, 1986.

Steiner W, Fontaine R: Toxic reaction following the combined administration of fluoxetine and L-tryptophan: Five case reports. Biol Psychiatry *21*: 1067, 1986.

30.2.24 / Valproic Acid

Valproic acid and sodium valproate (both Depakene) and sodium divalproex (Depakote) are carboxylic acid-derivative anticonvulsants. Valproic acid is an anticonvulsant that joins the ranks of two other anticonvulsants—carbamazepine (Tegretol) (Section 30.2.10) and clonazepam (Klonopin) (Section 30.2.5)—as a potentially effective drug for the treatment of bipolar disorder (Figure 30.2.24-1). Lithium and carbamazepine remain the first-line drugs for bipolar disorder, but valproic acid joins clonazepam and verapamil (Calan, Isoptin) (Section 30.2.9) as alternatives if lithium or carbamazepine is ineffective or cannot be tolerated by a particular patient.

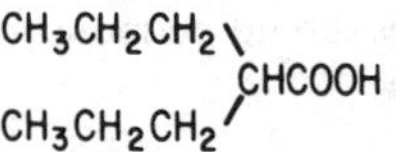

Figure 30.2.24-1. Molecular structure of valproic acid.

PHARMACOLOGICAL ACTIONS

Sodium valproate is converted into valproic acid in the stomach and is then almost completely absorbed by the gastrointestinal (GI) tract. Peak plasma levels are reached in one to two hours if the drug is taken when the stomach is empty and in four to five hours if the drug is taken when the stomach is full. The presence of food, however, does not affect the amount of drug absorbed. The half-life of valproic acid is about eight hours, thus making three times daily dosing necessary to maintain stable plasma concentrations. The therapeutic effects of valproic acid for seizure control are probably mediated by a decrease in the catabolism of γ-aminobutyric acid (GABA), resulting in increased central nervous system (CNS) GABA concentrations. Whether this is the mechanism involved in the therapeutic effects for bipolar disorder is unknown.

INDICATIONS

Bipolar Disorder

Valproic acid has been effective in the treatment of both manic and depressive episodes in bipolar disorder patients. Valproic acid is also an effective prophylactic treatment in the control of manic and depressive episodes; however, it should be reserved for the treatment of patients who either do not respond to or cannot tolerate lithium or carbamazepine. Additional alternative drugs for the treatment of bipolar disorder include clonazepam and verapamil. Some studies have reported that the addition of valproic acid to lithium can convert a lithium-nonresponsive patient into a drug-responsive patient. Other reports have suggested that valproic acid may be especially effective in the treatment of rapid-cycling bipolar disorder and in mania or depression resulting from organic brain disease.

Other Disorders

A few reports have indicated that valproic acid may be effective in controlling psychotic symptoms of schizophrenic patients and organic mental disorder patients. The coadministration of valproic acid and antipsychotics may increase the plasma concentrations of both drugs. The effectiveness of valproic acid in drug-induced akathisia and atypical depression with marked hypersomnia has also been noted in some case reports.

CLINICAL GUIDELINES

Valproic acid is available in 250 mg tablets. It is best to initiate drug treatment gradually, so as to minimize the common adverse effects of nausea, vomiting, and sedation. The dose on the first day should be 250 mg administered with a meal. The dosage can be raised up to 250 mg orally (PO) three times daily over the course of three to six days. Plasma levels can be taken in the morning before the first daily dose of the drug is administered. Therapeutic plasma levels for the control of seizures are between 50 and 100 μg per mL, although some physicians use up to 125 μg per mL. It is reasonable to use the same range for the treatment of psychiatric disorders, although the data to support this practice are not yet available. Most patients attain these plasma levels on a dosage of valproic acid between 1,200 and 1,500 mg a day in divided doses. The drug should not be administered to patients with hepatic disease or to pregnant or nursing women.

ADVERSE EFFECTS

The most common adverse effects are nausea, vomiting, and sedation, although tolerance to these effects often develops. These adverse effects can be minimized by increasing the dosage slowly and by taking the drug with meals. Other uncommon neurological adverse effects include hand tremor, asterixis, and, more rarely, ataxia, headache, anxiety, and depression. Also uncommon are thrombocytopenia and platelet dysfunction, occurring most commonly at high doses and resulting in the prolongation of bleeding times. Alopecia and generalized pruritus have been reported as rare adverse dermatological effects.

Serious adverse effects involve the pancreas and the liver. Rare cases of pancreatitis have been reported, occurring most often in the first six months of treatment and occasionally resulting in death. Transient increases in transaminases and lactate dehydrogenase occur in approximately 25 percent of patients. These laboratory abnormalities usually do not evidence themselves clinically and usually resolve in the first six months of treatment. Rare cases of hepatitis have been reported, occurring in approximately 1 in 20,000 patients. Hepatitis occurs most often in the first three to six months of treatment in children with severe seizure disorders who are treated with multiple drugs. A modest increase seen in liver function tests does not correlate with the development of hepatitis; however, the emergence of malaise, anorexia, jaundice, lethargy, or weakness should prompt the clinician to evaluate the patient's hepatic status immediately.

DRUG-DRUG INTERACTIONS

There are complex drug-drug interactions between valproic acid and other anticonvulsants. The clinician should consult the treating neurologist before adding valproic acid to an existent antiepileptic drug regimen. Valproic acid has additive depressant effects with CNS depressants, including alcohol. The hematological effects of valproic acid may potentiate the anticoagulant effects of aspirin and warfarin (Coumadin). Valproic acid also interferes with at least two laboratory tests, resulting in falsely elevated urine ketones and abnormal thyroid test results.

References

Calabrese J R, Delucchi G A: Spectrum of efficacy of valproate in 55 patients with rapid-cyclic bipolar disorder. Am J Psychiatry *147*: 431, 1990.

Kahn D, Stevenson E, Douglas C J: Effect of sodium valproate in three patients with organic brain syndromes. Am J Psychiatry *145*: 1010, 1988.

McElroy S L, Keck P E, Pope H G: Sodium valproate: Its use in primary psychiatric disorders. J Clin Psychopharmacol *7*: 16, 1987.

McElroy S L, Keck P E, Pope H G, Hudson J I: Valproate in the treatment of rapid-cycling bipolar disorder. J Clin Psychopharmacol *8*: 275, 1988.

Pies R, Adler D A, Ehrenberg B L: Sleep disorders and depression with atypical features: Response to valproate. J Clin Psychopharmacol *9*: 352, 1989.

Pope H G, McElroy S L, Satlin A, Hudson J, Keck P E, Kalish R: Head injury, bipolar disorder, and response to valproate. Compr Psychiatry *29*: 34, 1988.

Post R M, ed.: Emerging perspectives on valproate in affective disorders. J Clin Psychiatry *50*(3, Suppl): 2, 1989.

Wassef A, Watson D J, Morrison P, Bryant S, Flack J: Neuroleptic-valproic acid combination in treatment of psychotic symptoms: A three-case report. J Clin Psychopharmacol *9*: 45, 1989.

30.3 / Electroconvulsive Therapy

Electroconvulsive therapy (ECT) is an effective treatment for patients with depression, mania, and, in some circumstances, schizophrenia. Public misconceptions and biases have caused what is seen by many clinicians as the underutilization of ECT. Because ECT requires the use of electricity and the production of a seizure, many laypersons, patients, and patients' families are understandably frightened by ECT. Perhaps more important, there have been many inaccurate reports of permanent brain damage resulting from ECT. Although these reports have been largely disproved, the specter of ECT-induced brain damage remains. Widespread misinformation and inflammatory articles in the public press may be partly responsible for the skewed distribution of patients who do receive ECT. Patients treated with ECT are usually white and middle-class and are treated most often in private institutions. These epidemiological data suggest that ECT is not equally available as a treatment for poor, nonwhite patients in public institutions. In spite of this, its use is increasing as psychiatrists and others recognize its value as a treatment for severe depression.

The decision to suggest ECT to a patient, as with all treatment recommendations, should be based on both the treatment options and the risk-benefit considerations of ECT. The major alternatives to ECT are usually pharmacotherapy and psychotherapy, both of which have their own risks and benefits. ECT has been an effective treatment; clinicians should not allow their biases to deprive patients of this effective treatment.

HISTORY

In April 1938 in Rome, Ugo Cerletti and Lucio Bini administered the first electroconvulsive treatment. Initially, the treatment was referred to as electroshock therapy (EST) but later became known as ECT. Although Cerletti and Bini had been doing research on animal models of epilepsy, their work with humans was influenced primarily by the work of Lazlo von Meduna in Budapest. In 1934 von Meduna had reported the successful treatment of catatonia and other acute schizophrenic symptoms with pharmacologically induced seizures. Von Meduna began by using intramuscular injections of camphor suspended in oil but quickly switched to intravenously administered pentylenetetrazol (Metrazol). Von Meduna had attempted this treatment method on the basis of two observations. First, it had been clinically observed that schizophrenic symptoms often decreased after a seizure. Seizures were often accidentally or iatrogenically induced in psychiatric patients secondary to withdrawal from medications (e.g., barbiturates). Second, there was the incorrect belief that schizophrenia and epilepsy could not coexist in the same patient. They reasoned, therefore, that the induction of seizures might rid the patient of the schizophrenia. Pentylenetetrazol-induced seizures had been used as an effective treatment for four years before the introduction of electrically induced seizures.

The major problems associated with ECT were the patients' discomfort from the procedure and fractures resulting from the seizures' motor activity. These problems were eventually eliminated by the use of general anesthetics and muscle relaxants during the treatments. Interestingly, an American psychiatrist, A. E. Bennett, had helped develop the method of extracting curare from plant material. Bennett had suggested the use of spinal anesthetics during ECT and the use of curare to paralyze the muscles so as to prevent fractures. In 1951 succinylcholine was introduced and became the most widely used muscle relaxant for ECT. In 1957 hexafluorinated diethylether (Indokolon) was introduced as a new pharmacological means of inducing seizures, administering the compound as a gas. The lack of superiority to ECT, together with the introduction of antidepressant drugs in the 1950s, led to the removal of Indokolon from the market and to a decline in the number of patients given ECT.

CLASSIFICATION

ECT can be conducted with either bilaterally or unilaterally placed electrodes. Bilateral electrodes, which were introduced first, are applied with one stimulating electrode over each hemisphere of the brain. Unilateral ECT involves both electrodes over the nondominant hemisphere. Although controversial, bilateral ECT may produce clinical improvement more rapidly and may be somewhat more effective than unilateral ECT, especially for seriously ill patients. However, bilateral ECT is also more closely associated with adverse cognitive effects. In sum, unilateral ECT is probably as effective as bilateral ECT for most depressed patients and is associated with less severe adverse cognitive effects.

Another way of classifying ECT is by the shape of the electric current, as projected by an oscilloscope. The two major shapes are the sine wave and the brief pulse. The brief-pulse method of stimulus delivery induces a seizure by using less energy than is used in the sine-wave method. The administration of less electrical current is associated with fewer adverse cognitive effects. A reasonable approach may be to initiate treatment with unilateral brief-pulse wave forms that are slightly above the threshold necessary to induce a seizure. If initial signs of clinical improvement are not noted after the first three to six treatments, bilateral or sine-wave treatments may be instituted.

Two other variations in ECT are (1) the threshold-dosage schedule and (2) the placement of the two electrodes within a hemispheric region. Both variations in treatment are aimed at reducing the adverse cognitive effects associated with the treatment. A threshold-dosage schedule adjusts the current for each treatment session to just above the amount needed to produce the seizure. Because the amount of current needed to induce a seizure increases with the number of treatments, the current setting should be low at the initiation of treatment and increased during the course of treatment. Whether threshold-dosage schedules are as effective as constant-dosage schedules and whether they are associated with fewer adverse effects are matters currently not known and under investigation. Unfortunately, varying the placement of the two electrodes within a hemisphere does not seem to be associated with any reduction in adverse cognitive effects.

MECHANISM OF ACTION

The induction of a bilateral generalized seizure is necessary for both the beneficial and the adverse effects of ECT. The two main research approaches to finding the relationship between these seizures and the reduction of psychiatric symptoms have been neurochemical and neurophysiological.

The neurochemical hypotheses suggest that the clinical improvement from a series of ECT sessions results from changes in neurotransmitter function. A series of ECT sessions results in a downregulation of postsynaptic β-adrenergic receptors, the same receptor change observed with long-term antidepressant treatment. The effects of ECT on serotonergic neurons remains a controversial area of research. Various research reports have found an increase in postsynaptic 5-hydroxytryptamine (5HT) receptors, no change in postsynaptic 5HT receptors, or a change in the presynaptic regulation of serotonin release. ECT has also been shown to downregulate the number of muscarinic acetylcholine receptors. Some investigators suggest that the balance among noradrenergic, serotonergic, and cholinergic transmission is important, rather than the change in any individual neurotransmitter system. There is some research evidence that ECT may decrease the synthesis and release of γ-aminobutyric acid (GABA) and increase endogenous opioid activity.

The neurophysiological approach to idiopathic epilepsy has demonstrated that brain regions that are metabolically hyperactive during the seizure are quite hypoactive immediately after the seizure. This change has been demonstrated by positron emission tomography (PET) scans and cerebral blood flow imaging and is consistent with computed topographic maps of brain electrical activity. An observation that perhaps relates the neurochemical and neurophysiological findings is that ECT acts as an anticonvulsant; that is, repeated treatments with ECT raise the patient's seizure threshold.

INDICATIONS

Patients with bipolar disorder account for about 70 percent of patients who receive ECT; patients with schizophrenia account for about 17 percent. The three clearest indications for ECT are depression, mania, and, in some instances, schizophrenia.

Major Depression

The most common indication for ECT is major depression. Most clinicians believe that ECT results in more rapid improvement and at least the same degree of clinical improvement as standard antidepressant pharmacotherapy. Recently, the old studies that compared ECT with pharmacotherapy have been questioned. In spite of that, very few clinicians would doubt that ECT and pharmacotherapy are at least equal in their efficacy and response times.

ECT is effective for both major depression and bipolar disorder. It has long been thought that delusional or psychotic depression is particularly responsive to ECT; however, recent studies have suggested that psychotic depression is no more responsive to ECT than nonpsychotic depression. Nevertheless, since delusional depression is poorly responsive to antidepressant pharmacotherapy alone, ECT should be considered much more often as the first-line treatment for patients with the disorder. Depressions with features of melancholia (such as markedly severe symptoms, psychomotor retardation, early morning awakening, diurnal variation, decreased appetite and weight, and agitation) are thought to be very likely to respond to ECT. Old patients tend to respond to ECT more slowly than young patients. ECT, however, is a treatment for an episode of depression and does not provide prophylaxis. The question of maintenance ECT treatments to sustain clinical remission is an active area of research investigation.

Mania

There is now firm research evidence that ECT is an effective treatment for acute mania. In several studies, ECT has been shown to be as effective as lithium. In fact, some data suggest that ECT results in clinical improvement more quickly than lithium, although the same degree of clinical improvement is reached with both therapies after approximately two months of treatment. However, because the pharmacological management of mania is so effective and because lithium or carbamazepine (Tegretol) is often required for prophylaxis, ECT is most often used only when there is a specific contraindication to the pharmacological approach.

Schizophrenia

Approximately 15 to 20 percent of patients receiving ECT are being treated for schizophrenia. Schizophrenic patients with acute, catatonic, or affective symptoms are the most likely to respond. The efficacy of ECT in such patients is approximately equal to that of antipsychotics; however, ECT is effective in only 5 to 10 percent of patients with chronic schizophrenia.

Other Indications and Considerations

In countries outside the United States, ECT has been reported effective in treating delirium tremens and conversion disorder. ECT is probably the safest treatment in some special circumstances, including pregnancy, the elderly, and the presence of extreme symptoms requiring immediate relief. In medically ill and elderly patients ECT has less cardiotoxicity than currently available pharmacological treatments.

CLINICAL GUIDELINES

Patients and their families are often fearful and apprehensive about ECT; therefore, its beneficial and adverse effects, as well as alternative treatment approaches, must be explained to them. This informed consent process should be documented in the patient's medical record. The use of involuntary ECT is rare today and should be reserved for patients for whom the treatment is urgent and for whom a legally appointed guardian has agreed to its use. Relevant local, state, and federal laws must always be known.

Pretreatment Evaluation

Pretreatment evaluation should include a standard physical examination and medical history, blood and urine chemistries, a chest X-ray, and an electrocardiogram (ECG). Spine and skull X-rays, computed tomography (CT) scan, magnetic resonance imaging (MRI), or electroencephalogram (EEG) may be indicated in special circumstances.

The patient's ongoing medications should be carefully assessed for possible drug interactions with the adjunctive agents used with ECT. Anticholinesterase ophthalmic solutions, monoamine oxidase inhibitors (MAOIs), and lithium may alter succinylcholine metabolism. Hypotensive collapse with reserpine and increased CNS sequelae with lithium have been reported. Sedative-hypnotic drugs and anticonvulsants interfere with the electricity's ability to induce the seizure. The issue of whether to continue a patient's antidepressant or antipsychotic medications during ECT remains unsettled. Most clinicians, however, discontinue antidepressants before administering ECT.

Premedication, Anesthesia, and Muscular Relaxation

Thirty minutes before the actual treatment, an anticholinergic agent (e.g., atropine) is administered to minimize secretions and to create a mild tachycardia, which helps prevent treatment-related bradycardia. Some ECT centers have stopped the routine use of anticholinergics as a premedication. Their use is still indicated in patients on β-adrenergic blocking drugs and in patients with ventricular ectopic beats.

The administration of ECT requires general anesthesia, muscular relaxation or paralysis, and oxygenation. ECT patients are usually given oxygen from the onset of anesthesia to the resumption of adequate spontaneous respiration, except for the brief interval of electrical stimulation.

The depth of anesthesia should be as light as possible, not only to minimize adverse effects but also to avoid elevating the seizure threshold associated with many anesthetics. In most settings, methohexital (Brevital) or thiopental (Pentothal) is used. The former is probably preferable, as it is associated with fewer incidents of ECT-associated cardiac arrhythmias. A typical dose of methohexital for a medium-sized adult is 60 mg, although the range is from 30 to 160 mg.

After the onset of anesthetic effect, usually within a minute, the muscle relaxant is injected intravenously. Succinylcholine, an ultra-fast-acting depolarizing blocking agent, has gained virtually universal acceptance for this purpose. The optimal succinylcholine dose provides enough relaxation to stop most but not all major ictal body movements. A typical starting dose is 60 mg for a medium-sized adult. Because succinylcholine is a depolarizing blocking agent, its action is marked by the presence of muscle fasciculations, which move in a rostrocaudal progression. The disappearance of these movements indicates that maximal relaxation has been achieved. If musculoskeletal or cardiac disease necessitates the use of total relaxation, curare (3 to 6 mg intravenously) may be given several minutes before the anesthetic, along with an increased succinylcholine dosage. If necessary, a peripheral nerve stimulator can be used to ascertain the presence of a complete neuromuscular block.

Because of the short half-life of succinylcholine, the duration of apnea after its administration is generally shorter than the delay in regaining consciousness caused by the anesthesia and the postictal state. In cases of inborn or acquired pseudocholinesterase deficiency and when the metabolism of succinylcholine is disrupted by drug interaction, a prolonged apnea may occur, and the treating physician should always be prepared to manage this problem.

Stimulus Electrode Placement

As mentioned previously, there are two types of electrode placement, bilateral and unilateral. Because unilateral ECT appears to be associated with fewer adverse cognitive effects, some clinicians now routinely use it first and switch to bilateral placement if no significant improvement appears after five or six treatments.

Traditional bilateral ECT places electrodes bifrontotemporally, each with its center approximately one inch above the midpoint of an imaginary line drawn from the tragus of the ear to the external canthus of the eye. With unilateral ECT, one stimulus electrode is typically placed over the nondominant frontotemporal area. Although several locations for the second stimulus electrode have been proposed, placement on the nondominant centroparietal scalp, just lateral to the midline vertex, appears to provide a configuration associated with a relatively low seizure threshold.

Which cerebral hemisphere is dominant can generally be determined by a simple series of performance tasks (e.g., handedness, footedness, stated preference). Right body responses correlate very highly with left brain dominance. If the responses are mixed or if they clearly indicate left body dominance, clinicians should alternate the polarity of unilateral stimulation during successive treatments. They should also monitor the time that it takes for patients to recover consciousness and to answer simple orientation and naming questions. The side of stimulation associated with less rapid recovery and return of function is considered dominant.

Electrical Stimulus

ECT machines operate on either a constant current or a constant voltage. Which type of machine is preferable is not clear. The two main types of stimulation are sine wave and brief pulse. The brief-pulse method can evoke a seizure with about one-third as much energy as that needed with sine-wave stimulation. The brief-pulse method is now the preferred method in the United States. The precise stimulus settings depend on the machine used and the individual patient's seizure threshold. The resultant seizure should last for 30 to 60 seconds. Seizures of more than 60 seconds sometimes indicate that the stimulus intensity is suprathreshold and can be diminished at a later treatment session. At other times, however, even a small decrease in stimulus intensity can lead to no seizure at all. If no seizure is produced after about 20 seconds, a higher intensity setting should be tried. Waiting too long before restimulation may cause the effects of the anesthetic or muscle relaxant agents to wear off.

Induced Seizure

A brief muscular contraction, usually strongest in the jaw and facial muscles, is seen concurrently with the flow of stimulus current, regardless of whether a seizure occurs. The first behavioral sign of the seizure is often a plantar extension, which lasts 10 to 20 seconds and marks the tonic phase. This phase is then followed by rhythmic (i.e., clonic) contractions that decrease in frequency and finally disappear. The tonic phase is marked by high-frequency, sharp EEG activity on which may be superimposed an even higher-frequency muscle artifact. During the clonic phase, bursts of polyspike activity occur simultaneously with the muscular contractions but usually persist for at least a few seconds after the clonic movements stop. There is often some postictal transient suppression and occasionally even an apparent absence of background EEG activity. Such suppression is much less likely to occur with unilateral ECT, particularly over the nonstimulated hemisphere.

It is important to have an objective measure that there actually has been a bilateral generalized seizure after the stimulation. The physician should be able to observe either some evidence of tonic-clonic movements or to detect electrophysiological evidence of seizure activity from the EEG or electromyogram (EMG). Seizures with unilateral ECT are asymmetrical, demonstrating higher ictal EEG amplitude over the stimulated hemisphere. Occasionally, unilateral seizures are induced, and, for this reason, it is important that at least a single pair of EEG electrodes be placed over the contralateral hemisphere when using unilateral ECT.

Prolonged seizures (seizures lasting more than five minutes) or status epilepticus can be terminated either with additional doses of the anesthetic agent or with intravenous diazepam (Valium). Management of such complications should be accompanied by intubation, because the oral airway is insufficient to maintain adequate ventilation over an extended apneic period. In clinical practice a more common problem is difficulty in generating a seizure. This problem can be resolved by using hyperventilation, less anesthetic, a low-intensity stimulus before a high-intensity stimulus, or additional stimulating agents (such as premedication with intravenous caffeine).

Number and Spacing of ECT Treatments

Rather than use a fixed number of treatments, the clinician should determine the length of the ECT course on the basis of clinical response. Patients being treated for depression typically show some signs of improvement after the first few treatments, with maximum responses after 5 to 10 treatments. Depressed patients are usually treated with two to three treatments a week. Manic and schizophrenic patients may require more frequent treatments (sometimes daily) and more treatments (up to as many as 25).

Maintenance Treatment

A short-term course of ECT induces a remission but does not, in itself, prevent relapse. Post-ECT maintenance treatment should always be considered. Generally, this maintenance therapy is pharmacological, as the effectiveness of maintenance ECT has not yet been clarified.

ADVERSE EFFECTS

Contraindications

There are no absolute contraindications to ECT, only situations in which there is increased risk. Patients with intracranial masses and evolving strokes are likely to deteriorate neurologically with ECT because of an ECT-associated transient breakdown of the blood-brain barrier and an increase in intracranial pressure. ECT for such patients should be done only in the presence of measures (e.g., antihypertensives, steroids, and careful monitoring) designed to minimize these potential adverse sequelae. The presence of a recent myocardial infarction increases the risk of further cardiac decompensation with ECT because of the increased cardiovascular demands associated with the procedure. Severe underlying hypertension can be a concern, because ECT markedly increases blood pressure. Bringing the blood pressure into a normal range at the time of each treatment is essential in such cases.

Mortality

The mortality rate with ECT has been variously estimated to be between 1 in 1,000 and 1 in 10,000 patients, roughly the same as the mortality rate associated with brief general anesthesia itself. Death is usually from cardiovascular complications and is most likely to occur in patients whose cardiac status is already compromised.

Central Nervous System Effects

The greatest concern of both professional and lay groups regarding ECT is the potential adverse central nervous system effects, especially memory function. Although memory impairment during a course of treatment is almost the rule, follow-up data indicate that almost all patients are back to their cognitive baseline after six months. Some patients, however, do complain of persistent memory difficulties. The degree of cognitive impairment during treatment and the time it takes to return to baseline are related in part to the amount of electrical stimulation used during the treatment. Some research data have suggested that the degree to which the electrical dosage exceeds the dosage necessary to induce a seizure is correlated with the emergence of adverse effects. This hypothesis is being actively tested in several research centers.

Systemic Effects

Occasional, although usually quite mild, transient cardiac arrhythmias occur during ECT, particularly in patients with existent cardiac disease. These arrhythmias are usually a byproduct of the brief postictal bradycardia and, therefore, can often be prevented by increasing the dosage of anticholinergic premedication. At other times, arrhythmias may be secondary to a tachycardia present during the seizure and may occur as the patient returns to consciousness. The prophylactic administration of propranolol (Inderal) can be useful in such cases. As mentioned earlier, an apneic state may be prolonged if the metabolism of succinylcholine is impaired. Toxic or allergic reactions to the pharmacological agents used in the ECT procedures have rarely been reported.

References

Fox H A, Rosen A, Campbell R J: Are brief pulse and sine wave ECT equally efficient? J Clin Psychiatry *50*: 432, 1989.

King B H, Liston E H: Proposals for the mechanism of action of convulsive therapy: A synthesis. Biol Psychiatry *27*: 76, 1990.

Klein D F, ed.: Electroconvulsive therapy. Neuropsychopharmacology *3*: 73, 1990.

Pande A C, Krugler T, Haskett R F, Greden J F, Grunhaus L J: Predictors of response to electroconvulsive therapy in major depressive disorder. Biol Psychiatry *24*: 91, 1988.

Rifkin A: ECT versus tricyclic antidepressants in depression: A review of the evidence. J Clin Psychiatry *49*: 3, 1988.

Sackheim H A, Decina P, Kanzler M, Kerr B, Malitz S: Effects of electrode placement on the efficacy of titrated, low-dose ECT. Am J Psychiatry *144*: 1449, 1987.

Schoups A A, Beeckman N, Lauwers M-C, De Potter W P: Evaluation of the role of pre- and postsynaptic serotonergic receptors in electroconvulsive shock therapy. Biol Psychiatry *23*: 807, 1988.

Small J G, Klapper M H, Kellams J J, Miller M J, Milstein V, Sharpley P H, Small I F: Electroconvulsive treatment compared with lithium in the management of manic states. Arch Gen Psychiatry *45*: 727, 1988.

Thienhaus O J, Margletta S, Bennet J A: A study of the clinical efficacy of maintenance ECT. J Clin Psychiatry *51*: 141, 1990.

Thompson J W, Blaine J D: Use of ECT in the United States in 1975 and 1980. Am J Psychiatry *144*: 557, 1987.

30.4 / Other Organic Therapies

LIGHT THERAPY

The major indication for light therapy is seasonal affective disorder (SAD), also called seasonal pattern mood disorder, a type of major depressive episode characterized by symptoms that appear on a seasonal basis, usually in the fall and winter. In light therapy, also called phototherapy, the patient is exposed to a bright artificial light source on a daily basis.

Mechanism of Action

Human circadian rhythms result from the entrainment of endogenous pacemakers by exogenous *zeitgebers*. The suprachiasmatic nucleus of the hypothalamus is thought to be the major endogenous pacemaker; the light-dark cycle is thought to be the major exogenous *zeitgeber*. The rhythms of the body exhibit a biological feature called a *phase response curve*, which is based on a 24-hour unit. Perturbations, such as exposure to light, have a differential effect on bodily rhythms (e.g., sleep, hormone secretion), depending on what time of the day, hence where on the phase response curve, the perturbation is administered. Exposure to light in the morning results in a phase advance—that is, rhythms are shifted to an earlier time; exposure to light in the evening results in a phase delay—that is, rhythms are shifted to a later time. Therefore, the entrainment of the endogenous pacemakers by light is the result of a phase advance at dawn and a phase delay at dusk. Melatonin is secreted by the pineal gland during the night. It is stopped by exposure to light during the night but is not stimulated by exposure to darkness during the day.

More than 25 controlled studies have shown that light therapy is effective, although it is not known how it works. The most accepted theory is that exposure to bright artificial light in the morning causes a phase advance of biological rhythms that effectively treats the delayed circadian rhythms that are associated with SAD. This hypothesis is supported by the observations of several investigators that non-SAD types of depression do not appear to be responsive to phototherapy. The initial theory that light exposure worked by affecting melatonin secretion has not been supported by subsequent experiments. It is also quite certain that the light must be bright to achieve therapeutic effects; exposure to dim light has not been effective. Most studies support the notion that two hours of exposure is more effective than 30 minutes. It is undetermined whether light should be administered in the morning, in the evening, or at both times to achieve maximal benefit. Administration of light in the morning fits with the theoretical mechanism of action, and, in fact, a majority of studies have found that morning light is more effective than evening light. It is currently known that full-spectrum light is effective, whereas narrow-spectrum light is ineffective. It is not known, however, whether an intermediate spectrum of light would be effective. Studies are underway in several research centers to determine whether exposure to the ultraviolet light in full-spectrum light is necessary for effective treatment, since exposure to ultraviolet light can have harmful effects on the eyes and skin.

Indications

The major indication for light therapy is SAD, seen predominantly (80 percent) in women. The mean age of presentation is 40, although this age may decrease with better recognition of the disorder. The symptoms usually appear during the winter and remit spontaneously in the spring, although sometimes symptoms appear in summer. The most common symptoms include depression, fatigue, hypersomnia, hyperphagia, carbohydrate craving, irritability, and interpersonal difficulties. One-third to one-half of patients with seasonal pattern mood disorder have not previously sought psychiatric help. The remainder have most often been previously classified as having a mood disorder. Over 50 percent of patients with SAD have a first-degree relative with a mood disorder. There is some recent evidence that persons with mild, subsyndromal symptoms of SAD may also experience some relief with phototherapy.

Clinical Guidelines

The treatment requires exposure to bright light (2,500 lux) that is approximately 200 times brighter than usual indoor lighting. The initial experiments exposed patients to the light for two to three hours before dawn and, possibly, an additional two to three hours after dusk every day. The patients were instructed not to look directly into the light but to glance at it only occasionally. Patients usually respond after two to four days of treatment and relapse in two to four days after the treatment is stopped. The only adverse effects reported with any frequency are irritability, headache, and eye strain. These adverse effects can usually be managed by reducing the length of time that the patient is exposed to the light.

SLEEP DEPRIVATION AND ALTERATIONS OF SLEEP SCHEDULES

One night's sleep deprivation results in a dramatic reduction of depressive symptoms in approximately 60 percent of all patients with depressive disorders. Unfortunately, the beneficial effects last only one day. The depressive symptoms can often be brought back even more quickly if the patient takes even a short nap after the night of sleep deprivation. This finding has caused some researchers to hypothesize that there may be some sleep-related depressogenic process that is temporarily aborted by the sleep deprivation. Some studies have reported that preventing only rapid eye movement (REM) sleep has the same effects as preventing all sleep, causing some researchers to hypothesize that a REM-related process may be related to maintaining or even causing depression.

It has also been shown that phase advancing the sleep cycle—that is, going to bed and waking up earlier—may have antidepressant effects in some depressed patients, especially when used as an adjuvant to pharmacotherapy. In contrast to the single-day improvement associated with sleep deprivation, the beneficial effects from sleep phase advance sometimes last for up to one week.

DRUG-ASSISTED INTERVIEWING

To facilitate gathering information during a psychiatric interview, some psychiatrists advocate drug-assisted interviewing. The common use of an intravenous injection of sodium amobarbital (Amytal) led to the popular name of "Amytal interview" for this technique. Narcotherapy or narcoanalysis consists of a series of drug-assisted psychotherapy sessions. Both sedatives (e.g., barbiturates, benzodiazepines) and stimulants (e.g., methylphenidate [Ritalin]) have been used. Narcotherapy was thought to benefit patients by allowing them to experience the catharsis of having a repressed memory or thought brought to conscious awareness. Although narcotherapy is rarely used in modern psychiatry, there has been renewed interest in it. Some noted psychiatrists have proposed that methylenedioxymethamphetamine (MDMA, ecstasy) may be beneficial when used as an agent for drug-assisted psychotherapy.

Indications

Although there is much literature on drug-assisted interviewing, it consists mainly of uncontrolled studies and anecdotal reports, thus making difficult a definitive statement about its indications. Furthermore, several controlled trials have shown that the use of drugs does not guarantee that patients will tell the truth, in spite of the popular misconception that sodium amobarbital is a truth serum. A few studies have shown, in fact, that drug-assisted interviews are no better at eliciting information than an empathic interviewer, hypnosis, or the administration of a placebo.

The most common reasons for drug-assisted interviews in modern practice are uninformative or mute patients, catatonia, and supposed conversion disorders. Although drug-assisted interviews often elicit information sooner, there is no evidence that this technique has a positive effect on the therapeutic outcome. Patients may be silent because of excessive anxiety about recounting a traumatic event (e.g., rape, accident), and drug-assisted interviews have been used in such cases. But hypnosis, daytime sedation, an empathic and supportive approach, and time also help elicit information without the risks of drug-assisted interviewing.

Mute patients with a psychiatric disorder may have catatonic schizophrenia or a conversion disorder or be malingering. Barbiturates or benzodiazepines help in temporarily activating catatonic patients; therefore, catatonic schizophrenia may be a reasonable indication for using a drug-assisted interview. Patients with any type of conversion disorder or malingering may or may not improve during a drug-assisted interview. The commonly held but controversial belief is that a functional disorder improves during a drug-assisted interview, whereas an organic disorder does not improve or even worsens. If patients do improve, there is no indication that this technique facilitated their treatment; and, if they do not improve or even worsen, the information gained from the interview is of little help in guiding the patients' treatment.

Another indication for drug-assisted interviewing is the differential diagnosis of confusion, based on the assumption that functional confusion will clear during the procedure and that organic confusion will not. False positives occur when a confused patient is withdrawing from alcohol or barbiturates and when a patient has an epileptic disorder. False negatives occur when the interviewer uses too much drug and sometimes when the patient has a conversion disorder or is a malingerer. Another proposed indication for drug-assisted interviewing is to differentiate between schizophrenia and depression. It had been thought that, when given sodium amobarbital, schizophrenic patients would recall more bizarre material, and depressed patients would recall more depressed material. This hypothesis has not been confirmed in controlled studies. Sodium amobarbital has also been suggested as an adjuvant in supportive therapy. In this procedure the drug is used to reinforce a therapeutic suggestion (e.g., you will stop smoking). However, hypnosis has been found to be more effective in this regard. Furthermore, muscle relaxation has been found to be more powerful than sodium amobarbital as an adjuvant in behavior therapy.

Clinical Guidelines

A 10 percent solution of sodium amobarbital is administered at a rate of about 0.5 to 1.0 mL a minute. The rate and the total dose should be adjusted for each patient. The total dose may vary between 0.25 and 0.5 g, although occasionally some patients need up to 1 g. The end point is a state of mild sedation but not sleep. The benzodiazepines (e.g., diazepam [Valium]) are just as effective and less dangerous than the barbiturates.

Barbiturates should not be given to patients with liver, renal, and cardiopulmonary diseases or to patients with porphyria and a history of sedative abuse. Patients may have allergic reactions or respiratory suppression during barbiturate interviews, and the clinician must be prepared for both these possibilities. Furthermore, the use of what patients may perceive as a truth serum may increase their paranoia and interfere with transference.

PSYCHOSURGERY

Psychosurgery involves surgical modification of the brain with the goal of reducing the symptoms of the most severely ill psychiatric patients who have not responded adequately to less radical treatments. Psychosurgical procedures lesion specific brain regions (e.g., lobotomies, cingulotomies) or their connecting tracts (e.g., tractotomies, leukotomies). Psychosurgical techniques are also used in the treatment of neurological disorders, such as epilepsy and chronic pain syndromes.

History

In 1935, after the demonstration by Jacobsen and Fulton at Yale University that frontal lobe ablation in a monkey had a calming effect, Moniz and Lima, working in Portugal, severed frontal lobe white matter in 20 psychotic patients and reported a decrease in their tension and psychotic symptoms. In 1936 Freeman and Watts at George Washington University introduced the psychosurgical technique of prefrontal lobotomy to the United States. Although earlier procedures required burr holes or other exposure of the brain, Freeman eventually developed the technique of transorbital leukotomy, which involved the introduction and lateral movement of a sharp instrument (actually an ice pick) through the eye socket as a method of sectioning the white matter of the frontal lobes. By the late 1940s psychosurgery was being performed worldwide, and an estimated 5,000 patients were being operated on each year. In 1949 Egas Moniz won the Nobel Prize for his work in developing psychosurgical techniques. Shortly thereafter, the introduction of antipsychotic drugs and the increasing public concern about the ethics of psychosurgery led to a near abandonment of these techniques for the treatment of psychiatric patients, although psychosurgical approaches to pain and epilepsy continued to be used. The interest in psychosurgical approaches to psychiatric disorders has only recently been rekindled. This renewed interest is based on a number of factors, including much improved techniques that allow the neurosurgeon to make more exact stereotactically placed lesions, better preoperative diagnoses, more comprehensive preoperative and postoperative psychological assessments, and more complete follow-up data.

Modern Psychosurgical Techniques

Stereotactic neurosurgical equipment now allows the neurosurgeon to place discrete lesions in the brain. Radioactive implants, cryoprobes, electrical coagulation, proton beams, and ultrasonic waves are used to make the actual lesion. Bilateral cingulotomies, the most frequently performed procedure for the treatment of depression, affect frontolimbic communication, thus, presumably, interrupting the communication of abnormal emotions.

Indications

The major indication for psychosurgery is the presence of a debilitating, chronic psychiatric disorder that has not responded to any other treatment. A reasonable guideline is that the disorder should have been present for five years, during which a wide variety of alternative treatment approaches were attempted. Chronic intractable depression and, possibly, obsessive-compulsive disorder are the two disorders most responsive to psychosurgery. The presence of vegetative symptoms and marked anxiety further increases the likelihood of success. Whether psychosurgery is a reasonable treatment for intractable and extreme aggression is still controversial. Psychosurgery is not indicated for the treatment of schizophrenia, and the data regarding mania are controversial.

Therapeutic and Adverse Effects

When patients are carefully selected, between 50 and 70 percent have significant therapeutic improvement with psychosurgery. Fewer than 3 percent become worse. Continued improvement is often noted for one to two years after surgery, and patients are often more responsive than they were before psychosurgery to traditional pharmacological and behavioral treatment approaches. Postoperative seizures are present in fewer than 1 percent of patients, and these are usually controlled with diphenylhydantoin. As measured by intelligence quotient (I.Q.) scores, cognitive abilities improve after surgery, probably because of an increased ability to attend to cognitive tasks. Undesired changes in personality have not been noted with the modern limited procedures.

PLACEBOS

Placebos are substances that have no known pharmacological activity. Although it is usually thought that placebos act through suggestion, rather than biological action, this idea is based on an artificial distinction between the mind and the body. Virtually every treatment modality is accompanied by poorly understood factors affecting its outcome (e.g., the taste of a medicine, emotional response to a physician). Indeed, these poorly understood factors and the effects of placebos might better be called nonspecific therapeutic factors. For example, it has recently been demonstrated that naloxone (Narcan), an opioid antagonist, can block the analgesic effects of a placebo, thus suggesting that a release of endogenous opioids may explain some placebo effects.

Chronic treatment with placebos should never be undertaken when patients have clearly stated an objection to such treatment. Furthermore, deceptive treatment with placebos seriously undermines the patients' confidence in their physicians. Finally, placebos should never be used when an effective therapy is available, as placebos can lead to both a dependence on pills and various adverse effects.

ACUPUNCTURE AND ACUPRESSURE

An ancient Chinese treatment, acupuncture is the stimulation of specific points on the body with electrical stimulation or the twisting of a needle. Acupressure is the stimulation of these same points with pressure; however, acupressure was not a legitimate part of traditional Chinese medicine. The stimulation of specific points is associated with the relief of certain symptoms and is identified with particular organs. Many Chinese doctors have reported therapeutic success with these treatments in combination with herbal treatment (given orally, topically, or intradermally) for a variety of disorders, including psychiatric disorders. Several American investigators have reported that acupuncture is an effective treatment for some patients with depression or chemical addictions (e.g., nicotine, caffeine, cocaine, heroin). Although it is difficult to approach these Eastern treatments with a Western mind, it is also true that history has demonstrated that many ancient remedies have a firm biological basis.

ORTHOMOLECULAR THERAPY

Megavitamin therapy is treatment with large doses of niacin, ascorbic acid, pyridoxine, folic acid, vitamin B_{12}, and various minerals. Special diets and hormone treatments are often part of these treatment protocols as well. Uncontrolled reports of successful treatment of schizophrenia with niacin have not been replicated in controlled, collaborative studies. Despite claims to the contrary, megavitamin and diet therapies currently have no proved clinical use in psychiatry. However, a balanced diet reasonably supplemented with vitamins is a good prescription for all patients and physicians.

HISTORICAL TREATMENTS

A variety of treatments were used before the introduction of effective pharmacological agents. Although most never underwent controlled therapeutic trials, many clinicians report that the treatments were, in fact, quite effective. But because most of them were associated with unpleasant or dangerous adverse effects, they have been virtually supplanted by pharmacotherapy.

Subcoma Insulin Therapy

Psychiatrists used to inject small doses of insulin to induce mild hypoglycemia and the resultant sedative effects. Because of the possible complications of this treatment and the introduction of sedating drugs, this treatment has been abandoned.

Coma Therapy

Insulin coma therapy was introduced in 1933 by Manfred Sakel after his observation that schizophrenic patients who went into coma appeared to have less severe psychiatric symptoms after the coma. Insulin was used to induce a comatose state lasting 15 to 60 minutes. The risk of death and intellectual impairment and the introduction of antipsychotic drugs led to the abandonment of this treatment in the United States.

Atropine sulfate was first used in 1950 to induce coma in psychiatric patients. The atropine-induced comas lasted for six to eight hours, and the patients took warm and cold showers after awakening. Atropine coma is no longer used in the United States.

Carbon Dioxide Therapy

Carbon dioxide therapy was first used in 1929 and involved having the patient inhale carbon dioxide, resulting in an abreaction with severe motor excitement after removing the breathing mask. This treatment was used principally for neurotic patients, and there was doubt even when it was in use that the treatment was effective. Carbon dioxide therapy is no longer used in the United States.

Electrosleep Therapy

Electrosleep therapy involves applying a low level of current through electrodes applied to the patient's head. The patient usually feels a tingling sensation at the sites of electrode placement, but sleep is not necessarily induced. This treatment is applied to a wide variety of disorders, with mixed reports of efficacy, but it is not used in the United States.

Continuous Sleep Treatment

Continuous sleep treatment is a symptomatic method of treatment in which the patient is sedated with any of a variety of drugs to induce 20 hours of sleep a day, sometimes for as long as three weeks for severely agitated patients. Klaesi introduced the name in 1922 and used barbiturates to obtain a fairly deep narcosis. This treatment is not used in the United States.

References

Ballantine H T, Bouckoms A J, Thomas E K, Giriunas I E: Treatment of psychiatric illness by stereotactic cingulotomy. Biol Psychiatry *22*: 807, 1987.

Blehar M C, Rosenthal N E: Seasonal affective disorders and phototherapy. Arch Gen Psychiatry *46*: 469, 1989.

Brody H: The lie that heals: The ethics of giving placebos. Ann Intern Med *97*: 112, 1982.

Czeisler C A, Kronauer R E, Allan J S, Duffy J F, Jewett M E, Brown E

N, Ronda J M: Bright light induction of strong (Type 0) resetting of the human circardian pacemaker. Science *244*: 1328, 1989.

Dysken M W, Chang S S, Casper R C: Barbiturate-facilitated interviewing. Biol Psychiatry *14*: 421, 1979.

Kasper S, Rogers S L B, Yancey A, Schulz P M, Skwerer R G, Rosenthal N E: Phototherapy in individuals with and without subsyndromal seasonal affective disorder. Arch Gen Psychiatry *46*: 837, 1989.

Roy-Byrne P P, Uhde T W, Post R M: Effects of one night's sleep deprivation on mood and behavior in panic disorder. Arch Gen Psychiatry *43*: 895, 1986.

Sachdev P, Smith J S, Matheson J: Is psychosurgery antimanic? Biol Psychiatry *27*: 363, 1990.

Sack D A, Nurnberger J, Rosenthal N E: Potentiation of antidepressant medications by phase advance of the sleep-wake cycle. Am J Psychiatry *142*: 606, 1985.

Sack R L, Lewy A J, White D M, Singer C M, Fireman M J, Vandiver R: Morning vs evening light treatment for winter depression. Arch Gen Psychiatry *47*: 343, 1990.

Tippin J, Henn F A: Modified leukotomy in the treatment of intractable obsessional neurosis. Am J Psychiatry *139*: 1601, 1982.

Wu J C, Bunney W C: The biological basis of an antidepressant response to sleep deprivation and relapse: Review and hypothesis. Am J Psychiatry *147*: 14, 1990.

31

Child Psychiatry: Assessment, Examination, and Psychological Testing

The psychiatric assessment of a child, as with an adult, is aimed at revealing psychopathology and psychodynamics. Toward these ends, the examiner must be familiar with normal development, because behaviors that are normal at a young age can be deviant later on. Because normal immaturities prevent the child from detailing a psychiatric history, data must be sought from parents, guardians, teachers, and others.

There are currently three types of methods for the psychiatric assessment of children: (1) clinical interviews, (2) structured interviews using rating scales and questionnaires, and (3) standardized tests.

ASSESSMENT

Interview with Parents or Guardians

The first step in the psychiatric examination of a child is an interview with the child's parents or caretakers; however, adolescents should be given the choice of being seen first or being present during the initial interview with their parents. During the interview the onset, duration, and severity of the problem should be clarified. Any prior evaluations should be reviewed, and a detailed developmental history should be taken, as well as a family history of psychiatric (including cognitive and developmental) problems.

Historical or factual data (e.g., age, sex, race, legal status, birth history information, developmental milestones, previous illnesses) are best gathered by asking specific questions, whereas data about feelings and relationships are best elicited by an open-ended and indirect approach. Parents frequently recall historical dates incorrectly, although they may offer comparisons of their children (e.g., "David was much slower in getting toilet trained than Susan was.") To ensure the accuracy of the historical information, the examiner should gather data from as many objective sources as possible (e.g., school reports, hospital records, previous test reports) and from various observers (e.g., mother, father, siblings). Under special circumstances of child abuse, neglect, broken home, physical or mental illness, or institutionalization, the information provided by adults other than the child's parents is important to the examination and assessment.

Table 31-1 is a suggested outline for a complete assessment of the child, including the interview with parents and a history-taking guide.

Interview and Observation of the Child or Adolescent

The clinician's strategy and manner during the interview should be flexible and adjusted to the child's age, developmental stage, and the types of presenting problems. The clinician, however, has to make every effort to provide children with a comfortable emotional and physical setting in which they can easily interact to facilitate the children's verbal expressions and the interviewer's observations.

Clinical interviews with infants and young children. The parents of infants should be present to share in the observation and to learn. The parents' presence also allows the examiner to observe the parent–child interactions. An evaluation of the parents' child-rearing skills is particularly important to the assessment of an infant. Information should be gathered about the parents' physical health, self-esteem, competence, flexibility, and ability to provide a safe, nurturing, and appropriately stimulating environment for the child. Particular attention has to be paid to the parents' perception of and sensitivity to the infant's needs; the identification of the infant's temperamental characteristics to determine the goodness of fit between parent and child; the parents' ability to respond rapidly to the infant's expressed needs; the quality of play between parent and infant; and the amount of support, encouragement, and assistance (scaffolding) that the parent can provide for the child. The parents' ability to provide a stimulus shelter to prevent the child from being overwhelmed should also be evaluated. Observation of infants under the age of 18 months in spontaneous free play, using such games as peek-a-boo and pat-a-cake, should immediately follow the clinical interview. Children between 18 months and 3 years of age can participate more readily in regular unstructured play interviews. The play items should look reasonably realistic, as children at this age have a limited capacity for abstraction and symbolic play. A more thorough and detailed assessment requires the use of standardized developmental scales and psychological tests.

Clinical interviews with school-age children. Interviews with school-age children usually require a minimum of 45 to 60 minutes for each session. The examination room should be open and spacious enough to allow the physical activity required in the assessment but not so large as to reduce a reasonably intimate contact between the examiner and the child. Toys and materials should be available to suit children of different ages, sexes, and interests. Only necessary and appropriate play items should be made available, as too great a choice may be overstimulating or distracting, and too little choice may fail to accommodate important fantasies or interests.

The unstructured play sessions help the examiner make

Table 31-1
Outline for Interview with Parents

Child's history:
- Parents' main concerns about the child (chief complaint or presenting problem)
- Course of symptoms and current adjustment
- Past developmental, medical, social, and psychological history, including peer and school adjustments
- Child's relationships with siblings and each parent

Parents' marital history

Parents' personal history:
- Parents' primary family, past and present
- School and vocational adjustment
- Social and avocational interests and activities
- Review of any specific medical or psychological problems suffered by either parent

Other family problems:
- Other children
- Previous marriages
- In-laws
- Neighbors

Parents' opinions about possible causes and a review of their feelings about various treatments that may be proposed

Table based on J E Simmons: *The Psychiatric Examination of Children.* Lea & Febiger, Philadelphia, 1969, with permission.

further inferences about the child's intrapsychic life, such as wishes, fears, impulses, conflicts, defenses, affects, and capacity to relate to others. At the beginning of the interview, the clinician should ask the child what his or her understanding is of the reason for the visit, and the clinician should tell the child his or her own understanding. Next, the clinician should tell the child what will take place in the interview. The clinician should avoid taking notes during the interview, as it may not only inhibit the child but also interfere with the clinician's ability to observe. Leading questions or any kind of demanding interrogation is unproductive and may inhibit the play and communication. Open-ended questions are better than leading questions or questions that require only a single-word answer.

Clinical interviews with adolescents. Interviews with adolescents require an even more open and explicit approach. The clinician may tell the adolescent of his or her parents' having come to see the clinician to discuss their concerns, but the clinician wants to learn directly the adolescent's views of what his or her parents have said or what the problem is. The clinician should show genuine interest, acceptance, and candor and give the adolescent undivided and uninterrupted attention. If the adolescent talks in terms of a third person, the clinician should answer matter-of-factly, in the same third-person way.

Many adolescents are rejecting, even hostile, on the first few visits. The clinician should be patient and not jump to any conclusions. This rejection is often a test of how much the clinician can be trusted, a defense against anxiety, or a transference phenomenon. Silence should not be allowed to continue for too long, however, as it may start a power game to see who can hold out longer. Similarly, it is important not to be rigid about the length of the interview session.

Eventually, the clinician must inquire about such sensitive areas as suicidal thoughts, hallucinations, use of drugs, and sexual experiences. This should be done in a matter-of-fact, straightforward manner.

Limit setting. At the outset the clinician must set certain limits so as to avoid amplifying anxiety and guilt feelings. Therefore, destructive or unduly regressive behavior may have to be restrained—directly but compassionately—at the beginning of the interview.

Confidentiality. In child psychiatric practice, the younger the child, the more information will have to be shared between the psychiatrist and the parents as to what the child has said and done. Latency-age and preadolescent children, as well as adolescents, can rightfully expect the therapist to keep confidential some private information (e.g., masturbatory fantasies, sexual and aggressive urges and actions, and oedipal wishes). Absolute confidentiality is unrealistic with young children, but a reasonably trusting relationship can be achieved with them. Whenever possible and appropriate, the child and the adolescent should be informed of the extent or limits of confidentiality, particularly in the case of a court-referred or court-remanded psychiatric evaluation.

Countertransference. During clinical interviews with children and adolescents, the clinician should be aware of possible countertransference and transference phenomena. A predisposition to side with either the child or the parents can interfere with needed objectivity. Such problems as defiance and sexual conflicts in young patients can arouse strong countertransference feelings in the interviewer.

Mental Status Examination

How and what the child plays, says, and does constitute the raw data for the mental status examination. An outline of the mental status examination is presented in Table 31-2.

Another useful organizing principle is to keep in mind the major categories of psychopathology that should be covered. A list of such categories is shown in Table 31-3.

The presenting symptoms and history may indicate important areas for close attention. Clinicians should use their clinical judgment about what they should look for and how fast and in what detail they should proceed. They should also consider, when assessing a response, the age and developmental level of the infant, child, or adolescent.

Physical appearance. The child's size, stature, head size, physical stigmata, bruising, nutritional state, level of anxiety—manifested by hyperalertness and other behavioral signs—attention span, gait, dress, and conflicts are expressed in attitudes, behavior, dress, and mannerisms.

Table 31-2
Mental Status Examination

Outline	
1. Physical appearance	10. Quality of thinking and perception
2. Separation	11. Fantasies and inferred conflicts
3. Manner of relating	12. Affects
4. Orientation to time, place, and person	13. Object relations
5. Central nervous system functions	14. Drive behavior
6. Reading and writing	15. Defense organization
7. Speech and language	16. Judgment and insight
8. Intelligence	17. Self-esteem
9. Memory	18. Adaptive capacities
	19. Positive attributes

Table 31-3
Categories of Psychopathology

Developmental delay
Organic brain dysfunction
Thought disorder
Anxiety and neurotic conflict
Mood disorder
Temperament and personality (character) problems
Psychophysiological disorder
Mental retardation
Reaction to unfavorable environment

Separation. Too much ease in separating may indicate superficial relationships associated with frequent separations or maternal deprivation. Difficulty in separating may indicate an ambivalent parent-child relationship.

Manner of relating. Most children relate to the interviewer cautiously at first. Indiscriminate friendliness and shallow relatedness may indicate deprivation or child abuse. Autistic children appear to look through people or may avoid eye contact altogether.

Orientation to time, place, and person. Impairments in time, place, and person indicate organic brain factors, low intelligence, anxiety, or a thought disorder.

Central nervous system functions. Soft (nonfocal) neurological signs in such areas as speech, gross or fine motor coordination, right-left discrimination, decreased muscle tone, strabismus, nystagmus, asymmetry of muscle tone or reflexes, laterality, handedness, footedness, tremors, eye tracking, motor overflow, and activity level should be explored.

Reading and writing. Some children may struggle to read or write and may spell poorly. At the same time, many normal first-graders (6-year-olds) reverse letters. Clinicians should look for signs of general reading backwardness, with a broadly retarded reading level (2 to 2.5 years below the predicted level) and specific reading retardation. Children exhibiting reading and writing disorders should be evaluated further by means of standardized tests.

Speech and language. Children who do not use words by 18 months or phrases by 2.5 to 3 years but who have a history of normal babbling and who understand commands and can use and respond to nonverbal cues are probably developing normally. However, delays beyond these ages or disturbances in these and other forms of communication should be evaluated further.

Intelligence. An approximate idea of the child's intelligence may be assessed by his or her general vocabulary, responsiveness, level of comprehension and curiosity, drawing ability, and richness of fantasy and may be confirmed by a standardized intelligence test.

Memory. Between ages 6 and 8, normal children can count five digits forward and two or three digits backward; at age 10, they can count six digits forward and four digits backward. Minor difficulties may simply reflect anxiety. But very poor performance on the digit-span test may indicate brain damage (particularly left-hemisphere damage) or mental retardation. The child should also be able to repeat three items five minutes after they have been presented.

Quality of thinking and perception. Three major clinical dimensions in the thinking process should be evaluated: actual thought content, speed of thinking, and ease of flow. A variation in any of these dimensions may be of such a degree and duration as to constitute a thought disorder. In 5- to 8-year-old children, deviances in these areas are particularly difficult to evaluate, given the presence of normative cognitive immaturities.

Hallucinations in childhood are almost always pathological and may also be secondary to drug intoxication, seizure disorder, metabolic disorder, infection, immaturity, stress, anxiety, mood disorder, and schizophrenia.

Fantasies and inferred conflicts. Fantasies and inferred conflicts can be assessed by direct questioning about the child's dreams, drawings, doodles, or spontaneous play.

Affects. The interviewer should observe affects such as anxiety, depression, apathy, guilt, and anger. Suicidal risk may be part of a major depression. Whenever suicidal ideation is suspected, suicidal fantasies, actions, the presence or absence of previous suicidal behavior, motivation, the child's experiences and concept of death, nature of depression, other affects, and the family and environmental situations should be carefully explored.

Object relations. The interviewer may discuss the child's relations with family, peers, and teachers.

Drive behavior. Basic drive behavior in sexual and aggressive areas may be explored.

Defense organization. Defense organization may be studied by assessing the presence or absence of phobias, obsessive-compulsive behavior, denial, and reaction formation.

Judgment and insight. To assess the child's judgment and insight, the examiner should explore the following: what the child thinks caused his or her problem, how upset the child appears to be about the problem, what the child thinks may help solve the problem, and how the child thinks the clinician can help.

Self-esteem. The child who has low self-esteem often makes such remarks as, "I can't do that" or "I am no good at all."

Adaptive capacities. The child may be adept at many different kinds of problem-solving activities.

Positive attributes. Positive attributes include physical health, attractive appearance, normal height and weight, normal vision and hearing, even temperament, normal intelligence, appropriate emotional responses without extreme mood swings, recognition of feelings and fantasies, good command of language and capacity to verbalize thoughts and feelings, good academic and social performance at school, age-appropriate interests, and special talents.

DIAGNOSIS AND CLASSIFICATION

According to David Shaffer, a child can be said to have a psychiatric disorder when behavior or emotions interfere with the child's educational or social opportunities or when they cause the child or those who care for or live with the child sustained or repeated distress. Most psychiatrically disturbed children fall into one of the following general groups:

1. Children whose behavior does not conform to social norms and is troublesome to others (the disruptive behavior or conduct disorders).
2. Children who experience repeated and excessive depression, anxiety, or other states of personal distress (sometimes termed the internalizing or emotional disorders).
3. Children whose cognitive or neuromotor development is not proceeding normally (the developmental disorders).

A few children or adolescents present with specific symptom patterns, such as autistic disorder, anorexia nervosa, Tourette's disorder, and obsessive-compulsive disorder. Although it is not unusual for the same child to have symptoms of more than one of these three broad groups of disorders, the disorders themselves are in many respects quite distinct, differing from one another not only in symptoms but also in different demographic characteristics, prognoses, and family backgrounds. It is no longer reasonable, therefore, to refer to a generally disturbed child; instead, a behaviorally appropriate diagnosis is required.

The Committee on Child Psychiatry of the Group for the Advancement of Psychiatry (GAP) proposed a diagnostic classification that divides childhood and adolescent disorders into 10 major diagnostic categories (Table 31-4). It is the first system to include healthy responses as a diagnostic category. This system points out the need to recognize when signs that may cause concern are manifestations of adaptation and do not indicate failure to maintain mental growth. The first six categories, arranged more or less in ascending order of seriousness, deal essentially with the total personality, following as closely as possible the unitary view underlying the system. In contrast, the next three categories reflect end organ or organ system responses, even though the personalities of children with such disorders are almost always significantly involved.

Anna Freud's system of classification divides the psychiatric disorders of children into two major groups (Table 31-5). Her definitions are more narrowly defined than those of the GAP system. For Anna Freud, symptoms were only those manifestations of disorder that result from the failure of an essential step in mental development to take place at the normal time. She defined symptoms in terms of the specific step that failed and the point at which the child's development took its pathological turn.

In the revised third edition of *Diagnostic and Statistical Manual of Mental Disorders* (DSM-III-R), all childhood disorders are grouped under the heading of disorders usually first evident in infancy, childhood, or adolescence. These disorders include such categories as developmental disorders, disruptive behavior disorders, and anxiety disorders of childhood or adolescence.

Table 31-4
Group for the Advancement of Psychiatry Classification

1. Healthy responses
2. Reactive disorders
3. Developmental deviations
4. Psychoneurotic disorders
5. Personality disorders
6. Psychotic disorders
7. Psychosomatic disorders
8. Brain syndromes
9. Mental retardation
10. Other disorders

Table based on Group for the Advancement of Psychiatry: *Psychopathological Disorders in Childhood*, Report 62. Group for the Advancement of Psychiatry, New York, 1966, with permission.

Table 31-5
Anna Freud's System of Classification

Symptoms

Symptoms resulting from initial nondifferentiation between somatic and psychological processes: psychosomatics

Symptoms resulting from compromise formation between id and ego: neurotic symptoms

Symptoms resulting from the irruption of id derivatives into the ego: psychotic or delinquent symptoms if complete irruption, borderline symptoms if partial irruption

Symptoms resulting from changes in the libido economy or direction of cathexis: symptoms of some personality disorders and hypochondriasis

Symptoms resulting from changes in the quality or direction of aggression: inhibited or destructive symptoms

Symptoms resulting from undefended regressions: infantile symptoms

Symptoms resulting from organic causes

Other signs of disturbance and other reasons for a child's referral

Fears and anxieties

Delays and failures in development

School failures

Failures in social adaptation

Aches and pains

DEVELOPMENTAL AND PSYCHOLOGICAL TESTING

Psychological testing may not always be necessary for an effective examination. However, it is valuable in determining an infant's or child's developmental status, level of intelligence, and revelation of inner states otherwise obscured by defenses or inhibitions in communication. Psychological testing is particularly indicated when there are questions pertaining to learning difficulties, mental retardation, brain damage, severe disturbances of thinking, or behavioral problems related to a personality disorder (Table 31-6).

Table 31-6
Selected Developmental and Psychological Tests

Test Category	Age Range	Test Description
Developmental assessments		
Gesell Infant Scale	8 wk–3½ yr	Mostly motor development in the first year, with some social and language assessment
Catell Infant Scale		
Bayley Infant Scale of Development	8 wk–2½ yr	Motor and social
Denver Developmental Screening Test	2 mo–6 yr	Screening
Yale Revised Developmental Schedule	4 wk–6 yr	Gross motor, fine motor, adaptive, personal-social, language
Individual intelligence tests		
Stanford-Binet (ed 4)	2–24 yr	Verbal reasoning, abstract visual reasoning, qualitative reasoning, short-term memory composite score (I.Q. equivalent)
Wechsler Intelligence Scale for Children-Revised (WISC-R)	6–17 yr	Verbal, performance, and full-scale I.Q.
McCarthy Scales of Children's Abilities	2½–8 yr	General cognitive index (I.Q. equivalent) Score for: Verbal Quantitative Memory Motor Laterality
Kaufman Assessment Battery for Children	2½–12½ yr	Sequential processing Simultaneous process Achievement Mental processing Composite score (I.Q. equivalent)
Motor skills		
Bruininks-Oseretsky Test of Motor Proficiency	4½–14½ yr	Eight subtests Gross and fine motor balance
Perceptual and perceptuomotor		
Bender Visual-Motor Gestalt Test	4–12 yr	
Draw-a-Person	All ages	
Benton Visual Retention Test (BVRT)	8 yr–adult	
Beery Test of Visual Motor Integration (VMI)	2–15 yr	
Speech and language		
Peabody Picture Vocabulary	2½ yr–adult	Screening
Test of Early Language Development (TELD)	3–8 yr	
Clinical Evaluation of Language Fundamentals-Revised (CELF-R)	7–15 yr	
Personality		
Rorschach test	3 yr–adult	
Thematic Apperception Test (TAT)	6 yr–adult	
Children's Apperception Test (CAT)	2½ yr–adult	
Roberts Apperception	Latency age	
Social maturity behavior		
Vineland Adaptive Behavior Scales—Survey Form	0–adult	Interview with parent or caretaker on communication, motor skills, daily living socialization, and leisure time
Vineland Adaptive Behavior Scales—Survey Form—Classroom (Revised)	3–12½ yr	As above Teacher complete
School grade level skills		
Wide Range Achievement Test-Revised (WRAT-R)	5 yr–adult	Reading, spelling, math
Peabody Individual Achievement Test	5–18 yr	Word identification Spelling Math Reading comprehension
Kaufman Test of Educational Achievement	Grades 1–12	General information Reading decoding Spelling Reading comprehension Math application Math computation
Gray Oral Reading Test-Revised (GORT-R)	Grades 1–12	Oral reading and comprehension

Table by Melvin Lewis, M.B., B.S. (London), F.R.C. Psych, D.C.H.

Intelligence Tests

Infant and preschool child testing. Tests applicable to preschool children are divided into (1) developmental tests designed for infants ages 18 to 24 months and (2) preschool tests for children ages 24 to 60 months. In the infant tests the clinician's speech is of little or no use in giving test instructions, although the child's own speech development provides relevant developmental data. Most of the infant tests are controlled observations of the infant's sensorimotor development, especially in the first year, with some additional social and language assessment. In contrast, preschool children can actively participate in the test because of their ability to walk, sit at a table, manipulate test objects, and communicate verbally with the tester.

The Gesell Developmental Schedules cover ages 8 weeks to 3.5 years. Data are obtained by direct observation of the child's responses to standard toys and other controlled stimulus objects and are supplemented by developmental information provided by the mother or primary caretaker. The schedules yield scores indicating the child's level of development in four separate areas: motor, adaptive, language, and personal and social.

A test-oriented approach is the Cattell Infant Scale for Intelligence, applicable to infants and children ages 2 to 30 months. This scale was developed as a downward extension of the Stanford–Binet test and also includes some items from the Gesell schedules.

School-age testing. Intelligence tests for school-age children measure primarily those abilities essential to academic achievement. They are often more accurately described as tests of scholastic aptitude.

In the United States the earliest intelligence test was the Stanford–Binet test, adapted from the original Binet–Simon scales. The Stanford–Binet test relies heavily on verbal performance and covers the ages of 2 years to adulthood. It yields both a mental age and an intelligence quotient (I.Q.). Objects, pictures, and drawings are used mostly at the youngest ages; and printed, verbal, and numerical materials are used more at the older ages.

Another individual intelligence test, perhaps currently the most widely used test for children ages 6 to 17 years, is the Wechsler Intelligence Scale for Children–Revised (WISC-R). This scale provides verbal and performance subscale scores, as well as a full-scale I.Q. score.

Both the Stanford–Binet and the WISC-R require a highly trained tester and are administered individually to each subject. Group tests are designed for mass testing. Most group tests enable a single examiner to test a large group in one session, and they are relatively easy to administer and score. They are mainly for screening purposes and are useful when a crude index of intellectual level suffices or when more extensive individual testing is not available.

Long-term stability of intelligence. Most children's I.Q.s remain fairly constant throughout the developmental periods. In theory, if a child's biological, social, and psychological givens all remain stable, his or her I.Q. also remains the same. However, scores on infant tests are not reliable in predicting the child's intelligence in late childhood or adolescence. Infant tests are valuable only for the early detection of developmental deviations, including mental retardation and other developmental disorders of hereditary or adverse environmental origin. Infant tests rely heavily on sensorimotor functions, which bear little significance to the later-developing verbal, social, and other abstract functions that constitute intelligence in later years.

In reality, the I.Q. scores do fluctuate to some degree. Large shifts in I.Q. are usually associated with the child's motivation, emotional independence, cultural milieu, and home emotional climate. The I.Q. scores of children in socioeconomically disadvantaged environments tend to decrease with age; those in superior environments tend to increase.

Aptitude tests. Because most intelligence tests concentrate on the abstract verbal and numerical abilities, there is also a need for tests measuring the concrete and practical intellectual skills. Mechanical aptitudes were among the first for which special tests were developed. Tests of clerical aptitude, measuring chiefly perceptual speed and accuracy, and tests of musical and artistic aptitudes followed.

Multiple-aptitude batteries provide a profile of scores on separate tests. An example is the Differential Aptitude Tests (DAT), which yields scores in eight abilities: verbal reasoning, numerical ability, abstract reasoning, clerical speed and accuracy, mechanical reasoning, space relations, spelling, and grammar. Multiple-aptitude batteries are most useful in testing older children and adolescents.

Educational Tests

Readiness tests. Readiness tests are designed to assess a child's qualifications for schoolwork. The importance of prior learning is paramount, as the acquisition of simple concepts equips the child for learning more complex concepts at any age.

Special emphasis is placed on those abilities found to be most important in learning to read; some attention is also given to the prerequisites of numerical thinking and to the sensorimotor control required in learning to write. Among the functions covered are visual and auditory discrimination, motor control, verbal comprehension, vocabulary, quantitative concepts, and general information. A well-known example is the Metropolitan Readiness Tests.

Tests of special education disabilities. Reading tests are customarily classified as survey and diagnostic tests. Survey tests indicate the general level of the child's achievement in reading. These tests mainly screen children in need of remedial instruction. Diagnostic tests are designed to analyze the child's performance and identify specific sources of difficulty. These tests yield more than one score, and some include detailed checklists of specific types of errors. Information about possible emotional difficulties and a complete case history are essential.

Educational achievement batteries. Achievement tests measure the effects of a course of study. Many achievement tests gauge the attainment of relatively broad educational goals, cutting across subject matter specialties. An outstanding example is the Sequential Tests of Educational Progress (STEP). These tests are available at several levels, extending from the fourth grade of elementary school to the sophomore year of college and beyond. At each level there are seven tests: multiple-choice tests in reading, writing, mathematics, science, social studies, and listening and an essay-writing test. The main emphasis is on the application of learned skills to the solution of new problems.

Creativity tests. The growing recognition that creative talent is not synonymous with intelligence as measured by traditional intelligence tests has been accompanied by vigorous efforts to develop specialized tests of creativity. The tests involve various aspects of fluency, flexibility, and originality. An example of a test that is effective with young children is the improvements test, in which the child is given toys—such as a nurse kit, a fire truck, and a stuffed dog—and is asked to think of ways of changing each toy so that it will be more fun to play with.

Personality Tests

In comparison with tests of ability, personality tests are much less satisfactory with regard to norms, reliability, and validity. Any information obtained from personality tests should be verified and supplemented by other sources, such as interviews with the child's parents, direct observation of behavior, and case history.

Self-report inventories. Self-report inventories are a series of questions concerning emotional problems, worries, interests, motives, values, and interpersonal traits. Several inventories designed for children and adolescents are basically checklists of personal problems. The questions pertain directly to the information that the examiner wishes to elicit about the child's feelings and actions, and the responses are accepted at face value. A clear example of this approach is the Mooney Problem Check List. The problem areas covered in the junior high school form include health and physical development, school, home and family, money, work and the future, boy-girl relations, relations with people in general, and self-centered concerns. Personality inventories find their major usefulness in screening and identifying children in need of further evaluation.

Projective techniques. In projective techniques the person is assigned an unstructured task that permits an almost unlimited variety of possible responses. The test stimuli are typically vague and equivocal, and the instructions are brief and general. These techniques are based on the hypothesis that the way in which the person perceives and interprets the test materials reflects basic characteristics of his or her personality. The test stimuli thus serve as a screen on which the person projects his or her own ideas.

One of the most widely used projective techniques is the Rorschach test, in which the person is shown a set of bilaterally symmetrical inkblots and asked to tell what he or she sees or what the blot represents. Rorschach norms have been developed for children between the ages of 2 and 10 years and for adolescents between the ages of 10 and 17.

A somewhat more structured test is the Children's Apperception Test (CAT), an adaptation of the Thematic Apperception Test (TAT). In the CAT, pictures of animals are substituted for pictures of people, on the assumption that children respond more readily to animal characters. The pictures are designed to evoke fantasies relating to problems of feeding and other oral activities, sibling rivalry, parent–child relations, aggression, toilet training, and other childhood experiences. Another example is the Blacky Pictures, a set of cartoons showing a small dog, his parents, and a sibling. Based on a psychoanalytic theory of psychosexual development, the cartoons depict situations suggesting various types of sexual conflicts. Still another type of picture test is illustrated by the Rosenzweig Picture–Frustration Study. This test presents a series of cartoons in which one person frustrates another. In a blank space provided, the child writes what the frustrated person may reply.

Drawings, toy tests, and other play techniques represent other applications of projective methods. Play and dramatic objects—such as puppets, dolls, toys, and miniatures—have also been used. The objects are usually selected because of their associative value and often include dolls representing adults and children, bathroom and kitchen fixtures, and other household furnishings. Play with such articles is expected to reveal the child's attitudes toward his or her family, sibling rivalries, fears, aggressions, and conflicts. They are particularly useful in eliciting sexual abuse problems in children.

When evaluated as standardized tests, most projective techniques have fared quite poorly and thus should be regarded not as tests but as aids for the clinical interviewer.

References

Call J D: Toward a nosology of psychiatric disorders in infancy. In *Frontiers of Infant Psychiatry,* J D Call, E Galenson, and R L Tyson, editors, p 117. Basic Books, New York, 1983.

Caplan R, Guthrie D, Fish B, Tanguay P E, David-Lando G: The kiddie formal thought disorder rating scale: Clinical assessment, reliability, and validity. J Am Acad Child Adolesc Psychiatry *28*: 408, 1989.

Gittleman R: The role of psychological tests for differential diagnosis in child psychiatry. J Am Acad Child Psychiatry *19*: 413, 1980.

Gutterman E M, O'Brien J D, Young J G: Structured diagnostic interviews for children and adolescents: Current status and future directions. J Am Acad Child Adolesc Psychiatry *26*: 621, 1987.

Kashani J G, Beck N C, Hoeper E W, Fallahi C, Corcoran C M, McAllister J A, Rosenberg T K, Reid J C: Psychiatric disorders in a community sample of adolescents. Am J Psychol *144*: 584, 1987.

Kaufman A S, Kaufman N L: *Kaufman Assessment Battery for Children: Interpretive Manual.* American Guidance Service, Circle Pines, MN, 1983.

Kazdin A E: Assessment techniques for childhood depression: A critical appraisal. J Am Acad Child Psychiatry *20*: 358, 1981.

Lewis M: Psychiatric examination of the infant, child, and adolescent. In *Comprehensive Textbook of Psychiatry,* ed 5, H I Kaplan and B J Sadock, editors, p 1716. Williams & Wilkins, Baltimore, 1989.

Ollendick T H, Herensen M, eds.: *Handbook of Child Psychopathology.* Plenum, New York, 1983.

Pilowsky D, Chambers W, eds.: *Hallucinations in children.* American Psychiatric Press, Washington, DC, 1986.

Psychopharmacology Bulletin: Rating scales and assessment instruments for use in pediatric psychopharmacology research. Psychopharmacol Bull *21*: (4), 1985.

Puig-Antich J, Chambers W J, Tabrizi M A: The clinical assessment of current depressive episodes in children and adolescents: Interviews with parents and children. In *Affective Disorders in Childhood and Adolescence: An Update,* D P Cantwell and G A Carlson, editors, p 157. S P Medical & Scientific Books, New York, 1983.

Sattler J M: *Assessment of Children's Intelligence,* ed 2. Saunders, Philadelphia, 1982.

Shaffer D: Introduction and overview. In *Comprehensive Textbook of Psychiatry,* ed 5, H I Kaplan and B J Sadock, editors, p 1689. Williams & Wilkins, Baltimore, 1989.

Shapiro T: The psychoanalytic formulation in child and adolescent psychiatry. J Am Acad Child Adolesc Psychiatry *28*: 675, 1989.

Simmons J E: *Psychiatric Examination of Children,* ed 2. Lea & Febiger, Philadelphia, 1974.

Young J G, O'Brien J B, Gutterman E M, Cohen P: Research on the clinical interview. J Am Acad Child Adolesc Psychiatry *26*: 613, 1987.

32

Mental Retardation

Mental retardation is not a unitary disorder. The histories, personalities, and life experiences of those with mental retardation vary greatly, necessitating a careful individualized approach in diagnosis and treatment. There are likewise many varied causes, and, although recent years have brought discoveries like fragile X syndrome, the cause of mental retardation in many cases is still unknown.

There are two major conceptual approaches in defining mental retardation: the biomedical and the sociocultural adaptational models. The adherents of the biomedical model, particularly in the United States, maintain that the presence of basic changes in the brain is essential to the diagnosis of mental retardation. Alternatively, the proponents of the sociocultural adaptational model emphasize social functioning and general ability to adapt to accepted norms.

Table 32-1 focuses on the developmental impairment in infancy and preschool years, learning difficulties in school age, and poor social-vocational adjustment in adulthood. This table includes the criteria of both the revised third edition of *Diagnostic and Statistical Manual of Mental Disorders* (DSM-III-R) and the American Association of Mental Deficiency (AAMD). According to the 1983 AAMD definition, mental retardation refers to significantly subaverage general intellectual functioning resulting in or associated with concurrent impairments in adaptive behavior and manifested during the developmental period. The AAMD definition is virtually identical with the DSM-III-R definition, which describes the essential features of mental retardation as (1) significantly subaverage general intellectual functioning, accompanied by (2) significant deficits or impairments in adaptive functioning, with (3) onset before the age of 18. See Table 32-2 for the DSM-III-R criteria for mental retardation. The diagnosis is made regardless of whether there is a coexisting physical or other mental disorder.

General intellectual functioning is determined by the results of a standardized test of intelligence, and the term "significantly subaverage" is defined as an intelligence quotient (I.Q.) of approximately 70 or below or two standard deviations below the mean for the particular test. The category of borderline mental retardation (between one and two standard deviations below the test mean) was eliminated in 1973.

NOMENCLATURE

The term "mental retardation" is often used interchangeably with "mental deficiency." The World Health Organization (WHO) has recommended the term "mental subnormality," which includes two separate and distinct categories: mental retardation and mental deficiency. Mental retardation, according to WHO nosology, is reserved for subnormal functioning secondary to identifiable underlying pathological causes, whereas mental deficiency is often used as a legal term, applied to persons with an I.Q. of less than 70.

The term "feeble-mindedness" was often used in the past, especially in American literature, and is still in use in Great Britain, where it generally denotes the mild forms of mental retardation. "Oligophrenia" is commonly used in the Soviet Union, Scandinavia, and other western European countries. "Amentia" is no longer used in modern psychiatry, except occasionally to refer to a terminal stage of a degenerative illness.

CLASSIFICATION

The degrees or levels of mental retardation are expressed in various terms. DSM-III-R presents four types of mental retardation, reflecting the degree of intellectual impairment: mild mental retardation, moderate mental retardation, severe mental retardation, and profound mental retardation. The degrees of mental retardation by I.Q. range are indicated in Table 32-3.

In addition, DSM-III-R lists unspecified mental retardation as a type reserved for those persons who are strongly suspected of having mental retardation but cannot be tested by standard intelligence tests or are too impaired or uncooperative to be tested. This type may be applicable to infants whose significantly subaverage intellectual functioning is clinically judged but for whom the available tests (e.g., Bayley, Cattell) do not yield numerical I.Q. values. This type should not be used when the intellectual level is presumed to be above 70.

EPIDEMIOLOGY

The prevalence of mental retardation at any one time is estimated to be about 1 percent of the population. The

Table 32-1
Developmental Characteristics of the Mentally Retarded

Degree of Mental Retardation	Preschool Age 0–5 Maturation and Development	School Age 6–20 Training and Education	Adult 21 and over Social and Vocational Adequacy
Profound	Gross retardation; minimal capacity for functioning in sensorimotor areas; needs nursing care; constant aid and supervision required	Some motor development present; may respond to minimal or limited training in self-help	Some motor and speech development; may achieve very limited self-care; needs nursing care
Severe	Poor motor development; speech minimal; generally unable to profit from training in self-help; little or no communication skills	Can talk or learn to communicate; can be trained in elemental health habits; profits from systematic habit training; unable to profit from vocational training	May contribute partially to self-maintenance under complete supervision; can develop self-protection skills to a minimal useful level in controlled environment
Moderate	Can talk or learn to communicate; poor social awareness; fair motor development; profits from training in self-help; can be managed with moderate supervision	Can profit from training in social and occupational skills; unlikely to progress beyond second-grade level in academic subjects; may learn to travel alone in familiar places	May achieve self-maintenance in unskilled or semiskilled work under sheltered conditions; needs supervision and guidance when under mild social or economic stress
Mild	Can develop social and communication skills; minimal retardation in sensorimotor areas; often not distinguished from normal until later age	Can learn academic skills up to approximately sixth-grade level by late teens; can be guided toward social conformity	Can usually achieve social and vocational skills adequate to minimum self-support but may need guidance and assistance when under unusual social or economic stress

Adapted from *Mental Retardation Activities of the U.S. Department of Health, Education and Welfare*, p 2. United States Government Printing Office, Washington, D.C., 1983, with permission. DSM-III-R criteria are adapted essentially from this chart.

Table 32-2
Diagnostic Criteria for Mental Retardation

A. Significantly subaverage general intellectual functioning: an I.Q. of 70 or below on an individually administered I.Q. test (for infants, a clinical judgment of significantly subaverage intellectual functioning, since available intelligence tests do not yield numerical I.Q. values).

B. Concurrent deficits or impairments in adaptive functioning (i.e., the person's effectiveness in meeting the standards expected for his or her age by his or her cultural group in areas such as social skills and responsibility, communication, daily living skills, personal independence, and self-sufficiency).

C. Onset before the age of 18.

Table from DSM-III-R, *Diagnostic and Statistical Manual of Mental Disorders*, ed 3, revised. Copyright American Psychiatric Association, Washington, DC, 1987, with permission.

Table 32-3
Severity of Mental Retardation by I.Q. Range

Severity of Mental Retardation	I.Q. Range	Retarded Population (%)
Mild	50–55 to approx. 70	85
Moderate	35–40 to 50–55	10
Severe	20–25 to 35–40	3–4
Profound	Below 20 or 25	1–2

Adapted from DSM-III-R, *Diagnostic and Statistical Manual of Mental Disorders*, ed 3, revised. Copyright American Psychiatric Association, Washington, DC, 1987, with permission.

incidence of mental retardation is difficult to calculate accurately because of the impossibility of stating when mental retardation is diagnosed in a person. In many cases, retardation may be latent for a long time before the person's limitations are recognized, or, because of good adaptation, the formal diagnosis is not warranted at a particular point in the person's life. The highest incidence is in school-age children, with the peak at ages 10 to 14. Mental retardation is approximately 1½ times more common among men than among women. In older populations, prevalence is less, as those with severe or profound mental retardation have high mortality rates resulting from the complications of associated physical disorders.

ETIOLOGY

On the basis of current knowledge, approximately 25 percent of all cases of mental retardation are known to be caused by biological abnormalities. Chromosomal and metabolic disorders—such as Down's syndrome, fragile X syndrome, and phenylketonuria (PKU)—are the most common disorders manifesting mental retardation. Mental retardation associated with these disorders is usually diagnosed at birth or relatively early in childhood, and the severity is generally moderate to profound.

No specific biological causes can be identified in the remaining 75 percent of the cases. The level of intellectual impairment of a person with no known cause is usually mild, with an I.Q. between 50 and 70. The diagnosis of mild retardation is not usually made before grade school. In mild mental retardation, a familial pattern is often seen in parents and siblings.

The low socioeconomic groups are overrepresented in the cases of mild retardation, and the significance of this is not clear. However, psychosocial deprivation—such as deprivation in social, linguistic, and intellectual stimulation—has been suspected of contributing to mental retardation without a known biological cause. Current knowledge suggests that three sets of causative factors are involved, either singly or in combination: genetic factors, environmental biological factors (e.g., malnutrition), and early child-rearing experiences.

Prenatal Factors

Important prerequisites for the overall development of the fetus include the mother's physical, psychological, and nutritional health during pregnancy. Maternal chronic illnesses and conditions affecting the normal development of the fetus's central nervous system include uncontrolled diabetes, anemia, emphysema, hypertension, and long-term use of alcohol and narcotic substances. Maternal infections during pregnancy, especially viral infections, have been known to cause fetal damage and mental retardation. The degree of fetal damage depends on variables such as the type of viral infection, the gestational age of the fetus, and the severity of the illness. Although numerous infectious diseases have been reported to affect the fetus's central nervous system, the following three infectious disorders have been definitely identified as high-risk conditions for mental retardation: rubella (German measles), cytomegalic inclusion disease, and syphilis.

Rubella (German measles). Rubella has replaced syphilis as the major cause of congenital malformations and mental retardation caused by maternal infection. The children of affected mothers may present a number of abnormalities, including congenital heart disease, mental retardation, cataracts, deafness, microcephaly, and microphthalmia. Timing is crucial, as the extent and the frequency of the complications are inversely related to the duration of the pregnancy at the time of the maternal infection. When mothers are infected in the first trimester of pregnancy, 10 to 15 percent of the children are affected, but the incidence rises to almost 50 percent when the infection occurs in the first month of pregnancy. The situation is often complicated by subclinical forms of maternal infection, which often go undetected. Maternal rubella can be prevented by immunization.

Cytomegalic inclusion disease. In many cases, cytomegalic inclusion disease remains dormant in the mother. Some children are stillborn, and others have jaundice, microcephaly, hepatosplenomegaly, and radiographic findings of intracerebral calcification. Children with mental retardation from this disease frequently have cerebral calcification, microcephaly, or hydrocephalus. The diagnosis is confirmed by positive throat and urine cultures of the virus and the recovery of inclusion-bearing cells in the urine.

Syphilis. Syphilis in pregnant women used to be the main cause of various neuropathological changes in their offspring, including mental retardation. Today, the incidence of syphilitic complications of pregnancy fluctuates with the incidence of syphilis in the general population. Some recent alarming statistics from several major cities in the United States indicate that there is still no room for complacency.

Other diseases. Brain damage caused by toxoplasmosis transmitted from the pregnant mother to the fetus is another universally recognized but relatively rare complication of pregnancy that often results in mental retardation and a variety of brain malformations. Damage to the fetus from maternal hepatitis has also been reported.

Currently, acquired immune deficiency syndrome (AIDS) has become an important public health issue, and extensive research is being conducted to study its effects on fetuses and newborn infants. The pregnancy of a woman who has a confirmed case of AIDS results in fetal death, stillbirth, spontaneous abortion, or death of the baby within a few years, although some survive longer. Neurological symptoms in AIDS-infected children include developmental delay and retrogression. The brain can be invaded by the AIDS virus and by opportunistic infections.

The role of other maternal infections during pregnancy—such as influenza, common-cold viruses, pneumonia, and urinary tract infections—in causing mental retardation is being investigated, and the results are not yet conclusive.

Complications of pregnancy. Toxemia of pregnancy and uncontrolled maternal diabetes present hazards to the fetus and sometimes result in mental retardation. Maternal malnutrition during pregnancy often results in prematurity and other obstetrical complications. Vaginal hemorrhage, placenta previa, premature separation of the placenta, and prolapse of the cord may damage the fetal brain by causing anoxia.

The potential teratogenic effect of pharmacological agents administered during pregnancy was widely publicized after the thalidomide tragedy (the drug produced a high percentage of deformed babies when given to pregnant women). So far, with the exception of metabolites used in cancer chemotherapy, no usual doses are known to damage the fetus's central nervous system, but caution and restraint in prescribing drugs to pregnant women are certainly indicated. The use of lithium during pregnancy was recently implicated in some congenital malformations, especially of the cardiovascular system (e.g., Ebstein's syndrome).

Substance abuse. Many infants have been exposed to alcohol and drugs during the mother's pregnancy. Those born with fetal alcohol syndrome may be retarded and have physical stigmata, such as midfacial hypoplasia, short palpebral fissures, cardiac defects, and possibly microcephaly. Those born addicted to cocaine and heroin may be developmentally delayed, with the long-term prognosis yet unknown.

Chromosomal Abnormalities

Abnormalities in autosomal chromosomes are associated with mental retardation, although aberrations in sex chromosomes are not always associated with mental retardation (such as Turner's syndrome with XO and Klinefelter's syndrome with XXY, XXXY, and XXYY variations). Some children with Turner's syndrome have normal to superior intelligence.

Down's syndrome. Down's syndrome was first described by the English physician Langdon Down in 1866 and was based on the physical characteristics associated with subnormal mental functioning. Since then, Down's syndrome has remained the most investigated and the most discussed syndrome in mental retardation. The children with this syndrome were originally called *mongoloid* because of their physical characteristics of slanted eyes, epicanthal folds, and flat nose.

Despite a plethora of theories and hypotheses advanced in the past 100 years, the cause of Down's syndrome is still unknown. There is agreement on very few predisposing factors in chromosomal disorders—among them, the increased age of the mother, possibly the increased age of the father, and X-ray radiation. The problem of cause is complicated even further by the recent recognition of three types of chromosomal aberrations in Down's syndrome:

1. Patients with trisomy 21 (three of chromosome 21, instead of the usual two) represent the overwhelming majority; they have 47 chromosomes, with an extra chromosome 21. The mothers' karyotypes are normal. A nondisjunction during meiosis, occurring for yet unknown reasons, is held responsible for this disorder.
2. Nondisjunction occurring after fertilization in any cell division results in mosaicism, a condition in which both normal and trisomic cells are found in various tissues.
3. In translocation there is a fusion of two chromosomes, mostly 21 and 15, resulting in a total of 46 chromosomes, despite the presence of an extra chromosome 21. The disorder, unlike trisomy 21, is usually inherited, and the translocation chromosome may be found in unaffected parents and siblings. These asymptomatic carriers have only 45 chromosomes.

The incidence of Down's syndrome in the United States is about 1 in every 700 births. In his original description Down mentioned the frequency of 10 percent among all mentally retarded patients. Today, around 10 percent of patients with Down's syndrome are in institutions for the mentally retarded. For a middle-aged mother (more than 32 years old), the risk of having a Down's syndrome child with trisomy 21 is about 1 in 100 births, but, when translocation is present, the risk is about one in three. These facts assume special importance in genetic counseling.

Amniocentesis, in which a small amount of amniotic fluid is removed from the amniotic cavity transabdominally between the 14th and the 16th weeks of gestation, has been useful in diagnosing various infant abnormalities, especially Down's syndrome. Amniotic fluid cells, mostly fetal in origin, are cultured for cytogenetic and biochemical studies. Many serious hereditary disorders can be predicted with this method, and therapeutic abortion is the only method of prevention. Amniocentesis is recommended for all pregnant women over the age of 35. Fortunately, most chromosomal anomalies occur only once in a family.

Chorionic villus sampling (CVS) is a new screening technique to determine fetal abnormalities. It is done at 8 to 10 weeks of gestation, which is six weeks earlier than amniocentesis. Results are available in a short time (hours or days), and, if the result is abnormal, the decision to terminate the pregnancy can be made within the first trimester. There is a miscarriage risk of between 2 and 5 percent as a result of the procedure.

Mental retardation is the overriding feature of Down's syndrome. The majority of patients belong to the moderately and severely retarded groups, with only a minority having an I.Q. above 50. Mental development seems to progress normally from birth to 6 months of age. I.Q. scores gradually decrease from near normal at 1 year of age to about 30 at older ages. This decline in intelligence may be real or apparent. It could be that infantile tests do not reveal the full extent of the defect, which may become manifest when more sophisticated tests are used in early childhood. According to many sources, patients with Down's syndrome are placid, cheerful, and cooperative, which facilitates their adjustment at home. The picture, however, seems to change in adolescents, especially those in institutions, who may develop various emotional difficulties, behavior disorders, and (rarely) psychotic illnesses.

The diagnosis of Down's syndrome is made with relative ease in an older child but is often difficult in newborn infants. The most important signs in a newborn include general hypotonia, oblique palpebral fissues, abundant neck skin, a small flattened skull, high cheekbones, and a protruding tongue. The hands are broad and thick, with a single palmar transversal crease, and the little fingers are short and curved inward. Moro's reflex is weak or absent. More than 100 signs or stigmata are described in Down's syndrome, but rarely are all found in one person.

Life expectancy used to be about 12 years. With the advent of antibiotics, however, few young patients succumb to infections, but most of them do not live beyond the age of 40, when they already have many signs of senescence, which are similar to those of Alzheimer's disease. Despite numerous therapeutic recommendations, no treatment has proved effective.

Cat-cry (cri-du-chat) syndrome. Children with cat-cry syndrome are missing part of the fifth chromosome. They are severely retarded and show many stigmata often associated with chromosomal aberrations, such as microcephaly, low-set ears, oblique palpebral fissues, hypertelorism, and micrognathia. The characteristic catlike cry—caused by laryngeal abnormalities—that gave the syndrome its name gradually changes and disappears with increasing age.

Other syndromes of autosomal aberrations associated with mental retardation are much less prevalent than is Down's syndrome. Various types of autosomal and sex chromosome aberration syndromes are included in Table 32-4.

Fragile X syndrome. Fragile X, a recently discovered syndrome, is a known genetic cause of retardation. Second only to Down's syndrome, it occurs in 0.5 to 1 in every 1,000 male births. The fragile site on the X chromosome is expressed when cells are cultured in a folate-poor medium. The typical phenotype includes a large head and ears, a long and narrow face, short stature, and postpubertal macroorchidism. The child's intellectual level ranges from low average to severely retarded. Many children have symptoms of attention-deficit hyperactivity disorder and specific developmental disorders. Female carriers are usually less impaired than males with fragile X, but female carriers can manifest the typical physical characteristics and can be mildly retarded.

Rett's syndrome. In 1966 Dr. Andreas Rett from Vienna reported on 22 girls with a serious neurological disability characterized by a deterioration of hand skills and stereotyped hand movements. Autisticlike symptoms, ataxia, facial grimacing, teeth grinding, and loss of speech were noted. There was progressive spasticity, scoliosis, difficulty with gait (if walking had occurred), and onset of seizures. To date, the longest survival age has been 34 years, but the complete description of the spectrum is still being established.

Genetic Factors

Phenylketonuria. Phenylketonuria (PKU) was first described by Asbjörn Fölling in 1934 as the paradigmatic inborn error of metabolism. PKU is transmitted as a simple recessive autosomal Mendelian trait and occurs in approximately 1 in every 10,000 to 15,000 live births. To the parents who have already had a child with PKU, the chance of having another child with PKU is one in every four to five successive pregnancies. Although the disease is reported predominantly in people of north European origin, a few cases have been described in blacks, Yemenite Jews, and Asians. The frequency among institutionalized defectives is about 1 percent.

The basic metabolic defect in PKU is an inability to convert phenylalanine, an essential amino acid, to paratyrosine because of the absence or inactivity of the liver enzyme phenylalanine hydroxylase, which catalyzes the conversion. Two

Table 32-4
Thirty-Five Important Syndromes with Multiple Handicaps

Syndrome	Diagnostic Manifestations					
	Craniofacial	Skeletal	Other	Mental Retardation	Short Stature	Genetic Transmission
Aarskog-Scott syndrome	Hypertelorism; broad nasal bridge, anteverted nostrils, long philtrum	Small hands and feet; mild interdigital webbing; short stature	Scrotal shawl above penis		+	X-linked semidominant
Apert's syndrome (acrocephalosyndactyly)	Craniosynostosis; irregular midfacial hypoplasia; hypertelorism	Syndactyly; broad distal thumb and toe		±		Autosomal dominant
Cerebral gigantism (Sotos syndrome)	Large head; prominent forehead; narrow anterior mandible	Large hands and feet	Large size in early life; poor coordination	±		?
Cockayne's syndrome	Pinched facies; sunken eyes; thin nose; prognathism; retinal degeneration	Long limbs, with large hands and feet; flexion deformities	Hypotrichosis; photosensitivity; thin skin; diminished subcutaneous fat; impaired hearing	+	+	Autosomal recessive
Cohen syndrome	Maxillary hypoplasia with prominent central incisors	Narrow hands and feet	Hypotonia; obesity	+	±	? Autosomal recessive
Cornelia de Lange syndrome	Synophrys (continuous eyebrows); thin down-turning upper lip; long philtrum; anteverted nostrils; microcephaly	Small or malformed hands and feet; proximal thumb	Hirsutism	+	+	?
Cri-du-chat syndrome	Epicanthic folds, slanting palpebral fissues; round facial contour; hypertelorism; microcephaly	Short metacarpals or metatarsals; four-finger line in palm	Catlike cry in infancy	+	+	?
Crouzon's syndrome (craniofacial dysostosis)	Proptosis with shallow orbits; maxillary hypoplasia; craniosynostosis					Autosomal dominant
Down's syndrome	Upward slant to palpebral fissures; mid-face depression; epicanthic folds; Brushfield spots; brachycephaly	Short hands; clinodactyly of fifth finger; four-finger line in palm	Hypotonia; loose skin on back of neck	+	+	Trisomy 21
Dubowitz syndrome	Small facies; lateral displacement of inner canthi; ptosis; broad nasal bridge; sparse hair; microcephaly		Infantile eczema; high-pitched hoarse voice	±	+ +	? Autosomal recessive
Fetal alcohol syndrome	Short palpebral fissures; mid-facial hypoplasia; microcephaly		± Cardiac defect; fine motor dysfunction	+	+	
Fetal hydantoin syndrome (Dilantin)	Hypertelorism; short nose; occasional cleft lip	Hypoplastic nails, especially fifth	Cardiac defect	±	±	

Table 32-4
Continued

Syndrome	Diagnostic Manifestations: Craniofacial	Diagnostic Manifestations: Skeletal	Diagnostic Manifestations: Other	Mental Retardation	Short Stature	Genetic Transmission
Goldenhar's syndrome	Malar hypoplasia; macrostomia; micrognathia; epibulbar dermoid, lipodermoid; malformed ear with preauricular tags	± Vertebral anomalies				?
Incontinentia pigmenti	± Dental defect; deformities of ears; ± patchy alopecia		Irregular skin pigmentation in fleck, whorl, or spidery form	±		? Dominant, X-linked ? Lethal in males
Laurence-Moon-Bardet-Biedl syndrome	Retinal pigmentation	Polydactyly; syndactyly	Obesity; seizures; hypogenitalism	+	±	Autosomal recessive
Linear nevus sebaceus syndrome	Nevus sebaceus, face or neck		+/− Seizures	+	±	?
Lowe's syndrome (oculocerebrorenal syndrome)	Cataract	Renal tubular dysfunction	Hypotonia	+	+	X-linked recessive
Möbius' syndrome (congenital facial diplegia)	Expressionless facies; ocular palsy	± Clubfoot; syndactyly		±	±	?
Neurofibromatosis	± Optic gliomas; acoustic neuromas	± Bone lesions; pseudarthroses	Neurofibromas; café-au-lait spots; seizures	±		Autosomal dominant
Noonan's syndrome	Webbing of posterior neck; malformed ears; hypertelorism	Pectus excavatum; cubitus valgus	Cryptorchidism; pulmonic stenosis	±	+	?
Prader-Willi syndrome	± Upward slant to palpebral fissures	Small hands and feet	Hypotonia, especially in early infancy; then polyphagia and obesity; hypogenitalism	+	+	?
Robin complex	Micrognathia; glossoptosis; cleft palate, U-shaped		± Cardiac anomalies			?
Rubella syndrome	Cataract; retinal pigmentation; ocular malformations		Sensorineural deafness; patent ductus arteriosus	±	±	

Rubinstein-Taybi syndrome	Slanting palpebral fissures; maxillary hypoplasia; microcephaly	Broad thumbs and toes	Abnormal gait	+	+	?
Seckel syndrome	Facial hypoplasia; prominent nose; microcephaly	Multiple minor joint and skeletal abnormalities		+	+	Autosomal recessive
Sjögren-Larsson syndrome		Spasticity, especially of legs	Ichthyosis	+	+	Autosomal recessive
Smith-Lemli-Opitz syndrome	Anteverted nostrils, ptosis of eyelid	Syndactyly of second and third toes	Hypospadias; cryptorchidism	+	+	Autosomal recessive
Sturge-Weber syndrome	Flat hemangioma of face, most commonly trigeminal in distribution		Hemangiomas of meninges with seizures	±		?
Treacher Collins' syndrome (mandibulofacial dysostosis)	Malar and mandibular hypoplasia; downslanting palpebral fissures; defect of lower eyelid; malformed ears					Autosomal dominant
Trisomy 18	Microstomia; short palpebral fissures; malformed ears; elongated skull	Clenched hand, second finger over third; low arches on fingertips; short sternum	Cryptorchidism; congenital heart disease	+	+	Trisomy 18
Trisomy 13	Defects of eyes, nose, lips, ears, and forebrain of holoprosencephaly type	Polydactyly; narrow hyperconvex fingernails	Skin defects, posterior scalp	+	+	Trisomy 13
Tuberous sclerosis	Hamartomatous pink to brownish facial skin nodules	± Bone lesions	Seizures; intracranial calcification	±		Autosomal dominant
Waardenburg syndrome	Lateral displacement of inner canthi and puncta		Partial albinism; white forelock; heterochromia of iris; vitiligo; +/− deafness			Autosomal dominant
Williams syndrome	Full lips; small nose with anteverted nostrils; iris dysplasia	Mild hypoplasia of nails	± Hypercalcemia in infancy; supravalvular aortic stenosis	+	+	?
Zellweger syndrome (cerebrohepatorenal syndrome)	High forehead; flat facies		Hypotonia; hepatomegaly; death in early infancy			

Table from L Syzmanski, A Crocker, and adapted from D W Smith: Patterns of malformation. In *Nelson Textbook of Pediatrics*, ed 11. V C Vaughan III, R J McKay Jr, and R E Behrman, editors, p 2035. Saunders, Philadelphia, 1979, with permission.

other types of hyperphenylalaninemia have recently been described. One is due to a deficiency of an enzyme, dihydropteridine reductase, and the other to a deficiency of a cofactor, biopterin. The first defect can be detected in fibroblasts, and biopterin can be measured in body fluids. Both of these rare disorders carry a high risk of fatality.

The majority of patients with PKU are severely retarded, but some are reported to have borderline or normal intelligence. Eczema, vomiting, and convulsions are present in about a third of all cases. Although the clinical picture varies, typical PKU children are hyperactive and exhibit erratic, unpredictable behavior, which makes them difficult to manage. They frequently have temper tantrums and often display bizarre movements of their bodies and upper extremities and twisting hand mannerisms, and their behavior sometimes resembles that of autistic or schizophrenic children. Verbal and nonverbal communication is usually severely impaired or nonexistent. Their coordination is poor, and they have many perceptual difficulties.

This disease was previously diagnosed on the basis of a urine test: phenylpyruvic acid in the urine reacts with ferric chloride solution to yield a vivid green color. However, this test has its limitations, as it may not detect the presence of phenylpyruvic acid in urine before the baby is 5 or 6 weeks old, and it may give positive responses with other aminoacidurias. Currently, a more reliable screening test that is widely used is the Guthrie inhibition assay, which uses a bacteriological procedure to detect blood phenylalanine.

Early diagnosis is important, as a low phenylalanine diet, in use since 1955, significantly improves both behavior and developmental progress. The best results seem to be obtained with early diagnosis and the start of dietary treatment before the child is 6 months of age.

Dietary treatment, however, is not without risk. Phenylalanine is an essential amino acid, and its omission from the diet may lead to such severe complications as anemia, hypoglycemia, edema, and even death. Dietary treatment of PKU should be continued indefinitely. Children who receive a diagnosis before the age of 3 months and are placed on an optimal dietary regimen may have normal intelligence. For untreated older children and adolescents with PKU, a low phenylalanine diet does not influence the level of mental retardation. However, the diet does decrease their irritability and abnormal EEG changes and does increase their social responsiveness and attention span.

The parents of PKU children and some of these children's normal siblings are heterozygous carriers. The disease can be detected by a phenylalanine tolerance test, which may be important in the genetic counseling of these people.

Maple syrup urine disease (Menkes' disease). The clinical symptoms of Menkes' disease appear during the first week of life. The infant deteriorates rapidly and has decerebrate rigidity, seizures, respiratory irregularity, and hypoglycemia. If untreated, most patients die in the first months of life, and the survivors are severely retarded. Some variants have been reported with transient ataxia and only mild retardation.

Treatment follows the general principles established for PKU and consists of a diet very low in the three involved amino acids—leucine, isoleucine, and valine.

Other enzyme deficiency disorders. Several enzyme deficiency disorders associated with mental retardation have been identified, and still more diseases are being added as new discoveries are made. Some of these include Hartnup disease, galactosemia, and glycogen storage disease. Thirty important syndromes with inborn errors of metabolism, hereditary transmission patterns, defective enzymes, clinical signs, and relationship to mental retardation are listed in Table 32-5.

Acquired Childhood Diseases

Occasionally, a child's developmental status changes dramatically as a result of a specific disease or physical trauma. In retrospect, it is sometimes difficult to ascertain the full normality of the child's developmental progress before the insult, but the adverse effects on the child's development or skills undoubtedly have a new origin.

Infection. The most serious infections affecting cerebral integrity are encephalitis and meningitis. Measles encephalitis has been virtually eliminated by the universal use of measles vaccine, and the incidences of other bacterial infections of the central nervous system have been markedly reduced with antibacterial agents. Most episodes of encephalitis are caused by viral organisms. It is sometimes necessary to retrospectively assess a probable encephalitic component in a past obscure illness that had high fever and lasting encephalopathy. Meningitis that was diagnosed late and followed by antibiotic treatment or obstructive complications can seriously affect a child's cognitive development. Thrombotic and purulent intracranial phenomena secondary to septicemia are rarely seen today except in small infants.

Head trauma. The best-known causes of head injury in children that produce developmental handicaps, including seizures, are motor vehicle accidents. More head injuries, however, are caused by household accidents, such as falls from tables, from open windows, and on stairways. Child abuse is also a cause of head injury.

Other issues. Brain damage from cardiac arrest during anesthesia is rare. One cause of complete or partial decortication is asphyxia associated with near drowning. Chronic exposure to lead is a well-established cause of compromised intelligence and learning skills. Intracranial tumors of various types and origins in themselves or from the effects of surgery and chemotherapy can also adversely affect brain function.

Environmental and Sociocultural Factors

It is well known that mild retardation is significantly more prevalent among persons of culturally deprived, low socioeconomic groups and that many of the family members or relatives are affected with similar degrees of mental retardation. No biological causes have been identified in these cases.

In any case it is clear that children in poor, socioculturally deprived families are subjected to potentially pathogenic and developmentally adverse conditions. The prenatal environment is compromised by poor medical care and poor maternal nutrition. Teenage pregnancies are frequent and are associated with obstetrical complications, prematurity, and low birth weight. Poor postnatal medical care, malnutrition, exposure to such toxic substances as lead, and physical traumata are frequent. Family instability, frequent moves, and multiple but inadequate caretakers are common. Furthermore, the mothers in such families are often poorly educated and ill equipped to give the child appropriate stimulation.

Another unresolved issue is the influence of severe parental mental illness. It has been hypothesized that such illness adversely affects the child's care and stimulation and other aspects of the environment, thus putting the child at a developmental risk. Children of parents with mood disorder and

Table 32-5
Thirty Important Syndromes with Inborn Errors of Metabolism

Name of Disorder	Hereditary Transmission*	Enzyme Defect	Prenatal Diagnosis	Mental Retardation	Clinical Signs
		I. LIPID METABOLISM			
Niemann-Pick disease Group A, infantile Group B, adult	A.R.	Sphingomyelinase	+	±	Hepatosplenomegaly
Groups C and D, intermediate		Unknown	–	+	Pulmonary infiltration
Infantile Gaucher disease	A.R.	β-Glucosidase	+	±	Hepatosplenomegaly, pseudobulbar palsy
Tay-Sachs disease	A.R.	Hexosaminidase A	+	+	Macular changes, seizures, spasticity
Generalized gangliosidosis	A.R.	β-Galactosidase	+	+	Hepatosplenomegaly, bone changes
Krabbe disease	A.R.	Galactocerebroside β-Galactosidase	+	+	Stiffness, seizures
Metachromatic leukodystrophy	A.R.	Cerebroside sulfatase	+	+	Stiffness, developmental failure
Wolman disease	A.R.	Acid lipase	+	–	Hepatosplenomegaly, adrenal calcification, vomiting, diarrhea
Farber lipogranulomatosis	A.R.	Acid ceramidase	+	+	Hoarseness, arthropathy, subcutaneous nodules
Fabry disease	X.R.	α-Galactosidase	+	–	Angiokeratomas, renal failure
		II. MUCOPOLYSACCHARIDE METABOLISM			
Hurler's syndrome MPS I	A.R.	Iduronidase	+	+	
Hunter's disease II	X.R.	Iduronate sulfatase	+	+	
Sanfilippo disease III	A.R.	Various sulfatases (types A-D)	+	+	Varying degrees of bone changes, hepatosplenomegaly, joint restriction, etc.
Morquio disease IV	A.R.	*N*-Acetylgalactosamine-6-sulfate sulfatase	+	–	
Maroteaux-Lamy disease VI	A.R.	Arylsulfatase B	+	±	
		III. OLIGOSACCHARIDE AND GLYCOPROTEIN METABOLISM			
I-cell disease	A.R.	Glycoprotein *N*-acetylglucosaminyl-phosphotransferase	+	+	Hepatomegaly, bone changes, swollen gingivae
Mannosidosis	A.R.	Mannosidase	+	+	Hepatomegaly, bone changes, facial coarsening
Fucosidosis	A.R.	Fucosidase	+	+	Same as above
		IV. AMINO ACID METABOLISM			
Phenylketonuria	A.R.	Phenylalanine hydroxylase	–	+	Eczema, blonde hair, musty odor
Homocystinuria	A.R.	Cystathionine β-synthetase	+	+	Ectopia lentis, Marfanlike phenotype, cardiovascular anomalies
Tyrosinosis	A.R.	Tyrosine amine transaminase	–	+	Hyperkeratotic skin lesions, conjunctivitis
Maple syrup urine disease	A.R.	Branched chain ketoacid decarboxylase	+	+	Recurrent ketoacidosis
Methylmalonic acidemia	A.R.	Methylmalonyl-CoA mutase	+	+	Recurrent ketoacidosis, hepatomegaly, growth retardation
Proprionic acidemia	A.R.	Proprionyl-CoA carboxylase	+	+	Same as above

Table 32-5
Continued

Name of Disorder	Hereditary Transmission*	Enzyme Defect	Prenatal Diagnosis	Mental Retardation	Clinical Signs
Nonketotic hyperglycinemia	A.R.	Glycine cleavage enzyme	+	+	Seizures
Urea cycle disorders	Mostly A.R.	Urea cycle enzymes	+	+	Recurrent acute encephalopathy, vomiting
Hartnup disorder	A.R.	Renal transport disorder	–	–	None consistent
		V. OTHERS			
Galactosemia	A.R.	Galactose-1-phosphate uridyltransferase	+	+	Hepatomegaly, cataracts, ovarian failure
Wilson hepatolenticular degeneration	A.R.	Unknown factor in copper metabolism	–	±	Liver disease, Kayser-Fleischer ring, neurological problems
Menkes kinky-hair disease	X.R.	Same as above	+	–	Abnormal hair, cerebral degeneration
Lesch-Nyhan disease	A.R.	Hypoxanthine guanine phosphoribosyltransferase	+	+	Behavioral abnormalities

Table by L Syzmanski, A Crocker, and adapted from J G Leroy: Heredity, development, and behavior. In *Developmental-Behavioral Pediatrics*, Levine et al., editors, p 315. Saunders, Philadelphia, 1983, with permission.
*A.R. = autosomal recessive transmission. X.R. = X-linked recessive transmission.

schizophrenia are known to be at risk for these and related disorders. Recent studies also suggest a high prevalence of motor and other developmental delays among these children but not necessarily frank retardation.

MENTAL DISORDERS AND MENTAL RETARDATION

Personality and Behavioral Patterns

The most common misconception among professionals and the general public has been the belief that mentally retarded persons are a behaviorally homogeneous group. In fact, retarded persons display more personality styles and behaviors than do the nonretarded. For example, a mildly retarded person who is living independently with some supervision and who is partially self-supporting has more in common with a nonretarded coworker than with a profoundly retarded person who is totally dependent on others' care. Another misconception is the belief that the maladaptive behaviors of retarded persons are the result of mental retardation and organicity, rather than their life experiences.

All behaviors and personality patterns exhibited by retarded persons are seen also in nonretarded persons. However, certain behavioral patterns may be expected to be more frequently associated with mental retardation because of retarded persons' cognitive and other deficits and life experiences. Egocentricity and concreteness of thinking are often seen in retarded persons and are related to cognitive deficits, particularly difficulties in concept formation and abstract thinking.

Organicity—that is, definite neurological abnormalities—usually cannot be readily linked to behavioral patterns, especially in mildly or moderately impaired persons. Such neurological abnormalities are more common in profoundly retarded persons. They may be associated with motor hyperactivity and short attention span. Contrary to another misconception, aggressive behavior is not organically based and is not an especially common behavioral feature of retarded persons.

Environmental and experiential influences are probably the main factors responsible for the retarded person's behavior. Impersonal, dehumanizing, and understaffed custodial institutions have been the most pathogenic in this respect. The institution's staff often reward passivity, compliance, and lack of initiative. Some patients, however, thrive on the staff's negative attention, which they can elicit through inappropriate behaviors, including aggression. Overprotection by caretakers, especially parents, is often responsible for the retarded person's dependency, low frustration tolerance, sense of inadequacy, and low self-esteem.

Vulnerability to Mental Disorders

Negative self-image and low self-esteem are probably almost universal personality features of retarded persons, particularly the mildly and moderately retarded. They are well aware of being different from others, of not meeting their parents' and society's expectations, and of progressively falling behind their peers and even their younger siblings.

Defenses against an intolerable sense of inadequacy, low self-image, and anxiety may often be maladaptive and pathological and may lead to inappropriate behavior. Some retarded adolescents and young adults may resort to delinquency and aggressive behaviors.

The conflict between the expected self-image and the real self-image may be a source of lifelong stress and anxiety among mildly retarded persons who are aware of their handicap. Prolonged dependence on care and support by others prevents most retarded persons from developing a self-image as a separate person and, in a sense, prevents true separation-individuation. Communication difficulties further increase such persons' vulnerability to feeling inadequate and frustrated. Inappropriate behaviors, such as withdrawal, are common. The low self-esteem of mildly and moderately retarded persons may predispose them to depression.

No reliable data are available on the incidence of psychiatric disorders in mentally retarded persons, mainly because of methodological difficulties. However, several reports indicate a very high risk of psychiatric illness in such persons, with the incidence ranging from 40 to 75 percent.

Among mildly and moderately retarded adults, the most frequent diagnoses are adjustment disorders, mood disorders, and psychoses; among children, the most frequent diagnoses are mood disorders, anxiety disorders, and pervasive developmental disorders.

DIAGNOSIS

History

In most cases the history from the parents and primary caretaker is the only source of information about the retarded person, and so every effort and caution should be taken to ensure its accuracy. The history of the pregnancy, labor, and delivery; the consanguinity of the parents; and the presence of hereditary disorders in their families deserve particular attention. The parents may also provide information about the child's developmental milestones. This area is especially subject to distortions because of parental bias and anxiety. A history is particularly helpful in assessing the emotional climate of the family and their sociocultural background, which are important in the evaluation of clinical findings.

Psychiatric Interview

Two factors are of paramount importance when interviewing the patient: the interviewer's attitude and the manner of communication with the patient. The interviewer should not be guided by the patient's mental age, as it cannot fully characterize the person. A mildly retarded adult with a mental age of 10 is not a 10-year-old child. When addressed as if they were children, some retarded persons become justifiably insulted, angry, and uncooperative. Passive and dependent persons, alternatively, may assume the child's role that they think is expected of them. In both cases, no valid diagnostic data can be obtained.

The patient's verbal abilities, including receptive and expressive language, should be assessed as soon as possible by observing the verbal and nonverbal communication between the caretakers and the patient and from the history. In this regard it is often helpful to see the patient and the caretakers together. If the patient uses sign language, the caretaker may have to stay during the interview as an interpreter.

Retarded persons have the lifelong experience of failing in many areas, and they may be quite anxious before seeing an interviewer. The interviewer and the caretaker should attempt to give such patients a clear, supportive and concrete explanation of the diagnostic process, particularly those patients with sufficient receptive language. Giving patients the impression that their bad behavior is the cause of the referral should be avoided. Support and praise should be offered in language appropriate to the patient's age and understanding. Leading questions should be avoided, as retarded persons may be suggestible and wish to please others. Subtle directiveness, structure, and reinforcements may be necessary to keep them on the task or topic.

The child's control over motility patterns should be ascertained, and clinical evidence of distractibility and distortions in perception and memory may be evaluated. The use of speech, reality testing, and the ability to generalize from experiences are important to note.

The nature and the maturity of the child's defenses—particularly exaggerated or self-defeating uses of avoidance, repression, denial, introjection, and isolation—should be observed. Sublimation potential, frustration tolerance, and impulse control—especially over motor, aggressive, and sexual drives—should be assessed. Also important are self-image and its role in the development of self-confidence, as well as the assessment of tenacity, persistence, curiosity, and the willingness to explore the unknown.

In general, the psychiatric examination of the retarded child should reveal how the child has coped with the stages of personality development. In regard to failure or regression, it is possible to develop a personality profile that allows the logical planning of management and remedial approaches.

Physical Examination

Various parts of the body may have certain characteristics that are commonly found in the mentally retarded and have prenatal causes. For example, the configuration and the size of the head offer clues to a variety of conditions, such as microcephaly, hydrocephalus, and Down's syndrome. The patient's face may have some of the stigmata of mental retardation, which greatly facilitate the diagnosis. Such facial signs are hypertelorism, a flat nasal bridge, prominent eyebrows, epicanthal folds, corneal opacities, retinal changes, low-set and small or misshapen ears, a protruding tongue, and a disturbance in dentition. Facial expression, such as dull appearance, may be misleading and should not be relied on without other supporting evidence. The color and the texture of the skin and hair, a high-arched palate, the size of the thyroid gland, and the size of the child and his or her trunk and extremities are further areas to be explored. The circumference of the head should be measured as part of the clinical investigation. The clinician should bear in mind during the examination that mentally retarded children, particularly those with associated behavioral problems, are at increased risk for child abuse.

Dermatoglyphics or the handprinting patterns may offer another diagnostic tool, as uncommon ridge patterns and flexion creases are often found in retarded children. Abnormal dermatoglyphics may be found in chromosomal disorders and in children who were infected prenatally with rubella. Table 32-5 lists the multiple handicaps associated with the syndromes discussed.

Neurological Examination

When neurological abnormalities are present, their incidence and severity generally rise in direct proportion to the degree of retardation. However, many severely retarded children have no neurological abnormalities; conversely, about 25 percent of all children with cerebral palsy have normal intelligence.

Disturbances in motor areas are manifested in abnormalities of muscle tone (spasticity or hypotonia), reflexes (hyperreflexia), and involuntary movements (choreoathetosis). A smaller degree of disability in this area is revealed in clumsiness and poor coordination.

Sensory disturbances may include hearing difficulties, ranging from cortical deafness to mild hearing deficits. Visual disturbances may range from blindness to disturbances of spatial concepts, design recognition, and concept of body image.

The infants with the poorest prognosis are those who manifest a combination of inactivity, general hypotonia, and exaggerated response to stimuli. In older children, hyperactivity, short attention span, distractibility, and a low frustration tolerance are often hallmarks of brain damage.

In general, the younger the child is at the time of investigation, the more caution is indicated in predicting future ability, as the recovery potential of the infantile brain is very good. Following the child's development at regular intervals is probably the most reliable approach.

Skull X-rays are usually taken routinely but are illuminating only in a relatively few conditions, such as craniosynostosis, hydrocephalus, and others that result in intracranial calcifications (e.g., toxoplasmosis, tuberous sclerosis, cerebral angiomatosis, and hypoparathyroidism). Computed tomography (CT) scans and magnetic resonance imaging (MRI) have become important tools for uncovering central nervous system pathology associated with mental retardation. The occasional findings of internal hydrocephalus, cortical atrophy, or porencephaly in a severely retarded, brain-damaged child are not considered important to the general picture.

An electroencephalogram (EEG) is best interpreted with caution in cases of mental retardation. The exceptions are patients with hypsarhythmia and grand mal seizures, in whom the EEG may help establish the diagnosis and suggest treatment. In most other conditions a diffuse cerebral disorder produces nonspecific EEG changes, characterized by slow frequencies with bursts of spikes and sharp or blunt wave complexes. The confusion over the significance of the EEG in the diagnosis of mental retardation is best illustrated by the reports of frequent EEG abnormalities in Down's syndrome, which range from 25 percent to the majority of patients examined.

Laboratory Tests

Laboratory tests include examination of the urine and the blood for metabolic disorders. Enzymatic abnormalities in chromosomal disorders, particularly Down's syndrome, promise to become useful diagnostic tools. The determination of the karyotype in a suitable genetic laboratory is indicated whenever a chromosomal disorder is suspected.

Hearing and Speech Evaluations

Hearing and speech evaluations should be done routinely. The development of speech may be the most reliable criterion in investigating mental retardation. Various hearing impairments are often present in the mentally retarded; however, in some instances the impairments may simulate mental retardation. Unfortunately, the commonly used methods of hearing and speech evaluation require the patient's cooperation and, thus, are often unreliable in the severely retarded.

Psychological Assessment

Examining physicians may use several screening instruments for infants and toddlers. As in many areas of mental retardation, there is a heated controversy over the predictive value of infant psychological tests. The correlation of abnormalities during infancy with later abnormal functioning is reported by some as very low and by others as very high. It is generally agreed that the correlation rises in direct proportion to the age of the child at the time of the developmental examination.

Copying geometric figures, the Goodenough Draw-a-Person Test, the Kohs Block Test, and geometric puzzles—all may be used as quick screening tests of visual-motor coordination.

Psychological testing, performed by an experienced psychologist, is a standard part of an evaluation for mental retardation. The Gesell, Bayley, and Cattell tests are most commonly used with infants. For children the Stanford–Binet and the Wechsler Intelligence Scale for Children-Revised (WISC-R) are the most widely used in this country. Both tests have been criticized for penalizing the culturally deprived child, for being culturally biased, for testing mainly potential for academic achievement and not for adequate social functioning, and for their unreliability in children with I.Q.s of less than 50. Some people have tried to overcome the language barrier of the mentally retarded by devising picture vocabulary tests, of which the Peabody Vocabulary Test is the most widely used.

The tests often found useful in detecting brain damage are the Bender–Gestalt and the Benton Visual Retention tests (See Figures 5.2-1 and 5.2-2 in Section 5.2, "Neuropsychological Assessment of Adults"). These tests are also useful for mildly retarded children. In addition, a psychological evaluation should assess perceptual, motor, linguistic, and cognitive abilities. Information about motivational, emotional, and interpersonal factors is also important.

A clinical case example follows:

A psychiatrist specializing in patients with mental retardation received a call from a pediatric colleague referring a 17-year-old girl. She was described as "cured from depression" and needing only follow-up medication.

The patient's arrival created a commotion in the waiting room. She was a small, slender person, markedly agitated and restless, who screamed unintelligibly in a high-pitched voice while her anxious parents tried to calm her. She looked far from being cured.

The parents provided the following history. When the girl was under 1 year of age, she received a diagnosis of severe mental retardation. Extensive diagnostic evaluations failed to determine the cause of the retardation. She had always been physically healthy. The patient was an only child, was reared at home, and attended special classes in public schools. She was cheerful, friendly, and affectionate. She was nonverbal but managed to communicate through gestures and vocalizations. She learned some household tasks and liked to help her mother around the house.

The patient had never been separated from her parents until six months previously, when her parents went to Europe for a week and left her with a housekeeper. On their return they found her agitated, unresponsive to their requests, and uninterested in her usual activities. She cried frequently, slept poorly, ate little, and spent most of the time roaming around the house aimlessly. The parents felt guilty about having gone away and tried to make amends. They spent all their time with the girl and tried to do things with her that would make her happy.

The patient's parents wondered if she was physically ill, but examinations and tests by her pediatrician had all shown her to be well. The pediatrician gave her an antianxiety drug—diazepam (Valium), 2 mg three times a day—but it had no effect. The school psychologist thought that the girl's behavior was an attention-getting device reinforced by her parents' indulgence. The psychologist suggested setting firm limits and referred them to a child guidance clinic. There they were informed by the child psychiatrist that the girl was punishing them for abandoning her when they went on their vacation. The child psychiatrist suggested giving the patient unlimited attention and affection.

When this regimen only made matters worse, another psychiatrist was consulted. He thought that the patient was depressed and started her on an antidepressant, imipramine (Tofranil). The patient did not improve. In desperation, the parents called every psychiatric hospital in the area, trying to have her admitted, but none were willing to take her. As one admitting social worker explained, psychiatric hospitals generally have no experience in treating retarded, nonverbal patients. The patient was finally hospitalized on a pediatric ward, where an extensive medical evaluation failed to disclose the cause of her condition.

During the diagnostic interview with the specialist, the patient was extremely agitated. She screamed often in a high-pitched voice, would not sit in one place, and tugged at her mother's arm, indicating she wanted to go home.

Discussion. This case illustrates the difficulty in treating people with severe mental retardation who are unable to describe their subjective experiences. The patient seemed depressed and agitated but could not talk about a persistent depressed mood. It seemed reasonable to make a provisional diagnosis of major depression, based on her crying, uninterested attitude, decreased appetite, insomnia, and psychomotor agitation, even though she had not consistently responded to antidepressant medication.

DSM-III-R Diagnosis:
Axis I: Major depression, single episode, severe
Axis II: Severe mental retardation

DIFFERENTIAL DIAGNOSIS

Children who come from deprived homes that provide inadequate stimulation may manifest motor and mental retardation that can be reversed if an enriched, stimulating environment is provided in early childhood. A number of sensory handicaps, especially deafness and blindness, may be mistaken for mental retardation if, during testing, no compensation for the handicap is allowed. Speech deficits and cerebral palsy often make a child seem retarded, even in the presence of borderline or normal intelligence.

Chronic, debilitating diseases of any kind may depress the child's functioning in all areas. Convulsive disorders may give an impression of mental retardation, especially in the presence of uncontrolled seizures.

Chronic brain syndromes may result in isolated handicaps, failure to read (alexia), failure to write (agraphia), failure to communicate (aphasia), and several others that may exist in a person of normal and even superior intelligence.

In children with specific developmental disorders, which can coexist with mental retardation, there is a delay or failure of development in a specific area, such as reading or language, but the children develop normally in other areas. In contrast, children with mental retardation show general delays in many areas of development.

Mental retardation and pervasive developmental disorder often coexist, with 70 to 75 percent of those with pervasive developmental disorder having an I.Q. of less than 70. A pervasive developmental disorder results in the distortion of the timing, rate, and sequence of many basic psychological functions necessary for social development. Because of their general level of functioning, children with pervasive developmental disorder have more problems with social relatedness and have more deviant language than those with mental retardation. In mental retardation, generalized delays in development are present, but mentally retarded children behave as if they were passing through an earlier normal developmental stage.

A most difficult differential diagnostic problem concerns children with severe retardation, brain damage, autistic disorder, schizophrenia with childhood onset, or, according to some, Heller's disease. The confusion stems from the fact that details of the child's early history are often unavailable or unreliable. In addition, when the children are evaluated, many with these conditions display similar bizarre and stereotyped behavior, mutism, echolalia, or functioning on a retarded level. By the time these children are usually seen, it does not matter from a practical point of view whether the child's retardation is secondary to a primary early infantile autism or schizophrenia or whether the personality and behavioral distortions are secondary to brain damage or retardation. When ego functions are delayed in development or are atrophic because of other reasons, the physician must first concentrate on overcoming the child's unrelatedness. A relationship with the child must be established before remedial education measures can be successful.

TREATMENT

Mental retardation is associated with several heterogeneous groups of disorders and a multitude of psychosocial factors. The best treatment of mental retardation is the preventive medicine model of primary, secondary, and tertiary prevention.

Primary Prevention

Primary prevention refers to efforts and actions taken to eliminate or reduce the factors and conditions that lead to the development of the disorders associated with mental retardation. Such measures include (1) education to increase the general public's knowledge and awareness of mental retardation, (2) continuing efforts of health professionals to ensure and upgrade public health policies, (3) legislation to provide optimal maternal and child health care, and (4) the eradication of the known disorders associated with central nervous system damage. Family and genetic counseling helps reduce the incidence of mental retardation in a family with a history of a genetic disorder with mental retardation. For the children and mothers of low socioeconomic status, proper prenatal and postnatal medical care and various supplementary enrichment programs and social service assistance may help minimize medical and psychosocial complications.

Secondary and Tertiary Prevention

Once a disorder or condition associated with mental retardation has been identified, the disorder should be treated so as to shorten the course of the illness (secondary prevention) and to minimize the sequelae or consequent handicaps (tertiary prevention).

Hereditary metabolic and endocrine disorders, such as PKU and hypothyroidism, can be effectively treated in an early stage by dietary control or hormone replacement therapy.

Mentally retarded children frequently have emotional and behavioral difficulties requiring psychiatric treatment. These children's limited cognitive and social capabilities require modified psychiatric treatment modalities based on the children's level of intelligence. Play therapy and opportunities for social group interaction often help them express their inner conflicts.

Behavior therapy, especially positive reinforcement, has proved effective in modifying some maladaptive behaviors. Occasionally, psychotropic medication can help remove or modify some target behavioral symptoms, such as hyperactive and impulsive behavior, anxiety, and depression. Lithium or propranolol (Inderal) are sometimes useful for the management of aggressive behaviors. Naltrexone (Trexan) has reduced self-injurious behaviors in some retarded persons. In some institutions insufficient staffing and poor monitoring of medication result in the unnecessary use or excessively high dosaging of medication.

The parents need continuous counseling or, if indicated, family therapy. The parents should be allowed opportunities to express their feelings of guilt, despair, anguish, recurring denial, and anger regarding the child's disorder and future. The psychiatrist should be prepared to give the parents all the basic and current medical information regarding causes, treatment, and other pertinent areas (such as special training and the correction of sensory defects).

References

Brown W T: The fragile X syndrome. Neurol Clin *7*: 107, 1989.

Burd L, Martsolf J T: Fetal alcohol syndrome: Diagnosis and syndromal variability. Physiol Behav *46*: 39, 1989.

Crocker A C: The causes of mental retardation. Pediatr Ann *18*: 623, 1989.

Davis E, Fennoy I: Growth and development in infants of cocaine abusing mothers. Am J Dis Child *144*: 426, 1990.

Diamond G W: Developmental problems in children with HIV infection. Ment Retard *27*: 213, 1989.

Dosen A: Diagnosis and treatment of mental illness in mentally retarded children: A developmental model. Child Psychiatr Hum Dev *20*: 73, 1989.

Hagberg B A: Rett syndrome: Clinical peculiarities, diagnostic approach, and possible cause. Pediatr Neurol *5*: 75, 1989.

Hurley A D: Individual psychotherapy with mentally retarded individuals: A review and call for research. Res Dev Disabil *10*: 261, 1989.

Spreat S, Behar D, Reneski B, Miazzo P: Lithium carbonate for aggression in mentally retarded persons. Compr Psychiatry *30*: 505, 1989.

Szymanski L S, Crocker A C: Mental retardation. In *Comprehensive Textbook of Psychiatry*, ed 5, H I Kaplan and B J Sadock, editors, p 1728. Williams & Wilkins, Baltimore, 1989.

33

Pervasive Developmental Disorders

Pervasive developmental disorder (PDD) was first described in 1980 in the third edition of *Diagnostic and Statistical Manual of Mental Disorders* (DSM-III). Before that, in the second edition of *Diagnostic and Statistical Manual of Mental Disorders* (DSM-II), children with the symptoms of PDD were considered a subgroup of childhood schizophrenia. In the revised edition of DSM-III (DSM-III-R), there are two subgroups: autistic disorder, also known as infantile autism and Kanner's syndrome, and pervasive developmental disorder not otherwise specified (PDDNOS).

In these disorders there are delays and deviancies in multiple areas of development. The diagnostic criteria include three major clusters of developmental and behavioral problems: (1) impairments in reciprocal social interaction, (2) impairments in communication and imaginative activity, and (3) a markedly restricted repertoire of activities and interests. In the diagnosis of autistic disorder, DSM-III-R requires specifying the age at onset of autistic disorder: infantile (before 36 months), childhood (after 36 months), or age unknown or not otherwise specified.

The category of PDDNOS is reserved for cases that meet the general description of PDD but that have symptoms that fall short in number and severity of the specific criteria for autistic disorder. Some children, described by Hans Asperger as having severe problems with social relatedness but less impairment in language development, gave rise to the diagnosis of Asperger's syndrome.

The DSM-III-R criteria for the diagnoses of autistic disorder and PDDNOS are presented in Tables 33-1 and 33-2, respectively.

AUTISTIC DISORDER

History

Henry Maudsley (1867) was the first psychiatrist who paid serious attention to very young children with severe mental disorders involving a marked deviation, delay, and distortion in the developmental processes. Initially, all such disorders were considered psychoses. In 1943 Leo Kanner, in his classic paper "Autistic Disturbances of Affective Contact," coined the term "infantile autism" and provided a clear and comprehensive account of the early childhood syndrome. He described children who exhibited extreme autistic aloneness, failure to assume an anticipatory posture, delayed or deviant language development with echolalia and pronominal reversal (using "you" for "I"), monotonous repetitions of noises or verbal utterances, excellent rote memory, limited range in the variety of spontaneous activities, stereotypies and mannerisms, anxiously obsessive desire for the maintenance of sameness and a dread of change and incompleteness, and abnormal relationships with people and a preference for pictures and inanimate objects. Kanner suspected the syndrome to be more frequent than it seemed and suggested that some children had been misclassified as mentally retarded or schizophrenic.

There has been confusion about whether infantile autism is the earliest possible manifestation of schizophrenia or a discrete clinical entity, but the evidence points toward infantile autism and schizophrenia as separate entities.

Epidemiology

Prevalence. Autistic disorder occurs at a rate of 4 to 5 cases per 10,000 children (0.04 to 0.05 percent) under age 12 or 15. If severe mental retardation with some autistic features is included, the rate can rise as high as 20 per 10,000. In most cases autism begins before 36 months but may not be evident to parents, depending on their awareness and the severity of the disease.

Sex distribution. Infantile autism is found more frequently in boys than in girls. Three to five times more boys than girls have autism. But autistic girls tend to be more seriously affected and more likely to have family histories of cognitive impairment.

Socioeconomic status. Early studies suggested that a high socioeconomic status was common in families with autistic children; however, those findings were probably based on referral biases. Over the past 25 years, an increasing proportion of cases have been found in the low socioeconomic groups. This may well be due to an increased awareness of the syndrome and the increased availability of child mental health workers for poor children.

Etiology and Pathogenesis

Autistic disorder is a developmental behavioral disorder. Although autistic disorder was first considered to be psychosocial or psychodynamic in origin, much evidence has accumulated to support a biological substrate.

Psychodynamic and family factors. In his initial report Kanner noted that few parents of autistic children were really warmhearted and that, for the most part, the parents and other family members were preoccupied with intellectual abstractions and tended to express little genuine interest in their children. This finding, however, has not been replicated over

Table 33-1
Diagnostic Criteria for Autistic Disorder

At least eight of the following 16 items are present, these to include at least two items from A, one from B, and one from C.
Note: Consider a criterion to be met *only* if the behavior is abnormal for the person's developmental level.

A. Qualitative impairment in reciprocal social interaction as manifested by the following:
(The examples within parentheses are arranged so that those first mentioned are more likely to apply to younger or more handicapped, and the later ones, to older or less handicapped, persons with this disorder.)
(1) marked lack of awareness of the existence or feelings of others (e.g., treats a person as if he or she were a piece of furniture; does not notice another person's distress; apparently has no concept of the need of others for privacy)
(2) no or abnormal seeking of comfort at times of distress (e.g., does not come for comfort even when ill, hurt, or tired; seeks comfort in a stereotyped way, e.g., says "cheese, cheese, cheese" whenever hurt)
(3) no or impaired imitation (e.g., does not wave bye-bye; does not copy mother's domestic activities; mechanical imitation of others' actions out of context)
(4) no or abnormal social play (e.g., does not actively participate in simple games; prefers solitary play activities; involves other children in play only as "mechanical aids")
(5) gross impairment in ability to make peer friendships (e.g., no interest in making peer friendships; despite interest in making friends, demonstrates lack of understanding of conventions of social interaction, for example, reads phone book to uninterested peer)

B. Qualitative impairment in verbal and nonverbal communication, and in imaginative activity, as manifested by the following:
(The numbered items are arranged so that those first listed are more likely to apply to younger or more handicapped, and the later ones, to older or less handicapped, persons with this disorder.)
(1) no mode of communication, such as communicative babbling, facial expression, gesture, mime, or spoken language
(2) marked abnormal nonverbal communication, as in the use of eye-to-eye gaze, facial expression, body posture, or gestures to initiate or modulate social interaction (e.g., does not anticipate being held, stiffens when held, does not look at the person or smile when making a social approach, does not greet parents or visitors, has a fixed stare in social situations)
(3) absence of imaginative activity, such as playacting of adult roles, fantasy characters, or animals; lack of interest in stories about imaginary events
(4) marked abnormalities in the production of speech, including volume, pitch, stress, rate, rhythm, and intonation (e.g., monotonous tone, questionlike melody, or high pitch)
(5) marked abnormalities in the form or content of speech, including stereotyped and repetitive use of speech (e.g., immediate echolalia or mechanical repetition of television commercial); use of "you" when "I" is meant (e.g., using "You want cookie?" to mean "I want a cookie"); idiosyncratic use of words or phrases (e.g., "Go on green riding" to mean "I want to go on the swing"); or frequent irrelevant remarks (e.g., starts talking about train schedules during a conversation about sports)
(6) marked impairment in the ability to initiate or sustain a conversation with others, despite adequate speech (e.g., indulging in lengthy monologues on one subject regardless of interjections from others)

C. Markedly restricted repertoire of activities and interests, as manifested by the following:
(1) stereotyped body movements (e.g., hand flicking or twisting, spinning, head banging, complex whole-body movements)
(2) persistent preoccupation with parts of objects (e.g., sniffing or smelling objects, repetitive feeling of texture of materials, spinning wheels of toy cars) or attachment to unusual objects (e.g., insists on carrying around a piece of string)
(3) marked distress over changes in trivial aspects of environment (e.g., when a vase is moved from usual position)
(4) unreasonable insistence on following routines in precise detail (e.g., insisting that exactly the same route always be followed when shopping)
(5) markedly restricted range of interests and a preoccupation with one narrow interest (e.g., interested only in lining up objects, in amassing facts about meteorology, or in pretending to be a fantasy character)

D. Onset during infancy or childhood.
Specify if childhood onset (after 36 months of age).

Table from DSM-III-R, *Diagnostic and Statistical Manual of Mental Disorders*, ed 3, revised. Copyright American Psychiatric Association, Washington, DC, 1987, with permission.

Table 33-2
Diagnostic Criteria for Pervasive Developmental Disorder Not Otherwise Specified

This category should be used when there is a qualitative impairment in the development of reciprocal social interaction and of verbal and nonverbal communication skills, but the criteria are not met for autistic disorder, schizophrenia, or schizotypal or schizoid personality disorder. Some people with this diagnosis will exhibit a markedly restricted repertoire of activities and interests, but others will not.

Table from DSM-III-R, *Diagnostic and Statistical Manual of Mental Disorders*, ed 3, revised. Copyright American Psychiatric Association, Washington, DC, 1987, with permission.

the past 45 years. Other theories, such as parental rage and rejection and parental reinforcement of autistic symptoms, have also not been substantiated. Recent studies comparing parents of autistic children with parents of normal children have not shown significant differences in infant- and child-rearing skills. There has been no satisfactory evidence that any particular kind of deviant family functioning or psychodynamic constellation of factors leads to the development of autistic disorder. Nevertheless, some autistic children respond to psychosocial stressors, such as the birth of a sibling or the move to a new home, with an exacerbation of symptoms.

Organic-neurological-biological abnormalities. Autistic disorder and autistic symptoms are associated with conditions that have neurological lesions, notably congenital rubella, phenylketonuria (PKU), tuberous sclerosis, and Rett's syndrome. Autistic children show more evidence of perinatal complications than do comparison groups of normal children and those with other disorders.

Perinatal stress seems to increase the risk of infantile autism. The finding that autistic children have significantly more minor congenital physical anomalies than do their siblings and normal controls suggests that complications of pregnancy in the first trimester are significant. Four to 32 percent of autistic persons have grand mal seizures at some point in life, and about 20 to 25 percent of autistic persons show ventricular enlargement on computed tomography scans. Various electroencephalogram (EEG) abnormalities are found in 10 to 83 percent of autistic children, and, although no EEG finding is specific to infantile autism, there is some indication of failed cerebral lateralization. Recently, one magnetic resonance imaging (MRI) study revealed hypoplasia of cerebellar vermal lobules VI and VII, and another MRI study revealed cortical abnormalities, particularly polymicrogyria, in some autistic patients. These abnormalities may reflect abnormal cell migrations in the first six months of gestation. An autopsy study revealed decreased Purkinje cell counts, and in another study there was increased diffuse cortical metabolism during positron emission tomography (PET) scanning.

Biochemical abnormalities. In some autistic children, increased cerebrospinal fluid (CSF) homovanillic acid (HVA, the major dopamine metabolite) is associated with increased withdrawal and stereotypies. There is some evidence that symptom severity decreases as the ratio of CSF 5-hydroxyindoleacetic acid (5-HIAA, metabolite of serotonin) to CSF HVA increases. CSF-5-HIAA may be inversely proportional to blood serotonin levels; these are increased in one-third of autistic persons, a nonspecific finding that is also found in mentally retarded persons.

Genetic factors. In several surveys between 2 and 4 percent of siblings of autistic persons have been found to be afflicted with autistic disorder, a rate 50 times greater than in the general population. The concordance rate of autistic disorder in the two largest twin studies was 36 percent in monozygotic pairs versus 0 percent in dizygotic pairs in one study and about 96 percent in monozygotic pairs versus about 27 percent in dizygotic pairs in the second study. In the second study, however, zygosity was confirmed in only about one-half of the sample. Clinical reports and studies suggest that the nonautistic members of the families share various language or other cognitive problems with the autistic person but have them in a less severe form. Fragile X syndrome (see Chapter 32, "Mental Retardation") appears to be associated with autistic disorder, but the number of persons with both autistic disorder and fragile X syndrome is unclear.

Immunological factors. Some evidence indicates that immunological incompatibility between the mother and the embryo or fetus may contribute to autism. The lymphocytes of some autistic children react with maternal antibodies, raising the possibility that embryonic neural or extraembryonic tissues may be damaged during gestation.

Clinical Features

Physical characteristics

Appearance. Kanner was struck by autistic children's intelligent and attractive appearance. They also tend to be shorter between the ages of 2 and 7 than the normal population.

Handedness. There is a failure of lateralization in many autistic children because of a developmental lag. That is, they remain ambidextrous at an age when cerebral dominance is established in normal children. There is also a greater incidence of abnormal dermatoglyphics (e.g., fingerprints) than in the general population, which may suggest a disturbance in neuroectodermal development.

Intercurrent physical illness. There is a higher incidence of upper respiratory infections, excessive burping, febrile seizures, constipation, and loose bowel movements in young autistic children than in controls. Many autistic children react differently to illness than do normal children, which may reflect an immature or abnormal autonomic nervous system. Autistic children may not have elevated temperatures with infectious illnesses, may not complain of pain either verbally or by gesture, and may not show the malaise of ill children. Their behavior and relatedness may improve to a noticeable degree when they are ill, and in some cases this may be a clue to physical illness.

Behavioral characteristics

Failure to show relatedness (autism). All autistic children fail to show the usual relatedness to their parents and other people. As infants, many lack a social smile and anticipatory posture for being picked up as an adult approaches. Abnormal eye contact is a common finding. The social development of autistic children is characterized by a lack (but not always a total absence) of attachment behavior and a relatively early failure of person-specific bonding. These children often do not seem to recognize or differentiate the most important people in their lives—parents, siblings, and teachers. And they may show virtually no separation anxiety on being left in an unfamiliar environment with strangers.

When autistic children have reached school age, their withdrawal may have diminished or not be as obvious, particularly in the better-functioning children. Instead, their failure to play with peers and to make friends, their social awkwardness and inappropriateness, and, particularly, their failure to develop empathy are observed.

In late adolescence, those autistic persons who make the most progress often have a desire for friendships. However, their ineptness of approach and inability to respond to another's interests, emotions, and feelings are major obstacles in developing friendships. Autistic adolescents and adults have sexual feelings, but their lack of social competence and skills prevents most of them from developing a sexual relationship. It is extremely rare for autistic persons to get married.

Disturbances of communication and language. Gross deficits and deviances in language development are among the principal criteria for diagnosing infantile autism. Autistic children are not simply reluctant to speak, and their speech abnormalities are not due to lack of motivation. Language deviance, as much as language delay, is characteristic of autistic disorder. In contrast to normal and mentally retarded children, autistic children make little use of meaning in their memory and thought processes. When autistic persons do learn to converse fluently, they lack social competence, and their conversations are not characterized by reciprocal responsive interchanges.

In the first year of life, the autistic child's amount and pattern of babbling may be reduced or abnormal. Some children emit noises—clicks, sounds, screeches, and nonsense syllables—in a stereotyped fashion with no seeming intent at communication.

Unlike normal young children, who always have better

receptive language skills and understand much before they can speak, verbal autistic children may say more than they understand. Words and even entire sentences may drop in and out of a child's vocabulary. Autistic children may use a word once and then not use it again for a week, a month, or years. Their speech is usually in the form of echolalia, both immediate and delayed, or stereotyped phrases out of context. These abnormalities are often associated with pronominal reversal; that is, the girl asks, "Do you want the toy?" when she means she wants it. Difficulties in articulation are also noted. The use of peculiar voice quality and rhythm is observed clinically in many cases. About 50 percent of all autistic children never have useful speech. Some of the brighter children show a particular fascination with letters and numbers. A few literally teach themselves to read at a preschool age (hyperlexia), often astonishingly well. In virtually all cases, however, these children read without any comprehension whatsoever.

Abnormalities in play, stereotypies and ritualistic behaviors, insistence on sameness, and resistance to change. In the first years of an autistic child's life, much of the normal child's exploratory play is absent or minimal. Toys and objects are often manipulated in a way that was not intended, with little variety, creativity, and imagination and few symbolic features. Autistic children cannot imitate or use abstract pantomime. The activities and play, if any, of the autistic child are rigid, repetitive, and monotonous. Ritualistic and compulsive phenomena are common in early and middle childhood. They often spin, bang, and line up objects and become attached to inanimate objects. In addition, many autistic children, particularly those who are the most intellectually impaired, exhibit various abnormalities of movements. Stereotypies, mannerisms, and grimacing are most frequent when the child is left alone and may decrease in a structured situation. Autistic children are resistant to transition and change. Moving to a new house, moving furniture in a room, and having breakfast before a bath when the reverse was the routine may result in panic or temper tantrums.

Response to sensory stimuli. Autistic children may be overresponsive or underresponsive to sensory stimuli (e.g., to sound and pain). They may selectively ignore spoken language directed at them, and so they are often thought to be deaf. However, they may show unusual interest in the sound of a wristwatch. Many have a heightened pain threshold or an altered response to pain. Indeed, these children may injure themselves rather severely and not cry.

Many autistic children seem to enjoy music. They frequently hum a tune or sing a song or commercial before saying words or using speech. Some particularly enjoy vestibular stimulation—spinning, swinging, and up and down movements.

Other behavioral symptoms. Hyperkinesis is a common behavior problem in young autistic children. Hypokinesis is less frequent, and, when present, it often alternates with hyperactivity. Aggressiveness and temper tantrums are observed, often for no apparent reason, or are prompted by change or demands. Self-injurious behavior includes head banging, biting, scratching, and hair pulling. Short attention span, a complete inability to focus on a task, insomnia, feeding and eating problems, enuresis, and encopresis are also frequent.

A clinical case example follows:

A firstborn child aged 3½ was referred at the request of his parents because of his uneven development and abnormal behavior. Delivery had been difficult, and he had needed oxygen at birth. His physical appearance, motor development, and self-help skills were all age-appropriate; but his parents had been uneasy about him from the first few months of life because of his lack of response to social contact and the usual baby games. Comparison with their second child, who enjoyed social communication from early infancy, confirmed their fears.

The boy appeared to be self-sufficient and aloof from others. He did not greet his mother in the morning or his father when he returned from work, though, if left with a baby-sitter, he tended to scream much of the time. He had no interest in other children and ignored his younger brother. His babbling had no conversational intonation. At 3 years he could understand simple practical instructions. His speech consisted of echoing some words and phrases he had heard in the past, with the original speaker's accent and intonation; he could use one or two such phrases to indicate his simple needs. For example, if he said, "Do you want a drink?" he meant he was thirsty. He did not communicate by facial expression or use gesture or mime, except for pulling someone along and placing the person's hand on an object he wanted.

He was fascinated by bright lights and spinning objects and would stare at them while laughing, flapping his hands, and dancing on tiptoe. He also displayed the same movements while listening to music, which he had liked from infancy. He was intensely attached to a miniature car, which he held in his hand, day and night; but he never played imaginatively with this or any other toy. He could assemble jigsaw puzzles rapidly (with one hand because of the car held in the other), whether the picture side was exposed or hidden. From age 2 he had collected kitchen utensils and arranged them in repetitive patterns all over the floors of the house. These pursuits, together with occasional periods of aimless running around, constituted his whole repertoire of spontaneous activities.

The major treatment problem was the boy's intense resistance to any attempt to change or extend his interests. Removing his toy car, disturbing his puzzles or patterns, retrieving an egg whisk or a spoon for cooking, or trying to make him look at a picture book precipitated temper tantrums that could last an hour or more, with him screaming, kicking, and biting himself or others. These tantrums could be cut short by restoring the status quo. Otherwise, playing his favorite music or a long car ride was sometimes effective.

His parents had wondered if the boy was deaf, but his love of music, his accurate echoing, and his sensitivity to some very soft sounds, such as those made by unwrapping a chocolate in the next room, convinced them that this was not the cause of his abnormal behavior. Psychological testing gave him a mental age of 3 years in nonlanguage-dependent skills (fitting and assembly tasks) but only 18 months in language comprehension.

Discussion. The boy demonstrated marked impairment in reciprocal social interaction and in verbal and nonverbal communication and a marked restricted repertoire of activities, all beginning in the first few months of life. He did not seem interested in other children and never wanted to play baby games with his parents. His speech was limited and peculiar (echoing words and phrases of others), and his play was abnormal in that he never engaged in imaginative play. His interests were markedly restricted and stereotyped, and he became wildly upset if anyone interfered with his routines. These behaviors, beginning in infancy (much more rarely in childhood), are the characteristic signs of autistic disorder.

Intellectual functioning. About 40 percent of the children with infantile autism have intelligence quotient (I.Q.) scores below 50 to 55 (moderate, severe, or profound retardation); 30 percent have scores of 50 to approximately 70 (mild retardation); and 30 percent have scores of 70 or more. Epidemiological and clinical studies show that the risk of autistic disorder increases as the I.Q. decreases. About one-fifth of autistic children have a normal nonverbal intelligence. The I.Q. scores of autistic children tend to show problems with verbal sequencing and abstraction skills, rather than with visuospatial or rote memory skills, suggesting the importance of defects in language-related functions.

Unusual or precocious cognitive or visuomotor abilities are present in some autistic children. These may exist even within the overall retarded functioning and are referred to as splinter functions or islets of precocity. Perhaps the most striking examples are the idiot savants who have prodigious rote memories or calculating abilities. Here, the specific abilities usually remain beyond the capabilities of normal peers. Other precocious abilities in young autistic children include hyperlexia, an early ability to read well (although they are not able to understand what they read), memorizing and reciting, and musical abilities (singing tunes or recognizing different musical pieces).

Course and Prognosis

Autistic disorder has a chronic course and a guarded prognosis. A subgroup of autistic children suffer a loss of some or all of their preexisting speech. This occurs most often between 12 and 24 months of age. As a general rule, the autistic children with high I.Q.s (above 70) and those who use communicative language by ages 5 to 7 have the best prognoses. Adult outcome studies indicate that approximately two-thirds of autistic adults remain severely handicapped and live in complete dependence or semidependence, either with their relatives or in long-term institutions. Only 1 or 2 percent acquire a normal and independent status with gainful employment, and 5 to 20 percent achieve a borderline normal status. The prognosis is improved if the environment or home is supportive and capable of meeting the excessive needs of such a child.

Although a decrease of symptoms is noted in many cases, severe self-mutilation or aggressiveness and regression may develop in others. Approximately 4 to 32 percent develop grand mal seizures in late childhood or adolescence, and these seizures adversely affect the prognosis.

Differential Diagnosis

The major differential diagnoses are schizophrenia with childhood onset, mental retardation with behavioral symptoms, developmental receptive language disorder, congenital deafness or severe hearing disorder, psychosocial deprivation, and disintegrative (regressive) psychoses.

Because children with a pervasive developmental disorder usually have many concurrent problems, Michael Rutter suggested a stepwise approach to use in the differential diagnosis (Table 33-3).

Table 33-3
Procedure for Differential Diagnosis on a Multiaxial System

1. Determine intellectual level.
2. Determine level of language development.
3. Consider whether child's behavior is appropriate for
   (i) chronological age
   (ii) mental age
   (iii) language age
4. If not appropriate, consider differential diagnosis of psychiatric disorder according to
   (i) pattern of social interaction
   (ii) pattern of language
   (iii) pattern of play
   (iv) other behaviors
5. Identify any relevant medical conditions.
6. Consider whether there are any relevant psychosocial factors.

Table from M Rutter, L Hersov: *Child and Adolescent Psychiatry: Modern Approaches*, ed 2. Blackwell, Oxford, England, 1985, with permission.

Schizophrenia with childhood onset. Whereas there is a wealth of literature on infantile autism, there are few data on children under age 12 who meet the DSM-III-R criteria for schizophrenia. Schizophrenia is rare in children under the age of 5. It is accompanied by hallucinations or delusions, with a lower incidence of seizures and mental retardation and a more even I.Q. than that of autistic children.

Mental retardation with behavioral symptoms. About 40 percent of autistic children are moderately, severely, or profoundly retarded, and retarded children may have behavior symptoms that include autistic features. DSM-III-R states that, when both disorders are present, both should be diagnosed. The main differentiating features between autistic disorder and mental retardation are that (1) mentally retarded children usually relate to adults and other children in accordance with their mental age; (2) they use the language they do have to communicate with others; and (3) they have a relatively even profile of retardedness without splinter functions.

Developmental receptive language disorder. A group of children have autisticlike features and may present a diagnostic problem. Table 33-4 summarizes the major differences.

Acquired aphasia with convulsion. Acquired aphasia with convulsion is a rare condition and is sometimes difficult to differentiate from autistic disorder or disintegrative psychosis. Children with this condition are normal for several years before losing both their receptive and their expressive language over a period of weeks or months. Most of them have a few seizures and generalized EEG abnormalities at the onset, which usually do not persist. A profound disorder of language comprehension then follows, characterized by a deviant speech pattern and speech impairment. Some children recover but with considerable residual language impairment.

Congenital deafness or severe hearing impairment. Because autistic children are often mute or show a selective disinterest in spoken language in infancy, they are often thought to be deaf. The following may be differentiating features: Autistic children may babble only infrequently, whereas deaf infants have a history of relatively normal babbling that then gradually tapers and may stop from 6 months to 1 year of age. Deaf children respond only to loud sounds, whereas autistic children may ignore loud or normal sounds and respond to soft or low sounds. Most important, audiogram or auditory evoked potentials indicate significant hearing loss in deaf children. Unlike autistic children, deaf children usually relate to their parents, seek their affection, and, as infants, enjoy being held.

Psychosocial deprivation. Severe disturbances in the physical and emotional environment (such as maternal dep-

Table 33-4
Infantile Autism versus Developmental Receptive Language Disorder

Criteria	Infantile Autism	Developmental Receptive Language Disorder
Incidence	2–4 in 10,000	5 in 10,000
Sex ratio (M : F)	3–4 : 1	Equal or almost equal sex ratio
Family history of speech delay or language problems	Present in about 25 percent of cases	Present in about 25 percent of cases
Associated deafness	Very infrequent	Not infrequent
Nonverbal communication (gestures, etc.)	Absent or rudimentary	Present
Language abnormalities (e.g., echolalia, stereotyped phrases out of context)	More common	Less common
Articulatory problems	Less frequent	More frequent
Level of intelligence	Often severely impaired	Though may be impaired, less frequently severe
Patterns of I.Q. tests	Uneven, lower on verbal scores than dysphasics; lower on comprehension subtest than dysphasics	More even, though verbal I.Q. lower than performance I.Q.
Autistic behaviors, impaired social life, stereotypies and ritualistic activities	More common and more severe	Absent or, if present, less severe
Imaginative play	Absent or rudimentary	Usually present

Table from M Campbell, W H Green: Pervasive developmental disorders of childhood. In *Comprehensive Textbook of Psychiatry*, ed 4, H I Kaplan and B J Sadock, editors, p 1681. Williams & Wilkins, Baltimore, 1985, with permission.

rivation, psychosocial dwarfism, hospitalism, and failure to thrive) can cause children to appear apathetic, withdrawn, and alienated. Language and motor skills can be delayed. Children with these signs almost always rapidly improve when placed in a favorable and enriched psychosocial environment, which is not the case with an autistic child.

Disintegrative (regressive) psychoses. The disintegrative psychoses usually begin between ages 3 and 5. These conditions are even rarer than infantile autism. The child's development in these disorders is usually within normal limits until the onset of illness, when there is severe regression and decline in intelligence and all areas of behavior, accompanied by stereotypies and mannerisms. The illness progresses over a period of a few months. It may follow a mild illness or a known viral infection. In others, a lipoidosis, leukodystrophy, or Heller's disease (dementia infantilis) is found at autopsy. Rett's syndrome (see Chapter 32) is often manifested by autisticlike symptoms.

Treatment

The goals of treatment are to decrease behavioral symptoms and to aid in the development of delayed, rudimentary, or nonexistent functions, such as language and self-care skills. In addition, the parents, often distraught, need support and counseling.

Insight-oriented individual psychotherapy has proved ineffective. Educational and behavioral methods are currently considered the treatments of choice.

Structured classroom training in combination with intrusive behavioral methods is the most effective treatment method for many autistic children and is superior to other types of behavioral approaches. Well-controlled studies indicate that gains in the areas of language and cognition and decreases in maladaptive behaviors are achieved by using this method. Careful training and individual tutoring of parents in the concepts and skills of behavior modification and the resolution of parents' problems and concerns, within a problem-solving format, may yield considerable gains in the child's language, cognitive, and social areas of behavior. However, the training programs are rigorous and require a great deal of the parents' time. The autistic child requires as much structure as possible, and a daily program for as many hours as feasible is desirable.

Although no drug has been found to be specific to autistic disorder, psychopharmacotherapy is a valuable adjunct to comprehensive treatment programs. Administration of haloperidol (Haldol) both reduces behavioral symptoms and accelerates learning. The drug decreases hyperactivity, stereotypies, withdrawal, fidgetiness, abnormal object relations, irritability, and labile affect. There is supportive evidence that, when used judiciously, haloperidol remains an effective long-term drug. Although tardive and withdrawal dyskinesias do occur with haloperidol treatment in autistic children, to date there is evidence that these dyskinesias can resolve when haloperidol is discontinued. Fenfluramine (Pondimin), which reduces blood serotonin levels, is effective in few autistic children. Improvement does not seem to be associated with reduction in blood serotonin level. Naltrexone (Trexan), an opiate antagonist, is currently being investigated in the hope that blocking endogenous opioids will reduce autistic symptoms. Lithium can be tried for aggressive or self-injurious behaviors when other medications fail.

PERVASIVE DEVELOPMENTAL DISORDER NOT OTHERWISE SPECIFIED

Pervasive developmental disorder not otherwise specified (PDDNOS) should be diagnosed when a child manifests a qualitative impairment in the development of reciprocal social interaction and verbal and nonverbal communication skills but does not meet the criteria for autistic disorder, schizophrenia, or schizotypal or schizoid personality disorder. Some children with this diagnosis exhibit a markedly restricted repertoire of activities and in-

Table 33-5
Infantile Autism versus Schizophrenia with Childhood Onset

Criteria	Infantile Autism	Schizophrenia (with Onset before Puberty)
Age of onset	Before 36 months	Not under 5 years of age
Incidence	2–4 in 10,000	Unknown, possibly same or even rarer
Sex ratio (M : F)	3–4 : 1	1.67 : 1 (nearly equal, or slight preponderance of males)
Family history of schizophrenia	Not raised or probably not raised	Raised
Socioeconomic status (SES)	Overrepresentation of upper SES groups (artifact)	More common in lower SES groups
Pre- and perinatal complications and cerebral dysfunction	More common in autism	
Behavioral characteristics	Failure to develop relatedness; absence of speech or echolalia; stereotyped phrases; language comprehension absent or poor; insistence on sameness and stereotypies	Hallucinations and delusions; thought disorder
Adaptive functioning	Usually always impaired	Deterioration in functioning
Level of intelligence	In majority of cases subnormal, frequently severely impaired (70 percent ≤ 70)	Usually within normal range, mostly dull normal (15 percent ≤ 70)
Pattern of I.Q.	Marked unevenness	More even
Grand mal seizures	4–32 percent	Absent or lower incidence

Table by Magda Campbell, M.D., and Wayne Green, M.D.

terests. This condition usually shows a better outcome than does autistic disorder. Asperger described a group of children whose relatedness and activities were autisticlike but whose language development was relatively intact.

Treatment

The approach is basically the same as in autistic disorder. Mainstreaming in school may be possible. Compared with autistic children, those with PDDNOS generally have better language skills and more self-awareness, so they are better candidates for psychotherapy.

SCHIZOPHRENIA WITH CHILDHOOD ONSET

Beginning with DSM-III, schizophrenia with childhood onset was formally separated from autistic disorder. This change reflected evidence accrued during the 1960s and 1970s that the clinical picture, the family history, the age of onset, and the course of the two disorders were quite different. After the separation of the disorders, two controversies ensued. In the first, a minority of researchers remained of the opinion that a group of autistic children go on to develop schizophrenia. There is evidence that a few autistic children do develop schizophrenia, but assertions that these children constitute a large group are unsubstantiated. In general, schizophrenia is easily differentiated from autistic disorder (Table 33-5). The majority of autistic children are impaired in all areas of adaptive functioning, from early life onward. The onset is almost always before the age of 3 years, whereas the onset of schizophrenia is usually in adolescence or young adulthood. There are practically no reports of an onset of schizophrenia before the age of 5 years. The second controversy concerned the application of DSM-III and later DSM-III-R adult criteria for schizophrenia to children, as there are no separate criteria in the manuals for children. Several reports indicate that some children present with hallucinations, delusions, and thought disorders typical of schizophrenia. However, normal developmental immaturities in language development and in separating reality from fantasy sometimes make it difficult to diagnose this disorder in children ages 5 to 7 years.

With regard to treatment, few reports deal with either the psychological or the pharmacological treatment of schizophrenia in childhood or in adolescence. Two double-blind, placebo-controlled studies have shown the effectiveness of various antipsychotics in adolescents. In schizophrenia with childhood onset, antipsychotics are the drugs of choice, but double-blind, placebo-controlled studies are needed.

References

Anderson L T, Campbell M, Adams P, Small A M, Perry R, Shell J: The effects of haloperidol on discrimination learning, and behavioral symptoms in autistic children. J Autism Dev Disord *19*: 227, 1989.

Balottin V, Bejor M, Cecchini A, Martelli A, Polazzi S, Lanzi G: Infantile autism and CT brain-scan findings: Specific versus nonspecific abnormalities. J Autism Dev Disord *19*: 109, 1989.

Bryson S E, Smith I M, Eastwood D: Obstetrical suboptimality in autistic children. J Am Acad Child Adolesc Psychiatry *27*: 418, 1988.

Caplan R, Guthrie D, Fish B, Tanguay P E, David-Lando G: The kiddie formal thought disorder rating scale: Clinical assessment, reliability, and validity. J Am Acad Child Adolesc Psychiatry *28*: 408, 1989.

Cook E H: Autism: Review of neurochemical investigation. Synapse *6*: 292, 1990.

Courchesne E, Yeung-Courchesne R, Press G A, Hesselink J R, Jernigan T L: Hypoplasia of cerebellar vermal lobules VI and VII in autism. N Engl J Med *318*: 1349, 1988.

Dworkin R H, Green S R, Small N E, Warner M L, Cornblatt B A, Erlenmeyer-Kimling L: Positive and negative symptoms and social competence in adolescents at risk for schizophrenia and affective disorder. Am J Psychiatry *147*: 1234, 1990.

Folstein S E, Rutter M L: Autism: Familial aggregation and genetic implications. J Autism Dev Disord *18*: 3, 1988.

Goodman R: Infantile autism: A syndrome of multiple primary deficits? J Autism Dev Disord *19*: 409, 1989.

Lovaas O I: Behavioral treatment and normal educational and intellectual functioning in young autistic children. J Consult Clin Psychol *55*: 3, 1987.

Mesibov E B, Schopler E, eds.: *Neurobiological Issues in Autism*. Plenum Press, New York, 1987.

Payton J B, Steele M W, Wenger S L, Minshew N J: The fragile X marker and autism in perspective. J Am Acad Child Adolesc Psychiatry *28*: 417, 1989.

Petty L, Ornitz E M, Michelman J D, Zimmerman E G: Autistic children who become schizophrenic. Arch Gen Psychiatry *41*: 129, 1984.

Pilowsky D, Chambers W, eds.: *Hallucinations in Children*. American Psychiatric Press, Washington, DC, 1986.

Pisen J, Berthier M L, Sharkstein S E, Nehme E, Pearlson G, Folstein S: Magnetic resonance imaging: Evidence for a defect of cerebral cortical development in autism. Am J Psychiatry *147*: 734, 1990.

Realmuto G M, Erickson W D, Yellin A M, Hopwood J H, Greenberg L M: Clinical comparison of thiothixene and thioridazine in schizophrenic adolescents. Am J Psychiatry *141*: 440, 1984.

Reiss A L, Freund L: Fragile X syndrome, DSM-III-R, and autism. J Am Acad Child Adolesc Psychiatry *29*: 885, 1990.

Rogers S J, Di Lalla D L: Age of symptom onset in young children with pervasive developmental disorders. J Am Acad Child Adolesc Psychiatry *29*: 863, 1990.

Russell A T, Bott L, Sammons C: The phenomenology of schizophrenia occurring in childhood. J Am Acad Child Adolesc Psychiatry *28*: 399, 1989.

Rutter M: Infantile autism and other pervasive developmental disorders. In *Child and Adolescent Psychiatry: Modern Approaches*, ed 2. M Rutter and L Hersov, editors, p 545. Blackwell, Oxford, England, 1985.

Warren R P, Cole P, Odell D, Pingree C B, Warren W L, White E, Yonk J, Singh V K: Detection of maternal antibodies in infantile autism. J Am Acad Child Adolesc Psychiatry *29*: 873, 1990.

34

Specific Developmental Disorders

34.1 / Developmental Arithmetic Disorder

Developmental arithmetic disorder, like the other specific developmental disorders, received little attention from psychiatrists before the publication of the third edition of *Diagnostic and Statistical Manual of Mental Disorders* (DSM-III) in 1980. In the revised edition of DSM-III (DSM-III-R), developmental arithmetic disorder is one of the academic skills disorders contained in the category of specific developmental disorders. In the past this disorder has been called acalculia, Gerstmann's syndrome, congenital arithmetic disability, dyscalculia, and arithmetic disorder.

Developmental arithmetic disorder has the following clinical characteristics and criteria: The person's performance in daily activities requiring arithmetic skills is markedly below the person's intellectual capacity, and these impaired arithmetic skills and performance are confirmed by an individually administered standardized test (Table 34.1-1).

Table 34.1-1
Diagnostic Criteria for Developmental Arithmetic Disorder

A. Arithmetic skills, as measured by a standardized, individually administered test, are markedly below the expected level, given the person's schooling and intellectual capacity (as determined by an individually administered I.Q. test).

B. The disturbance in A significantly interferes with academic achievement or activities of daily living requiring arithmetic skills.

C. Not due to a defect in visual or hearing acuity or a neurological disorder.

Table from DSM-III-R, *Diagnostic and Statistical Manual of Mental Disorders*, ed 3, revised. Copyright American Psychiatric Association, Washington, DC, 1987, with permission.

According to DSM-III-R, a number of different types of skills may be impaired in developmental arithmetic disorder, including linguistic skills (such as understanding or naming mathematical terms, understanding or naming mathematical operations or concepts, and translating written problems into mathematical symbols), perceptual skills (such as recognizing or reading numerical symbols or arithmetic signs and clustering objects into groups), attention skills (such as copying figures correctly, remembering to add in carried numbers, and observing operational signs), and mathematical skills (such as following sequences of mathematical steps, counting objects, and learning multiplication tables).

EPIDEMIOLOGY

The prevalence of developmental arithmetic disorder is not known but is estimated to be about 6 percent of school-age children. It is probably less common than developmental reading disorder and is more common in boys than in girls. It is commonly accepted that some children are born with exceptional mathematical talents and display advanced mathematical competence from early childhood. This phenomenon suggests that persons may also be born with an inability to learn arithmetic skills.

ETIOLOGY

The cause of developmental arithmetic disorder is not known. An early theory proposed a neurological deficit in the right cerebral hemisphere, particularly in the occipital lobe areas. These regions are responsible for processing visual-spatial stimuli that, in turn, are responsible for mathematical skills. However, the validity of this theory has received little support in subsequent neuropsychiatric studies.

The current view on cause is multifactorial. Maturational, cognitive, emotional, educational, and socioeconomic factors account in varying degrees and combinations for developmental arithmetic disorder. Compared with reading, arithmetic abilities seem more dependent on the amount and the quality of instruction.

CLINICAL FEATURES

Most children with developmental arithmetic disorder can be classified during the second and third grades in elementary school. The affected child's performance in handling basic number concepts, such as counting and adding even one-digit numbers, is significantly below the age-expected norms, whereas the child shows normal intellectual skills in other areas.

During the first two or three years of elementary school, a child with developmental arithmetic disorder may appear to make some progress in mathematics by relying on rote memory. But soon, as arithmetic progresses into more complex and higher levels requiring discrimination and manipulation of spatial and numerical relationships, the presence of the disorder becomes conspicuous.

Some investigators have classified developmental arithmetic disorder into several categories: (1) difficulty in learning to count meaningfully, (2) difficulty in mastering cardinal and ordinal systems, (3) difficulty in performing arithmetic operations, and (4) difficulty in envisioning clusters of objects as groups. In addition, there may be difficulties in associating auditory and visual symbols, understanding the conservation of quantity, remembering sequences of arithmetic steps, and choosing principles for problem-solving activities. Children with these problems are, however, presumed to have good auditory and verbal abilities.

Developmental arithmetic disorder often coexists with other specific developmental disorders affecting the following skills: reading, expressive writing, coordination, and expressive and receptive language. Spelling problems, deficits in memory or attention, and emotional or behavioral problems may be present. Young grade-school children with developmental arithmetic disorder often present first with other specific developmental disorders and should be checked for developmental arithmetic disorder. Children with cerebral palsy may have developmental arithmetic disorder with normal overall intelligence.

The relationship between developmental arithmetic disorder and other language and academic skills disorders is not yet clear. Although children with developmental receptive language disorder and developmental expressive language disorder are not necessarily affected by developmental arithmetic disorder, the conditions often coexist, as they are associated in terms of sharing impairments in both decoding and encoding processes.

COURSE AND PROGNOSIS

Developmental arithmetic disorder is usually apparent by the time the child is 8 years old (third grade). In some children the disorder is apparent as early as 6 years (first grade), and in others it may not occur until age 10 (fifth grade) or later. Thus far, not much longitudinal study data have been available to present clear patterns of developmental and academic progress of children who were classified as having this disorder in early school grades. However, untreated children with a moderate developmental arithmetic disorder and those children whose arithmetic difficulties cannot be resolved by intensive remedial interventions may develop complications, which include continuing academic difficulties, poor self-concept, depression, and frustration. These complications may then lead to a reluctance to attend school, outright truancy, or a conduct disorder.

DIAGNOSIS

In a typical case of developmental arithmetic disorder, a careful inquiry into school performance history reveals the child's earlier difficulties with arithmetic subjects. The definite diagnosis can be made only after the child takes an individually administered standardized arithmetic test and scores markedly below the expected level, considering the child's schooling and intellectual capacity as measured by a standardized intelligence test. A pervasive developmental disorder or mental retardation should also be ruled out before confirming the primary diagnosis of developmental arithmetic disorder.

DIFFERENTIAL DIAGNOSIS

Arithmetic difficulties seen in mental retardation are accompanied by a generalized impairment in overall intellectual functioning. In unusual cases of mild mental retardation, arithmetic skills may be significantly below the expected level, given the person's schooling and level of mental retardation. In such cases the additional diagnosis of developmental arithmetic disorder should be made, as treatment of the arithmetic difficulties can be particularly helpful to the child's chances for employment in adulthood. Inadequate schooling, however, can often cause the child's poor arithmetic performance on a standardized arithmetic test. If so, it is likely that most of the other children in the same class have similarly poor arithmetic performances. Conduct disorder and attention-deficit hyperactivity disorder may be present with developmental arithmetic disorder, and in these cases both diagnoses should be made.

TREATMENT

The current most effective treatment of developmental arithmetic disorder is remedial educational intervention. Controversy continues as to the comparative effectiveness of various remedial educational treatments. However, the current consensus is that the treatment methods and materials are useful only when they fit the particular child, the type of the disorder, and the severity and feasibility of the particular teaching plans. Project MATH, a multimedia self-instructional or group-instructional in-service training program, has been successful for some children with developmental arithmetic disorder. Computer programs can be helpful and can increase compliance with remediation efforts. Poor coordination may accompany the disorder, so physical therapy and sensory integration activities may be helpful.

References

Badian N A: Dyscalculia and nonverbal disorders of learning. In *Progress in Learning Disabilities*, vol 5, H R Myklebust, editor, p 235. Grune & Stratton, New York, 1983.

Fleischner J E, Garnett K, Silver L B: Developmental arithmetic disorder. In *Comprehensive Textbook of Psychiatry*, ed 5, H I Kaplan and B J Sadock, editors, p 1800. Williams & Wilkins, Baltimore, 1989.

Johnson D, Myklebust H: *Learning Disabilities: Educational Principles and Practices*. Grune & Stratton, New York, 1967.

Kose L: Neuropsychological implications of diagnoses and treatment of mathematical learning disabilities. Top Lang Learn Disord *1*: 19, 1981.
Lerner J W: Educational interventions in learning disabilities. J Am Acad Child Adolesc Psychiatry *28*: 326, 1989.
McCleod T M, Crump W D: The relationship of visuospatial skills and verbal ability to learning disabilities in mathematics. J Learn Disabil *11*: 237, 1978.
Rourke B P, Strang J D: Subtypes of reading and arithmetic disabilities: A neuropsychological analysis. In *Developmental Neuropsychiatry*, M Rutter, editor, p 473. Guilford, New York, 1983.
Share D L, Moffitt T E, Silva P A: Factors associated with arithmetic-and-reading disability and specific arithmetic disability. J Learn Disabil *21*: 313, 1988.
Vogel S A: Gender differences in intelligence, language, visual motor abilities, and academic achievement in students with learning disabilities: A review of the literature. J Learn Disabil *23*: 44, 1990.
Yule W, Lansdown R, Urbanowicz M: Predicting educational attainment for WISC-R in a primary school sample. Br J Psychol *21*: 43, 1982.

34.2 / Developmental Expressive Writing Disorder

Developmental expressive writing disorder is often associated with other specific developmental disorders, but, since expressive writing is a skill that is acquired and mastered later than language and reading, the disorder is diagnosed somewhat later. Writing requires multimodal sensorimotor coordination and information processing. If the disorder persists through grade school, high school, and adulthood, it can jeopardize the affected person's access to the most gainful and intellectually productive occupations. Developmental expressive writing disorder is a new diagnostic entity in the revised third edition of *Diagnostic and Statistical Manual of Mental Disorders* (DSM-III-R). Until recently, it had been little studied.

DSM-III-R defines developmental expressive writing disorder as an academic skills disorder first occurring during childhood, characterized by poor performance in writing and composition (spelling words and expressing thoughts) considering the level of the person's schooling and intellectual capacity. That level is measured by a standardized test on which the person scores below the expected level.

This disorder is not due to a defect in visual or hearing acuity or a neurological disorder (Table 34.2-1). Rather, this diagnosis is made only if the impairment significantly interferes with academic achievement or with activities of daily living that require expressive writing skills.

EPIDEMIOLOGY

The prevalence of developmental writing disorder is not known but has been estimated at 3 to 10 percent of school-age children. The male-to-female ratio is also unknown. There are some indications that affected children are more frequently from families with a history of this disorder.

Table 34.2-1
Diagnostic Criteria for Developmental Expressive Writing Disorder

A. Writing skills, as measured by a standardized, individually administered test, are markedly below the expected level, given the person's schooling and intellectual capacity (as determined by an individually administered I.Q. test).

B. The disturbance in A significantly interferes with academic achievement or activities of daily living requiring the composition of written texts (spelling words and expressing thoughts in grammatically correct sentences and organized paragraphs).

C. Not due to a defect in visual or hearing acuity or a neurologic disorder.

Table from DSM-III-R, *Diagnostic and Statistical Manual of Mental Disorders*, ed 3, revised. Copyright American Psychiatric Association, Washington, DC, 1987, with permission.

ETIOLOGY

One hypothesis holds that developmental expressive writing disorder results from the combined effects of one or more of the following disorders: developmental expressive language disorder, developmental receptive language disorder, and developmental reading disorder. This view suggests the possible existence of neurological and cognitive defects or malfunctions somewhere in the central information-processing areas.

Hereditary predisposition to the disorder has been suggested on the basis of empirical findings that most children with developmental expressive writing disorder have relatives with the disorder.

Temperamental characteristics may play some role in developmental expressive writing disorder, especially such characteristics as short attention span and easy distractibility.

CLINICAL FEATURES

Children with developmental expressive writing disorder present difficulties very early in grade school in spelling words and expressing their thoughts according to age-appropriate grammatical norms. Their spoken and written sentences contain an unusually large number of grammatical errors or poor paragraph organization. During and after the second grade, these children commonly make simple grammatical errors in writing a short sentence. For example, they frequently fail, despite constant reminders, to start the first letter of the first word in a sentence with a capital letter and to end a sentence with a period.

As they grow older and progress toward higher grades in school, such children's spoken and written sentences become more conspicuously primitive, odd, and inferior to what is expected of students in their grade level. Their word choices are erroneous and inappropriate; their paragraphs are disorganized and not in proper sequence; and spelling correctly becomes increasingly more difficult as their vocabulary becomes more abstract and larger in number and characters.

Associated features of developmental expressive writing disorder include refusal or reluctance to go to school and to do assigned written homework, poor academic performance in other areas (such as mathematics), general disinterest in school work, truancy, and conduct disorder.

Most children with this disorder become frustrated and angry over their feelings of inadequacy and failure in their academic performance. They may have a chronic depression as a result of their growing sense of isolation, estrangement, and despair.

Adults with developmental expressive writing disorder who do not receive remedial intervention continue to have difficulties in social adaptation involving writing skills and a continuing sense of incompetence, inferiority, isolation, and estrangement. Some of them even try to avoid or procrastinate writing a response letter or a simple greeting card for fear that their writing incompetence will be exposed. When their coping mechanism fails, the severity of their psychopathology is likely to be increased. Most adults with the disorder choose occupations that require minimal writing skills, such as in trade, custodianship, and other menial work; seldom do they achieve or hold a socially desirable occupational position requiring a high level of expressive writing. Common associated disorders are developmental reading disorder, developmental expressive and receptive language disorders, developmental arithmetic disorder, developmental coordination disorder, and disruptive behavior disorders.

COURSE AND PROGNOSIS

Because writing, language, and reading disorders often coexist and a child normally speaks well before learning to read and reads well before writing well, a child with all three disorders has the language disorder diagnosed first and the writing disorder diagnosed last. In severe cases a developmental expressive writing disorder is apparent by age 7 (second grade); in less severe cases the disorder may not be apparent until age 10 (fifth grade) or later. Most persons with mild and moderate developmental expressive writing disorder fare rather well if they receive timely remedial educational intervention early in grade school. Severe developmental expressive writing disorder requires continual extensive remedial treatment through the late part of high school and even into college.

The prognosis depends on the severity of the disorder, the age or grade when the remedial intervention was started, the length and continuity of treatment, and the presence or absence of associated or secondary emotional or behavioral problems.

Those persons who later become well compensated or who recover from developmental expressive writing disorder are usually from families of favorable socioeconomic backgrounds.

DIAGNOSIS

The diagnosis of developmental expressive writing disorder is made on the basis of the person's consistently poor performance on the composition of written text. Performance is markedly below the person's intellectual capacity, as confirmed by an individually administered standardized expressive writing test. The presence of a major disorder, such as pervasive developmental disorder or mental retardation, obviates the diagnosis of developmental expressive writing disorder. Other disorders to be differentiated from developmental expressive writing disorder are developmental expressive and receptive language disorders, developmental reading disorder, and impaired vision and hearing.

Dyslexia is characterized by an inability to read and dysgraphia by an inability to write. From a diagnostic procedural viewpoint, it is important that any person suspected of having developmental expressive writing disorder first be given a standardized intelligence test, such as the Revised Wechsler Intelligence Scale for Children (WISC-R) or the Revised Wechsler Adult Intelligence Scale (WAIS-R) to determine the person's intellectual capacity before administering a standardized expressive writing test.

TREATMENT

Developmental expressive writing disorder responds to treatment. The best treatment to date is remedial educational intervention. Although controversy continues as to the effectiveness of various remedial expressive writing modalities, an intensive and continuous administration of individually tailored one-to-one expressive and creative writing therapy appears to show the most favorable treatment outcomes. Teachers in some special schools devote as much as two hours a day to such writing instruction.

The treatment of this disorder requires an optimal patient-therapist relationship, as in psychotherapy. The success or failure in sustaining the patient's motivation greatly affects the treatment's long-term efficacy.

Associated and secondary emotional and behavioral problems should be given prompt attention, with appropriate psychiatric treatment and parental counseling.

References

Houck C K, Billingsley B S: Written expression of students with and without learning disabilities: Differences across the grades. J Learn Disabil *22*: 561, 1989.

Johnson D, Myklebust H: *Learning Disabilities: Educational Principles and Practices*. Grune & Stratton, New York, 1967.

Oliver C E: A sensorimotor program for improving writing readiness skills in elementary-age children. Am J Occup Ther *44*: 111, 1990.

Orton S: *Reading, Writing, and Speech Problems in Children*. Norton, New York, 1937.

Outhred: Word processing: Its impact on children's writing. J Learn Disabil *22*: 262, 1989.

Persell C H: *Education and Inequality: A Theoretical and Empirical Synthesis*. Free Press, New York, 1977.

Shepherd M J, Charnow D A, Silver L B: Developmental expressive writing disorder. In *Comprehensive Textbook of Psychiatry*, ed 5, H I Kaplan and B J Sadock, editors, p 1796. Williams & Wilkins, Baltimore, 1989.

Weiss C E, Lillywhite H S: *Communicative Disorders: Prevention and Early Intervention*. Mosby, St. Louis, 1981.

34.3 / Developmental Reading Disorder

Developmental reading disorder has received much attention over the past decades, as evidenced by the number of names for it: alexia, dyslexia, reading backwardness, learning disability, specific reading disability, and developmental word blindness. Developmental reading disorder is characterized by a marked impairment in the development of word recognition skills and reading comprehension that cannot be explained by mental retardation or inadequate schooling and that is not due to a manifest visual, hearing, or neurological disorder. According to the revised third edition of *Diagnostic and Statistical Manual of Mental Disorders* (DSM-III-R), the diagnosis should be made only if this impairment significantly interferes with academic achievement or with activities of daily living that require reading skills. This disorder is also referred to as dyslexia.

EPIDEMIOLOGY

An estimated 2 to 8 percent of school-age children in the United States are affected by this disorder. Developmental reading disorder is two to four times more common in boys than in girls. In the adult form (reading backwardness or reading retardation) there is no difference in incidence between men and women.

ETIOLOGY

Developmental reading disorder tends to be more prevalent among family members of persons affected by the disorder than in the general population, leading to the speculation that the disorder may have a genetic origin. However, family and twin studies have not supplied definitive evidence to support this theory.

Studies in the 1930s attempted to explain developmental reading disorder with the cerebral hemispheric function model, which suggested positive correlations of reading disorder with left-handedness, left-eyedness, or mixed laterality. But subsequent epidemiological studies did not find any consistent association between reading disorder and laterality of handedness or eyedness. However, right-left confusion has been shown to be associated with reading difficulties. The reversal of cerebral asymmetry may result in the transference of language lateralization to a cerebral hemisphere that is less differentiated to accommodate language function, thereby leading to a developmental reading disorder. A few recent studies of patients with developmental reading disorder (computed tomography [CT] scan, magnetic resonance imaging [MRI], and on autopsy) have shown abnormal symmetries in the temporal or parietal lobes.

Many attribute developmental reading disorder to subtle deficits that are either visual or verbal (i.e., auditory). There is more evidence for the latter; thus, developmental reading disorder is considered to be part of an oral language disorder.

Reading requires a brain that is mature enough and sufficiently intact to integrate information arriving through various processing systems and to relegate disturbing stimuli to the background. In addition, reading requires sufficient freedom from conflict to permit the investment of energy in the task and a sociocultural value system that views reading as basic to survival.

There tends to be a high incidence of developmental reading disorder among children with cerebral palsy who are of normal intelligence. A slightly increased incidence of developmental reading disorder is also seen among epileptic children. Complications during pregnancy; prenatal and perinatal difficulties, including prematurity; and low birth weight are common in the histories of children with reading disorders.

Secondary reading disorders may be seen in children with postnatal brain lesions in the left occipital lobe resulting in right visual field blindness. They may also be seen in children with lesions in the splenum of the corpus callosum that block the transmission of visual information from the intact right hemisphere to the language areas of the left hemisphere.

Developmental reading disorder may be one manifestation of developmental delay or maturational lag. Temperamental attributes have been reported to be closely associated with developmental reading disorder. Compared with nonreading-disordered children, children with developmental reading disorder often have more difficulty in concentrating and a shorter attention span.

Some studies suggest an association between malnutrition and cognitive function. Children who were malnourished for a long time during early childhood show subaverage performances in various cognitive tests. Their cognitive performances are lower than those of their siblings who grew up in the same family environment but who were not subjected to the same degree of malnutrition.

Severe developmental reading disorder is often associated with psychiatric problems. Developmental reading disorder may be the result of a preexisting psychiatric disorder or the cause of emotional and behavior disorders; however, it is not always easy to ascertain the causal relationship between a developmental reading disorder and a coexisting psychiatric disorder.

CLINICAL FEATURES

Developmental reading disorder is usually apparent by age 7 (second grade). In severe cases, evidence of reading difficulty may be apparent as early as age 6 (first grade). Sometimes developmental reading disorder is compensated for in the early elementary grades, particularly when it is associated with high scores on intelligence tests. In this case the disorder may not be apparent until age 9 (fourth grade) or later.

Reading-disordered children make many errors in their oral reading. The faulty reading is characterized by omissions, additions, and distortions of words. Such children have difficulty distinguishing between printed letter characters and sizes, especially those that differ only in spatial orientation and length of line. The problems in managing printed or written language may pertain to individual letters, sentences, and even a whole page. The children's reading speed is slow, often with minimal comprehension. Most children with developmental reading disorder have an age-appropriate ability to copy from written or printed text, but nearly all are poor spellers.

Associated problems include language difficulties, shown often as impaired sound discrimination and difficulties in properly sequencing words. The reading-disordered child may start a word in the middle or at the end of a printed or written sentence. At times such children transpose letters that are to be read because of poorly established left-to-right tracking sequence. Failures in both memory recall and sustained elicitation result in poor recall of letter names and sounds.

Most children with developmental reading disorder dislike reading and writing and avoid them. Their anxiety is heightened when they are confronted with demands that involve printed language.

Most reading-disordered children who do not receive remedial education have a sense of shame and humiliation from their continuing failure and subsequent frustration. These feelings become more intense as time progresses. Older children tend to be angry and depressed, and their aggression may be directed against society, perhaps leading to the development of a conduct disorder.

COURSE AND PROGNOSIS

Even without any remedial assistance, many reading-disordered children acquire a little information about printed language during their first two years in grade school. By the end of the first grade, some have learned how to read a few words. If no remedial educational intervention is given by the third grade, however, these children remain reading-impaired. Under the best circumstances, a child is classified as being at risk for a reading disorder during the kindergarten year or early in the first grade.

When remediation is instituted early, it can sometimes be discontinued by the end of the first or second grade. In severe cases and depending on the pattern of deficits and strengths, remediation may be continued into the middle and high school years. Most children who have either compensated satisfactorily or recovered from early developmental reading disorder are from families with socioeconomically advantaged backgrounds.

DIAGNOSIS

The main diagnostic feature of a developmental reading disorder is a markedly decreased performance in reading skills that are below the person's intellectual capacity. Other characteristic features include difficulties with the recall, evocation, and sequencing of printed letters and words; with the processing of sophisticated grammatical constructions; and with the making of inferences (Table 34.3-1). Clinically, the observer is impressed by the interaction between emotional and specific features. The experience of school failure seems to confirm preexisting doubts that some children have about themselves. The energy of some children is so bound to their conflicts that they are unable to exploit their assets. The psychiatric evaluation should assess the need for psychiatric intervention and decide on an appropriate treatment.

Table 34.3-1
Diagnostic Criteria for Developmental Reading Disorder

A. Reading achievement, as measured by a standardized individually administered test, is markedly below the expected level, given the person's schooling and intellectual capacity (as determined by an individually administered I.Q. test).

B. The disturbance in A significantly interferes with academic achievement or activities of daily living requiring reading skills.

C. Not due to a defect in visual or hearing acuity or a neurologic disorder.

Table from DSM-III-R, *Diagnostic and Statistical Manual of Mental Disorders*, ed 3, revised. Copyright American Psychiatric Association, Washington, DC, 1987, with permission.

The diagnosis of developmental reading disorder cannot be established without confirmation by a standardized reading achievement test, and pervasive developmental disorders and mental retardation must be ruled out.

DIFFERENTIAL DIAGNOSIS

Deficits in expressive language and speech discrimination are usually present in developmental reading disorder and may be severe enough to warrant the additional diagnosis of developmental expressive language disorder or developmental receptive language disorder. Developmental expressive writing disorder is often present. In some cases there is a discrepancy between verbal and performance intelligence scores. Visual perceptual deficits are seen in only about 10 percent of cases.

Reading difficulties may be primarily caused by the generalized impairment in intellectual functioning seen in mental retardation, which can be checked by administering a standardized intelligence test.

Inadequate schooling resulting in poor reading skills can be determined by finding out whether other children in the same school have similarly poor reading performances on standardized reading tests.

Hearing and visual impairments should be ruled out with screening tests.

Developmental reading disorder often accompanies other emotional and behavioral disorders, especially attention-deficit hyperactivity disorder, conduct disorder, and depression, particularly in older children and adolescents.

PSYCHOEDUCATIONAL TESTS

In addition to standardized intelligence tests, psychoeducational diagnostic tests should be administered. The diagnostic battery may include a standardized spelling test, the writing of a composition, assessment of the processing and use of oral language, and design copying, a judgment of the adequacy of pencil use. A screening projective battery may include human-figure drawings, picture-story tests, and sentence completion. The evaluation should also include a systematic observation of behavior variables.

TREATMENT

There is a general consensus that the treatment of choice for developmental reading disorder is a remedial educational approach; however, there is considerable controversy as to the relative efficacy of various remedial teaching strategies.

One frequently used method, developed by Samuel Orton, urges therapeutic attention to the mastery of simple phonetic units, followed by the blending of those units into words and sentences. An approach that systematically engages the several senses is recommended. The rationale for this and similar methods is that children's difficulties in managing letters and syllables are basic to their failures to learn to read; therefore, if they are taught to cope with graphemes, they will learn to read.

As in psychotherapy, the therapist–patient relationship is important to a successful treatment outcome in remedial educational therapy.

Reading-disordered children should be placed in a grade as close as possible to their social functional level and given special remedial work in reading. Coexisting emotional and behavioral problems should be treated by appropriate psychotherapeutic means. Parental counseling may also be helpful.

References

Badian N A: The prediction of good and poor reading before kindergarten entry: A nine-year follow-up. J Learn Disabil *21*: 88, 1988.

Duane D D: Neurobiological correlates of learning disorders. J Am Acad Child Adolesc Psychiatry *28*: 314, 1989.

Duffy F H, Geschwind N: *Dyslexia: A Neuroscientific Approach to Clinical Evaluation*. Little, Brown, Boston, 1985.

Felton R H, Wood, F B: Cognitive deficits in reading disability and attention deficit disorder. J Learn Disabil *22*: 3, 1989.

Galaburda A M: Learning disability: Biological, societal or both? A response to Gerald Coles. J Learn Disabil *22*: 238, 1989.

Geschwing N: Asymmetries of the brain: New development. Bull Orton Soc *29*: 67, 1979.

Hyrid G W, Semrod-Clikeman E: Dyslexia and neurodevelopmental pathology: Relationships to cognition, intelligence, and reading skill acquisition. J Learn Disabil *22*: 204, 1989.

LaBuda M C, DeFries J C: Cognitive abilities in children with reading disabilities and controls: A follow-up study. J Learn Disabil *21*: 562, 1988.

Lerner J W: Educational interventions in learning disabilities. J Am Acad Child Adolesc Psychiatry *28*: 326, 1989.

Shepherd M J, Charnow D A, Silver L B: Developmental reading disorder. In *Comprehensive Textbook of Psychiatry*, ed 5, H I Kaplan and B J Sadock, editors, p 1790. Williams & Wilkins, Baltimore, 1989.

Silver A A, Hagin R A: *A Scanning Instrument for the Identification of Learning Disability*. Walker Educational Book, New York, 1980.

Smith S D, Pennington B F, Kimberling W J, Ing P S: Familial dyslexia: Use of genetic linkage data to define subtypes. J Am Acad Child Adolesc Psychiatry *29*: 204, 1990.

34.4 / Developmental Articulation Disorder

Developmental articulation disorder is relatively common but usually benign unless its persistence and severity lead to teasing and reduced self-esteem. Through the years it has been called baby talk, lalling, dyslasia, functional speech disorder, infantile perseveration, infantile articulation, delayed speech, lisping, lazy speech, specific developmental speech disorder, and oral inaccuracy. Most cases are mild, and recovery is spontaneous. In serious cases speech may be unintelligible, requiring lengthy, rigorous treatment. By definition, developmental articulation disorder is characterized by frequent and recurrent misarticulations of speech sounds, resulting in abnormal speech. Language development is within normal limits.

The revised third edition of *Diagnostic and Statistical Manual of Mental Disorders* (DSM-III-R) characterizes developmental articulation disorder as a consistent failure to make correct articulations of speech sounds at the developmentally appropriate age. The condition cannot be accounted for by pervasive developmental disorder; mental retardation; impairment of the oral speech mechanism; or neurological, intellectual, or hearing impairments. The disorder is manifested by frequent misarticulations, substitutions, or omissions of speech sounds, giving the impression of baby talk (Table 34.4-1). It is not due to any anatomical, structural, physiological, auditory, or neurological abnormalities. The disorder refers to a number of different articulation difficulties, ranging in severity from mild to severe. Speech may be completely intelligible, partially intelligible, or unintelligible. Only one speech sound or phoneme (the smallest sound unit) or many speech sounds may be affected.

EPIDEMIOLOGY

The prevalence of developmental articulation disorder is conservatively estimated to be approximately 10 percent

Table 34.4-1
Diagnostic Criteria for Developmental Articulation Disorder

A. Consistent failure to use developmentally expected speech sounds. For example, in a 3-year-old, failure to articulate p, b, and t, and in a 6-year-old, failure to articulate r, sh, th, f, z, and l.

B. Not due to a pervasive developmental disorder, mental retardation, a defect in hearing acuity, disorders of the oral speech mechanism, or a neurologic disorder.

of children below 8 years of age and approximately 5 percent of children 8 years of age and above. The disorder is two to three times more common in boys than in girls. It is also more common among the first-degree relatives of patients with the disorder than in the general population.

ETIOLOGY

The cause of developmental articulation disorder is not yet known. It is generally believed that a simple developmental lag or maturational delay in the neurological process underlying speech, rather than an organic dysfunction, is at fault.

A disproportionately high frequency of developmental articulation disorder has been found among children from large families and from low socioeconomic status families, suggesting the possible causal effects of inadequate speech stimulation and reinforcement in these families.

Constitutional factors, rather than environmental factors, seem to be of major importance in determining whether a child has developmental articulation disorder. The high proportion of children with the disorder who have relatives with a similar disorder suggests that the disorder may have a genetic component.

Poor motor coordination, laterality, and handedness have been proved not to contribute to developmental articulation disorder.

CLINICAL FEATURES

In severe cases this disorder is first recognized at about 3 years of age. In less severe cases the disorder may not be apparent until the age of 6 years. The essential features of developmental articulation disorder include articulation that is judged to be defective when compared with the speech of children at the same age level and that cannot be attributed to abnormalities in intelligence, hearing, or physiology of speech mechanism. In very mild cases only one phoneme may be affected. Single phonemes are usually affected, most commonly those acquired late in the normal language acquisition process.

According to DSM-III-R, the speech sounds that are most frequently misarticulated are those acquired late in the developmental sequence *(r, sh, th, f, z, l,* and *ch)*. But in more severe cases and in young children, sounds such as *b, m, t, d, n,* and *h* may be mispronounced. One or many speech sounds may be affected, but vowel sounds are not among them.

The child with developmental articulation disorder is not able to articulate certain phonemes correctly and may distort, substitute, or even omit the affected phonemes. With omissions, the phonemes are absent entirely—for example, "bu" for "blue," "ca" for "car," or "whaa?" for "what's that?" With substitutions, difficult phonemes are replaced with incorrect ones—for example, "wabbit" for "rabbit," "fum" for "thumb," or "whath dat?" for "what's that?" With distortions, the correct phoneme is approximated but is articulated incorrectly. Rarely do additions, usually of the vowel "schwa" or "uh," occur—for example, "puhretty" for "pretty," "what's uh that uh?" for "what's that?"

Omissions are thought to be the most serious type of misarticulation, with substitutions the next most serious type, and distortion the least serious type. Omissions are most frequently found in the speech of young children and usually occur at the end of words or in clusters of consonants ("ka" for "car," "scisso" for "scissors"). Distortions, which are found mainly in the speech of older children, result in a sound that is not part of the speaker's dialect. Distortions may be the last type of misarticulation remaining in the speech of children whose articulation problems have mostly remitted. The most common types of distortions are the *lateral slip*—in which the child pronounces *s* sounds with the air stream going across the tongue, producing a whistling effect—and the *palatal lisp*—in which the *s* sound is formed with the tongue too close to the palate, producing a *shh* sound effect. The misarticulations of children with developmental articulation disorder are often inconsistent and random. A phoneme may be pronounced correctly in one situation and incorrectly another time. Misarticulations are most common at the ends of words, in long and syntactically complex sentences, and during rapid speech.

Omissions, distortions, and substitutions also occur normally in the speech of young children learning to talk. However, whereas young normal children soon replace these misarticulations, children with developmental articulation disorder do not. Even as children with developmental articulation disorder grow and finally acquire the correct phoneme, they may use it only in newly acquired words and may not correct earlier learned words that they have been mispronouncing for some time.

Most children eventually outgrow developmental articulation disorder, usually by the third grade. After the fourth grade, however, spontaneous recovery is unlikely, and so it is important to try to remediate the disorder before the development of complications.

In most mild cases, recovery from developmental articulation disorder is spontaneous, and often the child's beginning kindergarten or school precipitates the improvement. Speech therapy is clearly indicated for those children who have not shown a spontaneous improvement by the third or fourth grade. For those children whose articulation is significantly unintelligible and are clearly troubled by their inability to speak clearly, speech therapy should be initiated at an early age.

According to DSM-III-R, other specific developmental disorders are commonly present, including developmental expressive language disorder, developmental receptive language disorder, developmental reading disorder, and developmental coordination disorder. Functional enuresis may also be present.

A delay in reaching speech milestones (such as first word and first sentence) has been reported in some children with developmental articulation disorder, but most children with this disorder begin speaking at the appropriate age.

Children with developmental articulation disorder may have various concomitant social, emotional, and behavioral problems. About one-third of children with this condition have a psychiatric disorder, such as attention-deficit hyperactivity disorder, separation anxiety disorder, avoidant disorder of childhood or adolescence, adjustment disorder, and depression. Those children with a severe degree of articulation impairment or whose disorder is chronic and nonremitting are the ones most likely to suffer from psychiatric problems.

PROGNOSIS

Recovery is frequently spontaneous, particularly in children whose misarticulations involve only a few phonemes. Spontaneous recovery is rare after the age of 8 years.

Table 34.4-2
Differential Diagnosis of Articulation Disorders

Criteria	Articulation Disorder Due to Structural or Neurological Abnormalities (Dysarthria)	Articulation Disorder Due to Hearing Impairment	Developmental Articulation Disorder	Articulation Disorder Associated with Mental Retardation, Infantile Autism, Developmental Dysphasia, Acquired Aphasia, or Deafness
Language development	Within normal limits	Within normal limits unless hearing impairment is serious	Within normal limits	Not within normal limits
Examination	Possible abnormalities of lips, tongue, or palate; muscular weakness, incoordination, or disturbance of vegetative functions, such as sucking or chewing	Hearing impairment shown on audiometric testing	Normal	
Rate of speech	Slow; marked deterioration of articulation with increased rate	Normal	Normal; possible deterioration of articulation with increased rate	
Phonemes affected	Any phonemes, even vowels	*F, th, sh,* and *s*	*R, sh, th, ch, dg, j, f, v, s,* and *z* are most commonly affected	

Table by Lorian Baker, Ph.D., and Dennis Cantwell, M.D.

DIAGNOSIS

The essential feature of developmental articulation disorder is an articulation defect characterized by the consistent failure to use developmentally expected speech sounds of certain consonants, including omissions, substitutions, and distortions of phonemes, which are generally late-learned phonemes. The disorder cannot be attributed to structural or neurological abnormalities and is accompanied by normal language development.

DIFFERENTIAL DIAGNOSIS

The differential diagnostic process for developmental articulation disorder involves three steps: First, determine that the misarticulations are severe enough to be considered abnormal, and rule out the normal misarticulations of young children. Second, determine that there are no physical abnormalities to account for the articulation errors, and rule out dysarthria, hearing impairment, and mental retardation. And third, establish that expressive language is within normal limits, and rule out developmental language disorder and pervasive developmental disorders.

A rough guideline for a clinical assessment of children's articulation is that normal 3-year-olds correctly articulate *m, n, ng, b, p, h, t, k, q,* and *d;* normal 4-year-olds correctly articulate *f, y, ch, sh,* and *z;* and normal 5-year-olds correctly articulate *th, s,* and *r.*

Neurological, oral structural, and audiometric examinations may be necessary to rule out physical factors that may cause certain types of articulation disorders.

Children with dysarthria, an articulation disorder caused by structural or neurological abnormalities, differ from children with developmental articulation disorder in that dysarthria is very difficult and sometimes impossible to remedy. Drooling, slow or uncoordinated motor behavior, abnormal chewing or swallowing, and awkward or slow protrusion and retraction of the tongue are indications of dysarthria. A slow rate of speech is another indication of dysarthria (Table 34.4-2).

TREATMENT

Speech therapy is considered the most successful treatment for most articulation errors. Speech therapy is indicated when the child's articulation intelligibility is poor; when the affected child is over 8 years of age; when the speech problem is apparently causing problems with peers, learning, and self-image; when the articulation impairment is so severe that many consonants are misarticulated; and when errors involve omissions and substitutions of phonemes, rather than distortions.

Monitoring of the child's peer relationships, school behavior, and parental counseling may be necessary for the timely implementation of psychiatric treatment when the need arises.

References

Beitchman J H, Hood J, Rochon J, Peterson M: Empirical classification of speech/language impairment in children: II. Behavioral characteristics. J Am Acad Child Adolesc Psychiatry *28*: 118, 1989.

Bloodstein O: *Speech Pathology: An Introduction*. Houghton Mifflin, Boston, 1979.

Carroll J L, Fuller G B, Lindley K E: Visual-motor ability of children with articulation disorders. Percept Mot Skills *69*: 32, 1989.

Fey M, Leonard L, Wilcox K: Speech style modification in language-impaired children. J Speech Hear Disord *46*: 91, 1981.
Freeman F J, Silver L B: Developmental articulation disorder. In *Comprehensive Textbook of Psychiatry*, ed 5, H I Kaplan and B J Sadock, editors, p 1804. Williams & Wilkins, Baltimore, 1989.
Kertesz A: Hemispheric dominance: Its development and relation to speech disorders. Folia Phoniatr *41*: 61, 1989.
Metter J E: *Speech Disorders: Clinical Evaluation and Diagnosis*. SP Medical & Scientific Books, New York, 1985.
Paul R, Shriberg L: Associations between phonology and syntax in speech delayed children. J Speech Hear Res *25*: 536, 1982.
Sander, E R: When are speech sounds learned? J Speech Hear Disord *37*: 55, 1972.
Weiss C E, Lillywhite H S: *Communicative Disorders: Prevention and Early Intervention*. Mosby, St. Louis, 1981.
Wiig E, Semel E: *Clinical Evaluation of Language Functions*. Merrill, Columbus, OH, 1980.
Wintz H: *Articulatory Acquisition and Behavior*. Prentice-Hall, Englewood Cliffs, NJ, 1969.

34.5 / Developmental Language Disorders

Language disorders are categorized into three major types: (1) failure to acquire any language, (2) an acquired language disability secondary to trauma or neurological disorder, and (3) delayed language acquisition, also called developmental language disorder. The most common language disorder is developmental language disorder. The revised third edition of *Diagnostic and Statistical Manual of Mental Disorders* (DSM-III-R) divides developmental language disorder into two types: developmental expressive language disorder and developmental receptive language disorder.

DEVELOPMENTAL EXPRESSIVE LANGUAGE DISORDER

According to DSM-III-R, the essential feature of developmental expressive language disorder is marked impairment in the development of expressive language that cannot be explained by mental retardation or inadequate schooling and that is not due to a pervasive developmental disorder, hearing impairment, or a neurological disorder. The diagnosis should be made only if this impairment significantly interferes with academic achievement or with activities of daily living that require the expression of verbal or sign language (Table 34.5-1).

Epidemiology

The prevalence of developmental expressive language disorder ranges from 3 percent to 10 percent of school-age children. The disorder is two to three times more common in boys than in girls. The disorder is also more prevalent among children whose relatives have a family history of developmental articulation disorder or other developmental disorders.

Table 34.5-1
Diagnostic Criteria for Developmental Expressive Language Disorder

A. The score obtained from a standardized measure of expressive language is substantially below that obtained from a standardized measure of nonverbal intellectual capacity (as determined by an individually administered I.Q. test).

B. The disturbance in A significantly interferes with academic achievement or activities of daily living requiring the expression of verbal (or sign) language. This may be evidenced in severe cases by use of a markedly limited vocabulary, by speaking only in simple sentences, or by speaking only in the present tense. In less severe cases, there may be hesitations or errors in recalling certain words, or errors in the production of long or complex sentences.

C. Not due to a pervasive developmental disorder, defect in hearing acuity, or a neurologic disorder (aphasia).

Etiology

The cause of developmental expressive language disorder is not known. Subtle cerebral damage and maturational lags in cerebral development have been postulated as being the underlying causes, but no evidence supports these theories. Left-handedness or ambilaterality appears to increase the risk.

Unknown genetic factors have been suspected to have a role because the relatives of children with developmental learning disorders have a relatively high incidence of developmental expressive language disorder.

Clinical Features

Severe forms of the disorder usually occur before the age of 3 years. Less severe forms may not occur until early adolescence, when language ordinarily becomes more complex. The essential feature of the child with developmental expressive language disorder is a marked impairment in the development of age-appropriate expressive language, which results in the use of verbal or sign language that is markedly below the expected level, considering the child's nonverbal intellectual capacity. The child's language understanding (decoding) skills remain relatively intact.

The disorder becomes conspicuous by about the age of 18 months when the child fails to utter spontaneously or even to echo single words or sounds. Even simple words, such as "mama" and "dada," are absent from the child's active vocabulary, and the child points or uses gestures to indicate desires. The child seems to want to communicate, maintains eye contact, relates well to the mother, and enjoys games such as pat-a-cake and peek-a-boo.

The child's repertoire of vocabulary is severely limited. At 18 months the child can, at most, comprehend simple commands and can point to common objects when they are named. When the child finally begins to speak, the language deficit becomes more apparent. Articulation is usually immature.

Numerous articulation errors are present but are inconsistent, particularly with such sounds as *th, r, s, z, y,* and *l,* which are either omitted or are substituted for other sounds.

By the age of 4, most children with this disorder can speak in short phrases, but they appear to forget old words as they learn new ones. After beginning to speak, they acquire language more slowly than do normal children. Their use of various grammatical structures is also markedly lower than the age-expected level. Their developmental milestones may also be slightly delayed. Developmental articulation disorder is often present. Developmental coordination disorder and functional enuresis are common associated features.

Complications

Emotional problems involving poor self-image, frustration, and depression may develop in school-age children. Children with the disorder may also have a learning impairment, manifested by reading retardation, that may result in serious difficulties in various academic subjects. The major learning difficulties are in perceptual skills and skills of recognizing and processing symbols in the proper sequence.

Other behavioral symptoms and problems that may appear in children with developmental expressive language disorder include hyperactivity, short attention span, withdrawing behavior, thumb sucking, temper tantrums, bed wetting, disobedience, accident proneness, and conduct disorder. Neurological abnormalities have been reported in a number of children. These associated features include soft neurological signs, depressed vestibular responses, and electroencephalogram (EEG) abnormalities.

Course and Prognosis

In general, the prognosis for developmental expressive language disorder is favorable. The rapidity and the degree of recovery depend on the severity of the disorder, the child's motivation to participate in therapies, and the timely institution of speech and other therapeutic interventions. The presence or absence of other factors—such as moderate to severe hearing loss, mild mental retardation, and severe emotional problems—also affects the prognosis for recovery. As many as 50 percent of children with a mild developmental expressive language disorder recover spontaneously without any sign of language impairment, but children with a severe developmental expressive language disorder may later display the features of mild to moderate impairment.

Diagnosis

The presence of markedly below-age-level verbal or sign language, accompanied by a low score on standardized expressive verbal and performance tests, is diagnostic. The disorder is not caused by a pervasive developmental disorder, as the child shows a desire to communicate. If there is any language, it is severely retarded; vocabulary is limited; grammar is simple; and articulation is variable. Inner language or the appropriate use of toys and household objects is present.

To confirm the diagnosis, the clinician should have the child tested with standardized expressive language and nonverbal intellectual tests. Observations of the disordered child's verbal and sign language patterns in various settings (e.g., in the school yard, classroom, home, and playroom) and during interactions with other children help ascertain the severity and the specific areas of the child's impairment and aid in the early detection of behavioral and emotional complications.

A careful family history should include the presence or absence of developmental expressive language disorder among relatives.

An audiogram is indicated for very young children and for those children whose hearing acuity appears to be impaired.

Differential Diagnosis

In mental retardation, there is an overall impairment in intellectual functioning, as shown in below-normal intelligence test scores in all areas. The nonverbal intellectual capacity and functioning of children with developmental expressive language disorder are within normal limits.

In developmental receptive language disorder, comprehension of language (decoding) is markedly below the expected age-appropriate level, whereas in developmental expressive language disorder, language comprehension remains within normal limits.

In pervasive developmental disorders, in addition to the cardinal cognitive characteristics, the affected children have no inner language, symbolic or imagery play, appropriate use of gesture, or capacity to form warm and meaningful social relationships. Moreover, there is little or no frustration with the inability to communicate verbally. In contrast, all these characteristics are present in children with developmental expressive language disorder.

Children with acquired aphasia or dysphasia have a history of an early normal language development, and the disordered language had its onset after head trauma or other neurological disorders (e.g., seizure disorders).

Children with elective mutism have a history of normal language development, and their speech is limited only to certain family members (e.g., mother, father, and siblings). More girls than boys are affected by elective mutism, and the affected children are mostly shy and withdrawn outside the family.

Treatment

Language therapy should be started immediately after diagnosis of the disorder. Such therapy consists of behaviorally reinforced exercises and practice with phonemes (sound units), vocabulary, and sentence construction. The goal is to increase the number of phrases by using block-building methods and conventional speech therapies.

Psychotherapy is not usually indicated unless the language-disordered child shows signs of concurrent or secondary behavioral or emotional difficulties.

Interpretive and supportive parental counseling may be indicated in some cases. The parents may need help to reduce intrafamilial tension arising from difficulties in rearing the language-disordered child and to increase their awareness and understanding of the child's disorder.

DEVELOPMENTAL RECEPTIVE LANGUAGE DISORDER

According to DSM-III-R, the essential feature of developmental receptive language disorder is marked impairment in the development of language comprehension that cannot be explained by mental retardation or inadequate schooling and that is not due to a pervasive developmental disorder, hearing impairment, or neurological disorder. The diagnosis should be made only if this impairment significantly interferes with academic achievement or with activities of daily living that require the comprehension of verbal or sign language (Table 34.5-2).

Epidemiology

The prevalence of developmental receptive language disorder ranges from 3 to 10 percent of school-age children. No familial pattern is known. The disorder is about two to three times more common in boys than in girls.

Etiology

The cause of this disorder is not known. Early theories listed perceptual dysfunction, subtle cerebral damage, maturational lag, and genetic factors as probable causative factors, but there is no definitive supporting evidence for these theories. Several studies suggest the possible presence of underlying impairment of auditory discrimination, as most children with developmental receptive language disorder are more responsive to environmental sounds than to speech sounds. As with developmental expressive language disorder, left-handedness or ambilaterality seems to increase the risk.

Clinical Features

The disorder typically appears before the age of 4 years. Severe forms are apparent by age 2; mild forms may not become evident until age 7 (second grade) or older, when language becomes more complex. Children with developmental receptive language disorder show markedly delayed and below-normal ability to comprehend (decode) verbal or sign language, although they do have age-appropriate nonverbal intellectual capacity. In most cases of the disorder, verbal or sign expression (encoding) of language is also impaired. The clinical features of developmental receptive language disorder in children between the ages of 18 and 24 months are almost indistinguishable from those of developmental expressive language disorder: the child fails to make spontaneous utterances of a single phoneme (sound unit) or to mimic another person's words.

Table 34.5-2
Diagnostic Criteria for Developmental Receptive Language Disorder

A. The score obtained from a standardized measure of receptive language is substantially below that obtained from a standardized measure of nonverbal intellectual capacity (as determined by an individually administered I.Q. test).

B. The disturbance in A significantly interferes with academic achievement or activities of daily living requiring the comprehension of verbal (or sign) language. This may be manifested in more severe cases by an inability to understand simple words or sentences. In less severe cases, there may be difficulty in understanding only certain types of words, such as spatial terms, or an inability to comprehend longer or more complex statements.

C. Not due to a pervasive developmental disorder, defect in hearing acuity, or a neurologic disorder (aphasia).

Table from DSM-III-R, *Diagnostic and Statistical Manual of Mental Disorders*, ed 3, revised. Copyright American Psychiatric Association, Washington, DC, 1987, with permission.

Many children with developmental receptive language disorder have auditory sensory difficulties or are unable to process visual symbols, such as the meaning of a picture. There are deficits in integrating both auditory and visual symbols—for example, recognizing the basic common attributes of a toy truck and a toy passenger car. Whereas a child with developmental expressive language disorder at 18 months can comprehend simple commands and can point to familiar household objects when told to do so, the child of the same age with developmental receptive language disorder is not able either to point to common objects or to obey simple commands. A child with developmental receptive language disorder usually appears to be deaf; however, the child does hear and responds normally to nonlanguage sounds from the environment but not to spoken language. If the child starts to speak at a later time, the speech contains numerous articulation errors, such as omissions, distortions, and substitution of a phoneme or phonemes. Language acquisition is much slower for the children with developmental receptive language disorder than for normal children.

Developmental receptive language–disordered children also have difficulty recalling earlier visual and auditory memories and recognizing and reproducing symbols in proper sequence. In some cases bilateral EEG abnormalities are seen. Most children with developmental receptive language disorder have a partial hearing defect for true tones, increased threshold of auditory arousal, and inability to localize sound sources. Seizure disorder and reading disorder are more common among relatives of children with developmental receptive language disorder than they are in the general population.

Associated features include developmental articulation disorder, developmental expressive language disorder, and academic skills disorder. Less commonly present are functional enuresis, developmental coordination disorder, attention-deficit hyperactivity disorder, and other social and behavioral problems.

Course and Prognosis

The overall prognosis for developmental receptive language disorder is less favorable than that for developmental expressive language disorder. The prognosis is fair in mild cases. In severe cases with auditory perceptual problems and difficulties in sensory integration, memory recall, and sequencing, the prognosis is guarded.

Diagnosis

The presence of a markedly below-age-appropriate level of comprehension of verbal or sign language with

Table 34.5-3
Differential Diagnosis of Language Disorders*

	Hearing Impairment	Mental Retardation	Infantile Autism	Developmental Expressive Language Disorder	Developmental Receptive Language Disorder	Elective Mutism	Developmental Articulation Disorder
Language comprehension	−	−	−	+	−	+	+
Expressive language	−	−	−	−	−	Variable	+
Audiogram	−	+	+	+	Variable	+	+
Articulation	−	−	− Variable	− Variable	− Variable	+	−
Inner language	+	+ (Limited)	−	+	+ (Slightly limited)	+	+
Uses gestures	+	+ (Limited)	−	+	+	+ Variable	+
Echoes	−	+	+ (Inappropriate)	+	+	+	+
Attends to sounds	Loud or low frequency only	+	−	+	Variable	+	+
Watches faces	+	+	−	+	+	+	+
Performance I.Q.	+	−	+	+	+	+	+

Table by Lorian Baker, Ph.D., and Dennis Cantwell, M.D.
*+ = normal; − = abnormal.

fairly intact age-appropriate nonverbal intellectual capacity, the confirmation of the language difficulties by standardized receptive language tests, and the absence of pervasive developmental disorders confirm the diagnosis of developmental receptive language disorder. In most cases developmental receptive language disorder coexists with developmental expressive language disorder. Therefore, standardized tests for both receptive and expressive language abilities should be given to any child suspected of having developmental receptive language disorder.

An audiogram is indicated in all suspected developmental receptive language–disordered children to rule out or confirm the presence of deafness and to determine the types of auditory deficits.

A careful history of the child and the family and observation of the child in various settings help clarify the diagnosis.

Differential Diagnosis

In developmental expressive language disorder, comprehension of spoken language (decoding) remains within age norms. Children with developmental articulation disorder or stuttering and cluttering have normal expressive and receptive language competence, despite their having speech impairments. Hearing impairment should be ruled out. Most children with developmental receptive language disorder have a history of variable and inconsistent responses to sounds; that is, they respond more often to environmental sounds than to speech sounds (Table 34.5-3).

Mental retardation, acquired aphasia, and pervasive developmental disorders should also be ruled out.

Treatment

Speech and language therapy is indicated for children with developmental receptive language disorder. The form of such treatment is still being debated. Some therapists believe that such children should be isolated in a nondistracting setting and should be taught single specific linguistic structures. Others believe that such children should learn in a natural setting with a group of children and should be taught several language structures simultaneously.

Psychotherapy is often necessary because these children frequently have emotional and behavioral problems. Particular attention should be paid to improving the child's self-image and social skills. Family counseling in which parents are taught appropriate patterns of interaction with the child can also be helpful.

References

Beitchman J H, Hood J, Rochin J, Peterson M: Empirical classification of speech/language impairment in children: II. Behavioral characteristics. J Am Acad Child Adolesc Psychiatry *28*: 118, 1989.

Bishop D V: Autism, Asperger's syndrome and semantic-pragmatic disorder: Where are the boundaries? Br J Disord Commun *24*: 107, 1989.

Cantwell D P, Baker L: Psychiatric and learning disorders in children with communication disorders. Adv Learn Behav Disabil *4*: 511, 1984.

Cohen N J, Davine M, Meloche-Kelly M: Prevalence of unsuspected language disorders in a child psychiatric population. J Am Acad Child Adolesc Psychiatry *28*: 107, 1989.

Gibbs D P, Cooper E B: Prevalence of communication disorders in students with learning disabilities. J Learn Disabil *22*: 60, 1989.

Laney M: *Reading in Childhood Language Disorders*. Wiley, New York, 1978.

Mazziotta J C, Metter E J: Brain cerebral metabolic mapping of normal and abnormal language and its acquisition during development. Res Publ Assoc Res Nerv Ment Dis *66*: 245, 1988.

Moore V, Law J: Copying ability of preschool children with delayed language development. Dev Med Child Neurol *32*: 249, 1990.
Rapin I, Allen D A: Syndromes in developmental dysphasia and adult aphasia. Res Publ Assoc Res Nerv Ment Dis *66*: 57, 1988.
Richardson S O: Developmental language disorder. In *Comprehensive Textbook of Psychiatry*, ed 5, H I Kaplan and B J Sadock, editors, p 1812. Williams & Wilkins, Baltimore, 1989.
Rothenberg J J: An outcome study of an early intervention for specific learning disabilities. J Learn Disabil *23*: 317, 1990.
Scarborough H S, Dobrich W: Development of children with early language delay. J Speech Hear Res *33*: 70, 1990.

34.6 / Developmental Coordination Disorder

The revised third edition of *Diagnostic and Statistical Manual of Mental Disorders* (DSM-III-R) includes developmental coordination disorder for the first time as a specific developmental disorder. It is also included in the ninth revision of the International Classification of Diseases (ICD-9).

There are relatively few studies of children with developmental coordination disorder, fewer than those for other developmental disorders, such as developmental language and academic skills disorders. It is not a well-documented condition.

According to DSM-III-R, the essential feature of developmental coordination disorder is a marked impairment in the development of motor coordination that cannot be explained by mental retardation and that is not due to a known physical disorder. This diagnosis should be made only if this impairment significantly interferes with academic achievement or with activities of daily living (Table 34.6-1).

Table 34.6-1
Diagnostic Criteria for Developmental Coordination Disorder

A. The person's performance in daily activities requiring motor coordination is markedly below the expected level, given the person's chronological age and intellectual capacity. This may be manifested by marked delays in achieving motor milestones (walking, crawling, sitting), dropping things, "clumsiness," poor performance in sports, or poor handwriting.

B. The disturbance in A significantly interferes with academic achievement or activities of daily living.

C. Not due to a known physical disorder, such as cerebral palsy, hemiplegia, or muscular dystrophy.

Table from DSM-III-R, *Diagnostic and Statistical Manual of Mental Disorders*, ed 3, revised. Copyright American Psychiatric Association, Washington, DC, 1987, with permission.

EPIDEMIOLOGY

The prevalence of developmental coordination disorder is not known but has been estimated at approximately 6 percent of school-age children. The male-to-female ratio is also not known. As with most developmental disorders, more boys than girls have developmental coordination disorder. Reports in the literature of the male-to-female ratio have ranged from 2 to 1 to 4 to 1.

ETIOLOGY

The mechanisms and causes of developmental coordination disorder are not yet known. Among the hypothesized factors that may be involved are neonatal problems (especially hypoxia, undernutrition), understimulation, inadequate establishment of cerebral dominance, delayed or incomplete cerebral maturation, neurochemical abnormalities in the brain, and structural lesions in the parietal lobes. The evidence for any of these postulated factors is inconclusive. It appears that developmental coordination disorder may have a multifactorial cause.

CLINICAL FEATURES

The clinical signs suggesting the existence of developmental coordination disorder are evident as early as infancy, when the affected child begins to attempt tasks requiring motor coordination. The essential clinical feature is the child's markedly impaired performance in motor coordination. The difficulties in motor coordination may vary with the child's age and developmental stage.

In infancy and early childhood the disorder may be manifested as delays in normal developmental milestones, such as turning over, crawling, sitting, standing, walking, buttoning shirts, and zipping up pants. Between the ages of 2 and 4 years, clumsiness appears in almost all activities requiring motor coordination. The children cannot hold objects and drop them easily; their gait is unsteady; they often trip over their own feet; and they may bump into other children while attempting to go around them.

In older children the impaired motor coordination may be shown in table games, such as putting together puzzles or building blocks, and in any type of ball game. Although no specific features are pathognomonic of developmental coordination disorder, developmental milestones are frequently delayed. Many children with this disorder may also have a speech disorder. Older children may also have secondary problems of school difficulties, including behavioral and emotional problems, that require appropriate therapeutic interventions.

COURSE AND PROGNOSIS

No reliable data are available on the prospective longitudinal outcomes of both treated and untreated children with developmental coordination disorder. Some studies suggest a favorable outcome for those children who have an average or above-average intellectual capacity, because they are able to learn to compensate for their coordination deficits. In general, the clumsiness persists into adolescence and adult life.

In very severe cases that remain untreated, there may be a number of secondary complications, such as repeated failures in both nonacademic and academic school tasks, repeated problems in attempting to integrate with a peer group, and inability to play games and sports. These problems may lead to low self-esteem, unhappiness, withdrawal, and, in some cases, increasingly severe behavioral problems as a reaction to the frustration engendered by the disability. All levels of adaptive functioning can be expected in the children. Commonly associated features include delays in nonmotor milestones, developmental articulation disorder, and developmental receptive language disorder and developmental expressive language disorder.

DIAGNOSIS

The diagnosis of developmental coordination disorder requires a careful history of the child's early motor behavior, including the direct observation of motor activities. Informal screening for developmental coordination disorder can be done by asking the child to perform tasks involving gross motor coordination (e.g., hopping, jumping, standing on one foot), fine motor coordination (e.g., finger tapping, shoelace tying), and hand-eye coordination (e.g., catching a ball, copying letters). The diagnosis is supported by below-normal scores on the performance subtests of standardized intelligence tests and by normal or above-normal scores on the verbal subtests. Specialized tests of motor coordination can be useful, such as the Bender-Gestalt Visual Motor test, the Frostig Movement Skills Test Battery, and the Bruininks-Oseretsky Test of Motor Development. The child's chronological age and intellectual capacity must be taken into account, and there should be no known neurological or neuromuscular disorder. However, slight reflex abnormalities and other soft neurological signs may occasionally be found on examination.

DIFFERENTIAL DIAGNOSIS

In mental retardation there is an overall decrease in performance involving both verbal and nonverbal motor areas. Pervasive developmental disorders should be ruled out; motor coordination difficulties, such as an abnormal gait and delays in motor milestones, are sometimes present in these disorders. Neurological and neuromuscular disorders—such as cerebral palsy, muscular dystrophy, and hemiplegia—may be associated with problems in coordination, and a conventional neurological examination reveals definite neural damage and abnormal findings.

TREATMENT

The various treatments include perceptual motor training, neurophysiological techniques of exercise for motor dysfunction, and modified physical education methods. The Montessori technique (developed by Maria Montessori) may be useful with many preschool children, as it emphasizes the development of motor skills. No single exercise or training method seems to be more advantageous or effective than another. Secondary behavioral or emotional problems and coexisting language and speech disorders must be managed by appropriate treatment methods.

There are no large-scale controlled studies on the effects of treatment, although small studies have suggested that exercises in rhythmic coordination, practicing motor movements, and learning to use typewriters are all somewhat helpful.

Parental counseling helps reduce the parents' anxiety and guilt over the child's impairment and increases their awareness, giving them confidence to cope with the child.

Table 34.6-2
Diagnostic Criteria for Specific Developmental Disorder Not Otherwise Specified

Disorders in the development of language, speech, academic, and motor skills that do not meet the criteria for a specific developmental disorder. Examples include aphasia with epilepsy acquired in childhood ("Landau syndrome") and specific developmental difficulties in spelling.

Table from DSM-III-R, *Diagnostic and Statistical Manual of Mental Disorders*, ed 3, revised. Copyright American Psychiatric Association, Washington, DC, 1987, with permission.

SPECIFIC DEVELOPMENTAL DISORDER NOT OTHERWISE SPECIFIED

This DSM-III-R residual category covers disorders in the development of language, speech, academic, and motor skills that cannot be classified as any of the specific developmental disorders discussed previously in this chapter. See Table 34.6-2 for the diagnostic criteria and examples of specific developmental disorder not otherwise specified.

References

Arnheim D D, Sinclair W A: *The Clumsy Child*. Mosby, St. Louis, 1975.

Baker L: Developmental coordination disorder. In *Comprehensive Textbook of Psychiatry*, ed 5, H I Kaplan and B J Sadock, editors, p 1818. Williams & Wilkins, Baltimore, 1989.

Breaner M W, Gillman S, Zangwill O L, Farrell M: Visuo-motor disability in school children. Br Med J *4*: 259, 1967.

Drillien C M: Etiology and outcome in low-birth-weight infants. Dev Med Child Neurol *14*: 563, 1972.

Gordon N: *Pediatric Neurology for the Clinician*. Heinemann, Philadelphia, 1976.

Prechtl H F, Stemmer C J: The choreiform syndrome in children. Dev Med Child Neurol *4*: 119, 1962.

Stott D H: A general test of motor impairment for children. Dev Med Child Neurol *8*: 523, 1966.

Disruptive Behavior Disorders

35.1 / Conduct Disorder

DIAGNOSIS

The essential feature of conduct disorder is a repetitive and persistent pattern of conduct in which either the basic rights of others or major age-appropriate societal norms or rules are violated. The conduct is more serious than the ordinary mischief and pranks of children and adolescents. DSM-III-R lists three types of conduct disorder: solitary aggressive type, group type, and undifferentiated type. The DSM-III-R diagnostic criteria for conduct disorder are listed in Table 35.1-1. This diagnosis is given only to persons below the age of 18 years.

As the criteria are a list of various infractions of societal norms, one must remember to explore for signs and symptoms of other psychopathology and neurological impairments, which are often associated with conduct disorder.

Table 35.1-1
Diagnostic Criteria for Conduct Disorder

A. A disturbance of conduct lasting at least six months, during which at least three of the following have been present:
   - (1) has stolen without confrontation of a victim on more than one occasion (including forgery)
   - (2) has run away from home overnight at least twice while living in parental or parental surrogate home (or once without returning)
   - (3) often lies (other than to avoid physical or sexual abuse)
   - (4) has deliberately engaged in fire-setting
   - (5) is often truant from school (for older person, absent from work)
   - (6) has broken into someone else's house, building, or car
   - (7) has deliberately destroyed others' property (other than by fire-setting)
   - (8) has been physically cruel to animals
   - (9) has forced someone into sexual activity with him or her
   - (10) has used a weapon in more than one fight
   - (11) often initiates physical fights
   - (12) has stolen with confrontation of a victim (e.g., mugging, purse-snatching, extortion, armed robbery)
   - (13) has been physically cruel to people

   Note: The above items are listed in descending order of discriminating power based on data from a national field trial of the DSM-III-R criteria for disruptive behavior disorders.

B. If 18 or older, does not meet criteria for antisocial personality disorder.

Table from DSM-III-R, *Diagnostic and Statistical Manual of Mental Disorders*, ed 3, revised. Copyright American Psychiatric Association, Washington, DC, 1987, with permission.

EPIDEMIOLOGY

Conduct disorder is fairly common during childhood and adolescence. It is estimated that approximately 9 percent of boys and 2 percent of girls under the age of 18 years have the disorder. The disorder is more common among boys than among girls, and the ratio ranges from 4 to 1 to 12 to 1. Conduct disorder is more common in children of parents with antisocial personality and alcohol dependence than it is in the general population. The prevalence of conduct disorder and antisocial behavior is significantly related to socioeconomic factors.

ETIOLOGY

No single factor can account for children's antisocial behavior and conduct disorder. Rather, a variety of biopsychosocial factors contribute to their development.

Parental Factors

It has long been recognized that some parental attitudes and faulty child-rearing practices influence the development of children's maladaptive behaviors. Chaotic home conditions are associated with conduct disorder and delinquency. However, broken homes per se are not causatively significant; it is the strife between the parents that contributes to conduct disorder. Parental psychopathology, child abuse, and negligence often contribute to conduct disorder. Sociopathy, alcoholism, and substance abuse in parents are associated with conduct disorder in their children. Parents may be so negligent that care of the child is shared by relatives or assumed by foster parents. Many such parents were scarred by their own upbringings and tend to be abusive, negligent, or engrossed in getting their own personal needs met. In the 1980s, particularly in urban areas, cocaine abuse and acquired immune deficiency syndrome (AIDS) increased family dysfunction. Recent studies suggest that many parents of conduct disorder children suffer from serious psychopathology, including psychoses. Psychodynamic hypotheses suggest that children with conduct disorder unconsciously act out their parents' antisocial wishes.

Sociocultural Factors

Current theories suggest that socioeconomically deprived children, unable to achieve status and obtain material goods through legitimate routes, are forced to resort to socially unacceptable means to reach those goals and that such behavior is normal and acceptable under circumstances of socioeconomic deprivation, as the children are adhering to the values of their own subculture.

Psychological Factors

Children brought up in chaotic, negligent conditions generally become angry, disruptive, demanding, and unable to progressively develop the tolerance for frustration necessary for mature relationships. As their role models are poor and often frequently changing, the basis for developing both an ego-ideal and a conscience is lacking. The children are left with little motivation to follow societal norms and are relatively remorseless.

Neurobiological Factors

Neurobiological factors in conduct disorder have been little studied. However, ADHD research yields some important findings, and conduct disorder and ADHD often coexist. In some conduct-disordered children a low level of plasma dopamine-β-hydroxylase, an enzyme that converts dopamine to norepinephrine, has been found. This finding supports a theory of decreased noradrenergic functioning in conduct disorder. Some conduct-disordered juvenile offenders have increased blood serotonin (5-hydroxytryptamine [5HT]) levels. There is some evidence that blood 5HT levels correlate negatively with levels of the 5HT metabolite 5-hydroxyindoleactic acid (5-HIAA) in the cerebrospinal fluid (CSF) and that low CSF 5-HIAA correlates with aggression and violence.

Other Factors

ADHD, central nervous system (CNS) dysfunction or damage, and early extremes of temperament can predispose a child to conduct disorder. Propensity to violence correlates with CNS dysfunction and signs of severe psychopathology, such as paranoid tendencies. Longitudinal temperament studies suggest that many behavioral deviations are initially a straightforward response to a poor fit between, on the one hand, a child's temperament and emotional needs and, on the other hand, parental attitudes and child-rearing practices.

DIFFERENTIAL DIAGNOSIS

Isolated acts of antisocial behavior do not justify a diagnosis of conduct disorder. Rather, antisocial behavior should be repetitive and persistent for a period of six months or more to justify a diagnosis of conduct disorder. Children with conduct disorder usually have chronically impaired social and school functioning.

Oppositional defiant disorder includes some of the features of conduct disorder, such as disobedience and defiant and oppositional behavior to authority figures. However, unlike conduct disorder, oppositional defiant disorder does not violate the basic rights of others and major age-appropriate societal norms or rules. Bipolar disorder must also be ruled out. The irritability and antisocial behavior associated with manic episodes are usually brief, whereas the symptoms of conduct disorder tend to persist over time. ADHD and specific developmental disorders are common associated diagnoses of conduct disorder, and these should be noted when present. Impulsive ADHD children are sometimes aggressive, but their aggression usually has a driven quality devoid of the anger and vengefulness found in conduct disorder.

TYPES

Solitary Aggressive Type

Clinical features. Children with the solitary aggressive type of conduct disorder commit solitary, rather than group, acts of aggression. The aggressive antisocial behavior may take the form of bullying, physical aggression, and cruel behavior toward peers. The children may be hostile, verbally abusive, impudent, defiant, and negativistic toward adults. Persistent lying, frequent truancy, and vandalism are common. In severe cases there is often destructiveness, stealing, and physical violence. The children usually make little attempt to conceal their antisocial behavior. Sexual behavior and the regular use of tobacco, liquor, or nonprescribed drugs begin unusually early for such children and adolescents. Suicidal thoughts, gestures, and acts are not infrequent.

Many of the children with this type of conduct disorder fail to develop social attachment, as manifested by their difficulty in or lack of sustained normal peer relationships. Such children are often socially withdrawn or isolated. Some of them may befriend a much older or younger person or have superficial relationships with other antisocial youngsters. Most of them have low self-esteem, although they may project an image of toughness. Characteristically, they do not put themselves out for others, even if it has an obvious immediate advantage. Their egocentrism is shown by their readily manipulating others for favors without any effort to reciprocate. They lack concern for the feelings, wishes, and welfare of others. They seldom have feelings of guilt or remorse for their callous behavior and try to blame others.

Not only have these children frequently encountered unusual frustrations, particularly of their dependency needs, but they also have escaped any consistent pattern of discipline. Their deficient socialization is revealed in their excessive aggressiveness and in their lack of sexual inhibition, which is frequently expressed aggressively and openly. Their general behavior is unacceptable in almost any social setting. They are generally viewed as bad kids and are frequently punished.

Unfortunately, such punishment almost invariably increases their maladaptive expression of rage and frustration, rather than ameliorating the problem.

In evaluation interviews, solitary aggressive conduct-disordered children are typically uncooperative, hostile, and provocative. Some have a superficial charm and compliance until they are urged to talk about their problem behaviors. Then they may angrily deny any problems. If the interviewer persists, conduct-disordered children may attempt to justify their misbehavior or become suspicious and angry about the source of the examiner's information and perhaps bolt from the room. Most often, they become angry at the examiner and express their resentment of the examination with open belligerence or sullen withdrawal. Their hostility is not limited to adult authority figures but expressed with equal venom toward their age-mates and younger children. In fact, they often bully those who are smaller and weaker than they. By boasting, lying, and expressing little interest in the listener's response, such children reveal their profoundly narcissistic orientation.

Evaluation of the family situation often reveals severe marital disharmony, which initially may center on disagreements concerning management of the child. Because of a tendency toward family instability, parent surrogates are often in the picture. Many children with this type of conduct disorder are only children of unplanned or unwanted pregnancies. The parents, especially the father, often have antisocial personality disorder or alcoholism.

The solitary aggressive child and the child's family demonstrate a stereotyped pattern of impulsive and unpredictable verbal and physical hostility. The child's aggressive behavior rarely seems directed toward any definable goal and offers little pleasure, success, or even sustained advantages with peers or authority figures.

Treatment. Multimodality treatment is often necessary and can include individual psychotherapy, family therapy, special schooling, pharmacotherapy, homemaking services, and residential placement. Treatment is difficult, given the child's and the family's pathology. Both the child and the family can undermine therapy, and frequently the conduct-disordered child proceeds to delinquency in adolescence and to antisocial behavior in adulthood. The age at which treatment begins is important to its success, not only because of the tendency of this behavioral pattern to become increasingly internalized and fixed in the face of the counterhostility that these youngsters engender in others but also because of the greater ease with which overt aggressiveness can be managed in a young child. Most therapists find it difficult to be patient with and sympathetic to these hostile youngsters.

Whenever feasible, the family should be involved in treatment. Unless the parents can come to feel some acceptance of and warmth toward the youngster and provide consistent guidelines for acceptable behavior, even the most intensive work with the child will probably not be helpful. Conjoint marital therapy and family therapy with these families is demanding. The therapist often feels overwhelmed by the intensity of the hostile interactions among the family group members and frustrated by the parents' inability to reach and follow through on their decisions regarding their child. The therapist is often faced with a confusing barrage of accusations, verbal attacks, and manipulations aimed at forcing the therapist into an alliance with one family member against another. Countertransference reactions of irritation, confusion, and helplessness are understandable. Firmness and impartiality are essential but difficult to maintain in the atmosphere of mutual recrimination and contradictory accounts of family interactions. Occasionally, the entire family achieves a temporary united front, but all too often it is based on a shared desire to attack the therapist.

To treat the child effectively, the therapist often finds it necessary to remove the child from the home. Even in a placement in a foster home or institution, the youngster can be expected to continue the extraordinary aggressiveness, testing of limits, and provocation. Those who are entrusted with caring for the solitary aggressive child must be prepared to offer acceptance and affection for long periods of time with very little positive feedback. Expectations for more socialized behavior from the youngster are initially minimal and are only gradually increased.

Behavior modification in a hospital setting has had some success, with varying degrees of lasting effect.

Medications are generally used in the conduct-disordered child to quell aggressive, assaultive behavior. Once under control, the child may be able to learn more in school and may be more amenable to psychotherapy. Lithium and haloperidol (Haldol) have proved effective with inpatients and with some outpatients. Carbamazepine (Tegretol) has benefited some in open trials.

Group Type

Clinical features. The DSM-III-R criteria for the group type of conduct disorder list the predominant feature as conduct problems occurring mainly as a group activity in the company of friends who have similar problems and to whom the child is loyal. Physical aggression may be included in this condition.

The group antisocial behavior invariably occurs outside the home. It includes repeated truancy, vandalism, and serious physical aggression or assault against others, such as mugging, gang fighting, and beating.

Children with this disorder usually have age-appropriate friendships. They are likely to show concern for the welfare of their friends or own gang members and are unlikely to blame them or inform on them.

In most cases there is a history of adequate or even excessive conformity during early childhood that ended when the youngster became a member of the delinquent peer group, usually in preadolescence or during adolescence. Also present in the history is some evidence of earlier problems, such as marginal or poor school performance, mild behavior problems, and neurotic symptoms.

Some degree of family social or psychological pathology is usually evident. Patterns of paternal discipline are rarely ideal and may vary from harshness and excessive strictness to inconsistency or relative absence of supervision and control. The mother has often protected the child from the consequences of early mild misbehavior but does not seem to actively encourage delinquency. Delinquency, also called juvenile delinquency, is most often associated with conduct disorder but may also be the result of other psychological or neurological disorders. There is usually evidence of a relatively warm relationship between the mother and the child, especially in infancy and early childhood. Some degree of marital disharmony may be present, and there is typically an absence of genuine family cohesion and comfortable interdependence. The group delinquent is likely to be from a large family living in poor economic circumstances.

The children's misdeeds usually occur in the company of a peer group. The parents often recognize the role of the peer group in the youngsters' difficulties and complain of the children's wish to spend all their time with their friends. Frequently, the parents use this accurate observation to discount the predisposing factors within the family and the community that underlie such children's selection of unsuitable companions.

The important and constant dynamic features in this condition are the significant influence of the peer group on such youngsters' behavior and their extreme dependency needs to maintain membership in the gang.

Course and prognosis. Very few youngsters with the group type of conduct disorder remain delinquent beyond adolescence; they may even give it up during adolescence. They may relinquish their delinquent behavior in response to fortuitous positive happenings, such as academic or athletic success, romantic attachments, and role modeling of an interested adult. Other youngsters may be dissuaded from the repetitive pattern through the unpleasantness of arrest and appearance in a juvenile court. Such occurrences may also awaken the family to their responsibilities toward the child.

Treatment. Traditional individual psychotherapy alone has proved to be relatively ineffective, partly because of adolescents' common resistance to this type of therapy. Some delinquent youngsters respond better to the accepting, permissive, and dynamically oriented counseling approach. A cognitive approach in a group setting has shown favorable results. The groups use a core of reformed delinquents who understand the rationalizations, denials, and self-justifications of the gang member seeking help and who vigorously confront youngsters with the realities of their behavioral predicament and the inevitability of negative consequences. The relatively high success rate in treating delinquent youngsters with the group-oriented approach is explained by the group conduct–disordered youngsters' natural tendency to turn to peers for advice and emotional support. Occasionally, such youngsters need to be separated from their previous peer group and to be transplanted to an entirely new environment, as in training schools, Outward Bound, and therapeutic camping programs.

Many youngsters with the group type of conduct disorder do not receive psychiatric treatment at all but are, instead, remanded to training schools or reformatories. A high percentage of these youngsters improve spontaneously as they become interested in heterosexual relationships, assume family responsibilities, and secure employment. Because their basic capacity for human relatedness is intact, they often discover their own passage out of delinquency.

Therapeutic optimism is very much warranted in this group of youngsters. Any approach that alters the attitudes of the entire group or that separates the youngsters from their delinquent peer group and offers them contact with strong adult leaders and less delinquent peers is likely to improve the group's antisocial or criminal behavior.

Undifferentiated Type

The undifferentiated type of conduct disorder is a category reserved for children or adolescents with a conduct disorder with clinical features that cannot be classified as either a solitary aggressive type or a group type.

References

Apter A, Bleich A, Plutchik R, Mendelsohn S, Tyano S: Suicidal behavior, depression and conduct disorder in hospitalized adolescents. J Am Acad Child Adolesc Psychiatry *27*: 696, 1988.

Berger M: Personality development and temperament. In *Temperamental Differences in Infants and Young Children*, R Porter and G M Collins, editors, p 176. Pitmann, London, 1982.

Farrington, D P: The family backgrounds of aggressive youths. In *Aggression and Antisocial Behavior in Childhood and Adolescence*, L Herzov, M Berger and D Shaffer, editors. Oxford, England, 1978.

Lamb M E: Parental influences on early socioemotional development. J Child Psychol Psychiatry *23*: 185, 1982.

Lewis D O, ed.: *Vulnerabilities to Delinquency*. Spectrum, New York, 1981.

Lewis D O, Lovely R, Yeager C, Ferguson G, Friedman M, Sloane G, Friedman H, Pincus J H: Intrinsic and environmental characteristics of juvenile murderers. J Am Acad Child Adolesc Psychiatry *27*: 582, 1988.

Lewis D O, Shanok S S, Lewis M L, Unger L, Goldman C: Conduct disorder and its synonyms: Diagnosis of dubious validity and usefulness. Am J Psychiatry *141*: 514, 1984.

Maziade M, Caron C, Côté R, Boutin P, Thivierge J: Extreme temperament and diagnoses. Arch Gen Psychiatry *47*: 477, 1990.

McAuley R: Annotation: Training parents to modify conduct problems in their children. J Child Psychol Psychiatry *23*: 335, 1982.

Pliszka S R, Rogness G A, Renner P, Sherman J, Broussard T: Plasma neurochemistry in juvenile offenders. J Am Acad Child Adolesc Psychiatry *27*: 588, 1988.

Robins L: *Deviant Children Grown Up*. Williams & Wilkins, Baltimore, 1966.

Stewart J T, Myers W C, Burket R C, Lyles W B: A review of the pharmacotherapy of aggression in children and adolescents. J Am Acad Child Adolesc Psychiatry *29*: 269, 1990.

Szatmari P, Boyle M, Offord D R: ADDH and conduct disorder: Degree of diagnostic overlap and differences among correlates. J Am Acad Child Adolesc Psychiatry *28*: 865, 1989.

35.2 / Attention-Deficit Hyperactivity Disorder

Attention-deficit hyperactivity disorder (ADHD) is composed of symptoms in three areas: short attention span, impulsivity, and hyperactivity. For the diagnosis to be made, the behavioral disturbances must have been present for at least six months and must first have appeared before the age of 7. The revised third edition of *Diagnostic and Statistical Manual of Mental Disorders* (DSM-III-R) diagnostic criteria for attention-deficit hyperactivity disorder are presented in Table 35.2-1.

Various terms have been used to describe this disorder: hyperkinetic reaction of childhood, hyperkinetic syndrome, hyperactive child syndrome, minimal brain dysfunction, minimal cerebral dysfunction, minimal brain damage, minor cerebral dysfunction, and, by the third edition of *Diagnostic and Statistical Manual of Mental Disorders* (DSM-III), attention deficit disorder with or without hyperactivity.

EPIDEMIOLOGY

Reports on the incidence of ADHD in the United States have varied from 2 to 20 percent of grade school children. However, a more conservative figure is about 3 to 5 percent of prepubertal elementary school children. In Great Britain the incidence is lower, less than 1 percent. There is a greater incidence in boys than in girls, with the ratio being from 3 to 1 to 5 to 1. It is most common in firstborn boys. The parents of children with ADHD show an increased

Table 35.2-1
Diagnostic Criteria for Attention-Deficit Hyperactivity Disorder

Note: Consider a criterion met only if the behavior is considerably more frequent than that of most people of the same mental age.

A. A disturbance of at least six months during which at least eight of the following are present:
   (1) often fidgets with hands or feet or squirms in seat (in adolescents, may be limited to subjective feelings of restlessness)
   (2) has difficulty remaining seated when required to do so
   (3) is easily distracted by extraneous stimuli
   (4) has difficulty awaiting a turn in games or group situations
   (5) often blurts out answers to questions before they have been completed
   (6) has difficulty following through on instructions from others (not due to oppositional behavior or failure of comprehension) (e.g., fails to finish chores)
   (7) has difficulty sustaining attention in tasks or play activities
   (8) often shifts from one uncompleted activity to another
   (9) has difficulty playing quietly
   (10) often talks excessively
   (11) often interrupts or intrudes on others (e.g., butts into other children's games)
   (12) often does not seem to listen to what is being said to him or her
   (13) often loses things necessary for tasks or activities at school or at home (e.g., toys, pencils, books, assignments)
   (14) often engages in physically dangerous activities without considering possible consequences (not for the purpose of thrill-seeking) (e.g., runs into street without looking)

Note: The above items are listed in descending order of discriminating power based on data from a national field trial of the DSM-III-R criteria for disruptive behavior disorders.

B. Onset before the age of 7.

C. Does not meet the criteria for a pervasive developmental disorder.

Table from DSM-III-R, *Diagnostic and Statistical Manual of Mental Disorders*, ed 3, revised. Copyright American Psychiatric Association, Washington, DC, 1987, with permission.

incidence of hyperkinesis, sociopathy, alcoholism, and conversion disorder. Although the onset is usually by the age of 3, the diagnosis is generally not made until the child is in elementary school and the formal learning situation requires structured behavior patterns, including developmentally appropriate attention span and concentration.

ETIOLOGY

Neurobiological Factors

The majority of children with ADHD do not show evidence of gross structural damage or disease in the central nervous system (CNS) when examined by conventional neurological methods. Conversely, most children with neurological disorders or brain injuries do not display any specific features of hyperactivity. Research efforts to find a neurophysiological or neurochemical basis have not yielded any definite findings. Nevertheless, some children with the disorder may have minimal and subtle brain damage from adverse circulatory, toxic, metabolic, or mechanical insults to the CNS during fetal and perinatal periods. That may account for the association of learning disorders in children with ADHD.

Hypersensitivity and idiosyncratic responses to food additives (such as colorings and preservatives) have been suggested as causes of the disorder, but these claims have not been scientifically validated.

Genetic Factors

A genetic basis of ADHD has been suggested by data that show a greater concordance rate in monozygotic twins than in dizygotic twins. Siblings of hyperactive children are also at a greater risk for hyperactivity than are half siblings.

Alcoholism, antisocial personality disorder, and Briquet's syndrome are more common in parents of children with ADHD, even in biological parents of adopted-away ADHD children, than in parents of other children.

Brain Damage

It has long been speculated that some of the children affected by ADHD may have received minimal and subtle brain damage to the CNS during fetal and perinatal periods. The brain damage may have been caused by adverse circulatory, toxic, metabolic, mechanical assault, and other effects and by stress and physical insult to the brain during early infancy, caused by infection, inflammation, and trauma. This minimal, subtle, and subclinical severity of brain damage may be responsible for the genesis of learning disorders and ADHD. Nonfocal (soft) neurological signs are frequent.

To date, there are no consistent computed tomographic (CT) scan abnormalities. A cerebral blood flow study showed frontal hypoperfusion. A positron emission tomography (PET) scan study of adults having a history of childhood attention-deficit disorder with hyperactivity showed depressed metabolic rates in many areas of the brain, particularly in the premotor and somatosensory cortex. Both these studies are supportive of a theory linking frontal lobe dysfunction and disinhibition with ADHD. Studies of cognitive impairments of ADHD children have yielded conflicting results relative to this theory.

Neurochemical Factors

Numerous studies of monoamines and their metabolites in urine, blood, and cerebrospinal fluid (CSF) fail to implicate a single neurotransmitter as producing ADHD. Noradrenergic dysfunction has the most support. Dextroamphetamine (Dexedrine) and desipramine (Norpramin) reduce urinary 3-methoxy-4-hydroxyphenylglycol (MHPG), which correlates with clinical improvement.

Maturational Lag

The human brain normally undergoes major growth spurts at several ages: 3 to 10 months, 2 to 4 years, 6 to 8 years, 10 to 12 years, and 14 to 16 years. Some children have a maturational delay in this developmental sequence and may show a clinical picture of ADHD that is temporary and disappears as maturational lags catch up to normal milestones at around puberty.

Psychosocial Factors

Children in institutions are frequently overactive and have poor attention spans. These symptoms result from prolonged emotional deprivation and disappear when deprivational factors are removed, such as through placement in a foster home or adoption. Stressful psychic events, a disruption of family equilibrium, and other anxiety-inducing factors contribute to the initiation or perpetuation of ADHD. Predisposing factors may include the child's temperament, genetic-familial factors, and the demands of society to adhere to a routinized way of behaving and performing. Socioeconomic status does not seem to be a predisposing factor.

CLINICAL FEATURES

The disorder may have its onset in infancy. Infants with ADHD are unduly sensitive to stimuli and are easily upset by noise, light, temperature, and other environmental changes. At times, the reverse occurs, and the children are placid and limp, sleep much of the time, and appear to develop slowly in the first months. It is more common, though, for infants with ADHD to be active in the crib, sleep little, and cry a great deal. ADHD children are far less likely than normal children to reduce their locomotor activity when their environment is structured by social limits. In school, ADHD children may rapidly attack a test but answer only the first two questions. They may be unable to wait to be called on in school and may respond for everyone else, and at home they cannot be put off for even a minute.

These children are often explosively irritable. This irritability may be set off by relatively minor stimuli, which may puzzle and dismay them. They are frequently emotionally labile, easily set off to laughter or to tears, and their mood and performance are apt to be variable and unpredictable. Impulsiveness and an inability to delay gratification are characteristic. They are often accident-prone.

Concomitant emotional difficulties are frequent. The fact that other children grow out of this kind of behavior and that ADHD children do not grow out of it at the same time and rate, the variability of their performance, and the general nuisance and inexplicability of their behavior—all may lead to adults' dissatisfaction and pressure. The resulting negative self-concept and reactive hostility are worsened by the children's frequent recognition that they are not right inside.

The characteristics most often cited are, in order of frequency, (1) hyperactivity, (2) perceptual motor impairment, (3) emotional lability, (4) general coordination deficit, (5) disorders of attention (short attention span, distractibility, perseveration, failure to finish things, inattention, poor concentration), (6) impulsivity (action before thought, abrupt shifts in activity, lack of organization, jumping up in class), (7) disorders of memory and thinking, (8) specific learning disabilities, (9) disorders of speech and hearing, and (10) equivocal neurological signs and electroencephalographic (EEG) irregularities.

Approximately 75 percent of children with ADHD fairly consistently show behavioral symptoms of aggression and defiance. But, whereas defiance and aggression are generally associated with adverse intrafamily relationships, hyperactivity is more closely related to developmental lags in sensorimotor coordination, language, and impaired performance on cognitive tests requiring concentration. Some studies claim that some relatives of hyperactive children show features of antisocial personality.

School difficulties, both learning and behavorial, are common, sometimes coming from concomitant developmental language disorders or academic skills disorders or from the children's distractibility and fluctuating attention, which hamper their acquisition, retention, and display of knowledge. These difficulties resemble specific developmental disorders, especially when evaluated on group tests. The adverse reactions of school personnel to the behavior characteristic of ADHD and the lowering of self-regard because of felt inadequacies may combine with the adverse comments of peers to make school a place of unhappy defeat. This, in turn, may lead to acting-out antisocial behavior and self-defeating, self-punitive behaviors. A clinical case example follows:

A 9-year-old boy was referred to a child psychiatrist at the request of his school because of the difficulties he created in class. He had twice been suspended for a day in the school year. His teacher complained that he was so restless that the other students were unable to concentrate. He was hardly ever in his seat but roamed around the class, talking to other children while they were working. He never seemed to know what he was going to do next and might suddenly do something quite outrageous. His most recent suspension had been for swinging from the fluorescent light fitting over the blackboard, where he had climbed in the transition from one class to the next; since he had been unable to climb down again, the class was in an uproar.

His mother said that the boy's behavior had been difficult since he was a toddler, and that, as a 3-year-old, he had been unbearably restless and demanding. He had always required little sleep and was awake before anyone else. When he was small, "he got into everything," particularly in the early morning, when he would awaken at 4:30 or 5:00 A.M. and go downstairs by himself. His parents would awaken to find the living room or kitchen "demolished." When he was 4, he managed to unlock the door of the apartment and wander off into a busy main street but, fortunately, was rescued from oncoming traffic by a passerby. He was rejected by a preschool program because of his difficult behavior; eventually, after a very difficult year in kindergarten, he was placed in a special behavioral program for first- and second-graders. He was in a regular class for most subjects but spent a lot of time in a resource room with a special teacher.

Psychological testing had shown the boy to be of average ability, and his achievements were only slightly below the expected level. His attention span was described by the psychologist as "virtually nonexistent." He had no interest in TV and disliked games or toys that required any concentration or patience on his part. He was not popular with other children and at home prefered to be outdoors, playing with his dog or riding his bike. If he did play with toys, his games were messy and destructive, and his mother could not get him to keep his things in any order.

He was also quite disobedient and in the preceding year or so had been provocative and defiant at school and, to some extent, at home. He had stolen small sums of money from home and school, and other children had complained because he had taken small toys that they had brought to school.

The boy had been treated with a stimulant, methylphenidate (Ritalin), in a small dosage (5 to 10 mg a day); but this had been discontinued in the previous year, apparently because it was having no effect on his defiance and conduct problems. When he was taking the drug, he was much easier to manage at school; he was less restless and possibly more attentive, even though other aspects of his behavior were unsatisfactory.

Discussion. The boy's behavior graphically demonstrated the characteristic inattention, impulsivity, and hyperactivity of attention-deficit hyperactivity disorder. He had difficulty remaining seated, fidgeted, could not follow through on instructions, could not sustain attention, often did not seem to listen to what was being said to him, shifted from one activity to another, had difficulty playing quietly, and often engaged in physically dangerous activities without considering the consequences. Because he almost certainly had the other symptoms of attention-deficit hyperactivity disorder (such as difficulty waiting his turn, blurting out answers to questions, talking excessively, and interrupting others) and because his symptoms significantly interfered with his functioning at home and at school, it was noted that the disorder was severe.

DIAGNOSIS

The principal sign of hyperactivity should alert clinicians to the possibility of ADHD. A detailed prenatal history of the child's early developmental patterns and direct observation usually reveal excessive motor activity. Hyperactivity may be seen in some situations (e.g., school) but not in others (e.g., one-to-one interviews, watching television), and it may be less obvious in structured situations than in unstructured situations. However, it should not be an isolated, brief, and transient behavioral manifestation under stress but should have been present over a long time. Other distinguishing features of ADHD are short attention span and easy distractibility. In school these children cannot follow instructions and often demand extra attention from their teachers. At home they often do not follow through on their parents' requests. They act impulsively, show emotional lability, and are explosive and irritable.

Specific developmental disorders—such as those involving reading, arithmetic, language, and coordination—may be found in association with ADHD. The history is important, as it may give clues to prenatal (including genetic), natal, and postnatal factors that may have affected the CNS structure or function. Rates of development, deviations in development, and parental reactions to significant or stressful behavioral transitions should be ascertained, as they may help determine the degree to which parents have contributed to or reacted to the child's inefficiencies and dysfunctions.

School history and teachers' reports are important in evaluating whether the children's difficulties in learning and school behavior are primarily due to their attitudinal or maturational problems or to their poor self-image because of felt inadequacies. This information may also reveal how the children have handled these problems. How they have related to siblings, to peers, to adults, and to free and structured activities gives valuable diagnostic clues to the presence of ADHD and helps identify the complications of the disorder.

The mental status examination may show a secondarily depressed mood but no thought disturbance, impaired reality testing, or inappropriate affect. There may be great distractibility, perseveration, and a concrete and literal mode of thinking. There may be indications of visual-perceptual, auditory-perceptual, language, or cognition problems. Occasionally, there is evidence of a basic, pervasive, organically based anxiety, often referred to as body anxiety.

A neurological examination may reveal visual-motor-perceptual or auditory-discriminatory immaturity or impairments without overt signs of disorders of visual or auditory acuity. The children may show problems with motor coordination and difficulties with copying age-appropriate figures, rapid alternating movements, right-left discrimination, ambidexterity, reflex asymmetries, and a variety of subtle nonfocal neurological signs (soft signs). A clinician should obtain an EEG to recognize the child with frequent bilaterally synchronous discharges resulting in short absence spells. Such a child may react in school with hyperactivity out of sheer frustration. The child with an unrecognized temporal lobe seizure focus can present a secondary behavior disorder. In these instances several features of the ADHD are often present. Identification of the focus requires an EEG obtained in drowsiness and in sleep.

COURSE AND PROGNOSIS

The course of ADHD is highly variable. Symptoms may persist into adolescence or adult life; they may remit at puberty; or the hyperactivity may disappear, but the decreased attention span and impulse control problems may persist.

The overactivity is usually the first symptom to remit, and distractibility the last. Remission is not likely before the age of 12. If it does occur, it is usually between the ages of 12 and 20. Remission may be accompanied by a productive adolescence and adult life, satisfying interpersonal relationships, and few significant sequelae. The majority of patients with ADHD, however, undergo partial remission and are vulnerable to antisocial and other personality disorders and mood disorders. Learning problems often continue.

In about 15 to 20 percent of cases, the symptoms of ADHD persist into adulthood. Those with the disorder may show diminished hyperactivity but remain somewhat impulsive and accident-prone. Although their educational attainment is lower than that of persons without ADHD, their early employment history is not different from those with a similar education.

Many children with ADHD become delinquent in adolescence or develop antisocial personality disorder in adulthood or both. This progression has been reported in upward of 25 percent of all children with ADHD, but in such studies many children appear to have had a concomitant conduct disorder or oppositional defiant disorder. Some evidence indicates that, when ADHD children receive multimodality treatment—that is, medication combined with psychosocial, individual, and family therapies—long-term social deviance can be diminished.

DIFFERENTIAL DIAGNOSIS

A temperamental constellation consisting of high activity level and short attention span should be first considered. It is often difficult to differentiate these temperamental characteristics from the cardinal symptoms of ADHD before age 3, mainly because of the overlapping features of a normally immature nervous system and the emerging signs of visual-motor-perceptual impairments frequently seen in ADHD.

Anxiety in the child needs to be evaluated. Anxiety may accompany ADHD as a secondary feature, and anxiety by itself may be manifested by overactivity and easy distractibility.

Many children with ADHD have secondary depression in reaction to their continuing frustration over their failure to learn and their consequent low self-esteem. This condition must be distinguished from a primary depressive disorder, which is more likely to be distinguished by hypoactivity and withdrawal.

The various types of conduct disorder with overactivity and aggression may be confused with ADHD, which is often associated with and secondary to these disorders. Frequently, conduct disorder and ADHD coexist, and so both must be diagnosed.

TREATMENT

Pharmacotherapy

The pharmacological agents for ADHD are the CNS stimulants, primarily dextroamphetamine (Dexedrine), methylphenidate, and pemoline (Cylert). The Food and Drug Administration (FDA) approves of dextroamphetamine in children 3 years and older and methylphenidate in those 6 years and older; these two are the most commonly used drugs.

The mechanism of action of the stimulants is unknown, but it is no longer widely believed to work paradoxically. These drugs are controversial because they may suppress growth slightly. However, drug holidays over school vacation periods apparently result in rebounds in growth. In one study, early adolescents did not experience growth suppression after 6 to 12 months on methylphenidate.

There is also a debate about the potential for abuse and habit formation with these drugs. One should be particularly careful in determining the potential for abuse in an adolescent or adult being considered for stimulant medication. When used judiciously and within the recommended dosage range, the stimulants have benefits that outweigh their risks for abuse.

Antidepressants, particularly imipramine (Tofranil), have been tried with some success in ADHD. They are particularly helpful for ADHD plus depression or anxiety. Desipramine (Norpramin) has been effective in several controlled studies and has benefited some ADHD children who failed to improve when given stimulants. It can also be used to treat ADHD with associated tics and when stimulant treatment of an ADHD child has precipitated or worsened preexisting tics. However, sudden death has been reported in three children receiving desipramine. Antidepressants work by blocking the reuptake of catecholamines. They should be used with great care in children because of their potential cardiotoxic effects.

Psychotherapy

Medication alone rarely satisfies the comprehensive therapeutic needs of ADHD children and is usually but one facet of a multimodality regimen. Individual psychotherapy, behavior modification, parent counseling, and treatment of any coexisting specific developmental disorder may be necessary.

When given medication, ADHD children should be given the opportunity to explore the meaning of the medication to them, helping dispel misconceptions (such as, "I'm crazy") because medication is used and making it clear that the medication is only an adjuvant. These children need to understand that they need not always be perfect.

When ADHD children are not only allowed but also helped to structure their environment, their anxiety diminishes. Thus, their parents and teachers should set up a predictable structure of reward and punishment, using a behavior therapy model and applying it to the physical, temporal, and interpersonal environment. An almost universal requirement is to help the parents recognize that permissiveness is not helpful to their child. They should also be helped to recognize that, in spite of their children's deficiencies in some areas, they face the normal tasks of maturation, including the need to introject standards and to form a normal, flexible superego. Therefore, children with ADHD do not benefit from being exempted from the requirements, expectations, and planning applicable to other children.

Evaluation of Therapeutic Progress

Monitoring starts with the initiation of medication. Because school performance is most markedly affected, special attention and effort should be given to establishing and maintaining a close collaborative working relationship with the children's school.

In most patients, stimulants reduce overactivity, distractibility, impulsiveness, explosiveness, and irritability. There is no evidence that the medications directly improve any existing impairments in learning, although, when the attention deficits diminish, the children can learn more effectively. In addition, medication can improve self-esteem when the ADHD children are no longer constantly reprimanded for their behavior.

UNDIFFERENTIATED ATTENTION-DEFICIT DISORDER

DSM-III-R includes undifferentiated attention-deficit disorder as a residual category for disturbances in which the predominant feature is the persistence of develop-

Table 35.2-2
Diagnostic Criteria for Undifferentiated Attention-Deficit Disorder

This is a residual category for disturbances in which the predominant feature is the persistence of developmentally inappropriate and marked inattention that is not a symptom of another disorder, such as mental retardation or attention-deficit hyperactivity disorder, or of a disorganized and chaotic environment. Some of the disturbances that in DSM-III would have been categorized as attention deficit disorder without hyperactivity would be included in this category. Research is necessary to determine if this is a valid diagnostic category and, if so, how it should be defined.

mentally inappropriate and marked inattention that is not a symptom of another disorder, such as mental retardation or ADHD, or of a disorganized and chaotic environment (Table 35.2-2).

In adults, residual signs of the disorder include impulsivity and attention deficit (for example, difficulty in organizing and completing work, inability to concentrate, increased distractibility, and sudden decision making without a thought of consequences). Many patients with the disorder suffer from a secondary depression that is associated with low self-esteem related to their impaired performance and affects both occupational and social functioning. The treatment of this disorder is the use of amphetamines (5 to 40 mg a day) or methylphenidate (5 to 60 mg a day). Signs of a positive response are an increased attention span, decreased impulsiveness, and improved mood. Psychopharmacological therapy may need to be continued indefinitely. Because of the abuse potential of these drugs, clinicians should carefully monitor drug response and patient compliance.

References

Biederman J, Baldessarini R J, Wright V, Knee D, Harmatz J S: A double-blind placebo controlled study of desipramine in the treatment of ADD: I. Efficiency. J Am Acad Child Adolesc Psychiatry *28*: 777, 1989.

Biederman J, Munir K, Knee D, Armentano M, Auter S, Waternaux C, Tsuang M: High rate of affective disorders in probands with attention deficit disorder and in their relatives: A controlled family study. Am J Psychiatry *144*: 330, 1987.

Hechtman L: Attention-deficit hyperactivity disorder in adolescence and adulthood: An updated follow-up. Psychiatr Ann *19*: 597, 1989.

Jacobvitz D, Sroufe L A, Stewart M, Leffert N: Treatment of attentional and hyperactivity problems in children with sympathicomimetic drugs: A comprehensive review. J Am Acad Child Adolesc Psychiatry *29*: 677, 1990.

Klein R G, Landa B, Mattes J A, Klein D: Methylphenidate and growth in hyperactive children. Arch Gen Psychiatry *45*: 1127, 1988.

Klorman R, Brumaghim J T, Fitzpatrick P A, Borgstedt A D: Clinical effects of a controlled trial of methylphenidate on adolescents with attention deficit disorder. J Am Acad Child Adolesc Psychiatry *29*: 702, 1990.

Loge D V, Staton D, Beatty W W: Performance of children with ADHD on tests sensitive to frontal lobe dysfunction. J Am Acad Child Adolesc Psychiatry *29*: 540, 1990.

Loney J, Kramer J, Milich R: The hyperkinetic child grows up: Predictors of symptoms, delinquency, and achievement at follow-up. In *Psychosocial Aspects of Drug Treatment for Hyperactivity*, K D Gadow and J Loney, editors, p 381. Westview Press, Boulder, CO, 1981.

Rogeness G A, Maas J W, Javors M A, Macedo C A, Harris W R, Hoppe S K: Diagnoses, catecholamine metabolism and plasma dopamine-β-hydroxylase. J Am Acad Child Adolesc Psychiatry *27*: 121, 1988.

Taylor E: Syndromes of overactivity and attention deficit. In *Child and Adolescent Psychiatry: Modern Approaches*, ed 2, M Rutter and L Hersov, editors, p 424. Blackwell, Oxford, England, 1985.

Vincent J, Varley C K, Leger P: Effects of methylphenidate on early adolescent growth. Am J Psychiatry *147*: 501, 1990.

Zametkin A J, Nordahl T E, Gross M, King A C, Semple W E, Rumsey J, Hamburger S, Cohen R M: Cerebral glucose metabolism in adults with hyperactivity of childhood onset. N Engl J Med *323*: 1361, 1990.

Zametkin A J, Rapoport J L: Neurobiology of attention deficit disorder with hyperactivity: Where have we come in 50 years. J Am Acad Child Adolesc Psychiatry *26*: 676, 1987.

35.3 / Oppositional Defiant Disorder

DIAGNOSIS

The essential feature of oppositional defiant disorder is a pattern of negativistic, hostile, and defiant behavior, often directed toward parents or teachers. These actions, however, do not include the more serious violations of the basic rights of others seen in the various conduct disorders. The revised third edition of *Diagnostic and Statistical Manual of Mental Disorders* (DSM-III-R) diagnostic criteria for oppositional defiant disorder are given in Table 35.3-1.

Table 35.3-1
Diagnostic Criteria for Oppositional Defiant Disorder

Note: Consider a criterion met only if the behavior is considerably more frequent than that of most people of the same mental age.

A. A disturbance of at least six months during which at least five of the following are present:
 (1) often loses temper
 (2) often argues with adults
 (3) often actively defies or refuses adult requests or rules, e.g., refuses to do chores at home
 (4) often deliberately does things that annoy other people, e.g., grabs other children's hats
 (5) often blames others for his or her own mistakes
 (6) is often touchy or easily annoyed by others
 (7) is often angry and resentful
 (8) is often spiteful or vindictive
 (9) often swears or uses obscene language

 Note: The above items are listed in descending order of discriminating power based on data from a national field trial of the DSM-III-R criteria for disruptive behavior disorders.

B. Does not meet the criteria for conduct disorder, and does not occur exclusively during the course of a psychotic disorder, dysthymia, or a major depressive, hypomanic, or manic episode.

EPIDEMIOLOGY

Oppositional, negativistic behavior may be developmentally normal in early childhood. Epidemiological studies of negativistic traits in nonclinical populations found them in between 16 and 22 percent of school-age children. Although the disorder can begin as early as 3 years of age, it typically begins by 8 years of age and usually not later than adolescence.

DSM-III-R states that the disorder is more prevalent in boys than in girls before puberty and that the sex ratio is probably equal after puberty. Another authority suggests that girls may be classified as having oppositional disorder more frequently than boys (using the third edition of DSM [DSM-III] criteria), as boys are more often given the diagnosis of conduct disorder.

There are no distinct family patterns, but almost all parents of oppositional defiant disorder children are themselves overconcerned with issues of power, control, and autonomy. Some families contain several obstinate children, controlling and depressed mothers, and passive-aggressive fathers. In many cases the patients were unwanted children.

ETIOLOGY

Asserting one's own will and opposing that of others is crucial to normal development. It is related to establishing one's autonomy, forming an identity, and setting inner standards and controls. The most dramatic example of normal oppositional behavior peaks between 18 and 24 months, the terrible twos, when the toddler behaves negativistically as an expression of growing autonomy. Pathology begins when this developmental phase persists abnormally, authority figures overreact, or oppositional behavior recurs considerably more frequently than in most children of the same mental age.

Children may have constitutional or temperamental predispositions to strong will, strong preferences, or greater assertiveness. If power and control are issues for the parents or if they exercise authority for their own needs, a struggle can ensue that sets the stage for the development of an oppositional defiant disorder. What begins for the infant as an effort to establish self-determination becomes transformed into a defense against overdependency on the mother and a protective device against intrusion into the ego's autonomy. In later childhood, environmental traumata, illness, or chronic incapacity, such as mental retardation, may trigger oppositionalism as a defense against helplessness, anxiety, and loss of self-esteem. Another normative oppositional stage occurs in adolescence as an expression of the need to separate from the parents and to establish an autonomous identity.

Classic psychoanalytic theory implicates unresolved conflicts that developed during the anal period. Behaviorists have suggested that oppositionalism is a reinforced, learned behavior through which the child exerts control over authority figures—for example, by having a temper tantrum when some undesired act is requested, the child coerces the parents to withdraw their request. In addition, increased parental attention—for example, long discussions about the behavior—many reinforce the behavior.

CLINICAL FEATURES

DSM-III-R notes that children with this disorder often argue with adults; lose their temper; swear; and are angry, resentful, and easily annoyed by others. They frequently actively defy adults' requests or rules and deliberately annoy other people. They tend to blame others for their own mistakes and difficulties. Manifestations of the disorder are almost invariably present in the home but may not be present at school or with other adults or peers. In some cases, features of the disorder from the beginning of the disturbance are displayed outside the home; in other cases they start in the home but are later displayed outside the home. Typically, symptoms of the disorder are most evident in interactions with adults or peers whom the child knows well. Thus, children with the disorder are likely to show little or no sign of the disorder when examined clinically. Usually, they do not regard themselves as oppositional or defiant but justify their behavior as a response to unreasonable circumstances. The disorder appears to cause more distress to those around the children than to the children themselves.

Chronic oppositional defiant disorder almost always interferes with interpersonal relationships and school performance. The children are often friendless and perceive human relationships as unsatisfactory. Despite adequate intelligence, they do poorly or fail in school, as they withhold participation, resist external demands, and insist on solving problems without others' help.

Secondary to these difficulties are low self-esteem, poor frustration tolerance, depressed mood, and temper outbursts. Adolescents may abuse alcohol and illegal psychoactive agents. Often this disturbance evolves into a conduct disorder or a mood disorder.

DIFFERENTIAL DIAGNOSIS

Because oppositional behavior is both normal and adaptive at specific developmental stages, these periods of negativism must be distinguished from oppositional defiant disorder. Developmental-stage oppositional behavior is of shorter duration than oppositional defiant disorder and is not considerably more frequent or more intense than that of other children of the same mental age.

Oppositional defiant behavior that occurs temporarily in reaction to a severe stress should be diagnosed as an adjustment disorder.

When features of oppositional defiant disorder appear during the course of a conduct disorder, schizophrenia, or a mood disorder, the diagnosis of oppositional defiant disorder should not be made.

Oppositional and negativistic behaviors may also be present in attention-deficit hyperactivity disorder, organic mental syndromes, and mental retardation. Whether a concomitant diagnosis of oppositional defiant disorder should be given depends on the severity, pervasiveness, and duration of such behavior.

TREATMENT

The primary treatment for this disorder is individual psychotherapy for the child with counseling and direct training of the parents in child management skills.

Behavior therapists emphasize teaching parents how to alter their behavior to discourage their child's oppositional behavior and to encourage appropriate behavior. Behavior therapy focuses on selectively reinforcing and praising appropriate behavior and ignoring or not reinforcing undesired behavior.

Clinicians who treat patients with individual psychotherapy note that family patterns are rigid and difficult to alter unless the children themselves have a new type of object relationship with the therapist. Within the therapeutic relationship, children can relive the autonomy-threatening experiences that produced their defenses. In the safety of a noncontrolling relationship, they can understand the self-destructive nature of their behavior and risk expressing themselves directly. Their self-esteem must be restored before their automatic defenses against external control can be relinquished. In this way independence may replace habitual defenses against intrusion and control. Once a therapeutic relationship has been formed on the basis of respect for the patient's separateness, the patient is ready to understand the source of the defenses and to try new coping behaviors.

References

Doke L A, Flippo J R: Aggressive and oppositional behavior. In *Handbook of Child Psychopathology*, T Ollendick, editor, p 222. Plenum, New York, 1982.

Farrington D P: The family backgrounds of aggressive youths. In *Aggression and Antisocial Behavior in Childhood and Adolescence*, L Herzov, M Berger, and D Shaffer, editors. Pergamon, Oxford, England, 1978.

Glueck S, Glueck E: *Unraveling Juvenile Delinquency*. Commonwealth Fund, New York, 1950.

Group for the Advancement of Psychiatry: *Psychopathological Disorders in Childhood: Theoretical Considerations and a Proposed Classification*. Group for the Advancement of Psychiatry, New York, 1966.

Levy D M: Oppositional syndromes and oppositional behavior. In *Psychopathology of Childhood*, P Hoch and J Zubin, editors, p 204. Grune & Stratton, New York, 1955.

Lewis D O, Shanok S S, Grant M, Ritvo E: Homicidally aggressive young children: Neuropsychiatric and experiential correlates. Am J Psychiatry *140*: 148, 1983.

Lewis D O, Shanok S S, Lewis M L, Unger L, Goldman C: Conduct disorder and its synonyms: Diagnosis of dubious validity and usefulness. Am J Psychiatry *141*: 514, 1984.

Rey J M, Bashir M R, Schwarz M, Richards I N, Plapp J M, Stewart A W: Oppositional disorder: Fact or fiction. J Am Acad Child Adolesc Psychiatry *27*: 157, 1988.

Robins L: *Deviant Children Grown Up*. Williams & Wilkins, Baltimore, 1966.

36

Anxiety Disorders of Childhood or Adolescence

Anxiety disorders in children and adolescents were first divided into three disorders in the third edition of *Diagnostic and Statistical Manual of Mental Disorders* (DSM-III) in 1980. In the previous edition, DSM-II, there was one category of overanxious reaction of childhood or adolescence subsumed under the rubric of behavior disorders. The fact that children with one anxiety disorder according to the revised third edition (DSM-III-R) often have symptoms of another anxiety disorder contributes to an ongoing controversy about the validity of the three disorders as distinct clinical entities.

Anxiety disorders of childhood or adolescence include three disorders in which anxiety is the predominant clinical feature. In separation anxiety disorder and avoidant disorder of childhood or adolescence, the anxiety is focused on specific situations. In overanxious disorder the anxiety is generalized to a variety of situations. (See Table 36-1 for a description of the anxiety disorders discussed in this chapter.) These disorders account for many outpatient referrals. Children and adolescents may also present with the following anxiety disorders described in the adult section of DSM-III-R: simple phobia, panic disorder, obsessive-compulsive disorder, and posttraumatic stress disorder.

SEPARATION ANXIETY DISORDER

In a child with separation anxiety disorder, anxiety can reach calamitous proportions during separation or while anticipating separation from a major caretaker. The extent of the anxiety is beyond that expected at the child's developmental level. School avoidance may occur.

According to DSM-III-R, a diagnosis of separation anxiety disorder should not be made if the anxiety occurs exclusively during the course of another disorder, such as pervasive developmental disorder.

Epidemiology

This disorder is common in early childhood and occurs equally in the two sexes. The onset may be as early as preschool years, but many cases begin around 11 or 12 years, especially the most extreme form of the disorder—refusing to go to school.

Etiology

Psychosocial factors. Young children, immature and dependent on a mothering figure, are particularly prone to anxiety related to separation. Because children undergo a series of developmental fears—fear of losing the mother, fear of losing the mother's love, fear of bodily damage, fear of their impulses, and fear of the punishing anxiety of the superego and of guilt—most have transient experiences of separation anxiety based on one or another of these fears. However, separation anxiety disorder occurs when there is a disproportionate fear of mother-loss. A frequent dynamic is the child's disavowal and displacement of angry feelings toward the parents onto the environment, which then becomes overly threatening. Fears of personal harm and of danger to one's parents are persistent preoccupations; the child can feel safe and secure only in the parent's presence. The syndrome is common in childhood, especially in mild forms that do not reach the physician's office. It is only when the symptoms have become established and disturb the child's general adaptation to family life, peers, and school that they come to the attention of professionals.

The character structure pattern in many children who develop this disorder includes conscientiousness, eagerness to please, and a tendency toward conformity. Families tend to be close-knit and caring, and the children often seem to be spoiled or the objects of parental overconcern.

External life stresses often coincide with the development of the disorder. The death of a relative, illness in the child, a change in the child's environment, or a move to a new neighborhood or a new school is frequently noted in the histories of children with this disorder.

Learning factors. Phobic anxiety may be communicated from parents to children by direct modeling. If a parent is fearful, there is a great likelihood that the child will develop a phobic adaptation to new situations, especially to the school environment. Some parents appear to teach their children to be anxious by overprotecting them from expected dangers or by exaggerating the dangers. For example, the parent who cringes in a room during a lightning storm teaches a child to do the same. The parent who is frightened of mice or insects conveys the affect of fright to the child. Conversely, the parent who becomes angry at a child during an incipient phobic concern about animals may inculcate a phobic concern in the child by the very intensity of the anger expressed.

Genetic factors. There is probably a genetic basis for the intensity with which separation anxiety is experienced by individual children. Family studies have shown that the biological offspring of adults with anxiety disorder are prone to suffer in childhood from separation anxiety disorder. Parents who have panic disorder and agoraphobia appear to have an

Table 36-1
Common Characteristics of Anxiety Disorders of Childhood or Adolescence

Criteria	Separation Anxiety Disorder	Avoidant Disorder of Childhood or Adolescence	Overanxious Disorder
Minimum duration to establish diagnosis	More than two weeks	At least six months	At least six months
Age of onset	Preschool to 18 years	2½ to 18 years	3 years or older
Precipitating stresses	Separation from significant parental figures, other losses, travel	Pressure for social participation	Unusual pressure for performance, damage to self-esteem, feelings of lack of competence
Peer relations	Good when no separation is involved	Tentative, overly inhibited	Overly eager to please, peers sought out and dependent relationship established
Sleep	Difficulty in falling asleep, fear of dark, nightmares	Difficulty in falling asleep at times	Difficulty in falling asleep
Psychophysiological symptoms	Stomachaches, nausea, vomiting, flulike symptoms, headaches, palpitations, dizziness, faintness	Blushing, body tension	Stomachaches, nausea, vomiting, lump in the throat, shortness of breath, dizziness, palpitations
Differential diagnosis	Overanxious disorder, schizophrenia, depressive disorder, conduct disorders, pervasive developmental disorder, major depression, panic disorder with agoraphobia	Adjustment disorder with withdrawal, overanxious disorder, separation anxiety disorder, major depression, dysthymia, avoidant personality disorder, borderline personality disorder	Separation anxiety disorder, attention-deficit hyperactivity disorder, avoidant disorder, adjustment disorder with anxious mood, obsessive-compulsive disorder, psychotic disorder, mood disorder

Table adapted from Sidney Werkman, M.D.

increased risk of having a child with separation anxiety disorder. There is also an overlap between separation anxiety disorder and depression in children, and some clinicians view this disorder as a variant of depression.

Clinical Features

According to DSM-III-R, the essential feature of separation anxiety disorder is extreme anxiety precipitated by separation from parents, home, or other familiar surroundings. The child's anxiety may approach terror or panic. The distress is greater than that normally expected for the child's developmental level and cannot be explained by any other disorder. In many cases the disorder is a kind of phobia, although the phobic concern is a general one and not directed to a particular symbolic object. Because the disorder is associated with childhood, it is not included among the phobic disorders of adulthood, which imply a much greater structuralization of the personality.

Morbid fears, preoccupations, and ruminations are characteristic of this disorder. Children with the disorder become fearful that someone close to them will be hurt or that something terrible will happen to them when they are away from important caring figures. Many children worry that they or their parents will have an accident or become ill. Fears about getting lost and about being kidnapped and never again finding their parents are common.

Adolescents may not directly express any anxious concern about separation from a mothering figure. Yet their behavior patterns often reflect a separation anxiety in that they express discomfort about leaving home, engage in solitary activities, and continue to use the mothering figure as a helper in buying clothes and entering social and recreational activities.

Separation anxiety disorder in children is often manifested at the thought of travel or in the course of travel away from home. Such children may refuse to go to camp, a new school, or even a friend's house. Frequently, there is a continuum between mild anticipatory anxiety before separation from an important figure and pervasive anxiety after the separation has occurred. Premonitory signs include irritability, difficulty in eating, whining, staying in a room alone, clinging to parents, and following the parent everywhere. Often, when a family moves, the child displays separation anxiety by intense clinging to the mother figure. Sometimes geographic relocation anxiety is expressed in feelings of acute homesickness or psychophysiological symptoms that break out when the child is away from home or is going to a new country. The child yearns to return home and becomes preoccupied with fantasies of how much better the old home was. Integration into the new life situation may become extremely difficult.

Sleep difficulties are frequent and may require that someone remain with the children until they fall asleep. Children often go to their parents' bed or even sleep at the parents' door when the bedroom is barred to them. Nightmares and morbid fears are other expressions of this anxiety.

Associated features include fear of the dark and imaginary, bizarre worries. Children may see eyes staring at them and become preoccupied with mythical figures or monsters reaching out for them in their bedrooms.

Many children are demanding and intrusive in adult affairs and require constant attention to allay their anxieties. Symptoms emerge when separation from an important parent figure becomes necessary. If separation is threatened, many children with this disorder do not experience interpersonal difficulties. They may, however, look sad and cry easily. They sometimes complain that they are not loved, express a wish to die, or complain that siblings are favored over them. They frequently develop gastrointestinal symptoms of nausea, vomiting, or stomachaches and have pains in various parts of the body, sore throats, and flulike symptoms. In older children, typical cardiovascular and respiratory symptoms of palpitations, dizziness, faintness, and strangulation are reported.

Course and Prognosis

The long-term prognosis is unclear. Most follow-up studies have methodological problems and are of hospitalized, school-phobic children, not of children with separation anxiety disorder per se. Little is reported about the outcome of mild cases, whether seen in outpatient treatment or receiving no treatment. Notwithstanding the limitations of the studies, some children with severe school phobia continue to resist attending school for many years.

During the 1970s it was reported that many adult agoraphobic women suffered separation anxiety in childhood. Although research indicates that many children with an anxiety disorder are at increased risk for an adult anxiety disorder, the specific link between separation anxiety disorder in childhood and agoraphobia in adulthood has not been clearly established. It is clearer from studies that anxious parents are at increased risk to have children with anxiety disorders. In addition, in recent years some cases have been reported of children presenting with both panic disorder and separation anxiety disorder.

Diagnosis

The diagnosis of separation anxiety disorder is made when any of the primary symptoms listed in Table 36-2 are present for at least two weeks. The disorder is considered to be mild when the child shows more than occasional concerns about separating from parents or home but can function in a new situation in spite of evidence of anxiety. The disorder is considered to be moderate when the child has panic reactions to separation but can perform adequately for a while, although acute symptoms develop intermittently; for example, the child may have to be picked up from school or camp or be accompanied on errands. In severe separation anxiety disorder, the child has panic reactions to threatened or actual separation and refuses to go to school or to stay home alone.

The history frequently reveals important episodes of separation in the child's life, particularly because of illness and hospitalization, illness of the parent, loss of a parent, or geographic relocation. The period of infancy should be scrutinized for evidence of separation-individuation disorders or lack of an adequate mothering figure. The use of fantasies, dreams, and play materials and observation of the child are of great help in making the diagnosis. Not only the content of thought but also the way in which thoughts are expressed should be examined. For example, children may express fears that their parents will die, even when their behavior does not show evidence of motor anxiety. Similarly, their difficulty in describing events or their bland denial of obviously anxiety-provoking events may indicate the presence of a separation anxiety disorder. Difficulty with memory in expressing separation themes or patent distortions in the recital of such themes may give clues to the disorder's presence.

Table 36-2
Diagnostic Criteria for Separation Anxiety Disorder

A. Excessive anxiety concerning separation from those to whom the child is attached, as evidenced by at least three of the following:
   (1) unrealistic and persistent worry about possible harm befalling major attachment figures or fear that they will leave and not return
   (2) unrealistic and persistent worry that an untoward calamitous event will separate the child from a major attachment figure (e.g., the child will be lost, kidnapped, killed, or the victim of an accident)
   (3) persistent reluctance or refusal to go to school in order to stay with major attachment figures or at home
   (4) persistent reluctance or refusal to go to sleep without being near a major attachment figure or to go to sleep away from home
   (5) persistent avoidance of being alone, including "clinging to" and "shadowing" major attachment figures
   (6) repeated nightmares involving the theme of separation
   (7) complains of physical symptoms (e.g., headaches, stomachaches, nausea, or vomiting, on many school days or on other occasions when anticipating separation from major attachment figures)
   (8) recurrent signs or complaints of excessive distress in anticipation of separation from home or major attachment figures (e.g., temper tantrums or crying, pleading with parents not to leave)
   (9) recurrent signs of complaints of excessive distress when separated from home or major attachment figures (e.g., wants to return home, needs to call parents when they are absent or when child is away from home)

B. Duration of disturbance of at least two weeks

C. Onset before the age of 18

D. Occurrence not exclusively during the course of a pervasive developmental disorder, schizophrenia, or any other psychotic disorder

Table from DSM-III-R, *Diagnostic and Statistical Manual of Mental Disorders,* ed 3, revised. Copyright American Psychiatric Association, Washington, DC, 1987, with permission.

Differential Diagnosis

According to DSM-III-R, some degree of separation anxiety is a normal phenomenon, and clinical judgment must be used in distinguishing this from separation anxiety disorder. In overanxious disorder, anxiety is not focused on separation. In pervasive developmental disorders and schizophrenia, anxiety about separation may occur but is viewed as caused by these conditions, rather than as a separate disorder. In depressive disorder occurring in children, the diagnosis of separation anxiety disorder should also be made when the criteria for both disorders are met; the two diagnoses often coexist. Panic disorder with agoraphobia is uncommon before age 18, and the fear is of being incapacitated by a panic attack, rather than of separation from parental figures. In some adult cases, however, many of the symptoms of separation anxiety disorder may be present. In conduct disorder, truancy is common, but the child stays away from home and does not have anxiety about separation. School refusal is a frequent symptom in separation anxiety disorder but is not pathognomonic of it. Children with other diagnoses, such as phobic disorders, can present with school refusal, and in these disorders, the age of onset may be later and the school refusal more severe than in separation anxiety disorder.

Treatment

Anxiety disorders in general respond to psychotherapy directed toward increasing the child's autonomy by exploring the unconscious meaning of symptoms. Family therapy helps the parents understand the need for consistent, supportive love and the importance of preparing for any important change in life, such as illness, surgery, or geographic relocation.

School phobia associated with separation anxiety disorder may present as a psychiatric emergency. A comprehensive treatment plan involves the child, the parents, and the child's peers and school. The child should be encouraged to attend school, but if a return to a full school day is overwhelming, a program should be arranged for the child to progressively increase his or her time spent at school. Graded contact with an object of anxiety is a form of behavior modification that can be applied to any type of separation anxiety. In some severe cases of school refusal, hospitalization (i.e., parentectomy) is required.

Pharmacotherapy is useful for panic and separation anxiety disorders. The tricyclic and tetracyclic antidepressants, such as the tricyclic imipramine (Tofranil), are usually begun in dosages of 25 mg daily, increased by additional 25-mg doses up to a total of 150 to 200 mg daily, until a therapeutic effect is noted. If no effect is noted with 200 mg daily, the plasma levels of imipramine and its active metabolite, desmethylimipramine, should be studied to determine whether a therapeutic blood level has been attained. Aside from its antidepressant effect, imipramine has been postulated to yield results that reduce panic and fear related to separation. Diphenhydramine (Benadryl) can be used to break a dangerous cycle of sleep disturbances.

AVOIDANT DISORDER OF CHILDHOOD OR ADOLESCENCE

In avoidant disorder of childhood or adolescence, the patient shows a persistent and excessive shrinking from contact with unfamiliar people that is of sufficient severity to interfere with social functioning in peer relationships, is of at least six months' duration, and is coupled with a clear desire for social involvement with familiar people, such as family members and peers the person knows well. Relationships with family members and other familiar figures are generally warm and satisfying. This diagnosis should not be made if the person is 18 or older.

Epidemiology

Avoidant disorder of childhood or adolescence is not common, and the male-to-female ratio is unknown. The syndrome may develop as early as 2½ years of age, after stranger anxiety or a normal developmental phenomenon should have disappeared. Modeling of a shy, retiring parent is frequently noted in such situations, and girls may go through many years of avoiding social situations without overt anxiety if parents support their shyness. Boys, however, are frequently expected to be more independent and aggressive. Therefore, if shyness is a predominant characteristic in their personality makeup, boys begin to suffer symptoms earlier than girls. Anxiety disorders are more common in the mothers of children with avoidant disorder of childhood or adolescence than in the general population.

Etiology

Temperamental differences may account for some of the predisposition to this disorder, particularly if a parent supports the child's shyness and withdrawal. Avoidant behaviors and diagnoses of anxiety disorders are more common in the offspring of parents suffering from panic disorder and agoraphobia than in the general population.

Devastating losses early in childhood, sexual traumas, and other kinds of physical abuse or neglect may also contribute to avoidant disorder of childhood or adolescence. Children who have chronic medical problems in childhood, such as rheumatic fever and orthopedic handicaps, may not learn the age-related social skills shared by their peers because they have not been involved in typical social interactions with their age-mates. Likewise, children who have grown up in foreign countries or have moved a great deal may not learn the necessary social skills that allow them to integrate effectively into the social world of their peers.

Clinical Features

Children with avoidant disorder of childhood or adolescence hold back excessively from establishing interpersonal contacts or satisfactory relationships with strangers to an extent that noticeably interferes with their peer functioning. The avoidance of involvement with strangers persists even after prolonged exposure to new relationships. These children are slow to warm up, although many of them participate actively in social groups that offer considerable support and structure. Typically, these children relate warmly and naturally in their home situations. However, they may be clinging, whining, and overly demanding with caretakers, making great demands on those who are with them.

Embarrassment and timidity are conveyed in their voices, and they may tend to whisper and stand behind people or hide behind furniture in an attempt not to be noticed. Blushing, difficulties in speech, and easy embarrassment are characteristic. Underneath these behaviors—and often expressed in close relationships—are anger, sullen resentment, rage, or grandiosity. There is no evidence of a pattern of intellectual impairment or fundamental difficulty in communication, even when such children seem inarticulate.

When pressured into social participation, children with avoidant disorder of childhood or adolescence may become tearful and anxious. They may cling to their caretakers and refuse to become involved in new activities. In adolescence the long delay in the development of psychosexual maturity may be evidenced by difficulty in peer relationships and in the establishment of appropriate social, sexual, and aggressive adolescent activities. Extreme inhibition in recreational activities is common, and a great deal of support is necessary to encourage participation. At times, shyness and inhibition complicate the learning process. In such cases a child's true abilities become apparent only under extremely favorable educational conditions.

Diagnosis

The diagnosis should not be made before the age of 2½ years, when the normal stranger anxiety phase has passed. The disorder is diagnosed on the basis of excessive shrinking from contact with unfamiliar people for a period of six months or longer. Children with avoidant disorder of childhood or adolescence may have great difficulty in separating from a parent figure, especially to meet unfamiliar persons. Often the parent must come into the examination room at the beginning of the session, because the child demands to know exactly where the parent is during the session. See Table 36-3 for the DSM-III-R criteria for avoidant disorder of childhood or adolescence.

Differential Diagnosis

Quiet and withdrawn children and adolescents can be found in many diagnostic categories. Those with separation anxiety disorder specifically avoid separations from their caretakers and do not avoid contact with unfamiliar people. In overanxious disorder, anxiety-laden situations are avoided, not contact with unfamiliar people. In adjustment disorder with withdrawal, a clear precipitant leads to avoidance.

Avoidance of social contact also characterizes children with pervasive developmental disorder; of these, some highly functioning children may have to be differentiated from children with avoidant disorder of childhood or adolescence. In pervasive developmental disorder, all relationships are abnormal, even those with familiar adults. This is also a differentiating characteristic between patients with avoidant disorder of childhood or adolescence and those children or adolescents with schizoid personality traits.

Avoidant disorder of childhood or adolescence often shades into the realm of avoidant personality disorder and borderline personality disorder. The avoidant personality disorder is diagnosed only after the behavior pattern has persisted for many years. In contrast to avoidant disorder of childhood or adolescence, borderline personality disorder has more serious character pathology and a greater and more diffuse variety of symptoms, which are not characterized primarily by the avoidance of contact with strangers and new situations. In major depression and dysthymia, the patient is withdrawn but generally from all persons, including familiar ones.

Table 36-3
Diagnostic Criteria for Avoidant Disorder of Childhood or Adolescence

A. Excessive shrinking from contact with unfamiliar people, for a period of six months or longer, sufficiently severe to interfere with social functioning in peer relationships.

B. Desire for social involvement with familiar people (family members and peers the person knows well), and generally warm and satisfying relations with family members and other familiar figures.

C. Age at least 2½ years.

D. The disturbance is not sufficiently pervasive and persistent to warrant the diagnosis of avoidant personality disorder.

Table from DSM-III-R, *Diagnostic and Statistical Manual of Mental Disorders,* ed 3, revised. Copyright American Psychiatric Association, Washington, DC, 1987, with permission.

Treatment

Psychotherapy with the explicit approval of the parent figure is the treatment of choice at the start. A great deal of work is directed toward helping the child separate from the parent and recognize that independent activity can be safe and fulfilling. In working with the parents, the therapist should show empathically and sensitively how the child is controlling the parent by means of shyness. The parent can then give the child opportunities to experience manageable anxiety and thus be able to give up some of the secondary gains of shyness. The development of skills in dancing, music performance, singing, or writing may be valuable ego supports for the children.

On occasion, antianxiety medication on a short-term basis may decrease anxiety in order to overcome the avoidant behavior. What is most needed, however, is a restructuring of relationships in a supportive therapeutic environment that directs the child toward facing new situations and mastering anxiety in order to achieve a higher level of independent functioning.

Parents often require therapy because they may be unwilling to support the newly assertive child, especially if shyness fulfilled unconscious needs in the parents to keep the child infantilized.

OVERANXIOUS DISORDER

According to DSM-III-R, the essential feature of overanxious disorder is excessive and unrealistic anxiety or worry for a period of six months or longer. Children with this disorder tend to be extremely self-conscious, to worry about future events (such as examinations, the possibility of injury, and inclusion in peer group activities) or about meeting expectations (such as deadlines, keeping appointments, and performing chores), and to be concerned about the discomforts or dangers of a variety of situations. For example, routine visits to the doctor may be anticipated with excessive worry about minor procedures. The children may also be overly anxious about competence in a number of areas, especially about what others think of them. In general, the patient with the disorder presents a picture of excessive worrying and fearful behavior.

Epidemiology

Some evidence suggests that overanxious disorder is most common in small families of upper socioeconomic status and in firstborn children. Although both boys and girls have this disorder, some workers believe that it is more common in boys than in girls; however, DSM-III-R describes the disorder as equally common in boys and girls. It may also be more common in urban areas than in rural areas.

Etiology

There is some evidence of a familial pattern, in that children with overanxious disorder are likely to have mothers who also suffer from anxiety disorders. Unconscious conflicts related to fixations at the oedipal psychosexual phase of development have been postulated. The disorder is often associated with situations in which there is great concern about performance, even when the child is functioning at an adequate level. The children come to believe that they must meet their parents' high expectations.

Clinical Features

According to DSM-III-R, the principal characteristics of the disorder are that the children are always worried, especially about future events that require meeting expectations (such as examinations, parties, and sports). They are greatly concerned about their competence and about being judged negatively. At times, these worries may have an obsessive or ruminative pattern. Physical signs and symptoms (such as insomnia, nail biting, palpitations, and respiratory and gastrointestinal distress) are common. The children may always appear nervous or tense.

Associated features include social and simple phobias. Children with this disorder may refuse to attend school because of their anxiety there. They often seem hypermature because of their precocious concerns. Perfectionist tendencies, with obsessional self-doubt, may be evident; the children may be excessively conformist and overzealous in seeking approval. They may be reluctant to engage in age-appropriate activities in which there are demands for performance, such as sports. Many of these children are accident-prone and seem to exaggerate the extent of pain, deformity, or potential handicap that may result from illness or accidents, and they may have unnecessary medical examinations as a result.

Course and Prognosis

Because of the high level of verbal and intellectual abilities of many children with overanxious disorder, the relatively effective mothering experiences in their lives, and their strong desires to relate, the course of the disorder is often benign. However, unusually stressful life experiences may contradict such a prognosis. Rarely does the disorder result in an inability to meet at least the minimal demands of school, home, and social life, but youngsters with overanxious disorder may have a great deal of inner stress that persists into adult life as an anxiety disorder, such as generalized anxiety disorder or social phobia.

Diagnosis

The symptoms include the presence of persistent anxiety and worrying about future events, together with a concern about competence in a variety of areas. Difficulty in falling asleep, frightening dreams, and somatic complaints—such as headaches, gastrointestinal symptoms, and respiratory symptoms for which no medical basis can be established—are typically noted. The disorder must be present for at least six months and must not be a symptom of another disorder, such as separation anxiety disorder, avoidant disorder of childhood or adolescence, phobic disorder, obsessive-compulsive disorder, depressive disorder, schizophrenia, or a pervasive developmental disorder. Table 36-4 lists the DSM-III-R diagnostic criteria for overanxious disorder.

Table 36-4
Diagnostic Criteria for Overanxious Disorder

A. Excessive or unrealistic anxiety or worry, for a period of six months or longer, as indicated by the frequent occurrence of at least four of the following:
   (1) excessive or unrealistic worry about future events
   (2) excessive or unrealistic concern about the appropriateness of past behavior
   (3) excessive or unrealistic concern about competence in one or more areas (e.g., athletic, academic, social)
   (4) somatic complaints, such as headaches or stomachaches, for which no physical basis can be established)
   (5) marked self-consciousness
   (6) excessive need for reassurance about a variety of concerns
   (7) marked feelings of tension or inability to relax

B. If another Axis I disorder is present (e.g., separation anxiety disorder, phobic disorder, obsessive-compulsive disorder), the focus of the symptoms in A is not limited to it. For example, if separation anxiety disorder is present, the symptoms in A are not exclusively related to anxiety about separation. In addition, the disturbance does not occur only during the course of a psychotic disorder or a mood disorder.

C. If 18 or older, does not meet the criteria for generalized anxiety disorder.

D. Occurrence not exclusively during the course of a pervasive developmental disorder, schizophrenia, or any other psychotic disorder.

Table from DSM-III-R, *Diagnostic and Statistical Manual of Mental Disorders*, ed 3, revised. Copyright American Psychiatric Association, Washington, DC, 1987, with permission.

Differential Diagnosis

Overanxious disorder is distinct from separation anxiety disorder, which emphasizes separation from a familiar person. Panic disorder is characterized by recurrent panic attacks and a fear of future attacks. Obsessive-compulsive disorder has more highly structured obsessions and compulsions than does overanxious disorder.

Overanxious disorder can coexist with many other disorders, including other anxiety disorders, depression, functional enuresis, and learning disabilities. Overanxious disorder should not be diagnosed when the anxiety is a symptom of a psychotic disorder or a mood disorder.

Treatment

Although the use of antianxiety medication in the treatment of overanxious disorder has not been systematically studied, such medications as diazepam (Valium) may be tried when a child is experiencing extreme anxiety. In treating overanxious disorder adolescents, however, one must keep in mind the addictive potential of antianxiety medication. Buspirone (BuSpar), an antianxiety drug with apparently no risk for abuse, is promising. In one report an overanxious adolescent was treated successfully with buspirone. Acute anxiety accompanied by insomnia can be effectively treated by the short-term use of such sedatives as diphenhydramine. When children complain of psychophysiological symptoms, they should be given the benefit of a thorough medical or pediatric examination. If the findings of such an examination are normal, their symptoms should be discussed and treated as somatic equivalents of anxiety. The patient should be assured that such symptoms will disappear when the basis for anxiety is resolved.

Children with overanxious disorder are excellent candidates for insight-oriented therapy, either individually or with their families. Many clinicians believe this to be the treatment of choice. Themes of sibling rivalry, wishes to excel, and oedipal struggles tend to emerge. The prognosis with treatment is usually excellent.

References

Alessi N E, Magen D R: Panic disorder in psychiatrically hospitalized children. J Am Psychiatr Assoc *145*: 1450, 1988.

Bell-Dolan D J, Last C G, Strauss C C: Symptoms of anxiety disorders in normal children. J Am Acad Child Adolesc Psychiatry *29*: 759, 1990.

Bernstein G A, Garfinkel B D, Borchardt C M: Comparative studies of pharmacotherapy for school refusal. J Am Acad Child Adolesc Psychiatry *29*: 773, 1990.

Black B, Robbins D R: Case study: Panic disorder in children and adolescents. J Am Acad Child Adolesc Psychiatry *29*: 36, 1990.

Bowlby J: *Attachment and Loss,* 3 vols. Basic Books, New York, 1969, 1973, 1980.

Freud S: Introductory lectures on psychoanalysis. In *Standard Edition of the Complete Psychological Works of Sigmund Freud,* vol 16, p 393. Hogarth Press, London, 1963.

Gittelman R, ed.: *Anxiety Disorders of Children.* Guilford, New York, 1986.

Kashani J H, Orveschel H: A community study of anxiety in children and adolescents. Am J Psychiatry *147*: 313, 1990.

Kranzler H R: Use of buspirone in an adolescent with overanxious disorder. J Am Acad Child Adolesc Psychiatry *27*: 789, 1988.

Last C G, Strauss C C: School refusal in anxiety-disordered children and adolescents. J Am Acad Child Adolesc Psychiatry *29*: 31, 1990.

Rosenbaum J F, Biederman J, Gersten M, Hirshfeld D R, Meminger S R, Herman J B, Kagan J, Reznick J S, Snidman N: Behavioral inhibition in children of parents with panic disorder and agoraphobia. Arch Gen Psychiatry *45*: 463, 1988.

Sheehan K H, Sheehan D N, Shaw K R: Diagnosis and treatment of anxiety disorders in children and adolescents. Psychiatr Ann *18*: 146, 1988.

Silverman W K, Cerny J A, Welles W B, Burke A E: Behavior problems in children of parents with anxiety disorders. J Am Acad Child Adolesc Psychiatry *27*: 779, 1988.

37 Eating Disorders

37.1 / Pica

DIAGNOSIS

Pica is the repeated ingestion of nonnutritive substances, such as dirt, clay, plaster, and paper. The revised third edition of *Diagnostic and Statistical Manual of Mental Disorders* (DSM-III-R) diagnostic criteria are given in Table 37.1-1.

EPIDEMIOLOGY

Pica rarely occurs in adults. DSM-III-R states that it is occasionally seen in young children, in persons with mental retardation, and in pregnant women. However, pica may be more common than this statement implies. Several studies report that between 10 percent and 32.3 percent of children between 1 and 6 years of age have pica. The incidence diminishes with age, and the disorder is apparently seen equally frequently in the two sexes.

Clay eating (geophasia) and starch (e.g., Argo starch) eating appear to have an increased incidence among pregnant women in some cultures. In one study 55 percent of pregnant women in Georgia had geophasia, and in another, 41 percent of pregnant black women ate starch, and 27 percent ate clay.

Table 37.1-1
Diagnostic Criteria for Pica

A. Repeated eating of a nonnutritive substance for at least one month

B. Does not meet the criteria for either autistic disorder, schizophrenia, or Kleine-Levin syndrome

Table from DSM-III-R, *Diagnostic and Statistical Manual of Mental Disorders,* ed 3, revised. Copyright American Psychiatric Association, Washington, DC, 1987, with permission.

ETIOLOGY

There are three commonly suggested causes of pica: (1) an inadequate mother–child relationship that results in unsatisfied oral needs expressed in the persistent search for inedible substances: (2) a specific nutritional deficiency, causing the indiscriminate ingestion of nonfood items; and (3) cultural factors suspected to be important to geophasia (earth or clay eating) and starch eating by some pregnant women.

CLINICAL FEATURES

Eating nonedible substances after 18 months of age is usually considered abnormal. The onset of pica is usually between ages 12 and 24 months, and the incidence declines with age. The specific substances ingested vary somewhat with their accessibility, and they increase with the child's mastery of locomotion and the resultant increased independence and decreased parental supervision. Typically, young children ingest paint, plaster, string, hair, and cloth; older children have access to dirt, animal feces, stones, and paper.

Clinical implications may be benign or life-threatening, according to the objects ingested. Among the most serious complications are lead poisoning, usually from lead-based paint; intestinal parasites after the ingestion of soil or feces; anemia and zinc deficiency after the ingestion of clay; severe iron deficiency after the ingestion of large quantities of starch; and intestinal obstruction from the ingestion of hair balls, stones, or gravel.

Except in the case of mentally retarded persons, pica usually remits by adolescence. Pica associated with pregnancy is usually limited to the pregnancy itself.

COURSE AND PROGNOSIS

The prognosis of pica is variable. In children, pica usually resolves with increasing age; in pregnant women, pica is usually limited to the term of the pregnancy. However, in some adults, especially in the mentally retarded, pica may continue for years. Follow-up data on these populations are too limited to permit conclusions.

DIFFERENTIAL DIAGNOSIS

DSM-III-R notes that nonnutritive substances may be eaten by patients with autistic disorder, schizophrenia, and certain physical disorders, such as Kleine–Levin syndrome, and that in such cases pica should not be noted as an additional diagnosis. Some clinicians believe that to be unfortunate, because only a small minority of autistic and schizophrenic persons ingest nonedible items.

The eating of bizarre and sometimes potentially dangerous substances (such as animal food, toilet water, and garbage) is a frequent behavioral abnormality among children with psychosocial dwarfism.

TREATMENT

There is no definitive treatment for pica. Treatments basically emphasize psychosocial, environmental, behavioral, and family guidance approaches.

An effort should be made to ameliorate any significant psychosocial stressors that are present. When lead is present in the surroundings, it must be eliminated or rendered inaccessible, or the child must be moved to new surroundings.

Several behavioral techniques have been used with some effect. The most rapidly successful seems to be mild aversion therapy or negative reinforcement (e.g., a mild electric shock, an unpleasant noise, or an emetic drug). Positive reinforcement, modeling, behavioral shaping, and overcorrection treatment have also been used.

Increasing parental attention, stimulation, and emotional nurturance may have positive results. One study found that pica was negatively correlated with involvement with play materials and occurred most frequently in impoverished environments.

In some patients, correction of an iron or zinc deficiency has resulted in the elimination of pica.

Medical complications (e.g., lead poisoning) that develop secondarily to the pica must also be treated.

References

Blinder B J, Chaitin B, Goldstein R, eds.: *The Eating Disorders*. Pergamon, New York, 1987.

Cooper M: *Pica*. Thomas, Springfield, IL, 1957.

Danford D E, Smith C J, Huber A M: Pica and mineral status in the mentally retarded. Am J Clin Nutr *35*: 958, 1982.

Lourie R S, Millican F K: Pica. In *Modern Perspectives in International Child Psychiatry,* J G Howells, editor, p 445. Brunner/Mazel, New York, 1971.

Millican F K, Dublin C C, Lourie R. S: Pica. In *Basic Handbook of Child Psychiatry,* J D Noshpitz, editor, vol 2. p 660. Basic Books, New York, 1979.

Millican F K, Lourie R S, Laymen E M: Emotional factors in the etiology and treatment of lead poisoning. Am J Dis Child *91*: 144, 1956.

Provence S, Lipton R C: *Infants and Institutions*. International Universities Press, New York, 1962.

37.2 / Rumination Disorder of Infancy

Rumination is an extremely rare but fascinating illness that has been recognized for hundreds of years. This regurgitation disorder, which can be fatal, occurs predominantly in infancy and seldom in adults. An awareness of the disorder is important, so that it be correctly diagnosed and so that unnecessary surgical procedures or inappropriate treatment can be avoided.

"Rumination" is derived from the Latin word *ruminare,* meaning to chew the cud. The Greek equivalent is *merycism,* which describes the act of regurgitating food from the stomach into the mouth, rechewing the food, and reswallowing it.

DIAGNOSIS

The revised third edition of *Diagnostic and Statistical Manual of Mental Disorders* (DSM-III-R) criteria for rumination disorder of infancy are given in Table 37.2-1. DSM-III-R notes that the essential feature of this disorder is repeated regurgitation of food, with weight loss or failure to gain expected weight, developing after a period of normal functioning. Partially digested food is brought up into the mouth without nausea, retching, disgust, or associated gastrointestinal disorder. The food is then ejected from the mouth or reswallowed. A characteristic position of straining and arching the back, with the head held back, is observed. The infant makes sucking movements with the tongue and gives the impression of gaining considerable satisfaction from the activity. An associated feature that is usually present is that the infant is generally irritable and hungry between episodes of rumination.

EPIDEMIOLOGY

Rumination is a rare disorder. It seems to be most common among infants between 3 months and 1 year of age and among mentally retarded children and adults.

Table 37.2-1
Diagnostic Criteria for Rumination Disorder of Infancy

A. Repeated regurgitation, without nausea or associated gastrointestinal illness, for at least one month following a period of normal functioning

B. Weight loss or failure to make expected weight gain

Table from DSM-III-R, *Diagnostic and Statistical Manual of Mental Disorders,* ed 3, revised. Copyright American Psychiatric Association, Washington, DC, 1987, with permission.

Adults with rumination usually maintain a normal weight. It is apparently equally common in boys and girls. There are no reliable figures on predisposing factors or familial patterns.

ETIOLOGY

Several causes have been proposed. In mentally retarded ruminators, the disorder may simply be self-stimulatory behavior. In nonretarded ruminators, psychodynamic theories hypothesize various disturbances in the mother-child relationship. The mothers of infants with the disorder are usually immature, involved in a marital conflict, and unable to give much attention to the baby. This results in insufficient emotional gratification and stimulation for the infant, who thus seeks gratification from within. The rumination is interpreted as an attempt by the infant to recreate the feeding process and provide gratification that the mother does not provide. Overstimulation and tension have also been suggested as causing rumination.

A dysfunctional autonomic nervous system has also been implicated. As more sophisticated and accurate investigative techniques are refined, a substantial number of children classified as ruminators are shown to have gastroesophageal reflux or a hiatal hernia.

Behaviorists attribute rumination to the positive reinforcement of the pleasurable self-stimulation and to the attention the baby receives from others as a consequence of the disorder.

CLINICAL FEATURES

Initially, rumination may be difficult to distinguish from the regurgitation that frequently occurs in normal infants. In the fully developed case, however, the diagnosis is obvious. Food or milk is regurgitated without nausea, retching, or disgust and is subjected to what appears to be innumerable pleasurable sucking and chewing movements. The food is then reswallowed or ejected from the mouth.

Although spontaneous remissions are common, severe secondary complications may develop, such as progressive malnutrition, dehydration, and lowered resistance to disease. Failure to thrive, with growth failure and developmental delays in all areas, may occur. Mortality as high as 25 percent has been reported in severe cases.

An additional complication is that the mother or caretaker is often discouraged by the failure to feed the infant successfully and may become alienated, if not already so. Further alienation often occurs as the noxious odor of the regurgitated material leads to avoidance of the infant.

COURSE AND PROGNOSIS

Rumination disorder of infancy is believed to have a high rate of spontaneous remission. Indeed, it is possible that many cases of rumination in infants develop and remit without ever being diagnosed. Only limited data are available regarding the prognosis of rumination in adults.

DIFFERENTIAL DIAGNOSIS

Rumination must be differentiated from congenital anomalies and infections of the gastrointestinal tract that may cause regurgitation of food. Pyloric stenosis is usually associated with projectile vomiting and is evident before 3 months of age.

TREATMENT

The effectiveness of treatments is difficult to evaluate, as most reports are single-case studies and are not randomly assigned to controlled studies. Any concomitant medical complications must also be treated.

Treatments include improvement of the child's psychosocial environment, more tender loving care from the mother or caretakers, and psychotherapy for the mother or both parents.

When anatomical abnormalities such as hiatal hernia are present, surgical repair may be necessary.

Behavioral techniques have also been used effectively. Aversive conditioning involves administering a mild electric shock or squirting an unpleasant substance (such as lemon juice) in the mouth whenever rumination occurs. This appears to be the most rapidly effective treatment; rumination is eliminated within three to five days. In the aversive-conditioning reports on rumination, the infants were doing well at 9- or 12-month follow-ups, with no recurrence of the rumination and with weight gains, increased activity levels, and greater general responsiveness to people.

One study showed that, if the infants were allowed to eat as much as they wanted, the rate of rumination decreased.

References

Blinder B J, Chaitin B, Goldstein R, eds.: *The Eating Disorders*. Pergamon, New York, 1987.

Davis P K, Cuvo A J: Chronic vomiting and rumination in intellectually normal and retarded individuals: Review and evaluation of behavioral research. Behav Res Severe Dev Disabil *1*: 31, 1980.

Flanagan C H: Rumination in infancy: Past and present: With a case report. J Am Acad Child Psychiatry *16*: 40, 1977.

Humphrey F J, Mayes S D, Bixler E O: Variables associated with frequency of rumination in a boy with profound mental retardation. J Autism Dev Disord *19*: 435, 1989.

Linscheid T R, Cunningham C E: A controlled demonstration of the effectiveness of electric shock in the elimination of chronic infant rumination. J Appl Behav Anal *10*: 500, 1977.

Mayes S D, Humphrey F J, Handford H A, Mitchell J F: Rumination disorder: Differential diagnosis. J Am Acad Child Adolesc Psychiatry *27*: 300, 1988.

Rast, J, Johnston J M, Drum C, Conrin J: The relation of food quantity to rumination behavior. J Appl Behav Anal *14*: 221, 1981.

Stunkard A J, Stellar E, eds.: *Eating and Its Disorders*. Raven Press, New York, 1984.

37.3 / Anorexia Nervosa and Bulimia Nervosa

ANOREXIA NERVOSA

In anorexia nervosa, food and dieting are all-consuming preoccupations. There is a significant disturbance in body image; anorexic patients feel fat even when emaciated.

For the diagnosis of anorexia nervosa to be made, there must be no known physical illness to account for the weight loss. Moreover, weight loss or failure to maintain expected weight is marked—for example, weighing less than 85 percent of the expected body weight. Anorexia nervosa patients refuse to maintain body weight over a minimal normal weight for their age and height. Such patients diet incessantly and often abuse diuretics and laxatives. In women there is amenorrhea. It is one of the few psychiatric illnesses that may have a course that leads to death.

Those with anorexia nervosa are sometimes referred to as restricters, as they, unlike bulimic bingers, restrict food intake. However, anorexia nervosa and bulimia nervosa often coexist.

Epidemiology

Anorexia nervosa occurs in 0.5 to 1.0 percent of adolescent girls and is 10 to 20 times more frequent in women than in men. The onset is usually in adolescence. The incidence is greatest in the high socioeconomic groups, in high-achieving women, and in professions, like modeling and ballet, in which there is a special premium on thinness. More cases are being discovered in minority groups, but, here also, those affected tend to be upwardly mobile. Anorexia nervosa is rare in men, and those afflicted may show effeminate tendencies.

Etiology

Biological, psychological, and environmental factors are implicated in the etiology of anorexia nervosa, although many findings to date require confirmation. There is some evidence of higher concordance rates in monozygotic twins than in dizygotic twins. Sisters of anorexia nervosa patients are likely to be afflicted, but this may reflect environmental influences more than genetic factors. Major mood disorders are more common in family members than in the general population. Neurochemically, diminished norepinephrine turnover and activity are suggested by the reduced 3-methoxy-4-hydroxyphenylglycol (MHPG) in the urine and cerebrospinal fluid (CSF) of some anorexia nervosa patients. There is also an inverse relationship between MHPG and depression in patients with anorexia nervosa: an increase in MHPG is associated with a decrease in depression.

It has been hypothesized that endogenous opioids contribute to the denial of hunger in anorexia nervosa patients. Preliminary studies show dramatic weight gains in some patients administered opiate antagonists. Starvation results in many biochemical changes, some of which are also present in depression, such as hypercortisolemia and nonsuppression by dexamethasone. Thyroid function is also suppressed. These abnormalities are corrected by realimentation. Starvation also results in amenorrhea, which reflects lowered hormonal levels (luteinizing, follicle-stimulating, and gonadotropin-releasing hormones). However, some anorexia nervosa patients become amenorrheic before significant weight loss. Several computed tomographic (CT) studies reveal enlarged CSF spaces (enlarged sulci and ventricles) in anorexia nervosa patients during starvation, a finding that is reversed by weight gain. In one positron emission tomographic (PET) scan study, caudate nucleus metabolism was higher in the anorectic state than after realimentation.

Environmentally, anorexia nervosa patients find support for their practices in society's emphasis on thinness and exercise. No family constellations are specific to anorexia nervosa. However, there is some evidence that anorexia nervosa patients have close but troubled relationships with their parents and, with their illness, tend to draw attention away from strained marital relationships in their homes.

Psychologically, anorexia nervosa appears to be a reaction to demands on adolescents for more independence and increased social and sexual functioning. Patients with this illness substitute their preoccupations with eating and weight gain for other, normal adolescent pursuits. These preoccupations are similar to obsessions.

Clinical Features

The onset of anorexia nervosa occurs between the ages of 10 and 30 years. The onset is uncommon before age 10 and after age 30. Those patients outside this age range are not typical, and so their diagnoses should be questioned. After the age of 13 years, the frequency of onset increases rapidly, with the maximum frequency at 17 to 18 years of age. About 85 percent of all anorexia nervosa patients have the onset of the illness between the ages of 13 and 20 years. Some anorexia nervosa patients, before age 10, were picky eaters or had frequent digestive problems.

Most of the aberrant behavior directed toward losing weight occurs in secret. Anorexia nervosa patients usually refuse to eat with their families or in public places. They lose weight by a drastic reduction in their total food intake, with a disproportionate decrease in high-carbohydrate and fatty foods.

Unfortunately, the term "anorexia," meaning loss of appetite, is a misnomer because the loss of appetite is usually rare until late in the illness. Evidence that the patients are constantly thinking about food is their passion for collecting recipes and preparing elaborate meals for others. Some patients cannot continuously control their voluntary restriction of food intake, and so they have eating binges. These binges usually occur secretly and often at night. Self-induced vomiting frequently follows the eating binge. Patients abuse laxatives and even diuretics to lose weight. Ritualistic exercising, extensive cycling, walking, jogging, and running are common activities.

Patients with this disorder exhibit peculiar behavior regarding food. They hide food all over the house and frequently carry large quantities of candies in their pockets and purses. While eating meals, they try to dispose of food in their napkins or hide it in their pockets. They cut their meat into very small pieces and spend a great deal of time rearranging the food items on their plate. If the patients are confronted about their peculiar behavior, they often deny that their behavior is unusual or flatly refuse to discuss it.

An intense fear of gaining weight and becoming obese is present in all patients with this disorder and undoubtedly contributes to their lack of interest in and even resistance to therapy.

Obsessive-compulsive behavior, depression, and anxiety are the other psychiatric symptoms in anorexia nervosa most frequently noted in the literature. Patients tend to be rigid and perfectionist. Somatic complaints, especially epigastric discomfort, are usual. Compulsive stealing, usually of candies and laxatives but occasionally of clothes and other items, is common.

Poor sexual adjustment is frequently described in patients with this disorder. Many adolescent anorexia nervosa patients have delayed psychosocial sexual development, and adults often have a markedly decreased interest in sex accompanying the onset of the illness. An unusual minority group of anorexia nervosa patients have a premorbid history of promiscuity or drug abuse or both, and during the illness they do not show a decreased interest in sex.

Patients usually come to medical attention when their weight loss becomes apparent. As the weight loss becomes profound, physical signs such as hypothermia (as low as 35°C), dependent edema, bradycardia, hypotension, and lanugo (the appearance of neonatallike hair) appear, and there are a variety of metabolic changes (Figure 37.3-1). Some female anorexia nervosa patients come to medical attention because of amenorrhea, which often appears before their weight loss is noticeable.

Some anorexia nervosa patients induce vomiting or abuse purgatives and diuretics, causing concern about hypokalemic alkalosis. Impaired water diuresis may be noted.

Electrocardiographic (ECG) changes—such as flattening or inversion of the T waves, ST segment depression, and lengthening of the QT interval—have been noted in the emaciated stage of anorexia nervosa. ECG changes may also occur as a result of potassium loss, which may lead to death. Gastric dilation is a rare complication of anorexia nervosa. In some patients, aortography has shown a superior mesenteric artery syndrome.

Other medical complications of eating disorders are listed in Table 37.3-1.

Course and Prognosis

The course of anorexia nervosa varies greatly—spontaneous recovery without treatment, recovery after a variety of treatments, a fluctuating course of weight gains followed by relapses, a gradually deteriorating course resulting in death caused by complications of starvation. In general, the prognosis is not good. In those who have regained sufficient weight, preoccupation with food and body weight often continues, social relationships are often poor, and many are depressed. The short-term response of patients to almost all hospital treatment programs is good. Studies have shown a range of mortality rates from 5 to 18 percent.

Indicators of a favorable outcome are the admission of hunger, less denial, less immaturity, and improved self-esteem. Such factors as childhood neuroticism, parental

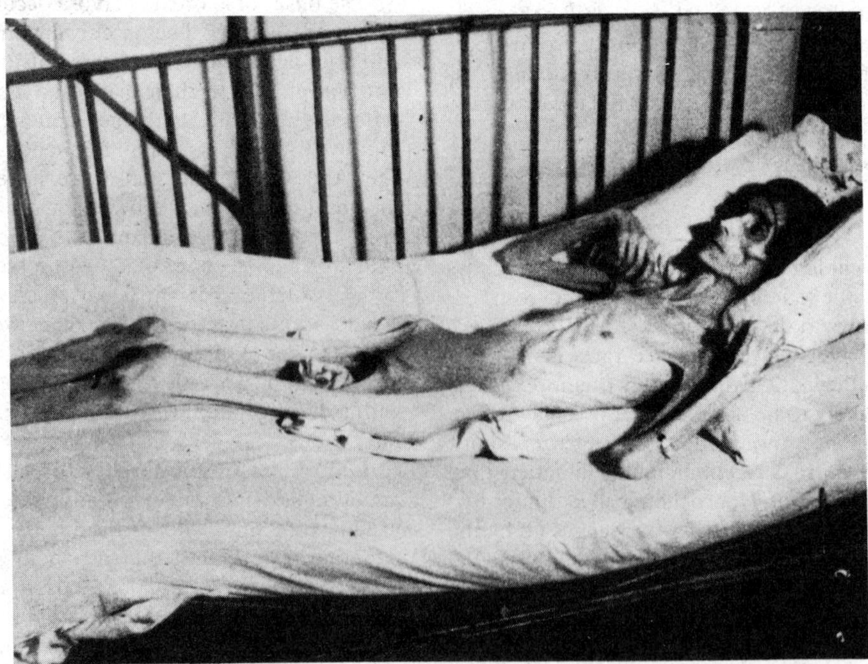

Figure 37.3-1. Patient with anorexia nervosa. (Courtesy Katherine Halmi, M.D.)

Table 37.3-1
Medical Complications of Eating Disorders

Related to weight loss:
Cachexia: Loss of fat, muscle mass, reduced thyroid metabolism (low T_3 syndrome), cold intolerance and difficulty maintaining core body temperature
Cardiac: Loss of cardiac muscle, small heart, cardiac arrhythmias including atrial and ventricular premature contractions, prolonged His bundle transmission (prolonged QT interval), bradycardia, ventricular tachycardia, sudden death
Digestive-gastrointestinal: Delayed gastric emptying, bloating, constipation, abdominal pain
Reproductive: Amenorrhea, low levels of luteinizing hormone (LH) and follicle-stimulating hormone (FSH)
Dermatological: Lanugo (fine babylike hair over body), edema
Hematological: Leukopenia
Neuropsychiatric: Abnormal taste sensation (?zinc deficiency), apathetic depression, mild organic mental symptoms
Skeletal: Osteoporosis

Related to purging (vomiting and laxative abuse):
Metabolic: Electrolyte abnormalities, particularly hypokalemic, hypochloremic alkalosis; hypomagnesemia
Digestive-gastrointestinal: Salivary gland and pancreatic inflammation and enlargement with increase in serum amylase, esophageal and gastric erosion, dysfunctional bowel with haustral dilatation
Dental: Erosion of dental enamel (perimyolysis), particularly of front teeth, with corresponding decay
Neuropsychiatric: Seizures (related to large fluid shifts and electrolyte disturbances), mild neuropathies, fatigue and weakness, mild organic mental symptoms

Table from J Yager: Eating disorders. In *Clinical Psychiatry for Medical Students,* A Stoudemire, editor, p 324. Lippincott, Philadelphia, 1990, with permission.

conflict, bulimia, vomiting, laxative abuse, and various behavioral manifestations (such as obsessive-compulsive, hysterical, depressive, psychosomatic, neurotic, and denial symptoms) have been related to poor outcome in some studies but have not been significant in affecting outcome in other studies.

Thirty to 50 percent of anorexia nervosa patients have the symptoms of bulimia nervosa, and usually the bulimic symptoms occur within 1½ years after the beginning of anorexia nervosa. Sometimes, the bulimic symptoms precede anorexia nervosa.

Diagnosis

The diagnosis of anorexia nervosa should be made only after finding the features listed in Table 37.3-2. Patients with this disorder are often secretive, deny their symptoms, and resist treatment. In almost all cases, relatives or intimate acquaintances must confirm the patient's history. The mental status examination usually shows a patient who is alert and very knowledgeable on the subject of nutrition and who is also preoccupied with food and weight.

The patient must have a thorough general physical and neurological examination. If the patient is vomiting, a hypokalemic alkalosis may be present. Because most patients are dehydrated, the clinician must obtain serum electrolytes initially and then again periodically during hospitalization.

Table 37.3-2
Diagnostic Criteria for Anorexia Nervosa

A. Refusal to maintain body weight over a minimal normal weight for age and height (e.g., weight loss leading to maintenance of body weight 15 percent below that expected; or failure to make expected weight gain during period of growth, leading to body weight 15 percent below that expected).

B. Intense fear of gaining weight or becoming fat, even though underweight.

C. Disturbance in the way in which one's body weight, size, or shape is experienced (e.g., the person claims to "feel fat" even when emaciated, believes that one area of the body is "too fat" even when obviously underweight).

D. In females, absence of at least three consecutive menstrual cycles when otherwise expected to occur (primary or secondary amenorrhea if her periods occur only following hormone [e.g., estrogen] administration.)

Table from DSM-III-R, *Diagnostic and Statistical Manual of Mental Disorders,* ed 3, revised. Copyright American Psychiatric Association, Washington, DC, 1987, with permission.

Differential Diagnosis

The clinician must ascertain that the patient does not have a medical illness that can account for the weight loss (e.g., brain tumor, cancer). Weight loss, peculiar eating behavior, and vomiting can occur in several psychiatric illnesses. Depressive disorders and anorexia nervosa have several features in common, such as depressed feeling, crying spells, sleep disturbance, obsessive ruminations, and occasional suicidal thoughts. These disorders, however, have several distinguishing features. Generally, a patient with a depressive disorder has a decreased appetite, whereas an anorexia nervosa patient claims to have a normal appetite and to feel hungry. Only in the severe stages of anorexia nervosa does the patient actually have a decreased appetite. In contrast to depressive agitation, the hyperactivity seen in anorexia nervosa is planned and ritualistic. The preoccupation with the caloric content of food, recipes, and the preparation of gourmet feasts is typical of the anorexia nervosa patient and is not present in the patient with a depressive disorder. And in depressive disorder, there is no intense fear of obesity or disturbance of body image, as there is in anorexia nervosa.

Weight fluctuations, vomiting, and peculiar food handling may occur in somatization disorder. On rare occasions a patient fulfills the criteria for both somatization disorder and anorexia nervosa; in such a case both diagnoses should be made. Generally, the weight loss in somatization disorder is not as severe as that in anorexia nervosa, nor does the patient with somatization disorder express a morbid fear of becoming overweight, as is common in the anorexia nervosa patient. Amenorrhea for three months or longer is unusual in somatization disorder.

Delusions about food in schizophrenia are seldom concerned with the caloric content of food. A patient with schizophrenia is rarely preoccupied with a fear of becoming obese and does not have the hyperactivity that is seen in the anorexia nervosa patient. Schizophrenic patients have bizarre eating habits and not the entire syndrome of anorexia nervosa.

Anorexia nervosa must be differentiated from bulimia nervosa, a disorder in which episodic binge eating—followed by depressive moods, self-deprecating thoughts, and often self-induced vomiting—occurs while patients maintain their weight within a normal range. Furthermore, in bulimia nervosa there is seldom a 15 percent weight loss. The two conditions frequently coexist.

Treatment

The immediate aim of treatment in anorexia nervosa is to restore the patient's nutritional state to normal, because the complications of emaciation, dehydration, and electrolyte imbalance may cause death. Usually, a hospitalized treatment program that provides considerable environmental structure is necessary for the weight restoration stage of treatment. Hospitalization of two to six months is often required.

The general management of anorexia nervosa patients during a hospitalized treatment program should take into account the following: Each patient should be weighed daily early in the morning after emptying the bladder. The daily fluid intake and urine output should be recorded. If vomiting is occurring, the hospital staff must obtain serum electrolytes regularly and watch for the development of hypokalemia. Because food is regurgitated after meals, it is possible to control the vomiting by making the bathroom inaccessible for at least two hours after meals or by having an attendant in the bathroom to prevent such activities. Constipation in anorexia nervosa patients is relieved when they begin to eat normally. Occasionally, it may be necessary to give stool softeners but never laxatives. If diarrhea occurs, it usually means that the patient is surreptitiously taking laxatives. Because of the rare complication of stomach dilation and the possibility of circulatory overload if the patient immediately starts eating an enormous number of calories, it is advisable to start to give patients about 500 calories over the amount required to maintain their present weight (usually 1,500 to 2,000 calories a day). It is wise to give these calories in six equal feedings throughout the day, so that the patients do not have to eat a large amount of food in one sitting. There may be an advantage in starting to give patients a liquid food supplement, such as Sustagen, because they may be less apprehensive about gaining weight slowly with the formula than by eating food.

After patients are discharged from the hospital, the clinician usually finds it necessary to continue some type of outpatient supervision of whatever problems are identified in the patients and their families.

Most patients are uninterested in and even resistant to psychiatric treatment and are brought to a doctor's office unwillingly by agonizing relatives or friends. The patients rarely accept the recommendation of hospitalization without arguing and criticizing the program being offered. Emphasizing the benefits, such as relief of insomnia and depressive signs and symptoms, may help persuade the patients to admit themselves willingly to the hospital. The relatives' support and confidence in the doctor and the treatment team are essential when firm recommendations must be carried out. The patients' families should be warned that the patients will resist admission and, for the first several weeks of treatment, will make many dramatic pleas for the family's support to obtain release from the program. Only when the risk of death from the complications of malnutrition is likely should a compulsory admission or commitment be obtained. On rare occasions patients may prove wrong the doctor's statements about the probable failure of outpatient treatment. Such patients may gain a specified amount of weight by the time of each outpatient visit; however, this behavior is uncommon, and usually a period of inpatient care is necessary.

A nursing treatment program is available that contains many of the positive reinforcements and privileges used in behavior therapy programs. In this program total bed rest is instituted and then progressively relaxed through a series of rewards as the patients cooperate and gain weight.

Behavioral conditioning has been used along with family therapy. Family therapy has been used to examine the interactions among family members and the possible secondary gain for the patient as a result of the disorder. The usefulness of behavioral contingencies in conjunction with other therapies in treating anorexia nervosa has become widely recognized.

Pharmacological studies have yet to yield a drug that is beneficial to many anorexia nervosa patients. Perhaps the most promising is cyproheptadine (Periactin), which has antihistaminic and antiserotonergic properties. Serotonin is thought to suppress appetite. Some nonbinging anorexia nervosa patients gain weight on cyproheptadine. Some also benefit from the antidepressant amitriptyline (Elavil), but, so far, antidepressants have not been shown to be of much help. Antipsychotics, such as chlorpromazine (Thorazine), may be tried, but there is a risk in the emaciated patient of increased hypotension and hypothermia.

In some cases electroconvulsive therapy (ECT) has been reported to be successful, especially when there is a strong depressive component.

The classic psychodynamically oriented therapy approach has not been effective in anorexia nervosa, particularly in inducing weight gain or in changing the abnormal eating behavior. Notwithstanding this, individual outpatient psychotherapy is usually a component of treatment.

BULIMIA NERVOSA

Bulimia nervosa is characterized by episodic, uncontrolled, compulsive, and rapid ingestion of large quantities of food over a short period of time (binge eating). Physical discomfort, such as abdominal pain or feelings of nausea, terminates the bulimic episode, which is followed by feelings of guilt, depression, or self-disgust. The person with the disorder regularly uses laxatives or diuretics or induces vomiting through other artificial or extreme means of purging.

Epidemiology

Bulimia nervosa, like anorexia nervosa, is much more common in women than in men. It usually begins somewhat later in adolescence than anorexia nervosa or begins in early adult life. It is much more prevalent than anorexia nervosa, occurring in as many as 40 percent of college women. No familial incidence has been noted, but obesity may be found in other family members. Obesity in adolescence may predispose to the disorder in adulthood.

Etiology

Biological, psychological, and social factors are associated with bulimia nervosa. Attempts have been made to associate cycles of binging and purging with various neurotransmitters. Because antidepressants often benefit patients with the disorder, serotonin and norepinephrine have been implicated.

Plasma endorphin levels are raised in some vomiting bulimia nervosa patients, leading to the possibility that the feelings of well-being experienced by some of these patients after vomiting may be mediated by raised endorphin levels.

Patients with bulimia nervosa, like those with anorexia nervosa, tend to be high achievers and respond to the same societal pressures to be thin. As with anorexia nervosa patients, many bulimia nervosa patients are depressed, and there is increased familial depression. The families of such patients, however, are generally different from those of anorexia nervosa patients. Families of bulimia nervosa patients are less close and more conflictual than the families of anorexia nervosa patients. Bulimia nervosa patients describe their parents as being neglectful and rejecting.

Psychologically, patients with bulimia nervosa, like those with anorexia nervosa, have difficulties with adolescent demands, but bulimia nervosa patients are more outgoing, angry, and impulsive than anorexia nervosa patients. Alcoholism, shoplifting, and emotional lability (including suicide attempts) are associated with bulimia nervosa. The bulimia nervosa patients generally experience their uncontrolled eating as more ego-dystonic than do anorexia nervosa patients, so bulimia nervosa patients more readily seek help.

Clinical Features

According to the revised third edition of *Diagnostic and Statistical Manual of Mental Disorders* (DSM-III-R), the essential features of bulimia nervosa are recurrent episodes of binge eating; a feeling of lack of control over eating behavior during the eating binges; self-induced vomiting, the use of laxatives or diuretics, strict dieting, fasting, or vigorous exercise to prevent weight gain; and persistent overconcern with body shape and weight. Binging usually precedes vomiting by about one year.

Vomiting is common and is usually induced by sticking a finger down the throat, although some patients are able to vomit at will. Vomiting decreases the abdominal pain and feeling of being bloated and allows the patients to continue eating without fear of gaining weight. Depression often follows the episode and has been called postbinge anguish. During their binges the patients eat food that is sweet, high in calories, and generally of smooth texture or soft, such as cakes and pastry. The food is eaten secretly and rapidly and is sometimes not even chewed.

Most bulimia nervosa patients are within their normal weight range, but some may be either underweight or overweight. Bulimia nervosa patients are concerned about their body image and their appearance, worry about how others see them, and are concerned about their sexual attractiveness. Most bulimia nervosa patients are sexually active compared with anorexia nervosa patients, who are not interested in sex. Pica and struggles during meals are sometimes revealed in the histories of bulimia nervosa patients. A clinical case example follows:

The patient, a 17-year-old who lived with her parents, insisted that she be seen because of binge eating and vomiting. She had achieved her greatest weight of 180 pounds at 16 years of age. Her lowest weight since she had reached her height of 5 feet 9 inches was 150 pounds, and her weight when examined was about 160 pounds.

The patient stated she had been dieting since age 10 and said she had always been very tall and slightly chubby. At age 12 she had started binge eating and vomiting. She was a serious competitive swimmer at that time, and it was necessary for her to keep her weight down. She would deprive herself of all food for a few days and then get an urge to eat. She could not control this urge and would raid the refrigerator and cupboards for ice cream, pastries, and other desserts. She would often do this at night, when nobody was looking, and might eat in one sitting a quart of ice cream, an entire pie, and any other desserts she could find. While binging, she would feel that her eating was totally out of control, and she would stop only when she felt physical discomfort. She would then become depressed and fearful of gaining weight, so she would self-induce vomiting by sticking her finger deep into the back of her mouth until she gagged.

The patient had always been very concerned about the effect this behavior was having on her weight and constantly fretted about being overweight, occasionally resorting to dextroamphetamine (Dexedrine) to help her lose weight. When she was 15, she was having eating binges and vomiting four days a week. Since age 13 she had gone through only one period of six weeks without gaining weight or going on eating binges or vomiting. She had quit school at age 17 for five months; during that period she just stayed home, binge eating and vomiting several times a day. She then went back to school and tried to do better in her schoolwork. She obtained average or below-average grades in junior high and high school.

For the preceding two years the patient had been drinking wine and beer on weekends. She drank mostly with girlfriends; she dated infrequently. She stated that she wanted to date but was ashamed of the way she looked. Several months before the interview she had been hospitalized for two weeks to control her binge eating. During that time she was very depressed and cut her wrists several times while hospitalized.

The patient was neatly dressed and well oriented and answered inquiries rationally. During the interview she indicated that she realized she had a serious problem with binge eating and vomiting but felt helpless about getting the behavior under control.

Discussion. The patient clearly had a gross disturbance in her eating behavior. She had recurrent episodes of binge eating, in which she rapidly consumed a large quantity of food over a discrete period. The food she ate during the binges was typically high in carbohydrates (ice cream, pastries, and other desserts); she ate it in secret (at night when nobody was looking). During the binges she experienced a feeling of lack of control over her eating behavior, so that only the physical discomfort caused by the binge allowed her to stop eating. To keep from gaining weight as a result of this overeating, she regularly engaged in self-induced vomiting and occasionally used dextroamphetamine to help her lose weight. Because of her frequent fluctuations in weight caused by the binges, dieting and the control of her weight were chronic preoccupations. Her eating binges were frequent, sometimes as often as several times a day, warranting the diagnosis of bulimia nervosa.

Course and Prognosis

Little is known about the long-range course of bulimia nervosa, but it currently appears to have a better prognosis than anorexia nervosa. The usual course of bulimia nervosa is chronic over a period of many years, with occasional remissions. Bulimia nervosa is rarely incapacitating except in a few persons who spend the entire day in binge eating and self-induced vomiting, which can lead to dehydration and electrolyte imbalance (hypochloremia and hypokalemia) and to metabolic alkalosis, which may require hospitalization. Frequent vomiting also causes dental caries, salivary gland enlargement, elevated serum amylase, and esophagitis.

Diagnosis

The diagnostic criteria for bulimia nervosa are listed in Table 37.3-3.

Differential Diagnosis

A diagnosis of bulimia nervosa cannot be made if anorexia nervosa is present, but episodic bulimic symptoms can occur in anorexia nervosa. If a patient meets all the criteria for the diagnosis of anorexia nervosa, a diagnosis of anorexia nervosa should be given. Bulimia nervosa does not lead to a severe weight loss, and amenorrhea is rare, two symptoms that are necessary for a diagnosis of anorexia nervosa.

Bulimia nervosa should not be diagnosed if the patient meets positive criteria for schizophrenia. The clinician must ascertain that the patient has no neurological disease, such as epileptic-equivalent seizures, central nervous system tumors, Klüver-Bucy-like syndromes, and Kleine-Levin syndrome. The pathological features manifested by Klüver-Bucy syndrome are visual agnosia, compulsive licking and biting, examination of objects by the mouth, inability to ignore any stimulus, placidity, altered sexual behavior (hypersexuality), and altered dietary habits, especially hyperphagia. This syndrome is exceedingly rare and is unlikely to cause a problem in differential diagnosis. Kleine-Levin syndrome consists of periodic hypersomnia, lasting for two to three weeks, and hyperphagia. As in bulimia nervosa, the onset is usually during adolescence, but this syndrome is more common in men than in women. Borderline personality disorder patients sometimes binge eat, but the eating is associated with the other signs of the borderline syndrome.

Table 37.3-3
Diagnostic Criteria for Bulimia Nervosa

A. Recurrent episodes of binge eating (rapid consumption of a large amount of food in a discrete period of time).

B. A feeling of lack of control over eating behavior during the eating binges.

C. The person regularly engages in either self-induced vomiting, use of laxatives or diuretics, strict dieting or fasting, or vigorous exercise in order to prevent weight gain.

D. A minimum average of two binge eating episodes a week for at least three months.

E. Persistent overconcern with body shape and weight.

Table from DSM-III-R, *Diagnostic and Statistical Manual of Mental Disorders,* ed 3, revised. Copyright American Psychiatric Association, Washington, DC, 1987, with permission.

Treatment

The treatment of bulimia nervosa consists of psychotherapy or pharmacotherapy or a combination of both. Psychotherapy is frequently stormy and may be prolonged. Some obese bulimia nervosa patients who have had prolonged psychotherapy do surprisingly well. Effective positive reinforcement, informational feedback, and contingency contracting with bulimic women with anorexia nervosa are useful. A program of desensitization to the thoughts and feelings that bulimia nervosa patients have just before binge eating, in conjunction with a behavioral contract, may be a promising approach to the treatment of the disorder. Cognitive therapy has also been reported helpful.

Pharmacologically, various antidepressants (imipramine [Tofranil], desipramine [Norpramin], trazodone [Desyrel]) have been shown to be of benefit in bulimia nervosa, and others (monoamine oxidase inhibitors [MAOIs] and fluoxetine [Prozac]) appear to be promising.

Bulimia nervosa patients who vomit may require hospitalization for electrolyte and metabolic disturbances.

EATING DISORDER NOT OTHERWISE SPECIFIED

The DSM-III-R diagnostic classification of eating disorder not otherwise specified is a residual category used for eating disorders that do not meet the criteria for a specific eating disorder. The DSM-III-R diagnostic criteria and examples are given in Table 37.3-4.

Table 37.3-4
Diagnostic Criteria for Eating Disorder Not Otherwise Specified

Disorders of eating that do not meet the criteria for a specific eating disorder.
Examples:
(1) a person of average weight who does not have binge eating episodes, but frequently engages in self-induced vomiting for fear of gaining weight
(2) all of the features of anorexia nervosa in a female except absence of menses
(3) all of the features of bulimia nervosa except the frequency of binge eating episodes

Table from DSM-III-R, *Diagnostic and Statistical Manual of Mental Disorders,* ed 3, revised. Copyright American Psychiatric Association, Washington, DC, 1987, with permission.

References

Artmann H, Grau H, Adelmann M, Scleiffer R: Reversible and non-reversible enlargement of cerebrospinal fluid spaces in anorexia nervosa. Neuroradiology *27*: 304, 1985.

Blinder B J, Chaitin B, Goldstein R, eds.: *The Eating Disorders*. Pergamon, New York, 1987.

Crisp A H, Hsu L K G, Harding B, Hartshorn J: Clinical features of anorexia nervosa: A study of 102 cases. J Psychosom Res *24*: 179, 1980.

Fairburn C G: The current status of the psychological treatments for bulimia nervosa. J Psychosom Res *32*: 635, 1988.

Fava M, Copeland P M, Schweiger W, Herzog D B: Neurochemical abnormalities of anorexia nervosa and bulimia nervosa. Am J Psychiatry *146*: 963, 1989.

Garfinkel P E, Garner D M, Rose J, Darby P L, Brandes O S, O'Hanlon J, Walsh N: A comparison of characteristics in the families of patients with anorexia nervosa and normal controls. Psychol Med *13*: 821, 1983.

Hudson J E, Pope H G Jr, eds.: *The Psychobiology of Bulimia*. American Psychiatric Press, Washington, DC, 1987.

Kassett J A, Gwirtsman H E, Kaye H K, Brandt H A, Jimerson D C: Pattern of onset of bulimic symptoms in anorexia nervosa. Am J Psychiatry *145*: 1287, 1988.

Marchi M, Cohen P: Early childhood eating behaviors and adolescent eating disorders. J Am Acad Child Adolesc Psychiatry *29*: 112, 1990.

Pope H G, Keok P E, McElroy S L, Hudson J I: A placebo-controlled study of trazodone in bulimia nervosa. J Clin Psychopharmacol *9*: 254, 1989.

Toner B B, Garfinkel P E, Garner D M: Cognitive style of patients with bulimic and diet-restricting anorexia nervosa. Am J Psychiatry *144*: 510, 1987.

Walsh B T, Kissileff H R, Cassidy S M, Dantzic S: Eating behavior of women with bulimia. Arch Gen Psychiatry *46*: 54, 1989.

Wamholdt F S, Kaslow N J, Swift W J, Ritholz M: Short-term course of depressive symptoms in patients with eating disorders. Am J Psychiatry *144*: 362, 1987.

Yager J: The treatment of eating disorders. J Clin Psychiatry *49*: 137, 1988.

Yates A: Current perspectives on the eating disorders: I. History, psychological and biological aspects. J Am Acad Child Adolesc Psychiatry *28*: 813, 1989.

Yates A: Current perspectives on the eating disorders: II. Treatment, outcome, and research directions. J Am Acad Child Adolesc Psychiatry *29*: 1, 1990.

Gender Identity Disorders

Gender identity disorders is a category first described in the third edition of *Diagnostic and Statistical Manual of Mental Disorders* (DSM-III). As noted in DSM-III and its revision (DSM-III-R), the disorders are probably at the severe end of a continuum of difficulties that many children have in reconciling their anatomical sex with their gender identity.

Gender identity refers to one's sense of oneself as being male or female. The person with a healthy gender identity is able to say with certainty, "I am male" or "I am female." *Gender role* is the public expression of gender identity. According to DSM-III-R, gender role is everything that one says or does to indicate to others or to oneself the degree to which one is male or female. These concepts must be distinguished from *sex*, which is strictly limited to the anatomical and physiological characteristics (e.g., penis, vagina) that indicate whether one is a male or a female.

According to DSM-III-R, gender identity disorders are classified under the heading of disorders first appearing during childhood or adolescence. Even though persons who present clinically with gender identity problems may be of any age, most cases begin in childhood.

DSM-III-R provides three diagnoses for males and females with gender identity disorders: (1) gender identity disorder of childhood, (2) transsexualism, and (3) gender identity disorder of adolescence or adulthood, nontranssexual type (GIDAANT). Persons with gender identity disorder feel persistent discomfort that their assigned gender is inappropriate. Those persons with a persistent preoccupation with and a desire to have sex-reassignment surgery (SRS) or to use hormones to achieve that end are labeled transsexuals; those without that persistent preoccupation are labeled nontranssexuals. Gender identity disorder not otherwise specified (NOS) is the classification for those who do not fit into the other diagnostic categories (Table 38-1).

Table 38-1
Diagnostic Criteria for Gender Identity Disorder Not Otherwise Specified

Disorders in gender identity that are not classifiable as a specific gender identity disorder.

Examples:

(1) children with persistent cross-dressing without the other criteria for gender identity disorder of childhood
(2) adults with transient, stress-related cross-dressing behavior
(3) adults with the clinical features of transsexualism of less than two years' duration
(4) people who have a persistent preoccupation with castration or peotomy without a desire to acquire the sex characteristics of the other sex

EPIDEMIOLOGY

There is almost no information about the prevalence of gender identity disorders among children, teenagers, and adults. Most estimates of prevalence are based on the number of people seeking SRS, and that indicates a male preponderance. The ratios of boys to girls reported in three child gender identity clinics were 30 to 1, 17 to 1, and 6 to 1, indicating little experience with girls. This disparity may indicate a great male vulnerability to gender identity disorder or a greater sensitivity to and worry about cross-gender-identified boys than cross-gender-identified girls. According to DSM-III-R, the estimated prevalence of transsexualism is 1 per 30,000 for males and 1 per 100,000 for females.

Studies of boys referred for outpatient psychiatric treatment revealed that up to about 50 percent had a significant amount of effeminate behavior. The boys were not referred primarily for problems with gender identity, and it is unclear how many met the criteria for DSM-III-R gender identity disorders.

ETIOLOGY

Biological Factors

For mammals, the resting state of tissue is initially female; as the fetus develops, a male is produced only if androgen (set off by the Y chromosome) is added. That implies that maleness and masculinity depend on fetal and perinatal androgens. Lower animals' sexual behavior is governed by sex steroids, and, as one ascends the evolutionary scale, this effect diminishes. Sex steroids influence the expression of sexual behavior in the mature man or woman; that is, testosterone can increase libido and aggressiveness in females, and estrogen can decrease libido and aggressiveness in males. But masculinity, femininity, and gender identity are more products of postnatal life events than of prenatal hormonal organization.

Psychosocial Factors

Children develop a gender identity consonant with their sex of rearing (also known as assigned sex). The formation of gender identity is influenced by the interaction of the temperament of the child and the qualities and attitudes of the parents. There are culturally acceptable gender roles: Boys are not expected to be effeminate, and girls are not expected to be tomboys. There are boys' games (e.g., cops and robbers) and girls' games (e.g., dolls and doll houses). These roles are learned, although some investigators believe that some boys are temperamentally more delicate and sensitive and that some girls are more aggressive and energized—traits that stereotypically are known in today's culture as feminine and masculine, respectively.

Sigmund Freud believed that gender identity problems resulted from conflicts experienced by the child within the oedipal triangle. These conflicts were fueled by both real family events and the child's fantasies. Whatever interfered with the child's loving the opposite-sex parent and identifying with the same-sex parent interfered with normal gender identity.

The onset of DSM-III-R gender identity disorders is usually between the ages of 2 and 4 years. The quality of the mother-child relationship in the first years of life is paramount in establishing gender identity. During this period mothers normally facilitate their children's awareness of and pride in their gender. The child is valued as a little boy or girl. At the same time, the separation-individuation process is unfolding. Devaluing, hostile mothering can result in gender problems. When these problems become associated with separation-individuation problems, the result can be the use of sexuality to remain in relationships characterized by shifts between a desperate infantile closeness and a hostile, devaluing distance.

Some children are given the message that they would be more valued if they adopted the gender identity of the opposite sex. Rejected or abused children may act on the belief that they would be better treated if they were the other sex. Gender identity problems can also be triggered by the death, extended absence, or depression of the maternal figure, to which a young boy may react by totally identifying with her—that is, becoming a mother to replace her.

The role of the father is also important in these early years. His presence normally helps the separation-individuation process. The absence of a father figure risks the mother and child's remaining in an overly close bond. For the female child, the father is normally the prototype of future love objects; for the male child, the father is a model for male identification.

GENDER IDENTITY DISORDER OF CHILDHOOD

According to DSM-III-R, the essential feature of gender identity disorder of childhood is a persistent and intense distress in a child about the child's assigned sex and the desire to be or insistence that he or she is of the other sex. Girls and boys show an aversion to normative stereotypical feminine or masculine clothing and repudiate their respective anatomical characteristics. Table 38-2 lists the DSM-III-R criteria for this disorder.

At the extreme of gender disorder in children are those boys who, by the standards of their cultures, are as feminine as are the most feminine of girls and those girls who are as masculine as are the most masculine of boys. No sharp line can be drawn on the continuum of gender disorder between children who should receive a formal diagnosis and those who should not. The disorder's prevalence is, therefore, unknown. DSM-III-R comments that girls with this disorder regularly have male companions and an avid interest in sports and rough-and-tumble play; they show no interest in dolls or playing house (unless they play the father or another male role). More rarely, a girl with this disorder refuses to urinate in a sitting position, claims that she has or will grow a penis, does not want to grow breasts or to menstruate, and asserts that she will grow up to become a man (not merely in role). According to DSM-III-R, boys with this disorder are usually preoccupied with female stereotypical activities. They may have a preference for dressing in girls' or women's clothes or

Table 38-2
Diagnostic Criteria for Gender Identity Disorder of Childhood

For females:

A. Persistent and intense distress about being a girl, and a stated desire to be a boy (not merely a desire for any perceived cultural advantages from being a boy), or insistence that she is a boy.

B. Either (1) or (2):
  (1) persistent marked aversion to normative feminine clothing and insistence on wearing stereotypical masculine clothing (e.g., boys' underwear and other accessories)
  (2) persistent repudiation of female anatomical structures, as evidenced by at least one of the following:
    (*a*) an assertion that she has, or will grow, a penis
    (*b*) rejection of urinating in a sitting position
    (*c*) assertion that she does not want to grow breasts or menstruate

C. The girl has not yet reached puberty.

For males:

A. Persistent and intense distress about being a boy and an intense desire to be a girl or, more rarely, insistence that he is a girl.

B. Either (1) or (2):
  (1) preoccupation with female stereotypical activities, as shown by a preference for either cross-dressing or simulating female attire, or by an intense desire to participate in the games and pastimes of girls and rejection of male stereotypical toys, games, and activities
  (2) persistent repudiation of male anatomical structures, as indicated by at least one of the following repeated assertions:
    (*a*) that he will grow up to become a woman (not merely in role)
    (*b*) that his penis and testes are disgusting and will disappear
    (*c*) that it would be better not to have a penis or testes

C. The boy has not yet reached puberty.

Table from DSM-III-R, *Diagnostic and Statistical Manual of Mental Disorders,* ed 3, revised. Copyright American Psychiatric Association, Washington, DC, 1987, with permission.

may improvise such items from available material when the genuine articles are not available. (The cross-dressing typically does not cause sexual excitement, as in transvestic fetishism.) They often have a compelling desire to participate in the games and pastimes of girls. Female dolls are often their favorite toys, and girls are regularly their preferred playmates. When playing house, such boys take the role of a female. Their gestures and actions are often judged against a standard of cultural stereotype to be feminine, and such boys are usually subjected to male peer group teasing and rejection, whereas that rarely occurs among girls until adolescence. Boys with this disorder may assert that they will grow up to become women (not merely in role). In rare cases a boy with this disorder claims that his penis or testes are disgusting or will disappear or that it would be better not to have a penis or testes at all.

Some children refuse to attend school because of teasing or pressure to dress in attire stereotypical of their assigned sex. Most children with this disorder deny being disturbed by it, except that it brings them into conflict with expectations of their family or peers.

Course and Prognosis

The prognosis for gender disorder depends on the age of onset and the intensity of the symptoms. Boys begin to have the disorder before the age of 4 years, and peer conflict develops during the early school years, at about the age of 7 or 8 years. Grossly feminine mannerisms may lessen as the boy grows older, especially if attempts are made to discourage such behavior. Cross-dressing may be part of the disorder, and 75 percent of boys who cross-dress begin to do so before age 4. The age of onset is also early for girls, but most give up masculine behavior by adolescence.

In both sexes homosexuality is likely to develop in one-third to two-thirds of cases, although fewer girls than boys develop a homosexual orientation, for reasons that are not clear. S. Levine reported that follow-up studies of gender-disturbed boys consistently indicated that homosexual orientation, not transsexualism, was the usual adolescent outcome. Transsexualism occurs in less than 10 percent of cases. Retrospective data on homosexual men indicate a high frequency of cross-gender identifications and feminine gender role behavior during childhood.

Treatment

Gender disorders and other mental illness, particularly borderline personality disorder, often coexist; in those cases, attention needs to be directed to both conditions. Attempts to inculcate culturally acceptable behavioral patterns in boys by role modeling adults or peers have been successful in some cases.

For treatment, Richard Green uses a one-to-one play relationship with the child and parental counseling in conjunction with group meetings of children with the same problem and their parents. Parents' encouragement of the child's atypical behavior (such as dressing a boy in girl's clothing or not giving him haircuts) needs to be examined in therapy. It is important to note ethical considerations in regard to the attempt to modify such behavior.

TRANSSEXUALISM

According to DSM-III-R, the essential features of transsexualism are a persistent discomfort and sense of inappropriateness regarding one's assigned sex in a person who has reached puberty. In addition, there is a persistent preoccupation, for at least two years, with getting rid of one's primary and secondary sex characteristics and acquiring the sex characteristics of the other sex. Therefore, the diagnosis of transsexualism should not be made if the disturbance is limited to brief periods of stress. The wish to live as a member of the other sex is always present (Table 38-3).

Most retrospective studies of transsexuals report gender identity problems during childhood; however, prospective studies of children with gender identity disorder indicate that very few become transsexuals. Transsexualism is much more common in men (1 per 30,000 men) than in women (1 per 100,000 women).

The diagnosis is easily made clinically. As DSM-III-R notes, people with this disorder usually complain that they are uncomfortable wearing the clothes of their assigned sex and, therefore, dress in clothes of the other sex. They engage in activities associated with the other sex. These people find their genitals repugnant, which may lead to persistent requests for SRS. That desire may override all other wishes, and, in time, they attempt the following: Men take estrogen to create breasts and other feminine contours; have electrolysis to remove their male hair; and have SRS, which includes removal of the testes and penis and the creation of an artificial vagina. Women bind their breasts or have a double mastectomy, a hysterectomy, and an oophorectomy; take testosterone to build up their muscle mass and deepen the voice; and have SRS, in which an artificial phallus is created. These procedures may make the transsexual indistinguishable from members of the other sex. Some investigators describe behavior in sex-reassigned persons that is almost a caricature of male and female roles.

Course and Prognosis

Transsexualism, which usually begins in childhood, is chronic. Impaired social and occupational functioning as a result of the person's wanting to participate in the desired (and opposite) gender role is common. Depression is also a common problem, especially if the person feels hopeless about obtaining a sex change with surgery or hormones. Male transsexuals have been known to castrate themselves, not as a suicide attempt but as a way of forcing a surgeon to deal with their problem.

Types

DSM-III-R defines three transsexual types according to sexual orientation: (1) asexual, referring to persons who give

Table 38-3
Diagnostic Criteria for Transsexualism

A. Persistent discomfort and sense of inappropriateness about one's assigned sex.

B. Persistent preoccupation for at least two years with getting rid of one's primary and secondary sex characteristics and acquiring the sex characteristics of the other sex.

C. The person has reached puberty.

Specify history of sexual orientation: **asexual, homosexual, heterosexual,** or **unspecified.**

Table from DSM-III-R, *Diagnostic and Statistical Manual of Mental Disorders,* ed 3, revised. Copyright American Psychiatric Association, Washington, DC, 1987, with permission.

no history of sexual activity or pleasure derived from the genitals; (2) homosexual, in which there is sexual arousal from same-sex partners; and (3) heterosexual. Persons in the homosexual group often deny they are homosexual because they believe themselves to be members of the opposite sex. Thus, a man claims he is not a homosexual because he feels like a woman and, thus, is heterosexual if defined by his identity. But if defined by his anatomy and that of his male partner, he is homosexual.

Like transsexual men, transsexual women do not deny their anatomical sex but are preoccupied with the sense of really being men who are attracted to women; they, too, are classified as asexual, homosexual, and heterosexual.

Despite the detailed subdivision in DSM-III-R, the overwhelming majority of transsexuals believe themselves to be heterosexual. The common statement in this group is, "I am a woman trapped in a man's body" or vice versa.

Treatment

A psychiatric evaluation to determine the presence of another mental disorder is essential. Some clinicians believe that the transsexual's belief of being of the opposite sex should be classified as a delusion. According to DSM-III-R, however, the insistence by persons that they are of the other sex is not a delusion, because what is invariably meant is that they *feel like* a member of the other sex, rather than truly believing that they are a member of the other sex.

Other illnesses may accompany transsexualism. Personality disorders, especially borderline personality disorder, are highly represented in this group. Depression is also common. Psychotherapy is useful for those conditions; however, so far, no reported psychological treatment will make transsexuals satisfied with their anatomical sex. The psychiatrist can either do nothing or comply with the patient's wish for a sex change. SRS is more successful male to female than female to male, mainly because of the surgical techniques. Surgical treatment is definitive, and, because there is no turning back, careful standards preceding the surgery have been developed, which include the following: (1) There must be a trial of cross-gender living for at least three months and sometimes up to one year. For some transsexuals the real-life test may make them change their minds, because they find it uncomfortable to relate to friends, workers, and lovers in that role. (2) They must receive hormone treatments, with estradiol and progesterone in male-to-female change and testosterone in female-to-male change. Many transsexuals like the changes in their bodies that occur as a result of this treatment, and some stop at that point. About 50 percent of transsexuals who meet the above criteria go on to SRS. Outcome studies are highly variable in terms of how success is defined and measured (e.g., successful intercourse, body image satisfaction).

About 70 percent of male-to-female and 80 percent of female-to-male SRS patients report satisfactory results. Unsatisfactory results correlate with a preexisting mental disorder. Suicide in postoperative SRS patients has been reported in up to 2 percent of all cases. SRS is a highly controversial measure that is undergoing much scrutiny.

GENDER IDENTITY DISORDER OF ADOLESCENCE OR ADULTHOOD, NONTRANSSEXUAL TYPE

DSM-III-R has a new diagnosis to describe persons with gender disorders who are not interested in changing their anatomical sex or in acquiring the characteristics of the other sex but who are uncomfortable with their assigned sex; it is called gender identity disorder of adolescence or adulthood, nontranssexual type (GIDAANT). An essential feature of this disorder is cross-dressing, either in fantasy or in reality (Table 38-4).

According to DSM-III-R, cross-dressing phenomena range from occasional solitary wearing of female clothes to extensive feminine identification in males and masculine identification in females and involvement in a transvestic subculture. More than one article of clothing of the other sex is involved, and the person may dress entirely as a member of the opposite sex. The degree to which the cross-dressed person appears as a member of the other sex varies, depending on mannerisms, body habitus, and cross-dressing skill. When not cross-dressed, these persons usually appear as unremarkable members of their assigned sex.

Table 38-4
Diagnostic Criteria for Gender Identity Disorder of Adolescence or Adulthood, Nontranssexual Type (GIDAANT)

A. Persistent or recurrent discomfort and sense of inappropriateness about one's assigned sex.

B. Persistent or recurrent cross-dressing in the role of the other sex, either in fantasy or actuality, but not for the purpose of sexual excitement (as in transvestic fetishism).

C. No persistent preoccupation (for a least two years) with getting rid of one's primary and secondary sex characteristics and acquiring the sex characteristics of the other sex (as in transsexualism).

D. The person has reached puberty.

Specify history of sexual orientation: **asexual, homosexual, heterosexual,** or **unspecified.**

Table from DSM-III-R, *Diagnostic and Statistical Manual of Mental Disorders,* ed 3, revised. Copyright American Psychiatric Association, Washington, DC, 1987, with permission.

This disorder differs from transvestic fetishism in that the cross-dressing is not for the purpose of sexual excitement. It differs from transsexualism in that there is no persistent preoccupation (for at least two years) with getting rid of one's primary and secondary sex characteristics and acquiring the sex characteristics of the other sex.

Some people with this disorder once had transvestic fetishism but no longer become sexually aroused by cross-dressing. Other people with this disorder are homosexuals who cross-dress. This disorder is common among female impersonators.

INTERSEXUAL DISORDERS

Intersexual disorders include a variety of syndromes that produce persons with gross anatomical or physiological aspects of the opposite sex. Although not an official DSM-III-R category, "intersexual disorders" is the term used by clinicians, and such patients should be classified on Axis III (physical disorders and conditions).

Turner's Syndrome

In Turner's syndrome, one sex chromosome is missing (XO). The result is an absence (agenesis) or minimal development (dysgenesis) of the gonads; no significant sex hormones, male or female, are produced in fetal life or postnatally. The sexual tissues remain in a female resting state. Because the second X chromosome, which seems responsible for full femaleness, is missing, these girls have an incomplete sexual anatomy and, lacking adequate estrogens, develop no secondary sex characteristics without treatment. They often suffer other stigmata, such as web neck, low posterior hairline margin, short stature, and cubitus valgus. The infant is born with normal-appearing female external genitals and so is unequivocally assigned to the female sex and is so reared. All these children develop as unremarkably feminine, heterosexually oriented girls; however, later medical management is necessary to assist them with their infertility and absence of secondary sex characteristics.

Klinefelter's Syndrome

A person (usually XXY) with Klinefelter's syndrome has a male habitus, under the influence of the Y chromosome, but this effect is weakened by the presence of the second X chromosome. Although the patient is born with a penis and testes, the testes are small and infertile, and the penis may also be small. Beginning in adolescence, some of these patients develop gynecomastia and other feminine-appearing contours. Their sexual desire is usually weak. Sex assignment and rearing should lead to a clear sense of maleness, but these patients often have gender disturbances, ranging from a complete reversal, as in transsexualism, to homosexuality or an intermittent desire to put on women's clothes. As a result of lessened androgen production, the fetal hypogonadal state in some patients seems to have interfered with the completion of central nervous system organization that should underlie masculine behavior. In fact, many of these patients have a wide variability of psychopathology, ranging from emotional instability to mental retardation.

Congenital Virilizing Adrenal Hyperplasia (Adrenogenital Syndrome)

Congenital virilizing adrenal hyperplasia results from an excess of androgen acting on the prenatal fetus. When the condition occurs in females, excessive adrenal fetal androgens from the adrenal gland cause androgenization of the external genitals, ranging from mild clitoral enlargement to external genitals that look like a normal scrotal sac, testes, and a penis; but hidden behind these external genitals are a vagina and a uterus. These patients are otherwise normally female. At birth, if the genitals look male, the child is assigned to the male sex and is so reared. The result is a clear sense of maleness and unremarkable masculinity; but, if the child is assigned to the female sex and is so reared, a sense of femaleness and femininity results. If the parents are uncertain to which sex their child belongs, a hermaphroditic identity results. The resultant gender identity reflects the rearing practices, but androgens may help determine behavior; those children raised unequivocally as girls have a tomboy quality more intense than that found in a control group. The girls nonetheless do have a heterosexual orientation.

Pseudohermaphroditism

Infants may be born with ambiguous genitals, which is an obstetrical emergency, because the sex assignment determines gender identity. Male pseudohermaphroditism is incomplete differentiation of the external genitals, even though a Y chromosome is present. Testes are present but rudimentary. Female pseudohermaphroditism is virilized genitals in a person who is XX, the most common cause being the adrenogenital syndrome described above.

The genitals' appearance at birth determines the sex assignment, and the core gender identity is male, female, or hermaphroditic, depending on the family's conviction as to the child's sex. Usually, a panel of experts determine the sex of rearing, basing their decision on buccal smears, chromosome studies, and parental wishes. Assignment should usually be made within 24 hours, so that the parents can adapt accordingly. If surgery is necessary to correct the genital deformity, it is generally done before the age of 3 years.

True hermaphroditism is characterized by the presence of both testes and ovaries in the same person, a rare condition.

Androgen Insensitivity Syndrome

Androgen insensitivity syndrome, a congenital X-linked recessive trait disorder—also known as testicular feminization syndrome— results from an inability of target tissues to respond to androgens. Unable to respond, the fetal tissues remain in their female resting state, and the central nervous system is not organized as masculine. The infant at birth appears to be an unremarkable female, although she is later found to have cryptorchid testes, which produce the testosterone to which the tissues do not respond, and minimal or absent internal sexual organs and vagina. Secondary sex characteristics at puberty are female because of the small but sufficient amounts of estrogens typically produced by the testes. The patients invariably sense themselves as females and are feminine.

References

Blanchard R, Steiner B W, eds.: *Clinical Management of Gender Identity Disorders in Children and Adults*. American Psychiatric Press, Washington, DC, 1990.

Bleiberg E, Jackson L, Ross J L: Gender identity disorder and object loss. J Am Acad Child Psychiatry *25*: 58, 1986.

Coates S, Person E S: Extreme boyhood femininity: Isolated behavior or pervasive disorder. J Am Acad Child Psychiatry *24*: 702, 1985.

Galenson E, Fields B: Gender disturbance in a 3½-year-old boy. In *The Significance of Infant Observational Research for Clinical Work with Children, Adolescents, and Adults,* S Dowling and A Rothstein, editors. International Universities Press, Madison, Conn, 1989.

Green R: Gender identity in childhood and later sexual orientation: Followup of 78 males. Am J Psychiatry *142*: 399, 1985.

Levine S B: Gender identity disorders of childhood, adolescence, and adulthood. In *Comprehensive Textbook of Psychiatry*, ed 5, H I Kaplan and B J Sadock, editors, p 1061. Williams & Wilkins, Baltimore, 1989.

Lothstein L M: *Female to Male Transsexualism: Historical, Clinical, and Theoretical Issues*. Routledge Kegan Paul, Boston, 1982.

Lothstein L M, Levine S B: Expressive psychotherapy with gender dysphoric patients. Arch Gen Psychiatry *38*: 924, 1981.

Pauley I B, Edgerton M T: The gender identity movement: A growing surgical-psychiatric liaison. Arch Sex Behav *15*: 315, 1986.

Pleak R R, Meyer-Bahlburg H F L, O'Brien J D, Bowen H A, Morganstein A: Cross-gender behavior and psychopathology in boy psychiatric outpatients. J Am Acad Child Adolesc Psychiatry *28*: 385, 1989.

Sreenivasan V: Effeminate boys in a child psychiatric clinic: Prevalence and associated factors. J Am Acad Child Psychiatry *24*: 689, 1985.

Stoller R J: *Presentations of Gender*. Yale University Press, New Haven, CT, 1986.

Walker P, Berger J, Green R, Laub D, Reynolds C, Wollman L: Standards of care: The hormonal and surgical reassignment of gender dysphoric persons. Arch Sex Behav *14*: 79, 1985.

Zucker K J, Green R: Treatment of the gender identity disorder of childhood. In *APA Task Force on the Treatment of Psychiatric Disorders,* T B Karasu, editor. American Psychiatric Press, Washington, DC, 1987.

39

Tic Disorders

In the revised third edition of *Diagnostic and Statistical Manual of Mental Disorders* (DSM-III-R), the tic disorders include Tourette's disorder, chronic motor or vocal tic disorder, transient tic disorder, and tic disorder not otherwise specified (NOS). In recent years the biological underpinnings of Tourette's disorder and the associations among obsessive-compulsive disorder, attention-deficit hyperactivity disorder, stimulant medication, and Tourette's disorder have attracted much attention from researchers.

Tics are involuntary, sudden, rapid, recurrent, nonrhythmic, stereotyped motor movements or vocal productions. They are experienced as irresistible but can be voluntarily suppressed for varying lengths of time, from minutes to hours. DSM-III-R notes the following: Both motor and vocal tics may be classified as either simple or complex, although the boundaries are not well defined. Common simple motor tics are eye blinking, neck jerking, shoulder shrugging, and facial grimacing. Common simple vocal tics are coughing, throat clearing, grunting, sniffing, snorting, and barking. Common complex motor tics are facial gestures, grooming behaviors, hitting or biting self, jumping, touching, stamping, and smelling an object. Common complex vocal tics are repeating words or phrases out of context, coprolalia (use of socially unacceptable words, frequently obscene), palilalia (repeating one's own sounds or words), and echolalia (repeating the last-heard sound, word, or phrase of another person or a last-heard sound). Other complex tics include echokinesis (imitation of the movements of someone who is being observed).

Stresses, such as intense self-consciousness and anxious anticipation, may exacerbate tics. Alternatively, absorption in an activity may attenuate tics. Although most authorities state that tics disappear during sleep, one recent study suggests that at least some persons with Tourette's disorder continue to have tics during sleep.

EPIDEMIOLOGY

Tics appear to be more common in the families of persons with tic disorders than in the general population. They are about three times more frequent in males than in females.

ETIOLOGY

Dysregulation of the neurochemical systems of the central nervous system (CNS) is probably the most important causative factor in the majority of tics. Head trauma also may sometimes precipitate the onset of a tic disorder. Other causes have been proposed, including psychoanalytic explanations, which postulate various psychodynamic mechanisms, and learning theory explanations, which invoke drive-reducing conditioned avoidance responses and classic operant conditioning models.

Stimulants may exacerbate existing tics or cause new tics, probably as a result of the release of dopamine from nigrostriatal dopaminergic nerve terminals. In addition, the dopamine blockers—haloperidol (Haldol) and pimozide (Orap)—are effective in treating tics. The combination of these two factors suggests a dysregulation of dopamine, resulting in a relative hyperdopaminergia in the etiologv of tics. In recent years some patients have developed Tourette's disorder while being treated with antipsychotics. This phenomenon is called tardive Tourette's disorder, and its cause is thought to be similar to that of tardive dyskinesia.

Abnormalities in noradrenergic regulation have also been implicated by the favorable response of some cases of Tourette's disorder to clonidine (Catapres), a noradrenergic blocker, and the worsening of tics caused by anxiety and stress.

Although there is increasing evidence of genetic and disturbed neurochemical functioning, biological heterogeneity (which results in a similar final pathway of symptom expression) must still be considered. No one explanation satisfactorily accounts for the variations in clinical course, response to pharmacological treatment, and family history.

DIAGNOSIS

DSM-III-R emphasizes precise and specific symptom patterns, time frameworks, and age of onset in classifying the tic disorders. Although similar to the third edition of *Diagnostic and Statistical Manual of Mental Disorders* (DSM-III) criteria used for these disorders, the DSM-III-R criteria are different enough to cause confusion and to make it difficult or impossible to compare studies using the different diagnostic criteria.

The exact relationships among the tic disorders are not yet known. DSM-III-R and many therapists postulate a continuum of severity, beginning with transient tics and progressing to Tourette's disorder. Although this is clearly true for many cases, it is uncertain whether all transient tics, which develop and usually disappear during childhood, are related to Tourette's disorder or whether some of them are primarily determined by psychological conflicts or are learned responses.

DIFFERENTIAL DIAGNOSIS

Tics must be reliably differentiated from other disordered movements (e.g., dystonic, choreiform, athetoid, myoclonic, and hemiballismic movements) and the neurological diseases of which they are characteristic (e.g., Huntington's chorea, parkinsonism, Sydenham's chorea, and Wilson's disease), as described in Table 39-1. Tremors, mannerisms, and a stereotypy or habit disorder (e.g., head banging or body rocking) must also be distinguished from tic disorders. The voluntary nature of stereotypy or habit disorder and the fact that such movements do not cause subjective distress differentiate it from tic disorders. Compulsions also are intentional behaviors.

Both autistic and mentally retarded children may exhibit symptoms similar to those seen in the tic disorders, including Tourette's disorder. Tardive dyskinesia must also be considered in those patients who are receiving or have received medications that may cause this untoward effect. Before instituting antipsychotic medication, the clinician must make a careful baseline evaluation of preexisting abnormal movements, as such medication can mask abnormal movements. If these movements occur later, they can be mistaken for tardive dyskinesia.

Stimulant medications (such as methylphenidate [Ritalin], amphetamines, and pemoline [Cylert]) have been reported to exacerbate preexisting tics and to precipitate the development of new tics and Tourette's disorder. This has been reported primarily in some children and adolescents being treated for attention-deficit hyperactivity disorder. In most but not all cases, after the drug was discontinued, the tics remitted or returned to premedication levels. Some authorities believe that stimulants should not be used to treat a child with attention-deficit hyperactivity disorder if the child has or has had tics or Tourette's disorder, that they should be used very cautiously if there is a family history of tics or Tourette's disorder, and that they should be discontinued immediately if the child begins to have tics. Other experts suggest that children and adolescents who develop tics while on stimulants are probably predisposed genetically and would have developed tics regardless of their treatment with stimulants. Until the situation is clarified, there should be great caution and frequent clinical monitoring of children at risk for tics who are given stimulants.

TRANSIENT TIC DISORDER

Diagnosis

The DSM-III-R criteria for establishing the diagnosis of transient tic disorder are as follows: (1) The tics are single or multiple motor or vocal tics; (2) the tics occur many times a day nearly every day for at least two weeks but for no longer than 12 consecutive months; (3) there is no history of Tourette's disorder or chronic motor or vocal tic disorder; (4) the onset is before age 21; and (5) the tic does not occur exclusively during psychoactive substance intoxication or known CNS disease. The diagnosis should also specify whether there has been a single episode or recurrent episodes (Table 39-2).

Transient tic disorder can be distinguished from chronic motor or vocal tic disorder and Tourette's disorder only by following the symptoms' progression over time.

Epidemiology

Transient, ticlike habit movements or nervous muscular twitches are common in children. From 5 to 24 percent of school-age children have a history of tics. The prevalence of tics as defined here is unknown.

Etiology

Transient tics probably have either organic or psychogenic origins, with some tics combining elements of both. Organic tics are probably most likely to progress to Tourette's disorder and have an increased family history of tics, whereas psychogenic tics are most likely to remit spontaneously. Those tics that progress to chronic motor or vocal tic disorder are most likely to have components of both.

Clinical Features

The average age of onset of tics is 7 years, but they may occur as early as 2 years. The most common tic is an eye blink or another facial tic. The most common tics involve the face and then the neck, with a descending gradient of frequency to the feet.

The most commonly described tics are as follows: (1) face and head: grimacing; puckering of forehead; raising eyebrows: blinking eyelids: winking: wrinkling nose; trembling nostrils; twitching mouth; displaying teeth; biting lips and other parts; extruding tongue; protracting lower jaw; nodding, jerking, or shaking the head; twisting neck; looking sideways; and head rolling; (2) arms and hands: jerking hands, jerking arms, plucking fingers, writhing fingers, and clenching fists; (3) body and lower extremities: shrugging shoulders; shaking foot, knee, or toe; peculiarities of gait; body writhing; and jumping; and (4) respiratory and alimentary: hiccuping, sighing, yawning, snuffing, blowing through nostrils, whistling inspiration, exaggerated breathing, belching, sucking or smacking sounds, and clearing throat.

Course and Prognosis

Most persons with transient tic disorder do not progress to a more serious tic disorder. Their tics either disappear permanently or recur during periods of special stress. Only a small percentage go on to chronic motor or vocal tic disorder or Tourette's disorder.

Table 39-1
Differential Diagnosis of Tic Disorders

Disease or Syndrome	Age at Onset	Associated Features	Course	Predominant Type of Movement
Hallervorden-Spatz	Childhood–adolescence	May be associated with optic atrophy, club feet, retinitis pigmentosa, dysarthria, dementia, ataxia, emotional lability, spasticity, autosomal recessive inheritance	Progressive to death in 5 to 20 years	Choreic, athetoid, myoclonic
Dystonia musculorum deformans	Childhood–adolescence	Autosomal recessive inheritance commonly, primarily among Ashkenazi Jews; a more benign autosomal dominant form also occurs	Variable course, often progressive but rare remissions	Dystonia
Sydenham's chorea	Childhood, usually 5–15 years	More common in females, usually associated with rheumatic fever (carditis elevated ASLO titers)	Usually self-limited	Choreiform
Huntington's chorea	Usually 30–50 years, but childhood forms are known	Autosomal dominant inheritance, dementia, caudate atrophy on CT scan	Progressive to death in 10 to 15 years after onset	Choreiform
Wilson's disease (hepatolenticular degeneration)	Usually 10–25 years	Kayser-Fleischer rings, liver dysfunction, inborn error of copper metabolism; autosomal recessive inheritance	Progressive to death without chelating therapy	Wing-beating tremor, dystonia
Hyperekplexias (including latah, myriachit, jumping Frenchman of Maine)	Generally in childhood (dominant inheritance)	Familial; may have generalized rigidity and autosomal inheritance	Nonprogressive	Excessive startle response; may have echolalia, coprolalia, and forced obedience
Myoclonic disorders	Any age	Numerous causes, some familial, usually no vocalizations	Variable, depending on cause	Myoclonus
Myoclonic dystonia	5–47 years	Nonfamilial, no vocalizations	Nonprogressive	Torsion dystonia with myoclonic jerks
Paroxysmal myoclonic dystonia with vocalization	Childhood	Attention, hyperactive, and learning disorders; movements interfere with ongoing activity	Nonprogressive	Bursts of regular, repetitive clonic (less tonic) movements and vocalizations
Tardive Tourette's disorder syndromes	Variable (after antipsychotic medication use)	Reported to be precipitated by discontinuation or reduction of medication	May terminate after increase or decrease of dosage	Orofacial dyskinesias, choreoathetosis, tics, vocalization
Neuroacanthocytosis	Third or fourth decade	Acanthocytosis, muscle wasting, parkinsonism, autosomal recessive inheritance	Variable	Orofacial dyskinesia and limb chorea, tics, vocalization
Encephalitis lethargica	Variable	Shouting fits, bizarre behavior, psychosis, Parkinson's syndrome	Variable	Simple and complex motor and vocal tics, coprolalia, echolalia, echopraxia, palilalia

Table 39-1
Continued

Disease or Syndrome	Age at Onset	Associated Features	Course	Predominant Type of Movement
Gasoline inhalation	Variable	Abnormal EEG; symmetrical theta and theta bursts frontocentrally	Variable	Simple motor and vocal tics
Postangiographic complications	Variable	Emotional lability, amnestic syndrome	Variable	Simple motor and complex vocal tics, palilalia
Postinfectious	Variable	EEG: occasional asymmetrical theta bursts before movements, elevated ASLO titers	Variable	Simple motor and vocal tics, echopraxia
Posttraumatic	Variable	Asymmetrical tic distribution	Variable	Complex motor tics
Carbon monoxide poisoning	Variable	Inappropriate sexual behavior	Variable	Simple and complex motor and vocal tics, coprolalia, echolalia, palilialia
XYY genetic disorder	Infancy	Aggressive behavior	Static	Simple motor, vocal tics
XXY and 9_p mosaicism	Infancy	Multiple physical anomalies, mental retardation	Static	Simple motor, vocal tics
Duchenne muscular dystrophy (X-linked recessive)	Childhood	Mild mental retardation	Progressive	Motor, vocal tics
Fragile X syndrome	Childhood	Mental retardation, facial dysmorphism, seizures, autistic features	Static	Simple motor, vocal tics, coprolalia
Developmental and perinatal disorders	Infancy, childhood	Seizures, EEG and CT abnormalities, psychosis, agressivity, hyperactivity, Ganser syndrome, compulsivity, torticollis	Variable	Motor and vocal tics, echolalia

Table adapted from A K Shapiro, E Shapiro, J G Young, T E Feinberg: *Gilles de la Tourette Syndrome,* ed 2. Raven Press, New York, 1987, with permission.

Table 39-2
Diagnostic Criteria for Transient Tic Disorder

A. Single or multiple motor and/or vocal tics.

B. The tics occur many times a day, nearly every day for at least two weeks, but for no longer than 12 consecutive months.

C. No history of Tourette's or chronic motor or vocal tic disorder.

D. Onset before age 21.

E. Occurrence not exclusively during psychoactive substance intoxication or known central nervous system disease, such as Huntington's chorea and postviral encephalitis.

Specify: single episode or **recurrent.**

Table from DSM-III-R, *Diagnostic and Statistical Manual of Mental Disorders,* ed 3, revised. Copyright American Psychiatric Association, Washington, DC, 1987, with permission.

Treatment

It is initially unclear whether the tics will disappear spontaneously, progress, or become chronic. As focusing attention on tics may exacerbate them, it is often recommended to the family that, at first, they disregard them as much as possible. But if the tics are so severe as to impair the patient or if they are accompanied by significant emotional disturbance, complete psychiatric and pediatric neurological examinations are recommended. Treatment depends on the results of the evaluations. Psychopharmacology is not recommended unless the symptoms are unusually severe and disabling. Several studies have found that behavioral techniques, particularly habit reversal treatments, have been effective in treating transient tics.

CHRONIC MOTOR OR VOCAL TIC DISORDER

Diagnosis

The DSM-III-R criteria for establishing the diagnosis of chronic motor or vocal tic disorder are (1) the presence of either motor or vocal tics but not both, as in Tourette's disorder; (2) the tics' occurrence many times daily nearly every day or intermittently for more than one year; (3) onset before age 21; and (4) occurrence not exclusively during psychoactive substance intoxication or known CNS disease (Table 39-3).

This diagnosis is composed of two mutually exclusive diagnoses—those for chronic motor tic disorder and those for chronic vocal tic disorder.

Epidemiology

The combined incidence of chronic motor tic disorder and Tourette's disorder has been estimated at 1.6 percent of the population.

Chronic tic disorders are less well studied and may be rarer than Tourette's disorder.

Course and Prognosis

The onset appears to be in early childhood. The types of tics and their locations are similar to those in transient tic disorder. Chronic vocal tic disorder is considerably rarer than chronic motor tic disorder. Chronic vocal tics are usually much less conspicuous than those in Tourette's disorder. They often are not loud or intense and consist of grunts or other noises caused by thoracic, abdominal, or diaphragmatic contractions; the tics are not primarily from the vocal cords.

Children whose tics start between the ages of 6 and 8 years seem to have the best outcomes. Symptoms usually last for four to six years and stop in early adolescence. Those children whose tics involve the limbs or the trunk tend to do less well than those with only facial tics.

Treatment

The treatment depends on the severity and the frequency of the tics; the subjective distress; the effects of the tics on school or work, job performance, and socialization; and the presence of any other concomitant psychiatric disorder.

Psychotherapy may be indicated to focus on what may be the primary emotional conflict or to minimize the secondary emotional problems caused by the tics. Several studies have found that behavior techniques, particularly habit reversal treatments, have been effective in treating chronic tic disorder. Minor tranquilizers have not been successful. Haloperidol has been helpful in some cases, but the risks must be weighed against the possible clinical benefits because of the adverse effects of this drug, including the development of tardive dyskinesia.

Table 39-3
Diagnostic Criteria for Chronic Motor or Vocal Tic Disorder

A. Either motor or vocal tics, but not both, have been present at some time during the illness.

B. The tics occur many times a day, nearly every day, or intermittently throughout a period of more than one year.

C. Onset before age 21.

D. Occurrence not exclusively during psychoactive substance intoxication or known central nervous system disease, such as Huntington's chorea and postviral encephalitis.

Table from DSM-III-R, *Diagnostic and Statistical Manual of Mental Disorders,* ed 3, revised. Copyright American Psychiatric Association, Washington, DC, 1987, with permission.

TOURETTE'S DISORDER

Gilles de la Tourette first described a patient with what came to be known as Tourette's disorder in 1885 while studying under Jean-Martin Charcot at the Salpêtrière Clinic in Paris.

Clinical Features and Diagnosis

The DSM-III-R criteria for diagnosing Tourette's disorder are as follows: (1) the presence of both multiple motor and one or more vocal tics at some time during the illness, not necessarily concurrently; (2) the tics' occurrence many times daily (usually in bouts) nearly every day or intermittently for more than one year; (3) a change in the tics' anatomical location, number, frequency, complexity, and severity over time; (4) age of onset before 21 years; and (5) occurrence not exclusively during psychoactive substance intoxication or known CNS disease (Table 39-4). A clinical case example follows:

A 46-year-old married man was referred for evaluation in 1966 because of unremitting tics. At age 13 he had a persistent eye blink, soon followed by lip smacking, head shaking, and barkinglike noises. In spite of these symptoms, he functioned well academically and eventually graduated from high school with honors. He was drafted during World War II. In the army his tics subsided significantly but were still troublesome and eventually resulted in a medical discharge. He married, had two children, and worked as a semiskilled laborer and foreman. At the age of 30, his symptoms included tics of the head, neck, and shoulders; hitting his forehead with his hand and various objects; repeated throat clearing; spitting; and shouting out, "Hey, hey, hey; la, la, la." Six years later, noisy coprolalia started; he would emit a string of profanities—such as "Fuck you, you cocksucking bastard"—in the middle of a sentence and then resume his conversation.

From 1951 to 1957, various treatments, all without benefit, were tried: insulin shock therapy, electroshock treatment, and the administration of various phenothiazines and antidepressants. The patient's social life became increasingly constricted because of his symptoms. He was unable to go to church or to the movies because of the cursing and noises. He worked at night to avoid social embarrassment. His family and friends became increasingly intolerant of his symptoms, and his daughters refused to bring friends home. He was depressed because of his enforced isolation and the seeming hopelessness of finding effective treatment. At the age of 46, he sought a

Table 39-4
Diagnostic Criteria for Tourette's Disorder

A. Both multiple motor and one or more vocal tics have been present at some time during the illness, although not necessarily concurrently.

B. The tics occur many times a day (usually in bouts), nearly every day or intermittently throughout a period of more than one year.

C. The anatomic location, number, frequency, complexity, and severity of the tics change over time.

D. Onset before age 21.

E. Occurrence not exclusively during psychoactive substance intoxication or known central nervous system disease, such as Huntington's chorea and postviral encephalitis.

Table from DSM-III-R, *Diagnostic and Statistical Manual of Mental Disorders,* ed 3, revised. Copyright American Psychiatric Association, Washington, DC, 1987, with permission.

prefrontal lobotomy; but, after psychiatric evaluation, his request was denied. That led to the 1966 referral.

Discussion. This patient had the characteristic features of Tourette's disorder: onset before age 21, multiple motor and one or more vocal tics (involuntary cursing or shouting), the tics' occurring many times a day (usually in bouts) nearly every day or intermittently throughout a period of more than one year, and changes over time in the anatomical location, number, frequency, complexity, and severity of the tics.

It is largely for historical reasons that this disorder is classified as a mental disorder, rather than a neurological disorder. Originally, the coprolalia and other bizarre symptoms were thought to represent pregenital conversion symptoms. Now most investigators believe that the cause of the disorder is organic and that whatever psychological disturbance may be present is best understood as a reaction to the chronic, incapacitating symptoms. In this case, when the symptoms of Tourette's disorder were brought under control, the patient was no longer depressed.

When the patient was evaluated, he was described as being "depressed because of his enforced isolation and the seeming hopelessness of finding effective treatment." This raised the question of adjustment disorder with depressed mood or of major depression. The concept of adjustment disorder generally does not include situations in which patients are distressed because of the consequences of the symptoms of their mental disorder or the reaction of others to the disorder. Such distress is commonplace in chronic illnesses and is better thought of as an associated feature of the illness, rather than an adjustment disorder. However, if the depression were so severe as to meet the criteria for major depression, the additional diagnosis of major depression would be appropriate. In this case there was no information about the other features of a depressive syndrome that would be necessary to make such a diagnosis.

Epidemiology

The prevalence of full-blown Tourette's disorder has been estimated to be minimally 1 per 2,000 (0.05 percent). If Tourette's disorder and multiple tics are considered to be part of a genetically determined spectrum, one review estimates the prevalence of this diathesis would approach 1 per 200 to 300 persons.

Sons of mothers with Tourette's disorder appear to have the highest risk of the disorder. There is evidence for a genetic association between Tourette's disorder and obsessive-compulsive disorder and some evidence for a genetic association between Tourette's disorder and attention-deficit hyperactivity disorder. The ratio of males to females with this disorder is approximately 3 to 1.

Etiology

Tourette's disorder is basically an organic illness. Relatives of Tourette's disorder patients are at an increased risk for Tourette's disorder or another tic disorder. In a sample of 43 twin pairs, there was a concordance rate of 53 percent in the monozygotic twins, as compared with 8 percent in the dizygotic pairs. Some researchers believe that Tourette's disorder is inherited as an autosomal dominant genetic disorder.

Visuomotor problems are common in Tourette's disorder. An estimated 10 to 65 percent of patients have nonspecific electroencephalogram (EEG) findings. Computed tomography (CT) scan studies of the brain reveal that approximately 10 percent of those with Tourette's disorder have a nonspecific abnormality. Evidence supportive of central dopamine dysregulation includes the benefits of antidopaminergic agents like haloperidol; reduced homovanillic acid in the plasma or cerebrospinal fluid (CSF) of some with Tourette's disorder; and exacerbation and possibly precipitation of Tourette's disorder with dopaminergic stimulant medication.

Course and Prognosis

Typically, prodromal behavioral symptoms—such as irritability, attention difficulties, and poor frustration tolerance—are evident before or coincide with the onset of tics. Over 25 percent of the persons in some studies received stimulants for a diagnosis of attention-deficit hyperactivity disorder before receiving a diagnosis of Tourette's disorder.

The first tics usually begin between the ages of 2 and 10 years and almost always before the age of 14 years. The mean age of onset is between 7 and 8 years. The most frequent initial symptom is an eye-blink tic, followed by a head tic or facial grimace. Most of the complex motor and vocal symptoms emerge several years after the initial symptoms. Coprolalia (obscene words) usually begins in early adolescence and occurs in about one-third of all cases. Mental coprolalia—in which there is a sudden, intrusive, socially unacceptable thought or obscene word—may also occur. In some severe cases, physical injuries, including retinal detachment and orthopedic problems, have resulted from severe tics.

Obsessions, compulsions, attention difficulties, impulsivity, and personality problems have been associated with Tourette's disorder. Attention difficulties often precede the onset of tics, whereas obsessive-compulsive symptoms often occur after the onset of tics. It is still being debated whether these problems usually develop secondarily to the patient's tics or are caused primarily by the same underlying pathobiological condition.

Many tics have an aggressive or sexual component, which may result in serious social consequences for the tiqueur. Phenomenologically, the tics resemble a failure of censorship, both conscious and unconscious, with increased impulsivity and a too-ready transformation of thought into action.

Untreated, Tourette's disorder is usually a chronic, lifelong disease with relative remissions and exacerbations. Initial symptoms may decrease, persist, or increase, and old symptoms may be replaced by new ones. Severely afflicted persons may have serious emotional problems, including major depression. Some of these difficulties appear to be associated with the disorder, whereas others result from severe social, academic, and vocational consequences, which are frequent sequelae of the disorder. In some cases despair over the disruption of social and occupational functioning is so severe that the persons contemplate and attempt suicide. On a more positive note, some children with Tourette's disorder have satisfactory peer relations, function well in school, and have adequate self-esteem; they may need no treatment and can be monitored by their pediatrician.

Treatment

Pharmacological treatments are most effective for Tourette's disorder, but those with mild cases may not require medication. Psychotherapy is usually ineffective as a primary treatment modality, although it may help the patient cope with the symptoms of this disorder and any concomitant personality and behavioral difficulties that arise.

Several behavioral techniques—including massed (negative) practice, self-monitoring, incompatible response training, presentation and removal of positive reinforcement, and habit reversal treatment—were reviewed by S. A. Hobbs. He reported that tic frequencies were reduced in many cases, particularly with habit reversal treatment, but relatively few studies have reported clinically significant change. In general, behavioral treatments were most effective in treating transient and chronic tic disorders, but relatively few cases of Tourette's disorder responded favorably. Behavior therapy currently seems most useful in reducing stresses that may aggravate Tourette's disorder. Whether there is a synergistic effect when behavior therapy is combined with pharmacotherapy has not been sufficiently investigated.

Pharmacotherapy. Haloperidol is the most frequently prescribed drug for Tourette's disorder. Up to 80 percent of patients have a favorable response; their symptoms decrease by as much as 70 to 90 percent of baseline frequencies. Follow-up studies, however, suggest that only 20 to 30 percent of patients continue on long-term maintenance. Discontinuation is often based on adverse effects of the drug.

Haloperidol appears to be most effective at relatively low dosages. The initial daily dosage for adolescents and adults is usually between 0.25 mg and 0.5 mg of haloperidol. Haloperidol is not approved for use in children under 3 years of age. For children between 3 and 12, it is recommended that a total daily dosage of between 0.05 mg per kg and 0.075 mg per kg be administered in divided doses either two or three times a day. Thus, this dosage imposes a daily limit of 3 mg of haloperidol for a 40-kg child. The dosage for all patients should be increased slowly, to minimize the likelihood of an acute dystonic reaction. The maximum effective dosage in adolescents and adults is often in the range of 3 to 4 mg a day, but some patients require higher dosages of up to 10 to 15 mg a day.

Patients and their parents, when appropriate, must be made aware of the drug's possible immediate and long-term adverse effects. It is particularly important to forewarn them of the possibilities of acute dystonic reactions and parkinsonian symptoms. Although prophylactic use of an anticholinergic agent is not recommended, it is appropriate to prescribe diphenhydramine (Benadryl) or benztropine (Cogentin) to the patient, so that it is available should an acute dystonic reaction or parkinsonian effects occur at home or on vacation. Other effects of special concern are cognitive dulling, which can impair school performance and learning, and the risk of developing tardive dyskinesia. School phobias in children and disabling social phobias in adults have been reported during the early phase of treatment, but the phobias usually remit within a few weeks after discontinuing haloperidol.

Pimozide, an inhibitor of postsynaptic dopamine receptors, is also effective in treating Tourette's disorder. In a recent large study haloperidol was somewhat more effective than pimozide. Pimozide, like haloperidol, should not be used to treat simple tics. Pimozide is an antipsychotic and has adverse effects similar to those of other antipsychotics. Furthermore, adverse cardiac effects are unusually frequent, and deaths have occurred at high dosages. Notwithstanding this, pimozide appears to be safe at recommended dosages, with cardiotoxicity limited to prolonged QT wave intervals. Electrocardiograms must be performed at baseline and periodically during treatment. There is little experience in administering this drug to children under age 12 years.

The initial dosage of pimozide is usually 1 to 2 mg daily in divided doses and may be increased every other day. Most patients are maintained at less than 0.2 mg per kg a day or 10 mg a day, whichever is less. It is recommended that a dosage of 0.3 mg per kg a day or 20 mg a day never be exceeded.

Although not presently approved for use in Tourette's disorder, clonidine, a noradrenergic antagonist, has been reported in several studies to be efficacious; 40 to 70 percent of patients benefited from this medication. It has been used by some clinicians after they have carefully considered its risks and benefits and fully informed the patient and, when appropriate, the parents of the situation. Clonidine has a slower onset of action than does haloperidol, and improvement may continue for more than a year in some cases. In addition to the improvement in tic symptoms, patients may experience less tension, a greater sense of well-being, and a longer attention span.

Children suffering from tics and severe attention-deficit hyperactivity disorder can be treated with desipramine for

Table 39-5
Diagnostic Criteria for Tic Disorder Not Otherwise Specified

Tics that do not meet the criteria for a specific tic disorder. An example is a tic disorder with onset in adulthood.

Table from DSM-III-R, *Diagnostic and Statistical Manual of Mental Disorders,* ed 3, revised. Copyright American Psychiatric Association, Washington, DC, 1987, with permission.

their attention problems. The benzodiazepines may be useful in diminishing anxiety in some patients, but they do not appear to significantly reduce the frequency of tics.

TIC DISORDER NOT OTHERWISE SPECIFIED

Tic disorder not otherwise specified (NOS) is a residual category for tics that do not meet the criteria for a specific tic disorder (Table 39-5). All tic disorders with onset after age 21 must be diagnosed as tic disorder NOS.

References

Caine E D, McBride M C, Chiverton P, Bamford K A, Rediess S, Shiao J: Tourette's syndrome in Monroe County school children. Neurology *38*: 472, 1988.

Cohen D J, Leckman J F, Shaywitz B A: The Tourette's syndrome and other tics. In *The Clinical Guide to Child Psychiatry,* D Shaffer, A A Ehrandt, and L L Greenhill, editors, p 3. Free Press, New York, 1985.

Friedhoff A J, Chase T N, eds.: *Gilles de la Tourette Syndrome.* Raven Press, New York, 1982.

Hobbs S A, Dorsett P G, Dahlquist L M: Tic disorders. In *Behavior Therapy with Children and Adolescents: A Clinical Approach,* M Hersen and V B Van Hasselt, editors, p 241. Wiley, New York, 1987.

Leckman, J F, Walkup J T, Riddle M A, Toubin K E, Cohen D J: Tic disorders. In *Psychopharmocology: The Third Generation of Progress,* H Y Meltzer, editor. Raven Press, New York, 1987.

Pauls D L, Hurst C R, Kruger S D, Leckman J F, Kidd K K, Cohen D J: Gilles de la Tourette's syndrome and attention deficit disorder with hyperactivity. Arch Gen Psychiatry *43*: 1177, 1986.

Pauls D L, Toubin K E, Leckman J F, Zahmer G E P, Cohen D J: Gilles de la Tourette's syndrome and obsessive-compulsive disorder. Arch Gen Psychiatry *43*: 1180, 1986.

Price R A, Kidd K K, Cohen D J, Pauls D L, Leckman J F: A twin study of Tourette's syndrome Arch Gen Psychiatry *43*: 815, 1985.

Riddle M A, Hardin M T, Cho S C, Woolston J L, Leckman J F: Desipramine treatment of boys with attention-deficit hyperactivity disorder and tics: Preliminary clinical experience. J Am Acad Child Adolesc Psychiatry *27*: 811, 1988.

Riddle M A, Leckman J F, Anderson G M, Ort S I, Hardin M T, Stevenson J, Cohen D J: Tourette's syndrome: Clinical and neurochemical correlates. J Am Acad Child Adolesc Psychiatry *27*: 409, 1989.

Robertson M M: The Gilles de la Tourette syndrome: The current status Br J Psychiatry *154*: 147, 1989.

Segal N L, Dysken M W, Bouchard T J, Petersen N L, Eckert E D, Heston L L: Tourette's disorder in a set of reared-apart triplets: Genetic and environmental influences. Am J Psychiatry *147*: 196, 1990.

Shapiro A K, Shapiro E: Tic disorders. In *Comprehensive Textbook of Psychiatry,* ed 5, H I Kaplan and B J Sadock, editors, p 1865. Williams & Wilkins, Baltimore, 1989.

Shapiro E, Shapiro A K, Fulop G, Hubbard M, Mendell J, Nordie J, Phillips R: Controlled study of haloperidol, pimozide and placebo for the treatment of Gilles de la Tourette's syndrome. Arch Gen Psychiatry *46*: 722, 1989.

Elimination Disorders

In elimination disorders the biopsychosocial determinants of behavior intermingle in complex patterns. Toilet training is affected by a child's maturational level and intellectual capacity, cultural attitudes, and the psychological makeup of each parent-child dyad.

Bowel control and bladder control usually develop gradually and sequentially. The normal sequence of attaining these milestones is (1) the development of nocturnal fecal continence, (2) the development of diurnal fecal continence, (3) the development of diurnal bladder control, and (4) the development of nocturnal bladder control.

FUNCTIONAL ENCOPRESIS

Diagnosis

Functional encopresis is fecal soiling past the time that bowel control is physiologically possible and after toilet training should have been accomplished. The revised third edition of *Diagnostic and Statistical Manual of Mental Disorders* (DSM-III-R) criteria for functional encopresis are given in Table 40-1. The feces may be of normal, near normal, or liquid consistency. This permits the inclusion of some but not all cases of overflow incontinence, the cause of the majority of functional encopresis seen by pediatricians. DSM-III-R states that the child's chronological and mental age must be at least 4 years and that fecal mishaps must have occurred at least once monthly for at least six months.

DSM-III-R also specifies a primary type and a secondary type of functional encopresis. Encopretic children are classified as primary type if the encopresis continues after both chronological and mental ages have reached at least 4 years and there has not been a prior period of fecal continence lasting at least one year. Encopresis that develops anytime after a yearlong period of continence is termed secondary encopresis.

Table 40-1
Diagnostic Criteria for Functional Encopresis

A. Repeated passage of feces into places not appropriate for that purpose (e.g., clothing, floor), whether involuntary or intentional. (The disorder may be overflow incontinence secondary to functional fecal retention.)

B. At least one such event a month for at least six months.

C. Chronologic and mental age, at least 4 years.

D. Not due to a physical disorder, such as aganglionic megacolon.

Specify primary or secondary type.

Primary type: the disturbance was not preceded by a period of fecal continence lasting at least one year.
Secondary type: the disturbance was preceded by a period of fecal continence lasting at least one year.

Table from DSM-III-R, *Diagnostic and Statistical Manual of Mental Disorders,* ed 3, revised. Copyright American Psychiatric Association, Washington, DC, 1987, with permission.

Epidemiology

In Western culture, bowel control is established in more than 95 percent of children by the fourth birthday and in 99 percent by the fifth birthday. Thereafter, frequency decreases to virtual absence by age 16. After age 4, functional encopresis at all ages is three to four times as common in boys as in girls. By ages 7 to 8, frequency is 2.3 percent in boys and 0.7 percent in girls. By ages 10 to 12, once-a-month soiling occurs in 1.3 percent of boys and in 0.3 percent of girls.

Etiology

Lack of appropriate toilet training or inadequate training may delay the child's attainment of continence. There is also evidence that some encopretic children suffer from lifelong inefficient and ineffective gastrointestinal motility. Either of these factors alone but especially the two in combination offer an opportunity for a power struggle between the child and the parent over issues of autonomy and control; such battles often aggravate the disorder, frequently causing secondary behavioral difficulties. Many encopretic children, however, do not have behavioral problems. When behavioral problems do occur, they are the social consequences of soiling.

Encopretic children who are clearly able to control their bowel function adequately and who deposit feces of relatively normal consistency in abnormal places usually have a psychiatric difficulty.

Functional encopresis may be associated with other neurodevelopmental problems, including easy distractibility, short attention span, low frustration tolerance, hyperactivity, and poor coordination. Occasionally, the child has a special fear of using the toilet. Functional encopresis may also be precipitated by life events, such as the birth of a sibling or a move to a new home.

Secondary encopresis sometimes appears to be a regression after such stresses as the birth of a sibling, a parental separation, a change in domicile, or the start of school.

Psychogenic megacolon. Many encopretic children also retain feces and become constipated either voluntarily or secondary to painful defecation. In these cases there is no clear evidence that preexisting anorectal dysfunction contributes to the constipation. The resulting chronic rectal distention from large, hard fecal masses may cause loss of tone in the rectal wall and desensitization to pressure. Thus, many children become unaware of the need to defecate, and overflow encopresis occurs, usually with relatively small amounts of liquid or soft stool leaking out. Olfactory accommodation may diminish or eliminate sensory cues.

Clinical Features

Long-term studies are lacking, but in many cases encopresis is self-limiting, rarely continuing beyond middle adolescence.

Encopresis is a particularly repugnant symptom to most people and may lead to severe intrafamilial tensions and social ostracism. The encopretic child is often scapegoated and ridiculed by peers and shunned by adults. Psychologically, the patient may appear blunted to the effect of the disorder on other people, but most encopretic children have abysmally low self-esteem and realize that they are unwanted.

Differential Diagnosis

In overflow incontinence, constipation can begin as early as the first year, peaking between the second and fourth years. Soiling usually begins at age 4. There are frequent liquid stools and hard fecal masses in the colon and rectum on abdominal palpation and rectal examination. Complications include impaction, megacolon, and anal fissures.

Overflow incontinence, resulting from constipation, can be caused by faulty nutrition; structural disease of the anus, rectum, and colon; medicinal side effects; or nongastrointestinal medical (endocrine or neurological) disorders. The chief differential problem is that of aganglionic megacolon or Hirschprung's disease, in which the patient may have an empty rectum and no desire to defecate but may still have an overflow of feces. It occurs in 1 in 5,000 children, with signs appearing shortly after birth.

Treatment

By the time a child is brought in for treatment, there is considerable family discord and distress. Family tensions regarding the symptom must be reduced, and a nonpunitive atmosphere must be created. Similar efforts should be made to reduce the child's embarrassment at school. Multiple changes of underwear with a minimum of fuss should be arranged.

Psychotherapy is useful for easing family tensions, for treating the encopretic children's reactions to their symptoms (such as low self-esteem and social isolation), for addressing the psychodynamic causes present in those children who have bowel control but continue to deposit their feces in inappropriate locations, and for treating those cases of secondary encopresis that are reactions to psychological stressors. A good outcome occurs when the child feels in control of life events. Coexisting behavior problems predict a poor outcome.

Behavioral techniques have been used with great success, including such behavior reinforcers as star charts, in which the child places a star on a chart for dry or continent nights.

A pediatrician should be consulted in cases of overflow incontinence secondary to fecal retention. First, the bowel must be cleared and then stool frequency maintained with stool softeners or laxatives. Proper bowel habits should be taught. Biofeedback techniques can be of help.

FUNCTIONAL ENURESIS

Diagnosis

Functional enuresis is manifested as a repetitive and inappropriate passage of urine. The voiding may be involuntary or voluntary. For instance, persons may intentionally fail to inhibit the reflex to pass urine, and at night some admit to being awake and choosing to urinate in bed, rather than get up and go to the toilet. A minimum chronological age of 5 years and a minimum mental age of 4 years are required. The DSM-III-R criteria for the diagnosis of functional enuresis are given in Table 40-2.

Functional enuresis is characterized as primary if the child has never been continent for a minimum of one year and secondary if the enuresis began after one year of dryness. The clinician should further note whether the enuresis is diurnal—that is, occurring during the daytime—or nocturnal, the most common form, or both. These classifications have practical diagnostic and therapeutic applications.

Table 40-2
Diagnostic Criteria for Functional Enuresis

A. Repeated voiding of urine during the day or night into bed or clothes, whether involuntary or intentional.

B. At least two such events per month for children between the ages of 5 and 6, and at least one event per month for older children.

C. Chronologic age at least 5, and mental age at least 4.

D. Not due to a physical disorder, such as diabetes, urinary tract infection, or a seizure disorder.

Specify primary or secondary type.

Primary type: the disturbance was not preceded by a period of urinary continence lasting at least one year.
Secondary type: the disturbance was preceded by a period of urinary continence lasting at least one year.

Specify nocturnal only, diurnal, or **nocturnal and diurnal**.

Table from DSM-III-R, *Diagnostic and Statistical Manual of Mental Disorders,* ed 3, revised. Copyright American Psychiatric Association, Washington, DC, 1987, with permission.

Epidemiology

Prevalence rates vary depending on the population studied and methods used in collecting the data. Reporting is influenced by the tolerance of symptoms in various cultures and socioeconomic groups. It seems clear, however, that there is a high incidence in institutions and in low socioeconomic groups. The incidence in boys outnumbers that in girls two to one in all studies.

There is a sharply decreasing prevalence up to age 4 and a gradual decline thereafter: 82 percent of 2-year-olds, 49 percent of 3-year-olds, 26 percent of 4-year-olds, 7 percent of 5-year-olds, 3 percent of 10-year-olds, and 1½ percent of 14-year-olds are enuretic. The adult prevalence is given at about 1 percent.

Psychiatric problems are present in only about 20 percent of enuretic children and are most common in enuretic girls and in children who wet both day and night.

Etiology

Normal bladder control is acquired gradually and is influenced by neuromuscular and cognitive development, socioemotional factors, toilet training, and, possibly, genetic factors. Difficulties in one or more of these areas may delay urinary continence. Although an organic cause precludes a diagnosis of functional enuresis, the correction of an anatomical defect or the cure of an infection does not always cure the enuresis, suggesting that the cause may be functional in some of those cases.

In a longitudinal study of child development, those children who were enuretic were about twice as likely to have concomitant developmental delays as were dry children.

About 75 percent of enuretic children have a first-degree relative who is or was enuretic. The concordance rate is higher in monozygotic twins than in dizygotic twins. Although there may be a genetic component, much could be accounted for by tolerance of enuresis in these families and by other psychosocial factors.

Some studies report that enuretic children have a bladder with a normal anatomical capacity when anesthetized but a functionally small bladder, so that there is an urge to void with little urine in the bladder. Other studies report that bedwetting occurs because the bladder is full and there is an absence of the high levels of a nighttime antidiuretic hormone. These factors allow for a higher than usual urine output. Enuresis does not appear to be related to a specific stage of sleep or time of night; rather, bed-wetting appears randomly. In most cases the quality of sleep is normal. There is little evidence that enuretic children sleep more soundly than other children.

Psychosocial stressors appear to precipitate some cases of secondary enuresis. In young children this disorder has been particularly associated with the birth of a sibling, hospitalization between the ages of 2 and 4, the start of school, the breakup of a family because of divorce or death, and a move to a new domicile.

Clinical Features

Functional enuresis is usually self-limited. The child can eventually remain dry without psychiatric sequelae. Most enuretic children find their symptom ego-dystonic and have enhanced self-esteem and improved social confidence when they become continent.

About 80 percent of affected children have primary enuresis, never having achieved a yearlong period of dryness. Secondary enuresis usually begins between ages 5 and 8 years; if it occurs much later, especially during adulthood, organic causes must be investigated. There is some evidence that secondary enuresis in children is more frequently associated with a concomitant psychiatric difficulty than is primary enuresis. Relapses occur in enuretics who are becoming dry spontaneously and in those who are being treated.

The significant emotional and social difficulties of enuretic children usually result from the primary symptom and include poor self-image, decreased self-esteem, social embarrassment and restriction, and intrafamilial conflict.

Differential Diagnosis

Although the large majority of enuretic cases are functional, possible organic causes must be ruled out. Organic features are found most often in children with both nocturnal and diurnal enuresis combined with urinary frequency and urgency. The organic features include (1) genitourinary pathology—structural, neurological, and infectious—such as obstructive uropathy, spina bifida occulta, and cystitis; (2) other organic disorders that may cause polyuria and enuresis, such as diabetes mellitus and diabetes insipidus; (3) disturbances of consciousness and sleep, such as seizures, intoxication, and somnambulism during which the person urinates; and (4) side effects from treatment with antipsychotics (for example, thioridazine [Mellaril]).

Treatment

Because there is usually no identifiable cause in functional enuresis and because it tends to remit spontaneously, even if not treated, some success has been achieved by a number of methods.

Appropriate toilet training. Appropriate toilet training with parental reinforcement should have been attempted, especially in primary enuresis. If toilet training was not attempted, the parents and the patient should be guided in this undertaking. Record keeping is helpful in determining a baseline and following the child's progress and may itself be a reinforcer. A star chart may be particularly helpful. Other useful techniques include restricting fluids before bed and night lifting to toilet train the child.

Behavior therapy. Classic conditioning with the bell (or buzzer) and pad apparatus is generally the most effective treatment for functional enuresis. Dryness results in over 50 percent of cases. This treatment is equally effective in children with and without concomitant psychiatric disorders, and there is no evidence of symptom substitution. Difficulties may include child and family noncompliance, improper use of the apparatus, and relapse.

Bladder training—encouragement or reward for delaying micturition for increasing lengths of time during waking hours—has also been used. Although sometimes effective, this method is decidedly inferior to the bell and pad.

Pharmacotherapy. Drugs should rarely be used to treat enuresis and then only as a last resort in intractable cases causing serious socioemotional difficulty for the sufferer. Imipramine (Tofranil) is efficacious and has been approved for use in treating childhood enuresis, primarily on a short-term basis. Initially, up to 30 percent of enuretics stay dry, and up to 85 percent wet less frequently. This success, however, does not often last. Tolerance often develops after six weeks of therapy. Once the drug is discontinued, relapse and enuresis at former frequencies usually occur within a few months. A more serious problem is the adverse effects of the drug, which include cardiotoxiocity. Desmopressin, an antidiuretic compound that is administered as an intranasal spray, has shown some initial success in reducing functional enuresis.

Psychotherapy. Although there have been many psychological and psychoanalytic theories regarding enuresis, controlled studies have found that psychotherapy alone is not an effective treatment of enuresis. Psychotherapy, however, may be useful in dealing with the emotional and family difficulties that arise secondary to the symptom and with coexisting psychiatric problems.

References

Friman P C, Matthews J R, Finney J W, Christophersen E R, Leibowitz J M: Do encopretic children have clinically significant behavior problems? Pediatrics *82*: 407, 1988.

Fournier J-P, Garfinkel B D, Bond A, Becuchesne H, Shapiro S K: Pharmacological and behavioral management of enuresis. J Am Acad Child Adolesc Psychiatry *26*: 849, 1987.

Hatch T F: Encopresis and constipation in children. Pediatr Clin North Am *35*: 257, 1988.

Hersov L: Faecal soiling. In *Child and Adolescent Psychiatry: Modern Approaches,* ed 2, M Rutter and L Hersov, editors, p 482. Blackwell, Oxford, England, 1985.

Kisch E H, Pfeffer C R: Functional encopresis: Psychiatric inpatient treatment. Am J Psychother *38*: 264, 1984.

Landman G B: Locus of control and self-esteem in children with encopresis. J Dev Behav Pediatr *7*: 11, 1986.

LaVietes R L: Functional enuresis. In *Comprehensive Textbook of Psychiatry,* ed 5, H I Kaplan and B J Sadock, editors, p 1883. Williams & Wilkins, Baltimore, 1989.

Loening-Baucke V: Modulation of abnormal defecation dynamics by biofeedback treatment in chronically constipated children with encopresis. J Pediatr *116*: 214, 1990.

Nørgaard J P, Rittig S, Djurkuus J C: Nocturnal enuresis: An approach to treatment based on pathogenesis. J Pediatr *114*: 705, 1989.

Rushton H G: Nocturnal enuresis: Epidemiology, evaluation, and currently available treatment options. J Pediatr *114*: 691, 1989.

Shaffer D: Enuresis. In *Child and Adolescent Psychiatry: Modern Approaches,* ed 2. M Rutter and L Hersov, editors, p 465. Blackwell, Oxford, England, 1985.

Steinhausen H-C, Göbel D: Enuresis in child psychiatric clinic patients. J Am Acad Child Adolesc Psychiatry *28*: 279, 1989.

41

Speech Disorders Not Elsewhere Classified

41.1 / Cluttering

Cluttering is a new classification in the revised third edition of *Diagnostic and Statistical Manual of Mental Disorders* (DSM-III-R). It is defined as a disorder of the rate and rhythm of speech resulting in rapid and jerky spurts of speech (Table 41.1-1).

Table 41.1-1
Diagnostic Criteria for Cluttering

A disorder of speech fluency involving both the rate and the rhythm of speech and resulting in impaired speech intelligibility. Speech is erratic and dysrhythmic, consisting of rapid and jerky spurts that usually involve faulty phasing patterns (e.g., alternating pauses and bursts of speech that produce groups of words unrelated to the grammatical structure of the sentence).

Table from DSM-III-R, *Diagnostic and Statistical Manual of Mental Disorders,* ed 3, revised. Copyright American Psychiatric Association, Washington, DC, 1987, with permission.

EPIDEMIOLOGY

Although its prevalence is unknown, cluttering appears to be a rare condition that has generated very little research. It appears to be more common in males than in females and is less common than stuttering.

ETIOLOGY

The cause of cluttering is not known. There appears to be higher rate of clutterers among the family members of the affected person than among the general population. Some clinical reports indicate that this condition may be present among elementary school children learning English as a second language.

CLINICAL FEATURES AND COURSE

The onset of the disorder is between ages 2 and 8 years. It develops over a period of weeks or months and worsens under emotional stress or pressured situations. Speech is fast, and at times the rapid and jerky spurts make speech sounds unintelligible. Between the rapid bursts of words are pauses that are unrelated to the completion of the sentence, thereby making the presentation of sentences fragmented and incomplete.

About two-thirds of children may recover spontaneously as they approach early adolescence. Cluttering is associated with other DSM-III-R academic skills disorders and language and speech disorders. It is less associated with social isolation, tics, and depression than stuttering. In a small number of severe cases, secondary emotional disorders may result because of poor peer interaction or negative familial response to the child.

DIAGNOSIS AND DIFFERENTIAL DIAGNOSIS

Except in children younger than 2 years, the fully developed disorder is manifested as described in Table 41.1-1.

Cluttering should be differentiated from stuttering, a speech disorder that is characterized by frequent repetitions or prolongations of sounds or syllables, thereby markedly impairing the fluency of speech. A major differential diagnostic feature is that clutterers are usually unaware of their altered fluency. In contrast, most stutterers are painfully aware of their speech difficulties.

TREATMENT

In most moderate to severe cases, speech therapy is indicated. Psychotherapy is indicated when the affected child shows frustration, anxiety, depression, and difficulties in social adjustment with peers and in school. Family therapy may be helpful in enabling the parents to understand their reactions to the disorder and to be supportive of the child.

The long-term effects of speech therapy and various psychotherapeutic approaches are not yet documented; however, such therapies should ameliorate the condition.

References

Bloom L, Lahey M: *Language Development and Language Disorders.* Wiley, New York, 1978.

Chess S, Rosenberg M: Clinical differentiation among children with initial language complaints. J Autism Child Schizophr *4*: 99, 1974.
Pitluk N: Aspects of the expressive language of cluttering and stuttering with school children. S Afr J Commun Disord *29*: 77, 1982.
Weiss D A: *Cluttering*. Prentice-Hall, Englewood Cliffs, NJ, 1964.
Wolk L: Cluttering: A diagnostic case report. Br J Disord Commun *21*: 199, 1986.

41.2 / Stuttering

According to the revised third edition of *Diagnostic and Statistical Manual of Mental Disorders* (DSM-III-R), stuttering is a speech disorder characterized by frequent repetitions or prolongation of sounds or syllables, markedly impairing the fluency of speech. Unusual hesitations and pauses disrupt the rhythmic flow of speech. The cause of the condition is not known. The term "stammering" is used synonymously with "stuttering."

EPIDEMIOLOGY

The percentage of the population who have stuttered is accepted as 3 percent (i.e., 2.5 to 4.5 percent). The percentage of the population currently affected is approximately 1 percent (i.e., 0.8 to 1.5 percent). All studies have indicated a strong sex link, with approximately four males for each female with the disorder.

ETIOLOGY

Although precise causative factors are not known, many theories have been proposed: (1) theories that explain the stuttering block, (2) theories related to conditions under which the disorder has its onset, (3) learning theories, (4) a cybernetic model theory, and (5) brain function theories.

Stuttering Block Theories

Stuttering block theories can be grouped into three areas: genogenic, psychogenic, and semantogenic.

The basic premise of the genogenic model is that the stutterer is biologically different from the nonstutterer. An example is the theory of cerebral dominance, which states that children are predisposed to stutter by a conflict between the two halves of the cerebrum for control of the speech organs' activity. The current consensus is that there may be some sort of constitutional predisposition toward stuttering but that environmental stresses work together with this somatic variant to produce stuttering.

Most psychogenic theories emphasize obsessive-compulsive mechanisms and a variety of psychosocial factors, such as a dysfunctional family. Stuttering is seen as a neurosis caused by the persistence into later life of early pregenital oral-sadistic and anal-sadistic components.

According to the semantogenic theories, stuttering is a learned pathological response to the mislabeling of normal early syllable and word repetitions.

Onset Theories

Onset theories fall into three groups: the breakdown, the repressed-need, and the anticipatory-struggle theories.

The breakdown theories view stuttering as a momentary failure of the complicated coordinations involved in speech. Most such theories regard constitutional or organic factors—that is, the genogenic factors discussed above—as the causes of the breakdown.

The repressed-need theory is based on psychoanalytic concepts and defines stuttering as a neurotic symptom rooted deeply in unconscious needs. Early theories suggested that stuttering satisfies oral gratifications or reflects oral-aggressive or anal-aggressive concerns.

The theme of the anticipatory-struggle theory is that stutterers interfere in some manner with the way they talk because of their belief in the difficulty of speech; that is, stutterers anticipate difficulty with speech.

Learning Theories

Learning theories use feedback models. The stimulus-response theories of learning use the relatively precise language of behavioral science to define the process by which stuttering is learned and maintained by identifying the stimulus variables and reinforcing conditions. One of the central problems in applying learning principles to stuttering is to explain the nature of the reinforcement that causes it to persist, despite repeated punishment.

Cybernetic Model Theory

In the cybernetic model, speech is seen as an automatic process that depends on feedback for regulation. Stuttering may be caused by a breakdown in feedback or in the sensor receptors of this feedback. The observations that stuttering is reduced by white noise and that delayed auditory feedback produces artificial stuttering in normal speakers support this view.

Brain Function Theories

Research on cerebral hemispheric lateralization and specialization suggests that incomplete lateralization of language may result in stuttering. Several studies using electroencephalography report that stuttering males demonstrated right hemisphere alpha suppression across stimulus words and tasks, as contrasted with left hemisphere alpha suppression for nonstuttering males and females. The earlier concern that forcing left-handed children to use the right hand caused stuttering has not been validated.

Recent family and twin studies strongly suggest that stuttering is a genetically inherited neurological disorder. However, the available data are not conclusive at this time.

CLINICAL FEATURES AND COURSE

Stuttering usually appears before the age of 12 years, in most cases between 18 months and 9 years, with two sharp peaks of onset between the ages of 2 to 3½ and 5 to 7 years. Some but not all stutterers have other speech and language problems, such as developmental articulation disorder and developmental expressive language disorder. Stuttering does not suddenly begin; it typically occurs over a period of weeks or months with a repetition of initial consonants, whole words that are usually the first words of a phrase, or long words. As the disorder progresses, the repetitions become more frequent, with consistent stuttering on the most important words or phrases. Even after it develops, stuttering may be absent during oral readings, singing, and talking to pets or inanimate objects.

Four gradually evolving phases in the development of stuttering have been identified.

Phase 1 occurs during the preschool period. Initially, the difficulty tends to be episodic, appearing for periods of weeks or months between long interludes of normal speech. There is a high percentage of recovery from these periods of stuttering. During this phase children stutter most often when excited or upset, when they seem to have a great deal to say, and under other conditions of communicative pressure.

Phase 2 usually occurs in the elementary school years. The disorder is chronic, with few if any intervals of normal speech. Such children become aware of their speech difficulty and regard themselves as stutterers. In this phase the stuttering occurs mainly on the major parts of speech–nouns, verbs, adjectives, and adverbs.

Phase 3 is usually seen after age 8 and up to adulthood. It occurs most often in late childhood and early adolescence. During this phase, the stuttering comes and goes largely in response to specific situations, such as reciting in class, speaking to strangers, making purchases in stores, and using the telephone. Some words and sounds are regarded as more difficult than others.

Phase 4 is typically seen in late adolescence and adulthood. Stutterers show a vivid, fearful anticipation of stuttering. They fear words, sounds, and situations. Word substitutions and circumlocutions are common. Stutterers avoid situations requiring speech and show other evidence of fear and embarrassment.

The course of stuttering is usually long-term, with some periods of partial remission lasting for weeks or months and exacerbations occurring most frequently when the stutterer is under pressure to communicate. Fifty to 80 percent of all children with stuttering, most with mild cases, recover spontaneously.

In chronic cases of stuttering by school-age children, impairment in peer relationships may be a result of teasing and social ostracism. The children may face academic difficulties if they avoid speaking in class. Later major complications include the affected person's limitations in occupational choice and advancement.

The disorder is more common among family members of the affected child than in the general population.

Stutterers may have associated clinical features: vivid, fearful anticipation of stuttering, with avoidance of particular words, sounds, or situations in which stuttering is anticipated; eye blinks; tics; and tremors of the lips or jaw. Frustration, anxiety, and depression are common among chronic stutterers.

DIAGNOSIS

The diagnosis of stuttering is not difficult when the clinical features are apparent and well developed and each of the four phases can be readily recognized. Diagnostic difficulties may arise, however, when trying to determine the existence of stuttering in young children, as some preschool children experience a period of transient dysfluency. It may not be clear whether this nonfluent pattern is part of normal speech and language development, or whether it represents the initial state in the development of stuttering. If incipient stuttering is suspected, referral to a speech pathologist is indicated. Table 41.2-1 presents the DSM-III-R diagnostic criteria for stuttering.

DIFFERENTIAL DIAGNOSIS

Normal speech dysfluency in the preschool years is difficult to differentiate from incipient stuttering. In stuttering there are more nonfluencies, part-word repetitions, sound prolongations, and disruptions in voice airflow through the vocal track.

Spastic dysphonia is a stutteringlike speech disorder and is distinguished from stuttering by the presence of an abnormal pattern of breathing.

Cluttering is a speech disorder characterized by erratic and dysrhythmic speech patterns of rapid and jerky spurts of words and phrases. In cluttering, the affected persons are usually unaware of the disturbance, whereas, after the initial phase of the disorder, stutterers are acutely aware of their speech difficulties.

TREATMENT

Until the end of the 19th century, the most common treatments for stuttering were distraction, suggestion, and relaxation. More recent approaches using distraction include teaching stutterers to talk in time to rhythmic movements of the arm, hand, or fingers. Stutterers are also advised to speak slowly in a sing-song or monotone. These approaches, however, remove the stuttering only temporarily. Suggestion techniques, such as hypnosis, also stop stuttering but, again, only temporarily. Relaxation techniques are based on the premise that it is almost impossible to be relaxed and at the same time to stutter in the usual manner. Because of their lack of long-term benefits, distraction, suggestion, and relaxation approaches as such are not currently used.

Classic psychoanalysis, insight-oriented psychotherapy, group therapy, and other psychotherapeutic modalities have not been successful in treating stuttering. However, if stutterers have a poor self-image, are anxious or depressed, or show evidence of an established neurotic process or another emotional disability, individual psychotherapy is indicated and effective for the associated condition. In one study the reaction of nonstuttering lis-

Table 41.2-1
Diagnostic Criteria for Stuttering

Frequent repetitions or prolongations of sounds or syllables that markedly impair the fluency of speech

Table from DSM-III-R, *Diagnostic and Statistical Manual of Mental Disorders*, ed 3, revised. Copyright American Psychiatric Association, Washington, DC, 1987, with permission.

teners to stutterers who acknowledged their stuttering was much more positive than to stutterers who did not acknowledge their stuttering.

Family therapy should also be considered if there is evidence of family dysfunction, family contribution to the stutterer's symptoms, or family stress caused by trying to cope with or to help the stutterer.

Most of the modern treatments of stuttering are based on the view that stuttering is essentially a learned form of behavior that is not necessarily associated with a basic neurotic personality or neurological abnormalities. These approaches work directly with the speech difficulty to minimize the issues that maintain and strengthen the stuttering, to modify or decrease the severity of the stuttering by eliminating the secondary symptoms, and to encourage the stutterer to speak, even if stuttering, in a relatively easy and effortless fashion, thereby avoiding fears and blocks.

One example of this approach is the self-therapy proposed by the Speech Foundation of America. Self-therapy is based on the premise that stuttering is not a symptom but a behavior that can be modified. Stutterers are told that they can learn to control their difficulty partly by modifying their feelings about and attitudes toward stuttering and partly by modifying the deviant behaviors associated with their stuttering blocks. This approach includes desensitization, reducing the emotional reaction to and fears of stuttering, and substituting positive action to control the moment of stuttering. The basic principle is that stuttering is something one is doing and that stutterers can learn to change what they are doing.

Recently developed therapies focus on the restructuring of fluency. The entire pattern of speech production is reshaped, with emphasis on a variety of target behaviors, including rate reduction, easy or gentle onset of voicing, and smooth transitions between sounds, syllables, and words. With adults, the approaches have met with substantial success in establishing perceptually fluent speech. However, maintenance of fluency over long periods of time and relapses remain a problem of concern for all involved in adult-stuttering treatment.

Whichever therapeutic approach is used, individual and family assessments and supportive interventions may be helpful. A team assessment of the child or adolescent and his or her family should be made before any approaches to treatment are begun.

References

Adams M R: Fluency, nonfluency, and stuttering in children. J Fluency Disord *7*: 171, 1982.

Andrew G, Guitar B, Howie P: Meta-analysis of the effects of stuttering treatment. J Speech Hear Disord *45*: 287, 1980.

Collins C R, Blood G W: Acknowledgement and severity of stuttering as factors influencing nonstutterers' perceptions of stutterers. J Speech Hear Disord *55*: 75, 1990.

Costello J M, ed.: *Speech Disorders in Children: Recent Advances*. College-Hill Press, San Diego, 1984.

Cullata R, Leeper L: Dysfluency isn't always stuttering. J Speech Hear Disord *53*: 486, 1988.

Freeman F J, Silver L B: Speech disorders not elsewhere classified. In *Comprehensive Textbook of Psychiatry,* ed 5, H I Kaplan and B J Sadock, editors, p 1810. Williams & Wilkins, Baltimore, 1989.

Koller W C: Dysfluency (stuttering) in extrapyramidal disease. Arch Neurol *40*: 175, 1983.

Metter J E: *Speech Disorders: Clinical Evaluation and Diagnosis*. S P Medical and Scientific Books, New York, 1985.

Nippold M A: Concomitant speech and language disorders in stuttering children: A critique of the literature. J Speech Hear Disord *55*: 51, 1990.

Rosenfield D B, Derman H S: Physician referral patterns for stutterers. J Otolaryngol *19*: 19, 1990.

Ryan B P: *Programmed Therapy for Stuttering in Children and Adults*. Thomas, Springfield, IL, 1974.

Van Riper C: *The Nature of Stuttering*, ed 2. Prentice-Hall, Englewood Cliffs, NJ, 1982.

42

Other Disorders of Infancy, Childhood, or Adolescence

42.1 / Elective Mutism

DIAGNOSIS

Elective mutism is characterized by a persistent refusal to talk in one or more major social situations, including at school, despite the ability to comprehend spoken language and to speak. The revised third edition of *Diagnostic and Statistical Manual of Mental Disorders* (DSM-III-R) criteria for elective mutism are given in Table 42.1-1.

EPIDEMIOLOGY

There is no clear-cut duration of symptoms in the diagnostic criteria. The prevalence data are not consistent; however, it is clear that elective mutism is uncommon, probably affecting fewer than 1 in 1,000 children. It is present in less than 1 percent of patients referred to child mental health-related services. Unlike other speech and language disorders, elective mutism is more common in girls than in boys.

ETIOLOGY

Elective mutism is a psychologically determined inhibition or refusal to speak. However, many children with elective mutism have histories of delayed onset of speech or speech abnormalities that may be contributory. Parental discord, maternal depression, and heightened dependency needs are noted in many of the families. These factors result in maternal overprotection and an overly close but ambivalent relationship between the mother and her electively mute child. Children with elective mutism usually speak freely at home; they have no significant biological disability. Some children seem predisposed to elective mutism after early emotional or physical trauma, and so some clinicians refer to this phenomenon as traumatic mutism, rather than elective mutism.

Table 42.1-1
Diagnostic Criteria for Elective Mutism

A. Persistent refusal to talk in one or more major social situations (including at school)

B. Ability to comprehend spoken language and to speak

Table from DSM-III-R, *Diagnostic and Statistical Manual of Mental Disorders*, ed 3, revised. Copyright American Psychiatric Association, Washington, DC, 1987, with permission.

CLINICAL FEATURES, COURSE, AND PROGNOSIS

Although children with elective mutism are often abnormally shy in the preschool years, the onset of the disorder is usually at age 5 or 6. The most common pattern is that the children speak almost exclusively at home with the nuclear family but not elsewhere, especially not at school. Consequently, they may have significant academic difficulties and even failure. Children with elective mutism are generally shy, anxious, and depressed. They may not form social relationships, and teasing and scapegoating by peers may cause them to refuse to go to school. Frequently, these children display at home compulsive traits, negativism, temper tantrums, and oppositional and aggressive behavior.

Some children with elective mutism communicate with gestures, such as nodding or shaking the head or saying "umm-hum" or "no." Most cases last only a few weeks or months, but some may persist for years. In one follow-up study, about half the children improved within 5 to 10 years. Children who do not improve by age 10 appear to have a long-term course and a worse prognosis than children who do improve by age 10.

Some mute children appear to have negativistic and sadistic relationships with adults and use their defiant muteness to punish them. This behavior seems to improve concomitantly with increasing speech in the environments where the child had previously been mute.

DIFFERENTIAL DIAGNOSIS

Very shy children may exhibit a transient muteness in new, anxiety-provoking situations. These children often have a history of not speaking in the presence of strangers and of clinging to their mothers. Most of the children who are mute on entering school improve spontaneously and may be described as having transient adaptational shyness.

Elective mutism must also be distinguished from mental retardation, pervasive developmental disorders, and developmental expressive language disorder. In those disorders, however, the symptoms are more widespread, and there is not one situation in which the child communicates essentially normally; there may be an inability to speak, rather than a refusal to speak. In mutism secondary to conversion disorder, the mutism is also pervasive.

Children introduced into an environment where a different language is spoken may be reticent to begin using the new language. Elective mutism should be diagnosed only when children also refuse to converse in their native language and when they have gained communicative competence in the new language.

TREATMENT

A multimodal approach using individual, behavioral, and family interventions is most likely to be successful. In the preschool years, counseling or psychotherapy for the parents may be indicated. The preschool child may also benefit from a therapeutic nursery. For the school-age child, individual psychotherapy or behavior therapy may be indicated. When a child's independence is being thwarted, marital counseling or psychotherapy for the parents is paramount.

References

Atoynatan T H: Elective mutism: Involvement of the mother in the treatment of the child. Child Psychiatry Hum Dev *17*: 15, 1986.

Hassleman S: Elective mutism in children 1877–1981: A literary summary. Acta Paedopsychiatry *49*: 297, 1983.

Hayden T L: Classification of elective mutism. J Am Acad Child Psychiatry *19*: 18, 1980.

Kolvin I, Fundudis T: Elective mute children: Psychological development and background factors. J Child Psychol Psychiatry *22*: 219, 1981.

Lesser-Katz M: Stranger reaction and elective mutism in young children. Am J Orthopsychiatry *56*: 458, 1986.

Wilkins R: A comparison of elective mutism and emotional disorders in children. Br J Psychiatry *146*: 198, 1985.

Wright H H, Miller M D, Cook M A, Littman J R: Early identification and intervention with children who refuse to speak. J Am Acad Child Psychiatry *24*: 739, 1985.

Wright H L: A clinical study of children who refuse to talk in school. J Am Acad Child Psychiatry *7*: 603, 1968.

42.2 / Identity Disorder

DIAGNOSIS

The revised third edition of *Diagnostic and Statistical Manual of Mental Disorders* (DSM-III-R) defines identity disorder as severe subjective distress about an inability to reconcile aspects of the self into a relatively coherent and acceptable sense of self. The disturbance is manifested by uncertainty about a variety of identity issues, including long-term goals, career choice, friendship patterns, values, and loyalties. These symptoms last for at least three months. A diagnosis of identity disorder is not valid when the condition is symptomatic of a mood disorder, psychotic disorder, or borderline personality disorder.

Little mention has been made of identity disorder in the psychiatric literature. This lack of discussion is probably caused by the fact that many adolescents experiencing symptoms of identity disorder are actually suffering from a different disorder. Also, it is thought that many adolescents suffering from identity disorder do not come to the attention of professionals. The DSM-III-R diagnostic criteria for identity disorder are given in Table 42.2-1.

EPIDEMIOLOGY

There is no reliable information on predisposing factors, familial pattern, sex ratio, or prevalence. It appears, however, that problems with identity formation are a result of life in modern society. Today there is great instability of family life, increased problems with identity formation, increased conflicts between adolescent peer values and the values of parents or society, and increased exposure through the media and education to a variety of moral, behavioral, and life-style possibilities.

ETIOLOGY

The cause of identity disorder is hypothesized to be psychological. Adolescents are unable to effectively use the intrapsychic and social moratoriums provided by society and do not achieve ego identity in the Eriksonian sense. The normal intrapsychic transformations necessary for ego mastery result in persistent regressive phenomena, leading to crisis formation and, if not relieved by adequate growth responses, identity diffusion.

Table 42.2-1
Diagnostic Criteria for Identity Disorder

A. Severe subjective distress regarding uncertainty about a variety of issues relating to identity, including three or more of the following:
   (1) long-term goals
   (2) career choice
   (3) friendship patterns
   (4) sexual orientation and behavior
   (5) religious identification
   (6) moral value systems
   (7) group loyalties

B. Impairment in social or occupational (including academic) functioning as a result of the symptoms in A.

C. Duration of the disturbance of at least three months.

D. Occurrence not exclusively during the course of a mood disorder or of a psychotic disorder, such as schizophrenia.

E. The disturbance is not sufficiently pervasive and persistent to warrant the diagnosis of borderline personality disorder.

CLINICAL FEATURES, COURSE, AND PROGNOSIS

The onset of identity disorder is most frequently in late adolescence, as the teenager separates from the nuclear family and attempts to establish an independent identity and value system. The onset is usually manifested by a gradual increase in anxiety, depression, regressive phenomena—such as loss of interest in friends, school, or activities—irritability, sleep difficulties, and changes in eating habits.

The essential features seem to revolve around the question "Who am I?" According to DSM-III-R, there is severe subjective distress regarding the inability to integrate aspects of the self into a relatively coherent and acceptable sense of self. In particular, there is confusion and ambivalence about long-term goals, sexuality, career choice, religious matters, morality, friendship patterns, and group loyalties. These conflicts are experienced as irreconcilable aspects of the self that the adolescent is unable to integrate into a coherent identity. If the symptoms are not recognized and resolved, a full-blown identity crisis may develop. As Erikson described, youth manifests severe doubting and an inability to make decisions (abulia), a sense of isolation and inner emptiness, a growing inability to relate to others, disturbed sexual function, a distorted time perspective and a sense of urgency, and the assumption of a negative identity.

The associated features frequently include marked discrepancy between the adolescent's self-perception and the views that others have of the adolescent; moderate anxiety and depression, usually related to inner preoccupation, rather than external realities; and self-doubt and uncertainty about the future, with either difficulty in making choices or impulsive experiments in an attempt to establish an independent identity. Some persons with identity disorder are apt to join cultlike groups, but the association between the disorder and cult membership is unclear.

The course is usually relatively brief, as developmental lags are responsive to support, acceptance, and the provision of a psychosocial moratorium. An extensive prolongation of adolescence with continued identity disorder may lead to the chronic state of identity diffusion that usually indicates disturbance of early developmental stages and the presence of borderline personality disorder, mood disorder, or schizophrenia. Identity disorder usually resolves by the mid-20s. If it persists, the person with identity disorder may be unable to make career commitments or lasting attachments.

DIFFERENTIAL DIAGNOSIS

Identity disorder should not be diagnosed if the identity problems are secondary to another mental disorder (such as borderline personality disorder, schizophreniform disorder, schizophrenia, or mood disorder). At times, what initially appears to be an identity disorder may be the prodromal manifestations of one of those disorders.

Intense but normal conflicts associated with maturing, such as adolescent turmoil and mid-life crisis, may be confusing, but they are usually not associated with marked deterioration in school, vocational, or social functioning or with severe subjective distress. There is considerable evidence, however, that adolescent turmoil is often not a phase that is outgrown but is indicative of true psychopathology.

TREATMENT

Individual psychotherapy directed toward encouraging growth and development is usually considered the therapy of choice. Adolescents, particularly in the regressed state of an identity disorder, often react as do borderline personality disorder patients to the psychotherapeutic technique in which the transference is permitted to develop in the context of a controlled regression without gratifying or infantilizing the patient. The patients' feelings and wishes are recognized, and the patients are encouraged to examine their longings and feelings of deprivations and to try to understand, with the empathic help of the therapist, what is happening to them.

References

Blos P: *On Adolescence*. Free Press, Glen Cove, NY, 1962.

Egan J: Etiology and treatment of borderline personality disorder in adolescents. Hosp Community Psychiatry *37*: 6, 1986.

Erikson E H: The problems of ego identity. J Am Psychoanal Assoc *4*: 428, 1956.

Galanter M: Cults and zealous self-help movements: A psychiatric perspective. Am J Psychiatry *147*: 543, 1990.

Masterson J F: *The Psychiatric Dilemma of Adolescence*. Little, Brown, Boston, 1967.

Petti T A, Vela R M: Borderline disorders of childhood: An overview. J Am Acad Child Adolesc Psychiatry *29*: 327, 1990.

Robson K S: *The Borderline Child: Approaches to Etiology, Diagnosis, and Treatment*. McGraw-Hill, New York, 1983.

Soloff P H, George A, Nathan R S, Schulz P M: Progress in pharmacotherapy of borderline disorders. Arch Gen Psychiatry *43*: 7, 1986.

Stone M H: *The Borderline Syndromes*. McGraw-Hill, New York, 1980.

42.3 / Reactive Attachment Disorder of Infancy or Early Childhood

DIAGNOSIS

Reactive attachment disorder of infancy or early childhood is essentially a new diagnosis that covers a broad range of conditions and causes. The revised third edition of *Diagnostic and Statistical Manual of Mental Disorders* (DSM-III-R) criteria for reactive attachment disorder of infancy or early childhood are given in Table 42.3-1.

EPIDEMIOLOGY

There are no specific data on the prevalence, sex ratio, or familial pattern at this time. Although patients with

Table 42.3-1
Diagnostic Criteria for Reactive Attachment Disorder of Infancy or Early Childhood

A. Markedly disturbed social relatedness in most contexts, beginning before the age of 5, as evidenced by either (1) or (2):
   (1) persistent failure to initiate or respond to most social interactions (e.g., in infants, absence of visual tracking and reciprocal play, lack of vocal imitation or playfulness, apathy, little or no spontaneity; at later ages, lack of or little curiosity and social interest)
   (2) indiscriminate sociability (e.g., excessive familiarity with relative strangers by making requests and displaying affection)

B. The disturbance in A is not a symptom of either mental retardation or a pervasive developmental disorder, such as autistic disorder.

C. Grossly pathogenic care, as evidenced by at least one of the following:
   (1) persistent disregard of the child's basic emotional needs for comfort, stimulation, and affection. *Examples:* overly harsh punishment by caregiver: consistent neglect by caregiver
   (2) persistent disregard of the child's basic physical needs, including nutrition, adequate housing, and protection from physical danger and assault (including sexual abuse)
   (3) repeated change of primary caregiver so that stable attachments are not possible (e.g., frequent changes in foster parents)

D. There is a presumption that the care described in C is responsible for the disturbed behavior in A; this presumption is warranted if the disturbance in A began following the pathogenic care in C.

Note: If failure to thrive is present, code it on Axis III.

Table from DSM-III-R, *Diagnostic and Statistical Manual of Mental Disorders,* ed 3, revised. Copyright American Psychiatric Association, Washington, DC, 1987, with permission.

reactive attachment disorder of infancy or early childhood come from all socioeconomic (SES) groups, studies of some patients (such as infants with failure to thrive) suggest an increased vulnerability among the low SES groups. This finding is congruent with the likelihood of psychosocial deprivation, single-parent households, family disorganization, and economic difficulties in families in low SES groups.

It is also important to realize that a caretaker may be fully satisfactory for one child but that another child under the same care may develop a reactive attachment disorder of infancy or early childhood.

ETIOLOGY

The cause is included in the disorder's definition. It is presumed that grossly pathogenic care of the infant or young child by the caretaker causes the markedly disturbed social relatedness usually evident. The emphasis is on the unidirectional cause; that is, the caretaker does something inimical or neglects to do something essential for the infant or child. However, in evaluating a patient for whom such a diagnosis is appropriate, the clinician should consider the contributions of each member of the caretaker-child dyad, as well as their interactions. Thus, such things as infant and child temperament, deficient or defective bonding, a developmentally disabled or sensorially impaired child, and a particular caretaker-child mismatch should be weighed. The likelihood of neglect increases with parental mental retardation; lack of parenting skills because of personal upbringing, social isolation, or deprivation and lack of opportunities to learn about caretaking behavior; and premature parenthood (during early and middle adolescence), in which the parents are unable to respond to and care for the infant's needs and in which the parents' own needs take precedence over their infant's or child's needs.

Frequent changes of the primary caretaker—as may occur in institutionalization, repeated lengthy hospitalizations, or multiple foster home placements—may also cause a reactive attachment disorder of infancy or early childhood.

CLINICAL FEATURES

Children with reactive attachment disorder of infancy or early childhood often first come to the attention of their pediatrician. The clinical picture varies greatly according to the child's chronological and mental ages. Perhaps the most typical clinical picture of the infant with this disorder is the nonorganic failure to thrive. In these infants hypokinesis, dullness, listlessness, and apathy with a poverty of spontaneous activity are usually seen. They look sad, unhappy, joyless, and miserable. Some infants also appear frightened and watchful, with a radarlike gaze. In spite of this, the infants may exhibit delayed responsiveness to a stimulus that would elicit fright or withdrawal in a normal infant.

Most of the infants appear significantly malnourished, and many have protruding abdomens (Figures 42.3-1 and 42.3-2). Occasionally, foul-smelling, celiaclike stools are reported. In unusually severe cases a clinical picture of marasmus appears. The infant's weight is often below the third percentile and markedly below their appropriate weight for height. If serial weights are available, it may be noted that weight percentiles have progressively decreased because of an actual weight loss or a failure to gain weight as height increases. Head circumference is usually normal for the age. Muscle tone may be poor. The skin may be colder and paler or more mottled than the normal child's skin. Laboratory findings are usually within normal limits, except those abnormal findings coincident with any malnutrition, dehydration, or concurrent illness. Bone age is usually retarded. Growth hormone levels are usually normal or elevated, suggesting that growth failure in these children is secondary to caloric deprivation and malnutrition. The children improve physically and gain weight rapidly after hospitalization.

Socially, the infants usually show little spontaneous activity and a marked diminution of both initiative toward others and a lack of reciprocity in response to the caretaking adult or examiner. Both the mother and the infant may be indifferent to their separation on hospitalization or termination of subsequent hospital visits. The infants frequently show none of the normal upset, fretting, or

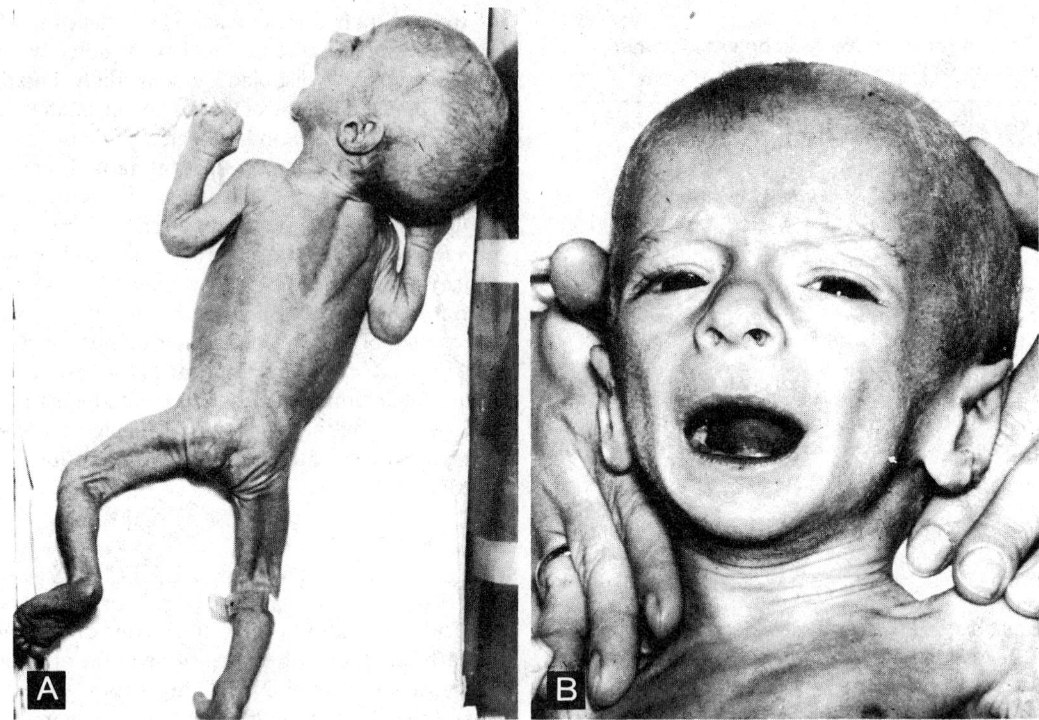

Figure 42.3-1. Three-month-old baby boy suffering from failure to thrive secondary to caloric deprivation. Weight is only 1 ounce over birth weight. (Courtesy of Barton Schmitt, M.D., Children's Hospital, Denver, CO.)

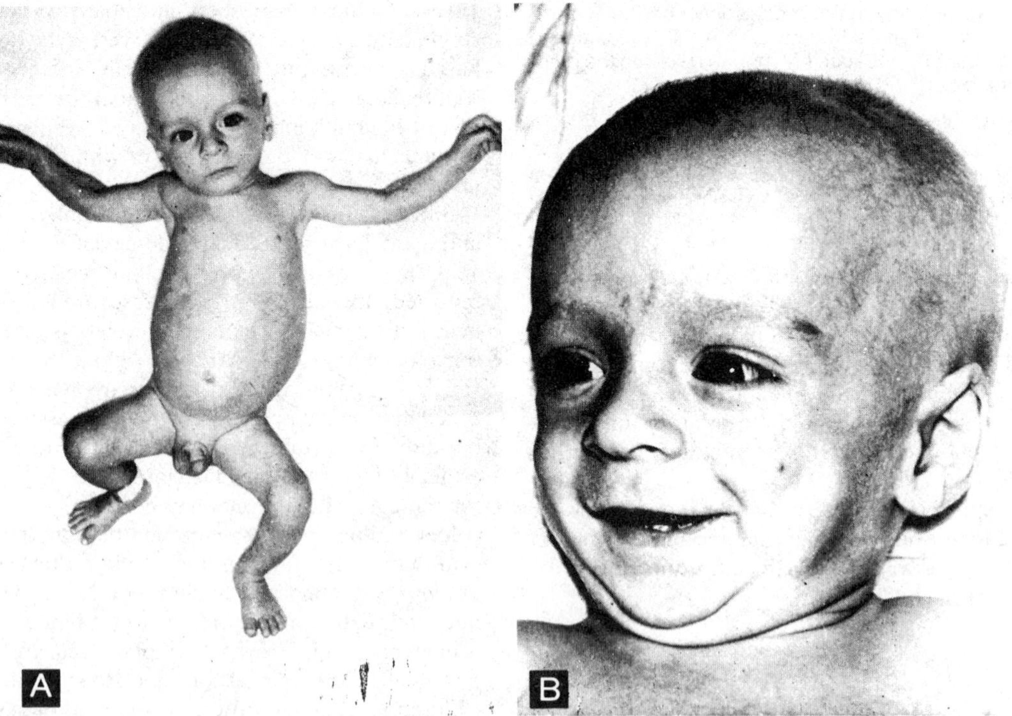

Figure 42.3-2. The same infant as in Figure 42.3-1, three weeks later, after hospitalization. (Courtesy of Barton Schmitt, M.D., Children's Hospital, Denver, CO.)

protest about hospitalization. Older infants usually show little interest in their environment. They may have little interest in playing with toys, even if encouraged. However, they rapidly or gradually take an interest in and relate to their caretakers in the hospital.

Classic psychosocial dwarfism or psychosocially determined short stature is a syndrome that is usually first manifested in children 2 to 3 years of age. The children typically are unusually short and have frequent growth hormone abnormalities and severe behavioral disturbances. All these symptoms are the result of an inimical caretaker-child relationship, and the symptoms resolve without any medical or psychiatric treatment after the child is removed from the home and placed in a more favorable domicile.

There is evidence that the affectionless character may appear when there is a failure or lack of opportunity to form attachments before age 2 to 3 years. The affectionless character is unable to form lasting relationships, and this is sometimes accompanied by a lack of guilt, an inability to obey rules, and a need for attention and affection. Some such children are indiscriminately friendly. This disorder is usually not reversible.

DIFFERENTIAL DIAGNOSIS

Pervasive developmental disorders, mental retardation, various severe neurological abnormalities, and psychosocial dwarfism are the primary considerations in the differential diagnosis. Autistic children are typically well nourished and of age-appropriate size and weight. They are generally alert and active, despite their impairments in reciprocal social interactions. Moderate, severe, or profound mental retardation is present in about 50 percent of autistic children, whereas most children with reactive attachment disorder of infancy or early childhood are only mildly retarded or have normal intelligence. There is no evidence that autistic disorder is caused by parental pathology, and most parents of autistic children do not differ significantly from the parents of normal children. Unlike most children with reactive attachment disorder, autistic children do not improve rapidly if they are removed from their homes and placed in a hospital or other more favorable environment.

Mentally retarded children may show delay in all social skills. These children, unlike children with reactive attachment disorder, are usually adequately nourished, their social relatedness is appropriate to their mental age, and they show a sequence of development similar to that seen in normal children.

PROGNOSIS

The prognosis depends on the severity of the pathological caretaking of the infant or child and the length of time spent in the inimical environment. If the patient remains in or returns to the home after evaluation, the adequacy of the corrective measures to change caretaking behavior must also be considered. Outcomes range from the extremes of death to the normal development of the child. In general, the longer the child stays in the inimical environment without adequate intervention, the worse the prognosis is. For those children who have multiple problems stemming from the abnormal caretaking, physical recovery is usually more complete than emotional or educational recovery.

TREATMENT

There are some general principles of treatment. Often, the first decision is whether to hospitalize an infant or child or to attempt treatment while the child remains in the home. Usually, the severity of the child's physical and emotional state or the severity of the pathological caretaking determines the strategy. The overriding choice must be for the child's safety. The patient must be given appropriate psychological and, if necessary, pediatric treatment. Concomitantly, the treatment team must begin to alter the unsatisfactory relationship between the caretaker and the child. This usually requires extensive and intensive long-term psychological therapy with the mother or, in intact households, both parents whenever possible.

Possible interventions include but are not limited to the following: (1) psychosocial support services, including hiring a homemaker, improving the physical condition of the apartment or obtaining more adequate housing, improving the family's financial status, and decreasing the family's isolation; (2) psychotherapeutic interventions, including individual psychotherapy, psychotropic medications, and family or marital therapy; (3) educational-counseling services, including mother-infant or mother-toddler groups, and counseling to increase awareness and understanding of the child's needs and to increase parenting skills; and (4) provisions for close monitoring of the progression of the patient's emotional and physical well-being. Should these interventions be unfeasible, be inadequate, or fail, placement with relatives or in foster care, adoption, or a group home or residential treatment facility must be considered.

References

Ainsworth M D S: The development of infant-mother attachment. In *Review of Child Development Research,* vol 3, B M Caldwen and H N Ricciuhi, editors, p 1. University of Chicago Press, Chicago, 1973.

Bowlby J: *Attachment and Loss,* 3 vols. Basic Books, New York, 1969, 1973, 1980.

Campbell M, Green W H, Caplon R, David R: Psychiatry and endocrinology in children: Early infantile autism and psychosocial dwarfism. In *Handbook of Psychiatry and Endocrinology,* P J V Beumont and G D Burrows, editors, p. 15. Elsevier, Amsterdam, 1982.

Ferholt J B: A psychodynamic study of psychosomatic dwarfism. J Am Acad Child Psychiatry *14*: 49, 1985.

Green W H, Campbell M, David R: Psychosocial dwarfism: A critical review of the evidence. J Am Acad Child Psychiatry *23*: 39, 1984.

Greenspan S I: *Psychopathology and Adaptation in Infancy and Early Childhood: Principles of Clinical Diagnosis and Preventive Intervention.* International Universities Press, New York, 1981.

Klaus M H, Kennell J M: *Parent–Infant Bonding,* ed 2. Mosby, St. Louis, 1982.

Lamb M E: Social development. Pediatr Ann *18*: 292, 1989.

Rutter M: *Maternal Deprivation Reassessed*, ed 2. Penguin Books, Middlesex, England, 1981.

42.4 / Stereotypy and Habit Disorder

DIAGNOSIS

Stereotypy and habit disorder is a diagnosis that first appeared in the revised third edition of *Diagnostic and Statistical Manual of Mental Disorders* (DSM-III-R). The diagnostic criteria are given in Table 42.4-1. Habit disorders include thumb or finger sucking, nail biting, and nose

Table 42.4-1
Diagnostic Criteria for Stereotypy and Habit Disorder

A. Intentional, repetitive, nonfunctional behaviors, such as hand-shaking or -waving, body-rocking, head-banging, mouthing of objects, nail-biting, picking at nose or skin.

B. The disturbance either causes physical injury to the child or markedly interferes with normal activities (e.g., injury to head from head-banging; inability to fall asleep because of constant rocking).

C. Does not meet the criteria for either a pervasive developmental disorder or a tic disorder.

or skin picking. There is a criterion of severity—namely, that the disorder must cause physical injury or markedly interfere with normal activities; thus, mild nail biting is precluded from this diagnosis.

Tic disorder and pervasive developmental disorder are exclusion criteria. It is unclear why the diagnosis of stereotypy and habit disorder is not allowed in DSM-III-R in pervasive developmental disorder but is allowed in mental retardation. Stereotypies are prevalent in both these disorders, and it seems as important and useful in planning treatment to know that a child with a pervasive developmental disorder has a coexisting severe stereotypy and habit disorder as it is to know that a mentally retarded person has such a coexisting disorder.

EPIDEMIOLOGY

The diagnosis is a compilation of many different symptoms and various groups—head bangers, body rockers, repetitive hand movers, and nail biters—that have to be studied separately to obtain data concerning prevalence, sex ratio, and familial patterns. It is clear, however, that stereotypy and habit disorders are most prevalent in the mentally retarded, in males, and in persons with severe sensory impairments, such as blindness and deafness. Some studies suggest that low socioeconomic status correlates with some stereotypies (e.g., head banging).

The provisions that the disorder must cause physical injury or markedly interfere with normal activities may cause some confusion. In one pediatric clinic up to 20 percent of the children had a history of rocking, head banging, or swaying in one form or another. Deciding which cases are severe enough to confirm a diagnosis may be difficult. Injury in some cases depends more on parental care and supervision and the quality of the environment (e.g., a padded crib) than on the intensity of the stereotypy.

ETIOLOGY

The causes of these disorders are essentially unknown, but there are several theories. Many of the behaviors may be associated with normal development. For example, up to 80 percent of all normal children show rhythmic activities that phase out by the age of 4 years. These rhythmic patterns seem to be purposeful, to provide sensorimotor stimulation and tension release, and to be satisfying and pleasurable to the children. The movements may increase at times of frustration, boredom, or tension.

The progression from what are perhaps viscissitudes of normal development to stereotypy and habit disorder is thought to reflect disordered development, as in mental retardation (or pervasive developmental disorder), or psychological conflict. It has also been suggested that such behaviors as head banging may result from maternal neglect or abuse and lack of psychosocial and physical stimulation.

Stereotypic movements appear to be associated with dopamine activity. Dopamine agonists induce or increase stereotypies, whereas dopamine antagonists decrease them. In one report four children with attention-deficit hyperactivity disorder were treated with stimulant medication and began to bite their nails and fingertips. The nail biting ceased when the medication was eliminated. Endogenous opioids have also been implicated in the production of self-injurious behaviors.

CLINICAL FEATURES

Affected persons may suffer from one or more symptoms of stereotypy and habit disorder; thus, the clinical picture varies considerably. Most commonly, one symptom predominates. The presence of several severe symptoms tends to occur among the most severely afflicted persons with mental retardation or pervasive developmental disorder. These persons frequently have other significant psychiatric disorders, especially behavioral disorders.

DSM-III-R notes that, in extreme cases, severe mutilation and life-threatening injuries may result, and secondary infection and septicemia may follow self-inflicted trauma.

Head Banging

Head banging is an example of a stereotypy disorder. The reported incidence varies between 3.3 and 19 percent. Typically, head banging begins during infancy, between 6 and 12 months of age. The infant strikes the head with a definite rhythmic and monotonous continuity against the crib or other hard surface. Infants appear to be absorbed in the activity, which may persist until they become exhausted and fall asleep. The head banging is transitory in many children, but in some cases it may persist into middle childhood.

Head banging that is a component of temper tantrums is different and ceases once the tantrums and their secondary gains are controlled.

Nail Biting

Nail biting, an example of a habit disorder, may begin as early as 1 year of age and increase in incidence until age 12. Usually, all the nails are bitten. Most cases are not sufficiently severe to meet the DSM-III-R diagnostic criteria. The others are those that cause physical damage to the fingers themselves, usually by associated biting of the cuticles and by secondary infections of the fingers and nail beds. Nail biting seems to occur or increase in intensity when the person is either anxious or bored. Some of the most severe nail biting occurs in the severely and profoundly mentally retarded and in some paranoid schizophrenic patients. Some nail biters, however, have no obvious emotional disturbance.

DIFFERENTIAL DIAGNOSIS

DSM-III-R notes that these symptoms cannot be caused by a more pervasive disorder, such as autistic disorder. This is likely to be the most difficult differential diagnosis among moderately, severely, and profoundly mentally retarded persons who have associated autistic symptoms. DSM-III-R also notes that this diagnosis should not be used if the symptoms arise during the course of a tic disorder. Stereotypy and habit disorder is distinguishable from tics in that the movements are voluntary and are not spasmodic. Moreover, unlike children with a tic disorder, those with stereotypy and habit disorder are not distressed by the symptoms.

It can be extremely difficult to differentiate dyskinetic movements from stereotypic movements. Because antipsychotic medication can suppress stereotypies, the clinician must note any stereotypic movements before initiating treatment with an antipsychotic.

Stereotypy and habit disorder may be diagnosed concurrently with psychoactive substance (e.g., amphetamine)-induced organic mental disorder, severe sensory impairments, central nervous system and degenerative disorders (e.g., Lesch-Nyhan syndrome), severe schizophrenia, and obsessive-compulsive disorder.

TREATMENT

Treatment should be related to the specific symptom or symptoms being treated, their causes, and the patient's mental age.

The psychosocial environment should be changed for those infants, young children, and mentally retarded persons for whom lack of adequate caretaking, little opportunity for physical expression, boring inactivity, and self-stimulation seem to be important causes. In these cases increased nurturance and stimulation may be helpful. Such measures as padding hard surfaces may be important for severe head bangers.

Behavioral techniques, including reinforcement and behavioral shaping, are successful in some cases. A large, specialized literature addresses these problems in the seriously retarded.

Psychotherapy has been used primarily in older, mentally normal persons in whom intrapsychic conflict or interpersonal difficulties seem prominent.

Finally, for those cases in which severe physical damage occurs, especially in the severely retarded, psychopharmacology must be considered. Phenothiazines have been the most frequently used drugs; however, the psychiatrist must be particularly aware of adverse effects, including tardive dyskinesia and impairment of cognition. Opiate antagonists have reduced self-injurious behaviors in some patients without exposing them to tardive dyskinesia or impaired cognition.

References

Barrett R P, Feinstein C, Hole W T: Effects of naloxone and nalotrexone on self-injury: A double-blind, placebo controlled analysis. Am J Ment Retard *93*: 644, 1989.

Cerny R: Thumb and finger sucking. Aust Dent J *26*: 167, 1981.

Coid J, Allolio B, Rees L H: Raised plasma metenkephalin in patients who habitually mutilate themselves. Lancet *2*: 545, 1983.

Evans J: Rocking at night. J Child Psychol Psychiatry *2*: 71, 1961.

Green W H: Stereotypy and habit disorder. In *Comprehensive Textbook of Psychiatry*, ed 5, H I Kaplan and B J Sadock, editors, p 1903. Williams & Wilkins, Baltimore, 1989.

Matthews L H, Leibowitz J M, Matthews J R: Tics, habits and mannerisms. In *Handbook of Clinical Child Psychology,* C E Walker and M C Roberts, editors, p 406. Wiley, New York, 1983.

Meiselas K D, Spencer E K, Oberfield R, Peselow E D, Angrist B, Campbell M: Differentiation of stereotypies from neuroleptic-related dyskinesias in autistic children. J Clin Psychopharmacal *9*: 207, 1989.

Schroeder S R, Schroeder C S, Rojahn J, Mulick J A: Self-injurious behavior: An analysis of behavior management techniques. In *Handbook of Behavior Modification with the Mentally Retarded,* p 61. Plenum, New York, 1981.

Silberstein R M, Blackman S, Mandell W: Autoerotic head banging: A reflection of the opportunism of infants. J Am Acad Child Psychiatry *5*: 235, 1966.

Sokol M S, Campbell M, Goldstein M, Kriechman A M: Attention deficit disorder with hyperactivity and the dopamine hypothesis: Case presentations with theoretical background. J Am Acad Child Adolesc Psychiatry *26*: 428, 1987.

Werry J, Corlielle J, Fitzpatrick J: Rhythmic motor activities in children under five: Etiology and prevalence. J Am Acad Child Psychiatry *22*: 329, 1983.

43 Child Psychiatry: Special Areas of Interest

43.1 / Mood Disorders

The criterion for mood disorders in childhood and adolescence is a disturbance of mood, such as depression or elation. In addition, irritability is a sign of mood disorder in children and adolescents. Depressive disorders in childhood and adolescence are more common than mania and hypomania, which are very rare before the onset of puberty. Mood disorders in adults are reviewed in detail in Chapter 16. Consequently, only those issues that pertain specifically to children and adolescents are considered here.

Suicidal ideation, gestures, and attempts are frequently associated with depression, and these phenomena, particularly in adolescence, are a growing public mental health problem.

DIAGNOSIS

Major Depressive Episode

The revised third edition of *Diagnostic and Statistical Manual of Mental Disorders* (DSM-III-R) diagnostic criteria for children and adolescents differ from those for adults in two of the nine symptoms that are given as indicative of major depressive episode (Table 43.1-1). Symptom 1, the depressed mood that must be present most of the day, nearly every day for at least two weeks in adults, may be an irritable mood in children and adolescents, rather than a depressed mood. Symptom 3, significant weight gain or loss and decrease or increase in appetite nearly every day may be reflected in children as a failure to make expected weight gains. The amount of weight that most children are expected to gain over a two-week period is too insignificant to measure accurately in most situations. Thus, in clinical practice this becomes a useful diagnostic criterion primarily in depressions of longer duration.

Table 43.1-1
Symptoms of Major Depressive Episode

1. Depressed mood (or can be irritable mood in children and adolescents) most of the day, nearly every day, as indicated either by subjective account or observation by others
2. Markedly diminished interest or pleasure in all, or almost all, activities most of the day, nearly every day (as indicated either by subjective account or observation by others of apathy most of the time)
3. Significant weight loss or weight gain when not dieting (e.g., more than 5% of body weight in a month), or decrease or increase in appetite nearly every day (in children, consider failure to make expected weight gains)
4. Insomnia or hypersomnia nearly every day
5. Psychomotor agitation or retardation nearly every day (observable by others, not merely subjective feelings of restlessness or being slowed down)
6. Fatigue or loss of energy nearly every day
7. Feelings of worthlessness or excessive or inappropriate guilt (which may be delusional) nearly every day (not merely self-reproach or guilt about being sick)
8. Diminished ability to think or concentrate, or indecisiveness, nearly every day (either by subjective account or as observed by others)
9. Recurrent thoughts of death (not just fear of dying), recurrent suicidal ideation without a specific plan, or a suicide attempt or a specific plan for committing suicide

Table adapted from DSM-III-R, *Diagnostic and Statistical Manual of Mental Disorders,* ed 3, revised. Copyright American Psychiatric Association, Washington, DC, 1987, with permission.

Dysthymia (Depressive Neurosis)

DSM-III-R notes that the boundary between dysthymia and major depression is unclear, particularly in children and adolescents. The onset is usually during childhood, adolescence, or early adulthood and was referred to in the past as depressive personality. There are two significant differences in the diagnostic criteria for dysthymia in children and adolescents and those in adults. Children and adolescents may exhibit an irritable mood instead of or in addition to the depressed mood required for adults. And the mood disturbance in children and adolescents must be present for only one year, rather than two years. DSM-III-R also directs that early onset be specified for children and adolescents. If major depression develops while dysthymia is still present, both diagnoses should be given.

Occasionally, youngsters fulfill the criteria for dysthymia except that their episodes last only two weeks to several months, with symptom-free intervals lasting for two to three months. These minor mood presentations in children are likely to indicate more severe mood disorder episodes in the future. Current knowledge suggests that the longer, the more recurrent, the more frequent, and perhaps the less related to environmental stress these episodes are, the greater likelihood there is of severe mood disorder in the future.

An important exception to this is that, when minor depressive episodes follow a significant stressful life event by less than three months, they do not indicate future mood disorder episodes, and so they should be diagnosed as an adjustment disorder with depressed mood or uncomplicated bereavement.

Cyclothymia

The only difference in criteria for this disorder is that, in child or adolescent cyclothymia, a period of one year of numerous mood swings is necessary, instead of the adult criterion of two years. It is likely that most cyclothymic adolescents go on to bipolar disorder.

Schizoaffective Disorder

The DSM-III-R criteria for schizoaffective disorder in children and adolescents are identical to those in adults. Although some adolescents and probably some children do fit the criteria for schizoaffective disorder, little is now known about the natural course of their illness, family history, psychobiology, and treatment.

EPIDEMIOLOGY

Mood disorders in preschool-age children are extremely rare. In school-age children the prevalence of depressive disorders is approximately 2 percent, and in adolescents the prevalence is approximately 5 percent. The prevalence is greater for school-age boys than for school-age girls, but this difference disappears in adolescence.

It has been conservatively estimated that, on general child and adolescent services in general hospitals, about 5 percent of prepubertal children and 15 percent of adolescents have mood disorders of all types.

ETIOLOGY

Considerable evidence indicates that the mood disorders are the same fundamental disease or disease group, regardless of age of onset. Both genetic and environmental factors appear to be important.

Genetic Factors

Mood disorders in children, adolescents, and adult patients tend to cluster in the same families. An increased incidence of mood disorders is generally found in the children of mood-disordered parents and in the relatives of mood-disordered children. However, in one study, depression was equally elevated in the parents of both depressed and nondepressed children and adolescent inpatients and outpatients. However, having one depressed parent probably doubles the risk for the offspring. Having both parents depressed probably quadruples the risk of a child's developing a mood disorder before age 18 when compared with the risk in children with two unaffected parents.

Some evidence indicates that the number of recurrences of parental depression does increase the likelihood that their children will be affected, but this may be related, at least in part, to the affective loading of that parent's own family tree. Similarly, children with the most severe episodes of depressive disorder have shown much evidence of dense and deep familial aggregation for major depression.

Environmental Factors

The finding that identical twins do not have a 100 percent concordance rate suggests a role for nongenetic factors. So far, there is little evidence that parental marital status, number of siblings, socioeconomic status, parental separation, divorce, marital functioning, or familial constellation or structure plays much of a role in causing depressive disorders in children. There is, however, some evidence that boys whose fathers died before they were 13 years old are more likely than are controls to have depression.

The psychosocial deficits that are found in depressed children improve after sustained recovery from the depression. These deficits appear to have been secondary to the depression itself and to have been compounded by the long duration in this age group of most dysthymic or depressive episodes, during which poorly or unaccomplished developmental tasks accumulated. It is likely that among preschoolers, in whom depressive clinical presentations are described, the role of environmental influence will receive more experimental support in the future.

Biological Factors

Studies of prepubertal major depression and adolescent mood disorders have revealed biological abnormalities.

Prepubertal children in an episode of major depression have been shown to secrete significantly more growth hormone during sleep than do normal children and those with nondepressed emotional disorders. They also secrete significantly less growth hormone in response to insulin-induced hypoglycemia than do nondepressed patients. Both abnormalities have been found to remain abnormal and basically unchanged after at least four months of full, sustained clinical response, the last month in a drug-free state.

In contrast, there exist conflicting data concerning cortisol hypersecretion during major depression. Some workers report hypersecretion, and some report normal secretion. The dexamethasone-suppression test (DST) is not sensitive or specific in childhood or adolescence.

Sleep studies are inconclusive in depressed children and adolescents. Polysomnography shows either no change or changes characteristic of adults with major depression: reduced rapid eye movement (REM) latency and increased numbers of REM periods.

CLINICAL FEATURES AND COURSE

The onset of a major depressive episode in children tends to be insidious and retrospectively difficult to pinpoint. When the first episode occurs during adolescence, it is likely to have a more clearly delineated or acute onset. Mania, hypomania, and cyclothymia are rarely seen before puberty, but there is evidence that childhood precursors to these states include depression, hyperactivity, dysregulation of affect, and aggression. The classic symptoms of mania have also been reported in some children.

Adolescent onset of mood disorder may be difficult to diagnose when first seen if there have been attempts at self-medication with illicit drugs or alcohol. In a recent study 17 percent of the youngsters with mood disorder first presented to medical attention as substance abusers. Only after detoxification could the psychiatric symptoms be properly assessed and the correct mood disorder diagnosis be made.

A major depressive episode in prepubertal children is likely to be manifested by somatic complaints, psychomotor agitation, and mood-congruent hallucinations. Anhedonia is also frequent, but it—as well as hopelessness, psychomotor retardation, and delusions—is more common in adolescent and adult episodes of major depression. Adults have more problems with sleep and appetite than do depressed children and adolescents. In adolescence negativistic or frankly antisocial behavior and the use of alcohol or illicit drugs may be present and justify the additional diagnoses of oppositional defiant disorder, conduct disorder, or psychoactive substance abuse or dependence. Feelings of restlessness, grouchiness, aggression, sulkiness, reluctance to cooperate in family ventures, withdrawal from social activities, and a desire to leave home are all common in adolescent depression. School difficulties are likely. There may be inattention to personal appearance and increased emotionality, with particular sensitivity to rejection in love relationships.

Children can be reliable reporters about their own behavior, emotions, relationships, and difficulties in psychosocial functions. They may, however, refer to dysphoria by many names. Thus, it is necessary to ask about feeling sad, empty, low, down, blue, very unhappy, or like crying or having a bad feeling inside that is there most of the time. Depressed children usually identify one or more of these terms as the persistent dysphoric feeling they have had. The duration and the periodicity of the depressive mood should be carefully assessed to differentiate relatively universal, short-lived, and sometimes frequent periods of sadness, usually after a frustrating event, from true, persistent depressive mood. The younger the child, the more imprecise his or her time estimates are likely to be.

Mood disorders tend to be chronic if they have begun early. Childhood onset may represent the most severe forms of mood disorder and tends to appear in families with a high incidence of mood disorder and alcoholism. The children are likely to have such secondary complications as conduct disorder, alcoholism, psychoactive substance abuse, and antisocial behavior.

Functional impairment associated with a depressive syndrome in childhood extends to practically all areas of the child's psychosocial world; school performance and behavior, peer relationships, and family relations—all suffer. Only highly intelligent and academically oriented children with no more than a moderate depression can compensate for their difficulties in learning by substantially increasing their time and effort. Otherwise, school performance is invariably affected by a combination of difficulty in concentrating, slowed down thinking, lack of interest and motivation, fatigue, sleepiness, depressive ruminations, and preoccupations. Depression in a child may be misdiagnosed as a learning disability. Learning problems secondary to depression, even when long-standing, correct themselves rapidly after recovery from the depressive episode.

Children and adolescents with a major depressive syndrome may have hallucinations and delusions. In most cases these psychotic symptoms are thematically consistent with the depressed mood, occur within the depressive episode (usually at its worst), and do not include certain types of hallucinations, such as conversing voices and a commenting voice, which are more specific to schizophrenia. Depressive hallucinations usually consist of a single voice speaking to the person from outside his or her head, with derogatory or suicidal content. Depressive delusions center on themes of guilt, physical disease, death, nihilism, deserved punishment, personal inadequacy, or sometimes persecution. These delusions are rare in prepuberty, probably because of cognitive immaturity, but are present in about half of all psychotically depressed adolescents.

A parallel situation exists for psychotic mania. Delusions and hallucinations may involve grandiose evaluations of the patient's own power, worth, knowledge, family, or relationships; persecutory delusions; or flight of ideas with gross impairment of reality testing.

Suicide

Suicidal phenomena in childhood and adolescence are discussed in Section 28.1. Suicidal ideation, gestures, and attempts occur frequently in depressed children and adolescents and are a frequent precipitant to hospitalization. Suicide is rare in children, but it has become the second leading cause of death in adolescents. Male adolescents are more likely to commit suicide, whereas female adolescents are more likely to have suicidal ideation, gestures, and attempts. Abuse of alcohol or drugs, a loss of social supports, and a history of physical or sexual abuse have all been associated with suicide. Direct questioning of children and adolescents about suicidal thoughts is necessary, because studies have consistently shown that parents are frequently unaware of such ideas in their children.

PROGNOSIS

The prognosis of mood disorders in children and adolescents is unclear and awaits findings from prospective studies. The impression is that depressive disorders are likely to recur and, if not successfully treated, produce considerable short-term and long-term difficulties and complications: poor academic achievement, arrest or delay in psychosocial development patterns, suicide, drug and alcohol abuse as a means of self-medication, and conduct disorders. Follow-up studies to date indicate a continued risk for mood disorders.

DIFFERENTIAL DIAGNOSIS

Psychotic forms of depression, mania, and schizoaffective disorders must be differentiated from schizophrenia. Organic mood syndromes can sometimes be differentiated from the mood disorders only after detoxification. Anxiety symptoms and conduct-disordered behavior can coexist with depression and can frequently pose problems in differentiating these disorders from nondepressed emotional and conduct disorders.

Of particular importance is the distinction between agitated depression or mania and attention-deficit hyperactivity disorder, in which the persistent excessive activity and restlessness can cause confusion. Prepubertal children do not present with classic forms of agitated depression, such as hand wringing and pacing. Instead, their inability to sit still and their frequent temper tantrums are the most common symptoms. Sometimes the correct answer becomes evident only after the depressive episode has remitted. If the child has no difficulty in concentrating and is not hyperactive while recovered from the depressive episode in a drug-free state, it is highly unlikely that an attention-deficit hyperactivity disorder was present.

TREATMENT

Hospitalization

The important immediate consideration is often whether hospitalization is indicated. When the patient is suicidal, hospitalization is indicated to provide maximum protection against the patient's own self-destructive impulses and behavior. This consideration may also be important when there is coexisting drug abuse, dependency, or addiction.

Psychotherapy

Child psychotherapy as generally practiced does not appear to be very effective in treating the depressive symptoms or any other aspect of the child's psychopathology as long as the youngster is severely depressed.

It is usually prudent to defer a decision for psychotherapeutic intervention until after the youngster has recovered from the depressive disorder. The best indication for individual or group treatment is the lack of spontaneous gradual improvement in relationships after the mood disorder has remitted. Other times, familial crises are precipitated by the child's recovery, indicating that the patient's illness had fulfilled certain family needs and that the family's psychodynamic equilibrium has been upset by the recovery. The indication for family therapy in such cases is clear.

Pharmacotherapy

There is, as yet, no clear evidence from double-blind, placebo-controlled studies that antidepressants are of benefit in child and adolescent depressive disorders. Moreover, antidepressants have yet to receive Food and Drug Administration (FDA) approval for use in depressed children. Nonetheless, if after careful consideration a trial of antidepressants is indicated, the following should be kept in mind: The use of antidepressants requires careful baseline studies, gradual titration of the drug, and monitoring of electrocardiogram (ECG) changes, blood pressure, side effects, and, whenever possible, serum levels. Because toxicity produces serious cardiac arrhythmias, seizures, coma, and death and the therapeutic-toxicity ratio is low, extremely careful monitoring is essential. The clinical response may be correlated with plasma level. In one uncontrolled study using imipramine (Tofranil) to treat prepubertal major depression, there was good response when blood levels were above 140 to 150 ng per mL. Because antidepressants have not yet been approved for use in depressed children and because of their potentially serious side effects and toxicity, it is recommended that clinicians use antidepressants in children only after careful study or consultation with a clinician experienced in their use.

Mania and hypomania in childhood and adolescence are treated with lithium with good results.

References

Carlson G A, Kashani J H: Phenomenology of major depression from childhood through adulthood: Analysis of three studies. Am J Psychiatry *145*: 1222, 1988.

Casat C D, Arana G W, Powell K: The DST in children and adolescents with major depressive disorder. Am J Psychiatry *146*: 505, 1989.

Emslie G J, Rush A J, Weinberg W A, Rintelmann J W, Roffwarg H P: Children with major depression show reduced rapid eye movement latencies. Arch Gen Psychiatry *47*: 119, 1990.

Harrington R C: Depressive disorder in children and adolescents. Br J Hosp Med *43*: 108, 1990.

Kazdin A E: Childhood depression. J Child Psychol Psychiatry *31*: 121, 1990.

Mitchell J, McCauley E, Burke P, Calderon R, Schloredt K: Psychopathy in parents of depressed children and adolescents. J Am Acad Child Adolesc Psychiatry *28*: 352, 1989.

Mitchell J, McCauley E, Burke P, Moss S J: Phenomenology of depression in children and adolescents. J Am Acad Child Adolesc Psychiatry *27*: 12, 1988.

Puig-Antich J, Dahl R, Ryan N, Novacento H, Goetz D, Goetz R, Tworrey J, Klepper T: Cortisol secretion in prepubertal children with major depressive disorder. Arch Gen Psychiatry *46*: 801, 1989.

Puig-Antich J, Perel J M, Lupatkin W, Chambers W, Tabrizi M A, King J, Goetz R, Davies M, Stiller R L: Imipramine in prepubertal major depressive disorders. Arch Gen Psychiatry *44*: 81, 1987.

Varanka T M, Weller R A, Weller E B, Fristad M A: Lithium treatment of manic episodes with psychotic features in prepubertal children. Am J Psychiatry *145*: 1557, 1988.

Velez C N, Cohen P: Suicidal behavior and ideation in a community sample of children: Maternal and youth reports. J Am Acad Child Adolesc Psychiatry *27*: 349, 1988.

Walker M, Moreau D, Weissman M M: Parents' awareness of children's suicide attempts. Am J Psychiatry *147*: 1364, 1990.

Zahn-Waxler C, Mayfield A, Radke-Yarrow M, McKnew D H, Cytryn L, Davenport Y B: A follow-up investigation of offspring of parents with bipolar disorder. Am J Psychiatry *145*: 506, 1988.

43.2 / Child Abuse

The alarmingly high number of reported cases of physical and sexual abuse of children probably reflects both an increasing incidence and a higher level of reporting of these grave problems.

Child abuse ranges from the deprivation of food, clothing, shelter, and parental love to incidents in which children are physically abused and mistreated by an adult, resulting in obvious trauma to the child and often leading to death. Many victims of physical abuse are also abused sexually. Child abuse is a medical-social disease that is assuming epidemic proportions. It is considered by some to be one aspect of the social violence that is insidiously creeping into society.

EPIDEMIOLOGY

The National Center on Child Abuse and Neglect in Washington, DC, has estimated that 1 million children are maltreated each year. There are 2,000 to 4,000 deaths annually in the United States caused by child abuse and neglect. There are 150,000 to 200,000 new cases of sexual abuse reported each year. The actual occurrence rates are likely to be higher than these estimates, because many maltreated children go unrecognized. Of those children physically abused, 32 percent are under 5 years of age; 27 percent are between 5 and 9 years; 27 percent are between 10 and 14 years; and 14 percent are between 15 and 18 years. More than 50 percent of all abused and neglected children were born prematurely or had low birth weights.

ETIOLOGY

Many abused children are perceived by their parents as being different, slow in development or mentally retarded, bad, selfish, or hard to discipline. Children who are hyperactive are particularly vulnerable to abuse, especially if born to parents with limited capacities for nurturant behavior.

The perpetrator of the battered child syndrome is more often the woman than the man. One parent is usually the active batterer, and the other passively accepts the battering. Of the perpetrators studied, 80 percent were regularly living in the homes of the children they abused. More than 80 percent of the children studied were living with married parents, and approximately 20 percent were living with a single parent. The average age of the mother who abused her children is reported to be around 26 years; the average age of the father is 30 years. Most abused children come from poor homes, and the families tend to be socially isolated.

The abusive parents have inappropriate expectations of their children, with a reversal of dependency needs. The parent deals with the child as if the child were older than the parent. The parent often turns to the child for reassurance, nurturing, comfort, and protection and expects a loving response. Ninety percent of these parents were severely physically abused by their own mothers or fathers. Sexual abuse is usually by men, although women acting in concert with men or alone have also been involved, especially in child pornography.

DIAGNOSIS OF PHYSICAL ABUSE

A maltreated child often presents no obvious signs of being battered but has multiple minor physical evidences of emotional and, at times, nutritional deprivation, neglect, and abuse. The maltreated child is often taken to a hospital or private physician and has a history of failure to thrive, malnutrition, poor skin hygiene, irritability, withdrawal, and other signs of psychological and physical neglect. The severely abused children are seen in hospital emergency rooms with external evidences of body trauma, bruises, abrasions, cuts, lacerations, burns, soft tissue swellings, and hematomas. Hypernatremic dehydration, after periodic water deprivation by psychotic mothers, has been reported as a form of child abuse. Inability to move certain extremities, because of dislocations and fractures associated with neurological signs of intracranial damage, can also indicate inflicted trauma. Other clinical signs and symptoms attributed to inflicted abuse may include injury to the viscera. Abdominal trauma may result in unexplained ruptures of the stomach, bowel, liver, or pancreas, with manifestations of an acutely injured abdomen. Those children with the most severe maltreatment injuries arrive at the hospital or physician's office in coma or convulsions, and some arrive dead.

SEXUAL ABUSE OF CHILDREN

The sexual abuse and exploitation of children has become an increasingly widespread type of child abuse, with psychosocial, legal, and medical implications. Most cases of sexual abuse involving children are never revealed because of the victim's guilt feelings, shame, ignorance, and tolerance, compounded by some physicians' reluctance to recognize and report sexual abuse, the court's insistence on strict rules of evidence, and the families' fears of dissolution if the sexual abuse is discovered.

Sexual abuse has been reported in schools, day-care centers, and group homes, where adult caretakers have been found to be the major offenders. The incidence of sexual abuse and child pornography is much higher than previously assumed.

Children may be sexually abused as early as infancy and through adolescence. Approximately 50 percent of abuse is by family members, with incest the principal form of sexual abuse. The most common abuse is by fathers, stepfathers, uncles, and older siblings. Mother-son incest is associated with more overtly severe maternal psychopathology than that seen in father-daughter incest. Features of father-daughter incest that have been described as common in many homes include a passive, sick, absent, or in some other way incapacitated mother; a daughter who takes on the maternal role in the family; alcohol abuse in the father; and overcrowding (Table 43.2-1).

The psychological and physical effects of sexual or physical abuse can be devastating and long-lasting. Children who are stimulated sexually by an adult feel anxiety and overexcitement, lose confidence in themselves, and become mistrustful of adults. Seduction, incest, and rape are important predisposing factors to later symptom formations, such as phobias, anxiety, and depression. The abused children tend to be hyperalert to external aggression, as shown by an inability to deal with their own aggressive impulses toward others or with others' hostility directed toward them.

DIAGNOSIS OF SEXUAL ABUSE

The diagnosis of sexual abuse in children is full of pitfalls. An estimated 2 to 8 percent of the allegations of sexual abuse are false. A much higher percentage of cases cannot be substantiated. Many investigations are done hastily or by inexperienced evaluators. In custody cases an allegation of sexual abuse can be used as a maneuver to limit a parent's visitation rights. Alleged sexual abuse of preschool-age children is particularly difficult to evaluate because of the child's immature cognitive and language development. The use of anatomically correct dolls has grown in popularity, but the use of such dolls is controversial. Patient and careful evaluations by experienced objective professionals are necessary; leading questions must be avoided. Children under the age of 3 years are unlikely to produce a verbal memory of past trauma or abuses; however, their experiences may be reflected in their play or fantasies. Some abused children meet the revised third edition of *Diagnostic and Statistical Manual of Mental Disorders* (DSM-III-R) criteria for posttraumatic stress disorder.

Table 43.2-1
Sexual Abuse of Children

Reported cases in U.S., 1985*	123,000
Prevalence of male abuse	3–31 percent
Prevalence of female abuse	6–62 percent
Perpetrators	
Father or stepfather	7–8 percent
Uncles or older siblings	16–42 percent
Friends	32–60 percent
Strangers	1 percent
Sexual activity	
Coitus	16–29 percent
Oral sex and intercourse	3–11 percent
Touching genitals	13–33 percent
Age	Peak between ages 9 and 12 25 percent below age 8
High-risk factors	Child living in single-parent home Marital conflict History of physical abuse Increase in sexual abuse
Reported motivation of abuser	Pedophilic impulses No other sexual object Inability to delay gratification

Table data from D Finklehor: The sexual abuse of children: Current research reviewed. Psychiatr Ann *17*: 4, 1987. Figures may total more than 100 percent because of overlapping studies.
*Current estimates are 150,000 to 200,000 new cases each year.

PHYSICIAN'S RESPONSIBILITY

In cases of suspected child abuse and neglect, the physician should diagnose the suspected maltreatment; secure the child's safety by admitting the child to a hospital or by arranging out-of-home placement; report the case to the appropriate social service department, child protection unit, or central registry; make an assessment with history, physical examination, skeletal survey, and photographs; request a social worker's report and appropriate surgical and medical consultations; confer within 72 hours with members of a child abuse committee; arrange a program of care for the child and the parents; and arrange for social service follow-up.

TREATMENT

Child

Ideally, each abused child should be given the benefit of an intervention plan based on the assessment of (1) the factors responsible for the parent's psychopathology; (2) the overall prognosis for the parents' achieving adequate parenting skills; (3) the time estimated to achieve meaningful change in the parent's ability to parent; (4) an estimate of whether the parent's dysfunction is confined to this child or involves other children; (5) the extent to which the parent's overall malfunctioning, if this is the case, is short-term or long-term (reflects a lifelong pattern); (6) the extent to which the mother's malfunctioning is confined to infants, as opposed to older children (that is, the incidence of abuse is inversely related to the child's age); (7) the parent's willingness to participate in the intervention plan; (8) the availability of personnel and physical resources to implement the various intervention strategies; and (9) the risk of the child's sustaining additional physical abuse by remaining in the home.

Parents

On the basis of the information obtained, several options can be selected to improve the parents' functioning: (1) eliminate or diminish the social or environmental stresses; (2) lessen the adverse psychological effects of the social factors on the parents; (3) reduce the demands on the mother to a level that is within her capacity through day-care placement of the child or provision of a housekeeper or baby-sitter; (4) provide emotional support, encouragement, sympathy, stimulation, instruction in maternal care, and aid in learning to plan for, assess, and meet the needs of the infant (supportive case work); and (5) resolve or diminish the parents' inner psychic conflicts (psychotherapy).

PREVENTION

In general, child abuse prevention and treatment programs should try to (1) prevent the separation of parents and child if possible, (2) prevent the placement of children in institutions, (3) encourage the parents' attainment of self-care status, and (4) encourage the family's attainment of self-sufficiency. As a last resort and to prevent further abuse and neglect, it may be necessary to remove children from families who are unwilling or unable to profit from the treatment program. In regard to sexual abuse, the licensing of day-care centers and the psychological screening of those persons who work in them should be mandatory to prevent further abuses. Education of the medical profession and members of allied health fields, as well as all who come in contact with children, will aid in early detection. And providing support services to stressed families will aid in preventing the problem in the first place.

References

American Academy of Child and Adolescent Psychiatry: Guidelines for the clinical evaluation of child and adolescent sexual abuse. J Am Acad Child Adolesc Psychiatry *27*: 655, 1988.

Benedek E P, Schetsky D H: Problems in validating allegations of sexual abuse: Part 1. Factors affecting perception and recall of events. J Am Acad Child Adolesc Psychiatry *26*: 912, 1987.

Benedek E P, Schetsky D H: Problems in validating allegations of sexual abuse: Part 2. Clinical evaluation. J Am Acad Child Adolesc Psychiatry *26*: 916, 1987.

Everson M D, Boat B W: False allegations of sexual abuse by children and adolescents. Am J Psychiatry *28*: 230, 1989.

Fontana V J: *The Maltreated Child: The Maltreatment Syndrome in Children*, ed 4. Thomas, Springfield, IL, 1979.

Herman J L, Perry C, Van der Kolk B A: Childhood trauma in borderline personality disorder. Am J Psychiatry *146*: 490, 1989.

Kempe C H, Silverman F N, Steele B N, Droegemueller W, Silver H K: The battered child syndrome. JAMA *181*: 17, 1962.

McLear S V, Deblinger E, Atkins M S, Foa E B, Raphe D L: Posttraumatic stress disorder in sexually abused children. J Am Acad Child Adolesc Psychiatry *27*: 650, 1988.

O'Brien J D: The effects of incest on female adolescent development. J Am Acad Psychoanal *15*: 83, 1987.

Realmuto G M, Jensen J B, Wescoe S: Specificity and sensitivity of sexually anatomically correct dolls in substantiating abuse: A pilot study. J Am Acad Child Adolesc Psychiatry *29*: 743, 1990.

Terr L: What happens to early memories of trauma? A study of twenty children under age 5 at the time of documented traumatic events. J Am Acad Child Adolesc Psychiatry *27*: 96, 1988.

Psychiatric Treatment of Children and Adolescents

44.1 / Individual Psychotherapy

THEORETICAL ASSUMPTIONS

The choice of intervention with an individual child should be based on the clinician's understanding of the child's problem and should stem from an individualized assessment of the child and the family. Regardless of how individualized such an evaluation is, any rational assessment requires that the data of observation be organized within a coherent framework. Typically, such systematizing schemata are derived from the therapist's preferred theory of personality development and organization, rendering it vital that the clinician be vigilant that these theories not distort the clinical observations or inappropriately influence the therapeutic interventions. Currently, four major theoretical systems underlie the bulk of child psychotherapy: (1) psychoanalytic theories of the evolution and resolution of emotional disturbance, (2) social-learning-behavioral theories, (3) family systems-oriented transactional theories of psychopathology and treatment, and (4) developmental theories.

Classic Psychoanalytic Theory

Classic psychoanalytic theory conceives of exploratory psychotherapy's working, with patients of all ages, by reversing the evolution of psychopathological processes. A principal difference noted with advancing age is a sharpening distinction between psychogenetic and psychodynamic factors. The younger the child, the more the genetic and the dynamic forces are intertwined.

The development of these pathological processes is generally thought to begin with experiences that have proved to be particularly significant to the patient and have affected him or her adversely. Although in one sense the experiences were real, in another sense they may have been misinterpreted or imagined. In any event, for the patient they were traumatic experiences that caused unconscious complexes. Being inaccessible to conscious awareness, these unconscious elements readily escape rational adaptive maneuvers and are subject to a pathological misuse of adaptive and defensive mechanisms. The end result is the development of conflicts leading to distressing symptoms, character attitudes, or patterns of behavior that constitute the emotional disturbance.

Increasingly, the psychoanalytic view of emotional disturbances in children has assumed a developmental orientation. Thus, the maladaptive defensive functioning is directed against conflicts between impulses that are characteristic of a specific developmental phase and environmental influences or the child's internalized representations of the environment. In this framework the disorders are the result of environmental interferences with maturational timetables or conflicts with the environment engendered by developmental progress. The result is difficulty in achieving or resolving developmental tasks and achieving the capacities specific to later phases of development, which can be expressed in various ways, such as Anna Freud's lines of development and Erik Erikson's concept of sequential psychosocial capacities.

The goal of therapy is to help develop good conflict resolution skills in the child, so that the child can function at the appropriate developmental level. Therapy may again be necessary as the child faces the challenges of subsequent developmental periods.

Psychoanalytic psychotherapy is a modified form of psychotherapy that is expressive and exploratory and that endeavors to reverse the evolution of emotional disturbance through a reenactment and desensitization of the traumatic events by the free expression of thoughts and feelings in an interview-play situation. Ultimately, the therapist helps the patient understand the warded-off feelings, fears, and wishes that have beset him or her.

Whereas the psychoanalytic psychotherapeutic approach seeks improvement by exposure and resolution of buried conflicts, suppressive-supportive-educative psychotherapy works in an opposite fashion. It aims to facilitate repression. The therapist, capitalizing on the patient's desire to please, encourages the patient to substitute new adaptive and defensive mechanisms. In this type of therapy, the therapist uses interpretations minimally; instead, the therapist emphasizes suggestion, persuasion, exhortation, operant reinforcement, counseling, education, direction, advice, abreaction, environmental manipulation, intellectual review, gratification of the patient's current dependent needs, and similar techniques.

Behavioral Theories

All behavior, regardless of whether it is adaptive or maladaptive, is a consequence of the same basic principles of behavior acquisition and maintenance. It is either learned or unlearned, and what renders behavior abnormal or disturbed is its social significance.

Although the theories and their derivative therapeutic intervention techniques have become increasingly complex over the years, it is still possible to subsume all learning within two global basic mechanisms. One is classic respondent conditioning, akin to Ivan Pavlov's famous experiments, and the second is operant instrumental learning, which is associated with B. F. Skinner, even though it is basic to both Edward Thorndike's law of effect regarding the influence of reinforcing consequences of behavior and to Sigmund Freud's pain-pleasure principle. Both of these basic mechanisms assign the highest priority to the immediate precipitants of behavior, deemphasizing those remote underlying causal determinants that are important in the psychoanalytic tradition. The theory asserts quite simply that there are but two types of abnormal behavior: behavioral deficits that result from a failure to learn and deviant maladaptive behaviors that are a consequence of learning inappropriate things.

Such concepts have always been an implicit part of the rationale underlying all child psychotherapy. Intervention strategies derive much of their success, particularly with children, from rewarding previously unnoticed good behavior, thereby highlighting it and making it more frequent.

Family Systems Theories

Although families have long been an interest of child psychotherapists, their understanding of transactional family processes has been greatly enhanced by conceptual contributions from cybernetics, systems theory, communications theory, object relations theory, social role theory, ethology, and ecology.

The bedrock premise entails the family's functioning as a self-regulating open system that possesses its own unique history and structure. Its structure is constantly evolving as a consequence of the dynamic interaction between the family's mutually interdependent systems and persons who share a complementarity of needs. From this conceptual foundation, a wealth of ideas has emerged under rubrics such as the family's development, life cycle, homeostasis, functions, identity, values, goals, congruence, symmetry, myths, rules, roles (spokesperson, symptom bearer, scapegoat, affect barometer, pet, persecutor, victim, arbitrator, distractor, saboteur, rescuer, breadwinner, disciplinarian, nurturer), structure (boundaries, splits, pairings, alliances, coalitions, enmeshed, disengaged), double bind, scapegoating, pseudomutuality, and mystification. Increasingly, it is being noted that appreciation of the family system sometimes explains why a minute therapeutic input at a critical junction may result in far-reaching changes, whereas in other situations huge quantities of therapeutic effort appear to be absorbed with minimal evidence of change.

Developmental Theories

Underlying child psychotherapy is the assumption that, in the absence of unusual interferences, children mature in basically orderly, predictable ways that are codifiable in a variety of interrelated psychosociobiological sequential systematizations. The central and overriding role of a developmental frame of reference in child psychotherapy distinguishes it from adult psychotherapy. The therapist's orientation should entail something more than knowledge of age-appropriate behavior derived from such studies as Arnold Gesell's descriptions of the morphology of behavior. It should encompass more than psychosexual development with ego-psychological and sociocultural amendments, exemplified by Erikson's epigenetic schema. It extends beyond familiarity with Jean Piaget's sequence of intellectual evolution as a basis for acquaintance with the level of abstraction at which children of various ages may be expected to function or for assessing their capacities for a moral orientation.

TYPES OF PSYCHOTHERAPY

Among the common bases for classification of child therapy is identification of the element presumed to be helpful for the young patient. Isolating a single therapeutic element as the basis for classification tends to be somewhat artificial, because most, if not all, of the factors are present in varying degrees in every child psychotherapeutic undertaking. For example, there is no psychotherapy in which the relationship between therapist and patient is not a vital factor; nevertheless, child psychotherapists commonly talk of relationship therapy to describe a form of treatment in which a positive, friendly, helpful relationship is viewed as the primary, if not the sole, therapeutic ingredient. Probably one of the best examples of pure relationship therapy is found outside a clinical setting in the work of the Big Brother Organization.

Remedial, educational, and patterning psychotherapy endeavors to teach new attitudes and patterns of behavior to children who persist in using immature and inefficient patterns, which are often presumed to be due to a maturational lag.

Supportive psychotherapy is particularly helpful in enabling a well-adjusted youngster cope with the emotional turmoil engendered by a crisis. It is also used with disturbed youngsters whose less than adequate ego functioning may be seriously disrupted by an expressive-exploratory mode or by other forms of therapeutic intervention. At the beginning of most psychotherapy, regardless of the patient's age and the nature of the therapeutic interventions, the principal therapeutic elements perceived by the patient tend to be the supportive ones, a consequence of therapists' universal efforts to be reliably and sensitively responsive. In fact, some therapy may never proceed beyond this supportive level, whereas others develop an expressive-exploratory or behavioral modification flavor on top of the supportive foundation.

Release therapy, described initially by David Levy, facilitates the abreaction of pent-up emotions. Although abreaction is an aspect of many therapeutic undertakings, in release therapy the treatment situation is structured to encourage only this factor. It is indicated primarily for preschool-age children who are suffering from a distorted emotional reaction to an isolated trauma.

Preschool-age children are sometimes treated through the parents, a process called filial therapy. The therapist using this strategy should be alert to the possibility that apparently successful filial treatment can obscure a significant diagnosis because the patient is not directly seen. The first case of filial therapy was that of Little Hans, reported by Sigmund Freud in 1905. Hans was a 5-year-old phobic child who was treated by Hans's father under Freud's supervision.

Psychotherapy with children is often psychoanalytically oriented, which means that it endeavors through the vehicle of self-understanding to enable the child's potential to develop further. This development is accomplished by liberating for more constructive use the psychic energy that is presumed to be expended in defending against fantasied dangers. Children are generally unaware of these unreal dangers, their fear of them, and the psychological defenses they use to avoid both the danger and the fear. With the awareness that is facilitated, patients can evaluate the usefulness of their defensive maneuvers and relinquish the unnecessary ones that constitute the symptoms of their emotional disturbance.

Child psychoanalysis—a more intensive, less common form of psychoanalytic psychotherapy—works on unconscious resistance and defenses during three to four sessions a week. Under these circumstances the therapist anticipates unconscious resistance and allows transference manifestations to mature to a full transference neurosis, through which neurotic conflicts are resolved.

Interpretations of dynamically relevant conflicts are emphasized in psychoanalytic descriptions. This does not, however, imply the absence of elements that are predominant in other types of psychotherapies. Indeed, in all psychotherapy the child should derive support from the consistently understanding and accepting relationship with the therapist. Remedial educational guidance is provided when necessary.

Probably the most vivid examples of the integration of psychodynamic and behavioral approaches, even though they are not always explicitly conceptualized as such, are to be found in the milieu therapy of child and adolescent psychiatric inpatient, residential, and day treatment facilities. Behavioral change is initiated in these settings, and its repercussions are explored concurrently in individual psychotherapeutic sessions, so that the action in one arena and the information stemming from it augment and illuminate what transpires in the other arena.

Cognitive therapy has been used with children, adolescents, and adults. This approach attempts to correct cognitive distortions, particularly negative conceptions of oneself, and is used mainly in depression.

DIFFERENCES BETWEEN CHILDREN AND ADULTS

Logic suggests that psychotherapy with children, who are generally more flexible than adults and have simpler defenses and other mental mechanisms, should consume less time than comparable treatment of adults. Experience does not usually confirm this expectation, because of the relative absence in children of some elements that contribute to successful treatment.

A child, for example, typically does not seek help. As a consequence, one of the first tasks for the therapist is to stimulate the child's motivation for treatment. Children commonly begin therapy involuntarily, often without the benefit of true parental support. Although the parents may want their child helped or changed, this desire is often generated by frustrated anger with the child. Typically, this anger is accompanied by relative insensitivity to what the therapist perceives as the child's need and the basis for a therapeutic alliance. Thus, whereas adult patients frequently perceive advantages in getting well, children may envision therapeutic change as nothing more than conforming to a disagreeable reality, which heightens the likelihood of perceiving the therapist as the parent's punitive agent. This is hardly the most fertile soil in which to nurture a therapeutic alliance.

Children tend to externalize internal conflicts in search of alloplastic adaptations and to find it difficult to conceive of problem resolution except by altering an obstructing environment. The passive, masochistic boy who is the constant butt of his schoolmates' teasing finds it inconceivable that this situation could be rectified by altering his mode of handling his aggressive impulses, rather than by someone's controlling his tormentors, a view that may be reinforced by significant adults in his environment.

The tendency of children to reenact their feelings in new situations facilitates the early appearance of spontaneous and global transference reactions that may be troublesome. Concurrently, the eagerness that children have for new experiences, coupled with their natural developmental fluidity, tends to limit the intensity and the therapeutic usefulness of subsequent transference developments.

Children have a limited capacity for self-observation, with the notable exception of some obsessive children who resemble adults in this ability. These obsessive children, however, usually isolate the vital emotional components. In the exploratory-interpretative psychotherapies, development of a capacity for ego splitting—that is, simultaneous emotional involvement and self-observation—is most helpful. Only by means of identification with a trusted adult and in alliance with that adult are children able to approach such an ideal. The therapist's sex and the relatively superficial aspects of the therapist's demeanor may be important elements in the development of a trusting relationship with a child.

Regressive behavioral and communicative modes can be wearing on child therapists. Typically motor-minded, even when they do not require external controls, children may demand a degree of physical stamina that is not of consequence in therapy with adults. The age appropriateness of such primitive mechanisms as denial, projection, and isolation hinders the process of working through, which relies on a patient's synthesizing and integrating capacities, both of which are immature in children. Also, environmental pressures on the therapist are generally greater in psychotherapeutic work with children than in work with adults.

Although children compare unfavorably with adults in many of the qualities that are generally considered desirable in therapy, children have the advantage of active maturational and developmental forces. The history of psychotherapy for children is punctuated by efforts to harness these assets and to overcome the liabilities. Recognition of the importance of play constituted a major forward stride in these efforts.

PLAYROOM

The structure, design, and furnishing of a playroom suitable for child psychotherapy is most important. Some therapists say that the toys should be few, simple, and carefully selected to facilitate the communication of fantasy. Others suggest that a wide variety of playthings be available to increase the range of feelings the child may express. These contrasting recommendations have been attributed to differences in therapeutic methods. Some therapists tend to avoid interpretation, even of conscious ideas, whereas others recommend the interpretation of unconscious content directly and quickly. Therapists tend to change their preferences in equipment as they accumulate experience and develop confidence in their abilities.

Although special equipment—such as genital dolls, amputation dolls, and see-through anatomically complete (except for genitalia) models—have been used in therapy, many therapists have observed that the unusual nature of such items risks making children wary and suspicious of the therapist's motives. Until the dolls available to the children in their own home include genitalia, the psychic content that these special dolls are designed to elicit may be more available at the appropriate time with conventional dolls.

Although the choices of play materials vary from therapist to therapist, the following equipment can constitute a well-balanced playroom or play area: multigenerational families of flexible but sturdy dolls of various races; additional dolls representing special roles and feelings, such as policemen, doctor, and soldier; dollhouse furnishings with or without a dollhouse; toy animals; puppets; paper, crayons, paint, and blunt-ended scissors; a spongelike ball; clay or something comparable; tools like rubber hammers, rubber knives, and guns; building blocks, cars, trucks, and airplanes; and eating utensils. These toys should enable children to communicate through play. It is wise to avoid toys and materials that are fragile or break easily, which can result in physical injury to the child or can increase the child's guilt.

A special drawer or box should be available, space permitting, to each child in which to store items the child brings to the therapy session or to store projects, such as drawings and stories, for further retrieval. Limits have to be set, so that this private storage capacity is not used to hoard communal play equipment, depriving the therapist's other patients. Some therapists assert that an absence of such arrangements evokes material about sibling rivalry; however, others feel that this is a rationalization for not respecting the child's privacy, inasmuch as there are other ways of facilitating the expression of such feelings.

INITIAL APPROACH

A variety of approaches can be derived from the therapist's individual style and perception of the child's needs. The range extends from those in which the therapist endeavors to direct the child's thought content and activity—as in release therapy, some behavior therapy, and certain educational patterning techniques—to those exploratory methods in which the therapist endeavors to follow the child's lead. Even though the child determines the focus, it remains the therapist's responsibility to structure the situation. Encouraging children to say whatever they wish and to play freely, as in exploratory psychotherapy, establishes a definite structure. The therapist has created an atmosphere in which to get to know all about the child—the good side, as well as the bad side, as children would put it. The therapist may communicate to the child that the child's response will not elicit either anger or pleasure, only understanding from the therapist. Such an assertion does not imply that therapists do not have emotions, but it assures the young patient that the therapist's personal feelings and standards are subordinate to understanding the youngster.

THERAPEUTIC INTERVENTIONS

Therapeutic interventions with children encompass a range comparable to those used with adults in psychotherapy. If the amount of therapist activity is used as the basis for a classificatory continuum of interventions, at the least active end are the questions posed by the therapist requesting elaboration of the patient's statements or behavior. Next on the continuum of therapeutic activity are the exclamations and confrontations in which the therapist more pointedly directs attention to some data of which the patient is cognizant. Then there are interpretations, designed to expand the patient's conscious awareness of himself or herself by making explicit those elements that have previously been implicitly expressed in his or her thoughts, feelings, and behavior. Beyond interpretation, the therapist may educatively offer the patient information that is new because the patient has not been exposed to it previously. At the most active end of the continuum, there is advising, counseling, and directing, designed to help the patient adopt a course of action or a conscious attitude.

Nurturing and maintaining a therapeutic alliance may require some education of the child regarding the process of therapy. Another educational intervention may entail assigning labels to affects that have not been part of the youngster's past experience. Rarely does therapy have to compensate for a real absence of education regarding acceptable decorum and playing games. Usually, children are in therapy not because of the absence of educational efforts but because repeated educational efforts have failed. Therefore, therapy generally does not need to include additional teaching efforts, despite the frequent temptation to offer them.

Adults' natural educational fervor with children is often accompanied by a paradoxical tendency to protect them from learning about some of life's realities. In the past, this tendency contributed to the stork's role in childbirth, the dead having taken a long trip, and similar fairy-tale explanations for natural phenomena about which adults were uncomfortable in communicating with children. Although adults are more honest with children today, therapists can find themselves in a situation in which their overwhelming urge to protect the hurt child may be as disadvantageous to the child as was the stork myth. Alternatively, information given to the child must take into account individual problems and developmental levels.

The temptation to offer oneself as a model for identification may stem also from helpful educational attitudes toward children. Although there are instances in which this may be an appropriate therapeutic strategy, therapists should not lose sight of the pitfalls in this apparently innocuous strategy.

PARENTS

Psychotherapy with children is characterized by the need for parental involvement. This involvement does not necessarily reflect parental culpability for the youngster's emotional difficulties but is a reality of the child's dependent state. This fact cannot be stressed too much because of what could be considered an occupational hazard shared by many who work with children. This hazard is the motivation to rescue children from the negative influence of their parents, sometimes related to an unconscious competitive desire to be a better parent than the child's or one's own parents.

There are varying degrees of parental involvement in child psychotherapy. With preschool-age children the entire therapeutic effort may be directed toward the parents, without any direct treatment of the child. At the other extreme, children can be seen in psychotherapy without any parental involvement beyond the payment of fees and perhaps transporting the child to the therapy sessions. However, the majority of practitioners prefer to maintain an informative alliance with the parents for the purpose of obtaining additional information about the child.

Probably the most frequent arrangements are those that were developed in child guidance clinics—that is, parent guidance focused on the child or on the parent-child interaction or therapy for the parents' own individual needs concurrent with the child's therapy. The parents may be seen by the child's therapist or by someone else. In recent years there have been increasing efforts to shift the focus from the child as the primary patient to the concept of the child as the family's emissary to the clinic. In such family therapy, all or selected members of the family are treated simultaneously as a family group. Although the preferences of specific clinics or practitioners for either an individual or a family therapeutic approach may be unavoidable, the final decision as to which therapeutic strategy or combination to use should be derived from the clinical assessment.

CONFIDENTIALITY

Consideration of parental involvement highlights the question of confidentiality in psychotherapy with children. There are advantages to creating an atmosphere in which the child can feel that all words and actions will be viewed by the therapist as simultaneously both serious and tentative. In other words, the child's communications do not bind the therapist to a commitment; nevertheless, they are too important to be communicated to a third party without the patient's permission. Although such an attitude may be conveyed implicitly, there are occasions in which it is wise to explicitly discuss confidentiality with the child. It can be risky to promise a child that the therapist will not tell parents what transpires in therapeutic sessions. Although the therapist has no intention of disclosing such data to the parents, the bulk of what children do and say in psychotherapy is common knowledge to the parents. Therefore, should the child be so motivated, it is easy for the child to manipulate the situation so as to produce circumstantial evidence that the therapist has betrayed a confidence. Accordingly, if confidentiality requires specific discussion during treatment, the therapist may not want to go beyond indicating that the therapist is not in the business of telling parents what goes on in therapy, as the therapist's role is to understand children and to help them.

It is also important to try to enlist the parents' cooperation in respecting the privacy of the child's therapeutic sessions. This respect is not always readily honored, as parents quite naturally are curious about what transpires and may be threatened by the therapist's apparently privileged position.

Routinely reporting to children the essence of communications with the third parties regarding the child underscores the therapist's reliability and respect for the child's autonomy. In certain types of treatment, this report may be combined with soliciting the child's guesses about these transactions. Also, it may be fruitful to invite children, particularly older ones, to participate in discussions about them with third parties.

INDICATIONS AND CONTRAINDICATIONS

The present level of knowledge does not permit the compilation of a meaningful list of the multifaceted indications for child psychotherapy. Existing diagnostic classifications cannot serve as the basis for such a list because of invariable deficiencies in nosological specificity and comprehensiveness. In general, psychotherapy is indicated for children with emotional disorders that appear to be permanent enough to impede maturational and developmental forces. Psychotherapy may also be indicated when the child's development is not impeded but is inducing reactions in the environment that are considered pathogenic. Ordinarily, such disharmonies are dealt with by the child with parental assistance, but, when these efforts are persistently inadequate, psychotherapeutic interventions may be indicated.

Psychotherapy should be limited to those instances in which there are positive indicators pointing to its potential usefulness. For the child to benefit from psychotherapy, the home situation must provide a certain amount of nurturance, stability, and motivation for therapy. The child must have adequate cognitive resources to participate in and profit from the process. If psychotherapy, despite contraindications, is invariably recommended after every child psychiatric evaluation by a particular therapist or clinic, this fact suggests not only unsatisfactory professional practice and a disservice to patients but also an indiscriminate use of psychotherapy.

Psychotherapy is contraindicated if the emotional disturbance is judged to be an intractable one that will not respond to treatment. This is an exceedingly difficult judgment but one that is essential, considering the excess of the demand for psychotherapy over its supply. Because the potential for error in such prognostic assessments is great, therapists should bring to them both professional humility and a readiness to offer a trial of therapy. There are times when the essential factor in intractability is the therapist. Certain patients may elicit a reaction from one therapist that is a contraindication for psychotherapy with that therapist but not necessarily with another.

Another contraindication is evidence that the therapeutic process will interfere with reparative forces. A difficult question is posed by suggestions that the forces mobilized as a consequence of psychotherapy may have dire social or somatic effects. An example is the circumstance in which psychotherapy may upset a precarious family equilibrium, thereby causing more difficulty than the original problem posed.

References

Abrams S: The psychoanalytic process in adults and children. Psychoanal Study Child *43*: 245, 1988.

Adams P L: *A Primer of Child Psychotherapy*. Little, Brown, Boston, 1982.

Berlin L N: Some transference and countertransference issues in the playroom. J Am Acad Child Adolesc Psychiatry *26*: 101, 1987.

Dulcan M K: Brief psychotherapy with children and their families: The state of the art. J Am Acad Child Adolesc Psychiatry *25*: 544, 1984.

Glenn J, ed.: *Child Analysis and Therapy*. Aronson, New York, 1978.

Looney J G: Treatment planning in child psychiatry. J Am Acad Child Psychiatry *23*: 529, 1984.

Rutter M: Psychological therapies in child psychiatry: Issues and prospects. Psychol Med *12*: 723, 1982.

Shapiro T, Esman A H: Psychotherapy with children and adolescents. Psychiatr Clin North Am *8*: 909, 1985.

Sholevar G P, Burland J A, Frank J L, Etezady M H, Goldstein J: Psychoanalytic treatment of children and adolescents, J Am Acad Child Adolesc Psychiatry *28*: 685, 1989.

Solnit A J: A psychoanalytic view of play. Psychoanal Study Child *42*: 205, 1987.

Werry J S, Wollerheim J P: Behavior therapy with children and adolescents: A twenty-year overview. J Am Acad Child Adolesc Psychiatry *28*: 1, 1989.

44.2 / Group Therapy

The characteristics of developmental stages have influenced the growth of group psychotherapy techniques perhaps more than any other factor.

PRESCHOOL-AGE AND EARLY-SCHOOL-AGE GROUPS

Work with a preschool-age group is usually structured by the therapist through the use of a particular technique, such as puppets or artworks, or is couched in terms of a permissive play atmosphere. In therapy with puppets, the children project their fantasies onto the puppets in a way not unlike ordinary play. The main value lies in the cathexis afforded the children, especially if they show difficulty in expressing their feelings. Here the group aids the child less by interaction with other members than by action with the puppets.

In play group therapy the emphasis rests on the interactional qualities of the children with each other and with the therapist in the permissive playroom setting. The therapist should be a person who can allow the children to produce fantasies verbally and in play but who can also use active restraint when the children undergo excessive tension. The toys are the traditional ones used in individual play therapy. The children use the toys to act out aggressive impulses and to relive with the group members and with the therapist their home difficulties. The children catalyze each other and obtain libido-activating stimulation from this catalysis and from their play materials. The therapist interprets a child to the group in the context of the transference to the therapist and to other group members.

The children selected for group treatment show in common a social hunger, the need to be like their peers and to be accepted by them. Usually, the therapist excludes the children who have never realized a primary relationship, as with their mothers, inasmuch as individual psychotherapy can better help those children. The children selected usually include those with phobic reactions, effeminate boys, shy and withdrawn children, and children with primary behavior disorders.

Modifications of these criteria have been used in group therapy for autistic children, along with parent group therapy and art therapy.

A modification of group therapy has been used for physically handicapped toddlers who showed speech and language delays. This experience of twice-a-week group activities involved the mothers and their children in a mutual teaching-learning setting. The experience proved effective to the mothers, who received supportive psychotherapy in this group experience; their formerly hidden fantasies about the children emerged, to be dealt with therapeutically.

LATENCY-AGE GROUPS

Activity group therapy assumes that poor and divergent experiences have led to deficits in appropriate personality development in the behavior of children; therefore, corrective experiences in a therapeutically conditioned environment will modify them. Because some latency-age children present deep disturbances involving neurotic traits (fears, high anxiety levels, and guilt), an activity-interview group psychotherapy modification evolved. This format uses interview techniques, verbal explanations of fantasies, group play, work, and other communications.

In this type of group therapy, as with pubertal and adolescent groups, the children verbalize in a problem-oriented manner, with the awareness that problems brought them together and that the group aims to change them. They report dreams, fantasies, and daydreams, as well as traumatic and unpleasant experiences. Both these experiences and the group behavior undergo open discussion. Therapists vary in their use of time, cotherapists, food, and materials. Most groups meet after school and last at least one hour, although some group leaders prefer 90 minutes. Some therapists serve food in the last 10 minutes, and others prefer serving times when the children are more together for talking. Food, however, does not become a major feature, never becoming central to the group's activities.

PUBERTAL AND ADOLESCENT GROUPS

Similar group therapy methods can be used with pubertal children, who are often grouped monosexually, rather than mixed. Their problems resemble those of late latency-age children, but they are also beginning, especially the girls, to feel the effects and pressures of early adolescence. In a way these groups offer help during a transitional period. The group appears to satisfy the social appetite of preadolescents, who compensate for feelings of inferiority and self-doubt by the formation of groups. This form of therapy puts to advantage the influence of the process of socialization during these years. Because children of this age experience difficulties in conceptualizing, pubertal therapy groups tend to use play, drawing, psychodrama, and other nonverbal modes of expression. The therapist's role is now active and directive, as opposed to the older, more passive role assigned to the therapist.

Activity group psychotherapy has been the recommended type of group therapy for latency-age and pubertal children who do not have significantly neurotic personality patterns. The children, usually of the same sex and in groups of not more than eight, freely engage in activities in a setting especially designed and planned for its physical and milieu characteristics. Samuel Slavson, one of the pioneers in group psychotherapy, pictured the group as a substitute family in which the passive, neutral therapist becomes the surrogate for parents. The therapist assumes different roles, mostly in a nonverbal manner, as each child interacts with the therapist and with other group members. Recent therapists, however, tend to see the group as a form of peer group, with its attendant socializing processes, rather than as a reenactment of the family. Late adolescents, 16 years of age and up, may be included in groups of adults when indicated. Group therapy has been very useful in the treatment of substance abuse problems. Combined therapy (the use of group and individual therapy) has also been used successfully with adolescents.

OTHER GROUP THERAPY SITUATIONS

Some residential and day treatment units frequently use group therapy techniques in their work. Group therapy in schools for underachievers and for the underprivileged has relied on reinforcement and on modeling theory, in addition to traditional techniques, and has been supplemented by parent groups.

With the opportunity for more controlled conditions, residential treatment units have been used for specific studies in group therapy, such as behavioral contracting. Behavioral contracting with reward-punishment reinforcement provides positive reinforcements among preadolescent boys with severe concerns in basic trust, low self-esteem, and dependency conflicts. Somewhat akin to formal residential treatment units are social group work homes. The children undergo many psychological assaults before placement, so that supportive group therapy offers ventilation and catharsis, but more often it succeeds in letting these children become aware of the enjoyment of sharing activities and developing skills.

Public schools—also a structured environment, although usually not considered the best site for group therapy—have been used by a number of workers. Group therapy as group counseling readily lends itself to school settings. One such group used gender- and problem-homogeneous selection for groups of six to eight students, who met once a week during school hours over a time span of two to three years.

INDICATIONS

From the foregoing one can gather that there are many indications for the use of group psychotherapy as a treatment modality. Some indications can be described as situational; the therapist may work in a reformatory setting, where group psychotherapy has seemed to reach the adolescents better than individual treatment. Another indication is time economics; more patients can be reached within a given time span by the use of groups than by individual therapy. Using groups best helps the child at a given age and developmental stage and with a given type of problem. In the young age group the children's social hunger and their potential need for peer acceptance help to determine their suitability for group therapy. Criteria for unsuitability are controversial and have been progressively loosened.

PARENT GROUPS

In the group treatment, as with most treatment procedures for children, parental difficulties present obstacles. Sometimes uncooperative parents refuse to bring a child or to participate in their own therapy. The extreme of this situation reveals itself when severely disturbed parents use the child as their channel of communication in working out their own needs. In such circumstances the child is in an intolerable position of receiving positive group experiences that seem to create havoc at home.

Parents groups, therefore, can be a valuable aid to the group therapy of their children. The parent of a child in therapy often has difficulty in understanding the nature of his child's ailment, of discerning the line of demarcation between normal and pathological behavior, in relating to the medical establishment, and in coping with feelings of guilt. A parents' group assists them in these areas and helps the members formulate guidelines for action.

References

Abramowitz C V: The effectiveness of group psychotherapy with children. Arch Gen Psychiatry *33*: 320, 1976.

Blotcky M, Sheinbein M, Wiggins K, Forgotson J: A verbal group technique for ego-disturbed children: Action to words. Int J Psychoanal Psychother *8*: 203, 1980.

Bromfield R, Pfeifer G: Combining group and individual psychotherapy: Impact on the individual treatment experience. J Am Acad Child Adolesc Psychiatry *27*: 220, 1988.

Kraft I A: Group therapy. In *Basic Handbook of Child Psychiatry,* J D Noshpitz, editor, vol 3, p 159. Basic Books, New York, 1979.

Kraft I A: Some special considerations in adolescent group psychotherapy. Int J Group Psychother *2*: 196, 1961.

Scheidlinger S: Group treatment of adolescents. Am J Orthopsychiatry *55*: 102, 1985.

Scheidlinger S: Short-term group psychotherapy for children: An overview. Int J Group Psychother *34*: 573, 1984.

Slavson S R, Schiffer M: *Group Psychotherapies for Children*. International Universities Press, New York, 1985.

Yalom I D: *Inpatient Group Psychotherapy*. Basic Books, New York, 1983.

44.3 / Residential, Day, and Hospital Treatment

RESIDENTIAL TREATMENT

More than 20,000 emotionally disturbed children are in residential treatment centers in the United States, and that number is increasing. Deteriorating social conditions, particularly in cities, often make it impossible for a child with a serious psychiatric problem to live at home. In these cases residential treatment centers serve a very real need. They provide a structured living environment where children may form strong attachments to and receive commitments from the staff. The purpose of these centers is to provide treatment and special education for the children and treatment of their families.

Staff and Setting

Staffing patterns include various combinations of child care workers, teachers, social workers, psychiatrists, pediatricians, nurses, and psychologists, making the cost of residential treatment very high.

The Joint Commission on the Mental Health of Children made the following structural and setting recommendations:

In addition to space for therapy programs, there should be facilities for a first-rate school and a rich evening activity program, and there should be ample space for play, both indoors and out. Facilities should be small, seldom exceeding 60 in capacity, with 100 a maximum limit, and should make provision for children to live in small groups. The centers should be located near the families they serve and be readily accessible by public transportation. They should be located for ready access to special medical and educational services and to various community resources, including consultants. They should be open institutions whenever possible; locked buildings, wards, or rooms should only rarely be required. In designing residential programs, the guiding principle should be this: Children should be removed the least possible distance—in space, in time, and in the psychological texture of the experience—from their normal life setting.

Indications

Most children who are referred for residential treatment have already been seen by one or more professional persons, such as a school psychologist, pediatrician, or members of a child guidance clinic, juvenile court, or state welfare agency. Attempts at outpatient treatment and foster home placement usually precede residential treatment. Sometimes the severity of the child's problems or the inability of the family to provide for the child's needs prohibit sending a child home. Many children sent to residential treatment centers have conduct disorders. The age range of the children varies from institution to institution, but most children are between 5 and 15 years of age. Boys are referred more frequently than girls.

An initial review of the data enables the intake staff to determine whether a particular child is likely to benefit from their treatment program. Often, for every one child accepted for admission, three are rejected. The next step is usually interviews with the child and parents by various staff members, such as a therapist, a group living worker, and a teacher. Psychological testing and neurological examinations are given when indicated if they have not already been done. The child and parents should be prepared for these interviews.

Group Living

Most of the children's time in a residential treatment setting is spent in group living. The group living staff consists of child care workers who offer a structured environment that constitutes a therapeutic milieu. The environment places boundaries and limitations on the children. Tasks are defined within the limits of the children's abilities; incentives, such as additional privileges, encourage them to progress, rather than regress. In milieu therapy the environment is structured, limits are set, and a therapeutic atmosphere is maintained.

The children often select one or more staff members with whom to form a relationship through which they express, consciously and unconsciously, many of their feelings about their parents. The child care staff should be trained to recognize such transference reactions and to respond to them in a way that is different from the children's expectations, based on their previous or even current relationship with their parents.

To maintain consistency and balance, the group living staff must communicate freely and regularly with one another and with the other professional and administrative staff members of the residential setting, particularly the children's teachers and therapists. The child care staff members must recognize any tendency toward becoming the good (or bad) parent in response to a child's splitting behavior. This tendency may be manifested as a pattern of blaming other staff members for a child's disruptive behavior. Similarly, the child care staff must recognize and avoid such individual and group countertransference reactions as sadomasochistic and punitive behavior toward a child.

The structured setting should offer a corrective emotional experience and opportunities for facilitating and improving the children's adaptive behavior, particularly when such deficiencies as speech and language deficits, intellectual retardation, inadequate peer relationships, bed-wetting, poor feeding habits, and attention deficits are present. Some of these deficits are the basis of the children's poor school academic performance and unsocialized behavior, including temper tantrums, fighting, and withdrawal.

Behavior modification principles have also been used, particularly in group work with children. Behavior therapy is part of the residential center's total therapeutic effort.

Education

Children in residential treatment frequently have severe learning disabilities, as well as disruptive behavior. Usually, they cannot function in a regular community school and, consequently, need a special on-grounds school setting. The educational process in residential treatment is complex, and Table 44.3-1 shows some of its components.

A major goal of the on-grounds school is to motivate the children to learn.

Table 44.3-1
Educational Process in Residential Treatment

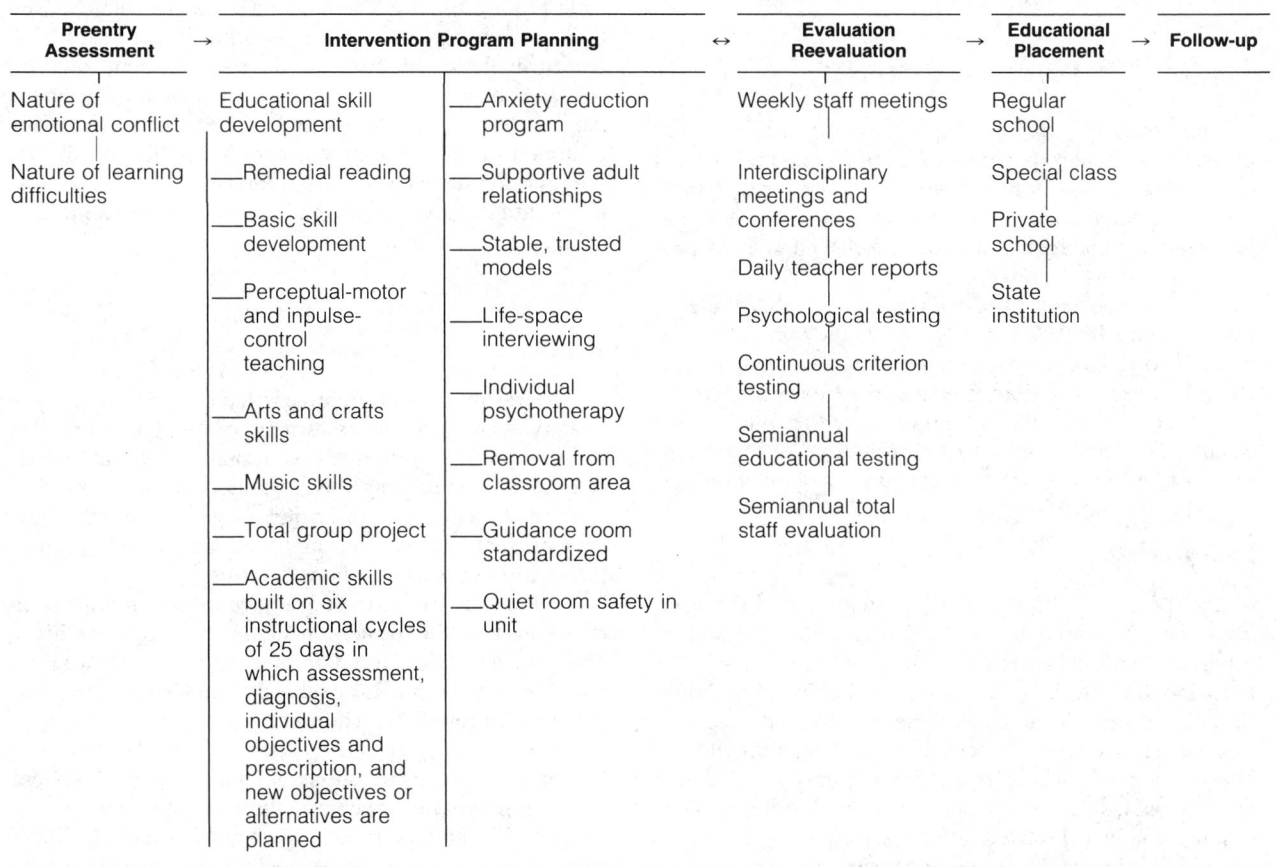

Preentry Assessment →	Intervention Program Planning ↔		Evaluation Reevaluation →	Educational Placement →	Follow-up
Nature of emotional conflict	Educational skill development	Anxiety reduction program	Weekly staff meetings	Regular school	
Nature of learning difficulties	Remedial reading	Supportive adult relationships	Interdisciplinary meetings and conferences	Special class	
	Basic skill development	Stable, trusted models	Daily teacher reports	Private school	
	Perceptual-motor and inpulse-control teaching	Life-space interviewing	Psychological testing	State institution	
	Arts and crafts skills	Individual psychotherapy	Continuous criterion testing		
	Music skills	Removal from classroom area	Semiannual educational testing		
	Total group project	Guidance room standardized	Semiannual total staff evaluation		
	Academic skills built on six instructional cycles of 25 days in which assessment, diagnosis, individual objectives and prescription, and new objectives or alternatives are planned	Quiet room safety in unit			

Table by Melvin Lewis, M.B., B.S., (London), F.R.C. Psych, D.C.H.

Therapy

Traditional modes of psychotherapy have a place in residential treatment, including intensive, individual psychotherapy with the child; group therapy with selected children; individual or group therapy or both for parents; and, in some cases, family therapy. However, several modifications need to be kept in mind.

The child relates to the total staff of the setting and, therefore, needs to know that what transpires in the therapist's office is shared with all professional staff members. The therapist informs the child that what they discuss and do in individual therapy will not be revealed to other family members or to other children in the residential center but will be shared with the professional staff members within the setting itself.

Parents

Concomitant work with the parents is essential. The child usually has a strong tie to the parent, no matter how disturbed the parent is. Sometimes the child idealizes the parent, who repeatedly fails the child. Sometimes the parent has an ambivalent or unrealistic expectation that the child will return home. In some instances the parent must be helped to enable the child to live in another setting when that is in the child's best interests. Most residential treatment centers offer individual or group therapy with the parents, couples or marital therapy, and in some cases conjoint family therapy.

DAY TREATMENT

The concept of daily comprehensive therapeutic experiences without removing the children from their homes or families derived in part from experiences with a therapeutic nursery school. The development of day hospital programs for children followed, and the number of programs continues to grow.

The main advantage of day treatment is that the children remain with their families, and so the families can be more involved in the treatment. Day treatment is also much less expensive than is residential treatment. At the same time, the risks of day treatment are the child's social isolation and confinement to a narrow band of social contacts within the program's disturbed peer population.

Indications

The primary indication for day treatment is the need for a more structured, intensive, and specialized treatment program than can be provided on an outpatient basis. At the same time, the home in which the child is living should be able to provide an environment that is at least not destructive to the child's development. Children who are likely to benefit from day treatment may have a wide range of diagnoses, including infantile autism, borderline conditions, conduct disorder, attention-deficit hyperactivity disorder, and mental retardation. Exclusion symptoms include behavior that is likely to be destructive to the children themselves or to others under the treatment conditions. Thus, some children who threaten to run away, set fires, attempt suicide, hurt others, or disrupt to a significant degree the life of their family while they are at home may not be suitable for day treatment.

Programs

The same ingredients that lead to a successful residential treatment program apply to day treatment. These ingredients include clear administrative leadership, team collaboration, open communication, and an understanding of the children's behavior. Indeed, there are advantages in having a single agency offer both residential and day treatment.

A major function of the child care staff in day treatment for psychiatrically disturbed children is to provide positive experiences and a structure that will enable the children and their families to internalize controls and to function better in regard to themselves and to the outside world. Again, the methods used are essentially similar to those found in the full residential treatment program.

Because the age, needs, and range of diagnoses of children who may benefit from some form of day treatment vary, a broad spectrum of day treatment programs has developed. Some programs specialize in the special educational and structured environmental needs of mentally retarded children. Others offer the special therapeutic efforts required to treat autistic or schizophrenic children. Still other programs provide the total spectrum of treatment usually found in full residential treatment, of which they may be a part. The children may then move from one part of the program to another and may be in residential treatment or day treatment according to their needs. The school program is always a major component of day treatment, and the psychiatric treatment varies according to the child's needs and diagnosis.

Results

The results of day treatment have not yet been adequately evaluated. The assessment of the long-term effectiveness of day treatment is fraught with difficulties, whether one is making the assessment from the point of view of the child's maintenance of gains, the therapist's view of what has been accomplished, or society's concerns for such matters as cost-benefit ratios.

At the same time, the advantage of day treatment has encouraged further development of these programs. Moreover, the lessons learned from day treatment programs have moved the mental health disciplines toward having the services follow the children, rather than perpetuating discontinuities of care. The experiences of day treatment for the psychiatric conditions of children and adolescents have also encouraged pediatric hospitals and departments to adapt this model for the medical nursing care of children with physical disorders, particularly those with chronic physical illnesses.

HOSPITAL TREATMENT

Begun in the 1920s, inpatient psychiatric treatment of children includes two types of units: acute-care hospital units and long-term hospital units. Acute-care units generally accept children manifesting dangerous—that is, suicidal, assaultive, or psychotically disorganized—behavior. Diagnosis, stabilization, and the formulation and initiation of a treatment plan are the goals of these units. Disposition is usually to home, to residential treatment centers, or to long-term (usually state) hospital units for continued care. Acute-care hospitalization generally lasts from 6 to 12 weeks and is often extended because of the wait for beds in residential treatment centers and state hospitals. Long-term hospitalization generally lasts many months to years. The staffs on inpatient units are interdisciplinary, including psychiatrists, psychologists, social workers, nurses, activity therapists, and teachers.

References

Evangelakis M G: *A Manual for Residential and Day Treatment of Children.* Thomas, Springfield, IL, 1974.

Hunger D S, Webster C D, Konstantareas M M, Sloman L: Ten years later: What becomes of the psychiatrically disturbed child in day treatment. J Child Care *1*: 45, 1982.

Lewis M, Brown T E: Child care in the residential treatment of the borderline child. Child Care Q *9*: 41, 1980.

Lewis M, Lewis D O, Shanok S S, Klatskin E, Osborn J R: The undoing of residential treatment. J Am Acad Child Psychiatry *19*: 160, 1980.

Lyman R D, Prentice-Dunn S, Gabel S, eds.: *Residential and Inpatient Treatment of Children and Adolescents.* Plenum, New York, 1989.

Nurcombe B: Goal-directed treatment planning and the principles of brief hospitalization. J Am Acad Child Adolesc Psychiatry *28*: 26, 1989.

Pfeiffer S I, Strzelecki S C: Inpatient psychiatric treatment of children and adolescents: A review of outcome studies. J Am Acad Child Adolesc Psychiatry *29*: 847, 1990.

Prentice-Dunn S, Wilson D R, Lyman R D: Client factors related to outcome in a residential and day treatment program for children. J Clin Child Psychol *10*: 188, 1981.

Zang L D: The antisocial aggressive school-age child: Day hospitals. In *Handbook of Treatment of Mental Disorders and Adolescence.* B Wolman, J Egan and A Ross, editors, p 317. Prentice-Hall, Englewood Cliffs, NJ, 1978.

44.4 / Organic Therapies

Medications in pediatric psychopharmacology are used with the treatment of either specific diagnostic categories or with target symptoms, such as aggression. In either case, medication is given to decrease maladaptive behaviors and to promote adaptive behaviors. Special consideration must be given to medicinal side effects, such as cognitive dulling, that interfere with a child's or adolescent's developmental tasks. Medication is never used alone; it is always used as an adjunct to other forms of therapy.

THERAPEUTIC CONSIDERATIONS

First, a thorough assessment must be conducted (Table 44.4-1). Does the child have a disorder or syndrome of a type and severity that warrants organic therapy? Other medical or social conditions causing such symptoms should be investigated. Equally important are an evaluation and an understanding of the patient's social and family context, which may influence the choice of therapy. A parent's ability to administer the child's medication may be hampered by a psychiatric disorder exhibited by the parent. Often, it is necessary to intervene in the parent's problem before medicating the child. Parental or school opposition to medication can also prevent its use. The parents' beliefs about the cause of the child's illness may color their attitudes toward medication. The history of drug response in other family members may be helpful in assessing the risk-benefit ratio and in selecting which member of a particular class of drugs to choose.

CHILDHOOD PHARMACOKINETICS

Because children are more efficient metabolizers of psychoactive drugs than adults, more rapid hepatic biotransformation and renal clearance can be expected. Therefore, children may require or tolerate slightly higher dosages than adults on a milligram-per-kilogram of body weight basis. This is clearly the case with lithium, which in one study had a shorter half-life and a higher renal clearance in children than in adults. One explanation for the differential effects is the greater liver-body weight ratio in children (e.g., 30 percent greater for a 6-year-old than for an adult). Stimulants seem to have a somewhat shorter half-life in children than in adults. Children convert imipramine (Tofranil) to desmethylimipramine more actively than do adults. Although children clear imipramine more rapidly through demethylation, their clearance of the sum of imipramine and desmethylimipramine after imipramine administration is at a rate similar to that of adults.

Studies of the serum levels of both lithium and antidepressants demonstrate wide variability of serum levels among persons receiving the same milligram-per-kilogram dosage. Similarly, this same variation has been seen in adults with these drugs and with most other psychotherapeutic agents. With imipramine, depressed children require the same plasma levels associated with a favorable response in adults.

INDICATIONS

Attention-Deficit Hyperactivity Disorder

The best-documented indication for pharmacological treatment in child psychiatry is attention-deficit hyperac-

Table 44.4-1
Stepwise Process of Organic Therapy

1. Diagnostic evaluation
2. Symptom measurement
3. Risk-benefit ratio analysis
4. Establishment of a contract for therapy
5. Periodic reevaluation
6. Termination and tapered drug withdrawal

tivity disorder (ADHD). The first choice among organic therapies is a stimulant, of which there are three: methylphenidate (Ritalin), dextroamphetamine (Dexedrine), and pemoline (Cylert). The dosage of the stimulant can be titrated about every three to five days (every week in the case of pemoline) until either a therapeutic benefit is achieved or side effects prohibit a further increase. The physician should use the lowest effective dosage. Doses are usually limited to the day, with their frequency based on the drug's half-life. Compared with the long half-lives of the antidepressants and antipsychotics, all the stimulants are short-acting. Of the three drugs, methylphenidate has the shortest half-life (2½ hours is about the mean). As a consequence, it is frequently administered twice daily. The half-life of pemoline is the longest (about 12 hours), and that of amphetamines is intermediate.

Decreased restlessness and impulsivity and increased attention span, concentration, and compliance with commands are the hallmarks of treatment response. About 75 percent of patients with ADHD respond to either amphetamine or methylphenidate. Some children respond to one stimulant but not to another. Although many of these drugs' pharmacological properties are known, the mechanism of action has not been elucidated. The actions of stimulants are not specific to hyperactive children. Normal children show similar behavioral responses, and so stimulant responsiveness does not confirm a diagnosis of ADHD.

Stimulants are contraindicated in children with thought disorder or psychosis, as they may exacerbate those conditions. Stimulants are also contraindicated for tiqueurs and highly anxious children. They have been associated with precipitation or aggravation of Tourette's disorder. The common side effects of stimulants are listed in Table 44.4-2.

Tricyclic antidepressants, such as imipramine, can be tried if stimulants are not effective in treating ADHD or if the side effects are severe. Desipramine (Norpramin) has been used with success in ADHD; however, sudden death in three children receiving desipramine has been reported. Tricyclic antidepressants are also indicated when ADHD is accompanied by depression or anxiety. Those children who respond to antidepressants do so rapidly (within one or two days); however, the response may be short-lived and not as striking as that with stimulants. The dosage used is lower than that for antidepressant activity. Antipsychotics, such as haloperidol (Haldol), have also been tried, but the risk of tardive dyskinesia must be considered.

The dietary management of hyperactivity has received a great amount of public attention, but controlled studies have not substantiated its benefit. Similarly, in most controlled studies, caffeine was not found superior to a placebo for ADHD.

Table 44.4-2
Common Dose-Related Side Effects of Stimulants

1. Insomnia
2. Decreased appetite
3. Irritability or nervousness
4. Weight loss

Tourette's Disorder

Because of its response to haloperidol, Tourette's disorder is one of the clearest indications for pharmacotherapy. The suggested dosage range for 3- to 12-year-old children is 0.2 mg per kg a day. Haloperidol is now the standard treatment against which other proposed treatments should be judged. Recently, improvements have been demonstrated with pimozide (Orap), a calcium-channel-binding antipsychotic, which, like haloperidol, is strongly antidopaminergic. In a large study, haloperidol was slightly superior to pimozide. Pimozide prolongs the QT interval, making electrocardiogram (ECG) monitoring necessary. Clonidine (Catapres), a presynaptic α-adrenergic blocking agent, has shown some efficacy in Tourette's disorder; it is less effective than haloperidol or pimozide, but its use avoids the side effects of antipsychotics.

Autistic Disorder

In autistic disorder, haloperidol is of proved efficacy in short-term and long-term treatment. Stereotypic behavior, hyperactivity, withdrawal, temper tantrums, aggression, and self-abusive behaviors often diminish on nonsedating dosages. Fenfluramine (Pondimin), a sympathomimetic amine with antiserotonergic properties, has not been demonstrated in controlled studies to be better than a placebo. However, it may be helpful in some cases. Naltrexone (Trexan), an opiate antagonist, is currently being studied in autistic children.

Schizophrenia

Children with signs and symptoms comparable with those found in adult schizophrenia probably benefit from antipsychotics, but there have been no controlled studies in this area. In two studies with schizophrenic adolescents, antipsychotic medication was effective. There is evidence that antipsychotics cause the same toxic side effects in children as in adults, including tardive dyskinesia. Consequently, the risk-benefit ratio is high, and great care must be taken to determine the need for continued antipsychotic use. Schizophrenia with onset in late adolescence is treated like the adult disorder.

Mood Disorders

Major depression has recently been recognized to occur in children and adolescence, not just in adulthood. However, no double-blind placebo-controlled study has, as yet, demonstrated the efficacy of antidepressants in this population. Depressed children with endogenous features may respond, with improvement in mood, to imipramine in dosages ranging from 1.0 to 2 mg per kg a day. The side effects are similar to those experienced by adults. The margin of benefit over a placebo is not as clear as it is in adults. Whether monoamine oxidase (MAO) inhibitors are any better has not yet been determined. There is no current indication for electroconvulsive therapy (ECT) in children.

Bipolar disorder patients' retrospective accounts indicate that a sizable minority (30 percent) first become ill in adolescence or earlier. Although lithium has had very limited study, a trial is warranted in those who meet the revised third edition of *Diagnostic and Statistical Manual of Mental Disorders* (DSM-III-R) criteria for the disorder and have not responded to more conservative treatment. Dosages of lithium to achieve blood levels of 0.6 to 1.2 mEq per liter, similar to that for adult patients, are suggested, and dosages may approximate adult dosages to achieve this. Side effects and complications are similar to those seen in adults.

Conduct Disorder

Many children with conduct disorder also have ADHD. Those who are medicated with stimulants sometimes show an improvement in their aggressive behaviors. However, for the aggressive conduct disorder-ADHD child or for the pure conduct disorder patient, haloperidol and lithium are the more proven drugs of choice. Both have been effective in treating hospitalized assaultive, conduct-disordered children. The less potent antipsychotics may decrease the severity of aggression, but their use is limited by sedation and possible cognitive impairment.

The older anticonvulsants do not appear beneficial, even in those who also have seizure disorders. There have been some claims supporting the efficacy of carbamazepine (Tegretol) and proparanolol (Inderal), but they need further study.

Functional Enuresis

Tricyclic antidepressants, particularly imipramine, control enuretic symptoms but do not provide a cure. They are indicated in some situations as adjunctive therapy in children 6 years or older. Initially, an oral dose of 25 mg a day given one hour before bedtime should be tried. The dosage may be increased to 50 mg in those children under 12 and 75 mg in those over 12 but should not exceed 2.0 mg per kg a day. The action that relieves the symptoms is not known. What is known is that the anticholinergic effect is irrelevant to enuresis control, as other peripherally acting anticholinergics are not efficacious. After a seven-day trial with an adequate amount of the drug, 60 percent or more of the children experience relief, but this effect may wear off, and tolerance may occur in half of the responders. The use of bell-and-pad conditioning is preferable, as the risk is minimal, and it produces long-lasting results.

Mental Retardation

Recent surveys have found that roughly half of all institutionalized mentally retarded persons receive antipsychotic drugs, which most likely reflects their overuse because of a lack of other therapies or services. Mental retardation by itself is not an indication for psychotropic drug use; some behaviors, such as hyperactivity and stereotypy, may be alleviated by stimulants or antipsychotics. Low dosages of haloperidol appear to offer the greatest benefit with the least cognitive impairment.

Thioridazine (Mellaril) and haloperidol may be useful in reducing unwanted behavior, such as self-stimulation, aggression, and motor activity. However, besides the risk of tardive dyskinesia, antipsychotics may impair the effectiveness of behavioral training and other rehabilitative efforts, such as workshop performance, if the patient has side effects that produce somnolence. Some aggressive retarded patients are benefited by lithium and β-blockers. Some self-abusive retarded patients are benefited by naltrexone.

Anxiety Disorders of Childhood or Adolescence

Imipramine has been shown to be useful as an adjunct in the treatment of school-phobic children, and it may be useful in separation anxiety in general. There are not enough anecdotal reports of school-phobic children's benefiting from chlordiazepoxide (Librium) and from amphetamine to justify their use in clinical practice. Antianxiety agents are overprescribed in these disorders.

Imipramine is the medication of choice in separation anxiety disorder. There have been several recent reports of panic disorder in children and adolescents who responded to antidepressants. Antianxiety medications have been little studied in children but can be tried in overanxious disorder children. Buspirone (BuSpar) may have a place in the treatment of overanxious disorder adolescents because it apparently has no abuse potential.

Sleep Terror Disorder

Sleep terror disorder consists of repeated episodes of abrupt awakening with intense anxiety marked by autonomic arousal. It occurs during stage 4 sleep. The child, who appears confused and disoriented, does not usually respond to comfort measures during the episode. Diazepam (Valium), in 2 to 5 mg doses, reduces the proportion of stage 4 sleep and has been shown to be helpful.

Obsessive-Compulsive Disorder

Obsessive-compulsive disorder is a rare condition in children. Clomipramine (Anafranil) has proved effective in the treatment of childhood obsessive-compulsive disorder, and there is some evidence that fluoxetine (Prozac) is successful in the same population.

Specific Developmental Disorders

No pharmacological agent has been shown to make a clinically significant improvement in any specific developmental disorder. However, many children with psychiatric disorders also have learning disabilities, and many who have learning disabilities also have behavioral problems. This, as well as the importance of school and learning in children's lives, raises questions about the cognitive ef-

Table 44.4-3
Effects of Psychotropic Drugs on Cognitive Tests of Learning Functions*

	Test Function					
Drug Class	**Continuous Performance Test (Attention)**	**Matching Familiar Figures (Impulsivity)**	**Paired Associates (Verbal Learning)**	**Porteus Maze (Planning Capacity)**	**Short-Term Memory***	**WISC (Intelligence)**
Stimulant	↑	↑	↑	↑	↑	↑
Antidepressants	↑	0		0	0	0
Neuroleptics	⇅		↓	↓	↓	0

Table adapted from M G Aman: Drugs, learning and the psychotherapies. In *Pediatric Psychopharmacology: The Use of Behavior Modifying Drugs in Children,* J S Werry, editor. Bruner/Mazel, New York, 1978.
↑ Improved, ⇅ inconsistent, ↓ worse, 0 no effect.
*Various tests; digit span, word recall, etc.

fects of psychotropics. Table 44.4-3 summarizes the effects of drugs on cognitive tests of learning functions.

In children with learning disabilities but no other psychiatric diagnosis, methylphenidate has been shown to facilitate performance on several standard cognitive, psycholinguistic, memory, and vigilance tests but has shown no improvement in academic achievement ratings or teacher ratings. Cognitive impairment from psychotropic drugs, especially antipsychotics, may be an even greater problem in mentally retarded persons.

Eating Disorders

Various antidepressants have proved to be effective in bulimia nervosa, but patients with anorexia nervosa appear to respond preferentially to cyproheptadine (Periactin) and not to the conventional antidepressants.

MEDICATION EFFECTS AND COMPLICATIONS

Antidepressants

The side effects of antidepressants in children are usually similar to those in adults and result from the antidepressant's anticholinergic properties. The side effects include dry mouth, constipation, palpitations, tachycardia, loss of accommodation, and sweating. The most serious side effects are cardiovascular, although, in children, diastolic hypertension is more common, and postural hypotension occurs more rarely than in adults. ECG changes are most apt to be seen in children receiving high dosages. Slowed cardiac conduction (PR interval >0.20 seconds or QRS interval >0.12) may necessitate lowering the dosage. Food and Drug Administration (FDA) guidelines limit dosages to a maximum of 5 mg per kg a day. The drug can be very toxic in an overdose, and, in small children, ingestions of 200 to 400 mg can be fatal. When the dosage is lowered too rapidly, withdrawal effects are manifested mainly by gastrointestinal symptoms: cramping, nausea, vomiting, and sometimes apathy and weakness. The treatment is a slower tapering of the dosage.

Antipsychotics

The best studied of the antipsychotics given to pediatric age groups are chlorpromaxine (Thorazine), thioridazine, and haloperidol. It is widely held in adult psychiatry that high- and low-potency antipsychotics differ in their side-effect profiles. The phenothiazine derivatives (chlorpromazine and thioridazine) have the most pronounced sedative and atropinic actions, whereas the high-potency antipsychotics are more commonly thought to be associated with extrapyramidal reactions, such as parkinsonian symptoms, akathisia, and acute dystonias. Caution is warranted in assuming that this is also true in children. In particular, when comparisons are made at low-dosage levels of equivalent potency, differences may not be detected.

Even if the frequency of these side effects differs among the medications, they are always caused by antipsychotics. Demonstrations in children of impaired cognitive function and, most important, of tardive dyskinesia, call for great caution in the use of drugs. Tardive dyskinesia—which is characterized by persistent abnormal involuntary movements of the tongue, face, mouth, or jaw and which may also involve the extremities—is a known hazard of giving antipsychotics to patients of all age groups. There is no known effective treatment. Tardive dyskinesia has not been reported in patients taking less than 375 to 400 g of chlorpromazine equivalents. Because nonpersistent choreiform movements of the extremities and trunk are common after an abrupt discontinuation of antipsychotics, it is important to distinguish these symptoms from persistent dyskinesias.

It is recommended that, whenever clinically feasible, children receiving antipsychotics be periodically withdrawn from the medication so that the clinician can assess the patient's current clinical need and the possible development of tardive dyskinesia.

Stimulants

Problems with retarded growth associated with taking stimulants have been reported, although there is little evidence for the problems. The current thinking is that any growth suppression is temporary and that children taking stimulants will eventually reach their normal height.

OTHER ORGANIC THERAPIES

There is little convincing evidence that dietary manipulation is a successful treatment for childhood psychiatric disorders, but it would be premature to dismiss it without good research. Studies of starvation and protein caloric malnutrition emphasize the importance of adequate nutrition to growth and development and suggest that infant malnutrition does have behavioral sequelae. Concepts such as dietary self-selection as a reflection of metabolic differences and oligoantigenic diets are now being studied.

ECT has been used in the past with children and adolescents, and some have reportedly benefited. Most reports have been confined to children with psychotic disorders, rather than children with mood disorders. Whether there is any indication for ECT in this age group has not been documented with controlled trials. No side effects or complications unique to childhood have been reported.

There is no accepted indication in child psychiatry for psychosurgery.

Table 44.4-4 lists a comprehensive overview of representative psychoactive drugs with their indications, dosages, adverse reactions, and monitoring.

Table 44.4-4
Common Psychoactive Drugs in Childhood and Adolescence

Drugs	Indications	Dosage	Adverse Reactions and Monitoring
Antipsychotics—also known as major tranquilizers, neuroleptics. Divided into (1) high potency, low dosage, e.g., haloperidol (Haldol), trifluoperazine (Stelazine), Thiothixene (Navine) and (2) low potency, high dosage (more sedating), e.g., chlorpromazine (Thorazine), thioridazine (Mellaril).	In general, for agitated, aggressive, self-injurious behaviors in mental retardation (MR), pervasive development disorder (PDD), conduct disorder (CD), and schizophrenia. Studies support following specific indications: haloperidol-PDD, CD, with severe aggression, Tourette's disorder.	All can be given in two to four divided doses or combined into one dose after gradual build up. Haloperidol—0.5–16 mg a day. Triothixene—5–42 mg a day. Chlorpromazine and thioridazine—10–400 mg.	Sedation, weight gain, hypotension, lowered seizure threshold, constipation, extrapyramidal symptoms, jaundice, agranulocytosis, dystonic reaction, tardive dyskinesia. Monitor; blood pressure, complete blood count (CBC), liver function tests (LFTs), electroencephalogram, if indicated. With thioridazine, pigmentary retinopathy is rare but dictates ceiling of 800 mg in adults and proportionately lower in children.
Stimulants Dextroamphetamine (Dexedrine) FDA-approved for children 3 years and older. Methylphenidate (Ritalin) and pemoline (Cylert) FDA-approved for children 6 years and older.	In attention-deficit hyperactivity disorder (ADHD) for hyperactivity, impulsivity, and inattentiveness.	Dextroamphetamine and methylphenidate are generally given at 8 AM and noon (the usefulness of sustained-release preparations is not proved). Dextroamphetamine—2.5–40 mg a day up to 0.5 mg per kg a day. Methylphenidate—10–60 mg a day or up to 1.0 mg per kg a day. Pemoline—37.5–112.5 mg given at 8 AM.	Insomnia, anorexia, weight loss (and possibility growth delay), tachycardia, precipitation or exacerbation of tic disorders. With pemoline, monitor LFTs, as hepatotoxicity is possible.
Lithium—considered an antipsychotic drug, also has antiaggressive properties.	Studies support use in MR and CD for aggressive and self-injurious behaviors. Can be used for same in PDD. Also indicated for early-onset bipolar disorder.	600–2,100 mg in two or three divided doses. Keep blood levels to 0.4–1.2 mEq per L.	Nausea, vomiting, headache, tremor, weight gain. Experience with adults suggests thyroid and renal function monitoring.
Antidepressants Imipramine (Tofranil) has been used in most child studies. Clomipramine (Anafranil) is effective in child obsessive-compulsive disorder (OCD). Fluoxetine (Prozac) may also be used in OCD.	Major depressive disorder, separation anxiety disorder, bulimia nervosa, functional enuresis. Sometimes used in ADHD, anorexia nervosa, somnambulism, and sleep terror disorder. OCD—clomipramine, fluoxetine.	Imipramine—start with dosage of about 1.5 mg per kg a day; can build up to not more than 5 mg per kg a day. Start with two or three divided doses; eventually combine in one dose.	Dry mouth, constipation, tachycardia, drowsiness, postural hypotension. Electrocardiogram (ECG) monitoring is needed because of risk of cardiac conduction slowing. Consider lowering dosage if PR interval > 0.20 seconds or QRS interval > 0.12 seconds. Baseline EEG is advised, as it can lower seizure threshold. Blood levels of drug are sometimes useful.

Table 44.4-4
Continued

Drugs	Indications	Dosage	Adverse Reactions and Monitoring
		Not FDA-approved for children except for functional enuresis; dosage is usually 50–100 mg before sleep. Clomipramine — start at 50 mg a day; can raise to not more than 3 mg per kg a day or 200 mg a day. Fluoxetine dosage not established in children.	
Carbamazepine (Tegretol)—an anticonvulsant.	Aggression or dyscontrol in MR or CD.	Start with 10 mg per kg a day and can build to 20–30 mg per kg a day. Therapeutic blood level range appears to be 4–12 mg per L.	Drowsiness, nausea, rash, vertigo, irritability. Monitor: CBC and LFTs for possible blood dyscrasias and hepatotoxicity. Blood levels are necessary.
Anxiolytics—have been insufficiently studied in childhood and adolescence.	Sometimes effective in parasomnias: somnambulism or sleep terror disorder. Can be tried in overanxious disorder.	Parasomnias: diazepam (Valium) 2–10 mg before bedtime.	Benzodiazepines can cause drowsiness, dyscontrol, and can be abused.
Fenfluramine (Pondimin)—an amphetamine congener.	Well studied in autistic disorder. Generally ineffective, but some patients show improvement.	Gradually increase to 1.0–1.5 mg per kg a day in divided doses.	Weight loss, drowsiness, irritability, loose bowel movements.
Propanolol (Inderal)—a β-adrenergic blocker.	Aggression in MR, PDD, and organic brain dysfuncton. Awaits controlled studies.	Effective dosage in children and adolescents is not yet established. Range is probably 40–320 mg a day.	Bradycardia, hypotension, nausea, hypoglycemia, depression. Avoid in asthma.
Clonidine (Catapres)—a presynaptic α-adrenergic blocking agent.	Tourette's disorder	0.1–0.3 mg a day; 3–5.5 μg per kg a day.	Orthostatic hypotension, nausea, vomiting, sedation, elevated blood glucose.
Cyproheptadine (Periactin)	Anorexia nervosa	Dosages up to 8 mg four times a day.	Antihistaminic side effects, including sedation and dryness of the mouth.
Naltrexone (Trexan)	Self-injurious behaviors in MR and PDD. Currently being studied in PDD.	From 0.5–2.0 mg per kg a day.	Sleepiness, aggressivity. Monitor LFTs, as hepatotoxicity has been reported in adults at high dosages.

Table by Richard Perry, M.D.

References

Bertagnoli M W, Borchardt C M: A review of ECT for children and adolescents. J Am Acad Child Adolesc Psychiatry *29*: 302, 1990.

Campbell M: Drug treatment of infantile autism: The past decade. In *The Third Generation of Progress,* H Y Meltzer, editor. p 225. Raven Press, New York, 1987.

Campbell M, Green W H, Deutsch S I: *Child and Adolescent Psychopharmacology*. Sage Publications, Beverly Hills, CA, 1985.

Campbell M, Small A M, Green W H, Jennings S J, Perry R, Bennett W G, Anderson L: Behavioral efficacy of haloperidol and lithium carbonate: A comparison in hospitalized aggressive children with conduct disorder. Arch Gen Psychiatry *41*: 650, 1984.

Campbell M, Spencer K: Psychopharmacology in child and adolescent psychiatry: A review of the past five years. J Am Acad Child Adolesc Psychiatry *27*: 269, 1988.

Coffey B J: Anxiolytics for children and adolescents: Traditional and new drugs. J Child Adolesc Psychopharmacol *1*: 57, 1990.

DeLong G R, Aldershaf A L: Long-term experience with lithium treatment in childhood: Correlation with clinical diagnosis. J Am Acad Child Adolesc Psychiatry *26*: 389, 1987.

Evans R W, Clay T H, Gualtieri C T: Carbamezepine in pediatric psychiatry. J Am Acad Child Adolesc Psychiatry *26*: 2, 1987.

Gittelman-Klein R: Pharmacotherapy of childhood hyperactivity: An update. In *The Third Generation of Progress,* H Y Meltzer, editor. Raven Press, New York, 1987.

Gualtieri C T, Quade D, Hicks R E, Mavo J P, Schroeder S R: Tardive dyskinesia and other clinical consequences of neuroleptic treatment in children and adolescents. Am J Psychiatry *141*: 20, 1984.

Kaplan S L, Busner J, Kupietz S, Wasserman E, Segal B: Effects of methylphenidate on adolescents with aggressive conduct disorder and ADHD: A preliminary report. J Am Acad Child Adolesc Psychiatry *29*: 719, 1990.

Medical Letter of Drugs and Therapeutics: Sudden death in children treated with a tricyclic antidepressant *32*: 53, 1990.

Popper C W, Elliott G R: Sudden death and tricyclic antidepressants: Clinical considerations for children. J Child Adolesc Psychopharmacol *1*: 125, 1990.

Psychopharmacology Bulletin: Special feature: Rating scales and assessment instruments for use in pediatric psychopharmacology research Psychopharmacol Bull *21*: 765, 1985.

Ryan N D: Heterocyclic antidepressants in children and adolescents. J Child Adolesc Psychopharmacol *1*: 21, 1990.

Stewart J T, Myers W C, Burket R C, Lyles W B: A review of the phar-

macotherapy of aggression in children and adolescents. J Am Acad Child Adolesc Psychiatry *29*: 269, 1990.
Vitello B, Behar D, Malone R, Delaney M A, Ryan P J, Simpson G M: Pharmacokinetics of lithium carbonate in children. J Clin Psychopharmacol *8*: 355, 1988.

44.5 / Psychiatric Treatment of Adolescents

Puberty and the stress of adolescence can precipitate psychiatric illness in vulnerable adolescents and can color their clinical presentations. It is a unique time of life that requires special treatment approaches.

DIAGNOSIS

Adolescents can be assessed in both their specific stage-appropriate functions and their general progress in accomplishing the tasks of adolescence. For almost all adolescents in today's culture, at least until their late teens, school performance is the prime barometer of healthy function. Intellectually normal adolescents who are not functioning satisfactorily in some form of schooling are demonstrating significant psychological problems whose nature and causes should be identified.

Questions to be asked in regard to adolescents' stage-specific tasks are: What degree of separation from their parents have the adolescents achieved? What sort of identities are evolving? How do they perceive their past? Do they perceive themselves as being responsible for their own development or as being only the passive recipients of their parents' influences? How do they perceive themselves with regard to the future, and how do they anticipate their future responsibilities for themselves and others? Can they think about the differing consequences of different ways of living? How do they express their sexual and affectionate interests? These tasks occupy all adolescents and normally are performed at different times.

Adolescents' object relations must be evaluated. Do they perceive and accept both the good and the bad qualities in their parents? Do they see their peers and boyfriends or girlfriends as separate persons with needs and identities of their own, or do they exist only for the patients' own needs?

A respect for and, if possible, some actual understanding of the adolescent's subcultural and ethnic background are essential. For example, in some groups, depression is acceptable, but in others, overt depression is a sign of weakness and is masked by antisocial acts, drug misuse, and self-destructive risks. It is not true, however, that a psychiatrist must be of the same race or group identity as the adolescent to be effective. Respect and knowledgeable concern are human qualities, not group-restricted ones.

INTERVIEWS

Whenever circumstances permit, both the adolescent and the parents should be interviewed. Other family members may also have to be included, depending on their degree of involvement in the youngster's life and difficulties. It is advisable, however, to see the adolescent first; this preferential treatment helps avoid the appearance of being the parents' agent.

In psychotherapy of the older adolescent, there is often little contact between the therapist and the parents after the initial part of therapy, because ongoing contact inhibits the adolescent's desire to open up.

Interview Techniques

All patients test and mistrust, but in adolescents these manifestations are likely to be crude, intense, provocative, and prolonged. Clinicians must establish themselves as trustworthy and helpful adults, so as to promote a therapeutic alliance. They should have the adolescents tell their own stories, without interrupting to check out discrepancies, as that will sound like correcting and disbelief. They should obtain explanations and theories from the patients about what happened, why these behaviors or feelings occur, when things changed, and what caused the identified problems to begin when they did.

Sessions with adolescents generally follow the adult model of the therapist's sitting across from the patient. However, in early adolescence, board games (e.g., checkers) may be helpful in stimulating conversation in an otherwise quiet, anxious adolescent.

Language is crucial. Even when a teenager and a doctor come from the same socioeconomic group, their language is seldom the same. Psychiatrists should use their own language, explain any specialized terms or concepts, and ask for an explanation of unfamiliar in-group jargon or slang.

Many adolescents do not talk spontaneously about drugs and suicidal tendencies but do respond honestly to the therapist's questions. It may be necessary to ask specifically about each drug and the amount and frequency of its use.

Adolescents' sexual histories and current sexual activities are increasingly important information for adequate evaluation. The nature of adolescents' sexual behavior is often a vignette of their whole personality structures and ego development. It may, however, take a long time in therapy before adolescents begin to talk about their sexual behavior.

TREATMENT

Usually, no single therapy is specific to a particular disorder. The best choice, then, is often what best fits the characteristics of the individual adolescent and the family or social milieu. Adolescents' real dependency needs may press clinicians to strive harder to maintain even the sickest youngster in a satisfactory home. But for the same reason, clinicians may be forced to remove adolescents from pathogenic homes, even when the severity of their illness alone does not dictate it, because the youngsters are not developmentally capable of handling the double burden of working to overcome their illness and being traumatized at home. Also, adolescents' striving for autonomy may so complicate problems of compliance with therapy that they force involuntary inpatient treatment of difficulties for which such treatment may not be necessary at a different stage of life. Thus, the following discussion is less a set of guidelines than a brief summary of what each treatment modality can or should offer.

Individual Psychotherapy

Few, if any, adolescent patients are trusting or open without considerable time and testing, and so it is helpful to anticipate this by letting the patients know that this is to be expected and is natural and healthy. Pointing out the likelihood of therapeutic problems—for instance, impatience and disappointment with the psychiatrist, with the therapy, with the time required, and with the often-intangible results—may help keep the problems under control. Therapeutic goals should be stated in terms that adolescents understand and value. Although they may not see the point in exercising self-control, enduring dysphoric emotions, or forgoing impulsive gratification, they may value feeling more confident and gaining more real control over their lives and the events that affect them.

Typical adolescent patients need a real relationship with a therapist whom they can perceive as a real person. The therapist becomes another parent, because adolescents still need appropriate parenting or reparenting. Thus, the professional who is impersonal and anonymous is a less useful model than is the one who can accept and respond rationally to an angry challenge or confrontation without fear or false conciliation, can impose limits and controls when the adolescents cannot, can admit mistakes and ignorance, and can openly express the gamut of human emotions. The failure to take a stand regarding self-damaging and self-destructive behavior or a passive response to manipulative and dishonest behavior is perceived as indifference or collusion.

Countertransference reactions can be quite intense in psychotherapeutic work with an adolescent, and the therapist must be aware of them. The adolescent often expresses hostile feelings toward adults, such as their parents and teachers. The therapist may react with an overidentification with the adolescent or with the parents. Such reactions are determined, at least in part, by the therapist's own experiences during adolescence or, when applicable, by the therapist's own experiences as a parent.

Individual outpatient therapy is appropriate for adolescents whose problems are manifested in conflicted emotions and nondangerous behavior, who are not too disorganized to be maintained outside a structured setting, and whose family or other living environment is not so disturbed as to negate the influence of therapy. Such therapy characteristically focuses on intrapsychic conflicts and inhibitions; on the meanings of emotions, attitudes, and behavior; and on the influence of the past and the present.

Antianxiety agents can be considered in adolescents whose anxiety may be high at certain times during psychotherapy. However, the adolescent's potential for abusing these drugs must be carefully weighed.

Group Therapy

In many ways group therapy is a natural setting for adolescents. Most are more comfortable with peers than with adults. A group diminishes the sense of unequal power between the adult therapist and the adolescent patient. Participation varies, depending on the adolescent's readiness. Not all interpretations and confrontations need come from the parent-figure therapist; group members are often adept at picking up symptomatic behavior in one another, and adolescents may find it easier to hear and consider critical or challenging comments from their peers.

Group therapy usually addresses interpersonal and present life issues. But some adolescents are too fragile for group therapy or have symptoms or social traits too likely to elicit peer group ridicule, and so they need individual therapy to attain enough ego strength to struggle with peer relationships. Conversely, others need to resolve interpersonal issues in a group before they can tackle intrapsychic issues in the intensity of one-to-one therapy.

Family Therapy

Family therapy is the primary modality when the adolescent's difficulties are mainly a reflection of a dysfunctional family (e.g., simple school phobics, runaways). The same may be true when developmental issues, such as adolescent sexuality and striving for greater autonomy, trigger family conflict. Or the family pathology may be more severe, as in cases of incest and child abuse. In these instances the adolescent usually needs individual therapy as well, but family therapy is mandatory if the adolescent is to remain in or return to the home. Serious character pathology, such as that underlying antisocial and borderline personality disorders, often develops out of highly pathogenic early parenting. Family therapy is strongly indicated whenever possible in such disorders, but most authorities consider it adjunctive to intensive individual psychotherapy when individual psychopathology has become so internalized that it persists regardless of the current family status.

Treatment in Institutional Settings

Residential treatment schools are often preferable for long-term therapy, but hospitals are more suitable for acute emergencies, although some adolescent inpatient hospital units also provide educational, recreational, and occupational facilities for longer-term patients. Adolescents whose families are too disturbed or incompetent, who are dangerous to themselves or others, who are out of control in ways that preclude further healthy development, or who are seriously disorganized require, at least temporarily, the external controls of a structured environment.

Long-term inpatient therapy is the treatment of choice for those severe disorders that are considered wholly or largely psychogenic in origin, such as major ego deficits that are caused by early massive deprivation and that respond poorly or not at all to medication. Severe borderline personality disorder, for example, regardless of the behavioral symptoms, requires a full-time corrective environment in which regression is possible and safe and failed ego development can take place. Psychosis in adolescence often requires hospitalization, but psychotic adolescents also often respond to appropriate medication, so that therapy is usually feasible in an outpatient setting except during acute exacerbations. Schizophrenic adolescents who show a chronic, deteriorating course may require hospitalization periodically.

Day Hospitals

In day hospitals, which have become increasingly popular, the adolescent spends the day in class, individual and group psychotherapy, and other programs but goes home in the evenings. Compared with full hospitalization, day hospitals are less expensive and are usually preferred by the patient.

CLINICAL PROBLEMS

Atypical Puberty

Pubertal changes that occur 2½ years earlier or later than the average age are within the normal range. But body image is so important to adolescents that extremes of the norm may be terribly distressing to some, either because markedly early maturation may subject them to social and sexual pressures for which they are unready or because late maturation may make them feel inferior and may exclude them from some peer activities. Medical reassurance, even if based on examination and testing to rule out pathophysiology, may be insufficient. The adolescents' distress may show as sexual or delinquent acting out, withdrawal, or problems at school of such a degree as to warrant therapeutic intervention. Therapy may also be prompted by similar disturbances in some adolescents who fail to achieve the peer-valued stereotypes of physical development, despite normal pubertal physiology.

Drug Use

Some experimentation with drugs is almost ubiquitous among adolescents, certainly if one includes alcohol. But the majority do not become abusers, particularly of prescription or illegal drugs.

Regular drug use of any degree represents disturbance. Drug abuse is sometimes self-medication against depression or schizophrenic deterioration and is sometimes a sign of characterological disorder in teenagers whose ego deficits render them unequal to the stresses of puberty and the tasks of adolescence. However, many drugs, especially cocaine, have a physiologically reinforcing action that acts independently of preexisting psychopathology. Regardless of why the abuse developed, it becomes a problem in itself. Ego development depends on confronting and learning to cope adaptively with reality. Drugs become both a substitute for and an avoidance of reality, thus impairing ego development and perpetuating their use to conceal even poorer coping skills.

When drug use covers an underlying illness or is a maladaptive response to current stresses or disturbed family dynamics, treatment of the underlying cause may take care of the drug use. Outpatient psychotherapy, however, is generally useless with long-term abusers, who require a structured setting where drugs are not available.

Suicide

Suicide is now the second leading cause of death among adolescents. Many hospital admissions of adolescents result from suicidal ideation or behavior. Suicide is the final common pathway for a number of disorders, and its high incidence reflects grave psychopathology. Some authorities consider that in adolescence, in contrast to adulthood, schizophrenia more often underlies suicide than major mood disorders. Among adolescents who are not psychotic, the highest suicidal risks occur in those adolescents who have a history of parental suicide, who are unable to form stable attachments, who display impulsive behavior or episodic dyscontrol, and who abuse drugs or alcohol. Many adolescent suicides show a common pattern of long-standing family and social problems throughout childhood and the escalation of subjective distress under the pressures and stresses of puberty and adolescence, followed by a suicide attempt precipitated by the sudden real or perceived loss of some person or social support felt to be the one source of meaning or closeness.

Normal developmental losses—of childhood dependency, of the parents of childhood—can also cause psychogenic depression in adolescents. The more rapid and extreme mood swings in adolescence, coupled with the adolescent's difficulty in seeing beyond the intensity of the moment, contribute to catastrophic despair and impulsive suicide attempts over losses that adults could weather. Moreover, drugs or alcohol can decrease the resistance to suicidal impulses. Normally persistent magical thinking may impair the sense of permanency of one's own death, allowing adolescents to contemplate suicide more lightly than adults.

Both during evaluation and treatment, suicidal thoughts, plans, and past attempts must be discussed directly when the concern arises and information is not volunteered. Chronic or recurring thoughts should be taken seriously, and an agreement or contract should be negotiated with the adolescent not to attempt suicide without first calling and talking about it with the psychiatrist. Adolescents are usually honest about making and keeping, or refusing, such agreements; if they refuse, closed hospitalization is indicated. This sign of serious, protective concern may be as therapeutic as is the opportunity to conduct or plan further treatment in a safe environment.

References

Blos P: *On Adolescence*. Free Press, New York, 1962.

Davis M, Raffe I H: The holding environment in the inpatient treatment of adolescents. Adolesc Psychiatry *12*: 434, 1985.

Erikson E H: The problem of ego identity. J Am Psychoanal Assoc *4*: 56, 1966.

Feldman L B: Integrating individual and family therapy in the treatment of symptomatic children and adolescents. Am J Psychother *42*: 272, 1988.

Freud A: Adolescence. Psychoanal Study Child *16*: 225, 1958.

Gartner A F: Countertransference issues in the psychotherapy of adolescents. J Child Adolesc Psychother *2*: 187, 1985.

Group for the Advancement of Psychiatry: *Normal Adolescence*, vol 6, Report 68, Group for the Advancement of Psychiatry, New York, 1968.

Kazdin A E: Psychotherapy for children and adolescents. Annu Res Psychol *41*: 21, 1990.

Lyman R D, Prentice-Dunn S, Gabel S: *Residential and Inpatient Treatment of Children and Adolescents*. Plenum, New York, 1989.

Peterson A C, Taylor B: The biological approach to adolescence. In *Handbook of Adolescent Development,* J Adelson, editor. Wiley, New York, 1980.

Schowalter J E, Anyan W R: *The Family Handbook of Adolescence*. Knopf, New York, 1979.

Sholevar G P, Burland A, Frank J L, Etezady M H, Goldstein J: Psychoanalytic treatment of children and adolescents. J Am Acad Child Adolesc Psychiatry *28*: 685, 1989.

Geriatric Psychiatry

Geriatric psychiatry (geropsychiatry) is that branch of medicine concerned with the prevention, diagnosis, and treatment of the physical and psychological disorders in the elderly and with the promotion of longevity. It is the fastest growing field in psychiatry and was declared an official subspecialty by the American Board of Psychiatry and Neurology (ABPN) in 1989. The first examination for certification was given in 1991, which resulted in the first group of certified geropsychiatrists. The term "geriatric" stems from the Greek *geras*, meaning old age, and *iatros*, meaning physician, and so "geriatric" refers to the medical treatment or healing of the aged.

PSYCHIATRIC ASSESSMENT

The same general principles of psychiatric history taking and mental status examination that apply to young adults also apply to geriatric patients. Care should be taken to establish rapport, to make the patient comfortable, and to maintain privacy and confidentiality. The psychiatrist should determine whether the patient understands the nature and the purpose of the examination. When the patient is cognitively impaired, the history is obtained from a family member either before or after examining the patient. However, the psychiatrist must see the patient alone, even if there is clear evidence of impairment, to preserve the privacy of the doctor-patient relationship. Certain signs and symptoms related to suicidal thoughts, paranoid ideation, and cognitive impairment may be impossible to elicit in the presence of family members.

Psychiatric History

The psychiatric history includes the preliminary identification (name, age, sex, marital status), chief complaint, history of the present illness, history of previous illnesses, past history, and family history. A careful review of medications (including over-the-counter medications) that the patient may be using currently or used in the recent past is also important. Drug effects can impair cognition and interfere with obtaining the history.

The geriatric psychiatrist must understand changes in the cognitive process in normal aging to accurately diagnose a cognitive disorder. The majority of patients over age 65 have subjective complaints of minor memory impairment, such as not remembering names of persons or misplacing objects. This age-associated memory impairment is of no significance. Minor cognitive problems may also occur because of anxiety in the interview situation. The term "benign senescent forgetfulness" has been used to describe these phenomena.

The past medical history should note all major illnesses, especially the presence of seizure disorder, loss of consciousness, headaches, visual problems, and hearing loss. A history of alcohol use should be ascertained. Although substance abuse is less of a problem in the aged than in young adults, a history of prolonged substance abuse may account for the current deficits observed by the clinician.

The childhood and adolescent history is often overlooked in the geriatric examination. It can provide information about personality organization and give important clues about coping strategies and defense mechanisms that the aged person may use under stress. A history of learning disability or minimal cerebral dysfunction is significant.

The psychiatrist should inquire about friends, sports, hobbies, social activity, and work. The occupational history should include the patient's feelings about work, relationships with peers, problems with authority, and attitudes toward retirement. The patient should also be questioned about plans for the future. What are the patient's hopes and fears?

The family history should include a patient's description of parents' attitudes and adaptation to their old age and, if applicable, information about the causes of their deaths. Alzheimer's disease is transmitted as an autosomal dominant trait in 10 to 30 percent of the offspring of parents with Alzheimer's disease, and depression and alcoholism run in families. The current social situation should be evaluated: Who cares for the patient; are there children; and what are the characteristics of the parent-child relationships? A financial history is essential to evaluate the role of economic hardship in the patient's illness and to make realistic treatment recommendations.

The marital history includes a description of the spouse and the characteristics of the relationship. If the patient is a widow or a widower, the psychiatrist should explore how grieving was handled. If the loss of the spouse occurred within the past year, the patient is at high risk for an adverse physical or psychological event.

Young clinicians may have to overcome their own biases about taking a sex history in the aged; however, it represents an important area of concern for many geriatric patients, who welcome the chance to talk about their sexual feelings and attitudes. A sex history includes sexual activity, orientation, libido, masturbation, extramarital affairs, and sexual symptoms (such as impotence and anorgasmia).

Mental Status Examination

The mental status examination is a cross-sectional view of how the patient thinks, feels, and behaves during the examination. In the aged patient, the psychiatrist may not be able to rely on a single examination to answer all diagnostic questions. Repeat mental status examinations may have to be performed, because there are fluctuating changes in the mental status. The longitudinal history from the patient or the patient's family is important.

General description. A general description of the patient includes appearance, psychomotor activity, attitude toward the examiner, and speech activity.

The examiner should note disturbances in motor activity, such as shuffling gait, stooped posture, pill-rolling movements of the fingers, tremors, and body asymmetry. The examiner should also note whether the patient is agitated and anxious. Involuntary movements of the mouth or tongue may be side effects of phenothiazine medication. Many depressed patients appear slow in speech and movement. A masklike facies occurs in Parkinson's disease.

The patient's speech may be pressured in agitated, manic, or anxious states. Tearfulness or overt crying are seen in depression and organic brain disease, especially if the patient feels frustrated about being unable to answer one of the examiner's questions. The presence of a hearing aid or some other indication that the patient has a hearing problem, such as requesting the repetition of questions, should be noted.

The patient's attitude toward the examiner—cooperative, suspicious, guarded, ingratiating—can give clues about possible transference reactions. Elderly patients can react to younger physicians as if the physicians were parent figures, in spite of the age difference, because of transference distortions.

Mood, feelings, and affect. Suicide is a leading cause of death in the elderly, and a careful evaluation of suicidal ideation is essential. Feelings of worthlessness, helplessness, and hopelessness are symptoms of depression. The examiner should specifically ask the patient about any thoughts of suicide, whether the patient feels life is no longer worth living, whether one is better off dead or, when dead, less of a burden to others. Such thoughts—especially when associated with alcoholism, living alone, recent death of a spouse, physical illness, and somatic pain—are indicative of a high suicidal risk.

An expansive or euphoric mood may indicate a manic episode or be part of an organic mental disorder. Frontal lobe dysfunction often produces *witzelsucht*, which is the tendency to make puns and jokes and then to laugh aloud at them.

The patient's affect may be flat, blunted, constricted, shallow, or inappropriate, which can indicate depression, schizophrenia, or an organic mental disorder. It is an important abnormal finding, even though it is not pathognomonic of a specific disorder. Dominant lobe dysfunction causes dysprosody, an inability to express emotional feeling through intonation of speech.

Perceptual disturbances. Hallucinations and illusions in the elderly may be transitory phenomena resulting from decreased sensory acuity. But sometimes they indicate a serious disturbance. The examiner should note whether the patient is confused about time or place during the hallucinatory episode, which points to an organic condition. Distorted perceptions of the body are particularly important to ask about in the elderly.

Agnosia (the inability to recognize and interpret the significance of sensory impressions) is a particular disturbance associated with organic brain disease. The examiner should note the type of agnosia—denial of illness (anosognosia), the denial of a body part (autotopagnosia), the inability to recognize objects (visual agnosia) or faces (prosopagnosia).

Language output. This category of the geriatric mental status examination covers the aphasias, which are disorders of language output related to organic lesions of the brain. The best described are (1) nonfluent or Broca's aphasia, (2) fluent or Wernicke's aphasia, and (3) global aphasia, a combination of fluent and nonfluent aphasias.

In nonfluent or Broca's aphasia, understanding remains intact but the ability to speak is lost. The patient is unable to pronounce "Methodist Episcopalian." In this type of aphasia, speech is generally mispronounced and may be telegraphic in nature. The patient may also be unable to blow out the cheeks or whistle (buccolingual aphasia). In Wernicke's aphasia there is a loss of ability to comprehend the meaning of words or the use of objects. A simple test for Wernicke's aphasia is to point to some common objects—such as a pen or pencil, a doorknob, and a light switch—and ask the patient to name them. The patient may be unable to demonstrate the use of simple objects, such as a key and a match (ideomotor apraxia).

Thought process. Disturbances in thinking include neologisms, word salad, circumstantiality, tangentiality, loosening of associations, flight of ideas, clang associations, and blocking. The loss of the ability to appreciate nuances of meaning (abstract thinking) is an early sign of an organic mental disorder. Thinking is then described as concrete or literal.

Thought content should be examined for phobias, obsession, somatic preoccupations, and compulsions. Ideas about suicide or homicide should be discussed. The examiner should determine if delusions are present and how such delusions affect the patient's life. Patients who are hard of hearing may be mistakenly classified as paranoid or suspicious. Ideas of reference or of influence should be described.

Sensorium and cognition. Sensorium is a general term that refers to the functioning of the special senses; cognition refers to information processing and intellect. The survey of both areas is known as the neuropsychiatric examination and consists of the assessment done by the clinician and a comprehensive battery of psychological tests.

Consciousness. A sensitive indicator of an organic mental disorder is an altered state of consciousness in which the patient does not appear to be alert, shows fluctuations in levels of awareness, or appears to be lethargic. In severe cases the patient is somnolescent or stuporous.

Orientation. Impairment in orientation to time, place, and person indicates a cognitive disorder, most often caused by an organic mental disorder but not always. Cognitive impairment is often observed in mood disorders, anxiety disorders, factitious disorders, conversion disorder, and personality disorders, especially during periods of severe physical or environmental stress.

The examiner should test for orientation to place by asking the patient to describe the present location. Orientation to person may be approached in two ways: Does the patient know his or her own name, and are nurses and doctors identified as such? Time is tested by asking the patient the date, year, month, and day of the week. Also, the patient should be asked about the length of time spent in the hospital, during what season of the year, and how the patient knows these facts. Greater significance is given to difficulties concerning person than to difficulties of time or place, and more significance is given to place than to time.

Memory. Memory is usually evaluated from the point of view of immediate, recent, and remote memory. Immediate retention and recall are tested by giving the patient six digits to repeat forward and backward. The examiner should record the result of the patient's capacity to remember. Patients with unimpaired memory can usually recall six digits forward and five or six backward. The clinician should be aware that the ability to do well on digit span is impaired in extremely anxious patients. Remote memory can be tested by asking the patient for the location and date of birth, mother's name before she was married, and names and birthdays of the patient's children.

Recent memory deteriorates first in organic mental impairment. Recent memory assessment can be approached in a number of ways. Some examiners give the patient the names of three items early in the interview and ask for recall later. Others prefer to tell a brief story and ask the patient to repeat it verbatim. Memory of the recent past can also be tested by asking for the patient's place of residence, including the street number; the method of transportation to the hospital; and some current events.

If the patient has a deficit in memory, such as amnesia, careful testing should be done to see if it is retrograde (loss of memory before an event) or anterograde (loss of memory after the event). Retention and recall can also be tested by having the patient retell a simple story. Patients who confabulate make up new material in the retelling of the story.

Intellectual tasks, information, and intelligence. A number of intellectual tasks may be presented to estimate the patient's general fund of knowledge and intellectual functioning.

Counting and calculation can be tested by asking the patient to subtract 7 from 100 and to continue subtracting 7 from the result until the number 2 is reached. The examiner records the responses as a baseline for future testing. The examiner can also ask the patient to count backward from 20 to 1, recording the time necessary to complete the exercise. The patient can also be asked to do simple arithmetic—for example, to state the number of nickels in $1.35.

The patient's general fund of knowledge is related to intelligence. The patient can be asked to name the President of the United States, name the three largest cities in the United States, give the population of the United States, and give the distance from New York to Paris. The examiner must take into account the patient's educational level, socioeconomic status, and general life experience in assessing the results of some of these tests.

Reading and writing. It may be important for the clinician to examine the patient's reading and writing and to determine whether there is a specific speech deficit. The examiner may have the patient read a simple story aloud or write a short sentence to test for a reading or writing disorder. It should be noted whether the patient is right-handed or left-handed.

Judgment. The patient's judgment should also be tested by asking some pertinent questions. Does the patient show impaired judgment? What would the patient do if a stamped, sealed, addressed envelope was found in the street? What would the patient do if smoke was smelled in a theater? Can the patient discriminate? What is the difference between a dwarf and a boy? Why are persons required to get a marriage license?

Neuropsychological assessment. A thorough neuropsychological examination includes a comprehensive battery of tests that can be replicated by different examiners and can be repeated over time to assess the course of a specific illness. The most popular test of gross cognitive functioning is the Mini-Mental State Examination (MMSE), which assesses orientation, registration, attention, calculation, memory, language, and visuospatial abilities (Table 45-1).

The assessment of intellectual abilities is performed with the Wechsler Adult Intelligence Scale—Revised (WAIS-R), which gives verbal, performance, and full-scale intelligence quotient (I.Q.) scores. Some tests, such as vocabulary, hold up as aging progresses; others, such as similarities and digit symbol substitution, do not. The performance part of the WAIS-R is a more sensitive indicator of brain damage than the verbal part.

Visuospatial functions are sensitive to the normal aging process. The Bender-Gestalt Test is one of a large number of instruments used to test these functions; another is the Halstead-Reitan Battery, the most complex battery of tests covering the entire spectrum of information processing and cognition.

Table 45-1
Mini-Mental State Examination (MMSE) Questionnaire

Orientation (score 1 if correct)	
Name this hospital or building.	____
What city are you in now?	____
What year is it?	____
What month is it?	____
What is the date today?	____
What state are you in?	____
What county is this?	____
What floor of the building are you on?	____
What day of the week is it?	____
What season of the year is it?	____
Registration	
Name three objects and have the patient repeat them. Score number repeated by the patient. Name the three objects several more times if needed for the patient to repeat correctly (record trials ___).	____
Attention and calculation	
Subtract 7 from 100 in serial fashion to 65. Maximum score = 5	____
Recall	
Do you recall the three objects named before?	____
Language tests	
Confrontation naming: watch, pen = 2	____
Repetition: "No ifs, ands, or buts" = 1	____
Comprehension: Pick up the paper in your right hand, fold it in half, and set it on the floor = 3	____
Read and perform the command "close your eyes" = 1	____
Write any sentence (subject, object, verb) = 1	____
Construction	
Copy the design below = 1	____
Total MMSE questionnaire score (maximum = 30)	____

Table adapted from M F Folstein, S Folstein, P R McHugh: Mini-mental state: A practical method for grading the cognitive state of patients for the clinician. J Psychiatr Res *12*: 189, 1975, with permission.

MENTAL DISORDERS OF OLD AGE

Mental disorders of old age result from the complex interplay of organic, psychological, and social factors. According to the National Institute of Mental Health (NIMH), the most common disorders of old age are depression, cognitive impairment, phobia, and alcoholism. Suicide risk increases with age. About 20 percent of all suicides are committed by persons over 65 years of age.

Many mental disorders of old age can be prevented, ameliorated, or even reversed. Of special importance are the reversible causes of delirium and dementia. If not diagnosed accurately and treated in a timely fashion, these conditions can progress to an irreversible state requiring that the patient be institutionalized.

Many drugs can cause psychiatric symptoms in the elderly. These symptoms occur as a result of age-related alterations in drug absorption, if the drug is prescribed in too large a dose, if the patient does not follow the instructions for its use and takes too much, if the patient is particularly sensitive to the medication, or if conflicting regimens are presented by several physicians. Common symptoms include confusion, delirium, disorientation, depression, anxiety, hallucinations, and delusions. Almost the entire spectrum of mental disorders can be caused by drugs.

Psychiatric symptoms usually stop after the offending drug is identified and withdrawn, but the clinician must also be alert to withdrawal reactions to a drug, especially if the drug is stopped abruptly.

Dementing Disorders

Dementias have been classified as cortical or subcortical, depending on the site of the cerebral lesion. A subcortical dementia is seen in Huntington's chorea, Parkinson's disease, normal pressure hydrocephalus, multi-infarct dementia, and Wilson's disease. The subcortical dementias are associated with movement disorders, gait apraxia, psychomotor retardation, apathy, and akinetic mutism that can be confused with catatonia. The cortical dementias are seen in Alzheimer's disease, Creutzfeldt-Jakob disease, and Pick's disease, which frequently manifest aphasia, agnosia, and apraxia. In clinical practice there is great overlap between the two types of dementia, and in most cases an accurate diagnosis can be made only by autopsy.

Alzheimer's disease. Alzheimer's disease affects 10 percent of people over age 65, with that figure rising to about 45 percent of those over age 85. According to the National Institute on Aging, by the year 2050 there will be 14 million persons with Alzheimer's disease. The disorder accounts for over half of the 1.3 million aged persons in nursing homes and is associated with more than 100,000 deaths in the United States each year. It is the most common cause of dementia in elderly patients.

The disorder is characterized by clinical features of dementia, such as disturbances of orientation, memory, calculation, and judgment. Personality changes—such as depression, obsessiveness, and suspiciousness—occur. Outbursts of anger are common, and violent acts are a risk. Disorientation leads to wandering, and the patient may be found far from home in a dazed condition. Loss of initiative is common. Neurological defects—such as gait disturbances, aphasia, apraxia, and agnosia—eventually occur.

The disease has an insidious onset and is progressive, with death (usually from a secondary infection) occurring 10 years after onset. The diagnosis is made on the basis of a history and a mental status examination. Brain-imaging techniques are currently of limited use.

Etiology. The cause of the disease is unknown, although various theories exist. There is a dysregulation of the neurotransmitter system in the brain, and specific acetylcholine deficiencies have been demonstrated. Structural neuronal degeneration occurs, producing characteristic neurofibrillary tangles and amyloid deposits (Figures 45-1 and 45-2). Abnormal central nervous system (CNS) protein metabolism and an amyloid precursor protein gene have been demonstrated as well.

Causative theories involving viruses and environmental toxins have also been proposed. Aluminum deposits may be present in Alzheimer's brain lesions but are not believed to be causative. A genetic transmission has been reported in about 10 to 30 percent of cases. Because Down's syndrome (trisomy 21) patients invariably develop Alzheimer's disease by age 40, attempts are being made to demonstrate an abnormal gene, possibly on chromosome 21.

Treatment. There is no known prevention or cure. Treatment is palliative, consisting of proper nutrition and exercise. Anxiety and depression respond to pharmacological agents, and agitation has been successfully managed with haloperidol (Haldol).

Multi-infarct dementia. Multi-infarct dementia is the second most common cause of dementia in the elderly and can occur in conjunction with Alzheimer's disease. It is characterized by a variable rate of dementia, with stepwise or patchy deterioration and focal neurological signs. The disorder results from repeated cerebral infarctions at various brain sites and is associated with hypertension and cardiac arrhythmias. There is no specific treatment except for methods that prevent or ameliorate further cerebral insults, such as lowering blood pressure and decreasing platelet aggregation with salicylates. The onset is more abrupt than Alzheimer's disease, an important sign in differentiating between the two disorders.

Pick's disease. Pick's disease is a slowly progressing dementia. It is associated with focal cortical lesions, primarily of the frontal lobe, producing aphasia, apraxia, and agnosia. The disease lasts from 2 to 10 years, with an average duration of five years. Clinically, Pick's disease is difficult to distinguish from Alzheimer's disease. On autopsy, however, the brain reveals intraneuronal inclusions called Pick bodies, which are different from the neurofibrillary tangles of Alzheimer's disease. Pick's disease is much rarer than Alzheimer's disease, and there is no treatment.

Creutzfeldt-Jakob disease. This diffuse degenerative disease affects the pyramidal and extrapyramidal systems. Creutzfeldt-Jakob disease begins in the fourth and fifth decades of life, and the usual course is about one year. The terminal stage is characterized by extreme dementia, generalized hypertonicity, and profound speech disturbance. It is caused by a slow-growing infectious virus. Some cases have been traced to the transplant of the cornea of an infected person to a previously noninfected person.

Huntington's chorea. This hereditary disease is associated with progressive degeneration of the basal ganglia and

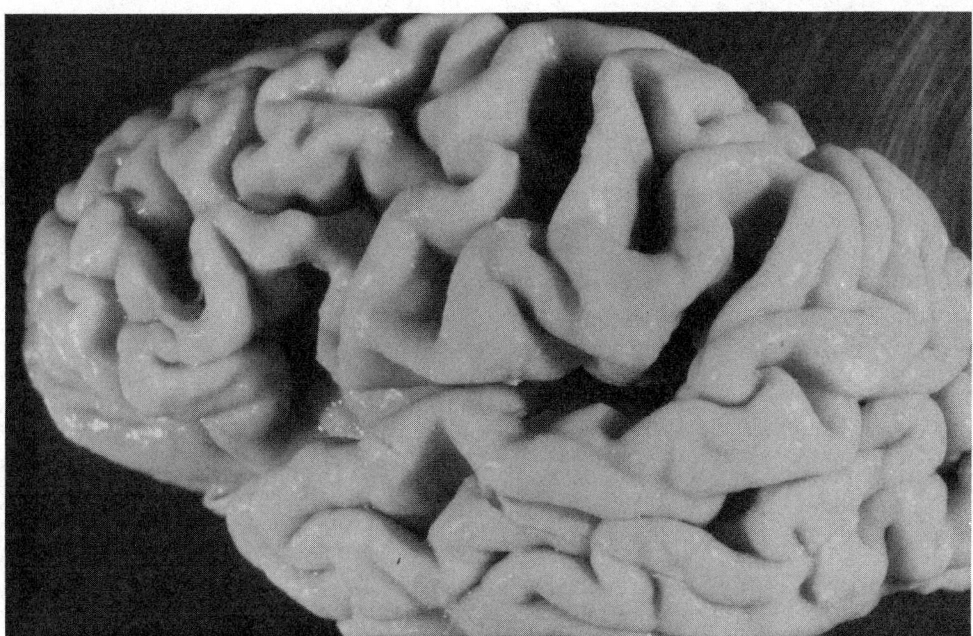

Figure 45-1. Gross external appearance of the brain of a patient who had primary degenerative dementia of the Alzheimer type, senile onset. The leptomeninges have been removed so that the generalized atrophy may be fully appreciated. (Courtesy of Daniel Perl, M.D.)

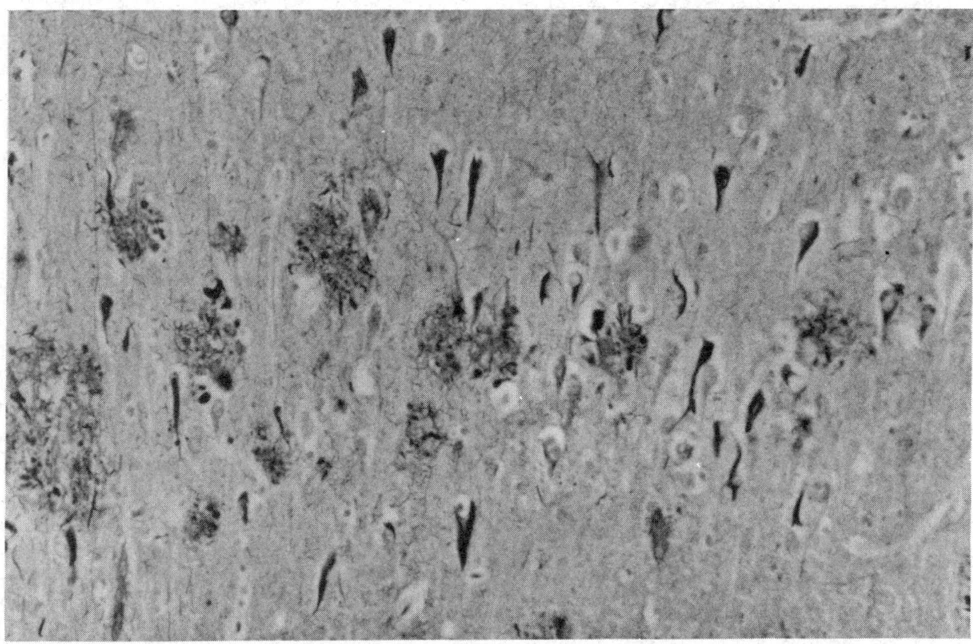

Figure 45-2. Microscopic appearance of the hippocampus from a patient with Alzheimer's disease, showing large numbers of neurofibrillary tangles and senile plaques (modified Bielschowsky's stain, original magnification × 190. (Courtesy of Daniel Perl, M.D.)

cerebral cortex. Huntington's chorea is transmitted as an autosomal dominant gene (traced to the G8 fragment of chromosome 4), with each offspring of an affected parent having a 50 percent chance of getting the disease. Everyone with the gene eventually has the disease. There is now a genetic screening test for the disorder. Currently, 25,000 Americans have Huntington's chorea, and about 125,000 children are at risk. The onset of Huntington's chorea is between 35 and 50 years and is characterized by progressive dementia, muscular hypertonicity, and bizarre choreiform movements; death usually occurs 15 to 20 years after onset. There is no treatment.

Normal pressure hydrocephalus. In the elderly, normal pressure hydrocephalus causes gait disturbances (unstable or shuffling gait), urinary incontinence, and dementia. Enlargement of the ventricles without increased cerebrospinal fluid (CSF) pressure is found.

Depression

Depressive disorders in the elderly are a significant concern for the geriatrician. Estimates of depression vary from 5 to 10 percent in those over 65. There is an increased rate for those over 80, for the poor, and for the unmarried. Up to 20 percent of general medical outpatients are depressed. The onset of most depression occurs between 55 and 65 in men and between 50 and 60 in women. Most episodes of depression are recurrent if not treated.

Common signs and symptoms include reduced energy and concentration, sleep problems (especially early morning awakening and multiple awakenings), decreased appetite, weight loss, and somatic complaints.

A particular syndrome unique to the elderly is melancholia, which is a type of depression. Melancholia is characterized by depression, hypochondriasis, low self-esteem, feelings of worthlessness, and self-accusatory trends (especially about sex and sinfulness), with paranoid and suicidal ideation.

Cognitive impairment in depressed geriatric patients is called pseudodementia, which can easily be confused with true dementia. In true dementia intellectual performance is usually global in nature, and impairment is consistently poor; in pseudodementia, deficits in attention and concentration are variable. Distinguishing between the two disorders is difficult. Pseudodementia occurs in about 15 percent of depressed elderly patients, and 25 to 50 percent of patients with dementia are depressed. Because depression responds to treatment, it is important to identify when it is present. Table 10-7 in Chapter 10, "Organic Mental Syndromes and Disorders," compares dementia of organic disease and pseudodementia. The causes of depression in the elderly are varied. Psychological factors include adaptation to loss, especially the loss of a loved one; disengagement from friends and work; and feelings of helplessness about being able to maintain control of one's life. Biological vulnerability to depression is increased as a result of the dysregulation of brain neurotransmitter regulation—in particular, reduced levels of serotonin, norepinephrine, and dopamine and increased levels of monoamine oxidase (MAO), which further reduce catecholamine levels.

Finally, depression may be associated with physical illness and the medications used for treating a particular illness. For example, depression is a side effect of propranolol (Inderal), which is used in the treatment of hypertension. The clinician needs to be aware of the many pharmacological agents that are common causes of depression (see Table 16.1-14 in Section 16.1, "Depressive and Bipolar Disorders").

Bipolar Disorder

Bipolar disorder with mania usually begins in middle adulthood, although the lifetime prevalence of 1 percent remains steady throughout life. A vulnerability to recurrences remains, so the patient with a history of bipolar disorder may present with a manic episode in late life. In most instances a first episode of manic behavior after age 65 should alert the clinician to search for an associated physiological or organic cause, such as the side effects of medication or an early dementia.

Signs and symptoms of mania in the elderly are similar to those in younger adults and also include an elevated, expansive, or irritable mood; a decreased need for sleep; distractibility; impulsivity; and, often, excessive alcohol intake. Hostile or paranoid behavior is usually present. The presence of cognitive impairment, disorientation, or fluctuating levels of awareness should make the clinician suspicious of an organic cause for the disorder.

Lithium remains the treatment of choice for mania; however, its use by elderly patients must be carefully monitored, because their reduced renal clearance makes lithium toxicity a significant risk. Neurotoxic effects are also more common in the elderly than in younger adults.

Schizophrenia

Although schizophrenia usually begins in late adolescence or young adulthood, it persists throughout life. It is rare to have a first episode diagnosed after age 65; however, a late-onset type beginning after age 45 has been described. It is characterized by suspiciousness, delusional episodes, and occasional hallucinatory activity in the absence of cognitive impairment. About 20 percent of schizophrenic persons show no active symptoms by age 65; 80 percent show varying degrees of impairment. Psychopathology becomes less marked as the patient ages.

A residual type of schizophrenia occurs in about 30 percent of all schizophrenic persons. Signs and symptoms include emotional blunting, social withdrawal, eccentric behavior, and illogical thinking. Delusions and hallucinations are not common. Since most residual schizophrenic persons are unable to care for themselves, long-term hospitalization is required.

Aged persons with schizophrenic symptoms respond well to antipsychotic drugs. Medication must be judiciously administered, so as not to reduce marginal cerebral competence, cause orthostatic hypotension, or produce extrapyramidal or anticholinergic side effects.

Delusional Disorder

The age of onset of delusional disorder is usually between 40 and 55; however, it can occur at any time in the geriatric period. Delusions can take many forms, the most common being persecutory in nature—the patient believes that he or she is being spied on, followed, poisoned, or harassed in some way. Delusional disorder persons may become violent against their supposed persecutors. In some cases they lock themselves in their rooms and live a reclusive life. Somatic delusions, in which the persons believe they have a fatal illness, may also occur in this age group. In one study of persons over 65, pervasive persecutory ideation was present in 4 percent of those sampled.

Delusional disorders occur under physical or psychological stress in vulnerable persons and may be precipitated by the death of the spouse, loss of a job, retirement, social isolation, adverse financial circumstances, debilitating medical illness or surgery, visual impairment, and deafness. Delusions may also accompany other disorders—such as Alzheimer's disease, alcoholism, schizophrenia, depressive disorders, and bipolar disorder—which need to be ruled out. Delusional syndromes may also result from prescribed medications or from early signs of a brain tumor.

The prognosis is fair to good in most cases, with best results achieved through a combination of psychotherapy and pharmacotherapy.

A late-onset delusional disorder called paraphrenia is characterized by persecutory delusions. It develops over several years and is not associated with dementia. Some workers believe the disorder to be a variant of schizophrenia that first becomes manifest after age 60. There is an increase in paraphrenia in patients with a family history of schizophrenia.

Anxiety Disorders

The anxiety disorders of old age, sometimes called late-onset neurosis, include panic disorder, phobias, obsessive-compulsive disorder, generalized anxiety disorder, and posttraumatic stress disorder (PTSD). The lifetime prevalence of these disorders is between 10 and 15 percent. Most begin in early or middle adulthood, but some appear for the first time after age 60.

Phobias are among the most common disorders in the elderly. In general, the signs and symptoms of each disorder are less severe than those that occur in younger persons, but the effects are equally, if not more, debilitating in the aged patient.

Existential theories help explain anxiety when there is no specifically identifiable stimulus for a chronically anxious feeling. The aged person has to come to grips with death. The person may deal with the thought of death with a sense of despair and anxiety, rather than with equanimity and Erik Erikson's sense of integrity.

The fragility of the autonomic nervous system in the aged may account for the development of anxiety after a major stressor (PTSD). PTSD is often more severe in the elderly than in younger persons because of concurrent physical disability in the aged.

Obsessions and compulsions may appear for the first time in the aged person, although one usually finds signs of this disorder in the personalities of patients who, when younger, were orderly, perfectionist, punctual, and parsimonious. When symptomatic, these patients become excessive in their desire for orderliness, rituals, and sameness. They may also develop compulsions to check things over and over, becoming generally inflexible and rigid.

Treatment of the spectrum of anxiety disorders must be individually tailored to the patient, taking into account the biopsychosocial interplay producing the disorder. Both pharmacotherapy and psychotherapy are required.

Somatoform Disorders

This broad category of disorders characterized by physical symptoms resembling medical diseases is relevant to geriatric psychiatry, because somatic complaints are common among the aged. Over 80 percent of the aged have at least one chronic disease—usually arthritis or cardiovascular problems. After 75 years, 20 percent have diabetes and an average of four diagnosable chronic illnesses that require medical attention.

Hypochondriasis is very common in patients over 60, although the peak incidence is in the 40-to-50-year-old age group. The disorder is usually chronic, and the prognosis is guarded. Repeated physical exams are useful in reassuring patients that they do not have a fatal illness; however, invasive and high-risk diagnostic procedures should be avoided unless medically indicated.

Telling patients that their symptoms are imaginary usually meets with resentment and is counterproductive. The clinician should acknowledge that the complaint is real, that the pain is really there and perceived as such by the patient, and that a psychological or pharmacological approach to the problem is indicated.

Alcoholism and Drug Dependence

Aged alcoholics with psychiatric problems usually give a history of excessive drinking that began in young or middle adulthood. They are usually medically ill, primarily with liver disease, and are either divorced, widowers, or men who never married. Many have arrest records and are numbered among the homeless poor. A large number have chronic dementing illnesses, such as Wernicke's encephalopathy and Korsakoff's syndrome. Prolonged institutional placement is often the only adequate management of the condition; 20 percent of nursing home patients are alcoholics.

Overall, alcohol and drug abuse account for 10 percent of all emotional problems in the aged, and dependence on drugs—such as hypnotics, anxiolytics, and narcotics—is more common in old age than is generally recognized. Drug-seeking behavior—characterized by crime, manipulativeness, and antisocial behavior—is relatively rare in this age group compared with younger adults. Elderly patients may abuse anxiolytics to allay chronic anxiety or to insure sleep. The maintenance of the chronically ill cancer patient with narcotics prescribed by the physician produces dependence; however, the need to provide pain relief takes precedence over the possibility of narcotic dependence and is entirely justified.

The clinical presentation of elderly alcoholics and drug abusers is varied. It includes falls, confusion, poor personal hygiene, depression, malnutrition, and the effects of exposure. The sudden onset of delirium in elderly persons hospitalized for medical illness is most often caused by alcohol withdrawal.

Over-the-counter (OTC) drugs, including nicotine and caffeine, may also be misused by the elderly. OTC analgesics are the most common offenders (used by 35 percent), followed by laxatives (used by 30 percent). Unexplained gastrointestinal, psychological, or metabolic problems should alert the clinician to OTC abuse.

Other Conditions

Sleep and insomnia. Elderly persons do not require more sleep than do younger persons (in many cases they require less); however, the quality of sleep changes with age, and complaints about sleeplessness are common. The amount of rapid eye movement (REM) sleep and the percentage of deep sleep (stages 3 and 4) remain about the same. Sleep disturbances have many causes: general inactivity during the day; the need for frequent medications that awakens the person; taking daytime naps that interfere with sleep at night; and pain from chronic illnesses, such as arthritis, gastroesophageal reflux, and prostratic hypertrophy. Other causes are anxiety, which prevents sleep, and depression, which causes multiple awakenings or early morning awakening. The patient who has taken small doses of anxiolytics or hypnotics on a regular basis for an extended period may have become psychologically dependent on them. It may be necessary to wean the patient from the medication and establish proper bedtime habits. If anxiety or depression is the cause, appropriate antianxiety or antidepressant medication may solve the problem. Often reassurance is sufficient, especially for patients who are worried about not getting enough sleep.

Vertigo. Feelings of vertigo or dizziness, a common complaint in the elderly, cause many elderly persons to become inactive because they fear falling. The causes of vertigo are varied and include anemia, hypotension, cardiac arrhythmia, cerebrovascular disease, basilar artery insufficiency, middle ear disease, acoustic neuroma, and Ménière's disease. There is a strong psychological component to most cases of vertigo, and the clinician should ascertain any secondary gain from the symptom. The overuse of anxiolytics can cause dizziness and daytime somnolence. Treatment with meclizine (Antivert), 25 to 100 mg daily, has been successful in many cases of vertigo.

Syncope. The sudden loss of consciousness associated with syncope results from a reduction of cerebral blood flow and brain hypoxia. A thorough medical workup is required to rule out the various causes listed in Table 45-2.

PSYCHOPHARMACOLOGICAL TREATMENT OF GERIATRIC DISORDERS

In the elderly certain guidelines should be followed regarding the use of all drugs. A pretreatment medical evaluation is essential, including an electrocardiogram (ECG). It is especially useful to have the elderly patient or the family bring in all currently used medications, because multiple drug usage may be contributing to the symptoms.

Most psychotropic drugs should be given in equally divided doses three or four times over a 24-hour period. Elderly patients may not be able to tolerate a sudden rise in drug blood level resulting from one large daily dose. Any changes in blood pressure and pulse rate and other side effects should be watched. For patients with insomnia, however, giving the major portion of an antipsychotic or antidepressant at bedtime takes advantage of its sedating and soporific effects. Liquid preparations are useful for elderly patients who cannot or who refuse to swallow tablets. Patients should be frequently reassessed to determine the need for maintenance medication, changes in dosage, and the development of side effects.

If the patient is taking psychotropic drugs at the time of the evaluation, it is helpful, if possible, to discontinue those medications and, after a washout period, to reevaluate the patient during a drug-free baseline state.

The elderly use the greatest number of medications of any age group, with 25 percent of all prescriptions written for those over age 65. Adverse drug reactions caused by medications result in the hospitalization of nearly 250,000 persons in the United States each year. Psychotropic drugs are among the most commonly prescribed, along with cardiovascular and diuretic medications; 40 percent of all hypnotics dispensed in the United States each year are to those over age 65, and 70 percent of elderly patients use OTC medications, compared with only 10 percent of young adults.

Table 45-2
Common Causes of Syncope

Epilepsy
Cerebral ischemia
Coronary artery insufficiency; valvular disease
Anemia
Carotid sinus syndrome
Cardiac arrhythmia
Stokes-Adams conduction defect
Hyperventilation
Hypoglycemia
Anxiety attack
Cerebrovascular accident; vertebral-basilar insufficiency

Principles

Individualization of dosage is the basic tenet of geriatric psychopharmacology. Alterations of drug dosages are required because of the physiological changes that occur as the person ages. Renal disease is associated with decreased renal clearance of drugs; liver disease results in a decreased ability to metabolize drugs; cardiovascular disease and reduced cardiac output can affect both renal and hepatic drug clearance; and gastrointestinal disease and decreased gastric acid secretion influence drug absorption. As a person ages, the ratio of lean-to-fat body mass also changes. With normal aging, lean body mass decreases, and body fat increases. Changes in the lean-to-fat body mass ratio that accompany aging affect the distribution of drugs. Many lipid-soluble psychotropic drugs are more widely distributed in fat tissue, thus prolonging the drug action more than expected. Similarly, changes in end-organ or receptor-site sensitivity need to be taken into account. The increased risk of orthostatic hypotension in the elderly from psychotropic drugs is related to reduced functioning of blood-pressure-regulating mechanisms. As a general rule, the lowest possible dose should be used to achieve the desired therapeutic response. The clinician must know the pharmacodynamics, pharmacokinetics, and biotransformation of each drug prescribed and the effects of the interaction of the drug with other drugs that the patient is taking.

Antidepressants and Drugs Used to Treat Depression

Among the antidepressants of potential use in the elderly, those most frequently preferred are the secondary amines, including desipramine (Norpramin) and nortriptyline (Aventyl, Pamelor), partly because they produce less hypotension than the tertiary amines. In comparison with other antidepressants, desipramine has few anticholinergic side effects. This is an advantage, because the elderly are known to have decreased cholinergic neurotransmitter functioning and are believed to be particularly sensitive to anticholinergic side effects. Nortriptyline is also frequently considered a drug of choice for the elderly because it is well-tolerated and because of the ability to monitor a therapeutic window of blood levels in relation to clinical response. Fluoxetine (Prozac) is a relatively new antidepressant compound that blocks serotonin reuptake as its primary effect. It is usually nonsedating and has relatively few side effects. Fluoxetine is well-tolerated and produces good results, especially if there are obsessions or agitation associated with the depressive disorder. It also has a low lethal potential. Only one case of suicide by using fluoxetine has been reported.

Antidepressant drugs should be prescribed in small dosages at first and should be gradually increased according to the patient's response and development of side effects. Careful cardiac monitoring is nevertheless mandatory. Cardiovascular side effects include increased heart rate, hypotension, prolonged cardiac conduction, and, rarely, cardiac arrhythmias. The antidepressants, like other psychotropic drugs, have more side effects in old patients than in young patients. Elderly patients vary in regard to the optimal dosage and the development of side effects. Patients who do not respond to one antidepressant may respond to another. At least four weeks of treatment should be allowed for an adequate trial before switching. There is no need to measure levels of tricyclic antidepressants in plasma on any regular basis. Table 45-3 lists the geriatric dosages for commonly used tricyclic and tetracyclic antidepressants.

Monoamine oxidase inhibitors (MAOIs) are also useful in treating depression, because MAO decreases in the aging brain and may account for diminished catecholamines and a resultant depression. Tranylcypromine (Parnate) and phenelzine (Nardil) are representative drugs that should be used cautiously in patients prone to hypertension. A tyramine-free diet is necessary to avoid hypertensive crises. Table 45-4 lists the geriatric dosages for the MAOIs.

Table 45-4
Geriatric Dosages for Monoamine Oxidase Inhibitors (MAOIs)

Generic Name	Trade Name	Geriatric Dosage Range (mg a day)
Isocarboxid	Marplan	10–30
Phenelzine	Nardil	15–45
Tranylcypromine†	Parnate	10–20

†Persons taking MAOIs should be on a tyramine-free diet.
Not recommended in persons over 60 because of pressor effects.

Psychostimulants

This class of drugs, which are also called analeptics, includes amphetamine (e.g., dextroamphetamine [Dexedrine]), methylphenidate (Ritalin), and pemoline (Cylert). In selected cases they can improve the mood, apathy, and anhedonia of the depressed elderly patient, especially when caused by some associated chronic medical illness, such as rheumatoid arthritis or multiple sclerosis. Amphetamine may also augment analgesia in patients who require pain medication. The use of psychostimulants is controversial because of the risk of abuse; however, when prescribed judiciously in small doses, they are of value. Table 45-5 lists the geriatric dosages for the psychostimulants.

Table 45-5
Geriatric Dosages for Psychostimulants

Generic Name	Trade Name	Geriatric Dosage Range (mg a day)
Dextroamphetamine	Dexedrine	2.5–10
Pemoline	Cylert	18.75–37
Methylphenidate	Ritalin	2.5–20

Lithium and Drugs Used to Treat Bipolar Disorder

The use of lithium in aged patients is more hazardous than its use in young patients because of the common occurrence of age-related morbidity and physiological changes of the heart, thyroid, and kidneys. Lithium is excreted by the kidneys, and decreased renal clearance and renal disease can increase the risk of toxicity. Thiazide diuretics decrease renal clearance of lithium; consequently, the concomitant use of these medications can necessitate adjustments in lithium dosage. Other medications may also interfere with lithium clearance. Lithium may cause CNS effects to which the elderly may be more sensitive. Because of these factors, frequent serum monitoring of lithium levels is recommended in the elderly. In addition, cardiac, kidney, and thyroid workups are essential before initiating therapy. Table 45-6 lists the geriatric dosages for drugs used in bipolar disorder.

Table 45-3
Geriatric Dosages for Commonly Used Tricyclic and Tetracyclic Antidepressants

Generic Name	Trade Name	Geriatric Dosage Range (mg a day)
Imipramine	Tofranil	25–300
Desipramine	Norpramine, Pertofrane	10–300
Trimipramine	Surmontil	25–300
Amitriptyline	Elavil	25–300
Nortriptyline	Pamelor, Aventyl	10–150
Protriptyline	Vivactil	10–40
Doxepin	Adapin, Sinequan	10–300
Maprotiline	Ludiomil	25–150

Exact range may vary among laboratories.

Table 45-6
Geriatric Dosages for Drugs Commonly Used to Treat Bipolar Disorder

Class	Generic Name	Trade Name	Geriatric Dosage Range (mg a day)
Lithium salts	Lithium carbonate	Eskalith, Lithane, Lithotabs	75–900
Anticonvulsants	Carbamazepine	Tegretol	200–1,200
	Valproic acid	Depakene, Depokate	250–1,000
	Clonazepam (a benzodiazepine)	Klonopin	0.5–1.5

Antipsychotics

In addition to treating overt signs of psychosis, such as hallucinations and delusions, antipsychotics have also been used to deal effectively with violent, agitated, and abusive geriatric patients.

In general, psychosis in the elderly frequently responds to much lower dosages of medication than those used in young patients. The elderly are also much more sensitive to many of the side effects of antipsychotic medications than young patients, specifically to the extrapyramidal (parkinsonian) side effects. Elderly patients have been known to stop speaking, ambulating, and swallowing as a result of these side effects. The same dosages of medication are not likely to produce significant problems in young patients.

Neurological side effects of antipsychotic drugs. The most common side effects are extrapyramidal signs, such as akathesia and acute dystonia. Akathesia may be misinterpreted as psychotic agitation, and the acute dyskinesias (especially of the face, tongue, and neck) may simulate the bizarre movements of schizophrenia. Parkinsonian symptoms are a later complication of drug therapy. The dyskinesias, manifested mainly by buccolingual movements, are noted late in the course of high-dosage antipsychotic therapy, especially in the elderly. Autonomic side effects are particularly troublesome because they may upset the homeostasis of organs innervated by the autonomic nervous system, such as the bladder, gastrointestinal tract, and cardiovascular system. Alterations in sleep—such as insomnia, bizarre dreams, and somnambulism—can occur. The toxic confusional state may occur with all drugs with anticholinergic properties, which may also cause mydriasis and blurring of vision. Other drugs have adrenergic properties causing miosis.

Hip fracture resulting from falls, in part associated with medication use, is a major cause of morbidity in the elderly and can be a proximal or distal factor associated with demise. Consequently, to minimize the potential deleterious and even life-threatening side effects, the clinician should carefully monitor drug use. Hip fractures are least often associated with short half-life anxiolytics and most often associated with antipsychotics.

Clinical experience indicates that the therapeutic effects of antipsychotic medications in the elderly may not become evident on a given dosage of medication for four weeks or longer. Because of the therapeutic factors and risks, the dictum in treating psychosis in the elderly is to "start low and go slow." As in younger patients, side-effect profiles should help determine the choice of medication; however, there is no consensus regarding the choice or dosage level of antipsychotics for the elderly. There is no need to administer prophylactic antiparkinsonian agents on a regular basis when prescribing antipsychotics. The anticholinergic aspects of those drugs can create unwanted side effects, especially memory impairment. Table 45-7 lists the geriatric dosages for commonly used antipsychotic agents.

Anxiolytics

The geriatric patient with mild or moderate anxiety can benefit from this class of drugs. The benzodiazepines are the drugs of first choice because of their rapid onset of action, relatively short half-life, and safety. Most patients are treated for brief periods, although some may have to be maintained on small dosages for long periods. The long-term use of benzodiazepines is controversial, however, because they are controlled substances with a potential for abuse. Benzodiazepines with short half-lives, such as triazolam (Halcion), are preferable for use as hypnotics. The

Table 45-7
Geriatric Dosages for Commonly Used Antipsychotics

Generic Name	Trade Name	Geriatric Dosage Range (mg a day)
Phenothiazines		
Aliphatic		
Chlorpromazine	Thorazine	30–300
Triflupromazine	Vesprin	1–15
Piperazine		
Perphenazine	Trilafon	8–32
Trifluoperazine	Stelazine	1–15
Fluphenazine	Prolixin, Permitil	1–10
Piperidine		
Thioridazine	Mellaril	25–300
Mesoridazine	Serentil	50–400
Thioxanthenes		
Chlorprothixene	Taractan	30–300
Thiothixene	Navane	2–20
Dibenzoxazepine		
Loxapine	Loxitane	50–250
Dihydroindole		
Molindone	Moban	50–225
Butyrophenone		
Haloperidol	Haldol	2–20

benzodiazepines may cause short periods of memory impairment, such as anterograde amnesia, which may aggravate an already existing cognitive disorder in the elderly patient. Some elderly patients accumulate the long-acting benzodiazepines (such as diazepam [Valium]) in adipose tissues, increasing such unwanted effects as ataxia, insomnia, and confusion (sundowner syndrome). This effect can be avoided if the smallest possible dosage is prescribed and intake is carefully monitored until a therapeutic response is achieved.

Barbiturates may be substituted for the benzodiazepines in the few patients who do not respond to the latter. The geriatric patient is particularly prone to paradoxical dysphoria and cognitive disorganization, which can result from barbiturates. There is also a higher abuse potential with the barbiturates compared with the benzodiazepines. Barbiturates are controlled substances (schedule II, DEA), and there are constraints on their use.

Buspirone (BuSpar) is an anxiolytic drug without sedative properties. It has a longer onset of action—up to three weeks—than either the benzodiazepines or the barbiturates and does not cause cognitive impairment. Moreover, it does not have any potential for abuse. A summary of geriatric dosages for drugs used to treat anxiety and insomnia is presented in Table 45-8.

The reader is referred to Chapter 30, "Biological Therapies," for a comprehensive survey of these and other pharmacological agents, including a detailed discussion of dosages.

PSYCHOTHERAPY OF THE AGED

The full range of psychotherapeutic interventions—such as insight-oriented psychotherapy, supportive psychotherapy, cognitive therapy, group therapy, and family therapy—should be available to the geriatric patient. According to Sigmund Freud, persons over 50 years of age are not suited for psychoanalysis because they lack elasticity of the mental processes. But in the view of many who followed Freud, psychoanalysis is possible after that age. Advanced age certainly limits the plasticity of the personality, but, as Otto Fenichel stated: "It does so in varying degrees and at very different ages so that no general rule can be given." Insight-oriented psychotherapy may be tried for removing a specific symptom, even with old persons. It is of most benefit if there are possibilities for libidinal and narcissistic gratification, but it is contraindicated if it would bring only the insight that life has been a failure and there is no opportunity to make up for it.

Age-related issues in therapy involve the need to adapt to recurrent and diverse losses (such as the death of friends and loved ones), the need to assume new roles (such as the adjustment to retirement and the disengagement from previously defined roles), and the need to accept one's mortality.

Psychotherapy helps the aged to deal with those issues and the emotional problems surrounding them and to understand their behavior and the effects of their behavior on others. In addition to improving interpersonal relations, psychotherapy increases self-esteem and self-confidence, decreases feelings of helplessness and anger, and improves the quality of life. As described by Alvin Goldfarb, psychotherapy of the aged has the general aim of assisting the old person to have minimal complaints, to help him or her make and keep friends of both sexes, and to have sexual relationships where there is still interest and capacity. Psychotherapy helps relieve tension of biological and cultural origins and helps old persons work and play within the limits of their functional status and as determined by their past training, activities, and self-concept in society.

In general, the therapist is more active, supportive, and

Table 45-8
Geriatric Dosages for Drugs Commonly Used to Treat Anxiety and Insomnia

Generic Name	Trade Name	Geriatric Dosage Range (mg a day)
Benzodiazepines		
Alprazolam	Xanax	0.5–6
Chlordiazepoxide	Librium	15–100
Chlorazepate	Tranxene	7.5–60
Diazepam	Valium	2–60
Flurazepam	Dalmane	15–30
Halazepam	Paxipam	60–160
Lorazepam	Ativan	2–6
Oxazepam	Serax	30–120
Prazepam	Centrax	20–60
Temazepam	Restoril	15–30
Triazolam	Halcion	0.125–0.25
Nonbenzodiazepines		
Buspirone	BuSpar	5–60
Secobarbital	Seconal	50–300
Carbamate	Miltown	400–800
Chloral hydrate	Noctec	500–1,000
β-Adrenergic blocking agents		
Propranolol	Inderal	40–160
Atenolol	Tenormin	25–100

flexible in conducting therapy with the aged person than with the young adult. The therapist must be prepared to act decisively at the first sign of an incapacity that requires the active involvement of another physician, such as an internist, or the need to consult or enlist the aid of a family member.

The aged person comes to therapy wanting the therapist's unqualified and unlimited support, reassurance, and approval. The most important irrational attitude the patient brings to the therapeutic situation is the expectation that the therapist is all-powerful, all-knowing, and able to effect a magical cure. Most patients eventually learn to recognize that the therapist is human and that they are engaged in a collaborative effort. In some cases, however, the therapist may have to assume the idealized role, especially when the patient is unable or unwilling to test reality effectively. With the help of the therapist, the patient deals with problems that were previously avoided. Direct encouragement, reassurance, and advice can be offered, increasing the patient's self-confidence as conflicts are resolved.

Transference

In most cases the elderly patient parentifies the younger psychiatrist and transfers the infantile responses from the past relationship with the parent to the present relationship with the physician. A childlike dependence can then develop, or, conversely, a childlike defiance and disobedience may appear. The patient can be shown how this infantile behavior is at work now in relation to the psychiatrist and to others in the patient's life. Other transferential reactions include the patient's reacting to the therapist as a brother, sister, uncle, or even grandparent. In patients with impaired cognition, psychotherapy can produce remarkable gains in both physical and mental symptoms. In one study conducted in an old-age home, 43 percent of the patients receiving psychotherapy showed decreased urinary incontinence, improved gait, greater mental alertness, improved memory, and better hearing than before psychotherapy.

Group Therapy

Group therapy with the aged provides an opportunity for mutual support and is an aid in helping patients deal with the stresses of adapting to declining resources. Group members provide new friendships at a time when there has been a loss of old friends by death. Patients have the opportunity to be of help to one another, increasing self-esteem. Even patients with mild to moderate dementia can be helped to remain stimulated, active, and oriented through group interaction.

Family Therapy

It is frequently desirable and often necessary for the psychiatrist to engage the patient's family in treatment. Issues in family therapy are myriad. They include the distribution of family resources in providing care for the patient, the attitudes of the children toward their parent and their parent's need for therapy, the grandparenting role, and the examination of family conflicts.

Brief Therapy

Short-term therapy approaches, such as cognitive therapy, help the aged by correcting distortions in thinking, especially self-induced prejudices about the aging process. Persons who think they are too old for sports, sex, learning new things, acquiring new skills, helping others, and working at new jobs can have those cognitive distortions modified by direct therapeutic interventions. Patients can learn to use adaptive defense mechanisms and can be persuaded to make an effort to fight phobic avoidances and other inhibitions.

INSTITUTIONAL CARE OF THE AGED

The placement of the aged person in an institution is often viewed as a failure in management. It is, however, often a carefully thought out and executed treatment option that improves the person's quality of life. There are several types of institutions:

1. Old-age homes and board-and-care homes are voluntary nonprofit institutions in which old persons are expected to live together for the rest of their lives, with no attempt to rehabilitate them for discharge. Instead, they are helped to adjust to the protective setting and to have a better social life than they could in their own homes.
2. Nursing homes and extended-care facilities are institutions for the long-term care of chronically ill or permanently impaired persons. These institutions emphasize the admission of short-term convalescent patients and persons with potential for rehabilitation to community life. However, only 50 percent stay less than three months, and 50 percent stay on as permanent residents. Nursing homes are divided into skilled nursing facilities and intermediate-care facilities by the government. Seventy percent are proprietary, and 30 percent are nonproprietary or governmental. In 1988 the average cost to stay in a nursing home was $22,000 a year. A total of $38 billion is spent annually on nursing home care; half of that is paid by the government (through Medicaid). An increasing number of private insurance companies now offer long-term-care insurance to help cover nursing home costs.
3. Day-care centers and community centers for the aged are places for elderly persons to congregate, to enjoy socializing experiences, and to deal with feelings of depression, anxiety, boredom, and loneliness.

The state psychiatric hospitals used to have a large geriatric population with various organic mental syndromes. Today these hospitals exclude aged persons with dementia unless the dementia is mild or reversible and the patient is not likely to become a permanent resident. As a result, both old-age homes and nursing homes have received patients who are similar to the disorganized, bizarre, and violent patients formerly in mental hospitals. The likelihood that these brain-damaged old persons will ever be discharged from these long-term care facilities is slim, because even willing and effective families cannot cope with the multiple around-the-clock needs of these patients.

A new trend to help avoid institutionalization is the so-called retirement community composed of relatively healthy old persons who live and work together. These communities are usually run on a nonprofit basis and may have an associated medical facility for the treatment of medical problems. Increasingly, profit-making companies are establishing retirement communities.

Restraints

Restraints are belts and vests that keep patients from falling out of bed and wheelchairs or from wandering away.

For some patients (such as patients who would pull out feeding or oxygen tubes) these are necessary, but for most patients, they are used excessively. Some federal surveys have found that about 40 percent of all nursing home residents are put in restraints each year. Alternatives include tilted recliners, safe wandering paths, and floor alarms. Patients without restraints have better muscle tone from the exercise of walking and, psychologically, have less rage and a greater sense of mastery than patients in restraints.

Psychosocial Therapy

The institution can provide a total-push approach to the patient that involves a variety of professional staff members, including psychologists; social workers; psychiatric aides; occupational, vocational, and activity therapists; nutritionists; and exercise therapists. Each has skills that, when brought to bear on the institutionalized resident either individually or in a group, can markedly improve the patient's quality of life.

Psychiatrists who work with the aged must be especially aware of their own attitudes toward the aging process and aged persons, particularly their own parents and grandparents. If they have unresolved resentments or unconscious anger toward the aged in their own lives, they are likely to have countertransference problems that interfere with their ability to do good psychotherapy. Similarly, if they have unresolved fears of death, dying, or chronic illness, they may have blind spots that interfere with therapy. Finally, they must have an optimistic view of this last stage in the life cycle and a genuine belief that aged persons have a rightful place in society and a reservoir of wisdom from their accumulated years of experience that enables them to change.

References

Francis J, Kapoor W N: Delirium in hospitalized elderly. J Gen Intern Med *5*: 65, 1990.

Goldberg R: Geriatric consultation/liaison psychiatry. Adv Psychosom Med *19*: 138, 1989.

Jenike M A: Treatment of affective illness in the elderly with drugs and electroconvulsive therapy. J Geriatr Psychiatry *22*: 77, 1989.

Koenig H G, Breitner J C: Use of antidepressants in medically ill older patients. Psychosomatics *31*: 22, 1990.

Kohn R R: Cause of death in very old people. JAMA *247*: 2703, 1982.

Onofrij M, Gambi D, Malatesta G, Ferracci F, Fulgente T: Electrophysiological techniques in the assessment of aging brain: Lacunar state and differential diagnosis. Eur Neurol *29*: 44, 1989.

Ramsdell J W, Rothrock J F, Ward H W, Volk D M: Evaluation of cognitive impairment in the elderly. J Gen Intern Med *5*: 55, 1990.

Salzman C: Practical considerations in the pharmacologic treatment of depression and anxiety in the elderly. J Clin Psychiatry *51*: 40, 1990.

Ulhmann R, Larson E: Relationship of hearing impairment to dementia and cognitive dysfunction in older adults. JAMA *261*: 1916, 1989.

Williams G O: Management of depression in the elderly. Prim Care *16*: 451, 1989.

46

Forensic Psychiatry

At various stages in their historical development, psychiatry and the law have converged. Both disciplines are concerned with the social deviant who, by violating the rules of society, adversely affects the functioning of the community. Traditionally, the psychiatrist's efforts are directed toward elucidation of the causes and, through prevention and treatment, reducing the self-destructive elements of harmful behavior. The lawyer, as the agent of society, is concerned with the fact that the social deviant represents a potential threat to the safety and security of other people. Both psychiatry and the law seek to implement their respective goals through the application of pragmatic techniques based on empirical observations. The intermix of the law and psychiatry is called forensic psychiatry.

PSYCHIATRISTS AND THE COURTS

Most psychiatric work with patients is based on the principle of the alliance between the doctor and the patient, but the legal model works from an adversarial position. The complexity of medicolegal matters is inevitably divided (or, more often, polarized) into two sides, which pull against each other in an effort to place the truth in the hands of the fact finder (judge or jury). For the clinician exposed to merciless cross-examination scenes in all media, this fundamental element of the American legal system is apt to evoke fear, revulsion, and dismay. But these feelings may be tempered somewhat by insights into the process.

From the clinician's viewpoint an important distinction must first be made regarding the clinician's role as witness. In ever-increasing numbers, psychiatrists are being called into court to offer testimony on a wide variety of topics, not only forensic matters but also broadly medicolegal topics. The earliest point to establish in sorting out the clinician's role is what kind of witness the psychiatrist will be.

Witness of Fact

The first type of witness is the witness of fact. As a witness of fact, the psychiatrist functions no differently from laypersons generally, such as observers of an accident on the street. That is, the witness's input—the facts—represent direct observations and material from direct scrutiny. A witness of fact in this context may be a psychiatrist who reads portions of the past or present medical record aloud to bring it into the legal record and thus make it available for testimony. In theory, any psychiatrist at any level of training could fulfill this role.

Expert Witness

In contrast, a psychiatrist under certain circumstances may be qualified as an expert. The qualifying process, however, consists not of proved recognition in one's clinical field but of being accepted by the court and both sides of the case as suitable to perform expert functions. Thus, the term "expert" has particular legal meaning and is independent of any actual or presumed expertise the clinician may have in a given area. In the context of the courtroom, an expert witness is one who may draw conclusions from data—for example, that a patient meets the required criteria for commitment or for an insanity defense under the standards of a jurisdiction.

The most common role of a psychiatrist in court proceedings is as an expert. When psychiatrists are asked to serve as experts, they are usually asked to do it for one of the sides in the case; rarely are clinicians independent examiners reporting directly to the court. The implication is that material to be offered is brought out by the hiring attorney in that part of the presentation known as the direct examination. The opposing attorney then draws out additional material through cross-examination.

Cross-examination. Few experiences can be as demoralizing for the clinician as cross-examination by an eager, aggressive, and sarcastic attorney for the opposing side. This segment of the total experience, more than any other, makes many clinicians leery of appearing in the courtroom in any role. For the clinician in this situation, certain principles may be helpful to keep in mind.

First, the clinician should listen closely to the question being asked and always pause a moment before answering, not only to replay the question mentally for clarity but to allow the other side to object.

Second, the clinician should keep sharply in mind the limits of his or her field and should be particularly careful about "always," "never," and so on as those words identify predictions the clinician is asked to make. If pressed to give a yes or no answer to a complex question, the clinician should recall that he or she is permitted to answer, "That question cannot be answered with a yes or no."

Third, one should not be afraid or reluctant to say, "I don't know" when that is the true response; not all questions that attorneys ask have answers.

Fourth, the clinician should insist on pretrial preparation

by the hiring attorney as an absolute necessity. Few situations are as needlessly traumatic as being sent into court unprepared.

In general, the attorneys in a case guide the psychiatrist, functioning either as fact witness or as expert, in proper courtroom procedure and the admissibility of various sorts of testimony. Attorneys are free to object at any point in the examination if they feel certain lines of inquiry, types of evidence, or content are inappropriate for the court's consideration.

Court-mandated evaluations. In several legal situations clinicians are asked to be consultants to the court, which raises the issue of for whom they work. Because clinical information may have to be revealed to the court, clinicians may not enjoy the same confidential relationship with their patients in those situations that they have in private practice. Clinicians who make such court-ordered evaluations are under an ethical and, in some states, a legal obligation to so inform the patients at the outset of the examinations and to make sure that the patients understand this condition.

Evaluation of witnesses' credibility. It is up to the trial judge to grant a psychiatric examination requested by one of the parties to the action. Before ordering such an examination, the trial judge asks for evidence showing that such an examination is necessary to determine the merits of the case and that the imposition on or inconvenience to the witness does not outweigh the examination's value. Many courts limit psychiatric examinations to complaining witnesses in rape and other sex-offense cases, in which corroborative proof is nearly always circumstantial. In incest cases, for example, the father and the daughter may jointly deny the incest that the mother persistently alleges; the father may steadfastly deny the act, and in some cases the mother may support his denial; or, after accusing her father, the daughter may retract her accusation. Psychiatrists say that only a thorough psychiatric examination of the family can eliminate the confusion. Recognizing that false sex charges may stem from the psychic complexes of a victim who appears normal to a layperson, the courts permit psychiatrists to expose mental defects, hysteria, and pathological lying in complaining witnesses. The liberal attitude in this area is probably due to the gravity of the charge or to the general lack of corroborating evidence.

PRIVILEGE AND CONFIDENTIALITY

Privilege

Privilege is the right to maintain secrecy or confidentiality in the face of a subpoena. This privilege belongs to the patient, not to the physician, and so it can be waived by the patient. Currently, 38 of the 50 states have statutes providing some kind of physician-patient privilege. Psychiatrists, who are licensed to practice medicine, may claim medical privilege, but they have found that the privilege is so riddled with qualifications that it is practically meaningless. Purely federal cases have no psychotherapist-patient privilege. Moreover, the privilege does not exist at all in military courts, regardless of whether the physician is military or civilian or whether the privilege is recognized in the state where the court-martial takes place. There are numerous exceptions to the privilege, which are often viewed as implied waivers. In the most common exception, patients are said to waive the privilege by injecting their condition into the litigation, thereby making the condition an element of their claim or defense. Another exception involves proceedings for hospitalization, in which the interests of both the patient and the public are said to call for a departure from confidentiality. Yet another exception is made in child custody and child protection proceedings in regard to the best interest of the child. Furthermore, the privilege does not apply to actions between a therapist and a patient. Thus, in a fee dispute or a malpractice claim, the complainant's lawyer can obtain the necessary therapist's records to resolve the dispute.

Confidentiality

A long-held premise of medical ethics binds the physician to hold secret all information given by a patient. This obligation is what is meant by confidentiality. Understanding confidentiality requires an awareness that it applies to certain populations and not to others. That is, one can identify a group that is within the circle of confidentiality, meaning that sharing information with the members of this group does not require specific permission from the patient. Within this circle are other staff members treating the patient, clinical supervisors, and consultants. Parties outside the circle include the patient's family, attorney, and previous therapist. Sharing information with such people does require the patient's permission. Nevertheless, there are innumerable instances in which the psychiatrist may be asked to divulge information imparted by the patient. Although it is a court demand for information that worries psychiatrists most, the most frequent demand is by someone, such as an insurer, who cannot compel disclosure but who can withhold a benefit without it. Apart from statutory disclosure requirements and judicial compulsion, there is no legal obligation to furnish information, even to law enforcement officials.

Generally, the patient makes disclosures or authorizes the psychiatrist to make them so as to receive a benefit, such as employment, welfare benefits, or insurance.

Third-party payers and supervision. Increased insurance coverage for health care is precipitating the concern about confidentiality and the conceptual model of psychiatric practice. Today insurance covers about 70 percent of all health care bills, and, to provide coverage, an insurance carrier must be able to obtain information with which it can assess the administration and cost of various programs.

Quality control of care necessitates that confidentiality not be absolute; it also requires a review of individual patients and therapists. The therapist in training must breach a patient's confidence by discussing the case with a supervisor. Also, institutionalized patients who have been ordered by a court to get treatment must have their individualized treatment programs submitted to a mental health board.

Writing about patients. In general, professionals have multiple loyalties: to clients, to society, and to the profession. Through their writings, they can share their acquired knowledge and experience, providing information that may be valuable to other professionals and to the public. But it is not easy to write about a psychiatric patient without breaching the confidentiality of the relationship. Unlike physical ailments, which can be discussed without anyone's recognizing the patient, a psychiatric history usually entails a discussion of distinguishing characteristics. Psychiatrists have an obligation not to disclose identifiable patient information (and, perhaps, any descriptive patient information) without appropriate informed consent.

Child abuse. It is now legally required in all states that psychiatrists, among others, who have reason to believe that a child has been the victim of physical or sexual abuse make an immediate report to an appropriate agency. In this situation, confidentiality is decisively limited by legal statute on the grounds that potential or actual harm to vulnerable children outweighs the value of confidentiality in a psychiatric setting. Although many complex psychodynamic nuances accompany the required reporting of suspected child abuse, it is generally agreed that such reports are ethically justified.

DISCLOSURE TO SAFEGUARD

In some situations the physician must report to the authorities, as it is specifically required by law. The classic example of mandatory reporting involves a patient with epilepsy who operates a motor vehicle. Another example of mandatory reporting—one in which penalities are imposed for failing to report—involves child abuse. By law, therapists are obliged to report suspected cases of child abuse to public authorities. Expanded definitions of what constitutes child abuse under the law have been amended in some jurisdictions to include both emotional and physical child abuse. Under this legislation practitioners who learn that a patient is engaged in sexual activity with a child are obliged to report it, although nothing may be gained by notifying the authorities. Other examples of mandatory reporting include many dangerous and contagious diseases, firearm and knife wounds, and patients in drug abuse treatment programs. In the absence of a specific statute that mandates reporting, a report is optional. As a general principle, a person has no duty to come to the aid of another unless there is a special relationship that mandates this duty.

Tarasoff I

Does the establishment of a therapist–patient relationship obligate the therapist to care for the safety of not only the patient but also others? This issue was raised in the case of *Tarasoff v. Regents of University of California* in 1974 (now known as Tarasoff I). In this case, Prosenjit Poddar, a student and a voluntary outpatient at the mental health clinic of the University of California, told his therapist his intention to kill a student readily identified as Tatiana Tarasoff. Realizing the seriousness of the intention, the therapist, with the concurrence of a colleague, concluded that Poddar should be committed for observation under a 72-hour emergency psychiatric detention provision of the California commitment law. The therapist notified the campus police both orally and in writing that Poddar was dangerous and should be committed.

Concerned about the breach of confidentiality, the therapist's supervisor vetoed the recommendation and ordered all records relating to Poddar's treatment destroyed. At the same time the campus police temporarily detained Poddar but released him on his assurance that he would "stay away from that girl." Poddar stopped going to the clinic when he learned from the police of his therapist's recommendation to commit him. Two months later he carried out his previously announced threat to kill Tatiana. The young woman's parents thereupon sued the university for negligence.

As a consequence, the California Supreme Court, which deliberated the case for the unprecedented time of some 14 months, ruled that a physician or a psychotherapist who has reason to believe that a patient may injure or kill someone must notify the potential victim, the victim's relatives or friends, or the authorities.

The discharge of the duty imposed on the therapist to protect intended victims against danger may take one or more various steps, depending on the case. Thus, said the court, it may call for the therapist to warn the intended victim or others likely to notify the victim of the danger, to notify the police, or to take whatever other steps are reasonably necessary under the circumstances.

The Tarasoff decision has not drastically affected psychiatrists, as it has long been their practice to warn the appropriate persons or law enforcement authorities when a patient presents a distinct and immediate threat to someone. According to the American Psychiatric Association, confidentiality may, with careful judgment, be broken in the following ways: (1) A patient will probably commit murder, and the act can be stopped only by the psychiatrist's notification of the police. (2) A patient will probably commit suicide, and the act can be stopped only by the psychiatrist's notification of the police. (3) A patient, such as a bus driver or airline pilot, who has potentially life-threatening responsibilities, shows marked impairment of judgment.

The Tarasoff ruling does not require therapists to report fantasies; rather, it requires a therapist to report an intended homicide; it is the therapist's duty to exercise good judgment.

Tarasoff II

In 1976 the California Supreme Court issued a second ruling in the case of *Tarasoff v. Regents of University of California* (Tarasoff II), which broadened its earlier ruling, the duty to *warn*, to include the duty to *protect*.

The Tarasoff II ruling has stimulated perhaps the most intense debates in the medicolegal field. Lawyers, judges, and expert witnesses argue the definition of prevention, the nature of the relationship between the therapist and the patient, and the balance between public safety and individual privacy.

Clinicians argue that the duty to protect hinders treatment because the patient may not trust the doctor if confidentiality is not maintained. Furthermore, because it is not easy to determine if a patient is dangerous enough to justify long-term incarceration, unnecessary involuntary incarceration because of defensive practices may occur.

As a result of such debates in the medicolegal field, since 1976 there has not been a uniform interpretation of the Tarasoff II ruling (the concept of the duty to protect) by the state courts.

HOSPITALIZATION

Civil Commitment

It is preferable to have a patient voluntarily enter a mental hospital or the psychiatric inpatient service of a general hospital, rather than to force hospitalization. However, all states provide for some form of involuntary hospitalization. Such action is usually taken when psychiatric patients present a danger to themselves and to others in their environment to the degree that their urgent need for treatment in a closed institution is evident.

The statutes governing hospitalization of the mentally ill have generally been designated as commitment laws. However, psychiatrists have long considered the term an undesirable one because commitment legally means a warrant for imprisonment. The American Bar Association and the American Psychiatric Association have recommended that the term be replaced by the less offensive and more accurate "hospitalization," which has been adopted by most of the states. Although this change in terminology does not correct the attitudes of the past, the emphasis on hospitalization and treatment is more in keeping with psychiatrists' views.

Procedures of Admission

Four procedures of admission to psychiatric facilities have been endorsed by the American Bar Association as safeguarding civil liberties and insuring that no person can be railroaded into a mental hospital. Although each of the 50 states has the power to enact its own laws regarding psychiatric hospitalization, the procedures outlined are gaining much acceptance.

Informal admission. Informal admission operates on the general hospital model, in which the patient is admitted to a psychiatric unit of a general hospital on the same basis as a medical or surgical patient may be admitted. Under such circumstances the ordinary doctor-patient relationship applies, with the patient free to enter and to leave, even against medical advice.

Voluntary admission (operates in psychiatric hospitals). In voluntary admission, patients apply in writing for admission to a psychiatric hospital. They may come to the hospital on the advice of their personal physician, or they may seek help on the basis of their own decision. In either case the patients are examined by a psychiatrist on the staff of the hospital and are admitted if that examination reveals the need for hospital treatment.

Temporary admission (emergency admission or certificate of one physician). Temporary admission is used for patients who are so senile or confused that they require hospitalization and are not able to make decisions of their own and for patients who are so acutely disturbed that they must be immediately admitted to a psychiatric hospital on an emergency basis.

Under this procedure a person is admitted to the hospital on the written recommendation of one physician. Once the patient has been brought to the psychiatric hospital, the need for hospitalization must be confirmed by a psychiatrist on the hospital staff.

This procedure is temporary because patients cannot be hospitalized against their will for more than 15 days.

Involuntary admission (certificate of two physicians). Involuntary admission involves the question of whether the patients are a danger to themselves, such as suicidal patients, or a danger to others, such as homicidal patients. Because these persons do not recognize their need for hospital care, the application for admission to a hospital may be made by a relative or friend.

Once the application is made, the patients must be examined by two physicians, and, if they confirm the need for hospitalization, the patients can then be admitted.

There is an established procedure for written notification to the next of kin whenever involuntary hospitalization is involved. Furthermore, the patients have access at any time to legal counsel, who can bring the case before a judge. If the judge does not think that hospitalization is indicated, the patient's release can be ordered.

Involuntary admission allows the patient to be hospitalized for 60 days. After that time, if the patient is to remain hospitalized, the case must be reviewed periodically by a board consisting of psychiatrists, nonpsychiatric physicians, lawyers, and other citizens not connected with the institution. In New York State this board is called the Mental Health Information Service. The power of the state to commit mentally ill persons in need of care is known as *parens patriae*, also known as police power, in that it prevents mentally ill persons from doing harm to themselves or to others.

Despite the clear-cut procedures and safeguards for hospitalization available to patients, to their families, and to the medical and legal professions, involuntary admissions are viewed by some as an infringement of civil rights.

Persons who have been hospitalized involuntarily and who believe that they should be released have the right to file a petition for a writ of *habeas corpus*. Under law, a writ of *habeas corpus* may be proclaimed by those who believe they have been illegally deprived of liberty. This legal procedure asks a court to decide whether hospitalization has been accomplished without due process of law. The case must be heard by a court at once, regardless of the manner or form in which the motion is filed. Hospitals are obligated to submit these petitions to the court immediately.

Involuntary Discharge

Under a variety of circumstances, patients may have to be discharged from a hospital against their will—if they have intentionally broken a major hospital rule (for example, smuggled drugs, assaulted another patient), refused treatment, or been restored to health but still wish to remain hospitalized. Some people may wonder why many patients wish to remain in a psychiatric hospital. For some patients, such a protective environment is preferable to the streets, jail, or the family's home. Although the focus here is on discharge from an inpatient unit, similar issues are involved in unilateral termination with an outpatient.

Abandonment as cause of action. For the clinician the potential pitfall of involuntary discharge or involuntary termination is the charge of abandonment. This claim can be a particularly fertile ground for malpractice litigation when the inevitable bad feelings are combined with a bad result. The clinician's vulnerability in this context is augmented by the jury's tendency to project a prejudicial distaste for the mentally ill person onto the physician, viewing the doctor as someone who probably wants to get rid of the patient and be free to play golf. This popular perception places an additional onus on the clinician to exercise special care in this charged situation.

Ending the relationship. An involuntary discharge entails all the pain of the termination process with far less opportunity for perspective, healing, and growth. Most important, in this situation the clinician directly opposes the patient's proclaimed wishes, thereby severely straining the therapeutic alliance.

Consultation and documentation of the rationale for the action are the two safeguards against liability.

Going the extra mile means smoothing the way for the patient to obtain care in the future. Termination does not mean abandonment when a good-faith transfer of services is made through an appropriate referral to another hospital or therapist. Furthermore, when possible, the patient should be told that the door is open for a negotiated return at some future time after restitution has been made or the problem has otherwise been redressed.

Emergencies. The one circumstance in which the clinician cannot terminate a patient is a state of emergency. A typical example is a patient who attacks a therapist. The therapist cannot terminate the patient's care, no matter how severe the assault, until the emergency situation has been resolved (e.g., by hospitalizing the patient or arranging for seclusion or restraint). Only then can the therapist terminate the relationship and transfer the patient.

RIGHT TO TREATMENT

Among the rights of patients, the right to the standard quality of care is fundamental. It has been litigated in much-publicized cases in recent years under the slogan of "right to treatment."

In 1966 Judge David Bazelon, speaking for the District of Columbia Court of Appeals in *Rouse v. Cameron*, noted that the purpose of involuntary hospitalization is treatment and concluded that the absence of treatment draws into question the constitutionality of the confinement. Treatment in exchange for liberty is the logic of the ruling. In that case the patient was discharged on a writ of *habeas corpus*, the basic legal remedy to ensure liberty.

Alabama Federal District Court Judge Frank Johnson was more venturesome in the decree he rendered in 1971 in *Wyatt v. Stickney*. The Wyatt case was a class-action proceeding, brought under newly developed rules that sought not release but treatment. Judge Johnson ruled that persons civilly committed to a mental institution have a constitutional right to receive such individual treatment as will give each of them a reasonable opportunity to be cured or to have their mental condition improved. Johnson set out minimum requirements for staffing, specified physical facilities and nutritional standards, and required individualized treatment plans. Shortly thereafter, Texas Federal District Judge William Justice set out standards for state training schools.

The new codes, more detailed than the old ones, include the right to be free from excessive or unnecessary medication; the right to privacy and dignity; the right to the least restrictive environment; the unrestricted right to be visited by attorneys and private physicians; and the right not to be subjected to lobotomies, electroconvulsive treatments, or other procedures without fully informed consent. Patients can be required to perform therapeutic tasks but not hospital chores unless they volunteer for them and are paid the federal minimum wage. This requirement is an attempt to eliminate the practice of peonage, in which psychiatric patients were forced to work at menial tasks, without payment, for the benefit of the state.

In a number of states today, medication or electroshock therapy cannot be forcibly administered to a patient without first obtaining court approval, which may take as long as 10 days. The right to refuse treatment is a legal doctrine that holds that a person cannot be forced to have treatment against his or her will unless it is a life-and-death emergency.

In the 1976 case of *O'Connor v. Donaldson*, the U.S. Supreme Court ruled that harmless mental patients cannot be confined against their will without treatment if they can survive outside. According to the Court, a finding of mental illness alone cannot justify a state's confining persons in a hospital against their will. Instead, involuntarily confined patients must be considered dangerous to themselves or others. Questions have been raised about psychiatrists' ability to accurately predict dangerousness and about the risk to psychiatrists, who may be sued for monetary damages if a person is thereby deprived of his or her civil rights.

The ethical controversy over applications of the law to psychiatric patients came to the fore through Thomas Szasz, a professor of psychiatry at the State University of New York. In his book *The Myth of Mental Illness*, Szasz argued that the various psychiatric diagnoses are totally devoid of significance and contended that psychiatrists have no place in the courts of law and that all forced confinements because of mental illness are unjust. Szasz's opposition to suicide prevention and the imposition of treatment, with or without confinement, is interesting but is viewed by the psychiatric community with strong misgivings.

SECLUSION AND RESTRAINT

Seclusion refers to the placement and retention of an inpatient in a bare room for the purpose of containing a clinical situation that may result in a state of emergency. Restraint refers to measures designed to confine a patient's bodily movements, such as the use of leather cuffs and anklets or straitjackets. The use of seclusion and restraint raises important issues of safety. The American Psychiatric Association's *Task Force Report on Seclusion and Restraint* provides standards for the use of these interventions. Clinicians practicing in institutions that use such measures should be familiar with this report and with local statutes. Finally, clinicians facing a genuine emergency should act conservatively. A patient can always be released from restraints or seclusion, whereas the harm caused by uncontained violence may be irreversible.

INFORMED CONSENT

Lawyers representing an injured claimant now invariably add to a claim of negligent performance or procedures (malpractice) an informed consent claim as another possible area of liability. Ironically, it is one claim under which the requirement of expert testimony may be avoided. The usual claim of malpractice requires the litigant to produce an expert to establish that there was a departure from accepted medical practice. But in a case in which there was no informed consent, the fact that the treatment was technically well performed and effected a complete cure is immaterial. However, as a practical matter, unless there are adverse consequences, a complainant will not get very far with a jury in an action based only on an allegation that the treatment was performed without consent.

In classical tort (a tort is a wrongful act) theory an intentional touching to which one has not given consent is a battery. Thus, the administration of electroconvulsive therapy or chemotherapy, though it may be therapeutic, is a battery when done without consent. Indeed, any unauthorized touching outside conventional social intercourse constitutes a battery. It is an offense to the dignity of the person, an invasion of his or her right of self-determination, for which punitive and actual damages may be imposed. Justice Benjamin Cardozo wrote: "Every human being of adult years and sound mind has a right to determine what shall be done with his own body; and a surgeon who performs an operation without his patient's consent commits [a battery] for which he is liable in damages."

According to Cardozo, it is not the effectiveness or the timeliness of the treatment that allows taking care of another but the consent to it. Thus, a mentally competent adult may refuse treatment, even though it is effective and of little risk. But, for example, when gangrene sets in and the patient is psychotic, treatment—even of such momentous proportions as amputation—may be ordered to save the patient's life. The state is also said to have a compelling interest in preventing its citizens from committing suicide.

In the case of minors, the parent or guardian is the person legally empowered to consent to medical treatment. However, most states by statute list specific diseases or conditions that a minor can consent to have treated—venereal disease, pregnancy, drug dependence, alcoholism, and contagious diseases. And in an emergency a physician can treat a minor without parental consent. The trend is to adopt what is referred to as the mature minor rule, allowing minors to consent to treatment under ordinary circumstances. As a result of the U.S. Supreme Court's 1967 Gault decision, all juveniles must now be represented by counsel, must be able to confront witnesses, and must be given proper notice of any charges. Emancipated minors have the rights of an adult when it can be demonstrated that they are living as adults with control over their own lives.

In the past, to obviate a claim of battery, physicians needed only to relate what they proposed to do and obtain the patient's consent thereto. However, simultaneously with the growth of product liability and consumer law, the courts began to require that physicians also relate sufficient information to allow the patient to decide whether such a procedure is acceptable in light of the risks and benefits and the available alternatives, including no treatment at all. This duty of full disclosure gave rise to the phrase "informed consent is no consent." In general, informed consent requires that there be (1) an understanding of the nature and the foreseeable risks and benefits of a procedure, (2) a knowledge of alternative procedures, (3) awareness of the consequences of withholding consent, and (4) the recognition that the consent is voluntary (Figure 46-1).

Consent Forms

The consent form is a written document proving that informed consent has been obtained. However, there are several problems inherent in its design and use. Consent forms are usually designed by attorneys whose aim is to protect the institution from liability. Therefore, such forms are often exhaustive and require a level of reading comprehension that is beyond that of many patients. Paradoxically, if such a form truly covered all possible eventualities, it would probably be too long to be comprehensible, and, if it were short enough to be comprehensible, it might be incomplete. Some theorists have recommended that the form be replaced by a standardized discussion and a progress note.

CHILD CUSTODY

The action of a court in a child custody dispute is now predicated on the best interests of the child. The maxim reflects the idea that a natural parent does not have an inherent right to be named as the custodial parent, but the presumption, although a bit eroded, remains in favor of the mother in the case of young children. By a rule of thumb, the courts presume that the welfare of a child of tender years is generally best served by maternal custody when the mother is a good and fit parent. The best interest of the mother may be served by naming her as the custodial parent, as a mother may never resolve the effects of the loss or death of a child, but her best interest is not to be equated *ipso facto* with the best interest of the child. Care and protection proceedings refer to the court's intervention in the welfare of a child when the parents are unable to do so.

More and more fathers are asserting custodial claims. In about 5 percent of all cases, they are named custodians. The movement supporting women's rights is also enhancing the chances of paternal custody. With more and more women going outside the home to work, the traditional rationale for maternal custody has less force than it did in the past.

Every state today has a statute allowing a court, usually a juvenile court, to assume jurisdiction over a neglected or abused child and to remove the child from parental custody. Most states provide several grounds for assuming jurisdiction, such as parental abuse, an injurious environment, and the danger of the child's being brought up to lead an idle, dissolute, or immoral life. If the court removes the child from parental custody, it usually orders that the care and custody of the child be supervised by the welfare or probation department.

TESTAMENTARY AND CONTRACTUAL CAPACITY AND COMPETENCE

Psychiatrists may be asked to evaluate patients' testamentary capacity—that is, their competence to make a will. Three psychological abilities are necessary to demonstrate this competence. Patients must know (1) the nature and extent of their bounty (property); (2) that they are making a will; and (3) who their natural beneficiaries are—that is, the spouse, children, and other relatives.

Quite often, when a will is being probated, one of the

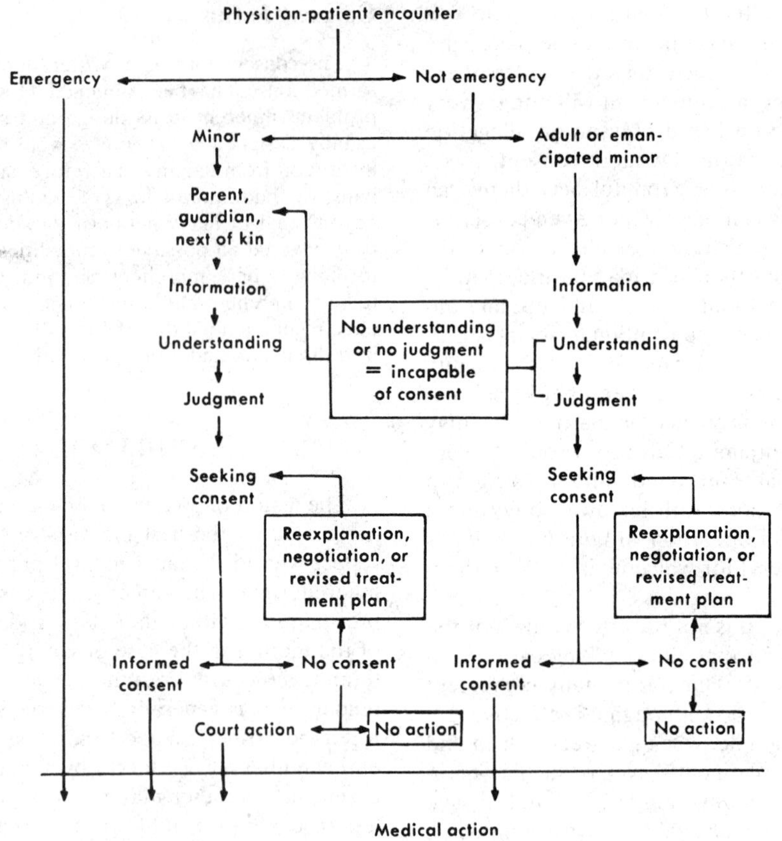

Figure 46-1. Seeking and obtaining informed consent. (From J E Groves, J M Vacarino: Legal aspects in consultation. In *Massachusetts General Hospital Handbook of General Hospital Psychiatry*, ed 2, T P Hackett and N H Cassem, editors. PSG Publishing, Littleton, MA, 1987, with permission.)

heirs or some other person challenges its validity. A judgment in such cases must be based on a reconstruction of what the testator's mental state was at the time the will was written. The expert gathers evidence for this reconstruction from persons who knew the testator at the time the will was written, from data from documents, and from expert psychiatric testimony.

An incompetence proceeding and the appointment of a guardian may be considered necessary when a member of the family is spending the family's assets. The guardianship process may be used when property is in danger of dissipation, as in the case of the aged, the retarded, the alcoholic, and the psychotic. The issue is whether such persons are capable of managing their own affairs. However, a guardian appointed to take control of the property of one deemed incompetent cannot make a will for the ward. When one is unable or does not exercise one's right to make a will, the law in all states provides for the distribution of one's property to the heirs; if there are no heirs, the estate goes to the public treasury. Witnesses at the signing of the will, which may include a psychiatrist, may attest that the testator was rational at the time the will was executed. In unusual cases the lawyer may videotape the signing to safeguard the will from attack.

Competence is determined on the basis of a person's ability to make a sound judgment. The diagnosis of a mental disorder is not, in itself, sufficient to warrant a finding of incompetence. Rather, the mental disorder must cause an impairment in judgment regarding the specific issues involved. Once declared incompetent, persons are deprived of certain rights: they cannot make contracts, marry, start a divorce action, drive a vehicle, handle their own property, or practice their profession. Incompetence is decided at a formal courtroom proceeding, and the court usually appoints a guardian who will best serve the patient's interests. Another hearing is necessary to declare the patient competent. Admission to a mental hospital does not automatically mean the person is incompetent; a separate hearing for that is usually required.

Competence is also essential in contracts, as a contract is an agreement between parties to do some specific act. The contract is declared invalid if, when it was signed, one of the parties was unable to comprehend the nature of his or her act. The marriage contract is subject to the same standard and, thus, can be voided if either party did not understand the nature, duties, obligations, and other characteristics entailed at the time they were married. In general, however, the courts are unwilling to declare a marriage void on the basis of incompetence.

Whether the competence is related to wills, contracts, or the making or breaking of marriages, the fundamental concern is the person's state of awareness and capacity to comprehend the significance of the particular commitment made.

Competence to Inform

Competence to inform is a relatively new concept involving the patient's interaction with the clinician and is useful in ambiguous situations that may have a poor outcome. The clinician first explains to the patient the value of being honest with the clinician and then attempts to determine whether the patient is competent to weigh the risks and benefits of withholding information about suicidal or homicidal intent. This process must be documented.

A conservator handles a person's fiscal or contractual affairs but not medical or surgical treatment.

Competence to Stand Trial

The U.S. Supreme Court stated that the prohibition against trying someone who is mentally incompetent is fundamental to the U.S. system of justice. Accordingly, the Court has approved a test of competence that seeks to ascertain whether a criminal defendant "has sufficient present ability to consult with his lawyer with a reasonable degree of rational understanding—and whether he has a rational as well as factual understanding of the proceedings against him."

Competence to Be Executed

One of the new areas of competence to emerge in the interface between psychiatry and the law is the question of the patient's competence to be executed. This requirement for competence has been thought to rest on three general principles. First, the patient's awareness of what is happening is supposed to heighten the retributive element of the punishment. Punishment is held as meaningless unless the patient is aware of what it is and to what it is a response. The second element is a religious one: Competent persons about to be executed are thought to be in the best position to make whatever peace is appropriate with their religious beliefs, including confession and absolution. Finally, the competent person about to be executed preserves until the last the possibility (admittedly slight) of recalling some forgotten detail of the events or crime that may prove exonerating.

The need to preserve competence was most recently supported in the Supreme Court case of *Ford v. Wainwright*. But no matter how the courts struggle with this question, most medical bodies have gravitated toward the position that it is unethical for any clinician to participate, no matter how remotely, in state-mandated executions, as the physician's duty to preserve life transcends all other competing requirements. Thus, it is unlikely that the average psychiatrist will lack for ethical guidance on this point. However, ethical dilemmas are readily predictable. A psychiatrist who examines a patient slated for execution may find the person incompetent on the basis of mental illness but may incur a medical obligation to recommend a treatment plan, which, if implemented, would ensure that person's fitness to be executed. There is room for a difference of opinion as to whether treatment under these circumstances is humane or inhumane.

CRIMINAL LAW

Criminal Responsibility

According to criminal law, a socially harmful act is not the sole criterion of a crime. Rather, the objectionable act must have two components: voluntary conduct (*actus reus*) and evil intent (*mens rea*). There cannot be a *mens rea* if the offender's mental status is so deficient, so abnormal, or so diseased as to have deprived the offender of the capacity for rational intent. The law can be invoked only when an illegal intent is implemented. Neither behavior, however harmful, nor the intent to do harm is, in itself, grounds for criminal action.

Until quite recently, in most American jurisdictions, persons could be found not guilty by reason of insanity if they suffered from a mental illness, did not know the difference between right and wrong, and did not know the nature and consequences of their acts.

M'Naghten rule. The precedent for determining legal responsibility was established in the British courts in 1843. The so-called M'Naghten rule, which has until recently determined responsibility in most of the United States, holds that people are not guilty by reason of insanity if they labored under a mental disease such that they were unaware of the nature, quality, and consequences of their act or if they were incapable of realizing that their act was wrong. Moreover, to absolve people from punishment, a delusion has to be one that, if true, would be an adequate defense. If the deluded idea does not justify the crime, then presumably such persons are to be held responsible, guilty, and punishable. The M'Naghten rule is known commonly as the right-wrong test.

The M'Naghten rule derives from the famous M'Naghten case dating back to 1843 (Figure 46-2). At that time Edward Drummond, the private secretary of Sir Robert Peel, was murdered by Daniel M'Naghten. M'Naghten had been suffering from delusions of persecution for several years. He had complained to many people about his delusional persecutors, and finally he decided to correct the situation by murdering Sir Robert Peel. When Drummond came out of Peel's home, M'Naghten shot Drum-

Figure 46-2. Daniel M'Naghten. His 1843 murder trial led to the establishment of rules still generally observed in legal insanity pleas. (Courtesy of Culver Pictures.)

mond, mistaking him for Peel. M'Naghten was later adjudged insane and committed to a hospital. The case aroused great interest, causing the House of Lords to debate the problems of criminality and insanity. In response to questions about what guidelines could be used to determine whether a person should plead insanity as a defense against criminal responsibility, the English judiciary wrote:

1. To establish a defense on the ground of insanity it must be clearly proved that, at the time of committing the act, the party accused was laboring under such a defect of reason, from disease of the mind, as not to know the nature and quality of the act he was doing, or if he did know it, he did not know he was doing what was wrong.
2. Where a person labors under partial delusions only and is not in other respects insane and as a result commits an offense he must be considered in the same situation as to responsibility as if the facts with respect to which the delusion exists were real.

The jury, as instructed under the prevailing law, found M'Naghten not guilty by reason of insanity.

The M'Naghten rule does not ask whether the accused knows the difference in general between right and wrong; it asks whether the defendant understood the nature and quality of the act and if the defendant knew the difference between right and wrong with respect to the act. It asks specifically whether the defendant knew the act was wrong or, perhaps, thought the act was correct—that is, was a delusion causing the defendant to act in legitimate self-defense.

Irresistible impulse. In 1922 a committee of jurists in England reexamined the M'Naghten rule and suggested broadening the concept of insanity in criminal cases to include the concept of the irresistible impulse. This means that a person charged with a criminal offense is not responsible for an act if the act was committed under an impulse that the person was unable to resist because of mental disease. The courts have chosen to interpret this law in such a way that it has been called the policeman-at-the-elbow law. In other words, the court grants the impulse to be irresistible only if it determines that the accused would have gone ahead with the act even if a policeman had been at the accused's elbow. To most psychiatrists this law is unsatisfactory because it covers only a small and very special group of those who are mentally ill.

Durham rule. In 1954 in the case of *Durham v. United States*, a decision was handed down by Judge David Bazelon, a pioneering jurist in forensic psychiatry in the District of Columbia Court of Appeals, that resulted in the product rule of criminal responsibility: An accused is not criminally responsible if his unlawful act was the product of mental disease or mental defect.

In the Durham case Judge Bazelon expressly stated that the purpose of the rule was to get good and complete psychiatric testimony. He sought to release the criminal law from the theoretical straitjacket of the M'Naghten test. However, judges and juries in cases using the Durham rule became mired in confusion over the terms "product," "disease," and "defect." In 1972, some 18 years after its adoption, the Court of Appeals for the District of Columbia, in *United States v. Brawner*, discarded the rule. The court—all nine members, including Judge Bazelon—decided in a 143-page opinion to throw out its Durham rule and to adopt in its place the test recommended in 1962 by the American Law Institute in its model penal code, which is the law in the federal courts today.

Model penal code. In its model penal code the American Law Institute recommended the following test of criminal responsibility: (1) Persons are not responsible for criminal conduct if at the time of such conduct, as a result of mental disease or defect, they lacked substantial capacity either to appreciate the criminality [wrongfulness] of their conduct or to conform their conduct to the requirement of the law. (2) As used in this article, the terms "mental disease or defect" do not include an abnormality manifested only by repeated criminals or otherwise antisocial conduct.

There are five operative concepts in subsection 1 of the American Law Institute rule: (1) mental disease or defect, (2) lack of substantial capacity, (3) appreciation, (4) wrongfulness, and (5) conformity of conduct to the requirements of law. The second subsection of the rule, stating that repeated criminal or antisocial conduct is not of itself to be taken as mental disease or defect, aims to keep the sociopath or psychopath within the scope of criminal responsibility.

The test of criminal responsibility and other tests grading criminal liability refer to the time of the offense's commission, whereas the test of competence to stand trial refers to the time of the trial.

Although much has been written on the insanity plea, it is actually asserted as a defense in only a small percentage of cases, and it is upheld in only a fraction of those.

The 1982 verdict of a District of Columbia jury—finding the would-be assassin of President Ronald Reagan, John W. Hinckley, Jr., not guilty by reason of insanity—ignited moves to limit or abolish this special plea. Hinckley's trial by jury also turned out to be a trial of law and psychiatry. The psychiatrists and the law allowing their testimony were made the culprits for the unpopular verdict. "The psychiatrists spun sticky webs of pseudo-scientific jargon," wrote a prominent columnist, "and in these webs the concept of justice, like a moth, fluttered feebly and was trapped." The American Bar Association and the American Psychiatric Association quickly issued statements calling for a change in the law. Over 40 bills were introduced in the Congress to amend the law, but none was passed. However, they helped defuse the public criticism. At present, Hinckley is hospitalized indefinitely at the federal St. Elizabeth's Hospital in Washington, D.C.

Attempts at reform have included the plea of guilty but mentally ill, which is already used in some jurisdictions. This standard has the advantage of identifying guilt while allowing some adaptation to psychiatric conditions. For example, it allows for treatment in restricted settings while permitting the courts to maintain an active role.

The American Medical Association proposed yet another reform: limiting the insanity exculpation to cases in which the person is so ill as to lack the necessary criminal intent (*mens rea*). This approach would all but eliminate the insanity defense and place a burden on the prisons to accept large numbers of mentally ill persons.

The American Bar Association and the American Psychiatric Association in their statements of 1982 recommended a defense of nonresponsibility, which focuses solely on whether the defendant, as a result of mental disease or defect, is unable to appreciate the wrongfulness of his or her conduct. These proposals would limit evidence of mental illness to cognition and exclude it on control (but there would apparently still be a defense available under a not-guilty plea—such as extreme emotional disturbance, automatism, provocation, or self-defense—that could be established without psychiatric testimony on mental illness). The American Psychiatric Association also urged that "mental illness" be limited to severely abnormal mental conditions. These proposals remain controversial, and it is likely that this issue will rise again with each sensational case in which the insanity defense is used.

MALPRACTICE

Malpractice is the term commonly used to refer to professional negligence. It has also been loosely used to cover intentional or willful invasion of another's legally protected interest, such as battery or treatment without consent. An action based on negligence, whatever the specific situation, involves basic problems of the relation among the parties, risk, and reason.

Four Elements of Malpractice

To claim malpractice, the patient or plaintiff must be able to demonstrate that four elements of malpractice are present. These elements can be mnemonically summarized as the four D's of malpractice: Dereliction (negligence) of a Duty Directly causing Damages.

In negligence (1) a standard of care requisite under the particular circumstances must exist, (2) a duty must have been owed by the defendant or by someone for whose conduct the defendant is answerable, (3) the duty must have been owed to the plaintiff, and (4) a breach of the duty must be the legal cause of the plaintiff's asserted damage or injury.

The requisite standard of care under the circumstances may be established in the federal or state constitution, statutes, administrative regulations, court decisions, or the custom of the community. However, the law, with few exceptions, does not specifically define the particular duties. And it is not possible to define the way in which a person ought to act under various circumstances and conditions. As a general rule, professionals have the duty to exercise the degree of skill ordinarily used under similar circumstances by other similar professionals.

Complainants in a malpractice action must prove their allegations by a preponderance of evidence. To sustain the burden of proof, the plaintiff must show (1) an act or omission on the part of the defendant or of someone for whose conduct the defendant is answerable, (2) a causal relation between the conduct and the damage or injury allegedly suffered by the plaintiff, and (3) the negligent quality of the conduct. Because most professional conduct is not within the common knowledge of the layperson, expert testimony must usually provide such information.

In relative frequency of malpractice suits, psychiatry ranks eighth among the medical specialties, and in almost every suit for psychiatric malpractice in which liability was imposed, tangible physical injury was demonstrated. The number of suits against psychiatrists is said to be small because of the patient's reluctance to expose a psychiatric history, the skill of the psychiatrist in dealing with the patient's negative feelings, and the difficulty in linking injury with treatment. Psychiatrists have been sued for malpractice for faulty diagnosis or screening, improper certification in commitment, suicide, harmful effects of electroconvulsive treatments and psychotropic drugs, improper divulgence of information, and sexual intimacy with patients (Figure 46-3).

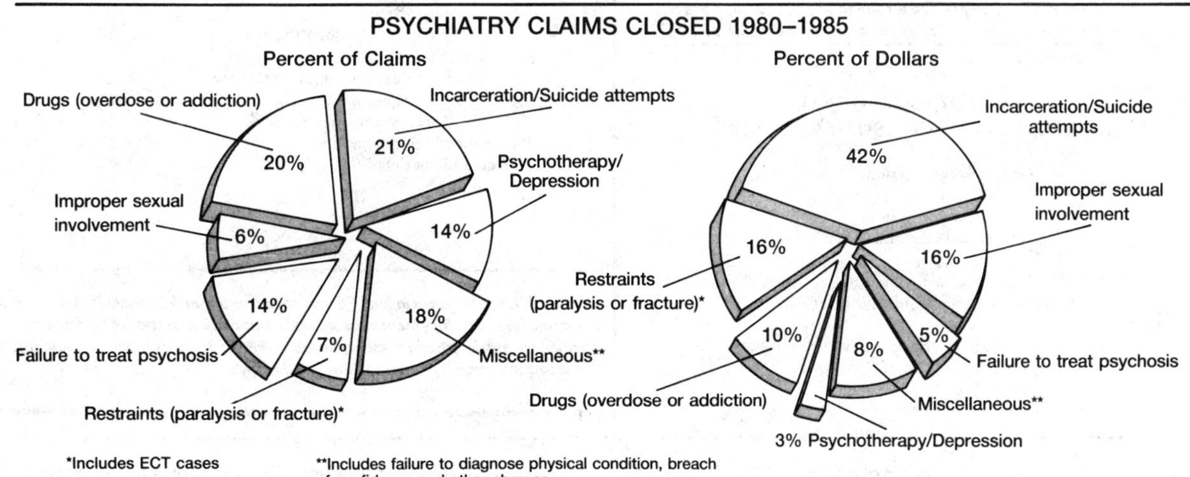

Figure 46-3. Figure from American Psychiatric Association: Psychiatric News *22*: 12, 1987, with permission.

Respondeat Superior

This Latin phrase expresses the axiom, "Let the master answer for the deeds of the servant." This doctrine holds that a person occupying a higher position in a chain or hierarchy of responsibility is liable for the actions of a person in a lower position. A typical example is the psychiatric attending physician who supervises a resident. By the same reasoning, when a state hospital, say, is named in a lawsuit, the list of cited defendants may extend upward to include the commissioner of mental health and the governor of the state. After this traditional first response, the attorneys usually weed out the less relevant defendants.

A few critical issues should be noted here. First, consultation from outside the line of clinical responsibility often does not fit this model. The consultant is an adviser, not a superior. Second, the question of the particular defendant's authority (whether that person can hire and fire, censure, or control subordinates in the system) is relevant to the assignment of blame. Third, as a rule, psychiatrists should remove themselves from situations in which they bear responsibility (liability) for the practice of other professionals but cannot control the activity of those persons or perform their own assessment of the patients. In addition, psychiatrists should clarify ambiguities of responsibility at the point of entry into a system.

Sexual Relations with Patients

Although this problem is not a common form of malpractice, it is not rare enough. The most common form of this activity is heterosexual relations occurring in an outpatient context between a male therapist and a female patient, but all other permutations have come to light—and to litigation.

Sexual relations with a patient is considered a breach of the fiduciary (trust-based) relationship of physician to patient, as well as a negligent failure by the physician to work correctly with transference-countertransference issues in a manner consistent with the standard of care. The usual harms identified are failure to provide treatment during the affair, misuse of time that might be spent in treatment elsewhere, creation of severe difficulties for future therapy, and the direct emotional harms of guilt, depression, anxiety, shame, humiliation, and suicidal intent.

A

PROFESSIONAL THERAPY NEVER INCLUDES SEX!

This brochure was developed pursuant to Senate Bill 1004 (Senator Diane Watson). Under this law, psychotherapists are required to provide a copy to any patient who has been the victim of sexual exploitation by another psychotherapist.

STATE OF CALIFORNIA
DEPARTMENT OF CONSUMER AFFAIRS

George Deukmejian, Governor

Shirley Chilton
Secretary, State and Consumer Services Agency

Michael A. Kelley
Director, Department of Consumer Affairs

John C. Lungren, Jr.
Deputy Director, Division of Consumer Services

1990

B

Table of contents

	Page
Introduction	4
Definitions	4
Warning signs	5
What if it's me?	6
Where to start	6
What you can do -- Options for action	
Reporting options	7
Administrative action	7
Criminal action	9
Civil action	9
Professional association action	10
Options for help	
Individual and/or group therapy	11
Self-help support groups	11
Therapy mediation sessions	11
Frequently asked questions	12
Client bill of rights	13

I foolishly put my trust in him. I assumed he was the professional. He told me that a body massage, touching me in intimate areas, was a legitimate part of therapy and that it helped release deep feelings and emotions. When I felt uneasy about it, I told myself that it was my hangup getting in the way of therapy.

Figure 46-4. Title page (*A*) and table of contents (*B*) of a booklet that must be given to any patient in California who reports a past history of sexual involvement with a therapist. (Produced by the State of California Department of Consumer Affairs, used with permission.)

As grounds for malpractice, engagement in sexual relations with patients poses many extremely complex conundrums about the nature of adult consent, transference and transference love, countertransference, confidentiality, mutuality, and exploitation. Such situations may represent neurotic acting out by a therapist whose marriage is in difficulty, successful seduction by a patient, exploitative or psychopathic manipulation of a vulnerable patient by the therapist, the development of true love, or false (groundless) accusations by a vengeful borderline personality disorder patient expressing sadistic transference. These issues are too extensive to be explored here, but some general points can be offered.

The consensus, drawn from case law and the codes of practice espoused by national professional organizations, quite clearly dictates that sexual relations with a patient under any circumstances (usually including ex-patients) is unethical, a deviation from the standard of care, and, therefore, proscribed. Numerous social activities that are not overtly sexual are highly suspect (one famous case involved a therapist taking tea with a patient). As a form of liability prevention, they should also be avoided.

Several questions are often raised on this subject. First, is there some rule of limitations specifying that, after a certain period of time has elapsed, an ex-patient can properly be dated? While some states have defined time limits, the short answer is "probably not": once a patient, always a patient, as far as this issue is concerned. The judgment calls are more difficult in the case of a colleague's patient or a patient seen for a one-time evaluation, but a conservative approach is recommended.

Second, what counts as sexual relations? Hugging? Hand holding? There is no way to tell what a court of law may consider sexual activity, but handshakes under appropriate circumstances should probably represent the limit of physical contact between parties. Clinicians who perform physical examinations of their patients should have them chaperoned, just as in medical practice.

Third, can a therapist refer and then date a patient, so that the patient's clinical needs are addressed and the therapist is not pretending to offer treatment while being paid and leaving the patient without psychiatric care? At this point in malpractice law, the answer must again be "no." The transference relationship with the original therapist is still thought to cloud the autonomy of the patient's consent. However, the therapist whose feelings of love (or hate, for that matter) toward the patient become unmanageable and do not respond to the usual means of countertransference resolution should terminate and refer the patient elsewhere in the interests of sound, objective care.

The problem of sexual relations with patients is such a serious issue that certain governmental authorities require that psychotherapists give a publication that explains their rights to those patients who report having been involved in sexual relations with a previous therapist (Figure 46-4).

Preventing Liability

Although it is impossible to eliminate malpractice, some preventive approaches have proved valuable in clinical practice. (1) Clinicians should provide only those kinds of care that they are qualified to offer. They should not overload their practices or overstretch their abilities; they should take reasonable care of themselves; and they should treat their patients with respect. (2) The documentation of good care is a strong deterrent to liability. Such documentation should include the decision-making process, the clinician's rationale for treatment, and an evaluation of costs and benefits. (3) A consultation affords protection against liability, because it allows the clinician to obtain information about the peer group's standard of practice. It also provides a second opinion, enabling the clinician to submit any judgment to the scrutiny of a peer. A clinician who takes the trouble to obtain a consultation in a difficult and complex case is unlikely to be viewed by a jury as careless or negligent. (4) The informed consent process involves a discussion of the inherent uncertainty of psychiatric practice. Such a dialogue helps prevent a liability suit.

References

American Psychiatric Association: *The Principles of Medical Ethics*. American Psychiatric Press, Washington, DC, 1981.

American Psychoanalytic Association: *Principles of Ethics for Psychoanalysts*. American Psychoanalytic Association, New York, 1983.

Benson P R, Roth L H, Winslade W J: Informed consent in psychiatric research: Preliminary findings from an ongoing investigation. Soc Sci Med *20*: 1331, 1985.

Bloch S, Chodoff P, eds.: *Psychiatric Ethics*. Oxford University Press, Oxford, England, 1984.

Culver C, Gert B: *Philosophy in Medicine*. Oxford University Press, New York, 1982.

Dyer A R: *Ethics and Psychiatry: Toward Professional Definition*. American Psychiatric Press, Washington, DC, 1987.

Eichelman B, Wikler D, Hartwig A: Ethics and psychiatric research: Problems and justification. Am J Psychiatry *141*: 400, 1984.

Gutheil T G: Legal issues in psychiatry. In *Comprehensive Textbook of Psychiatry*, ed 5, H I Kaplan and B J Sadock, editors, p 2107. Williams & Wilkins, Baltimore, 1989.

Gutheil T G, Appelbaum P S: *Clinical Handbook of Psychiatry and the Law*. McGraw-Hill, New York, 1982.

Gutheil T G, Bursztajn H, Brodsky A: Liability prevention through informed consent: Some new approaches for the clinician. Risk Management Foundation Forum *7*: 8, 1986.

Gutheil T G, Bursztajn H, Brodsky A: Malpractice prevention through the sharing of uncertainty: Informed consent and the therapeutic alliance. N Engl J Med *311*: 49, 1984.

Hofling C K, ed.: *Law and Ethics in the Practice of Psychiatry*, Brunner/Mazel, New York, 1981.

Jonsen A R, Siegler M, Winslade W J: *Clinical Ethics*, ed 2. Macmillan, New York, 1986.

Karasu T B: The ethics of psychotherapy. Am J Psychiatry *137*: 1502, 1980.

Katz J: *The Silent World of Doctor and Patient*. Free Press, New York, 1985.

Kentsmith D K, Sallady S A, Miga P A: *Ethics in Mental Health Practice*. Grune & Stratton, Orlando, FL, 1986.

Lakin M: *Ethical Issues in the Psychotherapies*. Oxford University Press, New York, 1988.

Lidz C, Meisel A, Zerubavel E, Carter M, Sestak R, Roth L: *Informed Consent*. Guilford, New York, 1984.

McGarry A L: *Competency to Stand Trial and Mental Illness*. National Institute of Mental Health, Rockville, MD, 1973.

Rachlin S: *Legal Encroachment on Psychiatric Practice*. Jossey-Bass, San Francisco, 1985.

Simon R: *Clinical Psychiatry and the Law*. American Psychiatric Press, Washington, DC, 1987.

Soloff P H, Gutheil T G, Wexler D H: Seclusion and restraint in 1985: A review and update. Hosp Community Psychiatry *36*: 652, 1985.

Stone A A: Law and psychiatry section. In *Psychiatry 1982: Annual Review and Update*. American Psychiatric Press, Washington, DC, 1982.

Stone A A: *Law, Psychiatry and Morality: Essays and Analysis*. American Psychiatric Press, Washington DC, 1984.

Tardiff K, ed.: Seclusion and restraint. American Psychiatric Association Task Force Report No 22, American Psychiatric Association, Washington, DC.

47

Ethics in Psychiatry

Ethics in psychiatry is a complex, controversial, often ambiguous and confusing topic. Clinical and research psychiatrists bring their own values to their work, but they must also deal with the values of their colleagues and patients. This intermixing of values sometimes leads to potential or actual value conflicts. These conflicts arise about confidentiality, informed consent, involuntary hospitalization, right to treatment, right to refuse treatment, duties to third parties, and regulation of psychiatric research.

Since ethics involves a set of principles guiding a person in deciding what is right or wrong, good or bad, physicians are often tempted to seek answers in the law or in professional codes of ethics to problems they encounter. However, these approaches do not necessarily solve problems. Laws may change, as they have in regard to involuntary hospitalization and treatment, or may be ambiguous, as they are in regard to the limits of patient confidentiality. Codes of ethics are also subject to change and are also often ambiguous. For example, does the rule "do no harm" help when trying to decide whether to force hospitalization on a patient in order to protect society? Does the rule mean no harm to the patient or no harm to society?

ETHICAL PRINCIPLES

Most ethical issues find their source in two major ethical theories: utilitarian theory and autonomy theory.

Utilitarian Theory

Utilitarian theory holds that one's fundamental obligation when making decisions is to try to produce the greatest possible happiness for the greatest number of people. When one is considering which decisions to make, laws to enact, or policies to follow, utilitarian theory requires the following: (1) Consider all the available evidence relevant to decisions about the consequences of alternative courses of action. (2) On the basis of that evidence, make the decision, law, or policy most likely to produce the greatest happiness in society. When alternative courses of action are dismal, one acts in ways that produce the least amount of pain. Sometimes the predictions about consequences are difficult to make and are controversial. For example, part of the debates about mandatory human immunodeficiency virus (HIV) testing and reporting and about mandatory drug-testing, center on the question of whether mandatory policies discourage persons from seeking medical treatment and, thus, have counterproductive consequences. For utilitarian theory there are no fundamental rights to truth, to informed consent, or to confidentiality. Truth telling, confidentiality, and informed consent are recognized only when and if they result in the most happiness or the least pain. Utilitarianism has also been used to justify medical paternalism, which is described below.

Utilitarian approaches to the physician-patient relationship are being replaced by approaches based on the second of the important ethical theories—autonomy theory. However, utilitarian theory is still used as the basis for making macro decisions about the allocation of society's resources for treatment and medical research.

Paternalism. Paternalism may be defined as performing actions for someone's benefit without that person's consent. Paternalism in medicine takes two forms: state paternalism and individual paternalism. Requirements that patients go to licensed practitioners for treatment and that certain drugs be given only through prescriptions are examples of state paternalism. Individual paternalism has been the traditional model for the physician-patient relationship. In this model the physician is supposed to treat the patient as a caring parent would treat a young child. The physician has a duty of *beneficence* (the principle of doing good and avoiding harm) to the patient, just as a parent has a duty of beneficence toward a child. The physician or parent is presumed to know what is best for the patient or child and has no obligation to explain each decision or to ask permission to perform actions that may benefit the patient or child. The physician, like a parent, is presumed to have knowledge that the patient may be incapable of understanding or, in the physician's judgment, is better off not knowing.

Autonomy Theory

Based on the writings of Immanuel Kant, autonomy theory conceives of the relationship between the physician and the normal adult patient as a relationship between two responsible persons, rather than as one between a parent and a child. This relationship is deontological, implying a moral obligation between the two parties.

The normal adult patient is presumed to have the ability and the right to make rational and responsible life decisions. The patient is autonomous (self-governing) and has rights to self-determination that must be respected, even if the physician believes that a decision will work against the patient's best interests. The law's assumption of adults' competence, the right to informed consent in treatment and research, the right to refuse treatment, and the limitations on the ability of psychiatrists to involuntarily hospitalize and involuntarily treat persons may all be seen as examples of the law's growing recognition of adults' fundamental rights to self-determination in medical decision making.

Autonomy theory accepts the idea that there are obligations to produce happiness and diminish pain. However, unlike utilitarian theory, it prohibits using persons to achieve those goals without their consent. For example, to lie to normal adults, even for their benefit, is to show a lack of respect for their ability to be responsible self-determined beings. For another example, autonomy theory claims that to use persons as research subjects without their consent is to treat them as things, rather than as persons, and is absolutely wrong. Utilitarian theory permits such research if it produces happiness in society.

Autonomy theory also holds that paternalistic treatment of a person is justified only when that person lacks the capacity to be autonomous—for example, young children, the profoundly retarded, and some psychotic persons.

Further Ethical Principles

Ethical principles can both support and further the goals of psychiatric practice and research. In particular situations, awareness of the relevance and conscious application of these principles can help clarify treatment options and justify particular decisions.

Justice. An ethical principle that is especially relevant to the ethics of mental health policy is *justice*, understood in this context as a fair distribution and application of psychiatric services. Justice in the sense of fair procedures enters into the justification for involuntary hospitalization and treatment of persons who, as a result of mental illness, are dangerous to themselves or others. The rules of procedural justice are central in this context because involuntary treatment restricts both the liberty and the choices of such persons.

Respect. An additional ethical principle is *respect* for persons, displayed through efforts to restore or maximize patients' competence or other capacities. The more that psychiatric treatment moves toward restoration of capacity to function, the more the treatment approximates the ethical ideal of respect for persons. This task is difficult, however, when patients suffer from enduring or permanent disabilities. Consider the difficulties of dealing with adult autistic persons whose capacity for insight, motivation, and judgment is permanently impaired. It is tempting to institutionalize such persons, to control their behavior by forcing them to function within a highly structured and sheltered environment. For some persons it may be the best treatment option. For others, despite their autistic tendencies and habits, a living situation may be possible that combines therapy and behavioral management with those preferences of the patient that, though eccentric, are socially permissible. Treatments that maximize patients' capacities and choices are clearly ethically preferable to treatments that are designed primarily for the convenience of caretakers.

PROFESSIONAL CODES

Most professional organizations and many business groups have codes of ethics. Such codes reflect a consensus about the general standards of appropriate professional conduct. The American Medical Association's *Principles of Medical Ethics* with annotations especially applicable to psychiatry and the American Psychiatric Association's *Principles of Ethics for Psychoanalysts* articulate ideal standards of practice and professional virtues of practitioners. They include exhortations to use skillful and scientific techniques, self-regulation of misconduct within the profession, and respect for the rights and needs of patients, families, colleagues, and society. Such exhortations are reinforced by ethical principles, such as beneficence, utility, autonomy, respect for the persons, and justice.

In recent years there has been increased interest in the use of professional codes of ethics as a standard of criticism and as a means to regulate professional misconduct. Local chapters of psychiatric societies and psychoanalytic institutes have strengthened their enforcement mechanisms for dealing with complaints against their members. For example, much attention has been given to complaints against psychiatrists who have allegedly exploited their patients, especially through sexual contact. This behavior is both unethical and illegal. The action of professional ethics committees does not prevent patients from pursuing legal actions against their psychiatrists, and some patients have done so successfully.

Many critics of professional ethics note, however, that professional ethics codes, in psychiatry and in other professions, have little effect on education, on advanced training, or on routine professional practice. And others question the efficacy of the enforcement mechanism for the codes because of the lack of sanctions against or public disclosures about psychiatrists who have acted unethically. At the same time, psychiatrists who are brought before ethics committees sometimes feel badly treated by their colleagues, especially if they have already been legally penalized for misconduct.

INFORMED CONSENT

Informed consent is the cornerstone of autonomy theory. Adult patients are assumed to have the right to consent or refuse to consent to treatment. U.S. law reflects strong popular beliefs about deep cultural commitments to self-determination. To permit competent adults to make important personal choices about life-styles, careers, relationships, and other values is one way to demonstrate respect for persons. However, the disabling effects of illness, especially mental illness, confuse the issue. How is it possible for psychiatrists to show respect for persons whose capacity to choose is compromised by the very condition for which the treatment is offered?

A document of informed consent serves only as a record of the completion of a process. That process should include enough uncoerced time and information to make an informed choice about treatment. Information about the diagnosis, prognosis, and risks and benefits of accepting or rejecting alternative courses of treatment enables patients to make informed choices.

As physicians, psychiatrists are educated to respond to persons in need of help, often in emergency or crisis situations. Quite often, persons in need of medical care do not want to make choices; they want physicians to take care of them and to tell them what to do to get well. The psychological authority of psychiatrists, in particular, is well documented. Patients often regress in response to mental and physical illness and may become especially vulnerable to influence and exploitation. It is understandable, then, why psychiatrists must guard against the tendency to dominate their patients' decision making.

The legal doctrine of informed consent is a reminder that psychiatrists must respect the rights of patients, including their right to be informed and to make treatment choices. The law does not, however, provide guidance about the complex and subtle ethical responsibility to show respect for one's patients, especially when their competence is, to some degree, compromised by their illness. The psychiatrist's first ethical task relates to the manner in which the patient is treated. To show respect is to listen, to try to understand, and to avoid stereotyping and a premature diagnosis. Respect is further conveyed by the way the psychiatrist talks, tries to explain, and seeks to provide realistic options to patients, even questionably competent ones.

Physicians must take precautions against presuming that patients are incompetent to decide for themselves until proved otherwise or protected by courts. Respect for patients is achieved by reciprocity, communication, and concern, not domination. Respect can be shown for severely mentally disordered and disorganized patients, as illustrated in the case reports of the British neurologist Oliver Sacks, through painstaking assessment of fragmentary communications. Even with patients with minimal mental disorders who are undergoing psychotherapy, it is not primarily informed consent that displays respect for them; instead, respect is manifested more in the attentive and sensitive response of psychiatrists to the nuances of their patients' verbal and nonverbal behavior.

RIGHT TO DIE

The patient's right to refuse treatment is part of the rationale used to support seriously ill patients' right to forgo life-sustaining treatment. That is, it has been recognized that patients who believe that their quality of life would be compromised by continued treatment have the right to demand that such treatment be withheld or withdrawn. Patients who are expected to lose their capacity to make decisions may express their wishes on a prospective basis, usually through the use of an advanced directive or living will. These directives have full legal standing in some states and may be used as evidence about a patient's wishes in the states that do not recognize them. However, living wills present problems because they are often too general, making it impossible to cover all the eventualities in the course of a serious illness.

On June 25, 1990, the U.S. Supreme Court made a determination in the right to die issue raised by *Cruzan v. Missouri Board of Health*. The Court upheld the right of a competent person to have "a constitutionally protected liberty interest in refusing unwanted medical treatment." The Supreme Court applied this principle to all patients who have made their wishes clearly known, whether or not they ever regain consciousness.

In the case of *Cruzan v. Missouri Board of Health*, the issue under dispute was who has the right to determine the care of an unconscious person who has not previously made his or her wishes known. The Supreme Court found that, when a permanently unconscious person has left no clear instructions, a state may carry out its interest in "the protection and preservation of human life" by denying a request by others, including family members, to withhold treatment. However, it was later determined that Cruzan had indicated to family and friends that she did not want life support, and she died in December 1990.

This ruling makes it possible for each state to decide the rigor of the evidentiary standards it wishes to apply when asked to withhold or withdraw treatment from a person in a persistent vegetative state who has not previously stated his or her wishes. Physicians are encouraged to consider the laws pertaining to the preservation of life in the states in which they practice before advising patients about writing a living will. The lack of clear documentation of a patient's wishes may cause those wishes to be set aside by surrogate decision makers or by the state.

SURROGATE DECISION MAKING

Sometimes a surrogate is designated to make treatment decisions for patients who have lost decisional capabilities. The surrogate may be designated by the patient before losing capacity or may be chosen by the courts. Sometimes states allow surrogates to be designated by the hospital. The designated surrogate is usually a next of kin, although next of kin may not always be the appropriate decision makers. Relatives may have psychological and other agendas that interfere with their ability to make just decisions. In the past, surrogates made decisions for patients on a best-interests principle. The surrogate was supposed to decide which treatments could be reasonably expected to be in the patient's best interests. Present autonomy-based legal approaches require surrogates to decide on the basis of what the patient would have wished, known as substituted judgment. The surrogate should be familiar with the patient's values and attitudes. Substituted judgments present problems because it may be difficult to determine whether a surrogate is really able to determine what the patient would have wished. If a substituted judgment cannot be made, the surrogate is to use the best-interests approach.

INVOLUNTARY PSYCHIATRIC TREATMENT

The principle of beneficence is invoked to justify treatment of some persons against their will. If a person has a mental disorder that is dangerous to self or others, the law permits involuntary treatment. The legal ground for treatment of persons dangerous to others is to protect public safety; the legal basis for treatment of suicidal or gravely disabled persons is to protect their lives or safety. In both cases the ethical basis is to benefit the patient by treating the mental disorder.

There are legal and ethical limits to involuntary hospitalization. Involuntarily hospitalized patients have a right to a judicial review of the grounds for their confinement and treatment. Because involuntary treatment restricts a person's liberty and personal choice, the law requires that it be done for good reasons. Moreover, the hospitalization may not be indefinite, as it was before the late 1960s. From an ethical perspective, involuntary treatment is permitted on a time-limited trial basis to determine if the treatment is beneficial. The law usually permits a longer duration of involuntary treatment for persons dangerous to others than it does for patients dangerous to themselves. In both cases the benefits of treatment must accrue within a finite time. A voluntary and consenting patient, however, can be treated as long as it is deemed medically necessary.

Some mentally disordered, disruptive, and dangerous patients cannot benefit from treatment unless their behavior and the underlying psychoses can be brought under control. Sedation or restraint may be unavoidable. At the same time, behavior control alone is not a sufficient goal of ethical psychiatric care. It may, in some instances, be all that can be achieved; sometimes mental illness defies psychiatry's best efforts to control it. But treating the mental illness, restoring competence and ability to function, and helping the mentally ill person cope with or even conquer mental illness are the ultimate goals of psychiatric intervention.

LIAISON PSYCHIATRY

Liaison psychiatrists are often called on to evaluate a patient's ability to make decisions about medical care. A physician may request a psychiatric consultation because a patient is refusing to consent to a procedure. Such evaluations often present ethical and conceptual problems. Under law, adult persons are considered competent until proved otherwise. That presumption of competence is reflected in the law's recognition that patients have the right to consent or refuse to consent to medical treatment. Incompetence is a legal concept and can only be established by the courts, but psychiatrists are often given leeway to establish whether a patient has decisional capacity. If a psychiatrist evaluates a patient as decisionally incapable, the burden of disproof effectively rests with the patient. It is then up to the patient to ask a patient advocate or lawyer to request a competence hearing before a court.

In such cases the autonomy ethic, backed by both the law and contemporary psychiatric diagnosis, is clear: No matter how beneficial a physician believes a treatment will be, no matter how dangerous the probable consequences of rejecting that treatment, a patient has a presumptive right to reject that treatment. Refusal of treatment is not sufficient justification for claiming that the patient is decisionally incapacitated. What is at question in that evaluation is really the patient's ability to given informed consent. That is, can the patient understand and appreciate the diagnosis, the prognosis, and the risks and benefits of accepting or rejecting the offered treatment? If the patient can do so, the patient has the right to refuse treatment.

PUBLIC HEALTH POLICY

Right to Health Care

After years of debate about the right to health care, public and professional opinions remain divided. Some believe that health care is a right to which all persons are equally entitled. Others think that health care is a privilege that must be privately purchased. Still others believe that some amount of health care should be provided for those with significant health care needs who are unable to obtain them with their own resources—if not as a matter of right, as an act of benevolence. Various proposals for national health insurance, catastropic health insurance, and health insurance of the indigent, among others, have been considered, and some coverage for certain categories of needy persons in the United States is made available through Medicare, Medicaid, and other special programs. However, many persons' medical and psychiatric needs are covered inadequately or not at all. Moreover, current political trends do not appear to be moving toward better provision of psychiatric services for underserved populations or even the middle class. Instead, psychiatric services, both inpatient and outpatient, are restricted by federal and state programs. Private insurance also seems to be moving toward reductions of psychiatric coverage. The trends are toward less outpatient coverage, fewer visits, and reduced long-term care.

Most commentators on the ethics of allocation of psychiatric services are critical of the injustice of mental health policies and pessimistic about the prospect of much improvement. Many indigent persons and even people with moderate financial resources who have serious and chronic psychiatric needs will go untreated. Only patients with substantial private wealth will have ready access to psychiatric care.

Abortion

Abortion is among the most controversial ethical issues confronting physicians, lawmakers, and the general public.

In *Roe v. Wade* the Supreme Court, basing its decision on common law precedents that gave no legal standing to early-stage fetuses, ruled that there are no legal obligations toward fetuses in the early stages of development. Early abortions, therefore, can be regulated only for the purpose of ensuring the safety of the pregnant woman. The Court ruled that common law precedents give limited obligations to the fetus once it becomes viable. Therefore, states were permitted to regulate late-stage abortions.

Since *Roe v. Wade*, antiabortion advocates have tried various ways of trying to limit abortions. In the case of *Missouri v. Reproductive Services*, the Supreme Court ruled that, because states have no constitutional obligation to provide any health care at all, they can choose not to provide publicly funded abortions.

The U.S. Supreme Court in 1990 upheld two state laws requiring an unmarried minor to give her parents advance notice of her intention to have an abortion. An Ohio law, debated in *Ohio v. Akron Center for Reproductive Health*, requires that a parent be notified 24 hours before an abortion. A Minnesota law, *Hodgson v. Minnesota*, requires that both biological parents be given 48 hours notice of a minor's abortion. It also provides that the minor may petition the court for permission to have an abortion without telling her parents, a provision known as judicial bypass.

References

Adler G, Beckett A: Psychotherapy of the patient with an HIV infection: Some ethical and therapeutic dilemmas. Psychosomatics *30*: 202, 1989.

Conte H R, Plutchik R, Picard S, Karasu T B: Ethics in the practice of psychotherapy: A survey. Am J Psychother *43*: 32, 1989.

Fink P J: On being ethical in an unethical world. Am J Psychiatry *146*: 1097, 1989.

Jonsen A R, Siegler M, Winslade W J: *Clinical Ethics*, ed 2. Macmillan, New York, 1986.

Kant I: *Foundations of the Metaphysics of Morals*, L W Beck, trans. Bobbs-Merrill, Indianapolis. 1959.

Kantor J E: *Medical Ethics for Physicians-in-Training*. Plenum, New York, 1989.

Kluft R P: Treating the patient who has been sexually exploited by a previous therapist. Psychiatr Clin North Am *12*: 1483, 1989.

Mill J S: *Essential Works of John Stuart Mill*, Max Lerner, editor. Bantam, New York, 1961.

Oppenheimer K, Swanson G: Duty to warn: When should confidentiality be breached? J Fam Pract *30*: 179, 1990.

Schwartz I M: Hospitalization of adolescents for psychiatric and substance abuse treatment: Legal and ethical issues. J Adolesc Health Care *10*: 473, 1989.

Stone, A: *Law, Psychiatry and Morality*, American Psychiatric Press, Washington, DC, 1984.

Weiner I B: On competence and ethicality in psychodiagnostic assessment. J Pers Assess *53*: 827, 1989.

Winslade W J: Ethics in psychiatry. In *Comprehensive Textbook of Psychiatry*, ed 5, H I Kaplan and B J Sadock, editors, p 2124. Williams & Wilkins, Baltimore, 1989.

48

History of Psychiatry

Psychiatry is the branch of medicine that deals with the diagnosis, understanding, and treatment of mental disorders. Table 48-1 shows how the recorded history of psychiatry originated in both medicine and philosophy; psychiatry was influenced by the ideas of Hippocrates—the father of medicine—and the ideas of the philosophers Plato and Aristotle. For most of its history, psychiatry has been influenced by physicians and by persons from diverse areas of thought.

In the past two centuries, psychiatry has become a specialty of medicine, mainly influenced by the work of individual physicians. The entries in this table also show that the history of psychiatry has been reflected in events or trends in which the names of persons have become secondary or anonymous. This, in part, is because psychiatry has become more scientific and dependent for its advances on the work of scientific research organizations and scientific networks. Moreover, psychiatry has maintained its humanistic tradition, with a continuing and intellectually productive dialogue between feminism and psychoanalysis; with new ideas about envy, love, and creativity; and with new books on the history of psychiatry and psychohistory.

Table 48-1
Historical Figures and Events and Their Relation to Psychiatry*

Person or Event	Date	Country	Publications	Significance
Hippocrates of Cos (ca. 460 B.C.–370 B.C.)		Greece	*Hippocratic Writings* (Pelican Classics, Baltimore, 1978)	Diseases caused by imbalance in four humors (blood, phlegm, yellow bile, black bile); melancholia caused by excess black bile; hysteria caused by wandering uterus; looked for natural causes of epilepsy, the sacred disease; dietary treatment of illness
Plato (427 B.C.–347 B.C.)		Greece	*The Dialogues of Plato* trans. B. Jowett (Random House, New York, 1937)	In *Timaeus*, *Phaedrus*, and *The Republic*, described two kinds of madness: that in which the appetitive soul lost the domination of the rational soul and madness inspired by the gods, divine madness
Aristotle (384 B.C.–322 B.C.)		Greece	W. D. Ross, *Aristotle*, ed 6, 1955	In *De Anima* and other psychological works, described the affections of desire, anger, fear, courage, envy, joy, hatred, and pity
Galen of Pergamum (A.D. 130–A.D. 200)		Asia Minor (Turkey) in the Roman Empire	*On the Affected Parts*, trans. and ed. Rudolph Siegel (Karger, Basel, 1976)	Consolidated the thoughts of Hippocrates, Plato, and Aristotle; idea that depression was caused by excess of black bile was influential until the 19th century
St. Augustine (354–430)		Tageste (Numidia, North Africa)	*Confessions*, trans. E. B. Pusey (Modern Library, New York, 1949)	His *Confessions* was the first book centering on psychological introspection
Avicenna (980–1037)		Persia	*A Treatise on the Canon of Medicine of Avicenna* (Grunner, London, 1930)	His *Canon of Medicine* recognized that certain physical diseases were caused by emotional upsets and was widely read by Christian and Mohammedan physicians
Constantius Africanus (ca. 1010–1087)		Carthage, North Africa	Constantino L'Africano, *Della melancolia* (Rome, 1959)	His *Melancholia* made observations on delusional thinking, and from the first medical school at Salerno spread Galenic ideas on depression throughout Western Europe

Table 48-1
Continued

Person or Event	Date	Country	Publications	Significance
Bartholomaeus Anglicus (13th century)	1250?	Paris, France	*De proprietatibus rerum* (London, 1535)	One of the earliest attempts to localize mental diseases and functions to different parts of the brain
Henry Kramer and James Sprenger (15th century)	1486	Germany	*Malleus maleficarum (Witches' Hammer)*	Influential in causing persecution of persons for witchcraft
Paracelsus (ca. 1493–1541)	1520	Austria	*Diseases Which Lead to a Loss of Reason*	Psychiatric illnesses are not caused by demons but are natural diseases, new classification of diseases, treatment of diseases with chemicals (absence of psychotherapy)
Juan Luis Vives (1492–1540)	1538	Spain	*De anima et vita (Of Soul and Life)*	Described the importance of psychological associations and their influence in forming emotions; a forerunner of Freud
Johann Weyer (1515–1588)	1563	Holland	*De prestigiis daemonum (The Deception of Demons)*	Influential in refuting *Malleus maleficarum*
Juan Huarte de San Juan (ca. 1530–1592)	1574	Spain	*The Examination of Men's Wits*	An early account of differences in temperaments and dispositions
Timothy Bright (?1551–1615)	1586	England	*A Treatise of Melancholia*	The first treatise by an English physician on mental illness; divided melancholy into that caused by humoral imbalance and that caused by psychological factors; similar to present-day classification
Giambattista Porta (1535–1615)	1586	Italy	*De humana physiognomia*	Gave to physiognomy the role of at least a pseudoscience
Felix Plater (1536–1614)	1602, 1614	Switzerland	*Practice of Medicine, Observations of Diseases Injurious to Body and Mind*	New classification of diseases based on symptoms, causes, and treatments; careful description of all known psychiatric and organic diseases; the first physician to separate medicine from philosophy and make it a branch of natural science
Edward Jorden (1569–1632)	1603	England	*A Brief Discourse of a Disease Called the Suffocation of the Mother*	First book in English by a physician that delineated hysteria as a disease caused by the uterus, a sex-linked disease, imitating other diseases
Robert Burton (1577–1640)	1621	England	*The Anatomy of Melancholy*	The most famous book on psychiatry in the 17th century. A comprehensive presentation of all previous medical-psychological thought on melancholy, also drawing on the nonmedical literature of Western civilization
William Harvey (1578–1657)	1628	England	*De motu cordis (The Motion of the Heart)*	In his discovery of the circulation of the blood, Harvey emphasized that mental emotions affect the movements of the heart
Paolo Zacchia (1584–1659)	1621–1650	Italy	*Questiones medico-legales*	He held that a physician, rather than a priest or lawyer, should evaluate a patient's responsibility for disturbed behavior; the beginning of forensic psychiatry
Thomas Sydenham (1624–1689)	1682	England	"Dissertatio epistolaris . . ." in *The Entire Works of Dr. Thomas Sydenham Newly Made English,* 1742	Gave a comprehensive picture of the many symptoms of hysteria, believing that, in the form of hypochondriacal complaints, it could exist in males and that it was caused by disturbed animal spirits

Table 48-1
Continued

Person or Event	Date	Country	Publications	Significance
Thomas Willis (1621–1675)	1683	England	*Two Discourses Concerning the Soul of Brutes*	Summarized what was known about major psychiatric illnesses; recognized differences in illnesses when there was gross brain disease and when the brain seemed normal, attributing latter to disturbed animal spirits; attributed hysteria to disturbed animal spirits acting on the brain, not to a wandering uterus
Georg Ernst Stahl (1660–1734)	1707, 1708	Germany	*Theoria medica vera, De animi morbis*	Theory of animism; the soul, anima, maintains functions of body in health and disease; psychiatric illness is caused either by inhibitions of anima or diseases of body
George Chyne (1671–1743)	1773	England	*The English Malady or, a Treatise of Nervous Diseases*	Depression (the English malady) thought to be caused by gluttony and intemperance
Simon Andre Tissot (1728–1797)	1758	Switzerland	*Onanism*	First medical discussion of masturbation, emphasizing the pathological effects of excess
William Battie (1703–1776)	1758	England	*A Treatise of Madness*	First physician who made insanity his full work, raised "the mad business" to a respected specialty, and first used "madness" in the title of his book
Boissier de Sauvages (1706–1767)	1763–1770	France	*Nosologia methodica*	Nosology divided diseases into classes based on symptoms; although speculative and artificial, it stimulated a rethinking of concepts of disease
John Aiken (1747–1822)	1771	England	*Thoughts on Hospitals*	First book on hospitals in which lunatic hospitals were discussed
Franz Anton Mesmer (1734–1815)	1779	Austria, France	*Memoire sur la découverte du magnetism animal*	Showed that, when a mental therapist used so-called animal magnetism, it could cure cases of psychiatric illness; this led to the discovery of hypnosis
Vincenzo Chiarugi (1759–1820)	1789	Italy	*Regulations of the Hospitals of Santa Maria Nuova and of Bonifazio*	One of the first attempts to treat the insane inmates of asylums humanely and without restraints
William Cullen (1710–1790)	1800	Scotland	*Nosology, or a Systematic Arrangement of Diseases*	A great 18th century nosologist who first used the terms "neurosis" and "neurotic" to describe mental diseases
Philippe Pinel (1745–1826)	1801	France	*A Treatise on Insanity in Which Are Contained the Principles of a New and More Practical Nosology of Mental Disorders*	Classified mental illness into four main forms and established a new humane treatment for inmates of insane asylums, which he called the moral treatment of insanity
Johann Reil (1759–1813)	1803	Germany	*Rhapsodies about the Application of Psychotherapy to Mental Disturbances*	The founder of rational psychotherapy, recognizing the therapeutic value of institutional surroundings, music, psychodrama, and occupational therapy; first used the word "psychiatry" and founded the first psychiatric journal
Benjamin Rush (1745–1813)	1812	USA	*Medical Inquiries and Observations upon the Diseases of the Mind*	First general book on psychiatry in America; Rush was regarded as the father of American psychiatry and the most famous American physician of his time; signer of the Declaration of Independence
Thomas Sutton (?1767–1835)	1813	England	*Tracts on Delirium Tremens*	First description of alcoholic delirium tremens

Table 48-1
Continued

Person or Event	Date	Country	Publications	Significance
William Tuke (1732–1822); Samuel Tuke (1784–1847), grandson of William Tuke; Daniel Hack Tuke (1827–1895), youngest son of Samuel Tuke; John Charles Bucknill (1817–1895)	1796–1858	England	*Description of the Retreat, an Institution near York, for Insane Persons of the Society of Friends,* by Samuel Tuke (York, 1813); *A Manual of Psychological Medicine Containing the History, Nosology, Description, Statistics, Diagnosis, Pathology, and Treatment of Insanity,* by Daniel Tuke and Bucknill (London, 1858)	William Tuke founded the York Retreat, for the moral treatment of mentally ill Quakers, in 1796; Samuel Tuke's *Description of the Retreat* influenced asylum treatment in England, Europe, and the USA; the *Manuel* of Daniel Tuke and Bucknill was the first comprehensive textbook of psychiatry
Joseph Adams (1756–1818)	1814	England	*A Treatise on the Supposed Hereditary Properties of Diseases . . . Particularly in Madness and Scrofula*	First book on the hereditary properties of diseases; argued it was not a disease that was inherited but a susceptibility to disease; therefore, prevention and cure were possible
Franz Joseph Gall (1758–1828), Johann Gaspar Spurzheim (1776–1832)	1815	Austria, Germany	*The Physiognomical System of Drs. Gall and Spurzheim; founded on an anatomical and physiological examination of the nervous system in general and of the brain in particular*	The beginning of phrenology, with its mapping parts of the brain, defining their psychological functions, and then making psychological and psychotherapeutic predictions
Johann Christian Heinroth (1773–1843)	1818	Germany	*Disturbances of the Mind*	First systematic textbook of psychiatry that attempted to formulate an actual clinical system of psychotherapy; Heinroth was the first to use the word "psychosomatic" and the first to hold a chair in psychological medicine at the University of Leipzig
Robert Gooch (1784–1830)	1829	England	*An Account of . . . Diseases Peculiar to Women*	First account of postpartum psychosis
Amariah Brigham (1798–1849)	1832	USA	*Remarks on the Influence of Mental Cultivation upon Health*	Pioneer in social psychiatry, supervised patient activity programs (today called recreational or occupational therapy); founded and edited *American Journal of Insanity*, 1844 (today *American Journal of Psychiatry*)
James Cowles Pritchard (1786–1848)	1835	England	*A Treatise on Insanity and Other Disorders Affecting the Mind*	Standard textbook of psychiatry covering all the literature on all known diseases; described moral insanity, later called psychopathic personality
Jean Etienne Dominique Esquirol (1782–1840)	1838	France	*Des maladies mentales considérées sous les rapports médicals, hygiéniques et médico-légals*	Coined the term "hallucination," described idiocy, classified insanities into monomania (partial insanity) and general delirium, and recognized both emotional and organic causes of illness
Isaac Ray (1807–1881)	1838	USA	*Treatise on Medical Jurisprudence of Insanity*	Founded American forensic psychiatry
James Braid (1795–1860)	1843	England	*Neurypnology; or, the Rationale of Nervous Sleep . . .*	This entirely separated hypnotism from animal magnetism and began the study of hypnotic phenomena
Wilhelm Griesinger (1817–1868)	1845	Germany	*Mental Pathology and Therapeutics*	Proclaimed that psychiatric diseases are brain diseases and that psychiatry had become a medical specialty; founded specialty of neuropsychiatry

Table 48-1
Continued

Person or Event	Date	Country	Publications	Significance
J. Moreau de Tours (1804–1884)	1845	France	*Du haschich et de l'aliénation mentale*	Described the effects of his taking hashish and became the first psychiatrist to experience a drug-induced psychosis
Pliny Earle (1809–1892)	1848	USA	*History, Description and Statistics of the Bloomingdale Asylum for the Insane*	Established a pattern of reporting the statistics on asylum inmates that was followed by other asylums
Walter Cooper Dendy (1794–1871)	1853	England	"Psychotherapeia, or the Remedial influence of Mind" in J Psychol Med Ment Pathol 6: 268, 1853	First introduced the term "psychotherapeia" (today "psychotherapy"), which he defined as prevention and remedy [of disease] by psychical influence and which he predicted would become valuable in psychiatry
Jean-Pierre Falret (1794–1870), Jules Baillarger (1809–1890)	1854	France	First Baillarger, "La folie à double forme"; then Falret "La folie circulaire", two weeks later, both in Bulletin de l'académie imperiale de medecine, 1853–1854, *19*, 340–352, 382–400	The association of melancholia and mania in the same patient had been observed but not named by an American psychiatrist, Rufus Wyman, 1830; in 1896 Kraepelin named this illness manic-depressive psychosis
Thomas Kirkbride (1809–1883)	1854	USA	*On the Construction, Organisation, and General Arrangements of Hospitals for the Insane*	Set a standard for mid-19th century care of the chronically insane that still commands respect today
John Conolly (1794–1866)	1856	England	*The Treatment of the Insane Without Mechanical Restraints*	Conolly's work for the nonrestraint system marked the success of a movement that began with Pinel and created a new approach to treating insanity throughout the civilized world
George Robinson (1821–1875)	1859	England	*On the Prevention and Treatment of Mental Disorders*	First book that introduced the idea of looking beyond the precincts of the asylum to prevent mental illness
Gustav Theodor Fechner (1801–1887)	1860	Germany	*Elements of Psychophysics*	Established the relationship between the intensity of stimuli and sensory reactions; was called the founder of experimental psychology
Benedict-Augustin Morel (1809–1873)	1860	France	*Traité des maladies mentales*	Cases of insanity and other mental illnesses caused by inherited mental degeneration, becoming worse from one generation to the next
Thomas Laycock (1812–1876)	1860	England	*Mind and Brain . . .*	Mentioned unconscious functional activity of the brain but did not further develop this idea
Forbes B. Winslow	1860	England	*On Obscure Diseases of the Brain and Disorders of the Mind*	First to mention psychical diagnostic tests (psychological tests) and the psychiatric interview
Cesare Lombroso (1835–1909)	1864	Italy	"Genio e follia" *(Genius and Insanity)*, prefazione al corso di clinica psichiatrica Milano (Chiusi, 1864)	Emphasized the relation between genius and abnormal mental traits
Henry Maudsley (1835–1918)	1867	England	*The Physiology and Pathology of the Mind*	Attempted to integrate psychology, reflex neurophysiology, and psychiatry into a synthetic whole
Ewald Hecker (1843–1909)	1871	Germany	"Die Hebephrenie," Archive für Pathologische Anatomie und Physiologie, *52*: 1871	First description of hebephrenia (later a subgroup of dementia precox)

Table 48-1
Continued

Person or Event	Date	Country	Publications	Significance
Jean M. Charcot (1825–1893)	1871	France	*L'Hystérie; Textes chosis et presentes par E. Trillat*	Vivid presentation of hysterical symptoms, including their occurrence in men, as well as women
Karl Kahlbaum (1828–1899)	1874	Germany	*Die Katatonie oder das Spannungsirresein* (Berlin, 1874)	First description of catatonia (later a subgroup of dementia precox)
George Miller Beard (1840–1883)	1880	USA	*A Practical Treatise on Nervous Exhaustion (Neurasthenia)*	Neurasthenia—a disease of mental and physical exhaustion—replaced the diagnosis of hypochondriasis; became prevalent in the American and European middle classes
Richard von Krafft-Ebing (1840–1902)	1886	Germany	*Psychopathia sexualis*	Described homosexuality and sex perversions, coining terms "sadism" and "masochism," claiming some were caused by degeneration; stimulated research in sex
Herman Emminghaus (1845–1904)	1887	Germany	*Psychic Disturbances of Childhood*	First textbook of child psychiatry
Sergei Korsakoff (1853–1900)	1890	Russia	"Eine Psych. Storung Combiniert mit Multipler Neuritis," Allgol-Z Psych, 46: 1890	Korsakoff's psychosis, commonly caused by chronic alcoholism; manifested by multiple neuritis, disorientation, and loss of memory with pseudoreminiscences
Emil Kraepelin (1856–1926)	1899	Germany	*Psychiatrie: Ein Lehrbuch für Studerende und Aerzte,* ed 6	The major psychoses were divided into two groups: dementia precox, which deteriorated to dementia, and manic-depressive psychosis, which did not deteriorate
John Hughlings Jackson (1834–1911)	1870–1900	England	*Selected Writings of John Hughlings Jackson* (London, 1931–1932)	For several decades he developed the thesis that psychiatric symptoms are a regression from higher functions that are the products of evolution; the symptoms resulted from activating more primitive functions
Sigmund Freud (1856–1939)	1900–1905	Austria	*The Interpretation of Dreams, Three Essays on the Theory of Sexuality*	Discovered the manifestations of the unconscious and how to use these in treating psychiatric patients; infantile sexuality and how it accounted for adult sexual dysfunctions; founded psychoanalysis
Morton Prince (1854–1929)	1905	USA	*The Dissociation of a Personality*	Early account of a multiple personality; emphasized techniques of hypnosis and manifestations of the unconscious
Clifford Beers (1876–1943)	1908	USA	*A Mind That Found Itself*	Account of experiences in psychiatric hospitals that stimulated the mental hygiene movement in the United States
Pierre Janet (1859–1947)	1910	France	*Les névroses (The Neuroses)*	Originated the concept of psychasthenia, a weakness in the nervous system that resulted in parts of consciousness being split off and forming dissociative, hysterical, or obsessive-compulsive symptoms
Eugen Bleuler (1857–1939)	1911	Switzerland	*Dementia Praecox or the Group of Schizophrenias*	Coined name "schizophrenia" and described its symptoms
Hideyo Noguchi (1876–1928)	1913	USA	H. Noguchi and J. W. Moore, "A demonstration of the *Treponema pallidum* in the brain in cases of general paralysis," J Exp Med, *17*	The definitive demonstration, after a century of controversy, that the syphilitic organism causes general paresis, the first time that the cause of a major psychosis became known

Table 48-1
Continued

Person or Event	Date	Country	Publications	Significance
William Alanson White (1870–1937), Smith Ely Jelliffe (1866–1945)	1915	USA	*Diseases of the Nervous System: A Textbook of Neurology and Psychiatry*	Represented an important new view, integrating neurological, biological, psychiatric, and psychoanalytic concepts; it went through many editions and was standard in many medical schools; Jelliffe was called the father of psychosomatic medicine
Alfred Adler (1870–1937)	1917	Austria	*Study of Organ Inferiority and Its Psychical Compensations*	First psychoanalytic defector from Freud; founded the school of individual psychology and coined the terms "life style" and "inferiority complex"
Hermann Rorschach (1884–1922)	1921	Switzerland	*Psychodiagnostik*	Rorschach's inkblot test revealed unconscious motivations and ego defenses against them and was used for psychiatric diagnosis; it stimulated the development of other projective diagnostic tests
Elmer Ernest Southard (1876–1920)	1922	USA	*The Kingdom of Evils: Psychiatric Social Work . . . with a Classification of Social Evils,* by Southard and Mary C. Jarrett (social worker)	Emphasized that a psychiatrist should know the entire social environment, both past and present, of the patient and that for this the aid of a social worker is needed
Ernst Kretschmer (1888–1964)	1924	Germany	*Constitution und Character*	Linked two body types to psychoses: leptosome (aesthenic) to schizophrenia, pyknic (rotund) to manic-depressive
Julius Wagner-Jauregg (1857–1940)	1917–1927	Austria	*Therapeutic Malaria,* 1927, by G. de Rudolf	During the decade 1917–1927, he showed that general paresis patients underwent remissions when malaria was induced; for the time it was the most successful organic treatment of a psychosis; for this he became, in 1927, the first psychiatrist to receive the Nobel Prize; in the 1940s, penicillin became the treatment of choice for paresis
Ivan Petrovich Pavlov (1849–1936)	1903–1936	Russia	*Lectures on Conditioned Reflexes,* ed. H. Gantt, 1941	In the last years of his life, he attempted to show how conditioned reflexes influence normal and pathological thought; in America this influenced the work of J. B. Watson, the father of behaviorism
Karen Horney (1885–1952)	1937	Germany up to 1932, then USA	*The Neurotic Personality of Our Time*	Opposed Freud's theory of the castration complex in women and his emphasis on the oedipal complex and sexuality as influencing neurosis; argued that neurosis was influenced by the society in which one lived
Albert Deutsch (1905–1961)	1937	USA	*The Mentally Ill in America: A History of Their Care and Treatment from Colonial Times*	In its time the most scholarly and influential history of the subject that had appeared
Franz Kallman (1897–1965)	1938	Germany and, after the 1930s, USA	*The Genetic Theory of Schizophrenia*	Indicated that the hereditary factor is relevant in schizophrenia and established the first full-time genetic department in a psychiatric institution in America

Table 48-1
Continued

Person or Event	Date	Country	Publications	Significance
Ugo Cerletti (1877–1963), Lucio Bini (1908–1964)	1938	Italy	"Old and new information about electroshock," Am J Psychiatry *107*: 1950 (Cerletti)	Electroshock was first used in 1938 as a way of producing convulsions, which it was hoped would alleviate psychosis: first in schizophrenia and then in manic-depressive psychosis; it was soon observed to be more effective in the latter illness and (with modifications) is still in use today
Führer decree (1939)	1939–1945	Germany	"The Nazi Doctors," Chapter 2 in "*Euthanasia*": *Direct Medical Killing* by Robert Jay Lifton. (Basic Books, New York, 1986); *By Trust Betrayed: Patients, Physicians, and the License to Kill in the Third Reich,* by Hugh Gregory Gallagher (Henry Holt, New York, 1990).	In October 1939, soon after the outbreak of World War II, a Führer decree ordered doctors to kill patients who had incurable medical illnesses (this grew out of the Nazi doctrine of preserving racial purity by eliminating those who were "biologically unfit"). After this, during the course of the war, about 270,000 mental patients were killed by physicians and medical personnel
Gregory Zilboorg (1890–1959)	1941	Russia to 1918, then USA	*A History of Medical Psychology,* in collaboration with George W. Henry, 1941	The first comprehensive history of psychiatry in English by two American historians
Leo Kanner (1894–1981)	1943	Austria, USA	"Austistic disturbances of affective content," Nerv Child *2*: 217, 1943	The first account of early infantile autism; in 1935 published *Child Psychiatry,* the first textbook on the subject in English
Helene Deutsch (1884–1982)	1945	Europe up to 1935, then USA	*The Psychology of Women*	Her two-volume work was for several decades the most comprehensive Freudian view of the life cycle of woman; she also named and described the psychology of the as-if personality: an apparently normal person who gives a good semblance of adaptation to reality, yet is actually devoid of genuine emotion
Melanie Klein (1882–1960), Anna Freud (1895–1982)	1932–46	Austria, then England since 1930s	*The Psycho-Analysis of Children,* Klein, 1932; *The Psycho-Analytical Treatment of Children,* Anna Freud, 1946	Two different ways of applying psychoanalysis to children that have stimulated present-day English and American schools of child psychiatry
John Cade (1912–1981)	1949	Australia	"Lithium salts in the treatment of psychotic excitement," Med J Aust *36*: 349, 1949	Cade was the first to observe that lithium quieted manic patients and that their mania returned when lithium was stopped; after methods were developed to control lithium's toxicity by measuring blood levels, it became used in the treatment of manic-depressive disease
Erik H. Erikson (1902–)	1950	Europe, USA since 1930s	*Childhood and Society*	In this book Erikson restated in a new way Freud's concepts of infantile sexuality and developed concepts of adult identity, identity vs. role diffusion, and identity crisis; applied psychoanalytic concepts to American cultural life and American political history

Table 48-1
Continued

Person or Event	Date	Country	Publications	Significance
Donald Winnicott (1896–1971)	1951	England	"Transitional objects and transitional phenomena," in Winnicott: *Collected Papers: Through Paediatrics to Psychoanalysis* (Tavistock, London, 1958)	The transitional things that a baby becomes deeply attached to and that provide a bridge between the inner and outer worlds and that then influence the development of play, creativity, and cultural life in general
Jean Delay (1907–1987), Pierre Deniker (1917–)	1952	Paris, France	Delay and Deniker: "Le traitement des psychoses par une méthode neurolytique dérivée de l'hibernothérapie," C. R. Congrès Med Alién. Neurol. France *50*: 497	In their first reports on chlorpromazine to French psychiatrists, Delay and Deniker emphasized how patients were quieted, like animals in hibernation, and called the drug "hibernotherapie"; chlorpromazine then became a factor in reducing the number of asylum patients and served as the prototype of future antipsychotic drugs
Maxwell Jones (1907–)	1953	England	*Therapeutic Community* (Basic Books, New York, 1953)	In this book Jones delineates the interactions of the mental patient with the communities in and outside the hospital and the need for support from groups of patients and patients' families; it heralded a period of psychiatric advance that was called social psychiatry, which was the title of the English edition of Jones's book
Harry Stack Sullivan (1892–1949)	1943	USA	*The Interpersonal Theory of Psychiatry*, ed. H. S. Perry and M. L. Gawel	The interpersonal theory holds that a person's impulses and strivings cannot be studied in and for themselves but only as they are made manifest in an interpersonal situation; also coined the terms "participant observer" (the therapist needs to be aware not only of the overt and covert behavior of the patient but also of the therapist's own reactions); "consensual validation" (the awareness by both patient and therapist of the terminology they are using); "parataxic distortion" (the patient's distortion of the real person of the therapist out of the necessities of the patient's personality structure)
Carl Gustav Jung (1875–1961)	1921–55	Switzerland	*Psychological Types*, 1921; *Two Essays on Analytical Psychology*, 1912–28; *The Structure and Dynamics of the Psyche*, 1916–52; *The Archetypes and the Collective Unconscious*, 1934–55	After separating from Freud, Jung founded the school of analytical psychology, developing new psychotherapeutic approaches and concepts of the unconscious (especially the collective unconscious) and new personality types, such as introvert and extrovert
Adolf Meyer (1866–1950)	1957	USA	*Psychobiology: A Science of Man* by Adolf Meyer, ed. E. Winters and E. M. Bowers, 1957	Psychobiology views the patient as a biological and psychological unity who became mentally ill because of internal pathology and maladaptations to the environment; in *Common Sense Psychiatry*, he treated patients with psychotherapy administered by psychiatrists and social workers in community clinics; used the term *ergasia* (based on the Greek root for "work") to designate mentally

Table 48-1
Continued

Person or Event	Date	Country	Publications	Significance
				integrated activity and then an ergasia terminology to describe diseases; foreshadowed the dynamic community psychiatry of contemporary America
Joint Commission on Mental Illness and Mental Health (1955–1961)	1961–63	USA	*Action for Mental Health,* 1961; *Community Mental Health Centers Act of 1963*	*Action for Mental Health* recommended psychiatric deinstitutionalization of the care of the mentally ill: that their care be shifted from large mental hospitals into community mental health clinics; deinstitutionalization then became a reality with the passage of the Community Mental Health Centers Act of 1963.
Classification of mental disorders	1952–1968	USA	First edition of *Diagnostic and Statistical Manual of Mental Disorders* (DSM-I), prepared by the Committee on Nomenclature and Statistics of the American Psychiatric Association (APA), George N. Raines, Chair (Mental Hospital Service, Washington, DC, 1952); second edition of *Diagnostic and Statistical Manual of Mental Disorders* (DSM-II), prepared by the Committee on Nomenclature and Statistics of the APA, Ernest Gruenberg, Chair (APA, Washington, DC, 1968)	DSM-I replaced several outdated classifications of mental disorders and for the first time provided a glossary of definitions of psychiatric conditions; it was not universally accepted in America and most other countries Although DSM-II diagnosed new disease entities, including disorders of childhood and adolescence, its diagnostic methods and criteria were criticized by several leading psychiatrists
Margaret Mahler (1897–1985)	1975	Central Europe up to 1938, then USA	*The Psychological Growth of the Human Infant,* by Margaret Mahler, Fred Pine, and Anni Bergman (Basic Books, New York, 1975)	Describes the separation–individuation process of the infant's gradual intrapsychic separation from the mother and the correlative understanding of the infant's self as a distinct person, along with other equally distinct persons
Jacques Lacan (1901–1981), "the French Freud"	1968–78	France	*The Language of the Self: The Function of Language in Psychoanalysis,* by Lacan, trans. A. Wilden 1968; *Psychoanalytic Politics: Freud's French Revolution,* trans. Sherry Turkle, 1978	Lacan emphasized language and the need to make contact with the prelanguage period in the unconscious and rejected the standard 50-minute analysis for sessions that were sometimes 10, 5, or even 3 minutes; founded his own school of psychoanalysis, described as a return to Freud; at the time of his death, there were reportedly about 5,000 Lacanian analysts in France; he was the most influential figure in French psychiatry. His ideas influenced literature, language, linguistics, economics, and mathematics; he was an integral part of the political left
Daniel Levinson (1920–)	1978	USA	*The Seasons of a Man's Life,* by Daniel Levinson in collaboration with Charlotte Darrow, Edward Klein, Maria H. Levinson, and Braxton McKee (Ballantine Books, New York, 1978)	Documents the mid-life transition that many men go through between the ages of 38 and 45 and shows that this is an adult developmental crisis

Table 48-1
Continued

Person or Event	Date	Country	Publications	Significance
Heinz Kohut (1913–1981)	1971–79	Austria until 1940, then USA	*The Analysis of the Self* (1971), *The Restoration of the Self* (1977), "The two analyses of Mr. Z," Int J Psychoanal *60*: 3, 1979; "Heinz Kohut's self psychology: An overview," H. Baker and M. Baker, *Am J Psychiatry 144*: 1, 1987	Kohut originated the psychoanalytic school of self-psychology, which delineated a new group of developmental needs and three new views of transferences: mirroring, idealizing, and alter-ego
Roger Sperry (1913–)	Early 1960s–1982	USA	"Some effects of disconnecting the cerebral hemispheres," Science, *217*: 1223, 1982	In 1981 Sperry shared the Nobel Prize in Medicine for his work demonstrating that the left brain hemisphere contains the primary speech capacity, that the right hemisphere is involved with short-term memory, and that the two hemispheres function independently of one another when the connection between them is cut; this work, which was funded by grants from the National Institute of Mental Health, suggested that such psychotic states as autism and delusions may sometimes be caused by disturbances in the connections between the hemispheres
Behavioral medicine and biofeedback	1970s and 1980s	USA	N. E. Miller; "Applications of learning and biofeedback to psychiatry and medicine," Section 4.9, in *Comprehensive Textbook of Psychiatry (CTP)-III,* 1980	"Behavioral medicine," a term originated by Birk in 1973, refers to the application of principles of behavior therapy to the diagnosis and treatment of a wide variety of medical, psychiatric, and psychosomatic disorders; largely developed by Neal E. Miller, biofeedback is a technique that, through instrumentation, signals persons about their normal involuntary biological processes, so that they may adjust their behavior and modify those processes; biofeedback (along with relaxation techniques) has been used to treat a wide variety of psychosomatic disorders; its efficacy is still being evaluated
Stanley Jackson (1920–)	1986	USA	*Melancholia and Depression: From Hippocratic Times to Modern Times* (Yale University Press, New Haven, 1986)	The most comprehensive history in English of the many different theories of and treatments for depression; the relationships between depression and such mental states as grief, love, melancholy, nostalgia, neurasthenia, hypochondriasis, and lycanthropy (the belief that a man takes the form of a wolf)
National Alliance for the Mentally Ill (NAMI) and National Alliance for Research on Schizophrenia and Depression (NARSAD).	1979–1987	USA	*NAMI: We are Family,* 10-page brochure describing work of NAMI (NAMI, Arlington, VA); *NARSAD Research,* 11-page brochure, describing NARSAD's research activities (NARSAD, Chicago, 1989)	NAMI, founded in 1979 as an organization of schizophrenic patients and their family members, has developed new approaches to working with families—counseling, individual family therapy, multiple-family therapy groups, and psychoeducational programs—and has probably become the most vigorous citizens group in America, advocating the problems of the mentally ill to legislators and the public.

Table 48-1
continued

Person or Event	Date	Country	Publications	Significance
				Since its formation in 1986, NARSAD has probably become the leading private association in America that gives grants and prizes to researchers in schizophrenia and depression; in 1987 it gave the first Lieber Prize (the largest psychiatric research prize in America) to Dr. Benjamin Bunney for his elucidation of mechanisms in the brain that appear to explain the action of antipsychotic drugs
Classification of mental disorders	1980–1987	USA	Third edition of *Diagnostic and Statistical Manual of Mental Disorders* (DSM-III), APA Task Force on Nomenclature and Statistics, Robert Spitzer, Chair (APA, Washington, DC, 1980); revised third edition of *Diagnostic and Statistical Manual of Mental Disorders* (DSM-III-R), Robert Spitzer, Chair, Work Group to Revise DSM-III, Janet Williams, Text Editor (APA, Washington, DC, 1987)	DSM-III involved a reorganization of the entire system of classifying diseases, leading to a more detailed, precise, and clearer delineation of symptoms and a more medical and less psychoanalytic view of these symptoms; DSM-III was widely read and accepted in America and became the common language used by workers in psychiatry DSM-III-R was published because data from new studies were inconsistent with some of the previous diagnostic criteria and because of the need to constantly review these criteria—along with systematic descriptions of diseases—for clarity and conceptual accuracy
Discoveries of genetic variations as a cause of mental illness	1983–1987	Mainly USA; also France, Israel, Italy, Venezuela, and West Germany	"A polymorphic DNA marker genetically linked to Huntington's disease," J. F. Gusella and associates, Nature *306*: 234, 1983; "The genetic defect causing familial Alzheimer's disease maps on chromosome 21," P. H. St. George-Hyslop and associates, Science *235*: 885, 1987; "Bipolar affective disorders linked to DNA markers on chromosome 11," J. A. Egeland, and associates, Nature *325*: 783, 1987; "Genetic linkage between X-chromosome markers and bipolar affective illness," M. Baron and associates, Nature *326*: 289, 1987	Discovery of the specific chromosomal locations of the genes causing Huntington's chorea and Alzheimer's disease and of the genes causing two distinct forms of bipolar disorder; further research in the area of these latter discoveries should lead to a better understanding of the cause and treatment of bipolar disorder
John Bowlby (1907–1990)	1969–1988	England	*Attachment* (Basic Books, New York, 1969); *Separation* (Basic Books, New York, 1973); *Loss* (Basic Books, New York, 1980); *A Secure Base* (Basic Books, New York, 1988)	A detailed psychological study of how infants attach to and then separate from their mothers and how they experience losses, mourning, and depression

Table 48-1
Continued

Person or Event	Date	Country	Publications	Significance
Psychology of women and feminism	1976–1988	USA, England, France	*Towards a New Psychology of Women,* J. B. Miller (Beacon Press, Boston, 1976); *Women: The Longest Revolution: Essays in Feminism, Literature and Psychoanalysis,* J. Mitchell (Virago Press, London, 1984); *Women Analyze Women: In France, England, and the United States,* ed. E. H. Baruch and L. J. Serrano (New York University Press, New York, 1988)	In these books women psychotherapists (representing different schools of psychotherapy) delineate some of the major mental conflicts experienced by contemporary American, English, and French women who, under the influence of the feminist movement, have tried to realize their intellectual and emotional potentials and who, at times, have also tried to achieve power in jobs and careers
Psychology and neurophysiology of dreams	1977–1988	USA	"The brain as a dream state generator: An activation-synthesis hypothesis of one dream process," J. A. Hobson and R. W. McCarley, Am. J. Psychiatry *134*: 1335, 1977; *The Dreaming Brain,* J. A. Hobson (Basic Books, New York, 1988)	Hobson–McCarley activation–synthesis hypothesis of dream formation, based on neurophysiological research, postulates that dreams are caused by two reciprocally interacting groups of brain stem neurons; this neurally determined hypothesis is considerably different from Freud's psychological hypothesis, which postulates that dreams are caused by psychic conflict
Theories on the psychology of love	1987–1988	USA	*The Anatomy of Loving,* M. S. Bergmann (Columbia University Press, New York, 1987); *The Triangle of Love: Intimacy, Passion, Commitment,* R. J. Sternberg (Basic Books, New York, 1987); *The Psychology of Love,* ed. R. J. Sternberg and M. L. Barnes (Yale University Press, New Haven, 1988); *Passionate Attachments: Thinking about Love,* ed. W. Gaylin and E. Person (Free Press, New York, 1988); *Dreams of Love and Fateful Encounters: The Power of Romantic Passion,* E. Person (Norton, New York, 1988)	These books, which appeared within one year, differ in their accounts of the nature of love; no one dominant theory emerges, yet each book offers new information and ideas on the phenomenology of love
Antidepressant drugs	1958–1989	USA, England, Europe	"The treatment of depressive states with G 22355 (imipramine hydrochloride)," Roland Kuhn, Am J Psychiatry *115*: 459, 1958; "Antidepressant drugs," J. H. Davis, A. H. Glassman, Section 31.4, in *CTP-V,* 1989; *Prozac, Fluoxetine Hydrochloride, Comprehensive Monograph* (Dista Products, Indianapolis, 1988)	After the tricyclic drug imipramine (Tofranil) was found to be effective as an antidepressant, other tricyclics, monoamine oxidase inhibitors (MAOIs), fluoxetine, and other drugs were found to be antidepressants; today, these drugs more than double the chance that a patient will recover from depression within one month, and they have provided clues about the biological causes of depression

Table 48-1
Continued

Person or Event	Date	Country	Publications	Significance
Drug treatment of panic disorders	Early 1960s–1989	USA	*Diagnosis and Drug Treatment of Psychiatric Disorders,* D. F. Klein and J. M. Davis (Williams & Wilkins, Baltimore, 1969); *Psychiatric Case Studies: Treatment, Drugs, and Outcome,* D. F. Klein (Williams & Wilkins, Baltimore, 1972); "Panic and generalized anxiety disorders," J. C. Nemiah, T. W. Uhde, Section 18.1, in *CTP-V,* 1989	During the 1960s Donald Klein and other psychiatrists reported that tricyclic and MAOI antidepressants were effective in treating patients with panic disorders; this has been confirmed by double-blind, placebo-controlled studies, and two benzodiazepines—alprazolam (Xanax) and clonazepam (Klonopin)—have been found to be effective in the treatment of these disorders
Revolution in neurochemistry	Mid-1960s–1989	USA, England, Europe	*The Broken Brain: The Biological Revolution in Psychiatry,* N. C. Andreasen (Harper & Row, New York, 1984); *Molecules of the Mind: The Brave New Science of Molecular Psychology,* J. Franklin (Atheneum, New York, 1987); "Receptors, monoamines, and amino acids," J. M. Baraban, J. T. Coyle, "Neuropeptides: Biology and regulation," S. J. Watson, H Akil: "Intraneuronal biochemical signals," J. A. Grebb, M. D. Browning: Sections 1.4–1.6, in *CTP-V,* 1989.	Knowledge of the many chemicals involved in the interactions between neuromessengers and receptors in the brain and the patterns of normal neurotransmissions has led to new approaches to assessing neurotransmission in mental illnesses and to developing drugs to treat these illnesses; advances in neurochemistry have become one of the cutting edges of psychiatry
Diagnosis and classification of homosexuality	1973–1989	USA	*Homosexuality and American Psychiatry: The Politics of Diagnosis,* R. Bayer (Basic Books, New York, 1981); *Male Homosexuality: A Contemporary Psychoanalytic Perspective,* R. C. Friedman (Yale University Press, New Haven, 1988)	In 1973, in the light of new clinical information and under political pressure from the National Gay Task Force, the APA changed its diagnosis of homosexuality from a disease to a condition that could be considered a disease only if it was subjectively disturbing to the person; APA members protested this decision, but in a 1974 APA referendum it was sustained by a 58 per cent vote; at this time, some of the factors that influence a person to have a homosexual orientation are known (biology, family-cultural environment, intrapsychic psychodynamics), but other factors remain unknown
Eric Kandel (1929–)	1979–1989	Austria, after 1938 USA	"Psychotherapy and the single synapse: The impact of psychiatric neurobiological research," N Engl J Med, *301*: 1028, 1979; "From metapsychology to molecular biology: Explorations into the nature of anxiety," Am J Psychiatry, *140*: 1277, 1983; *Principles of*	Kandel has shown the connections between psychiatry and neurobiology; research of the central nervous system of the snail *Aplysia*; has developed an experimental system and a set of conceptual approaches for studying the biological basis of simple forms of learning and memory and has demonstrated that "learning produces changes in neuronal architecture, changes that result from learned alterations in gene expression"; has

Table 48-1
Continued

Person or Event	Date	Country	Publications	Significance
			Neural Science, ed 2, E. Kandel and J. H. Schwartz (Elsevier, New York, 1985); "Genes, nerve cells, and the remembrance of things past," J Neuropsychiatry, *1*: 103, 1989	"suggested that normal learning, the learning of neurotic behavioral patterns and the unlearning of such detrimental behaviors through psychotherapeutic intervention might involve long-term functional and structural changes in the brain that result from alterations in gene expression"
Otto Kernberg (1928–)	1975–1990	Chile, after 1959 USA	*Borderline Conditions and Pathological Narcissism* (Aronson, New York, 1975); *Severe Personality Disorders: Psychotherapeutic Strategies* (Yale University Press, New Haven, 1984)	Development of psychoanalytic concepts for understanding and diagnosing narcissistic and borderline personality disorders and psychotherapeutic techniques for treating these disorders
Brief psychotherapy	1976–1989	USA, England	*A Study of Brief Psychotherapy*, D. Malan (Plenum, New York, 1976); *A Casebook in Time-Limited Psychotherapy*, J. Mann and R. Goldman (McGraw-Hill, New York, 1982); *Short-Term Dynamic Psychotherapy*, H. Davanloo (Aronson, New York, 1980); *Short-Term Dynamic Psychotherapy Evaluation and Technique*, P. Sifneos (Plenum, New York, 1979)	Brief psychotherapy aims at producing insight and personality changes in a patient in a short, cost-limited time; includes the following techniques: limiting time devoted to therapy, focusing on a particular problem, actively involving the therapist, anxiety-provoking confrontations, past-present link interpretations, problem solving, recapitulating patient's resistances, emphasizing change and progress, early termination
Aaron Beck (1921–)	1976–1990	USA	*Cognitive Therapy and the Emotional Disorder* (International Universities Press, New York, 1976); *Cognitive Therapy of Depression*, A. Beck, A. J. Rush, B. F. Shaw, and G. Emery (Guilford Press, New York, 1979)	As formulated by Beck, cognitive therapy is a system of psychotherapy based on a theory of psychopathology and a set of therapeutic principles and techniques that emphasize the rearrangement of a person's maladaptive processes of thinking, perceptions, and attitudes
Epidemic of acquired immune deficiency syndrome (AIDS) and of persons infected with AIDS virus (human immunodeficiency virus [HIV])	1981–present	Worldwide; in 1990 in the USA, there were 100,000 persons with AIDS and about 2 million with HIV infection	"Psychiatric aspects of AIDS," M. E. Faulstich, Am J Psychiatry, *144*: 551, 1987; *Psychological, Neuropsychiatric, and Substance Abuse Aspects of AIDS*, ed. P. T. Bridge, A. E. Mirsky, F. K. Goodwin (Raven Press, New York, 1988)	Some of the problems that American psychiatrists confront in the AIDS epidemic are differentiating organic symptoms from functional symptoms of HIV infection in the brain, the social stigmas of AIDS and HIV infection, the fear of contamination by HIV virus, the psychiatric treatment of dying AIDS patients and their families, the organization of AIDS-HIV care units in hospitals and clinics, and the counseling of other health care professionals about AIDS

*Table prepared by Ralph Colp, Jr., M.D.

References

Ackernecht E H: *A Short History of Psychiatry*. Hafner, New York, 1968.
Alexander F G, Selesnick S T: *The History of Psychiatry*. Harper & Row, New York, 1966.
Barton W E: *The History and Influence of the American Psychiatric Association*. American Psychiatric Press, Washington, DC, 1987.
Colp R: History of psychiatry. In *Comprehensive Textbook of Psychiatry*, ed 5. H I Kaplan and B J Sadock, editors, p 2132. Williams & Wilkins, Baltimore, 1989.
Ducey C, Simon B: Ancient Greece and Rome. In *World History of Psychiatry*, J G Howell, editor. Brunner/Mazel, New York, 1975.
Ellenberger H F: *The Discovery of the Unconscious: The History and Evolution of Dynamic Psychiatry*. Basic Books, New York, 1970.
Gay P: *Freud: A Life for Our Time*. Norton, New York, 1988.
Grob G N: The care and treatment of the mentally ill. Essay review. Bull Hist Med *62*: 104, 1988.
Grob G N: *Mental Illness and American Society: 1875–1940*. Princeton University Press, Princeton, NJ, 1983.
Grob G N: *Mental Institutions in America: Social Policy to 1875*. Free Press, New York, 1973.
Harms E: *Origins of Modern Psychiatry*. Thomas, Springfield, IL, 1967.
Hunter R, Macalpine I, eds.: *Three Hundred Years of Psychiatry, 1535–1860: A History Presented in Selected English Texts*. Oxford University Press, London, 1964.
Jackson S W: *Melancholia and Depression: From Hippocratic Times to Modern Times*. Yale University Press, New Haven, CT, 1986.
Kravis N M: James Braid's psychophysiology: A turning point in the history of dynamic psychiatry. Am J Psychiatry *145*: 1191, 1988.
McGovern C M: *Masters of Madness: Social Origins of the American Psychiatric Profession*. University Press of New England, Hanover, NH, 1985.
Porter R: *Mind-Forg'd Manacles*. Harvard University Press, Cambridge, MA, 1988.
Porter R: *A Social History of Madness: Stories of the Insane*. Weidenfeld & Nicolson, London, 1987.
Roazen, P: *Encountering Freud: The Politics and Histories of Psychoanalysis*. Transaction, New Brunswick, NJ, 1990.
Scull A: *Decarceration: Community Treatment and the Deviant: A Radical View*. Rutgers University Press, New Brunswick, NJ, 1984.
Thompson C: *The Origins of Modern Psychiatry*. Wiley, New York, 1987.

Index

Page numbers followed by t and f indicate tables and figures, respectively.
Page numbers in **boldface** indicate main discussions.

D

G